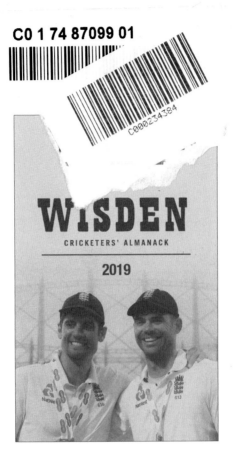

A Taste of Wisden 2019

She once recalled her mother telling her: "You'll never meet nice men if you play cricket." Rheinberg said: "She was quite right in a way. I won't say I didn't meet nice men – but I didn't marry."
The Netta Rheinberg diaries, page 45

* * *

He was starring in his own show,
Joseph and the Amazing Technicolor Dream Kit.
Five Cricketers of the Year, page 92

* * *

For the new batsman, trying to hit Garner's yorker
for eight an over was like trying to bench-press gravity.
The 1979 World Cup, page 122

* * *

Sometimes cricket seems a game so in love with its past, and so worried about its future, it forgets to appreciate the present.
Cricket in the Media in 2018, page 148

* * *

The fate of the ball that had been changed at Lord's remained
a subject of conjecture. Many assumed it was locked in a
filing cabinet in the Pavilion, never to be seen again.
In fact, it was on his mantelpiece in Cleethorpes.
Obituaries, page 225

* * *

In an unusual attempt to preserve moisture, the groundstaff
at Edgbaston treated their outfield with seaweed.
Ultimately, it was India who needed kelp.
England v India in 2018, page 317

* * *

The conditions were a gift to Mohammad Abbas, a loaves-and-fishes kind of bowler, able to do so much with so little.
Pakistan v Australia in 2018-19, Second Test, page 938

* * *

This contest had it all: on-field scuffles, off-field altercations,
ambush marketing, expulsions and sackings, a resignation,
a retirement, a rewriting of the history
books – and a small piece of sandpaper.
South Africa v Australia in 2017-18, page 985

LIST OF CONTRIBUTORS

Timothy Abraham
Ujjwal Acharya
Jules Akel
Andrew Alderson
Tanya Aldred
Elizabeth Ammon
Chris Aspin
Mike Atherton
Philip August
Vaneisa Baksh
Greg Baum
Benedict Bermange
Scyld Berry
Edward Bevan
Paul Bird
Paul Bolton
Daniel Brettig
Liam Brickhill
Gideon Brooks
Colin Bryden
Mark Bussell
Ian Callender
Nick Campion
Nazvi Careem
Brian Carpenter
Daniel Cherny
David Clough
Adam Collins
James Coyne
Craig Cozier
Liam Cromar
Jon Culley
John Curtis
Debashish Datta
Martin Davies
Geoffrey Dean
Tim de Lisle
William Dick
George Dobell
Rory Dollard
Paul Edwards
Syd Egan
Vithushan Ehantharajah

Mark Eklid
Matthew Engel
Peter English
John Etheridge
Melinda Farrell
Fidel Fernando
Warwick Franks
Alan Gardner
Mark Geenty
Richard Gibson
Haydn Gill
Gideon Haigh
Kevin Hand
David Hardy
Shahid Hashmi
Richard Heller
Douglas Henderson
Andrew Hignell
Paul Hiscock
Richard Hobson
Tristan Holme
Ben Horne
Jon Hotten
Nick Hoult
Steve James
Nishant Joshi
Miles Jupp
Abid Ali Kazi
Jarrod Kimber
Richard Latham
Geoff Lemon
Jonathan Liew
Andrew McGlashan
Will Macpherson
Neil Manthorp
Vic Marks
Ali Martin
Alex Massie
Mazher Arshad
Peter Miller
Mohammad Isam
R. Mohan
Sidharth Monga

Firdose Moonda
Benj Moorehead
K. R. Nayar
Paul Newman
Raf Nicholson
Peter Oborne
Mark Pennell
Snehal Pradhan
Paul Radley
Richard Rae
Charles Reynolds
Barney Ronay
Osman Samiuddin
Neville Scott
Utpal Shuvro
Revatha Silva
Rob Smyth
Richard Spiller
Fraser Stewart
Andy Stockhausen
Chris Stocks
Bharat Sundaresan
Pat Symes
Bruce Talbot
Sa'adi Thawfeeq
Huw Turbervill
Sharda Ugra
Tunku Varadarajan
Anand Vasu
Waleed Khan
Phil Walker
John Ward
David Warner
Chris Waters
Tim Wellock
Isabelle Westbury
Freddie Wilde
Simon Wilde
Marcus Williams
Dean Wilson
Robert Winder
Alex Winter
Lungani Zama

Photographers are credited as appropriate. Special thanks to Graham Morris. **Cartoons** by Nick Newman. Contributors to the **Round the World** section are listed after their articles.

The editor also acknowledges with gratitude assistance from the following: Robin Abrahams, Phil Agius, Aslam Siddiqui, Mike Bechley, Trevor Bedells, Derek Carlaw, Stephen Chalke, Henry Cowen, Brian Croudy, Stephen Cubitt, Prakash Dahatonde, Robin Darwall-Smith, Nigel Davies, Charles Davis, Gulu Ezekiel, M. L. Fernando, Ric Finlay, Alan Fordham, Patrick Foster, Graeme Fowler, David Frith, Nagraj Gollapudi, David Graveney, Clive Hitchcock, Julia and John Hunt, Nasser Hussain, David Kendix, Rajesh Kumar, Neil Leitch, Edward Liddle, Roger Long, Nirav Malavi, Mahendra Mapagunaratne, Peter Martin, Suresh Menon, André Odendaal, Michael Owen-Smith, Francis Payne, Mick Pope, Qamar Ahmed, Danny Reuben, Andrew Samson, Christopher Sandford, Clare Skinner, John Stern, Steven Stern, Claire Taylor, Christopher Travers, Ben Walker, Chris Walmsley, Charlie Wat, Chris and Jean Whipps, Alan Williams.

The production of *Wisden* would not be possible without the support and co-operation of many other cricket officials, county scorers, writers and lovers of the game. To them all, many thanks.

PREFACE

This book loves a niche stat: most Test runs by a left-hander at Chittagong, most T20 wickets under a full moon on a Tuesday – that sort of thing. So in a stab at simplification, this year's *Wisden* has introduced a page of all-format records. It is refreshing to be able to say, without caveat, that Graham Gooch is cricket's leading run-scorer (67,057), and Wilfred Rhodes its leading wicket-taker (4,187). Second, respectively, are Graeme Hick and Tich Freeman; there's even a non-England player among the two top tens. The full list appears on page 1248.

As ever, we have tweaked here and there. The profile of the Leading Woman Cricketer in the World, won by the Indian opener Smriti Mandhana, joins her male counterpart at the front of the book. Her compatriot Virat Kohli, wins for an unprecedented third year in a row. Meanwhile, the captain of Afghanistan has changed his name from Asghar Stanikzai to Asghar Afghan; because the change took place in August, both versions appear in the pages that follow.

Two northern powerhouses have written their last reports for the Almanack. David Warner, known to the world as "Plum", has stepped down after 21 years covering Yorkshire, while Tim Wellock has been a fixture ever since Durham assumed first-class status in 1992. In both cases, it feels like the end of an era; they will be missed.

With Afghanistan and Ireland playing more often, and full Twenty20 status given to the ICC's 93 Associate Members (Botswana can't have made many headlines in *Wisden* before), there is more cricket than ever to squeeze in. The editorial team were unfazed: my gratitude goes to Hugh Chevallier, who kept the show on the road, and to the tireless trio of Harriet Monkhouse, Steven Lynch and Richard Whitehead. Others are just as invaluable: consultant publisher Christopher Lane; our unflappable production co-ordinator, Peter Bather; Charles Barr, who proofreads; and Alan Williams, who offers legal advice. The typesetting team at DLXML, led by Gary Holmes and James Parsisson, put the pages together, patiently and skilfully.

At Bloomsbury, the support of Charlotte Croft, Lizzy Ewer and Katherine Macpherson is always welcome. Clare Skinner organised the annual Wisden–MCC photograph competition (now in need of a sponsor) with her customary efficiency. Thanks, too, to the judges, chaired by Chris Smith.

This job devours time, and my colleagues at the *Daily Mail* and *The Mail on Sunday* – Lee Clayton, Marc Padgett, Paul Newman, Richard Gibson, Alison Kervin and Mike Richards – were as generous as ever in respecting that.

No thanks are enough for my wife, Anjali, who treated my antisocial hours with patience and understanding. All my love to her, and to our toddler, Aleya, who likes to grab random Almanacks from the shelf, browse briefly, then return to *The Tiger Who Came to Tea*.

LAWRENCE BOOTH
Barnes, February 2019

CONTENTS

Part One – Comment

Part Two – The Wisden Review

Part Three – English International Cricket

Part Four – English Domestic Cricket

STATISTICS

SPECSAVERS COUNTY CHAMPIONSHIP

Review and statistics 397

ONE-DAY COUNTY COMPETITIONS

OTHER ENGLISH CRICKET

Part Five – Overseas Cricket

GLOBAL TOURNAMENTS

CRICKET IN AFGHANISTAN

CRICKET IN AUSTRALIA

Part Six – Overseas Domestic Twenty20 Cricket

Part Seven – Women's Cricket

Part Eight – Records and Registers

Features of 2018   1197

RECORDS

BIRTHS AND DEATHS

REGISTER

Part Nine – The Almanack

SYMBOLS AND ABBREVIATIONS

*	In full scorecards and lists of tour parties signifies the captain. In short scorecards, averages and records signifies not out.
†	In full scorecards signifies the designated wicketkeeper. In averages signifies a left-handed batsman.
‡	In short scorecards signifies the team who won the toss.
MoM/PoM	In short scorecards signifies the Man/Player of the Match.
MoS/PoS	In short scorecards signifies the Man/Player of the Series.
DLS	Signifies where the result of a curtailed match has been determined under the Duckworth/Lewis/Stern method.

Other uses of symbols are explained in notes where they appear.

First-class matches Men's matches of three or more days are first-class unless otherwise stated. All other matches are not first-class, including one-day and T20 internationals.

Scorecards Where full scorecards are not provided in this book, they can be found at Cricket Archive (www.cricketarchive.co.uk) or ESPNcricinfo (www.cricinfo.com). Full scorecards from matches played overseas can also be found in the relevant *ACS Overseas First-Class Annuals*. In Twenty20 scorecards, the second figure in a bowling analysis refers to dot balls, and not maidens (as in first-class or List A games).

Records The entire Records section (pages 1215–1359) can now be found at www.wisdenrecords.com. The online Records database is regularly updated and, in many instances, more detailed than in *Wisden 2019*. Further information on past winners of tournaments covered in this book can be found at www.wisden.com/almanacklinks.

PART ONE

Comment

Wisden Honours

THE LEADING CRICKETERS IN THE WORLD

Virat Kohli (page 100)
Smriti Mandhana (page 65)

The Leading Cricketers in the World are chosen by the editor of *Wisden* in consultation with some of the world's most experienced writers and commentators. Selection is based on a player's class and form shown in all cricket during the calendar year, and is guided by statistics rather than governed by them. There is no limit to how many times a player may be chosen. A list of notional past winners, backdated to 1900, appeared on page 35 of *Wisden 2007*.

THE LEADING TWENTY20 CRICKETER IN THE WORLD

Rashid Khan (page 1128)

This award mirrors those above, but is based solely on performances in Twenty20 cricket, both international and domestic – and may be won by a male or female player.

FIVE CRICKETERS OF THE YEAR

Tammy Beaumont (page 87)
Rory Burns (page 89)
Jos Buttler (page 91)
Sam Curran (page 93)
Virat Kohli (page 95)

The Five Cricketers of the Year are chosen by the editor of *Wisden*, and represent a tradition that dates back to 1889, making this the oldest individual award in cricket. Excellence in and/or influence on the previous English summer are the major criteria for inclusion. No one can be chosen more than once. A list of past winners can be found on page 1459.

WISDEN SCHOOLS CRICKETER OF THE YEAR

Nathan Tilley (page 742)

The Schools Cricketer of the Year, based on first-team performances during the previous English summer, is chosen by *Wisden's* schools correspondent in consultation with the editor and other experienced observers. The winner's school must be in the UK, play cricket to a standard approved by *Wisden* and provide reports to this Almanack. A list of past winners can be found on page 741.

WISDEN BOOK OF THE YEAR

Steve Smith's Men by Geoff Lemon (page 141)

The Book of the Year is selected by *Wisden's* guest reviewer; all cricket books published in the previous calendar year and submitted to *Wisden* for possible review are eligible. A list of past winners can be found on page 142.

WISDEN–MCC CRICKET PHOTOGRAPH OF THE YEAR

was won by Phil Hillyard (whose entry appears opposite page 64)

The Wisden–MCC Cricket Photograph of the Year is chosen by a panel of independent experts; all images on a cricket theme photographed in the previous calendar year are eligible.

WISDEN'S WRITING COMPETITION

was won by Nick Campion (page 85)

Wisden's Writing Competition is open to anyone (other than previous winners) who has not been commissioned to write for, or has a working relationship with, the Almanack. Full details appear on page 86.

Full details of past winners of all these honours can be found at www.wisdenalmanack.com

NOTES BY THE EDITOR

The view from the 29th floor of Millbank Tower is, as cricketers like to say, right up there. London spreads out in every direction. You are among the people, but not quite *of* them. As the light pierces the clouds towards the west, there is a hint of sunny uplands. It's almost… intoxicating. And it was here in January 2019 that the ECB chief executive, Tom Harrison, sought to explain why the 100-ball tournament scheduled to start next year really was the saviour of the English game.

In fact, there had been plenty to relish in 2018. The England men's Test side beat India at home, and Sri Lanka away, and for a while moved second in the rankings. The one-day team went top, broke their own world-record total and trounced Australia; they entered World Cup year as favourites, and were comfortable with the status. The women saw off South Africa and New Zealand, destroying the Twenty20 world-record total en route. Crowds flocked to the T20 Blast, and the ECB's All Stars initiative – aimed at introducing youngsters to the sport – thrived. Cricket was aglow.

Yet, all the while, The Hundred hung over the English game like the sword of Damocles, suspended only by the conviction of a suited few. Some preferred a modern analogy: this was cricket's Brexit, an unnecessary gamble that had overshadowed all else, gone over budget and would end in tears. But the analogy was imperfect: where Brexit had plenty of advocates, it was difficult to find anyone beyond a small group within the ECB's offices who believed that cricket – its fixture list already unfathomable – needed a fourth format. Harrison baulked at that description, preferring "a competition designed to do a certain job for a certain period of the season". It sounded like the new overseas spinner, not the future of English cricket.

The original plan, a city-based Twenty20 tournament, had logic, since not all counties were making a success of the Blast. But as its audiences grew, so The Hundred's *raison d'être* shrank. In private, some county executives are ambivalent, at best. In public, their support was lukewarm: after all, they are being paid to play host. A disaster suits no one, yet few envisage a triumph.

It is hard to be sanguine about stuffing another quart into the pint pot. Even if The Hundred succeeds – and the early signs were not good, with projected audiences of around 12,000 in stadiums capable of holding twice as many – then what of the other formats? Twenty20 will take a hit, years after the world agreed it was the way ahead. The 50-over competition, its fixtures clashing with the new tournament, will smack of the Second XI, just when England have become good at one-day cricket. And the Championship will be shoved deeper into the cupboard under the stairs. Then there's the growing divide between the eight counties who will stage the competition and the ten who won't. Worcestershire's Daryl Mitchell, who doubles as chairman of the Professional Cricketers' Association, spoke for many: "If it doesn't work, then we're all in trouble."

If only someone at the ECB had been on hand last year to explain why they thought it a good idea to stake cricket's wellbeing on a form of the game played nowhere else in the world. It's true that this approach worked in 2003, when Twenty20's arrival met with scepticism. Yet these grand schemes come off once a generation. And the public have to be convinced over time, not drip-fed careless soundbites. Of course, it all boiled down to money: a lucrative TV deal that guarantees almost daily action for Sky, and – thank goodness – some live cricket for a free-to-air channel. But at what cost to the game's credibility?

At first, amid a shambolic launch, existing fans were made to feel like outcasts. Eoin Morgan, England's white-ball captain – and one of only three players included in the ECB's "consultation process" – mocked the hand that fed him: "I have a lot of friends outside cricket who would never come to a match, but have said they enjoy that there is a bit of noise around [The Hundred], because it's upsetting people who already come to a game, and that is the point of the product." To alienate your core constituency was a curious marketing ploy.

It was sensible to entice women and children; less so to patronise them. Women, went the argument, would be better able to follow a game of 100 balls than 120. And on the day it was announced that 50,000 kids had signed up as All Stars, the ECB chairman, Colin Graves, was lamenting that "the younger generation are just not attracted to cricket". At this point, the board might have considered introducing their right hand to their left.

As the clumsiness of the PR strategy dawned on them, the ECB changed tack. First they quietly suggested that, on top of the new audience they hope to attract, they wanted to engage English cricket's lapsed fans too, presumably those excluded by the disappearance of live coverage from terrestrial channels. Then, at Millbank, Harrison threw open his embrace: The Hundred was for everyone! By then, however, many cricket lovers didn't want to know.

Of the market research the board said they had carried out to establish enthusiasm for the venture, not a peep was heard (though there were mutterings nothing new had been commissioned since a 2016 survey revealed more British youngsters were able to recognise an American wrestler than Alastair Cook.) The media filled the void. On the same morning, two newspapers ran exclusives which sounded mutually exclusive: one said the new tournament would be 12-a-side, the other 15-a-side. The fact that both ideas had been batted about, then leaked, summed up the chaos: no idea was too daft. And while the ECB talked about simplifying the game, it wasn't clear how giving bowlers the option of sending down five consecutive deliveries or ten would make things easier to follow.

Harrison admits mistakes have been made. He speaks with passion, and is right to fret about cricket's future. Despite what some think, he really does care. He is correct when he says cricket hates change – often to its detriment – and he has a point when he says The Hundred, thanks to the TV deal, has already paid for itself. But when he denies the game is taking an almighty punt, you wonder whether ambition has clouded his judgment.

Our sport is preparing for the summer of its life: not since 1975 have England hosted a World Cup and an Ashes. Imagine the joy if they win one, or even both – then consider whether this artificial stimulus is needed. Instead, this could go down as the moment the administrators flew too close to the sun.

The tomorrow people

Quite what a 100-ball tournament will do to England's search for a Test top order does not bear thinking about. Their openers were once the envy of the world; gutsy, stoical, pragmatic, they may even have embodied a certain Britishness. Now, it's a pleasant surprise when one survives until lunch.

England's response has been to pick sides which compensate for the weakness. Occasionally, there have been thrills: Sam Curran's counter-attacks from No. 8 were central to the 4–1 victory over India, and the depth of the batting helped them win 3–0 in Sri Lanka. There was breathless talk of "total cricket" and fluid line-ups, and praise for Ed Smith, who brought an open mind to the role of national selector. Jos Buttler was recalled to the Test team because of his form at the IPL, Adil Rashid in spite of a white-ball-only contract with Yorkshire (where the grumbling confirmed Smith was spot on). Curran's cameos extended into the winter. These were imaginative picks, beyond the daring of Smith's predecessors.

But there was a sense of fun-while-it-lasted, a problem deferred. Whatever the merits of England's strategy, it was not sustainable. And when the caravan moved to the Caribbean, Keaton Jennings was predictably exposed by the West Indies quicks, having scored a red-herring hundred against Sri Lanka's slow bowlers at Galle. The chalice passed to Joe Denly, a solid county pro but no regular opener, not even for Kent in Division Two; in Antigua, he was lucky to avoid a pair on debut. In St Lucia, the chalice passed back to Jennings, who edged it to slip.

Then there was No. 3. Between the start of 2018 and the end of the West Indies series, six were tried there (plus Jennings at Pallekele, behind a nightwatchman). Only one had more than six innings: Root, who wanted to bat at No. 4 (and soon did). And only one made a hundred: Jonny Bairstow, who wanted to bat at No. 7 (ditto). Moeen Ali's technique was too loose, but he got five innings; Ben Stokes's was deemed tight, but he got only one. It was as if the team analyst had been replaced by a roulette wheel.

The uncertainty seeped down the order. Stuart Broad was dropped in Barbados to accommodate Curran's batting at No. 9, while Curran himself went from new-ball bowler, to second-change, to drinks carrier. Not until that game, which they won, did England pick a balanced side.

In Sri Lanka, Root had boldly taken a leaf out of Morgan's white-ball book: when in doubt, attack. But a team aspiring to be the best in the world must also, if they are to be taken seriously, adapt. Even after West Indies' Darren Bravo ground out the slowest Test fifty since 1982, in Antigua, England refused to take note. Once, Kevin Pietersen was mocked for protesting: "It's the way I play." These days, that mantra seems a prerequisite. And it is encouraged by the ECB, who have highlighted the "responsibility to be playing exciting cricket for future generations to connect with". The mood, from boardroom to dressing-room, points in one direction: England's Test batsmen are in it for a good time, not a long time.

Since the Melbourne Test at the end of 2017, their highest score in 16 first innings has been 396 for seven; in nine, they failed to reach 300; twice, at

Auckland and Bridgetown, they were dismissed in double figures. They can be entertaining. But too often, when England fall behind, they are swept away, as if battling today will deny them the chance to do something special tomorrow. In the Caribbean, tomorrow didn't come until it was too late.

It is not easy to see what can be done while the domestic schedule treats four-day cricket as an inconvenience. And if the bowlers are handed a lively batch of Dukes balls, as they have been over the past two summers, the carnage will continue. In 2018, the average runs per wicket in the County Championship was under 27, the lowest figure of the four-day era. English batsmen used to clamour to go in early. Now they all seek comfort away from the new ball's glare. Unless the Championship can reclaim the turf of high summer, the flow of hopeful young openers will slow to a trickle.

Up where you belong

Not long ago, Root was being bracketed with Virat Kohli, Steve Smith and Kane Williamson. But while Kohli has entered another dimension, and Williamson stays classy, Root has dropped down a tier. In the Caribbean, his ranking slipped below Smith and David Warner, despite both being banned for their part in Australia's ball-tampering pickle, and his average fell below 50, for the first time in years.

Root remains England's best batsman, as he reminds us now and again: back-to-back one-day hundreds against India, a Test century at The Oval, a stunning piece of improvisation at Pallekele, then the relief of runs in St Lucia. He has converted his last three Test fifties into hundreds, after converting none of his previous 11. He even developed a taste for statesmanship, calmly reproving West Indies fast bowler Shannon Gabriel for making a homophobic remark. But, with the bat, Root has been trying to do too much, too quickly, as if staying in second gear were for wimps. And he is apparently determined to conquer Twenty20, which will help his bank balance but not his legacy.

If there was any doubt that slow and steady can still win the race, Cheteshwar Pujara dispelled it over the winter, inspiring India to their first series win in Australia by spending more than 31 hours at the crease, facing 1,258 balls, and chugging along at a strike-rate of 41. Test diehards warm to this stuff, because they understand that skill comes in many forms. Root's challenge is to rediscover the art of the Test-tempo hundred – and rejoin the elite.

Going down in style

Wisden has never needed much excuse to query the health of Test cricket. So when the ICC chairman, Shashank Manohar, warned at the start of 2019 that it was "dying", it was hard to quibble. His timing, though, was awry. For a while, fans have bemoaned the lack of away wins. Then, in late 2018, England's victory in Sri Lanka was followed by triumph for New Zealand in the UAE against Pakistan (including a four-run win), and India's success in Australia. Before all that, we had maiden Tests for Ireland's men and Afghanistan; after it, the West Indian wins over England in Barbados and Antigua, and an

England win in St Lucia inspired by the pulse-quickening pace of Mark Wood. To crown it all, Sri Lanka became the first Asian side to win in South Africa; one ratings system deemed Kusal Perera's unbeaten 153 at Durban the best Test innings ever. We haven't even mentioned the summer-long duel between Kohli and Jimmy Anderson, two all-time giants. Manohar was right in one sense: the size of crowds at non-England games does suggest imminent demise. But there is still nothing to get the blood pumping quite like a Test match.

A modern great, in case you hadn't noticed

Until the last, opponents reckoned they had a chance against Alastair Cook. The four overthrows that brought up his farewell Test century at The Oval were typical: Jasprit Bumrah was trying to run him out as he strolled a leisurely single. That was the thing about Cook – there was more to him than met the eye. He enjoyed the illusion, and fashioned a career out of it.

Sluggish between the wickets, he was fitter than anyone. Possessing only three strokes against the seamers – the cut and the pull grew scarce as bowlers cottoned on, leaving the nudge off the hip – he made more Test runs than any other left-hander or opener. And he took his only Test wicket while impersonating Bob Willis. When Radio 4's "World At One" cut to a clip of Cook "doing what he did best", that wicket is what they came up with, as if his 12,472 runs had passed them by.

But in one respect Cook was no paradox: for mental strength, England has never seen anyone like him. Even his parting shot – 71 and 147 against the world's No. 1 side – required him to rediscover the edge he said had deserted him. We shouldn't have been surprised.

He was in danger towards the end of being defined by the groaning weight of his numbers: the average might have been falling, but look at the aggregate! No one wanted to admit it, but he was becoming harder to celebrate. Then came the Fifth Test against India. This is an age when applause has been devalued, but the standing ovations that greeted his entrances and exits rang true. And the respect shown by his opponents was genuine. His swansong reminded spectators of the kind of batsman the English game craves. Cook was an everyday cricketer. People responded to that and, at The Oval, he gave them a memory to take home. There has not been a warmer send-off – or an England player more deserving.

Elite hypocrisy

The strangest emotion of the Australia's sandpaper fiasco was the pity momentarily directed towards David Warner, despite his apparent determination to become cricket's answer to life in the Middle Ages: nasty, brutish and short. The pity arose around Christmas, when Steve Smith and Cameron Bancroft – his co-conspirators at Cape Town – made it clear where they thought the blame lay. Smith said he had turned a blind eye to Warner's scheme; Bancroft said he went along with it to fit in, perhaps revealing more than he intended. For once, Warner kept quiet. It was almost dignified – but his silence was part of the problem.

Asked in its immediate aftermath whether Cape Town had been Australia's first tampering transgression, Warner declined to answer, which was probably sensible. "No" would have raised a chuckle both in England, who suspected he had been up to no good during the 2017-18 Ashes (but, having lost 4–0, did not want to be whingeing Poms), and in South Africa. An inquiry by Cricket Australia felt more like a whitewash: there had been no previous tampering, and only three players were involved. Fancy that…

The outrage was disproportionate: fiddling with the ball, if not rubbing it with sandpaper, happens. But there was more to it than outrage. Australia had been undone by the hubris-nemesis one-two, which has kept playwrights in business since Ancient Greece. With their prattle about the line – where it should be drawn (just beyond whatever the Australians had just done) and by whom (the Australians, naturally) – Smith's side forfeited the last drop of goodwill. This wasn't just English tittering: many of their compatriots were sick of them too. To cheat so brazenly confirmed a widely held suspicion: Australia believed they were above the law.

CA had made their own bed when, shortly before the 2013 Ashes, they appointed Darren Lehmann as head coach, in place of Mickey Arthur, who had twigged that something was rotten in the dressing-room. As a player, Lehmann had shouted a racist obscenity after being dismissed by Sri Lanka; and, months after replacing Arthur, he encouraged Australian fans to send Stuart Broad home in tears from that winter's Ashes (which didn't stop him complaining about the behaviour of South African fans). Lehmann was useful to his bosses as long as he was allowing Warner and his mates off the leash – but written off as a liability as soon as they were exposed. It was the kind of ruling-classes hypocrisy thought to be an English disease.

Deep down, did anything change? The new coach, Justin Langer, said he would have followed any orders as a player. An ex-captain, Michael Clarke, suggested the team "were not going to win shit" if they pursued the new captain Tim Paine's policy of treating the opposition with respect. And the Australians invited ridicule when buzzwords decorated their dressing-room walls. One was "elite honesty". To borrow from Australian comedian Hannah Gadsby, the rest of the world may have concluded their nose was being lectured by a fart. At least Paine wants to do something about the stench. Whether Australia will back him is another matter.

The wife isn't fine…

Amid the mayhem and the machismo stood Candice Warner, regarded by South African crowds as collateral damage in their bid to needle husband David. During the Second Test at Port Elizabeth, masks were distributed of a rugby star she had briefly been involved with, before her relationship with Warner. Two officials from Cricket South Africa thought it would be fun to pose, grinning, with fans who were wearing them. And so Candice was forced to relive the emotions she had experienced years earlier when she had become a tabloid headline. Soon after the tour, she suffered a miscarriage.

Sexism isn't unique to cricket. But that isn't to say cricket should tolerate it. It was alarming that CSA employees didn't understand how cruel the masks were, but maybe not surprising. The bubble in which cricket operates – the bubble that allowed the Australians to seek victory at any cost – is a long way from bursting.

Let's face it: this stuff is part of the sport's mythology. In 2017, a poll conducted by a county sponsor suggested that the best sledge of all time came during an apocryphal exchange between Rod Marsh and Ian Botham. Marsh: "How's your wife and my kids?" Botham: "The wife is fine, but the kids are retarded." The legend lives on, held up as proof of cricket's wit, yet confirmation of a damaging credo: when it comes to riling men, women are fair game.

Snappier, happier

It was fair of the ECB's Cricket Discipline Commission to rule that Ben Stokes had already served his time, while also finding him guilty of bringing the game into disrepute for his part in a late-night brawl in September 2017. He had missed two one-dayers against West Indies, a tour of Australia (including a Twenty20 tri-series), and a Test against India – a total of 17 internationals, at the peak of his career. He was then found not guilty of affray by a Bristol jury. Yes, the fight was ugly – but further punishment, beyond the £30,000 fine imposed by the CDC, would have been excessive. It was reasonable to hold both views.

Stokes has to adapt to life after acquittal – to relocate the on-field mongrel that once helped him score 258 at Cape Town, but otherwise to behave like a puppy. The worry is his batting has become too domesticated, as if he's trying to prove how responsible he can be.

By the end of the Tests in the West Indies, he was averaging 28 since his return, seven lower than before; his strike-rate dropped, too, from 63 to 46. And while his one-day average had risen, he was scoring less quickly: 98 runs per 100 balls before his ban, 76 between his return and the start of the series in the Caribbean. His bowling, especially in Tests, has been as good as ever, but it is an all-rounder's batting that reveals his state of mind. If England are going to win the World Cup, they need to remind Stokes that it's OK to hit out, as long as you choose the right target.

Treading water

Last year, *Wisden* introduced a piece on the environment. Some may have rolled their eyes. What good is composting cucumber sandwiches if China keeps burning coal? And isn't cricket supposed to be an escape from reality?

The first objection is defeatist, the second valid only until reality intrudes on cricket. The sport *does* have a role to play. If it chooses otherwise, there can be no complaints when it is limited to the countries which are still habitable in

50 years' time. That may not include Australia, where night-time temperatures in December in New South Wales never fell below 35°C; it may not include India, where swathes of land risk becoming desert; or Bangladesh, which may be under water; or the Caribbean islands, continually flattened by hurricanes. As for mild English summers and lush greentops, forget it.

Climate change is the biggest long-term issue facing cricket but, to judge by its collective response, you wouldn't know. There are notable exceptions, such as MCC's sustainability manager, Russell Seymour. But when Tanya Aldred, who writes our environment article, invited the boards of the 12 Test nations to declare their green credentials, the responses ranged from dispiriting to non-existent, with more in the second category.

Hiding behind government policy is no solution, since politicians don't view ecology as a vote-winner. Cricket should look to its cousin – baseball's New York Yankees recently appointed an "environmental science advisor" – and take its own conservation more seriously.

Put your foot down!

There was uproar when West Indies captain Jason Holder was banned for the Third Test against England in St Lucia because of his side's latest over-rate infraction. But some of the arguments in his defence were condescending. If the captain can't persuade his bowlers to keep up – despite allowances made for drinks breaks, the fall of wickets, DRS referrals and stewards walking in front of the sightscreen – then it is irrelevant how good a guy he is, or whether the world game needs a strong West Indies.

When Kraigg Brathwaite, the stand-in captain, hurried through a few overs of off-breaks to keep the officials off his back, the dullness of the cricket was seized on by Holder apologists: much better, they said, to enjoy the stirring sight of Shannon Gabriel and Kemar Roach, even at 11 overs an hour. But just as many fans say they feel short-changed when another day ends with eight overs unbowled.

There is a tactical consideration, too. If a team bowl only 51 overs by tea, as West Indies did on the first day in Antigua, it takes the load off their attack: the fresher they are, the harder they charge in. You can see why a captain might not urge his fast bowlers back to their mark – and why the ICC owe it to the game to take action.

Much at stake

You won't have heard of Patrick Foster, a seam bowler who was briefly at Northamptonshire. But he may have set an important ball rolling. In March 2018, he contemplated jumping on to the tracks at Slough station. He had racked up gambling debts of more than £150,000, and had just staked another £50,000 on the favourite, Might Bite, to win the Cheltenham Gold Cup. It came second. Patrick called his brother, Sam, who talked him back from the edge. Foster, who recently turned 32, now works for Epic, who help problem gamblers, and has built on the project they started in 2017, telling his story to county cricketers. He's clear about what he's found: the English game has a gambling issue, and the players aren't talking about it.

Foster is a shining example of the work done by the Professional Cricketers' Trust (previously the PCA Benevolent Fund), which supports players in trouble, and backed him – emotionally and financially – at his lowest ebb. And by opening up about his experience, he hopes to encourage others to open up about theirs – much as Marcus Trescothick, a Trust director, broke down taboos about mental health. Foster is brave and contrite, and admits lying to his creditors, who thought he needed to pay his taxes or repair the car. "Others will find it easier to forgive me than I do," he says. He could be any of us.

Cricket needs to listen, not judge. After touring the counties, Foster is concerned. Our administrators need to urge greater regulation of the adverts that swamp the game, though at least the gambling industry recently agreed to ban pre-9pm ads during most live TV sports coverage. They need to spot cricketers vulnerable to addictive behaviour. They need to encourage young players – with time on their hands after a first-baller, perhaps, or more money after a new contract – to come forward if they fear succumbing to gambling's grip. And their ears should prick up when Foster admits he would have accepted payment, at the height of his addiction, to bowl a no-ball.

He has come through the other side, but with baggage. His debts mean he can barely secure a mobile-phone contract, let alone a mortgage; he will be paying them off for many years. But at least he is still there.

Grass ceiling

At Malahide in May, as Ireland followed on in their first men's Test, against Pakistan, a miracle was threatening to unfold. Kevin O'Brien hit a century to set a target of 160 and, within a few overs, the Pakistanis were 14 for three. Excitement was in the air, and it lingered even after the Irish had gone down to a five-wicket defeat. They were not the only Test newcomers in 2018, though they were at least given a fair craic: Afghanistan began in India, tried to run before they could walk, and lost in two days. Ireland also proved a point many had been making for years – high-quality cricket is not the preserve of a favoured few.

There was a but. The ICC's decision to limit the 2019 World Cup to ten teams meant only two outside the top eight in the rankings could join them. One was West Indies, although – another reminder of the sport's strength in depth – they needed a dodgy lbw to elbow out Scotland. Afghanistan also qualified, so the chance to keep cricket in Irish minds after Malahide was lost. The ICC say they want to grow the game, but have a funny way of showing it.

Later this year, rugby will host its ninth World Cup, in Japan. Cricket's 12th edition will already have taken place, in dear old England, which hosted the first three (and whose one-day team beat everyone last year – except Scotland). Rugby's World Cup will feature 20 teams, including Georgia and Uruguay: it will be a global jamboree, not a closed shop. The ICC suggested they were open to expansion by granting Twenty20 international status to all 93 Associate Members. Yet their flagship event is more exclusionist than ever.

The mother of farewells

Alastair Cook's final Test was widely recognised as the best of finales. But was it? Step forward Enid Bakewell. Against West Indies at Edgbaston in 1979, she began by scoring 68, before taking three cheap wickets to help England to a narrow lead. Then she carried her bat for 112 out of a total of 164, or 68%. Almost unnoticed, she had beaten Test cricket's oldest record: Charles Bannerman's 165 out of Australia's 245 (or 67%) in the very first Test, at Melbourne in March 1877. Finally, she skittled West Indies with a career-best seven-for, completing match figures of ten for 75. Now that's how to say goodbye.

Spot the difference

At the end of India's Twenty20 win at Old Trafford in early July, many of their supporters stayed behind to watch the England footballers' World Cup shoot-out against Colombia on the giant screens. When Eric Dier scored the winning penalty, they jumped around with as much gusto as the England fans who had been shouting for Eoin Morgan's team. The fact they had cheered for India at cricket and for England at football confirmed that the question of national identity is complex. But at a time when some seem hell-bent on division, it was a glimpse of unity.

Look back in wonder

Did you know that the man who drew the record crowd at the MCG was American evangelist Billy Graham? Or that the two-minute silence on Remembrance Day was inspired by a Test cricketer? Were you aware of the leg-spinner who took part in what he called "the biggest anticlimax in athletics history" – the race after Roger Bannister broke the four-minute mile? That a county wicketkeeper escorted "Duckface" up the aisle in *Four Weddings and a Funeral*? Or that the last surviving England player from Jim Laker's 1956 Old Trafford Test was told of his call-up by a member of the Hastings constabulary? The obituaries in this year's Almanack contain as many gems as ever, throwing up reasons to grin, as well as to grieve.

ALASTAIR COOK RETIRES

Oh, it's such a perfect end…

SCYLD BERRY

Parting is such sweet sorrow, according to the Bard in *Romeo and Juliet*. In professional cricket, however, it is almost invariably plain sorrow: bitterness at the thought of what might have been, resentment at what was not, and even rage against the dying of the light. So Alastair Cook's farewell to the international game, in being the sweetest there could be, defied all precedent.

Nobody at Joe Root's press conference at The Oval, the day before the Fifth Test against India, had really believed him when he said a Cook century might be "written in the stars". But most cricketers' final Tests, when announced in advance, have been a disappointment. The nervous energy required to reach peak performance has drained away; even 99% is not enough in Test cricket.

Farewells at The Oval, in particular, have been more sorrow than joy. England's oldest Test ground had never seen a departure, by any cricketer from any country, to match the grandeur of the setting: no one has made a major contribution while seeing his side to victory in both match and series.

Jack Hobbs had started the tradition in 1930, on his home ground, when the Australians – led by Bill Woodfull – gave him three cheers as he walked out to bat, and Hobbs had replied: "Thank you very much, you chaps." He did not, however, shake Woodfull's hand: modest Jack thought it would be showing off to the crowd, and he lived to regret it.

The protocol was thus in place for Don Bradman's last Test, 18 years later. The sole survivor of Hobbs's last, Bradman knew the form, as did Norman Yardley, who led England in giving him three cheers – and two balls at the wicket. Hobbs scored 47 and nine, Bradman nought. In more recent Oval farewells, Viv Richards was carried off the field in 1991 by his players, his proud record of never captaining West Indies in a losing Test series intact – but England had won the game. Curtly Ambrose was warmly saluted in 2000, though West Indies were already steep in decline. The following summer, Michael Atherton scored 13 and nine, before being Warned and McGrathed one final time. Andrew Flintoff ran out Ricky Ponting with his famous final fling in 2009, but apart from that it was only a few runs and one wicket.

Cook had been struggling too. He had gone into a downward spiral, apart from his marathon double-centuries at Edgbaston against West Indies the previous summer and at Melbourne the previous winter. The two-Test series in New Zealand early in 2018 had not been environmentally friendly: 23 runs, one for every 1,000 miles travelled. Technically, Cook looked all right, better than ever at times, because his warm-up routines now began with underarm throws from ten yards, which got his front foot moving, and he drove through mid-off as never before. But after an hour or two he would play a big shot and get out, as if he had lost concentration, one of his greatest virtues.

Anthony Devlin, PA Photos

Quitting at the top: Alastair Cook acknowledges The Oval after being dismissed for 147.

Less than a week after The Oval, I chaired a Q&A session with Moeen Ali, who had been promoted to No. 3 and shared a long stand with Cook that wore India down on the first day. "The thing was, he didn't want to make nought in either innings," said Ali. No, you would not want to go the same way as Bradman. Then he illuminated Cook's struggles since Root had taken over, the difference in styles, and the tension – not personal but strategic. "The difference between the two captains is: Rooty is all about 'Let's go out there and put pressure on them,' not carefree or anything, but it's all about scoring runs. Cooky was all about earning the right: fight for runs, grind them down, build partnerships and get the bowlers tired – almost the opposite."

Hence, perhaps, Cook's drive in the Fourth Test at Southampton, where he had done an hour and a half's hard work. Had he still been captain, he would have soldiered on, nudging off his hip and cutting anything short – although those days had almost vanished, as bowlers had wised up, aiming full, often from round the wicket. But, in loyalty to the new team directive, he threw his bat and was gone. Cook's mentor, Graham Gooch, had in his last year of Test cricket batted as well as ever to reach 20 or 30, but could not carry on. Why expect anything different from his pupil? His scores against India before the Fifth Test had been 13, 0, 21, 29, 17, 17 and 12.

But in the first innings at The Oval, Cook reached 71, very acceptable given how much India's pace bowlers had hooped the new and old balls around all series: it was the first fifty by an opening batsman on either side. Point made: he could still do it, and his reflexes were still working, which was reinforced by his catching, safer than any of his team-mates in the cordon. Second slips came and went, from Dawid Malan to Jos Buttler and back to Root, all shelling half the chances that came their way.

In the final innings of his 161st Test, Cook again went to the well, and on this occasion it was not dry. But even though he reached 46 by the close on the third evening, surely the stars were not aligned? Ishant Sharma, who had tormented him as much as anyone in Test cricket, and dismissed him three times in the series alone, damaged his left ankle in the first over next morning. India were left with two quicks and a spinner. The pitch flattened out, and batting became easier than at any time in the summer. Cook played, and middled, all his shots. And no century has ever been made without good fortune: he reached 97 with a jab towards deep point, where a tired Jasprit Bumrah took aim at the non-striker's stumps and missed by such a margin that the ball went for four overthrows. Three minutes of unadulterated applause and appreciation ensued. Then more fine strokes in his 147, such as his cover-drive, if not a six (there were only 11 in his whole Test career).

It is futile to compare Cook with W. G. Grace or Hobbs or Len Hutton. Hobbs, after the First World War, enjoyed the highest-scoring era of Test cricket. Hutton, after the Second, faced another new ball after 55 overs. The pertinent point is that England have had two types of opening batsman. There was the attacker, such as Hobbs, or the pre-war Hutton before he injured his left arm, or Gooch against West Indies when they were world champions. And there was the defender, the accumulator, who did not try to dominate the bowling – most notably Geoffrey Boycott and Cook.

A nice symmetry was observed: Cook made a fifty and a hundred in both his first Test and his last. But, truth be told, his six-hour hundred on debut at Nagpur delayed England's declaration, so that there was no time for a second new ball, and India held on with four wickets left. His 33rd century, by contrast, gave England exactly what they wanted: almost four sessions to bowl India out on a more sporting pitch.

Andrew Strauss called Cook the greatest of all England cricketers, because of the qualities required to play 161 Tests, all bar two in a row. His loyalty towards a former opening partner was admirable. But objectivity will not accept such a judgment. To cite just three players more worthy of the accolade: Grace made cricket what it is today, the first mass spectator sport; Hobbs scored 12 Test centuries against Australia, the acid test through the ages; and Ian Botham regularly overwhelmed them.

What can be said unequivocally was that Cook was a model Test cricketer. His last two years in the England side came at a time when mendacity has never had it so good in public life, whether in the Brexit debate, or in Donald Trump's tweets. Decency, good manners, straightforwardness (honesty is sometimes impossible if you are a Test captain and asked if one of your players is going to be dropped): when politicians and other public figures seemed to have forgotten their worth, Cook preserved these anachronisms.

COOKING BY NUMBERS

Cook against the world

	M	I	NO	Runs	HS	100	50	Avge
v Australia	35	64	2	2,493	244*	5	11	40.20
v Bangladesh	6	11	1	490	173	2	1	49.00
v India	30	54	3	2,431	294	7	9	47.66
v New Zealand	15	27	0	1,047	162	3	4	38.77
v Pakistan	20	36	1	1,719	263	5	8	49.11
v South Africa	19	36	0	1,263	118	2	9	35.08
v Sri Lanka	16	28	4	1,290	133	3	7	53.75
v West Indies	20	35	5	1,739	243	6	8	57.96
	161	291	16	12,472	294	33	57	45.35

Cook opened in all but seven Tests

	M	I	NO	Runs	HS	100	50	Avge
As opener	154	278	14	11,845	294	31	55	44.86
No. 3	7	12	1	578	127	2	2	52.54
No. 7	(1)	1	1	49	49*	0	0	–

Cook batted at No. 7 on one occasion, because of injury.

How he fared in comparison with his opening partners

	M	I	NO	Runs	HS	100	50	Avge
A. N. Cook	154	278	14	11,845	294	31	55	44.86
A. J. Strauss	68	117	4	4,249	169	10	20	37.60
M. D. Stoneman	11	20	1	526	60	0	5	27.68
K. K. Jennings	12	22	0	486	112	1	1	22.09
N. R. D. Compton	9	17	2	479	117	2	1	31.93
A. D. Hales.	11	20	0	479	86	0	4	23.95
J. E. Root	6	11	1	417	180	1	2	41.70
M. A. Carberry	6	12	0	345	60	0	1	28.75
M. P. Vaughan	6	12	0	338	87	0	3	28.16
S. D. Robson	7	11	0	336	127	1	1	30.54
A. Lyth	7	13	0	265	107	1	0	20.38
H. Hameed	3	5	0	160	82	0	1	32.00
I. J. L. Trott	4	8	0	155	64	0	2	19.37
B. M. Duckett.	2	4	0	92	56	0	1	23.00
M. M. Ali	3	5	0	73	35	0	0	14.60
K. P. Pietersen	1	1	0	12	12	0	0	12.00

This excludes the seven Tests at home in 2006 in which Cook did not open, and the second innings against Sri Lanka at Lord's in 2016, when he went in at No. 7.

Performance of all openers in Cook's Tests

	M	I	NO	Runs	HS	100	50	Avge
Cook when opening ...	154	278	14	11,845	294	31	55	44.86
Cook's partner	154	278	8	8,412	180	16	42	31.15
The opposition openers .	154	574	24	19,587	199	43	93	35.61
The other three openers .	154	852	32	27,999	199	59	135	34.14

Excludes matches in which Cook did not open, but the opposing openers are included for the matches in which Cook did not open in the second innings.

Most runs by openers in Tests

	M	I	NO	Runs	HS	100	50	Avge
A. N. Cook (E)	**154**	**278**	**14**	**11,845**	**294**	**31**	**55**	**44.86**
S. M. Gavaskar (I)	119	203	12	9,607	221	33	42	50.29
G. C. Smith (SA/World)	114	196	12	9,030	277	27	36	49.07
M. L. Hayden (A)......	103	184	14	8,625	380	30	29	50.73
V. Sehwag (I/World) ...	99	170	6	8,207	319	22	30	50.04
G. Boycott (E)	107	191	23	8,091	246*	22	42	48.16
G. A. Gooch (E).......	100	184	6	7,811	333	18	41	43.88
M. A. Taylor (A)	104	186	13	7,525	334*	19	40	43.49
C. G. Greenidge (WI)...	107	182	16	7,488	226	19	34	45.10
M. A. Atherton (E).....	108	197	6	7,476	185*	16	45	39.14
D. L. Haynes (WI).....	116	201	25	7,472	184	18	39	42.45
C. H. Gayle (WI)	99	173	10	7,028	333	15	36	43.11
A. J. Strauss (E).......	97	171	6	6,741	169	20	27	40.85
L. Hutton (E)	76	131	12	6,721	364	19	31	56.47

Innings in which the player did not open are excluded.

Highest scores in final Test innings

258	S. M. Nurse..........	West Indies v New Zealand at Christchurch	1968-69
206	P. A. de Silva	Sri Lanka v Bangladesh at Colombo (PSO)......	2002
201*	J. N. Gillespie	Australia v Bangladesh at Chittagong	2005-06
187	M. Leyland	England v Australia at The Oval	1938
182	G. S. Chappell........	Australia v Pakistan at Sydney................	1983-84
154	V. M. Merchant......	India v England at Delhi	1951-52
147	**A. N. Cook**	**England v India at The Oval**................	**2018**
146	R. A. Duff	Australia v England at The Oval	1905

The most runs in a player's last Test is 375, by A. Sandham (325 and 50) for England v West Indies at Kingston in 1929-30. Cook (71 and 147) lies sixth on that list.

Captain Cook

	M	I	NO	Runs	HS	100	50	Avge
Cook as captain	59	111	7	4,844	263	12	24	46.57
Cook in the ranks	102	180	9	7,628	294	21	33	44.60

Year by year

	M	I	NO	Runs	HS	100	50	Avge
2006	13	24	2	1,013	127	4	3	46.04
2007	11	21	0	923	118	3	5	43.95
2008	12	21	0	758	76	0	8	36.09
2009	14	24	3	960	160	3	4	45.71
2010	14	24	2	1,287	235*	5	4	58.50
2011	8	11	0	927	294	4	2	84.27
2012	15	29	3	1,249	190	4	3	48.03
2013	14	27	0	916	130	2	6	33.92
2014	8	13	1	390	95	0	3	32.50
2015	14	26	1	1,364	263	3	8	54.56
2016	17	33	3	1,270	130	2	7	42.33
2017	11	20	1	899	244*	2	2	47.31
2018	10	18	0	516	147	1	2	28.66

John Walton, PA Photos

A piece of the action: the Oval crowd record Alastair Cook striding out for his last Test innings.

He did it without confrontation. Like Strauss, whom he had long observed, Cook would not get into an argument. He preferred to win a long-term battle rather than a short-term row. He read the newspapers, taking note and using the criticisms as motivation to prove people wrong, by which he meant commentators and journalists. In the end he won, most handsomely, by going out on his own terms, on the highest of highs.

As a captain, too, Cook could not have been more decent, towards his own men or opponents or umpires. I never saw him confront anyone on the field. If a bowler was ineffectual, he put him out to grass, as if back on his farm. If an opponent tried sledging, he walked away, head held high. If an umpire made an unpalatable decision against England's bowlers, Cook showed him respect in their conversation before resuming the game. He suffered the slings and arrows in defeat, and never gloated when England won.

He inherited the safe style of Strauss, focusing on man-management and the conservation of runs as the chief strategy, without much interest in tactics, though in the second half of his reign he was ready to try funkier fields. His forte as captain? Defending a target with outward calm, most notably against Australia at Trent Bridge in 2013, when he drew the best out of James Anderson, and led England home by 14 runs.

Cook's values – old-fashioned duty and service first, never mind the ego – were exemplified until the end. When he reached his hundred, he did not milk the applause: eventually he tried to signal to the crowd that the match should carry on. When he got out, top-edging his cut at an off-break, he walked off with a couple of turnarounds to acknowledge the spectators – not too much, not too little. And when Anderson sought his 564th Test wicket on the last day, to go past Glenn McGrath's record for the most by a pace bowler, Cook subsumed his desire to be the man who took the catch. They had, after all, taken more Test wickets than any other English pair of fielder and bowler.

WHAT WISDEN SAID ABOUT COOK

Alastair Cook, aged 14, won a place in the [Bedford] side after scoring an undefeated 102 against the school; MCC had been a player short. *Wisden 2000*

Cook's feat of scoring five hundreds in consecutive innings for Bedford School (and seven in the season) hinted at impressive powers of concentration. *Wisden 2003*

It was Cook, another teenager, who made the biggest impression. A tall, left-handed batsman, he was thrust into opening for the last three Championship games – and responded with a fifty in each. *Wisden 2004, from the Essex review*

The day after being named Young Player of the Year by the Cricket Writers' Club, Cook hit an inspirational double-century, as Essex ran up 502 runs to increase Australia's bowling worries before the showdown at The Oval. *Wisden 2006*

Despite a long journey from the Caribbean and a bout of illness on arrival, Cook gave an extraordinary display of tenacity in Nagpur, scoring 60 and an unbeaten 104; he was the youngest player to score a century for England since 1939. *Wisden 2007 on Cook's Test debut*

Cook, with a mature ability to focus on the next ball rather than dwell on the last, became the first England player since Botham to score a third hundred in his first seven Tests. *Wisden 2007 on the Second Test against Pakistan at Old Trafford*

Meanwhile, Cook was achieving something that had eluded every other Englishman throughout the series: a hundred. He batted six hours, hit some breathtaking drives off the back foot, and provided the only solace for a weary touring team. This was Cook's seventh Test century, reached three days before his 23rd birthday. Only three other players have scored so many centuries at such a tender age: Sir Donald Bradman, Javed Miandad and Sachin Tendulkar. Which suggests that Cook might become quite a good player. *Wisden 2008, after Cook makes 118 in the Third Test against Sri Lanka at Galle*

Instead of looking back at his bat as the bowler ran in, to start a complicated series of trigger movements, he watched the ball and hit it. *Wisden 2011, on his career-salvaging century against Pakistan at The Oval*

… Cook, digging in once again, to play the innings that was both to seal the series and to establish him as an Ashes phenomenon. *Wisden 2011, after Cook finishes the 2010-11 Ashes with 766 runs*

This was accumulation rather than artistry, but Cook wore the weight of his numbers lightly. *Wisden 2012, after Cook's career-best 294 against India at Edgbaston*

Cook's air of calm, whether in adversity or triumph, his pragmatic approach to coaxing the best out of the eclectic mix of characters under him, and his desire to succeed meant the post-Strauss transition took place more smoothly than anyone could have dreamed. *Wisden 2013, after Cook leads England to victory in India*

Even Cook, a famous non-sweater, had some beads on his forehead when he removed his helmet. But not losing as much fluid as other players allowed him to bat for more than two days in the ferocious heat without cramping. *Wisden 2016, after Cook makes 263 in 836 minutes in the First Test against Pakistan at Abu Dhabi*

After 83 runs in his first six innings of the series, Cook went into the Boxing Day Test – the day after his 33rd birthday – fending off questions about his future. He ended it five days later after fending off everything the Australians could hurl at him. *Wisden 2018, after Cook carries his bat for 244 at Melbourne*

Popperfoto, Getty Images

Exit The Master: Jack Hobbs is saluted by the Australians in his final Test, The Oval, August 1930.

Though they were the best of team-mates, Cook said it was the right outcome when Anderson flattened the middle stump of Mohammed Shami, because that image would live longer in the memory.

Cook's farewell was superlative – to match his feat of being England's highest Test run-scorer, leading century-maker, longest-serving captain, and most prolific slip catcher – because it was the most joyous farewell of any English cricketer. The one to beat was another Essex and England captain, not his batting mentor, Gooch, but his mentor on media matters, Nasser Hussain. After scoring an unbeaten 103 at Lord's in 2004 against New Zealand, Hussain had run off the field and finalised his decision to retire, with the applause still in his ears – and before the selectors could drop him. A batsman had to go for the next Test, because Strauss on debut had made himself undroppable, and Hussain, as the oldest, was the most vulnerable. So he got his retirement in first.

But Cook retired in his own time, at the right time. Was it all self-indulgent? No. If the series had stood at 2–2 after Southampton, he would not have rocked the boat by announcing the Oval Test would be his last: that would have distracted the team from their task of beating the world's No. 1 side. Instead, at 3–1, it was only right for once that the individual should be as big as the team.

It has to be added that Cook's handsomeness – of face and physique, that is, not his batting – added to the poignancy that many onlookers felt as he climbed the pavilion steps for the final time. Not every eye at The Oval was dry.

Scyld Berry is the cricket correspondent of The Daily Telegraph.

THE 2014 PESHAWAR SCHOOL TERRORIST ATTACK

How cricket helped me live again

WALEED KHAN

It is more than four years since seven terrorists attacked my school in Peshawar, in the north-west of Pakistan. They killed 149 people, mostly students. Many of my best friends died. I thought I was going to die too. I was 12 years old.

Of all the memories that remain, one sticks out. I was lying near the school library, bleeding and exhausted after being shot eight times. I looked up and saw some birds fly from a tree. I remember thinking how lucky they were. In that moment, I so wanted to be a bird.

But I also knew I had to survive. My worry was that if I lost consciousness, whoever came to rescue the survivors would think I was dead, and ignore me. So I punched the bullet wound on my leg, again and again. Only the pain would stop me drifting off and being placed with the other corpses.

Things didn't go to plan. I had taken six bullets to my face, swallowed my teeth and lost so much blood that no one realised I was still breathing. And I was so weak that I was unable to show I was alive. But I was conscious of everything around me, and determined not to die. By taking deep breaths, I created bubbles of blood around my mouth. Those bubbles saved my life: a nurse noticed them, and I was taken to hospital, where I stayed in a coma for eight days. On the sixth, the doctors told my family they would turn off the ventilator if I didn't wake up in the next 48 hours. Just in time, I woke up.

Was it a miracle? I didn't believe in miracles, but I now think they are more likely to happen if you believe in yourself. And I've always had self-belief.

My school was affiliated to the army, who paid for surgery in the UK. Six months later, after an operation at the Queen Elizabeth Hospital in Birmingham, I turned up at the Forward Drive Cricket Academy, five minutes from Edgbaston. I was on crutches, and my doctors had told me to take it easy. I could hardly blame them: my jaw had been rebuilt using bone from my left shin, so any physical activity, let alone landing on my left foot to bowl, was not recommended. To everyone's astonishment, I insisted on having a bowl. I did my best to take a run-up on my crutches, and sent down an over. There was no batsman, but I didn't care. I had done something I was told I would never do again: I had played cricket.

In the months that followed, cricket would help me recover from that terrible day. It had been my passion for as long as I could remember. I used to drive my mum crazy as a small boy, breaking things in the living room as I practised my favourite shot, the cover-drive. Four days before the terrorists came, I had captained our school – the Army Public School – to victory in a tournament. We were all dancing and shouting. We were happy. In many ways, cricket was my life. Now it became my lifeline.

Even holding a bat was a form of therapy. I kept one in my bedroom at my new home in Selly Oak, Birmingham and whenever I felt depressed I would

Vanley Burke

Waleed Khan.

pick it up and practise my strokes. I also watched as much as I could on the telly. But the moments cricket helped me most came when I was on the field.

Because I am so passionate about the game, I can't think of anything else when I'm batting or bowling. Cricket is the thing I do to forget what happened. Sometimes my dad, Gulzar, who travelled with me to the UK, comes along to matches for my school (the University of Birmingham School) or my club (Weoley Hill) and brings drink, food and my medicines. I get so immersed in the match that I tell him I don't have time to eat or drink, but he insists. Asian fathers have a reputation for being strict, but my dad has become my best friend. He comforts me when I'm feeling low, and supports me in everything I do. He also helps me when I miss my mum, Rabina, and sister, Hafsa, who are back in Peshawar.

Cricket didn't just help me forget. It made my recovery easier. The attack happened not long before the 2015 World Cup, and news of my situation reached the Pakistan team. One day in hospital, I was visited by some of the players, including Misbah-ul-Haq and Younis Khan, who brought me a shirt signed by New Zealand captain Kane Williamson. It was so strange. These guys were my heroes, and now they were telling me I was *their* hero.

I was also visited twice by Shahid Afridi, my favourite player because of his aggressive batting – I've tried to copy him, which means I don't play many defensive shots. I should also confess that the best cover-drive in the world belongs to Virat Kohli. He is Indian, and I am Pakistani – but I can't let the rivalry between our two countries get in the way of the truth.

And that is another thing I love about cricket. Unlike the terrorists, it treats people the same. There is no black or white on the field, no Muslim or Hindu or Christian. We are all the same. Cricket brings us together. I know that, because I was welcomed so warmly by the people in England – especially after they had seen me bowl in the nets at school. I took a wicket first ball, and was immediately made captain of the First XI. My fastest ball has been measured at 82mph, and I recently had trials with Warwickshire.

My injuries still cause me trouble. I take painkillers before every game, and I must still undergo some operations. But the discomfort is worth it. During the attack, I had managed to drag myself 50 or 60 metres out of the auditorium where we had been receiving a lecture about first aid, and where the terrorists killed my friends. A group of terrified students ran past me, and I tried to put my hand on a shoulder for support. But I fell down, and got trampled: my right wrist was broken. When I went for surgery, I was worried I might never play cricket again. It just made me more determined.

The truth was, I was just thankful to be alive. On the day itself, we heard some loud noises, but the teachers said they were nothing to worry about. Then the noises – like thumps – got louder. One of the terrorists was trying to kick down a door. He succeeded. Without saying a word, he started shooting.

I was stunned. Why were these people here? What were they doing? As head boy, I was standing on the stage, and for a moment I couldn't move. About 20 yards away, across the room, I saw another terrorist. He was aiming a gun at my face. He pulled the trigger, and I fell to the ground in agony. As I lay there, I could see my friends, helpless, covered in blood. There was nothing I, or any of us, could do.

After a while, the auditorium fell silent. The terrorists were walking around, looking for survivors. I knew I had to keep quiet, but I was in so much pain that I was crying out. One walked over, and shot me again – five times in the face, once in the hand, once in the leg. I was praying to God. All I wanted was to see my mum one last time. The terrorists finally left to look for more victims. Those who had played dead got up and ran for their lives.

Moments before the gunmen burst in, the army officer giving the lecture taught us the ABC of first aid: airways, breathing, circulation. At the end, he asked us what "A" stood for. Everyone was in a silly mood, and one of my friends put his hand up and said: "Apple".

We all giggled. It would be the last giggle we shared. But cricket has helped me smile again.

Waleed Khan is a member of the British Youth Parliament, and is a motivational speaker. He was talking to Lawrence Booth.

AUSTRALIA'S BALL-TAMPERING FARRAGO

"It beggars belief"

GIDEON HAIGH

On January 8, 2018, Steve Smith's Australian team, wreathed in smiles, gathered on what resembled a corny parade float at the Sydney Cricket Ground to celebrate a 4–0 eclipse of England. Smith held the Waterford crystal, flanked by vice-captain David Warner and wicketkeeper Tim Paine; leaning in from the right was Warner's opening partner, Cameron Bancroft. It is the sort of image that might hang in a cricketer's home, appear on the cover of a souvenir book, or form part of the opening sequence of a sports-panel show.

Yet its future reproduction will be pervaded by pathos. Here was a glory that could hardly have been more fleeting, pride that could scarcely have come before a steeper fall. Eleven weeks later, revealed to have been part of a scheme to doctor a ball with sandpaper, Smith, Warner and Bancroft would be pariahs; Paine, who 18 months earlier had virtually turned his back on the game, would be captain. Most people had by then forgotten the float, a brainstorm of Cricket Australia's marketing department. Yet, in hindsight, its jeering naffness looked like the hubris that invites nemesis to spit in its eye.

The toll nemesis took at CA may be the heaviest of any controversy in Australian cricket's annals. Within nine months, Sandpapergate had, directly

Before the fall: the dramatis personae (and others) in jubilant mood, January 2018.

Cameron Spencer, Getty Images

or indirectly, curtailed the careers of coach Darren Lehmann, chief executive James Sutherland, chairman David Peever, performance chief Pat Howard, integrity officer Iain Roy, and senior directors Bob Every and Mark Taylor. It had lent Australian cricket the look of English cricket in the 1990s – anxious, introspective, joyless, vulnerable. As their home summer opened in November 2018, Australia were ranked fifth in Tests and sixth in one-day internationals, despite an expensive corporate commitment to ruling the world in all formats. Once the envy of everyone, their system looked as dysfunctional and de-moralised as any.

In some eyes, the Australians had been snagged by the sense of exceptionalism cultivated under Taylor, Steve Waugh and Ricky Ponting. Long experience of being top dog, it was argued, and its associations with pushing the boundaries of acceptable aggression, were corrupting. But there was also the simple fact that Australia had turned into rather an ordinary team.

When the ballast of experience provided by Michael Clarke, Brad Haddin, Ryan Harris, Shane Watson and Chris Rogers went overboard in 2015, Australia undertook a remaking for which they seemed to have relatively little patience, aping the structure of XIs past, but without the substance. Taking cues from their coach, players became vigorous proponents of "the Australian way", espoused like a brand, and of "the line", a one-dimensional expression of cricket politesse notable for its flexibility. Smith and Warner were the leading performers; they were also among Australia's most frequent transgressors of the ICC's Code of Conduct.

In 2017, CA engineered a protracted and mainly pointless confrontation with the players' trade union over their next collective bargain. The campaign, which aimed to end the Australian Cricketers' Association's long-standing direct share in revenue, was closely associated with businessman Peever, and Kevin Roberts, Sutherland's No. 2. It soured to the degree that male and female players were locked out for two months. An uneasy summer ensued. Against England, Smith and Warner piled up 1,128 runs; there were record crowds and ratings. But, as much as anything, that spoke of the consolations of the Ashes in time of turmoil. Market research for CA discerned an ongoing weakening in the players' recognisability and likability; long-time broadcast partners, the Nine Network and Network 10, were conservative about cricket's prospects; sponsors were ever less whelmed by their treatment and their returns.

The Australians started their tour of South Africa in late February 2018 full of confidence. In the countries' two preceding series, reverse swing had been a decisive factor, the Australians suspicious of South Africa's efforts to expedite it. This time, Lehmann felt relaxed: "Obviously there's techniques used by both sides to get the ball reversing. That's just the way the game goes. I have no problem with it. Simple." Mitchell Starc duly showed himself a master of the craft at Durban, with a match-winning nine for 109.

Victory, however, was soured by gross behaviour on both sides of the boundary, from the Kingsmead crowds toward the Australians, and from the Australians towards their opponents, with the two arguably related. In his familiar role as the team's provocateur, Warner went about unsettling Quinton de Kock, who appeared to complain to the umpires. Electronic eavesdropping captured the aftermath as the players left the field for tea: an effects mike heard Warner decry de Kock as a "fucken sook"; a CCTV camera in the stairwell leading to the dressing-rooms caught Warner responding angrily to a retort from de Kock which apparently referred to an old incident involving Warner's wife, Candice, and the rugby star Sonny Bill Williams.

At Port Elizabeth, where South Africa squared the series thanks to Kagiso Rabada's own mastery of reverse swing, fans sporting Sonny Bill masks were at first turned away by security, then allowed in by two officers of Cricket South Africa, Clive Eksteen and Altaaf Kazi. Australians seethed again when CSA successfully appealed against a suspension imposed on Rabada for a needless skirmish with Smith. The Australians went to Cape Town feeling frustrated, embattled, and vaguely paranoid – but just because one is paranoid, as they say, doesn't mean one is mistaken. Warner was right to suspect that the local broadcaster SuperSport had singled him out for scrutiny of his preparatory rituals of the ball; he

More conspiracy than cock-up: Cameron Bancroft disposes of the evidence.

Ashley Vlotman, Gallo Images/Getty Images

THE COMEBACK TRAIL: SMITH AND WARNER IN CANADA

Of all the rehab joints in all the towns…

BEN HORNE

Just three months after it was decided Steve Smith and David Warner couldn't share the same flight home from South Africa, they both stayed at the Airport Marriott in Toronto for about a fortnight. It cannot have been straightforward, though it was a first step: in the wake of the ball-tampering scandal that tore Australian cricket to shreds, many wondered if the two prodigies from Sydney, whose lives had intertwined ever since they were teenagers, would ever share a dressing-room again.

Before all that came an unlikely appearance in late June at Yashi Sports, a shop-cum-indoor-cricket facility on the northern edge of Toronto. The sign outside read: "We repair bats". In walked Smith and Warner to one of cricket's unlikelier outposts. Having enrolled for the inaugural Canadian Global T20 League, a tournament not covered by their year-long bans, they took guard inside a tiny warehouse, and began their long journey back from the brink.

The eager guys at Yashi, part of Ontario's large South Asian community, normally spend their summers rolling grips and – as the sign says – repairing bats. But now they found themselves lining up to bowl to two of the best batsmen of the modern era.

While their Australian team-mates prepared to take on England in a Twenty20 game at Edgbaston, Smith and Warner prepared to become the grandstand performers at a ground with no grandstand. The white-flowered weeds flourishing in the outfield of King City's Maple Leaf Cricket Club might have reminded Warner of his humble roots in housing-commission flats in Sydney's east, though not of anything he had witnessed in professional cricket. And while Smith, like so many of Australia's batting greats, had nurtured his skills in the backyard, a ground sharing a fence with an old lady who refused to throw the ball back was perhaps a novel experience.

On the first day of the tournament, Smith carved out a 41-ball 61 for Toronto Nationals to unburden himself of some of the enormous weight he had been carrying on his shoulders since the sky caved in on his career in Cape Town. "It's been quite therapeutic," he said afterwards, though the Nationals would finish bottom of the six-team group.

Batting on a pitch that, since only a couple were used all tournament, got more traffic than the long motorway leading to the ground, Warner took longer to find his groove for Winnipeg Hawks. But after the dark times that had followed Sandpapergate, he too found solace in the middle. "At the end of the day, it was a big thing that happened, and you've got to handle it in your individual way," he said. "This has been good. I'm extremely grateful for cricket and what it's brought me. The game owes me nothing."

Spies inside the Airport Marriott spotted Smith and Warner sharing coffee in a breakfast room filled with cricket superstars and weary travellers. There was nothing particularly close about their interaction, but when you realise just how small the cricket world can be, it pays to say hello.

Ben Horne is chief cricket writer for Sydney's Daily Telegraph.

was wrong to think that merely passing his duties on would fix the problem. His locum was caught in the act.

Smith's attempt to head off the issue in a press conference with Bancroft began badly, grew worse, and ended disastrously: they were open *and* evasive, naive *and* cynical; they were clearly embarrassed, without being obviously penitent. Australians awoke to the news that their team had cheated in a Test match with the approval of a captain who still thought himself the "right person for the job". By the afternoon, those who differed included prime minister Malcolm Turnbull: "How can our team be engaged in cheating like this? It beggars belief."

From time to time, Australian teams have courted unpopularity with their uncompromising competitiveness, but usually there have been some supporters, with clichés about it being "a tough game" and "not tiddlywinks". The public had now drawn their own line: the Australians – and CA – found themselves on its wrong side. In partial atonement, the board stood Smith and Warner down; when play resumed on the fourth day, Paine was in charge, Howard and Roy en route.

Carrying out his interviews in the aftermath of Australia's 322-run defeat, Roy recommended charges against captain, vice-captain and Bancroft; although he spared Lehmann, Howard conveyed to the coach that his position was untenable, and he would have to see out his contract at Brisbane's National Cricket Centre. Institutional and personal sponsors invoked *force majeure* clauses to sever their ties; the IPL found Smith and Warner too hot to hold; theories abounded for the moral turpitude and the public indignation.

When Sutherland arrived in Johannesburg, the scene was set for drastic action: Smith and Warner were banned for 12 months each, Bancroft for nine. Denied their team gear like court-martialled officers stripped of their epaulettes, the three returned to Australia, where they faced media inquisitors in sorrow and contrition. Having foreshadowed "an independent review into the conduct and culture of our Australian men's team", chairman Peever announced "a review of the wider context of the event", in case "wider cultural, organisational and/or governance issues needed to be addressed". In the same breath, however, he said he was planning to stay a further three-year term, while Sutherland had the board's "full support".

This curious pre-emption effectively put CA's future on a collision course with their past. While Simon Longstaff of the Ethics Centre began his investigation, the game went through the motions of incremental advance. A broadcast rights deal with the Seven Network and the pay television venture Foxtel worth $A1.18bn was a boost for morale. Paine was confirmed as captain, Justin Langer anointed coach. In a one-day series in England, a T20 engagement in Zimbabwe and a Test series against Pakistan in the Gulf, there were more snakes than ladders, but at least they were largely out of sight.

Behind the scenes at Jolimont, alliances were shifting. On May 4, without any public explanation or even announcement, CA's senior-most director Bob Every, a spiky septuagenarian, stepped down, critical in his leaked resignation letter of Peever's "substandard" chairmanship; four months elapsed before replacement Lachlan Henderson was appointed. On June 5, Sutherland

Suits you, sir: Kevin Roberts, Cricket Australia's new CEO, is congratulated by his predecessor, James Sutherland. Chairman David Peever oversees the photo op.

announced his own resignation, with a notice period of up to a year; four months, including a global search with headhunters Egon Zehnder, were necessary to identify Roberts, his chief operating officer, as his successor, despite his being in the next-door office. Roy accepted a redundancy package; reasons were not given. Howard said he would not seek a further extension of his controversial role, due to end the following year. His decision was said by a spokesman to be "in no way connected to the reviews".

So what was? Apparently CA's annual meeting, which fell on October 25, in a baffling order. Twenty minutes after the state associations had unanimously re-elected Peever, they were offered the Ethics Centre's review to read – heavily redacted, but in an overall sense unsparing: "CA is perceived to say one thing and do another. The most common description of CA is as 'arrogant and controlling'. The core complaint is that the organisation does not respect anyone other than its own."

The Centre concluded that the attitude instilled – "winning is the only thing that matters" – had "led players and support staff to 'redefine' certain forms of cheating as merely 'playing hard to win'". Newlands was therefore "not an aberration", but "an extreme example of a latent tendency growing out of the prevailing culture of men's cricket in Australia", and the result of the grafting on to CA of "a corporate model designed exclusively to generate a profit for the sport's 'shareholders'".

When Peever made the review public three days after his re-election, he struggled to explain how the kind of cultural change the Ethics Centre seemed to be mandating could be achieved without a significant change in personnel –

and also why the review, substantially complete for many weeks save for the redactions, had not been available to the state associations in order that they could vote in an informed fashion. A maladroit television interview probably sealed Peever's fate, inciting a no-confidence push from Cricket NSW's chairman John Knox – a close friend of Sutherland.

"It is the unfortunate lot of the leader that he or she may sometimes be called upon to sacrifice themselves for the greater good," the Ethics Centre had noted. On November 1, Peever took the hint, followed the next week by Taylor, wearied by the turn of events. Victorian Earl Eddings, a businessman, became acting-chairman.

As the Australian team took tentative steps into the future, CA took dramatic strides into theirs. Roberts placed his stamp on the board by not only hurrying Howard out of the door, but axing commercial chief Ben Amarfio. Leafing through CA's 2017-18 annual report, one would hardly have known that the Ashes had been won: Smith's name was mentioned once in terms of "events in South Africa", Warner's and Bancroft's not at all. And it was now the photographs of the board and executive that were inscribed with pathos: just ten days after the report's publication, five of the 19 faces depicted were gone.

Gideon Haigh is the author of Crossing the Line: How Australian cricket lost its way.

THE NETTA RHEINBERG DIARIES

History girls

RAF NICHOLSON

"The menu provided for the women's cricket match at the Sydney Cricket Ground yesterday was the same as the one usually served to men Test players, with one exception. There was no beer." So said Australia's *Daily Telegraph* on December 5, 1948.

The match in question was an England XI against New South Wales, during the first post-war women's tour. England won by five wickets, though the paper provided no details. Instead, it explained that lunch consisted of "oysters, turkey and ham salad, fruit salad and cream" – not quite the goji berry and quinoa requested by Alastair Cook's team 65 years later. There were other pressing matters: "The English players did not worry about make-up when they came off the field. Their manageress (Miss Netta Rheinberg) said they all have English complexions, and she has never seen them use cosmetics while playing."

Rheinberg was unimpressed. "I found a simply awful article," she wrote in her diary. "I recognised in it about four remarks I'd actually made to the reporter, and the rest was pure fabrication!" Later on the tour, she said on New Zealand radio that she and another player were "immediately convulsed by being asked whether we bowl underarm! When we say no, [the interviewer] says she thought overarm bowling deformed women's shoulders!"

Even so, the tour – five months long, with 30 matches, including four Tests, all on famous grounds – kept making history. During the Sydney Test, the players were permitted to change in the men's dressing-rooms for the first time. When England captain Molly Hide, the premier batsman of the day, made a century, her photo was hung at the ground – the first woman to be honoured in such a way. And they were the first women allowed into the members' stand at the Gabba.

Public interest could scarcely have been higher. In November 2017, the women's Ashes Test at the North Sydney Oval produced an aggregate crowd of 12,600, and was proclaimed as a high point for the women's game. But the crowd at Adelaide in January 1949 totalled 17,025 across three days – still the largest for a women's Test in Australia. The match with the beer-free menu was attended by 5,000. Rheinberg records that some male spectators had travelled over 100 miles for England's practice game at Ballarat in February. "It's been the experience of a lifetime," she later wrote.

That was one of the last entries in a surprisingly candid tour diary, written by a woman whose force of personality dominated English women's cricket after the war. Of the 17 tourists, only Cecilia Robinson is still alive. On being reminded of Rheinberg in 2014, she smiled wryly: "She was a great character." Cecilia's own diary of the trip details a broken team curfew – 10pm – by her room-mate, Aline Brown: "After dinner about nine of us go aboard *Harpalia*,

S&G/PA Photos

Cameo appearance: Netta Rheinberg, the secretary of the Women's Cricket Association who answered the call to play a Test, in 1948-49.

which is due to sail for England tomorrow. Given drinks and eats by crew, including ice cream, champagne, cherry brandy, beer etc. Get back at 10.45, but Aline stays out with chief steward, causes stir, and Netta and Molly furious, have to wait up and tell her to go into them when she returns… Molly, Netta and I give up waiting at 12, but I'm still awake when Aline comes in at 12.35." Aline's fate went unrecorded.

Rheinberg was born in 1911 in Brondesbury, north London, the daughter of Julius Rheinberg, a wealthy export merchant. She attended South Hampstead High School, and went to secretarial college. She then worked for the family business, where she was at the time of the 1948-49 tour. She learned her cricket at school, and represented her local club, Gunnersbury, and Middlesex. Primarily a batsman, she was never a great one: her main contributions were as an administrator and writer. She served as secretary of the Women's Cricket Association between 1948 and 1958, edited *Women's Cricket* magazine between 1950 and 1967, later wrote a regular column for *The Cricketer* and for more than 30 years covered the women's game for *Wisden*. She is thought to be the only Jewish woman to have played in the Ashes, and was later awarded an MBE.

Never intended for publication, Rheinberg's diaries were donated to the WCA archive on her death in 2006. I discovered them five years later, in an outbuilding in a remote corner of Lancashire, more usually home to cows, where the farmer husband of ex-England all-rounder Carole Cornthwaite (née Hodges) had agreed to store them. The Lord's library acquired the archive in 2018. It seems a fitting home: in 1999, Rheinberg was among the first ten women given MCC membership.

The tour was quite an undertaking for the women's game. In 1945, the WCA had reported that there were only 18 functioning women's clubs left in England, down from 105 in 1939. The war had also put paid to two attempts to follow up the first women's tour, in 1934-35: plans for a repeat in 1939-40 were cancelled, and 1947-48 was ruled out because it was apparently impossible to get accommodation on any ship to Australia amid the chaos of demobilisation, though Wally Hammond's side had managed perfectly well a year earlier. One anonymous letter in *Women's Cricket* in September 1948 reflected a certain attitude: "Women should occupy themselves in doing things for which they are fitted, and avoid trying to act and dress as men do. It is a most ridiculous thing for females to waste their time in going overseas to play at cricket."

Then there was the money. England's players had to raise £200 each (about £7,000 today) for their boat passage, plus a minimum £50 spending money. A tour fund was established, and women's clubs spent two years holding jumble sales, dances, whist drives and raffles. MCC contributed £250.

The 16-strong squad, plus Rheinberg, consisted of seven teachers, three army officers, two civil servants, an agricultural worker (Hide), a personnel officer, a secretary, an ambulance driver and a student. Everyone was single, though Brown – sister of Freddie, who would captain England for the first time in July 1949 – married three months after her return, and spent some of her honeymoon playing cricket at the WCA's Cricket Week at Colwall. Rheinberg never married. She once recalled her mother telling her: "You'll never meet nice men if you play cricket." Rheinberg said: "She was quite right in a way. I won't say I didn't meet nice men – but I didn't marry."

The team set sail on October 14 on the passenger ship RMS *Orion*. A fortnight into an eventful four-week journey, Rheinberg wrote: "So many passengers know us now, and are coming to watch our various matches, that I have asked the purser to pin one of our itineraries up on the official notice board." The team exercised most days, and played deck cricket against the ship's officers.

Rationing was still in force in England, but there was plenty of food on board. "One can get as much slab chocolate as one likes at the shop, and sweets of all sorts," wrote Rheinberg. "It's really fantastic to be transported into the pre-war era in a matter of a few hours or so." Team-mate Grace Morgan wrote that Rheinberg celebrated her birthday on the voyage with a gin sling: "We all had drinks of different kinds, there were cigarettes, and Molly and Netta had a cigar each. Apparently they are both rather partial to them!" By April 1949, on the return voyage, Rheinberg conceded there had been some overindulgence: "We have nearly all gained a stone in weight."

It was also an opportunity for Rheinberg, an ardent imperialist, to encounter remote corners of the crumbling British Empire. En route to Australia, the boat docked at Colombo, Ceylon for a practice match. They were taken sightseeing, enjoyed lunch with the president and honorary secretary of the Ceylon cricket board, and played in front of 7,000 spectators against a team made up of six European women and five Ceylonese, including a 15-year-old schoolgirl. Hide scored a century, seamer Megan Lowe took a hat-trick, and England won by 117 runs.

The team had already disembarked at Port Said in Egypt, at the northern end of the Suez Canal, where Rheinberg prepared to conceal her Jewish background. "We were told to have our religion ready," she wrote. "In view of circumstances and the country being at war with the Jews, I was ready to say 'C of E', but was not asked."

After docking at Fremantle on November 9, the players were hurried to the town hall to meet the mayor. And so it began: weeks of being whisked from one function to another, a whirlwind of social events – from visiting a koala sanctuary via polo matches to a tour of a migrant camp – with cricket squeezed in. Rheinberg reckoned she gave 84 speeches, took part in 50 radio broadcasts and signed over 1,000 autographs.

Lindsay Hassett pranced around in Rheinberg's hat of pale blue feathers, then autographed it

Something of a snob, she complained bitterly in her diary about the accommodation provided by the Australian Women's Cricket Council – hotels during the Tests, cricketers' homes in between. She described their hotel at Melbourne as "a hole", because "we have to use the same knives for toast and marmalade as for bacon and eggs". She also grumbled when two of her players were billeted in the house of a dustman.

For the most part, though, England were treated as VIPs, meeting both the Australian and New Zealand prime ministers; Rheinberg noted that high commissioners "seem to be two a penny". They also mingled with some of Australia's leading men cricketers, and were introduced to the Victorian and South Australian sides in the Melbourne dressing-rooms, where Lindsay Hassett apparently pranced around in Rheinberg's hat of pale blue feathers before autographing it. And they had lunch with the Australian Test batsman Sid Barnes in Sydney. Rheinberg was not complimentary: "He is very unpopular over here – he is an eccentric and very conceited." The greatest honour came at the MCG on New Year's Day. "At lunch the great thrill occurred," she wrote. "Don Bradman attended. He had just been knighted and it was a great occasion. He sat next to Molly, who was thrilled."

Rheinberg had an inflated sense of her own importance, and everyone appeared to shore up her feelings of English superiority. "Most people here seem to have some link with England and are very loyal, and love hearing about the Mother Country," she wrote. "We constantly get the almost sob-stuff attitude of all we went through in the war and how magnificent we'd been – and they lay it on with gusto."

Everyone, that is, bar the Australian and New Zealand teams. Meeting with Dot Mummery, the secretary of the AWCC, Rheinberg wrote that she had "heard all the latest intrigue, which is rife here", and described Mummery as "a snake in the grass". The New Zealanders also incurred disapproval: "I don't

Charm offensive: the England women's team meet Peter Fraser, New Zealand's prime minister.
Molly Hide is centre left; Netta Rheinberg nearest the camera on the right.

care either for the New Zealand captain, Mrs Lamason, or the chairman of New
Zealand, Mrs Symonds. I wouldn't trust either of them round the next corner."

These tensions were reflected on the field. Rheinberg, like many at the top
of England women's cricket back then, was opposed to competitive sport,
preferring the old idea that it mattered not who won or lost, but how you
played the game. Against Western Australia, Hide refused to enforce the
follow-on, for fear of making things too one-sided. "The team has shown the
good English spirit of not being all out for a win," wrote Rheinberg.

The WCA's rules stated that "no member of any affiliated County
Association or Club shall institute or take place in any cricket challenge cup or
prize competition". But the Australians had different ideas. Eighteen months
after the tour, the WCA wrote to the AWCC – one of their member bodies –
objecting to a decision to allow the presentation of trophies to individual
players, which was not "in accordance with our principles". The Australians
appear to have ignored them.

Perhaps such moralising comforted England, who had suffered a shock
on the field. In 1934-35, they had won two of the three Tests with ease; in
1948-49, it was a different story. Australia romped home in the First Test at
Adelaide by 186 runs, thanks to a century and nine wickets from Betty Wilson.
In the Second at the MCG, Australia made 265 batting first; England collapsed
to 118, but held on for a draw. Hide hit a sparkling century in the drawn Third
Test at Sydney, watched by an admiring Neville Cardus, whom Rheinberg
thought "a most amusing raconteur". In *World Sports* magazine, Cardus wrote:
"It is extremely difficult to distinguish Molly Hide from a bats*man* of the finest

county class. She delightfully reminds me of Denis Compton." Australia won the series, but England did salvage some pride in New Zealand, winning a one-off Test at Eden Park by 185 runs. But, then as now, it was results against Australia that carried most weight.

Rheinberg put on a brave face, writing after Adelaide: "I am delighted to see such an important loss taken in such sporting and good spirit." Two days before Sydney, she was again sanguine. "We have tried our best here to instil into the Aussies the advantage of playing cricket merely for the love of the game, as it is done in England, and not for points altogether, as is the case throughout Australia. This competitive spirit leads to jealousy and rivalries and personal animosities which are unknown in England."

On another matter, she was less relaxed. Though her official designation was player–manager, no one – least of all herself – expected her to take the field. But shortly before the Adelaide Test, Joan Wilkinson developed ulcers on her eye. Rheinberg was in. Morgan documented the Australian reaction: "When Dot Mummery heard who was substitute, her face was a picture, and she said: 'What? Not in a Test!'" Rheinberg made a pair – stumped in the first innings, bowled first ball by Wilson in the second. "I use every swear word imaginable beneath my breath and feel utterly disgusted," she wrote.

The team left New Zealand for England on April 12, arriving home a month later. Rheinberg's last duty was a speech to the other passengers the day before disembarking. "I thanked them for their tolerance in putting up with 17 boisterous women." Just a few days later she was back at her desk, typing up letters and answering phone calls as meticulously as she had recorded life in her tour diary. She never played for England again.

Raf Nicholson is a women's cricket writer and historian, currently working on a history of the women's game in Britain. She is editor of the women's cricket website www.crickether.com

CRICKET'S WINDRUSH GENERATION

The ship that sailed

ROBERT WINDER

The unjust treatment of the *Windrush* generation was one of the stories of 2018. And if the term itself was loose, most people knew it referred to the Caribbean migrants who came to Britain in the 1950s and '60s, in the wake of the original *Windrush* pioneers of 1948. They had worked, married, brought up families and grown old in the so-called mother country. Now they found themselves on the wrong end of a hostile atmosphere whipped up by panicky modern politics. Some had actually been deported back to the homes they had left behind.

It was a clear scandal. The early travellers encountered racism at every turn, whether they were looking for a house, a job, a drink or just a chat. For that cold tone to be echoed now, in official government policy, was a shock.

This is not the place to debate whether the episode was an assault on human liberty or merely a bureaucratic bungle (it has been said that one should not ascribe to malevolence what can be put down to stupidity). According to the historian and documentary maker David Olusoga, it was both. It was, he says, an "unexploded bomb" left by clumsy legislative initiatives in the 1960s and '70s; but it was also shaped by lingering racial animosity. "Britain in those years accepted thousands of displaced people," said Olusoga, "but panicked at the thought of migrants from the West Indies."

Mike Phillips, who with his brother Trevor wrote *Windrush: The Irresistible Rise of Multi-Racial Britain*, agreed it was a dismaying shock, but believed the offspring of the *Windrush* generation were now too integrated to feel badly threatened. "When they go to the Caribbean, they stand out as obviously British," he said. "They saw it as wrong, obviously – but not enough to make them fear for their grandparents."

This may not have been a cricketing matter, but it did bring to mind an absence in the English game: the loss of its rich West Indian thread. It was almost as if, having failed to give England its own Sobers or Richards, a whole society was being sent home. Since 2005, only two men of Caribbean descent – Michael Carberry and Chris Jordan – have played Test cricket for England. Jofra Archer, the Barbados-born fast bowler with an English father and British passport may soon become the third. The team that took the field at Adelaide ten years earlier included three alone. Phillip DeFreitas struck an exhilarating second-innings 88. Devon Malcolm bowled with stomach-lurching power to remove Mark Taylor, Michael Slater and Steve Waugh. Chris Lewis knocked over the tail. (Also in the tour party was Joey Benjamin.)

Many players with similar backgrounds had also represented England: Roland Butcher, Norman Cowans, Wilf Slack, Monte Lynch, Gladstone Small, Syd Lawrence, Mark Ramprakash. In 1993, there were more than 30 players

Potent force: Jofra Archer and Chris Jordan form an accomplished partnership at Sussex.

of West Indian descent in county cricket: the children of the *Windrush* looked set to be a reliable nursery for the English game.

What happened? A decade later, the well seemed to have run dry. The audience had melted away, too. "There was hardly a Caribbean fan in sight to witness the capitulation of Brian Lara's team," wrote *Wisden,* after the West Indians' lame showing in England in 2004. "Just a few mournful elders staring into their drinks." The decline was put down to various things, starting with the weakening of West Indies cricket itself: as the Lloyd–Holding–Marshall–Richards era faded, so did the game's grip. But it was also said that English stuffiness, and regulations designed to suppress noise in grounds (soon scuppered by the Barmy Army), had silenced the exuberant Caribbean voice. It was mooted that the Americanisation of sport in the region – the rise of basketball and athletics – was fraying the heritage of leather and willow. Even food habits were blamed, fish and vegetables supplanted by cheeseburgers and chips.

The biggest reason, though, lay not in the Caribbean, but in the texture of English life. The West Indians had settled in the run-down areas of England's crowded inner cities: Brixton or Notting Hill in London, Handsworth in Birmingham, St Paul's and Toxteth in Bristol and Liverpool. Chance played a role. The first Windrushians were billeted in the Clapham Shelter, a disused wartime hostel. The nearest Labour Exchange was in Brixton, so that is where they went, and where they stayed.

The consequences were inevitable. The West Indian migrants slowly became assimilated into the inner-city mainstream, which meant football, not cricket.

Their arrival coincided with the disappearance of cricket pitches – so much easier to put down jumpers for goals and play football instead. A vibrant sporting stream was diverted, like the tributary of a river, into a new channel.

It took a while. The Nottingham-born Viv Anderson broke new ground in 1978, when he became the first black footballer to play for England, and was pelted with bananas for his pains. Times have changed, though there have been recent incidents, including a banana. A modern English cricket team may lack a West Indian accent, but the football World Cup squad in 2018 boasted eight players of Caribbean descent: Few raised an eyebrow.

For Phillips, this alteration coincided with the decline of cricket as a hub or rallying post. "It was so important, gathering at the cricket, watching West Indies. It was a social reference point. And we didn't want to watch other teams. We wanted to see ourselves – or, in the case of Sobers and Worrell, brilliant versions of ourselves. They gave us dignity. Maybe we stopped needing that."

Phillip DeFreitas recalls the Adelaide Test as one of the few times he felt able to bat for England with the zest of which he was capable. When the sixth second-innings wicket fell, they led by only 115. "I think we'd almost written off the chance of winning," he recalls. "The feeling in the dressing-room was that only two results were possible – a defeat or a draw."

His batting record was undistinguished: he finished with a Test average below 15 – not great for a man who would rack up nearly 11,000 first-class runs. But now he pummelled 22 off a single over from Craig McDermott to send flutters through the crowd, and the seagulls grazing at deep midwicket. In an era when run-a-ball batting was looked on much like the four-minute mile, DeFreitas went on to his highest Test score, a late flurry of boundaries shifting the mood of the match; England had set a worthwhile target, for once, and the game was afoot.

DeFreitas had come a long way since arriving in Britain from Dominica at the age of seven. He retains little of that childhood beyond an image of himself jumping into the sea on sunny mornings. There wasn't much of that in Willesden, north-west London; he became a fidgety and uncertain schoolboy who found refuge in sport. He was a useful enough footballer to have trials with Luton Town, but his first love was cricket – and cricket loved him back. At the end of the day he would go to Lord's and hang around the indoor school, bowling at anyone who didn't throw him out. He went on to win a place on the MCC groundstaff.

He does not recall playing in the Caribbean, but it was a fact of life in his family: "My father and my brother loved it, talked about it all the time – West Indies *and* England." Willesden High had a cricket pitch, a length of astroturf laid on cement, and that is where DeFreitas started to play. He was a quick learner. Signed by Leicestershire in 1985, he took three for three on debut as Oxford University were bowled out for 24; the following year he claimed 94 first-class wickets and scored a maiden century, against a Kent side including Graham Dilley, Terry Alderman and Derek Underwood. People noticed.

The way we were: lads play a makeshift game of cricket in Basing Street, Notting Hill, 1970.

DeFreitas is useful to quizmasters – the only player to take a five-for against all 18 first-class counties, and one of a handful to have made 10,000 first-class runs and taken 1,000 wickets. He may also be the most dropped player ever – 14 times by England, he believes. "Someone came to me recently and pointed out that every time I took fewer than three wickets, I was dropped. I don't know if that's true – but it certainly felt like it." The most hurtful occasion was in 1993. Recalled at short notice for the First Ashes Test at Old Trafford, he dismissed Slater and David Boon, and had Allan Border and Taylor dropped. After the match, he raced to play a four-day game at Essex, and was netting when he heard on the radio that he was not in the side for Lord's.

"I was very upset," he says. "No one ever said a word." Lord's was his spiritual home – part of his childhood, and the symbol of his success as a young boy making a fresh start in a new country. But he did not then, and does not now, suspect a racial motive lurked in this shoddy treatment. "I honestly never thought that. It's true I played a lot of games for England without ever feeling part of the team. But that's how selection was back then. You never felt safe." The most severe racism he encountered came when he played club cricket in South Africa, for Boland. People saw only his colour, and treated him coldly, until they learned he was an English cricketer. The shift was frightening.

Devon Malcolm was born in 1963 in Kingston, Jamaica – the port from which the MV *Empire Windrush* set sail. The ship herself was a migrant: originally a German troop carrier, the *Monte Rosa*, she was seized in the Baltic in 1945, and renamed after a Cotswold river. His father followed what was fast becoming a Caribbean tradition, supporting the family from afar, in England.

Devon lost his mother when he was six, and was raised by his grandmother until he joined his father in Sheffield at 17.

He was a student rather than a talked-about cricketer. But back in Jamaica he had tried, like everyone, to imitate the action of Michael Holding, and in one of his first matches it seemed he had taken all ten wickets. "Yes," he remembers. "The scorecard looked pretty good... but a lot of that was down to my cousin Danville at the other end. He was quick too."

A few non-cricketing years went by before he joined Sheffield Caribbean CC. And he soon impressed everyone with his thunderbolts. One Friday, he skipped college to play for Yorkshire Schools, and was at once snapped up to represent a Yorkshire League XI against the county. In his first over, he bowled Martyn Moxon; in his second, he was too much for Geoff Boycott. The Yorkshire-born policy meant he had no chance in his adopted county, but the following Monday he was invited to trials at Derbyshire, whose overseas player was... Michael Holding. Who said life couldn't be poetic? Before long he was the fast-bowling answer to England's prayers. Then, like DeFreitas, he was by turns picked and discarded. "That's how it was. They changed bowlers at the drop of a hat. They were happy when you did well, but one bad session and you knew you might be out."

Steve Waugh was one of many to express bewilderment when Malcolm was not selected – on the simple grounds that he was a match-winner. "We were amazed when his name wasn't on the teamsheet," he said. "Dev could bowl one ball that would go down the leg side for four wides, but the next would be a perfect outswinger at 100 miles an hour... and the next would be at your throat. That was hard."

Malcolm clearly recalls the final innings in Adelaide. "It was one of those days where it felt good from the start – the run-up, the ball coming out of the hand, a bit of movement. And I remember Slater. He hadn't hooked all series, but I bowled a flimsy bouncer at Boon and he hooked it, and I saw Slater smile. And I thought: he might have a go. Next chance I got I bowled him a *proper* bouncer, and he top-edged it."

He yields to no one, however, in his admiration for the great West Indies teams of the past. "A lot of kids playing now, even in the Caribbean, don't realise what West Indies cricket is, where it came from. I don't care who you are, England, Australia, wherever – everyone was influenced by those teams and those players." And he sees the decline as "mainly a generational thing". Watching his own 12-year-old son progress through junior cricket in England, he is struck by how orderly and expensive it has become. "I used to just run around, copy my heroes, bowl as fast as I could and have fun. I sometimes worry that it's all a bit methodical now."

When Chris Lewis came to London from Guyana at the age of ten, he had never played a cricket match. He had batted and bowled in the street ("I never kicked a football till I came to England"), but he had never been part of a real team, on a real pitch. His first encounter with London was memorable. "I can still see it. It was March 10, 1978, and I thought the whole world was going to be like the place I'd left. But it was cold and grey." Things looked up when his

Leonard Burt, Central Press/Hulton Archive/Getty Images

Lording it: West Indian supporters celebrate a total of 652 for eight declared. Rohan Kanhai's 1973 team went on to win by an innings and 226.

family settled in west London, and Lewis attended the same Willesden school as DeFreitas. He would follow him into the Leicestershire and England dressing-rooms, too.

A photograph taken after the Adelaide Test shows those two, and Malcolm, dangling their feet in a swimming pool and smiling into the camera. It looks like a happy moment, the completion of three long journeys. But it was not something Lewis fully appreciated. "Looking back, I feel I should have been more aware of it. At the time, it was mainly just a thrill to be there."

He hadn't actually been selected for the tour. "There were a few injuries, and I happened to be in Australia, so I was drafted in. I just felt so lucky and proud." He had second-innings figures of four for 24. It was a high point in a career of intermittent flashes. But he gives much of the credit to DeFreitas's batting. "That turned things round," he recalls. "We were going down. But when we came out to bowl we were buoyant."

Lewis had talent: he played in a World Cup final, scored a Test century in India, and bagged three five-wicket hauls. But he was never a fixture in the team. There were behind-the-hand mutterings about punctuality and attitude – and a fair few front-of-the-hand mutterings, too. "It's true there was no continuity back then," he says. "But it's all very easy to say, 'Oh, if only I'd had a two-year run, like they do now, how well might I have done?' There's no knowing. It was the same for everyone. No one felt secure."

Having said that, he *was* sensitive to racial condescension, and sometimes detected it even in admiring remarks. He would wince at the notion that he was a "natural" athlete, as if anything he achieved was a matter of racial luck rather than effort. When David Gower played a lackadaisical stroke, it was an aristocratic lapse; when Lewis did the same, it was an idiotic mistake.

Lewis is, of course, now known for something he would rather forget – a six-year prison sentence for attempting to carry cocaine through Gatwick airport in 2008. In his autobiography, *Crazy*, he stresses that the most painful aspect of the episode is that, having spent his professional life rejecting the stereotypes afflicting Caribbean men, he ended up reinforcing them. It is another reminder that migration is rarely a smooth story. Rather like cricket itself.

In July 1995 – six months after Adelaide – DeFreitas, Malcolm and Lewis found themselves judged defective by a sour article in *Wisden Cricket Monthly,* which argued that players from their background could never feel as English as their native-born team-mates, and thus burned with a weaker flame.

They issued libel writs, which were dropped when the publication apologised in court, and financial settlements made to the satisfaction of all three. Malcolm is adamant there was not a grain of truth in the slur. "I felt – we all felt – completely at one with the team. A hundred per cent. And I loved England. People used to say, oh, you must miss the sunny Caribbean, but I loved the seasons, the green summers. I never would have been a professional cricketer if I had stayed in the Caribbean. I was just proud to be selected. We all were."

The article betrayed a persistent unease in certain quarters at the racial changes symbolised by the *Windrush* and her children – no matter how much they gave to the national cause.

Pool of talent: Chris Lewis, Phil DeFreitas and Devon Malcolm, Adelaide, January 1995.

And yet, despite the Test win over England early in 2019, West Indies cricket feels like a fading force: the modern game is fed by Asian, rather than West Indian, energy. That need not be cause for sadness or self-reproach. It may just be the natural way of things. "I'm not sure it's right to think it's a falling-off," says Lewis. "It was always going to happen as the West Indian generation grew more assimilated. We can look back all we like, but the children of the children of the children – they are English." It is not only in England that the West Indian flame is dwindling. "Last time I was there, I walked around for days and never saw anyone playing cricket. No one. Their heroes no longer play for Somerset: they play for Manchester City."

Which brings us to the final reason the West Indian voice in English cricket has grown fainter: the great sell-off of school sports grounds, which has left generations of children with nowhere to play. In a sports-loving country, it is bewildering.

The Platform Initiative was launched last year by Daniel Bell-Drummond, the Kent opener who – like Ebony Rainford-Brent, the first woman of Caribbean descent to play for England – was born in south London. Bell-Drummond's father arrived from Jamaica; now Daniel hopes to rekindle the passion in places where cricket has been allowed to die. He wants to see it back on the curriculum, and puts on accessible after-school sessions in public parks. Thanks to his own experience – he grew up in Lewisham, before enjoying a cricketing education at Millfield, then joining Kent – he is keenly aware of the gulfs in English society. "I was privileged to get the best of everything, but a lot of talented friends weren't." The reason those friends were not able to advance in cricket, he feels, was simple: "Lack of opportunity."

The drop-off has, he agrees, been "astonishing… most of the urban areas where the [West Indian] population is haven't *ever* played cricket, as it is not taught in schools". But he is convinced there is still a "latent" West Indian feeling for the game, even if the first love of the youngsters he meets is football. The response so far has been "brilliant": some 700 boys and girls attended his tournament in Deptford Park.

It is a worthy cause, reminiscent of the Haringey Cricket College run by Reg Scarlett (also ex-Jamaica). That produced several first-class cricketers, including Mark Alleyne. But it was a finishing school; Bell-Drummond is addressing an even more basic issue. Malcolm feels this is the key: "The thing about cricket is, you have to love it. That's where it all has to start."

History, like cricket, moves in mysterious ways. It would be ironic if, in coming to England, the grandchildren of the *Windrush* generation have been stripped of their love of cricket. Maybe it is not too late to put it back.

Robert Winder is the author of The Little Wonder: the Remarkable History of Wisden, *and* Bloody Foreigners: The Story of Immigration to Britain.

THE SECRET LIFE OF THE GROUNDSMAN

Eight hours of magic, five days of torture

JON HOTTEN

It was one of those days at Lord's. The pitch looked a belter, but above the Pavilion full-bellied clouds had stalled in the skies. The air felt heavier. Mohammad Azharuddin, India's captain, was wondering what to do if he won the toss, when he spotted the head groundsman, Mick Hunt.

"Bat first?" asked Azhar. Hunt looked at him: "You know what it's like here: if it's overcast it does swing. Fresh pitch, first day, bit of seam…" Azharuddin won the toss – and bowled. England declared almost two days later on 653 for four. Graham Gooch made 333. That evening, Azharuddin walked past Hunt again, and muttered something that rhymed with his surname. Nearly three decades later, Hunt allows himself a long chuckle. "That was one of my more memorable cock-ups."

Hunt began working at Lord's in 1969, "doing a bit of fetching and carrying". Peter Parfitt was captain of Middlesex, Harold Wilson prime minister, and the Krays on their way to jail. He had grown up within earshot of cricket itself, and raised his family – two sons and two daughters – in the groundsman's house by the North Gate. His wife, a nurse, worked at the Wellington Hospital just over the road. "In the morning, she went out one door, I went out the other."

On a crystalline September day, soon after his final fixture, he was facing up to leaving not just a cricket ground, but a way of life. "After 49 years it's a hell of a wrench. I was born in St John's Wood. I've lived here 44 years. I don't know anything else, which is sad in some respects. My wife's taking it quite bad, to tell you the truth."

Hunt became head groundsman after Jim Fairbrother died in 1984, and since then has prepared pitches for 60 Tests, 49 one-day internationals (including the 1999 World Cup final), ten Twenty20 internationals, two women's World Cup finals, numerous domestic finals, and more Championship and limited-overs games than he can remember. The demands of the fixture card are as unerringly regular as the taxman. "I got to the stage I was taking it home with me," he says. "I'd wake up at ridiculous times thinking, 'Christ, has it stopped raining out there yet?' I won't miss the stress or the pressure."

A diagnosis a decade ago of cancer, from which he is still recovering, and the passing seasons, have made him reflective. "I missed out big time. I wasn't selfish in terms of personal gain, but I was selfish towards the kids: dad never took them out to the pictures or the seaside because dad was always working until September. Everything revolved around cricket. So this is a bit of payback time."

Cricket remains an elemental game, dependent on leather and willow, the soil and the weather. The cut strip, unchanged in length since 1744, is its terra

Clare Skinner, MCC

One man went to mow: Mick Hunt at Lord's, 2010.

incognita, conjured with what Gary Barwell, head groundsman at Edgbaston, calls only half-jokingly "the dark arts". A pitch is essentially simple, the earth rolled hard and held together by grass, yet no one – not even those preparing it – knows exactly how it will behave. Its mystery is innate, a sublime variation that can shape matches and careers.

Lord's was once so notorious for its stone-pitted wicket that W. G. Grace received an ovation for keeping out three shooters in a row. And for many years the ground was so vulnerable to rain that heavy weather became known as "beer clouds": an early close was inevitable. But a drainage system installed in 2001 proved a marvel of engineering, with a filtration rate of an inch of water per hour. "What you're looking at," says Hunt, waving a brawny arm at his outfield, "is the biggest golf green in the world."

It is a golf green that was kept short by sheep until the arrival of the mower in the middle of the 19th century. But the pitch remained treacherous for decades: George Summers died in 1870 when a ball struck a stone, then his head. As the County Championship took shape, so did the notion of a specialist groundsman. At Trent Bridge, "Fiddler" Walker introduced top-dressing with fertiliser, and pitches were properly rolled and cut. Even so, it was perhaps not until Harry Brind persuaded the Surrey committee to allow him to dig up the Oval square in the late 1970s, transforming its sluggish surfaces by underlaying them with Ongar loam trucked in from the construction of the M11, that science began to have its way.

For the groundsman, technology has become a reassuring presence. The Clegg Hammer looks a bit like the dynamite detonator from a kids' cartoon, and measures the pitch's hardness. A tensiometer, or soil moisture sensor, does what it says on the tin. These numbers – ideally around 240–260 on the Clegg, and 28–30% moisture – offer empirical evidence to soothe a feverish brow. Yet groundsmen are still subject to the whims of nature and the players, on whom perception of their work so often depends.

Every pitch in the English professional game will receive a grade from a cricket liaison officer, known as the "CLO" – a position Hunt, in what may be a Freudian slip, calls "the PLO". The CLO's sanctions include a points deduction. Playing time lost is money lost, and the quality of the wicket is a commercial imperative. Hunt remembers when county pitches could be like the Wild West. "One or two were at it," he smiles. "Notts were notorious, with Hadlee and Rice. I've heard stories of visiting teams who couldn't tell where the pitch was, there was so much grass. Other grounds were green at one end and bare at the other. I was told by one coach he'd seen someone using wire brushes on a spinner's length. Stories used to go around about home sides – if they'd batted first, they'd put a flat sheet down that night, and you get the greenhouse effect. Those days are over."

Gary Barwell began at Grace Road on the Youth Training Scheme, earning £30 a week. He had fallen in love with groundsmanship during a placement at Leicester City's Filbert Street, hallowed turf for a lifelong fan. Leicestershire sent him to agricultural college, where he studied greenkeeping, as there was no course specifically for cricket ("I'm qualified to rake a bunker on the European Tour"). His first job was painting sightscreens and dressing-rooms. Then came his first nets, cut on the outfield, that turned like a Hyderabad dustbowl: "They looked white, but this lad called Carl Crowe, a batter who bowled a bit, ragged it square. It taught me a lot." Next was the new second-team ground at Hinckley, where he worked under Andy Ward and Andy Whiteman. He moved to Trent Bridge as a deputy, before getting the Edgbaston job in 2011.

As he speaks, he gives the sense of an industry slowly pulling itself together. A few days earlier, he had been in Madrid at a meeting that included counterparts from Arsenal, Wimbledon and the Hurlingham Club. Barwell has a strapping medium-pacer's physique, a sharp intelligence and a strong sense of duty. He mentions his wife, a deputy head teacher, often.

"Emotionally, you go up and down," he says. "When I was at Leicester, we were playing Yorkshire. They're four for three, Vaughan's out, McGrath's out. But you know in your heart there's nothing wrong with the pitch. Andy Ward is pacing up and down, but Andy Whiteman's reading a broadsheet newspaper. I spoke to him about it later, and he said: 'I might have been sitting down, but inside I was totally drained.' I learned from him that if I got in charge, whatever happened on a pitch, I would put on me, not hand it down to my staff."

A groundsman's nightmares are populated by cataclysms of the past. There was Headingley's Fusarium Test during the 1972 Ashes, a rare sporting occasion named after a fungus; the abandonment at Sabina Park in 1997-98 on a pitch apparently relaid, wrote Mike Selvey, "by a cowboy gang of tarmac layers"; even Edgbaston 1995, when England lost 20 wickets in 75 overs after Curtly Ambrose's first ball sailed off a length, over Mike Atherton's head, and all the way to the boundary.

Earth science: Alastair Cook, Gary Barwell, Trevor Bayliss (crouching), Ottis Gibson and Paul Farbrace consider the pitch, Birmingham, July 2015.

The pressure can be all-consuming. The first session of a Test is about as bad as it gets. "Terrible," says Hunt. "And then five days of torture." Barwell says he feels physically sick before the first ball: "You have the weight of the world on your shoulders."

If the arts remain dark, cricketers still like to think they know a little about them. Like amateur golfers borrowing the pros' routines from TV, cricketers stare at the grass, assess its length and colour, look for telltale patches or cracks – even, in the long dry summer of 2018, for dust. Perhaps they'll bang a heel into it, or rub the back of their hand against it, offering a pithy "road", or a sage "might do a bit".

But how good a judge is the average player? "Oh, useless, absolutely," says Hunt, tongue only partially in cheek. "They haven't got a clue. I could pull my mum out there – she's 94 and she'd have more idea." He recalls the last game of the season, played on a used strip with some cracks, but ones not even the roller could move. "So the players come out, and they start on the cracks with their bats. I mean, that's brainless. It's like a Formula One driver taking a hammer to his engine. Doesn't make sense."

Barwell remembers an exchange with Robin Smith, towards the end of his career. "He was an absolute legend to me as a kid. Hampshire were at Grace Road, and I went over, second day of the game. I was 18, hadn't had six months' experience. I asked him: 'Which roller would you like?' He said: 'Which one do you reckon?' And I said: 'Look, I'm just a kid.' He said: 'Well you probably know better than me.' This is Robin Smith, one of the bravest, strongest players to have represented England. So I'd say about 20% know what it is to do a pitch."

Hunt's eyes twinkle when he talks about the players he has known, the long relationships with successive Middlesex captains, maintained through fair weather and foul. He and Mike Brearley once watched the covers float down the hill to the Tavern. Mike Gatting was a maestro at talking to Hunt within earshot of the umpires. "If he was in a winning position when it rained, he'd march out – 'Mick, I can't believe what a great job you've done here.' If he was in a losing position, it'd be: 'Ah dear, look at this, can't believe how much rain we've had.'"

Barwell recalls a conversation with Ian Bell, who explained how it felt when the ball wasn't quite coming on to the bat. "He wants to see it leave the hand and play his shot. I just thought, if it's slower, it's easier to hit. It's all about communicating with your players."

When you see all the tweets, it's a joy to come to work

The summer of 2018 began in the deep chill of April, but became the hottest on record, interspersed with biblical downpours. Village outfields burned to the colour of autumn leaves. Barwell pumped 46,000 litres of water on to Edgbaston every 36 minutes, the length of his sprinkler cycle. Hunt dared not contemplate the bill MCC received from their water supplier.

It was a classic batsman's summer, and yet the ball was dominant. The Edgbaston and Lord's Tests against India were remarkable pieces of theatre. Birmingham featured a deathless duel between Virat Kohli and James Anderson, when Kohli's bat seemed enchanted in so many ways; at Lord's, England won in 170.3 overs, their third-shortest home Test in a century. "Poor India, it just swung, they didn't have a chance," says Hunt. "It was bizarre, almost like the Bob Massie conditions in 1972. Then the sun came out for England: different ball game."

Barwell walks out on to Edgbaston, talking about the Test and the summer. In the grand stillness of an empty stadium, he is almost transported as he remembers Kohli. "I was privileged to produce a pitch that Virat Kohli scored 149 on," he says. "It was a great game, and when you see all the tweets and people talk about the wicket, it's a joy to come to work."

The Edgbaston square seems to stretch out like a pleasure beach: it has 24 pitches, 17 for first-class cricket. Eight are TV pitches, with cameras directly behind each end. They are one of the banes of a groundsman's life, putting even more pressure on a square that is in almost constant use.

"Next year will be the busiest ever," says Barwell, referring to 2019. "We've got eight TV pitches – and five World Cup games, an Ashes Test and T20 finals day. That's not including any Warwickshire TV games. On top of that, you've got pressure from the ICC – they want particular ones. Last year, we had home quarter- and semi-finals in the Royal London Cup which needed TV pitches…"

Like a schoolboy doing his times tables, Barwell can recite his routine. "Getting moisture in the pitch starts 14 days before. We start rolling 13 days out. We generally don't lose more than 7% moisture in that period. Put your

Edgbaston, we have lift-off... The first ball of the 1995 Test, bowled by Curtly Ambrose, rockets over Mike Atherton and West Indies keeper Junior Murray on its way to the boundary.

heavy roller on – just under three ton – at the start for two hours. Twelve days out, another two hours. Then the regular roller. It's like a plasterer doing a wall. He'll skim it with water, then smooth it. If we can roll a pitch for eight hours or more, it'll be pretty good. Anything under, it seems to lack a little bit. I call it the 'magic eight hours'. Nine days to go, we bring out a combi-brush – a little rake that stands the grass up and dries out the moisture."

Barwell has hit on a method of keeping the grass longer, which adds carry and pace to the pitch but leaves it dry, avoiding the dreaded greentop. In his office, tucked away under the stands by the storage space for his gleaming rows of mowers and rollers, he keeps his notes: the readings, scores, results and marks of every pitch he's made.

Hunt performed a similar juggling act on the Lord's square, from which he summoned two Test pitches a year in addition to the Middlesex schedule. He could squeeze in 20 and still maintain – just – the 50-yard boundary demanded by playing regulations. Each Test wicket had a three-week no-go zone around it. "Maybe the Test is on pitch ten, then you've got people running up and down pitch 11 for five days, so you have to put a one-day game on that one."

When Hunt began, even the Test wicket was seen up close by the players and umpires alone. Now it is examined by ultra-HD cameras and super slo-mo replays, and may be pressed and tapped and car-keyed by squadrons of former players from the commentary box. Media scrutiny is harsh and sapping; groundsmen, like elephants, never forget.

"Three balls into the India Test, Ebony Rainford-Brent is saying there's nothing in this pitch," recalls Barwell, evenly. "How can you make an assumption like that? I've got no problem if they say: 'Well, nothing's happened to the first two or three balls.' But everyone listening has already heard it. I'll always protect my pitch. The first year we were here, we had the wettest summer on record. Nasser Hussain stood on the square, on the mike, and said: 'We're not starting because the run-ups are wet.' I asked why he said that. He replied: 'Well, it sounds better than the outfield's wet.' Usually, the better players will talk. Shane Warne will always walk over and ask about the pitch. The wife says: 'Oh, you spoke to them today, didn't you? What they've just said is exactly what you'd say.'"

Hunt concedes: "They've got to talk about something, I suppose. What is frustrating is they set their stall out after three or four overs. We've got 90 overs a day. And they won't admit they're wrong: 'Oh, the sun's out now, it's got a bit more pace.' And some of the stuff in the papers – you wonder if the guy was actually here…"

Hunt has been honoured with life membership of MCC ("I'll be here shouting: 'Get on with it!'"), and one thing is certain: no other groundsman will have a career like his, when arcane knowledge was transformed into the scientific application of an ancient art. He has been left with a thousand stories, every one a jewel: the time Viv Richards defended his pitch from media criticism after England's batsmen got out gloving and fending West Indies' quicks; Brearley arguing on the outfield with Imran Khan while Wayne Daniel bowled at the speed of light ("He started his run-up in the top tier of the Pavilion"); Kapil Dev, in that long-ago Test where Azharuddin got his bum steer, lifting four sixes in a row to avoid the follow-on.

Maybe he should think about a one-man show. "You know what I'd like? Wherever I end up, if there's a little club, I'll just sneak along: 'Do you mind if I sit on your roller for a couple of hours, help you out?'" He laughs once again. "They'll go, 'Oi lads, we've got one here. Says he used to be head groundsman at Lord's…'"

Jon Hotten is the author of The Meaning of Cricket.

THE WISDEN–MCC CRICKET PHOTOGRAPH OF 2018   Phil Hillyard wins the award for his picture of Moises Henriques, playing for Sydney Sixers in the BBL, catching Melbourne Stars' Nick Larkin at the Sydney Cricket Ground, December 27.

The ninth Wisden–MCC Cricket Photograph of the Year attracted around 550 entries. First prize was £2,000; the two runners-up received £1,000, and the eight other shortlisted entries £250 each. Any image with a cricket theme taken during 2018 was eligible. The independent judging panel, chaired by former *Sunday Times* chief photographer Chris Smith, comprised award-winning photographers Patrick Eagar, Adrian Murrell and Kevin Cummins, broadcaster Diana Keen and Nigel Davies, the former art director of *The Cricketer*. For more details, go to www.lords.org/photooftheyear

THE WISDEN–MCC CRICKET PHOTOGRAPH OF 2018   Matthew Lewis is one of two runners-up, for his photograph of Sri Lanka's Nilakshi de Silva celebrating a catch with Yashoda Mendis during the women's World T20, November 14.

THE WISDEN–MCC CRICKET PHOTOGRAPH OF 2018 The second runner-up is Syed Mahabubul Kader, an amateur photographer from Bangladesh. It shows dockyard workers' children – some of whom also work on the boats – playing cricket in Keraniganj, Dhaka, in March.

UTTER DETERMINATION   Amir Hussain lost his arms, and Ramesh Shukla his legs, but nothing stops them playing.

RANDOM FANDOM Rangana Herath bids farewell to Test cricket at Galle in November, surrounded by lookalikes. At Sydney, admirers adopt a different pose for Virat Kohli.

EXTREME CONDITIONS   A moorland fire rages at Micklehurst near Stalybridge, Manchester, in June. In late August, the club staged a match to raise funds and thank the rescue services. Lord's had been blanketed by February snow.

David Rowe

HAMPIONS 2018

ONE IN THE EYE – AND THE EYELINE Ollie Pope gets more champagne than he bargains for as Surrey celebrate their Championship in September, while a Mumbai batsman has to cope with a silly mid-off.

S. L. Shanth

THE LEADING WOMAN CRICKETER IN THE WORLD Smriti Mandhana

LEADING WOMAN CRICKETER IN THE WORLD IN 2018

Smriti Mandhana

RAF NICHOLSON

In August 2018, Somerset decided to live-stream one of Western Storm's Kia Super League matches. An unprecedented experiment, it attracted 26,000 viewers globally – a huge success. Those who were paying attention, though, noticed something peculiar: 29 minutes in, after the fall of Storm's second wicket, viewing figures dropped dramatically. Not all the 26,000, it appeared, cared about the denouement. They just wanted to watch Smriti Mandhana.

Who could blame them? Her silky-smooth strokemaking has been a sight to behold ever since her international debut in April 2013, when she top-scored with 39 as India beat Bangladesh in a T20 match at Vadodara. And 2018 was her most prolific year yet. With 1,291 runs across the two limited-over formats, she finished the year as the world's leading scorer. Success came early and often – a third ODI century, against South Africa at Kimberley in February, was followed by six 50-over half-centuries in eight innings against Australia, England and Sri Lanka. In all, Mandhana passed 50 eight times in 12 ODI innings, two unbeaten, and another five times in T20 internationals.

Across July and August, she dominated the KSL: it was not so much Western Storm as Smriti Storm. Bowlers cowered as she broke one record after another: most runs in a season (421), most sixes (21), highest strike-rate (174). She missed finals day, which clashed with a BCCI training camp, and Western Storm fell at the penultimate hurdle, but there was only ever going to be one Player of the Tournament. She ended the year by helping India to the semi-finals of the World Twenty20; her 83 off 55 balls formed the backbone of their win in Guyana against Australia, the eventual champions.

Mandhana grew up in Maharashtra, playing with her father and brother, both district-level cricketers. By 11, she was representing the state Under-15s; by 16, her country. In 2015, she became one of the first batch of women to be awarded an annual contract by the BCCI.

She regards as her career-defining moment the five months spent away from the game in 2017, courtesy of a knee injury sustained during the Women's Big Bash League. It altered her approach to batting. "I wasn't able to walk," she says. "I spent two months on crutches. I used to feel like not scoring runs is the worst thing in life, but I started thinking, no, at least I'm getting to go out on the field wearing the Indian jersey. Not many get to do that. I am lucky. Now, if I get runs or don't get runs, I'm just going out there trying to enjoy my cricket." Her equanimous approach to the defeat by England in the 2017 World Cup final is a case in point: "I only thought about it for half an hour." The results speak for themselves.

After 2017, some doubted whether India's women could remain in the spotlight. Mandhana ensured they did – for all the right reasons.

THE TALE OF THE CENTURY

250 years and counting

JONATHAN LIEW

In his 1977 book *The Domestication of the Savage Mind*, the anthropologist Jack Goody visits the LoDagaa people of northern Ghana, who possess a unique system of counting. While large items such as cows are numbered singly, smaller items – particularly the cowrie shells that are used as common currency – are not. The locals first take a handful of three, then of two, and make a pile of five. Four piles of five make 20, and five piles of 20 make 100. When Goody asks the LoDagaa how they count, he is met with bafflement. "Count what?"

In other societies, numbers are tied to objects. In some of the Fijian islands, ten is *bola* when describing boats, *boro* when describing coconuts. The Tsimshians of north-west Canada have different words for three: *gulal* for men, *galtskan* for trees, *guant* for garments. And the Nivkh of Sakhalin Island in eastern Russia have over 30 classes of number, each pertaining to an – often maritime-themed – object. The number five could be *thory* (referring to people), *thovr* (places), *thosk* (poles for drying fish), *thor* (bundles of dried salmon slices), or plenty else.

We like to think of numbers as natural, abstract, objective and the same for everyone. In fact, they are man-made, and invariably laden with context, history and heritage. Even English is littered with words – quartet, dozen, score – that evoke a number but are not directly interchangeable with it. We can talk about a brace of pheasants, even a brace of goals, but walk into your local railway station and ask for a brace of singles to Swindon, and you will likely be invited to rephrase yourself.

All of which brings us to the batsman's century, which in 2019 celebrates its 250th birthday: one arbitrary measure of commemoration marking another, you might think. We've come a long way in the quarter of a millennium since John Minshull recorded 107 notches for the Duke of Dorset's XI against Wrotham, a period in which the simple act of scoring 100 runs has assumed totemic significance: not simply a measure of achievement or a basic unit of sporting currency, but an article of faith, perhaps even a yardstick of cricketing citizenship. Scoring ten or 30 or 80 means nothing beyond itself. Make a century, on the other hand, and – even if you do nothing else in your career – you have inducted yourself into a special fraternity.

We know little about Minshull's century. We don't know what the weather was like, what the pitch was doing, who won the toss, who bowled, how many Wrotham scored, or who won. What we do know is that, at some point on August 31, 1769, during "second hands", as the second innings was known, the first wicket fell, and Minshull stepped out to join his employer, the Duke of Dorset.

24

LONG SCORES.

The following high scores of 100 or more have been made by the gentlemen and players in great matches since the commencement of 1850:—

1850.
July 5. Tunbridge Wells, for Sussex v. Kent, Wisden 21 and 100.
Sept. 16. Brighton, for A.E.E. v. 16 of Sussex, G. Parr 118.

1853.
August 15. Canterbury, for England v. Kent, Julius Caesar 101.

1854.
April 17. Trent Bridge Ground, for Players and Gentlemen of Notts v. Gentlemen of Notts, G. Parr 116.

1855.
August 27. Sheffield, for Sussex v. Yorkshire, Wisden 148.

1856.
July 31. Luton, for U.A.E.E. v. 22 of Luton, Caffyn 104.
August 4. Brighton, for Sussex v. Kent, John Lillywhite 138.
August 7. Manchester, for North v. South, Hunt 102.
August 14. Canterbury, for Gentlemen of England v. Gentlemen of Kent and Sussex, Hon. S. Ponsonby 168.

1857.
July 20. Southgate, for Southgate v. Surrey Club, Mr. F. Walker 170.
August 24. Gravesend, for Sussex v. Kent, John Lillywhite 24 and 118 (not out).
For Surrey v. Oxford, Caffyn 107.

1858.
July 22. Oval, for Surrey v. England, Caffyn 102.
July 22. Reading, for Gentlemen of Berks v. Gentlemen of Sussex, Mr. S. Austen Leigh 13 and 133 (not out).
August 16. Brighton, for Gentlemen of Sussex v. Gentlemen of Berks, Mr. W. Napper 116.

1859.
May 26. Cambridge, for Surrey v. 16 of Cambridge University, Caffyn 157.
June 20. Redruth, for A.E.E. v. 22 of Cornwall, G. Parr 101.
July 11. Lord's, for England v. 16 of Oxford University, J. Grundy 103.
July 14. Lord's, for Gentlemen of Kent v. Gentlemen of England, Mr. F. H. Norman 103.

25

LONG SCORES.

July 14. Oval, for Notts v. Surrey, G. Parr 130.
July 14. Brighton, for Gentlemen of Berks v. Gentlemen of Sussex, Mr. S. Austen Leigh 112.
July 21. Oval, for England v. Surrey, Mr. V. E. Walker 20 (not out) and 108.
August 4. Southgate, for U.A.E.E. v. Mr. J. Walker's 16, Caffyn 124 and 30.

1860.
June 21. Manchester, for 20 of Broughton v. A.E.E., Mr. G. Makinson 104.
July 5. Oval, for Players v. Gentlemen, Carpenter 119.
July 9. Oval, for Gentlemen of Surrey Club v. Gentlemen of Midland Counties, Mr. C. M. Harvey 101.
July 9. Maidenhead, for Gentlemen of Berkshire v. Gentlemen of Sussex, Mr. E. Austen Leigh 190; and Mr. S. Austen Leigh 119.
July 9. Lord's, for Players v. Gentlemen, T. Hayward 132.
July 12. Oval, for Gentlemen of the South v. Gentlemen of the North, Mr. F. P. Miller 133.
July 16. Brighton, for Surrey v. Sussex, Mr. F. P. Miller 105.

1861.
May 20. Cambridge, for Surrey v. Cambridgeshire, Caffyn 103. For Cambridgeshire v. Surrey, Hayward 112.
June 17. Walsall, for A.E.E. v. 22 of Walsall, Daft 114.
June 27. Oval, for Surrey v. Cambridgeshire, Julius Caesar 50 and 111.
For Cambridgeshire v. Surrey, T. Hayward 108 and 48; and Carpenter 100 and 15.
July 4. Oval, for Players v. Gentlemen, Carpenter 106.
July 8. Oval, for Gentlemen of the Surrey Club v. Gentlemen of the Midland Counties, Mr. T. A. Raynes 116.

1862.
May 22. Portsmouth, for U.A.E.E. v. 22 of Hants, Carpenter 122.
July 17. Lord's, for Gentlemen of the North v. Gentlemen of the South, Mr. R. Fabian 106.
July 21. Lord's, for the North v. South, Daft 118.
July 24. Lord's, for South Wales Club v. M.C.C. and Ground, Mr. E. M. Grace 118.
August 11. Oval, for Middlesex v. Surrey Club, Mr. J. D. Walker 19 and 102.
August 13. Canterbury, for Gentlemen of M.C.C. v Gentlemen of Kent, Mr. E. M. Grace 192 (not out).
August 18. Brighton, for M.C.C. v Sussex, Hearne 20 and 133.

Modesty doesn't forbid... In 1864, in his first Almanack, John Wisden includes a list of "long scores" from the previous 14 seasons. His name appears twice.

Minshull was a gardener in the country house of Knole in Kent, supplementing his eight shillings a week by playing in the Duke's matches. He would have been in his late twenties, and according to John Nyren was "a thick-set man, standing about five feet nine, and not very active". Nor was he elegant or self-effacing. As Nyren recalled in *The Cricketers of my Time*: "His position and general style were both awkward and uncouth; yet he was as conceited as a wagtail." But over the course of what we can assume was an afternoon, Minshull scored four fours, nine threes, 15 twos and 34 singles: all run, and all from rolled or lobbed underarm deliveries slapped with a curved bat. It is the first surviving stroke-by-stroke record of a match: a rare written artefact in an age when the primary method of scorekeeping was carving notches into wood.

Minshull's century might not, in fact, have been the first. The previous summer, the *Reading Mercury* reported that John Small "fetched above seven score notches off his own bat" for Hambledon against Kent – though it's impossible to say whether this was over one innings or two. In any case, cricket in the pre-Victorian age was a leisure pursuit rather than a codified sport: what survives of it today is probably a fraction of what existed. Minshull's achievement did not appear in newspapers, which suggests such feats were either unremarkable or largely unrecorded. Had the historian John Goulstone not happened upon it in archives in 1959, it might have remained forgotten. And so, much as "first-class cricket", "Test cricket" or "the Ashes" only really emerged *ex post facto*, reverse-engineered in the service of an existing mythology, it wasn't until the late 20th century that Minshull's hundred came to be regarded as the first – despite the fact that it was more than 200 years later, and that Minshull himself might have been blissfully unaware he was doing anything momentous at all.

To explain how this came about, we need to understand how numbers function in societies: what significance they take on, and why. Minshull's is also a story of cricket's evolution from a game of untamed fields and betting ledgers, where the only statistic of relevance was who won and lost, to a game in which the upkeep and pursuit of personal statistics and milestones became a sport-within-a-sport – a development without which, dare we imagine it, *Wisden* might not exist.

There's a common assumption that the reason we count to ten is because we have ten fingers. Yet base-ten has been just one of many counting systems. The ancient Babylonians used base-60, the Mayans base-20. "People generally fancy that, if a child was raised by wolves, he would come to the idea of counting just by looking at his hands," writes the archaeologist Denise Schmandt-Besserat in *Before Writing: From Counting to Cuneiform*. "Cross-cultural linguistic and anthropological studies on numbers show, however, that in all parts of the world, many societies could survive without having number words beyond 'three'."

Certainly Britain in the imperial, pre-industrial 18th century, a place still wedded to furlongs and bushels, seems to have borne no affinity for powers of ten: the *Mercury's* description of Small's 1768 innings – "above seven score notches" – is telling. Leaf through contemporary newspapers, and "century" is deployed solely as a period of time.

Ton up: WG celebrates in style.

It's not until around 100 years later that the concept of a century as a hundred runs begins to take hold. The phrase is barely seen at all in a sporting context until the 1860s, and even then it often sits within quotation marks, denoting its quirky status. "Another great feature of the month has been the wonderful play of Mr W. G. Grace," trills *The Graphic* in August 1870, "his scores far more regularly exceeding 'a century' than falling short of that number."

So what happened in the interim? For one thing, centuries became more common. The advent of roundarm bowling kept scores low until the mid-19th century, at which point batsmen began to adjust, and broke free. It took 66 years to record

Popperfoto/Getty Images

the 100th first-class hundred of the 19th century, another six to record the 200th. As the game tilted in batsmen's favour, a new argot grew up around them. At its centre was a simple, heroic achievement that prince and pauper alike could understand: the "century".

There were broader forces at work, too. A large portion of the general population in Minshull's time was innumerate. The Industrial Revolution changed that. A firm grasp of arithmetic had long been a requirement for the ruling and military classes, given the importance of navigation, cartography, ballistics and architecture. But the following decades would see a partial democratisation of numbers. "By around 1800," notes Professor Tom Archibald, a maths historian from Simon Fraser University in Canada, "the demand for people who could do accurate reckoning was high. A good knowledge of basic mathematics was a key to social mobility for those not born into wealth." It was also around this time, Archibald notes, that scoring games, such as cricket, began to take precedence over more traditional sports, such as boxing or cockfighting.

Cricket now had a numerically engaged audience, interested in more than who won or lost. The migration of scorekeeping from knife and wood to pen and paper allowed for all sorts of statistics. In 1846, Lord's introduced its first telegraph scoreboard and sold its first scorecards. Until then, the only way for spectators to divine the score – unless they kept it themselves – was when both scorers ceremonially stood up to indicate the sides were level.

This wasn't just about keeping score. It was about creating a mythology, birthing a culture, negotiating the tokens and totems that would sustain cricket through its growth years and beyond. As the sport mushroomed in the 1860s, hastened by the spread of the railways, fuelled by the publishing boom and nourished by the emergence of Grace, the century was incorporated into cricket's epic narrative: rare enough to be heroic, common enough to keep drawing crowds, simple enough that anybody could grasp it, and resonant enough that people could bond over it.

Newspapers began to publish scores and averages; the arrival of almanacs such as *Wisden* and *Lillywhite's* fulfilled the mid-Victorian thirst for record-keeping and statistical ephemera. By the time Grace became the first player to record a 100 hundreds, in 1895 – an event commemorated with a leader in *The Times* and a letter from the Prince of Wales – the pursuit of the century had woven itself into cricket's culture. Like the LoDagaa's cowries or the Nivkh's fish-drying poles, the century elevated itself above other methods of counting by simple virtue of what was being counted.

For much of the summer of 2008, a small but dedicated press corps traipsed up and down the country hoping to see Mark Ramprakash score his 100th first-class hundred. His 98th had come in the middle of April, his 99th at the start of May. And yet, as July became August, he was still waiting: irritation turned to bemusement turned to frustration turned to mild anger. After being dismissed in a Twenty20 game at the Rose Bowl in June, Ramprakash had taken exception to a Sky cameraman tracking him back to the pavilion, and lashed out with a fusillade of four-letter words, forcing Surrey staff to intervene.

Patrick Eagar, Popperfoto/Getty Images

Five times a hundred times a century… is a lot of runs. Mark Ramprakash, John Edrich, Geoff Boycott, Dennis Amiss and Graham Gooch, who all scored 100 hundreds, in August 2008.

Though he finally got there on August 2 at Headingley, he had been labouring under one of the oldest ailments in the game. If scoring 100 constitutes a form of batting perfection, then 99 may be its polar opposite: the least satisfying number on which to be marooned, with its sense of incompleteness. Such is the weight of the century that even to approach it is to subject oneself to its unique and turbulent gravitational field. A hundred years earlier, Tom Hayward had merrily hewn his way to 99 centuries, before grinding to a halt. For more than a year between 1912 and 1913, he toiled away in search of the 100th, only to come unstuck 46 times in a row. "It is said that he has even worried himself about the crowning of his many batting triumphs in the way that he desired," reported the *Athletic News*.

The nervous nineties, then, is no recent phenomenon. In 1897, K. S. Ranjitsinhji was lamenting the tendency of batsmen to get anxious as they neared a milestone, which he attributed to the institution of "talent money", an early form of performance bonus. "Most counties give their representatives a sovereign for every 50 runs they make," he wrote in *The Jubilee Book of Cricket*. "Naturally this makes them all the more anxious when they approach the required totals. That sovereign causes innumerable run-outs and rash strokes."

Talent money may no longer feature, but the incentive to hit three figures remains as strong as ever. As numerous studies by psychologists and behavioural economists have proven, the brain gets lazy when processing numbers. It knows the digit on the left is the most important, so that's where it starts reading. This is why, towards the end of the 19th century, American businesses realised that pricing goods with ".99" on the end made the cost look smaller. And in sport, the eye is similarly drawn to round numbers: 100 uses more digits than 99, and therefore looks more imposing. This partly explains why the century has assumed such worth. But 100 runs also feels like a satisfactory measure of batsmanship: it generally means batting against at least four different bowlers, for at least a couple of hours – a test not simply of skill and patience, but of stamina and adaptability.

You might surmise then, as Ranji did, that batsmen edging towards the milestone are more susceptible to mistakes. Yet the reverse is true: the evidence suggests that batsmen in the nineties tend to play more cautiously. A Test batsman who reaches 95 is almost 10% more likely to be dismissed between 100 and 104 than between 95 and 99. The contrast is even more pronounced in one-day internationals, where the disparity is almost 50%. Meanwhile, a 2015 study by researchers at Queensland University of Technology discovered that batsmen's strike-rates slow as they approach their century, then speed up again once they pass it.

Perhaps our attachment to centuries speaks to something quintessentially human in us. In the 250 years since Minshull, the achievement has gone from an unfathomable pinnacle to a regular occurrence. Still, though, it beguiles us, subverts the rational and gnaws at the emotional, spins us into its web of numbers, plays on our craving for neatness.

One of the virtues of short-form cricket is the way it has returned the century to a realm of wonder it hasn't inhabited since the early 1800s. There were just 36 centuries in the first 14 years of T20 international cricket, and even if they're arriving at a quickening rate, they still feel cherishably rare.

As scoring rates rise, as boundaries creep inwards, as public culture demands ever more constant commemoration, ever more perpetual memorialisation, ever greater meaning – remember the confected hoo-ha a few years back over Sachin Tendulkar's 100th international century? – perhaps T20 will act as a sort of natural corrective, the format that put the century back on its pedestal.

Meanwhile, there's an irony in the fact that in 2018, when the ECB were casting around for a shiny gimmick that would distinguish their new short-form competition and simplify the game for a new audience, they settled on The Hundred: 100 balls a side, a scoring system so universally resonant that even the LoDagaa, the Tsimshians or the Nivkh would grasp it. In more than one sense, we may be coming full circle.

Jonathan Liew is the chief sportswriter at The Independent.

COUNTY CRICKET AFTER THE WAR: A CENTURY ON

Out of the wreckage

Richard Hobson

Nearly five years after the lamps went out all over Europe, the County Championship returned to life on a crisp morning in mid-May. It was 1919. Across the Channel, world leaders were plodding towards a peace deal at Versailles. Further east, the Red Army were consolidating Bolshevism in Russia. Back at The Oval, and to rather less fuss, roughly 6,000 spectators watched Jack Hobbs score twin half-centuries for Surrey against Somerset, while half that number saw Middlesex and Nottinghamshire share 438 runs and 15 wickets at Lord's on the first day alone. "The famous ground looked all the better for its long rest," said *The Times*.

In truth, Lord's had not enjoyed much more rest than other cricket grounds during the First World War. The Long Room had been used to make string haynets for horses, and stretchers for casualties on the Western Front. Elsewhere, pavilions had been used as hospitals: 3,553 wounded servicemen were treated at Trent Bridge, while Old Trafford needed fumigating to get rid of the stench of the sick. Taunton had become a farm, Grace Road a training ground for mules. For those grim years, cricket understood its place.

With 407 first-class players decorated for gallantry, no team lacked a returning hero. On that first day at Lord's, Nottinghamshire's Arthur Carr, trapped for three hours under a dead horse during early skirmishes at Mons, was bowled by Captain Nigel Haig, a recipient of the Military Cross. Harry Lee, the Middlesex opener, had been declared dead in 1915, and a memorial service held in his name; in fact, he had been discovered alive by the Germans between the lines three days after being shot. "I was lucky," he wrote. "Many splendid men were given no second innings." In all, 289 first-class cricketers perished. Hampshire alone lost 24, but every county mourned at least three. "These men do not die," wrote *The Times*, "for their fame is immortal." It was a nice line, but sooner or later clubs had to be pragmatic; immortality does not score runs or take wickets.

The countdown to a resumption of the Championship began a day after the signing of the Armistice, on November 12, 1918, when MCC summoned a meeting of the Advisory County Cricket Committee. They had plenty to ponder. A piece in *The Times* proposed banning left-handed batsmen for being "a thorough nuisance and a cause of waste of time". While accepting the style and brilliance of Frank Woolley, the piece continued: "No child surely is so left-handed that he cannot learn to play right-handed if he starts young enough." *The Manchester Guardian* observed: "Some [ideas] have been temperate, others wild and fantastic to the point of madness."

Delegates gathered on December 16 at the Midland Hotel in St Pancras, where the meeting was said by one critic to lack "the calm and judicial

Sport & General/PA Photos

The human cost: Abe Waddington cradled fellow Yorkshireman, Major Booth, as he died on the first day of the Somme.

atmosphere of the Committee Room at Lord's". The counties decided to return to the normality of peacetime by way of the abnormal, agreeing to shorten matches from three days to two: 11.30 to 7.30 on the first day, 11 to 7.30 on the second, the ultimate goal being brighter, quicker cricket. Tea lasted ten minutes, and refreshments were taken on the field. Lancashire proposed the motion, and Lord Hawke, the MCC president who chaired the meeting, pleaded unsuccessfully with counties to oppose it: "What amateur is going to arrive at his hotel for dinner at nine o'clock?"

This being English cricket, the meeting proved merely a staging-post. A month later, Plum Warner predicted "disaster and discontent", describing the two-day format as "almost Prussian" in its demands on the players. As concern mounted, the counties had a rethink, this time at the Sports Club in St James's Square. They huffed and puffed, before sticking with plan A, making a sole concession to the arduous playing hours by extending tea to 15 minutes. Warner remained unconvinced: "It seems to be too much of an American hustle." Meanwhile, Lord Harris, still the most influential figure at MCC, took a Machiavellian approach that has remained in fashion in cricket administration ever since: abject failure would be a small price if it means the idea is kicked into touch.

Squads assembled in April, with Lancashire's preparations hampered by snow. Yorkshire remained best equipped, boasting 40 amateurs and professionals. Finances were relatively sound: enough members had stayed loyal through the conflict, even with play no more than a dream. Only

Worcestershire of the 16 pre-war contestants opted out (Glamorgan didn't gain first-class status until 1921). Because of the lop-sided fixture list, placings were calculated on the percentage of wins; Yorkshire played 26 games, the poorer-resourced Somerset and Northamptonshire 12.

Of the newcomers, Herbert Sutcliffe was much the most successful; for others, careers proved short. Having taken a wicket with his first ball, Kent's Gerald Hough soon realised that war wounds restricted his off-spin, and he never struck again. Arthur Denton of Northamptonshire was permitted to bat with a runner, having lost a leg in 1917 (a cork and leather replacement allowed only limited mobility). But Colonel Alexander Johnston found less charity. Wounded four times, mentioned in despatches five, and a recipient of the *Croix de Guerre* for action at the Somme, he made one limping appearance for Hampshire, before being drummed out of the county game.

Entertainment became a watchword. Although 1890–1914 has been described as cricket's Golden Age, it had lost some of its glint because of slow play. Counties feared crowds would diminish further after losing the habit. The object of the game, as Old Etonian Sir Home Gordon said before the season began, was "not to occupy the wickets as passively as though the batsmen were in the trenches". When Derbyshire and Leicestershire managed a combined 392 for 16 on the first day, in August, the *Times* headline still read: "Dull Play at Chesterfield."

The most colourful and contentious incident of the season involved Harold Heygate, an opener who had last appeared for Sussex in 1905. Now 34, and wracked by rheumatism, he found himself in Taunton, with Sussex a man short to face Somerset. Having been dismissed for a duck by Jack White on the first day, Heygate – who batted at No. 11 and didn't bowl – spent the second, according to David Foot, sitting "morosely in his blue suit, rubbing his throbbing knee and hoping his county would not need him".

They did. Requiring 105 to win, Sussex lost their ninth wicket on 104 – and there was no sign of the last man. Just as umpire Alfred Street drew the stumps, Heygate hobbled into view, bad leg dragging behind good, still wearing blue serge jacket and trousers, plus waistcoat and watch chain. Street reinserted the stumps, only for Somerset's senior professionals, led by Len Braund, to persuade White – the amateur captain – to cry foul. Street felt he had no option but to call an end to proceedings for the second time, and declare a tie. Heygate, having taken four minutes to reach the crease, could only wince and retrace his steps. With no specific timed-out law back then, debate raged for several days on the sportsmanship of the incident, before MCC ruled that Street had acted correctly. The tie stood, and Heygate's career was over.

Concerns about the public appetite were assuaged, with people grateful for a diversion after wartime austerity. Outside cricket, heavily starched collars were starting to loosen, and a mood for greater equality continued to grow. Women, or at least some of those over 30, had been given the vote in 1918. David Lloyd George's coalition government had been returned to power on a programme of reform in public health, education and housing. Strikes became common, and the upper classes bemoaned a dearth of domestic servants. But social change in cricket was harder to detect: if the crowd at the second

215

NOTES BY THE EDITOR.

The long nightmare of the War has come to an end, and in the coming summer first-class cricket will again be in full swing. I have a very strong opinion that a grave mistake has been made in not letting the game alone. The restriction of all county matches to two days strikes me as being a sad blunder. I can see most weighty objections to the scheme, little or nothing in its favour. Let no one in future repeat the stale old fable that the County Championship was only kept in existence for the benefit of the newspapers. By their recent action the Advisory Committee have made an absolute fetish of the Championship, risking on its behalf famous county matches that can boast a tradition of over fifty years. There was the less reason to take such a drastic step as county cricket in 1919, after a blank of four seasons, was bound to be a very speculative and experimental business. To my thinking it would have been far better to drop the Championship entirely for one year, allowing all the counties to make such arrangements as seemed best fitted to their own needs, while the game was being gradually brought back to its old footing.

Trenchant: Sydney Pardon ascends the pulpit in *Wisden 1919*.

day of the Eton–Harrow centrepiece at Lord's appeared slightly down on the first, it was primarily due to its clash with a garden party at Buckingham Palace (the King had dropped in to see the match on the opening morning).

Despite increased admission charges caused by the widely loathed entertainment tax, more than 100,000 watched play over the Spring Bank Holiday. In August, around 18,000 at The Oval saw the first day of Hobbs's benefit game, postponed in 1914 when the military took over the ground. Cricket had faced criticism in those early weeks. That summer's Championship was not brought to an immediate close upon declaration of war – only later, when the loss of players to action made selection unfeasible, and public opinion hardened, shaped not least by W. G. Grace.

Come 1915, players scarcely used the Oval nets because they were afraid of jeers from men on the passing trams. Yet some of the most famous names, including Hobbs, continued to turn out in a strong Bradford League, well away from what Wilfred Owen described as "the monstrous anger of the guns". Hobbs, who opted to serve on the home front, was quickly forgiven.

Cricket in 1919 became a barometer for the health and cohesion of the nation, and the Canterbury Festival in August drew particular attention. "One

New beginning: Nottinghamshire captain Arthur Carr cover-drives against Middlesex at Lord's on the day the Championship restarted, May 16, 1919.

by one, the old pleasures that the war banished for five years are coming back," said *The Times*, noting the marquees ringing the ground, flags and Chinese lanterns in surrounding streets, and the Old Stagers performing their 74th season at the Theatre Royal. Ladies Day was deemed a success: "The skirts of today do not trail, and whether they cover age or youth they are uniformly short and brilliant and diaphanous." Work on a memorial to the Kent and England left-arm spinner Colin Blythe, who died at Ypres, was not finished in time, and it had to be unveiled a fortnight later.

By then, Kent were Yorkshire's strongest challengers. They had beaten Sussex in a day at Tonbridge, and were praised for their conduct during Hobbs's benefit game, when Surrey needed 95 to win in 42 minutes. Kent not only continued to play in heavy drizzle, but refused to slow the over-rate, and were in the 13th when Surrey won with ten minutes to spare. The title was decided only in the final minutes of the season. Yorkshire's draw against Sussex meant Kent had to beat Middlesex at Lord's. Rain allowed only 90 minutes on the first day, and made for a treacherous pitch on the second. Having stretched their total to 196, Kent dismissed Middlesex for 87, then reduced them to 86 for eight following on, with 15 minutes to claim the last two. Middlesex held firm, enabling Yorkshire to win the first of 12 titles in the 21 interwar years.

Poignantly, one of their new stars was left-arm seamer Abe Waddington; three years earlier, on the opening day of the Somme, he had sheltered in a crater, wounded by shrapnel, to comfort his childhood hero Major Booth as he died in his arms. Another leading light of Yorkshire's 1919 team, Roy Kilner, had sat in agony behind the lines receiving treatment on a wrist shattered only minutes earlier. Booth had been best man at Kilner's wedding.

Alongside the Championship, an Australian Imperial Forces touring team played 28 games, underwritten by the military authorities (hopes for a three-match Ashes were scrapped because of a lack of time). Herbie Collins soon replaced the quarrelsome Charlie Kelleway as captain, while other distinctive names included Jack Gregory, the fastest bowler of the season and future scourge of England, and Bert Oldfield, the long-serving wicketkeeper who had been found semi-conscious and partially buried near Ypres in 1917 in an attack that killed three of his comrades.

When the tour ended with defeat at Scarborough by C. I. Thornton's XI, inspired by Hobbs and Wilfred Rhodes, some thought back to the Melbourne Test of 1911-12, when the same pair put on 323 for the first wicket. But the fitness and consistency of the Australians warned of the series in 1920-21 and 1921, when they beat England 5–0 and 3–0. Australia had suffered fewer losses during the war, and MCC had turned down an invitation to tour there in 1919-20 because they did not feel ready. As *The Guardian* said presciently: "It is certain that we shall find our work cut out to keep the Ashes from changing hands."

By September, the same newspaper felt able to declare that cricket "has triumphed over the organised attempt to dethrone it". New, or nearly new, players had stamped a mark, including Cec Parkin, Tich Freeman and Sutcliffe, while the likes of Hobbs, Rhodes and Woolley continued to match pre-war standards.

But the physical demands of two-day cricket proved too much. "It has turned a pleasant, invigorating sport into a laborious, exacting and exhausting task," said Hobbs, noting how inferior batsmen took easy runs off tired bowlers and fielders. A lack of pace was especially conspicuous. And so, even before the season had ended, the counties accepted their error and voted to return to three-day cricket for 1920. Lord Harris could smile as the hands were counted.

Richard Hobson is a freelance cricket writer. He covered the game for more than 20 years at The Times, *and now gives guided tours of Oxford.*

THE QUESTION OF MOTIVATION

Why be a cricketer?

TIM DE LISLE

An up-and-coming player, representing England but not yet established, goes to the World Cup for the first time. This is it: the big stage, the chance to make a name. It goes pretty well – a good fifty, top score in a narrow defeat, followed by a first international hundred, which turns a classic England collapse into a cakewalk. For the team, things go less well. "I'd done OK," says the player, many years later. "I'd cemented my position, but we didn't even make the semi." The experience prompts some hard thinking. "I watched the World Cup final, and I was convinced that I wanted to be the best batsman in the world. I came home and made that statement to my coach and myself."

So that was Claire Taylor's motivation, for years, after the 2000 World Cup: to be No. 1. "In 2005, in South Africa, I was going to prove it. England were going to lift the World Cup, everyone was going to be a hero. I had an OK tournament, but we got a semi-final at Potch, spicy pitch, we were three down in the first few overs, I got nicked off by Fitzpatrick." For a duck. "That properly burst my bubble."

She had given up the day job, taken an 80% pay cut and moved back in with her mother. "I went back to my old coach and my old technique, and I started trying to be better motivated by what I could do for the team. Instead of trying to dominate, I tried to anchor." In case she forgot this, she would write "anchor" on the inside of her forearm. "My motivation changed markedly: it became much more intrinsic. With hindsight – and this is all a narrative that we create around our careers – by focusing on what the team needed, I was taking care of myself." When the ICC launched women's ODI rankings in 2008, she was No. 1. A year later, she became the first woman to be picked as one of *Wisden's* Five.

Motivation is a slippery thing, whether you're in sport or not. It's there under our noses all the time, which means, as Orwell observed, that we struggle to see it. In fact, there may be as many types of motivation as there are members of a team, and more than one may be exerting a force on the same player – who may or may not be aware of them.

1 The will to win The novelist Philip Pullman, who used to be a teacher, has said that in any class there are archetypal roles that have to be filled, whether it's the kingpin or the clown. Teams have those roles too – the joker, the talisman, the sergeant major. One of them is the type who just has to win, who can't bear not to have the last word.

Graeme Fowler, who opened the batting for England in the mid-1980s, has confessed to being so competitive as a young man that he couldn't enjoy his cricket. "When I look back," he says now, "I didn't really enjoy anything. It was not about enjoyment, it was about winning." So that was his motivation. "Yes, but I didn't know it. I was just compelled to do it, it was just part of me. I understood that it didn't enamour me to my friends – this is when I was 11, 12, 13 – but I thought if you couldn't keep up, it wasn't my fault."

Not all cricketers are driven by their competitive natures, but look at how they relax – by playing golf, or on the Xbox. Their idea of taking a breather from the relentless competition of the day job is to do more competing.

England's No. 1 anchor: Claire Taylor in 2008.

2 Making the best of what you've got Nasser Hussain is in Antigua, fronting the women's World T20 for Sky Sports. He's in a hotel, slightly distracted as he waits for his luggage to catch up with him. But when he's asked about his motivation in his playing days, it is clear, even in his voice, that those gimlet eyes are narrowing. "My motivation was probably – definitely – to make sure that I ended my career not saying 'what if'. 'What if I'd practised a bit harder, what if I'd trained a bit harder?' So that, when I finished, I would know I got the most out of my ability. I played 96 Tests, which was way above what I thought I would play. At no stage now do I think: 'Crikey, I could have done better.'"

He's aware this answer wouldn't be everybody's. "You could argue that if I'd relaxed a bit more, I might have been a better cricketer. But it was the cricketer I was, and the person I was."

3 Fear of failure After making his Test debut at 21, Hussain took more than six years to establish himself. Alastair Cook, by contrast, was an automatic pick at 21, a man who never discovered how it felt to be dropped (except from the one-day side). Always playing the same few shots, barely breaking sweat, he batted as if he resented the fact that only bowlers were labelled as metronomes. When he retired, Cook did two things that seemed out of character. He signed up to become a pundit, with Sky and *The Sunday Times*; and, in his first column, he said something revealing.

"Can I make the next tour? That was what drove me, the fear of failure," he told his ghostwriter. "It drove me more than others because I wasn't the most talented cricketer. I genuinely enjoyed the fight, not to prove others wrong, but to prove to myself that I could survive for as long as I chose to." He did prove it, just: the lean spells lengthened as time went on, but Cook left on his own terms after having much the longest Test career, in terms of matches, in England's history.

4 Money   "Some players were motivated by money, even back then, when it was very little," says Graeme Fowler of the 1980s. "I remember a semi-final with Lancashire, and the last thing anyone said before we left the dressing-room was: 'Come on, fellas, we're playing for a month's mortgage.' That upset me, not at the time, but when I thought about it afterwards."

In 2018, Mike Atherton wrote: "Most [players] of my acquaintance, would have gladly performed for nothing." But some are at least partly motivated by money, even if this is the drive that dare not speak its name. In Fowler's time, three England captains, former or future – Graham Gooch, Mike Gatting and John Emburey (twice) – signed up for rebel tours of apartheid South Africa, a move that could only be justified by wanting security for their families. Today, some young players target Twenty20, where the big bucks are; some older ones stick around because they have alimony to pay, or a benefit on the horizon. And few sportsmen of any age turn down the easy money that comes from endorsements, whether for motorbikes in India or hair-loss treatment in England.

5 Fame   When today's children are asked what they want to be when they grow up, they often say "famous". One of the few cricketers who have said it is Sanjay Manjrekar, the pundit and former India batsman. "I loved it," he told ESPNcricinfo in January 2019 about playing cricket as a boy, "and I wanted to be famous and well-known."

With other players, a thirst for fame shows up in their actions. Most long to be on the honours board. Some, like Ben Stokes, play more intensely at big moments, which may spring from a desire to dominate or to make their mark. Others, like Ian Botham when he flirted with Hollywood, ask for second helpings of fame. Some retire and head straight for "Strictly Come Dancing", where they are seen by about nine million more of their countrymen than they ever were in an Ashes Test.

6 Loyalty   If you had asked an international cricketer of the 1950s about motivation, he might have been surprised by the question – self-consciousness was foreign to him – and given a simple answer. "To represent your country, that's the highest honour." These days, it's not simple at all.

There's an entry in every player's ESPNcricinfo profile that has become more and more telling. It's the fourth line, and the first morsel of information that wouldn't be in the player's passport: "Major teams". For Alec Stewart, who retired 16 years ago, it says "England, Surrey". For Brendon McCullum, another international wicketkeeper-batsman-captain, still playing, it says "New Zealand, Brisbane Heat, Canterbury, Chennai Super Kings, Glamorgan, Gujarat Lions, Kochi Tuskers Kerala, Kolkata Knight Riders, Lahore Qalandars, New South Wales, Otago, Royal Challengers Bangalore, Sussex, Trinbago Knight Riders, Warwickshire". Not surprisingly, they missed a few: Kandahar Kings, Middlesex, New South Wales and Rangpur Riders.

Stewart was a one-club man. Whether playing for Queen or county, he took the field with his roots showing. McCullum is an 18-club man. This is not to doubt the commitment of someone who has done as much for New Zealand

Single-minded: Nasser Hussain in thoughtful mode, 1999.

cricket as anyone. It is just to point out that deep-seated loyalty is slipping into the mists of time. Today's globe-trotting cricketer, who may only be with a team for a month or two, is not really playing for the badge.

7 Grievance   It was a peculiar sight: a Test hundred not being celebrated. Belatedly restored after injury to England's red-ball team in Colombo last November, Jonny Bairstow batted at No. 3 for the first time. But when he reached three figures, the usual joy was replaced by anger. He seemed to have been seething with indignation that his place had ever been questioned. The fact that it barely had been was neither here nor there: Bairstow had turned his fury into fuel.

Two months later, Geoffrey Boycott called West Indies' Test team "very ordinary, average cricketers". They proceeded to hand out the heaviest defeat England had suffered in the Caribbean. Perhaps Boycott had forgotten what happened when Tony Greig flagged up his intention to make West Indies grovel. Being written off is always grist to a sportsman's mill, but Boycott and Greig were both, no doubt inadvertently, tapping into a deeper, darker, sadder seam – the vicious injustice visited, for centuries, by white people on black, in the form of slavery. "Whenever we come here," Jimmy Anderson had said a day or two before Boycott's blast, "you get the feeling West Indies really want to beat England. It's something that has been ingrained in them. You can see it in the players' eyes." The "mother" country, the former slave masters: that's motivation all right.

Revenge doesn't have to be a dish eaten quite so cold. England have managed to win four home Ashes series in the past 30 years (2005, 2009, 2013 and 2015) – and three have prompted Australian revenge missions that have turned into routs (5–0, 5–0, 4–0). Hell hath no fury like an Aussie scorned.

8 Sheer dislike   Revenge can even be served piping hot. When England were touring the West Indies in 1993-94, Curtly Ambrose developed what he, or his ghost, later called "an irrational dislike" of Andy Caddick. "I would probably say it was because he had an action quite similar to Sir Richard Hadlee's," Ambrose writes in his memoirs. "I always admired Hadlee as a truly great bowler and I figured, 'Man, you shouldn't be trying to bowl like Richard Hadlee, you're not in the same class.'" In the Third Test at Port-of-Spain, with West Indies only 171 ahead in the third innings, Ambrose had a big heave at Caddick and was bowled, presenting him with his first five-for in Tests. Back in the dressing-room, Ambrose received what was surely a rare dressing-down. So he was now angry with Caddick, angry with himself, and either angry with his team-mates or guilty about letting them down. The rest is history: England 46 all out, Ambrose six for 24.

9 Pleasing yourself   Graeme Fowler is talking about his early days as a player – which were not easy. A year before his Test debut, Botham's Ashes were unfolding, and Fowler was playing for Lancashire Seconds. Motivation, though, was never a problem. "It wasn't a word that existed in my vocabulary. All my mates would have 18th-birthday parties, 21sts, and I'd miss them. I'd say 'I have a game', they'd say 'it's only a club game', I'd say 'you don't understand'. When in fact *I* didn't understand. I was so driven. Selfish – no, self-centred is the word: so engrossed in my own little world."

When did he move beyond it? "I can tell you – 2, 3, 4 August 1994." He was 37. "My last season at Durham, second team, first game ever at the Riverside, I was captain. Katherine Elizabeth was born early in the morning, at twenty to four or something. I remember driving at six to my parents, who had brought their caravan up. I was driving towards the caravan park and thinking: 'Thank fuck, my life's not about me any more. I'm not Graeme Fowler, I am Kate Fowler's dad. Everything's not about me any more.' And that was such a relief."

Nasser Hussain makes a similar point in a different way. "When you have a young family, your motivation changes. To keep your focus is very difficult. Having a family helped – it did give me a sense of perspective. You've stuck 'em in at Brisbane, you're changing nappies at bedtime and this littl'un doesn't give a toss. Have something away from the game – Ath [Mike Atherton] used to read the *Racing Post*. It's a cliché, but you can want it too much."

10 Pleasing others   To reach the top in a sport, you have to please a lot of people, from the coach of the Under-9s to the selectors of the national team. And the first person most of us ever wanted to please was a parent. Joe Hussain, Nasser's dad, was also a coach, which may have doubled his impact. "Probably through my dad, every single game I played mattered to me, whether it was a benefit or a Test match," Nasser says. "With my family and me, it's about a little bit more than a game – it's being the best you can be. If I got 20, I could have got 30; if I got 40, I could have got 50. As a batsman you can never have

Philip Brown, Popperfoto, Getty Images

Pumped up: Jonny Bairstow gives vent on reaching a hundred at Colombo, November 2018.

enough, you're never completely satisfied. Even when Philip Tufnell bowled me round my legs for 99, you'd spend the next five days thinking about the one run you didn't get, not the 99 you did."

The grown man or woman, standing at the non-striker's end, lost in their own thoughts, may not be thinking about a parent (though more and more players seem to have mum and dad there, as at a school game). If they're trying to please anyone, it may be their team-mates. Often, when they reach a hundred, the first jab of the bat goes towards the players' balcony. It's said that soldiers in war are seldom thinking of the principles that were cited by the politicians sending them there: they're risking their lives for their mates.

There's another group players may be trying to please: the supporters, especially in away matches. Travelling fans, radiating commitment themselves, tend to inspire it in sportsmen. For some cricketers, there is a section of the crowd they feel particularly beholden to. "We've got big support, especially in the Asian community, whether it's Bradford, Birmingham or Pakistan," Adil Rashid said in October 2018. "In your younger days, you play for yourself, but as you represent England you go all around the world and realise it's a bit bigger than that. People look up to you, and it's about setting a good example, so when they're coming through, they see that and know it's achievable."

11 Fun Many great cricketers have appeared in the Under-19 World Cup, but none have done what an Australian leg-spinner with long red hair did in January 2018. Playing against England, Lloyd Pope took eight wickets in 9.4

overs, six with his wrong'un. After England had subsided from 47 for none to 96 all out, Pope came out with a statement you don't often hear at a press conference: "I've always played cricket for fun." Keith Miller would have approved.

Fun is the simplest motivation, the most childlike; but it also chimes with academic thinking on the subject. Claire Taylor, who now gives talks about getting the best out of yourself, mentions Mihaly Csikszentmihalyi, a Hungarian-American professor of psychology whose theme is that motivation should come from within. "He's written about the zone and flow," Taylor says. "The aim is to get into a flow-like state – you don't become nervous, and you lose yourself in the performance. He's for intrinsic motivation: the outcome is less important than the process." In other words, come on fellas, forget about the mortgage, let's have some fun.

Tim de Lisle, a former editor of Wisden, *is the author of* How to Write Well.

WISDEN WRITING COMPETITION WINNER IN 2018

An implicit language

Nick Campion

One sunny afternoon on the school playing fields in 1982, the nine-year-old me came face-to-face with my dad. In a father–son relationship founded in the old rules of stiff upper lips and unspoken affection, cricket was the medium through which we communicated, a way into a conversation where we could interact warmly, passionately even, without awkwardness. This was how we expressed our affection – and we accepted it. He knew no different, I knew no better.

As school drifted into the joyous last few days of the academic year, nine-year-old me walked to the wicket, heart thumping, ears alive to the cheers of encouragement from the boundary. Suddenly, I became so self-conscious that even walking felt complex and mechanical, but I made it to the middle, and took guard in the annual Fathers v Sons match. The umpire confirmed my Viv Richards-inspired leg-stump guard. I tapped my bat – my first, a size four Gunn & Moore – and looked up to see my dad at the end of his run.

It was rare for him to go to a school event. But this was a special occasion. Mum had bought a picnic and a summer dress. While other dads who were playing wore jeans, tracksuits and trainers, mine was in his whites.

Dad bowled off-spin. I watched him begin his familiar, curved trot to the wicket, left shoulder dipping, before a short delivery stride and a surprisingly delicate pivot on his left foot. The ball hung in the air. So slow, so hittable. I swung as hard as I ever had, the shouts of "Go on, Nick, show your dad!" and "Six! Six! Six!" spiking a surge of adrenaline.

As I swung my bat, I became aware that the expected moment of impact had come and gone. There was that instant between missing the ball and hearing it hit the stumps when you manage to generate a nanosecond of optimism, before the sound of leather on ash crashes through your hopes. My devastation was immediate and, I learned later, so was my dad's. He had thrown up a ball of innocuous gentleness, an offering from father to son, a delivery designed to ensure the moment belonged to me, not to him. The tears prickling my eyes would not be swallowed away. The jeers and boos directed at my dad made me feel better – and worse. My dad prepared to bowl his next ball, utterly crestfallen.

In the weeks before he died, when his world had shrunk to the edges of his hospice bed, his digital radio became the fire around which we gathered, while his heart counted down its remaining beats.

We listened, and agreed on enough to feel the warmth of our shared understanding, and disagreed on enough to maintain the fragile paternal carapace on which his dignity could rest. As consciousness became more fleeting, the mumbling of the radio alone, no matter what the words, was the blanket we wrapped ourselves in and huddled under, while the cricket continued to wash over us with reassuring timelessness.

Nick Campion is a freelance copywriter and psychotherapist in training. As a club cricketer, he has reached the stage of his career that might be described as crepuscular.

THE COMPETITION

Wisden received almost 100 entries for its seventh writing competition. They poured in from around the world and, as ever, the standard was high. Wisden remains appreciative of the industry, imagination and inventiveness of all entrants. The first articles arrived in April, almost eight months before the end-of-November deadline; others arrived with December only seconds away. All were equally welcome, and all read by the editorial team. The business of judging, however, becomes no easier. The prize remains the same: publication, adulation, and an invitation to the launch dinner, held at Lord's in April.

The rules are also unchanged. Anyone who has never been commissioned by Wisden can take part. Entries, which should not have been submitted before (and are restricted to a maximum of two per person), must be:

1. the entrant's own work
2. unpublished in any medium
3. received by the end of 30 November, 2019
4. between 480 and 500 words (excluding the title)
5. neither libellous nor offensive
6. related to cricket, but not a match report.

Articles should be sent to almanack@wisdenalmanack.com, with "Writing Competition 2019" as the subject line. (Those without access to email may post their entry to Writing Competition 2019, John Wisden & Co, 13 Old Aylesfield, Golden Pot, Alton, Hampshire GU34 4BY, *though email is much preferred*.) Please provide your name, address and telephone number. All entrants will be contacted by the end of 2019, and the winner informed by the end of January 2020. (Please contact Wisden if your entry has not been acknowledged by the end of December.) Past winners of this competition, Bloomsbury staff and those who in the editor's opinion have a working relationship with Wisden are ineligible. The editor's decision is final. Once again, we much look forward to receiving your contributions: they never fail to contain surprises.

THE 2018 ENTRANTS

Robert Bartram, Mike Battrum, David Beales, Jamie Beck, Andrew Bruce, Nick Campion, Carlos Castro, Paul Caswell, James Chadwick, Mohit Choudhary, Tom Churton, Paul Clifford, Oliver Colling, Matthew Cooper, Michael Cooper, Matthew Cowman, David Cuffley, Stephen Dansie, Dibyadarshan Das, Will Dawes, Jay Dhingra, Louie Elmer, Philip Evans, David Fraser, Scott Fraser, Deu Gaichor, Mark Gannaway, Nick Gormack, Steve Green, Michael Gyles, Mitchell Hall, Philip Hardman, Nick Hayhoe, John Heaton, Peter Hill, Jason Hobbs, Sameer Hussain, Alia Juman, Sam Juthani, Asmi Kartikeya, John Kirby, Simon Lamb, Huw Lloyd, Patrick Mackerras, Ian Marshall, Rory Mathews, Stephen Mellick, Tim Mickleburgh, Anthony Morrissey, Richard Naisby, Simon Parham, M. Pawan, Roy Pearce, Stephen Pickles, David Potter, Gordon Price, Noel Rajive, Richard Reardon, Miles Reucroft, John Rigg, Kenneth Rignall, Darryl Robinson, Phil Rose, Michael Rudling, Abdul Shakoor, Priya Sharma, Christopher Sharp, Alan Sharps, Simon Sheldon, David Sim, Daniel Skrzynski, John Sleigh, Dr Jane Smillie, Peter Stone, Seth Thomas, James Thomson, Dave Thornton, Alan Wainwright, David Walsh, Stephen Ward, Alan Warner, Ben Watson, Martin Whitton, Tim Wye, Mahmud Zeeshan.

WINNERS

2012	Brian Carpenter	2016	John Pitt
2013	Liam Cromar	2017	Robert Stanier
2014	Peter Casterton	**2018**	**Nick Campion**
2015	Will Beaudouin		

FIVE CRICKETERS OF THE YEAR

The Five Cricketers of the Year represent a tradition that dates back in Wisden *to 1889, making this the oldest individual award in cricket. The Five are picked by the editor, and the selection is based, primarily but not exclusively, on a player's influence on the previous English season. No one can be chosen more than once. A list of past Cricketers of the Year appears on page 1459.*

Tammy Beaumont

Adam Collins

On the joyous July evening when England's women won the 2017 World Cup, Tammy Beaumont had somewhere to go. With two medals round her neck – she was also Player of the Tournament – she headed for the white benches on the top deck of the Lord's Pavilion. There, four years earlier, after failing in a one-day game against Australia, she had wept alone, knowing she would be dropped again. Looking out over the home of cricket, she asked herself whether she was good enough. It was a question that would continue to haunt her.

The first seven years of Beaumont's international career produced little. Rock bottom came in 2014 at the World Twenty20 in Bangladesh, where she made ten runs in four innings. Doubt grew into a full-blown crisis. "I wasn't in the best place with cricket," she says. "I hated it." She told England's assistant coach, Carl Crowe, that she was considering quitting. Instead, she gave it one more go and – having batted in every position except No. 4 – set a goal of turning herself into the best opener in the world.

Central contracts had come along, so Beaumont could invest in her game. "I've been in the right place at the right time," she says. "A few years earlier, I would definitely have been lost to the system, as I would have needed to get a job. I wasn't good enough at that point." Returning to that bench as a world champion, she snapped a photo and sent it to Crowe: "Remember this?!"

There were still points to prove. In June 2018, England were thrashed in the first one-day international by South Africa at Worcester, and Beaumont made six off 26 balls. "I felt responsible for the whole innings. I didn't play anything like I wanted to for England." Three days later at Hove, she drove her first ball down the ground for four. "I was determined to go out and show what I could do." She finished with 101, and did not leave a single delivery. Three days after that, at Canterbury, she hit 105 to seal a chase and a 2–1 win. Then, in a T20 game at Taunton, Beaumont made it three international hundreds in nine days, getting there in 47 balls, the fastest by an England woman; a total of 250 was comfortably a world record. She followed that with 71 in another T20 against the South Africans, then one-day scores of 40, 67 and 53 against New Zealand. Her tally of 628 runs at 57 was a record for England in a home summer, beating Jan Brittin's 595 in 1984.

Beaumont is now a homeowner and part-time commentator – a world away from the days when she was struggling to get a sports-massage business off the ground. In the two years after England coach Mark Robinson backed her at the top of the order, she made 1,579 one-day international runs at nearly 51. She credits him with allowing her to flourish, even at the expense of Charlotte Edwards, pensioned off to create space for emerging players. Edwards had been Beaumont's "hero and role model" from an early age. "On the one hand you are devastated for Lot, and appreciate everything she has done," she says. "But at the same time it was the chance for someone like me to step forward."

In June 2016, Beaumont did just that: in successive innings against Pakistan, she made 70 (her first international fifty, nearly seven years after her debut), then 104 and 168 not out. As she completed the first hundred, her parents – watching at 4am in Boston, where they have lived since she was 20 – broke down. "They haven't missed too many games after that," she laughs.

TAMSIN TILLEY BEAUMONT was born in Dover on March 11, 1991. Her mother, Julie, smoothed the way for her first game of hard-ball cricket, aged eight. Her brother, Michael, was captain of an Under-11 side coached by her father, Kevin, a research scientist and dedicated club player. "My mum tells the story quite proudly," says Tammy. "They were struggling for numbers. I sat on dad's armchair, looked at his notes and said: 'But I bowl better than him and I bat better than him! Why can't I play?' Dad looked at mum, who said: 'She's right.' So then they had to pick me."

Her passion was nurtured on a challenging pitch in the back garden and, in the colder months, in the living-room, with a miniature bat and ball, as she tried to avoid getting into trouble with her mother. "Dad had to take the flak because it was his idea." Beaumont followed in his academic footsteps, studying chemistry and sports science at Loughborough University, while Michael got a PhD in organic chemistry. Some of her best memories come from the time all three turned out for Sandwich Town Second XI, where her dad was a cagey off-spinner. "Michael was a very good fielder, so he'd be at cow corner and I'd be keeping," she says. "The number of times it was 'stumped or caught Beaumont, bowled Beaumont' was ridiculous."

She wasn't selected for Kent Under-11 because she was a head shorter than her peers, a consequence of food allergies that slowed her growth. "My coach called me the Mighty Atom, because I was tiny," she says. "I started gymnastics because my mum thought I was so weak I needed to build up some muscle. I grew out of it when I was about eight, but I was always shorter than everyone."

Even so, Beaumont's technical prowess shone through. A Kent debut came in May 2007 at 16, leading to selection in the Super 4s, then a bridge to international cricket. By August, she was off to the Netherlands on an England development tour. Two years later came her first cap.

She still has a way to go. "I don't think I'm the best opener in the world. But that's still the goal, and I want to do it for as long as possible." After that, she would love to deploy her experience – the bad and the good – in a leadership role. "One day I would like to be in some kind of position of responsibility. That would be amazing. But if it doesn't happen, I'd like to be part of one of the most successful teams in England history."

Rory Burns

PHIL WALKER

In a year of daring selections, the elevation of Rory Burns to the top of England's Test order was as straightforward as they come. Nobody disputed it was his time. The question was why it had taken so long.

In 2018, everything fell into place. For the fifth season in a row, he passed 1,000 first-class runs, his tally of 1,359 the most in the Championship, 270 ahead of Somerset's James Hildreth. Three of his four centuries were over 150, his rate of 125 balls per dismissal was – according to CricViz – higher than anyone's, and his average of 64.71 the best by any opener. In his first year as Surrey captain, he oversaw ten wins out of 14, and the club's first Championship in 16 years. As his mentor Alec Stewart, Surrey's director of cricket, said in September: "If Rory is not in the Test squad for Sri Lanka, I'll have plenty to say on it." He need not have worried.

It had been a long apprenticeship. In 2015, Kumar Sangakkara – reflecting on a prosperous first season with Surrey – remarked that, if England were looking for an opener, "Rory Burns should be right up there as one of the top contenders." And yet, for the next two years, Burns would be overlooked, even for the Lions, as others with inferior records but more eye-catching techniques bustled past.

His left-handed idiosyncrasies may have held him back. Most notable, as the bowler gathers, is the pronounced bob of the head towards midwicket, as if he's tracking the path of a swallow flying across the pitch at an awkward moment. The crouched stance, elaborate backlift and distinct trigger movements come straight from the Alastair Cook school of studious functionality.

"I think the way my technique is, and the nuances with it – there may have been some scepticism about whether it could work," he says. "The unorthodox nature of my game probably played a part in why it took so long for the call to happen."

The bob of the head has a logical foundation. "I'm left-eye dominant," he explains, "so basically I want to get the left eye on the ball as much as possible. The fact that it's now a twitch is just a rhythm thing. Sangakkara had his own little taps and bounces. You've got to have your own routine to attune yourself to face the ball."

Stocky, nuggety, an excellent leaver and good off his pads, Burns sounds easy to pigeonhole. But there is more to him than the clichés usually reserved for left-handers. Against Yorkshire in late June, in a pivotal clash at Scarborough, he struck 156 runs, with 27 fours, across the two innings. A fortnight earlier, he had breezed to 151 in 204 balls against Hampshire. And a month before that, in conditions suiting the seamers, he had battled for eight minutes short of nine hours to make 193 against Worcestershire. Burns plays the situation as well as anybody in the county game.

The captaincy came at just the right time, and he believes it aids his batting. "It has probably been a stepping stone that has helped my game. In the past

I might have nicked off at 11am, and I'm sitting back in the changing-room with my pads still on, having a coffee. But now I'm talking to others, asking how they can be helped – rather than stewing over my own performance with a towel over my head."

RORY JOSEPH BURNS was born in Epsom on August 26, 1990, and educated at City of London Freemen's School and Cardiff Metropolitan University. Despite having been with Surrey since the age of eight, he was not offered a professional contract until he scored a century *against* them, for Hampshire Second XI. With an offer from Hampshire also on the table, he opted for his home club, and made his Championship debut in 2012, keeping wicket and batting at No. 7.

Burns regards Academy coach Neil Stewart, the least decorated of the Surrey clan, as his most important influence. "Even as a kid, he had his own way of playing," says Stewart. "He looked a massive lbw candidate playing across his front pad, except that he never missed the ball, just kept whacking it through the leg side time and time again. He was always unassuming and determined. We had a long chat before he started the captaincy, and he was very clear how he wanted to go about it. That's just him – a simple, straightforward lad. No airs and graces, no huge ego."

After a summer of unbroken fruitfulness, Burns returned to earth on Test debut in November. On the first morning at Galle, he was strangled down the leg side; in the second innings, he ran himself out. "Yeah," he concedes, "that one was slightly anticlimactic."

But in the next Test, at Pallekele, he made 43 and a 66-ball 59 full of decisive sweeps – an innings that set the example for others that followed. As an English opening batsman reared on seam, his assurance against spin surprised some. But not Sangakkara: "When I look at a young player I look at their overall game," he said back in 2015. "Burns is great against pace and very good against spin – he sweeps, he paddles, has a great defence and a very positive mindset."

Even so, Burns knew he had missed out at Pallekele. "I was really pleased with how I played. I should have got more: if anything I relaxed slightly – that could have been a big statement score. But at the same time, on that pitch, to make a contribution was important."

A series haul of 155 runs at 25 might have contained no statement score, but there was enough to suggest Burns had the game for Test cricket. A second-innings 84 at Bridgetown in January confirmed as much. If anything, the wait solidified his self-belief. "I'd felt good enough to do it for a couple of years. Whether others thought so, that's a matter of opinion. But I felt ready. It's a red pill, there's a cricket bat in my hand – get on with it." Was he nervous? "I was nervous to get off the mark, but not really. You build it up to be this massive thing, but at the end of the day it's just cricket, isn't it?"

Jos Buttler

TIM DE LISLE

Cricket is a game of a thousand swearwords. Most are routine outbursts of frustration or antagonism, instantly forgotten. Hardly any are written down – which makes this one more distinctive. Inked on the end of a bat handle, it sits on the parallel lines like notes on a sheet of music. It says, in full: "Fuck it".

It is England's most significant expletive since Mike Gatting addressed Shakoor Rana in 1987. That was a hand grenade, whereas this is a note to self. It was made famous by a cameraman during the Headingley Test, as Jos Buttler's bat leaned on his helmet. "It's just something that reminds me of my best mindset, when I'm playing cricket, and probably in life as well," he said. "It puts cricket in perspective: when you nick off, does it really matter?"

For Buttler, 2018 was one purple patch after another. Opening for Rajasthan Royals, he equalled Virender Sehwag's IPL record of five successive fifties. Summoned from the Test wilderness by Ed Smith, he kept turning the tide with a judicious sixty. Facing Australia's depleted white-ball teams, he racked up 336 for three times out. From his Test recall to England's triumph in Sri Lanka, he reached fifty 13 times in 32 international innings. Two things had been glaringly absent from his glittering record: a Test century, and consistency. In 2018, he achieved both, while still emptying bars.

Buttler finished the year starring for Sydney Thunder. He and his wife, Louise, pregnant with their first child, shared a house with Joe, Carrie and Alfie Root. "It's a bit more real living in a house," Buttler says. "In the England squad, there's lots of friendships, so it's nice to live together in a new city."

Ed Smith's England often seem to be playing 15-a-side, yet nobody wears more hats than Buttler, who doesn't even bowl. In 50-over cricket, he's a lethal finisher, racing along at 116 runs per hundred balls, polishing the scoop and the ramp, making Botham and Flintoff look like amateurs. In Twenty20, he's a swashbuckling opener. In Tests, he's the adult clearing up the mess when England collapse. In white-ball games, he's the wicketkeeper. In every format, he's the vice-captain, valued by two very different bosses – the buccaneering Eoin Morgan, the more tentative Root.

JOSEPH CHARLES BUTTLER was born in Taunton on September 8, 1990, and grew up in the village of Wedmore. The sporting gods gave him a phenomenal eye, big hands, whippy wrists, and older siblings. His cricket began in the back garden with James, seven years his elder. "I'd be the annoying younger brother," says Jos, who tends to see others' point of view. At Cheddar CC, his Under-13 coach was his mother, Patricia. "It was a bit embarrassing sometimes, my mum telling me what to do," he once said. "She would inevitably ask why I played that silly shot. She still does."

When Jos was eight, the World Cup came to Taunton. He was riveted as Ganguly and Dravid put on 318 for India against Sri Lanka. "Watching these guys smashing Murali into the river," he has said, "was probably my earliest fanboy moment." It may have been the best thing that happened to England in the tournament. At nine, he was Somerset Under-13 tennis champion. He had offers of sports scholarships from King's College, Taunton, and Millfield. His parents chose King's, further from Wedmore but closer to the county ground. Jos was amazed to find the school allowed him to net at lunchtime. In 2008, riled by missing out on a Somerset contract, he made 227 in an opening stand of 340 with Alex Barrow. In 2010, he was the Wisden Schools Cricketer of the Year. "I looked up who else had won it, Jonny Bairstow and James Taylor, and thought: 'These guys are on the path I want to be on.'"

By then, he had already tasted T20 in India, when Somerset reached the Champions League. After making his name with some white-ball fireworks, he played T20 cricket for England at the age of 20, ODIs at 21, and Tests at 23. His Test career started serenely against M. S. Dhoni's Indians in 2014, then stalled in the following summer's Ashes. "Until the last year," he says, "I never understood my red-ball game. I'm desperate to reach my potential." His 106 in the Trent Bridge Test against India, his 194th international innings, was the first of at least 150 balls. The man who had twice broken the record for England's fastest one-day hundred had discovered his inner classicist.

A few months earlier, Buttler was playing in any colour, as long as it wasn't white: the blue and orange of England, the red of Lancashire, the green of Sydney Thunder, the blue of Rajasthan Royals, the red of Comilla Victorians. He was starring in his own show, Joseph and the Amazing Technicolor Dream Kit. But he was a Test exile. James Whitaker's selection panel placed more faith in Tom Westley, James Vince and Dawid Malan. Buttler could have given up red-ball, like his friend Alex Hales; instead, he earmarked August 2018 as the time to make some Championship runs for Lancashire.

That never happened because he sailed back into Test cricket, propelled by the four winds: his IPL form, an Ashes drubbing, Ed Smith's lateral thinking, and a prod from Shane Warne, the Royals' official mentor. "He had a big influence," Buttler says. "You start off in awe of him, but we really clicked, whether it was on the bus or at the bar. He said: 'Test cricket should still be your aim.' That gave me confidence. He's an incredible cricket brain to learn from. You pinch yourself: I'm talking to Shane Warne about cricket!"

Rumours of the death of players talking shop may have been exaggerated. "One of England's strengths," he reckons, "is that everyone talks about cricket." And, among the franchises, "cricket is the common interest". Buttler, who used to suffer from nerves, now seems calm. "I've got a deep-down desire to win, but I try and enjoy having a clear head." He mentions two role models, Dhoni and Morgan: "They always look in control. You don't often make the right decision if you're not calm."

Buttler's superpower, though, is creativity. In Sri Lanka, he changed his game more in a week – sweeping everything in Pallekele, using his feet to straight-drive in Colombo – than Alastair Cook had in 12 years. "I always want to try every shot," he says. "That's one of the fun parts of practice, trying to learn new skills." His favourite stroke is "probably the ramp". Because it's the trickiest? "No – because it's effective. There's never a fielder behind the wicketkeeper. Even if you don't play it, the bowler is factoring in that you might." There he goes again: seeing the other point of view.

Sam Curran

Simon Wilde

Rarely has English cricket seen a player so young display such talent for shaping big matches as Sam Curran in 2018. Chosen as a bowling all-rounder, two days before his 20th birthday, he was reckoned by some to be too short, at 5ft 9in, and too slow, at 80mph, to succeed at the highest level.

Within weeks, the doubts were forgotten, after he emerged as an all-round match-winner in a taut First Test against India at Edgbaston. Despite missing the Third to make way for Ben Stokes, available again after his court case, Curran still finished with 272 runs, 11 wickets and the series award. Forty-eight hours later, he joined his Surrey team-mates at Worcester to celebrate their first title since 2002. Among England-qualified players, and excluding wartime schoolboys, only Jack Crawford, at 20 years four months, has been a Wisden Cricketer of the Year at an earlier age.

Curran continued to show remarkable match-awareness in Sri Lanka, playing important innings at No. 8 in the first two Tests, before sitting out the last with a side strain; he was also promoted to the new ball, though spin-friendly conditions limited his impact. In all, he had appeared in seven Tests, and won the lot, and arguably established himself as the most effective young Test cricketer England had ever produced. No one under the age of 21 had managed more than his 404 runs or three fifties, all brought up with sixes (a Test record); only Bill Voce, another left-armer, had bettered his 14 wickets. He had also hit 14 sixes, the third-most in Tests in 2018. The icing came when Kings XI Punjab handed him an IPL contract worth over £800,000.

Back in May, Curran had impressed Joe Root, the England Test captain, dismissing him cheaply while taking ten for 101 as Surrey beat Yorkshire by an innings. Even so, the feeling was that, for all his aggression and passion, he was 12 months from Test selection. But an injury to Stokes led to his late call-up against Pakistan at Leeds. Curran felt underprepared, having not played red-ball cricket for over a fortnight, but by Edgbaston he was more confident. By then he had played his first one-day international, against Australia, taken seven wickets for the Lions against India A, and struck 70 against a Nottinghamshire attack led by Stuart Broad.

Curran's influence on two of the India Tests was profound. In the First, he took three top-order wickets in eight balls; then, with England facing defeat, he became their first left-hander to attack Ravichandran Ashwin en route to a quick 63 that gave his side a total to defend. Restored to the team at the Rose Bowl, and with England again in trouble, he scored 78 and 46, and claimed the prize wicket of Virat Kohli. "It's like having two Ben Stokes," said Root.

It was a minor regret that Curran and the oldest brother, Tom, sidelined by a chest injury, did not team up during Surrey's Championship charge. But on August 30, Sam played for England, Tom for Surrey, and Ben – the middle brother – for Northamptonshire. And a long-held ambition was fulfilled in

October, when Sam and Tom, who had made his international debut in 2017, played together in an ODI in Colombo, the first brothers to appear for England since Adam and Ben Hollioake, also of Surrey, in 1999.

A simple explanation for Sam's precocity lay in the genes: his father Kevin was a match-shaping all-rounder for Zimbabwe, Gloucestershire and Northamptonshire whose own father, also Kevin, had represented Rhodesia against George Mann's MCC tourists in 1948-49. By spending half his young life in Zimbabwe, half in England, Sam became adaptable. Those who saw his first net ahead of the Tests in Sri Lanka weren't backing him to make runs against spin, but he devised a method.

SAMUEL MATTHEW CURRAN was born in Northampton on June 3, 1998. Kevin was nearing the end of his career at Wantage Road, where he had formed a close alliance with Allan Lamb, still a near neighbour and family friend. In 2004, Kevin joined Zimbabwe's coaching staff, and the Currans headed for Harare, where he would occupy various roles, including national coach. "There was cricket on in the house 24/7," says Sam. "He taught us about working hard, about fighting until the end. We watched him coach, we were around teams, we saw how guys batted, how they moved."

The boys soon emerged from their cricketing chrysalises. They attended St George's, where discipline was strictly enforced. They flourished. Tom was then sent to Durban's Hilton College, where he was spotted by Ian Greig, who recommended him to Surrey, his former county. With their help, Tom secured a scholarship to Wellington College in Berkshire.

When tragedy struck and Kevin died of a heart attack in October 2012 at the age of 53, the two younger boys and their mother, Sarah, from whom Kevin had separated, returned to England. With Lamb's help, they joined Tom at Wellington, also on scholarships. The three were there together for 18 months. "Wellington was my biggest kick-on in terms of development – that and the Surrey age-groups," says Curran. "Once I came over and saw the cricketing structures, it hooked me even more to the game." Dan Pratt, the cricket master, said the most competitive thing he saw at the school was the Currans netting together: "There was no love lost."

In his first summer, Curran played for Surrey Seconds; two years later, in 2015, aged 17, he marked his first-class debut, against Kent, by sharing the new ball with Tom and taking a five-for. The Currans claimed 55 wickets in six Championship matches together, including all ten in an innings against Northamptonshire. The following winter, Sam represented England at the Under-19 World Cup in Bangladesh. In 2016, the year he left school, nine Championship matches brought 472 runs and 27 wickets, including a career-best seven for 58 against Durham; his reward was a Lions tour to Sri Lanka. His returns dipped in 2017 but, after a winter of domestic Twenty20 in New Zealand, and Lions and North–South one-day series in the West Indies, came his remarkable summer.

Curran had achieved a lot, but a maiden hundred remained elusive. It was surely only a matter of time. "I've been telling people since Sam was 13 that he had the potential to be a top-six batsman," said Lamb, who remains a key adviser. "The self-belief is amazing. Nothing really fazes him."

Virat Kohli

TUNKU VARADARAJAN

Among the many beguiling memories from the Summer of Virat, there is one that does not feature his batting. On the opening day of the First Test of a mouth-watering series, England were in control on a balmy Birmingham afternoon. Jonny Bairstow, batting with Joe Root in an unruffled century stand, had worked an off-break to midwicket, where Kohli gave chase. The batsmen set off for what seemed like a humdrum two, before Root, halfway back, glanced at Kohli – and knew his day was done.

Kohli, as fit and fast a fielder as any India have produced, caught up with the ball, swivelled balletically, and threw down the stumps at the bowler's end. As a diving Root dusted himself off and trudged back to the pavilion, Kohli bade him adieu with a series of kisses blown off an upturned palm. The kisses were delicious mischief. To those who say they were gratuitous, just try watching a replay: one cannot quite imagine that run-out, now, without those kisses.

That wicket caused England to subside from 216 for three to a below-par 287. How would India respond? In the depressing modern manner, Kohli's side had come into the First Test with little preparation. He himself had not played a Test for more than six months, having missed the one-off encounter with Afghanistan in June – initially because he was planning to play for Surrey, though a neck injury scuppered that.

Kohli is a man of adamant ambition: he wants to be dominant – not merely successful – against all teams, in all conditions. Barring Pakistan, where he and every Indian cricketer his age or younger have yet to play, England was the only land in which he had failed. On his previous tour, in 2014, he had failed spectacularly, scoring 134 runs in ten innings. Comfortable against no England bowler, Kohli was thoroughly exposed by one in particular: James Anderson dismissed him four times, and would probably have had him twice as often had others not dismissed him first.

In an interview with Nasser Hussain on England's tour of India in 2016-17, Kohli revealed he had "put too much pressure" on himself that summer, and "wasn't able to get out of that desperation. You need to have a perfectly clear head to score runs in England." He was, he told Hussain, "expecting the inswinger too much". In the event, he nicked inswingers and outswingers alike, and lost much of his swagger.

And so it was that he returned in 2018, bearing a thick file from the Department of Unfinished Business. On the second day at Edgbaston, he came in at 54 for two, and was last out, at 274. He scored 149, more in one innings than he had managed in 2014 in ten. By the end of the series, he had 593 runs at 59, with two hundreds, three fifties, and 67 crunching fours; it was not his fault India lost 4–1.

At Trent Bridge, he was out for 97, wafting lazily at Adil Rashid. As if to atone for a century squandered, he scored 103 in the second innings, giving him precisely 200 for the match – a quirky reprise of the First Test, where Kohli followed that 149 with 51.

He might never have rewritten his personal history, nor found redemption, had Dawid Malan caught him on 21 at Edgbaston. India were 100 for five, and Anderson, bowling beautifully, induced an edge as if it were 2014. Malan dropped a catch only a few shades more taxing than a sitter, and Kohli was to deny Anderson his wicket for the rest of the series. He would be the last to say he mastered him, but there can be no doubt Kohli blunted him.

Born in Delhi on November 5, 1988, VIRAT KOHLI is often regarded as an embodiment of modern India. There is some truth in this assertion, but it is also misleading. He is certainly brash and hot-headed, as urban India has become, but he is the best in the world at what he does. Much of modern India, by contrast, is mired in mediocrity.

Kohli was born into middle-class surroundings, and his childhood was secure, but scarcely luxurious. His family ensured he received the best coaching their modest means could buy, and the investment bore rich fruit: shining for Delhi at age-group cricket, he captained India's Under-19 team to World Cup success in 2008, and made his one-day international debut later that year. He played his first Test in 2011, in a modest series in the West Indies, and did not score a century until his eighth – a gutsy 116 at Adelaide in January 2012, one of the few bright spots for India on a dismal tour. He was beginning to outgrow the tag hasty critics had thrust upon him, that of one-day specialist. And while he continued to thrive in limited-overs internationals – and remains the game's most ruthless chaser – he made no secret of the fact that Test cricket was his first love.

This has been a propaganda gift to the game's oldest form. He is articulate and passionate, speaks his mind, and has little time for platitudes. By the end of the 2018 series, it was his disarming post-match candour, as much as his irrepressible batting, that won him the respect of England's cricket-watching public. Later in the year, in Australia, he won more than that – India's first Test series victory there in more than 70 years of trying.

Ramachandra Guha, the Indian game's foremost historian, wrote that "in all formats and in all situations, Virat Kohli might already be India's greatest-ever batsman". This caused a flutter, but no great consternation: India has outgrown Sachin Tendulkar – the man most would have expected Guha to anoint – and is now in complete thrall to Kohli. Certainly, there is a belief that opponents fear him more than they have any Indian cricketer. Tendulkar commanded great respect, as did Sunil Gavaskar, the champion opener, and the all-rounder Kapil Dev, but none was feared. They were all much too nice, though Gavaskar had an edge.

By contrast, Kohli on song can make adversaries panic. Comparisons with Vivian Richards are made with increasing frequency. Before last summer, those comparisons sounded excessive, if not foolish. Now, they do not seem unreasonable. Late last year, Richards said of Kohli: "I also played the same game. Can you imagine Viv and Virat playing in the same team?" Pity the bowlers.

FIVE CRICKETERS OF THE YEAR, AND THE LEADING CRICKETER IN THE WORLD   Virat Kohli

FIVE CRICKETERS OF THE YEAR   Tammy Beaumont

FIVE CRICKETERS OF THE YEAR   Rory Burns

FIVE CRICKETERS OF THE YEAR   Jos Buttler

FIVE CRICKETERS OF THE YEAR   Sam Curran

IN-FLIGHT ENTERTAINMENT   Kent's Heino Kuhn is run out by Gareth Berg of Hampshire in the Royal London Cup final. In another Lord's final, Charles Janczur of Liphook & Ripsley enjoys the departure of Stuart Stocks, but Folkton & Flixton win *The Cricketer* Village Cup.

Sebastian Daly

SPRING CLEANING   A Munster Premier Division match between County Kerry and Cork Harlequins at the Oyster Oval, Tralee, Co Kerry, and an impromptu game in a block in Dhaka, Bangladesh.

Md Sariul Amin

TICKET TO THE CRICKET   The ingenious art of Jules Akel.

THE ART AND CRAFT OF THE LORD'S TICKET

Making an entrance

JULES AKEL

The total had reached 130. Not runs in an innings, but postcard-sized pieces of paper that opened the gates to the home of cricket. To some, perhaps, they were simply an entry ticket, a mundane record of a financial transaction. But, 25 years ago, I realised they could be more than that. And so this story began.

Back in 1992, Colin Maynard, MCC ticket office manager, saw a map I had created for The All England Lawn Tennis Club, at Wimbledon; it spurred him to commission something similar for Lord's. He must have been happy, as he promptly asked me to design the 1993 Ashes tickets, so starting a fruitful association. The commission was renewed, and extended to other major matches. By 2016, the number of tickets had reached three figures.

But what is a ticket, beyond a fragile and ephemeral item, casually discarded after the event? For me, it is far more than a token for admission. It's a store of value, which can play a substantial role in sustaining the reputation of the venue. It carries with it the eager anticipation of a day with friends, and later becomes a souvenir. From my seat I have heard them discussed (favourably), and some have been framed after the game. Usually purchased months in advance, a Test match ticket is also a significant outlay. So, from the start, I sought to make it a precious and crafted object in its own right – a symbol of the investment, and what it would unlock.

As with banknotes, the first tickets were produced using a technique that allowed fine-line work, which is a challenge for both designer and printer.

Indeed, these tickets were valuable in themselves: they contained all the necessary information – seat and row number, plus date – which meant each was unique and immediately valid. Consequently, they were delivered and stored as though they were cash, checked and double-checked and kept under lock and key at the ground. The similarity to currency went as far as the paper, with some of the early tickets printed on the Crane's Crest stock used for the US dollar bill. Later, with the advent of online booking, full-colour printing became possible. Tickets were designed so that details such as price, date, seat, row and stand could be overprinted by MCC immediately prior to despatch.

Then there was the challenge of keeping the designs fresh. My thoughts turned to the Test nations, their cultures and religious traditions, which offer abundant visual inspiration. Sri Lanka is predominantly Buddhist, India Hindu, and Pakistan Muslim. For South Africa and Zimbabwe, I could explore the richness of tribal art; for Australia and New Zealand, Aboriginal and Maori painting, and for West Indies, the vibrant colours of the Caribbean.

All this emphasis on the visiting nation did not go unnoticed by the ECB, who in 2010 suggested the designs could be more, well, jingoistic. To my mind the quality of the game is of greater importance than the victor, but I listened, and the ticket for the one-day international against Pakistan was my response. It showed a ball comprising the cross of St George breaking stumps of Pakistani green.

A year later, my design for the ODI against India caused a rumpus. The manager of the visiting team persuaded the Indian high commissioner to complain, even though the tickets had for several months been sold in their thousands to supporters of both sides. But now an irate diplomat rang Maynard, who was enjoying a sunny Sunday morning in a deckchair in his garden.

Exception had been taken because the ticket showed an arrow, made up of a stump and red-and-white flights, embedded in the centre of the Indian flag.

A ticket from 2008, before the addition of individual details.

Trouble was, the centre of the Indian flag shows a wheel – the Ashoka Chakra – revered by millions. Maynard swiftly composed an emollient letter to the high commissioner, mentioning the combative nature of cricket, and smoothing ruffled feathers. Even so, designs for matches involving India were in future more sensitive, to the relief of the Maynard household.

It was different when the Australians visited. In the spring of 2012, I started work on the tickets for the 2013 Ashes Test. In a prophetic moment, I depicted St George on his stallion, poking a supine kangaroo with his bat. Sure enough, England won by 347 runs. Did my gentle sledging affect the outcome?

Surprisingly, perhaps, I have no particular favourite, though the seven reproduced here (in this article and the colour section) give a flavour of 25 years' work.

With the arrival of e-ticketing, the pictorial printed ticket, with all its creative ideas, is at an end, my small canvas rendered obsolete by the march of the machines. The new system may be efficient, but perhaps lacking in soul. Still, all things considered, and with appreciation to MCC for their loyalty, the whole experience was entrancing.

Jules Akel is a designer of brands. His book, Cricket Tickets, *is published by Christopher Saunders.*

THE LEADING CRICKETER IN THE WORLD IN 2018

Virat Kohli

The image of Virat Kohli celebrating another hundred – chest out, teeth bared, a vision of furious fulfilment – was already one of the international game's staples. But in 2018 a familiar pose assumed even greater significance. Faced with Test series in South Africa, England and Australia – so often graveyards for Indian batsmen – Kohli rose to each challenge as if he had a score to settle. India's results were mixed, but his batting was supreme. Including a home series against West Indies, he scored five Test hundreds, totalling 1,322 runs, nearly 300 more than anyone else. For an unprecedented third successive year, he was *Wisden's* leading international cricketer in the world.

Hundreds at Centurion in January and at Perth in December underlined his growing comfort in South African and Australian conditions. But the real breakthrough – the only one he still needed to make – came in England. There, he put his 2014 nightmare behind him, averaging 59 and taking India to within touching distance of victories at Edgbaston and Southampton in a series they lost, unflatteringly, 4–1. Time and again, his was the pivotal wicket, yet the pressure never cowed him; if anything, it drove him on.

In Australia, he was able to marry personal and team success. While his 123 at Perth came in defeat, a patient 82 at Melbourne helped his side to a 2–1 lead. At Sydney, where rain robbed India, they completed the first series win in Australia by an Asian team. Kohli said it was the greatest moment of his career.

It almost went without saying that his one-day batting was in a class of its own. In 14 ODI innings, he racked up 1,202 runs and six hundreds – three in a row against West Indies – averaged 133 and had a strike-rate of 102. Forget Bradman: this was Superman. Only in Twenty20 internationals did he fail to stand out. But his tally of 2,735 across the formats was, as in 2017, more than 700 clear of second-placed Joe Root.

Not everyone warmed to Kohli's combative demeanour, and his tête-à-têtes with Australian captain Tim Paine occasionally threatened to distract from the cricket. But, over the top or not, his passion for the Test game was not to be sniffed at. And when a video of him batting in the Adelaide nets was viewed, within hours, over a million times on Twitter, it confirmed modern-day truth: when Kohli is batting, you daren't look away.

THE LEADING CRICKETER IN THE WORLD

2003	Ricky Ponting (Australia)	2011	Kumar Sangakkara (Sri Lanka)
2004	Shane Warne (Australia)	2012	Michael Clarke (Australia)
2005	Andrew Flintoff (England)	2013	Dale Steyn (South Africa)
2006	Muttiah Muralitharan (Sri Lanka)	2014	Kumar Sangakkara (Sri Lanka)
2007	Jacques Kallis (South Africa)	2015	Kane Williamson (New Zealand)
2008	Virender Sehwag (India)	2016	Virat Kohli (India)
2009	Virender Sehwag (India)	2017	Virat Kohli (India)
2010	Sachin Tendulkar (India)	**2018**	**Virat Kohli (India)**

A list of notional past winners from 1900 appeared in Wisden 2007, *page 32.*

IMRAN KHAN, PRIME MINISTER OF PAKISTAN

In charge again

Richard Heller and Peter Oborne

Sir Alec Douglas-Home played twice for Middlesex and became prime minister after Harold Macmillan resigned in 1963. West Indies fast bowler Wes Hall was made minister for tourism and sports in Barbados. Sachin Tendulkar serves in the Indian senate. But Imran Khan is the first case of an outstanding Test cricketer going on to lead his country. The nearest sporting equivalent is the footballer George Weah, who became president of Liberia in January 2018.

Imran was elected prime minister of Pakistan, a nation of over 200m people, last August. He faced a daunting task. Pakistan is bedevilled by long-standing cross-border tensions with India. Terrorism, while sharply down, remains a threat. Right-wing religious parties maintain an ugly grip on many areas of social policy. Endemic corruption and mismanagement hold back economic growth.

To an outsider these problems appear insurmountable. Yet Imran was convinced he could tackle them – echoes of his appointment as national cricket captain amid disarray in 1982. Back then, he was resented by rivals, and thought by many to be temperamentally unsuited. Yet he proved one of

Man of destiny: Imran Khan at Pakistan's moment of victory in the 1992 World Cup.

Pakistan's finest leaders, restoring fortunes so effectively that he led them to victory in the 1992 World Cup. Can he repeat the trick in high office?

The problems facing him now are far more complex. Yet there is no disputing that his playing career proved a useful training ground. Pakistan cricket has regularly exhibited many features of contemporary politics: factional cliques, backbiting, patronage, public rows, synthetic media storms and fake news. And it has mirrored many of the country's major problems.

Cricket gave Imran a prodigious work ethic. It taught him endurance in adversity, ignoring the pain of an unrecognised shin fracture to bowl flat out on hard pitches, then recovering after the injury should have ended his career. It taught him to improve constantly, to reinvent himself late in his career, and to learn from others. Above all, cricket made him a leader: previously shy and introverted, he unearthed qualities as a communicator and a mentor.

He also led by example. Few players can show such an improved performance as captain. Before his appointment for the tour of England in 1982, he played 37 Tests, scoring 1,330 runs at an average of 25; in 51 Tests from then on, including a three-match tour by Sri Lanka in 1985-86, when

Fury at self-seeking corruption and patronage drove him into politics

Imran was returning from injury, and the captaincy had passed briefly to Javed Miandad, he scored 2,477 runs at 51. His bowling enjoyed a similar curve: 158 wickets at 26 before that tour of England, followed by 204 at under 20. He rose to the occasion, and turned a factious team into a cohesive fighting unit.

Imran demanded, and met, high standards of integrity. He was deeply loyal to players he admired – leg-spinners Abdul Qadir and Mushtaq Ahmed, batsman Inzamam-ul-Haq, and his own fast-bowling successors, Wasim Akram and Waqar Younis. They all helped him reinvent Pakistan cricket. He was lucky to have the support of Javed, his predecessor, a great batsman and skilled tactician who willingly handed back the leadership. And in managing his country's cricket bureaucracy, he was helped by the great survivor of the Pakistan game, Intikhab Alam. Does Imran's government now have a Javed or an Intikhab?

Cricket gave him one other asset that may prove crucial in forging peace on the subcontinent: a greater knowledge of India, and more friends and admirers there, than any other Pakistan politician. It remains to be seen whether the Pakistan army or Narendra Modi's BJP government, increasingly influenced by militant Hinduism, will let him achieve any détente with India, over cricket or anything else.

Imran, who has been a politician for over 20 years, could have settled for a comfortable celebrity life, but has won respect, particularly from younger voters, for attempting to achieve more for his country. In his book *Pakistan: A Personal History*, he explains what drove him into politics, principally his fury at the self-seeking corruption and patronage which imbued Pakistan's political parties, who had buried their duty to meet the people's needs. In raising funds for his cancer hospital in memory of his mother, he experienced this at first hand. His major rivals, the Sharif and Bhutto-Zardari dynasties, are

The face of Pakistan: Imran addresses an election rally in July 2018.

reported to have enriched themselves. Imran has made nothing from politics – another source of strength. A recent list of opulent Pakistanis placed him below Shahid Afridi, a less successful but more commercially astute cricketer.

Imran has written of the heavy price he has paid for his political career: physical danger, personal hatred, media lies – which he blames for the destruction of his first marriage, to Jemima Goldsmith – and a short spell in prison under Pakistan's military ruler General Pervez Musharraf. In 2013, he was seriously injured in an accident at a campaign rally.

For years his Pakistan Tehreek-e-Insaf (Movement for Justice) party made little headway outside young, well-educated voters in Pakistan's major cities. But in 2013, he led them to third place in the National Assembly, and to the major share in the provincial government of Khyber Pakhtunkhwa. There, the party are credited with real improvements in health and schools, and in making public servants more accountable. They also planted millions of trees to reverse decades of catastrophic deforestation. Critics attacked him for doing too little to change the lives of women, especially over stalled legislation against domestic violence. Yet in 2018, the party were re-elected in the province with an absolute majority.

Imran has been a persistent critic of Pakistan's acquiescence in American drone strikes against suspected Taliban leaders, and of the army's efforts to suppress terrorism in Khyber Pakhtunkhwa and neighbouring tribal areas. His calls for a settlement with the government earned him the mocking nickname "Taliban Khan", and accusations of being soft on terrorism. His answer is that the drone strikes have caused unnecessary civilian suffering, and that military expeditions have a long record of local failure since the days of the British

CRICKETING PRIME MINISTERS

Selected, then elected

STEVEN LYNCH

Imran Khan is the sixth former first-class cricketer to become a prime minister. But none of the other five matched his 88 Test appearances, or secured a World Cup victory:

Grantley Adams
Played one match for Barbados in 1925-26, scoring 15 runs and making a stumping against British Guiana. Adams was the first premier of Barbados in 1953, and prime minister of the West Indies Federation from 1958 until it broke up in 1962. The airport near Bridgetown is named after him.

Francis Bell
Played two matches for Wellington in the 1870s, scoring two in the first and bagging a pair in the second, against Nelson. After two terms as mayor of Wellington, Bell became the first home-born prime minister of New Zealand, in 1925, serving for just 16 days after the death of William Massey.

Alec Douglas-Home
Played twice for Middlesex (as "Lord Dunglass") in the 1920s, and had eight other matches for various amateur teams, including three for MCC against Argentina on a tour of South America in 1926-27. He took a dozen wickets; Gubby Allen, the England captain who was a contemporary at Eton, thought him a decent swing bowler. In October 1963, Douglas-Home became prime minister after Harold Macmillan resigned through ill health, serving for a year until defeated in a general election. He retained a love of cricket, and was president of MCC in 1966.

Kamisese Mara
Kamisese Kapaiwai Tuimacilai Mara played two matches on a Fijian tour of New Zealand in 1953-54, accorded first-class status years later after persistent lobbying from the diplomat Philip Snow, who played on a similar Fijian tour six years before. Mara took seven wickets against Otago, and scored 44 against Canterbury. By the time he was confirmed as a first-class cricketer, he was prime minister of Fiji, an office he held from 1970 to 1992, apart from a month in 1987. He then became their president.

Nawaz Sharif
Made a duck in his only first-class match, for Railways against PIA in 1973-74. Much later he played in one of England's warm-up games in Lahore before the 1987 World Cup, and was bowled by Phillip DeFreitas for a single. In November 1990, he embarked on the first of three separate terms as Pakistan's prime minister, which amounted to around nine years in all. In 2018, he was given a ten-year prison sentence for money-laundering and corruption.

New Dawn: the Pakistani press react to Imran's election.

Empire. But it has called into question his relationship with fundamentalist Islam in Pakistan.

In his book, Imran set out his vision of Islam as a tolerant, liberating faith in which he and others can achieve self-identity and fulfilment in a mystical relationship with Allah. And while he was scathing about the organised-religious parties and the rigid prescriptive forms of Islam they sought to impose, he has courted their supporters. Most importantly, his new government are heavily dependent on financial support from Saudi Arabia, the principal exporter of fundamentalist Islam to the world.

There is a general fear that Imran's government cannot and will not deliver the promises made at the 2018 elections. This is not his fault. He inherited a virtually empty Treasury, with a broken tax system and barely two months' foreign-exchange reserves. Pakistan faces the prospect of economic vassalage to its creditors, especially Saudi Arabia and China. In preparation for yet another bailout of external debts, the government hiked up the prices of power and fuel, bearing most heavily on the poor. Even if they succeed in repatriating a large part of the capital Pakistanis have sent overseas, they will have few resources to spare for new social-welfare or job-creation policies.

Imran may have more success cracking down on corruption and privilege. He made a popular symbolic beginning by ordering a mass sale of official cars and cutting back on the politicians' cavalcades that regularly paralyse Pakistan's traffic. But critics have picked on his cabinet choices. Some have a high reputation for competence, as does his much-praised choice as the new head of the Pakistan Cricket Board, Ehsan Mani. However, other appointees are retreads from governments he had denounced as corrupt.

Critics have also accused him of making too many compromises to gain power, so that he will govern only on licence from forces who want no change in Pakistan, or want to change it for the worse. Most importantly, they accuse him of accepting power on terms set by the army, who have provided four rulers, covering 30 years of the country's 72-year history. Since the fall of the last, General Musharraf, in 2008, the army have veiled their power behind civilian governments, while retaining control of key areas of policy, especially relations with India and Afghanistan, and with any arms supplier, plus internal security and the defence budget, which has always exceeded the combined budget of health and education. The army are also a huge economic interest group in Pakistan, owning large tracts of valuable property (recently estimated at 12% of the country's land mass) and a swathe of major businesses.

For many years it has been dangerous for journalists, bloggers, political candidates, pressure groups and even judges to challenge them. Broadcast media disliked by the army were suddenly taken off air, and newspapers starved of advertising. To his credit, Imran promised new laws to guarantee media freedom. Even so, he faced multiple accusations of being the army's puppet. Hameed Haroon, chief executive of the publishers of *Dawn*, the newspaper established by Pakistan's founder, M. A. Jinnah, has spoken bluntly of "an unprecedented assault on press freedom", and of an attempt to patch up a coalition which would rule with direction from the deep state. Such accusations reinforce the key message: Imran will have to change the way Pakistan governs itself even more thoroughly than he changed the way it played cricket.

There are encouraging signs. He cuts a dashing figure on the international stage, unlike his long-term predecessor Nawaz Sharif. And he has already made his mark as one of the few global leaders to stand up publicly to US president Donald Trump – a display of courage which put others, including Modi and Theresa May, to shame.

In 1992, Imran Khan told his team to fight like "cornered tigers". The task that faces him today is yet more awesome. But, as his many vanquished opponents on the field will testify, if anyone can achieve the impossible, it is the new prime minister of Pakistan.

Richard Heller and Peter Oborne are the joint authors of White on Green: Celebrating the Drama of Pakistan Cricket. *Oborne also wrote* Wounded Tiger: A History of Cricket in Pakistan.

THE 2018 WISDEN DINNER SPEECH

One more thing to worry about

MILES JUPP

Thank you very much. It's always a thrill to visit what I like to think of as London's second-best Test venue. And it's a pleasure to be invited to come out for the evening and talk at great length about cricket, given the frosty reception I tend to receive for it at home – my wife sadly and erroneously believing that discussing the difference between Graham Gooch's batting average pre- and post-captaincy is less important than simply getting some sleep.

I fell in love with cricket in 1991, absolutely out of nowhere. I'd played it at school, played matches for my school. I even used to have nets here at the indoor school. But I didn't love it; I just did it. Like all the other things you're obliged to do at private school, from learning Latin verbs to cultivating a sense of unjustified superiority.

In 1991, as a result of some sort of alchemy, it happened. An interesting enough summer: Bryan Adams's "(Everything I do) I do it for you" riding high in the charts and presumably blasting out of R. A. Smith's dressing-room boom box throughout; a drawn series against a good West Indies side; the last Test of I. V. A. Richards; the debuts of G. A. Hick and M. R. Ramprakash ("Strap in!" we thought); the return of I. T. Botham; the leg-over incident.

Miles Jupp.

I was rewarded, that Christmas, with a series of cricket-related books – my parents no doubt delighted that I had suddenly, in my 12th year, actually taken an interest in something. They'd taken to poking me with a stick every few months just to see if I was sentient. It was a slightly unusual collection, mainly scoured from the second-hand bookshops of Lincolnshire. Certainly, no one else went back to school that term with their own hardback copy of the autobiography of the Bishop of Liverpool. Their loss – crikey, he knew how to dish the dirt. The best of the lot, though, was a brand new copy of the 1991 edition of *Wisden*, that fabulous yellow brick of hard facts. Imagine my disappointment, however, when I opened its covers and found that 1991 referred not to the year of the cricket it described, but to the year of its publication. I wanted to relive that glorious summer. What did I care or know of 1990? Who were these people? Who was J. E. Morris batting at No. 3? Who was this E. E. Hemmings? I read it, of course, from cover to cover. And, actually, not a bad year. At least I now understood why some people at school had bats with 333 branded on them. I'd assumed that, like most things at private school, it was some sort of reference to their fathers' Masonic connections.

Cricket to me had a kind of magic. It seemed to be a game where grittiness and stubbornness had their place. It's all very well people skipping up the wicket or heaving blockhole filth over cow corner. I like them to be rewarded for just about getting out of the way of a rising short ball, or thick-edging wide of fourth slip for a scampered single. I love that it can end in a draw. My dream day of Test cricket wouldn't involve Sehwag or Gilchrist smashing people to all corners; it would be Atherton and the less-gifted Waugh blocking out Warne and Ambrose all day for a draw.

I was now the proud owner of the autographs of Peter Bowler and Ole Mortensen

I was at The Oval on September 12, 2005. Kevin Pietersen played the most amazing innings I have ever seen in the flesh – in just his fifth Test. But if I could have been anyone on the pitch that day, it would have been Ashley Giles gutsing it out at the other end, forcing it through the covers off the back foot and smiling drily at sledges. And yes, it ended in a draw. Perfect.

The 1990s was my period for cricket. A lot of people my age remember the 1990s for Britpop – Blur, Oasis, that crowd. I remember it too, of course, but to me they were the soundtrack to the on-field exploits of M. A. Atherton, A. J. Stewart, D. Gough, G. A. Gooch, G. P. Thorpe, A. R. C. Fraser, D. E. Malcolm, C. C. Lewis, all too briefly D. I. Gower and – generally for one glorious Test at the tail end of each home summer in advance of a disastrous winter tour – Philip Clive Roderick Tufnell.

The first Test I ever went to was against Australia in 1993 at The Oval, England winning – Atherton's first victory in his second Test as leader. Atherton became my hero that summer, making scores of 19, 25, 80, 99, 11, 9, 55, 63, 72, 28, 50 and – that's right – 42. I know you all wanted to chant along with me.

It wasn't just the fancy venues I went to, though, the bustling stadia of our metropolises. The first professional cricket I actually saw was at the Racecourse Ground in Derby. It looked less like a first-class sporting arena than the sort of place people exercise their dogs. I saw Kim Barnett reach a century against the touring Australians. Has anyone else ever seen Wayne Holdsworth take a hat-trick at Derby? I didn't realise that *I* had, until I read about it in the paper the next day. I was happy enough, though. I was now the proud owner of the autographs of both Peter Bowler and Ole Mortensen. Not a bad haul for my first day, I thought.

I loved collecting autographs. The end of a day's play wasn't the end of the day for me. It was the start of my autograph hunting. In 1995, I spent three

NOTES ON USE

Usually, Autograph Books consist of a few blank pieces of paper. As signatures are not always easy to read, you may have difficulty, after a year or so, remembering whose a particular signature is.

This new style Autograph Book is designed to enable you to record a few useful details about the person (or persons) and the occasion on which you obtained the Autographs.

Record, on the page concerned:—

   the date you obtained the autograph.

   the occasion concerned (i.e. which sporting event or other event)

   the name of the Sports Star in BLOCK CAPITALS in the space provided, so that you can still read it clearly years later.

   the Sport played by the Star or the Team he or she plays for (if a Team sport) or record both Team and Sport.

Time signature: the cover and opening page of Miles Jupp's autograph book.

days watching Middlesex play Northamptonshire at Uxbridge. I got every single player's autograph – either when they were fielding at fine leg, or bustling between the pavilion and their sponsored cars with their names on the side, or round the back smoking B&H. When I got the last one, David Ripley I think it was, it was every bit as satisfying to me as having got Brian Lara's three days earlier at The Oval.

I have here something that I retrieved from a box under my desk last night. It's my autograph book from 1996 – all the signatures in it collected on one August evening on the Harleyford Road. Inside the front cover there are notes and advice on its use: "Record the name of the sports star in BLOCK CAPITALS in the space provided, so that you can still read it clearly years later," etc. It also says: "Sometimes, you will ask for an autograph, but be refused. A special section is provided at the back of the book to record these disappointments." I'd quite forgotten this feature, and so I eagerly looked at the back page and laughed for about ten minutes when I saw that the first two names on it were Cork and Boycott.

But never mind that. Listen to the names of the ones who did sign. I sometimes put extra details about them in brackets. "Robert Croft (debut), Ian Salisbury (also England A), John Crawley (smokes Marlboro Lights), Nick Knight, Alan Mullally, Alec Stewart, Nasser Hussain, Michael Atherton." I remember two things most vividly about acquiring the autograph of Michael Atherton that day. [Atherton is sitting feet away, laughing, as Jupp speaks.] The first was his modesty. The second was the state of his car. Astonishing. At that time in my life I had never witnessed a car so messy. I now have five children under the age of nine, and I have still never seen a car that messy. If he didn't sleep in it, something did. If the art department had borrowed his car when they were making the film version of Alan Bennett's *The Lady in the Van,* you'd have thought: "Oh, they've overdone it a bit here."

But there are other names that show just how much I loved cricket as a whole. It wasn't just the players, it was anyone associated with the game: Jonathan Agnew, Mervyn Kitchen, Peter van der Merwe. When I got the autograph of Alan Lee of *The Times*, I could not have been happier. Everything I learned about cricket when I started following it, I learned from him.

You see, I have an envy for people who can make a living from this great game – perhaps because I've always been absolutely dreadful at it. Once, at the age of 12, I scored 52 for my prep school Second XI. That form has never returned. I'd never done anything like that before, either. I was in the bubble for just one afternoon of my life.

The strange thing is, I do still find myself playing. I support the Lord's Taverners, which – as I hope many of you will know – is a charity that does a lot of work helping young people with disadvantages and disabilities. And one of the things they do is ask me to play in games in which you're on a team made up of professional cricketers and people off the telly and radio. So you end up out there in your whites, and standing at slip are Devon Malcolm and Gus Fraser, only next to them is Chris Tarrant. Lulu's keeping wicket. Bernie Clifton and his ostrich are patrolling the boundary. The whole thing's a bit like a fever dream.

What's interesting is that some of the ex-pros take it very seriously, whereas some of them don't. Ashley Giles – up for a laugh, enjoying an excuse to get out into the middle and swing the bat about for old time's sake. Andy Caddick – Christ, I faced one over from him, and he could not have put more into it if he thought there was one place left on the plane to Australia and he was still in contention. I even played in that *TMS* 60th-anniversary T20 game which was shown live on the BBC as a red-button extra, and has consequently given rise to the terrifying statistic that I have played more cricket on terrestrial television than Joe Root.

This envy for people who make a living from the game got the better of me in late 2005. I don't know if any of you saw *Jack and the Beanstalk* at His Majesty's, Aberdeen, that Christmas, but professionally, I felt dissatisfied. This was when I decided to become a cricket journalist. I figured I had two options. Get a qualification in journalism, then gradually acquire sufficient experience over a number of years to be able to break into the extremely competitive sports-writing world. Or the quicker way – and the one I chose – which was to acquire a press pass, go on an England tour, get access to the press box, and then pretend.

So before England travelled to India in early 2006, I got hold of the number of a sports producer for BBC Radio Scotland. I thought, what I'll do is, I'll ring her up, and I'll lie to her. "Hello, it's Miles Jupp here, I'm going out to India for a job, and I can't help noticing that while I'm out there, England are playing a Test series. Could I offer my services as your cricket correspondent?"

And she said, very politely: "Well, we don't carry a *lot* of cricket coverage, but keep in touch while you're out there and we'll see what happens." And I said: "Gosh, the thought occurs if I am going to do any work for you, I'd probably need some sort of press pass or something, wouldn't I? Oh, here's an idea: why don't you write a quick letter on BBC Scotland notepaper, saying 'to whom it may concern', that sort of thing, 'Miles Jupp is our cricket correspondent.' And then, you know, if anything comes up, I could use that."

And she did! So as soon as the letter on headed notepaper arrived, I rang the England and Wales Cricket Board, and I said: "Hi there, it's Miles Jupp, the *chief* cricket correspondent for BBC Scotland. Would it be possible to sort out accreditation for the India tour?"

Yes it would! My mistake, though, was to think getting in would be the hard part. Unfortunately, that was the easy part. The hard part was actually looking like you knew what you were doing once you got in there. I hadn't realised it was a real job. When I was in India, I knew fairly early on that I wasn't cut out to be a cricket journalist. I didn't fit in, I stuck out, I was unusual; Nasser Hussain even bought me a drink one night, and you don't get much more unusual than that.

Cigarette card: John Crawley, as memorable for his choice of tobacco as his maiden hundred.

But this all seems so long ago, and the game so very different. I am only – an admittedly not-very-young-looking – 38. But the game I loved then and the game played today seem like distant cousins.

What a year we've had. The England team playing exciting cricket, not just in the one-day game but also in the Test arena, where they've pioneered a brand of cricket so dynamic and exhilarating that the outcome of matches can be decided in the first session, sometimes the first 15 minutes. I don't know why it always seems so much more difficult to play Down Under. People talk about the pitches, the crowds, the Kookaburra ball. Personally, I would never rule out the sheer demoralising effect of simply being in Australia.

It's good to have Jonny Bairstow with us tonight, representing the rest of the England team in their absence, much as he does so often at the crease. What's remarkable is how quickly we all seem to have accepted it. I still remember the days when an Ashes thrashing would lead to a post-mortem, a formal review and the immediate jettisoning of the batsman with the highest average. But we seem to be much more relaxed about this latest Ashes defeat. As Trevor Bayliss says, we have to regard it as simply another staging post on the way to the 2021 Champions Trophy.

And we've welcomed Ben Stokes back with open arms. Which is frankly the best way to greet him. So that he can see you're not a threat. I think we can all agree it was disgraceful behaviour from Stokes. And totally unnecessary.

You're in Bristol, you've won a game. Don't go out drinking until 2am. You're in Brunel country, go and see a viaduct! Young people have no idea how to enjoy themselves.

But 4–0 in the Ashes. (Of course, I'd like to talk about some of the highlights of the one-day international season too, but as usual within 15 minutes of any of the games finishing they've become impossible to remember.) I mean, yes, it was 4–0. On paper. But, knowing what we know now, that result should probably have an asterisk beside it. Subsequent events mean we have no idea whether the Australians were bowling at all times with something recently retrieved from an Alsatian's mouth.

Really, the most extraordinary series of events. And what a turnaround. You look at footage of Smith and Bancroft in the headbutt press conference, and they're giggling about like Jeremy Clarkson and Richard Hammond. Then you see them sitting there at Cape Town, and suddenly they look like Michael Gove and Boris Johnson the morning after the EU referendum: two men beginning to realise that their actions have had consequences, that at least one of them is going to actually have to do some thinking, and that their lies might not stand up to scrutiny for ever.

Still, at least Smith and Bancroft have apologised. And Warner. Tricky one, that. They say you can judge a man by his enemies. Well, given that so many Australians seem to hate him now, I find myself really warming to the man.

Steve Smith's press conference was certainly very difficult to watch. Especially as a parent. As a rather tired father of five young children, I had briefly allowed myself to luxuriate in the thought that once they've all left home your job is pretty much done. Now it turns out I might have to pick up the pieces in their late twenties when they're done for ball-tampering. It's just one more thing to worry about, isn't it?

And these bans. Not just from international cricket and from the Sheffield Shield, but from the IPL as well. Which to me seems like a missed opportunity – who, after all, cares about the spirit of cricket when there's money to be made? This to me seemed like the perfect opportunity for the IPL to team up with a sandpaper manufacturer and every couple of overs pause the action for a "B&Q Moment of Tampering".

Bancroft won't even appear in the County Championship. Which is a relief. The County Championship simply doesn't need that sort of hullabaloo. The County Championship is an important reminder, much needed in this day and age, that life isn't always about things actually happening. Inevitably, nothing is held to be sacred. There's been some excitable chat about reorganising the County Championship, an opportunity to boost its popularity back to where it used to be, before the Boer War came along and spoiled it all.

And I must say I find the prospect of the new competition extremely exciting, and I don't just say that because the ECB have threatened to sue me otherwise. Although if I'm honest, that is most of the reason. The new franchises, I think, will make all the difference, especially in terms of getting youngsters into the game. You talk to any small child about cricket and ask them if there's anything that puts them off about it, and they will always reply: "Its ongoing association with the historic administrative divisions of England. Bruv."

I am – terrifyingly – probably one of the youngest people here. But even I cannot believe quite how much the game has changed since I've been following it, and the ructions that have occurred. When I was watching Pietersen's 158 at The Oval back in 2005, there's no way I could possibly have foreseen that his last game as a professional would not occur in England colours in front of a home crowd, but wearing bright golden pads playing for the Zappa Crackers in the Hula Hoops Whack Off, or whatever it is.

When I was lying to people in India, I was blown away not just by how knowledgable the journalists were about cricket, but by how much they *cared* about it. I don't watch anything like as much cricket as I used to. Cricket is a big business, and I am no longer one of its big

Star signing: Mike Atherton, whose autograph is neater than his car.

customers. I listen to quite a lot of cricket. But mainly I read about it. That's always been how I have connected with the game most.

I think that those people who write honestly, critically and insightfully about this game have always really been its custodians. And that's why I was as delighted to find Alan Lee's signature in this book as any of them.

So thank you for inviting me, thank you for listening to me, and thank you for being my heroes, or for writing about them.

The Long Room, Lord's
April 11, 2018

Miles Jupp is an actor, writer and comedian who would have given anything to have had just one summer turning out semi-regularly for Surrey Seconds.

THE 1979 WORLD CUP

When Collis was King

ROB SMYTH

Mike Hendrick will never forget one delivery from the 1979 World Cup final. He has never seen a replay – doesn't want to, doesn't need to. He knows what happened when he bowled that ball to Viv Richards, and he knows the impact it had. Hendrick's last delivery to Richards that day, flicked magically for six, is the defining image of the match. Yet it is the first ball Hendrick bowled to Richards in his second spell that is his most vivid memory of the World Cup.

"It went down the slope, and Viv moved across his stumps: big whack on the pad, big shout," he says. "Barrie Meyer said not out. I couldn't believe it. The lads who weren't playing must have seen a replay, because they all came out on the balcony to signal it was out."

Richards, on 22 at the time, went on to make a regal 138 not out, and Hendrick's appeal is one of a few moments in that final – some beyond England's control, others well within it – which left them wrestling with life's most bittersweet question: what if?

Forty years on, there are still two interpretations of a tournament in which England reached the final on home soil for the only time. The first is that West Indies were as near as dammit unbeatable. The second is that England came tantalisingly close, far closer than the margin of defeat suggested, to stunning the world, as India would in 1983.

History can be written by the vanquished, too – it's just that fewer people want to read their version. Most of the England squad felt that, while the result did not necessarily lie, it was economical with the truth. As Bob Willis put it: "No one will ever convince me that we were 92 runs the poorer side."

The second World Cup was short and sharp, spanning 15 days in June and 15 matches. In one sense, it could have been played on paper. West Indies began as even-money favourites, and the last four were as predicted (Pakistan and New Zealand also qualified). India, still four years from their limited-overs epiphany, lived down to expectations. Even the tournament's biggest shock, Sri Lanka's win over the Indians, didn't strain the eyebrows.

The 2019 World Cup will have as much in common with the 1979 version as the iMac Pro with the Atari 800. Much of the time it wasn't even called the World Cup, but the Prudential Cup. Each innings lasted 60 overs; group matches were played simultaneously, as were the semi-finals. There were no floodlights, fielding restrictions or coloured clothing, though Australia's Gary Cosier wore his shirt undone to the belly button.

Most of the England squad played in the Benson and Hedges Cup quarter-finals three days before the start, and the team assembled less than 48 hours ahead of their first game. As ever, Ian Botham was headline news. "Botham in

Patrick Eagar Collection/Getty Images

Sidelines: The eight teams on the Lord's turf – Sri Lanka, Pakistan, West Indies, England, Australia, New Zealand, India and Canada.

stag do rumpus", screamed the *Daily Mirror*. "For three hours a crowd of 200 men drank and laid bets on films of horse racing, before two strippers came on." At one stage a fight broke out, though Botham denied involvement. One onlooker told the *Mirror* it was "like a scene from a Wild West film".

The World Cup launch was a little more sedate: a reception at Buckingham Palace and a familiar photograph at Lord's, in which the eight squads lined up side by side. Some famous faces were missing, including the Chappell brothers, Dennis Lillee, Rodney Marsh, Alan Knott and Derek Underwood: England and Australia had excluded their Packer players. West Indies and Pakistan picked theirs.

Australia set the tone in their first game, against England at Lord's – after ten overs they were 14 for none. This was comfortably the most bowler-friendly World Cup, with the lowest average runs per wicket (25) and per over (3.54). No team scored 300, and England reached 200 only once; neither Australia nor India managed even that. There were 28 sixes. The first part of each innings was like a Test match, with two or three slips, and orthodox openers trying to see off the shine. The West Indies manager Clyde Walcott said his side would play themselves in for the first 30 overs, before having a dash in the last 30. On average, there were 13 maidens a game.

With Pakistan most people's second-favourites, England against Australia at Lord's was seen as a quarter-final. Chasing 160, England won comfortably, despite an early wobble. Geoff Boycott managed more wickets (two) than runs (one), and his bowling became a feature of the tournament, to the surprise of everyone except his captain, Mike Brearley. With the World Cup in mind, he had phoned Boycott during the winter to ask him to practise his slow-medium swingers, which he sent down, often from round the wicket, with his cap on (though not, as legend has it, reversed). They were integral to three of England's four victories. It was his chance to have some fun. He had a smile on his face almost throughout – almost – and Boycott the bowler became a cult hero. Some of the lustiest cheers came when he took a wicket.

Then there was Derek Randall's fielding. He pulled off four run-outs – more on his own than any other country managed in total – and probably would have had more with the aid of TV replays. Randall didn't buy a run in the group stages, but justified his place by prowling at cover or midwicket and scrambling batsmen's judgment of a safe single. England's fielding and skilful seam bowling were their strongest suits.

There wasn't exactly World Cup fever – this was the 1970s – but Randall and Boycott in particular elicited public goodwill, and the England players embraced the usual photo opportunities. Botham and Hendrick posed during a celebrity clay-pigeon shoot at Ducks Hill Road in Ruislip. On the day of the Pakistan game, Boycott joined a craze that briefly swept the nation by hanging a teaspoon on his nose.

England's second group game was against Canada, one of two Associates; the other, Sri Lanka, were still two years from Test status. The qualifying tournament, the ICC Trophy, had been played in England just before the World Cup, too late to stop the press: the official programme's list of teams on the cover included "Associates A&B".

Canada's qualification was joyously unexpected. Their left-arm seamer John Valentine said to Willis: "It's the biggest thrill of my life to be over here playing against you guys." In all, Valentine dismissed Majid Khan, Mike Brearley and Rick Darling, while Glenroy Sealy hit four consecutive fours off Australia's Rodney Hogg. In one of the few vignettes that would not look out of place in 2019, Canada were 33 for none after three overs.

They lost all three games comfortably, however, and were skittled for 45 by England. Twenty-one of those came from Franklyn Dennis, who eventually ducked into a Willis bouncer that left him spreadeagled on the stumps. Chris Old had figures of 10–5–8–4. Canada's innings lasted 40.3 overs, and the match dragged on to a second evening because of rain, a feature of the tournament. At one stage it looked as if England might be frustrated by a no-result, as West Indies would be against Sri Lanka, despite each match having two reserve days. But they raced to their target of 46 in near darkness to win with a reserve day to spare. It was day/night cricket without the floodlights.

Pakistan also beat Canada and Australia, so they and England qualified with a match in hand. But their meeting at Headingley was no dead rubber: to the victor, it was rightly assumed, New Zealand in the semi-finals; to the loser, West Indies at The Oval. Both sides were open about their desire to top the group for that reason alone. England won by 14 runs, thanks to unlikely heroism from Willis and Boycott. On a dodgy pitch, Willis's perky 24 – which would remain his ODI best – dragged them to 165 for nine. It looked inadequate as Pakistan raced to 27 for none. Then, for a few magical minutes, the gods

Bob Thomas, Getty Images

If the cap fits: Geoff Boycott bowls in the semi against New Zealand. John Langridge is the umpire.

smiled on Hendrick. His career was defined by batsmen playing and missing, but against Pakistan he took four for three in eight balls. "I probably had a bit of luck for once."

He would finish as the tournament's leading wicket-taker, with ten at under 15, and an economy-rate of 2.66. "Apart from bowling yorkers at the death, I didn't change my style from one-day cricket to Tests," he says. "I just did what I did. I was never a star, but I was a pretty good back-up. It was often said that I bowled too short, and that if I pitched it up I'd have got more people out. The one thing I would say is: 'How does anybody know that?!'"

Pakistan's powerful lower order regrouped – Imran Khan was at No. 9 – before Brearley gave the ball not to Phil Edmonds but Boycott, who took the last two wickets. Wasim Bari was excellently caught behind by Bob Taylor, otherwise having a poor competition; then Sikander Bakht, who needed only to support Imran, had a risible swipe and was caught spectacularly at deep mid-off by Hendrick. The tension spilled over into crowd trouble, with Denis Compton in the *Daily Express* lamenting some "soccer-type rowdyism". Bottles, cans and punches were thrown; 11 were injured, and £1,400 stolen from a turnstile operator.

There had been another incident during the tournament opener between West Indies and India at Edgbaston, where Gordon Greenidge suffered a sore neck after being manhandled by well-meaning supporters on reaching his century. "The next thing we know they'll be dashing out every time someone hits a six," said Clive Lloyd. "And our batsmen enjoy doing that."

England's batsmen were struggling to score runs of any kind. Only Gooch and Brearley totalled 100 in the tournament, Gower and Botham were quiet, while the partnership of Brearley and Boycott came in for stick. The media consensus was that the in-form Gooch, who top-scored in England's first four games from No. 4, should open, as he did for Essex. England did change the top order against New Zealand – but only by bringing in Wayne Larkins, making his international debut in a World Cup semi-final, at No. 3. He replaced Edmonds, with Randall dropping to No. 7. It meant Boycott, with support from Gooch and possibly Larkins, was now the fifth bowler rather than the sixth.

England got off to their usual false start, but a dogged 53 from Brearley and a thumping 71 from Gooch helped them to 221 for eight, their best of the competition. New Zealand began strongly before Randall, who had made a useful unbeaten 42, brilliantly ran out top-scorer John Wright and captain Mark Burgess. Boycott and Gooch were more economical than the four main bowlers, with combined figures of 12–2–32–1. Despite some desperate lower-order hitting from Warren Lees and Lance Cairns, Hendrick held his nerve, and England won by nine runs. "That was a really tough game," he says. "I was absolutely drained at the end, mentally and physically. The pressure was really on me to get my yorkers in."

For a long time, Pakistan were in control of the second semi-final. Chasing 294, they were 176 for one with 20 overs to go, before Colin Croft produced a furious three-wicket spell. Richards prised out the middle order, and West Indies won by 43 runs. It was the kind of scare which sharpens a team's focus.

Before the final, England's players dispersed to spend 24 hours with their families. Willis was fretting after he twisted his knee against New Zealand. In a fitness test on the morning of the match, he bowled sharply at Brearley, who along with chairman of selectors Alec Bedser decided to leave the decision to Willis. The heart said yes, the head said maybe, the knee said no. Willis decided, "with a reluctance close to grief", to tell Bedser he was unfit. "I felt the tears immediately flood into my eyes, and sought the privacy of the shower-room for a couple of minutes to regain my composure."

England brought back Edmonds and kept the same balance as the semi-final, with only four specialist bowlers. When some of Boycott's team-mates told him the XI as he walked from the nets to the dressing-room, he said the decision to have him as the fifth bowler was "crackers". West Indies had four of their own: Croft, Andy Roberts, Michael Holding and Joel Garner. "It is difficult," wrote John Arlott in *The Guardian*, "to imagine any twist of events, conditions or weather that could deny those four fast bowlers."

The newspaper coverage that day was low-key, with no cheerleading or pictures of Botham draped in the Union Jack. The front pages were devoted to former Liberal leader Jeremy Thorpe's acquittal of conspiracy to murder his ex-lover Norman Scott. The match was televised live on BBC1's *Grandstand*, though it had to battle with racing from Ascot, the final of the Colgate International women's tennis from Eastbourne, and the fourth round of the Sedan Products Open Rally Championship.

England won the toss and bowled, reasoning that if the pitch was going to do anything it would be early on. They were right. West Indies slipped to 99 for four – and it might have been worse, the ball repeatedly beating the bat. In *Wisden Cricket Monthly,* Willis reckoned England could have had it won by lunch. Though Richards moved towards a half-century, he was batting like a

Caribbean flourish: Collis King hits out during the Lord's final.

mortal. He edged Old a fraction wide of leg stump, survived that huge appeal from Hendrick, then reached 50 with a nick at catchable height through second slip off Botham.

Richards had gone 50 innings without a century in all formats, and worried whether he could still make big scores. He was also struggling to move the fingers on his left hand, after being attacked with iron bars in Antigua two months earlier. Before he even said good morning to his room-mate Desmond Haynes, Richards announced: "There's going to be a lot of people at Lord's today. It would be a really good time to turn it on." He loved the big stage, even more so in England, with thousands of expats watching. "We felt it was our duty to make sure they were happy. When we were touring England, and West Indies were successful, they felt in my opinion more comfortable in society."

The pressure of a World Cup stimulated rather than cowed him. As wickets fell, Richards's determination grew. But he knew that, when Lloyd was fourth out, West Indies were in trouble. "We're really struggling," he said to Dickie Bird. "This is serious. If they get another wicket now, we've had it." In the dressing-room, Holding was so nervous he couldn't watch for the next hour. West Indies had the dangerous but erratic Collis King at No. 6, followed by a relatively weak lower order. As it transpired, the last four would not score a run between them.

At the age of 28, King was an unfulfilled talent. Six one-day international innings had brought an average of 14. He was wearing no helmet or cap, and

Haynes's boots. As he walked down towards the Long Room, he realised one of his gloves contained a miniature bottle of brandy, a few of which he kept in his kit bag for emergencies. He knocked it back, and strode out to play the innings of his life.

King started briskly and was 19 not out at lunch, with West Indies 125 for four from 34 overs. In the hour after the interval, King and Richards took the World Cup away from England at dizzying speed. In an astonishing partnership of 139 in 21 overs, King was the driver (and puller and cutter). He caned 86 from 66 balls, with three brutal sixes – including two in a row off Larkins – and ten fours, treating every ball like a free hit. Richards had initially struggled, but King middled almost everything. Given the context, and the probable consequences of an early dismissal, the audacity was outrageous. It takes something to overshadow a hundred from Richards in a Lord's final, but King did just that. It was the only half-century of his one-day international career.

At first Richards told him to calm down. When he realised that was futile, he decided to play a supporting role, rather than try to match him. "Kingdom just went to work," he said, "and the result was pretty satisfactory." Richards had an eye on the bigger picture, and vowed to stay in until West Indies had at least 200. King just saw the ball and belted it. His last 41 runs came at 21st-century speed, from 17 deliveries.

Both treated England's part-timers savagely. "There was a silly little smirk on Boycott's face as he ran up to bowl," said Richards. "It soon vanished as the ball kept disappearing around the ground." The last ten overs from Boycott, Gooch and Larkins disappeared for 83. Brearley said he felt "close to impotence… like attacking tanks with pea-shooters". When Larkins's second over disappeared for 16, Brearley turned to Boycott, who conceded 15. Jim Laker, the BBC commentator and *Mirror* writer, said later that Bedser wanted to play Geoff Miller rather than Larkins, but must have been overruled. "England weakened their stronger suit to strengthen their weaker one," wrote John Woodcock in *The Cricketer*. "This seldom works and it did not on this occasion." The fact that it *had* worked in the semi-final had been forgotten.

When King holed out off Edmonds, England's most economical bowler with two for 40, the total was 238. Richards, content that West Indies had a workable total, went into overdrive and scored 42 of the last 48. Few will forget his stroke off the final ball of the innings, when he walked across his stumps to lift an attempted yorker from Hendrick over square leg and into the Mound Stand. As he left the field, Richards thought: "That shot is my invention."

It is also, in many ways, Hendrick's legacy. He has the best average (19.45) and economy-rate (3.27) in England's one-day history (from a minimum of 120 overs). Yet the first thing most people remember is a ball that was hit for six. "Viv was already 132 not out," he says. "He's a great player and he hit the last ball for six. So what!" In a parallel universe, Hendrick dismissed Richards for 22 and is the hero of England's only World Cup victory. "It's one of those things. I won't go to my grave wittering about it."

On paper, Richards's 138 not out from 157 balls looks like a typical masterpiece. Yet it was effectively three innings in one: a fight for survival and

Bob Thomas, Getty Images

Smiles all round: Desmond Haynes and Collis King are congratulated by Mike Hendrick, Chris Old and David Gower.

form, then an ego-free supporting role, and finally the Master Blaster *in excelsis*. The strokes at the end looked effortless, but only because he had worked like a beast early on. "It's such a relief," he said, "to know I can still play a big innings."

At the 1979 World Cup, all the major teams used their Test opening batsmen. Some were more naturally attacking than others. West Indies had Greenidge and Haynes; New Zealand had Wright and Bruce Edgar. England had Brearley and Boycott – combined age 75, combined ODI career strike-rate 39. "Not even at a pinch," wrote Scyld Berry in *Wisden 1999*, "could you have called them hitters." Their opening partnerships in the tournament were four, three, nought and 13, and now they had to face Holding, Roberts, Garner and Croft. Although it took Boycott 17 overs to reach double figures, he and Brearley looked good on an increasingly benign pitch, taking England to 79 for none off 25 at tea. Compton wrote that he had never seen Brearley play so confidently; Laker said he had never seen him play better, full stop.

During the interval, the England dressing-room were optimistic. Brearley drank lemon squash before sitting down for tea and rock cake. He suggested they should now try to score at least six an over, and target the last six overs from West Indies' fifth bowler, either Richards or King. He was talked out of it, with Botham and Randall – "Carry on, skip, it's magic" – especially insistent that England should keep playing as they were.

Brearley and Boycott were at the crease for another 13 overs after tea, adding 50 more. The hundred came up in the 32nd, only two more than it took West Indies. But somewhere along the way, an admirable partnership became a problem. Croft said to Garner he hoped West Indies did not take a wicket, and when Lloyd dropped Boycott, a simple chance at mid-on, many thought it deliberate. "I could have watched them all day, because I knew every over they batted was another nail in their coffin," said Lloyd. "A lot of people suggested I put it down purposefully, just to keep him in. It's not true, but it wouldn't have been a bad tactic." He later said he would have opened with Brearley and Gooch.

Eventually England's openers started to hit out, but were unable to significantly lift the run-rate. Brearley said he was thinking of a "very strategic retired hurt". After a partnership of 129 in 38 overs, both fell in quick succession to Holding.

England went into the last 20 needing 151. And though Randall and Gooch (32 from 28 balls) added 48 in seven, it was fraught with risk. Once Randall was dismissed, the innings crumbled in astonishing fashion, the last eight wickets falling for 11 runs in 26 balls. For the new batsman, trying to hit Garner's yorker for eight an over was like trying to bench-press gravity – especially as the light was fading, and his hand was above the sightscreen at the Nursery End and coming out of the trees. Garner took out Gooch, Gower and Larkins in his tenth over, Old and Taylor in his next. Four were bowled. Croft claimed the last wicket by castling Hendrick, who grabbed a stump and charged off in an attempt to beat the pitch invasion. Dickie Bird pulled a muscle as he sprinted for the Pavilion.

West Indies

C. G. Greenidge run out (Randall)	9	
D. L. Haynes c Hendrick b Old	20	
I. V. A. Richards not out	138	
A. I. Kallicharran b Hendrick	4	
*C. H. Lloyd c and b Old	13	
C. L. King c Randall b Edmonds	86	
†D. L. Murray c Gower b Edmonds	5	
A. M. E. Roberts c Brearley b Hendrick	0	
J. Garner c Taylor b Botham	0	
M. A. Holding b Botham	0	
C. E. H. Croft not out	0	
B 1, lb 10	11	

1/22 (1) 2/36 (2)   (9 wkts, 60 overs) 286
3/55 (4) 4/99 (5) 5/238 (6)
6/252 (7) 7/258 (8) 8/260 (9) 9/272 (10)

Botham 12–2–44–2; Hendrick 12–2–50–2; Old 12–0–55–2; Boycott 6–0–38–0; Edmonds 12–2–40–2; Gooch 4–0–27–0; Larkins 2–0–21–0.

England

*J. M. Brearley c King b Holding	64	
G. Boycott c Kallicharran b Holding	57	
D. W. Randall b Croft	15	
G. A. Gooch b Garner	32	
D. I. Gower b Garner	0	
I. T. Botham c Richards b Croft	4	
W. Larkins b Garner	0	
P. H. Edmonds not out	5	
C. M. Old b Garner	0	
†R. W. Taylor c Murray b Garner	0	
M. Hendrick b Croft	0	
Lb 12, w 2, nb 3	17	

1/129 (1) 2/135 (2) 3/183 (3)   (51 overs) 194
4/183 (4) 5/186 (5) 6/186 (7)
7/188 (6) 8/192 (9) 9/192 (10) 10/194 (11)

Roberts 9–2–33–0; Holding 8–1–16–2; Croft 10–1–42–3; Garner 11–0–38–5; Richards 10–0–35–0; King 3–0–13–0.

Umpires: H. D. Bird and B. J. Meyer.

The teams mingled and shared champagne, first on the balcony, then in the dressing-rooms. Garner threw his size 15 boots into the crowd, and West Indies staged an impromptu Caribbean carnival with their supporters in St John's Wood. Richards, whose hackles were briefly raised when an overzealous fan tried to steal his cap, poking him in the eye, led the way: "I drowned myself in champagne. I promised myself I would get into a hell of a state, and that's just what I did."

Richards regards this as the turning point in West Indies' history. By winning the World Cup a second time, they proved to themselves that they could win anything – and to outsiders that the first had not been a fluke. "I may be wrong, but I sense that winning an ultimate contest like this is more important for a black person than anyone else," he said. "It feels like a vindication – the sense of pride is phenomenal."

Two months later, he and Garner returned to Lord's to play an equally big part in Somerset's first trophy – Richards scored another century, Garner went one better, with six wickets.

The following winter, when England played West Indies in a triangular tournament in Australia, Boycott played a series of exhilarating attacking innings which evoked his famous century in the 1965 Gillette Cup final. He said he was not playing with greater intent than in the World Cup final, only that he was in better form.

The story of the 1979 final is generally told in those two partnerships, between Richards and King, then Brearley and Boycott. That feels unfair given the context of both, never mind that England's openers were talked out of accelerating – and by Botham, of all people. More than that, West Indies had plenty to defend. No team scored as many as 287 against them in limited-overs cricket until Pakistan in October 1988; England were the next to manage it, in 1995.

"We could never make enough runs against them," says Boycott. "If we had picked one more quality bowler, we would have been chasing around 250, which might have been gettable. John Woodcock was correct when he said we picked the wrong team. Boycott, Gooch and Larkins bowling 12 overs in a World Cup final was crazy. To me, the story of the 1979 final was the partnership between Richards and King." Boycott and Gooch overachieved in the earlier games, making England think they could get away with it one last time. "We'd done well on some dodgy pitches, but Lord's was completely flat and there was no swing. We were decent net bowlers and, at best, an occasional sixth bowler."

He thinks his opening partnership with Brearley is judged by modern standards. "Life is very easy with hindsight. It's nearly impossible to judge the past – especially as most people don't remember the rules, or how people thought 40 years ago. There were no pinch-hitters, and every team tried to build a platform without losing wickets.

"West Indies were probably the best Test side of all time, and every ODI team since would be hard pressed to beat them. Most people have no conception of how difficult it was to score runs against that attack. All these modern shots

Comment

– the reverse sweep, the scoop, hitting over the top – would be almost impossible against Joel Garner and the other guys. Try ramping when nearly every ball jumps from a length at your heart or your ribs. Their speed and accuracy were exceptional."

There will always be plenty of what-ifs. What if England had played a fifth bowler? What if Brearley had not been talked out of his plan to attack after tea? What if Botham, in the middle of an astonishing purple patch in Test cricket, had not mislaid his cape for a fortnight? What if King hadn't borrowed it for the final? And, what if, in the context of the 1979 World Cup final, "Hendrick to Richards" meant something else entirely?

Rob Smyth is a freelance writer based in Orkney.

The Wisden Review

CRICKET BOOKS IN 2018

Morality play

TANYA ALDRED

As November hit December, and the good ship Brexit overshadowed even England's win in Sri Lanka, life in the UK slouched into gloom. Then lo, from the East (well, London) a jiffy bag of light relief arrived on the doorstep: Derek Pringle's **Pushing the Boundaries**, a preposterous cricketing tale of shagging and boozing through the 1980s.

Never one to toe the line, Pringle embarks on a jolly romp through the decade of big hair and seismic societal change, in which cricket slowly moved from a sport for frisky dilettantes to something requiring Cromwellian discipline. Picked for England while a student at Cambridge, Pringle caught the eye of the press because of his earring and erroneous rumours that he was squiring two of the chief selector's daughters. Before he had even played, he was fielding requests from *Vogue* that he and his university team-mates pose in those "sexy cable-knit sweaters".

His selection didn't go down so well with die-hard cricket fans, but luckily our hero has a thick skin. He yomps across the years, discovering with delight the aphrodisiac that comes when you pull on an England shirt, and achieving an insight into the mind of a professional sportsman, with his "ability to compartmentalise one's feelings so they don't bleed into each other".

Very quickly, his era seems the distant past – a time when Pringle's decision to play in his second Test, against India at Old Trafford, instead of the Varsity Match, could raise eyebrows in the broadsheets; when Ian Botham could miss the first half of a tour because of panto commitments; and when a cricketer was used to advertise Nike's new football boots (Botham again). There is also a reminder of the ugliness of the age: when West Indian Norbert Phillip wasn't playing for Essex, a small group of spectators would stand by the River End sightscreen at Chelmsford carrying a placard that read "Keith Fletcher's white, white army". And when Pringle objected to some racist abuse, he was reminded by Essex's general secretary that "members should be respected at all times".

There is a sensitive chapter on Botham – though even Pringle stayed away when he took to downing jugs of whisky and ice cream – and a lot of love for Essex under "Flooch", an amalgam of Fletcher and Gooch coined by Matthew Engel, then *The Guardian's* cricket correspondent. And the reader is blessed by Pringle's urge, long before smartphones, to document – ridiculous letters sent to fellow players are saved for posterity, from the obscene to the prosaic. "Dear Ray East," read one. "I have long been an admirer of your left-arm spin bowling. You are a real asset to Essex CC. Please can you get me Graham Gooch's autograph?"

Pringle's forensic memory also records the moment, during an England A-tour of Zimbabwe, when the eternally enthusiastic Mark Nicholas announced to

Robert Mugabe that meeting him was "the greatest day of my life". Trouble was, deadpans Pringle, "MCJ had already had two greatest days of his life that trip". Pringle hung up his boots to climb the steps of the press box when shuttle-runs started to replace self-expression, leaving the muscle-flexing – and the money – to those who came after. He took in his pocket, though, the best stories.

Shane Warne stares out from the cover of **No Spin**. His ghost is the aforementioned Mark Nicholas, who describes the book as a stream of consciousness. And that's exactly what you get, along with gallons of self-justification, a soupçon of self-knowledge and fistfuls of exclamation marks. Whoa!

He was an ingénu to accept $5,000 from a random man in a casino

The usual suspects are nailed: John Buchanan and Steve Waugh get it in the neck – the famous loss in Kolkata in 2000-01 was Waugh's fault – as does both men's deification of the Baggy Green. Off-spin is decried as "limited and predictable", while Indians are "thoughtful and kind by nature". Warne's brush occasionally runs a little broad.

In many ways, he is old-fashioned, despite the friendship with the Packers, the private planes and the jet skis. He adores his children, believes in the school of hard knocks, and thinks today's cricketers have it too easy. He also has a bee in his bonnet about good manners, which unfortunately did not translate on to the field. In fact it is striking that Warne, who had the world at his fingertips, felt so impelled to casual cruelty in the name of tactics. When he first bowls to Kevin Pietersen, he greets him with: "Everyone on this field hates you. Even the non-striker thinks you're a prick. I don't know what's wrong with you, but you must be a fuckwit." There is no shame, and there are many similar confrontations.

That apart, Nicholas has things rattling along with his usual light touch. The book is fascinating on the intricacies of leg-spin, with its head-fizzing permutations, and on the thought and trickery behind it: the set-up, the angles, the revs, the patience. There are a few home truths for the English reader, too. While Warne loomed huge in our psyches, few England players made an impression on him, and the Ashes grew insignificant as Australian victory followed victory followed victory.

Scandals are skimmed over: he was an ingénu to accept $5,000 from a random man he met in a casino, naive not to have checked the contents of a diuretic that led to a drugs ban. His libido has a starring role (there must be something in the literary water), thanks to various blowsy trysts, and an unlikely relationship with Elizabeth Hurley. His attitude to booze, perhaps to life, is as enthusiastic: to borrow from Mike Brearley, shit or bust: "And by the way I'm no slouch, I can drink most people under the table." Bowled, Shane.

You pick up **Cricket: A Political History of the Global Game, 1945–2017** with trepidation. First, because of its unforgivingly academic feel; second, my god, the cost! At £115 it pretty much prices itself out of the market, which is a shame, because Stephen Wagg chews thoughtfully on the bone of post-war cricket (though the ebook is much cheaper).

His approach can be a bit dry, and the myriad notes at the end of each chapter rather daunting. But, as you close the book for a final time, you hear the clangour and scrape of cricket breaking the chains of colonialism and throwing itself, cluelessly, into the new globalism. The radical legacy of Mike Marqusee, whom Wagg honours in the dedication for speaking "truth to power", is stitched through, as he puts cricket's development in its political and social context, whether in national case studies or more thematically. It is in the second half of the book that Wagg really takes his gloves off, tackling toxic masculinity, "where ungentlemanly conduct becomes fierce competitiveness", the rise and rise of the mass media, and an astute chapter on coaching. Wagg's conclusion is optimism-despite-the-odds: "Cricket has already survived a number of obituaries."

Cricket:
A POLITICAL HISTORY OF THE GLOBAL GAME, 1945–2017
Stephen Wagg
ROUTLEDGE RESEARCH IN SPORTS HISTORY

Moeen Ali's autobiography, **Moeen**, is co-written by Mihir Bose who, like Nicholas, is a big enough draw to get his name on the cover. Ali is a captivating character, whose good nature, modesty and *joie de vivre* hide a steely interior: remember he wore a "Save Gaza" wristband during a Test.

This book gives us a better understanding of why English cricket's most popular beard is the player he is, and what makes him tick. It is no surprise that Ali came to the sport from a different pipeline – but the sheer soap opera of his background is revealing. His paternal grandparents, Shafayat and Betty, met in Birmingham in the late 1940s. Shafayat had come over from Kashmir to find work in a factory. Betty was a widow – her first husband was killed in the war – with two small children. They broke all conventions, and Betty converted to Islam. Shafayat then decided their children should have an Islamic education, so Ali's father, Munir, was packed off to Kashmir aged two, staying until he was ten. Betty spent long periods in Dadyal, learning Urdu and living like a local. The marriage eventually broke up, and the children returned to England. Munir and his twin brother Shabir married sisters, and the two families raised a cricketing dynasty – Moeen, brother Kadeer, cousin Kabir – by an esoteric mixture of superstition, sacrifice, dedication and improbable triumph.

If some of the later chapters slip towards formulaic match reports, the book is very good on Moeen's upbringing in Sparkhill, an inner-city area prone to the usual bedfellows of drugs, crime and violence. Cricket, he believes, saved him from the miserable fate that befell some of his friends. He writes passionately about the sheer joy of those shared cricket experiences, during which he perfected his lip-smacking cover-drive. "That Stoney Lane upbringing where cricket was so central has left me with great memories… That time in my life, those days were so special. I know I shall never again experience that wonderful bliss."

There is candour. Ali admits to feeling trapped by people's assumptions about his identity. He is clear that South Asian cricketers get a bad deal. Allegations that an Australian cricketer had called him "Osama" during the 2015 Ashes led to a brief investigation last autumn by their board. He also tells of his spiritual awakening, thanks to a random encounter with Ray Walee, a man he spotted out of the dressing-room window one rainy day at Edgbaston.

From this implausible meeting came the answers he had been looking for since he started questioning the purpose of life at 16. It is not the sort of philosophical introspection you expect from a teenage sporting prodigy. But Ali is not an average anything. "Living the selfish life of a modern sportsman, there's a contentment in my heart when I feel like I'm contributing to the wellbeing of society for a change."

He would make a textbook study for Mike Brearley, who follows up 2017's *On Form* with **On Cricket**, a collection of old articles, interspersed with 25 or so new ones. Most of the chapters stand the test of time and, if you've not read them before, are as good as new. A couple of thousand words of thoughtful observation on this and that, full of anecdote – a lovely one on Len Hutton watching Graham Gooch at Lord's in 1990 – and wisdom. Three pieces stand out: one, on the nature of heroism and the pressures of expectation, in which he remembers being touched when a man on Greenwich High Street greeted him as "my captain"; one on Steve Smith and ball-tampering, influenced by the thoughts of the Freud Museum; and, my favourite, entitled *In my opinion*. Ostensibly on the nature of masculinity, it is really a love letter to Mr Viv Richards, alpha male. Brearley wilts. "One can't imagine a woman not being fascinated. As a man (am I one?), older, in every sense paler, I am charmed, but also a tad intimidated." Wonderful.

> It is really a love letter to Mr Viv Richards, alpha male

Another book that interlinks cricket with social history is Simon Wilde's **England: The Biography 1877–2018**. At 614 pages, it's a tome and a half, and Wilde admits that the sheer quantity of evidence he trawled through was sometimes overwhelming.

It's a great yarn, though, a potted history of English (men's) cricket, with all the idiosyncrasies of an imperial game trying to live in the modern world but always falling at least one step behind. Run generally by double-breasted ex-public schoolboys, English cricket – imbued with a superiority complex – gets a frog in its throat at almost every turn. It struggles with the end of the amateur–professional divide; is preoccupied by attracting the right sort; is far too closely entangled with apartheid South Africa; and does not understand that players might actually like to be financially secure. There are many befuddling episodes. As Wilde points out, those at the top – men who were perfectly capable stockbrokers or captains of industry – found themselves in some kind of high-church tangle when having to manage the English game.

Wilde has an easy style, arranges his sources in a readable way, and enjoys an idiosyncratic table. Did you know that 10% of England's Test players have been closely related to one another? You do now.

English cricket is not, the book fairly illustrates, some uber-winning machine, like the All Blacks or the 1980s West Indians or Bradman's Australians. It's a team famous as much for their laughable failures as their rabbit-from-the-hat triumphs, a reflection of Britain's diminishing role on the world stage. And it is a history all the more absorbing for that.

The dog days of summer bring **The Test**, a first novel by Nathan Leamon, who for nine years was an analyst for the England team. Cricket is peculiarly unsuited to fiction – perhaps such a complex game ends up sucking the lifeblood out of authors as they strive for description – but Leamon pitches it just right. He deftly avoids the clichés of green and pleasant land, or plucky

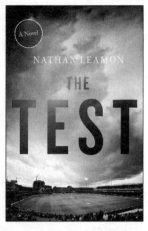

but hopeless amateurs, and uses his expertise to bring both technical and emotional insight.

What is ostensibly the story of stand-in captain James McCall leading England into the final Test of an Ashes series becomes a meditation on kinship and responsibility, love and death. It is excellent on the disconnect between the travelling cricketer and the family left behind, the silent distance that comes with countless days away, how the daddy-shaped hole gets filled by time. The hatred and distrust the players have for the media is all too believable. And the book gives a scathing portrayal of MCC – who won't be happy with their description as a bunch of thick, fat alcoholics.

Leamon's dressing-room job was to scrutinise, but this is not the cold novel of an analyst – it has true heart. If the lines of poetry occasionally seem a little shoehorned in, this reader shed big, plopping tears.

Eleven Gods and a Billion Indians is another doorstop, this time in five parts. It is an enlightening look into India's cricket history, written neither by nor for the curious eye of a foreigner. If this sometimes leaves the British reader struggling under a deluge of unfamiliar detail, it brings a valuable perspective when West looks East. The IPL is an example of "atypical globalisation", while Eden Gardens 2001 – VVS and Dravid on drips in the dressing-room – is cast as a turning point for Indian cricket, a rebirth after Cronjegate, and the moment at which TV really took notice.

Boria Majumdar opens with match-fixing, and deals an early blow to morale when he mentions in passing that Mohammad Azharuddin and Ajay Jadeja have been cleared by the courts and now work as TV pundits. Crikey, how did I miss that? It concentrates the mind as we go on a long journey deep into India's culture and past. The British obviously stuck their oar in (and how), but as the two countries pulled apart, so did their relationships with cricket –

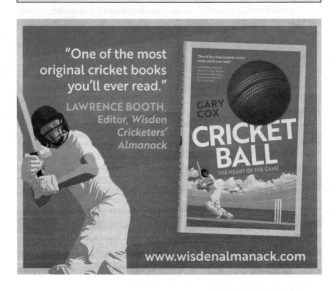

the British falling out of love, head turned by football, the Indians head over heels, wooed by television.

Majumdar's scope is huge, from the days of the Bombay Pentangular to the dizzying change in Indian society over the past 30 years and the aggressive cricket nationalism that accompanied it. He examines the various personal battles – Ganguly v Chappell, Ganguly v Buchanan, Kohli v Kumble, Kohli v social media – the overarching power of the IPL, monkeygate, buffoons at the BCCI… and so it goes on.

There's a brain-aching chapter on broadcasting rights, and a riveting one touching on TV coverage of elections to the Cricket Association of Bengal. This small provincial election somehow became primetime fodder, and involved one channel mocking up images of the two candidates, Jagmohan Dalmiya and Prasun Mukherjee, in full military armour crossing swords. (I can see Colin Graves and Giles Clarke going for this.) About the same time, four channels ran polls on whether or not Sourav Ganguly was a traitor.

Occasionally, Majumdar goes a little fanboy – he's known the Indian inner circle for 25 years, and the freshly scrubbed Ganguly in his handsome white kurta sometimes seems to get an easy ride. But, by the end, my eyes had been opened.

Last summer James Taylor was appointed a full-time selector by Ed Smith and was regularly spotted around county grounds. It might have slipped people's minds as to why, in April 2016, he finished playing cricket at the tender age of 26. The opening lines of **Cut Short** soon act as an aide-memoire: "By rights, I shouldn't be writing this book. I should have been found dead at the bottom of a flight of stairs. Or in the passenger seat of a car. Or on a cold wooden bench in a distant dressing-room far from friends and family."

> A fast-paced tale of what happens when the future is ripped from under your feet

Bang, between the eyes. From there, Taylor – and his ghost, John Woodhouse – narrate a fast-paced tale of what happens when the future is ripped from under your feet. Taylor was a talented sportsman from an early age – football, rugby, cricket, you name it – and we learn about his journey from brash teen through the Lions to becoming a near-fixture in the England team the winter before he had to retire because of a rare heart disease. Taylor doesn't spare himself: he was a cocksure schoolboy sports-brat. Teased for being small, he becomes obsessed with looking good. But, in the end, it is the obsession that saves him: lifting more weights, doing more reps, having the best six-pack, get him through a condition which the doctors later explain kills 80% of those affected.

The chapters on Taylor's diagnosis and recovery are painful. He spares nothing in his devastation at the ending of his career, the loss of his once-designer torso, his fears for the future and his fury with the ECB for their initial intransigence over his loss of earnings. His gradual acceptance of what happened, determination to move on and lack of self-pity are poignant, as is the dedication of his wife Jose, who writes her own chapter.

Godspeed James. As he says: "Perspective is a great thing. I might not have my life as it was. But I still have everything. Arrhythmogenic right ventricular

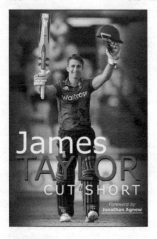

cardiomyopathy – those words are attached to me for ever. But at least I'm still here."

Bharat Sundaresan's **The Dhoni Touch** is smaller than the other biographies, and a breezy read. It's quite a thing, an opening chapter of a cricket book where the author's main concern is the length of his hair compared with his hero's. The world indeed is changing. "*Baal kaatlo, yaar.*" (Cut your hair, mate.)

Sundaresan tries to get to know the real Dhoni by tracking down his childhood friends in Ranchi, as Dhoni is often elsewhere, leading the kind of megastar life no England cricketer could dream of. Sundaresan finds his old school, where the shy introvert smashed windows from the cricket pitch, his old coach, his old kit supplier. Even at a prosaic level, the price of immense fame seems far too high: there are petty squabbles over who spends most time with the great man, and jealousy over his WhatsApp communications.

The book is charming, but there is little forensic scrutiny, and the sharpest criticism comes from Dhoni's friend Colonel Shankar: "MS is not too great at long-distance running." By the end, he remains an enigma – a cricketing colossus who advertises mobile phones but never answers them, speaks in riddles, smiles silently in response to questions about spot-fixing, and is attributed the mind-reading qualities of a demigod.

A few smaller books sit on top of the pile, teetering towards the dusty void under the bed, but I was glad to rescue **Women at the Wicket**, an engrossing volume by Adam McKie on women's cricket in interwar England. It follows the battle for supremacy between the English Women's Cricket Federation and the Women's Cricket Association, then examines the tightrope the victorious WCA had to walk between proselytising and the social mores of the time.

Having seen how sticking its neck out went for women's football – banned by the FA from using their grounds in December 1921 – the WCA swung towards decorum: white stockings, skirts to the knee, no tournaments or payments. Yet they were revolutionary in other ways: completely self-sufficient, they were run by and for women; men could only ever have an honorary role.

The book traces how attitudes to women and physical exercise changed during the early 20th century, how the experience of the First World War led the authorities to worry about the health of the working classes (after all, they needed cannon fodder), and how it suddenly became fashionable for women to be fit so that they could propagate the British race. Women's bodies have never stopped being a male concern.

By 1937, a crowd of 7,000 attended the women's Ashes Test at The Oval – and many factories, especially those of well-known philanthropists, had female teams. I fell in love with the idea of games between the "icing, chocolate, sugar wafers, cake and packing departments" at Huntley & Palmers. After the war, women's cricket struggled. As McKie book points out, universal suffrage arrived in 1928, but it wasn't until 1998 that women became members of MCC.

Enid Bakewell: Coalminer's Daughter by Simon Sweetman is another ACS publication. Bakewell is an intriguing character, more than deserving of a book, and there are plenty of cracking anecdotes about her early life in Newstead, a Nottinghamshire colliery village, where Len, her "almost a communist" father, trained in a bit of midwifery, and Enid ran around with the boys. She also, excruciatingly, had all her teeth, because "it cost nothing if you were under 21". It is quite a ride, though her cricketing exploits are slightly lost in a sea of scores. And – oh my eyes! – the microscopic print of both books is rather a strain.

Less cottage industry than industrial giant is Stephen Fay and David Kynaston's painstakingly researched, very readable and rather brilliant **Arlott, Swanton and the Soul of English Cricket**. A biography-cum-social-history, it moves seamlessly from the early 20th century to the millennium through the words and lives of arch-Establishment *Telegraph* man E. W. Swanton and liberal poet and *Guardian* writer John Arlott. As the years tick by, the young boys – born in 1907 (Swanton) and 1914 (Arlott) – become men, survive the Second World War and emerge blinking into a battered country with a ravenous appetite for first-class cricket.

Linked by a hatred of racism and a love of cricket, they were as colourfully different as any biographer could wish. What's more, they developed a healthy disregard for each other while becoming Voices of Cricket, working for *Test Match Special* and worrying about the game's survival in the face of commercialism. The son of a stockbroker who "never quite became 'something in the City'", Swanton spent the war years famously imprisoned in a Japanese POW camp with his 1939 *Wisden*, practising the art of survival. Arlott, the product of an adoring and aspirational working-class mother, walked out of school on a whim, became a policeman (despite a dislike of authority), befriended poets and – even though his Hampshire tones that offended delicate ears – got his own poetry programme on the radio, before being offered a chance to cover cricket.

The pictures painted of the two men – drawing on judicious quotation – are beautifully done: Swanton towering and boom-voiced, Arlott the romantic with a touch of sourness. Frank Keating goes to visit him on his 70th birthday, and finds the "old spaniel soft-boiled eyes shining bright".

The authors admit to being Arlott men, but also to a growing admiration for Swanton, despite his ridiculous pomposity, fixation with amateurism, and hilarious self-regard; he was to ponder whether the Bodyline crisis might have been averted if only he had been on the tour and had a quiet word with Douglas Jardine. We learn that, as Swanton aged, he mellowed, perhaps through a late and happy marriage, perhaps through an increasing awareness of his own bombast. He also watched cricket with a realistic eye, seeing – where Arlott did not – the need for faster scoring and a limited-overs game. Nor are the authors blind to the faults of Arlott, a prodigious talent and autodidact, who also grew fond of the sound of his own voice, and who in the end festered under the pull of the cellar.

Arlott at Tilbury docks, waving Harold Larwood off to his new life in Australia

The two formed a link to a past now sailing out of sight: EWS with his connections to Bradman; Arlott at Tilbury docks, waving Harold Larwood off to his new life in Australia. Which brings us, in roundabout fashion, to the cricket story of 2018: Sandpapergate, tackled in their different ways by Gideon Haigh and Geoff Lemon.

Both examine the poison at the heart of the Australian game, the obsession with the line, which became more mythical – and more fluid – with each mention. Whether the Australians were teetering close to it, nudging it or headbutting it, you could be sure they were never crossing it, even as their shadows danced merrily on the other side.

Crossing the Line, a small book written in a hurry, plays to all Haigh's strengths. Subtitled "How Australian cricket lost its way", it is an unsparing examination of the minutiae of authority, full of intelligent analysis and trademark fearlessness. The rationale behind the book was noble: "Nobody goes to bed honest and wakes up a cheat." Suspicious of Cricket Australia's cultural review, Haigh undertakes his own – interviewing 50 unnamed people whose views he respects. The first unattributable quote describes CA as "bullies and sycophants". Their reputation does not improve from there.

Under Haigh's guidance, we watch a morality play unfold at the offices at Jolimont. We learn of the slow erosion of the status quo, as CA change from a small old-fashioned organisation almost crippled by decision-making into a secretive, money-making, corporate bully – more like an events-management company than a sports governing body. It's a complex tale: on the one hand, CA became more open, welcoming women's and Aboriginal cricket, but they also became more lost in dollar bills and procedure and the desire for control. Dissent is quashed, player complaints are ignored. The rampant passion for aggressive cricket/language/performance is exemplified when Darren Lehmann opens a presentation to coaches on the Australian Way with an opening slide reading "WTBC" – watch the ball, cunt. Warnings – what warnings?

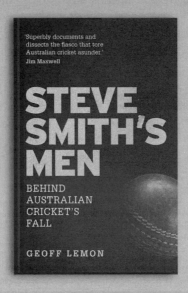

It's a super book. As Haigh, an expert on governance, turns on his Dictaphone and traipses through the labyrinth, he wonders whether the big cricket he watches has become "less precious, less special, less representative". The players, he concludes, are the fall guys: "At Jolimont, success has a thousand fathers, failure is the players' alone."

Lemon's **Steve Smith's Men** is a different animal, more emotional, more soulful. From a pulsating introductory chapter to an almost wistful epilogue, Lemon retraces the steps that led to the pants-down denouement at Cape Town. The book, he says, casts no moral judgment, but I envisage him scratching his poetic curls as he plots the long line in the sand – the crazy scheduling, the CA-sanctioned whipping-up of David Warner, the long-time fetishising of nastiness.

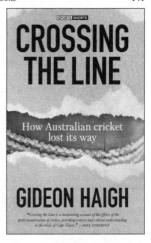

Lemon was physically present through pretty much the whole mess, and if his on-the-spot reporting has a hint of swagger, his writing is touched by a golden pen and an eye for detail – as when he watches Smith and Bancroft cross the turf on the way to the press box that fateful Cape Town evening, "shoulders rounded and feet slow"; or the farcical Lehmann press conference held in a store-room basement in a Sandton hotel, "like we were meeting someone under witness protection".

There is empathy, there is sympathy and there is despair. The chapters on the individual players work best, titled simply David, Steven, Cameron, Timothy [Paine, the new captain]. The four men were linked by nothing more, nothing less, than a Baggy Green.

Smith, the ultimate illustration of C. L. R. James's what-do-they-know line, is "impressively dull" – a cricket geek, desperate to be good, handed the leadership without showing any aptitude, inheriting a team shorn of senior men, and unable to put a leash on Warner. Warner himself is a hero–villain, a useful idiot willing to do the team's dirty work, and a young man lacking guidance, one who was driven to madness by the vilification of his adored wife, Candice. She was tormented and devastatingly, at the end of the whole sorry saga, when the game was up, when Warner was sent home, had a miscarriage. "The abstract figure people thought they were attacking turned out to be a real human, flesh and blood, tough and fragile," writes Lemon. "In no world, under no justification, should she ever have been forced into the middle of this mess."

The tale is yet raw – Lemon admits this is a first take. A different story will emerge as players retire and the *omerta* fractures. But the emotional power of this book lingers long after the last page: cricketers who wilted under the pressure of succeeding, suits who became immune to right and wrong, and – something that appears time after time in this year's books – a true unpleasantness at the heart of international cricket. For its first-hand account of hubris (theirs), and *Schadenfreude* (ours), *Steve Smith's Men* is the Wisden Book of the Year.

Tanya Aldred is a freelance writer and editor.

WISDEN BOOK OF THE YEAR

Since 2003, *Wisden's* reviewer has selected a Book of the Year. The winners have been:

OTHER AWARDS

The Cricket Society Literary Award has been presented since 1970 to the author of the cricket book judged best of the year. The 2018 award, made by the Cricket Society in association with MCC, was won in April by Harry Pearson for **Connie: The Marvellous Life of Learie Constantine** (Little, Brown); he received £3,000. In June, Steve Neal won the cricket category at the British Sports Book Awards for **Over and Out: Albert Trott** (Pitch).

BOOKS RECEIVED IN 2018

GENERAL

Battersby, David **My Summer of 1977** (limited edition paperback; more details from dave@talbot.force9.co.uk)
Battersby, David **The Forgotten Floodlit Encounter** Gloucestershire v The Australians at the Prince of Wales Stadium, Cheltenham, September 2, 1981 (privately published booklet; details as above)
Battersby, David **The Pakistan Tour to the UK 1978** (privately published booklet; details as above)
Brearley, Mike **On Cricket** (Constable, £20)
Cawkwell, Tim **Compleat Cricket** Eight Days in September (Sforzinda Books, paperback, £15.50) *An account of the Division One relegation battle in the 2017 County Championship.*
Cooke, David **Was Grace Better Than Bradman?** A new way to rank Ashes cricketers   Foreword by Geoffrey Boycott (Ockley Books, paperback, £10.99)

Cox, Gary **The Cricket Ball** The Heart of the Game (Bloomsbury Academic, £20)

Crabtree, James **The Billionaire Raj** A Journey through India's new Gilded Age (Oneworld, £18.99)

Dyson, Paul, comp. **Who's Who of The Yorkshire County Cricket Club** Foreword by Martyn Moxon (Great Northern Books, £19.99)

English, Ross **Cricket and England Through Five Matches** Class, War, Race & Empire 1900–1939 (privately published, paperback, £9.99)

Evans, Chris, ed. **Fifty Years of Surrey Championship Cricket** (available as a download from www.surreychampionship.com)

Fay, Stephen and Kynaston, David **Arlott, Swanton and the Soul of English Cricket** (Bloomsbury, £20)

Ferriday, Patrick **In Tandem** Cricket's Great Pace Pairs (Von Krumm, £17)

Haigh, Gideon **Crossing the Line** How Australian cricket lost its way (Slattery Media, paperback, £19.99)

Halford, Brian and Hignell, Andrew **The Daffodil Blooms** The glorious rise of Glamorgan CCC to County Champions in 1948 (ACS, paperback, £15)

Harragan, Bob and Hignell, Andrew **Whites On Green** A history of cricket at St Helen's, Swansea (ACS, paperback, £18)

Hignell, Andrew **Front Foot to Front Line** Welsh Cricket and the Great War (St David's Press, paperback, £16.99)

Hiscock, Paul and McDonald, Tony **Essex County Cricket Club Memories** Foreword by Graham Gooch (Inside Edge Books, £30)

Lemon, Geoff **Steve Smith's Men** Behind Australian cricket's fall (Hardie Grant, paperback, £16.99)

Lloyd, David **Around the World in 80 Pints** My Search for Cricket's Greatest Places (Simon & Schuster, £20)

McKie, Adam **Women at the Wicket** A History of Women's Cricket in Interwar England Foreword by Alison Mitchell (ACS, paperback, £18)

Majumdar, Boria **Eleven Gods and a Billion Indians** The on and off the field story of cricket in India and beyond (Simon & Schuster, £18.99)

Memon, Taher and Parvez, Salim **Another Perspective** Pakistan Cricket History: 1977–98: The Untold Story of Development Foreword by Zaheer Abbas (Matador, £17.99)

Odendaal, André, Reddy, Krish and Merrett, Christopher **Divided Country** The History of South African Cricket Retold, 1914–1950s (BestRed, paperback, £19.50)

Peel, Mark **Ambassadors of Goodwill** MCC Tours 1946/47–1970/71 (Pitch, £18.99)

Peel, Mark **Playing the Game?** Cricket's Tarnished Ideals from Bodyline to Present (Pitch, £18.99)

Rogers, Martin **Cricket in the Genes** George Bailey (Academy Publications, $A29.95)

Wagg, Stephen **Cricket: A Political History of the Global Game, 1945–2017** (Routledge, £115)

Westendorp, Tjebbe A. **1978–2018** Forty Years of Parliamentary Cricket – De Binnenhof and the Lords and Commons (privately published, paperback, £20 + £3 p&p; more details from tj.westendorp@gmail.com)

Wilde, Simon **England, The Biography** The Story of English Cricket 1877–2018 Foreword by Ed Smith (Simon & Schuster, £25)

BIOGRAPHY

Addis, Ian and Radd, Andrew, with Steele, David **The Bank Clerk Who Went To War** Memories of a Professional Cricketer (Chequered Flag, £20)

Battersby, David **Edward Sainsbury** The Lost Years of 1889 and 1890 (privately published booklet; more details from dave@talbot.force9.co.uk)

Battersby, David **Glamorgan CCC's first ever game** Glamorgan v Warwickshire at Cardiff Arms Park, June 21 and 22, 1889 (paperback, £12 inc p&p; details as above)

Battersby, David **My Summer of 1977** A nostalgic look back at a memorable summer (paperback, £12 inc p&p; details as above)

Battersby, David **Woofy** The Life & Times of W. A. Woof (paperback, £12 inc p&p; details as above)

Booth, Keith and Jennifer **The Haywards** The Biography of a Cricket Dynasty Foreword by Alec Stewart (Chequered Flag, paperback, £14)

Bradbury, Anthony **Reverend E. S. Carter** A Yorkshire Cricketing Cleric (ACS, paperback, £15)

Evans, Richard **Teddy** The Life and Times of Major E. G. Wynyard DSO, OBE (Chequered Flag, paperback, £14.99)

Kelly, Rob **Hobbsy** A Life in Cricket Foreword by Graham Gooch (Von Krumm, £16) *Biography of Robin Hobbs.*

Lonsdale, Jeremy **Tom Emmett** The Spirit of Yorkshire Cricket (ACS, paperback, £15)

Nicholls, J. L. **Sydney F. Barnes** The Legendary Cricket Genius   Foreword by Sydney Francis Barnes (UK Book Publishing, £14.99)

O'Brien, Christopher **Cardus Uncovered** Neville Cardus: The Truth, the Untruth and the Higher Truth (Whitethorn Range Publishing, paperback, £10)

Rowe, Mark **Young Bradman** (ACS, paperback, £18)

Sundaresan, Bharat **The Dhoni Touch** Unravelling the Enigma that is Mahendra Singh Dhoni (Penguin, paperback, £9.99)

Sweetman, Simon **Enid Bakewell** Coalminer's Daughter (ACS, paperback, £15)

AUTOBIOGRAPHY

Ali, Moeen, with Bose, Mihir **Moeen** (Atlantic, £20)

Arif Ali Khan Abbasi **Not a Gentleman's Game**   Introduction by R. V. C. Robins; foreword by Ehsan Mani (Ushba Publishing International, £20)

Nash, Malcolm, with Bentley, Richard **Not Only, But Also** My Life in Cricket (St David's Press, paperback, £19.99)

Pringle, Derek **Pushing the Boundaries** Cricket in the Eighties: Playing Home and Away (Hodder & Stoughton, £20)

Taylor, James with Woodhouse, John **Cut Short**   Foreword by Jonathan Agnew (White Owl, £20)

Warne, Shane, with Nicholas, Mark **No Spin** My Autobiography (Ebury, £20)

Wilkins, Alan **Easier Said Than Done** A Life in Sport   Foreword by Sunil Gavaskar (St David's Press, £20)

ILLUSTRATED

Levison, Brian **Remarkable Village Cricket Grounds** (Pavilion Books, £25)

Wellsteed, Geoff **Pavilions in Splendour** The Cricket Pavilions and Grounds of Cheshire   Forewords by Paul Allott, Neil Fairbrother and Bob Barber (Max Books, £25)

FICTION

Leamon, Nathan **The Test** (Constable, £16.99)

STATISTICAL

Bryant, John, ed. **First-Class Matches: Pakistan 1975/76 to 1979/80** (ACS, paperback, £25)

Lawton Smith, Julian, ed. **The Minor Counties Championship 1912** (ACS, paperback, £16)

Percival, Tony **Suffolk Cricketers** (ACS, paperback, £15)

Walmsley, Keith, ed. **West Indies: Internal first-class matches in Trinidad and Guyana 1958/59 to 1989/90** (ACS, paperback, £15)

HANDBOOKS AND ANNUALS

Bailey, Philip, ed. **ACS International Cricket Year Book 2018** (ACS, paperback, £32)

Bryant, John, ed. **ACS Overseas First-Class Annual 2018** (ACS, paperback, £70)
    Full scorecards for first-class matches outside England in 2017-18.

Bryden, Colin, ed. **South African Cricket Annual 2018** (Blue Weaver, R250, info@blueweaver.co.za)

Clayton, Howard, ed. **First-Class Counties Second Eleven Annual 2018** (ACS, paperback, £13)

Colliver, Lawrie, ed. **Australian Cricket Digest 2018-19** (paperback, $A30 plus p&p; more from lawrie.colliver@gmail.com)

Marshall, Ian, ed. **Playfair Cricket Annual 2018** (Headline, paperback, £9.99)

Moorehead, Benj, ed. **The Cricketers' Who's Who 2018** Foreword by Daryl Mitchell (Jellyfish, £19.99, ebook £10)

Payne, Francis and Smith, Ian, ed. **2018 New Zealand Cricket Almanack** (Upstart Press, $NZ55)

Piesse, Ken, ed. **Pavilion 2019** (Australian Cricket Society, paperback, $A10, www.cricketbooks.com.au)

REPRINTS AND UPDATES

Brearley, Mike **On Form** (Constable, paperback, £10.99)
Campbell, Charlie **Herding Cats** The Art of Amateur Cricket Captaincy Foreword by Mike Brearley (John Wisden, paperback, £9.99)
Lewis, Chris, with Pitman, Jed **Crazy** My Road to Redemption (The History Press, paperback, £9.99)

PERIODICALS

The Cricketer (monthly) ed. Simon Hughes (The Cricketer Publishing, £6.50; £44.99 for 12 print issues, £44.99 digital, £49.99 print & digital. Subscriptions: www.thecricketer.com)
The Cricket Paper (weekly) ed. Alex Narey (Greenways Publishing, £1.50; £20 for ten issues inc p&p, £49.99 for one year digital, www.thecricketpaper.com)
The Cricket Statistician (quarterly) ed. Simon Sweetman (ACS, £3 to non-members)
The Journal of the Cricket Society ed. Nigel Hancock (twice yearly) (from D. Seymour, 13 Ewhurst Road, Crofton Park, London, SE4 1AG £5 to non-members, www.cricketsociety.com)
The Nightwatchman The Wisden Cricket Quarterly ed. Tanya Aldred, Jon Hotten and Benj Moorehead (Cricket Properties, £10 print, £5 digital; £29.95 for four print issues exc p&p, £15 digital, www.nightwatchman.net)
Wisden Cricket Monthly ed. Phil Walker (Cricket Properties, £4.95; £39.99 for 12 print issues, £17.99 digital. Subscriptions: www.wisdensubs.com)

CRICKET IN THE MEDIA IN 2018

Worse than Brexit

ALEX MASSIE

As an aperitif for the English summer, few things could be better, or more surely lift the spirits, than an Australian scandal. If nothing else, the Australian ball-tampering disgrace offered some distraction from England's own troubles, on and off the field.

Forget about the spirit of cricket or the ICC's code of conduct, wrote Dean Wilson in the *Daily Mirror*, "the Australian cricket team is here to tell everyone where the line is, which if you didn't know is the point just beyond where Australia operate". The idea they could be "in any way the upholders of standards is quite laughable"; protestations to the contrary were "hypocritical claptrap". More charitably, *The Sun's* John Etheridge allowed: "You would need a heart of stone not to feel some sympathy for Steve Smith." Even Etheridge, though, felt a year's ban from international cricket was a "proportionate" sentence.

In general, however, following a winter in which Joe Root's team had been dismantled by the Australians, England seemed a stony-hearted place. The *Daily Mail* had a pertinent question, as well: "England players are left wondering… did they cheat in the Ashes too?" According to the paper, "the tourists were mystified as to how the home attack were able to produce such lavish reverse swing in comparison to that extracted by their own renowned exponents such as James Anderson and Chris Woakes, and at venues not routinely associated with it". As so often, David Warner was the supposed villain. If this became less of a controversy than it might have done, it was only because the gap between the sides was so vast that cheating seemed superfluous.

Mike Atherton, the most reasonable and generous, as well as the best, of the ex-players in the press box, wrote about the affair from a position of experience: "As I know to my cost, the level of moral indignation stirred up by accusations of ball-tampering far outweighs the nature of the crime." The crime, he reminded readers of *The Times*, is "serious… but not that serious". He too alluded to the obvious hypocrisy of Australia's position, but Atherton was also astute enough to appreciate that public discontent with this generation of Australian cricketers predated this embarrassment. Citing the late Peter Roebuck, he noted "it is possible to love a country and not its cricket team, a widespread feeling among supporters right now".

If the Australian response occasionally seemed hysterical, England supporters were left to reflect that at least the national team were a front-page story Down Under. The contrast with England is acute and, for some, depressing. The British media had some fun with it too, but the two most prominent cricketers in England last year were Ben Stokes (on trial for affray)

Site screen: Yorkshire and Surrey organised quality online coverage of their clash at Scarborough.

and Graeme Swann (the latest cricketer to appear on "Strictly Come Dancing"). The game itself? Not so prominent.

As has been the case for more than half a century, an element of foreboding and fretfulness ran through the cricket coverage. Sometimes it seems a game so in love with its past, and so worried about its future, it forgets to appreciate the present.

England returned to action in Edinburgh where, remarkably, they lost to Scotland. This was a "red-faced, humiliating experience", according to Etheridge, but also, wrote Atherton, "the kind of day when it felt good to be at a cricket ground". And it was one in the eye for the ICC, whose decision to make this year's World Cup a ten-team affair owed everything to commercialism and nothing to the wider interests of the global game.

"Gone are the days," noted Duncan Smith in *The Scotsman*, "when these occasional glamour games would come with a gentleman's agreement that the 'big' team would bat first," the better to ensure a full day's cricket. In conditions fit to break any bowler's heart, Scotland – smarting from their narrow failure to qualify for the World Cup – raced to 371, the highest score by an Associate nation against a Full Member. England lost by six runs. *Schadenfreude* is a dish best served at any time, so Sydney's *Daily Telegraph* were pleased to wade in: "We've had a ball-tampering scandal, lost our captain and VC, but at least we didn't lose to Scotland." On the other hand, Australia then lost 5–0 to the team that lost to Scotland.

In Dublin, history was made too, even if Ireland's debut as a Test nation was marked in traditional Irish style: with a downpour that washed out the first day of the one-off game against Pakistan. But it couldn't dampen spirits. Malachy Clerkin, writing in *The Irish Times*, observed that an affection for cricket had previously been considered the mark of "a subversive of some sort". It has been thought a sport "for weirdos and Brit-lickers", but, as he remarked, even weirdos and Brit-lickers can have their moment.

Off-field matters – or, rather, the organisation of the game – dominated discussion. ECB chairman Colin Graves, the "blazered Terminator" (Marina Hyde, *The Guardian*), had a near-Ratner moment: if cricket isn't crap, it's very nearly crap. According to Graves: "The younger generation, whether you like it or not, are just not attracted to cricket." They want something different. "They want more excitement, they want it shorter and simpler to understand." On balance, then, they would prefer it if cricket were not cricket.

Never let it be said the ECB does not listen to the people. A public confused by three versions of the game will, from 2020, be offered four. Plans for a new city-based competition, named The Hundred, considered doing away with the lbw, presumably on the grounds that it gets in the way. The Hundred would be a cricket competition for people who do not like cricket, a gateway drug to the real thing. As marketing strategies go, this one seemed curious.

And yet there was logic. "What nobody should doubt is the seriousness of the issues facing the game," wrote ESPNcricinfo's George Dobell. "Without the oxygen of publicity, the game has been suffocating for years. It is a crisis. Something needed to be done." And if it is nothing else, The Hundred is at least something – or, as Michael Henderson put it in *The Spectator*, "a gaudy mess knocked up by people who no longer know what cricket is". In the *Mail*, Paul Newman concurred, demanding that Graves "resign now and let people who know what they are doing sort out the mess that The Hundred threatens to create". Matthew Engel struck a still more apocalyptic note in *The Guardian*, where he feared that 2019 threatened to be "the last summer".

> Ammon, though, already likes cricket, and so may be part of the problem, not the solution

According to Andrew Strauss, then the director of English cricket, "we're looking at mums and kids in the summer holidays". But, complained Lizzy Ammon in *The Times*, even mums "with their tiny post-baby brains" aren't actually "a special subset of the population who need things explaining more slowly". There is "a fine line between targeted marketing and being downright patronising". Ammon, though, already likes cricket, and so may be part of the problem, not the solution. Then again, asking cricket people to get behind a competition designed for non-cricketing folk always seemed a big ask. No wonder, with only a hint of despair, Steve James wondered in *The Times* if it was time to "bring back Kevin Pietersen" and other "legends" to be the face of the new competition. At least the public knew who they were.

"Viewed in isolation," wrote *The Observer's* Vic Marks, the proposals for domestic cricket from 2020 "display rare common sense". But, with the wisdom of an old bird who has seen it all before, he added: "The problems arise when all the packages outlined are put together." Indeed, since "excellence in the shortest of formats" will be the obvious route into professional cricket,

THE LIFE AND DEATH OF THE COUNTY CORRESPONDENT
Press release

MARK EKLID

Neville Cardus never wrote a live blog, and no one asked J. M. Kilburn to sub copy while keeping an eye on play. They belonged to another era, when the regional newspaper correspondent was as much a part of a county summer as outgrounds and brisk over-rates, and thousands of readers relied on their reports because there were so few other sources of news. Life is very different for their successors in the digital age.

The number of cricket specialists at regional newspapers has been falling for many years, but the decline has grown sharper. When I took over as county cricket correspondent of the *Derby Telegraph* in 2002, the top regional papers still had a reporter at all home matches, and most – if not all – away games. Last season, if those papers were ever represented at all, even at their home grounds, it was often by journalists still keen enough to go in their time off. "I saw less cricket than at any time in the previous 17 years," said Simon Walter of the *Southern Echo*. It is a familiar complaint.

Only *The Yorkshire Post* remain committed to the old levels of coverage. At other publications, writers who until recently were sent regularly to matches have been made redundant, been reassigned, or have left altogether. Any coverage that does appear in print or online is tolerated by editors rather than welcomed. "I still try to get a Lancashire page-lead in the paper every day during the summer and put everything online, but now I often don't have the time," said Chris Ostick of the *Manchester Evening News*. "No one encourages me to put it on and, if I don't, no one asks why not – and it doesn't get done."

Should it trouble anyone that the regional press have all but stopped staffing county coverage? Or is it evolution, to be accepted with the shrug we might offer the video-recorder salesman or the knocker-upper? There are, after all, more ways now than ever to read about cricket. The trend is unlikely to be reversed.

Regional-press priorities have turned on their head over the last decade. Struggling circulation figures, with single-figure annual percentage falls considered almost acceptable, have left owners needing to recoup revenue from advertising that is going elsewhere. A stronger digital presence is the prize they now pursue. Mindsets had to change. Old-fashioned news sense is no longer enough. A journalist's story is deemed worthy only if it induces the reader to click on a link: a click is a hit, and hits pay the bills. Cricket, we are told, does not get enough hits.

"The reason I was given for being taken off cricket was that low web traffic meant they could no longer justify me spending a day at cricket, even though I always wrote my football copy from the ground as well," said Stuart Rayner of *The Journal* in Newcastle, which was the ECB's regional newspaper of the year in 2015. "I would have loved to take them around the ground to point out how many people were reading the paper."

The struggle between enthusiastic writers and unsympathetic editors is nothing new, but the analytics are. The old counter-arguments – a sport watched by few but followed by many, an older demographic which still prefers print – no longer wash. They are supposition. The figures show that football gets the hits, so the call is for more football news, however facile or unsubstantiated. Faced with increasingly limited resources, even the most supportive bosses have bowed to the inevitable.

Dwindling coverage has made it easier for the role of county correspondent to be scrapped. The ECB reporters' network, introduced in 2014 with financial support from the board when the Press Association declared they could no longer maintain their own service, aimed to provide eyewitness coverage of every day of county cricket. And it has been a success. The free copy has been snapped up by the smaller publications, which previously carried little or no county cricket, and is widely used by the titles which, traditionally, gave cricket a stronger presence. Yet it has provided an excuse for editors with stretched budgets: "Why should we pay to send when we can get this for free?"

The analytics are undeniable, they say, but the increased traffic reported by the counties on their official websites tells a different story. Even this, though, comes with a health warning. By expanding their own websites, clubs can claim the ground previously held by newspapers, and have emerged victorious without much of a battle. Counties no longer rely on the papers to keep their supporters informed, though there are signs the relationship is still valued. Some, including Warwickshire, Essex and Surrey, have recognised the worth in the accumulated knowledge of the former correspondents, and are using it to their advantage.

"Our main concern was that the papers were not going to focus on cricket any more, and that was a big blow for us," said Warwickshire's head of media relations, Tom Rawlings, who recruited former *Birmingham Post* cricket writer Brian Halford in 2016. "That is why we took Brian into our media team, and we are pleased with how it has worked out. The papers gave up on cricket too easily."

If the clubs now largely control the source of the news, that means they also control what gets reported. "Nobody calls them to account any more," said Bruce Talbot, who has covered Sussex cricket as a freelance and for *The Argus* for 30 seasons. "There are no breaking stories."

But the clubs have shown that the audience for county writing is still there. Some regional publications – primarily *The Yorkshire Post* and the *Sunday Independent* in the West Country – have found the readership will stay faithful if you provide articles worth reading, beyond the reporters' network and regurgitated press releases. Too many others have abandoned the fight. That may be their loss, as well as the readers'.

Mark Eklid is Wisden's *Derbyshire correspondent.*

"the longer formats, which now include 50-over cricket, will be of secondary importance". This is justified on the grounds that "the presence of a handful of matches of the new competition on terrestrial TV will somehow transform the fan base of the game. It is easier to believe in a harmonious Brexit."

Mercifully, there was some on-field action, too. The new chief selector, Ed Smith, was said to be a believer in the school of data-driven analytics, but his initial choices – notably recalling Jos Buttler – seemed driven by good old-fashioned hunches. Smith impressed the *Mail's* Nasser Hussain by "making brave decisions for the benefit of the England team, not for the benefit of himself". This, Hussain felt, distinguished him from previous selectors – which is, you may feel, a low threshold.

More controversial was the selection of Adil Rashid who, having opted out of red-ball cricket for Yorkshire, was recalled to the Test ranks for the India series. It spawned a fresh outbreak of that perennial summer favourite, Yorkshire-on-Yorkshire bloodletting. Michael Vaughan, never short of – or slow with – a view, declared the situation "ridiculous" and a "stab in the back for county cricket". Rashid, resisting the temptation to dwell on Vaughan's own commitment to the domestic game, contented himself by calling the criticisms "stupid". Be that as it may, Geoffrey Boycott wrote in *The Daily Telegraph* that Rashid was behaving "like a spoilt child" – a subject in which unkind critics might suggest the great man has some expertise – and should be ashamed of "trashing a great England captain". In any case, "in ten years nobody will remember Adil's Test match performances".

County cricket enjoyed a modest, perhaps unlikely, resurgence fuelled by new technology. Almost all teams now stream their Championship fixtures online. Fixed cameras mean only the cut strip is visible, giving the viewer the sense of glimpsing the action through a hole in a fence – and thereby reinforcing the sweet feeling that Championship cricket is watched on stolen time. But as many as 5,000 a day might log in, at least for a time.

Surrey's fixture with Yorkshire at Scarborough was given a more professional treatment – four cameras, chats with players and so on – and was viewed, on the first day, from a reported 15,000 different devices. A small beginning, maybe, but one that will grow, complementing the BBC's radio coverage of every county fixture. Who knows: promoting cricket as cricket could catch on.

The game is opening up, anyway, recognising that new platforms are key to building a new audience and keeping enthusiasts happy. It all offers the blissful prospect of "days of hypnotic fixed-camera drama", according to Alan Tyers in the *Telegraph*, and in 2018 gave the chance to see the likes of Paul Collingwood, James Foster and Jonathan Trott in action one last time before they slipped into retirement.

The best piece on retirement, however, came from Dobell, on Worcestershire seamer Jack Shantry: "You could see and feel the struggle with Jack. It was obvious he wasn't the most talented, and you could see how much the game meant to him. He was the underdog having his day in the sun; the journeyman rubbing shoulders with stars. And never, not for a moment, did he forget where he came from." If cricket really does have a spirit, this is part of it.

Border skirmish: England's defeat is given detailed coverage by *The Scotsman*.

Though Sky's coverage remains admirable, yet somehow tired – too many ex-captains can dull the broth – cracks were apparent elsewhere. When Talksport won the rights to England's winter tours, it prompted a response "somewhere on the spectrum between regret, dismay and a great swirling fudge of mawkish, cake-fondling, doily-clutching, Middle England horror", wrote Barney Ronay in *The Guardian*. "This is worse than Brexit," one fan told Jonathan Agnew on Twitter.

The BBC responded with The Cricket Social, "A *Test Match Special*-without-the-cricket format", according to Ronay, which proved an entertaining success and, more worryingly, entirely in keeping with the voguish theory that cricket itself is the obstacle to winning an audience for cricket. Yet cricket is more progressive than sometimes supposed: the presence of female commentators at football's World Cup prompted an eruption of disagreeable harrumphing, in marked contrast to cricket's embrace of Alison Mitchell, Isa Guha, Ebony Rainford-Brent and others, whose professionalism and talent are as obvious as they are appreciated.

Disruption is the name of the modern game, however, and old monopolies are threatened everywhere. In Australia, Channel Nine lost its exclusive rights for the first time in more than 40 years; then Adam Collins, a freelance journalist, picked up the rights for audio coverage of Australia's series against Pakistan, available on wisden.com. It felt like a significant moment.

Guerilla Cricket, the successor to Test Match Sofa, continued to provide an irreverent but knowledgable alternative to the BBC and Talksport. Fittingly, Daniel Norcross, an amateur-turned-professional broadcaster who has made the transition from one TMS (Sofa) to the other (Special) with increasing assurance, was in the box when Alastair Cook reached a century in his last Test innings: "What a magnificent moment," he purred. "The crowd just giving waves and waves of applause, everyone on their feet. You couldn't write it: a fifty and a hundred in his first Test, a fifty and a hundred in his last Test. I think this applause might go on to lunchtime."

If Cook's batting was not always loved, the service he gave his country was, the warmth of the send-off a reflection of the crowd's recognition that, as Atherton put it: "Scoring runs for Cook was never an easy task, every innings a draining one. If anything, he got runs in spite of his technique rather than because of it." But he got more runs as an opener than anyone in Test history. Quite a thing, that, and a thing that ended gloriously.

Cook's departure inevitably felt like the end of an era. Not just for him and England, but for a particular style of cricket. Indeed batting averages slumped across the world in 2018, falling to levels not seen in generations. Gideon Haigh, in *The Australian*, ascribed this to the demands made of batsmen asked to play three forms of cricket. The early years of this century might be "the culmination of a long phase of relative stability, an equipoise between five-and one-day cricket, leading to a bubble economy that fetishised big scores". Now, he went on, "there is already an underestimated gap between T20 and one-day cricket," while "Test cricket is exponentially more complicated".

Looking to the future, Haigh saw trouble: a World Test Championship "in which everyone prepares decks to give their own bowlers a chance of taking 20 wickets will soon pall. And an average game will not generate those extraordinary accomplishments that, even if it is only every now and again, Test cricket needs to verify its uniqueness." The future, you see, is always cloudy.

Alex Massie writes about politics for The Times *and* The Spectator, *and plays, when required, for Selkirk CC in the East of Scotland League.*

CRICKET AND BLOGS IN 2018

What, no hagiography?

BRIAN CARPENTER

Cricket has too often inhabited a rarefied vantage point from which to observe the moral failings of the wider world – a romanticised arbiter of a kind of fair play which, if it ever existed, went out with the Ark. The events of 2018 were a reminder that, regardless of its attachment to nostalgia, cricket can create and embrace controversy along with the best of them.

When Steve Smith, David Warner and Cameron Bancroft wrote the latest grim chapter in the sport's long history of rule bending, Jon Hotten (**theoldbatsman.blogspot.com**) harked back almost 40 years to Dennis Lillee throwing his aluminium bat across the WACA, and contrasted the absence of disciplinary action with the sanctions imposed on that trio.

"Imagine… Warner hurling his Kaboom 40 yards across the field because it wouldn't pass through the bat gauge," he wrote. "The thought that he might not be banned is actually an unthinkable one: he'd be more likely to face criminal charges. This is not simply a function of changing mores and morals. It's clear, from the Ben Stokes case and now the Sandpaper Three (or four, if we count Darren Lehmann), that the essential substance of such issues is being affected by the surrounding culture, specifically social media. The shape of them, their actual outcomes, are distorted in and by real time." The episode was endlessly debated in mainstream and social media, but few had the perceptiveness to examine the broader context, as Hotten did.

In the United Kingdom, though, there were other issues. Throughout 2018, Brexit became a prism through which all sorts of moral, ethical and political issues were viewed. Not to be outdone by the poor judgment of politicians, the ECB (the England and Wales Cricket Board, not the European Central Bank) blundered into this atmosphere of discontent with typical clumsiness when they proposed a new form of the game, and insisted it would go ahead in 2020. Brexit continued to have advocates, but the concept of The Hundred appeared to be disliked by everyone.

For reasons too opaque to unfold here, Peter Casterton (aka Tregaskis) at **dropinpitch.wordpress.com** slipped an oblique reference to the birth of Augustine of Hippo into a forensic dissection of how the ECB concocted The Hundred with a minimum of logical thought and a contemptible lack of consultation with the players and fans. Like Danny Frankland (**beingoutsidecricket.com**), Casterton also took aim at the sexism inherent in an interview in which Andrew Strauss sought to defend the new format because it would be easy for women and children to understand. And Casterton voiced the widespread doubts among those who already liked cricket in its various forms: "The 100-ball format does not exist anywhere else in the cricketing world, which is too interested in celebrating, marketing and profiting from the

CRICKET AND TWITTER IN 2018

Exaggerated rumours

NISHANT JOSHI

Not for the first time, cricket's presence on Twitter confirmed the suspicion that the lifeblood of social media is #outrage. If Ravi Bopara were to tweet a story about rescuing a cat from a tree, the first response would be to remind him that he failed to score the winning runs off the last ball against Sri Lanka at the 2007 World Cup. The second would ask him why he saves cats instead of dogs. And the third would be a request to retweet a fraudulent charity appeal.

Not even the most famous cricketer in the world is immune. In a year in which Virat Kohli was lauded again and again, he still managed to attract Twitter's ire. During a promotional video Q&A on his feed, he replied to an Indian user who had suggested Kohli was "overrated", and who said he preferred to watch overseas batsmen. Kohli replied: "Why are you living in our country and loving other countries? I don't mind you not liking me, but I don't think you should live in our country and like other things."

The initial responses to Kohli's retort were prickly and, for the first time in a while, he found himself on the back foot. Memes and columns fought for space in a feeding frenzy of epically pointless proportions. Commentators were quick to jump on the bandwagon, with Harsha Bhogle tweeting: "Virat Kohli's statement is a reflection of the bubble that most famous people either slip into or are forced into. The voices within it are frequently those that they wish to hear. It is a comfortable bubble and that is why famous people must try hard to prevent it from forming."

As the frenzy faded, Kohli tried to clarify his stance, as if it would change minds: "I guess trolling isn't for me guys, I'll stick to getting trolled! I'm all for freedom of choice. Keep it light guys and enjoy the festive season. Love and peace to all."

If you're a professional cricketer, you should know the Twitter playbook by now: things get misinterpreted. Just ask Ben Duckett, who tweeted: "RCB are a joke!" In context, it was clear Duckett was admiring the quality of Royal Challengers Bangalore. But Twitter does not do context. "Woken up to... horrible messages," tweeted Duckett. "Yesterday I referred to RCB as a 'joke', meaning they have such a good side with the likes of de Kock, de Villiers, Kohli, McCullum and lots of other world-class players. These types of messages are not acceptable."

Sometimes, confusion is deliberate. "I am alive and kicking more than ever before. Not sure where this news has come from but this is fake. Love you all." So tweeted Nathan McCullum, the former New Zealand off-spinner, after it was confidently announced by a fan page on Facebook that he had passed away. The post even had a funereal black and white picture.

In a swirl of unsubstantiated and malicious rumour-mongering, his younger brother Brendon came across the offending posts. He was understandably distressed: "Tonight someone decided via social media to release that my brother passed away! I'm on a flight back to NZ and my heart broke! None of it is true! Whoever put this out there, I'll find you! Somewhere, somehow." The fan page in question promised that such an incident would "never happen again", which was presumably of great reassurance to the McCullums.

Nishant Joshi is a medical doctor, and host of the sports podcast Radio Cricket.

99.94
Considered Cricket Analysis From Beyond the Boundary

About the Authors

England Player Ratings for Posted by: shootingtrumpet | November 27, 2018
Sri Lanka Test series

Keaton Jennings (233 runs
at 47, 8 catches)

His outstanding 146* set up
the crucial series opening
win in Galle, though he
struggled thereafter. Won
the dubious award of fielding
at short leg for his career
after a run of sensational
catches off the spinners.
Grade B

Yeah, 48 wickets between them in three Tests.

RECENT POSTS

• England Player Ratings for
  Sri Lanka Test series
• Five County Cricketers of the
  Year – 2018
• The Final Over of the Week
  in County Cricket – 28
  September 2018
• The Final Over of the Week
  in County Cricket – 24
  September 2018
• The Final Over of the Week
  in County Cricket – 16
  September 2018
• England Test Match Report
  Card – Summer 2018
• The Final Over of the Week
  in County Cricket – 8

exponential success of T20. The ECB may have just invented the Betamax of
cricket formats when VHS cricket has already captured the market."

There were, though, two things most could agree on: Virat Kohli is a
great batsman, and Alastair Cook, in his quiet way, was a phenomenon whose
long career defined an era in English cricket. Gary Naylor, at 99.94
(**nestaquin.wordpress.com**), paid tribute to Kohli's masterpiece in the First
Test at Edgbaston: "In these hours we would see greatness embraced,
established, underlined as Kohli fought to get himself into a match that was
sliding rapidly away from the grip of his iron will… but the application of
skill, the control of temperament and the calling upon of immense reserves of
concentration got him through."

The Test series between England and India was compelling, and Hotten
provided a memorable image from Lord's. Writing about Cheteshwar Pujara,
India's No. 3, he described him as "radiating innocence in his usual way. He
bears the look of someone whose dad still drives him to the game while the
cool kids sit together on the coach." Whatever his mode of transport, Pujara
can really bat, as his century at Southampton later in the series showed.

In the days either side of Cook's Test retirement, as the professional media
overflowed with tributes bordering on the hagiographic, the blogosphere was
more nuanced. At **thefulltoss.com**, where Cook was always assured of a
critical reception, James Morgan wrote a superbly balanced, fair and moving
appreciation. Elsewhere, while acknowledging many of Cook's virtues and
achievements, Casterton was a good deal harsher. And the American Matt
Becker, whose return at **limitedovers.wordpress.com** was one of the more
welcome aspects of the year, wove his memories of Cook together with
recollections of his own life in typically ambitious but eloquent fashion.
"Through it all: Cook has been there. And later this year in Sri Lanka, when

England's openers walk out in the heat, it won't be Alastair Cook. It will be someone else. And that thought makes me almost intolerably sad. For me, as a cricket fan, considering when it all started, England is Cook, and Cook is England. But. Now. No more. For good or for bad, that's the new reality."

The human instinct to recall better times was reflected by Stephen Hope at **bythesightscreen.com**, where he relived summer days at seaside grounds no longer graced by county cricket: Clarence Park at Weston-super-Mare, the United Services Ground at Portsmouth, Bournemouth's Dean Park. Hope's writing captured the essence of outground cricket, and was enhanced by sepia-toned photographs.

From the days when The Hundred was simply a batting milestone, here was Viv Richards, in all his muscular majesty, for Somerset against Hampshire at Weston in 1978, forcing the ball through the leg side with a stroke that exists in the memory as his leitmotif. Or his West Indian confrère Gordon Greenidge taking the applause of the Bournemouth crowd, a thrilling John Player League century to his name. In a year when cricket's internal dialogue often seemed to match the chaotic state of British politics, Hope's evocations of more stable times were worth clinging to.

Brian Carpenter blogs at differentshadesofgreen.blogspot.com. In 2013, he was the inaugural winner of Wisden's *writing competition.*

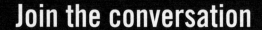

RETIREMENTS IN 2018

Cheery, simple and unfussy

STEVE JAMES

They do not make too many like **Jonathan Trott** any more. For several years, he was England's old-fashioned Test rock at No. 3. He was fidgety, intense, superstitious and forever scratching his mark. But until he left the 2013-14 Ashes with a stress-related illness, he was a reassuring presence, a throwback to an era when crease occupation was paramount. England's struggle to replace him merely emphasised his value.

Born in Cape Town, Trott made Birmingham and Warwickshire his home, scoring a century on first-class debut, against Sussex in 2003, then repeating the trick in Test cricket during the 2009 Ashes decider at The Oval, which England won.

His unusual method of advancing towards the bowler was borne of early problems with the low bounce and slowness of English pitches, but his balance made him a magnificent player off his legs. Only late in his career – most famously during that 2013-14 Ashes against Mitchell Johnson at Brisbane – did the short ball become a problem, but by then Trott had left his mark. He was the ICC's Cricketer of the Year in 2011, and made a heap of one-day international runs. His strike-rate of 77 attracted criticism, but his average of 51 – and the fact that England mostly won when he prospered – drew admiration.

Clive Rose, Getty Images

Keeping it so simple: Paul Collingwood and the World Twenty20 trophy England won in 2010.

Paul Collingwood was a throwback too, and was christened "Brigadier Block" for his defensive qualities, once batting two and a half hours for an unbeaten 26 to save a Test at Centurion, then holding out for more than four and a half to make 40 and do the same at Cape Town. But, unlike Trott, whose fear of failure was often evident, he was the most straightforward of cricketers.

As a young Durham batsman with a short backlift and dominant bottom hand, there was little indication of the success to come. But he squeezed every drop from his talent to become a Test batsman with an average of 40 – six higher than in his other first-class games – an energetic medium-pacer and a brilliant fielder. In a one-dayer against Bangladesh at Trent Bridge in 2005, he scored a hundred and took six wickets. And he did everything in a cheery, simple, unfussy way. He was an Ashes winner three times, scoring a double-century at Adelaide, and remains the only man to captain England to a global trophy, the World T20 in the West Indies in 2010, when he hit the winning runs in the final against Australia.

One wonders what might have been for **James Foster**, had he not broken his arm in the Essex nets in 2002. He was England's Test wicketkeeper at the time, with six caps, and it looked as if Alec Stewart's stint with the gloves was over. But Foster's misfortune gave Stewart another chance, and Foster played only one more Test (Stewart was injured), in Australia that winter. When Stewart retired in 2003, England returned to Chris Read, before opting for Geraint Jones and then Matt Prior.

Foster was as pure a gloveman as the game has seen, good enough to be recalled for the 2009 World Twenty20, when he pulled off three electric stumpings. But to categorise him as a specialist keeper who missed opportunities because he could not bat would be unfair. He averaged 36 in first-class cricket, with 23 centuries and a best of 212. He was simply unfortunate, in the wrong place at the wrong time.

It would have been harsh had **Ed Joyce** never played a Test, given that he averaged nearly 48 in first-class cricket, with nearly 18,500 runs and 47 centuries, as well as over 10,000 List A runs, and 18 more hundreds. So it was fitting that he played in Ireland's inaugural Test against Pakistan, then promptly retired. A classy left-hander who was prolific through the off side, he had moved to England in search of that Test goal, proving mightily effective for both Middlesex and Sussex. But he had to settle for the England one-day side, scoring a memorable century against Australia at Sydney in February 2007. It meant he had the curious distinction of playing for England at the 2007 World Cup, then for Ireland in the 2011 and 2015 editions.

Like Trott, **Nick Compton** – who did not play in 2018 – was South African-born and a complicated, intense character. The grandson of Denis, he made more than a decent fist of upholding the family name. He played 16 Tests, forged a successful opening partnership with Alastair Cook during England's monumental win in India in 2012-13, and later that winter scored centuries in successive innings in New Zealand, displaying great determination, despite a rather upright and stiff method.

James Tredwell did not play first-team cricket in 2018 either, but his solid off-breaks gave him a 17-year career with Kent (plus a few Championship games on loan to Sussex in 2014), and some success in two Tests and 62 white-ball internationals with England. He was well regarded, even captaining his country in a Twenty20 game against New Zealand at The Oval in 2007; it rained after two balls. He bowled more slowly than most at the top level, but with skill and nous. Polite and unassuming – he enjoyed time on his allotment, and made his own chutney and jam – he was often underestimated.

To say that Worcestershire's **Jack Shantry** had an unusual action would be only the half of it. A tall left-arm seamer of little more than medium-pace, his method of delivery – a whirlwind of limbs, apparently off the wrong foot – seemed to defy description, though his older brother Adam, another county left-armer, called it "a cry for help". Before a back injury became too much, Jack took 266 first-class wickets at 29 and, despite a lowly position in the order, made two first-class centuries.

Even for a wicketkeeper, **Niall O'Brien** was a chirpy cricketer, and a confident, combative left-hand batsman. He was a popular player with Kent, Northamptonshire and Leicestershire, but it was with Ireland he made his name, particularly at the 2007 World Cup, when his 72 was instrumental in the shock victory over Pakistan in Jamaica. He too bowed out after their inaugural Test.

Jimmy Adams was a fine opening batsman for Hampshire, whom he also captained. Another left-hander, he had a mountainous backlift. Adams was a late developer, but totalled over 14,000 first-class runs at an average of 37. Lesser players have been capped by England.

The day before Adams retired, **Sean Ervine**, another Hampshire stalwart, stepped down while on loan to Derbyshire. An all-rounder who bowled brisk awayswingers and batted left-handed with plenty of aggression, Ervine played five Tests and 42 one-day games for Zimbabwe, the last in 2004. He made Hampshire his home for 14 seasons, during which they won six white-ball trophies.

Steve Magoffin was unlucky never to play international cricket. A tall, slight fast bowler from Queensland, he made a significant impression in county cricket. After one game for Surrey in 2007, he spent 2008 with Worcestershire, where he ended his career. In between, from 2012, he had five full seasons with Sussex, and finished with 597 first-class wickets at 23 – remarkable figures.

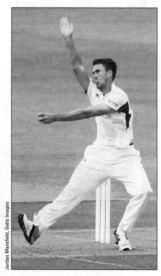

Jordan Mansfield, Getty Images

Action man: Jack Shantry bowling for Worcestershire in 2015.

Another foreigner to become a county favourite was **Johann Myburgh**. Good enough to become the youngest South African to score a first-class double-century, at the age of 17, he sought cricket in New Zealand when opportunities became limited at home, before heading to England. He played for Hampshire, Durham, then Somerset, where he was much liked, especially for his explosive Twenty20 performances.

Jim Allenby had left Somerset in 2017 after playing for Leicestershire and Glamorgan, but could not find another employer. Born in Australia, he was a more than useful all-rounder, especially in the one-day game. **Andrew Hodd** was a superb specialist wicketkeeper, who was mainly an understudy, but still managed to win four County Championship medals, two with Sussex (2006 and 2007) and two with Yorkshire (2014 and 2015). He also played for Surrey.

A lively seamer and hard-hitting batsman, **Steven Crook** had spells at Lancashire and Middlesex before finding most success at Northamptonshire, where he helped win T20 titles in 2013 and 2016. He also hit an unbeaten 142 against his native Australia in a first-class game at Wantage Road in 2015. **Will Gidman**, another well-travelled all-rounder, finished his career at Kent, having turned out for Durham, Gloucestershire and Nottinghamshire. His medium-pacers were particularly effective for Gloucestershire between 2011 and 2014, when he twice took 50 first-class wickets, and averaged 21 for three consecutive seasons.

Matt Hunn was a promising fast bowler with Kent, who took five wickets against the 2015 touring Australians. But he retired aged 24 after injuries hampered his progress.

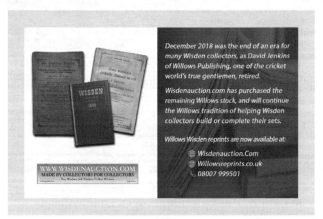

CAREER FIGURES

Players not expected to appear in county cricket in 2019

(minimum 40 first-class appearances)

BATTING

	M	I	NO	R	HS	100	Avge	1,000r/ season
J. H. K. Adams	233	409	30	14,134	262*	25	37.29	5
K. R. Brown	85	140	6	3,572	132	2	46.06	–
M. A. Carberry	208	363	25	13,868	300*	35	41.02	4
P. D. Collingwood	306	527	52	16,938	206	35	35.65	3
N. R. D. Compton	194	338	37	12,168	254*	27	40.42	6
S. P. Crook	106	146	19	4,043	145	5	31.83	–
E. J. H. Eckersley	108	193	12	5,779	158	14	31.92	1
S. M. Ervine	229	358	43	11,390	237*	22	36.15	1
J. S. Foster	289	427	52	13,761	212	23	36.69	1
J. E. C. Franklin	206	321	46	9,780	219	22	35.56	–
W. R. S. Gidman	83	125	21	3,673	143	5	35.31	1
A. J. Hodd	114	163	25	3,809	123	4	27.60	–
R. A. Jones	59	90	17	895	62	–	12.26	–
S. C. Kerrigan	104	122	42	1,058	62*	–	13.22	–
S. J. Magoffin	160	217	57	2,657	79	–	16.60	–
J. G. Myburgh	108	190	23	6,841	203	16	40.96	–
K. Noema-Barnett	84	126	19	3,086	108	3	28.84	–
M. L. Pettini	178	296	42	8,933	209	15	35.16	1
J. D. Shantry	92	118	32	1,640	106	2	19.06	–
J. C. Tredwell	177	247	31	4,727	124	4	21.88	–
I. J. L. Trott	281	468	47	18,662	226	46	44.32	9
G. C. Wilson	104	161	22	4,761	160*	3	34.25	–

BOWLING

	R	W	BB	Avge	5I	10M	Ct/St
J. H. K. Adams	721	13	2-16	55.46	–	–	189
K. R. Brown	65	2	2-30	32.50	–	–	52
M. A. Carberry	1,081	17	2-85	63.58	–	–	94
P. D. Collingwood	6,396	166	5-52	38.53	2	–	352
N. R. D. Compton	229	3	1-1	76.33	–	–	98
S. P. Crook	8,211	207	5-48	39.66	3	–	36
E. J. H. Eckersley	67	2	2-29	33.50	–	–	175/3
S. M. Ervine	11,901	280	6-82	42.50	5	–	195
J. S. Foster	128	1	1-122	128.00	–	–	839/62
J. E. C. Franklin	13,504	479	7-14	28.19	14	1	107
W. R. S. Gidman	5,156	219	6-15	23.54	10	1	38
A. J. Hodd	21	0	0-7	–	–	–	278/23
R. A. Jones	5,320	163	7-115	32.63	5	–	22
S. C. Kerrigan	9,844	322	9-51	30.57	13	3	36
S. J. Magoffin	14,091	597	8-20	23.60	27	4	35
J. G. Myburgh	2,160	45	4-56	48.00	–	–	61
K. Noema-Barnett	4,422	130	4-20	34.01	–	–	47
M. L. Pettini	263	1	1-72	263.00	–	–	120
J. D. Shantry	7,783	266	7-60	29.25	12	2	30
J. C. Tredwell	15,438	426	8-66	36.23	12	3	196
I. J. L. Trott	3,487	70	7-39	49.81	1	–	223
G. C. Wilson	89	0	0-2	–	–	–	189/5

CRICKETANA IN 2018

From W. G. Grace to Ed Sheeran

Marcus Williams

The hot summer revealed many archaeological features that had lain hidden in the British landscape for hundreds of years. So it was apt that 2018 also saw the resurfacing of an item from cricket's earliest days. It was a curved bat, dating from the first half of the 18th century, and looked more like a hockey stick. The curve vanished later in the century, when lob bowling replaced grubbers.

The museum in the Oval pavilion houses the bat recognised as the oldest in existence. Dated 1729, it weighs 2lb 4oz and belonged to James Chitty, of Knaphill, Surrey. The one offered by Shropshire auctioneers Mullock's weighed 3lb, not unlike some modern versions, though significantly heavier than a hockey stick. Like the Chitty bat, the side that is flat suggests it was used by a left-hander.

Unsurprisingly, given its age, it has signs of wear. Marks indicate it might have been used to knock stumps into the ground, and there are screws at the bottom of the shaft where a plaque was attached. Undeterred, the successful bidder paid £12,400 (all prices include buyer's premium and VAT). Its exact provenance is uncertain, but it is possible it was crafted in Surrey by the Clapshaws, a noted early bat-making family who later had a workshop in west London. Aquila Clapshaw was born in 1714, so this might be a fairly close contemporary of the Chitty. Some believe early players made their own bats – there's a thought for today's pros.

The Clapshaws were granted a royal warrant from Prince Albert, and the business survived until 1976. Mullock's also offered one of their later bats, a "Superior" model dating from around 1900 and made by Aquila Clapshaw and Salmon, as the firm had become. It carried the trademarked – though faded – image of W. G. Grace, but realised a modest £37.

WG material is not unusual in cricketing sales, but every now and again something out of the ordinary comes along. A rare, probably unique, presentation copy of his 1891 book

Grace and savour: the buyer of a presentation copy of *Cricket*, by WG, paid almost £4,500.

Morphets

"Minding Me Dad's Pint", painted by Brian Shields in his Lowryesque style, fetched £14,520.

Cricket, inscribed and signed "With the author's compliments", sold far above estimate for £4,464 at Knights in Leicester. The elaborate binding, by G. T. Bagguley of Newcastle under Lyme, was described in the catalogue as "Dark green full calf, the front, back and spine finely tooled with elaborate borders inlaid in caramel coloured calf. Bright red cricket balls motifs to the centre and in each corner." Then there are the "wonderful gauffered [patterned and gilded] page block edges". One for the true bibliophile.

Contemporary admirers of WG could buy leatherbound subscribers' copies of the same book, also bearing his signature. These were limited to 652 volumes, and are also collectable; a couple were recently on the market at around £500–600. A standard edition, in fine condition, was listed at £75.

While Grace's celebrity came from his exploits on the field, he was also a practising doctor. A letter of support he wrote in this capacity – on behalf of a patient having difficulty with a life insurance payment – realised £123 at Forum Auctions in London.

A posed image of Grace playing a cut with the Lord's Pavilion in the background formed part of a fascinating collection of more than 300 glass magic-lantern slides. Others included views of grounds from around the world, as well as players and teams of the Victorian era. The package, which also comprised 80 pages of accompanying notes and two magic lanterns, had been used by an unnamed cricketing devotee to deliver lectures on the history of the game, and sold at Knights for £3,224, more than three times the estimate.

In November, an oil painting by the late Liverpudlian artist Brian Shields (nicknamed Braaq, apparently after the French cubist Georges Braques) sold for a smidgen more than the curved bat. The painting, entitled "Minding Me Dad's Pint" and depicting crowds – including Braaq himself – attending a match at Aigburth, realised £14,520 at Morphets of Harrogate.

Among a range of interesting photographic items was an album compiled by Lord Hawke during a tour to Australia in 1887, which fetched £2,356 at Mellors & Kirk in Nottingham. It contained general and cricketing views taken both on the voyage out and after the players had arrived. Having played only three first-class matches, Hawke, who was the captain, had to return home in early December after the death of his father. This tour has some importance in the history of the game, since a rival English team, Arthur Shrewsbury's XI, were in Australia at the same time, prompting *Wisden 1889* to venture that "such a piece of folly will never be perpetrated again".

CHASING LEATHER

This is the 25th edition of the Almanack to be available in a special leather binding. The tradition began in 1995, when all 100 copies were immediately snapped up. The next year numbers were increased to 150, and have remained unchanged ever since.

Each copy bears its own number, from one to 150, though sales are in reality limited to 145, since Nos 1–5 are reserved for the Cricketers of the Year, and are often presented at the launch dinner, held each April in the Long Room at Lord's. All 150 are signed by the editor.

Few sets of leatherbound *Wisdens* have appeared on the market, though Chris Ridler, who runs WisdenAuction.com, oversaw the sale of a run of 23 identically numbered copies (1995–2017) for £6,250. A 22-volume set involving mixed numbers – the 1995 edition not matching the rest – fetched £5,950 in 2016. Meanwhile, the record for an individual volume of *Wisden 1995* was achieved at Knights in 2014, when the purchaser paid £2,284, including commission and VAT.

Two volumes have breached the £3,000 barrier, and each has a story. In 2011, only four Cricketers of the Year were selected, and the unallocated No. 5 was sold in 2016 for £3,100 (see pages 162–3 of *Wisden 2017*). A year later, another No. 5 made £3,000: Dermot Reeve, a Cricketer of the Year in 1996, felt compelled by financial hardship to sell his leatherbound. But in a heart-warming tale, a friend of Reeve bought it – and promptly gave it back to him.

Every limited-edition *Wisden* is bound in brown Morocco leather, finished with gilt to a high spec, and with gold lettering. In addition, each copy is imprinted with its individual number, and housed in a slip case. Purchasers of the current year's leatherbound always have first refusal on the same number when the next edition is published.

More details are available from almanack@wisdenalmanack.com, or John Wisden & Co Ltd, 13 Old Aylesfield, Golden Pot, Alton, Hampshire GU34 4BY.

Fin de siècle: Lord's in 1899.

Graham Budd Auctions in London sold a striking illuminated montage of
eight photos from the 1899 England v Australia Test at Lord's, featuring some
action from the game, spectators promenading on the field, and net practice. It
sold for £605 – around double its estimate. A star of that match was Victor
Trumper, who hit an undefeated century in only his second Test. His popularity
was reflected in a public reception at Sydney Town Hall in 1902; a scarce,
though slightly tattered, souvenir programme of the occasion made £868
at Mullock's.

Souvenirs of a more modern Ashes encounter went under the hammer too.
Two lots, both including menus from dinners to mark the 1977 Centenary
Test, proved popular. The first, from the Australian Cricket Board bash, was
signed by around 135 Ashes cricketers, including Bradman, Compton, Miller,
Barrington, Wyatt, Voce, Ryder and Laker; together with three miniature
bats autographed by England touring sides and five signed England tour
sheets, they fetched £440 at the Sussex auctioneers Toovey's. A second
menu, for the Melbourne CC dinner and signed by more than 60 players
from both sides (plus the astronomer and cricket fan Patrick Moore), made
£273 at Mullock's. And there were team autographs galore on a bat from the
one-off – and long-forgotten – 1985 Benson & Hedges World Championship
of Cricket, contested in Australia by the then seven Test-playing nations and
won by India. The bat realised £682 at Mullock's.

Some unusual county-related material also reached the salerooms. The best
was Worcestershire's scorebook recording, in various hands, matches played
between 1882 and 1893, before the club acquired first-class status. It fetched

Graham Budd Auctions

£2,108 at Knights, having been bought for "a pittance" at a junk shop 40 years earlier. Two volumes of Gloucestershire scores from 1870 to 1904, together with a banquet menu marking WG's 100th century and a Cheltenham Week scrapbook, made £626 at Gorringe's of Lewes. Warwickshire's 20-page annual report from 1903 sold for £126 at Midlands Sports Auctions of West Bromwich, while four medals, given to Worcestershire bowler Brian Brain for his appearances in one-day finals, made £665.

A remarkable volume emerged at a Knights sale. Compiled by F. S. Ashley-Cooper, an indefatigable historian and researcher, Pelham Warner's "Cricket Record 1888–1919" ran to 233 handwritten pages. Contained within were Warner's scores, averages, season-by-season statistics and summaries, covering his career with Harrison College in Barbados, Rugby School, Oxford University, Middlesex and England, plus other miscellaneous matches. Selling for £2,976, it doubled its estimate. To think that such detailed information can now be found at the click of a mouse.

As ever, *Wisdens* were in plentiful supply at auctions and dealers, but few expected the frenetic bidding that set a record for a single volume. At Christie's in July, an 1869 edition changed hands for £32,500, but because it was part of a stellar sale of rare books and manuscripts, which in total realised over £6m, it attracted little attention. More than 40 other lots fetched higher sums.

Two would-be owners fought tooth and nail for a volume that, unusually, had not been rebound. Although the original paper covers were slightly worn, the fact they were still there, on the second-scarcest edition, made the difference. Christie's upper estimate of £9,500 had long since come and gone when the bidding passed the highest for an 1869 in original binding (£16,000),

and then for any volume. That record had been established in 2006, when Karl Auty's copy of *Wisden 1875* – the holy grail – made $48,000, the equivalent of £25,731 (see *Wisden 2007*, page 1608).

At the same London sale, a rebound copy of 1875 sold for £16,250, and an 1864 in original covers £13,750. At Knights, meanwhile, a volume from 1897, the second produced with boards, went for £12,400, and the highly collectable 1916 for £6,696. For those without such deep pockets, the limited-edition reprints produced since 1983 by Willows Publishing have been welcome substitutes. They have, though, acquired a value of their own: at a Lawrence's of Crewkerne sale, a run of Willows reprints from 1879 to 1919 went for £1,290.

Willows have published reprints of every *Wisden* from 1864 to 1946, selling around 36,000, but the founder, David Jenkins, decided at the end of 2018 to call it a day. He could reflect on a job well done, and the profound gratitude of many happy collectors.

And finally, in the *Wisden* spirit of unusual occurrences, here are a few offbeat lots from salerooms around the country:

- A four-carriage Midland Mainline model train, whose locomotive is named "Leicestershire County Cricket Club" (£68).
- A Royal Household CC striped blazer, belonging to a Buckingham Palace footman (£37).
- One of Imran Khan's Sussex sweaters, together with a poster of a tiger, signed "That's me, Imran Khan" (£190).
- A penny slot-machine, updated in 1953 to reflect England's Ashes victory, with names such as Compton, Hutton and Evans (£198).
- Ed Sheeran's replica 2015 World Cup trophy, in a leather case (£233).
- The W. H. Smith interdepartmental cricket cup, contested from 1919 to 1964 (£434).
- A bottle of 12-year-old Highland single malt whisky, produced to "celebrate a century for the North of Scotland Cricket Association" (£508).

CRICKET AND THE WEATHER IN 2018

The good omen of Friday 13?

ANDREW HIGNELL

In 2018, southern counties tended to be the wettest, though it was Yorkshire, with 40, who lost most home hours in the Championship. The trend began with the season, when remnants of a weather system dubbed the "Beast from the East" blighted the University fixtures. Heavy rain also prompted Worcestershire to leave a soggy New Road for the Royal Grammar School.

On the day the Championship began – Friday, April 13 – six games totalled 142.3 overs, none of which came at Leeds, where Essex were defending their title. But when the second round started a week later, thermometers read the upper twenties – their highest in April since 1949 – and thunderstorms interrupted play. A blocking anticyclone then developed, a pattern lasting four months. Temperatures were the warmest since records began in 1910 (matched only by 1976). The game between Essex and the Indians at Chelmsford was reduced to three days, partly because of concerns about injury on the abrasive outfield, partly because of the debilitating heat so close to the Tests.

In meteorological terms, the summer was the driest since 1969. All told, 647 playing hours were lost in the Championship: since the millennium, only 2011, with 555, had a lower total. Rain returned, though, in September (strictly autumn) as Storms Ali and Bronagh swept the country. Winds prompted Kent to stow away their advertising boards during their game with Glamorgan, while at Taunton the covers were blown away, preventing play on the last day against Surrey. A draw guaranteed Somerset, who lost no time away from home in 2018, would finish second.

HOURS LOST TO THE WEATHER IN THE 2018 CHAMPIONSHIP

	Home	Away	2018	2017	Difference
Derbyshire	8.50	26.50	35.00	**86.75**	**−51.75**
Durham	**6.75**	34.75	41.50	50.75	−9.25
Essex	9.75	**43.50**	53.25	47.50	5.75
Glamorgan	9.50	27.75	37.25	38.50	−1.25
Gloucestershire	20.25	29.75	50.00	53.25	−3.25
Hampshire	18.50	24.25	42.75	71.25	−28.50
Kent	19.75	3.00	22.75	69.50	−46.75
Lancashire	16.50	1.25	**17.75**	54.25	−36.50
Leicestershire	21.50	1.75	23.25	39.25	−16.00
Middlesex	32.00	6.25	38.25	67.50	−29.25
Northamptonshire	29.50	28.75	**58.25**	50.75	**7.50**
Nottinghamshire	8.00	24.00	32.00	50.50	−18.50
Somerset	25.50	**0.00**	25.50	61.25	−35.75
Surrey	7.75	24.75	32.50	60.50	−28.00
Sussex	15.25	17.25	32.50	**28.75**	3.75
Warwickshire	17.25	4.50	21.75	37.50	−15.75
Worcestershire	16.75	9.00	25.75	44.00	−18.25
Yorkshire	**40.50**	16.50	57.00	50.25	−6.75
	323.50	323.50	647.00	962.00	−315.00

CRICKET PEOPLE

Irish coffee

RICHARD WHITEHEAD

On the third day of Ireland's inaugural men's Test, at Malahide, **Aideen Rice** took a break from the glad-handing, and settled down to watch the cricket. "Then someone tapped me on the shoulder to say that Mick Jagger had just arrived." For the president of Cricket Ireland, it was back to work.

Ireland's battle with Pakistan nearly turned into an epic. But it was always about much more than a game of cricket. Rice, the first woman to hold the job, began her year in office only 12 days before the Test, and knew she was destined for a hectic time. "I was speaking at lunches, entertaining guests in the marquees. We had the Pakistani ambassador, the chairman of the Pakistan Cricket Board, and lots of other visitors." The occasion was given a grand seal of approval when the Irish president, Michael D. Higgins, arrived on the third morning and stayed for five hours. Rice had not long waved him off when Jagger turned up, in town ahead of a Rolling Stones gig at Croke Park.

She was phlegmatic about the weather, which washed out the first day. Touring the soggy hospitality area that afternoon, she spotted a forlorn-looking Pakistani ambassador. "I said to him, 'You know, you don't really have to stay all day'. I think it was what he wanted to hear."

Transforming the homely surroundings of Malahide was not the least of the challenges facing Cricket Ireland. "It's a beautiful ground, but it has to become a pop-up stadium," says Rice. The temporary stands, dressing-rooms and marquees were left in place for the Twenty20 internationals against India in June. "The cricket was disappointing, but the atmosphere was sensational."

The 65-year-old Rice has been involved with cricket at the YMCA Dublin club since the early 1980s. She played for a while, but made her biggest impact running the club's flourishing youth section. And she emphasises that the year has not all been about the men's team. Rice attended the women's World T20 in Guyana, and made two trips to the Netherlands and countless visits to Belfast to forge closer relationships with clubs in the North. She regards contracts for the women players as a major gain.

The morning regulars at Coffee on the Crescent in Hyde Park, Leeds, are not concerned about the backstory of the man making their espressos or flat whites. Lecturers and students en route to university mix with locals, and only cricket lovers on their way to Headingley, less than a mile away, might notice something familiar about the proprietor as he dispenses caffeine and bonhomie.

"I find this far harder than playing cricket, and I found playing cricket really hard," says **Tim Linley**. "I'm judged on my coffee and on my shop, not as an ex-professional cricketer." Linley took 200 first-class wickets, mainly for Surrey: he was their leading wicket-taker as they returned to Division One in

2011. As he battled an injury to his right knee in 2015, they allowed him to speak to other counties, and a three-year contract with Leicestershire was on the table. Then his life turned upside down: a specialist told him he risked serious damage if he carried on.

"About three months after the news I hit an unbelievable low," he says. "It was brutal. I lost my sense of identity." He spoke to the Professional Cricketers' Association, who sent him to a therapist. With the PCA, he had already been through barista training and a course in accounting. Then he was awarded a PCA personal development scholarship, which helped him set up his business.

Coffee on the Crescent opened in May 2018. "It has been unbelievably challenging in ways I did not contemplate. I'm super proud of the shop, but there is a lot more work to make it a fully functioning business. It's more than just wanting to own a coffee shop – I have to be a businessman."

Linley was a tea drinker until he signed his first contract with Surrey, and used his new affluence to spend time in coffee shops. He became so fascinated he began to use independent shops as a way of discovering new areas of London. "Being a former cricketer does not make me immune from the challenges faced by anyone in this business. As a sportsman you have that confidence to think you are going to smash it from day one. But the sportsman's mentality is also an advantage – you have to keep going."

After 27 seasons as the public address announcer for Lancashire, **Matt Proctor** had wanted to go quietly, if that is not a contradiction when your job involves a microphone. "I was 75 in August," he says, "and I noticed during the season that my concentration levels were dipping slightly. Concentration is one thing you can't afford to lose."

He did not tell Lancashire until the end of the second day of the club's last home game of the season, against Worcestershire at Southport. But his hopes of slipping away unnoticed went unfulfilled. At lunch, a presentation was made in front of the pavilion by the chairman and chief executive. At the close – after a stirring home victory – he was summoned to the dressing-room and presented with a shirt signed by all the squad. On his way out, the groundstaff ambushed him with more gifts. "I held it together until I got home, and then the emotions flooded out."

A sports journalist who worked for BBC Radio Manchester, Piccadilly Radio and Manchester United's in-house station, Proctor took on the Lancashire role in 1992. He survived a first-day prank by captain Neil Fairbrother, who told him Kent were batting, only for Lancashire openers Gehan Mendis and Graeme Fowler to walk out. When David Lloyd was coach, Proctor found it best to double-check any requests from the dressing-room for an announcement.

Proctor relished his close relationship with the scorers and scoreboard operators in adjoining rooms at Old Trafford. He believes that "concentration and knowing the game" are the main attributes required. Tact was also vital. "If a batsman was out cheaply, I would always wait until he reached the steps of the pavilion before announcing the details of the dismissal."

CRICKET IN THE COURTS IN 2018

Doughnuts – but not peanuts

MINOR COUNTY CAPTAIN JAILED IN SEX CASE

Lee Dixon, 31, who captained Cheshire in 2016 and 2017, was jailed for two years at Chester Crown Court on February 16, after he admitted having sex with a student at a school where he worked. By chance, Dixon met the 17-year-old girl at a nightclub, where a routine conversation became flirtatious and led to sex that night, and on two further occasions. Dixon, who had special responsibility for troubled children at the school, also pleaded guilty to perverting the course of justice by telling the girl to say that only heavy petting took place. Gareth Roberts, defending, argued for a suspended sentence, saying Dixon was highly regarded, and "thoroughly ashamed, embarrassed and remorseful".

CLUB TREASURER GETS SEVEN YEARS FOR FRAUD

Financial advisor Gary Sams, 52, the treasurer of Annfield Plain CC, County Durham, was jailed for seven years for stealing nearly £80,000 from the club, and more than £300,000 from friends, mainly by falsely promising to invest their cash. He admitted one offence of theft from the cricket club, but denied five other charges – on which he was found guilty by a jury at Newcastle Crown Court on August 2. Prosecutor Ian West said the club was on the brink of insolvency. Sams had used the money to fund luxuries, including an executive box at Riverside, Durham's HQ.

LEAGUE TREASURER ESCAPES JAIL

Ann Gilfoyle, 54, stole £22,000 over a three-year period from the Lancashire-based Northern Premier League in her capacity as treasurer. She pleaded guilty, but was spared imprisonment on June 11 after Preston Crown Court heard she had been "clinically depressed" because her partner and both parents had just died within a short period. She was sentenced to 200 hours' unpaid work.

GUN POINTED AT BOY CRICKETERS

Two brothers, aged 16 and ten, had a "terrifyingly realistic" air revolver pointed at them as they played cricket in a back alley in Stockton-on-Tees by a man who said "I'm going to kill you." Christopher Jones, 49, a factory manager, racially abused Sharyaar and Tamoor Khan, then followed them into their yard. "It's like something out of a *Dirty Harry* movie," said Judge Sean Morris at Teesside Crown Court on June 5. "These two lads were doing no more than playing our national sport." Jones, who had been drinking, was

THE TRIAL OF BEN STOKES
A Bristol brawl

GEORGE DOBELL

At a time when cricket struggles to make the back pages, the trial of Ben Stokes brought it to the front. Detailed accounts of a drunken night out and a street brawl were accompanied by video footage of Stokes throwing multiple punches, and later handcuffed in the back of a police car. For a sport attempting to appeal to a family audience, it was deeply damaging.

Stokes had been arrested in the early hours of September 25, 2017, after helping England defeat West Indies in a one-day international in Bristol and going out with team-mates to celebrate. Around 2.30am, he became embroiled in a fight with Ryan Ali, a security guard, and Ryan Hale, an ex-soldier. All three were arrested and later charged with affray; the case was heard at Bristol Crown Court from August 6.

As the prosecution laid out their case, there was some ugly press coverage. Alongside details of the injuries sustained by Ali, including a broken eye socket, the three defendants were described by one witness as acting "like football hooligans". A bouncer, Andrew Cunningham, accused Stokes of "bullying" and "mimicking" William O'Connor and Kai Barry, two gay men he had met outside the Mbargo nightclub in the Clifton area. Stokes, the prosecution alleged, had been infuriated by being denied entry by Cunningham, and gone looking for trouble.

As holes in the prosecution case became apparent. There were inconsistencies in Cunningham's testimony; more importantly, footage suggested the violence had started when Ali hit Barry with a bottle. Ali accepted he had taken Stokes in a headlock, as Hale – having recovered from an earlier blow – ran back towards the fray with a metal bar wrenched from a road sign. Four days into the trial, however, the judge, Peter Blair QC, instructed the jury to find Hale not guilty because of lack of evidence. Later, Stokes's barrister, Gordon Cole QC, raised the possibility that Ali's eye injury had been caused not by a punch from Stokes, but by a kick from England team-mate Alex Hales, who was there when the trouble began. In footage, Hales could be seen telling police he hadn't been present at the incident.

Stokes did not deny throwing "numerous" punches at Ali and Hale. But he insisted he had used reasonable force, fearing for his and others' safety. In particular, he claimed he intervened to protect O'Connor and Barry; neither gave evidence, though through the media they did corroborate his version of events. On the seventh day of the trial, the jury took two and a half hours to reach not guilty verdicts on Stokes and Ali.

While Stokes's wife, Clare, and his manager, the former England batsman Neil Fairbrother, broke down in tears of relief – they had sat through every minute of the hearing – Stokes momentarily shut his eyes, then offered his hand to Ali, who accepted it. Within hours, Stokes was added to England's squad for the Third Test against India at Nottingham.

sentenced to four years in jail after admitting possession of an air weapon with intent to cause fear of harm, and a racially aggravated public-order offence. Alex Bousfield, defending, said Jones was a hard-working father of two who was "mortified" by his behaviour.

DRIVER PUNISHED FOR PITCH INVASION

Members of Truro CC, Cornwall, tackled a man who drove on to their pitch one evening and began skidding doughnuts on the field. The players locked a gate and wrestled him to the ground. Jarrod Westlake, 27, who had no driving licence, pleaded guilty to criminal damage and threatening behaviour before Truro magistrates on October 1. He was given a 12-month community order and a three-month weekend curfew, ordered to pay a total of £437 – and banned from the cricket ground.

NEWSPAPERS ATTACK PAY-OUT TO GAYLE

The Australian news group Fairfax Media were ordered to pay $A300,000 (about £175,000) to West Indian cricketer Chris Gayle following his victory in a libel case in 2017 (see *Wisden 2018*, page 165). Three daily papers had printed stories accusing Gayle of exposing himself to a masseuse in Sydney during the 2015 World Cup. On December 3, Justice Lucy McCallum made the award, which was described as being at the lower end of the scale by the standards of recent cases in New South Wales. "The award merely confirms the appalling burden of defamation laws in this country," said a Fairfax spokesperson.

DRUNK HURLED ADVERTISING BOARD

A drunken man being ejected from Trent Bridge during the Test against India hurled an advertising board which hit two spectators. Nottingham magistrates ordered farm worker David Marshall to pay each £50 in compensation. His solicitor, Devon Edwards, said Marshall was "just feeling frustrated", and promised the court: "He will not be attending the cricket ground any time in the near future."

CRICKET AND THE LAWS IN 2018

The spice of life

FRASER STEWART

The ball-tampering saga in Cape Town trod well-worn ground. Accusations have been ten a penny, yet most boil down to whether Law 41.3 has been breached by the application of sugary-sweet saliva to the ball, or by throwing it in on the bounce. The Australians' use of sandpaper, though, was flagrant.

It was curious, then, that the ball was not changed, and no penalty runs were awarded to South Africa. According to the Law, both should have happened. The offence was noticed only after the event, when the third umpire saw TV replays, and the on-field umpires inspected the ball, deciding it was in an acceptable condition. Regardless, though, the Law states that the ball must be changed, and five penalty runs awarded. South Africa won by 322, so the result was unaffected, but it remains unclear why the penalty was not applied.

David Warner, one of the trio suspended from all matches played under the auspices of Cricket Australia, was in the news again in October when playing club cricket for Randwick-Petersham against Western Suburbs in Sydney. He took offence at a fielder's comment and, with his score 35, reportedly told the umpires he was removing himself from the game. He then walked off the field. Play was held up for a few minutes, before Warner was persuaded to resume, with the blessing of the Western Suburbs captain. The approval was key: Law 25.4 states that, if a player retires for a reason other than illness or injury, he or she can continue only with the consent of the opposition captain. No other batsman had taken the field, so Warner could carry on. It was a sporting gesture – especially as he went on to 157.

Sri Lanka's Kamindu Mendis caused a stir during England's visit late in the year, when he proved he could bowl off-breaks as proficiently as his more regular left-arm spin. He is one of a growing number of players who can deliver high-quality bowling with either arm, joining Pakistan's Yasir Jan, Bangladesh's Shaila Sharmin, India's Akshay Karnewar and Australia's Jemma Barsby. As long as the bowler informs the umpire of a change in action, it is entirely lawful to switch arm.

Some fielders are ambidextrous, too, while the usually left-handed Warner swapped his batting stance, hitting 14 as a right-hander off his first three deliveries in a Bangladesh Premier League game in early 2019. It is right that such skill is allowed, and it is a great spectacle – as long as time is not wasted by repeated changes.

So, were Warner to face Mendis, stalemate might ensue: Warner might think, "I'll bat right-handed if he's bowling right-handed," prompting Mendis to change arm, and Warner to change back, and so on. Baseball wrote a rule to cover this: the pitcher has to state how he'll throw the ball, and the batter can then choose which way to stand. Cricket does not yet have such a firm

Law but, in light of these developments, guidelines were in the process of being drafted.

In November, Uttar Pradesh left-arm spinner Shiva Singh performed a 360-degree twirl during his run-up in an Under-23 match. The batsman seemed unperturbed, but the umpire signalled dead ball as the delivery was mid-air. The Laws do not specify how conventional the bowler's approach should be, but Law 41.4 states: "It is unfair for any fielder deliberately to attempt to distract the striker while he/she is preparing to receive, or receiving, a delivery." And, if such an attempt is made, dead ball should be called.

The offence is the attempt to distract rather than actual distraction. So it was for the umpire to decide if Singh's tactic was such an attempt. Considerations may include whether the twirl was part of the bowler's normal run-up, or if there were any advantage to be gained from it – unlike, for example, when the bowler (lawfully) varies the width of the release point, or the length of the run-up. If the batsman is distracted, he/she is entitled to withdraw from the stance. And if the umpire feels there has been a deliberate attempt at distraction, Law 41.4 kicks in, including the awarding of five penalty runs.

On the second afternoon of the Second Test between Sri Lanka and England at Pallekele in November, Joe Root's team were awarded five penalty runs. Sri Lanka, it emerged, had been punished after Roshen Silva played Jack Leach down to third man, and jogged towards the bowler's end, before stopping, presumably thinking the ball had gone for four. It had not – and Silva, at least a yard short of the popping crease, realised that his partner, Akila Dananjaya, was heading back for a second. Without grounding his bat, Silva ran back to the striker's end.

Marais Erasmus consulted his colleague at square leg, Sundaram Ravi, before calling dead ball and, under the rarely applied Law 18.5, awarded England the penalty runs. Erasmus believed the run had deliberately been short: as a result, no runs were allowed from the delivery, and five added retrospectively to England's first-innings total. The Law is there to stop batsmen deliberately running short to try to get one run (where two would not be possible) and keep a batsman on strike. This is distinct from an accidental short run, where only one run is deducted.

The vast majority of the Law changes made in October 2017 were well received. But the new full-toss Law, in which stricter penalties were invoked, did not land so well: too many bowlers, especially youngsters, were removed from the attack for deliveries which breached the Law, but should probably not have been classed as dangerous. The Law was set to change when a second edition of the 2017 Code came into effect on April 1, 2019. Full details of these changes are available on www.lords.org, where there is also a new eLearning tool aimed at educating players, officials and coaches on the risks of concussion.

Fraser Stewart is Laws Manager at MCC.

CRICKET AND TECHNOLOGY IN 2018

A scorer's lot is quite an 'appy one

Liam Cromar

It is 26 years since the introduction of computerised scoring in English first-class cricket, which finally did away with the need to phone the numbers through every few minutes. But while external media requirements were the primary driver of innovation in the 1990s, it is now the demands of the game itself – such as over-rate or DLS calculations – that must be met.

One influential scoring package has been Code27's **Total Cricket Scorer**, which most counties were using by 2017, bringing easier information flow between scorers, team analysts, coaches, players and scoreboard operators. Even greater consolidation has been achieved with the arrival of **Play-Cricket Scorer Pro**, developed in close association with scorers. Already used in its native New Zealand under the name of **Feedback Cricket – Live Scoring Edition**, it was in use by all first-class county scorers from 2018, with rollout expected throughout all levels of the English game.

Thanks to the advent of tablets, however, electronic scoring's greatest impact may be at recreational level, where demands on modern club scorers are considerable. Relatively few handle multi-day matches, but Twenty20's pace, along with a chronic lack of trained colleagues, leaves minimal time to perform necessary checks. The benefits of scoring apps are clear. They promise – if you believe the blurb – a golden age of innings auto-synchronisation, instant player analysis and scorecard accuracy.

Scoring is fundamentally (and often literally) a digital activity, comprised of recording and adding a sequence of numbers. Delegating tedious calculation to an electronic device is an obvious time-saver. Electronic records tempt players with statistical analysis. And automatic transmission of match results to league bodies, electronic scoreboards and Twitter opens up an audience at a distance.

Tablets also increase the accessibility of the job. Andrew Hignell, chairman of the Association of County Cricket Scorers, believes electronic scoring is attracting a younger breed. Well-designed apps make it easier, even attractive, for players, parents and spectators to step in and lend a finger. A tablet can be less intimidating than a scorebook: no arithmetical skill is required.

PLAY-CRICKET SCORER PRO.

Laptop scoring software, designed by scorers for scorers.

PLAY-CRICKET

PLAY-CRICKET SCORER PRO

Play-Cricket Scorer Pro delivers powerful free laptop scoring software for recording and analysing cricket matches at international, domestic and recreational level.

Even so, electronic scoring introduces its own issues. First, hardware: access is needed to an electronic device, whether laptop, tablet or smartphone. Scoring in bright sunlight – perhaps not a major concern in England – can be trickier. And a reliable internet connection is also needed for integration with external sources, such as league databases. Most obvious is the need for power: without it, there is a danger of failing to record every ball. The ACCS advise their members to keep a written record, even at Lord's: the St John's Wood substation has been known to retire hurt. As David Kendix, the international-match scorer there, points out: "You can't stop a game because the scorer's computer isn't working."

The second issue is out of the scorers' hands, yet at their fingertips: software. Whereas there is little difference between two brands of scorebook, app differs from app in usability, functionality and reliability. Bugs may crawl out in extreme situations: in a 2014 Under-19 match between New South Wales and Northern Territory, the **Statsmaster** program crashed during an 18-ball over.

Scorers also have to cope with developer troubles. The last two years have witnessed particular upheaval. **CricHQ**, one of the biggest names, fell out with the ECB over licensing issues. Whether the ECB were prescient or intransigent is debatable: CricHQ went into receivership in 2017, and resurfaced only after a restructuring deal was agreed. Yet the scorers on the frontline were inconvenienced: users of new versions of Total Cricket Scorer (taken over by CricHQ) were unable to directly upload matches into the ECB's recreational database.

CricHQ could at least take pride in their software. By contrast, the ECB's **Play-Cricket Scorer** for phones and tablets, released in early 2018, copped plenty of chat around the bat, thanks to its interface and teething problems. (Despite the name, it was produced by a different company to its laptop stablemate, the well-received Play-Cricket Scorer Pro.) While bugs in new software are inevitable, this app was based on the same platform as Cricket Australia's established app **MyCricket**, making the faults less excusable.

At time of writing, Play-Cricket Scorer had notched up just 2.8 out of five stars on the Google Play Store, comparing unfavourably with the competition. One alternative, **nxCricket**, available for Apple iOS, is notable for its statistical output; another, **CricHeroes**, boasts high satisfaction among Android users, and is popular in India. Whatever software is chosen, however, two major concerns remain.

First, some player data could well be classifed as personal. It may be a matter of time before a batsman asks to delete a golden duck. Also, app developers may be looking to exploit that data: essentially, users could unwittingly be paying for a free app with their data.

Second, to protect users becoming chained to a particular app, an open standard for match data – possibly based on Stephen Rushe's Cricsheet XML format – needs to be established, allowing any conforming app to use it. Should manufacturers collapse, change terms or stop updates, scorers could still be confident of transferring to another system.

But electronic scoring does not remove the need for scorers to be trained in the Laws. Sue Drinkwater, who manages scorer education on behalf of the

One woman and her log: Polly Rhodes, Somerset scorer, and the fruits of her labours.

ECB, is keen that those using electronic devices grasp the underlying principles of the job, and understand what their button taps mean. Scoring should not become a black box, where input is magically transformed into output with no comprehension of the internal processes.

Traditionalists need not fear: Hignell is confident electronic scoring will never replace paper. The attraction of a tangible book persists: the best practitioners elevate paper scoring to an art form, with sheets full of colour and calligraphy. Both approaches can happily flourish, since Law 3.1 mandates two scorers. What better way to meet its requirements than asking one to input, and the other to inscribe?

CRICKET AND THE ENVIRONMENT IN 2018

The heat is on

Tanya Aldred

The UN Intergovernmental Panel on Climate Change reported in October that the world had 12 years to prevent the catastrophe which will result from temperature rises of more than 1.5°C. Action, they said, would have to be "urgent and unprecedented". Meanwhile, the World Bank warned that unmitigated climate change could cause internal displacement of 143m people by 2050, including 40m in South Asia. Yet for cricket's authorities, it was mostly business as usual.

Wisden repeatedly contacted the boards of all the Test-playing countries to ask for their sustainability policies and plans, but heard back from only New Zealand and England. New Zealand were brutally honest: "NZC doesn't have a climate-change policy. We acknowledge man-made climate change, but have not yet discussed a workable strategy or best practice as a response. We don't do a carbon audit or measure our carbon footprint. We envisage these measures, eventually, will be inevitable and anticipate multi-ministry and cross-party guidance on the best way forward."

The islands that make up the West Indies sit on the front line of climate change, and have found themselves at the mercy of storms hitting the Caribbean with increasing force and frequency. A charity match between West Indies and a World XI at Lord's in May raised $500,000 towards repairing Windsor Park cricket stadium in Dominica and Ronald Webster Park in Anguilla, both ripped apart by hurricanes. There was no mention of climate change in the pre-match publicity.

The Caribbean islands are worried about ocean plastics injuring wildlife, the destruction of coral by rising sea temperatures, and the arrival of stinking sargassum seaweed on their white-sand beaches – a bad look (and smell) for a region so reliant on tourism. Caribbean leaders have pleaded with Donald Trump to rejoin the Paris Agreement, which in late 2015 had promised a low-carbon future.

At matches in the West Indies, spectators produce little waste compared with other major countries; few buy heavily packaged food, and most carry their own water. Sponsors tend to steer clear of plastic tat: handouts are flags, T-shirts and bandanas, all likely to be reused. "We'd be hugely supportive of the ICC acting on climate change, because of its effects on the people of the Caribbean, irrespective of the cricket," said Johnny Grave, CEO of Cricket West Indies.

"Our team probably fly the most in the world, because we are two long-haul flights away from most others, and players fly a lot regionally. But we've not got many indoor nets, many of our facilities are very basic compared with the rest of the world, and the average monthly wage in somewhere like Guyana is

On the front line: Windsor Park in Dominica, soon after Hurricane Maria struck in September 2017.

$US300. The majority of people are living basic lives, so our carbon footprint is comparatively tiny. We certainly believe cricket needs to do its bit, and be a platform for good."

In January 2019, the ECB released the headline announcements of their strategy for 2020–24. Within it was a pledge to invest £50m in first-class stadium infrastructure, and an undefined sum in facilities for the recreational game. While detail was light, sources suggested sustainability would be a key part of the investment. There was no feedback from the BCCI though, on the eve of the 2018 IPL final, they and UN Environment signed an agreement to promote "green cricket" in India.

It was another year of climate silence from the ICC, but an environmental audit was under way at the headquarters in Dubai. There are still no targets for member countries, nor any encouragement for them to arrange tours in a greener way. However, the ICC were due to launch a new global strategy in the spring, incorporating environmental sustainability. As with the ECB and the BCCI, we wait and watch.

These developments apart, most environmental leadership came from individual stadiums. At the MCG, Peter Wearne, the Melbourne Cricket Club's facilities general manager, talked about a "moral obligation" to reduce their carbon footprint: 83% of the stadium's rubbish is now recycled. And at the Holkar Stadium in Indore, occasional home to Kings XI Punjab, they have introduced a "green protocol", replacing plastic cheer sticks with cloth flags and banners, ensuring shirts and practice balls are made out of reclaimed ocean plastics, branding all recycled cloth material, and increasing recycling.

In the UK, the slow death of the beer snake may have begun, as many counties start to cut back on single-use plastics. Lord's took the lead, with cups "deliberately designed to be as functional and unattractive as possible", to dissuade people from taking them home as souvenirs. For the summer of 2019,

MCC plan to install more water points, and to reduce single-use plastics below the 1.5m pieces removed in 2018; sachets of ketchup and tiny cartons of milk are likely to disappear, along with other catering and retail packaging.

After a raft of eye-catching pre-season announcements in 2018, The Oval are aiming to be plastic-free by 2020. They hope to improve their waste separation for the new season, introduce different bins and bring in a new mixed recycling compactor. At Sophia Gardens, Glamorgan aim to install permanent water fountains on the concourse; at Warwickshire, excess food is regularly donated to Let's Feed Brum, and more fountains are in place. A few years after Lord's and The Oval, Edgbaston too is powered by renewable energy sources. As part of a Greater Manchester strategy, Old Trafford has pledged to be free of single-use plastics by 2020.

Cricket is the pitch sport most likely to be affected by climate change

It was hoped that this summer's World Cup might have sustainability at its core, to match other inter-national federations, such as UEFA and the IOC. Indeed, a sustainability plan was written for the ICC in 2016, but never implemented. Yet the ICC claim they "considered environmental sustainability at every stage". They also claim they fully engaged with The British Association for Sustainable Sport (BASIS), and implemented their suggestions; BASIS were not aware of a formal approach being made, nor advice sought.

The ICC say they are introducing renewable energy at the tournament – but this seems only to mean they are using stadiums which are already powered by renewable energy. They are using the Eco-Cup brand for the World Cup, though this in itself doesn't make environmental sense, since it takes six to eight times more resources to produce an Eco-Cup than a single-use cup. The benefit comes because it can be washed and reused 100 times. However, those not taken away by spectators at the end of the tournament will be recycled – far sooner than the end of their potential life.

Let's hope lessons have been learned from the 2017 Champions Trophy, when cups were branded differently for each venue, so more had to be made, then recycled after less usage. Overall, this is a worse solution than just using the renewable cups already in place at venues such as Lord's and The Oval, or going for single-use cups and trying to recycle as many as possible.

On the plus side, Nissan electric cars will be used for the trophy tour, ticketing and publications will be increasingly online, and all unused and redundant kit will go to the Lord's Taverners.

The publication of the Climate Coalition report in February 2018, which named cricket as the pitch sport most likely to be affected by climate change, led to more media attention. Mike Atherton covered the topic in *The Times*, and there were articles in *The Independent*, *The Guardian*, *The Cricket Paper* and *The Cricketer*, as well as discussion on *Test Match Special* and on the "Today" programme on Boxing Day. A Twitter feed, @TheNextTest, was set up for cricket lovers working for a greener game. BASIS met at Salford's Media City in the spring, where representatives of the ECB heard Lord Deben, chairman of the UK's committee on climate change, tell the room: "I don't

CRICKET AND ELECTRIC VEHICLES

Plugging away

Hugh Chevallier

For 100 days starting in February 2019, the ICC planned to parade the World Cup trophy throughout England and Wales. The distances are huge, but not the CO_2 spewed into the atmosphere, as the cup is being strapped into a Nissan Leaf, described by its manufacturers as "our hero electric vehicle". The ICC are making a song and dance about it, though the car itself is almost silent.

Hugh Chevallier

On the charge: an EV bay near Lord's.

With a host of countries having announced target dates for when petrol and diesel cars may no longer be sold, any such gesture, even as modest as this, is welcome. Like it or not, it is the direction of travel. As so often, the focus of commercial attention is India, where in 2016 the government announced that, from 2030, every car sold would be powered by a battery. The UK's more cautious target is 2040. But in neither country has the interest been as widespread as expected.

The major brakes on EV sales are range, cost and availability of charge-points. With modern EVs capable of up to 200 miles or more, that first issue is fading. The other two are not, and this is reflected in the way EVs have – or have not – been taken up in the UK.

Wisden asked all 18 first-class counties, as well as the ECB and MCC, of their plans for EVs, and whether anyone had taken the plunge and gone electric. It is probably no coincidence that the most encouraging response came from one of the wealthier clubs. Early in 2019, Surrey became the first county to install a charge-point, for two cars, at the Vauxhall end of The Oval. This may increase, in part because Kia, a major Surrey sponsor, are planning their own zero-emission vehicle.

MCC knew the location of their nearest charging stations – there is at least one lamp-post charge-point just metres from the Grace Gates, plus three double bays within five minutes' walk – but had no plans to install their own. Three counties – Glamorgan, Northamptonshire and Nottinghamshire – could all identify the nearest locations, though none was within a mile of Sophia Gardens or Trent Bridge, or within two of Wantage Road. Durham responded quickly, even if it was to say they had no idea where an EV could be plugged in, and did not envisage it being an issue in the coming 12 months. From the other clubs and the ECB, there was no reply. If there is a player driving a Tesla, Leaf or similar car, they are keeping it quiet.

care if you believe in climate change or not – the world does. One thing that is certain is we are moving to a low-carbon future."

In the UK, extreme weather focused minds. The Beast from the East was followed by the country's joint-hottest summer on record – including a six-week spell when daytime temperatures in parts of the country were higher than 30°C. This brought about a parasol-waving announcement at Lord's in July: "Due to the abnormally warm temperatures, MCC has decided to dispense with the requirement for gentlemen to wear jackets in the Pavilion and arrive wearing one."

Yet the heatwave was nothing compared with the drought in Cape Town, which in late January 2018 led to the cancellation by the Western Province Cricket Association of the remainder of their club and school matches. The touring Indian team, together with the South African side, donated 100,000 Rand (just over £5,500) to the Gift of the Givers foundation, to go towards bottled water and drilling boreholes.

There was little progress on other matters, such as meat consumption at matches, carbon emissions from flying, microfibres from sports clothes adding to microplastic pollution in the oceans, pointless ephemera at games, and the dubious sustainability of a constant push for growth: more cricket, bigger audiences, more tournaments, and so on. At the end of the year, a sports climate-action framework was signed at the UN Climate Change conference in Katowice, Poland. Signatories included the Tokyo 2020 Olympics, Roland-Garros, the Rugby League World Cup, and Forest Green Rovers FC. Cricket was nowhere to be seen.

Tanya Aldred is a freelance cricket writer and founder of @TheNextTest.

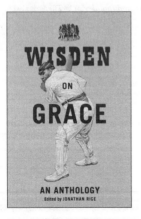

OBITUARIES

AAMER WASIM, who died of tuberculosis on September 26, aged 57, was a slow left-armer who took 242 wickets in an 18-year career for various domestic teams in Pakistan. His best return was seven for 169, for Railways against the Pakistan National Shipping Corporation in Multan in 1995-96. In October 2000, by now captaining Sialkot, he took eight for 68 against Okara in the Quaid-e-Azam Trophy – but this was a second-division match without first-class status. The Test player Shoaib Malik, born in Sialkot, was one of several local players mentored by Wasim.

ABED, SULAIMAN, died on January 19, aged 74. The youngest of five sporting brothers from Cape Town, "Dik" Abed followed Basil D'Oliveira in forging a professional career in England, since he was barred from first-class cricket in South Africa by the colour of his skin. Abed jumped at the chance to sign for the Lancashire club Enfield in 1967, even though he had to pay his own way there: local administrator Benny Bansda organised a series of fund-raisers, as he had for D'Oliveira. Abed stayed at Enfield for ten years, a record for a Lancashire League professional, beating Learie Constantine's nine at Nelson. He collected more than 5,000 runs and 855 wickets, predominantly with brisk leg-cutters delivered from an unusual grip. "Enfield's batting was fairly strong," he remembered, "but their bowling tended to be on the thin side. And so there was one sentence I never uttered to my captain: 'Sorry, I'm tired!' When I was given that ball, I bowled and bowled and bowled. I hated making way for anyone else."

In his second season, Enfield won their first title for 25 years, with Abed collecting 120 wickets at nine; three years later, when they won again, it was 101 at under eight. "He was one of the great pros," said David Lloyd, who played against him for Accrington. "He quickly adapted to bowling cutters at a decent pace, and batted well too. A wonderful chap." Abed had a fondness for Ramsbottom's batsmen: in a fortnight in June 1968, he took nine for 33 and nine for 29 against them, then three years later added nine for 26.

Unlike D'Oliveira, Abed never made the leap to county or Test cricket, despite playing a few second-team games (and scoring a century for Surrey in his first). Some suggested the powers that be at Lord's had discouraged counties from signing him, to avoid a repeat of the D'Oliveira Affair. He did, however, come closer than most non-white cricketers of his time to playing for South Africa. In 1971-72, in an attempt to salvage the planned tour of Australia, the South African board sounded out Abed and slow left-armer Owen Williams about joining the trip. But they declined. "We made it clear we would not be prepared to be used for window-dressing purposes to save the tour," said Abed. The pro-apartheid government said they would have banned the initiative anyway; the tour was eventually cancelled.

A few years later, Abed did finally get a taste of international cricket. He had moved to the Netherlands after marrying a Dutch woman, and captained their side in the 1982 ICC Trophy – the qualifying tournament for the World Cup – in the English Midlands. They narrowly missed a place in the semi-finals. The following year, rising 40, he scored 65 and took four for 32 against Denmark.

AFZALUR REHMAN SINHA, who died on August 8, aged 68, was the chairman of the Bangladesh Premier League, and a director of the national board. He had been a freedom fighter in the war of independence from Pakistan in 1971, forged a successful business career and joined the Bangladesh Cricket Board in 1998.

ALLINSON, CHRISTOPHER ANDREW, who died of complications from epilepsy on November 8, aged 28, was an attacking left-hander and tidy off-spinner who was briefly on the books at Leicester after a stint at the Yorkshire Academy. In 2008, he captained an ECB Elite Player Development XI containing Jonny Bairstow, Sam Northeast, James Taylor and Luke Wells. He represented several clubs in the North Yorkshire & South Durham League, hitting 194 for Marske against Bishop Auckland in 2011. Two years later he made 49 and dismissed Keaton Jennings as the League XI defeated Durham Seconds in a Twenty20 match. He was also a highly ranked squash player. Bairstow spoke of his sadness at Allinson's death, after scoring a century in Third Test against Sri Lanka in Colombo in December.

ALLSOP, DAVID, CBE, died on November 1, aged 74. Dave Allsop was a stalwart of The Cricket Society for many years, and a much-admired chairman from 1992 until 2003. "Dave was a driving force," said the current chairman, Nigel Hancock. "He knew how to manage meetings – and people." His wife, Christine, ran the society shop and organised events. Though he never went to university, Allsop rose to become a senior civil servant, respected for his knowledge of occupational pensions.

ANAND, K. N., who died on July 21 aged 66, was a sportswriter for *The Hindu* newspaper and India's *Sportstar* magazine. Although his main sport was athletics, he also wrote widely on cricket, and was a regular contributor to the old *Indian Cricket* annual.

ARENHOLD, JOHN ADOLF, who died on September 30, 2017, aged 86, was a Rhodes scholar who won a Blue at Oxford in 1954 after taking six for 37 against Middlesex in the Parks, where his victims included Leslie Compton and Fred Titmus for ducks, and Bill Edrich for a single. A tall seamer, Arenhold had made his debut the previous year, bowling the Australian opener Colin McDonald for a duck in his second match. In 1955, he managed only eight wickets in six outings, and was passed over for the Varsity Match, but claimed seven for 97 *against* the university, for Douglas Jardine's XI at Eastbourne. Arenhold later worked for Shell Oil in Ceylon, and played in two unofficial Tests against India in November 1956, when his only victim was Subhash Gupte. He did rather better in the annual Gopalan Trophy match, in April 1957, taking 11 wickets as Madras were skittled for 56 and 161 on a greenish pitch. Arenhold also played rugby for Ceylon, but eventually returned to his native South Africa, and represented Orange Free State in the Currie Cup in 1959-60. He enjoyed a successful business career, and was the regional marketing director of Nissan when they were major sponsors of South African cricket in the 1980s.

ARMSTRONG, DAVID JOHN MICHAEL, who died on February 16, aged 81, was an assiduous secretary of the Minor Counties Cricket Association from 1984 to 2007. A teacher, he had previously been Norfolk's secretary for 18 years, and was later their president. In his younger days he was a good enough batsman to play for Surrey's Second XI. He wrote *A Short History of Norfolk County Cricket* in 1990. Armstrong's brother, Chris, recalled how he disliked on-field banter: "The constant chatter, handclapping and shouts from all quarters sounded more moronic than motivational to David. The best part of his fulminations was that they were expressed with such volume they tended to drown out the noise about which he was complaining."

BAILEY, JACK ARTHUR, died on July 12, aged 88. MCC's bicentenary in 1987 should have been a grand celebration. Instead, a civil war was being fought in the corridors of the Lord's Pavilion. When the smoke cleared, Jack Bailey was the chief casualty. He had been one of the club's leading administrators for 20 years, and secretary since 1974. But his refusal to give way in negotiations with the TCCB (now the ECB) cost him his job.

Tensions came to a head at a committee meeting in late 1986, aimed at forging a better working relationship between the two organisations. Colin Cowdrey, the new MCC president, asked Bailey to leave the room before the meeting began so his position could be discussed. Soon after, his retirement was announced. Bailey left Lord's at the end of January 1987, treasurer David Clark joining him in protest. But it was not the end of the row. The members refused to accept the club's annual report and accounts, and a special general meeting was called. By then, Cowdrey had undergone heart surgery, missing both the meeting and the showpiece bicentenary match in August.

The disputes between MCC and the TCCB ranged from the staging of major matches to who should meet the Queen when she visited Lord's. In his office high above the ground,

Bailey saw it as his job to defend the interests of MCC members. He did so doggedly, and came into conflict with Donald Carr, his opposite number at the TCCB. Bailey regarded his treatment by Cowdrey and Carr as a betrayal.

He was born in Brixton, the son of a policeman, and attended Christ's Hospital school in Sussex, before reading geography at University College, Oxford. Imposingly tall, he bowled lively fast-medium, making good use of his height. On his debut for Essex in August 1953, he took seven second-innings wickets against Nottinghamshire at Southend. "No single achievement on the cricket field filled me with more wonder or more joy," he wrote. With 25 at 13, he finished top of the first-class averages. He followed it up in 1954 with 69 Championship wickets. At Oxford, he appeared in the Varsity Match three times, and was captain in 1958, losing by 99 runs to Ted Dexter's Cambridge.

He did not play much after that, moving into teaching, then a business career. In his one first-class appearance in 1966, he took 13 for 57 for MCC against Ireland at Dublin. As a job application, it was well timed: in 1967, he became assistant secretary at

The height of his powers: Jack Bailey in the Essex nets, 1955.

Lord's, with responsibility for marketing and publicity. Soon after, the D'Oliveira Affair brought MCC an avalanche of bad press. Though viewed as a staunch traditionalist, Bailey showed sharp commercial acumen. He negotiated improved television deals with the BBC, and was involved in the creation of the John Player League and the Benson and Hedges Cup.

But he was not always a moderniser: players at Lord's had to practise in whites and admission to the playing area was strictly controlled. The rules brought him into conflict with Dennis Lillee when some of the 1981 Australians turned up without permission during the Eton–Harrow match. Lillee broke another of Bailey's regulations by walking back from the Nursery Ground around the edge of the boundary, waving to the crowd. When Bailey remonstrated, Lillee threw orange juice over him.

BEST BOWLING ON CHAMPIONSHIP DEBUT

9-35	J. E. B. B. P. Q. C. Dwyer...	Sussex v Derbyshire at Hove	1906
8-70†	G. A. Wilson	Worcestershire v Yorkshire at Worcester	1899
8-94	C. J. Kortright	Essex v Warwickshire at Birmingham	1895
8-187	H. H. Jarrett	Warwickshire v Leicestershire at Hinckley	1932
7-24	W. Rhodes	Yorkshire v Somerset at Bath	1898
7-32†	**J. A. Bailey**	**Essex v Nottinghamshire at Southend**	**1953**
7-36	K. Higgs	Lancashire v Hampshire at Manchester	1958
7-44	R. G. Hardstaff	Nottinghamshire v Yorkshire at Nottingham	1894
7-46	J. E. Walsh	Leicestershire v Northamptonshire at Leicester	1938
7-50	P. M. Hutchison	Yorkshire v Hampshire at Portsmouth	1997
7-50†	S. P. Kirby	Yorkshire v Kent at Leeds	2001

† *First-class debut. Performances in 1890, the first official Championship season, are excluded if the bowlers concerned had previous county experience.*

By historic arrangement, MCC also held key positions in the International Cricket Conference, so Bailey was closely involved in the Packer affair in 1977. It meant plenty of air miles: one meeting with Packer's representatives took place in a hotel in New York's Upper East Side to guard against tapped phones. When Packer struck a peace deal with the Australian Cricket Board in 1979, Bailey was unimpressed. "It was hard to avoid the sense of being hijacked twice in a couple of years," he wrote. "First by Packer, now by the ACB."

The formation of the TCCB in 1968 came about because, as a private club, MCC could not access public funds and thus could no longer continue as the governing body. After Bailey's departure he wrote a biography of his former Essex team-mate Trevor Bailey, and *Conflicts in Cricket*, about the controversies he had seen at first hand. He also covered cricket and rugby for *The Times*. He was a more genial figure in the press box than he had sometimes been at Lord's, living up to his long-time nickname of "Jolly Jack". For *Wisden*, he wrote about the ICC and, for a few years in the 1990s, the review of umpiring. And he was eventually reconciled with MCC, returning to give his expertise on committees. Asked to describe how he viewed his time as secretary, he replied: "Possessive, proprietorial, proud, conscious of a great heritage."

BAIRAMIAN, ROBERT, died on September 7, aged 83. Bob Bairamian excelled in several sports, particularly cricket: he had two first-class matches in 1957 for Cambridge University, where he also won a hockey Blue, and later played much club cricket, for the Bluemantles and MCC, among others. Of Armenian descent, he was born in Cyprus while his mother was teaching there; his father later became Lord Chief Justice of Sierra Leone. Married four times, Bairamian was a hyper-enthusiastic prep-school master (and headmaster) for more than 60 years, teaching the Classics. He liked to pepper his conversation with Latin phrases, and enlivened long car journeys by asking his passengers to translate pub signs. His pupils included Shane McGowan, the lead singer of The Pogues, and the current president of Ghana.

BARNARD, HENRY MICHAEL, died on December 18, aged 85. On a Saturday morning in May 1954, Mike Barnard was at Northlands Road in Southampton to watch the opening day of Hampshire's Championship match against Middlesex when a phone call changed his life. It was Charles Knott, their amateur off-spinner, to say he had been detained at his fishmonger's business. Barnard, just 20, was told to get changed.

It was his third first-class match, though he had made an inauspicious start: four and nought against Glamorgan in 1952, a pair against Warwickshire in 1953. Now Hampshire were 48 for eight, before Barnard launched a counter-attack from No. 10. "Whereas the other members of the side had made batting seem an agonising impossibility, Barnard made it enjoyable and relatively easy," wrote Tony Pawson in *The Observer*. He hit 39, and added an unbeaten 24 in the second innings. The game proved a turning point.

In his next, against the Pakistanis in his home city of Portsmouth, watched by his brothers and father, he scored an unbeaten second-innings hundred. He rarely looked back, although he was sometimes let down by his concentration, a failing he ruefully admitted. But as a reliable middle-order batsman and superb slip fielder, Barnard became a valued member of the Hampshire side for the next 11 seasons. He spent his winters playing top-flight football for Portsmouth.

His sporting potential had been noted at Portsmouth Grammar School, where he excelled at cricket, football and rugby. He came to Hampshire's attention at Easter nets, and in 1949 was a member of the county's first colts side. A team-mate was Peter Sainsbury, and in the mid-1950s they were among a group of local youngsters promoted to reinvigorate the Hampshire team. "We were too young for anything to be ingrained in us about being a struggling side," said Barnard. Unusually for county cricket, he was Jewish.

They finished third in 1955, but three years later, under the bold leadership of Colin Ingleby-Mackenzie, were in the running to win their first title. Their hopes received a setback in an extraordinary defeat by Derbyshire at Burton-on-Trent, where they were bowled out for 23 and 55, Barnard top-scoring twice – with five and 16. Hampshire finished second, but in 1961 were finally crowned champions. Barnard had a moderate season until a back injury to Ingleby-Mackenzie gave him another chance. He scored an unbeaten hundred in the win over Warwickshire – "the best innings he has ever played, and the most important," said the Hampshire handbook – then 59 against Leicestershire, and 77 against Nottinghamshire, before the potentially decisive match against Derbyshire at Bournemouth.

On the final morning, with the outcome in the balance, he and Sainsbury put on 99 in just over an hour to set up a declaration. Barnard made 61, and their running between the wickets was electrifying. Derek Shackleton then took six for 39, and Hampshire were champions. Flushed with confidence, Barnard had his best season in 1962, passing 1,000 runs (without a century). He came close to that milestone in each of the next three summers, and in 1964 scored a hundred as an opener against the Australians. He made his final appearance in 1966. His 312 catches put him tenth on the club's all-time list.

Before the call: Mike Barnard, April 1954.

He had joined Portsmouth FC in 1951, just after they had become the first club to win successive League championships since Arsenal in the mid-1930s. In 1954-55, they finished third, and Barnard was a regular member of the forward line. He made 127 appearances and scored 26 goals before deciding to concentrate on cricket in 1959.

He had been earmarked for the role of Second XI coach with Hampshire, but broke his neck in a road accident in West Germany in 1969. The after-effects troubled him for the rest of his life, but he recovered sufficiently to take charge of sport at the Merchant Navy School of Navigation. He was also a regular summariser on cricket and football for local radio. "He was an indelible part of Hampshire cricket history," said the county chairman, Rod Bransgrove.

BARNES, DAVID JOHN, who died on June 6, aged 80, was associated with the Wolverhampton club for around 65 years as player, chairman and president. His finest hour was captaining them to victory in the national club final at Lord's in 1973, when he hit the winning boundary against The Mote, from Kent; 15 years later, he was back in the final, still in the ranks at 50, although Wolverhampton lost that one, held at Edgbaston after a washout at Lord's. An off-spinner and handy batsman, Barnes also played for Staffordshire, and later Shropshire, taking seven for 22 in his first match for them, against Somerset II at Oswestry in 1964.

BARRETT, ARTHUR GEORGE, who died on March 6, aged 73, was a tidy Jamaican leg-spinner whose opportunities were limited by Lance Gibbs, often the only slow bowler chosen as West Indies concentrated on pace. But Barrett was hard to ignore when Jamaica won the Shell Shield for the first time in 1968-69: he took six for 18 against a powerful Barbados batting line-up at Bridgetown. Club-mates rated his stylish batting so highly they nicknamed him "Trumper", but Barrett managed only one first-class century, against the Combined Islands in St Lucia in March 1970, to go with ten wickets in the match. Told he was the first to manage such a double in regional cricket in the West Indies, Barrett joked that "obviously Garry Sobers never played regionally". He made his Test debut against India under Sobers early in 1971, but won just five more caps, spread over three series. He did claim three wickets in each innings against England in Kingston in

1973-74, but had to send down 93 overs to do so, and failed to dislodge Dennis Amiss, whose unbeaten 262 ensured a draw. Barrett's best first-class figures were seven for 52, for Jamaica against a strong International Cavaliers XI at Sabina Park in February 1970, when his victims included Colin Cowdrey, Ted Dexter and Mushtaq Mohammad.

BELL, NEIL, who died of cancer on March 11, aged 61, was a popular reporter for BBC South East, and known as "a supreme sporting story-teller". He eventually covered many sports, but started in 1987 by commentating on Kent's matches; many years earlier, he had obtained his first autograph – Brian Johnston – at the St Lawrence ground.

BENNEWORTH, ANTHONY JOHN, died on March 10, aged 68, when he and another man drowned in a boating accident at Ansons Bay, on the north-east coast of Tasmania. He was universally known as "Benny", and his combative batting and bustling medium-pacers were a conspicuous part of Tasmania's belated entry into the Sheffield Shield in 1977-78. His best match that summer came against South Australia at Hobart, where he took five for 115 from 41 eight-ball overs, and hit 54 and 42. Next season, his last at state level, he made 75 as an unlikely No. 3 as Tasmania chased down 357 to beat Western Australia at Devonport. Earlier, he had played for Lowerhouse in the Lancashire League, collecting 794 runs and 84 wickets as their professional in 1974. Benneworth represented Bass in the Tasmanian House of Assembly from 1992 to 1998, and stood unsuccessfully for election to the federal parliament in 2001.

BHALEKAR, RAJENDRA BALKRISHNA, died on April 14, aged 66. Raju Bhalekar was a consistent scorer in a long Ranji Trophy career for Maharashtra, latterly as captain. He hit seven centuries, the highest an undefeated 207 against Saurashtra at Pune in 1981-82. The diminutive Bhalekar came close to Test selection in 1976-77: chosen for West Zone against Tony Greig's England tourists, he made the most of being dropped twice by top-scoring with 66, but fell away later in the season. His off-spin often came in useful to break a partnership: he took four for 60 against eventual Ranji champions Bombay in 1979-80.

BHATIA, PREM, who died on March 13, aged 78, played 56 first-class matches in a 15-year career in Indian domestic cricket, mainly for Delhi. He was involved in a strange incident in the first Irani Trophy match (between the Ranji champions, Bombay, and the Rest of India) in March 1960. The 20-year-old Bhatia was the Rest's twelfth man, but because their captain, Lala Amarnath, wanted to see him bat with a view to Test selection, Bhatia was allowed to go in: he scored 22 and 50 – "a fine, forceful innings," according to *Indian Cricket*. Amarnath, meanwhile, bowled but did not bat: "Only dad could have pulled this off," said his son Rajender. Bhatia's long career also closed in peculiar fashion: 25 years later, while managing North Zone in the one-day Deodhar Trophy in January 1985, he was forced to play against South Zone after several players were caught in heavy traffic. North won, but he did not bat, bowl or hold a catch. His highest score was 151 for Delhi against Southern Punjab in 1962-63, which was his best season – 532 runs at 53 – but India had no Tests, and his chance disappeared. Bhatia had started as a handy off-spinner, and took three for 69 against the 1960-61 Pakistan tourists, including Mushtaq Mohammad for a duck.

BIDLA, SONWABILE, who died suddenly on October 5, aged 37, was president of Blind Cricket South Africa. He played in three Blind World Cups between 2012 and 2017.

BINNS, ALFRED PHILLIP, died on December 29, 2017, aged 88. The Jamaican Allie Binns was one of several wicketkeepers tried by West Indies in the 1950s, after Clyde Walcott gave up the gloves to spare his back for batting. Binns was noted for his quick hands, which brought several stumpings, and won his first cap against India in 1952-53, not long after hitting a career-best 157 against British Guiana at Georgetown. He conceded no byes as India amassed more than 700 in the match at Port-of-Spain, but missed four chances on a nervy first day, earning catcalls from a Trinidadian crowd who wanted their own man, Ralph Legall, in the side instead. Binns failed twice with the bat, and was replaced by Legall. Two years later, an aggressive 151 against an Australian attack containing Lindwall, Miller, Davidson and Benaud – in a sixth-wicket partnership of 277 with Collie Smith after Jamaica had been 81 for five – earned Binns a Test recall, but again he did little with the bat. In all, he made four first-class centuries, but his highest score in five Tests was 27. He eventually moved to the United States, and became a teacher.

BLAND, KENNETH COLIN, died on April 14, nine days after his 80th birthday. There had been outstanding fielders before Colin Bland, but perhaps no one who became known primarily for that reason. The sight of Bland prowling in the covers for South Africa, or patrolling square leg, was unfailingly menacing. He elevated what many viewed as a chore into compelling theatre. Nicknamed "the Golden Eagle", Bland swooped on the ball as if it were prey; his throws usually zeroed in on the stumps. "He took our fielding to another dimension," said Peter Pollock.

Bland stood 6ft 1in, a strong, athletic figure – he was offered a rugby scholarship as a boy – and a graceful mover who covered the ground in swift strides. He was quiet and undemonstrative, but his impact was profound. "He led by example, and the whole team wanted to become better fielders," said Pollock. "We realised that runs saved could make a big difference." Sometimes, during a dull passage of play, Bland would produce an explosive pick-up, followed by a bullet throw. As he said, "People would think something was happening and it would wake up all the buggers dozing off, including the fielders. It was just a bit of showmanship."

At Lord's in 1965, England were threatening a match-winning lead when Ken Barrington, on 91, set off for a single towards midwicket. Bland pounced from in front of the square-leg umpire, picked up the ball one-handed, swivelled, and hit the stumps at the bowler's end. In *The Observer*, Alan Ross called it "staggering". Barrington said: "I knew Colin was great, but he's greater than I thought." Two days later, his run-out of Jim Parks was even better. Fred Titmus tickled a ball off his pads, and Parks called him for a single, but Titmus – spotting that Bland was in pursuit – sent him back. Parks attempted to put his body between the wickets and the ball, but Bland hit them anyway. "Here, for sure, is one of cricket's greatest entertainers," wrote John Woodcock in *The Times*.

The Test was drawn, before South Africa won at Trent Bridge, then secured only their second series victory in England with a draw at The Oval. But not even Bland could earn selection on fielding alone: in his primary role in the middle order, he was South Africa's second-highest run-scorer, with 286 (five behind Graeme Pollock) at nearly 48. He liked to hit hard and high down the ground, but in the second innings of the final Test he curbed his instincts to make 127 in four and a half hours, blunting England's hopes of squaring the series. Along with the Pollock brothers, he was named a Wisden Cricketer of the Year.

Bland was born in Bulawayo, Rhodesia, and pushed hard by his father, an accountant who had been a hockey international. His

Summer exhibition: Colin Bland demonstrates the art of fielding, Canterbury, July 1965.

Hart/Evening News/REX/Shutterstock

HIGHEST TEST BATTING AVERAGES FOR SOUTH AFRICA

		T	I	NO	Runs	HS	100
60.97	R. G. Pollock	23	41	4	2,256	274	7
55.25	J. H. Kallis	165	278	39	13,206	224	45
53.81	A. D. Nourse	34	62	7	2,960	231	9
50.66	A. B. de Villiers	114	191	18	8,765	278*	22
49.08	**K. C. Bland**	**21**	**39**	**5**	**1,669**	**144***	**3**
48.88	B. Mitchell	42	80	9	3,471	189*	8
48.70	G. C. Smith	116	203	13	9,253	277	27
47.33	H. M. Amla	122	211	16	9,231	311*	28
45.96	A. K. Markram	15	27	0	1,241	152	4
45.74	E. J. Barlow	30	57	2	2,516	201	6
45.27	G. Kirsten	101	176	15	7,289	275	21

Minimum 15 Tests. As at January 14, 2019.

work ethic was ingrained early: he graduated from throwing stones at telegraph poles to hurling six balls at three stumps spaced apart in front of a hockey goal. He trained intensively. "No one frowned upon the practice I did," he said. "But no one wanted to do it with me either."

Aged 18, he made his first-class debut for Rhodesia against MCC in November 1956, and top-scored in both innings against an attack led by Frank Tyson and Peter Loader. In 1961-62, he made 261 runs in two matches for Rhodesia against the New Zealanders to earn his first Test call (Rhodesians were then eligible to represent South Africa). He played in all five Tests and showed his potential as a batsman, though without making any significant scores. But a brilliant low diving catch in the covers to dismiss John Reid in the Fourth Test at Johannesburg announced his arrival. The Australian writer R. S. Whitington considered the great fielders he had seen, including Jack Hobbs and Learie Constantine: "I very seriously doubt whether any of the miracles of agility they performed measure up to the catch Bland held at the Wanderers." Even Reid joined in the applause.

Bland returned to Australia in 1963-64 and astonished his team-mates in the Second Test at Melbourne by putting down a sitter at silly mid-on, with the debutant Ian Redpath yet to score. Redpath went on to hit 97, and Australia won by eight wickets. But Bland made up for it with the bat, finishing a drawn series with 367 runs at 61. In the Fifth Test at Sydney, he scored 126, including a six on to the roof of the Noble Stand. When England visited South Africa a year later, he ran out Mike Brearley in a tour match after tricking him by ambling towards the first few balls hit in his direction. It made England wary. "He was more a deterrent than an instrument of destruction," said Woodcock. He was also the leading run-scorer on either side, with 572 at 71, and his unbeaten 144 saved the Second Test at the Wanderers after South Africa followed on.

He was married in 1965, on the day Rhodesian prime minister Ian Smith proclaimed independence from Britain; Smith, a family friend, sent a telegram, and some guests arrived late for the wedding, having attended the proclamation. Political tensions between the countries were such that Bland was denied entry at Heathrow when invited by Garry Sobers to play for a World XI at Scarborough in 1968. By then, his Test career was over. In the First Test of the 1966-67 series against Australia at the Wanderers, he was chasing a ball when his knee gave way and he fell heavily into the boundary fence. After that, he lost his speed and athleticism, although he carried on playing for Rhodesia, then for Eastern Province and Orange Free State until 1973-74, reinventing himself as a slip fielder. In 21 Tests, he made 1,669 runs at 49. In all, he scored 7,249 at just under 38. In the late 1990s, he moved to England to be near his two sons, and was recruited as a fielding coach by MCC.

Bland's reputation had been burnished at Canterbury in 1965 in the tour match against Kent that followed the Lord's Test. With a wet outfield delaying the start, a big crowd in the ground and the BBC having no cricket to show, Colin Cowdrey persuaded a reluctant

Bland to give a fielding exhibition. Picking up balls on the run, he hit the stumps 12 times out of 15. "They spoiled me by giving me three stumps to aim at," he said. "I always practise with one." Bland recalled: "The best part was at the end, when the cameraman wanted a close-up of the wicket exploding. They gave six balls to Graeme Pollock. He stood about three yards away and missed all six."

In 1999, when *Wisden* appointed a panel of 100 to vote for their Five Cricketers of the Century, his former Test captain Peter van der Merwe nominated Bland: "He revolutionised the attitude to fielding and set a standard not yet equalled."

BOOTH, ROY, who died on September 23, eight days before his 92nd birthday, was the wicketkeeper in the Worcestershire team that won successive Championships in the mid-1960s. Tall, lean and well groomed, he kept with equal efficiency to seamers and spinners. As player, stand-in captain, committee man and president, he became such a fixture at New Road that it was easy to forget he had begun his career at Yorkshire; his wife, Joyce, supervised the teas in the Ladies' Pavilion.

Booth might never have ended up in Worcester but for Cyril Washbrook. On taking over as captain in 1956, Peter Richardson approached Lancashire's Frank Parr about replacing the retiring Hugo Yarnold behind the stumps. Parr, a tousled jazz musician, had been frozen out at Old Trafford by the autocratic Washbrook, who warned Worcestershire that he would be a "grave social risk". They opted for Booth instead. He made his debut against the 1956 Australians – Neil Harvey was his first victim – and was not displaced until he retired in 1968. "Roy was a very fit guy," said his team-mate Duncan Fearnley. "I never remember him missing a match. John Elliott was his understudy for years, and hardly ever played."

Born in Marsden, near Huddersfield, Booth made his Yorkshire debut in 1951. By 1954, he seemed to have established himself, but the emergence of Jimmy Binks led to a straight fight for the gloves. Binks won. Booth was not bitter, and quickly relished the more

"What the game is all about": Roy Booth bats against Middlesex at Lord's, watched by keeper Ernie Clifton and slip Peter Parfitt. Worcestershire won by an innings.

relaxed regime at Worcester: "You're never too pressured by captains or committees here." He registered 101 dismissals in 1960 – Binks and John Murray also reached three figures that season – and was part of a formidable team assembled, piece by piece, at New Road. In 1962, they had already drunk the champagne when Yorkshire pipped them to the title, but two years later they were champions for the first time, after seven wins in their final eight matches. Booth took 90 catches and ten stumpings, 22 ahead of any rival; no one has claimed 100 victims in a season since. He stumped Gloucestershire's Ken Graveney off Norman Gifford to wrap up the win that secured the title, although Worcestershire had to wait an hour and three quarters before it was confirmed by Warwickshire's defeat by Hampshire. The following summer, the club's centenary, they retained the Championship with another thrilling late surge. In the deciding match, at Hove, Booth made a calm 38 in a fraught chase.

"Our wickets were very sporting, to say the least," he said. "They were made that way because Len Coldwell and Jack Flavell were as good as any pair of opening bowlers in the country." In 1968, his final full summer, he often led the team while Tom Graveney was on Test duty, though he made a four-match comeback in 1970 in response to an injury crisis. He finished with 1,016 dismissals for Worcestershire, a record since surpassed by Steve Rhodes. His career tally of 1,126 puts him 14th on the all-time list. Not that he would have needed to look it up – he could always reel off his statistics.

He remained deeply proud of his roots. He relished meeting anyone from the Huddersfield area, and devoured newspaper cuttings on the progress of Lightcliffe, his former Bradford League club. "He represented what the game is all about," said Fearnley.

BOSE, GOPAL KRISHNA, who died on August 26, aged 71, was a tenacious Bengal batsman who came close to Test selection for India in the 1970s. His maiden century – 113 for East Zone in the Duleep Trophy final in February 1971 – came just before the team to tour the West Indies were announced. Bose was overlooked, and the young Sunil Gavaskar nailed down a spot. A career-best 170 for the Rest of India against Ranji Trophy champions Bombay in 1973-74, followed by a century in an unofficial Test in Sri Lanka – where he shared an opening stand of 194 with Gavaskar – earned Bose a trip to England in 1974, but he missed out on the Tests. There was the consolation of his only one-day international, at The Oval, where he went in at No. 3 and made 13. The following winter he looked set to make his debut against West Indies, as the only specialist opener in the squad for the Fourth Test after Gavaskar was injured – but the selectors promoted Eknath Solkar to go in first with Farokh Engineer. Bose played on for Bengal until 1978-79. He later became a coach, and managed the Indian team, led by Virat Kohli, which won the Under-19 World Cup in 2007-08. He died after a heart attack while on holiday with his family in England during the Test series against India.

BUGGINS, BRUCE LEONARD, who died on December 5, aged 83, was keeping wicket for South Perth's first-grade side when he was only 14. Five years later, in 1954-55, he was playing for Western Australia, reportedly impressing Don Bradman during his debut, at Adelaide. Buggins was reliable and undemonstrative, and kept for WA for nine successive seasons and 63 matches. His dogged resistance often stiffened the lower order – he made an important 60 not out as Victoria were overcome at the MCG in 1961-62 – but he was eventually dropped for Gordon Becker, a better batsman.

BUNYARD, GRAHAM STUART, who died on May 10, aged 78, was a fast bowler who took seven wickets on first-class debut, for Transvaal against Border at East London in 1957-58 when he was 18. Two years later, he claimed a career-best five for 35 – including four Test players – against Rhodesia at Bulawayo. He narrowly missed selection for the 1960 tour of England, and was mentioned when a replacement was discussed for Geoff Griffin, who had been repeatedly called for throwing; in the event, no one was called up. Bunyard did make it to England in 1961, with the South African Fezelas (a forerunner of today's A-team), alongside the likes of Eddie Barlow and Peter Pollock. But he played only one more first-class match, for Rhodesia in 1962-63. He became a tobacco farmer.

BYFORD, Sir LAWRENCE, CBE, QPM, DL, who died on February 10, aged 92, changed the face of Yorkshire cricket after succeeding Len Hutton as president in 1991. One of Britain's most senior policemen, he rose to become Her Majesty's Inspector of Constabulary, and led the inquiry into the bungled hunt for the Yorkshire Ripper. After taking over at Headingley – he soon became chairman too – he warned the membership he would not be "hands-off". He was as good as his word. In June 1991, Byford persuaded them that, with results worsening and finances deteriorating, the Yorkshire-only rule should be abandoned. There was little grassroots disagreement, though Fred Trueman called it "a bloody disgrace". Byford phoned him to explain his thinking. "Like the great man he is, he decided to swallow his pride and support me," he said. Craig McDermott was their first choice but, when he withdrew through injury, Yorkshire signed the 19-year-old Sachin Tendulkar. He could not reverse the county's fortunes, but the decline in membership was halted, and commercial income grew. Byford had been an all-rounder in the Wakefield police team, and his wife, Muriel, a junior member of the county: "A condition of our courtship was that I went with her to Yorkshire matches – we did most of our courting at Bradford, Headingley and the Scarborough festival." Byford served as Yorkshire chairman until 1998, and as president until 1999.

CAFFYN, ALAN MORRIS, who died on April 4, aged 84, was Sussex's chairman from 1990 to 1996. A director of a car dealership whose head office overlooked the Saffrons ground, he was a keen cricketer, and captained the Eastbourne club. Caffyn remained involved in cricket after leaving the Sussex committee, and loved entertaining current and former players. One of them, John Snow, when asked what he wanted for breakfast one morning, replied: "Just a brandy for me."

CALLAGHAN, DAVID BERNARD, who died on March 12, aged 63, was the voice of Yorkshire cricket. Dave Callaghan reported on more than 400 Championship matches home and away for BBC radio stations across the county, achieving the tricky balance of earning the players' respect while maintaining his audience's trust. He managed not to lose his cheery demeanour, however cramped the press box or tight the schedule; he was even forgiven for being born in Manchester. Callaghan spent 43 years in sports journalism. "He understood the pressures and challenges that sports people have, so there was always that sympathetic slant to his reporting," said Martyn Moxon, Yorkshire's director of cricket. He had worked on Radio Leeds in the late 1980s and early '90s, for the Rugby Football League, and as a TV producer for "Look North". In recent years, he had also taken on ball-by-ball commentary, as well as his regular bulletins. Jonny Bairstow said: "He had a big impact on the current side – we had all grown up with him." He was remembered at the Cricket Writers' Club's annual lunch, not just in words, but in the choice of dessert: Cally's classic treacle tart.

CASS, GEORGE RODNEY, died on August 17, aged 78. A polished wicketkeeper and useful batsman, Rodney Cass had to move around to earn a living in county cricket. In his native Yorkshire, Jimmy Binks seemed immovable behind the stumps, so Cass soon tried his luck at Chelmsford – but failed to dislodge the popular Brian "Tonker" Taylor. He played most of 1966 as a batsman, managing a solitary fifty, and hit a maiden century after opening against Warwickshire the next year. Then he moved to Worcester, and finally had a run with the gloves after Roy Booth retired. Although he was capped in 1970, he injured his back the following season, and traded places for a while with Gordon Wilcock, before Cass regained a regular spot in 1975 after a career-best unbeaten 172 against Leicestershire – but that proved to be his last county season.

"He was a brave keeper, standing up a lot to the stumps," said John Elliott, later Worcestershire's chairman but a wicketkeeper at New Road around the same time. Cass played on for Shropshire, for Len Hutton's old club Pudsey St Lawrence in Yorkshire, and for MCC. His travels were not confined to England: he played a few matches for Tasmania while coaching in their pre-Sheffield Shield days, and also coached in South Africa and New Zealand.

He was an accomplished musician – before cricket, he had earned a living playing the trumpet – and later started a cricket equipment company, Arcass. Always smartly dressed, he had a good sense of humour, although it was tested in 1970-71, when the England team stopped off in Hobart. "He'd been the groomsman at my wedding," said the Yorkshire slow left-armer Don Wilson. "On Christmas Eve, I bowled him a long full toss, and he hit it straight back at me: Cassy caught and bowled for nought, and none too happy."

In the shadows: Tony Catt, 1958.

Dennis Oulds, Central Press/Hulton Archive/Getty Images

CATT, ANTHONY WALDRON, died on August 6, aged 84. When Tony Catt began his career as a wicketkeeper for Kent, Godfrey Evans was in his pomp. By the time he ended it, ten years later, Alan Knott had just abandoned off-spin to take up the gloves. To complicate matters, Catt was not always the first-choice understudy, because of the excellent Derek Ufton.

Catt was born in Ipswich, the son of a chauffeur, and came to Canterbury for a trial after a spell with MCC. With Ufton keen to forge a career as a batsman, he went straight into the team against Oxford University. He performed well, and that summer made more appearances than Ufton. It set the tone for the next few seasons, as both tried to escape Evans's long shadow. "When you are No. 2 to the greatest, you never find out how good you are yourself," said Ufton.

In Catt's second season, during the first innings at Northampton, he conceded 48 byes, and blamed having to keep to Doug Wright's leg-spin while suffering from sunstroke. With Ufton recovered from a shoulder injury, Catt was usually third choice until 1958, when Ufton became Second XI captain. But Evans retired in 1959, and Catt started the season in possession – only to lose form, and the gloves to Ufton, in June.

He did not play again until 1962, when he had a productive season with the bat. A good hooker and puller, he had often hinted at potential – he once made a double-century for the Seconds – without translating it into runs. But after going in as nightwatchman against Leicestershire at Maidstone, he scored a brilliant attacking 162, his maiden hundred, hitting 121 before lunch on the second day, and putting on 177 with Peter Richardson. Briefly promoted to open, he shared two more century partnerships with Richardson before

MOST BYES IN A FIRST-CLASS INNINGS

Byes	Total	Wicketkeeper		
57	539	C. W. Wright	Yorkshire v Cambridge University at Cambridge .	1884
54	529	J. S. Stephen†	W. C. Shepherd's XI v B. Guiana at Georgetown	1909-10
50	723-8d	Khalid Alvi	Karachi v PIA at Karachi	1977-78
49	197	T. A. Anson	Cambridge University v MCC at Cambridge	1842
49	409	F. T. Welman	Middlesex v Gloucestershire at Lord's	1888
48	**374**	**A. W. Catt**	**Kent v Northamptonshire at Northampton**. . . .	**1955**
47	441	J. E. Blackman . . .	West Indies XI v MCC at Georgetown	1912-13
47	592-4d	B. W. Quaife	Worcestershire v Lancashire at Worcester	1929
47	328-9d	T. M. Pistorius . . .	Limpopo v Mpumalanga at Duiwelskloof.	2006-07

† *Stephen was replaced by W. C. Shepherd (at 155-2), then by M. H. Hector (186-2).*

the end of the season. Catt's best year behind the stumps was 1963 – when he completed 65 catches and 13 stumpings – but his batting collapsed. And when Knott made his debut the following summer, the writing was on the wall. "A good wicketkeeper has no chance against a great one," wrote R. L. Arrowsmith in his history of the county. Catt emigrated to South Africa, where he made 12 first-class appearances for Western Province.

CHISHOLM, SAMUEL HEWLINGS, who died on July 9, aged 78, was twice at the centre of TV revolutions that changed cricket for ever. An abrasive New Zealander with a gift for one-liners, he was recruited by Kerry Packer in the 1970s, and saw at close quarters how the sport was repackaged during World Series Cricket, including multi-camera coverage, player close-ups, more replays and coloured clothing. He later became CEO of the Nine Network, then decamped to London in 1989 to head up Rupert Murdoch's nascent Sky. They were losing money at such a rate that it threatened the entire Murdoch empire; soon after Chisholm's arrival, a merger with rivals British Satellite Broadcasting meant the losses were even higher. "Sky and BSB had simply spent themselves into oblivion," he said. "It hadn't just been a failure: it had been an appalling failure." Using the acquisition of sports rights as his main weapon, Chisholm turned Sky's fortunes around. Initially, to fill gaps in the schedule, he paid for the rights to the 1989-90 series in the West Indies, the first live coverage of an England tour; interest grew when Graham Gooch's team unexpectedly won the First Test. It was the start of Sky's regular coverage of England trips, and led to the exclusive rights to their home matches in 2006.

CLAYTON, GEOFFREY, died on September 19, aged 80. A thatch of black hair, allied to a simian crouch behind the stumps, inspired Geoff Clayton's Lancashire team-mates to nickname him "Chimp". He was their regular wicketkeeper for six seasons from 1959, before falling out with the committee – like others around the time – after a slow innings in a one-day game he felt was a lost cause.

Weather eye: Ken Grieves and Geoff Clayton watch the clouds as Lancashire coach Stan Worthington looks on, 1961.

Clayton had made an impressive start to his county career, with 647 runs and 59 dismissals in his first season, and was asked to play for MCC in the traditional early-season match against the champions, Yorkshire, at Lord's in 1960. But there was a problem. His county team-mate Bob Barber explained: "A sad, sad case. He went from being a very nice young boy into a fellow who just wanted to keep on tipping drink down himself." Clayton reported for his big day at Lord's after getting into a fight at a greyhound track: "We had a one-eyed wicketkeeper," said Barber. Clayton still clung on to six catches but, when MCC played the South Africans a month later, Jim Parks wore the gloves, and kept them for the Tests. Clayton's moment had passed.

In 1965, he moved to Taunton, where he had three productive years. He made his only century in one of his early matches for Somerset, against Middlesex at the old Imperial Tobacco ground in Bristol, and in his first season there completed 85 dismissals (then 84 the following year). Seamer Roy Palmer remembered Clayton fondly: "The two Man of the Match awards I won in 1966 were a result of what he did for me," he told the *Somerset County Gazette*. "I hadn't played in the Championship match against Yorkshire, but was due to play in the Gillette Cup the next day, so when the three-day game ended as a draw, Geoff said he wanted me out in the middle to prepare for tomorrow. He did this for the quarter-final against Lancashire too, and both times I got the award."

Clayton left Somerset in 1967, after a difference of opinion with his captain, Colin Atkinson. He returned to the north, and resumed friendships at Old Trafford. Lancashire's historian, the Rev. Malcolm Lorimer, recalled: "I conducted a few funerals of former players, and Geoff always turned up in his tatty old raincoat looking like Columbo, walking down the middle of the chapel with a copy of the *Racing Post* stuffed in his pocket." He became a greyhound trainer, and also ran a grocery store, but latterly was in straitened circumstances; Lancashire contributed towards the costs of his funeral.

COBHAM, MICHAEL DAVID, died on March 25, aged 87. David Cobham was a noted author and conservationist, and a film-maker best remembered for the popular 1979 feature *Tarka the Otter*, which he scripted and directed. He had already produced "The Vanishing Hedgerows", an early environmental programme, as part of the BBC series "The World About Us". It showed, among other things, the devastating effects of pesticides on native birds. He later set up the Hawk and Owl Trust which, along with his books, aimed to protect Britain's birds of prey. In his youth, the lanky Cobham had been a useful seamer, taking part in schools matches at Lord's and becoming a playing member of MCC. He came close to a Blue at Cambridge, and in 1953 did appear in one first-class match at Fenner's, for the Free Foresters *against* the University, dismissing their openers after they had put on 126. He also played for Berkshire.

CONGDON, BEVAN ERNEST, OBE, died on February 10, the day before his 80th birthday. Not many players thrown into Test captaincy do well, but the quietly determined Bevan Congdon was an exception. When Graham Dowling suffered career-ending back trouble during New Zealand's tour of the West Indies in 1971-72, Congdon took over for the Third Test. He had just scored 166 not out at Port-of-Spain, the highest score of a modest career that until then had produced only one other century in 33 Tests. But in 17 as captain, he made four more, including 176 and 175 in successive innings in England in 1973.

His bowling was even more transformed. Previously a fill-in with just 18 wickets, he became an important third or fourth seamer, and picked up a further 33 while captain. He ceded the captaincy to Glenn Turner in 1975, as he was unavailable for the first World Cup, in England, and in his first Test back in the ranks, against the Indians at Auckland, took only five-for.

Although some found his captaincy defensive and unimaginative, New Zealand underwent a transformation of their own under his stewardship. Previously international cricket's whipping boys, they became hard to beat, and even caused the odd upset. Congdon led them to their first Test win over Australia, at Christchurch in 1973-74, and was still playing when they beat England for the first time – after 48 years of trying – at

Square jaw-jaw: Bevan Congdon (standing) with Ken Wadsworth and Brian Hastings, Sydney, 1974.

Wellington in 1977-78: in a low-scoring game, he made an important 44. He admitted he was helped by having some world-class players at his disposal: "I think 1973 to England was a defining tour, in that Glenn Turner made 1,000 runs in May, and Richard Hadlee started his career. We could have won two Tests out of three, which was unusual for us."

The First Test at Trent Bridge had seen Congdon lead an epic rearguard: needing a Test-record 479 to win, New Zealand fell just 38 short. Congdon was hit on his resolutely square jaw early on by John Snow, but that only sharpened his concentration. "Those so-and-sos are not going to get me out," he said at the end of the third day, before batting for most of the fourth: he was eventually dismissed for 176 after nearly seven hours. The so-and-sos struggled to get him out at Lord's, too, where his 175 swallowed eight and a half hours. New Zealand led by almost 300, but England clung on for a draw. Despite Brian Johnston pointing out that "he seems to have a problem in the 170s", Congdon was a shoo-in as one of the Five Cricketers of the Year.

He started life in sleepy Motueka, a coastal town at the northern tip of New Zealand's South Island, whose cricketers struggled for recognition from the bigger associations. A near contemporary was Denis Hulme, the 1967 world motor racing champion, who was born in Motueka in 1936. Bevan was the youngest of six brothers ("I was supposed to be the girl"), and was soon immersed in sport – and music, becoming an accomplished trumpeter who once joined in with the band during a tour function in England.

He made his debut for Central Districts over Christmas in 1960, but did not score a century for four years. When it came, it was well timed: 112 on Boxing Day 1964 helped set up an innings victory over Wellington, who were led by New Zealand's captain John Reid. The following month, Congdon made his Test debut, against Pakistan, and was soon off on a globe-trotting tour which included Tests in India (he and Barry Sinclair had to clear nesting birds out of their hotel room), Pakistan (he made a rare Test stumping by a substitute), and England, where he often opened.

When England visited after the 1965-66 Ashes, Congdon's maiden century – 104 at Christchurch – cemented his place until 1978, when he made a fourth tour of England at

HIGHEST TEST SCORES FOR NEW ZEALAND IN ENGLAND

206	M. P. Donnelly	Lord's	1949	120	C. S. Dempster	Lord's	1931
176	**B. E. Congdon**	**Nottingham . .**	**1973**	120	B-J. Watling	Leeds	2015
175	**B. E. Congdon**	**Lord's . . . .**	**1973**	119	J. G. Wright	The Oval.	1986
154*	L. R. P. L. Taylor	Manchester . . .	2008	117	S. P. Fleming	Nottingham . . .	2004
142	M. D. Crowe	Lord's	1994	116	V. Pollard	Nottingham . . .	1973
132	K. S. Williamson	Lord's	2015	115	M. D. Crowe	Manchester . . .	1994
123	G. P. Howarth	Lord's	1978	110	J. G. Bracewell	Nottingham . . .	1986

In all, New Zealand have scored 26 Test centuries in England.

---

the age of 40. He was proud he never missed a Test or first-class match through injury. In 1968-69, he made a career-best 202 not out for Central Districts against Otago at Nelson, the nearest first-class ground to his birthplace. And in 1974-75, he hit 101 in a one-day international against England: his ODI average of 56 remains New Zealand's highest.

When Walter Hadlee, Richard's father, picked an all-time New Zealand XI for his 1993 autobiography, he wasn't sure who to put at No. 3. "Glenn Turner would be my preferred choice," he mused. "But if the opposition had bowlers of real pace, I would replace him with Bevan Congdon – one of the best players of fast bowling, as he positioned himself well on the back foot and into line with the ball, whereas Turner tended to slash outside off stump."

After retirement, Congdon had a spell as a Test selector, worked as a sales manager for the Wills tobacco company, and made forays into radio commentary, exhibiting the common sense of his playing days. The Australian publisher Ronald Cardwell brought out a slim volume about him not long before his death. He recalled that, although Congdon's memory was fogged by dementia, his handshake was still firm.

CORKERY, MICHAEL, QC, who died on June 22, aged 92, was a colourful barrister who was involved in some of Britain's most famous criminal trials, notably the prosecution of former government minister John Stonehouse in 1976, and the 1984 case of two of the Brink's-Mat robbers, who had stolen three tons of gold worth £26m from a warehouse near Heathrow Airport. Corkery always loved cricket, his infatuation probably dating from the day in 1938 when, as a 12-year-old at Bickley Hall prep school in Kent, he bowled to Don Bradman and the Australian touring team. He lived with cancer for more than 30 years, once storing his chemotherapy drugs in the hotel minibar during a long case in Hong Kong. When it ended, he was so delighted that he bowled an imaginary cricket ball down the hotel corridor – and injured his shoulder so badly the flight home was spent in agony.

COSTELLO, DELWYN ANNE, who died on August 4, aged 58, was an economical medium-pacer who played one Test for New Zealand, taking two wickets against India in Ahmedabad in 1984-85, and seven one-day internationals. In January 1982, during her first season for Canterbury, she had figures of 4.3–3–4–4 as Otago were skittled for 24.

DAGNIN, IVAN, who died on May 6, aged 80, opened the batting for Western Province's non-white team in four matches later given first-class status. He also played representative football. "He was a seriously good all-rounder," said André Odendaal, the cricket historian and former chief executive of the WP Cricket Association.

DAVIS, PERCY VERE, who died on November 28, aged 96, joined the Kent staff at 16, in 1938, and made a good impression in the Second XI. Opening the batting, he scored 512 runs at 25; only Godfrey Evans managed more. Davis joined the RAF and rose to flight lieutenant, seeing service in Italy and the Middle East. In 1945, he toured England with a Desert Air Force XI (a team photograph appears in *Wisden 1946*), hitting 51 against the Royal Australian Air Force and an unbeaten 114 against a strong Bomber Command side at Trent Bridge. The following summer he made ten first-class appearances. He performed modestly for Kent in the Championship, but for Combined Services against

Oxford University in the Parks he hit 136, batting with John Dewes, Don Kenyon and Leo Harrison. Davis decided to stay in the RAF rather than pursue a cricket career.

DICKINSON, THOMAS EASTWOOD, died on June 25, aged 87. Tom Dickinson was born in Sydney, but his parents were from Lancashire, where they returned after the war. He played a few Lancashire League games as a schoolboy, and had four matches – with little success – as an amateur for Lancashire in 1950 (when they shared the title with Surrey) and 1951. After national service and teacher training he joined the staff at Queen's College, Taunton, and in 1957 took seven for 17 for Somerset's Second XI against Cornwall. That earned him a call-up to the first team: he claimed five for 36 on debut, against Glamorgan at Weston-super-Mare in August, but teaching commitments allowed only four more appearances, all during that season. He was an unconventional batsman who, according to the Somerset chronicler David Foot, would occasionally switch to being a left-hander in the middle of an over. Despite this, or perhaps because of it, he failed to reach double figures in his nine first-class matches. Dickinson remained at Queen's College for 29 years.

DICKINSON, VERNON EDWARD JOHN, who died on July 30, aged 85, was a slow left-armer who made 20 appearances for Rhodesia from 1955-56, three years after playing for South African Schools. He found plenty of turn on helpful pitches, and his best figures came in 1960-61, when he took seven for 22 – including the 16-year-old Graeme Pollock – against Eastern Province at Port Elizabeth, and finished with ten in the match. In his final game, in 1964-65, Dickinson took five for 44 to seal victory over Worcestershire, who had stopped off in Rhodesia as part of an ambitious world tour following their first Championship title.

DOGGART, GEORGE HUBERT GRAHAM, OBE, died on February 16, aged 92. Hubert Doggart was not the only England batsman bewildered by Sonny Ramadhin and Alf Valentine in the summer of 1950. In four innings, they each took his wicket twice, but his potential was such that, after scores of 29, 22 and 25 (plus a duck), he might have expected further opportunities. At the end of the season, however, he began a career in teaching, effectively turning his back on top-level cricket – although he later captained Sussex in 1954.

But Doggart was not lost to the game. He became a tireless supporter of schools cricket, firing the enthusiasm and nurturing the talent of scores of youngsters – Tiger Pataudi was a protégé – and was later the president of MCC. Yet the weight and style of his early run-scoring made it tempting to wonder how good he might have been.

After serving in the Coldstream Guards at the end of the war, he went up to Cambridge and announced himself spectacularly at the start of the 1948 season. On his first-class debut, against Lancashire at Fenner's, Doggart hit 215 in just under six hours, driving beautifully on the off side against an attack led by Test seamers Dick Pollard and Ken Cranston. By the end of term, he had made 794 runs at 44, and added hundreds against Northamptonshire and Free Foresters, although he was less successful in ten Championship appearances for Sussex.

HIGHEST SECOND-WICKET PARNERSHIPS IN ENGLAND

465*	J. A. Jameson/R. B. Kanhai	Warwickshire v Gloucestershire at Birmingham .	1974
451	W. H. Ponsford/D. G. Bradman .	Australia v England at The Oval..............	1934
450	N. R. D. Compton/J. C. Hildreth	Somerset v Cardiff MCCU at Taunton Vale.....	2012
429*	J. G. Dewes/G. H. G. Doggart .	Cambridge University v Essex at Cambridge..	1949
417	K. J. Barnett/T. A. Tweats	Derbyshire v Yorkshire at Derby	1997
403	G. A. Gooch/P. J. Prichard	Essex v Leicestershire at Chelmsford	1990
398	A. Shrewsbury/W. Gunn.........	Nottinghamshire v Sussex at Nottingham.......	1890
385	E. H. Bowley/M. W. Tate......	Sussex v Northamptonshire at Hove...........	1921
382	L. Hutton/M. Leyland..........	England v Australia at The Oval.............	1938
382	S. R. Dickson/J. L. Denly	Kent v Northamptonshire at Beckenham	2017

Paul Popper, Popperfoto/Getty Images

Peace mission: in April 1956, E. W. Swanton led a tour to the Caribbean to mend fences after the MCC's bad-tempered trip in 1953-54. *Standing:* Micky Stewart, Robin Marlar, David Blake, Swaranjit Singh, Alan Oakman, Colin Ingleby-Mackenzie, Roger Kimpton and Gamini Goonesena. *Seated:* Swanton, Frank Tyson, Hubert Doggart, Colin Cowdrey, John Warr and Tom Graveney.

He was soon back in the headlines. In Cambridge's second match in 1949, against Essex at Fenner's, he put on an unbeaten 429 in a day with John Dewes, a domestic second-wicket record that lasted until 1974. Doggart's share was 219. That summer, he passed 2,000 runs at 45. In his final year, he captained a Cambridge XI blessed with a formidable batting line-up – Dewes, David Sheppard and Peter May completed the top four – and exceeded 1,000 runs for the third successive season. He also captained The Rest in a Test trial at Bradford, where his team were bowled out for 27 by Jim Laker; he failed twice, though was still selected for the First Test at Old Trafford. But after West Indies' crushing victory in the Second, at Lord's, he was dropped. They were busy times: that academic year, he was also captain of football, squash and racquets, and won a half Blue for Rugby fives. He found time to get a second in history.

Doggart was born into a sporting family in Earls Court. His father, Graham, an accountant, had played for Cambridge and Middlesex, and captained England at football against Belgium in 1923: he was later president of the Football Association, and died of a heart attack at their AGM in 1963. Doggart and his younger brother, Peter, went to Winchester College, where Hubert was captain of cricket, football and racquets. He returned to teach Classics in 1950, and stayed until 1972, when he became headmaster of King's School, Bruton, in Somerset. He was credited with transforming its fortunes.

In 1954, he was given time off to captain Sussex. The county had finished second under Sheppard the previous summer, but now slipped to ninth. "Doggart, though competent, lacked the inspiration of his predecessor," said *Wisden*. He scored two centuries against Oxford University and one against the Pakistanis, but only one in the Championship. He made his final appearance in 1961.

President of MCC in 1981-82, he was asked to fill the role in the bicentenary year of 1987 after Colin Cowdrey fell ill; he continued as treasurer until 1992. For 35 years, he was president of the English Schools Cricket Association and was responsible for selecting the teams for MCC schools matches. He also wrote and edited a number of cricket books, including a history of Oxford and Cambridge cricket with George Chesterton, and a tribute to the historian H. S. Altham.

Doggart was fastidious to the point of pedantry on matters of grammar, and in his distinctive tones was fond of quoting the Classics – to the bemusement of some. At

Fenner's, his calling was said to be so loud it often led to run-outs in matches on nearby Parker's Piece.

DOMAN, MICHAEL EDWARD, who died of complications from diabetes on July 30, aged 57, was a batsman and occasional leg-spinner who played 14 matches later given first-class status for Western Province's non-white side. He was part of the team, also including Saait Magiet (see below) and Vince Barnes (later South Africa's bowling coach), which won the Howa Bowl in 1979-80, the first of five successive triumphs. Doman's 64 against Transvaal in Cape Town that season remained the highest score of a career curtailed by a back injury. He became a news reporter for the *Cape Herald*, and later a cricket writer and sports editor with the *Cape Argus*.

DONALD, DAVID LINDSAY, who died on October 3, 2016, aged 83, was an opening batsman from Manawatu who came to the attention of the New Zealand selectors after a patient 106 – his only first-class century – for Northern Districts against Canterbury in January 1959. England were about to arrive for two Tests after the Ashes, and two new openers were needed, but a double failure against Auckland, for whom Roger Harris made 82 and 68, cooked Donald's goose; Harris opened with Bruce Bolton, another new cap, in the Tests. Donald lost form the following season, although he did make 56 for Northern Districts against a strong Australian touring team. By the time New Zealand played another Test, in 1961-62, his first-class career was over.

DOUGHTY, RICHARD JOHN, who died on February 6, aged 57, was an enthusiastic fast bowler for Gloucestershire and Surrey. After leaving school in his native Yorkshire, Dickie Doughty had started his professional career on the MCC groundstaff as a wicketkeeper-batsman. But things changed in 1981, when the two Australians sent for scholarships at Lord's were Wayne Phillips and Tim Zoehrer, both future Test keepers. It meant that Doughty – and Dermot Reeve, there at the same time – had few opportunities behind the stumps, and took up bowling instead. A slingy action generated decent pace, and Doughty made his Gloucestershire debut that season, joining them full-time the following year. For a while he was living it up, after marrying an American socialite: "My first wife is George Bush's cousin," he told *The Times* in 2006. "So my life wasn't quite your average one. Grav [David Graveney, then Gloucestershire's captain] used to get pissed off with me because I'd roll into the County Ground in a BMW convertible. I'd go off to California at the end of the season or go skiing in Aspen."

After leaving Gloucestershire – where his aggressive batting also brought him three hundreds for the Seconds – Doughty's best bowling figures of six for 33 came in one of his earliest games for Surrey, against Warwickshire at The Oval in 1985. He took 34 wickets at 25 that year, but was released after one wicketless match in 1987: "They told me two weeks after the end of the season that they weren't going to renew my contract, by which time all the other counties had finalised their squads. There was no help in finding a job. I was 26 and going through a divorce." After leaving Surrey he suffered from depression, but overcame it to become a counsellor for the PCA and the Prince's Trust. Already diabetic, he had a brush with cancer, but died in his sleep while on holiday in Malaysia.

DRABU, KHURSHID HASSAN, CBE, who died on April 20, aged 72, was Britain's first Muslim judge; he had been called to the Bar in 1977, six years after arriving in England as an impecunious student from northern India. In 1990, he became the Commission for Racial Equality's deputy legal director, and undertook a review of the 1976 Race Relations Act. He was, said *The Independent*, "one of the most influential and respected of all British Muslims." Before all this, Drabu had played in the Ranji Trophy for Jammu & Kashmir, often opening, sometimes keeping wicket, later captaining. One of India's weakest teams at the time, they lost 20 of the 22 matches in which he played, 14 by an innings. He averaged just over ten, with a highest score of 49 against Services at Srinagar in 1966-67.

EDEN, GEOFFREY PHILIP, died on January 4, aged 66. Philip Eden was a meteorologist with a lifelong enthusiasm for his subject, which he conveyed with a light touch to listeners and readers, most regularly those of BBC 5 Live and the *Daily* and *Sunday Telegraph*. His reports were full of quirky facts and sharp phrases: he once called Mother Nature a "sadistic old crone". He was also a cricket lover, and contributed *Wisden's* Cricket and the Weather feature from 1999 to 2015. This incorporated his own system for assessing the weather in all the first-class counties from one summer to the next. Though he was always keen to debunk media-driven myths, his research supported the theory that the four wettest, most westerly counties (Glamorgan, Gloucestershire, Lancashire and Somerset) are disadvantaged in the Championship, having won only four between them since 1935. He lived at Whipsnade, next to the zoo, in a small house lined with *Wisdens* and meteorological tomes. He was hit by a rare form of dementia.

FELSINGER, HERBERT CLEMEN, died on April 29, aged 83. Herbie Felsinger was one of the umpires for Sri Lanka's inaugural Test, against England in Colombo in February 1982. He stood in five further Tests and 11 one-day internationals. He had been a good club batsman, sharing an opening partnership of 351 with Makkin Salih for Moors in the Sara Trophy in 1952-53; soon after, he toured India with a Ceylon team. His brother, Alane, was also a first-class umpire, who stood in one Test; they officiated together in a representative match against the West Indian tourists in 1978-79.

FLINT, DERRICK, who died on July 22, aged 94, made ten first-class appearances as a leg-spinner for Warwickshire in 1948 and 1949, without posing a serious threat to Eric Hollies. Flint took 12 wickets, with a best of four for 67 on debut against Cambridge University; Trevor Bailey and Doug Insole were among his victims. His father, Benjamin, had played 13 games for Nottinghamshire after the First World War. But his name became more widely known in 1971, when he married the England women's captain, Rachael Heyhoe. His career may have been a footnote, but he was not forgotten: when the couple arrived for a Warwickshire former players' day, they spotted a group of autograph hunters. As she searched in her handbag for a pen, they made a beeline for her husband.

FRENCH, KEITH, who died on April 1, aged 76, captained Rawtenstall when they achieved the Lancashire League championship and Worsley Cup double in 1976. He scored 3,644 runs for them between 1955 and 1977.

GALE, ROBERT ALEC, died on April 20, aged 84. With Eric Russell, Bob Gale formed one of the most aesthetically pleasing opening partnerships in county cricket. They both made their Middlesex debuts in 1956, although it was not until the retirement of Syd Brown, and Jack Robertson's decision to drop down the order, that they became regulars. Gale was in the Bedford Modern School XI for five years, before Middlesex offered him a three-year contract, but they had to wait until after he had done his national service.

Gale played regularly in 1957, passing 1,000 runs for the first of six times, and scoring his maiden hundred, against Sussex at Lord's. A tall, bulky left-hander, he was an attractive strokemaker, though *Wisden* noted that his "big scores were interspersed with periods when he did little of note". He scored more heavily in the next two seasons, and was spoken of as a candidate for England's tour of the West Indies in 1959-60. He first opened with Russell against Leicestershire at Grace Road in July 1958: they put on 96 and 113.

"They made a classical opening pair," said team-mate Peter Parfitt, "although Bob was no flyer between the wickets." Like the new Middlesex captain J. J. Warr, Gale was a stockbroker, and the pair socialised regularly during the winter, usually still wearing their City-uniform top hats. He scored consistently into the early 1960s, and in 1962 made 2,211 runs at 38. But his appearances tailed off, and he left permanently for the office halfway through the summer of 1965. He later returned to Middlesex as chairman of the cricket committee, and was president between 2001 and 2003.

Chaps about town: Ian Bedford, Bob Gale, Martin Young, Tom Pugh and Colin Ingleby-Mackenzie, September 1961.

Gale's finest moment had come against Glamorgan at Newport in 1962, when he made 200 in five hours. But the opposing captain, Wilf Wooller, did not allow him to savour it. "That's the worst double-hundred I've ever seen," he told him as he walked off.

GARDINER, HOWARD ARTHUR BRUCE, died on June 10, aged 74. Howie Gardiner was a 6ft 5in wicketkeeper from Rhodesia who could also bat destructively, preferring chunky drives to cross-batted shots. He came to prominence by smacking five sixes in a 58-minute 86 during a two-day game against Bob Simpson's 1966-67 Australian tourists. Shortly afterwards, in Rhodesia's first-class match against Simpson's side, he hit six sixes in an 81. Runs became scarcer when the faster bowlers started to push him on to the back foot, but he did make 99 – his highest first-class score – after coming in at 74 for seven against Western Province in Salisbury in 1974-75. A maiden century disappeared when he was stumped for the only time in his first-class career.

Gardiner was already an important part of Rhodesia's strong Currie Cup team, who were often inspired by Mike Procter. When Procter hammered 254 against Western Province in 1970-71 – his sixth successive first-class century – Gardiner scored 63 in a stand of 166; no one else passed 17. By the time back trouble forced him to retire in 1975-76, he had made 1,700 runs for Rhodesia, plus 156 dismissals as a neat and reliable keeper, despite his height. In later life he became chief executive of the British Oxygen Company in Zimbabwe, served as a national selector, and was one of the early ICC match referees.

GERA, AMAN LAJPAT, who died of cancer on June 26, aged 49, was an off-spinner who played nine Ranji Trophy matches for Uttar Pradesh, taking five for 133 against Haryana at Faridabad in 1996-97.

GRAHAM, WILLIAM FRANKLIN, KBE, died on February 21, aged 99. In a career that started in 1947, the Christian evangelist Billy Graham preached to total crowds estimated to exceed 210m worldwide, in addition to countless millions on television. In 1959, he drew the record attendance for any event at the Melbourne Cricket Ground – more than 130,000 (one source suggests 143,750). The record for a cricket match there is 93,013, for the 2015 World Cup final; the 1970 Australian Rules grand final attracted 121,696.

GUEST, COLIN ERNEST JOHN, who died on December 8, aged 81, was a seamer whose sole Test appearance came in the third match of the 1962-63 Ashes, at Sydney. The selectors were looking to replace Ken Mackay's medium-pacers with an injection of actual pace, and Guest had just taken six wickets in Victoria's three-day demolition of New South Wales, including the in-form Bob Simpson; he also snared Test players Norman O'Neill, Neil Harvey and Brian Booth. But Guest failed to take a wicket in the Test; although Lindsay Hassett had praised his "beautiful outswinger", it never appeared at Sydney. Bill O'Reilly noted he had "trouble in controlling his direction". Mackay was back for the Fourth Test – his final appearance – before Neil Hawke was tried in the Fifth.

Guest had first made a mark in 1958-59, when he was selected for Victoria after only a handful of first-grade games for Melbourne, in one of which he took six for seven against Collingwood. He claimed nine wickets (six bowled) in his third Sheffield Shield match, against Queensland, including Mackay and Peter Burge in both innings, but was then sidelined after breaking his ankle playing baseball for Victoria. He returned to Shield action in 1961-62, and the following season took 47 wickets, leading to that Test cap, including a career-best seven for 95 in a Western Australian total of 473 at the MCG. But he lost form, and moved to Perth. He made more of an impression with his batting, notably during his highest score of 74 against his old Victorian team-mates. The Australians wore black armbands in his memory on the first day of the First Test against India at Adelaide in December 2018.

GUY, RICHARD HENRY, died on May 16, aged 81. Eight matches for New South Wales spread over eight seasons in the 1960s was a poor reflection of Dick Guy's skills. His 26 inexpensive wickets showed he was comfortable against the strong batting in the Sheffield Shield – but, as a leg-spinner, he was up against Test players Richie Benaud, Bob Simpson, Peter Philpott and Kerry O'Keeffe for a place in the state side. However, Guy's 786 wickets in 18 seasons for Gordon in the Sydney grade competition proved his ability and durability. He was a state selector for 16 years, and part of the national panel which chose off-spinner Peter Taylor, seemingly out of nowhere, for the last Test of the 1986-87 Ashes. After a career in the NSW police force, Guy ran a successful cleaning business.

HALLEBONE, JEFFREY, died on October 18, aged 89. In February 1952, Jeff Hallebone hit 202 in a non-Sheffield Shield game for Victoria against Tasmania at Melbourne, becoming only the third Australian to make a double-century on first-class debut. (The others were Norman Callaway in 1914-15, in his only match, and Sam Loxton in 1946-47; no one has done it since.) Two seasons later – a summer with no home Tests – Hallebone established himself as Colin McDonald's opening partner, hitting two Shield centuries, and 99 against a New Zealand touring team. Against Queensland at the Gabba, he batted through the last day to stave off an innings defeat. He made 143, with only seven fours, but larruped left-arm spinner Mick Raymer for six sixes. It was, observed the Brisbane *Courier-Mail*, "a mixture of Ken Mackay at his dourest and Richie Benaud at his brightest". After Hallebone's previous efforts against the pace of Ray Lindwall and Keith Miller, the influential journalist Ray Robinson tagged him a serious contender for the 1954-55 Ashes, but he failed to reach 20 all season. The following year, for work reasons, Hallebone left Australia temporarily – and first-class cricket permanently. He played for another decade with his grade team, South Melbourne, and had a spell with Victor Trumper's old club, Paddington, while working in Sydney.

GREAT WAR OBITUARY – 100 YEARS ON

The rest is silence

HANDS, CAPT. REGINALD HARRY MYBURGH, died of wounds on April 20, 1918, aged 29. Reginald Hands made his debut for South Africa in the last Test before the outbreak of the First World War, but did not live to see international cricket's resumption. He had an inauspicious match, stumped twice by Herbert Strudwick at Port Elizabeth, for nought and seven. England wrapped up a 4–0 win, although the game was a collector's item. Hands played alongside his brother Philip, and also Herbie and Dan Taylor. It was the first time two pairs of brothers had appeared in a Test.

Hands was gassed during the German spring offensive, and died a month later at Boulogne. His death might have been just one more statistic amid the slaughter, but it had a lasting resonance. His father, Sir Harry Hands, was the mayor of Cape Town, and ordered a three-minute pause on the firing of the noon gun on Signal Hill (later reduced to two): one minute to remember those who died, one in gratitude for the survivors. Sir Percy FitzPatrick, a South African writer and politician who had also lost a son in the conflict, was moved by the gesture. A suggestion that it be more widely adopted was forwarded to King George V, who was enthusiastic. "All locomotion should cease, so that in perfect stillness, the thoughts of everyone may be concentrated on reverent remembrance of the glorious dead," he wrote in a proclamation. After a meeting of the War Cabinet, the silence was introduced with only six days' notice in 1919, and has been observed on Remembrance Day ever since.

Reginald Hands in 1908, when a member of the University College, Oxford, First XI.

The Master and Fellows of University College, Oxford

Before the war, Hands had made a few appearances for Western Province. He hit an unbeaten 79 on his debut against Orange Free State at Newlands, and 67 against Natal at Durban, but did little else to warrant a Test call-up. Philip, who also served on the Western Front, played in seven Tests and toured England in 1924; a third brother, Kenneth, who was in the Royal Engineers, had a long first-class career and made two appearances for Oxford University in 1912. All three attended Diocesan College in Cape Town, and went to Oxford as Rhodes scholars. Reginald, the eldest, read jurisprudence and was called to the Bar at Middle Temple in 1911. He excelled at a number of sports. In 1910, he won two caps for England in rugby's Five Nations championship – in the wins over France in Paris, and Scotland in Edinburgh.

Wisden first published an obituary for Reginald Hands in 1919. An updated appreciation of a player who died in the Great War has appeared in each of the last five Almanacks, 100 years after the original notice.

HARRIS, ALWYN, who died on March 11, aged 82, was a left-handed opener who played 49 matches for Glamorgan in the first half of the 1960s after doing well in club cricket for Ynysygerwyn. His best season was 1962, when he was one of a record seven Glamorgan batsmen to pass 1,000 runs. Harris's 1,049 at 23 included his only two centuries: 110 against Warwickshire at Swansea, then 101 in a victory over the Pakistan tourists at Cardiff Arms Park. But in 18 more matches after that season, he never reached 50, and was released at the end of 1964.

HECHT, ERNEST, OBE, who died on February 13, aged 88, launched his publishing career with a biography of Len Hutton, produced in his parents' spare bedroom. It taught him an early lesson: "We sold 5,000 but I'd printed 10,000. I hadn't understood the mechanics." Hecht was rarely caught napping again. Souvenir Press, the company he founded in 1951 with a £250 loan from his father, remained defiantly independent until Ernest's death. He operated from a chaotic office directly opposite the British Museum, where some of the titles in his eclectic list were on display in a shop window. Hecht had arrived from Moravia in Czechoslovakia on the *Kindertransport*. He was the last of the great émigré publishers, a group that included George Weidenfeld, Paul Hamlyn and André Deutsch. Hecht loved football – he was once Pelé's literary agent – and especially Arsenal, but he also performed an important service for cricket bibliophiles. He got to know the writer Margaret Hughes, who was Neville Cardus's literary executor, and in the 1980s published a string of his anthologies, which she edited. They sold well, and introduced Cardus to a new audience.

HILL, LEON TREVOR, who died on January 22, aged 81, played for South Australia for three seasons from 1958-59 as a forthright batsman who also bowled off-breaks. He hit 100 in a lost cause against Victoria at Adelaide in 1959-60. His business career took him to Brisbane, where he played twice for Queensland in 1962-63, then to Melbourne, where he turned out for the Fitzroy club. From 1996 to 2004 he served on the council of the City of Stonnington in Melbourne's suburbs, and was their mayor in 2001-02.

HILL-WOOD, PETER DENIS, who died on December 28, aged 82, was best known as the chairman of Arsenal, succeeding his father in 1982 and lasting until 2013, a few years after overseeing their move from Highbury to the Emirates Stadium. He was also a first-class cricketer, by virtue of an appearance for the Free Foresters against Cambridge University at Fenner's in 1960, when he scored 30 after catching the future England captain Tony Lewis. Hill-Wood had represented Eton against Harrow at Lord's for three years from 1952, returning a frugal 19–11–16–2 with his medium-pacers in 1953. He was a merchant banker, and became vice-chairman of Hambros Bank.

HOFMEYR, MURRAY BERNARD, who died on May 17, aged 92, was a talented all-round sportsman from Pretoria who played rugby union for England while a Rhodes scholar at Oxford. He was a consistent run-scorer for the University XI, forming a strong opening partnership with Brian Boobbyer, who played rugby for England alongside him; they put on 131 in 1950 as Yorkshire were beaten at Oxford for the second year in a row. Hofmeyr had twice carried his bat the previous summer, first for 95 – "after five hours of stolidness", according to the journalist Alan Mitchell – as the New Zealanders slipped to their only defeat of a long tour, and then for 64 out of 169 in the 1949 Varsity Match, which Oxford lost deep in the final session. The following season, the middle of his three as a Blue, was Hofmeyr's best: he made 1,063 runs at 55 with four centuries, including a career-high 161 when he outscored Gloucestershire (155) on his own in the Parks. He later captained North Eastern Transvaal, scoring 125 against Griqualand West in his last Currie Cup match, in January 1953. He had a successful business career, initially for the Anglo American Corporation, looking after their mining interests in Africa, then for Charter Consolidated, running their London office.

HOLMES, DAVID, died on January 7, aged 54. A stalwart of the Instonians club in Belfast, "Wee Davy" Holmes wrote about cricket in Ireland for several outlets, including the *Ulster Star* and the *Belfast Telegraph*. "I liked his desire to cover cricket at all levels, not just senior," said Cricket Ireland's former media manager, Barry Chambers. "He would travel the length and breadth of the country to help promote the game."

HUNT, MOLLIE ELAINE, who died on February 2, aged 81, played three Tests for England, all in South Africa in 1960-61. She scored 29 in the drawn Second Test at Johannesburg, having returned figures with her off-breaks earlier in the tour of 23–11–27–6 and 7.2–2–12–7 against Western Province, who were shot out for 32 in their second innings. She married soon after arriving home, and never represented England again, although – now Mollie Buckland – she remained involved with the Women's Cricket Association.

JADEJA, MULABHA V., who died on June 12, aged 87, played 31 Ranji Trophy matches, mainly for Saurashtra. Usually an opener, he made two centuries: 102 against Gujarat at Rajkot in 1955-56, and 110 as Saurashtra followed on against Bombay two seasons later. His son, Bimal Jadeja, also played for Saurashtra.

JADEJA, MANOHARSINHJI PRADYUMANSINHJI, who died on September 27, aged 82, played 14 times for Saurashtra under his princely name of the Yuvraj of Rajkot, usually as captain. No mere figurehead, he scored 144 in 1957-58 against a Gujarat side containing four present or future Test players, after making 59 on debut against them two years earlier. He succeeded his father – who had captained Kathiawar in the 1948-49 Ranji Trophy match they conceded when Bhausaheb Nimbalkar reached 443 not out for Maharashtra – as the 15th Thakore Saheb of Rajkot in 1973. He was active in local politics, and in 2010 secured the return from a German museum of the "Star of India", a saffron-yellow Rolls-Royce Phantom originally built for his grandfather in 1934.

JAFFEY, DR ISAAC MERVYN, who died on December 18, 2014, aged 85, spent five years in the Dublin University XI while a medical student at Trinity, and played in the annual first-class match against Scotland in 1953. He was a handy batsman and a good, if unorthodox, wicketkeeper: he preferred to take the ball in his left glove only, which meant he was often strangely positioned behind the stumps. He emigrated to the United States, and changed his name to Mervyn Jeffries, which explains why his death had escaped the notice of cricket historians for some time.

JAMSHEED MARKER, who died on June 21, aged 95, was a long-serving Pakistani diplomat who made the *Guinness Book of Records* for being posted to more countries than anyone else during a long career: he was an ambassador in ten major capitals, plus the United Nations. According to *The Hindu*, Marker "wore many hats and wore them all with poise, dignity, grace and distinction. He was a true Parsi gentleman of Karachi." Before joining the diplomatic corps, he had indulged his passion for cricket as one of Pakistan's earliest radio commentators, forming a popular double act with Omar Kureishi. They teamed up during Pakistan's first home Test series, against India in 1954-55, starting from a table on the fine-leg boundary at Karachi – although they were soon moved nearer the pavilion, after the crowd pelted them with oranges.

KALIA, SUMIT, drowned on July 8, after getting into difficulty in deep water in the Gobind Sagar Lake in India's Himachal Pradesh. He was 30. Kalia, who had performed with some success for Punjab's age-group teams before taking up coaching, made two appearances for the state's Twenty20 side. A slow left-armer, he also played in the Indian Cricket League (the short-lived rival to the IPL), taking four for 20 – all Pakistan Test players – for Ahmedabad Rockets against Lahore Badshahs in March 2008.

KASSAMALI, SIBTAIN, who died on October 27, aged 55, was a hard-hitting batsman from Mombasa who represented Kenya in two ICC Trophy competitions. In 1993-94, he was part of the team which finished runners-up at home, and qualified for the World Cup early in 1996, although he had dropped out of the squad by then. Kassamali played one first-class match, for Kenya against a touring Pakistan Starlets side, captained by Shoaib Mohammad. He later coached the national team, and also worked in Tanzania.

KEEN, SHEILA MARY, who died on April 27, aged 78, was prominent in women's cricket throughout the 1960s and '70s, returning figures of 16–5–19–6 for Molly Hide's XI against Surrey Women in 1978, when she was almost 39. Sixteen years earlier, she had taken five for 30 for Surrey against Middlesex. She turned to umpiring, standing in the 1987 Ashes Test in which Australia's Denise Annetts scored a then-record 193 not out.

KEMSLEY, JEREMY NEIL, died on February 16, aged 84. Born in Australia but schooled in Aberdeen, Neil Kemsley played ten matches for Scotland in the 1950s, eight first-class. He scored 103 against MCC – captained by Freddie Brown, who eventually caught and bowled him – at Aberdeen in 1957, having made an undefeated 100 in a two-day game at Lord's the previous year. He played club cricket for Grange and Clydesdale, and also represented Scotland at badminton.

KERLY, MARK ROBERT, who died in September 2017, aged 56, was for many years the busiest scorer in Auckland. He started young, keeping the book for England's Test at Eden Park in 1977-78; he was 16, and had to ask permission to miss school. He helped redesign the linear scorebook, although he sometimes preferred to leave the book to others and operate the scoreboard. He was private and reclusive: after a suspected heart attack, his body lay undiscovered in his flat for several months.

KOWALICK, JEFFREY PETER, died on February 28, aged 71. Seamer "Cuddles" Kowalick received his only call-up for South Australia in 1966-67, when Eric Freeman – soon to be a Test player – had to work. He took a solitary wicket, but it was a good one: Colin Milburn had pounded 129 for Western Australia when Kowalick bowled him. Later he turned to coaching at his old club, Sturt, in Adelaide.

LAWTON, JAMES, who died on September 27, aged 75, was one of British journalism's most prolific sports columnists. Jim Lawton's versatility extended to long stints as chief

Viv is angry, so better listen… Jim Lawton gets an earful, while Mark Ryan, Steve Whiting (in doorway) and Matthew Engel (hat) tune in.

sportswriter of the *Daily Express* and *The Independent*. And though he was an old-school Fleet Street man to his core, he spent seven years as a columnist on *The Vancouver Sun*. Returning home in 1986, he was for the next 27 years a regular at major cricketing occasions – most famously in Antigua in 1990, when Viv Richards, who should have been leading his team on to the field, stomped instead up to the press box, where he subjected the mild-mannered and cherubic Lawton to a bizarre harangue ("Vivi's mad!" said Richards), complete with veiled threats. The *casus belli* was a press conference the previous day where Lawton had asked about a V-sign to the crowd, which was followed by the *Express's* front-page headline "Captain Viv blows his top" – which was true when written, and became even truer when the page arrived by fax just before play began that morning. Richards made peace two tours later: the incident had been a PR disaster for him, since Lawton was much liked and admired by his colleagues. His genial manner, however, disguised a surprisingly intense workaholism. (He once described his working methods: "The coffee pot's half full, the ashtray overflowing…") Though he reluctantly retired, to Italy in 2013, he kept writing. He died suddenly, having just filed a column to a Dublin paper – a firm but fair-minded denunciation of Jose Mourinho's stewardship of Manchester United.

LEWIS, DESMOND MICHAEL, who died on March 25, aged 72, was a wicketkeeper who had a rapid rise to Test cricket, but faded equally quickly. In only his second home match for Jamaica, he made what remained a career-best 96 after opening against the 1970-71 Indian tourists, and was chosen to replace Mike Findlay for the Third Test at Georgetown. Lewis started with an unbeaten 81 after being dropped early at slip: he survived for three and a half hours, and shared an unlikely ninth-wicket partnership of 84 with Lance Gibbs. In the Fourth Test, he made 88 after being promoted to open, then 72 in the Fifth, to finish with 259 runs at 86 – which turned out to be his final average. Findlay, a smoother gloveman, was preferred when New Zealand toured the following year. "It was easily one of the worst selection blunders in West Indies cricket," wrote Lewis's friend and club-mate Karl Goodison. "But Desmond did not allow the disappointment to consume him, as he said his father told him there was enough bitterness in the world."

Any chance of a recall disappeared when Deryck Murray – who had been studying in England – returned to the Caribbean. Lewis struggled to regain his best form with the bat, although he did sign off his first-class career with 53 against the next Indian touring team, in 1975-76. Around the same time, noting an unusually large crowd for a club game in Kingston, he was told they had come to watch Lawrence Rowe and Michael Holding lock horns. "Well, it's me they're gonna see, all day," said Lewis, who made a century after Holding had dismissed Rowe cheaply. Soon after, he went to live in the United States.

McHUGH, FRANCIS PREST, died on February 21, aged 92. Discarded by his native Yorkshire after two matches, Frank McHugh found success with Gloucestershire. He stood 6ft 3in and began as an out-and-out fast bowler, but enjoyed better results when he cut down

LOWEST FIRST-CLASS BATTING AVERAGES

		M	I	NO	Runs	HS	
2.63	F. P. McHugh	95	111	43	179	18	1949 to 1956
3.15	B. Aislabie	56	100	29	224	15	1808 to 1841
3.25	T. A. V. H. K. Ranaweera	96	142	70	234	11	1995-96 to 2006-07
3.33	B. J. Griffiths	177	138	51	290	16	1974 to 1986
3.59	K. B. S. Jarvis	260	199	87	403	32	1975 to 1990
3.71	C. S. Martin	192	244	115	479	25	1997-98 to 2012-13
3.83	D. Buchanan	62	106	39	257	27	1850 to 1881
3.88	J. N. Graham	189	178	73	408	23	1964 to 1977
3.97	I. J. Jones	198	213	84	513	21	1960 to 1968
4.01	M. A. Robinson	229	259	112	590	27	1987 to 2002

Minimum: 100 innings.

his speed. He had taken the new ball with Alec Coxon for Yorkshire in 1949, but Fred Trueman also made his debut that summer, and the county were not short of pace. McHugh first played for Gloucestershire in 1952, his alliance with George Lambert giving them a cutting edge they had not had for years. His best season was 1954, when he topped the county's averages with 92 wickets at 20. He followed that in 1955 with 75 at 26, including a career-best seven for 32 against Yorkshire at Huddersfield, where his victims included Frank Lowson, Doug Padgett, Ray Illingworth and Norman Yardley. But illness forced him to miss most of 1956, and he was not re-engaged. McHugh was almost certainly the most hopeless batsman on the circuit: 111 first-class innings produced an average of 2.63 and a highest score of 18, one of only four times he reached double figures. He sent in reminiscences of former colleagues for the Lives Remembered section of *The Times*, and enjoyed recounting his conversations with Keith Miller. "Keith would say: 'At least we'll always be in *Wisden*, Frank,' and I'd reply: 'Which part?' 'The obituaries, Frank.'"

MAGIET, SAAIT, who died on July 17 while on holiday in Malaysia, aged 66, was a gifted all-rounder who played 67 matches subsequently given first-class status for non-white teams for South Africa. Most were for Western Province, for whom he took six for 24 against Natal in 1974-75, although his highest score of 128 came for The Rest against Eastern Province at Lenasia in April 1986. "He was probably our greatest cricketer after Basil D'Oliveira," said local administrator Norman Arendse. "He could easily have also played in England, or sold out and gone to play on the other side. But he stuck to his guns." His brother, Rushdi Magiet, had a spell as South Africa's convenor of selectors.

MELVILLE-BROWN, ARTHUR, died on August 30, aged 87. "Mel-Brown" was a keen philatelist whose company, Stamp Publicity, dealt in cricket stamps and labels, and first-day covers. A keen painter and illustrator, he also designed several stamps. His stall was a familiar sight at Test grounds in England, while the company's adverts featured regularly in cricket magazines.

METCALFE, STANLEY GORDON, who died on September 16, 2017, aged 85, was a Yorkshireman who played 17 matches for Oxford University between 1954 and 1956, winning a Blue in his final year, after innings of 70 and 75 against MCC at Lord's. Earlier that summer he had top-scored in both innings against the Australian tourists in the Parks, with 40 and 64. Metcalfe later played several first-class matches for the Free Foresters, scoring two centuries against his old university, and adding 159 against them in 1969, by which time the match no longer had first-class status. He worked for Rank Hovis McDougall from 1959, later becoming their chairman, and repelling hostile takeover bids, despite what *The Independent* called "an air of slightly crumpled affability".

MORGAN, REV. PHILIP RICHARD LLEWELYN, who died on January 12, 2017, aged 89, was a gifted all-round athlete who played one first-class match while at Oxford, against the Indian tourists of 1946. There was little scope for his leg-breaks in a rain-affected game, and he scored a single. In 1992, aged 65 but now bowling seamers, he took four for 23 for Salisbury Diocese against Oxford in the Church Times Cup final. Morgan was better known as an athlete: he beat the future Olympic champion Chris Brasher in the Varsity three-mile event in 1951, and three years later ran in what he called "the biggest anticlimax in athletics history" – the race that immediately followed Roger Bannister's four-minute mile. He became chaplain at Haileybury, and later headmaster of their junior school.

MUNDEN, DAVID JOHN, who died on March 10, aged 60, was a prominent photographer, running his own agency – and covering several England tours – until forced to retire by parkinson's disease. He had been a talented leg-spinner, playing for Leicestershire's age-group teams and touring the West Indies in 1976 with England Under-19, captained by Chris Cowdrey; he took eight wickets against the Leeward Islands. His father, Vic, had a long career with Leicestershire, which helped enliven dull sessions at the cricket. "Some photographers weren't always good to sit with, but Dave was great.

It was that daft sense of humour I will remember," said Patrick Eagar. "We would compare our fathers' performances when Hampshire played Leicestershire – Munden c Eagar b Knott 4 (May 1953), or Eagar b Munden 36 (August 1954)."

MURRAY, JOHN THOMAS, MBE, died on July 24, aged 83. It was at Edgbaston in 1961, in his first Test, that John Murray realised what sort of wicketkeeper he wanted to be. Observing Australia's Wally Grout at close quarters, he was riveted. "Godfrey Evans was unique – he used to jump around everywhere – but Wally Grout was the man I looked up to. He was always stylish in the way he took the ball, and always perfectly balanced. He was never tumbling around. I decided that's the way I wanted to do it."

Murray – known as JT – became the supreme wicketkeeping stylist, but he did not lack substance. In a career spanning 24 seasons and 635 first-class matches, he made 1,527 dismissals, behind only Bob Taylor's 1,649. Relaxed, graceful and immaculately turned out, he took the ball with reassuring calm, fingers pointing down, hands relaxed. "He could not do anything clumsily," said his friend and Middlesex team-mate Peter Parfitt. Murray had a pre-delivery routine: a touch of the cap, and a half-circle described with each hand, an action he repeated before crouching. He was agile, but only when he had to be, and did not believe in wasting time chasing wayward throws. With off-spinner Fred Titmus he

Bob Thomas, Getty Images

Murray mitts: England's John and West Indies' Deryck – both Murrays and both keepers – talk shop at Arundel, 1963.

formed a prolific double act. "JT and Fred had a telepathic relationship," said Parfitt. "But there was no doubt John was the senior partner."

Injuries, and competition from Jim Parks and Alan Knott at either end of his career, restricted Murray to 21 Test appearances, though the selectors also felt he did not score enough runs. But in the Fifth Test against West Indies at The Oval in 1966, with England in trouble in Brian Close's first match as captain, Murray put on 217 for the eighth wicket with Tom Graveney, looking "every bit as good" as him, according to *Wisden*. Murray batted almost four and a half hours for 112, becoming the second No. 9, after Gubby Allen, to make a Test hundred for England. It was the second time that summer – having played for MCC against the tourists at Lord's – he had taken a century off Hall, Griffith, Sobers and Gibbs. "He was one of the rare people I have seen who could make the hooking of a fast bouncer truly elegant," wrote Tony Lewis. Murray was named a Wisden Cricketer of the Year in 1967.

He was born in North Kensington, the son of a council worker. There were no sports facilities at his school, but a local boys' club, sponsored by Rugby School, gave him a route into cricket, football and boxing. He came to the attention of Arsenal, signing as an

THE WICKETKEEPER'S DOUBLE

1,000 runs and 100 dismissals in a season:

	Runs	HS	100	Avge	Dis	Ct	St	Year
L. E. G. Ames (Kent)	1,919	200	4	35.53	122	70	52	1928
L. E. G. Ames (Kent)	1,795	145	5	35.90	128	79	49	1929
L. E. G. Ames (Kent)	2,482	180	9	57.72	104	40	64	1932
J. T. Murray (Middlesex)	**1,025**	**120**	**1**	**19.71**	**104**	**82**	**22**	**1957**

amateur, and Middlesex, who offered him a place on the staff at 14. To his dismay, the school-leaving age was raised, and he had to wait a year. He was a batsman who bowled, until the regular wicketkeeper broke a finger, and Murray took over. He had little coaching – and proved a natural.

One morning in 1953, his father was dumbstruck to open the door to Tommy Lawton, the great England centre-forward who was then player–manager of Brentford. John was offered professional terms, but opted for cricket. He had made his debut in May 1952, aged 17, at Grace Road, replacing the injured Leslie Compton – and dropped Maurice Tompkin, who went on to a hundred. His first victim was Gerald Smithson, caught off Jack Young. But Murray's progress was held up by national service, and he had to wait until 1956 to become Compton's permanent successor.

Despite a team of stellar names, Middlesex were usually also-rans in the Championship. "Until Bill [Edrich] and Denis [Compton] finished in about '58, we never set out to win a Championship," Murray told the writer John Stern. He would never win a trophy – a lasting regret – and Middlesex lost both one-day finals in his farewell season. "Titmus always blamed me," Murray recalled. "I came here in 1950, and Middlesex had won the Championship in 1949. I left in 1975, and then we won it again in 1976."

Parks and Roy Swetman were given chances to become Godfrey Evans's permanent replacement in the Test side, but in the Ashes summer of 1961 Murray played in all five matches. It was his only full major series. He had to fly home from India the following winter for an operation on varicose veins, and did not regain his place, from Geoff Millman, until the middle of 1962. Alan Smith was his rival in Australia in 1962-63, playing in the first two Tests before Murray returned at Sydney. But in completing a brilliant leg-side catch to dismiss Bill Lawry off Len Coldwell, he injured his shoulder. With England facing defeat, he batted one-handed, and having taken 74 minutes to get off the mark, survived 100 balls in total while making an unbeaten three – in vain. But he did not play again until the First Test of the subsequent series in New Zealand. By 1967, the emergence of Knott signalled the end of Murray's international career; he equalled the

Stooping to conquer: John Murray catches Surrey's Geoff Howarth, at Lord's on May 31, 1975, the day he thought he had broken the record for wicketkeeping dismissals. Roland Butcher and Clive Radley are the slips.

then Test record of six dismissals in an innings, against India, but finished with a pair against Pakistan at Lord's.

And yet, as a batsman he was good enough to score 1,000 runs in a season six times, and 16 hundreds. "People have said he had a laissez-faire approach to batting, but there were plenty of times he dug us out of trouble," said Parfitt. In 1957, he completed a double matched only by Les Ames: 1,000 runs and 100 dismissals. He also opened on occasions (including in a Test in South Africa in 1964-65), but felt that pressure to score runs would undermine his main role. He served as Middlesex vice-captain under Titmus and Parfitt; when he took charge, he was a bold, attacking leader.

Murray was 40 when he retired at the end of the 1975 season. "He had strong views," said Mike Brearley. "He thought cricket should be played attractively, and the umpire's decision respected. He had a London spontaneity about him. He was charming, genial, interesting and lively." Murray had already begun his new career, selling squash courts for a company run by the cricket promoter Derrick Robins; later, he worked for Slazenger. He was an England selector, but resigned when Roger Tolchard's batting earned him a place as Bob Taylor's deputy on the 1978-79 Ashes tour. Murray believed in choosing the best wicketkeeper.

He had marvellous recall, and was a regular port of call for writers and cricket historians. He had been collaborating on a biography with the author Christopher Sandford. On the day he died, Murray was at Lord's watching Middlesex secure a narrow Championship victory over Warwickshire. He rang his wife to say he had enjoyed the day, and was heading home when he collapsed by the Harris Garden behind the Pavilion.

In 1975, he passed Bert Strudwick's record, set in 1927, for the most first-class dismissals. Even at the time, there was confusion about the record; *Wisden 1976* firmly stated that it was broken in the next match, at Southampton, and on the basis of later corrections to the figures it was at Old Trafford. Murray thought it had happened on the first day of the Championship game against Surrey, on May 31, when – apparently needing three – he took smart catches to remove Geoff Howarth and Younis Ahmed, then a more regulation edge from Dudley Owen-Thomas, all off Tim Lamb. Titmus, who had given one of the umpires a camera at the start of play, recorded the celebrations. Murray remembered: "Dudley Owen-Thomas of KCS Wimbledon and Cambridge University, bowled by the Honourable Timothy Lamb of Shrewsbury School and Oxford University, caught by John Murray of St John's Church of England School, Notting Hill. And Titmus always asked: 'Who's the odd man out?'"

NAPIER, DAVID CHARLES, who died on December 5, aged 85, played 18 matches for Rhodesia over a dozen years. A dual-purpose bowler able to start at a decent pace, then throttle back to send down serviceable spin, he took 28 wickets, but never bettered his four for 39 on debut against Griqualand West at Salisbury in 1954-55. He had little sight in one eye, so played in thick glasses, which hindered his batting – he averaged less than five, with a highest score of 15 not out. He was later a popular manager of the national team.

NAVED CHEEMA, who died on April 4, aged 74, played three first-class matches, spread across 11 years, for three different sides in Pakistan. A medium-pacer, his only two wickets came in his last game, in 1973-74, for Customs against a Karachi Whites side including the 16-year-old Javed Miandad, who made 50. Cheema's brother, Pervez, also played first-class cricket.

NEL, JOHN DESMOND, died on January 13, aged 89. A stylish right-hander, Jack Nel had a rapid ascent to Test cricket: after only three first-class matches – and a highest score of 42 – he was thrust into the South African team for their home series against Australia in 1949-50. It was a tough assignment. Although 21-year-old Nel was a good player of fast bowling, he was up against the world's most potent new-ball attack in Ray Lindwall and Keith Miller. And his selection raised hackles locally, as he was preferred to the popular Bruce Mitchell who, aged 40, had made a painful 69 from 102 balls against the tourists just before the First Test. Nel played in all five matches of the series, starting at No. 3 and later opening, but managed only 139 runs at 15, with a best of 38; Australia won 4–0.

He finally completed a first-class century in January 1952, making 139 and putting on 173 with Clive van Ryneveld for Western Province against Transvaal; later that year, he added a career-best 217 not out against Eastern Province. But his work as a quantity surveyor started to intrude, and he played little first-class cricket, though he did hit 110 in November 1957 against Natal, whose captain Jackie McGlew was also in charge of the Test side. Nel was recalled to face the Australians in the First Test at the Wanderers, but failed twice and was dropped for good; he made only two more first-class appearances. In later life he combined business with occasional stints behind the microphone as a summariser for South African radio at Newlands.

OAKMAN, ALAN STANLEY MYLES, who died on September 6, aged 88, was at home in Hastings one July evening in 1956 when a policeman popped by with an urgent message from England's chairman of selectors. Gubby Allen had enlisted the Sussex constabulary after discovering Oakman was not on the phone. Tom Graveney was injured, and Oakman was needed at Old Trafford for the Fourth Ashes Test. He gathered his kit, and drove north to take his place in cricket history.

Stationed in the leg trap, he had a close-up view as Jim Laker collected 19 for 90, the greatest figures in first-class history. He took five catches and, thanks to the television and newsreel commentaries, became for ever linked with Laker's achievement. "When Jim and I met up afterwards, he would always say: 'Are you still living off those five catches?'" They were just as well: Oakman had been given only eight overs in Australia's second innings, and made ten from No. 7. His second Test was his last – there were no more visits from the Hastings police. He was the final survivor of the England team from Old Trafford.

But Oakman was not the sort to dwell on his thwarted career. As an opening batsman and prolific off-spinner, he was a significant figure at Sussex: ninth on their all-time list of appearances, 11th for runs, 17th for wickets – and second for catches by a non-wicketkeeper. After leaving Hove, he coached Warwickshire, winning the Championship in 1972. The next quip was never far away: Keith Cook, then Warwickshire's membership secretary, said Oakman could make you laugh while proof-reading the fixture list.

He had joined Sussex straight from school in 1947, initially as a bowler, and made his debut that summer, aged 17. His second wicket, on his second appearance, earned a "well bowled" from his victim, Denis Compton. But it was not until 1950 that Oakman had a run of games, and not until 1951 that he was established. The following season, he took

Making history: Alan Oakman catches Keith Miller at Old Trafford in 1956. Tony Lock, who took the only wicket that evaded Jim Laker, folds his arms at leg gully.

S&G/PA Photos

83 wickets at 27, including a hat-trick against Somerset at Hove. And after working assiduously on his batting, he passed 1,000 runs for the first time. Gradually, he moved up the order, and became a regular opener.

At 6ft 6in, with a mop of blond hair, he was hard to miss. "As a batsman he was steady," said team-mate Jim Parks. "With his height he had a long reach, which meant he was strong driving off the front foot." His best year with the ball was 1954, when a late-summer purple patch took him to 99 wickets at 20, including a career-best seven for 39 against Glamorgan at Eastbourne. "He was interesting to keep to, because he really made it bounce on hard wickets, and he was quite a big spinner of the ball," said Parks.

Early in 1956, Oakman underlined his potential by making 80 for MCC against a strong Australian attack at Lord's. He was called up for the Third Test at Headingley and, batting at No. 3, was not overawed. After Colin Cowdrey was dismissed by Ron Archer in the fourth over, he was surprised to find the new boy passing him before he was halfway back to the pavilion. "There was this great, lanky chap strolling out to the middle, as unconcerned as though he was walking down a Sussex country lane." But Oakman made just four in England's only innings, and didn't bowl.

He was dropped for Old Trafford, only for Graveney's finger injury to grant him another chance. Despite his reputation as a sharp close catcher, he started at mid-on. Accounts vary as to whether it was David Sheppard, concerned about his own reflexes, or Laker who suggested a switch. Either way, Oakman was soon standing perilously close at short square leg. "Jim was so accurate that you didn't worry too much, particularly on that pitch," Oakman recalled. "I fielded closer than usual, and I knew I didn't have much chance of being hit. Keith Miller said to me: 'Oakie, that's a dangerous position. If I middle it, they will have to carry you off.' Three balls later he pushed forward and I caught him low by my ankle." Miller was his second catch of the first innings, following Ken Mackay; in the second, he caught Colin McDonald, Mackay again, and Archer. His record of five catches off the same bowler has been surpassed only by Mahela Jayawardene's six off Muttiah Muralitharan for Sri Lanka against Pakistan at Peshawar in 1999-2000.

That winter, Oakman was chosen to tour South Africa, but did not play in the Tests, and suffered a serious back injury which meant he missed most of the 1957 season. He retired in 1968 after 497 first-class appearances for Sussex, spent one year on the first-class umpires list, and in 1972 took charge of the one-day international against Australia at Edgbaston, stepping in at the last minute, when Arthur Fagg was unwell. At the same ground in 1973, he walked out alongside Dickie Bird on the third morning of the Test against West Indies, after Fagg refused to take the field in protest at verbal abuse from Rohan Kanhai; Fagg appeared at the end of the first over.

Oakman became a much-loved figure at Warwickshire, especially as Second XI coach. "He was a great encourager," said Bob Willis. "So many of the players he fostered helped us win the Sunday League in 1980. He instilled a positive attitude and ferocious fielding. Handling a Second XI was a difficult balancing act – not allowing the youngsters to be affected by the cynicism of the old pros who are out of the first team." In a eulogy at his funeral, John Claughton, one of his former players, said: "He created a team and a culture and a world in which we all felt we belonged. We loved playing for him, and one of the reasons was that he behaved like a dashing, slightly untrustworthy uncle taking his teenage nephews on an outing."

OSLEAR, DONALD OSMUND, who died on May 10, aged 89, had a short but eventful career as an international umpire. His five Tests included two of in Botham's Ashes series in 1981, while the 1983 World Cup match between England and Pakistan – one of his eight one-day internationals – had him wrestling a streaker.

But it was a match in 1992 in which he was not in the middle that earned Oslear lasting fame – and two appearances in court. At the tail-end of a rancorous summer, England's one-day international against Pakistan at Lord's had been extended by rain into a second day. The umpires, John Hampshire and Ken Palmer, believed Pakistan's bowlers had tampered with the ball. At lunch, they showed it to Oslear, the third umpire, and match referee Deryck Murray. The ball was changed. Pakistan won a thrilling victory, but the ICC announced no action would be taken. Oslear's typically thorough report was quietly shelved.

The issue of how Wasim Akram and Waqar Younis achieved prodigious reverse swing had been rumbling for weeks. In the *Daily Mirror*, Allan Lamb – in his final season as an England batsman – fuelled the flames by accusing them of roughing up one side of the ball, and suggested that Sarfraz Nawaz, his former Northamptonshire team-mate, had invented the method. Sarfraz sued Lamb for libel, and in 1993 the case was heard. In court, Oslear said: "In my opinion it is not possible to scour the ball like that by legal means."

The case was dropped, but the story would not go away. Three years later, Oslear was back in court when Lamb and Botham sued Imran Khan for libel, after he said they were ill-educated and had made racially motivated remarks about him. Oslear duelled with the ferocious libel lawyer George Carman, correcting him for calling him a referee, and pointing out that cricket had laws not rules. By then, Oslear's career was over. He had been forced to retire at the end of the 1993 season, blaming the bad publicity from the ball-tampering row. But the TCCB insisted he had been told months earlier that he would be retiring around his 65th birthday. "I had to admire Don Oslear for giving evidence," wrote Lamb, "because I knew what pressure had been put on him by the TCCB."

Oslear was born in Cleethorpes and worked as a quayside filleter in his father's fishing business. He was reserve goalkeeper for Grimsby Town under the management of Bill Shankly, although not in the Football League. He also played cricket for Cleethorpes and, after discovering a talent for umpiring club games in Lincolnshire, set about moving up the ladder: "I was never remotely good enough." He joined the umpires list in 1975, and was appointed to the international panel five years later, earning the respect of the players. Some, however, thought his inflexibility stemmed from not having played the game: Henry Blofeld called him a "highly tiresome stickler for the rules".

The seeds of the 1992 dispute had been sown the previous summer, when he reported Surrey for altering the condition of the ball in matches in which Waqar was bowling. He was open with reporters about what he had done, and criticised the TCCB for taking no action. Nor did he endear himself to the board when, in 1993, on the introduction of coloured clothing in the Sunday League, he walked out at Grace Road in the new blue umpires' jacket carrying a few bottles and crying "Milko".

The cheek of it: Don Oslear with a milk carrier at Leicester in 1993. Ten years later, he grapples with a streaker at Manchester, to the amusement of Pakistan's Sarfraz Nawaz. The photographer at Leicester was David Munden, whose obituary appears on page 218.

Oslear wrote *Tampering with Cricket* with Jack Bannister, and *The Wisden Book of Cricket Laws* with Don Mosey; in the introduction, Colin Cowdrey called him "the most committed and dedicated umpire in the game". The fate of the ball that had been changed at Lord's remained a subject of conjecture. Many assumed it was locked in a filing cabinet in the Pavilion, never to be seen again. In fact, it was on Oslear's mantelpiece in Cleethorpes.

PALMER, ROLAND JOHN, died on February 25, aged 82. Johnny Palmer was the regular opening bowler for the Sidmouth club in Devon for 40 years, taking around 2,000 wickets. He reached 1,000 in 1967 but, said his wife, "stopped counting when he got to 1,500". John Harris, later a first-class umpire, captained Sidmouth, and recalled: "He bowled a good length at a decent pace and he bowled it straight – if the batsman missed there was a good chance Johnny would hit."

PEARCE, MICHAEL LUPTON, who died on October 7, aged 88, was a familiar sight in the Oval press box, providing statistical nuggets to grateful reporters. In 1946, he became a junior member at The Oval, and in 1948 witnessed Don Bradman's final Test innings. An actuary, Pearce was a founding member of the Surrey Cricket Research Group, and later became The Cricket Society's bibliographical officer, assisting E. W. Padwick with his monumental 1977 *Bibliography of Cricket*.

PHILLIPS, EDWARD JOHN, died on January 9, aged 84. Ted Phillips was a talented striker, known for his powerful shooting, who was part of the Ipswich Town team managed by Alf Ramsey which won the Football League in 1961-62, the year after winning the Second Division. He scored a club-record 46 goals in 1956-57, and 28 in the title-winning season. Phillips was also a useful cricketer who played for the Colchester & East Essex club, and for Suffolk. An inveterate joker, he began the second day of a Minor County game against Nottinghamshire Seconds by bowling a bright red apple; the umpires reported him to Lord's. "Suffolk captain Bob Cunnell had some explaining to do," said the *East Anglian Daily Times*, "but what chance had he of controlling Ted when the task even proved beyond Alf Ramsey?"

PITHEY, DAVID BARTLETT, who died on January 21, aged 81, was a parsimonious Rhodesian off-spinner who played eight Tests for South Africa in the 1960s. Five also featured his older brother Tony, a batsman; and a rather more celebrated fraternal combination, Graeme and Peter Pollock. After going wicketless in his first three matches, in Australia in 1963-64, Pithey opened his account when the team moved on to New Zealand, and had match figures of seven for 64 in a damp draw at Dunedin. He played two further Tests at home in 1966-67, against Australia, but failed to take a wicket. Oddly, his best first-class figures – seven for 47 – had come in what *Wisden* called a "devastating spell" against the Australians for Oxford University in 1961. According to *The Times*, "he perplexed the batsmen with his command of length and judicious use of off-spin".

Pithey had come to prominence at Oxford, although he missed a Blue in 1960, his first summer, because of injury (he did win one for hockey). After leaving university he played a few matches for Northamptonshire in 1962 – and appeared in the last Gentlemen v Players match at Lord's – before returning home and rejoining Rhodesia. He also had seasons with Natal, winning the Currie Cup in 1966-67, and Transvaal.

Like his brother, Pithey was serious-minded. His humour was probably not improved when, in January 1958, he was stranded on 99 and denied a maiden hundred as Rhodesia's last three batsmen all made ducks against North Eastern Transvaal. He made them pay nearly five years later with a career-best 166, one of his three centuries.

POPE, ANTHONY VARDY, died on November 6, aged 84. Tony Pope never rose to the cricketing heights of his father, Alf, or uncle George, who both made over 200 appearances for Derbyshire and featured in their only Championship-winning side, in 1936. But he was a club cricketer for around 60 years, mainly for Alvaston & Boulton; he also played 522 matches for MCC, taking 813 wickets with his deceptive slow left-armers. "Young players would walk past his tweakers like lemmings," said a team-mate. An engineer, Pope claimed to have had the idea, now widely used, of switching sightscreens to advertisements when the bowling was at the other end.

PRETLOVE, JOHN FREDERICK, who died on April 1, aged 85, was indispensable during Kent's all-too-frequent crises in the 1950s. He may have been a Cambridge-educated amateur, but he was no dilettante: Pretlove relished a battle. He first played for Cambridge in 1954, leading the averages with 779 runs at 38, and hitting four hundreds. Against an Essex attack led by Trevor Bailey, he made 137. *Wisden* approved: "A left-handed bat, rather small in stature, he scored many runs with a brilliantly crisp, almost square, cut which showed perfect timing." He was less successful the following summer, but did produce one notable all-round performance: against Middlesex at Fenner's, he scored a hundred and took nine wickets with his left-arm spin. His potential was underlined with a hundred in the Varsity Match.

Pretlove was born in Herne Hill, south London, and played for Surrey Amateurs and the Second XI in 1954. But he qualified by residence for Kent and was offered the role of assistant secretary – a common device to pay amateurs. By chance, his Championship debut, straight after the 1955 Varsity Match, was at The Oval, where he ran into hostility from both sides. To mutterings from his team-mates, he had replaced Alan Dixon, a popular professional with a family to support; and when he walked out to bat, the Surrey fielders greeted him with "Here comes the traitor." In his final year at Cambridge he played less often, but still led the averages, with 409 at 40.

His best year for Kent was 1957, when he passed 1,000 runs for the only time. By now he had won over the professionals. "If we were in a tight spot, I would put money on him getting his team-mates out of it," said Derek Ufton. Perhaps sensing his career would be short, Pretlove then changed his style. "I was a poker and a pusher," he said. "I took to

Starting out: the Alleyn's first team from 1947 numbers John Pretlove (back row, far left) and Micky Stewart (front row, second from right).

using a long-handled bat and whacking the ball straight over the bowler. I remembered what my schoolteacher used to say: 'It's the most undefended part of the ground.'" He used the long handle to good effect in a memorable victory over Surrey at Blackheath, leading an all-out attack on Peter Loader and Tony Lock.

Pretlove was also in good form in 1959, but in July opted to join an all-amateur MCC tour of Canada and the United States, and did not play for Kent again – though he made four more first-class appearances for MCC. He contemplated becoming a professional, but decided to pursue a career in sales and marketing in the building industry. He was Kent's president in 1999.

The son of a hardware-shop owner, Pretlove attended Alleyn's School, where he became good friends with Micky Stewart, and was best man at his wedding. He was an outstanding sportsman – captain of the cricket XI in his final year, and a left-winger in the football team. At Cambridge he won two football Blues and also played for Pegasus and Corinthian-Casuals. But it was at Rugby fives that he excelled. He won the public-school singles title twice, the national amateur singles title four times, and the doubles title seven times; Dennis Silk, later the TCCB chairman, was a regular partner. The fives courts at Alleyn's are named after him.

On arrival at Canterbury in 1955, he filled out a form to join the Band of Brothers, Kent's famed nomadic amateur team, but discovered that his background of Alleyn's and Cambridge cut no ice. "I'm sorry John, but your father's in trade."

PROUTON, RALPH OLIVER, who died on September 12, aged 92, was Hampshire's regular wicketkeeper in 1952, after the retirement of Neil McCorkell and before the long-serving Leo Harrison settled in. Exactly half the Southampton-born Prouton's 52 first-class appearances came that summer: he was a safe catcher standing back to Derek Shackleton and Vic Cannings, and finished the season with 59 dismissals. He managed only 357 runs, although that did include an unbeaten 51 in a last-wicket stand of 117 with Reg Dare – who made his only century – against Worcestershire at Portsmouth. His highest score of 90 came the following season, against Leicestershire, but by then Harrison – a better batsman – was in favour. Prouton was also a useful footballer, playing 13 league games for Swindon after a spell on Arsenal's books. He took up umpiring, and stood in numerous Minor County matches between 1957 and 1969.

PUNJABI, PAPAN RAMCHAND, died on February 25, aged 89. Ram Punjabi was an umpire from Hyderabad who officiated in 37 first-class matches in India, including seven Tests between 1978-79 and 1981-82, as well as two one-day internationals. Sunil Gavaskar scored 107 in Punjabi's first Test, and 172 in his last. But three Indians received what they thought were poor decisions in that game, as did England's captain Keith Fletcher – who was disciplined after gently knocking off the bails on being adjudged caught behind – and Punjabi was not called on again.

RAJINDER PAL, who died on May 9, aged 80, was a tireless Indian seamer who had a long first-class career, mainly for Delhi and North Zone. On often unresponsive pitches, he took 337 wickets at 21, including eight for 27 for Southern Punjab against Jammu & Kashmir at Srinagar in 1966-67. Three years earlier he won his only Test cap, against England at Bombay, apparently at the request of the captain, Tiger Pataudi. The experiment was not a success: he bowled 13 overs without a wicket, and never played again, partly because he later fell out with Pataudi. Rajinder, who represented Haryana towards the end of his career, was credited there with broadening Kapil Dev's repertoire after taking up coaching. "He taught me inswing in three weeks," said Kapil. "I was told by old-timers that he was one of the finest new-ball bowlers, but unfortunately did not get the kind of exposure he deserved." His brother, Ravinder Pal, also played for Delhi: they opened the bowling together in one match in 1964-65, then the following season – after Rajinder had moved to Southern Punjab – shared 15 wickets in the game on opposite sides.

REID, JAMES JEFFREY, died on September 27, aged 91. Born in Blackburn, Jim Reid was a consistent scorer for East Lancashire over 16 seasons from 1942. He made a century against Haslingden in 1950, two years after hitting 104 for Lancashire's Second XI against Cheshire. Around this time he was apparently asked to play for the county's first team, but declined as he was making more money in the leagues. He wasn't asked again. "He never said so, but I think he always regretted it," said his son, John. In 1957, the Reids moved to California, where Jim immersed himself in the cricket scene. He represented the USA in the annual match against Canada five years running from 1963, captaining them to victory in 1966. At the time he was skippering a Pasadena side which sometimes included Mike Brearley, who was undertaking postgraduate research at a nearby university. Reid later became president of the USA Cricket Association, while John played for the United States in the ICC Trophy.

SCOTT, HUGH WILSON, died on April 17, aged 90. A well-built seamer, Wilson Scott forced his way into the Ireland side in 1958 with figures of 26–15–27–5 in the annual North v South match in Belfast. He played four times for the national team, taking five wickets in two games against the New Zealand tourists, but all four were badly affected by rain, including his only first-class appearance, against Scotland. He was Ireland's oldest cricketer when he died.

SHAHID ASHRAF DAR was shot dead by Indian troops during a protest in Drubgam, in southern Kashmir, on April 30. He was 28. Two others who died were known militants, but Shahid was described as a "stone pelter", with five previous public-order offences, and was apparently caught in crossfire. Over a thousand mourners attended the funeral of a man the *Kashmir Reader* said was "a brilliant cricketer who led his team to victories in several tournaments".

SHARMEEN KHAN, who died of pneumonia on December 12, aged 46, was one of the pioneers of women's cricket in Pakistan. She and her sister, Shaiza, decided to establish a national side after they watched the 1993 women's World Cup final at Lord's – and did so, in the face of indifference and occasional opposition from the Pakistan authorities. Sharmeen herself played in Pakistan's first two Tests, against Sri Lanka and Ireland: fittingly, she bowled their first delivery, and soon took their first wicket. She also appeared in 26 one-day internationals, including the 1997-98 World Cup in India, and was a playing member of MCC.

SHAW, JOHN HILARY, who died on August 5, aged 86, was a nephew of the Australian captain Lindsay Hassett, and like him was educated at St Joseph's College in Geelong. The writer Ray Robinson spotted similarities in their batting, and suggested Shaw "give freer rein to his well-timed strokes". He first played for Victoria in 1953-54, but was set back a couple of years later after being hit on the temple by a Pat Crawford bouncer against New South Wales. He recovered to exceed 500 runs in each of the next four Sheffield Shield seasons, but his only representative call was for a trip to New Zealand in 1959-60 (with no Tests, it would now be considered an A-team tour). Shaw's first-class career ended at the MCG on Boxing Day 1960 when, having scored 56, he trod on his stumps after being hit under the right eye by Western Australia's Des Hoare.

SHEHADIE, SIR NICHOLAS MICHAEL, AC, OBE, who died on February 11, aged 91, enjoyed a long political career after playing 30 rugby internationals for Australia. Later, when president of the Australian union, he was a major advocate of the rugby World Cup, which finally came to pass in 1987. His two-year term as Lord Mayor of Sydney included the official opening of the Opera House by the Queen in 1973. Five years later, he was invited to become a trustee of the Sydney Cricket Ground, and was its chairman from 1990 until retiring in 2001. In his final year, the SCG's Walk of Honour was opened, featuring 33 plaques commemorating former sporting champions – including Shehadie.

SISSONS, THOMAS MICHAEL BESWICK, died on August 24, aged 83. Michael Sissons was a literary agent, associated with the influential PFD agency for over 40 years, representing Margaret Drabble, Max Hastings and Simon Schama – and, according to *The Times*, "enough generals to form a small army". A cricket lover, he chaired MCC's arts and library sub-committee, and ran his own team in Oxfordshire, the Reverend Frederick Pickersgill Memorial XI, named after an imaginary Yorkshire vicar.

SMITH, WILLIAM ALBERT, died on September 18, three days after his 81st birthday. Left-hander Bill Smith was on the fringes of Surrey's first team throughout the 1960s, often filling in when Ken Barrington and John Edrich were on Test duty. He made 103 in only his fifth match, against Gloucestershire at The Oval in June 1963, but managed just one more century in 139 further appearances, against Essex in 1967. Smith's batting might have been unspectacular, but his fielding was not. "He was a brilliant cover point," said team-mate Roger Harman. "We used to say he had elastic hands." By the time Surrey won the title in 1971, Smith was turning out for his native Wiltshire and plying his trade as a carpenter, mixed with some coaching. His son Andy also played for Surrey, and scored 202 not out against Oxford University in 1994; he is now the ECB's cricket operations manager.

STRAUSS, RUTH (*née* McDonald), who died on December 29, aged 46, was the wife of the former England captain Andrew Strauss. He called a halt to a successful spell as England's director of cricket to help nurse her through the final stages of her illness, a rare form of lung cancer which can afflict non-smokers. She was born in Ballarat, and met Strauss when he was playing club cricket in Australia; they married in 2003, and had two sons. Even before her husband became Test captain, she was an important part of the backroom set-up. "It is hard to think any woman has done more for the England men's team behind the scenes, given her ability to tune into everyone's wavelength, which translated into making every new player's wife or partner feel integrated," wrote the former *Wisden* editor Scyld Berry, who came to know the family well while assisting Strauss with his book about England's 2009 Ashes victory.

STRETTON, TERRY KEITH, who died on December 12, aged 65, was a seamer on the fringes of the strong Leicestershire side of the mid-1970s. He played only six first-class matches, the last in 1975 – the year of their first Championship – when, not long after he took eight for 38 for the Second XI against Nottinghamshire, they beat the touring Australians. Stretton took over 400 wickets for the Leicester Nomads club.

Clive Brunskill, Getty Images

Tireless work behind the scenes: Ruth Strauss and husband Andrew, July 2015.

SUBRAMANYAM, PETER, who died on May 4, aged about 83, was a London-based representative of the Indian newspaper *The Hindu*. His various duties included looking after the owners' property and horse-racing interests, and also reporting on cricket: he was a regular in the Lord's press box for more than 30 years from the early 1970s. He played one first-class match, alongside several future Test players, for Indian Universities against the Pakistan tourists at Poona in 1960-61, and dismissed Hanif Mohammad (for 222).

THOMAS, BERNARD WILLIAM, who died on January 12, aged 92, was the England physiotherapist for 17 years and – long before the proliferation of backroom staff – a familiar figure on the Test circuit. On tour, when he was often assistant manager, his duties extended to baggage man, administrator and agony uncle. He was less popular when handing out fines or autograph sheets.

At Auckland early in 1975, he played a vital role in a terrifying incident. When New Zealand No. 11 Ewen Chatfield deflected a Peter Lever bouncer from his glove to his temple, he fell to the floor and lost consciousness. As he lay on the ground, twitching and moaning, the players frantically summoned help. Thomas hesitated: "I was aware I was a guest, and it was a New Zealand Cricket situation." But he raced to the middle, only to learn Eden Park had no resuscitation equipment. He gave Chatfield the kiss of life and ordered an ambulance man to pump his chest. "It's the worst case I have seen, and I never want to see another," Thomas said. "Ewen's heart had stopped beating, and technically that's the sign of dying." In the West Indies in 1980-81, Thomas was in the next room when Ken Barrington suffered a fatal heart attack. Alerted by the shouts of Barrington's wife, Ann, he rushed in, but realised nothing could be done.

Chatfield was stabilised and, still unconscious, taken to hospital. He had a hairline fracture of the skull, but went on to have a successful Test career. "New Zealand didn't even have a physio," Chatfield recalled. "If it hadn't been for Bernard, there's a good chance I wouldn't be around today."

Thomas had become Warwickshire physio in the 1960s, and was first invited to take on the England duties for the 1968-69 tour of South Africa cancelled after the row over Basil D'Oliveira. He earned the respect of the players because of his physical fitness and previous involvement in sport: he coached gymnastics and had represented Great Britain.

He began dealing with cricketers' fitness after setting up the Edgbaston Health Clinic. "It was state of the art for its time," said Bob Willis. "Bernard always had the latest gizmos." And it was successful enough for Thomas to buy a Rolls-Royce with a personalised number plate – EHC 7 – advertising the clinic.

Fitness work was restricted to stretching on the outfield before play, but he was seldom short of injuries to treat. In 1974-75, that meant a succession of broken bones and bruises caused by Dennis Lillee and Jeff Thomson. In Calcutta on Christmas Day 1976, he discovered Keith Fletcher lying on a hotel trolley outside his room, covered by a tablecloth. He had cracked a bone in his ankle while out drinking with Mike Selvey. It was on that tour that Thomas suggested Willis and John Lever put gauze smeared with Vaseline on their foreheads to stop sweat running into their eyes. Although the idea did not work, India were cheaply dismissed twice, and their captain, Bishan Bedi, claimed it had been done to alter the condition of the ball.

In Australia in 1970-71, he became a diplomatic bridge between the poles-apart pair of captain Ray Illingworth and tour manager David Clark. "He always did the rooming list, keeping apart people who were likely to collide," said Willis. "It was vital to get the right mix." Willis credits Thomas with extending his career, and believes others were grateful for his presence: "He was a confidant and a shoulder to cry on for lots of players."

Gerry Armes, *Birmingham Mail*/Popperfoto/Getty Images

Home stretch: Bernard Thomas ensures Warwickshire bowler Bob Willis is ready for the 1979 Edgbaston Test.

THOMAS, HENRY JOHN, who died on November 13, aged 79, was a prominent club cricketer, mainly for Midsomer Norton, in Somerset. A left-hander, he scored centuries in six different decades – the first as a 17-year-old in 1957, and the last in 2000. He played for Somerset Second XI, and for the county Over-50 and Over-60 teams.

TURNBULL, JOHN ASHLEY, who died on February 13, aged 82, was a tall off-spinner from unfashionable Gisborne who caused a stir on his debut for Auckland, over Christmas 1955, with seven for 54 in victory over Central Districts at Eden Park. The following week, he took five for 90 against Canterbury. But a new star had not been discovered: six further first-class matches produced only eight wickets.

TURNER, JOHN NEVILLE, died on April 19, aged 81. Neville Turner spread his talents wide: a barrister and jazz pianist, he was fluent in seven languages, including Latin and classical Greek, and loved football, attending every World Cup from 1986 to 2010. But his greatest passion was first-class cricket (anything shorter than the three-day game, he said, was "a facile perversion of a great art form"). It took him to Tests at 44 different grounds around the world, while he watched first-class matches at over 100. Born in Lancashire, Turner was devoted to the Red Rose, even after he emigrated to Australia in 1965. To gain his full endorsement, you had to know the genealogy of the Tyldesleys, and be able to tell Harry Makepeace from Harry Pilling. In 2010, the historian Bernard Whimpress preserved some of Turner's best writing in *Addicted to the Game: Essays on Cricket*. He was a long-term advocate of the legal protection of children, and had been president of OzChild, the oldest children's charity in Victoria.

ULYATE, CLIVE ANTHONY, who died on March 18, aged 84, was an energetic all-rounder who made his first-class debut for Transvaal in 1955-56 – the only wicket for his seamers was the Test player Trevor Goddard – and three more appearances almost a decade later, scoring 55 for Eastern Province against North Eastern Transvaal at Port Elizabeth. In between, he won seven rugby caps for South Africa at fly-half, including all four Tests against the 1955 British Lions. In the last, at Port Elizabeth, Ulyate scored a try and kicked a penalty as his side won 22–8 to tie the series.

VAN OORDT, GEORGE, who died on October 4, 2017, aged 68, was a seamer who took 56 wickets in 22 matches for Western Province's non-white team, with a best of five for 50 against Eastern Province in 1977-78. He became a noted administrator, and a contractor who repaired club pitches and outfields. Van Oordt was long associated with the Tygerberg club in Cape Town, where Vernon Philander played as a youngster.

VAN RYNEVELD, ANTHONY JOHN, died on August 29, aged 92. Better known as a rugby player in his native South Africa, Tony van Ryneveld appeared in one first-class match, for Oxford University, scoring 50 against the Free Foresters in the Parks in 1947. He died seven months after his younger brother, Clive (see below), who had followed him to Oxford as a Rhodes scholar; they played together in two Varsity rugby matches.

VAN RYNEVELD, CLIVE BERRANGE, died on January 29, aged 89. If Clive van Ryneveld had been an international sportsman and nothing else, his career would have been distinguished enough. As a cricketer, he played 19 Tests for South Africa, captaining them in two series, including a famous comeback against England in 1956-57. In rugby, he appeared in the Five Nations for England while at Oxford University, scoring three tries. But sport wasn't the half of it. As a politician, he helped form a rebel party to oppose apartheid; as a lawyer, he defended black political protesters.

Tall, athletic and languid, van Ryneveld cut a Corinthian figure. He came from a privileged background, but was not blind to the injustices in his homeland. His captaincy was strictly principled. Against Australia at Durban in 1957-58, he refused to run out Neil Harvey after the batsmen stopped, assuming the ball had gone for four. Later in the series, at Port Elizabeth, he withdrew Neil Adcock and Peter Heine from the attack when they ignored his one-bouncer-per-over edict.

For and against: Clive van Ryneveld had played for England at rugby, but in 1951 was part of the South African Test squad to play cricket against England.

Van Ryneveld's ancestors had arrived in southern Africa in 1759, and quickly became involved in government and administration. (The family house, Groote Schuur, was later the official home of the prime minister.) His father, also Clive, played rugby for South Africa, while Jimmy Blanckenberg, an uncle, took 25 wickets against England in 1922-23. Van Ryneveld attended Cape Town's Diocesan College, a mile from Newlands: sport mattered, but he also learned the values that were to guide his later work. The master in charge of cricket was Pieter van der Bijl, who made 125 and 97 in the Timeless Test against England at Durban in 1938-39 (van der Bijl's son, Vintcent, the former Natal and Middlesex fast bowler, was van Ryneveld's godson). An attractive, predominantly off-side batsman, a brilliant fielder in any position, and an occasionally destructive leg-spinner, van Ryneveld clearly had potential. Aged 18, he made his debut for Western Province against Rhodesia in 1946-47, and hit a match-winning unbeaten 90 in the second innings. Later in 1947, he left Cape Town for Oxford, after earning a Rhodes scholarship to University College.

He read law, although the college, said van Ryneveld, was "tolerant of students whose sporting activities were time-consuming". He went straight into the Oxford XV, appearing in the first of three Varsity Matches (he missed five penalties), and played cricket in 1948, taking on Bradman's Invincibles – though not Bradman – and claiming seven for 57 as Oxford won the Varsity Match at Lord's. By tradition, the captain for the following summer was elected after the second day: with the support of the colonial players, van Ryneveld won.

A dashing centre with superb hands and a lethal burst of pace, against Cambridge at Twickenham in December he ran almost the length of the pitch for a try that entered the fixture's folklore. He came through England trials for the Five Nations, and played in all four matches. "I don't think they worried too much about qualifications then," he said. "I certainly didn't quibble." He had to bring his own shorts – and hand back his shirt after each game. Team talks were restricted to a visit from the RFU president: "Tackle hard, chaps." On his 21st birthday, he scored two tries against Scotland at Twickenham, earning a gentle rebuke from *The Times* for diving over the line "in the manner of the storybooks".

He became Oxford cricket captain in 1949, when they beat four counties and the New Zealanders – the tourists' only defeat of the summer. Van Ryneveld scored a hundred against Worcestershire, and his fielding was electrifying. "He took horizontal catches at mid-on and mid-off that only a rugby player could have taken," said team-mate Derek Henderson. *Wisden* praised his "spirited" captaincy. Oxford were strong favourites for the Varsity Match, but lost by seven wickets. Selected for the Gentlemen against the Players at Lord's, he top-scored in the second innings with 64. But he wanted to do well in his finals, so ruled himself out of the 1950 Five Nations. Exams also meant little cricket, though he did take five for 78 against Cambridge.

Back home, he resumed his career with Western Province, returning to England with South Africa in 1951. He struggled on damp pitches, but hit a career-best 150 against Yorkshire at Bramall Lane, and a Test-best 83 at Headingley. There, he took his only Test wicket of the tour – Len Hutton, bowled playing for non-existent turn. That year, he was admitted to the Cape Bar, and had just established his legal practice when the squad for Australia and New Zealand in 1952-53 were selected. To his later regret, he declined the chance to be Jack Cheetham's vice-captain.

Such were the demands of work that he made only three first-class appearances between the England tour and the First Test against New Zealand at Durban in December 1953, yet still topped South Africa's series averages, with 234 runs at 46. Although he did not tour England in 1955, he was chosen for the eagerly awaited series against Peter May's team in 1956-57. An hour before the start, at Johannesburg, Jackie McGlew withdrew with a shoulder injury, propelling van Ryneveld into the captaincy. South Africa were soundly beaten, and lost again after McGlew returned for the Second Test. By the Third, van Ryneveld was back in charge, but had already told the selectors he was soon to be married and would miss the final two matches. With McGlew ruled out, he was persuaded to change his mind, and the newly-weds ended their honeymoon early. By way of compensation, the board flew his wife to Johannesburg to watch the Fourth Test, although she could not stay in the same hotel as her husband.

The Third had been drawn, before Hugh Tayfield's 13 wickets got South Africa back into the series at the Wanderers, where he and van Ryneveld were carried off by jubilant spectators. Then, on a shocking pitch at Port Elizabeth, against an injury-hit England, they made it 2–2. "We were lucky to draw the series," van Ryneveld wrote later.

By the time Ian Craig's Australians toured the following year, he had been elected to the South African parliament as an MP for the United Party, who opposed the brutal legislation of H. F. Verwoerd's ruling National Party. Van Ryneveld's constituency in East London was 600 miles from his home but – despite maintaining his legal practice – he declared himself available for selection. "Frankly, I hadn't made 50 runs before the Tests started," he said. "That's no way to take on the Australians." He missed the drawn First Test with a hand injury, but took charge for the next four, three of them lost heavily. It was in the last that he withdrew Heine and Adcock, to their disgust (though Adcock later forgave him). Van Ryneveld had been influenced by seeing New Zealand's Bert Sutcliffe hit by Adcock in 1953-54, and struck a pre-series agreement with Craig, though he later felt he could have allowed more liberal use of the short ball. He made just two more first-class appearances, almost five years later.

Van Ryneveld was one of 11 United MPs who felt the party too weak in their opposition to apartheid. They resigned en masse to form the Progressive Party, but in 1961 all but one (Helen Suzman) lost their seat at a general election, and van Ryneveld returned to the law in Cape Town. In 1962, he co-defended five black protesters charged with instigating a march that led to violent riots in Paarl. Three were sentenced to death. Van Ryneveld called the judgment "an awful indictment of the system".

His sporting status did not prevent him falling foul of the authorities. After finding legal work elusive, he went into merchant banking. In 1970, the broadcaster Charles Fortune asked him into the commentary box at a Test match, but was swiftly told to withdraw the invitation: "We can't have that Prog on air. Make an excuse."

In 2012, the Newlands CEO André Odendaal began staging reunions of former players on the field during the New Year Test: van Ryneveld was among the first to hold the Western Province flag. "He was one of a few prominent figures from the old racial cricket Establishment who wasn't dragged whingeing and complaining into the new order after unity and democracy," said Odendaal. "He displayed integrity and his characteristic old-world gentlemanly respect and humility to the end."

WADEKAR, AJIT LAXMAN, died on August 15, aged 77. In the second over of the final morning of the decisive Oval Test in August 1971, with India 97 from a first series victory in England, Ajit Wadekar hesitated while attempting a single, and was run out. It left his side three down. Wadekar returned to the dressing-room, lay on a bench, and fell asleep. As he dozed, his team carved a niche in the history of Indian cricket: he was woken to be told they had won by four wickets.

Earlier in the year, under his quietly authoritative captaincy, India had won a series for the first time in the West Indies. Now they had shrugged off decades of deference and defeats to win in England. Eighteen months later, they beat them at home to complete a memorable hat-trick: almost 40 years after their first Test, India had announced themselves on the world stage. Wadekar was fortunate to inherit a group purged of factionalism by his predecessor, Tiger Pataudi. He also came armed with the greatest spin-bowling arsenal the game had seen and, in the Caribbean, was stiffened by the emergence of Sunil Gavaskar. He was cool under pressure and tactically sharp, while a new emphasis on close catching benefited the spinners. "I thought, if I am going to prove to the selectors that they have a proper replacement for Pataudi," he said, "the only way is to start winning, and outside the country."

Wadekar was no prodigy: his father thought the game would distract him from a career in engineering, though he did once present him with a new bat after an impressive algebra result. And he became a cricketer almost by accident. While a student at Elphinstone College in Bombay, he shared a bus journey with future Test player Baloo Gupte, who invited him to be twelfth man for the college team. Wadekar was reluctant, but a match fee of three rupees sealed the deal. His left-handed elegance caught the eye of Madhav Mantri, a former Test wicketkeeper, and his first-class debut for Bombay came in the quarter-final of the 1958-59 Ranji Trophy. In the final, he scored 85 as they beat Bengal. He was soon joined in a powerful line-up by Farokh Engineer, who remembered: "In those days it was more difficult to get into the Bombay team than the India team."

It was the start of 18 Ranji Trophy wins in 19 seasons for Bombay, with Wadekar taking over the captaincy in 1968-69. He owed the launch of his Test career to Mantri, who persuaded Pataudi his batting would be an asset. Wadekar made his debut against West Indies in 1966-67, struggled, and was dropped after one game. Recalled at Madras, he began the second innings on a pair but quickly hit Wes Hall for six and four, and justified Mantri's faith by top-scoring with 67. In England in 1967, despite Pataudi's enterprising leadership, India lost 3–0. But Wadekar finished second in the averages, having hit 91 as India followed on in the First Test at Headingley.

He was dismissed for 99 at the MCG during another whitewash, in Australia in 1967-68, and when the tour moved on to New Zealand he made 328 runs at nearly 47, scoring 143 at Wellington – his only Test century. "He was definitely a much better batsman than his figures suggest," said Bishan Bedi. Wadekar felt his place was in jeopardy for the tour of the West Indies in 1970-71, but instead of the axe he was handed the captaincy. Vijay Merchant, the chairman of selectors, had been left with the casting vote, and opted for Wadekar's calmness ahead of Pataudi's charisma. "He thought Pataudi was too flamboyant," said Engineer.

Leonard Burt, Central Press/Getty Images

Making a point: Ajit Wadekar, captain of the first Indian team to win a Test in England, bats at The Oval in 1971. Brian Luckhurst and Alan Knott are slip and keeper.

Wadekar was with his wife, buying curtains for their new home in the State Bank employees' apartments. When they returned, a crowd of well-wishers and journalists were waiting outside. "My first thought was that some guy in the building had been promoted," he recalled. "Little did I realise that it was me."

India left for the Caribbean weakened by the absence of Pataudi, who had withdrawn, and Engineer, left out because he was not resident in India. And they were still haunted by memories of their previous visit, in 1961-62, when they were thrashed 5–0, and terrorised by Hall and (in a tour game) Charlie Griffith. Wadekar was determined to avoid a repeat. In the first tour match, in Jamaica, he was hit on the hand by pace bowler Uton Dowe, but ignored blood seeping into his glove to make 70. He also introduced a more aggressive approach. In the First Test at Sabina Park, he enforced the follow-on, against the wishes of his batsmen, who wanted more time in the middle as the game headed for a draw. "I went straight to the dressing-room and said it a bit loudly: 'Garry [Sobers], I think you are batting. I am enforcing the follow-on.'" India won the Second Test by seven wickets, their first victory over West Indies at the 25th attempt. Thereafter, quicker pitches were prepared, but India – with Gavaskar averaging 154 and Srinivas Venkataraghavan taking 22 wickets – were not to be denied.

There was an ecstatic welcome at Bombay airport, and an audience with prime minister Indira Gandhi, but many felt the forthcoming trip to England would provide a sterner test of India's new self-esteem. Two key decisions were made: Engineer came out of temporary exile to be Wadekar's vice-captain, and leg-spinner Bhagwat Chandrasekhar was recalled. The Indians won five of their eight warm-up matches before the First Test at Lord's. After beating Hampshire at Bournemouth, they arrived in London to find themselves booked into a fly-blown hotel. Wadekar struck an important blow for *esprit de corps* by successfully demanding better accommodation.

He made another statement on the second day of the match, hooking John Snow fearlessly on his way to 85, the highest score of the Test. "From the moment he came in,

Wadekar mounted a stirring counter-offensive, driving, hooking and cutting," wrote John Arlott in *The Guardian*. Rain ended play on the final afternoon, with India, eight down, needing 38. At Old Trafford, the weather spared them almost certain defeat, so it was 0–0 going to the final Test at The Oval. Again, India struggled, conceding a first-innings deficit of 71, but Chandrasekhar took six for 38 to turn the match in their favour.

It had been a triumph for the undemonstrative leadership qualities Merchant had divined. "He didn't make big speeches and I don't recall him ever giving anyone a big bollocking," said Engineer. The emphasis on fielding proved crucial. "We hardly dropped any catches in the West Indies and in England," Wadekar recalled. "After batting in the nets, I used to get fielding and catching done for one or two hours. I saw to it that the specialist fielders trained properly. I was a good slip fielder and I knew exactly the kind of anticipation and reflexes you require." And he struck up a fruitful relationship with his deputy. "We had a really good rapport," said Engineer. "We did not really have to talk about bowling changes and field placings."

Victory in England increased interest back home, and the visit of Tony Lewis's side in 1972-73 was eagerly awaited. England won the First Test, at Delhi, but India fought back to claim the five-match series 2–1, Chandrasekhar and Bedi sharing 60 wickets. From that high point, Wadekar's fall was swift. On India's return to England in 1974, they were thumped 3–0, including 42 all out at Lord's, and – having led them in their first ODI – he lost the captaincy. An innings defeat at Edgbaston proved his final Test, and he played just one more first-class match. Memories were short: a giant bat erected in Indore to commemorate the 1971 wins was defaced, and stones were thrown at Wadekar's Bombay home. He returned to his career in banking, but in the early 1990s proved a success as India's first permanent head coach, and also had a spell as chairman of selectors. "For me, he was always 'captain'," said Gavaskar. When news of his death reached the Indian touring team in England in 2018, the players wore black armbands during the Third Test at Trent Bridge.

WALMSLEY, PETER GAUNTLETT, who died on April 1, aged 87, led the Norfolk attack in the Minor Counties Championship almost throughout the 1950s. A nippy left-armer, he took 329 wickets at 21, with a best of eight for 40 against Buckinghamshire in 1954; four years later he destroyed Middlesex Seconds with eight for 43. Around this time he was offered terms by Kent, but preferred to concentrate on his career with the Norwich Union, for whose team he once started a club game against Dereham with a hat-trick, and ended the innings with another.

WAPAKHABULO, YONA NAMAWA, who died of a heart attack on August 6, aged 46, was said to be the first Ugandan cricketer to score a double-century – 212 for Kampala's Wanderers club in a league match in 1992 – and was also a handy pace bowler. He was a big hitter who, one team-mate recalled, "was responsible for a surge in repair expenses for some of the nearby buildings". His father had been a government minister, and Speaker of the Ugandan parliament. The president attended Yona's funeral.

WATSON, WILLIAM JOHN, died on December 29, aged 87. New South Wales opener Bill Watson had a rapid rise to international cricket. After making 82 on debut against South Australia in February 1954, he hit 155 in his second match, against Len Hutton's MCC tourists in November. His six-hour innings at the SCG had Bill O'Reilly admiring his cover-drives, "stamped unmistakably with the hallmark of artistry".

With the Ashes already surrendered to England, the slightly built Watson was called up for the final Test. In only his fifth first-class match, he did little in a rain-affected game at Sydney, but was retained for the West Indian tour that followed, where he won three further caps without passing 30. As it turned out, his international career was over at 24, not helped by the scarcity of Tests then (Australia had none at home between his 1954-55 appearance and the 1958-59 Ashes). Watson made a career-best 206 against Western Australia at Perth in 1956-57, after a pep talk from Don Bradman over the breakfast table, and added a match-saving 198 against Queensland later that season, but never quite scored the runs to guarantee him a place in the strong NSW side – they won ten Sheffield Shields out of 11 around this time – let alone the Australian team.

He remained a formidable presence in Sydney club cricket, where he scored over 10,000 first-grade runs in more than 20 seasons, most of them for St George, Bradman's old team. Their star-studded line-up included Test batsmen Norman O'Neill and Brian Booth, who recalled Watson's "amazing ability to pierce the gaps in the field".

Watson worked in, and later managed, the family business at the Sydney Produce Markets, where his early starts caused his team-mates to joke that he had already done a day's work by the time he reported for the cricket. He owed his nickname of "Blinks" to Keith Miller, who forgot his name when presenting the NSW team to the Duke of Edinburgh in 1954, and took his cue from a nervous habit of Watson's.

WEBB, RUPERT THOMAS, who died on August 27, aged 96, was for more than a decade an effervescent presence behind the stumps for Sussex. He was an old-fashioned specialist: he kept with nimble efficiency to the spinners, but never scored a fifty. His first and last victims were stumped: Gloucestershire's Tom Graveney at Bristol in 1948, and Lancashire's Tommy Greenhough at Hastings in 1960.

As well as a useful county cricketer, Webb was a wartime photographer, businessman, photographic model and actor. His third wife was the actress Barbara Whatley, who had allegedly once refused a marriage proposal from Elvis Presley, and he landed a walk-on part in *Four Weddings and a Funeral*. The stories – and there were plenty – flowed until his final days.

Webb grew up amid real hardship in Harrow. He might have gone to university, but had to look for work. He joined Kodak to train as a photographer, and soon found himself in the works cricket team. In 1940, he was due to play for Harrow in a charity match against an XI that included Patsy Hendren, but was switched to Hendren's team and kept tidily to the former England leg-spinner Jim Sims. Afterwards, Hendren sought him out. "If we both survive the war and you still want to play, come and see me."

Colorsport/REX/Shutterstock

Three of the 1954 Sussex team appear in the obituaries. *Standing:* Ted James, Don Smith, Alan Oakman, George Washer (scorer), Ian Thomson, Rupert Webb, Jim Parks and Ken Suttle. *Seated:* Jim Wood, John Langridge, Hubert Doggart, Robin Marlar and George Cox.

Webb served as a photographer in the Navy before returning to Kodak. Though reluctant to give up secure employment, he paid Hendren a visit. "I can't remember your name, but you're a wicketkeeper, aren't you?" Webb spent the summer of 1947 playing for various Middlesex teams. His polish was admired, but he was quietly told that club politics meant he would never displace Leslie Compton. Hendren, by now coaching Sussex, welcomed him to Hove. As Webb prepared for his debut at Bristol, he was approached by his Gloucestershire counterpart, Andy Wilson. "First match? Well, keep down. We always call this a knees-and-ankles wicket." He succeeded Billy Griffith as regular keeper in 1950.

His favourite captain was David Sheppard, who took charge for one summer in 1953. "He always had time for everybody," Webb told the writer Stephen Chalke. "If you had anything on your mind, he'd walk round the ground and listen to you." Under Sheppard, Sussex mounted an unlikely Championship challenge, before finishing second. When they finally won their first title, in 2003, Robin Marlar's celebratory piece in *Wisden* recalled the near miss. "I was personally convinced we were going to win in 1953, until Rupert Webb missed a vital catch behind the stumps at Hastings against Yorkshire," he wrote. "There may be an element of bias here since I was bowling at the time." The batsman was Vic Wilson, who made an unbeaten 84 on the last day to thwart Sussex. Webb was furious. "The batsman got a thick edge and it dropped short of first slip," he said. "I had nothing to do with it. It wasn't even a chance." The *Guardian* report, however, noted that Wilson's "escape at the wicket off Marlar when 65, and the score 172, proved a crucial factor".

Sussex, second, still had 11 matches to make up for any lapse. *Wisden* editor Matthew Engel wrote a mollifying letter to Webb, who was eventually reconciled with Marlar at a Sussex dinner. Webb's career as first-choice wicketkeeper had in fact ended under Marlar's captaincy. Against Yorkshire at Worthing in 1958, Marlar handed the gloves to Jim Parks, and told Webb he was not playing. He appeared intermittently for two more seasons before retiring in 1960. Of his 448 dismissals, sixth on the county's list, 127 were stumped. His top score was 49 not out against Lancashire at Hove in 1955, when he denied Ted James's run-out for denying him a fifty. His benefit in his final summer raised £4,000, but he had to argue not to share it with a team-mate. He was even warned that the split would not be 50–50. "You're more intelligent – you'll have a higher earning potential when you retire."

Webb had a successful career in business, but unexpected opportunities emerged in modelling after his marriage to Whatley. He appeared in ads for *The Independent*, Nestlé and Panasonic; the couple were known as "Rhubarb" by the agencies that booked them. One day, he dropped his wife off at Shepperton, where she was auditioning for a part in *Four Weddings*. She introduced him to the director, Mike Newell: she did not get a part, but he was cast as the father of Henrietta ("Duckface"), played by Anna Chancellor, and led her up the aisle for the final wedding. Scenes in which he had a speaking role were cut, but Webb relished the on-set catering. Other roles included an art dealer in an episode of "French and Saunders", an angry farmer in a Conservative Party broadcast, and a Specsavers advert. He was also involved in a real-life drama when, aged 91, he employed his walking stick to break up a dispute between a motorist and a traffic warden. He was grateful for the arrival of a police car.

WEIR, ROBERT SCOTT, died on October 4, aged 65. Tall and talented, and usually sporting a luxuriant moustache cultivated during his days as an RAF helicopter pilot, Scott Weir played 26 matches for Scotland, four first-class, from 1975. He hit 61 and 102 not out in a Varsity game against MCC at Lord's in 1982. Weir captained Clydesdale to three Scottish Cup wins, and the league title in 1995. Team-mates fondly recalled his answer to criticism of their late arrival for one Sunday friendly: "Look, pal, this game starts whenever we arrive – and finishes whenever we've won."

WELLUM, GEOFFREY HARRY AUGUSTUS, DFC, died on July 18, aged 96. The Schools section of *Wisden* in the late 1930s charted the progress of Geoffrey Wellum at Forest School in Essex. In 1936, he was second in the batting averages, with 233

Derbyshire dash: Chris Wilkins and bat head
north from Heathrow.

Ray Brigden, *Daily Mail*/REX/Shutterstock

runs at 25. The following summer his average
shot up to 47, and he was praised as a "most
consistent opening bat". In 1939, his final
year, he was "as good a captain as Forest has
had for some years". He soon had other
things on his mind – flying Spitfires in the
Battle of Britain. Wellum was 18, the
youngest of "the few" who fought overwhelming odds in the skies over southern
England. His first combat experience came
at Dunkirk, and he recalled being motivated
by a sense of duty, and anger that the Nazis
were trying to shatter English life. "I thought,
'What are you doing over here – you're
interfering with the cricket.' England was a
peaceful place. All I wanted to do was watch
England play Australia at Lord's."

WILKINS, CHRISTOPHER PAUL, died
on October 1, aged 74. When the County
Championship was opened up to instant-
registration overseas players in 1968, the
prize signings were the likes of Garry Sobers,
Rohan Kanhai and Barry Richards. Derbyshire, with less to splash, did not enter the
market until 1970 – and when they did, the
uncapped South African Chris Wilkins was
hardly a household name in Durban, let
alone Derby. But he shook up the County
Ground with superb fielding, useful swing bowling and, particularly, his aggressive batting,
which produced more than 1,600 first-class runs that season. "He was the most successful
newcomer in the history of Derbyshire cricket," enthused *Wisden*. "He gave the batting a
lustre it had never possessed in post-war years."

He had two further successful summers at Derby, crashing a career-best 156 against
Lancashire at Old Trafford in 1971, before returning to South Africa, where he enhanced
his name as a big hitter. He scored well for Eastern Province, then in 1980-81, after
moving to Natal (he eventually ran a farm there), led the Currie Cup run-lists with 595,
just ahead of Jimmy Cook and Allan Lamb. The future international batsman Dave
Callaghan recalled him as a schoolboy hero: "If we knew Eastern Province were batting,
we'd jump on our bikes and ride down to St George's Park to watch Wilkins. He was
incredibly exciting to watch, really ahead of his time. He would have no worry about
trying to hit the first ball of the innings for six if it was there to be hit."

Wilkins was a natural for limited-overs cricket, although it was in its infancy in South
Africa when he was at his peak. He reached 400 one-day runs in each of his three seasons
with Derbyshire, and pummelled a century at home against Orange Free State in 1977-78;
he also dismantled Western Province with five for 40 at Port Elizabeth in 1974-75. And he
would undoubtedly have been a major star in the Twenty20 era. "Viv Richards hit me
back over my head for six once or twice," said the ferocious fast bowler Garth le Roux,
"but the player who tried it most often was Chris Wilkins. He was particularly good at it.
He'd move right back on his stumps and hit straight. This also gave him more time to
hook and pull anything a bit short. He was the most annoying batsman to bowl at."

WINTER, JOHN, who died on April 12, aged 86, was president of the Lancashire League
from 1993 to 1997. He played for Haslingden for 30 years from 1947, scoring 7,659
league runs; a career highlight was opening with Clive Lloyd when he was the club's
professional in the late 1960s.

The obituaries section includes those who died, or whose deaths were notified, in 2018. Wisden always welcomes information about those who might be included: please send details to almanack@wisden.com, or to John Wisden & Co, 13 Old Aylesfield, Golden Pot, Alton, Hampshire GU34 4BY.

BRIEFLY NOTED

The following, whose deaths were noted during 2018, played or umpired in a small number of first-class (fc) matches.

	Died	*Age*	*Main team(s)*
BHAVANARAYANAN, M. G.	29.8.2018	90	Madras

Defensive batsman and handy medium-pacer; eight fc matches, 71 against Ceylon in 1952-53.

| **CAPON**, Stephen | 3.3.2017 | 89 | Kent |

Mote Park seamer; one wicketless fc match, at Nottingham in 1950.

| **DAVIES**, Peter John | 10.3.2018 | 60 | Victoria |

Prolific Waverley batsman; six fc matches, 57 v South Australia at Adelaide in 1981-82.

| **DICK**, Alexander Williamson | 31.1.2018 | 95 | Western Australia |

Perth seamer; one wicketless fc match, against Victoria at the MCG in 1948-49.

| **ENEBERG**, Alfred | 7.11.2016 | 87 | South Australia |

Port Adelaide all-rounder; one fc match, against Western Australia at Perth in 1951-52.

| **HINKSON**, Ernest Stephen | 14.1.2016 | 74 | Barbados |

Fast bowler for Wanderers and Carlton clubs; one fc match, against Guyana in 1973-74.

| **HOBSON**, Barry Sinton | 9.4.2017 | 91 | Cambridge University |

Opening bowler; seven fc games in 1946, including Varsity Match; cricket master at Millfield.

| **HUSKINSON**, Geoffrey Mark Clement | 7.3.2018 | 82 | Free Foresters |

Son of former Nottinghamshire player; one fc match against Oxford University in 1959.

| **ILLMAN**, Brian Keith | 4.8.2018 | 80 | South Australia |

Seamer for Glenelg, where he played with Ian Chappell; six fc matches in 1960-61, 3-5 v Tasmania.

| **JAIRAM**, Hiralal | 25.6.2018 | 84 | Transvaal |

Off-spinner who played eight fc matches for Transvaal's non-white side; 5-57 v Natal in 1971-72.

| **JOHNSON**, Peter Lovell | 11.7.2017 | 90 | Cambridge University |

One fc match v Middlesex in 1947 (scored 19 and 40), and another for Combined Services in 1950.

| **LONGNEY**, Geoffrey Wallace | 26.9.2018 | 83 | Victoria |

Long-serving Melbourne CC wicketkeeper; five dismissals in only fc match, in Adelaide in 1956-57.

| **LYONS**, Rodney Bernard | 19.7.2013 | 89 | Queensland |

Batsman from Cairns; 19 fc matches, 102 on debut, against Victoria at Brisbane in 1955-56.

| **MANVILLE**, David Walter | 26.8.2015 | 81 | Sussex |

Wicketkeeper who made his Second XI debut at 16; three fc matches in 1956.

| **RANGANNA**, Kunigal Srikantia | 10.2.2018 | 85 | Orissa |

Off-spinning all-rounder; 49 and 4-59 against Assam at Gauhati in 1960-61.

| **REID**, Alan Walter | 9.5.2012 | 80 | Queensland |

Wicketkeeper who broke his thumb during only fc match, against Western Australia in 1957-58.

| **RILEY**, John Christopher William | 30.1.2017 | 82 | Cambridge University |

Wicketkeeper from Uppingham who played one fc match in both 1955 and 1956.

| **SHAH**, Rajendra | 28.9.2018 | 68 | Saurashtra |

Left-arm wrist-spinner; two wickets in five fc matches in 1970s. Later a state selector.

| **SHAUKAT ABBAS** | 13.1.2016 | 71 | Sargodha |

Only three fc matches, but scored 103 in the second, against Multan in 1975-76.*

| **WILSON**, Norman Rowley | 28.3.2018 | 87 | Northern Districts |

Stalwart of NZ's Northland region; three wickets in five fc matches as leg-spinner from 1957-58.

| **WORRAD**, Damian Jo Lomax | 31.7.2018 | 43 | Dorset |

Seamer who played in the Minor Counties Championship.

A LIFE IN NUMBERS

	Runs	Avge	Wkts	Avge		Runs	Avge	Wkts	Avge
Aamer Wasim	1,227	14.78	242	26.61	Hill-Wood, P. D.	30	30.00	1	20.00
Arenhold, J. A.	403	10.07	82	27.14	Hofmeyr, M. B.	3,178	44.76	1	11.00
Bailey, J. A.	641	5.82	347	21.62	Jadeja, M. V.	1,373	26.92	1	79.00
Bairamian, R.	45	22.50	1	6.00	Jadeja, P. M.	614	29.23	5	58.40
Barnard, H. M.	9,314	22.07	16	35.18	Jaffey, I. M.	–	–	–	–
Barrett, A. G.	**1,086**	**17.51**	**169**	**31.21**	Kassamali, S.	24	12.00	–	–
Benneworth, A. J.	580	23.20	26	38.92	Kemsley, J. N.	285	20.35	–	–
Bhalekar, R. B.	3,877	39.16	35	44.11	Kowalick, J. P.	0	–	1	88.00
Bhatia, P.	2,548	30.69	36	30.88	**Lewis, D. M.**	**1,623**	**31.82**	–	–
Binns, A. P.	**1,446**	**37.07**	–	–	McHugh, F. P.	179	2.63	276	24.84
Booth, R.	10,134	18.90	0	–	Magiet, S.	2,650	29.12	171	12.99
Bose, G. K.	3,757	30.79	72	26.97	Metcalfe, S. G.	1,200	25.53	9	39.11
Buggins, B. L.	1,192	14.36	1	1.00	Morgan, P. R. L.	1	1.00	0	–
Bunyard, G. S.	192	13.71	48	22.54	**Murray, J. T.**	**18,872**	**23.59**	**6**	**40.50**
Cass, G. R.	4,304	21.84	–	–	Napier, D. C.	75	4.68	28	44.50
Catt, A. W.	3,123	17.25	0	–	Naved Cheema	47	11.75	2	63.50
Clayton, G.	6,154	17.63	–	–	**Nel, J. D.**	**1,839**	**31.70**	–	–
Cobham, M. D.	0	0.00	2	27.00	Oakman, A. S. M.	21,800	26.17	736	27.63
Congdon, B. E.	**13,101**	**34.84**	**204**	**30.02**	**Pithey, D. B.**	**3,430**	**23.33**	**240**	**30.78**
Dagnin, I.	58	8.28	0	–	Pretlove, J. F.	5,115	26.78	43	30.67
Davis, P. V.	276	16.23	–	–	Prouton, R. O.	982	14.44	–	–
Dickinson, T. E.	21	3.50	20	20.95	**Rajinder Pal**	**1,040**	**11.06**	**337**	**21.89**
Dickinson, V. E. J.	308	11.00	54	24.77	Scott, H. W.	–	–	0	–
Doggart, G. H. G.	**10,054**	**31.51**	**60**	**34.28**	Shaw, J. H.	3,276	40.44	1	55.00
Doman, M. E.	483	21.00	13	17.38	Smith, W. A.	5,024	22.42	0	–
Donald, D. L.	930	23.25	0	–	Stretton, T. K.	20	5.00	4	84.50
Doughty, R. J.	845	20.60	89	33.55	Subramanyam, P.	0	–	2	67.00
Drabu, K. H.	422	10.04	–	–	Turnbull, J. A.	78	6.00	22	32.31
Flint, D.	33	4.71	12	38.75	Ulyate, C. A.	110	15.71	5	35.60
Gale, R. A.	12,505	29.35	47	37.19	van Oordt, G.	411	13.70	56	16.01
Gardiner, H. A. B.	1,700	22.97	–	–	van Ryneveld, A. J.	69	34.50	0	–
Gera, A. L.	132	18.85	16	39.43	**van Ryneveld, C. B.**	**4,803**	**30.20**	**206**	**30.24**
Guest, C. E. J.	**922**	**19.20**	**115**	**27.13**	**Wadekar, A. L.**	**15,380**	**47.03**	**21**	**43.23**
Guy, R. H.	92	9.20	25	27.88	Watson, W. J.	1,958	32.09	0	–
Hallebone, J.	1,192	41.10	–	–	Webb, R. T.	2,685	11.72	1	43.00
Harris, A.	1,698	19.29	0	–	Weir, R. S.	187	31.16	–	–
Hill, L. T.	584	18.83	8	51.50	Wilkins, C. P.	10,966	32.63	142	35.30

Test players are in bold; their career figures can be found on page 1360.

Binns made 48 catches and 17 stumpings; Booth 948 and 178; Buggins 148 and 19; Cass 213 and 28; Catt 284 and 37; Clayton 605 and 65; Drabu five and two; Gardiner 137 and 19; Jaffey one and one; Lewis 67 and 11; Murray 1,268 and 259; Prouton 84 and 13; Webb 324 and 129; Wilkins 211 and six.

PART THREE

English International Cricket

THE ENGLAND TEAM IN 2018

Smith's vision takes form

ALI MARTIN

The contrast could scarcely have been greater. England's opening Test of 2018 had concluded with Joe Root downed in the Sydney dressing-room by a bout of viral gastroenteritis that left him incapable of witnessing the final rites of a 4–0 Ashes defeat. Yet by late November he was basking in series wins over India and in Sri Lanka, where England achieved their first 3–0 clean sweep away from home since 1962-63. His team had started to play in his own sparky image.

The last nine of England's 13 Tests of the year yielded eight victories, their best sequence since 11 out of 12 under Michael Vaughan in 2004. It lifted them to second in the rankings. With Eoin Morgan's one-day side claiming top spot in early May, following wins in Australia and New Zealand, and later

ENGLAND IN 2018

	Played	Won	Lost	Drawn/No result
Tests	13	8	4	1
One-day internationals	24	17	6	1
Twenty20 internationals	9	4	5	–

NOVEMBER		
DECEMBER	5 Tests and 5 ODIs (a) v Australia	(see *Wisden 2018*, page 349)
JANUARY		
FEBRUARY	Trans-Tasman T20 tri-series (in Australia and New Zealand)	(page 260)
MARCH	2 Tests and 5 ODIs (a) v New Zealand	(page 269)
APRIL		
MAY	2 Tests (h) v Pakistan	(page 289)
JUNE	1 ODI (a) v Scotland	(page 304)
	5 ODIs and 1 T20I (h) v Australia	(page 306)
JULY		
AUGUST	5 Tests, 3 ODIs and 3 T20Is (h) v India	(page 317)
SEPTEMBER		
OCTOBER	3 Tests, 5 ODIs and 1 T20I (a) v Sri Lanka	(page 359)
NOVEMBER		
DECEMBER		

Oli Scarff, AFP/Getty Images

Out of the box: Sam Curran and Jos Buttler took the Test team by storm.

extending their run of bilateral series triumphs to nine (either side of a shock defeat by Scotland), both teams were well-positioned ahead of a home World Cup and Ashes. Only the Twenty20 side, still used as a proving ground, failed to shine.

The upturn in Root's second year as Test captain owed a little to winning eight successive tosses, but far more to his growing authority and to the willingness of his players to buy into an approach that was bolder and more squad-focused. It was also significant that a new national selector, Ed Smith, was delivering inventive choices: in particular, Jos Buttler returned and was fast-tracked to the vice-captaincy, while Sam Curran made an ebullient arrival.

Neither had been at Sydney, though that game was not rock bottom. Two months later in Auckland, a weary England were torn apart for 58 by Trent Boult, Tim Southee and the pink Kookaburra, having threatened the all-time Test nadir of 26. Defeat prompted frank discussions before the Second Test at Christchurch, where they produced their best showing in five months on the road, but still fell two wickets short of squaring the series.

Root referenced this turning point after the win in Sri Lanka, where England made good on a vow to do things differently in Asia. The XI was packed with all-rounders, yet still included three frontline spinners (who shared 48 of the 60 wickets), while the batsmen were granted licence to attack. At first they did so too liberally: at lunch on the opening day of the series at Galle, England were 113 for five, only to be bailed out by a to-the-manner-born 107 from debutant wicketkeeper Ben Foakes. But a balance was soon found, and a series run-rate of 3.66 met the brief. The attacking elan peaked in the Second Test at Pallekele, led by Root's audacious second-innings 124. Callow opposition did not detract from a watershed tour.

Root was unapologetic about his muse: as a linchpin of Morgan's trend-setting one-day team (for whom he scored back-to-back centuries against India), he had learned the importance of taking, where possible, the positive option. It was noticeable that the Test team appeared fully his only after the retirement of his predecessor, Alastair Cook. That came at The Oval in September, when he signed off with an innings of 147 heavy in emotion and ovation. And while James Anderson and Stuart Broad ploughed on – Anderson passing Glenn McGrath's record 563 Test victims for a seamer with the final wicket of Cook's farewell, Broad flickering upwards after remodelling his action before New Zealand – a new senior core of Root, Buttler and Ben Stokes was now in charge.

Progress was not evident by the start of the summer, when Pakistan exploited seaming conditions to inflict a heavy defeat at Lord's. But England levelled the series in style at Headingley – and Root's run had begun. India, their captain Virat Kohli bristling with intent, were then overcome by a 4–1 scoreline that reflected the hosts' ability to seize the clutch moments.

At Edgbaston and again at the Rose Bowl, Curran rescued a scoreline of 86 for six with a carefree half-century. A third, at Pallekele, also turned a game in England's favour, and contained six of the 14 sixes he hit in his seven Tests, all won. Add 14 wickets at 25 for his bustling left-arm swing, plus the fact that England's sole defeat after his debut came when he was dropped for Stokes at Trent Bridge, and Curran's first year was hugely promising.

If his fearlessness stood out among England's seven Test newcomers in 2018, then Smith's opening gambit after being appointed in April – Buttler's return as a specialist No. 7 – was his truest statement of intent. Having emerged ahead of Andy Flower, Derek Pringle and Mike Selvey from an interview process that required a presentation entitled "Selection: Art or science?", Smith nudged the tiller towards science, placing greater emphasis on analytics, and working on the basis that form can transcend format.

Mainly unfulfilled during 18 previous Tests, and seemingly locked into the gilded cage of white-ball specialism, Buttler had scorched an IPL-record five successive half-centuries, for Rajasthan Royals. The switch from Twenty20's great *tamasha* to Test cricket had an inauspicious start, when he wafted to slip against Pakistan at Lord's. But he soon settled into the task, a string of seven 50-plus scores including a maiden Test century, at Trent Bridge. Versatility summed up Buttler 2.0, never more so than in Sri Lanka: a crucial first-innings 38 in Galle offered stoic defence; 97 across two innings at Pallekele a flurry of sweeps, orthodox and reverse; and a second-innings 64 in Colombo nimble footwork. Buttler delivered the one-day knock of the summer, too. After England had slipped to 114 for eight against Australia at Old Trafford, he made an ice-cool 110 to chase down 206 and complete a unique 5–0 annihilation.

But initial grumbles about his jump from 20-over to five-day cricket were dwarfed when Smith named Adil Rashid – who had paused his first-class career at Yorkshire – in the Test squad to face India. The voices from Headingley were angriest and loudest. England declared that, from now on, players must have a county contract in the corresponding format. And while Rashid had a quiet series against India – save for a couple of magical deliveries,

Stu Forster, Getty Images

Renaissance men? Ed Smith and Trevor Bayliss oversee England's success in Sri Lanka.

to Kohli in the Headingley one-dayer, and K. L. Rahul in the Oval Test – the opprobrium eventually felt worth it: in Colombo, his five for 49, in tandem with a fiery Stokes, helped secure the whitewash.

Even so, Rashid was still the luxury item among the three spinners deployed in that series, with Moeen Ali and Jack Leach claiming 18 wickets apiece to his 12. Leach's summer had been ruined by untimely injuries, but in Sri Lanka he transferred the skills learned on the spinning pitches of Taunton to excellent effect, and always offered control. For Ali, so meek in Australia that he was dropped midway through the tour of New Zealand, it was proof his off-breaks could thrive abroad; he had already underlined his prowess at home with nine Indian wickets during his comeback Test at Southampton.

It was Foakes who emerged as the player of the Sri Lanka series, however, top-scoring and exhibiting the silken glovework many county observers had long purred over. He was originally flown out as cover after Jonny Bairstow twisted an ankle playing football, but England liked what they saw, and Bairstow did not return until the Third Test, despite being fit for the Second. Even then, it was as a specialist No. 3; the century he scored on the first day in Colombo proved a point he didn't want to have to make.

Three months earlier, Bairstow had railed against batting at No. 4 in Southampton, after he had broken a finger, and the gloves passed to Buttler. He had enjoyed two solid years behind the stumps, but many believed his destiny lay higher up the order; after all, in a year in which only Root and Buttler averaged over 40 among the top six, it was not wicketkeepers that were lacking. To highlight the batting shortfall, Bairstow's Colombo hundred was the first in 51 innings by an England No. 3; in 2018 alone, six batsmen were used there.

It was unquestionably a year for the bowlers: eight averaged in the twenties, with the evergreen Anderson outstanding once more, claiming 43 wickets at 22. So much of the focus was on an underperforming top four. Mark Stoneman, James Vince and Dawid Malan, all tourists during the Antipodean winter, were despatched early in Smith's tenure. Ollie Pope, who with Curran, Dom Bess and Mason Crane made it four debutants aged 20 or younger in 2018, struggled at No. 4. Keaton Jennings somehow survived a second chastening home summer, averaging 19 from ten innings, but repaid this faith with an unbeaten 146 at Galle, even if he didn't quite dampen concerns against the new ball; his short-leg fielding, on the other hand, reached unexpected heights.

The strong attacks of Pakistan and India, and a batch of Dukes that moved prodigiously, had made it tough at the top during the summer, with the all-rounders frequently required to post competitive totals. England's depth came to the fore against India at Lord's, where Chris Woakes – a temporary replacement for Stokes – set up victory with a maiden Test century from No. 7.

Stokes was busy answering a charge of affray in Bristol, two days after his four-wicket haul, Kohli included, had polished off India at Edgbaston. He was found not guilty following his part in a brawl the previous September, but the saga did not end there. He and Alex Hales – also present during the incident but not prosecuted – each accepted two disrepute charges at an ECB cricket discipline commission hearing scheduled between tours in December. They received fines, backdated suspensions and warnings as to their future conduct. Stokes publicly apologised and, having previously lost the Test vice-captaincy and missed the Ashes tour, spoke of a lesson learned.

Meanwhile, the ECB were in the final stages of recruiting Ashley Giles as a replacement for Andrew Strauss, who had stepped down as director of cricket in October because his wife, Ruth, was seriously ill; two months later, she died. His decision to prioritise the one-day team under Morgan and head coach Trevor Bayliss continued to pay dividends. Their fourth year of 50-over collaboration saw everyone swept aside bar a Calum MacLeod-inspired Scotland, as England won 17 games from 24 and plundered records. A line-up led by Bairstow's 1,025 runs and strike-rate of 118 made six an over a non-negotiable. Thirteen centuries was England's most in a calendar year, and Jason Roy's 180 at the MCG a national record.

Such was their strength that Hales, the previous record-holder, felt an overqualified reserve at times (Roy had pinched his place after Bristol). But his 147 at Trent Bridge, plus 139 from Bairstow, shattered England's own world-record total by taking a barbaric 481 for six off Australia. In their first series since the sandpaper affair, the Australians were no match for England, who found a greater challenge from India and, before securing a 2–1 win, had to decode the left-arm wrist-spinner Kuldeep Yadav. When Sri Lanka were despatched 3–1 in a soggy October series, Bayliss revealed he was already using the phrase "World Cup favourites" to reduce its impact.

There was an irony to all the cross-format success. Strauss had begun his job in 2015 espousing the need for a greater separation of the Test and one-day teams. By the end of his tenure, they had seldom felt closer by way of personnel, style or results.

ENGLAND PLAYERS IN 2018

LAWRENCE BOOTH

The following 35 players (there were 33 in 2017, and 32 in 2016) appeared in 2018, when England played 12 Tests, 24 one-day internationals and nine Twenty20 internationals. Statistics refer to the full year, not the 2018 season.

MOEEN ALI   Worcestershire

Forever protesting he was a batsman who bowled, Ali spent much of the year performing like a bowler who batted – not very well. A lone half-century from 34 innings across the formats was a desperate return, though he was as amenable as ever in accepting the No. 3 Test role; the experiment merely showcased his looseness, and lasted five innings. Instead, it was his off-breaks that made headlines. Dropped for six Tests after a disastrous 2017-18 in Australia and New Zealand, Ali came back refreshed. He took 30 wickets at 21 in his next five Tests, including six hauls of four or better, four of them in the fourth innings. In Sri Lanka, where he enjoyed the insurance of Jack Leach's accuracy, he slowed his pace and aimed fuller. And he was meaner than anyone in the 50-over team. Now it was time to start batting properly again.

7 Tests: 268 runs @ 19.14; 32 wickets @ 28.81.
24 ODIs: 277 runs @ 17.31, SR 89.93; 29 wickets @ 34.48, ER 5.10.
3 T20Is: 33 runs @ 16.50, SR 173.68; 1 wicket @ 119.00, ER 14.28.

JAMES ANDERSON   Lancashire

It seemed harsh on Anderson that one of the highlights of the Test year anywhere in the world was his five-match battle with Virat Kohli, which yielded mutual respect but not a single wicket. Against everyone else, he was more magnificent than a 36-year-old had any right to be, picking up 33 in seven home Tests against Pakistan and India at 18 apiece. The last of them, Mohammed Shami at The Oval, was his 564th in all, taking him past Glenn McGrath as Test cricket's most prolific seamer. And he earned a game off in Colombo after Sri Lanka's turning pitches made him feel like "a bowling machine". For every wicket, there was exactly one run, none more important than the 19 he managed at Pallekele: in a 57-run win, he took part in two tenth-wicket stands totalling 101.

12 Tests: 43 runs @ 7.16; 43 wickets @ 22.51.

JONNY BAIRSTOW   Yorkshire

When it came to proving a point, Bairstow remained in a league of his own. Still learning the role of one-day opener, he blazed three hundreds in a row, and four in six innings, finishing the year with 31 sixes – ten more than any team-mate. But his tendency to stay leg side of the ball crept into his Test game. That, plus a broken finger, hindered him against India; to Bairstow's undisguised chagrin, he briefly lost the gloves to Buttler. Then came a twisted ankle playing football in Sri Lanka. His replacement, Foakes, sparkled on debut at Galle, and Bairstow's only route back was as a specialist No. 3. Having been ignored at Pallekele, he responded with an angry hundred in Colombo. Just as typically, he took the chance to rail against his doubters, of whom there were fewer than he imagined. But perhaps that was the point.

11 Tests: 609 runs @ 30.45; 29 catches as wicketkeeper, 2 stumpings.
22 ODIs: 1,025 runs @ 46.59, SR 118.22.
4 T20Is: 67 runs @ 22.33, SR 163.41.

SAM BILLINGS   Kent
Seven white-ball games, including one for an ICC World XI against West Indies, produced a best of 29, and the sense of a talent going nowhere. Inventiveness, Billings was discovering, was not enough to sustain an international career.

2 ODIs: 23 runs @ 11.50, SR 11.50; 2 catches as wicketkeeper.
5 T20Is: 61 runs @ 12.20, SR 107.01.

STUART BROAD   Nottinghamshire
Spurred on by a "rubbish" Ashes – his word – Broad remodelled his action before the visit to New Zealand. His wrist moved fully behind the ball, which helped relocate the awayswinger to the right-hander; with the seam now upright, he had the confidence to hit a fuller length. The reward was instant: a six-for at Christchurch. The summer had its moments too, notably six economical wickets in the Headingley win over Pakistan, and a trademark destructive four-for against India at Lord's. Despite suffering more than his share of dropped catches, he was now among Test cricket's top ten wicket-takers. But his absence from the first two Tests in Sri Lanka was a reminder that reputation counted only for so much. It prompted him to work on a shorter run-up – a suggestion from Richard Hadlee. At 32, Broad was preparing for the final phase of his career.

11 Tests: 35 wickets @ 28.28; 143 runs @ 8.41.

RORY BURNS   Surrey
England's first new opener of the post-Cook era enjoyed some success in Sri Lanka, mainly during the Second Test at Pallekele, where he totalled 102 and set the tone for a sweep-at-all-costs second innings – not bad for a player said by some to be frail against spin. There were misjudgments, but enough promise to suggest his apprenticeship in county cricket had been well spent.

3 Tests: 155 runs @ 25.83.

JOS BUTTLER   Lancashire
No one better embodied England's versatility. Traditionalists recoiled when he earned a Test recall because of success at the IPL, then fell quiet as the evidence mounted: Buttler was good enough to blend in wherever necessary, whatever the format. Few had questioned his attacking credentials, but a sensible rearguard hundred against India at Trent Bridge advertised other qualities. Among them was an intelligence that earned him the Test vice-captaincy and, in Sri Lanka, played a part in a change of plan, from sweeping (at Pallekele) to using his feet (in Colombo) after watching footage of Michael

Clarke taking on Graeme Swann. His white-ball batting simply confirmed his all-round gifts – his 15 scores of 50-plus was bettered only by Root – and his unbeaten century to seal a one-wicket win over Australia at Old Trafford was one of England's innings of the year.

10 Tests: 760 runs @ 44.70; 1 catch as wicketkeeper.

23 ODIs: 671 runs @ 51.61, SR 113.53; 26 catches, 9 stumpings.

9 T20Is: 246 runs @ 27.33, SR 135.91; 4 catches, 1 stumping.

ALASTAIR COOK
Essex

Even before he had gone, team-mates knew they would miss him. In his 161st and final Test, against India at The Oval, Cook made 71 and 147 – a flourish that belied his struggles on juicy pitches earlier in the year, in both New Zealand and at home. Others wondered whether international retirement at the age of 33 was premature; Cook matter-of-factly explained that his edge had gone. In truth, opening in England was becoming more precarious. He generally looked in decent touch, but conditions – and excellent Indian seam bowling, often from round the wicket – kept interfering. No one, though, could begrudge him his farewell, a reminder of the mental strength that had brought him more Test runs (12,472) and hundreds (33) than any England batsman in history. And he became Sir Alastair in the New Year's honours list.

10 Tests: 516 runs @ 28.66.

SAM CURRAN
Surrey

Few sights in English cricket in 2018 were more uplifting than Curran on the charge. Three counter-attacks from No. 8 – at Edgbaston, Southampton and Pallekele – turned Tests England's way, and on each occasion he reached his fifty with a six. In all, he cleared the ropes 14 times, twice as often as any of his team-mates, and personified the team's ever-growing sense of freedom. By the time he missed Colombo in late November with a side strain, he had played seven Tests and won the lot. The upshot was an IPL contract worth over £800,000. His left-armers were used sparingly, but – when the ball swung – effectively, and he demolished India's top order at Edgbaston. Such were his talismanic qualities that it came as a surprise when he was dropped at Trent Bridge; naturally, England lost.

7 Tests: 404 runs @ 36.72; 14 wickets @ 25.14.

2 ODIs: 17 runs @ 8.50, SR 58.62; 2 wickets @ 45.00, ER 7.50.

TOM CURRAN
Surrey

The older Curran was a combative, if not always economical, addition to England's white-ball attack, at his trickiest when running through his variations. A five-for in January 2018 at Perth raised expectations, which were not always met. But in their quest to build a World Cup squad, the selectors had at least identified another option.

1 Test: 62 runs @ 62.00; 1 wicket at 82.00.

10 ODIs: 71 runs @ 71.00, SR 114.51; 17 wickets at 26.64, ER 6.23.

4 T20Is: 6 runs @ 6.00, SR 300.00; 1 wicket at 134.00, ER 10.30.

BEN FOAKES   Surrey

On the island once known as Serendip, England found a new wicketkeeper by accident, with happy consequences for almost everyone. Bairstow's football injury persuaded the selectors to fast-track Foakes ahead of Buttler in Galle, where his first act was a faultless hundred to rescue a familiar top-order stumble. His keeping was pristine too – as Surrey fans knew it would be – and Foakes confirmed the good impression with important second-innings runs at Pallekele and Colombo, ending as Man of the Series. Bairstow was obliged to reinvent himself, and England looked a stronger side.

  3 Tests: 277 runs @ 69.25; 8 catches, 2 stumpings.

ALEX HALES   Nottinghamshire

Hales's plight summed up England's 50-over strength. Suspended in September 2017 – and later found guilty of bringing the game into disrepute – because of his Bristol night out with Stokes, he lost his opener's spot to Roy. Subsequent selection came with caveats: he would bat mainly at No. 3, and only if another member of the top six was absent. A 92-ball 147 during the world-record 481 for six against Australia at Trent Bridge was a reminder of his power. But when he did get another chance as opener in Sri Lanka, he failed to grasp it, making 16 runs in three innings. Since he had quit red-ball cricket with his county, there was little room for manoeuvre.

  14 ODIs: 457 runs @ 35.15, SR 91.76.
  9 T20Is: 222 runs @ 27.75, SR 142.30.

KEATON JENNINGS   Lancashire

His second crack at Test cricket came sooner than anyone expected – and was prolonged by the retirement of Cook. But, after averaging 19 on lively English pitches against Pakistan and India, Jennings justified his selection for Sri Lanka, sweeping and reverse-sweeping his way to 192 runs for once out at Galle. The runs tailed off, but at short leg he moved from wallflower to Venus flytrap – improbably, for a man measuring 6ft 4in. But he still needed to prove he could prosper against fast bowling.

  9 Tests: 425 runs @ 28.33.

CHRIS JORDAN   Sussex

One of five ever-presents in the Twenty20 team, Jordan remained perhaps the most niche of England's regulars, picked essentially for his late yorkers and athleticism. Both were as eye-catching as ever.

  9 T20Is: 34 runs @ 11.33, SR 141.66; 9 wickets @ 34.22, ER 8.88.

DAWID MALAN   Middlesex

The memory of his successful 2017-18 Ashes faded quickly: three Tests into the summer, Malan was gone, a victim of his tendency to get stuck in the crease, and Ed Smith's decisiveness. (Dropping Kohli on 21 at Edgbaston did not help.) Malan was, said Smith, "better suited to overseas conditions", though that was sugaring the pill, since he was referring specifically to the bouncier tracks of Australia and South Africa. In England, where eight Tests since his debut in 2017 had produced an average of 20, he simply didn't use his feet to counter swing or seam. His disappearance from the Twenty20 side made less sense, after he reached 50 in three of his four innings in Australia and New Zealand.

6 Tests: 219 runs @ 19.90; no wicket for 9 runs.
4 T20Is: 172 runs @ 43.00, SR 140.98; 1 wicket @ 27.00, ER 13.50.

EOIN MORGAN   Middlesex

Morgan's remark in October that he would drop himself for the World Cup if form demanded it seemed to sharpen his focus. The comment was unnecessary in any case – but 197 runs for once out, at better than a run a ball, during the 3–1 one-day win in Sri Lanka quashed what little debate there was. And it allowed England's white-ball captain to end a memorable year on a high. In May, they had gone top of the 50-over rankings for the first time since 2013, while the victory in Sri Lanka was their ninth bilateral series triumph in a row, punctuated only by a blip against Scotland. The idea that the man behind England's white-ball revolution might miss the party after inflating the balloons was ludicrous.

22 ODIs: 756 runs @ 42.00, SR 93.79.
7 T20Is: 158 runs @ 26.33, SR 141.07.

LIAM PLUNKETT   Yorkshire

A hamstring injury and marriage to his American fiancée, Emeleah, which coincided with the tour of Sri Lanka, limited Plunkett's contributions. But his value as a mid-innings wicket-taker remained beyond doubt. There were ODI four-fors against Australia at Cardiff and India at Lord's, plus a miserly spell in the Cardiff T20 against the Indians. Few members of the team did their job so unfussily.

12 ODIs: 66 runs at 16.50, SR 83.54; 19 wickets at 27.47, ER 6.32.
16 T20Is: 19 runs at 9.50, SR 135.71; 4 wickets at 48.00, ER 9.29.

ADIL RASHID   Yorkshire

Rashid finished the Test series in Sri Lanka as international cricket's leading wicket-taker in 2018, with 76 (and as the world's best No. 9). He had been overtaken by the New Year, but his progress from a limited-overs specialist to a leg-spinner capable of Test-winning spells was heart-warming. Initially, he angered those who saw a contradiction: unwilling to play first-class cricket for Yorkshire, he agreed to an unforeseen Test return after being cajoled by Ed Smith, who cherished his ability to turn it both ways, and insisted talks had begun *before* Rashid bowled Kohli with the ball of the summer in the Headingley ODI. His leg-breaks remained crucial to England's white-ball strategy, though he took a while to earn Root's trust in Tests: against

India at Lord's, he didn't bowl (or bat) at all. But he kept chipping in, and a first-innings five-for in Colombo vindicated Smith's hunch.

  8 Tests: 232 runs @ 23.20; 22 wickets @ 29.40.
  24 ODIs: 111 runs @ 13.87, SR 80.43; 42 wickets @ 27.47, ER 5.41.
  9 T20Is: 18 runs @ 9.00, SR 112.50; 12 wickets @ 20.50, ER 6.83.

JOE ROOT   Yorkshire

By the time Root led England to a Test whitewash of Sri Lanka in late November, only Kohli had scored more than his 1,938 international runs in 2018. Beneath the headline, though, lurked complexity. His Test average was his lowest in a calendar year since 2013, partly because of a selflessness that bordered on recklessness: so keen was Root to set an attacking example that he always gave bowlers hope, especially outside off stump. For a while, mid-series against India, he even looked out of form. But centuries at The Oval and Pallekele helped answer a long-standing complaint about his poor conversion-rate, and his captaincy grew in stature once Cook went. His one-day batting shone too, not least during back-to-back hundreds at Lord's and Leeds to see off India. And if his fight for his Twenty20 place had a touch of Yorkshire stubbornness, it also underlined his constant desire to improve. Root ended the year believing the best was yet to come.

  13 Tests: 948 runs @ 41.21; 3 wickets @ 47.66.
  24 ODIs: 946 runs @ 59.12, SR 83.93; 2 wickets @ 140.00, ER 6.26.
  3 T20Is: 44 runs @ 14.66, SR 125.71.

JASON ROY   Surrey

Roy began 2018 determined not to lose the opening slot he had only recently regained from Hales: an England-record 180 at Melbourne brooked little argument. But it paved the way for a curiously lop-sided year: he averaged 55 in ten ODIs against Australia, and 28 in 12 against everyone else. Two quirks held him back. His aggressive nature meant he fell in the first over six times; he also fell six times in the forties, when he ought to have been set. But his strokeplay could be as pure as anyone's, and no team-mate matched his 15 Twenty20 sixes, each played with a flourish worthy of Kevin Pietersen.

  22 ODIs: 894 runs @ 40.63, SR 105.05.
  9 T20Is: 271 runs @ 30.11, SR 169.37.

BEN STOKES   Durham

Injuries and a court hearing, in which he was acquitted of affray, deprived Stokes of momentum, but seemed to bring out a more responsible side. Test rearguards at Auckland and Nottingham proved in vain, while his one-day strike-rate was comfortably the lowest of England's regulars. Instead, it was with ball in hand that he shook things up, seizing the moment on the final morning of the Edgbaston Test against India, then banging in round-the-wicket bouncers to Sri Lanka in Colombo's sapping heat. In the field, he was a force of nature. Not for the first time, the numbers didn't reflect his influence. But the truth was that, when Stokes was missing, England felt less combative.

  10 Tests: 537 runs @ 26.85; 22 wickets @ 27.36.
  13 ODIs: 313 runs @ 44.71, SR 76.90; 5 wickets @ 72.20, ER 5.91.
  2 T20Is: 40 runs @ 20.00, SR 108.10; no wicket for 11 runs, ER 5.50.

MARK STONEMAN **Surrey**

A pair of fifties in New Zealand augured well for the summer, but a pair of failures against Pakistan at Lord's was enough for the selectors to pounce. Stoneman had the shots, but lacked any sense of permanence. At 31, and with a Test average of 27, his time had probably gone.

4 Tests: 198 runs @ 24.75.

JAMES VINCE **Hampshire**

Like Malan and Stoneman, Vince was swept away by Ed Smith's new broom, and told to score big runs for Hampshire. But his most unignorable effort – an unbeaten 201 at Taunton – was badly timed, since the selectors had already decided to leave him out of the Test squad to take on Pakistan. It meant he was unable to build on the 76 with which he finished his winter, at Christchurch, and he was limited to a couple of white-ball matches. Two run-outs in those games added to concerns about his concentration.

2 Tests: 137 runs @ 34.25.
1 ODI: 27 runs @ 27.00, SR 100.00.
2 T20Is: 31 runs @ 15.50, SR 110.71.

DAVID WILLEY **Yorkshire**

Willey kept plugging away, and was now trusted by Morgan to bowl in the middle and at the end of an innings, as well as in the powerplay. He also made progress with the bat, twice ticking off ODI-bests: an unbeaten 35 repaired a creaking run-chase against Australia at The Oval, while a 30-ball half-century took England out of reach of India at Lord's. But a back injury prevented him from travelling to Sri Lanka.

11 ODIs: 118 runs @ 23.60, SR 111.32; 13 wickets @ 34.15, ER 5.34.
8 T20Is: 77 runs @ 15.40, SR 154.00; 8 wickets @ 30.37, ER 8.52.

CHRIS WOAKES **Warwickshire**

When fitness permitted, Woakes barely put a foot wrong. The problems were his knee and thigh, which restricted him to three home Tests out of seven. His performance against India at Lord's was almost worth the aggravation: a working-over of Kohli and a maiden Test hundred. That was no great surprise, after he began the year with 170 runs from 145 balls for once out from three one-day innings in Australia. And he was always a threat with the new white ball. But when he carried the drinks during the Test series in Sri Lanka, it confirmed the suspicion after he was dropped after Auckland in March: with the red ball overseas, he was no longer an automatic pick.

4 Tests: 223 runs @ 44.60; 12 wickets @ 28.91.
13 ODIs: 205 runs @ 41.00, SR 107.89; 19 wickets @ 26.63, ER 5.11.

MARK WOOD **Durham**

Two Tests at Christchurch and Lord's brought little except a maiden fifty, before a heel injury intervened, others prospered, and white-ball cricket became the ceiling of his ambitions. He lengthened his run-up in Sri Lanka, an attempt to ease the strain on his body, but only twice in 16 one-day internationals all year did he manage more than one wicket. At 29, youthful pace and promise were becoming a memory – until he ran through West Indies in St Lucia in February 2019 with the quickest spell by an England bowler for years.

2 Tests: 72 runs @ 18.00; 4 wickets @ 48.75.
16 ODIs: 7 runs @ 3.50, SR 70.00; 13 wickets @ 57.92, ER 5.70.
2 T20Is: 10 runs without being dismissed, SR 83.33; 3 wickets @ 25.66, ER 10.26.

AND THE REST...

Dom Bess (Somerset; 2 Tests) was a feisty presence against Pakistan, knuckling down for runs and collecting a cheap three-for with his off-breaks at Leeds. His time would come again. **Ollie Pope** (Surrey; 2 Tests) rose quickly, perhaps too quickly: at No. 4 in the Test side, he was two places higher than his county role. But there were flickers of promise, and a tour of Sri Lanka. With the bat, **Craig Overton** (Somerset; 1 Test, 1 ODI) helped avert the embarrassment of the lowest Test total, at Auckland in March, but his bowling lacked zip, and he drifted out of contention. **Mason Crane** (Hampshire; 1 Test) was unable to build on his lone Test cap at Sydney because of a stress fracture of the back. At Dambulla in October, **Olly Stone** (Warwickshire; 4 ODIs) bounced out Niroshan Dickwella with his seventh ball in international cricket, but couldn't quite breach the Test team, despite his pace. **Jake Ball** (Nottinghamshire; 2 ODIs, 2 T20Is) did little except keep Buttler company in the one-wicket ODI win against Australia at Old Trafford. Firmly on the periphery of the white-ball teams, **Liam Dawson** (Hampshire; 2 ODIs, 2 T20Is) was not helped by a side strain which cut short his tour of Sri Lanka. **Joe Denly** (Kent; 1 T20I) opened the bowling with his leg-breaks in his first England appearance for over eight years, and took four for 19 in Colombo, winning the match award.

ENGLAND TEST AVERAGES
IN CALENDAR YEAR 2018

BATTING AND FIELDING

		T	I	NO	R	HS	100	50	Avge	SR	Ct/St
1	B. T. Foakes	3	6	2	277	107	1	1	69.25	56.30	8/2
2	T. K. Curran	1	2	1	62	39	0	0	62.00	59.04	0
3	J. C. Buttler	10	18	1	760	106	1	6	44.70	68.10	9
4	C. R. Woakes	4	6	1	223	137*	1	1	44.60	65.01	3
5	J. E. Root	13	24	1	948	125	2	6	41.21	53.19	9
6	D. M. Bess	2	3	0	111	57	0	1	37.00	51.62	1
7	†S. M. Curran	7	12	1	404	78	0	3	36.72	57.87	0
8	C. Overton	1	2	1	36	33*	0	0	36.00	83.72	0
9	J. M. Vince	2	4	0	137	76	0	1	34.25	50.00	3
10	J. M. Bairstow	11	20	0	609	110	2	2	30.45	53.51	29/2
11	†A. N. Cook	10	18	0	516	147	1	2	28.66	44.06	19
12	†K. K. Jennings	9	16	1	425	146*	1	0	28.33	47.59	12
13	†B. A. Stokes	10	20	0	537	66	0	4	26.85	46.09	11
14	†R. J. Burns	3	6	0	155	59	0	1	25.83	54.38	1
15	†M. D. Stoneman	4	8	0	198	60	0	2	24.75	43.90	1
16	A. U. Rashid	8	13	3	232	35	0	0	23.20	56.58	1
17	†D. J. Malan	6	11	0	219	62	0	2	19.90	37.56	7
18	†M. M. Ali	7	14	0	268	50	0	1	19.14	42.47	5
19	M. A. Wood	2	4	0	72	52	0	1	18.00	77.41	1
20	O. J. D. Pope	2	3	0	54	28	0	0	18.00	54.54	2
21	†M. J. Leach	4	7	1	55	16	0	0	9.16	36.91	2
22	†S. C. J. Broad	11	18	1	143	38	0	0	8.41	55.42	4
23	†J. M. Anderson	12	18	12	43	12	0	0	7.16	29.45	3
24	M. S. Crane	1	2	0	6	4	0	0	3.00	54.54	0

BOWLING

		Style	O	M	R	W	BB	5I	Avge	SR
1	J. M. Anderson	RFM	391.4	113	968	43	5-20	1	22.51	54.65
2	M. J. Leach	SLA	193.4	34	498	20	5-83	1	24.90	58.10
3	S. M. Curran	LFM	106.5	15	352	14	4-74	0	25.14	45.78
4	B. A. Stokes	RFM	179.2	31	602	22	4-40	0	27.36	48.90
5	S. C. J. Broad	RFM	331.2	79	990	35	6-54	1	28.28	56.80
6	M. M. Ali	OB	265	34	922	32	5-63	1	28.81	49.68
7	C. R. Woakes	RFM	108	20	347	12	3-55	0	28.91	54.00
8	A. U. Rashid	LB	186	17	647	22	5-49	1	29.40	50.72
9	D. M. Bess	OB	31.4	1	121	3	3-33	0	40.33	63.33
10	J. E. Root	OB/LB	49.4	9	143	3	1-13	0	47.66	99.33
11	M. A. Wood	RFM	70.3	20	195	4	2-45	0	48.75	105.75
12	C. Overton	RFM	25	7	70	1	1-70	0	70.00	150.00
13	T. K. Curran	RFM	25	3	82	1	1-82	0	82.00	150.00
14	M. S. Crane	LB	48	3	193	1	1-193	0	193.00	288.00
15	K. K. Jennings	RM	2	0	0	0	0-4	0	–	–
16	D. J. Malan	LB	4	1	9	0	0-9	0	–	–

ENGLAND ONE-DAY INTERNATIONAL AVERAGES IN CALENDAR YEAR 2018

BATTING AND FIELDING

		M	I	NO	R	HS	100	50	Avge	SR	Ct/St
1	T. K. Curran	10	6	5	71	35	0	0	71.00	114.51	4
2	J. E. Root	24	24	8	946	113*	3	5	59.12	83.93	12
3	J. C. Buttler........	23	18	5	671	110*	2	4	51.61	113.53	26/9
4	J. M. Bairstow......	22	22	0	1,025	139	4	2	46.59	118.22	5
5	†B. A. Stokes........	13	10	3	313	67	0	3	44.71	76.90	11
6	†E. J. G. Morgan......	22	22	4	756	92	0	7	42.00	93.79	5
7	C. R. Woakes	13	7	2	205	78	0	2	41.00	107.89	4
8	J. J. Roy	22	22	0	894	180	3	1	40.63	105.05	13
9	A. D. Hales.........	14	14	1	457	147	1	3	35.15	91.76	6
10	J. M. Vince	1	1	0	27	27	0	0	27.00	100.00	0
11	†D. J. Willey	11	8	3	118	50	0	1	23.60	111.32	3
12	†M. M. Ali	24	17	1	277	46	0	0	17.31	89.93	5
13	L. E. Plunkett	12	6	2	66	47*	0	0	16.50	83.54	2
14	A. U. Rashid........	24	10	2	111	22	0	0	13.87	80.43	6
15	S. W. Billings	2	2	0	23	12	0	0	11.50	71.87	3
16	†S. M. Curran	2	2	0	17	15	0	0	8.50	58.62	0
17	L. A. Dawson	2	1	0	4	4	0	0	4.00	100.00	1
18	M. A. Wood	16	5	3	7	3*	0	0	3.50	70.00	4
19	J. T. Ball	2	2	1	1	1*	0	0	1.00	8.33	1
20	O. P. Stone	4	1	1	9	9*	0	0	–	128.57	0
21	C. Overton..........	1	–	–	–	–	–	–	–	–	2

BOWLING

		Style	O	M	R	W	BB	4I	Avge	SR	ER
1	L. A. Dawson	SLA	6	0	26	1	1-26	0	26.00	36.00	4.33
2	C. R. Woakes	RFM	99	5	506	19	3-26	0	26.63	31.26	5.11
3	T. K. Curran	RFM	72.4	2	453	17	5-35	1	26.64	25.64	6.23
4	L. E. Plunkett	RFM	82.3	2	522	19	4-46	2	27.47	26.05	6.32
5	A. U. Rashid.......	LB	213	1	1,154	42	4-36	2	27.47	30.42	5.41
6	D. J. Willey........	LFM	83	2	444	13	4-43	1	34.15	38.30	5.34
7	M. M. Ali	OB	195.5	3	1,000	29	4-46	1	34.48	40.51	5.10
8	S. M. Curran.......	LFM	12	0	90	2	2-44	0	45.00	36.00	7.50
9	M. A. Wood	RFM	132	6	753	13	2-46	0	57.92	60.92	5.70
10	B. A. Stokes	RFM	61	0	361	5	2-42	0	72.20	73.20	5.91
11	O. P. Stone	RF	16	0	97	1	1-23	0	97.00	96.00	6.06
12	J. E. Root	OB	44.4	0	280	2	2-31	0	140.00	134.00	6.26
13	J. T. Ball..........	RFM	15	0	87	0	0-29	0	–	–	5.80
14	C. Overton	RFM	7	0	55	0	0-55	0	–	–	7.85

ENGLAND TWENTY20 INTERNATIONAL AVERAGES IN CALENDAR YEAR 2018

BATTING AND FIELDING

		M	I	NO	R	HS	50	Avge	SR	4	6	Ct/St
1	L. A. Dawson	2	1	0	10	10	0	10.00	**333.33**	1	1	0
2	T. K. Curran	4	1	0	6	6	0	6.00	**300.00**	0	1	0
3	†M. M. Ali	3	3	1	33	27	0	16.50	**173.68**	2	3	1
4	J. J. Roy	9	9	0	271	69	2	30.11	**169.37**	28	15	2
5	J. M. Bairstow.	4	4	1	67	28	0	22.33	**163.41**	2	6	0
6	†D. J. Willey.	8	7	2	77	29*	0	15.40	**154.00**	6	4	1
7	A. D. Hales.	9	9	1	222	58*	1	27.75	**142.30**	23	10	5
8	C. J. Jordan	9	7	4	34	16*	0	11.33	**141.66**	1	2	4
9	†E. J. G. Morgan.	7	7	1	158	80*	1	26.33	**141.07**	11	8	3
10	†D. J. Malan	4	4	0	172	59	3	43.00	**140.98**	14	9	0
11	J. C. Buttler.	9	9	0	246	69	2	27.33	**135.91**	30	7	4/1
12	L. E. Plunkett	6	4	2	19	9	0	9.50	**135.71**	1	1	2
13	J. E. Root	3	3	0	44	35	0	14.66	**125.71**	4	0	1
14	J. L. Denly	1	1	0	20	20	0	20.00	**117.64**	3	0	0
15	A. U. Rashid	9	4	2	18	8*	0	9.00	**112.50**	3	0	1
16	S. W. Billings	4	4	0	57	29	0	14.25	**111.76**	6	1	3
17	J. M. Vince	2	2	0	31	21	0	15.50	**110.71**	2	1	0
18	†B. A. Stokes	2	2	0	40	26	0	20.00	**108.10**	3	1	1
19	M. A. Wood	2	2	2	10	5*	0	–	**83.33**	1	0	0
20	J. T. Ball	2	–	–	–	–	–	–	**–**	–	–	1

BOWLING

		Style	O	Dots	R	W	BB	4I	Avge	SR	ER
1	J. L. Denly.	LB	4	13	19	4	4-19	1	4.75	6.00	**4.75**
2	B. A. Stokes	RFM	2	4	11	0	0-11	0	–	–	**5.50**
3	A. U. Rashid	LB	36	79	246	12	3-11	0	20.50	18.00	**6.83**
4	L. A. Dawson	SLA	6	13	50	1	1-27	0	50.00	36.00	**8.33**
5	D. J. Willey	LFM	28.3	74	243	8	3-28	0	30.37	21.37	**8.52**
6	C. J. Jordan	RFM	34.4	76	308	9	3-42	0	34.22	23.11	**8.88**
7	L. E. Plunkett	RFM	20.4	45	192	4	2-34	0	48.00	31.00	**9.29**
8	M. A. Wood	RFM	7.3	20	77	3	2-51	0	25.66	15.00	**10.26**
9	T. K. Curran	RFM	13	17	134	1	1-32	0	134.00	78.00	**10.30**
10	J. T. Ball	RFM	7	7	83	2	1-39	0	41.50	21.00	**11.85**
11	D. J. Malan	LB	2	2	27	1	1-27	0	27.00	12.00	**13.50**
12	M. M. Ali	OB	8.2	4	119	1	1-58	0	119.00	50.00	**14.28**

Billings and T. S. Mills also played one T20 international for the ICC World XI v West Indies. Billings scored four runs; Mills did not bat, but had figures of 3–13–13–0.

TRANS-TASMAN T20 TRI-SERIES IN 2017-18

Rory Dollard

1 Australia   2 New Zealand   3 England

This tournament broke new ground – the first Twenty20 tri-series between Full Members – although it concluded with more questions raised than lessons learned. Scheduled in place of the 50-over Chappell–Hadlee Trophy between Australia and New Zealand, with England joining the party between bilateral tours either side of the Tasman, it felt like a symptom of the identity crisis afflicting a three-format sport.

On the eve of the tournament, England's captain Eoin Morgan declared himself "a massive fan" of the triangular set-up, before – in his next breath – doubting its practicality. "If we could play more [tri-series] we would," he said. "But I don't think it's viable with travel schedules around the world." By the time England were knocked out, with just one win from four matches, their head coach Trevor Bayliss was questioning the purpose not just of tri-series in general, but of all Twenty20 internationals. In advocating a franchise-only future for cricket's cash cow, he was merely repeating a long-held personal view. But to do so after England's 100th match, and ahead of a heavily hyped final in Auckland, was significant.

How the suggestion went down with Bayliss's employers, or the short-form specialists in his squad, was another matter. But his New Zealand counterpart, Mike Hesson, described Twenty20s as both "incredibly meaningful" and financially critical to his country. For a player such as Martin Guptill, who outscored allcomers with 258 and hit a wonderful century in a record-breaking run-fest with Australia, they also represent a chance to catch the eye.

Australia's position was better judged by actions than words. They deservedly won all five of their matches, using the old-fashioned virtues of superior batting, bowling and fielding. They moved from seventh in the world rankings to second, failing to dislodge Pakistan at the top by a fraction. Things can happen quickly in T20 cricket.

Yet the Australians might have been absent had a clash of commitments not been waved through by administrators. The Test squad headed to South Africa, though David Warner delayed his departure to lead the Twenty20 side. But the selectors needed only to dip into the thriving Big Bash League to summon replacements. Billy Stanlake, Kane Richardson and Andrew Tye made the notion of a depleted Australian attack appear comical. Ashton Agar re-emerged as the wiliest white-ball spinner on show, and D'Arcy Short's big-hitting bravado transferred effortlessly to the international arena.

Between the first and second games, Short joined Alex Carey and Travis Head in a late dash to the BBL final, scrambling between Sydney, Adelaide and Hobart in an attempt to honour Cricket Australia's domestic showpiece. It was the latest logistical limbo act required to keep the show on the road, and support an entertaining but inconclusive innovation.

NATIONAL SQUADS

Australia *D. A. Warner, A. C. Agar, A. T. Carey, B. J. Dwarshuis, A. J. Finch, T. M. Head, C. A. Lynn, G. J. Maxwell, K. W. Richardson, D. J. M. Short, B. Stanlake, M. P. Stoinis, A. J. Tye, A. Zampa. *Coach:* D. S. Lehmann.

England *E. J. G. Morgan, S. W. Billings, J. C. Buttler, S. M. Curran, T. K. Curran, L. A. Dawson, A. D. Hales, C. J. Jordan, D. J. Malan, L. E. Plunkett, A. U. Rashid, J. J. Roy, J. M. Vince, D. J. Willey, M. A. Wood. *Coach:* T. H. Bayliss.
    J. E. Root was originally named, but decided to take a break and was replaced by S. M. Curran. B. A. Stokes was also originally selected, but was ruled out by a court appearance in England. J. T. Ball was temporarily added to the squad as cover after hamstring injuries to Jordan and Plunkett.

New Zealand *K. S. Williamson, T. A. Blundell, T. A. Boult, T. C. Bruce, M. S. Chapman, C. de Grandhomme, M. J. Guptill, A. K. Kitchen, C. Munro, S. H. A. Rance, M. J. Santner, T. L. Seifert, I. S. Sodhi, T. G. Southee, L. R. P. L. Taylor, B. M. Wheeler. *Coach:* M. J. Hesson.
    Chapman and Seifert replaced Blundell and Bruce after the first match.

AUSTRALIA v NEW ZEALAND

At Sydney, February 3, 2018 (floodlit). Australia won by seven wickets (DLS). Toss: Australia. Twenty20 international debuts: A. T. Carey, D. J. M. Short.
    Australia found new match-winners with ball and bat, brushing aside their neighbours and co-hosts. The 6ft 8in Billy Stanlake, reappearing a year after a muted first stint at the highest level, produced a compelling opening spell which boasted too much pace, bounce and quality for Munro and Guptill – who fell to his first two balls – and Bruce. New Zealand, playing their first T20 international in Australia for nine years, were 16 for three. They never recovered, with Agar's control ensuring they remained mired in dot balls: the first 14 overs produced only three boundaries. De Grandhomme briefly raised the tempo, but Tye's variations scattered the tail, yielding a career-best four for 23. The chase, recalibrated to 95 from 15 overs after rain, endured a false start, as debutant opener D'Arcy Short and stand-in captain Warner fell cheaply. That left Lynn, a Big Bash bully, in charge, and he made 44. He put on 77 with Maxwell, whose take-no-prisoners approach ushered Australia home with 21 deliveries unused.
    Man of the Match: B. Stanlake.

New Zealand

		B	4/6
1 M. J. Guptill *b 11*	5	5	1
2 C. Munro *c 5 b 11*	3	3	0
3 *K. S. Williamson *c 1 b 8*	8	21	0
4 T. C. Bruce *c 10 b 11*	3	3	0
5 L. R. P. L. Taylor *c 5 b 7*	24	35	1
6 †T. A. Blundell *c 10 b 9*	14	16	0
7 C. de Grandhomme *not out*	38	24	1/3
8 M. J. Santner *c 1 b 8*	1	4	0
9 T. G. Southee *c 6 b 8*	9	6	0/1
10 I. S. Sodhi *b 8*	0	3	0
B 2, lb 4, w 6	12		

6 overs: 29-3   (20 overs) 117-9

1/11 2/11 3/16 4/34 5/60 6/90 7/92 8/114 9/117

11 T. A. Boult did not bat.

Richardson 4–12–28–0; Stanlake 4–15–15–3; Agar 4–9–22–1; Tye 4–11–23–4; Zampa 3–8–21–1; Stoinis 1–4–2–0.

Australia

		B	4/6
1 *D. A. Warner *c 4 b 11*	6	8	1
2 D. J. M. Short *c 5 b 9*	4	4	1
3 C. A. Lynn *c 10 b 11*	44	33	6/1
4 G. J. Maxwell *not out*	40	24	5/1
5 †A. T. Carey *not out*	0	0	0
W 2	2		

5 overs: 36-2   (11.3 overs) 96-3

1/10 2/10 3/87

6 M. P. Stoinis, 7 A. C. Agar, 8 A. J. Tye, 9 A. Zampa, 10 K. W. Richardson and 11 B. Stanlake did not bat.

Boult 3–11–14–2; Southee 2.3–7–27–1; Santner 2–6–20–0; Sodhi 3–4–24–0; de Grandhomme 1–0–11–0.

Umpires: C. M. Brown and S. D. Fry.   Third umpire: G. A. Abood.
Referee: J. Srinath.

Advertisement

AUSTRALIA v ENGLAND

At Hobart, February 7, 2018 (floodlit). Australia won by five wickets. Toss: Australia.

Maxwell continued his gleeful reclamation of centre stage after being relegated by Australia's selectors from Big Show – his nickname – to no show. Unwanted during the Ashes, chosen only for the last of the five one-day internationals against England, and told to "train smarter" by Steve Smith, Maxwell had begun this tournament with a point to prove. He left the Bellerive Oval having emphatically made it. His first contribution came with his off-breaks, which accounted for Malan, Morgan and Willey, as England frittered away a buoyant start. From 60 for one after six overs, and 96 for three after ten, they went into a tailspin, losing six for 28 before Jordan and Wood stopped the rot. Willey's first-over removal of Warner and Lynn added intrigue but, as long as Maxwell was there, a target of 156 was always too slight. He was dropped by Hales when 40, and earned a more controversial reprieve at 59, when Roy's stooping catch – and the on-field soft signal – was overturned by third umpire Chris Brown. But there was no doubt about the *coup de grâce*, a six off Wood to bring up a 58-ball century, making Maxwell the first Australian to score two Twenty20 international hundreds.

Man of the Match: G. J. Maxwell.

England

		B	4/6
1 J. J. Roy *c 9 b 10*	9	7	1
2 A. D. Hales *c and b 8*	22	15	4
3 D. J. Malan *c 9 b 4*	50	36	5/2
4 *E. J. G. Morgan *c 1 b 4*	22	14	2/1
5 †J. C. Buttler *c 4 b 5*	5	7	0
6 S. W. Billings *c and b 8*	10	9	1
7 D. J. Willey *st 7 b 4*	3	6	0
8 C. J. Jordan *not out*	16	11	0/1
9 A. U. Rashid *c 5 b 11*	1	4	0
10 T. K. Curran *c 1 b 9*	6	2	0/1
11 M. A. Wood *not out*	5	9	0
Lb 4, w 4	6		

6 overs: 60-1   (20 overs) 155-9

1/16 2/60 3/94 4/109 5/122 6/126 7/126 8/127 9/137

Stanlake 4–11–43–1; Richardson 4–10–27–1; Tye 4–6–28–1; Stoinis 2–4–16–1; Agar 3–7–15–2; Head 1–1–14–0; Maxwell 2–6–10–3.

Australia

		B	4/6
1 *D. A. Warner *c 2 b 7*	4	2	1
2 D. J. M. Short *c and b 9*	30	20	2/2
3 C. A. Lynn *b 7*	0	2	0
4 G. J. Maxwell *not out*	103	58	10/4
5 M. P. Stoinis *c 6 b 11*	6	11	1
6 T. M. Head *b 7*	6	13	0
7 †A. T. Carey *not out*	5	5	0
Lb 4, w 3	7		

6 overs: 59-2   (18.3 overs) 161-5

1/4 2/4 3/82 4/98 5/127

8 A. C. Agar, 9 A. J. Tye, 10 K. W. Richardson and 11 B. Stanlake did not bat.

Willey 3–8–28–3; Wood 3.3–11–26–1; Jordan 4–7–34–0; Curran 4–3–39–0; Rashid 4–12–30–1.

Umpires: G. A. Abood and S. D. Fry.   Third umpire: C. M. Brown.
Referee: J. Srinath.

AUSTRALIA v ENGLAND

At Melbourne, February 10, 2018 (floodlit). Australia won by seven wickets. Toss: Australia.

Australia beat England for the second time in four days, booking a place in the final at the earliest opportunity. Warner pursued a familiar pattern, winning the toss for the third game in a row, and watching his well-balanced attack set up the game. England, who had lost Eoin Morgan to a groin strain – in came Vince and Dawson, while Mark Wood missed out – then lost their top three inside four overs. The manner of Malan's departure, run out taking on Warner from close quarters, hinted at a desperation to get things moving. Stand-in skipper Buttler mustered 46, but it was an unusually joyless effort; Stoinis got through four overs for 18, and Australia's precision and variety were too much. Needing only 138, they swaggered home. Warner's lean run continued at the hands of Willey, but then came a parade of punishing blows from Short, Lynn and Maxwell. It fell to the fit-again Finch to apply the finishing touches: he thumped Willey for a towering straight six, then upper-cut the next delivery high over third man.

Man of the Match: K. W. Richardson.

England

		B	4/6
1 J. J. Roy *c 7 b 10*	8	7	1
2 A. D. Hales *c 5 b 11*	3	3	0
3 D. J. Malan *run out (1)*	10	10	1
4 J. M. Vince *b 9*	21	21	2
5 *J. C. Buttler *c 8 b 10*	46	49	3
6 S. W. Billings *c 1 b 11*	29	23	4/1
7 D. J. Willey *c 1 b 10*	10	6	2
8 C. J. Jordan *not out*	1	1	0
B 2, w 7	9		

6 overs: 42-3   (20 overs) 137-7

1/12 2/16 3/34 4/70 5/113 6/133 7/137

9 L. A. Dawson, 10 A. U. Rashid and 11 T. K. Curran did not bat.

Richardson 4–9–33–3; Stanlake 4–12–28–2; Stoinis 4–12–18–0; Tye 4–9–29–1; Agar 4–7–27–0.

Australia

		B	4/6
1 *D. A. Warner *c 5 b 7*	2	4	0
2 D. J. M. Short *not out*	36	33	3/1
3 C. A. Lynn *c 5 b 8*	31	19	4/2
4 G. J. Maxwell *c 5 b 8*	39	26	3/2
5 A. J. Finch *not out*	20	5	2/2
Lb 2, w 8	10		

6 overs: 52-2   (14.3 overs) 138-3

1/2 2/51 3/116

6 M. P. Stoinis, 7 †A. T. Carey, 8 A. C. Agar, 9 A. J. Tye, 10 K. W. Richardson and 11 B. Stanlake did not bat.

Willey 3.3–15–30–1; Curran 2–2–23–0; Jordan 3–8–26–2; Rashid 4–7–34–0; Dawson 2–3–23–0.

Umpires: C. M. Brown and S. J. Nogajski.   Third umpire: S. D. Fry.
Referee: J. Srinath.

NEW ZEALAND v ENGLAND

At Wellington (Westpac Stadium), February 13, 2018 (floodlit). New Zealand won by 12 runs. Toss: England. Twenty20 international debut: T. L. Seifert.

After finally leaving Australia, more than three months after setting off for the Ashes, England arrived in New Zealand, and brought their Twenty20 travails with them. Events pivoted on the fifth over, when Wood – having just removed Munro – botched a chance to run out Williamson before he had scored, despite plenty of time to aim at all three stumps. Williamson went on to crack an unforgiving 72. Guptill had let rip at the head of the innings, while debutants Mark Chapman – a former Hong Kong international – and wicketkeeper Tim Seifert shared four late sixes. England's response kept up the entertainment: nine wickets, eight sixes and two run-outs. When Hales was dominating the powerplay they had a chance but, once he miscued Sodhi to deep midwicket, self-belief tangibly waned. Malan was impressive again, though Roy fell in single figures for the fifth Twenty20 international in a row. The result left England needing Australia to beat New Zealand at Auckland to keep alive their own interests.

Man of the Match: K. S. Williamson.

New Zealand

		B	4/6
1 M. J. Guptill *c 9 b 10*	65	40	6/3
2 C. Munro *c 6 b 11*	11	13	2
3 *K. S. Williamson *b 8*	72	46	4/4
4 C. de Grandhomme *c 8 b 10*	0	1	0
5 M. S. Chapman *c 6 b 11*	20	13	0/2
6 L. R. P. L. Taylor *not out*	1	1	0
7 †T. L. Seifert *not out*	14	6	0/2
B 1, lb 5, w 7	13		

6 overs: 50-1   (20 overs) 196-5

1/39 2/121 3/121 4/169 5/181

8 M. J. Santner, 9 T. G. Southee, 10 I. S. Sodhi
and 11 T. A. Boult did not bat.

Willey 4–9–36–0; Wood 4–9–51–2; Jordan
4–10–34–1; Plunkett 4–7–33–0; Rashid
4–3–36–2.

England

		B	4/6
1 J. J. Roy *c 11 b 9*	8	8	2
2 A. D. Hales *c 4 b 10*	47	24	6/3
3 D. J. Malan *c 11 b 8*	59	40	6/2
4 J. M. Vince *run out (3)*	10	7	0/1
5 *J. C. Buttler *c 9 b 10*	2	4	0
6 S. W. Billings *c 10 b 8*	12	11	1
7 D. J. Willey *run out (7)*	21	10	0/2
8 C. J. Jordan *b 11*	6	6	1
9 L. E. Plunkett *b 11*	0	1	0
10 A. U. Rashid *not out*	8	6	1
11 M. A. Wood *not out*	5	3	1
B 2, lb 2, w 2	6		

6 overs: 60-1   (20 overs) 184-9

1/14 2/79 3/95 4/109 5/129 6/158 7/168 8/168
9/172

Boult 4–10–46–2; Santner 4–11–29–2;
Southee 4–10–30–1; Sodhi 4–7–49–2; Munro
2–6–11–0; de Grandhomme 2–3–15–0.

Umpires: S. B. Haig and W. R. Knights.   Third umpire: P. Wilson.
Referee: J. Srinath.

NEW ZEALAND v AUSTRALIA

At Auckland, February 16, 2018 (floodlit). Australia won by five wickets. Toss: New Zealand.

Records tumbled at Eden Park, where Australia brushed aside their costliest bowling display to complete the largest successful chase in Twenty20 history. Auckland's come-hither straight boundaries and docile track proved a heady combination: there were 32 sixes in all, equalling the international record (West Indies v India at Lauderhill, Florida, in August 2016), while the match aggregate of 488 was only one short of the record (Lauderhill again). Guptill piled on 132 with Munro inside 11 overs, and reached a hundred in 49 balls; Guptill also overhauled Brendon McCullum's tally of 2,140 runs to become the leading scorer in T20 internationals. It was a dizzying assault, though Australia belatedly stemmed the bleeding, taking four for 37 in the last four overs. Despite New Zealand equalling their own highest score, they might have done better. Even so, Tye nursed figures of two for 64, Australia's most expensive in the format. Needing more than two a ball,

HIGHEST SUCCESSFUL TWENTY20 RUN-CHASES

Total	Overs		
245-5	**18.5**	**Australia v New Zealand (243-6) at Auckland**	**2017-18**
236-6	19.2	West Indies v South Africa (231-7) at Johannesburg	2014-15
230-8	19.4	England v South Africa (229-4) at Mumbai	2015-16
226-3	18.3	Sussex v Essex (225-3) at Chelmsford	2014
225-5	19.1	Nottinghamshire v Yorkshire (223-5) at Nottingham	2017
224-5	19.4	Cape Cobras v Titans (222-4) at Centurion	2010-11
224-5	20	Glamorgan v Essex (219-4) at Chelmsford	2017
223-8	20	Hobart Hurricanes v Melb. Renegades (222-4) at Melbourne (Docklands)	2016-17
220-4	18	Somerset v Hampshire (216-5) at Taunton	2010
220-4	19	Central Districts v Otago (219-4) at Dunedin	2005-06

The highest total in the second innings of any T20 match is Central Districts' 248-4 to lose to Otago (249-3) at New Plymouth in 2016-17.

Warner and Short swung with impunity to blaze 91 in six overs. Neither went as big as Guptill, but Lynn, Maxwell and Finch all took turns. The game began to resemble a variety show: Short smashed a hospitality-box window, another six knocked a beer from a spectator's hand, and a fan earned $NZ50,000 for a one-handed catch. Somebody had to pay for the merriment, and Wheeler footed the bill, removed from the attack for a second beamer after conceding an eye-watering 64 from 19 legal deliveries. Appropriately, the match finished with one last six, as Finch deposited de Grandhomme over long-on.

Man of the Match: D. J. M. Short.

New Zealand

		B	4/6
1 M. J. Guptill *c 4 b 9*	105	54	6/9
2 C. Munro *c 4 b 9*	76	33	6/6
3 †T. L. Seifert *c 5 b 8*	12	6	1/1
4 M. S. Chapman *hit wkt b 11*	16	14	1
5 C. de Grandhomme *b 10*	3	4	0
6 L. R. P. L. Taylor *not out*	17	6	0/2
7 *K. S. Williamson *c 9 b 10*	1	2	0
8 B. M. Wheeler *not out*	1	2	0
Lb 3, w 8, nb 1	12		

6 overs: 67-0   (20 overs) 243-6

1/132 2/155 3/212 4/220 5/222 6/224

9 T. G. Southee, 10 I. S. Sodhi and 11 T. A. Boult did not bat.

Richardson 4–10–40–2; Stalnake 4–8–43–1; Tye 4–5–64–2; Stoinis 4–5–50–0; Agar 3–5–24–1; Short 1–0–19–0.

Australia

		B	4/6
1 *D. A. Warner *b 10*	59	24	4/5
2 D. J. M. Short *c 3 b 11*	76	44	8/3
3 C. A. Lynn *c 1 b 5*	18	13	1/1
4 G. J. Maxwell *b 9*	31	14	3/2
5 A. J. Finch *not out*	36	14	3/3
6 M. P. Stoinis *run out (8/3)*	4	5	0
7 †A. T. Carey *not out*	1	1	0
W 18, nb 2	20		

6 overs: 91-0   (18.5 overs) 245-5

1/121 2/143 3/199 4/217 5/238

8 A. C. Agar, 9 A. J. Tye, 10 K. W. Richardson and 11 B. Stalnake did not bat.

Boult 3.5–8–42–1; Wheeler 3.1–4–64–0; Southee 4–5–48–1; Sodhi 4–6–35–1; de Grandhomme 3.5–2–56–1.

Umpires: S. B. Haig and P. Wilson.   Third umpire: W. R. Knights.
Referee: J. Srinath.

NEW ZEALAND v ENGLAND

At Hamilton, February 18 (floodlit). England won by two runs. Toss: New Zealand.

Even in victory, England were robbed of the chance to celebrate. New Zealand stumbled at the line, but still did enough to reach the final. It all came down to net run-rate which remained in the hosts' favour. England again leaned heavily on Malan's ability to extract maximum value from low-risk strokeplay, as he reeled off a fourth half-century in five Twenty20 internationals. But he was outdone by his captain, as Morgan relocated his muse to make 80 not out, and lead a frenetic four-over finale containing 61 runs and three wickets. New Zealand required 195 to win, but 175 to pip England to the final. Munro showed no sign of compromising, heaving seven sixes in an 18-ball 50 before falling to Rashid's googly. Eight successive overs of disciplined spin from Rashid and Dawson, costing 49, put England back in the fight, before Jordan's yorkers and Tom Curran's steely final over sealed a two-run success. De Grandhomme had to hit the last ball for four, but managed only a single. Yet England still trudged from the field, after Chapman's sparky innings had taken New Zealand through. "It didn't feel like a win," said Morgan. "We had absolutely no right to be in the final. We played terribly."

Man of the Match: E. J. G. Morgan.

England

	B	4/6
1 J. J. Roy *c 3 b 11*	21	13 3/1
2 A. D. Hales *c 3 b 9*	1	4 0
3 D. J. Malan *c 4 b 6*	53	36 2/5
4 *E. J. G. Morgan *not out*	80	46 4/6
5 †J. C. Buttler *st 7 b 10*	2	5 0
6 S. W. Billings *b 11*	6	8 0
7 D. J. Willey *c 1 b 9*	10	5 2
8 L. A. Dawson *c 1 b 11*	10	3 1/1
9 C. J. Jordan *not out*	6	1 0/1
W 4, nb 1	5	

6 overs: 41-2   (20 overs) 194-7

1/22 2/24 3/117 4/123 5/165 6/176 7/187

10 A. U. Rashid and 11 T. K. Curran did not bat.

Boult 4–9–50–3; Santner 2–3–32–0; Southee 4–9–22–2; de Grandhomme 4–8–32–1; Williamson 1–0–16–0; Sodhi 4–12–31–1; Munro 1–0–11–0.

New Zealand

	B	4/6
1 M. J. Guptill *b 3*	62	47 3/4
2 C. Munro *c 7 b 10*	57	21 3/7
3 *K. S. Williamson *b 8*	8	13 0
4 M. S. Chapman *not out*	37	30 2/2
5 L. R. P. L. Taylor *c 4 b 11*....	7	6 1
6 C. de Grandhomme *not out*	8	5 1
B 1, lb 8, w 2, nb 2	13	

6 overs: 77-0   (20 overs) 192-4

1/78 2/100 3/164 4/173

7 †T. L. Seifert, 8 M. J. Santner, 9 T. G. Southee, 10 I. S. Sodhi and 11 T. A. Boult did not bat.

Willey 3–9–33–0; Curran 3–5–32–1; Jordan 4–8–42–0; Rashid 4–6–22–1; Dawson 4–10–27–1; Malan 2–2–27–1.

Umpires: C. M. Brown and P. Wilson.   Third umpire: S. B. Haig.
Referee: J. Srinath.

QUALIFYING TABLE

	P	W	L	Pts	NRR
AUSTRALIA	4	4	0	8	1.71
NEW ZEALAND	4	1	3	2	–0.55
England	4	1	3	2	–1.03

FINAL

NEW ZEALAND v AUSTRALIA

At Auckland, February 21, 2018 (floodlit). Australia won by 19 runs (DLS). Toss: New Zealand.
To no great surprise, Australia left Eden Park with a fifth straight win, and another slab of silverware to take back to Melbourne. Any other result would have felt like an injustice. The manner of their victory was in contrast to the extravaganza between the same sides on the same strip five days earlier, as the bowlers extracted a measure of revenge. Munro and Guptill flexed their muscles against the new ball but, once they departed, Australia – in particular left-arm spinner Agar, who returned career-best figures – seized the initiative. Agar made Williamson pay for an ungainly smear, pinned Chapman on the sweep two balls later, then drew a mis-hit from de Grandhomme. Taylor lingered long enough to avert disaster, but did no lasting damage. Rain prevented Australia finishing things as they would have liked, but there was little room for doubt. Short reached 50 from 28 balls after accelerating fiercely and, despite Sodhi's best efforts, stiff blows from Maxwell and Finch left the DLS par in the rear-view mirror. Agar was promoted to No. 3 after Lynn dislocated his right shoulder in the field.
Man of the Match: A. C. Agar.   *Man of the Series:* G. J. Maxwell.

New Zealand

		B	4/6
1 M. J. Guptill *c 1 b 11*........	21	15	2/1
2 C. Munro *c 3 b 10*...........	29	14	3/2
3 *K. S. Williamson *b 3*.......	9	9	1
4 M. S. Chapman *lbw b 3*.....	8	9	1
5 L. R. P. L. Taylor *not out*	43	38	2/1
6 C. de Grandhomme *c 4 b 3*....	10	6	1
7 M. J. Santner *c 8 b 9*	0	1	0
8 †T. L. Seifert *b 7*............	3	8	0
9 T. G. Southee *c 4 b 10*.......	5	3	1
10 I. S. Sodhi *b 9*	13	16	0/1
11 T. A. Boult *not out*..........	1	1	0
Lb 3, w 5.................	8		

6 overs: 63-2   (20 overs)   150-9

1/48 2/59 3/72 4/73 5/91 6/93 7/101 8/110 9/148

Stanlake 4–8–37–1; Richardson 4–12–30–2;
Tye 4–9–30–2; Agar 4–7–27–3; Stoinis
4–10–23–1.

Australia

		B	4/6
1 *D. A. Warner *b 10*	25	23	2
2 D. J. M. Short *c 4 b 2*........	50	30	6/3
3 A. C. Agar *st 8 b 7*..........	2	5	0
4 G. J. Maxwell *not out*........	20	18	0/1
5 A. J. Finch *not out*	18	13	0/1
B 4, lb 1, nb 1	6		

6 overs: 55-0   (14.4 overs)   121-3

1/72 2/78 3/84

6 C. A. Lynn, 7 M. P. Stoinis, 8 †A. T. Carey,
9 A. J. Tye, 10 K. W. Richardson and 11 B.
Stanlake did not bat.

Boult 3–7–27–0; Sodhi 4–14–21–1; Southee
2–3–21–0; Santner 3.4–8–29–1; Munro
2–2–18–1.

Umpires: C. M. Brown and W. R. Knights.   Third umpire: S. B. Haig.
Referee: J. Srinath.

NEW ZEALAND v ENGLAND IN 2017-18

Review by Simon Wilde

One-day internationals (5): New Zealand 2, England 3
Test matches (2): New Zealand 1, England 0

England's tour of New Zealand, completing a tramp around the Antipodes that began in late October and spanned 160 days, confirmed the impression created by the trip to Australia: they were a limited Test team, but a 50-over side blessed with rare quality. A heavy loss in Auckland in the equivalent of three days, followed by a failure to drive home their advantage in Christchurch, left England nursing a first Test series defeat by New Zealand since 1999, and the first in New Zealand since 1983-84. Five defeats and two draws also confirmed their most unproductive winter: they had failed to win any of their seven Tests in 1987-88 or 2008-09, but did manage 11 draws. How such tedium would have been welcomed now.

If this all added up to a chastening start to Joe Root's career as a touring captain, Eoin Morgan's one-day team went from strength to strength. New Zealand had boasted a formidable 50-over record at home. But England fought back after losing the first game, and claimed the decider at Hagley Oval with a ruthlessness that left their superiority in no doubt. Following their 4–1 triumph in Australia, it meant they had won bilateral one-day series against two major opponents in the same winter for the first time.

Key three: Kane Williamson hit hundreds in both series, while Tim Southee and Trent Boult shared 27 wickets in the two Tests.

England's Test team have often outperformed their one-day side, but rarely has it been so emphatically the other way round. By the time the squad finally headed home – this was the longest trip since 1962-63, when the players last travelled to Australia by boat – the question was whether the decision by Andrew Strauss, the director of England cricket, to give the white-ball formats greater priority was responsible for the Test decline. There was plainly a lack of quality in the Test squad, and nothing like the competition for places enjoyed by the one-day group. Yet a suspicion nagged: England were losing interest in the longest format.

Trevor Bayliss, who unlike any of the players was involved throughout the winter, had been brought in as coach to bring about a white-ball renaissance, but how much desire did he have left for the two Tests that rounded off the campaign? And how angry did he get when England were dismissed for 58 on the first day at Auckland? Without a win in 13 Tests away from home since October 2016, there was hardly room for complacency. But at the end of the tour, Bayliss praised his players' work ethic, and predicted few changes come summer.

Change, however, was already on its way. Between the one-dayers and the Tests, it was announced that James Whitaker was stepping down as national selector, and his replacement – later revealed to be Ed Smith – would oversee a process with a fresh emphasis on talent identification. The message was clear: the old system had not always unearthed the right players.

Unlike in Australia, England could now count on their pivotal all-rounder, Ben Stokes. Having suspended him following an incident outside a Bristol nightclub in September 2017, the ECB counter-intuitively decided he was free to play after the police charged him with affray. His presence as an undoubted boon to the one-day side: he contributed 141 runs at 47, five wickets and seven catches, and won the match award after closing out the chase at Mount Maunganui.

But he developed a back problem which prevented him from bowling in the Auckland Test, and allowed only ten overs in Christchurch. While he was playing as a specialist batsman, the Test side lacked the balance the management craved. To accommodate a fourth seamer at Auckland, James Vince was dropped, and Root moved to No. 3, a position he had previously avoided as captain; when that did not work, Vince was recalled and the bowling attack reduced from five to four. Stokes still played England's best innings in Auckland as they scrapped in vain for a draw, defending solidly for almost four and a half hours.

Their desperation to find a way of taking 20 wickets was evident from the reconfiguration for the Second Test. They dropped Moeen Ali for the first time, and Chris Woakes, despite ten wickets at 20 in the ODIs. Faith in both as overseas Test bowlers had collapsed: Ali averaged 85 abroad since the start of the India tour in 2016-17, and Woakes 61 over his career. They were replaced by Jack Leach, the uncapped Somerset slow left-armer, who arrived during the build-up after Hampshire leg-spinner Mason Crane was ruled out by a stress fracture, and Mark Wood.

To an extent, events conspired against England. Modern itineraries leave little time for meaningful preparation, which for the eight members of the

Michael Bradley, AFP/Getty Images

Back in the saddle: Ben Stokes hits out in the second one-dayer, where his all-round performance helped secure an England win.

Ashes squad flying in for the Tests – and some had not played since Sydney – lent importance to the warm-up week in Hamilton. As the Auckland Test was a day/nighter, a pair of two-day games had been scheduled, the first under lights. In both, England would bowl and bat for a day each, regardless of wickets lost. Several players batted more than once in the same innings; it was an unhelpful mess.

The Tests were staged in late season. Rain wiped out most of the second and third days in Auckland, and low temperatures made the evening sessions tough for spectators. And the Christchurch Test was the latest ever on the South Island. The clocks even went back by an hour during the game, though the start was advanced by only 30 minutes. Bad light intervened on the last two evenings – to England's cost.

Perhaps it ought not have been a surprise that they were slow out of the blocks. Even so, their awfulness on the first afternoon at Eden Park was shocking. Faced with terrific bowling from the left-armer Trent Boult, who pitched the ball up and was rewarded with enough movement to cause chaos against leaden-footed batsmen, England's players could barely get their pads on fast enough as nine wickets tumbled in 12 overs. At 23 for eight, they had still needed four to beat the lowest Test score of all time; at 27 for nine, they might have recorded their own lowest by a distance had James Anderson edged a first-ball swish.

Their batting took the brunt of the criticism, but the bowling was sterile. A meticulous innings from Kane Williamson – who would convert his unbeaten

91 at stumps into a New Zealand-record 18th Test century – set the seal on what was numerically the worst opening day on which England had batted first. The weather gave them a chance of escape, and they battled valiantly, but Neil Wagner's short-ball aggression prised out three of the four who made fifty; England paid him the compliment of picking Wood to perform a similar role in Christchurch.

There, they improved, although they again started badly by losing five for 94, before Jonny Bairstow began a fightback, scoring his third international century in 25 days. Other England sides of recent vintage might have driven home the win, but this one had little self-belief: New Zealand were allowed to recover from 36 for five to 278, the batting lacked positivity in the push for third-innings runs, and several chances were spilled as the hosts negotiated nearly 125 overs to safety. A major recipient of those lapses was Ish Sodhi, whose eighth-wicket stand with Wagner spanned 31. It was the closest England came to winning a Test all winter.

FIVE STATS YOU MAY HAVE MISSED

BENEDICT BERMANGE

- Auckland, England were the fifth team to be bowled out in the first session of a Test:

Australia (53)	v England at Lord's	1896
India (76)	v South Africa at Ahmedabad	2007-08
New Zealand (45)	v South Africa at Cape Town	2012-13
Australia (60)	v England at Nottingham	2015
England (58)	**v New Zealand at Auckland**	**2017-18**
Bangladesh (43)	v West Indies at North Sound	2018

- Kane Williamson became the first batsman to outscore the opposition by the end of the second session of a Test: he had 59* to England's 58. In July 2018, Devon Smith (48*) followed suit for West Indies v Bangladesh in Antigua. The highest score by the end of the second session for the team batting second is 67*, by Sanath Jayasuriya for Sri Lanka against Bangladesh (all out for 90) at Colombo's SSC in 2001-02.

- For only the fourth time, England conceded a lead of more than 300 in consecutive Tests:

v Australia at Leeds (384) and The Oval (380)	1934
v Australia at Brisbane (504) and Sydney (404)	1946-47
v Pakistan at The Oval (331), and Australia at Brisbane (445)	2006 and 2006-07
v Australia at Sydney (303) and New Zealand at Auckland (369)	**2017-18**

   In the first four matches, D. G. Bradman scored 304, 244, 187 and 234.

- Christchurch, Ben Stokes became the ninth England player to appear in an overseas Test in the city of his birth, following G. O. B. Allen (Sydney), D. R. Jardine (Bombay), D. E. Malcolm (Kingston), C. C. Lewis (Georgetown), A. R. Caddick (Christchurch), A. J. Strauss (Johannesburg), I. J. L. Trott (Cape Town) and M. J. Prior (Johannesburg).

- Stuart Broad took wickets with the first two balls of a day's play, only the fourth such instance in Test cricket:

L. O. Fleetwood-Smith	Australia v England at Melbourne (fifth day)	1936-37
G. Onions	England v Australia at Birmingham (second)	2009
J. M. Anderson	England v West Indies at Leeds (third)	2017
S. C. J. Broad	**England v New Zealand at Christchurch (fifth)**	**2017-18**

   Fleetwood-Smith dismissed W. Voce and K. Farnes to end the Fifth Test, and win the Ashes.

Stu Forster, Getty Images

Striking success: one of the few positives for England was the form of Jonny Bairstow.

The flawed fielding was one of several unhappy aspects of their performance. The one-day side had looked sharper, typified by four run-outs at Mount Maunganui, and a brilliant running catch on the boundary at Hagley Oval by Bairstow. Even here, though, Bayliss sensed room for improvement.

It was hard to argue that any England Test player, except Bairstow, had enhanced his reputation. Vince again showed glimpses of talent without producing the breakthrough innings, while Mark Stoneman appeared the least sure of his place. After flourishing in Australia, Dawid Malan was rusty. Their fragility added pressure on the established run-getters, Alastair Cook and Root. Cook was plucked from the crease by Boult with the ease of a fisherman shucking oysters: his 23 runs in four innings represented the least productive series of his career. Root fell twice to Boult in Auckland, and again failed to convert starts: he ended the Test winter with seven fifties but no hundreds, the figures of a player failing to fulfil his potential.

The bowling remained as reliant on Anderson and Stuart Broad as it had been in Australia (though New Zealand were heavily dependent on Boult and Tim Southee, who took all ten first-innings wickets in both Tests). Broad was in danger of losing the new ball and, had the batting not failed so catastrophically, might have done so. In the event, although he – like Anderson – did not pitch the ball up as Boult had done, neither Woakes nor Craig Overton made a case for usurping him. Then, in the Second Test, everything clicked, and Broad's solitary work in the nets on his wrist position paid dividends. His six for 54 was his best since blowing away South Africa at Johannesburg in January 2016. Leach made a commendable Test debut in returning figures of 51–18–113–2, a performance that merited further outings, without suggesting he could solve England's spin-bowling crisis at a stroke.

The one-day series win had been all the more encouraging, as England were without Liam Plunkett, their leading wicket-taker of the previous 12 months.

Initially, Woakes shared the death overs with the inexperienced Tom Curran, who offered an array of variations. Between them, Woakes and Curran closed out a low-scoring game in Wellington. With Bairstow established as Jason Roy's opening partner, and Stokes returning, Alex Hales's future looked uncertain, even after he filled in for the injured Roy in the final match. He scored 61, but was overshadowed by the brilliant Bairstow, who struck the fastest hundred by an England opener.

England might even have won the two games they lost, but were thwarted by a pair of superb hundreds from Ross Taylor, whose absence from the decider was crucial. At Hamilton, they lost by three wickets in the final over. At Dunedin, they could have made many more than 335; for once, the supercharged batting imploded. Three days later, they committed no such slip-ups, cruising to their ninth win in ten bilateral series.

ENGLAND TOURING PARTY

*J. E. Root (Yorkshire; T/50), M. M. Ali (Worcestershire; T/50), J. M. Anderson (Lancashire; T), J. M. Bairstow (Yorkshire; T/50), S. W. Billings (Kent; 50), S. C. J. Broad (Nottinghamshire; T), J. C. Buttler (Lancashire; 50), A. N. Cook (Essex; T), M. S. Crane (Hampshire; T), T. K. Curran (Surrey; 50), B. T. Foakes (Surrey; T), A. D. Hales (Nottinghamshire; 50), M. J. Leach (Somerset; T), L. S. Livingstone (Lancashire; T), D. J. Malan (Middlesex; T), E. J. G. Morgan (Middlesex; 50), C. Overton (Somerset; T/50), A. U. Rashid (Yorkshire; 50), J. J. Roy (Surrey; 50), B. A. Stokes (Durham; T/50), M. D. Stoneman (Surrey; T), J. M. Vince (Hampshire; T), D. J. Willey (Yorkshire; 50), C. R. Woakes (Warwickshire; T/50), M. A. Wood (Durham; T/50).

Morgan captained in the ODIs. L. E. Plunkett (Yorkshire) was originally selected for the 50-over squad, but aggravated a hamstring injury in the preceding T20 tri-series, and was replaced by Overton. Leach was called up for the Tests after Crane was diagnosed with a lumbar stress fracture.

Coach: T. H. Bayliss (T). *Assistant coach:* P. Farbrace (T). *Batting coach:* G. P. Thorpe (T), M. R. Ramprakash (50). *Fast-bowling coach:* C. E. W. Silverwood (T/50). *Spin-bowling coach:* S. C. G. MacGill (T). *Fielding coach:* P. D. Collingwood (T/50). *Operations manager:* P. A. Neale (T/50). *Analyst:* N. A. Leamon (T/50). *Doctor:* M. G. Wotherspoon (T/50). *Physiotherapist:* C. A. de Weymarn (T), S. Griffin (50). *Masseur:* M. Saxby (T/50). *Strength and conditioning:* P. C. F. Scott (T/50). *Security manager:* R. C. Dickason (T/50). *Head of team communications:* D. M. Reuben (T/50).

ONE-DAY INTERNATIONAL REPORTS BY PAUL NEWMAN

NEW ZEALAND v ENGLAND

First One-Day International

At Hamilton, February 25, 2018 (day/night). New Zealand won by three wickets. Toss: New Zealand.

After a Twenty20 triangular tournament that failed to capture the public imagination, this five-match series got off to a thrilling start as New Zealand snatched victory from England's grasp. All the talk had been of Stokes's first game back for England, five months to the day since the fracas in Bristol that landed him in court on a charge of affray. For a while, it looked as if he would bend the match to his will. Despite losing Munro in the second over – Woakes's 100th ODI wicket – New Zealand were cruising home, needing 80 off 62 balls with seven wickets in hand, only for Stokes to remove Latham and de Grandhomme in successive overs. With Tom Curran adding Nicholls in between, 205 for three became 215 for six. Taylor put on 178 with Latham (a New Zealand fourth-wicket record against England – for ten days, before the same pair broke it again), but when he was stumped for a superb 113, the pendulum had swung. If Buttler had completed a second stumping to dismiss Southee next ball, it might have been game over. But Santner had other ideas, clattering Rashid for successive sixes, and finishing with another, off Woakes, as New Zealand hurried home with four balls to spare. England had been indebted to late impetus from Buttler, who top-scored with 79 off 65, including five sixes, on a slow pitch. Earlier, Root was undone by Munro's knuckle ball after a classy 71. But New Zealand's victory – their ninth in consecutive ODIs – was set up by their death bowling: England managed only 67 from their last ten overs.

Man of the Match: L. R. P. L. Taylor.

England

J. J. Roy b Santner	49		D. J. Willey not out		11
J. M. Bairstow c Taylor b Boult	4		T. K. Curran not out		0
J. E. Root b Munro	71		B 1, lb 4, w 6		11
*E. J. G. Morgan c Southee b Sodhi	8				
B. A. Stokes c Taylor b Santner	12		1/10 (2) 2/89 (1)	(8 wkts, 50 overs)	284
†J. C. Buttler run out (Southee)	79		3/104 (4) 4/139 (5)		
M. M. Ali b Guptill b Sodhi	28		5/181 (3) 6/228 (7)		
C. R. Woakes c and b Boult	11		7/253 (8) 8/284 (6)	10 overs: 41-1	

A. U. Rashid did not bat.

Southee 10–1–47–0; Boult 10–0–64–2; Santner 10–0–54–2; de Grandhomme 4–0–20–0; Sodhi 10–0–63–2; Munro 6–0–31–1.

New Zealand

M. J. Guptill c Stokes b Woakes	13		M. J. Santner not out		45
C. Munro c Buttler b Woakes	6		T. G. Southee not out		8
*K. S. Williamson c Buttler b Willey	8		Lb 5, w 8		13
L. R. P. L. Taylor st Buttler b Rashid	113				
†T. W. M. Latham c Root b Stokes	79		1/6 (2) 2/27 (3)	(7 wkts, 49.2 overs)	287
H. M. Nicholls c Roy b Curran	0		3/27 (1) 4/205 (5)		
C. de Grandhomme c Buttler b Stokes	2		5/206 (6) 6/215 (7) 7/244 (4)	10 overs: 28-3	

I. S. Sodhi and T. A. Boult did not bat.

Willey 6–1–26–1; Woakes 8.2–0–47–2; Curran 10–0–65–1; Stokes 8–0–43–2; Ali 5–0–30–0; Rashid 10–0–55–1; Root 2–0–16–0.

Umpires: S. B. Haig and R. S. A. Palliyaguruge.   Third umpire: R. J. Tucker.
Referee: R. S. Madugalle.

NEW ZEALAND v ENGLAND

Second One-Day International

At Mount Maunganui, February 28, 2018 (day/night). England won by six wickets. Toss: England.

Stokes stamped his authority on the Bay of Plenty, taking two wickets, running out two batsmen, then hitting an unbeaten 63 to take England home with a flourish, and scupper New Zealand's hopes of equalling the national record of ten straight one-day victories. His dynamism played a big part in what was arguably England's best fielding performance under Trevor Bayliss: in all, they pulled off four run-outs – only the fourth time they had done so in an ODI – and three outstanding catches, as New Zealand limped to 223. The spin of Rashid and Ali conceded just 65 in 20 overs. And it would have been worse for the hosts without a ninth-wicket stand of 69 between Santner, the hero of Hamilton, who scored a maiden one-day international half-century, and Ferguson. The early casualties included left-hander Mark Chapman, in his first ODI for New Zealand after two for his native Hong Kong. Boult quickly removed Roy and Root, with de Grandhomme's catch to dismiss Root – low to his right at short midwicket – even better than anything England managed. Stokes ensured there would be no serious alarms, though he might have been run out before he had scored: de Grandhomme sidefooted the ball wide of the stumps. England's best batting came from Morgan, who timed the ball sweetly from the start, and added 88 in 15 overs with Stokes to break the back of a chase completed with 73 balls to spare. "I was quite emotional walking off," said Stokes. "It made me understand how much of a privilege it is to represent your country."

Man of the Match: B. A. Stokes.

New Zealand

M. J. Guptill c Roy b Ali	50	*T. G. Southee run out (Stokes/Butler)	6
C. Munro c Buttler b Woakes	1	L. H. Ferguson c Rashid b Stokes	19
M. S. Chapman c Willey b Woakes	1	T. A. Boult run out (Stokes/Woakes)	2
L. R. P. L. Taylor run out (Willey/Buttler)	10	Lb 5, w 5	10
†T. W. M. Latham c Curran b Ali	22		—
H. M. Nicholls c Roy b Stokes	1	1/6 (2) 2/9 (3) 3/48 (4) (49.4 overs)	223
C. de Grandhomme run out (Bairstow/ Buttler)	38	4/79 (1) 5/82 (6) 6/108 (5) 7/141 (7) 8/147 (9) 9/216 (10)	
M. J. Santner not out	63	10/223 (11)	10 overs: 34-2

Willey 5–0–16–0; Woakes 7.4–1–42–2; Rashid 10–0–32–0; Curran 9–0–53–0; Ali 10–0–33–2; Stokes 8–0–42–2.

England

J. J. Roy c Santner b Boult	8	†J. C. Buttler not out	36
J. M. Bairstow c sub (T. D. Astle) b Ferguson	37	Lb 2, w 8	10
J. E. Root c de Grandhomme b Boult	9		—
*E. J. G. Morgan c and b Munro	62	1/15 (1) 2/47 (3) (4 wkts, 37.5 overs)	225
B. A. Stokes not out	63	3/86 (2) 4/174 (4)	10 overs: 47-2

M. M. Ali, C. R. Woakes, D. J. Willey, A. U. Rashid and T. K. Curran did not bat.

Southee 7–0–55–0; Boult 8–1–46–2; Santner 7.5–0–40–0; Ferguson 8–0–48–1; de Grandhomme 2–0–11–0; Munro 5–0–23–1.

Umpires: W. R. Knights and R. J. Tucker. Third umpire: R. S. A. Palliyaguruge.
Referee: R. S. Madugalle.

NEW ZEALAND v ENGLAND

Third One-Day International

At Wellington (Westpac Stadium), March 3, 2018 (day/night). England won by four runs. Toss: New Zealand.

England's first one-day international win at the Westpac Stadium in five attempts was almost ruined by Williamson. While he was there, New Zealand – even without the injured Ross Taylor – looked destined for victory, despite sliding from 80 for one to 103 for six against Ali and Rashid, a collapse triggered by Stokes's masterful leap at midwicket to see off Munro. The game might have turned on a controversial reprieve for Santner, who had made only two of his eventual 41 when Roy, diving forward at midwicket, was deemed not to have completed a catch; foreshortened TV images

---

FASTEST TO 5,000 RUNS IN ONE-DAY INTERNATIONALS

I		*I*	
101	H. M. Amla (South Africa)	121	C. G. Greenidge (West Indies)
114	V. Kohli (India)	124	A. B. de Villiers (SA/Africa)
114	I. V. A. Richards (West Indies)	126	S. C. Ganguly (India)
118	B. C. Lara (West Indies)	128	D. M. Jones (Australia)
119	**K. S. Williamson (New Zealand)**	131	G. C. Smith (SA/Africa)

---

did him no favours. Santner, the series' unlikely batting star, added 96 with his captain, but fortune finally favoured England when Woakes, attempting a return catch, deflected a Williamson drive on to the stumps, with Santner out of his ground. Southee didn't last long but, with 22 needed off two overs, Williamson reached his 11th one-day hundred with a boundary off Curran. The rest of the over produced only three singles, however, as Curran repaid Morgan's faith with a string of clever slower balls. When Williamson took ten from the first four deliveries of the final over, from Woakes, including a six over midwicket, New Zealand required five off two. Having failed to close out a tight game at Hamilton, Woakes now kept Williamson scoreless, and England were celebrating a 2–1 lead. On a slow, two-paced surface of uneven bounce, their own innings had yielded nine double-figure scores, but nothing higher than Morgan's 48. Stokes's 39 off 73 balls summed up the struggle. But a far-from-perfect total of 234 helped produce a perfect finish.

Man of the Match: M. M. Ali.

England

J. J. Roy c Guptill b Boult	15	A. U. Rashid run out (Boult) 11
J. M. Bairstow b Sodhi	19	T. K. Curran not out 2
J. E. Root c Sodhi b de Grandhomme	20	M. A. Wood run out (Nicholls/Boult) 1
*E. J. G. Morgan b Southee	48	B 2, lb 2, w 7 11
B. A. Stokes c Munro b Sodhi	39	
†J. C. Buttler c Latham b Sodhi	29	1/25 (1) 2/53 (3) 3/68 (2) (50 overs) 234
M. M. Ali run out (de Grandhomme/		4/139 (4) 5/168 (5) 6/184 (6)
Southee)	23	7/215 (8) 8/222 (7) 9/231 (9)
C. R. Woakes c Williamson b Boult	16	10/234 (11) 10 overs: 36-1

Southee 10–0–48–1; Boult 10–1–47–2; Santner 2–0–12–0; de Grandhomme 10–1–24–1; Sodhi 10–0–53–3; Munro 8–0–46–0.

New Zealand

M. J. Guptill c Curran b Woakes	3	T. G. Southee c Stokes b Woakes 7
C. Munro c Stokes b Rashid	49	I. S. Sodhi not out 2
*K. S. Williamson not out	112	Lb 1, w 4 5
M. S. Chapman c Morgan b Ali	8	
†T. W. M. Latham lbw b Ali	0	1/12 (1) 2/80 (2) (8 wkts, 50 overs) 230
H. M. Nicholls lbw b Rashid	0	3/97 (4) 4/97 (5)
C. de Grandhomme c Woakes b Ali	3	5/98 (6) 6/103 (7)
M. J. Santner run out (Woakes)	41	7/199 (8) 8/210 (9) 10 overs: 47-1

T. A. Boult did not bat.

Woakes 10–1–40–2; Wood 6–0–36–0; Curran 7–0–49–0; Stokes 6–0–27–0; Rashid 10–1–34–2; Ali 10–1–36–3; Root 1–0–7–0.

Umpires: W. R. Knights and R. S. A. Palliyaguruge.   Third umpire: R. J. Tucker.
Referee: R. S. Madugalle.

NEW ZEALAND v ENGLAND

Fourth One-Day International

At Dunedin, March 7, 2018. New Zealand won by five wickets. Toss: New Zealand.

Not long ago, England could only have dreamed of scoring 335 – yet the sense at the break was that they had blown it. Bairstow can rarely have played better for his 138 of 106 balls, three of his seven sixes disappearing over various roofs at the University Oval; Root, meanwhile, finally reached three figures – his 11th ODI hundred – having not converted his previous 12 international fifties. But the pair received no support and, from 267 for one in the 38th over, eight wickets tumbled for 46, handing Sodhi a career-best four for 58. Only a late flurry from Curran stemmed the bleeding. When Munro and Guptill went for ducks, England looked set to get away with their carelessness. Instead, Taylor embarked on an epic innings, all the more remarkable because he aggravated the thigh injury that had kept him out at Wellington. After receiving treatment on 109, he made the rest of his monumental unbeaten 181 – from 147 balls – virtually on one leg. Latham provided admirable

FALSE STARTS

Teams winning a one-day international after losing both openers for ducks:

India (S. M. Gavaskar and K. Srikkanth) v Zimbabwe at Tunbridge Wells............ 1983
India (M. Prabhakar and S. R. Tendulkar) v West Indies at Bombay 1994-95
Pakistan (Aamir Sohail and Zahoor Elahi) v Australia at Hobart.................... 1996-97
India (V. Sehwag and S. C. Ganguly) v Sri Lanka at Colombo (SSC) 2001
India (S. B. Bangar and P. A. Patel) v Zimbabwe at Adelaide...................... 2003-04
South Africa (G. C. Smith and L. E. Bosman) v India at Port Elizabeth 2006-07
England (M. J. Prior and L. J. Wright) v India at Lord's 2007
Sri Lanka (H. D. R. L. Thirimanne and T. M. Dilshan) v Afghanistan at Dunedin 2014-15
Zimbabwe (P. J. Moor and C. J. Chibhabha) v Afghanistan at Sharjah 2015-16
New Zealand (M. J. Guptill and C. Munro) v England at Dunedin................. **2017-18**

HIGHEST ODI SCORES FOR NEW ZEALAND

237*	M. J. Guptill	v West Indies at Wellington (Westpac)..........	2014-15
189*	M. J. Guptill	v England at Southampton.....................	2013
181*	**L. R. P. L. Taylor**	**v England at Dunedin**	**2017-18**
180*	M. J. Guptill	v South Africa at Hamilton....................	2016-17
172	L. Vincent.............	v Zimbabwe at Bulawayo	2005-06
171*	G. M. Turner...........	v East Africa at Birmingham...................	1975
170*	L. Ronchi.............	v Sri Lanka at Dunedin	2014-15
166	B. B. McCullum	v Ireland at Aberdeen	2008
161	J. A. H. Marshall........	v Ireland at Aberdeen	2008

support in a stand of 187, again beating New Zealand's fourth-wicket record against England. Nicholls hit the winning six with three balls to spare. It sealed their biggest successful chase against England, surpassing 306 for seven at the Rose Bowl in 2015, and set up a decider in Christchurch.

Man of the Match: L. R. P. L. Taylor.

England

J. J. Roy c Santner b Sodhi	42	T. K. Curran not out	22
J. M. Bairstow c Southee b Munro	138	M. A. Wood not out	3
J. E. Root c Latham b Southee	102		
†J. C. Buttler c and b Sodhi............	0	Lb 1, w 4	5
*E. J. G. Morgan c Munro b Boult	5		
B. A. Stokes c Nicholls b Sodhi	1	1/77 (1) 2/267 (2) (9 wkts, 50 overs)	335
M. M. Ali c Southee b Sodhi...........	3	3/267 (4) 4/274 (5)	
C. R. Woakes c Boult b Munro..........	3	5/276 (6) 6/280 (7) 7/288 (8)	
A. U. Rashid b Boult.................	11	8/305 (3) 9/313 (9) 10 overs: 77-0	

Southee 10–0–87–1; Boult 10–0–56–2; de Grandhomme 2–0–23–0; Santner 10–0–57–0; Sodhi 10–1–58–4; Munro 8–0–53–2.

New Zealand

M. J. Guptill c Stokes b Woakes	0	H. M. Nicholls not out.................	13
C. Munro lbw b Wood................	0	Lb 4, w 2	6
*K. S. Williamson c Buttler b Stokes	45		
L. R. P. L. Taylor not out	181	1/0 (2) 2/2 (1) (5 wkts, 49.3 overs)	339
†T. W. M. Latham c Ali b Curran	71	3/86 (3) 4/273 (5)	
C. de Grandhomme c Woakes b Curran ...	23	5/303 (6) 10 overs: 44-2	

M. J. Santner, T. G. Southee, I. S. Sodhi and T. A. Boult did not bat.

Woakes 8–2–42–1; Wood 8–0–65–1; Rashid 10–0–74–0; Curran 8.3–0–57–2; Stokes 7–0–45–1; Ali 8–0–52–0.

Umpires: S. B. Haig and R. J. Tucker.   Third umpire: R. S. A. Palliyaguruge.
Referee: R. S. Madugalle.

NEW ZEALAND v ENGLAND

Fifth One-Day International

At Christchurch, March 10, 2018. England won by seven wickets. Toss: England.

Billed as the perfect chance for England to test themselves under the pressure of a must-win game, the final match of a superb series turned into a stroll in Hagley Park. They were in control from the start. New Zealand failed to get going on a blameless pitch at this most picturesque of grounds, before Bairstow made light work of the chase. Woakes, superb again with the new ball, was named Man of the Series, and there was turn once more for Rashid and Ali. New Zealand sorely missed the injured Ross Taylor and, when they limped to 93 for six, it looked as though the capacity crowd might be short-changed. Santner excelled yet again, putting on 84 with Nicholls to lift them to the relative respectability of 223, even if it never looked enough. Bairstow had batted brilliantly in a losing cause in Dunedin, but now made the quickest one-day century by an England opener – in 58 balls – at the time their third-fastest in all. His second fifty needed just 20 deliveries, before his innings ended in anticlimax: giving himself room to carve Boult through the off side, he whacked his leg stump. Earlier, he collected a one-handed diving boundary catch to dismiss Southee – the best, he said, of his career. Hales had been given an unexpected opportunity when Jason Roy pulled out with a back spasm, and marked his first appearance of the series by contributing 61 and sharing an opening stand of 155 inside 21 overs. Stokes helped finish the job with more than 17 in hand, earning England a sixth successive one-day series win.

Man of the Match: J. M. Bairstow. *Man of the Series:* C. R. Woakes.

New Zealand

M. J. Guptill c Stokes b Rashid	47	I. S. Sodhi c Stokes b Curran		5
C. Munro c Buttler b Woakes	0	T. A. Boult not out		2
*K. S. Williamson b Wood	14			
†T. W. M. Latham c Stokes b Rashid	10	W 7		7
M. S. Chapman b Ali	0			
H. M. Nicholls c Morgan b Curran	55	1/1 (2) 2/26 (3) 3/60 (4)	(49.5 overs)	223
C. de Grandhomme c Curran b Rashid	6	4/61 (5) 5/79 (1) 6/93 (7)		
M. J. Santner c Hales b Woakes	67	7/177 (6) 8/213 (8) 9/214 (9)		
T. G. Southee c Bairstow b Woakes	10	10/223 (10)	10 overs: 27-2	

Woakes 10–1–32–3; Wood 8–0–26–1; Stokes 4–0–23–0; Rashid 10–0–42–3; Ali 10–1–39–1; Root 2–0–15–0; Curran 5.5–0–46–2.

England

J. M. Bairstow hit wkt b Boult	104
A. D. Hales c Williamson b Santner	61
J. E. Root not out	23
*E. J. G. Morgan c de Grandhomme b Sodhi	8
B. A. Stokes not out	26
Lb 4, w 3	7

1/155 (1) 2/177 (2)   (3 wkts, 32.4 overs)   229
3/192 (4)   10 overs: 65-0

†J. C. Buttler, M. M. Ali, C. R. Woakes, A. U. Rashid, T. K. Curran and M. A. Wood did not bat.

Southee 5–1–20–0; Boult 6–0–50–1; de Grandhomme 4–0–33–0; Santner 10–0–44–1; Sodhi 7.4–0–78–1.

Umpires: W. R. Knights and R. S. A. Palliyaguruge.   Third umpire: R. J. Tucker.
Referee: R. S. Madugalle.

> **❝** Even though the Tuc Cup was designed to reflect its snack-related sponsor, the first match was not exactly a cracker.**”**
> Pakistan v Australia in 2018-19, First Twenty20 International, page 941

At Hamilton, March 14–15, 2018 (day/night). **Drawn. ‡New Zealand XI 376-9** (90 overs) (T. A. Blundell 131*, K. A. Jamieson 101*; J. M. Anderson 4-56); **England XI 319-14** (90 overs) (L. S. Livingstone 88, J. E. Root 50*; S. H. A. Rance 3-62, D. A. J. Bracewell 3-33, S. C. Kuggeleijn 4-50, N. G. Smith 3-45). *The home side selected from 12 players, and the tourists from 13. The NZ XI were 30-5 in the first session of this floodlit warm-up, but Tom Blundell and Kyle Jamieson put on 165* for the seventh wicket before both retired hurt. Three New Zealanders batted twice, and next day five Englishmen – Mark Stoneman was out for one and two. Joe Root, however, made 50* at the second attempt, a few hours after falling lbw for one. As early wickets tumbled, Ben Stokes (who was resting a sore back and did not play) had to go and fetch Moeen Ali from the nets. The most impressive display came from Liam Livingstone, who hit 13 fours and a six in almost three hours, though he still missed out on a Test cap.*

At Hamilton, March 16–17, 2018. **Drawn. ‡New Zealand XI 287-13** (90 overs) (M. J. Guptill 73; M. M. Ali 3-67, J. E. Root 3-23); **England XI 353-9** (90 overs) (J. E. Root 115; S. C. Kuggeleijn 3-67). *The home side selected from 12 players, and the tourists from 13. The England XI shaped better in their second warm-up game, restricting the New Zealanders to 287, even though four of their batsmen went in twice. Root took three late wickets, and next day added a patient century.*

NEW ZEALAND v ENGLAND

First Test

Mike Atherton

At Auckland, March 22–26, 2018 (day/night). New Zealand won by an innings and 49 runs. Toss: New Zealand.

For England, it turned into a good week to bury bad news. Two days after they flirted with the lowest score in Test history, the eyes of the sport were diverted by another game, half a world away in South Africa, where Australia were imploding after three players were charged with ball-tampering. By the time England went down to defeat on the final evening in Auckland – just their tenth in 102 Tests against New Zealand – the result hardly registered on cricket's Richter scale.

ENGLAND'S LOWEST TEST TOTALS

45	v Australia at Sydney	1886-87		58	v New Zealand at Auckland	2017-18
46	v West Indies at Port-of-Spain	1993-94		61	v Australia at Melbourne	1901-02
51	v West Indies at Kingston	2008-09		61	v Australia at Melbourne	1903-04
52	v Australia at The Oval	1948		62	v Australia at Lord's *(2nd inns)*	1888
53	v Australia at Lord's *(1st inns)*	1888		64	v New Zealand at Wellington	1977-78

New Zealand were used to being overlooked, but deserved better here: under Williamson's leadership, they continued to look smart, savvy and adaptable. After England's appalling ineptitude in their first innings, when they were whistled out for 58 in 20.4 overs, only bad weather took the game the distance. Heavy rain was a dampener in more ways than one. The two most affected days were expected to be the best attended: on Friday, the second day, only 23.1 overs were possible; on Saturday, only 17 balls. But this was also a day/night Test – the ninth worldwide, and the first in New Zealand. It was a risky enterprise, given the cost to the home board of around $NZ500,000 to rent Eden

Stu Forster, Getty Images

Boult action: Ben Stokes falls to a masterly piece of deception by Trent Boult.

Park. They needed a daily attendance of around 10,000 to break even, yet the rain-free first and fourth days produced a combined attendance of 18,300.

The jury remained out on floodlit Test cricket. It was never going to be a revolutionary development in any case, more a tinkering at the edges of a form of the game challenged on all fronts. Some spectators dislike the inability to discuss the day's events over dinner, but others enjoy both the tactical nuances caused by the change in conditions around twilight, and the visibility of the pink ball. Not that England's batsmen sighted it too well, even in broad daylight. Despite this experiment, the long-term future of Tests in New Zealand was still likely to be characterised by boutique venues – this was Auckland's first Test for four years – and scarcity.

Given the amount of white-ball cricket between the teams beforehand, it was gratifying to hear Boult say that the two Tests were the games he was most excited about. Throughout, this eagerness was evident. New Zealand looked sharp and skilful, while England looked laboured – like a team, in fact, that had been on the road for over five months. The scheduling had landed them with a further complication: their Test-only batsmen were short of match practice. Cook had returned home after the Ashes, and a modest warm-up in Hamilton barely prepared England for New Zealand's intensity. It is a confused sport that can send a team on the road for so long, yet render them ill-prepared for their most challenging encounters.

The presence of Boult and his partner in destruction, Southee, encouraged Williamson to bowl first, and he was quickly vindicated. Left-arm and right-arm, waspish of pace and with canny variations of swing and angle, they proved far too good. Boult took a career-best six for 32, Southee four for 25. For the first time a pair of New Zealanders had bowled unchanged through a completed innings. They are an exceptional combination, among the best – if not *the* best – their country has produced.

Some of the out-cricket was spectacular, too – nothing better than the catch Williamson held in the gully to dismiss Broad, a stunning one-hander to his left to make it 27 for nine.

Moments earlier, when Southee bowled Ali for the fourth of England's five ducks (equalling their own record for a Test innings), they had been 23 for eight and in danger of undercutting the Test nadir of 26, by New Zealand against England on this ground in 1954-55. It needed a punchy unbeaten 33 from Overton to take them past their own lowest score. They did, though, break one record: this was their worst against New Zealand, below 64 at Wellington in 1977-78.

England's batting was lamentable. They were unable to cope with the late swing, their hard hands and lack of footwork a painful reminder of technical aspects of the game over which English players once had mastery. Overton aside, only Stoneman made double figures. For James Vince, dropped to accommodate Stokes on his return to Test cricket following his absence from the Ashes, it turned into a good game to miss. "We've been on the other side of scores like that, and it's euphoria," said coach Trevor Bayliss. "This is the opposite. Someone sneezes and the rest of the guys catch a cold."

The dismissal of Stokes illustrated better than any the challenge posed by Boult. Having set him up with a number of balls that swung away, Boult darted one back to clatter into off stump. It looked initially as if Stokes had been beaten for pace, but in truth he had failed to spot the variation, and was almost leaving the ball, before belatedly attempting to keep it out. It was a brilliant piece of bowling.

A high-class 102 from Williamson and a career-best unbeaten 145 from Nicholls ensured New Zealand a significant first-innings lead, as England failed to learn from the error of their ways in Australia: they picked a one-paced, right-arm seam attack, plus

---

LAST PAIR DOUBLING THE SCORE IN A TEST

From	To			
92-9	209-9	P. Willey/R. G. D. Willis	England v West Indies at The Oval	1980
21-9	47	P. M. Siddle/N. M. Lyon	Australia v South Africa at Cape Town .	2011-12
117-9	280	P. J. Hughes/A. C. Agar	Australia v England at Nottingham	2013
27-9	**58**	**C. Overton/J. M. Anderson** .	**England v New Zealand at Auckland**	**2017-18**

---

the off-breaks of Ali, who was short on confidence. Broad improved on his Ashes form, courtesy of some technical tweaks, and became the 15th bowler to take 400 Test wickets when he removed Latham. But at no stage did England match New Zealand's verve and energy.

Williamson's 18th Test hundred was an emotional one, taking him past the national-record by the late Martin Crowe and team-mate Taylor. Barring floods, pestilence and plague, he will make many more, because he is a batsman for all conditions and formats. Despite not having played a first-class innings since early December, he adapted superbly and found the ideal tempo, cutting risk from his game, yet always putting away the bad ball. When Williamson was dismissed by Anderson, Nicholls – watchful and well-controlled – assumed responsibility. The threat of rain encouraged Williamson to declare with a lead of 369 – New Zealand's biggest on first innings over England, surpassing 298 at Lord's in 1973 – and a minimum of 143 overs to go.

Cook went early, but England made a better fist of things. How could they not? There were four half-centuries, including yet another for Root, though no one made more than Stokes's 66, and too often wickets fell on the cusp of a break. Root was out-thought by Boult from what became the last ball of the fourth day, Ali was leg-before to the same bowler just before the end of the first session on the last, and Stokes fell to Wagner just before the end of the second. New Zealand never stopped trying; England took the game an hour into the final session, though the rain had helped them get there.

Wagner – the workhorse-cum-battering-ram, full of vigour and self-belief – allowed Williamson to adopt different tactics when the swing stopped. Hammering the ball into unforgiving surfaces requires strength and stamina, too, and Wagner was short of neither.

Catching their attention: Kane Williamson takes a blinder to dismiss Stuart Broad, and England are 27 for nine.

He took three vital wickets, all batsmen who were well set – Stoneman hooking, Stokes cutting, Woakes fending a bouncer off his nose. New Zealand's catching was excellent.

The key wicket, though, was Root, who the night before had set his sights on leading a last-day rearguard. Increasing his pace, Boult harried him with clever short-pitched bowling, then induced a faint glove. It was superbly taken by Watling, high and fast to his left – and summed up the hosts' cricket. With the floodlights gleaming, the pink ball luminous against the green baize of the outfield, and New Zealand sensing the moment, it was also a spectacular piece of theatre.

Man of the Match: T. A. Boult.

Close of play: first day, New Zealand 175-3 (Williamson 91, Nicholls 24); second day, New Zealand 229-4 (Nicholls 49, Watling 17); third day, New Zealand 233-4 (Nicholls 52, Watling 18); fourth day, England 132-3 (Malan 19).

England

A. N. Cook c Latham b Boult	5	– c Watling b Boult	2
M. D. Stoneman c Watling b Southee	11	– c Boult b Wagner	55
*J. E. Root b Boult	0	– c Watling b Boult	51
D. J. Malan c Watling b Boult	2	– c Latham b Southee	23
B. A. Stokes b Boult	0	– c Southee b Wagner	66
†J. M. Bairstow c and b Southee	0	– c Williamson b Astle	26
M. M. Ali b Southee	0	– lbw b Boult	28
C. R. Woakes b Boult	5	– c Nicholls b Wagner	52
C. Overton not out	33	– b Astle	3
S. C. J. Broad c Williamson b Southee	0	– not out	1
J. M. Anderson c Nicholls b Boult	1	– c Boult b Astle	1
Lb 1	1	B 8, lb 2, w 1, nb 1	12
	58		**320**

1/6 (1) 2/6 (3) 3/16 (4)   (20.4 overs)   1/6 (1) 2/94 (2)   (126.1 overs)
4/18 (2) 5/18 (5) 6/18 (6)   3/132 (3) 4/142 (4)
7/23 (8) 8/23 (7) 9/27 (10) 10/58 (11)   5/181 (6) 6/217 (7) 7/300 (5)
                                       8/304 (9) 9/319 (8) 10/320 (11)

Boult 10.4–3–32–6; Southee 10–3–25–4. *Second innings*—Boult 27–9–67–3; Southee 26–4–86–1; de Grandhomme 24–10–40–0; Wagner 32–11–77–3; Astle 16.1–5–39–3; Williamson 1–0–1–0.

New Zealand

J. A. Raval c Bairstow b Anderson 3	T. G. Southee c and b Root 25
T. W. M. Latham c Woakes b Broad. 26	N. Wagner not out. 9
*K. S. Williamson lbw b Anderson . . 102	
L. R. P. L. Taylor c Woakes b Anderson . . 20	B 4, lb 9, w 6 19
H. M. Nicholls not out. 145	
†B-J. Watling c Bairstow b Broad. 31	1/8 (1) 2/92 (2) (8 wkts dec, 141 overs) 427
C. de Grandhomme c Bairstow b Overton . 29	3/123 (4) 4/206 (3)
T. D. Astle b Broad 18	5/260 (6) 6/309 (7) 7/341 (8) 8/413 (9)

T. A. Boult did not bat.

Anderson 29–10–87–3; Broad 34–9–78–3; Overton 25–7–70–1; Woakes 33–9–107–0; Ali 17–1–59–0; Root 3–0–13–1.

Umpires: B. N. J. Oxenford and P. R. Reiffel.   Third umpire: M. Erasmus.
Referee: R. B. Richardson.

NEW ZEALAND v ENGLAND

Second Test

VIC MARKS

At Christchurch, March 30–April 3, 2018. Drawn. Toss: New Zealand. Test debut: M. J. Leach.

This was a throwback Test. It took place at the idyllic, grass-banked Hagley Oval, as autumnal trees in the background shed their leaves. The players respected and applauded each other throughout; the only controversy stemmed from the application of the bad-light regulations, and whether play should have been added at the start or the end of the last day. And it was a draw, an outcome seldom seen in the 21st century – unless a Test is scheduled during the monsoon.

The old-fashioned nature of this game was put in sharper relief by the inquest into the Australian ball-tampering saga. The humiliation of Steve Smith, David Warner and Cameron Bancroft in Cape Town and beyond remained a distraction in Christchurch, and a talking point among players, punters and pressmen. The players were appropriately restrained in their reactions, at least in public. One of the match referees in South Africa, Jeff Crowe, said he had never seen "such animosity between two teams". In Christchurch, by contrast, all was sweetness and (occasionally bad) light.

The Cape Town story captivated newsrooms around the globe, overshadowing some ugly statistics prompted by England's failure to force a win. This was only their fourth defeat by New Zealand in a Test series, their second away. More strikingly, it was the 13th consecutive Test overseas without a win, their longest sequence. Of those, ten had been lost.

At least they managed to exorcise some of the horrors of Auckland. Indeed they dominated most of the match but, with four wickets required in the final session, were thwarted by a determined New Zealand tail, and hampered by their own fielding. The frailties of some of England's newer batsmen extended beyond the crease: the catching of Vince and Stoneman in particular was fallible. On an increasingly benign surface, England needed to snatch all the chances that came their way, but were not good enough, or sufficiently relaxed, to do so.

New Zealand had made one enforced change, with Sodhi replacing fellow leg-spinner Todd Astle, who was injured. While Sodhi's contribution with the ball was negligible, his

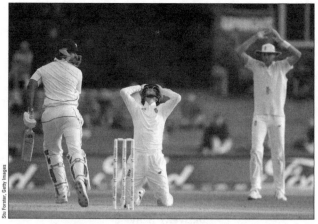

On their knees: Joe Root and Stuart Broad rue their luck as Ish Sodhi survives. England adopt an attacking field for Jack Leach, but the breakthrough does not come.

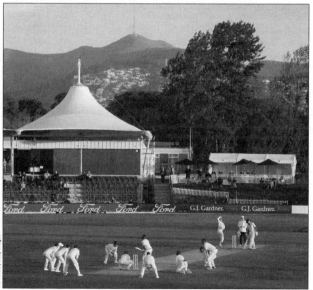

batting on the final day was skilful and significant. England made three changes, none enforced; by the standards of a side reluctant to tinker, this constituted a radical overhaul. As ever, even after the Auckland collapse, it was the bowlers who suffered. Out went Chris Woakes, Moeen Ali – dropped for the first time in his 50-Test career – and Craig Overton. In came Vince (back at No. 3 after Root's short-lived experiment), Wood and Somerset slow left-armer Jack Leach, making a Test debut despite not being in the original touring party.

England were asked to bat and, within 38 overs, were 94 for five. Cook was dismissed cheaply yet again by Boult, who would end up disposing of him all four times in the series. As usual Vince promised a little, and Root a lot – but both succumbed to Southee. Stokes got stuck in until he was caught down the leg side, a common dismissal on this trip. Bairstow fashioned a recovery, grateful for help from Wood and Leach. Wood struck the ball with remarkable freedom and power for a maiden Test fifty, after which he endearingly admitted: "The trouble is, when I get to 20 I start to think I'm Don Bradman." Leach calmly hung around for Bairstow to make his fifth Test century, and again demonstrate how adroitly he bats with the tail.

New Zealand's start was more calamitous than England's: 17 for four inside ten overs, 36 for five inside 20. Their tormentor was Broad. Following speculation he would be required to give up the new ball, he strode to the crease with renewed purpose, and a determination to bowl slightly fuller. After his disappointing Ashes ("I was rubbish"), he

DELIVERY SERVICE

The most balls in Tests by fast bowlers:

		T	Wkts	Avge
31,746	**J. M. Anderson (England)**	145	565	26.98
30,019	C. A. Walsh (West Indies)	132	519	24.44
29,248	G. D. McGrath (Australia)	124	563	21.64
27,740	Kapil Dev (India)	131	434	29.64
25,341	**S. C. J. Broad (England)**	124	433	29.04
24,353	S. M. Pollock (South Africa)	108	421	23.11
23,438	W. P. U. J. C. Vaas (Sri Lanka)	111	355	29.58
22,627	Wasim Akram (Pakistan)	104	414	23.62
22,103	C. E. L. Ambrose (West Indies)	98	405	20.99
21,918	R. J. Hadlee (New Zealand)	86	431	22.29
21,815	I. T. Botham (England).	102	383	28.40

As at January 14, 2019.

had spent time re-evaluating his method. It paid off: figures of six for 54, his first Test five-for in over two years, were a tangible reward for his good sense and humility in recognising something was wrong.

But New Zealand fought back, via the efforts of the battling Watling and, more improbably, a long defensive innings by de Grandhomme. They added 142 in 50 overs. De Grandhomme often scores at a run a ball, even in Tests, but – after a fast start when he kept hooking Wood – he delighted in the pleasures of blocking and exasperating England's attack. His 72 occupied 151 deliveries, an eternity for him. After Southee battered 50 in 48 balls, England's first-innings lead was a precarious 29. At this stage, just two bowlers on each side – Boult and Southee, Anderson and Broad – had taken a wicket, only the third occasion this had happened in Tests after two completed first innings (and the first not to include S. F. Barnes).

England batted sufficiently well in their second to allow Root a rare declaration, even if there were a few stutters along the way on a surface which stubbornly refused to deteriorate. Vince top-scored, which meant his winter had been bookended by his two highest Test innings – leaving the selectors none the wiser. Stoneman made 60, a Test-best, but failed to convince anyone he was the long-term answer to England's top-order problems. Root scored another half-century without advancing to a hundred; and Malan – who became the first England batsman in the match to fall to a bowler other than Boult or Southee – his first of the series.

New Zealand were set 382, a target that might have been feasible but for bad light on the fourth evening, when they sat comfortably on 42 without loss. However the first two deliveries of the fifth day ensured that a draw, and a much-coveted series victory, would be no formality. Raval clipped Broad's innocuous loosener to square leg, and Williamson edged a much better delivery to Bairstow, to collect his first golden duck in a Test.

Leach claimed his first Test wicket when Taylor top-edged a sweep to Cook, cunningly placed in no-man's land behind square on the leg side. And Nicholls fell to Anderson, so that New Zealand were four down by lunch. But de Grandhomme, first with Latham and then a resourceful tail, was obstinate once more. When Leach, in an encouraging debut, struck again – Latham mistiming a sweep – England had more than 50 overs, including a second new ball, to take the final four wickets.

De Grandhomme and Sodhi resisted for 26 of them, before de Grandhomme was caught hooking Wood, but the half-chances did not stick, and New Zealand inched towards the finishing line. Sodhi and Wagner defended resolutely for a further 31, no matter how many bowling changes Root tried, no matter whether the ball was old or new. Shortly after six, with darkness descending, Wagner was dismissed by Root. but it proved the last ball of the match.

For Root, a hard-fought draw was a source of some satisfaction at the end of an arduous winter. "We kept asking questions of New Zealand throughout the day, but unfortunately it did not go our way," he said. "It's frustrating. We can get a lot out of this week, but we are nowhere near where we want to be."

This sounded like a rare candid admission of how fast the expectations of England's Test side had diminished: a thrashing in Australia and a series defeat in New Zealand were no longer regarded as a calamity. A tough rebuilding process was in prospect as a new set of selectors was sought to invigorate a team overdependent on an ageing bowling attack and containing three or four batsmen whose Test futures were far from secure. However badly the winter had begun, it was not meant to end like this.

Man of the Match: T. G. Southee.   *Man of the Series:* T. A. Boult.

Close of play: first day, England 290-8 (Bairstow 97, Leach 10); second day, New Zealand 192-6 (Watling 77, Leach 13); third day, England 202-3 (Root 30, Malan 19); fourth day, New Zealand 42-0 (Latham 25, Raval 17).

England

A. N. Cook b Boult		2	– c Watling b Boult		14
M. D. Stoneman c Latham b Southee		35	– c Watling b Southee		60
J. M. Vince lbw b Southee		18	– c Taylor b Boult		76
*J. E. Root b Southee		37	– c Watling b Wagner		54
D. J. Malan b Boult		5	– c Nicholls b de Grandhomme		53
B. A. Stokes c Watling b Boult		25	– c Raval b de Grandhomme		12
†J. M. Bairstow c Taylor b Boult		101	– c Nicholls b Wagner		36
S. C. J. Broad c Sodhi b Southee		5	– c Sodhi b de Grandhomme		12
M. A. Wood b Southee		52	– b de Grandhomme		9
M. J. Leach c Watling b Southee		16	– not out		14
J. M. Anderson not out		0			
B 9, lb 5, w 1, nb 1		16	B 4, lb 3, w 2, nb 3		12

1/6 (1) 2/38 (3) 3/93 (4)   (96.5 overs) 307
4/94 (5) 5/94 (2) 6/151 (6)
7/164 (8) 8/259 (9) 9/307 (10) 10/307 (7)

1/24 (1)   (9 wkts dec, 106.4 overs) 352
2/147 (2) 3/165 (3)
4/262 (5) 5/262 (4) 6/282 (6)
7/300 (8) 8/312 (9) 9/352 (7)

Boult 28.5–5–87–4; Southee 26–7–62–6; de Grandhomme 17–4–44–0; Wagner 20–5–69–0; Sodhi 5–0–31–0. *Second innings*—Boult 28.5–5–89–2; Southee 19–4–65–1; de Grandhomme 26–2–94–4; Wagner 22.4–5–51–2; Sodhi 11–0–46–0.

New Zealand

J. A. Raval c Bairstow b Anderson	5	– (2) c Stoneman b Broad	17
T. W. M. Latham c Bairstow b Broad	0	– (1) c Vince b Leach	83
*K. S. Williamson c Bairstow b Anderson	22	– c Bairstow b Broad	0
L. R. P. L. Taylor c Cook b Broad	2	– c Cook b Leach	13
H. M. Nicholls lbw b Broad	0	– c Cook b Anderson	13
†B-J. Watling b Anderson	85	– c Anderson b Wood	19
C. de Grandhomme c Bairstow b Broad	72	– c Leach b Wood	45
T. G. Southee b Anderson	50	– (10) not out	0
I. S. Sodhi c Bairstow b Broad	1	– (8) not out	56
N. Wagner not out	24	– (9) c Vince b Root	7
T. A. Boult c Malan b Broad	16		
Lb 1	1	Lb 2, nb 1	3

1/0 (2) 2/14 (1) 3/17 (4)   (93.3 overs) 278   1/42 (2)   (8 wkts, 124.4 overs) 256
4/17 (5) 5/36 (3) 6/178 (7)   2/42 (3) 3/66 (4)
7/226 (6) 8/231 (9) 9/239 (8) 10/278 (11)   4/91 (5) 5/135 (6)
                                                          6/162 (1) 7/219 (7) 8/256 (9)

Anderson 24–5–76–4; Broad 22.3–5–54–6; Wood 21–3–69–0; Leach 19–3–52–0; Root 1–0–9–0; Stokes 6–2–17–0. *Second innings*—Anderson 26–8–37–1; Broad 24–6–72–2; Wood 22–10–45–2; Leach 32–15–61–2; Root 12.4–5–28–1; Stokes 4–3–2–0; Malan 4–1–9–0.

Umpires: M. Erasmus and B. N. J. Oxenford.   Third umpire: P. R. Reiffel.
Referee: R. B. Richardson.

ENGLAND v PAKISTAN IN 2018

REVIEW BY JOHN ETHERIDGE

Test matches (2): England 1, Pakistan 1

Pakistan were superb in one Test and rubbish in the other. Ditto England. Not surprisingly, the series was shared. Without the runs and nous of Younis Khan and Misbah-ul-Haq, who had starred during the Pakistanis' memorable 2–2 draw in England two years earlier but had since retired, this was quite an achievement. When you add victory in Ireland's historic first men's Test, and a couple of Twenty20 successes in Scotland, a young and inexperienced squad could be satisfied with the tour.

At Lord's, they became the first visiting team since Australia in 1921 to win a Test in England that started and finished in May – a result which briefly heaped pressure on head coach Trevor Bayliss. His place in the spotlight was inevitable: Ed Smith had only just been installed as national selector, while Joe Root had been captain for little over a year. The white-ball part of Bayliss's job was not under threat – he had helped transform England's one-day fortunes – but defeat in the Second Test might have persuaded the ECB to split the coaching roles. England won at Headingley to put that debate on hold.

Smith had succeeded James Whitaker and, long fascinated by American sport, was expected to bring a more data-driven approach to the job. In fact, the two left-field selections for his first match were based on youth and a

Irresistible: Mohammad Abbas removes Alastair Cook in the second innings at Lord's.

Philip Brown, Getty Images

hunch. Somerset off-spinner Dom Bess was handed a debut, aged 20, because his county team-mate Jack Leach had broken a thumb the day before the squad was announced, while Jos Buttler was recalled to Test cricket – following a string of explosive performances in the IPL – as a specialist No. 7 with a licence to attack. At Lord's, the pair combined in a second-innings stand of 126 – England's only substantial partnership of the match – while Ben Stokes was selected for his first home game since his arrest in Bristol the previous September. He took three wickets in Pakistan's first innings, and put Babar Azam out of the series with a broken arm.

Generally, though, it was an uncomfortable few days for Smith: watching England being demolished for 184 in their first innings was not what he had in mind. Among a flurry of poorly judged shots, Root played the worst, recklessly chasing a wide ball. It was not a propitious start to his latest stint at No. 3, after months of gentle coaxing from Bayliss, and by the end of the summer, he was back at No. 4. His decision to bat first might have been a statement of intent after a miserable winter. But most thought it an error, and it backfired: England lost by nine wickets.

> You don't want to look back and wonder what you were doing

Mohammad Abbas, in particular, exploited favourable conditions with fingertip control that found swerve in the air and nibble from the surface; he finished with ten wickets at 14 in the two Tests, and was named Player of the Series. Mohammad Amir was persistently dangerous, while the hustling, bustling Hasan Ali celebrated his wickets in style with a trademark star-shaped gesture. Pakistan batted with patience, discipline and an appreciation of the conditions England never managed.

Before the Second Test, Root warned his players about avoiding regret: "If we're lucky, we have ten to 15 years of international cricket. They are the best years of your life and you have to enjoy that challenge and pressure and make the most of it. You don't want to look back and wonder what you were doing worrying about this or that." He also tried to instil a greater intensity in training, a response to a winless winter. And he saw Stokes as the man to lead the cranked-up practice regime. But Stokes's absence from the Second Test after tweaking a hamstring meant he had missed 11 of England's last 29, either through injury or suspension.

Leeds was almost the exact opposite of Lord's. Sarfraz Ahmed, Pakistan's ebullient captain, could easily have bowled first as his team chased their first series win in England since 1996 – although his decision to bat was less obviously flawed than Root's the previous week, since the pitch looked decent. Stuart Broad and James Anderson shared 11 wickets, and Pakistan totalled 308, losing in three days. For England, Buttler scored a destructive 80 not out, the sort of cameo for which he had been chosen. Bess, going in as nightwatchman at No. 4, added 49 to the 57 he made at Lord's, and took his first international wickets. He plainly had the temperament for the highest level.

This was only the second Test series without a player from either team scoring a century or taking a five-for. (The other instance was Bangladesh

Stu Forster, Getty Images

Back in service: Jos Buttler repays the faith shown in him by new national selector, Ed Smith.

against South Africa in 2015, when both games were ruined by rain.) The standard of batting was poor, an indication of why this was in effect a play-off to avoid seventh place in the rankings. Even so, it was a shame the two boards couldn't have arranged a Third Test: this was the 25th series between the sides, but only the second – after 2001, also drawn – of just two matches.

Broad was perhaps motivated by comments made by his first England captain, Michael Vaughan, now a media pundit, who floated the idea both in print and on radio that he or Anderson might be dropped. The team, he suggested, had become too cosy. A curious but rancorous spat developed. At his media conference on the first evening, Broad revealed he had phoned Vaughan to complain, and claimed he had little insight into the dressing-room because players rarely spoke to them. This seemed unlikely, since Root regards him as a mentor. In turn, Vaughan expressed surprise that Broad divulged details of a private conversation, and suggested Broad thought he was immune from criticism. (Less than six months earlier, the pair had been among a group who shared a house on a brief mid-Ashes holiday on Australia's west coast.) Within a couple of weeks, they appeared to have made up.

Pakistan's tour created none of the animosity or controversy that had scarred previous visits. They were an energetic squad, eager to learn, and their shrewd, articulate coach Mickey Arthur helped improve areas such as fielding. During the First Test, a couple of players were asked by an ICC anti-corruption officer to remove their smart-watches – which could potentially access the internet or send and receive messages – and they did so without question and with good grace. All that was missing from the trip was a decider.

FIVE STATS YOU MAY HAVE MISSED

Benedict Bermange

- At Lord's, Imam-ul-Haq became only the second player to be batting at the moment of victory in each of his first two Tests. The first was Sammy Jones of Australia, in two matches against England at Sydney in 1881-82.

- Aged 20, Dom Bess became England's second-youngest specialist spinner, after 19-year-old Ian Peebles at the Old Wanderers ground in Johannesburg in 1927-28.

- Sam Curran was dismissed for 20 on his 20th birthday in the Second Test at Leeds. The only other man to score his age on his birthday in a Test was Geoff Pullar, with 26 for England against Australia at Manchester in 1961. In one-day internationals, Andrew Strauss made 34 on his 34th birthday as England lost to Ireland at Bangalore during the 2011 World Cup.

- Usman Salahuddin became the 11th player to make his Test debut in his 100th first-class match. England's Allen Hill did so in the first-ever Test, at Melbourne in 1876-77. The others were England's James Cranston (1890), Doug Wright (1938) and Mike Selvey (1976); Amir Elahi of India (1947-48); Australians Greg Chappell (1970-71) and John Maclean (1978-79); Reece Young (2010-11) and Kruger van Wyk (2011-12) of New Zealand; and Sri Lanka's Kaushal Silva (2011-12).

- By the end of the series Pakistan had played 22 successive Tests without a draw, winning ten and losing 12. The only longer sequences were by Zimbabwe, with 26 between 2004-05 and 2017-18 (three wins and 23 defeats), and Australia, with 23 between 1999-2000 and 2001 (20 wins and three defeats).

Benedict Bermange is the cricket statistician for Sky Sports.

PAKISTAN TOURING PARTY

*Sarfraz Ahmed, Asad Shafiq, Azhar Ali, Babar Azam, Fahim Ashraf, Fakhar Zaman, Haris Sohail, Hasan Ali, Imam-ul-Haq, Mohammad Abbas, Mohammad Amir, Rahat Ali, Saad Ali, Sami Aslam, Shadab Khan, Usman Salahuddin.
Coach: J. M. Arthur. *Batting coach:* G. W. Flower. *Bowling coach:* Azhar Mahmood. *Fielding coach:* S. J. Rixon. *Manager:* Talat Ali Malik. *Analyst:* Talha Ejaz. *Physiotherapist:* W. A. Deacon. *Masseur:* D. D. Albert. *Fitness coach:* G. Luden. *Security manager:* Azhar Arif. *Media manager:* Aun Mohammad Zaidi.

KENT v PAKISTANIS

At Canterbury, April 28–May 1. Drawn. Toss: Pakistanis.
Kent's dominance, coupled with heavy spring showers that washed out the second and third days, meant Pakistan took little away in terms of Test preparation. Their top order looked all at sea against the seaming ball: after Sarfraz Ahmed chose to bat, his side were bundled out in less than 56 overs. Imam-ul-Haq did survive for 165 minutes before falling to Gidman, who completed his maiden five-wicket haul for Kent in what proved his penultimate game before retiring. Kent started their reply towards the end of the first day, but could not resume until after lunch on the fourth. They had just enough time to edge into the lead, thanks to acting-captain Denly's unbeaten 113. He and Dickson put on 160, a record for Kent's second wicket against the Pakistanis, beating 106 by Charles Rowe and Chris Tavaré in 1978.
Close of play: first day, Kent 39-1 (Dickson 24, Denly 12); second day, no play; third day, no play.

Pakistanis

Sami Aslam lbw b Podmore	13	Mohammad Amir lbw b Gidman	4
Azhar Ali b Gidman	15	Hasan Ali c Haggett b Podmore	24
Imam-ul-Haq lbw b Gidman	61	Rahat Ali not out	0
Haris Sohail lbw b Gidman	5	Lb 6, nb 1	7
Asad Shafiq b Thomas	17		
Babar Azam c Rouse b Haggett	11	1/28 (2) 2/28 (1) 3/53 (4) (55.2 overs)	168
*†Sarfraz Ahmed c Rouse b Gidman	4	4/111 (5) 5/129 (6) 6/129 (3)	
Shadab Khan b Haggett	7	7/136 (8) 8/140 (7) 9/151 (9) 10/168 (10)	

Podmore 14.2–5–35–2; Thomas 13–3–32–1; Gidman 15–3–47–5; Haggett 11–4–41–2; Riley 2–0–7–0.

Kent

D. J. Bell-Drummond lbw b Hasan Ali	1	†A. P. Rouse not out	12
S. R. Dickson lbw b Shadab Khan	74	B 1, lb 2, nb 3	6
*J. L. Denly not out	113		
A. J. Blake b Mohammad Amir	3	1/1 (1) 2/161 (2) (4 wkts, 64 overs)	209
Z. Crawley b Shadab Khan	0	3/174 (4) 4/175 (5)	

W. R. S. Gidman, C. J. Haggett, A. E. N. Riley, H. W. Podmore and I. A. A. Thomas did not bat.

Mohammad Amir 15–4–45–1; Hasan Ali 15–5–28–1; Rahat Ali 12–1–32–0; Shadab Khan 18–3–88–2; Haris Sohail 4–0–13–0.

Umpires: J. W. Lloyds and S. J. O'Shaughnessy.

NORTHAMPTONSHIRE v PAKISTANIS

At Northampton, May 4–7. Pakistanis won by nine wickets. Toss: Northamptonshire. County debut: R. S. Vasconcelos.

With Northamptonshire choosing a strong batting line-up, and Pakistan gearing up for the inaugural men's Test in Ireland, this was a proper, intense contest, which the home side took deep into the fourth day. Rossington's combative 90 ensured Northamptonshire, who made 259, were not blown away on the first, despite a career-best from the 19-year-old leg-spinner Shadab Khan. After the tourists made an uncertain start, Asad Shafiq was dropped in the gully when 13, a simple chance to Ricardo Vasconcelos, a 20-year-old left-hander from Johannesburg with a Portuguese passport – he later took the gloves when Rossington injured a calf. Dropped again on 62, Shafiq extended his 20th first-class century to an unbeaten 186, which gave Pakistan a lead of 169. Northamptonshire's resistance was led by Newton, who made 118 in 341 minutes, despite a nasty knock on the finger from Mohammad Abbas. Newton was still there on the fourth morning but, after he fell to Abbas, Shadab mopped up, and finished with his maiden ten-for. Needing 133, the Pakistanis' only casualty was Azhar Ali, run out after a mid-pitch collision with Imam-ul-Haq.

Close of play: first day, Pakistanis 6-0 (Azhar Ali 3, Imam-ul-Haq 3); second day, Pakistanis 357-7 (Asad Shafiq 135, Mohammad Amir 12); third day, Northamptonshire 240-5 (Newton 102, Keogh 8).

Northamptonshire

*R. I. Newton c Sarfraz Ahmed b Shadab Khan	35	– lbw b Mohammad Abbas	118
B. M. Duckett lbw b Rahat Ali	26	– c Sarfraz Ahmed b Rahat Ali	15
L. A. Procter run out (Haris Sohail/Shadab Khan)	1	– lbw b Rahat Ali	1
R. E. Levi lbw b Shadab Khan	31	– b Shadab Khan	9
†A. M. Rossington st Sarfraz Ahmed b Shadab Khan	90	– c Shadab Khan b Mohammad Abbas	42
J. J. Cobb b Shadab Khan	7	– b Shadab Khan	52
R. I. Keogh lbw b Shadab Khan	0	– b Mohammad Abbas	23
S. P. Crook c Fahim Ashraf b Rahat Ali	10	– lbw b Mohammad Abbas	0
R. S. Vasconcelos b Shadab Khan	30	– not out	24
B. A. Hutton b Haris Sohail	8	– lbw b Shadab Khan	6
G. Wade not out	1	– lbw b Shadab Khan	0
B 4, lb 12, nb 4	20	B 1, lb 3, w 5, nb 2	11

1/36 (2) 2/41 (3) 3/104 (4)   (73.4 overs) 259
4/105 (1) 5/132 (6) 6/143 (7)
7/168 (8) 8/248 (9) 9/249 (5) 10/259 (10)

1/35 (2) 2/48 (3)   (95.5 overs) 301
3/57 (4) 4/113 (5)
5/207 (6) 6/270 (1) 7/270 (8)
8/279 (7) 9/301 (10) 10/301 (11)

Mohammad Amir 13–3–40–0; Mohammad Abbas 13–2–34–0; Rahat Ali 10–4–25–2; Fahim Ashraf 13–3–50–0; Shadab Khan 19–1–77–6; Asad Shafiq 1–0–1–0; Haris Sohail 4.4–0–16–1. *Second innings*—Mohammad Amir 14–3–37–0; Mohammad Abbas 18–3–62–4; Shadab Khan 31.5–6–80–4; Asad Shafiq 2–0–5–0; Haris Sohail 7–0–21–0; Rahat Ali 13–2–53–2; Fahim Ashraf 10–2–39–0.

Pakistanis

Azhar Ali lbw b Wade	9	– run out (†Vasconcelos)	10
Imam-ul-Haq lbw b Keogh	11	– not out	59
Haris Sohail c Crook b Keogh	79	– not out	55
Asad Shafiq not out	186		
Babar Azam c †Vasconcelos b Keogh	57		
*†Sarfraz Ahmed b Hutton	8		
Shadab Khan c Newton b Crook	3		
Fahim Ashraf c Newton b Crook	10		
Mohammad Amir b Crook	16		
Mohammad Abbas lbw b Crook	1		
Rahat Ali c Levi b Keogh	14		
B 12, lb 15, w 1, nb 6	34	B 8, nb 2	10

1/15 (1) 2/41 (2) 3/177 (3)   (116.3 overs) 428
4/287 (5) 5/308 (6) 6/311 (7)
7/321 (8) 8/364 (9) 9/372 (10) 10/428 (11)

1/14 (1)   (1 wkt, 27 overs) 134

Hutton 21–4–55–1; Wade 19–4–75–1; Procter 13–2–48–0; Keogh 32.3–6–111–4; Crook 26–2–89–4; Cobb 5–0–23–0. *Second innings*—Wade 9–0–43–0; Hutton 4–1–14–0; Procter 3–0–22–0; Keogh 5–0–31–0; Cobb 6–1–16–0.

Umpires: I. N. Ramage and M. J. Saggers.

At Malahide, May 11–15. PAKISTAN beat IRELAND by five wickets (see Cricket in Ireland, page 900). *Ireland's inaugural men's Test match.*

At Leicester, May 19–20 (not first-class). Drawn. ‡**Pakistanis 321-9 dec** (89.5 overs) (Azhar Ali 73, Fakhar Zaman 71, Usman Salahuddin 69*); **Leicestershire 226-6** (75 overs) (A. Javid 54). County debuts: B. W. M. Mike, T. A. I. Taylor. *Openers Azhar Ali and Fakhar Zaman made a bright start in this two-day practice game against a virtual Second XI (only three had so far featured for Leicestershire in the 2018 Championship). They put on 121 in 28 overs, but Usman Salahuddin was the only other man to pass 17. Next day, Leicestershire had few problems against an uninspiring bowling attack (Mohammad Abbas, who played for them either side of Pakistan's tour, took 1-42 from 12 overs), although Ateeq Javid was the only one to reach 50, at which point he retired out.*

ENGLAND v PAKISTAN

First Specsavers Test

O SMAN S AMIUDDIN

At Lord's, May 24–27. Pakistan won by nine wickets. Toss: England. Test debut: D. M. Bess.

In ordinary life, away from the unordinary world of sport, in which comparisons are inescapable, you might never put Mohammad Abbas and Mohammad Asif in the same sentence. Asif had hair from the heavens and wrists from the gods; Abbas has, well, hair and wrists. Invite Asif to a party, and he would be the life and soul; invite Abbas, and he would disappear into the crowd. But hand them a ball and you couldn't tell them apart – especially if viewed through the prism of the speed gun, Hawk-Eye or the pitch map. Eight wickets on his Lord's debut meant Abbas had more after one Test there than Asif in two (against Australia and England, both in 2010), but it was clear whose spirit he was channelling.

The tone for Pakistan's emphatic, joyous and slightly unexpected triumph – though it was their eighth win over England in 11 Tests – was set by Abbas. Root had chosen to bat, despite grass underfoot and clouds overhead. His coach, Trevor Bayliss, later said it was a 50–50 call; Sarfraz Ahmed said he would have bowled anyway. As if to vindicate that thought, Abbas began by working over Stoneman so thoroughly that Asif would have been proud: one way, then the other, against the slope, with it – and eventually bowled between bat and pad, all in just 12 balls.

There are glitzier bowlers in this Pakistan line-up, and they briefly took over. Hasan Ali introduced Lord's to his wilder, skiddier fare, and the explosive star celebration. Fahim Ashraf gave the attack something it hadn't had in over a decade: an all-round option to bring relief to the main quicks, but sufficient intent to qualify him as a bowler in his own right. He took just one wicket, but it was Bairstow, creator of rearguards, instigator of counter-attacks and, since 2016, a thorn in Pakistan's side. It was a beautiful piece of bowling, the ball straightening as Ashraf went slightly wider on the crease.

An unhelping hand… Dawid Malan and Ben Stokes make a mash of a slip catch.

ENGLAND'S LEAST SUCCESSFUL OPENING PAIRS

Avge		I	Runs	Best	100	50
18.75	**A. N. Cook/M. D. Stoneman**	**20**	**375**	**58**	**0**	**2**
26.63	A. N. Cook/J. E. Root	11	293	68	0	1
27.10	B. Wood/D. L. Amiss	10	271	80	0	2
27.80	P. E. Richardson/T. E. Bailey	15	417	115	1	2
28.30	L. Hutton/W. J. Edrich.	10	283	60	0	2
29.38	J. H. Edrich/B. W. Luckhurst.	13	382	94	0	3
30.92	A. Lyth/A. N. Cook	13	402	177	1	0
32.25	A. N. Cook/M. A. Carberry	12	387	85	0	4
32.27	A. N. Cook/S. D. Robson.	11	355	66	0	2
32.40	**A. N. Cook/K. K. Jennings**	**22**	**713**	**103**	**1**	**5**
32.68	G. A. Gooch/R. T. Robinson	19	621	79	0	4

*Minimum: 10 innings. The highest average of the 40 opening pairs who meet this quali-
fication for England is 87.81, by J. B. Hobbs and H. Sutcliffe (38 innings, 3,249 runs,
15 hundred partnerships).*

To Mohammad Amir went prime slot on the highlights reel. He had begun poorly: not
quite full enough, then too full – the leitmotif of this second phase of his Test career. But
he did get it right, never more so than when he removed Cook. The line and length were
perfect, and there was shape away. It was the delivery of the day, not only for aesthetic
reasons, but because it rid Pakistan of England's batsman of the day. Cook had 70, and
was batting with a rare fluency. With his dismissal, the dam burst: he was the first of six
wickets to fall for 35 in little more than ten overs. Three went to Abbas, who was gluing
this performance together. There was no great pace and only hints of swing; there was a
little bit off the surface and impeccable accuracy. Lines, yes, but also those lengths Asif
once specialised in, where for the batsman neither going forward nor hanging back is the
right answer.

Having skittled England for 184, Pakistan closed a triumphant day on 50 for the loss of
Imam-ul-Haq, leg-before to Broad in the sixth over. The only other blemish came when it
emerged that anti-corruption officials had spoken to Asad Shafiq and Babar Azam to
remind them that players could not wear smart-watches, which have internet access, on
the field.

The success of Pakistan's bowlers in these conditions was no surprise. That they batted
so well next day certainly was. Barring Azhar Ali, Shafiq and Sarfraz, this was a callow
line-up. A year earlier, they had lost Younis Khan and Misbah-ul-Haq; since then, they
had played only three Tests and, on the benign surfaces of the UAE against the benign
bowling of Sri Lanka, their last three totals were 114, 262 and 248. Here, they faced
Anderson and Broad. And yet, as if taking their lead from Abbas's unfussy excellence,
Pakistan's batsmen put together one of their finest away performances in years.

Azhar left more than he ordinarily would, and instead of attacking straight balls, went
after those offering width. Shafiq got further forward than usual to combat the swing, but
still played the ball right under his eyes. They ran with intent. Neither managed the big
score their seniority demanded, but these were significant hands, and they allowed Babar
to play arguably his best Test innings to date. Hugely gifted, but until now successful only
in white-ball formats, his 68 was a coming of age, following on from 59 in the nervy chase
against Ireland. He was dropped after lunch, on ten, by Cook at first slip off Anderson, but
otherwise looked as if he was playing on a different surface against different bowlers.
Some of his shots, in particular his punches off the back foot, were not those of a man
averaging below 25. It was a cruel blow when Stokes broke his left arm, forcing him out
of the tour.

England did not bowl badly. Anderson, from the Pavilion End, was unable to locate the
in-between length on the second morning that Pakistan had on the first day. But later, from
the Nursery End, he looked more dangerous. Broad was a consistent threat, and Wood had

Star performer: Hasan Ali celebrates the wicket of Joe Root for four.

his moments. In the first 15 overs, in fact, Pakistan played and missed more than England. And on that second afternoon, Stokes put together a ferocious spell, first with the old ball, then with the new, which he took ahead of Anderson.

But England were let down by their fielding. Depending on your interpretation of a chance, between five and seven were missed, mainly in the slips. They had been poor for a while, taking just 71% of their slip catches since the start of 2015, according to CricViz. Only Ireland (after one Test) and Bangladesh were worse. Among the beneficiaries were Shadab Khan and Ashraf, the two all-rounders who changed the nature of Pakistan's line-up, and who fought back after Babar's injury, when the lead was a fragile 62. In days past, Pakistan's lower order would have folded, but they put on 72 in quick time, an appropriate sequel to their match-tilting partnership against the Irish. At 19 years 233 days, Shadab was the second-youngest to score a Test fifty at Lord's, behind Jeff Stollmeyer (18 years 105 days) for West Indies in 1939.

Once Pakistan had taken the lead to 179, only the details of their triumph remained. This time Amir and Shadab joined Abbas in reducing England to 110 for six. Abbas quickly trapped Cook, but it was Amir's interventions that warmed the heart, in particular an over in which he dismissed Malan and Bairstow. The delivery to Bairstow was the left-arm dream, swinging and nipping in to take the off bail. Up in the media centre, Wasim Akram was purring for hours.

After Root fell for 68, there was resistance in the shape of an intelligent 126-run stand in 38 overs between Buttler and the debutant Dom Bess. Buttler's innings was revelatory. This was his first Test, and only his fifth first-class game, since December 2016. But there is something to be said for form, whatever colour the ball: including the IPL, he scored his sixth fifty in eight innings. The 20-year-old Bess compiled an elegant 57 – making him the fourth-youngest England batsman to hit a Test half-century, after Jack Crawford, Denis Compton and Haseeb Hameed. Buttler compared his back-foot punches and cover-drives to Root's.

The resistance, ultimately, was futile. It took the game into the fourth morning, but the last four fell for six runs in 18 balls to Abbas and Amir; Broad completed his first Test pair, at the same venue and against the same opposition as he had made a career-best 169 eight years earlier. Anderson bowled Azhar Ali, but Imam and Haris Sohail rattled to a target of 64, and Pakistan had their fifth Test win at Lord's; among visiting teams, only Australia, with 17, had more.

This one was every bit as exuberant as Pakistan's last, in 2016, when the squad performed press-ups in front of the Pavilion. For England, who had lost the opening Test of their home summer for the first time since the visit of West Indies in 1995, there was more introspection after a troubled winter. Their batsmen, said Bayliss, needed to take a "good hard look at themselves". The Second Test was suddenly more crucial than anyone could have imagined.

Man of the Match: Mohammad Abbas. *Attendance:* 102,580.

Close of play: first day, Pakistan 50-1 (Azhar Ali 18, Haris Sohail 21); second day, Pakistan 350-8 (Mohammad Amir 19, Mohammad Abbas 0); third day, England 235-6 (Buttler 66, Bess 55).

England

A. N. Cook b Mohammad Amir	70	– lbw b Mohammad Abbas	1
M. D. Stoneman b Mohammad Abbas	4	– b Shadab Khan	9
*J. E. Root c Sarfraz Ahmed b Hasan Ali	4	– lbw b Mohammad Abbas	68
D. J. Malan c Sarfraz Ahmed b Hasan Ali	6	– c Sarfraz Ahmed b Mohammad Amir	12
†J. M. Bairstow b Fahim Ashraf	27	– b Mohammad Amir	0
B. A. Stokes lbw b Mohammad Abbas	38	– c sub (Fakhar Zaman) b Shadab Khan	9
J. C. Buttler c Asad Shafiq b Hasan Ali	14	– lbw b Mohammad Abbas	67
D. M. Bess c Asad Shafiq b Mohammad Abbas	5	– b Mohammad Amir	57
M. A. Wood c Mohammad Amir b Hasan Ali	7	– c Sarfraz Ahmed b Mohammad Amir	4
S. C. J. Broad lbw b Mohammad Abbas	0	– c Sarfraz Ahmed b Mohammad Abbas	0
J. M. Anderson not out	0	– not out	0
B 1, lb 6, w 1, nb 1	9	B 4, lb 9, w 2	15

1/12 (2) 2/33 (3) 3/43 (4) (58.2 overs) 184
4/100 (5) 5/149 (1) 6/168 (6)
7/168 (7) 8/180 (8) 9/180 (10) 10/184 (9)

1/1 (1) 2/31 (2) (82.1 overs) 242
3/91 (4) 4/91 (5)
5/104 (6) 6/110 (3)
7/236 (7) 8/241 (9)
9/242 (8) 10/242 (8)

Mohammad Amir 14-3-41-1; Mohammad Abbas 14-7-23-4; Fahim Ashraf 9-2-28-1; Shadab Khan 6-0-34-0. *Second innings*—Mohammad Amir 18.1-3-36-4; Mohammad Abbas 17-3-41-4; Fahim Ashraf 9-2-31-0; Hasan Ali 19-3-58-0; Shadab Khan 19-2-63-2.

Pakistan

Azhar Ali lbw b Anderson	50	– b Anderson	4
Imam-ul-Haq lbw b Broad	4	– not out	18
Haris Sohail c Bairstow b Wood	39	– not out	39
Asad Shafiq c Malan b Stokes	59		
Babar Azam retired hurt	68		
*†Sarfraz Ahmed c Wood b Stokes	9		
Shadab Khan c Bairstow b Stokes	52		
Fahim Ashraf b Anderson	37		
Mohammad Amir not out	24		
Hasan Ali c Buttler b Anderson	0		
Mohammad Abbas c Bairstow b Wood	5		
Lb 14, w 1, nb 1	16	B 3, lb 2	5

1/12 (2) 2/87 (3) 3/119 (1) (114.3 overs) 363
4/203 (4) 5/227 (4) 6/318 (8)
7/332 (7) 8/337 (10) 9/363 (11)

1/12 (1) (1 wkt, 12.4 overs) 66

In the first innings Babar Azam retired hurt at 246-5.

Anderson 26–6–82–3; Broad 25–9–61–1; Wood 24.3–6–74–2; Stokes 22–5–73–3; Bess 17–0–59–0. *Second innings*—Anderson 3–0–12–1; Broad 3–1–13–0; Bess 3.4–0–29–0; Wood 3–1–7–0.

Umpires: P. R. Reiffel and R. J. Tucker. Third umpire: B. N. J. Oxenford.
Referee: J. J. Crowe.

ENGLAND v PAKISTAN

Second Specsavers Test

CHRIS WATERS

At Leeds, June 1–3. England won by an innings and 55 runs. Toss: Pakistan. Test debuts: S. M. Curran; Usman Salahuddin.

Joe Root's pre-match message could hardly have been more passionate or patriotic had he been puffing on a cigar and evoking fights on beaches. "I want the guys to stand up and be counted this week, and show how important it is to play for England," was his Churchillian cry. There was anger, too, after the defeat at Lord's, a result that stirred speculation about the position of head coach Trevor Bayliss. "I don't see why there's a need for a change," said Root, himself under pressure after six defeats – and no wins – in the previous eight Tests. Not for over nine years had England lost three series in a row.

From the sharp catch he held at third slip to dismiss Imam-ul-Haq off the 12th ball of the match, to the one he held to dismiss Mohammad Abbas and seal victory with over seven sessions in hand, England were as professional in Leeds as they had been pitiful at

Devon's finest: Dom Bess embodies a far better England fielding performance when he catches Haris Sohail.

Stu Forster, Getty Images

Lord's. Some wondered why England – not for the first time under Bayliss – had needed a debacle to rouse the lion.

They might have needed a dose of criticism, too. Broad had been piqued by Michael Vaughan's suggestion that England should consider dropping him or Anderson to "ruffle the feathers" of a "comfortable" team. In the event, they omitted Mark Wood and were without Ben Stokes, who injured a hamstring two days before the start. Back came Woakes, and there was a debut for Surrey left-armer Sam Curran, five Tests after older brother Tom's, at Melbourne; two days short of his 20th birthday, Curran was England's seventh teenage Test cricketer (Pakistan had picked 52). For Pakistan, Usman Salahuddin won his first cap, replacing the injured Babar Azam.

Pakistan were duped into batting by a straw-coloured pitch and by the sun, which disappeared behind cloud straight after the toss. The first six overs from Anderson and Broad yielded one run, and included the dismissal of Imam by Broad, who then trapped

ENGLAND'S YOUNGEST TEST DEBUTANTS

Years	Days			Years	Days		
18	149	D. B. Close	1949	20	229	A. Flintoff	1998
19	32	J. N. Crawford	1905-06	20	237	L. E. Plunkett	2005-06
19	83	D. C. S. Compton . .	1937	20	269	P. A. J. DeFreitas . . .	1986-87
19	269	B. C. Holliaoke	1997	20	273	J. B. Statham	1950-51
19	297	H. Hameed	2016-17	20	281	N. S. Mitchell-Innes .	1935
19	338	I. A. R. Peebles	1927-28	20	296	J. M. Anderson	2003
19	**363**	**S. M. Curran . . . . .**	**2018**	**20**	**306**	**D. M. Bess . . . .**	**2018**
20	156	W. Voce	1929-30	20	307	J. W. Hearne	1911-12
20	210	G. R. Dilley	1979-80	**20**	**320**	**M. S. Crane . . . . . .**	**2017-18**
20	**219**	**O. J. D. Pope . . . . .**	**2018**	20	324	G. MacGregor.	1890
20	225	F. R. Brown	1931	20	325	C. M. W. Read	1999
20	226	M. W. Gatting.	1977-78	20	342	S. T. Finn	2009-10

Azhar Ali with one that nipped back. He later pinned Salahuddin, and finished with three for 38. Central to his success was his length, the fullest he had bowled with the new ball in a home Test. Anderson took longer to catch on, but had played his part during England's miserly start.

It was an instant indication that Root – who would have batted, too – had contributed as much by losing the toss as by delivering his pre-game rhetoric. Anderson and Woakes, who shook off some rust while conceding five an over, also claimed three each, before Curran, having initially struggled with the slope, wrapped up the innings. From 79 for seven, Pakistan were grateful to Shadab Khan's counter-attacking 56 for reaching 174.

England closed on 106 for two. Jennings had looked good on his return, but edged behind for 29, before Cook – making his 154th consecutive Test appearance, beating Allan Border's record – gloved a pull down the leg side shortly before stumps. That evening, Broad called Vaughan's criticism "unfair", ascribing his punditry to "personal columns and radio shows that need likes and airtime".

The action off the field began to vie with the entertainment on it. Rain delayed the start on the second day until 2.45, and Vaughan helped fill the time by telling radio listeners that Broad had probably reacted "because the frustration has been building up". He added: "I got the sense it was: 'You can't criticise me, I'm Stuart Broad.'" Broad hit back in his newspaper column: "Everyone is entitled to their opinion, but surely that also means players have the right to respond to comments made about them?" After that it was presumably pistols at dawn behind the back of Headingley's half-built rugby stand, whose construction had shrunk capacity to around 12,500. One thing was clear: Vaughan had lost none of his capacity for motivation, and Broad none of his facility for penetration.

They really do win matches: Joe Root catches Mohammad Abbas, and England square the series.

Root's demeanour, however, had remained infectiously upbeat, as if he had undergone an injection of energy somewhere between London and Leeds. When he came to the crease on the first evening, he did not so much stride out as sprint, a man keen to back up his words with deeds. At stumps he had 29, and gave Bess – "desperate" to get out there as nightwatchman, Root said – a prolonged hug as they left the field. It was a snapshot of a happier day for the captain and his team.

Once play finally got under way on the second afternoon, Root was caught behind five short of a seemingly inevitable half-century, lured into a drive by Mohammad Amir. Malan came and went for 28, also undone outside off by Amir, while Bess was no less frustrated with himself when he fell for 49 after nearly two and a half hours. Having played some handsome shots through mid-on, cover and point, he was caught at slip off a ball of extra bounce from leg-spinner Shadab. His technique had looked as good – if not better – than some top-order batsmen England had picked in recent years.

No sooner had one son of the West Country departed than another appeared. Buttler had flourished on his comeback at Lord's, where he had been on the front foot in more ways than one, batting outside his crease in an effort to negate movement and make deliveries more driveable. It was an approach England collectively followed here, to the extent that Jennings was spoken to by the umpires for disturbing the danger zone normally breached by bowlers.

When Buttler is on song, the danger zone for opponents is anywhere within reach of the bat, and his innings comprised three distinct phases. First, he attacked Shadab, hitting three fours in an over, though the second burst through the butterfingers of Hasan Ali at midwicket when England, five down, were only 46 ahead. Then he reined himself in until stumps, taken at 302 for seven, before finally exploding, Twenty20-style, with the tail on the third morning. He crashed 35 from his last 11 balls to finish unbeaten on 80 – five short of his Test-best – and give England a lead of 189. Buttler drew gasps with one straight six off Fahim Ashraf, over the sightscreen and into the construction site and out again, as Richie Benaud might have put it. Two of the game's best shots, however, had been provided by Curran in the final over the previous evening: a pull for four off Hasan, then a drive down the ground, his pose held for the photographers.

Bess had already shown he could bat. But could he bowl? The answer came with three wickets in Pakistan's second innings, which was even less substantial than their first. After Anderson and Broad reduced them to 42 for three before lunch – including a sensational catch from Bess, leaping high to his left at mid-off to snare Haris Sohail – he trapped Imam with his sixth delivery. He later had Ashraf caught off a top-edged hoick, then

Salahuddin taken at mid-on. England's catching, particularly in the slips, was vastly improved from their display at Lord's.

They had emphatically heeded Root's plea, and avoided the embarrassment of a third successive series loss, after defeats by Australia and New Zealand. It was not quite their finest hour, perhaps, but – as their captain put it, briefly dispensing with the need to sound like Churchill – "a really great step in the right direction".

Man of the Match: J. C. Buttler. *Attendance:* 36,972.

Man of the Series: Mohammad Abbas.

Close of play: first day, England 106-2 (Root 29, Bess 0); second day, England 302-7 (Buttler 34, Curran 16).

Pakistan

Azhar Ali lbw b Broad	2	– b Anderson	11
Imam-ul-Haq c Root b Broad	0	– lbw b Bess	34
Haris Sohail c Malan b Woakes	28	– c Bess b Anderson	8
Asad Shafiq c Cook b Woakes	27	– c Bairstow b Broad	5
Usman Salahuddin lbw b Broad	4	– c Root b Bess	33
*†Sarfraz Ahmed b Anderson	14	– lbw b Woakes	8
Shadab Khan c Jennings b Curran	56	– c Cook b Curran	4
Fahim Ashraf lbw b Anderson	0	– c Malan b Bess	3
Mohammad Amir c Bairstow b Anderson	13	– not out	7
Hasan Ali c and b Woakes	24	– c Cook b Broad	9
Mohammad Abbas not out	1	– c Root b Broad	1
Lb 5	5	B 5, lb 5, nb 1	11

1/0 (2) 2/17 (1) 3/49 (3) (48.1 overs) 174
4/62 (4) 5/78 (6) 6/78 (5)
7/79 (8) 8/113 (9) 9/156 (10) 10/174 (7)

1/20 (1) 2/30 (3) (46 overs) 134
3/42 (4) 4/84 (2)
5/97 (6) 6/102 (7) 7/111 (8)
8/115 (5) 9/124 (10) 10/134 (11)

Anderson 15–6–43–3; Broad 15–6–38–3; Woakes 11–1–55–3; Curran 7.1–0–33–1. *Second innings*—Anderson 10–2–35–2; Broad 12–2–28–3; Curran 7–2–10–1; Woakes 6–0–18–1; Bess 11–1–33–3.

England

A. N. Cook c Sarfraz Ahmed b Hasan Ali	46	S. M. Curran c Asad Shafiq b Mohammad Abbas	20
K. K. Jennings c Sarfraz Ahmed b Fahim Ashraf	29	S. C. J. Broad c Mohammad Abbas b Fahim Ashraf	2
*J. E. Root c Sarfraz Ahmed b Mohammad Amir	45	J. M. Anderson c Haris Sohail b Hasan Ali	5
D. M. Bess c Asad Shafiq b Shadab Khan	49		
D. J. Malan c Haris Sohail b Mohammad Amir	28	B 8, lb 13	21
†J. M. Bairstow c Sarfraz Ahmed b Fahim Ashraf	21		
J. C. Buttler not out	80	1/53 (2) 2/104 (1) (106.2 overs) 363	
C. R. Woakes c Sarfraz Ahmed b Mohammad Abbas	17	3/138 (3) 4/200 (5)	
		5/212 (4) 6/260 (6) 7/285 (8)	
		8/319 (9) 9/344 (10) 10/363 (11)	

Mohammad Amir 23–5–72–2; Mohammad Abbas 26–8–78–2; Hasan Ali 20.2–4–82–2; Fahim Ashraf 20–4–60–3; Shadab Khan 17–2–50–1.

Umpires: B. N. J. Oxenford and R. J. Tucker.   Third umpire: P. R. Reiffel.
Referee: J. J. Crowe.

At Edinburgh, June 12. PAKISTAN beat SCOTLAND by 48 runs (see Cricket in Scotland, page 1103).

At Edinburgh, June 13. PAKISTAN beat SCOTLAND by 84 runs (see Cricket in Scotland, page 1103).

Jane Barlow, PA Photos

Scottish play: Calum MacLeod middles another during his dramatic unbeaten 140.

SCOTLAND v ENGLAND IN 2018

One-Day International

CHRIS STOCKS

At Edinburgh, June 10. Scotland won by six runs. Toss: England. One-day international debut: D. E. Budge.

On the weekend the Rolling Stones played Murrayfield, it was Calum MacLeod who proved Edinburgh's real headline act. England had travelled north newly installed at the top of the one-day rankings, while Scotland – 12 places back – were still smarting from their near miss at the World Cup Qualifier in Zimbabwe. It ought to have been a procession. Yet an astonishing day ended with pipers sounding a full-blooded rendition of "Flower of Scotland", and the crowd invading the outfield. MacLeod, who eight days earlier had been playing for Bexley in the Kent Premier League, was the architect of England's downfall, with an electrifying unbeaten 140 from 94 balls. But this was no one-man show. On a flat pitch, and with the boundaries shortened to accommodate temporary stands and outside-broadcast units, Cross and Coetzer began with 103 inside 14 overs after Morgan opted to bowl. Munsey contributed a maiden one-day half-century; Dylan Budge, Wisden Schools Cricketer of the Year in 2014, made 11 on international debut. Scotland's 371 for five was their highest one-day total, beating 341 for nine against Canada at Christchurch in 2013-14, while England had conceded more only three times. But Bairstow gave them a blistering start: his 54-ball hundred was their third-fastest, and made him the first England player to score three successive ODI centuries. At 220 for two in the 27th over, they were cruising. But Hales called Root for a non-existent single, and five fell for 56, Hales compounding his error when he was dismissed the ball after Morgan. Ali and Plunkett revived the chase with a stand of 71 but, with 25 needed from 28 deliveries, Ali holed out to long-on. Another run-out, as Rashid failed to make his ground coming back for a second, left the last pair needing ten. And a stunning win was sealed when Sharif trapped Wood with a yorker to spark scenes of unbridled joy. It was Scotland's first over England in five attempts, including the a no-result, and the first by an Associate nation over the team ranked No. 1. "It sends a message," said their coach Grant Bradburn. "And it maybe confirms that there's not only ten teams in the world that are reasonable at cricket."

Man of the Match: C. S. MacLeod.

SCALING THE HEIGHTS

Highest ODI totals for Associate nations against Test countries:

371-5	**Scotland v England (365) at Edinburgh**	**2018**
331-8	Ireland v Zimbabwe (326) at Hobart....................................	2014-15
329-7	Ireland v England (327-8) at Bangalore	2010-11
318-8	Scotland v Bangladesh (322-4) at Nelson..............................	2014-15
317-6	Scotland v Zimbabwe (272) at Edinburgh	2017
312-4	Zimbabwe v Sri Lanka (313-7) at New Plymouth	1991-92

Afghanistan scored 333-5 against Zimbabwe (179) at Sharjah in February 2018 – after becoming a Full Member, but before playing a Test.

Scotland

†M. H. Cross c Billings b Plunkett	48	M. A. Leask not out...................	10
*K. J. Coetzer c Billings b Rashid.........	58	Lb 5, w 5	10
C. S. MacLeod not out	140		
R. D. Berrington c Root b Plunkett......	39	1/103 (2) 2/107 (1) (5 wkts, 50 overs)	371
H. G. Munsey c Wood b Rashid	55	3/200 (4) 4/307 (5)	
D. E. Budge b Wood	11	5/360 (6)	10 overs: 70-0

S. M. Sharif, M. R. J. Watt, A. C. Evans and C. B. Sole did not bat.

Wood 10–0–71–1; Willey 10–0–72–0; Rashid 10–0–72–2; Plunkett 10–0–85–2; Ali 10–0–66–0.

England

J. J. Roy c and b Watt	34	A. U. Rashid run out (Leask/Sharif)	5
J. M. Bairstow c Munsey b Berrington 105		M. A. Wood lbw b Sharif	1
A. D. Hales c Evans b Berrington	52		
J. E. Root run out (Watt/Leask).........	29	W 7	7
*E. J. G. Morgan c Coetzer b Evans	20		
†S. W. Billings c Coetzer b Watt.........	12	1/129 (1) 2/165 (2) (48.5 overs)	365
M. M. Ali c Munsey b Watt	46	3/220 (4) 4/245 (5) 5/245 (3)	
D. J. Willey c Cross b Evans...........	7	6/263 (6) 7/276 (8) 8/347 (7)	
L. E. Plunkett not out.................	47	9/362 (10) 10/365 (11)	10 overs: 107-0

Sharif 9.5–0–71–1; Sole 8–0–72–0; Watt 10–0–55–3; Leask 4–0–50–0; Evans 8–1–50–2; Berrington 9–0–67–2.

Umpires: M. Erasmus and D. A. Haggo. Third umpire: H. D. P. K. Dharmasena.
Referee: R. S. Madugalle.

ENGLAND v AUSTRALIA IN 2018

Gideon Brooks

One-day internationals (5): England 5, Australia 0
Twenty20 international (1): England 1, Australia 0

Before the first one-day international, ambush marketeers for an online investment company and a DIY store handed out "4" and "6" cards, upsetting the authorities, who confiscated them as spectators filed into The Oval. The numbers were printed on yellow sandpaper. While the decision might have spared Australia's boundary fielders endless mockery – though one or two cards did make it through – nothing could stop Tim Paine's side being roughed up by England. Their first series since the ball-tampering scandal in Cape Town a couple of months earlier proved chastening.

Speaking at Edgbaston after England's victory in the solitary Twenty20 game had condemned his side to six defeats out of six, Australia's new coach Justin Langer surprised even himself: "England are showing our young guys what you have to do to be successful at international cricket. I can't believe I am saying that. Hopefully it will add layers to their character, not scars." Twenty-one Tests and a one-day international against the old enemy as a player had brought only five defeats, spread across a decade; now he had coached Australia to six in the space of a fortnight. England's 5–0 whitewash in the one-day series was their first over them in any format.

Langer, though, was comforted by the thought of the names set to return for the 2019 World Cup: Steve Smith and David Warner, after their ball-tampering bans, plus the injured fast-bowling trio of Mitchell Starc, Josh Hazlewood and Pat Cummins. And within their inexperienced group there were one or two straws to clutch at. Travis Head reached 50 in each of the last three one-day

TOTAL ECLIPSE

How the record total in one-day internationals has gone up:

	Overs		
191-5	34.6†	Australia v England (*190*) at Melbourne	1970-71
226-4	49.1	England v Australia (*222-8*) at Manchester	1972
240-5	51.3	Australia v England (*236-9*) at Lord's	1972
265-5	35†	Australia v New Zealand (234-6) at Christchurch	1973-74
266-6	51.1	England v India (265) at Leeds	1974
334-4	60	England v India (132-3) at Lord's‡	1975
338-5	60	Pakistan v Sri Lanka (288-9) at Swansea‡	1983
360-4	50	West Indies v Sri Lanka (169-4) at Karachi‡	1987-88
363-7	55	England v Pakistan (165) at Nottingham	1992
398-5	50	Sri Lanka v Kenya (254-7) at Kandy‡	1995-96
438-9	49.5	South Africa v Australia (*434-4*) at Johannesburg	2005-06
443-9	50	Sri Lanka v Netherlands (248) at Amstelveen	2006
444-3	50	England v Pakistan (275) at Nottingham	2016
481-6	**50**	**England v Australia (239) at Nottingham**	**2018**

† *Eight-ball overs.*   ‡ *World Cup.*
A score in italics indicates that the existing record was broken earlier in the match.

Swing into action: Eoin Morgan powers to the fastest fifty for England, from 21 balls, at Nottingham.

internationals, while Shaun Marsh hit hundreds at Cardiff and Chester-le-Street. There was the combativeness of Aaron Finch, the all-round ability of Ashton Agar, and the pace of Billy Stanlake, who put down a marker for the Ashes, let alone the World Cup.

But the tourists were unable to live with a near flawless display from England, who earlier in the year had won 4–1 in Australia. Langer talked about his young team having "walked into the jungle". England's big beasts were irresistible, scarily so in the third one-day international at Trent Bridge, where they threatened to reach 500 before settling for 481 for six – which still comfortably beat their own world record.

Jos Buttler had come back from a third stint at the IPL with his confidence bursting, after he was promoted to open for Rajasthan Royals and responded with five successive half-centuries. If that confidence had been evident during his return to Test cricket, against Pakistan, it now went through the roof. He struck 275 runs from 244 balls, was out only twice, and kept wicket impeccably. His best innings came in a low-scoring affair at Old Trafford, where his unbeaten 110 helped England chase down 206 after they had been 114 for eight, and secure the clean sweep. Paine called Buttler "the best white-ball wicketkeeper-batsman in the world". It was hard to disagree.

Jason Roy was also in the form of his life, scoring 120, 82 and 101 in successive innings, while his opening partner Jonny Bairstow weighed in with 300 runs and a strike-rate of 133 – the highest on either side. Eoin Morgan showed glimpses of his destructive best, hammering a whip-crack fifty from 21 balls, England's fastest in ODIs, in Nottingham; there, Alex Hales reminded the selectors of his power with 147. Without the injured Ben Stokes, there was room for growth. In all, England hit 33 sixes to Australia's 25, and 164 fours to 105.

They outbowled them, too, especially the spinners. Australia's warm-up games against Sussex and Middlesex had hinted at their weakness against slow bowling, and it was exploited by Adil Rashid and Moeen Ali, who took 12 wickets each. Liam Plunkett remained the most skilful of the quicker men, with eight in four matches.

It all helped England, who stayed top of the rankings, to their first 5–0 whitewash since beating Zimbabwe in 2001-02, and their first back-to-back one-day series wins against Australia since 1977. Rough times indeed for the world champions.

AUSTRALIA TOURING PARTY

*T. D. Paine (50), A. C. Agar (50/20), A. T. Carey (50/20), A. J. Finch (50/20), T. M. Head (50/20), N. M. Lyon (50), N. J. Maddinson (20), S. E. Marsh (50), G. J. Maxwell (50/20), M. G. Neser (50), J. A. Richardson (50/20), K. W. Richardson (50/20), D. J. M. Short (50/20), B. Stanlake (50), M. P. Stoinis (50/20), M. J. Swepson (20), A. J. Tye (50/20), J. D. Wildermuth (20). *Coach:* J. L. Langer.

J. R. Hazlewood was originally selected for the 50-over squad, but withdrew with a back injury and was replaced by Neser. Finch captained in the Twenty20 international.

At Hove, June 7 (day/night). **Australians won by 57 runs. Australians 277-9** (50 overs) (A. J. Finch 78, M. P. Stoinis 110; J. C. Archer 3-62); ‡**Sussex 220** (42.3 overs) (P. D. Salt 62, L. J. Evans 57; A. C. Agar 3-64). *In their first match since the fractious tour of South Africa, the Australians eased to victory in front of a full house thanks to 110 from 112 balls by Marcus Stoinis. He entered after a rapid opening stand of 74 in 10.3 overs between Aaron Finch and D'Arcy Short, and stayed until the 47th. With the Australian pacemen looking short of a gallop, Sussex were on course at 180-4 in the 34th, but lost their last six for 40. Phil Salt – dropped twice on nought by Short at square leg – top-scored with 62 from 49, including four sixes, two in succession off Ashton Agar to pass 50. Agar recovered to take three wickets later on.*

At Lord's, June 9. **Australians won by 101 runs.** ‡**Australians 283-6** (50 overs) (T. M. Head 106, A. J. Finch 54; T. E. Barber 3-62); **Middlesex 182** (41 overs) (M. D. E. Holden 71; K. W. Richardson 3-31). *Travis Head's 133-ball century, much of it in a second-wicket stand of 114 with Shaun Marsh, underpinned the Australians' innings – but they could not break loose later against a disciplined Middlesex attack. The former England Under-19 captain Max Holden sent down ten overs of brisk – but very occasional – off-breaks, taking 1-29, then gave Middlesex's chase a bright start with a run-a-ball 71. But Australia's seamers worked their way through the batting, sharing eight wickets. The only serious resistance down the order came from the Antipodean pair of Hilton Cartwright and James Franklin, who both made 31.*

ENGLAND v AUSTRALIA

First Royal London One-Day International

At The Oval, June 13 (day/night). England won by three wickets. Toss: Australia. One-day international debut: M. G. Neser.

Three days after their humbling experience north of the border against Scotland (see page 304), England restored their white-ball momentum with victory in south London. But if they got home with time to spare – six overs were still in the tank when Willey drilled debutant seamer Michael Neser straight for six – they made heavy weather of a modest chase. Australia's 214 was under par, the credit going largely to Ali and Rashid, who tightened the tourniquet and took five for 79 between them. Ali was on by the ninth over, removing Finch with his fourth ball and Marsh with his eighth; only when the dangerous Maxwell hit his last over for 14 did Australia treat his off-breaks with anything other than suspicion. But Plunkett removed Maxwell for 62 after he and Agar had rebuilt from 90 for five with a stand of 84, and Australia were dismissed with three overs unused. A cakewalk beckoned. Instead, Roy went second ball, bowled by the hostile Stanlake, and when the in-form Bairstow pulled Kane Richardson to deep square leg it was 38 for three. It took a partnership of 115 in 21 overs between Root and Morgan – after just one half-century in 15 one-day international innings – to put England back on track. But in 19 balls, Morgan and Buttler fell to the variations of Tye, and Root to Stanlake. Six down, England still needed 52. Ali and Willey knocked off 34 before Ali holed out to deep midwicket, but the run-rate was never an issue, and Willey kept his head on the way to his highest ODI score. The game had begun with handshakes between the sides at the instigation of Paine, keen to move on from the nastiness of Australia's series in South Africa.

Man of the Match: M. M. Ali.   *Attendance:* 23,464.

Australia

A. J. Finch c Wood b Ali	19	K. W. Richardson c Root b Wood		1
T. M. Head c Bairstow b Willey	5	B. Stanlake not out		0
S. E. Marsh b Ali	24			
M. P. Stoinis c Buttler b Rashid	22	W 4		4
*†T. D. Paine c Wood b Ali	12			—
G. J. Maxwell c Bairstow b Plunkett	62	1/7 (2) 2/47 (1) 3/52 (3) (47 overs)		214
A. C. Agar lbw b Rashid	40	4/70 (5) 5/90 (4) 6/174 (6)		
M. G. Neser c Root b Plunkett	6	7/193 (7) 8/197 (8) 9/208 (10)		
A. J. Tye c Buttler b Plunkett	19	10/214 (9)	10 overs: 51-2	

Wood 8–1–32–1; Willey 8–0–41–1; Ali 10–1–43–3; Rashid 10–0–36–2; Root 3–0–20–0; Plunkett 8–0–42–3.

England

J. J. Roy b Stanlake	0	D. J. Willey not out		35
J. M. Bairstow c Head b Richardson	28	L. E. Plunkett not out		3
A. D. Hales lbw b Neser	5	W 2		2
J. E. Root c Paine b Stanlake	50			—
*E. J. G. Morgan c Paine b Tye	69	1/0 (1) 2/23 (3) (7 wkts, 44 overs)		218
†J. C. Buttler c Richardson b Tye	9	3/38 (2) 4/153 (5)		
M. M. Ali c sub (D. J. M. Short) b Neser	17	5/163 (6) 6/163 (4) 7/197 (7)	10 overs: 48-3	

A. U. Rashid and M. A. Wood did not bat.

Stanlake 10–1–44–2; Neser 8–1–46–2; Richardson 9–1–49–1; Tye 10–1–42–2; Agar 5–0–28–0; Maxwell 2–0–9–0.

Umpires: R. J. Bailey and H. D. P. K. Dharmasena.   Third umpire: M. Erasmus.
Referee: R. S. Madugalle.

ENGLAND v AUSTRALIA

Second Royal London One-Day International

At Cardiff, June 16. England won by 38 runs. Toss: Australia. One-day international debut: D. J. M. Short.

The absence of Eoin Morgan, who pulled out with a back spasm before the toss, did little to halt England. Roy's 97-ball century and an unbeaten 91 from 70 by Buttler helped them to 342, their highest total against Australia – for three days, at least – and the highest in a one-day international at Cardiff. It proved beyond the tourists, despite the best efforts of Marsh, who struck 131 from 116, his first ODI century since 2013, at a ground he knew from his time with Glamorgan. But after he was bowled by Plunkett, with 50 still required from 27 deliveries, the chase ran out of steam. It completed a miserable day for Australian sport, after their rugby union team had lost to Ireland in Melbourne, and their footballers to France at the World Cup in Russia. Earlier, England's batsmen had again demonstrated their brutish power. After a steady start, Bairstow smashed 27 in eight balls, then edged Kane Richardson. And while Hales and Root made relatively stodgy contributions, the fireworks resumed when stand-in captain Buttler joined Roy. (For the first time in any international between these sides, both were led by wicketkeepers.) At the venue where he had been dropped a year earlier for the Champions Trophy semi-final, Roy battered his fifth ODI hundred. Buttler ensured his work did not go to waste, as Australia's bowlers – minus Billy Stanlake because of a toe injury – belatedly realised the pitch rewarded cutters and slower balls. Uniquely in a one-day international, England had registered a stand of at least 50 for each of the first five wickets. Paine ended Roy's innings with an excellent catch down the leg side three deliveries after he was struck in the mouth when the ball bounced awkwardly. It cost him a tooth, while his team's chances in the series were hanging by a thread.

Man of the Match: J. J. Roy.   *Attendance:* 15,010.

England

J. J. Roy c Paine b Tye	120	L. E. Plunkett run out (Short/Tye)	1
J. M. Bairstow c Paine b K. W. Richardson	42	A. U. Rashid not out	0
A. D. Hales b J. A. Richardson	26	Lb 5, w 5	10
J. E. Root c Short b Stoinis	22		
*†J. C. Buttler not out	91	1/63 (2) 2/113 (3) (8 wkts, 50 overs) 342	
S. W. Billings b Tye	11	3/179 (4) 4/239 (1)	
M. M. Ali c Agar b J. A. Richardson	8	5/289 (6) 6/300 (7)	
D. J. Willey c and b K. W. Richardson	11	7/325 (8) 8/332 (9) 10 overs: 71-1	

M. A. Wood did not bat.

J. A. Richardson 10–0–64–2; K. W. Richardson 8–0–56–2; Agar 9–0–52–0; Stoinis 10–0–60–1; Tye 9–0–81–2; Short 4–0–24–0.

Australia

T. M. Head c Hales b Wood	19	J. A. Richardson c Roy b Plunkett	2
D. J. M. Short c Root b Ali	21	K. W. Richardson not out	0
S. E. Marsh b Plunkett	131		
M. P. Stoinis b Plunkett	9	Lb 13, w 7	20
A. J. Finch lbw b Rashid	0		
G. J. Maxwell c Willey b Ali	31	1/24 (1) 2/77 (2) 3/99 (4) (47.1 overs) 304	
A. C. Agar st Buttler b Rashid	46	4/110 (5) 5/164 (6) 6/260 (7)	
*†T. D. Paine c Rashid b Plunkett	15	7/292 (8) 8/293 (3) 9/303 (9)	
A. J. Tye c Billings b Rashid	10	10/304 (10) 10 overs: 60-1	

Willey 7–0–40–0; Wood 9–1–57–1; Plunkett 9.1–1–53–4; Ali 10–0–47–2; Root 4–0–24–0; Rashid 8–0–70–3.

Umpires: M. Erasmus and A. G. Wharf.   Third umpire: H. D. P. K. Dharmasena.
Referee: R. S. Madugalle.

ENGLAND v AUSTRALIA

Third Royal London One-Day International

At Nottingham, June 19 (day/night). England won by 242 runs. Toss: Australia.

If Paine had been in the wars beforehand, sporting a cut lip from Cardiff, he must have left Nottingham feeling as if he had gone the distance with Anthony Joshua. Three hours after he opted to field, England had laid waste not only to his bowlers, but to their own world-record total. Morgan later said the performance was "as close as we've ever been to a perfect day". Two years after posting 444 for three against Pakistan, also at Trent Bridge, England sailed past that with 27 balls to go, Hales swinging Jhye Richardson over square leg on his way to 147 from 92. The next target was 500. Had Hales and Morgan stayed together, instead of falling to consecutive deliveries in the 48th over, they might have made it. But that six was England's last boundary off the bat, and they had to be content with 481 – "a missed opportunity", said Morgan. Roy and Bairstow – who made his fourth hundred in six ODIs – had got things going with a stand of 159 inside 20 overs, ended only when Roy risked a second and was run out for 82 from 61. Morgan then crashed 67 from 30. Even allowing for the short boundaries, particularly to leg from the Radcliffe Road End, the brutality meted out to Tye, who went for 100 from nine overs, Richardson (92 from ten) and Stoinis (85 from eight) was relentless. Australia were just ahead of England after ten overs, but had lost Short – and the wickets kept falling. Rashid and Ali were in clover, bowling with a huge cushion and against

FIGURES OF FUN

STEVEN LYNCH

481 The highest total in 4,011 one-day internationals.

242 Australia's heaviest defeat by runs – previously 206 by New Zealand at Adelaide in 1985-86. And England's biggest victory by runs – previously 210 over New Zealand at Birmingham in 2015.

138 Alex Hales's strike-rate in ODIs at Nottingham; 90 elsewhere.

100 Runs conceded by Andrew Tye. Only Mick Lewis had conceded more for Australia, with 10–0–113–0 against South Africa at Johannesburg in 2005-06. Just two – Zimbabwe's Brian Vitori (105) and India's Vinay Kumar (102) – have conceded more than Tye in nine overs.

62 Boundaries hit by England – 41 fours and 21 sixes – beating 59, set by Sri Lanka against the Netherlands at Amstelveen in 2006, and equalled by England against Pakistan at Nottingham in 2016.

37 The margin by which England bettered the old record. The only bigger improvement came in the first match of the 1975 World Cup, when England made 334-4 against India at Lord's, beating the previous mark (set by England v India at Leeds the year before) by 68. At Johannesburg in 2005-06, Australia scored 434-4, breaking the existing record by 36, only for South Africa (438-9) to surpass it later that day.

33.1 Overs required for England to reach 300, beaten only by South Africa (32.2) against Australia at Johannesburg in 2005-06.

21 Balls for Eoin Morgan's fifty, the fastest for England – bettering Jos Buttler's 22 against Pakistan at Nottingham in 2016. Morgan, who also scored 744 runs for Ireland, overhauled Ian Bell's England record of 5,416.

21 Sixes in England's innings, a national record (previously 16 against Pakistan at Nottingham in 2016, and Scotland at Edinburgh in 2018). Only New Zealand, with 22 against West Indies at Queenstown in 2013-14, have hit more.

2 Centuries by England, for only the second time against Australia, after Graham Gooch and David Gower at Lord's in 1985. Alex Hales's 62-ball hundred was the sixth-fastest for England; Jonny Bairstow's (69) the joint-eighth.

1 Higher total in List A cricket: 496-4 by Surrey v Gloucestershire at The Oval in 2007.

opponents hell-bent on boundaries: they mopped up seven between them in 15 overs at a cost of 75. Rashid was the pick, bowling Finch and taking a smart return catch to get rid of Agar. Australia's coach Justin Langer suggested his side "can't have had a worse day". For England, the series in the bag, attention turned to a whitewash.

Man of the Match: A. D. Hales.   *Attendance*: 17,007.

England

J. J. Roy run out (Short/Paine)	82	D. J. Willey not out		1
J. M. Bairstow c Richardson b Agar	139			
A. D. Hales c Agar b Richardson	147	B 1, lb 8, w 7, nb 3		19
†J. C. Buttler c Finch b Richardson	11			
*E. J. G. Morgan c Paine b Richardson	67	1/159 (1) 2/310 (2)	(6 wkts, 50 overs)	481
M. M. Ali run out (Paine)	11	3/335 (4) 4/459 (3)		
J. E. Root not out	4	5/459 (5) 6/480 (6)	10 overs: 79-0	

L. E. Plunkett, A. U. Rashid and M. A. Wood did not bat.

Stanlake 8–0–74–0; Richardson 10–1–92–3; Agar 10–0–70–1; Tye 9–0–100–0; Maxwell 2–0–21–0; Stoinis 8–0–85–0; Finch 1–0–7–0; Short 2–0–23–0.

Australia

D. J. M. Short c Ali b Willey	15	A. J. Tye not out	5
T. M. Head c and b Ali	51	B. Stanlake st Buttler b Rashid	1
S. E. Marsh c Plunkett b Ali	24		
M. P. Stoinis run out (Bairstow/Buttler)	44	Lb 10, w 6	16
A. J. Finch b Rashid	20		
G. J. Maxwell c Plunkett b Willey	19	1/27 (1) 2/95 (2) 3/100 (3) (37 overs) 239	
*†T. D. Paine c Hales b Rashid	5	4/152 (5) 5/173 (4) 6/190 (7)	
A. C. Agar c and b Rashid	25	7/194 (6) 8/230 (8) 9/236 (9)	
J. A. Richardson st Buttler b Ali	14	10/239 (11) 10 overs: 83-1	

Wood 7–0–38–0; Willey 7–0–56–2; Root 2–0–19–0; Ali 5–0–28–3; Plunkett 6–0–41–0; Rashid 10–0–47–4.

Umpires: H. D. P. K. Dharmasena and R. T. Robinson.   Third umpire: M. Erasmus.
Referee: R. S. Madugalle.

ENGLAND v AUSTRALIA

Fourth Royal London One-Day International

At Chester-le-Street, June 21 (day/night). England won by six wickets. Toss: Australia. One-day international debut: C. Overton.

A century apiece for Finch, restored as opener, and Marsh, plus the loss of just one wicket in their first 39 overs, should have taken Australia to an imposing total on a gorgeous summer afternoon in Durham. But well as the pair batted, they lacked urgency, and the innings did not achieve lift-off. A target of 311 was within easy reach of England, who romped to a 4–0 lead with 32 balls unused. It was their second-highest successful chase – behind 350 against New Zealand at Trent Bridge in 2015 – and never really looked in doubt. Australia's innings had been poorly paced, with Root, on as early as the ninth over, allowed to fire down ten for just 44; only four boundaries were scored between the 11th and 33rd. In contrast, England were sent towards victory with a rattling opening partnership of 174 between Roy and Bairstow. Roy reached his sixth ODI hundred, from his 81st ball, with a six over long-on off Lyon, playing his first game of the series. Bairstow settled for a 66-ball 79, before Buttler, with an unbeaten 54 from 29, took England to their target. Roy was also involved in the best moment in the field, initiating a superb effort on the long-on boundary to dismiss Marsh – the second of four wickets in eight balls for Willey. Roy caught him but, with his momentum carrying him over the ropes, he picked out the debutant Craig Overton, 20 yards away.

Man of the Match: J. J. Roy. *Attendance:* 13,912.

Australia

A. J. Finch lbw b Wood	100	J. A. Richardson not out	5
T. M. Head c Willey b Rashid	63	N. M. Lyon not out	3
S. E. Marsh c Overton b Willey	101	Lb 3, w 4	7
M. P. Stoinis b Wood	1		
A. C. Agar c Buttler b Rashid	19	1/101 (2) 2/225 (1) (8 wkts, 50 overs) 310	
A. T. Carey c Overton b Willey	6	3/227 (4) 4/256 (5)	
*†T. D. Paine lbw b Willey	3	5/296 (6) 6/296 (3)	
M. G. Neser c Buttler b Willey	2	7/299 (8) 8/305 (7) 10 overs: 61-0	

B. Stanlake did not bat.

Wood 9–1–49–2; Willey 7–0–43–4; Root 10–0–44–0; Overton 7–0–55–0; Rashid 10–0–73–2; Ali 7–0–43–0.

England

J. J. Roy c Marsh b Lyon.............. 101	†J. C. Buttler not out.................. 54
J. M. Bairstow c Paine b Stanlake....... 79	B 1, w 2, nb 1 4
A. D. Hales not out 34	
J. E. Root b Agar.................... 27	1/174 (1) 2/183 (2) (4 wkts, 44.4 overs) 314
*E. J. G. Morgan c Paine b Agar......... 15	3/228 (4) 4/244 (5) 10 overs: 76-0

M. M. Ali, D. J. Willey, C. Overton, A. U. Rashid and M. A. Wood did not bat.

Neser 8.4–0–74–0; Stanlake 8–0–54–1; Lyon 7–0–38–1; Richardson 7–0–58–0; Agar
8–0–48–2; Stoinis 6–0–41–0.

Umpires: M. Erasmus and M. A. Gough.   Third umpire: H. D. P. K. Dharmasena.
Referee: R. S. Madugalle.

ENGLAND v AUSTRALIA

Fifth Royal London One-Day International

At Manchester, June 24. England won by one wicket. Toss: Australia. One-day international debut:
S. M. Curran.

Buttler had batted more fluently, but rarely can he have batted more maturely, clinching a game
which, he admitted, England "had no right to win". At 114 for eight in pursuit of 206, they looked
likely to miss out on a whitewash, yet Buttler – facing 100 balls in a one-day international for the
first time – calmly shepherded them to victory in front of a sell-out crowd already buoyed by
England's 6–1 demolition of Panama in the football World Cup. He finished with an unbeaten 110
in a low-scoring game that silenced those who argue one-day cricket lacks tension. Buttler had
already proved his worth with the gloves, pulling off a surgical stumping of Marsh – one of a
career-best four wickets for Ali – then brilliantly running out Paine, throwing down the non-
striker's stumps while performing a full pirouette. That had left Australia 100 for five and, though

Nerveless: Jos Buttler lofts Marcus Stoinis for six to reach his hundred.

IT'S NEVER OVER...

Most runs after the fall of the eighth wicket to win a one-day international:

	From	To		
136	107-8	243-9	Sri Lanka v Australia (239-8) at Melbourne	2010-11
101	166-8	267-9	West Indies v Pakistan (266-7) at Birmingham†	1975
94	**114-8**	**208-9**	**England v Australia (205) at Manchester**	**2018**
79	132-8	211-9	Afghanistan v Scotland (210) at Dunedin†	2014-15
74	258-8	332-8	New Zealand v Australia (331-5) at Christchurch	2005-06
73	135-8	208-8	Australia v England (204-8) at Port Elizabeth†	2002-03
71	147-8	218-8	West Indies v England (217) at The Oval‡	2004

† *World Cup.*   ‡ *Champions Trophy final.*   *Research: Andrew Samson*

Carey and Short helped double the score, they were dismissed with more than 15 overs remaining. But the pace of Stanlake quickly reduced England to 27 for four and, when Kane Richardson removed Sam Curran (on his one-day debut) and Plunkett with successive balls, they were eight down and still 92 adrift. Buttler had 47, but there were 20 overs to play with, and Rashid knuckled down for 16 of them in a stand of 81 – an England record for the ninth wicket against Australia. Then, with 11 needed, Rashid was superbly caught by Stanlake, diving forward at fine leg. Buttler calmly hit the next ball back over Stoinis's head for six to bring up his sixth – and, from 117 deliveries, slowest – ODI hundred. Amid rising tension, Ball played out a maiden from Agar, then blocked three balls from Richardson. Buttler turned down an easy single that would have guaranteed England a tie, before carving Stoinis through cover two balls later. It was their second one-wicket win over Australia, eight years on from another Old Trafford thriller. "That stung," said Paine. "We've been taught a lesson by a world-class outfit."

Man of the Match: J. C. Buttler.   *Attendance:* 23,506.

Man of the Series: J. C. Buttler.

Australia

A. J. Finch b Ali	....	22
T. M. Head c Morgan b Plunkett	....	56
M. P. Stoinis c Ball b Ali	....	0
S. E. Marsh st Buttler b Ali	....	8
A. T. Carey c Buttler b Curran	....	44
*†T. D. Paine run out (Buttler)	....	1
D. J. M. Short not out	....	47
A. C. Agar b Curran	....	0
K. W. Richardson run out (Ali/Buttler)	....	14

N. M. Lyon lbw b Rashid	....	1
B. Stanlake b Ali	....	2
Lb 3, w 7	....	10

1/60 (1) 2/60 (3) 3/90 (2) (34.4 overs) 205
4/97 (4) 5/100 (6) 6/159 (5)
7/159 (8) 8/181 (9) 9/193 (10)
10/205 (11)   10 overs: 79-2

Ball 5–0–29–0; Curran 6–0–44–2; Root 3–0–32–0; Ali 8.4–0–46–4; Plunkett 4–0–19–1; Rashid 8–0–32–1.

England

J. J. Roy b Agar	....	1
J. M. Bairstow b Stanlake	....	12
A. D. Hales c Paine b Richardson	....	20
J. E. Root c Marsh b Stanlake	....	1
*E. J. G. Morgan b Stanlake	....	0
†J. C. Buttler not out	....	110
M. M. Ali c Lyon b Stoinis	....	16
S. M. Curran c Paine b Richardson	....	15
L. E. Plunkett c Paine b Richardson	......	0

A. U. Rashid c Stanlake b Stoinis	....	20
J. T. Ball not out	....	1
Lb 7, w 5	....	12

1/2 (1) 2/19 (2) (9 wkts, 48.3 overs) 208
3/23 (4) 4/27 (5)
5/50 (3) 6/86 (7) 7/114 (8)
8/114 (9) 9/195 (10)   10 overs: 34-4

Agar 10–2–34–1; Stanlake 10–1–35–3; Lyon 10–0–32–0; Richardson 9–0–51–3; Stoinis 8.3–0–37–2; Short 1–0–12–0.

Umpires: R. J. Bailey and H. D. P. K. Dharmasena.   Third umpire: M. Erasmus.
Referee: R. S. Madugalle.

ENGLAND v AUSTRALIA

First Vitality Twenty20 International

At Birmingham, June 27 (floodlit). England won by 28 runs. Toss: Australia. Twenty20 international debut: M. J. Swepson.

A capacity crowd witnessed the final act of a one-sided fortnight. With Buttler promoted to open – stand-in coach Paul Farbrace reasoned that the best players should face as many balls as possible – it was no surprise England got off to a flyer. Roy smashed the first delivery, from Stanlake, through midwicket, and it was 70 without loss after the powerplay. Roy was dropped on 27 by Kane Richardson off Agar – a sitter at long-off which formed part of a personal nightmare: his first over had already gone for 23, and he later made a golden duck. By the time Buttler pulled leg-spinner Mitchell Swepson to deep midwicket, he had registered England's fastest T20 half-century (22 balls, beating Ravi Bopara, against Australia at Hobart in 2013-14, by one), and there were 95 on the board. Demoted below Morgan, Hales instantly threatened to beat the new record, only to fall for a 24-ball 49 thanks to Stoinis's lightning reflexes. Root made a patchy 35, but Bairstow hammered a pair of late sixes, and England had their highest T20 score against Australia, cruising past 209 for six at the Rose Bowl in 2013. On that occasion, they had fallen well short thanks to Finch's murderous 156, and for a while it looked as if he might scupper them again, despite two wickets in the ninth from Rashid, reducing Australia to 72 for five. Finch went down guns blazing, taking 16 off three balls from Ali. But when he departed, caught at long-on off Rashid aiming for a seventh six, the game – and Australia's miserable tour – was up.

Man of the Match: A. U. Rashid.   *Attendance:* 24,227.

England		B	4/6
1 J. J. Roy *c 2 b 11*	44	26	6/0
2 †J. C. Buttler *c 1 b 10*	61	30	6/5
3 *E. J. G. Morgan *c 8 b 10*	15	8	1/1
4 A. D. Hales *c and b 6*	49	24	5/2
5 J. E. Root *run out (5/8)*	35	24	4
6 J. M. Bairstow *not out*	14	8	0/2
7 M. M. Ali *not out*	0	0	0
Lb 1, w 2	3		

6 overs: 70-0   (20 overs) 221-5

1/95 2/108 3/132 4/204 5/215

8 D. J. Willey, 9 L. E. Plunkett, 10 C. J. Jordan and 11 A. U. Rashid did not bat.

Stanlake 3–5–44–1; Agar 4–8–34–0; Swepson 4–6–37–2; Richardson 4–3–59–0; Tye 4–8–37–0; Stoinis 1–2–9–1.

Australia		B	4/6
1 D. J. M. Short *c 7 b 9*	16	12	3
2 *A. J. Finch *c 10 b 11*	84	41	7/6
3 G. J. Maxwell *b 10*	10	7	1
4 T. M. Head *c 4 b 7*	15	10	1
5 †A. T. Carey *b 11*	3	3	0
6 M. P. Stoinis *c 1 b 11*	0	2	0
7 A. C. Agar *b 10*	29	23	3/1
8 A. J. Tye *c 9 b 8*	20	11	0/2
9 K. W. Richardson *c 4 b 10*	0	1	0
10 M. J. Swepson *not out*	3	4	0
11 B. Stanlake *c 3 b 9*	7	5	0/1
B 1, w 4, nb 1	6		

6 overs: 59-2   (19.4 overs) 193

1/17 2/33 3/64 4/72 5/72 6/158 7/174 8/174 9/184

Willey 4–8–31–1; Jordan 4–6–42–3; Plunkett 3.4–8–34–2; Rashid 4–11–27–3; Ali 4–3–58–1.

Umpires: M. A. Gough and A. G. Wharf.   Third umpire: R. J. Bailey.
Referee: R. S. Madugalle.

ENGLAND v INDIA IN 2018

REVIEW BY JONATHAN LIEW

Twenty20 internationals (3): England 1, India 2
One-day internationals (3): England 2, India 1
Test matches (5): England 4, India 1

For most of June and July, England enjoyed one of the hottest and driest summers on record. An uncharacteristic northward shift of the jet stream had created strong anticyclones that sent temperatures soaring for weeks on end. Wildfires raged in the North-West and Wales. Parts of the South-East saw no rain. July was central England's fourth-hottest month since records began in the 17th century. Unfortunately for India, the Test series began on August 1.

Within a week, the heatwave gave way to a cooler, danker spell that swaddled the rest of the tour like a clammy blanket. The result was a moist microclimate that could scarcely have been more conducive to swing and seam, at venues already heavily irrigated in anticipation of continuing drought. In an unusual attempt to preserve moisture, the groundstaff at Edgbaston treated their outfield with seaweed. Ultimately, it was India who needed kelp.

The series was largely dominated by the ball, and frequently by the new ball. The Indians reached 350 only once and, until the final Test on a pristine Oval surface, no opener on either side passed 44. In all, there were 45 lbws, a

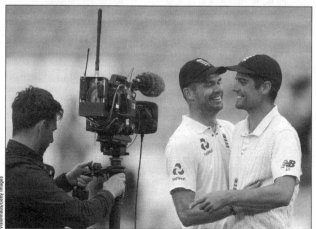

A fine bromance: England record-holders Jimmy Anderson (most wickets) and Alastair Cook (most runs) at the end of the Oval Test.

MOST LBWs IN A TEST SERIES

	T		
45	5	**England (took 25) v India (20) in England**	**2018**
43	3	Pakistan (22) v England (21) in the UAE.	2011-12
43	5	England (27) v West Indies (16) in England	2000
43	6	England (22) v Australia (21) in England.	1981
42	4	West Indies (15) v Australia (27) in the West Indies	1998-99
40	6	England (10) v Australia (30) in England.	1989
37	5	England (18) v South Africa (19) in England.	1955
36	6	India (17) v West Indies (19) in India.	1983-84
35	5	West Indies (17) v Australia (18) in the West Indies	1990-91
34	5	South Africa (20) v England (14) in South Africa	1927-28

record for any series. How might the tourists have fared had the weather held, or the games taken place a few weeks earlier? Idle counterfactuals, perhaps, given that a side ranked No. 1, in pursuit of their first win in England since 2007, were subjected to their heaviest defeat for almost seven years. England, meanwhile, having lost 4–0 in India in 2016-17, won four in a series for the first time since whitewashing them in 2011. It was as if the concept of home advantage was getting out of control.

And yet: India recorded more centuries and five-wicket hauls, boasted the two highest individual innings, as well as the more consistent seam attack. Virat Kohli, spectacularly laying to rest his demons from the 2014 tour, was comfortably the leading run-scorer, 244 clear of Jos Buttler. If the scoreline suggested India had been flattened, then England – who were spooked by their thrashing in the Third Test at Trent Bridge – were certainly flattered.

How did a hard-fought series end in a drubbing? Luck played a big role. The dry conditions of early summer would have favoured India's batsmen and spinners, the two areas in which, on paper, they looked superior. They were doubly unlucky at Lord's, losing the toss under grey clouds, which lifted when England batted. In fact, the importance of Joe Root winning all five tosses – the first Test captain this century to do so – could not be overestimated.

A more honest summary, then, would read: one trouncing apiece, and three close finishes, all of which – roared on for the most part by partisan capacity crowds – England managed to seize. Indeed, on the fourth day of the Fourth Test at Southampton, with India 123 for three in pursuit of 245, they looked capable of turning 0–2 into 3–2, a comeback achieved only by Bradman's 1936-37 Ashes winners. "You have to be doing some things right to be in a position where victories are possible for both sides," Kohli said. "We don't see a massive portion that we have to correct." And he was right, in a way. Instead, it was the small things that lost his side this series, an accumulation of marginal flaws – poor preparation, poor shots, poor catching, poor captaincy – that led to a mauling.

The first of these oversights was perhaps the biggest. India were hardly ignorant of the challenge awaiting them: their Under-19 squad had toured England the previous year, they had encouraged their players to take on county contracts (even if only Cheteshwar Pujara, at Yorkshire, and Ishant Sharma, at Sussex, did so), and their A-team were in town. So it should have come as no

Fly-bye: batsman Moeen Ali and Rishabh Pant are beaten by a ball from Mohammed Shami. The series included 153 byes.

surprise that a single three-day game against Essex – curtailed from four at India's request – proved inadequate preparation for a gruelling six-week churn.

It wasn't so much that they couldn't play the moving ball, more that they rarely gave themselves a chance. The imperious Kohli, and Pujara at times, showed what was possible when you arrived at the crease with a strategy. But, marshalled by the magnificent James Anderson – who with the final ball of the series passed Glenn McGrath to become Test cricket's most prolific fast bowler – England took wickets in clusters. India's 21 ducks were the most in a Test series in England.

Perhaps India were hoping that the two limited-overs series which preceded the Tests would provide ample acclimatisation. These went according to form. England asserted their primacy in the 50-over game, after confirming their relative meekness in Twenty20, where centuries for K. L. Rahul and Rohit Sharma underlined England's glaring weakness in the shortest format: a preference for pretty cameos over match-winning knocks. A single century in 13 years of T20 cricket – the same as Hong Kong, Scotland or the UAE – was an anomalous feature of their white-ball revolution.

Meanwhile, three events in the one-day series would have a significant impact on the Tests. First, England learned to play Kuldeep Yadav, whose left-arm wrist-spin had sung their batsmen to two shipwrecks: five wickets in the first T20 game at Old Trafford, six in the first one-day international at Trent Bridge. But in the second, at Lord's, Root played him brilliantly on his way to a century – nudging the ones, picking the twos, peppering the off-side boundary. It was the moment England appeared to realise that the best way to meet unorthodoxy was with orthodox aggression and proper cricket shots. Kuldeep played in only one Test, did not take another wicket on tour, and left before the end.

Second, in the one-day decider at Headingley, Kohli was bowled by Adil Rashid. It was a lovely delivery – pitching leg, hitting off – and was capped by Kohli's wide-eyed, slow-motion wonderment as he looked back up the pitch. Almost immediately, a clamour began for Rashid to be restored to the Test side, even though he had forsaken red-ball cricket with Yorkshire. It worked: Rashid resumed his first-class career at Edgbaston, becoming arguably the only player to win a Test cap on the strength of a batsman's facial expression – though national selector Ed Smith denied he had been chosen for one ball alone. Third, India's attack leader Bhuvneshwar Kumar

---

MOST BYES IN A TEST SERIES

198	South Africa (conceded 83) v England (115)	1922-23
192	South Africa (110) v England (82)	1909-10
174	South Africa (99) v England (75)	1905-06
171	Australia (52) v England (119)	1911-12
169	England (72) v Australia (97)	1905
164	South Africa (86) v England (78)	1913-14
163	West Indies (52) v England (111)	2008-09
158	West Indies (88) v England (70)	1929-30
153	**England (47) v India (106)**	**2018**
150	South Africa (86) v England (64)	1927-28

All series had five Tests except for West Indies v England in 1929-30, which had four.

---

exacerbated a back injury in that game at Headingley, and missed the Tests. His absence felt crucial.

All the while, Kohli was plotting an elegant retribution for his 2014 humiliation, when he had been undone by Anderson and the moving ball. Rewatching the footage, he noticed a kink in his alignment: his right hip too square, his front foot angled towards cover. This time he stood more side-on, and often two feet outside his crease to smother the swing. He averaged 59, compared with 13 last time, and never fell to Anderson: another challenge complete, another frontier conquered. His 149 and 51 at Edgbaston, where he almost won the game on his own, was one of the great efforts in a losing cause.

If only he had received a little help from his friends. For sure, there was the odd exception: Pujara's unbeaten century at Southampton, and a spirited rearguard at The Oval by Rahul and the precocious Rishabh Pant. But they were rescue acts rather than game-changers. In a lean summer for top-order batsmen, India's were particularly disappointing: Murali Vijay was jettisoned from the squad before the series was out, and finished the season at Essex, trying to get to grips with English conditions; Shikhar Dhawan was flighty and impermanent; Ajinkya Rahane subdued and struggling for fluency.

England's seamers again demonstrated they have few peers when the Dukes ball is moving around, which it continued to do well into its lifespan. Sam Curran – picked at the urging of Smith – enjoyed a breakthrough summer with bat and ball, and was England's Man of the Series, despite being dropped at Trent Bridge to make way for Ben Stokes, who had missed Lord's to attend court; Stuart Broad chipped away without ever quite looking at his best; and Stokes himself produced his venomous late inswinger at wildly opportune moments.

As ever, though, Anderson was king of the jungle, with new ball and old, the only blemish his failure to capture the scalp he really wanted. Kohli faced 271 balls from him without dismissal, despite not always being in control.

CAPTAIN WINNING ALL FIVE TOSSES IN A TEST SERIES

Hon. F. S. Jackson	England v Australia in England	1905
M. A. Noble	Australia v England in England	1909
H. G. Deane	South Africa v England in South Africa	1927-28
J. D. C. Goddard	West Indies v India in India	1948-49
A. L. Hassett	Australia v England in England	1953
M. C. Cowdrey	England v South Africa in England	1960
Nawab of Pataudi jnr	India v England in India	1963-64
G. S. Sobers	West Indies v England in England	1966
G. S. Sobers	West Indies v New Zealand in the West Indies	1971-72
C. H. Lloyd	West Indies v India in the West Indies	1982-83
M. A. Taylor	Australia v England in Australia	1998-99
J. E. Root	**England v India in England**	**2018**

For England in the West Indies in 1959-60, P. B. H. May won the toss in the first three Tests, and M. C. Cowdrey in the other two.

"Why can't he nick the ball like anyone else?" moaned Anderson. In fact, he did – on 21 and 51 in the first innings at Edgbaston – but Dawid Malan shelled both at second slip. England's chance to reopen a four-year-old scar at the first opportunity had gone.

Their batsmen, too, had issues. Having announced his intention to quit international cricket, Alastair Cook made a rousing century at The Oval, but it masked a poor series, and he admitted his "edge" had gone. Root at No. 3 was thus cast into the role of makeshift opener, though he eventually moved down to his preferred No. 4 midway through the Southampton Test. Keaton Jennings, Cook's partner, looked adrift, a fish not merely out of water but gutted, scaled and served with cheese sauce. Cook's retirement, which ensured countless standing ovations, probably saved Jennings's Test career.

And despite winning, England never did hit upon a satisfactory batting formula. Whether it was by giving Malan one last chance at Birmingham, or replacing him with Ollie Pope, who was dropped after two Tests, or shifting Moeen Ali to No. 3 mid-match, their top order retained the feel of a Sunday night stew, a concoction of whatever happened to be in the fridge, thrown together with little foresight or expertise.

It was their lower order who proved the difference. While the likes of Ravichandran Ashwin and Hardik Pandya struggled, Chris Woakes, Sam

Well armed: Jasprit Bumrah and Mohammed Shami, leading members of India's hostile attack.

Curran and Buttler sat proudly atop England's batting averages, having scored 770 at 42 between them. Woakes's unbeaten 137 at Lord's was higher than all 11 Indians managed in either innings. Curran's 63 at Birmingham and 78 at Southampton, both beginning amid the wreckage of 86 for six, were supreme, momentum-shifting efforts, without which India might well have won. Buttler's marvellous maiden Test century, at Nottingham, was a refined symphony in an album of pop bangers. Together, they hauled England to totals that, while never impregnable, were competitive enough.

It wasn't all chagrin for India. Coach Ravi Shastri's claim that this was their best-ever pace attack bore a customary ring of hyperbole, but at times it seemed plausible. Mohammed Shami bowled far better than his modest numbers – 16 wickets at 38 – suggested; Jasprit Bumrah, returning from injury at Trent Bridge, provided the X-factor; and Sharma displayed wonderful control of the new ball, consistently troubling England's left-handers from round the wicket. Even Pandya, the all-rounder, had his moment in the sun, with a five-for at Trent Bridge.

There were exciting discoveries, too. Hanuma Vihari scored a battling fifty on debut at The Oval, where Pant – who had got off the mark in Test cricket with a six after replacing Dinesh Karthik behind the stumps at Trent Bridge – hit a stunning maiden century. Late swing, though, made wicketkeeping perilous: no team had ever conceded more byes in a Test series in England than India's 106.

But India's selections often verged on the queer. Ashwin, perhaps their biggest disappointment, looked short of fitness and should probably have been

FIVE STATS YOU MAY HAVE MISSED

BENEDICT BERMANGE

- Edgbaston, Adil Rashid returned to first-class cricket after almost a year. Five players have had longer absences before a Test appearance for England:

Days

652	A. J. Fothergill	1887 to 1888-89
599	V. A. Barton	1890 to 1891-92
479	Hon. Ivo Bligh	1881 to 1882-83
472	S. F. Barnes	1907-08 to 1909
364	A. F. Giles	2005-06 to 2006-07
327	**A. U. Rashid**	**2017 to 2018**

- Joe Root's run of at least one score of 50 or more in each of his Tests against India came to an end at Lord's. He appears twice on a list of those with a fifty in eight or more consecutive Tests against one opponent from the start of a career:

12	**J. E. Root**	**England v India**
9	K. D. Walters	Australia v West Indies
8	W. Bardsley	Australia v South Africa
8	M. A. Taylor	Australia v England
8	J. E. Root	England v South Africa

- James Anderson dismissed two batsmen for pairs at Lord's, only the fourth instance in Tests:

W. J. O'Reilly	A v NZ (C. G. Rowe/L. A. Butterfield) at Wellington	1945-46
J. C. Laker	E v A (R. N. Harvey/K. D. Mackay) at Manchester	1956
D. W. Steyn	SA v NZ (M. R. Gillespie/I. E. O'Brien) at Centurion	2007-08
J. M. Anderson . . .	**E v I (M. Vijay/K. Yadav) at Lord's**	**2018**

- At Southampton, India fielded an unchanged side for the first time since Virat Kohli took over as captain in 2014-15. Only one Test captain had presided over more matches without an unchanged side from the start of his career – Graeme Smith (excluding one Test leading the ICC World XI):

43	G. C. Smith (South Africa)	2003 to 2006-07
38	**V. Kohli (India)**	**2014-15 to 2018**
28	S. C. Ganguly (India)	2000-01 to 2002-03
26	Inzamam-ul-Haq (Pakistan)	2000-01 to 2006-07

- Kohli ended the series with 593 runs, 244 more than the next highest. The only bigger difference between the top-scorer in a series and the next-best also came from the losing side: Brian Lara made 688 in Sri Lanka in 2001-02, with Hashan Tillekeratne next on 403, but West Indies still lost all three Tests.

left out at Southampton. Ravindra Jadeja, their leading bowler according to the world rankings, was curiously sheathed for the first four Tests. The top three were shuffled between Edgbaston and Lord's, then again before Trent Bridge. The slip cordon saw more changes than The Temptations. It was these minor infelicities, rather than any fundamental flaw, that cost India victory.

And so, as the curtain came down on a wild and weird series, a weary Kohli sat in the dimly lit bowels of the Oval indoor school, fielding yet more questions about his side's inability to win away from home. "Of course we can play," he argued. "But can we capitalise on the important moments better than the opposition? At the moment, no, we haven't done that." Rahul Dravid, the last captain to lead India to victory in England, was more surgical in his diagnosis: "We have to be better prepared."

England were busy toasting their triumph on the outfield, in front of what was left of the crowd. The clouds had settled over south London, and a spot of rain hung in the air, like an unuttered thought. A chilly September breeze whipped over the Peter May Stand, ruffling the flags on the old brick pavilion. Darkness was settling. It felt like the end of the summer, and in more ways than one.

INDIA TOURING PARTY

*V. Kohli (T/50/20), R. Ashwin (T), Bhuvneshwar Kumar (50/20), J. J. Bumrah (T), Y. S. Chahal (50/20), D. L. Chahar (20), S. Dhawan (T/50/20), M. S. Dhoni (50/20), S. S. Iyer (50), R. A. Jadeja (T), K. D. Karthik (T/50/20), S. Kaul (50/20), Mohammed Shami (T), K. K. Nair (T), M. K. Pandey (20), H. H. Pandya (T/50/20), K. H. Pandya (20), R. R. Pant (T), A. R. Patel (50), C. A. Pujara (T), A. M. Rahane (T), K. L. Rahul (T/50/20), S. K. Raina (50/20), I. Sharma (T), R. G. Sharma (50/20), P. P. Shaw (T), S. N. Thakur (T/50), G. H. Vihari (T), M. Vijay (T), K. Yadav (T/50/20), U. T. Yadav (T/50/20).

A. T. Rayudu was originally selected for the 50-over series, but failed a fitness test and was replaced by Raina. Bumrah broke his left thumb in Ireland; Chahar came in for the T20s in England, and Thakur for the ODIs. M. S. Washington Sundar was originally selected for both white-ball squads, but injured an ankle in training and went home; K. H. Pandya and Patel were called up as cover. Bhuvneshwar Kumar had been expected to be in the Test party, but aggravated a back injury during the ODIs and returned home. Shaw and Vihari replaced Vijay and K. Yadav after the Third Test.

Coach: R. J. Shastri. *Assistant coach:* S. B. Bangar. *Bowling coach:* B. Arun. *Fielding coach:* R. Sridhar. *Team manager:* S. Subramaniam. *Analyst:* C. K. M. Dhananjai. *Physiotherapist:* P. J. Farhart. *Masseurs:* A. Kanade, R. Kumar. *Strength and conditioning:* S. Basu. *Media manager:* M. Parikh. *Social media official:* R. Arora.

TEST MATCH AVERAGES

ENGLAND – BATTING AND FIELDING

	T	I	NO	R	HS	100	50	Avge	Ct/St
C. R. Woakes	2	3	1	149	137*	1	0	74.50	0
†S. M. Curran	4	7	0	272	78	0	2	38.85	0
J. C. Buttler	5	9	0	349	106	1	2	38.77	5
†A. N. Cook	5	9	0	327	147	1	1	36.33	13
J. E. Root	5	9	0	319	125	1	1	35.44	3
†M. M. Ali	2	4	0	119	50	0	1	29.75	1
J. M. Bairstow	5	9	0	230	93	0	2	25.55	14/1
†B. A. Stokes	4	8	0	200	62	0	1	25.00	2
A. U. Rashid	5	8	2	119	33*	0	0	19.83	1
†K. K. Jennings	5	9	0	163	42	0	0	18.11	3
O. J. D. Pope	2	3	0	54	28	0	0	18.00	2
†J. M. Anderson	5	7	6	15	11	0	0	15.00	1
†S. C. J. Broad	5	7	0	87	38	0	0	12.42	3

Played in one Test: †D. J. Malan 8, 20 (3 ct).

BOWLING

	Style	O	M	R	W	BB	5I	Avge
J. M. Anderson	RFM	183.4	56	435	24	5-20	1	18.12
C. R. Woakes	RFM	58	10	167	8	3-75	0	20.87
M. M. Ali	OB	76	9	252	12	5-63	1	21.00
S. M. Curran	LFM	77.4	11	259	11	4-74	0	23.54
B. A. Stokes	RFM	116.2	17	408	14	4-40	0	29.14
S. C. J. Broad	RFM	151.5	37	475	16	4-44	0	29.68
A. U. Rashid	LB	87	10	309	10	3-101	0	30.90

Also bowled: K. K. Jennings (RM) 2–0–4–0; J. E. Root (OB) 9–1–26–0.

INDIA – BATTING AND FIELDING

	T	I	NO	R	HS	100	50	Avge	Ct
V. Kohli	5	10	0	593	149	2	3	59.30	4
C. A. Pujara	4	8	1	278	132*	1	1	39.71	0
K. L. Rahul	5	10	0	299	149	1	0	29.90	14
†R. R. Pant	3	6	0	162	114	1	0	27.00	15
A. M. Rahane	5	10	0	257	81	0	2	25.70	4
H. H. Pandya	4	8	1	164	52*	0	1	23.42	0
R. Ashwin	4	8	2	126	33*	0	0	21.00	1
†S. Dhawan	4	8	0	162	44	0	0	20.25	2
M. Vijay	2	4	0	26	20	0	0	6.50	0
I. Sharma	5	9	1	42	14	0	0	5.25	0
K. D. Karthik	2	4	0	21	20	0	0	5.25	5
Mohammed Shami	5	10	0	27	10*	0	0	3.00	2
J. J. Bumrah	3	5	2	6	6	0	0	2.00	1

Played in one Test: †R. A. Jadeja 86*, 13; G. H. Vihari 56, 0; †K. Yadav 0, 0; U. T. Yadav 1*, 0*.

BOWLING

	Style	O	M	R	W	BB	5I	Avge
G. H. Vihari	OB	10.3	1	38	3	3-37	0	12.66
I. Sharma	RFM	151	36	437	18	5-51	1	24.27
H. H. Pandya	RFM	64.1	7	247	10	5-28	1	24.70
U. T. Yadav	RF	24	3	76	3	2-20	0	25.33
J. J. Bumrah	RFM	133.2	31	363	14	5-85	1	25.92
R. Ashwin	OB	139.4	30	360	11	4-62	0	32.72
R. A. Jadeja	SLA	77	3	258	7	4-79	0	36.85
Mohammed Shami	RFM	172.4	25	622	16	4-57	0	38.87

Also bowled: K. Yadav (SLW) 9–1–44–0.

At Malahide, June 27. INDIA beat IRELAND by 76 runs (see Cricket in Ireland, page 905).

At Malahide, June 29. INDIA beat IRELAND by 143 runs.

TWENTY20 INTERNATIONAL REPORTS BY DAVID CLOUGH

ENGLAND v INDIA

First Vitality Twenty20 International

At Manchester, July 3 (floodlit). India won by eight wickets. Toss: India.
England faced a sterner test of their white-ball credentials after the 6–0 dismissal of Australia – and were undone by the left-arm wrist-spin of Kuldeep Yadav and the blade of K. L. Rahul. The midsummer heatwave was unrelenting by the time India opened their tour, after a two-match

Twenty20 stopover in Ireland. They had lost key seamer Jasprit Bumrah to a broken thumb but, at an old Old Trafford, let loose Kuldeep – to devastating effect. Buttler and Roy began with 50 in five overs, and Buttler finished with his seventh half-century in eight T20 innings dating back to the IPL. But Hales made a painful eight from 18 balls before Kuldeep bowled him round his legs, and in his next over Morgan miscued a slog-sweep. It was the first of three wickets in four deliveries, as Bairstow and Root were both stumped first ball – Root a record 33rd stumping for Dhoni in T20 internationals, one ahead of Pakistan's Kamran Akmal. The wicket of Buttler gave Kuldeep a career-best five for 24, and England – after only the openers and No. 8 Willey had reached double figures – seemingly short of par. So it proved: Rahul added 123 for the second wicket with Sharma, and went on to his first international hundred since the 2016-17 Chennai Test against England. Kohli, when eight, became the fourth player to score 2,000 runs in T20 internationals, after the New Zealanders Martin Guptill and Brendon McCullum, and Shoaib Malik of Pakistan. India were cheered all the way by their sea-of-blue support, who turned Manchester into a home venue.

Man of the Match: K. Yadav.   *Attendance:* 23,002.

England

		B	4/6
1 J. J. Roy *b 9*		30	20 5
2 †J. C. Buttler *c 4 b 10*		69	46 8/2
3 A. D. Hales *b 10*		8	18 0
4 *E. J. G. Morgan *c 4 b 10*		7	6 0
5 J. M. Bairstow *st 6 b 10*		0	1 0
6 J. E. Root *st 6 b 10*		0	1 0
7 M. M. Ali *c 5 b 7*		6	8 1
8 D. J. Willey *not out*		29	15 2/2
9 C. J. Jordan *c and b 9*		0	1 0
10 L. E. Plunkett *not out.*		3	4 0
Lb 2, w 5		7	

6 overs: 53-1   (20 overs) 159-8

1/50 2/95 3/106 4/107 5/107 6/117 7/141 8/149

11 A. U. Rashid did not bat.

Bhuvneshwar Kumar 4–8–45–0; U. T. Yadav 4–12–21–2; Chahal 4–7–34–0; Pandya 4–10–33–1; K. Yadav 4–13–24–5.

India

		B	4/6
1 S. Dhawan *b 8*		4	4 1
2 R. G. Sharma *c 4 b 11*		32	30 3/1
3 K. L. Rahul *not out*		101	54 10/5
4 *V. Kohli *not out*		20	22 0/1
Lb 2, w 4		6	

6 overs: 54-1   (18.2 overs) 163-2

1/7 2/130

5 S. K. Raina, 6 †M. S. Dhoni, 7 H. H. Pandya, 8 Bhuvneshwar Kumar, 9 U. T. Yadav, 10 K. Yadav and 11 Y. S. Chahal did not bat.

Willey 4–7–30–1; Jordan 4–11–27–0; Plunkett 4–9–42–0; Rashid 4–10–25–1; Ali 2.2–0–37–0.

Umpires: R. J. Bailey and A. G. Wharf.   Third umpire: R. T. Robinson.
Referee: D. C. Boon.

ENGLAND v INDIA

Second Vitality Twenty20 International

At Cardiff, July 6 (floodlit). England won by five wickets. Toss: England. Twenty20 international debut: J. T. Ball.

England were instantly in must-win territory. But this time they had the chance to chase, and they took it, mainly thanks to a measured unbeaten fifty from Hales, who admitted he had spoken to himself "quite harshly" following his tortured innings in Manchester. India's batsmen had been unconvincing on a surface which surprised everyone with extra pace and bounce. There was no half-century – a hard-working Kohli came closest – and the varying skills of Yorkshire trio Willey, with his tightest figures in Twenty20 internationals, Plunkett and Rashid held sway. England then managed to tame Kuldeep. After netting against their spin-bowling machine, Merlyn, and a couple of young left-arm wrist-spinners plucked from club cricket, they either stayed right back or used their feet. Kuldeep looked human again: Hales launched him into the River Taff, while Bairstow slog-swept successive sixes. But this was no seamless chase. When an out-of-sorts Root was bowled by Chahal's googly, England were 44 for three in the seventh over, and Hales was grateful for support from Morgan and Bairstow. In the end, he was left to his own devices. Bhuvneshwar Kumar had conceded only seven runs in his first three overs, and England needed 12 off his last for victory. But Hales advanced to hit the first delivery straight over his head and back into the river, and three balls later it was 1–1.

Man of the Match: A. D. Hales.   *Attendance:* 15,089.

India

		B	4/6
1 R. G. Sharma *c 2 b 11*	5	9	1
2 S. Dhawan *run out (1/5)*	10	12	1
3 K. L. Rahul *b 9*	6	8	0
4 *V. Kohli *c 3 b 7*	47	38	1/2
5 S. K. Raina *st 2 b 10*	27	20	2/1
6 †M. S. Dhoni *not out*	32	24	5
7 H. H. Pandya *not out*	12	10	0/1
B 4, lb 2, w 2, nb 1	9		

6 overs: 31-3   (20 overs) 148-5

1/7 2/22 3/22 4/79 5/111

8 Bhuvneshwar Kumar, 9 U. T. Yadav, 10 K. Yadav and 11 Y. S. Chahal did not bat.

Willey 4–12–18–1; Ball 4–44–44–1; Plunkett 4–14–17–1; Jordan 4–6–34–0; Rashid 4–10–29–1.

England

		B	4/6
1 J. J. Roy *b 9*	15	12	2/1
2 †J. C. Buttler *c 4 b 9*	14	12	3
3 J. E. Root *b 11*	9	10	0
4 A. D. Hales *not out*	58	41	4/3
5 *E. J. G. Morgan *c 2 b 7*	17	19	2
6 J. M. Bairstow *c 10 b 8*	28	18	0/2
7 D. J. Willey *not out*	3	6	0
Lb 4, w 1	5		

6 overs: 42-2   (19.4 overs) 149-5

1/16 2/33 3/44 4/92 5/126

8 C. J. Jordan, 9 L. E. Plunkett, 10 A. U. Rashid and 11 J. T. Ball did not bat.

U. T. Yadav 4–12–36–2; Bhuvneshwar Kumar 3.4–11–19–1; Pandya 4–6–28–1; Chahal 4–10–28–1; K. Yadav 4–9–34–0.

Umpires: M. A. Gough and R. T. Robinson.   Third umpire: A. G. Wharf.
Referee: D. C. Boon.

ENGLAND v INDIA

Third Vitality Twenty20 International

At Bristol, July 8. India won by seven wickets. Toss: India. Twenty20 international debut: D. L. Chahar.

The backdrop to this decider was Stokes's latest return to international cricket – in the city where he had ended up in a late-night brawl ten months earlier. At Cardiff, he had made it as far as the dugout, following a month-long absence with a hamstring injury. Now, something had to give, and Root was dropped for the first time in any format since the 2013-14 Sydney Test. India sprang a surprise by leaving out Kuldeep, later citing Nevil Road's short boundaries; Bhuvneshwar Kumar was injured, and seamers Siddharth Kaul and Deepak Chahar had just one cap between them. But, as in Manchester, England's batting failed to fulfil the promise of Roy and Buttler. They powered to 94 inside eight overs, Roy hitting England's joint-second-fastest T20 half-century, from 23 deliveries. His 31-ball 67 included seven sixes, equalling the England record held jointly by Morgan (twice) and Ravi Bopara. But Pandya, who went for 22 in his first over, finished with a career-best four for 38, and England lost five wickets in a manic final 15 balls, as Dhoni held a record five catches in a T20 international. After passing 2,000 runs in the format, Sharma unfurled some wonderful shots, and became only the second man – after New Zealand's Colin Munro – to hit three hundreds in T20 internationals. Kohli helped him add 89 for the third wicket, before Pandya capped a series-sealing contribution with six boundaries in 14 balls.

Man of the Match: R. G. Sharma.   *Attendance:* 13,831.
Man of the Series: R. G. Sharma.

England

		B	4/6
1 J. J. Roy *c 7 b 8*	67	31	4/7
2 †J. C. Buttler *b 10*	34	21	7
3 A. D. Hales *c 7 b 5*	30	24	3/2
4 *E. J. G. Morgan *c 7 b 5*	6	9	0
5 B. A. Stokes *c 4 b 5*	14	10	2
6 J. M. Bairstow *c 7 b 5*	25	14	2/2
7 D. J. Willey *b 9*	1	2	0
8 C. J. Jordan *run out (7)*	3	3	0
9 L. E. Plunkett *c 7 b 10*	9	4	0/1
10 A. U. Rashid *not out*	4	3	1
Lb 4, nb 1	5		

6 overs: 73-0   (20 overs) 198-9

1/94 2/103 3/134 4/140 5/177 6/181 7/183 8/194
9/198

11 J. T. Ball did not bat.

Chahar 4–10–43–1; Yadav 4–9–48–1; Kaul
4–9–35–2; Pandya 4–11–38–4; Chahal
4–9–30–0.

India

		B	4/6
1 R. G. Sharma *not out*	100	56	11/5
2 S. Dhawan *c 11 b 7*	5	3	1
3 K. L. Rahul *c 8 b 11*	19	10	1/2
4 *V. Kohli *c and b 8*	43	29	2/2
5 H. H. Pandya *not out*	33	14	4/2
W 1	1		

6 overs: 70-2   (18.4 overs) 201-3

1/21 2/62 3/151

6 S. K. Raina, 7 †M. S. Dhoni, 8 D. L. Chahar,
9 U. T. Yadav, 10 S. Kaul and 11 Y. S. Chahal
did not bat.

Willey 3–6–37–1; Ball 3–3–39–1; Jordan
3.4–9–40–1; Plunkett 3–2–42–0; Stokes
2–4–11–0; Rashid 4–6–32–0.

Umpires: R. J. Bailey and R. T. Robinson.   Third umpire: M. A. Gough.
Referee: D. C. Boon.

ONE-DAY INTERNATIONAL REPORTS BY DEAN WILSON

ENGLAND v INDIA

First Royal London One-Day International

At Nottingham, July 12. India won by eight wickets. Toss: India. One-day international debut:
S. Kaul.

Despite their defeat in the Twenty20 series, England arrived at Trent Bridge feeling bullish. Top
of the one-day rankings, they had scored 444 and 481 in their last two completed matches in
Nottingham – both world records. By the end, though, their confidence had taken a knock, and they
left with only one man on their mind: Kuldeep Yadav. He had already announced himself with five
wickets in the first Twenty20 international, but his return of six for 25 elevated his stock still further.
It might have been even worse had England not begun their innings against the pace of Umesh
Yadav and Kaul: by the time Kuldeep bowled his first over, the 11th, Roy and Bairstow had put on
71. He removed Roy with his second ball, courtesy of a miscued reverse sweep, Root with his
seventh, and Bairstow, who misread a googly, with his 11th. The innings never found top gear again,

BEST ONE-DAY BOWLING FIGURES AGAINST ENGLAND

7-20	A. J. Bichel (Australia) at Port Elizabeth†	2002-03
7-33	T. G. Southee (New Zealand) at Wellington†	2014-15
7-36	Waqar Younis (Pakistan) at Leeds	2001
6-14	G. J. Gilmour (Australia) at Leeds†	1975
6-15	C. E. H. Croft (West Indies) at Arnos Vale	1980-81
6-19	H. K. Olonga (Zimbabwe) at Cape Town	1999-2000
6-23	A. Nehra (India) at Durban†	2002-03
6-25	**K. Yadav (India) at Nottingham**	**2018**
6-27	C. R. D. Fernando (Sri Lanka) at Colombo (RPS)	2007-08
6-29	S. T. Jayasuriya (Sri Lanka) at Moratuwa	1992-93
6-42	Umar Gul (Pakistan) at The Oval	2010
6-55	S. Sreesanth (India) at Indore	2005-06

† *World Cup.*

and Stokes reached a 102-ball half-century, England's slowest for more than a decade, before reverse-sweeping the next to backward point. That gave Kuldeep five wickets – he had already removed Buttler, for a more fluent fifty – and Willey's heave made it six. Kuldeep's were the best ODI figures by a left-arm spinner, beating Murali Kartik's six for 27 for India against Australia at Mumbai in October 2007, and the best by any spinner in England, beating Shahid Afridi's five for 11 for Pakistan against Kenya at Edgbaston during the 2004 Champions Trophy. A target of 269 on a good pitch posed no problems. Sharma finished with an unbeaten 137 from 114 balls – his 18th ODI century, and the highest score for India away to England – and put on 167 for the second wicket with Kohli. Victory came with nearly ten overs to spare.

Man of the Match: K. Yadav.   *Attendance:* 17,007.

England

J. J. Roy c U. T. Yadav b K. Yadav	38		L. E. Plunkett run out (Raina/Dhoni)	10
J. M. Bairstow lbw b K. Yadav	38		M. A. Wood not out	0
J. E. Root lbw b K. Yadav	3			
*E. J. G. Morgan c Raina b Chahal	19		Lb 5, w 5	10
B. A. Stokes c Kaul b K. Yadav	50			
†J. C. Buttler c Dhoni b K. Yadav	53		1/73 (1) 2/81 (3) 3/82 (2)	(49.5 overs) 268
M. M. Ali c Kohli b U. T. Yadav	24		4/105 (4) 5/198 (6) 6/214 (5)	
D. J. Willey c Rahul b K. Yadav	1		7/216 (8) 8/245 (7) 9/261 (9)	
A. U. Rashid c Pandya b U. T. Yadav	22		10/268 (10)	10 overs: 71-0

U. T. Yadav 9.5–0–70–2; Kaul 10–0–62–0; Chahal 10–0–51–1; Pandya 7–0–47–0; K. Yadav 10–0–25–6; Raina 3–1–8–0.

India

R. G. Sharma not out	137
S. Dhawan c Rashid b Ali	40
*V. Kohli st Buttler b Rashid	75
K. L. Rahul not out	9
W 8	8

1/59 (2) 2/226 (3)   (2 wkts, 40.1 overs) 269
10 overs: 74-1

S. K. Raina, †M. S. Dhoni, H. H. Pandya, U. T. Yadav, K. Yadav, S. Kaul and Y. S. Chahal did not bat.

Wood 6–0–55–0; Willey 5–0–25–0; Ali 8.1–0–60–1; Plunkett 6–0–31–0; Stokes 4–0–27–0; Rashid 10–0–62–1; Root 1–0–9–0.

Umpires: R. S. A. Palliyaguruge and R. T. Robinson.   Third umpire: B. N. J. Oxenford.
Referee: D. C. Boon.

ENGLAND v INDIA

Second Royal London One-Day International

At Lord's, July 14. England won by 86 runs. Toss: England.

For the first time in a one-day international since August 2016, Morgan chose to bat – and, on his home turf, he knew this was the time to make the switch. As in Nottingham, Roy and Bairstow flew out of the traps; as in Nottingham, Kuldeep Yadav bowled the 11th, and took a wicket with his second ball, Bairstow dragging on a sweep. Roy soon followed, slog-sweeping hard to deep midwicket, but from there the game took on a life of its own, moulded in the main by Root. Without a hundred in any format all season, he mastered Kuldeep's threat, and collected his 12th in one-day internationals. He and Morgan added 103 and, when England slipped to 239 for six in the 42nd over, Willey took over, muscling a maiden international fifty from 30 balls. Defending 322, the home bowlers went efficiently about their business, and in the case of their spinners did a good job, Ali and Rashid taking a combined three for 80. Kohli, the finest chaser in the game, was neutralised by Ali, leaving too much for Dhoni. He did pass 10,000 one-day international runs – the fourth Indian to do

ENGLAND'S MOST PROLIFIC ONE-DAY PARTNERSHIPS

Runs		I	Best	100	Avge
2,409	E. J. G. Morgan/J. E. Root	62	198	9	**41.53**
2,118	I. R. Bell/A. N. Cook	54	178	3	40.73
1,847	A. D. Hales/J. E. Root	31	248	5	**59.58**
1,725	N. V. Knight/M. E. Trescothick..........	46	165	5	37.50
1,615	P. D. Collingwood/A. Flintoff	43	174	2	41.41
1,598	N. V. Knight/A. J. Stewart	46	165	2	34.73
1,525	I. R. Bell/K. P. Pietersen	36	140	2	46.21
1,497	N. Hussain/N. V. Knight	33	165	5	48.29
1,466	P. D. Collingwood/K. P. Pietersen	41	136	2	37.58
1,411	A. D. Hales/J. J. Roy	42	256*	3	**34.41**
1,396	J. M. Bairstow/J. J. Roy	26	174	5	**53.69**

As at December 31, 2018.

---

so, after Tendulkar, Ganguly and Dravid. But his sluggish 59-ball 37 drew boos, many from Indian fans, and Plunkett finished with four wickets as the game petered out. The result kept England top of the one-day rankings.

Man of the Match: J. E. Root.   *Attendance:* 27,967.

England

J. J. Roy c U. T. Yadav b K. Yadav	40		D. J. Willey run out (Dhoni)	50
J. M. Bairstow b K. Yadav	38			
J. E. Root not out..................	113		Lb 1, w 3, nb 2................	6
*E. J. G. Morgan c Dhawan b K. Yadav....	53			
B. A. Stokes c Dhoni b Pandya..........	5		1/69 (2) 2/86 (1) (7 wkts, 50 overs)	322
†J. C. Buttler c Dhoni b U. T. Yadav.....	4		3/189 (4) 4/203 (5)	
M. M. Ali c Sharma b Chahal	13		5/214 (6) 6/239 (7) 7/322 (8) 10 overs: 69-0	

A. U. Rashid, L. E. Plunkett and M. A. Wood did not bat.

U. T. Yadav 10–0–63–1; Kaul 8–0–59–0; Pandya 10–0–70–1; Chahal 10–0–43–1; K. Yadav 10–0–68–3; Raina 2–0–18–0.

India

R. G. Sharma b Wood	15		S. Kaul lbw b Plunkett................	1
S. Dhawan c Stokes b Willey	36		Y. S. Chahal c Stokes b Willey	12
*V. Kohli lbw b Ali..................	45			
K. L. Rahul c Buttler b Plunkett	0		Lb 2, w 13	15
S. K. Raina b Rashid	46			
†M. S. Dhoni c Stokes b Plunkett	37		1/49 (1) 2/57 (2) 3/60 (4) (50 overs)	236
H. H. Pandya c Buttler b Plunkett.......	21		4/140 (3) 5/154 (5) 6/191 (7)	
U. T. Yadav c Buttler b Rashid	0		7/192 (8) 8/215 (6) 9/217 (10)	
K. Yadav not out...................	8		10/236 (11) 10 overs: 57-2	

Wood 5–0–31–1; Willey 10–0–48–2; Plunkett 10–1–46–4; Stokes 5–0–29–0; Ali 10–0–42–1; Rashid 10–0–38–2.

Umpires: B. N. J. Oxenford and A. G. Wharf.   Third umpire: R. S. A. Palliyaguruge.
Referee: D. C. Boon.

ENGLAND v INDIA

Third Royal London One-Day International

At Leeds, July 17. England won by eight wickets. Toss: England.

Morgan had regularly bemoaned the fact that bilateral limited-overs contests rarely replicate tournament cricket – hence his preference for tri-series. So, with the World Cup less than a year away, a decider was ideal. England had coped better with Kuldeep at Lord's after using the Merlyn bowling

The face that relaunched a Test career: Virat Kohli gapes at Adil Rashid after being bowled.

machine, but in the nets before this game they faced 16-year-old left-arm wrist-spinner Sam Wisniewski, a Yorkshire Academy bowler who had just taken his GCSEs. It clearly helped: for the first time in the series, Kuldeep went wicketless. And, after they were put in, it was India who made slow headway against spin. Rashid bowled Kohli for a run-a-ball 71 with a stunning leg-break that left Kohli gobsmacked, and he and Ali cost only 96 between them. Willey rounded off a good series, his three victims including Dhoni, who was sluggish once more. A target of 257 looked way below par, especially after Bairstow had slapped seven of the 13 balls he faced to the fence. Vince, given another chance because Jason Roy had split his right little finger at Lord's, was run out for 27 but, for England, 74 for two was as shaky as it got. Root's confidence was sky-high as he strode out on his home ground, and he didn't disappoint the locals. He scored precisely 100 in an unbroken partnership of 186 with Morgan – an England record for any wicket against India, one more than Marcus Trescothick and Nasser Hussain added at Lord's in 2002. Once Root's final blow had crossed the boundary, to overhaul Trescothick as England's leading one-day century-maker, with 13, he celebrated in the modern manner. His bat drop was a variation on the mic drop usually reserved for singers or comedians – and Barack Obama – to signify an exceptional performance. He earned scoffing from team-mates and, with Kohli watching closely after suffering his first defeat in nine bilateral one-day series as captain, scorn from opponents; Root later said it was one of the most embarrassing things he had done. For the moment, though, England could celebrate their first 50-over series win over India in five attempts.

Man of the Match: A. U. Rashid. *Attendance:* 13,487.

Man of the Series: J. E. Root.

India

R. G. Sharma c Wood b Willey	2	S. N. Thakur not out	22
S. Dhawan run out (Stokes)	44		
*V. Kohli b Rashid	71	Lb 6, w 5	11
K. D. Karthik b Rashid	21		
†M. S. Dhoni c Buttler b Willey	42	1/13 (1) 2/84 (2) (8 wkts, 50 overs) 256
S. K. Raina c Root b Rashid	1	3/125 (4) 4/156 (3)
H. H. Pandya c Buttler b Wood	21	5/158 (6) 6/194 (7)
Bhuvneshwar Kumar c Bairstow b Willey	21	7/221 (5) 8/256 (8) 10 overs: 32-1

K. Yadav and Y. S. Chahal did not bat.

Wood 10–2–30–1; Willey 9–0–40–3; Plunkett 5–0–41–0; Ali 10–0–47–0; Stokes 6–0–43–0; Rashid 10–0–49–3.

England

J. M. Vince run out (Pandya/Dhoni)	27
J. M. Bairstow c Raina b Thakur	30
J. E. Root not out	100
*E. J. G. Morgan not out	88
B 3, lb 6, w 5, nb 1	15

1/43 (2) 2/74 (1) (2 wkts, 44.3 overs) 260

10 overs: 78-2

B. A. Stokes, †J. C. Buttler, M. M. Ali, D. J. Willey, A. U. Rashid, L. E. Plunkett and M. A. Wood did not bat.

Bhuvneshwar Kumar 7–0–49–0; Pandya 5.3–0–39–0; Thakur 10–0–51–1; Chahal 10–0–41–0; Yadav 10–0–55–0; Raina 2–0–16–0.

Umpires: M. A. Gough and B. N. J. Oxenford.   Third umpire: R. S. A. Palliyaguruge.
Referee: D. C. Boon.

At Chelmsford, July 25–27 (not first-class). **Drawn.** ‡**Indians 395** (100.2 overs) (M. Vijay 53, V. Kohli 68, K. L. Rahul 58, K. D. Karthik 82, H. H. Pandya 51; P. I. Walter 4-113) **and 89-2** (21.2 overs); **Essex 359-8 dec** (94 overs) (T. Westley 57, M. S. Pepper 68, P. I. Walter 75; U. T. Yadav 4-35, I. Sharma 3-59). *The solitary warm-up game was originally scheduled to last four days, but the Indians asked for it to be reduced to three because they wanted an extra day in Birmingham ahead of the First Test. The game had already lost its first-class status after the tourists opted to use all their 18-man squad (Essex chose from 16). The dry conditions led to lots of boundaries: the Indians' top-scorer Dinesh Karthik hit 14 fours in his 82, while Virat Kohli and K. L. Rahul stroked 12 apiece, and later 20-year-old Michael Pepper's 68 was made up of 15 fours and eight singles. Essex's left-arm seamer Paul Walter followed four wickets with a three-hour 75.*

ENGLAND v INDIA

First Specsavers Test

LAWRENCE BOOTH

At Birmingham, August 1–4. England won by 31 runs. Toss: England.

The appeal was heartfelt, the review little better than hopeful. When on a tense fourth morning technology confirmed that Stokes had trapped Kohli, a game that had hung in the balance was reaching its climax. Three balls later, he removed Mohammed Shami; the final two wickets didn't last long. England, having flirted with defeat the previous afternoon, had won. Relief filled the air.

No one deserved to lose, least of all Kohli. As he exchanged warm words with Root, both victor and vanquished seemed happy to have been part of something special. On the occasion of England's 1,000th men's Test, the players had obliged with a nerve-jangler, if not always in the manner intended. Each side dropped important catches, and England's first-innings 287 was the highest total; for India, only Kohli passed 31. Yet his brilliance – he scored 48% of their runs off the bat – the effervescence of Sam Curran, and the non-stop swing of the pendulum contributed to the best game at Edgbaston since the 2005 Ashes. Amid the anger surrounding the ECB's proposed 100-ball tournament, this was a chance to wallow in the pleasure, and torment, of Test cricket.

There were caveats. The first two days attracted fewer than 35,000 spectators. Warwickshire cited the Wednesday start, though that had hardly been a secret. And, in a city with more Indian-born residents than any in the UK outside London or Leicester, the tourists attracted worryingly little support.

Until some second-innings heroics from Curran woke the Hollies Stand from its slumber, the atmosphere among the mainly England-supporting crowd was subdued. The problem was Kohli. After running out Root on the first afternoon to set in motion an England collapse, he dominated India's reply with a superb 149 (next best was Dhawan's 26). And when Kohli was still there at stumps on the third evening, with India five down and needing 84, Anderson said England would be dreaming of his demise. Kohli was everywhere in this game, even in the minds of others, even in the dead of night.

ENGLAND'S FIRST 1,000 TESTS

	W	L	D	
1–100	45	38	17	1876-77 to 1909

The Ashes are born in 1882. England's first 100 Tests took more than 32 years.

101–200	41	25	34	1909 to 1932-33

Three new countries join the Test club. England resort to Bodyline to deal with Bradman.

201–300	30	27	43	1933 to 1952

England beat all-comers – except Bradman's Australia.

301–400	44	21	35	1953 to 1963-64

Three successive Ashes victories helped towards more than twice as many wins as defeats.

401–500	30	15	55	1963-64 to 1974

A grey period in which more than half England's Tests ended in draws.

501–600	32	26	42	1974 to 1983-84

Cricket is changing: the first World Cup, the Packer schism, and Botham's Ashes (1981).

601–700	19	46	35	1984 to 1993-94

The worst hundred for results, with West Indies and Australia rampant.

701–800	29	35	36	1993-94 to 2002-03

Five thumping Ashes defeats skew the figures.

801–900	46	26	28	2002-03 to 2010

The most wins for any hundred, including the epic 2005 Ashes.

901–1,000	42	38	20	2010 to 2018

Eighty outright results is the most of any hundred since the first.

1–1,000	**358**	**297**	**345**	

Curran was pretty busy too. His debut against Pakistan at Headingley in June had been underwhelming. But with India's first innings going well on the second day, his left-arm swing collected three wickets in eight balls. On the third, with England in effect 100 for seven, he belted 63 from 65, transforming the target from a piece of cake to a banana skin. By the end, Root was gratefully likening him to Stokes, who was about to miss the Second Test at Lord's to answer a charge of affray.

Drama had preceded the game, as well. The recall of Rashid, 20 months after his previous Test, provoked outrage in Yorkshire, where he had declined to play Championship cricket. Moeen Ali had been taking wickets for Worcestershire, so Somerset's Dom Bess, a fellow off-spinner, failed to make the squad. Meanwhile, left-armer Jack Leach, Bess's county colleague, was deemed short of overs. In the event, both teams played only one slow bowler – Rashid for England, Ashwin for India, who preferred Rahul at No. 3 to Cheteshwar Pujara.

Root chose to bat, and England soon lost Cook, bowled by Ashwin's lavish off-break. Jennings was dropped on nine at fourth slip off Sharma, but ran out of luck after lunch when he played on against Shami via a back-foot defensive prod and his boot. And when Shami

Costly slip: Dawid Malan drops Virat Kohli on 21 off James Anderson.

pinned the motionless Malan, England were 112 for three, neither in the clear nor out of the woods. Busily repairing the damage with Bairstow, Root moved past 6,000 Test runs; the pitch remained helpful, but India were looking ragged. Another hour of these two, and England would have control.

Instead, Bairstow turned Ashwin to leg and called for a second. Root responded, but couldn't match his partner's speed. Running back from short midwicket, Kohli picked up the ball and, off-balance, hurled down the non-striker's stumps. Distraught, Root was out for 80 – his 11th Test half-century without a hundred since August 2017. Kohli's response was pure theatre: he blew two kisses, put his finger to his lips, and dropped an imaginary microphone, just as Root had his bat after sealing the one-day series. On that occasion, Kohli had watched closely. Now, he finished with an obscenity, earning a chat with match referee Jeff Crowe.

England's innings never recovered from the shock. Bairstow fell for 70, chopping on against Umesh Yadav, Buttler played round his second ball, from Ashwin, who then accepted a tame return catch from Stokes. Early next morning, seven had fallen for 71; Ashwin finished with four. India looked jaunty, especially when their openers flourished against an off-line Anderson and an off-colour Broad.

Curran now enacted the first of the innings' three dramatic vignettes. Two balls after swinging one into the pads of Vijay – and overturning umpire Aleem Dar's decision on review – he bowled Rahul off the inside edge, and soon had Dhawan prodding to second slip: 50 without loss had become 59 for three.

The second vignette, spanning 22 balls, took place with the score marooned on 100. Stokes had Rahane smartly held by Jennings at third slip, then flattened Karthik's middle stump – his 100th Test wicket. Immediately, he won an lbw shout against Pandya, who reviewed successfully: it was missing leg. Moments later, Kohli was dropped low down at second slip by Malan on 21 – the last ball of a spell from Anderson that would have been 15 overs had Rashid not bowled one before lunch. Anderson had troubled Kohli repeatedly, recalling 2014. The significance of the drop was lost on no one, and England were still contemplating it when Cook put down Pandya next ball, off Stokes. It was a mesmerising passage of play, Test cricket at its best.

Kohli gathered himself. He added 48 with Pandya, whose boot then intercepted a swinging yorker from Curran. Yet there was still time before tea for Malan to drop Kohli again, on 51 off Stokes – a tougher one as he dived to his right. Anderson took care of Ashwin and Shami, but from 182 for eight – still 105 behind – Kohli went into one-day mode.

Cue the third vignette: in a ninth-wicket stand of 35, Sharma made five; in a last-wicket stand of 57, Yadav made one not out. Kohli, whose previous Test-best in England was 39, scored more in one go than he had in ten attempts four years earlier, before eventually cutting Rashid to backward point. Against Anderson, he had parked his ego, making 18 from 74 balls; against the rest, he had indulged his genius, making 131 from 151. All the while, he had stood further out of his crease to negate the swing, yet still played the ball late – a skilful balancing act beyond any of his colleagues. India trailed by just 13.

The game had become a one-innings shoot-out, and there was a casualty before stumps, Ashwin again bowling Cook, for a duck – the only time he had been bowled twice in a Test. England resumed on the third morning 22 ahead, but Ashwin quickly did for Jennings and Root, caught in the leg trap, and it was 70 for four when Sharma turned Malan inside out. Then, either side of lunch, Sharma broke the heart of England's batting. Bairstow edged to first slip, and Stokes to third; after the break, Buttler aimed an ambitious back-foot force and was caught behind. Sharma had three in an over, and four in 17 balls; England were 87 for seven, and on the brink.

But this Test kept confounding notions of finality. Curran survived a hard chance at first slip on 13 to Dhawan, who then dropped an easier one off Rashid. Runs began to flow, the skies to grow dark. The lights came on, but the players trooped off for 20 minutes. On resumption, Yadav bowled Rashid, with England's lead 148. Curran moved up a gear, hitting Ashwin for six and four in two balls, and out of the attack. Even more thrillingly, he brought up a maiden Test fifty with six over extra cover off Sharma. Broad helped him add 41 before becoming Sharma's fifth victim that day, and when Curran nibbled at Yadav, India needed 194. On paper, it was within reach, but England's last three wickets had put on 93: the psychology of the game had shifted.

Sure enough, in the 36 overs before stumps, India wobbled to 110 for five. Broad, on the mend, bagged the openers, Rahul nicked Stokes, Rahane feathered Curran, and Anderson was too good for Ashwin. But Kohli was still there, holding the fate of the Test like Lady Justice.

EDGBASTON NOTES AND QUOTES

The build-up to the Test had been full of anger in Yorkshire, following England's selection of Adil Rashid, who had opted out of red-ball cricket for his county. Michael Vaughan described his selection as "ridiculous", saying it "stabbed the county game in the back". That prompted the normally mild-mannered Rashid to retort: "A lot of people have got no interest in what he says. His opinions do not matter to anyone." In weighed Geoffrey Boycott, who labelled Rashid a "spoilt child". Yorkshire's chief executive Mark Arthur did not hold back either: "I hope that England know what they're doing to Adil and the county game."

Before play started on the first day (Yorkshire Day, as it happened), ECB chairman Colin Graves walked out to accept a silver bear and ragged staff, the Warwickshire emblem, to celebrate England's 1,000th men's Test. He dropped it. For those seeking a metaphor for the board's handling of the proposed 100-ball tournament in 2020, this was a gift.

Joe Root took a relaxed view of Virat Kohli's mockery of the mic-drop celebration after Kohli had run him out on the first day. "It actually adds to the theatre of the game," said Root next morning. "I thought it was quite funny."

At lunch on the third day, with England stuttering at 86 for six in their second innings, Root, Alastair Cook and James Anderson took to the outfield after being chosen in an all-time England XI selected by 6,000 members of the public. A line-up of Cook, Hutton, Gower, Pietersen, Root, Botham, Knott, Swann, Trueman, Anderson and Willis meant no room for Hobbs, Hammond, Barnes, WG, Compton or… Each player selected received an artist's caricature; Anderson looked unimpressed with his.

All Notes and Quotes compiled by Will Macpherson

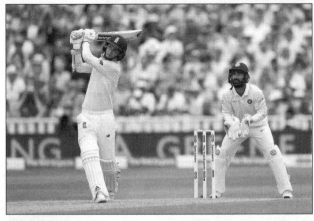

Six sense: Sam Curran collars Ravichandran Ashwin in England's second innings.

The fourth morning dawned bright, butterflies in stomachs. Off the sixth delivery, Karthik edged Anderson, and this time Malan did hold on. Root rotated his bowlers, and inertia gave way to a flurry – 20 runs from 12 balls. India were 53 short when Kohli, on 51, moved across his stumps in Stokes's first over back. Time stood still. Up went Dar's finger. By 12.30, when Stokes removed Pandya, it was done. Root called the match "a fabulous advert for Test cricket". Kohli agreed it was "the best format". England had won, and India had lost, but the result mattered less than the wider truth.

Man of the Match: S. M. Curran. *Attendance:* 75,676.

Close of play: first day, England 285-9 (Curran 24, Anderson 0); second day, England 9-1 (Jennings 5); third day, India 110-5 (Kohli 43, Karthik 18).

England

A. N. Cook b Ashwin	13	– b Ashwin	0
K. K. Jennings b Mohammed Shami	42	– c Rahul b Ashwin	8
*J. E. Root run out (Kohli)	80	– c Rahul b Ashwin	14
D. J. Malan lbw b Mohammed Shami	8	– c Rahane b Sharma	20
†J. M. Bairstow b Yadav	70	– c Dhawan b Sharma	28
B. A. Stokes c and b Ashwin	21	– c Kohli b Sharma	6
J. C. Buttler lbw b Ashwin	0	– c Karthik b Sharma	1
S. M. Curran c Karthik b Mohammed Shami	24	– c Karthik b Yadav	63
A. U. Rashid lbw b Sharma	13	– b Yadav	16
S. C. J. Broad lbw b Ashwin	1	– c Dhawan b Sharma	11
J. M. Anderson not out	2	– not out	0
B 9, lb 4	13	B 10, lb 2, nb 1	13

1/26 (1) 2/98 (2) 3/112 (4)	(89.4 overs) 287	1/9 (1) 2/18 (2) (53 overs) 180
4/216 (3) 5/223 (5) 6/224 (7)		3/39 (3) 4/70 (4)
7/243 (6) 8/278 (9) 9/283 (10) 10/287 (8)		5/85 (5) 6/86 (6) 7/87 (7)
		8/135 (9) 9/176 (10) 10/180 (8)

Yadav 17–2–56–1; Sharma 17–1–46–1; Ashwin 26–7–62–4; Mohammed Shami 19.4–2–64–3; Pandya 10–1–46–0. *Second innings*—Mohammed Shami 12–2–38–0; Ashwin 21–4–59–3; Sharma 13–0–51–5; Yadav 7–1–20–2.

India

M. Vijay lbw b Curran	20	– lbw b Broad	6
S. Dhawan c Malan b Curran	26	– c Bairstow b Broad	13
K. L. Rahul b Curran	4	– c Bairstow b Stokes	13
*V. Kohli c Broad b Rashid	149	– lbw b Stokes	51
A. M. Rahane c Jennings b Stokes	15	– c Bairstow b Curran	2
†K. D. Karthik b Stokes	0	– (7) c Malan b Anderson	20
H. H. Pandya lbw b Curran	22	– (8) c Cook b Stokes	31
R. Ashwin b Anderson	10	– (6) c Bairstow b Anderson	13
Mohammed Shami c Malan b Anderson	2	– c Bairstow b Stokes	0
I. Sharma lbw b Rashid	5	– lbw b Rashid	11
U. T. Yadav not out	1	– not out	0
B 4, lb 11, w 1, nb 4	20	B 1, lb 1	2

1/50 (1) 2/54 (3) 3/59 (2)   (76 overs) 274   1/19 (1) 2/22 (2)   (54.2 overs) 162
4/100 (5) 5/100 (6) 6/148 (7)   3/46 (3) 4/63 (5)
7/169 (8) 8/182 (9) 9/217 (10) 10/274 (4)   5/78 (6) 6/112 (7) 7/141 (4)
                                                 8/141 (9) 9/154 (10) 10/162 (8)

Anderson 22–7–41–2; Broad 10–2–40–0; Curran 17–1–74–4; Rashid 8–0–31–2; Stokes 19–4–73–2. *Second innings*—Anderson 16–2–50–2; Broad 14–2–43–2; Stokes 14.2–2–40–4; Curran 6–0–18–1; Rashid 4–1–9–1.

Umpires: Aleem Dar and C. B. Gaffaney.   Third umpire: M. Erasmus.
Referee: J. J. Crowe.

ENGLAND v INDIA

Second Specsavers Test

R I C H A R D   W H I T E H E A D

At Lord's, August 9–12. England won by an innings and 159 runs. Toss: England. Test debut: O. J. D. Pope.

The sight of Kohli, a colossus at Edgbaston, lying on the Lord's turf on Sunday afternoon while a physio tended to his aching back, summed up India's decline in the eight days since the First Test. There, they had been narrowly outpointed. Here, they were reverting to the stereotypes of 2011 and 2014: sickly travellers, underprepared and unable to adapt, supine in the face of England's mastery of conditions. Pre-series talk of drawing a line under past failures rang hollow.

At Birmingham, Kohli had dragged his team along in his wake, but even he looked broken. When he gingerly resumed after treatment, Broad exploited his discomfort with short-pitched balls, and he was gone before the painkillers kicked in: at 61 for five in their second innings, still miles behind, there was no way back. India's two innings eventually lasted a total of 82.2 overs – less than a day's play. Thrashings are rarely more comprehensive.

But there was mitigation. After an opening-day washout – the first of any day at Lord's since 2001 – India were put in beneath skies that posh paint manufacturers might call "mole's breath" or "cool arbour". They came unstuck against a cohesive effort from the England seamers, and tumbled to their lowest Lord's total since 1979, when Ian Botham helped hustle them out for 96. But the sun shone for most of the Saturday, and England – in spite of their recurring top-order frailty – established a stranglehold. When the players returned next morning, it was grey again: between showers, Root's team unfussily took a 2–0 lead.

Lord of all he purveys: Chris Woakes combined four cheap wickets with an unbeaten century.

India had made life harder for themselves by picking the wrong Yadav: fast bowler Umesh was replaced by left-arm wrist-spinner Kuldeep, England's tormentor in two of the white-ball matches. Deploying an extra slow bowler seemed reasonable after weeks of baking sunshine, but by Thursday morning the barometer had fallen. The rain came before the toss, so India had spurned the opportunity for a rethink.

It took five balls on Friday for their dressing-room to experience that feeling of slamming the front door with the keys on the hall table. Anderson bowled Vijay with a late outswinger so perfect it should have been cryogenically preserved. He then removed Rahul, promoted to open after Shikhar Dhawan was dropped, to leave India ten for two. But Anderson barely had time to resume his heavyweight bout with Kohli before the first shower arrived.

After a delay of just over two hours, the umpires fitted in another few minutes – enough time for a slapstick wicket, though Indian supporters did not see the funny side. More rain had sent the players hurrying off, only to ease as the batsmen reached the Pavilion. Back they came. Two balls later, Pujara – recalled after missing Edgbaston – nudged Anderson to point and set off. Kohli responded, then reconsidered, leaving Pujara stranded. Ollie Pope's first deed as a Test cricketer was to collect the ball and calmly remove the bails. It then began to pour, forcing a Keystone Kops dash from the field.

As lakes formed near the Mound Stand, Mick Hunt – MCC's soon-to-retire head groundsman – might have reflected that, when he took over in 1985, play would have been abandoned. But the drainage these days is miraculous, and floodlights are available: Hunt

MOST TEST WICKETS ON ONE GROUND

Wkts	T		
166	24	M. Muralitharan	Colombo (SSC)
117	16	M. Muralitharan	Kandy
111	15	M. Muralitharan	Galle
103	**23**	**J. M. Anderson**	**Lord's**
102	**19**	**H. M. R. K. B. Herath**	**Galle**
84	**14**	**H. M. R. K. B. Herath**	**Colombo (SSC)**
83	19	H. H. Streak	Harare
83	**21**	**S. C. J. Broad**	**Lord's**
82	14	D. K. Lillee	Melbourne
80	21	W. P. U. J. C. Vaas	Colombo (SSC)

cheerfully supervised the clearing-up, and the game resumed less than three and a half hours later. Anderson and Kohli butted heads, and there was the sense of a pivotal moment when Root rested his new-ball pair. However, Woakes, recalled while Ben Stokes was otherwise engaged at Bristol Crown Court, and Curran kept India under the cosh. Woakes curled the ball deliciously away or maintained a ramrod-straight off-stump line. In his third over he got the wicket England craved, when Kohli edged to Buttler at second slip, one delivery after he had dropped a similar chance. In Woakes's next over, it happened again, Buttler clinging on to the ball after dropping Pandya. If Buttler was making mistakes in his new role, at least he was learning quickly.

I'D LIKE TO THANK MY COLLEAGUES

Players on the winning side in a Test who did not bat, bowl or take a catch:

A. P. F. Chapman	England v South Africa at Lord's	1924
B. H. Valentine	England v South Africa at Durban	1938-39
W. A. Johnston	Australia v West Indies at Georgetown	1954-55
W. A. Johnston	Australia v West Indies at Kingston	1954-55
N. J. Contractor	India v New Zealand at Madras	1955-56
A. G. Kripal Singh	India v New Zealand at Madras	1955-56
C. J. McDermott	Australia v England at Lord's	1993
Asif Mujtaba	Pakistan v New Zealand at Wellington	1993-94
N. D. McKenzie	South Africa v Bangladesh at Chittagong	2002-03
A. G. Prince	South Africa v Zimbabwe at Cape Town	2004-05
G. J. Batty	England v Bangladesh at Lord's	2005
J. A. Rudolph	South Africa v England at The Oval	2012
W. P. Saha	India v New Zealand at Indore	2016-17
A. U. Rashid	**England v India at Lord's**	**2018**

Johnston was injured in the field on both occasions before having a chance to bowl; these were the last two Tests of his career. McDermott was taken ill early on. Saha was keeping wicket.

Encouraged by an unusually vocal Lord's crowd – Anderson thought the rain breaks had left them "well-oiled" – England finished the job. Curran bowled Karthik with a beauty and, after some uncomplicated resistance from Ashwin, Anderson completed the cheapest of his six Lord's five-fors; for the first time since his debut year, in 2003, his Test average dipped below 27. Seven wickets had fallen in two hours, the last perfectly timed so England's openers did not face an uncomfortable few minutes before the close.

India's gloomy mood did not improve when Cook and Jennings made an uncharacteristically assured start on the third morning, although England's progress was checked once Sharma and Mohammed Shami tuned their radars. The openers departed in short order and, with Dawid Malan dropped after Edgbaston, out walked a rosy-cheeked debutant – Test cricket's first Oliver, but England's second Pope, after Derbyshire's George in 1947. He hit his second ball for four, and looked unfazed until he fell to Pandya, wasting a review, as Jennings had earlier. When Root followed him for a scratchy 19 in the last over before lunch, England were 89 for four, and India glimpsed a way back.

Bairstow overcame a skittish start to ease England into the lead with a straight-drive off Shami, then hit him for successive fours. In a tacit admission of error, Ashwin did not come on until the 39th over, while Kuldeep was rarely seen at all. Buttler departed soon after lunch – a third leg-before victim for Shami – to leave England 131 for five, still seeking the partnership which would propel their lead beyond retrieval. It came when Woakes joined Bairstow. His colleague was already into his stride, so Woakes was able to reconnoitre before going on the offensive. He did not hang about: by tea the lead was 123, and both had passed 50. Nor did Woakes lose anything by artistic comparison; for a period after the break, he and Bairstow seemed engaged in a private battle to hit the shot of the day.

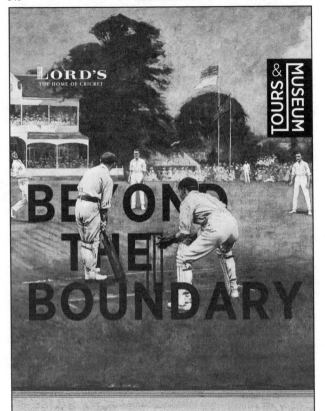

LORD'S NOTES AND QUOTES

James Anderson prepared for the Test in unusual fashion. While being filmed by Stuart Broad on a team golf day, he walloped a ball against a tree trunk, from which it rebounded into his face. His bowling proved more accurate than his chipping: Anderson finished with match figures of nine for 43.

After Adil Rashid became the first England player to get through a completed Test without batting, bowling or taking a catch since Gareth Batty against Bangladesh at Lord's in 2005, Joe Root described his contribution as a "TFC" – thanks for coming. Rashid did field the ball more than 20 times, but the closest he got to proper action came when Root declared at the fall of the seventh wicket, with Rashid due in next.

Alec Stewart, Surrey's director of cricket, made the pre-match cap presentation to England's fresh-faced debutant Ollie Pope. He couldn't resist a joke, recalling the moment "I gave you your Surrey Under-9s Player of the Year [award] – two years ago".

There was something familiar about one of the volunteers selling radios at the Nursery End on the second morning. Arjun Tendulkar, teenage son of Sachin, had been bowling at Virat Kohli in the nets in the build-up to the Test. Now Arjun, who had made his debut for India Under-19s the previous month, and been working with MCC's Young Cricketers, pitched in to help shift commentary radios. He went largely unrecognised, although his father's former team-mate Harbhajan Singh complimented him on his sales technique.

It was a busy final Test for groundsman Mick Hunt, who began working at Lord's in 1969 and was presented with a signed bat by Joe Root, and honorary life membership by MCC. "His place in the history of Lord's is assured," said assistant secretary John Stephenson.

Woakes completed his first Test hundred when he pulled Pandya towards midwicket and scampered three. In Australia during the winter he had toiled under the burden of replacing Stokes, but here proved every bit as capable. The warmth of his reception and the delight of his team-mates were testament to his status as English cricket's ideal son-in-law. He became the fifth player on all three Lord's honours boards (centuries, five-wicket innings and ten-wicket matches) after Gubby Allen, Keith Miller, Botham and Broad. Bairstow looked certain to follow him to three figures, but on 93 drove loosely at Pandya, and Karthik took a magnificent diving catch. The stand of 189 was England's best for the sixth wicket against India, passing 171 by Botham and Bob Taylor at Bombay in 1979-80.

Some muttered at Root's decision to prolong the innings when play resumed under grey skies on Sunday, the lead already 250. It did at least give the opportunity for Curran to smite Shami over square leg for six with an extraordinary overhead smash that was more Federer than Flintoff. But India's stay of execution did not last long. They were batting before midday, and the deficit of 289 had not been reduced when Anderson completed Vijay's pair – his 550th Test wicket, and his 100th at Lord's. Before a lunch break extended by more rain, he also removed Rahul.

In the afternoon, he retired to the wings while his new-ball partner took centre stage. Root revealed later that Broad had told him after a few deliveries that he felt the planets were aligned for one of his trademark spells of destruction. The forecast proved accurate: in eight overs of sustained pace, he took four for nine. It was compelling fare, particularly the inswinging yorker that detonated Pujara's off stump. Despite his reduced mobility, Kohli stroked Broad and Curran to the boundary with textbook cover-drives. He survived England's appeal – and review – for a catch down the leg side, but could not avoid Broad's next ball, a rib-tickler, as Pope plunged forward from deepish short leg. Again Kohli reviewed, but this time there was no reprieve. Karthik was then trapped in front first ball. When he also sent the decision upstairs, it was the first time three successive deliveries had been reviewed in a Test. In each instance, umpire Aleem Dar's verdict was upheld.

Gareth Copley, Getty Images

Cover dive: players and umpires run pell-mell towards the Pavilion as the heavens open.

Pandya and Ashwin briefly put the top-order struggles into perspective with a defiant stand of 55, Ashwin top-scoring in both innings, but it merely delayed the inevitable. Woakes trapped Pandya with the first ball of a new spell, Anderson collected two more easy scalps, and Woakes completed the rout when Sharma guided him into the hands of Pope at leg slip. Kohli refused to blame technical shortcomings for India's humbling, but conceded his batsmen needed to improve swiftly. With a visit to England's happy hunting ground at Trent Bridge a few days away, the word "whitewash" was beginning to crop up.

Man of the Match: C. R. Woakes.   *Attendance:* 81,806.

Close of play: first day, no play; second day, India 107; third day, England 357-6 (Woakes 120, Curran 22).

India

M. Vijay b Anderson	0	– c Bairstow b Anderson	0
K. L. Rahul c Bairstow b Anderson	8	– lbw b Anderson	10
C. A. Pujara run out (Pope)	1	– b Broad	17
*V. Kohli c Buttler b Woakes	23	– (5) c Pope b Broad	17
A. M. Rahane c Cook b Anderson	18	– (4) c Jennings b Broad	13
H. H. Pandya c Buttler b Woakes	11	– lbw b Woakes	26
†K. D. Karthik b Curran	1	– lbw b Broad	0
R. Ashwin lbw b Broad	29	– not out	33
K. Yadav lbw b Anderson	0	– b Anderson	0
Mohammed Shami not out	10	– lbw b Anderson	0
I. Sharma lbw b Anderson	0	– c Pope b Woakes	2
Lb 5, nb 1	6	B 6, lb 6	12

1/0 (1) 2/10 (2) 3/15 (3)   (35.2 overs) 107   1/0 (1) 2/13 (2)   (47 overs) 130
4/49 (4) 5/61 (6) 6/62 (7)   3/35 (4) 4/50 (3)
7/84 (5) 8/96 (9) 9/96 (8) 10/107 (11)   5/61 (5) 6/61 (7) 7/116 (6)
                                                               8/121 (9) 9/125 (10) 10/130 (11)

Anderson 13.2–5–20–5; Broad 10–2–37–1; Woakes 6–2–19–2; Curran 6–0–26–1. *Second innings*—Anderson 12–5–23–4; Broad 16–6–44–4; Woakes 10–2–24–2; Curran 9–1–27–0.

England

A. N. Cook c Karthik b Sharma 21	S. M. Curran c Mohammed Shami b Pandya 40
K. K. Jennings lbw b Mohammed Shami . . 11	
*J. E. Root lbw b Mohammed Shami 19	B 11, lb 10, w 1, nb 1 23
O. J. D. Pope lbw b Pandya. 28	
†J. M. Bairstow c Karthik b Pandya 93	1/28 (2) (7 wkts dec, 88.1 overs) 396
J. C. Buttler lbw b Mohammed Shami 24	2/32 (1) 3/77 (4)
C. R. Woakes not out 137	4/89 (3) 5/131 (6) 6/320 (5) 7/396 (8)

A. U. Rashid, S. C. J. Broad and J. M. Anderson did not bat.

Sharma 22–4–101–1; Mohammed Shami 23–4–96–3; Yadav 9–1–44–0; Pandya 17.1–0–66–3; Ashwin 17–1–68–0.

Umpires: Aleem Dar and M. Erasmus.   Third umpire: C. B. Gaffaney.
Referee: J. J. Crowe.

ENGLAND v INDIA

Third Specsavers Test

GEORGE DOBELL

At Nottingham, August 18–22. India won by 203 runs. Toss: England. Test debut: R. R. Pant.

By the time India completed a crushing victory, it seemed the tide had turned. England still left Nottingham with a series lead but, such was the margin of defeat, it felt as if India had struck a decisive blow. In the space of a few days, talk of a clean sweep after Lord's had given way to English concern that they might instead become only the second side in Test history to lose a series after going 2–0 up.

It took India just 17 deliveries on the final day to wrap up the win – their seventh in England and, according to head coach Ravi Shastri, their best overseas during his two stints in the role. It was Kohli's 22nd Test victory as captain, taking him past Sourav Ganguly in the national pantheon; only M. S. Dhoni, with 27, lay ahead. More than that, the Indians were finally acclimatising to local conditions. What might they have achieved in the first two Tests with better preparation?

Certainly their seamers proved far more effective than at Lord's. Strengthened by the return of Bumrah, who missed the first two Tests through injury and now replaced the ineffective Kuldeep Yadav, they claimed 19 wickets between them; only the 20th fell to spin. Both Bumrah and Pandya recorded five-wicket hauls. It led a cocksure Shastri to describe India's pace attack as their best ever, "by a mile".

But this was no one-dimensional victory. It saw a vastly improved performance by their slip fielders, a promising first cap for 20-year-old Rishabh Pant – who claimed seven dismissals, a Test record for a debutant Indian wicketkeeper, and got off the mark second ball with a six – and a batting display not exclusively reliant on Kohli. He still totalled exactly 200, as he had at Edgbaston, but this time enjoyed plenty of support. The extra runs helped India cope with a groin injury to Ashwin that would have more serious consequences as the series progressed. But, that setback apart, this was as complete an Indian display away from home as most could remember. Forty-seven years on from their first Test win in England, at The Oval, their players wore black armbands for the captain in that game, Ajit Wadekar, who had died three days earlier.

The game also showed England at something approaching their worst. They squandered the new ball in the first innings, produced two feeble efforts with the bat – other than a second-innings partnership between Stokes and Buttler – and remained porous in the slips. Most damaging was a first-innings collapse in which they lost all ten wickets in a session for the third time in two years. The previous instance had taken place in 1938.

Stu Forster, Getty Images

A little glancing is a dangerous thing: Ollie Pope flicks Ishant Sharma to Rishabh Pant, who holds the third of his five catches in England's first innings.

Root was obliged to resolve two issues before a ball was bowled. The first, and more controversial, was to recall Stokes in place of Sam Curran, a decision Root described as "one of the most difficult" of his captaincy. But with Stokes deemed fit, mentally and physically, to rejoin the squad just 48 hours after being cleared of affray, someone had to make way. It was poor reward for Curran, two games after he had been named Man of the Match, and left England's seam attack stocked with four right-armers. But they wanted to retain a spin option, so Rashid stayed, and the claims of Broad (on his home turf), Anderson (on the ground where nine Tests had yielded seven five-fors) and Woakes (Man of the Match at Lord's) all proved persuasive.

The second big call was to insert India. Overhead conditions encouraged Root, and there was movement on offer for the seamers. But, not for the first time, Broad and Anderson bowled too short to exploit it, and India's openers cashed in, with Dhawan, back in place of Murali Vijay, who was dropped after a pair at Lord's, and Rahul both disciplined. Kohli revealed he would have batted anyway.

Woakes briefly showed his seniors how it should be done, dismissing both openers in quick succession, and following up with the wicket of Pujara, caught on the hook at deep backward square the over before lunch – to his disbelief and Kohli's. But, from 82 for three, Kohli and Rahane added 159 at almost four an over. Broad and Anderson improved substantially, but a rusty Stokes pitched too short, and Rashid was loose. Anderson dropped Rahane on 57 at backward point off Woakes, before Cook snaffled a blinder at first slip, from Broad, to see him off for 81. (Broad's mood later took a turn for the worse, when Jennings bungled a simple chance at third to reprieve Pandya.) The value of the Kohli–Rahane partnership was underlined once it was over. Kohli, when 97, edged a drive off Rashid, and walked off cursing his misjudgment, before Pandya became Anderson's 100th Test wicket against India; only Muttiah Muralitharan had got there before him. Next morning, he and Broad ensured the last four tumbled for six; Broad was fined 15% of his match fee and given a demerit point for a send-off to Pant.

But it was nothing compared with the collapse to come. Cook and Jennings compiled their first fifty partnership of the series, but after lunch fell to successive deliveries to trigger an avalanche. Pope was strangled down the leg side, and Root undone by Pandya's first ball, which he poked low to second slip. Generating sharp movement from a probing length, Pandya – who had never claimed more in a Test innings than the three he managed at Lord's – collected five in 29 deliveries. Two were caught by Pant, who had replaced Dinesh Karthik behind the stumps and became only the third player – after Australians Brian Taber and John Maclean – to make five dismissals in his first Test innings with the gloves. England had lost all ten wickets in 159 balls, and trailed by 168. For the second summer in a row, following their meltdown against South Africa, they were enduring a nightmare in Nottingham.

India were not going to let their advantage slip. After another first-wicket partnership of 60 – the first time since 1986 their openers had shared two half-century stands in a Test in England – Kohli and Pujara batted their opponents out of the contest. Kohli compiled the fourth-slowest of his 23 Test centuries, from 191 balls, and Pujara gave steadfast support in his first innings of substance of the summer, having averaged just 13 in all first-class cricket for his county, Yorkshire, and his country. Pandya added a run-a-ball 52.

For England, the cracks were starting to show. The most painful was suffered by Bairstow, who was struck on the left middle finger taking a delivery from Anderson; he was later found to have a fracture, forcing him to give the gloves to Buttler for the rest of this Test and the whole of the next. Stokes, who had been unable to train during his trial, was limping, having sent down a short-pitched barrage in an attempt to unlock the batting. Meanwhile, England's catching troubles continued. Buttler, at second slip, missed Pujara on 40, and Jennings, at fourth, missed Kohli on 93 – both off the deserving Anderson. Assistant coach Paul Farbrace described the drops as "soul-destroying".

India's declaration, 520 ahead, sentenced England's openers to nine overs on the third evening, which they survived. But in the first next morning, Jennings was drawn into fiddling at one that left him from the relentless Sharma, who in his next removed Cook for the 11th time in Tests. When Root and Pope both flashed at balls they could have left, four had fallen for 35. The end looked nigh.

Then came the resistance. Buttler and an unusually becalmed Stokes put on 169, England's highest fourth-innings partnership since Cook and Ian Bell added 170 at Perth in 2006-07. Buttler registered his maiden Test century and the first by a member of

Paul Ellis, AFP/Getty Images

Ups and downs: Joe Root nicks Hardik Pandya's first ball low to slip, and England are 86 for four.

TRENT BRIDGE NOTES AND QUOTES

The selection of Ben Stokes, who joined the squad two days after being found not guilty of affray in Bristol, was described by coach Trevor Bayliss as "for his own well-being". But he also called on Stokes to make a public apology. It was not forthcoming.

The Test saw the first Saturday start in England since 1955, a curious piece of scheduling made more so by the fact that the following weekend included a bank holiday – the only weekend during the series not to contain any international cricket.

England's unlikely destroyer with the ball was India's answer to Stokes, Hardik Pandya – who, it turned out, did not want to be anyone's answer to anything. He also made a half-century, and bristled when compared with Indian all-rounders of the past: "I don't want to be Kapil Dev. Let me be Hardik Pandya. I'm good at being Hardik Pandya."

Host county Nottinghamshire had been set to charge £10 for tickets on the final day, which began with India needing only one wicket. "Great," tweeted BBC cricket correspondent Jonathan Agnew. "So a crowd of 0, then." Nottinghamshire reversed their decision, allowing spectators in for free, and providing a full refund to the 2,000 fans who had bought tickets in advance. "We've slept on the day-five pricing policy," they tweeted at 8.25 on the last morning. "Frankly, we got it wrong." A couple of hundred turned up.

Agnew was soon unhappy again, tweeting his dismay at being denied a post-match interview with Virat Kohli by India's media manager Moulin Parikh. Agnew accused Parikh of failing to "appreciate that he has a duty to the game", adding a Donald Trumpish "Great shame."

England's top six in the series. Belying their reputation as strokemakers, they repeatedly left the ball, played resolutely straight, and provided an example to their colleagues.

It was never going to be enough, though. The new ball, expertly utilised by Bumrah, who was quicker than any of England's bowlers, accounted for both and, with Bairstow bowled first ball and Woakes dismissed by a bouncer for the second time in the match, England lost four for ten. Had Rashid not survived two close shaves – bowled by a Bumrah no-ball on two, and dropped at third slip by Kohli on 22 – the game would have been over in four days. Instead, he put on 50 with Broad, who followed Richard Hadlee, Kapil Dev, Shane Warne and Shaun Pollock to the Test double of 3,000 runs and 400 wickets before providing Bumrah with his fifth wicket of the innings, and Rahul with his seventh catch of the match. The game dribbled into the final day but, once it dawned bright and sunny, there was to be no English escape.

Man of the Match: V. Kohli.   *Attendance:* 58,665.

Close of play: first day, India 307-6 (Pant 22); second day, India 124-2 (Pujara 33, Kohli 8); third day, England 23-0 (Cook 9, Jennings 13); fourth day, England 311-9 (Rashid 30, Anderson 8).

India

S. Dhawan c Buttler b Woakes	35	– st Bairstow b Rashid	44
K. L. Rahul lbw b Woakes	23	– b Stokes	36
C. A. Pujara c Rashid b Woakes	14	– c Cook b Stokes	72
*V. Kohli c Stokes b Broad	97	– lbw b Woakes	103
A. M. Rahane c Cook b Broad	81	– b Rashid	29
H. H. Pandya c Buttler b Anderson	18	– (7) not out	52
†R. R. Pant b Broad	24	– (6) c Cook b Anderson	1
R. Ashwin b Broad	14	– (9) not out	1
I. Sharma not out	1		
Mohammed Shami c Broad b Anderson	3	– (8) c Cook b Rashid	3
J. J. Bumrah b Anderson	0		
B 12, lb 6, w 1	19	B 1, lb 9, w 1	11

1/60 (1) 2/65 (2) 3/82 (3)   (94.5 overs) 329   1/60 (2)   (7 wkts dec, 110 overs) 352
4/241 (5) 5/279 (4) 6/307 (6)   2/111 (1) 3/224 (3)
7/323 (7) 8/326 (8) 9/329 (10) 10/329 (11)   4/281 (4) 5/282 (6) 6/329 (5) 7/349 (8)

Anderson 25.5–8–64–3; Broad 25–8–72–3; Stokes 15–1–54–0; Woakes 20–2–75–3; Rashid 9–0–46–1. *Second innings*—Anderson 22–7–55–1; Broad 16–3–60–0; Woakes 22–4–49–1; Stokes 20–3–68–2; Rashid 27–2–101–3; Root 3–0–9–0.

England

A. N. Cook c Pant b Sharma	29	– c Rahul b Sharma	17
K. K. Jennings c Pant b Bumrah	20	– c Pant b Sharma	13
*J. E. Root c Rahul b Pandya	16	– c Rahul b Bumrah	13
O. J. D. Pope c Pant b Sharma	10	– c Kohli b Mohammed Shami	16
†J. M. Bairstow c Rahul b Pandya	15	– (7) b Bumrah	0
B. A. Stokes c Rahul b Mohammed Shami	10	– (5) c Rahul b Pandya	62
J. C. Buttler c sub (S. N. Thakur) b Bumrah	39	– (6) lbw b Bumrah	106
C. R. Woakes c Pant b Pandya	8	– c Pant b Bumrah	4
A. U. Rashid c Pant b Pandya	5	– not out	33
S. C. J. Broad lbw b Pandya	0	– c Rahul b Bumrah	20
J. M. Anderson not out	1	– c Rahane b Ashwin	11
B 4, lb 1, w 1, nb 2	8	B 2, lb 16, nb 4	22

1/54 (1) 2/54 (2) 3/75 (4)   (38.2 overs) 161   1/27 (2) 2/32 (1)   (104.5 overs) 317
4/86 (3) 5/108 (6) 6/110 (5)   3/62 (3) 4/62 (4)
7/118 (8) 8/128 (9) 9/128 (10) 10/161 (7)   5/231 (6) 6/231 (7) 7/241 (8)
     8/241 (5) 9/291 (10) 10/317 (11)

Mohammed Shami 10–2–56–1; Bumrah 12.2–2–37–2; Ashwin 1–0–3–0; Sharma 9–2–32–2; Pandya 6–1–28–5. *Second innings*—Bumrah 29–8–85–5; Sharma 20–4–70–2; Ashwin 22.5–8–44–1; Mohammed Shami 19–3–78–1; Pandya 14–5–22–1.

Umpires: M. Erasmus and C. B. Gaffaney.   Third umpire: Aleem Dar.
Referee: J. J. Crowe.

ENGLAND v INDIA

Fourth Specsavers Test

HUGH CHEVALLIER

At Southampton, August 30–September 2. England won by 60 runs. Toss: England.

A change, so they say, is as good as a rest. And though Sam Curran and Moeen Ali must have smarted at being dropped, they roared back to the fold at Southampton. In an unputdownable contest full of unlikely twists and turns, those two proved the difference between evenly matched sides. Victory gave England an unassailable 3–1 lead: India, ranked No. 1 and boasting their fiercest-ever pace attack, had been beaten. True, it was yet another series won by the home team, but compelling skirmishes and set-piece battles created a Test more *War and Peace* than *Da Vinci Code*.

Despite pocketing the match award in the First Test and barely putting a foot wrong in the Second, Curran had been omitted once fellow all-rounders Stokes and Chris Woakes were available. Ali had been unwanted since Auckland in March, though his form for Worcestershire – he had just become the eighth player in Championship history to combine a double-hundred with a six-for – gave the selectors a prod too sharp to ignore, especially after England's heavy defeat at Nottingham; Ollie Pope made way after two caps. The door reopened for Curran when a quad injury ruled out Woakes, though he would probably have replaced him anyway.

There was one other enforced change. Bairstow was nursing a hairline fracture to his left middle finger and reluctantly agreed to hand over the gloves to Buttler, the one-day keeper, and move up to No. 4. The upshot was that England fielded just three specialist batsmen, and five whose attacking instincts made them better suited to the lower half of

Graham Morris

Simply staggering: Keaton Jennings pays the price for misreading a delivery from Jasprit Bumrah.

the middle order. While England tinkered, India trusted the team who had triumphed by the Trent – and for the first time in 46 Tests made no changes. Even more constant was Root's luck at the toss: an encouraging forecast, and a belief that the pitch at its youngest would be most placid, persuaded him to bat.

Openers had struggled all series, and it took just 13 balls for the curse to strike again. Bumrah has a style all his own, a clippity-clop run-up borrowed from the horseless knights of *Monty Python and the Holy Grail* that culminates in a delivery of whirring rods and levers. Yet it was Jennings who looked the numpty. Troubled at Nottingham by the ball that Bumrah angled across him, and determined not to fall for the ploy, he left several outswingers, only to ignore the one that tailed in. Jennings leapt in ungainly horror as he was struck by the ball – and by the folly of not playing a shot.

India's bright start came within a pixel or two of brilliance. Root missed one that straightened, convincing both Bumrah and Kohli – though not umpire Oxenford – of an lbw appeal. DRS showed it hitting leg, but also the squeakiest of no-balls. England would have been three for two. But against a pace quartet revelling in the conditions, it was simply a stay of execution. Sharma accounted for Root, toppling slightly, Bumrah found Bairstow's reckless edge, and Pandya's luck was in when Cook steered loosely to slip. Just 27 runs between them. If some painted England as a team of all-rounders, few could deny the top four were at sixes and sevens.

But their sixes and sevens fancied themselves as the top four. Stokes, exhibiting new sobriety since his acquittal, knuckled down. As the ball boomed for Bumrah and shaped for Sharma and Mohammed Shami, Buttler seemed similarly determined to sell his wicket dear, only to depart to a rush-of-blood flash shortly after lunch. And when Stokes followed his captain by burning a review for lbw, India were rampant. Could the momentum gained a week earlier sweep them to a series-levelling victory? England were 86 for six – just as they had been at Edgbaston when Curran came to the crease and hit a match-winning 63.

LONGEST TEST DUCKS FOR INDIA

Balls	Mins			
29	**47**	**R. R. Pant**	**v England at Southampton**	**2018**
29	39	S. K. Raina	v England at The Oval	2011
29	35	I. K. Pathan	v Pakistan at Bangalore	2004-05
28	34	M. M. Patel	v West Indies at St John's.............	2005-06
25	35	S. V. Manjrekar	v South Africa at Durban	1992-93
24	34	V. V. S. Laxman	v England at Mohali	2008-09
21	25	K. D. Ghavri..............	v Australia at Melbourne	1980-81

The longest duck for which the number of balls is unknown was 38 minutes by P. Roy against Pakistan at Dacca in 1954-55.

Then as now, he showed no fear. Unfazed by the roadkill that littering the carriageway behind him, Curran cut and drove with an authority unnatural for his 20 years. He put on 81 with Ali and 63 with Broad – and became only the fourth player to reach his first two Test fifties with a six when he deposited Ashwin over wide long-on. An unsung hero for England was Extras: as the ball swung extravagantly and late, Pant dived more than a colony of gannets, if with less success. Curran had yanked the game back from perdition, though four toothless overs from the opening pair before the close was not what Root had ordered.

Next morning, India made it to 37 before Broad – zip and zest relocated – nipped one back into Rahul. He removed Dhawan as well and, at 50 for two, honours felt even. Steadily, though, the nous of Pujara and the self-belief of Kohli gained the upper hand. It was not plain sailing. Pujara looked hesitant against the short ball, while an uncontrolled edge took Kohli to 6,000 Test runs in his 119th innings (for India, only Sunil Gavaskar had been quicker). By lunch, the pair were celebrating a fifty partnership; within an hour, the score was 142 for two, the game drifting towards India. But out of the drift came forth the ball that wrenched England back into contention: Curran landed it just outside off, and Kohli nibbled, wary of deliveries that had swung in. Cook snaffled a smart catch at slip. It was the hallmark of the Test: each time the batsmen threatened to take control, a wicket – maybe two – stopped them in their tracks.

Root had been so protective of Stokes's knee he had turned first to Jennings's anodyne medium-pace. But when Stokes did bowl, gingerly and off a short run-up, he promptly posed problems. In his third over, an inswinger removed Rahane; in his fifth, he clonked Pujara on the helmet. The greatest threat, though, came from Ali. Not a man to radiate confidence, he had rarely looked so at ease with the ball in his hand. On the stroke of tea he trapped Pant, who had squirmed through a torturous 29-ball duck, and soon after deceived Pandya with flight and turn. And when a red-faced Ashwin (attempting an ambitious reverse sweep) and a bemused Shami (misreading the line) departed to successive deliveries, Ali – at the ground where he collected eight against India in 2014 – had snatched four for eight in 16 balls. India were 195 for eight, and disintegrating.

Which was when England decided the prospect of removing the new batsman was so enticing they would give up trying to dismiss Pujara, now on 78. Better, apparently, to contain him with incessant short-pitched deliveries and buy an over at the tailender. Trouble was, they weren't any good at it: the ninth wicket put on 32, before Ali removed Sharma to claim his fifth wicket, and the last 46. Shielding his No. 11 like a hen her chick, Pujara took a single off the fifth or sixth ball on six occasions, as well as cracking fours through far-flung fields. His 15th Test century was only his second outside the subcontinent. When Bumrah – whose batting average at the start of this innings was 0.80 – eventually gave Cook his third catch, Pujara had battled almost six hours, and India led by 27.

England negotiated four overs – as India had the previous evening – then set about overturning the jinx on openers. They failed. Cook was undone by leaden feet and a slip catch from Rahul, who grasped it at the third juggle. In came Ali, his unexpected elevation the result of Root's preference for No. 4. There was sense in the move, but it too failed.

Turning point: India's hopes start to unravel when Alastair Cook catches Virat Kohli off Moeen Ali.

Whether Jennings's 36 constituted another failure was debatable, though not the horror waft that brought Bairstow a second golden duck in three innings. Wickets had fallen to Shami immediately before and after lunch, leaving England 92 for four. Such were the fluctuating fortunes it was impossible to determine whose noses were in front.

India thought they could scent victory, however, when a muddle between Root and Stokes spelled the end of a fluent 48 from the captain: five down and just 95 to the good. After Ali's success on the second day, it seemed certain Ashwin would run amok on a turning pitch. Though he later denied it, he bowled as if hampered by the hip injury that had troubled him at Nottingham (he would miss The Oval). His solitary success came when the stoic Stokes nicked his 110th ball to Rahane. India had other problems: Sharma was warned twice for running on the pitch, forcing Kohli to use him sparingly, while Pant threw up after being struck on the throat by a ball that spat out of the rough.

By contrast, there are few sweeter sounds in world cricket than the ball ringing from the bat of an on-song Buttler. He began scratchily, but with Curran – who maintained his record of always reaching 20 – took the advantage to 206 before he was dismissed by Sharma. The third day ended a delivery early when Rashid departed for 11, and the fourth started with Broad falling first ball. It meant that, for the second time in the innings, the consistently excellent Shami was on a protracted hat-trick. Curran's spirited knock eventually foundered on some shambolic running: it meant India needed a mouth-watering 245 to square the series, England ten wickets to win it.

Such a compelling, knife-edge Test required a dramatic denouement, but it briefly looked as if the pitch might scupper that: Rahul was sunk by one from Broad that scuttled into the base of the stumps. Anderson, more himself than on day two, then trapped Pujara and had Dhawan smartly held at gully: 22 for three.

Salvation, were it to happen, would involve Kohli. With the score 41 and the recovery still inchoate, a ball from Ali rapped him on the pad. A forest of arms and a cacophony of shrieks demanded blood, yet won only a shake of the head from Dharmasena. Cue the review. Third umpire Joel Wilson was unsure whether UltraEdge revealed bat on ball, or bat on pad, or both, and saw no reason to overturn the verdict – unlike countless armchair

ROSE BOWL NOTES AND QUOTES

There was more bad news for the ECB's proposed 100-ball tournament when *Wisden Cricket Monthly* publicised an interview with Virat Kohli, who sounded distinctly unenthused by the plans. "I feel somewhere the commercial aspect is taking over the real quality of cricket, and that hurts me," he said. "I don't want to be a testing sort of a cricketer for any new format."

Jonny Bairstow was forced to accept that, if he wanted to play through the pain of a broken left middle finger – sustained in the field at Trent Bridge – he would not be able to keep wicket. He said he was "desperate to try to keep my place as the keeper", and used stats to back his case up: he averaged 42 in Tests in which he had the gloves, and 27 when he didn't. A journalist threw back a different stat: when he kept wicket, his first-innings Test average was 59 if England batted first, and 28 if they batted second. But Bairstow said he hadn't seen that one.

Promoted to No. 4 – at least for the first innings, before Moeen Ali moved up to No. 3 mid-match – Bairstow ended up making six and nought, prompting Michael Vaughan to accuse him of having a strop. "I'm not sure where Jonny's mentality is," he said on *Test Match Special*. "It looks like he's got the 'poor old mes' because he wants to be keeping." Geoffrey Boycott, covering his first Test since quadruple heart-bypass surgery in June, said: "Bairstow is a No. 7 at Test level. He's not good enough to bat higher than that."

umpires up and down the land, whose muttered curses grew louder once Hawk-Eye showed the ball hitting leg. In fact, all the officials put in cracking performances, especially Wilson. His deliberations were quick, clear and – mercifully – never included a request for technicians to "just rock-and-roll that for me, please".

Neither time nor the weather was an issue, so Kohli and Rahane batted patiently. They milked Rashid for singles as though in a one-day international and, as tea neared, reached a century partnership. Half the runs were in the bank.

Then Ali changed everything: he spun one in to Kohli, who gloved a straightforward catch to short leg. Kohli scowled, looked at his forearm and asked for a review. There was no reprieve – neither for him nor for India. Lion-hearted resistance evaporated in the September sun. Rahane made a fifty, but Ali continued his love affair with Southampton, taking his record there to 17 wickets in two Tests. The last word of an epic tussle, though, went to Curran, who removed Ashwin – the 14th lbw victim of the Test, equalling the record in England. It was fitting: Curran's fight on the first day had kept his side afloat.

Man of the Match: M. M. Ali.   *Attendance:* 55,676.

Close of play: first day, India 19-0 (Dhawan 3, Rahul 11); second day, England 6-0 (Cook 2, Jennings 4); third day, England 260-8 (Curran 37).

England

A. N. Cook c Kohli b Pandya	17	– c Rahul b Bumrah	12
K. K. Jennings lbw b Bumrah	0	– lbw b Mohammed Shami	36
*J. E. Root lbw b Sharma	4	– (4) run out (Mohammed Shami)	48
J. M. Bairstow c Pant b Bumrah	6	– (5) b Mohammed Shami	0
B. A. Stokes lbw b Mohammed Shami	23	– (6) c Rahane b Ashwin	30
†J. C. Buttler c Kohli b Mohammed Shami	21	– (7) lbw b Sharma	69
M. M. Ali c Bumrah b Ashwin	40	– (3) c Rahul b Sharma	9
S. M. Curran b Ashwin	78	– run out (Sharma/Pant)	46
A. U. Rashid lbw b Sharma	6	– c Pant b Mohammed Shami	11
S. C. J. Broad lbw b Bumrah	17	– c Pant b Mohammed Shami	0
J. M. Anderson not out	0	– not out	1
B 23, lb 9, nb 2	34	B 7, lb 2	9

1/1 (2) 2/15 (3) 3/28 (4)   (76.4 overs) 246   1/24 (1) 2/33 (3)   (96.1 overs) 271
4/36 (1) 5/69 (6) 6/86 (5)   3/92 (2) 4/92 (5)
7/167 (7) 8/177 (9) 9/240 (10) 10/246 (8)   5/122 (4) 6/178 (6) 7/233 (7)
                                                      8/260 (9) 9/260 (10) 10/271 (8)

Bumrah 20–5–46–3; Sharma 16–6–26–2; Pandya 8–0–51–1; Mohammed Shami 18–2–51–2; Ashwin 14.4–3–40–2. *Second innings*—Ashwin 37.1–7–84–1; Bumrah 19–3–51–1; Sharma 15–4–36–2; Mohammed Shami 16–0–57–4; Pandya 9–0–34–0.

India

S. Dhawan c Buttler b Broad	23	– c Stokes b Anderson	17
K. L. Rahul lbw b Broad	19	– b Broad	0
C. A. Pujara not out	132	– lbw b Anderson	5
*V. Kohli c Cook b Curran	46	– c Cook b Ali	58
A. M. Rahane lbw b Stokes	11	– lbw b Ali	51
†R. R. Pant lbw b Ali	0	– (7) c Cook b Ali	18
H. H. Pandya c Root b Ali	4	– (6) c Root b Stokes	0
R. Ashwin b Ali	1	– lbw b Curran	25
Mohammed Shami b Ali	0	– (10) c Anderson b Ali	8
I. Sharma c Cook b Ali	14	– (9) lbw b Stokes	0
J. J. Bumrah c Cook b Broad	6	– not out	0
B 9, lb 1, w 4, nb 3	17	Lb 1, w 1	2

1/37 (2) 2/50 (1) 3/142 (4)   (84.5 overs) 273   1/4 (2) 2/17 (3)   (69.4 overs) 184
4/161 (5) 5/181 (6) 6/189 (7)   3/22 (1) 4/123 (4)
7/195 (8) 8/195 (9) 9/227 (10) 10/273 (11)   5/127 (6) 6/150 (7) 7/153 (5)
                                                             8/154 (9) 9/163 (10) 10/184 (8)

Anderson 18–2–50–0; Broad 18.5–5–63–3; Curran 16–4–41–1; Jennings 2–0–4–0; Rashid 7–0–19–0; Ali 16–1–63–5; Stokes 7–1–23–1. *Second innings*—Anderson 11–2–33–2; Broad 10–2–23–1; Ali 26–3–71–4; Stokes 12–3–34–2; Curran 3.4–2–1–1; Rashid 7–3–21–0.

Umpires: H. D. P. K. Dharmasena and B. N. J. Oxenford.   Third umpire: J. S. Wilson.
Referee: A. J. Pycroft.

ENGLAND v INDIA

Fifth Specsavers Test

Steven Lynch

At The Oval, September 7–11. England won by 118 runs. Toss: England. Test debut: G. H. Vihari.

After England clinched the series at the Rose Bowl, this might have been an anticlimax. But Alastair Cook's retirement added meaning, and the match built up from a sedate start into a gripping affair, one of the most momentous of the 101 men's Tests at England's oldest international ground. The crowds gave him a series of standing ovations, and were captivated until the last ball, when the festivities ended with another record for Jimmy Anderson, and another ovation for his pal Cook.

The first round of applause came as he walked out to bat through an Indian guard of honour after Root had won the toss yet again. "I think I need a coin with two heads," lamented Kohli. The opening day, though, gave little indication of the excitement to come. In the ninth over, Cook cut and pulled Bumrah for fours, an early sign that the release of pressure had helped his game. Shortly before lunch, after a stand of 60 – England's highest for the first wicket all summer – Jennings pushed straight to leg slip. The bowler, the piratical Jadeja, had replaced the injured Ravichandran Ashwin, while Hanuma Vihari, a batsman from Andhra with a first-class average of 59, came in for all-rounder Hardik Pandya. England were unchanged, though Bairstow reclaimed the gloves from Buttler after recovering from his broken finger.

Up at No. 3, Ali enjoyed a charmed life. In one spell, he played and missed a dozen times in 26 balls from Mohammed Shami, but somehow survived a scratchy second

Visionhaus/Getty Images

Steady as he goes: Alastair Cook leaves Test cricket on a high.

session in which he scored 21 of England's 55 runs. Cook also needed luck, dropped by Rahane in the gully when 37, before reaching the first fifty of the series by an opener.

England were creeping along at barely two an over when an old-fashioned day took an unexpected turn. First Cook inside-edged Bumrah into his stumps, and was cheered off for 71, then Root was trapped in front, and Bairstow caught behind off Sharma – his third duck in four innings. Ali continued to live dangerously, and reached a four-hour fifty before finally nicking one, off Sharma. When Curran fell for a duck, England had lost six for 48. It could have been worse: Buttler, when eight, was given lbw to Shami. He reviewed more in hope than expectation, and was pleasantly surprised when the technology showed a thin edge.

Buttler made the most of his reprieve next morning, his 28th birthday. He was helped by Broad, who shrugged off a blow from Bumrah which, it transpired, cracked a rib. Mixing chipped drives with the occasional slash, Broad helped add 98; Buttler then clouted two sixes off Bumrah before flicking Jadeja to slip on 89. England's 332 – their last three wickets had added 151 – looked imposing, more so when Dhawan missed a straight one in Broad's first over, which took him past Richard Hadlee's Test haul of 431.

Anderson was in one of his grumpier moods, especially when, after persuading the umpires to change the ball, he confounded Rahul three times and saw Pujara reprieved from lbw by a faint edge in the same over. Cook dropped Pujara, a tough chance at short leg, off Ali – the next delivery was pulled savagely for four – and India reached tea at 53

COOK'S LAST SHIFT

A giant in the dark

BARNEY RONAY

As the sun dipped below the curve of the OCS Stand, a mob of fond, bedraggled voices rang around the booze-soaked bleachers. "Ali Cook, Ali Cook, Ali, Ali Cook," they sang over and over, to the inappropriately jaunty tune of "Give It Up" by KC and the Sunshine Band. Two hours earlier, England's highest Test run-scorer had walked up the pavilion steps for the last time as an international player, bathed in his umpteenth standing ovation of an increasingly fuzzy, loved-up match.

The Oval is English cricket's traditional elephants' graveyard, a place of last things and late-summer goodbyes. Yet even it can't have seen many like this. Cook had reached a valedictory Test hundred 20 minutes before lunch on the fourth day, bunting a half-volley from Ravindra Jadeja to deep point, and looking on as Jasprit Bumrah hurled the return for four overthrows. The crowd stood and clapped for three full minutes, delaying the game as Cook shrugged, waved bashfully, then waved again.

It was one of those moments when the normal rules dissolve. Cook could be seen spanking the ball through square cover with a dreamy, Essex-calypso flourish, finding new gears deep into the final knockings of his final knock. And, by stumps, the good wishes had come pouring in to an otherwise routine dead-rubber Test, from the prime minister Theresa May, and the watching Mick Jagger, to a multitude of fond and tearful goodbyes from the public.

The feeling of warmth was infused with a slight sense of bafflement. Who knew all this love was out there? One of the most notable things about Cook had always been his basic anonymity, a giant in the dark. Every one of his England runs came behind the TV paywall, invisible to the unconverted.

Cook had announced his departure after the Fourth Test, and arrived in south London as the headline story, guest of honour at his farewell picnic. When Bumrah dismissed him for 71 in the first innings, the bowler raised his arms to celebrate, then let them fall in an attitude of apology – evidence of his sporting nature, but also of the protective atmosphere around Cook, of a tenderly staged benefit match.

Retirement had been a long time coming. Despite a late falling away, his record reads like a sporting life three or four times over, with 12,472 runs, 33 hundreds, 57 fifties, 1,442 fours and 11 long-forgotten sixes. An early mention, in the 2006 *Wisden*, referred to an "expansive left-hander". As it turned out, his style was more about contraction. Yet his final hundred was marked by his fullest range of shots, from cut, to nudge, to block – the highlight that familiar off-side flay, like an arthritic under-gardener swatting a cloud of midges with a broom.

One of the more remarkable sights at the end of the game was the otherwise taciturn Jimmy Anderson, speaking about his best friend's retirement, welling up during a TV interview. And around the ground there was a note of sadness buried within the applause, a sense of wider adieus. Cook remained an analogue cricketer, an embodiment of something slower and more studied – and not just in English cricket, which continues to turn itself inside out in pursuit of a hypothetical new audience. One thing does seem certain: it is unlikely to produce another Cook any time soon.

CENTURY IN FIRST AND LAST TEST

	First	Last	
R. A. Duff (A).........	104 v E, Melbourne .	146 v E, The Oval...	1901-02 to 1905
W. H. Ponsford (A)....	110 v E, Sydney	266 v E, The Oval ...	1924-25 to 1934
G. S. Chappell (A)......	108 v E, Perth	182 v P, Sydney	1970-71 to 1983-84
M. Azharuddin (I)	110 v E, Calcutta ...	102 v SA, Bangalore	1984-85 to 1999-2000
A. N. Cook (E)	**104* v I, Nagpur** ...	**147 v I, The Oval**...	**2005-06 to 2018**

Ponsford made centuries in his first two and last two Tests.

for one. As on the first day, though, the ball moved around more in the final session. Curran trimmed Rahul's bails, then Anderson was convinced he had pinned Kohli. England reviewed but, though the ball was flattening the stumps, the impact on pad was umpire's call. Anderson vented his spleen at Kumar Dharmasena, earning a 15% match-fee fine and a demerit point, but he cheered up when Pujara and Rahane fell in his next three overs.

Broad immediately had an lbw shout against Vihari turned down, and did not review the decision, though replays showed it was out. In his next over, Vihari *was* given out, only to be saved on review. He initially galloped a grateful single to get off the mark. Kohli whisked 14 in a Curran over but, one short of another half-century and 20 minutes short of the close, edged Stokes to second slip. After Stokes added Pant, India ended the day six down and still 158 behind.

The sun shone on the third morning, and Vihari overcame his jitters to reach a fifty. He feathered a catch behind just before lunch, but Jadeja farmed the strike well, especially with last man Bumrah, who faced only 14 balls out of 59 in a stand of 32. Jadeja was left with 86, but had reduced the deficit to 40.

Back came Cook for his final innings, to yet more applause. It took him five overs to score a run, clipping Bumrah to the square-leg boundary, and he joined a not very exclusive club by playing and missing at Shami. But, by the 12th over, Kohli had wasted both reviews after optimistic shouts from Jadeja (one exasperated Indian fan suggested a different captain for tosses and reviews). Jennings soon fell anyway, leaving one that nipped back – remarkably, a first wicket of the match for Shami. Jadeja bowled Ali through the gate, but by stumps England's lead had swelled to 154.

Even though it was a Monday, the fourth day was a near sell-out, in anticipation of the final episode of Cook's curtain call. A leg-side clip off Bumrah took him past 50, and next over a lip-smacking cover-drive off Jadeja reinforced the feeling that this was the day for a Chef Special. The milestones didn't stop. Up came the hundred partnership, before Cook passed Kumar Sangakkara (12,400) to go fifth on the all-time Test run-list, the leading left-hander. Root then reminded spectators of his presence by going down the track and lifting Jadeja for six. Cook clunked Bumrah straight for four, in the manner of his monumental Melbourne double-century the previous December.

A nudge took him to 96, before another off-side push seemed to have brought a single. But Bumrah unaccountably shied at the bowler's end: with no one backing up, the ball

MOST TEST WICKETS AGAINST INDIA

		T	Balls	Runs	BB	Avge
110	**J. M. Anderson (England)**........	27	**6,037**	2,858	**5-20**	25.98
105	M. Muralitharan (Sri Lanka)	22	7,020	3,425	8-87	32.61
94	Imran Khan (Pakistan).............	23	5,078	2,260	8-60	24.04
85	**N. M. Lyon (Australia)**	18	**5,117**	2,771	**8-50**	32.60
76	M. D. Marshall (West Indies)	17	3,507	1,671	6-37	21.98
70	**S. C. J. Broad (England)**	20	**3,864**	1,797	**6-25**	25.67
67	A. M. E. Roberts (West Indies)	14	3,030	1,454	7-64	21.70
65	W. W. Hall (West Indies)	13	2,774	1,221	6-49	18.78
65	C. A. Walsh (West Indies).........	15	3,124	1,316	6-62	20.24
65	D. W. Steyn (South Africa)	14	2,721	1,400	7-51	21.53
65	R. J. Hadlee (New Zealand)	14	3,106	1,493	7-23	22.96

Winning number: Mohammed Shami becomes the 564th victim for James Anderson, and England seal a 4–1 series victory.

scudded away to the boundary. Just as he had in a career-saving innings at The Oval in 2010 (when Pakistan's Mohammad Asif was the obliging fielder), Cook had reached his century thanks to an overthrow. The crowd went wild. Cook gazed to the heavens for the 33rd and last time in Test cricket, then to the stands and his heavily pregnant wife, Alice. The ovation went on and on.

After lunch, with Sharma missing because of an injured ankle, the stand reached 200 – Cook's tenth – just before Root completed his first Test century for 28 innings. England were 361 in front when Root slogged a gentle off-break from Vihari to deep midwicket. Then, to general disbelief, Cook tickled the next ball to Pant. Off he trudged, to yet more acclaim, for a superb 147. Bairstow and Buttler fell cheaply, but Stokes tucked in, and the declaration set India 464.

They had 18 overs to survive before stumps, and it briefly looked as if they might not manage even that. In the third, Anderson trapped Dhawan and Pujara. He could hardly wait to get at Kohli – but never had the chance. Kohli had scored 593 runs in the series from 1,024 deliveries, and not been caught behind (or dismissed by Anderson). But now he pushed limply at Broad, and was caught by Bairstow. Kohli's bowlers had beaten the bat 40-odd times in the match, yet he managed to nick his first ball. India were two for three, and the noise was incredible. Rahul counter-attacked, collecting four fours off Anderson, and somehow India reached the close without further loss. But it seemed all over, bar quite a lot more shouting.

A final-day crowd of 9,000 expected a quick finish, especially when Rahane toe-ended a sweep to midwicket and, next over, Vihari flinched Stokes to the keeper to make it 121 for five. But this absorbing series had one final twist. Rahul skipped through the nineties in a hectic over from Stokes, briefly sidelining the silky strokeplay that had taken him to 87 by smashing a tennis-style six over cover, then top-edging and swatting fours. Pant also tucked in, larruping Ali for a one-handed straight six.

By lunch Rahul had 108 of India's 167, but afterwards left-hander Pant played the aggressor in a session that set English nerves jangling. Driving and cutting crisply, he surged to a maiden fifty, and cracked three fours in an over to take the target below 200 as Stokes simmered. And when Rashid returned, Pant crashed him into the Bedser Stand; next over, he clattered another six to reach three figures from 117 balls (one quicker than

MOST CATCHES BY FIELDER OFF ONE BOWLER IN TESTS

Ct	T	Fielder	Bowler	
77	96	D. P. M. D. Jayawardene	M. Muralitharan	Sri Lanka
55	107	R. Dravid	A. Kumble	India
51	66	M. A. Taylor	S. K. Warne	Australia
51	95	R. Dravid	Harbhajan Singh	India
40	**130**	**A. N. Cook**	**J. M. Anderson**	**England**
39	60	G. S. Sobers	L. R. Gibbs	West Indies
39	69	M. L. Hayden	S. K. Warne	Australia
39	103	M. E. Waugh	S. K. Warne	Australia
36	85	R. T. Ponting	S. K. Warne	Australia

Rahul). A firm-footed technique behind the stumps, where he leaked 40 byes in this match alone, had invited ridicule. But now he became the first Indian wicketkeeper to score a Test century in England, and – at 20 – the youngest player to make one at The Oval (David Gower was about four months older in 1978). A further six just after tea raised the 300.

However, there were signs Pant was not picking Rashid, who was targeting the rough from wide round the wicket. Anderson was on at the other end in anticipation of the new ball, but Root shrewdly left Rashid with the old. In the 82nd over, he pitched one way outside leg that fizzed across, waspishly Warne-like, to tickle Rahul's off bail, and end a stand of 204, a sixth-wicket record in this fixture. With more experience, Pant might have taken stock – but instead he went for another big hit in Rashid's next over. It spiralled to long-off, where Ali made a tricky catch look simple. England breathed again, and the crowd relocated party mode.

With seven down, the question now was whether Anderson could claim the wicket he needed to become the leading fast bowler in Tests. When Curran removed Sharma and

OVAL NOTES AND QUOTES

In a Test dominated by the farewell to Alastair Cook, it emerged that the statement announcing his retirement – released four days before the start – had been drafted by Jonathan Agnew, who had learned of the news during the Southampton Test.

Tributes flowed and gifts poured in. The Professional Cricketers' Association produced a video with messages from 70 of Cook's 74 Test team-mates. The absentees were Michael Carberry, Andrew Flintoff, Darren Pattinson and Kevin Pietersen, although Pietersen did tweet his congratulations after Cook had made 147 in the second innings.

Surrey gave Cook a bottle of Bordeaux from 2006, the year of his Test debut. Jonny Bairstow organised a bottle of champagne for each Test century Cook had scored: 32 at the start of the game, 33 by the end.

The print media had a similar idea. Dean Wilson, cricket correspondent of the *Daily Mirror*, bought 33 bottles of beer from around the world the night before the Test began (the 33rd being a sensible insurance). Each was given a new label, bearing the details of one of the hundreds, as well as a personal message from a journalist who had witnessed it. Under the guise of asking the final question at the press conference on the fourth evening, Wilson thanked Cook and presented the beer.

There was time for one last presentation. Joe Root handed over a pair of his pads – "they have had a lot of hammer this summer" – to the Press Association's long-serving cricket correspondent David Clough, who had reported on his final Test before taking up a job covering horse racing.

No one had a more expensive week than Mick Jagger. A lifelong cricket fan, he had pledged to donate £20,000 for every century or five-wicket haul, and £10,000 for every fifty or three-for. The beneficiaries were Chance to Shine, the charity who in 2018 introduced their four millionth child to cricket. Jagger ended up forking out £190,000.

Jadeja in successive overs it looked doubtful – but Anderson, in the 14th over of a spell that had begun before tea, finally flattened Shami's middle stump. It was his 564th wicket, one more than Glenn McGrath (whose 563rd, in 2006-07, had been Anderson).

The crowd cranked out one more hearty roar, then another as Anderson and Cook led the players off. The final result felt closer than the 118-run margin suggested, as did England's 4–1 series triumph. And as they prepared for a world without Cook, the man himself reflected on "the most surreal few days of my life".

Man of the Match: A. N. Cook. *Attendance:* 98,097.

Men of the Series: England – S. M. Curran; India – V. Kohli.

Close of play: first day, England 198-7 (Buttler 11, Rashid 4); second day, India 174-6 (Vihari 25, Jadeja 8); third day, England 114-2 (Cook 46, Root 29); fourth day, India 58-3 (Rahul 46, Rahane 10).

England

A. N. Cook b Bumrah	71	– c Pant b Vihari	147
K. K. Jennings c Rahul b Jadeja	23	– b Mohammed Shami	10
M. M. Ali c Pant b Sharma	50	– b Jadeja	20
*J. E. Root lbw b Bumrah	0	– c sub (H. H. Pandya) b Vihari	125
†J. M. Bairstow c Pant b Sharma	0	– b Mohammed Shami	18
B. A. Stokes lbw b Jadeja	11	– c Rahul b Jadeja	37
J. C. Buttler c Rahane b Jadeja	89	– c Mohammed Shami b Jadeja	0
S. M. Curran c Pant b Sharma	0	– c Pant b Vihari	21
A. U. Rashid lbw b Bumrah	15	– not out	20
S. C. J. Broad c Rahul b Jadeja	38		
J. M. Anderson not out	0		
B 26, lb 9	35	B 14, lb 4, w 2, p 5	25

1/60 (2)   2/133 (1)   3/133 (4)   (122 overs) 332   1/27 (2)   (8 wkts dec, 112.3 overs) 423
4/134 (5)   5/171 (6)   6/177 (3)   2/62 (3)   3/321 (4)   4/321 (1)
7/181 (8)   8/214 (9)   9/312 (10)   10/332 (7)   5/355 (5)   6/356 (7)   7/397 (6)   8/423 (8)

Bumrah 30–9–83–3; Sharma 31–12–62–3; Vihari 1–0–1–0; Mohammed Shami 30–7–72–0; Jadeja 30–0–79–4. *Second innings*—Bumrah 23–4–61–0; Sharma 8–3–13–0; Mohammed Shami 25–3–110–2; Jadeja 47–3–179–3; Vihari 9.3–1–37–3.

India

K. L. Rahul b Curran	37	– b Rashid	149
S. Dhawan lbw b Broad	3	– lbw b Anderson	1
C. A. Pujara c Bairstow b Anderson	37	– lbw b Anderson	0
*V. Kohli c Root b Stokes	49	– c Bairstow b Broad	0
A. M. Rahane c Cook b Anderson	0	– c Jennings b Ali	37
G. H. Vihari c Bairstow b Ali	56	– c Bairstow b Stokes	0
†R. R. Pant c Cook b Stokes	5	– c Ali b Rashid	114
R. A. Jadeja not out	86	– c Bairstow b Curran	13
I. Sharma c Bairstow b Ali	4	– c Bairstow b Curran	5
Mohammed Shami c Broad b Rashid	1	– b Anderson	0
J. J. Bumrah run out (Broad/Bairstow)	0	– not out	0
B 4, lb 10	14	B 10, lb 16	26

1/6 (2)   2/70 (1)   3/101 (3)   (95 overs) 292   1/1 (1)   2/1 (3)   (94.3 overs) 345
4/103 (5)   5/154 (6)   6/160 (7)   3/2 (4)   4/120 (5)
7/237 (6)   8/249 (9)   9/260 (10)   10/292 (11)   5/121 (6)   6/325 (1)   7/328 (7)
   8/336 (9)   9/345 (8)   10/345 (10)

Anderson 21–7–54–2; Broad 20–6–50–1; Stokes 16–2–56–2; Curran 11–1–49–1; Ali 17–3–50–2; Rashid 10–2–19–1. *Second innings*—Anderson 22.3–11–45–3; Broad 12–1–43–1; Ali 17–2–68–1; Curran 9–2–23–2; Stokes 13–1–60–1; Rashid 15–2–63–2; Root 6–1–17–0.

Umpires: H. D. P. K. Dharmasena and J. S. Wilson.   Third umpire: B. N. J. Oxenford.
Referee: A. J. Pycroft.

SRI LANKA v ENGLAND IN 2018-19

Review by Neil Manthorp

One-day internationals (5): Sri Lanka 1, England 3
Twenty20 international (1): Sri Lanka 0, England 1
Test matches (3): Sri Lanka 0, England 3

Eyebrows were raised by England's pre-tour talk of a "brave and bold" approach to the Test series. But as a delighted Joe Root said afterwards: "We walked the talk, and it paid off with a victory we can all be very proud of for the rest of our careers." England were always favourites to claim the one-day games, but victory in the Tests seemed less likely. To win 3–0 surpassed most expectations, including many of their own.

There was almost constant collateral damage whenever they batted, but the loss of wickets was a price worth paying: their overall run-rate of 3.66 was their second-highest in a series on the subcontinent. With the exception of the famous victory at Mumbai in 2012-13, England had only ever won in Asia with patience and grind. Indeed, it was exactly the modus operandi suggested before this tour by Nasser Hussain, who had led his team to victories in Pakistan and Sri Lanka in 2000-01. But Root, inspired by the positivity of one-day captain Eoin Morgan, didn't simply challenge England's past approach: he challenged the traditional approach to Test cricket.

In all three matches, England won the toss, batted, and reached three figures by lunch, improving as they went on: 113 for five at Galle, 120 for four at Pallekele, 102 for two in Colombo. Even when they were five down in the First Test, it was obvious they had rattled Sri Lanka, who retreated into caution and defence, and allowed England – thanks to a superb debut century from Ben Foakes – to recover to 342. The tone had been set, the gauntlet laid down. It would have been understandable, even responsible, for the tourists to have changed course, but they remained committed to their strategy.

England did not maintain the tempo for the Second Test: they upped it. A plan to upset Sri Lanka's spinners produced over 200 sweeps, almost as many reverse as conventional. It was more than had been played in an entire series – by anyone, anywhere – since shot selection was first accurately recorded in 2006. Jos Buttler led the way, but nearly everyone followed. So comfortable was he in his apparent ambidexterity that he rarely appeared at risk. It became impossible for Sri Lanka to set a field, since bowling one side of the wicket was insufficient. Yet in the Third Test, Buttler might have been mistaken for a

---

ENGLAND'S OVERSEAS WHITEWASHES

	Captain	
3–0 in South Africa	Lord Hawke†	1895-96
3–0 in New Zealand	E. R. Dexter	1962-63
3–0 in Sri Lanka	**J. E. Root**	**2018-19**

Minimum: three matches. † *Sir Timothy O'Brien captained in the First Test.*

Reverse engineering: at Pallekele Jos Buttler sweeps Sri Lanka to distraction.

man unacquainted with a sweep of any sort. Instead, he advanced at the bowler and played straight to almost every delivery. Hundreds may win more Tests than thirties or sixties but, in a low-scoring, fast-moving series, Buttler's innings of 38, 35, 63, 34, 16 and 64 affected the course of each match.

In rescuing an inconsistent top order, however, he was far from alone. Foakes wasn't in the original tour party, but was called up as cover after Jonny Bairstow twisted his ankle playing football before the fourth one-day international. Even then, Buttler was expected to keep wicket. But coach Trevor Bayliss said it was vital to have "your best gloveman" when picking three spinners, and – to Buttler's dismay – Root agreed. It was the bravest of many bold decisions, and paid rich dividends. Foakes was named Man of the Series.

Moeen Ali batted at No. 3 at Galle, and Ben Stokes at Pallekele, but both were moved back down, leaving the spot as the only way back in for Bairstow. On the first day in Colombo, he scored a punchy hundred and then, oddly, claimed he had been "castigated" in the media for injuring himself. Typically, though, he had risen to a challenge, even if he insisted he was going to fight to regain the gloves. In the first two Tests, Sam Curran was preferred as the second seamer to Stuart Broad because of his batting, and produced match-changing innings of 48 and 64, adding 60 for the last wicket with James Anderson at Pallekele. England's lower-order strength was another area in which Sri Lanka couldn't compete.

In England's first series for 13 years without Alastair Cook, Rory Burns enjoyed only one good Test, while a career-best 146 not out at Galle for his

opening partner, Keaton Jennings, did not answer questions about his ability
against seam. There was none about his fielding, though: at short leg, he hung
on to four reflex chances, and cleverly knocked up another for Foakes.
"Everyone tells me it's a good job to do badly," he smiled. His success reflected
well on the training methods of assistant coaches Paul Farbrace and Paul
Collingwood, who spent many hours attempting to replicate what a 6ft 4in
man could expect when crouched at boot hill.

It would not be wholly accurate to say that every member of the team
chipped in at some point. In fact, virtually every member of the team made
at least one significant contribution, then chipped in elsewhere. Whenever

WHITEWASHES BY NON-ASIAN TEAMS IN ASIA

	Captain	
Australia beat Pakistan 3–0†	S. R. Waugh	2002-03
Australia beat Sri Lanka 3–0	R. T. Ponting	2003-04
England beat Sri Lanka 3–0	**J. E. Root**	**2018-19**

Minimum: three matches.   † *First Test in Sri Lanka, Second and Third in the UAE.*

England needed a breakthrough, someone produced a moment of genius,
and direct-hit run-outs by Stokes and Jack Leach changed the direction of
the last two Tests. Sri Lanka were sloppy, most damningly when spinner
Lakshan Sandakan was twice denied the wicket of Stokes in Colombo
because of overstepping.

More than that, England beat the hosts at their own game: not only did they
match Sri Lanka's spinners, but they outperformed them. Slow bowlers on
both sides claimed 100 of the 116 wickets to fall. The probing Dilruwan Perera
topped the list with 22, but next for Sri Lanka came fellow off-spinner Akila
Dananjaya, with ten. (Dananjaya's action was reported after Galle, and he
missed Colombo to have it tested at Brisbane's National Cricket Centre, where
it was deemed illegal.) By contrast, England's trio – left-armer Leach, off-
spinner Ali and leg-spinner Adil Rashid – prided themselves on working as a
team, celebrating others' wickets as much as their own. Leach was a model of
consistency, his economy-rate of 2.69 allowing Ali and Rashid to attack.
Between them, they collected 48 wickets. Ali took eight in Galle, and there
were five-fors for Leach in Pallekele and Rashid in Colombo.

If Sri Lanka were often a shambles on the field, they were even worse off it.
Their best cricketer, Angelo Mathews, had been omitted from the one-day
squad (which he had captained until September) to work on his fitness,
according to coach Chandika Hathurusinghe, who also muttered bleakly about
his running between the wickets. During the 50-over series, Sanath Jayasuriya,
a national hero and former chairman of selectors, was charged with two
offences by the ICC's anti-corruption unit in the days before the First Test,
though he denied any wrongdoing; two weeks later, bowling coach Nuwan
Zoysa was also charged, quickly followed by Dilhara Lokuhettige, a former
international all-rounder.

All good things… in his last Test, Rangana Herath is run out by Ben Foakes, in his first.

Another national hero, veteran spinner Rangana Herath, announced that the First Test, his 93rd, would be his last, and signed off by dismissing Root twice. Mathews, recalled for the Tests, contributed to the leadership vacuum by cutting a lone figure in the field, and signalled his dissatisfaction with his treatment by the selectors by pointing to his bat and making a chatting gesture after reaching both his half-centuries at Galle; unfortunately, Sri Lanka needed his bat to do more talking than 52 and 53.

When injury ruled Dinesh Chandimal out after Galle, the captaincy passed to fast bowler Suranga Lakmal, whose aptitude for it was matched by his peripheral role with the ball. Sri Lanka had their moments, but only Roshen Silva, opener Dimuth Karunaratne and Mathews averaged over 30 with the bat, and no one reached a hundred (England scored four). Losing all three tosses did not help. But it was hard to dispute that a side which had recently disposed of Australia and South Africa at home had been outplayed. Sri Lanka Cricket responded by sacking their entire selection panel during the Third Test.

The scheduling of the one-day games came in for criticism, with all five – plus the solitary Twenty20 international – affected by rain. Only the first, however, did not achieve a result. And while monsoon season is not the ideal time for a major series, critics were unable to point to a better slot in the crowded schedule; oddly, all five one-day internationals would have been rain-free had they been played a day later. You take your chances, as England do when hosting in September.

Morgan enjoyed a productive series with the bat, but his worth was most evident when he wasn't there. With England 3–0 up, he rested himself for the final match to give a game to team-mates in an oversized squad, and watched a rudderless, unbalanced XI fall to pieces amid bickering and finger-pointing. Niroshan Dickwella and Sadeera Samarawickrama carved an opening stand of

137, and the carnage continued as England's bowlers, under the temporary captaincy of Buttler, were unable to regroup. Their batting was equally dismal, and would have been worse but for 67 from a cramping Stokes.

It should probably be written off as an extremely bad day at the office, especially given the conviction with which England had already claimed the series. Yet it did provide a worrying insight into what might happen if Morgan were to miss a more important game. Scores of 14, 92, 58 and 31 – three unbeaten – were also a reminder of what an influential white-ball cricketer he remains. He was delightfully pragmatic about the weather, too. In the second ODI, Chris Woakes had reduced Sri Lanka to 31 for four. But voluptuous, dark-grey clouds were minutes away, so Ali and Liam Dawson galloped through their overs as quickly as possible until 20 had been bowled – the minimum required to constitute a match.

Joe Denly made his first England appearance for nearly nine years in the T20 game, and scored a handy 20 at No. 7, before taking the new ball with his leg-breaks and finishing with four for 19 and the match award. He had been widely tipped to fill the problem No. 3 spot in the Tests – and provide a fourth spin option – but was unconvincing in the two practice matches.

The tour was a significant success for England off the field as well. The travelling support had swelled from around 3,000 during the one-dayers to 8,000 for the Galle Test, and they truly made the occasion. When cynical agents demanded up to ten times the face value for a ticket, over 3,000 opted to watch from the walls of the 16th-century fort, where the sea breeze and elevated viewpoint often provided a more pleasant experience anyway.

FIVE STATS YOU MAY HAVE MISSED

BENEDICT BERMANGE

- At Galle, Rangana Herath (40 years 232 days) became the oldest player to take a Test wicket since Graham Gooch, 41, dismissed Michael Slater at Brisbane in 1994-95.

- Ben Foakes was the first England wicketkeeper to score a Test century in Asia. The previous highest was by Alan Knott, who had reached 96 against Pakistan at Karachi in 1968-69 when the match was abandoned after crowd disturbances.

- Foakes caught Dimuth Karunaratne from his second ball behind the stumps in a Test, equalling the record set by Australia's Peter Nevill, who caught Adam Lyth at Lord's in 2015. Roger Woolley of Australia (1982-83) and New Zealand's Robbie Hart (2002) both took a catch third ball. Against Australia at The Oval in 1884, W. G. Grace held a catch from his first ball keeping wicket in a Test (it was his fifth match), after taking over to allow the Hon. Alfred Lyttelton a bowl.

- Moeen Ali was out for a duck at Galle while batting at No. 3, the sixth position in which he had been dismissed for nought. This equalled the England record, shared by Mike Gatting and Derek Randall, but remained one behind the overall mark, shared by Mervyn Dillon of West Indies and Australia's Ian Johnson.

- Nine of England's second innings wickets at Pallekele were lbw (six) or bowled (three), only their second such instance after Kingston in 1959-60 (also six lbw and three bowled, against West Indies). The only team to lose all ten bowled or lbw were Don Bradman's Australians, against India at Adelaide in 1947-48 (six bowled, four lbw), though they ran up 674.

Around a hundred fans were then moved out of their luxury hotels in Kandy before the Pallekele Test, to accommodate late requests by Sri Lanka Cricket. Root signed personal letters to all affected, and arranged for a mass photograph with supporters and players on the outfield on the third morning. After each game, he led his team round the ground to applaud the fans.

The good mood was understandable. England had finished the year with five Test wins in a row, and eight out of their last nine, while Root was finally imposing his character on the side. For the first time, England had triumphed in all three formats on an overseas tour. And, perhaps more significantly, they had laid down a template for non-Asian teams on the subcontinent. A trip that might easily have been ticked off as just another home win ended up assuming an importance few thought possible.

ENGLAND TOURING PARTY

*J. E. Root (Yorkshire; T/50/20), M. M. Ali (Worcestershire; T/50/20), J. M. Anderson (Lancashire; T), J. M. Bairstow (Yorkshire; T/50/20), S. C. J. Broad (Nottinghamshire; T), R. J. Burns (Surrey; T), J. C. Buttler (Lancashire; T/50/20), S. M. Curran (Surrey; T/50/20), T. K. Curran (Surrey; 50/20), L. A. Dawson (Hampshire; 50), J. L. Denly (Kent; T/50/20), B. T. Foakes (Surrey; T), A. D. Hales (Nottinghamshire; 50/20), K. K. Jennings (Lancashire; T), C. J. Jordan (Sussex; 20), M. J. Leach (Somerset; T), E. J. G. Morgan (Middlesex; 50/20), L. E. Plunkett (Yorkshire; 50/20), O. J. D. Pope (Surrey; T), A. U. Rashid (Yorkshire; T/50/20), J. J. Roy (Surrey; 50/20), B. A. Stokes (Durham; T/50/20), O. P. Stone (Warwickshire; T/50/20), C. R. Woakes (Warwickshire; T/50/20), M. A. Wood (Durham; 50/20).

Morgan captained in the white-ball matches. Plunkett joined the tour late after his wedding, which he had arranged when the one-day games had been expected to follow the Tests. Dawson injured his side in the second ODI, and was replaced by Denly. Foakes was called up after Bairstow injured his ankle.

Coach: T. H. Bayliss (T/50/20). *Assistant coach:* P. Farbrace (T/50/20). *Batting coach:* M. R. Ramprakash (T). *Fast-bowling coach:* C. E. W. Silverwood (T/50/20). *Consultant coach:* P. D. Collingwood (T). *Wicketkeeping coach:* B. N. French (T). *Fielding coach:* C. D. Hopkinson (50). *Spin consultant:* Saqlain Mushtaq (T/50/20). *Operations manager:* P. A. Neale (T/50/20). *Analyst:* G. O. N. Lindsay (T), N. A. Leamon (50/20). *Doctor:* Moiz Moghal (T), M. G. Wotherspoon (50/20), G. Rae (50/20). *Physiotherapist:* C. A. de Weymarn (T/50/20). *Masseur:* M. Saxby (T/50/20). *Strength and conditioning:* P. C. F. Scott (T/50/20), D. Venness (50). *Security manager:* R. C. Dickason (T), S. Dickason (50/20). *Head of team communications:* D. M. Reuben (T/50/20).

TEST MATCH AVERAGES

SRI LANKA – BATTING AND FIELDING

	T	I	NO	R	HS	100	50	Avge	Ct/St
A. R. S. Silva	2	4	0	190	85	0	2	47.50	1
†F. D. M. Karunaratne	3	6	0	256	83	0	3	42.66	2
A. D. Mathews	3	6	0	223	88	0	3	37.16	2
B. K. G. Mendis	3	6	0	179	86	0	1	29.83	2
D. M. de Silva	3	6	0	168	73	0	2	28.00	8
†D. P. D. N. Dickwella.	3	6	0	128	35	0	0	21.33	7/1
P. M. Pushpakumara	2	4	1	60	42*	0	0	20.00	2
R. A. S. Lakmal	3	6	3	58	15*	0	0	19.33	0
†A. Dananjaya	2	4	1	47	31	0	0	15.66	0
M. D. K. Perera	3	6	0	73	30	0	0	12.16	0
J. K. Silva.	2	4	0	41	30	0	0	10.25	1

Played in one Test: L. D. Chandimal 33, 1 (1 ct); †M. D. Gunathilleke 18, 6 (1 ct); †H. M. R. K. B. Herath 14*, 5 (1 ct); P. A. D. L. R. Sandakan 2, 7 (1 ct).

BOWLING

	Style	O	M	R	W	BB	5I	Avge
M. D. K. Perera	OB	169	20	527	22	5-75	2	23.95
P. A. D. L. R. Sandakan.......	SLW	38	1	171	7	5-95	1	24.42
P. M. Pushpakumara	SLA	82	10	282	9	3-28	0	31.33
A. Dananjaya	OB	77.5	5	378	10	6-115	1	37.80
H. M. R. K. B. Herath	SLA	48	5	137	3	2-59	0	45.66
R. A. S. Lakmal	RFM	57	11	201	4	3-73	0	50.25

Also bowled: D. M. de Silva (OB) 35.1–3–110–0; M. D. Gunathilleke (OB) 2–0–5–0.

ENGLAND – BATTING AND FIELDING

	T	I	NO	R	HS	100	50	Avge	Ct/St
B. T. Foakes...............	3	6	2	277	107	1	1	69.25	8/2
†K. K. Jennings.............	3	6	1	233	146*	1	0	46.60	8
J. C. Buttler	3	6	0	250	64	0	2	41.66	3
J. E. Root	3	6	0	229	124	1	0	38.16	2
†S. M. Curran..............	2	4	1	112	64	0	1	37.33	0
†B. A. Stokes..............	3	6	0	187	62	0	2	31.16	9
A. U. Rashid..............	3	5	1	113	35	0	0	28.25	0
†R. J. Burns................	3	6	1	155	59	0	1	25.83	1
†J. M. Anderson.............	2	3	2	19	12	0	0	19.00	1
†M. M. Ali.................	3	6	0	78	33	0	0	13.00	3
†M. J. Leach...............	3	5	0	25	15	0	0	5.00	1

Played in one Test: J. M. Bairstow 110, 15; †S. C. J. Broad 0, 1 (1 ct).

BOWLING

	Style	O	M	R	W	BB	5I	Avge
B. A. Stokes................	RFM	31	4	102	5	3-30	0	20.40
M. J. Leach.................	SLA	142.4	16	385	18	5-83	1	21.38
M. M. Ali	OB	124	14	441	18	4-66	0	24.50
A. U. Rashid................	LB	99	7	338	12	5-49	1	28.16

Also bowled: J. M. Anderson (RFM) 41–6–105–1; S. C. J. Broad (RFM) 14–2–50–0; S. M. Curran (LFM) 15–2–50–1; J. E. Root (OB/LB) 16–0–46–1.

At Colombo (PSO), October 5, 2018. **England XI won by 43 runs** (DLS). ‡**Sri Lanka Board XI 287-9** (50 overs) (L. D. Chandimal 77, P. H. K. D. Mendis 61; M. M. Ali 3-42); **England XI 215-2** (35.3 overs) (J. E. Root 90*, E. J. G. Morgan 91*). *England recorded a comfortable victory in their first warm-up match, being well ahead of the DLS par score when the clouds unloaded. Moeen Ali dismissed both openers in his second over after a stand of 53, but Dinesh Chandimal made a bright 77. England's bowlers kept things tight, and the Board XI reached 287 only thanks to a late burst from Isuru Udana, who thumped three sixes in a 26-ball 40. England were 41-2 before Joe Root and Eoin Morgan took control in a stand eventually worth 174*. They had few problems, despite an unusual opponent in the ambidextrous Kamindu Mendis, barely 20, who followed a mature 61 by bowling slow left-arm to Root and right-arm off-breaks to the left-handed Morgan, finishing with tidy figures of 8–0–37–0.*

At Colombo (PSO), October 6, 2018. **Sri Lanka Board XI v England XI. Abandoned.**

LIMITED-OVERS INTERNATIONAL REPORTS BY NICK HOULT

SRI LANKA v ENGLAND

First One-Day International

At Dambulla, October 10, 2018 (day/night). No result. Toss: Sri Lanka. One-day international debut: O. P. Stone.

Only 15 overs were possible before the monsoon arrived, with England – already short of match practice because of the weather – 92 for two. During a 49-run opening stand, Roy and Bairstow became the first England partnership to reach 1,000 runs in a calendar year (Nick Knight and Marcus Trescothick came next, with 794 in 2002). But neither was at his most fluent: Bairstow edged a wide one and, four balls later, Roy misread the off-spin of Dananjaya. Earlier, Warwickshire seamer Olly Stone had been presented with his first one-day cap by Darren Gough, as England looked to add raw pace to their World Cup options. But the rain limited Stone to the pre-match game of football.

England

J. J. Roy c sub (W. S. R. Samarawickrama)	
b Dananjaya.	24
J. M. Bairstow c Dickwella b Fernando . . .	25
J. E. Root not out.	25
*E. J. G. Morgan not out	14
Lb 2, w 2	4

1/49 (2) 2/51 (1)　　　(2 wkts, 15 overs)　92
　　　　　　　　　　　10 overs: 55-2

B. A. Stokes, †J. C. Buttler, M. M. Ali, C. R. Woakes, L. A. Dawson, A. U. Rashid and O. P. Stone did not bat.

Malinga 5–0–37–0; Fernando 5–0–23–1; Dananjaya 5–0–30–1.

Sri Lanka

†D. P. D. N. Dickwella, W. U. Tharanga, *L. D. Chandimal, M. D. K. J. Perera, D. M. de Silva, N. L. T. C. Perera, M. D. Shanaka, A. Dananjaya, P. A. D. L. R. Sandakan, S. L. Malinga, A. N. P. R. Fernando.

Umpires: Aleem Dar and R. S. A. Palliyaguruge.　　Third umpire: P. R. Reiffel.
Referee: R. B. Richardson.

SRI LANKA v ENGLAND

Second One-Day International

At Dambulla, October 13, 2018. England won by 31 runs (DLS). Toss: Sri Lanka.

Malinga delivered a classic spell of death bowling, but it was not enough to affect the result of a rain-shortened match. He took five for 44, his best one-day international haul since August 2011, to prevent a late charge from England after they had been put in. But Morgan's well-crafted 92 from 91 balls had given his team a platform. Earlier in the week, he had admitted he could drop himself if he felt it would benefit the side but, on a typically slow Sri Lankan pitch, he proved he offered more than astute leadership. Morgan's first scoring shot was a straight six off Tissara Perera, and he manipulated the field with deft sweeps. At the other end, Root calmly took his sequence between

ODI dismissals to 309, an England record (previously 301 by Graeme Hick in January 1999). At 218 for four in the 42nd over, they were set for at least 300. But Malinga, who had removed Roy with the fourth ball of the match, ran through his repertoire. Morgan was caught off a leading edge, Ali bowled first ball with a dipping yorker – Malinga's 500th international wicket – and both Woakes and Dawson duped by slower-ball sleights of hand. An unbroken last-wicket stand of 24 between Rashid and Stone lifted England to 278. Dickwella ramped Woakes for four in a first over which also brought the wicket of Tharanga, but was then bounced out by the lively Stone, who touched 90mph. Woakes claimed three for 26 in a probing burst, before England's spinners whizzed through their overs to ensure the 20 needed to enact DLS. Despite some hefty blows from Tissara Perera, Sri Lanka were well behind when the rain swept in.

Man of the Match: E. J. G. Morgan.

England

J. J. Roy c Danajaya b Malinga	0	A. U. Rashid not out		19
J. M. Bairstow b Perera	26	O. P. Stone not out		9
J. E. Root c Danajaya b de Silva	71			
*E. J. G. Morgan c and b Malinga	92	Lb 3, w 4, nb 2		9
B. A. Stokes c de Silva b Danajaya	15			—
†J. C. Buttler b Fernando	28	1/0 (1) 2/72 (2)	(9 wkts, 50 overs)	278
M. M. Ali b Malinga	0	3/140 (3) 4/190 (5)		
C. R. Woakes lbw b Malinga	5	5/218 (4) 6/218 (7) 7/245 (6)		
L. A. Dawson b Malinga	4	8/249 (8) 9/254 (9)	10 overs: 54-1	

Malinga 10–1–44–5; Fernando 10–0–52–1; Dananjaya 10–0–64–1; N. L. T. C. Perera 7–0–37–1; Sandakan 9–0–59–0; de Silva 4–0–19–1.

Sri Lanka

†D. P. D. N. Dickwella c Buttler b Stone	9	N. L. T. C. Perera not out		44
W. U. Tharanga c Buttler b Woakes	0	B 1, lb 2, w 4		7
*L. D. Chandimal b Woakes	6			—
M. D. K. J. Perera c Roy b Dawson	30	1/9 (2) 2/16 (1)	(5 wkts, 29 overs)	140
M. D. Shanaka c Buttler b Woakes	8	3/20 (3) 4/31 (5)		
D. M. de Silva not out	36	5/74 (4)	10 overs: 38-4	

A. Dananjaya, P. A. D. L. R. Sandakan, S. L. Malinga and A. N. P. R. Fernando did not bat.

Woakes 5–0–26–3; Stone 6–0–23–1; Dawson 6–0–26–1; Ali 10–0–47–0; Rashid 2–0–15–0.

Umpires: R. E. J. Martinesz and P. R. Reiffel.   Third umpire: Aleem Dar.
Referee: R. B. Richardson.

SRI LANKA v ENGLAND

Third One-Day International

At Pallekele, October 17, 2018 (day/night). England won by seven wickets. Toss: England.

Tom Curran's slower balls and Rashid's wrist-spin helped England to a 2–0 lead in a game shortened by rain to 21 overs. The pair took the wind out of Sri Lanka's innings, before Morgan methodically led the chase. Heavy rain had delayed play by almost six hours, but the shrinking of the match did not close the gap between the sides. After a bright start, Sri Lanka failed to adapt to the conditions, holding back the dangerous Twenty20 hitters Tissara Perera and Shanaka. Dickwella and Samarawickrama had propelled them to 57 for no wicket in the sixth over, with England looking flustered. But Curran removed Dickwella, whose 36 included eight fours, with a back-of-the-hand delivery, and from there England had a grip on the scoring-rate; Rashid combined accuracy with penetration to claim four for 36. Chandimal's lack of urgency – he made 34 off 42 balls – put pressure on the others. Bairstow and Root fell early to slow left-armer Amila Aponso as England set about chasing 151, but Roy looked more comfortable against spin than in previous innings, and Morgan stroked the ball around. The best shots, however, came from Stokes, who had spent 45 minutes on the eve of the game working on his ramp. The preparation paid off when he scooped Nuwan Pradeep Fernando for six, and England cruised home with 15 balls to spare.

Man of the Match: A. U. Rashid.

Sri Lanka

†D. P. D. N. Dickwella c Woakes b Curran .	36	S. L. Malinga not out.	2
W. S. R. Samarawickrama c Woakes		M. A. Aponso run out (Buttler/Curran). . . .	0
b Rashid.	35		
B. K. G. Mendis b Rashid	0	B 2, lb 7, w 3	12
*L. D. Chandimal c Rashid b Curran	34		
N. L. T. C. Perera c Roy b Rashid.	0	1/57 (1)　2/59 (3)　　　(9 wkts, 21 overs) 150
D. M. de Silva c Roy b Curran	3	3/94 (2)　4/94 (5)
M. D. Shanaka b Rashid	21	5/110 (6)　6/138 (7)　7/146 (8)
A. Dananjaya run out (Bairstow/Buttler) . .	7	8/150 (4)　9/150 (10)
			4 overs: 45-0

A. N. P. R. Fernando did not bat.

Woakes 4–0–37–0; Stone 3–0–24–0; Curran 4–0–17–3; Ali 1–0–6–0; Rashid 5–0–36–4; Stokes 4–0–21–0.

England

J. J. Roy lbw b Dananjaya	41
J. M. Bairstow c Perera b Aponso	4
J. E. Root b Aponso.	8
*E. J. G. Morgan not out	58
B. A. Stokes not out.	35
Lb 2, w 5	7

1/18 (2)　2/34 (3)　　(3 wkts, 18.3 overs) 153
3/80 (1)　　　　　　4 overs: 35-2

†J. C. Buttler, M. M. Ali, C. R. Woakes, A. U. Rashid, T. K. Curran and O. P. Stone did not bat.

Malinga 4–0–39–0; Aponso 3.3–0–27–2; Dananjaya 4–0–33–1; de Silva 4–0–23–0; Fernando 2–0–21–0; Perera 1–0–8–0.

Umpires: Aleem Dar and R. R. Wimalasiri.　Third umpire: P. R. Reiffel.
Referee: R. B. Richardson.

SRI LANKA v ENGLAND

Fourth One-Day International

At Pallekele, October 20, 2018. England won by 18 runs (DLS). Toss: England.

England's preparations were hampered when Jonny Bairstow sustained an ankle-ligament injury playing football, but it did not stop them winning their ninth bilateral series in a row. Heavy clouds had gathered at the start of their pursuit of a notional 274, a target that was always going to be subject to DLS recalculations. Malinga's first over included two sets of four byes and cost 12 in all. And, thanks to Roy's hitting and Morgan's ability to find the gaps off the spinners, they recovered from the loss of Hales, Bairstow's replacement, to stay comfortably ahead. Sri Lanka thought they had dismissed the patient Root on 22, when he was caught on the sweep at short fine leg off de Silva, top-edging a full toss. But square-leg umpire Lyndon Hannibal had spotted there were too few fielders inside the ring, and called no-ball as the stroke was played. It was a lack of awareness that summed up Sri Lanka's series. Chandimal in desperation threw the ball back to Malinga, but England were in control when the rains came. Sri Lanka had at least batted with some consistency. Shanaka clouted five sixes in a run-a-ball 66, though he was missed on 24 by Hales, who parried an attempted catch at deep midwicket for six. After a wobble had reduced them to 102 for four, the fifth, sixth and seventh wickets all added at least 50. It represented progress, but it was not enough.

Man of the Match: E. J. G. Morgan.

Sri Lanka

†D. P. D. N. Dickwella lbw b Ali	52	A. Dananjaya not out	32
W. S. R. Samarawickrama c Buttler b Woakes	1	S. L. Malinga not out	4
*L. D. Chandimal b Ali	33	Lb 10, w 9	19
B. K. G. Mendis lbw b Rashid	5		
D. M. de Silva c Buttler b Curran	17	1/19 (2) 2/89 (3) (7 wkts, 50 overs)	273
M. D. Shanaka run out (Morgan/Woakes)	66	3/102 (1) 4/102 (4)	
N. L. T. C. Perera run out (Stokes/Buttler)	44	5/154 (5) 6/212 (6) 7/268 (7) 10 overs: 44-1	

M. A. Aponso and C. A. K. Rajitha did not bat.

Woakes 10–0–45–1; Stone 7–0–50–0; Curran 9–1–50–1; Ali 10–0–55–2; Rashid 10–0–36–1; Stokes 4–0–27–0.

England

J. J. Roy lbw b Dananjaya	45
A. D. Hales st Dickwella b Dananjaya	12
J. E. Root not out	32
*E. J. G. Morgan not out	31
B 8, w 3, nb 1	12
1/52 (2) 2/76 (1) (2 wkts, 27 overs)	132
10 overs: 54-1	

B. A. Stokes, †J. C. Buttler, M. M. Ali, C. R. Woakes, A. U. Rashid, T. K. Curran and O. P. Stone did not bat.

Malinga 5–0–15–0; Aponso 6–0–37–0; Rajitha 5–0–27–0; Dananjaya 7–0–27–2; de Silva 4–0–18–0.

Umpires: L. E. Hannibal and P. R. Reiffel.　Third umpire: Aleem Dar.
Referee: R. B. Richardson.

SRI LANKA v ENGLAND

Fifth One-Day International

At Colombo (RPS), October 23, 2018 (day/night). Sri Lanka won by 219 runs (DLS). Toss: Sri Lanka.

England slumped to their heaviest one-day defeat by runs, having made three changes to their series-winning side. Plunkett returned after cutting short his honeymoon, while Wood came in for Olly Stone – who had been expensive in the two games at Pallekele – and Morgan rested himself to make room for Sam Curran. He and Tom became the first brothers to play for England together since another Surrey duo, Adam and Ben Hollioake, in February 1999. But England, led by Buttler, were sloppy in the field, and their seamers poor; worse, on a humid night in Colombo, they at times lost their cool with each other. After putting on 137 in 19 overs for the first wicket with Samarawickrama, Dickwella was set for Sri Lanka's first one-day hundred of the year, but exhaustion set in and he holed out for 95. Chandimal was put down by Tom Curran off Ali on six, and recovered to make his first fifty of the series, while Kusal Mendis ended a horrible run by taking the aggressive option. He hit six sixes in a 33-ball 56, his first ODI half-century in 24 innings, a sequence that included ten scores of nought or one. Sri Lanka's 366 for six was their highest against England, beating 324 for two at Leeds in 2006. Within ten balls of the reply, England were reeling at four for three, after Rajitha and Chameera found new-ball movement that had been beyond the tourists. Roy was yorked, while Hales and Buttler fiddled outside off stump; Root soon poked at a wide one. Stokes offered resistance, before becoming one of four cheap victims for Dananjaya, but England were nine down and well beaten when the monsoon arrived. The result eclipsed a pair of 165-run defeats, by West Indies in St Vincent in March 1994, and by Pakistan at Karachi in December 2005.

Man of the Match: D. P. D. N. Dickwella.   *Man of the Series:* E. J. G. Morgan.

Sri Lanka

†D. P. D. N. Dickwella c Root b Ali	95	A. Dananjaya not out	18
W. S. R. Samarawickrama b Ali	54		
*L. D. Chandimal c Roy b T. K. Curran	80	B 4, lb 3, w 8	15
B. K. G. Mendis c Stokes b Plunkett	56		—
M. D. Shanaka c Roy b Rashid	18	1/137 (2) 2/168 (1) (6 wkts, 50 overs) 366	
N. L. T. C. Perera c Hales b T. K. Curran ..	11	3/270 (4) 4/300 (5)	
D. M. de Silva not out	19	5/328 (3) 6/328 (6) 10 overs: 72-0	

P. A. D. L. R. Sandakan, C. A. K. Rajitha and P. V. D. Chameera did not bat.

Wood 8–0–55–0; S. M. Curran 6–0–46–0; T. K. Curran 8–0–71–2; Ali 8–0–57–2; Rashid 10–0–52–1; Plunkett 5–0–44–1; Stokes 5–0–34–0.

England

J. J. Roy b Rajitha	4	L. E. Plunkett lbw b Dananjaya	5
A. D. Hales c Mendis b Chameera	0	T. K. Curran not out	1
J. E. Root c Samarawickrama b Chameera	10	Lb 1, w 1	2
*†J. C. Buttler c Dickwella b Chameera	0		—
B. A. Stokes c Perera b Dananjaya	67	1/4 (1) 2/4 (2) (9 wkts, 26.1 overs) 132	
M. M. Ali c Chandimal b Dananjaya	37	3/4 (4) 4/28 (3)	
S. M. Curran c Sandakan b de Silva	2	5/107 (6) 6/121 (7) 7/122 (5)	
A. U. Rashid b Dananjaya	4	8/129 (8) 9/132 (9) 10 overs: 41-4	

M. A. Wood did not bat.

Rajitha 5–0–21–1; Chameera 6–0–20–3; Perera 2–0–18–0; de Silva 4–0–18–1; Dananjaya 6.1–0–19–4; Sandakan 3–0–35–0.

Umpires: Aleem Dar and R. S. A. Palliyaguruge.   Third umpire: P. R. Reiffel.
Referee: R. B. Richardson.

SRI LANKA v ENGLAND

Twenty20 International

At Colombo (RPS), October 27, 2018 (floodlit). England won by 30 runs. Toss: Sri Lanka. Twenty20 international debut: P. H. K. D. Mendis.

More than eight years after his previous international, Joe Denly took four wickets with his reinvigorated leg-spin – and, after England eased to victory, the match award. Having hit 20 off 17 balls in an imposing total of 187 for eight, Denly opened the bowling, removed Kusal Mendis with his sixth ball and Dickwella with his 11th, and returned at the end to grab two more. He had missed 384 internationals since being ditched shortly before the 2010 World Twenty20; only West Indies' Rayad Emrit (396) had endured a longer gap between appearances. With the superb Rashid taking a career-best three for 11, the tourists' leg-spinners bagged seven; Tissara Perera's late blows were in vain. England's innings centred on Roy's mercurial 69. He was badly dropped in the deep three times – on 34, 41 and 53 – and ought to have persuaded Hales to review his lbw verdict; he also played a part in the run-out of Morgan. But Roy's strokeplay was a notch clear of anyone until Perera's fireworks, though Ali unfurled a bright cameo after a one-hour rain break. England dealt comfortably with the 20-year-old debutant Kamindu Mendis, who bowled slow left-arm to the right-handed Roy, and off-breaks to the left-handed Stokes. He looked a more natural left-armer, but there was little in it.

Man of the Match: J. L. Denly.

England

		B	4/6
1 J. J. Roy *c l b 11*	69	36	4/6
2 †J. C. Buttler *c 3 b 9*	13	7	3
3 A. D. Hales *lbw b 9*	4	3	1
4 *E. J. G. Morgan *run out (10/11)*	11	10	2
5 B. A. Stokes *b 10*	26	27	1/1
6 M. M. Ali *b 4*	27	11	1/3
7 J. L. Denly *c 2 b 10*	20	17	3
8 A. U. Rashid *b 8*	5	3	1
9 L. E. Plunkett *not out*	7	5	1
10 C. J. Jordan *not out*	2	1	0
Lb 1, w 2	3		

6 overs: 59-2   (20 overs) 187-8

1/41 2/45 3/60 4/107 5/145 6/173 7/173 8/185

11 T. K. Curran did not bat.

Malinga 4–13–30–2; Aponso 3–7–29–2; Udana 3–4–24–1; Sandakan 4–9–39–1; P. H. K. D. Mendis 3–5–27–0; Perera 1–1–15–0; de Silva 2–3–22–1.

Sri Lanka

		B	4/6
1 †D. P. D. N. Dickwella *b 7*	3	7	0
2 B. K. G. Mendis *b 7*	1	3	0
3 L. D. Chandimal *c 3 b 8*	26	20	4
4 D. M. de Silva *lbw b 8*	17	19	2
5 P. H. K. D. Mendis *c 3 b 8*	24	14	3/1
6 *N. L. T. C. Perera *c 1 b 7*	57	31	1/6
7 M. D. Shanaka *b 9*	10	13	0/1
8 I. Udana *c 5 b 10*	2	3	0
9 M. A. Aponso *b 10*	0	2	0
10 S. L. Malinga *b 7*	5	1	0
11 P. A. D. L. R. Sandakan *not out*	1	1	0
B 5, lb 5, w 1	11		

6 overs: 47-2   (20 overs) 157

1/7 2/16 3/49 4/77 5/77 6/110 7/119 8/119 9/156

Denly 4–13–19–4; Curran 4–7–40–0; Jordan 4–11–29–2; Rashid 4–14–11–3; Plunkett 2–5–24–1; Ali 2–1–24–0.

Umpires: R. E. J. Martinesz and R. R. Wimalasiri. Third umpire: R. S. A. Palliyaguruge.
Referee: R. B. Richardson.

At Colombo (Nondescripts), October 30–31 (not first-class). **Drawn.** ‡**Sri Lanka Board President's XI 392-9 dec** (89.5 overs) (J. K. Silva 62, W. S. R. Samarawickrama 58, S. M. A. Priyanjan 50, D. M. Sarathchandra 59*); **England XI 365-7** (90 overs) (J. E. Root 100, M. M. Ali 60; K. N. Peiris 3-108). *England chose from 14 players, and the home side from 15. The England bowlers toiled on the first day; Stuart Broad and Sam Curran both went wicketless. Three Sri Lankans retired after reaching 50, but, next day, Joe Root had no qualms in completing a 117-ball century before he, too, headed for the pavilion. In his first match for the full England side, Rory Burns made 47 from 79 balls to secure a Test spot. There was a worrying 20-minute delay after a Jos Buttler pull hit the short-leg fielder Pathum Nissanka, who was briefly knocked out and taken to hospital, where an MRI scan revealed no lasting damage (the ball rebounded to be caught by Angelo Mathews, dismissing Buttler for 44).*

At Colombo (CCC), November 1–2 (not first-class). **Drawn.** ‡**England XI 210-6 dec** (50 overs) (B. A. Stokes 53; C. B. R. L. S. Kumara 3-19); **Sri Lanka Board President's XI 200-7** (50 overs) (K. I. C. Asalanka 68). *This time England rotated 16 players, while the President's XI again used 15. After the first day was washed out, the sides agreed to bat for 50 overs each on the second. Joe Denly's chances of a Test debut faded when he bagged a second-ball duck, as did Ollie Pope. Jack Leach took 1-29 in 13 overs.*

SRI LANKA v ENGLAND

First Test

JARROD KIMBER

At Galle, November 6–9, 2018. England won by 211 runs. Toss: England. Test debuts: R. J. Burns, B. T. Foakes.

There was a coup in Sri Lanka. The president had sacked the prime minister, and installed the former president, Mahinda Rajapaksa. The minister for petroleum had been briefly arrested on charges relating to a murder. The people were angry, and there were warnings about staying away from crowds. In much of the Southern Province, Rajapaksa's image was everywhere, as if his re-emergence was less of a sudden coup than a careful

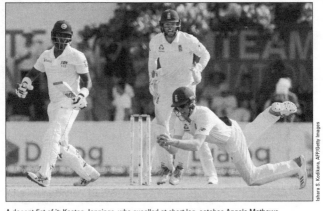

A decent fist of it: Keaton Jennings, who excelled at short leg, catches Angelo Mathews.

plan. He was grinning, impeccably groomed and wearing traditional clothes: an image-conscious politician.

Galle was also full of pictures of a man. He didn't look as polished. There were thank-yous, too, from banks, cricket boards, anyone who had the money to put up a poster. The man looked like a family guy, greying, slightly rotund, with a friendly face. It was clear he was no politician but, despite the cricket gear, he didn't look much of an athlete either. Rangana Herath never has – yet he turned himself into one of Sri Lanka's greatest cricketers. This was his last Test, and it was practically a testimonial. Even the weather behaved, as the monsoon that had left the pitch under water on the eve of the game stayed away.

It was also a party Ben Foakes never thought he'd be invited to. As he faced Dilruwan Perera in the 24th over, he might have been excused for thinking: "I'm not even supposed to be here." Foakes was not in England's original squad, but was brought in as back-up to the back-up keeper: an insurance policy dressed up as a tourist became England's first-choice gloveman. And, in a team full of No. 7s, he took that job too. Foakes was making his debut in Herath's backyard – and England were in trouble.

But Foakes had spent time in Sri Lanka, with England Under-19s and the Lions, and a couple of matches for Colombo's Colts CC. He had visited the place so many times he probably had a flat there. And that is how he played, as if these were his home conditions. While his team-mates attacked recklessly after Root had won the toss, Foakes batted like the only adult in the room. Rory Burns's maiden Test innings ended with a leg-side strangle off Lakmal, who then bowled Ali first ball. Root hit a busy 35 – too busy, thought many – before he yorked himself advancing at Herath. Then Perera bowled Jennings for 46, trying to cut a quicker one, and Stokes, moving too far across his stumps as he aimed a sweep for seven.

Foakes emerged shortly before lunch, and immediately played each ball on its merits. After 43, he had only nine. Then he started driving the spinners through cover. But mostly he waited for poor deliveries, which came often, and clinically put them away. By the end of the first day, he had turned 103 for five into 321 for eight, having added 61 with Buttler, 88 with his Surrey team-mate Curran, and 54 with Rashid.

Next morning, he moved to 91 with an effortless first-ball cover-drive. The only time his century looked anything but assured was when he had 95, and Leach was ninth out, a

CENTURY ON TEST DEBUT BY WICKETKEEPER

D. S. B. P. Kuruppu (201*).....	Sri Lanka v New Zealand at Colombo (CCC)	1986-87
R. S. Kaluwitharana (132*).....	Sri Lanka v Australia at Colombo (SSC)	1992-93
M. J. Prior (126*)	England v West Indies at Lord's.................	2007
T. A. Blundell (107*)	New Zealand v West Indies at Wellington	2017-18
B. T. Foakes (107)	**England v Sri Lanka at Galle.**.................	**2018-19**

fifth wicket for Perera. But Anderson survived the rest of the over, before Foakes hit two boundaries in three balls from Lakmal to pick up only the second hundred on debut by an England wicketkeeper, and believed to be the first by a bearded English debutant since W. G. Grace. Only Bryan Valentine (Bombay 1933-34), Alastair Cook (Nagpur 2005-06) and Jennings (Mumbai 2016-17) had previously made a Test-debut century for England in Asia. Foakes whacked the next ball for four, too, before one heave too many – but the last five wickets had added an imposing 239.

In reply to England's 342 – decent on a pitch which was already turning – Sri Lanka collapsed to 40 for four before lunch. Anderson removed Karunaratne with the second ball of the innings (the only wicket he claimed all series), and Curran swung one into the pads of Silva. Leach and Ali both struck too, leaving Sri Lanka in the hands of Mathews, who was back after missing the white-ball matches on fitness grounds, and Chandimal, who was hobbling after injuring his groin in the field. For a while, their two most seasoned batsmen played as sensibly as Foakes, until Chandimal charged at Rashid and was stumped – by Foakes. Mathews fell to Ali first ball after tea, and the tail offered little. Sri Lanka trailed by 139.

On the third morning, England moved to 60 for none before losing three for 14. Burns was run out after Sri Lanka moved the sluggish Herath from mid-on and replaced him with the more agile Karunaratne, who responded with a smart direct hit. When Ali was caught at mid-on for three, it was clear his brief spell at first drop would be discontinued. And, for the second time in the game, Root fell to Herath.

Jennings had looked the most composed top-order player in the first innings, and now cashed in. He is a peculiar batsman: he seems to have too many limbs, and plays fast bowling like it is booby-trapped, but he's superb against spin, even if his reverse sweep resembles a praying mantis going through puberty. And he manipulated an already chaotic Sri Lankan field: Chandimal was off injured, leaving the ineffectual Lakmal in charge; Herath occasionally weighed in, and Mathews moped.

They tested Jennings's patience with men out, hoping he would find one. But that was not his way: he nudged and reverse-nudged, and was happy to take singles to the fielders

200 WICKETS IN TESTS AFTER THE AGE OF 30

		T	Balls	Runs	Avge	BB	5I	10M
398	**H. M. R. K. B. Herath (Sri Lanka)**	81	23,598	10,953	27.52	9-127	34	9
388	M. Muralitharan (Sri Lanka/World)...	60	19,528	8,545	22.02	8-46	34	12
386	S. K. Warne (Australia)	73	20,039	9,791	25.36	7-94	22	6
343	A. Kumble (India)	71	21,735	10,627	30.98	8-141	19	5
341	C. A. Walsh (West Indies)	81	19,905	8,244	24.17	7-37	17	2
297	**J. M. Anderson (England)**	74	16,203	7,104	23.91	7-42	14	2
287	G. D. McGrath (Australia)	65	15,077	5,997	20.89	8-24	12	1
276	R. J. Hadlee (New Zealand)	51	12,971	5,373	19.46	9-52	25	6
228	G. P. Swann (England)...............	55	13,664	6,869	30.12	6-65	15	3
216	A. A. Donald (South Africa)	47	9,738	4,508	20.87	6-53	14	1
216	C. V. Grimmett (Australia)............	37	14,513	5,231	24.21	7-40	21	7
215	C. E. L. Ambrose (West Indies)........	56	11,751	4,430	20.60	6-24	13	1
215	L. R. Gibbs (West Indies).............	58	20,745	6,917	32.17	7-98	12	1

Grimmett made his Test debut at 33.   Swann played only five Tests before turning 30.

Launch site: Ben Foakes adds quick second-innings runs to his first-innings century.

on the boundary. There were only six fours in his hundred, his first in Tests since that debut at Mumbai, and his first score above 50 since his second Test, at Chennai. With Stokes contributing a solid 62, Buttler another thirty and Foakes a 34-ball 37 laced with three sixes, England were able to set Sri Lanka 462 in two days plus seven overs. They couldn't have chased it in two lifetimes.

England's spinners seemed to be picked via algorithms made for optimum variety. Leach is a specialist turning-pitch bowler, averaging 20 at Taunton but 32 everywhere else. He does nothing extravagant, but the simple things well. Rashid is a constant threat, an unplayable ball forever in his back pocket. Ali's huge revs compensate for his lack of accuracy. Together, they shared eight wickets, the pick a beauty from Leach to Chandimal that straightened and hit the top of middle and off. Ali had match figures of eight for 137, his best in an away Test. Only Mathews passed 50, though he was grateful for a terrible drop by Anderson at midwicket, when 18, during a battering-ram spell by Stokes.

Midway through the final session on the fourth day, England had ended a run of 13 overseas Tests without a win – the longest drought in their history – and secured their first victory at Galle.

As for Herath, he reached 100 wickets at the ground when he dismissed Root in the first innings, and passed Richard Hadlee's Test tally of 431 when he added him in the second. Think of those two: Root is one of the best players of his generation, while Hadlee spent a decade perfecting his action. Then think of Herath, who spent much of his career as back-up to Muttiah Muralitharan, and worked in a bank. His final wicket, Buttler, moved him to joint-eighth on the all-time list with Stuart Broad, who had been left out here, and one behind Kapil Dev. And his last act on a cricket field was playing one of his near-automatic reverse sweeps, then being run out by millimetres.

Mathews had made headlines for being dropped. Sanath Jayasuriya was in hot water for not handing his mobile phone over to the ICC's anti-corruption unit. And the minister for petroleum? That was Arjuna Ranatunga. Three of Sri Lanka's greatest cricketers were in the news, the country was in a constitutional crisis, and yet for a week the nation stopped to pay tribute to the wizard of Galle.

When Herath had come on to bowl on the first day, there were fireworks over the Galle Fort. It was touching, yet ridiculous: fireworks in the daytime can hardly be seen. When they finished, Herath bowled. Just as he let the ball go, and Jennings leaned forward, there was one last, huge firework. His career might have come late, but it came with a bang. After England had won, he quietly collected his trophies and headed back to the bank.

Man of the Match: B. T. Foakes.

Close of play: first day, England 321-8 (Foakes 87, Leach 14); second day, England 38-0 (Burns 11, Jennings 26); third day, Sri Lanka 15-0 (Karunaratne 7, Silva 8).

England

R. J. Burns c Dickwella b Lakmal	9	– run out (Karunaratne)	23
K. K. Jennings b Perera	46	– not out	146
M. M. Ali b Lakmal	0	– c Herath b Perera	3
*J. E. Root b Herath	35	– c Dickwella b Herath	3
B. A. Stokes b Perera	7	– b Perera	62
J. C. Buttler c Dickwella b Perera	38	– c Silva b Herath	35
†B. T. Foakes c de Silva b Lakmal	107	– c Mendis b Dananjaya	37
S. M. Curran c Chandimal b Dananjaya	48	– not out	0
A. U. Rashid c de Silva b Perera	35		
M. J. Leach c de Silva b Perera	15		
J. M. Anderson not out	0		
B 1, lb 1	2	B 4, lb 7, nb 2	13

1/10 (1) 2/10 (3) 3/72 (4)   (97 overs) 342   1/60 (1)   (6 wkts dec, 93 overs) 322
4/98 (2) 5/103 (5) 6/164 (6)   2/67 (3) 3/74 (4)
7/252 (8) 8/306 (9) 9/330 (10) 10/342 (7)   4/181 (5) 5/258 (6) 6/319 (7)

Lakmal 18–5–73–3; Perera 31–6–75–5; Dananjaya 20–2–96–1; Herath 25–4–78–1; de Silva 3–0–18–0. *Second innings*—Perera 30–3–94–2; Lakmal 9–2–30–0; Herath 23–1–59–2; Dananjaya 18.5–2–87–1; de Silva 12.1–2–41–0.

Sri Lanka

F. D. M. Karunaratne c Foakes b Anderson	4	– c and b Ali	26
J. K. Silva lbw b Curran	1	– lbw b Leach	30
D. M. de Silva b Ali	14	– c Root b Stokes	21
B. K. G. Mendis c Stokes b Leach	19	– c Ali b Leach	45
A. D. Mathews c Jennings b Ali	52	– c Buttler b Ali	53
*L. D. Chandimal st Foakes b Rashid	33	– b Leach	1
†P. D. P. D. N. Dickwella c Buttler b Ali	28	– c Stokes b Ali	16
M. D. K. Perera c Buttler b Leach	21	– c Stokes b Rashid	30
A. Dananjaya c Foakes b Ali	0	– c Stokes b Ali	8
R. A. S. Lakmal c Anderson b Rashid	15	– not out	14
H. M. R. K. B. Herath not out	14	– run out (Stokes/Foakes)	5
Lb 2	2	Lb 1	1

1/4 (1) 2/10 (2) 3/34 (4)   (68 overs) 203   1/51 (2) 2/59 (1)   (85.1 overs) 250
4/40 (3) 5/115 (6) 6/136 (5)   3/98 (3) 4/144 (4)
7/171 (7) 8/173 (9) 9/175 (8) 10/203 (10)   5/154 (6) 6/190 (7) 7/197 (5)
                                                        8/229 (9) 9/239 (8) 10/250 (11)

Anderson 10–0–26–1; Curran 6–1–16–1; Leach 18–2–41–2; Ali 21–4–66–4; Rashid 9–1–30–2; Stokes 4–0–22–0. *Second innings*—Curran 5–1–15–0; Anderson 12–2–27–0; Ali 20–2–71–4; Rashid 18.1–0–59–1; Leach 21–1–60–3; Stokes 8–2–16–1; Root 1–0–1–0.

Umpires: M. Erasmus and C. B. Gaffaney.   Third umpire: S. Ravi.
Referee: A. J. Pycroft.

SRI LANKA v ENGLAND

Second Test

LAWRENCE BOOTH

At Pallekele, November 14–18, 2018. England won by 57 runs. Toss: England.

Two hundred years after the Kandyan Wars ended local resistance to the colonial invaders, the English were making a nuisance of themselves in the hill country once more. Their approach was simple, but brutal: as if swinging machetes at the undergrowth, they swept, reverse-swept, then swept again – all the way to their first series win in Sri Lanka since Nasser Hussain's team 17 years earlier.

England's tactics peaked during a sparkling 124 from 146 balls by Root, batting as inventively as any of his compatriots can ever have done in Asia. Others needed little encouragement to follow their leader. In all, England's second innings produced 84 sweeps of various genres, for a return of 122 runs, of which Root contributed 47; only Curran, out first ball, and Rashid didn't play the shot. And while those 84 also included the first seven wickets, the rewards were clear: Sri Lanka spread the field in an attempt to plug the leaks, and ended up like boys with too few fingers in too many dykes. New gaps opened up, and England poured through. If the pragmatism was unsparing, the flair was outrageous. This was one of their most watchable wins in years.

Their spinners, too, rose to the occasion. For the first time since Jim Laker's Test at Old Trafford in 1956, England won without a wicket from a seamer. And the slow bowlers hunted as a pack: not since Derek Underwood, Geoff Miller, Chris Balderstone and an

MOST WICKETS IN A TEST BY ENGLAND SPINNERS

20	v A at Manchester . .	J. C. Laker 19, G. A. R. Lock 1	1956
19	v I at Kanpur	M. J. Hilton 9, R. Tattersall 8, J. D. B. Robertson 2	1951-52
19	v NZ at Leeds	G. A. R. Lock 11, J. C. Laker 8	1958
19	v I at Mumbai	M. S. Panesar 11, G. P. Swann 8	2012-13
19	**v SL at Pallekele**. . .	**M. J. Leach 8, M. M. Ali 6, A. U. Rashid 4, J. E. Root 1** . . .	**2018-19**
18	v WI at Manchester .	R. Berry 9, W. E. Hollies 8, J. C. Laker 1	1950
18	v A at Leeds.	J. C. Laker 11, G. A. R. Lock 7	1956
17	v I at Madras	H. Verity 11, J. Langridge 6	1933-34
17	v WI at Bridgetown .	J. C. Laker 9, R. Howorth 7, J. T. Ikin 1	1947-48
16	v SA at Lord's	D. V. P. Wright 10, D. C. S. Compton 4, W. E. Hollies 2	1947
16	v SA at Lord's	R. Tattersall 12, J. H. Wardle 4	1951
16	v WI at The Oval . . .	G. A. R. Lock 11, J. C. Laker 5	1957
16	**v SL at Galle**.	**M. M. Ali 8, M. J. Leach 5, A. U. Rashid 3**	**2018-19**

off-spinning Tony Greig at The Oval in 1976 had four English spinners taken a wicket in the same Test innings.

For Sri Lanka, the wounds were partly self-inflicted. Lakmal, their stand-in captain – Dinesh Chandimal was still nursing a groin injury – had asked for a turner, which against England would once have made sense. But the retirement of Rangana Herath had left the tourists with the more potent spin attack. Leach led the way, enacting lessons learned on the dry and dusty pitches of Taunton, and finishing with eight wickets. Ali's off-breaks claimed six, including the vital scalp of Mathews in the second innings, and Rashid four, including a pair of Warneian leg-breaks to remove de Silva and Mathews in the first. Root struck too, picking up one of the game's 15 lbws. Everywhere you looked, the ball was turning, and batsmen were sweeping. It was organised chaos – and England knew it was their best chance.

Homespun: Akila Dananjaya claimed six wickets, but was later ruled to have an illegal action.

Despite Jonny Bairstow having recovered from the twisted ankle that ruled him out at Galle, they were unchanged, save for one tweak: Stokes up to No. 3, Ali down to No. 6, a configuration that lasted one innings. Root won another toss and, again, England almost squandered the advantage. Jennings nibbled tamely at Lakmal (the only wicket in the Test for a seamer), and Stokes – unconvincing in his new position – was squared up by Perera. Root was bowled through the gate by Pushpakumara, who had replaced his fellow slow left-armer Herath, and it was 89 for four when Burns, after a promising 43, prodded Dananjaya to slip.

Buttler, though, played his shots before lunch, taken at a head-spinning 120 for four. After it, England ploughed ahead, like a tuk-tuk into the traffic, accidents be damned. Ali missed a hoick against Pushpakumara, who overturned Erasmus's not-out verdict, and Foakes was given out caught at slip, despite no evidence he had hit it (he thought he had, and declined a review). When Buttler, after an ingenious 63 that included 51 from sweeps, reverse-paddled Pushpakumara's slower ball to point, it was 171 for seven, and England's strategy on the brink.

Undeterred, Rashid crashed 31, but it was 225 for nine – still below par – when Anderson joined an unusually becalmed Curran, who had 16 from 65 deliveries. Curran was almost stranded: Anderson was given leg-before to Dananjaya from his first ball (but saved on review), and dropped by Dickwella from his second. It was the break Curran needed. From his next 38 deliveries, he plundered six sixes, moving to fifty with the fifth, a brutal pull off Dananjaya. That made him the first player to reach his first three Test half-centuries with a six; he also passed the Bangladeshi Mohammad Rafique's record of most sixes (five) in a Test innings before hitting a four. (Less than three weeks later, West Indies' Shimron Hetmyer trumped Curran, with eight against Bangladesh.) On 53, Curran was badly dropped by Pushpakumara at long-on, and had time for his sixth six – and finally that four (a sweep) – before driving Perera to long-off. England had added 60 for the last wicket in 11 overs, and Anderson had faced just 12 balls, a reflection of Curran's skill and Lakmal's tactics, which kept allowing a single late in the over. When, before stumps, Leach bowled Kaushal Silva with a beauty, England were on a high.

LEAVE IT WITH ME...

Opening the batting and the bowling for England in a Test since 1946:

W. J. Edrich..............	v West Indies at Manchester......................	1950
C. Washbrook.............	v New Zealand at Christchurch...................	1950-51
T. E. Bailey..............	v West Indies at Port-of-Spain...................	1953-54
T. E. Bailey..............	v West Indies at Kingston.......................	1953-54
T. E. Bailey..............	v Australia at Sydney...........................	1954-55
T. E. Bailey..............	v South Africa at Johannesburg.................	1956-57
T. E. Bailey..............	v South Africa at Port Elizabeth................	1956-57
G. A. Gooch..............	v Pakistan at Faisalabad........................	1987-88
M. J. Leach	**v Sri Lanka at Pallekele**.........................	**2018-19**

There were 35 instances before the Second World War.

Pushpakumara, the nightwatchman, fell early next morning, but Karunaratne and de Silva regrouped in style, exploiting the failure of England's spinners to locate a length. At 127 for two, with lunch in sight and Sri Lanka quietly in control, Stokes decided to shake things up. First he ran out Karunaratne from backward point, then he extended a telescopic left arm to catch Mendis at slip. Rashid soon ripped out de Silva and Mathews, and when Root trapped Dickwella on the sweep it was 211 for seven. But Roshen Silva, playing instead of Chandimal, took on the spinners, adding 41 with Perera and 56 with Dananjaya. Sri Lanka were ahead, England rattled.

But they were grateful for a curious incident which retrospectively added five penalty runs to their first-innings 285. From the first ball of the 86th over, Silva dabbed Leach to third man. Ali gave chase and limited the damage to two – or so it seemed. The umpires conferred, and Erasmus eventually invoked the obscure Law 18.5, ruling that Silva had deliberately failed to complete the first run. He docked two from Sri Lanka's total, and handed five to England's. Since Silva appeared simply to have got into a tangle after believing the ball had gone for four, this seemed harsh. When Rashid finally had him caught at mid-on for 85, Sri Lanka's lead was 46.

Out walked Leach to block one over before stumps. And though he went early next morning, Burns and Jennings settled English nerves with a stand of 73 at a rate of nearly 4.5 an over. Burns happily followed orders, sweeping his way to 59 from 66 balls. But Root took things to another level, relentlessly getting down on his front knee to disrupt Sri Lanka's spinners. Even in the over after Buttler had again fallen on the reverse sweep, Root played the shot three times. By tea, he had 98, and England a dizzying 259 for six in two sessions.

From the second ball after the break, Root moved to his 15th Test hundred, just his fourth overseas. Perhaps only in the 2015 Ashes opener at Cardiff had he made a more decisive century. By the time he was leg-before trying to reverse-sweep Dananjaya – under the threat of a ban after being reported for a suspect action at Galle – he had lifted his team past 300. But Dananjaya quickly took care of Curran and Rashid; when the first signs of an electrical storm ended play three-quarters of an hour early, England were 324 for nine from 76 overs. Sri Lanka had managed just three maidens. Only in their reviewing had England erred: both Burns and Stokes challenged plumb lbws, which meant Ali (hit outside the line) and Rashid (inside edge) had to swallow their fate.

Foakes, with the assurance of a veteran, and Anderson extended their last-wicket stand to 41 on the fourth morning, setting Sri Lanka 301 to square the series. And when, in a trice, Leach reduced them to 26 for three, it looked as if there wouldn't be a fifth. The first show of resistance came from Karunaratne and Mathews, who put on 77. Then, shortly after lunch, Karunaratne fell to an outrageous piece of work at short leg by Jennings. He had already snared de Silva, sticking out his left hand, while moving to his right. Now, he reacted to Karunaratne's paddle-sweep by moving to his left but, in attempting to complete the catch, parried the ball towards Foakes, alert to the rebound. The ricochet was lucky, but the anticipation world-class.

Stu Forster, Getty Images

X marks the shot: Joe Root makes good use of the sweep, en route to a hundred.

Sri Lanka refused to dwell on their misfortune. Silva added 73 with Mathews before Ali had him caught at slip on review via an inside edge, and tea came at 219 for five. Both sides fancied their chances. Instead, Ali immediately trapped Mathews for 88, and Leach pinned Perera. This time, the rain arrived even earlier, dragging the game into a final day, with Sri Lanka seven down and 75 adrift.

Root later said he had managed only three hours' sleep, though he needn't have fretted. Ali and Leach required barely half an hour to wrap things up, completing a Sri Lankan collapse of five for 22, and leaving Leach with a maiden Test five-for. "As soon as I got to the ground," said Root, "I felt very calm." Perhaps, after a frenzied Test, what he actually meant was exhausted.

Man of the Match: J. E. Root.

Close of play: first day, Sri Lanka 26-1 (Karunaratne 19, Pushpakumara 1); second day, England 0-0 (Leach 0, Burns 0); third day, England 324-9 (Foakes 51, Anderson 4); fourth day, Sri Lanka 226-7 (Dickwella 27, Dananjaya 0).

England

R. J. Burns c de Silva b Dananjaya	43	– (2) lbw b Pushpakumara	59
K. K. Jennings c Dickwella b Lakmal	1	– (3) c de Silva b Dananjaya	26
B. A. Stokes lbw b Perera	19	– (5) lbw b Perera	0
*J. E. Root b Pushpakumara	14	– lbw b Dananjaya	124
J. C. Buttler c Karunaratne b Pushpakumara	63	– (6) b Dananjaya	34
M. M. Ali lbw b Pushpakumara	10	– (7) lbw b Dananjaya	10
†B. T. Foakes c de Silva b Perera	19	– (8) not out	65
S. M. Curran c Karunaratne b Perera	64	– (9) b Dananjaya	0
A. U. Rashid lbw b Perera	31	– (10) lbw b Dananjaya	2
M. J. Leach b Dananjaya	7	– (1) lbw b Perera	1
J. M. Anderson not out	7	– b Perera	12
B 4, lb 3, p 5	12	B 4, lb 9	13

1/7 (2) 2/44 (3) 3/65 (4)   (75.4 overs) 290
4/89 (1) 5/134 (6) 6/165 (7)
7/171 (5) 8/216 (9) 9/225 (10) 10/285 (8)

1/4 (1) 2/77 (3)   (80.4 overs) 346
3/108 (2) 4/109 (5)
5/183 (6) 6/219 (7) 7/301 (4)
8/301 (9) 9/305 (10) 10/346 (11)

Lakmal 12–1–44–1; Perera 24.4–5–61–4; Pushpakumara 23–4–89–3; de Silva 2–0–4–0; Dananjaya 14–1–80–2. *Second innings*—Perera 20.4–2–96–3; Pushpakumara 27–1–101–1; Dananjaya 25–0–115–6; de Silva 4–0–7–0; Lakmal 4–0–14–0.

Sri Lanka

F. D. M. Karunaratne run out (Stokes)	63	– c Foakes b Rashid	57
J. K. Silva b Leach	6	– st Foakes b Leach	4
P. M. Pushpakumara c Burns b Ali	4	– (11) c and b Leach	1
D. M. de Silva c Foakes b Rashid	59	– (3) c Jennings b Leach	1
B. K. G. Mendis c Stokes b Leach	1	– (4) lbw b Leach	1
A. D. Mathews c Foakes b Rashid	20	– (5) lbw b Ali	88
A. R. S. Silva c Ali b Rashid	85	– (6) c Root b Ali	37
†D. P. D. N. Dickwella lbw b Root	25	– (7) c Stokes b Ali	35
M. D. K. Perera lbw b Leach	15	– (8) lbw b Leach	2
A. Dananjaya lbw b Ali	31	– (9) not out	8
*R. A. S. Lakmal not out	15	– (10) b Ali	0
B 6, lb 6	12	B 5, lb 4	9

1/22 (2) 2/31 (3) 3/127 (1)   (103 overs) 336
4/136 (5) 5/146 (4) 6/165 (6)
7/211 (8) 8/252 (9) 9/308 (10) 10/336 (7)

1/14 (2) 2/16 (3)   (74 overs) 243
3/26 (4) 4/103 (1)
5/176 (6) 6/221 (5) 7/226 (8)
8/240 (7) 9/240 (10) 10/243 (11)

Anderson 14–2–40–0; Curran 4–0–19–0; Leach 29–5–70–3; Ali 25–1–85–2; Rashid 22–2–75–3; Root 8–0–26–1; Stokes 1–0–9–0. *Second innings*—Anderson 5–2–12–0; Leach 28–2–83–5; Ali 19–2–72–4; Rashid 17–1–52–1; Root 5–0–15–0.

Umpires: M. Erasmus and S. Ravi.   Third umpire: C. B. Gaffaney.
Referee: A. J. Pycroft.

SRI LANKA v ENGLAND

Third Test

VITHUSHAN EHANTHARAJAH

At Colombo (SSC), November 23–26, 2018. England won by 42 runs. Toss: England.

England might have approached this game with one foot already on the plane. The series won, they often do. But their intensity in Colombo was on a par with Galle and Pallekele. Victory meant history was dotted and, arguably, selection matters crossed. England claimed their first whitewash in Asia in a series of three Tests or more, and only their third away from home.

With James Anderson rested, and Sam Curran missing because of a side injury, they had the luxury of bringing in replacements with 182 Tests between them. Both Broad and Bairstow had a point to prove. In Bairstow's case, it was done emphatically. He was no longer the first-choice wicketkeeper, but his right ankle had healed, and a fresh carrot dangled before him: the role of No. 3, fast becoming England's problem position, despite their attempts to depict the revolving door as a sign of flexibility. Twenty-four hours later, he had made the perfect start – and England were on their way.

Bairstow's sixth Test hundred was probably his most challenging. Colombo's sapping heat and minimal breeze tested both teams, so Root was relieved to win his eighth consecutive toss, one short of Colin Cowdrey's world record. Bairstow's arrival for his first innings in his new position came after Burns had tried to force Perera through the covers off the back foot and lost his off bail. A drive for four through extra cover from his first ball spoke of a purpose Bairstow carried through to lunch. His 42 from 58 deliveries included a slog-swept six off Pushpakumara, who had already removed Jennings, carelessly

Stu Forster, Getty Images

Line manager: Adil Rashid is close at hand as a direct hit from Jack Leach finds Kusal Mendis short of his ground, and England head for a 3–0 sweep.

turning the ball straight to leg slip. But a lunchtime score of 102 for two from 26 overs was England's best of a series in which they had consistently attacked the turning ball.

A stand of 100 came to an end when Root, on 46, top-edged a slog-sweep off left-arm wrist-spinner Sandakan, in the side for Akila Dananjaya, who was away having his action tested. A platform of 136 for three allowed Stokes to start slowly. He was lucky to survive a strong lbw appeal from Perera from his 14th delivery – Sri Lanka had carelessly used up both reviews – and finally got off the mark from his 15th. But he shook off the rust to bring up a half-century from his 78th. For Bairstow, a more significant milestone was round the corner.

A paddle to fine leg from his 165th delivery took him to three figures, followed by a celebration aimed, it seemed, at everyone and no one. He faced the press box as he ran through, three times screaming "Yes!" – once with his helmet removed – all while staring down the barrel of the cameras on the gantry. After a pointed jab of the bat in their direction, he saluted all corners of the ground, before throwing down his bat and helmet and embracing Stokes, who looked slightly bewildered. Bairstow later said he was driven by unjust criticism with tragedy back home – Chris Allinson, a former Yorkshire Second XI player, had died at the age of 28. Regardless, this was a superb century – the first by an England No. 3 since November 2016 (Root at Rajkot), and Bairstow's third in five innings against Sri Lanka.

But four balls later Stokes pushed Sandakan to slip, and it was 254 for five when Bairstow swung across the line. Less than 25 minutes into the second morning, England were all out for 336, their last seven having fallen for 101; Sandakan finished with a Test-best five for 95. It was their fifth successive total between 290 and 346; Sri Lanka would end the series with only one.

England's collapse looked particularly damaging while Karunaratne and de Silva took Sri Lanka to 173 for one. Both were dropped by Root at slip off Broad, Karunaratne on two, de Silva on 42. Broad had replaced Jimmy Anderson, who had half-smilingly complained of feeling like a bowling machine during the first two Tests. He summoned great pace, finding bounce where there supposedly was none, and movement through the air. But he ended the Test as he began it: with 433 Test wickets, the same as Herath. For Root, his drops formed part of one of his least convincing showings in the field; he even sent down his own novelty leg-spin before Rashid got a proper go from the 42nd over.

Root got it right eventually, with Rashid and Stokes in tandem. Stokes persisted with some testing short-pitched bowling, hitting Karunaratne in the ribs and Mendis on the right hand. Rashid ended a second-wicket stand of 142 shortly before tea as de Silva tickled him to Jennings at short leg. Karunaratne followed in the first over after the break and, as England grew in confidence, Sri Lanka lost their heads. In all, nine wickets tumbled for 67 in 18 overs, Rashid collecting his best Test figures of five for 49, and Jennings holding on to four close catches, the pick an instinctive grab low to his left at short leg to see off Roshen Silva. The mayhem was summed up by the run-out of Sandakan by Rashid, who misfielded at mid-off, before recovering to throw down the non-striker's stumps.

From nowhere, England led by 96, and added three runs in the four overs possible before rain forced an early conclusion to the second day. Ten overs into the third, their advantage was just as well. Perera pinned Jennings with the first ball of the morning, and quickly added

---

MOST WICKETS BY SPINNERS IN A THREE-TEST SERIES

100	**Sri Lanka (51) v England (49)**	**2018-19**
79	Sri Lanka (50) v New Zealand (29)	1997-98
78	Sri Lanka (54) v Australia (24)	2016
76	Sri Lanka (39) v Australia (37)	2003-04
75	Pakistan (48) v England (27) in the UAE	2011-12
71	Pakistan (43) v New Zealand (28)	1969-70
71	Sri Lanka (47) v India (24)	2008
69	India (46) v New Zealand (23)	1969-70
68	Bangladesh (49) v Zimbabwe (19)	2014-15
66	India (34) v Australia (32)	1956-57

Spinners took 109 wickets in the five-Test series between India (72) and England (37) in 1972-73.

Burns and Bairstow. Pushpakumara then gleefully held a return catch off Root: 39 for four. It would have been worse for England had Sandakan not overstepped twice – once when Stokes slapped him to cover on 29, then when he edged to slip on 32. Those were two of 13 uncalled no-balls Sky Sports picked up during Sandakan's spell. Stokes was eventually dismissed for 42, hitting Perera to long-on, but by then he and Buttler had added 89, quelling Sri Lanka's enthusiasm and tipping the game back England's way.

A lead of 224 still needed reinforcing, especially as the turn was getting slower and the bounce remained true. The explosions expected after Buttler brought up a clever 59-ball fifty, full of decisive footwork, did not quite materialise, though contributions from Ali, Foakes and Rashid ensured the lead was 326 when Perera wrapped up the innings, claiming his eighth five-wicket haul.

Sri Lanka's chase was hampered by a woeful start late on the third day. A probing spell from Ali accounted for both left-handed openers – Gunathilleke, who had come in for the out-of-form Kaushal Silva, caught at slip, and Karunaratne, bowled through the gate. In between, Leach nabbed de Silva for a duck. A comically poor piece of cricket from Mathews, who hooked Stokes tamely to Broad, meant Sri Lanka closed at 53 for four.

The nightwatchman Sandakan hung around for ten overs next morning, and Sri Lanka showed further resolve, Mendis and the classy Silva diligently adding 102 as England ran out of ideas. And it needed a rocket of a throw from deep square leg by Leach to end their alliance, as they came back for a second, only for Mendis to be caught short at the non-striker's end. Leach described the moment as the best of his career. It took the puff out of the hosts: soon it was 226 for nine, and victory beckoned with more than four sessions to spare.

Three's company: England spinners Moeen Ali, Jack Leach and Adil Rashid after England's Colombo triumph.

Instead, Pushpakumara threatened to knock England off kilter, thrashing 42 from 40 balls and leading Sri Lanka to tea with 43 needed. But the break allowed the tourists to take stock. Four balls after the restart, Leach trapped Lakmal, and the review proved in vain. The finale was a fitting microcosm of the series: England's spinners outbowled Sri Lanka's, while Sri Lanka's batsmen outcollapsed England's.

Man of the Match: J. M. Bairstow. *Man of the Series:* B. T. Foakes.

Close of play: first day, England 312-7 (Ali 23, Rashid 13); second day, England 3-0 (Burns 2, Jennings 1); third day, Sri Lanka 53-4 (Mendis 15, Sandakan 1).

England

R. J. Burns b Perera	14	– lbw b Perera	7
K. K. Jennings c Silva b Pushpakumara	13	– lbw b Perera	1
J. M. Bairstow b Sandakan	110	– c sub (J. K. Silva) b Perera	15
*J. E. Root c Gunathilleke b Sandakan	46	– c and b Pushpakumara	7
B. A. Stokes c de Silva b Sandakan	57	– c Pushpakumara b Perera	42
J. C. Buttler c and b Sandakan	16	– st Dickwella b Sandakan	64
M. M. Ali c Mathews b Perera	33	– c de Silva b Sandakan	22
†B. T. Foakes c Dickwella b Pushpakumara	13	– not out	36
A. U. Rashid not out	21	– c Dickwella b Pushpakumara	24
S. C. J. Broad b Sandakan	0	– c Mendis b Pushpakumara	1
M. J. Leach c Mathews b Perera	2	– c Dickwella b Perera	0
B 7, lb 3, nb 1	11	B 3, lb 4, w 1, nb 3	11

1/22 (1) 2/36 (2) 3/136 (4)   (92.5 overs) 336
4/235 (5) 5/254 (3) 6/265 (6)
7/294 (8) 8/328 (7) 9/329 (10) 10/336 (11)

1/3 (2) 2/20 (1)   (69.5 overs) 230
3/35 (3) 4/39 (4)
5/128 (5) 6/168 (6) 7/171 (7)
8/215 (9) 9/217 (10) 10/230 (11)

Lakmal 11–2–33–0; Perera 32.5–1–113–3; Pushpakumara 20–3–64–2; Sandakan 22–0–95–5; de Silva 5–0–16–0; Gunathilleke 2–0–5–0. *Second innings*—Perera 29.5–3–88–5; Pushpakumara 12–2–28–3; de Silva 9–1–24–0; Lakmal 3–1–7–0; Sandakan 16–1–76–2.

Sri Lanka

M. D. Gunathilleke c Jennings b Leach	18	– c Stokes b Ali	6
F. D. M. Karunaratne c Jennings b Rashid	83	– b Ali	23
D. M. de Silva c Jennings b Rashid	73	– lbw b Leach	0
B. K. G. Mendis c Stokes b Rashid	27	– run out (Leach)	86
A. D. Mathews c Foakes b Stokes	5	– c Broad b Stokes	5
A. R. S. Silva c Jennings b Rashid	3	– (7) lbw b Ali	65
†D. P. D. N. Dickwella c Foakes b Stokes	5	– (8) c Jennings b Leach	19
M. D. K. Perera c Foakes b Stokes	0	– (9) c Jennings b Ali	5
*R. A. S. Lakmal not out	3	– (10) lbw b Leach	11
P. A. D. L. R. Sandakan run out (Rashid)	2	– (6) c Stokes b Leach	7
P. M. Pushpakumara lbw b Rashid	13	– not out	42
Lb 7, w 1	8	B 8, w 5, nb 2	15

1/31 (1) 2/173 (3) 3/187 (2)	(65.5 overs) 240	1/15 (1) 2/24 (3)	(86.4 overs) 284
4/200 (5) 5/205 (6) 6/222 (7)		3/34 (2) 4/52 (5)	
7/222 (4) 8/222 (8) 9/224 (10) 10/240 (11)		5/82 (6) 6/184 (4) 7/214 (8)	
		8/225 (9) 9/226 (7) 10/284 (10)	

Broad 9–2–36–0; Leach 18–2–59–1; Ali 13–2–55–0; Rashid 13.5–2–49–5; Root 2–0–4–0; Stokes 10–1–30–3. *Second innings*—Broad 5–0–14–0; Ali 26–3–92–4; Leach 28.4–4–72–4; Stokes 8–1–25–1; Rashid 19–1–73–0.

Umpires: C. B. Gaffaney and S. Ravi.   Third umpire: M. Erasmus.
Referee: A. J. Pycroft.

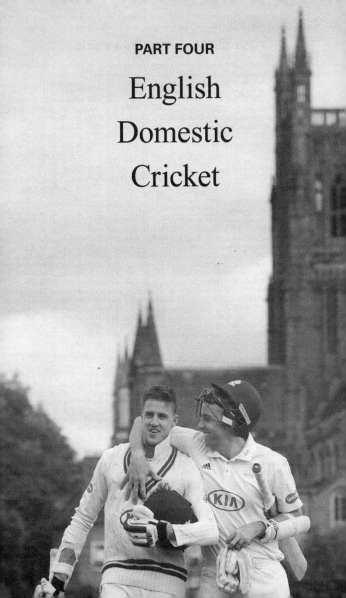

PART FOUR

English
Domestic
Cricket

FIRST-CLASS AVERAGES IN 2018

These include MCC v Essex at Bridgetown.

BATTING AND FIELDING (10 innings)

		M	I	NO	R	HS	100	50	Avge	Ct/St
1	O. J. D. Pope (*Surrey, Eng Lions & England*)	16	21	3	1,098	158*	4	2	61.00	26
2	†R. J. Burns (*Surrey & England Lions*)	15	24	1	1,402	193	4	7	60.95	11
3	V. Kohli (*Indians*)	5	10	0	593	149	2	3	59.30	4
4	I. R. Bell (*Warwicks*)	15	24	4	1,127	204	6	2	56.35	13
5	†S. G. Borthwick (*Surrey*)	9	13	2	619	175*	1	5	56.27	15
6	I. J. L. Trott (*Warwicks*)	15	24	4	1,046	170*	3	6	52.30	11
7	†M. T. Renshaw (*Somerset*)	6	11	1	513	112	3	1	51.30	5
8	B. C. Brown (*Sussex*)	15	25	4	1,031	119*	2	7	49.09	54/1
9	T. Köhler-Cadmore (*Yorks*)	6	11	2	414	106	2	2	46.00	4
10	J. C. Hildreth (*Somerset*)	14	26	2	1,089	184	3	6	45.37	13
11	S. R. Hain (*MCC & Warwicks*)	13	18	2	706	140*	1	6	44.12	9
12	J. C. Buttler (*Lancs & England*)	8	14	1	572	106	1	5	44.00	8
13	R. S. Bopara (*Essex*)	14	23	5	776	133*	2	4	43.11	8
14	†B. T. Slater (*Derbys & Notts*)	13	25	1	1,025	109	1	7	42.70	4
15	†W. M. H. Rhodes (*Warwicks*)	15	24	1	974	137	4	4	42.34	5
16	†A. N. Cook (*Essex, England & Eng Lions*)	14	25	0	1,041	180	2	6	41.64	22
17	T. B. Abell (*Somerset*)	14	26	4	883	132*	1	5	40.13	2
18	J. M. Vince (*Hants*)	14	25	1	962	201*	3	2	40.08	5
19	D. J. Vilas (*Lancs*)	15	24	2	879	235*	3	2	39.95	50/4
20	C. N. Ackermann (*Leics*)	14	24	2	876	196*	2	3	39.81	10
21	J. L. Denly (*Kent*)	16	26	2	954	119	4	3	39.75	3
22	S. S. Eskinazi (*Middx*)	13	23	1	874	134	1	5	39.72	16
23	†G. S. Ballance (*Yorks*)	12	23	0	906	194	3	4	39.39	4
24	†R. R. Pant (*India A & Indians*)	5	10	1	351	114	1	1	39.00	25
24	†W. D. Parnell (*Worcs*)	6	10	3	273	58*	0	3	39.00	1
26	†D. Elgar (*Surrey*)	7	10	0	387	110	1	2	38.70	6
27	W. L. Madsen (*Derbys*)	14	27	0	1,016	144	2	7	37.62	25
28	D. K. H. Mitchell (*Worcs*)	14	26	0	957	178	4	1	36.80	21
29	B. T. Foakes (*Surrey*)	12	18	1	624	90	0	4	36.70	37/1
30	†R. Rossouw (*Hants*)	10	18	3	550	120*	1	2	36.66	8
31	†K. K. Jennings (*Lancs & England*)	17	27	1	945	177	3	1	36.34	14
32	D. P. Sibley (*Warwicks*)	15	24	2	779	144*	4	1	35.40	18
33	†N. R. T. Gubbins (*Middx & England Lions*)	10	19	0	667	107	1	3	35.10	3
34	R. N. ten Doeschate (*Essex*)	14	23	3	702	173*	1	4	35.10	13
35	T. R. Ambrose (*Warwicks*)	15	21	2	666	103	1	3	35.05	58
36	†L. M. Reece (*Derbys*)	6	11	1	349	157*	1	1	34.90	2
37	N. J. Dexter (*Leics*)	12	20	3	585	87	0	3	34.41	9
38	J. M. Clarke (*Worcs*)	14	26	1	853	177*	3	1	34.12	8
39	†M. A. H. Hammond (*Glos*)	8	16	2	476	123*	2	2	34.00	6
40	H. G. Kuhn (*Kent*)	14	26	3	780	96*	0	6	33.91	21
41	†T. M. Head (*Worcs*)	6	11	1	339	62	0	3	33.90	2
42	L. R. P. L. Taylor (*Notts*)	8	15	0	506	146	1	4	33.73	13
43	J. Clark (*Lancs*)	11	16	0	538	82	0	5	33.62	2
43	D. Wiese (*Sussex*)	13	20	4	538	106	1	2	33.62	2
45	†C. D. J. Dent (*Glos*)	15	30	3	903	214*	1	4	33.44	11
46	J. M. Mennie (*Lancs*)	7	11	4	232	68*	0	2	33.14	1
47	†R. A. Whiteley (*Worcs*)	6	11	0	364	91	0	3	33.09	8
48	T. Westley (*Essex*)	15	26	1	825	134	2	3	33.00	2
49	†S. M. Davies (*Somerset*)	14	25	2	756	92*	0	5	32.86	38/3
50	S. P. Crook (*Northants*)	6	11	0	361	92	0	3	32.81	3
51	†K. Noema-Barnett (*Glos*)	9	16	6	327	73*	0	2	32.70	12
52	S. J. Croft (*Lancs*)	9	14	1	424	148*	1	2	32.61	10

	M	I	NO	R	HS	100	50	Avge	Ct/St
53 M. Vijay (*India A, Indians & Essex*)	6	11	0	357	100	1	3	32.45	3
54 J. A. R. Harris (*Middx*)	13	22	8	454	79*	0	3	32.42	6
55 A. J. A. Wheater (*Essex*)	10	16	3	420	68*	0	4	32.30	24/1
56 H. Z. Finch (*Sussex*)	15	25	0	802	103	1	6	32.08	25
57 ⎰ S. D. Robson (*Middx*)	14	25	1	768	135	2	2	32.00	7
⎱ †R. S. Vasconcelos (*Northants*)	11	20	1	608	140	1	4	32.00	15/1
59 †T. J. Haines (*Sussex*)	7	10	0	319	124	1	1	31.90	2
60 †J. H. K. Adams (*Hants*)	15	26	2	764	182*	2	1	31.83	15
61 J. A. Tattersall (*Yorks*)	7	12	1	350	70	0	2	31.81	19
62 R. Clarke (*Surrey*)	13	17	1	500	111	1	2	31.25	19
63 S. W. Billings (*Kent*)	8	14	2	370	85	0	2	30.83	20/2
64 Z. Crawley (*Kent*)	16	26	0	797	168	1	4	30.65	11
65 †T. P. Alsop (*Hants*)	8	14	1	397	99	0	4	30.53	22
66 D. M. Bess (*MCC, Somerset, Eng & E Lions*)	11	16	1	457	107	1	2	30.46	6
67 †J. R. Bracey (*Loughborough MCCU & Glos*)	16	30	3	819	125*	2	3	30.33	16
68 A. L. Davies (*Lancs*)	15	25	0	752	115	1	5	30.08	21/1
69 J. M. Bairstow (*Yorks & England*)	10	18	0	541	95	0	5	30.05	28/1
70 S. J. Mullaney (*Notts*)	11	20	0	601	130	1	4	30.05	11
71 †M. D. Stoneman (*Surrey & England*)	15	25	1	718	144	1	4	29.91	5
72 K. L. Rahul (*Indians*)	5	10	0	299	149	1	0	29.90	14
73 P. D. Salt (*Sussex*)	15	25	0	747	148	2	5	29.88	12
74 D. L. Lloyd (*Glam*)	10	18	2	474	119	1	1	29.62	3
75 J. E. Root (*Yorks & England*)	10	18	0	533	125	1	2	29.61	8
76 A. M. Rahane (*India A & Indians*)	6	12	0	354	81	0	2	29.50	4
77 M. G. K. Burgess (*Sussex*)	13	20	1	559	101*	1	2	29.42	4
78 S. R. Dickson (*Kent*)	16	28	1	793	134*	3	2	29.37	25
79 †T. J. Moores (*Notts*)	13	22	1	616	103	1	2	29.33	39
80 †M. D. E. Holden (*Middx*)	14	25	3	643	119*	1	3	29.22	4
81 †D. J. Malan (*Middx, England & Eng Lions*)	16	29	1	817	119	1	6	29.17	20
82 †R. S. Patel (*Surrey*)	10	15	3	350	48	0	0	29.16	4
83 C. T. Steel (*Durham*)	12	22	0	638	160	1	4	29.00	9
84 B. A. C. Howell (*Glos*)	14	25	1	693	89	0	5	28.87	9
85 A. G. Wakely (*Northants*)	14	22	1	600	106	1	4	28.57	4
86 †S. M. Curran (*Surrey, England & Eng Lions*)	13	19	1	513	78	0	3	28.50	3
87 M. H. Wessels (*Notts*)	12	23	3	568	75*	0	4	28.40	14
88 A. L. Hughes (*Derbys*)	14	27	1	737	103	1	5	28.34	9
89 P. J. Horton (*Leics*)	12	22	1	594	88	0	5	28.28	3
90 ⎰ M. J. J. Critchley (*Derbys*)	14	26	1	705	105	1	4	28.20	9
⎱ †N. L. J. Browne (*Essex*)	12	20	0	564	100	1	3	28.20	8
92 G. K. Berg (*Hants*)	10	14	2	335	84*	0	2	27.91	4
93 G. H. Roderick (*Glos*)	13	23	2	585	85*	0	5	27.85	49
94 G. A. Bartlett (*Somerset*)	6	11	0	306	110	1	0	27.81	2
95 A. M. Rossington (*Northants*)	12	21	1	551	90	0	4	27.55	34
96 G. C. Wilson (*Derbys*)	8	14	1	357	66	0	2	27.46	16
97 †A. Lyth (*Yorks*)	13	25	1	656	134*	1	2	27.33	16
98 †M. E. Trescothick (*Somerset*)	10	18	0	491	100	1	4	27.27	16
99 T. C. Fell (*Worcs*)	13	24	0	652	89	0	4	27.16	7
100 S. R. Harmer (*Essex*)	14	20	3	460	102*	1	1	27.05	13
101 H. R. Hosein (*Derbys*)	8	16	2	376	66*	0	3	26.85	12/1
102 J. A. Leaning (*Yorks*)	8	16	2	371	68	0	2	26.50	9
103 J. D. Libby (*Notts*)	14	27	2	662	100*	1	4	26.48	6
104 Azhar Ali (*Pakistans & Somerset*)	11	20	1	503	125	1	3	26.47	2
105 †B. A. Godleman (*Derbys*)	14	27	2	658	122	2	3	26.32	8
106 S. A. Northeast (*MCC & Hants*)	12	20	0	523	129	1	1	26.15	7
107 G. Stewart (*Kent*)	11	17	1	414	103	1	2	25.87	3
108 K. J. Abbott (*Hants*)	15	22	5	436	60*	0	2	25.64	0
109 S. R. Patel (*Notts*)	14	26	1	639	76	0	6	25.56	5
110 †L. W. P. Wells (*Sussex*)	15	25	1	613	102*	1	4	25.54	3
111 G. J. Harte (*Durham*)	8	15	0	382	114	2	0	25.46	4
112 †J. R. Murphy (*Glam*)	12	23	2	533	80	0	2	25.38	4

		M	I	NO	R	HS	100	50	Avge	Ct/St
113	R. E. Levi (*Northants*)	12	22	1	532	75	0	2	25.33	16
114	H. C. Brook (*Yorks*)	12	23	0	575	124	1	3	25.00	7
	S. W. Poynter (*Durham*)	11	20	1	475	170	1	1	25.00	34/1
	W. G. Jacks (*Surrey*)	7	10	1	225	53	0	1	25.00	8
117	†B. M. Duckett (*Northants & Notts*)	12	23	1	549	133	1	2	24.95	6
118	L. A. Dawson (*Hants*)	11	18	2	398	72	0	1	24.87	6
119	C. B. Cooke (*Glam*)	14	26	1	606	69	0	4	24.24	41/1
120	L. S. Livingstone (*Lancs*)	10	16	2	336	48*	0	0	24.00	15
121	R. F. Higgins (*Glos*)	15	25	3	526	105	1	2	23.90	6
122	†L. Wood (*Notts & Worcs*)	7	12	3	215	65*	0	1	23.88	5
123	J. M. R. Taylor (*Glos*)	11	20	1	452	112	1	0	23.78	4
124	†J. A. Simpson (*MCC & Middx*)	10	16	1	356	42*	0	1	23.73	27/4
125	C. A. Pujara (*Yorks & Indians*)	10	20	1	450	132*	1	1	23.68	4
126	K. S. Carlson (*Glam*)	13	25	1	567	152	1	1	23.62	5
127	E. G. Barnard (*Worcs*)	13	24	2	516	66	0	3	23.45	9
128	G. L. van Buuren (*Glos*)	8	15	1	327	83	0	3	23.35	2
129	D. W. Lawrence (*Essex*)	14	24	1	535	124	1	1	23.26	10
130	J. J. Weatherley (*Hants*)	13	22	1	486	126*	1	2	23.14	5
131	C. J. Jordan (*Sussex*)	8	13	0	299	68	0	2	23.00	5
132	C. D. Nash (*Notts*)	9	17	0	383	139	1	2	22.52	4
133	G. T. Griffiths (*Leics*)	12	18	8	225	40	0	0	22.50	2
134	†H. E. Dearden (*Leics*)	10	18	2	357	74	0	2	22.31	6
135	B. A. Raine (*Leics*)	11	17	0	371	65	0	1	21.82	5
136	M. J. Henry (*Kent*)	11	17	3	303	81	0	2	21.64	2
137	L. Gregory (*Somerset*)	12	21	2	411	65	0	3	21.63	12
138	†B. A. Stokes (*Durham & England*)	6	12	0	259	62	0	1	21.58	4
139	C. J. C. Wright (*Warwicks*)	15	18	2	342	72	0	2	21.37	3
140	N. J. Rimmington (*Durham*)	7	13	1	255	61	0	1	21.25	1
	A. G. Milton (*Cardiff MCCU & Worcs*)	9	14	2	255	104*	1	0	21.25	6/1
142	†L. A. Procter (*Northants*)	11	22	1	444	70	0	3	21.14	2
143	W. R. Smith (*Durham*)	9	17	0	357	90	0	2	21.00	5
144	M. J. Richardson (*Durham*)	10	18	0	377	115	1	1	20.94	3
145	G. Clark (*Durham*)	12	22	0	460	64	0	2	20.90	9
146	†E. J. Byrom (*Somerset*)	8	15	0	309	54	0	2	20.60	2
147	L. J. Wright (*Sussex*)	10	17	0	349	88	0	1	20.52	1
148	R. A. J. Smith (*Glam*)	7	14	2	246	52*	0	1	20.50	1
149	T. T. Bresnan (*Yorks*)	12	22	3	385	80	0	2	20.26	9
150	A. P. Rouse (*Kent & Surrey*)	10	14	2	242	55	0	1	20.16	28
151	M. E. Milnes (*Notts*)	6	10	5	100	43	0	0	20.00	4
152	†S. Chanderpaul (*Lancs*)	8	13	0	257	65	0	2	19.76	0
153	J. Overton (*Somerset*)	8	12	2	197	55	0	1	19.70	5
154	D. I. Stevens (*Kent*)	12	19	3	315	89	0	2	19.68	2
155	C. Overton (*Somerset*)	11	18	1	331	80	0	1	19.47	9
156	G. C. Viljoen (*Derbys*)	12	22	0	386	60*	0	1	19.30	1
157	L. D. McManus (*Hants*)	8	12	1	211	66	0	1	19.18	9
158	H. W. Podmore (*Kent*)	15	22	7	285	53	0	1	19.00	2
159	J. H. Davey (*Somerset*)	11	17	6	206	36	0	0	18.72	3
160	A. P. Palladino (*Derbys*)	12	23	6	317	32	0	0	18.64	1
161	S. A. Patterson (*Yorks*)	8	13	2	205	45*	0	0	18.63	2
162	J. K. Fuller (*Middx*)	8	16	3	242	71	0	1	18.61	3
163	L. J. Hill (*Leics*)	9	15	2	241	85	0	1	18.53	29
164	†M. J. Cosgrove (*Leics*)	14	24	0	440	75	0	3	18.33	6
	D. J. Bell-Drummond (*MCC & Kent*)	15	26	2	440	61	0	1	18.33	3
	E. J. H. Eckersley (*Leics*)	7	12	0	220	74	0	2	18.33	26
167	†K. H. D. Barker (*Warwicks*)	11	14	2	218	58	0	1	18.16	1
168	P. R. Stirling (*Middx*)	6	11	0	199	52	0	1	18.09	4
169	D. R. Briggs (*Sussex*)	12	20	7	234	46	0	0	18.00	5
170	O. B. Cox (*Worcs*)	12	22	1	372	65	0	2	17.71	35
171	P. M. Siddle (*Essex*)	7	11	2	158	33*	0	0	17.55	0
172	N. J. Selman (*Glam*)	12	23	0	403	42	0	0	17.52	21

		M	I	NO	R	HS	100	50	Avge	Ct/St
173	D. A. Payne (*Glos*)	7	11	6	86	31	0	0	17.20	1
174	J. C. Archer (*Sussex*)	8	13	3	170	33	0	0	17.00	6
175	B. O. Coad (*Yorks*)	9	15	7	135	33	0	0	16.87	0
176	T. van der Gugten (*Glam*)	10	18	5	217	60*	0	2	16.69	2
177	J. J. Cobb (*Northants*)	6	12	0	199	52	0	1	16.58	0
178	P. D. Collingwood (*MCC & Durham*)	12	21	0	344	47	0	0	16.38	12
179	†W. T. Root (*Notts*)	6	12	0	196	36	0	0	16.33	3
180	†S. A. Zaib (*Northants*)	7	11	1	163	57	0	1	16.30	0
181	J. T. Ball (*Notts*)	6	10	2	130	44*	0	0	16.25	1
182	†M. Morkel (*Surrey*)	11	14	2	194	29	0	0	16.16	1
183	†A. Z. Lees (*Yorks & Durham*)	10	19	0	306	69	0	1	16.10	4
184	J. A. Brooks (*Yorks*)	13	22	3	303	82	0	1	15.94	1
185	A. Javid (*Leics*)	6	10	0	157	58	0	1	15.70	2
186	H. W. R. Cartwright (*Middx*)	8	13	0	204	80	0	1	15.69	7
187	V. Chopra (*Essex*)	7	13	0	201	61	0	1	15.46	7
188	T. E. Bailey (*Lancs*)	15	22	2	308	66	0	1	15.40	6
189	O. E. Robinson (*Sussex*)	15	23	3	307	52	0	1	15.35	5
190	B. L. D'Oliveira (*MCC & Worcs*)	11	20	0	306	65	0	1	15.30	2
191	T. D. Groenewald (*Somerset*)	7	11	5	91	36*	0	0	15.16	2
192	A. G. Salter (*Glam*)	10	17	3	204	72*	0	1	14.57	8
193	C. F. Parkinson (*Leics*)	12	19	1	252	48	0	0	14.00	1
	S. J. Cook (*Essex*)	10	11	7	56	14	0	0	14.00	1
195	L. J. Fletcher (*Notts*)	13	23	1	304	43	0	0	13.81	4
196	I. G. Holland (*Hants*)	7	11	1	135	31	0	0	13.50	3
197	C. N. Miles (*Glos*)	14	20	5	201	38*	0	0	13.40	4
198	†T. J. Murtagh (*Middx*)	12	19	4	200	40	0	0	13.33	3
199	†M. J. Leach (*Somerset & England Lions*)	12	17	3	186	66	0	1	13.28	5
200	B. J. Twohig (*Worcs*)	7	13	2	145	35	0	0	13.18	1
201	J. C. Tongue (*Worcs*)	11	19	3	201	34	0	0	12.56	2
202	H. F. Gurney (*Notts*)	11	16	10	73	29*	0	0	12.16	1
203	I. Sharma (*Sussex & Indians*)	9	15	3	144	66	0	1	12.00	1
204	†S. C. J. Broad (*Notts & England*)	12	18	0	212	38	0	0	11.77	5
205	J. W. Dernbach (*Surrey*)	10	13	2	129	31	0	0	11.72	2
206	M. G. Hogan (*Glam*)	13	21	8	152	28	0	0	11.69	7
207	J. S. Patel (*Warwicks*)	14	19	3	184	32	0	0	11.50	4
208	O. P. Rayner (*Middx & Hants*)	12	17	2	172	28	0	0	11.46	16
209	B. J. McCarthy (*Durham*)	6	11	1	111	43	0	0	11.10	2
210	M. D. Taylor (*Glos*)	15	19	3	177	48	0	0	11.06	4
211	†E. J. G. Morgan (*Middx*)	6	11	0	121	76	0	1	11.00	4
212	E. R. Bamber (*Middx*)	6	10	3	76	27*	0	0	10.85	2
213	N. L. Buck (*Northants*)	9	15	2	135	20	0	0	10.38	0
214	R. G. White (*Middx*)	6	11	1	101	35	0	0	10.10	14
215	M. E. T. Salisbury (*Durham*)	10	19	5	141	37	0	0	10.07	1
216	B. A. Hutton (*Northants*)	13	22	2	198	27	0	0	9.90	9
217	H. Hameed (*Lancs*)	11	18	0	170	31	0	0	9.44	6
218	†S. J. Magoffin (*Worcs*)	6	10	3	65	43	0	0	9.28	0
219	G. Onions (*Lancs*)	13	19	4	135	41	0	0	9.00	1
	B. W. Sanderson (*Northants*)	13	21	13	72	36	0	0	9.00	3
221	G. S. Virdi (*Surrey*)	15	17	8	79	21*	0	0	8.77	5
222	D. Olivier (*Derbys*)	7	11	2	78	40*	0	0	8.66	0
223	D. Y. Pennington (*Worcs*)	8	14	3	94	37	0	0	8.54	4
224	†R. Rampaul (*Derbys*)	8	11	5	51	18*	0	0	8.50	2
225	C. R. Brown (*Glam*)	6	12	0	95	33	0	0	7.91	3
226	R. J. Gleeson (*MCC, Northants & Lancs*)	7	11	5	47	26	0	0	7.83	2
227	Mohammad Abbas (*Leics & Pakistanis*)	13	19	7	92	32*	0	0	7.66	2
228	C. Rushworth (*Durham*)	12	22	12	72	11*	0	0	7.20	2
229	F. H. Edwards (*MCC & Hants*)	16	20	9	75	14	0	0	6.81	4
230	J. A. Porter (*Essex & England Lions*)	16	20	4	108	31	0	0	6.75	3
231	L. H. Ferguson (*Derbys*)	5	10	2	51	16	0	0	6.37	4
232	M. W. Parkinson (*Lancs*)	7	11	5	35	9*	0	0	5.83	1

		M	I	NO	R	HS	100	50	Avge	Ct/St
233	†J. M. Anderson (*Lancs & England*).......	10	14	8	34	11	0	0	5.66	2
234	R. N. Sidebottom (*Warwicks*)	10	12	6	30	10*	0	0	5.00	5
235	Mohammed Shami (*Indians*).............	5	10	1	27	10*	0	0	3.00	2
236	I. A. A. Thomas (*Kent*)	13	14	8	17	4*	0	0	2.83	6

BOWLING (10 wickets in 5 innings)

		Style	O	M	R	W	BB	5I	Avge
1	B. D. Cotton (*Northants*)	RFM	44	13	101	10	5-48	1	10.10
2	O. P. Stone (*Warwicks*).............	RF	161.2	26	529	43	8-80	3	12.30
3	A. R. Patel (*Durham*)	SLA	99.4	33	235	18	7-54	1	13.05
4	M. Morkel (*Surrey*)................	RF	339.4	90	907	63	6-57	4	14.39
5	T. J. Murtagh (*Middx*)	RFM	359.5	95	888	58	5-38	2	15.31
6	M. J. Henry (*Kent*)	RFM	382.4	83	1,161	75	7-42	5	15.48
7	Z. J. Chappell (*Leics*)	RFM	76	13	255	16	6-44	1	15.93
8	R. J. Gleeson (*MCC, Northants & Lancs*)	RFM	180.3	42	548	34	6-79	2	16.11
9	B. O. Coad (*Yorks*)	RFM	272.5	87	784	48	6-81	3	16.33
10	P. M. Siddle (*Essex*)	RFM	234.4	47	607	37	5-37	3	16.40
11	T. K. Curran (*Surrey*)	RFM	120.4	30	312	19	5-28	1	16.42
12	K. H. D. Barker (*Warwicks*)	LFM	259.1	71	682	41	5-32	2	16.63
13	K. A. Maharaj (*Lancs*)	SLA	103.4	23	283	17	7-37	1	16.64
14	B. W. Sanderson (*Northants*)	RFM	422	112	1,002	60	5-16	2	16.70
15	L. M. Reece (*Derbys*)	LM	64.1	13	186	11	7-20	1	16.90
16	O. E. Robinson (*Sussex*)	RFM/OB	500.4	96	1,412	81	7-39	5	17.43
17	Mohammad Abbas (*Leics & Pakistanis*)	RFM	433.1	124	1,124	64	6-48	5	17.56
18	J. C. Archer (*Sussex*).............	RFM	273.5	67	750	42	5-69	1	17.85
19	J. L. Denly (*Kent*)	LB	160.1	28	426	23	4-36	0	18.52
20	R. F. Higgins (*Glos*)	RM	359.5	102	892	48	5-21	2	18.58
21	C. McKerr (*Surrey*)...............	RFM	67.2	13	246	13	4-26	0	18.92
22	D. I. Stevens (*Kent*).	RM	295.4	76	799	42	6-26	2	19.02
23	D. W. Steyn (*Hants*)	RFM	142.3	30	382	20	5-66	1	19.10
24	M. M. Ali (*Worcs & England*)	OB/RM	183.5	29	586	30	6-49	3	19.53
25	S. P. Crook (*Northants*)	RFM	58.2	7	235	12	4-51	0	19.58
26	M. A. Wood (*Durham & England*)....	RFM	136.4	31	374	19	6-46	2	19.68
27	T. E. Bailey (*Lancs*)	RFM	454.4	114	1,281	65	5-53	1	19.70
28	A. P. Palladino (*Derbys*)	RFM	369	94	1,006	51	6-29	3	19.72
29	M. K. Andersson (*Derbys & Middx*) .	RM	70	5	239	12	4-25	0	19.91
30	C. Rushworth (*Durham*)	RFM	386.4	83	1,201	60	8-51	3	20.01
31	R. K. Kleinveldt (*Northants*)	RFM	95.1	14	282	14	4-51	0	20.14
32	E. R. Bamber (*Middx*).	RFM	203.5	37	567	28	4-81	0	20.25
33	B. W. M. Mike (*Leics*)	RFM	87.2	10	385	19	5-37	1	20.26
34	W. J. Weighell (*Durham*)	RM	108.3	23	304	15	7-32	1	20.26
35	J. A. R. Harris (*Middx*)	RFM	384.5	67	1,253	61	7-83	2	20.54
36	C. N. Miles (*Glos*).	RFM	341.1	65	1,213	58	5-50	2	20.91
37	J. M. Anderson (*Lancs & England*) ...	RFM	337.4	99	887	42	5-20	1	21.11
38	J. M. Mennie (*Lancs*)	RFM	192.5	44	601	28	4-43	0	21.46
39	R. Clarke (*Surrey*).	RFM	363.1	87	1,012	47	5-29	1	21.53
40	S. M. Curran (*Surrey, Eng & Eng Lions*)	LFM	303	55	970	45	6-54	2	21.55
41	H. W. R. Cartwright (*Middx*)	RM	122.2	16	410	19	4-33	0	21.57
42	G. Onions (*Lancs*)................	RFM	398.3	81	1,275	59	6-55	2	21.61
43	D. J. Worrall (*Glos*).	RFM	119.1	33	348	16	4-45	0	21.75
44	T. van der Gugten (*Glam*).	RFM	287	69	936	43	7-42	2	21.76
45	O. J. Hannon-Dalby (*Warwicks*)	RFM	103.4	22	329	15	4-61	0	21.93
46	J. Leach (*Worcs*)	RFM	157.5	28	508	23	4-42	0	22.08
47	J. T. Ball (*Notts*)	RFM	171.5	38	623	28	5-43	2	22.25
48	H. J. H. Brookes (*Warwicks*)	RFM	142	22	470	21	4-54	0	22.38
49	B. A. Raine (*Leics*)	RFM	395.1	90	1,146	51	4-44	0	22.47
50	M. G. Hogan (*Glam*)	RFM	393.3	101	1,014	45	5-49	2	22.53
51	J. S. Patel (*Warwicks*)	OB	431.4	108	1,276	56	7-83	4	22.78
52	G. Stewart (*Kent*)	RFM	164.5	26	505	22	6-22	1	22.95

		Style	O	M	R	W	BB	5I	Avge
53	H. W. Podmore (*Kent*)	RM	353.4	85	1,037	45	6-36	1	23.04
54	K. J. Abbott (*Hants*)	RFM	348.3	70	1,182	51	6-39	4	23.17
55	E. G. Barnard (*Worcs*)	RFM	368.3	93	1,138	49	6-37	4	23.22
56	M. D. Taylor (*Glos*)	LM	358	66	1,186	51	5-15	2	23.25
57	S. C. J. Broad (*Notts & England*)	RFM	324.2	86	967	41	4-41	0	23.58
58	I. Sharma (*Sussex & Indians*)	RFM	265.3	55	783	33	5-51	1	23.72
59	M. de Lange (*Glam*)	RF	114.4	22	383	16	5-62	1	23.93
60	B. A. Stokes (*Durham & England*)	RFM	181.2	33	599	25	5-52	1	23.96
61	T. D. Groenewald (*Somerset*)	RFM	173	41	509	21	4-85	0	24.23
62	M. J. Leach (*Somerset & England Lions*)	SLA	262.4	57	757	31	8-85	3	24.41
63	S. R. Harmer (*Essex*)	OB	526.2	136	1,394	57	6-87	3	24.45
64	G. T. Griffiths (*Leics*)	RFM	269	67	882	36	6-49	1	24.50
65	H. H. Pandya (*Indians*)	RFM	64.1	7	247	10	5-28	1	24.70
66	S. A. Patterson (*Yorks*)	RFM	235	63	594	24	6-40	1	24.75
67	M. E. T. Salisbury (*Durham*)	RFM	293.1	54	1,090	44	6-37	1	24.77
68	J. Overton (*Somerset*)	RFM	177.3	34	646	26	4-25	0	24.84
69	L. Gregory (*Somerset*)	RFM	305.5	75	928	37	4-33	0	25.08
70	J. A. Porter (*Essex & England Lions*)	RFM	476.3	94	1,564	62	7-41	3	25.22
70	N. L. Buck (*Northants*)	RFM	196.5	22	782	31	4-51	0	25.22
72	K. A. Bull (*Glam*)	OB	85.4	14	278	11	3-36	0	25.27
73	J. C. Tongue (*Worcs*)	RFM	304.4	52	1,011	40	5-53	2	25.27
74	S. J. Cook (*Essex*)	RFM	219.3	60	684	27	5-28	1	25.33
75	J. H. Davey (*Somerset*)	RFM	290.4	73	862	34	5-65	1	25.35
76	D. Wiese (*Sussex*)	RFM	339.1	65	1,041	41	5-48	1	25.39
77	M. R. Quinn (*Essex*)	RFM	101	19	306	12	3-23	0	25.50
77	A. L. Hughes (*Derbys*)	RM	87	19	255	10	4-57	0	25.50
79	L. J. Fletcher (*Notts*)	RFM	347.3	86	977	38	5-27	1	25.71
80	R. N. Sidebottom (*Warwicks*)	RFM	187	40	644	25	6-35	1	25.76
81	T. B. Abell (*Somerset*)	RM	121.4	23	492	19	4-43	0	25.89
82	J. J. Bumrah (*Indians*)	RFM	133.2	31	363	14	5-85	1	25.92
83	I. G. Holland (*Hants*)	RFM	151	42	389	15	3-48	0	25.93
84	D. A. Payne (*Glos*)	LFM	204.2	42	573	22	4-25	0	26.04
85	Shadab Khan (*Pakistanis*)	LB	110.5	14	392	15	6-77	1	26.13
86	B. A. Hutton (*Northants*)	RFM	392.2	91	1,212	46	8-57	3	26.34
87	I. A. A. Thomas (*Kent*)	RFM	196	34	662	25	5-91	1	26.48
88	C. R. Woakes (*Warwicks, Eng & E Lions*)	RFM	144	52	514	19	3-55	0	27.05
89	H. F. Gurney (*Notts*)	LFM	325.3	52	1,137	42	6-25	2	27.07
90	D. R. Briggs (*Sussex*)	SLA	279.5	51	764	28	4-70	0	27.28
91	C. Overton (*Somerset*)	RFM	321.3	72	1,014	37	4-27	0	27.40
92	N. J. Dexter (*Leics*)	RM	169	40	494	18	3-17	0	27.44
93	D. Olivier (*Derbys*)	RFM	251.3	47	852	31	5-20	2	27.48
94	D. A. J. Bracewell (*Northants*)	RFM	93	19	304	11	4-71	0	27.63
95	S. Nadeem (*India A*)	SLA	105	16	332	12	3-42	0	27.66
95	J. E. Poysden (*Warwicks & Yorks*)	LB	75.4	3	332	12	5-29	1	27.66
97	T. T. Bresnan (*Yorks*)	RFM	279.5	48	969	35	5-28	1	27.68
98	F. H. Edwards (*MCC & Hants*)	RFM	388.2	60	1,530	55	6-50	2	27.81
99	J. A. Brooks (*Yorks*)	RFM	346.3	51	1,430	51	6-94	5	28.03
100	J. Clark (*Lancs*)	RM	217.1	28	730	26	5-58	1	28.07
101	R. A. Reifer (*West Indies A*)	LFM	89.3	15	311	11	5-50	1	28.27
102	M. W. Parkinson (*Lancs*)	LB	170.1	30	512	18	5-101	1	28.44
103	J. W. Dernbach (*Surrey*)	RFM	285.5	65	929	32	4-49	0	29.03
104	S. H. Lewis (*West Indies A*)	RFM	88.1	15	351	12	4-35	0	29.25
105	L. A. Procter (*Northants*)	RM	117.1	22	411	14	5-33	1	29.35
106	R. A. J. Smith (*Glam*)	RM	155.3	24	593	20	5-87	1	29.65
107	C. J. Jordan (*Sussex*)	RFM	191.1	32	598	20	3-23	0	29.90
108	J. K. Fuller (*Middx*)	RFM	227.2	25	845	28	4-49	0	30.17
109	A. U. Rashid (*England*)	LB	87	10	309	10	3-101	0	30.90
110	L. A. Dawson (*Hants*)	SLA	205.2	36	627	20	4-30	0	31.35
111	C. J. C. Wright (*Warwicks*)	RFM	378.2	68	1,292	41	5-32	1	31.51
112	G. S. Virdi (*Surrey*)	OB	383.3	47	1,263	40	6-105	1	31.57

		Style	O	M	R	W	BB	5I	Avge
113	G. C. Viljoen (*Derbys*)	RFM	356.1	55	1,225	38	4-51	0	32.23
114	W. D. Parnell (*Worcs*)	LFM	154.4	22	582	18	4-23	0	32.33
115	R. Ashwin (*Indians*)	OB	139.4	30	360	11	4-62	0	32.72
116	M. Carter (*Notts*)	OB	153.2	28	525	16	5-113	1	32.81
117	B. J. McCarthy (*Durham*)	RFM	130.3	21	460	14	4-58	0	32.85
118	L. H. Ferguson (*Derbys*)	RF	164.3	22	618	18	4-56	0	34.33
119	M. T. Coles (*Essex*)	RFM	147	31	485	14	5-123	1	34.64
120	D. Y. Pennington (*Worcs*)	RFM	187	34	778	22	4-53	0	35.36
121	S. J. Mullaney (*Notts*)	RM	114	21	402	11	4-68	0	36.54
122	S. J. Magoffin (*Worcs*)	RFM	202	55	593	16	3-70	0	37.06
123	D. M. Bess (*MCC, Som, Eng & E Lions*)	OB	285.5	59	891	24	6-51	1	37.12
124	M. J. J. Critchley (*Derbys*)	LB	285.5	14	1,218	32	6-106	1	38.06
125	Mohammed Shami (*Indians*)	RFM	172.4	25	622	16	4-57	0	38.87
126	B. T. J. Wheal (*Hants*)	RFM	114.5	17	462	11	2-46	0	42.00
127	A. G. Salter (*Glam*)	OB	245	45	759	18	4-80	0	42.16
128	G. K. Berg (*Hants*)	RFM	200.1	41	654	15	5-130	1	43.60
129	O. P. Rayner (*Middx & Hants*)	OB	218.5	52	530	12	4-54	0	44.16
130	L. J. Carey (*Glam*)	RFM	172	36	592	13	4-105	0	45.53
131	S. R. Patel (*Notts*)	SLA	305.5	66	896	19	6-114	1	47.15
132	L. Wood (*Notts & Worcs*)	LFM	142.1	21	519	11	3-66	0	47.18
133	M. E. Milnes (*Notts*)	RFM	153	26	527	11	4-44	0	47.90
134	R. Rampaul (*Derbys*)	RFM	183.3	35	651	13	3-53	0	50.07
135	N. J. Rimmington (*Durham*)	RFM	167.4	34	606	11	3-39	0	55.09
136	B. J. Twohig (*Worcs*)	SLA	161	18	598	10	2-47	0	59.80
137	C. F. Parkinson (*Leics*)	SLA	239	42	824	10	3-50	0	82.40

The following bowlers took ten wickets in fewer than five innings:

	Style	O	M	R	W	BB	5I	Avge
M. Siraj (*India A*)	RFM	85.5	14	266	15	4-64	0	17.73
S. Prasanna (*Northants*)	LB	72	7	247	10	4-49	0	24.70

BOWLING STYLES

LB	Leg-breaks (7)	**RF**	Right-arm fast (4)
LFM	Left-arm fast medium (7)	**RFM**	Right-arm fast medium (87)
LM	Left-arm medium (2)	**RM**	Right-arm medium (14)
OB	Off-breaks (11)	**SLA**	Slow left-arm (9)

Note: The total comes to 141 because M. M. Ali and O. E. Robinson have two styles of bowling.

INDIVIDUAL SCORES OF 100 AND OVER

There were **166** three-figure innings in 147 first-class matches in 2018, which was 53 fewer than in 2017, when 153 matches were played. Of these, six were double-hundreds, compared with 18 in 2017. The list includes 136 in the County Championship, compared with 181 in 2017.

I. R. Bell (6)
100 Warwicks v Durham MCCU, Birmingham
106*
115*} Warwicks v Glam, Birmingham
172 Warwicks v Kent, Tunbridge Wells
204 Warwicks v Glam, Colwyn Bay
112 Warwicks v Sussex, Hove

R. J. Burns (4)
193 Surrey v Worcs, The Oval
151 Surrey v Hants, Southampton
153 Surrey v Notts, Nottingham
122 Surrey v Worcs, Worcester

J. L. Denly (4)
113* Kent v Pakistanis, Canterbury
107 Kent v Glos, Bristol
119 Kent v Warwicks, Tunbridge Wells
106 Kent v Derbys, Derby

D. K. H. Mitchell (4)
118
163} Worcs v Lancs, Worcester
178 Worcs v Yorks, Scarborough
127 Worcs v Yorks, Worcester

O. J. D. Pope (4)
145 Surrey v Hants, The Oval
158* Surrey v Yorks, The Oval
117 Surrey v Somerset, Guildford
114 Surrey v Essex, The Oval

W. M. H. Rhodes (4)
100* Warwicks v Northants, Birmingham
118 Warwicks v Middx, Lord's
137 Warwicks v Glos, Birmingham
110 Warwicks v Kent, Birmingham

D. P. Sibley (4)
104 Warwicks v Kent, Tunbridge Wells
106 Warwicks v Leics, Leicester
144* Warwicks v Sussex, Hove
119 Warwicks v Kent, Birmingham

G. S. Ballance (3)
109 Yorks v Hants, Southampton
104 Yorks v Notts, Nottingham
194 Yorks v Worcs, Worcester

J. M. Clarke (3)
157 Worcs v Surrey, The Oval
105 Worcs v Essex, Worcester
177* Worcs v Notts, Nottingham

S. R. Dickson (3)
117 Kent v Glos, Bristol
133 Kent v Warwicks, Tunbridge Wells
134* Kent v Leics, Leicester

J. C. Hildreth (3)
111* Somerset v Worcs, Taunton
184 Somerset v Hants, Taunton
137 Somerset v Notts, Nottingham

K. K. Jennings (3)
109 Lancs v Somerset, Manchester
126 Lancs v Notts, Nottingham
177 Lancs v Worcs, Worcester

U. T. Khawaja (3)
125 Glam v Warwicks, Birmingham
126 Glam v Derbys, Swansea
103 Glam v Northants, Cardiff

M. T. Renshaw (3)
101* Somerset v Worcs, Taunton
112 Somerset v Yorks, Taunton
106 Somerset v Notts, Taunton

I. J. L. Trott (3)
111* Warwicks v Durham MCCU, Birmingham
170* Warwicks v Durham, Chester-le-Street
124 Warwicks v Sussex, Hove

D. J. Vilas (3)
235* Lancs v Somerset, Manchester
134 Lancs v Hants, Manchester
107* Lancs v Worcs, Southport

J. M. Vince (3)
201* Hants v Somerset, Taunton
103 Hants v Lancs, Manchester
147 Hants v Notts, Southampton

C. N. Ackermann (2)
186 Leics v Sussex, Leicester
196* Leics v Middx, Leicester

J. H. K. Adams (2)
182* Hants v Cardiff MCCU, Southampton
147 Hants v Yorks, Southampton

H. M. Amla (2)
112 Hants v Notts, Nottingham
107 Hants v Somerset, Taunton

G. J. Harte (2)
114 Durham v Derbys, Chester-le-Street
112 Durham v Middx, Chester-le-Street

R. S. Bopara (2)
118 Essex v Somerset, Chelmsford
133* Essex v Worcs, Chelmsford

T. Köhler-Cadmore (2)
106 Yorks v Notts, Nottingham
105* Yorks v Lancs, Leeds

J. R. Bracey (2)
120* Glos v Glam, Bristol
125* Glos v Middx, Lord's

V. Kohli (2)
149 India v England, Birmingham
103 India v England, Nottingham

B. C. Brown (2)
119* Sussex v Loughborough MCCU, Hove
116 Sussex v Derbys, Hove

W. L. Madsen (2)
144 Derbys v Warwicks, Birmingham
116 Derbys v Northants, Chesterfield

A. N. Cook (2)
180 England Lions v India A, Worcester
147 England v India, The Oval

S. D. Robson (2)
135 Middx v Durham MCCU, Northwood
134 Middx v Derbys, Lord's

B. A. Godleman (2)
122 Derbys v Sussex, Hove
105* Derbys v Middx, Lord's

P. D. Salt (2)
130 Sussex v Durham, Arundel
148 Sussex v Derbys, Hove

M. A. Hammond (2)
103 Glos v Sussex, Cheltenham
123* Glos v Middx, Bristol

T. Westley (2)
110* Essex v Notts, Nottingham
134 Essex v Surrey, The Oval

The following each played one three-figure innings:

T. B. Abell, 132*, Somerset v Yorks, Leeds; M. M. Ali, 219, Worcs v Yorks, Scarborough; S. W. Ambris, 128, West Indies A v India A, Beckenham; T. R. Ambrose, 103, Warwicks v Northants, Northampton; Asad Shafiq, 186*, Pakistanis v Northants, Northampton; Azhar Ali, 125, Somerset v Worcs, Worcester.

G. A. Bartlett, 110, Somerset v Lancs, Manchester; D. M. Bess, 107, MCC v Essex, Bridgetown; S. G. Borthwick, 175*, Surrey v West Indies A, The Oval; H. C. Brook, 124, Yorks v Essex, Chelmsford; S. S. J. Brooks, 122*, West Indies A v India A, Taunton; N. L. J. Browne, 100, Essex v Cambridge MCCU, Cambridge; M. G. K. Burgess, 101*, Sussex v Leics, Leicester; J. C. Buttler, 106, England v India, Nottingham.

K. S. Carlson, 152, Glam v Derbys, Swansea; R. Clarke, 111, Surrey v Notts, Nottingham; Z. Crawley, 168, Kent v Glam, Canterbury; M. J. J. Critchley, 105, Derbys v Middx, Lord's; S. J. Croft, 148*, Lancs v Loughborough MCCU, Loughborough.

A. L. Davies, 115, Lancs v Hants, Manchester; C. D. J. Dent, 214*, Glos v Leics, Bristol; B. M. Duckett, 133, Northants v Glam, Cardiff.

D. Elgar, 101, Surrey v West Indies A, The Oval; D. A. Escott, 175, Oxford Univ v Cambridge Univ, Oxford; S. S. Eskinazi, 134, Middx v Durham MCCU, Northwood.

H. Z. Finch, 103, Sussex v Middx, Hove.

N. R. T. Gubbins, 107, Middx v Sussex, Hove; M. J. Guptill, 111, Worcs v Lancs, Worcester.

S. R. Hain, 140*, MCC v Essex, Bridgetown; T. J. Haines, 124, Sussex v Durham, Arundel; S. R. Harmer, 102*, Essex v Surrey, The Oval; R. F. Higgins, 105, Glos v Durham, Cheltenham; M. D. E. Holden, 119*, Middx v Derbys, Lord's; A. L. Hughes, 103, Derbys v Glam, Swansea.

T. W. M. Latham, 147, Durham v Glos, Cheltenham; D. W. Lawrence, 124, Essex v Hants, Chelmsford; J. D. Libby, 100*, Notts v Worcs, Nottingham; D. L. Lloyd, 119, Glam v Glos, Bristol; A. Lyth, 134*, Yorks v Hants, Leeds.

D. J. Malan, 119, Middx v Sussex, Hove; S. E. Marsh, 111, Glam v Glos, Bristol; A. G. Milton, 104*, Worcs v Somerset, Worcester; T. J. Moores, 103, Notts v Somerset, Taunton; S. J. Mullaney, 130, Notts v Hants, Nottingham.

C. D. Nash, 139, Notts v Worcs, Nottingham; M. A. Naylor, 202, Oxford Univ v Cambridge Univ, Oxford; R. I. Newton, 118, Northants v Pakistanis, Northampton; S. A. Northeast, 129, Hants v Surrey, The Oval.

R. R. Pant, 114, India v England, The Oval; S. W. Poynter, 170, Durham v Derbys, Derby; C. A. Pujara, 132*, India v England, Southampton.

K. L. Rahul, 149, India v England, The Oval; L. M. Reece, 157*, Derbys v Middx, Derby; M. J. Richardson, 115, Durham v Derbys, Derby; J. E. Root, 125, England v India, The Oval; R. R. Rossouw, 120*, Hants v Lancs, Manchester; J. J. Roy, 128, Surrey v Essex, The Oval.

R. Samarth, 137, India A v West Indies A, Beckenham; P. P. Shaw, 188, India A v West Indies A, Beckenham; B. T. Slater, 109, Notts v Yorks, Nottingham; C. T. Steel, 160, Durham v Sussex, Chester-le-Street; G. Stewart, 103, Kent v Middx, Canterbury; M. D. Stoneman, 144, Surrey v Notts, The Oval.

J. M. R. Taylor, 112, Glos v Glam, Cardiff; L. R. P. L. Taylor, 146, Notts v Essex, Chelmsford; R. N. ten Doeschate, 173*, Essex v Somerset, Chelmsford; M. E. Trescothick, 100, Somerset v Lancs, Manchester.

R. S. Vasconcelos, 140, Northants v Middx, Northampton; M. Vijay, 100, Essex v Notts, Nottingham.

A. G. Wakely, 106, Northants v Derbys, Chesterfield; J. J. Weatherley, 126*, Hants v Lancs, Manchester; L. W. P. Wells, 102*, Sussex v Leics, Leicester; D. Wiese, 106, Sussex v Warwicks, Birmingham; C. R. Woakes, 137*, England v India, Lord's.

FASTEST HUNDREDS BY BALLS...

Balls

71	G. Stewart	Kent v Middlesex, Canterbury.
72	P. P. Shaw	India A v West Indies A, Beckenham.
86	M. T. Renshaw	Somerset v Yorkshire, Taunton.
87	P. D. Salt	Sussex v Derbyshire, Hove.
91	D. Wiese	Sussex v Warwickshire, Birmingham.
92	J. J. Roy	Surrey v Essex, The Oval.
93	B. M. Duckett	Northamptonshire v Glamorgan, Cardiff.
97	M. J. Guptill	Worcestershire v Lancashire, Worcester.
97	O. J. D. Pope	Surrey v Essex, The Oval.

...AND THE SLOWEST

Balls

277	J. M. Vince	Hampshire v Somerset, Taunton.
274	J. R. Bracey	Gloucestershire v Glamorgan, Bristol.
268	L. M. Reece	Derbyshire v Middlesex, Derby.
244	I. R. Bell	Warwickshire v Glamorgan, Birmingham.
234	K. K. Jennings	Lancashire v Somerset, Manchester.
234	D. P. Sibley	Warwickshire v Kent, Birmingham.
232	J. R. Bracey	Gloucestershire v Middlesex, Lord's.
232	D. P. Sibley	Warwickshire v Kent, Tunbridge Wells.

TEN WICKETS IN A MATCH

There were **23** instances of bowlers taking ten or more wickets in a first-class match in 2018, one more than in 2017. Twenty-two were in the County Championship.

M. J. Henry (3)
12-73   Kent v Durham, Chester-le-Street
10-122 Kent v Sussex, Canterbury
11-114 Kent v Northants, Canterbury

M. J. Leach (2)
10-112 Somerset v Essex, Taunton
12-102 Somerset v Lancs, Taunton

J. S. Patel (2)
10-170   Warwicks v Derbys, Birmingham
10-106   Warwicks v Glam, Colwyn Bay

The following each took ten wickets in a match on one occasion:

K. J. Abbott, 11-71, Hants v Somerset, Southampton.

E. G. Barnard, 11-89, Worcs v Somerset, Taunton.

B. O. Coad, 10-130, Yorks v Notts, Leeds; M. J. J. Critchley, 10-194, Derbys v Northants, Chesterfield; S. M. Curran, 10-101, Surrey v Yorks, The Oval.

G. T. Griffiths, 10-83, Leics v Durham, Chester-le-Street.

K. A. Maharaj, 11-102, Lancs v Somerset, Taunton; Mohammad Abbas, 10-52, Leics v Durham, Leicester.

D. Olivier, 10-125, Derbys v Durham, Chester-le-Street.

A. P. Palladino, 10-81, Derbys v Glam, Derby; J. A. Porter, 11-98, Essex v Worcs, Chelmsford.

O. E. Robinson, 10-67, Sussex v Leics, Hove; C. Rushworth, 12-100, Durham v Sussex, Chester-le-Street.

Shadab Khan, 10-157, Pakistanis v Northants, Northampton; R. N. Sidebottom, 10-96, Warwicks v Northants, Northampton; O. P. Stone, 11-96, Warwicks v Durham, Birmingham.

SPECSAVERS COUNTY CHAMPIONSHIP IN 2018

Neville Scott

Division One 1 *Surrey* 2 *Somerset*
Division Two 1 *Warwickshire* 2 *Kent*

For two years, a Championship review in the style of poor detective fiction (champo noir, perhaps) might risk the same, faux-weighty opening: "It all began at Guildford…" Banal, but true. What's more, both title bids then followed remarkably similar courses. On June 12, 2017, Essex beat Surrey at Woodbridge Road to start their unstoppable march to the prize. A year and ten days later, it was **Surrey** who strutted, seizing first place by trouncing a **Somerset** side that had led by a point but would finish runners-up, far behind. Not for a second, post-Guildford, did Essex or Surrey look back.

In an eight-team top division, with a quarter of sides destined for demotion, fear of the drop had again led to one side breaking free, another failing to stay in touch and the rest seeking only to survive. Where, in 2017, Kumar Sangakkara's runs had repeatedly made Surrey safe, they now forged ahead to claim wins. This pivotal victory at Guildford was the third of nine in succession, five by an innings.

COUNTY CHAMPIONSHIP TABLES

Division One

		M	W	L	T	D	Bonus pts Bat	Bonus pts Bowl	Pen	Pts
1	Surrey (**3**)	14	10	1	0	3	41	38	0	254
2	Somerset (**6**)	14	7	2	1	4	33	35	0	208
3	Essex (**1**)	14	7	4	0	2*	25	35	0	187
4	Yorkshire (**4**)	14	5	5	0	3*	25	33	0	158
5	Hampshire (**5**)	14	4	5	0	5	16	39	0	144
6	Nottinghamshire (**2**) . .	14	4	8	0	2	21	38	0	133
7	Lancashire (**2**)	14	3	7	1	3	23	40	1	133
8	Worcestershire (**1**) . . .	14	2	10	0	2	23	39	0	104

Division Two

		M	W	L	T	D	Bonus pts Bat	Bonus pts Bowl	Pen	Pts
1	Warwickshire (**8**)	14	9	2	0	3	41	42	0	242
2	Kent (**5**)	14	10	3	0	1	16	40	0	221
3	Sussex (*4*)	14	6	4	0	4	32	38	0	186
4	Middlesex (*7*)	14	7	4	0	3	14	38	0	179
5	Gloucestershire (*6*) . . .	14	5	4	0	5	15	37	0	157
6	Leicestershire (*10*) . . .	14	5	7	0	2	22	40	3	149
7	Derbyshire (*8*)	14	4	7	0	3	30	38	0	147
8	Durham (*9*)	14	4	7	0	2*	16	35	0	130
9	Northamptonshire (*3*)	14	4	8	0	1*	14	38	0	126
10	Glamorgan (*7*)	14	2	10	0	2	13	38	1	92

2017 positions are shown in brackets: Division One in bold, Division Two in italic.

* *Plus one match abandoned.*

Win = 16pts; tie = 8pts; draw = 5pts; abandoned = 5pts. *Penalties for slow over-rates.*

House of Stewart: director of cricket Alec Stewart and Morne Morkel at The Oval.

By his own admission, Morne Morkel – unfit for the first four games – still lacked rhythm when he joined Surrey, the most coveted Kolpak for years. Four other bowlers in a formidable squad had been responsible for earlier success, including Sam Curran who became, at 19 years 344 days, the youngest English player to 100 first-class wickets since Martin Bicknell (from Guildford, of course) in August 1988. But once things clicked for Morkel, he added 48 scalps at 13 in his last 15 innings.

Yet in a season where four-day wickets had never proved so cheap, it was Surrey's batting which was arguably more significant – helped by home pitches that actually promoted even contests. Among the first division batsmen who played a dozen or more Championship innings, only 13 averaged above 35 (it was more austere still in the lower tier). Four played for Surrey.

They were rare specimens. When war came between Charles V and Suleiman the Magnificent, prisoners proved so numerous that, in 1541, slaves at Algiers reportedly sold for an onion a head. Bowlers discovered similar bargains last year. Teams averaged less than 27 runs per wicket, the lowest for all 26 seasons since three-day matches were phased out, beating just under 29 in 1999. Wickets arrived more frequently than ever before, and only one in five games was drawn. Of the positive results in Division One, 60% were achieved in the overs equivalent of nine sessions or less; two games in nine failed to reach the equivalent of lunch on the third day. Life was even briefer in Division Two.

It was an odd summer. Deep snow lay heavy on many county squares weeks before the obligatory modern start in mid-April, and a third of the campaign was over by mid-May, often in conditions akin to a lottery. After a hiatus for

50-over cricket, the next tranche (another third) followed from mid-June to August 22, with a month surrendered to T20 en route, during weeks of record-breaking heat and aridity. It was as if the Pripet Marshes had given way to the Sahel Savannah. In truth, however, so much water was hosed on to pitches that seam movement remained and, with moisture drying under a baking sun, perturbed air also encouraged swing. So even such high-summer Championship cricket as T20 deigned to permit did not greatly help spin. The exception was at Taunton, and that was in early September: a controversial tie with Lancashire in what was effectively a slow bowlers' benefit match.

By then, the campaign was ending under uniformly murky autumn skies, occasionally enlivened by the remnants of Atlantic hurricanes, one of which ripped up the home covers to save Somerset from a likely second heavy defeat by Surrey. When warm weather mockingly returned for the final round, both promotion slots, plus **Worcestershire's** demise, had been settled. The one undecided issue – which other side would go down – was resolved on the second afternoon, amid nailbiting drama as **Nottinghamshire** escaped and **Lancashire** fell.

At Trent Bridge, Nottinghamshire were in tatters on 85 for five, destined to become 133 all out, when cheering from the crowd penetrated even the press box. Relief had come with news from Southampton that Lancashire's last three wickets had fallen in eight balls, leaving them 27 short of a third batting point. Had they achieved it, they would have survived: Nottinghamshire continued to massive defeat, after Somerset's Tom Abell and Craig Overton became the fourth pair in history to take hat-tricks for the same team, and Lancashire's eventual victory left the two sides equal on points, divided by a single win. It was cruel. With so few weather-dictated draws all season, and Nottinghamshire never really affected, Lancashire had probably been denied victory, over Surrey no less, by April rain in Manchester. And they lost the return match, one of the summer's best, by only six runs at The Oval in August, when twelfth man Will Jacks took a phenomenal reflex catch at short leg that confirmed Surrey were fated for the title. A fortnight later came that Taunton tie: the gods are not from Rawtenstall. But they may be fair. Had Lancashire not dallied in the home Roses match and incurred a one-point fine for their over-rate, they would have stayed up.

In the last five autumn rounds, half the completed first division innings failed to reach 200. But this was riches compared to the spring. Setting the tone on the season's second day, Kent were bowled out in 18.5 overs, the shortest Championship innings for five years. Yorkshire then managed 18.4 on May 4 when dismissed by Essex for 50. It was their lowest total since 1973; before 22 overs had been bowled on the first morning, four England Test batsmen (two on each side) had fallen for ducks. Heightening the absurdity, Yorkshire went on to win, only the second Championship side to revive from so paltry a first innings in 94 years.

Probably the most telling statistic of an unsubtle season was that, when Kent's New Zealand seam bowler Matt Henry reached 43 wickets in June by returning six for 58 at Bristol, his average rose by a fraction, from 9.59 to 9.60. These are figures from before the Great War. Henry's ultimate Championship tally was 75 at 15, one ahead of the next best, even though he missed three games. His wickets were harvested across the country, but most readily at Canterbury, where no match exceeded 240 overs. The visiting batsman's average life expectancy was 30 balls; for Kent, it was 36. Years before *The Origin of Species*, Charles Darwin had written a 684-page book on barnacles. Later, he confided to a friend: "I hate a barnacle as no man did before." This was the approximate attitude of top-order batsmen to English pitches. And probably to the seamers exploiting them.

All of which may unintentionally validate the Cricket Discipline Commission's derided refusal to penalise the pitch for that tie in Taunton. It was an even more exceptional result than was realised. The previous Championship tie, in 2003, one of just 24 in its history, required two declarations and a forfeiture. This was only the third in the last 63 years to arrive naturally, without a third-innings declaration. With spinners rampant, it was done and dusted inside 165 overs. Given that intent now has to be proved under amended protocols, it is hard to see how guilt could be established, short of uncovering incriminating emails. The Commission's report did offer an alarming reference to the dangers of "over-aggressive scarification", but it's unclear why a turning pitch should be any more culpable than the general run of excessively seam-friendly surfaces seen all summer. To a lesser degree, these were demanded by England for Test cricket.

If the weather had an obvious bearing, it is the ECB who consign red-ball cricket to the season's peripheries. Indeed, by apparent design, they are making

Backed by millions, Hampshire cheated relegation again

the form more marginal by the year. Ultimately, they may well welcome low-scoring early finishes. The decision that three sides will be promoted in 2019 and one relegated, to create a ten-team first division, compromises the integrity of the Championship: as in the lower tier last summer, each team will meet five competitors home and away, but the other four only

once. It would suit the ECB's seeming priorities to correct the imbalance by returning to three-day play, leaving yet more room for T20 cricket. At least a conference-based Championship, letting mediocrity off the hook, was once more rejected. But the key requirement, to establish genuine compensation for those poorer counties whose players are repeatedly poached, has still not been addressed – nor the need to financially hammer a reliance on imported talent, as the professional game's social base narrows ever further at home.

Essex, recovering well to finish third, and **Yorkshire**, overcoming both injuries and England calls to claim fourth, are largely beyond blame here. But in ten of their games, **Hampshire**, backed by the chairman's millions, fielded an entire pace attack raised abroad. They cheated relegation again.

Joining them in that attempt this summer may well be the two sides who ultimately found untroubled promotion, after an intense three-way fight seemed inevitable. With three rounds remaining, the leading trio were separated by a dozen points, and **Warwickshire** were still to meet rivals Sussex and Kent for a second time. There was poetic justice, perhaps, that Sussex had lost Jofra Archer and Chris Jordan to the IPL during the season's first third, for both

HIGHEST SCORE BY A WICKETKEEPER FOR EACH COUNTY

County	Score	Player, Match	Year
Kent	295	L. E. G. Ames v Gloucestershire at Folkestone	1933
Essex	286	J. R. Freeman v Northamptonshire at Northampton	1921
Surrey	271*	A. J. Stewart v Yorkshire at The Oval	1997
Warwickshire	254	G. W. Humpage v Lancashire at Southport	1982
Yorkshire	246	J. M. Bairstow v Hampshire at Leeds	2016
Nottinghamshire	240	C. M. W. Read v Essex at Chelmsford	2007
Lancashire	**235***	**D. J. Vilas v Somerset at Manchester**	**2018**
Somerset	219	M. D. Lyon v Leicestershire at Burton-on-Trent	1924
Derbyshire	216*	W. Storer v Leicestershire at Chesterfield	1899
Gloucestershire	214	J. H. Board v Somerset at Bristol	1900
Northamptonshire	209	D. Ripley v Glamorgan at Northampton	1998
Hampshire	203	N. T. McCorkell v Gloucestershire at Gloucester	1951
Sussex	201*	M. J. Prior v Loughborough UCCE at Hove	2004
Worcestershire	192	S. M. Davies v Gloucestershire at Bristol	2006
Middlesex	181	A. Lyttelton v Gloucestershire at Clifton	1883
Durham	**170**	**S. W. Poynter v Derbyshire at Derby**	**2018**
Glamorgan	146*	E. W. Jones v Sussex at Hove	1968
Leicestershire	144*	P. A. Nixon v Northamptonshire at Northampton	2006

were arguably filched from West Indies. But, after gaining five of their six wins at Hove, **Sussex** lost away to lowly Durham. They then inadvertently produced one of the season's few placid pitches, which brought stalemate on Warwickshire's visit. Warwickshire returned to base for a fifth Edgbaston win, each coming after they lost the toss and batted second. It secured the division title. **Kent**, overwhelmed, were left as runners-up.

The rest never challenged. **Middlesex**, fourth, were severely affected by injuries; **Gloucestershire** once more played above their ability, yet remained far off the pace. Behind them were **Leicestershire**, crashing back to earth with five defeats in their final six games, and **Derbyshire**, who sank from fourth to seventh in the last two rounds. For the first time since gaining first-class status in 1992, **Durham** won after following on, 256 behind Leicestershire. But, buffeted by 40mph gusts from Storm Ali, they were blown away in their return meeting at Leicester, for 61 and 66, their worst two totals yet. Storm Abbas would have been more apt: Mohammad Abbas ran through them twice, either side of lunch, to finish with ten for 52. A more welcome record was set in May at Derby, when Stuart Poynter made 170, the highest first-class score by a Durham wicketkeeper, seven days after Dane Vilas (235 not out) achieved the same for Lancashire, against Somerset. Another South African stumper proved less blessed: Derbyshire's Daryn Smit conceded 34 byes in an innings of 81 extras when his fast-bowling compatriots lost control at Chester-le-Street. Control was a commodity **Northamptonshire** sought in vain, with three of their eight defeats tight ones, but they avoided the wooden spoon, claimed (deservedly) by **Glamorgan's** foreign legion for the first time in 11 years.

Pre-season betting (best available prices): *Division One* – 7-2 Essex; 9-2 Lancashire; 11-2 SURREY; 7-1 Nottinghamshire and Yorkshire; 8-1 Hampshire; 14-1 Somerset; 20-1 Worcestershire. *Division Two* – 2-1 Middlesex; 5-1 WARWICKSHIRE; 11-2 Sussex; 7-1 Kent; 10-1 Northamptonshire; 16-1 Durham; 20-1 Glamorgan and Gloucestershire; 25-1 Derbyshire; 33-1 Leicestershire.

Prize money

Division One
£532,100 for winners: SURREY.
£221,020 for runners-up: SOMERSET.
£103,022 for third: ESSEX.
£32,121 for fourth: YORKSHIRE.
£24,000 for fifth: HAMPSHIRE.

Division Two
£111,050 for winners: WARWICKSHIRE.
£51,052 for runners-up: KENT.

Leaders: *Division One* – from April 16 Hampshire; April 23 Yorkshire; April 30 Nottinghamshire; June 12 Somerset; June 22 Surrey; Surrey became champions on September 13.
Division Two – from April 15 Middlesex; April 22 Warwickshire; Warwickshire became champions on September 26.

Bottom place: *Division One* – from April 23 Lancashire; April 30 Worcestershire; August 22 Lancashire; August 31 Worcestershire.
Division Two – from April 22 Durham; May 7 Northamptonshire; June 22 Gloucestershire; July 19 Glamorgan.

Scoring of Points

(a) For a win, 16 points plus any points scored in the first innings.

(b) In a tie, each side score eight points, plus any points scored in the first innings.

(c) In a drawn match, each side score five points, plus any points scored in the first innings.

(d) If the scores are equal in a drawn match, the side batting in the fourth innings score eight points, plus any points scored in the first innings, and the opposing side score five points, plus any points scored in the first innings.

(e) First-innings points (awarded only for performances in the first 110 overs of each first innings and retained whatever the result of the match):

    (i) A maximum of five batting points to be available: 200 to 249 runs – 1 point; 250 to 299 runs – 2 points; 300 to 349 runs – 3 points; 350 to 399 runs – 4 points; 400 runs or over – 5 points. Penalty runs awarded within the first 110 overs of each first innings count towards the award of bonus points.

    (ii) A maximum of three bowling points to be available: 3 to 5 wickets taken – 1 point; 6 to 8 wickets taken – 2 points; 9 to 10 wickets taken – 3 points.

(f) If a match is abandoned without a ball being bowled, each side score five points.

(g) The side who have the highest aggregate of points shall be the champion county of their respective division. Should any sides in the Championship table be equal on points, the following tie-breakers will be applied in the order stated: most wins, fewest losses, team achieving most points in head-to-head contests, most wickets taken, most runs scored.

(h) The minimum over-rate to be achieved by counties will be 16 overs per hour. Overs will be calculated at the end of the match, and penalties applied on a match-by-match basis. For each over (ignoring fractions) that a side have bowled short of the target number, one point will be deducted from their Championship total.

(i) Penalties for poor and unfit pitches are at the discretion of the Cricket Discipline Commission.

Under ECB playing conditions, two extras were scored for every no-ball bowled, whether scored off or not, and one for every wide. Any runs scored off the bat were credited to the batsman, while byes and leg-byes were counted as no-balls or wides, as appropriate, in accordance with Law 24.13, in addition to the initial penalty.

CONSTITUTION OF COUNTY CHAMPIONSHIP

At least four possible dates have been given for the start of county cricket in England. The first, patchy, references began in 1825. The earliest mention in any cricket publication in 1864, and eight counties have come to be regarded as first-class from that date, including Cambridgeshire, who dropped out after 1871. For many years, the County Championship was considered to have started in 1873, when regulations governing qualification first applied; indeed, a special commemorative stamp was issued by the Post Office in 1973. However, the Championship was not formally organised until 1890, and before then champions were proclaimed by the press; sometimes publications differed in their views, and no definitive list of champions can start before that date. Eight teams contested the 1890 competition – Gloucestershire, Kent, Lancashire, Middlesex, Nottinghamshire, Surrey, Sussex and Yorkshire. Somerset joined the following year, and in 1895 the Championship began to acquire something of its modern shape, when Derbyshire, Essex, Hampshire, Leicestershire and Warwickshire were added. At that point MCC officially recognised the competition's existence. Worcestershire, Northamptonshire and Glamorgan were admitted in 1899, 1905 and 1921 respectively, and are regarded as first-class from these dates. An invitation in 1921 to Buckinghamshire to enter the Championship was declined, owing to the lack of necessary playing facilities, and an application by Devon in 1948 was unsuccessful. Durham were admitted in 1992 and granted first-class status prior to their pre-season tour of Zimbabwe.

In 2000, the Championship was split for the first time into two divisions, on the basis of counties' standings in the 1999 competition. From 2000 onwards, the bottom three teams in Division One were relegated at the end of the season, and the top three teams in Division Two promoted. From 2006, this was changed to two teams relegated and two promoted. In 2016, two were relegated and one promoted, to create divisions of eight and ten teams. In 2019, one will be relegated and three promoted, to change the balance to ten teams in Division One and eight in Division Two.

COUNTY CHAMPIONS

The title of champion county is unreliable before 1890. In 1963, *Wisden* formally accepted the list of champions "most generally selected" by contemporaries, as researched by Rowland Bowen (see *Wisden 1959*, page 91). This appears to be the most accurate available list but has no official status. The county champions from 1864 to 1889 were, according to Bowen: 1864 Surrey; 1865 Nottinghamshire; 1866 Middlesex; 1867 Yorkshire; 1868 Nottinghamshire; 1869 Nottinghamshire and Yorkshire; 1870 Yorkshire; 1871 Nottinghamshire; 1872 Nottinghamshire; 1873 Gloucestershire and Nottinghamshire; 1874 Gloucestershire; 1875 Nottinghamshire; 1876 Gloucestershire; 1877 Gloucestershire; 1878 undecided; 1879 Lancashire and Nottinghamshire; 1880 Nottinghamshire; 1881 Lancashire; 1882 Lancashire and Nottinghamshire; 1883 Nottinghamshire; 1884 Nottinghamshire; 1885 Nottinghamshire; 1886 Nottinghamshire; 1887 Surrey; 1888 Surrey; 1889 Lancashire, Nottinghamshire and Surrey.

1890	Surrey	1926	Lancashire	1962	Yorkshire
1891	Surrey	1927	Lancashire	1963	Yorkshire
1892	Surrey	1928	Lancashire	1964	Worcestershire
1893	Yorkshire	1929	Nottinghamshire	1965	Worcestershire
1894	Surrey	1930	Lancashire	1966	Yorkshire
1895	Surrey	1931	Yorkshire	1967	Yorkshire
1896	Yorkshire	1932	Yorkshire	1968	Yorkshire
1897	Lancashire	1933	Yorkshire	1969	Glamorgan
1898	Yorkshire	1934	Lancashire	1970	Kent
1899	Surrey	1935	Yorkshire	1971	Surrey
1900	Yorkshire	1936	Derbyshire	1972	Warwickshire
1901	Yorkshire	1937	Yorkshire	1973	Hampshire
1902	Yorkshire	1938	Yorkshire	1974	Worcestershire
1903	Middlesex	1939	Yorkshire	1975	Leicestershire
1904	Lancashire	1946	Yorkshire	1976	Middlesex
1905	Yorkshire	1947	Middlesex	1977	{ Middlesex
1906	Kent	1948	Glamorgan		Kent }
1907	Nottinghamshire	1949	{ Middlesex	1978	Kent
1908	Yorkshire		Yorkshire }	1979	Essex
1909	Kent	1950	{ Lancashire	1980	Middlesex
1910	Kent		Surrey }	1981	Nottinghamshire
1911	Warwickshire	1951	Warwickshire	1982	Middlesex
1912	Yorkshire	1952	Surrey	1983	Essex
1913	Kent	1953	Surrey	1984	Essex
1914	Surrey	1954	Surrey	1985	Middlesex
1919	Yorkshire	1955	Surrey	1986	Essex
1920	Middlesex	1956	Surrey	1987	Nottinghamshire
1921	Middlesex	1957	Surrey	1988	Worcestershire
1922	Yorkshire	1958	Surrey	1989	Worcestershire
1923	Yorkshire	1959	Yorkshire	1990	Middlesex
1924	Yorkshire	1960	Yorkshire	1991	Essex
1925	Yorkshire	1961	Hampshire	1992	Essex

1993	Middlesex	2002	Surrey	2011	Lancashire
1994	Warwickshire	2003	Sussex	2012	Warwickshire
1995	Warwickshire	2004	Warwickshire	2013	Durham
1996	Leicestershire	2005	Nottinghamshire	2014	Yorkshire
1997	Glamorgan	2006	Sussex	2015	Yorkshire
1998	Leicestershire	2007	Sussex	2016	Middlesex
1999	Surrey	2008	Durham	2017	Essex
2000	Surrey	2009	Durham	2018	Surrey
2001	Yorkshire	2010	Nottinghamshire		

Notes: Since the Championship was constituted in 1890 it has been won outright as follows: Yorkshire 32 times, Surrey 19, Middlesex 11, Lancashire 8, Essex and Warwickshire 7, Kent and Nottinghamshire 6, Worcestershire 5, Durham, Glamorgan, Leicestershire and Sussex 3, Hampshire 2, Derbyshire 1. Gloucestershire, Northamptonshire and Somerset have never won.

The title has been shared three times since 1890, involving Middlesex twice, Kent, Lancashire, Surrey and Yorkshire.

Wooden spoons: Since the major expansion of the Championship from nine teams to 14 in 1895, the counties have finished outright bottom as follows: Derbyshire 16, Leicestershire 13, Somerset 12, Glamorgan and Northamptonshire 11, Gloucestershire 9, Nottinghamshire and Sussex 8, Worcestershire 6, Durham and Hampshire 5, Warwickshire 3, Essex and Kent 2, Yorkshire 1. Lancashire, Middlesex and Surrey have never finished bottom. Leicestershire have also shared bottom place twice, once with Hampshire and once with Somerset.

From 1977 to 1983 the Championship was sponsored by Schweppes, from 1984 to 1998 by Britannic Assurance, from 1999 to 2000 by PPP healthcare, in 2001 by Cricinfo, from 2002 to 2005 by Frizzell, from 2006 to 2015 by Liverpool Victoria (LV), and from 2016 by Specsavers.

COUNTY CHAMPIONSHIP – FINAL POSITIONS, 1890–2018

	Derbyshire	Durham	Essex	Glamorgan	Gloucestershire	Hampshire	Kent	Lancashire	Leicestershire	Middlesex	Northamptonshire	Nottinghamshire	Somerset	Surrey	Sussex	Warwickshire	Worcestershire	Yorkshire
1890	–	–	–	–	6	–	3	2	–	7	–	5	–	1	8	–	–	3
1891	–	–	–	–	9	–	5	2	–	3	–	4	5	1	7	–	–	8
1892	–	–	–	–	7	–	7	4	–	5	–	2	3	1	9	–	–	6
1893	–	–	–	–	9	–	4	2	–	3	–	6	8	5	7	–	–	1
1894	–	–	–	–	9	–	4	4	–	3	–	7	6	1	8	–	–	2
1895	5	–	9	–	4	10	14	2	12	6	–	12	8	1	11	6	–	3
1896	7	–	5	–	10	8	9	2	13	3	–	6	11	4	14	12	–	1
1897	14	–	3	–	5	9	12	1	13	8	–	10	11	2	6	7	–	4
1898	9	–	5	–	3	12	7	6	13	2	–	8	13	4	9	9	–	1
1899	15	–	6	–	9	10	8	4	13	2	–	10	13	1	5	7	12	3
1900	13	–	10	–	7	15	3	2	14	7	–	5	11	7	3	6	12	1
1901	15	–	10	–	14	7	7	3	12	2	–	9	12	6	4	5	11	1
1902	10	–	13	–	14	15	7	5	11	12	–	3	7	4	2	6	9	1
1903	12	–	8	–	13	14	8	4	14	1	–	5	16	10	11	2	7	6
1904	10	–	14	–	9	15	3	1	7	4	–	5	12	11	6	7	13	2
1905	14	–	12	–	8	16	6	2	5	11	13	10	15	4	3	7	8	1
1906	16	–	7	–	9	8	1	4	15	11	11	5	11	3	10	6	14	2
1907	16	–	7	–	10	12	8	6	11	5	15	1	14	4	13	9	2	2
1908	14	–	11	–	10	9	2	7	13	4	15	8	16	3	5	12	6	1
1909	15	–	14	–	16	8	1	2	13	6	7	10	11	5	4	12	8	3
1910	15	–	11	–	12	6	1	4	10	3	9	5	16	2	7	14	13	8
1911	14	–	6	–	12	11	2	4	15	3	10	8	16	5	13	1	9	7
1912	12	–	15	–	11	6	3	4	13	5	2	8	14	7	10	9	16	1
1913	13	–	15	–	9	10	1	8	14	6	4	5	16	3	7	11	12	2
1914	12	–	8	–	16	5	3	11	13	2	9	10	15	1	6	7	14	4

	Derbyshire	Durham	Essex	Glamorgan	Gloucestershire	Hampshire	Kent	Lancashire	Leicestershire	Middlesex	Northamptonshire	Nottinghamshire	Somerset	Surrey	Sussex	Warwickshire	Worcestershire	Yorkshire
1919	9	–	14		8	7	2	5	9	13	12	3	5	4	11	15	–	1
1920	16	–	9		8	11	5	2	13	1	14	7	10	3	6	12	15	4
1921	12	–	15	17	7	6	4	5	11	1	13	8	10	2	9	16	14	3
1922	11	–	8	16	13	6	4	5	14	7	15	2	10	3	9	12	17	1
1923	10	–	13	16	11	7	5	3	14	8	17	2	9	4	6	12	15	1
1924	17	–	15	13	6	12	5	4	11	2	16	6	8	3	10	9	14	1
1925	14	–	7	17	10	9	5	3	12	6	11	4	15	2	13	8	16	1
1926	11	–	9	8	15	7	3	1	13	6	16	4	14	5	10	12	17	2
1927	5	–	8	15	12	13	4	1	7	9	16	2	14	6	10	11	17	3
1928	10	–	16	15	5	12	2	1	9	8	13	3	14	6	7	11	17	4
1929	7	–	12	17	4	11	8	2	9	6	13	1	15	10	4	14	16	2
1930	9	–	6	11	2	13	5	1	12	16	17	4	13	8	7	15	10	3
1931	7	–	10	15	2	12	3	6	16	11	17	5	13	8	4	9	14	1
1932	10	–	14	15	13	8	3	6	12	10	16	4	7	5	2	9	17	1
1933	6	–	4	16	10	14	3	5	17	12	13	8	11	9	2	7	15	1
1934	3	–	8	13	7	14	5	1	12	10	17	9	15	11	2	4	16	5
1935	2	–	9	13	15	16	10	4	6	3	17	5	14	11	7	8	12	1
1936	1	–	9	16	4	10	8	11	15	2	17	5	7	6	14	13	12	3
1937	3	–	6	7	4	14	12	9	16	2	17	10	13	8	5	11	15	1
1938	5	–	6	16	10	14	9	4	15	2	17	12	7	3	8	13	11	1
1939	9	–	4	13	3	15	5	6	17	2	16	12	14	8	10	11	7	1
1946	15	–	8	6	5	10	6	3	11	2	16	13	4	11	17	14	8	1
1947	5	–	11	9	2	16	4	3	14	1	17	11	11	6	9	15	7	7
1948	6	–	13	1	8	9	15	5	1	3	17	14	12	2	16	7	10	4
1949	15	–	9	8	7	16	13	11	17	1	6	11	9	5	13	4	3	1
1950	5	–	17	11	7	12	9	1	16	14	10	15	7	1	13	4	6	3
1951	11	–	8	5	12	9	16	3	15	7	13	17	14	6	10	1	4	2
1952	4	–	10	7	9	12	15	3	6	5	8	16	17	1	13	10	14	2
1953	6	–	12	10	6	14	16	3	3	5	11	8	17	1	2	9	15	12
1954	3	–	15	4	13	14	11	10	16	7	7	5	17	1	9	6	11	2
1955	8	–	14	12	12	3	13	9	6	5	7	11	17	1	4	9	15	2
1956	12	–	11	13	3	6	16	2	17	5	4	8	15	1	9	14	9	7
1957	4	–	5	9	12	13	14	6	17	7	2	15	8	1	9	11	16	3
1958	5	–	6	15	14	2	8	7	12	10	4	17	3	1	13	16	9	11
1959	7	–	9	6	2	8	13	5	16	10	11	17	12	3	15	4	14	1
1960	5	–	6	11	8	12	10	2	17	3	9	16	14	7	4	15	13	1
1961	7	–	6	14	5	1	11	13	9	3	16	17	10	15	8	12	4	2
1962	7	–	9	14	4	10	11	16	17	13	8	15	6	5	12	3	2	1
1963	17	–	12	2	8	10	13	15	16	6	7	9	3	11	4	4	14	1
1964	12	–	10	11	17	12	7	14	16	6	3	15	8	4	9	2	1	5
1965	9	–	15	3	10	12	5	13	14	6	2	17	7	8	16	11	1	4
1966	9	–	16	14	15	11	4	12	8	12	5	17	3	7	10	6	2	1
1967	6	–	15	14	17	12	2	11	2	7	9	15	8	4	13	10	5	1
1968	8	–	14	3	16	5	2	6	9	10	13	4	12	15	17	11	7	1
1969	16	–	6	1	2	5	10	15	14	11	9	8	17	3	7	4	12	13
1970	7	–	12	2	17	10	1	3	15	16	14	11	13	5	9	7	6	4
1971	17	–	10	16	8	9	4	3	5	6	14	12	7	1	11	2	15	13
1972	17	–	5	13	3	9	2	15	6	8	4	14	11	12	16	1	7	10
1973	16	–	8	11	5	1	4	12	9	13	3	17	10	2	15	7	6	14
1974	17	–	12	16	14	2	10	8	4	6	3	15	5	7	13	9	1	11
1975	15	–	7	9	16	3	5	4	1	11	8	13	12	6	17	14	10	2
1976	15	–	6	17	3	12	14	16	4	1	2	13	7	9	10	5	11	8
1977	7	–	6	14	3	11	1	16	5	1	9	17	4	14	8	10	13	12
1978	14	–	2	13	10	8	1	12	6	3	17	7	5	16	9	11	15	4

Year	Derbyshire	Durham	Essex	Glamorgan	Gloucestershire	Hampshire	Kent	Lancashire	Leicestershire	Middlesex	Northamptonshire	Nottinghamshire	Somerset	Surrey	Sussex	Warwickshire	Worcestershire	Yorkshire
1979	16	–	1	17	10	12	5	13	6	14	11	9	8	3	4	15	3	7
1980	9	–	8	13	7	17	16	15	10	1	12	3	5	2		14	11	6
1981	12	–	5	14	13	7	9	16	8	4	15	1	3	6	2	17	11	10
1982	11	–	7	16	15	3	13	12	2	1	9	4	6	5	8	17	14	10
1983	9	–	1	15	12	3	7	12	4	2	6	14	10	8	11	5	16	17
1984	12	–	1	13	17	15	5	16	4	3	11	2	7	8	6	9	10	14
1985	13	–	4	12	3	2	9	14	16	1	10	8	17	6	7	15	5	11
1986	11	–	1	17	2	6	8	15	7	12	9	4	16	3	14	12	5	10
1987	6	–	12	13	10	5	14	2	3	16	7	1	11	4	17	15	9	8
1988	14	–	3	17	10	15	2	9	8	7	12	5	11	4	16	6	1	13
1989	6	–	2	17	9	6	15	4	13	3	5	11	14	12	10	8	1	16
1990	12	–	8	13	3	16	6	7	1	11	13	15	9	17	5	4	10	
1991	3	–	1	12	13	9	6	8	16	15	10	4	17	5	11	2	6	14
1992	5	18	1	14	10	15	2	12	8	11	3	4	9	13	7	6	17	16
1993	15	18	11	3	17	13	8	13	9	1	4	7	5	6	10	16	2	12
1994	17	16	6	18	12	13	9	10	2	4	5	3	11	7	8	1	15	13
1995	14	17	5	16	6	13	18	4	7	2	3	11	9	12	15	1	10	8
1996	2	18	5	10	13	14	4	15	1	9	16	17	11	3	12	8	7	6
1997	16	17	8	1	7	14	2	11	10	4	15	13	12	8	18	4	3	6
1998	10	14	18	12	4	6	11	2	1	17	15	16	9	5	7	8	13	3
1999	9	8	12	14	18	7	5	2	3	16	13	17	4	1	11	10	15	6
2000	**9**	**8**	2	3	4	7	**6**	**2**	**4**	*8*	*1*	7	5	**1**	9	6	*5*	**3**
2001	9	8	9	8	4	2	**3**	6	5	5	7	7	2	**4**	*1*	3	6	**1**
2002	6	9	1	5	8	**7**	3	**4**	5	2	7	3	8	1	**6**	2	4	9
2003	9	6	**7**	5	3	8	**4**	2	**9**	6	2	8	7	3	1	5	1	4
2004	8	9	5	3	**6**	2	2	8	6	**4**	9	1	4	3	5	1	7	7
2005	9	2	5	**9**	8	2	5	1	7	6	4	1	8	7	3	4	6	3
2006	5	7	3	8	7	3	5	2	4	9	6	8	9	1	1	4	2	6
2007	6	2	4	9	7	5	7	3	8	3	5	2	1	4	1	8	9	6
2008	6	1	5	8	9	3	8	5	7	3	4	2	4	9	6	1	2	7
2009	6	1	2	5	4	6	1	4	9	8	3	2	3	7	8	5	9	7
2010	9	5	9	3	5	7	8	4	4	8	6	1	2	7	1	6	2	3
2011	5	3	7	6	4	9	8	1	9	1	3	6	4	2	5	2	7	8
2012	1	6	5	6	9	4	3	8	7	3	8	5	2	7	4	1	9	2
2013	8	1	3	8	6	4	7	1	9	5	2	7	6	9	3	4	5	2
2014	4	5	3	8	7	1	6	8	9	7	9	4	6	5	3	2	2	1
2015	8	4	3	4	6	7	7	2	9	2	5	3	6	1	8	5	9	1
2016	9	4	1	8	6	8	2	7	7	1	5	9	2	5	4	6	3	3
2017	8	9	1	7	6	5	5	2	10	7	3	2	6	3	4	8	1	4
2018	7	8	3	10	5	5	2	7	6	4	9	3	1	3	1	8	4	

For the 2000–2018 Championships, Division One placings are in bold, Division Two in italic.

MATCH RESULTS, 1864–2018

County	Years of Play	Played	Won	Lost	Drawn	Tied	% Won
Derbyshire	1871–87; 1895–2018	2,573	629	951	992	1	24.44
Durham	1992–2018	437	119	182	136	0	27.23
Essex	1895–2018	2,537	748	731	1,052	6	29.48
Glamorgan	1921–2018	2,063	452	718	893	0	21.90
Gloucestershire	1870–2018	2,816	824	1,032	958	2	29.26
Hampshire	1864–85; 1895–2018	2,646	696	886	1,060	4	26.30
Kent	1864–2018	2,931	1,048	874	1,004	5	35.75
Lancashire	1865–2018	3,008	1,106	628	1,270	4	36.76

County	Years of Play	Played	Won	Lost	Drawn	Tied	% Won
Leicestershire......	1895–2018	2,503	558	917	1,027	1	22.29
Middlesex..........	1864–2018	2,713	987	690	1,031	5	36.38
Northamptonshire ...	1905–2018	2,270	571	776	920	3	25.15
Nottinghamshire.....	1864–2018	2,843	862	778	1,202	1	30.32
Somerset..........	1882–85; 1891–2018	2,545	619	977	945	4	24.32
Surrey.............	1864–2018	3,088	1,205	686	1,193	4	39.02
Sussex	1864–2018	2,982	854	1,010	1,112	6	28.63
Warwickshire......	1895–2018	2,518	706	716	1,094	2	28.03
Worcestershire.....	1899–2018	2,455	635	858	960	2	25.86
Yorkshire	1864–2018	3,111	1,344	553	1,212	2	43.20
Cambridgeshire	1864–69; 1871	19	8	8	3	0	42.10
		23,029	13,971	13,971	9,032	26	

Matches abandoned without a ball bowled are wholly excluded.

   Counties participated in the years shown, except that there were no matches in 1915–1918 and 1940–1945; Hampshire did not play inter-county matches in 1868–1869, 1871–1874 and 1879; Worcestershire did not take part in the Championship in 1919.

COUNTY CHAMPIONSHIP STATISTICS FOR 2018

County	For Runs	Wickets	Avge	Runs scored per 100 balls	Against Runs	Wickets	Avge
Derbyshire (7)........	6,943	255	27.22	53.88	7,212	228	31.63
Durham (8)..........	5,377	238	22.59	52.34	5,754	222	25.91
Essex (3)...........	5,851	199	29.40	56.78	5,921	232	25.52
Glamorgan (10)	5,470	253	21.62	55.34	6,113	208	29.38
Gloucestershire (5)....	5,937	233	25.48	48.34	5,490	215	25.53
Hampshire (5).......	6,147	227	27.07	50.20	6,018	207	29.07
Kent (2).............	6,024	225	26.77	60.95	5,286	252	20.97
Lancashire (7).......	5,621	226	24.87	55.00	6,484	255	25.42
Leicestershire (6)	5,605	227	24.69	52.78	6,419	234	27.43
Middlesex (4)	6,105	249	24.51	55.30	6,231	243	25.64
Northamptonshire (9)...	5,103	226	22.57	56.97	5,207	226	23.03
Nottinghamshire (6)...	6,390	246	25.97	58.81	6,667	211	31.59
Somerset (2)........	6,898	236	29.22	59.35	6,497	230	28.24
Surrey (1)..........	6,868	188	36.53	58.29	6,021	249	24.18
Sussex (3)..........	6,471	224	28.88	62.78	6,182	243	25.44
Warwickshire (1).....	6,845	196	34.92	55.20	5,986	255	23.47
Worcestershire (8)	6,605	252	26.21	58.89	7,138	227	31.44
Yorkshire (4).........	6,117	234	26.14	53.38	5,751	197	29.19
	110,377	4,134	26.69	55.68	110,377	4,134	26.69

2018 Championship positions are shown in brackets; Division One in bold, Division Two in italic.

ECB PITCHES TABLE OF MERIT IN 2018

	First-class	One-day			
Derbyshire..........	4.43	5.64	Surrey	5.40	5.58
Durham	4.33	5.31	Sussex	4.88	4.45
Essex	4.50	5.33	Warwickshire........	5.22	5.53
Glamorgan..........	4.63	5.75	Worcestershire.......	4.50	5.71
Gloucestershire	4.88	5.83	Yorkshire...........	5.00	5.46
Hampshire	5.22	6.00			
Kent	4.78	5.38			
Lancashire..........	4.88	5.17	Cambridge MCCU ...	5.00	
Leicestershire.......	4.67	5.40	Cardiff MCCU.......	5.33	
Middlesex	4.80	5.25	Durham MCCU......	5.50	
Northamptonshire	4.43	5.69	Leeds/Bradford MCCU	5.50	
Nottinghamshire	5.25	5.36	Loughborough MCCU	5.00	
Somerset	4.50	6.00	Oxford MCCU.......	4.50	

Each umpire in a match marks the pitch on the following scale: 6 – Very good; 5 – Good; 4 – Above average; 3 – Below average; 2 – Poor; 1 – Unfit.

The tables, provided by the ECB, cover major matches, including Tests, Under-19 internationals, women's internationals and MCCU games, played on grounds under the county's or MCCU's jurisdiction. Middlesex pitches at Lord's are the responsibility of MCC. The "First-class" column includes Under-19 and women's Tests, and inter-MCCU games.

Among the counties, Surrey had the highest mark for first-class cricket, while Hampshire and Somerset had the best for one-day cricket, though the ECB point out that the tables of merit are not a direct assessment of the groundsmen's ability. Marks may be affected by many factors, including weather, soil conditions and the resources available.

COUNTY CAPS AWARDED IN 2018

Essex	V. Chopra, S. R. Harmer.
Glamorgan*	T. van der Gugten.
Gloucestershire*	B. G. Charlesworth, R. F. Higgins, D. J. Worrall.
Hampshire	F. H. Edwards, C. P. Wood.
Kent	M. J. Henry, H. G. Kuhn.
Lancashire	T. E. Bailey, J. C. Buttler, K. K. Jennings, G. Onions, D. J. Vilas.
Leicestershire	Mohammad Abbas, B. A. Raine.
Middlesex	S. S. Eskinazi.
Northamptonshire	J. J. Cobb, B. W. Sanderson.
Nottinghamshire	K. C. Brathwaite, L. R. P. L. Taylor.
Somerset	T. B. Abell, R. E. van der Merwe.
Surrey	S. G. Borthwick, S. M. Curran, A. J. Finch, M. Morkel, O. J. D. Pope, M. D. Stoneman.
Sussex	I. Sharma.
Warwickshire	S. R. Hain.
Worcestershire*	M. J. Guptill, T. M. Head, A. G. Milton, W. D. Parnell, D. Y. Pennington, B. J. Twohig, O. E. Westbury, L. Wood.
Yorkshire	B. O. Coad.

* *Glamorgan's capping system is now based on a player's number of appearances. Gloucestershire now award caps to all first-class players. Worcestershire have replaced caps with colours awarded to all Championship players. Durham abolished their capping system after 2005.*

No caps were awarded by Derbyshire.

COUNTY TESTIMONIALS AWARDED FOR 2019

Durham	C. Rushworth.	Middlesex	D. J. Malan.
Glamorgan	G. G. Wagg.	Nottinghamshire	S. C. J. Broad.
Gloucestershire	I. A. Cockbain.	Surrey	J. W. Dernbach.
Kent	J. L. Denly	Worcestershire	J. D. Shantry.

None of the other ten counties awarded a testimonial for 2019.

DERBYSHIRE

Houghton to the rescue

MARK EKLID

Derbyshire's season finished with their seventh Championship defeat, leaving them seventh in Division Two. That followed failure to progress in either limited-overs competition. It was not a record to inspire much fondness, yet the end-of-term mood was closer to the optimism at the start of a new campaign than the grimness after a fruitless summer.

They had begun promisingly, beating Middlesex in the opening match – a first home Championship win in three and a half years – and winning four of their first six in the Royal London Cup. But fortunes unravelled in June, and reached crisis point at the start of July. Four days before the first Vitality Blast game, Kim Barnett resigned as cricket advisor, aiming a thinly veiled jab at the administrators. The same day, Nottinghamshire confirmed their intention to approach Ben Slater, then Derbyshire's leading run-scorer. Barnett's exit was a public embarrassment for the club, but of less long-term concern than the discord in the dressing-room, where there was a danger Slater would not be the last to leave. An old-fashioned Derbyshire meltdown seemed to be in the offing.

The poor results, a symptom of the problems rather than the cause, extended to defeats in the first four T20 matches – but there was to be no disintegration. Instead, several players signed contract extensions in September – with the core of the team committed to at least two more seasons – an emphatic statement of renewed harmony.

If this could be put down to any single factor, it was the decision at the end of August to bring back the former Zimbabwe captain Dave Houghton, who had been the Middlesex batting coach, as the new head of cricket. The appointment met with universal approval from the team, several of whom had played under him during two previous spells at Derby. From the brink of fragmentation, the club emerged with a sense of purpose and hope. They also appointed John Wright, their T20 coach, to an advisory role, and Steve Kirby, the former seamer who had been in charge of the MCC Young Cricketers at Lord's, as bowling coach.

Houghton's initial assessment was that Derbyshire were in better shape than at the start of his earlier stints and, either side of their mid-season slump, there were signs to encourage this view.

The best Championship performers were the two oldest regular players. Wayne Madsen passed 1,000 runs – one of only five in the country to do so – for the fifth time, and his two hundreds took him to 27, joint-fourth on Derbyshire's all-time list, behind Barnett (53), John Morris (33) and Denis Smith (30). Madsen will be 35 by the start of the new season, but agreed to stay on to the end of 2022. Seamer Tony Palladino began the summer with the

Matt Critchley

Nathan Stirk, Getty Images

double distraction of a testimonial year and bowling-coach duties, but still passed 50 first-class wickets. He also took ten in a match for the first time, at home to Glamorgan. At 35, he was given a new two-year deal, while the arrival of Kirby means he can concentrate on playing.

The 21-year-old Matt Critchley earned enthusiastic reviews in the North–South series in Barbados, and further plaudits for two heroic performances at Chesterfield, his home ground. First his leg-breaks conjured ten Northamptonshire wickets to clinch Derbyshire's first Championship victory at Queen's Park since 2008; then, a few days later, needing 19 off the final six balls of a T20 match against Yorkshire, Critchley belted 22 from five. This was comfortably his best all-round season.

Billy Godleman made a poor start, with only one fifty in his first 15 Championship innings, but finished with two centuries. He was also effective in the white-ball games, striking two hundreds in the Royal London Cup and, after being unavailable for the first four matches, three fifties in the Blast. Following Gary Wilson's decision to return to Ireland, Godleman will captain in all competitions in 2019.

Luis Reece was badly missed. He began the season with an unbeaten 157 against Middlesex, and ended it with seven for 20 – a career-best – against Gloucestershire. But in between he was out for three months with a broken foot.

Derbyshire's Championship shortcomings were not all down to misfortune. Selection was often erratic: 24 players were used across the 14 matches. The Kolpak new-ball pairing of Hardus Viljoen and Ravi Rampaul was inconsistent, although the overseas signing, South African fast bowler Duanne Olivier, was excellent during his half-season stay. He took 31 wickets from seven Championship appearances, including ten against Durham, and added 13 in the Royal London Cup. Few around the County Ground were surprised to see Olivier doing well for South Africa as 2019 began. In January, though, Viljoen decided not to fulfil the final year of his contract. Logan van Beck, a former Dutch all-rounder who recently represented New Zealand A, arrived to play in all formats.

The T20 overseas players were another pair of fast bowlers, New Zealander Lockie Ferguson and Wahab Riaz of Pakistan, although it was medium-pacer Alex Hughes who took the most wickets: 17 equalled Derbyshire's best in the competition. Scotland's Calum MacLeod, signed on a short-term deal, became only the third to score a T20 century for the county – and the first for eight years – but generally the batting was more miss than hit. A run of five wins out of six raised hopes of a quarter-final spot, but two defeats and two washouts from the last four scuppered that.

Championship attendance: 12,215.

DERBYSHIRE RESULTS

All first-class matches – Played 14: Won 4, Lost 7, Drawn 3.
County Championship matches – Played 14: Won 4, Lost 7, Drawn 3.

Specsavers County Championship, 7th in Division 2;
Vitality Blast, 7th in North Group; Royal London One-Day Cup, 5th in North Group.

COUNTY CHAMPIONSHIP AVERAGES, BATTING AND FIELDING

Cap		Birthplace	M	I	NO	R	HS	100	Avge	Ct/St
	†B. T. Slater	Chesterfield‡ . .	9	17	1	676	99	0	42.25	3
2011	W. L. Madsen	Durban, SA	14	27	0	1,016	144	2	37.62	25
	†L. M. Reece	Taunton	6	11	1	349	157*	1	34.90	2
2017	A. L. Hughes	Wordsley	14	27	1	737	103	1	28.34	9
	M. J. J. Critchley . . .	Preston	14	26	1	705	105	1	28.20	9
	G. C. Wilson	Dundonald, N. Ire . .	8	14	1	357	66	0	27.46	16
	T. C. Lace	Hammersmith . . .	4	8	0	219	43	0	27.37	1
	H. R. Hosein	Chesterfield‡ . . .	8	16	2	376	66*	0	26.85	12/1
2015	†B. A. Godleman	Islington	14	27	2	658	122	2	26.32	8
	D. Smit††	Durban, SA	4	8	2	129	45*	0	21.50	11
	G. C. Viljoen††	Witbank, SA	12	22	2	386	60*	0	19.30	1
2012	A. P. Palladino	Tower Hamlets . . .	12	23	6	317	32	0	18.64	1
	A. K. Dal	Newcastle-u-Tyne . .	4	7	0	107	25	0	15.28	2
	†S. M. Ervine	Harare, Zimbabwe .	2	4	0	51	26	0	12.75	2
	D. Olivier¶	Groblersdal, SA . . .	7	11	2	78	40*	0	8.66	0
	†R. Rampaul††	Preysal, Trinidad . .	8	11	5	51	18*	0	8.50	2
	L. H. Ferguson¶	Auckland, NZ	5	10	2	51	16	0	6.37	4
	Hamidullah Qadri . . .	Kandahar, Afg	4	8	2	33	15*	0	5.50	2

Also batted: M. K. Andersson (*Reading*) (1 match) 11, 0 (2 ct); †C. A. J. Brodrick (*Burton-upon-Trent*) (1 match) 0, 19 (2 ct); W. S. Davis (*Stafford*) (1 match) 6; M. H. A. Footitt (*Nottingham*) (cap 2014) (1 match) 0, 0* (1 ct); †A. F. Gleadall (*Chesterfield‡*) (1 match) 27*, 2; D. M. Wheeldon (*Nottingham*) (1 match) 33*, 2.

‡ *Born in Derbyshire.*   ¶ *Official overseas player.*   †† *Other non-England-qualified.*

BOWLING

	Style	O	M	R	W	BB	5I	Avge
L. M. Reece	LM	64.1	13	186	11	7-20	1	16.90
A. P. Palladino	RFM	369	94	1,006	51	6-29	3	19.72
A. L. Hughes	RM	87	19	255	10	4-57	0	25.50
D. Olivier	RFM	251.3	47	852	31	5-20	2	27.48
G. C. Viljoen	RFM	356.1	55	1,225	38	4-51	0	32.23
L. H. Ferguson	RF	164.3	22	618	18	4-56	0	34.33
M. J. J. Critchley	LB	285.5	14	1,218	32	6-106	1	38.06
R. Rampaul	RFM	183.3	35	651	13	3-53	0	50.07

Also bowled: M. K. Andersson (RM) 14–3–41–4; A. K. Dal (RM) 1–0–1–0; W. S. Davis (RFM) 11–3–39–2; S. M. Ervine (RFM) 18–0–65–0; M. H. A. Footitt (LFM) 15–2–57–1; A. F. Gleadall (RFM) 13.3–1–59–1; Hamidullah Qadri (OB) 78.1–7–319–8; W. L. Madsen (OB) 42.4–9–152–4; D. M. Wheeldon (RFM) 13–2–48–1.

LEADING ROYAL LONDON CUP AVERAGES (100 runs/4 wickets)

Batting	Runs	HS	Avge	SR	Ct
B. A. Godleman .	509	137	72.71	88.83	1
B. T. Slater	386	109*	55.14	101.31	2
L. M. Reece	174	92	43.50	88.32	2
W. L. Madsen . .	231	87	28.87	94.28	3
G. C. Wilson . . .	137	49	27.40	82.03	5
A. L. Hughes . . .	114	47	19.00	110.67	3
M. J. J. Critchley .	100	35	14.28	78.74	1

Bowling	W	BB	Avge	ER
L. M. Reece	8	3-37	18.00	5.14
D. Olivier	13	3-31	19.00	4.66
R. Rampaul	13	5-48	28.84	6.69
M. J. J. Critchley . .	8	3-35	40.37	6.87
A. L. Hughes	5	2-49	43.40	6.02
G. C. Viljoen	4	2-55	64.50	6.34

LEADING VITALITY BLAST AVERAGES (100 runs/15 overs)

Batting	Runs	HS	Avge	SR	Ct	Bowling	W	BB	Avge	ER
W. L. Madsen . . .	328	76*	32.80	142.60	3	L. H. Ferguson	16	4-26	19.93	6.64
Wahab Riaz	152	53	19.00	138.18	2	Wahab Riaz	15	3-27	20.86	7.27
B. A. Godleman . .	309	77	51.50	125.10	2	G. C. Viljoen	13	3-25	20.76	7.71
C. S. MacLeod . .	324	104	27.00	121.80	8	A. L. Hughes	17	4-42	19.05	8.10
M. J. J. Critchley .	154	38*	17.11	121.25	7	R. Rampaul	14	4-19	25.64	8.58
G. C. Wilson . . .	199	35	24.87	119.16	11					

FIRST-CLASS COUNTY RECORDS

Highest score for	274	G. A. Davidson v Lancashire at Manchester.	1896
Highest score against	343*	P. A. Perrin (Essex) at Chesterfield.	1904
Leading run-scorer	23,854	K. J. Barnett (avge 41.12).	1979–98
Best bowling for	10-40	W. Bestwick v Glamorgan at Cardiff	1921
Best bowling against	10-45	R. L. Johnson (Middlesex) at Derby	1994
Leading wicket-taker	1,670	H. L. Jackson (avge 17.11)	1947–63
Highest total for	801-8 dec	v Somerset at Taunton.	2007
Highest total against	677-7 dec	by Yorkshire at Leeds.	2013
Lowest total for	16	v Nottinghamshire at Nottingham.	1879
Lowest total against	23	by Hampshire at Burton-upon-Trent.	1958

LIST A COUNTY RECORDS

Highest score for	173*	M. J. Di Venuto v Derbys County Board at Derby	2000
Highest score against	158	R. K. Rao (Sussex) at Derby.	1997
Leading run-scorer	12,358	K. J. Barnett (avge 36.67).	1979–98
Best bowling for	8-21	M. A. Holding v Sussex at Hove.	1988
Best bowling against	8-66	S. R. G. Francis (Somerset) at Derby	2004
Leading wicket-taker	246	A. E. Warner (avge 27.13)	1985–95
Highest total for	366-4	v Combined Universities at Oxford	1991
Highest total against	369-6	by New Zealanders at Derby	1999
Lowest total for	60	v Kent at Canterbury.	2008
Lowest total against	42	by Glamorgan at Swansea.	1979

TWENTY20 COUNTY RECORDS

Highest score for	111	W. J. Durston v Nottinghamshire at Nottingham .	2010
Highest score against	158*	B. B. McCullum (Warwickshire) at Birmingham .	2015
Leading run-scorer	2,342	W. L. Madsen (avge 29.27, SR 131.79)	2010–18
Best bowling for	5-27	T. Lungley v Leicestershire at Leicester	2009
Best bowling against	5-14	P. D. Collingwood (Durham) at Chester-le-Street	2008
Leading wicket-taker	51	T. D. Groenewald (avge 27.52, ER 7.85)	2009–14
Highest total for	222-5	v Yorkshire at Leeds	2010
	222-5	v Nottinghamshire at Nottingham.	2017
Highest total against	249-8	by Hampshire at Derby	2017
Lowest total for	72	v Leicestershire at Derby	2013
Lowest total against	84	by West Indians at Derby	2007

ADDRESS

The Pattonair County Ground, Nottingham Road, Derby DE21 6DA; 01332 388 101; info@derby-shireccc.com; www.derbyshireccc.com.

OFFICIALS

Captain B. A. Godleman
(Twenty20) **2018** G. C. Wilson
Cricket advisor 2018 K. J. Barnett
Head of cricket 2019 D. L. Houghton
Head of development M. B. Loye
Twenty20 coach 2018 J. G. Wright
2019 D. G. Cork

Assistant and bowling coach 2019 S. P. Kirby
President 2018 E. Smith
Chairman R. I. Morgan
Chief executive 2018 S. Storey
2019 R. Duckett
Head groundsman N. Godrich
Scorer J. M. Brown

At Weetwood, Leeds, April 13–15. LEEDS/BRADFORD MCCU v DERBYSHIRE. Abandoned.

DERBYSHIRE v MIDDLESEX

At Derby, April 20–23. Derbyshire won by 101 runs. Derbyshire 21pts, Middlesex 3pts. Toss: uncontested. County debuts: D. Olivier, R. Rampaul.

After playing 23 first-class matches at home without a win since September 2014 – a whopping 1,306 days earlier – Derbyshire found victory especially sweet. Their domination was built on Duanne Olivier's eight wickets in the match (the most by a bowler on debut for Derbyshire since John O'Connor took ten at Old Trafford in 1900) and a second-innings opening stand of 219 between Slater and Reece, an all-wicket county record against Middlesex, overhauling 209 by Harry Storer and Denis Smith at Derby in 1932. That expanded a first-innings lead of 108, much of it due to late hitting from Viljoen, who reached his fifty with three sixes in an over from Rayner. By the third evening, Godleman was able to set his former county a target of 442. Middlesex's bowling had been severely restricted by injuries to Roland-Jones and Harris, but both managed to bat; from 95 for five, they played key roles in lower-order defiance which added another 245 and made Derbyshire work into the final session to complete their long-awaited win.

Close of play: first day, Middlesex 45-3 (Robson 15, Rayner 0); second day, Derbyshire 118-0 (Slater 63, Reece 47); third day, Middlesex 86-3 (Holden 37, Rayner 9).

Derbyshire

B. T. Slater b Harris	32	– c Holden b Rayner	99
L. M. Reece c Rayner b Murtagh	18	– not out	157
W. L. Madsen lbw b Murtagh	47	– c Cartwright b Stirling	52
A. L. Hughes c Simpson b Cartwright	15	– st Simpson b Stirling	5
*B. A. Godleman b Harris	17	– not out	1
†G. C. Wilson c White b Harris	6		
M. J. J. Critchley c Murtagh b Helm	14		
A. P. Palladino c Rayner b Harris	25		
G. C. Viljoen not out	60		
R. Rampaul c Rayner b Helm	2		
D. Olivier c Rayner b Helm	0		
B 9, lb 17, w 1, nb 2	29	B 3, lb 3, w 1, nb 12	19

1/31 (2) 2/75 (1) 3/117 (4)   (67 overs) 265
4/139 (5) 5/143 (3) 6/147 (6)
7/167 (7) 8/248 (8) 9/265 (10) 10/265 (11)

1/219 (1)   (3 wkts dec, 110 overs) 333
2/320 (3) 3/332 (4)

Murtagh 17–3–53–2; Roland-Jones 5–0–25–0; Harris 19–3–68–4; Helm 14–2–46–3; Cartwright 10–2–27–1; Rayner 2–0–20–0. *Second innings*—Murtagh 10–0–31–0; Harris 6–2–11–0; Cartwright 13–1–43–0; Helm 19–3–65–0; Rayner 35–5–84–1; Stirling 20–3–62–2; Holden 7–0–31–0.

Middlesex

*S. D. Robson lbw b Rampaul	19	– (2) lbw b Viljoen	5
M. D. E. Holden c Wilson b Rampaul	0	– (1) c Wilson b Viljoen	37
R. G. White c Critchley b Olivier	6	– lbw b Olivier	1
H. W. R. Cartwright c Hughes b Viljoen	10	– c Wilson b Olivier	29
O. P. Rayner lbw b Viljoen	2	– c Madsen b Olivier	18
P. R. Stirling lbw b Palladino	16	– c and b Reece	42
†J. A. Simpson b Olivier	32	– lbw b Madsen	24
J. A. R. Harris lbw b Olivier	21	– not out	64
T. S. Roland-Jones lbw b Palladino	10	– c Slater b Critchley	46
T. G. Helm c Madsen b Olivier	1	– lbw b Critchley	52
T. J. Murtagh not out	0	– b Olivier	5
B 13, w 21, nb 2	36	Lb 6, w 1, nb 10	17

1/1 (2) 2/23 (3) 3/45 (4)   (57.1 overs) 157
4/50 (1) 5/64 (5) 6/120 (7)
7/124 (6) 8/141 (9) 9/148 (10) 10/157 (8)

1/28 (2) 2/36 (3)   (111.3 overs) 340
3/69 (4) 4/95 (5)
5/95 (1) 6/160 (6) 7/166 (7)
8/223 (9) 9/329 (10) 10/340 (11)

Rampaul 13–3–43–2; Viljoen 19–8–47–2; Olivier 13.1–6–26–4; Palladino 12–6–28–2. *Second innings*—Rampaul 22–5–64–0; Viljoen 21–5–62–2; Olivier 23.3–2–82–4; Palladino 9–4–27–0; Madsen 13–7–26–1; Reece 7–1–22–1; Critchley 16–2–51–2.

Umpires: I. D. Blackwell and M. J. Saggers.

At Leicester, April 27–30. DERBYSHIRE drew with LEICESTERSHIRE.

At Birmingham, May 3–6. DERBYSHIRE lost to WARWICKSHIRE by eight wickets.

DERBYSHIRE v DURHAM

At Derby, May 11–14. Drawn. Derbyshire 10pts, Durham 11pts. Toss: uncontested. County debut: M. W. Dixon.

A record partnership comprehensively shifted the balance in Durham's favour on the third afternoon, though they could not convert the advantage into a second successive victory. Derbyshire had been on top for the first two days: Madsen had passed 9,000 first-class runs for the county on his way to 85, and on the third morning Durham were 175 for five, still 252 behind. Poynter's maiden Championship century – his 170 was a record for a Durham wicketkeeper – and Richardson's first for four years, changed all that. They added 278, Durham's highest stand for the sixth wicket, beating 249 by Gordon Muchall and Phil Mustard at Canterbury in 2006; their eventual first-innings lead was 93. Wood, who had returned early from the IPL to prepare for the First Test against Pakistan, found his rhythm on the final day, when he collected a career-best six for 46, and a Derbyshire defeat could not be ruled out. But dogged batting from tailenders Palladino, who survived an hour and a half, and Rampaul saw them to safety.

Close of play: first day, Derbyshire 301-4 (Madsen 80, Critchley 35); second day, Durham 115-2 (Steel 31, Clark 42); third day, Derbyshire 1-0 (Slater 0, Reece 1).

Derbyshire

B. T. Slater c Clark b Rimmington	55	– c Steel b Wood	42
L. M. Reece c Poynter b Weighell	48	– b Wood	12
W. L. Madsen lbw b Wood	85	– c Poynter b Wood	32
A. L. Hughes b Weighell	0	– c Poynter b Steel	17
*B. A. Godleman lbw b Dixon	61	– c Collingwood b Weighell	25
M. J. J. Critchley c and b Collingwood	64	– c Poynter b Steel	40
†D. Smit not out	45	– c Poynter b Wood	34
G. C. Viljoen lbw b Collingwood	9	– c Markram b Wood	12
A. P. Palladino b Steel	29	– not out	26
D. Olivier c Collingwood b Steel	0	– c Poynter b Wood	0
R. Rampaul lbw b Dixon	0	– not out	18
B 6, lb 21, nb 4	31	B 12, lb 5, nb 4	21

1/110 (1) 2/122 (2) 3/126 (4) (128.2 overs) 427   1/33 (2) (9 wkts, 79 overs) 279
4/240 (5) 5/318 (3) 6/346 (6)   2/88 (3) 3/97 (1)
7/360 (8) 8/422 (9) 9/426 (10)   4/114 (4) 5/177 (6) 6/185 (5)
10/427 (11)   110 overs: 393-7   7/213 (8) 8/236 (7) 9/242 (10)

Wood 29–4–91–1; Rimmington 13–4–46–1; Dixon 26.2–5–99–2; Weighell 33–10–82–2; Collingwood 17–7–40–2; Smith 3–0–10–0; Steel 6–2–19–2; Clark 2–0–13–0. *Second innings*—Wood 23–9–46–6; Weighell 14–3–39–1; Rimmington 10–1–40–0; Dixon 2–1–9–0; Smith 14–2–48–0; Steel 15–1–80–2; Markram 1–1–0–0.

Durham

C. T. Steel c Godleman b Olivier	31	N. J. Rimmington lbw b Madsen	3
A. K. Markram c Smit b Viljoen	30	M. W. Dixon not out	8
W. R. Smith b Viljoen	0		
G. Clark lbw b Palladino	63	B 24, lb 11, w 1, nb 6	42
*P. D. Collingwood c Smit b Rampaul	27		
M. J. Richardson lbw b Palladino	115	1/51 (2) 2/51 (3) (134.1 overs) 520	
†S. W. Poynter lbw b Olivier	170	3/115 (1) 4/169 (5) 5/175 (4)	
W. J. Weighell c Smit b Palladino	18	6/453 (7) 7/467 (6) 8/509 (9)	
M. A. Wood b Palladino	13	9/512 (10) 10/520 (8) 110 overs: 392-5	

Olivier 34–6–124–2; Rampaul 24–5–85–1; Viljoen 21–3–67–2; Critchley 17–0–85–0; Palladino 28.1–7–87–4; Madsen 2–0–10–1; Reece 8–0–27–0.

Umpires: P. K. Baldwin and R. A. Kettleborough.

At Chester-le-Street, June 9–12. DERBYSHIRE lost to DURHAM by 95 runs.

At Swansea, June 20–23. DERBYSHIRE drew with GLAMORGAN.

DERBYSHIRE v LEICESTERSHIRE

At Derby, June 25–27 (day/night). Leicestershire won by six wickets. Leicestershire 21pts, Derbyshire 4pts. Toss: uncontested.

Pakistan seamer Mohammad Abbas reduced Derbyshire to 17 for three under floodlights on the second night, and completed the job in blazing sunshine next day to help Leicestershire to their third victory in four Championship games. The pink ball moved substantially after dusk, but in the first innings neither side could harness it consistently enough to grasp control. Madsen made 80 for Derbyshire, while Leicestershire let Horton's good work slip as they lost their last nine for 129, restricting their lead to 52. They had to replace opener Dearden, who was struck on the helmet by Olivier, with Evans, a full substitute under the new concussion protocol; Olivier also hit Hill on the hand, but he was soon able to return. Abbas, however, ensured Derbyshire were four down before wiping out their deficit; only Critchley, with 86, offered much resistance before he became Abbas's sixth victim, leaving Leicestershire a target of 133. They eased home with 23 overs of the third day to spare.

Close of play: first day, Leicestershire 82-0 (Horton 48, Ackermann 14); second day, Derbyshire 43-3 (Hughes 15, Godleman 6).

Derbyshire

B. T. Slater lbw b Parkinson	46	– c Jones b Mohammad Abbas	7
H. R. Hosein c Hill b Mohammad Abbas	19	– lbw b Mohammad Abbas	4
W. L. Madsen lbw b Raine	80	– b Raine	2
A. L. Hughes lbw b Parkinson	0	– c Hill b Mohammad Abbas	30
*B. A. Godleman lbw b Parkinson	0	– b Mohammad Abbas	10
M. J. J. Critchley c Hill b Dexter	31	– c Griffiths b Mohammad Abbas	86
†D. Smit lbw b Jones	11	– b Raine	13
G. C. Viljoen c Hill b Griffiths	29	– c Ackermann b Parkinson	0
A. P. Palladino not out	11	– b Raine	8
D. Olivier lbw b Raine	0	– b Mohammad Abbas	9
R. Rampaul b Mohammad Abbas	0	– not out	0
B 4, lb 3, w 1, nb 10	18	B 13, lb 2	15

1/50 (2) 2/93 (1) 3/93 (4)	(66 overs) 245	1/10 (2) 2/15 (3) (60 overs) 184
4/93 (5) 5/155 (6) 6/184 (7)		3/17 (1) 4/47 (5)
7/232 (8) 8/236 (3) 9/236 (10) 10/245 (11)		5/86 (4) 6/128 (7) 7/131 (8)
		8/152 (9) 9/165 (10) 10/184 (6)

Raine 13–3–53–2; Mohammad Abbas 14–4–47–2; Jones 11–0–39–1; Griffiths 8–1–29–1; Parkinson 11–1–50–3; Dexter 9–2–20–1. *Second innings*—Raine 21–3–67–3; Mohammad Abbas 24–7–54–6; Griffiths 6–2–21–0; Parkinson 7–0–22–1; Jones 2–1–5–0.

Leicestershire

H. E. Dearden retired hurt	9			
*P. J. Horton lbw b Viljoen	88	– lbw b Olivier	48
C. N. Ackermann lbw b Palladino	32	– c Smit b Olivier	58
S. T. Evans c Smit b Olivier	29	– (1) c Hosein b Viljoen	2
M. J. Cosgrove c Madsen b Olivier	35	– (4) c Smit b Viljoen	4
N. J. Dexter lbw b Viljoen	0	– (5) not out	11
†L. J. Hill c Critchley b Rampaul	20	– (6) not out	3
B. A. Raine c sub (Hamidullah Qadri) b Palladino	10		
C. F. Parkinson c Madsen b Viljoen	34		
G. T. Griffiths b Palladino	10		
R. A. Jones b Palladino	0		
Mohammad Abbas not out	3		
B 1, lb 10, nb 16	27	B 1, lb 2, nb 4	7

1/105 (3) 2/168 (4) 3/174 (2)　　(103 overs) 297　　1/3 (1)　　(4 wkts, 29.4 overs) 133
4/174 (6) 5/196 (8) 6/225 (7)　　　　　　　　　　　　　2/100 (3) 3/105 (4)
7/256 (5) 8/271 (10) 9/273 (11)　　　　　　　　　　　　4/129 (2)
10/297 (9)

In the first innings Dearden retired hurt at 53–0; Hill, when 0, retired hurt at 179–4 and resumed at 196–5. Evans replaced Dearden, as a concussion substitute.

Olivier 29–8–85–2; Rampaul 17–3–62–1; Palladino 26–7–64–4; Viljoen 22–5–59–3; Critchley 9–1–16–0. *Second innings*—Olivier 10–1–37–0; Viljoen 10.4–1–48–2; Rampaul 3–0–16–0; Palladino 4–0–10–0; Critchley 2–0–19–0.

Umpires: S. J. O'Shaughnessy and B. V. Taylor.

DERBYSHIRE v NORTHAMPTONSHIRE

At Chesterfield, July 22–25. Derbyshire won by 39 runs. Derbyshire 21pts, Northamptonshire 5pts. Toss: Derbyshire. First-class debut: D. M. Wheeldon.

Matt Critchley and Hamidullah Qadri, two youngsters with 30 previous first-class appearances between them, spun Derbyshire to their first Championship victory at Queen's Park since 2008. The 21-year-old Critchley had scored a century at Chesterfield in 2017; this time he improved his best bowling figures, twice, and became the first Derbyshire leg-spinner to take ten in a match since Bert Rhodes in 1950. Wakely had led Northamptonshire to 227 for four chasing 314, before 17-year-old off-spinner Qadri bowled him on a rapidly wearing pitch, sparking a collapse of six for 47. In the first innings, Wakely's century – which took him past 6,000 first-class runs – had been largely responsible for Northamptonshire's 29-run lead, though he would have hoped for a bigger advantage during his 120-run stand with Crook. Sanderson's five wickets had restricted Derbyshire after they chose to bat, but on the third day a hundred by Madsen – his 27th hundred for the county, putting him equal fourth on their all-time list – and a fifty from Critchley helped set the challenging target.

Close of play: first day, Northamptonshire 74-3 (Buck 1, Wakely 12); second day, Derbyshire 147-4 (Madsen 52, Hosein 5); third day, Northamptonshire 174-3 (Wakely 48, Levi 22).

Derbyshire

B. T. Slater lbw b Sanderson	0	– c Duckett b Prasanna	53
*B. A. Godleman c Vasconcelos b Sanderson	10	– c Vasconcelos b Sanderson	16
W. L. Madsen b Sanderson	11	– c Levi b Sanderson	116
A. L. Hughes b Buck	12	– lbw b Prasanna	9
H. R. Hosein c Wakely b Sanderson	58	– b Prasanna	38
M. J. J. Critchley lbw b Buck	37	– (7) run out (Prasanna)	51
†G. C. Wilson b Buck	66	– b Buck	6
G. C. Viljoen c Vasconcelos b Sanderson	16	– (9) c Duckett b Prasanna	23
A. P. Palladino st Vasconcelos b Prasanna	1	– (10) c Vasconcelos b Hutton	0
D. M. Wheeldon not out	33	– b Sanderson	2
Hamidullah Qadri b Prasanna	6	– not out	1
B 6, lb 4	10	B 18, lb 5, nb 4	27

1/0 (1) 2/12 (3) 3/21 (2) (74.5 overs) 260
4/53 (4) 5/113 (6) 6/150 (5)
7/170 (8) 8/183 (9) 9/235 (10) 10/260 (11)

1/37 (2) 2/123 (1) (97.1 overs) 342
3/137 (4) 4/140 (5)
5/209 (6) 6/291 (3) 7/310 (8)
8/316 (7) 9/320 (10) 10/342 (9)

Sanderson 20–3–53–5; Hutton 18–2–68–0; Procter 3–0–7–0; Buck 17–1–62–3; Prasanna 16.5–1–60–2. *Second innings*—Sanderson 26–6–55–3; Hutton 16–1–52–1; Prasanna 31.1–3–104–4; Buck 13–1–59–1; Procter 9–0–31–0; Cobb 2–0–18–0.

Northamptonshire

L. A. Procter lbw b Viljoen	30	– c Madsen b Critchley	68
B. M. Duckett c Wilson b Palladino	29	– lbw b Wheeldon	16
†R. S. Vasconcelos b Palladino	0	– c Madsen b Hamidullah Qadri	10
N. L. Buck c Godleman b Critchley	12	– (9) c Madsen b Critchley	10
*A. G. Wakely c Madsen b Critchley	106	– (4) b Hamidullah Qadri	68
R. E. Levi b Viljoen	7	– (5) lbw b Critchley	29
S. P. Crook lbw b Palladino	60	– (6) c Hughes b Critchley	21
J. J. Cobb c and b Critchley	13	– (7) lbw b Critchley	9
S. Prasanna c Hughes b Critchley	14	– (8) b Critchley	27
B. A. Hutton b Palladino	2	– b Hamidullah Qadri	1
B. W. Sanderson not out	7	– not out	0
B 4, lb 4, w 1	9	B 8, lb 3, nb 4	15

1/53 (2) 2/53 (3) 3/59 (1) (68.2 overs) 289
4/101 (4) 5/118 (6) 6/238 (5)
7/260 (8) 8/280 (7) 9/280 (9) 10/289 (10)

1/29 (2) 2/48 (3) (69.3 overs) 274
3/123 (1) 4/187 (5)
5/227 (4) 6/229 (6) 7/256 (7)
8/265 (8) 9/266 (10) 10/274 (9)

Viljoen 21–1–94–2; Wheeldon 8–0–36–0; Palladino 15.2–5–33–4; Hamidullah Qadri 7–0–30–0; Critchley 17–0–88–4. *Second innings*—Palladino 6–0–28–0; Viljoen 16–0–51–0; Wheeldon 5–2–12–1; Hamidullah Qadri 18–2–66–3; Critchley 24.3–2–106–6.

Umpires: N. L. Bainton and B. J. Debenham.

At Hove, August 19–22. DERBYSHIRE lost to SUSSEX by 243 runs.

DERBYSHIRE v KENT

At Derby, August 29–September 1. Kent won by six wickets. Kent 23pts, Derbyshire 5pts. Toss: Kent. First-class debut: T. C. Lace.

Almost three years after his last Championship wicket, off-spinner Riley claimed seven to turn what looked like a high-scoring draw into a victory that put Kent back in the second promotion spot. Denly, dropped first ball, had completed his fourth first-class hundred of the summer, and Crawley narrowly missed the first of his career as they shared a second-wicket stand of 170; later, Stewart and

Henry, whose 81 was his highest score, added 119 for the eighth, helping Kent amass 561, their biggest total against Derbyshire since 1908. At 288 for two on the third day, the home side were also enjoying the benign surface. Then Riley, blighted by injuries and loss of form since touring South Africa with England Lions in 2014-15, trapped Madsen for 93. By stumps, he had dismissed him again as Derbyshire followed on, having lost eight for 112. He finished with four of the top six second time round, before Denly, off the field for most of the fourth morning because of illness, took the last four for a career-best. Hosein's unbeaten 66 ensured Kent would bat again, but they knocked off 110 inside 20 overs. Ervine later announced his retirement, after playing two games for Derbyshire on loan from Hampshire.

Close of play: first day, Kent 365-6 (Bell-Drummond 41, Stewart 14); second day, Derbyshire 210-2 (Madsen 60, Hughes 20); third day, Derbyshire 83-2 (Lace 28, Hughes 16).

Kent

S. R. Dickson lbw b Viljoen	4	– c Hosein b Ferguson	13
Z. Crawley lbw b Palladino	96	– c Madsen b Hamidullah Qadir	34
J. L. Denly b Viljoen	106	– (4) c and b Hamidullah Qadir	4
H. G. Kuhn lbw b Palladino	51	– (3) c Hamidullah Qadir b Critchley	24
D. J. Bell-Drummond c Hosein b Palladino	44	– not out	22
*†S. W. Billings lbw b Hughes	15	– not out	7
H. W. Podmore b Ferguson	3		
G. Stewart b Hughes	85		
M. J. Henry c Ervine b Palladino	81		
A. E. N. Riley c Godleman b Palladino	23		
I. A. A. Thomas not out	0		
B 22, lb 18, nb 8, p 5	53	B 4, nb 2	6

1/4 (1) 2/174 (2) 3/273 (4)   (131.4 overs) 561   1/20 (1)   (4 wkts, 19.2 overs) 110
4/283 (3) 5/320 (6) 6/331 (7)   2/77 (2) 3/81 (3)
7/393 (5) 8/512 (8) 9/561 (9)   4/87 (4)
10/561 (10)   110 overs: 440-7

Viljoen 26–2–104–2; Ferguson 31–5–103–1; Hughes 17–1–58–2; Palladino 30.4–5–113–5; Critchley 17–0–89–0; Ervine 6–0–23–0; Hamidullah Qadir 3–0–26–0; Madsen 1–1–0–0. *Second innings*—Ferguson 4–0–24–1; Palladino 3–0–15–0; Critchley 6.2–0–33–1; Hamidullah Qadir 6–0–34–2.

Derbyshire

T. C. Lace lbw b Thomas	40	– b Stewart	43
*B. A. Godleman b Thomas	71	– b Riley	26
W. L. Madsen lbw b Riley	93	– c and b Riley	5
A. L. Hughes c Denly b Riley	66	– c Billings b Henry	16
S. M. Ervine c Billings b Stewart	26	– c Kuhn b Riley	22
M. J. J. Critchley st Billings b Riley	15	– c Billings b Riley	1
†H. R. Hosein c Dickson b Denly	8	– not out	66
G. C. Viljoen c Kuhn b Stewart	5	– c Riley b Denly	23
A. P. Palladino run out (Henry)	18	– lbw b Denly	30
L. H. Ferguson c sub (O. G. Robinson) b Thomas	16	– c Riley b Denly	0
Hamidullah Qadir not out	15	– lbw b Denly	1
B 16, lb 5, nb 6	27	B 12, lb 12, nb 8, p 5	37

1/69 (1) 2/158 (2) 3/288 (3)   (126.3 overs) 400   1/51 (2) 2/57 (3)   (96.4 overs) 270
4/301 (5) 5/323 (6) 6/332 (7)   3/99 (4) 4/117 (1)
7/344 (8) 8/355 (5) 9/370 (9)   5/118 (6) 6/137 (5)
10/400 (10)   110 overs: 344-6   7/190 (8) 8/262 (9)
                                                                     9/268 (10) 10/270 (11)

Henry 22–1–95–0; Podmore 22–9–36–0; Stewart 13–2–40–2; Thomas 10.3–0–45–3; Denly 27–1–85–1; Riley 32–6–78–3. *Second innings*—Henry 19–5–40–1; Podmore 17–8–27–0; Riley 28–7–68–4; Thomas 10–0–39–0; Denly 14.4–4–36–4; Stewart 8–1–31–1.

Umpires: I. D. Blackwell and N. G. B. Cook.

DERBYSHIRE v GLAMORGAN

At Derby, September 4–6. Derbyshire won by 169 runs. Derbyshire 21pts, Glamorgan 3pts. Toss: uncontested. County debuts: M. K. Andersson; S. C. Cook.

Tony Palladino inflicted a fifth consecutive defeat on bottom-placed Glamorgan by tearing through their fragile batting. He completed the first ten-wicket haul of his 15-year career when last man Hogan skyed to midwicket. The previous day, Palladino's 300th victim for Derbyshire had started a collapse in which he claimed six, and Glamorgan lost their last eight for 38. It left them well adrift of a home total of 251 underpinned by Godleman's dogged 95. He batted for all but nine overs, though in the second innings he was caught behind for a duck. Glamorgan needed 302 to win in just over two days, but Palladino struck again before the close. Martin Andersson celebrated his 22nd birthday with his first four first-class wickets; he had joined his Middlesex Second XI team-mate Tom Lace on loan to Derbyshire following Sean Ervine's retirement. Cooke provided the only resistance, with 67, and none of his team-mates passed 11.

Close of play: first day, Glamorgan 20-0 (Cook 5, Brown 9); second day, Glamorgan 16-1 (Brown 7).

Derbyshire

T. C. Lace b van der Gugten	12	– lbw b Lloyd		24
*B. A. Godleman c Cooke b Wagg	95	– c Cooke b van der Gugten		0
W. L. Madsen c Cullen b Hogan	7	– b van der Gugten		14
A. L. Hughes c Cooke b van der Gugten	9	– c Brown b Smith		57
G. C. Wilson lbw b Lloyd	26	– c Hogan b Bull		15
M. J. J. Critchley lbw b Hogan	26	– c Brown b Bull		0
†H. R. Hosein st Cooke b Bull	10	– c Carlson b Hogan		31
M. K. Andersson lbw b Wagg	11	– c Cullen b Bull		0
A. P. Palladino not out	16	– c Brown b Smith		1
L. H. Ferguson lbw b Wagg	4	– not out		12
R. Rampaul c Cook b van der Gugten	18	– b Hogan		0
B 2, lb 9, nb 6	17	B 2, lb 7, nb 8		17

1/32 (1) 2/41 (3) 3/50 (4)   (73 overs) 251
4/102 (5) 5/143 (6) 6/176 (7)
7/205 (8) 8/214 (2) 9/224 (10) 10/251 (11)

1/5 (2) 2/29 (3)   (55.4 overs) 171
3/64 (1) 4/94 (5)
5/101 (6) 6/141 (4)
7/142 (8) 8/146 (9)
9/171 (6) 10/171 (11)

Van der Gugten 16–2–66–3; Smith 12–2–49–0; Hogan 17–3–48–2; Wagg 12–3–36–3; Lloyd 2–0–8–1; Bull 14–3–33–1. *Second innings*—van der Gugten 11–2–39–2; Hogan 6.4–2–18–2; Wagg 10–3–24–0; Smith 10–2–37–2; Lloyd 4–1–8–1; Bull 14–3–36–3.

Glamorgan

S. C. Cook c Wilson b Rampaul	9	– b Palladino		5
C. R. Brown b Ferguson	14	– c Hosein b Andersson		11
T. N. Cullen c Hosein b Palladino	20	– b Palladino		4
K. S. Carlson c Andersson b Palladino	23	– lbw b Palladino		4
D. L. Lloyd c Wilson b Palladino	25	– c Palladino b Ferguson		1
†C. B. Cooke lbw b Hughes	1	– b Ferguson		67
G. G. Wagg b Palladino	0	– c Madsen b Andersson		0
R. A. J. Smith b Palladino	0	– c Wilson b Andersson		9
T. van der Gugten b Palladino	9	– c and b Andersson		0
K. A. Bull b Ferguson	0	– not out		7
*M. G. Hogan not out	0	– c Ferguson b Palladino		11
B 2, lb 14, nb 4	20	Lb 9, nb 4		13

1/29 (2) 2/43 (1) 3/83 (4)   (44.3 overs) 121
4/86 (3) 5/89 (6) 6/90 (7)
7/94 (8) 8/104 (9) 9/121 (5) 10/121 (10)

1/16 (1) 2/22 (3)   (46.5 overs) 132
3/32 (4) 4/33 (5)
5/42 (2) 6/56 (7)
7/82 (8) 8/82 (9)
9/121 (6) 10/132 (11)

Ferguson 12.3–3–34–2; Rampaul 9–3–22–1; Andersson 5–1–16–0; Palladino 13–3–29–6; Hughes 5–2–4–1. *Second innings*—Palladino 19.5–8–52–4; Ferguson 13–5–25–2; Andersson 9–2–25–4; Rampaul 4–0–21–0; Critchley 1–1–0–0.

Umpires: B. J. Debenham and B. V. Taylor.

At Northampton, September 10–13. DERBYSHIRE beat NORTHAMPTONSHIRE by one wicket.

At Lord's, September 18–21. DERBYSHIRE lost to MIDDLESEX by 117 runs.

DERBYSHIRE v GLOUCESTERSHIRE

At Derby, September 24–26. Gloucestershire won by two wickets. Gloucestershire 19pts, Derbyshire 3pts. Toss: uncontested.

On his last appearance for Gloucestershire, Miles settled a close contest when he drove Critchley back over his head. It was a fitting way to sign off before leaving for Edgbaston; earlier in the game, he had picked up eight wickets, which took him to 255 since his county debut in 2011, at the age of 16. He had to share top billing with Reece, who had been out for nearly four months after breaking a metatarsal in his right foot. Reece started the second match of his comeback by making 59 – which remained the highest score of the game – then followed up with seven for 20, having never taken more than four in an innings. It earned Derbyshire a slender lead of 21. But their second innings was dismal: only Hughes, with an unbeaten 55, passed 17. Gloucestershire began their pursuit of a modest 179 on the second evening, but next day the pitch offered diminishing assistance to the bowlers. Howell's 58 carried them to 142 for four after lunch; Derbyshire's hopes revived when four wickets fell for 27, but Miles had the final word.

Close of play: first day, Gloucestershire 100-5 (Drissell 1, M. D. Taylor 0); second day, Gloucestershire 29-2 (Hammond 15, Drissell 7).

Derbyshire

L. M. Reece c Dent b Miles	59	– c Hammond b Higgins	7
*B. A. Godleman b Miles	8	– lbw b Payne	4
W. L. Madsen lbw b Higgins	14	– lbw b Higgins	14
T. C. Lace b Higgins	6	– lbw b Howell	17
A. L. Hughes lbw b Miles	22	– not out	55
M. J. J. Critchley c Howell b Miles	26	– b Drissell	10
†H. R. Hosein lbw b M. D. Taylor	11	– c Dent b Miles	2
A. K. Dal c M. D. Taylor b Miles	12	– c Howell b Higgins	11
G. C. Viljoen lbw b M. D. Taylor	0	– c Bracey b Miles	16
A. P. Palladino b M. D. Taylor	4	– c Dent b Miles	2
L. H. Ferguson not out	0	– c Bracey b M. D. Taylor	0
B 10, lb 8, w 2, nb 2	22	B 4, lb 13, nb 2	19

1/39 (2) 2/75 (3) 3/89 (1) (52 overs) 184
4/98 (4) 5/149 (6) 6/158 (5)
7/170 (7) 8/174 (9) 9/184 (10) 10/184 (8)

1/5 (2) 2/29 (3) (60.3 overs) 157
3/32 (1) 4/66 (4)
5/84 (6) 6/87 (7) 7/114 (8)
8/136 (9) 9/140 (10) 10/157 (11)

Payne 12–2–49–0; Miles 17–6–50–5; M. D. Taylor 12–2–32–3; Higgins 11–4–35–2. *Second innings*—Payne 12–2–28–1; Miles 15–3–46–3; Higgins 13–4–17–3; M. D. Taylor 8.3–1–17–1; Howell 5–3–12–1; Drissell 7–0–20–1.

Gloucestershire

M. A. H. Hammond b Palladino	4	– (2) c Madsen b Viljoen. 39
*C. D. J. Dent lbw b Reece	37	– (1) c Hosein b Ferguson 0
†J. R. Bracey lbw b Reece	26	– b Ferguson 2
B. A. C. Howell lbw b Reece	4	– (5) c Hughes b Critchley 58
B. G. Charlesworth lbw b Reece	3	– (6) lbw b Critchley 23
G. S. Drissell b Ferguson	6	– (4) lbw b Palladino. 16
M. D. Taylor c Ferguson b Reece	29	
J. M. R. Taylor c Hosein b Reece	4	– (7) c Godleman b Ferguson 16
R. F. Higgins c Madsen b Viljoen	12	– (8) c and b Ferguson. 5
C. N. Miles c Hosein b Reece	4	– (9) not out. 11
D. A. Payne not out	0	– (10) not out. 0
B 16, lb 8, w 10	34	Lb 4, w 1, nb 4 9

1/30 (1) 2/75 (3) 3/87 (4)   (64.1 overs) 163
4/99 (5) 5/100 (2) 6/121 (6)
7/135 (8) 8/153 (9) 9/158 (10) 10/163 (7)

1/0 (1)   (8 wkts, 53.5 overs) 179
2/19 (3) 3/54 (4) 4/95 (2)
5/142 (5) 6/149 (6) 7/158 (8) 8/169 (7)

Ferguson 13–3–30–1; Palladino 19–8–30–1; Hughes 10–4–25–0; Viljoen 8–1–34–1; Reece 14.1–6–20–7. *Second innings*—Ferguson 19–1–56–4; Palladino 16–4–48–1; Reece 8–2–18–0; Viljoen 6–0–24–1; Critchley 4.5–0–29–2.

Umpires: N. A. Mallender and D. J. Millns.

DURHAM

All change, please

TIM WELLOCK

There was a dramatic exodus at Riverside in 2018, with the retirement of captain Paul Collingwood, director of cricket Geoff Cook and chief executive David Harker, followed by the departure of head coach Jon Lewis. And the green shoots of recovery evident in mid-season withered in September: Durham recorded their two lowest first-class totals, 61 and 66, in a single day at Grace Road, just after the news that Collingwood and Cook were stepping down. Another defeat followed in the final game, leaving them eighth out of ten in the second division.

It was a disappointing end to Collingwood's sixth full season as captain but, at 42, a lack of form made retirement inevitable. Nor was Cook's exit a surprise: he had been a peripheral figure since a cardiac arrest in 2013, when Lewis replaced him as head coach. Former Australian Test batsman Marcus North – who appeared for Durham in 2004 – became director of cricket, and began a review of operations with the new chief executive, Tim Bostock, which led to Lewis leaving in December. Former New Zealand all-rounder James Franklin was appointed lead high performance coach in January 2019.

Bostock, who played for Cheshire and worked in banking and commerce, took charge in July, when Harker stood down after 18 years in the job. Like Cook, he had been with Durham since they achieved first-class status in 1992; he had planned to go five years earlier but, with financial worries mounting, was persuaded to stay on, and the ECB asked him to oversee the recovery following their 2016 bailout. While the cruelty of the accompanying sanctions continued to undermine the team, the accounts up to September 2017 showed an operating profit of £2.3m. The debt had fallen from £7.4m to £6m, and the county were forecast to break even in the following financial year.

In early and late season, the uncontested toss counted heavily against Durham in difficult conditions at Riverside, but the batting's lack of quality was confirmed in the calamity at Leicester. Cameron Steel was comfortably their top run-scorer in the Championship, with a meagre 638, and the only candidate for Player of the Year was Chris Rushworth. He missed just five games in all formats, took 60 first-class wickets, and earned a testimonial.

During their early struggles, Durham took the field with only three players who had been Championship regulars two years before. Still, a never-say-die spirit emerged as they extracted two four-day wins from deep within the jaws of defeat. Though they finished bottom of their Royal London Cup group, Durham turned a corner in the Vitality Blast, with a run to the quarter-finals – a surprise for a squad lacking big hitters.

The improving financial situation permitted some signings. Alex Lees arrived from Yorkshire in mid-August, alongside Indian spin-bowling all-rounder Akshar Patel; both played significant roles in a resounding Championship win at Cardiff. Seamer Matt Salisbury, along with ex-Kent and Somerset wicketkeeper Ryan Davies, had made a county debut in June; after a successful month on loan from Hampshire, Salisbury was signed full-time in July, while Davies became a T20 regular, although he rarely took the gloves as Stuart Poynter consolidated his position. Imran Tahir – joining his seventh county, a record – proved an inspired recruit for the T20 group games.

Harry Trump, Getty Images

Tom Latham

Less successful were Australian seamer Nathan Rimmington and South African opener Aiden Markram. Rimmington, a 35-year-old with a British passport, had been handed a two-year deal just after Graham Onions, a couple of months older, left Durham when his request for something similar had strings attached. Onions took 57 Championship wickets for his new county, Lancashire, while Rimmington managed 11, though he contributed 22 in the Blast.

Three weeks after scoring 152 in the Fourth Test against Australia at Johannesburg, Markram bagged a pair on his first day for Durham. After the second of his four scheduled appearances was washed out, he made a third duck, against Leicestershire. But his second-innings 94, in an opening stand of 152 with Steel, as Durham followed on, 256 behind, inspired them to a 46-run win. And they pulled off a similar turnaround in the next home game after Derbyshire dismissed them for 96.

In his second season at Riverside, the New Zealander Tom Latham took over as overseas player from mid-May to August, and captained the one-day side. After defeat in two of the first three T20 games, he and opening partner Graham Clark helped Durham to eight wins in the next nine. But the bubble burst; they were bowled out for 78 by Lancashire, and more limp batting followed in their home quarter-final against Sussex.

In September, the club announced that Sunderland-born Ben Raine would return from Leicestershire in 2019, while Brydon Carse signed a three-year contract despite missing the entire season with a knee injury. Raine bolstered a stable of seaming all-rounders, with Carse, James Weighell and Matty Potts expected to shine after growing pains – though Irish international Barry McCarthy was released. But the spin cupboard looked bare, with off-spinner Ryan Pringle given only one first-class appearance.

In August, Durham revealed that Cameron Bancroft would be their overseas player throughout 2019 subject to selection by Australia. (Latham was expected to play in the World Cup.) The press release did not mention his ban for ball-tampering in the Cape Town Test; inevitably, the media raised it with Bostock, who insisted Durham had signed "an outstanding young man".

Championship attendance: 21,011.

DURHAM RESULTS

All first-class matches – Played 13: Won 4, Lost 7, Drawn 2. Abandoned 1.
County Championship matches – Played 13: Won 4, Lost 7, Drawn 2. Abandoned 1.

Specsavers County Championship, 8th in Division 2;
Vitality Blast, quarter-finalists; Royal London One-Day Cup, 9th in North Group.

COUNTY CHAMPIONSHIP AVERAGES, BATTING AND FIELDING

Cap		Birthplace	M	I	NO	R	HS	100	Avge	Ct/St
	T. W. M. Latham¶ ..	Christchurch, NZ ..	4	8	0	366	147	1	45.75	8
	W. J. Weighell.....	Middlesbrough ..	3	5	0	185	84	0	37.00	1
	C. T. Steel	Greenbrae, USA..	12	22	0	638	160	1	29.00	9
	G. J. Harte	Johannesburg, SA .	8	15	0	382	114	2	25.46	4
	S. W. Poynter	Hammersmith	11	20	1	475	170	1	25.00	34/1
	A. K. Markram¶	Pretoria, SA	3	5	0	124	94	0	24.80	4
†A. R. Patel¶	Anand, India	4	7	1	147	95*	0	24.50	1
†A. Z. Lees	Halifax	6	11	0	256	69	0	23.27	3
	M. A. Wood§	Ashington	4	7	2	115	61*	0	23.00	1
	N. J. Rimmington†† ..	Redcliffe, Australia ..	7	13	1	255	61	0	21.25	1
	W. R. Smith.......	Luton	9	17	0	357	90	0	21.00	5
	M. J. Richardson ...	Port Elizabeth, SA ..	10	18	0	377	115	1	20.94	3
	G. Clark	Whitehaven	12	22	0	460	64	0	20.90	9
1998	P. D. Collingwood...	Shotley Bridge‡ ..	11	20	0	299	47	0	14.95	12
	B. J. McCarthy	Dublin, Ireland ..	6	11	1	111	43	0	11.10	2
†J. Coughlin	Sunderland‡.....	2	4	0	42	19	0	10.50	1
	M. E. T. Salisbury ...	Chelmsford.....	10	19	5	141	37	0	10.07	1
	C. Rushworth	Sunderland‡.....	12	22	12	72	11*	0	7.20	2
	R. C. Davies	Margate	3	6	0	27	20	0	4.50	7

Also batted: M. W. Dixon†† (*Subiaco, Australia*) (1 match) 8*; G. H. I. Harding (*Poole*) (1 match) 0, 7; M. A. Jones (*Ormskirk*) (1 match) 10, 3; M. J. Potts (*Sunderland‡*) (1 match) 15*, 36; R. D. Pringle (*Sunderland‡*) (1 match) 34, 3 (1 ct); †B. A. Stokes§ (*Christchurch, NZ*) (1 match) 3, 9 (2 ct).

‡ Born in Durham. § ECB contract. ¶ Official overseas player. ††Other non-England-qualified.

Durham ceased to award caps after 2005.

BOWLING

	Style	O	M	R	W	BB	5I	Avge
A. R. Patel	SLA	99.4	33	235	18	7-54	1	13.05
M. A. Wood.....................	RFM	109.1	24	293	17	6-46	2	17.23
C. Rushworth	RFM	386.4	83	1,201	60	8-51	3	20.01
W. J. Weighell	RM	108.3	23	304	15	7-32	1	20.26
M. E. T. Salisbury	RFM	293.1	56	1,090	44	6-37	1	24.77
B. J. McCarthy	RFM	130.3	21	460	14	4-58	0	32.85
N. J. Rimmington...............	RFM	167.4	34	606	11	3-39	0	55.09

Also bowled: G. Clark (LB) 13.5–0–51–2; P. D. Collingwood (RM) 49–15–116–6; J. Coughlin (RM) 35–3–139–3; M. W. Dixon (RFM) 28.2–6–108–2; G. H. I. Harding (SLA) 30–4–106–0; G. J. Harte (RM) 45.1–7–148–3; A. K. Markram (OB) 1.4–1–1–1; M. J. Potts (RFM) 5–0–37–1; R. D. Pringle (OB) 28–2–74–3; W. R. Smith (OB) 66.1–6–204–4; C. T. Steel (LB) 46.2–4–202–9; B. A. Stokes (RFM) 43–11–118–8.

LEADING ROYAL LONDON CUP AVERAGES (100 runs/4 wickets)

Batting	Runs	HS	Avge	SR	Ct/St
M. J. Richardson ..	392	111	49.00	82.35	4
G. J. Harte	140	48	35.00	85.36	0
W. R. Smith	266	119	33.25	80.60	2
T. W. M. Latham ..	255	86	31.87	80.18	2
G. Clark........	131	45	16.37	64.53	2
S. W. Poynter ...	110	36	13.75	79.71	6/1

Bowling	W	BB	Avge	ER
C. Rushworth	9	3-39	22.44	4.43
N. J. Rimmington .	9	3-36	32.77	5.56
M. W. Dixon	9	3-42	53.88	6.77
R. D. Pringle	4	2-39	59.00	4.45

LEADING VITALITY BLAST AVERAGES (100 runs/15 overs)

Batting	Runs	HS	Avge	SR	Ct/St	Bowling	W	BB	Avge	ER
R. C. Davies....	136	27	17.00	146.23	5	Imran Tahir......	15	4-14	13.53	6.34
G. Clark......	408	65	29.14	139.72	9	W. R. Smith	5	2-20	21.40	6.68
B. A. Stokes....	177	90*	59.00	138.28	1	B. G. Whitehead..	5	2-23	28.80	7.20
T. W. M. Latham	470	98*	36.15	136.62	11	C. Rushworth	11	3-22	29.63	7.58
S. W. Poynter...	177	31	44.25	131.11	13/3	P. D. Collingwood	10	3-25	32.40	7.71
P. D. Collingwood	257	50*	25.70	112.71	5	N. J. Rimmington.	22	4-28	18.54	8.96
W. R. Smith....	154	37*	17.11	111.59	4	W. J. Weighell ...	13	2-7	25.23	9.11

FIRST-CLASS COUNTY RECORDS

Highest score for	273	M. L. Love v Hampshire at Chester-le-Street	2003
Highest score against	501*	B. C. Lara (Warwickshire) at Birmingham........	1994
Leading run-scorer	**12,030**	**P. D. Collingwood (avge 33.98)**..............	**1996–2018**
Best bowling for	10-47	O. D. Gibson v Hampshire at Chester-le-Street ...	2007
Best bowling against	9-34	J. A. R. Harris (Middlesex) at Lord's	2015
Leading wicket-taker	527	G. Onions (avge 25.58).......................	2004–17
Highest total for	648-5 dec	v Nottinghamshire at Chester-le-Street	2009
Highest total against	810-4 dec	by Warwickshire at Birmingham................	1994
Lowest total for	**61**	**v Leicestershire at Leicester**..................	**2018**
Lowest total against	18	by Durham MCCU at Chester-le-Street	2012

LIST A COUNTY RECORDS

Highest score for	164	B. A. Stokes v Nottinghamshire at Chester-le-St ..	2014
Highest score against	174	J. M. Bairstow (Yorkshire) at Leeds	2017
Leading run-scorer	**6,007**	**P. D. Collingwood (avge 33.00)**..............	**1995–2018**
Best bowling for	7-32	S. P. Davis v Lancashire at Chester-le-Street	1983
Best bowling against	6-22	A. Dale (Glamorgan) at Colwyn Bay	1993
Leading wicket-taker	298	N. Killeen (avge 23.96).......................	1995–2010
Highest total for	353-8	v Nottinghamshire at Chester-le-Street	2014
Highest total against	361-7	by Essex at Chelmsford.......................	1996
Lowest total for	72	v Warwickshire at Birmingham.................	2002
Lowest total against	63	by Hertfordshire at Darlington	1964

TWENTY20 COUNTY RECORDS

Highest score for	108*	P. D. Collingwood v Worcestershire at Worcester .	2017
Highest score against	127	T. Köhler-Cadmore (Worcs) at Worcester	2016
Leading run-scorer	**3,207**	**P. Mustard (avge 25.05, SR 122.03)**............	**2003–16**
Best bowling for	5-6	P. D. Collingwood v Northants at Chester-le-St ...	2011
Best bowling against	5-16	R. M. Pyrah (Yorkshire) at Scarborough.........	2011
Leading wicket-taker	93	G. R. Breese (avge 21.56, ER 6.76)	2004–14
Highest total for	225-2	v Leicestershire at Chester-le-Street	2010
Highest total against	225-6	by Worcestershire at Worcester................	2016
Lowest total for	**78**	**v Lancashire at Chester-le-Street**.............	**2018**
Lowest total against	47	by Northamptonshire at Chester-le-Street........	2011

ADDRESS

Emirates Durham International Cricket Ground, Riverside, Chester-le-Street, County Durham DH3 3QR; 0191 387 1717; reception@durhamcricket.co.uk; www.durhamcricket.co.uk.

OFFICIALS

Captain 2018 P. D. Collingwood
 (limited-overs) **2018** T. W. M. Latham
Director of cricket 2018 G. Cook
 2019 M. J. North
First-team coach 2018 J. J. B. Lewis
High perf. coach 2019 J. E. C. Franklin

Academy coach J. B. Windows
Chairman Sir Ian Botham
Chief operating officer R. Dowson
Chief executive T. J. Bostock
Head groundsman V. Demain
Scorer W. R. Dobson

At Chester-le-Street, April 13–15 (not first-class). **Drawn. ‡Durham MCCU 194-3 dec** (50 overs) (M. J. Plater 76, W. A. R. Fraine 65*); **Durham 165-3** (47 overs). *County debut:* N. J. Rimmington. *Prolonged wet weather wiped out the first two days, and the teams batted half a day each on the third. Durham used eight bowlers but took only two bona fide wickets in 50 overs, with Matthew Plater retiring out for 76; his captain, Will Fraine, scored an unbeaten 65 in 74 balls. Similarly, Durham opener Cameron Steel retired out for 39 after seven student bowlers dismissed two of his team-mates between them.*

DURHAM v KENT

At Chester-le-Street, April 20–21. Kent won by nine wickets. Kent 19pts, Durham 3pts. Toss: uncontested. First-class debut: G. J. Harte. County debut: A. K. Markram.

Durham couldn't handle the relentless accuracy of New Zealand seamer Matt Henry after rain had washed out most of their pre-season preparations. Though the weather was now glorious, their first innings ended by lunch, and the match in five sessions. The surface was as good as could be expected, but Henry skidded the ball through from a perfect length; he claimed seven for 45 second time round and 12 for 73 in all, both career-bests. Aiden Markram, fresh from a successful Test series for South Africa against Australia, became the first player to make a pair on his first day of Championship cricket, and the regular top seven mustered 68 over two innings. Nightwatchman Potts steered them past 39 for seven in the second but, when he was eighth out at 75, they still needed three to make Kent bat again. Weighell thrashed 84 off 89 balls to leave a target of 93, and Kuhn confirmed there were no demons in the pitch, following up his first-day 54 with 36 not out.

Close of play: first day, Durham 13-1 (Smith 8, Potts 5).

Durham

W. R. Smith b Henry	3	– (2) c Dickson b Henry	12
A. K. Markram lbw b Henry	0	– (1) c Thomas b Henry	0
G. J. Harte lbw b Henry	16	– (4) b Henry	1
G. Clark c Dickson b Podmore	7	– (5) lbw b Stevens	0
*P. D. Collingwood c Rouse b Henry	4	– (6) c Kuhn b Stevens	0
M. J. Richardson lbw b Henry	15	– (7) c Rouse b Henry	7
†S. W. Poynter b Podmore	0	– (8) lbw b Henry	3
N. J. Rimmington c Crawley b Stevens	11	– (10) b Henry	25
W. J. Weighell c Rouse b Stevens	16	– c Podmore b Henry	84
M. J. Potts not out	15	– (3) lbw b Podmore	36
C. Rushworth c Bell-Drummond b Stevens	3	– not out	0
Lb 1	1	B 1, lb 1	2

1/3 (2) 2/4 (1) 3/27 (3) (30.4 overs) 91 1/0 (1) 2/17 (2) (43.1 overs) 170
4/31 (4) 5/37 (5) 6/46 (7) 3/23 (4) 4/24 (5)
7/46 (6) 8/62 (9) 9/77 (8) 10/91 (11) 5/24 (6) 6/35 (7) 7/39 (8)
8/75 (3) 9/129 (10) 10/170 (9)

Henry 11–1–28–5; Stevens 9.4–1–29–3; Podmore 8–3–23–2; Thomas 2–0–10–0. *Second innings*—Henry 14.1–4–45–7; Stevens 15–2–55–2; Thomas 5–1–21–0; Podmore 5–1–29–1; Denly 4–0–18–0.

Kent

D. J. Bell-Drummond lbw b Rushworth	0	– not out	45
S. R. Dickson c Markram b Potts	41	– c Clark b Rimmington	3
H. G. Kuhn c Rushworth b Smith	54	– not out	36
*J. L. Denly b Collingwood	8		
Z. Crawley b Rimmington	1		
D. I. Stevens lbw b Weighell	17		
W. R. S. Gidman b Weighell	19		
†A. P. Rouse c Poynter b Rimmington	1		
M. J. Henry b Rimmington	0		
H. W. Podmore not out	8		
I. A. A. Thomas c and b Weighell	0		
B 4, lb 4, nb 12	20	B 4, lb 1, nb 6	11

1/4 (1) 2/67 (2) 3/79 (4) (56.4 overs) 169   1/4 (2) (1 wkt, 23.1 overs) 95
4/80 (5) 5/112 (6) 6/141 (3)
7/142 (8) 8/142 (9) 9/169 (7) 10/169 (11)

Rushworth 17–6–37–1; Rimmington 16–7–39–3; Weighell 11.4–3–29–3; Potts 5–0–37–1; Collingwood 2–0–5–1; Harte 1–1–0–0; Smith 4–0–14–1. *Second innings*—Rushworth 6–1–28–0; Rimmington 8–2–28–1; Weighell 6–1–16–0; Smith 2–0–12–0; Harte 1.1–0–6–0.

Umpires: B. J. Debenham and R. T. Robinson.

At Northampton, April 27–30. NORTHAMPTONSHIRE v DURHAM. Abandoned.

DURHAM v LEICESTERSHIRE

At Chester-le-Street, May 4–7. Durham won by 46 runs. Durham 18pts, Leicestershire 6pts. Toss: Durham.

In their 27th first-class season, Durham recorded their first victory after following on – an extraordinary turnaround after slumping to 14 for four in reply to 440. Defeat still looked likely when Griffiths grabbed five for ten at the start of the final afternoon, leaving them 89 ahead with two wickets standing. Then Weighell stepped up. He hit 38 to lift the target to 148 in 44 overs, before destroying Leicestershire with a career-best seven for 32. They folded inside 30 overs, a gut-wrenching defeat after such dominance. The pitch had developed some uneven bounce, but Carberry initially read it better when he chose to toss; he lost, but was granted his wish to bat, and built an opening stand of 146 with Horton. Following on 256 adrift, Durham batted more resolutely. Steel shared century partnerships with Markram, whose run of two ducks ended with 94, and Will Smith, back at Durham after leaving Hampshire. From 323 for three, Griffiths tipped the balance again, improving his career-best for the second time in the match, which he finished with ten for 83 – only to be upstaged. Rushworth sparked Leicestershire's downfall with three wickets before injuring his groin, and Weighell did the rest.

Close of play: first day, Leicestershire 301-4 (Cosgrove 66, Hill 17); second day, Durham 142-7 (Clark 50, Rimmington 13); third day, Durham 233-1 (Steel 79, Smith 43).

Leicestershire

*M. A. Carberry lbw b McCarthy	73	– lbw b Weighell 22
P. J. Horton c Steel b Rimmington	75	– c Collingwood b Rushworth 9
C. N. Ackermann c Poynter b Weighell	36	– lbw b Rushworth 5
M. J. Cosgrove lbw b Weighell	75	– c Smith b Weighell 10
†E. J. H. Eckersley lbw b McCarthy	9	– (7) c Poynter b Weighell 15
L. J. Hill b McCarthy	26	– (5) lbw b Rushworth 5
N. J. Dexter not out	70	– (6) b Weighell 21
B. A. Raine b Smith	13	– c Markram b Weighell 4
C. F. Parkinson c Markram b Rushworth	19	– c Rimmington b Weighell 4
G. T. Griffiths c Poynter b Steel	6	– not out 1
V. R. Aaron lbw b Markram	8	– lbw b Weighell 0
B 1, lb 22, w 3, nb 4	30	B 1, lb 4 5

1/146 (2) 2/165 (1) 3/203 (3)   (150.4 overs) 440   1/19 (2) 2/29 (3)   (29.5 overs) 101
4/254 (5) 5/313 (4) 6/339 (6)   3/40 (4) 4/47 (5)
7/355 (8) 8/406 (10) 9/420 (10)   5/61 (1) 6/79 (7) 7/95 (8)
10/440 (11)   110 overs: 343-6   8/100 (6) 9/101 (9) 10/101 (11)

Rushworth 33–10–91–1; Rimmington 31–7–78–1; McCarthy 29–4–72–3; Weighell 35–5–106–2; Smith 12–0–39–1; Steel 10–1–30–1; Markram 0.4–0–1–1. *Second innings*—Rushworth 7.2–4–12–3; Rimmington 7–0–31–0; Weighell 9.5–1–32–7; Smith 3.4–1–7–0; McCarthy 2–0–14–0.

Durham

C. T. Steel b Aaron	0	– lbw b Raine 86
A. K. Markram b Raine	0	– lbw b Parkinson 94
W. R. Smith b Raine	4	– c Dexter b Griffiths 74
G. Clark b Griffiths	64	– c Ackermann b Parkinson 25
*P. D. Collingwood lbw b Raine	0	– c Ackermann b Griffiths 15
M. J. Richardson b Griffiths	17	– c Dexter b Griffiths 0
†S. W. Poynter b Griffiths	0	– lbw b Griffiths 13
W. J. Weighell b Griffiths	29	– b Griffiths 38
N. J. Rimmington lbw b Aaron	23	– c Horton b Griffiths 0
B. J. McCarthy c Eckersley b Dexter	14	– c and b Ackermann 16
C. Rushworth not out	1	– not out 2
B 10, lb 7, w 5, nb 10	32	B 18, lb 8, nb 14 40

1/5 (1) 2/5 (2) 3/10 (3)   (54.3 overs) 184   1/152 (2) 2/265 (1)   (129.4 overs) 403
4/14 (5) 5/51 (6) 6/51 (7)   3/309 (4) 4/323 (3)
7/112 (8) 8/157 (9) 9/178 (10) 10/184 (4)   5/325 (6) 6/330 (5) 7/345 (7)
                                                8/345 (9) 9/386 (10) 10/403 (8)

Aaron 17–2–72–2; Raine 15–3–39–3; Griffiths 12.3–3–34–4; Dexter 6–3–9–1; Parkinson 4–0–13–0. *Second innings*—Aaron 22–0–102–0; Raine 31–7–71–1; Griffiths 21.4–6–49–6; Dexter 14–3–41–0; Parkinson 37–12–101–2; Carberry 2–0–7–0; Ackermann 2–0–6–1.

Umpires: N. L. Bainton and P. R. Pollard.

At Derby, May 11–14. DURHAM drew with DERBYSHIRE.

DURHAM v DERBYSHIRE

At Chester-le-Street, June 9–12. Durham won by 95 runs. Durham 19pts, Derbyshire 4pts. Toss: uncontested. First-class debuts: M. A. Jones; A. F. Gleadall. Championship debuts: J. Coughlin; C. A. J. Brodrick.

Durham snatched another astonishing victory: their first after being dismissed for under 100 in their first innings. Steel took the reins of an unfamiliar side: five players, including Paul Collingwood, were injured, three were with England or Ireland, and there were two debutants plus Matt Salisbury, on loan from Hampshire. Only Rushworth and Clark had appeared in the county's Championship line-up in Division One two years earlier. But Gareth Harte, in his second first-class game, turned the match with an obdurate 218-ball century. Derbyshire needed 268, but only Slater resisted Rushworth, who picked up five wickets, and Salisbury, with four. Durham sealed victory by a slightly delayed lunch on the final day. That had seemed unlikely when Olivier dismissed them for 96 on a well-grassed pitch in overcast conditions, with his first five-wicket haul for Derbyshire. He soon completed his second – including Steel, obliged to bat at No. 8 by an arm injury. Steel had fallen to the ninth ball of the third day, at which point Durham led by just 50 with three wickets left; thanks to Harte, they added a further 217. Derbyshire's indiscipline conceded 81 extras: a total of 57 byes and leg-byes was the highest in a Championship innings since 1990.

Close of play: first day, Derbyshire 175-8 (Palladino 26, Gleadall 12); second day, Durham 155-6 (Harte 24, Steel 6); third day, Derbyshire 69-4 (Slater 41, Brodrick 9).

Durham

T. W. M. Latham lbw b Viljoen...............	6	– c Madsen b Olivier...................	67
*C. T. Steel c Smit b Olivier.................	1	– (8) c Smit b Olivier..................	6
M. A. Jones b Olivier.......................	10	– (2) b Viljoen.......................	3
G. Clark c Smit b Palladino.................	19	– c Brodrick b Hughes.................	22
W. R. Smith b Viljoen......................	2	– (4) b Brodrick b Viljoen..............	1
G. J. Harte b Gleadall......................	20	– c Critchley b Madsen................	114
†R. C. Davies c Madsen b Olivier.............	2	– (6) c Smit b Olivier.................	0
J. Coughlin b Viljoen.......................	19	– (7) lbw b Olivier...................	9
N. J. Rimmington b Madsen b Olivier..........	0	– lbw b Critchley....................	42
M. E. T. Salisbury lbw b Olivier.............	0	– b Olivier.........................	25
C. Rushworth not out.......................	7	– not out...........................	6
B 6, lb 3, w 1	10	B 34, lb 23, w 2, nb 22......	81

1/7 (2) 2/23 (1) 3/23 (3)   (43.3 overs) 96   1/29 (2) 2/84 (3)   (125.4 overs) 376
4/26 (5) 5/64 (6) 6/66 (4)   3/95 (4) 4/121 (1)
7/79 (7) 8/83 (9) 9/85 (10) 10/96 (8)   5/121 (6) 6/133 (7) 7/159 (8)
                                                                  8/263 (9) 9/362 (10) 10/376 (5)

Olivier 16–9–20–5; Viljoen 16.3–4–30–3; Palladino 6–1–17–1; Gleadall 5–1–20–1. *Second innings*—Olivier 40–8–105–5; Viljoen 31–9–63–2; Palladino 24–6–48–0; Hughes 9–1–17–1; Gleadall 8.3–0–39–0; Critchley 10.3–0–38–1; Madsen 2.4–0–9–1.

Derbyshire

B. T. Slater c Davies b Rimmington...........	32	– b Salisbury.......................	68
*B. A. Godleman b Rushworth.................	2	– b Salisbury.......................	10
W. L. Madsen lbw b Rushworth...............	36	– c and b Salisbury...................	0
A. L. Hughes b Salisbury...................	4	– lbw b Rushworth...................	4
M. J. J. Critchley b Coughlin...............	38	– lbw b Rushworth...................	0
C. A. J. Brodrick c Latham b Salisbury........	0	– c Davies b Rushworth...............	19
†D. Smit c Latham b Rimmington.............	0	– lbw b Salisbury....................	1
G. C. Viljoen lbw b Coughlin...............	5	– b Rimmington....................	10
A. P. Palladino c Davies b Salisbury..........	32	– not out.........................	29
A. F. Gleadall not out.....................	27	– b Rushworth......................	2
D. Olivier c Harte b Rushworth..............	5	– lbw b Rushworth..................	18
B 5, lb 10, w 5, nb 4.........	24	Lb 5, nb 6...........	11

1/3 (2) 2/61 (1) 3/79 (4)   (58.1 overs) 205   1/24 (2) 2/24 (3)   (58.3 overs) 172
4/93 (3) 5/108 (6) 6/122 (7)   3/35 (4) 4/35 (5)
7/122 (5) 8/135 (8) 9/192 (9) 10/205 (11)   5/85 (6) 6/86 (7) 7/108 (8)
                                                                  8/133 (1) 9/140 (10) 10/172 (11)

Rushworth 21.1–6–57–3; Salisbury 20–1–71–3; Coughlin 8–1–31–2; Rimmington 9–1–31–2. *Second innings*—Rushworth 19.3–1–47–5; Salisbury 14–8–69–4; Coughlin 8–2–18–0; Rimmington 9–3–23–1; Harte 1–0–6–0; Smith 2–1–1–0; Clark 1–0–3–0.

Umpires: P. J. Hartley and T. Lungley.

At Arundel, June 20–22. DURHAM lost to SUSSEX by an innings and 64 runs.

DURHAM v WARWICKSHIRE

At Chester-le-Street, June 25–28 (day/night). Warwickshire won by 86 runs. Warwickshire 23pts, Durham 4pts. Toss: Warwickshire.

With a heatwave sweeping the country, the pitch dried and Patel declared early on the final day before bagging a six-wicket haul which consolidated Warwickshire's grip at the top of Division Two. He was indebted to Trott for innings of 170 not out and 53. Following a one-day century here a few weeks earlier, he accumulated steadily, adding 135 for the fifth wicket with Ambrose – who went on to hold ten catches – to set up a commanding total. Durham responded with resolve: Steel shared an opening stand of 96 with Latham. But they were undermined by the loss of early wickets on the third day, when Hannon-Dalby finished with four for 61. More fluent in the second innings, Trott helped extend Warwickshire's lead to 279 by the end of day three, though he fell in the last session, the seventh wicket of the match for Salisbury, whose form soon prompted Durham to sign him full-time. On the final day, off-spinner Pringle – in his first Championship game since September 2017 – struck three times in an over. That merely confirmed spin would be decisive, and Patel got to work.

Close of play: first day, Warwickshire 297-5 (Trott 119, Barker 9); second day, Durham 138-2 (Steel 51, Clark 18); third day, Warwickshire 152-5 (Ambrose 18, Barker 22).

Warwickshire

W. M. H. Rhodes c Latham b Salisbury	14	– b Rimmington	9
D. P. Sibley lbw b Rushworth	27	– c Davies b Salisbury	18
I. R. Bell c Steel b Salisbury	23	– c Collingwood b Salisbury	4
I. J. L. Trott not out	170	– c Clark b Salisbury	53
A. J. Hose c Davies b Salisbury	17	– lbw b Rushworth	15
†T. R. Ambrose c Harte b Rushworth	67	– c Latham b Pringle	39
K. H. D. Barker c Davies b Salisbury	27	– not out	32
*J. S. Patel b Rushworth	15	– c Latham b Pringle	0
C. J. C. Wright c Davies b Harte	21	– c and b Pringle	0
O. J. Hannon-Dalby c Latham b Rushworth	13	– c Steel b Rushworth	0
R. N. Sidebottom lbw b Rimmington	6	– not out	2
B 14, lb 3, w 1, nb 6	24	B 12, lb 1	13

1/17 (1) 2/52 (3) 3/81 (2) (134 overs) 424
4/130 (5) 5/265 (6) 6/332 (7)
7/351 (8) 8/381 (9) 9/405 (10)
10/424 (11)

1/26 (2) (9 wkts dec, 52 overs) 185
2/32 (3) 3/38 (1)
4/102 (5) 5/119 (4) 6/179 (6)
7/179 (8) 8/179 (9) 9/182 (10)

110 overs: 352-7

Rushworth 38–9–101–4; Salisbury 35–9–111–4; Rimmington 25–5–81–1; Harte 15–2–54–1; Pringle 16–1–43–0; Collingwood 4–0–15–0; Clark 1–0–2–0. *Second innings*—Rushworth 14–3–44–2; Salisbury 16–3–57–3; Rimmington 10–1–40–1; Pringle 12–1–31–3.

Durham

T. W. M. Latham c Ambrose b Hannon-Dalby	50	– lbw b Patel	29
C. T. Steel c Ambrose b Sidebottom	51	– c Bell b Wright	2
W. R. Smith c Ambrose b Hannon-Dalby	2	– c Ambrose b Hannon-Dalby	35
G. Clark c Bell b Patel	32	– c Ambrose b Patel	17
*P. D. Collingwood lbw b Hannon-Dalby	9	– c Ambrose b Patel	4
G. J. Harte c Ambrose b Wright	45	– c Sibley b Sidebottom	18
†R. C. Davies c Bell b Patel	0	– c Ambrose b Patel	20
R. D. Pringle c Ambrose b Hannon-Dalby	34	– c Bell b Sidebottom	3
N. J. Rimmington c Bell b Wright	32	– b Patel	61
M. E. T. Salisbury not out	8	– c Ambrose b Patel	19
C. Rushworth c Rhodes b Patel	5	– not out	2
B 8, lb 8, w 5, nb 8	29	B 10, lb 4, nb 2	16

1/96 (1) 2/98 (3) 3/139 (2) (104 overs) 297
4/150 (5) 5/173 (4) 6/175 (7)
7/223 (8) 8/277 (9) 9/284 (6) 10/297 (11)

1/14 (2) 2/79 (3) (66 overs) 226
3/83 (1) 4/87 (5)
5/120 (4) 6/138 (6) 7/144 (7)
8/148 (8) 9/179 (10) 10/226 (9)

Barker 22–5–58–0; Wright 22–8–46–2; Hannon-Dalby 22–5–61–4; Sidebottom 16–2–70–1; Patel 22–9–46–3. *Second innings*—Barker 11–1–42–0; Wright 10–1–26–1; Sidebottom 12–4–31–2; Hannon-Dalby 8–0–30–1; Patel 25–8–83–6.

Umpires: G. D. Lloyd and C. M. Watts.

At Cheltenham, July 22–25. DURHAM lost to GLOUCESTERSHIRE by 41 runs.

At Cardiff, August 19–21. DURHAM beat GLAMORGAN by an innings and 30 runs.

DURHAM v NORTHAMPTONSHIRE

At Chester-le-Street, August 29–30. Northamptonshire won by seven wickets. Northamptonshire 19pts, Durham 3pts. Toss: uncontested. First-class debut: B. J. Curran.

Durham suffered their second two-day defeat at Riverside in 2018, the fragility of their batting exposed by Northamptonshire's five seamers on a responsive pitch. Going into the match with seven first-class wickets for the season, Procter took five in the first innings. Gleeson, in his first Championship game since April, bagged three in the second, and Sanderson had match figures of seven for 80. With 16 wickets falling on the first day, the runs scored by Wakely and Rossington proved crucial, though Rushworth should have had Wakely caught in the slips before he had scored: he was dropped first ball by Richardson, and second ball by Lees. Northamptonshire lost their last four in the first 22 deliveries of the second morning – Rushworth and Salisbury finished with four apiece – but had Durham five down by lunch. Though Steel dug in for a 113-ball fifty, they were all out for 133, leaving a target of just 65. On the second day, the three Curran brothers were all playing first-class cricket: Ben on debut here, Tom for Surrey at The Oval, and Sam for England against India at the Rose Bowl.

Close of play: first day, Northamptonshire 189-6 (Rossington 47).

Durham

C. T. Steel c Wakely b Sanderson		2	– b Sanderson	50
A. Z. Lees lbw b Procter		25	– lbw b Sanderson	9
G. J. Harte lbw b Sanderson		6	– b Sanderson	0
G. Clark lbw b Hutton		3	– c Hutton b Gleeson	6
M. J. Richardson b Sanderson		19	– b Gleeson	15
A. R. Patel b Procter		8	– b Gleeson	0
*P. D. Collingwood c Rossington b Procter		17	– b Buck	27
†S. W. Poynter b Hutton		28	– lbw b Buck	11
B. J. McCarthy c Rossington b Procter		0	– b Sanderson	4
M. E. T. Salisbury not out		5	– not out	4
C. Rushworth b Procter		4	– c Rossington b Buck	0
Lb 10, nb 2		12	Lb 7	7

1/6 (1) 2/12 (3) 3/35 (4)   (39.1 overs) 129   1/21 (2) 2/21 (3)   (47.1 overs) 133
4/50 (2) 5/68 (6) 6/72 (5)   3/39 (4) 4/65 (5)
7/102 (7) 8/102 (9) 9/124 (8) 10/129 (11)   5/73 (6) 6/112 (7) 7/118 (1)
                                     8/126 (9) 9/132 (9) 10/133 (11)

Sanderson 14–2–46–3; Hutton 11–7–11–2; Buck 4–0–29–0; Procter 10.1–1–33–5. *Second innings*—Sanderson 15–4–34–4; Hutton 15–4–35–0; Gleeson 9–2–26–3; Procter 3–1–16–0; Buck 5.1–2–15–3.

Northamptonshire

B. J. Curran c Steel b Rushworth	11	– c Steel b Rushworth	11
L. A. Procter lbw b Salisbury	21	– b Patel	21
R. S. Vasconcelos lbw b Salisbury	20	– lbw b Patel	8
*A. G. Wakely b Patel	60	– not out	10
R. E. Levi c Poynter b McCarthy	11	– not out	6
†A. M. Rossington lbw b Rushworth	47		
S. A. Zaib c Poynter b Salisbury	11		
N. L. Buck not out	6		
B. A. Hutton lbw b Rushworth	0		
R. J. Gleeson b Rushworth	0		
B. W. Sanderson c McCarthy b Salisbury	0		
Lb 11	11	B 4, lb 5	9

1/24 (2) 2/45 (1) 3/66 (3)　　　　　(57.3 overs) 198　1/26 (1)　　　(3 wkts, 16.2 overs) 65
4/97 (5) 5/163 (4) 6/189 (7)　　　　　　　　　　　　2/36 (2) 3/45 (3)
7/189 (6) 8/197 (9) 9/197 (10) 10/198 (11)

Rushworth 18–5–52–4; Salisbury 15.3–4–44–4; McCarthy 11–2–59–1; Patel 9–3–29–1; Harte 4–2–3–0. *Second innings*—Rushworth 8.2–2–22–1; Salisbury 4–0–16–0; Patel 4–0–18–2.

Umpires: N. L. Bainton and N. A. Mallender.

At Birmingham, September 4–7. DURHAM drew with WARWICKSHIRE.

DURHAM v SUSSEX

At Chester-le-Street, September 10–12. Durham won by 186 runs. Durham 19pts, Sussex 3pts. Toss: uncontested.

Rushworth ensured a decisive win with 12 wickets, including his 400th for Durham and his 50th of the season. Weather permitted only 27 overs on the first day, in which Durham slipped to 92 for seven; they were all out early on the second, with Robinson claiming his third successive five-wicket haul (he almost managed a fourth later on). But Rushworth exploited helpful conditions with unrelenting accuracy. He took seven in ten overs before lunch, and eight for 51 in all, restricting Sussex's lead to 19; at the close, the club announced he was being awarded a testimonial in 2019. Meanwhile, the sun came out and Steel changed the tempo. He shared an opening stand of 72 with Lees on the way to a serene century, and added 79 for the sixth wicket with Collingwood, before becoming opening batsman Haines's maiden first-class victim. Sussex needed 322, but lost three men for ducks by the third over. Patel polished off the innings in his final appearance for Durham, who had again displayed a knack for fighting back on home turf.

Close of play: first day, Durham 92-7 (Poynter 12, Rimmington 0); second day, Durham 220-4 (Steel 114, Patel 14).

Durham

C. T. Steel c Brown b Jordan	25	– c Robinson b Haines	160
A. Z. Lees c Salt b Archer	2	– c Brown b Robinson	43
W. R. Smith c Jordan b Robinson	1	– c Finch b Archer	4
G. Clark c Finch b Robinson	5	– lbw b Archer	21
M. J. Richardson c Finch b Wiese	23	– c Brown b Robinson	19
A. R. Patel b Wiese	8	– c Wiese b Briggs	14
*P. D. Collingwood b Wiese	5	– b Robinson	47
†S. W. Poynter lbw b Robinson	14	– b Briggs	21
N. J. Rimmington b Robinson	5	– c Briggs b Robinson	4
M. E. T. Salisbury b Robinson	0	– b Briggs	0
C. Rushworth not out	4	– not out	0
Lb 9, nb 2	11	B 1, lb 2, nb 4	7

1/10 (2) 2/15 (3) 3/23 (4)　　　　　(31.4 overs) 103　1/72 (2) 2/91 (3)　　　(108.5 overs) 340
4/65 (5) 5/69 (1) 6/75 (6)　　　　　　　　　　　　3/139 (4) 4/194 (5)
7/88 (7) 8/96 (8) 9/96 (10) 10/103 (9)　　　　　　5/221 (6) 6/300 (1) 7/336 (7)
　　　　　　　　　　　　　　　　　　　　　　　　8/336 (8) 9/336 (10) 10/340 (9)

Robinson 11.4–3–29–5; Archer 6–0–19–1; Jordan 6–0–25–1; Wiese 8–0–21–3. *Second innings—* Robinson 25.5–1–75–4; Archer 20–0–94–2; Jordan 19–3–51–0; Wiese 16–0–63–0; Haines 5–0–13–1; Briggs 21–7–34–3; Wells 2–0–7–0.

Sussex

T. J. Haines c Poynter b Rushworth	0	– lbw b Rushworth	40
P. D. Salt c Clark b Rushworth	20	– b Rushworth	0
L. W. P. Wells b Salisbury	9	– c Poynter b Salisbury	0
H. Z. Finch b Rushworth	12	– b Rushworth	0
M. G. K. Burgess c Clark b Rushworth	18	– b Rushworth	22
*†B. C. Brown lbw b Rushworth	10	– b Patel	11
D. Wiese lbw b Salisbury	25	– b Salisbury	24
C. J. Jordan c Smith b Rushworth	9	– lbw b Patel	9
J. C. Archer b Rushworth	0	– run out (Richardson)	0
O. E. Robinson c Collingwood b Rushworth	14	– c Steel b Patel	14
D. R. Briggs not out	4	– not out	4
B 1	1	Lb 11	11

1/0 (1) 2/29 (2) 3/29 (3) (25.2 overs) 122
4/51 (4) 5/65 (6) 6/72 (5)
7/86 (8) 8/86 (9) 9/110 (10) 10/122 (7)

1/5 (2) 2/10 (3) (32 overs) 135
3/11 (4) 4/51 (5)
5/72 (1) 6/78 (6) 7/102 (7)
8/110 (9) 9/122 (8) 10/135 (10)

Rushworth 13–3–51–8; Salisbury 9.2–0–47–2; Rimmington 3–0–23–0. *Second innings—* Rushworth 12–2–49–4; Salisbury 8–1–30–2; Rimmington 3–0–18–0; Patel 9–3–27–3.

Umpires: J. W. Lloyds and P. R. Pollard.

At Leicester, September 18–19. DURHAM lost to LEICESTERSHIRE by an innings and 194 runs. *On the second day, Durham are bowled out for 61 and 66, their lowest first-class totals.*

DURHAM v MIDDLESEX

At Chester-le-Street, September 24–26. Middlesex won by 57 runs. Middlesex 19pts, Durham 6pts. Toss: Middlesex.

Collingwood received a guard of honour from his own team at the start, and from the visitors when he batted, but Middlesex spoiled his swansong by coming from behind to win. It seemed they had done him a favour by claiming first use of the pitch – they were all out for 121, with a career-best six for Salisbury. In the end, however, Malan's reluctance to bat last proved sound. After a century from Harte guided Durham to a lead of 189, Gubbins and Eskinazi wiped that out by adding 159 for Middlesex's second wicket. Eskinazi was the more fluent, despite having been hit in the face while fielding in the slips. Harris was less fortunate, retiring hurt after McCarthy struck his helmet. A lengthy discussion about whether Rayner could be his concussion substitute (as an off-spinner, he was not a like-for-like replacement for a seamer) was resolved in Middlesex's favour only after the umpires left the field to ring the ECB for guidance. Wood wrapped up the tail with five wickets, including Andersson for a valuable 34, and Durham required 167. Steel batted obdurately for 142 minutes, but Collingwood's final innings ended when he was bowled by a shooter from Andersson for ten, and the lower order collapsed.

Close of play: first day, Durham 227-5 (Harte 76, Poynter 20); second day, Middlesex 255-2 (Gubbins 90, Malan 31).

Middlesex

S. D. Robson lbw b Salisbury	9	– (2) b Collingwood	36
N. R. T. Gubbins c Poynter b Salisbury	19	– (1) lbw b Rushworth	91
S. S. Eskinazi c Lees b Salisbury	19	– c Collingwood b Salisbury	96
*D. J. Malan b Rushworth	3	– c Richardson b Collingwood	43
M. D. E. Holden c Harte b Wood	17	– c Lees b Wood	1
†R. G. White lbw b Salisbury	0	– b Rushworth	1
J. A. R. Harris c Poynter b Wood	31	– retired hurt	12
M. K. Andersson not out	7	– b Wood	34
J. K. Fuller b Salisbury	3	– c and b Wood	9
E. R. Bamber lbw b Salisbury	0	– not out	14
T. J. Murtagh b Wood	0	– (12) c Rushworth b Wood	4
O. P. Rayner (did not bat)		– (11) b Wood	2
B 1, lb 10, nb 2	13	B 2, lb 4, nb 6	12

1/32 (2) 2/39 (1) 3/42 (4)   (28.5 overs) 121   1/56 (2) 2/215 (3)   (113.2 overs) 355
4/62 (3) 5/72 (6) 6/88 (5)   3/259 (1) 4/262 (5)
7/113 (7) 8/116 (9) 9/118 (10) 10/121 (11)   5/269 (6) 6/270 (4) 7/328 (8)
                                        8/339 (9) 9/349 (11) 10/355 (12)

In the second innings Harris retired hurt at 322-6. Rayner replaced Harris, as a concussion substitute.

Rushworth 9–0–41–1; Salisbury 12–3–37–6; Wood 5.5–0–23–3; McCarthy 2–0–9–0. *Second innings*—Salisbury 25.3–8–70–1; Rushworth 22–6–61–2; McCarthy 23.3–5–85–0; Wood 26.2–3–94–5; Collingwood 12–2–25–2; Steel 3–0–12–0; Harte 1–0–2–0.

Durham

C. T. Steel c White b Harris	21	– c Rayner b Bamber	23
A. Z. Lees lbw b Murtagh	25	– lbw b Murtagh	22
G. J. Harte c Eskinazi b Murtagh	112	– c White b Andersson	14
M. J. Richardson lbw b Murtagh	50	– c White b Fuller	3
*P. D. Collingwood lbw b Bamber	32	– b Andersson	10
R. C. Davies b Bamber	1	– run out (Fuller)	4
†S. W. Poynter c White b Bamber	26	– b Murtagh	23
M. A. Wood c Murtagh b Andersson	10	– c Rayner b Bamber	0
B. J. McCarthy b Fuller	13	– (11) not out	0
M. E. T. Salisbury not out	9	– (9) c Rayner b Murtagh	0
C. Rushworth c White b Murtagh	0	– (10) c Gubbins b Fuller	4
Lb 6, w 1, nb 4	11	Lb 2, nb 4	6

1/39 (2) 2/47 (1) 3/136 (4)   (91 overs) 310   1/27 (2) 2/45 (3)   (39.4 overs) 109
4/201 (5) 5/205 (6) 6/233 (7)   3/48 (4) 4/67 (5)
7/252 (8) 8/287 (9) 9/310 (3) 10/310 (11)   5/79 (6) 6/97 (1) 7/97 (8)
                                        8/98 (9) 9/105 (7) 10/109 (10)

Murtagh 21–7–56–4; Bamber 25–5–78–3; Harris 19–1–73–1; Andersson 10–0–45–1; Fuller 16–2–52–1. *Second innings*—Murtagh 12–3–29–3; Bamber 13–6–38–2; Fuller 6.4–1–25–2; Andersson 8–2–15–2.

Umpires: M. A. Gough and S. J. O'Shaughnessy.

ESSEX

Grateful for an Indian summer

PAUL HISCOCK

It was always going to be difficult for Essex to follow their unbeaten Championship-winning season of 2017. The start was not ideal – a washout at Headingley – and relegation looked a possibility until a late surge brought four wins from the last five matches, including the only defeat suffered all season by new champions Surrey. That lifted them to third, which represented quite a comeback.

The team's struggles in the first half of the season were clear from the stats. Ravi Bopara was the leading Championship run-maker, with 751, but of the others only Tom Westley and Ryan ten Doeschate topped 500. Varun Chopra scored freely in the one-day formats, but was out of sorts in the red-ball game, scraping 201 runs from 13 innings; neither he nor fellow opener Nick Browne made a Championship century. Westley managed just one fifty in his first ten games until finding his touch, while Dan Lawrence, who turned 21, passed 50 only twice and averaged 21 fewer in the Championship than in 2017 – although his 124 against Hampshire did set up an innings victory.

It was not until the late signing of opener Murali Vijay – discarded by the Indian tourists midway through the Test series – that Essex ended relegation worries. He played in the last three matches, all won, and provided stability with innings of 56, 100, 85 and 80. With Vijay at the helm, the rest seemed to find batting much easier: four other centuries were scored, as against three before his arrival. Even so, only he and Bopara averaged over 40.

The lack of top-order runs had placed a greater burden on the bowlers but, as in 2017, Jamie Porter and Simon Harmer performed superbly, taking 58 and 57 wickets respectively. It was the fourth season in a row Porter had reached 50 in the Championship.

Ten Doeschate continued to lead the team well in all three formats, often devising innovative field placings, particularly in four-day cricket. Fittingly, it was his half-century in an epic last match of the season – which Essex won by one wicket – that dented Surrey's record.

The overseas duties were shared. The Australian seamer Peter Siddle had seven matches, either side of three appearances from New Zealander Neil Wagner, before Vijay took over. Siddle endeared himself with his attitude, both on and off the field, and took 37 Championship wickets at just 16 apiece, and signed for another two years. Wagner remained popular, but was less effective than in the title-winning summer, and was left out of the T20 side.

For Anthony McGrath, in his first year as head coach after Chris Silverwood left to join the England set-up, it was a mixed season. Third in the Championship was a decent start, but he was disappointed by the lack of limited-overs success.

Ryan ten Doeschate

Harry Trump, Getty Images

Essex had signed the former England one-day all-rounder Dimitri Mascarenhas as McGrath's assistant. It had been hoped his white-ball nous would help get the best out of the side, but he left in December. Although they finished second in a competitive Royal London Cup group to gain a home quarter-final, a familiar loss of big-match nerve resurfaced as they were beaten by a makeshift Yorkshire.

The T20 Blast was an abject failure – just two wins, both over group wooden-spoonists Middlesex. Essex had opted for two overseas bowlers, but what they needed was a gung-ho gladiator to help Chopra with the batting. He scored 503 runs, twice as many as any of his colleagues. The Australian leg-spinner Adam Zampa looked good, and took 12 wickets before he decamped to the Caribbean Premier League once it was obvious Essex were not going to qualify for the knockouts. He was set to return for more Twenty20 action in 2019, alongside Cameron Delport, an experienced South African all-rounder with a UK passport. Essex also signed Pakistan fast bowler Mohammad Amir, who represented the club in 2017, for eight T20 group games.

Prospects for 2019 were improved when Alastair Cook – now, to local delight, Sir Alastair – committed himself to three years of county cricket after his emotional retirement from England duty. He is expected to underpin the batting. With Siddle also in the ranks, there are hopes of another Championship challenge.

There are some promising pace bowlers ready to support Siddle and Porter: Sam Cook made strides in 2018, while the England Under-19 seamer Jack Plom should get a run. But one long-time Essex stalwart will be missing. Even though he was 38, it was a shock when the county announced that James Foster was not being retained. He was still a superb wicketkeeper, and his runs often proved invaluable. Essex preferred Adam Wheater, but also have talented young keepers in Michael Pepper and Will Buttleman – so many were surprised Foster was not given a backroom role to assist all three. Instead, he will further his coaching career elsewhere, while continuing at Forest School, his and Nasser Hussain's old stamping ground.

Championship attendance: 33,251.

ESSEX RESULTS

All first-class matches – Played 15: Won 7, Lost 5, Drawn 3. Abandoned 1.
County Championship matches – Played 13: Won 7, Lost 4, Drawn 2. Abandoned 1.

Specsavers County Championship, 3rd in Division 1;
Vitality Blast, 7th in South Group; Royal London One-Day Cup, quarter-finalists.

COUNTY CHAMPIONSHIP AVERAGES, BATTING AND FIELDING

Cap		Birthplace	M	I	NO	R	HS	100	Avge	Ct/St
	M. Vijay¶	Madras, India	3	5	0	323	100	1	64.60	1
2005	R. S. Bopara	Forest Gate‡	13	22	4	751	133*	2	41.72	8
2006	R. N. ten Doeschate††	Port Elizabeth, SA . .	12	20	2	680	173*	1	37.77	13
2005	†A. N. Cook§	Gloucester	6	11	0	412	96	0	37.45	6
	A. J. A. Wheater	Leytonstone‡	8	13	3	340	68*	0	34.00	23/1
2013	T. Westley	Cambridge	13	23	1	687	134	2	31.22	2
2018	S. R. Harmer††	Pretoria, SA	13	20	3	460	102*	1	27.05	13
	†N. Wagner¶	Pretoria, SA	3	4	1	80	37	0	26.66	3
	M. R. Quinn††	Auckland, NZ	3	5	4	26	16	0	26.00	0
2015	†N. L. J. Browne	Leytonstone‡	10	17	0	414	86	0	24.35	8
2001	J. S. Foster	Leytonstone‡	4	7	0	165	69	0	23.57	13/1
2017	D. W. Lawrence	Leytonstone‡	12	21	1	468	124	1	23.40	10
	P. M. Siddle¶	Traralgon, Aust. . . .	7	11	2	158	33*	0	17.55	0
2018	V. Chopra	Barking‡	7	13	0	201	61	0	15.46	7
	S. J. Cook	Chelmsford‡	10	11	7	56	14	0	14.00	1
	M. S. Pepper	Harlow‡	2	4	0	53	22	0	13.25	0
	†M. T. Coles	Maidstone	4	5	1	37	10*	0	9.25	1
2015	J. A. Porter	Leytonstone‡	13	17	3	88	31	0	6.28	2

Also batted: †P. I. Walter (*Basildon*) (1 match) 7, 14.

‡ *Born in Essex.*   § *ECB contract.*   ¶ *Official overseas player.*   †† *Other non-England-qualified.*

BOWLING

	Style	O	M	R	W	BB	5I	Avge
P. M. Siddle	RFM	234.4	47	607	37	5-37	3	16.40
S. R. Harmer	OB	526.2	136	1,394	57	6-87	3	24.45
J. A. Porter	RFM	432.3	81	1,429	58	7-41	3	24.63
S. J. Cook	RFM	219.3	60	684	27	5-28	1	25.33
M. R. Quinn	RFM	101	19	306	12	3-23	0	25.50
M. T. Coles	RFM	124	27	393	13	5-123	1	30.23

Also bowled: R. S. Bopara (RM) 80.2–9–304–9; N. L. J. Browne (LB) 1–0–4–0; D. W. Lawrence (OB/LB) 3–0–15–0; N. Wagner (LFM) 109–9–421–9; P. I. Walter (LM) 11–1–39–2; T. Westley (OB) 26–9–65–3.

LEADING ROYAL LONDON CUP AVERAGES (100 runs/4 wickets)

Batting	Runs	HS	Avge	SR	Ct/St	**Bowling**	W	BB	Avge	ER
V. Chopra	528	160	66.00	86.98	2	J. A. Porter	12	4-29	14.16	4.23
R. S. Bopara	401	125	57.28	95.93	4	M. T. Coles	9	3-41	20.88	5.44
T. Westley	387	134	48.37	99.23	1	S. Snater	5	5-60	26.80	7.65
A. J. A. Wheater	390	88	43.33	97.25	12/1	R. S. Bopara	5	3-30	36.72	5.66
Ashar Zaidi	188	82	31.33	101.07	3	N. Wagner	12	3-40	37.08	6.35
D. W. Lawrence	241	115	30.12	88.92	2	S. R. Harmer	7	2-38	48.42	5.38
R. N. ten Doeschate	112	28	22.40	99.11	4	S. J. Cook	5	1-21	55.60	4.21

LEADING VITALITY BLAST AVERAGES (100 runs/15 overs)

Batting	Runs	HS	Avge	SR	Ct/St	Bowling	W	BB	Avge	ER
R. S. Bopara ...	240	45*	26.66	157.89	2	J. A. Porter......	3	2-26	57.00	7.65
D. W. Lawrence	233	86	29.12	157.43	4	A. Zampa......	12	3-17	20.75	7.90
A. J. A. Wheater	250	45	19.23	152.43	7/2	S. R. Harmer	7	2-43	36.71	8.86
P. I. Walter	128	40	18.28	143.82	2	R. S. Bopara	5	2-26	50.60	9.37
V. Chopra	503	67	38.69	128.97	2	P. M. Siddle....	3	1-21	50.66	9.50
R. N. ten Doeschate	216	43	19.63	127.81	0	S. J. Cook	4	1-27	46.00	9.68
T. Westley.....	124	26	20.66	119.23	0	M. T. Coles	5	2-33	52.60	11.51

FIRST-CLASS COUNTY RECORDS

Highest score for	343*	P. A. Perrin v Derbyshire at Chesterfield......	1904
Highest score against	332	W. H. Ashdown (Kent) at Brentwood........	1934
Leading run-scorer	30,701	G. A. Gooch (avge 51.77).................	1973–97
Best bowling for	10-32	H. Pickett v Leicestershire at Leyton.........	1895
Best bowling against	10-40	E. G. Dennett (Gloucestershire) at Bristol	1906
Leading wicket-taker	1,610	T. P. B. Smith (avge 26.68)................	1929–51
Highest total for	761-6 dec	v Leicestershire at Chelmsford	1990
Highest total against	803-4 dec	by Kent at Brentwood	1934
Lowest total for	20	v Lancashire at Chelmsford	2013
Lowest total against	14	by Surrey at Chelmsford	1983

LIST A COUNTY RECORDS

Highest score for	201*	R. S. Bopara v Leicestershire at Leicester	2008
Highest score against	158*	M. W. Goodwin (Sussex) at Chelmsford......	2006
Leading run-scorer	16,536	G. A. Gooch (avge 40.93)	1973–97
Best bowling for	8-26	K. D. Boyce v Lancashire at Manchester.....	1971
Best bowling against	7-29	D. A. Payne (Gloucestershire) at Chelmsford ..	2010
Leading wicket-taker	616	J. K. Lever (avge 19.04)	1968–89
Highest total for	391-5	v Surrey at The Oval	2008
Highest total against	373-5	by Nottinghamshire at Chelmsford	2017
Lowest total for	57	v Lancashire at Lord's	1996
Lowest total against	{ 41	by Middlesex at Westcliff-on-Sea	1972
	{ 41	by Shropshire at Wellington	1974

TWENTY20 COUNTY RECORDS

Highest score for	152*	G. R. Napier v Sussex at Chelmsford	2008
Highest score against	153*	L. J. Wright (Sussex) at Chelmsford	2014
Leading run-scorer	**3,114**	**R. S. Bopara (avge 27.80, SR 126.94)**	**2003–18**
Best bowling for	6-16	T. G. Southee v Glamorgan at Chelmsford	2011
Best bowling against	{ 5-11	Mushtaq Ahmed (Sussex) at Hove	2005
	{ 5-11	T. G. Helm (Middlesex) at Lord's	2017
Leading wicket-taker	123	G. R. Napier (avge 24.74, ER 8.02).......	2003–16
Highest total for	242-3	v Sussex at Chelmsford	2008
Highest total against	226-3	by Sussex at Chelmsford	2014
Lowest total for	74	v Middlesex at Chelmsford	2013
Lowest total against	82	by Gloucestershire at Chelmsford	2011

ADDRESS

The Cloudfm County Ground, New Writtle Street, Chelmsford CM2 0PG; 01245 252420;
administration@essexcricket.co.uk; www.essexcricket.org.uk.

OFFICIALS

Captain R. N. ten Doeschate
Head coach A. McGrath
President D. L. Acfield
Chairman J. F. Faragher

Chief executive D. W. Bowden
Chairman, cricket advisory group R. C. Irani
Head groundsman S. G. Kerrison
Scorer A. E. Choat

At Bridgetown, Barbados, March 27–29. ESSEX lost to MCC by an innings and 34 runs (see MCC section).

At Cambridge, April 7–9. ESSEX drew with CAMBRIDGE MCCU.

At Leeds, April 13–16. YORKSHIRE.v ESSEX. Abandoned.

ESSEX v LANCASHIRE

At Chelmsford, April 20–22. Essex won by 31 runs. Essex 19pts, Lancashire 3pts. Toss: uncontested. County debut: P. M. Siddle.

In 2017, the only side champions Essex failed to beat were runners-up Lancashire, but they put that right this time. A low-scoring match seemed in prospect when 18 wickets went down on the first day, only for conditions to ease. Essex's best stand on that opening day was 37 for the tenth wicket between Siddle, their Australian import (he later had to wait 20 overs for his first victim), and Porter, who then nipped the ball around to good effect himself. Porter and Harmer – who was capped, along with Chopra, at lunch on the second day – took five apiece as Lancashire were restricted to 144, and trailed by six. Wickets continued to fall regularly, and with Essex 208 for seven the match remained in the balance – but Foster and Harmer knuckled down for 25 overs and the game's only century partnership. Chasing 320, Lancashire lost Hameed in single figures for the second time in the match, before Davies dug in for 161 minutes. Half-centuries from Clark and Mennie, another Australian, kept Lancashire's hopes alive, until Porter removed them to finish with match figures of nine for 80.

Close of play: first day, Lancashire 141-8 (Clark 24); second day, Essex 313.

Essex

N. L. J. Browne b Mennie	23	– c Vilas b Mennie 17
V. Chopra lbw b Onions	6	– b Onions 32
T. Westley c Hameed b Bailey	17	– c Jennings b Parkinson 49
D. W. Lawrence c Jennings b Clark	14	– c Livingstone b Mennie 5
R. S. Bopara c Livingstone b Clark	7	– c Livingstone b Bailey 26
*R. N. ten Doeschate lbw b Mennie	14	– lbw b Onions 25
†J. S. Foster c Davies b Onions	7	– lbw b Bailey 69
P. I. Walter c Vilas b Mennie	7	– c Davies b Mennie 14
S. R. Harmer c Livingstone b Bailey	10	– c Davies b Onions 49
P. M. Siddle not out	33	– lbw b Bailey 0
J. A. Porter run out (Vilas)	4	– not out 0
Lb 8	8	B 12, lb 15 27

1/12 (2) 2/38 (1) 3/48 (3)   (50 overs) 150   1/48 (2) 2/58 (1)   (90.1 overs) 313
4/65 (5) 5/68 (4) 6/85 (7)   3/70 (4) 4/127 (5)
7/94 (8) 8/105 (6) 9/113 (9) 10/150 (11)   5/166 (3) 6/174 (6) 7/208 (8)
                              8/311 (9) 9/312 (10) 10/313 (7)

Bailey 12–4–19–2; Onions 15–3–43–2; Mennie 13–2–52–3; Clark 6–0–17–2; Parkinson 4–0–11–0. *Second innings*—Bailey 18.1–3–73–3; Onions 18–4–57–3; Mennie 18–4–47–3; Parkinson 18–1–49–1; Livingstone 7–0–20–0; Clark 11–1–40–0.

Lancashire

K. K. Jennings c Foster b Porter	2	– c Chopra b Siddle...............	24
H. Hameed c Foster b Porter	8	– b Porter......................	1
†A. L. Davies c ten Doeschate b Porter........	6	– lbw b Porter..................	71
*L. S. Livingstone c ten Doeschate b Harmer....	33	– c Foster b Walter..............	23
D. J. Vilas c ten Doeschate b Harmer	25	– (6) lbw b Siddle...............	22
S. Chanderpaul c Foster b Porter	8	– (5) lbw b Walter...............	1
J. Clark b Harmer	25	– b Harmer	59
T. E. Bailey st Foster b Harmer	10	– run out (Siddle)...............	9
J. M. Mennie c Bopara b Harmer	12	– b Porter......................	56
G. Onions b Porter	2	– c Foster b Harmer..............	1
M. W. Parkinson not out	0	– not out	4
B 10, lb 1, nb 2.....................	13	B 3, lb 10, nb 4.............	17

1/4 (1) 2/16 (3) 3/19 (2)   (47.1 overs) 144   1/7 (2) 2/32 (1)   (82.2 overs) 288
4/65 (4) 5/86 (5) 6/88 (6)   3/88 (4) 4/98 (5)
7/109 (8) 8/141 (9) 9/144 (10) 10/144 (7)   5/139 (3) 6/172 (6) 7/195 (8)
                                                       8/243 (7) 9/246 (10) 10/288 (9)

Porter 12–2–26–5; Siddle 13–2–40–0; Walter 5–0–18–0; Harmer 15.1–2–46–5; Bopara
2–0–3–0. *Second innings*—Porter 19.2–4–54–4; Siddle 20–4–55–2; Harmer 29–5–109–1; Walter
6–1–21–2; Bopara 8–0–36–0.

Umpires: R. J. Bailey and N. L. Bainton.

At Southampton, April 27–30. ESSEX drew with HAMPSHIRE.

ESSEX v YORKSHIRE

At Chelmsford, May 4–6. Yorkshire won by 91 runs. Yorkshire 19pts, Essex 3pts. Toss: Yorkshire.
   When Yorkshire were shot out on the first morning for 50 – their lowest first-class total for 45 years
– defeat looked inevitable. But six sessions later Essex were licking their wounds after a comeback
spearheaded by 19-year-old Harry Brook, who hit a superb maiden century to atone for a first-innings
duck. Early on the third morning, Essex – chasing 238 – still seemed on course at 114 for four, but
Coad and Patterson (who finished with a career-best six for 40) ripped out four wickets for no runs,
and Yorkshire roared home. On the first day, there had been early movement, and the pitch was a little
two-paced: Sam Cook took full advantage, his five for 28 including Root for a first-baller. Siddle
weighed in with four cheap wickets, and only Ballance – in what proved to be his last game as captain
– reached double figures. Essex were soon 12 for three, Alastair Cook and Westley both falling for
nought, before Lawrence counter-attacked before some late biffing from Harmer stretched the lead to 92
on a day on which 22 wickets fell. Bairstow, promoted to open, gave Yorkshire's second innings a

---

YOUNGEST YORKSHIRE FIRST-CLASS CENTURIONS

Yrs	Days			
18	33	L. Hutton (196)...........	v Worcestershire at Worcester...........	1934
18	112	Azeem Rafiq (100).........	v Worcestershire at Worcester...........	2009
18	283	C. W. J. Athey (131*)......	v Sussex at Leeds....................	1976
19	**72**	**H. C. Brook (124)**.........	**v Essex at Chelmsford**...............	**2018**
19	104	S. R. Tendulkar (100).......	v Durham at Durham	1992
19	180	A. U. Rashid (108).........	v Worcestershire at Kidderminster	2007
19	214	M. P. Vaughan (106*).......	v Oxford University at Oxford..........	1994
19	238	A. A. Metcalfe (122).......	v Nottinghamshire at Bradford	1983
19	358	A. Z. Lees (121)	v Leeds/Bradford MCCU at Leeds	2013

Maiden hundreds only. Hutton and Vaughan scored further centuries while under 20.

brisk start with 50 from 44 balls – and then came Brook. He put on 94 with Pujara and 86 with Root, and batted for a minute short of four hours, defending well and driving crisply. "The way he played through mid-off and through the covers, that was special," said Bairstow. By the second-day close, Essex were recovering from the loss of Westley (his third duck in seven balls) and Bopara without scoring. But Yorkshire's seamers proved irresistible next morning, as Essex slipped to their first Championship defeat since September 2016. Only once before had Yorkshire won after scoring fewer in their first innings: they made 42 against Sussex at Hove in 1922.

Close of play: first day, Yorkshire 161-2 (Brook 57, Pujara 22); second day, Essex 97-4 (Lawrence 22, ten Doeschate 27).

Yorkshire

A. Lyth c Foster b S. J. Cook	0	– c Harmer b Siddle	27
H. C. Brook c Harmer b S. J. Cook	0	– (3) c Westley b Harmer	124
C. A. Pujara lbw b Porter	9	– (4) b Siddle	41
J. E. Root c A. N. Cook b S. J. Cook	0	– (5) b Bopara	35
*G. S. Ballance c Browne b Siddle	22	– (6) b Bopara	3
†J. M. Bairstow b S. J. Cook	7	– (2) b Siddle	50
J. A. Leaning lbw b Siddle	7	– b Porter	29
T. T. Bresnan lbw b S. J. Cook	1	– lbw b Porter	0
S. A. Patterson c Foster b Siddle	2	– b Porter	7
J. A. Brooks c Browne b Siddle	0	– c Foster b Siddle	1
B. O. Coad not out	0	– not out	2
Nb 2	2	B 4, lb 6	10

1/0 (2) 2/9 (1) 3/9 (4) (18.4 overs) 50 1/77 (2) 2/96 (1) (94.3 overs) 329
4/11 (3) 5/22 (6) 6/41 (7) 3/190 (4) 4/276 (5)
7/42 (8) 8/45 (9) 9/45 (10) 10/50 (5) 5/288 (3) 6/290 (6) 7/290 (8)
 8/304 (9) 9/305 (10) 10/329 (7)

Porter 6–2–15–1; S. J. Cook 9–0–28–5; Siddle 3.4–0–7–4. *Second innings*—Porter 27.3–5–89–3; S. J. Cook 15–1–56–0; Siddle 25–7–65–4; Harmer 15–2–70–1; Bopara 11–3–33–2; Lawrence 1–0–6–0.

Essex

N. L. J. Browne b Coad	7	– b Patterson	10
A. N. Cook c Bairstow b Brooks	0	– b Patterson	26
T. Westley b Brooks	0	– lbw b Patterson	0
D. W. Lawrence lbw b Bresnan	48	– b Patterson	32
R. S. Bopara c Pujara b Patterson	9	– c Brook b Patterson	0
*R. N. ten Doeschate lbw b Bresnan	18	– lbw b Coad	34
†J. S. Foster b Bresnan	3	– c Bairstow b Coad	0
S. R. Harmer c Bresnan b Coad	36	– lbw b Coad	0
P. M. Siddle c Ballance b Brooks	15	– lbw b Bresnan	24
J. A. Porter lbw b Coad	0	– lbw b Patterson	3
S. J. Cook not out	3	– not out	5
Lb 3	3	B 8, lb 4	12

1/2 (2) 2/2 (3) 3/12 (1) (43.5 overs) 142 1/34 (2) 2/34 (3) (53 overs) 146
4/58 (5) 5/72 (4) 6/80 (7) 3/55 (1) 4/55 (5)
7/93 (6) 8/120 (9) 9/121 (10) 10/142 (8) 5/114 (6) 6/114 (7) 7/114 (8)
 8/114 (4) 9/126 (10) 10/146 (9)

Coad 14.5–4–27–3; Brooks 14–1–63–3; Patterson 8–2–23–1; Bresnan 7–1–26–3. *Second innings*—Coad 18–10–36–3; Brooks 6–0–27–0; Patterson 18–3–40–6; Bresnan 9–3–26–1; Root 2–1–5–0.

Umpires: R. A. Kettleborough and S. J. O'Shaughnessy.

At Worcester, May 11–13. ESSEX beat WORCESTERSHIRE by 32 runs.

At Manchester, June 9–11. ESSEX beat LANCASHIRE by five wickets.

ESSEX v NOTTINGHAMSHIRE

At Chelmsford, June 20–23. Nottinghamshire won by 301 runs. Nottinghamshire 23pts, Essex 3pts. Toss: Nottinghamshire.

From the moment Nash edged the third ball of the match to first slip, where Chopra dropped it, Essex were chasing the game. Nash went on to 51, then Taylor tucked in for 146, his 25th first-class century, but first for Nottinghamshire. Solid contributions down the order pushed the total to 380, before Chopra's miserable match continued with a 21-ball duck. Cook and Bopara both batted for more than two hours, but it needed a late flourish from Wagner to help Essex towards a bonus point.

ESSEX'S HEAVIEST FIRST-CLASS DEFEATS BY RUNS

470	by Hampshire at Southampton...	2014	309	by Australian Imperial Forces	
371	by Somerset at Ilford	1924		XI at Southend.............	1919
352	by Surrey at Southend	1907	307	by Middlesex at Chelmsford	1937
327	by South Africans at Leyton ..	1929	302	by Kent at Tunbridge Wells....	1930
317	by Gloucestershire at Bristol		301	by Notts at Nottingham	1910
	(Ashley Down).............	1947	**301**	**by Notts at Chelmsford**	**2018**

With Quinn bowling well in his first senior appearance for more than a year after a back injury, Nottinghamshire made heavy weather of building on their lead, until wicketkeeper Moores smacked a rousing 87, with seven sixes and seven fours. He was batting with a runner after turning his ankle practising before the third day; Second XI keeper Tom Keast was summoned, and arrived 16 overs into the final innings, when he replaced a relieved Wessels behind the stumps. Essex needed 441, but Cook was trapped in front for nought, and only a fourth-wicket stand of 55 held Nottinghamshire up. Both counties had stand-in captains: Westley in place of Ryan ten Doeschate, serving a two-match suspension for disciplinary breaches; and Nash in place of Steven Mullaney, who was leading the England Lions.

Close of play: first day, Nottinghamshire 311-6 (Moores 28, Fletcher 2); second day, Nottinghamshire 35-1 (Libby 20, Milnes 3); third day, Essex 88-4 (Bopara 33, Porter 0).

Nottinghamshire

*C. D. Nash lbw b Quinn........................	51	– c Wheater b Quinn..............	8
J. D. Libby b Quinn............................	5	– b Wagner	51
S. R. Patel lbw b Coles........................	20	– (4) c Wheater b Coles..........	15
L. R. P. L. Taylor c Wheater b Porter	146	– (5) b Coles	4
W. T. Root c Chopra b Harmer	32	– (6) c Cook b Harmer	28
M. H. Wessels lbw b Harmer....................	13	– (7) c Wheater b Wagner........	14
†T. J. Moores c Wheater b Porter................	28	– (9) c Wheater b Porter........	87
L. J. Fletcher c Coles b Wagner.................	19	– run out (Coles)...............	18
M. Carter c Wagner b Harmer...................	19	– (10) c Chopra b Quinn	14
M. E. Milnes c Wagner b Harmer................	22	– (3) b Quinn..................	3
H. F. Gurney not out	6	– not out	0
Lb 19	19	B 8, lb 8, w 2, nb 6.........	24

1/26 (2) 2/60 (3) 3/113 (1)   (115.1 overs) 380   1/21 (1) 2/35 (3)   (72.1 overs) 266
4/235 (5) 5/257 (6) 6/309 (4)   3/83 (4) 4/87 (5)
7/312 (7) 8/341 (9) 9/362 (8)   5/95 (2) 6/123 (7) 7/143 (6)
10/380 (10)   110 overs: 358-8   8/178 (8) 9/208 (10) 10/266 (9)

Porter 22–3–90–2; Quinn 19–3–52–2; Wagner 23–2–87–1; Coles 19–4–54–1; Harmer 32.1–10–78–4. *Second innings*—Porter 15.1–3–53–1; Quinn 12–3–23–3; Coles 14–5–40–2; Harmer 15–3–78–1; Wagner 15–1–43–2; Bopara 1–0–13–0.

Essex

V. Chopra lbw b Fletcher	0	– b Milnes	14
A. N. Cook c Carter b Gurney	33	– lbw b Milnes	0
*T. Westley lbw b Milnes	8	– b Fletcher	9
D. W. Lawrence c Nash b Fletcher	1	– c and b Patel	30
R. S. Bopara b Carter	69	– c sub (†T. G. Keast) b Milnes	39
†A. J. A. Wheater c Moores b Fletcher	24	– (7) b Gurney	16
S. R. Harmer lbw b Carter	0	– (8) b Gurney	6
M. T. Coles lbw b Fletcher	4	– (9) c sub (†T. G. Keast) b Milnes	9
N. Wagner c Fletcher b Carter	37	– (10) c Taylor b Patel	5
J. A. Porter not out	3	– (6) c sub (†T. G. Keast) b Fletcher	0
M. R. Quinn c Libby b Carter	16	– not out	5
B 6, lb 2, w 1, nb 2	11	Lb 2, nb 4	6

1/6 (1) 2/19 (3) 3/26 (4)   (59.3 overs) 206   1/6 (2) 2/15 (5)   (58.5 overs) 139
4/80 (5) 5/124 (6) 6/125 (7)   3/31 (3) 4/86 (4)
7/130 (8) 8/156 (5) 9/185 (9) 10/206 (11)   5/94 (5) 6/94 (6) 7/114 (8)
                               8/129 (7) 9/133 (9) 10/139 (10)

Fletcher 16–5–43–4; Milnes 9–1–20–1; Carter 15.3–8–34–4; Gurney 13–0–68–1; Patel 6–0–33–0. *Second innings*—Fletcher 11–5–28–2; Milnes 20–7–44–4; Gurney 14–3–43–2; Carter 9–4–21–0; Patel 4.5–3–1–2.

Umpires: N. J. Llong and B. V. Taylor.

ESSEX v SOMERSET

At Chelmsford, June 25–28 (day/night). Drawn. Essex 11pts, Somerset 10pts. Toss: Essex. First-class debut: M. S. Pepper.

Helped by a docile pitch, Essex's batsmen conquered the pink Kookaburra ball in a match that seemed destined for a draw from the start. Browne and Cook opened with a stand of 151, which was ended by a run-out, and it was a surprise when Cook fell in sight of a century during a 35-over spell from off-spinner Bess (Somerset sent down 98 in all on the first day). Bopara and ten Doeschate – back after suspension – then stretched their fifth-wicket stand to 294 on the second, the all-wicket record in this fixture. Ten Doeschate's unbeaten 173 was the highest of his 19 centuries for Essex (he had two doubles for the Netherlands). Somerset replied in equally determined fashion, passing 400 even though the highest individual contribution was Hildreth's 78. Essex did not start their second innings until near the third-day close and, although two quick wickets went down, Bopara stopped the rot next morning. Alastair Cook missed the third day with tonsillitis, came in at No. 7, and was out fourth ball. The eventual declaration set Somerset 319 in 50 overs: they made a bright start, but shut up shop after losing three wickets in 11 deliveries. If floodlit cricket was meant to bring in the crowds, nobody told Chelmsford: little more than 1,000 attended each of the first three days, and only a few hardy souls on the fourth.

Close of play: first day, Essex 298-4 (Bopara 37, ten Doeschate 46); second day, Somerset 140-2 (Byrom 53); third day, Essex 17-2 (Browne 5, Bopara 11).

Essex

N. L. J. Browne run out (Groenewald)	66	– c Bartlett b Trego	75
A. N. Cook lbw b Bess	96	– (7) c Overton b Trego	3
T. Westley c Abell b Gregory	21	– (2) lbw b Davey	0
M. S. Pepper b Bess	22	– (3) lbw b Gregory	1
R. S. Bopara b Trego	118	– (4) c Gregory b Bess	58
*R. N. ten Doeschate not out	173	– (5) b Bess	4
†A. J. A. Wheater not out	6	– (6) b Bess	20
S. R. Harmer (did not bat)		– not out	30
N. Wagner (did not bat)		– not out	9
Lb 9, nb 6	15	Lb 1, w 1, nb 6	8

1/151 (1) 2/176 (2)   (5 wkts dec, 150 overs) 517   1/0 (2)   (7 wkts dec, 53 overs) 208
3/204 (3) 4/212 (4)   2/1 (3) 3/107 (4)
5/506 (5)   110 overs: 360-4   4/111 (5) 5/149 (6) 6/152 (7) 7/180 (1)

J. A. Porter and S. J. Cook did not bat.

Gregory 16–1–70–1; Overton 22–1–110–0; Davey 23–8–67–0; Groenewald 12–0–48–0; Bess 49–10–132–2; Trego 20–6–43–1; Abell 8–1–38–0. *Second innings*—Gregory 9–4–25–1; Davey 9–2–19–1; Overton 5–0–19–0; Bess 17–2–81–3; Trego 13–0–63–2.

Somerset

E. J. Byrom c Wheater b Porter	54	– run out (ten Doeschate)	38
†S. M. Davies c Wheater b Wagner	41	– b Harmer	30
G. A. Bartlett b S. J. Cook	42	– c A. N. Cook b Wagner	25
J. C. Hildreth lbw b Harmer	78	– b Harmer	19
*T. B. Abell c Wheater b Bopara	41	– not out	21
P. D. Trego b Porter	39	– c A. N. Cook b Harmer	2
L. Gregory c Bopara b Wagner	22	– not out	15
D. M. Bess c Wheater b Wagner	35		
J. H. Davey c ten Doeschate b Harmer	13		
J. Overton c Bopara b Westley	35		
T. D. Groenewald not out	1		
Lb 2, nb 4	6	B 1	1

1/55 (2) 2/140 (3) 3/150 (1)	(127 overs) 407	1/64 (1) (5 wkts, 49 overs) 151
4/242 (5) 5/280 (4) 6/310 (6)		2/75 (2) 3/107 (4)
7/356 (8) 8/361 (7) 9/385 (9)		4/113 (3) 5/116 (6)
10/407 (10)	110 overs: 356-6	

Porter 23–4–87–2; S. J. Cook 19–4–66–1; Harmer 46–13–122–2; Wagner 32–1–122–3; Bopara 6–1–8–1; Westley 1–1–0–1. *Second innings*—Porter 6–1–33–0; S. J. Cook 3–1–15–0; Harmer 22–12–44–3; Wagner 14–1–56–1; Westley 2–1–1–0; Bopara 2–1–1–0.

Umpires: M. J. Saggers and R. J. Warren.

At Chelmsford, July 25–27. ESSEX drew with INDIANS (see Indian tour section).

At Taunton, August 19–22. ESSEX lost to SOMERSET by 45 runs.

ESSEX v HAMPSHIRE

At Chelmsford, August 29–September 1. Essex won by an innings and 52 runs. Essex 24pts, Hampshire 2pts. Toss: Essex.

Lawrence gave Essex control after a first-day washout, driving well during his only first-class century of an underwhelming season. He shared stands of 122 and 105 with ten Doeschate and Wheater, and was ninth out at 412. By then Siddle had made sure of the final batting point with two balls to spare, by clubbing Abbott for six. There was time for Cook to reach double figures for the first time, in his 16th match, and he then started Hampshire's decline by removing Adams for a single. Before long it was 110 for eight: the pitch offered modest help to the seamers, but there were some scatterbrained shots, and the only sustained resistance came from Vince, who survived more than two hours down at No. 3 after a stomach bug. Dawson and Abbott saved some face, but the deficit was still 263, which looked even steeper when Siddle reduced Hampshire to 24 for four in the follow-on. For the second time, the ninth-wicket partnership was their biggest, and with about an hour to spare Harmer wrapped up victory. Essex used a different wicketkeeper in each session on the third day. After Wheater was hit on the shoulder just before lunch, the Academy's Will Buttleman emerged after the interval. He was replaced at tea by Second XI keeper Michael Pepper.

Close of play: first day, no play; second day, Essex 363-6 (Lawrence 114, Harmer 0); third day, Hampshire 17-2 (Holland 1, Abbott 3).

Essex

N. L. J. Browne b Edwards	9	P. M. Siddle lbw b Abbott	8
V. Chopra lbw b Abbott	61	J. A. Porter not out	5
T. Westley b Abbott	40	S. J. Cook c Berg b Edwards	14
D. W. Lawrence c sub (A. H. T. Donald) b Holland	124	B 22, lb 18, nb 4	44
R. S. Bopara c Adams b Abbott	4	1/16 (1) 2/117 (3) (114.1 overs)	435
*R. N. ten Doeschate c Browne b Holland	55	3/120 (2) 4/124 (5) 5/246 (6)	
†A. J. A. Wheater b Dawson	52	6/351 (7) 7/394 (8) 8/408 (9)	
S. R. Harmer c Adams b Abbott	19	9/412 (4) 10/435 (11)	110 overs: 408-8

Edwards 18.1–2–97–2; Abbott 28–8–90–5; Holland 27–3–83–2; Dawson 24–6–56–1; Berg 17–4–69–0.

Hampshire

J. J. Weatherley lbw b Siddle	32	– b Siddle	0
J. H. K. Adams b Cook	1	– lbw b Siddle	8
I. G. Holland b Harmer	17	– b Siddle	2
S. A. Northeast c Lawrence b Siddle	1	– (6) c Chopra b Harmer	41
*J. M. Vince c Wheater b Bopara	26	– b Siddle	4
†T. P. Alsop b Cook	5	– (7) c sub (†M. S. Pepper) b Harmer	51
R. R. Rossouw c Browne b Harmer	12	– (8) c Browne b Harmer	14
G. K. Berg c Browne b Bopara	3	– (10) lbw b Harmer	37
L. A. Dawson b Porter	32	– c sub (†M. S. Pepper) b Siddle	13
K. J. Abbott not out	28	– (4) run out (sub P. I. Walter)	22
F. H. Edwards c sub (†M. S. Pepper) b Cook	6	– not out	4
B 1, lb 2, nb 6	9	B 8, lb 2, w 5	15
1/8 (2) 2/39 (3) 3/44 (4) (78.3 overs)	172	1/6 (1) 2/13 (2) (90.3 overs)	211
4/57 (1) 5/65 (6) 6/90 (7)		3/20 (3) 4/24 (5)	
7/99 (8) 8/110 (5) 9/146 (9) 10/172 (11)		5/63 (4) 6/91 (6) 7/114 (8)	
		8/131 (9) 9/183 (7) 10/211 (10)	

Porter 16–3–38–1; Cook 10.3–4–27–3; Siddle 14–3–22–2; Harmer 31–13–52–2; Bopara 7–0–30–2. *Second innings*—Porter 20–6–49–0; Siddle 22.7–7–48–5; Harmer 29.3–8–64–4; Cook 12–5–27–0; Bopara 4–0–9–0; Westley 2–2–0–0; Browne 1–0–4–0.

Umpires: R. J. Bailey and M. Burns.

ESSEX v SURREY

At Chelmsford, September 4–6. Surrey won by ten wickets. Surrey 22pts, Essex 2pts. Toss: Essex.
    The battle between the title-holders and the champions-elect was a one-sided affair, as Surrey completed their eighth successive victory with a day to spare, stretching their lead to 43 points. Yet there had been playing and missing galore as Surrey battled to lunch on the first day on a surface offering movement and bounce. Crucially, though, they lost only one wicket, and Burns and Elgar took charge in a stand of 148. Both batted for 253 minutes, with Burns becoming the first to 1,000 Championship runs for the season. Pope, who was to disappear on England duty after the second day, made 21, and Clarke thumped two sixes in an aggressive 56 as Surrey banked a third batting point. He was soon in action with the ball, too, as Essex were skittled for 126: Westley alone of the top eight reached double figures. Early on the third day, it was 31 for three in the follow-on, and only Bopara, who used his feet well during a fine unbeaten 81, held Surrey up; ten Doeschate fell to a blinding gully catch by Burns, but the tail did just enough to avert an innings defeat. Clarke grabbed four more wickets, to finish with match figures of eight for 75.
    Close of play: first day, Surrey 256-4 (Foakes 24, Jacks 15); second day, Essex 13-0 (Browne 5, Chopra 4).

Surrey

*R. J. Burns b Siddle	90	– not out	2
M. D. Stoneman c Westley b Cook	12	– not out	0
D. Elgar b Harmer	75		
O. J. D. Pope c Harmer b Siddle	21		
†B. T. Foakes b Porter	30		
W. G. Jacks c Lawrence b Siddle	16		
R. Clarke c ten Doeschate b Porter	56		
T. K. Curran c Lawrence b Harmer	26		
M. Morkel b Cook	1		
C. McKerr c Lawrence b Cook	0		
G. S. Virdi not out	0		
B 14, lb 6, nb 4	24		

1/30 (2) 2/178 (1) 3/200 (3) (119.2 overs) 351   (no wkt, 0.4 overs) 2
4/233 (4) 5/257 (6) 6/279 (5)
7/324 (8) 8/325 (9) 9/325 (10)
10/351 (7)   110 overs: 305-6

R. S. Patel replaced Pope, who left to join England's Test squad.

Porter 28.2–3–87–2; Cook 25–7–71–3; Siddle 29–6–86–3; Harmer 29–12–62–2; Westley 2–0–8–0; Bopara 6–1–17–0. *Second innings*—Harmer 0.4–0–2–0.

Essex

N. L. J. Browne c Elgar b Morkel	7	– c Patel b Clarke	21
V. Chopra c Clarke b Curran	3	– lbw b Curran	5
T. Westley c Burns b Clarke	49	– b Curran	7
D. W. Lawrence lbw b Curran	3	– c Burns b Clarke	3
R. S. Bopara c Foakes b Clarke	6	– not out	81
*R. N. ten Doeschate c Foakes b Clarke	2	– c Burns b Morkel	11
†M. S. Pepper b Curran	9	– c Stoneman b Clarke	21
S. R. Harmer lbw b Clarke	0	– c Elgar b Morkel	0
P. M. Siddle not out	21	– c Stoneman b Clarke	8
J. A. Porter lbw b McKerr	12	– c Jacks b Morkel	31
S. J. Cook c Pope b McKerr	2	– b Virdi	12
Lb 4, w 4, nb 4	12	B 9, lb 11, w 2, nb 4	26

1/10 (1) 2/10 (2) 3/20 (4) (37.2 overs) 126   1/16 (2) 2/28 (3) (70.3 overs) 226
4/47 (5) 5/53 (6) 6/86 (7)   3/31 (4) 4/60 (1)
7/86 (3) 8/87 (8) 9/122 (10) 10/126 (11)   5/86 (6) 6/139 (7) 7/140 (8)
                                                     8/157 (9) 9/208 (10) 10/226 (11)

Morkel 9–3–18–1; Curran 13–2–36–3; McKerr 6.2–0–40–2; Clarke 9–1–28–4. *Second innings*—Morkel 20–3–68–3; Curran 20–8–46–2; Clarke 17–3–47–4; Virdi 8.3–1–36–1; McKerr 5–1–9–0.

Umpires: J. H. Evans and N. J. Llong.

At Nottingham, September 10–13. ESSEX beat NOTTINGHAMSHIRE by eight wickets.

ESSEX v WORCESTERSHIRE

At Chelmsford, September 18–20. Essex won by an innings and 129 runs. Essex 24pts, Worcestershire 2pts. Toss: Worcestershire.

Essex wrapped up their home season with a flourish not long after lunch on the third day – a result that sealed Worcestershire's relegation. Five men bagged ducks as they were rolled for 94 on the first morning, four inflicted by Porter, who swung the ball around to finish with a career-best seven for 41. Three wickets fell in his second over, including a comedy run-out, when Westbury and Clarke found themselves at the same end: Wheater had to gather a wild throw from Porter, but still had time to send Westbury packing. Murali Vijay, the Indian opener hit a classy 85 during a stand of 129 with Westley, and Essex were already 158 in front by the end of the first day. Bopara then took charge, batting almost five and a half hours for an unbeaten 133, although he was dropped twice. Trailing by 380, Worcestershire immediately lost both openers to Porter again, which took him to 50 Championship wickets for the fourth season running. Clarke produced some fluent strokes in his 74, but also fell to Porter. Essex's former captain James Foster bade farewell to Chelmsford with a late spell as a substitute fielder.

Close of play: first day, Essex 252-5 (Bopara 36, Wheater 36); second day, Worcestershire 140-4 (Clarke 74, Tongue 0).

Worcestershire

*D. K. H. Mitchell c Wheater b Porter	6	– lbw b Porter	0
T. C. Fell b Porter	0	– b Porter	1
O. E. Westbury run out (Porter/Wheater)	4	– lbw b Coles	8
J. M. Clarke b Porter	28	– b Porter	74
A. G. Milton b Porter	0	– lbw b Harmer	38
†O. B. Cox lbw b Porter	12	– (7) b Harmer	9
E. G. Barnard b Porter	0	– (8) c Wheater b Porter	22
W. D. Parnell b Cook	20	– (9) not out	50
B. J. Twohig not out	17	– (10) c ten Doeschate b Harmer	18
J. C. Tongue c Lawrence b Cook	0	– (6) c Lawrence b Cook	12
D. Y. Pennington c Vijay b Harmer	0	– b Harmer	0
B 5, lb 2	7	B 18, lb 1	19

1/1 (2) 2/10 (1) 3/12 (3)   (25.3 overs)   94   1/1 (2) 2/4 (1)   (77.5 overs) 251
4/12 (5) 5/32 (6) 6/32 (7)   3/44 (3) 4/138 (5)
7/60 (8) 8/83 (4) 9/93 (10) 10/94 (11)   5/140 (4) 6/161 (7) 7/161 (6)
                                        8/212 (8) 9/251 (10) 10/251 (11)

Porter 10–1–41–7; Cook 8–1–30–1; Coles 4–0–15–0; Harmer 3.3–2–1–1. *Second innings*—Porter 18–5–57–4; Cook 12–4–38–1; Harmer 28.5–8–76–4; Coles 15–2–47–1; Westley 3–2–12–0; Bopara 1–0–2–0.

Essex

N. L. J. Browne b Parnell	5	M. T. Coles not out	10
M. Vijay b Tongue	85		
T. Westley c Cox b Barnard	55	B 30, lb 6, w 2, nb 6	44
D. W. Lawrence lbw b Barnard	1		
R. S. Bopara not out	133	1/9 (1) (7 wkts dec, 124 overs) 474
*R. N. ten Doeschate c Clarke b Pennington	18	2/138 (2) 3/139 (4)
†A. J. A. Wheater b Barnard	66	4/170 (3) 5/201 (6)
S. R. Harmer b Twohig	57	6/318 (7) 7/452 (8) 110 overs: 412-6

J. A. Porter and S. J. Cook did not bat.

Tongue 24–2–94–1; Parnell 21–1–95–1; Barnard 24–8–63–3; Pennington 24–5–57–1; Twohig 23–2–107–1; Mitchell 7–2–16–0; Westbury 1–0–6–0.

Umpires: I. J. Gould and B. V. Taylor.

At The Oval, September 24–27. ESSEX beat SURREY by one wicket. *Essex scrape home after taking a first-innings lead of 410.*

GLAMORGAN

Croft out on review

A wretched season ended with a packed members' forum demanding answers during the final game. Hugh Morris, the chief executive, announced an independent review into the club's affairs, undertaken by Huw Bevan, the former England fitness coach who is now a consultant to World Rugby. His recommendations were put to the board of directors, and within a week the head coach Robert Croft was on his way, after 32 years with Glamorgan, 25 as a player; he had been assistant coach before succeeding Toby Radford in charge in 2016. Morris remained CEO, but was no longer director of cricket. In December, their former captain and wicketkeeper Mark Wallace took the job.

Glamorgan had been poor, but they were also unlucky, and injuries blighted the summer. Marchant de Lange suffered a bad hamstring strain on May 23 and missed the rest of the season. Shaun Marsh, signed as the overseas player, then dislocated his shoulder in the second Twenty20 match, and returned to Australia after only four Championship outings.

The team's inexperience was continually exposed, with the young batsmen displaying an alarming lack of confidence. Glamorgan won their opening Championship match, at Bristol, and the last, against Leicestershire at Cardiff – but in between lost ten out of 12, four by an innings. Sussex shot them out for 85 and 88 in a day at Hove. For the first time since 2007, they came last in Division Two.

Things were almost as bad in the white-ball competitions. Glamorgan won only once in the Royal London Cup, finishing bottom of their group. And although they managed five consecutive wins in the Vitality Blast, three late defeats cost any chance of a repeat of the T20 finals-day appearance which had brightened up the 2017 season.

Usman Khawaja, originally signed for the T20s, was called up early to replace Marsh – who was taking part in Australia's one-day series in England – and played in four Championship matches. He boosted the fragile batting order, and created a club record with centuries in his first three games. But halfway through the Blast he was summoned home by Cricket Australia to prepare for an A-tour of India. Joe Burns became the third Aussie of a confusing season, but lasted only two T20 games before injuring his back. Finally Stephen Cook, the South African opener, was signed for the Championship run-in – but he also made little impression, averaging 15.

Overall, Glamorgan collected just 13 batting points, including seven in the two matches they won – the lowest in either division. Apart from Khawaja, no recognised batsman averaged 30, and there were only three other centuries to add to his trio. The opening partnership rarely flourished: Nick Selman, who had made four hundreds in 2017, averaged 17, without a fifty. Jack Murphy, who started as a left-arm seamer and worked his way up the order, showed promise, especially in the two games against Kent. First he carried his bat at Cardiff, standing alone on the burning deck as Glamorgan crashed from 57 without loss to 94 all out; then he made a spirited 80 at Canterbury, this time from No. 3. But they were his only two half-centuries in 23 innings.

Quinn Rooney, Getty Images

Usman Khawaja

Kiran Carlson struck 152 against Derbyshire at Swansea, where he put on 289 with Khawaja, but was otherwise disappointing; he did have the excuse of the distraction of studies at Cardiff University. Still only 20, Carlson has undoubted talent, which he showed off in a couple of limited-overs innings, notably at The Oval, where his 58 from 32 balls set up a thrilling T20 victory over Surrey.

Many were saddened by Aneurin Donald's decision to sign a two-year deal with Hampshire: he was a product of the Academy, and had been offered a three-year contract. He made a splash as a 19-year-old in 2016, with a rapid double-century against Derbyshire, but suffered a second underwhelming season, averaging less than 20 in all three formats. He said he was leaving as he wanted to play for England, and felt that "moving to a first division club would help". There was hollow laughter in Wales when he joined his new county and failed to make the team for their last five Championship matches. Billy Root, brother of the more famous Joe, will bolster the batting for 2019 after joining from Nottinghamshire, he is joined by the Doncaster-born Queensland batsman Charlie Hemphrey.

The bowling attack was again led by Timm van der Gugten and 37-year-old Michael Hogan, who shared 88 Championship wickets. Van der Gugten, a Sydney-born Dutch international, won the club's Player of the Year award for the second time in three years. Ruaidhri Smith had his moments as third seamer, but de Lange was badly missed, as were Craig Meschede, unavailable early on because of a calf injury, and the promising Lukas Carey, after an ankle problem. Andrew Salter was more effective in the white-ball games, while his fellow off-spinner Kieran Bull returned to Championship action after a three-year absence, and took 11 wickets in four matches in September.

There was some good news: the club's financial position continued to improve, after a £2.5m payment from the ECB in return for Glamorgan agreeing not to apply to host any Test matches between 2020 and 2024. The decision was not without controversy: two ECB non-executive directors, Surrey chairman Richard Thompson and former Somerset chairman Andy Nash, stepped down in protest. But the Good Governance Institute found no evidence that the payment was unconstitutional.

Championship attendance: 11,960.

GLAMORGAN RESULTS

All first-class matches – Played 14: Won 2, Lost 10, Drawn 2.
County Championship matches – Played 14: Won 2, Lost 10, Drawn 2.

Specsavers County Championship, 10th in Division 2;
Vitality Blast, 6th in South Group; Royal London One-Day Cup, 9th in South Group.

COUNTY CHAMPIONSHIP AVERAGES, BATTING AND FIELDING

Cap		Birthplace	M	I	NO	R	HS	100	Avge	Ct/St
	†U. T. Khawaja¶	Islamabad, Pakistan	4	8	0	420	126	3	52.50	2
	M. de Lange††	Tzaneen, SA	3	5	1	142	90	0	35.50	1
	D. L. Lloyd	St Asaph‡	10	18	2	474	119	1	29.62	3
	†S. E. Marsh¶	Narrogin, Australia .	4	7	0	203	111	1	29.00	1
	†J. R. Murphy	Haverfordwest‡. . . .	12	23	2	533	80	0	25.38	4
2016	C. B. Cooke	Johannesburg, SA . .	14	26	1	606	69	0	24.24	41/1
	K. S. Carlson	Cardiff‡.	13	25	1	567	152	1	23.62	5
	C. A. J. Meschede	Johannesburg, SA . .	4	8	1	151	55	0	21.57	0
	R. A. J. Smith	Glasgow	7	14	2	246	52*	0	20.50	1
	N. J. Selman	Brisbane, Australia . .	12	23	0	403	42	0	17.52	21
2018	T. van der Gugten†† .	Sydney, Australia . .	10	18	5	217	60*	0	16.69	2
	K. A. Bull	Haverfordwest‡. . . .	4	8	3	76	30	0	15.20	2
	S. C. Cook¶	Johannesburg, SA . .	4	8	0	120	36	0	15.00	3
	A. O. Morgan	Swansea‡	3	6	0	89	36	0	14.83	1
	A. G. Salter	Haverfordwest‡. . . .	10	17	3	204	72*	0	14.57	8
	P. Sisodiya	Cardiff‡.	2	4	1	41	38	0	13.66	1
2013	G. G. Wagg	Rugby	4	8	0	102	33	0	12.75	0
2013	M. G. Hogan††	Newcastle, Aust. . . .	13	21	8	152	28	0	11.69	7
	A. H. T. Donald	Swansea‡	4	7	1	67	27	0	11.16	2
	J. L. Lawlor	Cardiff‡.	3	6	0	49	21	0	8.16	3
	C. R. Brown	Caerphilly‡	6	12	0	95	33	0	7.91	9
	L. J. Carey	Carmarthen‡.	6	8	0	58	28	0	7.25	0
	T. N. Cullen	Perth, Australia	2	4	0	29	20	0	7.25	2

‡ *Born in Wales.* ¶ *Official overseas player.* †† *Other non-England-qualified.*

BOWLING

	Style	O	M	R	W	BB	5I	Avge
T. van der Gugten	RFM	287	69	936	43	7-42	2	21.76
M. G. Hogan	RFM	393.3	101	1,014	45	5-49	2	22.53
M. de Lange	RF	114.4	22	383	16	5-62	1	23.93
K. A. Bull	OB	85.4	14	278	11	3-36	0	25.27
R. A. J. Smith	RM	155.3	24	593	20	5-87	1	29.65
A. G. Salter	OB	245	45	759	18	4-80	0	42.16
L. J. Carey	RFM	172	36	592	13	4-105	0	45.53

Also bowled: K. S. Carlson (OB) 1–0–5–0; J. L. Lawlor (OB/RM) 29.1–3–110–4; D. L. Lloyd (RM) 105.3–19–343–9; C. A. J. Meschede (RM) 76–8–327–9; A. O. Morgan (SLA) 12.1–2–46–0; J. R. Murphy (LFM) 16.3–2–73–1; N. J. Selman (RM) 1–0–6–0; P. Sisodiya (SLA) 63.2–12–151–7; G. G. Wagg (SLA/LM) 82.4–13–258–8.

LEADING ROYAL LONDON CUP AVERAGES (125 runs/4 wickets)

Batting	Runs	HS	Avge	SR	Ct/St	Bowling		W	BB	Avge	ER
C. A. Ingram	402	95*	57.42	98.04	3	G. G. Wagg		9	2-33	38.66	5.52
C. R. Brown	163	98	54.33	63.67	1	M. de Lange		5	3-65	44.20	8.50
S. E. Marsh.	143	57	35.75	78.57	0	T. van der Gugten.		6	3-58	52.66	6.40
G. G. Wagg	210	49	30.00	106.06	1	C. A. Ingram		4	3-24	55.25	5.57
N. J. Selman	236	92	29.50	68.80	2	A. G. Salter		2	2-50	59.66	5.68
D. L. Lloyd	233	92	29.12	86.94	4	L. J. Carey.		5	2-57	64.20	5.56
C. B. Cooke	168	59	24.00	79.24	10/1						

LEADING VITALITY BLAST AVERAGES (125 runs/15 overs)

Batting	Runs	HS	Avge	SR	Ct/St		Bowling	W	BB	Avge	ER
C. A. Ingram ..	430	89	53.75	164.75	3		R. A. J. Smith ...	9	4-6	21.66	7.50
C. A. J. Meschede	247	77*	27.44	153.41	1		A. G. Salter	11	3-34	25.90	7.70
C. B. Cooke ...	238	60*	26.44	147.82	10/3		C. A. Ingram	4	2-15	37.75	8.01
G. G. Wagg....	130	53*	16.25	144.44	2		G. G. Wagg	14	2-17	23.64	8.74
K. S. Carlson ..	295	58	29.50	143.20	6		M. G. Hogan	13	3-31	32.00	9.04
A. H. T. Donald .	206	37	15.84	138.25	10		C. A. J. Meschede	6	3-21	48.00	9.29
U. T. Khawaja ..	168	44	24.00	136.58	1		T. van der Gugten	19	4-31	22.47	10.00

FIRST-CLASS COUNTY RECORDS

Highest score for	309*	S. P. James v Sussex at Colwyn Bay	2000
Highest score against	322*	M. B. Loye (Northamptonshire) at Northampton	1998
Leading run-scorer	34,056	A. Jones (avge 33.03)	1957–83
Best bowling for	10-51	J. Mercer v Worcestershire at Worcester.....	1936
Best bowling against	10-18	G. Geary (Leicestershire) at Pontypridd	1929
Leading wicket-taker	2,174	D. J. Shepherd (avge 20.95)...............	1950–72
Highest total for	718-3 dec	v Sussex at Colwyn Bay	2000
Highest total against	712	by Northamptonshire at Northampton	1998
Lowest total for	22	v Lancashire at Liverpool	1924
Lowest total against	33	by Leicestershire at Ebbw Vale	1965

LIST A COUNTY RECORDS

Highest score for	169*	J. A. Rudolph v Sussex at Hove.............	2014
Highest score against	268	A. D. Brown (Surrey) at The Oval...........	2002
Leading run-scorer	12,278	M. P. Maynard (avge 37.66)	1985–2005
Best bowling for	7-16	S. D. Thomas v Surrey at Swansea	1998
Best bowling against	7-30	M. P. Bicknell (Surrey) at The Oval	1999
Leading wicket-taker	356	R. D. B. Croft (avge 31.96)	1989–2012
Highest total for	429	v Surrey at The Oval	2002
Highest total against	438-5	by Surrey at The Oval	2002
Lowest total for	42	v Derbyshire at Swansea	1979
Lowest total against	{ 59	by Combined Universities at Cambridge....	1983
	{ 59	by Sussex at Hove	1996

TWENTY20 COUNTY RECORDS

Highest score for	116*	I. J. Thomas v Somerset at Taunton..........	2004
Highest score against	117	M. J. Prior (Sussex) at Hove	2010
Leading run-scorer	1,770	C. A. Ingram (avge 41.16, SR 161.64)	2015–18
Best bowling for	5-14	G. G. Wagg v Worcestershire at Worcester....	2013
Best bowling against	6-5	A. V. Suppiah (Somerset) at Cardiff	2011
Leading wicket-taker	100	D. A. Cosker (avge 30.32, ER 7.79)	2003–16
Highest total for	240-3	v Surrey at The Oval	2015
Highest total against	239-5	by Sussex at Hove	2010
Lowest total for	88	v Sussex at Hove	2018
Lowest total against	81	by Gloucestershire at Bristol	2011

ADDRESS

Sophia Gardens, Cardiff CF11 9XR; 029 2040 9380; info@glamorgancricket.co.uk; www.glamorgancricket.com.

OFFICIALS

Captain M. G. Hogan
2018 (limited-overs) C. A. Ingram
Head coach 2018 R. D. B. Croft
Interim head coach 2019 M. P. Maynard
Director of cricket 2019 M. A. Wallace
Head of talent development R. V. Almond

President 2018 A. Jones
Chairman G. Williams
Chief executive H. Morris
Head groundsman R. Saxton
Scorer/archivist A. K. Hignell

At Cardiff, April 13–15 (not first-class). **Drawn. Cardiff MCCU 249** (91 overs) (J. H. Ludlow 53, C. L. Herring 52, J. R. Turpin 57*; L. J. Carey 4-39, T. van der Gugten 3-65) **and 56-2** (29 overs); ‡**Glamorgan 217-5 dec** (68 overs) (K. S. Carlson 69*, A. G. Salter 51*; A. D. F. Brewster 3-46). *A potentially interesting final day was ruined by rain. Cardiff MCCU had struggled to 131-8 on the first, before Welshman Cameron Herring and No. 10 James Turpin (whose highest first-class score was five) put on 101. Glamorgan were also in a spot of bother at 55-4, but Kiran Carlson batted for nearly four hours, while David Lloyd (46) and Andrew Salter played more aggressively. Andrew Brewster, a York-born seamer who later appeared for Glamorgan's Second XI, took three for two in 18 balls.*

At Bristol, April 20–23. GLAMORGAN beat GLOUCESTERSHIRE by six wickets.

At Lord's, April 27–30. GLAMORGAN drew with MIDDLESEX.

GLAMORGAN v KENT

At Cardiff, May 4–6. Kent won by six wickets. Kent 19pts, Glamorgan 3pts. Toss: uncontested.

A remarkable first-day collapse all but handed this match to Kent. Glamorgan's openers made serene progress to lunch, reaching 57 without loss. But then, as the cloud cover increased, all ten wickets tumbled for 37 in 15.3 overs: Stevens finished with six for 26, and Henry four for 31. Jack Murphy carried his bat in only his third match as opener; his unbeaten 39 was the lowest such score for Glamorgan since 1922, when Tom "Stonewall" Morgan made 13 out of 42 against Lancashire. Kent also found it hard going, losing nine before the close, although a fourth-wicket stand of 78 between Denly and Crawley ensured a lead. Podmore stretched that to 80 next morning, before van der Gugten sealed career-best figures. Glamorgan's batsmen made a better fist of things on the second day, chiefly thanks to Murphy and Marsh, who added 126. But Henry claimed four more victims, the last three wickets fell for one against the second new ball, and Kent's target was a modest 195. The openers put on 77, then Kuhn guided them home with almost four sessions to spare. The third day's play started more than 90 minutes late after a drainage leak produced a wet patch near the pitch.

Close of play: first day, Kent 163-9 (Podmore 25, Thomas 0); second day, Glamorgan 273-9 (van der Gugten 0).

Glamorgan

N. J. Selman lbw b Stevens	33	– lbw b Stevens	11
J. R. Murphy not out	39	– c Kuhn b Henry	54
S. E. Marsh c Rouse b Henry	5	– run out (Gidman)	76
K. S. Carlson lbw b Stevens	1	– c Rouse b Gidman	30
A. H. T. Donald b Stevens	0	– lbw b Podmore	1
†C. B. Cooke lbw b Stevens	2	– c Rouse b Stevens	16
D. L. Lloyd c Rouse b Henry	4	– c Kuhn b Henry	46
A. G. Salter lbw b Stevens	4	– c Rouse b Henry	18
M. de Lange c Kuhn b Stevens	0	– lbw b Podmore	1
T. van der Gugten lbw b Henry	2	– not out	0
*M. G. Hogan b Henry	0	– c Dickson b Henry	1
Lb 2, w 2	4	B 9, lb 6, w 1, nb 4	20

1/57 (1) 2/66 (3) 3/67 (4)　　(46.4 overs)　94　　1/11 (1) 2/137 (3)　　(86.3 overs)　274
4/73 (5) 5/77 (6) 6/86 (7)　　　　　　　　　　　3/158 (2) 4/159 (5)
7/91 (8) 8/91 (9) 9/94 (10) 10/94 (11)　　　　5/191 (6) 6/228 (4) 7/260 (8)
　　　　　　　　　　　　　　　　　　　　　　8/273 (7) 9/273 (9) 10/274 (11)

Henry 13.4–6–31–4; Stevens 16–6–26–6; Podmore 8–2–10–0; Thomas 6–2–16–0; Gidman 2–1–2–0; Denly 1–0–7–0. *Second innings*—Henry 20.3–3–59–4; Stevens 18.4–5–57–2; Podmore 18.2–4–55–2; Thomas 13–4–39–0; Gidman 10–0–36–1; Denly 6–1–13–0.

Kent

D. J. Bell-Drummond lbw b van der Gugten	19	– lbw b van der Gugten	36
S. R. Dickson lbw b van der Gugten	6	– lbw b de Lange	39
H. G. Kuhn b Hogan	0	– not out	69
*J. L. Denly lbw b van der Gugten	43	– c sub (T. N. Cullen) b Salter	26
Z. Crawley lbw b Lloyd	33	– lbw b de Lange	11
D. I. Stevens c de Lange b van der Gugten	1	– not out	1
W. R. S. Gidman c Selman b Lloyd	7		
†A. P. Rouse b van der Gugten	4		
M. J. Henry c Hogan b van der Gugten	11		
H. W. Podmore not out	33		
I. A. A. Thomas c and b van der Gugten	2		
B 8, lb 2, w 1, nb 4	15	B 9, lb 2, nb 2	13

1/18 (2) 2/25 (3) 3/29 (1)   (50.5 overs) 174
4/107 (4) 5/111 (6) 6/115 (5)
7/118 (7) 8/137 (9) 9/141 (8) 10/174 (11)

1/77 (1)   (4 wkts, 48.5 overs) 195
2/102 (2) 3/173 (4)
4/193 (5)

De Lange 11–1–52–0; van der Gugten 19.5–7–42–7; Hogan 10–1–39–1; Lloyd 10–2–31–2. *Second innings*—de Lange 12–3–50–2; van der Gugten 9–1–29–1; Hogan 9–2–21–0; Lloyd 4–0–23–0; Salter 14.5–0–61–1.

Umpires: G. D. Lloyd and B. V. Taylor.

At Leicester, May 11–13. GLAMORGAN lost to LEICESTERSHIRE by three runs.

At Birmingham, June 9–12. GLAMORGAN lost to WARWICKSHIRE by four wickets.

GLAMORGAN v DERBYSHIRE

At Swansea, June 20–23. Drawn. Glamorgan 8pts, Derbyshire 11pts. Toss: Glamorgan. First-class debut: P. Sisodiya.

Glamorgan's hopes of a second Championship victory of the summer were thwarted by Derbyshire's ninth-wicket pair, who saw out the last 14.3 overs: Palladino survived 114 minutes, and Olivier 51. In fact, Derbyshire had made much of the running. Glamorgan were 52 for five on the first day, which did not start until 3.20 after overnight rain, but Cooke and Salter inspired the tail. Then, in the second innings, they were 48 for three – still 31 behind – before Khawaja (with a second century in two matches) added 289 with Carlson, the best in this fixture. Derbyshire had seemed set for a bigger lead after Hughes's patient century, but lost their last five for five in 30 madcap deliveries. Prem Sisodiya, a 19-year-old slow left-armer on debut, started the rot with a run-out, then claimed three of the wickets. The eventual target was 325 in 63 overs: Madsen rebuilt the innings after a poor start, but four wickets for Hogan left Derbyshire hanging on.

Close of play: first day, Glamorgan 175-7 (Salter 26, Sisodiya 10); second day, Derbyshire 207-3 (Hughes 67, Godleman 8); third day, Glamorgan 201-3 (Khawaja 79, Carlson 69).

Glamorgan

N. J. Selman lbw b Olivier	10	– lbw b Critchley	18
J. R. Murphy c Hosein b Palladino	19	– lbw b Hamidullah Qadri	27
A. O. Morgan c Wilson b Palladino	4	– b Hamidullah Qadri	3
U. T. Khawaja b Palladino	5	– c Madsen b Hughes	126
K. S. Carlson c Madsen b Rampaul	2	– b Palladino	152
†C. B. Cooke b Palladino	69	– c Slater b Hughes	13
D. L. Lloyd c Wilson b Rampaul	21	– not out	43
A. G. Salter not out	72	– c Hughes b Palladino	4
P. Sisodiya b Palladino	38	– not out	3
L. J. Carey c Godleman b Hamidullah Qadri	28		
*M. G. Hogan run out (Critchley)	6		
Lb 7, nb 2	9	B 6, lb 2, nb 6	14

1/27 (2) 2/31 (1) 3/35 (3)   (71 overs) 283   1/44 (2)   (7 wkts dec, 82 overs) 403
4/48 (4) 5/52 (5) 6/110 (7)   2/48 (1) 3/48 (3)
7/162 (6) 8/218 (9) 9/260 (10) 10/283 (11)   4/337 (5) 5/341 (4) 6/364 (6) 7/381 (8)

Rampaul 15–3–53–2; Olivier 17–2–94–1; Palladino 25–4–69–5; Critchley 11–0–49–0; Hamidullah Qadri 3–0–11–1. *Second innings*—Olivier 7–1–23–0; Rampaul 8–1–38–0; Hamidullah Qadri 23–2–101–2; Critchley 21–1–97–1; Madsen 9–1–47–0; Palladino 7–0–46–2; Hughes 7–0–43–2.

Derbyshire

B. T. Slater c Sisodiya b Salter	52	– lbw b Salter	15
H. R. Hosein b Salter	35	– b Hogan	0
W. L. Madsen c Carlson b Murphy	41	– c Salter b Sisodiya	55
A. L. Hughes run out (Hogan)	103	– c Madsen b Hogan	9
*B. A. Godleman lbw b Salter	24	– c Hogan b Sisodiya	0
†G. C. Wilson run out (Sisodiya)	44	– lbw b Carey	26
M. J. J. Critchley not out	54	– lbw b Hogan	0
A. P. Palladino b Sisodiya	0	– not out	30
Hamidullah Qadri c Cooke b Salter	0	– c Cooke b Hogan	0
D. Olivier lbw b Sisodiya	0	– not out	6
R. Rampaul c Selman b Sisodiya	1		
B 4, lb 4	8	Lb 2, nb 4	6

1/90 (2) 2/91 (1) 3/175 (3)   (127.5 overs) 362   1/4 (2) 2/18 (1)   (8 wkts, 63 overs) 147
4/257 (5) 5/265 (4) 6/357 (6)   3/76 (4) 4/77 (5)
7/358 (8) 8/359 (9) 9/360 (10)   5/88 (3) 6/93 (7) 7/125 (6) 8/128 (9)
10/362 (11)   110 overs: 303-5

Carey 26–11–65–0; Hogan 32–8–77–0; Lloyd 3.3–0–8–0; Sisodiya 21.5–1–54–3; Murphy 8.3–1–41–1; Salter 35–7–105–4; Morgan 1–0–4–0. *Second innings*—Carey 11–1–37–1; Hogan 20–6–43–4; Salter 16–8–46–1; Sisodiya 16–8–19–2.

Umpires: N. L. Bainton and P. K. Baldwin.

GLAMORGAN v NORTHAMPTONSHIRE

At Cardiff, June 25–28. Northamptonshire won by 233 runs. Northamptonshire 21pts, Glamorgan 5pts. Toss: Northamptonshire.

Northamptonshire wrapped up their second successive victory in convincing style, with Duckett's forthright century the main difference between the teams. Wakely's 82 – and fifties from the South Africans Vasconcelos (his first in the Championship) and Levi – had put them in a strong position on the first day, but from 275 for five they lost five for six as van der Gugten mopped up. Glamorgan also fell away: only Khawaja, last out after completing his third hundred in three matches, passed 29. Duckett then dominated an opening stand of 208 with Procter – a Northamptonshire record against Glamorgan – and reached his century in 93 balls; he eventually hit 22 fours. Ruaidhri Smith's seamers made inroads, but seventies from Vasconcelos and Crook boosted the lead past 400. Left with around 125 overs to bat, Glamorgan were going well shortly before the third-day close at 111 for two – but Sri Lankan Seekkuge Prasanna's leg-breaks claimed the crucial scalp of Khawaja thanks to a juggled catch at short leg, and also snared Morgan. With Hogan unavailable for family reasons, the remaining wickets went down before lunch on the final day, Prasanna finishing with four to justify Northamptonshire's decision to call him up a week before the T20 Blast began.

Close of play: first day, Glamorgan 21-0 (Selman 15, Murphy 2); second day, Northamptonshire 169-0 (Procter 50, Duckett 111); third day, Glamorgan 121-4 (Carlson 3, van der Gugten 2).

Northamptonshire

L. A. Procter c Cooke b Smith	15	– c Cooke b van der Gugten	70
B. M. Duckett c Selman b Hogan	6	– c Morgan b Smith	133
R. S. Vasconcelos c Cooke b van der Gugten	56	– c Selman b Smith	79
*A. G. Wakely c Khawaja b Smith	82	– c Selman b van der Gugten	1
R. E. Levi c Salter b van der Gugten	75	– lbw b Salter	20
†A. M. Rossington c Salter b Smith	7	– lbw b Smith	3
S. P. Crook lbw b Hogan	33	– b Smith	73
S. Prasanna c sub (L. J. Carey) b van der Gugten	0	– lbw b Sisodiya	1
B. A. Hutton c Khawaja b van der Gugten	3	– not out	5
N. L. Buck not out	0	– c Salter b Sisodiya	6
B. W. Sanderson b van der Gugten	0		
B 2, lb 2	4	B 6, lb 9	15

1/10 (2) 2/36 (1) 3/105 (3) (87 overs) 281   1/208 (1) (9 wkts dec, 99.3 overs) 406
4/223 (4) 5/231 (6) 6/275 (5)   2/214 (2) 3/215 (4)
7/275 (8) 8/279 (7) 9/281 (9) 10/281 (11)   4/243 (5) 5/246 (6)
6/393 (7) 7/394 (3)
8/398 (8) 9/406 (10)

Van der Gugten 18–5–45–5; Hogan 17–6–35–2; Murphy 5–1–15–0; Smith 17–1–73–3; Sisodiya 12–1–46–0; Salter 14–1–38–0; Morgan 4–0–25–0. *Second innings*—van der Gugten 22–4–103–2; Hogan 21–1–73–0; Smith 20–5–75–4; Salter 20–0–91–1; Murphy 3–0–17–0; Sisodiya 13.3–2–32–2.

Glamorgan

N. J. Selman c Rossington b Sanderson	29	– c Crook b Procter	15
J. R. Murphy lbw b Procter	21	– c Hutton b Buck	30
A. O. Morgan c Rossington b Procter	20	– c Levi b Prasanna	17
U. T. Khawaja c Levi b Hutton	103	– c Vasconcelos b Prasanna	38
K. S. Carlson lbw b Sanderson	19	– c Rossington b Hutton	32
†C. B. Cooke b Sanderson	0	– (7) b Hutton	22
A. G. Salter lbw b Hutton	19	– (8) not out	10
R. A. J. Smith c Rossington b Buck	9	– (9) lbw b Buck	4
P. Sisodiya b Buck	0	– (10) c Vasconcelos b Prasanna	0
T. van der Gugten b Buck	2	– (6) lbw b Prasanna	6
*M. G. Hogan not out	2	– absent	
B 4, lb 6, nb 20	30	B 7, lb 10, w 1, nb 8	26

1/40 (1) 2/72 (2) 3/87 (3) (65.3 overs) 254   1/40 (1) 2/54 (2) (65 overs) 200
4/156 (5) 5/156 (6) 6/195 (7)   3/111 (4) 4/118 (3)
7/206 (8) 8/208 (9) 9/216 (10) 10/254 (4)   5/126 (6) 6/174 (5) 7/187 (7)
8/199 (9) 9/200 (10)

Sanderson 16–6–30–3; Hutton 16.3–4–46–2; Buck 15–1–77–3; Crook 4–1–18–0; Procter 10–2–39–2; Prasanna 4–0–34–0. *Second innings*—Sanderson 16–5–34–0; Hutton 15–6–44–2; Procter 6–3–17–1; Buck 6–2–27–2; Crook 2–0–12–0; Prasanna 20–3–49–4.

Umpires: M. Burns and B. J. Debenham.

At Hove, July 22–23. GLAMORGAN lost to SUSSEX by an innings and 154 runs. *Glamorgan are bowled out twice on the second day.*

GLAMORGAN v DURHAM

At Cardiff, August 19–21. Durham won by an innings and 30 runs. Durham 21pts, Glamorgan 3pts. Toss: uncontested. County debuts: A. Z. Lees, A. R. Patel.

Glamorgan suffered a third successive heavy defeat, with Durham needing only 50 balls to complete victory on the third morning. After being bundled out for 85 and 88 in their previous match, Glamorgan fared little better in their first innings on an overcast opening day, and it needed a run-a-ball 36 from Ruaidhri Smith to ensure they reached three figures. He then claimed a maiden five-for with his medium-pace as Durham stuttered after an opening stand of 94. Alex Lees made 69 in his first match after moving from Yorkshire, and another Durham debutant, the Indian white-ball all-rounder Akshar Patel, started with a forthright unbeaten 95 from 99 balls. That stretched the lead to 141, which proved enough as Glamorgan – lacking any confidence – caved in again. The chief destroyer this time was Rushworth, with five for 28. Brown faced 29 deliveries before getting off the mark, but fell to Steel's first ball – one of five catches for wicketkeeper Poynter – and only a late shower prevented a two-day finish.

Close of play: first day, Durham 75-0 (Steel 22, Lees 53); second day, Glamorgan 79-7 (Meschede 4, Smith 8).

Glamorgan

N. J. Selman c Richardson b Rushworth	3	– c Poynter b McCarthy	26
J. R. Murphy c Richardson b Rushworth	17	– c Poynter b Rushworth	7
C. R. Brown c Poynter b Salisbury	1	– c Poynter b Steel	18
K. S. Carlson b Salisbury	33	– b Rushworth	2
D. L. Lloyd c and b Collingwood	31	– c Poynter b McCarthy	4
†C. B. Cooke c Collingwood b Salisbury	0	– c Poynter b Patel	2
C. A. J. Meschede c Poynter b McCarthy	6	– lbw b Rushworth	8
A. G. Salter not out	12	– lbw b Steel	4
R. A. J. Smith b Rushworth	36	– not out	25
L. J. Carey lbw b Patel	1	– b Rushworth	1
*M. G. Hogan b Patel	11	– b Rushworth	6
Lb 3	3	B 4, lb 2, nb 2	8

1/17 (2) 2/18 (3) 3/26 (1)	(49.1 overs) 154	1/31 (1) 2/33 (2)	(42.2 overs) 111
4/77 (4) 5/81 (6) 6/89 (5)		3/35 (4) 4/40 (5)	
7/91 (7) 8/141 (9) 9/142 (10) 10/154 (11)		5/54 (6) 6/64 (3) 7/70 (8)	
		8/95 (9) 9/101 (10) 10/111 (11)	

Rushworth 14–4–36–3; Salisbury 13–3–34–3; McCarthy 11–1–41–1; Harte 4–0–17–0; Collingwood 4–3–13–1; Patel 3.1–1–10–2. *Second innings*—Rushworth 12.2–3–28–5; Salisbury 7–1–32–0; McCarthy 7–3–11–2; Patel 11–4–21–1; Harte 3–1–6–0; Steel 2–0–7–2.

Durham

C. T. Steel b Smith	32	M. E. T. Salisbury b Hogan	6
A. Z. Lees lbw b Meschede	69	C. Rushworth b Hogan	4
G. J. Harte b Smith	13		
G. Clark c Selman b Smith	11	Lb 14, w 1	15
M. J. Richardson c Cooke b Smith	9		
*P. D. Collingwood lbw b Meschede	8	1/94 (1) 2/112 (3)	(73.2 overs) 295
A. R. Patel not out	95	3/124 (2) 4/133 (5)	
†S. W. Poynter c Lloyd b Smith	29	5/144 (6) 6/158 (6) 7/219 (8)	
B. J. McCarthy run out (Meschede)	4	8/237 (9) 9/284 (10) 10/295 (11)	

Carey 15–3–42–0; Smith 20–2–87–5; Hogan 18.2–2–66–2; Meschede 17–1–78–2; Salter 3–1–8–0.

Umpires: J. H. Evans and A. G. Wharf.

GLAMORGAN v WARWICKSHIRE

At Colwyn Bay, August 29–31. Warwickshire won by an innings and 35 runs. Warwickshire 23pts, Glamorgan 3pts. Toss: uncontested.

The scenery changed, with the annual trip to the North Wales coast, but Glamorgan's fortunes did not: they slumped to a fourth consecutive trouncing, the third in a row by an innings. Warwickshire, meanwhile, consolidated their position at the top of the table. Glamorgan's batting problems were all too familiar, and were exacerbated by helpful conditions for bowlers on the first morning. Selman's disappointing season continued with a 14-ball duck, and only an attacking half-century from No. 8 Meschede secured a rare batting point. But Bell soon put a total of 203 into perspective, bettering it on his own: it was his fourth double-century for Warwickshire, but the first for ten years (though he made 235 for England in 2011). Dropped twice – a straightforward chance to slip on 34, then a more difficult one at cover point on 55 – he batted for 455 minutes, facing 331 balls, and passed 20,000 first-class runs. After twin unbeaten hundreds against Glamorgan at Edgbaston, Bell took his season's average against them to 425. He had help all down the order, with Stone's 42 not out taking the lead to exactly 300. After Barker made early inroads, Patel took over, often zeroing in on the rough caused by left-armer Barker's follow-through. He finished with seven victims and match figures of ten for 106, which included his 800th first-class wicket. The last pair lashed out, putting on 63 in 38 balls. There were ten fours and a six in Smith's unbeaten 52, while Hogan thrashed three sixes, before swishing once too often at Patel.

Close of play: first day, Warwickshire 116-3 (Bell 43, Wright 4); second day, Warwickshire 445-8 (Barker 43, Stone 2).

Glamorgan

N. J. Selman c Ambrose b Barker	0	– c Bell b Patel	14
J. R. Murphy c Ambrose b Sidebottom	18	– lbw b Barker	8
C. R. Brown c Ambrose b Stone	4	– b Barker	33
K. S. Carlson b Patel	32	– lbw b Patel	49
D. L. Lloyd c Bell b Barker	19	– c Wright b Patel	26
†C. B. Cooke b Stone	31	– c Trott b Patel	12
G. G. Wagg lbw b Patel	3	– c Rhodes b Patel	7
C. A. I. Meschede not out	53	– c Ambrose b Wright	7
A. G. Salter b Stone	5	– c Rhodes b Patel	8
R. A. J. Smith c Bell b Stone	5	– not out	52
*M. G. Hogan b Patel	1	– b Patel	28
B 2, lb 25, w 5	32	B 10, lb 9, nb 2	21

1/10 (1) 2/28 (2) 3/38 (3)   (59.4 overs) 203
4/80 (4) 5/113 (5) 6/118 (7)
7/142 (6) 8/162 (9) 9/172 (10) 10/203 (11)

1/9 (2) 2/60 (3)   (77.4 overs) 265
3/81 (1) 4/137 (5)
5/144 (4) 6/169 (6) 7/170 (7)
8/182 (8) 9/202 (9) 10/265 (11)

Barker 12–4–30–2; Sidebottom 11–3–34–1; Stone 13–4–28–4; Wright 13–3–61–0; Patel 10.4–3–23–3. *Second innings*—Barker 12–5–21–2; Sidebottom 13–6–51–0; Wright 13–4–43–1; Stone 13–3–48–0; Patel 26.4–6–83–7.

Warwickshire

W. M. H. Rhodes c Cooke b Wagg	24	O. P. Stone not out	42
D. P. Sibley lbw b Meschede	7	R. N. Sidebottom lbw b Smith	3
I. R. Bell lbw b Salter	204		
I. J. L. Trott c Selman b Smith	28	B 5, lb 20, w 2, nb 8	35
C. J. C. Wright b Meschede	16		
S. R. Hain c Carlson b Smith	61	1/23 (2) 2/43 (1) (133.3 overs) 503
†T. R. Ambrose lbw b Lloyd	22	3/106 (4) 4/162 (5) 5/283 (6)
K. H. D. Barker c Hogan b Salter	58	6/345 (7) 7/435 (3) 8/442 (9)
*J. S. Patel lbw b Hogan	3	9/488 (8) 10/503 (11) 110 overs: 385-6

Smith 29.3–4–98–3; Hogan 27–8–75–1; Meschede 17–3–69–2; Wagg 22–1–81–1; Salter 26–3–113–2; Lloyd 11–3–37–1; Carlson 1–0–5–0.

Umpires: J. W. Lloyds and P. R. Pollard.

At Derby, September 4–6. GLAMORGAN lost to DERBYSHIRE by 169 runs.

GLAMORGAN v GLOUCESTERSHIRE

At Cardiff, September 10–13. Gloucestershire won by nine wickets. Gloucestershire 22pts, Glamorgan 2pts. Toss: uncontested.

Glamorgan's horror run continued, the writing on the wall as early as the 11th over when they were 21 for five. Cooke and Wagg put on 83 in 16 overs, but a total of 137 was insufficient. Gloucestershire stuttered too, and at 141 for six shortly after a delayed start on the second day only just had their noses in front. But a stand of 155 between Jack Taylor and 17-year-old Ben Charlesworth changed all that: before lunch next day the lead had stretched beyond 200. Almost immediately, Glamorgan crashed to six for three. Miles took the wickets in ten balls, the day his move to Warwickshire in 2019 was announced; he finished the match with eight for 90. Lloyd counter-attacked, biffing ten fours in a rapid 54, but at 101 for seven another three-day finish looked on the cards. Smith, Bull (who survived almost three hours) and a career-best unbeaten 60 from van der Gugten at least saved the innings defeat and prolonged the match into a fourth day, when Gloucestershire won inside an hour.

Close of play: first day, Gloucestershire 133-5 (J. M. R. Taylor 15, Higgins 15); second day, Gloucestershire 284-6 (J. M. R. Taylor 98, Charlesworth 65); third day, Glamorgan 235-9 (van der Gugten 58, Hogan 8).

Glamorgan

S. C. Cook c Roderick b Miles	11	– c Roderick b Miles	20
C. R. Brown lbw b Miles	1	– c Hammond b Miles	0
T. N. Cullen b Miles	5	– lbw b Miles	0
K. S. Carlson lbw b Payne	0	– c Roderick b Miles	0
D. L. Lloyd lbw b Payne	4	– c Higgins b M. D. Taylor	54
†C. B. Cooke c Roderick b Miles	60	– b Higgins	11
G. G. Wagg c J. M. R. Taylor b M. D. Taylor	5	– b M. D. Taylor	8
R. A. J. Smith c Roderick b Payne	5	– c Roderick b M. D. Taylor	34
T. van der Gugten b M. D. Taylor	0	– (10) not out	60
K. A. Bull not out	0	– (9) lbw b M. D. Taylor	30
*M. G. Hogan c Roderick b Payne	15	– b M. D. Taylor	17
Lb 3	3	B 5, lb 8, nb 4	17

1/4 (2) 2/16 (3) 3/17 (4) (38.1 overs) 137 1/0 (2) 2/0 (3) (79.3 overs) 251
4/17 (1) 5/21 (5) 6/104 (6) 3/6 (4) 4/37 (1)
7/116 (8) 8/117 (9) 9/122 (7) 10/137 (11) 5/72 (6) 6/90 (5) 7/101 (7)
8/150 (8) 9/223 (9) 10/251 (11)

Payne 12.1–3–25–4; Miles 10–2–42–4; Higgins 8–3–15–0; M. D. Taylor 8–1–52–2. *Second innings*—Payne 17–6–46–0; Miles 20.8–48–4; Higgins 10.3–3–38–1; M. D. Taylor 20.3–2–81–5; Charlesworth 5–3–9–0; Dent 4–3–2–0; Hammond 3–0–14–0.

Gloucestershire

M. A. H. Hammond lbw b Smith	15	– (2) lbw b van der Gugten	0
*C. D. J. Dent lbw b Hogan	4	– (1) not out	25
J. R. Bracey c Cooke b van der Gugten	33	– not out	10
B. A. C. Howell c Hogan b Bull	43		
†G. H. Roderick lbw b van der Gugten	0		
J. M. R. Taylor c Cooke b van der Gugten	112		
R. F. Higgins b Hogan	18		
B. G. Charlesworth c Bull b van der Gugten	72		
C. N. Miles b Wagg	14		
D. A. Payne c Hogan b Bull	31		
M. D. Taylor not out	0		
B 4, lb 8	12		

1/18 (2) 2/27 (1) 3/77 (3) (128.4 overs) 354 1/1 (2) (1 wkt, 7.5 overs) 35
4/77 (5) 5/115 (4) 6/141 (7) 7/296 (8)
8/307 (6) 9/354 (10) 10/354 (9) 110 overs: 304-7

Van der Gugten 38–13–66–4; Hogan 34–9–91–2; Wagg 23.4–3–65–1; Smith 9–2–30–1; Bull 19–2–67–2; Lloyd 5–0–23–0. *Second innings*—van der Gugten 4–0–19–1; Hogan 3.5–0–16–0.

Umpires: N. L. Bainton and I. D. Blackwell.

At Canterbury, September 18–20. GLAMORGAN lost to KENT by an innings and 172 runs. *Glamorgan's seventh successive defeat.*

GLAMORGAN v LEICESTERSHIRE

At Cardiff, September 24–26. Glamorgan won by 132 runs. Glamorgan 23pts, Leicestershire 3pts. Toss: uncontested.

Glamorgan ended the Championship season as they had begun it, with a victory. In between, though, they had not won at all. This welcome success – their first at Cardiff since beating the same opposition in June 2015 – was set up by a vastly improved batting performance. Led by Carlson's boundary-studded 83, and with van der Gugten spanking another half-century from No. 10, they banked four batting points for the only time all season. Leicestershire then declined from 48 for one to 59 for five, with Wagg having Ackermann and Cosgrove caught behind off consecutive deliveries either side of lunch, then snaring Hill for another duck. Dearden made 48, but Glamorgan eventually led by 227. With two days and a session to spare, Hogan waived the follow-on. Another indifferent batting display ensued, with the new-ball pair of Tom Taylor (in his first Championship match since leaving Derbyshire) and Ben Mike sharing seven wickets, but Leicestershire still needed an unlikely 403. They nosedived to 42 for five, and later were 102 for eight. Klein delayed the inevitable, crashing 15 fours and a six during stands of 72 with Parkinson and 96 with Griffiths, before falling just short of a maiden century with only 11 balls of the third day remaining.

Close of play: first day, Glamorgan 331-8 (Bull 14, van der Gugten 40); second day, Glamorgan 106-4 (Lawlor 21, Cooke 41).

Glamorgan

S. C. Cook lbw b Parkinson	36	– lbw b Taylor	5
N. J. Selman lbw b Taylor	14	– lbw b Klein	19
J. R. Murphy c Mike b Taylor	0	– c Hill b Klein	11
K. S. Carlson b Mike	83	– c Hill b Griffiths	0
J. L. Lawlor lbw b Klein	2	– b Taylor	21
†C. B. Cooke c Hill b Griffiths	27	– b Taylor	45
C. A. J. Meschede c Klein b Ackermann	55	– b Taylor	4
G. G. Wagg lbw b Parkinson	28	– c Klein b Mike	23
K. A. Bull c Hill b Griffiths	24	– not out	10
T. van der Gugten c Dearden b Griffiths	50	– b Mike	6
*M. G. Hogan not out	8	– c Hill b Mike	16
B 2, lb 7, w 3, nb 20	32	B 4, lb 5, nb 6	15

1/20 (2) 2/32 (3) 3/96 (1) (103.4 overs) 359
4/148 (4) 5/148 (5) 6/207 (6)
7/268 (8) 8/268 (6) 9/348 (10) 10/359 (9)

1/12 (1) 2/38 (2) (57.4 overs) 175
3/39 (3) 4/39 (4)
5/110 (5) 6/114 (7) 7/117 (6)
8/137 (8) 9/157 (10) 10/175 (11)

Griffiths 21.4–7–71–3; Taylor 22–4–77–2; Klein 18–5–60–1; Mike 16–2–80–1; Parkinson 19–4–51–2; Cosgrove 2–0–2–0; Ackermann 5–2–9–1. *Second innings*—Taylor 12–7–15–4; Mike 12.4–0–73–3; Griffiths 11–3–33–1; Klein 12–5–23–2; Parkinson 7–2–11–0; Ackermann 3–0–11–0.

Leicestershire

A. Javid c Murphy b van der Gugten	29	– lbw b Hogan	3
S. T. Evans b Hogan	1	– c Bull b van der Gugten	8
*C. N. Ackermann c Cooke b Wagg	26	– lbw b van der Gugten	0
M. J. Cosgrove c Cooke b Wagg	0	– c Murphy b Hogan	11
H. E. Dearden c and b van der Gugten	48	– c Cooke b Meschede	24
†L. J. Hill c Selman b Wagg	0	– c Cooke b Meschede	13
T. A. I. Taylor b Meschede	5	– c Cook b Hogan	26
B. W. M. Mike c Selman b Meschede	0	– c Lawlor b Bull	8
C. F. Parkinson c Lawlor b Bull	3	– b Hogan	31
D. Klein not out	14	– lbw b van der Gugten	94
G. T. Griffiths c Cooke b Hogan	0	– not out	38
Lb 2, nb 4	6	B 1, lb 8, w 1, nb 4	14

1/2 (2) 2/48 (3) 3/48 (4)   (48.3 overs) 132   1/3 (1) 2/4 (3)   (71.1 overs) 270
4/58 (1) 5/59 (6) 6/89 (7)   3/23 (2) 4/23 (4)
7/91 (8) 8/96 (9) 9/130 (5) 10/132 (11)   5/42 (6) 6/75 (5) 7/92 (7)
                                        8/102 (8) 9/174 (9) 10/270 (10)

Van der Gugten 12–2–37–2; Hogan 12.3–5–18–2; Meschede 10–1–30–2; Wagg 10–4–25–3; Bull 4–0–20–1. *Second innings*—van der Gugten 15.1–4–63–3; Hogan 16–7–30–4; Meschede 11–0–55–2; Wagg 5–0–27–0; Bull 16–3–58–1; Selman 1–0–6–0; Lawlor 7–2–22–0.

Umpires: I. D. Blackwell and J. W. Lloyds.

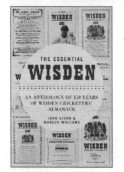

GLOUCESTERSHIRE

Starting again – again

ANDY STOCKHAUSEN

Gloucestershire's need to nurture young talent was again brought into focus by two notable departures at the end of the season. As had been feared, opening bowlers Liam Norwell and Craig Miles declined new contracts, and headed up the M5 to Edgbaston's bigger stage.

Head coach Richard Dawson and his assistant Ian Harvey are adept at unearthing and developing new players – which is just as well. As proof of continued progress, they can point to the emergence of another crop from the Academy conveyor belt. Without the resources to compete with wealthier rivals, Gloucestershire have little option but to mine their youth system, even in the knowledge that they are producing exceptional cricketers for the benefit of others.

Given opportunities that might not have been available elsewhere, Miles Hammond established himself as an opener of real ability, while fellow Academy product George Drissell profited from an equally steep learning curve, deploying his off-breaks in challenging conditions during the middle of the season. Drissell is part of a line of gifted cricketers to emerge from South Gloucestershire and Stroud College, one of the few state schools in the region to promote the sport.

Batsmen James Bracey and George Hankins further developed their game, and Hankins represented an ECB XI against India A at Headingley in June, before a serious knee injury ended his season. Ben Charlesworth, a 17-year-old all-rounder, was given permission to play by St Edward's School, Oxford, after the autumn term had begun, and made an encouraging start. In all, he appeared in six Championship matches, becoming – in the third, against Middlesex – the youngest Gloucestershire player to hit a fifty since 1890. No slouch with the ball, he claimed three wickets in the same match.

These players will form the nucleus of an ambitious, new-look side in 2019, again led by the experienced Chris Dent, whose captaincy improved as the season went on. Hamstrung by losses in excess of £500,000 for the previous financial year, Gloucestershire can at least find cause for optimism in their youth policy.

Regarded as no-hopers in the Championship, they made the doubters take stock when they won their opening fixture on a bowler-friendly track at Canterbury. A determined half-century from Gareth Roderick was instrumental in despatching Kent, who went on to promotion. It proved a false dawn: the next six games did not produce another victory, as injuries took their toll on a small squad. Forced to make do without strike bowler Norwell for almost all the season, and deprived of experienced left-armer David Payne for the first three months, Gloucestershire then lost their overseas signing Dan Worrall, a

Ryan Higgins

seamer from Victoria. A foot injury meant he returned to Australia after just four matches, though the county liked what they saw. His 16 first-class wickets suggested he could adapt to English conditions, and he was invited back for the whole of 2019. He will be joined by Stuart Whittingham, a Scottish international seamer recruited from Sussex.

When Hankins joined the list of long-term casualties, Gloucestershire were left to rely on emerging players to fill the void. Cheltenham provided the perfect stage for Hammond, a 22-year-old left-hander born in the town, to relaunch his career, five years after his debut. Promoted to open, he took a maiden hundred off a lively Sussex attack in front of a generous Festival crowd, though he could not prevent a narrow defeat. He followed it with an unbeaten 123 in a draw against Middlesex at Bristol in September.

Like Hammond, Ryan Higgins – who seemed to relish the big stage – also hit his first county hundred at Cheltenham as Gloucestershire overcame a Durham side that included Ben Stokes. Signed from Middlesex the previous winter, Higgins proved an excellent all-round addition, establishing himself as a model of consistency across the formats; he was alone in appearing in every game of the summer.

Back-to-back wins over Glamorgan and Essex were a promising start to the Royal London Cup, but a mixture of three defeats and three games ruined by rain washed away the optimism. The weather was particularly frustrating at Taunton, where Gloucestershire had fought hard to gain a winning position. All the same, the competition did provide a platform for Hankins to show his talents. He made 291 runs at 58 in his new role as an opener.

Aided by overseas hired hands Michael Klinger and Andrew Tye, and eager to make amends for a feeble 2017, Gloucestershire were once again a force in the T20 Blast, winning eight games and securing a top-four finish in the competitive South Group. But a quarter-final against Worcestershire at New Road proved a bridge too far.

In 2016, Gloucestershire's season had been knocked off course by defeat at the same stage of the competition. Two years later, however, they shook off their Worcester disappointment, and demonstrated far more resilience. Maintaining their focus and competitive edge to the last, they carved out convincing Championship victories over Leicestershire, Glamorgan and Derbyshire, and held their own in two draws. They eventually finished a satisfactory fifth in Division Two, their best since 2011.

Championship attendance: 25,768.

GLOUCESTERSHIRE RESULTS

All first-class matches – Played 15: Won 5, Lost 4, Drawn 6.
County Championship matches – Played 14: Won 5, Lost 4, Drawn 5.

Specsavers County Championship, 5th in Division 2;
Vitality Blast, quarter-finalists; Royal London One-Day Cup, 7th in South Group.

COUNTY CHAMPIONSHIP AVERAGES, BATTING AND FIELDING

Cap		Birthplace	M	I	NO	R	HS	100	Avge	Ct
2015	†K. Noema-Barnett††	Dunedin, NZ	8	14	5	323	73*	0	35.88	10
2010	†C. D. J. Dent	Bristol	14	28	3	851	214*	1	34.04	11
2013	†M. A. H. Hammond	Cheltenham‡	8	16	2	476	123*	2	34.00	6
2016	†J. R. Bracey	Bristol	14	27	3	785	125*	2	32.70	14
2012	B. A. C. Howell	Bordeaux, France	13	24	1	604	67	0	26.26	9
2018	†B. G. Charlesworth	Oxford	6	9	1	194	77*	0	24.25	2
2013	G. H. Roderick††	Durban, SA	12	22	1	500	67	0	23.80	48
2018	D. J. Worrall¶	Melbourne, Aust	4	5	1	94	50	0	23.50	2
2018	R. F. Higgins	Harare, Zimbabwe	14	24	2	482	105	1	21.90	6
2010	J. M. R. Taylor	Banbury	10	18	0	384	112	1	21.33	4
2016	G. L. van Buuren††	Pretoria, SA	7	14	1	275	83	0	21.15	2
2011	D. A. Payne	Poole	7	11	6	86	31	0	17.20	1
2011	C. N. Miles	Swindon	13	20	5	201	38*	0	13.40	3
2013	M. D. Taylor	Banbury	14	19	3	177	48	0	11.06	4
2017	G. S. Drissell	Bristol‡	5	9	0	76	19	0	8.44	0
2017	C. J. Liddle	Middlesbrough	2	4	2	11	6*	0	5.50	5

Also batted: I. A. Cockbain (*Liverpool*) (cap 2011) (1 match) 0 (1 ct); G. T. Hankins (*Bath*) (cap 2016) (1 match) 3, 10 (1 ct); L. C. Norwell (*Bournemouth*) (cap 2011) (1 match) 2, 1.

‡ *Born in Gloucestershire.*   ¶ *Official overseas player.*   †† *Other non-England-qualified.*

BOWLING

	Style	O	M	R	W	BB	5I	Avge
R. F. Higgins	RM	353.5	99	882	48	5-21	2	18.37
C. N. Miles	RFM	328.1	61	1,180	56	5-50	2	21.07
D. J. Worrall	RFM	119.1	33	348	16	4-45	0	21.75
M. D. Taylor	LM	344	61	1,171	46	5-81	1	25.45
D. A. Payne	LFM	204.2	42	573	22	4-25	0	26.04

Also bowled: B. G. Charlesworth (RM) 21.1–7–47–4; C. D. J. Dent (SLA) 4–3–2–0; G. S. Drissell (OB) 83–10–272–4; M. A. H. Hammond (OB) 3–0–14–0; B. A. C. Howell (RM) 28–5–122–4; C. J. Liddle (LFM) 31–5–99–2; K. Noema-Barnett (RM) 78–13–260–7; L. C. Norwell (RFM) 9–3–20–0; G. L. van Buuren (SLA) 72–8–246–4.

LEADING ROYAL LONDON CUP AVERAGES (100 runs/3 wickets)

Batting	Runs	HS	Avge	SR	Ct
I. A. Cockbain	208	106*	69.33	97.65	3
R. F. Higgins	195	81*	65.00	117.46	0
G. T. Hankins	291	92	58.20	78.43	5
G. H. Roderick	155	87*	51.66	91.17	5
C. D. J. Dent	225	80	45.00	108.17	1
B. A. C. Howell	165	68*	41.25	85.49	2
J. M. R. Taylor	146	54	36.50	94.19	2

Bowling	W	BB	Avge	ER
C. J. Liddle	13	4-57	25.92	6.74
C. N. Miles	6	3-31	27.00	6.99
D. J. Worrall	3	3-47	31.33	4.70
R. F. Higgins	4	1-11	52.50	5.52
B. A. C. Howell	5	2-24	59.60	5.41

LEADING VITALITY BLAST AVERAGES (100 runs/15 overs)

Batting	Runs	HS	Avge	SR	Ct	Bowling	W	BB	Avge	ER
J. M. R. Taylor ..	247	52	30.87	199.19	5	A. J. Tye.........	13	3-17	23.61	7.42
K. Noema-Barnett	198	57*	28.28	172.17	2	B. A. C. Howell ...	17	3-31	19.29	7.84
M. A. H. Hammond	313	51	24.07	155.72	9	D. A. Payne	18	3-29	24.22	8.54
I. A. Cockbain..	362	123	32.90	137.12	4	K. Noema-Barnett .	6	3-18	30.00	8.57
B. A. C. Howell .	137	28	17.12	130.47	7	T. M. J. Smith	9	3-39	26.00	8.72
R. F. Higgins....	240	55	24.00	129.03	4	R. F. Higgins	10	3-34	33.40	9.63
M. Klinger......	431	77*	35.91	114.93	8					

FIRST-CLASS COUNTY RECORDS

Highest score for	341	C. M. Spearman v Middlesex at Gloucester	2004
Highest score against	319	C. J. L. Rogers (Northants) at Northamptonshire .	2006
Leading run-scorer	33,664	W. R. Hammond (avge 57.05)	1920–51
Best bowling for	10-40	E. G. Dennett v Essex at Bristol	1906
Best bowling against {	10-66	A. A. Mailey (Australians) at Cheltenham	1921
	10-66	K. Smales (Nottinghamshire) at Stroud	1956
Leading wicket-taker	3,170	C. W. L. Parker (avge 19.43)	1903–35
Highest total for	695-9 dec	v Middlesex at Gloucester.	2004
Highest total against	774-7 dec	by Australians at Bristol	1948
Lowest total for	17	v Australians at Cheltenham	1896
Lowest total against	12	by Northamptonshire at Gloucester	1907

LIST A COUNTY RECORDS

Highest score for	177	A. J. Wright v Scotland at Bristol.............	1997
Highest score against	189*	J. G. E. Benning (Surrey) at Bristol	2006
Leading run-scorer	7,825	M. W. Alleyne (avge 26.89)	1986–2005
Best bowling for	7-29	D. A. Payne v Essex at Chelmsford	2010
Best bowling against	6-16	Shoaib Akhtar (Worcestershire) at Worcester. ...	2005
Leading wicket-taker	393	M. W. Alleyne (avge 29.88)	1986–2005
Highest total for	401-7	v Buckinghamshire at Wing	2003
Highest total against	496-4	by Surrey at The Oval....................	2007
Lowest total for	49	v Middlesex at Bristol...................	1978
Lowest total against	48	by Middlesex at Lydney	1973

TWENTY20 COUNTY RECORDS

Highest score for	126*	M. Klinger v Essex at Bristol	2015
Highest score against	116*	C. L. White (Somerset) at Taunton	2006
Leading run-scorer	2,633	H. J. H. Marshall (avge 27.71, SR 136.00)..	2006–16
Best bowling for	5-24	D. A. Payne v Middlesex at Richmond........	2015
Best bowling against	5-16	R. E. Watkins (Glamorgan) at Cardiff	2009
Leading wicket-taker	99	B. A. C. Howell (avge 18.95, ER 7.05).......	2012–17
Highest total for	254-3	v Middlesex at Uxbridge..................	2011
Highest total against	250-3	by Somerset at Taunton	2006
Lowest total for	68	v Hampshire at Bristol	2010
Lowest total against	97	by Surrey at The Oval....................	2010

ADDRESS

County Ground, Nevil Road, Bristol BS7 9EJ; 0117 910 8000; reception@glosccc.co.uk; www.gloscricket.co.uk.

OFFICIALS

Captain (first-class) C. D. J. Dent
(Twenty20) M. Klinger
Head coach R. K. J. Dawson
Assistant head coach I. J. Harvey
Head of talent pathway T. H. C. Hancock

President M. J. Journeaux
Chairman R. M. Cooke
Chief executive W. G. Brown
Head groundsman S. P. Williams
Scorer A. J. Bull

GLOUCESTERSHIRE v CARDIFF MCCU

At Bristol, April 1–3. Drawn. Toss: Cardiff MCCU. First-class debuts: H. A. J. Allen, B. N. Evans, J. H. Ludlow, L. Machado, S. J. Pearce, A. J. Woodland. County debut: R. F. Higgins.

Matt Taylor took advantage of seaming conditions and modest opposition to claim a career-best five for 15. He dismissed Cardiff's top three, including A. J. Woodland – the 2016 Wisden Schools Cricketer of the Year, and one of six students on first-class debut. The main resistance came from another, Sam Pearce, who fared better with the bat than his leg-spin (he had been removed from the attack in his fourth over for bowling beamers). Cardiff were shot out for 101 in reply to Gloucestershire's 359 for five, but Dent preferred batting practice to the follow-on. Howell had hit 70 in boundaries to warm a chilly audience on the opening day, while Roderick was less expansive; Brad Evans took four for 53. The students' wicketkeeper was Cameron Herring who, four years earlier, had hit his only first-class hundred, *for* Gloucestershire *against* Cardiff. There was no play on the second day.

Close of play: first day, Gloucestershire 359-5 (Higgins 44, Noema-Barnett 0); second day, no play.

Gloucestershire

B. A. C. Howell c Herring b Evans	89				
*C. D. J. Dent c Woodland b Evans	7	– (1) retired out			45
†G. H. Roderick retired not out	85				
G. T. Hankins b Evans	9	– (2) not out			54
J. M. R. Taylor c Herring b Evans	41	– (4) not out			27
G. L. van Buuren c Woodland b Turpin	52				
R. F. Higgins not out	44				
K. Noema-Barnett not out	0	– (3) lbw b Pike			4
B 16, lb 8, w 4, nb 4	32	B 1, lb 7, nb 2			10

1/32 (2) 2/145 (1)   (5 wkts dec, 80 overs) 359
3/161 (4) 4/241 (5) 5/352 (6)

1/79 (1)   (2 wkts, 35 overs) 140
2/83 (3)

C. N. Miles, C. J. Liddle and M. D. Taylor did not bat.

In the first innings Roderick retired not out at 263-4.

Brewster 16–3–59–0; Evans 17–5–53–4; Pike 14–5–39–0; Turpin 16.2–2–68–1; Pearce 3.4–0–32–0; Woodland 2–0–15–0; Allen 11–0–69–0. *Second innings*—Brewster 8–0–29–0; Evans 7–1–24–0; Pike 8–0–35–1; Turpin 6–3–12–0; Allen 5–0–28–0; Woodland 1–0–4–0.

Cardiff MCCU

J. H. Ludlow c Hankins b M. D. Taylor	19	J. R. Turpin c Noema-Barnett b Miles	5
H. A. J. Allen b M. D. Taylor	4	A. D. F. Brewster c Noema-Barnett b Liddle	7
A. J. Woodland c Miles b M. D. Taylor	1	O. L. Pike not out	0
*A. G. Milton c Roderick b Liddle	5	Lb 9	9
†C. L. Herring b Miles	9		
L. Machado lbw b M. D. Taylor	7	1/11 (2) 2/13 (3) 3/23 (4) (46.4 overs) 101	
S. J. Pearce c Hankins b Noema-Barnett	35	4/38 (1) 5/38 (5) 6/52 (6)	
B. N. Evans lbw b M. D. Taylor	0	7/60 (8) 8/65 (9) 9/95 (10) 10/101 (7)	

M. D. Taylor 14–5–15–5; Miles 13–4–33–2; Higgins 6–3–10–0; Liddle 9–2–23–2; Noema-Barnett 4.4–1–11–1.

Umpires: I. D. Blackwell and J. H. Evans.

At Canterbury, April 13–16. GLOUCESTERSHIRE beat KENT by five wickets.

GLOUCESTERSHIRE v GLAMORGAN

At Bristol, April 20–23. Glamorgan won by six wickets. Glamorgan 22pts, Gloucestershire 2pts. Toss: uncontested.

Wickets from de Lange and Hogan, and runs from Marsh – all schooled overseas – powered Glamorgan to a convincing win. There were Welsh-born contributors, too: Carey had seven victims, while Lloyd hit an unruffled career-best 119. On the opening day, the rangy de Lange snatched five for 62, his best figures for Glamorgan, to dismiss Gloucestershire for 236, a recovery from 86 for five. Norwell, Gloucestershire's spearhead throughout 2017, pulled up with a hamstring injury after nine overs, allowing Marsh to take centre-stage. He eased through the gears to reach a high-class century – on Championship debut for Glamorgan – and pave the way for Lloyd, who added 117 with de Lange, a club eighth-wicket record against Gloucestershire. Hogan declared, 290 ahead, on the third afternoon. Bracey, ten days shy of his 21st birthday, gave his seniors an object lesson in application, carving out an undefeated 120 over seven and a half hours. A string of scores from the bowlers – Higgins, Worrall (for the second time in the game) and Matt Taylor all made career-bests – slowed Glamorgan down, but in the end a target of 83 in 21 overs was insufficient. They made heavy weather of it before Donald brought victory with a four and a six.

Close of play: first day, Glamorgan 26-0 (Selman 17, Murphy 7); second day, Glamorgan 296-5 (Cooke 10, Lloyd 5); third day, Gloucestershire 133-5 (Bracey 34, Higgins 31).

Gloucestershire

B. A. C. Howell lbw b Carey	11	– (2) lbw b Carey		6
*C. D. J. Dent b Carey	6	– (1) c Salter b de Lange		12
†G. H. Roderick c Selman b Hogan	17	– c Donald b Carey		4
J. R. Bracey c Selman b de Lange	34	– not out		120
J. M. R. Taylor b de Lange	9	– c Carlson b de Lange		29
G. L. van Buuren lbw b Hogan	10	– lbw b de Lange		5
R. F. Higgins b Marsh b de Lange	43	– lbw b Hogan		61
K. Noema-Barnett lbw b Carey	46	– b Carey		12
D. J. Worrall not out	36	– b Carey		50
M. D. Taylor c Lloyd b de Lange	0	– c Cooke b Salter		48
L. C. Norwell c Cooke b de Lange	2	– c Cooke b Hogan		1
B 9, lb 3, nb 10	22	B 5, lb 6, w 1, nb 12		24

1/15 (2) 2/30 (1) 3/53 (3) (85.4 overs) 236
4/85 (5) 5/86 (4) 6/124 (6)
7/168 (7) 8/211 (8) 9/234 (10) 10/236 (11)

1/14 (2) 2/18 (3) (118 overs) 372
3/28 (1) 4/74 (5)
5/84 (6) 6/184 (7) 7/205 (8)
8/285 (9) 9/362 (10) 10/372 (11)

Carey 15–1–72–3; de Lange 20.4–4–62–5; Hogan 18–10–23–2; Lloyd 16–1–42–0; Salter 16–5–25–0. *Second innings*—de Lange 31–4–98–3; Carey 28–4–105–4; Hogan 27–7–74–2; Salter 23–3–62–1; Lloyd 9–2–22–0.

Glamorgan

N. J. Selman b Higgins	28	– c Bracey b M. D. Taylor		36
J. R. Murphy lbw b van Buuren	47	– c Roderick b M. D. Taylor		18
S. E. Marsh c Higgins b Worrall	111	– c Roderick b Worrall		0
K. S. Carlson c Roderick b Howell	45	– c Dent b M. D. Taylor		2
A. H. T. Donald c Roderick b Higgins	27	– not out		10
†C. B. Cooke c Howell b Worrall	43			
D. L. Lloyd c Roderick b Howell	119	– (6) not out		8
A. G. Salter c Howell b M. D. Taylor	4			
M. de Lange not out	50			
L. J. Carey lbw b Higgins	7			
*M. G. Hogan not out	7			
B 6, lb 8, w 2, nb 22	38	B 1, lb 5, w 1, nb 4		11

1/57 (1) 2/124 (2) (9 wkts dec, 153 overs) 526
3/235 (4) 4/263 (3)
5/287 (5) 6/349 (6) 7/379 (8)
8/496 (7) 9/510 (10)
110 overs: 335-5

1/51 (2) (4 wkts, 12.5 overs) 85
2/56 (3) 3/67 (4)
4/67 (1)

Worrall 33–13–91–2; M. D. Taylor 32–8–90–1; Norwell 9–3–20–0; Higgins 30–5–102–3; van Buuren 32–4–113–1; Noema-Barnett 7–1–42–0; Howell 10–1–54–2. *Second innings*—Worrall 6.5–0–54–1; M. D. Taylor 6–0–25–3.

Umpires: J. H. Evans and P. R. Pollard.

At Hove, April 27–30. GLOUCESTERSHIRE drew with SUSSEX.

At Lord's, May 11–14. GLOUCESTERSHIRE drew with MIDDLESEX.

GLOUCESTERSHIRE v KENT

At Bristol, June 9–12. Drawn. Gloucestershire 7pts, Kent 12pts. Toss: Kent.

After gaining just one batting point in four Championship matches, Kent made hay on the only true pitch they had encountered. Dickson hit their first Championship hundred of the season, Denly reached their second next day and, thanks to three half-centuries from the middle order, they declared at 582 for nine. Batting against Henry, in murderous form, was a more difficult proposition for Gloucestershire, who slumped to 82 for six. Then van Buuren and Noema-Barnett came together for the first of their two century stands. They could not prevent the follow-on, but did eat up 41 overs. Openers Dent and Howell made a hundred partnership of their own but, at 219 for six, 123 adrift, Gloucestershire were in trouble. Cue a repeat performance from van Buuren and Noema-Barnett, whose doggedness frustrated Kent for another 37 overs. Van Buuren eventually became a first senior victim for Bell-Drummond's rarely used seam, but Kent could not press home their advantage; after taking at least four wickets in each of his last seven innings, Henry claimed none.

Close of play: first day, Kent 297-4 (Denly 36, Stevens 11); second day, Gloucestershire 44-4 (J. M. R. Taylor 24, van Buuren 5); third day, Gloucestershire 73-0 (Dent 27, Howell 44).

Kent

D. J. Bell-Drummond c Dent b Miles	49	M. J. Henry c Roderick b Miles	24
S. R. Dickson b Miles	117	A. E. N. Riley not out	0
H. G. Kuhn c Bracey b van Buuren	38	B 7, lb 5, w 1, nb 2, p 5	20
*J. L. Denly c Roderick b Miles	107		
Z. Crawley c Dent b Higgins	30	1/124 (1) (9 wkts dec, 160.4 overs)	582
D. I. Stevens lbw b Noema-Barnett	89	2/216 (2) 3/220 (3)	
†A. P. Rouse c Roderick b van Buuren	55	4/279 (5) 5/440 (6) 6/459 (4) 7/555 (7)	
H. W. Podmore b van Buuren	53	8/564 (8) 9/582 (9) 110 overs: 366-4	

I. A. A. Thomas did not bat.

M. D. Taylor 29–7–98–0; Miles 30.4–5–122–4; Higgins 28–9–67–1; Noema-Barnett 21–1–89–1; Drissell 24–2–94–0; van Buuren 21–1–74–3; Howell 7–0–21–0.

Gloucestershire

B. A. C. Howell b Stevens	0	– (2) lbw b Podmore	67
*C. D. J. Dent b Stevens	1	– (1) c Rouse b Podmore	76
J. R. Bracey c Crawley b Podmore	12	– (4) c Rouse b Denly	27
†G. H. Roderick c Riley b Henry	0	– (3) lbw b Thomas	0
J. M. R. Taylor b Henry	33	– lbw b Denly	15
G. L. van Buuren c Kuhn b Henry	83	– c Kuhn b Bell-Drummond	59
R. F. Higgins b Henry	9	– c Dickson b Stevens	3
K. Noema-Barnett not out	73	– not out	42
C. N. Miles lbw b Henry	13	– not out	2
G. S. Drissell c Crawley b Henry	0		
M. D. Taylor c Rouse b Denly	9		
W 1, nb 6	7	B 11, lb 12, nb 8	31

1/1 (1) 2/2 (2) 3/5 (4)   (99.4 overs) 240   1/114 (2)   (7 wkts, 126.4 overs) 322
4/37 (3) 5/58 (5) 6/82 (7)   2/115 (3) 3/182 (1)
7/186 (6) 8/204 (9) 9/204 (10) 10/240 (11)   4/200 (4) 5/207 (5) 6/219 (7) 7/319 (6)

Henry 20–4–58–6; Stevens 21–5–42–2; Thomas 11–5–19–0; Podmore 13–2–37–1; Riley 23–9–46–0; Denly 11.4–1–38–1. *Second innings*—Henry 24.4–9–62–0; Stevens 18–6–40–1; Thomas 15–4–34–1; Denly 34–9–79–2; Podmore 16.4–6–55–2; Riley 14.2–5–28–0; Bell-Drummond 4–3–1–1.

Umpires: N. J. Llong and G. D. Lloyd.

HIGHEST FIRST-CLASS TOTALS BY TEAMS VISITING BRISTOL

774-7 dec	Australians	1948	603	Surrey	2005
746-9 dec	Northamptonshire	2002	592	Nottinghamshire	1911
626-6 dec	Surrey	2014	587-8 dec	Worcestershire	2006
615-7 dec	Glamorgan	2014	**582-9 dec**	**Kent**	**2018**
607	Nottinghamshire	1899	579	Surrey	1901

At Northampton, June 20–22. GLOUCESTERSHIRE lost to NORTHAMPTONSHIRE by ten wickets.

GLOUCESTERSHIRE v SUSSEX

At Cheltenham, July 16–19. Sussex won by 28 runs. Sussex 21pts, Gloucestershire 6pts. Toss: Sussex.

Archer and Robinson held their nerve to bowl promotion-chasing Sussex to victory in a thrilling encounter. Seemingly destined for heavy defeat after slumping to 38 for four in pursuit of 276, Gloucestershire took the contest to the wire thanks to the 21-year-old Bracey. He scored 87 in four hours, and added 138 with Roderick. But, once Briggs had broken the stand, the game tilted back towards Sussex – only for Bracey to whittle the target to 34 with three wickets left. Robinson snatched all three in 11 balls to pull the rug from beneath the hosts. Last to go was Bracey, held on the square-leg boundary. After Sussex had made a steady 286 on the first day, Hammond – asked to open in his first Championship game since 2015 – hit his maiden century (the first Hammond hundred at Cheltenham since 1937). He and Dent put on 182 for the first wicket and, at 295 for three, Gloucestershire looked set for a huge lead. But a catastrophic collapse that started on the second evening saw seven wickets cascade for 11 runs, including three for Archer in four balls. Finch made runs in both Sussex innings, falling on 98 in the second; Brown held six catches, and became the first Sussex wicketkeeper, after Harry Butt, to make six dismissals in an innings three times. Gloucestershire, who used two nightwatchmen on the third evening, stumbled to defeat.

Close of play: first day, Gloucestershire 42-0 (Hammond 27, Dent 12); second day, Gloucestershire 303-8 (Roderick 48); third day, Gloucestershire 30-2 (Drissell 5, Taylor 1).

Sussex

L. W. P. Wells c van Buuren b Miles	17	– c Roderick b Payne	5
P. D. Salt b Miles	57	– b Higgins	9
H. Z. Finch c and b Taylor	76	– c Roderick b Miles	98
L. J. Wright c Bracey b Miles	9	– c Higgins b Payne	48
M. G. K. Burgess lbw b Noema-Barnett	2	– b Payne	5
*†B. C. Brown c Higgins b Drissell	59	– lbw b Taylor	20
D. Wiese lbw b Noema-Barnett	7	– c Miles b Higgins	40
C. J. Jordan c Noema-Barnett b Drissell	0	– c Roderick b Miles	31
J. C. Archer c Noema-Barnett b Miles	21	– b Payne	5
O. E. Robinson not out	27	– c Dent b Taylor	19
D. R. Briggs lbw b Payne	7	– not out	0
B 1, lb 3	4	B 1, lb 12, w 2	15

1/74 (1) 2/80 (2) 3/90 (4)	(83 overs) 286	1/16 (2) 2/22 (1)	(73.4 overs) 295
4/97 (5) 5/210 (6) 6/219 (7)		3/103 (4) 4/119 (5)	
7/220 (8) 8/236 (3) 9/271 (9) 10/286 (11)		5/180 (6) 6/219 (3) 7/256 (7)	
		8/264 (9) 9/291 (8) 10/295 (10)	

Payne 15–4–41–1; Taylor 16–4–63–1; Higgins 15–6–38–0; Miles 18–1–68–4; Noema-Barnett 9–0–34–2; Drissell 10–1–38–2. *Second innings*—Payne 19–2–69–4; Higgins 19–5–59–2; Taylor 12.4–1–56–2; Miles 16–2–71–2; Drissell 5–0–20–0; van Buuren 2–0–7–0.

Gloucestershire

M. A. H. Hammond c Brown b Wiese	103	– (2) c Brown b Archer	11
*C. D. J. Dent c Archer b Briggs	65	– (1) c Brown b Archer	8
J. R. Bracey lbw b Jordan	34	– (5) c Briggs b Robinson	87
†G. H. Roderick not out	50	– (6) b Briggs	66
G. L. van Buuren b Wiese	11	– (7) c Finch b Jordan	14
G. S. Drissell b Archer	1	– (3) c Brown b Archer	5
R. F. Higgins b Archer	0	– (8) c Brown b Archer	12
K. Noema-Barnett c Brown b Archer	0	– (9) c Brown b Robinson	5
C. N. Miles lbw b Robinson	4	– (10) lbw b Robinson	1
D. A. Payne b Robinson	1	– (11) not out	2
M. D. Taylor b Archer	0	– (4) c Brown b Robinson	3
B 8, lb 17, nb 12	37	B 16, lb 13, nb 4	33

1/182 (2) 2/194 (1) 3/259 (3) (109.4 overs) 306
4/295 (5) 5/298 (6) 6/298 (7)
7/298 (8) 8/303 (9) 9/305 (10) 10/306 (11)

1/24 (1) 2/27 (2) (80.3 overs) 247
3/36 (4) 4/38 (3)
5/176 (6) 6/197 (7) 7/215 (8)
8/242 (9) 9/244 (10) 10/247 (5)

Archer 25.4–9–62–4; Robinson 23–5–67–2; Jordan 16–3–56–1; Wiese 18–3–56–2; Briggs 19–3–48–1; Wells 3–0–9–0. *Second innings*—Archer 21–8–29–4; Robinson 22.3–3–49–4; Jordan 14–0–46–1; Wiese 9–0–40–0; Briggs 12–0–47–1; Wells 2–0–7–0.

Umpires: B. J. Debenham and A. G. Wharf.

GLOUCESTERSHIRE v DURHAM

At Cheltenham, July 22–25. Gloucestershire won by 41 runs. Gloucestershire 23pts, Durham 5pts. Toss: Gloucestershire.

The Gloucestershire seamers combined to forge their first Championship win since the opening fixture. Set 340, Durham gained a solid start from the openers, and were well placed at 168 for two. But wickets fell as pressure told and, after Matt Taylor bowled Stokes and Poynter, they were a precarious 201 for six. Miles chipped away, as did Higgins, who delivered victory when Rushworth edged behind, leaving Wood unbeaten on 61. Higgins had a memorable all-round match. On the opening day, he hit his maiden hundred, a measured innings lasting three and a half hours; on the third, he finished with three for 41 to help secure a useful lead of 87, then struck a brisk 42 to keep Gloucestershire noses in front; on the last he added three more wickets. Durham were indebted to Latham, whose near-faultless 147 spanned their first innings, and to Stokes, whose eight wickets included his first county five-for since 2014.

Close of play: first day, Gloucestershire 315-7 (Miles 6); second day, Durham 219-5 (Latham 120, Poynter 21); third day, Durham 35-0 (Latham 10, Steel 23).

Gloucestershire

M. A. H. Hammond b Rushworth	51	– (2) c Stokes b Rushworth	4
*C. D. J. Dent lbw b Stokes	19	– (1) c Poynter b Salisbury	33
J. R. Bracey lbw b Rushworth	38	– b Rushworth	2
B. A. C. Howell c Steel b Stokes	4	– c Latham b Salisbury	43
†G. H. Roderick lbw b Salisbury	67	– c Poynter b Stokes	0
R. F. Higgins c Steel b Stokes	105	– c and b Smith	42
K. Noema-Barnett b Rushworth	7	– not out	69
C. N. Miles b Stokes	21	– c Poynter b Stokes	14
D. A. Payne not out	19	– c Clark	1
M. D. Taylor c sub (G. J. Harte) b Stokes	0	– c Poynter b Stokes	7
G. S. Drissell c Poynter b Salisbury	13	– c Stokes b Smith	16
Lb 12, nb 6	18	B 4, lb 5, nb 12	21

1/40 (2) 2/48 (4) 3/112 (1) (111 overs) 362
4/219 (5) 5/283 (3) 6/295 (7)
7/315 (6) 8/338 (8) 9/338 (10)
10/362 (11)

1/13 (2) 2/15 (3) (61.3 overs) 252
3/85 (4) 4/86 (5)
5/86 (1) 6/170 (6) 7/198 (8)
8/205 (9) 9/220 (10) 10/252 (11)

110 overs: 362-9

In the first innings Bracey, when 3, retired hurt at 44-1 and resumed at 219-4.

Rushworth 26–4–107–3; Salisbury 21–3–85–2; Stokes 25–8–52–5; Wood 6–3–4–0; Harding 24–4–76–0; Smith 8–0–23–0; Steel 1–0–3–0. *Second innings*—Rushworth 13–1–54–2; Salisbury 13–2–60–2; Harding 6–0–30–0; Stokes 18–3–66–3; Smith 5.3–0–10–2; Clark 6–0–23–1.

Durham

*T. W. M. Latham c Howell b Payne	147	– c Roderick b Taylor	45
C. T. Steel c Roderick b Miles	13	– lbw b Miles	62
W. R. Smith lbw b Miles	8	– lbw b Higgins	32
G. Clark lbw b Taylor	18	– c Roderick b Higgins	30
B. A. Stokes c Dent b Noema-Barnett	3	– b Taylor	9
M. J. Richardson c Howell b Higgins	21	– lbw b Miles	26
†S. W. Poynter b Miles	32	– b Taylor	8
M. A. Wood run out (Taylor)	11	– not out	61
M. E. T. Salisbury c Noema-Barnett b Higgins	3	– b Miles	1
G. H. I. Harding c Roderick b Higgins	0	– c Bracey b Taylor	7
C. Rushworth not out	2	– c Roderick b Higgins	2
Lb 7, nb 10	17	B 5, lb 4, w 2, nb 4	15

1/46 (2) 2/64 (3) 3/88 (4)   (96.4 overs) 275   1/94 (1) 2/126 (2)   (97 overs) 298
4/105 (5) 5/171 (6) 6/234 (7)   3/168 (4) 4/187 (3)
7/252 (8) 8/256 (9) 9/256 (10) 10/275 (1)   5/189 (5) 6/201 (7) 7/260 (6)
                                              8/262 (9) 9/280 (10) 10/298 (11)

Payne 19.4–5–42–1; Higgins 16–8–41–3; Taylor 18–3–67–1; Miles 24–4–88–3; Noema-Barnett 6–3–10–1; Drissell 13–4–20–0. *Second innings*—Payne 20–1–79–0; Miles 21–1–76–3; Higgins 20–3–44–3; Taylor 16–4–31–4; Drissell 15–2–42–0; Noema-Barnett 5–0–17–0.

Umpires: M. Burns and C. M. Watts.

At Birmingham, August 19–20. GLOUCESTERSHIRE lost to WARWICKSHIRE by an innings and 47 runs.

GLOUCESTERSHIRE v LEICESTERSHIRE

At Bristol, August 29–September 1. Gloucestershire won by 328 runs. Gloucestershire 20pts, Leicestershire 3pts. Toss: uncontested.
The third double-hundred of Dent's career propelled Gloucestershire to victory, their first at Bristol since beating Leicestershire in April 2017. Dent made an unbeaten 214 from 290 balls and shared century stands for the first three wickets of the second innings. He dominated the third – striking 118 from 101 balls as he and Howell put on 183 in 31 overs – and declared on 402 for four, setting a

---

GLOUCESTERSHIRE'S BIGGEST VICTORIES BY RUNS

342	v Oxford University at Oxford	1980
328	**v Leicestershire at Bristol**	**2018**
324	v Yorkshire at Cheltenham	1994
317	v Essex at Bristol	1947
316	v Somerset at Bristol	1947
313	v Cambridge University at Bristol	1959
313	v Cambridge University at Bristol	1994
307	v Nottinghamshire at Bristol	1896
300	v Yorkshire at Gloucester	1998

---

notional target of 494 and giving his bowlers more than four sessions to extract ten batsmen. Higgins then undermined the Leicestershire chase, removing two on the third evening and two more next morning. Apparently in a position of strength after Mohammad Abbas had taken five for 30 on the opening day, Leicestershire threw the initiative away by collapsing for 111: the top score came from nightwatchman Griffiths, and the last eight wickets fell for 49. Gloucestershire's first-innings 202 had brought an unexpected 91-run lead, which Dent made impregnable.

Close of play: first day, Leicestershire 11-1 (Horton 6, Griffiths 1); second day, Gloucestershire 152-1 (Dent 61, Bracey 17); third day, Leicestershire 117-6 (Cosgrove 42, Parkinson 4).

Gloucestershire

M. A. H. Hammond c Eckersley				
b Mohammad Abbas.	7	– (2) c Ackermann b Dexter	68
*C. D. J. Dent b Griffiths	28	– (1) not out.	214
J. R. Bracey lbw b Mohammad Abbas.	76	– c Eckersley b Dexter	43
B. A. C. Howell c Ackermann b Mohammad Abbas	0	– lbw b Ackermann.	56
†G. H. Roderick lbw b Mohammad Abbas	41		
J. M. R. Taylor lbw b Ackermann	21	– (5) c Mohammad Abbas b Ackermann	0
R. F. Higgins lbw b Raine	0		
B. G. Charlesworth lbw b Raine	2		
C. N. Miles not out.	1		
D. A. Payne c Eckersley b Raine	0		
M. D. Taylor c Cosgrove b Mohammad Abbas.	0		
B 15, lb 5, nb 6.	26	B 2, lb 7, w 2, nb 10.	21

1/50 (2)   2/50 (1)   3/50 (4)   (87.3 overs)   202   1/107 (2)   (4 wkts dec, 99.3 overs)   402
4/150 (5)   5/191 (6)   6/196 (7)   2/219 (3)   3/402 (4)
7/200 (8)   8/200 (3)   9/201 (10)   10/202 (11)   4/402 (5)

Mohammad Abbas 20.3–11–30–5; Raine 22–9–44–3; Klein 10–4–20–0; Griffiths 16–3–37–1; Parkinson 11–2–32–0; Dexter 5–2–16–0; Ackermann 3–0–3–1. *Second innings*—Mohammad Abbas 16–7–19–0; Raine 16–4–53–0; Griffiths 10–2–30–0; Klein 13–0–103–0; Dexter 15–2–53–2; Ackermann 8.3–1–26–2; Parkinson 21–1–109–0.

Leicestershire

H. E. Dearden c Hammond b Payne	4	– c Roderick b Miles.	5
*P. J. Horton c Roderick b Higgins	27	– lbw b Miles	10
G. T. Griffiths not out.	36	– (10) c Bracey b Higgins.	2
C. N. Ackermann b Higgins.	11	– (3) c Higgins b Payne.	2
M. J. Cosgrove b Miles	6	– (4) c Roderick b Higgins	52
N. J. Dexter c Roderick b Miles.	2	– (5) c Hammond b Higgins	4
†E. J. H. Eckersley c Roderick b Payne.	6	– (6) lbw b Higgins	8
B. A. Raine c Miles b M. D. Taylor.	8	– (7) c M. D. Taylor b Miles.	30
C. F. Parkinson lbw b Higgins.	2	– (8) lbw b M. D. Taylor.	17
D. Klein c Miles b Higgins	1	– (9) not out.	17
Mohammad Abbas lbw b M. D. Taylor.	0	– c Roderick b Charlesworth.	1
Lb 8	8	B 1, lb 6, nb 10.	17

1/10 (1)   2/48 (3)   3/62 (4)   (54.2 overs)   111   1/5 (1)   2/12 (3)   (67.1 overs)   165
4/70 (5)   5/78 (6)   6/85 (7)   3/24 (2)   4/42 (5)
7/105 (8)   8/108 (9)   9/110 (10)   10/111 (11)   5/52 (6)   6/112 (7)   7/141 (8)
                                                  8/145 (4)   9/155 (10)   10/165 (11)

Payne 18–3–52–2; Higgins 15–5–26–4; Miles 12–6–18–2; M. D. Taylor 9.2–4–7–2. *Second innings*—Payne 17–4–42–1; Miles 17–4–44–3; M. D. Taylor 17–5–44–1; Higgins 16–7–28–4; Charlesworth 0.1–0–0–1.

Umpires: M. J. Saggers and B. V. Taylor.

---

66 A piece in *The Times* proposed banning left-handers for being 'a thorough nuisance and a cause of waste of time'."
County Cricket after the War, page 72

GLOUCESTERSHIRE v MIDDLESEX

At Bristol, September 4–7. Drawn. Gloucestershire 9pts, Middlesex 8pts. Toss: uncontested.

A career-best 123 not out by Hammond effectively killed off Middlesex's hopes of promotion. An exciting finish had seemed in prospect on the final day, when Gloucestershire resumed their second innings 141 ahead with six wickets standing. If Middlesex had hoped to force the issue, they were hamstrung by the loss of their strike bowler, Murtagh, who missed the start of play after seeking emergency treatment for toothache. Dent then erred on the side of caution, batting past lunch before

---

YOUNGEST TO HIT A FIFTY FOR GLOUCESTERSHIRE

Yrs	Days		
16	54	W. W. F. Pullen (71) v Yorkshire at Cheltenham	1882
17	186	C. F. Belcher (60*) v Kent at Gloucester	1890
17	257	W. Troup (62) v Yorkshire at Gloucester.	1887
17	**290**	**B. G. Charlesworth (77*) v Middlesex at Bristol**	**2018**
17	314	C. J. Barnett (71) v Sussex at Hove	1928
18	54	M. W. Alleyne (116*) v Sussex at Bristol	1986
18	191	C. L. Townsend (95) v Somerset at Bristol	1895
18	254	L. D. Brownlee (66) v Somerset at Taunton.	1901
18	298	M. J. Procter (69) v South Africans at Bristol	1965
18	338	J. A. Pearson (51) v Northamptonshire at Bristol.	2002

Maiden scores of 50 or more only.

---

setting a target of 306 in 40 overs. He had hit a stubborn four-hour 82 on the opening day, but was upstaged by 17-year-old Ben Charlesworth, who became the youngest Gloucestershire player to score a first-class half-century since 1890. No one batted with fluency, though: the 110-over score was 237 for eight. Any chance Middlesex had of dictating terms departed with Malan, dismissed for 62; Charlesworth weighed in with three wickets for his seamers, as Gloucestershire led by 54. They had time to remove five opponents on the last afternoon, but no more.

Close of play: first day, Gloucestershire 208-7 (Charlesworth 18, Miles 4); second day, Middlesex 182-7 (Harris 6, Bamber 0); third day, Gloucestershire 87-4 (Hammond 43, J. M. R. Taylor 15).

Gloucestershire

M. A. H. Hammond c Malan b Fuller	23	– (2) not out.	123
*C. D. J. Dent c Gubbins b Malan	82	– (1) run out (Gubbins)	3
J. R. Bracey lbw b Fuller	3	– b Fuller.	15
B. A. C. Howell c Robson b Bamber.	17	– c Stirling b Murtagh.	1
†G. H. Roderick c Robson b Bamber.	30	– c Malan b Murtagh.	6
J. M. R. Taylor c Stirling b Harris	1	– c Eskinazi b Murtagh	43
R. F. Higgins c Stirling b Harris	24	– run out (Fuller)	23
B. G. Charlesworth not out	77	– c Fuller b Malan	10
C. N. Miles c Holden b Bamber.	14	– c Eskinazi b Fuller	9
D. A. Payne c Eskinazi b Bamber	1	– not out	8
M. D. Taylor lbw b Harris	17		
Lb 3, nb 4	7	B 4, lb 2, nb 4	10

1/63 (1) 2/77 (3) 3/106 (4)	(121 overs) 296	1/13 (1) (8 wkts dec, 94 overs) 251
4/149 (2) 5/158 (6) 6/162 (5) 7/196 (7)		2/48 (3) 3/51 (4)
8/235 (9) 9/238 (10) 10/296 (11)	110 overs: 237-8	4/59 (5) 5/153 (6)
		6/191 (7) 7/210 (8) 8/227 (9)

Murtagh 26–11–34–0; Harris 29.1–5–64–3; Bamber 27–6–81–4; Fuller 22.5–4–61–2; Stirling 1–0–7–0; Holden 7–0–25–0; Malan 8–2–21–1. *Second innings*—Murtagh 15–3–29–3; Bamber 24–6–47–0; Fuller 24–4–59–2; Holden 6–0–24–0; Malan 20–0–59–1; Robson 2–0–15–0; Stirling 3–0–12–0.

Middlesex

S. D. Robson c Roderick b Miles.............	10	– (6) not out........................	41
N. R. T. Gubbins lbw b Higgins	25	– lbw b Miles	5
†S. S. Eskinazi lbw b Charlesworth...........	45	– (7) not out........................	20
*D. J. Malan c Roderick b M. D. Taylor........	62	– (3) c J. M. R. Taylor b Payne	10
E. J. G. Morgan b M. D. Taylor..............	16	– (4) c Charlesworth b Payne	6
M. D. E. Holden lbw b Charlesworth..........	9		
P. R. Stirling c J. M. R. Taylor b Charlesworth....	4	– (1) run out (Bracey)	3
J. A. R. Harris c and b Payne	35		
E. R. Bamber not out	27		
J. K. Fuller c Roderick b Payne	3	– (5) lbw b Higgins	16
T. J. Murtagh b Bracey b Payne..............	0		
W 2, nb 4	6	B 5, lb 2, w 1, nb 2........	10

1/20 (1) 2/67 (2) 3/103 (3)   (96.3 overs) 242 1/3 (1)   (5 wkts, 31 overs) 111
4/124 (5) 5/155 (6) 6/161 (7)   2/13 (3) 3/18 (2)
7/181 (4) 8/234 (8) 9/238 (10) 10/242 (11)   4/29 (4) 5/56 (5)

Payne 23.3–6–51–3; Miles 18–4–59–1; M. D. Taylor 23–7–63–2; Higgins 19–3–44–1; Charlesworth 13–4–25–3. *Second innings*—Payne 8–1–20–2; Miles 10–1–46–1; M. D. Taylor 5–1–12–0; Higgins 5–0–14–1; Howell 3–1–12–0.

Umpires: G. D. Lloyd and R. J. Warren.

At Cardiff, September 10–13. GLOUCESTERSHIRE beat GLAMORGAN by nine wickets.

GLOUCESTERSHIRE v NORTHAMPTONSHIRE

At Bristol, September 18–21. Drawn. Gloucestershire 8pts, Northamptonshire 8pts. Toss: uncontested.
Ball dominated bat throughout the 114 overs that defied the worst of Storm Bronagh. The combination of an unusually green pitch and the damp weather meant no score above 43, and just one partnership above 33. Gloucestershire endured the worst of the conditions on day one, when the in-form Dent laboured almost two hours and faced 78 balls in scratching 15. Consistent in line and length, Hutton claimed four for 65, and Gloucestershire scraped past 100 only when the shine had left the ball, and the tail wagged. Payne and Miles proved awkward when Northamptonshire batted, and each claimed three wickets, though there was a brief passage of play, either side of lunch on the second day, when runs flowed: Levi and Rossington went for their shots, adding 72 in nine overs. They helped the visitors to a modest advantage that might have proved decisive, had Bronagh not swallowed all but five overs of the last two days.
Close of play: first day, Northamptonshire 4-1 (Curran 4, Newton 0); second day, Northamptonshire 173; third day, no play.

Gloucestershire

M. A. H. Hammond c Rossington b Hutton.......	0	– (2) not out	2
*C. D. J. Dent c Cotton b Hutton.............	15	– (1) not out	4
†J. R. Bracey c Rossington b Sanderson	8		
B. A. C. Howell c Levi b Sanderson	11		
I. A. Cockbain lbw b Buck...................	0		
J. M. R. Taylor c Levi b Cotton..............	17		
R. F. Higgins c Rossington b Hutton	10		
B. G. Charlesworth c Rossington b Hutton	1		
C. N. Miles b Buck........................	23		
D. A. Payne not out	23		
M. D. Taylor c Cotton b Buck	9		
B 2, lb 4, w 2	8		

1/1 (1) 2/16 (3) 3/32 (4)   (54.1 overs) 125   (no wkt, 5 overs) 6
4/32 (5) 5/54 (6) 6/61 (2)
7/63 (8) 8/68 (7) 9/101 (9) 10/125 (11)

Sanderson 15–7–16–2; Hutton 22–3–65–4; Buck 12.1–4–32–3; Cotton 5–2–6–1. *Second innings*—Sanderson 3–1–6–0; Hutton 2–2–0–0.

Northamptonshire

B. A. Hutton lbw b Payne	0	B. D. Cotton c Bracey b M. D. Taylor	7
B. J. Curran c Hammond b Miles	30	N. L. Buck c Howell b Payne	0
R. I. Newton lbw b M. D. Taylor	8	B. W. Sanderson not out	2
R. S. Vasconcelos c Cockbain b Payne	8	B 9, lb 11, nb 6	26
*A. G. Wakely c Bracey b Howell	17		
R. E. Levi c Charlesworth b Miles	30	1/0 (1) 2/30 (3) 3/50 (4) (55 overs) 173
†A. M. Rossington b Miles	43	4/70 (2) 5/76 (5) 6/148 (6)
S. A. Zaib b Higgins	2	7/161 (7) 8/165 (8) 9/171 (9) 10/173 (10)

Payne 11–3–29–3; Miles 16–6–52–3; M. D. Taylor 9–1–19–2; Higgins 16–6–30–1; Howell 3–0–23–1.

Umpires: M. Burns and P. R. Pollard.

At Derby, September 24–26. GLOUCESTERSHIRE beat DERBYSHIRE by two wickets.

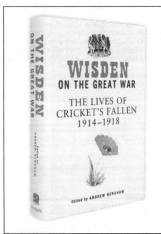

HAMPSHIRE

50 overs good, 20 overs bad

PAT SYMES

Any season that brings a trophy must be a success. By lifting the Royal London Cup in June, when an emphatic campaign culminated in a resounding defeat of Kent, Hampshire rediscovered their knack of winning limited-overs competitions. They could be content, too, with fifth in the Championship – especially after only one victory from their first eight games. But their performance in the Vitality Blast was abject. Hampshire won only two of their 14 matches, and were a shadow of the side who triumphed in 50-over cricket.

In that format, they were dominant. They prevailed in five of their seven completed group matches, their two defeats coming when they might – perhaps should – have won: they lost to Kent by one run, and to Somerset off the last delivery, despite defending 356. James Vince was in imperious form in the semi-final against Yorkshire, when he hit 171 from 126 balls; at Lord's, Rilee Rossouw, Tom Alsop and Sam Northeast took the total well beyond their opponents' reach. It was particularly satisfying for Northeast, Kent captain the summer before, who endured jeers from former supporters as he made a classy unbeaten 75. And for Rossouw, who won the match award for his 125, it was the highlight of a season that was patchy in the Championship and poor in the Blast.

Northeast's first summer at Southampton was interrupted by a broken finger, which meant Hampshire had to be over-reliant for runs on Vince, their captain. It was fortunate for them, if not Vince, that England decided they could manage without him. He made 962 Championship runs at 40, another 527 at 58 in the Royal London, but a disappointing 248 at 22 in the Blast, which helped explain the results.

Of Hampshire's four Championship wins, two came against Worcestershire, who finished last. The batsmen had to shoulder most blame: none of Alsop, Rossouw, Northeast, Joe Weatherley or the veteran Jimmy Adams strung together a convincing run of scores, and a total of 16 batting points was uncomfortably the lowest in the division. Hashim Amla hit two centuries in his five spring appearances, but Hampshire often needed the lower order to come to the rescue; Kyle Abbott and Gareth Berg did much of the baling. Supporters were mystified that the experienced Sean Ervine, in what proved his last season, was selected only once, and eventually loaned to Derbyshire.

Abbott struggled for rhythm in the first half of the season, when he managed only 14 wickets in the first seven Championship games. But something clicked, and in the next seven he grabbed 37, inspiring Hampshire to three victories in their last six: in those three games, he took an irresistible 25 at eight. He and Dale Steyn, at Southampton partly to improve his fitness, had taken the new

Fidel Edwards

ball together for South Africa; now they did so for Hampshire.

The bowling, though, wasn't solely made up of thirty-something South Africans: as well as Abbott, Steyn and Berg, there was Fidel Edwards, of Barbados. Despite turning 36 before the season, he snatched 54 Championship wickets in occasional spells of real hostility. Hampshire's attack may have been long in the tooth, but only Lancashire bettered their 39 bowling points.

Injuries did not help Hampshire's cause. Northeast, Brad Wheal, Brad Taylor, Mason Crane and Reece Topley were all absent for long spells. A stress fracture of the back ended Crane's season after he collected his winner's medal at Lord's – a fitting reward for 15 Royal London wickets. Sadly, though, the injury-prone Topley was again sidelined for most of the season, and he chose to leave at its end.

Quite what happened between June 30, when Hampshire won at Lord's, and July 6, when they suffered the first of nine defeats in the Vitality Blast, is uncertain. They recruited powerful New Zealand opening batsman Colin Munro and teenage Afghanistan spinner Mujeeb Zadran – and looked well equipped to mount a challenge. Mujeeb did fine: nine wickets in 12 matches with an economy-rate of just over seven. But although Munro topped the Hampshire averages – 211 runs at 26, with a decent strike-rate – he was 79th nationally, proof that the batting malfunctioned. Chris Wood, who nabbed 19 wickets at 17 and cost 7.6 an over, was a rare success. Liam Dawson performed respectably with bat and ball, but it was arguably Hampshire's worst T20 season.

At the end of a curious summer, the county moved to plug gaps. Aneurin Donald arrived from Glamorgan to deepen the batting, while proven seamers Keith Barker (Warwickshire) and James Fuller (Middlesex) should add nous to the bowling. Crane and Taylor are expected to have recovered from long-term injuries and to supplement Dawson's left-arm spin.

Adams and Ervine decided to call it a day after long careers. Adams had captained Hampshire, toured with England Lions, and amassed over 14,000 first-class runs in 17 seasons. Like Ervine, who gave up an international career with Zimbabwe to provide sterling service over 14 summers at the Rose Bowl, he had been a key component in Hampshire's many white-ball successes. Their departure will give greater opportunity to players such as all-rounder Tom Scriven and batsman Ollie Soames. Also on the move were Craig White, who chose to leave after two seasons as head coach, and groundsman Karl McDermott, who replaces Mick Hunt at Lord's.

Championship attendance: 20,052.

HAMPSHIRE RESULTS

All first-class matches – Played 15: Won 4, Lost 5, Drawn 6.
County Championship matches – Played 14: Won 4, Lost 5, Drawn 5.

Specsavers County Championship, 5th in Division 1;
Vitality Blast, 8th in South Group; Royal London One-Day Cup, winners.

COUNTY CHAMPIONSHIP AVERAGES, BATTING AND FIELDING

Cap		Birthplace	M	I	NO	R	HS	100	Avge	Ct
	H. M. Amla¶	Durban, SA	5	9	0	492	112	2	54.66	2
2013	J. M. Vince	Cuckfield	14	25	1	962	201*	3	40.08	5
	†R. R. Rossouw††	Bloemfontein, SA . . .	9	17	3	489	120*	1	34.92	8
	†T. P. Alsop	Wycombe	8	14	1	397	99	0	30.53	22
2016	G. K. Berg	Cape Town, SA	9	14	2	335	84*	0	27.91	4
2013	L. A. Dawson	Swindon	10	17	2	385	72	0	25.66	6
2017	K. J. Abbott††	Empangeni, SA	14	22	5	436	60*	0	25.64	0
	S. A. Northeast	Ashford, Kent	10	18	0	451	129	1	25.05	5
2006	†J. H. K. Adams	Winchester‡	14	25	1	582	147	1	24.25	15
	J. J. Weatherley	Winchester‡	12	21	1	459	126*	1	22.95	5
	L. D. McManus	Poole	7	12	1	211	66	0	19.18	9
2018	C. P. Wood	Basingstoke‡	3	5	1	56	26	0	14.00	2
	I. G. Holland‡‡	Stevens Point, USA . . .	7	11	1	135	31	0	13.50	3
	D. W. Steyn¶	Phalaborwa, SA	5	7	1	65	25	0	10.83	1
	B. T. J. Wheal††	Durban, SA	5	7	1	63	25*	0	10.50	7
	O. C. Soames	Kingston-u-Thames . . .	4	7	0	69	29	0	9.85	0
2018	F. H. Edwards††	St Peter, Barbados . .	14	20	9	75	14	0	6.81	3

Also batted: †S. M. Ervine (*Harare, Zimbabwe*) (cap 2005) (1 match) 8, 10; O. P. Rayner (*Fallingbostel, Germany*) (2 matches) 0, 0 (2 ct); B. J. Taylor (*Winchester‡*) (1 match) 5, 16.

‡ *Born in Hampshire.*   ¶ *Official overseas player.*   †† *Other non-England-qualified.*

BOWLING

	Style	O	M	R	W	BB	5I	Avge
D. W. Steyn	RFM	142.3	30	382	20	5-66	1	19.10
K. J. Abbott	RFM	348.3	70	1,182	51	6-39	4	23.17
I. G. Holland	RFM	151	42	389	15	3-48	0	25.93
F. H. Edwards	RFM	362.2	55	1,443	54	6-50	2	26.72
L. A. Dawson	SLA	205.2	36	627	20	4-30	0	31.35
B. T. J. Wheal	RFM	114.5	17	462	11	2-46	0	42.00
G. K. Berg	RFM	200.1	41	654	15	5-130	1	43.60

Also bowled: J. H. K. Adams (LM) 1–0–3–0; T. P. Alsop (SLA) 3–0–12–1; O. P. Rayner (OB) 72–17–196–5; B. J. Taylor (OB) 16–4–50–2; J. M. Vince (RM) 5–1–17–0; J. J. Weatherley (OB) 14–1–65–2; C. P. Wood (LFM) 72–13–268–6.

LEADING ROYAL LONDON CUP AVERAGES (150 runs/5 wickets)

Batting	Runs	HS	Avge	SR	Ct		**Bowling**	W	BB	Avge	ER
J. M. Vince	527	171	58.55	109.79	7		L. A. Dawson	7	4-47	21.00	5.25
T. P. Alsop	248	95	49.60	89.53	3		M. S. Crane	15	4-46	29.13	5.90
R. R. Rossouw . .	394	125	43.77	105.34	1		G. K. Berg	13	3-46	37.00	5.85
G. K. Berg	163	65	40.75	134.71	4		R. J. W. Topley . . .	7	4-40	41.57	5.24
J. J. Weatherley . .	250	105*	35.71	79.11	3		B. J. Taylor	6	2-35	49.00	4.81
B. J. Taylor	155	56	31.00	68.88	4		C. P. Wood	6	3-46	54.16	5.05

LEADING VITALITY BLAST AVERAGES (100 runs/15 overs)

Batting	Runs	HS	Avge	SR	Ct/St	Bowling	W	BB	Avge	ER
R. R. Rossouw .	217	50	18.08	**158.39**	9	D. W. Steyn	5	2-29	21.60	**7.04**
C. Munro	211	63	26.37	**154.01**	3	Mujeeb Zadran . .	9	2-31	35.33	**7.09**
J. M. Vince. . . .	248	74	22.54	**140.11**	3	L. A. Dawson . . .	9	2-22	37.22	**7.12**
L. A. Dawson. .	289	82	26.27	**129.59**	5	C. P. Wood	19	5-32	17.63	**7.61**
S. A. Northeast	256	73*	23.27	**106.22**	4	R. A. Stevenson .	9	2-28	32.11	**9.07**
T. P. Alsop	165	41	16.50	**105.09**	8/2	G. K. Berg	2	2-33	111.00	**10.09**

FIRST-CLASS COUNTY RECORDS

Highest score for	316	R. H. Moore v Warwickshire at Bournemouth .	1937
Highest score against	303*	G. A. Hick (Worcestershire) at Southampton . .	1997
Leading run-scorer	48,892	C. P. Mead (avge 48.84)	1905–36
Best bowling for	9-25	R. M. H. Cottam v Lancashire at Manchester . .	1965
Best bowling against	10-46	W. Hickton (Lancashire) at Manchester	1870
Leading wicket-taker	2,669	D. Shackleton (avge 18.23)	1948–69
Highest total for	714-5 dec	v Nottinghamshire at Southampton	2005
Highest total against	742	by Surrey at The Oval	1909
Lowest total for	15	v Warwickshire at Birmingham	1922
Lowest total against	23	by Yorkshire at Middlesbrough	1965

LIST A COUNTY RECORDS

Highest score for	178	J. M. Vince v Glamorgan at Southampton	2017
Highest score against	203	A. D. Brown (Surrey) at Guildford	1997
Leading run-scorer	12,034	R. A. Smith (avge 42.97)	1983–2003
Best bowling for	7-30	P. J. Sainsbury v Norfolk at Southampton	1965
Best bowling against	7-22	J. R. Thomson (Middlesex) at Lord's	1981
Leading wicket-taker	411	C. A. Connor (avge 25.07).	1984–98
Highest total for	371-4	v Glamorgan at Southampton	1975
Highest total against	**360-7**	**by Somerset at Southampton**	**2018**
Lowest total for	43	v Essex at Basingstoke.	1972
Lowest total against	{ 61	by Somerset at Bath	1973
	{ 61	by Derbyshire at Portsmouth	1990

TWENTY20 COUNTY RECORDS

Highest score for	124*	M. J. Lumb v Essex v Southampton	2009
Highest score against	116*	L. J. Wright (Sussex) at Southampton	2014
Leading run-scorer	**3,430**	**J. M. Vince (avge 32.05, SR 136.21)**	**2010–18**
Best bowling for	5-14	A. D. Mascarenhas v Sussex at Hove	2004
Best bowling against	**6-28**	**J. K. Fuller (Middlesex) at Southampton**. . . .	**2018**
Leading wicket-taker	119	D. R. Briggs (avge 19.40, ER 6.86).	2010–15
Highest total for	249-8	v Derbyshire at Derby	2017
Highest total against	220-4	by Somerset at Taunton	2010
Lowest total for	85	v Sussex at Southampton	2008
Lowest total against	67	by Sussex at Hove	2004

ADDRESS

The Ageas Bowl, Botley Road, West End, Southampton SO30 3XH; 023 8047 2002; enquiries@ageasbowl.com; www.ageasbowl.com.

OFFICIALS

Captain J. M. Vince   **President** N. E. J. Pocock
Cricket operations manager T. M. Tremlett   **Chairman** R. G. Bransgrove
Director of cricket G. W. White   **Chief executive** D. Mann
First-team coach 2018 C. White   **Head groundsman 2018** K. McDermott
           2019 A. V. Birrell   **2019** N. Gray
Head of player development C. R. M. Freeston   **Scorer** K. R. Baker

HAMPSHIRE v CARDIFF MCCU

At Southampton, April 7–9. Drawn. Toss: Cardiff MCCU. First-class debut: S. J. S. Assani. County debut: S. A. Northeast.

The 37-year-old Jimmy Adams batted throughout the first day, when Oliver Pike, a seam bowler from Bridgend (and a cousin of the Wales and Real Madrid winger Gareth Bale), felt his full force. In four balls Adams sprinted from 82 to a hundred, his 24th in first-class cricket. He shared century stands for the second wicket with Rossouw and for the fifth with Ervine; both made sixties on an easy surface. Cardiff's captain, Alex Milton, used eight bowlers, before the weather, which had snatched a dozen overs from the first day, washed out the remainder.

Close of play: first day, Hampshire 417-4 (Adams 182, Ervine 65); second day, no play.

Hampshire

J. J. Weatherley c Ludlow b Evans	27	S. M. Ervine not out		65
J. H. K. Adams not out	182	B 7, lb 10, nb 24		41
R. R. Rossouw c Assani b Pike	61			—
S. A. Northeast b Turpin	28	1/37 (1) 2/169 (3)	(4 wkts, 83 overs)	417
L. A. Dawson c Ludlow b Pearce	13	3/250 (4) 4/269 (5)		

†L. D. McManus, G. K. Berg, *K. J. Abbott, B. T. J. Wheal and F. H. Edwards did not bat.

Brewster 15–1–74–0; Evans 16–4–64–1; Pike 12–0–64–1; Turpin 8–0–49–1; Assani 8–2–41–0; Pearce 15–0–74–1; Woodland 8–0–30–0; Allen 1–0–4–0.

Cardiff MCCU

J. H. Ludlow, H. A. J. Allen, A. J. Woodland, *†A. G. Milton, L. Machado, S. J. Pearce, B. N. Evans, S. J. S. Assani, J. R. Turpin, A. D. F. Brewster, O. L. Pike.

Umpires: B. J. Debenham and B. V. Taylor.

HAMPSHIRE v WORCESTERSHIRE

At Southampton, April 13–16. Hampshire won by 196 runs. Hampshire 21pts, Worcestershire 4pts. Toss: uncontested. County debuts: H. M. Amla; T. M. Head.

Hampshire made an emphatic start to the Championship, defeating newly promoted Worcestershire with ease. The batting had been strengthened by the arrival of Amla and Northeast, though neither played a significant role. Leach chose to field in conditions that favoured seam throughout, but 75s from Vince and Berg saw Hampshire to 290. In reply, Worcestershire slipped to 127 for seven before Cox and Barnard helped limit the deficit to 79. Day three belonged to Abbott: after his half-century shored up Hampshire from their overnight 163 for eight and set Worcestershire an improbable 324, he struck three times before the close. Next morning, he grabbed another. Edwards marked the award of his Hampshire cap with five wickets, taken in hostile bursts redolent of his West Indies heyday. Leach, spirited in defeat, claimed seven for 97.

Close of play: first day, Worcestershire 40-2 (Mitchell 15, Tongue 4); second day, Hampshire 163-8 (Abbott 4, Wheal 2); third day, Worcestershire 59-3 (Mitchell 34, Tongue 0).

Hampshire

J. H. K. Adams lbw b Magoffin	33	lbw b Leach	19
†L. D. McManus c Cox b Leach	2	c Cox b Tongue	27
*J. M. Vince b Magoffin	75	c Mitchell b Magoffin	12
S. A. Northeast b Leach	17	b Leach	4
H. M. Amla lbw b Tongue	36	run out (Barnard)	36
R. R. Rossouw b Leach	0	b Magoffin	29
L. A. Dawson b Mitchell	24	b Leach	16
G. K. Berg not out	75	lbw b Tongue	10
K. J. Abbott lbw b Mitchell	0	c Rhodes b Barnard	51
B. T. J. Wheal lbw b Tongue	4	c Clarke b Barnard	19
F. H. Edwards c Cox b Leach	1	not out	3
B 8, lb 8, w 1, nb 6	23	B 10, lb 8	18

1/5 (2) 2/111 (1) 3/122 (3)   (75.4 overs) 290
4/158 (4) 5/164 (6) 6/193 (5)
7/233 (7) 8/233 (9) 9/242 (10) 10/290 (11)

1/47 (2) 2/47 (1)   (66.2 overs) 244
3/51 (4) 4/73 (3)
5/113 (6) 6/137 (7) 7/157 (8)
8/157 (5) 9/229 (10) 10/244 (9)

Leach 15.4–4–42–4; Magoffin 17–3–61–2; Barnard 15–2–54–0; Tongue 16–0–61–2; Head 7–1–35–0; Mitchell 5–0–21–2. *Second innings*—Leach 16–1–55–3; Magoffin 16–5–60–2; Tongue 17–4–40–2; Barnard 13.2–2–57–2; Mitchell 4–0–14–0.

Worcestershire

D. K. H. Mitchell c Northeast b Edwards	21	lbw b Abbott	35
B. L. D'Oliveira c Vince b Edwards	1	lbw b Abbott	1
T. C. Fell b Abbott	16	b Abbott	8
J. C. Tongue c Rossouw b Abbott	4	(5) c Wheal b Berg	4
J. M. Clarke b Berg	20	(4) lbw b Abbott	15
T. M. Head c Northeast b Berg	9	not out	45
G. H. Rhodes lbw b Abbott	12	c Amla b Edwards	1
†O. B. Cox c Adams b Wheal	65	b Wheal	0
E. G. Barnard c Wheal b Dawson	40	lbw b Edwards	4
*J. Leach c Berg b Wheal	2	c McManus b Edwards	0
S. J. Magoffin not out	4	c Vince b Dawson	6
B 4, lb 12, w 1	17	Lb 6, nb 2	8

1/4 (2) 2/36 (3) 3/40 (4)   (66.2 overs) 211
4/52 (1) 5/78 (6) 6/83 (5)
7/127 (7) 8/203 (8) 9/207 (10) 10/211 (9)

1/4 (2) 2/18 (3)   (49.5 overs) 127
3/50 (4) 4/67 (5)
5/67 (1) 6/95 (7) 7/96 (8)
8/101 (9) 9/101 (10) 10/127 (11)

Abbott 19–6–45–3; Edwards 16–4–45–2; Wheal 12–2–46–2; Berg 15.3–3–46–2; Dawson 4.2–0–13–1. *Second innings*—Berg 13–4–26–1; Abbott 17–6–45–4; Edwards 11–2–33–3; Wheal 5–1–15–1; Dawson 3.5–2–2–1.

Umpires: J. W. Lloyds and M. J. Saggers.

At The Oval, April 20–23. HAMPSHIRE lost to SURREY by 139 runs.

HAMPSHIRE v ESSEX

At Southampton, April 27–30. Drawn. Hampshire 11pts, Essex 10pts. Toss: uncontested.

Rain reduced this contest to a scramble for bonus points, with Hampshire – inserted under grey skies – faring slightly better. Play over the first three days totalled just 88 overs, and on the fourth it was so cold that Siddle bowled in a beanie hat. It did not impede him: with the second ball of the morning he broke Rossouw's bat, and with the fourth had him caught at second slip. But thanks to the diligence of Adams, who knuckled down in conditions that favoured the quicker bowlers, and the hitting of Abbott, Hampshire declared after banking four batting points. Alastair Cook, in his first match of the season, and Bopara both struck 84, and a late flourish from Foster steered Essex to 300.

Close of play: first day, Hampshire 41-0 (Weatherley 22, Adams 19); second day, Hampshire 154-2 (Adams 57, Amla 8); third day, Hampshire 241-4 (Rossouw 10, Dawson 0).

Hampshire

J. J. Weatherley c Browne b Siddle	29	K. J. Abbott c and b S. J. Cook	43
J. H. K. Adams lbw b Porter	87	C. P. Wood not out	10
*J. M. Vince c Foster b Harmer	47	B 7, lb 9, w 1, nb 6	23
H. M. Amla c Foster b Siddle	52		
R. R. Rossouw c Harmer b Siddle	10	(7 wkts dec, 108.4 overs)	351
L. A. Dawson not out	34	1/54 (1)	
†L. D. McManus c Foster b S. J. Cook	16	2/134 (3) 3/227 (4)	
		4/241 (2) 5/241 (5) 6/272 (7) 7/340 (8)	

B. T. J. Wheal and F. H. Edwards did not bat.

Porter 29–4–86–1; S. J. Cook 22–7–87–2; Siddle 29–7–62–3; Bopara 9.4–2–37–0; Harmer 18–3–59–1; Lawrence 1–0–4–0.

Essex

N. L. J. Browne c Adams b Wheal	26	S. R. Harmer not out	21
A. N. Cook c McManus b Wood	84		
T. Westley c Amla b Wheal	0	B 1, lb 8	9
D. W. Lawrence lbw b Abbott	6		
R. S. Bopara not out	84	(6 wkts, 70.5 overs)	300
*R. N. ten Doeschate lbw b Edwards	24	1/54 (1) 2/54 (3)	
†J. S. Foster b Dawson	46	3/61 (4) 4/148 (2)	
		5/175 (6) 6/251 (7)	

P. M. Siddle, J. A. Porter and S. J. Cook did not bat.

Abbott 17–3–42–1; Edwards 16–4–63–1; Wood 17–1–72–1; Wheal 12.5–3–63–2; Dawson 8–0–51–1.

Umpires: N. L. Bainton and P. K. Baldwin.

At Nottingham, May 4–7. HAMPSHIRE lost to NOTTINGHAMSHIRE by 203 runs.

At Taunton, May 11–14. HAMPSHIRE drew with SOMERSET. *James Vince hits 201*.*

HAMPSHIRE v SURREY

At Southampton, June 9–11. Surrey won by an innings and 58 runs. Surrey 23pts, Hampshire 3pts. Toss: Surrey.

Surrey's victory, accomplished inside three days, was their third in five starts, and briefly overtook Somerset at the top of the table. They met little resistance from Hampshire, who were forced to follow on and lost 20 wickets in 108 overs. Two South African stalwarts – with over 700 Test wickets between them – were making Championship debuts for a new county: Morkel for Surrey, Steyn for Hampshire. Morkel enjoyed greater success, claiming match figures of five for 70 on a sound surface, while Hampshire's spearhead turned out to be Edwards. Despite a reliable pitch, the only batsmen to bed themselves in were Burns and Foakes, who added 199 for Surrey's fourth wicket at a healthy lick. Burns's hundred was his fourth against these opponents in two years, taking his record against them to 908 runs at 90. The architect of Hampshire's first-innings downfall was Clarke, his five-for only the fifth of a career spanning 17 seasons. They did not help themselves in the follow-on: when patient defence was their only salvation, Vince was stumped and Weatherley run out.

Close of play: first day, Surrey 216-3 (Burns 109, Foakes 68); second day, Hampshire 135.

Surrey

*R. J. Burns b Taylor	151	J. W. Dernbach lbw b Steyn	6
M. D. Stoneman c Adams b Edwards	0	M. Morkel not out	4
S. G. Borthwick run out (Taylor)	0	G. S. Virdi b Edwards	0
R. S. Patel lbw b Taylor	34	Lb 10, w 1, nb 4	15
†B. T. Foakes lbw b Edwards	90		
O. J. D. Pope c McManus b Edwards	41	1/1 (2) 2/1 (3) 3/83 (4) (97 overs) 368
S. M. Curran c Adams b Steyn	13	4/282 (1) 5/282 (5) 6/312 (7)
R. Clarke c Rossouw b Edwards	14	7/345 (8) 8/364 (9) 9/364 (6) 10/368 (11)

Edwards 26–5–93–5; Steyn 26–2–91–2; Berg 12–2–39–0; Abbott 17–2–85–0; Taylor 16–4–50–2.

Hampshire

J. J. Weatherley c Clarke b Dernbach	9	– run out (Dernbach)	50
J. H. K. Adams lbw b Clarke	13	– lbw b Curran	2
*J. M. Vince c Borthwick b Clarke	14	– st Foakes b Virdi	28
S. M. Ervine c Foakes b Morkel	8	– c Clarke b Virdi	10
R. R. Rossouw c Pope b Morkel	46	– not out	39
†L. D. McManus b Curran	6	– b Morkel	1
G. K. Berg lbw b Clarke	8	– lbw b Clarke	6
B. J. Taylor c Borthwick b Clarke	5	– lbw b Clarke	16
K. J. Abbott b Curran	3	– lbw b Virdi	0
D. W. Steyn not out	8	– c Pope b Morkel	0
F. H. Edwards c Foakes b Clarke	1	– c Pope b Morkel	0
Lb 10, nb 4	14	B 1, lb 5, nb 2	8

1/12 (1) 2/41 (3) 3/54 (2)   (49.2 overs) 135   1/8 (2) 2/50 (3)   (58.4 overs) 175
4/60 (4) 5/83 (6) 6/117 (5)   3/76 (4) 4/106 (1)
7/121 (7) 8/124 (8) 9/134 (9) 10/135 (11)   5/107 (6) 6/117 (7) 7/151 (8)
                                                     8/170 (9) 9/175 (10) 10/175 (11)

Dernbach 11–2–30–1; Curran 13–5–31–2; Morkel 13–2–33–2; Virdi 1–0–2–0; Clarke 11.2–3–29–5. *Second innings*—Dernbach 10–3–29–0; Curran 15–6–26–1; Morkel 11.4–2–37–3; Clarke 13–0–54–2; Virdi 9–2–23–3.

Umpires: N. A. Mallender and B. V. Taylor.

HAMPSHIRE v YORKSHIRE

At Southampton, June 20–23 (day/night). Drawn. Hampshire 11pts, Yorkshire 10pts. Toss: Yorkshire. First-class debut: J. A. Tattersall. County debut: O. P. Rayner.

An hour into the last day, with Yorkshire 112 for four in their second innings, just 19 ahead, Hampshire sensed an opening. But Brook and Leaning put on a solid 108 in 38 overs, and were not prised apart until Berg deflected the ball on to the non-striker's stumps to dismiss Brook for 68 – and by then it was too late. On a lifeless wicket, Hampshire had struggled to overcome stubborn defence, especially from Leaning, unbeaten on 54 from 191 balls when the draw was agreed. On the first day, there had been an inevitability to Ballance's century, whose last five scores against Hampshire now read 120, 55, 108, 203 not out and 109. Steyn finished with five for 66. Hampshire's reply coalesced first round Adams, who hit his 22nd and last Championship hundred (his first had also come against Yorkshire in 2006) and then Berg. They enjoyed a 93-run advantage but, in a slow-scoring pink-ball contest, too much time had slipped by. Rayner, borrowed from Middlesex because Hampshire's spinners were injured or on England Lions duty, found enough turn to claim four victims.

Close of play: first day, Yorkshire 315-7 (Bresnan 33, Patterson 18); second day, Hampshire 245-3 (Adams 132, Alsop 62); third day, Yorkshire 91-2 (Pujara 14, Ballance 18).

Yorkshire

A. Lyth c Alsop b Berg	21	– c Alsop b Rayner	17
A. Z. Lees lbw b Edwards	0	– lbw b Rayner	39
C. A. Pujara b Steyn	0	– b Holland	32
G. S. Ballance c Northeast b Steyn	109	– c Alsop b Rayner	21
H. C. Brook lbw b Steyn	79	– run out (Berg)	68
J. A. Leaning b Edwards	39	– not out	54
†J. A. Tattersall c Rayner b Steyn	6	– b Rayner	22
T. T. Bresnan b Edwards	35	– not out	4
*S. A. Patterson c Steyn b Abbott	37		
J. A. Brooks c Rayner b Steyn	1		
B. O. Coad not out	13		
B 2, lb 4, nb 4	10	Lb 2, nb 4	6

1/1 (2) 2/10 (3) 3/21 (1)   (104.2 overs) 350   1/49 (1)   (6 wkts dec, 113 overs) 263
4/164 (5) 5/235 (4) 6/245 (7)   2/58 (2) 3/108 (4)
7/277 (6) 8/318 (8) 9/319 (10) 10/350 (9)   4/112 (5) 5/220 (5) 6/256 (7)

Edwards 23–2–109–3; Steyn 29–7–66–5; Berg 17–2–51–1; Abbott 13.2–3–58–1; Holland 13–2–35–0; Rayner 9–3–25–0. *Second innings*—Steyn 21–6–47–0; Edwards 13–2–53–0; Berg 14–8–26–0; Holland 17–7–44–1; Rayner 33–9–54–4; Abbott 14–5–34–0; Adams 1–0–3–0.

Hampshire

J. J. Weatherley lbw b Brooks	7	D. W. Steyn b Patterson	23
J. H. K. Adams c Tattersall b Bresnan	147	F. H. Edwards c Tattersall b Brooks	0
*J. M. Vince b Brooks	35		
S. A. Northeast b Patterson	4	B 1, lb 7, nb 6	14
†T. P. Alsop lbw b Brooks	63		
I. G. Holland c Tattersall b Brooks	31	1/9 (1) 2/63 (3) (144.4 overs) 443
G. K. Berg not out	84	3/68 (4) 4/247 (5) 5/286 (2)
O. P. Rayner c Tattersall b Patterson	0	6/309 (6) 7/310 (8) 8/384 (9)
K. J. Abbott c sub (J. A. Thompson) b Lyth	35	9/442 (10) 10/443 (11) 110 overs: 302-5

Coad 27–9–81–0; Brooks 30.4–3–124–5; Patterson 32–10–67–3; Bresnan 27–5–78–1; Lyth 19–3–54–1; Brook 1–0–8–0; Leaning 8–0–23–0.

Umpires: J. W. Lloyds and R. J. Warren.

At Manchester, June 25–28. HAMPSHIRE drew with LANCASHIRE.

HAMPSHIRE v NOTTINGHAMSHIRE

At Southampton, August 19–22. Hampshire won by 270 runs. Hampshire 21pts, Nottinghamshire 3pts. Toss: uncontested. County debut: K. C. Brathwaite.

After Hampshire coasted to victory, Vince reserved special praise for Abbott, whose return to form after an ankle injury had brought match figures of six for 66, as well as 88 across two unbeaten innings. The captain's gratitude might as easily have been for Edwards, whose six for 50 in Nottinghamshire's first innings contained spells of genuine pace and hostility, or even for Vince himself, after making 74 and 147 on a pitch still giving help to the quicker bowlers. Nottinghamshire, who had chosen to bowl, conceded a first-innings deficit of 111, despite Steyn sending down only 10.4 overs because of a groin injury. As batting became easier, Alsop contributed a patient 99. Vince's declaration challenged Nottinghamshire to make a notional 511 or bat out 156 overs. Chief resistance came from Mullaney and Wessels in a fifth-wicket stand of 88, but Abbott and Dawson – who had rescued Hampshire's first innings from 137 for seven on the opening day – shared eight wickets, and Nottinghamshire succumbed to their fifth defeat by lunch on the last.

Close of play: first day, Nottinghamshire 39-4 (Patel 6, Mullaney 8); second day, Hampshire 253-4 (Alsop 63, Rossouw 6); third day, Nottinghamshire 128-4 (Mullaney 29, Wessels 17).

Hampshire

J. J. Weatherley c Wessels b Footitt	9	– lbw b Milnes	18
J. H. K. Adams b Mullaney	22	– b Footitt	0
*J. M. Vince c Mullaney b Carter	74	– b Milnes	147
S. A. Northeast b Mullaney	0	– c Wessels b Mullaney	12
†T. P. Alsop b Mullaney	0	– c Carter b Footitt	99
R. R. Rossouw c Carter b Fletcher	13	– lbw b Fletcher	36
G. K. Berg lbw b Fletcher	0	– c Brathwaite b Footitt	9
L. A. Dawson b Carter	72	– not out	36
K. J. Abbott not out	60	– not out	28
D. W. Steyn c Mullaney b Carter	0		
F. H. Edwards run out (Brathwaite/Wessels)	1		
B 10, lb 8, w 2, nb 6	26	B 4, lb 1, w 3, nb 6	14

1/25 (1) 2/58 (2) 3/58 (4)   (74.5 overs) 277   1/0 (2)   (7 wkts dec, 104 overs) 399
4/62 (5) 5/137 (6) 6/137 (3)   2/24 (1) 3/73 (4)
7/137 (7) 8/270 (8) 9/270 (10) 10/277 (11)   4/244 (3) 5/319 (6) 6/327 (5) 7/336 (7)

Fletcher 16–3–54–2; Footitt 15–2–67–1; Milnes 14–1–40–0; Mullaney 14–3–43–3; Carter 10.5–2–34–3; Patel 5–1–21–0. *Second innings*—Fletcher 18–3–46–1; Footitt 15–2–69–3; Milnes 13–0–54–2; Mullaney 11–0–49–1; Carter 30–2–110–0; Patel 15–1–56–0; Brathwaite 2–0–10–0.

Nottinghamshire

K. C. Brathwaite c Adams b Edwards	5	– c Berg b Dawson	48
J. D. Libby b Edwards	16	– b Abbott	15
C. D. Nash c Alsop b Berg	1	– lbw b Dawson	2
M. E. Milnes b Edwards	2	– (10) not out	12
S. R. Patel lbw b Edwards	6	– (4) c Rossouw b Edwards	9
*S. J. Mullaney c Alsop b Berg	38	– (5) c Berg b Dawson	50
†M. H. Wessels lbw b Abbott	11	– (6) lbw b Abbott	69
W. T. Root c Edwards b Abbott	36	– (7) c Rossouw b Weatherley	8
L. J. Fletcher c Dawson b Edwards	43	– (8) c Adams b Abbott	4
M. Carter b Edwards	0	– (9) b Abbott	0
M. H. A. Footitt not out	4	– b Dawson	8
Lb 4	4	B 4, lb 4, w 5, nb 2	15

1/21 (1) 2/22 (3) 3/24 (2)   (44.1 overs) 166   1/31 (2) 2/34 (3)   (93.4 overs) 240
4/25 (4) 5/46 (5) 6/78 (7)   3/53 (4) 4/85 (1)
7/82 (6) 8/133 (9) 9/148 (10) 10/166 (8)   5/173 (5) 6/186 (7) 7/209 (8)
                                            8/209 (9) 9/229 (6) 10/240 (11)

Steyn 10.4–1–41–0; Edwards 16–2–50–6; Berg 7–1–25–2; Abbott 6.1–0–30–2; Dawson 4.2–2–16–0. *Second innings*—Edwards 19–3–72–1; Berg 14–3–42–0; Abbott 22–6–36–4; Dawson 35.4–8–80–4; Weatherley 3–1–2–1.

Umpires: I. D. Blackwell and R. J. Warren.

At Chelmsford, August 29–September 1. HAMPSHIRE lost to ESSEX by an innings and 52 runs.

At Worcester, September 4–6. HAMPSHIRE beat WORCESTERSHIRE by 114 runs.

HAMPSHIRE v SOMERSET

At Southampton, September 10–11. Hampshire won by six wickets. Hampshire 19pts, Somerset 3pts. Toss: Somerset.

Somerset were the losers in the Rose Bowl's first two-day result since 2004, while the beneficiaries were not simply Hampshire, who boosted their chances of avoiding relegation, but Surrey – now as good as champions. High-class pace bowling from the South Africans, Abbott and Steyn, accounted for all ten wickets in Somerset's second innings, and 18 in the match. On a wicket offering extravagant movement for the quicker bowlers, Somerset – despite winning the toss – were twice dismissed in exactly 37 overs. Abbott finished with 11 for 71, taking his haul from his past four matches to 30 at under ten. Only two batsmen made half-centuries: Northeast in helping Hampshire gain a handy first-innings lead, and Trescothick, who was last out in Somerset's second innings after eventually losing a tense duel with Steyn (almost 14 years earlier, he had been Steyn's first Test victim). Hampshire needed 75 for their third win in four, for Craig Overton to provoke jitters by reducing them to 21 for three; Adams steered them home before tea.

Close of play: first day, Hampshire 142-9 (Abbott 8, Edwards 4).

Somerset

M. E. Trescothick c Alsop b Abbott	13	– b Steyn	50
B. G. F. Green b Holland	26	– b Abbott	0
Azhar Ali lbw b Holland	12	– c Alsop b Abbott	7
J. C. Hildreth c Adams b Abbott	10	– lbw b Abbott	4
*T. B. Abell c Holland b Steyn	3	– b Abbott	2
†S. M. Davies b Abbott	4	– c Holland b Steyn	23
L. Gregory lbw b Abbott	2	– b Abbott	5
C. Overton c Alsop b Steyn	12	– c Alsop b Abbott	6
J. Overton lbw b Abbott	0	– c Dawson b Steyn	5
M. J. Leach c Alsop b Steyn	6	– b Steyn	5
J. H. Davey not out	3	– not out	0
B 10, lb 5	15	B 1, lb 8	9

1/17 (1) 2/45 (3) 3/64 (2)	(37 overs) 106	1/0 (2) 2/8 (3) 3/12 (4)	(37 overs) 116
4/71 (4) 5/71 (5) 6/74 (7)		4/20 (5) 5/61 (6) 6/72 (7)	
7/83 (6) 8/83 (9) 9/97 (8) 10/106 (10)		7/78 (8) 8/83 (9) 9/91 (10) 10/116 (11)	

Steyn 13–1–37–3; Abbott 10–3–31–5; Holland 8–5–5–2; Edwards 6–0–18–0. *Second innings*—Steyn 15–4–34–4; Abbott 13–3–40–6; Holland 5–1–12–0; Edwards 4–0–21–0.

Hampshire

J. J. Weatherley lbw b Gregory	4	– c Davies b C. Overton	11
O. C. Soames lbw b Davey	0	– c Davies b C. Overton	6
J. H. K. Adams c Davies b Davey	31	– not out	25
*J. M. Vince b Gregory	0	– c J. Overton b C. Overton	0
S. A. Northeast b J. Overton	53	– c Trescothick b J. Overton	12
†T. P. Alsop lbw b J. Overton	1	– not out	10
I. G. Holland b J. Overton	2		
L. A. Dawson c and b Green	31		
K. J. Abbott not out	10		
D. W. Steyn b Davey	5		
F. H. Edwards c and b C. Overton	8		
Lb 1, nb 2	3	B 4, lb 5, nb 2	11

1/0 (2) 2/12 (1) 3/12 (4)	(58.4 overs) 148	1/14 (2)	(4 wkts, 22.5 overs) 75
4/59 (3) 5/62 (6) 6/68 (7)		2/21 (1) 3/21 (4)	
7/124 (8) 8/126 (5) 9/135 (10) 10/148 (11)		4/46 (5)	

Gregory 6–1–12–2; Davey 17–5–40–3; C. Overton 12.4–2–44–1; J. Overton 13–4–22–3; Abell 4–1–21–0; Green 6–3–8–1. *Second innings*—Gregory 5–2–13–0; Davey 2.5–0–10–0; C. Overton 8–2–22–3; J. Overton 6–2–12–1; Green 1–0–9–0.

Umpires: S. J. O'Shaughnessy and A. G. Wharf.

At Leeds, September 18–21. HAMPSHIRE drew with YORKSHIRE. *Hampshire ensure survival in Division One.*

HAMPSHIRE v LANCASHIRE

At Southampton, September 24–26. Lancashire won by eight wickets. Lancashire 21pts, Hampshire 3pts. Toss: Lancashire. First-class debut: B. D. Guest.

Lancashire's emphatic victory, completed on the third morning, could not prevent relegation. They finished tied on points with Nottinghamshire, but had won three matches to their rivals' four. The crucial passage of play had come on the second afternoon, as Lancashire neared a third batting point that would – given how results fell – have saved them. They were 273 for seven, 27 from their immediate goal, when Bohannon edged Abbott to third slip. Next over, Edwards bowled Bailey and, just after two o'clock, trapped Mahmood, sowing despair in the Lancashire camp. It was especially hard on Rob Jones, who had batted resolutely for his 68, and on Bailey, whose four wickets in each innings took him to 64 for the season, the most in Division One. Trailing by 86, Hampshire fared little better second time round, though McManus did at least push the target past 100. Jennings and Livingstone completed the hollow victory. This was the end of Jimmy Adams's 17-season career on the south coast: he was given a guard of honour by his team-mates, and signed off with a seven – three runs plus four overthrows.

Close of play: first day, Lancashire 123-4 (Livingstone 46, Vilas 5); second day, Hampshire 178-8 (McManus 30, Abbott 21).

Hampshire

J. J. Weatherley c Davies b Gleeson	7	– c Davies b Gleeson 16
O. C. Soames b Mahmood	29	– c Vilas b Gleeson 3
J. H. K. Adams c Vilas b Bailey	0	– lbw b Gleeson 13
*J. M. Vince lbw b Bohannon	22	– c Davies b Bohannon 19
S. A. Northeast lbw b Bailey	42	– b Bohannon 11
L. A. Dawson c Jennings b Mahmood	10	– c Davies b Bailey 37
I. G. Holland b Gleeson	1	– b Bohannon 4
†L. D. McManus c Jennings b Gleeson	0	– not out 44
G. K. Berg c Jones b Bailey	21	– c Jennings b Bailey 4
K. J. Abbott not out	10	– b Bailey 21
F. H. Edwards c Livingstone b Bailey	14	– c Jones b Bailey 5
B 8, lb 13, nb 10	31	B 1, lb 15, w 5 21

1/15 (1) 2/20 (3) 3/63 (4) (56.5 overs) 187   1/4 (2) 2/27 (1) (57 overs) 198
4/87 (2) 5/101 (6) 6/112 (7)   3/38 (3) 4/65 (5)
7/112 (8) 8/152 (6) 9/163 (9) 10/187 (11)   5/84 (4) 6/88 (7) 7/131 (6)
                                            8/148 (9) 9/182 (10) 10/198 (11)

Bailey 18.5–4–57–4; Gleeson 15–5–34–3; Mahmood 15–4–39–2; Bohannon 8–0–36–1. *Second innings*—Bailey 19–5–43–4; Gleeson 16–5–57–3; Parry 6–1–18–0; Mahmood 6–0–18–0; Bohannon 10–2–46–3.

Lancashire

K. K. Jennings b Holland	48	– not out 40
†A. L. Davies b Edwards	3	– c Northeast b Edwards 12
B. D. Guest b Abbott	8	– b Edwards 0
*L. S. Livingstone b Edwards	46	– not out 48
S. D. Parry c McManus b Holland	0	
D. J. Vilas c and b Dawson	27	
R. P. Jones lbw b Holland	68	
J. J. Bohannon c Weatherley b Abbott	28	
T. E. Bailey b Edwards	16	
R. J. Gleeson not out	0	
S. Mahmood lbw b Edwards	0	
B 5, lb 11, nb 8, p 5	29	Lb 9, nb 4 13

1/13 (2) 2/30 (3) 3/111 (1) (82.4 overs) 273   1/40 (2) (2 wkts, 13 overs) 113
4/111 (5) 5/123 (4) 6/207 (6)   2/40 (3)
7/241 (7) 8/273 (8) 9/273 (9) 10/273 (11)

Edwards 15.4–2–72–4; Abbott 19–6–43–2; Berg 11–2–38–0; Holland 19–6–48–3; Dawson 18–3–51–1. *Second innings*—Abbott 4–0–41–0; Edwards 4–1–23–2; Dawson 2–0–18–0; Holland 2–0–10–0; Berg 1–0–12–0.

Umpires: R. J. Bailey and I. J. Gould.

KENT

No ordinary Joe

MARK PENNELL

In 2018, when not taking wickets or scoring runs, Joe Denly spent rare moments of free time helping extend his family's seaside home. The extra room proved useful come the close season, when he scooped an array of awards. He helped Kent end an eight-season stay in Division Two of the Championship, make their first Lord's final for a decade, and reach the Vitality Blast quarter-finals. Fourteen years after his first-class debut – and in the fourth summer of his second stint with the county of his birth – Denly was the outstanding performer in a rejuvenated side who were serious contenders in three competitions.

His batting showed style and maturity, while his burgeoning leg-spin had become unerringly accurate. A deep appreciation of technique enabled him to adapt to – and often dominate in – all formats. So it was no surprise he earned an England recall in October: in the Twenty20 international in Sri Lanka, he opened the bowling, and took four wickets.

In 16 first-class games for Kent, Denly hit 954 runs at a shade under 40. He made four hundreds, including a consummate 113 not out against the Pakistanis, and added 23 wickets at 18 each. He was as dynamic in the shorter formats, combining 492 one-day runs at 70 – including a club-record 150 not out against Glamorgan – with 14 wickets. And in the Vitality Blast, he was Kent's leading run-scorer and wicket-taker: 409 at 37, and 20 at 16. In all cricket, he hit seven centuries and grabbed 57 wickets.

Denly topped the overall Professional Cricketers' Association's most valuable player ranking (and both white-ball categories), and was voted PCA Players' Player of the Season. He also collected three trophies at the club's awards night, including Player of the Season. Kent could also thank Denly, a quiet man, for stepping into the breach when club captain Sam Billings was away at the IPL. He led effectively, if not effortlessly, saying the job caused him sleepless nights. His record, though, was good: after defeat in the opening Championship game by Gloucestershire came four wins and a draw, laying solid foundations for the promotion push.

The other factor behind Kent's improved form was the shrewd signing of New Zealand pace bowler Matt Henry, and – on a Kolpak deal – the South African batsman Heino Kuhn. Henry barely bowled a poor delivery in his 11 first-class matches, which were interrupted by a five-week New Zealand training camp. His skiddy pace proved too fiery for many Division Two batsmen, and he finished with 75 victims – the most in the country – at 15.

Kuhn, a compact, muscular right-hander, plundered four stunning hundreds and a fifty during Kent's run to the Royal London final, and brought urgency and focus to the fielding. But the lack of a Championship century was a

Matt Henry

disappointment, and in 2019 he will aim to better his 780 runs at 33. Indeed, Kent's first-innings batting proved their Achilles heel, almost costing them promotion. They managed only 16 batting points; Warwickshire, who went up with them, had 41.

Yet Kent found a way to win ten games. That was down to better batting in the second innings, and consistently strong seam bowling that brought 40 bonus points. Leading the attack with Henry were Harry Podmore, who in his first season since leaving Middlesex took 45 first-class wickets, and Darren Stevens, who collected 42, one for each of his years. There were useful contributions from Grant Stewart and from Ivan Thomas, though his season ended abruptly after he tore ligaments in his right knee in September. He was expected to miss the start of 2019.

Promotion meant the leadership group – coach Matt Walker, his assistant Allan Donald, interim chief executive Ben Green and new director of cricket Paul Downton – had achieved their primary ambition. They had collaborated brilliantly before the season, and ensured any recruits would be skilful and of good character – a policy that paid off with Kuhn and Podmore. It bore fruit in the Blast too, when Marcus Stoinis, Carlos Brathwaite and Adam Milne fitted in quickly.

Of the home-grown crop, top-order batsman Zak Crawley hit a maiden hundred, while England Under-19 wicketkeeper Ollie Robinson showed promise. Overall, though, Kent's success came down to team spirit. Billings and Denly led by example and, with support and backing from Walker's coaching unit, confidence blossomed. The defeat in the Royal London final, if a bitter pill, was treated as a blip, and the Vitality Blast quarter-final loss partially mitigated by the unhelpful – and inexplicable – preparation of a spin-friendly Canterbury pitch.

But Kent were determined not to sit on their laurels. Simon Storey joined from Derbyshire as chief executive, and Green departed. Nottinghamshire's 24-year-old seamer Matt Milnes and English-born left-armer Fred Klaassen, who plays for the Netherlands, were recruited for 2019. Kent also gave a first contract to Jordan Cox, an 18-year-old Academy wicketkeeper. Walker and opening bat Sean Dickson signed contract extensions, as did several others. All will need to be at their best in Division One.

A shoulder injury forced the departure of former captain James Tredwell after 177 first-class appearances had brought 426 wickets; he will turn to coaching and umpiring. Head groundsman Simon Williamson left for a quieter life in Scotland, while seamers Will Gidman and Matt Hunn also retired.

Championship attendance: 24,519.

KENT RESULTS

All first-class matches – Played 16: Won 10, Lost 3, Drawn 3.
County Championship matches – Played 13: Won 10, Lost 3, Drawn 1.

Specsavers County Championship, 2nd in Division 2;
Vitality Blast, quarter-finalists; Royal London One-Day Cup, finalists.

COUNTY CHAMPIONSHIP AVERAGES, BATTING AND FIELDING

Cap		Birthplace	M	I	NO	R	HS	100	Avge	Ct/St
2008	J. L. Denly	Canterbury‡	14	24	0	828	119	3	34.50	3
2018	H. G. Kuhn††	Piet Retief, SA	14	26	3	780	96*	0	33.91	21
	Z. Crawley	Bromley‡	14	24	0	755	168	1	31.45	11
2015	S. W. Billings	Pembury‡	8	14	2	370	85	0	30.83	20/2
	S. R. Dickson††	Johannesburg, SA . .	14	21	1	710	134*	3	28.40	25
	G. Stewart††	Kalgoorlie, Aust . . .	10	17	1	414	103	0	25.87	3
2018	M. J. Henry¶	Christchurch, NZ . .	11	17	3	303	81	0	21.64	2
2015	D. J. Bell-Drummond	Lewisham‡	13	24	2	436	61	0	19.81	3
2005	D. I. Stevens	Leicester	11	18	2	310	89	0	19.37	2
	H. W. Podmore	Hammersmith	14	22	7	285	53	0	19.00	2
	A. E. N. Riley	Sidcup‡	4	6	3	56	23	0	18.66	6
	A. P. Rouse	Harare, Zimbabwe .	7	11	0	187	55	0	17.00	24
	O. G. Robinson	Sidcup‡	3	4	0	59	26	0	14.75	1
	†C. J. Haggett	Taunton	2	4	0	53	31	0	13.25	0
	†W. R. S. Gidman . . .	High Wycombe	3	4	0	27	19	0	6.75	2
	I. A. A. Thomas	Greenwich‡	11	14	8	17	4*	0	2.83	6

Also batted: †M. E. Claydon (*Fairfield, Australia*) (1 match) 5, 0.

‡ *Born in Kent.*   ¶ *Official overseas player.*   †† *Other non-England-qualified.*

BOWLING

	Style	O	M	R	W	BB	5I	Avge
M. J. Henry	RFM	382.4	83	1,161	75	7-42	5	15.48
J. L. Denly	LB	160.1	28	426	23	4-36	0	18.52
D. I. Stevens	RM	295.4	76	799	42	6-26	2	19.02
G. Stewart	RFM	164.5	26	505	22	6-22	1	22.95
H. W. Podmore	RM	339.2	80	1,002	43	6-36	1	23.30
I. A. A. Thomas	RFM	183	31	630	24	5-91	1	26.25

Also bowled: D. J. Bell-Drummond (RM) 7–3–8–2; M. E. Claydon (RFM) 11.4–0–27–2; W. R. S. Gidman (RFM) 18.4–2–56–2; C. J. Haggett (RM) 18–7–44–4; A. E. N. Riley (OB) 134.2–33–334–9.

LEADING ROYAL LONDON CUP AVERAGES (100 runs/4 wickets)

Batting

	Runs	HS	Avge	SR	Ct
H. G. Kuhn	696	127	87.00	101.45	7
J. L. Denly	492	150*	70.28	94.61	5
D. J. Bell-Drummond	485	90	44.09	88.34	4
A. J. Blake	326	61	40.75	121.18	7
A. P. Rouse	114	70	38.00	82.60	3
S. R. Dickson . . .	173	68*	34.60	92.02	4

Bowling

	W	BB	Avge	ER
D. I. Stevens	16	6-25	26.31	4.51
J. L. Denly	14	4-56	30.78	5.90
M. J. Henry	16	3-37	34.43	5.55
H. W. Podmore . . .	6	4-57	37.83	6.67
C. J. Haggett	14	3-42	40.00	6.72
M. E. Claydon	8	3-73	50.25	6.48
I. Qayyum	6	2-45	60.66	5.51

LEADING VITALITY BLAST AVERAGES (100 runs/15 overs)

Batting	Runs	HS	Avge	SR	Ct/St	Bowling	W	BB	Avge	ER
A. J. Blake	161	57	17.88	**161.00**	6	A. F. Milne.	13	4-15	22.84	**7.15**
H. G. Kuhn. . . .	310	67*	31.00	**145.53**	6	J. L. Denly	20	3-25	16.75	**7.76**
D. J. Bell-Drummond	372	80	31.00	**145.31**	3	I. Qayyum.	10	3-40	29.60	**8.92**
J. L. Denly	409	102	37.18	**145.03**	7	C. R. Brathwaite. .	9	4-21	18.88	**9.44**
S. W. Billings . .	372	95*	53.14	**144.74**	9/4	C. J. Haggett . . .	11	2-26	31.72	**9.69**
S. R. Dickson . .	112	32	28.00	**115.46**	10	M. E. Claydon . .	8	2-36	38.87	**10.03**

FIRST-CLASS COUNTY RECORDS

Highest score for	332	W. H. Ashdown v Essex at Brentwood	1934
Highest score against	344	W. G. Grace (MCC) at Canterbury	1876
Leading run-scorer	47,868	F. E. Woolley (avge 41.77)	1906–38
Best bowling for	10-30	C. Blythe v Northamptonshire at Northampton .	1907
Best bowling against	10-48	C. H. G. Bland (Sussex) at Tonbridge	1899
Leading wicket-taker	3,340	A. P. Freeman (avge 17.64)	1914–36
Highest total for	803-4 dec	v Essex at Brentwood	1934
Highest total against	676	by Australians at Canterbury	1921
Lowest total for	18	v Sussex at Gravesend	1867
Lowest total against	16	by Warwickshire at Tonbridge	1913

LIST A COUNTY RECORDS

Highest score for	150*	**J. L. Denly v Glamorgan at Canterbury**	**2018**
Highest score against	167*	P. Johnson (Nottinghamshire) at Nottingham . .	1993
Leading run-scorer	7,814	M. R. Benson (avge 31.89)	1980–95
Best bowling for	8-31	D. L. Underwood v Scotland at Edinburgh	1987
Best bowling against	6-5	A. G. Wharf (Glamorgan) at Cardiff	2004
Leading wicket-taker	530	D. L. Underwood (avge 18.93)	1963–87
Highest total for	384-6	v Berkshire at Finchampstead	1994
	384-8	**v Surrey at Beckenham**	**2018**
Highest total against	371-8	by Somerset at Taunton	2014
Lowest total for	60	v Somerset at Taunton	1979
Lowest total against	60	by Derbyshire at Canterbury	2008

TWENTY20 COUNTY RECORDS

Highest score for	127*	J. L. Denly v Essex at Chelmsford.	2017
Highest score against	151*	C. H. Gayle (Somerset) at Taunton	2015
Leading run-scorer	3,358	**J. L. Denly (avge 30.25, SR 126.86)**	**2004–18**
Best bowling for	5-11	A. F. Milne v Somerset at Taunton	2017
Best bowling against	5-17	G. M. Smith (Essex) at Chelmsford	2012
Leading wicket-taker	119	J. C. Tredwell (avge 28.46, ER 7.32).	2003–17
Highest total for	231-7	v Surrey at The Oval	2015
	231-5	**v Somerset at Canterbury**	**2018**
Highest total against	250-6	**by Surrey at Canterbury**	**2018**
Lowest total for	72	v Hampshire at Southampton	2011
Lowest total against	82	by Somerset at Taunton	2010

ADDRESS

The Spitfire Ground, St Lawrence, Old Dover Road, Canterbury CT1 3NZ; 01227 456886; kent@ecb.co.uk; www.kentcricket.co.uk.

OFFICIALS

Captain S. W. Billings	**Chairman** S. R. C. Philip
Director of cricket P. R. Downton	**Chief executive 2018** B. Green
Head coach M. J. Walker	**2019** S. Storey
Assistant coach 2018 A. A. Donald	**Head groundsman** A. Llong
High performance director J. R. Weaver	**Scorer** L. A. R. Hart
President C. R. Swadkin	

KENT v OXFORD MCCU

At Canterbury, April 1–3. Drawn. Toss: Oxford MCCU. First-class debuts: H. R. D. Adair, S. R. Green, W. J. R. Robertson, J. C. Seward.

Only 33 overs, all on the first day, survived the weather. Opening for the first time, Crawley hit a steady 42, after Dickson – his more experienced partner – had shouldered arms to Alex Wilkinson and lost his off stump. Five members of the Oxford team were not born when Stevens, undefeated on five, made his first-class debut, 21 years earlier.

Close of play: first day, Kent 100-3 (Denly 13, Stevens 5); second day, no play.

Kent

S. R. Dickson b Wilkinson	. . . .	9
Z. Crawley c Seward b Pettman	. . . .	42
A. J. Blake c Webb b Robertson	. . . .	28
*J. L. Denly not out	. . . .	13
D. I. Stevens not out	. . . .	5
B 1, w 2	. . . .	3

1/37 (1) 2/68 (2)   (3 wkts, 33 overs) 100
3/95 (3)

W. R. S. Gidman, †A. P. Rouse, G. Stewart, A. E. N. Riley, M. D. Hunn and I. A. A. Thomas did not bat.

Lake 9–2–26–0; Heathfield 9–1–32–0; Pettman 7–2–16–1; Wilkinson 4–0–18–1; Robertson 3–1–7–1; Green 1–1–0–0.

Oxford MCCU

H. R. D. Adair, †J. C. Seward, J. S. D. Gnodde, A. J. W. Rackow, *M. B. Lake, L. A. Webb, W. J. R. Robertson, T. D. Heathfield, S. R. Green, T. H. S. Pettman, A. R. Wilkinson.

Umpires: B. J. Debenham and M. J. Saggers.

KENT v GLOUCESTERSHIRE

At Canterbury, April 13–16. Gloucestershire won by five wickets. Gloucestershire 19pts, Kent 3pts. Toss: uncontested. County debuts: M. J. Henry, H. G. Kuhn, H. W. Podmore; D. J. Worrall.

Kent made a disastrous start to the Championship season, losing in 809 legal deliveries, their quickest first-class defeat at Canterbury. After the first four sessions were lost to the weather, they were unceremoniously steamrollered for 64 in 91 minutes. Left-arm seamer Matt Taylor caused most havoc, and only Crawley – plus Extras – made double figures. Gloucestershire also struggled on a sporting early-season pitch marked above average by ECB cricket liaison officer Graham Cowdrey, though they did manage a 46-run lead thanks to Roderick's gritty half-century. Bell-Drummond decided the situation called for aggression, and belted ten fours and a six en route to 61, out of a total of 75, before he became the first of five wickets for Higgins, a winter arrival from Middlesex. There was some resistance lower down the order, but Gloucestershire were set only 108. They had reached 61 for one when rain ended play early on the third evening. Next morning, the score had progressed to 81 when Henry trapped Roderick, the first of three wickets to fall for three in eight balls, but Howell stopped the rot.

Close of play: first day, no play; second day, Gloucestershire 110-8 (Miles 7, Worrall 0); third day, Gloucestershire 61-1 (Howell 34, Roderick 11).

Kent

D. J. Bell-Drummond c Howell b M. D. Taylor ...	4	– lbw b Higgins	61
S. R. Dickson c Noema-Barnett b Worrall	8	– lbw b Worrall	5
H. G. Kuhn b Worrall	4	– lbw b M. D. Taylor	5
*J. L. Denly c Roderick b M. D. Taylor	0	– c Roderick b Higgins	0
Z. Crawley lbw b Higgins	15	– lbw b Worrall	32
D. I. Stevens lbw b M. D. Taylor	1	– lbw b Higgins	0
W. R. S. Gidman c Roderick b M. D. Taylor	0	– c Roderick b Miles	1
†A. P. Rouse c Higgins b Miles	8	– lbw b M. D. Taylor	21
M. J. Henry b Miles	4	– c Roderick b Higgins	14
G. Stewart c Roderick b Miles	7	– c Dent b Higgins	2
H. W. Podmore not out	2	– not out	0
Lb 4, w 5, nb 2	11	Lb 8, nb 4	12

1/12 (1) 2/19 (3) 3/24 (4)   (18.5 overs)   64
4/28 (2) 5/29 (6) 6/29 (7)
7/42 (8) 8/50 (9) 9/60 (5) 10/64 (10)

1/19 (2) 2/75 (1)   (48.3 overs)   153
3/75 (3) 4/79 (4)
5/83 (6) 6/89 (7) 7/132 (8)
8/147 (9) 9/153 (10) 10/153 (5)

Worrall 6–2–20–2; M. D. Taylor 6–0–20–4; Miles 3.5–0–11–3; Higgins 3–0–9–1. *Second innings*—Worrall 11.3–5–25–2; M. D. Taylor 15–3–49–2; Higgins 14–4–22–5; Miles 8–1–49–1.

Gloucestershire

B. A. C. Howell lbw b Henry	0	– (2) not out	52
*C. D. J. Dent lbw b Stevens	0	– (1) b Henry	6
†G. H. Roderick lbw b Podmore	51	– lbw b Henry	26
J. R. Bracey lbw b Henry	5	– c Gidman b Henry	0
J. M. R. Taylor lbw b Stevens	9	– lbw b Stevens	2
G. L. van Buuren c Kuhn b Stevens	2	– b Stevens	9
R. F. Higgins c Gidman b Stewart	3	– not out	0
K. Noema-Barnett lbw b Gidman	18		
C. N. Miles not out	7		
D. J. Worrall lbw b Henry	0		
M. D. Taylor c Dickson b Henry	0		
B 4, lb 11	15	B 1, lb 7, w 1, nb 4	13

1/0 (1) 2/8 (2) 3/19 (4)   (39 overs)   110
4/30 (5) 5/38 (6) 6/56 (7)
7/98 (8) 8/106 (3) 9/110 (10) 10/110 (11)

1/6 (1)   (5 wkts, 28.3 overs)   108
2/81 (3) 3/81 (4)
4/84 (5) 5/102 (6)

Henry 14–5–33–4; Stevens 10–4–19–3; Stewart 8–2–27–1; Podmore 3–2–6–1; Gidman 4–0–10–1. *Second innings*—Henry 14–3–37–3; Stevens 9–1–39–2; Stewart 2.2–0–10–0; Gidman 2.4–1–8–0; Podmore 0.3–0–6–0.

Umpires: N. L. Bainton and M. Burns.

At Chester-le-Street, April 20–21. KENT beat DURHAM by nine wickets. *Matt Henry takes 12-73.*

At Canterbury, April 28–May 1. KENT drew with PAKISTANIS (see Pakistan tour section).

At Cardiff, May 4–6. KENT beat GLAMORGAN by six wickets.

KENT v SUSSEX

At Canterbury, May 11–13. Kent won by 58 runs. Kent 20pts, Sussex 3pts. Toss: uncontested.

Matt Henry played the starring role in his 50th first-class appearance, which ended in a thrilling Kent victory late on the third evening. He claimed match figures of ten for 122 and hit a belligerent 55. Kent's first-day 215 was typical of the top-order underachievement that had characterised their spring – only Kuhn passed 31 – but it did bring their first batting point of the season. Wiese maintained his incisive form for Sussex with four wickets, before Henry, whose stellar Championship season had so far brought 27 at under nine, also grabbed four to help secure a handy 34-run lead. Only Brown and Burgess offered sustained resistance, but their stand ended when Stewart bowled Brown; three deliveries later he limped off with a hamstring strain, leaving the over to be completed by Thomas, who promptly despatched Robinson. A double-wicket maiden had been sent down by two different bowlers. When Kent batted again, Sharma and Robinson quickly exposed familiar weaknesses. Henry strode in at 146 for seven and smote a 47-ball half-century. The late flourish meant Sussex needed 270 in five sessions, but Henry quickly removed the openers – Wells was his 200th first-class victim – and only during a fifth-wicket stand of 82 between Wright and Brown did they look threatening.

Close of play: first day, Sussex 69-4 (Wright 28, Brown 20); second day, Kent 125-4 (Crawley 23, Rouse 10).

Kent

D. J. Bell-Drummond b Robinson	13	– c Brown b Sharma	2
S. R. Dickson lbw b Wiese	10	– b Sharma	8
H. G. Kuhn c Brown b Wiese	60	– c Finch b Wiese	47
*J. L. Denly c Brown b Wiese	26	– c Brown b Robinson	26
Z. Crawley c Brown b Robinson	7	– c Wiese b Sharma	24
†A. P. Rouse b Finch b Wiese	0	– b Salt b Sharma	18
C. J. Haggett b Robinson	31	– c Brown b Robinson	5
H. W. Podmore b Sharma	6	– not out	24
M. J. Henry c Wells b Sharma	8	– c Burgess b Robinson	55
G. Stewart b Sharma	31	– b Robinson	11
I. A. A. Thomas not out	4	– b Wiese	1
B 4, lb 9, nb 6	19	B 7, lb 3, nb 4	14

1/19 (1) 2/50 (2) 3/125 (4)   (74.1 overs) 215   1/4 (1) 2/31 (2)   (62.4 overs) 235
4/132 (3) 5/132 (6) 6/134 (5)   3/86 (4) 4/94 (3)
7/153 (8) 8/163 (9) 9/185 (7) 10/215 (10)   5/133 (5) 6/140 (6) 7/146 (7)
                                       8/220 (9) 9/234 (10) 10/235 (11)

Sharma 18.1–3–62–3; Robinson 19–8–51–3; Wiese 21–6–54–4; van Zyl 7–3–12–0; Briggs 8–1–19–0; Wells 1–0–4–0. *Second innings*—Sharma 17–1–52–4; Robinson 22–4–70–4; van Zyl 7–0–32–0; Wiese 14.4–2–59–2; Briggs 2–0–12–0.

Sussex

L. W. P. Wells c Rouse b Henry	3	– b Henry	9
P. D. Salt c Rouse b Podmore	3	– c Kuhn b Henry	11
S. van Zyl b Henry	9	– c Rouse b Thomas	38
H. Z. Finch c Dickson b Henry	5	– c Crawley b Haggett	13
L. J. Wright c Kuhn b Henry	35	– c and b Thomas	47
*†B. C. Brown b Stewart	30	– lbw b Henry	48
M. G. K. Burgess c Kuhn b Podmore	54	– b Henry	17
O. E. Robinson c Rouse b Thomas	0	– lbw b Podmore	3
D. Wiese c Crawley b Haggett	28	– not out	3
D. R. Briggs c Bell-Drummond b Haggett	5	– b Henry	8
I. Sharma not out	1	– b Henry	0
B 5, lb 1, nb 2	8	B 4, lb 8, nb 2	14

1/6 (2) 2/6 (1) 3/16 (4)   (43.5 overs) 181   1/23 (2) 2/30 (1)   (58 overs) 211
4/21 (3) 5/78 (5) 6/118 (6)   3/74 (3) 4/76 (4)
7/118 (8) 8/161 (9) 9/179 (10) 10/181 (7)   5/158 (5) 6/186 (7) 7/197 (8)
                                         8/201 (6) 9/211 (10) 10/211 (11)

Henry 18–4–69–4; Podmore 11.5–2–48–2; Stewart 6.5–1–15–1; Thomas 5.1–0–37–1; Haggett 2–0–6–2. *Second innings*—Henry 21–5–53–6; Podmore 16–1–80–1; Thomas 11–0–39–2; Haggett 9–1–26–1; Denly 1–0–1–0.

Umpires: R. J. Bailey and R. J. Warren.

At Bristol, June 9–12. KENT drew with GLOUCESTERSHIRE.

KENT v WARWICKSHIRE

At Tunbridge Wells, June 20–23. Kent won by 73 runs. Kent 19pts, Warwickshire 3pts. Toss: uncontested.

Kent moved within eight points of leaders Warwickshire after defeating them in a tense, fluctuating match that began with 20 wickets in a day. Again Kent failed to bank a batting point, though they came close, thanks to an elegant half-century from Denly; Barker's hit-deck seamers gathered five for 32. Talk of an underprepared pitch grew louder on the first evening, when the Kent attack sliced through Warwickshire. Trott stood firm, though not until Brookes arrived at 71 for eight did he find a partner of similar resilience. They added 54, but Kent led by 72 once Henry snatched the last two wickets in two balls – the ninth time in 11 innings he had taken four or more. On the second day, in far easier conditions, Dickson and Denly unfurled their strokes, putting on 208 – a Kent record for the third wicket against Warwickshire – and each hitting a second Championship hundred of the summer. Crawley chipped in with a career-best 93, allowing Denly to declare, 518 ahead, shortly before lunch on day three. Rhodes survived an hour, but Sibley and Bell batted for almost five in adding 260; both hit graceful centuries. At 304 for one, the mammoth target was starting to seem manageable. But Podmore prised out Sibley and Trott within six balls. Then Thomas trapped Bell with a shooter, and the initiative swung Kent's way. Hose kept Warwickshire hopes alive, but on a wearing pitch Denly's leg-breaks grabbed three for one in six balls to secure victory.

Close of play: first day, Kent 4-0 (Bell-Drummond 2, Dickson 2); second day, Kent 359-6 (Crawley 47, Podmore 13); third day, Warwickshire 229-1 (Sibley 82, Bell 102).

Kent

D. J. Bell-Drummond c Ambrose b Wright	7	c Ambrose b Barker	16
S. R. Dickson b Barker	1	lbw b Patel	133
H. G. Kuhn lbw b Hannon-Dalby	39	lbw b Barker	8
*J. L. Denly c Ambrose b Barker	59	lbw b Patel	119
Z. Crawley lbw b Hannon-Dalby	0	lbw b Hannon-Dalby	93
D. I. Stevens c Trott b Wright	27	c Ambrose b Barker	3
†A. P. Rouse c Sibley b Brookes	10	lbw b Barker	8
H. W. Podmore lbw b Barker	22	c Ambrose b Hannon-Dalby	24
M. J. Henry b Barker	2	not out	20
A. E. N. Riley not out	13	not out	4
I. A. A. Thomas lbw b Barker	3		
B 5, lb 1, nb 8	14	Lb 6, nb 12	18

1/9 (2) 2/15 (1) 3/66 (3)   (54.1 overs) 197   1/26 (1)   (8 wkts dec, 120 overs) 446
4/66 (5) 5/117 (6) 6/144 (7)   2/44 (3) 3/252 (2) 4/303 (4)
7/174 (8) 8/176 (9) 9/191 (8) 10/197 (11)   5/318 (6) 6/334 (7) 7/412 (8)
                                         8/423 (5)

Barker 13.1–1–32–5; Wright 14–0–69–2; Hannon-Dalby 15–4–50–2; Brookes 10–2–32–1; Patel 2–0–8–0. *Second innings*—Barker 17.2–1–64–4; Wright 22.4–1–92–0; Hannon-Dalby 23–3–85–2; Brookes 17–0–58–0; Patel 36–5–126–2; Rhodes 4–0–15–0.

Warwickshire

W. M. H. Rhodes b Henry	11	–	lbw b Podmore	25
D. P. Sibley c Rouse b Stevens	1	–	c Kuhn b Podmore	104
I. R. Bell c Riley b Henry	4	–	lbw b Thomas	172
I. J. L. Trott not out	51	–	c Rouse b Podmore	0
A. J. Hose lbw b Stevens	5	–	lbw b Denly	65
†T. R. Ambrose c Kuhn b Podmore	7	–	b Henry	9
K. H. D. Barker lbw b Podmore	0	–	c Dickson b Podmore	16
*J. S. Patel c Rouse b Podmore	4	–	c Riley b Henry	7
C. J. C. Wright b Podmore	8	–	lbw b Denly	14
H. J. H. Brookes c Crawley b Henry	28	–	not out	5
O. J. Hannon-Dalby c Rouse b Henry	0	–	c Kuhn b Denly	0
B 4, nb 2	6		B 10, lb 14, nb 4	28

1/12 (1) 2/16 (3) 3/20 (2) (36.4 overs) 125
4/34 (5) 5/55 (6) 6/57 (7)
7/61 (8) 8/71 (9) 9/125 (10) 10/125 (11)

1/44 (1) 2/304 (2) (140.1 overs) 445
3/308 (4) 4/336 (3)
5/355 (6) 6/392 (7) 7/405 (8)
8/440 (9) 9/441 (5) 10/445 (11)

Henry 12.4–2–54–4; Stevens 11–3–31–2; Podmore 8–1–26–4; Thomas 5–1–10–0. *Second innings*—Henry 38–4–128–2; Stevens 24–3–80–0; Podmore 28–5–84–4; Riley 18–1–48–0; Thomas 21–5–57–1; Denly 11.1–2–24–3.

Umpires: J. D. Middlebrook and S. J. O'Shaughnessy.

KENT v MIDDLESEX

At Canterbury, June 25–27 (day/night). Kent won by 342 runs. Kent 20pts, Middlesex 3pts. Toss: Kent. Championship debut: G. F. B. Scott.

This match was a triumph for Grant Stewart, Australian-born and playing on an Italian passport courtesy of his mother. In his fifth first-class appearance, he claimed six for 22 and hit a maiden hundred, from No. 10. Billings had chosen to bat but, despite having the best of the conditions, Kent managed only 241; with Stewart making a robust 38. The fastest, most incisive and most expensive member of the attack was Fuller, who removed Kent's top three scorers. Middlesex began their reply as the sun set, and had collapsed to 54 for nine by stumps as Stewart found prodigious swing. He was playing in the absence of Matt Henry, resting before the Royal London final, and Darren Stevens,

BIGGEST WINS BY RUNS FOR KENT

429	v Northamptonshire at Dover	1933	**342**	**v Middlesex at Canterbury**	**2018**
365	v Nottinghamshire at Nottingham	1899	340	v Cambridge Univ. at Cambridge	1994
354	v Somerset at Taunton	1906	334	v Gloucestershire at Canterbury	2017
354	v Somerset at Catford	1913	323	v Gloucestershire at Maidstone	1914
351	v Cambridge Univ. at Cambridge	1999	321	v Lancashire at Tunbridge Wells	1910

whose colour-blindness made it tricky to see the pink ball. (Indeed on the first evening, as the sun dazzled between the stands, no batsman could see anything, and the umpires briefly suspended play.) Stewart wrapped things up next day; the last seven had fallen for 12 in 13 overs, with Eskinazi alone reaching double figures. Armed with a lead of 185, Billings preferred to bat in daylight rather than enforce the follow-on. At 165 for eight, 350 ahead, Kent were in danger of leaving the door ajar. Then Stewart returned. He plundered 13 fours and five sixes in a 74-ball innings that sapped all hope from Middlesex. Needing 467, they folded again, the damage done by Podmore, their former seamer;

HEAVIEST DEFEATS BY RUNS FOR MIDDLESEX

390	by Australians at Lord's	1893	298	by Yorkshire at Lord's	1895
363	by Derbyshire at Derby	1996	281	by Yorkshire at Lord's	1906
361	by Lancashire at Manchester	1994	280	by Surrey at Guildford	1998
342	**by Kent at Canterbury**	**2018**	278	by South Africans at Lord's	1907
301	by Leicestershire at Lord's	1976	278	by Derbyshire at Derby	1934

Stewart picked up another couple. Middlesex head coach Richard Scott was unhappy about the continuing pink-ball trial, and the disproportionate value of the toss. "We are guinea pigs," he said. "The whole Championship system is being used for an experiment. It's a farce." Five days later, he stepped down after nine years in charge.

Close of play: first day, Middlesex 54-9 (Fuller 0); second day, Middlesex 22-2 (Robson 6, Patel 4).

Kent

D. J. Bell-Drummond lbw b Cartwright	17	–	lbw b Murtagh	14
S. R. Dickson lbw b Harris	5	–	lbw b Harris	4
H. G. Kuhn c Holden b Cartwright	11	–	c Simpson b Murtagh	57
J. L. Denly c Malan b Fuller	37	–	c Murtagh b Cartwright	2
*S. W. Billings c Cartwright b Murtagh	17	–	b Murtagh	29
Z. Crawley b Harris	5	–	st Simpson b Patel	25
†A. P. Rouse c Simpson b Fuller	42	–	lbw b Cartwright	20
C. J. Haggett c Simpson b Fuller	7	–	c Eskinazi b Patel	10
H. W. Podmore c sub (T. E. Barber) b Patel	32	–	lbw b Cartwright	4
G. Stewart c and b Fuller	38	–	c Malan b Patel	103
I. A. A. Thomas not out	0	–	not out	1
B 4, lb 13, w 5, nb 8	30		B 4, lb 8	12

1/16 (2) 2/46 (3) 3/59 (1)   (71.2 overs) 241   1/18 (2) 2/28 (1)   (79.4 overs) 281
4/99 (5) 5/106 (6) 6/114 (4)   3/47 (4) 4/105 (3)
7/134 (8) 8/185 (9) 9/228 (7) 10/241 (10)   5/110 (5) 6/145 (7) 7/158 (8)
                                     8/165 (9) 9/181 (6) 10/281 (10)

Murtagh 17–5–33–1; Harris 21–6–47–2; Fuller 15.2–1–86–4; Cartwright 10–0–41–2; Patel 7–3–16–1; Malan 1–0–1–0. *Second innings*—Murtagh 17–6–54–3; Harris 4–2–13–1; Cartwright 14–5–33–3; Fuller 17–1–88–0; Scott 12–3–23–0; Patel 15.4–4–58–3.

Middlesex

S. D. Robson c Dickson b Stewart	2	–	(2) c sub (A. E. N. Riley) b Stewart	11
M. D. E. Holden b Stewart	6	–	(1) c Rouse b Podmore	0
S. S. Eskinazi c Billings b Stewart	25	–	c Crawley b Podmore	5
*D. J. Malan c Dickson b Stewart	0	–	(5) c Rouse b Podmore	0
H. W. R. Cartwright c Dickson b Podmore	9	–	(6) lbw b Podmore	4
G. F. B. Scott b Stewart	3	–	c Dickson b Podmore	13
†J. A. Simpson c Rouse b Haggett	2	–	(8) c Rouse b Podmore	12
J. A. R. Harris b Thomas	1	–	not out	7
R. H. Patel b Thomas	0	–	(4) c Bell-Drummond b Stewart	13
J. K. Fuller not out	2	–	c Dickson b Thomas	8
T. J. Murtagh c Rouse b Stewart	0	–	b Thomas	40
Lb 3, w 1, nb 2	6		Lb 4, w 1, nb 6	11

1/7 (1) 2/19 (2) 3/19 (4)   (24 overs) 56   1/0 (1) 2/17 (3)   (33.5 overs) 124
4/44 (3) 5/44 (5) 6/50 (6)   3/27 (2) 4/36 (5)
7/54 (8) 8/54 (7) 9/54 (9) 10/56 (11)   5/40 (4) 6/48 (6) 7/68 (8)
                                     8/71 (7) 9/80 (10) 10/124 (11)

Podmore 8–1–28–1; Stewart 10–2–22–6; Haggett 4–4–0–1; Thomas 2–1–3–2. *Second innings*—Podmore 14–2–36–6; Stewart 11–1–36–2; Thomas 5.5–1–36–2; Haggett 3–2–12–0.

Umpires: Y. C. Barde and N. G. B. Cook.

KENT v LEICESTERSHIRE

At Canterbury, July 22–23. Leicestershire won by ten wickets. Leicestershire 20pts, Kent 3pts. Toss: uncontested.

A grassy, seaming pitch meant this Canterbury Week fixture lasted less than two days. It was only the fourth time – and the first since 2001 – that Leicestershire had left the St Lawrence ground victorious. Kent were without their overseas pace bowler Adam Milne, who had injured his ankle, but still picked five seamers and no frontline spinner. Even so, they were outgunned by Leicestershire's lively and youthful attack. Raine and Chappell led the way with three wickets each, and Kent were dismantled for 104. After holding five catches (and dropping a couple more) Eckersley starred with the bat. In a perfect demonstration of how to cope with the conditions, he left well, avoided risk and survived almost four hours in accumulating an invaluable 74 that helped Leicestershire to a lead of 125. Dickson also left well in compiling Kent's only fifty, but eventually became the sixth of Eckersley's eight catches. Leicestershire made short work of the Kent tail: Mohammad Abbas finished with four and Chappell another three. A target of 75 posed no problems, and allowed Dearden to hit his first half-century of a thin season.

Close of play: first day, Leicestershire 149-6 (Eckersley 45).

Kent

D. J. Bell-Drummond c Eckersley b Raine	9	– b Mohammad Abbas		0
S. R. Dickson c Eckersley b Griffiths	24	– c Eckersley b Raine		59
H. G. Kuhn b Raine	0	– c Cosgrove b Griffiths		29
J. L. Denly c Eckersley b Chappell	5	– lbw b Dexter		24
*†S. W. Billings b Chappell	10	– lbw b Mohammad Abbas		29
Z. Crawley c Eckersley b Chappell	5	– lbw b Mohammad Abbas		11
D. I. Stevens not out	38	– lbw b Chappell		6
H. W. Podmore lbw b Dexter	2	– c Eckersley b Chappell		6
G. Stewart lbw b Dexter	0	– c Dexter b Mohammad Abbas		12
M. E. Claydon c Eckersley b Mohammad Abbas	5	– c Eckersley b Chappell		0
I. A. A. Thomas lbw b Raine	0	– not out		4
B 2, lb 4	6	B 7, lb 4, nb 8		19

1/25 (1) 2/25 (3) 3/44 (4)   (37.5 overs) 104
4/48 (2) 5/58 (5) 6/65 (6)
7/77 (8) 8/77 (9) 9/103 (10) 10/104 (11)

1/0 (1) 2/71 (3)   (49.2 overs) 199
3/109 (4) 4/133 (2)
5/157 (5) 6/164 (6) 7/172 (7)
8/185 (8) 9/195 (10) 10/199 (9)

Mohammad Abbas 9–4–17–1; Raine 13.5–2–39–3; Chappell 7–2–14–3; Griffiths 5–1–17–1; Dexter 3–1–11–2. *Second innings*—Mohammad Abbas 16.2–3–55–4; Raine 12–1–47–1; Griffiths 4–0–23–1; Chappell 10–2–39–3; Dexter 6–0–23–1; Parkinson 1–0–1–0.

Leicestershire

H. E. Dearden c Billings b Podmore	0	– not out		55
*P. J. Horton c Billings b Thomas	21	– not out		15
C. N. Ackermann c Crawley b Stevens	5			
M. J. Cosgrove lbw b Stewart	22			
N. J. Dexter b Thomas	41			
†E. J. H. Eckersley b Bell-Drummond	74			
B. A. Raine c Dickson b Denly	9			
Z. J. Chappell c Dickson b Stewart	21			
C. F. Parkinson c Billings b Claydon	4			
G. T. Griffiths not out	9			
Mohammad Abbas b Claydon	2			
B 9, lb 9, w 1, nb 2	21	B 4, lb 1, w 1		6

1/0 (1) 2/17 (3) 3/47 (2)   (80.4 overs) 229
4/51 (4) 5/121 (5) 6/149 (7)
7/179 (8) 8/198 (9) 9/224 (6) 10/229 (11)

(no wkt, 15.4 overs) 76

Podmore 19–6–39–1; Stevens 19–7–30–1; Thomas 14.2–2–39–2; Stewart 12–1–53–2; Denly 4–0–21–1; Claydon 11.4–0–27–2; Bell-Drummond 1–0–2–1. *Second innings*—Podmore 6–1–22–0; Stevens 4–1–18–0; Stewart 3.4–0–24–0; Denly 2–1–7–0.

Umpires: J. H. Evans and T. Lungley.

At Leicester, August 19–21. KENT beat LEICESTERSHIRE by eight wickets.

At Derby, August 29–September 1. KENT beat DERBYSHIRE by six wickets.

KENT v NORTHAMPTONSHRE

At Canterbury, September 4–7. Kent won by 102 runs. Kent 19pts, Northamptonshire 3pts. Toss: uncontested.

Kent rallied from a poor start to secure an eighth win, which lifted them back above Sussex into second. On a helpful pitch, the Northamptonshire seamers had hustled them out for 137 to seize the initiative – only for their Kent counterparts to wrench it back. When bad light brought the first day to an early close, Northamptonshire had sunk to 71 for eight, with six for Henry. It had been even worse: the ninth-wicket pair of Hutton and Gleeson joined forces at 44. They batted throughout the second day – limited by the weather to 19 balls – before Henry prised them apart on the third to end a stand of 49. His seven for 42 was a career-best, and Kent enjoyed a lead of 32. In their second innings, there were fifties for Crawley and Denly, and also Billings, who had not reached 30 in first-class cricket since September 2017; the persevering Gleeson took six wickets for the first time, in his last match before joining Lancashire. Set an unlikely 320, Northamptonshire stumbled to 56 for three by stumps. Next day, Rossington scored his only half-century of the match; Henry finished with 11 for 114.

Close of play: first day, Northamptonshire 71-8 (Hutton 14, Gleeson 12); second day, Northamptonshire 76-8 (Hutton 16, Gleeson 15); third day, Northamptonshire 56-3 (Wakely 17, Levi 5).

Kent

Z. Crawley c Rossington b Hutton	6	– lbw b Hutton	63
S. R. Dickson lbw b Sanderson	7	– c Levi b Sanderson	10
J. L. Denly c Rossington b Gleeson	14	– (4) b Gleeson	81
H. G. Kuhn lbw b Buck	16	– (5) lbw b Gleeson	34
D. J. Bell-Drummond c Rossington b Gleeson	23	– (6) lbw b Gleeson	0
*†S. W. Billings c Rossington b Gleeson	18	– (7) c Levi b Sanderson	56
D. I. Stevens lbw b Sanderson	5	– (8) b Gleeson	14
H. W. Podmore not out	10	– (9) b Gleeson	3
G. Stewart b Sanderson	5	– (3) c Rossington b Sanderson	0
M. J. Henry b Buck	18	– c Rossington b Gleeson	2
I. A. A. Thomas lbw b Buck	0	– not out	0
B 4, lb 9, nb 2	15	B 11, lb 4, w 1, nb 8	24

1/13 (1) 2/15 (2) 3/53 (4) (47 overs) 137
4/65 (3) 5/93 (6) 6/98 (7)
7/106 (5) 8/113 (9) 9/137 (10) 10/137 (11)

1/23 (2) 2/23 (3) (71.2 overs) 287
3/134 (1) 4/198 (4)
5/198 (6) 6/223 (5) 7/255 (8)
8/259 (9) 9/275 (10) 10/287 (7)

Sanderson 14–4–37–3; Hutton 11–0–35–1; Procter 3–0–8–0; Buck 8–0–28–3; Gleeson 11–3–16–3. *Second innings*—Sanderson 10.2–2–44–3; Hutton 24–5–72–1; Buck 11–0–52–0; Gleeson 19–2–79–6; Zaib 1–1–0–0; Procter 6–0–25–0.

Northamptonshire

B. J. Curran b Henry	0	– lbw b Henry	18
L. A. Procter lbw b Stevens	13	– c Billings b Henry	4
R. S. Vasconcelos b Henry	5	– b Stewart	6
*A. G. Wakely b Henry	0	– c and b Thomas	38
R. E. Levi c Thomas b Henry	2	– lbw b Henry	14
†A. M. Rossington c Stewart b Henry	18	– c Kuhn b Podmore	56
S. A. Zaib c Billings b Stevens	3	– c Henry b Podmore	9
N. L. Buck b Henry	0	– c Billings b Henry	17
B. A. Hutton run out (Thomas)	27	– st Billings b Denly	21
R. J. Gleeson c Thomas b Henry	26	– b Denly	3
B. W. Sanderson not out	6	– not out	1
Lb 3, nb 2	5	B 6, lb 14, nb 10	30

1/2 (1) 2/18 (3) 3/20 (2)   (36.3 overs) 105
4/20 (4) 5/25 (5) 6/38 (7)
7/39 (8) 8/44 (6) 9/93 (10) 10/105 (9)

1/11 (2) 2/28 (1)   (71.4 overs) 217
3/28 (3) 4/83 (5)
5/105 (4) 6/132 (7) 7/180 (8)
8/207 (6) 9/212 (10) 10/217 (9)

Henry 16.3–6–42–7; *Stevens* 17–2–48–2; *Podmore* 2–0–8–0; *Stewart* 1–0–4–0. *Second innings—Henry* 22–4–72–4; *Stevens* 7–0–22–0; *Stewart* 14–3–36–1; *Podmore* 17–5–32–2; *Thomas* 5–0–28–1; *Denly* 6.4–2–7–2.

Umpires: M. Burns and P. R. Pollard.

At Lord's, September 10–12. KENT beat MIDDLESEX by three wickets.

KENT v GLAMORGAN

At Canterbury, September 18–20. Kent won by an innings and 172 runs. Kent 24pts, Glamorgan 3pts. Toss: Glamorgan.

A maiden first-class hundred for Crawley set Kent on their way to a resounding victory, their tenth, which clinched promotion after eight seasons in Division Two; they were now ahead of Warwickshire at the top of the table by virtue of more wins. It was a tenth defeat for Glamorgan, who could not escape the wooden spoon. Opting to bat despite cloud cover and a dewy 10.30 start, they were five down by lunch, and toppled for 186 shortly after tea. Only Murphy, a 6ft 7in left-hander with a penchant for the leg side, offered much resistance as Henry led the attack once more.

HIGHEST MAIDEN HUNDREDS FOR KENT

211	D. Nicholls	v Derbyshire at Folkestone		1963
193*	B. R. Edrich	v Sussex at Tunbridge Wells		1949
176	F. Marchant	v Sussex at Gravesend		1889
170*	J. M. Prodger	v Essex at Maidstone		1961
168	**Z. Crawley**	**v Glamorgan at Canterbury**		**2018**
162	P. R. Sunnucks	v Nottinghamshire at Nottingham		1937
162	A. W. Catt	v Leicestershire at Maidstone		1962
150	P. V. F. Cazalet	v Oxford University at Oxford		1928
146*	D. G. Aslett	v Hampshire at Bournemouth		1981
145	G. R. Cowdrey	v Essex at Chelmsford		1988

Crawley, like Colin Cowdrey and Ed Smith a product of Tonbridge School, made his century from his 141st ball, despite damaging his favourite bat on 95 and reaching the mark with a replacement, which he said didn't feel right. The old one was repaired during lunch on the second day, and he survived another two hours to make 168 – putting him fifth on the county's list of highest maiden century-makers. Billings chipped in with 85, Stevens passed 15,000 first-class runs, and Kent sped to full batting points. Buoyed by a lead of 250, they made short work of a feeble Glamorgan; Murphy top-scored again, while Stevens picked up his 21st five-for, and Kent claimed their only maximum-points win of the year. This was the final game before retirement for Simon Williamson, Kent's popular head groundsman.

Close of play: first day, Kent 93-2 (Crawley 56, Podmore 0); second day, Glamorgan 33-4 (Murphy 10).

Glamorgan

S. C. Cook c Robinson b Henry	20	– c Dickson b Stevens	14
N. J. Selman b Stevens	1	– c Kuhn b Stevens	0
J. R. Murphy c Kuhn b Henry	80	– not out	22
K. S. Carlson c Dickson b Henry	6	– b Denly	9
J. L. Lawlor c Podmore b Henry	15	– (6) c Billings b Stevens	3
†C. B. Cooke c Billings b Stewart	4	– (7) c Billings b Stevens	5
C. A. J. Meschede c Crawley b Stewart	16	– (8) b Henry	2
R. A. J. Smith c Henry b Stevens	19	– (9) c Billings b Henry	9
K. A. Bull b Stewart	5	– (5) c Dickson b Henry	0
T. van der Gugten c Dickson b Denly	8	– b Henry	8
*M. G. Hogan not out	0	– c Denly b Stevens	6
Lb 3, w 1, nb 8	12		

1/8 (2) 2/37 (1) 3/51 (4)	(67.1 overs) 186	1/12 (2) 2/15 (1)	(30.2 overs) 78
4/79 (5) 5/86 (6) 6/110 (7)		3/32 (4) 4/33 (5)	
7/152 (8) 8/165 (9) 9/186 (10) 10/186 (3)		5/36 (6) 6/42 (7) 7/45 (8)	
		8/59 (9) 9/69 (10) 10/78 (11)	

Henry 18.1–2–45–4; Stevens 15–5–38–2; Podmore 14–1–55–0; Stewart 14–3–34–3; Denly 6–3–11–1. *Second innings*—Henry 15–4–53–4; Stevens 13.2–6–24–5; Denly 2–1–1–1.

Kent

S. R. Dickson c Cook b van der Gugten	3	G. Stewart not out	24
Z. Crawley b Bull	168	M. J. Henry c Lawlor b Bull	31
J. L. Denly c Cooke b Bull	30		
H. W. Podmore c Cooke b Hogan	2	B 11, lb 15, nb 6	32
H. G. Kuhn c Cooke b Smith	9		
D. J. Bell-Drummond c Selman b Meschede	5	1/28 (1) 2/93 (3)	(105.4 overs) 436
*†S. W. Billings b Hogan	85	3/109 (4) 4/132 (5)	
O. G. Robinson c Cooke b Smith	17	5/162 (6) 6/294 (2) 7/338 (8)	
D. I. Stevens c Carlson b Lawlor	30	8/359 (7) 9/390 (10) 10/436 (11)	

Van der Gugten 20–3–67–1; Hogan 21–3–77–2; Smith 17–1–78–2; Meschede 21–3–95–1; Bull 18.4–3–64–3; Lawlor 8–1–29–1.

Umpires: J. H. Evans and R. J. Warren.

At Birmingham, September 24–26. KENT lost to WARWICKSHIRE by an innings and 34 runs.

LANCASHIRE

Bowling slow misses the point

PAUL EDWARDS

Lancashire's third relegation in the seven seasons since they won the title in 2011 was not confirmed until September 25, when they failed to gain a third bowling point in their final match, against Hampshire. Both the lateness and the manner of their demise reflected broader themes: Liam Livingstone's team had never been cut adrift from the rest of the first division, and their problems had been caused mainly by inadequate batting. Despite gaining 40 bowling points – more than any other side in the top tier – they won only three games, fewer than anyone except Worcestershire.

Victory at Southampton meant they finished equal on points with sixth-placed Nottinghamshire, but the argument that Lancashire were unfortunate to go down rang hollow. The case rested in part on a one-point deduction for a slow over-rate in the Roses match at Old Trafford, yet other counties could cite similar penalties over the years. Relegated sides in eight-team divisions are frequently unlucky; Lancashire were no more hard done by than anyone else.

A more persuasive explanation would begin with an analysis of the specialist batting. No one reached 800 Championship runs; only Dane Vilas, Alex Davies and Keaton Jennings managed 550. Even more damaging were the frequent collapses, not all on spring's seaming pitches. Lancashire were dismissed for under 200 in ten of their 24 Championship innings; few teams prosper when their batting is so fragile. The most troubling individual slump was suffered by Haseeb Hameed, who scored 165 in 17 innings at less than ten. Two years before, his average had been a fraction under 50.

It would be unfair to blame Lancashire's plight on a 21-year-old, and Livingstone carried his own share of the responsibility as he admitted the senior batsmen were letting the side down. In November, he resigned as captain, after a single season. He was succeeded by Vilas, the batsman least affected by the malaise, whose three centuries included an unbeaten 235 against Somerset and a match-winning 107 not out in a memorable run-chase against Worcestershire at Southport. Vilas's partner as Lancashire completed an unexpected win was Josh Bohannon, whose all-round ability and tenacious approach brightened the end-of-season gloom.

Even when Lancashire batted well in their first innings, they were rarely able to force victory. In early home games against Surrey and Somerset, they scored over 400, but were denied on the final afternoon. And when they batted badly, they almost invariably lost, though they bowled out Somerset for 77 to tie at Taunton, and at The Oval were only seven short of defeating Surrey, the eventual champions. By such margins are seasons shaped and contracts decided.

Relegation was poor reward for Tom Bailey, Division One's leading wicket-taker with 64, the most by a Lancashire bowler since Gary Keedy claimed 72

Tom Bailey

in 2004 (another summer that ended in demotion). Bailey may have thought the arrival of Graham Onions from Durham would limit his opportunities, but it proved a boon: the pair worked together superbly, with Onions close behind on 57 wickets. Their potency ensured a penetrative seam attack, even when Joe Mennie missed two Championship games after being hit on the head by a drive from Martin Guptill at Worcester, and with James Anderson limited to three appearances. Still, the signing of Blackpool-born Richard Gleeson from Northamptonshire in early September looked a shrewd move, particularly after all-rounder Jordan Clark – who had claimed a rare Roses hat-trick – announced he was moving to Surrey.

Gleeson was one of four bowlers signed by Lancashire late in the season, although Afghan spinner Zahir Khan and Scotland's Mark Watt played only T20 cricket. The most prominent was South African slow left-armer Keshav Maharaj, who took 17 wickets in three matches after Mennie had gone home, including 11 to secure the tie at Taunton. Leg-spinner Matthew Parkinson needed twice as many Championship games to bag 16, but continued his steady improvement and in the Royal London Cup took more wickets (18) than anyone in the country; he won a contract with Melbourne Stars in the Big Bash, though a back injury prevented him fulfilling it. Simon Kerrigan and Karl Brown (who had both played their part in the 2011 Championship triumph) were released at the end of their contracts, along with Arron Lilley, who joined Leicestershire. In December, the county unveiled Australians Joe Burns and Glenn Maxwell as their overseas players for 2019.

Lancashire won only three of their eight fixtures in the Royal London Cup, but began the Vitality Blast with five victories in six matches, and qualified for finals day by beating Kent at Canterbury in the quarter-final. Any hopes that the Twenty20 title might take their supporters' minds off first-class failures were snuffed out when, for the fourth time in seven finals-day appearances, Lancashire lost the morning semi.

All these problems made it a difficult first season as director of cricket for Paul Allott. Yet, in the aftermath of relegation, he restated a commitment to fielding a team containing at least seven locally produced players, and he deserved credit for watching as much age-group and Second XI cricket as his responsibilities permitted.

Championship attendance: 30,167.

LANCASHIRE RESULTS

All first-class matches – Played 15: Won 3, Lost 7, Tied 1, Drawn 4.
County Championship matches – Played 14: Won 3, Lost 7, Tied 1, Drawn 3.

Specsavers County Championship, 7th in Division 1;
Vitality Blast, semi-finalists; Royal London One-Day Cup, 6th in North Group.

COUNTY CHAMPIONSHIP AVERAGES, BATTING AND FIELDING

Cap		Birthplace	M	I	NO	R	HS	100	Avge	Ct/St
2018	†K. K. Jennings	*Johannesburg, SA* ..	10	16	1	709	177	3	47.26	9
2018	D. J. Vilas††.......	*Johannesburg, SA* ..	14	23	2	792	235*	3	37.71	50/4
	J. Clark	*Whitehaven*	10	16	0	538	82	0	33.62	2
	J. M. Mennie¶	*Coffs Harbour, Aust*	7	11	4	232	68*	0	33.14	1
	J. J. Bohannon	*Bolton‡*	5	9	1	255	78*	0	31.87	2
2017	A. L. Davies	*Darwen‡*	14	24	0	732	115	1	30.50	19/1
2017	L. S. Livingstone	*Barrow-in-Furness* ..	10	16	2	336	48*	0	24.00	15
2010	S. J. Croft	*Blackpool‡*	8	13	0	276	62	0	21.23	10
2010	†S. Chanderpaul†† ...	*Unity Village, Guy .*	8	13	0	257	65	0	19.76	6
	R. P. Jones	*Warrington*	5	8	0	137	68	0	17.12	5
2015	K. R. Brown	*Bolton‡*	2	4	0	67	43	0	16.75	1
2018	T. E. Bailey	*Preston‡*	14	22	2	308	66	0	15.40	5
	D. J. Lamb	*Preston‡*	4	6	2	57	20*	0	14.25	1
	K. A. Maharaj¶	*Durban, SA*	3	5	0	66	38	0	13.20	2
2016	H. Hameed	*Bolton‡*	10	17	0	165	31	0	9.70	6
2018	G. Onions	*Gateshead*	12	19	4	135	41	0	9.00	1
	M. W. Parkinson	*Bolton‡*	6	11	5	35	9*	0	5.83	1
2003	†J. M. Anderson§	*Burnley‡*	3	4	0	14	8	0	3.50	1
2015	S. D. Parry	*Manchester‡*	3	4	0	7	6	0	1.75	0

Also batted: J. C. Buttler§ (*Taunton*) (cap 2018) (1 match) 3, 59 (2 ct); R. J. Gleeson (*Blackpool‡*) (2 matches) 9*, 0*, 0*; B. D. Guest (*Manchester‡*) (1 match) 8, 0; †T. J. Lester (*Blackpool‡*) (1 match) 8, 8; A. M. Lilley (*Tameside‡*) (1 match) 28; S. Mahmood (*Birmingham*) (1 match) 0.

‡ *Born in Lancashire.* § *ECB contract.* ¶ *Official overseas player.* †† *Other non-England-qualified.*

BOWLING

	Style	O	M	R	W	BB	5I	Avge
K. A. Maharaj	SLA	103.4	23	283	17	7-37	1	16.64
R. J. Gleeson	RFM	57	15	196	10	3-34	0	19.60
T. E. Bailey	RFM	439.4	106	1,258	64	5-53	1	19.65
J. M. Mennie	RFM	192.5	44	601	28	4-43	0	21.46
G. Onions	RFM	379.3	72	1,241	57	6-55	2	21.77
J. Clark	RM	198.3	22	688	24	5-58	1	28.66
M. W. Parkinson	LB	155.1	23	481	16	5-101	1	30.06

Also bowled: J. M. Anderson (RFM) 100–29–280–9; J. J. Bohannon (RFM) 27–3–103–5; S. J. Croft (RFM/OB) 7–2–11–0; K. K. Jennings (RM) 14–0–92–0; R. P. Jones (LB) 6–0–19–1; D. J. Lamb (RFM) 28–1–146–0; T. J. Lester (LFM) 27.1–2–78–3; A. M. Lilley (OB) 28.3–6–89–2; L. S. Livingstone (LB) 86.5–18–214–7; S. Mahmood (RFM) 21–4–57–2; S. D. Parry (SLA) 97–14–274–3.

LEADING ROYAL LONDON CUP AVERAGES (100 runs/4 wickets)

Batting	Runs	HS	Avge	SR	Ct/St
K. K. Jennings .	375	136	75.00	95.41	3
L. S. Livingstone	362	90*	60.33	122.71	7
H. Hameed	113	55*	56.50	77.39	0
A. L. Davies ...	339	147	42.37	94.42	4/1
D. J. Vilas	210	83*	42.00	119.31	3/3
J. Clark	149	51	29.80	100.00	2

Bowling	W	BB	Avge	ER
M. W. Parkinson .	18	5-68	18.22	5.15
K. K. Jennings ...	5	2-19	21.00	5.52
S. D. Parry	7	2-20	29.85	5.07
G. Onions	5	2-31	30.20	5.39
J. M. Mennie	8	3-56	31.37	4.75
T. E. Bailey	6	2-16	33.33	6.66
L. S. Livingstone .	4	2-30	48.25	4.48

LEADING VITALITY BLAST AVERAGES (100 runs/15 overs)

Batting	Runs	HS	Avge	SR	Ct/St		Bowling	W	BB	Avge	ER
L. S. Livingstone	318	100	45.42	**188.16**	4		Zahir Khan	9	2-8	20.55	**7.02**
A. M. Lilley	246	47	18.92	**156.68**	7		M. W. Parkinson	25	3-19	16.60	**7.32**
K. R. Brown	204	61	29.14	**150.00**	4		J. P. Faulkner	20	3-24	17.60	**7.68**
J. Clark	191	41*	47.75	**143.60**	7		L. S. Livingstone	6	4-17	22.00	**8.25**
D. J. Vilas	192	30*	19.20	**134.26**	13/6		J. Clark	7	2-26	31.14	**8.77**
A. L. Davies	534	94*	53.40	**129.61**	5		T. J. Lester	15	4-25	22.33	**8.89**
K. K. Jennings	239	51*	59.75	**117.15**	2						
S. J. Croft	108	30	15.42	**112.50**	8						

FIRST-CLASS COUNTY RECORDS

Highest score for	424	A. C. MacLaren v Somerset at Taunton	1895
Highest score against	315*	T. W. Hayward (Surrey) at The Oval	1898
Leading run-scorer	34,222	E. Tyldesley (avge 45.20)	1909–36
Best bowling for	10-46	W. Hickton v Hampshire at Manchester	1870
Best bowling against	10-40	G. O. B. Allen (Middlesex) at Lord's	1929
Leading wicket-taker	1,816	J. B. Statham (avge 15.12)	1950–68
Highest total for	863	v Surrey at The Oval	1990
Highest total against	707-9 dec	by Surrey at The Oval	1990
Lowest total for	25	v Derbyshire at Manchester	1871
Lowest total against	20	by Essex at Chelmsford	2013

LIST A COUNTY RECORDS

Highest score for	162*	A. R. Crook v Buckinghamshire at Wormsley	2005
Highest score against	186*	C. G. Greenidge (West Indians) at Liverpool	1984
Leading run-scorer	11,969	N. H. Fairbrother (avge 41.84)	1982–2002
Best bowling for	6-10	C. E. H. Croft v Scotland at Manchester	1982
Best bowling against	8-26	K. D. Boyce (Essex) at Manchester	1971
Leading wicket-taker	480	J. Simmons (avge 25.75)	1969–89
Highest total for	381-3	v Hertfordshire at Radlett	1999
Highest total against	**379-7**	**by Yorkshire at Manchester**	**2018**
Lowest total for	59	v Worcestershire at Worcester	1963
Lowest total against	52	by Minor Counties at Lakenham	1998

TWENTY20 COUNTY RECORDS

Highest score for	103*	A. N. Petersen v Leicestershire at Leicester	2016
Highest score against	108*	I. J. Harvey (Yorkshire) at Leeds	2004
Leading run-scorer	3,161	**S. J. Croft (avge 29.26, SR 123.18)**	**2006–18**
Best bowling for	5-13	S. D. Parry v Worcestershire at Manchester	2016
Best bowling against	6-19	T. T. Bresnan (Yorkshire) at Leeds	2017
Leading wicket-taker	117	**S. D. Parry (avge 24.94, ER 7.17)**	**2009–18**
Highest total for	231-4	v Yorkshire at Manchester	2015
Highest total against	211-5	by Derbyshire at Derby	2017
Lowest total for	91	v Derbyshire at Manchester	2003
Lowest total against	53	by Worcestershire at Manchester	2016

ADDRESS

Emirates Old Trafford, Talbot Road, Manchester M16 0PX; 0161 282 4000; enquiries@lancashire-cricket.co.uk; www.lancashirecricket.co.uk.

OFFICIALS

Captain 2018 L. S. Livingstone
2019 D. J. Vilas
Director of cricket P. J. W. Allott
Head coach G. Chapple
Performance Director and assistant head coach M. J. Chilton
Academy director G. Yates

President Sir Howard Bernstein
Chairman D. M. W. Hodgkiss
Chief executive D. Gidney
Head groundsman M. Merchant
Scorer C. Rimmer

At Loughborough, April 7–9. LANCASHIRE drew with LOUGHBOROUGH MCCU.

LANCASHIRE v NOTTINGHAMSHIRE

At Manchester, April 13–16. Nottinghamshire won by six wickets. Nottinghamshire 20pts, Lancashire 3pts. Toss: uncontested. County debuts: J. M. Mennie; C. D. Nash, L. R. P. L. Taylor.

On a crazy final morning, 12 batsmen were out in 15 overs. Lancashire began the day on 58 for two, six runs behind, but lost their last eight for 15: backed up by excellent close fielding, Gurney bowled superbly on a soft pitch for a career-best six for 25. Then Nottinghamshire's top four fell in five overs – three of them to Australian seamer Joe Mennie on his county debut – before they reached ten. "Extraordinary is probably the right word," said their coach, Peter Moores. The quicker bowlers had exploited the cloudy conditions throughout, none more effectively than Ball, who took five in

STAGGERING HOME

Lowest successful chases losing four or more wickets:

10-4	**Nottinghamshire (set 10 to win) v Lancashire at Manchester**	**2018**
12-4	Kent (*11*) v Sussex at Town Malling....................................	1841
16-7	New South Wales (*16*) v Victoria at Melbourne........................	1855-56
18-5	Lancashire (*18*) v Kent at Catford................................	1875
20-4	Somerset (*20*) v Gloucestershire at Taunton	1907

Lancashire's first innings and four on the last morning. After a first-day washout, Vilas made 49, which would prove the game's highest score, before Ball wrapped up the innings for 158, but Nottinghamshire lost their last eight wickets in a 43-over evening session. Wessels and Tom Moores batted calmly next day to add 82, helping their side to a lead of 64; Moores displayed a sound technique against pace over 143 minutes, the longest innings of the match. Lancashire seemed to be back in it when their openers put on 49, only for the game to take its chaotic twist.

Close of play: first day, no play; second day, Nottinghamshire 127-6 (Wessels 18, Moores 0); third day, Lancashire 58-2 (Jennings 27, Livingstone 4).

Lancashire

K. K. Jennings c and b Gurney	11	– lbw b Gurney	27
H. Hameed lbw b Ball	3	– c Moores b Gurney..............	19
†A. L. Davies lbw b Wood....................	23	– c Moores b Gurney..............	0
*L. S. Livingstone b Wood....................	9	– c Moores b Ball	12
S. Chanderpaul c Libby b Fletcher...........	0	– c Taylor b Gurney..............	0
D. J. Vilas b Gurney.......................	49	– c Wessels b Ball	6
S. J. Croft c Wessels b Ball	6	– b Ball	0
J. Clark c Wood b Ball.....................	19	– c Nash b Ball	0
T. E. Bailey c Moores b Ball	0	– c Moores b Gurney..............	1
J. M. Mennie not out	4	– c Moores b Gurney..............	0
G. Onions c Wood b Ball....................	0	– not out	0
B 5, lb 15, w 1, nb 2.......................	23	B 4, lb 4	8

1/21 (2) 2/28 (1) 3/59 (4)   (61 overs) 158   1/49 (2) 2/51 (3)   (34.2 overs) 73
4/60 (3) 5/124 (5) 6/131 (6)   3/58 (1) 4/62 (5)
7/149 (7) 8/149 (9) 9/158 (8) 10/158 (11)   5/66 (4) 6/66 (7) 7/66 (8)
                                      8/73 (9) 9/73 (6) 10/73 (10)

Ball 17-7-43-5; Fletcher 15-7-23-1; Gurney 14-3-18-2; Wood 9-0-43-2; Mullaney 6-3-11-0. *Second innings*—Ball 10.5-5-14-4; Fletcher 6-1-16-0; Gurney 12.2-5-25-6; Patel 6-2-10-0.

Nottinghamshire

*S. J. Mullaney c Davies b Bailey	24	– c Onions b Mennie	1
J. D. Libby c Davies b Onions	15	– c Livingstone b Mennie	4
C. D. Nash lbw b Bailey	24	– c Hameed b Mennie	0
L. R. P. L. Taylor lbw b Bailey	9	– c Livingstone b Onions	0
S. R. Patel b Mennie	28	– not out	4
M. H. Wessels lbw b Livingstone	44	– not out	1
L. J. Fletcher c Davies b Mennie	2		
†T. J. Moores b Mennie	38		
L. Wood c Vilas b Livingstone	8		
J. T. Ball st Davies b Livingstone	9		
H. F. Gurney not out	0		
B 4, lb 15, nb 2	21		

1/20 (2) 2/62 (1) 3/75 (3)   (72.2 overs) 222   1/1 (1) 2/5 (3)   (4 wkts, 5 overs) 10
4/82 (4) 5/110 (5) 6/112 (7)   3/5 (2) 4/9 (4)
7/194 (6) 8/210 (9) 9/220 (8) 10/222 (10)

Bailey 19–7–26–3; Onions 15–5–46–1; Clark 8–0–35–0; Mennie 20–6–46–3; Livingstone 7.2–0–27–3; Jennings 2–0–21–0; Croft 1–0–2–0. *Second innings*—Onions 3–0–6–1; Mennie 2–1–4–3.

Umpires: G. D. Lloyd and N. A. Mallender.

At Chelmsford, April 20–22. LANCASHIRE lost to ESSEX by 31 runs.

LANCASHIRE v SURREY

At Manchester, April 27–30. Drawn. Lancashire 12pts, Surrey 8pts. Toss: uncontested.

Lancashire enforced the follow-on but were frustrated by Foakes and Pope on the final afternoon. After uninterrupted rain on the first day, the home side had been three down by the tenth over, before a series of useful partnerships – most importantly 118 between Mennie and Bailey, a ninth-wicket record for this fixture, which allowed Livingstone to declare an hour into the third day. Bailey reached a career-best 66 before becoming Virdi's fourth victim, and followed up with four wickets as Surrey collapsed from 131 for two. Onions also took four, including former Durham team-mates Stoneman and Borthwick; when he removed last man Virdi early on the last morning, Surrey were 204 behind and needed to bat out the day to save the game. They declined to 90 for four just before tea; had Vilas – keeping wicket after Davies injured his thumb – taken a simple catch offered by Pope, then 12, off Onions, Lancashire might have won. Instead, Foakes and Pope held out for 31 overs before both fell to Bailey with the new ball. Curran and Patel saw out the last half-hour.

Close of play: first day, no play; second day, Lancashire 352-8 (Mennie 35, Bailey 15); third day, Surrey 231-9 (Patel 4, Virdi 0).

Lancashire

K. K. Jennings lbw b Curran	15	J. M. Mennie not out	68
H. Hameed c Elgar b Dernbach	4	T. E. Bailey c Dunn b Virdi	66
†A. L. Davies c Dunn b Dernbach	4	B 1, lb 9, nb 6	16
*L. S. Livingstone lbw b Dernbach	48		
S. Chanderpaul c Borthwick b Virdi	65	1/15 (2) (9 wkts dec, 118.5 overs) 439
D. J. Vilas c Borthwick b Curran	13	2/23 (3) 3/23 (1) 4/111 (4)
S. J. Croft c Foakes b Virdi	62	5/128 (6) 6/206 (5) 7/252 (7)
J. Clark c Pope b Virdi	78	8/321 (8) 9/439 (10) 110 overs: 371-8

G. Onions did not bat.

Dernbach 29–6–93–3; Curran 26–0–106–2; Dunn 24–7–88–0; Patel 16–0–62–0; Virdi 23.5–2–80–4.

Surrey

*R. J. Burns c Davies b Bailey	28	– c Jennings b Livingstone	33
M. D. Stoneman b Onions	0	– c †Vilas b Bailey	29
S. G. Borthwick c Davies b Onions	79	– b Bailey	0
D. Elgar c †Vilas b Bailey	34	– c †Vilas b Clark	14
†B. T. Foakes lbw b Clark	34	– c †Vilas b Bailey	57
O. J. D. Pope b Bailey	17	– c Livingstone b Bailey	41
S. M. Curran lbw b Livingstone	9	– not out	9
R. S. Patel not out	4	– not out	9
J. W. Dernbach c Jennings b Bailey	7		
M. P. Dunn lbw b Onions	1		
G. S. Virdi c †Vilas b Onions	4		
B 8, lb 6, nb 4	18	Lb 7	7

1/2 (2) 2/100 (1) 3/131 (3) (89.4 overs) 235
4/171 (4) 5/202 (5) 6/217 (7)
7/218 (6) 8/228 (9) 9/231 (10)
10/235 (11)

1/53 (2) (6 wkts, 90.3 overs) 199
2/53 (3) 3/68 (1)
4/90 (4) 5/176 (5) 6/177 (6)

Bailey 22–5–54–4; Onions 19.4–6–49–4; Livingstone 18–4–36–1; Mennie 16–2–47–0; Clark 12–4–32–1; Croft 2–0–3–0. *Second innings*—Bailey 19–12–13–4; Onions 19–6–41–0; Clark 12–3–29–1; Mennie 15–5–44–0; Livingstone 22.3–5–59–1; Croft 3–1–6–0.

Umpires: P. J. Hartley and R. A. Kettleborough.

LANCASHIRE v SOMERSET

At Manchester, May 4–7. Drawn. Lancashire 11pts, Somerset 10pts. Toss: Somerset.

Lancashire fought their way to a 63-run advantage after two huge first innings, but were finally denied by Leach's career-best 66. On the opening day, Trescothick had batted imperiously to reach 95, then broke a metatarsal in his right foot; aided by a runner, he completed his 66th first-class century but was caught behind next ball. He had added 134 with Bartlett, 22 years his junior, who registered a maiden hundred that evening; next day Abell looked set to become Somerset's third centurion before he fell lbw to Mennie. In reply Jennings, who opened with Alex Davies after Hameed was dropped for the first time, made his first century since leaving Durham, during a 201-run stand with Vilas, only to be put in the shade. Vilas batted almost nine hours for 235 not out – a record for a Lancashire wicketkeeper, beating Luke Sutton's 151 against Yorkshire in 2006 (he had again taken the gloves from Davies, nursing his sore thumb, on the first afternoon). Last man Parkinson saw him to 200 after Abell's accurate medium-pace snatched three wickets in an over, earning a career-best four for 43 and shattering Lancashire's hopes of a larger lead. Even so, they scented victory when Parkinson reduced Somerset to 145 for six, only 82 ahead. Leach's determined half-century partnerships with Overton and Groenewald ensured the draw. Anderson took one wicket in his first match of the season, sporting a short-lived ash-blond hairstyle.

Close of play: first day, Somerset 321-5 (Abell 48); second day, Lancashire 217-2 (Jennings 91, Vilas 83); third day, Somerset 51-0 (Renshaw 20, Davies 22).

Somerset

M. E. Trescothick c †Vilas b Livingstone	100			
M. T. Renshaw c Clark b Bailey	21	– (1) c Bailey b Parkinson	20
G. A. Bartlett c Livingstone b Mennie	110	– lbw b Anderson	6
J. C. Hildreth c Clark b Mennie	5	– lbw b Parkinson	26
*T. B. Abell lbw b Mennie	99	– lbw b Parkinson	13
†S. M. Davies c †Vilas b Clark	15	– (2) c Croft b Parkinson	54
L. Gregory c Livingstone b Bailey	10	– (6) c Livingstone b Mennie	13
C. Overton c Anderson b Parkinson	28	– (7) lbw b Bailey	5
M. J. Leach c †Vilas b Parkinson	0	– (8) b Parkinson	66
T. D. Groenewald not out	7	– (9) not out	36
P. A. van Meekeren lbw b Parkinson	6	– (10) not out	0
B 8, lb 10, nb 10	28	B 12, lb 10, nb 8	30

1/65 (2) 2/199 (1) 3/215 (4)   (121.2 overs) 429   1/51 (1)   (8 wkts dec, 93 overs) 269
4/294 (3) 5/321 (6) 6/354 (7)   2/67 (3) 3/113 (2)
7/415 (8) 8/415 (5) 9/415 (9)   4/120 (4) 5/143 (6)
10/429 (11)   110 overs: 379-6   6/145 (5) 7/197 (7) 8/266 (8)

Anderson 26–7–91–0; Bailey 27–4–112–2; Mennie 27–8–82–3; Clark 11–0–34–1; Parkinson 26.2–5–80–3; Livingstone 4–1–12–1. *Second innings*—Bailey 15–7–33–1; Anderson 17–6–46–1; Parkinson 31–6–101–5; Livingstone 14–4–25–0; Mennie 11–4–24–1; Clark 5–0–18–0.

Lancashire

K. K. Jennings lbw b Leach	109	J. M. Anderson c Davies b Abell	0
†A. L. Davies c Davies b Groenewald	23	M. W. Parkinson c Overton b van Meekeren	9
*L. S. Livingstone c Gregory b Leach	6		
D. J. Vilas not out	235	B 13, lb 24, w 1, nb 2	40
S. Chanderpaul lbw b Overton	6		
S. J. Croft c Gregory b Leach	11	1/35 (2) 2/48 (3) 3/249 (1) (144 overs) 492
J. Clark b Abell	50	4/283 (5) 5/329 (6) 6/431 (7)
J. M. Mennie b Abell	1	7/437 (8) 8/443 (9) 9/443 (10)
T. E. Bailey lbw b Abell	2	10/492 (11) 110 overs: 367-5

Gregory 20–3–70–0; Overton 22–4–65–1; Groenewald 24–6–52–1; Leach 46–8–149–3; van Meekeren 20–3–67–1; Abell 10–2–43–4; Renshaw 2–1–9–0.

Umpires: N. G. B. Cook and B. J. Debenham.

At Nottingham, May 11–13. LANCASHIRE beat NOTTINGHAMSHIRE by an innings and 67 runs. *Lancashire's first Championship victory away from home since July 2015.*

LANCASHIRE v ESSEX

At Manchester, June 9–11. Essex won by five wickets. Essex 22pts, Lancashire 6pts. Toss: uncontested.

Porter enabled Essex to complete the double over Lancashire, exposing their top-order frailties in both innings to finish with 16 wickets across the two games. He started by dismissing the openers as Lancashire stumbled to 59 for five, before Chanderpaul and Clark added 131, and some late biffing by Bailey and Onions ensured these batting sums. The home seamers kept Essex's lead down to one, helped by smart fielding, including a brilliant pick-up-and-throw by wicketkeeper Vilas. His victim, ten Doeschate, caused such a ruckus on his return to the dressing-room that he was given three disciplinary points, taking him to nine, and triggering a two-game suspension. But the game's poise tilted decisively the visitors' way on the third day, when 19 wickets fell. After Bailey cleared away the Essex tail, Lancashire collapsed to 41 for seven against Porter and Harmer, then 105 all out. Onions did his best to derail the run-chase, with three early strikes, but a composed unbeaten 36 from Bopara settled Essex nerves. On the third morning, play was interrupted for 35 minutes when a member was taken ill; an air ambulance landed on the outfield, while three road ambulances parked by the pavilion to help administer treatment, but he later died.

Close of play: first day, Lancashire 297-9 (Bailey 36, Parkinson 1); second day, Essex 221-6 (Wheater 31, Harmer 7).

Lancashire

K. K. Jennings c Lawrence b Porter	19	– c Harmer b Porter	0
A. L. Davies c Harmer b Porter	2	– c A. N. Cook b S. J. Cook	0
H. Hameed c Wheater b Wagner	5	– c Wheater b Porter	4
*L. S. Livingstone c Harmer b S. J. Cook	11	– lbw b Porter	17
S. Chanderpaul b Harmer	58	– lbw b Harmer	10
†D. J. Vilas lbw b S. J. Cook	10	– c ten Doeschate b Harmer	4
J. Clark b Harmer	79	– lbw b Porter	0
J. M. Mennie lbw b S. J. Cook	15	– not out	32
T. E. Bailey c Wagner b Harmer	38	– c ten Doeschate b Harmer	16
G. Onions c Chopra b Wagner	41	– c A. N. Cook b Harmer	13
M. W. Parkinson not out	3	– b Porter	1
B 2, lb 7, w 1, nb 10	20	B 4, lb 2, nb 2	8

1/7 (2) 2/26 (1) 3/28 (3) (98.2 overs) 301
4/40 (4) 5/59 (6) 6/190 (5)
7/193 (7) 8/229 (8) 9/281 (10) 10/301 (9)

1/0 (1) 2/0 (2) (32.4 overs) 105
3/12 (3) 4/23 (4)
5/28 (6) 6/29 (7) 7/41 (5)
8/75 (9) 9/95 (10) 10/105 (11)

Porter 22–8–68–2; S. J. Cook 24–6–65–3; Wagner 21–4–91–2; Harmer 22.2–8–35–3; Bopara 9–1–33–0. *Second innings*—Porter 12.4–4–30–5; S. J. Cook 5–3–13–1; Harmer 11–1–34–4; Wagner 4–0–22–0.

Essex

V. Chopra b Onions	3	– b Onions	6
A. N. Cook c Vilas b Mennie	58	– c Hameed b Onions	9
T. Westley b Mennie	41	– c Vilas b Onions	14
D. W. Lawrence lbw b Onions	2	– b Mennie	3
R. S. Bopara c Livingstone b Mennie	6	– not out	36
*R. N. ten Doeschate run out (Vilas)	43	– c Davies b Parkinson	19
†A. J. A. Wheater lbw b Bailey	41	– not out	11
S. R. Harmer lbw b Bailey	29		
N. Wagner c Davies b Bailey	29		
J. A. Porter lbw b Bailey	0		
S. J. Cook not out	8		
B 13, lb 15, w 2, nb 12	42	Lb 4, nb 6	10

1/9 (1) 2/119 (2) 3/120 (3) (84.1 overs) 302
4/124 (4) 5/130 (5) 6/211 (6)
7/253 (8) 8/260 (7) 9/260 (10) 10/302 (9)

1/7 (1) (5 wkts, 28.5 overs) 108
2/22 (2) 3/39 (3)
4/41 (4) 5/93 (6)

Bailey 20.1–2–54–4; Onions 20–2–74–2; Mennie 24–6–83–3; Livingstone 4–2–8–0; Parkinson 12–1–39–0; Clark 4–0–16–0. *Second innings*—Bailey 7–1–23–0; Onions 7–0–29–3; Mennie 5–0–26–1; Parkinson 5.5–1–10–1; Livingstone 4–0–16–0.

Umpires: J. W. Lloyds and S. J. O'Shaughnessy.

> **"** Not often have an Australian attack looked so devoid of ideas and hope: an over from Khawaja could hardly have reached the other end more slowly had it been sent in the post."
> Australia v India in 2018–19, Fourth Test, page 835

At Worcester, June 20–23. LANCASHIRE lost to WORCESTERSHIRE by 202 runs. *Lancashire's Danny Lamb becomes the first concussion substitute in county cricket.*

LANCASHIRE v HAMPSHIRE

At Manchester, June 25–28. Drawn. Lancashire 11pts, Hampshire 10pts. Toss: Hampshire.

Dale Steyn, rested ahead of the Royal London Cup final two days later, may have been grateful to miss a high-scoring draw on a flat pitch. The teams shook hands at the earliest opportunity, and Hampshire set off to prepare for Lord's. Five players scored hundreds: Vince's 103 brightened the first day, and Rossouw's unbeaten 120 the second morning, when Onions – who warmed up in spotty boxer shorts, having tweeted that he would bowl in his underpants if Panama's football team didn't have a man sent off in their World Cup game with England – picked up his fifth wicket. Davies and Vilas made resilient centuries next day, putting on 138 before Vilas and Clark added 112, but Lancashire conceded a 40-run lead. With both sides near the foot of the table, neither was inclined to gamble on achieving a positive result, but there was time for Weatherley to make a maiden first-class hundred before the draw was agreed at 4.50pm. Hampshire would not play another Championship match for 52 days.

Close of play: first day, Hampshire 302-6 (Rossouw 54, Rayner 0); second day, Lancashire 140-3 (Davies 78, Vilas 37); third day, Hampshire 66-2 (Weatherley 29, Northeast 8).

Hampshire

J. J. Weatherley c Vilas b Onions	0	– not out	126
J. H. K. Adams b Onions	44	– lbw b Onions	4
*J. M. Vince b Parry	103	– c Vilas b Bailey	18
S. A. Northeast c Jones b Clark	41	– b Clark	10
†T. P. Alsop b Onions	15	– b Parry	33
R. R. Rossouw not out	120	– lbw b Clark	1
I. G. Holland c Vilas b Onions	24	– not out	26
O. P. Rayner lbw b Onions	0		
G. K. Berg c Lamb b Parry	49		
K. J. Abbott b Lilley	20		
F. H. Edwards c Vilas b Lilley	9		
B 4, lb 4, nb 18	26	B 5, lb 8, nb 6	19

1/7 (1) 2/114 (2) 3/187 (3)   (142.3 overs) 451   1/12 (2)   (5 wkts dec, 97 overs) 237
4/216 (5) 5/235 (4) 6/296 (7)   2/47 (3) 3/86 (4)
7/304 (8) 8/390 (9) 9/423 (10)   4/161 (5) 5/164 (6)
10/451 (11)   110 overs: 343-7

Bailey 27–5–68–0; Onions 31–6–96–5; Parry 38–6–101–2; Lamb 6–0–38–0; Lilley 15.3–3–52–2. *Second innings*—Bailey 18–7–32–1; Onions 13–3–41–1; Parry 25–7–50–1; Clark 14–5–18–2; Lilley 13–3–37–0; Lamb 13–0–45–0; Jones 1–0–1–0.

Lancashire

K. K. Jennings c Alsop b Berg	4	T. E. Bailey lbw b Abbott	6
A. L. Davies c Rossouw b Holland	115	G. Onions not out	0
H. Hameed b Edwards	13		
R. P. Jones b Abbott	1	B 6, lb 7, nb 6	19
*†D. J. Vilas lbw b Abbott	134		
J. Clark run out (Vince).	82	1/7 (1) 2/54 (3) (118.5 overs) 411
D. J. Lamb lbw b Rayner	3	3/70 (4) 4/208 (2) 5/320 (5)
A. M. Lilley c Alsop b Holland	28	6/327 (7) 7/385 (8) 8/394 (9)
S. D. Parry b Berg	6	9/411 (6) 10/411 (10) 110 overs: 394-7

Edwards 24–5–64–1; Berg 27–6–78–2; Abbott 19.5–1–89–3; Rayner 30–5–117–1; Holland 18–3–50–2.

Umpires: P. K. Baldwin and N. J. Llong.

LANCASHIRE v YORKSHIRE

At Manchester, July 22–24. Yorkshire won by 118 runs. Yorkshire 19pts, Lancashire 2pts (after 1pt penalty). Toss: Yorkshire. County debut: J. E. Poysden.

Jordan Clark became only the second Lancashire bowler to take a Roses hat-trick, but his team still lost this pell-mell game. Clark's victims – Root, Williamson and Bairstow – lay third, fourth and 16th in the Test rankings, leading some to rate his hat-trick the best in history. He took five wickets for the first time, and also ran out Bresnan when he got a touch to Lyth's fierce drive. Livingstone broke his thumb in the field, however, and Lancashire felt his absence: outstanding pace bowling

ROSES HAT-TRICKS

G. Freeman (Yorks) at Holbeck	1868		G. G. Macaulay (Yorks) at Manchester	1933
G. Ulyett (Yorks) at Sheffield	1883		K. Higgs (Lancs) at Leeds	1968
S. Haigh (Yorks) at Manchester	1909		**J. Clark (Lancs) at Manchester**	**2018**

The only Roses hat-trick in one-day cricket was taken by D. Gough (Yorkshire) at Leeds in 1998.

dismissed them for 109, still 83 behind, by the first-day close. Yorkshire were 21 for three next morning before Brook and Bairstow – dropped on 22 by Parkinson at mid-on off Onions – put on 133. Needing 323, Lancashire had their hopes raised when Buttler and Bailey added 80 for the sixth wicket, but they were dashed by Buttler's departure, caught down the leg side off Root's off-spin just before stumps. Root claimed three more next morning, finishing with a career-best four for five to outshine Poysden, the leg-spinner signed on loan from Warwickshire; Yorkshire had failed to persuade Adil Rashid to play, despite rumours of his imminent Test recall. Livingstone came out at No. 11 wearing a shin guard on his arm to protect his pinned thumb, but Anderson's dismissal spared him from having to face a ball. Lancashire were penalised one point for their slow over-rate, which was to cost them dearly come September. This was the last Championship match at Old Trafford in 2018, with two months of the season to run.

Close of play: first day, Lancashire 109; second day, Lancashire 194-6 (Bailey 38, Onions 0).

Yorkshire

A. Lyth c Jennings b Anderson	70	– c Vilas b Onions	4
H. C. Brook b Onions	6	– c Vilas b Bailey	55
J. E. Root lbw b Clark	22	– c Vilas b Anderson	3
K. S. Williamson lbw b Clark	0	– c Vilas b Onions	1
†J. M. Bairstow c Buttler b Clark	0	– c Buttler b Onions	82
G. S. Ballance b Onions	9	– c Vilas b Bailey	9
T. T. Bresnan run out (Clark)	0	– b Clark	18
*S. A. Patterson c Jennings b Bailey	22	– not out	45
J. A. Brooks c Hameed b Clark	14	– st Vilas b Parkinson	5
J. E. Poysden not out	20	– c Hameed b Parkinson	1
B. O. Coad b Clark	15	– b Clark	0
B 4, lb 6, nb 4	14	B 6, lb 8, nb 2	16

1/24 (2) 2/59 (3) 3/59 (4)   (57.1 overs) 192   1/5 (1) 2/18 (3)   (51.3 overs) 239
4/59 (5) 5/78 (6) 6/86 (7)   3/21 (4) 4/154 (2)
7/131 (8) 8/131 (6) 9/166 (9) 10/192 (11)   5/160 (5) 6/170 (6) 7/211 (7)
                                              8/230 (9) 9/238 (10) 10/239 (11)

Anderson 15–3–38–1; Bailey 12–4–22–1; Onions 13–3–48–2; Clark 12.1–1–58–5; Parkinson 5–1–16–0. *Second innings*—Anderson 9–0–52–1; Onions 12–0–44–3; Bailey 9–1–47–2; Clark 10.3–0–39–2; Jennings 3–0–20–0; Parkinson 8–2–23–2.

Lancashire

K. K. Jennings c Root b Bresnan	22	– lbw b Coad	30
A. L. Davies c Bairstow b Coad	51	– lbw b Bresnan	32
H. Hameed b Patterson	1	– c Bairstow b Patterson	31
†D. J. Vilas lbw b Patterson	0	– lbw b Poysden	1
J. C. Buttler c Bairstow b Bresnan	3	– c Williamson b Root	59
J. Clark c Bresnan b Brooks	15	– c Bairstow b Patterson	0
T. E. Bailey b Coad	0	– lbw b Patterson	45
G. Onions b Coad	0	– c Bairstow b Root	0
M. W. Parkinson not out	9	– c Lyth b Root	2
J. M. Anderson lbw b Brooks	8	– b Root	0
*L. S. Livingstone absent hurt		– not out	0
		B 1, lb 1, nb 2	4

1/46 (1) 2/55 (3) 3/55 (4)   (30.4 overs) 109   1/54 (2) 2/86 (1)   (60.4 overs) 204
4/66 (5) 5/92 (2) 6/92 (7)   3/87 (4) 4/110 (3)
7/92 (8) 8/92 (6) 9/109 (10)   5/110 (6) 6/190 (5) 7/194 (8)
                                                        8/196 (9) 9/204 (7) 10/204 (10)

Coad 9–3–28–3; Brooks 6.4–1–24–2; Patterson 8–3–34–2; Bresnan 7–1–23–2. *Second innings—* Coad 11–3–29–1; Brooks 8–0–50–0; Bresnan 9–2–43–1; Patterson 18–6–38–3; Poysden 7–0–37–1; Root 7.4–5–5–4.

Umpires: P. R. Pollard and A. G. Wharf.

At The Oval, August 19–22. LANCASHIRE lost to SURREY by six runs.

LANCASHIRE v WORCESTERSHIRE

At Southport, August 29–31. Lancashire won by four wickets. Lancashire 19pts, Worcestershire 4pts. Toss: Worcestershire. County debut: K. A. Maharaj.

Until the third afternoon, Worcestershire were strong favourites to follow their victory at Scarborough nine days previously with another at Southport. But, amid rising excitement, Vilas and Josh Bohannon added an unbroken 139 for the seventh wicket to reach 317, Lancashire's highest successful run-chase for 16 years (in June they had scored 399 in defeat at Worcester). The win lifted them out of the relegation zone. Vilas's third century of the summer was overshadowed by Bohannon, whose determination to attack was remarkable in a 21-year-old playing his second Championship match. Apart from D'Oliveira's half-century, the batting on the first two days was poor: Lancashire collapsed to 85 for five against Tongue on the first evening, with Vilas run out when Davies's drive was diverted on to the stumps by Tongue's boot. They trailed by 61 before their bowlers mounted yet another rescue, and Bailey registered match figures of seven for 94. But Worcestershire's last four wickets added 122, including 50 from Parnell, to leave Lancashire needing 314. Few at Trafalgar Road gave them a hope in hell.

Close of play: first day, Lancashire 96-5 (Lester 2, Clark 5); second day, Lancashire 8-0 (Lester 4, Hameed 0).

Worcestershire

D. K. H. Mitchell c Vilas b Lester	9	– lbw b Bailey	7
T. C. Fell lbw b Bailey	31	– c Davies b Bailey	22
J. M. Clarke c Vilas b Clark	36	– b Bailey	2
A. G. Milton run out (Maharaj)	0	– c Vilas b Maharaj	37
*B. L. D'Oliveira c Croft b Bailey	65	– c Vilas b Onions	14
†O. B. Cox lbw b Onions	14	– lbw b Maharaj	40
E. G. Barnard not out	24	– c Hameed b Onions	24
W. D. Parnell b Bailey	4	– c Jones b Maharaj	50
B. J. Twohig c Vilas b Lester	1	– c Vilas b Onions	14
J. C. Tongue c Vilas b Bailey	17	– c Davies b Lester	20
D. Y. Pennington c Vilas b Onions	2	– not out	15
B 1, lb 11, w 1, nb 6	19	B 4, lb 1, nb 2	7

1/20 (1) 2/55 (2) 3/62 (4)   (70.1 overs) 222
4/98 (3) 5/139 (6) 6/177 (5)
7/183 (8) 8/193 (9) 9/215 (10) 10/222 (11)

1/14 (1) 2/16 (3)   (73.1 overs) 252
3/31 (2) 4/56 (5)
5/117 (6) 6/130 (4) 7/174 (7)
8/200 (9) 9/226 (8) 10/252 (10)

Lester 14–1–51–2; Onions 18.1–3–53–2; Bailey 17–3–41–4; Maharaj 12–2–33–0; Clark 9–2–32–1. *Second innings*—Bailey 16–2–53–3; Onions 18–1–76–3; Clark 7–0–27–0; Lester 13.1–1–27–1; Maharaj 19–2–64–3.

Lancashire

A. L. Davies lbw b Tongue	47	– (3) c Cox b Pennington	30
H. Hameed c Clarke b Tongue	0	– c Cox b Barnard	14
R. P. Jones c Mitchell b Tongue	0	– (4) c Cox b Barnard	0
S. J. Croft c Twohig b Parnell	14	– (5) c Clarke b Tongue	36
*†D. J. Vilas run out (Tongue)	18	– (6) not out	107
T. J. Lester c Twohig b Tongue	8	– (1) run out (Barnard)	8
J. Clark c Pennington b Tongue	27	– c D'Oliveira b Twohig	31
J. J. Bohannon run out (Barnard)	13	– not out	78
T. E. Bailey c Cox b Parnell	4		
K. A. Maharaj c Cox b Parnell	0		
G. Onions not out	4		
B 8, lb 4, nb 14	26	B 4, lb 5, nb 4	13

1/2 (2) 2/4 (3) 3/27 (4)   (37.5 overs) 161
4/81 (5) 5/85 (1) 6/106 (6)
7/129 (8) 8/143 (9) 9/143 (10) 10/161 (7)

1/12 (1)   (6 wkts, 88.4 overs) 317
2/47 (2) 3/47 (4)
4/63 (3) 5/121 (5) 6/178 (7)

Parnell 12–2–42–3; Tongue 15.5–2–63–5; Pennington 5–0–33–0; Barnard 5–3–11–0. *Second innings*—Tongue 19.4–4–75–1; Parnell 18–2–70–0; Barnard 20–5–50–2; Pennington 11–2–42–1; Twohig 15–3–48–1; Mitchell 5–0–23–0.

Umpires: M. A. Gough and D. J. Millns.

At Taunton, September 4–5. LANCASHIRE tied with SOMERSET. *Lancashire bowl out Somerset for 77 to seal only their fourth Championship tie.*

At Leeds, September 10–13. LANCASHIRE lost to YORKSHIRE by 95 runs.

At Southampton, September 24–26. LANCASHIRE beat HAMPSHIRE by eight wickets. *Despite a comfortable victory, Lancashire miss out on a third batting point, which would have saved them from relegation.*

LEICESTERSHIRE

One rung at a time

RICHARD RAE

Under the effervescent leadership of coach Paul Nixon, there was a tangible improvement on the field for Leicestershire. But the departure in December of chief executive Wasim Khan – to take over as managing director of the Pakistan Cricket Board – cast a shadow. In four years in charge, he had upgraded facilities at Grace Road, improved the club's financial position, and boosted their profile. "I'll look back at my time here with great pride and fondness," he said. In January, it was announced that his replacement was Karen Rothery, whose previous roles had included commercial director at England Netball.

The challenge now is to keep moving forward. In the first half of the Championship season, Leicestershire looked to have discovered the right formula. After thumping promotion contenders Kent in two days at Canterbury, their fourth win in five matches, they were in fourth place in Division Two, just ten points off second. It would be an understatement to say they then faded. Five of the final six matches were lost – all heavily – and they finished sixth. It was considerably better than 2017's bottom place, but still felt like a disappointment. Injuries were always likely to take a toll on a small squad, and so it proved.

Nixon remained typically positive, emphasising that Leicestershire had almost doubled their points total from the previous year, won their highest number of matches since 2010, and taken 20 wickets in a match eight times – a feat not achieved once in 2017. As so often, however, holding on to talented players was impossible. All-rounder Ben Raine, who had a good season with the ball, asked to be released from the final year of his contract, and rejoined Durham, to be nearer his family. Zak Chappell, an exciting fast-bowling prospect, followed the path taken by Stuart Broad, Harry Gurney and James Taylor, and joined Nottinghamshire.

Tough decisions did not faze Nixon. After four Championship matches and two Royal London Cup games, the last of which ended in a heavy defeat by Nottinghamshire, Michael Carberry was relieved of the captaincy. Carberry, who had been on loan from Hampshire in 2017, then signed on a two-year contract, did not play for the county again. Nixon insisted he had wanted him to continue as a player. "He's a fantastic cricketer and a great pro," he said. "We just didn't feel the captaincy was the right thing for him." The negotiations over the termination of his contract, which involved the Professional Cricketers' Association, were not concluded until the end of the season, and were an uncomfortable distraction. The club said Carberry left "by mutual consent".

Paul Horton, who had been in discussions to take over the captaincy of the Second XI, was appointed as Carberry's successor, and proved a success, although his form fell away in the final weeks, and he missed the last two matches for personal reasons. He will be given a chance to carry on his good work, and his task should be considerably eased by the return of Pakistan seamer Mohammad Abbas. In his first season in county cricket, which included a break for his country's short Test series against England, he was outstanding. In ten first-class matches, he took 50 wickets at 17, leading the attack with skill and a work ethic which inspired the other seamers. When he lines up alongside Chris Wright, an arrival from

Jordan Mansfield, Getty Images

Mohammad Abbas

Warwickshire, Leicestershire should have a potent new-ball pair.

Abbas was not the only reason their 40 bowling points were level with second-placed Kent and bettered only by Division Two champions Warwickshire. Bowling coach Matt Mason, brought in by Nixon after he left Worcestershire, did valuable work in helping Gavin Griffiths remodel his action. Griffiths was rewarded with 36 wickets at 24, and was the most improved player at the club. The emergence of all-rounder Ben Mike, who took nine wickets on his debut and 19 in four Championship matches at the end of the season, was another bonus, and will go some way to offsetting the loss of Raine and Chappell.

But the success of the bowlers should not gloss over the failures of the batsmen. Colin Ackermann began the season in outstanding form, with 186 in the opener against Sussex and an unbeaten career-best 196 against Middlesex. But they were Leicestershire's only two first-class centuries of the season, and Ackermann's 876 runs at 39 was almost 300 more than the next man. Mark Cosgrove, who had passed 1,000 in each of his previous three seasons with the county, managed only 440. His contributions were seriously missed.

The Vitality Blast was a mixed bag. At home, Leicestershire were miserable, with just one win, even if it was against the eventual champions, Worcestershire. Away from Grace Road it was a different story. There were victories at Northampton, Edgbaston, Trent Bridge and Old Trafford, where overseas signing Mohammad Nabi, the Afghanistan all-rounder, played his only match-winning innings. There was less variety in the Royal London results: two wins out of eight lived down to gloomy expectations.

Along with Wright, the other new arrivals were Will Davis from Derbyshire, a pace bowler of promise, and all-rounder Arron Lilley from Lancashire. Departures included Rob Sayer, Tom Wells and Mark Pettini. Another to leave was wicketkeeper Ned Eckersley, who had been the club's longest-serving player.

Championship attendance: 9,757.

LEICESTERSHIRE RESULTS

All first-class matches – Played 14: Won 5, Lost 7, Drawn 2.
County Championship matches – Played 14: Won 5, Lost 7, Drawn 2.

Specsavers County Championship, 6th in Division 2;
Vitality Blast, 8th in North Group; Royal London One-Day Cup, 8th in North Group.

COUNTY CHAMPIONSHIP AVERAGES, BATTING AND FIELDING

Cap		Birthplace	M	I	NO	R	HS	100	Avge	Ct
	Z. J. Chappell	Grantham	4	5	2	145	40	0	48.33	1
	C. N. Ackermann††	George, SA	14	24	2	876	196*	0	39.81	10
	N. J. Dexter	Johannesburg, SA	12	20	3	585	87	0	34.41	9
	D. Klein††	Lichtenburg, SA	5	9	3	202	94	0	33.66	2
	†M. A. Carberry	Croydon	4	6	0	193	73	0	32.16	1
	P. J. Horton	Sydney, Australia	12	22	1	594	88	0	28.28	3
	G. T. Griffiths	Ormskirk	12	18	8	225	40	0	22.50	2
	†H. E. Dearden	Bury	10	18	2	357	74	0	22.31	6
2018	†B. A. Raine	Sunderland	11	17	0	371	65	0	21.82	5
	L. J. Hill	Leicester‡	9	15	2	241	85	0	18.53	29
2015	†M. J. Cosgrove††	Elizabeth, Aust	14	24	0	440	75	0	18.33	6
2013	E. J. H. Eckersley	Oxford	7	12	0	220	74	0	18.33	26
	A. Javid	Birmingham	6	10	0	157	58	0	15.70	2
	C. F. Parkinson	Bolton	12	19	1	252	48	0	14.00	1
	B. W. M. Mike	Nottingham	4	7	0	96	39	0	13.71	2
	S. T. Evans	Leicester‡	3	5	0	50	29	0	10.00	1
2018	Mohammad Abbas¶	Sialkot, Pakistan	10	15	6	84	32*	0	9.33	1
	V. R. Aaron¶	Jamshedpur, India	3	5	1	14	8	0	3.50	0

Also batted: U. Arshad (*Bradford*) (1 match) 9, 0; R. A. Jones (*Stourbridge*) (1 match) 0 (1 ct); †D. W. Sayer (*Huntingdon*) (1 match) 6, 21 (2 ct); T. A. I. Taylor (*Stoke-on-Trent*) (1 match) 5, 26.

‡ *Born in Leicestershire.* § *ECB contract.* ¶ *Official overseas player.* †† *Other non-England-qualified.*

BOWLING

	Style	O	M	R	W	BB	5I	Avge
Z. J. Chappell	RFM	76	13	255	16	6-44	1	15.93
Mohammad Abbas	RFM	345.1	101	886	50	6-48	5	17.72
B. W. M. Mike	RFM	87.2	10	385	19	5-37	1	20.26
B. A. Raine	RFM	395.1	90	1,146	51	4-44	0	22.47
G. T. Griffiths	RFM	269	67	882	36	6-49	1	24.50
N. J. Dexter	RM	169	40	494	18	3-17	0	27.44
C. F. Parkinson	SLA	239	42	824	10	3-50	0	82.40

Also bowled: V. R. Aaron (RM) 86–11–359–9; C. N. Ackermann (OB) 43.3–5–137–9; U. Arshad (RFM) 16–2–81–0; M. A. Carberry (OB) 2–0–7–0; M. J. Cosgrove (RM) 3–0–8–0; A. Javid (OB) 26.2–3–78–2; R. A. Jones (RFM) 13–1–44–1; D. Klein (LFM) 94–17–400–5; D. W. Sayer (LM) 5–1–28–0; T. A. I. Taylor (RFM) 34–11–92–6.

LEADING ROYAL LONDON CUP AVERAGES (150 runs/4 wickets)

Batting	Runs	HS	Avge	SR	Ct	Bowling		W	BB	Avge	ER
T. J. Wells	198	69	49.50	106.45	1	Z. J. Chappell		5	3-45	24.80	5.39
M. J. Cosgrove	317	84	45.28	95.77	1	N. J. Dexter		6	2-46	26.66	6.31
C. N. Ackermann	286	71*	40.85	89.09	5	G. T. Griffiths		8	4-30	27.87	6.96
P. J. Horton	284	103	35.50	79.55	4	B. A. Raine		7	3-31	40.71	5.41
C. S. Delport	174	122	34.80	95.60	3	V. R. Aaron		7	4-31	46.57	6.39
B. A. Raine	166	83	27.66	114.48	2						

LEADING VITALITY BLAST AVERAGES (100 runs/15 overs)

Batting	Runs	HS	Avge	SR	Ct	**Bowling**	W	BB	Avge	ER
B. A. Raine.....	332	113	25.53	**168.52**	4	Mohammad Nabi .	9	2-13	35.88	**7.28**
Mohammad Nabi	246	86*	24.60	**143.85**	2	C. F. Parkinson ..	15	4-20	21.53	**7.69**
C. N. Ackermann	343	74	31.18	**137.75**	6	G. T. Griffiths	5	3-28	34.20	**8.14**
N. J. Dexter	296	56	22.76	**137.03**	3	Mohammad Abbas	7	3-32	39.71	**8.96**
C. S. Delport....	177	33	19.66	**126.42**	4	Z. J. Chappell	12	3-23	28.50	**9.58**
M. J. Cosgrove ..	234	65	18.00	**113.59**	2	B. A. Raine	10	2-28	40.90	**10.71**

FIRST-CLASS COUNTY RECORDS

Highest score for	309*	H. D. Ackerman v Glamorgan at Cardiff......	2006
Highest score against	355*	K. P. Pietersen (Surrey) at The Oval	2015
Leading run-scorer	30,143	L. G. Berry (avge 30.32)	1924–51
Best bowling for	10-18	G. Geary v Glamorgan at Pontypridd	1929
Best bowling against	10-32	H. Pickett (Essex) at Leyton	1895
Leading wicket-taker	2,131	W. E. Astill (avge 23.18).................	1906–39
Highest total for	701-4 dec	v Worcestershire at Worcester.............	1906
Highest total against	761-6 dec	by Essex at Chelmsford	1990
Lowest total for	25	v Kent at Leicester.....................	1912
Lowest total against	{ 24	by Glamorgan at Leicester...............	1971
	{ 24	by Oxford University at Oxford............	1985

LIST A COUNTY RECORDS

Highest score for	201	V. J. Wells v Berkshire at Leicester.........	1996
Highest score against	201*	R. S. Bopara (Essex) at Leicester..........	2008
Leading run-scorer	8,216	N. E. Briers (avge 27.66).................	1975–95
Best bowling for	6-16	C. M. Willoughby v Somerset at Leicester ...	2005
Best bowling against	6-21	S. M. Pollock (Warwickshire) at Birmingham .	1996
Leading wicket-taker	308	K. Higgs (avge 18.80)	1972–82
Highest total for	406-5	v Berkshire at Leicester..................	1996
Highest total against	**458-4**	**by India A at Leicester**.................	**2018**
Lowest total for	36	v Sussex at Leicester	1973
Lowest total against	{ 62	by Northamptonshire at Leicester	1974
	{ 62	by Middlesex at Leicester	1998

TWENTY20 COUNTY RECORDS

Highest score for	113	**B. A. Raine v Warwickshire at Birmingham**.	**2018**
Highest score against	103*	A. N. Petersen (Lancashire) at Leicester.......	2016
Leading run-scorer	1,455	P. A. Nixon (avge 21.71, SR 115.75)	2003–11
Best bowling for	5-11	C. J. McKay v Worcestershire at Worcester ...	2017
Best bowling against	5-21	J. A. Brooks (Yorkshire) at Leeds	2013
Leading wicket-taker	69	C. W. Henderson (avge 26.95, ER 6.92)......	2004–12
Highest total for	**229-5**	**v Warwickshire at Birmingham**	**2018**
Highest total against	225-2	by Durham at Chester-le-Street	2010
Lowest total for	90	v Nottinghamshire at Nottingham	2014
Lowest total against	72	by Derbyshire at Derby	2013

ADDRESS

Fischer County Ground, Grace Road, Leicester LE2 8EB; 0116 283 2128; enquiries@leicester-shireccc.co.uk; www.leicestershireccc.co.uk.

OFFICIALS

Captain 2018 M. A. Carberry
2019 P. J. Horton
(Twenty20) C. N. Ackermann
Head coach P. A. Nixon
Assistant coach J. L. Sadler
Academy director A. P. Siddall

President D. W. Wilson
Chairman P. R. Haywood
Chief executive 2018 W. G. Khan
2019 K. Rothery
Head groundsman A. B. Ward
Scorer P. J. Rogers

At Leicester, April 13–15 (not first-class). **Drawn. Leicestershire 277-6 dec** (63.4 overs) (M. J. Cosgrove 91, N. J. Dexter 66*, B. A. Raine 50*; C. W. G. Sanders 3-82) **and 3-0** (0.2 overs); ‡**Loughborough MCCU 155** (62.5 overs) (G. T. Griffiths 4-44). *County debut: Mohammad Abbas. After a wet outfield caused the first day to be abandoned, a brisk 91 from Cosgrove saved Leicestershire from embarrassment. They had lost four wickets for 16 to the swing and seam of Loughborough opening pair Chris Sanders and William Pereira, but unbeaten half-centuries from Neil Dexter and Ben Raine completed the recovery. Gavin Griffiths then demonstrated the effectiveness of his remodelled action before the weather had the last word.*

LEICESTERSHIRE v SUSSEX

At Leicester, April 20–23. Drawn. Leicestershire 10pts, Sussex 9pts. Toss: Sussex. County debut: A. Javid. Championship debut: Mohammad Abbas.

A dry, pale pitch brought the early-season rarity of a toss. And after Raine bowled Wright and Robinson with consecutive balls to leave Sussex 240 for seven, Brown must have wondered if he had done the right thing in batting. A stand of 153 between Burgess, released by Leicestershire in 2016, and Sharma, with his maiden half-century, allayed those fears; Burgess completed his second first-class hundred. Leicestershire responded strongly, as Ackermann – dropped on 41 by Wright off Wiese – made 186, one short of his highest score. Unusually for April, leg-spinners Wells and Beer bowled in tandem and, despite a lack of encouragement from the pitch, Wells finished with a career-best four for 81, before Carberry declared on the third evening, 16 behind. Sussex still had to work to secure the draw, with Pakistan seamer Mohammad Abbas providing a searching examination. Wells was marooned on his overnight seven for 70 minutes, and it said much for his application that he progressed to an unbeaten century.

Close of play: first day, Sussex 254-7 (Burgess 7, Sharma 8); second day, Leicestershire 112-2 (Ackermann 61, Cosgrove 12); third day, Sussex 11-0 (Wells 7, Salt 3).

Sussex

L. W. P. Wells c Hill b Raine.............	2	– not out	102
P. D. Salt c Hill b Mohammad Abbas	21	– b Mohammad Abbas	17
S. van Zyl c Ackermann b Parkinson...........	44	– lbw b Griffiths	24
H. Z. Finch c Ackermann b Dexter	14	– lbw b Raine	22
L. J. Wright b Raine.................	88	– b Javid	29
*†B. C. Brown c Horton b Mohammad Abbas......	64	– not out	25
M. G. K. Burgess not out..................	101		
O. E. Robinson b Raine	0		
I. Sharma c Griffiths b Javid.............	66		
D. Wiese not out	19		
B 9, lb 8, nb 2	19	B 8, lb 10, nb 4........	22

1/23 (1) 2/25 (2) (8 wkts dec, 143 overs) 438 1/27 (2) (4 wkts dec, 83 overs) 241
3/52 (4) 4/115 (3) 5/234 (6) 2/63 (3) 3/119 (4)
6/240 (5) 7/240 (8) 8/393 (9) 4/179 (5)
110 overs: 315-7

W. A. T. Beer did not bat.

Mohammad Abbas 32–10–61–2; Griffiths 26–8–69–0; Raine 32–6–104–3; Dexter 16–5–63–1; Parkinson 24–4–81–1; Javid 13–0–43–1. *Second innings*—Mohammad Abbas 17–8–37–1; Raine 18–6–42–1; Parkinson 26–5–73–0; Griffiths 10–1–41–1; Javid 12–3–30–1.

Leicestershire

*M. A. Carberry lbw b Sharma...........	32	G. T. Griffiths not out	5
P. J. Horton lbw b Sharma..............	0	Mohammad Abbas not out	5
C. N. Ackermann c Finch b Wells........	186		
M. J. Cosgrove c and b Wells...........	64	B 12, lb 6, w 5, nb 8	31
A. Javid lbw b Wiese..................	13		
N. J. Dexter c Brown b Wells	34	1/7 (2) 2/73 (1) (9 wkts dec, 135 overs) 422
†L. J. Hill lbw b Wells................	8	3/214 (4) 4/253 (5)
B. A. Raine c Brown b Sharma	40	5/328 (6) 6/345 (7) 7/406 (3)
C. F. Parkinson c Brown b Beer	4	8/410 (8) 9/417 (9) 110 overs: 336-5

Sharma 29–5–85–3; Robinson 27–9–72–0; Wiese 23–5–63–1; Beer 26–3–88–1; van Zyl 3–0–15–0; Wells 27–2–81–4.

Umpires: P. K. Baldwin and A. G. Wharf.

LEICESTERSHIRE v DERBYSHIRE

At Leicester, April 27–30. Drawn. Leicestershire 11pts, Derbyshire 10pts. Toss: uncontested. County debut: V. R. Aaron.

After the weather stole seven sessions, the match became a scrap for bonus points. Leicestershire shaded it, but there was controversy when Godleman declared after Derbyshire passed 250, with two wickets in hand and six balls left, denying Leicestershire the chance of a further bowling point. They felt this contravened the regulation about extraordinary declarations, but the ECB disagreed. After being put in, Leicestershire had rattled along. Raine's clean striking looked set to earn full batting point, until he was run out in a mix-up with Klein, who might have sacrificed himself. Raine also shone in the field, taking two wickets and a pair of fine catches. Wilson took Derbyshire to a second batting point – and the declaration.

Close of play: first day, no play; second day, no play; third day, Leicestershire 267-5 (Eckersley 40, Dexter 22).

Leicestershire

*M. A. Carberry c Madsen b Reece	45	D. Klein not out	19
P. J. Horton c Madsen b Reece	66	G. T. Griffiths lbw b Davis	0
C. N. Ackermann b Critchley	65	V. R. Aaron lbw b Viljoen	1
M. J. Cosgrove c Slater b Reece	11		
†E. J. H. Eckersley c sub (C. A. J. Brodrick) b Rampaul	54	B 4, lb 5, nb 14	23
L. J. Hill c Wilson b Davis	3	1/94 (1) 2/157 (2) 3/179 (4) (96 overs) 381
N. J. Dexter b Olivier	47	4/210 (3) 5/219 (6) 6/301 (7)
B. A. Raine run out (Davis)	47	7/336 (5) 8/366 (8) 9/374 (10) 10/381 (11)

Rampaul 20–3–82–1; Viljoen 11–2–35–1; Davis 11–3–39–2; Olivier 20–1–94–1; Reece 16–2–64–3; Critchley 18–1–58–1.

Derbyshire

B. T. Slater c Eckersley b Raine	27	W. S. Davis c and b Ackermann	6
L. M. Reece lbw b Raine	0	R. Rampaul not out	3
W. L. Madsen lbw b Aaron	0		
A. L. Hughes b Dexter	42	Lb 11, nb 10	21
*B. A. Godleman lbw b Griffiths	7		
†G. C. Wilson not out	64	1/8 (2) 2/9 (3) (8 wkts dec, 68 overs) 251
M. J. Critchley c Raine b Griffiths	38	3/43 (1) 4/54 (5)
G. C. Viljoen c Raine b Ackermann	43	5/104 (4) 6/164 (7) 7/224 (8) 8/242 (9)

D. Olivier did not bat.

Aaron 17–5–54–1; Raine 16–1–65–2; Griffiths 11–3–29–2; Klein 9–1–36–0; Ackermann 6–0–36–2; Dexter 9–1–20–1.

Umpires: J. H. Evans and M. A. Gough.

At Chester-le-Street, May 4–7. LEICESTERSHIRE lost to DURHAM by 46 runs.

LEICESTERSHIRE v GLAMORGAN

At Leicester, May 11–13. Leicestershire won by three runs. Leicestershire 17pts (after 2pt penalty), Glamorgan 2pts (after 1pt penalty). Toss: Leicestershire.

Leicestershire clinched their first first-class win in 19 matches – since beating the same opponents in September 2016 – in storybook fashion, when Parkinson held a steepling catch at long-on to dismiss de Lange. His refusal to accept a lost cause had almost carried Glamorgan to an extraordinary victory. Coming in at seven down with 144 still needed, he launched a furious counter-attack. Several of his eight sixes cleared the stands; one smashed a window in the umpires' room. He put on 56 with van der Gugten and 52 with Hogan and sailed past his previous best of 65 before he perished attempting to hit a full toss for the winning boundary. "I'd been striking it so nicely," he said. Leicestershire had been indebted to Dexter's calm 87 on the first day after the Glamorgan seamers had reduced them to 67 for six. Glamorgan were cruising at 82 without loss, but lost all ten for 96. Half-centuries for Horton and Raine then lifted the target to 251, which appeared too many until de Lange's intervention. The match ended just before seven on the third day, but both teams were deducted points for a slow over-rate, even though Leicestershire had spent time in the final session looking for the ball behind the stands.

Close of play: first day, Glamorgan 82-0 (Selman 39, Murphy 32); second day, Leicestershire 119-2 (Ackermann 18, Cosgrove 25).

Leicestershire

*M. A. Carberry c Cooke b Hogan	1	– c Cooke b de Lange 20
P. J. Horton lbw b van der Gugten	7	– lbw b Lloyd 50
C. N. Ackermann c Hogan b van der Gugten	0	– c Lloyd b Hogan 22
M. J. Cosgrove lbw b de Lange	14	– c Cooke b Hogan 33
A. Javid c Cooke b Lloyd	13	– lbw b Hogan 1
N. J. Dexter c Murphy b Salter	87	– c Cooke b Hogan 4
†L. J. Hill b de Lange	13	– b van der Gugten 8
B. A. Raine b Hogan	2	– c Donald b de Lange 65
C. F. Parkinson c Selman b Hogan	30	– c Cooke b de Lange 9
V. R. Aaron lbw b de Lange	0	– (11) not out 5
G. T. Griffiths not out	0	– (10) c Cooke b Hogan 4
B 1, lb 14, w 1, nb 8	24	B 5, lb 9, nb 2 16

1/9 (2) 2/9 (3) 3/9 (1)   (69.1 overs) 191   1/62 (1) 2/76 (2)   (77 overs) 237
4/33 (4) 5/45 (5) 6/67 (8)   3/127 (3) 4/132 (4)
7/147 (9) 8/181 (7) 9/191 (10) 10/191 (6)   5/133 (5) 6/142 (6) 7/158 (7)
                                                            8/198 (9) 9/205 (10) 10/237 (8)

In the first innings Hill, when 3, retired hurt at 62-5 and resumed at 147-7.

Van der Gugten 15–5–42–2; Hogan 16.3–3–41–3; Lloyd 14–5–24–1; de Lange 18–6–56–3; Salter 6.1–3–13–1. *Second innings*—van der Gugten 17–4–54–1; Hogan 29–8–61–5; de Lange 22–4–65–3; Lloyd 6–2–28–1; Salter 3–0–15–0.

Glamorgan

N. J. Selman b Aaron	40	– c Hill b Raine 2
J. R. Murphy c Horton b Raine	32	– b Raine 34
S. E. Marsh c Hill b Aaron	7	– b Griffiths 0
K. S. Carlson c Cosgrove b Dexter	14	– c Hill b Griffiths 1
A. H. T. Donald b Griffiths	14	– b Aaron 15
†C. B. Cooke b Griffiths	6	– c Hill b Raine 39
D. L. Lloyd c Raine b Dexter	15	– lbw b Aaron 4
A. G. Salter lbw b Aaron	9	– lbw b Griffiths 9
M. de Lange b Aaron	1	– c Parkinson b Raine 90
T. van der Gugten not out	19	– lbw b Parkinson 22
*M. G. Hogan c Carberry b Raine	4	– not out 7
B 8, lb 1, w 6, nb 2	17	B 6, lb 5, w 2, nb 6, p 5 24

1/82 (2) 2/90 (3) 3/91 (1)   (58.2 overs) 178   1/6 (1) 2/24 (3)   (56.4 overs) 247
4/118 (5) 5/129 (4) 6/133 (6)   3/38 (4) 4/51 (2)
7/145 (7) 8/148 (9) 9/159 (8) 10/178 (11)   5/70 (5) 6/81 (7) 7/107 (8)
                                                           8/139 (6) 9/195 (10) 10/247 (9)

Raine 17.2–5–38–2; Aaron 16–3–65–4; Griffiths 10–5–27–2; Dexter 13–3–35–2; Parkinson 2–1–4–0. *Second innings*—Raine 14.4–4–44–4; Aaron 14–1–66–2; Griffiths 13–6–51–3; Parkinson 10–1–49–1; Dexter 5–0–21–0.

Umpires: M. Burns and P. J. Hartley.

At Leicester, May 19–20. LEICESTERSHIRE drew with PAKISTANIS (see Pakistan tour section).

At Northampton, June 9–11. LEICESTERSHIRE beat NORTHAMPTONSHIRE by six wickets.

At Leicester, June 19. LEICESTERSHIRE lost to INDIA A by 281 runs (see India A tour section).

LEICESTERSHIRE v MIDDLESEX

At Leicester, June 20–23. Middlesex won by one wicket. Middlesex 19pts, Leicestershire 7pts. Toss: Leicestershire.

Middlesex inched over the line in the final session when Harris hit Mohammad Abbas for four to complete a stirring comeback and scupper Leicestershire's hopes of winning a second home nailbiter in a row. They had appeared on course for a third successive Championship victory in the same season for the first time since they won six to take the title in 1998. But Middlesex transformed the game following a frank dressing-room meeting on the second evening, after conceding a lead of 194. They began the last day 82 for three, still needing 299, and a key moment came before Cartwright had scored: Griffiths seamed one through his defence, nudging the off stump but failing to dislodge a bail. Cartwright went on to make 80, though he was involved in a mix-up which cost Eskinazi his wicket for 97. But Harris survived two missed chances and, with last man Murtagh calmness personified, steered Middlesex to victory with 6.3 overs remaining. Leicestershire's formidable first-innings total was built around a career-best from Ackermann. Raine and Chappell then ensured a healthy advantage and, although Middlesex bowled much better second time around, a target of 381 appeared well beyond them.

Close of play: first day, Leicestershire 353-8 (Ackermann 151, Griffiths 18); second day, Leicestershire 0-1 (Dearden 0); third day, Middlesex 82-3 (Eskinazi 35, Patel 0).

Leicestershire

H. E. Dearden c Cartwright b Finn	13	– c Simpson b Murtagh	6
*P. J. Horton b Murtagh	8	– b Harris	0
C. N. Ackermann not out	196	– b Harris	3
M. J. Cosgrove c Malan b Cartwright	16	– lbw b Holden	23
N. J. Dexter c Simpson b Murtagh	66	– st Simpson b Murtagh	38
†L. J. Hill c Robson b Murtagh	3	– b Harris	4
B. A. Raine c and b Patel	37	– c Simpson b Murtagh	36
Z. J. Chappell b Murtagh	16	– not out	37
C. F. Parkinson c Simpson b Murtagh	1	– lbw b Finn	2
G. T. Griffiths c Cartwright b Harris	40	– c Simpson b Cartwright	14
Mohammad Abbas c Malan b Cartwright	1	– c Harris b Patel	7
B 13, lb 10, w 1, nb 6	30	Lb 13, w 1, nb 2	16

1/17 (2) 2/25 (1) 3/65 (4)	(120.2 overs) 427	1/0 (2) 2/8 (3)	(69.4 overs) 186
4/194 (5) 5/198 (6) 6/262 (7)		3/32 (1) 4/51 (4)	
7/304 (8) 8/306 (9) 9/398 (10)		5/66 (6) 6/115 (7) 7/128 (5)	
10/427 (11)		8/133 (9) 9/156 (10) 10/186 (11)	

110 overs: 391-8

Murtagh 28–11–60–5; Finn 27–5–91–1; Cartwright 17.2–2–61–2; Harris 29–5–107–1; Patel 19–1–85–1. *Second innings*—Murtagh 18–6–27–3; Harris 17–2–43–3; Finn 14–2–32–1; Holden 5–2–15–1; Cartwright 9–0–38–1; Patel 6.4–1–18–1.

Middlesex

S. D. Robson c Dexter b Raine	15	– (2) lbw b Griffiths	31
M. D. E. Holden lbw b Mohammad Abbas	16	– (1) c Hill b Raine	0
S. S. Eskinazi b Chappell	10	– run out (Raine)	97
*D. J. Malan not out	78	– c Hill b Raine	12
P. R. Stirling c Dearden b Raine	52	– (6) c Hill b Griffiths	4
H. W. R. Cartwright c Cosgrove b Chappell	33	– (7) lbw b Raine	80
†J. A. Simpson lbw b Griffiths	2	– (8) lbw b Griffiths	39
J. A. R. Harris lbw b Chappell	5	– (9) not out	58
S. T. Finn lbw b Chappell	0	– (10) c Hill b Mohammad Abbas	9
R. H. Patel b Griffiths	0	– (5) c Hill b Mohammad Abbas	20
T. J. Murtagh b Raine	8	– not out	3
B 2, lb 4, nb 8	14	B 13, lb 8, w 1, nb 8	30

1/30 (2) 2/40 (1) 3/60 (3)   (64.2 overs) 233   1/0 (1)   (9 wkts, 117.3 overs) 383
4/140 (5) 5/200 (6) 6/203 (7)   2/51 (2) 3/79 (4)
7/212 (8) 8/212 (9) 9/213 (10) 10/233 (11)   4/134 (5) 5/149 (6) 6/197 (3)
                                                            7/284 (8) 8/343 (7) 9/374 (10)

Raine 17.2–4–53–3; Mohammad Abbas 13–4–29–1; Griffiths 15–2–63–2; Chappell 14–0–65–4;
Dexter 5–0–17–0. *Second innings*—Raine 34–7–89–3; Mohammad Abbas 31.3–5–99–2; Chappell
16–4–50–0; Griffiths 25–4–81–3; Dexter 4–0–24–0; Parkinson 7–2–19–0.

Umpires: G. D. Lloyd and P. R. Pollard.

At Derby, June 25–27. LEICESTERSHIRE beat DERBYSHIRE by six wickets.

At Canterbury, July 22–23. LEICESTERSHIRE beat KENT by ten wickets.

LEICESTERSHIRE v KENT

At Leicester, August 19–21. Kent won by eight wickets. Kent 19pts, Leicestershire 4pts. Toss:
uncontested. First-class debut: O. G. Robinson.

Urged by bowling coach Allan Donald to up his pace and aggression, Ivan Thomas twice produced
career-best figures as Kent exacted revenge for their thrashing at Canterbury a month earlier. Life
was fraught for batsmen from the off, with heavy cloud contributing to lavish swing under floodlights;
a pitch previously used for a T20 Blast fixture also assisted seam movement, though Leicestershire
mounted a recovery from 119 for seven. Thomas took four for 35, but perhaps his most significant
deed was to hit Chappell on the helmet; he retired and was replaced by Klein as a concussion
substitute. Chappell's pace and bounce might have prospered in the conditions, but Mohammad
Abbas and Raine filled the gap. Abbas took six for 48 as Leicestershire secured a slender lead,
although Thomas – with his first five-for – ensured they could not turn it into a position of command.
Dearden's application at least gave Kent what appeared a tricky target of 253 but, after Abbas struck
two early blows, the skies cleared and batting became easier. Dickson's belligerent 134 in an
unbroken stand of 215 with Kuhn steered Kent home with a day to spare.

Close of play: first day, Kent 53-3 (Denly 0, Billings 1); second day, Leicestershire 126-5 (Dearden
61, Raine 15).

Leicestershire

H. E. Dearden lbw b Stevens	12	– c Dickson b Stevens	74
*P. J. Horton b Podmore	49	– lbw b Stewart	8
C. N. Ackermann lbw b Stewart	11	– lbw b Thomas	31
M. J. Cosgrove b Thomas	4	– c Dickson b Thomas	0
A. Javid c Dickson b Denly	8	– c Billings b Thomas	8
†E. J. H. Eckersley lbw b Podmore	17	– lbw b Thomas	0
B. A. Raine b Podmore	0	– c Billings b Podmore	23
Z. J. Chappell retired hurt	31		
C. F. Parkinson c Billings b Thomas	7	– (8) c Kuhn b Thomas	8
G. T. Griffiths not out	20	– not out	16
Mohammad Abbas c Billings b Thomas	20	– c Thomas b Denly	9
D. Klein c Stewart b Thomas	11	– (9) lbw b Denly	41
B 5, lb 21, nb 4	30	Lb 7, nb 2	9

1/23 (1) 2/47 (3) 3/56 (4)   (68.3 overs) 220
4/79 (5) 5/114 (6) 6/114 (7)
7/119 (2) 8/149 (9) 9/202 (11) 10/220 (12)

1/13 (2) 2/82 (3)   (62.5 overs) 227
3/84 (4) 4/106 (5)
5/106 (6) 6/135 (7) 7/152 (8)
8/188 (1) 9/207 (9) 10/227 (11)

In the first innings Chappell retired hurt at 163-8; Klein replaced him, as a concussion substitute.

Podmore 17–2–68–3; Stevens 16–7–29–1; Stewart 17–3–42–1; Thomas 12.3–2–35–4; Denly 4–0–15–1; Bell-Drummond 2–0–5–0. *Second innings*—Stewart 12–1–32–1; Stevens 10–2–32–1; Podmore 16–2–55–1; Thomas 20–1–91–5; Denly 4.5–1–10–2.

Kent

D. J. Bell-Drummond c Eckersley b Mohammad Abbas	10	– c Eckersley b Mohammad Abbas	6
S. R. Dickson c Cosgrove b Raine	15	– not out	134
H. G. Kuhn c Raine b Mohammad Abbas	12	– (4) not out	96
J. L. Denly lbw b Raine	62		
*†S. W. Billings c Eckersley b Mohammad Abbas	5		
Z. Crawley c Eckersley b Mohammad Abbas	10		
O. G. Robinson c Eckersley b Raine	26		
D. I. Stevens c Eckersley b Raine	0		
H. W. Podmore b Mohammad Abbas	16		
G. Stewart c Javid b Mohammad Abbas	12	– (3) b Mohammad Abbas	12
I. A. A. Thomas not out	2		
B 8, lb 15, nb 2	25	B 4, lb 1	5

1/24 (2) 2/37 (3) 3/46 (1)   (52.2 overs) 195
4/86 (5) 5/100 (6) 6/157 (7)
7/157 (8) 8/164 (9) 9/188 (9) 10/195 (10)

1/22 (1)   (2 wkts, 54.2 overs) 253
2/38 (3)

Mohammad Abbas 17.2–4–48–6; Raine 21–8–62–4; Griffiths 7–1–33–0; Klein 7–1–29–0. *Second innings*—Mohammad Abbas 14–4–50–2; Raine 11–4–25–0; Griffiths 6–1–45–0; Klein 8–0–37–0; Parkinson 11–0–72–0; Cosgrove 1–0–6–0; Ackermann 2–0–8–0; Javid 1.2–0–5–0.

Umpires: N. L. Bainton and J. W. Lloyds.

At Bristol, August 29–September 1. LEICESTERSHIRE lost to GLOUCESTERSHIRE by 328 runs.

At Hove, September 4–6. LEICESTERSHIRE lost to SUSSEX by 274 runs.

LEICESTERSHIRE v WARWICKSHIRE

At Leicester, September 10–12. Warwickshire won by an innings and 104 runs. Warwickshire 24pts, Leicestershire 3pts. Toss: uncontested. First-class debut: D. W. Sayer. County debut: U. Arshad.

With injury depriving them of six seamers, Leicestershire lacked more than confidence against the Division Two leaders. They gave debuts to 20-year-old David Sayer and triallist Usman Arshad, previously of Durham; Warwickshire, by contrast, included the fit-again Woakes. The outcome was predictably one-sided. Leicestershire were blown away – not helped by the run-out of Cosgrove – as Barker and Woakes relished helpful conditions, and Stone bowled faster than anyone at Grace Road all summer. Before the close, Sibley had eclipsed Leicestershire's score off his own bat, a skittish first fifty followed by more restrained progress to three figures. Rain restricted the second day, when Hain and Woakes helped Warwickshire towards maximum batting points, before the declaration. Leicestershire batted with more application, but Barker was almost unplayable, and Patel passed 50 wickets for the season to earn his team a day off. Victory took Warwickshire to the brink of promotion.

Close of play: first day, Warwickshire 190-3 (Trott 34, Hain 2); second day, Warwickshire 384-9 (Woakes 64, Patel 2).

Leicestershire

H. E. Dearden c Ambrose b Barker	3	– lbw b Patel	29
*P. J. Horton b Woakes	19	– b Barker	9
C. N. Ackermann lbw b Barker	12	– b Barker	16
M. J. Cosgrove run out (Woakes)	4	– lbw b Barker	0
N. J. Dexter c Ambrose b Woakes	1	– b Wright b Patel	15
A. Javid b Barker	0	– lbw b Patel	24
†E. J. H. Eckersley b Stone	13	– b Barker	23
B. W. M. Mike c Wright b Stone	23	– c Patel b Stone	39
U. Arshad c Woakes b Stone	9	– lbw b Patel	0
D. W. Sayer b Wright	6	– b Barker	21
Mohammad Abbas not out	0	– not out	0
B 4, lb 4, nb 2	10	B 9, lb 5, nb 6	20

1/10 (1) 2/26 (3) 3/42 (2) (32.1 overs) 100
4/42 (4) 5/43 (6) 6/45 (5)
7/76 (7) 8/94 (9) 9/95 (8) 10/100 (10)

1/21 (1) 2/41 (3) (60.4 overs) 196
3/41 (4) 4/69 (1)
5/78 (5) 6/123 (6) 7/145 (7)
8/158 (9) 9/195 (10) 10/196 (8)

Barker 11–4–23–3; Woakes 9–2–27–2; Stone 7–1–24–3; Wright 5.1–1–18–1. *Second innings*—Barker 15–4–40–5; Woakes 12–1–59–0; Wright 6–4–3–0; Patel 20–2–67–4; Stone 7.4–3–13–1.

Warwickshire

W. M. H. Rhodes lbw b Dexter	37	O. P. Stone b Mohammad Abbas	0
D. P. Sibley lbw b Mike	106	*J. S. Patel not out	9
I. R. Bell lbw b Mohammad Abbas	1		
I. J. L. Trott c Eckersley b Mike	42	B 3, lb 3, w 9, nb 8	23
S. R. Hain lbw b Mike	72		
†T. R. Ambrose c Eckersley b Ackermann	28	1/123 (1) (9 wkts dec, 109.4 overs) 400
C. R. Woakes not out	73	2/126 (3) 3/184 (2)
K. H. D. Barker c Sayer b Ackermann	9	4/214 (4) 5/269 (6) 6/344 (5)
C. J. C. Wright c Sayer b Mohammad Abbas	0	7/376 (8) 8/380 (9) 9/380 (10)

Mohammad Abbas 26–7–70–3; Sayer 5–1–28–0; Arshad 16–2–81–0; Mike 25.4–6–112–3; Dexter 26–7–72–1; Ackermann 11–2–31–2.

Umpires: P. K. Baldwin and G. D. Lloyd.

LEICESTERSHIRE v DURHAM

At Leicester, September 18–19. Leicestershire won by an innings and 194 runs. Leicestershire 22pts, Durham 3pts. Toss: uncontested.

Durham suffered the humiliation of losing 20 wickets in 52.3 overs and slumping to their two lowest first-class scores on the same day. "I'm struggling to find the words – it's just unacceptable," said head coach Jon Lewis after they were bundled out for 61 and 66. "It was embarrassing, and that's not a word I have had to use before." In his final appearance of the summer, a rampant Mohammad Abbas took ten for 52 to reach 50 Championship wickets and complete an outstanding first season for Leicestershire. Last man out to a poor stroke early on the second morning after a consistent performance in which his ten team-mates all reached double figures, he had promised to make amends with the ball. He was as good as his word, trapping Steel with his fourth delivery and taking three wickets in four balls in his sixth over to single-handedly reduce Durham to 18 for five.

LOWEST CHAMPIONSHIP AGGREGATES SINCE 1970

90	Glamorgan (24 and 66) v Leicestershire (209-8 dec) at Leicester	1971
103	Yorkshire (60 and 43) v Surrey (268-9 dec) at The Oval	1973
121	Sussex (67 and 54) v Kent (282-5 dec) at Hastings	1973
121	Sussex (54 and 67) v Glamorgan (172 and 183-9 dec) at Swansea	1997
126	Hampshire (70 and 56) v Nottinghamshire (180 and 218-5 dec) at Nottingham.	1982
127	**Durham* (61 and 66) v Leicestershire (321) at Leicester**	**2018**
129	Derbyshire* (42 and 87) v Lancashire (477-5) at Buxton	1975

* *One batsman absent ill.*

Bowling from the Bennett End with a strong wind behind him – though he denied it helped him – he added half a yard of pace to his customary mastery of swing and seam. Six successive maidens from Dexter maintained the pressure, and Durham were all out for 61, six short of their previous lowest score, against Middlesex at Lord's in 1996. Following on, they fared little better; opener Lees's first-innings 16 was their highest score of a dismal day. Abbas, who received his cap, announced his intention to return to Leicestershire in 2019.

Close of play: first day, Leicestershire 316-8 (Hill 42, Griffiths 21).

Leicestershire

A. Javid lbw b Rushworth	58	C. F. Parkinson c Poyner b Wood	13
S. T. Evans lbw b Rushworth	10	G. T. Griffiths b Salisbury	23
*C. N. Ackermann c Poyner b McCarthy. . .	18	Mohammad Abbas lbw b Salisbury	0
M. J. Cosgrove b Salisbury	38	B 7, lb 16	23
H. E. Dearden c Poyner b Wood	32		
N. J. Dexter lbw b Harte	43	1/31 (2) 2/66 (3) 3/118 (1) (97.5 overs) 321
†L. J. Hill not out.	43	4/139 (4) 5/216 (6) 6/216 (5)
B. W. M. Mike lbw b Harte.	20	7/256 (8) 8/292 (9) 9/319 (10) 10/321 (11)

Rushworth 21–7–66–2; Salisbury 18.5–2–79–3; McCarthy 18–2–61–1; Wood 19–5–35–2; Collingwood 9–2–18–0; Harte 9–1–26–2; Steel 3–0–13–0.

Durham

C. T. Steel lbw b Mohammad Abbas	0	– b Mohammad Abbas	5
A. Z. Lees c Dearden b Griffiths	16	– lbw b Dexter.	10
G. J. Harte c Dexter b Mohammad Abbas	5	– c Hill b Mohammad Abbas	5
G. Clark b Mohammad Abbas	4	– c Javid b Dexter	0
M. J. Richardson b Mohammad Abbas	0	– b Mohammad Abbas	8
*P. D. Collingwood c Ackermann b Mohammad Abbas .	0	– b Mohammad Abbas	5
†S. W. Poyner c Dearden b Dexter.	0	– c Evans b Dexter	4
M. A. Wood b Mike	5	– not out	15
B. J. McCarthy c Hill b Griffiths	14	– c Hill b Mike	1
M. E. T. Salisbury c Hill b Mike	2	– b Griffiths	5
C. Rushworth not out	4	– b Mohammad Abbas	7
B 4, lb 5, nb 2	11	B 1	1

1/0 (1) 2/14 (3) 3/18 (4)   (28 overs) 61   1/10 (1) 2/20 (2)   (24.3 overs) 66
4/18 (5) 5/18 (6) 6/21 (7)   3/20 (4) 4/20 (3)
7/30 (8) 8/48 (2) 9/53 (10) 10/61 (9)   5/29 (5) 6/34 (7) 7/38 (6)
                                           8/50 (9) 9/59 (10) 10/66 (11)

Mohammad Abbas 8–2–23–5; Dexter 7–6–1–1; Griffiths 7–3–10–2; Mike 6–0–18–2. *Second innings*—Mohammad Abbas 10.3–4–29–5; Dexter 7–3–17–3; Griffiths 5–2–11–1; Mike 2–0–8–1.

Umpires: N. L. Bainton and D. J. Millns.

At Cardiff, September 24–26. LEICESTERSHIRE lost to GLAMORGAN by 132 runs.

MIDDLESEX

Send for the Law

KEVIN HAND

After the shock of relegation in 2017, Middlesex – champions the previous year – were widely expected to make an instant return. But that never looked likely during a disappointing season that led to the departure of head coach Richard Scott after nine years. He was told midway through the summer that his contract would not be renewed, and decided to leave immediately. His swansong was defeat in a pink-ball match at Canterbury, which he described as a farce: "This hasn't been a fair game of cricket, because it was very much dependent on the toss."

By the time he departed, promotion was already improbable. It had been obvious for some time that change was needed: the 2017 defence of the title had been a non-starter, and the first half of 2018 tepid. Fortunes quickly improved under interim coach Richard Johnson, with a dramatic win over Warwickshire at Lord's, but the subsequent charge was too late.

The season had begun with news that Nick Compton, the former Test batsman, would not be considered for selection, even though it was his benefit year. To no surprise, he retired at the end of the summer, although he will continue to be associated with Middlesex in an ambassadorial role. There were times when his calm head might have been useful at the top of the order: Sam Robson averaged only 27 in the Championship, while the highly rated Nick Gubbins missed the first month with a hamstring injury. No one averaged more in four-day cricket than Stevie Eskinazi's 35, and there were just four centuries.

Some had doubts when Dawid Malan was appointed captain: he had been one of the few successes of England's Ashes tour, so seemed unlikely to feature much. Though rested for the first two four-day games, he was jettisoned from the Test side in August. The man he replaced, the 2016 title-winning skipper James Franklin, did not make a single Championship appearance, but did feature in most of the white-ball matches.

After failing to secure an IPL deal, Eoin Morgan had hoped to return to regular Championship action, but broke his hand in pre-season nets. He eventually appeared in six four-day games, and averaged 11. This, plus Malan's expected absence, caused Middlesex's embattled director of cricket, Angus Fraser, to backtrack on the original decision to do without an overseas player. Australia's Hilton Cartwright was signed primarily as a batsman, but struggled in early-season conditions. His bowling made more impression, until his penultimate Championship match against Leicestershire when – having survived on nought because the bails stayed put after the ball hit the stumps – he scored 80 to turn the game on its head; Middlesex scraped home by one wicket. Two months later, they pulled off an even more remarkable victory at Northampton, where – following on – they were only seven ahead with four wickets in hand. But a dull draw at Bristol in early September, when Gloucestershire stubbornly refused to manufacture a run-chase, ended faint hopes of going up.

Morgan was not the only one of the physio's table. Toby Roland-Jones was ruled out for the season after just the second match, at Derby, with a recurrence of the back stress fractures which had robbed him of an Ashes tour. James Harris also limped out of that game, although he recovered to take 61 Championship wickets, three more than the evergreen Tim Murtagh, now aged 37. It was probably at Derby that the players

Dawid Malan

first realised the second division was not going to be a pushover, as they faced an attack led by Duanne Olivier, Ravi Rampaul and Hardus Viljoen, all fast bowlers with Test experience.

White-ball cricket did not offer much encouragement. Along with Championship promotion, Fraser had targeted qualification from both limited-overs groups – but they fell well short in each. In the Royal London Cup, Middlesex burnished rather than buried their reputation as a "50–50 team" by winning four games and losing four, to finish sixth out of nine. And it was worse in the T20 Blast, where they finished rock bottom, with two wins to set against a dozen defeats.

Despite the improvement under Johnson, Fraser felt Middlesex needed a new broom. His search ended with the appointment of Stuart Law, the straight-talking Australian who cut short his time in charge of West Indies because he wanted to spend more time with his family, who had settled in England. His first signing was Afghanistan's teenage mystery spinner Mujeeb Zadran for the Blast. Law's arrival, as coach in all formats, also meant an early departure for New Zealander Daniel Vettori, after two years of a three-season deal in charge of the misfiring Twenty20 team; Johnson joined Surrey as bowling coach.

Reviving the spirit of 2016, and the upward curve that led to it, will be a priority. The first thing that needs to improve is the batting, no easy task given the preponderance of Championship fixtures on green, early-season pitches. But Law's approach will be keenly watched, as he tries to meld a team containing several current or aspiring internationals. The cast list remains roughly the same, although pace bowler James Fuller moved on to Hampshire, and slow left-armer Ravi Patel was released.

Championship attendance: 45,824.

MIDDLESEX RESULTS

All first-class matches – Played 15: Won 7, Lost 4, Drawn 4.
County Championship matches – Played 14: Won 7, Lost 4, Drawn 3.

Specsavers County Championship, 4th in Division 2;
Vitality Blast, 9th in South Group; Royal London One-Day Cup, 6th in South Group.

COUNTY CHAMPIONSHIP AVERAGES, BATTING AND FIELDING

Cap		Birthplace	M	I	NO	R	HS	100	Avge	Ct/St
2018	S. S. Eskinazi††	Johannesburg, SA . .	12	22	1	740	97	0	35.23	16
2016	†N. R. T. Gubbins	Richmond	9	17	0	585	107	1	34.41	2
2015	J. A. R. Harris	Morriston	12	22	8	454	79*	0	32.42	6
	†M. D. E. Holden	Cambridge	13	24	3	632	119*	1	30.09	4
2010	†D. J. Malan	Roehampton	12	22	1	613	119	1	29.19	12
2013	S. D. Robson	Paddington, Aust.. .	13	24	1	633	134	1	27.52	7
	T. G. Helm	Stoke Mandeville . .	4	6	2	102	52	0	25.50	2
2011	†J. A. Simpson	Bury	8	14	0	309	39	0	22.07	23/3
2012	T. S. Roland-Jones§ . .	Ashford‡	2	4	0	79	46	0	19.75	0
	J. K. Fuller††	Cape Town, SA . . .	8	16	3	242	71	0	18.61	3
2016	P. R. Stirling	Belfast, N. Ireland .	6	11	0	199	52	0	18.09	4
	M. K. Andersson	Reading	3	6	2	72	34	0	18.00	0
	H. W. R. Cartwright¶	Harare, Zimbabwe .	7	12	0	204	80	0	17.00	7
2008	†T. J. Murtagh††	Lambeth	11	19	4	200	40	0	13.33	3
2015	O. P. Rayner	Fallingbostel, Ger. .	9	15	2	172	28	0	13.23	14
2008	†E. J. G. Morgan§	Dublin, Ireland	6	11	0	121	76	0	11.00	4
	E. R. Bamber	Westminster‡	6	10	3	76	27*	0	10.85	2
2009	S. T. Finn	Watford	4	6	0	50	27	0	8.33	0
	R. H. Patel	Harrow‡	2	4	0	33	20	0	8.25	1
	R. G. White	Ealing‡	5	10	0	71	35	0	7.10	14

Also batted: T. E. Barber (*Poole*) (2 matches) 0*, 3, 0; G. F. B. Scott (*Hemel Hempstead*) (1 match)
3, 13.

‡ *Born in Middlesex.* § *ECB contract.* ¶ *Official overseas player.* †† *Other non-England-qualified.*

BOWLING

	Style	O	M	R	W	BB	5I	Avge
T. J. Murtagh	RFM	359.5	95	888	58	5-38	2	15.31
E. R. Bamber	RFM	203.5	37	567	28	4-81	0	20.25
J. A. R. Harris	RFM	384.5	67	1,253	61	7-83	3	20.54
H. W. R. Cartwright	RM	122.2	16	410	19	4-33	0	21.57
J. K. Fuller	RFM	227.2	25	845	28	4-49	0	30.17

Also bowled: M. K. Andersson (RM) 56–2–198–8; T. E. Barber (LFM) 34–4–131–0; S. T. Finn
(RFM) 108–9–395–9; T. G. Helm (RFM) 74.5–12–236–7; M. D. E. Holden (OB) 40–3–145–1;
D. J. Malan (LB) 48–3–145–3; R. H. Patel (SLA) 48.2–9–177–6; O. P. Rayner (OB)
146.5–35–334–7; S. D. Robson (LB) 4–0–27–0; T. S. Roland-Jones (RFM) 21–0–98–2; G. F. B.
Scott (RM) 12–3–23–0; P. R. Stirling (OB) 24–3–81–2.

LEADING ROYAL LONDON CUP AVERAGES (100 runs/4 wickets)

Batting	Runs	HS	Avge	SR	Ct/St
P. R. Stirling . . .	515	127*	73.57	89.25	5
J. E. C. Franklin .	148	62*	49.33	90.79	4
E. J. G. Morgan .	300	100	42.85	96.46	1
N. R. T. Gubbins	246	86	30.75	87.85	2
S. S. Eskinazi . . .	167	49	27.83	71.06	3
J. A. Simpson . . .	166	77	27.66	77.20	9/4
H. W. R. Cartwright	189	60*	27.00	94.97	1

Bowling	W	BB	Avge	ER
R. H. Patel	15	4-58	25.20	4.90
S. T. Finn	12	4-65	26.83	5.30
N. A. Sowter	10	3-43	29.80	4.91
T. G. Helm	13	4-49	33.92	6.66
J. E. C. Franklin . .	4	3-42	53.25	4.73

LEADING VITALITY BLAST AVERAGES (100 runs/22 overs)

Batting	Runs	HS	Avge	SR	Ct/St		Bowling	W	BB	Avge	ER
P. R. Stirling ..	498	109	35.57	160.12	8		D. J. Bravo	7	2-24	28.42	**8.91**
J. K. Fuller....	224	46*	37.33	158.86	8		N. A. Sowter....	3	1-24	73.66	**9.20**
D. J. Bravo....	131	38	26.20	148.86	1		S. T. Finn	9	3-21	24.00	**9.39**
E. J. G. Morgan	259	90	25.90	143.09	7		A. C. Agar	9	3-17	23.11	**9.45**
M. D. E. Holden	169	84	28.16	137.39	3		R. H. Patel	5	2-27	48.20	**9.64**
S. S. Eskinazi..	262	55	26.20	130.34	6		J. K. Fuller	15	6-28	31.86	**10.82**
J. A. Simpson .	246	62	22.36	130.15	4/2		T. E. Barber	9	4-28	30.33	**12.40**
N. R. T. Gubbins	123	25	15.37	126.80	3						

FIRST-CLASS COUNTY RECORDS

Highest score for	331*	J. D. B. Robertson v Worcestershire at Worcester	1949
Highest score against	341	C. M. Spearman (Gloucestershire) at Gloucester	2004
Leading run-scorer	40,302	E. H. Hendren (avge 48.81).................	1907–37
Best bowling for	10-40	G. O. B. Allen v Lancashire at Lord's........	1929
Best bowling against	9-38	R. C. Robertson-Glasgow (Somerset) at Lord's ..	1924
Leading wicket-taker	2,361	F. J. Titmus (avge 21.27)...................	1949–82
Highest total for	642-3 dec	v Hampshire at Southampton................	1923
Highest total against	850-7 dec	by Somerset at Taunton....................	2007
Lowest total for	20	v MCC at Lord's	1864
Lowest total against {	31	by Gloucestershire at Bristol	1924
	31	by Glamorgan at Cardiff	1997

LIST A COUNTY RECORDS

Highest score for	163	A. J. Strauss v Surrey at The Oval...........	2008
Highest score against	163	C. J. Adams (Sussex) at Arundel.............	1999
Leading run-scorer	12,029	M. W. Gatting (avge 34.96).................	1975–98
Best bowling for	7-12	W. W. Daniel v Minor Counties East at Ipswich	1978
Best bowling against	6-27	J. C. Tredwell (Kent) at Southgate...........	2009
Leading wicket-taker	491	J. E. Emburey (avge 24.68).................	1975–95
Highest total for	367-6	v Sussex v Hove.........................	2015
Highest total against	368-2	by Nottinghamshire at Lord's	2014
Lowest total for	23	v Yorkshire at Leeds	1974
Lowest total against	41	by Northamptonshire at Northampton	1972

TWENTY20 COUNTY RECORDS

Highest score for	129	D. T. Christian v Kent at Canterbury........	2014
Highest score against	**123**	**I. A. Cockbain (Gloucestershire) at Bristol ..**	**2018**
Leading run-scorer	2,828	D. J. Malan (avge 31.77, SR 125.13)........	2006–18
Best bowling for	**6-28**	**J. K. Fuller v Hampshire at Southampton...**	**2018**
Best bowling against	6-24	T. J. Murtagh (Surrey) at Lord's	2005
Leading wicket-taker	61	S. T. Finn (avge 22.40, ER 7.58)	2008–18
Highest total for {	221-2	v Sussex at Hove	2015
	221-5	**v Surrey at The Oval**	**2018**
Highest total against	254-3	by Gloucestershire at Uxbridge	2011
Lowest total for	92	v Surrey at Lord's	2013
Lowest total against	74	by Essex at Chelmsford	2013

ADDRESS

Lord's Cricket Ground, London NW8 8QN; 020 7289 1300; enquiries@middlesexccc.com; www.middlesexccc.com.

OFFICIALS

Captain D. J. Malan
Managing director of cricket A. R. C. Fraser
Head coach 2018 R. J. Scott
2019 S. G. Law
Twenty20 coach 2018 D. L. Vettori
Head of youth cricket R. I. Coutts

President 2017-2019 J. E. Emburey
Chairman M. O'Farrell
Secretary/chief executive R. J. Goatley
Head groundsman 2018 M. J. Hunt
2019 K. McDermott
Scorer D. K. Shelley

MIDDLESEX v DURHAM MCCU

At Northwood, April 7–9. Drawn. Toss: Middlesex. First-class debuts: E. W. F. Fenwick, C. Nicholls, J. Subramanyan. County debuts: H. W. R. Cartwright, R. G. White.

The early-season weather relented to allow Middlesex's batsmen to stretch their legs on the first day, but no further play was possible. Robson and Eskinazi helped themselves to untroubled centuries, and put on 220; both retired. Cartwright, the Zimbabwe-born Australian Test player, failed to take advantage, falling lbw first ball to Jhatavedh Subramanyan, an 18-year-old leg-spinner from Hong Kong.

Close of play: first day, Middlesex 367-4 (Simpson 42, White 30); second day, no play.

Middlesex

*S. D. Robson retired out	135		R. G. White not out		30
M. D. E. Holden c Macdonell b Cooke	11		B 2, lb 6, w 1, nb 6		15
S. S. Eskinazi retired out	134				
H. W. R. Cartwright lbw b Subramanyan	0		1/24 (2) 2/244 (1)	(4 wkts, 108 overs)	367
†J. A. Simpson not out	42		3/245 (4) 4/313 (3)		

J. A. R. Harris, T. S. Roland-Jones, O. P. Rayner, T. G. Helm and T. J. Murtagh did not bat.

McGrath 14–4–44–0; Fenwick 16–2–55–0; Ruffell 17–1–57–0; Cooke 15–2–35–1; Macdonell 13–0–50–0; Subramanyan 18–1–67–1; Graves 15–1–51–0.

Durham MCCU

J. D. Marshall, M. J. Plater, C. M. Macdonell, *W. A. R. Fraine, J. M. Cooke, B. W. M. Graves, F. W. A. Ruffell, A. H. McGrath, J. Subramanyan, †C. Nicholls, E. W. F. Fenwick.

Umpires: N. L. Bainton and C. M. Watts.

MIDDLESEX v NORTHAMPTONSHIRE

At Lord's, April 13–15. Middlesex won by 160 runs. Middlesex 20pts, Northamptonshire 3pts. Toss: uncontested. County debuts: D. A. J. Bracewell, B. A. Hutton. Championship debuts: H. W. R. Cartwright, R. G. White.

Persistent rain – and even some snow – over the previous four weeks had hampered the Lord's groundstaff, leading to a green, damp pitch. It was particularly spiteful on the second day, on which 26 wickets fell: Northamptonshire's first innings was derailed by a devilish spell of swing and seam from Harris, which brought him five for nine in 5.2 overs. Harris was fresh from top-scoring in Middlesex's first innings, which started on a truncated opening day when the Lord's floodlights were used for the first time in a Championship match. Against the county he had played for on loan in 2017, Holden gave the second innings a bright start as Middlesex looked to build on a lead of 143. But wickets continued to tumble: 54 for one became 57 for five, three to the New Zealand fast bowler Bracewell, before No. 11 Murtagh smacked 31 to set Northamptonshire 303. Newton survived for 102 minutes, but seam continued to hold sway next day: after going to lunch five down, they lost their last five in six overs. Murtagh took wickets in the match, a month before his Test debut for Ireland at 36, included his 700th in first-class cricket.

Close of play: first day, Middlesex 136-4 (Stirling 40, Simpson 31); second day, Northamptonshire 9-0 (Newton 4, Duckett 5).

Middlesex

*S. D. Robson lbw b Hutton	14	– (2) lbw b Sanderson	5
M. D. E. Holden c Hutton b Sanderson	8	– (1) c Rossington b Bracewell	33
R. G. White b Sanderson	0	– lbw b Bracewell	16
H. W. R. Cartwright b Hutton	30	– b Bracewell	0
P. R. Stirling c Rossington b Sanderson	44	– lbw b Procter	1
†J. A. Simpson lbw b Sanderson	32	– lbw b Gleeson	12
J. A. R. Harris not out	46	– c sub (R. I. Keogh) b Procter	18
T. S. Roland-Jones c Levi b Hutton	13	– c Duckett b Hutton	10
O. P. Rayner c Bracewell b Hutton	2	– b Procter	6
T. G. Helm c Hutton b Bracewell	4	– not out	16
T. J. Murtagh b Hutton	0	– b Gleeson	31
B 3, lb 12, nb 6	21	Lb 5, nb 6	11

1/21 (2) 2/21 (3) 3/54 (4)   (80.2 overs) 214   1/5 (2) 2/54 (1)   (38.3 overs) 159
4/63 (1) 5/141 (5) 6/142 (6)   3/56 (4) 4/57 (5)
7/174 (8) 8/180 (9) 9/201 (10) 10/214 (11)   5/57 (3) 6/85 (6) 7/102 (7)
8/106 (8) 9/112 (9) 10/159 (11)

Sanderson 19–5–42–4; Bracewell 23–6–61–1; Hutton 20.2–6–54–5; Gleeson 18–9–42–0. *Second innings*—Sanderson 7–3–21–1; Bracewell 9–2–31–3; Hutton 8–0–39–1; Procter 8–2–38–3; Gleeson 6.3–0–25–2.

Northamptonshire

R. I. Newton lbw b Murtagh	0	– c Simpson b Roland-Jones	44
B. M. Duckett c Stirling b Murtagh	6	– c Holden b Murtagh	9
L. A. Procter c Simpson b Roland-Jones	1	– (4) lbw b Harris	8
*A. G. Wakely lbw b Harris	12	– (5) lbw b Cartwright	26
R. E. Levi b Harris	20	– (6) c Helm b Harris	23
†A. M. Rossington lbw b Murtagh	0	– (7) lbw b Murtagh	2
J. J. Cobb b Murtagh	0	– (8) c and b Harris	7
D. A. J. Bracewell b Harris	0	– (9) c Rayner b Harris	6
B. A. Hutton c and b Harris	18	– (3) c Simpson b Murtagh	6
R. J. Gleeson b Harris	8	– not out	0
B. W. Sanderson not out	4	– lbw b Murtagh	0
Nb 2	2	Lb 7, nb 4	11

1/0 (1) 2/7 (3) 3/9 (2)   (21.2 overs) 71   1/13 (2) 2/25 (3)   (38.2 overs) 142
4/38 (5) 5/41 (6) 6/41 (4)   3/44 (4) 4/95 (1)
7/41 (8) 8/41 (7) 9/62 (10) 10/71 (9)   5/115 (5) 6/125 (7) 7/131 (6)
8/141 (9) 9/142 (8) 10/142 (11)

Murtagh 9–4–27–4; Roland-Jones 7–0–35–1; Harris 5.2–4–9–5. *Second innings*—Murtagh 11.2–1–36–4; Roland-Jones 9–0–38–1; Harris 10.2–2–39–4; Helm 6–1–18–0; Cartwright 2–0–4–1.

Umpires: P. K. Baldwin and R. T. Robinson.

At Derby, April 20–23. MIDDLESEX lost to DERBYSHIRE by 101 runs.

MIDDLESEX v GLAMORGAN

At Lord's, April 27–30. Drawn. Middlesex 6pts, Glamorgan 8pts. Toss: uncontested. First-class debut: T. E. Barber.

More awful weather allowed only 58 overs, with two days washed out. But there was time for Eskinazi, who had shaken off a virus, to hit 94, defying seam-friendly conditions that allowed Hogan and van der Gugten to share nine wickets. Murtagh took four in Glamorgan's brief innings, which included a lighter moment when Aneurin Donald was introduced over the PA as "Aneurin Bevan", the architect of the NHS; Donald fell first ball. His one previous innings at Lord's, for England

Schools in September 2013, also ended in a golden duck. After the match, Malan suggested that pink balls could be used to boost the chances of play in indifferent early-season conditions.

Close of play: first day, Middlesex 64-3 (Eskinazi 31, Cartwright 0); second day, no play; third day, Glamorgan 38-4 (Carlson 3, Cooke 0).

Middlesex

S. D. Robson b Hogan	17	T. G. Helm c Cooke b van der Gugten	4
M. D. E. Holden c Cooke b Carey	7	T. J. Murtagh c Selman b Hogan	0
S. S. Eskinazi c Cooke b van der Gugten	94	T. E. Barber not out	0
*D. J. Malan c Selman b Hogan	5	B 4, lb 1, nb 4	9
H. W. R. Cartwright b Hogan	5		
P. R. Stirling c Cooke b Hogan	1	1/14 (2) 2/34 (1) 3/58 (4) (42.1 overs)	194
†J. A. Simpson c Selman b van der Gugten	38	4/80 (5) 5/104 (6) 6/164 (3)	
O. P. Rayner b van der Gugten	14	7/189 (7) 8/193 (9) 9/194 (8) 10/194 (10)	

Van der Gugten 13–1–63–4; Carey 12–3–48–1; Hogan 13.1–1–49–5; Lloyd 4–0–29–0.

Glamorgan

N. J. Selman b Murtagh	21	†C. B. Cooke not out	0
J. R. Murphy lbw b Murtagh	4	Lb 4, w 2	6
S. E. Marsh lbw b Murtagh	4		
K. S. Carlson not out	3	1/17 (2) 2/23 (3) (4 wkts, 15.5 overs)	38
A. H. T. Donald c Simpson b Murtagh	0	3/34 (1) 4/34 (5)	

D. L. Lloyd, A. G. Salter, T. van der Gugten, L. J. Carey and *M. G. Hogan did not bat.

Murtagh 8–3–12–4; Barber 5–1–13–0; Helm 2.5–0–9–0.

Umpires: R. J. Bailey and I. J. Gould.

At Hove, May 4–7. MIDDLESEX lost to SUSSEX by three wickets.

MIDDLESEX v GLOUCESTERSHIRE

At Lord's, May 11–14. Drawn. Middlesex 12pts, Gloucestershire 8pts. Toss: uncontested.

A typically slow, low Lord's pitch ultimately condemned this match to a draw, as Gloucestershire – forced to follow on late on the third day – batted through the fourth. Bracey was undefeated after five and a half hours. Middlesex had amassed 455 by lunch on the second day, when rain ended play, with Gubbins falling one short of a second successive century when he gloved a lifter from the persistent Worrall after some attractive drives. There were also 76s for Malan and Morgan, in his first first-class match since July 2015. Middlesex still missed out on maximum batting points, unable to conjure four runs from the last 15 balls of the first 110 overs. Gloucestershire made a useful start but, once Dent and Bracey were separated after an opening stand of 72, the only serious resistance came from Howell, down at No. 7 after a stomach upset. Cartwright made up for his fourth duck in nine innings since joining Middlesex with four for 33, his best first-class figures. There were around 120 overs left when Malan enforced the follow-on. Although the restored Howell and Dent fell on the third evening, there were few alarms on the final day.

Close of play: first day, Middlesex 356-6 (Simpson 15, Harris 2); second day, Middlesex 455-8 dec; third day, Gloucestershire 66-2 (Roderick 6, Bracey 5).

Middlesex

S. D. Robson c Roderick b Worrall	36	O. P. Rayner not out		27
N. R. T. Gubbins c Roderick b Worrall	99	T. G. Helm not out		25
S. S. Eskinazi b c Noema-Barnett b Worrall	31	B 9, lb 20		29
*D. J. Malan lbw b M. D. Taylor	76			
E. J. G. Morgan lbw b Higgins	76	1/77 (1)	(8 wkts dec, 122 overs)	455
H. W. R. Cartwright c Dent b M. D. Taylor	0	2/165 (3) 3/186 (2)		
†J. A. Simpson c Roderick b Miles	32	4/318 (4) 5/320 (6) 6/353 (5)		
J. A. R. Harris c Worrall b Miles	24	7/396 (8) 8/397 (7)	110 overs: 398-8	

S. T. Finn did not bat.

Worrall 26–4–73–3; M. D. Taylor 27–2–116–2; Higgins 24–5–76–1; Miles 21–4–85–2; Noema-Barnett 7–0–24–0; van Buuren 17–3–52–0.

Gloucestershire

*C. D. J. Dent c Malan b Helm	66	– c Simpson b Helm	35
J. R. Bracey c Simpson b Cartwright	28	– (4) not out	125
†G. H. Roderick lbw b Cartwright	0	– c Simpson b Harris	48
G. L. van Buuren c Simpson b Rayner	22	– (6) not out	46
J. M. R. Taylor lbw b Finn	22	– b Harris	41
R. F. Higgins c and b Helm	5		
B. A. C. Howell c Cartwright b Rayner	47	– (2) b Harris	16
K. Noema-Barnett c Simpson b Helm	6		
C. N. Miles c Morgan b Cartwright	13		
D. J. Worrall lbw b Cartwright	6		
M. D. Taylor not out	1		
B 2, lb 4, nb 4	10	Lb 6, w 1, nb 8	15

1/72 (2) 2/72 (3) 3/90 (4)	(72.5 overs)	210	1/49 (2) (4 wkts, 111 overs) 326
4/117 (5) 5/130 (4) 6/141 (6)			2/54 (1) 3/152 (3)
7/153 (8) 8/185 (9) 9/199 (10) 10/210 (7)			4/243 (5)

Finn 15–0–54–1; Helm 14–1–48–3; Harris 15–5–42–0; Cartwright 11–1–33–4; Rayner 15.5–7–23–2; Malan 2–0–4–0. *Second innings*—Finn 14–0–53–0; Helm 19.5–5–50–1; Cartwright 16–1–68–0; Harris 25–5–60–3; Rayner 29–8–54–0; Malan 6–1–23–0; Robson 2–0–12–0.

Umpires: J. Blades and S. J. O'Shaughnessy.

At Lord's, June 9. MIDDLESEX lost to AUSTRALIANS by 101 runs (see Australian tour section).

At Leicester, June 20–23. MIDDLESEX beat LEICESTERSHIRE by one wicket. *Middlesex overhaul 381 after conceding a first-innings lead of 194.*

At Canterbury, June 25–27. MIDDLESEX lost to KENT by 342 runs. *Middlesex all out for 56.*

MIDDLESEX v WARWICKSHIRE

At Lord's, July 22–24. Middlesex won by 18 runs. Middlesex 20pts, Warwickshire 5pts. Toss: Middlesex.

Murtagh swung this match with an inspirational opening over just before lunch on the third day, as Warwickshire began their quest for 203 on a pitch better than the modest totals suggested. First Sibley was caught at slip off one that moved away down the slope, then Bell was gated second ball. Murtagh later trapped Trott, and some adhesive batting by Hain and Ambrose was to no avail. Finally the pacy Fuller bowled Wright, ending a 77-minute rearguard, and Middlesex could celebrate victory in their first Championship match since parting company with head coach Richard Scott. Fuller had been the unlikely batting star in their first innings, his 71 saving the day after six wickets crashed for 25 before lunch. Warwickshire scraped together a lead of 40, almost entirely thanks to opener Rhodes, who was last out after more than five hours for a career-best 118; he had 94 when No. 11

Sidebottom came in, but scored all the runs off the bat as the last wicket pilfered 27. Gubbins and Eskinazi then shared a century partnership, before the Middlesex batting misfired against Patel's off-spin, to set up an inviting target.

Close of play: first day, Warwickshire 152-4 (Rhodes 53, Wright 7); second day, Middlesex 183-6 (Rayner 0, Simpson 4).

Middlesex

P. R. Stirling c Bell b Wright	16	– c Trott b Woakes	16
N. R. T. Gubbins b Hannon-Dalby	26	– lbw b Patel	47
S. S. Eskinazi c Trott b Wright	9	– c Hain b Patel	73
*D. J. Malan c Ambrose b Sidebottom	6	– b Hannon-Dalby	28
E. J. G. Morgan b Hannon-Dalby	4	– lbw b Patel	3
M. D. E. Holden lbw b Patel	48	– c Sidebottom b Patel	8
†J. A. Simpson c Sibley b Sidebottom	0	– (8) b Patel	33
J. A. R. Harris c Sibley b Sidebottom	0	– (9) not out	15
J. K. Fuller b Hannon-Dalby	71	– (10) run out (Woakes)	0
O. P. Rayner c Ambrose b Wright	28	– (7) c Trott b Woakes	9
T. J. Murtagh not out	12	– b Hannon-Dalby	0
B 4, lb 9, w 1, nb 2	16	Lb 6, nb 4	10

1/17 (1) 2/51 (2) 3/53 (3)   (54.1 overs) 236
4/60 (5) 5/66 (4) 6/70 (7)
7/76 (8) 8/162 (6) 9/213 (10) 10/236 (9)

1/18 (1) 2/119 (2)   (80.3 overs) 242
3/152 (4) 4/167 (5)
5/179 (6) 6/179 (4) 7/213 (7)
8/236 (8) 9/239 (10) 10/242 (11)

Woakes 14-0-75-0; Wright 12-1-48-3; Hannon-Dalby 12.1-2-41-3; Sidebottom 8-0-34-3; Patel 8-0-25-1. *Second innings*—Woakes 16-3-64-2; Wright 7-2-29-0; Sidebottom 14-4-48-0; Hannon-Dalby 15.3-5-39-2; Patel 28-12-56-5.

Warwickshire

W. M. H. Rhodes c and b Harris	118	– b Harris	8
D. P. Sibley lbw b Harris	14	– c Rayner b Murtagh	0
I. R. Bell lbw b Murtagh	8	– b Murtagh	0
I. J. L. Trott lbw b Rayner	47	– lbw b Murtagh	32
S. R. Hain lbw b Murtagh	16	– b Harris	37
C. J. C. Wright c Simpson b Harris	14	– (9) b Fuller	19
C. R. Woakes c Simpson b Harris	7	– (6) lbw b Rayner	6
†T. R. Ambrose c Simpson b Murtagh	8	– (7) c Rayner b Fuller	41
*J. S. Patel lbw b Rayner	14	– (8) lbw b Murtagh	13
O. J. Hannon-Dalby b Fuller	6	– c Simpson b Fuller	4
R. N. Sidebottom not out	0	– not out	10
B 2, lb 17, w 1, nb 4	24	B 4, lb 10	14

1/20 (2) 2/29 (3) 3/114 (4)   (77.3 overs) 276
4/141 (5) 5/172 (6) 6/180 (7)
7/191 (8) 8/228 (9) 9/249 (10) 10/276 (1)

1/1 (2) 2/1 (3)   (55.5 overs) 184
3/21 (1) 4/57 (4)
5/64 (6) 6/108 (5) 7/151 (7)
8/153 (8) 9/162 (10) 10/184 (9)

Murtagh 18-3-43-3; Harris 19.3-3-84-4; Fuller 16-0-67-1; Rayner 22-3-55-2; Holden 2-0-8-0. *Second innings*—Murtagh 19-1-54-4; Harris 17-2-55-2; Rayner 9-2-21-1; Fuller 10.5-1-40-3.

Umpires: I. D. Blackwell and B. V. Taylor.

At Northampton, August 19–22. MIDDLESEX beat NORTHAMPTONSHIRE by 31 runs. *Middlesex win after following on.*

MIDDLESEX v SUSSEX

At Lord's, August 29–31. Middlesex won by 55 runs. Middlesex 19pts, Sussex 3pts. Toss: uncontested.

Middlesex's third successive win revived hopes of a promotion challenge. Sixteen wickets fell on the opening day in favourable conditions for the seamers. Holden made a mature fifty as Middlesex inched to 169, with Morgan scoring six in 78 balls, one of which he hit for four. Sussex struggled in turn: Harris took care of the middle order, and a lead of two turned the match into a one-innings shoot-out. Tenacious half-centuries from Eskinazi and Malan (who survived for 261 minutes) gave Middlesex the upper hand, although Archer dragged his side back into the game with his only five-for of the season. Needing 231, Sussex were undone by Fuller, Harris – whose first wicket (Finch) was his 50th of the season – and 19-year-old Ethan Bamber, in his second Championship match. They shared eight wickets, with only Haines and Wiese lasting more than an hour.

Close of play: first day, Sussex 120-6 (Brown 15, Jordan 8); second day, Middlesex 210-5 (Malan 69, Harris 24).

Middlesex

S. D. Robson lbw b Robinson	8	– (2) lbw b Robinson	15
N. R. T. Gubbins c Finch b Wiese	29	– (1) b Archer	8
†S. S. Eskinazi lbw b Archer	0	– c Brown b Robinson	60
*D. J. Malan lbw b Wiese	6	– c Brown b Robinson	70
E. J. G. Morgan c Robinson b Jordan	6	– b Jordan	4
M. D. E. Holden not out	50	– c Haines b Archer	4
J. A. R. Harris c Salt b Robinson	0	– lbw b Archer	26
J. K. Fuller b Jordan	17	– c Jordan b Archer	0
O. P. Rayner b Jordan	0	– not out	17
E. R. Bamber c Brown b Archer	6	– b Robinson	0
S. T. Finn b Archer	8	– c Haines b Archer	0
B 9, lb 20, nb 10	39	B 4, lb 10, nb 14	28

1/27 (1) 2/30 (3) 3/46 (2)   (62.5 overs) 169
4/57 (4) 5/99 (5) 6/100 (7)
7/123 (8) 8/141 (9) 9/157 (10) 10/169 (11)

1/19 (1) 2/29 (2)   (85.4 overs) 232
3/116 (3) 4/125 (5)
5/152 (6) 6/212 (4)
7/213 (8) 8/226 (7)
9/231 (10) 10/232 (11)

Archer 17.5–7–34–3; Robinson 19–3–49–2; Jordan 14–5–26–3; Wiese 12–2–31–2. *Second innings*—Robinson 25–6–59–4; Archer 21.4–3–69–5; Jordan 13–4–31–1; Wiese 13–2–32–0; Haines 6–1–13–0; Briggs 7–1–14–0.

Sussex

L. W. P. Wells c Harris b Bamber	24	– b Bamber	3
P. D. Salt c Malan b Finn	32	– c Eskinazi b Fuller	20
T. J. Haines c Rayner b Fuller	15	– c Malan b Fuller	23
H. Z. Finch b Fuller	17	– lbw b Harris	20
L. J. Wright lbw b Harris	0	– b Finn	0
*†B. C. Brown lbw b Harris	24	– c Eskinazi b Harris	31
D. Wiese lbw b Harris	6	– not out	37
C. J. Jordan b Harris	14	– c Eskinazi b Bamber	2
J. C. Archer not out	12	– b Bamber	0
O. E. Robinson c Morgan b Finn	9	– run out (Malan)	11
D. R. Briggs c Eskinazi b Bamber	5	– c Eskinazi b Fuller	20
B 4, lb 8, w 1	13	B 4, lb 4	8

1/45 (1) 2/63 (2) 3/87 (3)   (45.5 overs) 171
4/88 (5) 5/92 (4) 6/108 (7)
7/130 (8) 8/139 (6) 9/162 (10) 10/171 (11)

1/7 (1) 2/41 (2)   (44.5 overs) 175
3/58 (3) 4/59 (5)
5/86 (4) 6/111 (6)
7/114 (8) 8/114 (9)
9/128 (10) 10/175 (11)

Harris 18–4–61–4; Bamber 8.5–1–32–2; Finn 9–0–34–2; Fuller 10–0–32–2. *Second innings*—Harris 11–0–43–2; Bamber 12–0–50–3; Fuller 10.5–3–37–3; Finn 11–1–37–1.

Umpires: B. J. Debenham and J. H. Evans.

At Bristol, September 4–7. MIDDLESEX drew with GLOUCESTERSHIRE.

MIDDLESEX v KENT

At Lord's, September 10–12. Kent won by three wickets. Kent 19pts, Middlesex 3pts. Toss: uncontested.

Kent's victory left them one win away from promotion – and ended Middlesex's hopes. Some familiar faces did the damage. The evergreen Stevens took four wickets as Middlesex subsided in the first innings, and added three more in the second. And Podmore, who started his career at Lord's, twice took three for 35. Stevens also rescued Kent after they had dipped to 82 for seven (in all, 19 wickets went down on the first day). He put on 75 with Stewart, who had slammed a century in the earlier match between these sides, which Kent also won. Trailing by 31, Middlesex needed someone to bat long. Gubbins survived for nearly two hours, but the highest score was Robson's 36. That still left a ticklish target of 156, and the match was in the balance at 54 for four on the second evening. But Kuhn and Bell-Drummond applied themselves, and Billings carried his side home. After Tim Murtagh fell ill the night before the game, Middlesex sent out an SOS to Martin Andersson, who was on loan to Derbyshire and expecting to play at Northampton. Despite being involved in a minor accident on the M1, he made it in time to bat before lunch on the hectic first day.

Close of play: first day, Kent 189-9 (Stewart 60, Thomas 0); second day, Kent 104-4 (Kuhn 26, Bell-Drummond 27).

Middlesex

S. D. Robson lbw b Stevens	12	– (2) c Kuhn b Stevens	36
N. R. T. Gubbins c Dickson b Henry	17	– (1) lbw b Podmore	25
M. D. E. Holden run out (Henry)	7	– lbw b Stevens	3
*D. J. Malan c Crawley b Stevens	16	– lbw b Henry	32
†S. S. Eskinazi c Crawley b Podmore	16	– lbw b Stevens	22
E. J. G. Morgan lbw b Stevens	1	– c Stewart b Podmore	1
M. K. Andersson lbw b Podmore	2	– lbw b Podmore	3
J. K. Fuller not out	37	– not out	28
O. P. Rayner c and b Stevens	19	– c Kuhn b Henry	13
E. R. Bamber b Podmore	0	– c Billings b Henry	1
S. T. Finn b Denly	27	– lbw b Henry	6
B 4, lb 3	7	B 13, lb 3	16

1/27 (2) 2/39 (1) 3/42 (3) (45.2 overs) **161** 1/59 (2) 2/63 (3) (60.2 overs) **186**
4/69 (4) 5/73 (6) 6/73 (5) 3/101 (1) 4/101 (4)
7/80 (7) 8/119 (9) 9/120 (10) 10/161 (11) 5/102 (6) 6/114 (7) 7/156 (5)
  8/176 (9) 9/178 (10) 10/186 (11)

Henry 10–2–42–1; Stewart 9–2–23–0; Stevens 12–2–44–4; Podmore 12–4–35–3; Denly 1.2–0–5–1; Thomas 1–0–5–0. *Second innings*—Henry 18.2–6–40–4; Podmore 16–5–35–3; Stevens 15–4–46–3; Stewart 3–0–22–0; Thomas 8–2–27–0.

Kent

Z. Crawley lbw b Fuller	3	– c Malan b Bamber	4
S. R. Dickson lbw b Bamber	8	– c Rayner b Andersson	32
J. L. Denly lbw b Finn	9	– (4) lbw b Fuller	10
H. G. Kuhn b Andersson	19	– (5) lbw b Fuller	39
D. J. Bell-Drummond c Eskinazi b Fuller	6	– (6) lbw b Bamber	28
*†S. W. Billings c Eskinazi b Fuller	5	– (7) not out	31
D. I. Stevens b Andersson	64	– (8) lbw b Fuller	5
H. W. Podmore c Morgan b Finn	10	– (9) not out	1
G. Stewart b Fuller	63		
M. J. Henry c Eskinazi b Bamber	0	– (3) c Morgan b Finn	1
I. A. A. Thomas not out	0		
B 2, lb 3	5	Lb 6	6

1/9 (2) 2/20 (3) 3/29 (1) (49.5 overs) 192 1/12 (1) (7 wkts, 44 overs) 157
4/39 (5) 5/51 (6) 6/53 (4) 2/13 (3) 3/46 (4)
7/82 (8) 8/157 (7) 9/158 (10) 10/192 (9) 4/54 (2) 5/106 (6) 6/136 (5) 7/144 (8)

Bamber 15–2–31–2; Finn 11–1–55–2; Fuller 11.5–0–49–4; Andersson 12–0–52–2. *Second innings*—Bamber 16–3–34–2; Finn 7–0–39–1; Fuller 14–1–53–3; Andersson 7–0–25–1.

Umpires: M. J. Saggers and B. V. Taylor.

MIDDLESEX v DERBYSHIRE

At Lord's, September 18–21. Middlesex won by 117 runs. Middlesex 24pts, Derbyshire 5pts. Toss: uncontested.

On Mick Hunt's last pitch, after 49 years as a groundsman at Lord's, Middlesex continued a general upturn in form. They passed 400 for only the second time in the summer thanks to centuries from Robson and Holden, who reached his first for Middlesex during a rollicking last-wicket stand of 66 with Murtagh. Derbyshire wobbled to 62 for four in reply, but were rescued by Critchley, who hit his first hundred of the season, too; he would also claim six wickets with his leg-breaks. Leading by 128, Middlesex made heavy weather of their search for quick runs, with the in-form Robson taking his match total to 207 in more than seven hours. Derbyshire were left with a day to make 328, and skipper Godleman buckled down for a century against his first county. But no one else exceeded 22, and he ended up carrying his bat. The home seamers shared the spoils on a pitch of variable bounce: Bamber, Harris and Murtagh all took six wickets in the match.

Close of play: first day, Middlesex 350-8 (Holden 96, Bamber 5); second day, Derbyshire 222-6 (Critchley 87, Dal 19); third day, Middlesex 199-7 (Harris 5, Andersson 23).

Middlesex

S. D. Robson c Madsen b Palladino	134	– (2) run out (Critchley)	73
N. R. T. Gubbins lbw b Viljoen	20	– (1) hit wkt b Ferguson	19
S. S. Eskinazi lbw b Critchley	35	– st Hosein b Critchley	14
*D. J. Malan c Reece b Viljoen	16	– c Hughes b Critchley	13
M. D. E. Holden not out	119	– b Madsen	22
†R. G. White c Wilson b Palladino	0	– (7) c Madsen b Critchley	7
J. A. R. Harris lbw b Palladino	0	– (8) not out	5
M. K. Andersson lbw b Palladino	3	– (9) not out	23
J. K. Fuller c Critchley b Ferguson	17	– (6) c Wilson b Critchley	15
E. R. Bamber c Madsen b Ferguson	7		
T. J. Murtagh c Ferguson b Critchley	39		
B 10, lb 14, w 5, nb 4	33	B 4, lb 3, w 1	8

1/64 (2) 2/139 (3) 3/166 (4) (108.4 overs) 423 1/58 (1) (7 wkts dec, 46 overs) 199
4/298 (1) 5/298 (6) 6/304 (7) 2/89 (3) 3/126 (4)
7/308 (8) 8/341 (9) 9/357 (10) 10/423 (11) 4/127 (2) 5/163 (5) 6/170 (7) 7/171 (6)

Palladino 29–5–92–4; Ferguson 26–3–113–2; Hughes 12–4–29–0; Viljoen 18–0–74–2; Reece 2–0–10–0; Critchley 17.4–1–65–2; Madsen 4–0–16–0. *Second innings*—Palladino 6–2–19–0; Ferguson 10–0–55–1; Viljoen 10–1–35–0; Critchley 15–0–60–4; Madsen 5–0–23–1.

Derbyshire

L. M. Reece lbw b Murtagh	16	– c Bamber b Murtagh		12
*B. A. Godleman c Eskinazi b Andersson	28	– not out		105
W. L. Madsen lbw b Harris	19	– lbw b Harris		11
A. L. Hughes b Bamber	9	– c White b Andersson		11
†H. R. Hosein lbw b Bamber	0	– c White b Murtagh		10
M. J. J. Critchley c Eskinazi b Harris	105	– lbw b Bamber		8
G. C. Wilson lbw b Bamber	31	– b Harris		22
A. K. Dal c Robson b Harris	23	– lbw b Murtagh		14
G. C. Viljoen not out	31	– c and b Bamber		4
A. P. Palladino lbw b Harris	0	– c White b Bamber		1
L. H. Ferguson b Murtagh	16	– b Murtagh		2
B 4, lb 13	17	B 4, lb 6		10

1/26 (1) 2/49 (3) 3/62 (4)   (82.4 overs) 295   1/30 (1) 2/51 (3)   (61 overs) 210
4/62 (5) 5/127 (2) 6/187 (7)   3/90 (4) 4/108 (5)
7/243 (6) 8/246 (8) 9/252 (10) 10/295 (11)   5/123 (6) 6/173 (7) 7/192 (8)
    8/197 (9) 9/205 (10) 10/210 (11)

Murtagh 17.4–3–53–2; Bamber 14–2–35–3; Harris 23–3–83–4; Fuller 12–2–53–0; Andersson 12–0–38–1; Malan 2–0–9–0; Holden 2–0–7–0. *Second innings*—Murtagh 16–3–55–4; Bamber 16–2–35–3; Harris 12–1–48–2; Andersson 7–0–23–1; Fuller 8–0–34–0; Malan 2–0–5–0.

Umpires: B. J. Debenham and R. A. Kettleborough.

At Chester-le-Street, September 24–26. MIDDLESEX beat DURHAM by 57 runs.

NORTHAMPTONSHIRE

Darkness on the edge of town

ALEX WINTER

After relegation for Northampton Town FC and a lowly finish for the Northampton Saints rugby team, it was down to the cricketers to lift the pall of sporting gloom that hung over the town. Instead they made it worse. Next to bottom of the Championship, and feeble in the white-ball competitions – it was the lowest point since the horror show of 2014. Unlike his local counterparts, head coach David Ripley, quite rightly, did not pay with his job. But there was a recognition that things had to improve. The era of the chubsters – the name given to Northamptonshire's cheerfully overweight team – was over.

The squad will have a new look for Ripley's reboot. As so often, Northamptonshire proved unable to retain talented players. After a 12-year association with the county, Ben Duckett became one of a string of new signings by Nottinghamshire, while seamer Richard Gleeson joined Lancashire, his home county. Replacing his genuine pace may prove harder than finding a batsman to score Duckett's runs. Unearthing a cricketer who approaches the game with the same gusto as the retiring Steven Crook may be more difficult still. Crook spent 11 years at Wantage Road in two spells, and starred when the club won the T20 title and promotion in 2013.

The new arrivals have the potential to lift the mood. Temba Bavuma, the South African Test batsman, signed for eight Championship matches in 2019, and Blessing Muzarabani, the 6ft 6in Zimbabwe seamer, agreed a three-year Kolpak deal after retiring from international cricket at the age of 22. Pakistan all-rounder Fahim Ashraf will add stardust in the Vitality Blast. In February, it was announced that Jason Holder, who had just led West Indies to a Test series win over England in the Caribbean, would play two Championship matches and six in the Royal London Cup ahead of the World Cup.

Alex Wakely called 2018 the most difficult of his four years as captain. Just 19 points came in the first five Championship matches, before a mini-rally ended with defeats from winning positions against Derbyshire and Middlesex. The Middlesex game was particularly traumatic – Northamptonshire's first-ever loss after enforcing the follow-on. Missed opportunity was the story of the season: only in their second match, at home to Warwickshire, were they comprehensively outplayed.

This was largely thanks to the bowlers. Ben Sanderson took 60 wickets – only four in the country took more – at 16, and was awarded his county cap. At times he formed an irresistible new-ball pairing with Brett Hutton, who claimed 45 Championship wickets in his first season at the club. Nathan Buck chipped in with 31 at 25, and no bowler with ten wickets averaged over 28.

There was not much joy for the batsmen. Pre-season preparation was severely hampered by the late blast of cold, wet weather that left Wantage

Ben Sanderson

Road's relaid outfield muddy. Outdoor practice was often impossible. Even allowing for this, and some sporty early-season pitches, it took the frontline batsmen far too long to find any sort of form. Wakely's 600 runs was the highest tally, and there were only three centuries in the Championship. The most impressive performer was Ricardo Vasconcelos. A South African of Portuguese parentage, he had been signed as a back-up wicketkeeper. But he showed enough on debut, against the Pakistanis, to be given further opportunities in the Championship, and seized his chance. A diminutive left-hander, he had an appetite for occupying the crease and leaving the ball – welcome qualities in Northamptonshire's aggressive batting line-up. He was rewarded with a three-year contract.

As one South African began his career, another said farewell. Rory Kleinveldt's combative approach and indomitable character were much admired during his four summers with the club. In some ways he was a throwback to the old overseas player, able to commit for an entire season. His skill with the ball and brutal hitting played a key part in Northamptonshire's rebuilding after 2015.

But this proved a season too far. He arrived for the start of the Royal London Cup and immediately suffered an injury. He also bowled a traumatic last over in the opening Vitality Blast game when Leicestershire completed an unlikely victory after needing 112 from 42 balls. That set the tone for a miserable tournament in which the bowlers leaked far too many – 200 or more in four of the first five matches that went the distance. At Edgbaston, Northamptonshire notched their highest T20 total – and still had to settle for a tie. The nadir came when Worcestershire chased 188 in 13.1 overs. Their 50-over fortunes were little better: except for a tense home win against Lancashire, there was almost nothing to cheer.

An elbow injury for Gleeson restricted him to six T20 games, and Kleinveldt's struggles meant they had little penetration in the powerplay. That made life hard for the spinners, Sri Lanka's Seekkuge Prasanna and, especially, Graeme White, who in June retired from the first-class game to concentrate on white-ball cricket. Having been a T20 force for several summers, Northamptonshire did not register a win until their 11th game. It needed a victory in their final match, at Leicester, to avoid equalling their worst season.

The slump did at least give an opportunity to one newcomer. Ben Curran – younger than Tom, older than Sam – returned to the town of his birth, and made a good impression in five Championship and three T20 appearances. He signed a two-year contract, and there were hints he could go some way towards filling the vacancy left by Duckett.

Championship attendance: 6,367.

NORTHAMPTONSHIRE RESULTS

All first-class matches – Played 14: Won 4, Lost 9, Drawn 1, Abandoned 2.
County Championship matches – Played 13: Won 4, Lost 8, Drawn 1, Abandoned 1.

Specsavers County Championship, 9th in Division 2;
Vitality Blast, 9th in North Group; Royal London One-Day Cup, 7th in North Group.

COUNTY CHAMPIONSHIP AVERAGES, BATTING AND FIELDING

Cap		Birthplace	M	I	NO	R	HS	100	Avge	Ct/St
2013	S. P. Crook	Modbury, Australia .	5	9	0	351	92	0	39.00	2
	†B. J. Curran	Northampton‡.	5	9	1	251	83*	0	31.37	3
	†R. S. Vasconcelos†† .	Johannesburg, SA . .	10	18	0	554	140	1	30.77	14/1
2012	A. G. Wakely	Hammersmith	12	22	1	600	106	1	28.57	4
2017	R. I. Newton	Taunton	4	7	0	183	46	0	26.14	1
2017	R. E. Levi††	Johannesburg, SA . .	11	20	1	492	75	0	25.89	15
2016	†B. M. Duckett	Farnborough, Kent .	8	16	1	375	133	1	25.00	5
	A. M. Rossington	Edgware	11	19	1	419	58	0	23.27	34
	†L. A. Procter	Oldham	10	20	1	442	70	0	23.26	2
	D. A. J. Bracewell¶ . .	Tauranga, NZ	3	6	1	113	81	0	22.60	2
	C. O. Thurston	Cambridge	2	4	0	78	29	0	19.50	1
	†S. A. Zaib	High Wycombe . . .	7	11	1	163	57	0	16.30	0
	B. D. Cotton	Stoke-on-Trent	3	4	2	32	24*	0	16.00	2
2018	J. J. Cobb	Leicester	5	10	0	140	30	0	14.00	2
	S. Prasanna¶	Balapitiya, SL	2	4	0	42	27	0	10.50	0
	N. L. Buck	Leicester	9	15	2	135	20	0	10.38	0
	B. A. Hutton	Doncaster	12	20	2	184	27	0	10.22	4
	R. I. Keogh	Dunstable	4	7	0	69	29	0	9.85	3
2018	B. W. Sanderson	Sheffield	13	21	13	72	36	0	9.00	3
2016	R. K. Kleinveldt¶ . . .	Cape Town, SA . . .	3	5	0	45	21	0	9.00	1
	R. J. Gleeson	Blackpool	4	7	1	38	26	0	6.33	0

‡ *Born in Northamptonshire.*　　¶ *Official overseas player.*　　†† *Other non-England-qualified.*

BOWLING

	Style	O	M	R	W	BB	5I	Avge
B. D. Cotton	RFM	44	13	101	10	5-48	1	10.10
R. J. Gleeson	RFM	90.3	19	256	16	6-79	1	16.00
B. W. Sanderson	RFM	422	112	1,002	60	5-16	2	16.70
R. K. Kleinveldt	RFM	95.1	14	282	14	4-51	0	20.14
L. A. Procter	RM	101.1	20	341	14	5-33	1	24.35
S. Prasanna	LB	72	7	247	10	4-49	0	24.70
N. L. Buck	RFM	196.5	22	782	31	4-51	0	25.22
B. A. Hutton	RFM	367.2	86	1,143	45	8-57	3	25.40
D. A. J. Bracewell	RFM	93	19	304	11	4-71	0	27.63

Also bowled: J. J. Cobb (OB) 3.4–0–28–0; S. P. Crook (RFM) 32.2–5–146–8; R. I. Keogh (OB) 53–5–205–2; S. A. Zaib (SLA) 26.4–8–52–2.

LEADING ROYAL LONDON CUP AVERAGES (100 runs/4 wickets)

Batting

	Runs	HS	Avge	SR	Ct/St
R. E. Levi	127	90	42.33	90.71	0
J. J. Cobb	203	78	40.60	87.12	1
A. G. Wakely	280	79	40.00	86.68	6
A. M. Rossington . .	271	66	38.71	86.85	8/1
R. K. Kleinveldt. . .	132	41	26.40	126.92	1
G. G. White	119	41*	19.83	92.96	0
B. M. Duckett. . .	133	57	19.00	71.50	4

Bowling

	W	BB	Avge	ER
L. A. Procter	5	3-45	32.80	5.12
B. A. Hutton	6	2-37	37.33	6.52
R. K. Kleinveldt . .	6	2-39	39.50	5.15
G. G. White	8	3-63	41.50	5.26
B. W. Sanderson . .	6	2-60	59.16	6.01
N. L. Buck	4	2-70	69.50	6.04

LEADING VITALITY BLAST AVERAGES (100 runs/20 overs)

Batting	Runs	HS	Avge	SR	Ct/St	Bowling	W	BB	Avge	ER
R. E. Levi.....	233	95*	29.12	**150.32**	3	R. J. Gleeson....	7	2-21	28.57	**8.51**
J. J. Cobb	448	103	37.33	**147.36**	3	B. A. Hutton....	4	2-28	57.75	**8.66**
B. M. Duckett .	414	96	29.57	**144.75**	6/1	S. Prasanna.....	9	2-22	44.33	**8.67**
S. P. Crook....	128	33	14.22	**143.82**	3	N. L. Buck	11	3-38	30.90	**9.14**
S. Prasanna....	149	38	13.54	**134.23**	3	B. W. Sanderson	7	2-41	42.71	**10.31**
A. G. Wakely..	292	54*	26.54	**132.72**	3	R. K. Kleinveldt .	8	2-53	42.25	**11.39**

FIRST-CLASS COUNTY RECORDS

Highest score for	331*	M. E. K. Hussey v Somerset at Taunton	2003
Highest score against	333	K. S. Duleepsinhji (Sussex) at Hove	1930
Leading run-scorer	28,980	D. Brookes (avge 36.13)	1934–59
Best bowling for	10-127	V. W. C. Jupp v Kent at Tunbridge Wells.....	1932
Best bowling against	10-30	C. Blythe (Kent) at Northampton.............	1907
Leading wicket-taker	1,102	E. W. Clark (avge 21.26)..................	1922–47
Highest total for	781-7 dec	v Nottinghamshire at Northampton	1995
Highest total against	701-7 dec	by Kent at Beckenham	2017
Lowest total for	12	v Gloucestershire at Gloucester..............	1907
Lowest total against	33	by Lancashire at Northampton...............	1977

LIST A COUNTY RECORDS

Highest score for	172*	W. Larkins v Warwickshire at Luton.........	1983
Highest score against	184	M. J. Lumb (Nottinghamshire) at Nottingham .	2016
Leading run-scorer	11,010	R. J. Bailey (avge 39.46)	1983–99
Best bowling for	7-10	C. Pietersen v Denmark at Brøndby.........	2005
Best bowling against	7-35	D. E. Malcolm (Derbyshire) at Derby	1997
Leading wicket-taker	251	A. L. Penberthy (avge 30.45)..............	1989–2003
Highest total for	425	v Nottinghamshire at Nottingham	2016
Highest total against	445-8	by Nottinghamshire at Nottingham	2016
Lowest total for	41	v Middlesex at Northampton	1972
Lowest total against	56	by Leicestershire at Leicester...............	1964
	56	by Denmark at Brøndby....................	2005

TWENTY20 COUNTY RECORDS

Highest score for	111*	L. Klusener v Worcestershire at Kidderminster	2007
Highest score against	161	A. Lyth (Yorkshire) at Leeds................	2017
Leading run-scorer	**2,318**	**A. G. Wakely (avge 27.27, SR 120.72)**	**2009–18**
Best bowling for	6-21	A. J. Hall v Worcestershire at Northampton ...	2008
Best bowling against	5-6	P. D. Collingwood (Durham) at Chester-le-Street	2011
Leading wicket-taker	73	D. J. Willey (avge 19.45, ER 7.42).........	2009–15
Highest total for	**231-5**	**v Warwickshire at Birmingham**	**2018**
Highest total against	260-4	by Yorkshire at Leeds....................	2017
Lowest total for	47	v Durham at Chester-le-Street	2011
Lowest total against	86	by Worcestershire at Worcester.............	2006

ADDRESS

County Ground, Abington Avenue, Northampton NN1 4PR; 01604 514455; reception@nccc.co.uk; www.northantscricket.com.

OFFICIALS

Captain A. G. Wakely
Head coach D. Ripley
Academy director K. J. Innes
President Lord Naseby

Chairman G. G. Warren
Chief executive R. Payne
Head groundsman C. Harvey
Scorer A. C. Kingston

At Oxford, April 7–9. OXFORD MCCU v NORTHAMPTONSHIRE. Abandoned.

At Lord's, April 13–15. NORTHAMPTONSHIRE lost to MIDDLESEX by 160 runs.

NORTHAMPTONSHIRE v WARWICKSHIRE

At Northampton, April 20–22. Warwickshire won by an innings and 48 runs. Warwickshire 22pts, Northamptonshire 2pts. Toss: Northamptonshire.

Sidebottom's maiden five-wicket haul set Warwickshire on course for a thumping victory. Scoring was restricted by a relaid outfield that had not bedded down after the harsh winter and halted even the best-timed shots. But Northamptonshire made things worse by showing little of the discipline required on a slow, two-paced pitch, collapsing from 101 for three to 147. Warwickshire were in peril at 28 for three, but Rhodes and Hain put on 91, and Ambrose battled to his 17th first-class hundred; his partnership of 117 with 18-year-old Henry Brookes, who made 70 from No. 10, was a ninth-wicket record for this fixture. A lead of 266 heaped pressure on Northamptonshire, who initially batted with more resolve, but slipped from 87 for one to 160 for five, before Rossington put on 72 with Cobb. Sidebottom, unfazed by extra responsibility after Olly Stone had been injured in the warm-up at his old home ground, finished with ten in the match, before Brookes wrapped things up. "It was difficult to score on that pitch, but to get knocked over was another thing," said Northamptonshire coach David Ripley.

Close of play: first day, Warwickshire 113-3 (Rhodes 39, Hain 51); second day, Northamptonshire 41-0 (Newton 29, Duckett 10).

Northamptonshire

R. I. Newton c Ambrose b Brookes	24	– c Sibley b Wright	46
B. M. Duckett c Rhodes b Sidebottom	0	– c Ambrose b Sidebottom	12
*A. G. Wakely c Brookes b Wright	10	– lbw b Patel	25
R. E. Levi b Sidebottom	41	– c Trott b Patel	0
R. I. Keogh b Patel	23	– c Ambrose b Sidebottom	6
†A. M. Rossington c Ambrose b Sidebottom	8	– lbw b Sidebottom	58
J. J. Cobb c Trott b Patel	18	– c Ambrose b Wright	30
D. A. J. Bracewell c Bell b Sidebottom	4	– not out	15
B. A. Hutton not out	6	– b Sidebottom	7
R. J. Gleeson b Sidebottom	1	– b Brookes	0
B. W. Sanderson lbw b Sidebottom	0	– b Brookes	0
B 4, lb 6, nb 2	12	B 3, lb 9, w 1, nb 6	19

1/4 (2) 2/37 (3) 3/55 (1)   (48.4 overs) 147   1/52 (2) 2/87 (3)   (91.2 overs) 218
4/101 (5) 5/113 (4) 6/118 (6)   3/87 (4) 4/95 (1)
7/130 (8) 8/146 (7) 9/147 (10) 10/147 (11)   5/100 (5) 6/172 (7) 7/193 (6)
                                         8/209 (9) 9/210 (10) 10/218 (11)

Wright 13–1–36–1; Sidebottom 12.4–3–35–6; Brookes 7–1–21–1; Lamb 4–1–13–0; Patel 12–4–32–2. *Second innings*—Wright 18–4–38–2; Sidebottom 22–5–61–4; Patel 31–15–65–2; Brookes 18.2–5–33–2; Lamb 2–0–9–0.

Warwickshire

W. M. H. Rhodes b Bracewell	44	H. J. H. Brookes c sub (R. S. Vasconcelos)	
D. P. Sibley c Hutton b Gleeson	12	b Hutton	70
I. R. Bell c Levi b Sanderson	0	R. N. Sidebottom not out	4
I. J. L. Trott lbw b Gleeson	4	B 10, lb 7, nb 10	27
S. R. Hain c Bracewell b Sanderson	85		
M. J. Lamb b Bracewell	44	1/22 (2) 2/23 (3) (128.1 overs) 413
†T. R. Ambrose c Newton b Bracewell	103	3/28 (4) 4/119 (1) 5/167 (5)
*J. S. Patel b Sanderson	20	6/233 (6) 7/262 (8) 8/263 (9)
C. J. C. Wright b Hutton	0	9/380 (7) 10/413 (10) 110 overs: 326-8

Sanderson 29–9–62–3; Bracewell 27–2–101–3; Gleeson 27–3–68–2; Hutton 29.1–3–101–2; Keogh 15–0–60–0; Cobb 1–0–4–0.

Umpires: R. A. Kettleborough and R. J. Warren.

NORTHAMPTONSHIRE v DURHAM

At Northampton, April 27–30. Abandoned. Northamptonshire 5pts, Durham 5pts.

Heavy rain claimed the first two days, saturating the outfield. It was the first abandoned first-class match at Northampton since 1981, and their fifth at home overall.

At Northampton, May 4–7. NORTHAMPTONSHIRE lost to PAKISTANIS by nine wickets (see Pakistan tour section).

At Birmingham, May 11–13. NORTHAMPTONSHIRE lost to WARWICKSHIRE by six wickets.

NORTHAMPTONSHIRE v LEICESTERSHIRE

At Northampton, June 9–11. Leicestershire won by six wickets. Leicestershire 19 pts (after 1pt penalty), Northamptonshire 4pts. Toss: uncontested. Championship debut: R. S. Vasconcelos.

In his first Championship game of the season, Chappell took a career-best six for 44 to put Northamptonshire in a tailspin on the first day. They needed an eighth-wicket stand of 42 between Zaib and Buck to help them towards a batting point. Kleinveldt, also making his first red-ball appearance of the summer, responded with four wickets to limit Leicestershire's lead to 13. A limping Newton, who had pulled a calf muscle, and Wakely, with his first Championship fifty of 2018, then put Northamptonshire in a position of apparent command. They began the third day 152 ahead with seven wickets in hand, but were ambushed by the Leicestershire seamers, losing seven for 53 in 19 calamitous overs. When Dearden was bowled third ball by Kleinveldt, it looked as if Leicestershire might find a target of 217 testing. But Horton and Hill put on 148 and made batting look easier than at any time in the match. Hill fell for 85, but Leicestershire soon secured back-to-back Championship victories for the first time since 2010.

Close of play: first day, Leicestershire 64-3 (Ackermann 19, Griffiths 1); second day, Northamptonshire 165-3 (Wakely 51, Rossington 20).

Northamptonshire

R. I. Newton b Chappell	31	– b Mohammad Abbas	30
B. M. Duckett c Hill b Raine	14	– b Raine	17
R. S. Vasconcelos c Hill b Chappell	49	– c sub (R. A. Jones) b Raine	37
*A. G. Wakely c Cosgrove b Chappell	9	– run out (sub A. Javid)	74
†A. M. Rossington c Hill b Dexter	24	– c Dexter b Mohammad Abbas	29
R. I. Keogh c Hill b Chappell	0	– c Hill b Mohammad Abbas	3
S. A. Zaib c Chappell b Raine	34	– lbw b Raine	0
R. K. Kleinveldt b Chappell	21	– c sub (A. Javid) b Raine	3
N. L. Buck b Chappell	20	– c sub (A. Javid) b Griffiths	17
B. D. Cotton not out	1	– lbw b Griffiths	0
B. W. Sanderson lbw b Raine	0	– not out	2
Lb 1	1	B 8, lb 9	17

1/22 (2) 2/51 (1) 3/75 (4)   (69 overs) 204
4/128 (3) 5/128 (6) 6/128 (5)
7/155 (8) 8/197 (7) 9/203 (9) 10/204 (11)

1/23 (2) 2/70 (1)   (76.1 overs) 229
3/121 (3) 4/176 (5)
5/192 (6) 6/199 (7) 7/199 (8)
8/225 (9) 9/225 (10) 10/229 (4)

Mohammad Abbas 16–4–43–0; Raine 17–5–35–3; Griffiths 11–2–55–0; Chappell 14–2–44–6; Parkinson 4–2–10–0; Dexter 7–1–16–1. *Second innings*—Raine 22–5–54–4; Mohammad Abbas 20–7–46–3; Chappell 15–3–43–0; Parkinson 12–2–46–0; Griffiths 7.1–1–23–2.

Leicestershire

H. E. Dearden b Sanderson	17	– b Kleinveldt		0
*P. J. Horton c and b Sanderson	13	– c Rossington b Keogh		62
C. N. Ackermann b Cotton	44	– (4) not out		42
M. J. Cosgrove lbw b Cotton	13	– (5) c sub (W. J. Heathfield) b Zaib		0
G. T. Griffiths c Keogh b Kleinveldt	1			
N. J. Dexter c Rossington b Sanderson	45	– not out		10
†L. J. Hill c Vasconcelos b Keogh	7	– (3) lbw b Zaib		85
B. A. Raine c Keogh b Kleinveldt	20			
Z. J. Chappell b Kleinveldt	40			
C. F. Parkinson c Sanderson b Kleinveldt	6			
Mohammad Abbas not out	0			
B 5, lb 4, nb 2	11	Lb 10, nb 8		18

1/24 (2) 2/31 (1) 3/56 (4)   (64.4 overs) 217   1/0 (1)   (4 wkts, 66.4 overs) 217
4/66 (5) 5/111 (3) 6/140 (7)   2/148 (2) 3/198 (3)
7/146 (6) 8/191 (8) 9/208 (9) 10/217 (10)   4/200 (5)

Kleinveldt 16.4–1–51–4; Sanderson 18–5–57–3; Cotton 12–3–24–2; Buck 8–0–36–0; Keogh 10–2–40–1. *Second innings*—Kleinveldt 12–1–39–1; Sanderson 12–4–19–0; Cotton 7–3–13–0; Keogh 19–1–69–1; Buck 10–1–43–0; Zaib 6.4–0–24–2.

Umpires: P. K. Baldwin and N. G. B. Cook.

NORTHAMPTONSHIRE v GLOUCESTERSHIRE

At Northampton, June 20–22 (day/night). Northamptonshire won by ten wickets. Northamptonshire 21pts, Gloucestershire 3pts. Toss: uncontested.

The floodlights were rendered redundant by brilliant sunshine stretching to the 8.30 close. In contrast to the previous summer's pink-ball thriller against Leicestershire, Northamptonshire won in 32 minutes of the third day – not that their supporters were grumbling about a first Championship victory of the season. Gloucestershire, still without Liam Norwell and David Payne, bowled dreadfully at the start, and Northamptonshire raced to 97 in 16 overs. Duckett, who hit Taylor for five successive fours in the third, recorded his first Championship half-century of the summer, in 44 balls. Sanderson then took five wickets in Gloucestershire's third-lowest total in this fixture. Following on, they slumped again, and looked on course to lose inside two days until Roderick and Higgins put on 100 for the sixth wicket. Higgins's 63 was his highest first-class score, but a career-best eight for 57 from Hutton ensured Gloucestershire did not wriggle off the hook. Duckett needed just 18 balls to complete the chase, entirely off his own bat. Only Javed Burki, who hit 38 not out for the Pakistanis against Yorkshire at Leeds in 1967, had made more while scoring 100% of his team's runs in an innings than Duckett's unbeaten 32.

Close of play: first day, Gloucestershire 25-1 (Howell 14); second day, Gloucestershire 245-8 (Miles 34, Taylor 37).

Northamptonshire

L. A. Procter c Bracey b Taylor	70	– not out	0
B. M. Duckett c Roderick b Taylor	52	– not out	32
R. S. Vasconcelos c Noema-Barnett b Taylor	0		
*A. G. Wakely c and b Noema-Barnett	3		
R. E. Levi c Roderick b Higgins	63		
†A. M. Rossington c Noema-Barnett b Taylor	10		
S. P. Crook c Noema-Barnett b Higgins	35		
S. A. Zaib lbw b Noema-Barnett	6		
R. K. Kleinveldt lbw b Miles	9		
B. A. Hutton c Hankins b Higgins	12		
B. W. Sanderson not out	0		
B 5, lb 15, nb 2	22		

1/99 (2) 2/105 (3) 3/112 (4)   (80.5 overs) 282   (no wkt, 4 overs) 32
4/186 (1) 5/209 (6) 6/220 (5)
7/248 (8) 8/261 (9) 9/277 (7) 10/282 (10)

Taylor 12–1–70–4; Higgins 18.5–6–52–3; Miles 17–0–58–1; Liddle 13–1–47–0; Noema-Barnett 20–8–35–2. *Second innings*—Taylor 2–1–9–0; Miles 2–0–23–0.

Gloucestershire

B. A. C. Howell c Rossington b Sanderson	14	– (2) c Rossington b Kleinveldt	14
*C. D. J. Dent lbw b Crook	11	– (1) c Levi b Hutton	23
J. R. Bracey b Kleinveldt	0	– lbw b Hutton	13
G. T. Hankins b Sanderson	3	– c Levi b Hutton	10
†G. H. Roderick lbw b Sanderson	0	– c Duckett b Crook	46
G. L. van Buuren lbw b Sanderson	0	– lbw b Hutton	0
R. F. Higgins c Rossington b Sanderson	10	– c Rossington b Hutton	63
K. Noema-Barnett not out	8	– c Rossington b Hutton	0
C. N. Miles c Procter b Crook	1	– not out	38
M. D. Taylor b Crook	10	– c Levi b Hutton	38
C. J. Liddle b Hutton	5	– b Hutton	0
		Lb 3, nb 2	5

1/25 (2) 2/25 (1) 3/25 (3) 　　(31.5 overs) 62　1/23 (2) 2/42 (3) 　　(77.5 overs) 250
4/26 (5) 5/26 (6) 6/33 (4)　　　　　　　　　3/57 (1) 4/72 (4)
7/42 (7) 8/43 (9) 9/57 (10) 10/62 (11)　　　5/72 (6) 6/172 (7) 7/172 (5)
　　　　　　　　　　　　　　　　　　　　8/172 (8) 9/250 (10) 10/250 (11)

Kleinveldt 13–6–27–1; Sanderson 14–7–16–5; Crook 3–1–11–3; Hutton 1.5–0–8–1. *Second innings*—Kleinveldt 18–1–76–1; Sanderson 17–1–45–0; Hutton 18.5–6–57–8; Crook 11–1–54–1; Procter 6–2–10–0; Zaib 7–4–5–0.

Umpires: N. A. Mallender and C. M. Watts.

At Cardiff, June 25–28. NORTHAMPTONSHIRE beat GLAMORGAN by 233 runs.

At Chesterfield, July 22–25. NORTHAMPTONSHIRE lost to DERBYSHIRE by 39 runs.

NORTHAMPTONSHIRE v MIDDLESEX

At Northampton, August 19–22. Middlesex won by 31 runs. Middlesex 19pts, Northamptonshire 6pts. Toss: uncontested. First-class debut: E. R. Bamber.

A catastrophic implosion condemned Northamptonshire to their first defeat after enforcing the follow-on. Chasing 216, they had reached 94 for one in the best batting conditions of the match when Murtagh and 19-year-old seamer Ethan Bamber, on debut, induced a collapse of seven for 54. The lower order were unable to mount a rescue operation. "There are ways of winning games and finding a way over the line – we were doing it last season but have lost it this year," said coach David Ripley. His team had dominated Middlesex until the third afternoon. Vasconcelos made his first Championship century, equalling his career-best 140, before Northamptonshire's seamers thrived in helpful conditions. With a lead of 159 and the light murky towards the close on the second day, Wakely's decision to enforce the follow-on made sense. He seemed to have been vindicated when Middlesex were six down and just seven ahead. But as the clouds parted, Holden and Harris – who had taken seven for 83 in Northamptonshire's first innings – put on 121 for the seventh wicket, and Bamber helped Harris add another 54 for the ninth. In all, the last four wickets swelled the total by 208. It was Middlesex's first win after following on since 1924, and the fifth in their history.

Close of play: first day, Northamptonshire 332-8 (Zaib 21, Hutton 14); second day, Middlesex 32-1 (Robson 16, Eskinazi 5); third day, Middlesex 374-9 (Harris 79, Murtagh 4).

Northamptonshire

L. A. Procter lbw b Harris	26	– (2) c White b Bamber. 35
B. M. Duckett b Harris.	7	– (8) c sub (O. P. Rayner) b Bamber. . . 0
†R. S. Vasconcelos b Bamber	140	– c sub (O. P. Rayner) b Murtagh 52
*A. G. Wakely c White b Harris	18	– lbw b Murtagh 6
R. E. Levi c Malan b Murtagh	41	– c White b Fuller 18
S. P. Crook lbw b Harris	31	– lbw b Murtagh 5
S. A. Zaib c White b Harris	27	– (1) c and b Harris 5
R. K. Kleinveldt b Harris	7	– (7) lbw b Bamber 5
N. L. Buck c White b Harris	0	– c Fuller b Murtagh 20
B. A. Hutton b Harris	22	– b Murtagh 23
B. W. Sanderson not out	0	– not out 2
B 4, lb 12, w 11	27	B 4, lb 3, nb 2. 9

1/16 (2) 2/75 (1) 3/133 (4)   (103.1 overs) 346
4/210 (5) 5/273 (3) 6/301 (6)
7/312 (8) 8/312 (9) 9/339 (7) 10/346 (10)

1/19 (1) 2/94 (2)   (60.5 overs) 184
3/102 (3) 4/111 (4)
5/125 (6) 6/130 (7) 7/130 (8)
8/148 (5) 9/177 (9) 10/184 (10)

Murtagh 26–7–68–2; Harris 26.1–6–83–7; Bamber 18–2–68–1; Fuller 20–3–69–0; Holden 10–1–34–0; Malan 3–0–8–0. *Second innings*—Murtagh 17.5–5–38–5; Harris 15–0–60–1; Fuller 12–2–40–1; Bamber 15–2–38–3; Holden 1–0–1–0.

Middlesex

S. D. Robson c Vasconcelos b Kleinveldt	18	– (2) c Vasconcelos b Buck. 72
N. R. T. Gubbins b Sanderson.	32	– (1) lbw b Sanderson 8
S. S. Eskinazi c Duckett b Kleinveldt	8	– lbw b Buck 20
*D. J. Malan lbw b Kleinveldt	0	– b Kleinveldt 5
E. J. G. Morgan b Sanderson	4	– lbw b Kleinveldt. 0
M. D. E. Holden c Vasconcelos b Hutton	30	– c Levi b Hutton 94
†R. G. White c Vasconcelos b Buck	35	– c Kleinveldt b Hutton. 5
J. A. R. Harris c Crook b Buck	6	– not out 79
J. K. Fuller b Buck	4	– c sub (†A. M. Rossington)
		b Kleinveldt. 12
E. R. Bamber not out	2	– c sub (†A. M. Rossington) b Buck. . . 19
T. J. Murtagh c Vasconcelos b Buck	11	– b Kleinveldt 4
B 22, lb 15	37	B 28, lb 16, w 3, nb 4, p 5 . . .	56

1/57 (2) 2/70 (1) 3/87 (4)   (52.2 overs) 187
4/71 (3) 5/79 (5) 6/148 (6)
7/158 (7) 8/170 (9) 9/171 (8) 10/187 (11)

1/23 (1) 2/70 (3)   (110.3 overs) 374
3/84 (4) 4/92 (5)
5/143 (2) 6/166 (7) 7/287 (6)
8/313 (9) 9/367 (10) 10/374 (11)

Sanderson 14–4–31–2; Hutton 11–1–48–1; Buck 16.2–2–51–4; Kleinveldt 11–3–20–3. *Second innings*—Kleinveldt 24.3–2–69–4; Sanderson 24–4–60–1; Buck 19–3–73–3; Hutton 25–3–80–2; Procter 6–0–20–0; Zaib 12–3–23–0.

Umpires: P. R. Pollard and M. J. Saggers.

At Chester-le-Street, August 29–30. NORTHAMPTONSHIRE beat DURHAM by seven wickets.

At Canterbury, September 4–7. NORTHAMPTONSHIRE lost to KENT by 102 runs.

NORTHAMPTONSHIRE v DERBYSHIRE

At Northampton, September 10–13. Derbyshire won by one wicket. Derbyshire 20pts, Northamptonshire 5pts. Toss: uncontested. Championship debut: C. O. Thurston.

    Rampaul concluded a final day of high tension and fluctuating fortunes by flicking Buck to fine leg for the boundary that completed Derbyshire's victory – and inflicted a second morale-crushing defeat on Northamptonshire in successive home matches. The decisive role was played by wicketkeeper Hosein, who made a skilful, unbeaten 54 from No. 7. In pursuit of 233, Derbyshire had reached 116 for two, but the loss of Madsen prompted a flurry. Hosein found willing accomplices in Hughes and Dal; the target was down to single figures when the ninth wicket fell. Hosein paddle-swept Sanderson for four, and in the next over Rampaul's sole scoring shot completed the job. Ben Curran, son of the former Northamptonshire all-rounder Kevin and brother of Surrey and England's Tom and Sam, had hit a maiden fifty on his home Championship debut, and Zaib's 57 guided the hosts to a decent total. Hughes kept Derbyshire's deficit manageable, despite Hutton's hard-working five-for. But Northamptonshire appeared to be moving into an impregnable position when they reached 154 for two in their second innings, only to lose eight for 45. It was Derbyshire's eighth one-wicket victory, and their first since beating the Australians in 1997; for Northamptonshire, it was a tenth such defeat, and the first since losing to Kent in 1988.

Close of play: first day, Derbyshire 60-2 (Lace 19, Hughes 38); second day, Derbyshire 118-4 (Hughes 74, Critchley 0); third day, Northamptonshire 198-8 (Zaib 4, Buck 5).

Northamptonshire

B. J. Curran c Dal b Palladino	51	– c and b Rampaul	11
L. A. Procter lbw b Palladino	1	– c Hosein b Viljoen	21
R. S. Vasconcelos c Critchley b Palladino	3	– c Dal b Critchley	62
R. E. Levi c Lace b Hughes	25	– c Critchley b Rampaul	46
*†A. M. Rossington b Hughes	35	– b Rampaul	1
C. O. Thurston c Hosein b Viljoen	20	– c Hughes b Viljoen	25
J. J. Cobb c Viljoen b Hughes	1	– c Hosein b Viljoen	3
S. A. Zaib c Wilson b Rampaul	57	– not out	5
B. A. Hutton b Hughes	16	– c Godleman b Viljoen	0
N. L. Buck c Rampaul b Viljoen	17	– c Wilson b Palladino	5
B. W. Sanderson not out	1	– b Palladino	0
B 9, lb 17, w 2	28	B 14, lb 6	20

1/22 (2) 2/36 (3) 3/78 (4) (76.3 overs) 255 1/15 (1) 2/79 (2) (64 overs) 199
4/115 (1) 5/137 (5) 6/139 (7) 3/154 (4) 4/155 (3)
7/149 (6) 8/170 (9) 9/212 (10) 10/255 (8) 5/155 (5) 6/183 (6) 7/186 (7)
 8/192 (9) 9/199 (10) 10/199 (11)

Palladino 19–11–25–3; Rampaul 17.3–5–60–1; Viljoen 20–2–77–2; Hughes 18–5–57–4; Dal 1–0–1–0; Madsen 1–0–9–0. *Second innings*—Palladino 18–5–31–2; Rampaul 15–1–53–3; Viljoen 16–5–51–4; Hughes 9–2–22–0; Madsen 1–0–1–0; Critchley 5–0–21–1.

Derbyshire

T. C. Lace c Curran b Buck	38	– b Hutton	39
*B. A. Godleman lbw b Hutton	1	– b Sanderson	0
W. L. Madsen c Rossington b Sanderson	0	– lbw b Sanderson	62
A. L. Hughes c Rossington b Buck	75	– c Levi b Buck	28
G. C. Wilson c Curran b Hutton	3	– run out (Cobb)	1
M. J. J. Critchley b Sanderson	6	– c Vasconcelos b Sanderson	4
†H. R. Hosein lbw b Sanderson	30	– not out	54
A. K. Dal b Hutton	8	– b Procter	14
G. C. Viljoen c Rossington b Hutton	12	– lbw b Procter	12
A. P. Palladino c Thurston b Hutton	26	– b Buck	5
R. Rampaul not out	5	– not out	4
Lb 12, nb 6	18	B 1, lb 6, nb 4	11

1/11 (2) 2/12 (3) 3/94 (1) (84.3 overs) 222 1/4 (2) 2/98 (1) (9 wkts, 77 overs) 234
4/117 (5) 5/125 (4) 6/125 (6) 3/116 (3) 4/118 (5)
7/150 (8) 8/185 (9) 9/190 (7) 10/222 (10) 5/122 (6) 6/158 (4)
 7/196 (8) 8/210 (9) 9/224 (10)

Hutton 25.3–9–59–5; Sanderson 25–9–61–3; Buck 20–4–63–2; Procter 14–6–27–0. *Second innings*—Hutton 23–8–70–1; Sanderson 27–6–52–3; Buck 17–1–63–2; Procter 10–2–42–2.

Umpires: J. H. Evans and R. J. Warren.

At Bristol, September 18–21. NORTHAMPTONSHIRE drew with GLOUCESTERSHIRE.

NORTHAMPTONSHIRE v SUSSEX

At Northampton, September 24–25. Northamptonshire won by six wickets. Northamptonshire 19pts, Sussex 3pts. Toss: Sussex.

Northamptonshire closed a grim season with a two-day victory. A change of ball proved a turning point in both first innings. After raising eyebrows by batting, Sussex were 58 for one when the switch was made, and crashed to 118, with Sanderson exploiting helpful conditions. Northamptonshire were also well placed, but lost eight for 48 before Sanderson and Cotton added 60 for the last wicket. Trailing by 53, Sussex started badly, but Wells and Finch appeared to be giving them the upper hand, until both perished to loose strokes. Cotton marched through the breach to claim his first five-for. Even so, Jordan's 47 ensured Northamptonshire would have an awkward chase of 170, and the match was in the balance at 82 for four. Curran exuded maturity, however, and his unbeaten 83, with good support from Rossington, avoided another calamity.

Close of play: first day, Sussex 4-0 (Wells 0, Salt 4).

Sussex

L. W. P. Wells b Cotton	15	– c Wakely b Cotton	50
P. D. Salt c Wakely b Hutton	20	– b Hutton	5
L. J. Evans b Sanderson	34	– b Hutton	0
H. Z. Finch b Buck	0	– c Rossington b Sanderson	63
M. G. K. Burgess c Keogh b Cotton	11	– c Curran b Cotton	15
*†B. C. Brown c and b Sanderson	21	– c Rossington b Cotton	0
D. M. W. Rawlins c Vasconcelos b Sanderson	0	– b Cotton	0
C. J. Jordan lbw b Hutton	1	– run out (Hutton)	47
O. E. Robinson lbw b Sanderson	1	– c Rossington b Buck	23
D. R. Briggs lbw b Hutton	7	– b Cotton	5
A. Sakande not out	0	– not out	1
B 4, lb 4	8	Lb 11, nb 2	13

1/28 (2) 2/58 (1) 3/63 (4) (35.1 overs) 118
4/78 (5) 5/89 (6) 6/89 (7)
7/90 (8) 8/93 (9) 9/118 (6) 10/118 (10)

1/5 (2) 2/5 (3) (59.1 overs) 222
3/114 (4) 4/124 (1)
5/128 (6) 6/128 (7) 7/153 (5)
8/194 (9) 9/215 (10) 10/222 (8)

Sanderson 12–3–32–4; Hutton 12.1–3–41–3; Buck 5–0–27–1; Cotton 6–2–10–2. *Second innings—* Hutton 16–7–56–2; Sanderson 17–3–52–1; Buck 10.1–0–45–1; Cotton 14–3–48–5; Keogh 2–0–10–0.

Northamptonshire

B. J. Curran c Evans b Sakande	36	– not out	83
R. S. Vasconcelos c Finch b Jordan	0	– c Brown b Robinson	19
C. O. Thurston b Sakande	29	– b Brown b Robinson	4
*A. G. Wakely c Brown b Jordan	12	– c Finch b Jordan	6
L. A. Procter c Finch b Brown	6	– lbw b Robinson	1
†A. M. Rossington c Brown b Robinson	0	– not out	51
R. I. Keogh c Finch b Robinson	7		
B. A. Hutton c Brown b Robinson	9		
B. D. Cotton not out	24		
N. L. Buck c Robinson b Sakande	5		
B. W. Sanderson c Brown b Jordan	36		
Lb 5, nb 2	7	Lb 6, nb 2	8

1/6 (2) 2/63 (1) 3/67 (3) (50.3 overs) 171
4/79 (5) 5/87 (4) 6/87 (6)
7/103 (8) 8/104 (7) 9/111 (10) 10/171 (11)

1/53 (2) (4 wkts, 37.1 overs) 172
2/59 (3) 3/81 (4)
4/82 (5)

Robinson 17–2–55–4; Jordan 18.3–2–59–3; Sakande 12–1–44–3; Briggs 3–1–8–0. *Second innings—*Robinson 16–2–48–3; Jordan 8–0–50–1; Sakande 10–0–47–0; Briggs 2.1–0–11–0; Wells 1–0–10–0.

Umpires: B. J. Debenham and N. J. Llong.

NOTTINGHAMSHIRE

Too close for comfort

Jon Culley

When Nottinghamshire won three of their first four Championship games, it was interpreted by some as the precursor to an unexpected title challenge on their return to Division One. Instead, those early points in the bank acted as an insurance against relegation after a collapse in the second half of the season. They lost five of their last six – three by an innings – and avoided relegation only because they had won four games to Lancashire's three, after they finished level on points.

Nor was there any white-ball success to lift the mood. The two trophies won in 2017 were both surrendered at the quarter-final stage: to Kent at Trent Bridge in the Royal London Cup, to Somerset at Taunton in the Vitality Blast. Before the season, the coaching staff had set out cautious ambitions: stay in Division One, and challenge for a limited-overs title. Even so, the way things turned out was disappointing.

The management wasted no time in tackling the cause of the problem: the failure to secure a batting bonus point in half their 14 Championship matches. Before the season had ended – with a huge home defeat by Somerset – a string of new signings began to arrive. Ben Slater from Derbyshire, and Ben Duckett from Northamptonshire came initially on loan, before signing permanently. Slater played in the last four games, and marked his home debut with a century against Yorkshire, while Duckett made three appearances. The batting will also be bolstered by Joe Clarke from Worcestershire, and the bowling by Leicestershire's Zak Chappell.

Others moved on. Will Fraine was offered a renewal to the contract he signed in May, but opted for a three-year deal with has native Yorkshire. Billy Root was released, and joined Glamorgan. Perhaps the most surprising departure was Riki Wessels, who signed for Worcestershire after he and Nottinghamshire decided it was in their mutual interests to end his eight-year stay at Trent Bridge. Seamer Matt Milnes, who claimed the wickets of Alastair Cook, Varun Chopra and Ravi Bopara in the win over Essex, his second Championship appearance, was offered a new contract, but preferred a move to Kent. Ben Kitt, a fast bowler who took more than 100 Second XI and Academy wickets in 2016, was released after two seasons of injury problems.

All the comings and goings will mean a different Nottinghamshire in 2019. Paul Coughlin, the all-rounder who arrived from Durham before the start of the season, made just three T20 appearances, and could not bowl at all after injuring his right shoulder on England Lions duty in the Caribbean. A similar injury disrupted Chris Nash's first season at the club. And more should be seen of Stuart Broad, who has been granted a testimonial year, and has only brief international commitments before August.

As much as the summer was a let-down, there were mitigating circumstances. Coughlin and Nash were intended to be a major part of the rebuilding process, so to lose one for virtually the whole summer, and the other for a sizable chunk, was unfortunate. It was perhaps not a surprise that the batting struggled after the loss over two seasons of four proven performers: James Taylor, Brendan Taylor, Michael Lumb and Chris Read were tough acts to follow. And Nottinghamshire missed Brett Hutton, their leading Championship wicket-taker in 2017, following his move to Northamptonshire.

Laurence Griffiths, Getty Images

Tom Moores

Alex Hales signed a white-ball contract, further weakening the first-class batting line-up, although because of England commitments and his IPL contract with Sunrisers Hyderabad he made just nine limited-overs appearances. The setbacks mounted when Quinton de Kock, who was to have replaced New Zealander Ross Taylor in August, withdrew at the last moment at the behest of Cricket South Africa. West Indian opener Kraigg Brathwaite was swiftly recruited, and averaged 42 in four matches.

A number of normally reliable performers were below par. Wessels had his poorest season for several years in all formats. Samit Patel, the PCA's Most Valuable Player in 2017, fell well short of his usual standards in the Championship, suffering his lowest returns with both bat and ball since 2012. He was short of runs in the 50- and 20-over competitions as well. Trusting it was only a blip, Nottinghamshire gave him a contract extension until the end of 2020.

There are still plenty of reasons for optimism. In a difficult year, Steven Mullaney dealt well with his elevation to the Championship captaincy. Tom Moores, voted Player of the Season, had to wear Read's gloves, but was excellent in his first full season as wicketkeeper. He scored a maiden first-class hundred at Taunton in June, and was the county's leading run-scorer in the Blast, where Dan Christian's unbeaten 113 against Northamptonshire was a county record.

Members who mutter about new signings denying opportunities to home-grown talent were cheered when Lyndon James, a 19-year-old all-rounder from Worksop, took three wickets on his first-class debut, against Essex in September. And Nottingham-born seamer Jack Blatherwick, also 19, made his first appearance, in a Royal London match against Warwickshire. The attendance that day of 14,537 was a record for a county one-day game at Trent Bridge. With a T20 average home gate of 11,377 – also a record – it was a good summer for the marketing department, at least.

Championship attendance: 38,130.

NOTTINGHAMSHIRE RESULTS

All first-class matches – Played 14: Won 4, Lost 8, Drawn 2. Abandoned 1.
County Championship matches – Played 14: Won 4, Lost 8, Drawn 2.

Specsavers County Championship, 6th in Division 1;
Vitality Blast, quarter-finalists; Royal London One-Day Cup, quarter-finalists.

COUNTY CHAMPIONSHIP AVERAGES, BATTING AND FIELDING

Cap		Birthplace	M	I	NO	R	HS	100	Avge	Ct
	†B. T. Slater	Chesterfield	4	8	0	349	109	1	43.62	1
2018	K. C. Brathwaite¶. . . .	Belfield, Barbados. . . .	4	8	1	296	71	0	42.28	1
2018	L. R. P. L. Taylor¶. . . .	Lower Hutt, NZ	8	15	0	506	146	1	33.73	13
2013	S. J. Mullaney.	Warrington	11	20	0	601	130	1	30.05	11
	†T. J. Moores	Brighton	13	22	1	616	103	1	29.33	39
2014	M. H. Wessels.	Maroochydore, Aust . .	12	23	3	568	75*	0	28.40	14
	†B. M. Duckett	Farnborough, Kent . . .	3	5	0	133	80	0	26.60	1
	J. D. Libby	Plymouth	14	27	2	662	100*	1	26.48	6
2008	S. R. Patel	Leicester	14	26	1	639	76	0	25.56	5
	C. D. Nash	Cuckfield	9	17	0	383	139	1	22.52	4
	M. E. Milnes	Nottingham‡	6	10	5	100	43	0	20.00	4
	M. H. A. Footitt	Nottingham‡	3	5	3	38	21*	0	19.00	1
	†L. Wood	Sheffield	6	10	2	137	35*	0	17.12	5
	†W. T. Root	Sheffield	6	12	0	196	36	0	16.33	3
2016	J. T. Ball§	Mansfield‡	6	10	2	130	44*	0	16.25	1
2008	S. C. J. Broad§	Nottingham‡	5	8	0	123	38	0	15.37	2
2014	L. J. Fletcher	Nottingham‡	13	23	1	304	43	0	13.81	4
2014	H. F. Gurney	Nottingham‡	11	16	10	73	29*	0	12.16	1
	M. Carter	Lincoln	4	8	0	76	22	0	9.50	4

Also batted: W. A. R. Fraine (*Huddersfield*) (1 match) 19, 30; L. W. James (*Worksop*‡) (1 match) 1, 13.

‡ *Born in Nottinghamshire.* § *ECB contract.* ¶ *Official overseas player.* †† *Other non-England-qualified.*

BOWLING

	Style	O	M	R	W	BB	5I	Avge
S. C. J. Broad	RFM	117.3	31	352	18	4-41	0	19.55
J. T. Ball	RFM	171.5	38	623	28	5-43	2	22.25
L. J. Fletcher	RFM	347.3	86	977	38	5-27	1	25.71
H. F. Gurney	LFM	325.3	52	1,137	42	6-25	2	27.07
M. Carter	OB	153.2	28	525	16	5-113	1	32.81
S. J. Mullaney	RM	114	21	402	11	4-68	0	36.54
L. Wood	LFM	110.1	15	411	10	3-66	0	41.10
S. R. Patel	SLA	305.5	66	896	19	6-114	1	47.15
M. E. Milnes	RFM	153	26	527	11	4-44	0	47.90

Also bowled: K. C. Brathwaite (OB) 2–0–10–0; M. H. A. Footitt (LFM) 66.4–9–276–6; L. W. James (RFM) 15–1–68–3; J. D. Libby (OB) 11.5–0–40–1; C. D. Nash (OB) 22–1–66–3; W. T. Root (OB) 9.3–1–55–3.

LEADING ROYAL LONDON CUP AVERAGES (100 runs/4 wickets)

Batting	Runs	HS	Avge	SR	Ct
S. J. Mullaney . .	406	124	58.00	103.04	6
T. J. Moores . . .	263	76	37.57	101.54	8/2
M. H. Wessels . .	273	76	34.12	109.63	7
L. R. P. L. Taylor	235	58	33.57	87.68	10
L. J. Fletcher . . .	133	53*	33.25	107.25	2
S. R. Patel	208	100	29.71	96.29	1
C. D. Nash	169	56	24.14	70.41	1
W. T. Root	128	41	21.33	85.90	2

Bowling	W	BB	Avge	ER
M. Carter	13	4-40	15.23	4.60
H. F. Gurney	9	4-58	24.00	6.54
J. T. Ball	14	4-29	27.92	5.66
L. J. Fletcher	9	4-20	36.11	5.41
S. R. Patel	10	2-33	37.20	5.01
S. J. Mullaney	4	2-42	61.25	4.62

LEADING VITALITY BLAST AVERAGES (100 runs/15 overs)

Batting	Runs	HS	Avge	SR	Ct	Bowling	W	BB	Avge	ER
D. T. Christian ..	415	113*	41.50	172.91	10	H. F. Gurney.....	20	3-24	19.35	7.63
M. H. Wessels...	307	58	21.92	163.29	4	I. S. Sodhi	19	4-17	23.21	8.16
S. J. Mullaney ..	263	55	18.78	152.02	5	L. J. Fletcher ...	12	3-21	31.25	8.89
T. J. Moores	445	80*	34.23	146.86	5	S. R. Patel	8	2-26	49.12	9.17
J. D. Libby	284	58	35.50	142.71	1	J. T. Ball	3	3-40	53.00	9.26
A. D. Hales.....	173	71*	34.60	132.06	7	S. J. Mullaney ...	11	2-29	28.09	9.65
S. R. Patel......	228	52	19.00	118.75	4	D. T. Christian ...	10	3-34	35.40	10.06
W. T. Root	199	40	24.87	109.94	3					

FIRST-CLASS COUNTY RECORDS

Highest score for	312*	W. W. Keeton v Middlesex at The Oval	1939
Highest score against	345	C. G. Macartney (Australians) at Nottingham ..	1921
Leading run-scorer	31,592	G. Gunn (avge 35.69)	1902–32
Best bowling for	10-66	K. Smales v Gloucestershire at Stroud........	1956
Best bowling against	10-10	H. Verity (Yorkshire) at Leeds	1932
Leading wicket-taker	1,653	T. G. Wass (avge 20.34)	1896–1920
Highest total for	791	v Essex at Chelmsford.	2007
Highest total against	781-7 dec	by Northamptonshire at Northampton	1995
Lowest total for	13	v Yorkshire at Nottingham................	1901
Lowest total against	16	by Derbyshire at Nottingham..............	1879
	16	by Surrey at The Oval	1880

LIST A COUNTY RECORDS

Highest score for	187*	A. D. Hales v Surrey at Lord's.	2017
Highest score against	191	D. S. Lehmann (Yorkshire) at Scarborough. ...	2001
Leading run-scorer	11,237	R. T. Robinson (avge 35.33)	1978–99
Best bowling for	6-10	K. P. Evans v Northumberland at Jesmond	1994
Best bowling against	7-41	A. N. Jones (Sussex) at Nottingham	1986
Leading wicket-taker	291	C. E. B. Rice (avge 22.60)	1975–87
Highest total for	445-8	v Northamptonshire at Nottingham	2016
Highest total against	425	by Northamptonshire at Nottingham	2016
Lowest total for	57	v Gloucestershire at Nottingham	2009
Lowest total against	43	by Northamptonshire at Northampton	1977

TWENTY20 COUNTY RECORDS

Highest score for	113*	**D. T. Christian v Northants at Northampton**	**2018**
Highest score against	111	W. J. Durston (Derbyshire) at Nottingham	2010
Leading run-scorer	3,465	**S. R. Patel (avge 27.50, SR 127.15)**	**2003–18**
Best bowling for	5-22	G. G. White v Lancashire at Nottingham	2013
Best bowling against	5-13	A. B. McDonald (Leicestershire) at Nottingham	2010
Leading wicket-taker	148	**S. R. Patel (avge 26.12, ER 7.36).**	**2003–18**
Highest total for	227-3	by Derbyshire at Nottingham..............	2017
Highest total against	227-5	by Yorkshire at Leeds	2017
Lowest total for	91	v Lancashire at Manchester	2006
Lowest total against	90	by Leicestershire at Nottingham	2014

ADDRESS

County Cricket Ground, Trent Bridge, Nottingham NG2 6AG; 0115 982 3000; administration@ nottsccc.co.uk; www.nottsccc.co.uk.

OFFICIALS

Captain (Ch'ship/one-day) S. J. Mullaney	**Chairman** R. W. Tennant
(Twenty20) D. T. Christian	**Chief executive** L. J. Pursehouse
Director of cricket M. Newell	**Chairman, cricket committee** D. J Bicknell
Head coach P. Moores	**Head groundsman** S. Birks
President P. Wynne-Thomas	**Scorer** R. Marshall

At Cambridge, April 1–3. CAMBRIDGE MCCU v NOTTINGHAMSHIRE. Abandoned.

At Manchester, April 13–16. NOTTINGHAMSHIRE beat LANCASHIRE by six wickets. *Nottinghamshire lose four chasing a target of ten.*

At Leeds, April 20–23. NOTTINGHAMSHIRE lost to YORKSHIRE by 164 runs.

At Worcester, April 27–30. NOTTINGHAMSHIRE beat WORCESTERSHIRE by an innings and 41 runs.

NOTTINGHAMSHIRE v HAMPSHIRE

At Nottingham, May 4–7. Nottinghamshire won by 203 runs. Nottinghamshire 22pts, Hampshire 4pts. Toss: Nottinghamshire.

In his first home match since becoming club captain, Mullaney led Nottinghamshire to their third win in four, reinforcing their position as Championship leaders. His one error was dropping Amla in the slips early on the last morning, on 13; Amla punished him with a five-hour century, but was last out in the final session. Mullaney finished in credit, as his own assertive second-innings hundred had allowed him to set Hampshire a formidable 469. On a slow pitch which made dislodging batsmen difficult, every home bowler made a mark. Broad allied high skill to pace in several spells as good as any he had bowled for Nottinghamshire. Patel's economy (in all, he took four for 48 in 38 overs, compared with two for 140 in 31 from his fellow left-arm spinner Dawson) maintained pressure, frustrating Amla into giving away his wicket on the second day.

Close of play: first day, Hampshire 70-3 (Amla 27, Rossouw 24); second day, Nottinghamshire 136-0 (Mullaney 82, Libby 50); third day, Hampshire 111-3 (Amla 11, Wood 13).

Nottinghamshire

*S. J. Mullaney c Wheal b Abbott	11	– c Vince b Weatherley	130
J. D. Libby lbw b Edwards	0	– c Adams b Edwards	54
C. D. Nash c Weatherley b Edwards	11	– c McManus b Wheal	15
L. R. P. L. Taylor run out (Amla/McManus)	47	– b Wheal	83
S. R. Patel c Wheal b Edwards	73	– c Wheal b Dawson	36
M. H. Wessels c Dawson b Wheal	54	– c Weatherley b Wood	14
†T. J. Moores c Weatherley b Wood	29	– c †Vince b Edwards	34
S. C. J. Broad c Vince b Wheal	33	– c Wheal b Wood	1
L. J. Fletcher c McManus b Edwards	5	– b Edwards	9
J. T. Ball b Dawson	11	– not out	1
H. F. Gurney not out	16		
B 9, lb 3	12	B 4, lb 2, nb 6	12

1/11 (1) 2/26 (3) 3/27 (2)   (69.3 overs) 302   1/155 (2)   (9 wkts dec, 85.3 overs) 389
4/122 (4) 5/176 (5) 6/211 (7)   2/180 (3) 3/222 (1)
7/265 (8) 8/271 (9) 9/275 (6) 10/302 (10)   4/318 (5) 5/333 (4) 6/371 (7)
                                                 7/377 (8) 8/379 (6) 9/389 (9)

Edwards 21–5–84–4; Abbott 17–2–73–1; Wood 13–3–65–1; Wheal 11–2–51–2; Dawson 7.3–1–17–1. *Second innings*—Abbott 8–0–47–0; Edwards 16.3–1–60–3; Dawson 24–1–123–1; Wheal 22–2–80–2; Wood 12–0–56–2; Weatherley 3–0–17–1.

Hampshire

J. J. Weatherley c Taylor b Broad	12	– c Fletcher b Patel	56
J. H. K. Adams c Moores b Broad	0	– c Mullaney b Gurney	17
*J. M. Vince lbw b Fletcher	5	– lbw b Broad	5
H. M. Amla c Wessels b Patel	69	– c Taylor b Ball	112
R. R. Rossouw c Taylor b Broad	26	– (6) c Wessels b Broad	7
L. A. Dawson c Libby b Gurney	10	– (7) lbw b Gurney	8
†L. D. McManus c Mullaney b Fletcher	66	– (8) c Moores b Broad	2
K. J. Abbott c Mullaney b Patel	14	– (9) c Wessels b Ball	10
C. P. Wood b Patel	5	– (5) b Ball	13
B. T. J. Wheal c Mullaney b Ball	3	– c Taylor b Gurney	2
F. H. Edwards not out	1	– not out	0
Lb 8, nb 4	12	B 9, lb 18, nb 6	33

1/0 (2) 2/17 (1) 3/23 (3) (86.1 overs) 223
4/88 (5) 5/106 (6) 6/140 (4)
7/188 (8) 8/198 (9) 9/211 (10) 10/223 (7)

1/82 (1) 2/82 (2) (108.5 overs) 265
3/93 (3) 4/112 (5)
5/151 (6) 6/191 (8) 7/236 (9)
8/241 (7) 9/257 (10) 10/265 (4)

In the second innings Dawson, when 6, retired hurt at 161-5 and resumed at 236-7.

Ball 22–6–69–1; Broad 21–9–45–3; Fletcher 15.1–3–26–2; Gurney 11–1–50–1; Patel 17–7–25–3.
Second innings—Ball 23.5–9–64–3; Broad 21–5–57–3; Patel 21–9–23–1; Fletcher 13–3–32–0;
Gurney 28–8–57–3; Nash 2–0–5–0.

Umpires: R. J. Bailey and P. J. Hartley.

NOTTINGHAMSHIRE v LANCASHIRE

At Nottingham, May 11–13. Lancashire won by an innings and 67 runs. Lancashire 22pts,
Nottinghamshire 3pts. Toss: uncontested.

Lancashire avenged their defeat at Old Trafford four weeks earlier with their first Championship win
of the season – and first away from home for nearly three years – thanks to Jennings and Onions, their
signings from Durham. After Nottinghamshire had collapsed from 80 for three to 133 all out, Jennings
batted five and a half hours for a hundred that helped his side to a 205-run lead. He looked calm and
authoritative, choosing his shots judiciously on a pitch with plenty in it for bowlers – though, apart from
Broad, the home attack fell well below the previous game's standards. But Onions and Anderson were
in fine fettle, reducing Nottinghamshire's second innings to a calamitous one for three. Skilfully
exploiting the conditions, Onions dismissed Nash and Taylor with consecutive balls on his way to six
wickets and match figures of nine for 77. Only Libby showed the necessary application, batting for three
and a half hours, before Lancashire wrapped things up on the third morning.

Close of play: first day, Lancashire 157-4 (Jennings 52, Vilas 9); second day, Nottinghamshire
106-5 (Libby 38, Moores 5).

Nottinghamshire

*S. J. Mullaney c Livingstone b Onions	3	– b Anderson	0
J. D. Libby c Livingstone b Clark	34	– c Livingstone b Anderson	46
C. D. Nash c Croft b Onions	16	– b Onions	0
L. R. P. L. Taylor lbw b Onions	0	– lbw b Onions	0
S. R. Patel run out (Vilas)	27	– c Davies b Anderson	16
M. H. Wessels c Vilas b Anderson	9	– lbw b Onions	35
†T. J. Moores c Vilas b Anderson	1	– c Vilas b Onions	9
S. C. J. Broad c Davies b Bailey	20	– lbw b Onions	4
L. J. Fletcher b Bailey	5	– lbw b Anderson	0
J. T. Ball c Vilas b Bailey	2	– c Croft b Onions	4
H. F. Gurney not out	0	– not out	0
B 1, lb 7, nb 8	16	B 9, lb 14, nb 4	24

1/3 (1) 2/46 (3) 3/50 (4) (47.1 overs) 133
4/80 (2) 5/99 (6) 6/104 (5)
7/106 (7) 8/128 (8) 9/132 (10) 10/133 (9)

1/0 (1) 2/1 (3) (52.4 overs) 138
3/1 (4) 4/24 (5)
5/92 (6) 6/118 (7) 7/126 (8)
8/127 (9) 9/138 (2) 10/138 (10)

Anderson 15–6–27–2; Onions 11–4–22–3; Bailey 8.1–1–28–3; Clark 11–1–36–1; Jennings 2–0–12–0. *Second innings*—Anderson 18–7–26–4; Onions 17.4–4–55–6; Bailey 8–3–13–0; Clark 7–0–17–0; Livingstone 1–0–2–0; Jennings 1–0–5–0.

Lancashire

K. K. Jennings b Broad	126	T. E. Bailey c Moores b Ball	11
A. L. Davies b Fletcher	50	G. Onions not out	16
H. Hameed c Moores b Fletcher	0	J. M. Anderson c Moores b Broad	6
*L. S. Livingstone c Moores b Gurney	8	B 14, lb 4, w 1, nb 6	33
S. Chanderpaul lbw b Mullaney	23		
†D. J. Vilas c and b Broad	20	1/77 (2) 2/87 (3) 3/96 (4) (86 overs) 338	
S. J. Croft c Moores b Broad	5	4/143 (5) 5/180 (6) 6/196 (7)	
J. Clark c Fletcher b Ball	40	7/281 (8) 8/301 (9) 9/323 (1) 10/338 (11)	

Ball 19–0–101–2; Broad 20.7–7–41–4; Fletcher 14–2–41–2; Gurney 14–4–53–1; Mullaney 8–2–36–1; Patel 11–0–40–0.

Umpires: M. A. Gough and R. T. Robinson.

At Taunton, June 9–12. NOTTINGHAMSHIRE lost to SOMERSET by six wickets. *Nottinghamshire score 505 following on.*

At Chelmsford, June 20–23. NOTTINGHAMSHIRE beat ESSEX by 301 runs.

NOTTINGHAMSHIRE v WORCESTERSHIRE

At Nottingham, June 25–28 (day/night). Drawn. Nottinghamshire 12pts, Worcestershire 9pts. Toss: uncontested. First-class debut: D. Y. Pennington.

With Broad off the field for much of the final day, nursing a minor ankle injury, Nottinghamshire failed to secure a win that would have closed the gap on the new leaders, Surrey. On the opening day Nash, in charge while Mullaney was captaining England Lions, scored his first century since leaving Sussex; he later wound up Worcestershire's first innings with his off-breaks, but did not enforce the follow-on, despite a 212-run advantage. With hindsight, he may have questioned his decision, though he had to consider the different demands of day/night cricket and the pink Kookaburra ball. He provided the brisk 19-year-old seamer Dillon Pennington with a maiden first-class wicket, but a fluent hundred from Libby and 71 from Patel – who was run out after colliding with the bowler, Whiteley, but survived when visiting captain D'Oliveira withdrew the appeal – allowed Nottinghamshire to set a target of 462. Instead, Worcestershire batted out 115 overs, thanks in part to Broad's absence but far more to the stylish Clarke, who spent tea on 99 – like Nash on the first day – before reaching an accomplished unbeaten 177.

Close of play: first day, Nottinghamshire 336-5 (Wessels 12, Moores 8); second day, Worcestershire 215-7 (Whiteley 25, Pennington 8); third day, Worcestershire 43-0 (Mitchell 19, Guptill 18).

Nottinghamshire

*C. D. Nash lbw b Guptill	139	– lbw b Pennington	1
J. D. Libby c Mitchell b Twohig	88	– not out	100
S. R. Patel b Magoffin	76	– c Guptill b Twohig	71
L. R. P. L. Taylor c Whiteley b Magoffin	0	– b Mitchell	1
W. T. Root c Cox b Magoffin	0	– lbw b Pennington	13
M. H. Wessels not out	75	– not out	57
†T. J. Moores b Whiteley	56		
S. C. J. Broad c Guptill b D'Oliveira	23		
L. J. Fletcher c Whiteley b D'Oliveira	13		
M. E. Milnes b Mitchell	8		
Lb 18, w 1, nb 2	21	B 3, lb 3	6

1/164 (2) 2/310 (1)   (9 wkts dec, 135 overs) 499   1/1 (1)   (4 wkts dec, 55.2 overs) 249
3/311 (3) 4/311 (5)   2/122 (3) 3/123 (4)
5/312 (4) 6/395 (8) 7/455 (8)   4/144 (5)
8/484 (9) 9/499 (10)   110 overs: 395-6

H. F. Gurney did not bat.

Magoffin 25–7–70–3; Pennington 22–6–87–0; Morris 22–2–82–0; Twohig 21–1–104–1; Whiteley 16–2–39–1; Mitchell 14–1–43–1; D'Oliveira 12–1–44–2; Guptill 3–1–12–1. *Second innings*—Magoffin 4–0–11–0; Pennington 8–0–51–2; Morris 5–0–27–0; Twohig 9–0–33–1; Whiteley 6.2–0–28–0; D'Oliveira 11–0–51–0; Mitchell 11–2–37–1; Guptill 1–0–5–0.

Worcestershire

D. K. H. Mitchell c Wessels b Gurney	18	– c Moores b Gurney	33
M. J. Guptill c Milnes b Gurney	28	– c Taylor b Milnes	29
T. C. Fell c Moores b Fletcher	25	– c †Wessels b Nash	26
J. M. Clarke lbw b Fletcher	40	– not out	177
*B. L. D'Oliveira c Nash b Broad	24	– c Libby b Gurney	14
†O. B. Cox b Gurney	25	– c Root b Fletcher	27
R. A. Whiteley b Nash	76	– c †Wessels b Gurney	10
B. J. Twohig b Broad	2	– b Fletcher	35
D. Y. Pennington lbw b Gurney	16	– c †Wessels b Fletcher	0
C. A. J. Morris not out	9	– not out	2
S. J. Magoffin lbw b Nash	0		
B 3, lb 7, nb 14	24	B 2, lb 3, nb 10	15

1/43 (2) 2/64 (1) 3/107 (3)   (74 overs) 287   1/62 (1)   (8 wkts, 114.5 overs) 368
4/128 (5) 5/173 (6) 6/189 (5)   2/74 (2) 3/137 (3)
7/195 (8) 8/234 (9) 9/287 (7) 10/287 (11)   4/156 (5) 5/212 (6)
                                           6/266 (7) 7/346 (8) 8/354 (9)

Broad 14–2–52–2; Fletcher 13–1–54–2; Gurney 23–0–97–4; Milnes 11–2–46–0; Patel 10–1–24–0; Nash 3–1–4–2. *Second innings*—Broad 8–1–32–0; Fletcher 20.5–6–54–3; Gurney 29–7–91–3; Milnes 24–6–76–1; Patel 19–1–61–0; Nash 13–0–48–1; Root 1–0–1–0.

Umpires: I. D. Blackwell and J. W. Lloyds.

NOTTINGHAMSHIRE v SURREY

At Nottingham, July 22–24. Surrey won by an innings and 183 runs. Surrey 24pts, Nottinghamshire 3pts. Toss: uncontested. Championship debut: W. A. R. Fraine.

Championship leaders Surrey took just over seven sessions to thrash Nottinghamshire, who had started in second place. The home batting looked lightweight, with Chris Nash injured and Ross Taylor's stint as overseas player done, but they fielded their first-choice seam attack – Broad, Ball, Gurney and Fletcher – for only the fourth time in 2018; the first two had produced wins. This may have explained a verdant pitch, but the move backfired: with the first day overcast, Surrey chose to bowl. Their seamers dismissed Nottinghamshire in 54 overs, and Burns steered his side into the lead by stumps. Apart from an hour or so on the second morning, the home quartet bowled mostly too short, and Surrey briskly amassed 592, their biggest total of the season. Burns continued to state his case for a Test call-up, and Clarke scored a magnificent century, his first for six years. Trailing by 382, Nottinghamshire subsided meekly again: Morkel ended the match with his ninth wicket, hitting the lengths that had too often eluded his opponents.

Close of play: first day, Surrey 223-1 (Burns 97, Borthwick 19); second day, Nottinghamshire 57-1 (Mullaney 19, Fraine 17).

Nottinghamshire

*S. J. Mullaney c Foakes b Dernbach	0	– lbw b Curran	23
J. D. Libby c sub (R. S. Patel) b Morkel	28	– lbw b Morkel	18
W. A. R. Fraine c Pope b Morkel	19	– c Foakes b Curran	30
S. R. Patel lbw b Curran	5	– c Borthwick b Morkel	55
W. T. Root c Pope b Clarke	15	– c Burns b Morkel	22
M. H. Wessels c Clarke b Dernbach	23	– c Borthwick b Dernbach	5
†T. J. Moores lbw b Clarke	27	– c Pope b Virdi	10
S. C. J. Broad c Curran b Morkel	3	– lbw b Morkel	1
L. J. Fletcher b Morkel	21	– b Virdi	8
J. T. Ball b Curran	16	– c Curran b Morkel	13
H. F. Gurney not out	29	– not out	0
B 1, lb 12, w 3, nb 8	24	Lb 2, nb 12	14

1/0 (1) 2/59 (3) 3/60 (2)   (54 overs) 210   1/37 (2) 2/61 (1)   (47.5 overs) 199
4/74 (4) 5/90 (5) 6/121 (6)   3/108 (3) 4/153 (4)
7/129 (8) 8/165 (7) 9/165 (9) 10/210 (10)   5/160 (6) 6/166 (5) 7/172 (8)
                                             8/176 (7) 9/189 (9) 10/199 (10)

Dernbach 12–2–38–2; Curran 13–2–47–2; Morkel 14–4–60–4; Clarke 15–4–52–2. *Second innings*—Dernbach 10–3–47–1; Curran 11–0–34–1; Morkel 13.5–2–60–5; Clarke 7–3–21–1; Virdi 6–0–35–2.

Surrey

*R. J. Burns c Mullaney b Patel	153	J. W. Dernbach not out	27
M. D. Stoneman c Moores b Ball	86	G. S. Virdi c Broad b Root	9
S. G. Borthwick c Moores b Fletcher	24		
A. J. Finch c Ball b Broad	2	B 7, lb 13, w 2, nb 30	52
†B. T. Foakes c Wessels b Broad	0		
O. J. D. Pope c Moores b Gurney	30	1/147 (2) 2/235 (3) (119.3 overs) 592
S. M. Curran lbw b Patel	70	3/246 (4) 4/250 (5) 5/297 (6)
R. Clarke c Moores b Root	111	6/347 (1) 7/472 (7) 8/549 (8)
M. Morkel lbw b Root	28	9/564 (9) 10/592 (11) 110 overs: 535-7

Ball 23–2–128–1; Broad 19–4–80–2; Gurney 16–0–119–1; Fletcher 20–3–63–1; Mullaney 10–1–44–0; Patel 27–3–101–2; Root 4.3–0–37–3.

Umpires: D. J. Millns and R. J. Warren.

At Southampton, August 19–22. NOTTINGHAMSHIRE lost to HAMPSHIRE by 270 runs.

At The Oval, August 29–31. NOTTINGHAMSHIRE lost to SURREY by an innings and 125 runs.

NOTTINGHAMSHIRE v YORKSHIRE

At Nottingham, September 4–7. Drawn. Nottinghamshire 12pts, Yorkshire 12pts. Toss: uncontested. County debuts: B. M. Duckett; M. W. Pillans; J. A. Raval.

Both teams had an unfamiliar look. Nottinghamshire's new signings – West Indies' Kraigg Brathwaite, Slater (from Derbyshire) and Duckett (Northamptonshire) – made their home debuts, while Footitt played his first home game at Trent Bridge since 2007; Riki Wessels was dropped. Meanwhile Yorkshire, whose relegation fears were growing after two heavy defeats, introduced New Zealand opener Jeet Raval, plus Mat Pillans, a transfer from Surrey; with Steven Patterson and David

Willey injured, Lyth became their fifth captain of the summer. Nottinghamshire's new batsmen were an instant success, contributing 260 runs to help their side to five bonus points for the first time in 2018. Yorkshire responded in kind, comfortably exceeding their previous highest total of the season, thanks to centuries from Ballance and Köhler-Cadmore (his first for the county). When Patel bowled Köhler-Cadmore with the fourth ball of the 110th over, they needed five for maximum batting points themselves; Waite, in his third first-class game, came in and hit his first two balls for four. By then, however, it was the fourth day, after drizzle had wiped out two sessions on the third. Patel's six wickets took him to 300 for Nottinghamshire but, on a slow pitch, the match drifted to a draw.

Close of play: first day, Nottinghamshire 332-7 (Patel 4, Milnes 1); second day, Yorkshire 258-4 (Köhler-Cadmore 57, Tattersall 12); third day, Yorkshire 357-5 (Köhler-Cadmore 92, Bresnan 11).

Nottinghamshire

K. C. Brathwaite lbw b Waite	71	– not out	42
B. T. Slater c Tattersall b Waite	109	– b Poysden	39
J. D. Libby lbw b Waite	1	– not out	0
B. M. Duckett c Tattersall b Bresnan	80		
*S. J. Mullaney b Brooks	39		
†T. J. Moores c Raval b Bresnan	8		
S. R. Patel c Brooks b Poysden	54		
L. Wood c Tattersall b Brooks	9		
M. E. Milnes lbw b Poysden	43		
H. F. Gurney c Raval b Bresnan	14		
M. H. A. Footitt not out	1		
B 1, lb 12, nb 6	19	B 2, lb 2, nb 8	12

1/182 (2) 2/188 (3) 3/205 (2) (117.3 overs) 448   1/91 (2) (1 wkt dec, 31 overs) 93
4/292 (5) 5/318 (4) 6/321 (6)
7/331 (8) 8/421 (9) 9/434 (7)
10/448 (10)   110 overs: 412-7

Bresnan 33.3–5–93–3; Brooks 21–2–79–2; Waite 23–4–91–3; Pillans 22–5–98–0; Poysden 10–0–60–2; Brook 6–2–7–0; Lyth 2–0–7–0. *Second innings*—Bresnan 3–1–7–0; Pillans 8–0–32–0; Waite 3–1–6–0; Poysden 10–0–34–1; Lyth 7–1–10–0.

Yorkshire

*A. Lyth c Wood b Footitt	0	J. A. Brooks c Libby b Patel	1
J. A. Raval b Gurney	15	J. E. Poysden not out	2
H. C. Brook c Wood b Patel	47		
G. S. Ballance c Slater b Patel	104	B 11, lb 10, w 3, nb 18	42
T. Köhler-Cadmore b Patel	106		
†J. A. Tattersall c Moores b Gurney	51	1/0 (1) 2/59 (2)	(147.2 overs) 498
T. T. Bresnan c Footitt b Libby	80	3/137 (3) 4/232 (4) 5/334 (6)	
M. J. Waite c Milnes b Patel	42	6/395 (5) 7/469 (8) 8/484 (9)	
M. W. Pillans lbw b Patel	8	9/492 (10) 10/498 (7)	110 overs: 403-6

Footitt 22–2–79–1; Milnes 21–2–96–0; Wood 15–1–51–0; Gurney 33.5–4–114–2; Patel 47–12–114–6; Libby 8.3–0–23–1.

Umpires: R. J. Bailey and S. J. O'Shaughnessy.

NOTTINGHAMSHIRE v ESSEX

At Nottingham, September 10–13. Essex won by eight wickets. Essex 20pts, Nottinghamshire 3pts. Toss: Nottinghamshire. First-class debut: L. W. James. County debut: M. Vijay.

Nottinghamshire's disappointing finish to the season continued with a fourth defeat in five matches, mainly because of weak contributions from the middle order. They stumbled from 66 for two to 104 for eight in the first innings, and from 161 for one to 337 all out in the second, when only Mullaney's fifty held up Essex; Harmer's off-spin claimed six for 87. That left the visitors four sessions to accrue 282; they used only two, winning just before lunch on the final day. The chase featured hundreds for Indian Test batsman Murali Vijay, on his Essex debut, and Westley, who helped him add 204 for the second wicket. There were some positives for Nottinghamshire. Debutant Lyndon James, a 19-year-old seam-bowling all-rounder, took three wickets in 18 balls – culminating in Vijay – as they fought back on the first evening. Next day, the new opening pair Brathwaite and Slater put on 108, their third substantial partnership in four innings.

Close of play: first day, Essex 133-5 (ten Doeschate 11, Porter 8); second day, Nottinghamshire 116-1 (Brathwaite 47, Fletcher 6); third day, Essex 147-1 (Vijay 73, Westley 45).

Nottinghamshire

K. C. Brathwaite lbw b Porter	0	– lbw b Harmer	68
B. T. Slater b Coles	33	– lbw b Coles	54
J. D. Libby b Porter	9	– (4) b Harmer	15
B. M. Duckett c Wheater b Coles	21	– (5) lbw b Westley	17
*S. J. Mullaney c Wheater b Quinn	3	– (6) c Wheater b Harmer	53
†T. J. Moores lbw b Quinn	7	– (7) st Wheater b Harmer	15
S. R. Patel c Harmer b Quinn	19	– (8) lbw b Porter	11
L. W. James c Lawrence b Coles	1	– (9) c ten Doeschate b Harmer	13
L. Wood b Porter	27	– (10) not out	14
L. J. Fletcher c ten Doeschate b Porter	30	– (3) lbw b Harmer	39
M. H. A. Footitt not out	21	– c Wheater b Porter	4
B 1, lb 3, nb 2	6	B 4, lb 24, nb 6	34

1/0 (1) 2/16 (3) 3/66 (4)　　　　　　(58.1 overs) 177　　1/108 (2) 2/161 (1)　　(103 overs) 337
4/67 (2) 5/74 (5) 6/91 (6)　　　　　　　　　　　　　　3/194 (3) 4/199 (4)
7/96 (7) 8/104 (8) 9/132 (9) 10/177 (10)　　　　　　5/222 (5) 6/290 (7) 7/299 (6)
　　　　　　　　　　　　　　　　　　　　　　　　8/315 (9) 9/331 (8) 10/337 (11)

Porter 15.1–3–50–4; Quinn 19–6–37–3; Harmer 8–1–24–0; Coles 16–1–62–3. *Second innings—* Porter 26–5–77–2; Quinn 17–2–69–0; Coles 24–10–52–1; Bopara 2–0–12–0; Harmer 29–6–87–6; Westley 5–0–12–1.

Essex

N. L. J. Browne b Mullaney	24	– lbw b Footitt	11
M. Vijay c Moores b James	56	– b Patel	100
T. Westley lbw b James	16	– not out	110
D. W. Lawrence c Fletcher b James	0	– not out	29
R. S. Bopara c Patel b Mullaney	5		
*R. N. ten Doeschate lbw b Mullaney	32		
J. A. Porter lbw b Fletcher	8		
†A. J. A. Wheater c Moores b Mullaney	14		
S. R. Harmer b Wood	48		
M. T. Coles lbw b Wood	9		
M. R. Quinn not out	1		
Lb 10, nb 10	20	Lb 9, w 7, nb 16	32

1/56 (1) 2/93 (3) 3/93 (4)　　　　　　(66.1 overs) 233　　1/17 (1)　　(2 wkts, 69.4 overs) 282
4/102 (5) 5/118 (2) 6/134 (7)　　　　　　　　　　　　2/221 (2)
7/163 (8) 8/174 (6) 9/206 (10) 10/233 (9)

Fletcher 18–2–58–1; Footitt 6–2–12–0; Mullaney 22–5–68–4; Wood 8.1–3–31–2; James 12–1–54–3. *Second innings—*Fletcher 17–4–58–0; Footitt 8.4–1–49–1; Mullaney 16–2–57–0; Wood 11–3–31–0; James 3–0–14–0; Patel 13–3–60–1; Libby 1–0–4–0.

Umpires: N. G. B. Cook and T. Lungley.

❝ The conditions were a gift to Mohammad Abbas, a loaves-and-fishes kind of bowler, able to do so much with so little.❞
Pakistan v Australia in 2018–19, Second Test, page 939

NOTTINGHAMSHIRE v SOMERSET

At Nottingham, September 24–26. Somerset won by an innings and 146 runs. Somerset 24pts, Nottinghamshire 2pts. Toss: Somerset.

Needing five points to guarantee Division One status, Nottinghamshire managed only two – but survived when Lancashire failed to secure a third batting point at Southampton. They slumped to their fourth innings defeat in a dismal season; extraordinarily, since 2009 they had won only one out of 26 Championship matches in September. Meanwhile, Somerset took maximum points to make sure they were runners-up to Surrey. Their total of 463 might have been higher still but for Gurney

HAT-TRICKS BY TWO BOWLERS ON SAME TEAM

G. S. le Roux and C. E. B. Rice	South Africa v Australian XI at Johannesburg . .	1985-86
V. J. Wells and A. Sheriyar	Leicestershire v Durham at Durham	1994
D. W. Headley and M. J. McCague . . .	Kent v Hampshire at Canterbury	1996
T. B. Abell and C. Overton	**Somerset v Nottinghamshire at Nottingham** .	**2018**

WINNING COMBINATION

Hat-tricks for a wicketkeeper or fielder off one bowler:

†W. H. Brain* (off C. L. Townsend) . .	Gloucestershire v Somerset at Cheltenham	1893
G. J. Thompson (off S. G. Smith) . . .	Northants v Warwickshire at Birmingham	1914
†K. R. Meherhomji (off L. Ramji) . . .	Freelooters v Nizam's State Railway A at Secunderabad	1931-32
C. D. White (off R. Beesly)	Border v Griqualand West at Queenstown	1946-47
†G. O. Dawkes (off H. L. Jackson) . . .	Derbyshire v Worcestershire at Kidderminster . . .	1958
M. E. Trescothick (off C. Overton)	**Somerset v Nottinghamshire at Nottingham** . . .	**2018**

†   *Wicketkeeper.*   *   *All stumped.*

R. C. Russell and T. Frost also claimed wicketkeeping hat-tricks, but off more than one bowler.

checking their progress by dismissing Hildreth, for a four-hour century, Gregory and Davies in 21 deliveries just before the first-day close. Nottinghamshire were bowled out inside 36 overs first time round; asked to follow on, they were out again by lunch on the third day, losing their last nine for 70. Two bowlers took hat-tricks for Somerset: Abell's medium-pace accounted for the last three first-innings wickets, before Craig Overton removed Slater, Patel and Wessels in the first over of the third morning, all held at second slip by Trescothick – the first outfielder since George Thompson of Northamptonshire in 1914 to take catches from three consecutive deliveries in the Championship.

Close of play: first day, Somerset 353-7 (C. Overton 0); second day, Nottinghamshire 115-3 (Slater 45).

Somerset

M. E. Trescothick c Duckett b Gurney	71	J. H. Davey lbw b Fletcher	21
T. Banton lbw b Wood	3	M. J. Leach not out	5
Azhar Ali c Wessels b Gurney	19		
J. C. Hildreth c Moores b Gurney	137	B 5, lb 13, nb 4	22
*T. B. Abell c Mullaney b Carter	42		
†S. M. Davies c Moores b Gurney	55	1/8 (2) 2/75 (3) 3/146 (1) (115.5 overs) 463	
L. Gregory c Moores b Gurney	10	4/238 (5) 5/328 (4) 6/348 (7)	
C. Overton c Wood b Gurney	23	7/353 (6) 8/394 (8) 9/457 (10)	
J. Overton c Carter b Patel	55	10/463 (9) 110 overs: 429-8	

Fletcher 22–5–75–1; Wood 13–2–56–1; Gurney 30–4–106–6; Mullaney 3–1–14–0; Carter 30–2–131–1; Patel 17.5–3–63–1.

Nottinghamshire

J. D. Libby c C. Overton b Gregory	0	– c Hildreth b Davey	12
B. T. Slater b C. Overton	35	– c Trescothick b C. Overton	49
*S. J. Mullaney c Hildreth b C. Overton	18	– c Gregory b Leach	54
B. M. Duckett c Trescothick b C. Overton	0	– (5) lbw b Gregory	15
S. R. Patel c Davies b Gregory	16	– (6) c Trescothick b C. Overton	0
M. H. Wessels b C. Overton	4	– (7) c Trescothick b C. Overton	0
†T. J. Moores c Davies b Gregory	4	– (8) c Hildreth b Davey	17
L. Wood not out	35	– (9) c Davies b Gregory	4
L. J. Fletcher c Trescothick b Abell	12	– (4) c Gregory b J. Overton	0
M. Carter c Hildreth b Abell	0	– lbw b Davey	22
H. F. Gurney c C. Overton b Abell	0	– not out	4
Lb 7, nb 2	9	B 2, lb 3, nb 2	7

1/0 (1) 2/50 (3) 3/50 (4)   (35.3 overs) 133   1/17 (1) 2/114 (3)   (64.2 overs) 184
4/69 (2) 5/73 (5) 6/85 (6)   3/115 (4) 4/119 (2)
7/85 (7) 8/133 (9) 9/133 (10) 10/133 (11)   5/119 (6) 6/119 (7) 7/149 (5)
                                        8/157 (9) 9/171 (8) 10/184 (10)

Gregory 11.4–3–36–3; Davey 9–1–49–0; C. Overton 9–2–27–4; J. Overton 4.2–0–14–0; Abell 1.3–1–0–3. *Second innings*—Gregory 15–5–35–2; C. Overton 16–3–68–3; Davey 11.2–4–20–3; J. Overton 13–7–23–1; Abell 5–1–25–0; Leach 4–1–8–1.

Umpires: N. G. B. Cook and R. A. Kettleborough.

SOMERSET

The wicked pitch of the West

Richard Latham

For the fifth time since the turn of the century, Somerset had to be content with runners-up spot in the Championship. The quest for a first title will go into a 128th year. While no one at Taunton was disputing Surrey's credentials as champions, new director of cricket Andy Hurry and head coach Jason Kerr could reflect with great satisfaction on a first year in charge, during which the team also reached finals day in the Vitality Blast. A happy dressing-room brought the best out of the old hands, and allowed younger players to prosper.

They even managed to negotiate the fallout from the Australian ball-tampering scandal. After cancelling plans to hire Cameron Bancroft, Somerset turned to his countryman Matt Renshaw, who proved a more than adequate replacement. He hit centuries in the first two Championship games, including one before lunch against Yorkshire, averaged 51 in 11 innings, and proved popular on and off the field. When Renshaw was forced home by a finger injury, Hurry signed Azhar Ali, the Pakistan Test batsman, who also made a century on debut, at Worcester; he was set to return. With all-rounder Corey Anderson and seamer Jerome Taylor playing leading roles in the Blast, Somerset's overseas recruitment was impressive.

In the Championship, they won seven games, the most they had won in the first division, and one more than in 2010, when they finished level on points with champions Nottinghamshire. James Hildreth again demonstrated why many consider him the best contemporary batsman not to have represented England, scoring 1,089 runs at 45. Tom Abell, a wiser and more mature player in his second summer as captain, was the other batsman to average over 40. Marcus Trescothick's season was interrupted by a foot injury suffered while making a hundred at Old Trafford. But he still did more than enough to earn a new contract, which will see him playing on at the age of 43.

Pitches at Taunton again came under scrutiny, especially during the extraordinary tie with Lancashire in September, when Somerset failed to reach a target of 78. Twenty-five wickets fell to spin, and the surface was rated "below average" by ECB cricket liaison officer Dean Cosker. It was the second such rating in 12 months and, while Somerset escaped a points deduction this time, they were left in no doubt about the consequences of a further transgression.

Slow left-armer Jack Leach was a beneficiary of the spin-friendly pitches. After a summer in which two injuries suffered while batting – one in the nets – hit his hopes of England selection, he claimed career-best figures of 12 for 102 during the Lancashire game to help secure his place on the tour to Sri Lanka. But while Leach eventually prospered, it was a frustrating season for off-spinner Dom Bess, who was selected for only half the Championship

Harry Trump, Getty Images

Tom Abell

fixtures despite his sudden elevation to the England Test team against Pakistan, and finished with 11 wickets at 54. Away from home, Somerset relied on their seam attack, led by Lewis Gregory and Craig Overton. They were well supported by Josh Davey, Tim Groenewald, a resurgent Jamie Overton and Abell, who surprised perhaps even himself by taking 19 wickets. The arrival of Jack Brooks from Yorkshire will add to a wide array of seam options.

Two of Somerset's poorest performances came against Surrey. They were thrashed by an innings at Guildford, and looked set for another defeat in the return at Taunton, where an overnight storm before the final day lifted the covers and forced an abandonment. It was fortunate that Surrey were already assured of the Championship – and Somerset well placed in second.

No one was getting too excited about the Vitality Blast when Somerset lost three of their first six games. But a seven-match winning streak prompted talk of a first trophy since 2005. After finishing top of their group, they despatched Nottinghamshire in a home quarter-final in which Gregory bludgeoned 60 off 24 balls; he finished as the fastest-scoring batsman in the competition, with a strike-rate over 200. The ploy of opening the bowling with leg-spinner Max Waller also paid off: he claimed 16 wickets, with an economy-rate under seven. Jamie Overton developed variations in pace that brought 24 victims, and the wily Taylor took 22. But their tournament ended in the semi-final, when they lost to Sussex.

Johann Myburgh marked his last season by hammering a maiden T20 century, against Essex at Taunton. Anderson topped 500 runs in the Blast at an average of 42, striking 34 sixes, 15 more than Gregory, who rose to the challenge of captaining the side, and blossomed after signing a new three-year contract.

The only disappointment was the Royal London Cup. After victories over Surrey and Glamorgan raised hopes, Somerset lost three of their next four, and would almost certainly have been beaten by Gloucestershire at home but for the weather. Failure to reach the knockout stage was a shock, but there were still some brilliant individual performances: Hildreth hit 159 against Glamorgan, and the irrepressible Peter Trego clinched a white-ball contract for 2019 with a century in the final group match, at Southampton.

Championship attendance: 37,954.

SOMERSET RESULTS

All first-class matches – Played 14: Won 7, Lost 2, Tied 1, Drawn 4.
County Championship matches – Played 14: Won 7, Lost 2, Tied 1, Drawn 4.

Specsavers County Championship, 2nd in Division 1;
Vitality Blast, semi-finalists; Royal London One-Day Cup, 4th in South Group.

COUNTY CHAMPIONSHIP AVERAGES, BATTING AND FIELDING

Cap		Birthplace	M	I	NO	R	HS	100	Avge	Ct/St
	M. T. Renshaw¶	Middlesbrough . . .	6	11	1	513	112	3	51.30	5
2007	J. C. Hildreth	Milton Keynes	14	26	2	1,089	184	3	45.37	13
2018	T. B. Abell	Taunton‡	14	26	4	883	132*	1	40.13	2
	Azhar Ali¶	Lahore, Pakistan . .	7	13	1	402	125	1	33.50	2
2017	†S. M. Davies	Bromsgrove	14	25	2	756	92*	0	32.86	38/3
	G. A. Bartlett	Frimley	6	11	0	306	110	1	27.81	2
1999	†M. E. Trescothick	Keynsham‡	10	18	0	491	100	1	27.27	16
	D. M. Bess	Exeter	7	11	1	226	92	0	22.60	3
2015	L. Gregory	Plymouth	12	21	2	411	65	0	21.63	12
	†E. J. Byrom††	Harare, Zimbabwe .	8	15	0	309	54	0	20.60	2
	J. Overton	Barnstaple	8	12	2	197	55	0	19.70	5
2016	C. Overton	Barnstaple	11	18	1	331	80	0	19.47	9
	J. H. Davey††	Aberdeen	11	17	6	206	36	0	18.72	3
2016	T. D. Groenewald . . .	Pietermaritzburg, SA	7	11	5	91	36*	0	15.16	2
2017	†M. J. Leach	Taunton‡	11	16	2	174	66	0	12.42	5
2007	P. D. Trego	Weston-s-Mare‡ . .	2	4	0	46	39	0	11.50	1
	B. G. F. Green	Exeter	2	4	0	43	26	0	10.75	3

Also batted: T. Banton (*Chiltern*) (2 matches) 30, 4, 3 (1 ct); R. E. van der Merwe†† (*Johannesburg, SA*) (cap 2018) (1 match) 0; P. A. van Meekeren†† (*Amsterdam, Netherlands*) (1 match) 6, 0*; M. T. C. Waller (*Salisbury*) (1 match) 0.

‡ *Born in Somerset.* ¶ *Official overseas player.* †† *Other non-England-qualified.*

BOWLING

	Style	O	M	R	W	BB	5I	Avge
M. J. Leach	SLA	255.4	57	722	30	8-85	3	24.06
T. D. Groenewald	RFM	173	41	509	21	4-85	0	24.23
J. Overton	RFM	177.3	34	646	26	4-25	0	24.84
L. Gregory	RFM	305.5	55	928	37	4-33	0	25.08
J. H. Davey	RFM	290.4	73	862	34	5-65	1	25.35
T. B. Abell	RM	121.4	23	492	19	4-43	0	25.89
C. Overton	RFM	321.3	72	1,014	37	4-27	0	27.40
D. M. Bess	OB	204.1	51	602	11	3-81	0	54.72

Also bowled: Azhar Ali (LB) 11–3–20–1; G. A. Bartlett (OB) 3.2–0–27–0; E. J. Byrom (OB) 10–1–39–0; B. G. F. Green (RFM) 7–3–17–1; M. T. Renshaw (OB) 3–1–11–0; P. D. Trego (RFM) 41–7–146–3; R. E. van der Merwe (SLA) 51–13–143–5; P. A. van Meekeren (RFM) 20–3–67–1.

LEADING ROYAL LONDON CUP AVERAGES (100 runs/4 wickets)

Batting	Runs	HS	Avge	SR	Ct
J. C. Hildreth	438	159	62.57	98.20	4
P. D. Trego	376	100	47.00	89.52	1
R. E. van der Merwe	195	61	39.00	107.73	3
L. Gregory	151	60	37.75	102.72	0
J. G. Myburgh	218	75*	31.14	110.65	1
M. T. Renshaw . .	180	56	30.00	103.44	2
S. M. Davies	158	56	19.75	105.33	10

Bowling	W	BB	Avge	ER
T. D. Groenewald .	9	3-43	22.00	5.82
C. Overton	12	4-27	28.00	5.96
L. Gregory	6	2-41	31.00	5.63
P. D. Trego.	7	2-23	34.85	4.88
R. E. van der Merwe	6	2-64	47.83	6.91

LEADING VITALITY BLAST AVERAGES (150 runs/15 overs)

Batting	Runs	HS	Avge	SR	Ct/St	Bowling	W	BB	Avge	ER
L. Gregory	328	62	46.85	202.46	5	M. T. C. Waller ..	16	4-25	23.87	6.82
C. J. Anderson .	514	72	42.83	169.07	3	R. E. van der Merwe	12	2-26	41.83	8.58
J. G. Myburgh .	372	103*	26.57	151.21	6	J. E. Taylor......	22	5-15	16.63	8.92
S. M. Davies ..	213	60	15.21	141.05	8/1	L. Gregory	18	4-28	31.88	9.89
J. C. Hildreth .	403	57	28.78	139.93	5	J. Overton......	24	5-47	22.50	10.25
P. D. Trego....	328	72*	23.42	138.98	2					
T. B. Abell....	292	48	29.20	132.12	12					

FIRST-CLASS COUNTY RECORDS

Highest score for	342	J. L. Langer v Surrey at Guildford	2006
Highest score against	424	A. C. MacLaren (Lancashire) at Taunton	1895
Leading run-scorer	21,142	H. Gimblett (avge 36.96)	1935–54
Best bowling for	10-49	E. J. Tyler v Surrey at Taunton	1895
Best bowling against	10-35	A. Drake (Yorkshire) at Weston-super-Mare	1914
Leading wicket-taker	2,165	J. C. White (avge 18.03)	1909–37
Highest total for	850-7 dec	v Middlesex at Taunton.....................	2007
Highest total against	811	by Surrey at The Oval	1899
Lowest total for	25	v Gloucestershire at Bristol.................	1947
Lowest total against	22	by Gloucestershire at Bristol................	1920

LIST A COUNTY RECORDS

Highest score for	184	M. E. Trescothick v Gloucestershire at Taunton .	2008
Highest score against	167*	A. J. Stewart (Surrey) at The Oval	1994
Leading run-scorer	7,374	M. E. Trescothick (avge 36.87)...............	1993–2014
Best bowling for	8-66	S. R. G. Francis v Derbyshire at Derby.........	2004
Best bowling against	7-39	A. Hodgson (Northamptonshire) at Northampton	1976
Leading wicket-taker	309	H. R. Moseley (avge 20.03)	1971–82
Highest total for	413-4	v Devon at Torquay........................	1990
Highest total against	429-9	by Nottinghamshire at Taunton..............	2017
Lowest total for	{ 58	v Essex at Chelmsford......................	1977
	{ 58	v Middlesex at Southgate	2000
Lowest total against	60	by Kent at Taunton	1979

TWENTY20 COUNTY RECORDS

Highest score for	151*	C. H. Gayle v Kent at Taunton	2015
Highest score against	122*	J. J. Roy (Surrey) at The Oval................	2015
Leading run-scorer	3,359	J. C. Hildreth (avge 24.51, SR 123.81)........	2004–18
Best bowling for	6-5	A. V. Suppiah v Glamorgan at Cardiff	2011
Best bowling against	5-11	A. F. Milne (Kent) at Taunton	2017
Leading wicket-taker	137	A. C. Thomas (avge 20.17, ER 7.67)	2008–15
Highest total for	250-3	v Gloucestershire at Taunton	2006
Highest total for	231-5	**by Kent at Canterbury**	**2018**
Lowest total for	82	v Kent at Taunton	2010
Lowest total against	73	by Warwickshire at Taunton.................	2013

ADDRESS

Cooper Associates County Ground, St James's Street, Taunton TA1 1JT; 0845 337 1875; enquiries@somersetcountycc.co.uk; www.somersetcountycc.co.uk.

OFFICIALS

Captain T. B. Abell	**President** B. C. Rhodes
(Twenty20) L. Gregory	**Chairman** C. F. B. Clark
Director of cricket A. Hurry	**Chief executive** A. Cornish
Head coach J. I. D. Kerr	**Head groundsman** S. Lee
Academy director S. D. Snell	

At Taunton, April 13–15 (not first-class). **Somerset v Oxford MCCU. Abandoned.**

SOMERSET v WORCESTERSHIRE

At Taunton, April 20–22. Somerset won by 83 runs. Somerset 20pts, Worcestershire 3pts. Toss: uncontested. County debut: M. T. Renshaw.

Eighteen wickets fell on the opening day, but the moving ball held no terrors for Renshaw, Somerset's last-minute replacement for his compatriot Cameron Bancroft, whose contract had been cancelled after his part in Australia's ball-tampering scandal. Despite only one of his colleagues – Hildreth – passing ten, and five wickets for Barnard, Renshaw marked his debut with a battling century. His doggedness looked even more valuable when Worcestershire tumbled to 48 for five, although Barnard's 50 dragged them to within 23 of Somerset next day. Hildreth made an unbeaten hundred, while six wickets for Barnard improved his innings-best figures for the second time in the match. Worcestershire never looked likely to reach a target of 279, and Somerset completed victory with a day and a half to spare, although Worcestershire felt Renshaw had put a foot on the rope before throwing in the return that ran out last man Magoffin. The Taunton pitch was the subject of much speculation, but it had pace and helped the seamers throughout, in contrast to the spin-friendly surfaces of 2017.

Close of play: first day, Worcestershire 153-8 (Barnard 27, Tongue 7); second day, Somerset 255-9 (Hildreth 111, Groenewald 4).

Somerset

M. E. Trescothick lbw b Magoffin	1	– c Cox b Tongue 43
E. J. Byrom c Cox b Leach	4	– c Fell b Leach 0
M. T. Renshaw not out	101	– c Fell b Leach 7
J. C. Hildreth c Clarke b Barnard	48	– not out 111
*T. B. Abell lbw b Barnard	10	– c Rhodes b Barnard 27
†S. M. Davies c Mitchell b Leach	9	– lbw b Barnard 5
L. Gregory b Barnard	2	– c Head b Barnard 0
C. Overton c Cox b Barnard	0	– b Magoffin 22
J. H. Davey lbw b Barnard	4	– c Cox b Barnard 12
M. J. Leach c Cox b Tongue	4	– b Barnard 11
T. D. Groenewald c Cox b Tongue	2	– b Barnard 4
B 9, lb 5, w 1, nb 2	17	B 6, lb 3, nb 4 13

1/1 (1) 2/7 (2) 3/99 (4)   (56.1 overs) 202   1/1 (2) 2/11 (3)   (69.2 overs) 255
4/134 (5) 5/163 (6) 6/170 (7)   3/75 (1) 4/145 (5)
7/176 (8) 8/182 (9) 9/197 (10) 10/202 (11)   5/153 (6) 6/153 (7) 7/206 (8)
                                            8/223 (9) 9/239 (10) 10/255 (11)

Leach 15–3–61–2; Magoffin 10–4–26–1; Tongue 14.1–0–42–2; Barnard 16–3–52–5; Head 1–0–7–0. *Second innings*—Leach 15–2–61–2; Magoffin 16–2–58–1; Barnard 19.2–8–37–6; Tongue 14–0–67–1; Head 5–0–23–0.

Worcestershire

D. K. H. Mitchell c Hildreth b Gregory	5	– b Gregory 1
B. L. D'Oliveira b Gregory	3	– lbw b Davey 5
T. C. Fell lbw b Davey	21	– lbw b Gregory 41
J. M. Clarke lbw b Gregory	0	– lbw b Gregory 7
T. M. Head b Davey	49	– c Davies b Groenewald 9
G. H. Rhodes c Byrom b Overton	1	– c Renshaw b Groenewald 0
†O. B. Cox c Trescothick b Groenewald	21	– b Davey 23
E. G. Barnard b Overton	50	– not out 45
*J. Leach c Renshaw b Davey	8	– c Hildreth b Groenewald 6
J. C. Tongue c Abell b Gregory	10	– c and b Overton 34
S. J. Magoffin not out	0	– run out (Renshaw) 10
B 5, lb 6	11	Lb 4, w 2, nb 8 14

1/12 (1) 2/17 (2) 3/17 (4)   (44 overs) 179   1/4 (1) 2/16 (2)   (51.4 overs) 195
4/47 (3) 5/48 (6) 6/93 (7)   3/25 (4) 4/55 (5)
7/112 (5) 8/124 (9) 9/173 (10) 10/179 (8)   5/63 (6) 6/85 (3) 7/103 (7)
                                            8/121 (9) 9/164 (10) 10/195 (11)

Gregory 14–4–51–4; Overton 14–2–53–2; Davey 10–1–38–3; Groenewald 6–1–26–1. *Second innings*—Gregory 13–5–35–3; Davey 11–1–49–2; Overton 12–2–45–1; Groenewald 14–3–51–3; Leach 1.4–0–11–0.

Umpires: I. J. Gould and S. J. O'Shaughnessy.

SOMERSET v YORKSHIRE

At Taunton, April 27–30. Somerset won by 118 runs. Somerset 20pts, Yorkshire 3pts. Toss: uncontested.

Somerset began a Championship campaign with back-to-back wins for the first time since 1993. After a first-day washout, Renshaw made up for lost time with a century before lunch. He made light of a seaming pitch to hit 112 off 99 balls, getting off the mark and reached both his fifty and hundred with sixes. "I can't remember a Championship innings like it in April," said Yorkshire coach Andrew Gale. Even so, Brooks took five wickets as Somerset collapsed from 145 for one to 216, before Yorkshire were hustled out for 96. Somerset were batting again by the end of what was in effect the first day. Abell's 82 helped them to a lead of 320 on a pitch still offering assistance to the seamers. Somerset's attack again performed superbly. Abell broke a stubborn seventh-wicket partnership between Leaning and Bresnan, and suggested he had added a yard of pace over the winter.

Close of play: first day, no play; second day, Somerset 6-0 (Trescothick 2, Renshaw 4); third day, Yorkshire 49-1 (Lyth 25, Pujara 6).

Somerset

M. E. Trescothick c Brook b Brooks	4	– c Lyth b Coad	2
M. T. Renshaw c Hodd b Brooks	112	– b Brooks	8
G. A. Bartlett lbw b Coad	39	– c Hodd b Coad	4
J. C. Hildreth c Brook b Coad	0	– b Brooks	10
*T. B. Abell b Brooks	4	– c Lyth b Coad	82
†S. M. Davies c Hodd b Coad	6	– c Pujara b Coad	33
L. Gregory lbw b Brooks	8	– lbw b Waite	14
C. Overton not out	19	– c Backes b Waite	18
D. M. Bess c Hodd b Brooks	0	– c Lyth b Waite	14
J. H. Davey c sub (A. Z. Lees) b Bresnan	11	– c Ballance b Bresnan	11
T. D. Groenewald lbw b Bresnan	5	– not out	0
B 4, lb 1, w 1, nb 2	8	Lb 4	4

1/5 (1) 2/145 (3) 3/153 (4)   (47.1 overs) 216   1/6 (1) 2/10 (2)   (57.3 overs) 200
4/166 (5) 5/171 (2) 6/179 (7)   3/20 (4) 4/24 (3)
7/181 (6) 8/182 (9) 9/206 (10) 10/216 (11)   5/90 (6) 6/107 (7) 7/129 (8)
                                                          8/171 (9) 9/200 (10) 10/200 (5)

Coad 16–2–67–3; Brooks 15–3–57–5; Bresnan 6.1–0–36–2; Waite 8–0–41–0; Lyth 2–0–10–0.
Second innings—Coad 20.3–6–61–4; Brooks 15–4–44–3; Bresnan 13–2–43–1; Waite 9–1–48–2.

Yorkshire

A. Lyth run out (Bartlett/C. Overton)	0	– c Hildreth b Groenewald	34
H. C. Brook b Overton	32	– c Trescothick b Davey	15
C. A. Pujara lbw b Gregory	7	– c Davies b Gregory	6
*G. S. Ballance c and b Groenewald	11	– c Davies b Gregory	19
J. A. Leaning c Davies b Gregory	0	– c Renshaw b Overton	68
M. J. Waite c Trescothick b Groenewald	11	– c and b Overton	6
†A. J. Hodd c Trescothick b Groenewald	0	– lbw b Overton	1
T. T. Bresnan c Davies b Davey	22	– lbw b Abell	21
J. A. Brooks b Gregory	0	– c and b Groenewald	21
B. O. Coad b Overton	8	– c Trescothick b Abell	2
K. Carver not out	1	– not out	0
Lb 2, nb 2	4	B 2, lb 7	9

1/0 (1) 2/30 (3) 3/51 (4)   (49.4 overs) 96   1/26 (2) 2/49 (3)   (86.1 overs) 202
4/53 (2) 5/64 (6) 6/64 (7)   3/67 (4) 4/81 (4)
7/64 (5) 8/64 (9) 9/82 (10) 10/96 (8)   5/99 (6) 6/103 (7) 7/159 (8)
                                                       8/188 (9) 9/191 (10) 10/202 (5)

Gregory 13–4–30–3; Overton 15–6–38–2; Davey 12.4–6–14–1; Groenewald 9–4–12–3. *Second innings*—Gregory 23–7–59–2; Overton 21.1–7–43–3; Davey 7.5–4–12–1; Groenewald 19–5–51–2; Bess 9.1–5–13–0; Abell 6–2–15–2.

Umpires: M. Burns and A. G. Wharf.

At Manchester, May 4–7. SOMERSET drew with LANCASHIRE.

SOMERSET v HAMPSHIRE

At Taunton, May 11–14. Drawn. Somerset 13pts, Hampshire 9pts. Toss: Somerset.

Having won their first two home games on seaming pitches, Somerset picked two spinners on a drier surface. But it refused to break up. To make matters worse, Leach fractured a thumb while facing throwdowns from coach Jason Kerr on the final morning, ruling him out of the First Test against Pakistan at Lord's. On the first day, the home seamers made the most of what life there was in the wicket, Abell again demonstrating his progress as a bowler with three wickets. An injury to Abbott weakened the Hampshire attack, and Hildreth took full advantage with a masterful 184, his 43rd first-class century, after Edwards somehow dropped him on 24 at midwicket. Contributions from Craig Overton and Bess, who made 92 from No. 10, took Somerset past 500. But without Leach, they were powerless to prevent Vince and Amla securing a draw, with Vince making a chanceless double-century to press his claims to retain his Test place. At 437 balls and 514 minutes, it was the longest innings of his career, though to no avail: when England's squad was named next day, he wasn't in it – but Bess was.

Close of play: first day, Hampshire 198-8 (Abbott 5, Wheal 0); second day, Somerset 324-7 (Hildreth 125, Leach 22); third day, Hampshire 178-2 (Vince 63, Amla 86).

Hampshire

J. J. Weatherley lbw b Abell	28	– c Bartlett b Groenewald	11
J. H. K. Adams c Davies b Groenewald	23	– c Davies b Gregory	11
*J. M. Vince c Davies b Abell	44	– not out	201
H. M. Amla c Davies b Groenewald	4	– c Davies b Gregory	107
T. P. Alsop b Gregory	20	– c Hildreth b Groenewald	12
R. R. Rossouw c Leach b Bess	38	– not out	65
†L. D. McManus c Renshaw b Abell	21		
G. K. Berg lbw b Gregory	4		
K. J. Abbott c Hildreth b Groenewald	5		
B. T. J. Wheal not out	25		
F. H. Edwards c Davies b Overton	7		
Lb 3, w 1, nb 8	12	B 7, lb 9, w 1, nb 8	25

1/44 (2) 2/86 (1) 3/105 (3) (66.3 overs) 231
4/111 (4) 5/165 (5) 6/178 (6)
7/187 (8) 8/198 (7) 9/218 (9) 10/231 (11)

1/15 (2) (4 wkts dec, 150 overs) 432
2/39 (1) 3/233 (4)
4/256 (5)

Gregory 14–3–41–2; Overton 13.3–3–62–1; Groenewald 16–3–59–3; Abell 11–4–36–3; Leach 5–2–13–0; Bess 7–2–17–1. *Second innings*—Gregory 22–6–60–2; Overton 28.4–8–88–0; Groenewald 25–9–61–2; Leach 11–2–18–0; Abell 15–3–61–0; Bess 34–13–60–0; Byrom 10–1–39–0; Bartlett 3.2–0–27–0; Renshaw 1–0–2–0.

Somerset

M. T. Renshaw c Adams b Berg	36	D. M. Bess b Berg	92
E. J. Byrom b Edwards	10	T. D. Groenewald not out	25
G. A. Bartlett c Rossouw b Wheal	1		
J. C. Hildreth c Wheal b Alsop	184	B 11, lb 8, nb 2	21
*T. B. Abell c Edwards b Berg	0		
†S. M. Davies c Adams b Berg	33	1/39 (2) 2/40 (3) (113.1 overs) 506
L. Gregory b Wheal	2	3/71 (1) 4/71 (5) 5/134 (7)
C. Overton b Berg	80	6/267 (8) 7/285 (6) 8/327 (9)
M. J. Leach b Edwards	22	9/472 (4) 10/506 (10) 110 overs: 487-9

Davies, when 26, retired hurt at 131-4 and resumed at 267-6.

Berg 34.1–3–130–5; Edwards 30–5–144–2; Wheal 23–4–101–2; Weatherley 8–0–46–0; Vince 5–1–17–0; Abbott 10–0–37–0; Alsop 3–0–12–1.

Umpires: J. H. Evans and J. W. Lloyds.

SOMERSET v NOTTINGHAMSHIRE

At Taunton, June 9–12. Somerset won by six wickets. Somerset 22pts, Nottinghamshire 2pts. Toss: Somerset. County debut: M. E. Milnes.

Somerset went top of Division One with a third victory in five games to prompt excited talk among the locals of a first Championship. Renshaw's third century of the season – on his final home appearance – and an immaculate contribution from Davies were the highlights of a solid first innings, despite the best efforts of off-spinner Carter. Either side of lunch on the second day, Craig Overton claimed three wickets for four runs, generating the sort of pace more associated with his twin, Jamie. Nottinghamshire never recovered from 28 for five, and five of their top eight made ducks. But Abell's decision to enforce the follow-on looked questionable when Mullaney and Libby put on 145 for the first wicket, and Moores compiled a maiden century. With runs throughout the order, Nottinghamshire managed 505, setting Somerset 248. But, from 163 for four, Abell and Davies calmed any nerves, steering them home with just over an hour to spare.

Close of play: first day, Somerset 307-7 (Davies 59, Bess 7); second day, Nottinghamshire 112-0 (Mullaney 54, Libby 54); third day, Nottinghamshire 468-8 (Fletcher 7).

Somerset

M. T. Renshaw b Carter	106	– c Taylor b Carter	61
E. J. Byrom lbw b Mullaney	14	– c Moores b Mullaney	22
G. A. Bartlett c Taylor b Carter	29	– b Carter	43
J. C. Hildreth c Taylor b Carter	1	– c Root b Carter	21
*T. B. Abell c Wessels b Fletcher	57	– not out	46
†S. M. Davies not out	92	– not out	44
L. Gregory b Carter	16		
R. E. van der Merwe b Milnes	0		
D. M. Bess c Taylor b Patel	34		
C. Overton c Milnes b Carter	8		
J. H. Davey lbw b Patel	14		
B 7, lb 5, w 5, nb 4	21	B 8, lb 3, nb 2	13

1/62 (2) 2/117 (3) 3/127 (4)   (122.4 overs) 392   1/29 (2)   (4 wkts, 67.2 overs) 250
4/176 (1) 5/258 (5) 6/288 (7)   2/125 (3) 3/154 (1)
7/289 (8) 8/340 (9) 9/359 (10)   4/163 (4)
10/392 (11)   110 overs: 341-8

Fletcher 23–7–51–1; Milnes 16–4–54–1; Mullaney 17–3–58–1; Carter 37–6–113–5; Patel 26.4–5–92–2; Nash 2–0–5–0; Root 1–0–7–0. *Second innings*—Fletcher 7–1–21–0; Milnes 6–1–21–0; Mullaney 7–1–22–1; Carter 21–4–82–3; Patel 21–4–70–0; Root 3–1–10–0; Libby 2.2–0–13–0.

Nottinghamshire

*S. J. Mullaney lbw b Overton	19	– lbw b van der Merwe	94
J. D. Libby c Davies b Overton	0	– lbw b Davey	69
C. D. Nash b Gregory	0	– b Davey	66
L. R. P. L. Taylor c Davies b Overton	74	– b van der Merwe	5
S. R. Patel lbw b Overton	0	– lbw b van der Merwe	55
M. H. Wessels b Gregory	0	– lbw b van der Merwe	19
†T. J. Moores lbw b Abell	10	– lbw b Bess	103
W. T. Root c Renshaw b Abell	0	– b Bess	36
L. J. Fletcher lbw b van der Merwe	8	– b Davey	21
M. Carter run out (Bess)	1	– c Davies b Davey	20
M. E. Milnes not out	4	– not out	3
B 9, lb 2, w 5, nb 2	18	B 1, lb 13	14

1/10 (2) 2/15 (3) 3/19 (1)   (37.1 overs) 134   1/145 (2) 2/179 (1)   (146.1 overs) 505
4/27 (5) 5/28 (6) 6/68 (7)   3/191 (4) 4/299 (3)
7/68 (8) 8/100 (9) 9/103 (10) 10/134 (4)   5/299 (5) 6/338 (6) 7/456 (8)
                                                 8/468 (7) 9/502 (10) 10/505 (9)

Gregory 10–2–36–2; Overton 12.1–3–53–4; Davey 6–2–8–0; Abell 6–3–21–2; van der Merwe 3–1–5–1. *Second innings*—Gregory 19–2–66–0; Overton 24–2–82–0; Abell 5–0–14–0; Davey 22.1–4–76–4; van der Merwe 48–12–138–4; Bess 28–9–115–2.

Umpires: N. L. Bainton and R. K. Illingworth.

At Guildford, June 20–22. SOMERSET lost to SURREY by an innings and 69 runs.

At Chelmsford, June 25–28. SOMERSET drew with ESSEX.

At Worcester, July 22–25. SOMERSET beat WORCESTERSHIRE by 141 runs. *Azhar Ali makes a century on Somerset debut.*

SOMERSET v ESSEX

At Taunton, August 19–22. Somerset won by 45 runs. Somerset 22pts, Essex 3pts. Toss: Somerset.

Bowling 32 overs unchanged from the River End on the final day, Leach carried Somerset to a victory that kept their title hopes flickering with a career-best eight for 85. After a season of setbacks, it was a reminder to the England selectors of his effectiveness. In pursuit of 336, Essex looked well placed at 171 for one, but Leach removed the stubborn Browne, and in the next over Jamie Overton trapped Westley. Leach then gave ten Doeschate a thorough examination, eventually bowling him after he had completed his second fifty of the match. Once he had gone, Essex folded, losing their last six for 34. Trescothick, returning after a foot injury for his first appearance at Taunton since late April, had fallen five short of a first-innings century on becoming one of Siddle's five wickets, and there were also runs for Abell as Somerset took an early grip. Ten Doeschate apart, Essex struggled with the bat, and conceded a lead of 133. With Harmer extracting significant turn on a worn surface, it was clear a fourth-innings chase would not be easy – and so it proved.

Close of play: first day, Somerset 308-7 (Gregory 42, Overton 0); second day, Somerset 32-1 (Byrom 10, Bess 11); third day, Essex 147-1 (Browne 75, Westley 43).

Somerset

M. E. Trescothick c Browne b Siddle	95	– lbw b Cook	7
E. J. Byrom c Wheater b Siddle	16	– lbw b Harmer	42
Azhar Ali c Lawrence b Harmer	17	– (4) c Bopara b Harmer	23
J. C. Hildreth lbw b Porter	9	– (5) b Siddle	15
*T. B. Abell c Wheater b Bopara	70	– (6) c Bopara b Harmer	27
†S. M. Davies b Porter	45	– (7) c sub (M. R. Quinn) b Porter	29
L. Gregory b Siddle	47	– (8) c Chopra b Harmer	11
D. M. Bess c Lawrence b Siddle	8	– (3) c Harmer b Cook	12
J. Overton not out	3	– b Siddle	10
M. J. Leach b Siddle	2	– lbw b Westley	5
J. H. Davey c Chopra b Porter	6	– not out	10
Lb 6	6	B 2, lb 7, nb 2	11

1/38 (2) 2/63 (3) 3/104 (4)   (100.3 overs) 324   1/13 (1) 2/33 (3)   (66.3 overs) 202
4/180 (1) 5/244 (5) 6/285 (6)   3/85 (4) 4/96 (2)
7/298 (8) 8/313 (7) 9/317 (10) 10/324 (11)   5/118 (5) 6/142 (6) 7/154 (8)
                                                          8/169 (9) 9/183 (10) 10/202 (7)

Porter 24.3–5–82–3; Cook 11–2–40–0; Siddle 26–7–80–5; Harmer 32–5–88–1; Westley 4–2–11–0; Bopara 3–0–17–1. *Second innings*—Porter 11.3–2–44–1; Cook 12–6–23–2; Harmer 25–6–69–4; Siddle 15–1–49–2; Westley 3–1–8–1.

Essex

N. L. J. Browne c Davies b Davey	13	– c Overton b Leach	86
V. Chopra lbw b Gregory	16	– lbw b Leach	24
T. Westley b Davey	0	– lbw b Overton	56
D. W. Lawrence lbw b Leach	28	– b Leach	21
R. S. Bopara c Davies b Overton	15	– (6) b Leach	27
*R. N. ten Doeschate lbw b Overton	73	– (5) b Leach	50
†A. J. A. Wheater c Gregory b Leach	10	– c and b Leach	1
S. R. Harmer c and b Bess	4	– c Trescothick b Bess	4
P. M. Siddle c Gregory b Azhar Ali	12	– c Overton b Leach	6
J. A. Porter c Davies b Overton	2	– lbw b Leach	0
S. J. Cook not out	6	– not out	3
B 5, lb 7	12	B 4, lb 6, nb 2	12

1/25 (1) 2/29 (2) 3/29 (3)   (66.4 overs) 191   1/58 (2) 2/171 (1)   (106 overs) 290
4/54 (5) 5/106 (4) 6/132 (7)   3/171 (3) 4/225 (4)
7/137 (8) 8/174 (9) 9/180 (6) 10/191 (10)   5/256 (5) 6/258 (7) 7/281 (6)
                                                         8/281 (8) 9/287 (9) 10/290 (10)

Gregory 11–2–37–1; Davey 10–3–27–2; Leach 19–9–27–2; Overton 8.4–1–40–3; Bess 14–4–43–1; Azhar Ali 4–1–5–1. *Second innings*—Gregory 5–1–20–0; Davey 18–4–53–0; Bess 26–3–78–1; Leach 48–16–85–8; Overton 9–0–44–1.

Umpires: B. J. Debenham and D. J. Millns.
J. D. Middlebrook replaced Millns on the second day.

At Leeds, August 29–September 1. SOMERSET beat YORKSHIRE by 224 runs.

SOMERSET v LANCASHIRE

At Taunton, September 4–5. Tied. Somerset 11pts, Lancashire 11pts. Toss: Lancashire. First-class debut: B. G. F. Green.

An extraordinary match ended in the first Championship tie for 15 years, Lancashire's first since 1952, and Somerset's first in the competition since 1939. With Somerset needing just 78 for victory, and the scores level, last man Leach lofted Maharaj to deep midwicket, where Bailey was the only fielder not around the bat. Two overs earlier, on the same score, Bess had been stumped advancing down the pitch. Somerset had imploded spectacularly. But the shambles of their collapse, which all but ended their title hopes, could not detract from the mesmeric excellence of the South African slow left-armer Maharaj. In his second game for Lancashire, he took the new ball and bowled unchanged, finishing with seven for 37 (and 11 in the match). There was also a priceless contribution from Onions, who gave Somerset the jitters by removing Trescothick and Azhar Ali with successive balls in the fourth over; when he added Davies, it was 23 for five. "It kind of feels like a win for us," said Livingstone, Lancashire's captain. A dry surface on which 25 wickets fell to spin was rated "below average" by ECB cricket liaison officer Dean Cosker. After an inquiry, no

---

LOWEST FOURTH-INNINGS TOTAL TO TIE

70	Nelson v Wellington at Wellington	1873-74
74	Lancashire v Surrey at The Oval	1894
77	**Somerset v Lancashire at Taunton**	**2018**
93	Surrey v MCC at The Oval	1868
94	Burgher v Chilaw Marians at Katunayake	2017-18
104	Sussex v Somerset at Taunton	1919
107	MCC v Oxford and Cambridge Universities at Lord's	1839
117	Australians v Gloucestershire at Bristol	1930
121	Western Province v Eastern Province at Cape Town (Elfindale)	1984-85

---

points were deducted, but Somerset were warned they were "treading a very fine line". Twenty-two wickets had tumbled on the first day, with Leach taking five for 28 as Lancashire were brushed aside for 99, then putting on 55 for the last wicket – Somerset's highest stand of the match – with Gregory. Lancashire closed 86 behind with eight wickets in hand, then clawed their way to a slender advantage thanks to a battling 51 from Croft. Leach picked up seven to finish with career-best match figures of 12 for 102, but – with the bat – couldn't quite complete the job.

Close of play: first day, Lancashire 7-2 (Brown 1, Bailey 0).

Lancashire

K. R. Brown c Green b Gregory	13	– lbw b C. Overton		1
A. L. Davies c C. Overton b Leach	20	– b Leach		6
S. J. Croft st Davies b Leach	14	– (5) c Davies b C. Overton		51
*L. S. Livingstone c sub (R. E. van der Merwe) b J. Overton	1	– (6) c Bess b Leach		39
†D. J. Vilas c Davies b Leach	11	– (7) c Gregory b Leach		0
J. J. Bohannon c Trescothick b C. Overton	18	– (8) c Gregory b Leach		11
D. J. Lamb lbw b Leach	6	– (9) not out		20
T. E. Bailey b Leach	13	– (4) c Azhar Ali b C. Overton		14
K. A. Maharaj c Green b J. Overton	1	– (10) st Davies b Leach		9
G. Onions b J. Overton	0	– (11) c Bess b Leach		18
M. W. Parkinson not out	0	– (3) c Gregory b Leach		0
Lb 2	2	B 1		1

1/18 (1) 2/47 (3) 3/48 (4)   (39.1 overs) 99
4/48 (5) 5/69 (6) 6/79 (5)
7/94 (7) 8/99 (9) 9/99 (10) 10/99 (8)

1/7 (2) 2/7 (3)   (52.5 overs) 170
3/11 (1) 4/24 (4)
5/81 (6) 6/89 (7) 7/119 (8)
8/131 (5) 9/146 (10) 10/170 (11)

Gregory 7–3–27–1; C. Overton 10–5–10–1; J. Overton 10–2–32–3; Leach 12.1–2–28–5. *Second innings*—Leach 26.5–9–74–7; Bess 4–1–13–0; C. Overton 14–5–43–3; J. Overton 4–0–19–0; Gregory 4–1–20–0.

Somerset

M. E. Trescothick b Onions	9	– lbw b Onions 0
B. G. F. Green b Bailey	1	– c Brown b Maharaj 16
Azhar Ali b Onions	1	– c Croft b Onions 0
J. C. Hildreth c Vilas b Onions	32	– b Maharaj 7
*T. B. Abell lbw b Maharaj	14	– st Vilas b Maharaj 7
†S. M. Davies st Vilas b Maharaj	13	– lbw b Maharaj 2
L. Gregory not out	64	– lbw b Maharaj 12
D. M. Bess c Bohannon b Maharaj	0	– st Vilas b Maharaj 19
C. Overton lbw b Parkinson	4	– lbw b Maharaj 4
J. Overton b Maharaj	24	– not out 6
M. J. Leach c Croft b Livingstone	17	– c Bailey b Maharaj 0
B 8, lb 1, nb 4	13	Lb 4 4

1/9 (1) 2/11 (2) 3/19 (3)   (46 overs) 192   1/5 (1) 2/5 (3)   (26.4 overs) 77
4/60 (4) 5/62 (5) 6/81 (6)   3/12 (4) 4/20 (5)
7/97 (8) 8/104 (9) 9/137 (10) 10/192 (11)   5/23 (6) 6/37 (2) 7/56 (7)
                                              8/64 (9) 9/77 (8) 10/77 (11)

Bailey 7–0–41–1; Onions 12–2–40–3; Maharaj 19–2–65–4; Parkinson 4–0–31–1; Livingstone 4–2–6–1. *Second innings*—Maharaj 13.4–4–37–7; Onions 11–2–28–3; Parkinson 2–0–8–0.

Umpires: P. K. Baldwin and J. W. Lloyds.

At Southampton, September 10–11. SOMERSET lost to HAMPSHIRE by six wickets.

SOMERSET v SURREY

At Taunton, September 18–21. Drawn. Somerset 6pts, Surrey 13pts. Toss: Surrey. First-class debut: T. Banton.

Storm Bronagh blew away Surrey's bid to garland their Championship with a tenth successive victory, which would have eclipsed the club record of nine in a season, previously achieved in 1896, 1955 and 1957. They arrived on the final morning needing seven wickets, while Somerset were 171 runs short of an innings defeat. There seemed only one outcome. But gale-force winds had shifted the covers overnight, causing muddy tyre marks at one end, and exposing part of the pitch to torrential rain. An abandonment was inevitable. "This is an act of God and there is nothing we could do," said Somerset chief executive Andrew Cornish. Surrey's director of cricket Alec Stewart said he was "massively frustrated", and added: "Imagine if this game had been a Championship decider, which at one stage it looked like it might have been." On a pitch that was notably blander than the previous Championship match, Surrey's top order had enjoyed themselves, Elgar making a century against his former employers. Somerset were hustled out in under 45 overs, and were in peril again by the third-day close. Trescothick was dismissed twice by Morkel without scoring.

Close of play: first day, Surrey 368-4 (Elgar 72, Foakes 11); second day, Somerset 122-9 (Davey 22, Leach 8); third day, Somerset 168-3 (Azhar Ali 61, Abell 21).

Surrey

*R. J. Burns b Groenewald	78	C. McKerr lbw b Abell	6
M. D. Stoneman c C. Overton b J. Overton	85	G. S. Virdi not out	21
J. J. Roy lbw b J. Overton	63		
D. Elgar c Davies b Abell	110	B 9, lb 11, w 1, nb 2	23
O. J. D. Pope c J. Overton b Davey	44		
†B. T. Foakes b Groenewald	25	1/147 (2) 2/206 (1) (125.1 overs) 485
R. Clarke st Davies b Leach	18	3/263 (3) 4/345 (5) 5/414 (6)
T. K. Curran c Banton b Leach	5	6/446 (7) 7/446 (4) 8/458 (8)
M. Morkel c Davies b Abell	7	9/458 (9) 10/485 (10) 110 overs: 415-5

C. Overton 22–1–83–0; Davey 21–3–72–1; Leach 24–2–107–2; Groenewald 22–4–64–2; J. Overton 23–4–87–2; Abell 13.1–0–52–3.

Somerset

M. E. Trescothick c Clarke b Morkel	0	– b Morkel	0
T. Banton c Foakes b Virdi	30	– c Foakes b Curran	4
Azhar Ali c and b Morkel	2	– not out	61
J. C. Hildreth lbw b Curran	6	– c Foakes b Curran	60
*T. B. Abell c Foakes b Clarke	21	– not out	21
†S. M. Davies c Burns b McKerr	5		
C. Overton b McKerr	0		
J. Overton c Virdi b McKerr	9		
J. H. Davey c Stoneman b Morkel	36		
T. D. Groenewald lbw b Clarke	11		
M. J. Leach not out	15		
B 1, lb 9, w 1	11	B 13, lb 9	22

1/0 (1) 2/2 (3) 3/11 (4)   (44.2 overs) 146 1/0 (1)   (3 wkts, 42.2 overs) 168
4/37 (5) 5/42 (6) 6/42 (7)   2/4 (2) 3/107 (4)
7/53 (8) 8/84 (2) 9/109 (10) 10/146 (9)

Morkel 8.2–1–19–3; Curran 14–2–32–1; McKerr 7–1–20–3; Clarke 10–1–32–2; Virdi 5–0–33–1. *Second innings*—Morkel 8.2–4–16–1; Curran 9–1–44–2; Clarke 7–0–24–0; McKerr 11–3–38–0; Virdi 7–0–24–0.

Umpires: R. T. Robinson and A. G. Wharf.

At Nottingham, September 24–26. SOMERSET beat NOTTINGHAMSHIRE by an innings and 146 runs. *Somerset finish runners-up.*

SURREY

Home crop produces vintage year

RICHARD SPILLER

Surrey ended a 16-year wait by storming to the Championship with two games to spare. Five of their ten wins were by an innings, another by ten wickets; they won nine in a row, their best run since 1957 and a first division record. It might have been ten, but for Storm Bronagh's intervention at Taunton, before Essex dashed hopes of an unbeaten season in a gripping finale.

It was a triumphant summer for the new captain, Rory Burns, the outstanding county batsman of the year. He amassed 1,359 Championship runs in a season dominated by bowlers and, at last, forced the England selectors to pick him. Burns hit four centuries, three over 150. He was lucky he could marshal a formidable attack, led by the giant South African Morne Morkel, who signed a two-year Kolpak deal. Surrey were careful not to rush him after a rib injury in his Test farewell, and he repaid them with 59 wickets in ten Championship matches. Constantly threatening both the stumps and wellbeing of opponents, he was the spearhead lacking in recent seasons.

The emergence of a core of home-grown talent was welcome. Two 20-year-olds, Sam Curran and Ollie Pope, developed so quickly they featured in the Test side: Curran was Man of the Series against India. His older brother, Tom, had appeared in the previous winter's Ashes, although he missed much of the summer when a side strain followed an IPL stint. Pope averaged 70 in the Championship, with four sparky centuries, but found the step up to Test cricket a big one, not helped by being asked to bat higher than for Surrey.

When, following relegation, Alec Stewart became director of cricket in 2014, he bracketed team success alongside the development of international players. With the hard work of head coach Michael Di Venuto, who succeeded Graham Ford in 2016, both have been triumphantly achieved. Stewart also had high praise for academy director Gareth Townsend and his staff. Surrey have been criticised in the past for importing talent, but have now produced a largely home-cooked team capable of winning from almost any position.

There had been concern about how to replace Kumar Sangakkara. Australian all-rounder Mitchell Marsh withdrew to have ankle surgery, while the much-hyped signing of Virat Kohli came unstuck when he suffered a neck injury. But the adhesive left-hander Dean Elgar – and, briefly, his fellow South African Theunis de Bruyn – proved excellent choices. Elgar returns for 2019.

Victories over Hampshire and Yorkshire at The Oval – where groundsman Lee Fortis ensured batsmen found life harder than before – meant Surrey already had confidence and momentum when Morkel was ready to rumble. After that they were almost unstoppable, the main back-up coming from Rikki Clarke – the sole survivor of Surrey's most recent Championship-winning team, in 2002 – young off-spinner Amar Virdi, and seamer Jade Dernbach.

Add contributions from both Currans, 6ft 6in youngster Conor McKerr and Ryan Patel, who had a spell of six for five against Somerset at Guildford, and it was unsurprising no opponent reached 350 during a run of ten matches. It all reflected well on bowling coaches Geoff Arnold, who had returned to The Oval for a fourth spell, and Ryan Sidebottom.

Jordan Mansfield, Getty Images

Amar Virdi and Morne Morkel

Virdi, another 20-year-old, took the opportunity offered by an injury to Gareth Batty (who continued in white-ball game only, and coached the second team), and gave Burns a genuine attacking option with flight and turn. His celebratory wheel around the outfield after a wicket became familiar.

Surrey's bowlers owed much to wicketkeeper Ben Foakes and slips Clarke and Scott Borthwick. In fact, there were stunning catches all round the ground: Will Jacks's reflex effort at short leg to complete a grandstand six-run win over Lancashire was one of the summer's champagne moments.

Mark Stoneman's moderate winter for England and a poor start back home cost him his Test place, but he finished the season strongly for Surrey. Borthwick had a much improved summer, solid at No. 3 until he broke his wrist. Foakes scored consistently, while Clarke stiffened the lower order with 500 runs, which included his first century for Surrey since 2006.

Stewart's next target is white-ball improvement, after Surrey failed to reach the knockout stages of either competition. Defeats in the first two Royal London Cup matches made qualification unlikely, before a 220-run thrashing at Beckenham sealed their fate. One highlight was a magnificent maiden century by 19-year-old Jacks, against Gloucestershire at The Oval. But the bowling lacked discipline, and was badly hit by Tom Curran's absences.

In the T20 Blast, they were overdependent on Aaron Finch, whose nine innings harvested 589 runs at a dizzying strike-rate of 182. He was capable of clearing any boundary, but international commitments and a family bereavement cost him five matches, none of which was won. Nic Maddinson, another Australian, made a more modest impression.

Jason Roy could not find his best form – except when helping Finch lacerate Middlesex in a stand of 194 in 13.5 overs – and his frustration boiled over in bizarre fashion. After a T20 first-baller against Hampshire, he hurled his bat in the dressing-room: it rebounded into his face, keeping him out until two late Championship appearances, which included an attractive 128 against Essex.

A strong squad are likely to be contenders again in 2019, at least in the Championship. Anticipating more international calls, Stewart added fast bowler Liam Plunkett from Yorkshire (Mathew Pillans headed the other way) and Lancashire all-rounder Jordan Clark.

Championship attendance: 53,819.

SURREY RESULTS

All first-class matches – Played 15: Won 10, Lost 1, Drawn 4.
County Championship matches – Played 14: Won 10, Lost 1, Drawn 3.

Specsavers County Championship, winners of Division 1;
Vitality Blast, 5th in South Group; Royal London One-Day Cup, 5th in South Group.

COUNTY CHAMPIONSHIP AVERAGES, BATTING AND FIELDING

Cap		Birthplace	M	I	NO	R	HS	100	Avge	Ct/St
2018	O. J. D. Pope	Chelsea	13	16	2	986	158*	4	70.42	21
2014	†R. J. Burns	Epsom‡	14	22	1	1,359	193	4	64.71	11
2018	†S. G. Borthwick	Sunderland	8	12	1	444	83	0	40.36	13
	†D. Elgar¶	Welkom, SA	7	10	0	387	110	1	38.70	6
2016	B. T. Foakes	Colchester	12	18	1	624	90	0	36.70	37/1
2018	†M. D. Stoneman	Newcastle-u-Tyne	13	21	1	660	144	1	33.00	4
2005	R. Clarke	Orsett	13	17	1	500	111	1	31.25	19
	†R. S. Patel	Sutton‡	9	13	3	255	48	0	25.50	4
2018	†S. M. Curran	Northampton	7	10	1	209	70	0	23.22	2
	C. McKerr††	Johannesburg, SA	5	5	2	64	29	0	21.33	0
	W. G. Jacks	Chertsey‡	6	8	0	168	53	0	21.00	8
2016	T. K. Curran	Cape Town, SA	4	5	0	81	43	0	16.20	0
2018	†M. Morkel††	Vereeniging, SA	10	13	2	172	29	0	15.63	1
2011	J. W. Dernbach	Johannesburg, SA	10	13	2	129	31	0	11.72	2
	G. S. Virdi	Chiswick	14	16	8	68	21*	0	8.50	5

Also batted: T. B. de Bruyn¶ (*Pretoria, SA*) (2 matches) 0, 38, 8* (2 ct); †M. P. Dunn (*Egham‡*) (2 matches) 0, 9*, 1 (2 ct); A. J. Finch¶ (*Colac, Australia*) (cap 2018) (2 matches) 2, 43, 32 (1 ct); †A. Harinath (*Sutton‡*) (cap 2016) (2 matches) 48, 1, 7 (1 ct); S. C. Meaker (*Pietermaritzburg, SA*) (cap 2012) (1 match) 13 (1 ct); J. J. Roy§ (*Durban, SA*) (cap 2014) (2 matches) 63, 5, 128.

‡ *Born in Surrey.*   § *ECB contract.*   ¶ *Official overseas player.*   †† *Other non-England-qualified.*

BOWLING

	Style	O	M	R	W	BB	5I	Avge
M. Morkel	RF	315.4	82	845	59	6-57	4	14.32
T. K. Curran	RFM	120.4	30	312	19	5-28	1	16.42
C. McKerr	RFM	67.2	13	191	13	4-26	0	18.92
R. Clarke	RFM	363.1	87	1,012	47	5-29	1	21.53
S. M. Curran	LFM	192.2	37	608	25	6-54	1	24.32
J. W. Dernbach	RFM	285.5	65	929	32	4-49	0	29.03
G. S. Virdi	OB	360.3	46	1,184	39	6-105	1	30.35

Also bowled: S. G. Borthwick (LB) 18-1-67-0; M. P. Dunn (RFM) 44.3-10-171-3; S. C. Meaker (RF) 22-1-93-0; R. S. Patel (RM) 87.1-14-279-8.

LEADING ROYAL LONDON CUP AVERAGES (100 runs/4 wickets)

Batting	Runs	HS	Avge	SR	Ct	**Bowling**	W	BB	Avge	ER
D. Elgar	229	91	57.25	91.60	0	S. G. Borthwick	4	2-32	20.75	6.38
B. T. Foakes	279	86	55.80	81.10	8	T. K. Curran	8	4-33	23.50	6.26
O. J. D. Pope	119	57*	39.66	79.86	2	R. Clarke	13	4-48	27.07	5.77
R. J. Burns	270	68	38.57	86.53	2	M. Morkel	4	2-39	34.50	4.60
W. G. Jacks	254	121	36.28	118.13	1	S. M. Curran	7	2-37	34.57	5.90
J. J. Roy	181	86	36.20	119.07	4	J. W. Dernbach	6	2-57	53.66	6.33
						G. J. Batty	5	1-33	60.80	5.62

LEADING VITALITY BLAST AVERAGES (150 runs/15 overs)

Batting	Runs	HS	Avge	SR	Ct	Bowling	W	BB	Avge	ER
A. J. Finch	589	131*	147.25	**182.35**	3	G. J. Batty	11	3-36	30.00	**7.85**
J. J. Roy	163	84	23.28	179.12	4	R. Clarke	16	2-19	23.56	**8.34**
R. Clarke	235	50	47.00	176.69	9	J. W. Dernbach	12	3-31	32.08	**8.61**
O. J. D. Pope	159	34	39.75	167.36	3	M. Morkel	12	3-30	26.66	**9.41**
R. J. Burns	176	50	25.14	154.38	4	M. W. Pillans	10	3-20	23.80	**9.91**
B. T. Foakes	310	75*	38.75	149.03	8	T. K. Curran	12	3-30	23.33	**10.00**
N. J. Maddinson	245	70	35.00	138.41	4					

FIRST-CLASS COUNTY RECORDS

Highest score for	357*	R. Abel v Somerset at The Oval	1899
Highest score against	366	N. H. Fairbrother (Lancashire) at The Oval	1990
Leading run-scorer	43,554	J. B. Hobbs (avge 49.72)	1905–34
Best bowling for	10-43	T. Rushby v Somerset at Taunton	1921
Best bowling against	10-28	W. P. Howell (Australians) at The Oval	1899
Leading wicket-taker	1,775	T. Richardson (avge 17.87)	1892–1904
Highest total for	811	v Somerset at The Oval	1899
Highest total against	863	by Lancashire at The Oval	1990
Lowest total for	14	v Essex at Chelmsford	1983
Lowest total against	16	by MCC at Lord's	1872

LIST A COUNTY RECORDS

Highest score for	268	A. D. Brown v Glamorgan at The Oval	2002
Highest score against	187*	A. D. Hales (Nottinghamshire) at Lord's	2017
Leading run-scorer	10,358	A. D. Brown (avge 32.16)	1990–2008
Best bowling for	7-30	M. P. Bicknell v Glamorgan at The Oval	1999
Best bowling against	7-15	A. L. Dixon (Kent) at The Oval	1967
Leading wicket-taker	409	M. P. Bicknell (avge 25.21)	1986–2005
Highest total for	496-4	v Gloucestershire at The Oval	2007
Highest total against	429	by Glamorgan at The Oval	2002
Lowest total for	64	v Worcestershire at Worcester	1978
Lowest total against	44	by Glamorgan at The Oval	1999

TWENTY20 COUNTY RECORDS

Highest score for	**131***	**A. J. Finch v Sussex at Hove**	**2018**
Highest score against	116*	J. L. Denly (Kent) at The Oval	2017
Leading run-scorer	**2,977**	**J. J. Roy (avge 30.37, SR 149.67)**	**2008–18**
Best bowling for	6-24	T. J. Murtagh v Middlesex at Lord's	2005
Best bowling against	4-9	D. J. Willey (Northamptonshire) at Birmingham	2013
Leading wicket-taker	**103**	**J. W. Dernbach (avge 26.30, ER 8.31)**	**2005–18**
Highest total for	**250-6**	**v Kent at Canterbury**	**2018**
Highest total against	240-3	by Glamorgan at The Oval	2015
Lowest total for	88	v Kent at The Oval	2012
Lowest total against	68	by Sussex at Hove	2007

ADDRESS

The Kia Oval, Kennington, London SE11 5SS; 0844 375 1845; enquiries@surreycricket.com; www.surreycricket.com.

OFFICIALS

Captain R. J. Burns	**President** D. P. Stewart
(Twenty20) J. W. Dernbach	**Chairman** R. W. Thompson
Director of cricket A. J. Stewart	**Chief executive** R. A. Gould
Head coach M. J. Di Venuto	**Head groundsman** L. E. Fortis
Assistant head coach V. S. Solanki	**Scorer** P. J. Makepeace
Academy director G. T. J. Townsend	

At The Oval, April 13–15 (not first-class). **Drawn. ‡Surrey 466-9 dec** (97 overs) (R. J. Burns 76, R. S. Patel 55, S. G. Borthwick 108, A. Harinath 55, M. W. Pillans 81*; S. Handley 4-105) **and 119-1 dec** (33 overs) (O. J. D. Pope 68*); **Cambridge MCCU 215** (71.5 overs) (D. D. W. Brierley 52*; R. Clarke 3-40) **and 106-6** (34 overs) (J. W. Dernbach 3-22). *County debut:* W. G. Jacks. *A century from Scott Borthwick, then late hitting from Mathew Pillans and Jade Dernbach (35), took Surrey to a lofty total on the opening day. Drew Brierley survived two and a half hours on the second, but the students still faced a big deficit, which Ollie Pope rapidly widened. Set a fanciful 371, Cambridge lost six wickets, three to Dernbach, before bad light intervened.*

SURREY v HAMPSHIRE

At The Oval, April 20–23. Surrey won by 139 runs. Surrey 20pts, Hampshire 3pts. Toss: Surrey.

The match started on the hottest April day in London since 1949, but it took time for the batsmen on both sides to warm up. A ferocious opening spell from Edwards rocked Surrey, and he returned to spark a dizzying post-tea collapse, during which the last five wickets mustered just nine. For Hampshire, Amla showed his class on a pitch that continued to give occasional help to the bowlers, with Sam Curran and Clarke taking most advantage. Borthwick built on Surrey's unexpected lead of 64, but it was a fifth-wicket partnership of 131 that really turned the screw. Foakes made a

MOST LBWs IN A CHAMPIONSHIP MATCH

18	Gloucestershire v Sussex at Bristol	2010
18	Sussex v Middlesex at Hove	2010
18	Gloucestershire v Glamorgan at Cheltenham	2010
18	Worcestershire v Northamptonshire at Worcester	2013
18	**Surrey v Hampshire at The Oval**	**2018**
17	Glamorgan v Northamptonshire at Cardiff	1976
17	Northamptonshire v Essex at Luton	1995
17	Middlesex v Sussex at Lord's	1999
17	Middlesex v Glamorgan at Southgate	2000
17	Kent v Warwickshire at Canterbury	2010
17	**Kent v Gloucestershire at Canterbury**	**2018**

patient 81, while Pope first injected urgency, then dominated stylishly, as the lead grew from imposing to impregnable. This was his second first-class century; the first came during another big stand with Foakes against Hampshire, in September 2017. Off-spinner Virdi removed Amla and Vince in the same over, but Northeast's first hundred for his new county – and obduracy from the lower order – kept Surrey waiting until after tea to complete victory. It came when Foakes grasped his third magnificent catch of the game to end Northeast's resistance after 346 minutes.

Close of play: first day, Hampshire 52-3 (Vince 6); second day, Surrey 217-4 (Foakes 50, Pope 30); third day, Hampshire 116-4 (Northeast 14, Rossouw 19).

Surrey

*R. J. Burns c Northeast b Edwards	46	– c McManus b Abbott	10
M. D. Stoneman lbw b Edwards	4	– b Abbott	24
S. G. Borthwick lbw b Edwards	5	– lbw b Abbott	74
D. Elgar c McManus b Wood	44	– lbw b Wood	20
†B. T. Foakes lbw b Dawson	46	– b Edwards	81
O. J. D. Pope lbw b Abbott	34	– c Rossouw b Dawson	145
S. M. Curran c Wood b Dawson	5	– lbw b Dawson	13
R. Clarke c Wood b Dawson	5	– c Dawson b Edwards	7
J. W. Dernbach b Edwards	0	– c McManus b Edwards	8
M. P. Dunn c Rossouw b Dawson	0	– not out	9
G. S. Virdi not out	0		
B 4, lb 5, w 9, nb 4	22	B 9, lb 3, w 2, nb 2	16

1/8 (2) 2/23 (3) 3/110 (1) (73.1 overs) 211
4/114 (4) 5/187 (6) 6/202 (7)
7/203 (5) 8/210 (8) 9/211 (9) 10/211 (10)

1/20 (1) (9 wkts dec, 109.3 overs) 407
2/41 (3) 3/86 (4)
4/173 (4) 5/304 (5) 6/332 (7)
7/363 (8) 8/379 (9) 9/407 (6)

Abbott 18–1–61–1; Edwards 15–3–38–4; Wheal 15–3–54–0; Wood 14–7–19–1; Dawson 11.1–2–30–4. *Second innings*—Abbott 19–2–72–3; Edwards 23–1–130–3; Dawson 37.3–7–85–2; Wood 16–2–56–1; Wheal 14–0–52–0.

Hampshire

J. H. K. Adams c Foakes b Clarke	17	– c Stoneman b Clarke	21
†L. D. McManus lbw b Clarke	22	– b Dunn	4
C. P. Wood lbw b Curran	2	– (9) lbw b Curran	26
*J. M. Vince lbw b Clarke	6	– (3) lbw b Virdi	33
H. M. Amla lbw b Clarke	55	– (4) lbw b Virdi	21
S. A. Northeast c Foakes b Curran	6	– (5) c Foakes b Dunn	129
R. R. Rossouw lbw b Dunn	4	– (6) lbw b Virdi	29
L. A. Dawson c Foakes b Dernbach	6	– (7) b Dernbach	3
K. J. Abbott b Curran	23	– (8) c Burns b Virdi	29
B. T. J. Wheal lbw b Curran	0	– lbw b Dernbach	10
F. H. Edwards not out	0	– not out	5
B 2, lb 4	6	B 12, lb 6, nb 4	22

1/37 (2) 2/42 (1) 3/52 (3)　　　(50.2 overs) 147　　　1/29 (1) 2/29 (2)　　　(115.3 overs) 332
4/52 (4) 5/63 (6) 6/79 (7)　　　　　　　　　　　　　　3/83 (4) 4/84 (3)
7/116 (8) 8/147 (9) 9/147 (10) 10/147 (5)　　　　　　5/150 (6) 6/163 (7) 7/206 (8)
　　　　　　　　　　　　　　　　　　　　　　　　　　8/245 (9) 9/313 (10) 10/332 (5)

Dernbach 10–3–21–1; Curran 16–6–39–4; Clarke 15.2–6–39–4; Dunn 9–0–42–1. *Second innings*—Dernbach 27–6–86–2; Curran 16–5–44–1; Virdi 33–7–79–4; Clarke 21–7–46–1; Dunn 11.3–3–41–2; Borthwick 7–1–18–0.

Umpires: R. K. Illingworth and D. J. Millns.

At Manchester, April 27–30. SURREY drew with LANCASHIRE.

SURREY v WORCESTERSHIRE

At The Oval, May 4–7. Drawn. Surrey 9pts, Worcestershire 11pts. Toss: Surrey. First-class debut: B. J. Twohig.

Worcestershire had started the season with three defeats, but demonstrated great resilience to avoid a fourth. Patience was the most valuable quality on a lethargic pitch and, when Surrey batted first, Burns exhibited it in spades, dropping anchor for 532 minutes. Only Foakes was dominant, making an attractive 72. Leach persevered, finishing with four wickets, while Ben Twohig, a 20-year-old slow left-armer from Yorkshire, made a promising debut. The outfield had quickened up by the time Worcestershire set out on what became their highest total at The Oval. Mitchell and Fell both departed in the eighties – Fell's half-century was his first since September 2016 – before Joe Clarke tucked in with some authoritative strokes, finishing with 157 in almost six hours. Surrey's seamers toiled, but Virdi showed control as well as flight, and was rewarded with a career-best. The final day – the hottest Spring Bank Holiday on record – was not marked by sparkling cricket, as Worcestershire dallied with the bat when they might have been bowling. When they were finally all out, Borthwick put his struggles the previous summer behind him to ensure against any alarms.

Close of play: first day, Surrey 278-4 (Burns 137, Pope 18); second day, Worcestershire 135-1 (Mitchell 77, Fell 27); third day, Worcestershire 469-6 (Barnard 42, Twohig 4).

Surrey

*R. J. Burns c Mitchell b Morris	193	– c Barnard b Twohig	30
M. D. Stoneman run out (Barnard)	28	– lbw b Morris	20
S. G. Borthwick c Cox b Leach	10	– not out	82
R. S. Patel c Cox b Leach	10	– c Head b Morris	25
†B. T. Foakes c Cox b Barnard	72	– not out	11
O. J. D. Pope c Mitchell b Leach	32		
S. M. Curran b Leach	0		
R. Clarke lbw b Morris	38		
S. C. Meaker b Twohig	13		
C. McKerr not out	10		
G. S. Virdi c Mitchell b Tongue	11		
B 8, lb 3, nb 6	17	B 3, nb 2	5

1/50 (2) 2/87 (3) 3/99 (4)   (144.2 overs) 434   1/38 (2)   (3 wkts dec, 60 overs) 173
4/224 (5) 5/293 (6) 6/295 (7)   2/74 (1) 3/136 (4)
7/384 (8) 8/403 (1) 9/415 (9)
10/434 (11)   110 overs: 307-6

Leach 36–4–96–4; Barnard 25–4–73–1; Tongue 25.2–3–88–1; Morris 29–5–85–2; Twohig 20–2–60–1; Head 8–0–21–0; Mitchell 1–1–0–0. *Second innings*—Leach 4–2–11–0; Tongue 8–2–28–0; Twohig 22–3–62–1; Head 16–5–36–0; Morris 6–1–21–2; D'Oliveira 3–0–12–0; Mitchell 1–1–0–0.

Worcestershire

D. K. H. Mitchell lbw b Clarke	81	J. C. Tongue c and b Virdi	9
B. L. D'Oliveira lbw b Clarke	23	C. A. J. Morris not out	0
T. C. Fell c Meaker b Curran	88		
J. M. Clarke lbw b McKerr	157	Lb 8, w 3, nb 14	25
T. M. Head b Virdi	50		
†O. B. Cox lbw b Virdi	0	1/48 (2) 2/139 (1) (158.4 overs) 526	
E. G. Barnard c and b Virdi	66	3/256 (3) 4/336 (5) 5/336 (6)	
B. J. Twohig c Patel b Virdi	9	6/460 (4) 7/475 (8) 8/505 (9)	
*J. Leach c Borthwick b Virdi	18	9/523 (10) 10/526 (7) 110 overs: 353-5	

Curran 21–4–62–1; Clarke 33–10–90–2; Virdi 41.4–7–105–6; McKerr 16–1–76–1; Patel 17–3–57–0; Meaker 22–1–93–0; Borthwick 8–0–35–0.

Umpires: J. H. Evans and A. G. Wharf.

SURREY v YORKSHIRE

At The Oval, May 11–14. Surrey won by an innings and 17 runs. Surrey 24pts, Yorkshire 4pts. Toss: uncontested.

Yorkshire were consigned to their first Championship defeat by Surrey since 2002. Root captained in place of Gary Ballance, who pulled out the night before the match with what was described as a bug – but he later took a break from cricket, and gave up the captaincy. Root decided to bowl on a pitch with a touch of green, and offering bounce and movement. Surrey wobbled to 69 for four, but were saved by an adhesive innings from Elgar, which preceded a superb display by Pope, who gambolled to his third century in ten first-class matches. He stroked 27 fours, and put on 129 for the seventh wicket with Clarke, who passed 10,000 first-class runs during his fortnight 71. Only 21.4 overs were possible on the second day, but Sam Curran grabbed the spotlight on the third: swinging the ball at a lively pace, he claimed his 100th first-class wicket, and – still only 19 – received his county cap shortly afterwards. Bairstow unleashed some sparkling strokes, and threatened to avert the follow-on before falling for 95. Yorkshire were soon in trouble again. Pujara went to Curran for a duck, before Virdi produced a drifting, turning beauty to extract Root. Curran hastened the end on the fourth morning with three wickets in six balls, to finish with career-best match figures of ten for 101.

Close of play: first day, Surrey 366-7 (Pope 131, McKerr 27); second day, Yorkshire 40-3 (Root 14, Brook 1); third day, Yorkshire 142-5 (Bairstow 25, Leaning 13).

Surrey

*R. J. Burns c Pujara b Brooks	9
M. D. Stoneman lbw b Bresnan.	10
S. G. Borthwick c Lyth b Shaw.	5
D. Elgar b Root	61
†B. T. Foakes c Bairstow b Patterson	18
O. J. D. Pope not out	158
S. M. Curran c Bairstow b Patterson	19
R. Clarke c Lyth b Brooks.	71

C. McKerr c Pujara b Bresnan. 29
J. W. Dernbach c Root b Patterson 14
G. S. Virdi c Leaning b Bresnan 1
    B 4, lb 10, w 1, nb 4 19

1/15 (2) 2/19 (1) 3/40 (3)   (101.1 overs) 414
4/69 (5) 5/137 (4) 6/162 (7)
7/291 (8) 8/373 (9) 9/404 (10) 10/414 (11)

Bresnan 26.1–5–98–3; Brooks 18–0–91–2; Shaw 17–2–76–1; Patterson 27–2–107–3; Root 11–1–27–1; Brook 2–1–1–0.

Yorkshire

A. Lyth lbw b Curran.	6	– c Clarke b Virdi	58
A. Z. Lees c Elgar b Dernbach.	0	– c Borthwick b Dernbach	4
C. A. Pujara c Borthwick b Curran	17	– b Curran	0
*J. E. Root lbw b Curran	14	– b Virdi	23
H. C. Brook c Foakes b Curran	17	– lbw b Virdi.	8
†J. M. Bairstow c Clarke b Dernbach	95	– c Foakes b Clarke	29
J. A. Leaning lbw b Clarke	20	– lbw b Clarke	28
T. T. Bresnan c Borthwick b Curran	1	– c Foakes b Curran	1
S. A. Patterson c Pope b Clarke	5	– b Curran	0
J. Shaw c Elgar b Curran	29	– b Curran	0
J. A. Brooks not out	5	– not out	4
B 6, lb 7, w 1, nb 6.	20	B 1, lb 3, w 1, nb 8.	13

1/1 (2) 2/7 (1) 3/34 (3)   (57.2 overs) 229
4/41 (4) 5/88 (5) 6/155 (7)
7/158 (8) 8/183 (9) 9/203 (6) 10/229 (10)

1/9 (2) 2/10 (3)   (66.1 overs) 168
3/66 (4) 4/99 (1)
5/102 (5) 6/151 (6) 7/164 (8)
8/164 (9) 9/164 (10) 10/168 (7)

Dernbach 18–2–81–2; Curran 16.2–2–54–6; Clarke 16–2–47–2; McKerr 3–0–16–0; Virdi 4–1–18–0. *Second innings*—Dernbach 13–4–24–1; Curran 17–6–47–4; Clarke 17.1–3–41–2; Virdi 19–1–52–3.

Umpires: D. J. Millns and M. J. Saggers.

At Southampton, June 9–11. SURREY beat HAMPSHIRE by an innings and 58 runs.

SURREY v SOMERSET

At Guildford, June 20–22. Surrey won by an innings and 69 runs. Surrey 24pts, Somerset 2pts. Toss: uncontested. First-class debut: W. G. Jacks. County debut: T. B. de Bruyn.

Somerset arrived as Championship leaders, but were outplayed from the start by a rampant Surrey, who replaced them at the top by winning at Woodbridge Road for the first time in 16 years. It was their third successive innings victory, a sequence they last achieved in 1958. Abell decided to bowl, perhaps misled by a green pitch, but Borthwick and the recalled Harinath took advantage of the short boundaries. And then came Pope: one of four Guildford colts in the Surrey side, he enchanted a festival crowd basking in fine weather with his rare ability to play the ball late, collecting 19 fours. In reply, Byrom batted staunchly for 218 minutes, but Somerset imploded on the second evening. They were 169 for four before Byrom finally fell to Ryan Patel, who had taken only two wickets in his previous seven first-class games. But now his late movement transfixed the batsmen: his first five wickets came in 11 balls, and he ended with six for five. (Only Northamptonshire's David Hardy, with 3.4–0–11–6 against Nottinghamshire in 1908, had finished with six wickets in fewer balls in a Championship innings.) Five more went down in the follow-on inside the first hour next morning. Hildreth, who passed 15,000 runs during his long rearguard, prevented an even more emphatic defeat. Leach was hit on the head by Morkel during his brief first innings, and was replaced by Waller, a concussion substitute, in the second.

Close of play: first day, Surrey 351-5 (Pope 73, Jacks 15); second day, Somerset 18-0 (Renshaw 2, Byrom 11).

Surrey

*R. J. Burns lbw b Gregory	66	J. W. Dernbach c Leach b Groenewald	0
A. Harinath lbw b Abell	48	G. S. Virdi not out	0
S. G. Borthwick b Groenewald	83		
R. S. Patel c Davies b Abell	48	B 4, lb 11, w 1, nb 4	20
T. B. de Bruyn c Hildreth b Bess	0		
†O. J. D. Pope lbw b Groenewald	117	1/83 (2) 2/158 (1) (120.1 overs)	459
W. G. Jacks c Gregory b Davey	15	3/246 (3) 4/247 (5) 5/299 (4)	
R. Clarke lbw b Gregory	42	6/351 (7) 7/411 (6) 8/447 (9)	
M. Morkel b Groenewald	20	9/447 (10) 10/459 (8) 110 overs: 411-7	

Gregory 25.1–0–86–2; Davey 27–3–105–1; Groenewald 26–6–85–4; Abell 22–4–99–2; Bess 16–2–50–1; Leach 4–0–19–0.

Somerset

M. T. Renshaw c de Bruyn b Clarke	39	– lbw b Morkel	2		
E. J. Byrom lbw b Patel	52	– c Jacks b Morkel	19		
G. A. Bartlett lbw b Clarke	0	– c Pope b Dernbach	7		
J. C. Hildreth c Harinath b Clarke	2	– not out	89		
*T. B. Abell c Pope b Clarke	26	– lbw b Dernbach	5		
†S. M. Davies lbw b Patel	33	– c Borthwick b Clarke	9		
L. Gregory c Borthwick b Patel	4	– c Clarke b Morkel	32		
D. M. Bess not out	6	– b Clarke	6		
J. H. Davey c Clarke b Patel	0	– c Pope b Dernbach	21		
T. D. Groenewald lbw b Patel	0	– b Dernbach	0		
M. J. Leach lbw b Patel	0				
M. T. C. Waller (did not bat)		– (11) c Pope b Morkel	0		
B 4, lb 3, w 1, nb 10	18	B 9, lb 5, nb 6	20		

1/53 (1) 2/57 (3) 3/63 (4)	(59.5 overs) 180	1/18 (1) 2/33 (3)	(61.2 overs) 210
4/117 (5) 5/169 (2) 6/173 (7)		3/33 (2) 4/40 (5)	
7/174 (6) 8/174 (9) 9/174 (10) 10/180 (11)		5/69 (6) 6/121 (7) 7/145 (8)	
		8/209 (9) 9/209 (10) 10/210 (11)	

Waller replaced Leach, as a concussion substitute.

Morkel 12–4–39–0; Dernbach 15–4–35–0; Clarke 13–3–32–4; Virdi 16–1–62–0; Patel 3.5–2–5–6. *Second innings*—Morkel 15.2–6–36–4; Dernbach 15–4–49–4; Clarke 13–1–50–2; Patel 4–1–7–0; Virdi 12–0–44–0; Borthwick 2–0–10–0.

Umpires: I. D. Blackwell and N. G. B. Cook.

At Scarborough, June 25–28. SURREY beat YORKSHIRE by seven wickets.

At The Oval, July 16–18. SURREY drew with WEST INDIES A (see West Indies A tour section).

At Nottingham, July 22–24. SURREY beat NOTTINGHAMSHIRE by an innings and 183 runs.

SURREY v LANCASHIRE

At The Oval, August 19–22 (day/night). Surrey won by six runs. Surrey 20pts, Lancashire 4pts. Toss: Surrey. First-class debut: J. J. Bohannon.

A taut match was finally settled by the pace and hostility of Morkel, who took all five wickets to fall on the last day. A pitch offering seam movement throughout, plus occasional uneven bounce, amply compensated for lack of swing from the pink ball. Only Sam Curran in Surrey's first innings – when Bailey was rewarded for his persistence – and Vilas in the reply looked properly at home, though Josh Bohannon showed poise with a debut fifty to earn Lancashire a narrow lead. He followed it with the valuable wicket of Burns, who had been giving Surrey the upper hand. Dernbach's groin strain restricted his bowling, but his rousing partnerships with Morkel in both innings – 56 and 51 – proved priceless. Chasing 271, Lancashire were reduced to 125 for five by the accurate Virdi. But Croft and Bohannon got stuck in and, when the final day dawned, they needed 94. Morkel dismissed both after a stand of 78, and soon removed Mennie as well. Bailey and Onions, who hit the first delivery with the delayed second new ball for six, added 47 to take Lancashire to within 15 of victory. But Morkel had the last word: he bowled Onions and had Parkinson held at short leg, one of three sharp catches there by substitute Will Jacks.

Close of play: first day, Lancashire 134-6 (Chanderpaul 25, Bohannon 1); second day, Surrey 197-4 (Foakes 20, Curran 27); third day, Lancashire 177-5 (Croft 28, Bohannon 22).

Surrey

*R. J. Burns c Croft b Bailey	6	– b Bohannon	70
M. D. Stoneman c Jones b Bailey	14	– c Parkinson b Bailey	16
A. Harinath c Vilas b Bailey	1	– run out (Bailey)	7
A. J. Finch c Bailey b Parkinson	43	– lbw b Onions	32
†B. T. Foakes c Davies b Mennie	12	– †Vilas b Mennie	33
S. M. Curran c Davies b Bailey	40	– c †Vilas b Bailey	31
R. S. Patel c Croft b Mennie	12	– b Parkinson	14
R. Clarke run out (Hameed)	15	– lbw b Onions	19
M. Morkel c Mennie b Parkinson	23	– b Onions	29
J. W. Dernbach c Croft b Bailey	31	– not out	24
G. S. Virdi not out	0	– b Mennie	0
Lb 2, nb 12	14	B 9, lb 14, nb 8	31

1/14 (1) 2/21 (2) 3/28 (3)   (52.2 overs) 211
4/51 (5) 5/108 (4) 6/130 (6)
7/154 (8) 8/155 (7) 9/211 (9) 10/211 (10)

1/35 (2) 2/73 (3)   (91.5 overs) 306
3/114 (4) 4/162 (1)
5/204 (6) 6/226 (5)
7/240 (7) 8/254 (8)
9/305 (9) 10/306 (11)

Bailey 15.2–5–53–5; Onions 9–0–54–0; Mennie 10–1–46–2; Parkinson 16–4–51–2; Bohannon 2–0–5–0. *Second innings*—Bailey 24.5–5–78–2; Onions 24–3–91–3; Mennie 15.5–3–39–2; Parkinson 23–2–62–1; Croft 1–1–0–0; Bohannon 4–0–13–1.

Lancashire

†A. L. Davies c Clarke b Dernbach	0	– c sub (W. G. Jacks) b Virdi	35
H. Hameed b Morkel	22	– lbw b Morkel	20
R. P. Jones c Clarke b Morkel	10	– c sub (W. G. Jacks) b Virdi	48
*D. J. Vilas c Foakes b Curran	61	– lbw b Clarke	3
S. Chanderpaul run out (Burns)	45	– c Clarke b Virdi	2
S. J. Croft c Finch b Clarke	10	– c Foakes b Morkel	43
M. W. Parkinson lbw b Clarke	0	– (11) c sub (W. G. Jacks) b Morkel	7
J. J. Bohannon lbw b Virdi	52	– (7) c Burns b Morkel	32
J. M. Mennie c Foakes b Virdi	26	– (8) c Foakes b Morkel	1
T. E. Bailey not out	6	– (9) not out	20
G. Onions c Burns b Patel	4	– (10) b Morkel	29
B 6, lb 1, nb 4	11	B 4, lb 6, nb 14	24

1/0 (1) 2/34 (3) 3/41 (2)   (79.2 overs) 247
4/114 (4) 5/129 (6) 6/129 (7)
7/176 (5) 8/225 (9) 9/242 (8) 10/247 (11)

1/45 (1) 2/83 (2)   (93.1 overs) 264
3/97 (4) 4/104 (5)
5/125 (3) 6/203 (6)
7/204 (7) 8/209 (8)
9/256 (10) 10/264 (11)

Dernbach 9.4–2–31–1; Curran 17–1–69–1; Morkel 16–5–42–2; Clarke 16.2–7–42–2; Virdi 19–2–54–2; Patel 1.2–0–2–1. *Second innings*—Curran 11–0–49–0; Dernbach 1–0–5–0; Morkel 21.1–5–57–6; Clarke 21–2–45–1; Virdi 37–8–95–3; Patel 2–1–3–0.

Umpires: M. Burns and M. A. Gough.

SURREY v NOTTINGHAMSHIRE

At The Oval, August 29–31. Surrey won by an innings and 125 runs. Surrey 23pts, Nottinghamshire 3pts. Toss: uncontested. County debut: B. T. Slater.

Stoneman's only century of the season paved the way for Surrey to hammer Nottinghamshire by an innings for the second time in six weeks. Finally recovering the fluency which had earned him an Ashes tour, Stoneman prevented the visitors' seam-dominated attack from exploiting a good start on a rain-affected first day. Foakes and Jacks provided robust support, before play was held up for 15 minutes when Tom Curran was struck on the head by Milnes. First he was checked for concussion, then he tried half a dozen helmets before finding one that fitted. On 99 overnight, Stoneman went on the attack next morning. By contrast, Nottinghamshire's batsmen showed little application as Curran carved through the top order, employing a fuller length than most in a belated first Championship appearance of the summer after his IPL stint and a side strain. Only Moores showed much fight. Brathwaite battled bravely in the follow-on, making 60 despite being clonked on the head by both Morkel and McKerr, who found sharp lift in only his seventh first-class match. But after 220 minutes Brathwaite provided Foakes with one of his nine catches. Three overs after lunch on the third day, Surrey completed their seventh straight victory.

Close of play: first day, Surrey 256-6 (Stoneman 99, Curran 12); second day, Nottinghamshire 83-2 (Brathwaite 39, Patel 4).

Surrey

*R. J. Burns c Moores b Fletcher	10	
M. D. Stoneman c Moores b Wood	144	
D. Elgar lbw b Gurney	8	
R. S. Patel c Moores b Wood	0	
†B. T. Foakes c Patel b Wood	48	
W. G. Jacks b Milnes	48	
R. Clarke lbw b Fletcher	14	
T. K. Curran c Root b Milnes	43	
M. Morkel c Milnes b Gurney	5	
C. McKerr not out	19	
G. S. Virdi b Patel	19	
B 5, lb 4, w 2, nb 6	17	
	375	

1/18 (1)　2/35 (3)　3/36 (4)　(107.3 overs) 375
4/126 (5)　5/204 (6)　6/225 (7)
7/309 (8)　8/315 (9)　9/340 (2)　10/375 (11)

O. J. D. Pope replaced Jacks after being released from England's Test squad.

Fletcher 23–3–87–2; Wood 22–5–66–3; Gurney 26–3–101–2; Milnes 19–2–76–2; Patel 17.3–6–36–1.

Nottinghamshire

K. C. Brathwaite lbw b Curran	2	– c Foakes b McKerr	60	
B. T. Slater c Foakes b Curran	9	– c Clarke b McKerr	21	
J. D. Libby c Patel b Curran	12	– lbw b Virdi	17	
*S. R. Patel lbw b Morkel	5	– lbw b Morkel	15	
W. T. Root c Foakes b McKerr	6	– c Foakes b Morkel	0	
M. H. Wessels c Jacks b McKerr	12	– c Foakes b Morkel	0	
†T. J. Moores c Foakes b McKerr	29	– c Foakes b Curran	20	
L. Wood c Foakes b Morkel	8	– c Pope b Morkel	5	
L. J. Fletcher c Foakes b Curran	9	– run out (Curran)	1	
M. E. Milnes not out	0	– not out	3	
H. F. Gurney b Curran	0	– c Virdi b McKerr	1	
B 5, lb 1, w 1, nb 2	9	B 2, lb 2, nb 2	6	
	101		**149**	

1/12 (2)　2/13 (1)　3/20 (4)　　　(31.4 overs) 101
4/38 (3)　5/39 (5)　6/70 (6)
7/80 (8)　8/101 (7)　9/101 (9)　10/101 (11)

1/41 (2)　2/78 (3)　　　(61 overs) 149
3/109 (4)　4/109 (5)
5/111 (6)　6/122 (1)　7/132 (8)
8/135 (9)　9/148 (7)　10/149 (11)

Morkel 9–2–21–2; Curran 8.4–1–28–5; McKerr 7–1–21–3; Clarke 7–2–25–0. *Second innings*—Morkel 17–3–39–3; Curran 14–4–31–1; McKerr 12–6–26–4; Clarke 12–5–31–0; Patel 3–0–9–0; Virdi 3–0–9–1.

Umpires: S. J. O'Shaughnessy and R. T. Robinson.

At Chelmsford, September 4–6. SURREY beat ESSEX by ten wickets.

At Worcester, September 10–13. SURREY beat WORCESTERSHIRE by three wickets. *Surrey clinch the Championship with their ninth win in a row.*

At Taunton, September 18–21. SURREY drew with SOMERSET. *A violent overnight storm ends Surrey's run of victories.*

SURREY v ESSEX

At The Oval, September 24–27. Essex won by one wicket. Essex 22pts, Surrey 2pts. Toss: Surrey.

The clash of champions old and new appeared all but over when Surrey, after choosing to bat, were shot out just after lunch on the first day. Essex's seamers gained lavish assistance from a pitch covered for the previous two; Surrey's 67 was their lowest total since 1986, and their lowest at The Oval since 1962, when Warwickshire skittled them for 61. Vijay and Westley patiently built the lead as conditions eased, and Essex's advantage seemed complete when Wheater and Harmer – who reached his first county century by smacking Virdi into the pavilion – put on 159, a record for Essex's seventh wicket in this fixture. Wheater finally retired hurt after being struck on the thumb by Morkel (substitute Michael Pepper kept in the second innings), while Simon Cook was hit on the head by the ball from Dernbach which dismissed him; he failed a concussion test and was replaced by Matt Coles. Surrey batted again facing a huge deficit of 410 – no side had won a first-class match from such a position – but Stoneman and Roy led a thunderous response. Roy crunched his first Championship century for two years, then Pope showcased his rasping square cut as he motored to his fourth of the summer. By the time Jacks completed a maiden fifty, Surrey – who were chasing an unbeaten season – were in front, but Coles worked his way through the lower order. Essex needed only 132, but made a meal of it on an enthralling final day of the season. Morkel started the slide by bowling Vijay, before Dernbach and Virdi chipped in with two wickets apiece. It was left to ten Doeschate to take his side home. By then he had a nervous No. 11 for company; but Quinn somehow survived three snorters from Morkel, and then ten Doeschate collected the winning boundary off Dernbach.

Close of play: first day, Essex 197-2 (Westley 93, Lawrence 11); second day, Surrey 88-1 (Stoneman 41, Roy 23); third day, Surrey 477-5 (Jacks 52, Patel 20).

Surrey

*R. J. Burns c Harmer b Quinn	19	– c and b Porter	21
M. D. Stoneman c Wheater b Porter	2	– b Harmer	86
J. J. Roy lbw b Porter	5	– c sub (A. S. S. Nijjar) b Quinn	128
O. J. D. Pope c Bopara b Cook	26	– lbw b Coles	114
†B. T. Foakes lbw b Quinn	0	– lbw b Quinn	32
W. G. Jacks b Cook	0	– c Harmer b Coles	53
R. S. Patel lbw b Cook	5	– c sub (†M. S. Pepper) b Coles	38
R. Clarke lbw b Porter	0	– c sub (†M. S. Pepper) b Coles	39
M. Morkel c Wheater b Porter	1	– c Browne b Coles	0
J. W. Dernbach b Cook	4	– b Porter	2
G. S. Virdi not out	1	– not out	2
Lb 4	4	B 14, lb 5, w 1, nb 6	26

1/13 (2) 2/23 (3) 3/41 (1)   (27 overs) 67
4/41 (5) 5/48 (6) 6/54 (7)
7/55 (8) 8/57 (9) 9/62 (10) 10/67 (4)

1/63 (1) 2/244 (3)   (142.2 overs) 541
3/249 (2) 4/364 (5)
5/418 (4) 6/479 (6) 7/532 (8)
8/532 (9) 9/539 (7) 10/541 (10)

Porter 10–0–26–4; Cook 11–5–27–4; Quinn 6–2–10–2. *Second innings*—Porter 26.2–3–127–2; Quinn 28–3–115–2; Harmer 50–10–122–1; Coles 32–5–123–5; Bopara 1–0–17–0; Westley 4–0–13–0; Lawrence 1–0–5–0.

Essex

N. L. J. Browne b Morkel	2	– (2) c Clarke b Virdi	12
M. Vijay c Foakes b Dernbach	80	– (1) b Morkel	2
T. Westley c Foakes b Clarke	134	– c Clarke b Dernbach	20
D. W. Lawrence lbw b Clarke	17	– c Clarke b Dernbach	10
R. S. Bopara b Virdi	8	– c Jacks b Virdi	0
*R. N. ten Doeschate c Pope b Dernbach	27	– not out	53
†A. J. A. Wheater retired hurt	68	– c Patel b Morkel	11
S. R. Harmer not out	102	– c Foakes b Morkel	0
J. A. Porter lbw b Dernbach	1	– lbw b Morkel	4
S. J. Cook c Foakes b Dernbach	1		
M. R. Quinn not out	4	– not out	0
M. T. Coles (did not bat)		– (10) run out (Jacks)	5
B 7, lb 13, w 1, nb 12	33	B 4, lb 5, nb 8	17

1/12 (1) 2/158 (2) (8 wkts dec, 140.2 overs) 477
3/205 (4) 4/236 (5)
5/276 (6) 6/282 (3)
7/449 (9) 8/456 (10)
110 overs: 334-6

1/13 (1) (9 wkts, 32.2 overs) 134
2/25 (2) 3/42 (4)
4/47 (5) 5/55 (3) 6/97 (7)
7/97 (8) 8/111 (9) 9/124 (10)

In the first innings Wheater retired hurt at 441-6. Coles replaced Cook, as a concussion substitute.

Morkel 30–6–84–1; Dernbach 29.2–8–95–4; Clarke 29–7–65–2; Patel 25–3–92–0; Virdi 27–1–121–1. *Second innings*—Virdi 11–0–73–2; Morkel 12–3–28–4; Dernbach 9.2–2–24–2.

Umpires: M. J. Saggers and A. G. Wharf.

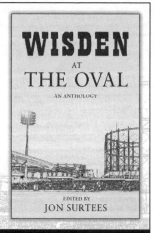

SUSSEX

Hove is where the heart is

BRUCE TALBOT

After several years of stagnation, Sussex were on the move again in 2018. In August they were in a promotion spot in the Championship after five wins out of six, and in September they reached the final of the Blast.

In both competitions they ran out of steam but, in his first season as head coach, Jason Gillespie fulfilled the main tasks of his remit: making Sussex competitive, and backing new talent. The players warmed to his relaxed approach, the youngsters he threw in generally made the most of their opportunities, and he formed a good relationship with Ben Brown, the captain, who said: "We came up short, but we definitely made progress. The whole atmosphere is a lot more positive, and the players enjoyed working under Jason. The youngsters will be a lot better for the experience."

In the driest summer for years, Sussex suffered four washouts in the Vitality Blast, but won their last three to qualify in third place. Their success was built around a strong bowling unit in which Jofra Archer's pace and Danny Briggs's slow left-arm were a regular threat, while Afghanistan leg-spinner Rashid Khan proved an inspired overseas signing. He took 17 wickets at 14, had an economy-rate of 6.59, and showed an enthusiasm for the club ethos, perhaps not seen since the days of Mushtaq Ahmed. The sight of the small local Afghan community cheering his every move became a colourful part of Twenty20 nights at Hove. But in August he rejoined Afghanistan, missing the T20 climax when – after a brilliant innings from Luke Wright had blown Somerset away in the semi – he might have enjoyed an exhausted pitch in the final. Laurie Evans made his seventh half-century and finished the leading run-scorer in the tournament, but Sussex were second best. And in 2019, there is the prospect that, under new registration rules, Archer will be spending time with England.

Seven of their T20 wins, including the quarter- and semi-final, came away from home, but it was their failure to make an impression outside Sussex that cost them in the Championship. Their one success was a tense 28-run victory at Cheltenham, and in their last three away games – all defeats – there were only two half-centuries. Brown said some of the pitches they encountered were awful, but too often the batting collectively struggled. After making 438 against Leicestershire in April, Sussex were dismissed for under 300 on 13 occasions. Their promotion challenge effectively ended at Riverside a few days before T20 finals day, when there was just one score above 25 across their two innings.

Brown's first-class form benefited from his omission from the T20 side. His wicketkeeping was always of a high standard, and his 912 runs at 43 made him the leading scorer. One of Gillespie's biggest achievements was turning Phil Salt into a credible four-day opener. Pigeonholed as a one-day dasher, he

Matthew Lewis, Getty Images

Laurie Evans

relished the chance to carve a niche in the longer format, and his glorious 148 in the win over Derbyshire was Sussex's best – and highest – Championship innings of the season. Harry Finch was given greater opportunity and reached 50 six times, though he converted only one into a maiden Championship century, against Middlesex. Michael Burgess's runs tailed off, though he may have been distracted by his role as keeper-batsman in the T20 team, while Luke Wells scored less than half the 1,292 he contributed in 2017. For a while near the end of the season he ceased to open, in an attempt to find form. His leg-spin, though, continued to improve.

The absence of Stiaan van Zyl for most of the summer was a blow. Despite the severity of his knee injury becoming clear, Sussex resisted the temptation to draft in an overseas replacement. The 19-year-old Academy graduate Tom Haines was a beneficiary, and his century against Durham at Arundel seemed to confirm the belief that he will be the mainstay of the top order for years to come.

After missing the early season because of IPL commitments, Archer and Chris Jordan formed an incisive pair. (Their absence partly explained Sussex's poor showing in the Royal London Cup.) When the mood took him, Archer was as quick as anyone in the country, though for consistency he could not match Ollie Robinson, who wholeheartedly embraced Gillespie's methods. Despite a patchy fitness record earlier in his career, he played in every Championship match. His 81 first-class wickets – including 28 in his last four games – were the most in the country. Just twice in 27 innings did he fail to strike. In September, he signed a new contract, and could yet push for England recognition. The attack will be further strengthened by the arrival of Pakistan left-arm quick Mir Hamza, who will be available for eight Championship matches from May to July.

David Wiese's all-round ability gave the side a healthy balance, while Briggs bowled reliably on unhelpful pitches. But George Garton, the left-arm seamer who had joined England's Ashes squad as cover in November 2017, suffered an injury-plagued summer. He desperately needs to stay fit if he is to fulfil his potential. The same went for Stuart Whittingham, who also played just once in the Championship; in December he joined Gloucestershire.

If Sussex's bowling resources remain well stocked, their batting is a concern: the top order must deliver dependable totals if they are to return to Division One. The glory years under Chris Adams may be a fading memory, yet there is a renewed optimism on the South Coast.

Championship attendance: 27,974.

SUSSEX RESULTS

All first-class matches – Played 15: Won 6, Lost 4, Drawn 5.
County Championship matches – Played 14: Won 6, Lost 4, Drawn 4.

Specsavers County Championship, 3rd in Division 2;
Vitality Blast, finalists; Royal London One-Day Cup, 8th in South Group.

COUNTY CHAMPIONSHIP AVERAGES, BATTING AND FIELDING

Cap		Birthplace	M	I	NO	R	HS	100	Avge	Ct/St
2014	B. C. Brown	Crawley‡	14	24	3	912	116	1	43.42	52/1
	D. Wiese††	Roodepoort, SA . . .	13	20	4	538	106	1	33.62	2
	†T. J. Haines	Crawley‡	7	10	0	319	124	1	31.90	2
	P. D. Salt	Bodelwyddan	14	24	0	739	148	2	30.79	11
	M. G. K. Burgess	Epsom	12	19	1	551	101*	1	30.61	4
	H. Z. Finch	Hastings‡	14	24	0	722	103	1	30.08	23
2016	†L. W. P. Wells	Eastbourne‡	14	24	1	607	102*	1	26.39	3
	†S. van Zyl††	Cape Town, SA . . .	5	9	0	237	45	0	26.33	1
2018	I. Sharma¶	Delhi, India	4	6	2	102	66	0	25.50	1
2014	C. J. Jordan	Lowlands, Barb . . .	8	13	0	299	68	0	23.00	5
2007	L. J. Wright	Grantham	9	16	0	338	88	0	21.12	1
	D. R. Briggs	Newport, IoW	12	20	7	234	46	0	18.00	5
2017	J. C. Archer††	Bridgetown, Barb . .	8	13	3	170	33	0	17.00	6
	O. E. Robinson	Margate	14	22	3	294	52	0	15.47	5

Also batted: W. A. T. Beer (*Crawley‡*) (1 match) did not bat; L. J. Evans (*Lambeth*) (1 match) 34, 0 (1 ct); †G. H. S. Garton (*Brighton‡*) (1 match) 22* (1 ct); †D. M. W. Rawlins (*Bermuda*) (1 match) 0, 0; A. Sakande (*Chester*) (1 match) 0*, 1*; S. G. Whittingham (*Derby*) (1 match) 0*.

‡ *Born in Sussex.*   ¶ *Official overseas player.*   †† *Other non-England-qualified.*

BOWLING

	Style	O	M	R	W	BB	5I	Avge
J. C. Archer	RFM	273.5	67	750	42	5-69	1	17.85
O. E. Robinson	RFM/OB	485	92	1,381	74	7-58	4	18.66
I. Sharma	RFM	114.3	19	346	15	4-52	0	23.06
D. Wiese	RFM	339.1	65	1,041	41	5-48	1	25.39
D. R. Briggs	SLA	279.5	51	764	28	4-70	0	27.28
C. J. Jordan	RFM	191.1	32	598	20	3-23	0	29.90

Also bowled: W. A. T. Beer (LB) 26–3–88–1; B. C. Brown (RM) 3–2–1–0; M. G. K. Burgess (RM) 6–1–14–0; G. H. S. Garton (LFM) 27–2–103–1; T. J. Haines (RM) 29–8–74–1; A. Sakande (RFM) 22–1–91–3; P. D. Salt (RM) 9–2–32–1; S. van Zyl (RM) 48–12–127–3; L. W. P. Wells (LB) 125.2–11–378–8; S. G. Whittingham (RFM) 16–2–61–2.

LEADING ROYAL LONDON CUP AVERAGES (100 runs/3 wickets)

Batting	Runs	HS	Avge	SR	Ct
L. J. Evans	243	107*	60.75	78.38	3
D. Wiese	214	67	53.50	118.23	1
L. J. Wright	229	105	45.80	106.01	1
H. Z. Finch	250	108	41.66	68.49	2
M. G. K. Burgess . .	162	58	32.40	122.72	3
B. C. Brown	131	73*	26.20	71.97	4
L. W. P. Wells . . .	121	62	20.16	69.54	2

Bowling	W	BB	Avge	ER
I. Sharma	8	3-47	26.50	4.81
O. E. Robinson	9	3-31	27.11	5.54
D. R. Briggs	9	3-23	30.88	4.87
C. J. Jordan	3	2-55	38.33	5.75
D. Wiese	6	3-46	41.00	5.12

LEADING VITALITY BLAST AVERAGES (100 runs/15 overs)

Batting	Runs	HS	Avge	SR	Ct/St	Bowling	W	BB	Avge	ER
P. D. Salt	355	74	25.35	**172.33**	4	Rashid Khan	17	3-9	14.35	**6.59**
L. J. Wright	452	92	37.66	**151.17**	2	D. R. Briggs	18	3-29	18.83	**7.06**
D. M. W. Rawlins	203	49	25.37	**146.04**	6	W. A. T. Beer	7	2-17	18.42	**7.58**
J. C. Archer	120	26*	20.00	**139.53**	3	C. J. Jordan	13	2-9	23.07	**7.92**
L. J. Evans	614	96	68.22	**135.84**	4	T. S. Mills	7	3-20	32.00	**8.45**
D. Wiese	167	52	20.87	**130.46**	4	J. C. Archer	22	3-24	19.90	**8.56**
M. G. K. Burgess	160	56	22.85	**128.00**	5/5	D. Wiese	7	5-24	40.71	**9.50**

FIRST-CLASS COUNTY RECORDS

Highest score for	344*	M. W. Goodwin v Somerset at Taunton	2009
Highest score against	322	E. Paynter (Lancashire) at Hove	1937
Leading run-scorer	34,150	J. G. Langridge (avge 37.69)	1928–55
Best bowling for	10-48	C. H. G. Bland v Kent at Tonbridge	1899
Best bowling against	9-11	A. P. Freeman (Kent) at Hove	1922
Leading wicket-taker	2,211	M. W. Tate (avge 17.41)	1912–37
Highest total for	742-5 dec	v Somerset at Taunton	2009
Highest total against	726	by Nottinghamshire at Nottingham	1895
Lowest total for	{ 19	v Surrey at Godalming	1830
	19	v Nottinghamshire at Hove	1873
Lowest total against	18	by Kent at Gravesend	1867

LIST A COUNTY RECORDS

Highest score for	163	C. J. Adams v Middlesex at Arundel	1999
Highest score against	198*	G. A. Gooch (Essex) at Hove	1982
Leading run-scorer	7,969	A. P. Wells (avge 31.62)	1981–96
Best bowling for	7-41	A. N. Jones v Nottinghamshire at Nottingham	1986
Best bowling against	8-21	M. A. Holding (Derbyshire) at Hove	1988
Leading wicket-taker	370	R. J. Kirtley (avge 22.35)	1995–2010
Highest total for	399-4	v Worcestershire at Horsham	2011
Highest total against	377-9	by Somerset at Hove	2003
Lowest total for	49	v Derbyshire at Chesterfield	1969
Lowest total against	36	by Leicestershire at Leicester	1973

TWENTY20 COUNTY RECORDS

Highest score for	153*	L. J. Wright v Essex at Chelmsford	2014
Highest score against	152*	G. R. Napier (Essex) at Chelmsford	2008
Leading run-scorer	3,718	**L. J. Wright (avge 32.33, SR 153.44)**	**2004–18**
Best bowling for	5-11	Mushtaq Ahmed v Essex at Hove	2005
Best bowling against	{ 5-14	A. D. Mascarenhas (Hampshire) at Hove	2004
	5-14	K. J. Abbott (Middlesex) at Hove	2015
Leading wicket-taker	**84**	**W. A. T. Beer (avge 27.27, ER 7.36)**	**2008–18**
Highest total for	242-5	v Gloucestershire at Bristol	2016
Highest total against	242-3	by Essex at Chelmsford	2008
Lowest total for	67	v Hampshire at Hove	2004
Lowest total against	85	by Hampshire at Southampton	2008

ADDRESS

The 1st Central County Ground, Eaton Road, Hove BN3 3AN; 0844 264 0202; info@
sussexcricket.co.uk; www.sussexcricket.co.uk.

OFFICIALS

Captain B. C. Brown
    (Twenty20) L. J. Wright
Director of cricket K. Greenfield
Head coach J. N. Gillespie
Academy director R. G. Halsall

President J. M. Abbott
Chairman R. Warren
**Chief executive and chairman, cricket
    committee** C. R. Andrew
Head groundsman A. Mackay
Scorer M. J. Charman

SUSSEX v LOUGHBOROUGH MCCU

At Hove, April 1–3. Drawn. Toss: Sussex. First-class debuts: N. A. Hammond, W. J. N. Pereira, J. A. J. Rishton, W. J. L. Rollings, C. W. G. Sanders, O. C. Soames.

Sussex slipped to 20 for two – then 98 for five – before Brown, having opted to bat, bailed them out. He added 85 with Finch and an unbroken 124 with Beer, who hit his maiden senior fifty; Brown survived a drop on 96 to reach his 14th first-class hundred. All four members of Loughborough's pace attack were making their first-class debut, but were not overawed. Backed up by left-arm spinner Adam Tillcock, they rattled through 103 overs on the first day, only for the second to fall prey to the weather, prompting Brown to declare. The damp conditions on the last proved ideal for Robinson, who hoovered up seven wickets for the first time. Loughborough rallied from 38 for six thanks to an undefeated 32 from Andy Rishton, born in Massachusetts, but could not save the follow-on. They fared better – and batted longer – at their second attempt.

Close of play: first day, Sussex 337-7 (Brown 119, Beer 50); second day, no play.

Sussex

L. W. P. Wells b Sanders	6	O. E. Robinson b Tillcock		13
P. D. Salt b Pereira	8	W. A. T. Beer not out		50
H. Z. Finch run out (Rishton)	80	B 8, lb 11, w 3, nb 8		30
M. G. K. Burgess c Soames b Pereira	8			
L. J. Evans c Bracey b Rishton	12	1/16 (2) 2/20 (1) (7 wkts dec, 103 overs)		337
L. J. Wright lbw b Sanders	11	3/41 (4) 4/81 (5)		
*†B. C. Brown not out	119	5/98 (6) 6/183 (3) 7/213 (8)		

S. G. Whittingham and A. Sakande did not bat.

Sanders 21–4–67–2; Pereira 19–2–55–2; Rishton 19–3–67–1; Rollings 17–2–61–0; Tillcock 24–3–53–1; Evans 1–0–3–0; Thurston 2–0–12–0.

Loughborough MCCU

S. T. Evans lbw b Robinson	0	– not out	33
Hassan Azad c Brown b Whittingham	4	– c Salt b Beer	17
†J. R. Bracey lbw b Robinson	16	– c Finch b Sakande	13
O. C. Soames b Whittingham	2		
C. O. Thurston c Finch b Robinson	9		
*A. D. Tillcock c Brown b Robinson	4		
N. A. Hammond b Beer	18		
J. A. J. Rishton not out	32		
C. W. G. Sanders b Robinson	6		
W. J. L. Rollings b Robinson	4		
W. J. N. Pereira lbw b Robinson	0		
Nb 4	4	B 8	8

1/0 (1) 2/4 (2) 3/22 (4)   (30.4 overs)   99   1/41 (2)   (2 wkts, 34.4 overs)   71
4/24 (3) 5/33 (5) 6/38 (6)   2/71 (3)
7/65 (7) 8/81 (9) 9/99 (10) 10/99 (11)

Robinson 9.4–2–23–7; Whittingham 9–0–56–2; Sakande 6–3–13–0; Beer 6–2–7–1. *Second innings*—Robinson 6–2–8–0; Sakande 9.4–3–25–1; Beer 8–3–9–1; Wells 11–3–21–0.

Umpires: M. Burns and R. A. White.

At Birmingham, April 13–16. SUSSEX drew with WARWICKSHIRE.

At Leicester, April 20–23. SUSSEX drew with LEICESTERSHIRE.

SUSSEX v GLOUCESTERSHIRE

At Hove, April 27–30. Drawn. Sussex 8pts, Gloucestershire 8pts. Toss: uncontested.

With Sussex needing four wickets and Gloucestershire 59 runs, the last day was set for an exciting climax, only for rain to cause a washout. There had been little hint of the drama to come when Sussex's opening pair – Salt finally looking the part in his new role – put on 86 with few alarms in the 21 overs possible on the first day. By lunch on the second, though, ten wickets had fallen for 59. A capricious pitch, persistent cloud cover (the floodlights were on throughout) and some injudicious shots were to blame; medium-pacer Higgins collected a career-best five for 21. Gloucestershire struggled too, with Wiese claiming his first Sussex five-for, but it needed an innings of gumption from Finch, who took several blows to the hands, to give the home bowlers something to defend. Van Zyl triggered a collapse of four for two in 17 balls as Gloucestershire sagged in pursuit of 167. A dreadful forecast made the teams keen to wrap things up on the third evening, but the umpires ruled it too gloomy even to face spin.

Close of play: first day, Sussex 86-0 (Wells 25, Salt 54); second day, Sussex 51-2 (van Zyl 23); third day, Gloucestershire 108-6 (Higgins 18, Noema-Barnett 6).

Sussex

L. W. P. Wells c Roderick b Higgins	27	– b Noema-Barnett	22
P. D. Salt c van Buuren b Higgins	63	– b Higgins	0
S. van Zyl c Bracey b Higgins	3	– c Roderick b Worrall	44
H. Z. Finch c Roderick b Worrall	5	– b Worrall	48
L. J. Wright c J. M. R. Taylor b Miles	13	– lbw b Higgins	0
*†B. C. Brown lbw b Higgins	0	– b M. D. Taylor	16
M. G. K. Burgess c Dent b Higgins	4	– c Roderick b M. D. Taylor	17
O. E. Robinson c Noema-Barnett b Higgins	0	– lbw b Higgins	10
D. Wiese b M. D. Taylor	0	– not out	27
D. R. Briggs c Worrall b Miles	11	– lbw b Worrall	1
I. Sharma not out	7	– lbw b Worrall	6
B 5, lb 7	12	B 9, lb 2, nb 2	13

1/92 (1) 2/97 (2) 3/105 (3)   (47 overs) 145
4/105 (4) 5/105 (6) 6/116 (7)
7/116 (8) 8/117 (9) 9/128 (10) 10/145 (5)

1/4 (2) 2/51 (1)   (58.5 overs) 204
3/79 (3) 4/80 (5)
5/117 (6) 6/135 (7) 7/154 (8)
8/184 (4) 9/188 (10) 10/204 (11)

Worrall 17–5–40–2; M. D. Taylor 11–0–43–1; Miles 9–2–29–2; Higgins 10–2–21–5. *Second innings*—Worrall 18.5–4–45–4; Higgins 22–7–65–3; M. D. Taylor 10–0–48–2; Noema-Barnett 3–0–9–1; Miles 5–0–26–0.

Gloucestershire

B. A. C. Howell lbw b Wiese	37	– (2) lbw b Robinson	45
*C. D. J. Dent b Robinson	14	– (1) b Robinson	13
†G. H. Roderick lbw b Robinson	23	– c Brown b van Zyl	10
J. R. Bracey b Robinson	15	– b van Zyl	0
J. M. R. Taylor c Sharma b Robinson	9	– c Brown b van Zyl	1
G. L. van Buuren c Brown b Wiese	21	– lbw b Briggs	9
R. F. Higgins b Robinson	15	– not out	18
K. Noema-Barnett c Wells b Briggs	31	– not out	6
C. N. Miles c Briggs b Wiese	0		
D. J. Worrall c Finch b Wiese	2		
M. D. Taylor not out	5		
Lb 3, nb 8	11	B 1, lb 3, nb 2	6

1/27 (2) 2/69 (1) 3/91 (4)   (57.1 overs) 183
4/102 (3) 5/107 (5) 6/129 (7)
7/144 (6) 8/144 (9) 9/150 (10) 10/183 (8)

1/24 (1)   (6 wkts, 43.2 overs) 108
2/69 (3) 3/69 (4)
4/69 (2) 5/71 (5) 6/95 (6)

Robinson 20–4–67–4; Sharma 14–1–53–0; Wiese 18–6–48–5; van Zyl 5–1–12–0; Briggs 0.1–0–0–1. *Second innings*—Robinson 11–1–25–2; Sharma 7–2–25–0; Wiese 6–0–21–0; van Zyl 11–6–16–3; Briggs 6–1–8–1; Wells 1.2–0–9–0.

Umpires: M. J. Saggers and R. J. Warren.

SUSSEX v MIDDLESEX

At Hove, May 4–7. Sussex won by three wickets. Sussex 22pts, Middlesex 4pts. Toss: Middlesex.
   Indifferent bounce kept batsmen on their toes, but made for an absorbing contest that would not have been out of place in Division One. An unbeaten 84 from Holden held Middlesex's first innings together, after Robinson – with his second seven-for of the season – had threatened to demolish

them. And although Gubbins and Malan would hit stylish centuries in their second, the innings that defined the match was Finch's maiden Championship hundred, compiled over the first two days, when conditions were trickiest. He battled hard, helped Sussex – despite stumbling to 127 for six – to a lead of 93, and invited comparisons with Mike Yardy, his mentor and batting coach. A stand of 234 between Gubbins and Malan then took them to 243 for two but, after Briggs removed them and Cartwright in five deliveries, they folded. Set 230, Sussex seemed destined for defeat when, still needing 102, they lost their sixth wicket. But Brown counter-attacked intelligently as the ball softened, and his yell when victory arrived would have been audible in Brighton. Savouring his first win as Sussex's head coach, Jason Gillespie said: "That's why I love county cricket."

Close of play: first day, Sussex 60-4 (Finch 26, Briggs 1); second day, Middlesex 64-2 (Gubbins 22, Malan 34); third day, Sussex 35-2 (van Zyl 12, Briggs 1).

Middlesex

S. D. Robson c Brown b Robinson	10	– (2) c Briggs b Wiese	4
N. R. T. Gubbins b Robinson	8	– (1) c Salt b Briggs	107
S. S. Eskinazi lbw b Robinson	38	– c Brown b Robinson	3
*D. J. Malan b Robinson	13	– st Brown b Briggs	119
H. W. R. Cartwright c Burgess b Robinson	4	– c Finch b Briggs	0
M. D. E. Holden not out	84	– b Briggs	29
†J. A. Simpson c Burgess b Briggs	26	– b Wiese	25
J. A. R. Harris c Garton b Briggs	1	– lbw b Wiese	0
O. P. Rayner lbw b Robinson	9	– b Wiese	6
T. J. Murtagh c Wright b Garton	26	– not out	13
T. E. Barber b Robinson	3	– run out (van Zyl/Finch/Brown)	0
B 1, lb 1, nb 6	8	B 11, lb 3, nb 2	16

1/13 (2) 2/24 (1) 3/67 (3)   (73 overs) 230   1/6 (2) 2/9 (3)   (99.2 overs) 322
4/75 (5) 5/76 (4) 6/132 (7)   3/243 (1) 4/244 (4)
7/135 (8) 8/169 (9) 9/220 (10) 10/230 (11)   5/245 (5) 6/303 (7) 7/303 (6)
                                                          8/303 (8) 9/312 (9) 10/322 (11)

Robinson 21–3–58–7; Wiese 18–5–54–0; Garton 15–1–46–1; van Zyl 4–0–13–0; Briggs 12–1–48–2; Wells 3–0–9–0. *Second innings*—Robinson 23–6–54–1; Wiese 23.2–7–70–4; Briggs 26–4–70–4; Garton 12–1–57–0; Wells 15–1–57–0.

Sussex

L. W. P. Wells c Robson b Murtagh	4	– c Rayner b Harris	10
P. D. Salt c Malan b Murtagh	0	– lbw b Harris	12
S. van Zyl c Eskinazi b Harris	15	– c Robson b Cartwright	45
H. Z. Finch lbw b Harris	103	– (5) c Simpson b Harris	11
L. J. Wright b Harris	9	– (6) c and b Cartwright	0
D. R. Briggs lbw b Cartwright	23	– (4) c Cartwright b Rayner	39
*†B. C. Brown b Cartwright	7	– not out	65
M. G. K. Burgess c Robson b Cartwright	45	– lbw b Malan	22
O. E. Robinson lbw b Harris	52	– not out	10
D. Wiese c Simpson b Harris	16		
G. H. S. Garton not out	22		
B 8, lb 5, w 4, nb 10	27	B 8, lb 6, w 2, nb 2	18

1/4 (1) 2/5 (2) 3/32 (3)   (93.1 overs) 323   1/11 (1)   (7 wkts, 73.3 overs) 232
4/50 (5) 5/106 (6) 6/127 (7)   2/24 (4) 3/113 (4)
7/221 (8) 8/242 (4) 9/270 (10) 10/323 (9)   4/125 (3) 5/125 (6) 6/128 (5) 7/215 (8)

Murtagh 23–6–72–2; Barber 19–2–81–0; Harris 24.1–3–86–5; Cartwright 13–2–45–3; Rayner 14–2–26–0. *Second innings*—Murtagh 13–4–24–0; Harris 19.3–3–74–3; Rayner 20–6–51–1; Barber 10–1–37–0; Cartwright 7–2–17–2; Malan 4–0–15–1.

Umpires: J. Blades and D. J. Millns.

At Canterbury, May 11–13. SUSSEX lost to KENT by 58 runs.

At Hove, June 7. SUSSEX lost to AUSTRALIANS by 57 runs (see Australian tour section).

SUSSEX v DURHAM

At Arundel, June 20–22. Sussex won by an innings and 64 runs. Sussex 24pts, Durham 3pts. Toss: uncontested.

Sussex pulled off an impressive win on a typically slow pitch, set up by maiden hundreds from Salt and Haines, aged 21 and 19. Haines had been playing for the Seconds at New Malden but, when Chris Jordan was called up by England Lions, his mother drove him to Arundel to make only his third Championship appearance. After early clouds dispersed, the pair put on 244, a second-wicket record for both the fixture and the ground. If Salt was more willing to play his shots, there was much to admire in his partner's footwork and placement. Burgess almost joined them in three figures, taking the score to 552, so it was no surprise that Durham – who began the third day at 202 for four with hopes of a competitive total – eventually wilted. In 70 deliveries they lost six for nine, Wiese the destroyer-in-chief with three wickets in seven balls, and followed on, 341 behind. Will Smith dug in for the second time, and Poynter played sensibly; otherwise resistance was sporadic. Boosted by some excellent catching, Sussex coasted home with 12 minutes of the third evening remaining.

Close of play: first day, Sussex 439-5 (Brown 50, Burgess 30); second day, Durham 202-4 (Smith 90, Harte 12).

Sussex

L. W. P. Wells c Latham b Salisbury	8	O. E. Robinson b Clark		24
P. D. Salt c Harte b Salisbury	130	D. R. Briggs not out		0
T. J. Haines c Collingwood b Steel	124			
H. Z. Finch c Poynter b Salisbury	56	B 1, lb 5, w 1, nb 6		13
L. J. Wright c Coughlin b Steel	32			
*†B. C. Brown c Poynter b Rushworth	52	1/9 (1) 2/253 (3)	(119.5 overs)	552
M. G. K. Burgess c Smith b Coughlin	88	3/283 (2) 4/350 (5) 5/364 (4)		
D. Wiese lbw b Rushworth	0	6/446 (6) 7/446 (8) 8/500 (9)		
J. C. Archer c Clark b Rushworth	17	9/552 (7) 10/552 (10)	110 overs: 509-8	

Rushworth 26–0–116–3; Salisbury 26–5–112–3; Rimmington 23.4–3–128–0; Coughlin 19–0–90–1; Smith 11.2–2–37–0; Harte 6–0–28–0; Steel 4.2–0–25–2; Clark 3.5–0–10–1.

Durham

T. W. M. Latham c Finch b Archer	2	– b Robinson		20
C. T. Steel c Archer b Briggs	20	– b Archer		8
W. R. Smith lbw b Briggs	90	– c Finch b Wiese		36
G. Clark b Wells	27	– lbw b Briggs		49
*P. D. Collingwood lbw b Wells	44	– lbw b Wiese		0
G. J. Harte c Brown b Briggs	13	– c Brown b Briggs		0
†S. W. Poynter b Wiese	0	– lbw b Briggs		84
J. Coughlin b Wiese	0	– c Finch b Wells		14
N. J. Rimmington c Brown b Wiese	0	– not out		49
M. E. T. Salisbury b Wiese	8	– b Robinson		4
C. Rushworth not out	0	– c and b Archer		4
Lb 5, nb 2	7	Lb 5, nb 4		9

1/2 (1) 2/43 (2) 3/96 (4)	(85.4 overs)	211	1/9 (2) 2/61 (1) (83 overs) 277
4/178 (5) 5/202 (3) 6/203 (7)			3/77 (3) 4/79 (5)
7/203 (8) 8/203 (9) 9/209 (6) 10/211 (10)			5/88 (6) 6/137 (4) 7/189 (8)
			8/268 (7) 9/272 (10) 10/277 (11)

Archer 18–5–50–1; Robinson 13–3–40–0; Wiese 15.4–4–33–4; Briggs 27–11–57–3; Wells 12–1–26–2. *Second innings*—Archer 14–2–65–2; Robinson 15–3–34–2; Briggs 24–4–71–3; Wiese 10–1–42–2; Haines 11–6–22–0; Wells 9–2–38–1.

Umpires: Y. C. Barde and M. Burns.

At Cheltenham, July 16–19. SUSSEX beat GLOUCESTERSHIRE by 28 runs.

SUSSEX v GLAMORGAN

At Hove, July 22–23 (day/night). Sussex won by an innings and 154 runs. Sussex 22pts, Glamorgan 3pts. Toss: Sussex.

Sussex's pace attack made outstanding use of the pink ball to rout a sorry Glamorgan twice in 62 overs. Archer was the spearhead, his match figures of eight for 46 helping deliver an innings victory in five sessions. After Sussex had hit 327, he grabbed four in 11 balls to leave Glamorgan in freefall at 15 for five – Robinson also pinched one in the mayhem – so a total of 85 almost represented a recovery. All the same, they followed on 242 behind, and fared little better; in both innings only two batsmen reached double figures. On a pitch offering bounce and good carry, they were as flummoxed by the relentless off-stump line of Jordan and Robinson as by Archer's high pace. Earlier, Wells had gone when seemingly set, and Sussex were grateful for lower-order runs. Last man Briggs dominated a 61-run stand with Archer, and then left it to the seamers. Sussex coach Jason Gillespie said their performance was as good as anything he had seen in county cricket.

Close of play: first day, Sussex 327.

Sussex

L. W. P. Wells c Murphy b Hogan	71	O. E. Robinson c Selman b van der Gugten	6
P. D. Salt c Cooke b Hogan	48	D. R. Briggs lbw b Lawlor	46
T. J. Haines c Selman b Carey	18		
H. Z. Finch c Cooke b Hogan	1	B 1, lb 5, nb 2	8
M. G. K. Burgess c Cooke b Lawlor	13		
*B. C. Brown c Cooke b Salter	49	1/73 (2) 2/114 (3)	(95.1 overs) 327
D. Wiese c Cooke b Lawlor	2	3/139 (4) 4/140 (1)	
C. J. Jordan b Hogan	46	5/163 (5) 6/171 (7) 7/254 (6)	
J. C. Archer not out	19	8/254 (8) 9/266 (10) 10/327 (11)	

Carey 25–4–97–1; van der Gugten 19–4–89–1; Hogan 25–9–39–4; Lawlor 14.1–0–59–3; Salter 12–1–37–1.

Glamorgan

N. J. Selman b Archer	9	– b Robinson	2
J. R. Murphy b Archer	2	– c Brown b Archer	0
C. R. Brown lbw b Robinson	0	– lbw b Archer	3
U. T. Khawaja c Brown b Archer	0	– c Salt b Wiese	19
K. S. Carlson c Salt b Archer	0	– b Robinson	22
†C. B. Cooke b Wiese	32	– c Salt b Jordan	6
J. L. Lawlor c Brown b Jordan	6	– b Jordan	2
A. G. Salter c Archer b Jordan	9	– c Brown b Archer	5
T. van der Gugten b Jordan	1	– lbw b Robinson	6
L. J. Carey run out (Briggs)	17	– b Archer	4
*M. G. Hogan not out	2	– not out	4
B 1, lb 3	4	Lb 6, w 7, nb 2	15

1/8 (2) 2/11 (1) 3/11 (4)   (28.4 overs) 85   1/7 (1) 2/8 (2)   (33.3 overs) 88
4/11 (3) 5/15 (5) 6/34 (7)   3/15 (3) 4/36 (4)
7/60 (8) 8/66 (9) 9/68 (6) 10/85 (10)   5/44 (6) 6/54 (7) 7/70 (5)
                                                      8/76 (8) 9/80 (9) 10/88 (10)

Robinson 7–0–24–1; Archer 10–3–15–4; Jordan 7.4–2–23–3; Wiese 4–1–19–1. *Second innings—* Robinson 10–2–20–3; Archer 9.3–3–31–4; Jordan 7–3–14–2; Wiese 7–2–17–1.

Umpires: J. W. Lloyds and J. D. Middlebrook.

SUSSEX v DERBYSHIRE

At Hove, August 19–22. Sussex won by 243 runs. Sussex 24pts, Derbyshire 7pts. Toss: uncontested. First-class debut: A. K. Dal. County debut: S. M. Ervine. Championship debut: L. H. Ferguson.

Sussex improved as the game wore on, but it took until after tea on the final day to overcome Derbyshire, and achieve their heaviest win against them by runs. Victory, their fourth in a row, was set up by Salt and Wells, who helped plunder 191 in a session on the third day, Salt batting in one-day mode to make 148 from 138 balls. Brown's declaration asked ten-man Derbyshire – Rampaul was absent after complaining of breathing problems on the first day – to make 405. It wasn't their only problem. On the second morning, a story appeared on the Nottinghamshire website prematurely announcing that Slater, though playing here, had signed a three-year contract; it was soon taken down. Slater's last innings for Derbyshire ended when he was hit on the helmet by Archer (leading to a first-class debut for concussion substitute Anuj Dal). And wicketkeeper Harvey Hosein dislocated a finger before the game began: Madsen kept until Smit arrived from Derby, in time to see Brown striking his 15th first-class hundred. Derbyshire had threatened to gain a first-innings lead, but subsided from a promising 285 for two.

Close of play: first day, Sussex 400-7 (Wiese 89, Archer 13); second day, Derbyshire 315-5 (Hughes 60); third day, Derbyshire 6-0 (Slater 0, Godleman 1).

Sussex

L. W. P. Wells c †Madsen b Rampaul	35	– c Hughes b Critchley	78
P. D. Salt c Ervine b Viljoen	15	– b Palladino	148
T. J. Haines c Critchley b Ferguson	8	– c Madsen b Critchley	27
H. Z. Finch b Palladino	82	– c Hughes b Viljoen	29
M. G. K. Burgess c †Madsen b Palladino	11	– b Viljoen	4
*†B. C. Brown lbw b Ferguson	116	– (8) not out	4
D. Wiese b Ferguson	93	– (6) c Smit b Critchley	12
C. J. Jordan b Viljoen	3		
J. C. Archer c sub (A. K. Dal) b Ferguson	15	– (7) not out	31
O. E. Robinson b Viljoen	15		
D. R. Briggs not out	17		
B 12, lb 12, nb 6	30	B 12, lb 4, w 2, nb 2	20

1/32 (2) 2/47 (3) 3/65 (1) 4/111 (5)   (113 overs) 440   1/191 (1)   (6 wkts dec, 61 overs) 353
5/214 (4) 6/356 (6) 7/379 (8)   2/247 (3) 3/270 (2)
8/404 (9) 9/409 (7) 10/440 (10)   110 overs: 432-9   4/287 (5) 5/306 (6) 6/318 (4)

Ferguson 26–2–106–4; Viljoen 21–1–97–3; Rampaul 16–3–52–1; Ervine 5–0–17–0; Palladino 22–3–59–2; Critchley 21–0–82–0; Madsen 2–0–3–0. *Second innings*—Ferguson 10–0–72–0; Viljoen 11–0–71–2; Critchley 22–0–133–3; Palladino 11–0–36–1; Ervine 7–0–25–0.

Derbyshire

B. T. Slater c Salt b Robinson	24	– retired hurt	40
*B. A. Godleman b Wells	122	– b Wiese	14
W. L. Madsen c Briggs b Jordan	72	– lbw b Jordan	0
A. L. Hughes c Salt b Robinson	77	– c Brown b Robinson	20
S. M. Ervine run out (Robinson)	2	– lbw b Briggs	1
G. C. Viljoen b Briggs	13	– (9) c Brown b Robinson	12
M. J. J. Critchley b Robinson	8	– (6) c Brown b Archer	7
†D. Smit not out	20	– (7) lbw b Briggs	5
A. P. Palladino c Jordan b Wiese	9	– (10) not out	14
L. H. Ferguson c Brown b Wiese	0	– (11) b Archer	1
R. Rampaul absent hurt		– absent hurt	
A. K. Dal (did not bat)		– (8) lbw b Briggs	25
B 5, lb 13, w 2, nb 22	42	B 8, lb 7, w 3, nb 4	22

1/70 (1) 2/200 (3) 3/285 (2)   (100.3 overs) 389   1/58 (2) 2/59 (3)   (70.2 overs) 161
4/296 (5) 5/315 (6) 6/343 (7)   3/77 (5) 4/84 (6)
7/348 (4) 8/389 (9) 9/389 (10)   5/89 (7) 6/109 (4)
                                                         7/140 (9) 8/158 (8) 9/161 (11)

In the second innings Slater retired hurt at 72-2. Dal replaced him, as a concussion substitute.

Archer 23–5–75–0; Robinson 19–2–77–3; Wiese 15.3–2–71–2; Jordan 15–1–59–1; Briggs 15–2–61–1; Haines 6–1–12–0; Wells 7–1–16–1. *Second innings*—Robinson 15–4–36–2; Archer 15.2–8–21–2; Wiese 12–3–53–1; Jordan 11–1–22–1; Briggs 15–2–41–3; Wells 2–1–1–0.

Umpires: G. D. Lloyd and B. V. Taylor.

At Lord's. August 29–31. SUSSEX lost to MIDDLESEX by 55 runs.

SUSSEX v LEICESTERSHIRE

At Hove, September 4–6. Sussex won by 274 runs. Sussex 23pts, Leicestershire 3pts. Toss: Sussex. First-class debut: B. W. M. Mike.

The day after signing a new contract, Robinson completed a maiden match haul of ten wickets. With Archer taking six, Sussex's pace attack overcame a brittle Leicestershire to claim a fifth win in six, briefly restoring them to second place. If there was a feeling that, despite four players passing 50, Sussex hadn't made the most of winning the toss, it was soon dispelled by Robinson and Archer, who reduced Leicestershire to 49 for nine inside 20 overs. The last pair fought hard to add 84, yet it

---

A CASE FOR PROMOTION?

Tenth-wicket partnerships forming the highest percentage of a Championship total:

83.51	228/273	R. Illingworth/K. Higgs	Leics v Northants at Leicester . .	1977
80.70	230/285	R. W. Nicholls/W. Roche	Middx v Kent at Lord's	1899
75.94	60/79	M. N. Malik/S. C. G. MacGill	Notts v Essex at Nottingham . .	2003
68.85	42/61	G. H. Hirst/D. Hunter	Yorks v Glos at Leeds	1894
66.07	111/168	A. Ward/A. W. Mold	Lancs v Leics at Manchester . .	1895
64.59	135/209	C. M. W. Read/R. D. Stemp	Notts v Hants at Southampton .	2001
63.55	68/107	P. I. Pocock/R. Harman.	Surrey v Somerset at Bath	1966
63.46	66/104	G. Geary/H. C. Snary	Leics v Kent at Leicester	1932
63.46	99/156	R. G. Duckfield/G. Davies	Glam v Surrey at Swansea	1932
63.15	**84/133**	**C. F. Parkinson/Mohammad Abbas**	**Leics v Sussex at Hove**	**2018**
61.93	192/310	H. A. W. Bowell/W. H. Livsey	Hants v Worcs at Bournemouth .	1921

Research: Andrew Samson

---

came as a surprise when, on the second afternoon, Brown declined to enforce the follow-on in ideal bowling conditions. Jordan top-scored for the second time, and Sussex set a notional target of 451. Leicestershire put up more resistance – Ackermann hit a sober fifty – though Robinson seized the first five wickets, and the rest came quietly. There was one bright spot for the visitors, however: 20-year-old seamer Ben Mike, son of former Nottinghamshire bowler Greg, took nine wickets on debut.

Close of play: first day, Sussex 323-8 (Jordan 52, Robinson 2); second day, Sussex 100-6 (Brown 9, Jordan 8).

Sussex

T. J. Haines c Raine b Mohammad Abbas	56	– c Eckersley b Raine	8
P. D. Salt c and b Mike	44	– c Eckersley b Klein	35
L. W. P. Wells c Eckersley b Dexter	58	– c Dexter b Mohammad Abbas	0
H. Z. Finch lbw b Raine	4	– lbw b Mike	35
L. J. Wright b Mike	27	– c Dexter b Mike	1
*†B. C. Brown c Eckersley b Raine	60	– c Eckersley b Raine	10
D. Wiese c Dearden b Mike	0	– lbw b Raine	0
C. J. Jordan c Dearden b Klein	68	– b Mike	54
J. C. Archer lbw b Raine	1	– c Dexter b Mike	33
O. E. Robinson b Mike	19	– b Mike	17
D. R. Briggs not out	13	– not out	7
B 9, lb 12, nb 2	23	B 1, lb 2, w 1, nb 6	10

1/79 (2) 2/126 (1) 3/140 (4) (102.3 overs) 373
4/188 (3) 5/204 (5) 6/204 (7)
7/314 (6) 8/320 (9) 9/347 (8) 10/373 (10)

1/13 (1) 2/18 (3) (50.3 overs) 210
3/68 (4) 4/70 (5)
5/88 (2) 6/91 (7) 7/103 (6)
8/173 (9) 9/195 (10) 10/210 (8)

Mohammad Abbas 27–5–83–1; Klein 8–0–41–1; Raine 20–1–73–3; Mike 13.3–1–57–4; Parkinson 19–3–56–0; Ackermann 3–0–7–0; Dexter 12–1–35–1. *Second innings*—Mohammad Abbas 13–1–46–1; Raine 11–2–49–3; Mike 11.3–1–37–5; Klein 9–1–51–1; Parkinson 6–0–24–0.

Leicestershire

H. E. Dearden c Brown b Archer	5	– c Brown b Robinson	21
*P. J. Horton c Jordan b Robinson	0	– b Robinson	10
C. N. Ackermann b Robinson	3	– lbw b Robinson	52
M. J. Cosgrove lbw b Robinson	0	– b Robinson	5
N. J. Dexter b Archer	16	– c Brown b Archer	30
†E. J. H. Eckersley c Jordan b Robinson	1	– b Robinson	0
B. A. Raine c and b Robinson	5	– c Archer b Briggs	22
B. W. M. Mike b Archer	2	– c Finch b Archer	4
C. F. Parkinson c Archer b Briggs	48	– not out	10
D. Klein c Salt b Jordan	5	– b Archer	0
Mohammad Abbas not out	32	– b Wiese	4
B 4, lb 12	16	B 5, lb 9, nb 4	18

1/0 (2) 2/8 (3) 3/8 (4)   (36.3 overs) 133
4/8 (1) 5/9 (6) 6/29 (7)
7/39 (5) 8/44 (8) 9/49 (10) 10/133 (9)

1/21 (2) 2/54 (1)   (62 overs) 176
3/62 (4) 4/121 (3)
5/121 (6) 6/156 (5) 7/158 (7)
8/163 (8) 9/167 (10) 10/176 (11)

Archer 13–2–28–3; Robinson 10–3–24–5; Jordan 5–0–22–1; Wiese 3–0–21–0; Briggs 5.3–0–22–1. *Second innings*—Robinson 16–3–43–5; Archer 20–5–44–3; Wiese 8–1–28–1; Jordan 7–2–19–0; Briggs 9–2–25–1; Wells 2–0–3–0.

Umpires: I. D. Blackwell and N. A. Mallender.

At Chester-le-Street, September 10–12. SUSSEX lost to DURHAM by 186 runs.

SUSSEX v WARWICKSHIRE

At Hove, September 18–21. Drawn. Sussex 9pts, Warwickshire 12pts. Toss: Warwickshire.

For a potential promotion decider – Sussex's only hope lay in victory – the teams might have expected a result pitch, but were given one whose only hazard was occasional indifferent bounce. Unsurprisingly, there were runs for Bell and Trott, and the game was drawn, guaranteeing promotion for Warwickshire, preventing it for Sussex. Trott's hundred was his seventh in the Championship against Sussex, taking his runs against them to 1,801 (706 more than against anyone else). Bell, too, now had more hundreds (five) and runs (1,515) than against any other county. They put on 230, a Warwickshire third-wicket record in this fixture. With Haines unable to bat for Sussex after injuring his ankle, three lbws in Barker's first 20 balls enhanced the prospect of enforcing the follow-on, before Brown and Wiese produced another rescue act, and limited the arrears to 97. With no incentive to make a game of it, Warwickshire batted through the last day, allowing Salt to claim a maiden first-class wicket, Burgess and Finch to take the gloves, and Sibley to grind to 144 over seven hours. Despite the placid pitch, Bell needed treatment on his thumb after Robinson found some unexpected lift.

Close of play: first day, Warwickshire 308-2 (Bell 108, Trott 86); second day, Sussex 224-5 (Brown 58, Wiese 66); third day, Warwickshire 141-0 (Rhodes 76, Sibley 43).

Warwickshire

W. M. H. Rhodes b Wiese	50	– lbw b Robinson	88
D. P. Sibley c Burgess b Briggs	44	– not out	144
I. R. Bell lbw b Briggs	112	– retired hurt	5
I. J. L. Trott c Finch b Wiese	124	– c Finch b Jordan	8
S. R. Hain b Robinson	53	– c †Finch b Salt	90
†T. R. Ambrose lbw b Briggs	14	– not out	5
K. H. D. Barker b Archer	6		
C. J. C. Wright b Archer	10		
O. P. Stone b Archer	0		
*J. S. Patel not out	1		
R. N. Sidebottom lbw b Archer	0		
B 3, lb 11, nb 12	26	B 23, lb 7, w 1, nb 10	41

1/96 (2) 2/102 (1) 3/332 (3)   (142.5 overs) 440   1/158 (1)   (3 wkts dec, 119 overs) 381
4/368 (4) 5/421 (5) 6/423 (6)   2/190 (4) 3/358 (5)
7/433 (7) 8/433 (9) 9/440 (8)
10/440 (11)   110 overs: 352-3

In the second innings Bell retired hurt at 168-1.

Robinson 29–3–89–1; Archer 22.5–3–66–4; Jordan 17–1–74–0; Wiese 23–5–62–2; Briggs 38–9–86–3; Haines 1–0–14–0; Wells 12–1–35–0. *Second innings*—Robinson 19–4–50–1; Archer 16–4–48–0; Briggs 28–2–82–0; Wells 20–2–47–0; Wiese 10–1–39–0; Jordan 8–2–38–1; Salt 9–2–32–1; Burgess 6–1–14–0; Brown 3–2–1–0.

Sussex

D. R. Briggs lbw b Barker	12	J. C. Archer c Sibley b Stone	16
P. D. Salt lbw b Barker	0	O. E. Robinson not out	8
L. W. P. Wells c Ambrose b Stone	26	T. J. Haines absent hurt	
H. Z. Finch lbw b Barker	0	B 4, lb 12, nb 12	28
M. G. K. Burgess b Stone	46		
*†B. C. Brown c Trott b Patel	99	1/11 (2) 2/14 (1) 3/14 (4) (87.4 overs) 343
D. Wiese b Wright	93	4/86 (5) 5/87 (3) 6/283 (7)
C. J. Jordan c Sidebottom b Patel	15	7/312 (6) 8/317 (8) 9/343 (9)

Barker 13–2–42–3; Wright 18–2–69–1; Patel 21–2–85–2; Stone 14.4–2–59–3; Sidebottom 12–0–42–0; Rhodes 9–3–30–0.

Umpires: P. K. Baldwin and N. J. Llong.

At Northampton, September 24–25. SUSSEX lost to NORTHAMPTONSHIRE by six wickets.

WARWICKSHIRE

Bearing up nicely

PAUL BOLTON

Satisfaction at winning Division Two and securing a swift return to the top flight was tempered by the departure of Ashley Giles, who replaced Andrew Strauss as the ECB's director of cricket. His second spell in charge at Edgbaston had begun calamitously in 2017, with relegation. But he successfully addressed the two most urgent issues: achieving promotion at the first attempt, and reshaping an ageing squad that was no longer fit for purpose. "We've been through a lot of change," he said, "but I truly believe we're back on the right track now." Paul Farbrace, who stepped down as England's assistant coach after the tour of the West Indies in early 2019, will take over.

His was not the only departure. In May, Jonathan Trott announced he would retire at the end of the season, and left with the warm wishes of everyone in the game. With 12,220 first-class runs for the club, he did not quite make it into their top 25, though he would have done so but for Test calls and fewer fixtures than many of those above him. Seamers Keith Barker and Chris Wright, two other members of the 2012 Championship-winning team, moved on to Hampshire and Leicestershire; with Boyd Rankin leaving, Warwickshire were set to start 2019 with only four survivors from that squad.

Promotion, which took priority over white-ball success, was confirmed in the penultimate round of matches, but the champagne was kept on ice for a week until Kent, who had gone up alongside them, had been routed inside three days at Edgbaston. It was a highly rewarding season for several members of the old guard. Ian Bell rediscovered his appetite for runs: after hitting only one first-class century in the previous two seasons, he scored six, including three in three innings against Glamorgan. Tim Ambrose, now 36, ignored speculation that Warwickshire were seeking a new wicketkeeper, and enjoyed a productive time either side of the stumps. He scored freely and positively, held 75 catches in all formats, and was rewarded with a one-year contract.

Jeetan Patel took on the captaincy in four-day and 50-over cricket without lowering his standards as a match-winning off-spinner. He claimed 56 Championship wickets and 21 in white-ball matches, and led the side by splendid example. Sadly, the same could not be said of his New Zealand compatriots in a disappointing Vitality Blast season, only a year after reaching the final. Grant Elliott, the T20 captain, produced modest returns with the bat, and Colin de Grandhomme's reputation for big hitting failed to compensate for shortcomings with the ball – five wickets at nearly 48.

His problems were symptomatic of the weakness of the whole attack. In four successive matches in July, Warwickshire conceded at least 220. Even Bell's maiden T20 century, against Northamptonshire, forced a tie rather than victory. They fared better than in 2017 in the One-Day Cup, but still missed out on the knockout stages.

The greatest pleasure came from the progress of Olly Stone, Will Rhodes and Dom Sibley. Mindful of the injury he suffered while celebrating a wicket for Northamptonshire in 2016, Warwickshire nursed Stone through the season so that he could be quick and destructive when needed. Giles urged the England selectors to be similarly careful, and he did not make his one-day international debut until the matches in Sri Lanka in the autumn. When he was ruled out of the tour of the West Indies in the new year with a stress fracture of his lower back, it was a reminder that he needed to be treated with the utmost care.

Nathan Stirk, Getty Images

Olly Stone

Rhodes, a left-handed batsman signed by Giles from Yorkshire, and Sibley, who arrived from Surrey in an exchange for Rikki Clarke halfway through 2017, each made four Championship centuries, in contrasting style. Rhodes was the more fluent and aggressive, but Sibley worked on technical issues to improve his balance, and was rewarded with three hundreds in four innings at the end of the season. The pair, who are housemates, put on 176 in the final game, against Kent, Warwickshire's best start to a Championship innings in seven years.

Inevitably, the success of some counted against others, including Andy Umeed, an obdurate opener who made a century on county debut in 2016, but became labelled a one-format player. Slow left-armer Sunny Singh was also released, having tinkered with his action during the winter, to the exasperation of the coaching staff. Injury and international calls meant little was seen of Chris Woakes.

There are hopes that Sam Hain will compensate for the absence of Trott. He may have Trott's mannerisms at the crease, but – for all his white-ball talent – not yet the same ability to play match-shaping innings against the red. He was awarded his county cap in late May, but failed to make a Championship century for the second successive season.

Before his departure for Lord's, Giles began the task of strengthening the squad for the challenge of Division One. While Jordan Clark, Ben Raine and Ben Duckett all turned down the chance to move to Edgbaston, Warwickshire did succeed in signing Liam Norwell and Craig Miles, two seamers from Gloucestershire. They face the unenviable task of replacing Wright and Barker, who were still effective enough to share 82 first-class wickets in their final season with the county.

Championship attendance: 19,190.

WARWICKSHIRE RESULTS

All first-class matches – Played 15: Won 9, Lost 2, Drawn 4.
County Championship matches – Played 14: Won 9, Lost 2, Drawn 3.

Specsavers County Championship, winners of Division 2;
Vitality Blast, 6th in North Group; Royal London One-Day Cup, 4th in North Group.

COUNTY CHAMPIONSHIP AVERAGES, BATTING AND FIELDING

Cap		Birthplace	M	I	NO	R	HS	100	Avge	Ct
2001	I. R. Bell	Walsgrave‡	14	23	4	1,027	204	5	54.05	13
	M. J. Lamb	Wolverhampton	3	4	1	151	79	0	50.33	1
2005	I. J. L. Trott	Cape Town, SA	14	23	3	935	170*	2	46.75	11
	†W. M. H. Rhodes	Nottingham	14	23	1	972	137	4	44.18	5
	D. P. Sibley	Epsom	14	23	2	777	144*	4	37.00	18
	S. R. Hain	Hong Kong	12	17	1	566	90	0	35.37	9
2018	T. R. Ambrose	Newcastle, Aust	14	20	1	656	103	1	34.52	57
2007	H. J. H. Brookes	Solihull‡	5	6	1	165	70	0	33.00	3
	A. J. Hose	Newport, IoW	3	6	1	126	65	0	25.20	1
2013	C. J. C. Wright	Chipping Norton . . .	14	18	2	342	72	0	21.37	3
2013	†K. H. D. Barker	Manchester	10	14	2	218	58	0	18.16	1
	O. P. Stone	Norwich	7	8	2	86	42*	0	14.33	0
2012	J. S. Patel¶	Wellington, NZ.	14	19	3	184	32	0	11.50	4
	R. N. Sidebottom†† . . .	Shepparton, Aust . . .	9	12	6	30	10*	0	5.00	5
	†O. J. Hannon-Dalby . . .	Halifax	4	7	0	29	13	0	4.14	0

Also batted: †J. E. Poysden (*Shoreham-by-Sea*) (1 match) 0; C. R. Woakes§ (*Birmingham*) (cap 2009) (2 matches) 7, 6, 73* (1 ct).

‡ *Born in Warwickshire.*   § *ECB contract.*   ¶ *Official overseas player.*   †† *Other non-England-qualified.*

BOWLING

	Style	O	M	R	W	BB	5I	Avge
O. P. Stone	RF	160.2	26	525	43	8-80	3	12.20
K. H. D. Barker	LFM	254.1	69	672	40	5-32	2	16.80
O. J. Hannon-Dalby	RFM	103.4	22	329	15	4-61	0	21.93
H. J. H. Brookes	RFM	142	22	470	21	4-54	0	22.38
J. S. Patel	OB	431.4	108	1,276	56	7-83	4	22.78
R. N. Sidebottom	RFM	185	40	637	25	6-35	1	25.48
C. J. C. Wright	RFM	373.2	67	1,279	41	5-32	1	31.19

Also bowled: M. J. Lamb (RFM) 6–1–22–0; J. E. Poysden (LB) 23.2–2–73–5; W. M. H. Rhodes (RFM) 56–12–182–1; C. R. Woakes (RFM) 51–6–225–4.

LEADING ROYAL LONDON CUP AVERAGES (100 runs/4 wickets)

Batting	Runs	HS	Avge	SR	Ct/St	Bowling	W	BB	Avge	ER
S. R. Hain	426	108	106.50	88.93	0	A. D. Thomason .	9	4-45	26.44	6.49
I. R. Bell	226	145*	56.50	86.59	2	J. S. Patel	10	4-33	26.60	4.75
I. J. L. Trott	271	102*	54.20	79.00	3	H. J. H. Brookes .	9	3-57	27.22	5.50
A. J. Hose	139	51	34.75	96.52	4	O. P. Stone	12	4-71	28.16	5.64
T. R. Ambrose .	123	75	24.60	96.09	6/2	I. J. L. Trott	4	4-65	29.50	6.80
E. J. Pollock . . .	127	56	21.16	144.31	2	K. H. D. Barker .	6	2-28	45.16	5.31

LEADING VITALITY BLAST AVERAGES (100 runs/18 overs)

Batting	Runs	HS	Avge	SR	Ct
E. J. Pollock	251	39	17.92	**185.92**	3
C. de Grandhomme	254	63*	36.28	**170.46**	6
A. J. Hose......	377	66*	31.41	**140.67**	9
I. R. Bell......	580	131	48.33	**139.08**	3
S. R. Hain......	371	95	33.72	**133.45**	6

Bowling	W	BB	Avge	ER
J. S. Patel........	11	2-17	38.18	**7.50**
G. D. Elliott.....	19	3-16	19.57	**7.91**
H. J. H. Brookes ..	7	2-28	24.28	**8.50**
O. P. Stone	7	3-22	23.28	**8.57**
O. J. Hannon-Dalby	16	4-20	18.87	**9.43**
C. de Grandhomme	5	2-24	47.80	**10.86**
A. D. Thomason ..	12	3-55	29.16	**11.66**

FIRST-CLASS COUNTY RECORDS

Highest score for	501*	B. C. Lara v Durham at Birmingham........	1994
Highest score against	322	I. V. A. Richards (Somerset) at Taunton......	1985
Leading run-scorer	35,146	D. L. Amiss (avge 41.64).................	1960–87
Best bowling for	10-41	J. D. Bannister v Comb. Services at Birmingham .	1959
Best bowling against	10-36	H. Verity (Yorkshire) at Leeds	1931
Leading wicket-taker	2,201	W. E. Hollies (avge 20.45)	1932–57
Highest total for	810-4 dec	v Durham at Birmingham	1994
Highest total against	887	by Yorkshire at Birmingham	1896
Lowest total for	16	v Kent at Tonbridge.....................	1913
Lowest total against	15	by Hampshire at Birmingham	1922

LIST A COUNTY RECORDS

Highest score for	206	A. I. Kallicharran v Oxfordshire at Birmingham	1984
Highest score against	172*	W. Larkins (Northamptonshire) at Luton......	1983
Leading run-scorer	11,254	D. L. Amiss (avge 33.79).................	1963–87
Best bowling for	7-32	R. G. D. Willis v Yorkshire at Birmingham ...	1981
Best bowling against	6-27	M. H. Yardy (Sussex) at Birmingham........	2005
Leading wicket-taker	396	G. C. Small (avge 25.48).................	1980–99
Highest total for	392-5	v Oxfordshire at Birmingham	1984
Highest total against	415-5	by Nottinghamshire at Nottingham	2016
Lowest total for	59	v Yorkshire at Leeds	2001
Lowest total against	56	by Yorkshire at Birmingham	1995

TWENTY20 COUNTY RECORDS

Highest score for	158*	B. B. McCullum v Derbyshire at Birmingham .	2015
Highest score against	100*	I. J. Harvey (Gloucestershire) at Birmingham ..	2003
Leading run-scorer	2,111	**I. R. Bell (avge 31.50, SR 128.56)**	**2003–18**
Best bowling for	5-19	N. M. Carter v Worcestershire at Birmingham ..	2005
Best bowling against	5-25	D. J. Pattinson (Nottinghamshire) at Birmingham	2011
Leading wicket-taker	124	**J. S. Patel (avge 23.25, ER 6.85)**	**2009–18**
Highest total for	242-2	v Derbyshire at Birmingham	2015
Highest total against	215-6	by Durham at Birmingham	2010
Lowest total for	73	v Somerset at Taunton	2013
Lowest total against	{ 96	by Northamptonshire at Northampton	2011
	{ 96	by Gloucestershire at Cheltenham	2013

ADDRESS

Edgbaston Stadium, Birmingham B5 7QU; 0844 635 1902; info@edgbaston.com; www.edgbaston.com.

OFFICIALS

Captain J. S. Patel	**President** Earl of Aylesford
Sport director 2018 A. F. Giles	**Chairman** N. Gascoigne
2019 P. Farbrace	**Chief executive** N. Snowball
First-team coach J. O. Troughton	**Head groundsman** G. Barwell
Elite development manager P. Greetham	**Scorer** M. D. Smith

WARWICKSHIRE v DURHAM MCCU

At Birmingham, April 1–3. Drawn. Toss: Durham MCCU. First-class debuts: M. J. Plater, F. W. A. Ruffell, A. M. C. Russell, V. V. S. Sohal, J. H. Sookias. County debut: W. M. H. Rhodes.

Bleak weather confined play to the first day, though there was time for centuries from Bell – his first in first-class cricket for two years – and Trott, plus a quick fifty for Hose. He hit three sixes off the left-arm spin of Benedict Graves, one on to the top tier of the pavilion. Earlier, Sibley had failed in his first game in charge; he was standing in for Jeetan Patel, who was playing for Wellington in New Zealand.

Close of play: first day, Durham MCCU 35-1 (Plater 9, Macdonell 22); second day, no play.

Warwickshire

W. M. H. Rhodes c Sookias b McGrath	2	†T. R. Ambrose not out		10
*D. P. Sibley c Sookias b Russell	2	Lb 4, nb 2		6
I. R. Bell c Sookias b Cooke	100			
I. J. L. Trott not out	111	1/2 (1) 2/10 (2) (4 wkts dec, 78 overs)		299
A. J. Hose c Plater b Graves	68	3/168 (3) 4/280 (5)		

K. H. D. Barker, O. P. Stone, C. J. C. Wright, Sukhjit Singh and R. N. Sidebottom did not bat.

McGrath 15–2–45–1; Russell 12–2–34–1; Cooke 11–2–26–1; Ruffell 10–0–39–0; Sohal 12–0–56–0; Graves 13–1–62–1; Macdonell 5–0–33–0.

Durham MCCU

J. D. Marshall c Ambrose b Barker	0
M. J. Plater not out	9
C. M. Macdonell not out	22
Lb 1, w 1, nb 2	4

1/0 (1)   (1 wkt, 13 overs)   35

*W. A. R. Fraine, J. M. Cooke, B. W. M. Graves, F. W. A. Ruffell, A. H. McGrath, V. V. S. Sohal, †J. H. Sookias and A. M. C. Russell did not bat.

Barker 5–2–10–1; Wright 5–1–13–0; Sidebottom 2–0–7–0; Stone 1–0–4–0.

Umpires: G. D. Lloyd and R. J. Warren.

WARWICKSHIRE v SUSSEX

At Birmingham, April 13–16. Drawn. Warwickshire 10pts, Sussex 12pts. Toss: uncontested. County debut: I. Sharma.

Two outstanding individual performances dominated a match that might have produced a fascinating conclusion had the weather not wiped out the first four sessions. After Warwickshire began with 299, Stone – who missed most of 2017 through injury – used pace and late swing to fillet the Sussex top order, taking five wickets in his first six overs, the first six in the innings, and a career-best eight for 80 in all. But the other Warwickshire seamers looked rusty, and Wiese – who had already taken four for 56 – capitalised when Stone was rested, flaying his maiden century in England, and the first Championship hundred of the season, from 91 balls before lunch on the final day. He put on 155 in 30 overs with Brown, an eighth-wicket record for Sussex in this fixture. Earlier, Ambrose piloted Warwickshire's first-innings recovery from 147 for six, then held six catches.

Close of play: first day, no play; second day, Warwickshire 284-9 (Ambrose 76, Wright 17); third day, Sussex 194-6 (Brown 43, Robinson 12).

Warwickshire

W. M. H. Rhodes c Salt b Sharma	10	– b Robinson	6
D. P. Sibley c Brown b Robinson	2	– not out	42
I. R. Bell c van Zyl b Wiese	70	– c Brown b Sharma	10
I. J. L. Trott c Robinson b Wiese	15	– lbw b Sharma	4
A. J. Hose lbw b Sharma	9	– not out	15
S. R. Hain lbw b Wiese	8		
†T. R. Ambrose c Brown b Barker	81		
K. H. D. Barker c Brown b Whittingham	25		
*J. S. Patel c Finch b Whittingham	0		
O. P. Stone c Finch b Wiese	2		
C. J. C. Wright not out	27		
B 5, lb 17, w 12, nb 16	50	Nb 10	10

1/14 (1) 2/20 (2) 3/80 (4)   (86.2 overs) 299
4/96 (5) 5/128 (6) 6/147 (3)
7/199 (8) 8/204 (9) 9/222 (10) 10/299 (7)

1/25 (1)   (3 wkts, 35 overs) 87
2/45 (3) 3/55 (4)

Sharma 20.2–4–53–3; Robinson 17–4–75–1; Wiese 21–3–56–4; van Zyl 11–2–27–0; Whittingham 14–2–56–2; Wells 3–0–10–0. *Second innings*—Sharma 9–3–16–2; Robinson 11–1–41–1; Wiese 10–4–16–0; Whittingham 2–0–5–0; Wells 3–0–9–0.

Sussex

L. W. P. Wells c Ambrose b Stone	29	D. Wiese lbw b Stone	106
P. D. Salt c Hose b Stone	29	I. Sharma b Stone	22
S. van Zyl c Ambrose b Stone	15	S. G. Whittingham not out	0
H. Z. Finch c Hain b Stone	8	B 2, lb 4, nb 8	14
L. J. Wright c Ambrose b Stone	0		
*†B. C. Brown c Ambrose b Barker	91	1/30 (2) 2/68 (3) 3/77 (1) (88.5 overs) 374
M. G. K. Burgess c Ambrose b Stone	48	4/77 (5) 5/88 (4) 6/166 (7)
O. E. Robinson c Ambrose b Barker	12	7/194 (6) 8/349 (6) 9/361 (9) 10/374 (10)

Barker 25–5–99–2; Wright 19–3–76–0; Stone 22.5–4–80–8; Patel 16–2–64–0; Rhodes 6–0–49–0.

Umpires: S. J. O'Shaughnessy and P. R. Pollard.

At Northampton, April 20–22. WARWICKSHIRE beat NORTHAMPTONSHIRE by an innings and 48 runs.

WARWICKSHIRE v DERBYSHIRE

At Birmingham, May 3–6. Warwickshire won by eight wickets. Warwickshire 23pts, Derbyshire 5pts. Toss: Derbyshire.

Warwickshire ruthlessly swept aside Derbyshire, who had little to offer after Madsen's first-day century. He played with composure, despite treatment for a cut neck when he was struck by a lifter from Brookes, but none of his colleagues followed his example. Too many sold their wickets cheaply when the pitch was at its best; though Warwickshire found themselves a bowler light after Sidebottom suffered a side strain. Lamb, selected to provide an extra seam option, did not bowl a ball – but did hit a valuable career-best 79. Warwickshire then handed out a lesson in how to build a match-winning total, with solid, steady progress against a persevering attack. Brookes topped and tailed Derbyshire again, while Patel unpicked the middle order to finish with ten in the match. Warwickshire wrapped up victory an hour into the final day. The last rites were witnessed by bemused cast members of the American TV series *Charmed*, who were attending a 20th anniversary convention in the ground's exhibition hall.

Close of play: first day, Warwickshire 32-1 (Rhodes 13, Wright 10); second day, Warwickshire 375-6 (Lamb 79, Ambrose 8); third day, Warwickshire 19-1 (Sibley 6, Bell 6).

Derbyshire

B. T. Slater c Sidebottom b Wright	16	– c Hain b Patel	68
L. M. Reece c and b Patel	20	– b Brookes	0
W. L. Madsen b Brookes	144	– c Patel b Brookes	4
A. L. Hughes c Rhodes b Patel	4	– lbw b Patel	38
*B. A. Godleman b Brookes	1	– c Bell b Patel	0
†G. C. Wilson c Trott b Wright	34	– lbw b Brookes	13
M. J. J. Critchley lbw b Patel	30	– lbw b Patel	6
G. C. Viljoen c Ambrose b Patel	7	– b Patel	44
Hamidullah Qadri c Sibley b Brookes	3	– c Brookes b Patel	7
D. Olivier not out	40	– b Brookes	0
M. H. A. Footitt b Brookes	0	– not out	0
B 4, lb 7, nb 8	19	B 4, lb 17, nb 8	29

1/28 (1) 2/72 (2) 3/80 (4)   (81.5 overs) 318
4/84 (5) 5/168 (6) 6/209 (7)
7/233 (8) 8/251 (9) 9/318 (3) 10/318 (11)

1/0 (2) 2/10 (3)   (67.2 overs) 209
3/98 (4) 4/100 (5)
5/138 (1) 6/138 (6) 7/170 (7)
8/198 (9) 9/199 (10) 10/209 (8)

Wright 18.4–2–81–2; Sidebottom 9.2–1–39–0; Rhodes 11–2–30–0; Brookes 15.5–5–0–63–4; Patel 27–3–94–4. *Second innings*—Wright 15–3–51–0; Brookes 18–5–56–4; Patel 30.2–13–76–6; Rhodes 4–2–5–0.

Warwickshire

W. M. H. Rhodes c Wilson b Footitt	50	– lbw b Olivier	4
D. P. Sibley c Critchley b Olivier	6	– lbw b Critchley	7
C. J. C. Wright b Critchley	72		
I. R. Bell lbw b Viljoen	44	– (3) not out	34
I. J. L. Trott c Critchley	76	– (4) not out	35
S. R. Hain lbw b Critchley	8		
M. J. Lamb c Godleman b Olivier	79		
†T. R. Ambrose c Footitt b Olivier	40		
*J. S. Patel c Godleman b Olivier	7		
H. J. H. Brookes c Wilson b Viljoen	9		
R. N. Sidebottom not out	4		
B 11, lb 9, w 8, nb 16	44	Lb 4, w 1, nb 4	9

1/18 (2) 2/95 (1) 3/172 (4)   (123.5 overs) 439
4/191 (3) 5/206 (6) 6/363 (5)
7/383 (8) 8/399 (9) 9/418 (10)
10/439 (8)   110 overs: 379-6

1/12 (1)   (2 wkts, 23.1 overs) 89
2/29 (2)

Viljoen 29–5–97–2; Olivier 32.5–1–134–4; Hamidullah Qadri 14–2–30–0; Critchley 22–2–68–3; Footitt 15–2–57–1; Reece 9–2–25–0; Madsen 2–0–8–0. *Second innings*—Olivier 9–2–28–1; Viljoen 2–0–5–0; Critchley 8–3–31–1; Hamidullah Qadri 4.1–1–21–0.

Umpires: R. K. Illingworth and N. A. Mallender.

WARWICKSHIRE v NORTHAMPTONSHIRE

At Birmingham, May 11–13. Warwickshire won by six wickets. Warwickshire 21pts, Northamptonshire 5pts. Toss: Northamptonshire.

Warwickshire held their nerve when it mattered, with a composed maiden century from Rhodes eventually bringing calm to a frenetic affair. The absence of Crook, who pulled up with a hamstring injury at the end of Warwickshire's first innings, hindered Northamptonshire, but their gung-ho batting on the first morning on a seamers' pitch proved more costly. They had rattled along at a run a minute in the first hour, but lost six wickets and helped Brookes improve his career-best bowling for the fifth successive innings. Northamptonshire's policy reaped at least some reward when Crook and Bracewell plundered 122 to equal their eighth-wicket record against Warwickshire and secure their first batting point of the season. The same pair then had Warwickshire in trouble but, for the second time in three weeks, Ambrose and Brookes frustrated Northamptonshire with a defiant ninth-wicket stand. Stone, developed by Northamptonshire, tormented his former team-mates by taking his second five-wicket haul in three innings. Warwickshire stumbled when Bell and Trott perished in a searching spell from Sanderson, but the unflappable Rhodes saw them home.

Close of play: first day, Warwickshire 100-4 (Bell 55, Lamb 1); second day, Northamptonshire 160-7 (Keogh 13, Bracewell 1).

Northamptonshire

L. A. Procter run out (Brookes/Ambrose)	19	– c Bell b Brookes	12
B. M. Duckett c Ambrose b Wright	4	– lbw b Patel	38
*A. G. Wakely b Brookes	3	– c Lamb b Stone	14
R. E. Levi c Trott b Brookes	0	– c Trott b Wright	21
J. J. Cobb c Hain b Stone	29	– c Ambrose b Stone	30
†A. M. Rossington c Ambrose b Stone	4	– lbw b Wright	23
R. I. Keogh lbw b Brookes	1	– c Brookes b Stone	29
S. P. Crook c Ambrose b Patel	92	– b Stone	1
D. A. J. Bracewell c Hain b Brookes	81	– c Ambrose b Stone	7
B. A. Hutton c Ambrose b Wright	5	– b Wright	1
B. W. Sanderson not out	7	– not out	4
B 4, lb 5, nb 2	11	B 4, lb 3	7

1/13 (2) 2/16 (3) 3/20 (4)   (60.5 overs) 256   1/39 (1) 2/52 (2)   (48.5 overs) 187
4/29 (1) 5/47 (6) 6/52 (7)   3/88 (3) 4/92 (4)
7/102 (5) 8/224 (8) 9/229 (10) 10/256 (9)   5/130 (6) 6/150 (5) 7/158 (8)
                                       8/178 (9) 9/179 (10) 10/187 (7)

Wright 16–0–65–2; Brookes 14.5–2–54–4; Stone 10–1–57–2; Patel 14–0–47–1; Rhodes 6–0–24–0. *Second innings*—Wright 19–4–58–3; Brookes 11–2–62–1; Patel 3–1–11–1; Stone 15.5–0–49–5.

Warwickshire

W. M. H. Rhodes c Levi b Bracewell	14	– not out	100
D. P. Sibley c Hutton b Bracewell	0	– c Procter b Sanderson	2
I. R. Bell c Hutton b Bracewell	61	– lbw b Sanderson	14
I. J. L. Trott lbw b Hutton	17	– lbw b Sanderson	1
S. R. Hain lbw b Crook	6	– c Hutton b Procter	17
M. J. Lamb lbw b Bracewell	5	– not out	23
†T. R. Ambrose c Rossington b Crook	78		
*J. S. Patel c Hutton b Crook	11		
C. J. C. Wright c Rossington b Crook	4		
H. J. H. Brookes lbw b Sanderson	50		
O. P. Stone not out	1		
B 1, lb 5, nb 4	18	B 5, lb 5, w 3, nb 10	23

1/0 (2) 2/25 (1) 3/53 (4)   (71 overs) 265   1/6 (2)   (4 wkts, 53.4 overs) 180
4/92 (5) 5/115 (6) 6/118 (3)   2/42 (3) 3/44 (4)
7/145 (8) 8/169 (9) 9/264 (7) 10/265 (10)   4/94 (5)

Sanderson 21.4–5–64–1; Bracewell 21–7–71–4; Hutton 16–4–65–1; Crook 12.2–2–51–4. *Second innings*—Bracewell 13–2–40–0; Sanderson 16–4–33–3; Hutton 10–2–37–0; Procter 7–1–28–1; Keogh 7–2–26–0; Cobb 0.4–0–6–0.

Umpires: N. L. Bainton and I. D. Blackwell.

WARWICKSHIRE v GLAMORGAN

At Birmingham, June 9–12. Warwickshire won by four wickets. Warwickshire 21pts, Glamorgan 4pts. Toss: Glamorgan. County debut: U. T. Khawaja.

Bell played two masterful but contrasting innings to achieve a pair of milestones and steer his team to victory. He became the first Warwickshire batsman to score twin hundreds since he himself did it at Old Trafford in 2004, the third after Dennis Amiss and Alvin Kallicharran to do it twice, and the second after Kallicharran in 1984 to be unbeaten in both innings. His efforts were the difference between the teams. In the first innings, Bell batted almost six and a quarter hours for his first Championship century in over two years; second time around he was more fluent in guiding

---

HUNDRED ON FIRST-CLASS DEBUT FOR GLAMORGAN

F. B. Pinch (138*)	v Worcestershire at Swansea	1921
R. C. Fredericks (145*)	v Nottinghamshire at Nottingham	1971
Javed Miandad (140*)	v Essex at Swansea	1980
Younis Ahmed (158*)	v Oxford University at Oxford	1984
M. P. Maynard (102)	v Yorkshire at Swansea	1985
I. V. A. Richards (119)	v Leicestershire at Cardiff	1990
M. J. Powell (200*)	v Oxford University at Oxford	1997
A. G. Wharf (100*)	v Oxford University at Oxford	2000
M. J. Cosgrove (114)	v Derbyshire at Cardiff	2006
B. B. McCullum (160)	v Leicestershire at Cardiff	2006
S. E. Marsh (111)	**v Gloucestershire at Bristol**	**2018**
U. T. Khawaja (125)	**v Warwickshire at Birmingham**	**2018**

Only Pinch, Maynard and Powell were making their overall first-class debuts. M. T. G. Elliott made 117 against Warwickshire at Birmingham in 2000 in his second match for Glamorgan, having not batted in the first.

Warwickshire to what had appeared a difficult target of 294 on a used pitch. Khawaja – who began his stint at his third county with an unflustered second-innings century – and Trott also provided quality in a match of otherwise indifferent batting. Leg-spinner Poysden made short work of Glamorgan's first innings with a career-best five for 29, which included Cooke, facing his first ball in Championship cricket since September 2016. Warwickshire also struggled against spin, with Salter, benefiting from a winter in New Zealand under the tutelage of opposing captain Patel, taking four wickets in an innings for the first time. But with Hogan and de Lange injured, Glamorgan lacked the firepower to dislodge Bell.

Close of play: first day, Warwickshire 24-2 (Bell 10, Trott 5); second day, Glamorgan 55-0 (Selman 37, Murphy 17); third day, Warwickshire 25-0 (Rhodes 15, Sibley 10).

Glamorgan

N. J. Selman c Hain b Patel	30	– c Sibley b Barker	42
J. R. Murphy lbw b Brookes	18	– b Brookes	25
C. R. Brown c Ambrose b Wright	9	– c Ambrose b Wright	1
U. T. Khawaja lbw b Barker	4	– lbw b Patel	125
A. O. Morgan lbw b Poysden	36	– lbw b Brookes	9
*†C. B. Cooke lbw b Poysden	34	– c Ambrose b Brookes	59
D. L. Lloyd c Ambrose b Patel	39	– lbw b Barker	11
A. G. Salter c Patel b Poysden	5	– lbw b Patel	7
R. A. J. Smith lbw b Poysden	22	– c Sibley b Wright	17
T. van der Gugten not out	9	– not out	9
L. J. Carey b Poysden	0	– c Sibley b Wright	0
B 8, lb 2, nb 4	14	Lb 6, nb 12	18

1/44 (2) 2/59 (3) 3/59 (1)	(76.2 overs) 220	1/64 (1) 2/67 (3)	(98.5 overs) 323
4/69 (4) 5/126 (6) 6/172 (5)		3/95 (2) 4/144 (5)	
7/182 (8) 8/190 (7) 9/220 (9) 10/220 (11)		5/259 (4) 6/284 (6)	
		7/284 (7) 8/312 (9)	
		9/322 (8) 10/323 (11)	

Barker 12–6–26–1; Wright 14–2–53–1; Brookes 12–5–21–1; Patel 25–8–81–2; Poysden 13.2–2–29–5. *Second innings*—Barker 20–6–59–2; Brookes 18–0–70–3; Patel 27–4–67–2; Wright 16.5–4–59–3; Poysden 10–0–44–0; Rhodes 7–1–18–0.

Warwickshire

W. M. H. Rhodes b Carey	0	– c Cooke b Salter	61
D. P. Sibley b van der Gugten	7	– c Smith b Salter	19
I. R. Bell not out	106	– not out	115
I. J. L. Trott run out (Lloyd)	57	– lbw b Lloyd	67
S. R. Hain c and b Salter	16	– b Lloyd	0
†T. R. Ambrose c Selman b Carey	12	– lbw b Salter	21
K. H. D. Barker b Carey	0	– c Selman b Salter	0
*J. S. Patel c and b Salter	4	– not out	4
C. J. C. Wright lbw b van der Gugten	29		
H. J. H. Brookes lbw b van der Gugten	3		
J. E. Poysden c Salter b van der Gugten	0		
B 8, lb 8	16	Lb 2, w 1, nb 4	7

1/0 (1) 2/18 (2) 3/99 (4) (93 overs) 250
4/127 (5) 5/164 (6) 6/164 (7)
7/173 (8) 8/242 (9) 9/250 (10) 10/250 (11)

1/68 (2) (6 wkts, 86.1 overs) 294
2/119 (1) 3/232 (4)
4/232 (5) 5/286 (6) 6/286 (7)

Carey 23–5–56–3; van der Gugten 20–7–65–4; Smith 11–5–29–0; Salter 30–8–65–2; Lloyd 6–2–12–0; Morgan 3–1–7–0. *Second innings*—Carey 17–4–70–0; van der Gugten 18–5–47–0; Salter 26–5–80–4; Smith 10–0–37–0; Lloyd 11–1–48–2; Morgan 4.1–1–10–0.

Umpires: Y. C. Barde and M. J. Saggers.

At Birmingham, June 17. WARWICKSHIRE beat WEST INDIES A by 131 runs (see West Indies A tour section).

At Tunbridge Wells, June 20–23. WARWICKSHIRE lost to KENT by 73 runs.

At Chester-le-Street, June 25–28. WARWICKSHIRE beat DURHAM by 86 runs.

At Lord's, July 22–24. WARWICKSHIRE lost to MIDDLESEX by 18 runs.

WARWICKSHIRE v GLOUCESTERSHIRE

At Birmingham, August 19–20. Warwickshire won by an innings and 47 runs. Warwickshire 21pts, Gloucestershire 3pts. Toss: Gloucestershire. First-class debut: B. G. Charlesworth.

Gloucestershire were dismissed twice in 77 overs in a contest that lasted two days and exposed the gap between the upper and lower reaches of Division Two. Depleted by injuries, they were unable to cope with the pressure applied by Warwickshire's seamers. On a murky first morning, Gloucestershire reached 52 without loss, before the innings unravelled, ten falling for 75 in less than 28 overs. The last six batsmen contributed three, as Wright took five for 32. Their seamers showed scarcely more discipline. By the close on the first day, Warwickshire were 44 in front, and Rhodes had raced to a century, though Miles – who would sign for them later in the season – led a fightback. His victims included Bell and Trott, but Rhodes proved immovable, occupying two overs more than Gloucestershire managed in total. Their second innings was a mix of panic and resignation, and there was no way back after three wickets fell with the score on 27.

Close of play: first day, Warwickshire 171-2 (Rhodes 101, Bell 0).

Gloucestershire

M. A. H. Hammond c Ambrose b Sidebottom	17	– (2) c Hain b Sidebottom	9
*C. D. J. Dent lbw b Patel	35	– (1) c Sibley b Sidebottom	16
J. R. Bracey lbw b Patel	28	– c Ambrose b Barker	1
B. A. C. Howell c Hain b Wright	26	– b Wright	32
†G. H. Roderick lbw b Wright	15	– b Barker	0
R. F. Higgins b Wright	0	– c Ambrose b Sidebottom	1
B. G. Charlesworth c Ambrose b Barker	1	– c Sibley b Hannon-Dalby	5
C. N. Miles c Sidebottom b Barker	2	– b Sidebottom	9
G. S. Drissell c Barker b Wright	0	– c Sibley b Rhodes	19
M. D. Taylor b Wright	0	– c Sidebottom b Wright	1
C. J. Liddle not out	0	– not out	6
B 2, lb 1	3	Lb 2, nb 2	4

1/52 (1)　2/52 (2)　3/101 (3)　　　　　(46 overs) 127　　1/10 (2)　2/27 (1)　　　　(31 overs) 103
4/106 (4)　5/108 (6)　6/113 (7)　　　　　　　　　　　　3/27 (3)　4/27 (5)
7/115 (8)　8/118 (9)　9/118 (10)　10/127 (5)　　　　　5/32 (6)　6/61 (7)　7/67 (4)
　　　　　　　　　　　　　　　　　　　　　　　　　　8/85 (8)　9/88 (10)　10/103 (9)

Barker 13–6–22–2; Wright 11–5–32–5; Patel 12–6–28–2; Sidebottom 6–1–33–1; Hannon-Dalby 4–2–9–0. *Second innings*—Barker 7–1–12–2; Sidebottom 10–3–42–4; Wright 9–1–33–2; Hannon-Dalby 4–1–14–1; Rhodes 1–1–0–1.

Warwickshire

W. M. H. Rhodes b Drissell	137	O. J. Hannon-Dalby c and b Miles	6
D. P. Sibley c Bracey b Higgins	65	R. N. Sidebottom c Bracey b Miles	0
C. J. C. Wright lbw b Liddle	1		
I. R. Bell b Miles	2	B 2, lb 5	7
I. J. L. Trott c Roderick b Miles	4		
S. R. Hain c Hammond b Liddle	25	1/161 (2)　2/166 (3)　　(87.4 overs) 277	
†T. R. Ambrose c Howell b Miles	3	3/178 (4)　4/182 (5)	
K. H. D. Barker not out	20	5/230 (6)　6/236 (7)　7/258 (1)	
*J. S. Patel b Taylor	7	8/268 (9)　9/277 (10)　10/277 (11)	

Taylor 19–3–59–1; Higgins 21–4–39–1; Miles 17.4–1–69–5; Liddle 18–4–52–2; Drissell 9–1–38–1; Charlesworth 3–0–13–0.

Umpires: P. K. Baldwin and P. J. Hartley.

At Colwyn Bay, August 29–31. WARWICKSHIRE beat GLAMORGAN by an innings and 35 runs. *Ian Bell reaches 20,000 first-class runs; Jeetan Patel 800 wickets.*

WARWICKSHIRE v DURHAM

At Birmingham, September 4–7. Drawn. Warwickshire 11pts, Durham 10pts. Toss: uncontested.

　　Warwickshire worked themselves into a winning position, but were frustrated by autumnal weather, which wiped out three sessions, and Durham resistance on a tense final day. Poynter and Salisbury, the ninth-wicket pair, clung on for 35 balls, despite nine close fielders. Durham's seamers had provided a thorough examination on a dank, truncated first day, Rushworth taking his 400th first-class wicket when he removed Sibley. But Trott showed class and tenacity, and better conditions on the second morning allowed Wright to push Warwickshire past 300 with an aggressive fifty. Stone then took seven wickets with pace and late swing as Durham finished 18 adrift on first innings, before rain prevented play after lunch on the third day. But the game sparked back to life when Warwickshire lost their last six inside ten overs as Hain looked on helplessly. Akshar Patel, the recently recruited Indian slow left-armer, grabbed a career-best seven for 54, including Sidebottom, caught and bowled after sweeping on to the helmet of Smith at short leg; he would have been not out until a recent change in the laws. Durham declined to chase 218 in 41 overs, but survival proved tough against a fired-up Stone, who finished with 11 for 96, the best figures in this fixture.

Close of play: first day, Warwickshire 184-6 (Trott 67, Patel 10); second day, Durham 224-7 (Collingwood 32, McCarthy 24); third day, Warwickshire 28-1 (Sibley 7, Bell 4).

Warwickshire

W. M. H. Rhodes c Smith b Patel	36	– lbw b Rushworth	16
D. P. Sibley c Clark b Rushworth	4	– b Patel	27
I. R. Bell lbw b McCarthy	12	– c Clark b Patel	10
I. J. L. Trott b Salisbury	79	– c Collingwood b McCarthy	13
S. R. Hain c Poynter b McCarthy	11	– not out	58
†T. R. Ambrose b Rushworth	15	– lbw b Patel	42
K. H. D. Barker c Lees b Salisbury	18	– b McCarthy	5
*J. S. Patel b McCarthy	26	– b Patel	7
C. J. C. Wright not out	54	– c Collingwood b Patel	15
O. P. Stone c Clark b McCarthy	38	– c McCarthy b Patel	0
R. N. Sidebottom lbw b Patel	0	– c and b Patel	1
B 11, lb 4, nb 2	17	Lb 3, nb 2	5

1/9 (2) 2/47 (3) 3/63 (1) (95.5 overs) 310
4/82 (5) 5/114 (6) 6/160 (7)
7/206 (4) 8/224 (9) 9/310 (10) 10/310 (11)

1/22 (1) 2/47 (3) (65.4 overs) 199
3/64 (2) 4/68 (4)
5/157 (6) 6/166 (7) 7/173 (8)
8/193 (9) 9/193 (10) 10/199 (11)

Rushworth 22–4–64–2; Salisbury 19–3–81–2; Patel 35.5–10–76–2; McCarthy 15.3–3–58–4; Collingwood 1–1–0–0; Steel 2–0–13–0; Smith 1–0–3–0. *Second innings*—Rushworth 14–2–37–1; Salisbury 12–2–55–0; Patel 27.4–12–54–7; McCarthy 12–1–50–2.

Durham

C. T. Steel c Ambrose b Stone	19	– c Ambrose b Wright	21
A. Z. Lees b Wright	35	– lbw b Barker	0
W. R. Smith c Ambrose b Stone	45	– c Sibley b Stone	8
G. Clark lbw b Sidebottom	14	– c Hain b Stone	23
M. J. Richardson lbw b Stone	23	– lbw b Stone	7
A. R. Patel b Stone	0	– b Barker	22
*P. D. Collingwood b Stone	32	– c Ambrose b Wright	13
†S. W. Poynter lbw b Stone	0	– not out	9
B. J. McCarthy lbw b Wright	43	– lbw b Stone	2
M. E. T. Salisbury b Stone	37	– not out	5
C. Rushworth not out	11		
Lb 29, nb 4	33	Lb 3, nb 2	5

1/46 (1) 2/72 (2) 3/105 (4) (94.1 overs) 292
4/152 (3) 5/156 (6) 6/165 (5)
7/165 (8) 8/224 (7) 9/266 (9) 10/292 (10)

1/9 (2) (8 wkts, 40.5 overs) 115
2/25 (1) 3/33 (3) 4/55 (5)
5/64 (4) 6/97 (6) 7/99 (7) 8/102 (9)

Barker 18–7–30–0; Sidebottom 15–4–54–1; Patel 22.1–3–59–7; Stone 22.1–3–59–7; Wright 21–1–83–2; Rhodes 8–3–11–0. *Second innings*—Barker 10–4–22–2; Sidebottom 7–1–16–0; Wright 11–2–30–2; Stone 10.5–1–37–4; Patel 2–0–7–0.

Umpires: M. A. Gough and M. J. Saggers.

At Leicester, September 10–12. WARWICKSHIRE beat LEICESTERSHIRE by an innings and 104 runs.

At Hove, September 18–21. WARWICKSHIRE drew with SUSSEX. *Warwickshire secure promotion.*

WARWICKSHIRE v KENT

At Birmingham, September 24–26. Warwickshire won by an innings and 34 runs. Warwickshire 23pts, Kent 2pts. Toss: Kent.

Division Two's title showdown turned into a no-contest as Warwickshire thumped Kent with over four sessions to spare. After the visitors were bundled out for 167, Trott was given a guard of honour when he arrived at the crease in his last first-class match, but was out 13 balls later, brilliantly caught at short midwicket by Stevens. Once victory had been secured, Trott led the team off, closely followed by Barker and Wright, also making their final appearances for the county. Kent's feckless batting on a blameless pitch, which had been used for T20 finals day nine days earlier, had handed the initiative to Warwickshire, whose seamers were a tight, aggressive unit. Contrasting centuries from Rhodes and Sibley, who put on 176 for the first wicket, their biggest partnership of the season, rammed home the advantage. Rhodes reached his hundred in 105 balls, the fastest of his four centuries in 2018, while Sibley's vigilance over more than six hours demoralised Kent. In their second innings, only Crawley and Billings kept Warwickshire's champagne on ice.

Close of play: first day, Warwickshire 148-0 (Rhodes 102, Sibley 37); second day, Kent 38-1 (Crawley 21, Riley 0).

Kent

S. R. Dickson lbw b Barker	9	– c Sibley b Stone		12
Z. Crawley c Ambrose b Wright	4	– lbw b Sidebottom		75
J. L. Denly c Sibley b Stone	30	– (4) b Barker		0
H. G. Kuhn c Sibley b Stone	15	– (5) c Ambrose b Stone		8
O. G. Robinson lbw b Stone	12	– (6) b Stone		4
*†S. W. Billings c Ambrose b Barker	17	– (7) lbw b Patel		46
D. I. Stevens lbw b Wright	8	– (8) lbw b Wright		1
G. Stewart c Ambrose b Wright	9	– (9) c Bell b Wright		0
H. W. Podmore b Barker	9	– (10) run out (Stone)		15
M. J. Henry not out	32	– (11) not out		0
A. E. N. Riley lbw b Sidebottom	11	– (3) c Sibley b Barker		5
B 3, lb 8	11	B 4, lb 7, nb 2		13

1/4 (2) 2/18 (1) 3/55 (4)		(59 overs)	167	1/34 (1) 2/56 (3) (56 overs) 179
4/78 (5) 5/89 (3) 6/102 (6)				3/56 (4) 4/68 (5)
7/108 (7) 8/121 (8) 9/125 (9) 10/167 (11)				5/90 (6) 6/133 (2) 7/134 (8)
				8/134 (9) 9/179 (7) 10/179 (10)

Barker 14–4–31–3; Wright 15–4–29–3; Stone 13–2–36–3; Sidebottom 8–0–22–1; Patel 9–1–38–0. *Second innings*—Barker 8.4–3–19–2; Wright 14–4–51–2; Patel 14–3–38–1; Stone 10.2–2–35–3; Sidebottom 9–3–25–1.

Warwickshire

W. M. H. Rhodes b Stewart	110	*J. S. Patel c Dickson b Denly	32
D. P. Sibley c Dickson b Henry	119	R. N. Sidebottom not out	0
I. R. Bell lbw b Podmore	16		
I. J. L. Trott c Stevens b Podmore	8	B 6, lb 14, nb 8	28
S. R. Hain lbw b Riley	3		
†T. R. Ambrose lbw b Riley	21	1/176 (1) 2/203 (3) (115.5 overs) 380
K. H. D. Barker lbw b Denly	2	3/223 (4) 4/236 (5) 5/284 (6)
C. J. C. Wright c and b Denly	38	6/293 (7) 7/317 (2) 8/324 (9)
O. P. Stone lbw b Podmore	3	9/379 (8) 10/380 (10) 110 overs: 365-8

Henry 20–3–75–1; Stevens 15–4–50–0; Stewart 20–4–54–1; Podmore 23–5–67–3; Riley 19–5–66–2; Denly 18.5–2–48–3.

Umpires: G. D. Lloyd and R. T. Robinson.

WORCESTERSHIRE

Golden Brown

JOHN CURTIS

It was possible to claim – without too much fear of contradiction – that Worcestershire were the leading white-ball side in the country in 2018. After ending their long wait to reach a first T20 finals day, they performed magnificently under Moeen Ali's inspired captaincy to win the trophy. In the words of head coach Kevin Sharp, they had "got a monkey off their backs". That followed an impressive 50-over campaign in which they topped the North group for a second successive season, before losing an enthralling semi-final to Kent.

But they could not translate that form to the Championship. It meant a sixth relegation since 2004 – though, on the bright side, they have made a speciality of bouncing back quickly. There had been a genuine belief among players and coaching staff that the squad were equipped to cope with life among the elite. But a failure to seize the moment in tight situations proved costly.

Against Essex at New Road, they had a first-innings lead, but failed to chase 215; at Southport against Lancashire, they were in charge until the third afternoon, before losing the initiative; and at home against Surrey, they fought hard, until a devastating burst by Morne Morkel took the visitors to the brink of the title. Dealing with these pressure situations ought to benefit the younger players.

Worcestershire's cause was not helped when captain Joe Leach suffered a stress fracture of his back in early June. He had taken 23 wickets in the opening five Championship fixtures, but sat out the rest of the season. Josh Tongue, who confirmed his enormous potential with 40 wickets at 25, was also absent in the middle of the summer with a foot injury. Eighteen of those wickets came in his final five games, underlining how much he had been missed. Worryingly, a recurrence ruled him out of England Lions' winter tour of the UAE.

Daryl Mitchell again led the batsmen, with four Championship hundreds. Only four others in Division One scored more than his 957 runs, and three of those played for the top two teams. Joe Clarke, whose departure for Nottinghamshire will leave a considerable void, was not far behind, with 853 runs and three centuries. But it was indicative of the team's batting problems that, of the other regulars, only stand-in wicketkeeper Alex Milton reached three figures, from No. 7 on debut at Taunton. Martin Guptill (one in two games) and Ali (with a dazzling double at Scarborough) were the other centurions.

The reshaping of the squad began early. Wayne Parnell, who prospered as an overseas recruit, became Worcestershire's first Kolpak signing since the Zimbabwean spinner Ray Price in 2007. Riki Wessels signed from Nottinghamshire on a three-year contract, and the Australian Callum Ferguson,

Stu Forster, Getty Images

Daryl Mitchell

who made an explosive impact in limited-overs matches, will play in all formats. Wessels is set to replace Clarke as a white-ball opener, and Ferguson to bat in the Championship middle order.

The Royal London and T20 results meant Worcestershire had now won three of their last four qualifying groups in the two competitions. Their Vitality Blast finals-day victories over Lancashire and Sussex were certainly no fluke. A team had been assembled which were not over-reliant on one or two individuals, and in which several home-grown players had already acquired big-match experience.

That was underlined on T20 finals day at Edgbaston when Ben Cox, who had been dropped for the preceding Championship game against Surrey, picked up two match awards. Much praise was lavished on seamer Pat Brown, still a student at the University of Worcester, who finished as the competition's leading wicket-taker, with 31. His slower-ball variations and calmness under fire were among the chief factors in Worcestershire's success. They were also well served by their overseas quartet: Guptill, Ferguson, Parnell and Travis Head. Guptill ended his stint with a 35-ball century at Northampton to win the Walter Lawrence Trophy for the fastest domestic hundred of the season.

Regaining Division One status, and this time staying up, is the first priority. Sharp has moved up from head coach to head of player and coaches' development, with his old job going to Alex Gidman, who was promoted from the Second XI. Gidman and bowling coach Alan Richardson were given much credit for the T20 success after taking charge of the white-ball sides. "It became apparent to me that they should have the responsibility of running first-team cricket," said Sharp. "They have both recently played the game, are tactically very smart, think outside the box, and are a great combination in the way they manage the players. The time was right, and they are ready."

In January 2019, a jury were unable to reach a decision on two counts of rape faced by Worcestershire all-rounder Alex Hepburn. A retrial was set for April.

Championship attendance: 24,344.

WORCESTERSHIRE RESULTS

All first-class matches – Played 14: Won 2, Lost 10, Drawn 2. Abandoned 1.
County Championship matches – Played 14: Won 2, Lost 10, Drawn 2.

Specsavers County Championship, 8th in Division 1;
Vitality Blast, winners; Royal London One-Day Cup, semi-finalists.

COUNTY CHAMPIONSHIP AVERAGES, BATTING AND FIELDING

Colours		Birthplace	M	I	NO	R	HS	100	Avge	Ct/St
2007	†M. M. Ali§	Birmingham	3	5	0	383	219	1	76.60	0
2018	M. J. Guptill¶	Auckland, NZ	2	4	0	170	111	1	42.50	3
2018	W. D. Parnell¶	Port Elizabeth, SA	6	10	3	273	58*	0	39.00	1
2005	D. K. H. Mitchell . . .	Badsey‡	14	26	0	957	178	4	36.80	21
2015	J. M. Clarke	Shrewsbury	14	26	1	853	177*	3	34.12	8
2018	†T. M. Head¶	Adelaide, Aust. . . .	6	11	1	339	62	0	33.90	2
2013	†R. A. Whiteley	Sheffield	6	11	0	364	91	0	33.09	8
2013	T. C. Fell	Hillingdon	13	24	0	652	89	0	27.16	7
2015	E. G. Barnard	Shrewsbury	13	24	2	516	66	0	23.45	9
2018	A. G. Milton	Redhill	7	13	2	250	104*	1	22.72	6/1
2009	O. B. Cox	Wordsley‡	12	22	1	372	65	0	17.71	35
2014	C. A. J. Morris	Hereford	4	7	5	31	9*	0	15.50	0
2012	B. L. D'Oliveira	Worcester‡	10	19	0	276	65	0	14.52	1
2018	B. J. Twohig	Dewsbury	7	13	2	145	35	0	13.18	3
2017	J. C. Tongue	Redditch‡	11	19	3	201	34	0	12.56	2
2018	O. E. Westbury	Dudley	2	4	0	49	22	0	12.25	1
2008	†S. J. Magoffin†† . . .	Corinda, Aust	6	10	3	65	43	0	9.28	0
2012	D. Y. Pennington . . .	Shrewsbury	8	14	3	94	37	0	8.54	4
2012	J. Leach	Stafford	5	9	0	66	18	0	7.33	1
2016	G. H. Rhodes	Birmingham	3	6	0	22	12	0	3.66	1

Also batted: P. R. Brown (*Peterborough*) (colours 2017) (1 match) 2* (1 ct); †L. Wood (*Sheffield*) (colours 2018) (1 match) 65*, 13.

‡ *Born in Worcestershire.*   § *ECB contract.*   ¶*Official overseas player.*   †† *Other non-England-qualified.*

BOWLING

	Style	O	M	R	W	BB	5I	Avge
M. M. Ali	OB/RM	107.5	20	334	18	6-49	2	18.55
J. Leach	RFM	157.5	28	508	23	4-42	0	22.08
E. G. Barnard	RFM	368.3	93	1,138	49	6-37	4	23.22
J. C. Tongue	RFM	304.4	52	1,011	40	5-53	2	25.27
W. D. Parnell	LFM	154.4	22	582	18	4-23	0	32.33
D. Y. Pennington	RFM	187	34	778	22	4-53	0	35.36
S. J. Magoffin	RFM	202	55	593	16	3-70	0	37.06
B. J. Twohig	SLA	161	18	598	10	2-47	0	59.80

Also bowled: P. R. Brown (RFM) 20–3–67–1; B. L. D'Oliveira (LB) 51–3–208–4; M. J. Guptill (OB) 4–1–17–1; T. M. Head (OB) 43–6–162–1; D. K. H. Mitchell (RM) 62–9–200–4; C. A. J. Morris (RFM) 108.4–15–372–9; O. E. Westbury (OB) 1–0–6–0; R. A. Whiteley (LM) 36.2–4–115–3; L. Wood (LFM) 32–6–108–1.

LEADING ROYAL LONDON CUP AVERAGES (150 runs/5 wickets)

Batting	Runs	HS	Avge	SR	Ct
C. J. Ferguson . . .	377	192	94.25	117.81	4
O. B. Cox	396	122*	79.20	107.02	18
E. G. Barnard . . .	153	50*	76.50	100.00	2
B. L. D'Oliveira . .	265	78	37.85	92.98	5
D. K. H. Mitchell . .	260	102*	37.14	82.53	4
J. M. Clarke	306	122	34.00	89.21	2
R. A. Whiteley . . .	195	66*	32.50	126.62	4

Bowling	W	BB	Avge	ER
M. M. Ali	11	4-33	21.18	4.95
E. G. Barnard	16	3-64	28.87	6.16
P. R. Brown	7	3-53	34.42	6.39
C. A. J. Morris	11	4-33	34.63	6.35
B. L. D'Oliveira . .	10	2-28	38.00	5.27
D. K. H. Mitchell . .	5	2-19	43.40	5.40
J. Leach	7	2-28	45.00	6.11

LEADING VITALITY BLAST AVERAGES (150 runs/15 overs)

Batting	Runs	HS	Avge	SR	Ct/St	Bowling	W	BB	Avge	ER
M. M. Ali	334	115	41.75	175.78	6	P. R. Brown	31	4-21	13.35	7.64
R. A. Whiteley	313	60	26.08	152.68	7	D. K. H. Mitchell	10	2-7	23.90	7.70
J. M. Clarke	396	76	28.28	151.72	6	W. D. Parnell	14	3-20	18.35	7.94
M. J. Guptill	253	102	36.14	147.09	6	L. Wood	8	2-20	41.00	8.06
B. L. D'Oliveira	171	64	19.00	143.69	3	B. L. D'Oliveira	8	4-26	33.62	8.40
C. J. Ferguson	390	102*	48.75	141.81	3	M. M. Ali	11	3-30	24.09	8.54
O. B. Cox	274	55*	27.40	120.70	9/5	E. G. Barnard	12	3-29	38.50	9.05

FIRST-CLASS COUNTY RECORDS

Highest score for	405*	G. A. Hick v Somerset at Taunton	1988
Highest score against	331*	J. D. B. Robertson (Middlesex) at Worcester	1949
Leading run-scorer	34,490	D. Kenyon (avge 34.18)	1946–67
Best bowling for	9-23	C. F. Root v Lancashire at Worcester	1931
Best bowling against	10-51	J. Mercer (Glamorgan) at Worcester	1936
Leading wicket-taker	2,143	R. T. D. Perks (avge 23.73)	1930–55
Highest total for	701-6 dec	v Surrey at Worcester	2007
Highest total against	701-4 dec	by Leicestershire at Worcester	1906
Lowest total for	24	v Yorkshire at Huddersfield	1903
Lowest total against	30	by Hampshire at Worcester	1903

LIST A COUNTY RECORDS

Highest score for	192	**C. J. Ferguson v Leicestershire at Worcester**	**2018**
Highest score against	{ 158	W. Larkins (Northamptonshire) at Luton	1982
	{ 158	R. A. Smith (Hampshire) at Worcester	1996
Leading run-scorer	16,416	G. A. Hick (avge 44.60)	1985–2008
Best bowling for	7-19	N. V. Radford v Bedfordshire at Bedford	1991
Best bowling against	7-15	R. A. Hutton (Yorkshire) at Leeds	1969
Leading wicket-taker	370	S. R. Lampitt (avge 24.52)	1987–2002
Highest total for	404-3	v Devon at Worcester	1987
Highest total against	399-4	by Sussex at Horsham	2011
Lowest total for	58	v Ireland v Worcester	2009
Lowest total against	45	by Hampshire at Worcester	1988

TWENTY20 COUNTY RECORDS

Highest score for	127*	T. Köhler-Cadmore v Durham at Worcester	2016
Highest score against	141*	C. L. White (Somerset) at Worcester	2006
Leading run-scorer	**2,224**	**M. M. Ali (avge 26.47, SR 137.53)**	**2007–18**
Best bowling for	5-24	A. Hepburn v Nottinghamshire at Worcester	2017
Best bowling against	6-21	A. J. Hall (Northamptonshire) at Northampton	2008
Leading wicket-taker	92	J. D. Shantry (avge 28.21, ER 8.07)	2010–17
Highest total for	227-6	v Northamptonshire at Kidderminster	2007
Highest total against	233-6	by Yorkshire at Leeds	2017
Lowest total for	53	v Lancashire at Manchester	2016
Lowest total against	93	by Gloucestershire at Bristol	2008

ADDRESS

Blackfinch New Road, Worcester WR2 4QQ; 01905 748474; info@wccc.co.uk; www.wccc.co.uk.

OFFICIALS

Captain J. Leach
   (Twenty20) M. M. Ali
Head coach 2018 K. Sharp
Head of player and coaches development 2019 K. Sharp
First-team coach 2019 A. P. R. Gidman
Assistant coach and bowling coach 2019 A. Richardson
Academy coach E. J. Wilson

President N. Gifford
Chairman 2018 S. D. Taylor
   2019 F. Hira
Chief executive M. J. Rawnsley
Head groundsman T. R. Packwood
Scorer S. M. Drinkwater and P. M. Mellish

WORCESTERSHIRE v LEEDS/BRADFORD MCCU

At Worcester RGS, April 1–3. Abandoned.

At Southampton, April 13–16. WORCESTERSHIRE lost to HAMPSHIRE by 196 runs.

At Taunton, April 20–22. WORCESTERSHIRE lost to SOMERSET by 83 runs. *Ed Barnard takes 11-89.*

WORCESTERSHIRE v NOTTINGHAMSHIRE

At Worcester, April 27–30. Nottinghamshire won by an innings and 41 runs. Nottinghamshire 22pts, Worcestershire 3pts. Toss: uncontested.

Nottinghamshire needed just five sessions to win the battle of the promoted teams and continue Worcestershire's miserable return to Division One. It took heroic work by the groundstaff to get New Road ready after it had been under water only three weeks earlier. Rain delayed the start until the third day, when Worcestershire found conditions even less to their liking than umpire Illingworth, who wore gloves. They were hustled out for 110 in 26.3 overs by the Nottinghamshire seamers, with Fletcher taking a career-best five for 27, his first five-for since September 2013; only three batsmen passed four. Taylor then showed it was possible to prosper in awkward conditions, before quick runs from Moores and Broad hastened the declaration, giving Nottinghamshire 80 overs to bowl out Worcestershire again. They didn't need even half that, Ball taking the honours.

Close of play: first day, no play; second day, no play; third day, Nottinghamshire 204-6 (Moores 19, Broad 5).

Worcestershire

D. K. H. Mitchell b Ball	0	– b Ball	3
B. L. D'Oliveira c Nash b Ball	3	– c Taylor b Ball	0
T. C. Fell lbw b Broad	0	– b Gurney	37
J. M. Clarke c Mullaney b Fletcher	42	– c Moores b Broad	4
T. M. Head lbw b Fletcher	33	– lbw b Ball	29
G. H. Rhodes b Fletcher	0	– c Moores b Fletcher	8
†O. B. Cox c Moores b Fletcher	3	– c Libby b Fletcher	11
E. G. Barnard b Broad	4	– c Moores b Ball	12
*J. Leach b Fletcher	12	– c Moores b Ball	6
J. C. Tongue not out	2	– b Gurney	21
C. A. J. Morris b Broad	3	– not out	9
B 1, lb 2, w 1, nb 4	8	B 5, lb 4	9

1/0 (1) 2/3 (3) 3/3 (2) (26.3 overs) 110   1/1 (2) 2/12 (1) (38.2 overs) 149
4/68 (4) 5/68 (6) 6/86 (7)   3/17 (4) 4/62 (5)
7/87 (5) 8/103 (8) 9/105 (9) 10/110 (11)   5/75 (6) 6/89 (7) 7/101 (3)
8/118 (9) 9/125 (8) 10/149 (10)

Ball 5–1–25–2; Broad 8.3–1–28–3; Fletcher 9–2–27–5; Gurney 4–0–27–0. *Second innings*—Ball 13–2–59–5; Broad 6–2–17–1; Fletcher 9–2–28–2; Gurney 10.2–2–36–2.

Nottinghamshire

*S. J. Mullaney lbw b Tongue	28	J. T. Ball lbw b Tongue	0
J. D. Libby c Mitchell b Leach	9	H. F. Gurney not out	1
C. D. Nash b Leach	26		
L. R. P. L. Taylor lbw b Tongue	50	Lb 16, w 4, nb 10	30
S. R. Patel lbw b Leach	12		
M. H. Wessels b Barnard	36	1/33 (2) (9 wkts dec, 70.5 overs) 300
†T. J. Moores c Cox b Tongue	43	2/44 (1) 3/122 (3)
S. C. J. Broad c Cox b Head	38	4/126 (4) 5/138 (5) 6/193 (6)
L. J. Fletcher not out	27	7/252 (7) 8/287 (8) 9/288 (10)

Leach 21–7–73–3; Barnard 14–0–62–1; Morris 12–2–38–0; Tongue 19.5–1–81–4; Head 4–0–30–1.

Umpires: R. K. Illingworth and D. J. Millns.

At The Oval, May 4–7. WORCESTERSHIRE drew with SURREY. *Worcestershire make 526, their highest total at The Oval.*

WORCESTERSHIRE v ESSEX

At Worcester, May 11–13. Essex won by 32 runs. Essex 19pts, Worcestershire 4pts. Toss: Essex.

Siddle's parting gift to Essex was a match-winning five-for that resurrected their title defence after defeat by Yorkshire. In the final appearance of an initial four-match stint (he would return later in the season), he took three early wickets to derail Worcestershire's pursuit of 215. There were also five for Harmer, whose victims included Head, last out after offering lonely resistance. Worcestershire, urged to "put on a performance for the members" by head coach Kevin Sharp after their capitulation against Nottinghamshire, could at least take some solace from the bowling of Tongue and the batting of Clarke. Tongue removed Lawrence, ten Doeschate and Bopara in 15 balls in the first innings and, showing maturity beyond his 20 years, finished with nine in the match. Clarke's classy century, meanwhile, was his second in successive games. With a first-innings lead of 61, Worcestershire looked well placed to end their wretched start to the season. But Alastair Cook and Lawrence, who put on a crucial 63 with Foster, ensured Essex scraped together enough to offer a challenging chase.

Close of play: first day, Worcestershire 47-0 (Mitchell 7, D'Oliveira 34); second day, Essex 143-4 (Lawrence 9, Porter 1).

Essex

V. Chopra c Barnard b Magoffin	10	– b Tongue	21
A. N. Cook c Twohig b Leach	37	– b Magoffin	66
T. Westley b Barnard	15	– b Leach	26
D. W. Lawrence b Tongue	20	– lbw b Tongue	71
R. S. Bopara c Mitchell b Tongue	7	– c Cox b Tongue	13
*R. N. ten Doeschate lbw b Tongue	1	– (7) c Fell b Leach	4
†J. S. Foster lbw b Barnard	16	– (8) c Cox b Tongue	24
S. R. Harmer c Mitchell b Barnard	22	– (9) c Leach b Tongue	23
P. M. Siddle b Leach	29	– (10) b Leach	2
J. A. Porter c Cox b Tongue	6	– (6) run out (Head/Cox)	9
S. J. Cook not out	2	– not out	0
Lb 8, nb 4	12	B 5, lb 5, nb 6	16

1/19 (1) 2/59 (3) 3/68 (2)　　　　(65.1 overs)　177　　1/58 (1) 2/106 (2)　　(82.5 overs)　275
4/88 (4) 5/90 (6) 6/101 (5)　　　　　　　　　　　　　　3/114 (3) 4/142 (5)
7/125 (7) 8/140 (8) 9/157 (10) 10/177 (9)　　　　　　5/158 (6) 6/170 (7) 7/233 (8)
　　　　　　　　　　　　　　　　　　　　　　　　　8/260 (4) 9/273 (10) 10/275 (9)

Leach 15.1–3–37–2; Magoffin 16–6–38–1; Barnard 19–8–49–3; Tongue 15–7–45–4. *Second innings*—Leach 20–2–72–3; Magoffin 20–4–67–1; Tongue 23.5–8–53–5; Barnard 11–3–53–0; Twohig 8–1–20–0.

Worcestershire

D. K. H. Mitchell lbw b Bopara	41	– c Bopara b Harmer	26
B. L. D'Oliveira c Bopara b Siddle	37	– c Foster b Siddle	11
T. C. Fell b Porter	5	– b Siddle	10
J. M. Clarke lbw b Bopara	105	– b Siddle	2
T. M. Head c Foster b Harmer	5	– c ten Doeschate b Harmer	62
†O. B. Cox b Siddle	0	– lbw b Siddle	9
E. G. Barnard c Harmer b Porter	2	– b Harmer	29
B. J. Twohig lbw b S. J. Cook	8	– c Porter b Harmer	1
*J. Leach b Harmer	9	– c ten Doeschate b Harmer	5
J. C. Tongue not out	12	– c Harmer b Siddle	3
S. J. Magoffin c ten Doeschate b Bopara	0	– not out	1
Lb 7, w 1, nb 6	14	B 8, lb 13, nb 2	23

1/51 (2) 2/56 (3) 3/142 (1)　　　　(72.4 overs)　238　　1/22 (2) 2/50 (3)　　(60.1 overs)　182
4/155 (5) 5/158 (6) 6/161 (7)　　　　　　　　　　　　3/52 (4) 4/68 (1)
7/188 (8) 8/207 (9) 9/237 (4) 10/238 (11)　　　　　　5/97 (6) 6/160 (7) 7/166 (8)
　　　　　　　　　　　　　　　　　　　　　　　　　8/173 (9) 9/180 (10) 10/182 (5)

Porter 19–3–70–2; S. J. Cook 14–3–46–1; Siddle 20–2–56–2; Bopara 6.4–0–30–3; Harmer 13–3–29–2. *Second innings*—Porter 13–2–50–0; Siddle 18–1–37–5; S. J. Cook 7–1–25–0; Harmer 21.1–3–43–5; Bopara 1–0–6–0.

Umpires: N. G. B. Cook and N. A. Mallender.

At Worcester, June 19. WORCESTERSHIRE lost to WEST INDIES A by 21 runs (see West Indies A tour section).

WORCESTERSHIRE v LANCASHIRE

At Worcester, June 20–23. Worcestershire won by 202 runs. Worcestershire 20pts, Lancashire 3pts. Toss: uncontested. First-class debut: D. J. Lamb. County debut: M. J. Guptill.

Outstanding performances by Mitchell, who scored twin centuries, and Barnard, who took nine wickets, earned Worcestershire their first victory of the summer. The third day was notable for the appearance of Lamb as a concussion replacement for Mennie, who had been struck on the head the previous day by a return drive from Guptill; it was the first time the regulation had been used. Worcestershire, led by D'Oliveira after Joe Leach's season-ending back injury, grabbed the initiative when Lancashire collapsed from 77 without loss to 130. Guptill, on his first appearance for Worcestershire, held a magnificent catch at midwicket to remove Davies, and Barnard then took four in 16 balls, inflicting five ducks on the middle order (it was the first time Nos 3–6 had all made nought for Lancashire in a Championship innings). Mitchell's first hundred had glued Worcestershire together after a probing spell by Mennie reduced them to 81 for five. His second followed an opening stand of 215 inside 33 overs with Guptill, who hit a rapid 111, and 137 for the second wicket with Fell. It was the fourth time Mitchell had scored two centuries in a match for Worcestershire, equalling the record of Graeme Hick. Set 602 on the third morning, Lancashire offered defiance until the penultimate session. Jennings batted for almost seven hours before playing down the wrong line to Brown.

Close of play: first day, Lancashire 86-5 (Jennings 42); second day, Worcestershire 361-4 (Clarke 5, D'Oliveira 2); third day, Lancashire 269-4 (Jennings 135, Vilas 7).

Worcestershire

D. K. H. Mitchell c Bailey b Clark	118	– c Vilas b Clark	163
M. J. Guptill c Vilas b Onions	2	– lbw b Bailey	111
T. C. Fell b Bailey	10	– b Jones	62
J. M. Clarke b Mennie	21	– (5) b Bailey	10
*B. L. D'Oliveira lbw b Mennie	8	– (6) lbw b Bailey	22
†O. B. Cox c Vilas b Mennie	0	– (7) not out	58
E. G. Barnard b Mennie	21	– (4) b Clark	1
R. A. Whiteley b Clark	32	– c Bailey b Clark	23
C. A. J. Morris c Vilas b Clark	0	– not out	8
S. J. Magoffin c sub (S. Mahmood) b Clark	0		
P. R. Brown not out	2		
B 6, lb 15, nb 12	33	Lb 12, w 2, nb 12	26

1/4 (2) 2/15 (3) 3/53 (4)   (63.5 overs) 247   1/215 (2)   (7 wkts dec, 96 overs) 484
4/81 (5) 5/81 (6) 6/147 (7)   2/352 (1) 3/354 (4)
7/226 (8) 8/232 (9) 9/240 (10) 10/247 (1)   4/354 (3) 5/384 (5) 6/391 (6) 7/439 (8)

Bailey 16–6–68–1; Onions 14–3–40–1; Mennie 12–2–43–4; Clark 15.5–3–56–4; Jennings 1–0–10–0; Parry 5–0–9–0. *Second innings*—Bailey 22–0–120–3; Onions 14–1–55–0; Mennie 4–0–18–0; Clark 18–0–96–3; Parry 23–0–96–0; Jennings 5–0–24–0; Jones 5–0–18–1; Lamb 5–0–45–0.

Lancashire

K. K. Jennings lbw b Magoffin	55	– b Brown	177
A. L. Davies c Guptill b Morris	43	– lbw b D'Oliveira	64
S. D. Parry c and b Barnard	0	– (9) lbw b Barnard	1
H. Hameed b Barnard	0	– (3) lbw b D'Oliveira	20
S. Chanderpaul c Brown b Barnard	0	– (4) c Cox b Morris	28
R. P. Jones lbw b Barnard	0	– (5) c Cox b Morris	10
*†D. J. Vilas lbw b Magoffin	3	– (6) b Morris	33
J. Clark lbw b Barnard	0	– (7) c Cox b Whiteley	33
J. M. Mennie not out	17		
T. E. Bailey c Clarke b Morris	8	– lbw b Barnard	0
G. Onions b Morris	0	– b Barnard	0
D. J. Lamb (did not bat)		– (8) not out	19
B 3, lb 1	4	B 9, lb 5	14

1/77 (2) 2/84 (3) 3/86 (4)   (46.4 overs) 130
4/86 (5) 5/86 (6) 6/95 (7)
7/96 (8) 8/112 (1) 9/130 (10) 10/130 (11)

1/126 (2) 2/184 (3)   (122.4 overs) 399
3/234 (4) 4/252 (5)
5/325 (6) 6/359 (1) 7/398 (7)
8/399 (8) 9/399 (10) 10/399 (11)

Lamb replaced Mennie, as a concussion substitute.

Magoffin 18–4–58–2; Morris 9.4–4–20–3; Barnard 16–4–34–5; Brown 3–0–14–0. *Second innings*—Magoffin 24–5–60–0; Morris 25–1–99–2; Barnard 30.4–8–95–4; Brown 17–3–53–1; D'Oliveira 17–2–68–2; Mitchell 5–2–8–0; Whiteley 4–2–2–1.

Umpires: B. J. Debenham and P. J. Hartley.

At Nottingham, June 25–28. WORCESTERSHIRE drew with NOTTINGHAMSHIRE.

WORCESTERSHIRE v SOMERSET

At Worcester, July 22–25. Somerset won by 141 runs. Somerset 22pts, Worcestershire 5pts. Toss: Worcestershire. County debut: Azhar Ali. Championship debut: A. G. Milton.

Somerset were made to wait for the win that lifted them to second place by a Worcestershire record tenth-wicket stand between Alex Milton, in his first Championship match, and Magoffin. They put on 136, beating 119 by William Burns and George Wilson, also against Somerset at New Road, in 1906. Milton, replacing the injured Ben Cox as wicketkeeper after 70 consecutive Championship appearances, made a patient, undefeated 104. Half-centuries from Hildreth, Abell and Davies had rebuilt Somerset's first innings after both openers departed swiftly. But Worcestershire fought back doggedly, and it needed a stand of 53 in seven overs between Craig and Jamie Overton to lift the total past 300. In his second Championship match of the season after injury, Jamie proved a handful with the ball as well and shared eight wickets with Davey. Worcestershire's plight would have been worse, but for an unbeaten 65 from Wood, on loan from Nottinghamshire. On his county debut, Pakistan's Azhar Ali hit a classy hundred as Somerset built an impregnable lead, despite Moeen Ali's first Championship five-for in five years. Jamie Overton then took another four wickets before Worcestershire's last-ditch resistance.

Close of play: first day, Somerset 324-9 (Davey 4, Leach 1); second day, Somerset 47-0 (Trescothick 33, Byrom 12); third day, Worcestershire 50-2 (Head 36).

Somerset

M. E. Trescothick lbw b Wood	6	– st Milton b Ali	71
E. J. Byrom c Milton b Magoffin	5	– lbw b Ali	28
Azhar Ali c Milton b Pennington	37	– c Milton b Ali	125
J. C. Hildreth b Pennington	57	– lbw b Ali	5
*T. B. Abell lbw b Magoffin	70	– b Magoffin	31
†S. M. Davies c Milton b Ali	72	– lbw b Ali	18
P. D. Trego lbw b Ali	1	– b Barnard	4
C. Overton c Mitchell b Ali	31	– run out (D'Oliveira)	29
J. Overton lbw b Barnard	28	– c Whiteley b Pennington	14
J. H. Davey not out	11	– not out	20
M. J. Leach c Whiteley b Barnard	7		
Lb 3, w 1, nb 8	12	B 11, lb 4, nb 2	17

1/11 (2) 2/11 (1) 3/110 (3)   (101.3 overs) 337
4/115 (4) 5/241 (6) 6/251 (7)
7/266 (5) 8/319 (8) 9/323 (9) 10/337 (11)

1/97 (2)   (9 wkts dec, 100.5 overs) 362
2/110 (1) 3/120 (4)
4/189 (5) 5/228 (6) 6/239 (7)
7/294 (8) 8/314 (9) 9/362 (3)

Magoffin 19–7–51–2; Wood 19.4–4–59–1; Pennington 17–2–83–2; Ali 22–6–63–3; Whiteley 2–0–17–0; D'Oliveira 1–0–2–0. *Second innings*—Magoffin 17–8–33–1; Wood 13–2–49–0; Barnard 16–5–47–1; Ali 33.5–3–107–5; Pennington 10–0–60–1; D'Oliveira 6–0–26–0; Head 2–0–10–0; Whiteley 2–0–8–0; Mitchell 1–0–7–0.

Worcestershire

D. K. H. Mitchell c Davies b C. Overton	5	– lbw b Davey	6
T. M. Head c C. Overton b Davey	2	– c Davies b J. Overton	46
M. M. Ali c Davies b J. Overton	30	– b J. Overton	7
J. M. Clarke c Byrom b Davey	16	– b Davey	5
*B. L. D'Oliveira lbw b J. Overton	22	– c Hildreth b J. Overton	6
E. G. Barnard b Davey	29	– c Trescothick b J. Overton	0
†A. G. Milton lbw b C. Overton	8	– not out	104
R. A. Whiteley b J. Overton	26	– c Davies b J. Overton	39
L. Wood not out	65	– c Trego b Leach	13
D. Y. Pennington b J. Overton	37	– c Davies b Leach	0
S. J. Magoffin c Azhar Ali b Davey	1	– c Davey b C. Overton	43
B 1, lb 8, w 1, nb 6	16	B 18, lb 7, w 5, nb 2	32

1/8 (2) 2/14 (1) 3/35 (4)   (63.5 overs) 257
4/77 (3) 5/82 (5) 6/120 (6)
7/120 (7) 8/166 (8) 9/250 (10) 10/257 (11)

1/21 (2) 2/50 (3)   (87 overs) 301
3/65 (4) 4/65 (2)
5/65 (6) 6/71 (5) 7/142 (8)
8/165 (9) 9/165 (10) 10/301 (11)

C. Overton 14–5–29–2; Davey 16.5–4–68–4; Abell 7–1–38–0; J. Overton 15–4–61–4; Trego 7–1–35–0; Leach 4–0–17–0. *Second innings*—C. Overton 19–3–55–1; Davey 19–5–43–3; J. Overton 19–2–82–4; Leach 22–2–76–2; Trego 1–0–5–0; Azhar Ali 7–2–15–0.

Umpires: R. J. Bailey and P. K. Baldwin.

At Scarborough, August 19–22. WORCESTERSHIRE beat YORKSHIRE by an innings and 186 runs.

At Southport, August 29–31. WORCESTERSHIRE lost to LANCASHIRE by four wickets.

WORCESTERSHIRE v HAMPSHIRE

At Worcester, September 4–6. Hampshire won by 114 runs. Hampshire 19pts, Worcestershire 3pts. Toss: Hampshire. County debut: O. C. Soames.

Hampshire took a significant step towards survival, and pushed Worcestershire closer to relegation, with a win completed 45 minutes into the third morning. Seventeen wickets fell to the overseas pace trio of Abbott, Steyn and Edwards, who overwhelmed the Worcestershire batting. Hampshire had looked well set at 81 for two at lunch on the first day, but Barnard's inspired spell of five for 21 in nine overs sent them tumbling to 126 for eight. Northeast's 48 restored some order, before 24 wickets fell on the second day as Hampshire moved to the brink of victory. They had threatened to throw away the advantage conferred by a lead of 71 when slumping to 25 for four, but Alsop made the only half-century of the match, and put on 77 for the seventh wicket with Dawson. Beginning their second innings after tea, Worcestershire were soon in dire straits. And when Abbott took the first Hampshire hat-trick of his career – Clarke, Tongue and Barnard – they were 72 for eight. It was the first Hampshire hat-trick since Billy Taylor against Middlesex at Southampton in 2006. They claimed the extra half-hour, but had to return the next morning to finish the job.

Close of play: first day, Worcestershire 68-4 (D'Oliveira 11, Cox 2); second day, Worcestershire 120-8 (Whiteley 37, Parnell 17).

Hampshire

J. J. Weatherley c Cox b Barnard	10	– c Fell b Tongue	3
O. C. Soames c Mitchell b Barnard	25	– b Tongue	0
J. H. K. Adams lbw b Tongue	31	– b Pennington	13
*J. M. Vince c Cox b Barnard	10	– c Mitchell b Barnard	9
S. A. Northeast c Mitchell b Parnell	48	– lbw b Parnell	12
†T. P. Alsop c Cox b Pennington	0	– b Parnell	64
I. G. Holland c Mitchell b Barnard	4	– b Tongue	15
L. A. Dawson c Whiteley b Barnard	4	– c Mitchell b Parnell	39
K. J. Abbott c and b Barnard	0	– c Cox b Tongue	1
D. W. Steyn c Cox b Parnell	25	– c Mitchell b Parnell	4
F. H. Edwards not out	1	– not out	0
B 13, lb 15, w 1, nb 4	33	B 9, lb 3, w 2, nb 2	16

1/21 (1) 2/80 (3) 3/83 (2)   (57.3 overs) 191
4/106 (4) 5/113 (6) 6/118 (7)
7/126 (8) 8/126 (9) 9/168 (10) 10/191 (5)

1/3 (2) 2/8 (1)   (53.1 overs) 176
3/25 (4) 4/25 (3)
5/69 (5) 6/92 (7) 7/169 (8)
8/170 (6) 9/176 (9) 10/176 (10)

Tongue 16–4–42–1; Parnell 13.3–4–31–2; Barnard 16–6–50–6; Pennington 12–3–40–1. *Second innings*—Tongue 11–2–38–4; Parnell 9.1–1–23–4; Barnard 14–4–34–1; Pennington 10–2–39–1; Whiteley 5–0–16–0; Mitchell 3–0–9–0; D'Oliveira 1–0–5–0.

Worcestershire

D. K. H. Mitchell c and b Edwards	41	– c Holland b Abbott	0
T. C. Fell c Alsop b Steyn	4	– b Steyn	2
J. M. Clarke lbw b Holland	1	– c Alsop b Abbott	33
A. G. Milton b Abbott	5	– b Steyn	7
*B. L. D'Oliveira c Weatherley b Steyn	15	– b Abbott	2
†O. B. Cox c Alsop b Edwards	6	– c Alsop b Edwards	4
R. A. Whiteley c Alsop b Abbott	14	– b Abbott	37
E. G. Barnard c Alsop b Steyn	0	– (9) lbw b Abbott	0
W. D. Parnell not out	21	– (10) c Adams b Steyn	26
J. C. Tongue b Holland	4	– (8) b Abbott	0
D. Y. Pennington run out (Soames)	1	– not out	4
B 1, lb 7	8	B 1, lb 13, nb 4	18

1/24 (2) 2/25 (3) 3/48 (4)   (41 overs) 120
4/66 (1) 5/76 (6) 6/78 (5)
7/78 (8) 8/108 (7) 9/113 (10) 10/120 (11)

1/0 (1) 2/10 (2)   (41.5 overs) 133
3/24 (4) 4/27 (5)
5/41 (6) 6/72 (3) 7/72 (8)
8/72 (9) 9/125 (7) 10/133 (10)

Edwards 11–2–27–2; Steyn 12–3–25–3; Holland 10–4–31–2; Abbott 8–1–29–2. *Second innings*—Abbott 14–4–39–6; Steyn 15.5–4–41–3; Holland 5–1–12–0; Edwards 7–1–27–1.

Umpires: N. G. B. Cook and R. A. Kettleborough.

WORCESTERSHIRE v SURREY

At Worcester, September 10–13. Surrey won by three wickets. Surrey 21pts, Worcestershire 6pts. Toss: Worcestershire. First-class debut: O. E. Westbury.

It fell to Morkel, one of the key figures in their success, to hit the runs that secured Surrey's 20th Championship. His thumping pull off Pennington sparked celebrations on the balcony, and completed a fraught chase after Worcestershire had refused to bend the knee. Even so, Surrey's ninth win in a row pushed the home team inexorably towards relegation. It was Morkel's stunning spell on the third afternoon that swung the contest. He took five for five in 38 balls either side of tea as Worcestershire slid from 154 for two – a lead of 222 – to 203 all out. By the close, set 272, Surrey were 70 without loss and apparently sailing home. The loss of four quick wickets on the final afternoon caused some anxiety, but the wise heads of Clarke, a member of Surrey's last title-winning team in 2002, and Morkel saw them over the line. "What took them so long?" said Morkel, who had claimed his 50th Championship wicket of the summer when bowling Parnell. "It's been competitive – there's been quality cricket played, but I've been blown away by this season." Worcestershire had made life difficult from the start, with Whiteley, promoted to No. 5, hitting 91, and solid contributions from Fell and Barnard. Burns's fourth hundred of the year dominated a below-par Surrey response. Fell's 89 appeared to have put Worcestershire on course to leave a formidable target – but Morkel had other ideas.

Close of play: first day, Worcestershire 288-6 (Barnard 63, Parnell 14); second day, Surrey 213-6 (Burns 103, Morkel 4); third day, Surrey 70-0 (Burns 33, Stoneman 37).

Worcestershire

*D. K. H. Mitchell c Burns b Dernbach	13	– c Burns b Clarke	15
T. C. Fell lbw b Clarke	69	– b Morkel	89
O. E. Westbury b Curran	22	– lbw b Virdi	15
J. M. Clarke c Clarke b Curran	0	– (8) c Jacks b Virdi	0
R. A. Whiteley c Pope b Morkel	91	– b Morkel	10
†A. G. Milton c Foakes b Morkel	7	– (4) c Pope b Morkel	24
E. G. Barnard b Morkel	63	– (6) lbw b Morkel	12
W. D. Parnell c Clarke b Virdi	42	– (7) b Morkel	2
B. J. Twohig c Foakes b Curran	2	– not out	7
J. C. Tongue c Virdi b Curran	5	– c Elgar b Curran	6
D. Y. Pennington not out	2	– lbw b Virdi	1
B 5, lb 7, w 2, nb 6	20	B 2, lb 8, w 4, nb 8	22

1/22 (1) 2/88 (3) 3/88 (4)   (116.4 overs) 336   1/65 (1) 2/91 (3)   (63.5 overs) 203
4/134 (2) 5/165 (6) 6/248 (5)   3/154 (4) 4/157 (2)
7/290 (7) 8/311 (9) 9/323 (10)   5/181 (5) 6/187 (6) 7/188 (8)
10/336 (8)   110 overs: 326-9   8/188 (7) 9/200 (10) 10/203 (11)

Dernbach 17–3–70–1; Curran 32–11–61–4; Virdi 19.4–4–65–1; Morkel 26–8–62–3; Clarke 22–6–66–1. *Second innings*—Curran 10–1–34–1; Dernbach 11–3–33–0; Morkel 17–8–24–5; Clarke 6–0–29–1; Virdi 19.5–2–73–3.

Surrey

*R. J. Burns c Parnell b Barnard	122	– b Pennington	66
M. D. Stoneman b Parnell	0	– b Parnell	59
D. Elgar c Barnard b Parnell	0	– b Tongue	21
O. J. D. Pope c Milton b Parnell	48	– b Pennington	49
W. G. Jacks b Twohig	17	– (6) c Westbury b Barnard	12
R. Clarke c Milton b Whiteley	33	– (7) not out	18
T. K. Curran c Whiteley b Tongue	0	– (8) c Whiteley b Pennington	7
M. Morkel b Tongue	16	– (9) not out	9
†B. T. Foakes c Fell b Pennington	13	– (5) c Whiteley b Parnell	22
J. W. Dernbach c Tongue b Pennington	6		
G. S. Virdi not out	0		
B 3, lb 10	13	B 1, lb 6, nb 4	11

1/4 (2)   2/4 (3)   3/101 (4)   (71.3 overs) 268   1/111 (2)   (7 wkts, 71.2 overs) 274
4/135 (5)   5/203 (6)   6/204 (7)   2/135 (1)   3/157 (3)
7/232 (8)   8/262 (9)   9/262 (1)   10/268 (10)   4/210 (5)   5/228 (6)   6/240 (4)   7/260 (8)

Tongue 16–0–63–2; Parnell 18–3–56–3; Barnard 14.2–2–48–1; Pennington 9.3–3–36–2; Twohig 11–2–44–1; Whiteley 1–0–5–1; Mitchell 2–0–3–0. *Second innings*—Tongue 11.2–2–36–1; Parnell 21–3–101–2; Twohig 11.2–2–36–0; Barnard 16–3–53–1; Pennington 12.2–3–41–3.

Umpires: M. Burns and N. A. Mallender.

At Chelmsford, September 18–20. WORCESTERSHIRE lost to ESSEX by an innings and 129 runs. *Worcestershire are relegated.*

WORCESTERSHIRE v YORKSHIRE

At Worcester, September 24–26. Yorkshire won by seven wickets. Yorkshire 24pts, Worcestershire 6pts. Toss: uncontested. First-class debut: J. E. G. Logan.

Two bonus points on the opening day guaranteed Yorkshire's survival – and they celebrated with a crushing victory. In a show-stopping farewell performance before joining Somerset, Brooks contributed six first-innings wickets and 82 in a match-defining stand with Ballance. It meant Worcestershire's season ended with a sobering five successive defeats. Yet they had been in the ascendancy for the first five sessions after Mitchell patiently compiled his fourth century of the summer. Yorkshire had to wait until the 84th over – when Brooks dismissed Barnard – to gain the point that secured their safety. It was his third five-for in five games since his departure had been announced. "He is one of the key reasons why we are still in Division One," said coach Andrew Gale. Against a weakened attack, Ballance played a lone hand for much of the second day. Yorkshire were still 108 behind when their eighth wicket fell, but he and Brooks put on 171 – a ninth-wicket record in this fixture – before Brooks fell to Ali, who had switched from off-spin to medium pace. Ali and Parnell offered the only resistance in Worcestershire's second innings.

Close of play: first day, Worcestershire 319-8 (Twohig 30, Tongue 20); second day, Yorkshire 417-9 (Ballance 189, Coad 2).

Worcestershire

D. K. H. Mitchell c Logan b Brooks 127	– c Tattersall b Brooks 5
T. C. Fell c Leaning b Bresnan 19	– c Lyth b Coad................. 21
*M. M. Ali c Köhler-Cadmore b Patterson 60	– c and b Patterson 67
J. M. Clarke b Brooks 8	– b Patterson 16
A. G. Milton c Köhler-Cadmore b Coad 1	– c Tattersall b Coad 10
†O. B. Cox lbw b Brooks..................... 9	– b Patterson 18
E. G. Barnard lbw b Brooks.................. 34	– c Leaning b Coad 0
W. D. Parnell b Lyth b Brooks............... 0	– (9) not out. 58
B. J. Twohig lbw b Coad 30	– (8) c Bresnan b Coad 1
J. C. Tongue not out....................... 30	– c Köhler-Cadmore b Bresnan...... 8
D. Y. Pennington c Tattersall b Brooks 7	– b Bresnan 9
B 4, lb 6, w 1, nb 4.................... 15	B 3, lb 3, nb 2............. 8

1/29 (2) 2/131 (3) 3/149 (4) (102 overs) 340
4/154 (5) 5/167 (6) 6/255 (7)
7/255 (8) 8/270 (1) 9/319 (10) 10/340 (11)

1/15 (1) 2/33 (2) (50 overs) 221
3/63 (4) 4/122 (3)
5/122 (5) 6/122 (7) 7/132 (8)
8/158 (6) 9/198 (10) 10/221 (11)

Coad 26–10–65–2; Brooks 22–3–94–6; Patterson 23–8–64–1; Bresnan 19–5–62–1; Logan 10–2–40–0; Leaning 2–0–5–0. *Second innings*—Coad 11–1–56–4; Brooks 13–0–69–1; Bresnan 10–1–48–2; Patterson 14–3–38–3; Logan 2–1–4–0.

Yorkshire

A. Lyth lbw b Parnell........................ 27	– c and b Barnard 20
J. A. Raval b Twohig 21	– b Pennington 13
J. A. Leaning b Tongue 13	– not out 22
G. S. Ballance c Pennington b Barnard 194	– c Pennington b Twohig 60
T. Köhler-Cadmore lbw b Twohig............. 8	– not out 8
†J. A. Tattersall b Tongue 19	
T. T. Bresnan c Mitchell b Pennington 7	
*S. A. Patterson b Tongue 6	
J. E. G. Logan lbw b Ali 6	
J. A. Brooks c Cox b Ali 82	
B. O. Coad not out 8	
B 22, lb 7, nb 8...................... 37	Lb 7, w 1, nb 6............. 14

1/30 (1) 2/45 (3) 3/83 (2) (90.5 overs) 428
4/117 (5) 5/161 (6) 6/184 (7)
7/193 (8) 8/232 (9) 9/403 (10) 10/428 (4)

1/39 (2) (3 wkts, 30.1 overs) 137
2/47 (3) 3/124 (4)

Parnell 14–1–84–1; Tongue 14–5–31–3; Barnard 13.5–0–76–1; Pennington 15–2–98–1; Ali 16–3–44–2; Twohig 15–2–47–2; Mitchell 3–0–19–0. *Second innings*—Barnard 11.1–3–31–1; Pennington 7–1–31–1; Ali 6–1–31–0; Twohig 6–0–37–1.

Umpires: R. K. Illingworth and R. J. Warren.

YORKSHIRE

A bumpy ride

DAVID WARNER

The final tables suggest a flat season of average achievement, but it was only in the closing weeks that Yorkshire put months of turbulence behind them. As in 2017, they finished fourth in the County Championship and fifth in the North Group of the T20 Blast, while in the Royal London One-Day Cup they went a stage further, reaching the semi-finals.

Yet, as late as September 10, Yorkshire looked relegation fodder in the Championship; had that happened, knives already sharpened would have been out of their sheaths. That day, they started the Roses match at Headingley in seventh, and by the close sixth-placed Lancashire seemed on top: 105 without loss replying to 209. But next morning Jack Brooks bowled fuller and straighter, to take five wickets and restrict the lead to 43, before the middle order supplied the backbone which allowed Brooks and Ben Coad to snuff out dispirited opponents. The rivals switched positions, and Yorkshire breathed more easily, getting the better of a rain-hit draw with Hampshire, and crushing Worcestershire to avenge a humiliating innings defeat at Scarborough.

Their problems had begun well before the first ball was bowled – and that was not until April 20. The curtain-raisers against Leeds/Bradford MCCU and champions Essex were submerged by a sea of mud, the first complete blanks in first-class cricket at Headingley since 1967.

It was easier to absorb the departures, arrivals and delays at Leeds station than to fathom the comings, goings and derailments at the club. At the AGM in March, director of cricket Martyn Moxon had the unenviable task of explaining to disgruntled members that leg-spinner Adil Rashid wished to concentrate solely on white-ball cricket. Moxon acknowledged that Rashid was an invaluable part of Yorkshire's one-day set-up – but in July, England controversially drafted him into their Test squad to play India, so he barely appeared in the Vitality Blast. Rashid later signed a deal agreeing to appear in all competitions in 2019.

Another serious blow came in mid-May. Captain Gary Ballance withdrew from the Championship side at The Oval because of stress symptoms; Joe Root stood in, the second of five players who would lead the team, the most since 1956. Though Ballance returned, he stepped down as captain. Steve Patterson took over, at first temporarily and then permanently when his contract was extended by two years. Patterson had his own problems, missing the season's start with one broken finger, and sidelined for a month by another.

It was a difficult summer for overseas players. Giant fast bowler Billy Stanlake was signed for the T20 Blast, but Cricket Australia pulled him out before he arrived, while New Zealand captain Kane Williamson's fourth season at Headingley was significantly reduced by his board. Indian batsman

Cheteshwar Pujara, at the start of the Championship, and New Zealand opener Jeet Raval, towards the end, scraped 256 between them in 19 innings. Pujara did better in the Royal London Cup, with consecutive scores of 82, 73, 101 and 75 not out before tailing off, and Williamson revealed his true self in the Blast and his last two Championship matches – after beginning with nought and one at Old Trafford.

Steve Patterson

Trying to patch gaps left by Rashid's absence and injuries to fast bowlers, Yorkshire recruited leg-spinner Josh Poysden from Warwickshire and South African seamer Mat Pillans from Surrey, both initially on loan but given three-year deals from 2019; neither achieved much. After plenty of contract discussions, David Willey and Tim Bresnan stayed put, but the 34-year-old Brooks – the top wicket-taker – moved to Somerset on a three-year deal that Yorkshire could not match, and Liam Plunkett joined Surrey. Brooks's departure will be more keenly felt, and he might have remained if negotiations had not dragged on. His first match after the die was cast was against Somerset: he claimed five in the first innings, and was to take 25 of his season's haul of 51 in the last five games. Coad continued where he left off in 2017, and would have outstripped Brooks had he not missed four matches through injury; he still managed 48 at 16.

Tom Köhler-Cadmore smashed 447 in the first five Royal London matches, was called up by the England Lions one-day team and, when he eventually appeared in the Championship, played a key role in preserving first-division status, with an unbeaten century against Lancashire. Out-of-touch Alex Lees moved to Durham, while off-spinner Azeem Rafiq and wicketkeeper Andrew Hodd were not retained. But one of the season's most encouraging aspects was the form of 23-year-old batsman Jonny Tattersall, given another chance after being released in 2015. He agreed to take up wicketkeeping, and his work with gloves and bat was exemplary.

In the new year, former all-rounder Paul Grayson, who had been working with the Yorkshire Diamonds women's team and Durham MCCU, joined the staff as a specialist batting coach, backing up Andrew Gale and bowling coach Rich Pyrah.

Off the field, club chairman Steve Denison resigned in July after a report claimed that, as a senior auditor at PricewaterhouseCoopers, he had failed to flag up major risks at department store BHS before it collapsed; Robin Smith returned for a second stint as chairman. It was all part and parcel of a season that was far from flat.

Championship attendance: 48,155.

YORKSHIRE RESULTS

All first-class matches – Played 13: Won 5, Lost 5, Drawn 3. Abandoned 2.
County Championship matches – Played 13: Won 5, Lost 5, Drawn 3. Abandoned 1.

Specsavers County Championship, 4th in Division 1;
Vitality Blast, 5th in North Group; Royal London One-Day Cup, semi-finalists.

COUNTY CHAMPIONSHIP AVERAGES, BATTING AND FIELDING

Cap		Birthplace	M	I	NO	R	HS	100	Avge	Ct
	T. Köhler-Cadmore....	Chatham	6	11	2	414	106	2	46.00	4
2011	J. M. Bairstow§.......	Bradford‡	3	6	0	263	95	0	43.83	9
2012	†G. S. Ballance.......	Harare, Zimbabwe ..	12	23	0	906	194	3	39.39	4
	K. S. Williamson¶.....	Tauranga, NZ ..	3	6	0	218	87	0	36.33	3
	J. A. Tattersall.......	Harrogate‡	7	12	1	350	70	0	31.81	19
2016	A. J. Hodd...........	Chichester	3	6	0	175	85	0	29.16	12
2010	†A. Lyth	Whitby‡	13	25	1	656	134*	1	27.33	16
2016	J. A. Leaning	Bristol	8	16	2	371	68	0	26.50	9
	H. C. Brook..........	Keighley‡	12	23	0	575	124	1	25.00	7
	J. Shaw.............	Wakefield‡.......	3	6	1	104	42	0	20.80	0
2006	T. T. Bresnan	Pontefract‡......	12	22	3	385	80	0	20.26	9
2012	S. A. Patterson	Beverley‡	8	13	2	205	45*	0	18.63	2
2018	B. O. Coad	Harrogate‡	9	15	7	135	33	0	16.87	0
2012	J. E. Root§..........	Sheffield‡........	3	6	0	97	35	0	16.16	2
	M. J. Waite	Leeds‡..........	4	6	0	96	42	0	16.00	0
2013	J. A. Brooks	Oxford	13	22	3	303	82	0	15.94	1
	C. A. Pujara¶	Rajkot, India	6	12	0	172	41	0	14.33	4
2016	†D. J. Willey§........	Northampton	2	4	1	42	34*	0	14.00	0
	M. D. Fisher	York‡..........	2	4	1	39	20*	0	13.00	1
	†J. A. Raval¶	Ahmedabad, India ..	4	7	0	84	21	0	12.00	3
	†J. E. Poysden	Shoreham-by-Sea ..	3	5	2	25	20*	0	8.33	1
2014	†A. Z. Lees..........	Halifax‡.........	4	8	0	50	39	0	6.25	1

Also batted: †K. Carver (*Northallerton‡*) (1 match) 1*, 0*; †J. E. G. Logan (*Wakefield‡*) (1 match) 6 (1 ct); M. W. Pillans†† (*Durban, SA*) (1 match) 8.

‡ *Born in Yorkshire.* § *ECB contract.* ¶ *Official overseas player.* †† *Other non-England-qualified.*

BOWLING

	Style	O	M	R	W	BB	5I	Avge
B. O. Coad	RFM	272.5	87	784	48	6-81	3	16.33
S. A. Patterson	RFM	235	63	594	24	6-40	1	24.75
T. T. Bresnan	RFM	279.5	48	969	35	5-28	1	27.68
J. A. Brooks	RFM	346.3	51	1,430	51	6-94	5	28.03

Also bowled: H. C. Brook (RM) 22.1–5–67–0; M. D. Fisher (RFM) 54–6–219–2; J. A. Leaning (OB) 19–3–57–1; J. E. G. Logan (SLA) 12–3–44–0; A. Lyth (OB) 68–8–246–4; M. W. Pillans (RFM) 30–5–130–0; J. E. Poysden (LB) 52.2–1–259–7; J. E. Root (OB) 20.4–7–37–5; J. Shaw (RFM) 63–5–265–4; M. J. Waite (RFM) 61–14–221–8; D. J. Willey (LFM) 67.2–13–217–6; K. S. Williamson (OB) 2–0–9–0.

LEADING ROYAL LONDON CUP AVERAGES (125 runs/4 wickets)

Batting	Runs	HS	Avge	SR	Ct/St
D. J. Willey	202	131	67.33	107.44	0
A. Lyth.........	433	144	54.12	99.08	1
C. A. Pujara	370	101	52.85	90.02	4
T. Köhler-Cadmore	472	164	52.44	101.50	11
G. S. Ballance .	247	91	49.40	100.40	0
J. A. Tattersall .	143	89	47.66	103.62	5/1
T. T. Bresnan ...	140	41	28.00	97.90	2

Bowling	W	BB	Avge	ER
D. J. Willey.....	11	4-47	11.81	5.45
A. U. Rashid.....	14	4-47	28.92	6.32
M. D. Fisher	9	3-40	29.77	5.56
B. O. Coad	9	2-40	30.11	5.01
S. A. Patterson ...	13	4-36	31.46	5.55
T. T. Bresnan	7	2-39	48.28	5.92

LEADING VITALITY BLAST AVERAGES (100 runs/15 overs)

Batting	Runs	HS	Avge	SR	Ct/St	Bowling	W	BB	Avge	ER
A. Lyth	401	92*	30.84	153.05	6	L. E. Plunkett. . . .	4	2-25	34.50	**7.66**
K. S. Williamson	280	77	40.00	148.14	2	J. A. Brooks.	9	3-21	29.77	**7.76**
H. C. Brook. . . .	165	44	27.50	144.73	0	S. A. Patterson . .	12	3-35	27.91	**7.97**
D. J. Willey	386	80	38.60	142.96	3	J. A. Thompson . .	8	3-23	24.00	**8.34**
G. S. Ballance . .	269	79	22.41	141.57	3	D. J. Willey	9	3-30	32.88	**8.45**
T. Köhler-Cadmore	321	73	24.69	140.17	4	Azeem Rafiq	8	2-28	41.75	**9.02**
J. A. Tattersall . .	165	53*	23.57	135.24	8/2	M. D. Fisher	7	2-26	33.71	**10.26**
T. T. Bresnan . .	106	28*	17.66	134.17	5	T. T. Bresnan	5	3-38	62.40	**10.45**

FIRST-CLASS COUNTY RECORDS

Highest score for	341	G. H. Hirst v Leicestershire at Leicester	1905
Highest score against	318*	W. G. Grace (Gloucestershire) at Cheltenham . . .	1876
Leading run-scorer	38,558	H. Sutcliffe (avge 50.20).	1919–45
Best bowling for	10-10	H. Verity v Nottinghamshire at Leeds	1932
Best bowling against	10-37	C. V. Grimmett (Australians) at Sheffield.	1930
Leading wicket-taker	3,597	W. Rhodes (avge 16.02)	1898–1930
Highest total for	887	v Warwickshire at Birmingham	1896
Highest total against	681-7 dec	by Leicestershire at Bradford	1996
Lowest total for	23	v Hampshire at Middlesbrough.	1965
Lowest total against	13	by Nottinghamshire at Nottingham.	1901

LIST A COUNTY RECORDS

Highest score for	191	D. S. Lehmann v Nottinghamshire at Scarborough	2001
Highest score against	177	S. A. Newman v Surrey) at The Oval	2009
Leading run-scorer	8,699	G. Boycott (avge 40.08)	1963–86
Best bowling for	7-15	R. A. Hutton v Worcestershire at Leeds	1969
Best bowling against	7-32	R. G. D. Willis (Warwickshire) at Birmingham . .	1981
Leading wicket-taker	308	C. M. Old (avge 18.96)	1967–82
Highest total for	411-6	v Devon at Exmouth	2004
Highest total against	375-4	by Surrey at Scarborough	1994
Lowest total for	54	v Essex at Leeds	2003
Lowest total against	23	by Middlesex at Leeds	1974

TWENTY20 COUNTY RECORDS

Highest score for	161	A. Lyth v Northamptonshire at Leeds.	2017
Highest score against	111	D. L. Maddy (Leicestershire) at Leeds	2004
Leading run-scorer	2,260	A. W. Gale (avge 25.39, SR 120.53)	2004–15
Best bowling for	6-19	T. T. Bresnan v Lancashire at Leeds.	2017
Best bowling against	4-9	C. K. Langeveldt (Derbyshire) at Leeds	2008
Leading wicket-taker {	110	A. U. Rashid (avge 24.25, ER 7.62)	2008–18
	110	T. T. Bresnan (avge 25.42, ER 8.09)	2003–18
Highest total for	260-4	v Northamptonshire at Leeds	2017
Highest total against	231-4	by Lancashire at Manchester.	2015
Lowest total for	90-9	v Durham at Chester-le-Street.	2009
Lowest total against	90	by Glamorgan at Cardiff	2016

ADDRESS

Emerald Headingley, Leeds LS6 3BU; 0843 504 3099; cricket@yorkshireccc; www.york-shireccc.com.

OFFICIALS

Captain 2018 G. S. Ballance/S. A. Patterson	**President** R. A. Hutton
2019 S. A. Patterson	**Chairman** R. Smith
Director of cricket M. D. Moxon	**Chief executive** M. A. Arthur
First-team coach A. W. Gale	**Head groundsman** A. Fogarty
2nd XI coach/Academy director I. M. Dews	**Scorer** J. T. Potter

YORKSHIRE v LEEDS/BRADFORD MCCU

At Leeds, April 7–9. Abandoned.

A waterlogged pitch led to the first washout of a first-class match at Headingley since 1967.

YORKSHIRE v ESSEX

At Leeds, April 13–16. Abandoned. Yorkshire 5pts, Essex 5pts.

Weeks of rain and snow left parts of the outfield a quagmire. It was Yorkshire's first abandonment in four-day cricket at any venue, and their first in the County Championship since 1987, at Hastings. Their last home Championship washout was in 1985, at Abbeydale Park in Sheffield; then, too, the visitors were the reigning champions Essex, who had not suffered a first-class abandonment since.

YORKSHIRE v NOTTINGHAMSHIRE

At Leeds, April 20–23. Yorkshire won by 164 runs. Yorkshire 21pts, Nottinghamshire 3pts. Toss: uncontested.

Yorkshire finally started their season after seven blank days, and secured a comfortable victory despite missing four fast bowlers (Patterson and Fisher were injured, Plunkett and Willey at the IPL) and two batsmen (England withheld Root and Bairstow). Their mainstays of 2017, Ballance and Coad, continued more or less where they had left off. Though he fell for a duck after a casual shot on the first morning – when Yorkshire slipped to 93 for five – Ballance atoned with a captain's knock in the second innings. After his 82 established a lead of 68, he shared a crucial fifth-wicket stand of 103 with Leaning that stretched their advantage to 266, before Bresnan pushed it past 400. Coad, just recovered from a hip injury, was a constant menace; he had taken eight in the Championship opener a year earlier, and went two better this time. For Nottinghamshire, Gurney collected six, including three in ten balls in the second innings, though only Taylor reached 50. Ballance claimed the extra half-hour on the third evening with the visitors 155 for seven; only one further wicket fell before play ended in bright sunshine at 7.40, but it was all over inside an hour next day.

Close of play: first day, Nottinghamshire 53-4 (Taylor 34, Wessels 8); second day, Yorkshire 189-4 (Ballance 76, Leaning 37); third day, Nottinghamshire 181-8 (Moores 10, Ball 8).

Yorkshire

A. Lyth lbw b Gurney	45	– c Moores b Wood	12
A. Z. Lees c Taylor b Ball	6	– lbw b Ball	0
C. A. Pujara lbw b Fletcher	2	– run out (Libby/Gurney)	18
*G. S. Ballance c Patel b Ball	0	– b Gurney	82
H. C. Brook b Wood	22	– b Ball	36
J. A. Leaning c Mullaney b Fletcher	12	– lbw b Gurney	37
†A. J. Hodd b Gurney	62	– lbw b Gurney	3
T. T. Bresnan lbw b Fletcher	10	– not out	68
J. Shaw c Moores b Gurney	17	– c Moores b Fletcher	6
J. A. Brooks not out	30	– c Moores b Ball	13
B. O. Coad c Patel b Fletcher	18	– c Mullaney b Fletcher	33
B 3, lb 18, w 5, nb 6	32	B 5, lb 17, nb 4	26

1/25 (2) 2/36 (3) 3/37 (4) (74.1 overs) 256
4/87 (1) 5/93 (5) 6/137 (6)
7/155 (8) 8/191 (9) 9/212 (7) 10/256 (11)

1/5 (2) 2/28 (3) (108.2 overs) 334
3/37 (1) 4/95 (5)
5/198 (6) 6/199 (4) 7/204 (7)
8/228 (9) 9/257 (10) 10/334 (11)

Ball 17–2–51–2; Fletcher 18.1–8–47–4; Gurney 20–4–46–3; Wood 13–0–70–1; Patel 6–1–21–0. *Second innings*—Ball 22–4–69–3; Fletcher 23.2–10–45–2; Gurney 27–4–86–3; Wood 19–1–63–1; Patel 15–4–45–0; Nash 2–0–4–0.

Nottinghamshire

*S. J. Mullaney b Brooks	0	– lbw b Coad	13
J. D. Libby lbw b Coad	6	– b Coad	38
C. D. Nash c Hodd b Brooks	0	– c Hodd b Bresnan	23
L. R. P. L. Taylor c Leaning b Coad	57	– c Hodd b Brooks	30
S. R. Patel lbw b Brooks	4	– b Coad	7
M. H. Wessels c Leaning b Bresnan	40	– c Hodd b Shaw	33
†T. J. Moores c Leaning b Coad	1	– (8) not out	40
L. Wood b Lyth b Bresnan	17	– (9) c Leaning b Coad	10
L. J. Fletcher run out (Brooks)	8	– (7) b Brooks	2
J. T. Ball not out	44	– b Coad	30
H. F. Gurney c Bresnan b Coad	2	– c Lyth b Coad	0
B 5, lb 2, nb 2	9	B 1, lb 10, w 1	12

1/0 (1) 2/6 (3) 3/6 (2)	(46.2 overs) 188	1/21 (1) 2/59 (3)	(58.4 overs) 238
4/39 (5) 5/100 (4) 6/102 (7)		3/81 (2) 4/101 (5)
7/127 (8) 8/130 (6) 9/179 (9) 10/188 (11)		5/135 (4) 6/143 (7) 7/151 (6)
		8/172 (9) 9/238 (10) 10/238 (11)

Brooks 14–3–58–3; Coad 13.2–4–49–4; Bresnan 13–3–45–2; Shaw 6–0–29–0. *Second innings*—Brooks 18–2–77–2; Coad 19.4–6–81–6; Shaw 10–0–46–1; Bresnan 8–2–19–1; Lyth 3–2–4–0.

Umpires: N. G. B. Cook and M. A. Gough.

At Taunton, April 27–30. YORKSHIRE lost to SOMERSET by 118 runs.

At Chelmsford, May 4–6. YORKSHIRE beat ESSEX by 91 runs. *Yorkshire are bowled out for 50 on the first morning.*

At The Oval, May 11–14. YORKSHIRE lost to SURREY by an innings and 17 runs.

At Southampton, June 20–23. YORKSHIRE drew with HAMPSHIRE.

YORKSHIRE v SURREY

At Scarborough, June 25–28. Surrey won by seven wickets. Surrey 21pts, Yorkshire 6pts. Toss: Yorkshire.

A capricious sea fret halted Surrey's first innings nine times before ending play early on the second evening. Next morning, Coad grabbed their last three batsmen in four balls, to leave them trailing by 75, but three quick wickets from Morkel soon left Yorkshire floundering. From then on it was plain sailing for the Division One leaders – who noted that the last five champions had all won at North Marine Road – while Yorkshire's third defeat put them in the relegation zone. With seven players called up by England or the Lions, their top order struggled. Lees's solitary run took him to 50 from eight innings; Pujara waited 70 minutes to get off the mark on the first day and joined the Indian tourists without a half-century in a dozen first-class knocks. Tattersall's spirited maiden fifty kept Yorkshire's first innings competitive, but Morkel and Dernbach were so troublesome second time around that only Patterson reached 25. Pope and Burns – Division One's leading run-scorers – batted splendidly; only a careless moment late on denied the clean-hitting Burns his third century of the season. With Stoneman and Borthwick, he blunted a home attack lacking a regular spinner. The one blot on Surrey's seaside trip was a five-run penalty after two Level One disciplinary offences by Dernbach and Stoneman; the runs were added to Yorkshire's first innings after it ended. While making no excuses, Surrey apparently linked their behaviour to a tense atmosphere after Ryan Patel was racially abused by a spectator.

Close of play: first day, Yorkshire 299-8 (Patterson 8, Brooks 9); second day, Surrey 219-7 (Pope 34, Morkel 18); third day, Surrey 89-0 (Burns 55, Stoneman 32).

Yorkshire

A. Lyth c de Bruyn b Morkel	42	– c Pope b Morkel	7
A. Z. Lees c and b Dernbach	0	– c Dernbach b Morkel	1
C. A. Pujara c Jacks b Virdi	23	– b Dernbach	17
G. S. Ballance b Clarke	54	– c Jacks b Morkel	15
H. C. Brook lbw b Virdi	0	– c Pope b Clarke	6
J. A. Leaning c Jacks b Dernbach	21	– c Pope b Morkel	15
†J. A. Tattersall c Borthwick b Morkel	70	– lbw b Morkel	23
T. T. Bresnan b Clarke	48	– c Pope b Patel	18
*S. A. Patterson b Dernbach	21	– not out	25
J. A. Brooks c Burns b Dernbach	27	– c Clarke b Dernbach	13
B. O. Coad not out	0	– b Dernbach	4
B 11, lb 6, nb 14, p 5	36	Lb 8	8

1/6 (2) 2/51 (1) 3/107 (3) (102.5 overs) 342
4/107 (5) 5/139 (4) 6/166 (6)
7/266 (8) 8/276 (7) 9/337 (10) 10/337 (9)

1/3 (2) 2/8 (1) (63.4 overs) 152
3/24 (4) 4/42 (5)
5/48 (3) 6/70 (6) 7/103 (8)
8/115 (7) 9/148 (10) 10/152 (11)

Morkel 26–7–63–2; Dernbach 24.5–3–104–4; Clarke 20–6–52–2; Patel 11–3–28–0; Virdi 20–1–69–2; Borthwick 1–0–4–0. *Second innings*—Morkel 16–4–39–5; Dernbach 13.4–5–34–3; Clarke 12–3–25–1; Virdi 18–6–32–0; Patel 4–1–14–1.

Surrey

*R. J. Burns c Tattersall b Coad	59	– c Lees b Bresnan	97
M. D. Stoneman c Tattersall b Coad	9	– lbw b Coad	32
S. G. Borthwick c Tattersall b Bresnan	20	– b Leaning	62
R. S. Patel c Brook b Bresnan	32	– not out	24
T. B. de Bruyn c Tattersall b Patterson	38	– not out	8
†O. J. D. Pope not out	69		
W. G. Jacks lbw b Patterson	7		
R. Clarke c and b Bresnan	0		
M. Morkel c Lyth b Coad	29		
J. W. Dernbach c Leaning b Coad	0		
G. S. Virdi b Coad	0		
Nb 4	4	Lb 4, nb 2	6

1/9 (2) 2/71 (3) 3/105 (1) (83.2 overs) 267
4/140 (4) 5/172 (5) 6/192 (7)
7/197 (8) 8/253 (9) 9/253 (10) 10/267 (11)

1/99 (2) (3 wkts, 66.1 overs) 229
2/146 (1) 3/220 (3)

Coad 20.2–5–53–5; Brooks 15–1–73–0; Patterson 26–7–61–2; Bresnan 21–2–77–3; Lyth 1–0–3–0. *Second innings*—Coad 17–6–47–1; Brooks 14–2–53–0; Patterson 14–4–39–0; Bresnan 9–0–51–1; Lyth 3–1–10–0; Leaning 8–3–16–1; Brook 1.1–0–9–0.

Umpires: P. J. Hartley and P. R. Pollard.

At Manchester, July 22–24. YORKSHIRE beat LANCASHIRE by 118 runs.

YORKSHIRE v WORCESTERSHIRE

At Scarborough, August 19–22. Worcestershire won by an innings and 186 runs. Worcestershire 24pts, Yorkshire 1pt. Toss: uncontested.

Bottom-of-the-table Worcestershire dominated from start to finish. A festival crowd totalling over 13,000 watched in stunned silence, though they gave standing ovations to Ali and Mitchell. Ali became the first player to score a double-century and take six in an innings in a Yorkshire match (George Hirst managed 232 not out and five for 43 against Surrey in 1905). Mitchell, meanwhile, shared a century stand with new opening partner Fell and 294 with Ali, a second-wicket record for this fixture, to set up Worcestershire's highest total against Yorkshire. For the hosts, Williamson showed his class with two half-centuries, but even he was troubled by 19-year-old paceman Dillon

CHAMPIONSHIP DOUBLE-HUNDRED AND SIX-WICKET RETURN

244	6-61	C. M. Wells	Middlesex v Nottinghamshire at Nottingham	1899
200*	7-44	E. G. Arnold	Worcestershire v Warwickshire at Birmingham . . .	1909
210*	9-47	J. W. H. T. Douglas . . .	Essex v Derbyshire at Leyton.	1921
202	6-65	J. W. Hearne	Middlesex v Warwickshire at Birmingham	1921
277*	6-78	T. F. Shepherd	Surrey v Gloucestershire at The Oval	1927
280*	6-31	E. H. Bowley	Sussex v Gloucestershire at Hove	1929
222*	7-69	W. J. Edrich	Middlesex v Northamptonshire at Northampton . . .	1946
219	**6-49**	**M. M. Ali**	**Worcestershire v Yorkshire at Scarborough**. . . .	**2018**

W. G. Grace scored 221* and took 6-45 for Gloucestershire v Middlesex at Clifton in 1885, before the formal establishment of the County Championship in 1890.

Pennington, who took a career-best four for 53 in his third first-class outing. This was Ali's match, however. Released from England's Test squad, he batted over six hours for 219 in 277 balls, the highest score against Yorkshire at North Marine Road; soon after, he was back in the thick of it, claiming the first four second-innings wickets, and he led his side to victory on the final morning – half an hour after England lost to India at Trent Bridge.

Close of play: first day, Worcestershire 39-0 (Mitchell 16, Fell 21); second day, Worcestershire 310-1 (Mitchell 140, Ali 107); third day, Yorkshire 140-6 (Tattersall 6, Willey 0).

Yorkshire

A. Lyth lbw b Barnard	20	– lbw b Ali	17
H. C. Brook c Pennington b Tongue	6	– c Tongue b Ali	16
K. S. Williamson b Ali.	87	– c Cox b Parnell	61
G. S. Ballance c Barnard b Pennington	3	– c Clarke b Ali	19
T. Köhler-Cadmore c Barnard b Pennington	0	– lbw b Ali	8
†J. A. Tattersall c Mitchell b Pennington	27	– not out	15
T. T. Bresnan c Fell b Pennington	2	– c Mitchell b Parnell	0
*D. J. Willey c Clarke b Ali.	0	– b Ali	5
M. D. Fisher not out	20	– c Cox b Ali	0
J. A. Brooks c and b Barnard	38	– b Pennington	9
J. E. Poysden c Fell b Barnard	1	– c Mitchell b Pennington.	1
B 2, lb 6, nb 4.	12	B 10, lb 5, nb 4	19

1/8 (2)	2/42 (1)	3/63 (4)	(61.4 overs) 216	1/37 (1) 2/40 (2) (62.1 overs) 170
4/63 (5)	5/151 (6)	6/153 (3)		3/92 (4) 4/116 (5)
7/155 (7)	8/155 (8)	9/211 (10) 10/216 (11)		5/136 (3) 6/138 (7) 7/149 (8)
				8/149 (9) 9/164 (10) 10/170 (11)

Parnell 12–0–47–0; Tongue 14–4–36–1; Barnard 12.4–3–32–3; Pennington 16–2–53–4; Ali 7–0–40–2. *Second innings*—Parnell 16–5–33–2; Tongue 10–2–28–0; Barnard 5–0–18–0; Pennington 8.1–3–27–2; Ali 23–7–49–6.

Worcestershire

D. K. H. Mitchell c Bresnan b Lyth	178	A. G. Milton not out	9
T. C. Fell lbw b Brooks	45	B 10, lb 14, w 1, nb 4	29
*M. M. Ali c Brook b Bresnan	219		
J. M. Clarke lbw b Lyth.	34	1/111 (2) (7 wkts dec, 139.2 overs) 572
†O. B. Cox lbw b Poysden	18	2/405 (1) 3/473 (4)
R. A. Whiteley c Bresnan b Poysden	6	4/522 (3) 5/525 (5)
E. G. Barnard c Fisher b Poysden	34	6/544 (6) 7/572 (7) 110 overs: 414-2

W. D. Parnell, J. C. Tongue and D. Y. Pennington did not bat.

Brooks 23–5–77–1; Willey 24–3–71–0; Fisher 26–5–84–0; Bresnan 22–3–91–1; Poysden 25.2–1–128–3; Lyth 19–1–97–2.

Umpires: N. A. Mallender and R. T. Robinson.

YORKSHIRE v SOMERSET

At Leeds, August 29–September 1. Somerset won by 224 runs. Somerset 23pts, Yorkshire 6pts. Toss: Yorkshire.

For the first time, Somerset recorded three consecutive wins against Yorkshire; the hosts were pushed back into the relegation zone, while Somerset strengthened their own hold on second place. Even when Brooks dismissed five of their batsmen, it was a promise of things to come; he had just confirmed he would be joining Somerset in 2019. Meanwhile Hodd, who had announced his imminent retirement, made an unexpected return for Yorkshire. Down in Taunton with the Seconds, he was called up when keeper Jonny Tattersall suffered a back spasm. Hodd held three catches and added 173 with Köhler-Cadmore in a recovery from 119 for five, though he later became the match's fifth batsman to fall in the eighties. At 29 for three, Somerset led by just 108, but Hildreth and Gregory made fifties again, and Abell stroked an unbeaten 132, his only century of the season. In a strong team effort, Gregory stood out, his runs and wickets coming exactly when needed. There was some resistance on the final morning, as nightwatchman Shaw kept Williamson company until ten minutes before lunch; Williamson passed 50 on his last appearance of the season for Yorkshire, but was one of six victims for the Overton twins as the wheels fell off.

Close of play: first day, Somerset 374-8 (J. Overton 8, Leach 3); second day, Yorkshire 292-7 (Hodd 84); third day, Yorkshire 8-2 (Shaw 4, Williamson 0).

Somerset

M. E. Trescothick c Lyth b Willey	4	– c Lyth b Willey	15
E. J. Byrom c Hodd b Brooks	1	– b Willey	4
Azhar Ali b Shaw	89	– c Ballance b Fisher	9
J. C. Hildreth c Köhler-Cadmore b Willey	81	– c Hodd b Lyth	72
*T. B. Abell c Hodd b Brooks	12	– not out	132
†S. M. Davies c Ballance b Brooks	80	– c Lyth b Fisher	6
L. Gregory c Williamson b Brooks	65	– c Williamson b Willey	57
C. Overton c Hodd b Shaw	15	– run out (Shaw/Hodd)	27
J. Overton c Leaning b Brooks	8		
M. J. Leach c Lyth b Willey	9		
J. H. Davey not out	13		
B 1, lb 17, nb 4	22	B 4, lb 10, w 1, nb 2	17

1/5 (2) 2/5 (1) 3/142 (4) (103.2 overs) 399 1/8 (2) (7 wkts dec, 70.1 overs) 339
4/170 (5) 5/229 (3) 6/343 (7) 2/28 (3) 3/29 (1)
7/343 (6) 8/369 (8) 9/375 (9) 10/399 (10) 4/164 (4) 5/184 (6) 6/277 (7) 7/339 (8)

Brooks 29–8–116–5; Willey 26.2–8–74–3; Fisher 14–0–55–0; Shaw 21–3–72–2; Lyth 6–0–32–0; Williamson 2–0–9–0; Brook 5–1–23–0. *Second innings*—Brooks 17.1–2–81–0; Willey 17–2–72–3; Fisher 14–1–80–2; Shaw 9–0–42–0; Brook 7–1–19–0; Lyth 5–0–18–1; Leaning 1–0–13–0.

Yorkshire

A. Lyth c Trescothick b Davey	45	– c Davies b Gregory	4
H. C. Brook b Gregory	2	– b Gregory	0
K. S. Williamson c Leach b C. Overton	18	– (4) c Davies b C. Overton	51
G. S. Ballance c Leach b C. Overton	37	– (5) b J. Overton	4
J. A. Leaning c and b Davey	4	– (7) b J. Overton	2
T. Köhler-Cadmore c Davies b Davey	81	– (6) b C. Overton	0
†A. J. Hodd c Hildreth b Gregory	85	– (8) b Gregory	24
M. D. Fisher lbw b Davey	0	– (9) c Gregory b J. Overton	19
*D. J. Willey c Hildreth b Davey	3	– (10) not out	34
J. A. Brooks c Davey b C. Overton	14	– (11) c Trescothick b J. Overton	4
J. Shaw not out	10	– (3) lbw b Gregory	42
Lb 11, nb 10	21	Lb 8, nb 2	10

1/5 (2) 2/52 (3) 3/111 (1) (97.2 overs) 320 1/3 (2) 2/4 (1) (78.3 overs) 194
4/119 (4) 5/119 (5) 6/292 (6) 3/94 (3) 4/99 (4)
7/292 (8) 8/296 (9) 9/296 (7) 10/320 (10) 5/103 (6) 6/103 (5) 7/124 (7)
8/143 (8) 9/188 (9) 10/194 (11)

Gregory 25–8–66–2; Davey 23–7–65–5; C. Overton 18.2–3–59–3; J. Overton 11–1–56–0; Abell 6–0–20–0; Leach 14–1–43–0. *Second innings*—Gregory 18–8–33–4; Davey 14–6–27–0; C. Overton 16–4–45–2; Leach 14–3–47–0; J. Overton 14.3–6–25–4; Abell 2–0–9–0.

Umpires: P. J. Hartley and G. D. Lloyd.

At Nottingham, September 4–7. YORKSHIRE drew with NOTTINGHAMSHIRE.

YORKSHIRE v LANCASHIRE

At Leeds, September 10–13. Yorkshire won by 95 runs. Yorkshire 20pts, Lancashire 5pts. Toss: uncontested. County debut: R. J. Gleeson.

Yorkshire's first Roses double since 2001 flung them a lifeline, while Lancashire were sucked closer to the second division. The home side started one point behind their opponents, with a game in hand. But the gap seemed to be growing on the first day: Lancashire reached 105 without loss in reply to a total of 209 relying heavily on Köhler-Cadmore's second century in successive innings. Fortunes began to shift, however, once Coad dismissed Brown with the opening delivery next morning. When Davies, who had taken advantage of loose bowling the previous evening, was snared by Brooks just after lunch, Lancashire were 166 for five, though a late assault from Maharaj earned two batting points and a 43-run lead. Again, Yorkshire's brittle top order let them down, but Ballance and Köhler-Cadmore steadied them with a fourth-wicket stand of 148, and the eventual target was 230. For the second day running, Brooks and Coad knocked the stuffing out of Lancashire. After removing Davies and Croft, who both fell to lazy strokes, they hit the stumps five times between them, and finished with 16 wickets as Yorkshire won early on the fourth morning.

Close of play: first day, Lancashire 105-0 (Brown 43, Davies 57); second day, Yorkshire 127-3 (Ballance 53, Köhler-Cadmore 42); third day, Lancashire 109-7 (Bohannon 6, Maharaj 6).

Yorkshire

A. Lyth c Vilas b Bailey	16	– c Vilas b Onions	7
J. A. Raval b Onions	8	– lbw b Bailey	10
H. C. Brook c Vilas b Bailey	3	– b Bailey	5
G. S. Ballance lbw b Bailey	5	– lbw b Maharaj	85
T. Köhler-Cadmore not out	105	– lbw b Maharaj	63
†J. A. Tattersall lbw b Onions	33	– c Vilas b Bailey	22
T. T. Bresnan c Vilas b Onions	0	– c and b Maharaj	20
M. J. Waite c Vilas b Onions	0	– lbw b Onions	15
*S. A. Patterson b Gleeson	17	– b Bailey	9
J. A. Brooks c Maharaj b Gleeson	6	– c Croft b Gleeson	1
B. O. Coad c Bohannon b Gleeson	12	– not out	7
B 2, lb 2	4	B 4, lb 20, nb 4	28

1/20 (2) 2/23 (3) 3/32 (1)   (60.4 overs) 209 1/17 (1) 2/19 (1)   (101.2 overs) 272
4/33 (4) 5/138 (6) 6/142 (7)   3/27 (3) 4/175 (5)
7/144 (8) 8/177 (9) 9/187 (10) 10/209 (11)   5/192 (4) 6/214 (6) 7/238 (8)
                                                    8/250 (9) 9/254 (7) 10/272 (10)

Bailey 14–4–18–3; Onions 21–6–76–4; Gleeson 15.4–2–74–3; Lamb 2–1–5–0; Maharaj 8–1–32–0. *Second innings*—Bailey 29–6–69–4; Onions 24–5–77–2; Gleeson 10.2–3–31–1; Maharaj 32–12–52–3; Lamb 2–0–13–0; Livingstone 1–0–3–0; Bohannon 3–1–3–0.

Lancashire

K. R. Brown c Tattersall b Coad	43	– lbw b Bresnan	10
A. L. Davies lbw b Brooks	87	– c Tattersall b Coad	8
S. J. Croft c Lyth b Brooks	11	– c Raval b Brooks	13
*L. S. Livingstone b Brooks	7	– b Brooks	28
†D. J. Vilas lbw b Brooks	0	– b Coad	10
J. J. Bohannon lbw b Brooks	10	– c Bresnan b Coad	13
D. J. Lamb c Tattersall b Bresnan	9	– lbw b Coad	0
T. E. Bailey c Tattersall b Waite	16	– b Coad	7
K. A. Maharaj c Patterson b Coad	38	– b Brooks	18
G. Onions b Waite	3	– b Brooks	4
R. J. Gleeson not out	9	– not out	0
B 13, lb 2, nb 4	19	B 2, lb 19, nb 2	23

1/105 (1) 2/145 (3) 3/153 (4)   (84.2 overs) 252
4/157 (5) 5/166 (2) 6/175 (6)
7/198 (8) 8/212 (7) 9/221 (10) 10/252 (9)

1/11 (2) 2/31 (1)   (48.1 overs) 134
3/66 (3) 4/81 (4)
5/87 (5) 6/87 (7) 7/95 (8)
8/122 (9) 9/134 (10) 10/134 (6)

Coad 17.2–5–57–2; Brooks 17–4–66–5; Patterson 22–6–40–0; Bresnan 17–3–58–1; Waite 11–5–16–2. *Second innings*—Coad 15.1–6–24–5; Brooks 15–4–47–4; Bresnan 7–0–17–1; Patterson 9–3–23–0; Waite 2–1–2–0.

Umpires: R. J. Bailey and D. J. Millns.

YORKSHIRE v HAMPSHIRE

At Leeds, September 18–21. Drawn. Yorkshire 8pts, Hampshire 8pts. Toss: uncontested.

Stormy weather wiped out much of the third day and all of the fourth, though a draw ensured Hampshire's survival and left Yorkshire needing only two more points. Had play continued, they might well have won, thanks to Bresnan and Lyth, who both ended lean spells. Although conditions were extremely difficult – on the second day, the wind was so strong it blew down an advertising board, which struck a spectator on the head – bowlers on both sides turned in economical figures. Bresnan claimed five for 28, his ninth five-wicket haul in first-class cricket and, surprisingly, a career-best; neither team managed a batting point. But the pitch eased, and in the second innings Lyth reached the game's first fifty. Well supported by Tattersall, he advanced on the third day to an unbeaten 134, his first first-class century since June 2017; he was put down on 80 and 94 by twelfth man Aneurin Donald, who kept wicket after Alsop broke his thumb standing up to Holland.

Close of play: first day, Hampshire 79-5 (Alsop 9, Abbott 2); second day, Yorkshire 172-4 (Lyth 60, Tattersall 14); third day, Yorkshire 287-5 (Lyth 134, Bresnan 4).

Yorkshire

A. Lyth c Dawson b Holland	23	– not out	134
J. A. Raval b Abbott	8	– c Alsop b Edwards	9
H. C. Brook b Edwards	0	– c Alsop b Dawson	28
G. S. Ballance lbw b Berg	30	– lbw b Dawson	11
T. Köhler-Cadmore b Berg	2	– c Alsop b Holland	33
†J. A. Tattersall b Holland	19	– c Adams b Dawson	43
T. T. Bresnan b Edwards	25	– not out	4
M. J. Waite c Alsop b Edwards	22		
*S. A. Patterson b Edwards	9		
J. A. Brooks b Abbott	14		
B. O. Coad not out	13		
B 4, lb 1, nb 14	19	B 7, lb 8, nb 10	25

1/21 (2) 2/22 (3) 3/70 (4)   (52.1 overs) 184
4/72 (5) 5/72 (1) 6/110 (6)
7/136 (8) 8/149 (7) 9/160 (9) 10/184 (10)

1/26 (2)   (5 wkts, 80 overs) 287
2/65 (3) 3/81 (4)
4/132 (5) 5/265 (6)

Abbott 14.1–4–50–2; Edwards 16–2–83–4; Holland 12–8–16–2; Berg 10–2–30–2. *Second innings*—Abbott 21–4–65–0; Edwards 11–1–37–1; Berg 8–1–42–0; Holland 15–2–43–1; Dawson 25–4–85–3.

Hampshire

J. J. Weatherley lbw b Brooks	21	I. G. Holland b Waite	9
O. C. Soames c Tattersall b Coad	6	G. K. Berg lbw b Coad	25
J. H. K. Adams c Brook b Brooks	0	F. H. Edwards not out	9
*J. M. Vince lbw b Bresnan	25	B 4, lb 4, nb 4	12
S. A. Northeast c Brook b Bresnan	8		
†T. P. Alsop c Lyth b Bresnan	24	1/29 (1) 2/33 (2) 3/33 (3) (66.4 overs)	157
K. J. Abbott lbw b Bresnan	8	4/63 (5) 5/68 (4) 6/96 (7)	
L. A. Dawson c and b Bresnan	10	7/107 (6) 8/110 (8) 9/140 (9) 10/157 (10)	

Coad 16.4–7–23–2; Brooks 15–3–60–2; Bresnan 13–4–28–5; Patterson 16–6–20–0; Lyth 1–0–1–0; Waite 5–2–17–1.

Umpires: M. A. Gough and G. D. Lloyd.

At Worcester, September 24–26. YORKSHIRE beat WORCESTERSHIRE by seven wickets.

VITALITY BLAST IN 2018

Review by Huw Turbervill

1 Worcestershire   2 Sussex   3= Lancashire, Somerset

Words like wizardry are usually reserved for spinners; rarely is a seamer hailed as a magician. But there were times last summer when Worcestershire's Pat Brown looked every bit the sorcerer. His 31 wickets at 13 apiece, with an economy-rate of 7.64, were pivotal to Worcestershire's maiden Twenty20 triumph. Falling only two short of Alfonso Thomas's tournament record, for Somerset in 2010, the 20-year-old Brown was reckoned by his captain Moeen Ali to be "very close" to an England call-up. In a summer when the debate over the ECB's proposed new tournament in 2020 at times threatened to overshadow the Blast, Brown was a welcome on-field success story.

In the semi-final against Lancashire, he claimed four for 21. And though he did not take a wicket in the final against Sussex, four captivating overs cost only 15. He is tall, a trickster, difficult to pick, and has a natural gift, for not everyone can bowl knuckle balls, as West Indies' World T20-winning captain Darren Sammy demonstrated on Sky. These made up about two-thirds of Brown's output. He also bowled off-cutters, cross-seamers and slower balls into the pitch, along with an 84mph stock delivery. There appeared to be more varieties than Shane Warne, though Brown bragged rather less. James Anderson hailed him "the find of the tournament". But he was not seeking lucrative global contacts just yet: instead, he was finishing off his degree in business studies (with a cricket scholarship) at the University of Worcester.

Worcestershire's triumph was not just about one man. There was Ali, leading a side full of keen colts. His mantra, according to Brown, was: "Let's be brave. If in doubt, take the positive option. If we play our best cricket, we will be the best team." Ali's languid batting brought him a pair of 41s on finals day, while his off-spin was ice-cool: he bowled Jos Buttler in the semi, then Sussex dangerman Luke Wright in the final, beautifully holding the ball back.

There was Ben Cox, who in the final channelled his frustration at being left out of the Championship side into a fearless unbeaten 46, helping to overhaul Sussex's 157. He had also hit 55 not out against Lancashire. There were the Antipodeans: Callum Ferguson (with a maiden T20 ton, against Nottinghamshire), Travis Head and Martin Guptill, who crashed a 35-ball century at Northampton. The 19-year-old Dillon Pennington was a sensation at the start of the tournament. Then, in the quarter-final against Gloucestershire, Brett D'Oliveira took four wickets with his leg-spin. Worcestershire fans felt they had made a point, since New Road will not be one of the venues for the new tournament. They also felt they had been written off before finals day, though this allowed them to slip under the radar. Their T20 title softened the blow – confirmed five days later – of relegation in the Championship.

It meant disappointment for Sussex, many people's tip for the title because of a stellar attack including Jofra Archer, Chris Jordan, Tymal Mills and – in

Stu Forster; Getty Images

Delivery charge: Pat Brown had a habit of making opponents pay.

the group stages – Afghanistan leg-spinner Rashid Khan. He took 17 wickets at just 14, with one of the lowest economy-rates (6.59) in the competition. How they missed him on finals day, when he was away on international duty. Archer's accuracy deserted him in the penultimate over against Worcestershire, and it was of little consolation that Laurie Evans's 52 made him the competition's highest scorer, with 614. Despite that, Archer had a fine campaign, with 22 wickets, including a hat-trick against Middlesex at Lord's; left-arm spinner Danny Briggs also bowled well, taking 19.

For Lancashire, Liam Livingstone smashed a 49-ball century against Derbyshire, but was limited to seven games by a fractured thumb, leaving Alex Davies to carry the batting, with six half-centuries among his 534 runs. Matt Parkinson's 25 wickets – only Brown claimed more – were a reminder of leg-spin's potency in white-ball cricket.

Somerset reached finals day after topping the South Group with ten wins, the most in the country. Captain Lewis Gregory shone in the late-middle order, with 328 runs and a strike-rate of 202. That included 62 off 26 balls (and four for 28) in the group stage against Middlesex, plus an unbeaten 60 off 24 in the quarter-final against Nottinghamshire. New Zealander Corey Anderson was their leading scorer (514), and West Indian Jerome Taylor their leading wicket-taker (22). That quarter-final was delayed by a day because of rain, and therefore not on Sky, prompting a social-media and streaming blitzkrieg by the club. Like Worcestershire, Somerset felt aggrieved to be overlooked as a venue for the new competition.

Surrey might have expected to make the last eight, especially with Aaron Finch in such devastating form. His 589 runs included a staggering unbeaten 131 off 79 balls at Hove and, a week later, 83 off 38 to lift Surrey to 250 against Kent, the third-highest total in English T20. But a narrow defeat at Bristol cost them dear. Glamorgan also missed out, after losing their last three games. In contrast to their four-day travails, they had white-ball potential, and their South African captain, Colin Ingram made 430 runs, despite missing two games with unexplained breathing problems.

Warwickshire failed to make the quarters, too, even after an unlikely renaissance from Ian Bell. Omitted from their T20 side in 2017, he demanded a recall with his Championship form, and made 580 runs, including a century in a thrilling tie against Northamptonshire. New Zealander Grant Elliott was typically smart with the ball, taking 19 wickets at the age of 39, before announcing his retirement.

Kent made the quarters and, in Joe Denly's leg-spin, possessed an unexpected weapon: among his 20 wickets was a hat-trick at The Oval, a match in which he also scored a century. But they were spun out in the quarter-finals by Lancashire on a Canterbury pitch described by captain Sam Billings as a "snot-heap". Paul Collingwood found form with bat and ball in his farewell season with Durham, who lost a home quarter-final against Sussex. But New Zealander

FINAL GROUP TABLES

North Group

		P	W	L	T	NR	Pts	NRR
1	WORCESTERSHIRE	14	9	4	0	1	19	0.59
2	DURHAM	14	9	4	0	1	19	0.55
3	LANCASHIRE	14	8	5	0	1	17	0.68
4	NOTTINGHAMSHIRE	14	8	6	0	0	16	0.07
5	Yorkshire	14	7	7	0	0	14	−0.03
6	Warwickshire	14	6	7	1	0	13	0.03
7	Derbyshire	14	5	7	0	2	12	−0.04
8	Leicestershire	14	5	8	0	1	11	−0.38
9	Northamptonshire	14	2	11	1	0	5	−1.39

South Group

		P	W	L	T	NR	Pts	NRR
1	SOMERSET	14	10	4	0	0	20	0.78
2	KENT	14	8	2	0	4	20	0.62
3	SUSSEX	14	7	3	0	4	18	0.73
4	GLOUCESTERSHIRE	14	8	4	0	2	18	0.38
5	Surrey	14	7	5	0	2	16	0.98
6	Glamorgan	14	7	6	0	1	15	−0.14
7	Essex	14	2	8	1	3	8	−1.03
8	Hampshire	14	2	9	1	2	7	−0.82
9	Middlesex	14	2	12	0	0	4	−1.12

Where counties finished tied on points, positions were decided by net run-rate.

Daniel Vettori paid the price for another limp Middlesex campaign, and – a month after being sacked as coach of the IPL's Royal Challengers Bangalore – was released with a season to go on his three-year contract; Stuart Law was appointed as Middlesex's new coach across all formats.

There were plenty of highlights in the group stages. Dan Christian hit a 37-ball hundred for Nottinghamshire at Northampton, the second-quickest in England. For Leicestershire, Ben Raine's exciting talent translated into the second-fastest by an Englishman – from just 41 – at Edgbaston. A few weeks after he had felled England at Edinburgh, Scotland's Calum MacLeod smacked a 58-ball century for Derbyshire to help see off Northamptonshire, who lost 11 of their 14 games; their Blast triumphs of 2013 and 2016 seemed an age ago.

Lancashire won a Roses thriller at Old Trafford by one run, thanks to Livingstone's 79, while the London derby at The Oval saw Finch and Jason Roy make light work of Middlesex's 221, hammering 194 for Surrey's first wicket inside 14 overs. Gloucestershire showed some of their old white-ball form to make the quarters, and Ian Cockbain's 123 from 61 balls against Middlesex in a total of 242 for four – their best at Bristol – made for a memorable evening.

The Blast faces an uncertain future, but the 2018 model worked well, with attendances steadily rising. Lord's and The Oval do not need the new tournament, since their crowds are already excellent, but there is scope for improvement at some venues. From 2020, the counties will need to fit in and around the new competition, and were told they could not have 16 group matches instead of 14. Finals day was on September 15: the ECB might consider staging it earlier, since dew and grey weather limited heavy scoring. Overall, though, the tournament was still a multi-coloured, flamboyant, noisy success story.

Prize Money

£256,060 for winners: WORCESTERSHIRE.
£123,934 for runners-up: SUSSEX.
£30,212 for losing semi-finalists: LANCASHIRE, SOMERSET.
£4,500 for losing quarter-finalists: DURHAM, GLOUCESTERSHIRE, NOTTINGHAMSHIRE, KENT
Match-award winners received £2,500 in the final, £1,000 in the semi-finals, £500 in the quarter-finals and £225 in the group games.

VITALITY BLAST AVERAGES

BATTING (300 runs, strike-rate of 140)

		M	I	NO	R	HS	100	50	Avge	SR	4	6
1	L. Gregory (*Somerset*)....	16	13	6	328	62	0	3	46.85	202.46	28	19
2	L. S. Livingstone (*Lancs*) .	7	7	0	318	100	1	1	45.42	188.16	31	21
3	A. J. Finch (*Surrey*)......	9	9	5	589	131*	2	3	147.25	182.35	60	31
4	†M. M. Ali (*Worcs*).......	9	8	0	334	115	1	1	41.75	175.78	37	18
5	D. T. Christian (*Notts*)....	15	14	4	415	113*	1	1	41.50	172.91	29	24
6	P. D. Salt (*Sussex*).......	15	14	0	355	74	0	4	25.35	172.33	42	16
7	†C. J. Anderson (*Somerset*).	16	15	3	514	72	0	3	42.83	169.07	31	34
8	B. A. Raine (*Leics*)	13	13	0	332	113	1	1	25.53	168.52	28	21
9	†C. A. Ingram (*Glam*).....	11	11	3	430	89	0	3	53.75	164.75	40	23

		M	I	NO	R	HS	100	50	Avge	SR	4	6
10	M. H. Wessels (*Notts*)....	14	14	0	307	58	0	2	21.92	**163.29**	29	22
11	P. R. Stirling (*Middx*)	14	14	0	498	109	1	4	35.57	**160.12**	61	21
12	†M. A. H. Hammond (*Glos*)	14	13	0	313	51	0	1	24.07	**155.72**	43	13
13	†A. Lyth (*Yorks*)	14	14	1	401	92*	0	3	30.84	**153.05**	37	20
14	†R. A. Whiteley (*Worcs*) ..	16	15	3	313	60	0	1	26.08	**152.68**	27	15
15	J. M. Clarke (*Worcs*)	15	15	1	396	76	0	2	28.28	**151.72**	47	14
16	J. G. Myburgh (*Somerset*).	16	16	2	372	103*	1	1	26.57	**151.21**	48	12
17	L. J. Wright (*Sussex*).....	13	12	0	452	92	0	5	37.66	**151.17**	47	15
18	B. T. Foakes (*Surrey*)	14	10	2	310	75*	0	3	38.75	**149.03**	32	9
19	J. J. Cobb (*Northants*)	14	14	2	448	103	1	4	37.33	**147.36**	31	28
20	†T. J. Moores (*Notts*).....	15	15	2	445	80*	0	3	34.23	**146.86**	35	25
21	H. G. Kuhn (*Kent*).......	13	12	2	310	67*	0	1	31.00	**145.53**	26	8
22	D. J. Bell-Drummond (*Kent*)	13	12	0	372	80	0	3	31.00	**145.31**	39	9
23	J. L. Denly (*Kent*)	13	12	1	409	102	1	2	37.18	**145.03**	48	11
24	†B. M. Duckett (*Northants*)	14	14	0	414	96	0	2	29.57	**144.75**	53	10
25	S. W. Billings (*Kent*).....	13	12	5	372	95*	0	3	53.14	**144.74**	33	12
26	†D. J. Willey (*Yorks*).....	10	10	0	386	80	0	4	38.60	**142.96**	27	22
27	W. L. Madsen (*Derbys*)...	13	12	2	328	76*	0	3	32.80	**142.60**	41	6
28	C. J. Ferguson (*Worcs*) ...	10	10	2	390	102*	1	2	48.75	**141.81**	36	7
29	A. J. Hose (*Warwicks*)....	14	14	2	377	66*	0	3	31.41	**140.67**	39	12
30	T. Köhler-Cadmore (*Yorks*)	13	13	0	321	73	0	3	24.69	**140.17**	32	12

The leading run-scorer in the tournament was L. J. Evans (Sussex), who hit 614 runs from 14 innings at an average of 68.22 and a strike-rate of 135.84.

BOWLING (12 wickets, economy-rate 8.60)

		Style	O	Dots	R	W	BB	4I	Avge	SR	ER
1	Imran Tahir (*Durham*)....	LB	32	65	203	15	4-14	2	13.53	12.80	**6.34**
2	Rashid Khan (*Sussex*) ...	LB	37	80	244	17	3-9	0	14.35	13.00	**6.59**
3	L. H. Ferguson (*Derbys*) .	RF	48	138	319	16	4-26	1	19.93	18.00	**6.64**
4	M. T. C. Waller (*Somerset*)	LB	56	101	382	16	4-25	1	23.87	21.00	**6.82**
5	D. R. Briggs (*Sussex*)	SLA	48	101	339	18	3-29	0	18.83	16.00	**7.06**
6	A. F. Milne (*Kent*).......	RF	41.3	106	297	13	4-15	1	22.84	19.10	**7.15**
7	Wahab Riaz (*Derbys*)	LFM	43	114	313	15	3-27	0	20.86	17.20	**7.27**
8	M. W. Parkinson (*Lancs*) .	LB	56.4	107	415	25	3-19	0	16.60	13.60	**7.32**
9	A. J. Tye (*Glos*).........	RFM	41.2	87	307	13	3-17	0	23.61	19.00	**7.42**
10	C. P. Wood (*Hants*)......	LFM	44	107	335	19	5-32	1	17.63	13.80	**7.61**
11	H. F. Gurney (*Notts*).....	LFM	50.4	119	387	20	3-24	0	19.35	15.20	**7.63**
12	P. R. Brown (*Worcs*)	RFM	54.1	143	414	31	4-21	1	13.35	10.40	**7.64**
13	J. P. Faulkner (*Lancs*)	LFM	45.5	100	352	20	3-24	0	17.60	13.70	**7.68**
14	C. F. Parkinson (*Leics*) ...	SLA	42	73	323	15	4-20	1	21.53	16.80	**7.69**
15	G. C. Viljoen (*Derby*)	RFM	35	90	270	13	3-25	0	20.76	16.10	**7.71**
16	J. L. Denly (*Kent*)	LB	43.1	88	335	20	3-25	0	16.75	12.90	**7.76**
17	B. A. C. Howell (*Glos*) ...	RM	41.5	77	328	17	3-31	0	19.29	14.70	**7.84**
18	A. Zampa (*Essex*)	LB	31.3	61	249	12	3-17	0	20.75	15.70	**7.90**
19	G. D. Elliott (*Warwicks*) ..	RM	47	60	372	19	3-16	0	19.57	14.80	**7.91**
20	C. J. Jordan (*Sussex*)	RFM	37.5	85	300	13	2-9	0	23.07	17.40	**7.92**
21	W. D. Parnell (*Worcs*)	LFM	32.2	88	257	14	3-20	0	18.35	13.80	**7.94**
22	S. A. Patterson (*Yorks*) ...	RFM	42	82	335	12	3-35	0	27.91	21.00	**7.97**
23	A. L. Hughes (*Derbys*) ...	RM	40	68	324	17	4-42	1	19.05	14.10	**8.10**
24	I. S. Sodhi (*Notts*)	LB	54	92	441	19	4-17	1	23.21	17.00	**8.16**
25	R. Clarke (*Surrey*)	RFM	45.1	72	377	16	2-19	0	23.56	16.90	**8.34**
26	D. A. Payne (*Glos*)	LFM	51	120	436	18	3-29	0	24.22	17.00	**8.54**
27	J. C. Archer (*Sussex*)	RFM	51.1	122	438	22	3-24	0	19.90	13.90	**8.56**
28	R. Rampaul (*Derbys*).....	RFM	41.5	98	359	14	4-19	1	25.64	17.90	**8.58**
29	R. E. van der Merwe (*Som*)	SLA	58.3	76	502	12	2-26	0	41.83	29.20	**8.58**

LEADING WICKETKEEPERS

Dismissals	M	
18 (12 ct, 6 st)	15	D. J. Vilas (*Lancs*)
16 (13 ct, 3 st)	14	S. W. Poynter (*Durham*)
14 (9 ct, 5 st)	16	O. B. Cox (*Worcs*)
13 (9 ct, 4 st)	13	S. W. Billings (*Kent*)
13 (10 ct, 3 st)	13	C. B. Cooke (*Glam*)

Dismissals	M	
12 (11 ct, 1 st)	14	T. R. Ambrose (*Warks*)
11 (11 ct)	14	G. H. Roderick (*Glos*)
10 (5 ct, 5 st)	15	M. G. K. Burgess (*Sussex*)
10 (8 ct, 2 st)	14	J. A. Tattersall (*Yorks*)

LEADING FIELDERS

Ct	M	
15	16	E. G. Barnard (*Worcs*)
13	16	M. T. C. Waller (*Somerset*)
12	16	T. B. Abell (*Somerset*)
11	14	T. W. M. Latham (*Durham*)
10	13	S. R. Dickson (*Kent*)

Ct	M	
10	13	A. H. T. Donald (*Glam*)
10	15	D. T. Christian (*Notts*)
10	16	J. Overton (*Somerset*)
10	16	R. E. van der Merwe (*Somerset*)

NORTH GROUP

DERBYSHIRE

At Derby, July 6 (floodlit). **Lancashire won by nine wickets. Derbyshire 161-4** (20 overs) (C. S. MacLeod 44, W. L. Madsen 76*); ‡**Lancashire 164-1** (14.3 overs) (A. L. Davies 50*, L. S. Livingstone 100). *MoM:* L. S. Livingstone. *County debuts:* L. H. Ferguson, C. S. MacLeod, Wahab Riaz (Derbyshire). *Attendance:* 4,205. *A 49-ball century from Liam Livingstone made light of Lancashire's task, their victory coming with 33 balls to spare. He and Alex Davies put on 160, a club record for the first wicket. Derbyshire had made a respectable 161-4 thanks to 76* from Wayne Madsen and 44 from Calum MacLeod, the hero of Scotland's ODI triumph over England the previous month. Left-arm seamer Toby Lester conceded ten runs from three overs.*

At Derby, July 8. **Worcestershire won by six wickets. Derbyshire 135-9** (20 overs) (B. T. Slater 33, A. K. Dal 35); ‡**Worcestershire 136-4** (18.4 overs) (M. J. Guptill 65). *MoM:* M. J. Guptill. *County debut:* A. K. Dal (Derbyshire). *Attendance:* 2,119. *The experienced Martin Guptill, formerly a Derbyshire favourite, adapted best to a grudging surface. By his standards, a run a ball was sedate, but Worcestershire had no need to hurry after limiting a hesitant Derbyshire to 135. Anuj Dal, from Newcastle under Lyme, had top-scored on debut – also his 22nd birthday – though Worcestershire's 19-year-old Dillon Pennington, in his first T20 outing, had the greater say, taking 2-22. In the battle of the Antipodean Fergusons, New Zealander Lockie (playing for Derbyshire), bowled Aussie Callum for ten.*

At Derby, July 13. **Nottinghamshire won by 39 runs** (DLS). **Nottinghamshire 175-8** (19 overs) (T. J. Moores 53, D. T. Christian 62; L. H. Ferguson 4-26); ‡**Derbyshire 139-9** (19 overs) (C. S. MacLeod 48; D. T. Christian 3-34). *MoM:* D. T. Christian. *Attendance:* 4,034. *A mid-innings charge from fifth-wicket pair Dan Christian and Tom Moores added 64 in 33 balls after a maiden four-for from Ferguson reduced Nottinghamshire to 59-4. A rain delay docked each team an over and raised Derbyshire's target to 179. Christian then took three wickets to derail the chase. Only MacLeod escaped the teens.*

At Chesterfield, July 28. **Derbyshire won by five wickets.** ‡**Yorkshire 166-8** (20 overs) (D. J. Willey 55, K. S. Williamson 35; R. Rampaul 4-19); **Derbyshire 170-5** (19.5 overs) (B. A. Godleman 71*, M. J. J. Critchley 38*). *MoM:* M. J. J. Critchley. *Attendance:* 4,517. *With Derbyshire needing 19 off the final over, from Tim Bresnan, Critchley struck 22 from five deliveries, including two sixes and two fours. Though Critchley, whose 38* spanned just 17 balls, was the hero, there were important contributions from Ravi Rampaul and Billy Godleman. It was Derbyshire's first home win.*

At Derby, August 3 (floodlit). **Derbyshire won by 16 runs.** ‡**Derbyshire 143-9** (20 overs) (C. S. MacLeod 39, G. C. Wilson 30*; G. D. Elliott 3-16); **Warwickshire 127-9** (20 overs) (I. R. Bell 65; Wahab Riaz 3-27). *MoM:* G. C. Viljoen. *Attendance:* 2,546. *A total of 143-9 gave Derbyshire's* *bowlers little margin for error, but they rose to the task. Wahab Riaz claimed 3-27, his best return of the season, while Hardus Viljoen – not always the tightest – had figures of 4–15–12–2. Ian Bell was the danger: he became Warwickshire's highest T20 scorer (passing Jonathan Trott's total of 1,911 runs), but when he fell for 65 at 107-6 in the 17th, the game was up.*

At Derby, August 8 (floodlit). **Northamptonshire won by seven wickets.** ‡Derbyshire **177-6** (20 overs) (B. A. Godleman 77, W. L. Madsen 38); **Northamptonshire 179-3** (18.2 overs) (B. M. Duckett 41, J. J. Cobb 73*). MoM: J. J. Cobb. *County debut*: B. J. Curran (Northamptonshire). *Attendance*: 2,337. *After nine defeats and a tie, Northamptonshire won their first match. Derbyshire, aiming for a sixth victory in seven, set a decent target thanks to a stand of 83 in 49 balls between Godleman, with a career-best 77, and Wayne Madsen. The in-form Josh Cobb then clobbered a 37-ball 73*, with seven sixes, to power Northamptonshire home. There was a quiet debut for Ben Curran, the middle of the three brothers: he made two.*

At Derby, August 11 (floodlit). **No result. Leicestershire 103-4** (14.3 overs) v ‡Derbyshire. *County debut*: H. M. Nicholls (Derbyshire). *Attendance*: 2,257. *Neither side could progress; rain ended the game as Colin Ackermann (24*) and Ateeq Javid (28*) were building a recovery from 50-4.*

Derbyshire away matches

July 14: lost to Lancashire by 12 runs.
July 19: beat Northamptonshire by 31 runs.
July 27: beat Leicestershire by six wickets.
July 30: beat Yorkshire by 77 runs.

August 2: lost to Nottinghamshire by nine runs.
August 9: lost to Worcestershire by 16 runs.
August 17: no result v Durham.

DURHAM

At Chester-le-Street, July 13 (floodlit). **Yorkshire won by ten runs.** ‡Yorkshire **157-6** (20 overs) (H. C. Brook 38, J. A. Tattersall 36; P. D. Collingwood 3-27); **Durham 147-6** (20 overs) (T. W. M. Latham 42, G. Clark 39). MoM: T. Bresnan. *Attendance*: 7,785. *Tim Bresnan proved the match-winner. First he hit 28* off 15 balls to lift Yorkshire to a respectable total. Then, with Durham needing 29 off three overs with seven wickets in hand, he removed Will Smith and Paul Collingwood with his first two balls, and ran out Stuart Poynter, finishing with 4–11–19–2.*

At Chester-le-Street, July 20 (floodlit). **Durham won by seven wickets. Worcestershire 121** (19.2 overs) (T. M. Head 40; B. A. Stokes 4-16); ‡**Durham 125-3** (14.4 overs) (G. Clark 55, B. A. Stokes 43). MoM: B. A. Stokes. *Attendance*: 3,807. *Ben Stokes, in the second of three group-match appearances, took a career-best 4-16, then hit 43 off 24 balls. He shared an opening stand of 77 in 8.2 overs with Graham Clark (55 off 39). Put in following afternoon rain, Worcestershire lost Moeen Ali third ball, and only Travis Head passed 17.*

At Chester-le-Street, July 28. **Durham won by seven wickets. Nottinghamshire 132-7** (20 overs) (S. R. Patel 32, S. J. Mullaney 38); ‡**Durham 136-3** (16.5 overs) (G. Clark 64, P. D. Collingwood 40*). MoM: G. Clark. *Attendance*: 3,648. *Durham completed a surprisingly easy double over the holders. Nottinghamshire were shackled on a sluggish pitch by tight bowling, led by Chris Rushworth's 2-13 from three overs. Clark's third half-century in four innings eased Durham towards victory.*

At Chester-le-Street, August 2 (floodlit). **Durham won by 75 runs. Durham 170-4** (20 overs) (P. D. Collingwood 50*); ‡**Northamptonshire 95** (17 overs) (Imran Tahir 4-16). MoM: Imran Tahir. *Attendance*: 4,678. *Durham's fifth successive win took them top of the group, and left Northamptonshire rooted to the bottom. Imran Tahir picked up 4-16 in his final appearance for Durham, his seventh county. Collingwood followed 40* against Nottinghamshire with 50*. Northamptonshire looked a shadow of the side who had beaten Durham in the 2016 final.*

At Chester-le-Street, August 8 (floodlit). **Durham won by 14 runs.** ‡**Durham 156-6** (20 overs) (T. W. M. Latham 52); **Leicestershire 142-6** (20 overs) (C. N. Ackermann 74, E. J. H. Eckersley 39*; N. J. Rimmington 3-23). MoM: T. W. M. Latham. *Attendance*: 4,442. *Durham reclaimed top spot with their seventh win in eight games, set up by Tom Latham's gritty half-century and rounded off by three wickets for Nathan Rimmington. In between, Colin Ackerman made 74 for Leicestershire, and put on 89 with Ned Eckersley, but they had too much to do from 33-5.*

At Chester-le-Street, August 12. **Lancashire won by 65 runs. Lancashire 143-6** (20 overs) (A. L. Davies 64; S. J. Croft 30; N. J. Rimmington 4-28); **‡Durham 78** (15.2 overs) (M. W. Parkinson 3-19). *MoM*: A. L. Davies. *Attendance*: 4,739. *Alex Davies helped Lancashire into the quarter-finals after they were put in under heavy cloud and slipped to 6-2. He eventually became Rimmington's fourth victim, off the last ball of the innings, after making 64 off 62, his sixth half-century of the competition. Durham were then reduced to 4-4 by James Faulkner (2–10–3–2) and Toby Lester (3–13–5–2), before slumping to 78, their lowest T20 total, undercutting 93 against Kent at Canterbury in 2009.*

At Chester-le-Street, August 17 (floodlit). **Durham v Derbyshire. Abandoned.** *The weather cost Durham the chance to stay top of the group. Worcestershire's win the same evening took them ahead by 0.039 of a run.*

Durham away matches

July 5: lost to Yorkshire by 44 runs.
July 6: beat Leicestershire by 33 runs.
July 15: beat Warwickshire by 18 runs.
July 17: beat Nottinghamshire by 34 runs.

August 3: lost to Worcestershire by three wickets.
August 7: beat Lancashire by four runs.
August 10: beat Northamptonshire by 12 runs.

LANCASHIRE

At Manchester, July 5 (floodlit). **Worcestershire won by five wickets. ‡Lancashire 188-6** (20 overs) (L. S. Livingstone 35, K. K. Jennings 50); **Worcestershire 190-5** (19.5 overs) (J. M. Clarke 42, C. J. Ferguson 35, B. L. D'Oliveira 37*). *MoM*: B. L. D'Oliveira. *County debut*: L. Wood (Worcestershire). *Attendance*: 5,516. *Lancashire should have defended 188 after Keaton Jennings's 33-ball 50, but Worcestershire got off to a scorching start, and reached 70-1 after six overs. They briefly slowed, but Brett D'Oliveira helped collect 66 from the last six overs to decide a game dominated by batsmen: of the 15 who reached the crease, only one was dismissed in single figures.*

At Manchester, July 8. **Lancashire won by eight wickets. ‡Northamptonshire 123-9** (20 overs) (R. E. Levi 40); **Lancashire 124-2** (16.1 overs) (A. L. Davies 64*). *MoM*: A. L. Davies. *Attendance*: 9,122. *Lancashire's slow bowlers condemned Northamptonshire to a third defeat in five days. Left-armer Stephen Parry and leg-spinners Liam Livingstone and Matt Parkinson conceded only 62 in taking six wickets from their combined 12 overs; Northamptonshire, who had been 62-1 in the sixth, limped to 123-9. Alex Davies's unbeaten half-century proved its inadequacy.*

At Manchester, July 14. **Lancashire won by 12 runs. ‡Lancashire 157-8** (20 overs) (A. L. Davies 31, L. S. Livingstone 44); **Derbyshire 145-7** (20 overs) (C. S. MacLeod 30, W. L. Madsen 34; T. J. Lester 4-25). *MoM*: T. J. Lester. *County debut*: M. H. McKiernan (Derbyshire). *Attendance*: 7,195. *Lancashire had the better of a low-scoring game thanks to Livingstone's 21-ball 44 and tight overs from their least experienced bowlers: Parkinson claimed 2-21, while the star was left-arm seamer Toby Lester, in his third T20 game. He took two wickets in his first three overs, then two in the last, when Derbyshire made just five of the 18 they needed. This was their fourth defeat in four.*

At Manchester, July 20 (floodlit). **Lancashire won by one run. Lancashire 176-2** (14 overs) (L. S. Livingstone 79, A. M. Lilley 42*, J. Clark 36*); **‡Yorkshire 175-4** (14 overs) (A. Lyth 60, J. E. Root 51*). *MoM*: L. S. Livingstone. *Attendance*: 22,515. *A match reduced to 14 overs had an explosive start when Livingstone clouted six sixes in his 37-ball 79. Arron Lilley and Jordan Clark maintained the momentum, but Yorkshire's batsmen were undeterred by the size of their target. Adam Lyth also cracked six sixes, Joe Root made a classy 51*, and the outcome was undecided until Kane Williamson managed only two off Lester's final delivery. After 148 consecutive appearances, Steven Croft was dropped by Lancashire, who became the first county to win 100 T20 matches.*

MOST CONSECUTIVE APPEARANCES FOR ONE T20 TEAM

158	**S. K. Raina (Chennai Super Kings)**	**2007-08 to 2017-18**
148	**S. J. Croft (Lancashire)**	**2006 to 2018**
144	V. Kohli (Royal Challengers Bangalore)	2007-08 to 2015-16
137*	**M. S. Dhoni (Chennai Super Kings)**	**2009-10–**
111	P. Mustard (Durham)	2008 to 2016
108*	**J. S. Patel (Warwickshire)**	**2011–**
107	R. Ashwin (Chennai Super Kings)	2009-10 to 2014-15
107	G. Gambhir (Kolkata Knight Riders)	2011-12 to 2016-17
104	J. H. K. Adams (Hampshire)	2009 to 2015
102	A. T. Rayudu (Mumbai Indians)	2009-10 to 2014-15
100	D. K. H. Mitchell (Worcestershire)	2007 to 2016
100*	**R. A. Jadeja (Chennai Super Kings)**	**2011-12–**

* *Unbroken at January 1, 2019.*

At Manchester, August 3 (floodlit). **Leicestershire won by five wickets.** ‡Lancashire 190-5 (20 overs) (A. L. Davies 94*); **Leicestershire 194-5** (18.4 overs) (B. A. Raine 44, C. N. Ackermann 45, Mohammad Nabi 86*). *MoM:* Mohammad Nabi. *County debut:* M. R. J. Watt (Lancashire). *Attendance:* 9,525. *An extraordinary 33-ball 86* from Mohammad Nabi, including eight sixes and four fours, transformed this game. Leicestershire were 92-5 in the 11th over when the onslaught began, and won with eight balls to spare; Ateeq Javid's contribution to a sixth-wicket stand of 102* was 15*. Nabi's huge blows, some out of the ground, rendered Alex Davies's more measured 94* a mere footnote.*

At Manchester, August 7 (floodlit). **Durham won by four runs.** ‡Durham 154-7 (20 overs) (W. R. Smith 37*); **Lancashire 150-9** (20 overs) (A. L. Davies 53; L. Trevaskis 4-16). *MoM:* L. Trevaskis. *County debut:* Zahir Khan (Lancashire). *Attendance:* 8,712. *Lancashire needed six off the final over with four wickets in hand, but slow left-armer Liam Trevaskis – selected mainly for his batting – took three wickets and conceded only a single to clinch an astonishing win. The 19-year-old Trevaskis was playing his eighth T20 game for Durham, but this was just the second time he had bowled. Earlier, he was the first victim for Afghan left-arm wrist-spinner Zahir Khan, also aged 19, who took 4–11–19–2 on debut to help restrict Durham to 154-7. Another fifty for Alex Davies, his fifth in eight T20 innings, then seemed to put Lancashire on course for victory.*

At Manchester, August 10 (floodlit). **Lancashire won by 37 runs.** ‡Lancashire 185-5 (20 overs) (K. R. Brown 61, J. Clark 41*; A. T. Thomson 4-35); **Warwickshire 148** (19.5 overs) (A. J. Hose 45, S. R. Hain 34; J. P. Faulkner 3-28, M. W. Parkinson 3-23). *MoM:* M. W. Parkinson. *Attendance:* 8,081. *On another turning pitch, Warwickshire off-spinner Alex Thomson took four wickets on his T20 debut, but could not prevent Lancashire following victory at Leeds the day before with another comfortable win that kept them third. Karl Brown made his second fifty in 24 hours, though Lancashire's success also owed much to the intelligent leg-spin of Parkinson, who bowled Colin de Grandhomme with a beauty.*

Lancashire away matches

July 6: beat Derbyshire by nine wickets.	August 9: beat Yorkshire by six wickets.
July 18: beat Leicestershire by eight wickets.	August 12: beat Durham by 65 runs.
July 27: lost to Notts by 16 runs (DLS).	August 15: lost to Warwickshire by seven wickets.
July 29: no result v Worcestershire.	

LEICESTERSHIRE

At Leicester, July 6 (floodlit). **Durham won by 33 runs. Durham 153-7** (20 overs) (P. D. Collingwood 36; Z. J. Chappell 3-23); ‡**Leicestershire 120** (18.3 overs) (N. J. Dexter 35; Imran Tahir 4-14). *MoM:* Imran Tahir. *Attendance:* 3,267. *Imran Tahir recorded his best figures in England to inspire Durham to victory. Leicestershire had looked well set at 83 for two, but in four balls Tahir* *had Neil Dexter stumped, and bowled Colin Ackermann. Durham owed much to Paul Collingwood, and were given late impetus by Stuart Poynter's 29* off 20.*

At Leicester, July 8. **Nottinghamshire won by 19 runs. Nottinghamshire 199-8** (20 overs) (T. J. Moores 51, S. R. Patel 52, D. T. Christian 47; Z. J. Chappell 3-25); ‡**Leicestershire 180-9** (20 overs) (C. S. Delport 33, N. J. Dexter 43, Mohammad Nabi 32). *MoM*: D. T. Christian. *Attendance*: 3,375. *A partnership of 97 between Samit Patel and Tom Moores formed the bedrock of Nottinghamshire's total. Dan Christian's 47 came from 29 balls. Leicestershire were in the game at 51-0 in the sixth over, but Steven Mullaney's brilliant catch to remove Mark Cosgrove proved pivotal. Nottinghamshire's attack deployed their experience wisely.*

At Leicester, July 18 (floodlit). **Lancashire won by eight wickets. Leicestershire 142** (19.4 overs) (N. J. Dexter 30, M. J. Cosgrove 31; L. S. Livingstone 4-17); ‡**Lancashire 146-2** (16.4 overs) (A. L. Davies 51*, K. K. Jennings 37*). *MoM*: L. S. Livingstone. *Attendance*: 2,277. *Leicestershire subjected their supporters to a familiar collapse, and slid to a third successive home defeat. They had advanced to 88-1 in the tenth over, before crashing to 106-6 in the 14th. Liam Livingstone reaped the benefits with a career-best 4-17. Alex Davies batted sensibly, allowing Livingstone (28 off 11) to go on the offensive. Keaton Jennings joined Davies to finish the job with a stand of 70*.*

At Leicester, July 27 (floodlit). **Derbyshire won by six wickets. Leicestershire 149-5** (20 overs) (M. J. Cosgrove 65); **Derbyshire 150-4** (18.5 overs) (B. A. Godleman 57*, G. C. Viljoen 32). *MoM*: B. A. Godleman. *Attendance*: 2,198. *Derbyshire never looked like slackening the grip they had established from the off. They conceded just four boundaries in the powerplay, and Leicestershire needed Cosgrove's 65 and Ackermann's 29* to set any sort of target. Billy Godleman unwittingly ran out the in-form Calum MacLeod in the first over, but recovered his composure to move to a calm fifty. Hardus Viljoen's 32 off 16 helped complete a comfortable win.*

At Leicester, August 2 (floodlit). **Warwickshire won by eight wickets. ‡Leicestershire 143** (19.3 overs) (N. J. Dexter 56; O. P. Stone 3-22); **Warwickshire 146-2** (14.2 overs) (I. R. Bell 34, A. J. Hose 66*). *MoM*: A. J. Hose. *Attendance*: 2,387. *Warwickshire strolled to a win that ended their slump and condemned Leicestershire to a fifth home defeat in five. Dexter alone coped with the pace of Olly Stone, who took a career-best. With Chris Woakes and Grant Elliott equally hard to get away, a total of 143 looked inadequate. Ian Bell oozed class before being run out, but Adam Hose and Sam Hain put on 95* to secure the points.*

At Leicester, August 10 (floodlit). **Leicestershire won by five runs. Leicestershire 155-9** (20 overs) (M. J. Cosgrove 33, B. A. Raine 32); ‡**Worcestershire 150-6** (20 overs) (C. J. Ferguson 69; G. T. Griffiths 3-28). *MoM*: G. T. Griffiths. *Attendance*: 2,281. *Callum Ferguson appeared to be steering Worcestershire to a fifth successive win – and a home quarter-final – when he failed to beat Mohammad Nabi's throw from long-on. Wayne Parnell and Ed Barnard were unable to maintain the momentum, handing Leicestershire an unlikely first home victory. Once again they had struggled to set a decent total. Ben Raine looked in destructive form, hitting Pat Brown for two sixes and two fours in an over, but he was stumped off a leg-side wide from Daryl Mitchell.*

At Leicester, August 17 (floodlit). **Northamptonshire won by four wickets. Leicestershire 148-7** (20 overs) (H. E. Dearden 61); ‡**Northamptonshire 154-6** (18.4 overs) (B. M. Duckett 37, J. J. Cobb 30). *MoM*: H. E. Dearden. *Attendance*: 2,442. *The basement battle was won by Northamptonshire thanks to some fine striking at the top of the order from Ben Curran, Ben Duckett and Josh Cobb. They raced to 90-1 in the 11th, which allowed them to survive the loss of five for 35. Leicestershire had made a wretched start, but Harry Dearden, on his T20 debut, hit 61 off 40 balls to pull things around. Gareth Wade, Northamptonshire's debutant seamer, was removed from the attack after bowling two beamers in his first three balls.*

Leicestershire away matches

July 4: beat Northamptonshire by four wickets.
July 13: beat Warwickshire by 100 runs.
July 20: beat Nottinghamshire by 17 runs.
July 31: lost to Yorkshire by 60 runs.

August 3: beat Lancashire by five wickets.
August 8: lost to Durham by 14 runs.
August 11: no result v Derbyshire.

NORTHAMPTONSHIRE

At Northampton, July 4 (floodlit). **Leicestershire won by four wickets. Northamptonshire 218-3** (20 overs) (B. M. Duckett 96, J. J. Cobb 56, A. G. Wakely 51*); ‡**Leicestershire 219-6** (19.4 overs) (N. J. Dexter 38, C. N. Ackermann 66*). *MoM*: B. M. Duckett. *County debut*: Mohammad Nabi (Leicestershire). *Attendance*: 2,291. *Colin Ackermann snatched victory from Northamptonshire's grasp in an enthralling season-opener. He blasted 66* from 31 as Leicestershire climbed off the canvas to win with two balls to spare. The evening had begun promisingly for Northamptonshire. Ben Duckett's career-best 96 included a stand of 111 for the second wicket with Josh Cobb. It was – briefly – the highest total made on the ground. Leicestershire had needed another 112 from 42 balls when Ackermann got to work. A penalty for a slow over-rate saw their last-over target shrink from 20 to 14, at which point Rory Kleinveldt began with a ball that went for five wides.*

At Northampton, July 6 (floodlit). **Nottinghamshire won by 58 runs. Nottinghamshire 219-6** (20 overs) (S. R. Patel 35, D. T. Christian 113*); ‡**Northamptonshire 161** (17.3 overs) (B. M. Duckett 88; H. F. Gurney 3-30, L. J. Fletcher 3-21). *MoM*: D. T. Christian. *County debut*: P. Coughlin (Nottinghamshire). *Attendance*: 3,487. *For the second successive home game, Northamptonshire were crushed by an all-out assault. With Nottinghamshire 81-4 in the tenth over, Dan Christian raced to the joint-second-fastest domestic T20 hundred in 37 balls – a record he held for three weeks. He hit seven fours and nine sixes in his 113*. Nottinghamshire's total equalled the ground record, set two days earlier by Leicestershire. Duckett again batted superbly, crashing 30 off a Samit Patel over, but lacked support.*

At Northampton, July 19 (floodlit). **Derbyshire won by 31 runs. Derbyshire 211-2** (20 overs) (C. S. MacLeod 104, W. L. Madsen 50*); ‡**Northamptonshire 180** (19.3 overs) (R. E. Levi 30, R. K. Kleinveldt 36; A. L. Hughes 4-42). *MoM*: C. S. MacLeod. *Attendance*: 1,976. *From the moment Billy Godleman came down the pitch to hit the first ball for four, Northamptonshire were on course to concede another big total. Calum MacLeod eased through the gears so that 75 runs came in the last six overs. He reached Derbyshire's third T20 hundred off 58 balls, equalling his career-best 104. It was their joint-second-highest T20 total. Northamptonshire struggled to cope with the pace and bounce generated by the Derbyshire attack. Alex Hughes had his best career figures.*

At Northampton, July 27 (floodlit). **Worcestershire won by nine wickets. Northamptonshire 187-9** (20 overs) (R. E. Levi 39, S. P. Crook 33; P. R. Brown 3-31); ‡**Worcestershire 189-1** (13.1 overs) (M. J. Guptill 102, J. M. Clarke 61*). *MoM*: M. J. Guptill. *County debut*: A. Carter (Worcestershire). *Attendance*: 2,630. *Martin Guptill hammered the second-fastest domestic T20 hundred on another*

ANARCHY IN THE UK

Fastest domestic Twenty20 hundreds, by balls faced:

34	A. Symonds (112)	Kent v Middlesex at Maidstone	2004
35	**M. J. Guptill (102)**	**Worcestershire v Northamptonshire at Northampton** . . .	**2018**
37	S. B. Styris (100*)	Sussex v Gloucestershire at Hove	2012
37	**D. T. Christian (113*)** . .	**Nottinghamshire v Northamptonshire at Northampton** . .	**2018**
40	D. J. Willey (100)	Northamptonshire v Sussex at Hove	2015
41	**B. A. Raine (113)**	**Leicestershire v Warwickshire at Birmingham**	**2018**
42	B. F. Smith (105)	Worcestershire v Glamorgan at Worcester	2005
42	B. B. McCullum (158*) . .	Warwickshire v Derbyshire at Birmingham	2015
42	Shahid Afridi (101)	Hampshire v Derbyshire at Derby	2017
43	T. Köhler-Cadmore (127)	Worcestershire v Durham at Worcester	2016

---

humbling evening for Northamptonshire. They thought they had posted a challenging total, but Guptill and Joe Clarke ridiculed that notion with 162 in ten overs. Worcestershire cruised home with 41 balls to spare. Guptill sprinted to his fifty in 20, and his hundred in 35, with 12 fours and seven sixes. At 51, he reached 6,000 T20 runs. It was the joint-fourth-fastest T20 century worldwide. On his Worcestershire debut, Andrew Carter equalled Imran Tahir's record of appearing for seven counties.

At Northampton, August 5. **Warwickshire won by 17 runs.** ‡**Warwickshire 187-7** (20 overs) (I. R. Bell 43, S. R. Hain 31, C. R. Woakes 57*); **Northamptonshire 170-7** (20 overs) (J. J. Cobb 103; G. D. Elliott 3-34). *MoM:* J. J. Cobb. *Attendance:* 2,676. *Chris Woakes was central to Northamptonshire's ninth defeat in ten. Despite a typically elegant contribution from the prolific Ian Bell, Warwickshire were stuck in second gear until Woakes arrived. He hit a career-best 57* from 23 after surviving a tough chance to Richard Gleeson on 12. Cobb scored his first T20 hundred – the fourth for Northamptonshire – but played a lone hand.*

At Northampton, August 10 (floodlit). **Durham won by 12 runs. Durham 174-7** (20 overs) (T. W. M. Latham 33, S. W. Poynter 31); ‡**Northamptonshire 162-9** (20 overs) (B. M. Duckett 40, S. Prasanna 38; C. Rushworth 3-22). *MoM:* C. Rushworth. *Attendance:* 1,844. *When they needed 34 from 20 with five wickets in hand, Northamptonshire had a chance of ending their miserable home run. But Seekkuge Prasanna holed out off Nathan Rimmington as three wickets fell in four balls, and Durham seized control. Their victory secured a quarter-final place, and consigned Northamptonshire to the wooden spoon.*

At Northampton, August 16 (floodlit). **Yorkshire won by seven wickets.** ‡**Northamptonshire 162-8** (20 overs) (J. J. Cobb 68*; D. J. Willey 3-30); **Yorkshire 165-3** (15.3 overs) (A. Lyth 66, D. J. Willey 79). *MoM:* D. J. Willey. *Attendance:* 2,508. *Northamptonshire's horrible season was concluded in familiar fashion with another thumping defeat. A superb all-round display by old boy David Willey provided a stark reminder of better times: after taking three late-order wickets, he arrived at the crease in the first over to hit 79 off 44, with seven sixes. The win maintained Yorkshire's hopes of reaching the quarter-finals.*

Northamptonshire away matches

July 8: lost to Lancashire by eight wickets.
July 13: lost to Worcestershire by 41 runs.
July 20: tied with Warwickshire.
August 2: lost to Durham by 75 runs.

August 3: lost to Yorkshire by six wickets.
August 8: beat Derbyshire by seven wickets.
August 17: beat Leicestershire by four wickets.

NOTTINGHAMSHIRE

At Nottingham, July 4 (floodlit). **Warwickshire won by eight wickets. Nottinghamshire 155-7** (20 overs) (M. H. Wessels 41, W. T. Root 33*); ‡**Warwickshire 159-2** (17.2 overs) (I. R. Bell 82*, S. R. Hain 45*). *MoM:* I. R. Bell. *Attendance:* 15,278. *Warwickshire fast bowler Henry Brookes opened his T20 career with a wicket-maiden, before Nottinghamshire collapsed from 46-1 to 68-5. Three sixes for Luke Fletcher (27 from 14) helped them towards respectability, but a majestic 82* from Ian Bell – his best T20 score in three years – and his partnership of 121* in 13.2 overs with Sam Hain saw Warwickshire home with 16 balls to spare.*

At Nottingham, July 17 (floodlit). **Durham won by 34 runs. Durham 184-5** (20 overs) (T. W. M. Latham 98*, G. Clark 33); ‡**Nottinghamshire 150** (18 overs) (M. H. Wessels 42, D. T. Christian 32; P. D. Collingwood 3-25). *MoM:* T. W. M. Latham. *Attendance:* 11,173. *Tom Latham, who hit 20 in an over from Dan Christian, fell just short of a maiden T20 hundred after finding himself at the non-striker's end for the last two deliveries of the Durham innings. Nottinghamshire were on course at 97-3 from ten overs, but lost their last seven for 53.*

At Nottingham, July 20 (floodlit). **Leicestershire won by 17 runs. Leicestershire 193-6** (20 overs) (N. J. Dexter 30, B. A. Raine 83; J. T. Ball 3-40); ‡**Nottinghamshire 176-9** (20 overs) (M. H. Wessels 58; Mohammad Abbas 3-32, C. F. Parkinson 3-28). *MoM:* B. A. Raine. *Attendance:* 14,950. *Ben Raine's 43-ball 83 – a week after hitting a hundred against Warwickshire – set Nottinghamshire too many, despite a 22-ball fifty from Riki Wessels. Clever bowling from Leicestershire's left-arm spinner Callum Parkinson helped bring about a collapse from 77-1 to 124-7, and a third consecutive home defeat.*

At Nottingham, July 27 (floodlit). **Nottinghamshire won by 16 runs** (DLS). **Nottinghamshire 196-9** (20 overs) (M. H. Wessels 33, W. T. Root 40, J. D. Libby 44, D. T. Christian 36*; T. J. Lester 3-33, J. P. Faulkner 3-34); ‡**Lancashire 139-8** (15 overs) (K. R. Brown 49). *MoM:* I. S. Sodhi. *Attendance:* 11,268. *Another explosive start by Wessels, who was bowled by Graham Onions after hitting him for four sixes in five balls, was followed by career-bests for Jake Libby and Billy Root. Set a revised target of 156 from 15 overs, group leaders Lancashire received a late boost from James*

Faulkner (23 from eight balls, following three economical wickets). But, when he was seventh out, they still needed 33 from 15, which proved too much. Ish Sodhi (2-17) gave little away with his leg-breaks.

At Nottingham, August 2 (floodlit). **Nottinghamshire won by nine runs.** ‡**Nottinghamshire 166-5** (20 overs) (T. J. Moores 48, D. T. Christian 39*); **Derbyshire 157-8** (20 overs) (Wahab Riaz 53; I. S. Sodhi 4-17). MoM: I. S. Sodhi. *Attendance:* 11,237. *Sodhi's competition-best 4-17 stifled Derbyshire. At 93-2 in the tenth over, they were in sight of Nottinghamshire's 166-5, but lost momentum after Sodhi's leg-breaks dismissed Wahab Riaz (53 off 31, his first half-century in all T20 cricket) and Gary Wilson in three deliveries. Nottinghamshire's total relied on Tom Moores's 48 off 34, then a stand of 73* in 7.4 overs between Christian and Root. Riaz claimed 1-17 from four tidy overs. Nottinghamshire became the second county, after Lancashire, to record 100 wins in domestic T20 cricket.*

At Nottingham, August 4 (floodlit). **Worcestershire won by 72 runs.** ‡**Worcestershire 206-2** (20 overs) (M. M. Ali 65, C. J. Ferguson 102*, R. A. Whiteley 32*); **Nottinghamshire 134** (17.2 overs) (S. J. Mullaney 55; W. D. Parnell 3-20, P. R. Brown 3-21). MoM: C. J. Ferguson. *Attendance:* 9,809. *Callum Ferguson completed a superb maiden T20 century from the penultimate ball of the Worcestershire innings, his 55th, after he and Moeen Ali (65 from 36) added a powerful 135 for the second wicket in 12.2 overs. Pat Brown and Wayne Parnell had shared six wickets as Nottinghamshire – with the exception of Steven Mullaney – fell away tamely. Worcestershire opened up a three-point lead at the top of the group.*

At Nottingham, August 10 (floodlit). **Nottinghamshire won by 63 runs.** ‡**Nottinghamshire 212-5** (20 overs) (J. D. Libby 58, T. J. Moores 80*); **Yorkshire 149-7** (20 overs) (T. Köhler-Cadmore 72, D. J. Willey 30; H. F. Gurney 3-24). MoM: T. J. Moores. *Attendance:* 12,277. *Nottinghamshire stayed in quarter-final contention after their highest home total of the season, and their most emphatic win. Moores (80* from 49) and Libby (58 from 33) made career-bests, adding 112 in 10.5 overs for the third wicket. In reply, Tom Köhler-Cadmore hit 72 from 50, but Yorkshire's runs dried up after he fell in the 15th over: only 20 came from the last five. Harry Gurney took 3-3 in his last ten balls.*

Nottinghamshire away matches

July 6: beat Northamptonshire by 58 runs.
July 8: beat Leicestershire by 19 runs.
July 13: beat Derbyshire by 39 runs (DLS).
July 28: lost to Durham by seven wickets.

August 9: lost to Warwickshire by six wickets.
August 12: beat Worcestershire by five wickets.
August 17: beat Yorkshire by eight wickets.

WARWICKSHIRE

At Birmingham, July 8. **Warwickshire won by eight wickets. Yorkshire 157-7** (20 overs) (G. S. Ballance 79; O. J. Hannon-Dalby 3-37); ‡**Warwickshire 158-2** (15.5 overs) (E. J. Pollock 39, I. R. Bell 50*, A. J. Hose 51*). MoM: E. J. Pollock. *Attendance:* 9,619. *Warwickshire's victory was based on a brutal assault from Ed Pollock, who flayed 26 of his season's-best 39 in an opening over from Matt Fisher that cost 33. They were then eased to victory with 25 balls to spare by a fourth-wicket partnership of 83* – Warwickshire's highest for any wicket against Yorkshire – between Ian Bell and Adam Hose. "I feel like a fan watching our guys bat," said coach Jim Troughton. Yorkshire had been 28-3, before Gary Ballance's 79 from 49 gave them something to bowl at.*

At Birmingham, July 13 (floodlit). **Leicestershire won by 100 runs. Leicestershire 229-5** (20 overs) (M. J. Cosgrove 42, B. A. Raine 113); ‡**Warwickshire 129** (15.2 overs) (C. F. Parkinson 4-20). MoM: B. A. Raine. *Attendance:* 8,593. *Ben Raine smashed the second-fastest T20 hundred by an Englishman, in 41 balls – one more than David Willey for Northamptonshire against Sussex in 2015. His eventual 113 was Leicestershire's highest score, and included ten sixes. "I knew I had it in me," he said. Their biggest total was also the biggest against Warwickshire. Raine then took the key wickets of Bell and Sam Hain in his first over, and held a good catch to remove Colin de Grandhomme.*

At Birmingham, July 15. **Durham won by 18 runs.** ‡**Durham 220-6** (20 overs) (T. W. M. Latham 58, G. Clark 65, P. D. Collingwood 37, W. R. Smith 34; G. D. Elliott 3-40); **Warwickshire 202-5** (20 overs) (S. R. Hain 95, C. de Grandhomme 63*). MoM: G. Clark. *Attendance:* 6,715.

Warwickshire's bowlers were again in a generous mood, helping Durham to their second-highest T20 total. Tom Latham and Graham Clark put on 126 in 68 balls, Durham's record opening stand and, although Warwickshire hit back, Paul Collingwood and Will Smith added a rapid 75. The reply started limply, but Hain and de Grandhomme put on 110 for the fourth wicket in 8.2 overs. De Grandhomme hit Imran Tahir for four successive sixes, and Hain took 29 off a Chris Rushworth over, but it was still not enough.

At Birmingham, July 20 (floodlit). **Tied. Northamptonshire 231-5** (20 overs) (R. E. Levi 95*, J. J. Cobb 61; A. D. Thomason 3-55); ‡**Warwickshire 231-5** (20 overs) (I. R. Bell 131, A. J. Hose 64; N. L. Buck 3-38). *MoM:* I. R. Bell. *Attendance:* 7,716. *Records tumbled on an exhilarating night, but both sides were left regretting missed chances. The aggregate of 462 runs was a record for a*

HIGHEST TWENTY20 MATCH AGGREGATES

497	Central Districts (249-3) beat Otago (248-4) at New Plymouth.................	2016-17
489	West Indies (245-6) beat India (244-4) at Lauderhill...........................	2016
488	**New Zealand (243-6) lost to Australia (245-5) at Auckland**	**2017-18**
469	Chennai Super Kings (246-5) beat Rajasthan Royals (223-5) at Chennai.........	2009-10
467	South Africa (231-7) lost to West Indies (236-6) at Johannesburg	2014-15
467	**Balkh Legends (244-6) beat Kabul Zwanan (223-7) at Sharjah**	**2018-19**
462	**Warwickshire (231-5) tied with Northamptonshire (231-5) at Birmingham**....	**2018**
459	South Africa (229-4) lost to England (230-8) at Mumbai	2015-16
459	**Kolkata Knight Riders (245-6) beat Kings XI Punjab (214-8) at Indore**.......	**2017-18**
457	Australia (248-6) beat England (209-6) at Southampton	2013
457	**Kent (231-5) beat Somerset (226-5) at Canterbury**	**2018**

domestic fixture, and a world record for a tie. Powered by Richard Levi's 95, Northamptonshire reached 50 in the fifth over and 100 in the ninth; he and Josh Cobb put on 129 for the second wicket. But they were eclipsed by Bell and Hose, who added 171 in 14 overs, a global record for the third wicket. Bell hit his first T20 hundred, in his 90th match, and struck 11 fours and seven sixes in his 131 off 62. Warwickshire needed ten off the final over, but Nathan Buck ensured they were one short.*

At Birmingham, August 9 (floodlit). **Warwickshire won by six wickets. Nottinghamshire 152-8** (20 overs) (S. R. Patel 41; O. J. Hannon-Dalby 3-30); ‡**Warwickshire 156-4** (16.2 overs) (I. R. Bell 54, C. de Grandhomme 49*). *MoM:* I. R. Bell. *Attendance:* 8,952. *Nottinghamshire's sixth defeat further loosened their grip on the trophy, but Warwickshire kept their quarter-final hopes alive. Their bowlers had operated efficiently, but were assisted by some feckless batting: only Samit Patel, who top-scored with 41, lasted more than 20 balls. Warwickshire lost two early wickets, but Bell saw them home, passing 500 runs for the season.*

At Birmingham, August 15 (floodlit). **Warwickshire won by seven wickets. ‡Lancashire 102** (19 overs) (O. J. Hannon-Dalby 4-20); **Warwickshire 105-3** (14.1 overs) (I. R. Bell 34, E. J. Pollock 36). *MoM:* O. J. Hannon-Dalby. *Attendance:* 8,759. *A dry, turning pitch made for a disappointing contest which was effectively over by the interval. Lancashire, already through to the last eight, slumped to their second-lowest T20 total. Oliver Hannon-Dalby's career-best figures made up for the absence of Henry Brookes, Olly Stone and Chris Woakes, and his mixture of slow and slower balls baffled the batsmen. Lancashire used five spinners, in vain.*

At Birmingham, August 17 (floodlit). **Worcestershire won by 15 runs. Worcestershire 209-5** (20 overs) (J. M. Clarke 32, M. M. Ali 115; J. E. Poysden 3-41); ‡**Warwickshire 194-7** (20 overs) (E. J. Pollock 36, A. J. Hose 45, C. de Grandhomme 31; W. D. Parnell 3-47). *MoM:* M. M. Ali. *Attendance:* 14,895. *Worcestershire secured a home quarter-final after Moeen Ali, released from England's Test squad at Trent Bridge, pummelled his maiden T20 century, from 51 balls. In all he hit 12 fours and seven sixes, making the most of being dropped twice before he had reached 50. He put on 80 with Joe Clarke and 74 with Callum Ferguson (13). His 115 was the highest score against Warwickshire, surpassing Raine's 113 a month earlier. Warwickshire's bowlers leaked 200 for the fifth time in 2018, having previously done so three times in 15 seasons. After the abandonment of Durham's match against Derbyshire, Worcestershire knew they had to restrict Warwickshire to under 203 to head the group. Wayne Parnell grabbed the key wicket of Bell, and Pat Brown bowled beautifully to make sure they did.*

Warwickshire away matches

July 4: beat Nottinghamshire by eight wickets.
July 6: lost to Worcestershire by four runs.
July 27: lost to Yorkshire by 31 runs.
August 2: beat Leicestershire by eight wickets.

August 3: lost to Derbyshire by 16 runs.
August 5: beat Northamptonshire by 17 runs.
August 10: lost to Lancashire by 37 runs.

WORCESTERSHIRE

At Worcester, July 6. **Worcestershire won by four runs. Worcestershire 192-7** (20 overs) (M. J. Guptill 51, J. M. Clarke 33, C. J. Ferguson 45, R. A. Whiteley 34); ‡**Warwickshire 188-9** (20 overs) (S. R. Hain 70; P. R. Brown 3-28, E. G. Barnard 3-29). *MoM:* P. R. Brown. *Attendance:* 4,161. *Luke Wood, on loan from Nottinghamshire, bowled a nerveless final over, conceding only seven to ensure Worcestershire edged a tense finish. Tim Ambrose and Oliver Hannon-Dalby had threatened to pilfer the win for Warwickshire with a last-wicket stand of 36*, after Sam Hain followed up two centuries for England Lions with 70 off 44 balls. Pat Brown and Ed Barnard responded with career-bests. Earlier, Martin Guptill – on his Worcestershire T20 debut – hit 51 off 40.*

At Worcester, July 13. **Worcestershire won by 41 runs.** Reduced to 9 overs a side. **Worcestershire 130-3** (9 overs) (T. M. Head 37, R. A. Whiteley 36*); ‡**Northamptonshire 89-6** (9 overs) (A. G. Wakely 54*; D. Y. Pennington 4-9). *MoM:* D. Y. Pennington. *Attendance:* 2,249. *On his home debut, 19-year-old seamer Dillon Pennington took four wickets in two overs as Worcestershire maintained their 100% start. Play began two hours late after a downpour, but Worcestershire raced along at more than 14 an over, Travis Head clubbing 37 off 14 on his competition debut for them. For Northamptonshire, only Alex Wakely made any headway.*

At Worcester, July 15. **Yorkshire won by 12 runs.** Yorkshire 179-7 (20 overs) (A. Lyth 35, H. C. Brook 33, G. S. Ballance 40; P. R. Brown 3-34); ‡**Worcestershire 167-8** (20 overs) (R. A. Whiteley 37; T. T. Bresnan 3-38, S. A. Patterson 3-35). *MoM:* T. T. Bresnan. *County debut:* J. A. Thompson (Yorkshire). *Attendance:* 2,871. *The last unbeaten record in the competition disappeared in the face of a fine all-round Yorkshire display. Gary Ballance's 40 off 21 balls included four sixes. Tim Bresnan grabbed the first of his three wickets by removing Guptill in the first over, and Worcestershire were never quite up with the rate, despite Ross Whiteley's 37 off 21.*

At Worcester, July 29. **Worcestershire v Lancashire. Abandoned.**

At Worcester, August 3. **Worcestershire won by three wickets.** Durham 194-7 (20 overs) (T. W. M. Latham 78, R. D. Pringle 35); ‡**Worcestershire 195-7** (19.4 overs) (M. M. Ali 42, C. J. Ferguson 39, R. A. Whiteley 60; B. J. McCarthy 4-31). *MoM:* R. A. Whiteley. *County debuts:* W. D. Parnell (Worcestershire); B. G. Whitehead (Durham). *Attendance:* 3,084. *Needing 70 off five overs, Worcestershire seemed set to become the latest victims of Durham's hot streak. Whiteley's 60 off 26 put the match back in the balance, but they still needed ten when he was dismissed off the first ball of the final over. Wayne Parnell, making his debut for his fourth county, got them in three deliveries off Nathan Rimmington. Barry McCarthy's 4-31 was a career-best. Tom Latham had boosted Durham's total with 78 off 49, including six sixes.*

At Worcester, August 9. **Worcestershire won by 16 runs.** ‡**Worcestershire 137-8** (20 overs) (J. M. Clarke 76; G. C. Viljoen 3-25); **Derbyshire 121-7** (20 overs) (B. A. Godleman 38, G. C. Wilson 35). *MoM:* J. M. Clarke. *Attendance:* 3,267. *A slow pitch made life awkward for most batsmen, but not Joe Clarke. After his 76 off 53, Parnell's 12 was Worcestershire's next highest score. Despite defiance from Billy Godleman and Gary Wilson, Derbyshire could not prevent the hosts from regaining top spot.*

At Worcester, August 12. **Nottinghamshire won by five wickets.** Worcestershire 191-6 (20 overs) (B. L. D'Oliveira 64); ‡**Nottinghamshire 194-5** (18.1 overs) (M. H. Wessels 55, J. D. Libby 37, T. J. Moores 30; P. R. Brown 3-28). *MoM:* M. H. Wessels. *Attendance:* 2,226. *Worcestershire's bid to secure a home quarter-final was thwarted by a brutal innings from Riki Wessels. After managing just a single from his first four balls, his next nine scoring shots were all sixes; in total, he faced only 18 balls. Jake Libby and Tom Moores helped take Nottinghamshire home with something to spare. Brown's first three balls had been hit for six by Wessels, but he finished with three wickets to become Worcestershire's most successful bowler in a season, surpassing Saeed Ajmal's 21 in 2015. Their total included Brett D'Oliveira's best T20 score.*

Worcestershire away matches

July 5: beat Lancashire by five wickets.
July 8: beat Derbyshire by six wickets.
July 20: lost to Durham by seven wickets.
July 27: beat Northamptonshire by nine wickets.

August 4: beat Nottinghamshire by 72 runs.
August 10: lost to Leicestershire by five runs.
August 17: beat Warwickshire by 15 runs.

YORKSHIRE

At Leeds, July 5 (floodlit). **Yorkshire won by 44 runs. Yorkshire 200-3** (20 overs) (A. Lyth 92*, H. C. Brook 44, J. A. Tattersall 53*); ‡**Durham 156-4** (20 overs) (B. A. Stokes 90*; J. A. Brooks 3-21). *MoM:* A. Lyth. *County debut:* Imran Tahir (Durham). *Attendance:* 7,879. *Adam Lyth and Ben Stokes both batted through 20 overs – in vain, in Stokes's case. Testing out his hamstring after a month on the sidelines, he took time to adjust but finished with eight fours and five sixes from 68 balls, though he was not helped by a bruised ankle. Competition newcomers Harry Brook (44 from 31) and Jonny Tattersall (53* from 27) gave Lyth (92* from 54) excellent support. Tidy bowling, led by Jack Brooks, in his first T20 game for three years, meant Durham were never in the hunt.*

At Leeds, July 27 (floodlit). **Yorkshire won by 31 runs** (DLS). ‡**Yorkshire 226-8** (20 overs) (A. Lyth 40, T. Köhler-Cadmore 73, K. S. Williamson 49, G. S. Ballance 35); **Warwickshire 176-4** (18 overs) (I. R. Bell 42, A. J. Hose 43, C. de Grandhomme 38*). *MoM:* T. Köhler-Cadmore. *Attendance:* 9,666. *In his first game since accepting England's invitation to resume his Test career, Adil Rashid produced three tight overs to stifle Warwickshire's hopes of reaching a revised target of 208 in 18 overs. Despite possessing a white-ball-only contract for Yorkshire, he was warmly received by the crowd. Chris Woakes and Boyd Rankin had been cannon fodder as the hosts thrashed their fourth-highest T20 score, Tom Köhler-Cadmore leading the assault with six sixes in a 30-ball 73.*

At Leeds, July 30 (floodlit). **Derbyshire won by 77 runs.** Derbyshire 179-7 (17 overs) (Wahab Riaz 42, W. L. Madsen 66; J. A. Thompson 3-23); ‡**Yorkshire 102** (14 overs) (L. H. Ferguson 3-21, A. L. Hughes 3-12, G. C. Viljoen 3-32). *MoM:* W. L. Madsen. *Attendance:* 4,979. *A rain-reduced match saw a slovenly Yorkshire fall to Derbyshire for the second time in three days. From 91-4, they lost six for 11 as Alex Hughes and Hardus Viljoen cleaned up; 102 was their lowest score against Derbyshire. After David Willey had bowled Billy Godleman with the first ball of the match, Wayne Madsen crashed a 28-ball 66, including a reverse-swept six; seamer Jordan Thompson claimed 3-23 on home debut.*

At Leeds, July 31 (floodlit). **Yorkshire won by 60 runs.** ‡**Yorkshire 187-5** (20 overs) (T. Köhler-Cadmore 53, D. J. Willey 31, K. S. Williamson 77); **Leicestershire 127-9** (20 overs) (J. A. Brooks 3-23). *MoM:* K. S. Williamson. *Attendance:* 8,643. *Brooks claimed three wickets in his first two overs to leave Leicestershire 49-5 and out of the contest. Köhler-Cadmore, dropped early on, had scored a well-constructed half-century for Yorkshire, but it was Kane Williamson who treated the home crowd to a masterclass, hitting five sixes in a 41-ball 77.*

At Leeds, August 3 (floodlit). **Yorkshire won by six wickets.** ‡**Northamptonshire 129-7** (20 overs) (C. O. Thurston 41); **Yorkshire 132-4** (18.4 overs) (K. S. Williamson 52*). *MoM:* K. S. Williamson. *Attendance:* 9,152. *Two fours and a six from Kane Williamson in the 18th over, bowled by Luke Procter, helped ease Yorkshire to a comfortable win, after Northamptonshire, still winless, fell short of a competitive total. Charlie Thurston, who earlier in the season had hit 53 here on his county debut in the Royal London Cup, was again impressive, but the visitors managed only 12 boundaries.*

At Leeds, August 9 (floodlit). **Lancashire won by six wickets.** ‡**Yorkshire 181-9** (20 overs) (T. Köhler-Cadmore 46, D. J. Willey 80; J. P. Faulkner 3-24); **Lancashire 185-4** (17.4 overs) (A. L. Davies 34, K. R. Brown 51, A. M. Lilley 47). *MoM:* K. R. Brown. *Attendance:* 13,260. *While Willey was thrashing a 43-ball 80 in a second-wicket stand of 129 with Köhler-Cadmore, Lancashire crumbled. Even when Willey departed in the 12th over, Yorkshire were handsomely placed at 130-2. But they lost momentum as the bowlers found their lengths, James Faulkner taking three wickets in a final over that cost just five. Lancashire openers Alex Davies and Karl Brown responded with 57 in 5.2, before Arron Lilley smacked a brutal, career-best 47 from 20 balls to help his side complete a Roses T20 double.*

At Leeds, August 17 (floodlit). **Nottinghamshire won by eight wickets.** ‡**Yorkshire 163-6** (20 overs) (A. Lyth 44, D. J. Willey 51, K. S. Williamson 44); **Nottinghamshire 169-2** (19 overs) (A. D. Hales 71*, J. D. Libby 30, T. J. Moores 43*). *MoM:* A. D. Hales. *Attendance:* 10,232.

A season's-best 71* from 56 balls by Alex Hales took Nottinghamshire into the quarter-finals at Yorkshire's expense. Yorkshire might have managed more than 96-1 after 12 overs, but Harry Gurney proved unhittable at the death: of the five scored from the 20th over, four were byes or leg-byes. Acting-captain Willey's second half-century in two days proved in vain.

Yorkshire away matches

July 8: lost to Warwickshire by eight wickets.
July 13: beat Durham by ten wickets.
July 15: beat Worcestershire by 12 runs.
July 20: lost to Lancashire by one run.

July 28: lost to Derbyshire by five wickets.
August 10: lost to Nottinghamshire by 63 runs.
August 16: beat Northamptonshire by seven wickets.

SOUTH GROUP

ESSEX

At Chelmsford, July 4 (floodlit). **Sussex won by 36 runs.** ‡**Sussex 181-6** (20 overs) (L. J. Evans 61, M. G. K. Burgess 56); **Essex 145** (19.4 overs) (V. Chopra 64; J. C. Archer 3-24, D. Wiese 5-24). *MoM:* D. Wiese. *Attendance:* 4,087. *County debuts:* A. Zampa (Essex); T. C. Bruce, Rashid Khan (Sussex). *After Sussex slipped to 32-3, Laurie Evans and Michael Burgess, who reached a 20-ball half-century in his first T20 innings (he hadn't batted in his only previous match, for Leicestershire in 2016), put on 81 in seven overs. It helped Sussex set a target that proved beyond Essex, whose last five wickets tumbled for two runs in eight balls. The Afghanistan leg-spinner Rashid Khan had tidy figures of 4–14–25–2 in his first county match.*

At Chelmsford, July 6 (floodlit). **Essex won by three wickets.** ‡**Middlesex 179-6** (20 overs) (S. S. Eskinazi 46, J. A. Simpson 46); **Essex 181-7** (19.5 overs) (A. J. A. Wheater 45, V. Chopra 38). *MoM:* A. J. A. Wheater. *Attendance:* 5,019. *Stevie Eskinazi and John Simpson shared a fourth-wicket stand of 92, then Hilton Cartwright (27*) cracked a six and three fours in the last over, from Ravi Bopara. Middlesex seemed to have enough but, with Dwayne Bravo proving expensive (3.5–3–53–1), Essex scrambled home thanks to Simon Harmer's four off the penultimate ball. Adam Wheater had kicked off the reply with 45 from 18.*

At Chelmsford, July 13 (floodlit). **Glamorgan won by two wickets. Essex 167** (20 overs) (A. J. A. Wheater 34, R. N. ten Doeschate 43); ‡**Glamorgan 171-8** (20 overs) (A. H. T. Donald 37, C. B. Cooke 60*; A. Zampa 3-17). *MoM:* C. B. Cooke. *Attendance:* 5,062. *Glamorgan looked dead in the water at 110-8 in the 16th over of the chase. But Chris Cooke hammered 60* from 29 balls – he and Timm van der Gugten (9*) reaped 61* from the last 4.2 overs – and sealed a remarkable victory by crashing the final delivery, from Neil Wagner, to the fence after a wide had tied the scores.*

At Chelmsford, July 21 (floodlit). **Tied.** ‡**Hampshire 170-5** (20 overs) (C. Munro 38, S. A. Northeast 73*, L. A. Dawson 32); **Essex 170-8** (20 overs) (D. W. Lawrence 49, R. S. Bopara 39; C. P. Wood 3-27). *MoM:* S. A. Northeast. *Attendance:* 4,790. *Essex needed the last over needing 13, and looked set for victory after Bopara clubbed Ryan Stevenson's first ball for six, was dropped off the second, and hit the fifth for four. But, needing two from the last, he was beaten by Colin Munro's throw from deep square, and the match was tied. Hampshire had earlier been becalmed, and were grateful that Sam Northeast struck four sixes, including one from the last ball of the innings in a Matt Quinn over costing 14.*

At Chelmsford, August 5. **Surrey won by six wickets. Essex 157-5** (20 overs) (V. Chopra 52); ‡**Surrey 159-4** (16.3 overs) (N. J. Maddinson 49*, R. Clarke 37*). *MoM:* R. Clarke. *Attendance:* 4,694. *Varun Chopra hit his fourth half-century of the competition, but received little support. Surrey's chase began badly, with Jason Roy stumped off the first delivery he faced, a wide from Ashar Zaidi, but Nic Maddinson and Rikki Clarke took them home with little fuss.*

At Chelmsford, August 10 (floodlit). **Essex v Gloucestershire. Abandoned.** *Essex's point lifted them off the bottom of the table.*

At Chelmsford, August 17 (floodlit). **Kent won by five wickets. Essex 201-6** (20 overs) (A. J. A. Wheater 40, V. Chopra 37); ‡**Kent 203-5** (19.5 overs) (J. L. Denly 45, D. J. Bell-Drummond 80, S. W. Billings 33). *MoM:* D. J. Bell-Drummond. *Attendance:* 4,811. *Essex had passed 200 for the first time in 2018 at Lord's the previous night – and now did so again, even though Adam Wheater's*

40 was the highest score. But it was not enough. Joe Denly spanked 45 in 23 balls during an opening stand of 98 with Daniel Bell-Drummond, who batted through to the final over for his 51-ball 80. Although he fell to Matt Coles with five wanted, Grant Stewart carved the winning boundary to guarantee Kent a home quarter-final. Bopara, playing his 300th T20 match, had earlier claimed his 200th wicket when he bowled Heino Kuhn.

Essex away matches

July 12: lost to Surrey by 39 runs.
July 20: no result v Gloucestershire.
August 2: lost to Kent by 28 runs.
August 3: lost to Somerset by ten wickets.

August 7: lost to Glamorgan by six runs.
August 12: no result v Hampshire.
August 16: beat Middlesex by six wickets.

GLAMORGAN

At Cardiff, July 8. **Sussex won by eight wickets.** ‡**Glamorgan 173-4** (20 overs) (C. A. Ingram 81*, D. L. Lloyd 33); **Sussex 177-2** (18.4 overs) (L. J. Wright 88, L. J. Evans 65*). *MoM: L. J. Wright. Attendance: 4,198. Colin Ingram's 44-ball 81* dragged Glamorgan to a reasonable total, but their bowlers then pitched too short. Luke Wright (88 from 53) and Laurie Evans (65* from 47) took advantage in a second-wicket stand of 123 that set Sussex up for a comfortable victory. Shaun Marsh, one of Glamorgan's overseas players, hurt his shoulder trying to stop a boundary and missed the rest of the season.*

At Cardiff, July 20 (floodlit). **Somerset won by 30 runs. Somerset 190-5** (20 overs) (J. C. Hildreth 56*, C. J. Anderson 59; T. van der Gugten 3-36); ‡**Glamorgan 160-9** (20 overs) (U. T. Khawaja 44, K. S. Carlson 33). *MoM: C. J. Anderson. Attendance: 6,613. County debut: J. A. Burns (Glamorgan). Somerset were rescued from 59-4 by James Hildreth and Corey Anderson, who muscled 97 in eight overs. Glamorgan then struggled against a varied attack, in which leg-spinner Max Waller claimed his 100th T20 wicket (Chris Cooke). Joe Burns, signed to replace his fellow Australian Marsh, made a disappointing start, dropping a catch and later being stumped for five.*

At Cardiff, July 29. **Glamorgan v Kent. Abandoned.**

At Cardiff, August 3 (floodlit). **Glamorgan won by two runs. Glamorgan 201-6** (20 overs) (A. H. T. Donald 31, C. A. J. Meschede 77*; B. A. C. Howell 3-39); ‡**Gloucestershire 199-9** (20 overs) (R. F. Higgins 37, J. M. R. Taylor 52; T. van der Gugten 3-54, M. G. Hogan 3-31). *MoM: C. A. J. Meschede. Attendance: 5,870. Gloucestershire entered the last five overs requiring another 75, but Jack Taylor's 52 from 21 balls put them back in the hunt. Andrew Tye needed three from the last delivery, but was bowled by Timm van der Gugten. Glamorgan's Graham Wagg was penalised five runs for "fake fielding", and later laid out by a fierce straight-drive from Taylor that hit him on the head. He took no further part in the game, but made a full recovery. Michael Hogan's third wicket (Gareth Roderick) was his 100th in T20 cricket.*

At Cardiff, August 7 (floodlit). **Glamorgan won by six runs. Glamorgan 198-7** (20 overs) (C. A. Ingram 89, G. G. Wagg 53*; M. R. Quinn 3-61); ‡**Essex 192-6** (20 overs) (V. Chopra 54, R. S. Bopara 45*). *MoM: C. A. Ingram. Attendance: 4,955. Glamorgan kept qualification hopes alive with their sixth victory of the summer, after Hogan remained calm in the final over, which started with Essex needing 24. After Ravi Bopara had thrashed a six and two fours, Hogan conceded only a single from the last two balls. Ingram had set up Glamorgan's big total with 89 from 47, and Wagg clubbed 53* from 28 as he and Ruaidhri Smith (22*) smashed 60 in the last three overs. They were particularly severe on Matt Quinn, who had 2-5 after two overs, but conceded 56 from his last two.*

At Cardiff, August 10 (floodlit). **Glamorgan won by eight wickets. Hampshire 151-8** (20 overs) (J. M. Vince 30, R. R. Rossouw 50; C. A. J. Meschede 3-21); ‡**Glamorgan 155-2** (15.5 overs) (C. A. J. Meschede 32, C. A. Ingram 71*, K. S. Carlson 31*). *MoM: C. A. Ingram. Attendance: 5,449. Another rapid knock from Ingram – 71* from 40 balls – set up Glamorgan's fifth win on the trot. It had looked unlikely when James Vince (30 from 13) and Rilee Rossouw (50 from 24) blazed away at the start: Hampshire were 90-1 after 7.5 overs, but Craig Meschede applied the brakes.*

At Cardiff, August 17 (floodlit). **Surrey won by 24 runs** (DLS). ‡**Glamorgan 183-8** (20 overs) (K. S. Carlson 35, D. L. Lloyd 39, C. B. Cooke 31; T. K. Curran 3-30); **Surrey 60-0** (5 overs) (A. J. Finch 44*). *MoM: A. J. Finch. Attendance: 5,215. The winners stood a chance of reaching the* *quarter-finals, if Sussex lost to Middlesex – but they won, rendering the result here academic. With rain threatening, Surrey shot out of the blocks, reaching 50 in the fourth over; when the weather closed in soon after, they were well ahead.*

Glamorgan away matches

July 6: beat Hampshire by 63 runs.
July 13: beat Essex by two wickets.
July 27: lost to Gloucestershire by 30 runs.
July 31: beat Surrey by four wickets.

August 5: beat Middlesex by seven wickets.
August 12: lost to Somerset by 29 runs.
August 14: lost to Sussex by 98 runs.

GLOUCESTERSHIRE

At Bristol, July 11 (floodlit). **Gloucestershire won by five runs. Gloucestershire 184-7** (20 overs) (K. Noema-Barnett 31, J. M. R. Taylor 42*); ‡**Kent 179-8** (20 overs) (H. G. Kuhn 44, S. R. Dickson 32). *MoM: J. M. R. Taylor. Attendance: 1,250. Gloucestershire's unheralded seam attack exploited a slow pitch to hinder Kent's more illustrious batting. Joe Denly suffered a rare failure, but Heino Kuhn hit 44 to sustain the visitors' chase, which went to the last ball. Earlier, Jack Taylor's pugnacious 42* gave the Gloucestershire innings a rousing finale. The match was brought forward to 3pm to avoid a clash with England's appearance in the semi-final of the football World Cup.*

At Bristol, July 13 (floodlit). **Gloucestershire won by four wickets. Somerset 114-8** (11 overs) (C. J. Anderson 40*; A. J. Tye 3-24); ‡**Gloucestershire 116-6** (10.1 overs) (I. A. Cockbain 43*). *MoM: I. A. Cockbain. Attendance: 9,832. In a match reduced by rain to 11 overs a side, Gloucestershire overhauled a target of 115 thanks largely to Ian Cockbain's 43* from 22 balls. Somerset, kept in check by some athletic fielding and three wickets for Andrew Tye, would have been in deeper trouble without a 17-ball 40* from Corey Anderson.*

At Cheltenham, July 20. **No result. Essex 172-7** (18.2 overs) (V. Chopra 61; T. M. J. Smith 3-39) **v ‡Gloucestershire.** *Attendance: 4,794. Essex began strongly after being inserted but, when Michael Klinger set in train a collapse of five for 32 with a brilliant run-out of Varun Chopra for 61, Gloucestershire seemed to have gained the upper hand. But their quest for a fourth straight win was frustrated by heavy rain.*

At Cheltenham, July 27. **Gloucestershire won by 30 runs. Gloucestershire 197-6** (20 overs) (M. A. H. Hammond 34, M. Klinger 77*, R. F. Higgins 30); ‡**Glamorgan 167-9** (20 overs) (U. T. Khawaja 33, C. A. Ingram 38; R. F. Higgins 3-34, A. J. Tye 3-17). *MoM: A. J. Tye. Attendance: 4,898. Gloucestershire's Australians were key in securing a convincing victory at a sold-out Cheltenham. Klinger cracked 20 from the last over, bowled by Michael Hogan, to finish on a well-judged 77*; Tye then claimed 3-17 to dismantle Glamorgan's middle order.*

At Bristol, August 9 (floodlit). **Gloucestershire won by 70 runs. Gloucestershire 242-4** (20 overs) (M. Klinger 44, I. A. Cockbain 123, K. Noema-Barnett 31); ‡**Middlesex 172-6** (20 overs) (E. J. G. Morgan 36, S. S. Eskinazi 51; K. Noema-Barnett 3-18). *MoM: I. A. Cockbain. Attendance: 3,260. Cockbain's maiden T20 hundred swept Gloucestershire to another win, their seventh in ten. Both their 242 and Cockbain's 123 had been bettered only once by Gloucestershire, while Tom Barber's 4–9–62–1 was the most expensive return for Middlesex. Cockbain, who hit 48 in fours and 48 in sixes, fell to the last ball of the innings, his 61st. Middlesex raced to 60-1 in the fifth over, but were undone by Kieran Noema-Barnett: he had miserly figures of 3-18 after earlier crashing 31 from 12 balls.*

GLOUCESTERSHIRE'S HIGHEST TWENTY20 TOTALS...

254-3	v Middlesex at Uxbridge	2011
242-4	**v Middlesex at Bristol**............................	**2018**
227-4	v Somerset at Bristol................................	2006
221-7	v Glamorgan at Bristol	2003
214-4	v Middlesex at Richmond.........................	2015

...AND THEIR TWENTY20 CENTURIES

126*	M. Klinger v Essex at Bristol..........................	2015
123	**I. A. Cockbain v Middlesex at Bristol**................	**2018**
119	K. J. O'Brien v Middlesex at Uxbridge.................	2011
108*	M. Klinger v Worcestershire at Bristol................	2013
104*	M. Klinger v Essex at Chelmsford.....................	2015
104*	M. Klinger v Glamorgan at Bristol....................	2015
102	H. J. H. Marshall v Middlesex at Uxbridge.............	2011
101	M. Klinger v Somerset at Taunton.....................	2016
101*	M. Klinger v Hampshire at Bristol....................	2017
100*	I. J. Harvey v Warwickshire at Birmingham.............	2003
100	H. J. H. Marshall v Worcestershire at Kidderminster......	2007

At Bristol, August 12. **Gloucestershire won by five runs. Gloucestershire 174-6** (20 overs) (K. Noema-Barnett 57*; M. Morkel 3-34); ‡**Surrey 169-7** (20 overs) (B. T. Foakes 59, R. Clarke 35; D. A. Payne 3-29, B. A. C. Howell 3-31). *MoM:* K. Noema-Barnett. *Attendance:* 2,699. David Payne bowled Ben Foakes round his legs for 59 in the penultimate over to take the wind from Surrey sails. Even so, they would have levelled the scores with a last-ball six, but managed only a single. For Gloucestershire, Noema-Barnett had hit his first T20 fifty outside his native New Zealand to repair damage inflicted by Morne Morkel and Rikki Clarke (2-27). Victory guaranteed them a place in the quarter-finals, with three to play, while Surrey's progress was no longer in their own hands.

At Bristol, August 16 (floodlit). **Sussex won by four wickets.** ‡**Gloucestershire 159-9** (20 overs) (M. Klinger 59; Rashid Khan 3-24); **Sussex 160-6** (19 overs) (P. D. Salt 60, H. Z. Finch 33, D. Wiese 38; B. A. C. Howell 3-37). *MoM:* P. D. Salt. *County debut:* J. B. Lintott (Gloucestershire). *Attendance:* 3,448. A buccaneering 30-ball 60 from Phil Salt proved decisive: he and Harry Finch put on 85 for the first wicket, allowing Sussex's assault on 160 to withstand a lurch to 87-3. Two of those wickets went to left-arm spinner Jake Lintott, on Gloucestershire debut. The hosts had also enjoyed a decent start – 41-0 in the fifth suggested riches that, despite a fifty from Klinger, never materialised; only three batsmen reached ten, as Rashid Khan proved a thorn in their side. Sussex maintained their hopes of joining Gloucestershire in the knockouts.

Gloucestershire away matches

July 6: lost to Somerset by six wickets.	August 5: beat Kent by eight wickets.
July 8: beat Middlesex by six wickets.	August 10: no result v Essex.
August 1: beat Sussex by four wickets.	August 17: lost to Hampshire by six wickets.
August 3: lost to Glamorgan by two runs.	

HAMPSHIRE

At Southampton, July 6 (floodlit). **Glamorgan won by 63 runs. Glamorgan 168-6** (20 overs) (C. A. Ingram 35, D. L. Lloyd 38*); ‡**Hampshire 105** (16.5 overs) (A. G. Salter 3-34). *MoM:* A. G. Salter. *County debuts:* Mujeeb Zadran, C. Munro (Hampshire). *Attendance:* 6,252. *Glamorgan's victory was their biggest by runs. Mujeeb Zadran, a 17-year-old mystery spinner from Afghanistan, bowled Usman Khawaja in his first over – a maiden – but conceded 19 in his next. Colin Munro struck Andrew Salter for six from the first ball of the reply, but he and fellow opener Rilee Rossouw had gone before the over was done. Six days after winning the Royal London Cup, Hampshire slumped to 32-7; an eighth-wicket stand of 54 saved a little face.*

At Southampton, July 12 (floodlit). **Sussex won by eight wickets. Hampshire 158-7** (20 overs) (C. Munro 30, J. M. Vince 30, T. P. Alsop 35*; J. C. Archer 3-26, D. R. Briggs 3-29); ‡**Sussex 161-2** (18.2 overs) (L. J. Wright 68, L. J. Evans 55*). *MoM:* L. J. Wright. *Attendance:* 5,518. *Against his old county, Danny Briggs dismissed three of Hampshire's top four after they had raced to 45-0 in four overs. They never regained their fluency. Luke Wright and Laurie Evans put on 96 for the second wicket as Sussex coasted to a third straight win.*

At Southampton, July 20 (floodlit). **Hampshire won by 21 runs.** ‡**Hampshire 184** (19.4 overs) (C. Munro 63, R. R. Rossouw 32; J. K. Fuller 6-28); **Middlesex 163-9** (20 overs) (M. D. E. Holden

36, D. J. Bravo 38). *MoM:* C. Munro. *Attendance:* 7,620. *When Dawid Malan tossed the ball to James Fuller – unused the night before against Somerset, and the eighth Middlesex bowler here – the score was 122-2 from 12 overs. He took two wickets in his first over, one in his second, two in his third and one in his last. Dismissed for 184 with two deliveries unbowled, Hampshire seemed to have missed a trick. But none of the Middlesex batsmen bedded in, and they came up well short. Hampshire's win ended a run of three defeats.*

TWENTY20 SIX-FOURS IN THE UK

6-5	A. V. Suppiah	Somerset v Glamorgan at Cardiff	2011
6-16	T. G. Southee	Essex v Glamorgan at Chelmsford	2011
6-19	T. T. Bresnan	Yorkshire v Lancashire at Leeds	2017
6-21	A. J. Hall	Northamptonshire v Worcestershire at Northampton	2008
6-24	T. J. Murtagh	Surrey v Middlesex at Lord's	2005
6-28	**J. K. Fuller**	**Middlesex v Hampshire at Southampton**	**2018**

All bowled four overs apart from Suppiah and Hall (both 3.4).

At Southampton, August 3 (floodlit). **Kent won by 51 runs.** ‡**Kent 139-7** (20 overs); **Hampshire 88** (16.1 overs) (A. F. Milne 3-14, M. P. Stoinis 4-17). *MoM:* M. P. Stoinis. *Attendance:* 7,845. *Kent swept to the top of the South Group with an emphatic win, in the process inflicting on Hampshire their second-lowest T20 total. Indeed a score of 88 represented a recovery after they languished at 7-3 in the third over, 20-5 in the fifth. No one on either side reached 30, though six Kent batsmen made double figures to Hampshire's three. Adam Milne and Marcus Stoinis did most damage.*

At Southampton, August 8 (floodlit). **Somerset won by six wickets.** Hampshire **129-8** (20 overs) (S. A. Northeast 30; J. E. Taylor 3-39); ‡**Somerset 130-4** (18.5 overs) (J. G. Myburgh 54*). *MoM:* J. G. Myburgh. *Attendance:* 8,091. *Johann Myburgh, who played for Hampshire in 2011, hit an unbeaten half-century and steered Somerset to an eighth win. Not that they faced an exacting target: although six Hampshire batsmen had a start, only Sam Northeast reached 20. Roelof van der Merwe (4–11–13–1) proved almost impossible to get away, and Hampshire managed only four boundaries between the end of the powerplay and the beginning of the final over.*

At Southampton, August 12. **No result.** Essex **72-4** (7.5 overs) v ‡**Hampshire.** *Already reduced to 18 overs a side, the match came to a halt in the eighth, when rain grew too heavy. Chris Wood had dismissed the Essex openers.*

At Southampton, August 17 (floodlit). **Hampshire won by six wickets.** Gloucestershire **144-8** (20 overs) (M. Klinger 43, R. F. Higgins 31; C. P. Wood 4-16); ‡**Hampshire 147-4** (16.5 overs) (R. R. Rossouw 42, S. A. Northeast 37, J. M. Vince 48*). *MoM:* C. P. Wood. *County debut:* T. A. R. Scriven (Hampshire). *Attendance:* 5,396. *Hampshire finished with a win, only their second of a wretched competition, thanks largely to Wood, whose four wickets lifted his tournament total to 19. Already guaranteed a quarter-final, Gloucestershire never came to terms with his left-arm seam. James Vince and Northeast added 66 for the third wicket to hasten a convincing victory.*

Hampshire away matches

July 13: lost to Kent by three runs.	August 1: lost to Somerset by 16 runs.
July 21: tied with Essex.	August 10: lost to Glamorgan by eight wickets.
July 26: lost to Middlesex by 22 runs.	August 15: lost to Surrey by seven wickets.
July 29: no result v Sussex.	

KENT

At Beckenham, July 13. **Kent won by three runs.** Kent **210-4** (20 overs) (D. J. Bell-Drummond 46, S. W. Billings 95*); ‡**Hampshire 207-6** (20 overs) (T. P. Alsop 41, L. A. Dawson 75*, L. D. McManus 38; J. L. Denly 3-37). *MoM:* S. W. Billings. *Attendance:* 3,075. *After Sam Billings had guided Kent beyond 200 with a format-best 95* from 54 balls, Hampshire slipped to 6-3 from seven: two wickets for Joe Denly and a golden duck for Sam Northeast. But Liam Dawson set up a* *grandstand finish. With seven required from three balls, Mitch Claydon fired in yorkers to keep Hampshire to three singles.*

At Canterbury, July 20 (floodlit). **No result.** ‡Surrey 250-6 (20 overs) (A. J. Finch 83, R. J. Burns 50, O. J. D. Pope 34; Imran Qayyum 3-40) v Kent. *Attendance: 6,321. Surrey's exhilarating batting counted for naught once a thunderstorm deluged the ground at the interval. Aaron Finch sped to fifty from 19 balls, while fellow opener Rory Burns took 27; the middle order scored freely. Carlos Brathwaite's three overs cost 55, but left-arm spinner Imran Qayyum took a career-best 3-40.*

HIGHEST TWENTY20 TOTALS IN THE UK

260-4	Yorkshire v Northamptonshire at Leeds...................	2017
254-3	Gloucestershire v Middlesex at Uxbridge	2011
250-3	Somerset v Gloucestershire at Taunton	2006
250-6	**Surrey v Kent at Canterbury.**	**2018**
249-8	Hampshire v Derbyshire at Derby	2017
248-6	Australia v England at Southampton	2013
242-2	Warwickshire v Derbyshire at Birmingham................	2015
242-3	Essex v Sussex at Chelmsford	2008
242-4	**Gloucestershire v Middlesex at Bristol**	**2018**
242-5	Sussex v Gloucestershire at Bristol	2016
240-3	Glamorgan v Surrey at The Oval	2015

At Canterbury, July 27 (floodlit). **No result.** Kent 99-2 (11.2 overs) (J. L. Denly 52) v ‡Sussex. *County debut:* M. P. Stoinis (Kent). *Attendance:* 4,597. *For the second game in a row, the weather spoiled the party. Denly had cracked a 36-ball 52, falling just before the rain.*

At Canterbury, August 2 (floodlit). **Kent won by 28 runs.** ‡Kent 191-4 (20 overs) (S. W. Billings 56*, M. P. Stoinis 47); Essex 163 (20 overs) (P. I. Walter 40, R. N. ten Doeschate 34, R. S. Bopara 42; A. F. Milne 4-15). *MoM:* S. W. Billings. *Attendance:* 3,828. *The setting sun halted play for 13 minutes, but could not stop Kent, whose last three games had fallen foul of the weather, from securing a fourth win; they went second, Essex stayed seventh. Billings and Marcus Stoinis, unable to take the field on county debut six days earlier, added 106 for the fourth wicket. The ploy of opening with Denly's leg-spin worked again when he bowled Adam Wheater with the second ball. The Essex middle order rallied, before Adam Milne brought the innings to an abrupt conclusion, scattering the last four for three from nine balls.*

At Canterbury, August 5. **Gloucestershire won by eight wickets.** ‡Kent 160-5 (20 overs) (J. L. Denly 99*); Gloucestershire 164-2 (19.2 overs) (M. A. H. Hammond 51, M. Klinger 46, I. A. Cockbain 32*). *MoM:* M. A. H. Hammond. *Attendance:* 4,362. *Miles Hammond's maiden T20 half-century, from 31 balls, underpinned a perfectly timed chase: league leaders Gloucestershire coasted home with four to spare. An accomplished 99* off 63 by Denly had papered over the cracks in a staccato Kent innings, before Hammond's poise at the top of the order, as well as three other calm contributions, won the day.*

At Beckenham, August 12. **Kent won by three wickets.** Middlesex 189-7 (20 overs) (D. J. Malan 36, P. R. Stirling 34; J. L. Denly 3-25); ‡Kent 191-7 (19.3 overs) (D. J. Bell-Drummond 62, A. J. Blake 57; J. A. R. Harris 3-32). *MoM:* A. J. Blake. *Attendance:* 2,108. *Denly's 3-25 held Middlesex in check after a six-over score of 71-0 suggested they would hurtle past 200. The Kent middle all made double figures, but a total of 189 felt like a missed opportunity. Daniel Bell-Drummond ensured a lively start to the Kent reply, and Alex Blake an even livelier finish: he cracked 20 from Tom Barber's last four balls of the 18th over to wrench the initiative from Middlesex.*

At Canterbury, August 16 (floodlit). **Kent won by five runs.** Kent 231-5 (20 overs) (D. J. Bell-Drummond 37, S. W. Billings 57*, A. J. Blake 42); ‡Somerset 226-5 (20 overs) (S. M. Davies 45, P. D. Trego 30, J. C. Hildreth 45, L. Gregory 44*). *MoM:* S. W. Billings. *Attendance:* 3,448. *In a strong batting display, Billings hit his third fifty of the tournament. Six of Kent's top seven reached 20 as they matched their highest total (231-7 v Surrey in 2015). Somerset then emulated Kent when six of their top seven reached 20 but, with six needed for a tie, Claydon nailed his last-ball yorker, and Tom Abell managed only a single. The scores would already have been level had Somerset not* *given away six penalty runs for a shoddy over-rate. This was Kent's tenth successive T20 victory over Somerset, a sequence unmatched in domestic cricket. The only longer run in the format is by Pakistan, whose record against Zimbabwe stands at 11.*

Kent away matches

July 6: beat Surrey by six runs.
July 8: beat Somerset by eight wickets.
July 11: lost to Gloucestershire by five runs.
July 29: no result v Glamorgan.

August 3: beat Hampshire by 51 runs.
August 10: no result v Sussex.
August 17: beat Essex by five wickets.

MIDDLESEX

At Lord's, July 5 (floodlit). **Middlesex won by three wickets.** ‡Surrey 158-6 (20 overs) (R. J. Burns 36, R. Clarke 50; P. R. Stirling 3-26); **Middlesex 161-7** (19 overs) (P. R. Stirling 66, H. W. R. Cartwright 38). *MoM:* P. R. Stirling. *Attendance:* 27,262. *County debuts:* D. J. Bravo (Middlesex); J. D. Smith (Surrey). *Paul Stirling made the difference, cracking 66 from 36 balls – with ten fours and two sixes – after taking three wickets, including both Surrey openers. It meant Middlesex had enough in hand to overcome a wobble when Morne Morkel removed Dwayne Bravo and Stevie Eskinazi with the first two balls of the 11th over.*

At Uxbridge, July 8. **Gloucestershire won by six wickets.** Middlesex 160-7 (20 overs) (D. J. Bravo 34, J. K. Fuller 33*); ‡Gloucestershire 165-4 (18.4 overs) (M. A. H. Hammond 36, M. Klinger 58). *MoM:* M. Klinger. *Attendance:* 2,143. *Outmatched on paper, Gloucestershire put in a superb performance. Middlesex's openers made a single between them, and only a 12-ball blitz from James Fuller lifted them to 160. Miles Hammond ignited the chase, smacking eight fours in his 36 from 21 balls, and Michael Klinger helped secure victory with 58 from 49.*

At Lord's, July 19 (floodlit). **Somerset won by four wickets.** ‡Middlesex 175-5 (20 overs) (M. D. E. Holden 84, D. J. Bravo 32*); Somerset 178-6 (18 overs) (J. G. Myburgh 46, P. D. Trego 32, C. J. Anderson 39). *MoM:* J. G. Myburgh. *Attendance:* 23,003. *County debut:* A. C. Agar (Middlesex). *Max Holden, whose previous-highest T20 score was 19, hurtled to 84 from 55 balls to set a steep target. But Somerset attacked from the start, and tamed an experienced attack.*

At Lord's, July 26 (floodlit). **Middlesex won by 22 runs.** Middlesex 165-8 (20 overs) (P. R. Stirling 60); ‡Hampshire 143 (18.5 overs) (C. Munro 58; S. T. Finn 3-21, A. C. Agar 3-17). *MoM:* A. C. Agar. *Attendance:* 20,162. *When Hampshire sprinted to 89-1 in the ninth over, chasing 166, there looked like only one result – but, from 127-4, they lost six for 16 in 24 balls. Ashton Agar, the Australian slow left-armer, returned his best T20 figures.*

At Lord's, August 2 (floodlit). **Sussex won by 12 runs.** ‡Sussex 168 (19.4 overs) (P. D. Salt 50, D. M. W. Rawlins 49; T. E. Barber 4-28, A. C. Agar 3-41); **Middlesex 156-7** (20 overs) (E. J. G. Morgan 90; J. C. Archer 3-25). *MoM:* J. C. Archer. *Attendance:* 19,311. *Phil Salt gave Sussex an electric start with 50 from 20 balls; one of his three sixes cleared the Mound Stand. Tom Barber's first T20 four-for reined in the later batsmen, but the loss of Stirling for a duck set Middlesex back. Eoin Morgan made a 56-ball 90 – surprisingly his highest T20 score – but fell in the final over, the first victim of a Jofra Archer hat-trick.*

At Richmond, August 5. **Glamorgan won by seven wickets.** Middlesex 131 (20 overs) (G. F. B. Scott 32, J. K. Fuller 46*; R. A. J. Smith 4-6, T. van der Gugten 4-31); ‡Glamorgan 135-3 (12.5 overs) (C. A. Ingram 46*, K. S. Carlson 40). *MoM:* R. A. J. Smith. *Attendance:* 3,325. *Another miserable effort by a batting side bereft of confidence allowed Glamorgan to coast to victory at Old Deer Park. Medium-pacer Ruaidhri Smith returned stunning figures of 4–19–6–4 as Middlesex slumped to 39-6 in the tenth over. Craig Meschede fell to the second ball of the chase, but there were no further alarms.*

At Lord's, August 16 (floodlit). **Essex won by six wickets.** Middlesex 210-3 (20 overs) (P. R. Stirling 78, E. J. G. Morgan 77*); ‡Essex 211-4 (19.2 overs) (V. Chopra 51, D. W. Lawrence 86, R. S. Bopara 31*). *MoM:* D. W. Lawrence. *Attendance:* 22,692. *Middlesex made 200 for the second time in 2018 – and lost for the second time. They looked secure after Stirling (who passed 4,000 T20 runs) and Morgan (whose 77* from 38 balls included eight sixes) put on 77 for the third wicket, but Essex replied in kind: Dan Lawrence spanked 86 from 46 to take them close, then Ravi Bopara and Ashar Zaidi (20* from eight) took them over the line, leaving Middlesex bottom of the group.*

Middlesex away matches

July 6: lost to Essex by three wickets.
July 20: lost to Hampshire by 21 runs.
July 29: lost to Somerset by 38 runs (DLS).
August 3: lost to Surrey by nine wickets.

August 9: lost to Gloucestershire by 70 runs.
August 12: lost to Kent by three wickets.
August 17: lost to Sussex by 31 runs.

SOMERSET

At Taunton, July 6. **Somerset won by six wickets. Gloucestershire 188-6** (20 overs) (R. F. Higgins 55, J. M. R. Taylor 34); ‡**Somerset 194-4** (16.5 overs) (S. M. Davies 60, P. D. Trego 72*). *MoM:* P. D. Trego. *Attendance:* 6,803. *Peter Trego's crowd-pleasing innings – including a stand of 90 in 7.1 overs with Steven Davies – ensured Somerset got off to a flying start. Gloucestershire were handicapped by the loss of Liam Norwell, who tweaked a hamstring after nine balls. A late assault by Ryan Higgins had allowed them to post a challenging total.*

At Taunton, July 8. **Kent won by eight wickets. Somerset 159-6** (20 overs) (J. C. Hildreth 57, T. B. Abell 36, C. J. Anderson 30*; C. R. Brathwaite 4-21); ‡**Kent 163-2** (16.3 overs) (D. J. Bell-Drummond 58, H. G. Kuhn 67*). *MoM:* H. G. Kuhn. *Attendance:* 5,571. *Kent extended their winning sequence against Somerset to nine, after Daniel Bell-Drummond and Heino Kuhn put on 101 in 10.3 overs. Somerset had looked well set at 120-4 after 15, but Carlos Brathwaite and Adam Milne prevented any acceleration. Earlier, James Hildreth passed 3,000 T20 runs in his 57.*

At Taunton, July 29. **Somerset won by 38 runs** (DLS). **Somerset 229-6** (20 overs) (P. D. Trego 60, T. B. Abell 31, C. J. Anderson 41*, L. Gregory 62; T. E. Barber 3-37); ‡**Middlesex 174-6** (18 overs) (P. R. Stirling 30, S. S. Eskinazi 55; L. Gregory 4-28). *MoM:* L. Gregory. *Attendance:* 5,129. *Lewis Gregory, Somerset's new T20 captain, produced a stellar performance in an easy win. They had been reeling at 29-3 after Tom Barber took three in an over. But Trego thrashed 60 off 31 – including 24 in an over from Ashton Agar – then Gregory took up the cudgels with 62 from 26, a career-best. Rain left Middlesex chasing 213 in 18 overs, but Gregory starred again, with four wickets. Ten-year-old Fin Bussey was taken to hospital after being struck on the head by a Stevie Eskinazi six. He recovered quickly, and was a guest at Somerset's next home game.*

At Taunton, August 1. **Somerset won by 16 runs. Somerset 197-7** (20 overs) (J. C. Hildreth 57, C. J. Anderson 32, R. E. van der Merwe 31*; C. P. Wood 5-32); ‡**Hampshire 181-9** (20 overs) (J. M. Vince 74, L. A. Dawson 82; J. E. Taylor 5-15, J. Overton 3-37). *MoM:* J. E. Taylor. *Attendance:* 5,759. *West Indian seamer Jerome Taylor took 5-15 after Somerset's middle order had ridden to the rescue again. Three wickets for Chris Wood in his first nine balls had silenced the Taunton crowd (he would finish with career-best 5-32), but Hildreth began the recovery, before Gregory and Roelof van der Merwe launched a late blitz. Hampshire's scorecard looked lopsided: James Vince and Liam Dawson batted superbly, but no one else made double figures.*

At Taunton, August 3. **Somerset won by ten wickets.** ‡**Essex 135-9** (20 overs) (V. Chopra 43; J. E. Taylor 3-28, J. Overton 3-23); **Somerset 136-0** (11.2 overs) (J. G. Myburgh 103*). *MoM:* J. G. Myburgh. *Attendance:* 6,942. *Four days before he announced his retirement, Johann Myburgh hit his first T20 century in an emphatic victory. His 103* came off 44 balls in a stand of 136* with Tom Banton (29*). Essex had been 82-2 in the 12th, but folded.*

At Taunton, August 10. **Somerset won by four wickets. Surrey 176-9** (20 overs) (W. G. Jacks 53, R. Clarke 32; J. Overton 4-24); ‡**Somerset 177-6** (19.1 overs) (P. D. Trego 70, C. J. Anderson 53; M. Morkel 3-30). *MoM:* P. D. Trego. *Attendance:* 6,996. *Somerset stayed top of the group, thanks to a stand of 104 in 10.3 overs between Trego and Corey Anderson, whose 53 included five sixes. Earlier, Jamie Overton took four wickets. Rory Burns was run out off the first ball of the match, but Surrey were boosted by a partnership of 69 in 5.5 overs from the teenage Will Jacks and the ageless Rikki Clarke.*

At Taunton, August 12. **Somerset won by 29 runs. Somerset 210-8** (20 overs) (S. M. Davies 36, J. C. Hildreth 47, C. J. Anderson 72); ‡**Glamorgan 181-9** (20 overs) (C. A. J. Meschede 35; M. T. C. Waller 4-25). *MoM:* C. J. Anderson and M. T. C. Waller. *Attendance:* 5,554. *Anderson treated the crowd to a stunning display of hitting, and secured Somerset's quarter-final place with their seventh successive win. His 72 off 30 balls included six sixes, one of which – off Graham Wagg – sailed over the scoreboard and into St James's churchyard. Leg-spinner Max Waller again made shrewd use of the new ball.*

Somerset away matches

July 13: lost to Gloucestershire by four wickets.   August 5: beat Sussex by three wickets.
July 19: beat Middlesex by four wickets.   August 8: beat Hampshire by six wickets.
July 20: beat Glamorgan by 30 runs.   August 16: lost to Kent by five runs.
July 27: lost to Surrey by nine wickets.

SURREY

At The Oval, July 6 (floodlit). **Kent won by six runs.** ‡Kent 173-6 (20 overs) (J. L. Denly 102, H. G. Kuhn 30; M. W. Pillans 3-22); **Surrey** 167 (18.5 overs) (R. J. Burns 39, B. T. Foakes 75*; J. L. Denly 3-31, A. F. Milne 3-22). *MoM:* J. L. Denly. *Attendance:* 23,693. *County debut:* C. R. Brathwaite (Kent). *Joe Denly's 102 from 63 balls underpinned a solid Kent total, although Surrey were on course at 98-1 in the ninth over. But Denly made a decisive intervention with his leg-breaks in the 13th, becoming the first to marry a hat-trick to a century in any senior limited-overs game. The West Indian T20 specialist Carlos Brathwaite weighed in with two quick wickets in his first match for Kent, and Ben Foakes was left with too much to do.*

HALF-CENTURY AND HAT-TRICK IN THE SAME T20 GAME

Yuvraj Singh (50, 3-22) ..	Kings XI Punjab v Royal Challengers Bangalore at Durban	2008-09
Jannisar Khan (55, 4-16)..	Peshawar Panthers v Quetta Bears at Karachi	2009-10
D. J. Willey (60, 4-9)	Northamptonshire v Surrey at Birmingham†	2013
J. L. Denly (102, 3-31). . .	**Kent v Surrey at The Oval**	**2018**

† *T20 Cup final. There have been seven such doubles in List A games, none involving a century.*

At The Oval, July 12 (floodlit). **Surrey won by 39 runs.** ‡**Surrey** 222-4 (20 overs) (A. J. Finch 58, B. T. Foakes 56, O. J. D. Pope 31*, R. Clarke 48*); **Essex** 183-7 (20 overs) (A. J. A. Wheater 30, V. Chopra 67; M. W. Pillans 3-34, G. J. Batty 3-36). *MoM:* R. Clarke. *Attendance:* 22,097. *County debut:* N. J. Maddinson (Surrey). Big hitting from Aaron Finch (58 from 33 balls), Foakes (56 from 35) and Rikki Clarke (48* from 20) put this match beyond Essex's grasp; only the Australian leg-spinner Adam Zampa (4–7–20–2) was able to keep a lid on the scoring. Varun Chopra prospered in reply, but Gareth Batty and Mat Pillans filleted the middle order.*

At The Oval, July 27 (floodlit). **Surrey won by nine wickets.** Somerset 99-6 (10 overs) (L. Gregory 50*); ‡**Surrey** 102-1 (6.4 overs) (A. J. Finch 43*). *MoM:* A. J. Finch. *Attendance:* 21,998. *County debut:* J. E. Taylor (Somerset). Surrey strolled home in a match reduced to ten overs a side by rain. Somerset were 46-5 after six, before Lewis Gregory biffed four sixes in a 23-ball 50*, briefly interrupted when three sprinklers showered the ground with more water. But the game was as good as over once Jason Roy and Finch blasted 69 from the first 22 deliveries of the reply.*

At The Oval, July 31 (floodlit). **Glamorgan won by four wickets.** ‡**Surrey** 194-4 (20 overs) (A. J. Finch 30, N. J. Maddinson 70); **Glamorgan** 195-6 (19 overs) (C. A. J. Meschede 43, K. S. Carlson 58, G. G. Wagg 46*). *MoM:* G. G. Wagg. *Attendance:* 20,070. Surrey looked favourites after Nic Maddinson's 45-ball 70, but Glamorgan strolled to their sixth victory in seven T20 matches at The Oval, chiefly thanks to Kiran Carlson's 32-ball 58.*

At The Oval, August 3 (floodlit). **Surrey won by nine wickets.** ‡**Middlesex** 221-5 (20 overs) (P. R. Stirling 109, S. S. Eskinazi 31, J. K. Fuller 37*); **Surrey** 222-1 (16 overs) (J. J. Roy 84, A. J. Finch 117*). *MoM:* A. J. Finch. *Attendance:* 21,839. Paul Stirling made the most of being dropped first ball to race to a maiden T20 century in 54 deliveries, with seven sixes. With James Fuller and James Franklin (21 from eight) caning the last four overs for 52, Middlesex reached their highest T20 total. But it was nowhere near enough, as Roy and Finch (who reached his hundred from 45 balls) plundered 18 fours and 15 sixes in an opening stand of 194 in 13.5 overs.*

At The Oval, August 9 (floodlit). **No result.** Sussex 159-2 (13 overs) (P. D. Salt 33, L. J. Wright 55, L. J. Evans 48*) v ‡**Surrey**. *Attendance:* 17,909. Luke Wright managed a 26-ball half-century, but rain ruined a game already reduced to 15 overs a side.*

At The Oval, August 15 (floodlit). **Surrey won by seven wickets. ‡Hampshire 133-7** (20 overs) (S. A. Northeast 37); **Surrey 136-3** (17.3 overs) (A. J. Finch 67*, N. J. Maddinson 41). *MoM:* A. J. Finch. *Attendance:* 17,680. *Hampshire struggled on a sluggish pitch, with Jade Dernbach (2-19) and Batty (1-18) keeping the scoring down. Surrey lost two quick wickets, but the Australian pair of Finch and Maddinson put on 92 to ensure victory.*

Surrey away matches

July 5: lost to Middlesex by three wickets.
July 13: beat Sussex by 52 runs.
July 20: no result v Kent.
August 5: beat Essex by six wickets.

August 10: lost to Somerset by four wickets.
August 12: lost to Gloucestershire by five runs.
August 17: beat Glamorgan by 24 runs (DLS).

SUSSEX

At Hove, July 13 (floodlit). **Surrey won by 52 runs. Surrey 192-3** (20 overs) (A. J. Finch 131*); **‡Sussex 140** (17.4 overs) (P. D. Salt 74; J. W. Dernbach 3-31, M. W. Pillans 3-20). *MoM:* A. J. Finch. *Attendance:* 6,310. *Aaron Finch, badly dropped on one by Jofra Archer, crashed 131*, Surrey's highest score in the format, though he had twice made more for Australia. He exploited a strong crosswind and a short leg-side boundary to crash seven sixes and ten fours from 79 balls. While the Sussex attack never adapted to a slow pitch, Sam Curran did: he started with 12 dot balls, and conceded just 14 in four overs. And although Phil Salt played enterprisingly for a career-best 74, Sussex were never in contention.*

At Hove, July 29. **Sussex v Hampshire. Abandoned.**

At Hove, August 1 (floodlit). **Gloucestershire won by four wickets. ‡Sussex 127-8** (20 overs) (L. J. Evans 46); **Gloucestershire 129-6** (18.2 overs) (M. A. H. Hammond 35). *MoM:* D. A. Payne. *Attendance:* 5,140. *There were groans from Sussex's speedy attack about another slow surface, which suited Gloucestershire's pace-off bowlers. Sussex slumped to 27-4 in the powerplay, and passed 100 only thanks to a responsible 46 from Laurie Evans. Gloucestershire never quite settled – Rashid Khan had figures of 4–12–14–2, and did not concede a boundary – but Jack Taylor thumped four fours in ten balls to hasten victory.*

At Hove, August 5. **Somerset won by three wickets. Sussex 169-5** (20 overs) (L. J. Evans 96); **‡Somerset 170-7** (19.3 overs) (T. B. Abell 30, R. E. van der Merwe 34*; Rashid Khan 3-29). *MoM:* L. J. Evans. *Attendance:* 4,577. *Well placed at 112-3 in the 13th, Somerset lost four for 22 and, needing 36 from 20 balls, were in danger of losing their way. But Roelof van der Merwe hit powerfully, and 16 came from the 18th over, bowled by David Wiese; from there it was a simple matter for Somerset to claim their seventh win in ten. Earlier, Evans had fallen from the penultimate ball, trying to bring up a maiden hundred by clearing midwicket. Only he – and later Rashid – kept Sussex in contention.*

At Hove, August 10 (floodlit). **Sussex v Kent. Abandoned.**

At Hove, August 14 (floodlit). **Sussex won by 98 runs. Sussex 186-5** (20 overs) (L. J. Evans 63*, D. M. W. Rawlins 35, M. G. K. Burgess 39); **‡Glamorgan 88** (13.3 overs) (T. S. Mills 3-20, Rashid Khan 3-9). *MoM:* L. J. Evans. *Attendance:* 5,499. *Tymal Mills took the tournament's second hat-trick by a Sussex bowler – Archer had grabbed one at Lord's a fortnight earlier – to turn Glamorgan's stumble into headlong decline. After reaching a promising 50-0 in the fifth over, they fell apart: the game was probably up at 87-5, but losing five wickets for a single in eight balls was calamitous. Mills put the innings out of its misery in the 14th over. Evans had helped set a demanding target with his fifth half-century in nine starts; Archer smashed 22* from six balls.*

At Hove, August 17 (floodlit). **Sussex won by 31 runs. Sussex 215-5** (20 overs) (P. D. Salt 66, L. J. Wright 74, L. J. Evans 36; J. K. Fuller 3-51); **‡Middlesex 184** (19.4 overs) (P. R. Stirling 58, J. A. Simpson 62). *MoM:* P. D. Salt. *County debut:* M. K. Andersson (Middlesex). *Attendance:* 5,850. *Sussex, who would reach the knockouts only if they won, were given an electric start by Salt: when he departed for a 25-ball 66, Luke Wright – no slouch – had 11, and the total was 79. Wright later outscored him, and the innings roared past 200. If Sussex thought they were home and dry, they had underestimated Paul Stirling and John Simpson, who added 122 in eight overs. But Will Beer, playing because Rashid was with Afghanistan in Ireland, snared both, and the remaining Middlesex batsmen went quietly.*

Sussex away matches

July 4: beat Essex by 36 runs.
July 8: beat Glamorgan by eight wickets.
July 12: beat Hampshire by eight wickets.
July 27: no result v Kent.

August 2: beat Middlesex by 12 runs.
August 9: no result v Surrey.
August 16: beat Gloucestershire by four wickets.

QUARTER-FINALS

At Canterbury, August 23 (floodlit). **Lancashire won by six wickets.** ‡Kent **133-9** (20 overs) (S. W. Billings 37; M. W. Parkinson 3-27); **Lancashire 134-4** (18.4 overs) (K. K. Jennings 46, D. J. Vilas 30*). *MoM*: M. W. Parkinson. *Attendance*: 5,519. *Kent were left to rue their pitch preparation after a turning wicket – described by home captain Sam Billings as a "slow snot-heap" – dealt Lancashire the aces. Against an attack brimming with spin, Kent produced an abject batting display. Matt Parkinson claimed 3-27, and, without some biffing from the tail, they might not have made three figures. For the fourth time in the competition, Joe Denly took a wicket in the opening over – the fact that it was Jos Buttler, stumped first ball, gave hope to a partisan crowd. Lancashire seemed deflated but, despite athletic fielding and intelligent captaincy, Keaton Jennings's classy 46 from 40 balls steered them towards finals day.*

At Chester-le-Street, August 24 (floodlit). **Sussex won by five wickets.** ‡Durham **140-7** (20 overs) (B. A. Stokes 34); **Sussex 144-5** (18.2 overs) (L. J. Evans 63*, D. M. W. Rawlins 42). *MoM*: L. J. Evans. *Attendance*: 5,840. *Sussex spinners Danny Briggs and Will Beer proved the difference, bowling superbly for combined figures of 8–19–36–4. Without Imran Tahir (on CPL duty) and Liam Trevaskis (glandular fever), Durham's first attempt at spin saw Will Smith struck for two fours by Delray Rawlins. His swashbuckling 42 off 29 balls formed part of a stand of 70 with Laurie Evans, who completed the chase with ease. Durham had opened up with 47 off 3.3 overs. Ben Stokes, playing as a batsman because of a troublesome left knee, hit six fours from his first 13 balls, including four in an over off Jofra Archer, but managed no more in a further ten, before he was lbw attempting to reverse-sweep Beer.*

At Taunton, August 26–27. **Somerset won by 19 runs.** Somerset **209-5** (20 overs) (J. C. Hildreth 52, T. B. Abell 46*, L. Gregory 60*); ‡Nottinghamshire **190** (20 overs) (A. D. Hales 45, J. D. Libby 41, T. J. Moores 36; J. Overton 5-47). *MoM*: L. Gregory. *Attendance*: 6,980. *Somerset ensured a sixth finals day appearance and ousted the holders in front of an ecstatic home crowd. But the outcome was in the balance until the 18th over, when Samit Patel, Luke Fletcher and Steven Mullaney all hoisted Jamie Overton into the leg side and were caught by Max Waller; Overton completed his first T20 five-for. After a washout, the match was played on Bank Holiday Monday. Somerset needed a stand of 81* in 5.3 overs from Tom Abell and Lewis Gregory to lift them to a challenging total. When Tom Moores hit 36 from 18, Nottinghamshire were poised to go through.*

At Worcester, August 25 (floodlit). **Worcestershire won by five wickets.** Gloucestershire **136-8** (20 overs) (M. A. H. Hammond 45, I. A. Cockbain 35; B. L. D'Oliveira 4-26); ‡Worcestershire **137-5** (18.4 overs) (C. J. Ferguson 64*). *MoM*: C. J. Ferguson. *Attendance*: 4,556. *Amid wild celebrations, Callum Ferguson steered Worcestershire to a first appearance at finals day. His composed 64* off 47 ensured there were no frayed nerves around New Road as the finishing line approached – a perfect gift to end his stay. He was helped by a calamitous 16th over, bowled by David Payne, which included two no-balls and two wides, and cost 22. Miles Hammond and Michael Klinger had hurried Gloucestershire to 65 in the eighth over. But Worcestershire found unlikely heroes in Daryl Mitchell, whose innocuous medium-pace went for just 15, and Brett D'Oliveira, who took a career-best 4-26 with his leg-spin.*

"This contest had it all: on-field scuffles, off-field altercations, ambush marketing, expulsions and sackings, a resignation, a retirement, a rewriting of the history books – and a small piece of sandpaper."

South Africa v Australia in 2017–18, page 985

FINALS DAY REPORTS BY RICHARD GIBSON

SEMI-FINALS

LANCASHIRE v WORCESTERSHIRE

At Birmingham, September 15. Worcestershire won by 20 runs. Toss: Lancashire.

And then there was one. Worcestershire's maiden appearance at finals day left only Derbyshire awaiting participation in domestic cricket's end-of-season stag do – and they revelled in the atmosphere of a full house. With overseas recruits Callum Ferguson and Martin Guptill unavailable, it was left to Ali, their captain, to provide early impetus after losing the toss. A clutch of boundaries took Worcestershire to 56 for one, which would be the best powerplay of the day, yet when Ali holed out to long-off for a 21-ball 41, they appeared on course for nothing more than a middling total. It was the first of three wickets in three deliveries: D'Oliveira was run out by Lester, and Fell stumped off the first ball of the next over, from Parkinson. But the fetters imposed by Parkinson and fellow wrist-spinner Zahir Khan were thrown off by Cox during the 19th over, which reaped 27 runs; Lester bowled it only because Faulkner had pulled a calf muscle, and Cox hit three sixes into the Hollies Stand. He brought up a 32-ball half-century in the final over. Fashionably late to the party, Worcestershire fielded like a team intent on hanging around until carriages. The second of two Barnard run-outs, to send back Vilas, left Lancashire five down, needing 51 from the last five overs. Ali completed a nerveless spell, which included the prize scalp of Buttler, before turning to the death specialist Brown. He took three in an over to finish with a career-best four for 21, and leave Jennings stranded.

Man of the Match: O. B. Cox. *Attendance (for all three matches on finals day):* 24,426.

Worcestershire

		B	4/6
1 J. M. Clarke *b 8*	5	7	0
2 *M. M. Ali *c 8 b 11*	41	21	7/1
3 T. C. Fell *st 4 b 10*	23	21	3
4 B. L. D'Oliveira *run out (9)*	0	0	
5 †O. B. Cox *not out*	55	34	3/3
6 R. A. Whiteley *b 10*	4	3	
7 D. K. H. Mitchell *lbw b 7*	6	10	0
8 E. G. Barnard *not out*	28	19	3
Lb 3, w 2, nb 2	7		

6 overs: 56-1   (20 overs) 169-6

1/37 2/70 3/70 4/70 5/82 6/97

9 W. D. Parnell, 10 L. Wood and 11 P. R. Brown did not bat.

Lester 4–8–53–0; Faulkner 2–4–8–1; Livingstone 1–0–23–0; Clark 4–8–27–1; Parkinson 4–6–23–2; Zahir Khan 4–7–24–1; Jennings 1–2–8–0.

Lancashire

		B	4/6
1 A. L. Davies *run out (8/5)*	9	9	2
2 *L. S. Livingstone *c 4 b 8*	30	18	3/2
3 A. M. Lilley *lbw b 2*	23	18	2/1
4 †J. C. Buttler *b 2*	12	13	0
5 K. K. Jennings *not out*	51	40	3/2
6 D. J. Vilas *run out (8/1)*	13	8	1
7 J. Clark *c 7 b 11*	3	5	0
8 J. P. Faulkner *c 3 b 11*	2	5	0
9 T. J. Lester *b 11*	0	1	0
10 M. W. Parkinson *c 3 b 11*	0	1	0
11 Zahir Khan *not out*	1	2	0
Lb 2, w 3	5		

6 overs: 55-1   (20 overs) 149-9

1/20 2/64 3/67 4/89 5/119 6/132 7/140 8/141 9/141

Wood 2–8–11–0; Parnell 3–7–36–0; Brown 4–14–21–4; Barnard 4–4–34–1; Ali 4–11–16–2; D'Oliveira 2–0–16–0; Mitchell 1–2–13–0.

Umpires: D. J. Millns and M. J. Saggers.   Third umpire: M. Burns.

SOMERSET v SUSSEX

At Birmingham, September 15. Sussex won by 35 runs. Toss: Sussex.

Wright was on course to become only the second batsman to register more than seven Twenty20 hundreds (Chris Gayle was way ahead, with 21), but had to settle for a 53-ball 92, the highest score in finals-day history. Sussex's match-winning total of 202 for eight was based around his fourth-wicket partnership of 120 in ten overs with Wiese, who clouted 52 off 29. But they might have plundered even more. When Wright, who hit seven sixes, fell to Anderson, Sussex were 193 for four with 16 balls to go, yet they managed only nine more runs, and failed to hit a boundary from any of the final 22 deliveries. Jerome Taylor, the Jamaican fast bowler, played a big part in Somerset's fightback, taking four for 20. Earlier, Jamie Overton had missed a chance to impress England's selectors ahead of the winter tours, conceding 31 from his third over. "They put us under a lot of pressure, and on the big stage there's some clouded thinking," said Somerset captain Gregory, who himself had leaked 27 in an over. Somerset then slipped to 48 for four after seven, only for Abell and Anderson to thrash 84 in the next seven, before Briggs's fingertips diverted a vicious return drive from Anderson on to the stumps, leaving Abell marooned. Jordan produced a maiden, Archer removed the dangerous Anderson to claim his third wicket, and Gregory fell soon after, handing Wright a 300th T20 appearance later in the evening. Among English players, only Ravi Bopara had beaten him to the landmark.

Man of the Match: L. J. Wright.

Sussex

		B	4/6
1 P. D. Salt *c 11 b 10*	13	7	3
2 *L. J. Wright *c 11 b 6*	92	53	5/7
3 L. J. Evans *lbw b 10*	8	8	1
4 D. M. W. Rawlins *c 2 b 11*	18	12	2/1
5 D. Wiese *c 1 b 10*	52	29	5/2
6 †M. G. K. Burgess *c 11 b 10* ...	2	7	0
7 J. C. Archer *run out (5)*	3	3	0
8 C. J. Jordan *c 12 b 7*	0	2	0
9 W. A. T. Beer *not out*	1	1	0
B 4, lb 2, w 3, nb 4	13		
6 overs: 55-2 (20 overs)	202-8		

1/15 2/44 3/73 4/193 5/197 6/197 7/199 8/202

10 D. R. Briggs and 11 T. S. Mills did not bat.

Waller 4–4–35–1; Taylor 4–14–20–4; Overton 3–4–50–0; Gregory 4–6–49–1; van der Merwe 3–3–31–0; Anderson 2–4–11–1.

Somerset

		B	4/6
1 J. G. Myburgh *c 4 b 7*	22	11	3/1
2 †S. M. Davies *c 10 b 7*	1	4	0
3 P. D. Trego *c 5 b 8.*	5	8	0
4 J. C. Hildreth *c 5 b 11*	15	12	3
5 T. B. Abell *run out (10).*	48	29	5/2
6 C. J. Anderson *c 11 b 7*	48	32	2/3
7 *L. Gregory *b 8*	7	14	0
8 R. E. van der Merwe *not out* ...	8	7	0
9 J. Overton *b 11*	5	3	1
10 J. E. Taylor *not out*	1	1	0
Lb 3, w 2, nb 2	7		
6 overs: 45-3 (20 overs)	167-8		

1/3 2/24 3/33 4/48 5/132 6/153 7/154 8/163

11 M. T. C. Waller did not bat.

12th man: C. Overton.

Archer 4–8–32–3; Mills 4–9–32–1; Jordan 4–14–17–2; Wiese 2–3–29–0; Briggs 3–6–31–1; Beer 3–2–23–0.

Umpires: M. Burns and A. G. Wharf.   Third umpire: M. J. Saggers.

FINAL

SUSSEX v WORCESTERSHIRE

At Birmingham, September 15 (floodlit). Worcestershire won by five wickets. Toss: Sussex.

This triumph for Worcestershire – 33–1 outsiders at the start of the tournament – was not the overnight success it appeared. Indeed, their former coaching duo of Steve Rhodes and Matt Mason had been spectators at Edgbaston in previous years, meticulously taking notes on the characteristics of the champion teams. Such dedication led to a post-match tribute by Ali, the victorious captain, to Rhodes, sacked earlier in the year following an internal disciplinary procedure: "I want to give a special mention to Bumpy, who put this team together and unfortunately is not here to see it."

Worcestershire were the youngest team in the competition, and it was their youngest player who proved a star turn once again. Hours earlier, Pat Brown, a 20-year-old undergraduate about to resume a business studies degree at the University of Worcester, had snared four Lancastrians. Now, such was his hold over Sussex, he seemed to possess half a dozen variations, although he modestly suggested his deceptive arts amounted to a knuckle ball and a slower off-cutter, plus an occasional slippery bouncer.

"I've just bowled the right ball at the right time," said Brown. "In 17 games, I've not had a single dropped catch off my bowling, and so I have counted my lucky stars." Ali called him "international standard", and Sussex, who finished with a modest 157 for six, were hardly in a position to argue after managing just 15 runs from his four overs. The surprise was that Brown went wicketless.

The Sussex attack had been lauded as the best in the tournament, but now lacked an X-factor component: leg-spinner Rashid Khan was at the Asia Cup with Afghanistan. And they could ill

Double top: Ben Cox swings his way to a second match award of the day, and Worcestershire to a first Twenty20 triumph.

afford the kind of slip provided by the pacy Archer. Cox, who had been dropped from Worcestershire's Championship side the previous week, put him under pressure when, with 41 needed off 23, he reverse-paddled a four. In his next over, Archer hurled down a beamer that flew to the fence, before Cox all but settled things by launching the free hit for a towering six. For the second time in the day, he was named Man of the Match – a finals-day first.

Worcestershire's players hurtled on to the outfield but Ali, who took a stray arm to the face in the dugout delirium, remained dignity personified. He had become the first player to total 50 runs and five wickets on finals day. Now he lifted the trophy. Birmingham-born, and still a resident of the city, he had enjoyed quite a homecoming.

Man of the Match: O. B. Cox.

Sussex

		B	4/6
1 P. D. Salt *run out (4)*	17	8	1/2
2 *L. J. Wright *b 2*	33	25	3/2
3 L. J. Evans *b 7*	52	44	4/2
4 D. M. W. Rawlins *c 11 b 2*	21	16	0/2
5 D. Wiese *b 2*	6	6	1
6 †M. G. K. Burgess *not out*	14	14	0/1
7 J. C. Archer *c 7 b 8*	7	8	0
Lb 2, w 3, nb 2	7		

6 overs: 43-1   (20 overs) 157-6

1/19 2/77 3/121 4/131 5/138 6/157

8 C. J. Jordan, 9 W. A. T. Beer, 10 D. R. Briggs and 11 T. S. Mills did not bat.

Wood 4–10–24–0; Parnell 3–7–32–1; Brown 4–13–15–0; Barnard 3–6–28–1; Ali 4–9–30–3; D'Oliveira 1–1–15–0; Mitchell 1–1–11–0.

Worcestershire

		B	4/6
1 J. M. Clarke *c 6 b 10*	33	27	4
2 *M. M. Ali *c 1 b 9*	41	27	6/1
3 T. C. Fell *c 2 b 9*	1	3	0
4 B. L. D'Oliveira *st 6 b 10*	10	9	1
5 †O. B. Cox *not out*	46	27	5/2
6 R. A. Whiteley *c 8 b 7*	14	17	2
7 E. G. Barnard *not out*	1	2	0
B 5, lb 2, w 3, nb 2	12		

6 overs: 53-0   (18.3 overs) 158-5

1/61 2/62 3/80 4/90 5/126

8 W. D. Parnell, 9 D. K. H. Mitchell, 10 L. Wood and 11 P. R. Brown did not bat.

Archer 3.3–5–36–1; Mills 3–8–26–0; Jordan 3–7–29–0; Wiese 1–2–9–0; Briggs 4–13–19–2; Beer 4–6–32–2.

Umpires: M. J. Saggers and A. G. Wharf. Third umpire: D. J. Millns.

ROYAL LONDON ONE-DAY CUP IN 2018

Review by Isabelle Westbury

1 Hampshire   2 Kent   3= Worcestershire, Yorkshire

Strong team spirit and a sprinkling of international magic – that, according to Kent's Joe Denly, was the formula for white-ball success. Not that it was infallible: it let them down in the final, where they lost to Hampshire, who claimed a trophy for the first time since 2012. For Kent, the wait went on: though they had lifted the Twenty20 Cup at Edgbaston in 2007, they had not won a Lord's final since 1978. And with the one-day climax shifting to Trent Bridge in 2020, time was running out.

Speaking before Lord's, Denly said Kent had a good mix of young and old. And though he admitted there were no superstars, there was a great deal of first-class experience – as well as what he called "togetherness" in the dressing-room. "We've been involved in some really close games, and that togetherness has seen us over the line on a few occasions." Denly, who had tasted defeat at the hands of Essex in Kent's last final, in 2008, might have been thinking of the group game at the Rose Bowl in late May. Somehow, Kent denied Hampshire, who began the 49th over with six needed and six wickets left.

Denly had been the all-round star of the tournament, thanks to sharpening his leg-spin. If it was little surprise that he averaged 85 with the bat in the group stage, few expected to see him finish with 14 wickets – only six took more. And yet he was eclipsed in Kent's top order by Heino Kuhn, a South African who

---

FOUR HUNDREDS IN A ONE-DAY TOURNAMENT IN ENGLAND

	M	I	NO	Runs	HS	Avge		
T. M. Moody (Worcs) .	16	15	2	917	160	70.53	Refuge Assurance League	1991
D. M. Jones (Derbys) ..	15	15	3	749	118	62.41	AXA Equity & Law Lge .	1996
M. W. Goodwin (Sussex)	18	18	3	731	129*	48.73	National League	2003
M. van Jaarsveld (Kent)	9	9	3	660	124	110.00	Friends Provident Trophy	2008
J. A. Rudolph (Yorks) .	13	13	4	861	124*	95.66	Clydesdale Bank 40.	2010
H. G. Kuhn (Kent) . . .	**11**	**11**	**3**	**696**	**127**	**87.00**	**Royal London Cup**	**2018**

---

had chosen the Kolpak route after a sobering Test tour of England in 2017. He began unspectacularly, hitting one half-century in five innings, then exploded, striking hundreds against Surrey and Gloucestershire, before whisking Kent through the knockouts with two more to become only the sixth player – all born outside the UK – to hit four in a one-day tournament in England.

But Hampshire had their own South African opener. And, crucially, Rilee Rossouw came good on the biggest stage, his 125 helping lay down the highest total in a county final at Lord's. He gained strong support from Sam Northeast, who had left Canterbury for Southampton the previous winter, and was subjected to jeers from some disgruntled Kent followers.

Sarah Ansell, Getty Images

London driver: Rilee Rossouw enjoys himself at Lord's.

Although England players were available for the final, neither county had anyone in the national side. And so the game resembled the rest of the tournament in having something of a low-key feel. Hardest done by, perhaps, were Yorkshire, who prevailed in the quarter-final over Essex, despite donating five players to England. Similarly weakened in the semi against Hampshire, Yorkshire couldn't pull off the trick twice.

So the stars tended to be those with experience of the top level, but who were now out of favour – and keen to make a point. Hampshire's James Vince conjured a sublime 126-ball 171 in that semi-final victory over Yorkshire, while few have made a county debut as emphatic as Callum Ferguson, unwanted by Australia but welcomed at Worcester. Leicestershire had just racked up 376 for four, their best against a first-class county, which simply gave Ferguson scope to make an entrance: his 192 from 143 balls delivered the highest successful chase in England. Four days later, he whipped Northamptonshire for an unbeaten 159.

Younger talent also grabbed a moment or two in the spotlight. Ferguson's Worcestershire colleague Ed Barnard confirmed his promise by claiming 16 wickets and hitting useful late-order runs; he gained a call-up to the England Lions. Tom Köhler-Cadmore – once of Worcestershire, now of Yorkshire – took 164 off Durham, and frequently made a strong statement at the top of the innings. There was an encouraging raft of young slow bowlers, too. Lancashire's leg-spinner, Matt Parkinson, still only 21 by the end of the season, led the way with 18 wickets (and an economy-rate of 5.15), while Middlesex's left-armer Ravi Patel, Hampshire's leggie Mason Crane and Matt Carter, an off-spinner from Nottinghamshire, thrust their way high up the averages.

Another welcome development from 2018 – and one set to continue – was the return of the county outground. Sookholme (also known as Welbeck), Eastbourne, Gosforth, Beckenham, Blackpool, Radlett and Oakham all staged matches, and some, especially the first four, attracted healthy crowds. In 2019, Nottinghamshire branch out to Grantham too.

Despite forecasts of its imminent demise, 50-over cricket isn't ready to roll over quite yet. And just like the performances of the England one-day team, there is a lot to like, whether in unfashionable Beckenham or – for one more year – swanky St John's Wood.

Prize Money

£154,000 for winners: HAMPSHIRE.
£72,000 for runners-up: KENT.
£23,150 for losing semi-finalists: WORCESTERSHIRE, YORKSHIRE.
There was no financial reward for winning individual matches.

FINAL GROUP TABLES

North Group

		P	W	L	NR	Pts	NRR
1	WORCESTERSHIRE....	8	6	2	0	12	0.26
2	NOTTINGHAMSHIRE ..	8	5	2	1	11	0.67
3	YORKSHIRE.........	8	5	2	1	11	0.51
4	Warwickshire......	8	4	2	1	10	0.44
5	Derbyshire........	8	4	4	0	8	-0.55
6	Lancashire........	8	3	4	0	7	0.96
7	Northamptonshire..	8	2	5	1	5	-0.33
8	Leicestershire....	8	2	6	0	4	-0.70
9	Durham............	8	2	6	0	4	-1.08

South Group

		P	W	L	NR	Pts	NRR
1	HAMPSHIRE.........	8	5	2	1	11	0.32
2	ESSEX.............	8	5	3	0	10	0.79
3	KENT..............	8	5	3	0	10	0.01
4	Somerset..........	8	4	3	0	9	0.54
5	Surrey............	8	4	3	1	9	-0.84
6	Middlesex.........	8	4	4	0	8	0.08
7	Gloucestershire...	8	2	3	2	7	-0.25
8	Sussex............	8	2	4	2	6	0.07
9	Glamorgan.........	8	1	7	0	2	-0.78

Where counties finished tied on points, positions were decided by (a) most wins, (b) net run-rate. Group winners were awarded a home semi-final, while second and third contested quarter-finals.

ROYAL LONDON ONE-DAY CUP AVERAGES

BATTING (300 runs at 40.00)

		M	I	NO	R	HS	100	50	Avge	SR	4	6
1	S. R. Hain (*Warwicks*)....	8	6	2	426	108	2	3	106.50	88.93	42	1
2	C. J. Ferguson (*Worcs*) ...	5	5	1	377	192	2	0	94.25	117.81	38	8
3	H. G. Kuhn (*Kent*).......	11	11	3	696	127	4	1	87.00	101.45	61	10
4	O. B. Cox (*Worcs*).......	9	8	3	396	122*	1	3	79.20	107.02	43	7
5	†K. K. Jennings (*Lancs*) ..	6	6	1	375	136	1	3	75.00	95.41	34	2
6	P. R. Stirling (*Middx*)	8	8	1	515	127*	3	1	73.57	89.25	49	10
7	†B. A. Godleman (*Derbys*) .	8	8	1	509	137	2	3	72.71	88.83	44	3

		M	I	NO	R	HS	100	50	Avge	SR	4	6
8	J. L. Denly (*Kent*)	11	11	4	492	150*	2	2	70.28	94.61	49	12
9	V. Chopra (*Essex*)	9	9	1	528	160	1	3	66.00	86.98	45	13
10	J. C. Hildreth (*Somerset*)	8	8	1	438	159	1	2	62.57	98.20	35	12
11	L. S. Livingstone (*Lancs*)	8	7	1	362	90*	0	4	60.33	122.71	29	17
12	J. M. Vince (*Hants*)	9	9	0	527	171	2	2	58.55	109.79	58	5
13	S. J. Mullaney (*Notts*)	8	7	0	406	124	1	3	58.00	103.04	34	11
14	†C. A. Ingram (*Glam*)	8	8	1	402	95*	0	3	57.42	98.04	35	11
15	R. S. Bopara (*Essex*)	9	8	1	401	125	1	4	57.28	95.93	26	9
16	†B. T. Slater (*Derbys*)	8	8	1	386	109*	1	5	55.14	101.31	45	5
17	†A. Lyth (*Yorks*)	9	9	1	433	144	2	0	54.12	99.08	54	5
18	C. A. Pujara (*Yorks*)	8	8	1	370	101	1	3	52.85	90.02	36	1
19	T. Köhler-Cadmore (*Yorks*)	9	9	0	472	164	1	3	52.44	101.50	42	17
20	M. J. Richardson (*Durham*)	8	8	0	392	111	1	2	49.00	82.35	35	2
21	T. Westley (*Essex*)	9	9	1	387	134	1	3	48.37	99.23	37	7
22	P. D. Trego (*Somerset*)	8	8	0	376	100	1	4	47.00	89.52	33	5
23	†M. J. Cosgrove (*Leics*)	7	7	0	317	84	0	4	45.28	95.77	28	6
24	D. J. Bell-Drummond (*Kent*)	11	11	0	485	90	0	4	44.09	88.34	50	3
25	†R. R. Rossouw (*Hants*)	9	9	0	394	125	2	1	43.77	105.34	38	6
26	A. J. A. Wheater (*Essex*)	9	9	0	390	88	0	4	43.33	97.25	44	4
27	†E. J. G. Morgan (*Middx*)	7	7	0	300	100	1	2	42.85	96.46	23	12
28	A. L. Davies (*Lancs*)	8	8	0	339	147	1	1	42.37	94.42	40	2
29	†A. J. Blake (*Kent*)	11	9	1	326	61	0	2	40.75	121.18	21	21

BOWLING (11 wickets)

		Style	O	M	R	W	BB	4I	Avge	SR	ER
1	D. J. Willey (*Yorks*)	LFM	23.5	2	130	11	4-47	2	11.81	13.00	5.45
2	J. A. Porter (*Essex*)	RFM	40.1	3	170	12	4-29	2	14.16	20.00	4.23
3	M. Carter (*Notts*)	OB	43	2	198	13	4-40	2	15.23	19.80	4.60
4	M. W. Parkinson (*Lancs*)	LB	63.4	3	328	18	5-68	2	18.22	21.20	5.15
5	D. Olivier (*Derbys*)	RFM	53	3	247	13	3-31	0	19.00	24.40	4.66
6	M. M. Ali (*Worcs*)	OB	47	1	233	11	4-33	1	21.18	25.60	4.95
7	R. H. Patel (*Middx*)	SLA	77	0	378	15	4-58	1	25.20	30.80	4.90
8	C. J. Liddle (*Glos*)	LFM	50	0	337	13	4-57	2	25.92	23.00	6.74
9	D. I. Stevens (*Kent*)	RM	93.1	4	421	16	6-25	0	26.31	34.90	4.51
10	S. T. Finn (*Middx*)	RFM	60.4	2	322	12	4-65	1	26.83	30.30	5.30
11	R. Clarke (*Surrey*)	RFM	61	1	352	13	4-48	1	27.07	28.10	5.77
12	J. T. Ball (*Notts*)	RFM	69	4	391	14	4-29	1	27.92	29.50	5.66
13	C. Overton (*Somerset*)	RFM	56.2	3	336	12	4-27	1	28.00	28.10	5.96
14	O. P. Stone (*Warwicks*)	RF	59.5	3	338	12	4-71	1	28.16	29.90	5.64
15	R. Rampaul (*Derbys*)	RFM	56	3	375	13	5-48	1	28.84	25.80	6.69
16	E. G. Barnard (*Worcs*)	RFM	75	0	462	16	3-64	0	28.87	28.10	6.16
17	A. U. Rashid (*Yorks*)	LB	64	1	405	14	4-47	1	28.92	27.40	6.32
18	M. S. Crane (*Hants*)	LB	74	0	437	15	4-46	1	29.13	29.60	5.90
19	J. L. Denly (*Kent*)	LB	73	2	431	14	4-56	2	30.78	31.20	5.90
20	S. A. Patterson (*Yorks*)	RFM	73.4	2	409	13	4-36	1	31.46	34.00	5.55
21	T. G. Helm (*Middx*)	RFM	66.1	2	441	13	4-49	1	33.92	30.50	6.66
22	M. J. Henry (*Kent*)	RFM	99.1	7	551	16	3-37	0	34.43	37.10	5.55
23	C. A. J. Morris (*Worcs*)	RFM	60	0	381	11	4-33	1	34.63	32.70	6.35
24	R. S. Bopara (*Essex*)	RM	71.2	4	404	11	3-30	0	36.72	38.90	5.66
25	G. K. Berg (*Hants*)	RFM	82.1	1	481	13	3-46	0	37.00	37.90	5.85
26	N. Wagner (*Essex*)	LFM	70	0	445	12	3-40	0	37.08	35.00	6.35
27	C. J. Haggett (*Kent*)	RFM	83.2	0	560	14	3-42	0	40.00	35.70	6.72

LEADING WICKETKEEPERS

Dismissals	M		Dismissals	M	
18 (18 ct)	9	O. B. Cox (*Worcs*)	11 (10 ct, 1 st)	8	C. B. Cooke (*Glamorgan*)
14 (14 ct)	8	D. Smit (*Derbyshire*)	10 (10 ct)	8	S. M. Davies (*Somerset*)
13 (9 ct, 4 st)	8	J. A. Simpson (*Middlesex*)	10 (8 ct, 2 st)	8	T. J. Moores (*Notts*)
13 (12 ct, 1 st)	9	A. J. A. Wheater (*Essex*)			

LEADING FIELDERS

Ct	M		Ct	M	
11	9	T. Köhler-Cadmore (*Yorkshire*)	7	9	J. M. Vince (*Hampshire*)
10	8	L. R. P. L. Taylor (*Nottinghamshire*)	7	11	A. J. Blake (*Kent*)
7	4	M. T. C. Waller (*Somerset*)	7	11	M. J. Henry (*Kent*)
7	8	L. S. Livingstone (*Lancashire*)	7	11	H. G. Kuhn (*Kent*)
7	8	M. H. Wessels (*Nottinghamshire*)			

NORTH GROUP

DERBYSHIRE

At Derby, May 23. **Derbyshire won by four wickets.** ‡**Durham 272-8** (50 overs) (T. W. M. Latham 66); **Derbyshire 273-6** (49.4 overs) (B. A. Godleman 60, L. M. Reece 92). *Attendance: 655. A career-best 92 from Luis Reece, batting for much of his innings with a runner because of a foot injury, formed the backbone of a Derbyshire chase that had threatened to crumble after three quick wickets had fallen to Nathan Rimmington. But they still needed a measured sixth-wicket partnership of 80 between Gary Wilson and Alex Hughes to secure victory. Durham had been well placed at 137-2 in the 27th over, but only Tom Latham made much headway after that.*

At Derby, May 25. **Derbyshire won by five runs. Derbyshire 211-9** (33 overs) (B. A. Godleman 64; V. R. Aaron 4-31); ‡**Leicestershire 206-7** (33 overs). *Attendance: 271. Leicestershire's position in a rain-reduced match appeared hopeless when they needed 38 runs off 12 balls, then 24 off six – less so when Tom Wells's clean striking reduced the requirement to eight off three. But Ravi Rampaul regained his nerve, and conceded only two singles to lift Derbyshire to the top of the group. Leicestershire had been 139-7 before Wells (49* from 28 balls) and Callum Parkinson put on 67*. Earlier, Derbyshire had declined from 163-4 against the pace of Varun Aaron. Leicestershire announced shortly before the start that Michael Carberry had been sacked as captain; Paul Horton took over.*

At Derby, May 30. **Yorkshire won by two wickets. Derbyshire 189-6** (24 overs) (B. T. Slater 109*; D. J. Willey 4-47); ‡**Yorkshire 192-8** (23.5 overs) (T. Köhler-Cadmore 81; R. Rampaul 5-48). *Attendance: 652. In a contest reduced to 24 overs, Ben Slater batted through the innings for 109*, and Rampaul took a one-day best 5-48, but neither could prevent a Yorkshire win. David Willey grabbed four wickets to stall Derbyshire momentum, Tom Köhler-Cadmore cracked four sixes in a 63-ball 81, and Matt Fisher hit 24* off eight to steal the win with a delivery to spare.*

At Derby, June 3. **Lancashire won by 25 runs. Lancashire 290-8** (50 overs) (L. S. Livingstone 86, J. Clark 51); ‡**Derbyshire 265-8** (50 overs) (B. A. Godleman 75, G. C. Viljoen 50*). *Attendance: 1,054. Lancashire's victory could not extend their interest in the competition, but dented Derbyshire's prospects. Liam Livingstone's 86 from 73 set up a strong total, which made Billy Godleman regret his decision to bowl. Derbyshire then fell away after an opening stand of 100 inside 19 overs between Godleman and Slater. Eight wickets tumbled for 96, before Hardus Viljoen's 34-ball 50* massaged the margin of defeat.*

Derbyshire away matches

May 17: beat Warwickshire by 57 runs.　　　　June 1: beat Northamptonshire by 51 runs.
May 19: lost to Worcestershire by 50 runs.　　June 7: lost to Nottinghamshire by eight wickets.

DURHAM

At Chester-le-Street, May 18 (day/night). **Yorkshire won by 142 runs.** ‡**Yorkshire 328-4** (50 overs) (T. Köhler-Cadmore 164, C. A. Pujara 82); **Durham 186** (40 overs) (A. U. Rashid 4-47). *MoM:* T. Köhler-Cadmore. *Attendance: 2,148. Durham had no answer to Tom Köhler-Cadmore's career-best 164, on his 50-over debut for Yorkshire; it came from 151 balls and included 15 fours and seven sixes, as he dominated a second-wicket stand of 176 with Cheteshwar Pujara. Adil Rashid shone on his seasonal debut after stepping down from red-ball cricket, as Durham were skittled with ten overs* *unused. Earlier, the club unveiled the Paul Collingwood Pavilion; the man himself produced tidy figures of 10–0–40–0 but, opening the innings, made only 12.*

At Gosforth, May 25. **Durham won by nine runs** (DLS). **Durham 209** (45.2 overs) (M. J. Richardson 64; C. A. J. Morris 4-33); ‡**Worcestershire 82-4** (15 overs). *Attendance: 1,214. Worcestershire's unbeaten start came to a halt. In pursuit of Durham's 209, they lost three early wickets and, when the rain arrived after 15 overs, were ten short of their DLS target. Gareth Harte scored a valuable 48 on his List A debut for Durham, before becoming part of Charlie Morris's career-best haul of four.*

At Chester-le-Street, June 1 (day/night). **Warwickshire won by five wickets. Durham 299-8** (50 overs) (M. J. Richardson 111, W. R. Smith 119); ‡**Warwickshire 300-5** (48.5 overs) (I. J. L. Trott 100, I. R. Bell 145*). *Attendance: 1,382. Four centuries were scored for the first time in a one-day game at Riverside (no one else passed 15). While Mark Richardson and Will Smith were putting on 161 for Durham's fourth wicket, it was clear the pitch was a belter. But they were upstaged by Jonathan Trott and Ian Bell, who added 202 for Warwickshire's third after both openers had fallen cheaply. Bell's 145* came from 144 balls; it was his second-highest one-day score, behind 158 for England Lions against India A at Worcester in 2010.*

At Chester-le-Street, June 3. **Nottinghamshire won by 31 runs. Nottinghamshire 255** (49.4 overs) (S. J. Mullaney 124); ‡**Durham 224** (48 overs) (M. J. Richardson 68; M. Carter 4-47). *Attendance: 1,505. Steven Mullaney's one-day best 124 lifted Nottinghamshire from 73-5, and culminated in three successive sixes off Matt Dixon in the final over; Dixon finished with 2-88, Durham's most expensive analysis. The hosts made only 26 in their first ten overs, but a fourth-wicket stand of 61 between Richardson and Smith left them needing 80 off 12. Mullaney capped an all-action performance by removing Richardson for 68, and wickets tumbled, keeping Nottinghamshire in the hunt for the quarter-finals.*

Durham away matches

May 20: lost to Lancashire by 192 runs.   May 27: beat Northamptonshire by five runs.
May 23: lost to Derbyshire by four wickets.   June 7: lost to Leicestershire by five wickets.

LANCASHIRE

At Manchester, May 17 (day/night). **Nottinghamshire won by nine runs.** ‡**Nottinghamshire 318** (49.5 overs) (C. D. Nash 52, L. R. P. L. Taylor 58, S. J. Mullaney 70; M. W. Parkinson 5-68); **Lancashire 309-9** (50 overs) (K. K. Jennings 136). *MoM: S. J. Mullaney. County debut: W. A. R. Fraine (Nottinghamshire). Attendance: 1,775. Keaton Jennings's third successive century in all formats could not quite engineer a Lancashire victory. Against the guile of the Nottinghamshire attack and Steven Mullaney's astute field placing, Lancashire subsided from a promising 243-3 after 40 overs. They needed 16 from Jake Ball's last, but managed only six. Earlier, Mullaney's 54-ball 70 had put vim into Nottinghamshire's innings, though five wickets for Matt Parkinson – all in the final seven overs – threatened to give Lancashire the momentum.*

At Manchester, May 20. **Lancashire won by 192 runs.** ‡**Lancashire 314-7** (50 overs) (K. K. Jennings 73, A. L. Davies 147); **Durham 122** (31.1 overs). *Attendance: 2,711. Alex Davies raced to his first white-ball century, from 88 balls, and put on 175 with Jennings, a first-wicket record in this fixture. Davies departed for 147, Lancashire's second-highest score (Andrew Crook hit 162* against Buckinghamshire in 2005). The innings ended on 314-7, despite four wickets falling for 12 in 21 balls as Lancashire slid to 238-5. Jordan Clark added late oomph with 48 from 34. Durham never threatened to make a game of it, and all five home bowlers claimed two wickets at modest cost.*

At Blackpool, May 25. **No result. Lancashire 50-1** (8.2 overs) v ‡**Warwickshire.** *County debut: J. J. Bohannon (Lancashire). The Blackpool weather, which had nipped an over out of the contest before play began, made an unwelcome return after 35 minutes.*

At Manchester, June 5. **Yorkshire won by 16 runs.** ‡**Yorkshire 379-7** (50 overs) (A. Lyth 144, D. J. Willey 131); **Lancashire 363** (49 overs) (K. K. Jennings 69, L. S. Livingstone 79; D. J. Willey 4-59). *Attendance: 2,814. A stand of 235 between Adam Lyth and David Willey was the best for the second wicket for Yorkshire, and an all-wicket Roses record. Both were dropped twice after passing 100 as Lancashire's outcricket disintegrated. Lyth hit 20 fours, Willey seven sixes and 11 fours; all seven bowlers cost at least seven an over. Jennings gave Lancashire's reply a bright start, and Liam*

Livingstone's 48-ball 79 raised the tempo. At 218-2 in the 26th, they were in with a shout but, despite useful runs down the order, Willey had the final say, claiming four wickets, including two in what became the last over.

Lancashire away matches

May 23: lost to Northamptonshire by two wickets.
May 27: lost to Worcestershire by three wickets (DLS).

May 31: beat Leicestershire by nine wickets.
June 3: beat Derbyshire by 25 runs.

LEICESTERSHIRE

At Leicester, May 23. **Nottinghamshire won by 93 runs. Nottinghamshire 409-7** (50 overs) (C. D. Nash 56, M. H. Wessels 76, T. J. Moores 76, S. R. Patel 100); ‡**Leicestershire 316-9** (50 overs) (T. J. Wells 69, C. F. Parkinson 52*; H. F. Gurney 4-58). Attendance: 926. *Michael Carberry watched in horror after inserting Nottinghamshire on a flat pitch. They had already laid the foundations for a big total when Samit Patel arrived to blast a 62-ball hundred, and their eventual 409-7 was the highest List A total against Leicestershire, and a record at Grace Road; both were eclipsed less than a month later by India A's 458-4. Carberry – stripped of the captaincy two days after this game – was bowled in the first over, and Leicestershire slumped to 93-5. Tom Wells and Callum Parkinson made the final margin a little more respectable.*

At Leicester, May 27. **Yorkshire won by nine wickets. ‡Leicestershire 293-9** (50 overs) (M. J. Cosgrove 84, E. J. H. Eckersley 50, N. J. Dexter 50*); **Yorkshire 295-1** (46.3 overs) (A. Lyth 132*, T. Köhler-Cadmore 74, C. A. Pujara 75*). Attendance: 2,772. *Yorkshire made short work of a total that never felt enough: on the pitch that had yielded 725 runs four days earlier, Leicestershire probably needed at least 350. Mark Cosgrove looked like taking them close, but was superbly caught on the boundary by Tom Köhler-Cadmore off Adil Rashid trying to hit his fourth six. Adam Lyth's 132* came off 127 balls.*

At Oakham, May 31. **Lancashire won by nine wickets. Leicestershire 172** (49 overs) (M. J. Cosgrove 52; M. W. Parkinson 4-30); ‡**Lancashire 175-1** (25.5 overs) (H. Hameed 55*, L. S. Livingstone 90*). Attendance: 874. *The return of county cricket to Oakham School after an 11-year absence was greeted by a misty morning which made the toss vital. Put in, Leicestershire were undermined by Joe Mennie and Graham Onions, then befuddled by Matt Parkinson's leg-spin. Lancashire seemed intent on leaving Rutland in a hurry: Liam Livingstone's 90* off 56 balls included seven sixes.*

At Leicester, June 7 (day/night). **Leicestershire won by five wickets. ‡Durham 240** (48.4 overs) (R. C. Davies 61*); **Leicestershire 243-5** (44.2 overs) (C. S. Delport 122, C. N. Ackermann 50). *County debuts: R. C. Davies, M. E. T. Salisbury (Durham). Attendance: 523. After taking seven wickets in their previous four matches, Leicestershire's bowlers reduced Durham to 137-8 on a flat pitch, before Ryan Davies and Barry McCarthy put on 100. Cameron Delport's first List A century for Leicestershire helped them end a run of six defeats.*

Leicestershire away matches

May 17: beat Northamptonshire by 72 runs.
May 25: lost to Derbyshire by five runs.

May 29: lost to Worcestershire by six wickets.
June 3: lost to Warwickshire by nine wickets.

NORTHAMPTONSHIRE

At Northampton, May 17. **Leicestershire won by 72 runs. Leicestershire 265-7** (50 overs) (P. J. Horton 103); ‡**Northamptonshire 193** (38.2 overs) (J. J. Cobb 56; G. T. Griffiths 4-30). Attendance: 634. *Northamptonshire missed a golden opportunity to kick off their white-ball season with a win after a series of poor top-order dismissals. Ben Raine (3-31), and Gavin Griffiths both had List A career-bests as the home team slid to 124-8, before Graeme White and Brett Hutton put on 64. Leicestershire had experienced their own slump, but Paul Horton's third one-day hundred proved decisive.*

At Northampton, May 23. **Northamptonshire won by two wickets. ‡Lancashire 279-8** (50 overs) (K. K. Jennings 69, A. L. Davies 59, D. J. Vilas 83*); **Northamptonshire 282-8** (49.5 overs) (J. J. Cobb 57, R. E. Levi 90). *Attendance: 820. Luke Procter hit the penultimate ball for four to settle a thrilling match. After Josh Cobb and Richard Levi put on 113 in 16.2 overs, Northamptonshire had been well placed. But the run-out of Alex Wakely began a collapse of three for five in four overs, and Procter's calming 43* off 38 balls against his former county was crucial. Lancashire had also begun with a big opening stand, but it took Dane Vilas's 83* to ensure a challenging total.*

At Northampton, May 27. **Durham won by five runs. Durham 256-7** (50 overs) (T. W. M. Latham 86); **‡Northamptonshire 251-9** (50 overs) (A. G. Wakely 79, A. M. Rossington 66). *Attendance: 1,652. Once again, Northamptonshire were in control of a modest chase, only to collapse – and this time there was no escape. Wakely and Adam Rossington put on 129 for fourth wicket, but four fell for 20 in 30 balls. Sixteen were needed off the last over and, although Rory Kleinveldt hit Nathan Rimmington's first ball for six, he was brilliantly yorked by the second. Durham had been 35-3, before Tom Latham's 86.*

At Northampton, June 1 (day/night). **Derbyshire won by 51 runs. ‡Derbyshire 265-2** (50 overs) (B. T. Slater 94, B. A. Godleman 125*); **Northamptonshire 214** (46 overs) (B. M. Duckett 57). *Attendance: 698. Billy Godleman's second century of the competition kept Derbyshire in contention for the knockouts. After they had chosen to bat on a slightly damp pitch, he and Billy Slater added 182 for the first wicket – a record for the fixture – with Godleman going on to 125*. Ben Duckett passed 50 for the first time in the season in any format, but Northamptonshire were never in the running.*

Northamptonshire away matches

May 20: beat Nottinghamshire by 49 runs.
May 30: no result v Warwickshire.

June 3: lost to Worcestershire by 34 runs.
June 7: lost to Yorkshire by four wickets.

NOTTINGHAMSHIRE

At Sookholme, May 20. **Northamptonshire won by 49 runs. Northamptonshire 339-9** (50 overs) (J. J. Cobb 78, A. G. Wakely 72, A. M. Rossington 50); **‡Nottinghamshire 290** (46.2 overs) (S. J. Mullaney 71). *Attendance: 2,943. Northamptonshire's first win in Nottinghamshire in any competition since 2003 came after left-arm spinner Graeme White struck three important blows as the home team fell well short of a testing target. Josh Cobb set things up for Northamptonshire with 78, before captain Alex Wakely (72 from 68), Adam Rossington (50 from 39) and Steven Crook (45* from 28) cashed in.*

At Nottingham, May 27. **Warwickshire won by 108 runs. ‡Warwickshire 295-9** (50 overs) (E. J. Pollock 56, S. R. Hain 72, A. J. Hose 51; M. Carter 4-40); **Nottinghamshire 187** (38.5 overs) (L. R. P. L. Taylor 56; A. D. Thomason 4-45). *Attendance: 14,537. County debut: J. M. Blatherwick (Nottinghamshire). A £1 admission fee on a warm Bank Holiday Sunday attracted a record crowd for a county limited-overs match at Trent Bridge. Nottinghamshire's tall off-spinner Matt Carter made an impressive List A debut, but Warwickshire built on a flying start from Ed Pollock (56 off 29 balls, with 52 in boundaries), and Sam Hain's good form continued with a neat 72. Nottinghamshire seldom looked likely to chase down 296, with seamer Aaron Thomason claiming a career-best 4-45.*

At Nottingham, June 1. **Nottinghamshire won by 38 runs. Nottinghamshire 202** (45.1 overs) (M. H. Wessels 50; M. M. Ali 4-33); **‡Worcestershire 164** (47.2 overs) (D. K. H. Mitchell 62; L. J. Fletcher 4-20). *Attendance: 3,367. Despite the return of Alex Hales from the IPL, Nottinghamshire – for whom defeat would have meant elimination – posted another poor total. But they secured an unlikely win through a combination of Worcestershire mistakes and incisive bowling, particularly from Luke Fletcher, who returned his best List A figures. Moeen Ali had done the same earlier, as Nottinghamshire subsided from 146-3 to 202.*

At Nottingham, June 7 (day/night). **Nottinghamshire won by eight wickets. ‡Derbyshire 110** (35 overs) (J. T. Ball 4-29); **Nottinghamshire 115-2** (11.5 overs) (M. H. Wessels 63). *Attendance: 3,597. Nottinghamshire qualified for the knockouts, dismissing an inept Derbyshire for their lowest total in the 2018 competition; they reached their target quickly enough to finish second in the North*

Division on net run-rate, and guarantee a home tie in the play-off. Riki Wessels (63 from 34) hit the first four deliveries of off-spinner Hamidullah Qadri's second over for six (and the last for four). Jake Ball bowled superbly, and Carter's three wickets gave him 12 from four matches.

Nottinghamshire away matches

May 17: beat Lancashire by nine runs.   May 25: no result v Yorkshire.
May 23: beat Leicestershire by 93 runs.   June 3: beat Durham by 31 runs.

WARWICKSHIRE

At Birmingham, May 17. **Derbyshire won by 57 runs. Derbyshire 357-8** (50 overs) (B. T. Slater 69, B. A. Godleman 137, W. L. Madsen 58; I. J. L. Trott 4-65); ‡**Warwickshire 300** (45.3 overs) (S. R. Hain 108). *County debut:* S. M. Sharif (Derbyshire). *Attendance: 1,523. Derbyshire's highest total against a first-class county was based around Billy Godleman's career-best 137. He put on 129 for the first wicket with Ben Slater, and 99 for the second with Wayne Madsen. Amid the carnage, Jonathan Trott collected his best figures in English limited-overs cricket. Duanne Olivier then dismissed the openers cheaply, leaving Sam Hain to fight a lone battle in compiling his sixth one-day hundred.*

HIGHEST ONE-DAY TOTALS BY DERBYSHIRE

366-4	v Combined Universities at Oxford (55 overs)	1991
365-3	v Cornwall at Derby (60 overs)	1986
357-8	**v Warwickshire at Birmingham (50 overs)**	**2018**
356-2	v Derbyshire Cricket Board at Derby (50 overs)	2000
340-5	v Hampshire at Derby (50 overs)	2014
334-8	v Yorkshire at Leeds (50 overs)	2017
327-8	v Sussex at Derby (60 overs)	1997
324-7	v Northamptonshire at Derby (60 overs)	1997
321-5	v Essex at Leek (40 overs)	2013
309-4	v Northamptonshire at Derby (48.4 overs)	2017

At Birmingham, May 30 (day/night). ‡**Warwickshire v Northamptonshire Abandoned.**

At Birmingham, June 3. **Warwickshire won by nine wickets.** ‡**Leicestershire 207** (43.1 overs) (M. J. Cosgrove 60, C. N. Ackermann 57); **Warwickshire 211-1** (37.4 overs) (I. J. L. Trott 102*, S. R. Hain 69*). *Attendance: 2,260. Leicestershire collapsed feebly on a good pitch after a fourth-wicket stand of 104 in 17 overs between Mark Cosgrove and Colin Ackermann. There were three wickets each for Olly Stone and Aaron Thomason. Trott passed 10,000 List A runs while compiling his 23rd – and final – hundred.*

At Birmingham, June 7 (day/night). **Worcestershire won by one wicket. Warwickshire 292-7** (50 overs) (S. R. Hain 68, T. R. Ambrose 75, W. M. H. Rhodes 69); ‡**Worcestershire 296-9** (45.4 overs) (M. M. Ali 114, O. B. Cox 80; O. P. Stone 4-71). *County debut:* D. Y. Pennington (Worcestershire). *Attendance: 2,324. In what was a straight knockout, Worcestershire scrambled home. They were in danger of wasting Moeen Ali's brilliant 64-ball century – his first in domestic List A cricket for five years (also 114 at Edgbaston) – when they slipped from 272-5 to 288-9 against the pace of Stone and Henry Brookes, still five short of victory. But a misfield from Keith Barker, turning a single into a boundary, all but clinched Worcestershire's home semi-final. Tim Ambrose and Will Rhodes had put on 133, a Warwickshire sixth-wicket record. Trott made eight in his final one-day innings.*

Warwickshire away matches

May 20: beat Yorkshire by five wickets.   May 27: beat Nottinghamshire by 108 runs.
May 25: no result v Lancashire.   June 1: beat Durham by five wickets.

WORCESTERSHIRE

At Worcester, May 19. **Worcestershire won by 50 runs.** ‡**Worcestershire 323-6** (50 overs) (T. C. Fell 56, O. B. Cox 56*, R. A. Whiteley 58); **Derbyshire 273** (46.3 overs) (L. M. Reece 62, W. L. Madsen 87). Attendance: 1,666. *On his first appearance of the season, Ross Whiteley showed the power that led to a winter playing for T20 franchises. He muscled Worcestershire towards an imposing total with 58 off 39 deliveries, hitting three sixes, and losing the ball each time. Tom Fell had already put them on a solid footing, before Ben Cox and Whiteley slammed 101 in ten overs. Luis Reece responded to being pushed up the order with a career-best 62, but Derbyshire's hopes faded when Wayne Madsen fell to Travis Head.*

At Worcester, May 27. **Worcestershire won by three wickets** (DLS). **Lancashire 254-9** (48 overs) (L. S. Livingstone 67); ‡**Worcestershire 255-7** (47.5 overs) (D. K. H. Mitchell 102*). Attendance: 1,409. *A composed innings by Daryl Mitchell carried Worcestershire to a rousing last-ball victory. Two were needed, but Joe Mennie bowled a wide, allowing Mitchell and Joe Leach to scramble the winning run. Mennie had looked like being the Lancashire hero after taking three early wickets, and it was 151-7 when Matt Parkinson removed Ed Barnard. Instead, Mitchell and Leach added 104*. Lancashire had been on course to set a bigger target, before Cox's brilliant full-length catch removed Liam Livingstone.*

At Worcester, May 29. **Worcestershire won by six wickets.** ‡**Leicestershire 376-4** (50 overs) (P. J. Horton 79, B. A. Raine 83, M. J. Cosgrove 70, C. N. Ackermann 71*); **Worcestershire 380-4** (47.2 overs) (J. M. Clarke 62, C. J. Ferguson 192, D. K. H. Mitchell 50, B. L. D'Oliveira 54*). *County debut: C. J. Ferguson (Worcestershire). Attendance: 1,766. Records lay strewn across New Road as Callum Ferguson ensured Worcestershire breezed past Leicestershire with 16 balls to spare. Both counties made their highest score against first-class opponents, and it was the highest successful chase in county cricket, surpassing a mark set by Nottinghamshire in 2017. Ferguson, starting his*

HIGHEST WINNING ONE-DAY CHASES

438-9	South Africa beat Australia (434-4) at Johannesburg	2005-06
402-3	Queensland beat Tasmania (398-1) at North Sydney	2014-15
392-2	Karachi beat Sialkot (391-5) at Sialkot	2003-04
385-6	Andhra beat Goa (383-7) at Bangalore (Rajinder Singh)	2011-12
380-4	**Worcestershire beat Leicestershire (376-4) at Worcester**	**2018**
378-6	Federal Areas beat Baluchistan (375-7) at Rawalpindi	2017
378-6	**Baluchistan beat Khyber Pakhtunkhwa (372-8) at Faisalabad**	**2018**
372-6	South Africa beat Australia (371-6) at Durban	2016-17
373-5	Nottinghamshire beat Essex (370-5) at Chelmsford	2017
366-3	**Punjab beat Baluchistan (365-3) at Faisalabad**	**2018**

All 50-over games.

---

spell with the county early after Head joined the Australian one-day squad, went to 50 in 44 balls, 100 in 87, and 150 in 120. In all, he hit 21 fours and five sixes, and went past Tom Moody's Worcestershire-record 180 against Surrey at The Oval in 1994. He put on 140 with Joe Clarke and 137 with Brett D'Oliveira. Leicestershire thought they had put themselves in a winning position when four batsmen passed 50 in an imposing total, but Ferguson had other ideas.

At Worcester, June 3. **Worcestershire won by 34 runs.** ‡**Worcestershire 348-5** (50 overs) (J. M. Clarke 122, C. J. Ferguson 159*); **Northamptonshire 314** (49.4 overs) (R. I. Newton 61, A. M. Rossington 63, R. I. Keogh 51). Attendance: 2,154. *Worcestershire maintained their 100% home record with a step closer to the semi-finals after another hectic day. Ferguson hit 159* – the county's sixth-highest List A score – and put on 239 with Clarke, a county record for the second wicket. Both men passed Worcestershire's previous highest innings against Northamptonshire – 120 by Graeme Hick in 2007. The visitors took up the challenge but lost three for 20 in the middle order.*

HIGHEST SCORE ON ONE-DAY DEBUT FOR A NEW TEAM

202*	A. Barrow............	Natal v South African African XI at Durban	1975-76
192	**C. J. Ferguson**	**Worcestershire v Leicestershire at Worcester** ...	**2018**
176*	Asif Zakir	Karachi v Sialkot at Sialkot	2003-04
175	T. M. Head	Yorkshire v Leicestershire at Leicester	2016
170*	G. F. J. Liebenberg	South Africa U-24 v Sri Lanka U-24 at Moratuwa ..	1995
167*	P. R. Carlstein	Transvaal v North Eastern Transvaal at Pretoria ..	1970-71
164	**T. Köhler-Cadmore**	**Yorkshire v Durham at Chester-le-Street**	**2018**
163*	B. M. Duckett........	England Lions v Pakistan A at Cheltenham........	2016
161*	M. D. K. J. Perera......	Kegalle v Puttalam at Katunayake	2016-17
161*	C. K. Kapugedera......	Victoria v Prime Bank at Fatullah	2014-15
161	**G. S. N. F. G. Jayasuriya**	Chilaw Marians v Galle at Katunayake	**2017-18**

Worcestershire away matches

May 23: beat Yorkshire by four runs.   June 1: lost to Nottinghamshire by 38 runs.
May 25: lost to Durham by nine runs (DLS).   June 7: beat Warwickshire by one wicket.

YORKSHIRE

At Leeds, May 20. **Warwickshire won by five wickets.** ‡**Yorkshire 247-9** (50 overs) (C. A. Pujara 73; J. S. Patel 4-33); **Warwickshire 248-5** (45.4 overs) (I. J. L. Trott 50, S. R. Hain 102*). *Attendance: 4,053. After a bright start, Yorkshire slid from 80-0 to 149-6 as they struggled against Jeetan Patel. Cheteshwar Pujara held firm for 73, but Warwickshire cantered to victory, with Jonathan Trott and Adam Hose (44) giving sound support to the unflappable Sam Hain. A faultless century – his second in four days – added substance to the claim made by Ashley Giles, Warwickshire's sport director, that he was one of the best 50-over batsmen in the country.*

At Leeds, May 23. **Worcestershire won by four runs. Worcestershire 350-6** (50 overs) (J. M. Clarke 61, T. M. Head 77, R. A. Whiteley 66*, O. B. Cox 50); ‡**Yorkshire 346-9** (50 overs) (T. Köhler-Cadmore 89, C. A. Pujara 101). *Attendance: 2,927. After hitting the penultimate ball of the match, from Charlie Morris, over long-on for six, Andrew Hodd needed six more from the last – but could manage only a single. Chasing the second-highest List A score they had conceded, Yorkshire had a sniff at 173-1 in the 30th over, thanks to Pujara (who went on to 101 from 94 balls) and Tom Köhler-Cadmore (89 from 85). Three wickets fell for 11, but the lower-middle order chipped in, setting up the grandstand finish. Yorkshire paid the price for a shoddy bowling performance, in which Adil Rashid's 10–0–86–2 were their second-most expensive figures, behind Tim Bresnan's 9–0–87–1 at Taunton in 2005. Four Worcestershire batsmen made fifties, with Ross Whiteley's 66* from 41 balls the most destructive; he and Ben Cox (50 off 33) thrashed 110 in 10.2 overs.*

At Leeds, May 25. **Yorkshire v Nottinghamshire. Abandoned.**

At Leeds, June 7 (day/night). **Yorkshire won by four wickets.** ‡**Northamptonshire 241** (47.5 overs) (C. O. Thurston 53); **Yorkshire 245-6** (49 overs) (D. J. Willey 71, G. S. Ballance 66, J. A. Tattersall 52*). *County debuts: B. D. Cotton, C. O. Thurston (Northamptonshire). Attendance: 2,913. Yorkshire qualified for the knockouts, but not quite as expected. It was assumed that victory would automatically give them a home quarter-final against Kent, but Nottinghamshire's demolition of Derbyshire meant they needed to win in 41 overs or fewer, a rate of scoring which was never on. Instead, they made it over the line with an over to spare, which meant a trip to Chelmsford. Perhaps unaware of the need for urgency, Yorkshire had seemed unworried as Northamptonshire recovered from 101-6, the resistance led with panache by debutant Charlie Thurston. David Willey batted powerfully for 71 but, when he fell, Yorkshire were five down, still needing 108. Gary Ballance and the nimble Jonny Tattersall, with a maiden half-century, steadied home nerves. Earlier, the Yorkshire mascot Vinnie helped tackle a pitch invader, who was escorted from the ground.*

Yorkshire away matches

May 18: beat Durham by 142 runs.   May 27: beat Leicestershire by nine wickets.
May 30: beat Derbyshire by two wickets.   June 5: beat Lancashire by 16 runs.

SOUTH GROUP

ESSEX

At Chelmsford, May 25 (day/night). **Essex won by 40 runs. Essex 313** (49.3 overs) (V. Chopra 160, R. S. Bopara 73); ‡**Somerset 273** (48.1 overs) (P. D. Trego 50, R. E. van der Merwe 61; S. Snater 5-60). *Attendance: 2,257. Varun Chopra, who batted through to the final over, set up Essex's big total: his 160, with six sixes, was the highest of his nine List A centuries, and he put on 141 for the fourth wicket with Ravi Bopara. After Neil Wagner (3-71) made early inroads, Somerset's chase was disrupted by Shane Snater, a Zimbabwe-born Dutch international seamer, who marked his home debut by dismissing all five batsmen who scored more than 23.*

At Chelmsford, May 27. **Surrey won by six wickets. Essex 294-9** (50 overs) (V. Chopra 61, T. Westley 54, R. S. Bopara 74); ‡**Surrey 295-4** (45 overs) (J. J. Roy 86, D. Elgar 87, B. T. Foakes 84*). *Attendance: 2,534. Essex paid for failing to hit the accelerator, scoring no boundaries between the 24th and 35th overs. Surrey had no such problems against a lacklustre attack: Jason Roy clouted 86 from 64 balls in a second-wicket partnership of 127 in 18 overs with Dean Elgar, who then admired Ben Foakes's strokeplay in a stand of 100.*

At Chelmsford, May 30. **Essex won by nine wickets. Glamorgan 200** (48.3 overs) (C. B. Cooke 59; J. A. Porter 4-29); ‡**Surrey 201-1** (31.3 overs) (V. Chopra 98*, A. J. A. Wheater 88). *Attendance: 2,052. Glamorgan were dismantled by Jamie Porter, who claimed his best one-day figures, and Matt Coles, in his first home game for his third county. From 100-6, Glamorgan had Chris Cooke and Andrew Salter (43) to thank for reaching 200, but Essex still cantered home, with openers Chopra and Adam Wheater piling on 189.*

At Chelmsford, June 6 (day/night). **Essex won by 153 runs. Essex 337-7** (50 overs) (D. W. Lawrence 115, R. S. Bopara 125); ‡**Kent 184** (37.5 overs) (S. R. Dickson 51; J. A. Porter 4-37). *Attendance: 2,946. Another sizable Essex total was set up by a fourth-wicket stand of 187 between Dan Lawrence, who hit his maiden List A century, and Bopara, whose 125 needed just 88 balls and contained 11 fours and six sixes. Kent soon dipped to 53-4, but Sean Dickson and Alex Blake (41) shored things up before the last six tumbled for 48 in eight overs. Essex's victory improved their net run-rate enough to leapfrog Kent and ensure a home quarter-final.*

Essex away matches

May 17: beat Middlesex by six wickets.   May 23: lost to Hampshire by six wickets.
May 20: lost to Gloucestershire by four wickets.   June 3: beat Sussex by four wickets.

GLAMORGAN

At Cardiff, May 18. **Gloucestershire won by eight wickets.** ‡**Glamorgan 264** (49.3 overs) (S. E. Marsh 57; C. J. Liddle 4-60); **Gloucestershire 265-2** (48.2 overs) (G. T. Hankins 85, C. D. J. Dent 80, B. A. C. Howell 68*). *Attendance: 1,090. Glamorgan looked in charge while Shaun Marsh and Colin Ingram were adding 98 for the third wicket in 16 overs, but the last five clattered for 26. Left-arm seamer Chris Liddle's third victim (Andrew Salter) was his 100th in List A matches. Gloucestershire were soon into their stride, George Hankins (opening in a county match for the first time) and Chris Dent putting on 147 by halfway; Benny Howell finished the job.*

At Cardiff, May 23 (day/night). **Middlesex won by two runs. Middlesex 304-6** (50 overs) (N. R. T. Gubbins 53, E. J. G. Morgan 57, J. E. C. Franklin 62*); ‡**Glamorgan 302-9** (50 overs) (D. L. Lloyd 92). *MoM: J. E. C. Franklin. Attendance: 862. A high-scoring match boiled down to the last ball: Timm van der Gugten needed to hit Tom Helm for six, but fell just short of the square-leg boundary. Middlesex were indebted to the seventh-wicket pair of James Franklin and Nathan Sowter (16*), who conjured 44* from the last 25 balls, including 20 from Marchant de Lange's wayward final* *over. Glamorgan looked in good shape at 222-3, with Ingram and David Lloyd (whose 75-ball 92 was a one-day best) going strong, but Steven Finn's accuracy restricted the later batsmen.*

At Cardiff, June 1. **Glamorgan won by six wickets. Sussex 277-8** (50 overs) (M. G. K. Burgess 58, D. Wiese 67); ‡**Glamorgan 281-4** (48.2 overs) (C. A. Ingram 95*, K. S. Carlson 59*). *Attendance: 855. A fifth-wicket stand of 98* in ten overs between Ingram and Kiran Carlson – who hit 59* from 40 balls in his first game of the season after university exams – spirited Glamorgan to their only win of the competition. Jofra Archer and Chris Jordan made little impression on their return from the IPL. Sussex had been rescued by Michael Burgess and David Wiese, who put on 120 for the sixth wicket in 16 overs.*

At Swansea, June 3. **Hampshire won by four wickets. Glamorgan 227** (48.4 overs) (C. A. Ingram 64; M. S. Crane 4-46); ‡**Hampshire 229-6** (43.2 overs) (B. J. Taylor 54*, G. K. Berg 52*). *Attendance: 1,509. Ingram was the only home batsman to prosper on a true pitch, some poor shot selection helping Mason Crane claim four wickets. Hampshire were wobbling at 144-6 in the 29th over, but Brad Taylor and Gareth Berg took them home – and into the knockouts.*

Glamorgan away matches

May 20: lost to Somerset by 83 runs.
May 25: lost to Kent by four wickets.

May 30: lost to Essex by nine wickets.
June 6: lost to Surrey by five wickets.

GLOUCESTERSHIRE

At Bristol, May 20. **Gloucestershire won by four wickets.** ‡**Essex 287-7** (50 overs) (R. S. Bopara 50, Ashar Zaidi 82; C. J. Liddle 4-57); **Gloucestershire 289-6** (48.1 overs) (G. T. Hankins 77, G. H. Roderick 87*). *Attendance: 1,563. Gareth Roderick steered Gloucestershire home with a cool 87*, first in partnership with George Hankins, then with Ryan Higgins, who walloped a 29-ball 47. The Essex innings had begun brightly, the openers putting on 74 in 11 overs. A second four-wicket return in three days for Chris Liddle hampered progress, though not until the last ball of the innings did he get the better of Ashar Zaidi, whose 82 was his best since joining Essex in 2016.*

At Bristol, May 25 (day/night). **Gloucestershire v Hampshire. Abandoned.**

At Bristol, May 27. **Gloucestershire v Sussex. Abandoned.**

At Bristol, June 6 (day/night). **Middlesex won by 33 runs. Middlesex 322-3** (50 overs) (P. R. Stirling 127*, E. J. G. Morgan 100, H. W. R. Cartwright 60*); ‡**Gloucestershire 289** (48.3 overs) (I. A. Cockbain 106*, R. F. Higgins 65). *Attendance: 1,655. Neither side reached the knockouts, but there was encouragement for England white-ball captain Eoin Morgan before the ODI series against Australia. He made a century, his first for Middlesex for two years, from 63 balls, and added 158 with fellow Irishman Paul Stirling for the third wicket. With Hilton Cartwright hitting a brisk 60*, Middlesex's 322-3 proved too much for Gloucestershire, especially after they slipped to 72-4. Ian Cockbain and Higgins fought back, but seamers Tom Helm and James Franklin, who shared six wickets, had the final say.*

Gloucestershire away matches

May 18: beat Glamorgan by eight wickets.
May 23: lost to Surrey by six wickets.

June 1: no result v Somerset.
June 3: lost to Kent by seven wickets.

HAMPSHIRE

At Southampton, May 21 (day/night). **Hampshire won by four wickets** (DLS). ‡**Surrey 262-7** (44 overs) (D. Elgar 91); **Hampshire 227-6** (32.5 overs) (R. R. Rossouw 90; R. Clarke 4-48). *MoM: R. R. Rossouw. Attendance: 1,714. Opener Rilee Rossouw struck a 68-ball 90 and Joe Weatherley a steadying 46 as Hampshire reached a revised target of 227 from 34 overs. Dean Elgar had put on a gritty 93 for Surrey's second wicket with Rory Burns, who became the first of three victims for Mason*

Crane's leg-spin. Rain interrupted the innings at 198-6 in the 38th over and, though Surrey added 64 after the resumption, it was not enough. Hampshire now had two wins, Surrey two defeats.

At Southampton, May 23. **Hampshire won by six wickets. Essex 303-6** (50 overs) (A. J. A. Wheater 70, T. Westley 66, R. S. Bopara 55, Ashar Zaidi 57*); ‡**Hampshire 304-4** (47.2 overs) (R. R. Rossouw 111, J. M. Vince 66, J. H. K. Adams 51*). *County debut:* S. Snater (Essex). *Attendance:* 1,886. *Hampshire went top of the group thanks to another strong performance from Rossouw, who hit 111 at a run a ball. Facing a stiff target after four Essex batsmen struck half-centuries, Hampshire strode ahead as Rossouw and Vince added 126 for the second wicket in 18 overs. The rate slowed a little, but Jimmy Adams oversaw the closing stages with 51*.*

At Southampton, May 27. **Kent won by one run. Kent 296-6** (50 overs) (D. J. Bell-Drummond 82, S. R. Dickson 68*); ‡**Hampshire 295-5** (50 overs) (J. J. Weatherley 105*, B. J. Taylor 56). *Attendance:* 2,233. *With two overs left, six runs needed and two well-set batsmen at the crease – Weatherley had 103 and Brad Taylor 56 – Hampshire seemed home and dry. But Calum Haggett dismissed Taylor, ending a stand of 133 for the fifth wicket, and conceded two from the 49th. Still, just four required from the last, and Weatherley facing. Matt Henry summoned four dot balls, then a single, heaping the pressure on new man Lewis McManus. He too could manage only a single, and Hampshire's unbeaten record had gone. All seven of Kent's batsmen had made at least 25, including Heino Kuhn, forced to retire after being hit on the arm by a fierce drive from Daniel Bell-Drummond; an unusually forthright Sean Dickson provided late momentum with 68* off 41.*

At Southampton, June 6 (day/night). **Somerset won by three wickets.** ‡**Hampshire 356-9** (50 overs) (T. P. Alsop 95, J. M. Vince 109, L. A. Dawson 76); **Somerset 360-7** (50 overs) (J. G. Myburgh 71, P. D. Trego 100, J. C. Hildreth 56). *County debut:* D. W. Steyn (Hampshire). *Attendance:* 2,350. *Hampshire made their highest score at the Rose Bowl, yet they lost to a spirited Somerset, who pulled off their highest successful chase. Thanks to a run-a-ball 100 from Trego, 11 were needed at the start of Chris Wood's final over, which became three from two when Overton was dropped; he ran a couple to tie the scores, then struck a four. A second-wicket stand of 186 between Tom Alsop and James Vince had given Hampshire an electric start, but poor fielding – and early rustiness from debutant Dale Steyn, who cost 80 – let them down. Despite the result, Hampshire finished top, and Somerset failed to progress.*

Hampshire away matches

May 19: beat Sussex by two wickets.
May 25: no result v Gloucestershire.

May 30: beat Middlesex by five wickets.
June 3: beat Glamorgan by four wickets.

KENT

At Canterbury, May 25. **Kent won by four wickets. Glamorgan 274** (49.3 overs) (N. J. Selman 92; J. L. Denly 4-56); ‡**Kent 278-6** (48.1 overs) (J. L. Denly 150*). *Attendance:* 1,801. *Acting-captain Joe Denly hit 150* to sweep Kent to their first victory; the next-highest contribution was a combative 41 from Alex Blake. Wearied by the previous evening's six-and-a-half-hour coach journey along congested motorways, Glamorgan tried seven bowlers in a bid to stem Denly's progress. Nick Selman's career-best 92 and a belligerent 49 from Graham Wagg had underpinned Glamorgan's innings, but again they ran into Denly, whose 4-56 was his List A best in the UK.*

HIGHEST ONE-DAY INNINGS FOR KENT

150*	J. L. Denly	v Glamorgan at Canterbury	**2018**
147	D. I. Stevens	v Glamorgan at Swansea	2017
146	A. Symonds	v Lancashire at Tunbridge Wells	2004
145	C. L. Hooper	v Leicestershire at Leicester	1996
144*	R. W. T. Key	v Netherlands at Tunbridge Wells	2013
143	C. J. Tavaré	v Somerset at Taunton	1985
143	S. W. Billings	v Derbyshire at Canterbury	2012
142	B. W. Luckhurst	v Somerset at Weston-super-Mare	1970
138	D. J. Bell-Drummond	v Sussex at Canterbury	2017
137	N. R. Taylor	v Surrey at The Oval	1988

At Canterbury, May 29 (day/night). **Kent won by 28 runs (DLS).** Somerset 221-9 (42 overs) (M. T. Renshaw 56, L. Gregory 60); ‡**Kent 88-1** (16 overs). *Attendance: 1,262. Rain brought a late start, an early finish, and plenty of swing and seam movement. After the game was reduced to 42 overs a side, half-centuries by Matt Renshaw and Lewis Gregory helped Somerset recover from 65-5; Matt Henry, capped before the match, and Calum Haggett shared six wickets. Daniel Bell-Drummond went to the third ball of the reply, but Heino Kuhn (36*) and Denly (44*) had put Kent ahead when the heavens opened.*

At Beckenham, June 1. **Kent won by 220 runs.** Kent 384-6 (50 overs) (H. G. Kuhn 117, J. L. Denly 78, A. J. Blake 59; T. K. Curran 4-75); ‡**Surrey 164** (30.1 overs) (J. J. Roy 68; D. I. Stevens 6-25). *Attendance: 3,069. This one-sided affair ended in Kent's biggest List A victory by runs, eclipsing their 198-run downing of Dorset at Canterbury in 1989; it was also Surrey's heaviest defeat. If Kuhn's first one-day hundred for Kent was the centrepiece, Blake's brutal 59 proved most eye-catching. It culminated in four sixes off Gareth Batty, who dismissed him as he attempted a fifth — some recompense for Batty, who endured figures of 9–0–96–1; Curran was perhaps flattered by his 4-75. Jason Roy and Rory Burns, with 42, did their best to answer back, but Surrey's reply became the Darren Stevens show. His medium-pace brought a career-best 6-25.*

KENT'S HIGHEST ONE-DAY TOTALS

384-6	v Berkshire at Finchampstead .	1994		349-8	v Staffordshire at Stone.......	1995
384-8	**v Surrey at Beckenham**	**2018**		341-6	v Norfolk at Horsford	2002
383-7	v Somerset at Taunton	2014		341	v Glamorgan at Swansea	2017
359-4	v Dorset at Canterbury	1989		340-5	v Notts at Nottingham........	2015
352-6	v Somerset at Taunton	2017		339	v Somerset at Taunton	2002

At Beckenham, June 3. **Kent won by seven wickets.** ‡Gloucestershire 322-8 (50 overs) (C. D. J. Dent 63, G. T. Hankins 92, I. A. Cockbain 68, J. M. R. Taylor 53); **Kent 323-3** (46.3 overs) (H. G. Kuhn 113, J. L. Denly 109*). *Attendance: 1,567. Another rousing batting display brought Kent their fifth victory in a row; only twice had they made more in a successful chase. On a Beckenham shirtfront, four Gloucestershire batsmen plundered half-centuries, George Hankins leading the way with a career-best 92. A seemingly tricky pursuit became simpler once Denly and Kuhn had added an all-wicket ground-record 186 in 28 overs to help sweep Kent into second place.*

Kent away matches

May 17: lost to Sussex by seven wickets.
May 20: lost to Middlesex by 70 runs.

May 27: beat Hampshire by one run.
June 6: lost to Essex by 153 runs.

MIDDLESEX

At Radlett, May 17. **Essex won by six wickets.** ‡Middlesex 250 (48.3 overs) (N. R. T. Gubbins 50); **Essex 253-4** (42.4 overs) (V. Chopra 59, T. Westley 134). *Attendance: 1,176. Tom Westley made the most of being dropped three times to anchor Essex to victory: 134 was the highest of his five one-day centuries. The fielding was symptomatic of an undistinguished Middlesex performance: eight batsmen reached double figures, but only Nick Gubbins made it to 50.*

At Radlett, May 20. **Middlesex won by 70 runs.** ‡Middlesex 313-9 (50 overs) (P. R. Stirling 125, E. J. G. Morgan 50); **Kent 243** (43.5 overs) (H. G. Kuhn 90; T. G. Helm 4-49). *Attendance: 1,187. The pitch at Middlesex's home-from-home in Hertfordshire was unpredictable: Matt Henry got one to leap from a full length to clunk Hilton Cartwright on the helmet, then bowled him for a duck. But Paul Stirling mastered it with a superb 125, which included 13 fours and five sixes. "The pace at which the ball was coming off his bat was ridiculous at times," said his admiring captain, Steven Finn. The Kent middle order was then dismantled by Tom Helm. Only Heino Kuhn scored freely, making 90 from 92 balls.*

At Northwood, May 30. **Hampshire won by five wickets.** ‡Middlesex 199-8 (45 overs) (R. J. W. Topley 4-40); **Hampshire 200-5** (38.4 overs) (J. M. Vince 56). *Attendance: 1,041. In a match reduced to 45 overs a side, Finn's decision to bat on an unreliable outground pitch backfired, as*

Reece Topley claimed four wickets for only the second time in his Hampshire career (the other one was also against Middlesex). Hampshire also found batting difficult, but James Vince buckled down for 56 to set them on course.

At Lord's, June 3. **Surrey won by five wickets.** ‡**Middlesex 234** (50 overs) (P. R. Stirling 67; T. K. Curran 4-33); **Surrey 238-5** (48.1 overs) (B. T. Foakes 86, O. J. D. Pope 57*). *Attendance:* 6,823. *A two-paced track bothered the Middlesex batsmen: Stirling alone prospered, although some handy lower-order contributions pushed the total to 234. Surrey made an uncertain start but, from 133-4, Ben Foakes and Ollie Pope added 98 to take them to the brink of victory.*

Middlesex away matches

May 23: beat Glamorgan by two runs.
May 25: beat Sussex by 74 runs.

May 27: lost to Somerset by 53 runs.
June 6: beat Gloucestershire by 33 runs.

SOMERSET

At Taunton, May 20. **Somerset won by 83 runs. Somerset 372-7** (50 overs) (P. D. Trego 56, J. C. Hildreth 159); ‡**Glamorgan 289** (46 overs) (C. A. Ingram 85). *Attendance:* 3,325. *James Hildreth continued his prolific start to the season with a superb career-best 159 in a comfortable victory – though he was dropped on 63 by Jack Murphy at deep midwicket off Colin Ingram. Hildreth, who passed 5,000 List A runs, faced 125 balls, and hit 13 fours and eight sixes. Ingram dragged Glamorgan back into the game after a poor start, but fell to a well-taken catch by Craig Overton.*

At Taunton, May 22. **Sussex won by 75 runs.** ‡**Sussex 341-7** (50 overs) (L. J. Wright 105, M. G. K. Burgess 56, D. Wiese 58*); **Somerset 266** (42.5 overs) (S. M. Davies 56, J. C. Hildreth 87, M. T. Renshaw 55). *Attendance:* 3,675. *The Somerset bandwagon was stopped in its tracks by a notable all-round effort from Sussex. Luke Wright took centre stage with his tenth List A hundred, from 87 balls, and fifties from Michael Burgess and David Wiese helped the visitors to a formidable total. Hildreth was fluent again, but Somerset lost their last six for 69 – and their first game of the season in any format.*

At Taunton, May 27. **Somerset won by 53 runs.** Reduced to 49 overs a side. **Somerset 283** (48.3 overs) (P. D. Trego 65, L. Gregory 56, R. E. van der Merwe 52; S. T. Finn 4-65); ‡**Middlesex 230** (40.1 overs) (J. A. Simpson 77). *Attendance:* 2,225. *Somerset's trio of all-rounders – Peter Trego, Lewis Gregory and Roelof van der Merwe – each made a fifty to lay the foundations of a victory that was less emphatic than had appeared likely. Middlesex were reeling on 84-6, before John Simpson's 77 saved them from embarrassment.*

At Taunton, June 1. **No result. Somerset 211** (40.1 overs) (P. D. Trego 74); ‡**Gloucestershire 39-0** (6 overs). *Attendance:* 3,235. *Gloucestershire appeared on course for victory when torrential rain turned the outfield into a lake. Somerset's innings was a catalogue of mistakes, with only Trego living up to his reputation.*

Somerset away matches

May 18: beat Surrey by eight wickets.
May 25: lost to Essex by 40 runs.

May 29: lost to Kent by 28 runs (DLS).
June 6: beat Hampshire by three wickets.

SURREY

At The Oval, May 18. **Somerset won by eight wickets. Surrey 129** (35.2 overs) (C. Overton 4-27); ‡**Somerset 131-2** (21.3 overs) (J. G. Myburgh 75*). *Attendance:* 7,262. *Surrey crashed to 58-6 in the 18th over and, although Sam Curran made 30, the eventual total never tested Somerset. Craig Overton returned his best List A figures, while Peter Trego's analysis was 10–3–23–2, with 43 dots. Johann Myburgh showed up the lack of demons in the pitch, cracking 13 fours in his 75* from 65.*

At The Oval, May 23. **Surrey won by six wickets. Gloucestershire 282-6** (50 overs) (B. A. C. Howell 60, J. M. R. Taylor 54, R. F. Higgins 81*); ‡**Surrey 286-4** (45.4 overs) (W. G. Jacks 121, D. Elgar 50, B. T. Foakes 50*). *Attendance:* 2,942. *A stand of 110 in 18.2 overs between Jack Taylor and Ryan Higgins cheered up the Gloucestershire innings from 131-5, but Will Jacks soon put Surrey* *in control. At 19, and playing only his third List A match, he became Surrey's youngest one-day centurion (previously Jason Roy, 21, in 2011). He hit 14 fours and four sixes from 100 balls, and put on 158 for the second wicket with Dean Elgar, after Roy departed for a first-over duck.*

At The Oval, May 29. **Surrey v ‡Sussex. Abandoned.** *County debut:* M. Morkel (Surrey). *Morne Morkel's debut was washed out by a fierce thunderstorm, but counted as an appearance because the toss had taken place. He first took the field for Surrey at Beckenham three days later.*

At The Oval, June 6 (day/night). **Surrey won by five wickets. Glamorgan 266-8** (50 overs) (C. R. Brown 98); **‡Surrey 269-5** (40.4 overs) (W. G. Jacks 80, R. J. Burns 68). *Attendance:* 5,166. *Glamorgan were 0-2 after ten balls, but Connor Brown – who entered in the first over and stayed to the last – took them to a respectable total, surviving 136 deliveries as he almost tripled his previous one-day best of 34. Surrey were always ahead of the game – Jacks clobbered 80 from 57 balls, with 60 in boundaries – but results elsewhere muted the celebrations, as they finished a point away from the knockouts.*

Surrey away matches

May 21: lost to Hampshire by four wickets (DLS).   June 1: lost to Kent by 220 runs.
May 27: beat Essex by six wickets.   June 3: beat Middlesex by five wickets.

SUSSEX

At Hove, May 17. **Sussex won by seven wickets. ‡Kent 188** (43.3 overs) (D. J. Bell-Drummond 90); **Sussex 189-3** (39.5 overs) (L. W. P. Wells 62, B. C. Brown 73*). *Attendance:* 1,628. *Luke Wells hit his first white-ball fifty, shared a third-wicket stand of 107 with his captain, Ben Brown, and steered Sussex towards a comfortable win. In fact, the hard work had already been done. The seamers topped and tailed the Kent innings, while spinners Wells and Danny Briggs with 5-53 from a combined 20 overs, undid the rest. Daniel Bell-Drummond ploughed a lone furrow: the only other double-figure contributions were from Alex Blake (29) and Extras (25).*

At Hove, May 19. **Hampshire won by two wickets. ‡Sussex 250** (49.3 overs) (L. J. Wright 56, H. Z. Finch 108); **Hampshire 253-8** (49.2 overs) (H. M. Amla 63, G. K. Berg 65). *Attendance:* 1,626. *When Hashim Amla departed at 133-6, Hampshire needed another 118 from 16 overs – a tough ask for the all-rounders. But Lewis McManus and Gareth Berg met the challenge, and added 61 from the next six overs. Berg, who fell with victory in sight, had earlier claimed three Sussex wickets, including Harry Finch after his first limited-overs hundred.*

At Hove, May 25. **Middlesex won by 74 runs. Middlesex 288-4** (50 overs) (P. R. Stirling 116, N. R. T. Gubbins 86); **‡Sussex 214** (43.5 overs) (D. Wiese 57; R. H. Patel 4-58). *Attendance:* 1,816. *This match was won by the Middlesex openers. Paul Stirling, who needed a runner for the second half of his innings after hurting his thigh, and Nick Gubbins put on 198, a first-wicket record between these teams. Despite the ideal platform, the scoring-rate barely increased on a slow pitch, but Middlesex had plenty. Steven Finn removed the Sussex openers and, although there were contributions down the card, they could not string a partnership together. Spinners Ravi Patel (with a career-best 4-58) and Nathan Sowter took seven.*

At Eastbourne, June 3. **Essex won by four wickets. Sussex 281-7** (50 overs) (H. Z. Finch 56, L. J. Evans 107*); **‡Essex 285-6** (48 overs) (A. J. A. Wheater 60, T. Westley 88). *Attendance:* 3,323. *Sussex were already out of contention for the knockouts, but Essex kept their hopes alive, thanks to well-paced innings from Adam Wheater and Tom Westley, who adapted to the slow Saffrons wicket. After surviving a couple of dropped chances, Westley's luck ran out when he was stranded mid-pitch after a mix-up with Dan Lawrence – but by then the result was clear. Sussex had scored steadily, thanks to Finch and Laurie Evans, if unspectacularly. Jofra Archer injected urgency with a 15-ball 33, but it came too late.*

Sussex away matches

May 22: beat Somerset by 75 runs.   May 29: no result v Surrey.
May 27: no result v Gloucestershire.   June 1: lost to Glamorgan by six wickets.

QUARTER-FINALS

At Nottingham, June 14. **Kent won by nine wickets. Nottinghamshire 255-8** (50 overs) (S. J. Mullaney 90, L. J. Fletcher 53*; H. W. Podmore 4-57); ‡**Kent 257-1** (35.5 overs) (D. J. Bell-Drummond 79, H. G. Kuhn 124*, J. L. Denly 52*). *Attendance: 2,627. Nottinghamshire's defence of the trophy ended in abject defeat: Heino Kuhn led Kent's march to the semis with an authoritative 124*, his third century of the competition. He was on 113 when, with the score 194, Daniel Bell-Drummond fell for 79, and the advent of a whirlwind allowed Kuhn to sit back: Joe Denly walloped 52* from 28 balls, and brought victory with his fifth six. Earlier, Harry Podmore, a late replacement for the injured Mitch Claydon, finished with a white-ball-best 4-57, having helped reduce Nottinghamshire to 23-4 in the tenth. Although Steven Mullaney and Luke Fletcher – whose 53* was also a white-ball-best – engineered a recovery, 255 was inadequate on a good surface.*

At Chelmsford, June 14 (day/night). **Yorkshire won by 25 runs.** ‡**Yorkshire 259-7** (50 overs) (G. S. Ballance 91, J. A. Leaning 57); **Essex 234** (49.1 overs) (A. J. A. Wheater 78; S. A. Patterson 4-36). *MoM: S. A. Patterson. Attendance: 2,564. Yorkshire may have been understrength, thanks to injuries and international calls, but those who remained put up a gritty performance to take them through. They were tottering at 45-4 after three strikes from Jamie Porter, before Gary Ballance orchestrated a recovery, putting on 129 with Jack Leaning. After they departed, Tim Bresnan and Matt Fisher belted 71 from 49 balls. Essex's batsmen had scored freely at Chelmsford during the group games, but now Ben Coad removed Alastair Cook and ran out Tom Westley. Slow left-armer Karl Carver teased out Varun Chopra, who finished with 528 runs from nine matches in the competition (only Kent's Heino Kuhn, with 696 from 11, would end with more). Then Scott Patterson, recently installed as Yorkshire's captain, turned the screw, finishing with four wickets as the later batsmen struggled.*

SEMI-FINALS

WORCESTERSHIRE v KENT

At Worcester, June 17. Kent won by two wickets. Toss: Worcestershire.

Heino Kuhn's fourth hundred in five matches steered Kent towards their first Lord's final for ten years, and consigned Worcestershire to a second successive semi-final defeat. But it was a close-run thing. Kent needed 11 off the final over, bowled by 19-year-old seamer Pat Brown. After a single off the first ball, Kuhn hit the next back over Brown's head for six, but was then caught at short midwicket off the third. Harry Podmore kept his nerve to slam Brown's fourth ball over mid-off for a match-clinching boundary. Kent had been 31 for three against an injury-weakened home attack, before Kuhn joined forces with Adam Rouse and Alex Blake in partnerships of 114 and 115. A pivotal moment came when Daryl Mitchell dropped a comfortable return catch when Kuhn was on 50. On a used pitch, Worcestershire felt their 306 was a challenging total. After an uncertain start, they were hauled out of trouble by Ben Cox, who reached his first List A hundred, in 101 balls. He put on 140 in 24 overs with Brett D'Oliveira then an unbroken 107 with Ed Barnard.

Man of the Match: H. G. Kuhn. *Attendance:* 2,983.

Worcestershire

G. H. Rhodes c Kuhn b Henry	2	E. G. Barnard not out	50
J. M. Clarke c Henry b Stevens	23		
*C. J. Ferguson lbw b Podmore	13	B 1, lb 3, w 6	10
D. K. H. Mitchell b Stevens	4		
B. L. D'Oliveira c Henry b Denly	78	1/8 (1) 2/27 (3) (6 wkts, 50 overs)	306
†O. B. Cox not out	122	3/41 (2) 4/48 (4)	
R. A. Whiteley b Podmore	4	5/188 (5) 6/199 (7) 10 overs: 41-3	

D. Y. Pennington, C. A. J. Morris and P. R. Brown did not bat.

Henry 10–1–60–1; Podmore 8–0–55–2; Stevens 10–1–33–2; Qayyum 5–0–26–0; Haggett 9–0–80–0; Denly 8–0–48–1.

Kent

D. J. Bell-Drummond b Pennington	1	H. W. Podmore not out	6
H. G. Kuhn c Mitchell b Brown	127	C. J. Haggett not out	0
*J. L. Denly c Ferguson b Pennington	0	B 4, lb 5, w 3, nb 4	16
S. R. Dickson c Ferguson b D'Oliveira	8		
†A. P. Rouse c Rhodes b Mitchell	70	1/2 (1) 2/8 (3) (8 wkts, 49.4 overs) 307
D. I. Stevens c Cox b Brown	10	3/31 (4) 4/145 (5)
A. J. Blake c D'Oliveira b Barnard	61	5/162 (6) 6/277 (7)
M. J. Henry c D'Oliveira b Brown	8	7/291 (8) 8/303 (2) 10 overs: 37-3

I. Qayyum did not bat.

Pennington 8–0–50–2; Morris 6–0–29–0; D'Oliveira 10–0–64–1; Barnard 8–0–59–1; Brown 7.4–0–53–3; Mitchell 10–0–43–1.

Umpires: N. G. B. Cook and N. A. Mallender.   Third umpire: S. J. O'Shaughnessy.

HAMPSHIRE v YORKSHIRE

At Southampton, June 18. Hampshire won by 107 runs. Toss: Yorkshire.

A match containing a magnificent innings limped to a dull conclusion. Yorkshire could point to five of their players helping England crush Australia, and might even have whispered, should Yorkshiremen possess the skill, that Hampshire preferred to buy talent rather than nurture it. But actions speak louder than whispers, and Vince, who first played for the Hampshire Cricket Academy aged 15, plundered 171 from 126 balls. Some of his 20 fours and three sixes were shots of real beauty and, on a true pitch, runs flowed. He and Northeast put on 142 at seven an over, with left-arm spinner Carver coming in for harshest treatment. A target of 349 demanded a platform better than 47 for three in the 12th over. Tattersall hit an impish 89 that augured well for the future, even if he could not save Yorkshire's bacon.

Man of the Match: J. M. Vince.   *Attendance:* 2,808.

Hampshire

J. H. K. Adams c Köhler-Cadmore b Coad	16	D. W. Steyn run out (Tattersall)	6
R. R. Rossouw c Pujara b Bresnan	32	R. J. W. Topley not out	6
*J. M. Vince c Köhler-Cadmore b Lyth	171		
S. A. Northeast c Patterson b Bresnan	58	Lb 2, w 2, nb 2	6
J. J. Weatherley b Coad	3		
L. A. Dawson c Lyth b Fisher	17	1/30 (1) 2/76 (2) (9 wkts, 50 overs) 348
†L. D. McManus c Leaning b Patterson	25	3/218 (4) 4/244 (5)
G. K. Berg not out	6	5/292 (6) 6/313 (3) 7/333 (7)
C. P. Wood b Patterson	2	8/336 (9) 9/342 (10) 10 overs: 58-1

Fisher 10–0–70–1; Coad 9–0–48–2; Bresnan 10–0–71–2; Patterson 10–0–56–2; Carver 6–0–60–0; Lyth 5–0–35–1.

Yorkshire

A. Lyth lbw b Wood	11	B. O. Coad c Vince b Wood	9
T. Köhler-Cadmore c Berg b Dawson	21	K. Carver not out	3
C. A. Pujara c Adams b Steyn	0		
G. S. Ballance c Northeast b Berg	25	Lb 2, w 5, nb 2	9
†J. A. Tattersall c Berg b Topley	89		
J. A. Leaning b Dawson	23	1/14 (1) 2/15 (3) (43.4 overs) 241
T. T. Bresnan b Wood	26	3/47 (4) 4/73 (2) 5/123 (6)
M. D. Fisher lbw b Dawson	25	6/173 (7) 7/223 (5) 8/227 (9)
*S. A. Patterson c McManus b Dawson	0	9/230 (8) 10/241 (10) 10 overs: 40-2

Steyn 7–0–34–1; Wood 8.4–0–46–3; Berg 8–0–59–1; Topley 10–0–53–1; Dawson 10–0–47–4.

Umpires: M. Burns and A. G. Wharf.   Third umpire: P. K. Baldwin.

FINAL

HAMPSHIRE v KENT

Lawrence Booth

At Lord's, June 30. Hampshire won by 61 runs. Toss: Kent.

Misfortunes are said to come in threes, but Rilee Rossouw was having none of it. Twelve days earlier, in the semi-final against Yorkshire, he lost two front teeth dropping a catch. On the eve of the final, he was stuck alone in a hotel lift for 80 minutes while his wife and baby waited in the lobby. A golden duck surely beckoned. Instead, after his high-class 125 from 114 balls set up victory for Hampshire – and extended Kent's losing sequence in one-day finals since 1978 to eight – Rossouw was in Panglossian mood: "I would take all the bad luck in the world to win a Lord's final."

Under a sweltering sun and on a flat pitch speckled green, he might have thought his fortunes had changed when Billings chose to bowl. Kent, Billings explained, preferred chasing, but Hampshire were unperturbed. By the time Alsop was stumped for 72 off the second ball from left-arm spinner Qayyum, he and Rossouw had put on 136 for the first wicket inside 23 overs. A crowd of almost 21,000 – not quite full, but enough to allay fears that county fans were losing interest in 50-over cricket – settled in to watch haymaking in the late-June sun.

Rossouw had been accelerating neatly, twice depositing Henry, the rapid New Zealander, for leg-side sixes, then lifting Qayyum high into the Warner Stand. At 193 for one from 30, then 270 for two after 41, Hampshire spied riches. They didn't quite materialise. Denly's 150 List A matches had yielded a modest 42 wickets, but now his leg-breaks picked up four for seven in 18 balls, and it needed a defiant unbeaten 75 from 60 by Northeast to fulfil Hampshire's early promise. Northeast had been booed to the crease by Kent fans still indignant about his move from Canterbury four months earlier, a reception Billings described as "not really cricket". And it didn't help Kentish moods that their former captain took Hampshire to 330 for seven, surpassing Warwickshire's 322 for five (from 60 overs) in the 1993 NatWest Trophy as the highest score in a domestic Lord's final. It was a curious record: weirdly inevitable in an era of inflated runs, yet less imposing than it might have been.

Still, Kent's batsmen had it all to do. And worse was to come. After four Royal London hundreds in ten innings, Kuhn was run out by Berg's underarm throw, ending an opening stand of 55 with Bell-Drummond. Denly, later named by the PCA as the tournament's Most Valuable Player, miscued a pull off Berg to make it 83 for two, and Dickson struggled against the combative left-arm spin of Dawson, whose first seven overs cost only 23. When Dickson finally fell to Crane, nursed through his final game of the season by an injection in his back, Kent needed 173 from 20 overs with seven wickets in hand.

It was feasible, if less so once Wood ended Bell-Drummond's polished 86 via an inside edge. Hampshire began to assert themselves. Crane's direct hit from deep backward point did for Blake, while Stevens – the only member of either team born when Kent last won a Lord's final – was furious at finding long-off. It was all down to Billings, out of form and running out of partners.

Steyn, one of five South African-born players on show, bounced out Henry, and Haggett's miserable day (his three overs had cost 34) continued when he couldn't make it back for a second. Podmore went the same way: four run-outs were the most in one innings of a Lord's final since Australia suffered five against West Indies in the 1975 World Cup. Billings flung his bat to the ground. Moments later, he was last to fall, his 75 from 60 mirroring Northeast.

As Hampshire lifted a trophy they had last won six years earlier, Rossouw was grinning from ear to ear. It was a smile to make his orthodontist proud.

Man of the Match: R. R. Rossouw.   *Attendance:* 20, 886.

Hampshire

T. P. Alsop st Billings b Qayyum	....	72
R. R. Rossouw c Blake b Denly	....	125
*J. M. Vince c Denly b Qayyum	....	23
S. A. Northeast not out	....	75
L. A. Dawson c Blake b Denly	....	8
†L. D. McManus c Dickson b Denly	....	6
J. J. Weatherley lbw b Denly	....	0

G. K. Berg b Haggett	....	9
D. W. Steyn not out	....	1
Lb 2, w 5, nb 4	....	11

1/136 (1) 2/193 (3)   (7 wkts, 50 overs)   330
3/270 (2) 4/287 (5)
5/297 (6) 6/297 (7) 7/323 (8)   10 overs: 58-0

C. P. Wood and M. S. Crane did not bat.

Podmore 9–0–54–0; Henry 9–0–64–0; Haggett 3–0–34–1; Stevens 10–0–59–0; Denly 10–1–57–4; Qayyum 9–0–60–2.

Kent

D. J. Bell-Drummond b Wood	86	H. W. Podmore run out (Wood)	1
H. G. Kuhn run out (Berg)	32	I. Qayyum not out	3
J. L. Denly c Vince b Berg	12		
S. R. Dickson c Rossouw b Crane	30	B 1, lb 4, w 1, nb 2	8
*†S. W. Billings c Steyn b Berg	75		
A. J. Blake run out (Crane)	9	1/55 (2) 2/83 (3) (47.1 overs) 269	
D. I. Stevens c Weatherley b Dawson	12	3/158 (4) 4/179 (1) 5/190 (6)	
M. J. Henry c Alsop b Steyn	0	6/217 (7) 7/218 (8) 8/241 (9)	
C. J. Haggett run out (Vince)	1	9/257 (10) 10/269 (5) 10 overs: 56-1	

Wood 9–0–43–1; Steyn 9–1–56–1; Berg 9.1–1–43–2; Dawson 10–1–48–1; Crane 7–0–53–1; Vince 3–0–21–0.

Umpires: N. G. B. Cook and D. J. Millns. Third umpire: M. J. Saggers.

INDIA A AND WEST INDIES A IN ENGLAND IN 2018

Steven Lynch

One-day tri-series: 1 India A   2 England Lions   3 West Indies A
A-team Tests (2): India A 1, West Indies A 0
A-team Test (1): England Lions 1, India A 0

Before the full England and India teams locked horns, their A-teams linked up with West Indies' for a one-day tri-series, plus three four-day matches. India A recovered from a slow start in the 50-over games to win the final, then beat the West Indians at Taunton, before coming unstuck in the one-off A-team Test at Worcester against the Lions, for whom Alastair Cook made 180.

With county cricket in T20 mode, Cook was playing to get in some practice ahead of what turned out to be his farewell Test series, to the amusement of Surrey's Rory Burns, who led the Lions to victory in his first match for them. "It was a bit bizarre captaining a team with all this experience," he said. "Cooky was the first one to pipe up about me making my debut as captain." Burns's side also included Chris Woakes and Sam Curran, who took seven for 60 in the match as the Lions completed a 253-run victory.

In the one-day tri-series, when the Lions were led by Steven Mullaney, their leading performer was Sam Hain of Warwickshire, whose 356 runs included two centuries, although his 108 in the Oval final was trumped by a good all-round performance by India A's batsmen. Prithvi Shaw and Mayank Agarwal had formed an effective opening pair in the preceding matches, and slammed centuries as their side scorched to 458 for four in the 50-over warm-up at Leicester.

For the four-day game against the Lions, the Indians had also included Ajinkya Rahane and Murali Vijay from their probable Test team, but they met with less success. Still, several of the squad featured in the full internationals that followed against England: seamer Deepak Chahar was whisked into the T20 team, batsman Shreyas Iyer and slow left-armer Akshar Patel joined the 50-over party, while Karun Nair, the captain, was named in the Test squad alongside wicketkeeper Rishabh Pant and Shardul Thakur, another seamer. Shaw and Hanuma Vihari were called up after a mid-series reshuffle, and Vihari played in the final Test, at The Oval. Later in the year, Shaw and Agarwal both made successful Test debuts.

The cast list may occasionally have been confusing, but the overall concept remained a significant marker for further honours. "A-tours are a step up from domestic cricket," said the Indians' coach, Rahul Dravid. "It is really a good barometer for them and the selectors to see whether they can perform or not."

Things were less rosy for the West Indians. Despite choosing an experienced side – more than half had played senior international cricket – they were outclassed in all four one-dayers, then lost the four-day series to India A, despite claiming big leads in both matches. One bright spot was the batting of their exotically named captain, Shamarh Shaqad Joshua Brooks, who followed

91 in the first four-day game with 122 in the second: he was chosen for the full Test squad to face England at home early in 2019, as was John Campbell, an aggressive opener from Jamaica. Sunil Ambris made 128 in the first match, in which the West Indian seamers also had some success, but the spinners – including the hulking Rahkeem Cornwall – posed few problems.

SQUADS

England Lions *R. J. Burns (Surrey; FC), E. G. Barnard (Worcestershire; 50), D. M. Bess (Somerset; FC), A. N. Cook (Essex; FC), S. M. Curran (Surrey; FC), L. A. Dawson (Hampshire; 50), M. D. Fisher (Yorkshire; FC/50), B. T. Foakes (Surrey; 50), N. R. T. Gubbins (Middlesex; FC/ 50), S. R. Hain (Warwickshire; 50), T. G. Helm (Middlesex; 50), C. J. Jordan (Sussex; 50), T. Köhler-Cadmore (Yorkshire; 50), M. J. Leach (Somerset; FC), L. S. Livingstone (Lancashire; 50), D. J. Malan (Middlesex; 50), S. J. Mullaney (Nottinghamshire; 50), C. Overton (Somerset; 50), M. W. Parkinson (Lancashire; 50), O. J. D. Pope (Surrey; FC), J. A. Porter (Essex; 50), R. J. W. Topley (Hampshire; 50), C. R. Woakes (Warwickshire; FC). *Coach:* M. R. Ramprakash.

Mullaney captained in the one-day games. Curran and C. Overton (Somerset) were originally chosen for the 50-over matches, but were called up to the full England team and replaced by Barnard and Jordan.

India A *K. K. Nair (FC), M. A. Agarwal (FC/50), K. K. Ahmed (50), A. R. Bawne (FC), D. L. Chahar (50), A. R. Easwaran (FC), S. Gill (50), K. Gowtham (50), R. N. Gurbani (FC), D. Hooda (50), S. S. Iyer (50), I. P. Kishan (50), P. M. Krishna (50), S. Nadeem (50), K. H. Pandya (50), R. R. Pant (FC/50), A. R. Patel (50), A. M. Rahane (FC), A. Rajpoot (FC), N. A. Saini (FC), R. Samarth (FC), V. Shankar (FC), P. P. Shaw (FC), M. Siraj (FC), K. Srikar Bharat (FC), S. N. Thakur (50), G. H. Vihari (FC/50), M. Vijay (FC), J. Yadav (FC). *Coach:* R. Dravid.

Iyer captained in the 50-over matches. S. V. Samson was originally selected for the one-day squad, but failed a fitness test and was replaced by Kishan. Rahane and Vijay joined the team briefly for some practice before the Tests.

West Indies A *S. S. J. Brooks (FC), S. W. Ambris (FC/50), J. Blackwood (FC/50), J. D. Campbell (FC), R. R. S. Cornwall (FC/50), D. C. Drakes (50), C. Hemraj (FC/50), C. K. Holder (FC/50), S. H. Lewis (50), A. M. McCarthy (50), J. N. Mohammed (50), K. M. A. Paul (50), R. Powell (50), R. A. Reifer (FC/50), R. Shepherd (FC), V. A. Singh (FC), O. F. Smith (FC), D. C. Thomas (FC/50), O. R. Thomas (FC/50), J. A. Warrican (FC/50). *Coach:* R. O. Estwick.

Mohammed captained in the 50-over matches.

At Leeds, June 17. **India A won by 125 runs. India A 328-8** (50 overs) (P. P. Shaw 70, S. S. Iyer 54, I. P. Kishan 50; R. F. Higgins 4-50); ‡**ECB XI 203** (36.5 overs) (D. L. Chahar 3-48). *An ECB XI made up of promising youngsters, and captained by the Lancashire wicketkeeper Alex Davies, were outgunned by a side brimming with IPL experience. Prithvi Shaw led the way with a 61-ball 70, and half-centuries followed for Shreyas Iyer, the captain, and wicketkeeper Ishan Kishan; they all fell to the Gloucestershire seamer Ryan Higgins. Regular wickets set back the chase, in which the Derbyshire all-rounder Matt Critchley top-scored with 40 from No. 7.*

At Birmingham, June 17. **Warwickshire won by 131 runs. Warwickshire 385-6** (50 overs) (D. P. Sibley 115, W. M. H. Rhodes 69); ‡**West Indies A 254** (40.3 overs) (J. N. Mohammed 102; D. A. Douthwaite 3-43, O. J. Hannon-Dalby 3-55, A. T. Thomson 3-53). *County debut:* D. A. Douthwaite. *The West Indians started their tour with a sobering defeat, after Warwickshire ran up a huge total, led by skipper Dom Sibley's 115 from 103 balls. There were 18 sixes in all; Oshane Thomas took 2-91 in ten overs, and left-arm seamer Dominic Drakes 2-74 in seven. Jason Mohammed retaliated with five sixes of his own in an 86-ball century, but no one else passed 30.*

At Leicester, June 19. **India A won by 281 runs. ‡India A 458-4** (50 overs) (P. P. Shaw 132, M. A. Agarwal 151*, S. Gill 86); **Leicestershire 177** (40.4 overs) (T. J. Wells 62; D. L. Chahar 3-24). *County debuts:* J. W. Dickinson, J. H. Funnell. *India A monstered an inexperienced county attack for what was, for a few hours, the second-highest total in all List A cricket, behind Surrey's 496-4* *against Glamorgan at The Oval in 2007. Remarkably, England bulldozed past it later in the day, with 481-6 against Australia, about 25 miles away at Trent Bridge. Shaw was the early aggressor, hitting 20 fours and three sixes during an opening stand of 221 in 26 overs with Mayank Agarwal, who went on to 151 from 106 balls before retiring. Shaw hit five sixes, as did Shubman Gill, as the total stretched far beyond 400. James Dickinson, a 19-year-old leg-spinner from Edinburgh, went for 87 in ten overs on his debut, although he did dismiss the dangerous Rishabh Pant for 13. Ateeq Javid's off-breaks were even more expensive, finishing with 2-91. Deepak Hooda made 38* from 25 balls, and later took a wicket (Aadil Ali) with his first delivery in a competitive match in England, ending up with 4–0–9–2. There was never any danger of Leicestershire getting close: Tom Wells, captain for the day, top-scored with a sedate 62 from 93 balls.*

At Worcester, June 19. **West Indies A won by 21 runs.** ‡**West Indies A 338-9** (50 overs) (J. Blackwood 119, J. N. Mohammed 142; D. Y. Pennington 5-67, R. A. Whiteley 4-58); **Worcestershire 317-8** (50 overs) (G. H. Rhodes 95, R. A. Whiteley 70; C. K. Holder 3-42). *County debuts: J. J. Dell, J. A. Haynes, A. G. Milton, M. T. Spencer, O. E. Westbury, Zain-ul-Hasan. The West Indians recorded their only victory of the tour, against a county side containing six debutants. Jermaine Blackwood and Mohammed both hit sprightly centuries, and added 238 for the third wicket. But Worcestershire's youngsters put up quite a fight: George Rhodes, the son of the club's former coach Steve, made a career-best 95 (his previous six List A games had produced just seven runs), and later Ross Whiteley spanked 70 from 45 balls. The tail, though, was left with too much to do.*

A-TEAM TRI-SERIES

At Derby, June 22. **England Lions won by seven wickets.** ‡**India A 232** (46.3 overs) (R. R. Pant 64; T. G. Helm 3-33, L. A. Dawson 4-30); **England Lions 236-3** (41.5 overs) (N. R. T. Gubbins 128*, S. R. Hain 54). *England Lions 4pts. The Indian batting misfired on a slow pitch, with left-arm spinner Liam Dawson removing Gill (37) and Iyer (42) when they looked well set. Dawson's eventual 4-30 included 42 dots. After Liam Livingstone dismissed top-scorer Pant, who made 64 from 55 balls, Tom Helm filleted the tail. Nick Gubbins anchored the chase, finishing with 128* from 132, and putting on 134 for the second wicket with Sam Hain, as India's spinners posed little threat.*

At Derby, June 23. **England Lions won by 87 runs.** ‡**England Lions 318-5** (50 overs) (T. Köhler-Cadmore 67, S. R. Hain 145*, S. J. Mullaney 58); **West Indies A 231** (44.4 overs) (J. N. Mohammed 52, R. Powell 55; R. J. W. Topley 3-54, C. J. Jordan 3-25, L. A. Dawson 4-27). *England Lions 5pts. Hain set up a big total with a superb 145*, his highest one-day score. He shared another important second-wicket partnership, 148 with Tom Köhler-Cadmore, after Gubbins fell for a duck in the first over, then posted 95 for the fifth with Steven Mullaney, and 62* in 26 balls for the sixth with Dawson (28* from 14). The West Indian openers Chandrapaul Hemraj (35) and Blackwood (40) put on 50, but Chris Jordan's first over (the ninth) was a double wicket-maiden. Dawson claimed four more victims, and Reece Topley cleaned up the last three – including top-scorer Rovman Powell – in eight balls as the Lions made it two out of two, this time with a bonus point.*

At Leicester, June 25. **India A won by seven wickets.** ‡**West Indies A 221** (49.1 overs) (D. C. Thomas 64*; D. L. Chahar 5-27); **India A 222-3** (38.1 overs) (M. A. Agarwal 112, S. Gill 58*). *India A 5pts. The West Indians never recovered from the loss of Blackwood for a duck, the first of five wickets for medium-pacer Deepak Chahar, who would make his T20I debut a fortnight later. Only a canny 64* from wicketkeeper Devon Thomas got them as far as 221. It was nowhere near enough against the side which had blazed 458-4 on this ground the previous week: after Shaw thrashed 27 from 16 balls, Agarwal flew to 112 off 102. He dominated a second-wicket stand of 148 with Gill who, with no need for fireworks, made 58* from 92 as his side claimed a bonus point.*

At Leicester, June 26. **India A won by 102 runs.** ‡**India A 309-6** (50 overs) (M. A. Agarwal 112, S. Gill 72, G. H. Vihari 69); **England Lions 207** (41.3 overs) (S. N. Thakur 3-53). *India A 5pts. "I've enjoyed batting here," said Agarwal after making 112 for the second day running – his third century at Grace Road in eight days – as India A avenged their first-match defeat. On an oven-hot day, he shared an opening stand of 165 with Gill, before Hanuma Vihari took the total past 300.*

The Lions lurched to 32-3, with Shardul Thakur dismissing the openers, and Prasidh Krishna up-rooting two of Hain's stumps, were behind the rate from then on. Although six men made it into the twenties, the top score was Dawson's 38.

At Northampton, June 28. **England Lions won by nine wickets. West Indies A 162** (44.3 overs) (R. J. W. Topley 4-16, L. A. Dawson 4-21); **‡England Lions 163-1** (25 overs) (T. Köhler-Cadmore 80*). *England Lions 5pts. The Lions made sure of a place in the final with a facile victory, cantering past West Indies A's inadequate total with half their overs unused. Topley claimed three wickets in 16 balls to start the slide, and only Devon Thomas (45) held the Lions up. Topley and Dawson (who did not concede a boundary in his ten overs) both finished with morale-boosting four-wicket hauls two days ahead of Hampshire's Royal London Cup final against Kent; they returned for the tri-series final after picking up winners' medals at Lord's. The Lions lost only one wicket – Gubbins to a run-out – as they strolled to victory. Köhler-Cadmore, dropped from two of his first three balls, made 80* from 70, and put on 120* with Hain (48*). He hit two enormous sixes, one out of the ground, one into the car park.*

At Northampton, June 29. **India A won by 203 runs. ‡India A 354-6** (50 overs) (P. P. Shaw 102, G. H. Vihari 147; C. K. Holder 3-70); **West Indies A 151** (37.4 overs) (A. R. Patel 4-34). *India A 5pts. Another hefty victory for India A ensured the West Indian finalists pointless. Agarwal was rested, and Pant and Iyer went cheaply – but then Shaw and Vihari (who hit 13 fours and five sixes) tucked in with a partnership of 160. Blackwood fell to the first ball of the chase, from Chahar, and wickets kept tumbling; slow left-armer Akshar Patel collected four. Hemraj top-scored with 43 in another insipid batting display by West Indies A, whose highest total in four matches was 231.*

India A 15pts, England Lions 14pts, West Indies A 0pts.

Final   At The Oval, July 2. **India A won by five wickets. England Lions 264-9** (50 overs) (S. R. Hain 108, L. S. Livingstone 83; D. L. Chahar 3-58, K. K. Ahmed 3-48); **‡India A 267-5** (48.2 overs) (R. R. Pant 64*). *The Lions were favourites at several points during a fluctuating day, but India A won out. Hain struck his fourth List A hundred of the season – he averaged 111 in all matches – and put on 152 with Livingstone, who muscled five sixes. But when they were separated, only 78 more came from the last 16 overs as the Indian seamers applied the brakes. Then, with Dawson again bowling well, the strong Indian batting line-up was reduced to 196-5 in the 39th. Shortly after, Topley – running in from long-on – dropped Pant on 35. He went on to share a match-winning stand of 71* with Krunal Pandya (34*).*

INDIA A v WEST INDIES A

First A-Team Test

At Beckenham, July 4–7. Drawn. Toss: India A.
    India A staged a remarkable comeback after being skittled for 133 on the first day, almost forcing a win after trailing by 250 on first innings. The initial damage was done by the lively West Indian new-ball pair of Chemar Holder and Sherman Lewis: after seven balls, India A were three for three, with both their prolific openers, Shaw and Agarwal, bagging golden ducks. Vihari, who batted for two and a half hours, averted a complete meltdown, but the total was paltry on a pitch usually known as a featherbed. West Indies A were ahead by stumps, and on the second day Brooks and Ambris took their stand to 152; a workmanlike 52 from Raymon Reifer stretched the total to 383. Seamer Ankit Rajpoot took four wickets, and also pulled off a run-out. Well behind, the Indians launched a stunning counter-attack. The openers piled on 181 inside 28 overs, before Agarwal fell for 68, which included 14 fours. Shaw careered to 188 from 169 balls, then Ravikumar Samarth and Karun Nair added 166, at which point they were 505 for two. Nair fell for 93 on the fourth morning before declaring, leaving a target of 360 in what became 76 overs. Now it was Hemraj's turn for a first-baller, and Brooks soon followed – but Blackwood and Ambris shored up the innings, and later Cornwall ensured there would be no late collapse with a solid 40.
    Close of play: first day, West Indies A 148-3 (Brooks 51, Ambris 24); second day, India A 159-0 (Shaw 101, Agarwal 56); third day, India A 536-4 (Nair 77, Shankar 6).

India A

P. P. Shaw b Holder	0	– c Hemraj b Lewis	188
M. A. Agarwal c Campbell b Lewis	0	– c Brooks b Lewis	68
R. Samarth c Cornwall b Holder	2	– c Thomas b Holder	137
*K. K. Nair lbw b Reifer	20	– c Warrican b Lewis	93
G. H. Vihari c Ambris b Lewis	37	– c Warrican b Thomas	10
V. Shankar lbw b Reifer	34	– c Cornwall b Lewis	13
†K. Srikar Bharat c Campbell b Lewis	2	– not out	33
J. Yadav c Campbell b Holder	0	– not out	10
S. Nadeem c Hemraj b Lewis	15		
N. Saini c Blackwood b Holder	4		
A. Rajpoot not out	0		
B 8, lb 1, w 1, nb 9	19	B 22, lb 2, w 14, nb 19	57

1/0 (1) 2/3 (3) 3/3 (2) 4/45 (4)   (42.1 overs) 133
5/105 (6) 6/108 (5) 7/108 (7)
8/109 (8) 9/119 (10) 10/133 (9)

1/181 (2)   (6 wkts dec, 111 overs) 609
2/339 (1) 3/505 (3)
4/521 (5) 5/564 (6) 6/566 (4)

Holder 13–0–57–4; Lewis 11.1–2–35–4; Reifer 12–4–20–2; Warrican 6–3–12–0. *Second innings*—Holder 31–2–148–1; Lewis 24–1–130–4; Reifer 18–1–92–0; Cornwall 11–0–66–0; Warrican 13–0–89–0; Thomas 14–1–60–1.

West Indies A

J. D. Campbell lbw b Rajpoot	2	– c Vihari b Rajpoot	44
C. Hemraj c Shankar b Nadeem	42	– b Saini	0
J. Blackwood c Srikar Bharat b Rajpoot	18	– (4) c Srikar Bharat b Nadeem	61
*S. S. J. Brooks c Nair b Rajpoot	91	– (3) b Yadav	9
S. W. Ambris c Srikar Bharat b Saini	128	– b Yadav	42
†D. C. Thomas c Agarwal b Nadeem	10	– c Shaw b Saini	22
R. A. Reifer c Srikar Bharat b Rajpoot	52	– not out	11
R. R. S. Cornwall c Srikar Bharat b Saini	0	– lbw b Nadeem	40
J. A. Warrican run out (Rajpoot)	3	– not out	4
S. H. Lewis c Srikar Bharat b Shankar	10		
C. K. Holder not out	5		
B 5, lb 7, nb 10	22	B 1, lb 10, nb 1	12

1/4 (1) 2/28 (3) 3/82 (2)   (101.2 overs) 383
4/234 (4) 5/269 (6) 6/341 (5)
7/341 (8) 8/347 (9) 9/372 (10) 10/383 (7)

1/0 (2) 2/28 (3)   (7 wkts, 76 overs) 245
3/77 (1) 4/143 (4)
5/188 (5) 6/188 (6) 7/236 (8)

Rajpoot 25.2–9–76–4; Saini 25–5–78–2; Shankar 17–0–71–1; Nadeem 19–1–87–2; Yadav 15–0–59–0. *Second innings*—Rajpoot 11–5–21–1; Saini 14–4–41–2; Nadeem 26–6–81–2; Yadav 21–4–73–2; Shankar 4–0–18–0.

Umpires: N. A. Mallender and R. A. White.

INDIA A v WEST INDIES A

Second A-Team Test

At Taunton, July 10–13. India A won by five wickets. Toss: West Indies A.

As in the previous match, India A bounced back from a big first-innings deficit – and this time made it count, completing a series-clinching victory before lunch on the final day. The West Indians had been in control throughout the first two. First they made 302, thanks mainly to 122 from their captain, Brooks. Then the seamers – led by left-armer Reifer – restricted a reshuffled Indian line-up to 192, of which 30 came from No. 11 Vijay Shankar. Early on the third day, West Indies A were sitting pretty at 125 for one, a lead of 235, but the wheels fell off: only Vishaul Singh of the remaining batsmen made more than six. Seamers Mohammed Siraj and Rajneesh Gurbani shared seven wickets, and India A needed 321. Just before the third-day close they had reached 214 for two, but Nair fell to the last ball, and next morning Ankit Bawne and Vihari also went quickly. But Pant tucked in, cracking 11 fours in an undefeated sixth-wicket stand of 99 with Jayant Yadav to take his side home.

Close of play: first day, West Indies A 301-9 (Brooks 121, O. R. Thomas 2); second day, West Indies A 96-1 (Campbell 43, Blackwood 23); third day, India A 214-3 (Vihari 65).

West Indies A

J. D. Campbell b Shankar	41	– c Pant b Siraj	61
†D. C. Thomas c Vihari b Gurbani	27	– c Pant b Gurbani	25
J. Blackwood b Nadeem	12	– b Gurbani	67
*S. S. J. Brooks not out	122	– c Pant b Siraj	2
S. W. Ambris lbw b Nadeem	0	– c sub (M. A. Agarwal) b Nadeem	5
V. A. Singh c Nair b Yadav	8	– c Samarth b Siraj	16
R. A. Reifer c Nadeem b Siraj	11	– c Easwaran b Gurbani	0
R. Shepherd b Siraj	5	– c Pant b Siraj	5
J. A. Warrican c Pant b Nadeem	5	– c sub (M. A. Agarwal) b Yadav	1
S. H. Lewis c Pant b Siraj	18	– b Yadav	0
O. R. Thomas c Pant b Siraj	2	– not out	6
B 17, lb 23, w 2, nb 9	51	B 7, lb 12, w 1, nb 2	22

1/49 (2) 2/86 (1) 3/114 (3)   (90.5 overs) 302
4/114 (5) 5/166 (6) 6/210 (7)
7/216 (8) 8/222 (9) 9/292 (10) 10/302 (11)

1/51 (2) 2/125 (1)   (57.3 overs) 210
3/137 (4) 4/160 (5)
5/180 (3) 6/180 (7) 7/203 (8)
8/204 (6) 9/204 (9) 10/210 (10)

Siraj 22.5–4–68–4; Gurbani 20–3–53–1; Shankar 6–0–20–1; Yadav 20–1–79–1; Nadeem 22–4–42–3. *Second innings*—Siraj 20–3–64–4; Gurbani 17–1–64–3; Yadav 7.3–2–23–2; Nadeem 13–2–40–1.

India A

R. Samarth c Blackwood b O. R. Thomas	10	– c D. C. Thomas b Reifer	18
A. R. Easwaran c D. C. Thomas b Reifer	23	– c D. C. Thomas b Shepherd	31
G. H. Vihari c D. C. Thomas b O. R. Thomas	4	– run out (Campbell/Warrican)	68
*K. K. Nair c D. C. Thomas b Reifer	42	– c Campbell b Warrican	55
A. R. Bawne not out	43	– b Lewis	1
†R. R. Pant c and b Shepherd	3	– not out	67
J. Yadav c Warrican b Lewis	0	– not out	23
S. Nadeem b Reifer	11		
M. Siraj b Reifer	0		
R. N. Gurbani c D. C. Thomas b Reifer	0		
V. Shankar c D. C. Thomas b O. R. Thomas	30		
B 14, lb 1, w 11	26	B 35, w 19, nb 4	58

1/36 (1) 2/40 (3) 3/48 (2)   (48 overs) 192
4/114 (4) 5/123 (6) 6/125 (7)
7/147 (8) 8/147 (9) 9/149 (10) 10/192 (11)

1/51 (1)   (5 wkts, 67.1 overs) 321
2/78 (2) 3/214 (4)
4/218 (5) 5/222 (3)

Lewis 11–2–31–1; O. R. Thomas 12–1–66–3; Reifer 16–2–50–5; Shepherd 9–1–30–1. *Second innings*—Lewis 16–2–64–1; O. R. Thomas 12–1–64–0; Reifer 18–2–49–1; Shepherd 9.1–1–57–1; Warrican 9–0–36–1; Campbell 3–0–16–0.

Umpires: N. L. Bainton and M. Newell.

ENGLAND LIONS v INDIA A

A-Team Test

At Worcester, July 16–19. England Lions won by 253 runs. Toss: India A.

India A had come from behind in both four-day games against the West Indians, but could not make it a hat-trick against a strong England Lions side, bolstered by the inclusion of Cook, Curran and Woakes ahead of the Tests. Cook made the most of his chance, batting serenely through the first day before falling for 180 after 408 minutes, with 26 fours: it was his first first-class hundred since carrying his bat for 244 in the Boxing Day Test at Melbourne in 2017. He shared stands of 155 and 181 with the Middlesex pair of Gubbins and Malan and, although the later batting was undistinguished, a total of 423 looked imposing. India A had included Vijay and Rahane from their Test party, but Vijay failed to take advantage, the first of three wickets inside three overs. Shaw made a snappy 62, then Rahane and Pant patiently added 96 – but from 189 for four, six tumbled for eight, four to Curran. Burns waived the follow-on and, with Malan and Pope adding 70 in even time, eventually set a lofty 421. Vijay failed again, and Shaw fell second ball: when nightwatchman Shahbaz Nadeem was castled early on the final morning it was 15 for four. Rahane and Pant shared another useful stand, but the Lions eased to a comfortable victory midway through the afternoon session.

Close of play: first day, England Lions 310-2 (Cook 154, Malan 59); second day, India A 144-4 (Rahane 26, Pant 37); third day, India A 11-3 (Nadeem 10).

England Lions

*R. J. Burns c Agarwal b Saini	5	– c Pant b Siraj	38
A. N. Cook b Rajpoot	180	– b Siraj	5
N. R. T. Gubbins c Vijay b Rajpoot	73	– c Pant b Siraj	9
D. J. Malan b Siraj	74	– b Nadeem	56
†O. J. D. Pope lbw b Nadeem	8	– not out	50
C. R. Woakes b Siraj	15	– c Agarwal b Saini	28
S. M. Curran c Pant b Siraj	12		
D. M. Bess c Vijay b Siraj	13		
M. J. Leach not out	12		
M. D. Fisher c Nair b Nadeem	6		
J. A. Porter b Nadeem	0		
B 13, lb 8, w 1, nb 3	25	B 5, lb 1, nb 2	8

1/9 (1) 2/164 (3) 3/345 (2)   (128.5 overs) 423   1/11 (2)   (5 wkts dec, 52 overs) 194
4/351 (4) 5/361 (5) 6/380 (7)   2/25 (3) 3/72 (1)
7/391 (6) 8/400 (8) 9/423 (10)   4/142 (4) 5/194 (6)
10/423 (11)

Rajpoot 24.5–7–64–2; Saini 29–6–109–1; Siraj 29–5–79–4; Yadav 28–4–93–0; Nadeem 15–3–46–3; Vijay 3–0–11–0. *Second innings—*Siraj 14–2–55–3; Saini 16–3–56–1; Yadav 12–2–41–0; Nadeem 10–0–36–1.

India A

P. P. Shaw c Malan b Curran	62	– (2) c Malan b Curran	0
M. Vijay lbw b Porter	8	– (1) b Porter	0
M. A. Agarwal c Pope b Fisher	0	– (4) lbw b Porter	1
*K. K. Nair c Curran b Fisher	4	– (5) c Gubbins b Woakes	13
A. M. Rahane c Pope b Curran	49	– (6) c Fisher b Bess	48
†R. R. Pant b Woakes	58	– (7) c Pope b Bess	61
J. Yadav b Woakes	5	– (8) c Porter b Leach	21
S. Nadeem lbw b Curran	0	– (3) c Curran b Woakes	10
M. Siraj lbw b Curran	1	– b Fisher	11
N. Saini lbw b Curran	0	– not out	1
A. Rajpoot not out	0	– absent hurt	
B 3, lb 5, nb 2	10	Lb 1	1

1/37 (2) 2/42 (3) 3/50 (4)   (66.5 overs) 197   1/0 (1) 2/0 (2)   (44 overs) 167
4/93 (1) 5/189 (6) 6/189 (5)   3/11 (4) 4/15 (3) 5/54 (5)
7/189 (8) 8/195 (7) 9/196 (10) 10/197 (9)   6/108 (6) 7/135 (7) 8/160 (8)
                                   9/167 (9)

Porter 15–4–36–1; Curran 11.5–3–43–5; Leach 5–0–22–0; Fisher 13–0–43–2; Woakes 13–5–28–2; Bess 9–2–17–0. *Second innings—*Porter 10–2–43–2; Curran 7–2–17–2; Fisher 12–2–29–1; Woakes 5–0–21–1; Bess 8–1–43–2; Leach 2–0–13–1.

Umpires: I. D. Blackwell and J. D. Middlebrook.

698 *English Domestic Cricket*

SURREY v WEST INDIES A

At The Oval, July 16–18. Drawn. Toss: Surrey. County debut: A. P. Rouse.

The West Indians wrapped up their tour with a match against the champions-elect. Borthwick entered in the third over and dominated the first day. His unbeaten 175 was only his second century since joining from Durham in 2017. Borthwick put on 131 with Patel, then shared useful stands down the order, including 93 for the sixth wicket with Adam Rouse, borrowed from Kent to allow Surrey's other wicketkeepers to rest minor niggles. The tourists' reply was underwhelming, with only left-hander Singh passing 30, but Tom Curran – captaining Surrey for the first time – did not enforce the follow-on, despite a lead of 188. He was playing as a batsman as he continued his recovery from a side strain, but faced only nine balls across the two innings. Set an unlikely 362 after a lunchtime declaration on the final day, West Indies A settled for the draw, with Campbell and Ambris making lively half-centuries.

Close of play: first day, Surrey 309-8 (Borthwick 153, Morkel 1); second day, Surrey 62-1 (Stoneman 23, Patel 30).

Surrey

A. Harinath c Smith b Shepherd	10	– c sub (J. A. Warrican) b Holder 7
M. D. Stoneman c Campbell b Lewis	1	– c Thomas b Shepherd............ 44
S. G. Borthwick not out	175	
R. S. Patel b Holder	47	– (3) c Thomas b Smith............ 48
W. G. Jacks c Brooks b Reifer	10	– (4) not out.................... 47
*T. K. Curran c Thomas b Holder	0	– (5) b Smith 2
†A. P. Rouse c Brooks b Campbell	36	– (6) not out 7
S. C. Meaker b Lewis	5	
M. W. Pillans c Thomas b Reifer	10	
M. Morkel c Thomas b Smith	22	
G. S. Virdi c Smith b Reifer	11	
B 14, lb 5, w 12, nb 8	39	B 9, lb 1, w 5, nb 3 18

1/9 (2) 2/34 (1) 3/165 (4) (98.3 overs) 366
4/184 (5) 5/185 (6) 6/278 (7)
7/285 (8) 8/308 (9) 9/350 (10) 10/366 (11)

1/9 (1) (4 wkts dec, 37 overs) 173
2/88 (2) 3/138 (3)

Lewis 19–5–64–2; Holder 18–2–57–2; Shepherd 14–1–54–1; Reifer 20.3–6–65–3; Smith 19–3–84–1; Campbell 8–1–23–1. *Second innings*—Lewis 7–3–27–0; Holder 11–0–50–1; Reifer 5–0–35–0; Campbell 1–0–6–0; Shepherd 8–2–30–1; Smith 5–0–15–2.

West Indies A

J. D. Campbell b Morkel	5	– lbw b Meaker 55
C. Hemraj c Borthwick b Morkel	19	– c Borthwick b Virdi 23
S. W. Ambris c Stoneman b Pillans	12	– not out 63
V. A. Singh c Rouse b Morkel	47	– b Morkel 26
†D. C. Thomas c Rouse b Pillans	28	– not out 22
R. A. Reifer c Meaker b Pillans	0	
R. Shepherd lbw b Meaker	19	
O. F. Smith b Borthwick	30	
S. H. Lewis not out	0	
C. K. Holder b Borthwick	8	
*S. S. J. Brooks absent hurt		
Lb 7, w 1, nb 2	10	B 1, lb 1, w 3 5

1/28 (1) 2/29 (2) 3/53 (3) (55.1 overs) 178
4/102 (5) 5/102 (6) 6/123 (7)
7/152 (4) 8/170 (8) 9/178 (10)

1/79 (2) (3 wkts, 50 overs) 194
2/79 (1) 3/127 (4)

Morkel 13–6–12–3; Pillans 12–2–29–3; Meaker 12–2–36–1; Patel 5–1–17–0; Virdi 9–1–42–0; Borthwick 4.1–0–35–2. *Second innings*—Morkel 11–2–50–1; Pillans 7–1–39–0; Meaker 7–2–29–1; Virdi 14–0–37–1; Borthwick 6–0–24–0; Patel 5–1–13–0.

Umpires: P. K. Baldwin and M. Burns.

THE UNIVERSITIES IN 2018

CAMBRIDGE MCCU v NOTTINGHAMSHIRE

At Cambridge, April 1–3. Abandoned.

Play was called off early on the second day after persistent rain. Nottinghamshire's first washout in a first-class match for ten years turned out to be particularly bad news for 19-year-old Tom Keast, who had been due to keep wicket. By the end of the season he had still not made his first-class debut.

At Bristol, April 1–3. CARDIFF MCCU drew with GLOUCESTERSHIRE.

At Canterbury, April 1–3. OXFORD MCCU drew with KENT. *Only 33 overs are possible.*

At Hove, April 1–3. LOUGHBOROUGH MCCU drew with SUSSEX.

At Birmingham, April 1–3. DURHAM MCCU drew with WARWICKSHIRE.

At Worcester (Royal Grammar School), April 1–3. WORCESTERSHIRE v LEEDS/BRADFORD MCCU. Abandoned.

CAMBRIDGE MCCU v ESSEX

At Cambridge, April 7–9. Drawn. Toss: Essex. First-class debuts: J. W. R. Bowers, J. Bulpitt, S. Handley, J. B. R. Keeping, B. M. A. Seabrook; J. H. Plom.

The terrible early-season weather relented briefly, allowing 66.3 overs, all after lunch on the first day. Browne grabbed the chance to make his 14th first-class century, from 122 balls, before retiring out, and Essex's other batsmen all had time in the middle before the clouds closed in again. Play was called off on the third day by 8.45. The England Under-19 seamer Jack Plom made his debut for Essex – but neither batted nor bowled.

Close of play: first day, Essex 283-4 (Bopara 25, ten Doeschate 14); second day, no play.

Essex

N. L. J. Browne retired out	100	*R. N. ten Doeschate not out	14
A. J. A. Wheater c Keeping b Guest	50	B 5, w 6, nb 2	13
T. Westley c and b Chapman	44		—
D. W. Lawrence c and b Rippington	37	1/122 (2) 2/169 (1) (4 wkts, 66.3 overs)	283
R. S. Bopara not out	25	3/227 (3) 4/244 (4)	

†J. S. Foster, P. I. Walter, S. R. Harmer, J. A. Porter and J. H. Plom did not bat.

Rippington 20–1–90–1; Bulpitt 12–3–32–0; Seabrook 6–1–25–0; Guest 5–0–28–1; Chapman 13–1–65–1; Handley 10.3–4–38–0.

Cambridge MCCU

H. J. Palmer, A. D. Greenidge, B. M. A. Seabrook, *C. J. Guest, J. B. R. Keeping, D. D. W. Brierley, S. Handley, †J. W. R. Bowers, L. J. Chapman, J. Bulpitt, S. E. Rippington.

Umpires: D. J. Millns and P. R. Pollard.

At Southampton, April 7–9. CARDIFF MCCU drew with HAMPSHIRE.

LOUGHBOROUGH MCCU v LANCASHIRE

At Loughborough, April 7–9. Drawn. Toss: Lancashire. County debuts: K. K. Jennings, G. Onions.

Lancashire's seamers, and two wickets for Parkinson's leg-breaks, reduced Loughborough to 135 for nine on the first day. But the last pair, Stockport-born Chris Sanders and his new-ball partner William Pereira, put on 85 – easily the highest stand of the innings – to take the students to the relative prosperity of 220. Hopes of a positive result diminished when rain cut the second day in half, and Lancashire's batsmen opted for practice on the third. Croft made a careful century, sharing stands of 116 with Vilas and an unbroken 133 with Jones. But Hameed, captaining Lancashire for the first time, missed out: Will Rollings rattled his stumps, shortly after doing the same to Davies.

Close of play: first day, Loughborough MCCU 191-9 (Sanders 45, Pereira 15); second day, Lancashire 145-3 (Vilas 49, Croft 10).

Loughborough MCCU

S. T. Evans lbw b Onions	2	C. W. G. Sanders c Davies b Clark	56
Hassan Azad lbw b Onions	33	W. J. L. Rollings c Bailey b Parkinson	0
†J. R. Bracey c Davies b Clark	5	W. J. N. Pereira not out	28
O. C. Soames b Mahmood	19	B 10, lb 9, w 1, nb 4	24
C. O. Thurston b Mahmood	6		—
*A. D. Tillcock c Jennings b Bailey	23	1/18 (1) 2/29 (3) 3/62 (4) (89.4 overs)	220
N. A. Hammond b Mahmood	1	4/72 (5) 5/78 (2) 6/87 (7)	
J. A. J. Rishton c Jones b Parkinson	23	7/117 (6) 8/127 (8) 9/135 (10) 10/220 (9)	

Onions 19–9–34–2; Mahmood 16–2–53–3; Clark 18.4–6–42–2; Bailey 15–8–23–1; Parkinson 15–7–31–2; Jones 1–0–1–0; Jennings 5–0–17–0.

Lancashire

K. K. Jennings c Rollings b Sanders	44	R. P. Jones not out	38
†A. L. Davies b Rollings	20	B 2, lb 11, nb 14	27
*H. Hameed b Rollings	5		—
D. J. Vilas c Bracey b Rishton	87	1/34 (2) 2/50 (3) · (4 wkts, 102 overs)	369
S. J. Croft not out	148	3/120 (1) 4/236 (4)	

J. Clark, T. E. Bailey, S. Mahmood, G. Onions and M. W. Parkinson did not bat.

Sanders 24–5–107–1; Pereira 23–3–83–0; Rollings 21–3–78–2; Tillcock 17–1–40–0; Rishton 16–2–44–1; Thurston 1–0–4–0.

Umpires: J. D. Middlebrook and R. T. Robinson.

At Northwood, April 7–9. DURHAM MCCU drew with MIDDLESEX.

At Leeds, April 7–9. YORKSHIRE v LEEDS/BRADFORD MCCU. Abandoned.

OXFORD MCCU v NORTHAMPTONSHIRE

At Oxford, April 7–9. Abandoned.

At Chester-le-Street, April 13–15 (not first-class). DURHAM MCCU drew with DURHAM.

At Cardiff, April 13–15 (not first-class). CARDIFF MCCU drew with GLAMORGAN.

At Weetwood, Leeds, April 13–15 (not first-class). LEEDS/BRADFORD MCCU v DERBYSHIRE. Abandoned. *All three of Leeds/Bradford's county games are washed out.*

At Leicester, April 13–15 (not first-class). LOUGHBOROUGH MCCU drew with LEICESTER-SHIRE.

At Taunton, April 13–15 (not first-class). SOMERSET v OXFORD MCCU. Abandoned. *Oxford's three-match county season amounts to 33 overs.*

At The Oval, April 13–15 (not first-class). CAMBRIDGE MCCU drew with SURREY.

THE UNIVERSITY MATCHES IN 2018

At Oxford, May 18. **Oxford University won by 83 runs. ‡Oxford University 214-6** (20 overs) (M. S. T. Hughes 53, J. S. D. Gnodde 76; K. Suresh 3-36); **Cambridge University 131-9** (20 overs) (A. C. H. Dewhurst 60). *An opening stand of 126 in 11 overs between Matt Hughes and Jamie Gnodde set up an imposing Oxford total. Gnodde faced 35 balls and hit 70 in boundaries (13 fours and three sixes). Hughes then removed Cambridge captain Darshan Chohan with the first ball of the reply. Ali Dewhurst stood alone – the next-best score was 17 – as Oxford ran out easy winners. Four of their bowlers took two wickets, while Harry McGhee hung on to four catches in the field. Oxford's win tied the overall score in the Varsity T20 match at 4–4 since the first in 2008 (two were abandoned and one was a no-result).*

At Lord's, June 23. **Oxford University won by five wickets. ‡Cambridge University 222-7** (50 overs) (D. Chohan 77, A. C. H. Dewhurst 35); **Oxford University 223-5** (39.5 overs) (M. S. T. Hughes 132*). *Oxford won the one-day Varsity Match for the sixth time running, giving them a 15–9 overall lead. First they kept things tight; opening bowler Toby Pettman had 44 dot balls in his 10–1–34–2. Then Hughes made light of the chase, hitting 20 fours in a magnificent 132* from 109 balls; his second six, off seamer Karthik Suresh, ended the match with more than ten overs to spare.*

OXFORD UNIVERSITY v CAMBRIDGE UNIVERSITY

At Oxford, July 2–5. Oxford University won by nine wickets. Toss: Oxford University. First-class debuts: M. J. Fanning, B. J. Leighton, J. D. Powe, O. J. W. Rogers; T. W. Balderson, T. P. Corner, J. O. Cross-Zamirski, E. R. B. Hyde, D. G. Murty, K. Suresh, S. A. Turner.

Oxford completed a clean sweep in all three formats, although they were made to wait by some staunch Cambridge batting in the follow-on, which lasted 132.1 overs. Oxford's huge first innings owed much to a partnership of 267 between skipper Dan Escott and Matt Naylor, who extended his maiden first-class century to 202 on the second morning – the highest score in this fixture by an English-born batsman. It was Oxford's best stand for the fifth wicket, breaking the record of 256, set by Abbas Ali Baig and Charles Fry against the Free Foresters in the Parks in 1959. Escott declared

DOUBLE-CENTURIES IN THE VARSITY MATCH

313*	S. S. Agarwal............	for Oxford at Cambridge	2013
247	S. Oberoi	for Oxford at Cambridge	2005
238*	Nawab of Pataudi snr.....	for Oxford at Lord's...........	1931
236*	J. W. M. Dalrymple.......	for Oxford at Cambridge	2003
211	G. Goonesena...........	for Cambridge at Lord's........	1957
202	**M. A. Naylor............**	**for Oxford at Oxford ....**	**2018**
201*	M. J. K. Smith...........	for Oxford at Lord's...........	1954
201	A. Ratcliffe	for Cambridge at Lord's........	1931
200	Majid Khan	for Cambridge at Lord's........	1970

at 533, Oxford's fourth-highest total against Cambridge (all scored since 2005). His counterpart, Darshan Chohan, put on 92 with Tom Colverd before they were separated by Toby Pettman, a lively seamer who went on to a maiden five-for as Cambridge slid to 199, a deficit of 334. Pettman claimed Colverd quickly in the follow-on, but Tom Corner dropped anchor for more than three hours, and Ali Dewhurst for nearly four. From 259 for five at the end of the third day, Cambridge's lower order survived another 49 overs on the fourth, with Sam Turner battling 175 minutes for 33, before Escott trapped him in front.

Close of play: first day, Oxford University 389-5 (Naylor 123, Powe 4); second day, Cambridge University 191-8 (Suresh 4, Balderson 0); third day, Cambridge University 259-5 (Turner 21, Winder 0).

Oxford University

M. S. T. Hughes c and b Cross-Zamirski	11	– b Cross-Zamirski	4
*D. A. Escott lbw b Suresh	175	– not out	1
J. S. D. Gnodde c Hyde b Suresh	18	– not out	4
A. J. W. Rackow b Balderson	16		
O. J. W. Rogers c Chohan b Cross-Zamirski	13		
M. A. Naylor c Chohan b Suresh	202		
†J. D. Powe c Hyde b Balderson	11		
T. H. S. Pettman not out	54		
B 12, lb 6, w 3, nb 12	33	Lb 1	1

1/11 (1) 2/57 (3) (7 wkts dec, 141 overs) 533 1/5 (1) (1 wkt, 2.1 overs) 10
3/84 (4) 4/111 (5)
5/378 (2) 6/412 (7) 7/533 (6)

M. J. Fanning, M. J. Dawes and B. J. Leighton did not bat.

Suresh 36–2–172–3; Cross-Zamirski 28–5–96–2; Winder 32–4–106–0; Balderson 35–8–91–2; Turner 10–0–50–0. *Second innings—*Suresh 1.1–1–1–0; Cross-Zamirski 1–0–8–1.

Cambridge University

T. P. Corner c Powe b Pettman	10	– lbw b Escott	46
T. G. L. Colverd c Gnodde b Pettman	63	– c Powe b Pettman	0
*D. Chohan b Leighton	67	– c Escott b Pettman	37
A. C. H. Dewhurst c Powe b Dawes	4	– c Escott b Gnodde	65
D. G. Murty c Gnodde b Leighton	4	– c Powe b Leighton	52
S. A. Turner lbw b Pettman	15	– lbw b Escott	33
†E. R. B. Hyde c Powe b Gnodde	0	– (8) b Escott	32
K. Suresh lbw b Pettman	5	– (9) c Powe b Rogers	18
N. J. Winder b Pettman	1	– (7) c Powe b Pettman	8
T. W. Balderson not out	2	– lbw b Gnodde	1
J. O. Cross-Zamirski b Escott	1	– not out	0
B 5, lb 9, w 1, nb 12	27	B 23, lb 14, w 2, nb 12	51

1/27 (1) 2/119 (2) 3/138 (4) (70.2 overs) 199 1/2 (2) 2/45 (3) (132.1 overs) 343
4/153 (5) 5/170 (3) 6/177 (7) 3/126 (1) 4/211 (4)
7/187 (6) 8/191 (9) 9/192 (8) 10/199 (11) 5/254 (5) 6/284 (7) 7/292 (6)
8/334 (8) 9/342 (10) 10/343 (9)

Pettman 21–8–41–5; Leighton 12–1–42–2; Dawes 15–6–41–1; Fanning 9–3–23–0; Gnodde 9–2–32–1; Rogers 2–0–6–0; Escott 2.2–2–0–1. *Second innings—*Pettman 35–15–72–3; Leighton 14–3–37–1; Dawes 30–9–73–0; Escott 20–3–52–3; Fanning 8–2–23–0; Gnodde 18–6–35–2; Hughes 2–0–7–0; Rogers 5.1–1–7–1.

Umpires: M. Newell and C. M. Watts.

Oxford University *D. A. Escott (*Winchester College and Lincoln*), M. J. Dawes (*City of London Freemen's School and St Hugh's*), M. J. Fanning (*St Joseph's Roman Catholic High School, Horwich, and St Anne's*), J. S. D. Gnodde (*Eton College and Pembroke*), M. S. T. Hughes (*Stockport Grammar School and Hertford*), B. J. Leighton (*Monmouth School and St Hugh's*), M. A. Naylor (*Finham Park School, Coventry, and Merton*), J. D. Powe (*Highgate School and Somerville*), A. J. W. Rackow (*Dulwich College and St Hilda's*), O. J. W. Rogers (*Eton College and St Edmund Hall*).

T. R. W. Gnodde (*Eton College and Pembroke*) replaced Fanning in the 50- and 20-over matches. E. A. J. Coombs (*Brighton College and Hertford*), H. McGhee (*King Edward VI School, Southampton, and Worcester*) and N. P. Taylor (*The Perse School and St Catherine's*) replaced Dawes, Naylor and Powe in the T20 game.

Cambridge University *D. Chohan (*Dulwich College and St Catharine's*), T. W. Balderson (*Cheadle Hulme High School and Downing*), T. G. L. Colverd (*Haberdashers' Aske's Boys' School and Robinson*), T. P. Corner (*The Skinners' School and Fitzwilliam*), J. O. Cross-Zamirski (*The Perse School and Corpus Christi*), A. C. H. Dewhurst (*St Paul's School and Robinson*), E. R. B.

Hyde *(Tonbridge School and Jesus)*, D. G. Murty *(Loughborough Grammar School, York University and Girton)*, K. Suresh *(Cranleigh School and Wolfson)*, S. A. Turner *(St Paul's School and Christ's)*, N. J. Winder *(Tonbridge School and Robinson)*.

A. G. M. Mathieson *(King Edward VI Aston School, Durham University and Wolfson)* replaced Corner in the 50- and 20-over matches. R. C. Triniman *(Canford School, Leeds University and Hughes Hall)* and K. S. Wilson *(Barnard Castle School and St Edmund's)* replaced Cross-Zamirski and Turner in the T20 game.

This was the 173rd University Match, a first-class fixture dating back to 1827. Cambridge have won 60 and Oxford 57, with 56 drawn. It was played at Lord's until 2000.

MCC UNIVERSITIES CHAMPIONSHIP

	P	W	L	First-innings W	L	D	Bonus pts	Pts
Loughborough (1)......	5	1	0	4	0	0	47	104
Durham (3)...........	5	0	0	3	1	1	32	67
Oxford (6)...........	5	0	0	2	3	0	41	61
Cambridge (5)........	5	0	1	2	2	0	37	57
Leeds/Bradford (4).....	5	0	0	1	2	2	26	46
Cardiff (2)...........	5	0	0	0	4	1	29	34

Outright win = 17pts; first-innings win in a drawn match = 10pts; no result on first innings = 5pts; abandoned = 5pts.

WINNERS

2001	Loughborough	2007	Cardiff/Glamorgan	2013	Leeds/Bradford
2002	Loughborough	2008	Loughborough	2014	Loughborough
2003	Loughborough	2009	Leeds/Bradford	2015	Cardiff
2004	Oxford	2010	Durham	2016	Loughborough
2005	Loughborough	2011	Cardiff	2017	Loughborough
2006	Oxford	2012	Cambridge	2018	Loughborough

MCC UNIVERSITIES CHALLENGE FINAL

At Lord's, June 20. **Durham MCCU won by 43 runs. Durham MCCU 213** (49.4 overs) (J. Subramanyan 45*; W. J. N. Pereira 4-30); ‡**Loughborough MCCU 170** (46 overs) (C. O. Thurston 62, O. C. Soames 53; A. H. McGrath 3-20). *For the third year running, Loughborough won the two-day Championship but lost the one-day Challenge. They had looked certain winners as Durham dipped to 118-8, but No. 10 Jhatavedh Subramanyan put on 81 with James Sookias (39), and pilfered 34 more for the last wicket with Mungo Russell (11). Russell then had Sam Evans caught behind by Sookias with the first ball of the chase, though Loughborough looked in control while Charlie Thurston and Ollie Soames were adding 87 for the third wicket. But no one passed 14 after they were parted and, with Hong Kong international Subramanyan taking two wickets in three balls with his leg-breaks, Durham surged to a comfortable victory.*

MCC IN 2018

STEVEN LYNCH

The new administrative team at Lord's bedded in during 2018. Guy Lavender, the secretary and chief executive, who had joined from Somerset, and Jamie Clifford (an assistant secretary, from Kent) did not have to grapple with quite as many arguments about redevelopment as their predecessors, although the issue did not entirely disappear. One idea floated by the Rifkind Levy Partnership, the owners of the land at the Nursery End, suggested selling off small parcels of the territory so interested parties could own a piece of Lord's.

The next stage of the stadium redevelopment, which members had agreed in 2017 should be funded by the club, will be the replacement of the Compton and Edrich Stands, either side of the media centre. The three-tier structures will house around 2,500 more spectators, restoring overall capacity to 31,000, a figure regularly reached during Australian summers before the 1980s, when several thousand sat on the grass. They will have better amenities – not difficult, as there were hardly any in the old stands, despite being opened as recently as 1991. Planning permission was granted in January 2019, and the cost estimated at £50m.

The sense of change was amplified at the end of the season by the retirement of Mick Hunt, who had worked at Lord's for 49 years; he succeeded Jim Fairbrother as head groundsman in 1985. His replacement is Irishman Karl McDermott, who had been in charge at the Rose Bowl in Hampshire, after 17 years at Clontarf in Dublin. He faces a challenging first season, with the World Cup final followed by Test matches against Ireland and Australia.

MCC's world cricket committee, chaired by Mike Gatting, continued as an influential think tank for the international game. In 2018 they called for better over-rates in Tests and Twenty20 matches, after noting they had dipped, and commissioned a survey into fans' views about how to safeguard the future of Test cricket. Rod Marsh stepped down from the committee after six years, and was replaced by Shane Warne.

Notable deaths during the year included Hubert Doggart, the former president and treasurer; Jack Bailey, the club's secretary between 1974 and 1987; and Tony Pope, whose 813 wickets in 522 matches for MCC was a record.

In all, MCC teams played more than 500 matches in 2018. At home, of 492 men's games, 227 were won, 87 drawn, three tied, 113 lost, and 62 abandoned or cancelled. There were 26 women's matches, of which 12 were won, two drawn and nine lost, with three abandoned. Club teams toured Brazil and Chile, Kenya, Sweden and Thailand, while a women's side visited Belgium.

A final indication that Lord's is moving with the times came at the staff Christmas party, with a special version of "Strictly Come Dancing", organised by ballroom dancer (and cricket fan) Anton du Beke. Reports of spinning noises near W. G. Grace's grave were unconfirmed.

MCC v ESSEX

At Bridgetown, March 27–29 (day/night). MCC won by an innings and 34 runs. Toss: Essex.

After eight years in Abu Dhabi, the English season's curtain-raiser moved to Barbados, but never had it felt more like an afterthought. The BBC packed up and went home after the North–South one-day series, and any hope of newspaper coverage was scuppered by Australia's ball-tampering scandal. The lack of intensity was compounded by county champions Essex fielding an understrength team because of fitness issues; injuries also forced changes on MCC, but they had 17 other county squads to choose from, and emerged even stronger. The match played out as expected: MCC victorious with a day (and night) of the pink-ball fixture to spare, and three of their team attracting what attention there was. Northamptonshire's 30-year-old seamer Gleeson used the first-day twilight to skittle the middle and lower order, grabbing a hat-trick in his five for 50 as Essex were bowled out for 187 after choosing to bat. Next day, as their bowlers toiled – though seven out of eight claimed a wicket – Hain's belligerence earned him his first first-class hundred since 2016, while Bess notched a maiden century, timing each of his 18 fours with a precision that suggested his future would be higher than No. 9. To underline his worth, he bowled MCC to an innings win, collecting six for 51 as Essex collapsed for 187 again. As the players faced an extra day on the beach, there was talk that in future this fixture might be replaced by a four-day North–South game. VITHUSHAN EHANTHARAJAH

Man of the Match: D. M. Bess.

Close of play: first day, MCC 73-2 (Northeast 35, Hain 5); second day, Essex 26-1 (Nijjar 5, Westley 19).

Essex

N. L. J. Browne c Simpson b Edwards	48	– c D'Oliveira b Gleeson	2
A. S. S. Nijjar c Edwards b Bess	20	– c Northeast b Gleeson	30
T. Westley lbw b Collingwood	32	– c and b Bess	62
D. W. Lawrence c Simpson b Gleeson	23	– c Gleeson b Bess	7
A. J. A. Wheater c and b Bess	7	– c Bess b Gleeson	23
*R. N. ten Doeschate c Simpson b Fisher	4	– b Fisher	4
†J. S. Foster c Simpson b Bess	34	– st Simpson b Bess	29
C. J. Taylor b Gleeson	0	– b Bess	0
M. T. Coles c Northeast b Gleeson	0	– not out	10
A. P. Beard lbw b Gleeson	0	– lbw b Bess	0
J. A. Porter not out	10	– lbw b Bess	10
B 4, lb 1, nb 4	9	B 5, lb 2, w 1, nb 2	10

1/53 (2) 2/89 (1) 3/112 (3)   (68 overs) 187
4/130 (4) 5/139 (5) 6/139 (6)
7/140 (8) 8/142 (9) 9/142 (10) 10/187 (7)

1/3 (1) 2/54 (2)   (60 overs) 187
3/77 (4) 4/115 (3)
5/122 (6) 6/157 (5) 7/158 (8)
8/171 (7) 9/171 (10) 10/187 (11)

Edwards 17–5–45–1; Gleeson 18–5–50–5; Fisher 13–5–27–1; Bess 15–2–57–2; Collingwood 5–3–3–1. *Second innings*—Edwards 9–0–42–0; Gleeson 15–3–46–3; Fisher 12–2–33–1; Bess 18–2–51–6; Collingwood 6–3–8–0.

MCC

*D. J. Bell-Drummond c Foster b Porter	3	D. M. Bess b Lawrence	107
B. L. D'Oliveira c and b Coles	30	R. J. Gleeson not out	0
S. A. Northeast c Taylor b Beard	44		
S. R. Hain not out	140	Lb 1, w 1, nb 4	6
D. M. W. Rawlins st Foster b Nijjar	28		
P. D. Collingwood c Foster b Lawrence	45	1/16 (1) 2/47 (2) (8 wkts dec, 114 overs) 408
†J. A. Simpson c Wheater b Westley	5	3/93 (3) 4/128 (5)
M. D. Fisher c Foster b Taylor	0	5/210 (6) 6/235 (7) 7/236 (8) 8/408 (9)

F. H. Edwards did not bat.

Porter 19–7–56–1; Coles 23–4–92–1; Beard 21–4–79–1; Taylor 11–0–59–1; Nijjar 16–4–48–1; Lawrence 19–2–63–2; Westley 2–0–3–1; ten Doeschate 3–0–7–0.

Umpires: J. W. Lloyds and D. J. Millns.

MCC TRIANGULAR TWENTY20 CHALLENGE

1= Nepal, Netherlands   3 MCC

Twenty20 international   At Lord's, July 29. **No result. Netherlands 174-4** (16.4 overs) (W. Barresi 44, R. N. ten Doeschate 38, M. J. G. Rippon 38*, S. A. Edwards 34*) **v** ‡**Nepal.** *T20I debuts:* D. S. Airee, L. N. Rajbanshi, A. K. Sah, A. Sheikh (Nepal); H. C. Overdijk (Netherlands). *Rain spoiled MCC's ambitious three-way tournament, stopping this match just before the end of a Netherlands innings already reduced to 18 overs. Wesley Barresi hit 44 from 24 balls, then Ryan ten Doeschate, taking a break from captaining Essex and playing his first official international since the 2011 World Cup, added 38 from 27. Michael Rippon and Tonga-born Scott Edwards piled on 61* in 26 balls before the weather closed in. MCC, captained by Mahela Jayawardene and including former Test players James Foster and Jonathan Trott, were the third team taking part: they had earlier lost to both the Netherlands and Nepal, also on July 29, in games restricted to six overs a side.*

ICC WORLD XI v WEST INDIES

Twenty20 International

ELIZABETH AMMON

At Lord's, May 31 (floodlit). West Indies won by 72 runs. Toss: ICC World XI. Twenty20 international debut: S. Lamichhane.

This charity fixture, staged to help rebuild West Indian cricket stadiums devastated by Hurricanes Irma and Maria in 2017, was given Twenty20 international status, but felt more like a good-spirited exhibition match. MCC made no charge for the use of Lord's, the players and coaches took no pay, and Sky Sports provided a free global feed; former England captain Nasser Hussain was on the field for the entire match as a roving reporter, interviewing the players between deliveries and providing footage from a mobile camera on his head. It added to the fun, not least because the ball seemed to follow him wherever he stood. The cricket itself was one-sided. The World XI – who included 17-year-old Nepali leg-spinner Sandeep Lamichhane, making his senior international debut – were comprehensively outplayed by the World Twenty20 champions. England's white-ball captain, Eoin Morgan, had been due to lead the World XI, but was forced out by a broken finger; Shahid Afridi, making another comeback two years after his last retirement, took over, in his 99th T20 international; now 38 and limping, he just about got through his four overs, picking up the wicket of Fletcher with his second delivery. Fletcher was the only West Indian batsman to fail, though Gayle struggled against the pace of Mills, who bowled ten successive dot balls after Afridi put them in. But the powerful hitting of Lewis, Samuels and Ramdin took West Indies to a hefty 199 for four. In reply, the World XI stuttered: the top four made six between them before falling to Russell and Badree. Only Tissara Perera, with 61 from 37 balls, prevented a farce. They were all out inside 17 overs, with Afridi using a runner (no longer officially permitted by ICC regulations) and Mills unable to bat after a quad strain in the field. But the result didn't matter. The match had raised more than $500,000 and awareness, the forecast rain never arrived, and a young and diverse crowd of 15,000 had seen some of their heroes.

Man of the Match: E. Lewis.

West Indies

		B	4/6
1 C. H. Gayle b 5	18	28	1
2 E. Lewis lbw b 8	58	26	5/5
3 A. D. S. Fletcher st 2 b 7	7	9	1
4 M. N. Samuels c 6 b 8	43	22	2/4
5 †D. Ramdin not out	44	25	3/3
6 A. D. Russell not out	21	10	0/3
Lb 3, w 5	8		

6 overs: 51-0   (20 overs) 199-4

1/75 2/87 3/100 4/152

7 *C. R. Brathwaite, 8 A. R. Nurse, 9 K. M. A. Paul, 10 K. O. K. Williams and 11 S. Badree did not bat.

McClenaghan 3–3–31–0; Mills 3–13–13–0; Shoaib Malik 3–9–31–1; Perera 2–1–27–0; Rashid Khan 4–8–48–2; Shahid Afridi 4–13–34–1; Lamichhane 1–1–12–0.

ICC World XI

		B	4/6
1 Tamim Iqbal c 2 b 6	2	8	0
2 †L. Ronchi lbw b 11	0	2	0
3 S. W. Billings c 7 b 6	4	6	1
4 K. D. Karthik c 2 b 11	0	5	0
5 Shoaib Malik lbw b 7	12	10	1
6 N. L. T. C. Perera c and b 10	61	37	7/3
7 *Shahid Afridi c 8 b 9	11	12	1
8 Rashid Khan lbw b 10	9	7	0/1
9 M. J. McClenaghan c 8 b 10	10	8	0/1
10 S. Lamichhane not out	4	5	0
11 T. S. Mills absent hurt			
B 4, lb 3, w 7	14		

6 overs: 30-4   (16.4 overs) 127

1/4 2/8 3/8 4/8 5/45 6/93 7/101 8/108 9/127

Badree 3–14–4–2; Russell 3–10–25–2; Williams 3.4–7–42–3; Paul 3–3–24–1; Brathwaite 2–5–14–1; Nurse 2–7–11–0.

Umpires: R. J. Bailey and A. G. Wharf.   Third umpire: P. K. Baldwin.

Referee: B. C. Broad.

The World XI (coached by A. Flower) also included S. M. Curran, Mohammed Shami and A. U. Rashid. E. J. G. Morgan, the original captain, withdrew with a broken finger, H. H. Pandya because of illness and Shakib Al Hasan for personal reasons. The West Indies squad (coached by S. G. Law) also included R. R. Emrit and R. Powell.

ECB NORTH–SOUTH SERIES IN 2018

Vithushan Ehantharajah

50-over matches (3): North 2, South 1

"We all grew up in a council house, now we want a cheque from Andrew Strauss!" For those who wondered how seriously this series was being taken, the chant emanating from the North dressing-room after the last game at Barbados's Three Ws Oval spoke volumes. After being whitewashed a year earlier, they now had the opportunity to rub southern noses in the dirt. The barracking had started before a ball was bowled: in the hotel, battle lines were drawn and separate dinner plans arranged; the sledging – exclusively from the North at first – kicked up a gear.

Strauss, the ECB director of cricket, and technical director Andy Flower watched, as assistant England coaches Mark Ramprakash and Paul Collingwood marshalled the sides and selectors Angus Fraser and Mick Newell took notes. All six were fairly hands-on; Flower thundered into the dressing-room to reprimand batsmen for rash dismissals. The series might have moved from the UAE to the Caribbean, but this was no jolly.

Beyond the jibes, the cricket flourished, as did players tipped for England caps. Worcestershire's Joe Clarke (229 in three innings) and Middlesex's Nick Gubbins (224 from two) led the run-charts, while Lancashire seamer Saqib Mahmood and Somerset off-spinner Dom Bess took 15 wickets between them. But arguably the find of the series was left-arm quick Tom Barber – released by Hampshire but picked up by Middlesex – who bowled with considerable pace and extracted bounce from some unrewarding surfaces.

It was a shame that the final match, which the North won to take the series, lacked the competitiveness of the first two. But this exercise was a success, especially off the field, where players had to meet Strauss, Newell and Fraser in a *Dragons' Den* set-up to pitch for their inclusion in the 2019 World Cup squad. Players and coaches left the Caribbean with more than a nice tan.

SQUADS

North *S. J. Mullaney (Nottinghamshire), Z. J. Chappell (Leicestershire), J. M. Clarke (Worcestershire), M. J. J. Critchley (Derbyshire), A. L. Davies (Lancashire), B. L. D'Oliveira (Worcestershire), M. D. Fisher (Yorkshire), R. J. Gleeson (Northamptonshire), †S. R. Hain (Warwickshire), A. J. Hose (Warwickshire), †K. K. Jennings (Lancashire), S. Mahmood (Lancashire), M. W. Parkinson (Lancashire). *Coach:* P. D. Collingwood. *Assistant coach:* P. J. Franks.

P. Coughlin (Nottinghamshire) was originally selected, but withdrew with a shoulder injury and was replaced by Critchley.

South *S. A. Northeast (Hampshire), T. E. Barber (Middlesex), †D. J. Bell-Drummond (Kent), D. M. Bess (Somerset), S. M. Curran (Surrey), L. J. Evans (Sussex), N. R. T. Gubbins (Middlesex), R. H. Patel (Middlesex), O. J. D. Pope (Surrey), J. A. Porter (Essex), D. M. W. Rawlins (Sussex), J. A. Simpson (Middlesex), P. I. Walter (Essex). *Coach:* M. R. Ramprakash. *Assistant coach:* A. Flower.

L. C. Norwell (Gloucestershire) was originally selected, but withdrew with a hamstring injury and was replaced by Patel.

† *Selected on PCA MVP rankings for the 2017 Royal London One-Day Cup. Eight players were automatically invited on this basis, but A. N. Cook and J. M. Vince were with England in New Zealand, G. S. Ballance and R. S. Bopara had other commitments, and S. J. Thakor was unavailable because of a criminal conviction.*

First match At Bridgetown, March 18, 2018. **South won by 63 runs. South 347** (49 overs) (D. J. Bell-Drummond 52, N. R. T. Gubbins 116, D. M. W. Rawlins 53; S. Mahmood 5-60); ‡**North 284** (47.1 overs) (S. J. Mullaney 57). MoM: N. R. T. Gubbins. *The South, who had won the inaugural series in the United Arab Emirates 3–0, began their defence in style. Put in, they scored the highest List A total at Kensington Oval, thanks to a top-order assault led by Nick Gubbins. He made 116 in 99 balls, despite cramp late on, while fifties from Daniel Bell-Drummond and Delray Rawlins helped them to 347 – even though Saqib Mahmood yorked five batsmen in his last three overs. It might have been a rout had Rawlins, at first slip, held two early catches off Sam Curran; reprieved, Joe Clarke and Alex Davies were among four players who passed 40, though only captain Steven Mullaney reached 50 as the North fell 63 short. Dom Bess (3-61) accounted for three of the top four, and Curran (3-51), the pick of the bowlers, wiped out the tail.*

Second match At Bridgetown, March 21, 2018. **North won by 46 runs. North 335-8** (50 overs) (J. M. Clarke 71, B. L. D'Oliveira 79, M. J. J. Critchley 64); ‡**South 289** (44.3 overs) (N. R. T. Gubbins 109, L. J. Evans 64). MoM: N. R. T. Gubbins. *The North pulled level in the most competitive match of the series. They had to fight back more than once. After Clarke and Davies (42) opened with 95, they slipped to 132-4, with Clarke departing for a classy 71. But Mullaney (also 42) and Brett D'Oliveira added 108 to put them back on course, before Derbyshire's Matt Critchley blitzed 64 from 37 balls. If the South had successfully chased a target of 336, it would have been another ground record, and that looked within reach at 203-2; Gubbins had completed another hundred, and Laurie Evans was giving an exhibition in clean hitting. But Richard Gleeson struck twice in three balls, giving the North a route back in, and Lancashire leg-spinner Matt Parkinson bagged 3-47 as he tied the tail in knots. Ollie Pope counter-attacked with 42 before he was last out, yorked by Mahmood.*

Third match At Bridgetown (Three Ws Oval), March 23, 2018. **North won by 92 runs. ‡North 296-8** (50 overs) (J. M. Clarke 112, S. R. Hain 51, S. J. Mullaney 52); **South 204** (44.2 overs) (O. J. D. Pope 68). MoM: J. M. Clarke. MoS: J. M. Clarke. *The odds shifted dramatically in favour of the North when Gubbins finally erred in judgment – but in the field, where he was sliding at deep cover, and damaged his right hamstring. He played no further part, while the North set about taking their share of the prize money to £40,000. Clarke did most of the damage with 112 from 98 balls, adding 143 for the second wicket with Sam Hain, though what might have been 400 ended up as 296 as the South pulled things back. Shorn of their leading run-scorer, they were never really in the chase. Despite a high-quality 68 from Pope, Mullaney was able to cycle through his bowlers, knowing he could wait for risks to be taken. Parkinson conceded only 27 in his ten overs as the South squirmed to 204 all out with nearly six overs to go.*

AUSTRALIAN ABORIGINAL XIs IN ENGLAND IN 2018

STEVEN LYNCH

To commemorate the pioneering 1868 tour of England by a team of Aboriginal cricketers, another side retraced their steps in 2018, and play in some of the same towns. To have played in all of them would have been quite an undertaking: in 1868 there were 47 matches, between May and October, with cricket on 99 days out of a possible 125. Last year's team made do with six, all 20-over games. And on June 8, exactly 150 years after the original tourists took on the Gentlemen of Sussex at the old Brunswick Ground in Hove, their successors locked horns with Sussex at the current county headquarters.

The side included two Australian white-ball players – the captain, Dan Christian, and seamer Scott Boland – and would have had another had D'Arcy Short not been chosen for the one-day series in England. At Hove they met up with Jason Gillespie, the first Australian Test cricketer from an Aboriginal background. He might have coached the tourists, but for the Sussex job, and said: "I'm absolutely pumped to be here at the same time as them."

Gillespie's county charges, virtually a first-choice team, stormed to victory by 99 runs, but the Aboriginals won their other matches: two at Arundel against MCC (Christian made 78 not out in the second), one at The Oval against a Surrey Championship side, and two against county XIs, at Derby and Nottingham.

There was a nice touch on the squad's kit, in traditional Australian one-day yellow, which bore the Indigenous names of the original tourists. Boland was joined in the party by his brother Nick, and they sported shirts with the names of 1868 siblings Yellanach (who toured under the supposedly comic English nickname of "Johnny Cuzens") and Grongarrong ("Mosquito"). The team also visited the grave, in London's Tower Hamlets, of Bripumyarrumin ("King Cole"), who died of tuberculosis during the original tour.

In a departure from the long-ago visit, the team doubled up with a women's side, captained by Ashleigh Gardner. An off-spinning all-rounder, she hammered an unbeaten 129 from 71 balls as a National Cricket Conference XI were overwhelmed by 137 runs in Derby. The tourists came unstuck in their final match, against a strong England Academy side captained by Fran Wilson, and also lost to Surrey and Sussex Women.

Both teams met up with the full Australian side at Lord's, where the national coach Justin Langer organised a rousing rendition of the team song in the dressing-room. Over in the museum, the Aboriginal team were shown artefacts from the 1868 tour, and mocked-up recreations of some of the memorabilia. Queensland fast bowler Brendan Doggett, another of the tourists, said: "To learn their story – what they did, and the courage it took for them to get on that boat and travel to England – was pretty powerful stuff."

For more details of the 1868 tour and the background to this one, see Wisden 2018, *page 97.*

THE MINOR COUNTIES IN 2018

Philip August

After completing a hat-trick of titles, **Berkshire** now have a clear target: to match the record four-in-a-row Devon side of the mid-1990s. They will be trying to win a competition on the cusp of a revolution. In a shake-up, announced after discussions lasting more than a year between the Minor Counties Cricket Association and the ECB, there will be significant structural change in 2020, and a new name: the National Counties Cricket Association. "It has long been felt that Minor Counties seemed a pejorative term," said chairman Nick Archer. "Other names were suggested, but they made us sound second-rate."

The fixture list will also look radically different. Each division will be split into two sections of five, with promotion and relegation, and four three-day matches instead of six. Teams will have to field eight under-25s, and eight who have a strong local connection with the county. "We'll have the best sides playing the best sides," said Archer. The 50-over trophy will have group stages, followed by quarter- and semi-finals, and there will be more Twenty20 matches. Scheduling of Second XI cricket by the first-class counties will be crucial. For years, minor counties have lost their best young talent to Second XI matches, and even age-group limited-overs games. This often leaves them unable to field the players they have developed.

On the field, Berkshire were outstanding in the Western Division, winning six out of six. They surrendered their 50-over title to Devon, but won the T20 competition to complete another double. The 37-year-old slow left-armer Chris Peploe was again pivotal. For the second season running, he was the leading wicket-taker, with 45 at 16. He bowled roughly a third of his team's overs, going for little more than two. Quick runs came from Waqas Hussain and Richard Morris.

There was a notable improvement by **Oxfordshire,** who climbed four places to finish runners-up. They were boosted by the arrival of Gareth Andrew, the former Worcestershire and Somerset seamer, who took 38 wickets at 15. He won the Frank Edwards Trophy for the best bowler. **Shropshire** finished third after the shrewd recruitment of former Netherlands and Worcestershire batsman Alexei Kervezee. He scored heavily – 748 at 74, and quicker than a run a ball. **Cornwall** were fourth, under their new captain Matthew Rowe. The highlight of their summer was a county-record chase against Devon at Werrington: 335 for four, with Jake Libby hitting an unbeaten 142.

A split-captaincy experiment worked reasonably well for **Cheshire**: white-ball captain Rick Moore led them to both limited-overs finals, and they won the 50-over competition after a superb contest with Devon. Against Herefordshire at Alderley Edge in their final Championship match, debutant Jamie Crawley (173) and Furqan Shafiq (207) put on 339 for the fourth wicket, a county record.

Wiltshire boasted a potent new-ball pair: Tahir Afridi took 35 wickets at 17, and Luke Evans 26 at 22. **Herefordshire** leaned heavily on all-rounder

Peter Burgoyne – 20 wickets and 460 runs – while **Devon** suffered availability issues, though they performed well in both white-ball competitions. Their solitary Championship victory, over Dorset, featured a stellar performance by Josh Bess, cousin of Somerset off-spinner Dom: he hit 203 not out and 70, claimed a cheap second-innings five-for, and held five catches.

After an encouraging 2017, **Dorset** had just one win and slumped to ninth. **Wales** were without a victory for the third successive season, but did make 456 for nine to force a draw against Cheshire.

The Eastern Division produced a thrilling battle, with eight points separating the top four sides. **Lincolnshire** completed a hat-trick of divisional titles after some imaginative captaincy by Carl Wilson and his Cumberland counterpart Jacques du Toit in their final game, at Carlisle. Two forfeits were needed before Lincolnshire won by 53 runs. Perhaps the highlight of their season, however, were two innings by Louis Kimber in the T20 double-header against Cumberland at Jesmond. He hit 162 off 55 balls, then 112 off 45, with 22 sixes in total.

Suffolk had been in pole position for a couple of hours on the last day after wrapping up victory over Cambridgeshire, before Lincolnshire denied them. Superbly led by wicketkeeper Adam Mansfield, whose 42 victims broke a 40-year-old county record, they thrashed Norfolk and Hertfordshire by an innings. Against Hertfordshire, Kyran Young and Jed Cawkwell put on a record 262 for the third wicket.

Staffordshire also had a chance going into the final round: they beat Northumberland easily, but it was not enough. Captain Kadeer Ali scored 581 at 52, and veteran slow left-armer Paul Byrne took 26 wickets at 26. The most improved side were **Buckinghamshire** who, after two seasons without a win, recorded four. Michael Payne became their first player to score three successive centuries, and leg-spinner Stephen Croft had a sensational debut, with eight for 23 against Hertfordshire.

Norfolk had the season's best batsman: Sam Arthurton's 822 runs at 82 earned him the Wilfred Rhodes Trophy for the highest average from six completed innings. Off-spinner Chris Brown retired after taking his 480th wicket on his 100th appearance. **Cambridgeshire** made a number of pre-season changes, including appointing James Williams as captain, but had a middling summer. There was high turnover at **Cumberland**, where Michael Slack was the sole survivor of their 2015 Championship-winning team. They did, though, have 13 players who had progressed from their youth programme.

A young **Hertfordshire** pulled off a fabulous victory in their first match, against Northumberland. They were 68 for six, before Alex Axon and Ben Cowell put on a county seventh-wicket record 242. Alfie Duke, a 19-year-old left-arm seamer, then took a five-for on debut. **Bedfordshire** avoided the wooden spoon, but have now won one Championship game in eight seasons; captain Andy Reynoldson held their batting together. **Northumberland** also failed to win a three-day game but, led by former England white-ball wicket-keeper Phil Mustard, had five T20 victories.

MINOR COUNTIES CHAMPIONSHIP IN 2018

Eastern Division	P	W	L	D	*Bonus points* Batting	Bowling	Pts	NRPW
1 LINCOLNSHIRE (1)......	6	4	1	1	21	18	107	15.03
2 Suffolk (2)............	6	4	1	1	16	21	105	5.91
3 Staffordshire (3).........	6	4	1	1	18	17	103	4.97
4 Buckinghamshire (8)......	6	4	2	0	14	21	99	6.58
5 Norfolk (5)............	6	3	2	1	14	20	86	7.38
6 Cambridgeshire (6).......	6	3	3	0	14	23	85	−1.06
7 Cumberland (4).........	6	2	3	1	16	19	71	−1.50
8 Hertfordshire (7)........	6	1	4	1	12	19	51	−10.05
9 Bedfordshire (9)........	6	0	4	2	10	21	39	−10.32
10 Northumberland (10)......	6	0	4	2	9	20	37	−15.56

Western Division	P	W	L	D	*Bonus points* Batting	Bowling	Pts	NRPW
1 BERKSHIRE (1).........	6	6	0	0	19	23	138	13.97
2 Oxfordshire (6)	6	5	1	0	12	23	115	3.00
3 Shropshire (4).........	6	4	1	1	21	24	113	3.43
4 Cornwall (8)...........	6	2	2	2	9	24	73	−0.23
5 Wiltshire (9)...........	6	2	3	1	9	24	69	−0.32
6 Cheshire (2)............	6	1	3	2	20	24	68	6.31
7 Herefordshire (7)	6	2	4	0	11	23	66	−5.56
8 Devon (5)............	6	1	3	2	14	23	61	2.55
9 Dorset (3)............	6	1	4	1	4	21	45	−9.78
10 Wales Minor Counties (10) .	6	0	3	3	8	23	43	−12.31

Win = 16pts; Draw = 4pts. NRPW is net runs per wicket (runs per wicket for, less runs per wicket against).

LEADING AVERAGES IN 2018

BATTING (350 runs at 40.00)

	M	I	NO	R	HS	100	50	Avge	Ct/St
1 J. C. Mickleburgh (*Suffolk*).........	4	6	1	487	173*	2	2	97.40	0
2 †E. D. Woods (*Berkshire*)...........	3	5	1	360	159	1	2	90.00	2
3 S. S. Arthurton (*Norfolk*)...........	6	12	2	822	155	3	4	82.20	7
4 Waqas Hussain (*Berkshire*)..........	5	9	1	648	192	2	4	81.00	2
5 A. N. Kervezee (*Shropshire*)	6	11	1	748	166	3	4	74.80	10
6 G. T. Park (*Buckinghamshire*).......	4	6	1	358	166	2	0	71.60	6
7 A. W. R. Barrow (*Devon*)	3	6	0	417	163	2	2	69.50	7
8 J. J. Bess (*Devon*)	6	11	1	677	203*	1	5	67.70	15
9 D. D. Freeman (*Lincolnshire*)	7	11	4	469	110*	1	4	67.00	4
10 M. J. Payne (*Buckinghamshire*)......	6	11	3	530	126	3	2	66.25	2
11 S. Kendall (*Lincolnshire*).........	7	12	1	667	230*	3	0	60.63	1
12 J. A. Cater (*Oxfordshire*)...........	4	8	1	417	114*	1	3	59.57	10/3
13 †A. M. Reynoldson (*Bedfordshire*)	6	12	1	606	159	1	4	55.09	9
14 †T. J. New (*Norfolk*)............	6	11	2	490	114*	2	2	54.44	6/1
15 K. Ali (*Staffordshire*).............	6	12	1	581	142	2	3	52.81	4
16 F. Shafiq (*Cheshire*).............	6	10	0	520	207	2	2	52.00	6
17 S. Kelsall (*Staffordshire*)..........	6	12	1	526	110	1	3	47.81	11
18 P. I. Burgoyne (*Herefordshire*)	5	10	0	460	79	0	4	46.00	6
19 R. P. Zelem (*Cumberland*)	6	10	0	436	86	0	4	43.60	5
20 †Masoor Khan (*Buckinghamshire*)	6	11	1	414	133	1	3	41.40	3
21 J. H. Voke (*Wales Minor Counties*) ..	6	12	0	493	132	1	4	41.08	10
22 B. M. Shafayat (*Lincolnshire*)........	6	11	2	367	134	2	0	40.77	3

BOWLING (20 wickets at 27.00)

		Style	O	M	R	W	BB	5I	Avge
1	G. M. Andrew (*Oxfordshire*)	RFM	205.5	47	582	38	8-40	3	15.31
2	D. A. Woods (*Cheshire*)	SLA	184.2	40	477	30	7-65	3	15.90
3	C. T. Peploe (*Berkshire*)	SLA	354.5	132	720	45	5-18	—	16.00
4	W. F. S. Fynn (*Shropshire*)	SLA	146.4	33	417	26	7-60	1	16.03
5	J. A. J. Rishton (*Berkshire*)......	RM	129	23	421	24	6-48	2	17.54
6	Tahir Afridi (*Wiltshire*)	LFM	227.4	62	615	35	6-47	1	17.57
7	O. S. Bocking (*Suffolk*).........	RFM	133.5	25	456	25	6-44	2	18.24
8	O. D. Clarke (*Oxfordshire*)	SLA	151.3	38	494	27	7-99	3	18.29
9	A. J. Willerton (*Lincolnshire*)....	RM	217	57	627	33	7-92	3	19.00
10	M. A. Comber (*Suffolk*)	RFM	140.1	33	403	21	3-18	0	19.19
11	A. C. Libby (*Cornwall*)	SLA	225.4	50	609	31	4-40	0	19.64
12	M. H. Rowe (*Cornwall*)	OB	143	22	474	24	6-69	3	19.75
13	B. S. Phagura (*Staffordshire*)	RM	122.1	29	401	20	5-41	1	20.05
14	B. A. Waring (*Hertfordshire*)....	SLA	187	37	559	26	7-144	2	21.50
15	A. C. F. Wyatt (*Shropshire*)	RFM	125.4	27	433	20	4-61	0	21.65
16	W. A. White (*Cheshire*)	RFM	201.5	35	612	28	5-78	1	21.85
17	L. A. Evans (*Wiltshire*).........	RFM	168.1	42	584	26	6-55	1	22.46
18	J. K. H. Naik (*Dorset*)	OB	222	56	638	28	5-70	2	22.78
19	R. J. Sayer (*Cambridgeshire*)	OB	163.3	30	547	24	8-66	3	22.79
20	A. M. Watson (*Norfolk*)	SLA	168	39	479	21	5-57	1	22.80
21	J. A. Stephens (*Devon*)	OB	196.2	40	664	29	7-58	2	22.89
22	J. J. Bess (*Devon*)	RFM	125.4	17	473	20	5-33	1	23.65
23	T. J. Dinnis (*Cornwall*)	RM	189.2	35	636	24	6-77	3	26.50
24	P. I. Burgoyne (*Herefordshire*) ..	OB	147.2	29	530	20	4-58	0	26.50
25	P. A. Byrne (*Staffordshire*)......	SLA	254.4	69	698	26	6-59	2	26.84

CHAMPIONSHIP FINAL

At Banbury, September 16–18. **Berkshire won by an innings and 32 runs. Lincolnshire 198** (60.5 overs) (N. S. Keast 42; A. M. C. Russell 5-57) **and 175** (62.4 overs) (J. P. Timby 42; J. A. J. Rishton 5-33, T. M. Nugent 3-36); **‡Berkshire 405-7 dec** (90 overs) (J. L. B. Davies 73, E. D. Woods 98, J. C. Morris 46; C. S. Free 4-91). *Berkshire made it three final victories out of three over Lincolnshire with an emphatic win. Hostile fast bowling from Mungo Russell reduced Lincolnshire to 84-6, before Nic Keast and Curtis Fell fought back, adding 52 for the eighth wicket. Berkshire were ahead in little more than 40 overs – and with eight wickets in hand – after Jack Davies and Euan Woods put on 139 for the second wicket. But they got bogged down, and needed quick runs from Stewart Davison and Tom Nugent before declaring. Lincolnshire started more promisingly, but subsided to Andy Rishton and Nugent. Chris Peploe was unable to bowl until noon, after being ill on the second day – but wrapped up the win with two wickets.*

T20 FINAL

At Wormsley, August 27. **Berkshire won by six wickets. ‡Cheshire 130-6** (20 overs) (W. A. White 36). **Berkshire 131-4** (18.4 overs) (C. T. Peploe 52). *Cheshire had scored 202-2 in their semi-final against Norfolk, but could not repeat the trick against disciplined Berkshire bowling. Chris Peploe made 52 off 46.*

TROPHY FINAL

At Wormsley, August 29. **Cheshire won by two runs. Cheshire 248-7** (50 overs) (W. J. Evans 45, C. Rowe 58, E. B. Fluck 54*; J. A. Stephens 4-53); **‡Devon 246-9** (50 overs) (J. E. Burke 95; S. Normanton 4-21). *Wormsley's long boundaries offered a challenge to batsmen. Cheshire's score seemed par, although they needed Ed Fluck's late 54* from 47 to get there. James Burke produced a classy response but, when he was sixth out, Devon faltered. They required 45 from 37 balls, which proved just beyond the tail in a thrilling finish.*

SECOND ELEVEN CHAMPIONSHIP IN 2018

	North Division	P	W	L	D	A	Bonus points Bat	Bonus points Bowl	Total points
1	Durham (8)............	9	6	1	2	0	26	26	158
2	Warwickshire (2)........	9	4	2	3	0	26	30	135
3	Lancashire (1).........	9	3	1	4	1	27	28	128
4	Nottinghamshire (6)......	9	3	3	3	0	29	32	124
5	Yorkshire (4)..........	9	3	1	5	0	27	22	122
6	Leicestershire (7).......	9	2	3	3	1	25	25	102
7	MCCYC (9)...........	9	2	3	3	1	21	25	98
8	Northamptonshire (10).....	9	2	5	2	0	22	32	96
9	Worcestershire (3).......	9	1	4	4	0	26	28	90
10	Derbyshire (5).........	9	1	4	3	1	21	21	78

	South Division	P	W	L	D	A	Bonus points Bat	Bonus points Bowl	Total points
1	Essex (10).............	8	6	0	2	0	27	30	163
2	Hampshire (1).........	8	4	1	3	0	22	27	128
3	Glamorgan (8).........	8	2	1	5	0	25	20	102
4	Surrey (3).............	8	2	2	4	0	24	23	99
5	Kent (4).............	8	2	3	3	0	17	23	87
6	Gloucestershire (7).......	8	1	3	4	0	24	18	78
7	Somerset (5)..........	8	0	2	6	0	22	23	75
8	Sussex (6)............	8	2	5	1	0	17	20	74
9	Middlesex (2)..........	8	0	2	6	0	18	21	69

Win = 16pts; draw/abandoned = 5pts. Penalties were for slow over-rates. MCC Universities did not take part in the 2018 Championship.

LEADING AVERAGES IN 2018

BATTING (480 runs)

		M	I	NO	R	HS	100	50	Avge	Ct/St
1	R. K. Patel (*Essex*)...............	9	15	2	988	151	5	3	76.00	2
2	J. A. Thompson (*Yorks*)...........	6	12	5	515	77*	0	5	73.57	7
3	I. G. Holland (*Hants*)...........	8	11	2	659	151	2	5	73.22	10
4	A. Kapil (*Sussex*).............	6	12	4	535	135*	2	3	66.87	3
5	P. I. Walter (*Essex*).............	6	11	2	592	219*	2	1	65.77	5
6	G. F. B. Scott (*Middlesex*).......	6	8	0	508	221	2	2	63.50	4
7	R. G. White (*Middlesex*)...........	8	12	0	744	155	3	4	62.00	11/4
8	A. T. Thomson (*Warwicks*).......	9	13	2	650	134*	3	1	59.09	3
9	O. E. Westbury (*Worcs*).........	9	14	2	656	127	3	3	54.66	6
10	F. S. Organ (*Hants*).............	8	12	1	549	189	3	0	49.90	9
11	H. J. Swindells (*Leics*)...........	7	13	2	531	110	1	4	48.27	13/1
12	S. M. Imtiaz (*MCCYC, Worcs, Yorks*)	9	16	1	693	173	2	3	46.20	19
13	N. R. Welch (*Surrey*).............	8	15	2	594	175*	2	2	45.69	5
14	B. J. Curran (*MCCYC, Northants*) ...	11	21	1	876	161	2	5	43.80	5
15	Kashif Ali (*Kent, MCCYC*).......	10	17	2	656	115	1	6	43.73	5
16	A. Harinath (*Surrey*).............	8	15	1	601	104*	2	4	42.92	2
17	S. Steel (*Durham*)..............	10	17	3	590	109	1	4	42.14	2
18	O. G. Robinson (*Kent*).............	8	15	1	589	223	1	3	42.07	20/3
19	R. C. Davies (*Durham*)..........	7	12	0	480	155	2	2	40.00	16/5
20	M. A. Jones (*Durham*).............	8	14	1	516	117*	1	1	39.69	5
21	J. J. Dell (*Worcs*).............	9	13	0	510	104	1	3	39.23	3
22	C. F. Gibson (*Northants*)........	9	16	0	557	148	2	2	34.81	8
23	M. D. Lezar (*Glos, MCCYC*).......	9	16	1	493	147	1	2	32.86	4
23	L. Trevaskis (*Durham*).............	10	17	2	493	93	0	5	32.86	6
25	T. W. Loten (*Yorks*)..............	9	16	0	500	131	1	2	31.25	0

BOWLING (17 wickets)

		Style	O	M	R	W	BB	5I	Avge
1	T. J. Lester (*Lancs*)	LFM	138.2	40	359	23	5-45	1	15.60
2	G. Stewart (*Kent*)	RFM	120	31	380	24	6-61	3	15.83
3	M. P. Dunn (*Surrey*)	RFM	80.4	17	270	17	7-31	1	15.88
4	P. I. Walter (*Essex*)	LM	123.2	17	450	26	4-15	0	17.30
5	I. G. Holland (*Hants*)	RFM	140.2	41	356	17	5-23	1	20.94
6	A. S. S. Nijjar (*Essex*)	SLA	277.1	80	819	39	5-47	3	21.00
7	B. D. Cotton (*Northants, Sussex*)	RFM	223	62	595	26	4-49	0	22.88
8	S. Snater (*Essex*)	RM	142.4	24	486	21	3-26	0	23.14
9	G. H. I. Harding (*Durham*)	SLA	178.4	45	443	19	5-27	1	23.31
10	A. T. Thomson (*Warwicks*)	OB	175.1	39	558	23	6-18	1	24.26
11	M. H. A. Footitt (*Notts*)	LFM	157.1	36	499	20	4-48	0	24.95
12	B. V. Sears (*MCCYC*)	RFM	119.4	13	494	19	5-69	2	26.00
13	F. J. Hudson-Prentice (*MCCYC*)	RFM	193.2	45	660	24	4-41	0	27.50
14	B. G. Whitehead (*Durham*)	LB	158.5	35	483	17	6-77	1	28.41
15	K. Carver (*Yorks*)	SLA	178.3	34	628	22	6-26	1	28.54
16	J. P. McIlroy (*Glam,Glos,MCCYC,Worcs*)	LFM	168.3	33	525	17	5-74	2	30.88
17	L. J. Hurt (*Lancs*)	RFM	179	36	587	19	5-17	1	30.89
18	J. H. Plom (*Essex*)	RFM	153.1	32	558	18	6-33	1	31.00
19	B. W. M. Mike (*Leics*)	RM	189.3	28	734	22	4-37	0	33.36
20	T. N. Walallawitta (*Middx*)	SLA	229.5	36	754	21	5-83	1	35.90
21	O. D. W. Birts (*MCCYC, Middx*)	SLA	193.3	27	707	18	3-18	0	39.27
22	K. T. van Vollenhoven (*MCCYC, Som*)	LB	194	19	807	20	4-52	0	40.35

SECOND ELEVEN CHAMPIONSHIP FINAL

At Chester-le-Street, September 4–7. **Drawn (Durham won on first innings). Essex 130** (49 overs) (R. K. Patel 32; J. Coughlin 4-37, G. H. I. Harding 4-20) **and 380** (113.5 overs) (P. I. Walter 36, A. P. Beard 124, F. I. N. Khushi 123, Extras 35; R. D. Pringle 4-30); ‡**Durham 263** (82 overs) (M. A. Jones 46, R. C. Davies 83, J. Coughlin 68; M. T. Coles 5-50, S. Snater 3-43) **and 144-9** (55 overs) (R. D. Pringle 30; M. R. Quinn 4-59, M. T. Coles 5-46). *When last-day rain relented, Essex had 27 overs in which to take three wickets. But Durham, despite lurching to 90-7 the previous evening, fought hard. There was stiff resistance from Chris McBride and, for 31 balls, from Josh Coughlin, who turned in a spirited all-round performance. When he became Matt Coles's tenth victim, however, a fluctuating game seemed Essex's. Instead, the last pair of McBride and Ben Whitehead held out for seven overs, and Durham's first-innings lead gave them the Championship.*

SECOND ELEVEN TROPHY FINAL

At Radlett, June 21. **Middlesex won by one wicket.** ‡**Somerset 250** (46.2 overs) (T. Banton 36, T. A. Lammonby 51, B. G. F. Green 52, F. R. Trenouth 45; T. E. Barber 3-50, N. A. Sowter 3-47); **Middlesex 251-9** (48.2 overs) (G. F. B. Scott 79, M. K. Andersson 54, T. C. Lace 32; J. Overton 3-48, M. T. C. Waller 3-39). *Middlesex were in control at 112-0 in the 18th, and well placed at 209-5 in the 40th. But a burst of four wickets in 18 balls – including three in three – left them reliant on Thilan Walallawitta and Tom Barber to squeeze past Somerset.*

SECOND ELEVEN TWENTY20 FINAL

At Arundel, August 9. **Lancashire won by 25 runs. Lancashire 66-9** (9 overs) (P. I. Walter 4-12); ‡**Essex 41-7** (9 overs) (T. Hartley 3-12). *Lancashire slipped to 6-3, before three of the middle order made it into the teens; they proved the only double-figure scores of a game reduced to nine overs on a damp finals day.*

LEAGUE CRICKET IN 2018

Albert Ross spreads his wings

GEOFFREY DEAN

One of the most dramatic finishes to a Premier League season came in Nottinghamshire. Going into the final round, Cuckney led Cavaliers & Carrington by three points, knowing that victory over bottom-placed Mansfield Hosiery Mills would clinch a second successive title. Set 245, they were three short with two wickets in hand when rain ended play. Cavaliers & Carrington, meanwhile, had bundled Attenborough out for 97, and romped home by six wickets to pinch the trophy from under Cuckney's noses.

Cavaliers & Carrington – winners of the League in 2013, when they were known as West Indian Cavaliers – were led by Bilal Shafayat, former England Under-19 captain and scorer of 14 first-class hundreds. "My brother was at Mansfield Hosiery's ground, and he gave a live commentary of the last nine overs to 90 or 100 people in our clubhouse," he said. "When we found out we'd won, we blew the roof off. We don't drink, but we turned the whole place upside down jumping on each other." Shafayat paid tribute to seamer Shahzada Khan who, despite being "basically on one leg", claimed six for 40 against Attenborough.

The Birmingham League also enjoyed a compelling conclusion. Knowle & Dorridge led Berkswell by 12 points when they met in the penultimate round. Thanks to an irresistible five for 11 from Tom Milnes, Knowle & Dorridge were shot out for 56, and lost by 102 runs. Berkswell had only to beat bottom club Wolverhampton in the final round to secure their second title in three years. They did so in style, Tom Lewis crashing a brilliant 104 from 58 balls, including 28 off one Zen Malik over, as they stormed to a 117-run triumph. Knowle & Dorridge, meanwhile, surprisingly lost to Dorridge, but finished runners-up. Ombersley paid the price of fielding Worcestershire's Ben Cox, who was ineligible, against Moseley, and were relegated.

A superb all-round season for Qaisar Ashraf, who combined 54 wickets with 454 runs, helped Wakefield Thornes to a third consecutive Yorkshire South Premier League title. York again won the northern equivalent, and were especially grateful to Dan Woods (81 wickets in all competitions) and Duncan Snell (1,715 runs). Mark Robertshaw was the only batsman to pass 1,000 in the Bradford League, helping Pudsey St Lawrence to their third title in four years, while Chris Batchelor of North Yorkshire & South Durham League champions, Great Ayton, amassed 1,020 runs. The winners of Yorkshire's four premier leagues met in play-offs to contest the county's championship final, which was won by Thornes, after they skittled Great Ayton for 97.

Werrington pipped local rivals Penzance to the Cornwall League by three points, despite losing to them in the penultimate round. This meant they had to beat Falmouth on the final Saturday, which they did by six wickets. "It was an

TALES OF AN AGEING CRICKETER
League of gentlemen

MARK BUSSELL

It's a Saturday evening in September. Tilford Green plays host to men in bulging whites. A gaggle of spectators watch from in front of The Barley Mow, where years ago that legend of English cricket, Silver Billy Beldham, was the publican. The watery sunlight shimmers against the Lutyens-designed village hall. It's a picture worthy of Constable – or at least a posh biscuit-tin lid. Tilford Thirds need 32 off four. Henry Newbolt is about to clear his throat: "Play up! Play up! And play the game."

It's in this corner of Surrey I play my cricket, for Tilford in the I'Anson League, which claims to be the oldest in the world. It's a place where cricketing stories become folklore. Like the time a Tilford bowler, a policeman, plodded back to his mark, only to break into a sprint, vault a hedge and arrest a burglar attempting a break-in. Or when a farm worker had to retire hurt after a ball struck his hip, and his trousers caught fire. The folly of batting with a box of Swan Vestas in your pocket.

For 15 years I had clogged up the innings at the top of the order with my array of leaves, nudges and nurdles, but in recent times these talents were in decreasing demand. There was only one thing for it. I would have to invent a new team to play in, so Tilford Thirds were formed. We were to play in Division Seven. Amid much talk of pyramids and pathways, this was the subterranean foundation of the pyramid, and a pathway so bumpy and overgrown it was hardly discernible.

I found I was not alone in ignoring Old Father Time. Former players, drawn like moths to the flame of past glories, signed up. With an average age of 58, our dressing-room was an apothecary's Aladdin's den. Deep Heat was applied, knee socks slid into place, ankle supports strapped on; ITV missed a trick when casting "Love Island."

And yet, despite our expanding waistlines and myriad infirmities, we were winning against teams much younger. Nous was triumphing over athleticism. Our 76-year-old leg-spinner delivered balls so slow, callow batsmen were caught in five minds. Our photocopier repairman's swingers were as repetitively accurate as one of his newly serviced machines. And our batsmen adhered to that age-old maxim of keeping out the straight ones and waiting for the bad (of which there many).

But back to Tilford Green. The Division Seven title may have been won the week before, but victory in this last match of the season would be the icing on the cake. Some lusty blows from our cardiac surgeon inched us closer. (Every Third XI should carry its own cardiac surgeon.) But village teams don't chase well, especially when they need north of 200.

There was to be no happy ending: defeat by 12 runs. That was followed by end-of-season photographs and frothy ales in the pub, and that warm glow of comradeship that a winning team radiates. And then, as more ales appeared, a notion started to ferment: we may just be the oldest team ever to win a competitive league.

unbelievable feeling to hit the runs to win the league," said captain Paul Smith, who drove down from Birmingham every weekend. "The fact that we've done it with a team of best mates means a hell of a lot. The last two years, we've been in mid-table, and at one stage we were 30-odd points behind, so to come out top at the end of the season is a remarkable achievement."

Blackheath also climbed from mid-table to the top, and won the Kent League for the first time since 1984. Fifth in 2017, they clinched the title emphatically in the final game: they made 278 against previous champions Beckenham, then routed them for 73. Skipper Chris Willetts praised the all-round performances of Tanveer Sikandar, who struck 145 off 134 balls and then took four for 45 in an important home win over runners-up Lordswood.

In the Surrey Championship, Weybridge similarly leaped from fifth to first. Reigate Priory led for much of the season but, after failing to beat Sutton and East Molesey, two of the weaker sides, in August they faced Weybridge in the penultimate round. Weybridge wheeled out two Curran brothers, Tom and Ben, as well as Surrey's Will Jacks. But it was their team-mate Jack Winslade who proved the match-winner: he castled five batsmen at a cost of 31. All the same, Weybridge slumped to 21 for four in pursuit of 120, and needed New Zealand T20 international Tom Bruce, with an unbeaten 63, to see them home. Another five-for from Winslade in the last match, against Sutton, underpinned their first title since 2004.

Chris Aspin writes: The Lancashire League's first season with 24 clubs – there were seven newcomers – determined the make-up of the two divisions for 2019. The title was decided on the final afternoon, when Walsden, a large village in West Yorkshire but historically part of Lancashire, became champions after winning 20 games and losing only to Darwen. The Second XI did even better, with a league and cup double, and the Third XI, captained by 67-year-old Albert Ross, also became champions, to complete a unique treble. Success owed much to the club's links with the local primary school, where nine members of the winning side first learned the game. A tenth, also a villager, attended a school two miles away. The club run a Friday crèche for boys and girls aged four to eight; afterwards, coaches guide youngsters at all levels. Walsden's only setbacks came in the Twenty20 competition, won by Burnley, and the Worsley Cup knockout, where Lowerhouse beat Burnley by three wickets in the final, with the crowd paying a record £6,469 at the gate.

Batsmen prospered during the heatwave, with nine sides topping 300 – Walsden four times. Amateur batsmen scored 36 centuries and the professionals 21, including three by Kaustubh Pawar when sub-pro for Rawtenstall and Todmorden. Josh Gale (Walsden) was the leading run-scorer with 817 at 40, and Mansoor Amjad, the Rishton pro, made 803 at 50. Umesh Karunaratne (Walsden) led the wicket-takers with 71 at 11, just ahead of Ramsbottom's Jon Fielding (65 at ten).

The most remarkable match was at Littleborough. They were 12 for three against Bacup, when professional Thomas Kaber and Joe Smith-Butler added an unbroken 258, a league record for the fourth wicket, and the third-highest

for any. Kaber made 134 and Smith-Butler 108. Undaunted, Bacup went for
the runs: opener Simon Newbitt hammered a club amateur record of 128 to
help them to a three-wicket victory, with five balls to spare.

Walsden amassed the season's highest total – 355 for eight – in a 173-run
win over Great Harwood, Karunaratne following 102 with seven for 39. Nelson
blasted 350 for three at Rawtenstall, where David Crotty hit 139 and sub-pro
Daryn Smit an unbeaten 108. Smit starred again when he stood in at Lowerhouse, who accumulated a club record 340 for three against Rishton. He made
138, and shared a third-wicket partnership of 189 with Francois Haasbroek
(113 not out).

Great Harwood stormed to 323 for four against Rishton, who took up the
challenge, but ended 22 short with the last pair at the wicket. The same
afternoon, Lowerhouse made 320 for four against Colne, professional Ockert
Erasmus scoring 106 and former pro Haasbroek 118 not out. Colne struggled
to 81 to give Lowerhouse victory by 239 runs, a club record. Walsden opener
Jake Hooson made an unbeaten 132 to help his side to 314 for five against
Middleton, and then took five for 19. Accrington plundered the Rishton attack,
posting 301 for four in a game reduced to 46 overs. Clitheroe reached 301 for
seven against Colne, with skipper Jack Dewhurst (130) and Sam Mulligan (83)
sharing a second-wicket stand of 211.

Walsden dismissed Milnrow for 35 in the 21st over, and needed less than
eight to win. There was another early finish when Nelson shot out Colne for
36 in the 16th: eight batsmen made nought or one, but 14 wides helped out;
Nelson won by ten wickets in 35 balls. But when Nelson were bowled out for
49 by Rochdale, seven batsmen failed to score.

Calvin Savage, Darwen's South African pro, made an unbeaten 170 off 112
balls against Clitheroe, hitting 11 sixes and 13 fours. Josh Gale (Walsden)
smashed the Bacup bowlers for 160 off 151 (22 fours, three sixes) to beat his
brother Joe's amateur record – 148 – made earlier in the season in a Lancashire
Knockout Cup game against Formby. Ben Pearson broke a Todmorden amateur
record when he made 152 not out against Milnrow; his third-wicket stand of
237 with professional Chris Schofield (88) was also a record. Lowerhouse
skipper Ben Heap cracked 144 off 124 balls against Milnrow. In totalling 564
runs, Graham Knowles, the Haslingden opener, overtook his father Bryan's
career aggregate of 13,086 to become the club's second-highest run-maker.
Mas Ahmed hit a half-century for Great Harwood against Bacup a month short
of his 57th birthday. Paddy Morton, the Lowerhouse off-spinner, took seven
Norden wickets for three runs in 6.3 overs.

The recall of overseas professionals, often weeks before the season ended,
again caused headaches. Fifteen went home early, and not all clubs were able
to recruit substitutes; four had to field all-amateur XIs. Zahir Khan became the
first Afghan to play in the league when he was sub-pro for Haslingden; he
claimed four for 35 in a narrow victory over Enfield.

Darwen won the Lancashire Knockout Cup, beating Clifton of the Greater
Manchester League by two wickets in the final. Alex Hartley, a member of the
England women's squad, took four for nine when Clitheroe selected her for a
Second XI game against Milnrow.

ECB PREMIER LEAGUE TABLES IN 2018

Birmingham & District Premier League

		P	W	L	Pts
1	**Berkswell**	22	14	3	**375**
2	Knowle & Dorridge	22	15	5	357
3	West Bromwich Dartmouth	22	11	5	318
4	Smethwick	22	10	7	305
5	Shrewsbury	22	9	9	270
6	Moseley	21	9	11	256
7	Walsall	22	8	8	241
8	Barnt Green	22	6	10	221
9	Dorridge	22	7	12	220
10	Kenilworth Wardens	22	5	10	213
11	Ombersley	22	7	11	211†
12	Wolverhampton	22	3	13	176

† *Deducted 20pts for fielding an ineligible player.*

Bradford Premier League

		P	W	L	Pts
1	**Pudsey St Lawrence**	22	17	4	**353**
2	New Farnley	22	17	5	350
3	Hanging Heaton	22	14	7	310
4	Woodlands	22	14	7	303
5	Methley	22	13	8	299
6	Farsley	22	14	7	295
7	Cleckheaton	22	10	11	253
8	Townville	22	10	11	250
9	Lightcliffe	22	7	14	194
10	Bradford & Bingley	22	4	18	172
11	East Bierley	22	2	19	100
12	Scholes	22	5	16	85†

† *Deducted 50pts.*

Cheshire County League Premier Division

		P	W	L	Pts
1	**Nantwich**	22	14	4	**416**
2	Chester Boughton Hall	22	13	4	402
3	Timperley	22	13	2	397
4	Neston	22	13	7	380
5	Toft	22	10*	6	350
6	Alderley Edge	22	8*	4	318
7	Cheadle	22	9	12	294
8	Oulton Park	22	8	11	284
9	Marple	22	6	15	222
10	Grappenhall	22	5	14	214
11	Bramhall	22	5	13	204
12	Didsbury	22	4	16	181

* *Plus one tie.*

Cornwall Premier Division

		P	W	L	Pts
1	**Werrington**	20	15	4	**313**
2	Penzance	20	14	3	312
3	Truro	20	13	4	303
4	St Austell	20	11	6	269
5	Redruth	20	10	8	258
6	St Just	20	8	8	240
7	Falmouth	20	8	7	231
8	Wadebridge	20	7	11	199
9	Grampound Road	20	6	12	195†
10	Callington	20	3	16	145
11	Camborne	20	1	18	133

† *Deducted 5 points for late submission of captain's report.*

Derbyshire Premier League

		P	W	L	Pts
1	**Ticknall**	22	16	3	**467**
2	Spondon	22	14	1	457
3	Sandiacre Town	22	12	2	420
4	Ockbrook & Borrowash	22	10	7	346
5	Eckington	22	9	7	323
6	Swarkestone	22	8	6	310
7	Chesterfield	22	6	9	287
8	Elvaston	22	5	10	258
9	Denby	22	4	10	237
10	Alvaston & Boulton	22	5	8	236
11	Wirksworth & Middleton	22	1	13	155
12	Rolleston	22	1	15	152

Devon Premier League

		P	W	L	Pts
1	**Sidmouth**	18	13	4	**280**
2	Exeter	18	13	4	275
3	Heathcoat	18	12	4	272
4	Plymouth	18	10	7	251
5	Exmouth	18	9	8	220
6	North Devon	18	7	11	197†
7	Bovey Tracey	18	7	10	194
8	Sandford	18	6	12	187
9	Bradninch	18	6	11	185
10	Hatherleigh	18	3	15	136

† *Deducted 2pts for showing dissent to an umpire.*

East Anglian Premier League

		P	W	L	Pts
1	**Sudbury**	22	16	4	**444**
2	Swardeston	22	15	4	443
3	Mildenhall	22	13	7	383
4	Frinton-on-Sea	22	8	7	344
5	Horsford	22	8	10	319
6	Copdock & Old Ipswichian	22	9	10	315
7	Great Witchingham	22	8	11	299
8	Cambridge Granta	22	7	11	296
9	Burwell & Exning	22	6	12	293
10	Vauxhall Mallards	22	9	10	290
11	Bury St Edmunds	22	7	12	270
12	Norwich	22	5	13	261

Essex League Premier Division

		P	W	L	Pts
1	**Hornchurch**	18	13	3	311
2	Wanstead & Snaresbrook .	18	12	5	289
3	Brentwood	18	10	5	267
4	Chingford.	18	9	6	247
5	Chelmsford	18	9	6	238
6	Billericay.	18	9	9	230
7	Hadleigh & Thundersley .	18	6	12	172
8	Ilford.	18	5	10	171
9	Shenfield	18	4	12	156
10	Southend-on-Sea.	18	3	14	100

Hertfordshire League Premier Division

		P	W	L	Pts
1	**Totteridge Millhillians** .	18	12	4	390
2	North Mymms	18	12	5	385
3	Welwyn Garden City. . . .	18	11	5	364
4	Potters Bar	18	8	5	326
5	Radlett.	18	7*	8	280
6	Hertford	18	7	8	272
7	West Herts	18	7*	9	262
8	Bishop's Stortford.	18	5	9	252
9	Harpenden	18	3	8	217
10	Letchworth.	18	2	15	132

Home Counties Premier League

		P	W	L	Pts
1	**Henley**	18	11	2	313
2	Slough.	18	12	4	307
3	Aston Rowant.	18	11	3	300
4	High Wycombe.	18	7	7	249
5	Banbury.	18	7	7	248
6	Tring Park	18	8	7	243
7	Finchampstead	18	6	8	209†
8	Horspath	18	3	8	183
9	Oxford.	18	4	9	172
10	Thame Town	18	1	15	104

† *Deducted 20pts for fielding an unregistered player.*

Kent League Premier Division

		P	W	L	Pts
1	**Blackheath**	18	12	5	250
2	Lordswood.	18	12	5	249
3	Tunbridge Wells	18	11	6	234
4	Sevenoaks Vine	18	10	7	222
5	Sandwich Town	18	10	7	216
6	Bickley Park	18	8	9	201
7	Bexley.	18	9	9	193
8	Beckenham	18	8	9	176
9	Tenterden.	18	4	13	132
10	Bromley Common.	18	2	15	103

Leics & Rutland League Premier Division

		P	W	L	Pts
1	**Kibworth**	22	15	3	426
2	Lutterworth	22	14	5	405
3	Barrow Town	22	13	6	395
4	Leicester Ivanhoe	22	12	6	368
5	Loughborough Town. . . .	22	10	9	359
6	Sileby Town.	22	9	9	335
7	Syston Town	22	10	7	323
8	Kegworth Town	22	10	8	319
9	Barkby United	22	7	12	273
10	Langtons	22	7	13	267
11	Uppingham Town	22	4	15	221
12	Market Harborough	22	1	19	97

Lincolnshire Cricket Board Premier League

		P	W	L	Pts
1	**Bracebridge Heath**	22	19	0	381
2	Grantham.	22	14	5	319
3	Sleaford.	22	12	7	282
4	Woodhall Spa.	22	11	7	270
5	Boston	22	10	8	240
6	Bourne.	22	10	8	229
7	Market Deeping	22	8	11	228
8	Lindum	22	7	10	223
9	Scunthorpe Town	22	6	10	213
10	Louth.	22	7	11	207
11	Alford	22	5	15	171
12	Grimsby Town	22	3	16	136

Liverpool & District Competition

		P	W	L	Pts
1	**Northern**.	22	16	2	413
2	Ormskirk	22	13	5	348
3	Formby	22	10	5	316
4	Bootle	22	9	7	284
5	Leigh	22	9	8	281
6	Rainhill	22	8	8	263
7	Lytham	22	8	7	247
8	Wallasey	22	7	10	247
9	Colwyn Bay	22	6*	9	236
10	New Brighton	22	7*	9	231
11	Rainford	22	4	15	189
12	Highfield	22	2	14	146

* *Plus one tie.*

Middlesex County League Division One

		P	W	L	Pts
1	**Richmond**	18	16	1	165
2	Ealing	18	11	6	122
3	North Middlesex	18	10	5	117
4	Teddington	18	7*	6	91
5	Shepherds Bush	18	7*	8	82
6	Hampstead	18	7	9	75
7	Twickenham.	18	6	10	65†
8	Finchley.	18	6	11	64
9	Brondesbury	18	3	10	50
10	Highgate	18	4	11	49

* *Plus one tie.* † *Deducted 1pt for failure to mark wicket.*

Northamptonshire League Premier Division

		P	W	L	Pts
1	**Finedon Dolben**	20	14	2	330
2	Old Northamptonians	20	12	3	305
3	Peterborough Town	20	10	5	271†
4	Horton House	20	8	7	249
5	Northampton Saints	20	9	8	249
6	Rushden Town	20	8	8	245
7	Oundle Town	20	6	9	200
8	Brixworth	20	6	9	195
9	Geddington	20	5	10	188
10	Brigstock	20	5	10	176‡
11	Wollaston	20	3	15	121

† *Deducted 10pts for failure to attend pre-season meeting.* ‡ *Deducted 1pt for fielding an ineligible player.*

N Staffs & S Cheshire League Premier Division

		P	W	L	Pts
1	**Porthill Park**	22	13	1	415
2	J & G Meakin	22	10	5	356
3	Blythe	22	10	5	332
4	Checkley	22	11	5	332
5	Stone	22	7	7	289
6	Longton	22	6	8	259†
7	Ashcombe Park	22	5	11	247
8	Leek	22	3	9	234
9	Whitmore	22	5	12	212
10	Hem Heath	22	6	12	211‡
11	Burslem	22	6	10	168§
12	Elworth	22	9	6	49¶

† *Deducted 9pts.* ‡ *Deducted 26pts.*
§ *Deducted 71pts.* ¶ *Deducted 238pts.*

North East Premier Division

		P	W	L	Pts
1	**South Northumberland**	22	16	0	471
2	Chester-le-Street	22	11	3	403
3	Hetton Lyons	22	11	6	362
4	Tynemouth	22	10	6	349
5	Newcastle	22	9	9	299
6	Whitburn	22	9	7	294
7	Benwell Hill	22	6	9	261
8	Eppleton	22	5	11	222
9	Durham Academy	22	4	9	221
10	Felling	22	5	10	206
11	Sacriston	22	5	12	195
12	Stockton	22	5	14	189

North Wales League Premier Division

		P	W	L	Pts
1	**Menai Bridge**	22	16	3	233
2	Brymbo	22	15*	4	220
3	Llandudno	22	15*	5	218
4	Bangor	22	11	9	177
5	Northop	22	12	8	169
6	St Asaph	22	10*	10	167
7	Gresford	22	10*	9	166
8	Pwllheli	22	10	10	155
9	Denbigh	22	9	11	145
10	Connah's Quay	22	6	12	113
11	Hawarden Park	22	2	16	61
12	Chirk	22	0	19	32

Northern Premier League

		P	W	L	Pts
1	**Blackpool**	22	14*	2	258
2	Netherfield	22	12	2	251
3	St Annes	22	11*	5	228
4	Leyland	22	9	5	207
5	Chorley	22	9	10	196
6	Garstang	22	10	10	190
7	Barrow	22	8	6	186
8	Penrith	22	7	9	165
9	Fleetwood	22	8	11	163†
10	Fulwood & Broughton	22	8	11	161
11	Morecambe	22	7	10	159
12	Preston	22	0	22	–11‡

* *Plus one tie.* † *Deducted 5pts.*
‡ *Deducted 18pts.*

N Yorks & S Durham League Premier Division

		P	W	L	Pts
1	**Barnard Castle**	22	13	4	385
2	Great Ayton	22	12	2	381
3	Richmondshire	22	11	4	361
4	Stokesley	22	10	6	317
5	Darlington	22	9	6	298
6	Thornaby	22	8	8	277
7	Marton	22	5	8	274
8	Hartlepool	22	6	11	238
9	Seaton Carew	22	7	10	234†
10	Middlesbrough	22	6	13	229
11	Marske	22	5	12	206‡
12	Bishop Auckland	22	4	12	193

† *Deducted 30pts.* ‡ *Deducted 10pts.*

Nottinghamshire Cricket Board Premier League

		P	W	L	Pts
1	**Cavaliers & Carrington**	22	14	3	342
2	Cuckney	22	12	4	339
3	Kimberley Institute	22	12	4	326
4	Plumtree	22	9	9	265
5	Wollaton	22	9	7	259
6	Farnsfield	22	8	8	251
7	Radcliffe-on-Trent	22	9	11	222
8	Papplewick & Linby	22	6	8	218
9	Hucknall	22	5	11	200
10	Attenborough	22	5	10	190
11	Caythorpe	22	3	10	187
12	Mansfield Hosiery Mills	22	3	10	168

Southern Premier League

		P	W	L	Pts
1	**St Cross Symondians**	17	11	4	307
2	Burridge	16	12	4	279
3	Hants CCC Academy	16	10	5	266
4	Basingstoke & North Hants	16	10	6	247
5	South Wilts	18	8	7	271
6	Havant	16	8	7	216
7	Bashley (Rydal)	18	6	10	216
8	Lymington	16	5*	8	173
9	Alton	17	4*	9	182
10	New Milton	16	1	15	67

Positions determined by average pts per game.
* *Plus one tie.*

South Wales Premier League Division One

		P	W	L	Pts
1	**Newport**	18	13	1	281
2	Neath	18	12	3	252
3	Cardiff	18	8	7	210
4	Ammanford	18	8*	5	207
5	St Fagans	18	7*	7	203
6	Pontarddulais	18	7	8	183
7	Port Talbot Town	18	5	10	168
8	Mumbles	18	5	10	156
9	Bridgend Town	18	5	10	150
10	Ynysygerwn	18	2**	11	105†

* *Plus one tie.* ** *Plus two ties.*
† *Deducted 22pts.*

Surrey Championship Premier Division

		P	W	L	Pts
1	**Weybridge**	18	12	2	301
2	Reigate Priory	18	11*	3	282
3	Ashtead	18	7	5	222
4	Wimbledon	18	7	6	214
5	Banstead	18	7	8	203
6	Sunbury	18	5	9	194
7	Sutton	18	5	9	173
8	East Molesey	18	5*	10	170
9	Normandy	18	5	8	163
10	Cranleigh	18	5	10	156

* *Plus one tie.*

Sussex League Premier Division

		P	W	L	Pts
1	**Roffey**	18	13	1	445
2	Eastbourne	18	10	6	393
3	Preston Nomads	18	10	4	381
4	East Grinstead	18	10	4	370
5	Horsham	18	10	6	357
6	Brighton & Hove	18	8	8	335
7	Cuckfield	18	7	8	297
8	Middleton-on-Sea	18	5	10	264
9	Hastings & St Leonards	18	2	15	170
10	Ifield	18	1	14	145

West of England Premier League

		P	W	L	Pts
1	**Clevedon**	18	14	3	309
2	Bath	18	11	5	277
3	Downend	18	11	6	258
4	Potterne	18	10	7	246
5	Bristol	18	10*	6	235
6	Bridgwater	18	8*	9	217
7	Bedminster	18	7	11	197
8	Taunton St Andrews	18	6	11	186
9	Frocester	18	4	12	171
10	Goatacre	18	3	14	156

* *Plus one tie.*

Yorkshire North Premier League

		P	W	L	Pts
1	**York**	22	10	2	165
2	Woodhouse Grange	22	12	3	156
3	Stamford Bridge	22	9	4	154
4	Sheriff Hutton Bridge	22	8	4	139
5	Yorkshire Academy	22	7	5	115
6	Scarborough	22	5	5	106
7	Harrogate	22	5	9	96
8	Castleford	22	6	8	94
9	Sessay	22	3	6	86
10	Clifton Alliance	22	4	8	84
11	Driffield Town	22	4	5	76
12	Acomb	22	0	16	17

Yorkshire South Premier League

		P	W	L	Pts
1	**Wakefield Thornes**	22	19	2	236
2	Sheffield Collegiate	22	15	5	200
3	Barnsley Woolley Miners	22	13	7	166
4	Treeton	22	13	8	166
5	Doncaster Town	22	10*	9	162
6	Cleethorpes	22	8	12	122
7	Aston Hall	22	8	12	118
	Hallam	22	8	12	118
	Wickersley Old Village	22	8	12	118
	Whitley Hall	22	7*	12	118
11	Appleby Frodingham	22	7	13	104
12	Whiston Parish Church	22	4	16	70

* *Plus one tie.*

LANCASHIRE LEAGUE TABLE IN 2018

		P	*W*	*L*	*Pts*
1	**Walsden**	23	20	1	240
2	Lowerhouse	23	19	2	234
3	Ramsbottom	23	19	3	228
4	Darwen	23	17	5	212
5	Church	23	14	7	187
6	Norden	23	12*	8	180
7	Burnley	23	13*	6	170
8	Clitheroe	23	13	7	167
9	Crompton	23	13	8	160
10	Accrington	23	12	9	160
11	Rochdale	23	10*	11	155
12	Todmorden	23	11	9	154
13	Nelson	23	12	9	150
14	Enfield	23	8*	12	129
15	Haslingden	23	8	10	114
16	Middleton	23	6	14	105
17	Littleborough	23	6	14	96
18	Colne	23	6*	14	94
19	Great Harwood	23	6	15	85
20	Rawtenstall	23	5	15	84
21	Bacup	23	5	15	82
22	East Lancashire	23	5*	15	73
23	Rishton	23	3	18	52
24	Milnrow	23	2	18	49

* *Plus one tie.*

The top 12 teams formed the first division for 2019, and the bottom 12 the second.

OTHER LEAGUE WINNERS IN 2018

Airedale & Wharfedale	Otley
Bolton	Walkden
Cambs & Hunts	Saffron Walden
Greater Manchester	Flixton
Huddersfield	Hoylandswaine
Norfolk Alliance	Fakenham
North Essex	Wivenhoe
North Lancs & Cumbria	Cockermouth
Northumberland & Tyneside Senior	Swalwell
Pembrokeshire	Neyland
Quaid-e-Azam	Keighley RZM
Ribblesdale	Oswaldtwistle Immanuel
Shropshire	Wem
South Wales Association	Gorseinon
Thames Valley	Wokingham
Two Counties	Worlington
Warwickshire	Bedworth
Worcestershire	Bewdley

ECB CITY CUP IN 2018

RICHARD WHITEHEAD

Bradford, birthplace of Jim Laker, Jonny Bairstow and Adil Rashid, added a new feather to its cricketing cap by winning the ECB City Cup, now in its tenth year, for the first time, beating Sheffield by 22 runs in an all-Yorkshire final at Grace Road.

The victory gave particular pleasure to Nasa Hussain, a key figure in the redevelopment of facilities at Bradford's historic Park Avenue ground. "It's great for Bradford that we've won the City Cup," said Hussain, who is also vice-chairman of the National Asian Cricket Council. "I have always said there's a lot of cricket talent in the city."

The competition, launched by former *Wisden* editor Scyld Berry in 2009, aims to unearth promising inner-city cricketers who have slipped under the radar of county development programmes. The players are aged 16 to 21; six of the XI have to be under 18. Twenty cities take part, and the competition has now been incorporated into the ECB's South Asian Action Plan.

Bradford's victory at Leicester was built on a half-century from 20-year-old captain Hamza Iqbal. Fittingly, he received the trophy from Lord Patel of Bradford, an ECB independent director. "It's been great experience for the lads, winning the regional finals at Park Avenue, getting through the semis in Birmingham and now this weekend in Leicester," said Hussain.

The squad were assembled after sessions on Park Avenue's all-weather nets. Their coaches have included former Yorkshire and England seamer Ajmal Shahzad, and Leicestershire's Usman Arshad, himself a Bradfordian. Hamza was one of 32 players – two from each team – who took part in sessions at Lord's in November.

Mohammed Arif, the ECB's national growth manager for diverse communities, said the tie-up with MCC offered the selected players "the chance for a range of coaches to look at their talent". Grace Road once again proved an excellent venue for the final, giving the players a chance to appear on a first-class ground. "We're really grateful to Leicestershire for making us feel so welcome," said Arif.

At Leicester, September 16. **Bradford won by 22 runs. Bradford 143-5** (20 overs) (Junaid Jamshed 32, Hamza Iqbal 50; Arsalan Tariq 3-20); ‡**Sheffield 121-8** (20 overs). *After being put in, Bradford shrugged off the loss of an early wicket to take command. Their total was built on captain Hamza Iqbal's 50 from 39 balls. Opener Junaid Jamshed proceeded more cautiously, but his 32 from 43 was also key to a challenging total. Arsalan Tariq was the sixth bowler Sheffield used, but proved the most impressive, with 3-20. Bradford's attack operated as a unit, and quickly exerted a tight grip. Junaid also starred with the ball, taking 2-14, Zeeshan Haider took 2-25, and Mohammed Haris's four overs went for just 16. Arsalan reduced the victory margin with 24 from 14, but Sheffield were well short.*

ROYAL LONDON CLUB CHAMPIONSHIP AND VITALITY CLUB T20 IN 2018

PAUL EDWARDS

The Yorkshire Cricket Board's Christmas dinner was not lacking in celebratory spirit. At the end of summer, the county had become the first to supply the winners of three national club competitions – and the board invited all three. Richmondshire (Royal London Club Championship) and Hanging Heaton (Vitality Club T20) were joined by Folkton & Flixton, winners of the Village Knockout, reflecting the strength of cricket in a county with over 700 clubs. Richmondshire had already been given a civic reception and named the *Northern Echo's* team of the year, while the Hanging Heaton players switched on Dewsbury's Christmas lights.

The accolades had been well earned. Richmondshire beat four previous winners en route to the final at Bristol, while Hanging Heaton followed up three trophies in 2017 by defeating Swardeston in their final, at Derby. Consolation for Swardeston, from Norfolk, came in a remarkable innings by Lewis Denmark, whose 122 not out off 56 balls in the semi against Nantwich was the highest score in the competition's 11-year history.

Both tournament winners were led by players with first-class experience. Richmondshire's Gary Pratt once played for Durham, and may be England's most famous substitute fielder; Hanging Heaton's Gary Fellows was a member of the Yorkshire side that won the Cheltenham & Gloucester Trophy in 2002. The Royal London also offers good experience to future professionals. Lancashire's Josh Bohannon played for 2017 runners-up Ormskirk, and Mattie McKiernan followed his season with Richmondshire by joining Derbyshire.

Good weather was a bonus for the organisers of both competitions, although it did not prevent elite clubs becoming bogged down in fixture backlogs. Richmondshire's quarter-final against Ormskirk was reduced to ten overs and played in pouring rain. Such problems are inevitable when some clubs enter six tournaments. There is good reason to prioritise the Club Championship in 2019: the final is returning to Lord's for the first time since 2008.

ROYAL LONDON CLUB CHAMPIONSHIP FINAL

RICHMONDSHIRE v STANMORE

At Bristol, September 23. Richmondshire won by five wickets (DLS). Toss: Stanmore.

Tight bowling on a tacky pitch, followed by a well-paced pursuit of a small total, earned Richmondshire the trophy for the first time. They got home with four balls to spare after rain reduced the match to 30 overs, and then to 28. None of Stanmore's batsmen stayed around long enough to anchor their innings. Leg-spinner Mattie McKiernan was miserly and took two wickets, while back-up came from Craig Swainston and captain Gary Pratt. Stanmore were 30 short of a challenging total, and their position looked hopeless when McKiernan and Bob Carr eased Richmondshire to 73 for one in the 19th over. They stumbled briefly, but the result was never in doubt. Steve Mather and Sam Wood put on an unbeaten 25 to wrap things up. "I did shed a little tear when we hit the winning runs," said Pratt, best known for his run-out of Ricky Ponting during the Trent Bridge Test of 2005. "This is up there with winning the Minor Counties with Cumberland, and that Ashes moment, too."

Man of the Match: M. H. McKiernan.

Stanmore

T. Azam c Pratt b Swainston	21	R. Mullahzada b McKiernan		0
S. J. Reingold run out (McKiernan)	24	T. Brock not out		13
A. Elech c T. Dowson b Pratt	13			
K. Patel b Swainston	0	Lb 11, w 4, nb 1		16
G. Reingold c and b West	1			
*T. Karia b McKiernan	16	1/31 (1) 2/65 (3)	(8 wkts, 28 overs)	120
S. Ratnakumaran lbw b Pratt	1	3/66 (4) 4/67 (2)		
M. S. Reingold not out	15	5/69 (5) 6/72 (7) 7/102 (6) 8/102 (9)		

†W. T. D. Hanson did not bat.

Wood 2–0–15–0; J. Dowson 4–0–19–0; Swainston 6–0–19–2; McKiernan 6–1–20–2; Pratt 6–0–19–2; West 4–0–17–1.

Richmondshire

R. J. Carr lbw b Karia	19	S. A. Wood not out		11
*G. J. Pratt b Mullahzada	9			
M. H. McKiernan run out (M. S. Reingold)	44	B 3, lb 2, w 1		6
M. L. Layfield st Hanson b S. J. Reingold	17			
M. T. Cowling c G. Reingold		1/17 (2) 2/73 (1)	(5 wkts, 27.2 overs)	125
b S. J. Reingold	3	3/94 (4) 4/98 (5)		
S. Mather not out	16	5/100 (3)		

†T. Dowson, J. Dowson, C. Swainston and R. West did not bat.

Mullahzada 6–0–23–1; Elech 4.2–0–17–0; Karia 6–0–19–1; M. S. Reingold 6–0–32–0; S. J. Reingold 5–0–29–2.

Umpires: N. Davies and J. Finch.

WINNERS 2005–2018

2005	Horsham	2012	York
2006	South Northumberland	2013	West Indian Cavaliers
2007	Bromley	2014	Sandiacre Town
2008	Kibworth	2015	Blackheath
2009	Chester-le-Street	2016	South Northumberland
2010	South Northumberland	2017	Wanstead & Snaresbrook
2011	Shrewsbury	2018	Richmondshire

A full list from the start of the competition in 1969 to 2004, appears in Wisden 2005, page 941.

VITALITY CLUB T20

First semi-final At Derby, September 16. **Swardeston won by 47 runs. Swardeston 212-4** (20 overs) (L. R. K. Denmark 122*, P. A. Lambert 46); ‡**Nantwich 165-5** (20 overs) (B. Johnston 65).

Second semi-final At Derby, September 16. **Hanging Heaton won by seven wickets.** ‡**Roffey 99-9** (20 overs) (T. Chippendale 3-18, D. A. Stiff 3-16); **Hanging Heaton 102-3** (17.3 overs) (J. Fraser 41*).

Final At Derby, September 16. **Hanging Heaton won by five wickets.** ‡**Swardeston 164-8** (20 overs) (J. G. Taylor 54); **Hanging Heaton 165-5** (19.3 overs) (G. M. Fellows 88*).

WINNERS

2008	South Northumberland	2014	Chester Boughton Hall
2009	Bournemouth	2015	Ealing
2010	Swardeston	2016	Swardeston
2011	Ealing	2017	South Northumberland
2012	Wimbledon	2018	Hanging Heaton
2013	Wimbledon		

THE CRICKETER VILLAGE CUP IN 2018

BENJ MOOREHEAD

On the face of it, this was another victory for Yorkshire, which had provided three of the previous four winners. But, refreshingly, this was the first time in five years the Village Cup was lifted by a club that had not won it before. There was a boyish charm about Folkton & Flixton, whose average age was 22: they were unassuming, wide-eyed cricketers, who could scarcely believe the course of events that led to their crowning at Lord's.

They were exactly the sort of club the Village Cup was meant for. The competition is open to villages with a population of no more than 10,000; Folkton & Flixton, who both sit at the foot of the Yorkshire Wolds in the district of Scarborough, have fewer than 1,000 between them. The club fare well in league cricket, playing in the tier below the elites of the Yorkshire Premier League North, but they had to rely on local donations to finance their trip to Lord's.

Folkton & Flixton were masters of the chase: they batted second in all but one of their eight matches before the final, having restricted the opposition to under 200 seven times. When they did bat first, against Moorsholm in the regional phase, they lost, but went through after their opponents were found to have fielded six ineligible players. At Lord's, they had fantastic travelling support from a conspicuous group calling themselves "Benidorm Corner", the name they give to a suntrap at their home ground, which is apparently as hot as the Costa Blanca coast.

While they had been trying to reach the Lord's final for more than four decades, Liphook & Ripsley, from Hampshire, managed it at the second attempt. They entered in 2017 after the decision to extend the population limit for competing villages beyond 5,000. Liphook lies on the border with West Sussex, with the cricket club based two miles south at Ripsley Park.

Apart from a seven-run win in the first round, they were dominant until the final. Ryan Covey scored 431 runs and took 13 wickets, while George Neave, 19, sparkled with a couple of match-winning fifties. But Liphook's league form plummeted as the summer wore on: by the time of the final they had lost eight in a row, and were relegated. This may have explained their twitchy batting display at Lord's.

This was the most open competition in years, with no previous winners among the 32 teams in the national rounds (so it was a shame it attracted no headline sponsor). Fillongley, from north Warwickshire, suffered their third semi-final defeat, despite the efforts of all-rounder Ahsan "Waqar" Sayed – 277 runs and 13 wickets, including a match-clinching hat-trick in the quarters against Pelsall, from the West Midlands. Falkland, from Fife, reached the last eight for the first time.

The unofficial player of the tournament was James Watson, who hit 500 runs in six innings, including three hundreds, for quarter-finalists Worlington, from Suffolk. Mayfield, of Sussex, who reached the last four, had the leading wicket-taker; left-arm spinner James Allen with 17.

Elsewhere, there were more uneven performances. During the match against Borstal in the Kent section, a Sibton Park seamer began his spell with seven consecutive wides and a no-ball. After being told to switch to off-spin, he took a wicket with his first legal delivery: a long hop which the batsman slapped straight back to him.

FINAL

FOLKTON & FLIXTON v LIPHOOK & RIPSLEY

At Lord's, September 16. Folkton & Flixton won by 72 runs. Toss: Liphook & Ripsley.

Liphook captain Charles Janczur admitted his batsman had suffered stage fright in front of a lively crowd of almost 2,000, but said it was still "the best defeat we've ever had". Cool heads were needed to chase a gettable 199 under clear skies, but Liphook's batting was frenetic. They reached 39 for one in the sixth over, before a succession of batsmen fell to injudicious shots. Only Ryan Covey, caught behind off a beauty from Connor Stephenson, was blameless. Any prospect of a mid-innings recovery was snuffed out by off-spinner Tom Norman's excellent spell, which included two wickets in his first two overs. A comfortable victory had appeared unlikely when Folkton & Flixton were put in under overcast skies, on a pitch tinged with green. They were up against it when captain Will Norman was brilliantly caught at gully by Suman Ganguly to make it 59 for four. But Will Hutchinson and Matthew Nesfield dug in to add 85. Harry Walmsley then hammered 35 from 17 balls, all but three in boundaries, including a straight-drive into the Pavilion for the only six of the day.

Man of the Match: M. Nesfield.

Folkton & Flixton

R. F. Malthouse b Janczur	8	J. Nesfield not out		2
S. J. Stocks b Janczur	1	J. Hatton not out		1
T. H. R. Norman c Nicklin b Neave	19			
W. Hutchinson b Neave	48	Lb 4, w 15, nb 1		20
*W. J. M. Norman c Ganguly b Neave	2			
M. Nesfield b Ganguly	60	1/10 (2) 2/19 (1)	(8 wkts, 40 overs)	198
H. L. Walmsley lbw b Ganguly	35	3/57 (3) 4/59 (5)		
C. Stephenson lbw b Covey	2	5/144 (4) 6/174 (6) 7/185 (8) 8/197 (7)		

†M. J. Ward did not bat.

Ganguly 8–1–37–2; Janczur 8–1–19–2; Covey 8–0–39–1; Neave 8–0–39–3; Elliott 5–0–30–0; Burton 3–0–30–0.

Liphook & Ripsley

R. J. Covey c Ward b Stephenson	9	S. A. A. Burton c Malthouse b Walmsley		4
R. C. Nicklin c Malthouse b Hatton	7	*C. F. Janczur c Hatton b Walmsley		14
H. P. Munt lbw b Stephenson	19	D. Elliott not out		1
S. S. Ganguly b T. H. R. Norman	16	B 2, lb 6, w 21		29
G. J. Neave c Hutchinson b Stephenson	0			
†G. D. Rouse c Malthouse b T. H. R. Norman	25	1/17 (1) 2/39 (2) 3/55 (3)	(29.3 overs)	126
J. R. Pryce lbw b T. H. R. Norman	0	4/55 (5) 5/75 (4) 6/77 (7)		
R. L. Williams lbw b Malthouse	2	7/99 (6) 8/99 (8) 9/112 (9) 10/126 (10)		

Stephenson 6–0–33–3; J. Nesfield 3–0–29–0; Hatton 3–0–19–1; T. H. R. Norman 8–2–18–3; Malthouse 8–2–18–1; Walmsley 1.3–0–1–2.

Umpires: T. F. Boston and N. P. Crickmore.

DISABILITY CRICKET IN 2018

P A U L   E D W A R D S

Pakistan and Bangladesh were the visitors in the summer for a Twenty20 tri-series against the England Physical Disability side. It was a tremendous success and, although England lost to Pakistan in the final, they were rewarded with the emergence of some exciting new talent: four players, all under 20, were given their first international chance. Ian Martin, the ECB's head of disability cricket, said: "For me, it's been about the standard of cricket, and how all three teams have developed since the last time they played, in Dubai in 2016."

On the opening day at Malvern, England lost to an impressive Pakistan by a resounding 78 runs, but then overcame Bangladesh by eight wickets. Alex Hammond anchored a pursuit of 195 with an unbeaten 81, after opening partner Liam Thomas had rattled off 57 from 25 balls. Debutant Liam O'Brien, a 19-year-old from Sussex who had made 60 against Pakistan, took two for 31.

The third day of the competition, at Old Elizabethans, Worcester, turned into a nailbiter for England after they lost to Bangladesh on the second. They beat Pakistan by six wickets with 15 balls to spare thanks to an unbeaten 64 from Callum Flynn. But they had to wait anxiously as Bangladesh came within four runs of a shock victory over Pakistan that would have denied them a place in the final. There, however, Pakistan were back to their dominant best, making 198 for seven, before reducing England to 42 for six. O'Brien ensured they went down fighting, with a sparkling 75 off 40 balls, but could not prevent a 45-run defeat.

In the tournament's finale, England beat a combined Pakistan–Bangladesh XI by 22 runs at New Road, a match played before Worcestershire's T20 Blast game against Northamptonshire. O'Brien's two fifties and six wickets in the competition earned him the Lord's Taverners Disabled Cricketer of the Year award, presented at the Cricket Writers' Club lunch in October. He had played for Sussex at age-group levels through his teens, but a lack of mobility cost him a place at their Academy. He was found to have bilateral talipes, often described as club foot, but his ambitions were revived when he was introduced to the disabled game. "He's probably been the stand-out performer for us in this tournament," said England Physical Disability head coach Ian Salisbury. "He's taken fantastic catches, he's scored runs at the hardest time and he's taken the most wickets."

Later in the year, there was a further reminder that the power in the game now lies on the subcontinent. After a young England Visually Impaired team had lost to the hosts India and Sri Lanka in a Twenty20 tri-series in October, captain Ed Hossell marvelled at the size of Indian crowds watching disability cricket. He was in no doubt that they had been beaten by the best team in the world. Preferring to focus on the T20 format, England had not taken part in the 50-over World Cup earlier in the year, when India beat Pakistan by two wickets in the final. Hossell took comfort from his team's showing, and his leadership was widely praised.

Nathan Stirk, ECB/Getty Images

Clean strike: Liam O'Brien, England's discovery of the summer, goes on the attack against Pakistan during the Physical Disability tri-series.

However, no one did more for the standing of the game in 2018 than Dan Bowser and Chris Edwards, of the England Learning Disability team. At the end of a match against an able-bodied Netherlands Under-17 side, England looked to have clinched a seven-run win, when an appeal for a catch behind off Alex Jervis was upheld. But Bowser, at first slip, was convinced the last man's bat had hit the ground, not the ball, and told Edwards, his captain, who withdrew the appeal.

England quickly took the last wicket to win by three runs, but their gesture did not go unnoticed, and later they were named as joint-winners of the Christopher Martin-Jenkins Spirit of Cricket Award. They were nominated by Mark Costin, their team's assistant coach. "I would go so far as to say that it is the best thing I have ever seen on a cricket field, and I certainly have never seen such a courageous sporting gesture," he said. There was also praise from MCC president Lord MacLaurin: "Dan and Chris have shown not only outstanding sportsmanship, but also superb character and judgment, and they are worthy winners of the CMJ Award."

The year ended with more good news, when Richard Hill, the ECB's disability cricket support officer, received an MBE in the New Year Honours list, in recognition of his service to the disabled game. Over more than 25 years, Hill has overseen the growth of disabled county cricket from 12 teams to more than 30, and has introduced clock cricket to care homes, in addition to trialling a wheelchair-only form of the game.

SENIOR CRICKET

At the end of three nip-and-tuck encounters, the England–Australia Over-70s one-day series came down to the last ball, with Australia needing four to tie, five to win. Colin Cooke launched a huge straight-drive off Barry Hart, which looked to be sailing for six, but instead landed in the upstretched hands of substitute fielder Stuart Bulger at long-on. England had sneaked home 2–1, revenge for a 3–0 whitewash on their tour of Australia in February and March. In extremely hot conditions, they had been soundly beaten in the internationals, but had three victories over provincial sides.

Australia arrived for their reciprocal visit in August, and won their first three matches comfortably, before losing by one run to a Chairman's XI. In the first ODI at Banbury, they recovered from a poor start thanks to a patient 43 from Vietnam veteran Stirling Hamman, who put on 57 with Alan Reid. With seven overs to go, they were 160 for six, before late-order hitting lifted them to 205 for seven. England were 26 for three after a testing opening spell by Ron Kasputtis. But the innings was rebuilt by Malcolm Wright and Hart, who added 61, then by the Sussex pair Peter Crees and wicketkeeper-batsman Martin Burgess, who added 79. Needing 32 from seven overs, England were favourites, but it came down to the last pair requiring 13 from three – and they finished five short.

At Horsham, opener Andy Barnes hit a superbly paced hundred to set England up for a series-levelling win. He put on 163 for the first wicket with captain Mike Swain, cashing in on an uncharacteristically sloppy Australian fielding performance. Barnes enjoyed a second profitable stand, with the belligerent Chris Swadkin, before retiring for 116. But Swadkin punished a tiring attack to make an undefeated 62 off 40 balls, as England reached 271.

That seemed plenty, but Australia raced to 50 in nine overs, and it needed Hart and Colin Breed, bowling in tandem, to put the brakes on. Thanks to some excellent fielding – including three stumpings by Burgess – England picked up wickets regularly, and won by 22 runs.

The decider at Sutton was played on a green pitch which, after heavy rain, tempted Australian captain Ian Petherick to bowl. It seemed like the wrong call when England reached 71 without loss after 20. They then accelerated gradually, and reached a challenging 251 for six.

Led by an outstanding innings from Petherick, Australia bustled along at a run a ball and, with wickets in hand, looked poised to steal the series. England clawed their way back but, when Petherick took 13 off the penultimate over, the odds favoured Australia again. Instead, Hart bowled a cool final over, and had Petherick caught at short midwicket off the third ball. That set the scene for Bulger's boundary heroics.

The focus will be on the England Under-60s in 2019, with visits from Australia and Pakistan. England will tour Australia in November.

Winners of the age-group competitions – Over-50 Championship **Yorkshire**. Over-60s **Lancashire**. Over-70s **Kent**.

ENGLAND UNDER-19 v SOUTH AFRICA UNDER-19 IN 2018

STEVEN LYNCH

Under-19 Tests (2): England 2, South Africa 0
Under-19 one-day internationals (3): England 0, South Africa 2

For England, the omens were unpromising. They had not won an Under-19 Test for more than five years and, already without several players on county duty in the Vitality Blast, were forced to change their captain after a late injury. And yet they won both Tests with a day to spare.

The standout performance came from a stand-in: Tom Banton took over the captaincy when his Somerset team-mate Tom Lammonby was injured, and crunched 137 to turn the tide in the First Test at Scarborough. Lammonby had missed the Under-19 World Cup in New Zealand in January 2018 with a hand injury; now he pulled out with a stress fracture of the heel. Banton's hundred helped England end a run of 11 Under-19 Tests without a victory, but others also came up trumps. Jack Plom of Essex took seven wickets in the First Test, while his new-ball partner, Worcestershire's Adam Finch, grabbed eight in the Second, when South Africa were dismantled for 90.

England's coach Jon Lewis had encouraged several players – including Harry Brook, Henry Brookes, Will Jacks, Dillon Pennington and Jamie Smith – to turn out in the T20 Blast, which allowed some precocious talent to surface here. Luke Hollman, a tall leg-spinning all-rounder from Middlesex, was one of five players in the squad aged 17 or under, and was highly praised by Lewis after the First Test.

It was a different story in the 50-over matches. South Africa won the first two comfortably, before the third was washed out. Jonathan Bird, an aggressive left-hander from Western Province, followed 51 in the first match with an unbeaten 142. The captain, Wandile Makwetu, made up for an indifferent Test series with scores of 36 and 53. And Thando Ntini bowled with pace reminiscent of his father, Makhaya, taking four wickets as England slumped at Riverside. For the hosts, an opening stand of 124 in the second game between two of their 17-year-olds, Jack Haynes and Ben Charlesworth, was another gleam of hope for the future.

SQUADS

England   *T. Banton (Somerset; T/50), L. Banks (Warwickshire; T/50), B. G. Charlesworth (Gloucestershire; T/50), S. Conners (Derbyshire; T/50), J. D. Cook (Nottinghamshire; 50), J. L. B. Davies (Middlesex; T/50), A. W. Finch (Worcestershire; T/50), A. F. Gleadall (Derbyshire; T/50), Hamidullah Qadri (Derbyshire; T), J. A. Haynes (Worcestershire; T/50), L. B. K. Hollman (Middlesex; T/50), N. J. H. Kimber (Nottinghamshire; 50), G. I. D. Lavelle (Lancashire; T), J. H. Plom (Essex; T/50), O. G. Robinson (Kent; T/50), H. D. Ward (Sussex; T/50). *Coach:* J. Lewis.

South Africa   *W. K. Makwetu (T/50), J. A. Bird (50), C. Campher (50), A. Cloete (T/50), J. P. de Klerk (T/50), J. F. du Plessis (T/50), J. Goncalves-Jardine (T), M. Khumalo (T/ 50), T. Khumalo (T/50), J. Miltz (T), K. Molefe (T/50), J. Niemand (T/50), M. Ntini (T/50), G. G. Peters (T/50), S. Qeshile (T/50), J. M. Richards (T/50), L. F. van Schalkwyk (T/50). *Coach:* L. Mahatlane.

ENGLAND v SOUTH AFRICA

First Under-19 Test

At Scarborough, July 8–10. England won by nine wickets. Toss: South Africa.

England began with a convincing three-day victory, set up by a superb innings from their captain, Tom Banton, who made the most of being dropped early on. His 137, which included 23 fours and two sixes, followed by 45 from No. 8 Luke Hollman, stretched England's lead to 73, after Hollman, a lanky leg-spinner, had taken four wickets to restrict South Africa to 232. Their innings owed much to adhesive half-centuries from Jacob Miltz and Jade de Klerk (53 in three hours). Led by the Essex seamer Jack Plom, England's bowlers made decisive inroads on the third morning, as South Africa declined to 81 for six. They almost doubled the score, but a target of 89 held few terrors for England. Fittingly, Banton was in at the end after openers Ben Charlesworth and Ollie Robinson crashed 69 inside eight overs. It was England's first victory in an Under-19 Test since January 2013 at Cape Town.

Close of play: first day, England Under-19 46-1 (Charlesworth 8, Banton 29); second day, South Africa Under-19 24-0 (Richards 9, Miltz 5).

South Africa Under-19

J. M. Richards c Davies b Plom	8	– run out (Banton)	19
T. Khumalo b Finch	2	– run out (Robinson)	12
J. Miltz lbw b Hollman	61	– c Gleadall b Plom	7
S. Qeshile lbw b Gleadall	15	– c sub (G. I. D. Lavelle) b Plom	9
*W. K. Makwetu c Robinson b Ward	4	– b Haynes b Hollman	17
†J. F. du Plessis lbw b Hollman	9	– c Davies b Gleadall	6
J. P. de Klerk b Plom	53	– c Hollman b Plom	18
A. Cloete c Gleadall b Hollman	29	– lbw b Plom	26
M. Khumalo st Davies b Hollman	0	– b Hollman	23
J. Goncalves-Jardine not out	33	– not out	8
G. G. Peters c Haynes b Plom	0	– c Haynes b Gleadall	0
B 6, lb 6, nb 6	18	B 4, lb 7, w 2, nb 3	16

1/12 (1) 2/26 (2) 3/77 (4)   (84.3 overs) 232   1/36 (1) 2/40 (3)   (62.5 overs) 161
4/87 (5) 5/97 (6) 6/121 (3)   3/53 (4) 4/62 (2)
7/169 (8) 8/178 (9) 9/227 (7) 10/232 (11)   5/73 (6) 6/81 (5) 7/116 (7)
                                          8/135 (8) 9/155 (9) 10/161 (11)

In the second innings T. Khumalo, when 9, retired hurt at 11-0 and resumed at 53-3.

Plom 14.3–3–45–3; Finch 15–4–41–1; Gleadall 15–3–47–1; Charlesworth 2–0–22–0; Hollman 25–5–39–4; Ward 13–2–26–1. *Second innings*—Plom 20–5–56–4; Finch 12–3–32–0; Hollman 22–9–30–2; Gleadall 7.5–0–24–2; Ward 1–0–8–0.

England Under-19

B. G. Charlesworth c Miltz b Goncalves-Jardine	8	– not out	41
L. Banks c Richards b Cloete	4		
*T. Banton c Richards b Peters	137	– not out	9
J. A. Haynes lbw b Peters	16		
O. G. Robinson c du Plessis b M. Khumalo	8	– (2) c du Plessis b M. Khumalo	34
H. D. Ward b Cloete	7		
†J. L. Davies lbw b Peters	26		
L. B. K. Hollman run out (sub J. Niemand)	45		
A. F. Gleadall c du Plessis b de Klerk	1		
A. W. Finch lbw b Peters	12		
J. H. Plom not out	1		
B 16, lb 3, nb 21	40	B 1, w 1, nb 3	5

1/8 (2) 2/46 (1) 3/93 (4)   (78 overs) 305   1/69 (2)   (1 wkt, 13.2 overs) 89
4/107 (5) 5/150 (6) 6/231 (7)
7/240 (3) 8/246 (9) 9/294 (10) 10/305 (8)

Cloete 13–1–53–2; Goncalves-Jardine 6–1–27–1; Peters 19–2–76–4; de Klerk 22–2–74–1; M. Khumalo 17–1–54–1; Richards 1–0–2–0. *Second innings*—Cloete 4–0–21–0; Peters 3–1–21–0; de Klerk 3–0–29–0; M. Khumalo 3.2–2–0–17–1.

Umpires: M. Burns and D. J. Millns.

ENGLAND v SOUTH AFRICA

Second Under-19 Test

At Chester-le-Street, July 16–18. England won by four wickets. Toss: South Africa.

A low-scoring match finished on a hectic third day, when 17 wickets went down. That included all ten in South Africa's second innings as they crashed to 90, and England completed a 2–0 series triumph. No one made a half-century in the match, although Sinethemba Qeshile and de Klerk hit 47 apiece on the first day, as a South African side showing four changes recovered from 20 for three to inch past 200. England's new-ball pair, Plom and Finch, did most of the damage. England struggled in turn: all out for 133, and a top score of just 28, by 17-year-old Jack Haynes. South Africa resumed with a lead of 76, but were derailed by a hat-trick of sorts in the ninth over. Josh Richards was bowled middle stump, and Louis van Schalkwyk run out first ball, trying a sharp single. Then Wandile Makwetu, South Africa's captain, feathered a catch to keeper Jack Davies. Finch joined in, chopping off the tail to finish with match figures of eight for 69. Needing just 167, England lost both openers by the third over. Banton went on the offensive, taking 17 off a Gideon Peters over before falling for 34 from 36 balls, trying to reverse-sweep slow left-armer Kgaudisa Molefe. But Banton had put his side on the front foot and, despite a wobble at 104 for five, a gritty partnership of 50 between Harrison Ward and Davies took England to the brink.

Close of play: first day, South Africa Under-19 118-5 (Niemand 8, de Klerk 1); second day, England Under-19 121-9 (Finch 5, Connors 1).

South Africa Under-19

J. M. Richards c Lavelle b Finch	7	– b Plom		11
J. Miltz c Haynes b Finch	2	– c Davies b Conners		11
L. F. van Schalkwyk c Davies b Plom	4	– run out (Plom)		0
*W. K. Makwetu lbw b Hollman	36	– c Davies b Plom		0
†S. Qeshile c Davies b Plom	47	– lbw b Ward		14
J. Niemand lbw b Plom	10	– lbw b Conners		14
J. P. de Klerk lbw b Finch	47	– c Lavelle b Finch		16
M. Ntini c Haynes b Charlesworth	2	– c Davies b Finch		4
M. Khumalo c Davies b Finch	0	– lbw b Finch		6
K. Molefe c Charlesworth b Hollman	21	– b Finch		0
G. G. Peters not out	1	– not out		1
B 12, lb 6, w 7, nb 7	32	B 7, lb 1, nb 5		13

1/7 (1) 2/12 (3) 3/20 (2)   (75.2 overs) 209   1/30 (1) 2/30 (3)   (36.4 overs) 90
4/83 (4) 5/108 (5) 6/124 (6)   3/30 (4) 4/35 (2)
7/143 (8) 8/151 (9) 9/208 (10) 10/209 (7)   5/51 (5) 6/72 (6) 7/82 (7)
                                         8/88 (8) 9/89 (9) 10/90 (10)

Plom 19–6–44–3; Finch 21.2–6–47–4; Charlesworth 11–3–26–1; Conners 5–0–32–0; Hollman 16–4–28–2; Ward 3–0–14–0. *Second innings*—Plom 10.3–3–25–2; Finch 8.4–0–22–4; Conners 10–2–20–2; Hollman 6–1–12–0; Ward 2–1–3–1.

England Under-19

B. G. Charlesworth lbw b Molefe	24	– c Qeshile b Peters	4
O. G. Robinson lbw b Ntini	1	– b Ntini	0
*T. Banton c Qeshile b Ntini	0	– lbw b Molefe	34
J. A. Haynes c Qeshile b Peters	28	– c Miltz b Khumalo	27
G. I. D. Lavelle lbw b Molefe	0	– c Miltz b Khumalo	25
H. D. Ward st Qeshile b Molefe	7	– c Miltz b Peters	27
†J. L. Davies c van Schalkwyk b de Klerk	17	– not out	32
L. B. K. Hollman c van Schalkwyk b Khumalo	25	– not out	11
A. W. Finch not out	16		
J. H. Plom b de Klerk	4		
S. Conners c van Schalkwyk b Peters	2		
Lb 7, w 1, nb 1	9	B 8, lb 2	10

1/6 (2) 2/6 (3) 3/38 (1)   (65.3 overs) 133   1/4 (2)   (6 wkts, 49.1 overs) 170
4/40 (5) 5/58 (6) 6/67 (4)   2/4 (1) 3/65 (3)
7/103 (8) 8/111 (7) 9/117 (10) 10/133 (11)   4/77 (4) 5/104 (5) 6/154 (6)

Peters 13.3–3–33–2; Ntini 10–5–18–2; Khumalo 8–1–24–1; Molefe 21–10–33–3; Niemand 2–0–9–0; de Klerk 11–7–9–2. *Second innings*—Peters 13–2–57–2; Ntini 11–2–42–2; Molefe 13.1–4–35–1; Khumalo 5–0–16–1; de Klerk 7–2–10–0.

Umpires: S. J. O'Shaughnessy and M. J. Saggers.

First Under-19 one-day international At Chester-le-Street, July 23. **South Africa won by 79 runs. South Africa** 229-9 (50 overs) (J. A. Bird 51; J. D. Cook 4-30); ‡**England** 150 (39.4 overs) (O. G. Robinson 54; M. Ntini 4-19). *MoM:* M. Ntini. *A disastrous start – 6-3 after three overs, and soon 43-5 – meant England were never on terms, despite Ollie Robinson's 54. Much of the damage was done by Thando Ntini, the son of former Test fast bowler Makhaya, who removed Ben Charlesworth with his first delivery and added three more cheap scalps. South Africa's total had owed much to the two newcomers to their squad after the Test series: Jonathan Bird clipped 51 from 47 balls, while Curtis Campher made 43* from 55 at No. 8. Nottinghamshire off-spinner Jordan Cook claimed four wickets.*

Second Under-19 one-day international At Gosforth (South Northumberland CC), July 26. **South Africa won by six wickets.** ‡**England** 251 (50 overs) (J. A. Haynes 74; L. F. van Schalkwyk 5-32); **South Africa** 255-4 (42 overs) (J. A. Bird 142*; W. K. Makwetu 53). *MoM:* J. A. Bird. *An opening stand of 124 in 28.5 overs between Jack Haynes and Charlesworth underpinned a better England batting performance, although five wickets for Louis van Schalkwyk's off-breaks restricted the late search for runs. Bird then put the total in perspective with a superb 142*, from 123 balls with 14 fours and a six; he and skipper Wandile Makwetu put on 129 for the fourth wicket in 20 overs to ensure a series-clinching victory with time to spare.*

Third Under-19 one-day international At Scarborough, July 29. **England v South Africa. Abandoned.** *South Africa took the 50-over series 2–0 after a washout.*

YOUTH CRICKET IN 2018

No one could accuse them of lacking ambition. In September, the ECB and the ICC unveiled a joint initiative to use the 2019 World Cup to introduce more than a million under-12s to cricket, some of them pre-school. The bid to ensure that the most was made of the opportunity is well and truly on.

At the centre of the plan is the Cricket World Cup Schools Programme. Launched in conjunction with Chance to Shine, the idea is to involve more than 700,000 children at 8,000 primary schools in cricket activities. Teachers have been invited to sign up to an online portal which has ideas for cricket-based lessons. But it is not centred on the classroom: schools will also be encouraged to organise World Cup Kwik Cricket competitions.

The scheme was launched at Lord's by England captain Heather Knight, all-rounder David Willey and former international players Isa Guha and Graeme Swann. As well as throwing balls around, they tried out one of the classroom sessions with local schoolchildren. Steve Elworthy, ICC's managing director of the World Cup, said: "We hope to be giving young people a chance to be part of sporting history."

There were three other parts to the strategy. Small grants have been made available to encourage clubs to become more family-friendly and diverse. It is hoped that 3,000 will stage World Cup-related events to coincide with the second weekend of the tournament, when matches include England v Bangladesh and India v Australia. There will be an expansion of the All Stars programme, now in its third year, and a World Cup theme to the activities. There will also be a concerted marketing initiative – in and away from grounds – to attract new fans to the sport.

ECB chief executive Tom Harrison said: "We must turn the excitement of a World Cup on home soil into a guaranteed route to draw more players and volunteers to recreational cricket."

The ECB aim to tap into the progress already made by the success of the All Stars programme. Testament to its impact was provided by Samantha Arnold, a teacher at Langley Primary School in Staffordshire. "We have had many more children taking part in activities, and many more children taking part in PE," she said. "It's really helped with their teamwork and working with each other."

Another board initiative unveiled during 2018 was the South Asian Action Plan, aimed at engaging those communities, and drawing more people into cricket, as well as forging closer links with existing lovers of the game. Children form an important part of the strategy: Chance to Shine hope to deliver cricket sessions to 6,000 primary schools in deprived urban areas.

Winners of age group competitions
Under-17 County Championship **Yorkshire**. Under-17 County Cup **Essex.** Under-17 Women's County Cup **Lancashire**. Under-15 County Cup **Yorkshire**. Under-15 Bunbury Festival **South & West**. Under-15 Women's County Cup **Yorkshire**. Under-15 Women's Twenty20 **Yorkshire**.

THE 2018 ECB DAVID ENGLISH BUNBURY FESTIVAL

In its 32nd year, there was a change of title for the Bunbury Festival, with the addition of its founder's name. But there was no slackening of its reputation as a hothouse of the country's best Under-15 talent. A second, more fundamental, change came when the ECB took over the event from the English Schools Cricket Association, incorporating it into their player pathway programme. But David Graveney, the ECB national performance manager and festival director, said: "We must keep the fun element that David English worked so hard to create."

On superb wickets at Millfield, there was a resurgence for the South & West, who had lost all three 50-over matches in 2017. After defeat in their first match, they pipped the Midlands to the 50-over title on net run-rate, and triumphed in the T20 competition. In South & West's lone defeat, Midlands' Anoop Chima and James Cronie made fifties to set up a total of 238. South & West appeared to have the chase under control, until all-rounder Jacob Bethell's left-arm spin grabbed three for 38, including a superb return catch to dismiss Alex Horton. In the other first-day match, the North beat London & East by seven wickets. Atharva Prasad, the London & East captain, hit the week's first hundred, but the North's spinners kept control, and solid batting saw them home with five overs to spare.

South & West soon shook off their disappointment. On the second day, they strolled to victory over the North. James Coles was the pick of their bowlers with four for 27. George Langston then hit an unbeaten 53 in a straightforward chase. The Midlands batted poorly in the other match, with the exception of 51 from Bethell. But Prasad was once again in terrific form, hitting 89 as London & East eased home by nine wickets.

The 50-over competition was intriguingly poised at the start of the final day. The Midlands produced a thumping 113-run win over the North, as Bethell – a year younger than most – made sure of the Player of the Tournament award. First, he hit 111 off 149 balls, while excellent contributions from Chima and Cronie took the Midlands to an imposing 321 for five. Then he took four for 28 as the North slumped to 208. South & West also won in commanding fashion, and scored swiftly enough to pinch the title. Hamdi Saleem took three for 37 as they bowled out London & East for 169. Will Naish's 84 and Langston's 66 not out gobbled up the target in 21.2 overs.

In the T20 semi-finals on the third day, South & West's bowlers were again outstanding, before Naish made a quick 56 as they passed the North's 188 in the 16th over. London & East joined them in the final after Nathan Khelawon's 56 not out saw off the Midlands. Rain marred the final: South & West made 139, then reduced London & East to 35 for five. They were in no position to chase a revised target.

The best players met up again at Loughborough later in August for matches in both formats. A combined South & West/London & East XI beat the Midlands/North in two tight contests.

SCHOOLS CRICKET IN 2018

REVIEW BY DOUGLAS HENDERSON

After the hottest and driest summer since 1976, it was hard to recall the wet start. Matches were called off days in advance, and the first two rounds of the National T20 Cup were ravaged. It might have turned into a glorious summer for schools cricket, had not the pressure of exams grown unbearable. The impression was that, though schools understandably pushed their students to work hard, it was in fact parents who drove the agenda. At one school, a senior master refused to let his son play, or even practise, for the first XI during the five-week GCSE period. Elsewhere, a cricket master, when asked whether parents were incensed at paying vast fees for a summer term which barely existed, said complaints only arose when he insisted pupils play matches. Many schools reported it was almost impossible to field their best XI. This, surely, is madness – though whether anyone is prepared to stop it is unclear. Another cricket master spoke for most, perhaps, when he wrote: "The season was as short as usual, and marred by other school withdrawals and exam disruption. But we soldier on in the hope that someone will save schools cricket one day!"

The last word goes to David Elstone, chairman of the school sports committee of the HMC (the body representing many of the UK's independent schools):

> It's a real crisis for the future of cricket in this country. Many cricketing schools in the north of England are now only playing 20-over matches – or 35 if they're lucky – even for Saturday fixtures. The all-day game, whether 50-over or declaration, is seriously threatened. There is pressure, from parents, and increasingly from pupils themselves, to play shorter games because of their busy social lives and their belief that they cannot spare time from their academic studies and examination preparation in the summer. They seem to want to reduce cricket to something more like a game of tiddlywinks!

The fine weather produced true pitches and plenty of runs. Eight players reached 1,000, while two, both from Sedbergh, came painfully close: George Hill made 999 and Sam Barrett 993. Leading the way was Jack Haynes of Malvern, who struck a magnificent 1,393, though he did have the advantage of 25 innings, rather more than most. The others to make four figures were Nathan Tilley (Reed's), Joshua Smith (Kimbolton), Ben Charlesworth (St Edward's), Ben Chapman-Lilley (Repton), Sanjay Patel (KCS Wimbledon), Jack Redman (Denstone) and Will Rigg (Solihull). As well as the Sedbergh pair, Simon Fernandes (Oundle), Henrique Pieterse (Queen's, Taunton), Sami Shori (Tiffin), and Tawanda Muyeye (Eastbourne) all passed 900.

Tilley was alone in averaging over 100 – he managed a Herculean 139 – though the unlucky Hill came within a whisker. Not far behind were Alex Oxley (Culford) and Fernandes, who both made it into the nineties.

Of the bowlers, Charterhouse's Prince Singh was comfortably the leading wicket-taker. He collected 58 with his genuine pace, including a return of five for ten, and also made a useful 483 runs at 23. Four other bowlers finished with 40 victims: Singh's colleague at Charterhouse, Aman Mahtani, Shrewsbury's Will Sissons, Alex Rennie of Bedford, and Jamie Curtis, from St Edward's. Ben Sutton (RGS Worcester) and Jack Grant (Dauntsey's) took 39.

Twenty-one bowlers with ten or more wickets also averaged ten or less. James Amos, from Rossall, Ellesmere's Harry Newton, Tom Bouttell from The Glasgow Academy, Ben Mills (St Edmund's) and William Atkinson, from Hymer's, all averaged under eight.

Selecting all-rounders is a less precise art, but those to marry success in both disciplines include Josh Lawrenson (Victoria College, Jersey), Harrison Ward from St Edward's, Josh de Caires of St Albans, Aaron Amin (Merchant Taylors', Northwood), Sedbergh's Sam Barrett and Winchester's Johnny Figy.

The National Schools T20 competition, nine years in its current format, endured a miserable start, with the early rounds widely rained off. But the weather relented, and a new name made their first appearance at Arundel for

---

WISDEN SCHOOLS CRICKETERS OF THE YEAR

2007	Jonathan Bairstow...................	St Peter's School, York
2008	James Taylor......................	Shrewsbury School
2009	Jos Buttler.......................	King's College, Taunton
2010	Will Vanderspar	Eton College
2011	Daniel Bell-Drummond..............	Millfield School
2012	Thomas Abell	Taunton School
2013	Tom Köhler-Cadmore................	Malvern College
2014	Dylan Budge	Woodhouse Grove
2015	Ben Waring.......................	Felsted School
2016	A. J. Woodland	St Edward's School, Oxford
2017	Teddie Casterton	RGS, High Wycombe
2018	**Nathan Tilley**....................	**Reed's School**

---

finals day. Charterhouse had enjoyed a fine season, thanks to their powerful bowling attack, led by Singh, and backed up by some excellent batting. But they lost in the final to Millfield, who proved unstoppable on the day. They prospered on the back of powerful contributions by Sam Young, Charlie Clist, Marcus Critchley and – above all – Tom Bevan, the captain, who crashed 53 not out from 29 balls. In the semi-finals, Sedbergh could not overcome Millfield, while Charterhouse were run close by Bedford.

Millfield, indeed, had the best season in terms of win-rate, followed by The Manchester Grammar School and Magdalen College School. Victoria College in Jersey – for whom arranging any fixtures is a logistical challenge – also triumphed in more than 80% of their games. Dollar were alone in recording an unbeaten season – a difficult task for those entering the National Schools T20, which is a knockout tournament. Other schools to make the 80% grade were Simon Langton Grammar and St Edmund's, both in Kent. Meanwhile, Mount Kelly, in Devon, won three-quarters of their matches. Neither they nor Simon Langton have a strong cricket tradition, and their success is especially welcome.

Surprisingly, no county has shown interest in the 2017 Wisden Schools Cricketer of the Year, Teddie Casterton, despite his 1,423 runs for RGS High

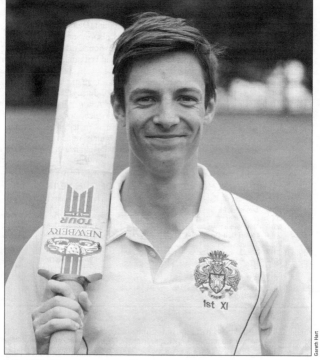

Gareth Hart

Nathan Tilley of Reed's School: the 12th Wisden Schools Cricketer of the Year.

Wycombe – more than any schoolboy in the last 20 years, perhaps ever. So much for the counties' scouting systems.

It is to be hoped that the 2018 winner, Nathan Tilley of Reed's, fares better. No great skill is needed to conclude he was the outstanding schools cricketer of the year, though Charterhouse's Singh deserves an honourable mention. Tilley has a voracious appetite for runs, and great stamina: in 2018, four of his six centuries reached 150. In his calmness at the crease and in his all-round game – his characteristic shots are a force through midwicket and a cover-drive – he reminded Malcolm Dunn, master in charge of cricket at Reed's, of Kane Williamson. Tilley possesses single-minded determination, and has worked industriously on playing the short ball, an area he felt required improvement. That determination is also a source of frustration to opponents aiming to get under his skin: he shuts out distractions and remains immune to sledging. A thoughtful captain, he is a fine slip fielder with large hands, and an ambidextrous bowler, able to mix up left-arm wrist-spin and right-arm seam.

Douglas Henderson is editor of Schools Cricket Online, where all schools reports from past Wisdens since 1887 can be browsed and searched.

MCC Schools v ESCA

At Lord's September 4. **ESCA won by 19 runs. ESCA 304-5** (50 overs) (J. M. de Caires 49, J. D. M. Evison 36, H. G. Duke 60*, L. Doneathy 113*); ‡**MCC Schools 285** (49 overs) (O. J. Price 60, E. A. Brookes 57; H. A. Sullivan 4-20).

ESCA *J. M. de Caires (*St Albans School*), H. T. Crocombe (*Bede's School*), R. J. Das (*Brentwood School*), L. Doneathy (*Prudhoe Community HS*), H. G. Duke (*QEGS, Wakefield*), J. D. M. Evison (*Stamford School*), F. E. H. Geffen (*Tonbridge School*), E. S. Kalley (*Barking Abbey School*), W. C. F. Smeed (*King's College, Taunton*), H. A. Sullivan (*Temple Moore Science College*), R. S. Wijeratne (*Harrow*).

MCC *E. N. Gay (*Bedford School*), B. J. Balmforth (*Huddersfield New College*), E. A. Brookes (*Solihull School*), J. J. Carson (*Hurstpierpoint College*), I. V. A. Dilkes (*St Lawrence College*), S. M. L. Fernandes (*Oundle School*), J. J. Figy (*Winchester College*), T. D. Gordon (*Bede's School*), A. E. King (*Stowe School*), O. J. Price (*Magdalen College School*), C. F. B. Scott (*St Albans School*).

The following tables cover only those schools listed in the Schools A–Z section.

SCHOOLS AVERAGES

BEST BATTING AVERAGE (5 completed innings)

		I	NO	Runs	HS	100	Avge
1	N. J. Tilley (*Reed's School*)	13	4	1,256	200	6	139.55
2	G. C. H. Hill (*Sedbergh School*)	19	9	999	125*	4	99.90
3	A. Oxley (*Culford School*)	13	6	691	109*	1	98.71
4	S. M. L. Fernandes (*Oundle School*)	15	5	947	181*	2	94.70
5	S. H. Patel (*King's College School, Wimbledon*)	18	6	1,074	118	5	89.50
6	R. M. Yates (*Warwick School*)	7	2	437	114*	1	87.40
7	J. J. Smith (*Kimbolton School*)	15	2	1,122	170	5	86.30
8	H. W. Pieterse (*Queen's College, Taunton*)	14	3	947	132	1	86.09
9	H. F. Houillon (*Sevenoaks School*)	9	4	416	129*	1	83.20
10	J. E. Nightingale (*Ratcliffe College*)	7	2	388	109	2	77.60
11	A. J. Eckland (*Millfield School*)	8	2	443	125	1	73.83
12	W. E. Rigg (*Solihull School*)	17	3	1,029	177	5	73.50
13	B. J. Chapman-Lilley (*Repton School*)	19	4	1,099	109	2	73.26
14	J. M. Cox (*Felsted School*)	16	5	793	167*	3	72.09
15	J. R. Jordan (*Dollar Academy*)	10	5	360	60*	0	72.00
16	E. B. Fluck (*Cheadle Hulme School*)	5	0	358	155	1	71.60
17	I. V. A. Dilkes (*St Lawrence College*)	13	2	775	163	2	70.45
18	W. E. L. Buttleman (*Felsted School*)	15	3	817	168*	3	68.08
19	S. Shori (*Tiffin School*)	16	2	939	145	1	67.07
20	J. A. Haynes (*Malvern College*)	25	4	1,393	177*	5	66.33
21	B. G. Charlesworth (*St Edward's School, Oxford*)	18	1	1,115	201	5	65.58
22	J. S. Hawkins (*Bishop's Stortford College*)	8	1	452	145	1	64.57
23	J. R. Redman (*Denstone College*)	21	5	1,033	103*	1	64.56
24	E. J. Fox (*Simon Langton GS*)	9	2	451	105*	2	64.42
25	A. Bassingthwaighte (*Bishop's Stortford College*)	7	2	322	81	0	64.40
26	J. J. Figy (*Winchester College*)	18	6	754	147*	3	62.83
27	J. A. D. Lawrenson (*Victoria College, Jersey*)	10	5	313	69*	0	62.60
28	O. T. Wright (*Portsmouth GS*)	6	0	373	149	1	62.16

		I	NO	Runs	HS	100	Avge
29	A. J. Neal (*Haileybury*)	13	2	680	97	0	61.81
30	T. J. Staveley-Parker (*Bloxham School*)	12	1	679	111*	1	61.72
31	B. J. J. Wells (*Monkton*)	12	2	611	103	1	61.10
32	T. Snell (*Ratcliffe College*)	13	1	724	99	0	60.33
33	O. G. F. Pooler (*Manchester GS*)	12	2	602	186	1	60.20

MOST RUNS

		I	NO	Runs	HS	100	Avge
1	J. A. Haynes (*Malvern College*)	25	4	1,393	177*	5	66.33
2	N. J. Tilley (*Reed's School*)	13	4	1,256	200	6	139.55
3	J. J. Smith (*Kimbolton School*)	15	2	1,122	170	5	86.30
4	B. G. Charlesworth (*St Edward's School, Oxford*)	18	1	1,115	201	5	65.58
5	B. J. Chapman-Lilley (*Repton School*)	19	4	1,099	109	2	73.26
6	S. H. Patel (*King's College School, Wimbledon*)	18	6	1,074	118	5	89.50
7	J. R. Redman (*Denstone College*)	21	5	1,033	103*	1	64.56
8	W. E. Rigg (*Solihull School*)	17	3	1,029	177	5	73.50
9	G. C. H. Hill (*Sedbergh School*)	19	9	999	125*	4	99.90
10	S. Barrett (*Sedbergh School*)	24	1	993	125	1	43.17
11	S. M. L. Fernandes (*Oundle School*)	15	5	947	181*	2	94.70
	H. W. Pieterse (*Queen's College, Taunton*)	14	3	947	132	1	86.09
13	S. Shori (*Tiffin School*)	16	2	939	145	1	67.07
14	T. S. Muyeye (*Eastbourne College*)	20	3	902	214*	2	53.05
15	H. D. Ward (*St Edward's School, Oxford*)	18	2	864	113	4	54.00
16	R. X. Clarke (*Shrewsbury School*)	21	1	845	126*	1	42.25
17	I. A. Malik (*Bradfield College*)	21	2	825	109*	2	43.42
18	W. E. L. Buttleman (*Felsted School*)	15	3	817	168*	3	68.08
19	C. J. Clist (*Millfield School*)	17	2	801	254*	1	53.40
20	J. M. Cox (*Felsted School*)	16	5	793	167*	3	72.09
21	J. Banton (*King's College, Taunton*)	17	2	786	116	2	52.40
22	P. A. Ades (*St Edward's School, Oxford*)	22	2	782	122	2	39.10
23	I. V. A. Dilkes (*St Lawrence College*)	13	2	775	163	2	70.45
24	J. H. Burslem (*Felsted School*)	19	2	774	136	2	45.52
25	R. N. Patel (*Dauntsey's School*)	18	3	773	105	1	51.53
26	M. G. Clarke (*Wellingborough School*)	16	3	768	129*	2	59.07
27	J. D. M. Evison (*Stamford School*)	15	2	760	100*	1	58.46
	R. A. J. Richardson (*Charterhouse*)	25	4	760	109*	1	36.19
29	J. J. Figy (*Winchester College*)	18	6	754	147*	3	62.83
30	D. W. Oldreive (*Gresham's School*)	17	2	751	151*	2	50.06

BEST BOWLING AVERAGE (10 wickets)

		O	M	R	W	BB	Avge
1	J. S. Amor (*Rossall School*)	30	12	69	12	7-10	5.75
2	H. Newton (*Ellesmere College*)	61	11	144	24	5-18	6.00
3	T. W. Bouttell (*The Glasgow Academy*)	29	7	78	11	3-3	7.09
4	B. C. Mills (*St Edmund's School, Canterbury*)	40.3	3	178	25	8-6	7.12
5	W. J. Atkinson (*Hymers College*)	34	8	117	16	6-10	7.31
6	Z. Jaftha (*Shebbear College*)	19.4	3	88	11	6-8	8.00
7	I. Philander (*Shebbear College*)	37	5	129	16	4-6	8.06
8	O. Norton (*Fettes College*)	18	1	83	10	4-31	8.30
9	J. A. D. Lawrenson (*Victoria College, Jersey*)	115	16	255	30	7-14	8.50
10	A. D. Hirani (*The John Lyon School*)	34.3	2	145	17	4-8	8.52
11	N. Aslam (*Dr Challoner's GS*)	39	4	155	18	4-9	8.61
12	C. J. Keatinge (*George Heriot's School*)	21	1	88	10	3-19	8.80
13	J. S. Cairns (*Dollar Academy*)	36	7	161	18	3-1	8.94
14	C. Hodges (*Aldenham School*)	16	1	90	10	6-56	9.00
15	D. J. Ahmed (*Queen Elizabeth's Hospital, Bristol*)	26.5	3	93	10	3-18	9.30
16	A. J. L. Khanna (*Eltham College*)	24.4	3	96	10	3-24	9.60
17	J. W. Dickenson (*Malvern College*)	27	3	108	11	4-14	9.81

		O	M	R	W	BB	Avge
18	N. Wolff (*Kirkham GS*)	32.2	4	109	11	5-18	9.90
19	A. C. Munro (*Newcastle under Lyme School*)	22.1	0	139	14	4-15	9.92
20	S. J. C. Ellis (*Ellesmere College*)	80	9	200	20	7-48	10.00
21	L. M. Theobald (*Prior Park College*)	22	1	110	11	4-19	10.00
22	K. B. Szymanski (*King's College, Taunton*)	80.1	15	252	25	5-23	10.08
23	A. D. Bhasin (*Hampton School*)	110	11	152	15	3-20	10.13
24	N. L. Ward (*Harvey GS, Folkestone*)	21	5	92	9	4-22	10.22
25	J. R. Clarke (*Wellingborough School*)	92	5	354	34	7-16	10.41
26	C. J. Creighton (*Shiplake College*)	63.1	9	282	27	4-36	10.44
27	M. E. Butler (*King's School, Rochester*)	28.3	1	106	10	4-34	10.60

MOST WICKETS

		O	M	R	W	BB	Avge
1	P. Singh (*Charterhouse*)	187	26	716	58	5-10	12.34
2	W. B. S. Sissons (*Shrewsbury School*)	112.3	5	526	40	4-7	13.15
	A. Mahtani (*Charterhouse*)	187	24	627	40	5-90	15.67
	A. I. Rennie (*Bedford School*)	224	30	677	40	6-6	16.92
	J. A. Curtis (*St Edward's School, Oxford*)	188.1	10	974	40	6-41	24.35
6	B. R. Sutton (*Royal GS, Worcester*)	167	34	615	39	5-22	15.76
	J. B. Grant (*Dauntsey's School*)	167.4	13	690	39	6-16	17.69
8	W. W. O. Middleton (*King's College, Taunton*)	130	12	506	37	6-21	13.67
	A. W. Garrett (*Shrewsbury School*)	169	23	625	37	4-19	16.89
10	C. W. Rogers (*Norwich School*)	105.3	11	530	36	5-50	14.72
11	F. J. Heldreich (*Framlingham College*)	143.4	21	501	35	7-34	14.31
	H. D. Ward (*St Edward's School, Oxford*)	159	26	543	35	7-35	15.51
13	J. R. Clarke (*Wellingborough School*)	92	7	354	34	7-16	10.41
	J. J. Figy (*Winchester College*)	181	22	536	34	5-35	15.76
15	T. N. S. Chesser (*Magdalen College School*)	112.5	17	367	33	4-13	11.12
	R. V. Parekh (*Lancaster Royal GS*)	120	23	372	33	6-15	11.27
	J. A. O'Callaghan (*Forest School*)	118	19	475	33	5-61	14.39
	K. K. Khanna (*Bradfield College*)	140.3	22	528	33	6-32	16.00
	T. S. Muyeye (*Eastbourne College*)	120.4	13	544	33	4-13	16.48
	J. M. de Caires (*St Albans School*)	131.3	14	597	33	6-7	18.09
	G. C. H. Barlow (*Charterhouse*)	174	24	636	33	4-10	19.27
	K. T. Peters (*Gresham's School*)	168.1	26	642	33	7-42	19.45
23	L. S. C. Brown (*Repton School*)	73	2	423	32	5-3	13.21
	O. B. G. Sheen (*Charterhouse*)	112	11	504	32	4-11	15.75
	L. R. Allen (*Royal GS, Worcester*)	148	16	642	32	5-28	20.06
	S. Barrett (*Sedbergh School*)	163.1	14	652	32	4-60	20.37
27	A. R. Amin (*Merchant Taylors', Northwood*)	102	10	384	31	5-15	12.38
28	J. A. D. Lawrenson (*Victoria College, Jersey*)	115	16	255	30	7-14	8.50
	S. White (*Monkton*)	104	10	399	30	4-20	13.30
	M. T. Roberts (*St Peter's School, York*)	103	12	443	30	4-29	14.76
	S. Swingwood (*Monmouth School*)	113.4	12	452	30	8-23	15.06
	J. R. Redman (*Denstone College*)	158	24	528	30	5-24	17.60
	W. A. J. Sharp (*Malvern College*)	130	15	545	30	5-23	18.16
	G. A. M. Freeman (*Christ's Hospital*)	124.3	12	576	30	7-61	19.20
	G. W. Griffiths (*Reed's School*)	171	21	600	30	6-43	20.00

OUTSTANDING SEASONS (minimum 7 matches)

	P	W	L	T	D	A	%W
Millfield School	18	16	2	0	0	1	88.88
The Manchester Grammar School	13	11	2	0	0	2	84.62
Magdalen College School	17	14	1	0	2	1	82.35
Victoria College, Jersey	16	13	3	0	0	0	81.25
Dollar Academy	15	12	0	0	3	3	80.00
Simon Langton Grammar School for Boys	15	12	2	0	1	0	80.00

	P	W	L	T	D	A	%W
St Edmund's School, Canterbury	10	8	2	0	0	0	80.00
Wellingborough School	19	15	2	0	2	1	78.95
Shrewsbury School	23	18	5	0	0	0	78.26
Bedford School	18	14	2	0	2	1	77.78
Durham School	17	13	3	0	1	1	76.47
Mount Kelly School	20	15	4	0	1	5	75.00
Sedbergh School	24	18	5	0	1	3	75.00
Oakham School	22	16	6	0	0	1	72.73
Shiplake College	18	13	4	0	1	0	72.22
Stowe School	18	13	4	0	1	1	72.22
Charterhouse	25	18	4	1	2	1	72.00
Berkhamsted School	14	10	3	0	1	4	71.43
Ratcliffe College	14	10	2	0	2	2	71.43
Eastbourne College	21	15	5	0	1	0	71.43
Tonbridge School	21	15	4	0	2	0	71.43
King's College, Taunton	20	14	6	0	0	0	70.00
Ellesmere College	10	7	3	0	0	0	70.00

SCHOOLS A–Z

In the results line, A = abandoned without a ball bowled. An asterisk indicates captain. The qualification for the averages (which now include Twenty20 games, but not overseas tour games) is 150 runs or ten wickets. Counties have been included for all schools. Since cricket does not follow the current complex system of administrative division, *Wisden* adheres to the county boundaries in existence before the dissolution of Middlesex in 1965. Those schools affected by the boundary changes of the last five decades – such as Eton College, which was removed from Buckinghamshire and handed to Berkshire – are listed under their former county.

Abingdon School *Berkshire*
P16 W4 L11 D1
Master i/c J. M. Golding	**Coach** Dr C. J. Burnand
Results were disappointing because of uncertain batting, though this improved as the season wore on. When the top order played with freedom, the team produced some irresistible cricket, and it was encouraging to see youngsters Thomas Owen and Freddie Smith demonstrate their talent.
Batting J. H. Coombs 186 at 31.00; F. E. H. Smith 402 at 26.80; M. E. M. Owen 344 at 22.93; J. A. T. Lawson 279 at 18.60; *O. J. Fountain 197 at 15.15.
Bowling S. H. C. Warren 13 at 18.15; O. J. Fountain 11 at 23.81; W. Webb 13 at 35.30.

Aldenham School *Hertfordshire*
P12 W6 L5 D1 A3
Master i/c L. J. Kirsten	**Coach** D. J. Goodchild
A promising first team won half their fixtures. Heman Hirani, Dan Travers and Louis Heap were the leading batsmen, while James Michelin, Prithvi Nakrani and Charlie Hodges all did well with the ball. Viren Patel looks a fine prospect.
Batting *H. Hirani 342 at 48.85; C. J. G. Eve-Raw 216 at 30.85; L. O. Heap 167 at 23.85; D. Travers 268 at 22.33.
Bowling C. Hodges 10 at 9.00; J. S. Michelin 13 at 19.30; P. Nakrani 11 at 23.72.

Alleyn's School *Surrey*
P12 W6 L4 D2 A1
Master i/c R. N. Ody	**Coach** P. E. Edwards
It proved another enjoyable season, and the team were well led by co-captains Daniel Smith and Benedict Clinch. A group of highly committed Year 13 students made major contributions, and will be much missed.
Batting Z. B. Wood 332 at 33.20; H. P. Chapman 213 at 23.66.
Bowling O. J. E. Mawdsley 14 at 13.07; M. Swanson 10 at 15.20.

Ampleforth College *Yorkshire*
P12 W5 L6 D1 A2
Master i/c C. M. Booth	**Coach** A. Shahzad
A positive approach from a young side ably captained by Arthur Campion produced fine individual and team performances. Top-order runs came from Campion, Joe Wright and Crispin Kerr-Dineen. Focus and intensity in the field helped left-arm spinners (and leading wicket-takers) Charlie Buchanan and Rory Stewart. Joe Browne, Tom Wade and Kit MacLellan shared the new ball with some success.

Batting *A. G. Campion 312 at 31.20; C. B. Kerr-Dineen 300 at 27.27; E. J. W. Wright 240 at 20.00; K. D. MacLellan 196 at 19.60.
Bowling R. C. Stewart 15 at 11.46; C. T. K. Buchanan 18 at 13.61; T. J. Browne 11 at 16.54.

Bancroft's School *Essex*   P14 W6 L7 D1
Master i/c C. G. Greenidge
Once again exam pressure made it difficult to field the first-choice team. Captain Sahil Handa and Alex Agedah hit most runs, and were well supported by all-rounders Deven Solanki and Max Sydenham. The 2019 season may be a challenge for an inexperienced side.
Batting *S. C. Handa 321 at 40.12; A. K. Agedah 299 at 33.22; N. H. A. Jani 164 at 32.80; D. V. Solanki 275 at 30.55; M. W. Sydenham 260 at 26.00; Z. A. Piracha 208 at 18.90; L. J. H. Whalley 159 at 15.90.
Bowling H. Vallance 10 at 24.00; A. S. Nanray 10 at 28.40; D. V. Solanki 14 at 29.50; S. C. Handa 12 at 29.66; M. W. Sydenham 11 at 36.54.

Bede's School *Sussex*   P16 W11 L4 T1 A2
Master i/c A. P. Wells   **Coaches** N. J. Lenham and R. J. Kirtley
A talented young XI had a solid season and retained the Langdale Cup. The summer ended on a high with good performances against Hurstpierpoint and Hampton. Alastair Orr, Henry Crocombe, Thomas Gordon and Scott Lenham (son of Neil and grandson of Les) all played for Sussex Seconds.
Batting A. G. H. Orr 654 at 40.87; *H. Scowan 346 at 38.44; T. D. Gordon 304 at 33.77.
Bowling F. S. Sheppard 18 at 22.55.

Bedford Modern School *Bedfordshire*   P13 W4 L7 D2
Master i/c P. J. Woodroffe
A very enjoyable term included fine wins and several narrow defeats. Robert Bassin had an excellent season, finishing top of both averages; Sam Pitkin led superbly.
Batting R. G. S. Bassin 365 at 33.18; S. O. Cruse 220 at 27.50; A. Vaidya 195 at 17.72; T. W. Saunders 209 at 16.07.
Bowling R. G. S. Bassin 16 at 14.31; A. Vaidya 11 at 21.54.

Bedford School *Bedfordshire*   P18 W14 L2 D2 A1
Master i/c I. G. S. Steer   **Coach** T. Brett
A magnificent season included an innings victory over Tonbridge in the two-day game, as well as the National Schools T20 finals day. The key performers were Emilio Gay, Gus Miller, Harry Gouldstone, Alex Rennie and Rahul Sheemar.
Batting A. H. Miller 526 at 58.44; E. N. Gay 552 at 50.18; H. O. Gouldstone 559 at 39.92; *R. Sheemar 327 at 32.70; A. Hassan 222 at 27.75; T. G. L. Blythman 156 at 19.50.
Bowling A. I. Rennie 40 at 16.92; T. O'Toole 10 at 18.10; R. Sheemar 18 at 23.05; A. Mehmood 17 at 25.17; E. N. Gay 10 at 29.00; A. H. Miller 13 at 29.53; S. H. Younis 14 at 32.14.

Berkhamsted School *Hertfordshire*   P14 W10 L3 D1 A4
Master i/c G. R. A. Campbell   **Coaches** D. J. Gibson and B. R. Mahoney
A wonderful summer saw Berkhamsted triumph in their last nine games to finish with ten wins from 14. Captain Freddie Thompson led from the front with 20 wickets and 375 runs, while opening batsmen Scott Rolfe and Sam Quinn both passed 400.
Batting S. J. T. Rolfe 449 at 40.81; S. A. J. Quinn 442 at 40.18; L. A. K. Golding 312 at 39.00; *F. A. Thompson 375 at 37.50; D. J. H. Young 331 at 33.10.
Bowling J. J. P. Baron 17 at 13.58; J. Abbott 13 at 18.46; F. A. Thompson 20 at 19.20; D. J. H. Young 11 at 20.81; J. J. Woodley 15 at 21.80; L. O. R. Snookes 16 at 25.56.

Bishop's Stortford College *Hertfordshire*   P10 W5 L4 D1 A1
Master i/c M. Drury   **Coach** N. D. Hughes
A positive season bought wins against Ipswich, The Perse and Colchester RGS. A young team played some excellent cricket following a successful pre-season tour to Cape Town.
Batting J. S. Hawkins 452 at 64.57; A. Bassingthwaighte 322 at 64.40; T. H. Snelling 202 at 28.85.
Bowling J. D. Woollerson 17 at 12.41; A. K. Ansell 11 at 17.36.

Freddie Thompson, Berkhamsted's captain, had a productive all-round season; Alex Rennie took 40 wickets for Bedford.

Bloxham School *Oxfordshire* — P18 W11 L6 D1 A2
Master i/c D. D. Finch

Bloxham had a rewarding season, thanks in part to the excellence of Toby Staveley-Parker with bat and ball. He and Ollie Morgan shared the captaincy, and helped foster a winning mentality. There are encouraging signs for the future.

Batting *T. J. Staveley-Parker 679 at 61.72; H. T. Denison-Smith 208 at 34.66; *O. J. Morgan 362 at 32.90; O. G. F. Woodcock 239 at 18.38; H. D. D. Hopkins 173 at 14.41; A. F. Din 167 at 13.91.

Bowling T. J. Staveley-Parker 26 at 14.38; B. E. Staveley-Parker 18 at 17.38; O. P. Maginnis 12 at 23.58; O. J. Maw 14 at 24.35.

Blundell's School *Devon* — P14 W4 L10 A1
Master i/c L. J. Lewis

The first team, whose average age was under 16, endured a tough season. But they battled hard against strong opposition, and made steady progress; several Year 10 pupils put in match-winning performances.

Batting T. E. Reynolds 248 at 20.66; *C. Fanous 248 at 20.66; J. R. Burnand 161 at 16.10; J. du'Gay 162 at 14.72.

Bowling W. Bucknell 13 at 14.23; G. Kitson 19 at 16.63; J. Hancock 16 at 21.18; T. E. Reynolds 13 at 27.76; W. C. Hall-Tomkin 12 at 28.50.

Bradfield College *Berkshire* — P22 W13 L5 D4 A7
Master i/c M. S. Hill   **Coaches** J. R. Wood and C. P. Ellison

Bradfield's success can be put down to the runs and captaincy of Imran Malik, and the effectiveness of the bowlers. The combined 61 wickets taken by Kamran Khanna and Tom Watson helped make up for a shortage of runs. Seven leavers will be difficult to replace in 2019.

Batting *I. A. Malik 825 at 43.42; D. R. A. McMurray 253 at 28.11; F. J. Brabham 451 at 23.73; E. J. S. Bray 169 at 21.12; E. J. A. Chapman 182 at 20.22; P. Khanna 300 at 20.00; T. A. W. Ettridge 247 at 17.64; J. R. J. Nichols 296 at 16.44; R. Patel 256 at 16.00.

Bowling E. J. S. Bray 18 at 14.33; K. K. Khanna 33 at 16.00; T. J. Watson 28 at 18.42; J. R. J. Nichols 19 at 21.52; T. A. W. Ettridge 12 at 21.83; F. J. Brabham 11 at 34.81.

Brentwood School *Essex* — P13 W6 L6 T1 A4
Master i/c S. Salisbury   **Coach** J. C. Mickleburgh

A young side containing only two Year 13s took notable strides. Robin Das showed great potential as a batsman, while William Steinberg bowled with real pace and made useful runs. Spinners Isaac Raj, Surya James and all-rounder Jack Levy are excellent prospects.

Batting R. J. Das 469 at 39.08; H. J. Deacon 153 at 30.60; J. S. Levy 205 at 20.50; W. Steinberg 170 at 17.00.

Bowling I. N. Raj 23 at 11.30; S. James 15 at 15.00; J. S. Levy 16 at 20.93.

Brighton College *Sussex*   P14 W7 L7

Master i/c M. P. Smethurst   **Coach** M. W. Machan

The college had a much-improved season, despite the youth of the side. Most will return for 2019, including Ravi Jadav, a Year 9 spinner who made his debut in 2018. Captain Jono Conolly was the leading bowler, with 23 wickets, but it was a genuine team effort.

Batting L. S. Smith 219 at 27.37; A. J. Bushell 195 at 21.66; T. J. Green 276 at 21.23; *J. M. Conolly 232 at 19.33; H. M. E. Moorat 204 at 15.69.

Bowling J. M. Conolly 23 at 15.69; L. D. Milne 17 at 18.41; A. J. Bushell 16 at 21.43; I. R. G. Christie 16 at 24.25.

Bristol Grammar School *Gloucestershire*   P19 W7 L11 D1 A2

Master i/c K. R. Blackburn

An unbeaten 180 by Sam Maskell against Wycliffe was the individual highlight of the season, while leg-spinner Om Reddy took consecutive five-fors. Matt Brewer was consistent with the bat. Fourteen regulars should return for 2019.

Batting M. J. M. Brewer 677 at 52.07; S. G. Maskell 329 at 36.55; T. H. J. Quinlan 327 at 20.43; *H. S. Canagarajah 286 at 20.42; E. J. Faulkner-Ellis 293 at 18.31; A. A. Hares 205 at 17.08; J. T. Winfield 175 at 14.58; H. B. R. Abel 176 at 11.73.

Bowling L. D. Nottage 10 at 19.00; T. H. J. Quinlan 25 at 20.20; O. S. M. Reddy 26 at 23.30; J. W. C. Cuthbert 16 at 23.37; W. E. Jones 11 at 25.72; A. A. Hares 11 at 41.00.

Bromsgrove School *Worcestershire*   P17 W8 L8 D1

Master i/c D. J. Fallows

Victory at New Road over Malvern in the Chesterton Cup final was the highlight of a challenging season. An impressive 90 from Fahd Janjua was the performance of the day. For the first time, the school reached the National ECB/ESCA Under-15s T20 Schools finals day.

Batting F. K. Janjua 299 at 27.18; *G. T. Hatfield 250 at 25.00; T. J. Maidment 172 at 24.57; A. Mohammed 284 at 21.84; A. J. Hinkley 326 at 20.37; D. E. Meredith 240 at 16.00.

Bowling T. J. Maidment 24 at 16.79; D. E. Meredith 26 at 17.34; G. T. Hatfield 14 at 18.78; A. Mohammed 21 at 21.47; H. J. Marshall 17 at 26.17; G. O. Marshall 10 at 46.20.

Bryanston School *Dorset*   P11 W4 L7

Master i/c S. J. Turrill   **Coach** P. J. Norton

Under the outstanding captaincy of Alex Sands, Bryanston enjoyed a sequence of nailbiting finishes against KES Southampton, Portsmouth Grammar School, Sherborne and Canford. Stars with bat and ball were Johnny Plimmer, in his last season, and 2019 captain Cameron Robertson.

Batting T. P. L. Barber 244 at 81.33; J. L. R. Plimmer 263 at 43.83; C. W. Robertson 283 at 31.44.

Bowling J. C. Guinness 17 at 14.05; E. A. H. Mackay 15 at 14.26; C. W. Robertson 15 at 18.06.

Canford School *Dorset*   P11 W6 L5 A2

Master i/c M. Keech

A young side excellently led by Max Mallinson gained much from a tough season, which included a superb win against the Leopards touring side.

Batting J. T. Taylor 230 at 38.33; M. J. Daubeney 230 at 32.85; T. J. Prest 203 at 29.00; W. J. Elwood 222 at 27.75; *M. W. Mallinson 190 at 21.11.

Bowling T. J. Prest 14 at 22.21; Z. H. Organ 11 at 38.27.

Caterham School *Surrey*   P16 W4 L11 D1 A1

Master i/c J. N. Batty

Caterham enjoyed victories over Lingfield College, Judd, Alleyn's and Old Caterhamians. Matthew Terry led the side capably and was well supported by vice-captain and leading run-scorer Louis Brown, and leading wicket-taker Ian Haywood.

Batting J. S. Ireland 206 at 34.33; M. S. Wilson 258 at 23.45; L. F. Brown 291 at 20.78; M. Santana 191 at 19.10; M. E. Ireland 199 at 16.58; *M. J. Terry 229 at 15.26; S. E. Dickson 162 at 13.50.

Bowling I. A. Haywood 20 at 16.70; M. J. Terry 19 at 19.26.

Cheadle Hulme's Ed Fluck hit 155 against King's Macclesfield; Alex Oxley of Culford made 691 runs at an average of 98.

Charterhouse *Surrey*   P25 W18 L4 T1 D2 A1
Master i/c M. P. Bicknell   **Coach** R. Woods

The school enjoyed their most successful year, winning 18 games and finishing runners-up in the National T20 final. Prince Singh took 58 wickets, and Ross Richardson scored 760 runs. The impressive captain George Barlow hit 570 runs and claimed 33 wickets.

Batting R. A. J. Richardson 760 at 36.19; *G. C. H. Barlow 570 at 27.14; P. Singh 483 at 23.00; A. Mahtani 374 at 22.00; C. A. M. Short 222 at 20.18; T. C. P. Rawlings 309 at 18.17; A. R. R. Wilman 270 at 16.87; A. A. Patel 257 at 14.27.

Bowling P. Singh 58 at 12.34; T. C. P. Rawlings 11 at 14.18; A. Mahtani 40 at 15.67; O. B. G. Sheen 32 at 15.75; G. C. H. Barlow 33 at 19.27; A. A. Patel 13 at 32.23.

Cheadle Hulme School *Cheshire*   P16 W9 L7 A7
Master i/c G. J. Clinton   **Coach** R. C. Kitzinger

The 2018 season was one of development for a young side. Ed Fluck scored a school-record 155 against King's Macclesfield, and there were four consecutive century opening stands, all featuring different sets of batsmen. Ollie Latter and Ted Vanderhook led the side admirably several times, and the runs of Dan Adams and Ben Staniforth will be missed. The season was rounded off at the Abingdon Festival and by an excellent win against MCC.

Batting *E. B. Fluck 358 at 71.60; B. J. Staniforth 483 at 34.50; D. J. Adams 294 at 32.66; O. Latter 349 at 26.84.

Bowling B. J. Staniforth 11 at 16.00; M. L. Madeira 16 at 20.25; O. Latter 17 at 29.58; A. J. Tittle 13 at 39.46.

Cheltenham College *Gloucestershire*   P15 W7 L7 T1 A5
Master i/c M. K. Coley   **Coach** M. P. Briers

The second half of the term saw wins over St Edward's Oxford, Marlborough and Winchester, to secure third place in the John Harvey Cup. Captain Jason Soames fared well with bat and ball, and left-arm spinner Felix Watson-Smyth took 25 wickets.

Batting *J. C. Soames 440 at 36.66; O. C. D. Butcher 261 at 29.00; J. R. J. Gunn 322 at 26.83; J. A. Clement 206 at 25.75; S. Blake 358 at 22.37; J. A. S. Boyle 227 at 20.63; D. J. Ward 188 at 13.42.

Bowling F. G. E. Watson-Smyth 25 at 15.44; J. A. Clement 15 at 16.53; C. J. A. Davison 12 at 17.41; J. R. J. Gunn 15 at 25.13; J. C. Soames 21 at 25.42.

Chigwell School *Essex*   P12 W4 L4 T1 D3 A2
Master i/c F. A. Griffith   **Coach** V. Chopra
A young and talented side had a mixed season. They faced up to many challenges, as they will need to in 2019. Ben Chillingworth, Ben Kearin, Haaris Usman and Harry Allen made the bulk of the runs. Kearin's spin accounted for ten wickets, and the remaining bowlers proved economical.
Batting B. D. Chillingworth 385 at 38.50; B. H. P. Kearin 291 at 36.37; H. Usman 195 at 21.66; H. W. Allen 152 at 16.88.
Bowling B. H. P. Kearin 10 at 16.60.

Chislehurst & Sidcup Grammar School *Kent*   P5 W2 L2 D1 A2
Master i/c R. A. Wallbridge   **Coach** B. Stock
An enthusiastic squad, led adroitly by Liam Buttery, enjoyed an encouraging summer. Robert Woods was the spearhead of the attack. The highlight was Buttery's unbeaten century against MCC to secure a comfortable (though rare) draw.
Batting *L. D. Buttery 196 at 65.33.
Bowling The leading bowler was R. S. Woods, who took six wickets at 14.83.

Christ's Hospital *Sussex*   P14 W9 L4 D1
Master i/c H. P. Holdsworth   **Coaches** T. E. Jesty and D. H. Messenger
This was a good season. Will Freeman led by example and was supported by his brother Gus, a useful leg-spinning all-rounder. There were excellent batting displays from Ben Kinnear and Solly Woodall. All four defeats might have been won, and there is promise for the future. Howard Holdsworth retires after 27 years in charge.
Batting *W. E. M. Freeman 445 at 44.50; B. E. Kinnear 496 at 41.33; G. A. M. Freeman 428 at 35.66; S. J. Woodall 353 at 35.30.
Bowling G. A. M. Freeman 30 at 19.20; W. E. M. Freeman 22 at 20.45; N. J. Cooper 17 at 21.17; W. A. Thwaites 12 at 23.33; H. T. Condron 11 at 28.09.

Churcher's College *Hampshire*   P11 W6 L5
Master i/c R. Maier
The 2018 vintage were enthusiastic, but injuries, exam pressure and limited availability denied them the results they might have expected. The 2019 squad will benefit from several good young players coming through the system.
Batting J. J. Paul 204 at 34.00.
Bowling C. Tuffin 11 at 17.82; M. J. Crane 10 at 18.30.

Claysmore School *Dorset*   P16 W8 L8
Master i/c D. O. Conway
James Miles's thoughtful, inclusive captaincy ensured that his young team had an enjoyable season. The team effort that brought the defeat of MCC was a fair reflection of their abilities.
Batting J. Gordon 357 at 32.45; J. C. A. Berry 233 at 21.18; G. Pratt 209 at 20.90; H. B. Morgan 189 at 15.75.
Bowling J. C. A. Berry 19 at 14.31; W. M. D. Perrin 11 at 16.45; G. Pratt 14 at 21.64; A. H. Ashmore 11 at 22.09.

Clifton College *Gloucestershire*   P21 W12 L7 D2
Master i/c J. C. Bobby   **Coach** J. R. A. Williams
At last, a summer of sunshine and plenty of cricket! The highlight for a youthful side – many of whom will have at least two more seasons in the XI – was the seven-run win over King's College, Taunton, in the knockout stages of the National Schools T20.
Batting *C. P. C. Griffith 439 at 36.58; R. E. Clarke 265 at 29.44; J. Lloyd 188 at 26.85; D. C. Goodman 491 at 25.84; O. J. Meadows 406 at 25.37; J. H. Millard 445 at 24.72; T. A. T. Thornycroft 190 at 23.75; J. J. Hughes 177 at 22.12; H. J. P. King 188 at 20.88; H. R. Ascherl 151 at 18.87.
Bowling O. J. Meadows 23 at 15.95; D. C. Goodman 28 at 17.14; I. Lloyd 20 at 19.55; H. R. Ascherl 21 at 20.57; C. P. C. Griffith 18 at 28.16; J. H. Millard 12 at 31.16.

Colston's School *Gloucestershire*   P15 W8 L6 D1 A2
Master i/c L. M. Evans   **Coach** P. B. Muchall
Colston's, superbly captained by Ed Webb, enjoyed a successful season. He and Sam Williams completed their fourth year in the team, and both hit hundreds: Webb against Dauntsey's, and Williams against the XL Club.

Batting *E. G. Webb 694 at 57.83; S. J. Williams 352 at 27.07; Z. S. Hamid 314 at 24.15; B. C. Miller 154 at 11.00.
Bowling S. J. Williams 23 at 11.34; S. J. Manning 23 at 20.13; M. I. Waite 13 at 21.46; J. W. Waite 11 at 23.72; B. C. Miller 12 at 32.25.

Cranleigh School *Surrey*   P12 W4 L5 D3 A2
Master i/c A. P. Forsdike   **Coach** S. D. Welch
Without eight first-team players from 2017, Cranleigh endured a year of rebuilding. Callum Job led the side well, and was leading run-scorer; the Ealham brothers – sons of former England all-rounder Mark – starred with the ball. All bar three of the regular XI return for 2019.
Batting *C. A. Job 262 at 32.75; S. D. G. Bugler 160 at 32.00; C. T. Pyle 179 at 22.37.
Bowling G. S. Ealham 18 at 17.50; T. M. Ealham 20 at 20.40; M. A. Bell 14 at 28.85.

Culford School *Suffolk*   P15 W10 L5 A2
Master i/c A. M. Northcote
The fantastic weather was matched by some superb performances, including victories over Norwich and New Hall. But the outstanding moment was winning the East Anglian Festival. Alex Oxley (Year 12) finished within a whisker of averaging 100.
Batting A. G. Oxley 691 at 98.71; O. Melville-Ross 424 at 35.33; *M. Whittaker 335 at 33.50; T. J. Auchterlonie 340 at 30.90; A. Packer 173 at 21.62; J. O. Walters 151 at 16.77; A. Cruickshank 165 at 16.50.
Bowling G. W. J. Southgate 15 at 20.53; A. Cruickshank 19 at 23.63; T. J. Auchterlonie 11 at 24.81; O. H. J. Riddick 19 at 30.63.

Dauntsey's School *Wiltshire*   P20 W12 L6 D2 A1
Master i/c A. J. Palmer   **Coach** J. R. Ayling
A young side, with only three Year 13s, retained the Monkhouse Intersport League title and played attractive cricket. The top three in the bowling averages were all spinners: leggie Jack Grant took 39 wickets, the best since 2011, including five against MCC. Openers Rahul Patel and Will Thomas ended their careers with aggregates of 2,110 and 1,933.
Batting R. N. Patel 773 at 51.53; A. Ayers 531 at 40.84; A. J. Ayling 351 at 29.25; *W. J. Thomas 465 at 29.06; G. M. Edwards 393 at 28.07; T. J. Swanton 186 at 26.57; J. B. Grant 186 at 18.60.
Bowling J. B. Grant 39 at 17.69; J. Williams 21 at 18.61; H. M. J. Cox 19 at 24.21; T. J. Swanton 23 at 24.26; G. M. E. Lishman 18 at 27.27; A. J. Ayling 10 at 37.00.

Dean Close School *Gloucestershire*   P10 W2 L7 D1 A3
Master i/c A. G. A. Milne   **Coach** M. J. Powell
Dean Close beat the Cathedral School, Llandaff, and King's Gloucester in May, but then lost six of their last seven games. Oliver Horne captained and topped the batting averages, while fast bowler Oscar Newcombe was the pick of the attack. Both return next year. Full colours were awarded to Oliver Horne, Henry Sleeman and James Humphreys.
Batting O. P. M. Horne 354 at 39.33; J. D. Humphreys 295 at 29.50; J. P. Gray 180 at 18.00.
Bowling O. H. D. Newcombe 12 at 21.75; J. D. Boden 11 at 26.09.

Denstone College *Staffordshire*   P21 W14 L7 A5
Master i/c T. A. H. Williams   **Coach** S. M. Guy
This was a much-improved season for the College, who won 14 of their 21 games, despite a tougher fixture list. Jack Redman led the way with bat and ball, and it is exciting that the entire squad will return in 2019.
Batting J. R. Redman 1,033 at 64.56; *M. A. Webber 488 at 34.85; D. M. Afford 516 at 34.40; A. W. O'Hara 497 at 33.13; J. J. Bailey 199 at 28.42; R. L. F. Gray 328 at 25.23; A. I. Cooper 346 at 23.06; D. J. Jones 160 at 11.42.
Bowling J. R. Redman 30 at 17.60; R. B. Hughes 18 at 21.00; A. I. Cooper 21 at 21.33; E. A. Gaffney 10 at 29.30; A. D. Billington 21 at 29.38; J. J. Bailey 17 at 30.17; R. C. Owens 19 at 43.21.

Dr Challoner's Grammar School *Buckinghamshire*   P11 W7 L4 A2
Master i/c N. J. S. Buchanan
The school enjoyed a rewarding season, playing plenty of exciting cricket. Henry Moore led by example, while leading wicket-taker Nouman Aslam finished four excellent years in the first team.
Batting L. E. F. Dawson 304 at 33.77; T. W. P. Lane 245 at 30.62; *H. J. Moore 312 at 28.36.
Bowling N. Aslam 18 at 8.61; J. H. Rance 11 at 14.72; H. J. Moore 13 at 25.69.

Dollar Academy *Clackmannanshire* P15 W12 D3 A3
Master i/c J. G. A. Frost
Dollar Academy, captained by Gus Warr, rounded off an unbeaten season by defeating Merchiston Castle in the final of the Scottish Independent Schools T20. Jonhli Jordan batted superbly, though it was the bowling, led by Lachlan Kelly and assisted by left-arm spinners Toby Douglas and Jamie Cairns, that provided the cornerstone of the team's success.
Batting J. R. Jordan 360 at 72.00; T. B. Douglas 213 at 30.43; I. A. Brett 179 at 17.90.
Bowling J. S. Cairns 18 at 8.94; T. B. Douglas 15 at 12.67; L. Kelly 16 at 14.13.

Dover College *Kent* P5 L3 D2 A5
Master i/c G. R. Hill
Rain and exams meant a frustrating season for a largely inexperienced team. Senior players worked hard, but could not make up for a lack of depth in the batting. The highlight was a tenacious draw against the Old Dovorian XI.
Batting The leading batsman was *J. Blair-Hickman, who hit 82 runs at 20.50.
Bowling The leading bowler was J. S. Hide, who took six wickets at 35.16.

Downside School *Somerset* P8 W3 L5
Master i/c A. Thomas
Downside School had an enjoyable 2018, entering the National T20 Cup and playing a range of fixtures in and around Somerset. Notable performers included Jack Smith and Alex Lowe; the team was well led by Hugo Morgan.
Batting J. Smith 166 at 23.71; *H. Morgan 150 at 21.43.
Bowling A. Lowe 10 at 16.20.

Durham School *County Durham* P17 W13 L3 D1 A1
Master i/c M. Fishwick
A fine summer brought 13 wins from 17 starts. The senior players performed well, and newcomers gave strong support. A good team ethic helped the side through some tough moments.
Batting S. J. D. Bell 259 at 64.75; *C. M. Fyfe 563 at 51.18; P. Pansare 189 at 47.25; J. J. Bushnell 414 at 34.50; W. D. Jewitt 243 at 22.09; S. M. E. North 238 at 21.63.
Bowling C. M. Fyfe 20 at 16.15; S. M. E. North 15 at 16.80; W. D. Jewitt 10 at 17.80; J. J. Bushnell 17 at 18.94; L. Giacomelli 13 at 23.15.

Eastbourne College *Sussex* P21 W15 L5 D1
Master i/c R. S. Ferley   **Coach** A. C. Waller
Four batsmen, all of whom return for 2019, scored centuries: Tawanda Muyeye's unbeaten 214 was the highlight. In a remarkable end to the season, Year 9 Danial Ibrahim took an all-bowled hat-trick to secure victory over Framlingham by one run.
Batting T. S. Muyeye 902 at 53.05; *J. A. Pocklington 504 at 45.81; F. J. Logan 209 at 41.80; O. J. Carter 745 at 41.38; H. A. Tagg 475 at 31.66; O. H. Streets 255 at 23.18.
Bowling L. J. Barron 22 at 15.95; T. S. Muyeye 33 at 16.48; J. A. Pocklington 27 at 17.11; T. S. Crathern 13 at 19.84.

Edinburgh Academy *Midlothian* P14 W2 L11 D1 A3
Master i/c R. W. Sales
The first team had a mixed season, losing most of the close matches they should have won; this is the area that demands greatest attention. They were well led by Harry O'Brien, who was the leading run-scorer; Sam Bell took most wickets and topped the batting averages.
Batting S. I. J. Bell 245 at 24.50; *H. J. O'Brien 288 at 20.57; C. F. Swanson 201 at 16.75; F. Riddle 160 at 14.54.
Bowling T. Holden 11 at 17.45; A. D. M. Carson 11 at 18.45; S. I. J. Bell 15 at 19.80; H. J. O'Brien 10 at 30.40.

Elizabeth College, Guernsey *Channel Islands* P16 W2 L13 D1 A2
Master i/c T. P. Eisenhuth
A character-building season ended with a much-deserved win. Many senior players have moved on, leaving a wonderful legacy for cricket.
Batting D. N. Le Messurier 278 at 21.38; *N. C. Guilbert 289 at 20.64.
Bowling N. J. Buckle 17 at 11.82; M. J. Sharpe 11 at 16.18.

Flashing blades at Felsted: Jordan Cox and Will Buttleman hit a combined 1,610 runs.

Ellesmere College *Shropshire* P10 W7 L3
Master i/c G. Owen   **Coach** R. Jones

Despite only one regular in Year 13, the team were highly competitive, and a series of promising performances from younger players gave encouragement for 2019. The side played particularly well in timed matches against adult opponents.

Batting J. W. Carter 195 at 48.75; J. D. Andrady 181 at 36.20; C. A. Davies 236 at 33.71; *S. J. C. Ellis 216 at 27.00.

Bowling H. Newton 24 at 6.00; S. J. C. Ellis 20 at 10.00.

Eltham College *Kent* P15 W10 L4 D1 A1
Master i/c J. L. D. Baldwin   **Coach** Yasir Arafat

The first team won ten of 14 completed matches, and reached the regional final of the National T20. Sam Smith proved an astute captain, and he and Nico Murlowski passed 500 runs. Ben Day enjoyed a fine all-round season.

Batting N. C. Murlowski 531 at 59.00; *S. Smith 517 at 51.70; B. Day 200 at 40.00.

Bowling A. J. L. Khanna 10 at 9.60; C. D. J. Fuller 14 at 10.64; B. Day 20 at 12.35; T. Gallo 16 at 17.62; O. P. Davies 16 at 18.56; N. C. Murlowski 15 at 20.73.

Emanuel School *Surrey* P15 W8 L7 A2
Master i/c T. Gwynne   **Coach** M. G. Stear

A promising season featured notable weekend victories against Westminster, Kingston Grammar, Colfe's and Latymer. Will Ellis and Sinan Mahmud hit most runs, while Ivan Barker and captain Robbie Hawken bowled especially well.

Batting W. A. Ellis 493 at 41.08; S. K. Mahmud 385 at 27.50; *R. C. Hawken 236 at 23.60; N. C. Hughes 230 at 19.16; I. P. Barker 239 at 18.38.

Bowling S. K. Mahmud 13 at 19.69; R. C. Hawken 11 at 26.90; A. G. E. Banks 11 at 29.63; B. S. Emery-Dickinson 11 at 34.00; I. P. Barker 11 at 34.54.

Epsom College *Surrey* P18 W8 L9 D1
Master i/c D. C. Shirazi

Hampered by long-term injuries, Epsom had an up-and-down season: all told, 29 players were used. Edward Hughes was a consistent batsman, while Liam Head, the captain, took 24 wickets. With many returning, hopes are high for 2019.

Batting E. D. Hughes 537 at 38.35; *L. A. Head 428 at 28.53; A. M. Koep 314 at 22.42; F. B. Savill 189 at 21.00; T. Allen 212 at 19.27.

Bowling A. M. Koep 15 at 16.13; C. E. Lansdown 16 at 17.62; L. A. Head 24 at 22.83.

Eton College *Buckinghamshire*   P18 W9 L7 D2 A2
Master i/c R. R. Montgomerie   **Coach** T. W. Roberts
Well led by Charlie Lyons, Eton had an enjoyable season, even though a strong all-round team won
only three of their 11 chases. On the other hand, they went undefeated when batting first. The
performance of the season was victory against Harrow at Lord's: Ben Elias followed 70 runs with
four for 11.
Batting B. M. Elias 620 at 41.33; H. A. M. Thistlethwayte 531 at 40.84; C. L. W. Adair 524 at
37.42; *C. E. M. Lyons 518 at 32.37; T. S. Lytle 251 at 20.91; C. D. G. Penny 231 at 17.76;
W. G. D. Lowther-Pilkington 211 at 15.07.
Bowling H. A. M. Thistlethwayte 10 at 19.10; S. Mathur 19 at 21.00; C. E. M. Lyons 12 at 21.16;
F. E. Butler 17 at 21.70; C. D. G. Penny 21 at 24.09; B. M. Elias 19 at 25.21; J. W. Gammell 17 at
28.94; J. B. Hardy 17 at 33.35.

Felsted School *Essex*   P17 W10 L6 D1
Master i/c J. E. R. Gallian   **Coaches** C. S. Knightley, A. Mohindru and N. J. Lockhart
Felsted improved as the term went on, winning ten of their 17 games. It was a good team effort, and
they were well led by Will Buttleman.
Batting J. M. Cox 793 at 72.09; *W. E. L. Buttleman 817 at 68.08; J. H. Burslem 774 at 45.52;
A. Akbar 157 at 31.40; O. W. S. Hills 170 at 18.88.
Bowling L. Simpson 26 at 19.30; O. W. S. Hills 26 at 22.46; W. E. L. Buttleman 25 at 26.76; E. J.
Snooks 15 at 33.00.

Fettes College *Midlothian*   P14 W6 L8 A3
Master i/c A. B. Russell
A flying start tailed off after the first month, when some established players became unavailable.
New captain Robert Edwards shone with the bat, while Finlay Young and Ben MacLeod shared
bowling honours.
Batting *R. A. Edwards 389 at 43.22; J. Brydon 211 at 21.10; O. Norton 206 at 20.60; D. Hood 168
at 18.66.
Bowling O. Norton 10 at 8.30; B. G. Sperling 11 at 14.63; F. M. Young 17 at 15.58; B. M. MacLeod
17 at 16.17; D. Hood 10 at 19.70; Z. Clayburn 12 at 20.00.

Forest School *Essex*   P19 W10 L6 D3
Master i/c J. Perham
A record number of senior boys participated, and the competition for places brought encouraging
results. The school beat all three local rivals – Chigwell, Bancroft's and Brentwood – and there were
positive performances against Haberdashers' (win), MCC (draw) and St Albans (defeat).
Batting H. C. Sewell 451 at 45.10; *E. G. Risby 492 at 37.84; J. H. Coughlan 418 at 32.15; M. H.
Manack 301 at 30.10; T. P. Dixon 152 at 12.66; F. G. Britt 154 at 11.84.
Bowling J. A. O'Callaghan 33 at 14.39; A. M. Bassi 12 at 31.25; A. P. Ragutharan 15 at 35.20.

Framlingham College *Suffolk*   P17 W11 L5 D1 A1
Master i/c M. J. Marvell   **Coach** C. D. Gange
Framlingham enjoyed an excellent season, thanks in part to Jack Hobbs (509 runs) and the stylish
Maaz Dehlvi (413). Fred Heldreich's wrist-spin collected 35 wickets, while the reliable Rory
Torrance and Harrison Stiles contributed 42 between them.
Batting *J. L. Hobbs 509 at 36.35; M. M. Dehlvi 413 at 34.41; B. P. Chapman 418 at 32.15; W. J. H.
Donsworth 191 at 27.28; H. G. Bureau 308 at 25.66; J. C. K. Lecompte 170 at 21.25; H. T. J. Bevan
249 at 19.15.
Bowling F. J. Heldreich 35 at 14.31; R. A. S. Torrance 24 at 17.25; H. J. Stiles 18 at 21.66; H. G.
Bureau 16 at 23.18; H. T. J. Bevan 15 at 23.86.

George Heriot's School *Midlothian*   P7 W3 L3 D1
Master i/c E. L. Harrison
Priyanshu Agrawal led an enthusiastic group of players in a rewarding summer. The highlight was a
last-ball win over The Glasgow Academy.
Batting The leading batsman was D. D. Blood, who hit 133 runs at 44.33.
Bowling C. J. Keatinge 10 at 8.80.

Framlingham's Fred Heldreich practises with England's Adil Rashid, a fellow leg-spinner.

George Watson's College *Midlothian*

P19 W11 L7 D1 A1

Master i/c M. J. Leonard   **Coach** A. D. W. Patterson

A strong squad performed well, with notable victories over Fettes, UCS Hampstead (in our festival) and Merchiston, as well as a winning draw against MCC. Murray Whitaker led astutely, and Callum Macleod excelled with the ball. Most players return for 2019, which is encouraging.

Batting *M. K. Whitaker 445 at 27.81; M. A. Brian 501 at 26.36; A. R. Young 221 at 18.41; F. C. Tait 159 at 17.66; R. H. Fontana 298 at 17.52; A. A. Cousin 314 at 17.44; F. J. Kinloch 279 at 16.41.

Bowling E. J. Burgess 15 at 12.66; J. A. Reid 19 at 16.73; A. R. Young 12 at 18.16; C. A. Macleod 11 at 19.45; A. A. Cousin 16 at 25.00; G. W. Carr 11 at 30.54; O. J. Snodgrass 17 at 31.82.

Giggleswick School *Yorkshire*

P13 W3 L9 D1 A2

Master i/c R. T. F. Bunday

The 2018 season was marked by a series of close contests. Batting was the school's strength, with Ryan Hodgson and Herbie Milton passing 400 runs. In three days at the Bruton festival, the team totalled over 750.

Batting R. Hodgson 496 at 49.60; H. G. Milton 445 at 37.08; *E. A. Leech 236 at 26.22; H. G. Snowden 226 at 18.83; F. J. H. Scott 181 at 18.10.

Bowling R. Hodgson 17 at 18.00; T. W. Lothian 14 at 22.85; O. R. West 13 at 28.30; F. J. H. Scott 11 at 34.18.

The Glasgow Academy *Lanarkshire*

P7 W1 L5 D1 A1

Master i/c P. J. W. Smith   **Coach** V. Hariharan

After the successes of recent years – and with senior players having left – it was always going to be difficult for a young team to match their predecessors. Even so, results did no justice to their abilities.

Batting The leading batsman was R. S. Heginbottom, who hit 127 runs at 42.33.

Bowling *T. W. Bouttell 11 at 7.09.

The High School of Glasgow *Lanarkshire*

P10 W4 L5 D1 A1

Master i/c S. C. Leggatt   **Coach** K. J. A. Robertson

The first team continued to show great potential, and began to hit their stride as an enjoyable season ended. An unbeaten 116 by Callum Coats against Gordonstoun was a highlight.

Batting *C. J. Coats 271 at 33.87; J. A. Greene 165 at 23.57; J. I. Chalmers 165 at 23.57.

Bowling J. Tyagi 10 at 11.40; G. H. Shafar 10 at 15.00; J. A. Greene 12 at 17.16.

Gordonstoun School *Morayshire*   P9 W4 L5
Master i/c R. Denyer
Magnificent weather matched the enthusiasm of a young team. Year 9 Gabriel Gallmann-Findlay top-scored and kept wicket brilliantly, while classmate Theo Barker took 18 wickets.
Batting The leading batsman was G. R. E. Gallmann-Findlay, who hit 134 runs at 19.14.
Bowling R. E. MacGregor 12 at 13.91; T. F. Barker 18 at 14.72; M. A. Cheyne 12 at 27.00.

Gresham's School *Norfolk*   P18 W11 L6 D1 A2
Master i/c D. J. Atkinson   **Coaches** A. Horsley and C. Brown
A marvellous season contained 11 victories. Declan Oldreive hit two centuries in his 751 runs and averaged 50. He gained valuable support from the captain, Billy Buckingham. Kieran Peters claimed 33 wickets to finish his first-team career with 97.
Batting D. W. Oldreive 751 at 50.06; *W. G. Buckingham 457 at 32.64; B. A. Wilcox 308 at 23.69; K. T. Peters 222 at 20.18; A. J. Sheridan 219 at 19.90; H. A. de Lucchi 208 at 13.00; F. C. Wilcox 180 at 12.00.
Bowling W. G. Buckingham 12 at 12.58; B. P. Withers 17 at 18.35; K. T. Peters 33 at 19.45; H. A. de Lucchi 18 at 24.05; C. A. G. Douds 17 at 24.41; C. O. Adams 11 at 24.81; D. W. Oldreive 19 at 27.15.

Haberdashers' Aske's Boys' School *Hertfordshire*   P19 W8 L7 D4 A4
Master i/c S. D. Charlwood   **Coaches** D. H. Kerry and J. P. Hewitt
The team were inconsistent, despite Naresh Rasakulasuriar, in his fifth year in the XI, leading by example. Opener Freddie Wright hit an unbeaten century against Old Haberdashers' CC, and the season ended with victory against Devon Under-16s. Stephen Charlwood completed 25 years as master in charge of cricket.
Batting V. Jegatheesan 492 at 41.00; H. J. J. Cobb 428 at 30.57; F. J. Wright 452 at 28.25; *N. Rasakulasuriar 387 at 27.64; L. T. Ignatius 320 at 26.66; A. S. Lakhani 279 at 21.46.
Bowling S. Singh 14 at 22.50; A. S. Lakhani 11 at 23.54; N. N. Chvada 10 at 30.90; J. P. Granger 12 at 31.25; C. Mullapudi 10 at 38.60; N. Rasakulasuriar 10 at 44.00; S. D. Shah 14 at 44.85.

Haileybury *Hertfordshire*   P14 W9 L2 D3 A1
Master i/c D. L. S. van Bunge   **Coach** C. E. Igolen-Robinson
Going unbeaten until deep into June illustrates the quality of the season, which included victories over Cheltenham, Felsted and MCC. Andrew Neal led intelligently and topped both averages. Bill Meacock, aged 15, hit his first half-century.
Batting *A. J. Neal 680 at 61.81; A. M. Whaits 245 at 49.00; H. Reid 200 at 22.22; H. C. Willgoss 228 at 20.72; W. G. Meacock 217 at 19.72.
Bowling A. J. Neal 16 at 21.87; I. K. Shah 12 at 23.33; J. E. Bridge 10 at 23.40.

Hampton School *Middlesex*   P16 W5 L10 D1 A3
Master i/c A. M. Banerjee   **Coach** C. P. Harrison
Results reveal a tough, yet encouraging, season, not helped by unavailability for exams. With 11 talented players from Year 11 or below representing the first XI, the near future looks bright.
Batting C. R. Campbell 402 at 50.25; *J. F. D. Wheeler 373 at 31.08; R. P. Desai 262 at 29.11; B. C. Cullen 251 at 25.10.
Bowling A. D. Bhasin 15 at 10.13; J. F. D. Wheeler 12 at 17.50; C. R. Campbell 14 at 24.28.

Harrow School *Middlesex*   P20 W9 L9 D2
Master i/c R. S. C. Martin-Jenkins   **Coach** S. A. Jones
A talented if inexperienced side won nine games, including an eight-wicket defeat of Wellington. Tej Sheopuri, aged 15, scored back-to-back hundreds, while the 16-year-old Rishi Wijeratne hit most runs. Another 16-year-old, James Langston, claimed two five-wicket hauls.
Batting T. N. Sheopuri 423 at 42.30; R. S. Wijeratne 575 at 33.82; L. B. H. Harrington-Myers 348 at 29.00; A. P. Ferreira 361 at 25.78; W. A. Falcon 176 at 25.14; H. H. Dicketts 337 at 24.07; J. E. Langston 156 at 19.50; *M. W. Ayliffe 153 at 9.00.
Bowling J. E. Langston 19 at 15.21; H. J. S. Maxwell 24 at 16.33; G. P. T. Gray 12 at 18.16; J. A. Chohan 26 at 20.07; W. A. Falcon 21 at 21.61; M. W. Ayliffe 10 at 34.10; M. S. Ali 13 at 37.23.

The Harvey Grammar School *Kent*   P7 W4 L3 A2
Master i/c G. Meers   **Coach** P. M. Castle
A youthful and enthusiastic team showed great promise, and were well captained by Nick Ward,
whose father had played for the school in 1984.
Batting J. McVittie 151 at 50.33.
Bowling The leading bowler was *N. L. Ward, who took nine wickets at 10.22.

Highgate School *Middlesex*   P5 W1 L4 A1
Master i/c A. S. Iga
Highgate fielded a relatively raw side, who developed as the season progressed under the astute
captaincy of Dempster Fawden.
Batting W. Bliss 165 at 55.00.
Bowling The leading bowler was W. Bliss, who took seven wickets at 12.71.

Hurstpierpoint College *Sussex*   P20 W6 L11 T1 D2
Master i/c N. J. K. Creed   **Coaches** J. P. Anyon and P. G. Hudson
After a demanding 2018, this young side will be better equipped for the future. Jack Carson and Will
Collard topped the averages, and they, as well as Mason Robinson, all played for Sussex Seconds;
Josh Wood turned out for Scotland.
Batting J. A. J. Wood 466 at 35.84; J. J. Carson 573 at 35.81; T. G. Bloomfield 175 at 25.00; J. A.
Gander 204 at 22.66; B. J. Caidan 289 at 19.26; M. L. Robinson 321 at 18.88; *W. C. H. P. Collard
282 at 18.80; L. D. Heath 230 at 13.52.
Bowling W. C. H. P. Collard 29 at 20.96; H. J. Drew 15 at 24.26; B. J. Caidan 25 at 25.84; J. A. J.
Wood 12 at 31.00; J. J. Carson 18 at 35.33.

Hymers College *Yorkshire*   P16 W11 L4 D1 A3
Master i/c G. Tipping
Hymers College turned in an outstanding set of results. All the players showed great commitment,
and thoroughly deserved their achievements.
Batting C. J. Rawlins 474 at 39.50; B. L. Renwick 344 at 34.40; S. J. Elstone 444 at 34.15; H. T. F.
Marsden 425 at 30.35; A. R. F. Brocklesby 324 at 23.14.
Bowling W. J. Atkinson 16 at 7.31; A. Gupta 14 at 10.64; G. Balaji 15 at 16.66; J. E. Davies 17 at
19.64; S. J. Elstone 12 at 30.75; B. L. Renwick 12 at 32.50.

Ibstock Place School *Surrey*   P19 W6 L13 A2
Master i/c R. S. Brown   **Coach** M. W. Costin
A young team sparkled at times: they snatched a one-wicket win against MCC, and Oscar Welton hit
a brutal 66 against KCS Wimbledon. Injuries caused problems, though, and the team will be hoping
for more luck as they mature in 2019.
Batting *O. M. Welton 548 at 34.25; I. J. King 455 at 25.27.
Bowling O. M. Welton 26 at 17.19; O. J. Thornbury 13 at 32.30.

Ipswich School *Suffolk*   P16 W5 L11
Master i/c B. H. Edmondson   **Coach** M. G. Cull
Although not the most successful season of recent times, 2018 included many close encounters. Luke
Froggatt and Joe MacGregor led well in the field and with the bat, while Andrew Whitehead was a
constant threat with ball in hand.
Batting J. L. H. MacGregor 380 at 34.54; G. F. Haines 152 at 30.40; *L. R. C. Froggatt 379 at
23.68; W. T. Main 280 at 33.33.
Bowling A. J. Whitehead 21 at 14.52; J. L. H. MacGregor 12 at 18.58; O. T. Taylor 11 at 24.27.

John Hampden Grammar School *Buckinghamshire*   P18 W9 L9 A3
Master i/c S. K. Parbery
A record 18 matches were played. The top five batsmen performed well, including a memorable 96
by Kieran Devereux against Wrekin College at the Bablake Festival. Young leg-spinner Toby Slater
took 27 wickets, including five for 17 against St George's, Weybridge.
Batting W. M. Shepherd 264 at 44.00; K. P. Devereux 426 at 38.72; *F. J. Clark 387 at 35.18;
W. C. S. Midwinter 183 at 30.50; W. A. Kidd 350 at 26.92.
Bowling T. J. B. Slater 27 at 10.92; F. R. B. Harmen 11 at 18.00; T. T. Lemon 12 at 21.00; K. P.
Devereux 11 at 30.09.

The John Lyon School *Middlesex*
P14 W8 L4 T1 D1 A2

Master i/c A. S. Ling
Coach C. T. Peploe

Defeat in the semi-final of the Middlesex County Cup was a rare disappointment for a team who showed great character. Abhay Hirani topped both averages, though Rahil Thapar was the pick of the bowlers. In his final game, Owen Marshall took his 100th first-team wicket.

Batting A. D. Hirani 302 at 30.20; *O. J. Marshall 237 at 21.54; Q. Y. D. Trevelyan 157 at 13.08.
Bowling A. D. Hirani 17 at 8.52; R. S. Bhatti 11 at 11.54; O. J. Marshall 28 at 14.96; R. K. Thapar 19 at 16.57; C. A. O. Rashid 12 at 23.16.

The Judd School *Kent*
P9 W2 L6 D1 A3

Master i/c R. M. Richardson

After a rewarding tour, several narrow defeats meant results did not fulfil the early promise. The team were led expertly by Callum Gallagher, who could rely on runs from Rory Easton and wickets from Archie Johnstone. The draw against MCC was especially memorable.

Batting *C. J. Gallagher 218 at 27.25; R. A. Easton 245 at 27.22.
Bowling A. R. M. Johnstone 11 at 17.36.

Kimbolton School *Huntingdonshire*
P15 W7 L8

Master i/c M. S. Gilbert
Coach A. J. Tudor

The summer was dominated by Joshua Smith, who hit a school-record 1,122 runs at 86, including a top score of 170 and four more centuries; he also claimed 24 wickets. Alex Kenyon, Oscar Bryden, Chris Oliver, Archie Carroll and Ben Szczepanski will hope to build on solid performances.

Batting *J. J. Smith 1,122 at 86.30; O. L. Bryden 257 at 21.41; J. P. Wilkins 156 at 19.50; A. C. Kenyon 264 at 17.60.
Bowling J. J. Smith 24 at 20.83; A. R. Carroll 12 at 34.91; B. D. Szczepanski 12 at 36.08; C. M. Oliver 17 at 38.00.

King Edward VI School, Southampton *Hampshire*
P14 W8 L3 D3

Master i/c D. Kent
Coach A. D. Penn

Another satisfying year included a 151-run win against Portsmouth Grammar School and ended with victory over Dauntsey's. The team were a mix of young and old, capably led by Jacob Fay, who finished his career with 99 not out in that final match.

Batting C. E. O. Harden 207 at 69.00; *J. L. Fay 333 at 47.57; B. M. D. Millar 214 at 35.67; J. Dhariwal 360 at 32.73.
Bowling J. Dhariwal 18 at 14.38; J. L. Fay 21 at 14.80; A. A. P. Millar 12 at 15.08; J. S. Gaunt 14 at 17.64.

King Edward's School, Birmingham *Warwickshire*
P19 W12 L7 A2

Master i/c L. M. Roll
Coach N. W. Round

Tanay Kulkarni led the school during an encouraging season. The side scored plenty of first-innings runs and, with only two boys leaving, hopes are high for even more success in 2019.

Batting S. S. Mangat 596 at 39.73; V. M. Sinha 514 at 36.71; *T. R. Kulkarni 401 at 33.41; A. Hussain 352 at 29.33; Y. Machani 365 at 24.33; A. A. Ali 203 at 22.55; S. Poshakwale 201 at 20.10.
Bowling H. Sohail 22 at 19.36; Y. Machani 10 at 24.60; T. R. Kulkarni 19 at 24.73; J. H. Taylor 11 at 26.18.

King's College School, Wimbledon *Surrey*
P24 W8 L14 D2 A1

Master i/c J. S. Gibson
Coaches B. T. Hudson and P. J. Scott

The 2018 season proved a curate's egg. Sanjay Patel's total of 1,074 runs (and five centuries) was a magnificent effort, and he provided the main impetus with the bat. Bobby Woodcock was leading wicket-taker, despite challenging bowling conditions.

Batting *S. H. Patel 1,074 at 89.50; D. Harish 253 at 21.08; A. R. Pillai 263 at 20.23; T. F. Huxtable 181 at 18.10; M. R. J. Ansell 280 at 17.50; C. A. King 259 at 17.26; D. H. Patel 150 at 16.66; F. B. Lamy 183 at 15.25.
Bowling R. E. Woodcock 25 at 25.08; O. H. Bekheit 11 at 29.63.

King's College, Taunton *Somerset*
P20 W14 L6

Master i/c R. J. Woodman
Coach P. D. Lewis

The college enjoyed another successful season, with plenty of rotation for senior players. A slip-up in the National Schools T20 did not overshadow a brilliant term, which was rounded off by winning the Woodard schools festival, hosted by Worksop College. Player of the season was Kazi Szymanski.

Batting J. Banton 786 at 52.40; *S. G. Wyatt 668 at 51.38; T. L. Harlow 400 at 33.33; W. C. F. Smeed 212 at 26.50; J. Whitemore 248 at 24.80; W. T. Smale 344 at 24.57; E. W. O. Middleton 186 at 20.66.
Bowling K. B. Szymanski 25 at 10.08; T. Hall 10 at 12.40; W. W. O. Middleton 37 at 13.67; M. Mejzner 18 at 17.77; J. Whitemore 12 at 34.08.

King's School, Bruton *Somerset*   P12 W5 L4 D3
Master i/c R. S. Hamilton   **Coach** M. R. Davies
There were high hopes for the season after many players returned from 2017, but the school did not quite fire on all cylinders, and lost or drew matches that could have been won. The performances of Arthur Harman with bat and ball are a testament to his hard work and passion for the game.
Batting M. J. Harvey 187 at 62.33; T. A. Rogers 257 at 51.40; A. L. Harman 255 at 28.33; *B. J. Latham 234 at 23.40.
Bowling P. J. Jenkins 10 at 13.10; A. L. Harman 17 at 22.64; S. Houldsworth 12 at 22.66.

The King's School, Canterbury *Kent*   P22 W9 L13 A4
Master i/c R. A. L. Singfield   **Coach** M. A. Ealham
After a good tour to the UAE, the first team had a tough start to the season, but came back well to secure some fine wins, including MCC and Band of Brothers. Isaac Rahman, the top run-scorer, was selected for Scotland Under-17s.
Batting I. A. Rahman 629 at 37.00; D. Gidoomal 394 at 28.14; *R. P. Heywood 471 at 24.78; W. J. Oates 355 at 19.72; S. Ravishankar 256 at 13.47; W. R. Sturges 177 at 10.41.
Bowling W. J. Oates 24 at 17.50; S. Ravishankar 18 at 19.16; Z. C. Barker 18 at 19.72; R. P. Heywood 18 at 23.44; G. T. C. Howard-Smith 18 at 26.83.

The King's School in Macclesfield *Cheshire*   P18 W11 L7 A2
Master i/c S. Moores   **Coach** A. J. Harris
A successful tour to Dubai was the precursor to a rewarding summer in which the XI reached the regional final of the National Schools T20. Owen Jones captained well, and there were strong performances from all-rounder Angus Thomson and Year 10 wicketkeeper Joey Chong.
Batting J. W. Chong 386 at 35.09; A. J. Thomson 507 at 31.68; G. J. C. Holden 219 at 24.33; S. S. Crosby 304 at 21.71; *O. R. Jones 255 at 19.61; H. H. S. Elms 257 at 18.35; S. J. Buckingham 229 at 15.26; T. R. Carter 152 at 12.66.
Bowling G. J. C. Holden 10 at 14.10; A. J. Thomson 19 at 17.52; O. R. Jones 18 at 20.16; S. H. Cheetham 11 at 21.00; G. F. Muirhead 15 at 21.20; W. Fosbrook 14 at 22.00; H. H. S. Elms 22 at 24.90.

King's School, Rochester *Kent*   P15 W5 L8 D2 A5
Master i/c C. H. Page   **Coach** D. A. Saunders
While no individual stood out, the collective efforts of a young team ensured a competitive season. Only one regular has left, so further progress is likely for 2019.
Batting T. D. J. Castle 355 at 23.66; R. J. Butler 238 at 19.83; *T. J. Miles 231 at 17.76; G. J. Taylor 195 at 17.72.
Bowling M. E. Butler 10 at 10.60; H. T. Fermor 15 at 13.53; R. J. Butler 10 at 22.60; T. D. J. Castle 15 at 22.66; T. J. Miles 11 at 25.45.

The King's School, Worcester *Worcestershire*   P20 W10 L10 A3
Master i/c S. D. Greenall   **Coach** A. A. D. Gillgrass
An excellent bowling unit gave the team a real edge, but the lack of runs meant winning games could be difficult. There were notable victories, however, against MCC and RGS Worcester.
Batting H. G. S. Armstrong 279 at 23.25; J. A. Hammond 351 at 21.93; O. K. Tsiquaye 254 at 19.53; *J. N. Sullivan 265 at 16.56; A. J. Robb 258 at 16.12.
Bowling O. K. Tsiquaye 16 at 14.00; A. J. Kite 12 at 15.75; F. J. Chance 18 at 17.22; J. A. Hammond 15 at 19.40; E. R. Burgoyne 21 at 21.76; T. W. Gidney 11 at 24.36; M. D. M. Richardson 18 at 26.11.

Kingswood School, Bath *Somerset*   P18 W9 L9 A1
Master i/c J. O. Brown   **Coach** J. Green
A promising season tailed off towards the end, though Oscar Kenyon and Matthew Hooper, young bowlers in their first season, both took more than 20 wickets. Al Mackenzie scored his maiden hundred, while stalwarts Henry Brearey and Harry Hodges enjoyed productive final seasons.

Batting A. F. G. Mackenzie 276 at 25.09; H. R. Brearey 318 at 24.46; O. B. Parry 344 at 21.50; W. Barnes 187 at 17.00; M. Kershaw 161 at 16.10; H. J. Walker 201 at 12.56; *O. G. Penney 197 at 11.58.

Bowling O. P. Kenyon 21 at 16.76; A. F. G. Mackenzie 11 at 18.09; M. W. R. Hooper 22 at 20.40; H. E. Hodges 17 at 22.58; H. R. Brearey 17 at 25.58.

Kirkham Grammar School *Lancashire* P10 W4 L4 T1 D1
Master i/c J. R. C. Lyon
The summer of 2018 was one of ups and downs. Nathan Wood proved a shrewd captain and, while several batsmen gained promising starts, none made a hundred.
Batting C. A. Doyle 152 at 19.00.
Bowling N. Wolff 11 at 9.90.

Lancaster Royal Grammar School *Lancashire* P18 W8 L9 D1 A3
Masters i/c I. W. Ledward and G. A. J. Mason   **Coach** I. Perryman
Ruairidh Barker led the school to their first success in the RGS Schools' Festival, with wins over Guildford, Worcester, Colchester and High Wycombe. Tom Anderton was Player of the Festival. Rohan Parekh was the leading bowler.
Batting T. E. J. Anderton 589 at 34.64; Y. S. Chabbra 363 at 24.20; J. A. Wills 300 at 23.07; H. Malik 272 at 20.92; *R. N. Barker 254 at 16.93.
Bowling T. E. J. Anderton 20 at 10.80; R. V. Parekh 33 at 11.27; R. N. Barker 14 at 22.14; J. A. Derham 16 at 23.00.

Lancing College *Sussex* P16 W9 L7 A1
Master i/c R. J. Maru
A young side, well captained by Oliver John, remained competitive all season. Thirteen-year-old Alice Capsey marked her debut, against Tiffin, with a wicket from her first ball, and finished with three for 20 from ten overs. Results were mixed, but there is much on which to build for 2019.
Batting L. Haddow 255 at 28.33; J. J. Coup 183 at 26.14; *O. J. John 341 at 22.73; E. Carniel 252 at 21.00.
Bowling W. H. Edgeler 19 at 21.05; M. G. E. Lee 17 at 24.35; H. A. Corney 17 at 25.11; O. J. John 18 at 29.77.

The Grammar School at Leeds *Yorkshire* P12 W7 L4 D1
Master i/c S. H. Dunn
Tyler Cant led with distinction. A lack of senior players gave many youngsters the chance to gain first-team experience. Sabir Mohammed (Year 7) showed great promise.
Batting E. Litvin 324 at 54.00; V. Sharma 203 at 50.75; B. R. Hemsley 294 at 29.40.
Bowling V. Sharma 14 at 15.57; B. R. Hemsley 12 at 26.75.

Leicester Grammar School *Leicestershire* P5 W1 L4 A5
Master i/c L. Potter
Summer had a frustrating start when four of the first five games were cancelled due to rain or a wet outfield. A school-record unbeaten 193 from Harry Pounds was an innings of class.
Batting H. Pounds 251 at 84.66.
Bowling The leading bowler was *D. R. Scudamore, who took five wickets at 21.00.

The Leys School *Cambridgeshire* P16 W9 L5 T1 D1 A1
Master i/c R. I. Kaufman   **Coach** W. J. Earl
Another successful season saw the school win most of their all-day fixtures. Andrew Bramley was the outstanding batsman, with 735 runs; Titus Waldock the most penetrative bowler, with 25 wickets.
Batting *A. S. Bramley 735 at 56.53; T. S. Waldock 298 at 42.57; O. P. L. Howell 424 at 32.61; J. S. Howlett 176 at 19.55; M. J. I. Aubrey 227 at 17.46.
Bowling T. S. Waldock 25 at 16.96; W. A. Latham 21 at 21.00; M. J. I. Aubrey 19 at 21.31; A. S. Bramley 20 at 22.85.

The Cathedral School, Llandaff *Glamorgan* P12 W5 L7 A3
Master i/c M. G. Barrington   **Coach** S. P. Jones
A fuller fixture card in the school's second season offered a challenge, while starting a two-day festival was a highlight; it was gratifying to reach the final. Will Youngs captained with maturity and drive, and Year 11 all-rounder Adam Khattak showed talent.

Jack Haynes, from Malvern College, the leading run-scorer in schools cricket in 2018. Eastbourne's Tawanda Muyeye claimed 33 wickets with his off-spin, and also hit an unbeaten 214.

Batting N. Satish 205 at 25.62; P. Saha 160 at 16.00; *W. J. Youngs 159 at 15.90; B. K. Das 173 at 15.72; A. Khattak 167 at 13.91.
Bowling A. Khattak 15 at 19.60.

Lord Wandsworth College *Hampshire* P13 W7 L5 D1 A1
Master i/c D. M. Beven
The most memorable moment of the year was the convincing defeat of MCC. The college had already played well, but in this match they were superior in every department.
Batting A. J. Brown 508 at 46.18; H. C. Trussler 350 at 29.16; *O. H. Hewetson-Brown 232 at 25.77; J. A. Young 232 at 25.77; T. E. C. H. Williams 177 at 13.61.
Bowling R. M. Lane 21 at 13.23; T. A. B. Leonard 17 at 16.52; S. M. Gilley 10 at 25.60; A. M. Lewis 12 at 25.75.

Loughborough Grammar School *Leicestershire* P17 W4 L12 D1
Master i/c M. I. Gidley
This was not a vintage summer. James O'Kelly and Dylan Church were sound openers, but had little support. Leg-spinner Chris Crowson took 25 wickets.
Batting J. W. O'Kelly 480 at 53.33; D. T. P. Church 507 at 29.82; M. L. R. Carr 354 at 25.28; *F. J. Towne 269 at 22.41; B. Thompson 267 at 17.80; L. Wales 209 at 17.41.
Bowling C. G. Crowson 25 at 23.00; B. Thompson 16 at 31.56.

Magdalen College School *Oxfordshire* P17 W14 L1 D2 A1
Master i/c C. Boyle **Coach** A. A. Duncan
This was an outstanding season, with 14 victories – over Bromsgrove, Malvern, Merchant Taylors', Bedford and others – in 17 matches. The team went unbeaten in 50-over cricket.
Batting *T. J. Price 550 at 45.83; A. T. Spittles 495 at 41.25; O. J. Price 473 at 39.41; J. M. Coles 179 at 22.37; F. H. Pietersen 159 at 15.90.
Bowling T. N. S. Chesser 33 at 11.12; O. J. Price 28 at 11.78; A. P. S. Chapman 19 at 13.63; H. J. R. Startin 13 at 19.30; T. J. Price 15 at 20.40.

Malvern College *Worcestershire*   P24 W16 L7 D1 A2
Master i/c M. A. Hardinges   **Coach** N. A. Brett

A youthful XI, boosted by true team spirit, achieved good wins against Shrewsbury, Harrow, Wellington and Bromsgrove, and made the quarter-finals of the National Schools T20. Jack Haynes proved an adept leader on and off the field, signed for Worcestershire and won selection for England Young Lions.

Batting *J. A. Haynes 1,393 at 66.33; C. E. Lea 723 at 32.86; S. Aggarwal 491 at 30.68; D. N. Holland 404 at 26.93; W. A. J. Sharp 173 at 17.30; M. Ahmed 227 at 16.21.

Bowling J. W. Dickenson 11 at 9.81; D. N. Holland 16 at 14.43; W. A. J. Sharp 30 at 18.16; J. O. Baker 28 at 18.57; J. A. Haynes 26 at 19.15; M. Ahmed 26 at 25.11; A. G. Tomson 24 at 26.66; L. A. Tulacz 15 at 26.80.

The Manchester Grammar School *Lancashire*   P13 W11 L2 A2
Master i/c M. Watkinson

The first XI prospered in 2018. Sam Perry, who hit three centuries, and Ollie Pooler, who broke the school record when he made 186 against Loughborough GS, hit the bulk of the runs. Several players represented county squads, and Perry was part of the Lancashire Academy.

Batting O. G. F. Pooler 602 at 60.20; *S. J. Perry 644 at 58.54; A. H. Makin 366 at 40.66; G. J. Bell 250 at 35.71; L. B. Poyser 237 at 33.85; A. Dooler 218 at 27.25.

Bowling G. W. Poyser 11 at 13.63; S. J. Perry 20 at 17.60; A. H. Makin 21 at 18.80; G. J. Valentine 10 at 39.10.

Marlborough College *Wiltshire*   P16 W1 L12 D3 A2
Master i/c M. P. L. Bush   **Coaches** M. W. Alleyne and J. P. Carroll

It proved a tough season for an inexperienced side, which included four of the Under-15 team who reached the Lord's Taverners semi-final. Dominic Coulson's leadership inspired a squad who have time on their side.

Batting W. E. B. Cook 307 at 34.11; B. R. L. Spink 351 at 31.90; T. J. Hargrove 176 at 25.14; H. J. Brooks 303 at 23.30; *D. H. Coulson 275 at 19.64; W. J. Hammersley 183 at 13.07.

Bowling F. O. Coen 10 at 26.60; O. C. J. Mace 12 at 29.41; J. A. Cleverly 14 at 32.07; D. H. Coulson 13 at 35.00.

Merchant Taylors' School, Crosby *Lancashire*   P16 W8 L8 A2
Master i/c S. P. Sutcliffe   **Coach** J. Cole

Tom Barker captained a cheerful team. Highlights included another win against MCC and good performances against Bolton and RGS Lancaster. The XI fared well in the Durham festival, beating The Perse and Newcastle Boys' School before falling four runs short of defeating the hosts in the final game. Kunal Mahambrey was the leading batsman, Jackson Darkes-Sutcliffe the leading bowler.

Batting R. F. Rankin 271 at 38.71; G. H. Politis 240 at 34.28; K. T. Mahambrey 409 at 31.46; J. Darkes-Sutcliffe 151 at 21.57; S. R. Bapu 229 at 19.08.

Bowling J. Darkes-Sutcliffe 23 at 19.47; H. J. Rankin 11 at 22.18.

Merchant Taylors' School, Northwood *Hertfordshire*   P18 W12 L4 D2 A2
Master i/c T. Webley

Another superb run in the National Schools T20 was the highlight of an impressive season. With most pitches taking spin, slow bowlers Ashane Wijesuriya, Aaron Amin and Sachin Shah proved too hot for opponents. Amin deserves special mention for taking 132 wickets in his first-team career.

Batting A. L. Wijesuriya 646 at 58.72; A. R. Amin 746 at 57.38; D. J. Burnell 657 at 46.92; A. Palmer 521 at 37.21; T. Steene 282 at 35.25; M. John 286 at 28.60.

Bowling A. R. Amin 31 at 12.38; S. Shah 28 at 13.39; R. Day 20 at 14.10; A. L. Wijesuriya 25 at 14.60; M. John 19 at 14.73; T. Steene 14 at 17.50.

Merchiston Castle School *Midlothian*   P14 W9 L5 A1
Master i/c R. D. McCann

A pleasing all-round summer for a youthful squad included a run of victories in the Scottish Schools T20 Cup that ended only in the final.

Batting D. J. Tidy 470 at 47.00; *T. Mackintosh Sabater 382 at 38.20; T. Martin 329 at 36.55.

Bowling M. Layton 16 at 14.87; R. Walker 13 at 28.76.

Mill Hill School *Middlesex*   P11 W4 L6 D1 A2
Master i/c S. Patel
This was a season of rebuilding, and the team were stretched. The biggest positive was that newly blooded players gained valuable experience.
Batting C. Plummer 153 at 30.60; J. Drage 221 at 27.62; S. Bogiatzis 155 at 17.22.
Bowling S. Bogiatzis 11 at 26.27.

Millfield School *Somerset*   P18 W16 L2 A1
Master i/c M. Garaway   **Coach** D. J. Helesfay
Millfield had another wonderful year, winning all but two matches in a strong fixture list and lifting the National Schools T20 Cup at Arundel in June. The Under-15 girls and Under-17 boys also won their national finals in September. Charles Clist made a school-record 254 not out against Canford, and Alex Eckland hit two centuries. Julius Sumerauer was the leading wicket-taker.
Batting A. J. Eckland 443 at 73.83; C. J. Clist 801 at 53.40; T. R. Bevan 603 at 50.25; L. P. Goldsworthy 251 at 50.20; M. Critchley 341 at 42.63; *S. J. Young 381 at 34.64.
Bowling J. T. S. Sumerauer 27 at 12.19; M. W. Hancock 12 at 12.42; L. P. Goldsworthy 15 at 15.93; T. R. Bevan 25 at 17.20; N. O. Leonard 12 at 24.83; W. D. J. Easterfield 26 at 26.23.

Monkton *Somerset*   P21 W10 L11 A1
Master i/c S. P. J. Palmer   **Coach** J. C. A. Leggett
A total of ten wins was the best in the school's history. Captaincy was shared between all-rounder Will Arney and wicketkeeper-batsman Ben Wells, who became the school's leading all-time run-scorer with 2,273. The highlight was retaining the Bath Schools' T20 Cup.
Batting *B. J. J. Wells 611 at 61.10; D. R. Call 330 at 23.57; *W. G. K. Arney 360 at 18.94; O. C. Shrubb 260 at 13.68; L. J. Walker 251 at 13.21.
Bowling S. White 30 at 13.30; L. J. Hunnisett 29 at 14.13; W. G. K. Arney 23 at 16.82; A. W. Parashar 29 at 17.06; O. A. A. Adeleye 17 at 21.64; D. R. Call 12 at 33.50.

Monmouth School *Monmouthshire*   P17 W8 L7 D2
Master i/c A. J. Jones
A strong second half of the summer showed the side's potential. There was a maiden first-team century by Harry Friend and an excellent eight for 23 from leg-spinner Sam Swingwood – both Year 10s. Angus McIntyre adroitly captained a young side, and was supported by Nathan Lee, who again passed 500 runs.
Batting N. J. Lee 569 at 40.64; H. Friend 364 at 36.40; *A. D. McIntyre 453 at 34.84; M. Burger 343 at 26.38; T. W. Franklin 168 at 24.00.
Bowling S. Swingwood 30 at 15.06; H. Friend 14 at 16.92; B. W. Skailes 16 at 21.00.

Mount Kelly School *Devon*   P20 W15 L4 D1 A5
Master i/c G. D. James
This was an exceptional season for a young and developing team intelligently led by Leon Horn. The XI – who enjoyed their first international tour – progressed to the later stages of the National Schools T20. Abraham Kopparambil hit 152 not out against Bristol Grammar to break the school record.
Batting *L. Horn 677 at 48.35; J. M. Brady 244 at 40.66; A. S. Kopparambil 574 at 35.87; T. Gerry 201 at 33.50; O. M. Allsop 429 at 33.00; A. Creasey 310 at 23.84.
Bowling B. E. Bruck-Jackson 13 at 16.46; A. S. Kopparambil 20 at 22.90; T. M. Douie 10 at 24.20; L. Horn 14 at 29.14; J. Staig 10 at 38.60.

New Hall School *Essex*   P18 W11 L7 A6
Master i/c P. M. Davidge
This was a season of firsts: winning 11 matches, entering the National Schools T20 and playing a two-day fixture – all uncharted territory for New Hall. Highlights were the two-day victory over St Albans by eight wickets, and recovering from 68 for seven to beat Eltham College.
Batting N. Khelawon 513 at 42.75; V. A. Gandhi 351 at 29.25; R. J. McKenna 266 at 24.18; *S. C. Sullivan 309 at 23.76; J. Hussain 155 at 17.22; C. M. Limrick 199 at 13.26.
Bowling F. E. Bright 16 at 11.62; A. Boparai 19 at 16.47; S. C. Sullivan 17 at 17.29; C. M. Limrick 21 at 18.90; N. Khelawon 10 at 21.60; V. A. Gandhi 17 at 22.17; A. D. Berry 11 at 32.09.

Newcastle under Lyme School *Staffordshire*

P14 W5 L8 D1 A3

Master i/c G. M. Breen   **Coaches** J. Allenby and J. F. Brown

Player availability was not an issue, though results did not noticeably pick up. Instead there was an enhanced team spirit, even against stronger schools. In the last-over draw with MCC, Rohan Hesketh and Eemeli Heiskanen (both Year 10) put on 86 for the first wicket, setting the scene for Peter Vickers to hit 66 from 73 balls, an immaculate innings which included six fours and four sixes.

Batting P. J. Vickers 222 at 31.71; P. E. Heiskanen 250 at 25.00; J. H. Wagg 216 at 19.63; O. J. Tinsley 187 at 14.38; *F. J. Meredith 155 at 12.91.

Bowling A. C. Munro 14 at 9.92; P. J. Vickers 15 at 14.46; R. G. Hesketh 13 at 19.23; W. D. Clarke 14 at 19.78; P. M. Clarke 11 at 23.36; O. J. Tinsley 12 at 26.25.

Norwich School *Norfolk*

P19 W13 L4 T1 D1 A3

Master i/c J. L. O. Cawkwell   **Coach** R. W. Sims

Norwich won 13 matches thanks to some superb cricket. All-rounders Alfie Cooper, Oscar Binny and Charlie Rogers made huge contributions to one of the strongest teams Norwich have produced; the squad can be proud of their hard work and dedication.

Batting O. R. Binny 731 at 56.23; C. W. Rogers 563 at 46.91; *A. J. H. Cooper 520 at 43.33; D. Long-Martinez 553 at 36.86.

Bowling O. R. Binny 15 at 13.33; C. W. Rogers 36 at 14.72; A. J. H. Cooper 25 at 14.72; D. G. Hastings 12 at 23.91; G. Angier 10 at 24.90; H. R. N. Williams 15 at 27.33; J. P. Hardy 14 at 32.57.

Nottingham High School *Nottinghamshire*

P15 W5 L10 A6

Master i/c M. Baker   **Coach** P. M. Borrington

In a term of highs and lows, inconsistency affected results. Haris Khalil performed well, and Eduardo Martin and Neel Badhe enjoyed strong debut seasons. The odd moment aside, the batting did not live up to potential.

Batting H. Khalil 278 at 27.80; B. J. R. Martindale 187 at 26.71; S. R. Menon 185 at 23.12.

Bowling N. Badhe 10 at 11.20.

Oakham School *Rutland*

P22 W16 L6 A1

Master i/c N. C. Johnson   **Coaches** T. G. Stokes and F. C. Hayes

A committed group of cricketers – perhaps including one or two emerging stars for 2019 – enjoyed a reasonably successful season. Against other schools, Oakham won 12 and lost five: the modern game allows no draws.

Batting B. N. Lewin 457 at 38.08; N. J. Kimber 557 at 34.81; R. N. Bell 472 at 29.50; H. J. Tyler 150 at 21.42; H. J. S. Tattersall 391 at 20.57; A. W. G. Jones 189 at 18.90; E. J. W. Siddle 224 at 18.66; *A. W. Grieve 364 at 18.20; A. P. Anthony 175 at 8.75.

Bowling N. J. Kimber 20 at 12.65; E. J. W. Siddle 16 at 14.62; H. J. Tyler 29 at 16.86; A. W. G. Jones 21 at 17.19; O. R. Drakard 23 at 21.13; C. F. Morley 26 at 21.61.

The Oratory School *Oxfordshire*

P15 W8 L6 D1

Master i/c S. C. B. Tomlinson

A callow XI performed maturely and played positively, with some fine team and individual performances in the second part of the season. Maturely led by Year 12 Jarryd Wallace, the entire team will return for 2019.

Batting *J. K. Wallace 268 at 33.50; J. C. Winterbottom 180 at 25.71; C. Thomas 164 at 18.22.

Bowling J. K. Wallace 17 at 12.94; J. C. Winterbottom 11 at 15.27; J. Mather 12 at 15.83; A. Baxter 10 at 20.40.

Oundle School *Northamptonshire*

P15 W8 L4 D3

Master i/c J. P. Crawley   **Coach** M. Genis

A tally of eight wins was fair reward for a team that blended youth and experience. The captain, Simon Fernandes, averaged 94 and scored more runs than the rest of the batting combined. Oundle did not fare well at the Silk Trophy, but played good – sometimes excellent – cricket. They bowled well as a unit, but more runs must be the target for 2019.

Batting *S. M. L. Fernandes 947 at 94.70; T. J. Simeons 348 at 49.71; T. D. P. Aubrey 172 at 28.67; J. I. Esler 179 at 19.89; W. G. de Capell Brooke 156 at 17.33.

Bowling H. J. Woodrow 20 at 15.35; T. D. P. Aubrey 17 at 16.06; T. J. Reyner 10 at 22.10; T. J. Simeons 11 at 25.36; P. J. O. Fisher 15 at 27.73; J. I. Esler 22 at 28.73.

Simon Fernandes of Oundle played for MCC Schools; Ben Chapman-Lilley hit 1,099 runs for Repton.

The Perse School *Cambridgeshire*   P12 W2 L8 D2 A5

Master i/c S. M. Park

There were opportunities for the most promising players of any age group to experience first-team cricket. Under-15 batsmen Nikhil Gorantla and Henry Howarth were outstanding.

Batting H. J. S. Howarth 212 at 35.33; N. V. Gorantla 231 at 33.00; D. F. Shaw 204 at 25.50; *T. R. Baldwin 247 at 24.70.

Bowling A. Tandon 10 at 23.50.

Pocklington School *Yorkshire*   P15 W10 L5

Master i/c D. Byas

Had there been better performances against Ampleforth and St Peter's, this would have been an outstanding season. Charlie Foster led the team astutely, and received excellent support from Jimmy Wraith and Rory Stephenson.

Batting R. Stephenson 462 at 42.00; W. D. Watts 448 at 40.72; J. A. Wraith 397 at 36.09; *C. B. Foster 387 at 27.64.

Bowling J. A. Wraith 28 at 15.50; C. B. Foster 16 at 16.31; R. Stephenson 17 at 21.58; E. R. Wraith 16 at 21.68; T. P. P. Kirby 11 at 23.81.

The Portsmouth Grammar School *Hampshire*   P12 W6 L5 D1

Master i/c S. J. Curwood   **Coach** S. D. Lavery

After a slow start, hampered by poor pre-season weather, the first XI improved throughout the summer. The side showed maturity beyond their years, learned from defeat as much as victory, and played quality cricket in June and July.

Batting O. T. Wright 373 at 62.16; C. M. Pratt 263 at 29.22; T. Wallis 237 at 26.33; J. J. McBride 260 at 26.00; *J. F. Kooner-Evans 208 at 26.00.

Bowling J. F. Kooner-Evans 14 at 18.71; M. Beckett 10 at 31.00.

Prior Park College *Somerset*   P16 W7 L9

Master i/c R. J. Pandya   **Coach** M. D. Bond

After a strong start, Prior Park struggled to close out matches. Will South was the top run-scorer, and Greg Harden headed the wicket count. Despite the tailing-off in form, this was a pleasing season.

Batting A. F. Parson 335 at 30.45; W. A. South 359 at 27.61; A. Wortlehock 256 at 21.33; G. C. Harden 157 at 19.62; E. A. Mortimer 263 at 17.53; *J. T. Avenell 163 at 16.30; T. Pitman 188 at 13.42; A. Bramwell 182 at 13.00.

Bowling L. M. Theobald 11 at 10.00; G. C. Harden 24 at 16.50; W. A. South 18 at 17.88; J. T. Avenell 17 at 19.52; T. Pitman 13 at 20.53.

Queen Elizabeth Grammar School, Wakefield *Yorkshire*   P11 W3 L8
Master i/c S. A. Wood
A small pool of senior cricketers and a lack of availability led to defeats in all longer-format games. However, there were two wins in the National Schools T20, victory in the Bradford GS Sixes competition, and a superb century against MCC by the captain, Harry Thompson.
Batting *H. D. Thompson 338 at 56.33; V. S. Patel 201 at 33.50; O. G. H. Appleyard 157 at 19.62.
Bowling The leading bowler was H. L. Dyke, who took seven wickets at 39.85.

Queen Elizabeth's Hospital, Bristol *Gloucestershire*   P12 W4 L8 A1
Master i/c P. E. Joslin   **Coach** D. C. Forder
Ed Wilson, captain for a second year, set a fine all-round example. Ben Jarman hit most runs, while Wilson's bowling was backed up by Fuzael Ahmed, Daaryoush Ahmed, Ben Yuen and Ben Harding.
Batting B. W. Jarman 258 at 32.25; *E. W. T. Wilson 239 at 29.87.
Bowling D. J. Ahmed 10 at 9.30; F. J. Ahmed 13 at 12.84; E. W. T. Wilson 14 at 14.14.

Queen Mary's Grammar School, Walsall *Staffordshire*   P14 W8 L6 A2
Master i/c B. T. Gibbons   **Coach** J. O. Hawkins
A youthful team produced several memorable victories, including those against Newcastle under Lyme, King Edward VI Camp Hill and John Hampden Grammar School. Captain Rohit Suglani hit most runs and claimed most wickets.
Batting *R. R. Suglani 387 at 35.18; J. J. Millerchip 384 at 32.00; H. J. Iqbal 239 at 23.90; D. Tandon 163 at 18.11.
Bowling R. R. Suglani 12 at 23.08; D. Tandon 10 at 23.10.

Queen's College, Taunton *Somerset*   P13 W8 L4 D1
Master i/c A. G. Hamilton   **Coach** J. B. Lintott
This was an excellent season for the first team. Only once in the school's 175-year history had a student scored more than Fionn Hand's 156; and at times his bowling was unplayable. Henrique Pieterse has a rare talent. He hit 947 runs and took 22 wickets.
Batting H. W. Pieterse 947 at 86.09; *F. Hand 341 at 56.83; T. Hazell-Evans 312 at 28.36; J. P. Duckering 311 at 23.92; M. Thompson 152 at 19.00.
Bowling F. Hand 17 at 11.94; H. W. Pieterse 22 at 15.68; M. Thompson 14 at 21.14; J. P. Duckering 11 at 26.55.

Radley College *Oxfordshire*   P18 W9 L8 D1 A4
Master i/c S. H. Dalrymple   **Coach** A. R. Wagner
A summer term slightly disrupted by injury included notable wins against Wellington in the National Schools T20, Charterhouse and Marlborough – and a thrilling last-over defeat by Harrow. The season ended at St Edward's with a fantastic stand of 149 between two Year 12s.
Batting H. J. A. Chapman 591 at 45.46; D. V. Brooke 564 at 40.28; H. W. Purton 333 at 25.61; F. J. R. Horler 383 at 25.53; *R. A. Betley 354 at 23.60.
Bowling L. L. F. Needham 14 at 17.92; H. W. Purton 20 at 20.25; W. C. K. Carr 10 at 22.40; W. G. Barker 16 at 28.18; H. J. A. Chapman 15 at 30.73; M. C. Martin-Zakheim 13 at 42.76.

Ratcliffe College *Leicestershire*   P14 W10 L2 D2 A2
Master i/c E. O. Woodcock
In a year of great success, the captain, Jack Nightingale, continued to play for Leicestershire Seconds. As he had in 2017, Toby Snell led the batting, while the bowling was dominated by the spin of Oliver Welch, George Morgan-Jones and Finley Back.
Batting *J. E. Nightingale 388 at 77.60; T. Snell 724 at 60.33; A. D. King 189 at 31.50; O. R. Welch 227 at 25.22; G. W. A. Morgan-Jones 150 at 15.00.
Bowling F. J. W. Back 10 at 12.40; T. Snell 20 at 13.35; O. R. Welch 23 at 17.69; G. W. A. Morgan-Jones 18 at 25.38.

Reading Blue Coat School *Berkshire*   P15 W6 L8 T1
Master i/c P. J. B. Davies   **Coach** P. D. Wise
The first team had a distinctly young look for much of the year, which will serve them well. The fixture list was altered to include some of the region's best cricketing schools.
Batting T. L. Greatwood 389 at 55.57; T. Price 236 at 26.22; J. Hill 213 at 19.36; *W. J. Perkin 184 at 16.73.
Bowling J. Harris 11 at 28.00; K. Shah 11 at 31.09.

Reed's School *Surrey*   P15 W8 L3 D4 A1
Master i/c M. R. Dunn   **Coach** K. T. Medlycott
Nathan Tilley dominated the batting, hitting six centuries (including four over 150) and ending the
summer with a school-record 1,256 runs at an average of almost 140. Max Hogben was the other
half of a productive opening pair. George Griffiths, the leading all-rounder, spun his way to 30
wickets, while Jack Kenningham again spearheaded the attack.
Batting *N. J. Tilley 1,256 at 139.55; N. J. L. Morgan 309 at 44.14; G. W. Griffiths 362 at 40.22;
M. D. Hogben 461 at 35.46; H. G. D. Alderson 280 at 35.00; S. G. Moldon 216 at 27.00.
Bowling G. W. Griffiths 30 at 20.00; J. D. Kenningham 18 at 20.55; N. J. L. Morgan 13 at 21.30;
H. P. R. Williams 10 at 38.10.

Reigate Grammar School *Surrey*   P13 W2 L8 D3 A7
Master i/c J. M. C. Leck   **Coach** J. E. Benjamin
The weather marred the start of the season, forcing the abandonment of fixtures that should have
built momentum. The inexperience of many players, plus the disappointing form of the seniors,
resulted in a summer of development and transition.
Batting M. G. Crighton 208 at 29.71; S. J. W. Hall 165 at 27.50; *A. Bhat 174 at 21.75; D. C. Grant
165 at 18.33; T. H. T. Guise 152 at 16.88.
Bowling J. M. V. Flanders 14 at 23.64; T. H. T. Guise 11 at 23.90.

Repton School *Derbyshire*   P21 W10 L8 D3 A2
Master i/c I. M. Pollock   **Coach** J. A. Afford
For the third year running, Repton finished with ten wins – an impressive feat on a com-
petitive circuit. Ben Chapman-Lilley became only the third Reptonian in over 150 years to pass
1,000 runs in a season; the others were England Test players Chris Adams (1,242) and Richard
Hutton (1,056).
Batting *B. J. Chapman-Lilley 1,099 at 73.26; W. A. Hobson 488 at 37.53; A. G. Bennett 225 at
25.00; S. Sayer 226 at 20.54; A. S. Chima 253 at 18.07; E. Berlusconi 167 at 13.91.
Bowling L. S. C. Brown 32 at 13.21; E. Berlusconi 12 at 22.08; B. J. Chapman-Lilley 24 at 23.12;
T. A. Buffin 27 at 23.22; W. A. Hobson 19 at 27.15; T. S. Jones 14 at 39.07.

Rossall School *Lancashire*   P8 W5 L2 D1 A4
Master i/c M. J. Kelly   **Coach** I. C. Bergh
Rossall enjoyed their most successful season in recent years, thanks to a small group of senior players
who were well supported by some talented youngsters. Wins against Giggleswick and Stonyhurst
were the highlights. Departing captain James Amor gave many years of fine service.
Batting W. Gair 153 at 76.50; C. Clark 169 at 33.80; C. Ardron 192 at 27.42; J. Hamnett 159
at 22.71.
Bowling *J. S. Amor 12 at 5.75; J. Hamnett 14 at 15.85.

Royal Grammar School, Guildford *Surrey*   P16 W10 L5 D1
Master i/c R. C. Black   **Coach** M. W. Barnes
A summer of superb Surrey weather was accompanied by a superb summer of cricket. A huge
positive for the 2019 squad is the emergence of so many good young players; should they work hard
in the off-season, they should reap the rewards.
Batting A. Gonella 732 at 56.30; *B. E. Thomas 652 at 50.15; H. S. M. Green 367 at 30.58; Y. S.
Hafiz 191 at 13.64.
Bowling F. P. Cousins 10 at 15.50; A. Gonella 19 at 15.52; A. Ashfaque 12 at 16.66; E. J. Milton-
Seall 25 at 17.68; T. J. Eves 21 at 20.38; Y. S. Hafiz 11 at 27.45.

Royal Grammar School, High Wycombe *Bucks*   P16 W3 L11 D2 A4
Master i/c B. T. R. Berryman
Rain gave the season a slow start, while poor availability made a tough fixture list even tougher.
Harry Cameron captained well and proved himself a capable all-rounder. Despite a difficult term,
there is optimism that a youthful team has a bright future.

Isaac Dilkes of St Lawrence College made an undefeated 150 against Eltham College; Josh de Caires, the son of Mike Atherton, topped the St Albans averages with bat and ball.

Batting Y. Rastogi 213 at 30.43; A. M. McDonald 179 at 25.57; F. G. Wells 157 at 19.63; Z. A. Khan 225 at 17.31; J. F. Baldwin 254 at 16.93; *H. M. E. Cameron 178 at 14.83.
Bowling J. C. T. D. Dalby 16 at 23.81; H. M. E. Cameron 15 at 25.60; S. Iqbal 10 at 29.80; Z. A. Khan 15 at 20.20.

Royal Grammar School, Newcastle *Northumberland*   P16 W8 L8
Master i/c M. J. Smalley   **Coach** D. Shurben
A callow side performed well at the RGS Festival in Lancaster and, with strong showings against the Grammar School at Leeds, Sedbergh and Durham, there is plenty to come in the next three years.
Batting M. D. Watts 387 at 35.18; R. J. Hanley 346 at 31.45; *P. Mannikar 258 at 25.80; A. Elder 258 at 19.84.
Bowling R. J. Hanley 21 at 12.86; M. F. Jennings 13 at 13.85; J. V. Boaden 17 at 14.82; A. Ramesh 15 at 15.80; C. J. Fletcher 13 at 24.00.

Royal Grammar School, Worcester *Worcestershire*   P21 W14 L7 A2
Master i/c M. D. Wilkinson   **Coach** P. J. Newport
Twice as many victories as defeats represented a successful term. The school were stronger in bowling, with spinners Ben Sutton (Year 10) and Luke Allen (Year 11) leading the way. There were many exciting wins, thanks in part to an indomitable team spirit. Four out of five at the RGS Festival was a great finish.
Batting *G. S. Cook 568 at 29.89; B. R. Llewellyn 178 at 25.42; B. R. Sutton 284 at 23.66; L. W. A. Dear 403 at 22.38; J. E. J. Rees 202 at 20.20; B. M. Hawkes 224 at 18.66; A. E. P. Rees 347 at 17.35; J. M. Corlett 281 at 16.52; B. O. Selby 247 at 15.43.
Bowling B. R. Sutton 39 at 15.76; L. R. Allen 32 at 20.06; W. A. Reading 16 at 20.06; O. J. N. Sankey 19 at 20.78; B. M. Hawkes 15 at 32.53; G. S. Cook 11 at 47.63.

Rugby School *Warwickshire*   P12 W3 L6 D3 A1
Master i/c A. E. L. Thomson   **Coach** M. J. Powell
Rugby improved as the days lengthened, despite a team of less experience than in recent years. The captain, Henry Anton, rounded off the summer with an excellent maiden century at Clifton College. Fourteen-year-old Jacob Bethell – an exciting prospect – was the leading wicket-taker.
Batting *H. J. R. Anton 394 at 43.78; J. G. Bethell 283 at 21.76; J. S. Z. Montfort Bebb 255 at 21.25; W. J. Hardman 227 at 20.63.
Bowling W. R. Gardener 17 at 19.12; J. G. Bethell 18 at 20.00.

Rydal Penrhos *Denbighshire*   P8 L8
Master i/c M. T. Leach
Llewellyn Cowell, captain (and part-time assistant groundsman) led by example. He got the best out of several young players, including Year 7 leg-spinner Arran Sen, who topped the bowling.
Batting *J. A. Jones 169 at 21.12.
Bowling A. Sen 14 at 17.92.

St Albans School *Hertfordshire*   P20 W13 L5 D2 A2
Master i/c M. C. Ilott
The school enjoyed their most successful season since first appearing in *Wisden* in 1916, with 13 wins. Josh de Caires and Charlie Scott had great seasons at the crease, while de Caires and fellow off-spinner Gus Laws-Mather frequently turned games on their head.
Batting J. M. de Caires 699 at 53.76; *C. F. B. Scott 696 at 49.71; B. E. Yurkwich 226 at 32.28; A. Laws-Mather 404 at 28.85; W. E. Thomson 282 at 21.69; B. Craig 167 at 13.91.
Bowling J. M. de Caires 33 at 18.09; A. Laws-Mather 15 at 19.66; H. E. Wilcox 17 at 20.29; J. Deanne 10 at 20.40; T. Gerrard 10 at 22.00; B. W. Warren 16 at 22.25; H. J. Craig 10 at 28.00.

St Benedict's School, Ealing *Middlesex*   P13 W5 L7 D1
Master i/c K. Newell
An excellent start, containing four wins in five matches, fell away, but Tomek Tsang continued to shine as an all-rounder. The backbone of the side remains for 2019, so hopes are high.
Batting T. J. L. Tsang 374 at 37.40; C. Pyne 309 at 25.75; T. J. Knight 218 at 19.81.
Bowling T. J. L. Tsang 12 at 16.25; J. M. L. Chippendale 12 at 18.66.

St Edmund's School, Canterbury *Kent*   P10 W8 L2
Master i/c A. R. Jones   **Coach** C. W. Bodle
A talented group of players achieved superb results. Fast bowler Ben Mills, who turned out for Kent Seconds, and batsman Joe Gordon led the way, though there were valuable contributions from many senior players.
Batting B. J. Croft 297 at 74.25; J. A. Gordon 366 at 52.28; M. A. Nordin 303 at 37.87.
Bowling B. C. Mills 25 at 7.12; L. P. V. N. Gray 12 at 12.58; *J. B. Nordin 12 at 18.58.

St Edward's School, Oxford *Oxfordshire*   P26 W13 L8 D5
Master i/c P. O. B. Swainson   **Coach** D. P. Simpkins
Despite some long-term injuries, the first team enjoyed another successful year, culminating in victory over Radley to win the John Harvey Cup for a record sixth time. Captain Harrison Ward and leading run-scorer Ben Charlesworth were selected for England Under-19.
Batting B. G. Charlesworth 1,115 at 65.58; *H. D. Ward 864 at 54.00; P. A. Ades 782 at 39.10; T. J. Kershaw 152 at 30.40; T. E. R. Powell 366 at 26.14; A. J. Horton 434 at 22.84; L. A. Charlesworth 215 at 21.50.
Bowling B. G. Charlesworth 16 at 10.81; H. D. Ward 35 at 15.51; J. E. Marsh 25 at 21.12; J. A. Curtis 40 at 24.35; T. E. R. Powell 18 at 30.27; L. A. Charlesworth 11 at 38.54.

St George's College, Weybridge *Surrey*   P13 W7 L6 A2
Master i/c O. J. Clayson   **Coach** R. Hall
The season was about teamwork, graft, learning and exciting cricket – as well as more wins than defeats. The main performers were Charlie Brennen, Arya Behl, Will Hilton and Harry Martin.
Batting H. Martin 230 at 25.55; M. Richardson 195 at 17.72; W. Hilton 170 at 15.45.
Bowling A. Behl 15 at 18.00; C. Brennen 16 at 18.68.

St John's School, Leatherhead *Surrey*   P12 W8 L3 D1 A1
Master i/c D. J. Hammond
A young side, led astutely by Ben Geddes, gave their all, winning eight out of 12 games. Highlights included maiden first-team centuries for Luke Trimming and Jordan Bond, and a hat-trick from Will Sanders. Robbie Dennis, a 13-year-old left-arm spinner, looks one for the future.
Batting J. H. L. Bond 364 at 40.44; L. C. Trimming 460 at 38.33; *B. B. A. Geddes 381 at 31.75; J. E. Potter 178 at 22.25; W. M. Farnsworth 221 at 18.41.
Bowling W. M. Farnsworth 10 at 11.00; W. E. Sanders 14 at 15.21; B. B. A. Geddes 13 at 18.00.

Angle of attack: Jamie Curtis took 40 wickets for St Edward's, Oxford, while his team-mate, Harrison Ward, played for England Under-19s.

St Joseph's College *Surrey*   P12 W4 L6 D2 A4
Master i/c E. M. Tyler
The season contained strong performances in red- and white-ball cricket. While some individuals stood out, much of the success derived from the desire to play as a team.
Batting *D. R. Shanks 290 at 48.33; H. D. Skinner 300 at 33.33; K. J. H. Waldock 215 at 19.55; J. P. Colcomb 162 at 16.20.
Bowling D. R. Shanks 13 at 16.23; O. W. Stace 13 at 16.69; G. J. S. Jones 14 at 20.57.

St Lawrence College *Kent*   P15 W10 L4 D1
Master i/c S. M. Simmons   **Coach** T. Moulton
In the best batting year since 1927, the first team recorded five hundreds, and two double-century stands, plus another of 190. Isaac Dilkes, whose initials mark him as a dashing batsman, played for Kent Seconds. Harrison Smith and Spencer Smith leave after distinguished service, but the rest return.
Batting *I. V. A. Dilkes 775 at 70.45; J. A. Mitchell 433 at 43.30; H. C. Smith 421 at 42.10; A. E. Ralph-Harding 192 at 27.42.
Bowling I. V. A. Dilkes 15 at 15.86; H. C. Smith 10 at 21.00.

St Paul's School *Surrey*   P12 W7 L3 D2 A4
Master i/c N. E. Briers
Notable wins included Dulwich, Hampton, RGS Guildford, The Leys, KCS Wimbledon and Fettes. Left-arm spinner Abdullah Nazir played for Sussex Seconds, while Anosh Malik turned out for Middlesex Under-17s, and Freddie Eltringham for Surrey Under-17s. In his first full season, Freddie Harrison took 21 wickets with his leg-spin.
Batting F. P. Eltringham 438 at 39.81; F. R. Walter 291 at 24.25; A. Malik 213 at 21.30; *A. Nazir 205 at 20.50.
Bowling F. W. J. Harrison 21 at 16.33; F. R. Walter 15 at 16.33; Z. J. L. Campbell 12 at 17.75; A. Nazir 12 at 21.00.

St Peter's School, York *Yorkshire*   P22 W13 L5 D4 A4
Master i/c G. J. Sharp
Under the strong leadership of Alex Liley, a young, talented and enthusiastic team had an excellent season; they reached the North final of the National Schools T20. Year 12 Christopher Wood will lead in 2019.

English Domestic Cricket

Batting M. Lodge 550 at 45.83; H. R. Contreras 640 at 45.71; C. D. S. Wood 538 at 41.38; *A. Liley 576 at 32.00; B. T. Lodge 448 at 26.35; M. T. Roberts 325 at 21.66; J. J. Amsden 251 at 20.91; H. Gration 192 at 17.45; I. N. Giannini 155 at 12.91.

Bowling J. J. Amsden 10 at 14.00; J. R. Bramley 10 at 14.10; M. T. Roberts 30 at 14.76; H. R. Contreras 13 at 18.07; C. D. S. Wood 21 at 19.19; H. Gration 22 at 24.54; I. P. Watson 10 at 25.10; I. N. Giannini 21 at 27.61; F. H. Southgate 10 at 39.00.

Sedbergh School *Yorkshire*   P24 W18 L5 D1 A3

Master i/c C. P. Mahon   **Coach** M. P. Speight

An inexperienced side had a magnificent season, winning the BOWS Festival and reaching the semi-final of the National Schools T20. Sam Barrett and George Hill were outstanding throughout: both came agonisingly close to 1,000 runs – particularly Hill, who fell one short of reaching four figures and averaging three. They also shared 56 wickets.

Batting G. C. H. Hill 999 at 99.90; *S. Barrett 993 at 43.17; A. M. Ebbin 397 at 30.53; L. S. Johnson 218 at 24.22; K. Hull 210 at 19.09; T. Aspinwall 169 at 18.77; T. J. Manihera 341 at 17.94; C. Park-Johnson 375 at 17.04; B. J. Davidson 187 at 17.00.

Bowling B. J. Davidson 16 at 14.50; M. A. Forde 21 at 17.28; G. C. H. Hill 24 at 18.45; B. B. G. Hickey 17 at 18.64; S. Barrett 32 at 20.37; T. Aspinwall 17 at 21.70; C. A. W. Jeffers 29 at 23.03.

Sevenoaks School *Kent*   P16 W10 L5 D1 A1

Master i/c C. J. Tavaré   **Coach** P. J. Hulston

After the first team lost their first three matches, the season looked up: under the shrewd leadership of Rhys Joseph, ten of the next 12 ended in victory. The outstanding performer was Harry Houillon, whose 129 not out overcame MCC. Joseph and Michael Procter took most wickets.

Batting H. F. Houillon 416 at 83.20; *R. L. Joseph 249 at 27.66; P. D. Nickols 373 at 24.86.

Bowling A. E. Marr-Johnson 11 at 15.00; O. E. Chaplin 11 at 18.36; M. L. Procter 15 at 24.20; R. L. Joseph 16 at 25.06; A. G. Sackville-West 10 at 32.00.

Shebbear College *Devon*   P10 W6 L4

Master i/c A. B. Bryan

Several overseas players helped ensure it was a year to remember: Siyo Nyawose made 116 in the victory over local rivals West Buckland, while Romario Brathwaite grabbed five in an eight-wicket defeat of MCC.

Batting R. Roach 179 at 35.80; I. Philander 202 at 33.66; S. Nyawose 245 at 24.50; E. Jones 185 at 23.12.

Bowling Z. Jaftha 11 at 8.00; I. Philander 16 at 8.06; R. Brathwaite 18 at 11.61; E. Jones 12 at 17.41.

Sherborne School *Dorset*   P15 W9 L6

Master i/c A. D. Nurton   **Coach** M. G. Pardoe

Sherborne totted up nine wins as the side made great strides. Harry Fisher was outstanding as wicketkeeper and batsman. The bowlers, all of whom played their part, shared the wickets around.

Batting H. S. Fisher 477 at 43.36; C. R. Millar 398 at 36.18; L. H. McLaughlin 315 at 28.63; P. J. R. Reynolds 244 at 18.76; S. H. W. Pope 210 at 17.50.

Bowling T. F. C. Clark 12 at 15.50; G. F. D. Whipple 17 at 16.41; *T. C. Perkins 17 at 20.76; J. E. B. Walliker 18 at 22.00; P. J. R. Reynolds 12 at 25.83; J. A. M. Pyman 14 at 25.85.

Shiplake College *Oxfordshire*   P18 W13 L4 D1

Master i/c J. H. Howorth   **Coach** C. Ellison

With 13 wins, including 12 in a row, this was perhaps Shiplake's best season. Eight players hit half-centuries, though the openers shone brightest: Oliver Brown and Matt Dalrymple both made 526 runs at a healthy rate. A good all-round attack was spearheaded by left-arm quick Callum Creighton; off-spinner Callum Theodorou gave strong support. Captain Joe Tucker will be a tough act to follow.

Batting O. H. N. Brown 526 at 40.46; J. Howard 316 at 39.50; M. R. Dalrymple 526 at 37.57; *J. W. Tucker 358 at 32.54; R. G. Stone 171 at 28.50.

Bowling C. J. Creighton 27 at 10.44; J. W. Roxburgh-Smith 19 at 16.21; C. Theodorou 22 at 20.18; F. G. T. Bowcock 14 at 23.42; L. G. Bishop 11 at 30.81.

Shrewsbury School *Shropshire*
P23 W18 L5

Master i/c A. S. Barnard **Coach** A. J. Shantry

A youthful first team, reliant on spin, made good progress, but didn't quite deliver in key fixtures. But with only George Garrett and Jamie Crawley leaving, prospects for 2019 appear good.

Batting R. X. Clarke 845 at 42.25; J. G. T. Crawley 610 at 35.88; D. J. Humes 690 at 32.85; W. B. S. Sissons 419 at 24.64; *G. A. Garrett 336 at 24.00; A. W. Garrett 163 at 16.30.

Bowling W. B. S. Sissons 40 at 13.15; G. A. Garrett 26 at 14.11; A. W. Garrett 37 at 16.89; R. X. Clarke 11 at 18.81; J. P. Pattenden 22 at 18.86; P. J. H. Clark 21 at 23.04.

Silcoates School *Yorkshire*
P10 W4 L6 A1

Master i/c G. M. Roberts **Coach** J. F. C. Leathley

An inexperienced squad were well captained by Year 12 Liam Webb. The high point of the summer was a nailbiting two-wicket victory against MCC.

Batting *L. J. Webb 234 at 29.25; M. A. Nawaz 196 at 28.00.

Bowling L. J. Webb 10 at 23.70.

Simon Langton Grammar School for Boys *Kent*
P15 W12 L2 D1

Master i/c J. K. R. Whitnell

An extremely rewarding term brought just one defeat by another school side (Charterhouse). The first XI retained both the Kent (Lemon) Cup and the Kent Schools T20 League. Tom Davis played frequently for Kent Seconds.

Batting E. J. Fox 451 at 64.42; *A. R. Beck 313 at 39.12; T. E. Davis 457 at 38.08; F. J. Coupe 293 at 36.62; B. A. Rutherford 385 at 35.00; J. S. Goldbacher 207 at 25.87; A. J. Hopkins 150 at 25.00.

Bowling W. T. D. Dibiase 18 at 15.66; E. J. Fox 13 at 17.46; B. A. Rutherford 12 at 18.66; J. S. Goldbacher 12 at 28.91.

Sir Thomas Rich's School *Gloucestershire*
P13 W7 L5 D1

Master i/c R. G. Williams **Coach** N. O'Neil

After a great start brought wins over RGS Worcester, Bristol Grammar and Wycliffe, the second half of the season was disappointing, with defeats by Gloucestershire Gipsies, MCC, Monmouth and KES Birmingham. The two-day game against Dean Close ended in a draw.

Batting L. E. Carr 175 at 43.75; *S. J. Price 301 at 37.62; S. R. J. Campbell 276 at 34.50; F. W. Elsey 347 at 31.54; T. J. Niblett 305 at 30.50.

Bowling W. R. D. Sanderson 14 at 11.07; S. A. McCormack 17 at 18.05; S. J. Price 18 at 20.72; L. J. Richards 12 at 25.00; R. J. Elsey 11 at 30.72.

Solihull School *Warwickshire*
P17 W9 L7 D1

Master i/c D. L. Maddy **Coach** D. Smith

Will Rigg, the captain, had a brilliant all-round season, scoring 1,029 runs (including five centuries) and taking 24 wickets (including two five-fors).

Batting *W. E. Rigg 1029 at 73.50; E. A. Brookes 349 at 49.85; A. A. Blundell 289 at 41.28; A. M. Chakrapani 267 at 38.14; T. E. Serle 365 at 26.07.

Bowling F. A. H. Roll 15 at 17.06; W. E. Rigg 24 at 20.50; A. A. Blundell 12 at 26.83; O. G. Nesbitt 15 at 29.73.

South Gloucestershire and Stroud College *Glos*
P12 W7 L4 T1

Master i/c S. G. Hinks

The college had another bright summer, becoming regional AOC College 20/20 champions, reaching the regional semi-finals of the National Schools T20 and seeing three players – Max Tryfonos, Joe Dryell and Lewis Shean – play for Gloucestershire Seconds.

Batting M. M. Tryfonos 372 at 37.20; *B. J. Parker 165 at 27.50; J. A. Dryell 316 at 26.33; V. Mamgai 194 at 24.25; J. H. Newman 248 at 22.54; M. Omar 150 at 21.42; C. W. Dangerfield 158 at 13.16.

Max Tryfonos and Lewis Shean have followed the path from South Gloucestershire and Stroud College to Gloucestershire CCC.

Bowling M. Omar 10 at 15.90; J. H. Newman 12 at 22.66; C. W. Dangerfield 11 at 24.27; M. M. Tryfonos 10 at 26.40; K. J. Slade 10 at 27.80; B. J. Parker 10 at 28.80.

Stamford School *Lincolnshire*   P18 W9 L7 T1 D1 A3
Master i/c C. A. R. Esson   **Coach** D. W. Headley
Stamford's young team, captained by Nick Green, enjoyed several good wins against major rivals, and made the last 16 in the National T20 competition.
Batting J. D. M. Evison 760 at 58.46; B. M. Woodward 177 at 44.25; *N. J. Green 499 at 38.38; J. R. Martin 354 at 25.28; P. J. Harrington 339 at 22.60; J. Baxter 161 at 20.12; S. S. Subramonian 203 at 15.61.
Bowling H. C. Z. Bell 27 at 17.59; C. K. Headley 19 at 18.57; S. Saleem 15 at 25.60; J. D. M. Evison 12 at 31.83; M. C. Saunders 16 at 45.87.

Stewart's Melville College, Edinburgh *Midlothian*   P17 W9 L6 D2 A4
Master i/c J. A. Beharrell   **Coach** A. Ranson
Given the number of new players, this was an encouraging season. Congratulations to Patrick Ritchie, Bahaudden Ali, and Freddie and Charlie Peet, who all played age-group cricket for Scotland.
Batting *P. G. F. Ritchie 447 at 40.63; T. S. C. Hughes 244 at 24.40; C. D. Peet 184 at 20.44; *M. I. C. Hay-Smith 269 at 17.93; H. S. Johnstone 171 at 15.54; Z. Thompson 163 at 14.81.
Bowling C. D. Peet 15 at 14.86; F. T. Peet 14 at 19.07; S. L. Tait 21 at 21.47.

Stonyhurst College *Lancashire*   P7 W3 L4
Master i/c G. Thomas   **Coach** S. Owen
The first team displayed outstanding commitment and attitude under the leadership of Oliver Foster, a Stonyhurst stalwart. The college bade farewell to long-standing head of cricket, Gareth Thomas.
Batting The leading batsman was G. Oyston, who hit 148 runs at 24.66.
Bowling B. J. Pickles 12 at 10.83; *O. B. J. Foster 11 at 17.36.

Stowe School *Buckinghamshire*
P18 W13 L4 D1 A1

Master i/c J. A. Knott
Coach P. R. Arnold

The school enjoyed 13 wins and a good run in the National Schools T20. Captain Adam King led the way with run-scoring and glovework, and represented Northamptonshire Seconds. Year 10 James Cronie had a good term, taking 20 wickets and hitting 353 runs; at the Bunbury Festival, he was the second-highest scorer.

Batting *A. E. King 586 at 45.07; T. J. Olsen 254 at 28.22; J. P. Cronie 353 at 27.15; J. F. Jackman 369 at 26.35; C. I. Renshaw 340 at 26.15.

Bowling J. P. Cronie 20 at 11.20; T. J. Olsen 21 at 14.04; A. S. A. Johnson 17 at 20.11; O. N. J. Taylor 17 at 20.64; R. E. A. Easdale 18 at 25.72.

Sutton Valence School *Kent*
P12 W5 L6 D1 A4

Master i/c V. J. Wells

An inexperienced team fared well under the captaincy of Michael Law. The bulk of the runs came from Rishi Roy-Mukherjee. Injuries to others gave Year 11 Max Savage greater responsibilities with the new ball; he gained useful support from a green attack.

Batting R. Roy-Mukherjee 458 at 57.25; J. J. Stanton-Gleaves 237 at 23.70; T. F. Aiken 158 at 22.57; T. B. S. Saltmarsh 177 at 22.12; T. E. Lazarides 163 at 20.37.

Bowling T. B. S. Saltmarsh 12 at 12.00; M. D. Savage 12 at 19.58.

Taunton School *Somerset*
P14 W7 L6 D1 A1

Master i/c P. N. Sanderson

Results steadily improved, with victories against Blundell's, Clifton, Colston's, King's Bruton and Millfield, as well as festival wins against Dulwich and Framlingham. Oscar Samuel, a Year 11, collected 326 runs and 13 wickets, including a hat-trick. Travis Green took most wickets, while Thomas Walsh managed a five-for.

Batting O. L. Samuel 326 at 40.75; *D. S. Court 214 at 35.66; C. J. Harding 255 at 31.87; T. E. Green 180 at 30.00.

Bowling H. F. M. Ledger 13 at 17.46; T. E. Green 16 at 21.68; O. L. Samuel 13 at 26.00; T. R. Walsh 11 at 28.27.

Tiffin School *Surrey*
P16 W4 L11 D1 A1

Master i/c M. J. Williams

This was a poor year for Tiffin, but disappointment was tempered by the excellence of the school's junior sides. First-team captain Sami Shori had a huge appetite for runs, though wickets proved harder to come by.

Batting *S. Shori 939 at 67.07; T. Sood 175 at 25.00; H. Morris 213 at 21.30.

Bowling P. Sivagnanasundaram 11 at 12.18; A. V. Joshi 15 at 22.40; S. Shori 11 at 24.18.

Tonbridge School *Kent*
P21 W15 L4 D2

Master i/c P. T. Sadler
Coaches I. Baldock and J. P. Arscott

An excellent year for a remarkably young side suggests a rosy future. A miserly spin quartet, led by 15-year-old Harry Bevan-Thomas and backed up by tigerish fielding and astute captaincy, meant most totals could be defended. Highlights included victory in all five Cowdrey Cup matches, and the Under-15s becoming national champions.

Batting J. J. O'Riordan 683 at 45.53; B. J. E. Robinson 650 at 36.11; *A. J. Moen 676 at 35.57; E. Owen-Browne 309 at 30.90; C. A. Winder 384 at 29.53; H. C. Bevan-Thomas 234 at 26.00; H. C. A. Weston 183 at 22.87; S. M. Hadfield 238 at 21.63; F. E. H. Geffen 175 at 19.44.

Bowling H. C. Bevan-Thomas 27 at 13.66; F. E. H. Geffen 24 at 13.70; S. T. S. Huggett 11 at 17.09; E. A. J. Surguy 19 at 17.78; A. J. Moen 15 at 24.53; J. J. O'Riordan 16 at 27.18; O. G. H. Nolan 12 at 27.41; S. M. Hadfield 14 at 30.28.

Trent College *Derbyshire*
P13 W4 L8 D1 A1

Master i/c S. A. J. Boswell
Coach P. Johnson

This proved a challenging term, though a strong performance against Worksop College brought encouragement. Mathew Kimmitt was a dangerous batsman who passed 650 runs, while Dan Blatherwick, a lively opening bowler, caused problems with his pace.

Batting *M. J. Kimmitt 679 at 56.58; A. D. Moore 502 at 41.83; D. L. Blatherwick 458 at 38.17; H. Whitworth 206 at 25.75.

Bowling F. S. Landa 13 at 12.85; D. L. Blatherwick 22 at 16.23; H. J. Rhodes 10 at 18.90; S. G. Westbrook 12 at 23.17; S. Q. Haider 11 at 25.09.

Trinity School *Surrey*
P14 W9 L3 T1 D1 A1

Master i/c S. D. Schofield **Coach** A. D. Brown

Trinity tasted success in 2018, winners of three county cups and runners-up in another. A record number of boys played for the school, and at least one in every age group represented Surrey or Kent.

Batting *A. Roberts 297 at 24.75; A. Sabesan 261 at 21.75; R. Hari 301 at 21.50; F. Baker 250 at 19.23.
Bowling F. Baker 25 at 21.60; A. Sabesan 17 at 25.17; M. Cadiz 14 at 32.57; E. Lilley 15 at 38.33.

University College School, Hampstead *Middlesex*
P16 W10 L5 D1

Master i/c D. J. Brown **Coaches** M. J. Lane and A. R. Wilkes

UCS enjoyed their best season for many years, thanks to some talented brothers. Julius and Henry Raschke scored centuries in the annual festival at George Watson's College, while the bowling was dominated by Daniel and Joel Grabinar, who shared 51 wickets.

Batting *J. F. Raschke 551 at 50.09; H. L. Raschke 346 at 28.83; D. A. S. Grabinar 258 at 25.80; J. A. Grabinar 169 at 21.12; S. F. Clarfield 180 at 13.84; L. H. Rehman 165 at 13.75.
Bowling D. A. S. Grabinar 26 at 10.69; J. A. Grabinar 25 at 12.28; N. R. Bor 20 at 20.25; V. Ramaswamy 10 at 24.10.

Uppingham School *Rutland*
P13 W1 L9 D3 A1

Master i/c C. M. W. Read **Coach** T. R. Ward

A tough summer for Uppingham brought just one victory for a team in transition. Several Year 11s made their debuts, and some – such as Sam Turberville Smith and Pip Jackson – caught the eye.

Batting S. R. Turberville Smith 346 at 34.60; *S. J. C. Wallis 253 at 21.08; M. A. Cunnington 219 at 15.64.
Bowling T. H. Regis 15 at 21.80; C. H. P. Jackson 12 at 24.83.

Victoria College, Jersey *Channel Islands*
P16 W13 L3

Master i/c M. D. Smith **Coach** M. Dixon

Victoria College enjoyed perhaps their most successful summer since the millennium, winning 13 of 16 fixtures and triumphing at the Castles Festival in Monmouth. Fifteen-year-old Josh Lawrenson took 30 wickets and hit 313 runs; David Bourne was again leading run-scorer, in his last year.

Batting J. A. D. Lawrenson 313 at 62.60; D. A. Bourne 484 at 48.40; J. A. Heward 337 at 37.44; E. J. W. Giles 233 at 25.88; P. B. Gouge 298 at 24.83; M. G. Donaldson 182 at 16.54.
Bowling J. A. D. Lawrenson 30 at 8.50; B. C. Le Gallais 18 at 13.38; C. V. Breese 18 at 14.50; E. J. W. Giles 18 at 17.50; D. A. Bourne 15 at 21.46.

Warwick School *Warwickshire*
P15 W7 L8 A3

Master i/c S. R. G. Francis

Warwick excelled at the 40-over game, winning six of eight weekend matches. Rob Yates finished his career by hitting four fifties and a century in his last five innings. Tom Hornby scored 104 and Henry Mortimer 99, both unbeaten. Slow left-armer Harrison Chambers bowled consistently well to take 26 wickets, including six for 20 against MCC.

Batting *R. M. Yates 437 at 87.40; H. W. Mortimer 293 at 32.55; M. Leatherdale 330 at 25.38; T. C. Hornby 212 at 21.20; H. R. Miles 162 at 18.00; E. J. W. Briggs 177 at 16.09.
Bowling H. J. Chambers 26 at 11.30; C. R. Curtis 14 at 27.50; W. J. Kelley 10 at 27.80; G. M. D'Souza 11 at 27.81.

Wellingborough School *Northamptonshire*
P19 W15 L2 D2 A1

Master i/c G. E. Houghton **Coach** L. M. Sharples

Wellingborough put in a true squad effort: each week different players proved match-winners. Joseph Stockdale captained intelligently, and fellow leaver Matthew Clarke hit two centuries. James Sales, an under-15 batsman, showed promise, while Jonny Clarke snatched 34 wickets.

Batting M. G. Clarke 768 at 59.07; J. J. G. Sales 565 at 43.46; J. W. Saxby 351 at 31.90; *J. T. Stockdale 284 at 31.55; N. J. Piper 273 at 24.81; O. R. Cousins 284 at 18.93; M. W. Mills 179 at 13.76.
Bowling J. R. Clarke 34 at 10.41; C. T. Blake 28 at 13.53; A. E. Davies 18 at 14.16; J. T. Stockdale 13 at 19.84; M. G. Clarke 13 at 28.84.

Wellington College *Berkshire*   P20 W10 L10 A1
Master i/c D. M. Pratt   **Coach** H. C. Grice
When the team were on song, they were formidable – but they did not produce their best as often as they should. No individual dominated with bat or ball, and they needed to fire together to achieve results.
Batting *J. L. B. Davies 608 at 50.66; A. R. Carter 580 at 36.25; M. A. C. Keast 444 at 31.71; T. J. Petrie 395 at 28.21; M. S. Bradbury 284 at 20.28; M. J. Watson 150 at 18.75; W. J. Sinfield 317 at 18.64.
Bowling A. S. Dale 26 at 14.19; M. S. Bradbury 16 at 24.56; G. A. Cooke 10 at 27.20; W. J. Sinfield 11 at 28.18; H. W. Petrie 15 at 29.80; T. J. Petrie 12 at 34.08; J. J. Henry 18 at 36.72.

Wells Cathedral School *Somerset*   P13 W5 L7 D1
Master i/c J. A. Boot   **Coach** D. M. J. Peck
The first team, predominantly made up of Year 12s, scrapped hard in many tight games. Highlights included a tense draw against MCC in cricket week, Jacob Potts's 96 against Prior Park and Hasnain Altaf's six for 11 against Clayesmore.
Batting H. J. Lindsay 326 at 27.16; J. Potts 326 at 25.07; W. Holley 176 at 22.00; *T. A. S. Connock 232 at 17.84; S. H. Pritchard 227 at 17.46; B. Ake 165 at 16.50; D. J. Hill 155 at 15.50.
Bowling A. J. Padgett 12 at 25.66; H. Altaf 10 at 28.00; J. Potts 14 at 32.42; T. A. S. Connock 10 at 35.20.

Westminster School *Middlesex*   P15 W8 L6 D1 A2
Master i/c J. D. Kershen   **Coach** S. K. Ranasinghe
An eventful year included a tour to Barbados, a fifth London Schools' Under-19 Cup victory and a sixth winning season in a row. Alex Benson, Alex Vinen and Lucas McConnell were the outstanding performers; there is more to come from Matthew Carver, Junaid Ahmed and Tarun Eapen.
Batting *A. C. Benson 355 at 44.37; A. S. Vinen 330 at 27.50; L. F. McConnell 298 at 27.09; J. F. Ahmed 187 at 20.77; T. M. Eapen 253 at 19.46; M. Y. J. Carver 194 at 14.92.
Bowling L. F. McConnell 19 at 14.57; A. S. Vinen 16 at 17.50; M. Zainuddin 12 at 20.00; A. C. Benson 15 at 21.60.

Whitgift School *Surrey*   P17 W11 L4 T1 D1 A2
Master i/c D. M. Ward   **Coach** P. R. Hindmarch
Whitgift won all but one Saturday fixture, and reached the last 16 of the National Schools T20. Jamie Smith, the captain, signed for Surrey. Nine players return for 2019, aiming to build on their success.
Batting *J. Smith 643 at 49.46; J. A. Cleaver 264 at 37.71; N. M. J. Reifer 414 at 37.63; B. P. M. Sewell 356 at 29.66; S. Nathan 378 at 27.00; H. J. Cutmore 262 at 21.83; N. Young 257 at 21.41.
Bowling H. J. Cutmore 25 at 14.68; W. G. Heaver 24 at 14.83; N. Young 13 at 18.00; W. Doyle 11 at 20.00; S. Eyre 12 at 32.08.

Wilson's School *Surrey*   P14 W5 L9 A3
Master i/c A. K. Parkinson   **Coach** C. K. Bullen
This was a time of transition for the first XI, which usually included five or more Under-15s. However, there were promising signs: Janaken Prabhakaran and 15-year-old Pranav Madan led the batting, while Prabhakaran took most wickets, followed by Aranan Sivakumar and Riley Jarrold.
Batting P. Madan 381 at 42.33; J. Prabhakaran 383 at 34.81; A. Srivastav 234 at 23.40.
Bowling A. Sivakumar 11 at 24.27; *R. D. Jarrold 11 at 25.45; J. Prabhakaran 13 at 28.07.

Winchester College *Hampshire*   P21 W10 L10 D1 A3
Master i/c G. E. Munn   **Coaches** P. N. Gover and J. M. Burridge
Highlights included wins against Marlborough (by ten wickets) and Bradfield. Johnny Figy was outstanding, hitting 103 against Radley, 147 against Old Wykehamists and 102 against I Zingari – all three unbeaten. He also claimed 34 wickets, including four for two against Marlborough and five for 25 against the XL Club.
Batting J. J. Figy 754 at 62.83; A. S. Lee 395 at 28.21; C. A. S. Byers 315 at 24.23; *S. G. Byers 274 at 18.26; F. J. Egleston 169 at 12.07.
Bowling J. T. F. Flatt 16 at 14.50; J. J. Figy 34 at 15.76; F. J. Egleston 12 at 18.58; J. S. Scull 17 at 20.41; H. L. Adams 21 at 21.09; T. W. Kidner 11 at 21.72; H. R. Vaughan 16 at 24.25; W. E. H. Richards 10 at 24.40.

Woodbridge School *Suffolk*   P9 W4 L5 A5
Master i/c I. J. Simpson   **Coach** D. Brous
The development of the team continued, and all players are available for 2019. Ben Harper and Dan Norman, captain and vice-captain, will be hoping for fewer abandonments.
Batting D. I. S. Norman 243 at 34.71; *B. E. Harper 284 at 31.55.
Bowling T. A. Harper 15 at 18.86; T. B. Stowe 10 at 22.70.

Woodhouse Grove School *Yorkshire*   P16 W7 L7 D2 A2
Master i/c R. I. Frost   **Coach** A. Sidebottom
Woodhouse Grove enjoyed a summer of progress that contained several notable victories. Owen Tennant made 716 runs at 55 in his first season, while captain Ali Ahmed marked the end of a five-year career with 307 runs and 23 wickets.
Batting O. T. Tennant 716 at 55.07; *A. H. Ahmed 307 at 30.70; L. Fairbank 388 at 24.25; M. A. Sheard 272 at 18.13; R. Newman 157 at 15.70; E. Horne 197 at 15.15.
Bowling J. Swarbrigg 10 at 11.80; A. H. Ahmed 23 at 19.86; T. Kaznowski 19 at 21.68; J. O. Stephenson 10 at 22.60; O. T. Tennant 13 at 23.46; D. J. Gallagher 10 at 31.90.

Worksop College *Nottinghamshire*   P13 W6 L7 A7
Master i/c N. J. Longhurst   **Coach** I. C. Parkin
Spring was ruined by the weather, with only one of the first eight fixtures taking place. Josh Porter was the most threatening bowler, but runs were in short supply. Defeat by one wicket from the penultimate ball against King's Taunton cost them the Woodard Festival.
Batting *R. A. Parker-Cole 427 at 35.58; O. M. Blackburn 196 at 32.66; J. D. Porter 240 at 26.66; N. S. Keast 279 at 25.36; N. A. Lowe 226 at 25.11; P. K. Delahunty 186 at 18.60.
Bowling J. D. Porter 18 at 13.27; D. J. D. Harris 17 at 16.58; N. S. Keast 20 at 17.15; R. A. Parker-Cole 11 at 24.27; A. R. Shannon 10 at 28.70.

Worth School *Sussex*   P16 W7 L5 D4
Master i/c R. Chaudhuri
Krishan Nayee led a young first XI through a decent season, hitting most runs and claiming most wickets. He gained batting support from Akshay Ramani and Anish Padalkar, and bowling support from Vikram Kohli, Mali Lewis and Ramani.
Batting *K. Nayee 602 at 43.00; A. Padalkar 329 at 27.41; A. Ramani 404 at 25.25; L. W. Wills 218 at 16.76.
Bowling V. Kohli 21 at 13.28; K. Nayee 22 at 16.63; A. Ramani 21 at 20.28; M. B. Lewis 10 at 25.30.

Wrekin College *Shropshire*   P18 W10 L7 D1 A1
Master i/c J. R. Mather   **Coach** D. A. Davies
Fine performances from Mathew Batkin and the captain, Henry Davies, produced good wins against Bablake, KES Stratford, Newcastle under Lyme and Dean Close. A squad dependent on Year 13s worked hard, sharing out the runs and the responsibilities.
Batting M. Batkin 604 at 37.75; *H. J. Davies 349 at 24.92; B. A. Harrison 157 at 17.44; O. G. Davies 230 at 15.33; B. E. Crump 161 at 14.63.
Bowling M. Batkin 26 at 15.88; H. J. Davies 29 at 17.41; O. G. Davies 11 at 24.63.

Wycliffe College *Gloucestershire*   P13 W1 L10 D2 A2
Master i/c M. J. Kimber
Though not apparent from the results, the first team, well led by Will Naish, showed glimpses of real promise. Oliver Wood displayed encouraging all-round ability, and Year 13 pupil Innes Pierce scored a well-deserved 106 not out against Gloucestershire Gipsies. Most of the squad return for 2019.
Batting M. C. Cole 153 at 38.25; O. Wood 268 at 24.36; *W. L. Naish 158 at 17.56; H. W. Murray 167 at 16.70; I. C. Pierce 167 at 16.70.
Bowling O. Wood 13 at 26.84.

PART FIVE

Overseas Cricket

Ireland v Pakistan
Inaugural Test Match
2018

ICC UNDER-19 WORLD CUP IN 2017-18

Snehal Pradhan

1 India   2 Australia   3 Pakistan

India won the tournament for a record fourth time with a dominant performance. The philosophy instilled by coach Rahul Dravid, and the preparation that backed it up, reaped a rich dividend: his team were light years ahead of the opposition. They were strong in batting – the top three scored 72% of their runs – with Shubman Gill, the player of the tournament, hitting 372 at 124. But it was their pace attack that really caught the eye, with Kamlesh Nagarkoti and Shivam Mavi bowling in excess of 90mph and earning themselves IPL deals with Kolkata Knight Riders.

Australia finished runners-up, but Greg Chappell, their national talent manager, admitted they were outplayed in the final; none of his charges featured in the team of the tournament. Meanwhile, **England** cruised through their group, but were ambushed by Australian leg-spin in the quarter-finals. And there were unwanted echoes of the off-field problems suffered by the seniors on the Ashes tour, when captain Harry Brook was dropped for the seventh-place play-off for disciplinary reasons.

After their defeat by West Indies in the 2016 final, India had drawn up a masterplan for recapturing the trophy. "The focus was to put a process in place where we could give opportunities to a lot more than 15 or 16 players," said Dravid. "We made a decision not to select boys for this World Cup who had played in the last one." Between the competitions, India played 17 matches spread over four series. It made them considerably more battle-hardened than their opponents; in the final, they boasted five first-class cricketers. Later Dravid insisted on a 50% pay cut to ensure equal reward for each of the coaching staff, including him.

But while India's game's acquired an air of predictability, a less obvious storyline was provided by **Afghanistan's** progress to the last four. They were led by Naveen-ul-Haq, who spoke with maturity about the terrorist attacks that hit Kabul and Jalalabad in the days before the quarter-final against hosts **New Zealand**. After they won that game by 202 runs, he said: "Someone told me, 'As underdogs you don't have anything to lose.' I said, 'We are not underdogs.' It's not like we are beating anyone by chance. Soon they won't call us underdogs or dark horses." Afghanistan were followed by a noisy and steadily increasing band of supporters, whose presence inspired rather than cowed the players. They finished fourth, denied a crack at third when their play-off was washed out: **Pakistan** edged ahead on net run-rate. Leg-spinner Qais Ahmad was Afghanistan's leading bowler with 14 wickets, the joint-most in the tournament with India's slow left-armer Anukul Roy and Canadian seamer Faisal Jamkhandi Haque.

Pakistan's 6ft 5in left-arm quick Shaheen Shah Afridi took 12 wickets in five games, while Bangladesh's Kazi Anik, another left-armer, bowled

Marty Melville, AFP/Getty Images

Hitting the deck: India fast bowler Kamlesh Nagarkoti can't quite catch Lloyd Pope in the final.

deceptive cutters at pace from around the wicket. And Jason Ralston, the Australian seamer, took seven for 15 against Papua New Guinea, briefly the best figures in the history of the competition. That was enough to put him top of the averages, though they were his only wickets of the tournament, and his record lasted four days: in the quarter-final, Australian leg-spinner Lloyd Pope bamboozled England with eight for 35. Gill topped the batting averages, but Brook and West Indies' Alick Athanaze also had three-figure averages. Athanaze, South Africa captain Raynard van Tonder and Sri Lanka's Hasitha Boyagoda all made two hundreds.

Group A

At Mount Maunganui, January 13, 2018 (day/night). **New Zealand won by eight wickets. West Indies 233-8** (50 overs) (K. A. Simmons 92*, K. S. Melius 78; M. J. Fisher 3-61, R. Ravindra 3-30); ‡**New Zealand 234-2** (39.3 overs) (J. J. N. P. Bhula 83, F. H. Allen 115*). *MoM:* F. H. Allen. *Defending champions West Indies were brushed aside by New Zealand, who had finished 12th at the previous Under-19 World Cup, in Bangladesh two years earlier. West Indies had looked set for a substantial total after openers Keagan Simmons – nephew of former Test player Phil – and Kimani Melius put on 123 inside 28 overs, but they managed only 110-8 after that, with Simmons batting through the innings for 92*. New Zealand were untroubled in reply, as Jakob Bhula and Finn Allen (115* off 100 balls) put on 163 for the second wicket.*

At Lincoln (No. 3), January 14, 2018. **South Africa won by 169 runs. ‡South Africa 341-7** (50 overs) (J. Pillay 62, R. van Tonder 143); **Kenya 172-7** (50 overs). *MoM:* R. van Tonder. *South African captain Raynard van Tonder butchered 143 from 121 deliveries to set up a crushing win. Chasing 342, the Kenyans were soon in trouble at 50-4 – one of the wickets falling to Thando Ntini, son of former Test fast bowler Makhaya – and never came close.*

At Christchurch, January 17, 2018. **New Zealand won by 243 runs. New Zealand 436-4** (50 overs) (J. J. N. P. Bhula 180, R. Ravindra 117, F. H. Allen 90); ‡**Kenya 193-4** (50 overs) (A. R. Gandhi 63). *MoM:* J. J. N. P. Bhula. *New Zealand bulldozed their way into the quarter-finals after an* *emphatic display from their top three. Bhula's 180 from 144 balls was, for six days, the highest score in an Under-19 ODI (beating Theo Doropoulos's 179* for Australia against England at Sydney in February 2003). And his stand of 245 with Rachin Ravindra (117 off 101) was a first-wicket record (beating 231 between Bangladesh's Anamul Haque and Amit Majumder against Zimbabwe at Bogra in November 2009). Bhula and Allen, who contributed a bruising 90 off 40, then thrashed 156 in 11.1 overs, before New Zealand lost three wickets in three balls – two to run-outs – on 401. Their eventual 436-4 was the second-highest in Under-19 ODIs, behind Australia's 480-6, also against Kenya, at Dunedin in January 2002. The Kenyans were content to bat out their overs.*

At Mount Maunganui, January 17, 2018 (day/night). **South Africa won by 76 runs. South Africa 282-8** (50 overs) (W. K. Makwetu 99*); ‡**West Indies 206** (45.3 overs) (A. S. Athanaze 76; H. Rolfes 4-33). *MoM*: W. K. Makwetu. *West Indies' title defence ended in another World Cup controversy, two years after their Under-19s had knocked out Zimbabwe with a Mankad. This time South African opener Jiveshan Pillay was given out obstructing the field after picking up the ball, which had come to rest by his stumps. West Indian captain and wicketkeeper Emmanuel Stewart appealed, in accordance with Law 37.4, which prohibits a batsman from returning the ball without the fielder's consent. "On reflection, I thought our appeal wasn't in the spirit of the game," Stewart admitted. "Moving forward, if I'm in such a situation, I'd withdraw the decision to go upstairs." It made little difference. South African wicketkeeper Wandile Makwetu made a run-a-ball 99* as his side plundered 58 off their final three overs. West Indies' last six fell for 29; seamer Hermann Rolfes finished with 4-33.*

At Lincoln (No. 3), January 20, 2018. **West Indies won by 222 runs.** ‡**West Indies 318-7** (50 overs) (K. S. Melius 60, A. S. Athanaze 116*, N. R. J. Young 57; A. S. Desai 3-54); **Kenya 96** (24.4 overs) (J. Royal 4-25, B. Yadram 5-18). *MoM*: A. S. Athanaze. *Both sides were already out – but there was still time for Kenya to suffer a third straight hammering. Alick Athanaze (116* off 93 balls) and Nyeem Young (57 off 45) transformed a moderate West Indies score of 198-6 into an imposing 318-7. Then Kenya collapsed from 51-0, losing all ten for 45 inside 15 overs. Spinners Jeavor Royal and Bhaskar Yadram shared nine.*

At Mount Maunganui, January 20, 2018 (day/night). **New Zealand won by 71 runs.** ‡**New Zealand 279-8** (50 overs) (R. Ravindra 76); **South Africa 208** (46.2 overs) (H. Rolfes 108, J. F. du Plessis 54; R. Ravindra 4-32). *MoM*: R. Ravindra. *Ravindra's all-round excellence ensured New Zealand finished top of the group, earning them a quarter-final in Christchurch against Afghanistan. His 76 had been the backbone of a decent 279-8, before his loopy left-arm spin collected 4-32 as South Africa fell well short, despite a century for Rolfes. Of the rest, only Jean du Plessis passed 15, leaving the South Africans with a tricky quarter-final against Pakistan.*

NEW ZEALAND 6pts, SOUTH AFRICA 4pts, West Indies 2pts, Kenya 0pts.

Group B

At Lincoln (No. 3), January 13, 2018. **Zimbabwe won by ten wickets.** Reduced to 20 overs a side. **Papua New Guinea 95** (20 overs) (W. Madhevere 3-19); ‡**Zimbabwe 98-0** (14 overs) (W. Madhevere 53*). *MoM*: W. Madhevere. *From 41-0 in the ninth over, Papua New Guinea lost ten for 54, and were thrashed. Wesley Madhevere was Zimbabwe's all-round destroyer-in-chief.*

At Mount Maunganui, January 14, 2018 (day/night). **India won by 100 runs.** ‡**India 328-7** (50 overs) (P. P. Shaw 94, M. Kalra 86, S. Gill 63; J. R. Edwards 4-65); **Australia 228** (42.5 overs) (J. R. Edwards 73; S. P. Mavi 3-45, K. L. Nagarkoti 3-29). *MoM*: P. P. Shaw. *India flexed their muscles in the tournament's first heavyweight clash. Openers Prithvi Shaw and Manjot Kalra put on 180, before Shubman Gill's late flourish – 63 off 54 balls – helped them recover from a fallow spell. The pace of Shivam Mavi and Kamlesh Nagarkoti, who each took three wickets, rocked Australia, and only Jack Edwards (who earlier claimed a four-for) averted total collapse.*

At Mount Maunganui, January 16, 2018 (day/night). **India won by ten wickets. Papua New Guinea 64** (21.5 overs) (A. S. Roy 5-14); ‡**India 67-0** (8 overs) (P. P. Shaw 57*). *MoM*: A. S. Roy. *The underdogs were crushed in a match lasting less than 30 overs. Mavi and Nagarkoti made the PNG batsmen hop around, but it was slow left-armer Anukul Roy who reaped the benefits, with five wickets in 6.5 overs, his best international figures. Shaw's second fifty of the competition swiftly administered the last rites.*

At Lincoln (No. 3), January 17, 2018. **Australia won by seven wickets. Zimbabwe 134** (33.2 overs) (X. Bartlett 3-20); ‡**Australia 135-3** (18.2 overs). *MoM*: X. Bartlett. *Australia put themselves in pole* *position to qualify alongside India. Xavier Bartlett's new-ball burst established the tone, removing Zimbabwe's top three inside 11 overs. Only Robert Chimhinya's 27 suggested defiance. Australia batted like men late for a meeting, racing to 46 in 4.2 overs. Max Bryant top-scored with 44.*

At Lincoln (No. 3), January 19, 2018. **Australia won by 311 runs. Australia 370-8 (50 overs)** (N. A. McSweeney 156, J. J. S. Sangha 88, P. Uppal 61); **‡Papua New Guinea 59** (24.5 overs) (J. T. Ralston 7-15). *MoM*: N. A. McSweeney. *A third humiliation for Papua New Guinea saw Australia ease into the last eight. Nathan McSweeney's savage 156 came off 111 balls, after opening partner Bryant had been bowled for a duck in the second over. Ralston's seven wickets, a tournament record, were crammed into 6.5 overs.*

BIGGEST WINS BY RUNS IN UNDER-19 INTERNATIONALS

430	Australia (480-6)	v Kenya (50) at Dunedin	2001-02
311	**Australia (370-8)**	**v Papua New Guinea (59) at Lincoln**	**2017-18**
311	**Sri Lanka (419-4)**	**v Kenya (108) at Dunedin**	**2017-18**
301	West Indies (402-3)	v Scotland (101) at Dunedin	2001-02
299	England (371-3)	v Fiji (72) at Chittagong	2015-16
282	**England (383-7)**	**v Canada (101) at Queenstown**	**2017-18**
277	Pakistan (348-7)	v Denmark (71-7) at Boksburg	1997-98
270	India (425-3)	v Scotland (155-8) at Dhaka	2003-04

At Mount Maunganui, January 19, 2018 (day/night). **India won by ten wickets. ‡Zimbabwe 154** (48.1 overs) (A. S. Roy 4-20); **India 155-0** (21.4 overs) (H. M. Desai 56*, S. Gill 90*). *MoM*: S. Gill. *India made changes, but still looked invincible as they eased to a victory that earned them a week off before their quarter-final. Roy took the eye again, and India employed four spinners as Zimbabwe toiled. Gill oozed class, and Harvik Desai, who kept wicket tidily, contributed 56.*

INDIA 6pts, AUSTRALIA 4pts, Zimbabwe 2pts, Papua New Guinea 0pts.

Group C

At Lincoln (Bert Sutcliffe Oval), January 13, 2018. **Bangladesh won by 87 runs. Bangladesh 190-4** (20 overs) (Mohammad Naim 60, Saif Hasan 84); **‡Namibia 103-6** (20 overs) (E. van Wyk 55). *MoM*: Saif Hasan. *In a game cut to 20 overs a side, a whirlwind 84 from Bangladesh captain Saif Hasan sped his team to 190. He hit five sixes, including three in the last over, before falling to the final ball, all told, 55 zipped from the last 24 deliveries. Namibia's reply began more slowly: from his first three overs, Kazi Anik (4–19–14–2) bowled 16 dots and claimed two wickets, reducing them to 12-4. Eben van Wyk's 55 off 52 balls preserved a little pride.*

At Lincoln (Bert Sutcliffe Oval), January 15, 2018. **Bangladesh won by 66 runs. Bangladesh 264-8** (50 overs) (Towhid Hridoy 122, Afif Hossain 50; F. J. S. Haque 5-48); **‡Canada 198** (49.3 overs) (A. S. Khan 63; Afif Hossain 5-43). *MoM*: Afif Hossain. *A fluent century from Towhid Hridoy and a fine all-round effort from Afif Hossain steered Bangladesh to another comfortable win. Five wickets for seamer Faisal Jamkhandi Haque had hampered their progress, but the Canadian batsmen could not mount a serious challenge: even at 170-4, the asking-rate was almost 12. Top-scorer Arslan Khan then departed, and the rest quickly followed; Afif's off-spin accounted for five.*

At Queenstown, January 15, 2018. **England won by eight wickets. ‡Namibia 196-9** (50 overs) (L. B. K. Hollman 3-41); **England 198-2** (24.1 overs) (H. C. Brook 59*, W. G. Jacks 73*). *MoM*: W. G. Jacks. *Namibia escaped humiliation, though not a trouncing. They began well enough, putting on 42 for the first wicket after winning the toss, but England's disciplined attack stifled their innings. Shaun Fouché hit a sober 44 from 75 balls before becoming the second of leg-spinner Luke Hollman's three wickets. There was little sobriety in England's response. The main fizz came from Will Jacks, who – like his captain, Harry Brook – walloped 12 fours. They added 130* in 15 overs.*

At Queenstown, January 18, 2018. **England won by seven wickets. ‡Bangladesh 175** (49.2 overs) (Afif Hossain 63; E. R. Bamber 3-19, E. D. Woods 3-26); **England 177-3** (29.3 overs) (H. C. Brook 102*). *MoM*: H. C. Brook. *Once again Brook cracked England to a decisive win after his bowlers split open the batting. By the fifth over, Bangladesh were 8-3; by the ninth, when Ethan Bamber's* *pace claimed a third wicket, they were 27-4. Afif and Aminul Islam shored things up with a stand of 96, but off-spinner Euan Woods dismissed them in quick succession. Bangladesh's 175 began to look competitive when England lurched to 49-3, but Brook and Woods (48*) put on 128* at better than a run a ball.*

At Lincoln (Bert Sutcliffe Oval), January 18, 2018. **Canada won by four wickets.** ‡**Namibia 193** (46 overs) (A. S. Gill 4-43); **Canada 197-6** (42 overs) (A. S. Khan 72, A. S. Gill 52, K. K. Singh 50*). MoM: A. S. Gill. *At 151-3 in the 34th over, Namibia looked set for a daunting total. But left-arm spinner Aran Pathmanathan broke through, and the balance tilted Canada's way. Seamer Akash Gill ended with four as the wickets tumbled – undoing the groundwork of the top five, who all reached 20. Leg-spinner Petrus Burger took the new ball for Namibia and quickly removed the openers, before fifties from the next three – including Gill – hastened Canada to victory.*

At Queenstown, January 20, 2018. **England won by 282 runs. England 383-7** (50 overs) (L. Banks 120, W. G. Jacks 102, J. L. Davies 57; F. J. S. Haque 3-68, P. C. Pretorius 3-69); ‡**Canada 101** (31.5 overs) (P. Sisodiya 3-23). MoM: L. Banks. *England demolished Canada to march into the quarter-finals, unbeaten and unstretched. After opener Tom Banton lay a spry 27, Jacks joined Liam Banks, and together they added 186 at almost seven an over. Jack Davies then crashed 57 from 36 balls to usher England to their highest one-day total. None of the bowlers could stem the flow, though Haque and off-spinner Tiaan Pretorius each claimed three victims. In reply, six Canadians failed to get off the mark. Prem Sisodiya picked up three – and sent down 54 dots with his left-arm spin.*

ENGLAND 6pts, BANGLADESH 4pts, Canada 2pts, Namibia 0pts.

Group D

At Whangarei, January 13, 2018. **Afghanistan won by five wickets.** ‡**Pakistan 188** (47.4 overs) (Rohail Nazir 81; Azmatullah Omarzai 3-34, Qais Ahmad 3-38); **Afghanistan 194-5** (47.3 overs) (Darwish Rasooli 76*). MoM: Darwish Rasooli. *Darwish Rasooli thumped 76* in 78 balls and sealed Afghanistan's win with a six; he had put on 75 with Ikram Ali Khil (46) to steer them away from an uncertain 50-3. Pakistan's total leaned heavily on opener Rohail Nazir, who scored 81 out of 146-4 before becoming the first of three victims in four overs for leg-spinner Qais Ahmad.*

At Whangarei, January 14, 2018. **Sri Lanka won by seven wickets.** Reduced to 48 overs a side. ‡**Ireland 207-8** (48 overs) (J. B. Grassi 75; P. H. K. D. Mendis 3-35); **Sri Lanka 208-3** (37.3 overs) (P. A. D. Lakshan 101*, P. H. K. D. Mendis 74*). MoM: P. A. D. Lakshan. *An inexperienced Irish team fell away after Jamie Grassi and Mark Donegan (36) had built a first-wicket stand of 73. There were three run-outs, and three wickets for Sri Lankan captain Kamindu Mendis, who alternated right-arm off-breaks with left-arm spin and went on to score a run-a-ball 74*. Opener Dhananjaya Lakshan reached a first international century after losing three partners cheaply, adding 157* with Mendis to hurry Sri Lanka to victory.*

At Whangarei, January 16, 2018. **Pakistan won by nine wickets. Ireland 97** (28.5 overs) (Shaheen Shah Afridi 6-15, Hasan Khan 3-16); ‡**Pakistan 98-1** (8.5 overs). MoM: Shaheen Shah Afridi. *Seventeen-year-old left-arm quick Shaheen Shah Afridi returned Pakistan's best figures in Under-19 ODIs; his first three victims were caught behind, his last three bowled. Ireland were poleaxed, and it would have been even worse but for a last-wicket stand of 20 between Josh Little, who hit 24* in 20 balls, and Max Neville (none from three). Zaid Alam romped to 43* in 19, completing Pakistan's win in the ninth over with a four and a six.*

At Whangarei, January 17, 2018. **Afghanistan won by 32 runs** (DLS). **Afghanistan 284-7** (50 overs) (Ibrahim Zadran 86, Ikram Ali Khil 55, Darwish Rasooli 63); ‡**Sri Lanka 202** (37.3 overs) (Naveen-ul-Haq 4-35). MoM: Ibrahim Zadran. *Afghanistan advanced to the quarter-finals with their second win. Their 284 was Group D's highest total, thanks to Ibrahim Zadran, who smashed five sixes; Ikram, who helped him add 115 for the second wicket; and Rasooli, with 63 in 44 balls. Rain interrupted Sri Lanka's chase at 108-3, revising their target to 235 in 38 overs. Naveen-ul-Haq struck twice after they resumed, and finished with 4-35, plus a run-out.*

At Whangarei, January 19, 2018. **Pakistan won by three wickets. Sri Lanka 188** (48.2 overs) (J. K. C. Daniel 53; Suleman Shafqat 3-29); ‡**Pakistan 190-7** (43.3 overs) (Ali Zaryab 59; T. R. Dilshan 3-47). MoM: Ali Zaryab. *A place in the quarter-finals was at stake; Pakistan sailed through when Musa Khan hit successive sixes in the 44th over of the chase. Ali Zaryab had kept them on course after early strikes from Thisaru Rashmika Dilshan, but they needed only 189. Sri Lanka had* *stumbled to 72-5 before Jehan Daniel and Ashen Bandara (37) doubled the total, only for their last five to fall for 40 as leg-spinner Suleman Shafqat mopped up.*

At Whangarei, January 20, 2018. **Ireland won by four runs. Ireland 225-8** (50 overs) (Wafadar Momand 3-50, Qais Ahmad 3-32); ‡**Afghanistan 221** (49.2 overs) (H. T. Tector 3-37). *MoM:* H. T. Tector. *A dead fixture provided the tournament's tightest result, and Ireland's first win. Their captain, Harry Tector (36), led them from 73-4 to 157-6, and Graham Kennedy struck 37* in 24 balls to lift the total to 225. Tector then extracted the Afghan middle order with his off-spin. Afghanistan started the final over nine down, needing seven; Max Neville donated a no-ball and a wide before claiming the last wicket with his second legitimate delivery.*

PAKISTAN 4pts, AFGHANISTAN 4pts, Sri Lanka 2pts, Ireland 2pts.

Quarter-finals

At Queenstown, January 23, 2018. **Australia won by 31 runs.** ‡**Australia 127** (33.3 overs) (J. J. S. Sangha 58; E. R. Bamber 3-31, D. Y. Pennington 3-27, W. G. Jacks 3-21); **England 96** (23.4 overs) (T. Banton 58; L. A. J. Pope 8-35). *MoM:* L. A. J. Pope. *Midway through the eighth over of England's reply, the match was surely sewn up: needing 128 to reach the semis, they were 47-0, with Tom Banton scoring freely. But everything changed when the flame-haired Lloyd Pope turned a leg-break past Liam Banks to have him stumped. Next ball, he bowled Harry Brook, and Australia had self-belief. Pope's line was infallible and – aided by athletic slip catching from Jason Sangha – he ran through a rattled England to take 8-35, the second-best figures in all Under-19 internationals. Defeat was hard on the English seam attack, who had the measure of everyone bar Sangha.*

MOST WICKETS IN AN UNDER-19 ONE-DAY INTERNATIONAL

7.5–3–16–9	I. K. Pathan	India v Bangladesh at Lahore	2003-04
9.4–2–35–8	**L. A. J. Pope**	**Australia v England at Queenstown**	**2017-18**
6.5–0–15–7	**J. T. Ralston**	**Australia v Papua New Guinea at Lincoln**	**2017-18**
9.2–1–19–7	B. M. A. J. Mendis	Sri Lanka v Zimbabwe at Christchurch	2001-02
9.3–2–19–7	Mujeeb Zadran	Afghanistan v Bangladesh at Sylhet	2017-18
8.1–1–20–7	T. A. Boult	New Zealand v Malaysia at Johor	2007-08
8.3–0–41–7	J. E. Bishop	England v West Indies at Chelmsford	2001

At Christchurch, January 24, 2018. **Pakistan won by three wickets. South Africa 189-9** (50 overs) (W. K. Makewu 60; Musa Khan 3-29); ‡**Pakistan 190-7** (47.5 overs) (Ali Zaryab 74*). *MoM:* Ali Zaryab. *At 111-5, Pakistan were on the verge of bungling their pursuit of a modest 190, but they were rescued by Ali Zaryab, who made 74* and added 65 with Saad Khan (26). A nervy victory came with 13 balls to spare. South Africa had been restricted by tidy seam bowling from Musa Khan and left-armer Shaheen Shah Afridi, who between them claimed 5-59 from 20 overs. Only Wandile Makewu, with 60 from 65 balls, made much headway – but it was not enough.*

At Christchurch, January 25, 2018. **Afghanistan won by 202 runs.** ‡**Afghanistan 309-6** (50 overs) (Rahmanullah Gurbaz 69, Ibrahim Zadran 68, Bahir Shah 67*, Azmatullah Omarzai 66); **New Zealand 107** (28.1 overs) (Mujeeb Zadran 4-14, Qais Ahmad 4-33). *MoM:* Azmatullah Omarzai. *Afghanistan stunned the hosts by sprinting into their first Under-19 World Cup semi. They were on top from the moment they won the toss. Four Afghan batsmen passed 65: openers Rahmanullah Gurbaz and Ibrahim Zadran ran up 117 in 20 overs, Bahir Shah held firm throughout the second half of the innings, and Azmatullah Omarzai raced to 66 in 23 balls, with seven sixes. Needing 310 to advance, New Zealand slumped to 20-4; the collapse had begun when Rachin Ravindra was run out without scoring. Only Katene Clarke (38) and Dale Phillips (31) passed 13, as spinners Mujeeb Zadran and Qais Ahmad wrapped up the innings in 28.1 overs.*

At Queenstown, January 26, 2018. **India won by 131 runs.** ‡**India 265** (49.2 overs) (S. Gill 86, A. Sharma 50; Kazi Anik 3-48); **Bangladesh 134** (42.1 overs) (K. L. Nagarkoti 3-18). *India set up a semi-final against Pakistan by winning a feisty encounter. Their batting was extended for the first time, but they still won by a thumping margin after another impressive effort from the bowlers, backed up by brilliant fielding. Shubman Gill starred again, with 86 but India were becalmed* *between the 20th and 40th overs, and needed Abhishek Sharma's 49-ball 50 to lift them to a challenging total. Ishan Porel strangled Bangladesh's reply, while Shivam Mavi and Kamlesh Nagarkoti engineered key run-outs.*

Semi-finals

At Christchurch, January 29, 2018. **Australia won by six wickets. ‡Afghanistan 181** (48 overs) (Ikram Ali Khil 80; J. A. Merlo 4-24); **Australia 182-4** (37.3 overs) (J. R. Edwards 72). *MoM:* J. R. Edwards. *Afghanistan's astonishing run came to an end against an efficient Australia. Apart from Ikram Ali Khil, who batted steadily for 119 balls, the Afghans struggled against the seamers, who claimed nine wickets, with four for Jonathan Merlo. The Australians then played confidently against the spinners, including Mujeeb, who took the new ball; Jack Edwards, dropped on eight, lifted him for two sixes. When Qais finally induced Edwards to drag on, Australia were 129-4, but Param Uppal (32*) and Nathan McSweeney (22*) calmly added the 53 required to book a place in their fifth Under-19 World Cup final.*

At Christchurch, January 30, 2018. **India won by 203 runs. ‡India 272-9** (50 overs) (S. Gill 102*; Arshad Iqbal 3-51, Musa Khan 4-67); **Pakistan 69** (29.3 overs) (I. C. Porel 4-17). *MoM:* S. Gill. *India surged into the final by thrashing their great rivals. Hasan Khan, the Pakistan captain, rued the fielding lapses that eased the pressure on India early in their innings, but that did not explain the gulf between the teams. Gill continued his rich run of form with a century, though openers Prithvi Shaw (41) and Manjot Kalra (47) both benefited from missed chances. Porel then produced an opening burst of 6–2–17–4. Mavi and Shaw held magnificent catches.*

FINAL

AUSTRALIA v INDIA

At Mount Maunganui, February 3, 2018 (day/night). India won by eight wickets. Toss: Australia.

At the game's halfway stage, Indian captain Prithvi Shaw gathered his team to issue some motivational words. They were in the driving seat after bowling Australia out for 216, but he wanted to be certain there was no complacency. He need not have worried: India galloped home with more than 11 overs to spare. Manjot Kalra had fallen short of a century in the group game against Australia, but made amends with an unbeaten 101 off 102 balls. It fell to wicketkeeper Harvik Desai, who scored a controlled 47, to hit the winning runs. Australian captain Jason Sangha said: "It was hard to set fields for the kind of batsmen India have." Slow left-armer Shiva Singh, retained for his economy despite not taking a wicket in the group games, had snared two victims (including Will Sutherland, son of Cricket Australia chief executive James) as Australia lost their last six for 33. Jonathan Merlo's 76 had provided the highlight of their innings.

Man of the Match: M. Kalra. *Man of the Tournament:* S. Gill.

Australia Under-19

J. R. Edwards c Nagarkoti b Porel	28	R. E. Hadley c Desai b Mavi	1
M. A. Bryant c Sharma b Porel	14	L. A. J. Pope not out	0
*J. J. S. Sangha c Desai b Nagarkoti	13		
J. A. Merlo c Shiva Singh b Roy	76	Lb 1, w 7	8
P. Uppal c and b Roy	34		
N. A. McSweeney c and b Shiva Singh	23	1/32 (2) 2/52 (1) (47.2 overs) 216	
W. J. Sutherland c Desai b Shiva Singh	5	3/59 (3) 4/134 (5) 5/183 (6)	
†B. J. H. Holt run out (Shiva Singh/Desai)	13	6/191 (7) 7/212 (4) 8/214 (9)	
Z. K. Evans b Nagarkoti	1	9/216 (8) 10/216 (10) 10 overs: 52-2	

Mavi 8.2–1–46–1; Porel 7–1–30–2; Shiva Singh 10–0–36–2; Nagarkoti 9–0–41–2; Sharma 6–0–30–0; Roy 7–0–32–2.

India Under-19

*P. P. Shaw b Sutherland		29
M. Kalra not out		101
S. Gill b Uppal		31
†H. M. Desai not out		47
Lb 1, w 10, nb 1		12

1/71 (1) 2/131 (3)   (2 wkts, 38.5 overs) 220
                        10 overs: 55-0

R. P. Das, A. Sharma, A. S. Roy, K. L. Nagarkoti, S. P. Mavi, Shiva Singh and I. C. Porel did not bat.

Hadley 7–0–37–0; Evans 5–1–30–0; Sutherland 6.5–0–36–1; Edwards 1–0–15–0; Pope 5–0–42–0; Merlo 4–0–21–0; Uppal 10–0–38–1.

Umpires: G. O. Brathwaite and S. George.   Third umpire: N. Duguid.
Referee: J. J. Crowe.

UNDER-19 WORLD CUP FINALS

1987-88	AUSTRALIA beat Pakistan by five wickets at Adelaide.	
1997-98	ENGLAND beat New Zealand by seven wickets at Johannesburg.	
1999-2000	INDIA beat Sri Lanka by six wickets at Colombo (SSC).	
2001-02	AUSTRALIA beat South Africa by seven wickets at Lincoln.	
2003-04	PAKISTAN beat West Indies by 25 runs at Dhaka.	
2005-06	PAKISTAN beat India by 38 runs at Colombo (RPS).	
2007-08	INDIA beat South Africa by 12 runs (D/L) at Kuala Lumpur.	
2009-10	AUSTRALIA beat Pakistan by 25 runs at Lincoln.	
2012	INDIA beat Australia by six wickets at Townsville.	
2013-14	SOUTH AFRICA beat Pakistan by six wickets at Dubai.	
2015-16	WEST INDIES beat India by five wickets at Mirpur.	
2017-18	INDIA beat Australia by eight wickets at Mount Maunganui.	

Third-place Play-off

At Queenstown, February 1, 2018. **Afghanistan v Pakistan. Abandoned.** *Pakistan were placed third as they had a better record in qualifying.*

Fifth-place Play-off

Semi-final At Christchurch, January 27, 2018. **South Africa won by 73 runs.** ‡**South Africa 284-6** (50 overs) (M. P. Breetzke 115, R. van Tonder 117); **New Zealand 211** (43.5 overs) (D. N. Phillips 74; G. W. Coetzee 5-32). *MoM:* R. van Tonder. *A second-wicket stand of 213 between Matthew Breetzke and skipper Raynard van Tonder – who both passed 1,000 runs in Under-19 ODIs – lifted South Africa to a total that always looked beyond the hosts, especially after Jakob Bhula fell for a duck in the first over. He was one of five victims for seamer Gerald Coetzee.*

Semi-final At Queenstown, January 28, 2018. **Bangladesh won by five wickets. England 216** (47.2 overs) (L. Banks 74, H. C. Brook 66; Hasan Mahmud 3-29, Afif Hossain 3-18); ‡**Bangladesh 220-5** (47.3 overs) (Saif Hasan 59, Afif Hossain 71). *MoM:* Afif Hossain. *Ten days earlier, England had crushed Bangladesh here with 20 overs to spare. Now, batting first, they failed to use their full 50, and paid the price. As in the quarter-final against Australia, they squandered a strong position: 143-1 in the 26th. Then a stunning relay catch on the long-off boundary by Towhid Hridoy and Robiul Haque despatched Banks for 74, promptly followed by most of the middle order as England lost five for 14. Steady batting saw Bangladesh home.*

Final At Queenstown, January 31, 2018. **South Africa won by eight wickets.** ‡**Bangladesh 178** (41.4 overs) (Afif Hossain 63, Shakil Hossain 61; F. A. Jones 5-33, A. Mnyaka 3-27); **South Africa 180-2** (38.3 overs) (R. van Tonder 82*). *MoM:* F. A. Jones. *Bangladesh slumped to 33-5 in the ninth over, with four of the wickets going to the nippy Fraser Jones. Afif Hossain (63 from 59 balls) and*

Shakil Hossain saved face with a stand of 96, but the eventual total did not test South Africa, who strolled to fifth place thanks to a stand of 117* between van Tonder and Hermann Rolfes.

Seventh-place Play-off

At Queenstown, January 30, 2018. **England won by 32 runs. ‡England 261-7** (50 overs) (T. Banton 112, J. L. Davies 63; L. I. Georgeson 3-29); **New Zealand 229** (47.1 overs) (F. H. Allen 87, K. D. Clarke 60; E. D. Woods 3-44, W. G. Jacks 3-41). *MoM:* T. Banton. *England won the battle of the demoralised – in the quarter-finals, New Zealand had been dismissed for 107 by Afghanistan, England for 96 by Australia – thanks to a fourth-wicket stand of 139 between Tom Banton and Jack Davies. New Zealand also depended on a productive fourth-wicket pairing and, at 201-3 in the 42nd, were favourites. But Will Jacks, captaining because Harry Brook had been dropped "for a disciplinary matter", removed both Finn Allen and Katene Clarke after they had added 113. The rest fell meekly.*

Ninth-place Play-off

Quarter-final   At Lincoln (No. 3), January 22, 2018. **Canada won by 80 runs. Canada 265-8** (50 overs) (A. S. Gill 120); **‡Papua New Guinea 185** (44.3 overs) (S. K. Atai 81; F. J. S. Haque 3-48, A. Pathmanathan 3-23). *MoM:* A. S. Gill. *A polished 120 from 115 balls by Akash Gill – Canada's first hundred at an Under-19 World Cup – proved too much for PNG. Chasing 266, they had a sniff at 140-2, but eight tumbled for 45.*

Quarter-final   At Lincoln (Bert Sutcliffe Oval), January 22, 2018. **Zimbabwe won by seven wickets. ‡Namibia 113** (40.1 overs); **Zimbabwe 114-3** (19.3 overs). *MoM:* W. Madhevere. *Zimbabwe survived a tremor at 6-2, but Wesley Madhevere soothed the tension with 47.*

Quarter-final   At Lincoln (Bert Sutcliffe Oval), January 23, 2018. **West Indies won by four wickets. ‡Ireland 278-8** (50 overs) (H. T. Tector 69, N. A. Rock 91; J. Royal 3-59); **West Indies 281-6** (48.2 overs) (B. Yadram 53, E. W. J. A. Stewart 50, N. R. J. Young 55*). *MoM:* N. R. J. Young. *Ireland reached their highest total yet in this tournament, but could not defend it against West Indies. Tector took first use of the pitch, and shared a fifth-wicket stand of 116 with Neil Rock, who fell in the final over nine short of a century. Bhaskar Yadram got West Indies' reply off to a rapid start, which was built on by the captain, Emmanuel Stewart, before Nyeem Young knocked 55 off 33 balls to ensure victory with ten deliveries in hand.*

Quarter-final   At Lincoln (No. 3), January 23, 2018. **Sri Lanka won by 311 runs. ‡Sri Lanka 419-4** (50 overs) (H. R. B. Boyagoda 191, K. N. M. Fernando 60, P. H. K. D. Mendis 53*); **Kenya 108** (35.5 overs) (P. H. B. Weerasinghe 4-27). *MoM:* H. R. B. Boyagoda. *Less than a week after New Zealand caned the Kenyans for 436, Sri Lanka piled up 419 – easily their highest total, and only the fifth instance of 400 in Under-19 ODIs. Hasitha Boyagoda faced 152 balls and hit 28 fours and two sixes in his 191, the highest individual innings at this level, beating Jakob Bhula's 180 against Kenya the week before. Sri Lanka's captain Kamindu Mendis rounded things off with a 21-ball 53*, which included 24 from the final over, bowled by his opposite number, Sachin Bhudia. Kenya were soon in trouble: apart from Thomas Ochieng (45), no one made more than 16.*

HIGHEST SCORES IN AN UNDER-19 ODI

191	H. R. B. Boyagoda	Sri Lanka v Kenya at Lincoln		2017-18
180	J. J. N. P. Bhula	New Zealand v Kenya at Christchurch		2017-18
179*	T. P. Doropoulos	Australia v England at Sydney		2002-03
177*	A. T. Rayudu	India v England at Taunton		2002
176	D. J. Pagon	West Indies v Scotland at Dunedin		2001-02
174	D. W. Lawrence	England v Fiji at Chittagong		2015-16
166	K. A. Simmons	**West Indies v Canada at Lincoln**		2017-18
164*	J. A. H. Marshall	New Zealand v Namibia at Pretoria		1997-98
164	S. P. Kremerskothen	Australia v Papua New Guinea at Orkney		1997-98
160	M. A. Agarwal	India v Australia at Hobart		2008-09
160	S. Gill	India v England at Mumbai		2016-17

Semi-final At Lincoln (Bert Sutcliffe Oval), January 25, 2018. **Sri Lanka won by five wickets. Zimbabwe 259-4** (50 overs) (D. Mlambo 52, J. T. Schadendorf 74, M. Shumba 62*); **‡Sri Lanka 260-5** (45.3 overs) (K. N. M. Fernando 109*, M. N. K. Fernando 68). *MoM:* K. N. M. Fernando. *Debutant Donald Mlambo dropped anchor for 52 from 104 balls and, after he departed in the 34th over, Jayden Schadendorf (74 off 78) and Milton Shumba (62* from 53) pressed the accelerator. Sri Lanka were 4-2 after seven deliveries, but Nishan Madushka Fernando's maiden Under-19 ODI century, and his fifth-wicket stand of 143 with Nuwanidu Fernando, settled matters.*

Semi-final At Lincoln (Bert Sutcliffe Oval), January 26, 2018. **West Indies won by 187 runs. ‡West Indies 323-8** (50 overs) (K. A. Simmons 166, A. S. Athanaze 87; A. S. Gill 4-54); **Canada 136** (47.3 overs) (K. Naress 61). *MoM:* K. A. Simmons. *West Indies squashed Canada after left-hander Keagan Simmons hustled 166 in 137 balls. He and Alick Athanaze put on 156 for the third wicket, though four wickets for Akash Gill checked the final charge. Canada were 5-3, before Kavian Naress batted for 41 overs, but only he and Arslan Khan reached double figures.*

Final At Lincoln (Bert Sutcliffe Oval), January 28, 2018. **Sri Lanka won by three wickets. West Indies 254-5** (50 overs) (A. S. Athanaze 110*); **‡Sri Lanka 255-7** (49.4 overs) (P. A. D. Lakshan 98, H. R. B. Boyagoda 116). *MoM:* H. R. B. Boyagoda. *Athanaze hit a run-a-ball 110*, his main support coming from Brad Barnes (37*) in a sixth-wicket stand of 102* in 15 overs. But Sri Lanka's openers Dhananjaya Lakshan and Boyagoda responded with a partnership of 218. Two quick run-outs induced panic, and seven wickets had gone down before a relieved Hareen Buddila Weerasinghe scraped the winning single in the final over.*

Eleventh-place Play-off

At Rangiora, January 28, 2018. **Zimbabwe won by 138 runs. ‡Zimbabwe 272-8** (50 overs) (W. Madhevere 93); **Canada 134** (37.5 overs) (A. S. Gill 60; W. Madhevere 4-24). *MoM:* W. Madhevere. *Wesley Madhevere's all-round form ensured Zimbabwe's victory. He scored a fluent 93 out of 150 in their first 30 overs, including an opening stand of 97 with Tanunurwa Makoni (30), and later claimed four wickets with his off-breaks. He also caught Gill, the only Canadian to pass 24.*

Thirteenth-place Play-off

Semi-final At Rangiora, January 25, 2018. **Ireland won by three wickets. ‡Papua New Guinea 121** (37.1 overs) (H. T. Tector 3-32, J. J. Garth 4-18); **Ireland 122-7** (41.5 overs) (J. J. Tau 4-45). *MoM:* J. J. Garth. *Igo Mahuru (45) and Heagi Toua (39) put on 78 for PNG's fourth wicket, but that was about it. Ireland dipped to 38-4 before Neil Rock, with 43, took them most of the way.*

Semi-final At Lincoln (No. 3), January 25, 2018. **Namibia won by eight wickets. Kenya 176** (46.5 overs) (A. R. Gandhi 52; B. Shikongo 3-29, P. Burger 5-24); **‡Namibia 180-2** (27 overs) (L. Louwrens 114). *MoM:* L. Louwrens. *Namibia's Lohan Louwrens clattered 114 off 76 balls to complete an easy win. Kenya had slipped from 85-1 to 176, with leg-spinner Petrus Burger collecting 5-24.*

Final At Lincoln (No. 3), January 27, 2018. **Ireland won by 102 runs. Ireland 288-6** (50 overs) (J. B. Grassi 51, H. T. Tector 101, N. A. Rock 55); **‡Namibia 186** (39.1 overs) (L. Louwrens 62; J. B. Little 3-33). *MoM:* H. T. Tector. *A maiden century for Tector set up a total that proved beyond Namibia, once a brave opening stand of 58 between Jurgen Linde and Louwrens was broken by left-arm seamer Josh Little.*

Fifteenth-place Play-off

At Rangiora, January 27, 2018. **Kenya won by 14 runs. ‡Kenya 176** (50 overs) (S. I. Kamea 3-24); **Papua New Guinea 162** (48.3 overs) (G. M. Mwendwa 4-37, J. R. Mepani 3-22). *MoM:* J. R. Mepani. *Kenya recovered from 84-7, Jayant Mepani top-scoring with 44* from No. 7. Then, after opening the bowling with his left-arm spin, he and his new-ball partner Gerard Mwendwa shared seven wickets as PNG fell just short.*

Final rankings

1 India 2 Australia 3 Pakistan 4 Afghanistan 5 South Africa 6 Bangladesh 7 England 8 New Zealand 9 Sri Lanka 10 West Indies 11 Zimbabwe 12 Canada 13 Ireland 14 Namibia 15 Kenya 16 Papua New Guinea

ICC WORLD CUP QUALIFIER IN 2017-18

Liam Brickhill

1 Afghanistan   2 West Indies

The World Cup Qualifier in Zimbabwe threw cricket's contrasts into stark relief. Never has there been more money in the global game; never have the Associate countries been more competitive in one-day cricket. Though ten of the 34 matches were televised, cost-cutting meant there was no DRS, while the coveted qualification was to a World Cup that excludes most of the world. If the cricket was of high quality and often breathtaking excitement, the abiding sentiment was of injustice.

Afghanistan added another chapter to their extraordinary story by staging one of the game's great comebacks, winning the tournament despite losing their first three matches. Twice they needed unlikely results elsewhere to progress – and the cricketing gods obliged. The teenage leg-spinner Rashid Khan finished as the joint-top wicket-taker with 17, alongside his even younger team-mate Mujeeb Zadran and Scotland's Safyaan Sharif. Afghanistan looked set to add value to this year's World Cup.

But that same World Cup, restricted to ten teams, is a slap in the face for the ICC's own development programme, and the ramifications of missing out for Zimbabwe, Ireland and Scotland were far-reaching and severe. Cast even further into the wilderness were **Hong Kong** and **Papua New Guinea**, who lost their one-day international status. The **Netherlands** had arrived with ODI status already secured by winning the World Cricket League in December, while Scotland and the **United Arab Emirates** did enough, by reaching the Super Six, to keep theirs. **Nepal** fell well short of qualification, but claimed one-day status for the first time.

Scotland had played a measly two ODIs against an established Test nation (Zimbabwe) since the 2015 World Cup, but turned out to be one of the most complete teams, with an unyielding spirit that made them better than the sum of their parts. While Afghanistan and West Indies were the favourites, it was Zimbabwe and Scotland who initially led the way. The Scots went into the Super Six unbeaten, after tying with Zimbabwe and beating Afghanistan, and then had West Indies on the ropes – and a World Cup place tantalisingly within reach – before a poor lbw decision and late-summer rain scuppered them.

Ireland were one of the oldest teams at the tournament, banking on the players who had served them so well, but some of their familiar vim and vigour were missing. Boyd Rankin's pace and bounce provided an X-factor, but Ireland lost the moments that counted. They left the tournament with their maiden Test match, against Pakistan in Malahide, to look forward to – but little else.

Amid all the drama, **West Indies** declared "mission accomplished" by reaching the final. A side missing several star names, who preferred the big money of global T20 leagues, made it through despite never quite firing. They lost twice to Afghanistan, and might have been knocked out by Zimbabwe or Scotland but for questionable umpiring decisions. But while Jason Holder's side shouldered considerable pressure in trying to qualify for a competition they had once dominated, they never let it show.

The same couldn't be said for the hosts, **Zimbabwe**, who pulled off a great escape to beat Afghanistan by two runs in the group stage, and "dodged a bullet" (in the words of their captain, Graeme Cremer) in that tie with Scotland. But, crucially and crushingly, they missed two bites at the cherry, against West Indies and, more surprisingly, the previously outclassed UAE. At the heart of Zimbabwe's campaign was all-rounder Sikandar Raza. Brendan Taylor outscored him with 457 runs, but Raza made 319 (next came West Indies' Evin Lewis, with 316) and bagged 15 wickets, often driving his side forward through sheer force of will. But he couldn't do it on his own. He was controversially given out off a no-ball against West Indies, and his dismissal three days later tilted the balance against the UAE. The rest wilted, falling four runs short, and Zimbabwe missed out on the World Cup for the first time since their debut in 1983, when Duncan Fletcher captained a squad including a teenage Graeme Hick.

The loss stunned a crowd of 13,000 at Harare Sports Club into silence, and sent shock waves through the local cricket community. The fallout spread far beyond the boundary: the Zimbabwean board fired every senior coach in the country – the national incumbent Heath Streak and his backroom staff, and even those in charge of the Under-19 and A-teams – while Cremer was sacked too. A month after the tournament, Zimbabwe Cricket's well-respected managing director Faisal Hasnain resigned, while Streak brought a $1m defamation suit against Tavengwa Mukuhlani, ZC's chairman, after allegations of racism.

Cricket has always produced winners and losers, but the modern game has created a gulf of inequality, with self-interest eroding much of the hard work done to globalise it. The moment which embodied cricket's embattled spirit below the top level took place off the field, when Raza accepted his Player of the Tournament award. Standing about ten feet from the ICC's chief executive Dave Richardson, Raza laid bare the disconnect at the heart of the game. "This trophy will serve as a painful reminder of the dreams we had," he said. "When I started playing cricket, I thought it was to unite countries, players of different backgrounds, coming together to play this beautiful sport. Unfortunately you'll see that is not going to happen in next year's World Cup."

Others shared his view. Cremer was just heartbroken. Ireland's captain William Porterfield was angry: "How is there only two teams going to a competition that's played every 208 weeks – and lasts six weeks, so two or three big teams can play nine games on TV, so the ICC can cash in with a big cheque?" Scotland's Kyle Coetzer was dignified and philosophical, despite the umpiring howlers that probably cost his side a place at the top table. Michael Vaughan used Twitter to sum it all up: "Let's be honest: Scotland, Ireland, Nepal and Zimbabwe should all be there. The ICC have made a huge mistake."

And so a qualifying tournament that had begun in hope ended in despair.

NATIONAL SQUADS

*   Captain.   †   Did not play.*

Afghanistan   *Asghar Stanikzai, Afsar Zazai, Dawlat Zadran, Gulbadeen Naib, Ihsanullah Janat, Javed Ahmadi, Mohammad Nabi, Mohammad Shahzad, Mujeeb Zadran, Najibullah Zadran, Nasir Ahmadzai, Rahmat Shah, Rashid Khan, Samiullah Shenwari, Shapoor Zadran, Sharafuddin Ashraf. *Coach:* P. V. Simmons.

Asghar Stanikzai missed the start of the tournament after an emergency appendix operation. He was replaced in the squad by Afsar Zazai (Rashid Khan stood in as captain), but returned when Zazai injured a hamstring.

Hong Kong   *Babar Hayat, Aizaz Khan, C. J. Carter, Ehsan Khan, Ehsan Nawaz, S. S. McKechnie, Nadeem Ahmed, Nizakat Khan, A. Rath, K. D. Shah, Shahid Wasif, Simandeep Singh, Tanveer Ahmed, Tanvir Afzal, Waqas Barkat. *Coach:* S. J. Cook.

Ahsan Ali was originally selected, but injured his knee in a warm-up game and was replaced by Shah.

Ireland   *W. T. S. Porterfield, A. Balbirnie, †P. K. D. Chase, G. H. Dockrell, E. C. Joyce, A. R. McBrine, B. J. McCarthy, T. J. Murtagh, K. J. O'Brien, N. J. O'Brien, W. B. Rankin, †J. N. K. Shannon, S. Singh, P. R. Stirling, G. C. Wilson. *Coach:* G. X. Ford.

Nepal   *P. Khadka, D. S. Airee, †L. S. Bhandari, S. P. Gauchan, S. Kami, K. C. Karan, S. Lamichhane, G. Malla, D. Nath, R. K. Paudel, L. N. Rajbanshi, B. Regmi, A. K. Sah, A. Sheikh, S. Vesawkar. *Coach:* J. Tamata.

Netherlands   *P. W. Borren, W. Barresi, B. N. Cooper, B. F. W. de Leede, S. A. Edwards, V. J. Kingma, F. J. Klaassen, M. P. O'Dowd, P. M. Seelaar, Sikander Zulfiqar, S. Snater, R. N. ten Doeschate, T. van der Gugten, R. E. van der Merwe, P. A. van Meekeren. *Coach:* R. J. Campbell.

S. J. Myburgh was originally selected, but injured his ankle before the tournament and was replaced by de Leede.

Papua New Guinea   *A. Vala, C. J. A. Amini, S. Bau, M. D. Dai, K. Doriga, J. Kila, V. V. Morea, A. Nao, D. Ravu, J. B. Reva, L. Siaka, C. A. Soper, T. P. Ura, N. Vanua, J. N. T. Vare. *Coach:* J. H. Dawes.

Scotland   *K. J. Coetzer, R. D. Berrington, M. H. Cross, A. C. Evans, M. A. Jones, M. A. Leask, C. S. MacLeod, H. G. Munsey, S. M. Sharif, C. B. Sole, T. B. Sole, C. D. Wallace, M. R. J. Watt, B. T. J. Wheal, S. G. Whittingham. *Coach:* G. E. Bradburn.

United Arab Emirates   *Rohan Mustafa, Adnan Mufti, Ahmed Raza, Amir Hayat, Ashfaq Ahmed, Chirag Suri, Ghulam Shabbir, Imran Haider, Mohammad Boota, Mohammad Naveed, Mohammad Usman, Qadeer Ahmed, Rameez Shahzad, Shaiman Anwar, Zahoor Khan. *Coach:* D. R. Brown.

West Indies   *J. O. Holder, D. Bishoo, C. R. Brathwaite, S. S. Cotterell, C. H. Gayle, S. O. Hetmyer, S. D. Hope, E. Lewis, N. O. Miller, J. N. Mohammed, A. R. Nurse, K. M. A. Paul, R. Powell, K. A. J. Roach, M. N. Samuels, K. O. K. Williams. *Coach:* S. G. Law.

Paul replaced Cotterell, who injured a hamstring in the first match.

Zimbabwe   *A. G. Cremer, T. L. Chatara, T. S. Chisoro, C. R. Ervine, K. M. Jarvis, H. Masakadza, S. F. Mire, P. J. Moor, B. Muzarabani, †R. Ngarava, Sikandar Raza, B. R. M. Taylor, B. V. Vitori, M. N. Waller, S. C. Williams, C. Zhuwao. *Coach:* H. H. Streak.

R. P. Burl and T. K. Musakanda were named in the original squad, but replaced by Williams and Zhuwao. Ngarava was called up when Vitori's bowling action was ruled illegal after the second match.

All matches were official one-day internationals, except those involving Nepal or the Netherlands.

Group A

At Harare (Old Hararians), March 4, 2018. **Ireland won by 93 runs** (DLS). **Ireland 268-7** (50 overs) (W. T. S. Porterfield 47, E. C. Joyce 32, A. Balbirnie 68, N. J. O'Brien 49; T. van der Gugten 3-59); ‡**Netherlands 149** (32.2 overs) (T. van der Gugten 33; T. J. Murtagh 3-28). *MoM:* A. Balbirnie. *Andy Balbirnie shrugged off a blow on the head from Ryan ten Doeschate (he continued batting, but did not field) to anchor Ireland's innings with 68. Tim Murtagh struck twice* *early on, and the Netherlands were soon 63-5. Rain meant the target was revised to 243 from 41, and they never got close.*

At Harare, March 4, 2018. **United Arab Emirates won by 56 runs** (DLS). **United Arab Emirates 221** (49.4 overs) (Rohan Mustafa 95, Ashfaq Ahmed 50; N. Vanua 4-39); ‡**Papua New Guinea 113** (25.5 overs) (Mohammad Naveed 5-28). *MoM:* Mohammad Naveed. *ODI debut:* J. Kila (PNG). *An opening stand of 91 between Rohan Mustafa and Ashfaq Ahmed seemed to have set the UAE up for a tall score, but they fizzled out, with Norman Vanua claiming four late wickets in 13 balls. PNG slumped to 23-4 after five overs – all to seamer Mohammad Naveed – and never recovered; a shower left them needing 170 from 28, which proved beyond them.*

At Harare, March 6, 2018. **Ireland won by four wickets. Papua New Guinea 235** (50 overs) (T. P. Ura 151; A. R. McBrine 3-38); ‡**Ireland 237-6** (49.1 overs) (W. T. S. Porterfield 111, E. C. Joyce 53). *MoM:* T. P. Ura. *Ireland won again despite a superb onslaught from Tony Ura, who blazed six sixes and 11 fours from 142 balls. But he got no support: the next highest was No. 9 Chad Soper's 25, while No. 10 Vanua hit the innings' only other boundary. In reply, William Porterfield reached his 11th ODI century, and was out within sight of victory.*

HIGHEST PERCENTAGE OF RUNS IN COMPLETED ODI INNINGS

69.48	I. V. A. Richards (189*/272-9) .	West Indies v England at Manchester	1984
65.78	Kapil Dev (175*/266-8)	India v Zimbabwe at Tunbridge Wells.	1983
65.34	R. G. Sharma (264/404-5). . . .	India v Sri Lanka at Kolkata	2014-15
64.25	**T. P. Ura (151/235).**	**Papua New Guinea v Ireland at Harare** .	**2017-18**
63.51	A. H. Jones (47/74)	New Zealand v Pakistan at Sharjah	1989-90
63.21	S. T. Jayasuriya (189/299-5) . . .	Sri Lanka v India at Sharjah.	2000-01
62.66	S. B. Styris (141/225)	New Zealand v Sri Lanka at Bloemfontein . .	2002-03
62.17	C. K. Coventry (194*/312-8). . . .	Zimbabwe v Bangladesh at Bulawayo.	2009
60.73	D. R. Martyn (116*/191).	Australia v New Zealand at Auckland	1999-2000
60.37	E. C. Joyce (160*/265-5).	Ireland v Afghanistan at Belfast.	2016
60.30	M. J. Guptill (237*/393-6).	New Zealand v West Indies at Wellington . . .	2014-15
60.28	R. A. Smith (167*/277-5)	England v Australia at Birmingham.	1993

Includes only innings in which teams were all out, or used up their allocation of overs.

At Harare (Old Hararians), March 6, 2018. **West Indies won by 60 runs.** ‡**West Indies 357-4** (50 overs) (C. H. Gayle 123, E. Lewis 31, S. O. Hetmyer 127, S. D. Hope 35*); **United Arab Emirates 297-6** (50 overs) (Chirag Suri 38, Rameez Shahzad 112*, Shaiman Anwar 64, Adnan Mufti 45; J. O. Holder 5-53). *MoM:* S. O. Hetmyer. *ODI debut:* Chirag Suri. *Chris Gayle made a blazing start, hitting 11 sixes in his 91-ball 123 – putting on 88 with Evin Lewis, and 103 in 11.2 overs with Shimron Hetmyer. It was Gayle's 23rd ODI century, and Hetmyer's first. Rohan Mustafa was the first to go in the reply, the 100th ODI wicket for Kemar Roach; skipper Jason Holder captured the other five to fall. Rameez Shahzad and Shaiman Anwar clubbed seven sixes and shared a fourth-wicket stand of 144, but it was a forlorn task.*

At Harare, March 8, 2018. **United Arab Emirates won by six wickets.** ‡**Netherlands 176** (46.3 overs) (W. Barresi 37, R. N. ten Doeschate 34; Rohan Mustafa 5-26); **United Arab Emirates 177-4** (44 overs) (Chirag Suri 78*, Mohammad Usman 36*). *MoM:* Rohan Mustafa. *The Netherlands were 50-0 after ten overs – but their innings was all downhill from there. Mustafa took five wickets with his off-breaks, and ran out Ben Cooper: the eventual 176 was underwhelming. The Dutch were in with a sniff when the UAE slipped to 84-4, but opener Chirag Suri and Mohammad Usman took them home with a stand of 93*.*

At Harare (Old Hararians), March 8, 2018. **West Indies won by six wickets.** ‡**Papua New Guinea 200** (42.4 overs) (T. P. Ura 37, A. Vala 57, M. D. Dai 35, N. Vanua 35; C. R. Brathwaite 5-27); **West Indies 201-4** (43 overs) (S. D. Hope 49*, J. O. Holder 99*). *MoM:* J. O. Holder. *After five wickets in the previous match, Holder, who finished one short of a maiden ODI hundred, dominated a fifth-wicket stand of 143* with Shai Hope – whose 49* occupied 115 balls – to ensure another victory. PNG's uneven innings included six single-figure dismissals (four inflicted by Carlos Brathwaite, who completed his maiden international five-for), while skipper Asad Vala faced 56 dot balls in his 57 from 89.*

At Harare, March 10, 2018. **West Indies won by 52 runs. West Indies 257-8** (50 overs) (S. O. Hetmyer 36, J. O. Holder 54, R. Powell 101; T. J. Murtagh 4-41); ‡**Ireland 205** (46.2 overs) (E. C. Joyce 63, N. J. O'Brien 34, K. J. O'Brien 38; K. A. J. Roach 4-27, K. O. K. Williams 4-43). *MoM:* R. Powell. *West Indies eased home – and into the Super Six – in this battle of the unbeaten teams. But they had made a hesitant start on a juicy pitch, and were rescued from 83-5 by Holder and Rovman Powell, who struck seven sixes in his maiden international hundred before falling in the final over. No West Indian had previously scored an ODI century from as low as No. 7. Ireland looked on course at 165-4 after 36 overs, but Ed Joyce and Kevin O'Brien fell in the next, from Roach, and seamer Kesrick Williams mopped up.*

At Harare (Old Hararians), March 10, 2018. **Netherlands won by 57 runs. Netherlands 216-8** (50 overs) (R. E. van der Merwe 38, Sikander Zulfiqar 53*); ‡**Papua New Guinea 159** (42.1 overs) (A. Vala 44, K. Doriga 32*; R. E. van der Merwe 4-46). *MoM:* R. E. van der Merwe. *Netherlands managed their first victory, leaving PNG winless. They kept their slim World Cup hopes alive mainly thanks to Roelof van der Merwe, who added four wickets to an important 38, and put on 56 with Sikander Zulfiqar. PNG's eventual total represented something of a comeback from 93-7.*

At Harare (Old Hararians), March 12, 2018. **Ireland won by 226 runs** (DLS). **Ireland 313-6** (44 overs) (W. T. S. Porterfield 92, P. R. Stirling 126, K. J. O'Brien 50*; Mohammad Naveed 3-84); ‡**United Arab Emirates 91** (29.3 overs) (W. B. Rankin 4-15, S. Singh 3-15). *MoM:* P. R. Stirling. *A national-record opening stand of 205 between Porterfield and Paul Stirling (who hit his seventh ODI hundred), and a 26-ball half-century from Kevin O'Brien, propelled Ireland past 300. Two early showers reduced this to a 44-over match: the UAE's target was revised slightly to 318, which was still way beyond them; Ireland's win was their biggest by runs in ODIs. The Netherlands' defeat elsewhere in Harare meant both these sides joined West Indies in the Super Six.*

At Harare, March 12, 2018. **West Indies won by 54 runs** (DLS). **West Indies 309-6** (48 overs) (C. H. Gayle 46, E. Lewis 84, M. N. Samuels 73*, R. Powell 52); ‡**Netherlands 167-6** (28.4 overs) (W. Barresi 64, R. N. ten Doeschate 67*). *MoM:* E. Lewis. *The Netherlands needed a thumping win to progress – but lost heavily when rain ended play with them well adrift of the DLS par score of 221. Gayle and Lewis had given West Indies a rapid start with 85 in 8.3 overs, before Samuels and Powell put on 99 for the sixth wicket. From 29-2 in the reply, Wesley Barresi and ten Doeschate added 113, but a flurry of wickets as the clouds gathered ended Dutch hopes.*

Group B

At Bulawayo (Athletic Club), March 4, 2018. **Scotland won by seven wickets. Afghanistan 255** (49.4 overs) (Mohammad Shahzad 30, Mohammad Nabi 92, Najibullah Zadran 67; B. T. J. Wheal 3-36, R. D. Berrington 3-42); ‡**Scotland 256-3** (47.2 overs) (C. S. MacLeod 157*, R. D. Berrington 67). *MoM:* C. S. MacLeod. *An imperious innings from Calum MacLeod, who stroked 23 fours and a six, carried Scotland to a comfortable victory over the fancied Afghans. From 21-2, he and Richie Berrington put on 208, a Scotland record for any wicket, beating 203 by openers Gavin Hamilton and Fraser Watts against Canada at Aberdeen in 2009. MacLeod passed 150 with successive fours off Rashid Khan, who turned disappointing figures of 9–0–68–1 to add to a first-ball duck as he became the first 19-year-old to captain in a one-day international. Earlier, Afghanistan had recovered from 71-4 thanks to a stand of 149 between Mohammad Nabi and Najibullah Zadran.*

HIGHEST ODI SCORES FOR SCOTLAND

175	C. S. MacLeod	v Canada at Christchurch	2013-14
157*	**C. S. MacLeod**	**v Afghanistan at Bulawayo (Athletic Club)**	**2017-18**
156	K. J. Coetzer	v Bangladesh at Nelson	2014-15
154	C. S. MacLeod	v Papua New Guinea at Port Moresby	2017-18
140*	**C. S. MacLeod**	**v England at Edinburgh**	**2018**
139*	P. L. Mommsen	v United Arab Emirates at Lincoln	2013-14
133	K. J. Coetzer	v Afghanistan at Sharjah	2012-13
127	K. J. Coetzer	v United Arab Emirates at Edinburgh	2016
123*	R. R. Watson	v Canada at Mombasa	2006-07
121*	N. F. I. McCallum	v Ireland at Benoni	2008-09

At Bulawayo, March 4, 2018. **Zimbabwe won by 116 runs.** ‡**Zimbabwe 380-6** (50 overs) (C. Zhuwao 41, S. F. Mire 52, B. R. M. Taylor 100, C. R. Ervine 34, Sikandar Raza 123); **Nepal 264-8** (50 overs) (G. Malla 32, P. Khadka 40, S. Vesawkar 52, A. Sheikh 50, R. K. Paudel 30; Sikandar Raza 3-48). *MoM:* Sikandar Raza. *The hosts overwhelmed Nepal in a run avalanche led by Sikandar Raza, who scorched to three figures in 59 balls and finished with 123* from 66, including nine sixes. He overshadowed a round 100 by Brendan Taylor, who faced only 91 balls himself; they put on 173 for the fifth wicket in 18 overs. Raza then ensured the match award, taking three wickets with his flattish off-breaks.*

At Bulawayo (Athletic Club), March 6, 2018. **Scotland won by four wickets. Hong Kong 91** (38.2 overs) (A. C. Evans 3-19, T. B. Sole 4-15); ‡**Scotland 92-6** (23.3 overs) (K. J. Coetzer 41*; Ehsan Khan 3-29). *MoM:* T. B. Sole. *Scotland made it two out of two, although their victory was not quite as straightforward as seemed likely after Hong Kong, from 46-0 in the 11th over, lost all ten for 45. Off-spinner Tom Sole struck twice in his first three deliveries, and finished with 10–5–15–4. Scotland were sailing home at 50-2 in the 13th, but three wickets for fellow off-spinner Ehsan Khan slowed them.*

At Bulawayo, March 6, 2018. **Zimbabwe won by two runs.** ‡**Zimbabwe 196** (43 overs) (B. R. M. Taylor 89, Sikandar Raza 60; Mujeeb Zadran 3-49, Rashid Khan 3-38); **Afghanistan 194** (49.3 overs) (Rahmat Shah 69, Mohammad Nabi 51; B. Muzarabani 4-47, Sikandar Raza 3-40). *MoM:* Sikandar Raza. An excited home crowd celebrated after a narrow victory that looked improbable when Zimbabwe were restricted to 196. Exactly half came in a fifth-wicket stand between Taylor and Raza; no one else reached 20, and there were four ducks. Afghanistan were cruising at 156-3, but the 21-year-old seamer Blessing Muzarabani trapped Rahmat Shah, and Raza had Nabi stumped. Afghanistan reached the last over needing four, but with only one wicket left: Brian Vitori had Shapoor Zadran caught behind third ball to spark the jubilation. "We say that the team that panics first will lose," said Raza. "We just kept our composure." It wasn't all good news for Zimbabwe: Vitori's action was reported for the third time in two years, and he was soon suspended from bowling in international cricket. Afghanistan's opener Mohammad Shahzad slammed his bat into the turf on dismissal, and received a demerit point that triggered a suspension: he missed the next two matches.

At Bulawayo (Athletic Club), March 8, 2018. **Hong Kong won by 30 runs** (DLS). **Hong Kong 241-8** (50 overs) (Babar Hayat 31, A. Rath 65; Mujeeb Zadran 3-26, Mohammad Nabi 3-48); ‡**Afghanistan 195-9** (46 overs) (Mohammad Nabi 38, Najibullah Zadran 32, Dawlat Zadran 40*; Ehsan Khan 4-33). *MoM:* Ehsan Khan. *Scatterbrained batting left Afghanistan on the brink of elimination, and reliant on other results. A disciplined 65 in 90 balls from Anshuman Rath had eased Hong Kong to their highest total of the tournament. Despite being without regular captain Asghar Stanikzai and suspended opener Shahzad, Afghanistan looked in decent shape at 132-4 in the 35th over, but then lost three for ten. A shower drove the players off at the end of the 43rd, and four overs were lopped off, which left Afghanistan needing 59 from 18 deliveries to reach a revised target of 226. It proved impossible. This was Hong Kong's first ODI victory over a Full Member nation.*

At Bulawayo, March 8, 2018. **Scotland won by four wickets.** ‡**Nepal 149** (47.4 overs) (P. Khadka 63; S. G. Whittingham 3-35); **Scotland 153-6** (41.3 overs) (K. J. Coetzer 88*). *MoM:* K. J. Coetzer. *Scotland ensured their place in the Super Six with a clinical despatch of Nepal, who at one stage were 39-5. Sussex seamer Stuart Whittingham, in his match of the tournament, took 3-35. Kyle Coetzer, Scotland's captain, anchored the chase with 88* from 136 balls.*

At Bulawayo (Athletic Club), March 10, 2018. **Afghanistan won by six wickets.** ‡**Nepal 194** (49.5 overs) (P. Khadka 75, D. S. Airee 32; Rashid Khan 3-45, Mohammad Nabi 4-33); **Afghanistan 195-4** (38.4 overs) (Rahmat Shah 46, Mohammad Nabi 34, Najibullah Zadran 52*). *MoM:* Mohammad Nabi. *Nepal, at one stage 105-1 with skipper Paras Khadka going strong, lost nine for 89, as spinners Rashid and Nabi shared seven. And so Afghanistan finally got off the mark, also boosting their net run-rate by winning with more than 11 overs to spare. But to advance they needed Nepal – who had now lost three out of three – to defeat Hong Kong, conquerors of Afghanistan earlier in the group.*

At Bulawayo, March 10, 2018. **Zimbabwe won by 89 runs. Zimbabwe 263-9** (50 overs) (C. Zhuwao 45, H. Masakadza 84, B. R. M. Taylor 46; Ehsan Nawaz 4-47); ‡**Hong Kong 174** (46.5 overs) (A. Rath 85; Sikandar Raza 3-30). *MoM:* H. Masakadza. *Zimbabwe ensured their place in the Super Six with a comfortable victory, led by Hamilton Masakadza, who put on 98 for the third wicket with the consistent Taylor. Rath was a lone beacon for Hong Kong: no one else reached 20 as Zimbabwe's spinners collected seven wickets.*

At Bulawayo (Athletic Club), March 12, 2018. **Nepal won by five wickets.** ‡Hong Kong 153 (48.2 overs) (Nizakat Khan 47; S. Lamichhane 3-17); **Nepal 155-5** (40.4 overs) (R. K. Paudel 48*, S. Kami 37*). MoM: R. K. Paudel. *Afghanistan pulled off the first part of their great escape, squeezing through to the Super Sixes on net run-rate after Nepal recorded their first win of the tournament. Hong Kong's batting misfired: there were three cheap wickets for 17-year-old leg-spinner Sandeep Lamichhane, who had recently signed for Delhi Daredevils in the IPL. But they reduced Nepal to 66-5, before 15-year-old Rohit Kumar Paudel and Sompal Kami settled nerves in Kathmandu and Kabul with a stand of 89*.*

At Bulawayo, March 12, 2018. **Tied.** ‡Zimbabwe 210 (46.4 overs) (S. F. Mire 35, B. R. M. Taylor 44, C. R. Ervine 57; S. M. Sharif 5-33, M. A. Leask 4-37); **Scotland 210** (49.1 overs) (K. J. Coetzer 39, R. D. Berrington 47; T. S. Chisoro 3-42, A. G. Cremer 3-23). MoM: S. M. Sharif. *When No. 10 Mark Watt hit successive fours and a two off Tendai Chatara to take Scotland within two of victory in the 49th over, it seemed that a seesaw match had finally been decided. But Watt holed out to the last delivery, leaving two needed from the final over. Muzarabani started with a wide, levelling the scores, but last man Brad Wheal snicked the next ball to keeper Taylor. It was the first tied ODI since Zimbabwe v West Indies, also at Bulawayo, 16 months previously.*

QUALIFYING TABLES

Group A

	P	W	T	L	Pts	NRR
WEST INDIES	4	4	0	0	8	1.17
IRELAND	4	3	0	1	6	1.47
UNITED ARAB EMIRATES	4	2	0	2	4	−1.17
Netherlands	4	1	0	3	2	−0.70
Papua New Guinea	4	0	0	4	0	−0.86

Group B

	P	W	T	L	Pts	NRR
ZIMBABWE	4	3	1	0	7	1.03
SCOTLAND	4	3	1	0	7	0.85
AFGHANISTAN	4	1	0	3	2	0.03
Nepal	4	1	0	3	2	−0.89
Hong Kong	4	1	0	3	2	−1.12

Teams carried through points gained against fellow qualifiers: West Indies 4, Scotland 3, Zimbabwe 3, Ireland 2, Afghanistan 0 and United Arab Emirates 0.

Super Six

At Harare, March 15, 2018. **Afghanistan won by three wickets.** ‡West Indies 197-8 (50 overs) (M. N. Samuels 36, S. D. Hope 43; Mujeeb Zadran 3-33); **Afghanistan 198-7** (47.4 overs) (Rahmat Shah 68, Mohammad Nabi 31; J. O. Holder 3-39). MoM: Mujeeb Zadran. ODI debut: K. M. A. Paul (West Indies). *Afghanistan ended West Indies' 100% record, with their spinners restricting the Caribbean strokemakers. Mujeeb Zadran, just 16, opened the bowling and took 3-33, including Chris Gayle for a single. Shai Hope top-scored, but his boundary-less 43 used up 94 balls. Afghanistan were 17-2 in the fifth over, but Rahmat Shah put on 66 with Samiullah Shenwari (27) and 49 with Mohammad Nabi to take his side close. Nerves cost a few wickets, but not the match.*

At Bulawayo, March 15, 2018. **Scotland won by 73 runs.** ‡Scotland 322-6 (50 overs) (M. H. Cross 114, K. J. Coetzer 43, C. S. MacLeod 78, R. D. Berrington 37*, H. G. Munsey 30; Rohan Mustafa 4-56); **United Arab Emirates 249** (47.4 overs) (Rohan Mustafa 32, Ashfaq Ahmed 30, Mohammad Usman 80, Ahmed Raza 50; C. B. Sole 4-68). MoM: M. H. Cross. *Matt Cross's second ODI hundred (the first, two months previously, was also against the UAE) lifted Scotland to a total that always looked enough. After an opening stand of 68 with Kyle Coetzer, Cross added 161 with Calum MacLeod. The UAE were rescued from 117-6 by Mohammad Usman and Ahmed Raza, who put on 105, but they were never on terms. Chris Sole claimed four wickets in his first match of the tournament after a hamstring strain. This was Richie Berrington's 211th official appearance for Scotland, breaking Majid Haq's record.*

At Harare, March 16, 2018. **Zimbabwe won by 107 runs. Zimbabwe 211-9** (50 overs) (Sikandar Raza 69*; T. J. Murtagh 3-36); ‡Ireland 104 (34.2 overs) (P. R. Stirling 41; T. S. Chisoro 3-22, A. G. Cremer 3-18). MoM: Sikandar Raza. *Zimbabwe remained undefeated – and boosted their net* *run-rate – with a thumping victory after Ireland's catastrophic collapse on a sluggish pitch. Apart from Paul Stirling, whose 41 ate up 70 deliveries before he was run out, only Gary Wilson (15) reached double figures as the spinners claimed eight wickets. Earlier, Zimbabwe were again indebted to Sikandar Raza, whose 69* ensured they passed 200 after being 139-7. They now needed to win one of their remaining two matches to reach the World Cup.*

At Harare, March 18, 2018. **Ireland won by 25 runs. Ireland 271-9** (50 overs) (A. Balbirnie 105, N. J. O'Brien 70, K. J. O'Brien 46; B. T. J. Wheal 3-43); ‡**Scotland 246** (47.4 overs) (K. J. Coetzer 61, R. D. Berrington 44, S. M. Sharif 34, M. R. J. Watt 31*; W. B. Rankin 4-63). *MoM:* A. Balbirnie. *Scotland's unbeaten run was ended by their oldest rivals – and, arguably, by the umpiring decision which reprieved Andy Balbirnie when he was pinned in front on one. But the former Australian Test player Paul Wilson declined Brad Wheal's appeal, and Balbirnie – whose previous four innings had all ended in single figures – took advantage with his second ODI century, and putting on 138 with Niall O'Brien. After reaching 94-1, Scotland wobbled to 132-6, and fell short, despite gritty innings from Berrington and Safyaan Sharif.*

At Harare, March 19, 2018. **West Indies won by four wickets.** ‡**Zimbabwe 289** (50 overs) (S. F. Mire 45, B. R. M. Taylor 138, S. C. Williams 34; K. A. J. Roach 3-55, J. O. Holder 4-35); **West Indies 290-6** (49 overs) (E. Lewis 64, S. D. Hope 76, M. N. Samuels 86). *MoM:* M. N. Samuels. *West Indies inflicted Zimbabwe's first defeat – and remained on course for qualification – by staying calm in the face of a sizeable total. It had been set up by Brendan Taylor's tenth ODI century, a superb 138 from 124 balls. West Indies had only ever successfully chased four higher scores, but looked in charge while Hope and Marlon Samuels were putting on 135 after Evin Lewis's lively start. But four wickets in 12 balls set hearts racing with 25 still needed. A leg-bye sealed the victory. Zimbabwe needed to win their final game, against the UAE, to qualify.*

At Harare (Old Hararians), March 20, 2018. **Afghanistan won by five wickets.** ‡**United Arab Emirates 177** (43 overs) (Shaiman Anwar 64, Mohammad Naveed 45; Dawlat Zadran 3-45, Rashid Khan 5-41); **Afghanistan 178-5** (34.3 overs) (Gulbadeen Naib 74*, Najibullah Zadran 63*). *MoM:* Gulbadeen Naib. *Afghanistan, with Asghar Stanikzai back in charge even though he had barely recovered from having his appendix out, kept their faint hopes alive – but they had to survive yet another scare. The UAE had struggled against Rashid Khan, freed of the cares of captaincy, and only a late flourish from Mohammad Naveed, whose 20-ball 45 included 40 in boundaries, got them as far as 177. Naveed then struck twice as the Afghans dipped to 54-5, but they surged to victory thanks to Gulbadeen Naib and Najibullah Zadran, who piled on 124* in 19 overs.*

At Harare, March 21, 2018. **West Indies won by five runs** (DLS). **West Indies 198** (48.4 overs) (E. Lewis 66, M. N. Samuels 51; S. M. Sharif 3-27, B. T. J. Wheal 3-34); ‡**Scotland 125-5** (35.2 overs) (R. D. Berrington 33, H. G. Munsey 32*). *MoM:* S. M. Sharif. *The winners were guaranteed a World Cup spot – and West Indies grabbed it. But their joy meant heartbreak for a well-organised Scottish side, who were particularly aggrieved at a late lbw decision: with storm clouds gathering, the sides were neck and neck on DLS when Berrington, Scotland's last recognised batsman, was given out by Paul Wilson to an Ashley Nurse delivery heading down leg. The rain arrived 22 balls later, with Scotland five adrift: had they been 125-4 instead they would have won, and reached the World Cup. "Clearly that decision is not sitting very well with us right now," said Coetzer. "It's not the first one in this tournament. Two critical moments in two critical games have potentially cost us." Earlier, Scotland had made the perfect start when Sharif dismissed Gayle with the first ball of the match, and Hope – also for a duck – with the first delivery of his next over. From 2-2, West Indies recovered through a stand of 121 between Lewis and Samuels, but the later batting fell away.*

At Harare, March 22, 2018. **United Arab Emirates won by three runs** (DLS). **United Arab Emirates 235-7** (47.5 overs) (Rohan Mustafa 31, Ghulam Shabbir 40, Rameez Shahzad 59, Shaiman Anwar 33; Sikandar Raza 3-41); ‡**Zimbabwe 226-7** (40 overs) (P. J. Moor 39, S. C. Williams 80, Sikandar Raza 34; Mohammad Naveed 3-40). *MoM:* Mohammad Naveed. *To reach the World Cup, Zimbabwe just needed to beat the UAE, who hadn't managed a win in the Super Six stage and had never beaten a Full Member. To the disbelief of a large home crowd, the Zimbabweans blew it, perhaps unsettled by a downpour which lopped ten overs off their innings. The hard-hitting Rameez Shahzad was the main contributor in a serviceable UAE batting performance, curtailed 13 balls early by rain. Zimbabwe's target was revised to 230 in 40 overs and, although they stumbled at the start – 18-2 after five – they were stabilised by Peter Moor (39 from 61 in his first match of the tournament) and Sean Williams, whose run-a-ball 80 ended when he holed out to the last delivery of the 37th. That left Zimbabwe needing 24 off 18 – but, after Cremer's ungainly swish at his first delivery, they came up just short.*

At Harare, March 23, 2018. **Afghanistan won by five wickets.** ‡**Ireland 209-7** (50 overs) (P. R. Stirling 55, N. J. O'Brien 36, K. J. O'Brien 41; Rashid Khan 3-40); **Afghanistan 213-5** (49.1 overs) (Mohammad Shahzad 54, Gulbadeen Naib 45, Asghar Stanikzai 39*; S. Singh 3-30). *MoM:* Mohammad Shahzad. *A sequence of unlikely results meant this final Super Six match turned into a shootout for the final World Cup spot – and Afghanistan completed their remarkable comeback with another narrow victory. Ireland's batsmen were shackled by the teenage spinners – Mujeeb Zadran whisked through his ten overs for 31, while Rashid took 3-40. Mohammad Shahzad then shot out of the blocks with 54 from 50 balls, but two wickets for off-spinner Simi Singh set the chase back. Stanikzai supervised the final push, despite being in pain from an appendectomy. "I only had my operation two weeks ago," he said. "I still feel pain inside, especially when I was playing big shots." Fittingly, it was Stanikzai who carved the first ball of the final over, from Barry McCarthy, for the boundary that confirmed a World Cup place – and eliminated Ireland.*

SUPER SIX TABLE

	P	W	T	L	Pts	NRR
WEST INDIES	5	4	0	1	8	0.47
AFGHANISTAN	5	3	0	2	6	0.30
Zimbabwe	5	2	1	2	5	0.42
Scotland	5	2	1	2	5	0.24
Ireland	5	2	0	3	4	0.34
United Arab Emirates	5	1	0	4	2	–1.95

Play-offs

Semi-final At Kwekwe, March 15, 2018. **Netherlands won by 44 runs.** ‡**Netherlands 174** (48.2 overs) (M. P. O'Dowd 62, P. W. Borren 31; Nadeem Ahmed 3-20); **Hong Kong 130** (43 overs) (Babar Hayat 52; R. E. van der Merwe 4-18). *MoM:* M. P. O'Dowd. *Hong Kong's disappointing batting performance meant they lost their ODI status after this tournament.*

Semi-final At Harare (Old Hararians), March 15, 2018. **Nepal won by six wickets. Papua New Guinea 114** (27.2 overs) (S. Lamichhane 4-29, D. S. Airee 4-14); ‡**Nepal 115-4** (23 overs) (D. S. Airee 50*). *MoM:* D. S. Airee. *Nepal's convincing victory, set up by teenage spinners Sandeep Lamichhane and Dipendra Singh Airee, confirmed they would have official ODI status for the first time – but Papua New Guinea lost theirs.*

Seventh place At Kwekwe, March 17, 2018. **Netherlands won by 45 runs.** ‡**Netherlands 189-9** (50 overs) (B. F. W. de Leede 39; S. Kami 5-24); **Nepal 144** (44.4 overs) (S. Kami 36; R. E. van der Merwe 4-20). *MoM:* R. E. van der Merwe. *Bas de Leede, the 18-year-old son of former Netherlands captain Tim, made the biggest contribution of a low-scoring encounter.*

Ninth place At Harare (Old Hararians), March 17, 2018. **Papua New Guinea won by 58 runs.** ‡**Papua New Guinea 200** (48.2 overs) (T. P. Ura 49, C. A. Soper 39, M. D. Dai 35; K. D. Shah 4-11); **Hong Kong 142** (35.2 overs) (Babar Hayat 37; N. Vanua 4-24, C. J. A. Amini 4-27). *MoM:* C. J. A. Amini. *ODI debut:* Simandeep Singh (Hong Kong). *This was the last official ODI for both sides, at least until after the qualifying competition for the 2023 World Cup.*

FINAL

AFGHANISTAN v WEST INDIES

At Harare, March 25, 2018. Afghanistan won by seven wickets. Toss: West Indies.

Afghanistan completed a roller-coaster tournament with a comfortable victory, their third win in four completed one-day internationals against West Indies. With the World Cup places decided, there was little riding on this match, and West Indies made a quiet start: when Holder was run out without facing in the 24th over, it was 101 for five. Hetmyer and Powell organised something of a recovery, but the total was still well below par on a true Harare Sports Club pitch. Nineteen-year-old Rashid Khan became the youngest to take 100 ODI wickets (beating Pakistan's Saqlain Mushtaq by around ten months), and also the quickest (in 44 matches, to Mitchell Starc's 52). When Afghanistan batted, Mohammad Shahzad all but settled the issue with a typically robust 84, then Mohammad Nabi finished the match with three successive sixes off Gayle.

Man of the Match: Mohammad Shahzad. *Man of the Tournament:* Sikandar Raza (Zimbabwe).

West Indies

C. H. Gayle c Sharafuddin Ashraf	
b Mujeeb Zadran .	10
E. Lewis c Mohammad Shahzad	
b Gulbadeen Naib.	27
†S. D. Hope lbw b Rashid Khan	23
M. N. Samuels c Rahmat Shah	
b Sharafuddin Ashraf.	17
S. O. Hetmyer c Mohammad Shahzad	
b Sharafuddin Ashraf.	38
*J. O. Holder run out (Rahmat Shah/	
Mohammad Nabi).	0
R. Powell b Mujeeb Zadran	44

C. R. Brathwaite c Asghar Stanikzai	
b Dawlat Zadran .	14
A. R. Nurse not out	26
K. M. A. Paul lbw b Mujeeb Zadran	0
K. A. J. Roach b Mujeeb Zadran	0
Lb 2, w 3	5

1/16 (1) 2/50 (2) 3/73 (4)   (46.5 overs) 204
4/99 (3) 5/101 (6) 6/138 (5)
7/163 (8) 8/204 (7) 9/204 (10)
10/204 (11)   10 overs: 43-1

Dawlat Zadran 7–0–26–1; Mujeeb Zadran 9.5–0–43–4; Gulbadeen Naib 5–0–28–2; Mohammad Nabi 9–1–37–0; Sharafuddin Ashraf 7–0–26–1; Rashid Khan 9–0–42–1.

Afghanistan

†Mohammad Shahzad c Holder b Gayle. . . .	84
Gulbadeen Naib c Gayle b Paul	14
Rahmat Shah st Hope b Gayle.	51
Samiullah Shenwari not out.	20
Mohammad Nabi not out.	27
Lb 2, w 8	10

1/58 (2) 2/148 (1)   (3 wkts, 40.4 overs) 206
3/170 (3)

                          10 overs: 59-1

*Asghar Stanikzai, Najibullah Zadran, Sharafuddin Ashraf, Rashid Khan, Dawlat Zadran and Mujeeb Zadran did not bat.

Roach 5–0–24–0; Holder 6–0–45–0; Brathwaite 6–0–37–0; Paul 8–0–29–1; Nurse 10–2–31–0; Gayle 5.4–0–38–2.

Umpires: S. D. Fry and M. A. Gough.   Third umpire: P. Wilson.
Referee: G. F. Labrooy.

Final standings

1 Afghanistan 2 West Indies 3 Zimbabwe 4 Scotland 5 Ireland 6 United Arab Emirates
7 Netherlands 8 Nepal 9 Papua New Guinea 10 Hong Kong

Afghanistan and West Indies qualified for the 2019 World Cup. Zimbabwe, Scotland, Ireland and the UAE retained official one-day international status; the Netherlands and Nepal acquired ODI status; Papua New Guinea and Hong Kong lost it.

AFGHANISTAN CRICKET IN 2018

Spinning a story

SHAHID HASHMI

Afghanistan were given a brutal introduction to the realities of Test cricket when their inaugural match ended in a two-day mauling by India. But they were not discouraged, and far from dismayed. Continuing their heady progress in the world game, they became a real threat to the established order in the white-ball formats. As the former Australia all-rounder Tom Moody, now a leading coach, said: "I can't wait to see how many teams Afghanistan roll in the World Cup."

Moody's comments came after Afghanistan had performed magnificently at the Asia Cup, held in the UAE in September. As expected, India were the winners, beating Bangladesh in the final, but in many ways the maverick Afghans were the team of the tournament. They inflicted heavy defeats on Sri Lanka and Bangladesh, and qualified for the second phase. From there, they lost narrowly to Pakistan, and to Bangladesh by three runs when only seven were needed off the final over. They signed off with a tie against India. "We

AFGHANISTAN IN 2018

	Played	Won	Lost	Drawn/No result
Tests	1	–	1	–
One-day internationals	20	12	7	1
Twenty20 internationals	7	7	–	–

JANUARY		
FEBRUARY	5 ODIs and 2 T20Is (in the UAE) v Zimbabwe	(page 803)
MARCH	World Cup Qualifier (in Zimbabwe)	(page 790)
APRIL		
MAY		
JUNE	3 T20Is (in India) v Bangladesh	(page 805)
	1 Test (a) v India	(page 877)
JULY		
AUGUST	3 ODIs and T20Is (a) v Ireland	(page 907)
SEPTEMBER	Asia Cup (in the UAE)	(page 1110)
OCTOBER		
NOVEMBER		
DECEMBER		

For a review of Afghanistan domestic cricket from the 2017-18 season, see page 807.

Wakil Kohsar, AFP/Getty Images

Happy homecoming: Afghanistan captain Asghar Afghan shows off the World Cup qualifying trophy in Kabul, with Mohammad Nabi and Rashid Khan.

can hold our heads high and take pride from this," said captain Asghar Afghan, who had changed his name from Asghar Stanikzai for patriotic reasons.

But that competition was not the highlight of their year. That came in March, with an against-the-odds triumph in the World Cup qualifying tournament. They looked to be heading home, after losing to Scotland, hosts Zimbabwe and Hong Kong. But Nepal upset Hong Kong, and Afghanistan sneaked into the second phase on net run-rate. They made the most of the reprieve but, to qualify for the World Cup, they still needed the winless UAE to beat Zimbabwe: remarkably, they did. By now convinced of their invincibility, Afghanistan strolled past West Indies in the final.

The competition underlined their reliance on a high-quality spin attack. Rashid Khan and Mujeeb Zadran were joint-leading wicket-takers (alongside Scotland seamer Safyaan Sharif) with 17. Mohammad Nabi took 12. Rashid was also the top bowler at the Asia Cup, with ten. More impressively still, in 2018 he took more wickets than anyone in ODIs, 48 at 14 in 20 matches, putting him ahead of India's Kuldeep Yadav and England's Adil Rashid. Mujeeb was fourth, with 37 at 19, and Nabi only just outside the top ten. In February, Rashid Khan had risen to No. 1 in the ODI rankings, a considerable feather in his country's cap. Afghanistan will take a strong bowling line-up into the World Cup if frontline seamers Shapoor Zadran and Dawlat Zadran are fit. Their ODI batting leaned on Rahmat Shah, who scored 722 runs at 38, and Mohammad Shahzad (607 at 35).

In two away series outside the key tournaments, they had wins against Zimbabwe (4–1 in the UAE) and Ireland (2–1). There was little Twenty20 cricket, though they won each of their three series, including a 3–0 whitewash of Bangladesh in their adopted home at the Rajiv Gandhi Stadium at Dehradun, in the Indian state of Uttarakhand. It was a first bilateral series win over Bangladesh.

The three spinners were in demand by T20 franchises, and gained invaluable experience in India, Australia, the West Indies, Bangladesh and England. Rashid was joint-leading wicket-taker at the Big Bash, and joint-second at the IPL. He was also voted Man of the Tournament in Afghanistan's first professional domestic T20 competition, held in Sharjah in October. The tournament was given wider publicity when Hazratullah Zazai, an opener for Kabul Zwana, hit six sixes in an over against Balkh Legends.

With such a wealth of good-news stories, it was unfortunate that Afghanistan's Test debut was such an anticlimax. In two painful days, they were utterly overwhelmed. India needed 66.3 overs to bowl them out twice, for totals that barely crept into three figures. Hashmatullah Shahidi was the only batsman to show an appreciation of the format's demands, taking 88 balls over his second-innings 36. Coach Phil Simmons said the only way to improve was to play more red-ball matches. "I think there has to be a lot more A-team cricket against big countries by some players in England, India, Bangladesh, Australia," he said. "That's the best way for us to close this gap."

The administration have developed, with Aziz Ullah Fazale, one of the pioneers of the game in the country, taking over as president of the board.

AFGHANISTAN v ZIMBABWE IN THE UAE IN 2017-18

K. R. NAYAR

Twenty20 internationals (2): Afghanistan 2, Zimbabwe 0
One-day internationals (5): Afghanistan 4, Zimbabwe 1

Afghanistan inched up the rankings in both white-ball formats with comfortable series wins over Zimbabwe in Sharjah. The teams used the games as a warm-up for the following month's World Cup Qualifier, hosted by Zimbabwe, but that did not mean they were tepid affairs: Afghanistan are yet to tire of beating established nations. The matches, watched by an enthusiastic band of Afghan expats, were a triumph for their spinners. Rashid Khan was irrepressible, with 21 wickets at eight in the seven games. But Afghanistan were not a one-man band: in the series-clinching one-day win, 16-year-old off-spinner Mujeeb Zadran became the youngest to take an ODI five-for.

In two low-scoring T20 contests, Mohammad Nabi hit 85 runs at a strike-rate of 160; in the 50-over games, Rahmat Shah was a model of consistency, with 272 at an average of 68. The return of Mohammad Shahzad, a local favourite, after a ban for a doping offence aroused much interest. He shook off the ring-rust to be Afghanistan's second-highest run-scorer in the ODIs. It all added up to a highly satisfactory first assignment for new coach Phil Simmons.

For Zimbabwe, Brendan Taylor led the one-day averages with 207 at 41 and made a century in the second game, their solitary win. But they were bedevilled by batting collapses. In the first T20, they slipped from 52 for none to 85 for eight; in the first ODI, 50 without loss became 136 for eight; and in the last, eight fell for 23.

ZIMBABWE TOURING PARTY

*A. G. Cremer, R. P. Burl, T. L. Chatara, T. S. Chisoro, C. R. Ervine, K. M. Jarvis, H. Masakadza, S. F. Mire, P. J. Moor, B. Muzarabani, Sikandar Raza, B. R. M. Taylor, B. V. Vitori, M. N. Waller. *Coach:* H. H. Streak.

First Twenty20 international At Sharjah, February 5, 2018 (floodlit). **Afghanistan won by five wickets. Zimbabwe 120-9** (20 overs) (S. F. Mire 34; Rashid Khan 3-19); ‡**Afghanistan 121-5** (14.4 overs) (Mohammad Nabi 40*). *MoM:* Mohammad Nabi. *T20I debuts:* Mujeeb Zadran (Afghanistan); R. P. Burl, S. F. Mire, B. Muzarabani, (Zimbabwe). *Zimbabwe got off to a flyer, powered past 50 in the sixth over by Hamilton Masakadza and Solomon Mire. But in seven balls they slumped from 65-1 to 68-4. Having inflicted flesh wounds, Afghanistan delivered a lethal blow by bringing on Rashid Khan. He took 3-19, and it was only Malcolm Waller's 27* from 16 that gave Zimbabwe a chance. On his return after a doping ban, Mohammad Shahzad hit two sixes in his 20, but Afghanistan were making hard work of the chase until Mohammad Nabi steadied the ship with 40* off 27.*

Second Twenty20 international At Sharjah, February 6, 2018 (floodlit). **Afghanistan won by 17 runs. Afghanistan 158-9** (20 overs) (Mohammad Nabi 45; T. L. Chatara 3-20); ‡**Zimbabwe 141-5** (20 overs) (Sikandar Raza 40, R. P. Burl 30). *MoM:* Mohammad Nabi. *A second successive match-winning display by Nabi secured a 2–0 win, taking Afghanistan above Sri Lanka in the rankings. Nabi's 45 included four sixes, and there were useful twenties from Karim Sadiq, Asghar Stanikzai and Najibullah Zadran. Afghanistan looked set to pass 180, but lost five wickets in ten* *balls to Kyle Jarvis and Tendai Chatara. Mujeeb Zadran then removed Masakadza for 29 to check Zimbabwe's early momentum, before a fourth-wicket partnership of 53 between Sikandar Raza and Ryan Burl made things interesting. But Afghanistan had Rashid up their sleeve: he despatched both to settle the issue.*

First one-day international   At Sharjah, February 9, 2018 (day/night). **Afghanistan won by 154 runs.** ‡**Afghanistan 333-5** (50 overs) (Mohammad Shahzad 36, Ihsanullah Janat 54, Rahmat Shah 114, Nasir Ahmadzai 31, Najibullah Zadran 81*; A. G. Cremer 3-47); **Zimbabwe 179** (34.4 overs) (S. F. Mire 34, C. R. Ervine 33; Rashid Khan 4-26). *MoM:* Rahmat Shah. *Afghanistan carried over their T20 momentum to secure their biggest ODI win by runs. They owed much to a superbly paced century from Rahmat Shah. Openers Shahzad and Ihsanullah Janat had begun with 90, but Rahmat had to rebuild after three quick wickets for Graeme Cremer's leg-spin, and finished with his highest ODI score. Najibullah joined in the fun with 81* in 51 balls, including five sixes. It was Afghanistan's second-highest ODI total, behind 338 against Ireland at Greater Noida in March 2017. In response, Masakadza and Mire raced to 50 by the eighth over, but the introduction of Rashid proved decisive. He grabbed 4-26 in 5.4 overs as Zimbabwe folded.*

Second one-day international   At Sharjah, February 11, 2018 (day/night). **Zimbabwe won by 154 runs.** ‡**Zimbabwe 333-5** (50 overs) (H. Masakadza 48, B. R. M. Taylor 125, Sikandar Raza 92); **Afghanistan 179** (30.1 overs) (Rahmat Shah 43, Mohammad Nabi 31, Dawlat Zadran 47*; T. L. Chatara 3-24, A. G. Cremer 4-41). *MoM:* B. R. M. Taylor. *Brendan Taylor made his ninth ODI century, and his first since returning to the team in October as Zimbabwe levelled the series. He shared two key partnerships: 85 for the second wicket with Masakadza, and 135 for the fourth with Raza. Taylor hit five fours and eight sixes in his 125; only Rashid and Nabi escaped punishment. The outcome was settled by the 11th over of Afghanistan's response, when they slumped to 36-5, Chatara making three early incisions. Later, there were four victims for Cremer, although Dawlat Zadran's defiant big hitting delayed the inevitable. The scores replicated the first match – but the other way around – unique in an ODI series.*

Third one-day international   At Sharjah, February 13, 2018 (day/night). **Afghanistan won by six wickets.** ‡**Zimbabwe 154** (34.3 overs) (C. R. Ervine 39, Sikandar Raza 38; Mujeeb Zadran 3-45, Rashid Khan 5-24); **Afghanistan 158-4** (27.3 overs) (Rahmat Shah 56, Nasir Ahmadzai 51). *MoM:* Rashid Khan. *Teenage spin twins Mujeeb and Rashid re-established Afghanistan's series lead. Zimbabwe never got going: Mujeeb, opening the bowling, took two early wickets, and Rashid laid waste to the middle order. Craig Ervine and Raza hung around, but were subsumed by Rashid's third ODI five-for. Afghanistan made a hesitant start, before Rahmat and Nasir Ahmadzai went on the attack, both passing 50 as they cruised home.*

Fourth one-day international   At Sharjah, February 16, 2018 (day/night). **Afghanistan won by ten wickets.** ‡**Zimbabwe 134** (38 overs) (B. R. M. Taylor 30, C. R. Ervine 54*; Mujeeb Zadran 5-50); **Afghanistan 135-0** (21.1 overs) (Mohammad Shahzad 75*, Ihsanullah Janat 51*). *MoM:* Mujeeb Zadran. *Thanks largely to a stunning performance by Mujeeb, Afghanistan clinched the one-day series – their fourth in five against Zimbabwe – and moved above their opponents to tenth in the rankings. Taking the new ball again, he removed openers Mire and Masakadza. Taylor counter-attacked – launching Mujeeb for two sixes in an over – and Craig Ervine made a dogged half-century, but Zimbabwe never recovered. At 16 years 325 days, Mujeeb grabbed the record for the youngest ODI five-for from Waqar Younis, who was 18 years 164 days when he took 6-26 for Pakistan against Sri Lanka, also in Sharjah, in April 1990. Shahzad and Ihsanullah were in no mood to hang around, reaching the target in a blizzard of boundaries. It was Afghanistan's first ten-wicket win.*

Fifth one-day international   At Sharjah, February 19, 2018 (day/night). **Afghanistan won by 146 runs.** ‡**Afghanistan 241-9** (50 overs) (Javed Ahmadi 76, Rahmat Shah 59; Rashid Khan 3-13); **Zimbabwe 95** (32.1 overs) (C. R. Ervine 34; Rashid Khan 3-13). *MoM:* Sharafuddin Ashraf. *MoS:* Rashid Khan. *Zimbabwe were blown away by an increasingly confident Afghanistan. This time, Rashid showed his worth with the bat, hitting 45 off 29 balls after they seemed to have frittered away a decent start, built on a partnership of 129 for the second wicket between Javed Ahmadi and Rahmat. In reply, Zimbabwe calmly reached 72-2, only to lose eight for 23. Rashid took three wickets in six balls in Afghanistan's second-largest ODI win by runs, ten days after the biggest. Sharafuddin Ashraf won the match award for a quick 21 and the big wickets of Taylor and Raza.*

AFGHANISTAN v BANGLADESH IN INDIA IN 2018

Sidharth Monga

Twenty20 internationals (3): Afghanistan 3, Bangladesh 0

Dehradun in Uttarakhand had never hosted any recognised matches before Afghanistan adopted the new Rajiv Gandhi International Cricket Stadium as their home for a three-match Twenty20 series in which they whitewashed Bangladesh. Close to 20,000 people cheered them on as they won the first game; the reaction was no less enthusiastic four days later for what turned out to be a thrilling finish to a dead rubber. Afghanistan's performance was all the more remarkable as the entire team were observing Ramadan in the unforgiving Indian summer – compared with only three of the Bangladeshis.

Both sides have been known for passionate cricket, and their coaches have often emphasised the need to calm their players down. But over three matches, Afghanistan showed how much they had matured since the teams' only previous encounter in this format, at the 2014 World Twenty20, when Bangladesh crushed them: they were calmer than their opponents and more deliberate, sussing out the conditions, clinically targeting weaker bowlers and tying up Bangladesh with a three-pronged spin attack.

Predictably, the pitch at a new ground in a hastily arranged series was slow and two-paced, making it near impossible to hit out against good spinners. Afghanistan were easily ahead in that department: Rashid Khan, Mujeeb Zadran and Mohammad Nabi took 14 wickets between them, with an economy rate of 4.82, whereas Bangladesh's five spinners managed eight wickets at 6.15. Rashid, who flew in the day before the opening match, following a charity Twenty20 international at Lord's, was Afghanistan's talisman, controlling the middle overs and bowling at the death. Eight for 49 in 11 overs earned him two match awards plus Man of the Series. Mujeeb did his bit, bowling nine powerplay overs, the maximum possible in three games, and in all conceded just five an over.

Meanwhile Afghanistan's batsmen, though still needing to learn to rotate the strike, defied their image, showing awareness of how to build a limited-overs innings, especially on low-scoring surfaces. It was just a pity the series was no sort of preparation for their maiden Test the following week, against India at Bangalore.

BANGLADESH TOURING PARTY

*Shakib Al Hasan, Abu Haider, Abu Jayed, Abul Hasan, Ariful Haque, Liton Das, Mahmudullah, Mehedi Hasan, Mosaddek Hossain, Mushfiqur Rahim, Nazmul Islam, Rubel Hossain, Sabbir Rahman, Soumya Sarkar, Tamim Iqbal. *Coach:* C. A. Walsh.

Mustafizur Rahman was originally selected, but injured his foot in the IPL and was replaced by Abul Hasan.

First Twenty20 international At Dehradun, June 3, 2018 (floodlit). **Afghanistan won by 45 runs. Afghanistan 167-8** (20 overs) (Mohammad Shahzad 40, Samiullah Shenwari 36); ‡**Bangladesh 122** (19 overs) (Liton Das 30; Shapoor Zadran 3-40, Rashid Khan 3-13). *MoM:* Rashid Khan.

Bangladesh's choice to bat second on a two-paced pitch against an effective spin attack could truly be explained by fear of dew, or by a lack of awareness of the opposition's strengths. Afghanistan would have been slight favourites even with 140 on the board, but Bangladesh were rattled, and ended up conceding 167. Mohammad Shahzad, usually a dasher, batted sensibly, his strike-rate hovering around a run a ball; by the time he fell, Afghanistan were 86-2 from 12 overs and ready for the final push. Bangladesh underbowled their part-time spinners, and their seamers were taken apart by Samiullah Shenwari and Shafiqullah Shinwari, who scored 60 off 26 between them. The chase was stillborn, with Tamim Iqbal trapped first ball by Mujeeb Zadran. Rashid did not come on until the 11th over, but then capitalised on the pressure created by Mujeeb and Mohammad Nabi, striking with his first two deliveries, before left-arm seamer Shapoor Zadran collected three in an over.

Second Twenty20 international   At Dehradun, June 5, 2018 (floodlit). **Afghanistan won by six wickets.** ‡**Bangladesh 134-8** (20 overs) (Tamim Iqbal 43; Rashid Khan 4-12); **Afghanistan 135-4** (18.5 overs) (Samiullah Shenwari 49, Mohammad Nabi 31*). *MoM:* Rashid Khan. *Bangladesh changed their strategy and batted first, but could not build a big enough total. In the recent IPL, Rashid's economy-rate against left-handers had been twice as many as against right-handers, so Bangladesh stacked their later order with left-hand batsmen. But it meant they felt obliged to hit out against him: three came unstuck trying to hit Rashid for six. They started the 16th over on 101-4, but Shakib Al Hasan and Tamim Iqbal fell swinging, while Mosaddek Hossain had no clue against a first-ball wrong'un; Rashid added a fourth wicket in his next over. Bangladesh had been courageous with the ball, opening with two slow bowlers and reverting to spin from the 12th over to the 18th, when the asking-rate crept up to ten. But Afghanistan did not panic and, when Bangladesh turned to the pace of Rubel Hossain, Nabi knocked off the 20 required in five balls.*

Third Twenty20 international   At Dehradun, June 7, 2018 (floodlit). **Afghanistan won by one run.** ‡**Afghanistan 145-6** (20 overs) (Samiullah Shenwari 33*); **Bangladesh 144-6** (20 overs) (Mushfiqur Rahim 46, Mahmudullah 45). *MoM:* Mushfiqur Rahim. *MoS:* Rashid Khan. *The closest match was clinched by an astonishing piece of fielding off the final delivery. Bangladesh needed four to win, and the ball seemed to be sailing over long-on – until a leaping Shafiqullah knocked it back, realised it was about to bounce over the boundary and slapped it in again a millisecond before stepping over the rope. A powerful throw from Nabi to Shahzad helped run out Mahmudullah as he went for a third, which would have forced a super over. Afghanistan had opted to bat, but could not force the pace, and Bangladesh were chasing only 146 in now-familiar conditions. Joining forces at 53-4, Mushfiqur Rahim and Mahmudullah kept their hopes alive, and wanted 30 from the last 12 balls. Asghar Stanikzai turned to the medium-pace of his younger brother, Karim Janat, a disastrous move: Mushfiqur took him apart, with five fours and a single, cheered on by his partner. The same pair had come within a couple of runs of beating India in the World Twenty20 two years before – but once again they failed. With nine required off the final over, from Rashid, Mushfiqur holed out first ball. Five runs came off edges, bringing the game to that heady finish as Shafiqullah – literally – rose to the occasion.*

DOMESTIC CRICKET IN AFGHANISTAN IN 2017-18

A few months after Afghanistan and Ireland became the ICC's 11th and 12th Full Members, in June 2017, the Afghans staged their inaugural first-class domestic competition. The Ahmad Shah Abdali Tournament, named after the 18th-century king regarded as the founder of modern Afghanistan, had been running for several years, but was awarded first-class status in the build-up to the national team becoming a Test nation.

Five regional sides – Amo, Band-e-Amir, Boost, Mis Ainak and Speen Ghar – played 20 four-day games between them, across three venues, leading to a five-day final between the top two in December. A couple of months later, they did it all again: this time there were six teams (with Kabul joining the other five) and 30 games before the final. Afghanistan's international cricketers were largely absent, playing Intercontinental Cup games and a one-day series with Ireland during the first competition, and winning the World Cup Qualifier in Zimbabwe during the second.

Both first-class titles went to **Band-e-Amir**, who had already won the Shpageeza T20 tournament in September. In the first final, they spent more than two days accumulating a total of 747 for nine against table leaders **Speen Ghar**, who were missing their star batsman – teenager Bahir Shah – and responded with a feeble 196; Band-e-Amir chose to bat again, and eventually won by 537 runs. Five months later, in the second final, they could not force a result against **Amo**, but took the trophy on the basis of a 127-run first-innings lead.

Band-e-Amir's monopoly did not extend to the 50-over Ghazi Amanullah Khan Tournaments (named after another king, from the 20th century). Staged in August 2017 and July 2018, both produced the same finalists, with **Speen Ghar** winning a low-scoring game in the first competition, and **Boost** having the better of a run-fest in the second.

Shah set an extraordinary clutch of records in his first few weeks of first-class cricket. He announced himself in the opening round, with an unbeaten 256 for Speen Ghar against Amo – at that time the second-highest score on debut, after 260 by Amol Muzumdar of Bombay in 1993-94 – and shared a fourth-wicket stand of 291 with Shawkat Zaman, the highest partnership between two first-class debutants. After a quiet second match, he made twin hundreds against Boost in the third, and followed up with 303 not out, also against Boost, in his next innings; at 18 years 261 days, he was the second-youngest to score a triple-century, after Javed Miandad (who did it for Karachi Whites in 1974-75 aged 17 years 311 days), and the first to reach double-hundreds twice in his first four matches.

It took him to 831 runs in his first six innings, beating Bill Ponsford's record of 741 – though Ponsford did it in four games spread across two years, rather than Bahir's three weeks. After a couple of half-centuries in his next two matches, he reached 1,000 first-class runs in his 11th innings, on the way to a fifth hundred; only Ponsford, with eight innings, had taken fewer. Bahir then set off for the Under-19 World Cup in New Zealand, missing Speen Ghar's last group game and the final, both of which they lost to Band-e-Amir. Once he was back, he could not regain his momentum, scraping together 100 runs in his next seven innings, though he returned to better form with two more fifties and his sixth century by the end of the season.

There were five more debutant centurions, including Haji Murad, who made 102 and 142 for Amo in the same match as Bahir's 256. Another Speen Ghar batsman, Zahidullah, also scored twin hundreds in April, and there were nine double-centuries in all, two from Amo's Darwish Rasooli. Shafiqullah Shinwari hit the fastest double in first-class cricket – 89 balls and 103 minutes, both records – for Kabul against Boost; it included 22 sixes, one short of Colin Munro's world record, which gave him 24 in all, the record for a match. Fourteen batsmen passed 1,000 first-class runs, and Zia-ul-Haq, the captain of Band-e-Amir, was the leading scorer with 1,616. Bowling returns were less startling, the best being eight for 76 (and 14 for 119 in the match) by Abdul Baqi for Boost against Amo. Slow left-armer Zia-ur-Rehman was the leading wicket-taker with 101; he was also one of three Mis Ainak batsmen given out obstructing the field – all in different games.

FIRST-CLASS AVERAGES IN 2017-18

BATTING (700 runs)

		M	I	NO	R	HS	100	Avge	Ct/St
1	Darwish Rasooli (*Amo*)	8	14	1	1,073	249	3	82.53	7
2	Bahir Shah (*Speen Ghar*)	14	25	4	1,504	303*	6	71.61	14/1
3	Zia-ul-Haq (*Band-e-Amir*)	17	31	4	1,616	148	8	59.85	10
4	†Shahidullah (*Mis Ainak*)	12	19	1	1,032	175	3	57.33	9
5	Rahmatullah Sahaq (*Mis Ainak*)	15	24	3	1,152	176*	4	54.85	12
6	†Hashmatullah Shahidi (*Band-e-Amir*)	8	15	1	749	163	3	53.50	8
7	Munir Ahmad (*Boost*)	18	32	2	1,496	210	5	49.86	40/5
8	Karim Janat (*Band-e-Amir/Kabul*)	16	29	3	1,237	211*	3	47.57	10
9	Najeeb Tarakai (*Amo/Speen Ghar*)	13	24	0	1,125	153	2	46.87	14
10	Karim Sadiq (*Boost*)	14	26	0	1,202	163	3	46.23	15
11	Imran Mir (*Mis Ainak*)	13	22	1	966	170	3	46.00	11
12	Haji Murad (*Amo*)	18	30	1	1,266	142	2	43.65	35/11
13	Fazal Niazai (*Mis Ainak*)	15	23	6	739	101*	1	43.47	2
14	Usman Ghani (*Band-e-Amir*)	15	28	0	1,165	117	1	41.60	18/1
15	Nasir Khan (*Boost/Speen Ghar*)	18	32	3	1,148	166	2	39.58	17
16	†Hazratullah Zazai (*Band-e-Amir*)	17	33	1	1,246	133	3	38.93	22
17	Younas Ahmadzai (*Band-e-Amir*)	13	23	1	852	210*	1	38.72	13
18	†Bahar Shinwari (*Boost/Kabul*)	11	21	0	793	108	1	37.76	3
19	Imran Janat (*Band-e-Amir/Kabul*)	15	27	0	1,019	200	2	37.74	11
20	Fazal Zazai (*Amo/Mis Ainak*)	16	27	0	988	155	4	36.59	14/1
21	Waheedullah Shafaq (*Speen Gh*)	15	24	2	803	87	0	36.50	14
22	Shawkat Zaman (*Kabul/Speen Ghar*)	17	29	0	929	169	3	32.03	10
23	Khaibar Omar (*Boost/Kabul*)	15	27	1	815	110	1	31.34	8
24	Mohammad Sardar (*Band-e-Amir*)	17	30	3	736	94	0	27.25	40/5

BOWLING (25 wickets)

		Style	O	M	R	W	BB	5I	Avge
1	Sharafuddin Ashraf (*Amo*)	SLA	166.3	51	407	30	7-38	2	13.56
2	Zia-ur-Rehman (*Mis Ainak*)	SLA	785.3	238	1,995	101	7-70	8	19.75
3	Rokhan Barakzai (*B-e-A/Boost*)	SLA	265.5	83	692	35	6-49	1	19.77
4	Hamza Hotak (*Band-e-Amir*)	SLA	514.2	126	1,404	67	6-33	5	20.95
5	Waqar Khan (*Band-e-Amir*)	LM	302.2	59	996	47	7-53	5	21.19
6	Zamir Khan (*Speen Ghar*)	SLA	203	46	585	27	5-46	2	21.66
7	Tariq Stanikzai (*Speen Ghar*)	SLA	199.5	51	605	27	6-22	2	22.40
8	Abdul Wasi (*Amo*)	LB	338	57	1,235	54	6-91	3	22.87
9	Qais Ahmad (*Speen Ghar*)	LB	288	48	1,038	41	6-74	2	25.31
10	Jamshid Khan (*Amo*)	SLW	469.1	105	1,551	61	6-69	4	25.42
11	Sayed Shirzad (*Boost*)	LM	282.1	43	1,177	44	6-45	4	26.75
12	Mohammad Alam (*Boost*)	SLA	337.4	74	1,019	38	7-76	3	26.81
13	Zahir Shehzad (*Speen Ghar*)	SLA	1,643	59	2,144	77	6-106	5	27.84
14	Inamullah Khan (*B-e-A/Kabul*)	SLA	469.1	113	1,534	54	6-89	3	28.40
15	Nawaz Khan (*Mis Ainak*)	RFM	340	50	1,341	42	5-57	1	31.92
16	Fazal Niazai (*Mis Ainak*)	RM	314.5	44	1,231	37	5-44	1	33.27
17	Fitratullah Khawari (*B-e-A/Sp Gh*)	LB	396.2	65	1,603	48	5-57	4	33.39
18	Nijat Masood (*Band-e-Amir*)	RM	266.3	28	1,267	37	6-55	2	34.24
19	Abdul Baqi (*Boost*)	LB	486.1	53	2,069	60	8-76	4	34.48
20	Fareed Ahmad (*Speen Ghar*)	LFM	234.4	25	935	26	4-47	0	35.96
21	Karim Janat (*Band-e-Amir/Kabul*)	RM	476.4	90	1,837	51	4-50	0	36.01
22	Karim Sadiq (*Boost*)	OB	314.4	44	1,233	32	6-96	1	38.53
23	Abdullah Mazari (*Amo/Kabul*)	SLA	599.1	136	2,166	54	5-116	3	40.11
24	Muslim Musa (*B-e-A/Speen Ghar*)	RM	388	66	1,442	31	5-104	1	46.51

AHMAD SHAH ABDALI FOUR-DAY TOURNAMENT IN 2017-18

	P	W	L	D	1st-inns pts	Pts
Speen Ghar	8	4	2	2	30	100
Band-e-Amir	8	3	2	3	36	99
Mis Ainak	8	2	1	5	24	87
Amo.	8	2	2	4	6	62
Boost	8	1	5	2	24	52

Outright win = 14pts; draw = 7pts; first-innings lead = 6pts.

Final At Ghazi Amanullah Khan Town, December 19–23, 2017. **Band-e-Amir won by 537 runs.** ‡**Band-e-Amir 747-9 dec** (Hashmatullah Shahidi 163, Younas Ahmadzai 210*) **and 265-4 dec** (Zia-ul-Haq 101*); **Speen Ghar 196** (Waqar Salamkheil 6-56) **and 279** (Inamullah Khan 6-89). *Band-e-Amir won Afghanistan's inaugural first-class tournament after amassing the country's first total of 700-plus. Younas Ahmadzai converted his maiden century into a double, before 16-year-old Waqar Salamkheil demolished Speen Ghar's line-up (minus the record-breaking Bahir Shah). Despite a lead of 551, Zia-ul-Haq waived the follow-on, and scored his own century before setting a target of 817. Slow left-armer Inamullah Khan collected six wickets, as he and Salamkheil needed only 12 deliveries to mop up Speen Ghar's last three on the fifth morning.*

ALOKOZAY AHMAD SHAH ABDALI
FOUR-DAY TOURNAMENT IN 2017-18

	P	W	L	D	1st-inns pts	Pts
Amo.	10	6	2	2	36	134
Band-e-Amir	10	4	2	4	48	132
Mis Ainak	10	4	2	4	39	123
Speen Ghar	10	4	3	3	18	95
Boost	10	1	6	3	27	62
Kabul	10	1	5	4	12	54

Outright win = 14pts; draw = 7pts; first-innings lead = 6pts; no decision on first innings = 3pts.

Final At Kandahar, May 8–12, 2018. **Drawn. Band-e-Amir won by virtue of their first-innings lead.** ‡**Amo 280** (Farmanullah Safi 5-60) **and 420-8 dec** (Fazal Zazai 155; Fitratullah Khawari 5-79); **Band-e-Amir 407** (Asif Musazai 134, Zia-ul-Haq 122) **and 180-5.** *Band-e-Amir won their third trophy of the season. Seventeen-year-old seamer Farmanullah Safi reduced Amo to 30-4 inside the first hour and, though the middle order fought back, a 227-run stand between Asif Musazai and Zia-ul-Haq helped Band-e-Amir build a substantial lead. Fazal Zazai led a far stronger second-innings effort from Amo, despite five wickets from leg-spinner Fitratullah Khawari, but they could not bowl out Band-e-Amir on the final day to snatch the title.*

GHAZI AMANULLAH KHAN REGIONAL TOURNAMENT IN 2017

50-over league plus knockout

	P	W	L	Pts	NRR
Band-e-Amir	4	4	0	8	0.59
Speen Ghar.	4	2	2	4	0.82
Amo	4	2	2	4	0.15
Boost	4	2	2	4	0.09
Mis Ainak	4	0	4	0	−1.74

Semi-finals Boost beat Band-e-Amir by six runs; Speen Ghar beat Amo by 61 runs.

Final   At Ghazi Amanullah Khan Town, August 19, 2017. **Speen Ghar won by five wickets. Boost 147** (43.2 overs) (Karim Janat 5-42); ‡**Speen Ghar 150-5** (23.1 overs). *In a low-scoring game, seamer Karim Janat ran through Boost's line-up, before Gulbadeen Naib retaliated by reducing Speen Ghar to 29-4, which soon became 63-5. But Darwish Rasooli (68* from 54 balls) steered Speen Ghar to victory with nearly 27 overs in hand, sharing a stand of 87* in 64 deliveries with Shafiqullah Shinwari (32*).*

GHAZI AMANULLAH KHAN REGIONAL TOURNAMENT IN 2018

50-over league plus final

	P	W	L	Pts	NRR
Speen Ghar	5	5	0	10	0.62
Boost	5	3	2	6	0.98
Band-e-Amir	5	3	2	6	0.94
Amo	5	2	3	4	−0.90
Mis Ainak	5	1	4	2	−0.66
Kabul	5	1	4	2	−0.94

Final   At Kabul, July 27, 2018. **Boost won by five wickets. Speen Ghar 320-8** (50 overs); ‡**Boost 325-5** (48.3 overs) (Munir Ahmad 108*). *Speen Ghar suffered their first defeat of the tournament after being asked to bat and running up 320, with Azmatullah Omarzai (66 in 45 balls) and Fareed Ahmad (41* in 30) adding 78 in 44 for the eighth wicket. Boost were undaunted, and Munir Ahmad, who hit 108* in 91, shared an even bigger partnership, 167 for the fifth wicket, with the captain, Najibullah Zadran (73); Najibullah fell with 14 required from four overs, and Munir completed victory with his third six.*

The Shpageeza T20 Tournament has its own section (page 1147).

AUSTRALIAN CRICKET IN 2018

Ashes to asses

DANIEL BRETTIG

Winning the Ashes at home, as Australia did in comprehensive fashion as 2018 began, has always been seen as the baseline for the national team and the system around it. So there was triumphalism – and relief – at the SCG when Steve Smith lifted the urn, against a garish backdrop of four raised Australian fingers and a closed English fist, to illustrate the 4–0 win. For Smith and his team, it looked as if the hard part was over, and the rest of the year would be relatively smooth sailing. How wrong that assumption was to prove.

Within three months, Smith, his vice-captain David Warner and opening batsman Cameron Bancroft had been slapped with long bans for their roles in

AUSTRALIA IN 2018

	Played	Won	Lost	Drawn/No result
Tests	10	3	6	1
One-day internationals	13	2	11	–
Twenty20 internationals	19	10	8	1

NOVEMBER		
DECEMBER	5 Tests and 5 ODIs (h) v England	(see *Wisden 2018*, page 349)
JANUARY		
FEBRUARY	Trans-Tasman T20 tri-series (h/a) v England and New Zealand	(page 260)
MARCH	4 Tests (a) v South Africa	(page 985)
APRIL		
MAY		
JUNE	5 ODIs and 1 T20I (a) v England	(page 307)
JULY	T20 tri-series (in Zimbabwe) v Zimbabwe and Pakistan	(page 1071)
AUGUST		
SEPTEMBER		
OCTOBER	2 Tests and 3 T20Is (in the UAE) v Pakistan	(page 933)
	1 T20I (a) v United Arab Emirates	(page 1108)
NOVEMBER	3 ODIs and 1 T20I (h) v South Africa	(page 815)
DECEMBER	4 Tests, 3 ODIs and 3 T20Is (h) v India	(page 820)
JANUARY		

For a review of Australian domestic cricket from the 2017-18 season, see page 841.

the Cape Town ball-tampering scandal. At home, the wider game writhed in the realisation that years of resentment – harboured within Australia and overseas – were now being unleashed upon the team and the governing body. For too long, Australian cricket had resolved to win by any means necessary, a statement as true of the decision to use sandpaper on the ball to try to gain reverse swing as it was of the abrasive behaviour favoured by several of Cricket Australia's senior executives and, for three years, their chairman David Peever. Smith, for example, revealed that one Test defeat in 2016 had resulted in James Sutherland, CA's chief executive, telling the players: "We don't pay you to play, we pay you to win." The backlash, when it finally came, was devastating.

It should not be forgotten that the behavioural problems in South Africa – which began with an ill-tempered Test in Durban, festered in Port Elizabeth, then exploded in Cape Town – had a cricketing origin. Parallel to the tale of the breakdown of the Australian team's leadership was the increasing supremacy of the South Africans, personified by A. B. de Villiers with the bat, and Kagiso Rabada, the ball. The riches of runs and wickets Australia had enjoyed in the Ashes were replaced by far more modest returns: Smith and Warner delivered the performances of fraying minds and fatigued bodies and, without their lead, the rest were unable to find a slipstream.

So when CA deemed Smith and Warner worthy of one-year bans – Bancroft was handed nine months – they sutured one wound, only to open up another. And the independent reviews of the team and governing body, commissioned when the baying for blood was loudest, also created trouble down the line.

At first, though, the major concern of Sutherland and the board was to get closure, to enable critical broadcast-rights negotiations to continue. Things calmed down just enough for him to announce a deal with News Corporation and Seven West Media, worth $A1.18bn – around double the previous contract – although the downside was that men's one-day and Twenty20 internationals would go behind a paywall for the first time. One hurdle had been successfully negotiated, but there were many more struggles to come.

In the wake of Darren Lehmann's tearful resignation as coach, his successor was unveiled as Justin Langer, the 100-Test opener who had become a disciplined and thoughtful coach. Fresh from Western Australia and the Perth Scorchers, he brought plenty of clear ideas to the job, but they were to be gradually eroded by the realities of managing a team without their two best batsmen, and without their best pacemen for much of the year, through injury. A one-day drubbing by England in June – the oldest enemy's first 5–0 whitewash over Australia in any format – gave Langer a sense of what he was in for. Ditto the new captain, wicketkeeper Tim Paine, whose eloquence and life experience could not make up for the hard currency of Smith's and Warner's runs.

That tour was the first to take place after Sutherland announced his intention to step down after 17 years, following long-running discussions with Peever that still left CA without a clear replacement. The chief operating officer Kevin Roberts, who had stepped off the board to join Sutherland's executive team late in 2015, was widely expected to be appointed – and duly was, leaving

Crisis management: James Sutherland announces his resignation in June; David Peever hoped to stay on, but in October he too stepped down.

plenty wondering just how closed the CA shop had become. One of the discontents was the former industrialist Bob Every, who resigned from the board in protest when Peever announced his intention to carry on as chairman for another three years under the pretence of continuity.

Langer's team, meanwhile, performed slightly better in a T20 tri-series in Zimbabwe, before preparing for the tricky tasks of Test series against Pakistan away and India at home. In the UAE, they were given a major injection of belief by Usman Khawaja's epic salvage operation in the First Test in Dubai, only to have it dissipate when Khawaja injured his knee in Abu Dhabi. Australia surrendered a strong first-day position there, and were soundly defeated as Pakistan took the series. That disappointment was a prelude to further ructions back home, as the independent reviews of Simon Longstaff (on the board) and Rick McCosker (on the national team) were merged into one highly damaging document.

At first Peever thought he might be able to tough out its release, which was delayed until a few days after he was formally re-elected to the board at an AGM that also served as Sutherland's final day at the Jolimont office. The state associations were miffed by the scheduling, more so when they were finally given a preview of the report's content a matter of minutes after the AGM concluded.

Anger came to the boil when Peever spoke woodenly and without apparent recognition of the gravity of the situation when the reviews were publicly released. Within days, the Cricket New South Wales chairman John Knox had withdrawn his support, forcing Peever's resignation. Long-term director Mark Taylor soon stepped down, too, and the new CEO Roberts made his presence felt by jettisoning Pat Howard, the high performance manager, and the commercial chief Ben Amarfio on the same day as CA's annual staff forum at the MCG.

Soon afterwards, the home international season began, with a white-ball series against South Africa and a full visit from India. The Australians were comfortably second-best in each contest, and questions were raised about a jumbled schedule which forced some players to switch formats as many as six times before the first Test of the summer, against Virat Kohli's tourists at Adelaide in December. Thanks mainly to Cheteshwar Pujara, India gained a foothold after losing early wickets to the seamers, and held on to it all the way to a narrow victory, despite the best efforts of the Australian tail. That result gained resonance when Paine enjoyed the first Test win of his captaincy on a flying Perth Stadium pitch, which rewarded the spin of Nathan Lyon most of all, despite the seamers' evident enjoyment.

The Australians thus reached Boxing Day all square, but found themselves struggling with the mental toll of a long series against more seasoned opponents. They were also hoping for a drop-in pitch more like Perth's high-tech and bouncy number than the sluggish one served up by Melbourne. This was a surface that rewarded methodical, consistent batting and bowling, a task seemingly beyond an Australian line-up that could not conjure a century in any of the four Tests. India's vast victory secured the Border–Gavaskar Trophy, and a mighty first innings at the SCG – led by Pujara's third century of the series – sealed things before rain ruined the last couple of days. It was Australia's first home defeat by an Asian side.

Just as Smith, Warner and the Australian team had placed a spotlight on CA's culture by their transgressions, so they did on the country's cricket system by their absence. And even as the time ticked down to the end of their bans – Langer and Paine had long since dispensed with any illusions about cultural hand-wringing over their return – news of Smith suffering an elbow injury in the Bangladesh Premier League provided a reminder of how tenuous things truly were. So much for an easier road beyond winning the Ashes.

AUSTRALIA v SOUTH AFRICA IN 2018-19

BEN HORNE

One-day internationals (3): Australia 1, South Africa 2
Twenty20 international (1): Australia 0, South Africa 1

Faf du Plessis must wonder how many times he can stand at the other end while Australian cricket self-destructs. On South Africa's previous visit, in late 2016, Australia's national selector Rod Marsh and half a dozen players were axed after the Test side were steamrollered in Hobart. That defeat, and the ensuing panic, led to the relaunch of their attack-dog approach. Chief executive James Sutherland and high-performance manager Pat Howard had marched into the dressing-room and stripped paint off the walls, pugnacious wicket-keeper Matthew Wade was recalled to bring back the mongrel and, in time, David Warner was encouraged to leave behind his new "Reverend" persona and relocate the "Bull".

The chickens had come home to roost in March 2018, when Warner, Steve Smith and Cameron Bancroft conspired to use sandpaper to alter the condition of the ball in the Third Test at Cape Town. Forget the 2016 crisis: *this* was a crisis. With Australia already flat out on the canvas, it was going to be difficult for du Plessis to inflict another knockout when he arrived for four limited-overs matches in November. But what he did prove by winning the 50-over games 2–1, as well as the lone Twenty20 match – reduced to ten overs by rain – was just how long the Australians' road to redemption might be.

There were other humiliations en route. Before the opening match, in Perth, Shaun Marsh – fighting for his international future – was ruled out because of an abscess on his backside. Cricket Australia's marketing department were also embarrassed when photos appeared on social media revealing the catchphrases plastered on the dressing-room wall. One of them, "elite honesty", created an internet storm and became yet another way to parody an organisation that, in the wake of their crushing independent cultural review, had done a pretty good job of it themselves.

Elite honesty was not supposed to be a marketing ploy, but a team catch-cry penned by the new coach, Justin Langer; it was never meant to be broadcast to the wider world. Most teams' buzzwords sound naff, but normally stay behind closed doors. Langer couldn't win. But what this episode did reinforce to CA – aside from their lack of self-awareness – was just how unpopular they had become with their public. The Australian game's recovery would have to be an organic process on the field, not an accelerated marketing push off it.

Once the cricket started, things didn't get much better. Batting first at Perth under a new one-day captain, Aaron Finch – Tim Paine had been jettisoned after the whitewash in England, along with his deputy, Mitchell Marsh – Australia didn't last 40 overs, let alone 50. In the second match, at Adelaide, they recovered some respect after their bowlers defended a mediocre total to end a seven-match losing streak. Ultimately South Africa were too good, but

Australia were far from disgraced in the decider at Hobart, clinched by du Plessis's spectacular hundred.

Both sides had an eye on the 2019 World Cup. On this evidence, Australia's chances of defending their crown appeared bleak, given the systematic failures of an unbalanced top order. The return of the banned Smith and Warner couldn't come quickly enough. South Africa also looked fragile: with A. B. de Villiers retired, they were too reliant for runs on du Plessis and David Miller.

SOUTH AFRICAN TOURING PARTY

*F. du Plessis, F. Behardien, Q. de Kock, B. E. Hendricks, Imran Tahir, H. Klaasen, A. K. Markram, D. A. Miller, C. H. Morris, L. T. Ngidi, A. L. Phehlukwayo, D. Pretorius, K. Rabada, T. Shamsi, D. W. Steyn. *Coach:* O. D. Gibson.

At Canberra, October 31, 2018 (day/night). **Prime Minister's XI won by four wickets. ‡South Africans 173** (42 overs) (A. K. Markram 47, D. A. Miller 45; J. P. Behrendorff 3-35, Usman Qadir 3-28); **Prime Minister's XI 174-6** (36.3 overs) (J. R. Philippe 57, G. J. Bailey 51*, J. J. Sangha 38). *MoM:* J. R. Philippe. *The first XI chosen in the name of Australia's new prime minister, Scott Morrison, took control in the first over, when Jason Behrendorff struck twice, and never let go. There were three wickets for Usman Qadir, the 25-year-old son of the great Pakistan leg-spinner Abdul Qadir; Usman now lives in Perth, and has played for Western Australia. Another WA player, 21-year-old Josh Philippe, made an attractive 53, and the experienced George Bailey took his side home with 51*.*

AUSTRALIA v SOUTH AFRICA

First One-Day International

At Perth Stadium, November 4, 2018. South Africa won by six wickets. Toss: South Africa.

When Dale Steyn broke down with a shoulder injury in Perth in November 2016, some feared he would never bowl in international cricket again. But two years later he made a triumphant return to the city, piloting South Africa to a rampant victory after du Plessis had unleashed his fast bowlers on the vulnerable Australians at the new Optus Stadium. Steyn removed Head and Short in the third over, and the Australians were all out after 38, Coulter-Nile top-scoring with 34 from No. 9. South Africa had also been struggling in limited-overs cricket, and arrived in Australia without Hashim Amla or J-P. Duminy, both injured. But they appeared on a different level from their opponents. Finch typified their crisis of confidence post-Sandpapergate when, despite being his side's best batsman, he declined the chance to review a contentious lbw. Technology showed the delivery from Ngidi was clearing the stumps, but Australia were eight for three in the sixth over. After ten, in which they failed to hit a boundary, they had just 19 runs – their lowest powerplay score at home. Their bowlers never got a look-in: de Kock and Hendricks set up a comfortable chase for South Africa with an opening stand of 94, and three wickets for Stoinis only massaged the margin of defeat. It was Australia's seventh in a row, beating a national record established in 1996.

Man of the Match: D. W. Steyn.   *Attendance:* 23,342.

Australia

T. M. Head c de Kock b Steyn	1		M. A. Starc lbw b Imran Tahir	12	
*A. J. Finch lbw b Ngidi	5		J. R. Hazlewood not out	6	
D. J. M. Short c du Plessis b Steyn	0				
C. A. Lynn c de Kock b Phehlukwayo	15		B 2, lb 4, w 3	9	
†A. T. Carey c de Kock b Imran Tahir	33			—	
G. J. Maxwell c Klaasen b Phehlukwayo	11		1/4 (1) 2/4 (3) 3/8 (2) (38.1 overs)	152	
M. P. Stoinis c Klaasen b Phehlukwayo	14		4/36 (4) 5/48 (6) 6/66 (7)		
P. J. Cummins run out (Miller)	12		7/89 (8) 8/107 (5) 9/140 (10)		
N. M. Coulter-Nile c Klaasen b Ngidi	34		10/152 (9)	10 overs: 19-3	

Steyn 7–1–18–2; Ngidi 8.1–3–26–2; Rabada 8–0–30–0; Phehlukwayo 6–0–33–3; Imran Tahir 9–0–39–2.

South Africa

†Q. de Kock c Hazlewood b Coulter-Nile...	47		D. A. Miller not out................		2
R. R. Hendricks c Lynn b Stoinis	44		B 1, lb 4, w 7		12
A. K. Markram b Stoinis	36				
*F. du Plessis not out.	10		1/94 (1) 2/122 (2) (4 wkts, 29.2 overs)		153
H. Klaasen c Finch b Stoinis	2		3/143 (3) 4/151 (5) 10 overs: 57-0		

A. L. Phehlukwayo, D. W. Steyn, K. Rabada, L. T. Ngidi and Imran Tahir did not bat.

Hazlewood 8–2–41–0; Coulter-Nile 3–0–26–1; Starc 8–0–47–0; Cummins 6–2–18–0; Stoinis 4.2–1–16–3.

Umpires: Aleem Dar and S. D. Fry.   Third umpire: M. A. Gough.
Referee: J. J. Crowe.

AUSTRALIA v SOUTH AFRICA

Second One-Day International

At Adelaide, November 9, 2018 (day/night). Australia won by seven runs. Toss: South Africa.
Australia had gone 288 days without a one-day win, but now pulled a backs-to-the-wall thriller out of the fire. Stoinis inspired them to defend an underwhelming total of 231 with three more wickets, including the crucial scalp of Miller. As so often, an apparently straightforward chase had produced a pulsating game, although it suggested both sides were miles off challenging for the 2019 World Cup. At the toss, du Plessis had tried to seize on Australia's plight, saying he had elected to bowl to play on his opponents' minds after their struggles at Perth. The plan seemed to work when Australia's top order again fell short of expectations, with Finch, Lynn and Carey – the last two part of a lively four-wicket haul for Rabada – all falling in the forties. They were grateful for a last-wicket stand of 27 between Zampa and Hazlewood. South Africa slipped to 68 for four, including Markram, run out chasing a third on Stoinis's arm. Du Plessis and Miller piled on 74 to give them the edge. But du Plessis chopped on against the economical Cummins, Miller was trapped on review by Stoinis after completing the first half-century of the series, and wickets tumbled to set up a decider at Hobart.
Man of the Match: A. J. Finch.   *Attendance:* 17,680.

Australia

*A. J. Finch b Pretorius................	41		A. Zampa c Miller b Rabada............		22
T. M. Head lbw b Ngidi	8		J. R. Hazlewood not out		10
S. E. Marsh c de Kock b Rabada.........	22				
C. A. Lynn c de Kock b Rabada	44		Lb 9, w 2		11
†A. T. Carey c de Kock b Rabada.........	47				
G. J. Maxwell c de Kock b Pretorius	15		1/12 (2) 2/66 (3) 3/96 (1) (48.3 overs)		231
M. P. Stoinis c Hendricks b Pretorius	2		4/133 (4) 5/166 (6) 6/170 (7)		
P. J. Cummins b Steyn.	3		7/179 (8) 8/187 (9) 9/204 (5)		
M. A. Starc c and b Steyn	6		10/231 (10) 10 overs: 58-1		

Steyn 10–1–31–2; Ngidi 9–0–67–1; Rabada 9.3–0–54–4; Pretorius 10–0–32–3; Imran Tahir 10–1–38–0.

South Africa

†Q. de Kock c Zampa b Starc	9		L. T. Ngidi not out.		19
R. R. Hendricks c Carey b Hazlewood	16		Imran Tahir not out		11
A. K. Markram run out (Stoinis/Carey)...	19				
*F. du Plessis b Cummins	47		B 1, w 11		12
H. Klaasen c Lynn b Stoinis	14				
D. A. Miller lbw b Stoinis.............	51		1/18 (1) 2/46 (3) (9 wkts, 50 overs)		224
D. Pretorius c Lynn b Hazlewood	14		3/48 (2) 4/68 (5)		
D. W. Steyn b Stoinis	3		5/142 (4) 6/174 (7) 7/184 (8)		
K. Rabada b Starc	9		8/187 (6) 9/202 (9) 10 overs: 48-2		

Starc 10–1–51–2; Hazlewood 10–0–42–2; Cummins 10–0–27–1; Zampa 9–0–57–0; Stoinis 10–0–35–3; Maxwell 1–0–11–0.

Umpires: G. A. Abood and M. A. Gough.   Third umpire: Aleem Dar.
Referee: J. J. Crowe.

AUSTRALIA v SOUTH AFRICA

Third One-Day International

At Hobart, November 11, 2018 (day/night). South Africa won by 40 runs. Toss: Australia.

Du Plessis etched another chapter into an extraordinary body of work against Australia to help secure a 2–1 series victory. He and his right-hand man Miller produced a scintillating partnership of 252, a South African fourth-wicket record, and the biggest Australia had conceded for any wicket (previously 237 for the first, by Sri Lanka's Marvan Atapattu and Sanath Jayasuriya at Sydney in 2002-03). Shaun Marsh's sixth ODI century gave the Australians a sniff of chasing down their mammoth target of 321, but the du Plessis–Miller blitz had been just too devastating. South Africa lost three early wickets after being put in, before both men scored centuries, then smashed a decisive 57 runs between the 47th and 49th overs. In all, they combined to hit 28 fours and six sixes; seven overs from Stoinis cost 70. For du Plessis, it was a seventh century against Australia out of 19 in all formats. Afterwards, he said he drew on extra reserves when facing them, and had been assisted by verbals after Starc struck him on the hand when he had nine: "That was my moment to wake me up. It is something that just gets me going." The hosts also rued the moment Carey, standing up to Maxwell, dropped du Plessis on 29. Australia were 34 runs ahead of South Africa after 35 overs, but needed Marsh to bat through. When he fell to Pretorius in the 42nd, the path became too steep. South Africa, by contrast, had thrashed 227 from their last 25, having moved cautiously to 93 for three at halfway. They easily beat their previous highest total away to Australia, 288 for six in Perth in 2008-09.

Man of the Match: D. A. Miller.   *Attendance:* 5,321.   *Man of the Series:* D. A. Miller.

South Africa

†Q. de Kock c Carey b Starc	4		D. Pretorius not out	1	
R. R. Hendricks c Carey b Stoinis	8		B 1, lb 2, w 7	10	
A. K. Markram c Carey b Starc	32				
*F. du Plessis c Marsh b Stoinis	125		1/4 (1) 2/26 (2)	(5 wkts, 50 overs)	320
D. A. Miller c Finch b Hazlewood	139		3/55 (3) 4/307 (4)		
H. Klaasen not out	1		5/318 (5)	10 overs: 27-2	

D. W. Steyn, K. Rabada, L. T. Ngidi and Imran Tahir did not bat.

Starc 10–1–57–2; Hazlewood 10–1–53–1; Cummins 10–2–67–0; Stoinis 7–0–70–2; Zampa 6–0–32–0; Maxwell 7–0–38–0.

Australia

C. A. Lynn c de Kock b Steyn	0		A. Zampa c du Plessis b Rabada	0	
*A. J. Finch c Rabada b Ngidi	11		J. R. Hazlewood not out	0	
S. E. Marsh c Klaasen b Pretorius	106				
T. M. Head c Markram b Rabada	6		Lb 2, w 8	10	
M. P. Stoinis c Markram b Pretorius	63				
†A. T. Carey c de Kock b Steyn	42		1/1 (1) 2/18 (2)	(9 wkts, 50 overs)	280
G. J. Maxwell c Hendricks b Steyn	35		3/39 (4) 4/146 (5)		
P. J. Cummins not out	7		5/226 (3) 6/256 (6) 7/278 (7)		
M. A. Starc c and b Rabada	0		8/278 (9) 9/278 (10)	10 overs: 39-2	

Steyn 10–0–45–3; Ngidi 10–0–56–1; Rabada 10–3–40–3; Imran Tahir 7–0–58–0; Pretorius 10–0–61–2; Markram 3–0–18–0.

Umpires: Aleem Dar and P. Wilson.   Third umpire: M. A. Gough.
Referee: J. J. Crowe.

AUSTRALIA v SOUTH AFRICA

Twenty20 International

At Carrara, November 17, 2018 (day/night). South Africa won by 21 runs. Toss: Australia.

In a town most famous in cricket for David Gower's Tiger Moth flypast in 1990-91, the international game came to the Gold Coast for the first time. Right on cue a deluge arrived, and this historic occasion at Metricon Stadium – which had recently hosted the Commonwealth Games – was

Chris Hyde, Getty Images

For my next trick… Glenn Maxwell throws the ball up before he crosses the rope – and completes the catch moments later.

transformed into a soggy ten-over shootout. The match might have gone down as one of the most forgettable ever played, but for a spectacular boundary catch from Maxwell. Du Plessis had zoomed to 27 when Maxwell held on at deep midwicket. Realising he would carry the ball over the boundary, he flicked it up with his right hand, stepped back on to the field and completed the catch. If such incidents are becoming more common, it was the ease of Maxwell's dexterity that was so impressive. But, needing 109, his team-mates were less inspired. Maxwell himself made 38 off 23, but of the rest only Lynn reached double figures; Shamsi's left-arm spin was hard to get away. South Africa had been given a turbo-boosted start when de Kock and Hendricks flailed 42 inside three overs.

Man of the Match: T. Shamsi.   *Attendance:* 12,866.

South Africa

		B	4/6
1 †Q. de Kock st 7 b 4.	22	16	0/2
2 R. R. Hendricks c 6 b 8	19	8	3/1
3 *F. du Plessis c 4 b 11	27	15	4
4 H. Klaasen c 4 b 8	12	6	2
5 D. A. Miller c 3 b 9	11	10	1
6 F. Behardien not out	3	2	0
7 C. H. Morris c 7 b 9	0	1	0
8 A. L. Phehlukwayo not out	2	3	0
Lb 7, w 4, nb 1	12		

3 overs: 42-1   (10 overs) 108-6

1/42 2/61 3/84 4/99 5/104 6/106

9 K. Rabada, 10 L. T. Ngidi and 11 T. Shamsi did not bat.

12th man: A. K. Markram.

Behrendorff 1–2–15–0; Stanlake 2–5–23–1; Coulter-Nile 2–6–19–2; Maxwell 2–5–14–1; Short 1–1–12–0; Tye 2–4–18–2.

Australia

		B	4/6
1 *A. J. Finch b 10	7	6	1
2 C. A. Lynn b 7	14	10	3
3 D. J. M. Short c 8 b 7	0	1	0
4 G. J. Maxwell c 6 b 10	38	23	2/2
5 M. P. Stoinis c 12 b 8	5	3	1
6 B. R. McDermott c 1 b 8	4	6	0
7 †A. T. Carey c 4 b 11	8	7	0
8 N. M. Coulter-Nile not out	2	4	0
Lb 5, w 4.	9		

3 overs: 27-3   (10 overs) 87-7

1/21 2/26 3/27 4/37 5/43 6/60 7/87

9 A. J. Tye, 10 J. P. Behrendorff and 11 B. Stanlake did not bat.

Rabada 2–4–21–0; Ngidi 2–6–16–2; Morris 2–6–12–2; Phehlukwayo 2–3–21–2; Shamsi 2–4–12–1.

Umpires: G. A. Abood and P. Wilson.   Third umpire: S. D. Fry.
Referee: J. J. Crowe.

AUSTRALIA v INDIA IN 2018-19

Gideon Haigh

Twenty20 internationals (3): Australia 1, India 1
Test matches (4): Australia 1, India 2
One-day internationals (3): Australia 1, India 2

The Border–Gavaskar Trophy has pretty much accompanied whichever team are touring, for handover at the end of the series, so ingrained has been home advantage, and so determined have administrators been that it should remain that way. The instalment of 2018-19, however, looked different from the start: Virat Kohli optimistic about India's prospects; Australia faintly cowed, with the banned Steve Smith and David Warner looking on, and their most permeable batting line-up in at least 40 years.

In the event, Kohli's team lost in Perth by looking at the pitch through green-coloured glasses and choosing an XI long on pace bowling but short on batting. Otherwise, their superiority was scarcely threatened after the first morning at Adelaide, and by Sydney was growing daily. Success in the subsequent one-day series – the Twenty20s at the start of the tour had been shared – confirmed their superiority. After 11 Test series in Australia since 1947-48 without victory, India could finally celebrate. The 2–1 margin flattered Tim Paine's side, for whom not one batsman averaged over 40, and only one bowler – Pat Cummins – under 30. Not since the 1890 Ashes had their highest individual score in a series of at least two Tests been lower than the 79 made by newcomer Marcus Harris at Sydney.

India, by contrast, had the outstanding batsman and bowler. Cheteshwar Pujara batted 31 hours and faced 1,258 deliveries, 50 of which he despatched for four, and two for six, but most of which he left. To Nathan Lyon, he used his feet and his front pad, skipping down the pitch when the ball was straight, kicking it away when the line allowed and, in the last two Tests, restricting the world's best finger-spinner to five for 328. This was despite being an ersatz opener, given the impermanence of K. L. Rahul and Murali Vijay, who in nine innings together managed only 106 runs.

The form of Jasprit Bumrah, meanwhile, was a revelation – fast, tireless, threatening both edges, perhaps slightly less effective when operating round the wicket to the left-handers, but at the stumps and hardly ever worked to leg. Twelve of his 21 wickets at 17 were unassisted, five caught at the wicket, three

---

SIX OF THE WORST

The lowest collective average for Australia's top six in a home series (three or more Tests):

	T				T		
21.37	5	v England	1884-85	26.96	5	v England	1954-55
22.34	4	v England	1882-83	**27.02**	**4**	**v India**	**2018-19**
24.37	6	v England	1978-79	27.12	5	v West Indies	1984-85
25.50	5	v England	1901-02	28.44	5	v England	1911-12
26.63	3	v England	1891-92	29.00	3	v New Zealand	1985-86

SEAM UP

How the pace attacks compared in 2018-19:

	O	R	W	BB	5I	10M	Avge
India's fast bowlers	433.5	1,177	50	6-33	2	0	23.54
Australia's fast bowlers	462	1,287	40	6-27	1	0	32.17

at slip. His baffling, dipping slower ball to dismiss Shaun Marsh in Melbourne was the most replayable instant of the series. By the end, some were prophesying that Bumrah would be the world's best all-format bowler within a year. Whatever the case, he, Mohammed Shami and Ishant Sharma constituted by far the best Indian pace-bowling combination to visit Australian shores – relentlessly disciplined, formidably fit.

Spin has possibly never played so small a role in an Indian attack against Australia, Ravichandran Ashwin being ruled out after a single Test with an abdominal strain, and Ravindra Jadeja and Hanuma Vihari filling a containing role. The balance was partly restored at Sydney, where Kuldeep Yadav's left-arm variations proved useful on a bare, little-altering surface.

Perhaps the most popular character on tour was Rishabh Pant, a 21-year-old jack-in-the-box, whose carefree unbeaten 159 at Sydney was the first Test century in Australia by an Indian wicketkeeper, and whose 20 catches were interspersed with some acrobatic interceptions and only a few errors. His on-field garrulity, meanwhile, gained a cult following via the newly open stump microphones. A photograph of him with Paine's wife and children – after Paine tried to distract him while he batted by wondering if he might babysit – was perhaps the social-media moment of the series, there now being informal competition for such titles. Even with M. S. Dhoni making three half-centuries in the 50-over matches, two to anchor successful chases, there were calls for Pant to assume the gloves in all formats.

Still more of a surprise packet was Mayank Agarwal, a preternaturally composed opening batsman flown in before the Melbourne Test. He looked as if he had 50 caps already, hitting 19 fours and five sixes in three fluent innings, and overshadowing the established Ajinkya Rahane and Rohit Sharma. India's tail looked vulnerable, but was hardly tested.

Australians loved hating and hated loving Kohli. If he did not quite

© Bonnie Paine/Instagram

Reaching out: Rishabh Pant proves a genuine all-rounder.

dominate with the bat – though he followed a hundred in the Perth Test with a typically effervescent century in the second ODI, at Adelaide – he was the most vivid personality on either side, always chivvying his team-mates, and only occasionally riling the home side as he had in the past. Sizeable contingents of Indian supporters attended each Test, uniformed in replica gear, equipped with standards and banners, and swooning at Kohli's every gesture. The rejoicings when he won the toss at Melbourne and Sydney were remarkable. Coach Ravi Shastri's word salads were, blessedly, barely intelligible.

For Australia, although half a million turnstile clicks were good news for the exchequer, it was a salutary series. There were some good personal performances: Lyon won the match award for his eight for 106 at Perth, Cummins a great deal of sympathy for his nine for 99 and second-innings 63

LONGEST TIME AT THE CREASE IN A FOUR-TEST SERIES

Mins	Runs			
1,869	521	C. A. Pujara	**India in Australia**	**2018-19**
1,861	602	R. Dravid	India in England	2002
1,814	619	R. B. Richardson	West Indies v India	1988-89
1,714	562	A. N. Cook	England in India	2012-13
1,701	496	R. Dravid	India in the West Indies	2005-06
1,695	712	J. H. Kallis	South Africa v West Indies	2003-04
1,669	569	S. V. Manjrekar	India in Pakistan	1989-90
1,640	706	R. T. Ponting	Australia v India	2003-04
1,637	619	R. Dravid	India in Australia	2003-04
1,620	769	S. P. D. Smith	Australia v India	2014-15

In three-Test series for Pakistan, Shoaib Mohammad batted for 1,689 minutes (507 runs) at home to New Zealand in 1990-91, and Mohammad Yousuf for 1,631 (665) at home to West Indies in 2006-07. S. M. Gavaskar played in four of India's five Tests in the West Indies in 1970-71, and scored 774 runs in 1,996 minutes. G. Boycott (England) played in three Tests of the 1977 Ashes, and scored 442 runs in 1,631 minutes. The record for any series is 2,283 minutes (839 runs) by M. A. Taylor for Australia in the 1989 Ashes (six Tests).

---

in a lost cause at Melbourne. But the batting turned into a source of local despair, notably the failure to convert starts, the inability to build partnerships, and the eccentric shot selection. Travis Head, in his second series, showed pluck, but fell five times in a row to flaky attacking strokes; Harris, in his first, did not look out of his class, although he was nonplussed by the short ball.

Most disappointing were Shaun Marsh and Usman Khawaja, who failed to fill even a portion of the breach left by Smith and Warner. Marsh played some attractive shots, Khawaja batted some long periods. But they hardly resembled senior cricketers, and the burden of leadership fell acutely on Paine, whose prominence was consolidated at no expense to his own game: he kept wicket immaculately, looked as assured at the crease as anyone, and developed helpfully cordial relations with the media. His coach, Justin Langer, followed more of a sine curve, at times feeling his embattlement.

Australia's pace bowling was persistent and persevering but, after the opening hour of the First Test, seldom threatened to break open an Indian

FEWEST LBWs FOR ONE SIDE IN A SERIES

Lbw	Wkts	T	Bowling side	
0	98	6	England in Australia	1970-71
0	52	4	England in Australia	1881-82
1	72	5	Australia v England	1884-85
1	67	4	England in Australia	1882-83
1	**62**	**4**	**Australia v India**	**2018-19**
1	52	5	Pakistan in India............................	1960-61
1	51	4	New Zealand in India........................	1964-65
1	43	4	New Zealand v England.......................	1929-30

Minimum: 4 Tests.

innings. Falling back on defensive lengths, Mitchell Starc and Josh Hazlewood barely threatened the stumps – the Australians obtained only one lbw all series. By the end, they and Cummins looked stale, as relieved as any by the rain and bad light that queered the last two days at Sydney, and by omission from the one-day squad. Many commented on the doleful and sour expressions the Australians wore at that Test's conclusion. But they were a long way second, and it smarted.

INDIAN TOURING PARTY

*V. Kohli (T/50/20), M. A. Agarwal (T), K. K. Ahmed (50/20), R. Ashwin (T), Bhuvneshwar Kumar (T/50/20), J. J. Bumrah (T/20), Y. S. Chahal (50/20), S. Dhawan (50/20), M. S. Dhoni (50), S. Gill (50), S. S. Iyer (20), R. A. Jadeja (T/50), K. M. Jadhav (50), K. D. Karthik (50/20), Mohammed Shami (T/50), M. K. Pandey (20), H. H. Pandya (T/50), K. H. Pandya (20), R. R. Pant (T/20), P. A. Patel (T), C. A. Pujara (T), A. M. Rahane (T), K. L. Rahul (T/50/20), A. T. Rayudu (50), V. Shankar (50), I. Sharma (T), R. G. Sharma (T/50/20), P. P. Shaw (T), M. Siraj (50), G. H. Vihari (T), M. Vijay (T), M. S. Washington Sundar (20), K. Yadav (T/50/20), U. T. Yadav (T/20). *Coach:* R. J. Shastri.

Shaw injured his ankle attempting a boundary catch in a warm-up game; he returned home during the Second Test and was replaced by Agarwal. H. H. Pandya was added to the squad at the same time after recovering from a back injury, but he and Rahul were sent home for disciplinary reasons after the first ODI, and replaced by Gill and Shankar.

TEST MATCH AVERAGES

AUSTRALIA – BATTING AND FIELDING

	T	I	NO	R	HS	100	50	Avge	Ct
†M. S. Harris	4	8	1	258	79	0	2	36.85	6
†T. M. Head	4	7	0	237	72	0	2	33.85	1
†U. T. Khawaja	4	8	1	198	72	0	1	28.28	6
†S. E. Marsh................	4	7	0	183	60	0	1	26.14	2
T. D. Paine	4	7	0	174	41	0	0	24.85	16
†M. A. Starc................	4	7	2	117	29*	0	0	23.40	4
P. J. Cummins	4	7	0	163	63	0	1	23.28	1
P. S. P. Handscomb	3	5	0	105	37	0	0	21.00	6
N. M. Lyon	4	7	3	83	38*	0	0	20.75	2
A. J. Finch	3	6	0	97	50	0	1	16.16	7
†J. R. Hazlewood............	4	7	2	51	21	0	0	10.20	0

Played in one Test: M. Labuschagne 38 (1 ct); M. R. Marsh 9, 10.

BOWLING

	Style	O	M	R	W	BB	5I	Avge
P. J. Cummins	RF	145	29	389	14	6-27	1	27.78
N. M. Lyon..................	OB	242.1	35	639	21	6-122	2	30.42
J. R. Hazlewood.............	RFM	152.1	51	398	13	3-52	0	30.61
M. A. Starc.................	LF	138.5	26	449	13	3-40	0	34.53

Also bowled: A. J. Finch (SLA) 2–0–8–0; T. M. Head (OB) 8–1–35–0; U. T. Khawaja (OB) 1–0–4–0; M. Labuschagne (LB) 16–0–76–0; M. R. Marsh (RFM) 26–4–51–0.

INDIA – BATTING AND FIELDING

	T	I	NO	R	HS	100	50	Avge	Ct
C. A. Pujara	4	7	0	521	193	3	1	74.42	3
M. A. Agarwal	2	3	0	195	77	0	2	65.00	3
†R. R. Pant.................	4	7	1	350	159*	1	0	58.33	20
V. Kohli....................	4	7	0	282	123	1	1	40.28	5
R. G. Sharma	2	4	1	106	63*	0	1	35.33	1
A. M. Rahane...............	4	7	0	217	70	0	2	31.00	6
†R. A. Jadeja	2	3	0	90	81	0	1	30.00	0
G. H. Vihari...............	3	5	0	111	42	0	0	22.20	1
M. Vijay...................	2	4	0	49	20	0	0	12.25	1
K. L. Rahul................	3	5	0	57	44	0	0	11.40	1
Mohammed Shami...........	4	5	2	6	6	0	0	2.00	1
J. J. Bumrah	4	4	2	4	4	0	0	2.00	0
I. Sharma	3	4	0	5	4	0	0	1.25	2

Played in one Test: R. Ashwin 25, 5; †K. Yadav did not bat (1 ct); U. T. Yadav 4*, 2.

BOWLING

	Style	O	M	R	W	BB	5I	Avge
J. J. Bumrah	RFM	157.1	48	357	21	6-33	1	17.00
K. Yadav	SLW	31.5	6	99	5	5-99	1	19.80
I. Sharma	RFM	103	21	262	11	4-41	0	23.81
R. Ashwin	OB	86.5	22	149	6	3-57	0	24.83
Mohammed Shami...........	RFM	136.4	28	419	16	6-56	1	26.18
R. A. Jadeja	SLA	89	25	200	7	3-82	0	28.57

Also bowled: G. H. Vihari (OB) 35–8–94–2; M. Vijay (OB) 9–1–31–0; U. T. Yadav (RF) 37–3–139–2.

TWENTY20 INTERNATIONAL REPORTS BY ANDREW McGLASHAN

AUSTRALIA v INDIA

First Twenty20 International

At Brisbane, November 21, 2018 (floodlit). Australia won by four runs (DLS). Toss: India.

A nervy Australia held on for victory after Pant and Karthik had threatened to overhaul the DLS target in a late onslaught following a miscalculation from Finch. Rain had reduced the contest to 17 overs a side but, at the start of India's 14th – with 60 still needed – Finch did not realise he had already used Stanlake's allocation (he could bowl only three overs, because two others had already bowled four). Instead, he had to give the ball to Tye, who sent down two wides in an over costing 25. Tye atoned by removing Pant in his next, before Stoinis was able to defend 13 off the last. "I just stuffed it up out there," admitted Finch. Stoinis's closing act completed a busy match after he made an unbeaten 33 off 19 balls in a six-over stand of 78 with Maxwell, who struck four sixes – three in succession – off slow left-armer Krunal Pandya. Miscuing an attempted fifth, he hit the Flying Fox camera suspended over the field, resulting in a call of dead ball. Dhawan's crisp innings led India's reply, but Zampa showed outstanding control, conceding one boundary in his four overs, and getting rid of Kohli, who sliced to short third man. When Dhawan was caught at third man for 76 off 42, Australia were on top, before Finch's poor maths helped provide a late twist.

Man of the Match: A. Zampa. *Attendance:* 31,186.

Australia

	B	4/6
1 D. J. M. Short c 9 b 11	7	12 1
2 *A. J. Finch c 11 b 9	27	24 3
3 C. A. Lynn c 8 b 9	37	20 1/4
4 G. J. Maxwell c 8 b 10	46	24 0/4
5 M. P. Stoinis not out	33	19 3/1
6 B. R. McDermott not out	2	3 0
B 1, w 5	6	

6 overs: 38-1   (17 overs) 158-4

1/24 2/64 3/75 4/153

7 †A. T. Carey, 8 A. Tye, 9 A. Zampa, 10 J. P. Behrendorff and 11 B. Stanlake did not bat.

Bhuvneshwar Kumar 3–10–15–0; Bumrah 3–7–21–1; Ahmed 3–5–42–1; Yadav 4–9–24–2; Pandya 4–5–55–0.

India

	B	4/6
1 R. G. Sharma c 2 b 10	7	8 0
2 S. Dhawan c 10 b 11	76	42 10/2
3 K. L. Rahul st 7 b 9	13	12 1
4 *V. Kohli c 3 b 9	4	8 0
5 †R. R. Pant c 10 b 8	20	16 1/1
6 K. D. Karthik c 10 b 5	30	13 4/1
7 K. H. Pandya c 4 b 5	2	4 0
8 Bhuvneshwar Kumar not out	1	1 0
9 K. Yadav not out	4	1 1
Lb 3, w 6, nb 3	12	

5 overs: 41-1   (17 overs) 169-7

1/35 2/81 3/94 4/105 5/156 6/163 7/163

10 J. J. Bumrah and 11 K. K. Ahmed did not bat.

Behrendorff 4–9–43–1; Stanlake 3–7–27–1; Tye 3–3–47–1; Zampa 4–11–22–2; Stoinis 3–4–27–2.

Umpires: S. D. Fry and P. Wilson.   Third umpire: G. A. Abood.
Referee: J. J. Crowe.

AUSTRALIA v INDIA

Second Twenty20 International

At Melbourne, November 23, 2018 (floodlit). No result. Toss: India.

Rain denied India the chance of a modest chase after Australia's batsmen struggled to break free in cold, windy conditions. Finch's first-ball dismissal, edging a drive, set the tone, and the hosts never found a foothold after stumbling to 40 for three in the powerplay. Krunal Pandya claimed revenge for his treatment at the hands of Maxwell at the Gabba, bowling him with a lovely delivery which gripped; his celebrations matched the excitement of the vast Indian contingent in the crowd. At 74 for six in the 14th over, Australia were sinking, but McDermott batted sensibly alongside some lusty hitting from Coulter-Nile, playing after Billy Stanlake twisted his ankle in the warm-ups. The rain came with an over of Australia's innings left. *Attendance:* 63,439.

Australia

		B	4/6
1 D. J. M. Short *b 11*	14	15	2
2 *A. J. Finch *c 5 b 8*	0	1	0
3 C. A. Lynn *c 7 b 11*	13	13	1/1
4 G. J. Maxwell *b 7*	19	22	1
5 M. P. Stoinis *c 6 b 10*	4	5	1
6 B. R. McDermott *not out*	32	30	2/1
7 †A. T. Carey *c 7 b 9*	4	6	0
8 N. M. Coulter-Nile *c 12 b 8*	18	9	1/2
9 A. J. Tye *not out*	12	13	2
B 1, lb 3, w 12	16		

6 overs: 40-3   (19 overs)   132-7

1/1 2/27 3/35 4/41 5/62 6/74 7/101

10 A. Zampa and 11 J. P. Behrendorff did not bat.

Bhuvneshwar Kumar 3–11–20–2; Ahmed 4–12–39–2; Bumrah 4–16–20–1; Yadav 4–12–23–1; Pandya 4–7–26–1.

India

1 R. G. Sharma, 2 S. Dhawan, 3 *V. Kohli, 4 K. L. Rahul, 5 †R. R. Pant, 6 K. D. Karthik, 7 K. H. Pandya, 8 Bhuvneshwar Kumar, 9 K. Yadav, 10 J. J. Bumrah and 11 K. K. Ahmed did not bat.

12th man: M. K. Pandey.

Umpires: G. A. Abood and S. D. Fry.   Third umpire: P. Wilson.
Referee: J. J. Crowe.

AUSTRALIA v INDIA

Third Twenty20 International

At Sydney, November 25, 2018 (floodlit). India won by six wickets. Toss: Australia.

Kohli steered India to a series-levelling victory with two balls to spare amid frenzied scenes at the SCG, as stands turned into a sea of blue shirts. He had been given breathing space in the chase by a rollicking start from Sharma and Dhawan, who added 67 in 33 balls. But Australia struck back when Starc, playing his first T20 international in over two years, pinned Dhawan on review, then Zampa started with a wicket-maiden as he skidded one through Sharma. Poor shot selection from Rahul and Pant built pressure, and India required 47 off 28 balls when Kohli took charge with a magnificent straight six off Tye. Karthik provided smart assistance – and put Tye into the second tier over square leg – before Kohli finished things with consecutive boundaries. Australia's innings had been a stop-start affair dominated by India's spin duo. Despite the hosts' attempts to counter Kuldeep Yadav with a reshuffled order, he tied them in knots, while Krunal Pandya fed off the panic, bagging the best T20I figures by a spinner in Australia, including Maxwell once more. Australia did not manage a six – for just the second time in a full 20-over innings – and only late scampering from Stoinis and Coulter-Nile got them as far as 164.

Man of the Match: K. H. Pandya.   *Attendance:* 37,339.
Man of the Series: S. Dhawan.

Australia

		B	4/6
1 D. J. M. Short *lbw b 7*	33	29	5
2 *A. J. Finch *c 7 b 9*	28	23	4
3 G. J. Maxwell *c 1 b 7*	13	16	2
4 B. R. McDermott *lbw b 7*	0	1	0
5 †A. T. Carey *c 3 b 7*	27	19	4
6 C. A. Lynn *run out (10)*	13	10	1
7 M. P. Stoinis *not out*	25	15	3
8 N. M. Coulter-Nile *not out*	13	7	2
B 1, lb 2, w 9	12		

6 overs: 49-0   (20 overs)   164-6

1/68 2/73 3/73 4/90 5/119 6/131

9 M. A. Starc, 10 A. J. Tye and 11 A. Zampa did not bat.

India

		B	4/6
1 R. G. Sharma *b 11*	23	16	1/2
2 S. Dhawan *lbw b 9*	41	22	6/2
3 *V. Kohli *not out*	61	41	4/2
4 K. L. Rahul *c 8 b 3*	14	20	0/1
5 †R. R. Pant *c 5 b 10*	0	1	0
6 K. D. Karthik *not out*	22	18	1/1
Lb 1, w 6	7		

6 overs: 67-1   (19.4 overs)   168-4

1/67 2/67 3/108 4/108

7 K. H. Pandya, 8 Bhuvneshwar Kumar, 9 K. Yadav, 10 J. J. Bumrah and 11 K. K. Ahmed did not bat.

Bhuvneshwar Kumar 4–7–33–0; Ahmed 4–10–35–0; Bumrah 4–5–38–0; Yadav 4–13–19–1; Pandya 4–5–36–4. | Starc 4–11–26–1; Coulter-Nile 3–5–40–0; Stoinis 1–1–22–0; Zampa 4–11–22–1; Maxwell 4–8–25–1; Tye 3.4–11–32–1.

Umpires: G. A. Abood and P. Wilson.   Third umpire: S. D. Fry.
Referee: J. J. Crowe.

Test Reports by Gideon Haigh

AUSTRALIA v INDIA

First Test

At Adelaide, December 6–10, 2018. India won by 31 runs. Toss: India. Test debut: M. S. Harris.

India secured victory in an enthralling match in the last over before tea on the fifth day when Hazlewood, after a painstaking tenth-wicket partnership of 32 in 67 balls with Lyon, nicked Ashwin low to second slip. Having lost a close game here four years earlier, Kohli had cause to be doubly satisfied: never had India started an away Test so badly, then won so well.

Having rejected a pink-ball Test in the afternoon and evening, India made a meal of the morning, sinking by noon on the first day to 41 for four in the face of some withering Australian pace; Kohli succumbed to a Khawaja catch in the gully resembling an airborne cartwheel. They were led from their crisis by Pujara, seven Tests on from his controversial exclusion against England at Edgbaston, and with an away average comparing palely to his home record. He turned a rout into an orderly retreat with Rohit Sharma, Pant and Ashwin, then a startling counter-attack with the tailenders, during which he hooked Hazlewood and cut Starc for unlikely sixes, and passed 5,000 Test runs.

Pujara's 16th Test century took 231 deliveries, and he repeatedly stepped out to Lyon like a man stamping on a spider. The only chance he offered was on 89, when Hazlewood and Paine might have reviewed a caught-behind decision: the Snickometer detected a spike. As it was, the Australians had to wait until the first day's final delivery, when he was run out trying to steal the strike for the following morning – another virtuoso piece of fielding, mid-on Cummins throwing down the stumps side-on while in mid-air. Mohammed Shami fell first ball next day, but Australia's innings had barely begun when Finch was bowled through a woolly drive, presaging a sketchy reply.

The pitch played superbly. It was Australia who were culpable, Marsh dragging a wide half-volley on to his off stump, Handscomb trying to run a ball down to third man, Marcus Harris on his Test debut feeling for one he might have left. Khawaja, who would spend a careworn three and a half hours over 36 runs in the game, leaned the other way. Head, the industrious local boy playing his first home Test, was alone in achieving the necessary balance of bustle and bristle, Cummins helping him assemble Australia's only half-century partnership of the match. Lyon's effective sweep limited the deficit to 15.

Second time round, Rahul and Vijay – playing because Prithvi Shaw had twisted an ankle in a warm-up game – laid a firmer foundation, although both perished wildly, and India again had need of Pujara's serenity. With Kohli, he added 71 in 32 overs, with

Rahane 87 in 30. By the time Pujara was fourth out, caught at silly point for 71 spread across nearly five hours, India were 249 in front – and in sight of safety. From this point, they faltered, losing seven for 73 to some impulsive strokes, Pant producing a T20 cameo of 28 in 16 deliveries. Four years after his match-winning seven for 152 on this ground against the same opponents, Lyon winkled out six for 122. Australia's target was 323, on a pitch of good character, with little rough or variable bounce. They faced mainly a battle with themselves.

Finch's was excruciating. On a pair, he was plumb lbw to the second delivery of the innings, only for third umpire Chris Gaffaney to detect a no-ball. He then declined to review a catch behind that Gaffaney would probably have confirmed had hit neither bat nor glove – a strangely sacrificial gesture from the last ball before tea on the fourth day. India struck twice in the next hour, Khawaja charging down the wicket, and raising the possibility of a hurried conclusion.

After six consecutive single-figure scores, however, Marsh provided firm defence and fluent drives, prolonging his resistance into the following morning, and reaching fifty with an exquisite stroke through midwicket. Ashwin wheeled away at the River End, while the pace bowlers took turns at the Cathedral End, but there was little assistance for anyone,

---

MOST BATSMEN OUT CAUGHT IN A TEST

Ct	Wkts		
35	40	**Australia (17/20) v India (18/20) at Adelaide**	**2018-19**
34	40	**South Africa (18/20) v Australia (16/20) at Cape Town**	**2017-18**
34	40	**South Africa (16/20) v Pakistan (18/20) at Johannesburg**	**2018-19**
33	36	Australia (15/16) v India (18/20) at Perth (WACA)	1991-92
32	35	New Zealand (18/20) v Pakistan (14/15) at Auckland	1993-94
32	37	Australia (13/17) v England (19/20) at Brisbane	2013-14
32	40	England (15/20) v Pakistan (17/20) at Leeds	1971
32	40	Zimbabwe (15/20) v Pakistan (17/20) at Harare	1994-95
32	40	Australia (13/20) v Pakistan (19/20) at Sydney	2009-10
32	40	West Indies (16/20) v Pakistan (16/20) at Bridgetown	2016-17

---

apart from a ball from Ishant Sharma that reared off a length and nearly decapitated Head. The lower order sold themselves dearly, Paine lasting two hours before skying a pull, Cummins two and a half before edging to slip. Bumrah, fast and awkward, was the difference, while Shami nicked off the dangerous Starc. At 259 for nine, Australia were 64 short, and India a wicket away from a series lead.

India still had to contend with Lyon, who had expressed optimism about Australia's prospects the night before, and whom fortune now favoured. He was dropped by Pant on seven off Bumrah – depriving Pant of a record 12th catch in a Test – and at 32 looked lbw to Ishant, only for umpire Dharmasena to call no-ball. A not-out decision would have stood, as the ball's predictive path involved a kiss of leg stump, but at the time it looked like a moment of built-in regret.

Every ball safely negotiated brought forth applause, every run cheers. Hazlewood defended stoutly until Ashwin drew him into a hazardous drive, Rahul completing the 35th catch of the match, a record for a Test. It also secured India's third-closest win by runs, and their first in the opening Test of a series in Australia. Lyon sank to his haunches, bereft. Pant described himself as "very nervous" in the final stages, Kohli himself relieved at the end: "I wouldn't say I was cool as ice, but you try not to show it." Paine was rueful: "We honestly feel we let that Test match slip."

Man of the Match: C. A. Pujara. *Attendance:* 112,868.

Close of play: first day, India 250-9 (Mohammed Shami 6); second day, Australia 191-7 (Head 61, Starc 8); third day, India 151-3 (Pujara 40, Rahane 1); fourth day, Australia 104-4 (Marsh 31, Head 11).

India

K. L. Rahul c Finch b Hazlewood	2	– c Paine b Hazlewood	44
M. Vijay c Paine b Starc	11	– c Handscomb b Starc	18
C. A. Pujara run out (Cummins)	123	– c Finch b Lyon	71
*V. Kohli c Khawaja b Cummins	3	– c Finch b Lyon	34
A. M. Rahane c Handscomb b Hazlewood	13	– c Starc b Lyon	70
R. G. Sharma c Harris b Lyon	37	– c Handscomb b Lyon	1
†R. R. Pant c Paine b Lyon	25	– c Harris b Starc	28
R. Ashwin c Handscomb b Cummins	25	– c Harris b Starc	5
I. Sharma b Starc	4	– c Finch b Starc	0
Mohammed Shami c Paine b Hazlewood	6	– b Lyon	0
J. J. Bumrah not out	0	– not out	0
Lb 1	1	B 21, lb 13, w 2	36

1/3 (1) 2/15 (2) 3/19 (4) (88 overs) 250
4/41 (5) 5/86 (6) 6/127 (7)
7/189 (8) 8/210 (9) 9/250 (5) 10/250 (10)

1/63 (2) 2/76 (1) (106.5 overs) 307
3/147 (4) 4/234 (3)
5/248 (6) 6/282 (7) 7/303 (8)
8/303 (5) 9/303 (10) 10/307 (9)

Starc 19–4–63–2; Hazlewood 20–3–52–3; Cummins 19–3–49–2; Lyon 28–2–83–2; Head 2–1–2–0. *Second innings*—Starc 21.5–7–40–3; Hazlewood 23–13–43–1; Cummins 18–4–55–0; Lyon 42–7–122–6; Head 2–0–13–0.

Australia

A. J. Finch b I. Sharma	0	– c Pant b Ashwin	11
M. S. Harris c Vijay b Ashwin	26	– c Pant b Mohammed Shami	26
U. T. Khawaja c Pant b Ashwin	28	– c R. G. Sharma b Ashwin	8
S. E. Marsh b Ashwin	2	– c Pant b Bumrah	60
P. S. P. Handscomb c Pant b Bumrah	34	– c Pujara b Mohammed Shami	14
T. M. Head c Pant b Mohammed Shami	72	– c Rahane b I. Sharma	14
*†T. D. Paine c Pant b I. Sharma	5	– c Pant b Bumrah	41
P. J. Cummins lbw b Bumrah	10	– c Kohli b Bumrah	28
M. A. Starc c Pant b Bumrah	15	– c Pant b Mohammed Shami	28
N. M. Lyon not out	24	– not out	38
J. R. Hazlewood c Pant b Mohammed Shami	0	– c Rahul b Ashwin	13
B 6, lb 10, w 1, nb 2	19	B 1, lb 6, nb 3	10

1/0 (1) 2/45 (2) 3/59 (4) (98.4 overs) 235
4/87 (3) 5/120 (5) 6/127 (7)
7/177 (8) 8/204 (9) 9/235 (6) 10/235 (11)

1/28 (1) 2/44 (2) (119.5 overs) 291
3/60 (3) 4/84 (5)
5/115 (6) 6/156 (4) 7/187 (7)
8/228 (9) 9/259 (8) 10/291 (11)

I. Sharma 20–6–47–2; Bumrah 24–9–47–3; Mohammed Shami 16.4–6–58–2; Ashwin 34–9–57–3; Vijay 4–1–10–0. *Second innings*—I. Sharma 19–4–48–1; Bumrah 24–8–68–3; Ashwin 52.5–13–92–3; Mohammed Shami 20–4–65–3; Vijay 4–0–11–0.

Umpires: H. D. P. K. Dharmasena and N. J. Llong. Third umpire: C. B. Gaffaney.
Referee: R. S. Madugalle.

AUSTRALIA v INDIA

Second Test

At Perth Stadium, December 14–18, 2018. Australia won by 146 runs. Toss: Australia.
The pitch is never merely scenery in the drama of cricket; every so often, it's virtually an actor. The first surface prepared for a Test at the giant new Optus Stadium, only Australia's tenth Test venue in 142 years, was among the most fascinating ever rolled, a

verdant drop-in laced with intricate cracks that its talkative groundsman, Brett Sipthorpe, described as a response to a "mandate for pace and bounce".

To this it lived up thoroughly, the ball travelling through at head height until the last day, although in other phases playing benignly. "A strange one," Hazlewood called it, but also "exciting". The stand-out bowler, in fact, was not a paceman at all: Man of the Match Nathan Lyon took eight for 106, including the venue's first five-for, to bowl Australia to their first Test victory since Durban at the start of March, and square the series.

India, by contrast, were seduced by the siren song of speed, choosing four pace bowlers when Ravichandran Ashwin reported unfit with a stomach strain. Bumrah, and Ishant Sharma, Mohammed Shami and Umesh Yadav were by some distance the slickest attack India had chosen for a Test, and probably also the longest tail, given that Rohit Sharma was also injured. But four right-arm quicks without a specialist spinner looked like too much of a good thing from the moment Australia proceeded rapidly past 50 without loss soon after drinks.

Paine had circumspectly chosen to bat on winning the toss; Kohli had not looked fussed. But in beginning with a century stand, the Victorian pair of Harris and Finch did for Australia – at the best possible time – what they had not previously done for their state. Four fell for 36, including Harris for 70, but in the evening Marsh and Head put on 84, tested by the pace but not particularly troubled. The most hostile spell the Australians withstood was with the second new ball, which Paine and Cummins saw out to finish a good day's work at 277 for six. The loss of the last four for 16 in 22 balls was then offset by the removal of India's openers before and after lunch.

India lost only one more wicket on that second day, as Kohli pervaded the crease as calmly as only a great batsman can on a challenging pitch, quick to pounce on errors of length, happy to leave imperiously. Another hour on the third day, and the first-innings lead might have been India's. But Lyon had Rahane caught at the wicket in the morning's first over, and Pant lacked the experience to rally the elongated tail once Kohli was given out to a low slip catch following his 25th Test century – the first of five wickets to subside for 32 as Lyon mopped up. Australia led by 43, which had swollen to 102 before India took a second-innings wicket, although Finch retired hurt on 25 when his finger was damaged by a lifter from Shami.

The heat, unrelieved by breezes, was fierce, the cricket red-blooded, at times a little reckless. Marsh edged tamely, Head contrived to be caught at deep third man for the second time in the match, Handscomb to stumble into a straight ball; Khawaja held firm and founded an alliance with Paine. Open stump mikes, allowed since the ICC's relaxed protocols earlier in the year, provided hints of short temper and mutual provocation. Late on the third day, Kohli was heard telling Paine he could not afford to fail, Paine that Kohli faced batting again. On the fourth morning, umpire Gaffaney chided the pair when Kohli nearly brushed chests with his rival at the non-striker's end: "Come on, play the game. You guys are the captains." More amusement was taken when the microphones overheard Ishant and sub fielder Ravindra Jadeja having a long contretemps in Hindi, laced with expletives.

The pitch seemed to settle on the fourth morning, perhaps thanks to the heavy roller. But, resuming on 190 for four after lunch, Australia lost five for 15 – four to the second new ball – with Shami heading for a career-best six for 56. The session saw the fall of eight for 68, despite a sprightly last-wicket partnership of 36 between Starc and Hazlewood, who between them removed Rahul and Pujara before tea.

With Kohli batting, the Australians were ever more talkative. "I know he's your captain, but you can't seriously like him as a bloke," Paine said to Vijay, Kohli's partner. "You couldn't possibly like him." Paine's advice to Lyon to "hit the hole" preluded Kohli's dismissal by a delivery bouncing from footmarks left by Ishant, the seventh time Lyon had removed him in Tests.

By now the pitch was playing tricks: finding an ideal length and speed to exploit them, Lyon bowled Vijay in his next over. India's selection looked worse still when Rahane flailed to point within sight of stumps, leaving them 98 for five chasing 287, with essentially four No. 11s in reserve. Once Vihari fell the following morning, Pant seemed perplexed, and holed out to Lyon, commencing a final crash of four for three. In two innings, India's last four batsmen had contributed only 11.

It was India's seventh away defeat in 2018, Australia's first win under coach Justin Langer and captain Paine. Asked about the confrontational air, neither skipper was concerned. "It's Test cricket at the end of the day – it has to be competitive," said Kohli. "You can't say that people aren't going to try and get you out in any way possible at all." Paine argued that it enriched the contest: "I enjoy watching him, I always have. I think he brings out the competitive spirit in a lot of people, which is great, and I'm sure it was great to watch." Unfortunately, fewer people watched than locals had hoped, the stadium most of the time being barely half-full – less than the game, and the pitch, deserved.

Man of the Match: N. M. Lyon. *Attendance:* 81,104.

Close of play: first day, Australia 277-6 (Paine 16, Cummins 11); second day, India 172-3 (Kohli 82, Rahane 51); third day, Australia 132-4 (Khawaja 41, Paine 8); fourth day, India 112-5 (Vihari 24, Pant 9).

Australia

M. S. Harris c Rahane b Vihari	70	– b Bumrah	20
A. J. Finch lbw b Bumrah	50	– c Pant b Mohammed Shami	25
U. T. Khawaja c Pant b Yadav	5	– c Pant b Mohammed Shami	72
S. E. Marsh c Rahane b Vihari	45	– c Pant b Mohammed Shami	5
P. S. P. Handscomb c Kohli b Sharma	7	– lbw b Sharma	13
T. M. Head c Mohammed Shami b Sharma	58	– c Sharma b Mohammed Shami	19
*†T. D. Paine lbw b Bumrah	38	– c Kohli b Mohammed Shami	37
P. J. Cummins b Yadav	9	– b Bumrah	1
M. A. Starc c Pant b Sharma	6	– b Bumrah	14
N. M. Lyon not out	9	– c Vihari b Mohammed Shami	5
J. R. Hazlewood c Pant b Sharma	0	– not out	17
B 4, lb 7, w 7, nb 1	19	B 8, lb 3, w 4	15
	326		**243**

1/112 (2) 2/130 (3) 3/134 (1)   (108.3 overs) 326   1/59 (1) 2/64 (4)   (93.2 overs) 243
4/148 (5) 5/232 (4) 6/251 (6)   3/85 (5) 4/120 (6)
7/310 (8) 8/310 (7) 9/326 (9) 10/326 (11)   5/192 (7) 6/192 (6) 7/198 (3)
    8/198 (8) 9/207 (10) 10/243 (9)

In the second innings Finch, when 25, retired hurt at 33-0 and resumed at 192-5.

Sharma 20.3–7–41–4; Bumrah 26–8–53–2; Yadav 23–3–78–2; Mohammed Shami 24–3–80–0; Vihari 14–1–53–2; Vijay 1–0–10–0. *Second innings—*Sharma 16–1–45–1; Bumrah 25.2–10–39–3; Mohammed Shami 24–8–56–6; Yadav 14–0–61–0; Vihari 14–4–31–0.

India

K. L. Rahul b Hazlewood	2	– b Starc	0
M. Vijay b Starc	0	– b Lyon	20
C. A. Pujara c Paine b Starc	24	– c Paine b Hazlewood	4
*V. Kohli c Handscomb b Cummins	123	– c Khawaja b Lyon	17
A. M. Rahane c Paine b Lyon	51	– c Head b Hazlewood	30
G. H. Vihari c Paine b Hazlewood	20	– c Harris b Starc	28
†R. R. Pant c Starc b Lyon	36	– c Handscomb b Lyon	30
Mohammed Shami c Paine b Lyon	0	– (10) not out	0
I. Sharma c and b Lyon	1	– c Paine b Cummins	0
U. T. Yadav not out	4	– (8) c and b Starc	2
J. J. Bumrah c Khawaja b Lyon	4	– c and b Cummins	0
B 4, lb 7, w 5, nb 2	18	B 6, w 3	9
	283		**140**

1/6 (2) 2/8 (1) 3/82 (3)   (105.5 overs) 283   1/0 (1) 2/13 (3)   (56 overs) 140
4/173 (5) 5/223 (6) 6/251 (4)   3/48 (4) 4/55 (2)
7/252 (8) 8/254 (9) 9/279 (7) 10/283 (11)   5/98 (5) 6/119 (6) 7/137 (7)
    8/139 (8) 9/140 (10) 10/140 (11)

Starc 24–4–79–2; Hazlewood 21–8–66–2; Cummins 26–4–60–1; Lyon 34.5–7–67–5. *Second innings*—Starc 17–3–46–3; Hazlewood 11–3–24–2; Cummins 9–0–25–2; Lyon 19–3–39–3.

Umpires: H. D. P. K. Dharmasena and C. B. Gaffaney.   Third umpire: N. J. Llong.
Referee: R. S. Madugalle.

AUSTRALIA v INDIA

Third Test

At Melbourne, December 26–30, 2018. India won by 137 runs. Toss: India. Test debut: M. A. Agarwal.

India won their first Melbourne Test since February 1981 – and more convincingly than the margin implied. In truth, Australia were out of it by the end of the first day, which the Indians finished at a hard-won 215 for two after winning the toss. By doing so, they retained the Border–Gavaskar Trophy retrieved in 2017, and achieved their 150th Test victory.

After the thrills and spills of Perth, the somnolence of the surface, the pace of the game and the extremity of the heat on the first two days suited Kohli's team to a tee. Bumrah then plagued the hosts with nine for 86, his best match figures, and the best by an Indian pace bowler in Australia. It was a triumph also at the selection table, setting previous miscalculations right with bold strokes. With Ravichandran Ashwin still unavailable, Jadeja displaced Umesh Yadav. India also omitted both openers in order to recall Rohit Sharma and whisk new cap Mayank Agarwal from the Ranji Trophy, shuffling Vihari to the top of the order. All the moves paid off: if Vihari made few runs, his survival for more than an hour in the first innings and almost an hour in the second formed a useful bulwark.

Agarwal made an instantly excellent impression, despite having just arrived from representing Karnataka against Gujarat on an outground in Surat. He was compact against pace, and decisive against spin, batting four hours and hitting a daring six off Lyon, before edging Cummins on the stroke of tea. Pujara and Kohli then ground out a 170-run partnership in five hours and 408 deliveries, negotiating a second new ball and eschewing heroics. It was archetypally disciplined Test batting on a pitch where timing was elusive. Two large Indian supporter camps gave them healthy support; several Australian fans had to be expelled for being part of coarse cries of "Show us your visas."

When both fell after lunch on the second day, Pujara for his 17th Test hundred, Australia briefly sensed a way through. But Rohit made a sensible fifty, and with Rahane and Pant prolonged India's innings into the early evening, when Kohli declared with six overs to bowl at a tense Harris and Finch. Australia had struggled all year batting second, and this would be no exception, batsmen used to forcing the pace double- and triple-guessing themselves against an attack focused on the stumps in search of inconsistencies in bounce.

Finch drove heedlessly to short midwicket, Harris hooked awkwardly to fine leg, Head and Mitchell Marsh – recalled in place of Peter Handscomb – went hard at deliveries they might have defended. Khawaja and Shaun Marsh could not stop the slide, Marsh the victim of a cunning slower one from Bumrah that dipped beneath the bat and hit him on the full. It was the last ball before lunch. The pace bowlers were explosive, and Jadeja so quickly through his overs that their advance seemed relentless. The innings' highest score was 22, its best partnership 36, the total of 151 Australia's poorest at Melbourne for eight years. Bumrah finished with a career-best six for 33.

Driving ahead: Cheteshwar Pujara strikes Travis Head on the ankle.

Armed with a lead of 292, but considerate of his bowlers, Kohli did not enforce the follow-on, allowing Australia's seamers to regain a smidgen of initiative by taking five for 16 in ten overs, four to Cummins. On his way to his best Test innings and match figures, he had Pujara and Kohli caught at leg gully for ducks in the same over. Yet India's lead already brooked little argument – if anything, the wickets simply brought Australia's chase closer. Agarwal applied himself for two and a half hours, and Pant played a responsible hand until Kohli declared, setting a target of 399, which was 168 more than any team had made to win in the fourth innings since the advent of drop-in pitches at the MCG.

It was more than enough. The Australians played like defeated men, beginning with Finch, who flailed at his fourth ball and was caught at slip, and continuing with Harris's hard-handed push to short leg. Khawaja looked good until he unsuccessfully reviewed an lbw; Shaun Marsh did the same; brother Mitch slog-swept a six, then spooned to cover; Head was pinned down, and dragged on trying to hit his way out.

As at Adelaide and Perth, the Australian tail rallied, this time around Cummins, who played with patience and sound technique in defence and attack: he followed a slog-sweep for six by stroking down the ground for a single. Paine, Starc and Lyon kept him company, the last helping him through the second new ball, and a final session extended by half an hour, to a career-best 63.

The sight of his handsome drives nourished fantasies of a dramatic final day. In fact, delayed by rain until 12.55, it lasted only 27 balls, Cummins nicking Bumrah to slip, and Lyon edging a Sharma bouncer to Pant, who made his 20th dismissal of the series – all catches – passing the Indian record shared by Naren Tamhane in 1954-55 and Syed Kirmani in 1979-80, both against Pakistan.

Kohli, who joined Sourav Ganguly as India's most successful captain abroad, with 11 wins, saw the result as a rightful reflection of his team's strength: "We always knew that we can do this. Although we are very happy, we are not shocked, we are not very surprised about what has happened."

Man of the Match: J. J. Bumrah.   *Attendance:* 176,539.

Close of play: first day, India 215-2 (Pujara 68, Kohli 47); second day, Australia 8-0 (Harris 5, Finch 3); third day, India 54-5 (Agarwal 28, Pant 6); fourth day, Australia 258-8 (Cummins 61, Lyon 6).

India

G. H. Vihari c Finch b Cummins	8	– c Khawaja b Cummins	13
M. A. Agarwal c Paine b Cummins	76	– b Cummins	42
C. A. Pujara b Cummins	106	– c Harris b Cummins	0
*V. Kohli c Finch b Starc	82	– c Harris b Cummins	0
A. M. Rahane lbw b Lyon	34	– c Paine b Cummins	1
R. G. Sharma not out	63	– c S. E. Marsh b Hazlewood	5
†R. R. Pant c Khawaja b Starc	39	– c Paine b Hazlewood	33
R. A. Jadeja c Paine b Hazlewood	4	– c Khawaja b Cummins	5
Mohammed Shami (did not bat)		– not out	0
B 15, lb 14, w 1, nb 1	31	B 5, lb 1, w 1	7

1/40 (1) 2/123 (2)   (7 wkts dec, 169.4 overs) 443
3/293 (4) 4/299 (3)
5/361 (5) 6/437 (6) 7/443 (8)

1/28 (1)   (8 wkts dec, 37.3 overs) 106
2/28 (3) 3/28 (4)
4/32 (5) 5/44 (6)
6/83 (2) 7/100 (8) 8/106 (7)

I. Sharma and J. J. Bumrah did not bat.

Starc 28–7–87–2; Hazlewood 31.4–10–86–1; Lyon 48–7–110–1; Cummins 34–10–72–3; M. R. Marsh 26–4–51–0; Finch 2–0–8–0. *Second innings*—Starc 3–1–11–0; Hazlewood 10.3–3–22–2; Lyon 13–1–40–0; Cummins 11–3–27–6.

Australia

M. S. Harris c I. Sharma b Bumrah	22	– c Agarwal b Jadeja	13
A. J. Finch c Agarwal b I. Sharma	8	– c Kohli b Bumrah	3
U. T. Khawaja c Agarwal b Jadeja	21	– lbw b Mohammed Shami	33
S. E. Marsh lbw b Bumrah	19	– lbw b Bumrah	44
T. M. Head b Bumrah	20	– b I. Sharma	34
M. R. Marsh c Rahane b Jadeja	9	– c Kohli b Jadeja	10
*†T. D. Paine c Pant b Bumrah	22	– c Pant b Jadeja	26
P. J. Cummins b Mohammed Shami	17	– c Pujara b Bumrah	63
M. A. Starc not out	7	– b Mohammed Shami	18
N. M. Lyon lbw b Bumrah	0	– c Pant b I. Sharma	7
J. R. Hazlewood b Bumrah	0	– not out	0
B 4, w 1, nb 1	6	B 2, lb 6, w 2	10

1/24 (2) 2/36 (1) 3/53 (3)   (66.5 overs) 151
4/89 (4) 5/92 (5) 6/102 (6)
7/138 (8) 8/147 (7) 9/151 (10) 10/151 (11)

1/6 (2) 2/33 (1)   (89.3 overs) 261
3/63 (3) 4/114 (4)
5/135 (6) 6/157 (5) 7/176 (7)
8/215 (9) 9/261 (8) 10/261 (10)

I. Sharma 13–2–41–1; Bumrah 15.5–4–33–6; Jadeja 25–8–45–2; Mohammed Shami 10–2–27–1; Vihari 3–2–1–0. *Second innings*—I. Sharma 14.3–1–40–2; Bumrah 19–3–53–3; Jadeja 32–6–82–3; Mohammed Shami 21–2–71–2; Vihari 3–1–7–0.

Umpires: M. Erasmus and I. J. Gould.   Third umpire: R. A. Kettleborough.
Referee: A. J. Pycroft.

> **"** If Paine had been in the wars beforehand, sporting a cut lip from Cardiff, he must have left Nottingham feeling as if he had gone the distance with Anthony Joshua."
> England v Australia in 2018, page 311

AUSTRALIA v INDIA

Fourth Test

At Sydney, January 3–7, 2019. Drawn. Toss: India.

India defeated Australia at the SCG everywhere but on the scoreboard, rain washing out all bar 25 overs of the last two days, even as the Australians followed on at home for the first time in more than 30 years. Still, the draw confirmed India's first series win in Australia. And, having twice been part of losing teams here, Kohli thought this the proudest moment of his storied career.

For Australia, who had dropped Aaron Finch for apprentice No. 3 and part-time leg-spinner Marnus Labuschagne, and included Handscomb for Mitchell Marsh a match after including Marsh for Handscomb, the game was a gruelling affair, with no consolations to speak of, aside from the rain.

After India won the toss and lost the recalled Rahul, back to replace Rohit Sharma (who had flown home to be at the birth of his first child), the first two days passed as if in a batting dream. Pujara's third hundred of the series was more expressive and less clinical than the other two, involving his facing 373 of 771 deliveries bowled while he was at the crease, and hitting 22 of them for four. Although his pad-first détente with Lyon continued,

INDIA'S HIGHEST TEST PARTNERSHIPS IN AUSTRALIA

Runs	Wkt		
353	4th	S. R. Tendulkar/V. V. S. Laxman at Sydney	2003-04
303	5th	R. Dravid/V. V. S. Laxman at Adelaide	2003-04
262	4th	V. Kohli/A. M. Rahane at Melbourne	2014-15
224	2nd	S. M. Gavaskar/M. Amarnath at Sydney	1985-86
204	**7th**	**R. R. Pant/R. A. Jadeja at Sydney**	**2018-19**
196	5th	S. R. Tendulkar/R. J. Shastri at Sydney	1991-92
193	2nd	S. M. Gavaskar/M. Amarnath at Perth	1977-78
191	1st	S. M. Gavaskar/K. Srikkanth at Sydney	1985-86
188	6th	V. S. Hazare/D. G. Phadkar at Adelaide	1947-48
185	3rd	M. Vijay/V. Kohli at Adelaide	2014-15
175	2nd	R. Dravid/V. V. S. Laxman at Sydney	2007-08
170	**3rd**	**C. A. Pujara/V. Kohli at Melbourne**	**2018-19**

Pujara also used his feet delightfully and decisively. Agarwal confirmed opinions formed in Melbourne, also taking Lyon on, until he holed out to deep mid-off, while Kohli's cameo kicked off with a cover-drive that was probably the shot of the Test.

But Pujara trumped them both for sparkling strokeplay. From his last dozen balls before tea, he plundered 21, including three fours in an over from Labuschagne; in the last session, he zoomed from 61 to 130. With Vihari he added 101, with Pant 89. On the second day, Pujara seemed guaranteed a double-century, until he pushed a tired return catch to Lyon, having brought his series batting time to 31 hours. But there was to be no respite for the hosts, as Pant and Jadeja added 204 in 224 balls, India's highest seventh-wicket partnership against Australia, and the highest Australia had conceded at home. They did it with ease, so neutered were the bowlers by the flat pitch and their flat morale.

Pant went to a second Test hundred, India's fifth of the series, and finished with an unbeaten 159 – among visiting wicketkeepers, only South Africa's A. B. de Villiers, with 169 at the WACA in 2012-13, had made more in a Test. Jadeja did as he pleased before he was bowled by Lyon for 81. Not often have an Australian attack looked so devoid of ideas and hope: an over from Khawaja could hardly have reached the other end more slowly had it been sent in the post.

Kohli's declaration ten overs from time made his hunger for victory clear, even if Pant marred his day by missing Khawaja before he had scored. With Harris playing some crisp and confident shots, and Labuschagne battling alongside him, at lunch on the third day the Australians looked reasonably fortified at 122 for one. But when Harris dragged on against Jadeja, he was the first of eight wickets to fall for 130 in 48 overs. Only Handscomb and Cummins for the seventh wicket, and Starc and Hazlewood for the last, delayed the Indians long, as the left-arm wrist-spinner Kuldeep Yadav, included for Ishant Sharma, threw the ball up gamely and took a rare first-innings five-for.

Shaun Marsh nicking meekly to slip somehow summed up the season's batting travails: tame, confused, exasperating. Had Vihari at mid-on held a slog from Hazlewood, the follow-on would have been enforced an hour earlier. As it was, Australia's second in-

INDIA'S HIGHEST TEST TOTALS AGAINST AUSTRALIA

705-7 dec	Sydney	2003-04	532	Sydney	2007-08
657-7 dec	Kolkata	2000-01	526	Adelaide	2007-08
633-5 dec	Kolkata	1997-98	523	Adelaide	2003-04
622-7 dec	**Sydney**	**2018-19**	520	Adelaide	1985-86
613-7 dec	Delhi	2008-09	517-5 dec	Bombay	1986-87
603-9 dec	Ranchi	2016-17	510-7 dec	Delhi	1979-80
600-4 dec	Sydney	1985-86	503	Hyderabad	2012-13
572	Chennai	2012-13	501	Chennai	2000-01

nings had barely begun when the umpires judged the light unfit; on the final day, rain and darkness rivalled one another to disrupt play, eventually declared a non-starter at 2.30.

Those who sacrificed a gold coin to enter the ground, most of them Indians, at least enjoyed the presentation ceremony, and Kohli sounding ominously sure of his team's confidence: "I don't say it in an arrogant way, but I am saying the truth when I say that we have so much belief in ourselves that we can beat anyone, anywhere."

Paine, describing the result as "really hard to take", sounded like his name: "We are really disappointed. We know we had some guys missing, but we honestly felt coming into the series that, in Australia in particular, we could beat India. But, throughout the series, more often than not, when those big moments came up, Virat has scored runs, Pujara has scored runs, Bumrah has bowled a great spell, and we couldn't quite get through those moments."

Man of the Match: C. A. Pujara.   *Attendance:* 125,905.

Man of the Series: C. A. Pujara.

Close of play: first day, India 303-4 (Pujara 130, Vihari 39); second day, Australia 24-0 (Harris 19, Khawaja 5); third day, Australia 236-6 (Handscomb 28, Cummins 25); fourth day, Australia 6-0 (Khawaja 4, Harris 2).

India

M. A. Agarwal c Starc b Lyon	77	R. A. Jadeja b Lyon	81
K. L. Rahul c Marsh b Hazlewood	9		
C. A. Pujara c and b Lyon	193	B 2, lb 13, w 5	20
*V. Kohli c Paine b Hazlewood	23		
A. M. Rahane c Paine b Starc	18	1/10 (2) (7 wkts dec, 167.2 overs)	622
G. H. Vihari c Labuschagne b Lyon	42	2/126 (1) 3/180 (4)	
†R. R. Pant not out	159	4/228 (5) 5/329 (6) 6/418 (3) 7/622 (8)	

K. Yadav, Mohammed Shami and J. J. Bumrah did not bat.

Starc 26–0–123–1; Hazlewood 35–11–105–2; Cummins 28–5–101–0; Lyon 57.2–8–178–4; Labuschagne 16–0–76–0; Head 4–0–20–0; Khawaja 1–0–4–0.

Australia

M. S. Harris b Jadeja	79	– (2) not out	2
U. T. Khawaja c Pujara b Yadav	27	– (1) not out	4
M. Labuschagne c Rahane b Mohammed Shami	38		
S. E. Marsh c Rahane b Jadeja	8		
T. M. Head c and b Yadav	20		
P. S. P. Handscomb b Bumrah	37		
*†T. D. Paine b Yadav	5		
P. J. Cummins b Mohammed Shami	25		
M. A. Starc not out	29		
N. M. Lyon lbw b Yadav	0		
J. R. Hazlewood lbw b Yadav	21		
B 4, lb 2, w 5	11		

1/72 (2) 2/128 (1) 3/144 (4)   (104.5 overs) 300   (no wkt, 4 overs)   6
4/152 (3) 5/192 (5) 6/198 (7)
7/236 (8) 8/257 (6) 9/258 (10) 10/300 (11)

Mohammed Shami 19–2–58–2; Bumrah 21–5–62–1; Jadeja 32–11–73–2; Yadav 31.5–6–99–5; Vihari 1–0–2–0. *Second innings*—Mohammed Shami 2–1–4–0; Bumrah 2–1–2–0.

Umpires: I. J. Gould and R. A. Kettleborough.   Third umpire: M. Erasmus.
Referee: A. J. Pycroft.

ONE-DAY INTERNATIONAL REPORTS BY ANDREW McGLASHAN

AUSTRALIA v INDIA

First One-Day International

At Sydney, January 12, 2019 (day/night). Australia won by 34 runs. Toss: Australia. One-day international debut: J. P. Behrendorff.

An incisive new-ball burst for Australia's inexperienced opening attack paved the way for victory, as Jason Behrendorff, making his ODI debut, and Jhye Richardson, in his fifth match, reduced India to four for three. Despite Sharma's defiant 133 from 129 balls, that proved too big a hurdle to overcome. Richardson's opening spell of 4–2–6–2 was especially eye-catching, both his wickets coming in his second over before he had conceded a run: Kohli caught at square leg – a juggling effort by Stoinis – and Rayudu beaten for pace. India had four sixes, three to Sharma, before they managed their first four, in the 21st over, as Sharma and Dhoni resurrected the chase with a stand of 137 in 28 overs. Dhoni soaked up 63 dot balls out of 96, but India remained in the game until he was lbw to Behrendorff, though replays showed the delivery had pitched outside leg stump; Rayudu had used up India's review. Sharma ploughed on to the fifth ODI century in his last 13 innings in Australia (there was also a 99), but with his dismissal – caught at deep midwicket – went India's last hope. Australia's innings had been workmanlike from their new-look middle order. Khawaja marked his first ODI for two years with 59, while Shaun Marsh moved on from his Test axing with 54; they added 92 for the third wicket. However, it was Handscomb, back in the one-day fold after an absence of 15 months, who shone, with 73 in 61. He and Stoinis helped manufacture 93 in the final ten overs in what proved a match-winning stand. Rayudu, who bowls off-breaks, was reported for a suspect action, and banned after failing to submit to a test within the required fortnight.

Man of the Match: J. A. Richardson.   *Attendance:* 37,556.

Australia

†A. T. Carey c Sharma b Yadav	24		G. J. Maxwell not out	11
*A. J. Finch b Bhuvneshwar Kumar	6			
U. T. Khawaja lbw b Jadeja	59		B 4, lb 2, w 6, nb 2	14
S. E. Marsh c Mohammed Shami b Yadav	54			
P. S. P. Handscomb c Dhawan			1/8 (2) 2/41 (1) (5 wkts, 50 overs) 288	
b Bhuvneshwar Kumar	73		3/133 (3) 4/186 (4)	
M. P. Stoinis not out	47		5/254 (5) 10 overs: 41-2	

J. A. Richardson, N. M. Lyon, P. M. Siddle and J. P. Behrendorff did not bat.

Bhuvneshwar Kumar 10–0–66–2; Ahmed 8–0–55–0; Mohammed Shami 10–0–46–0; Yadav 10–0–54–2; Jadeja 10–0–48–1; Rayudu 2–0–13–0.

India

R. G. Sharma c Maxwell b Stoinis	133	K. Yadav c Khawaja b Siddle	3
S. Dhawan lbw b Behrendorff	0	Mohammed Shami c Maxwell b Stoinis	1
*V. Kohli c Stoinis b Richardson	3	Lb 7, w 6, nb 1	14
A. T. Rayudu lbw b Richardson	0		
†M. S. Dhoni lbw b Behrendorff	51	(9 wkts, 50 overs)	254
K. D. Karthik b Richardson	12		
R. A. Jadeja c Marsh b Richardson	8		
Bhuvneshwar Kumar not out	29		

K. K. Ahmed did not bat.

1/1 (2) 2/4 (3) 3/4 (4) 4/141 (5) 5/176 (6) 6/213 (7) 7/221 (1) 8/247 (9) 9/254 (10)   10 overs: 21-3

Behrendorff 10–2–39–2; Richardson 10–2–26–4; Siddle 8–0–48–1; Lyon 10–1–50–0; Stoinis 10–0–66–2; Maxwell 2–0–18–0.

Umpires: M. A. Gough and P. Wilson.   Third umpire: R. A. Kettleborough.
Referee: A. J. Pycroft.

AUSTRALIA v INDIA

Second One-Day International

At Adelaide, January 15, 2019 (day/night). India won by six wickets. Toss: Australia. One-day international debut: M. Siraj.

On a sweltering day, with temperatures in the middle hitting the mid-40s, Marsh and Kohli traded exceptional hundreds. But it was Kohli who emerged victorious, as India's middle order – with Dhoni to the fore – secured victory with four balls to spare, and set up a decider at the MCG. Unlike at Sydney, India had made a solid start to their chase, and felt in charge throughout. Kohli compiled his 39th ODI hundred – his first fifty coming from 66 balls, his second from 42 – though he wasn't around to finish the job, caught at deep midwicket with 57 needed off 38. Dhoni was battling fatigue caused by the heat, but Karthik played a gem of an innings, and the pair scampered hard to keep the rate under control. Dhoni's second six (and second boundary), off the first ball of the last over, brought the scores level. Marsh's hundred, his fourth in eight ODIs (after none since September 2013), had been the centrepiece for Australia after another poor powerplay. Khawaja was run out by a brilliant direct hit from Jadeja, swooping at point, but Maxwell joined Marsh in a sixth-wicket stand of 94 off 65 balls. Marsh launched three sixes in six deliveries, and a total of 320 appeared possible, but both he and Maxwell fell in the 48th over to Bhuvneshwar Kumar, who finished with his best ODI figures in Australia.

Man of the Match: V. Kohli.   *Attendance:* 22,454.

Australia

†A. T. Carey c Dhawan b Mohammed Shami	18	N. M. Lyon not out	12
*A. J. Finch b Bhuvneshwar Kumar	6	P. M. Siddle c Kohli b Bhuvneshwar Kumar	0
U. T. Khawaja run out (Jadeja)	21	J. P. Behrendorff not out	1
S. E. Marsh c Jadeja b Bhuvneshwar Kumar	131		
P. S. P. Handscomb st Dhoni b Jadeja	20	Lb 4, w 6	10
M. P. Stoinis c Dhoni b Mohammed Shami	29		
G. J. Maxwell c Karthik b Bhuvneshwar Kumar	48	(9 wkts, 50 overs)	298
J. A. Richardson c Dhawan b Mohammed Shami	2		

1/20 (2) 2/26 (1) 3/82 (3) 4/134 (5) 5/189 (6) 6/283 (7) 7/283 (4) 8/286 (8) 9/286 (10)   10 overs: 38-2

Bhuvneshwar Kumar 10–0–45–4; Mohammed Shami 10–0–58–3; Siraj 10–0–76–0; Yadav 10–0–66–0; Jadeja 10–1–49–1.

India

R. G. Sharma c Handscomb b Stoinis	43	K. D. Karthik not out	25
S. Dhawan c Khawaja b Behrendorff	32	Lb 9, w 7	16
*V. Kohli c Maxwell b Richardson	104		
A. T. Rayudu c Stoinis b Maxwell	24	1/47 (2) 2/101 (1) (4 wkts, 49.2 overs)	299
†M. S. Dhoni not out	55	3/160 (4) 4/242 (3)	
		10 overs: 53-1	

R. A. Jadeja, Bhuvneshwar Kumar, K. Yadav, Mohammed Shami and M. Siraj did not bat.

Behrendorff 8.2–1–52–1; Richardson 10–0–59–1; Siddle 8–0–58–0; Lyon 10–0–59–0; Stoinis 9–0–46–1; Maxwell 4–0–16–1.

Umpires: R. A. Kettleborough and S. J. Nogajski.   Third umpire: M. A. Gough.
Referee: A. J. Pycroft.

AUSTRALIA v INDIA

Third One-Day International

At Melbourne, January 18, 2019 (day/night). India won by seven wickets. Toss: India. One-day international debut: V. Shankar.

Dhoni completed a series full of personal triumph, taking India to victory with an unbeaten 87, characteristically rounded off in the final over. On a sluggish pitch which made scoring difficult, the tourists had to work hard, but leg-spinner Chahal's career-best six for 42, in his first international in Australia, had given them the breathing space of a moderate target. Bhuvneshwar Kumar again set the tone, removing Finch cheaply for the third time in the series, but it was Chahal who derailed the innings. His second delivery had the in-form Marsh stumped off a leg-side wide, and three balls later

---

BEST ODI BOWLING FIGURES IN AUSTRALIA

6-42	A. B. Agarkar	India v Australia at Melbourne	2003-04
6-42	**Y. S. Chahal**	**India v Australia at Melbourne**	**2018-19**
6-43	M. A. Starc	Australia v India at Melbourne	2014-15
6-45	C. R. Woakes	England v Australia at Brisbane	2010-11
5-15	G. S. Chappell	Australia v India at Sydney	1980-81
5-15	R. J. Shastri	India v Australia at Perth	1991-92
5-16	C. G. Rackemann	Australia v Pakistan at Adelaide	1983-84
5-17	C. E. L. Ambrose	West Indies v Australia at Melbourne	1988-89
5-19	A. J. Bichel	Australia v South Africa at Sydney	2001-02
5-19	R. J. Harris	Australia v Pakistan at Perth	2009-10

---

he claimed a leading edge off Khawaja; Stoinis soon followed, caught at slip. Then, after Handscomb's second fifty of the series, Chahal returned to remove him and two others. Australia bowled well, but needed everything to run for them. Instead they missed numerous chances. Kohli was dropped on ten by Handscomb at slip off Stanlake, and Dhoni given a life first ball when Maxwell shelled a routine catch at point off Stoinis. Richardson claimed Kohli for the third innings in a row, but Jadhav, in his first game of the series, timed the ball sweetly in a 52-ball half-century. Dhoni was content for the asking-rate to touch nine, although there could have been a twist had he been held by Finch at mid-off, again off Stoinis, with 27 needed off 18 balls.

Man of the Match: Y. S. Chahal.   *Attendance:* 53,603.
Man of the Series: M. S. Dhoni.

Australia

†A. T. Carey c Kohli b Bhuvneshwar Kumar   5
*A. J. Finch lbw b Bhuvneshwar Kumar. . . .   14
U. T. Khawaja c and b Chahal.   34
S. E. Marsh st Dhoni b Chahal   39
P. S. P. Handscomb lbw b Chahal.   58
M. P. Stoinis c Sharma b Chahal.   10
G. J. Maxwell c Bhuvneshwar Kumar
                              b Mohammed Shami.   26
J. A. Richardson c Jadhav b Chahal   16

A. Zampa c Shankar b Chahal.   8
P. M. Siddle not out.   10
B. Stanlake b Mohammed Shami   0
          Lb 2, w 8   10

1/8 (1) 2/27 (2) 3/100 (4)   (48.4 overs) 230
4/101 (3) 5/123 (6) 6/161 (7)
7/206 (8) 8/219 (5) 9/228 (9)
10/230 (11)   10 overs: 30-2

Bhuvneshwar Kumar 8–1–28–2; Mohammed Shami 9.4–0–47–2; Shankar 6–0–23–0; Jadhav 6–0–35–0; Jadeja 9–0–53–0; Chahal 10–0–42–6.

India

R. G. Sharma c Marsh b Siddle   9
S. Dhawan c and b Stoinis.   23
*V. Kohli c Carey b Richardson   46
†M. S. Dhoni not out   87
K. M. Jadhav not out.   61
          Lb 1, w 7   8

1/15 (1) 2/59 (2)   (3 wkts, 49.2 overs) 234
3/113 (3)   10 overs: 26-1

K. D. Karthik, R. A. Jadeja, V. Shankar, Bhuvneshwar Kumar, Y. S. Chahal and Mohammed Shami did not bat.

Richardson 10–1–27–1; Siddle 9–1–56–1; Stanlake 10–0–49–0; Maxwell 1–0–7–0; Zampa 10–0–34–0; Stoinis 9.2–0–60–1.

Umpires: M. A. Gough and P. Wilson.   Third umpire: R. A. Kettleborough.
Referee: A. J. Pycroft.

DOMESTIC CRICKET IN AUSTRALIA IN 2017-18

PETER ENGLISH

Each season, Australia's traditional domestic game is pushed further towards the fringes. In 2016-17, the Sheffield Shield concluded in Alice Springs; a year later, the Australian football season squeezed it on to Brisbane's suburban Allan Border Field, where entry was by gold-coin (charity) donation. Despite the excellent value, only a sprinkling of supporters watched **Queensland** beating Tasmania to claim their eighth title, and first in six years.

Their success was a stunning return on the renovation undertaken by Wade Seccombe, the new coach, and Jimmy Peirson, who led the team once Usman Khawaja left for the Ashes. They headed the Shield table without many A-list performers; apart from Khawaja, only openers Matt Renshaw and Joe Burns had Test experience. In a difficult season for batsmen, Renshaw was the Shield's leading run-scorer with 804, including three centuries in consecutive games (concussion forced him out during the next match). But the team stood tall, with Burns, Marnus Labuschagne, Charlie Hemphrey (formerly of Kent, Derbyshire and Essex Second XIs) and Jack Wildermuth enjoying more than 500 runs apiece; Michael Neser, Luke Feldman and leg-spinner Mitchell Swepson passed 30 wickets, closely trailed by Wildermuth and newcomer Brendan Doggett.

Tasmania had a hit-and-miss campaign. After an unremarkable one-day tournament, they collapsed for 63 to lose the opening Shield game to Western Australia. But they recovered through the emergence of Jake Doran, who made 756 runs in his third season, and Matthew Wade, who scored three centuries in his debut summer for his native state after a decade with Victoria. Seamers Jackson Bird and Tom Rogers managed 37 wickets apiece, and a strong finish saw them reach the Shield final.

Their last-round win over **Victoria** ended the reigning champions' hopes of a fourth successive title. The old and the new were on show, with Glenn Maxwell powering to 278, Victoria's seventh-highest Shield score, against New South Wales, while 20-year-old Will Pucovski reached 188, his maiden century, against Queensland at the MCG. Marcus Harris and Cameron White also passed 500 runs. Chris Tremain was the Shield's leading wicket-taker with 51 at 21; he peaked with a ten-wicket haul in Perth, including a career-best seven for 82, and was named Sheffield Shield Player of the Year.

Western Australia won the one-day JLT Cup in October. In the final, captain Mitchell Marsh's unbeaten 80 guided a comfortable chase against South Australia, and his older brother Shaun was named Man of the Tournament for his 412 runs at 82. The Shield team often missed the Marshes and Cameron Bancroft, and were dismissed for 93 by Queensland in the penultimate round, when all three were touring South Africa with Australia. The coach, Justin Langer, took over the national side in May, after Darren Lehmann resigned at the end of that controversial Test series; Adam Voges succeeded Langer in Perth.

The loudest noise **New South Wales** made came when Nathan Lyon's burnt toast stopped play in Brisbane. With a fire alarm blaring, tea was taken early on the third day until the emergency services arrived. The attack was led by Trent Copeland's accurate seamers, but Mitchell Starc, playing a couple of games ahead of the Ashes, became the first player to take two hat-tricks in a Shield match, against Western Australia at Hurstville Oval. He was the eighth to achieve the feat in all first-class cricket, but the first to claim the last three wickets of both innings. Steve O'Keefe, suspended throughout the one-day competition for drunken off-field behaviour in April, took a career-best eight for 77 against Victoria at the Junction Oval.

After making the previous two Shield finals, **South Australia** were back at the bottom of the table. Their brightest lights were Callum Ferguson, Jake Weatherald and Travis Head, who each passed 700 runs. They were the only team beaten by the **Cricket Australia XI**, playing their third season in the one-day competition before being dropped for 2018-19.

FIRST-CLASS AVERAGES IN 2017-18

BATTING (550 runs)

		M	I	NO	R	HS	100	Avge	Ct/St
1	S. P. D. Smith (*New South Wales/Australia*)	8	13	2	955	239	4	86.81	17
2	†U. T. Khawaja (*Queensland/Australia*) ...	8	13	2	679	171	2	61.72	5
3	J. A. Burns (*Queensland*)	7	14	1	725	202*	2	55.76	6
4	*S. E. Marsh (*Western Australia/Australia*)	9	15	1	749	156	1	53.50	3
5	M. R. Marsh (*Western Australia/Australia*)	9	16	2	744	181	3	53.14	7
6	C. L. White (*Victoria*)	7	12	1	574	149	1	52.18	11
7	C. T. Bancroft (*W Australia/Australia*) ...	9	16	3	672	228*	1	51.69	13
8	G. J. Maxwell (*Victoria*)	8	15	1	707	278	1	50.50	6
9	C. J. Ferguson (*South Australia*)	9	18	2	780	182*	1	48.75	12
10	†D. A. Warner (*New South Wales/Australia*)	8	14	1	629	103	1	48.38	2
11	†D. J. Malan (*England*)	7	12	0	560	140	2	46.66	7
12	†T. M. Head (*South Australia*)	8	16	0	738	145	2	46.12	5
13	*M. T. Renshaw (*Queensland*)	11	21	3	804	170	3	44.66	7
14	†J. R. Doran (*Tasmania*)	11	17	0	756	114	1	44.47	12
15	C. R. Hemphrey (*Queensland*)	8	15	2	568	103*	1	43.69	10
16	*M. S. Wade (*Tasmania*)	11	17	2	654	139	3	43.60	37
17	*M. S. Harris (*Victoria*)	10	18	1	706	109	2	41.52	3
18	†D. P. Hughes (*New South Wales*)	10	19	3	661	98*	0	41.31	6
19	J. C. Silk (*Tasmania*)	8	15	1	566	104	1	40.42	6
20	M. Labuschagne (*Queensland*)	11	22	2	795	134	2	39.75	9
21	†J. B. Weatherald (*South Australia*)	10	20	0	765	152	2	38.25	10
22	†K. R. Patterson (*New South Wales*)	10	19	1	672	89	0	37.33	5
23	A. J. Turner (*Western Australia*)	10	19	1	650	101*	1	36.11	12
24	J. D. Wildermuth (*Queensland*)	11	18	2	551	95	0	34.43	2
25	G. J. Bailey (*Tasmania*)	11	18	0	602	106	1	33.44	10
26	A. J. Doolan (*Tasmania*)	11	20	3	555	247*	1	32.64	15
27	H. W. R. Cartwright (*Western Australia*) ..	10	20	1	617	111*	1	32.47	4

BOWLING (24 wickets)

		Style	O	M	R	W	BB	5I	Avge
1	T. S. Rogers (*Tasmania*)	RFM	213.4	42	679	37	4-9	0	18.35
2	M. A. Starc (*NSW/Australia*)	LF	235.2	46	734	39	8-73	2	18.82
3	N. P. Winter (*South Australia*)	LFM	220.3	41	670	34	5-48	4	19.70
4	G. T. Bell (*Tasmania*)	RM	167	39	475	24	4-38	0	19.79
5	C. P. Tremain (*Victoria*)	RFM	349.4	83	1,075	51	7-82	2	21.07
6	M. G. Neser (*Queensland*)	RFM	278	69	852	39	6-57	1	21.84
7	M. L. Kelly (*Western Australia*)	RFM	178.1	51	530	24	5-60	1	22.08
8	L. W. Feldman (*Queensland*)	RFM	261.2	64	761	34	6-32	2	22.38
9	J. R. Hazlewood (*NSW/Australia*)	RFM	223.5	58	617	27	5-48	1	22.85
10	J. M. Bird (*Tasmania/Australia*)	RFM	311.5	71	916	37	5-30	1	24.75
11	T. A. Copeland (*New South Wales*)	RFM	344	89	863	34	6-24	3	25.38
12	P. J. Cummins (*NSW/Australia*)	RF	262.1	61	743	29	4-39	0	25.62
13	N. M. Lyon (*NSW/Australia*)	OB	358.4	79	897	34	4-60	0	26.38
14	S. M. Boland (*Victoria*)	RFM	367.4	99	1,023	38	4-41	0	26.92
15	B. J. Doggett (*Queensland*)	RFM	216.1	42	776	28	5-77	2	27.71
16	J. D. Wildermuth (*Queensland*)	RFM	238.2	55	808	29	4-25	0	27.86
17	D. J. Worrall (*South Australia*)	RFM	316.5	72	973	34	5-72	1	28.61
18	S. L. Rainbird (*Tasmania*)	LFM	337.5	66	1,131	35	3-47	0	32.31
19	J. M. Mennie (*South Australia*)	RFM	344.1	69	1,017	30	4-39	0	33.90
20	S. P. Mackin (*Western Australia*)	RFM	279	50	990	28	6-43	1	35.35
21	M. J. Swepson (*Queensland*)	LB	296.1	21	1,183	32	5-142	1	36.96
22	Fawad Ahmed (*Victoria*)	LB	283.1	33	1,019	27	5-94	1	37.74
23	P. M. Siddle (*Victoria*)	RFM	317.4	81	952	24	3-21	0	39.66

SHEFFIELD SHIELD IN 2017-18

	P	W	L	D	Bonus pts Bat	Bowl	Pts
QUEENSLAND	10	6	1	3	7.40	8.6	55.00
TASMANIA	10	5	3	2	5.85	9.7	47.55
Victoria	10	3	2	5	8.11	8.8	39.91
Western Australia	10	3	5	2	8.19	8.9	37.09
New South Wales	10	3	5	2	6.47	7.9	34.37
South Australia	10	2	6	2	7.04	8.0	29.04

Outright win = 6pts; draw = 1pt. Bonus points awarded for the first 100 overs of each team's first innings: 0.01 batting points for every run over the first 200; 0.5 bowling points for the fifth wicket taken and for every subsequent two.

FINAL

QUEENSLAND v TASMANIA

At Brisbane (Allan Border Field), March 23–27, 2018. Queensland won by nine wickets. Toss: Tasmania.

The wet season and a roll-of-the-dice declaration delivered Queensland a surprise outright victory, though the destination of the Shield was rarely in doubt. On a ground draining like a sink full of porridge, the first day was abandoned, leaving Tasmania behind from the start in their quest to force a win. Wicketkeeper Matthew Wade held their innings together with a gritty century, until he became part of the second five-wicket haul of Brendan Doggett's career, but a total of 477 was not large enough to cause any panic. Queensland's patient batsmen, guided by seventies from Charlie Hemphrey and Jack Wildermuth, all reached double figures to establish a 39-run buffer late on the fourth day. More bad weather forced Alex Doolan and Jordan Silk to channel their Twenty20 technique, sending all fielders to the boundary as they desperately tried to set a challenging target. But a four-hour rain break forced Tasmania to declare only 127 ahead, with a minimum of 32 overs remaining. Matt Renshaw, just recalled by Australia to join their traumatic South African tour, muscled 12 fours and two sixes on the way to his first Shield title.

Man of the Match: M. S. Wade.

Close of play: first day, no play; second day, Tasmania 360-6 (Wade 92, Rogers 28); third day, Queensland 233-3 (Hemphrey 48, Heazlett 37); fourth day, Tasmania 10-0 (Silk 5, Doolan 5).

Tasmania

J. C. Silk c Feldman b Doggett	76	– c Swepson b Wildermuth	74
A. J. Doolan c Renshaw b Neser	2	– not out	82
B. J. Webster c Peirson b Wildermuth	10	– not out	3
J. R. Doran c Peirson b Doggett	34		
*G. J. Bailey run out (Neser)	51		
†M. S. Wade c Peirson b Doggett	108		
S. A. Milenko c Swepson b Doggett	50		
T. S. Rogers c Heazlett b Neser	28		
S. L. Rainbird b Feldman	57		
J. M. Bird c Neser b Doggett	13		
A. L. Fekete not out	25		
B 4, lb 14, w 2, nb 3	23	B 4, lb 3	7

1/7 (2) 2/65 (3) 3/120 (1)   (138.2 overs) 477   1/160 (1)   (1 wkt dec, 26 overs) 166
4/141 (4) 5/221 (5) 6/305 (7)
7/360 (8) 8/384 (6) 9/420 (10) 10/477 (9)

Neser 28–6–89–2; Feldman 26.2–9–78–1; Doggett 31–4–101–5; Wildermuth 23–5–99–1; Swepson 23–1–83–0; Renshaw 3–0–4–0; Labuschagne 3–1–2–0; Heazlett 1–0–3–0. *Second innings*—Neser 7–2–34–0; Feldman 8–1–31–0; Wildermuth 6–0–54–1; Doggett 4–0–34–0; Swepson 1–0–6–0.

Queensland

M. T. Renshaw c Wade b Bird	37	– not out	81
J. A. Burns lbw b Rogers	49	– c Bailey b Webster	41
M. Labuschagne b Rogers	32	– not out	5
C. R. Hemphrey c Wade b Bird	77		
S. D. Heazlett c Wade b Fekete	43		
J. D. Wildermuth c and b Milenko	73		
*†J. J. Peirson b Milenko	48		
M. G. Neser c Milenko b Webster	58		
M. J. Swepson c Wade b Webster	27		
B. J. Doggett b Webster	15		
L. W. Feldman not out	11		
B 15, lb 13, w 3, nb 15	46	Lb 1	1

1/59 (1) 2/128 (2) 3/133 (3)   (148.3 overs) 516   1/106 (2)   (1 wkt, 22.5 overs) 128
4/247 (5) 5/308 (4) 6/362 (6)
7/462 (8) 8/466 (7) 9/499 (10) 10/516 (9)

Bird 25–7–77–2; Fekete 27–2–81–1; Rainbird 27–3–117–0; Rogers 23–3–61–2; Milenko 21–4–69–2; Webster 25.3–4–83–3. *Second innings*—Bird 4–0–20–0; Fekete 6–0–21–0; Rainbird 4.5–0–37–0; Rogers 3–0–13–0; Milenko 3–0–27–0; Webster 2–0–7–1.

Umpires: G. A. Abood and S. J. Nogajski.   Third umpire: P. J. Gillespie.
Referee: P. L. Marshall.

SHEFFIELD SHIELD WINNERS

1892-93	Victoria	1928-29	New South Wales	1966-67	Victoria
1893-94	South Australia	1929-30	Victoria	1967-68	Western Australia
1894-95	Victoria	1930-31	Victoria	1968-69	South Australia
1895-96	New South Wales	1931-32	New South Wales	1969-70	Victoria
1896-97	New South Wales	1932-33	New South Wales	1970-71	South Australia
1897-98	Victoria	1933-34	Victoria	1971-72	Western Australia
1898-99	Victoria	1934-35	Victoria	1972-73	Western Australia
1899-1900	New South Wales	1935-36	South Australia	1973-74	Victoria
1900-01	Victoria	1936-37	Victoria	1974-75	Western Australia
1901-02	New South Wales	1937-38	New South Wales	1975-76	South Australia
1902-03	New South Wales	1938-39	South Australia	1976-77	Western Australia
1903-04	New South Wales	1939-40	New South Wales	1977-78	Western Australia
1904-05	New South Wales	1940–46	*No competition*	1978-79	Victoria
1905-06	New South Wales	1946-47	Victoria	1979-80	Victoria
1906-07	New South Wales	1947-48	Western Australia	1980-81	Western Australia
1907-08	Victoria	1948-49	New South Wales	1981-82	South Australia
1908-09	New South Wales	1949-50	New South Wales	1982-83	New South Wales*
1909-10	South Australia	1950-51	Victoria	1983-84	Western Australia
1910-11	New South Wales	1951-52	New South Wales	1984-85	New South Wales
1911-12	New South Wales	1952-53	South Australia	1985-86	New South Wales
1912-13	South Australia	1953-54	New South Wales	1986-87	Western Australia
1913-14	New South Wales	1954-55	New South Wales	1987-88	Western Australia
1914-15	Victoria	1955-56	New South Wales	1988-89	Western Australia
1915-19	*No competition*	1956-57	New South Wales	1989-90	New South Wales
1919-20	New South Wales	1957-58	New South Wales	1990-91	Victoria
1920-21	New South Wales	1958-59	New South Wales	1991-92	Western Australia
1921-22	Victoria	1959-60	New South Wales	1992-93	New South Wales
1922-23	New South Wales	1960-61	New South Wales	1993-94	New South Wales
1923-24	Victoria	1961-62	New South Wales	1994-95	Queensland
1924-25	Victoria	1962-63	Victoria	1995-96	South Australia
1925-26	New South Wales	1963-64	South Australia	1996-97	Queensland*
1926-27	South Australia	1964-65	New South Wales	1997-98	Western Australia
1927-28	Victoria	1965-66	New South Wales	1998-99	Western Australia*

1999-2000	Queensland	2006-07	Tasmania	2013-14	New South Wales
2000-01	Queensland	2007-08	New South Wales	2014-15	Victoria
2001-02	Queensland	2008-09	Victoria	2015-16	Victoria*
2002-03	New South Wales*	2009-10	Victoria	2016-17	Victoria
2003-04	Victoria	2010-11	Tasmania	2017-18	Queensland
2004-05	New South Wales*	2011-12	Queensland		
2005-06	Queensland	2012-13	Tasmania		

New South Wales have won the title 46 times, Victoria 31, Western Australia 15, South Australia 13, Queensland 8, Tasmania 3.

The tournament was known as the Pura Milk Cup in 1999-2000, and the Pura Cup from 2000-01 to 2007-08.

* *Second in table but won final. Finals were introduced in 1982-83.*

JLT ONE-DAY CUP IN 2017-18

50-over league plus play-off and final

	P	W	L	Bonus	Pts	NRR
WESTERN AUSTRALIA.............	6	5	1	2	22	0.88
SOUTH AUSTRALIA................	6	4	2	1	17	−0.01
VICTORIA	6	3	3	3	15	0.55
New South Wales....................	6	3	3	2	14	0.41
Queensland..........................	6	3	3	1	13	0.01
Tasmania	6	2	4	2	10	−0.42
Cricket Australia XI.................	6	1	5	0	4	−1.31

Win = 4pts; 1 bonus pt awarded for achieving victory with a run-rate 1.25 times that of the opposition, and 2 bonus pts for victory with a run-rate twice that of the opposition.

Play-off   At Hobart, October 19, 2017 (day/night). **South Australia won by 176 runs** (DLS). **South Australia 339-5** (48 overs) (J. B. Weatherald 116); ‡**Victoria 168** (35.5 overs) (D. J. Worrall 5-62). *Alex Carey (92) and Jake Weatherald put on 212 in 36 overs for South Australia's first wicket. After their innings was reduced to 48 overs, Victoria's target was increased to 345. Dan Worrall removed their openers cheaply and returned to run through the lower order.*

Final   At Hobart, October 21, 2017 (day/night). **Western Australia won by six wickets.** ‡**South Australia 248-9** (50 overs); **Western Australia 250-4** (43.4 overs). *Western Australia won their 13th List A title, an Australian record. Cameron Bancroft (76) and captain Mitchell Marsh (80*) put on 126 for their third wicket to set up victory with more than six overs to spare.*

The KFC T20 Big Bash League has its own section (page 1129).

BANGLADESH CRICKET IN 2018

The final frontier

UTPAL SHUVRO

It was a year of missed opportunities for Bangladesh. At the end of it, there was no end to the wait for a first international trophy. Three finals were reached, but all were lost, two in heartbreaking fashion. While Bangladesh remained a significant force in one-day internationals, their Test results fluctuated wildly; in Twenty20, one step forward was usually followed by two back.

But the overall picture was positive – 21 victories across all formats was a record – and the women's team succeeded where the men had failed, winning a tournament. And a new era was launched in June, when former England wicketkeeper Steve Rhodes was appointed as the men's coach, after a search that had lasted seven months.

At the start of 2018, the headlines were being made by his predecessor. Two months after stepping down, Chandika Hathurusinghe returned in January as the coach of Sri Lanka, for a tri-series also involving Zimbabwe, followed by two Tests and two Twenty20 internationals. Bangladesh were under the interim

BANGLADESH IN 2018

	Played	Won	Lost	Drawn/No result
Tests	8	3	4	1
One-day internationals	20	13	7	–
Twenty20 internationals	16	5	11	–

JANUARY	ODI tri-series (h) v Sri Lanka and Zimbabwe	(page 849)
FEBRUARY	2 Tests and 2 T20Is (h) v Sri Lanka	(page 852)
MARCH	T20 tri-series (in Sri Lanka) v India and Sri Lanka	(page 1026)
APRIL		
MAY	3 T20Is (in India) v Afghanistan	(page 805)
JUNE		
JULY	2 Tests, 3 ODIs and 3 T20Is (in the WI and the USA) v West Indies	(page 1053)
AUGUST		
SEPTEMBER	Asia Cup (in the UAE)	(page 1110)
OCTOBER	2 Tests and 3 ODIs (h) v Zimbabwe	(page 857)
NOVEMBER		
DECEMBER	2 Tests, 3 ODIs and 3 T20Is (h) v West Indies	(page 863)

For a review of Bangladesh domestic cricket from the 2017-18 season, see page 870.

care of Khaled Mahmud and Richard Halsall, but at first the absence of a full-time coach didn't seem to matter: they won their first three matches, one by a record margin over Sri Lanka, before falling in a heap against them in the final. What followed was also unpalatable: after a turgid First Test on a dead pitch at Chittagong, Sri Lanka won at Mirpur by showing more determination to get to grips with a spinning surface.

A failure at home was tough to take, but there was bitterness and rancour when Bangladesh visited Sri Lanka in March for the Nidahas Trophy, a Twenty20 tri-series marking the hosts' 70 years of independence. In what came down to a semi-final against the Sri Lankans, Bangladesh squeezed through after Mahmudullah crashed the penultimate ball for six. But the triumph was marred by ugly scenes on the field during the final over, and a smashed glass door in the Bangladesh dressing-room afterwards. The board did not dodge the issue. A statement criticised Shakib Al Hasan, the captain, and Nurul Hasan, a substitute who was on the field only to deliver a message to the batsmen. The pair were also fined and issued with demerit points by the ICC.

It did not appear to disrupt the players' focus in the final against India, where they were poised for a win until Dinesh Karthik hit the final ball of the match, bowled by Mustafizur Rahman, for six. "We haven't become a T20 side of calibre yet, but we have taken a step in the right direction," said Mushfiqur Rahim. "We will keep this hurt inside us so that we can go ahead."

But there was more agony off the last ball of the Asia Cup, when India's last pair scrambled a leg-bye to inflict Bangladesh's sixth defeat in a tournament final. Captain Mashrafe bin Mortaza spoke of the progress his team had made, but admitted to mistakes. There was consolation for Liton Das, whose polished century earned the match award.

Tight finishes held no perils for the women. In Kuala Lumpur in June, they won the Twenty20 Asia Cup in a thriller against India. They began the final over needing nine, and from the first five balls scored seven runs and lost two wickets. Jahanara Alam, at No. 8, coolly steered her first ball to midwicket and sprinted the two needed to complete a stirring victory. An online video of the men's squad watching the finale offered pleasing evidence of unity at the top of Bangladeshi cricket. The following month, the women also won the World Twenty20 qualifying tournament in the Netherlands, beating Ireland in the final. The good news stopped at the World Twenty20 itself, in the West Indies: they lost all four matches.

The Caribbean was also the venue for a sobering tour by the men. Rhodes had been in post for only a few days, so could hardly be blamed for two abject Test defeats. On the first day in Antigua, Bangladesh were blown away for 43, a record low, and they only just extended the match into a third day. They were more competitive in the Second Test in Jamaica, but defeat still came in three days. If Rhodes needed any convincing of his team's preference for the white ball, they then won the one-day and T20 series.

A far less encouraging T20 performance had come before that tour, when a visit to India to play Afghanistan in Dehradun ended in a 3–0 drubbing. Only one of the matches was close. But after a disappointing drawn Test series

Tharaka Basnayaka, NurPhoto/Getty Images

Smiles ahead: Mushfiqur Rahim gets a hug from Mahmudullah after his electrifying unbeaten 72 off 35 balls secures victory over Sri Lanka in the Nidahas Trophy.

against Zimbabwe, which included the picturesque Sylhet's inaugural Test, revenge was extracted over West Indies, with a 2–0 victory. The one-dayers were won, too, but Bangladesh missed the chance to win all three formats in a series for the first time when they lost the T20s.

Mushfiqur had an outstanding year, especially in white-ball matches. In all formats, he hit 1,657 runs, a national record, and established career-bests in each. His 219 in the Second Test against Zimbabwe at Mirpur was his country's highest score, and made him the first Bangladeshi to hit two Test doubles. Mominul Haque also had a good year, making four Test centuries – including, uniquely for Bangladesh, two in a Test, against Sri Lanka at Chittagong. Slow left-armer Taijul Islam, with 43 Test wickets, and off-spinner Mehedi Hasan, with 54 in all formats, were the pick of the bowlers. And there was the exciting emergence of 17-year-old off-spinner Nayeem Hasan: against West Indies at Chittagong, he became the third-youngest to take a five-for on debut.

BANGLADESH TRI-SERIES IN 2017-18

Mᴏʜᴀᴍᴍᴀᴅ Iꜱᴀᴍ

1 Sri Lanka   2 Bangladesh   3 Zimbabwe

Sri Lanka looked set to be dumped on the canvas, only to begin a fightback that led to an unexpected triumph. Defeat in their first two games of this 50-over tri-series in Dhaka suggested Chandika Hathurusinghe's appointment as coach had failed to galvanise them. But the revival was perfectly timed.

Bangladesh, the pre-tournament favourites, had won their first three games, but imploded in the final, losing by 79 runs against a cohesive Sri Lanka. And Hathurusinghe, who had been in charge of Bangladesh until November 2017, employed his knowledge of local conditions to good effect: his new charges showed greater nous in dealing with a lifeless Mirpur surface.

Sri Lanka's victory was given a sprinkling of fairy dust when Shehan Madushanka Kumara, a debutant 22-year-old seamer, clinched the trophy with a hat-trick. Yet it was far from a vintage competition, and attendances were below expectations. Some thought unseasonal chilly weather was to blame; others pointed to the quality of the cricket.

Bangladesh had looked formidable. They breezed past Zimbabwe in the opener, with Shakib Al Hasan hogging the limelight. He opened the bowling, took two wickets in his first over, then contributed to a brisk, unfussy run-chase. Next, they demolished Sri Lanka. Tamim Iqbal starred with 84, before Shakib added three wickets to his 67.

The Shakib and Tamim show continued in another stroll against Zimbabwe, but there was a warning they might not always have things their own way in the final group match, when a rejuvenated Sri Lanka administered a ten-wicket drubbing. "It is difficult to get back into this kind of tournament," said Dinesh Chandimal, who took over the captaincy when Angelo Mathews was injured in the opening game. The result knocked out Zimbabwe, who had earlier beaten Sri Lanka by 12 runs in the best game of the tournament. Tamim was the competition's highest run-scorer, with 252 at 63, while Tissara Perera underlined his value to Sri Lanka. He took 11 wickets at 17 – the best haul of the tournament – and hit 134 runs at a strike-rate of 154.

NATIONAL SQUADS

Bangladesh   *Mashrafe bin Mortaza, Abul Hasan, Anamul Haque, Imrul Kayes, Mahmudullah, Mehedi Hasan, Mithun Ali, Mohammad Saifuddin, Mushfiqur Rahim, Mustafizur Rahman, Nasir Hossain, Rubel Hossain, Sabbir Rahman, Sanjamul Islam, Shakib Al Hasan, Tamim Iqbal. *Coaches:* R. G. Halsall, Khaled Mahmud.

Sri Lanka   *A. D. Mathews, P. V. D. Chameera, L. D. Chandimal, A. Dananjaya, D. M. de Silva, P. W. H. de Silva, D. P. D. N. Dickwella, A. N. P. R. Fernando, D. A. S. Gunaratne, M. D. Gunathilleke, D. S. M. Kumara, R. A. S. Lakmal, B. K. G. Mendis, M. D. K. J. Perera, N. L. T. C. Perera, P. A. D. L. R. Sandakan, W. U. Tharanga. *Coach:* U. C. Hathurusinghe.

Mathews withdrew with a hamstring injury after Sri Lanka's opening game; Chandimal took over as captain. M. D. K. J. Perera suffered a side strain after their third, and was replaced by D. M. de Silva.

Zimbabwe *A. G. Cremer, T. L. Chatara, T. S. Chisoro, C. R. Ervine, K. M. Jarvis, H. Masakadza, B. A. Mavuta, S. F. Mire, P. J. Moor, C. B. Mpofu, R. C. Murray, B. Muzarabani, Sikandar Raza, B. R. M. Taylor, M. N. Waller. *Coach:* H. H. Streak.

At Mirpur, January 15, 2018 (day/night). **Bangladesh won by eight wickets. Zimbabwe 170** (49 overs) (Sikandar Raza 52, P. J. Moor 33; Shakib Al Hasan 3-43); ‡**Bangladesh 171-2** (28.3 overs) (Tamim Iqbal 84*, Shakib Al Hasan 37). *Bangladesh 5pts. MoM:* Shakib Al Hasan. *ODI debut:* B. Muzarabani (Zimbabwe). *Bangladesh's deployment of two left-arm spinners to open the bowling flummoxed Zimbabwe, who lost two wickets to Shakib Al Hasan's first four balls. They slumped to 81-5, and needed Sikandar Raza's careful 52 off 99 to drag them towards respectability. Raza's stand of 50 with Peter Moor was the only time Zimbabwe looked steady. But Bangladesh were never out of cruise control, with Tamim Iqbal hitting 84* and sharing 78 for the second wicket with Shakib. The struggles of the Zimbabwe attack were underlined by debutant Blessing Muzarabani, who bowled four no-balls in what became the penultimate over. The target was reached with more than 21 in hand.*

At Mirpur, January 17, 2018 (day/night). **Zimbabwe won by 12 runs. Zimbabwe 290-6** (50 overs) (H. Masakadza 73, S. F. Mire 34, B. R. M. Taylor 38, Sikandar Raza 81*; D. A. S. Gunaratne 3-37); ‡**Sri Lanka 278** (48.1 overs) (M. D. K. J. Perera 80, A. D. Mathews 42, L. D. Chandimal 34, N. L. T. C. Perera 64; T. L. Chatara 4-33). *Zimbabwe 4pts. MoM:* Sikandar Raza. *The Shere Bangla celebrated becoming the sixth venue to stage 100 ODIs – and in less time than the other five – with a thriller. Chasing an imposing 291, Sri Lanka were in contention while Tissara Perera was going well. But in the 47th over, with 16 needed, he heaved Tendai Chatara towards midwicket, where Raza ran in to hold a low catch. Chatara then rounded off the victory by removing Dushmantha Chameera – his fourth wicket. Raza had done most to forge a challenging total, with 81* off 67 balls, but opener Hamilton Masakadza's 73 was also key. Zimbabwe's previous ODI win against a Full Member at a neutral venue had also been against Sri Lanka, at Sharjah almost 15 years earlier. It was also their third victory in a row against them, following two at Hambantota in July 2017.*

At Mirpur, January 19, 2018 (day/night). **Bangladesh won by 163 runs.** ‡**Bangladesh 320-7** (50 overs) (Tamim Iqbal 84, Anamul Haque 35, Shakib Al Hasan 67, Mushfiqur Rahim 62; N. L. T. C. Perera 3-60); **Sri Lanka 157** (32.2 overs) (Shakib Al Hasan 3-47). *Bangladesh 5pts. MoM:* Shakib Al Hasan. *This was billed as a grudge match after Chandika Hathurusinghe's defection to coach Sri Lanka, but a commanding all-round display by Bangladesh turned it into an anticlimax. The victory margin was their biggest by runs, a total of 320 their joint-fifth-highest. The batting was led by Tamim, who made his second 84 in five days, and put on 71 with Anamul Haque and 99 with Shakib, as Sri Lanka's tactic of bowling short failed to pay off; Mushfiqur Rahim added a rapid 62. Sri Lanka's response was stalled by a miserly opening spell from Mashrafe bin Mortaza, before Dinesh Chandimal was brilliantly run out by Shakib, who then chipped away at the lower order.*

At Mirpur, January 21, 2018 (day/night). **Sri Lanka won by five wickets.** ‡**Zimbabwe 198** (44 overs) (B. R. M. Taylor 58, A. G. Cremer 34; A. N. P. R. Fernando 3-28, N. L. T. C. Perera 4-33); **Sri Lanka 202-5** (44.5 overs) (M. D. K. J. Perera 49, B. K. G. Mendis 36, L. D. Chandimal 38*, N. L. T. C. Perera 39*; B. Muzarabani 3-52). *Sri Lanka 4pts. MoM:* N. L. T. C. Perera. *Sri Lanka finally put points on the board, but their win was far from convincing, and a mid-innings stutter meant they missed a bonus point. At least their senior players contributed, with Tissara Perera making good use of the short ball to remove Zimbabwe's top four on his way to his best figures since June 2012. Only Brendan Taylor, despite treatment for a stiff back which meant he did not keep wicket, showed any mastery of the bowling or surface. Sri Lanka were strolling at 103-1 in the 22nd over, before Muzarabani took three wickets. When Asela Gunaratne fell to Kyle Jarvis, they still needed 54, but Chandimal and Perera saw them home.*

At Mirpur, January 23, 2018 (day/night). **Bangladesh won by 91 runs.** ‡**Bangladesh 216-9** (50 overs) (Tamim Iqbal 76, Shakib Al Hasan 51; K. M. Jarvis 3-42, A. G. Cremer 4-32); **Zimbabwe 125** (36.3 overs) (Sikandar Raza 39; Shakib Al Hasan 3-34). *Bangladesh 5pts. MoM:* Tamim Iqbal. *Presented with a chance to book a place in the final, Zimbabwe fluffed their lines; it left them hoping for a Bangladesh victory over Sri Lanka in the last group match. The day belonged to Tamim, whose 76 – his third successive half-century – made him the first Bangladeshi to reach 6,000 in ODIs, and* *the format's most prolific batsman at one venue, passing Sanath Jayasuriya's 2,514 at Colombo's R. Premadasa Stadium. Zimbabwe had been excellent with the ball, captain Graeme Cremer taking four wickets with his leg-spin (his best haul against a Full Member), and Jarvis three. Even Tamim and Shakib were confounded by a docile surface, and 12 overs went by without a boundary in their second-wicket partnership of 106; despite that, Bangladesh ought to have done far better from 147-2 in the 35th over. Zimbabwe's reply was derailed from the start: four wickets fell in the first ten overs, and Shakib finished with three for the third successive match.*

At Mirpur, January 25, 2018 (day/night). **Sri Lanka won by ten wickets.** ‡**Bangladesh 82** (24 overs) (R. A. S. Lakmal 3-21); **Sri Lanka 83-0** (11.5 overs) (M. D. Gunathilleke 35*, W. U. Tharanga 39*). *MoM:* R. A. S. Lakmal. *Sri Lanka 5pts. It took Sri Lanka less than three hours – and 36 overs – to wallop Bangladesh, and ease into the final at the expense of Zimbabwe. After Shakib was run out by a superb piece of work from Dhanushka Gunathilleke, and the previously infallible Tamim was undone by a nasty ball from Suranga Lakmal, the rest of the Bangladesh batting folded. Gunathilleke and Upul Thuranga blasted Sri Lanka to their target in 11.5 overs. It was their sixth ten-wicket win, and their third over Bangladesh (the other three had been over England).*

Bangladesh 15pts, Sri Lanka 9pts, Zimbabwe 4pts.

Final At Mirpur, January 27, 2018 (day/night). **Sri Lanka won by 79 runs.** ‡**Sri Lanka 221** (50 overs) (W. U. Tharanga 56, D. P. D. N. Dickwella 42, L. D. Chandimal 45; Rubel Hossain 4-46); **Bangladesh 142** (41.1 overs) (Mahmudullah 76; D. S. M. Kumara 3-26). *MoM:* W. U. Tharanga. *MoS:* N. L. T. C. Perera. *ODI debut:* D. S. M. Kumara (Sri Lanka). *Sri Lanka peaked when it mattered, chiselling out victory on a pitch offering nothing to strokemakers. After Chandimal won a vital toss, only Kusal Mendis – with 28 off nine balls – found any fluency, though Chandimal made a steady 45 after important contributions from Tharanga and Niroshan Dickwella. Rubel Hossain, with his best figures for more than four years, and Mustafizur Rahman bowled brilliantly at the death, as Sri Lanka lost seven for 63 in the last 15 overs. But a total of 221 still looked testing, especially with Shakib unable to bat after injuring his hand in the field. And when, either side of the run-out of Mithun Ali, a fired-up Chameera removed Tamim and Sabbir Rahman cheaply, Bangladesh were 22-3. Only Mahmudullah, with 76, got to grips with the conditions. Shehan Madushanka Kumara, a seamer picked on a hunch by Hathurusinghe after just six senior matches, wrapped things up with a hat-trick. Mashrafe was fined 20% of his match fee, and Gunathilleke reprimanded, for giving batsmen send-offs.*

BANGLADESH v SRI LANKA IN 2017-18

MAZHER ARSHAD

Test matches (2): Bangladesh 0, Sri Lanka 1
Twenty20 internationals (2): Bangladesh 0, Sri Lanka 2

Bangladesh's hard-won reputation as tough opponents at home was surrendered meekly to Sri Lanka. After losing the final of a one-day international tri-series also involving Zimbabwe, they were beaten in the Tests and Twenty20 matches. It was an unhappy few weeks that fractured much of the optimism generated over the previous few years by Test victories over England and Australia, and six successive home one-day series wins, before England triumphed in late 2016.

Sri Lanka struck a significant blow even before they arrived. The recruitment of their former Test player Chandika Hathurusinghe as coach in December, 2017, soon after he left the Bangladesh job, gave them inside knowledge of their opponents and conditions. "We had some strategic plans for some of the players," said Hathurusinghe. "We knew how they would react under pressure." The visitors had also gained an advantage when Shakib Al Hasan, Bangladesh's new Test captain, injured his hand in the tri-series final and missed the subsequent matches.

Shakib's injury meant the captaincy passed to Mahmudullah. The 35-year-old left-arm spinner Abdur Razzak, who had recently received an award for becoming the first Bangladeshi to 500 first-class wickets, was welcomed back for his first Test in four years.

The First Test in Chittagong was tough to watch, even for diehards. Bangladesh's squad contained six spinners, but the pitch emasculated them all. In five days, 1,533 runs were scored – the second-highest aggregate for a Test in Bangladesh – for the loss of only 24 wickets. Referee David Boon's damning report persuaded the ICC to issue the venue a demerit point.

When the action moved to Mirpur, the contrast was almost comical. The match rushed to a conclusion inside three days, this time for an aggregate of 681 – the second-lowest in Bangladesh. Sri Lanka won by 215, and added a potentially exciting new weapon to their armoury in off-spinner Akila Dananjaya, who took eight wickets on debut. Again Boon reported the pitch and another demerit point was handed out. The board's appeal was dismissed.

Sri Lanka's batting was built around Man of the Series Roshen Silva, who brought sound technique to the middle order and hit 235 runs at 117, and Kusal Mendis, who managed 271 at 90. Dhananjaya de Silva also passed 200. For Bangladesh, the major gain was the return to form of Mominul Haque. At Chittagong, he responded to being dropped twice in the previous year by becoming the first Bangladeshi to score two hundreds in a Test.

The two T20 matches were also a let-down for the hosts. The benefits that many expected to accrue from the Bangladesh Premier League were yet to be felt by the national team.

SRI LANKAN TOURING PARTY

*L. D. Chandimal (T/20), M. A. Aponso (20), P. V. D. Chameera (T), A. Dananjaya (T/20), D. M. de Silva (T), D. P. D. N. Dickwella (T/20), A. Fernando (20), P. L. S. Gamage (T), D. A. S. Gunaratne (20), M. D. Gunathilleke (T/20), H. M. R. K. B. Herath (T), F. D. M. Karunaratne (T), C. B. R. L. S. Kumara (T), D. S. M. Kumara (20), R. A. S. Lakmal (T), B. K. G. Mendis (T/20), B. M. A. J. Mendis (20), M. D. K. Perera (T), M. D. K. J. Perera (20), N. L. T. C. Perera (20), P. A. D. L. R. Sandakan (20), A. R. S. Silva (T), W. U. Tharanga (20), I. Udana (20), J. D. F. Vandersay (20). *Coach:* U. C. Hathurusinghe.

A. D. Mathews withdrew after being injured in the preceding one-day tri-series and Gunaratne on the eve of the T20 games.

BANGLADESH v SRI LANKA

First Test

At Chittagong, January 31–February 4, 2018. Drawn. Toss: Bangladesh. Test debut: Sanjamul Islam.

For a fleeting moment on the fourth morning of a run-soaked match came a hint that the tedium would lift, and a positive outcome ensue. Herath had just removed Mushfiqur Rahim with the last ball of the day to reduce Bangladesh to 81 for three in their second innings, still 119 behind, and Sri Lanka glimpsed an opening. But, on a last-day pitch that steadfastly refused to offer encouragement to the bowlers, Mominul Haque and Liton Das dug in and steered Bangladesh towards the draw that had looked likely from the start. Mominul made his second hundred of the match – the first to do so for Bangladesh – while Liton, after a golden duck on the opening day, fell six runs short of his first in Tests. Their 180-run stand slammed the door in Sri Lanka's face.

Play started at 9.30 because the sun set early, and any cracks refused to open. The Kookaburra ball also gave the spinners less assistance than the SG used against Australia and England. Just four wickets fell on the first day, when Mominul – after reaching a hundred in 96 balls – closed on 175. He celebrated ostentatiously, in what was interpreted as a message to Chandika Hathurusinghe, the new Sri Lanka coach, who had dropped him when in charge of Bangladesh. Mominul's stand of 236 with Mushfiqur helped them to 513, while Mahmudullah, leading the team for the first time, made an unbeaten 83. It was the largest Test total without a bye or a leg-bye.

But Sri Lanka made it look puny. Karunaratne fell to off-spinner Mehedi Hasan for a duck, only for Kusal Mendis – dropped on four – and Dhananjaya de Silva to put on 308, the eighth-highest for any Sri Lankan wicket. Both finished with career-bests. Mendis then added 107 with Roshen Silva, who would not have played his second Test if Angelo Mathews had been fit, and survived a stumping chance on one. Then, after Mendis fell four short of a double-century, Silva put on a further 135 with Chandimal. Dickwella's 61-ball 62 was the final meaty contribution to a total of 713 for nine, Sri Lanka's joint-fifth-highest. Taijul Islam took four wickets, but his 67.3 overs were the most in a Test innings by a Bangladesh bowler, and his 219 runs the most conceded.

Bangladesh began the final day perhaps anxiously remembering their defeat by New Zealand at Wellington in January 2017, when they racked up 595 for eight in their first innings, only to lose by seven wickets. But Mominul and Liton ate up more than 50 overs as Bangladesh moved into the lead, and the pitch refused to yield. When the captains shook hands on the draw 70 minutes before the scheduled close, only 24 wickets had fallen. Mahmudullah defended the surface, claiming it was a "good wicket for Test cricket". He then undermined his own argument, admitting that he thought "it might start turning from the second or third day, or the fourth or fifth". The truth was that, even after a sixth or a seventh, the players might still have been waiting.

Man of the Match: Mominul Haque.

Close of play: first day, Bangladesh 374-4 (Mominul Haque 175, Mahmudullah 9); second day, Sri Lanka 187-1 (Mendis 83, de Silva 104); third day, Sri Lanka 504-3 (Silva 87, Chandimal 37); fourth day, Bangladesh 81-3 (Mominul Haque 18).

Bangladesh

Tamim Iqbal b Perera	52	– c Dickwella b Sandakan	41
Imrul Kayes lbw b Perera	40	– c Chandimal b Perera	19
Mominul Haque c Mendis b Herath	176	– c Karunaratne b de Silva	105
Mushfiqur Rahim c Dickwella b Lakmal	92	– c Mendis b Herath	2
†Liton Das b Lakmal	0	– c Perera b Herath	94
*Mahmudullah not out	83	– not out	28
Mosaddek Hossain c Sandakan b Herath	8	– not out	8
Mehedi Hasan run out (Kumara/Dickwella)	20		
Sanjamul Islam st Dickwella b Sandakan	24		
Taijul Islam b Herath	1		
Mustafizur Rahman c Dickwella b Lakmal	8		
B 5, nb 4	9	B 3, lb 2, w 1, nb 4	10

1/72 (1) 2/120 (2) 3/356 (4)　　　(129.5 overs) 513　　1/52 (2)　　(5 wkts dec, 100 overs) 307
4/356 (5) 5/376 (3) 6/390 (7)　　　　　　　　　　　　2/76 (1) 3/81 (4)
7/417 (8) 8/475 (9) 9/478 (10) 10/513 (11)　　　　　4/261 (3) 5/279 (5)

Lakmal 23.5–4–68–3; Kumara 15–1–79–0; Perera 27–4–112–1; Herath 37–2–150–3; Sandakan 22–1–92–2; de Silva 5–0–12–0. *Second innings*—Herath 28–6–80–2; Lakmal 9–1–25–0; de Silva 12–0–41–1; Perera 26–5–74–1; Sandakan 18–2–64–1; Kumara 6–0–16–0; Mendis 1–0–2–0.

Sri Lanka

F. D. M. Karunaratne c Imrul Kayes b Mehedi Hasan	0	M. D. K. Perera lbw b Sanjamul Islam	32
B. K. G. Mendis c Mushfiqur Rahim b Taijul Islam	196	H. M. R. K. B. Herath lbw b Taijul Islam	24
		R. A. S. Lakmal b Taijul Islam	9
D. M. de Silva c Liton Das b Mustafizur Rahman	173	C. B. R. L. S. Kumara not out	2
A. R. S. Silva c Liton Das b Mehedi Hasan	109	B 11, lb 6, w 2	19
*L. D. Chandimal b Taijul Islam	87		
†D. P. D. N. Dickwella c Liton Das b Mehedi Hasan	62		

P. A. D. L. R. Sandakan did not bat.

1/0 (1)　　(9 wkts dec, 199.3 overs) 713
2/308 (3) 3/415 (2)
4/550 (4) 5/613 (5) 6/663 (6)
7/687 (7) 8/706 (9) 9/713 (8)

Mustafizur Rahman 32–6–113–1; Sanjamul Islam 45–2–153–1; Mehedi Hasan 49–4–174–3; Taijul Islam 67.3–13–219–4; Mosaddek Hossain 3–0–24–0; Mominul Haque 2–0–6–0; Mahmudullah 1–0–7–0.

Umpires: M. Erasmus and R. J. Tucker.　　Third umpire: J. S. Wilson.
Referee: D. C. Boon.

BANGLADESH v SRI LANKA

Second Test

At Mirpur, February 8–10, 2018. Sri Lanka won by 215 runs. Toss: Sri Lanka. Test debut: A. Dananjaya.

On a pitch that took spin from the start, providing a searching examination of technique, only one team were prepared to knuckle down. At the end of a hectic three-day contest, Sri Lanka's application – and the potency of their spinners – meant they took the spoils. "Truly, this was a very difficult series," said Chandimal. "The First Test was a nightmare for the bowlers, and this one was a nightmare for the batsmen."

But it was another lip-smacking game for statisticians: off-spinner Akila Dananjaya's eight for 44 were the best match figures by a Sri Lankan on debut; Silva equalled an obscure record with the bat; and Herath became the most successful left-arm bowler in history.

There was an indication of what was in store when Bangladesh opened with Mehedi Hasan and Abdur Razzak, only the second time two spinners have taken the new ball in the first innings of a Test. But Sri Lanka gained the initiative: Mendis made 68, and was ruthless when the bowlers dropped short, while Silva compiled a patient 56, giving a

MOST TEST WICKETS BY LEFT-ARMERS

		T	R	Avge	SR	
433	**H. M. R. K. B. Herath (SL)**.....	**93**	**12,157**	**28.07**	**60.03**	**1999-2000 to 2018-19**
414	Wasim Akram (P).............	104	9,779	23.62	54.65	1984-85 to 2001-02
362	D. L. Vettori (NZ/World).......	113	12,441	34.36	79.59	1996-97 to 2014-15
355	W. P. U. J. C. Vaas (SL)........	111	10,501	29.58	66.02	1994-95 to 2009
313	M. G. Johnson (A).............	73	8,891	28.40	51.12	2007-08 to 2015-16
311	Zaheer Khan (I)...............	92	10,247	32.94	60.40	2000-01 to 2013-14
297	D. L. Underwood (E)...........	86	7,674	25.83	73.60	1966 to 1981-82
266	B. S. Bedi (I)................	67	7,637	28.71	80.31	1966-67 to 1979
235	G. S. Sobers (WI).............	93	7,999	34.03	91.91	1953-54 to 1973-74
233	**T. A. Boult (NZ)**............	**59**	**6,501**	**27.90**	**56.57**	**2011-12 to 2018-19**

As at January 14, 2019. Herath, Vettori, Underwood and Bedi bowled spin, the others seam, and Sobers both.

textbook demonstration of playing late with soft hands, and squeezed out a critical 112 for the last four wickets. Slow left-armers Razzak and Taijul Islam shared eight.

But Bangladesh failed to show the same fight and, with Lakmal snaring three early victims to move to 100 Test wickets, they were soon in trouble. Mominul Haque, their hero from the First Test, was carelessly run out for a duck after failing to ground his bat. Any hopes of a recovery were dashed when the last five fell for three. Starting with a lead of 112, Sri Lanka were again indebted to Silva, whose unbeaten 70 was the sole score above 32. Only Australia's Herbie Collins, and Indian duo Sunil Gavaskar and Mohammad Azharuddin, had previously managed four scores of 50 or more in their first five Test innings. The Sri Lankans, 338 ahead, had more than enough.

Playing like men with a train to catch, Bangladesh were bowled out for 123 in less than 30 overs, this time the last six adding just 23. Dananjaya got the ball to lift steeply off an apparently innocuous length, and his five wickets came in five overs. Herath wrapped things up to move to 415 Test wickets, one clear of Pakistan's Wasim Akram among left-armers. The surface may have provided more entertainment than at Chittagong, but referee David Boon noted its uneven bounce and inconsistent turn, and imposed a demerit point. "We knew the pitch would get a result, but the batsmen let us down," said Mahmudullah. "Our intent was there, but we should have been choosy while playing the strokes."

Man of the Match: A. R. S. Silva. *Man of the Series:* A. R. S. Silva.

Close of play: first day, Bangladesh 56-4 (Liton Das 24, Mehedi Hasan 5); second day, Sri Lanka 200-8 (Silva 58, Lakmal 7).

Sri Lanka

B. K. G. Mendis b Abdur Razzak	68	– (2) lbw b Abdur Razzak........... 7
F. D. M. Karunaratne st Liton Das b Abdur Razzak	3	– (1) c Imrul Kayes b Mehedi Hasan .. 32
D. M. de Silva c Sabbir Rahman b Taijul Islam ...	19	– b Taijul Islam.................... 28
M. D. Gunathilleke c Mushfiqur Rahim		
b Abdur Razzak .	13	– lbw b Mustafizur Rahman 17
*L. D. Chandimal b Abdur Razzak	0	– lbw b Mehedi Hasan 30
A. R. S. Silva c Liton Das b Taijul Islam........	56	– not out 70
†D. P. D. N. Dickwella b Taijul Islam............	1	– c Mahmudullah b Taijul Islam...... 10
M. D. K. Perera c Mominul Haque b Taijul Islam .	31	– c Liton Das b Mustafizur Rahman ... 7
A. Dananjaya c Mushfiqur Rahim		
b Mustafizur Rahman.	20	– c Liton Das b Mustafizur Rahman ... 0
H. M. R. K. B. Herath c Mushfiqur Rahim		
b Mustafizur Rahman.	2	– (11) lbw b Taijul Islam............ 0
R. A. S. Lakmal not out	4	– (10) b Taijul Islam 21
Lb 5	5	Lb 4 4

1/14 (2) 2/61 (3) 3/96 (4)   (65.3 overs) 222   1/19 (2) 2/53 (3)   (73.5 overs) 226
4/96 (5) 5/109 (1) 6/110 (7)   3/80 (4) 4/92 (1)
7/162 (6) 8/205 (9) 9/207 (10) 10/222 (6)   5/143 (5) 6/170 (7) 7/178 (8)
                                                         8/178 (9) 9/226 (10) 10/226 (11)

Mehedi Hasan 13–0–54–0; Abdur Razzak 16–2–63–4; Taijul Islam 25.3–2–83–4; Mustafizur Rahman 11–4–17–2. *Second innings*—Abdur Razzak 17–2–60–1; Mustafizur Rahman 17–3–49–3; Taijul Islam 19.5–2–76–4; Mehedi Hasan 20–5–37–2.

Bangladesh

Tamim Iqbal c and b Lakmal	4	– lbw b Perera	2
Imrul Kayes lbw b Perera	19	– c Dickwella b Herath	17
Mominul Haque run out (de Silva/Dickwella)	0	– c Dickwella b Herath	33
Mushfiqur Rahim b Lakmal	1	– st Dickwella b Herath	25
†Liton Das b Lakmal	25	– c Mendis b Danajaya	12
Mehedi Hasan not out	38	– (5) c Dickwella b Danajaya	7
*Mahmudullah b Danajaya	17	– (6) c Karunaratne b Danajaya	6
Sabbir Rahman c Chandimal b Danajaya	0	– (7) c Mendis b Danajaya	1
Abdur Razzak c and b Danajaya	1	– st Dickwella b Danajaya	2
Taijul Islam run out (Mendis)	1	– c Gunathilleke b Herath	6
Mustafizur Rahman lbw b Perera	0	– not out	5
Lb 2, w 1, nb 1	4	B 6, lb 1	7

1/4 (1) 2/4 (3) 3/12 (4)	(45.4 overs) 110	1/3 (1) 2/49 (2)	(29.3 overs) 123
4/45 (2) 5/73 (5) 6/107 (7)		3/64 (3) 4/78 (5)	
7/107 (8) 8/109 (9) 9/110 (10) 10/110 (11)		5/100 (6) 6/102 (4) 7/102 (7)	
		8/104 (9) 9/113 (8) 10/123 (10)	

Lakmal 12–4–25–3; Perera 11.4–4–32–2; Danajaya 10–2–20–3; Herath 12–1–31–0. *Second innings*—Lakmal 3–0–11–0; Perera 10–0–32–1; Herath 11.3–1–49–4; Danajaya 5–1–24–5.

Umpires: R. J. Tucker and J. S. Wilson. Third umpire: M. Erasmus.
Referee: D. C. Boon.

First Twenty20 international At Mirpur, February 15, 2018 (floodlit). **Sri Lanka won by six wickets.** ‡**Bangladesh 193-5** (20 overs) (Soumya Sarkar 51, Mushfiqur Rahim 66*, Mahmudullah 43); **Sri Lanka 194-4** (16.4 overs) (B. K. G. Mendis 53, M. D. Gunathilleke 30, M. D. Shanaka 42*, N. L. T. C. Perera 39*). *MoM:* B. K. G. Mendis. *T20I debuts:* Afif Hossain, Ariful Haque, Nazmul Islam, Zakir Hasan (Bangladesh); D. S. M. Kumara (Sri Lanka). *Sri Lanka ended a run of eight T20 defeats with their highest second-innings total. Kusal Mendis, a late replacement for Kusal Perera, hit a brisk 53, but their progress was interrupted when his departure was swiftly followed by those of Upul Tharanga and Niroshan Dickwella. However, Dasun Shanaka (42* off 24) and Tissara Perera (39* off 18) steered them home with 20 balls in hand. Bangladesh's highest T20I total at the time included a first fifty in the format for Soumya Sarkar, and a career-best 66* for Mushfiqur Rahim.*

Second Twenty20 international At Sylhet, February 18, 2018 (floodlit). **Sri Lanka won by 75 runs. Sri Lanka 210-4** (20 overs) (M. D. Gunathilleke 42, B. K. G. Mendis 70, N. L. T. C. Perera 31, M. D. Shanaka 30*); ‡**Bangladesh 135** (18.4 overs) (Mahmudullah 41). *MoM:* B. K. G. Mendis. *MoS:* B. K. G. Mendis. *T20I debuts:* Abu Jayed, Mehedi Hasan snr (Bangladesh); M. A. Aponso (Sri Lanka). *Bangladesh's first men's international at Sylhet was one to forget as they conceded their second-highest T20 total, losing the match and the series. Mendis continued his fine tour with a career-best 70 off 42 balls, and put on 98 for the first wicket with Dhanushka Gunathilleke. Bangladesh's generosity in the field extended to dropping Gunathilleke twice, before Shanaka and Tharanga plundered 45 off 19 balls. Sri Lanka then struck three early blows to effectively settle the issue. Apart from Mahmudullah, run out for 41 off 31, the Bangladesh batsmen struggled.*

BANGLADESH v ZIMBABWE IN 2018-19

MOHAMMAD ISAM

One-day internationals (3): Bangladesh 3, Zimbabwe 0
Test matches (2): Bangladesh 1, Zimbabwe 1

When Bangladesh started in Test cricket, in 2000, matches against Zimbabwe were their best chance of an upset, especially in home conditions. Since then, victories had become routine, and recent home wins over England, Australia and Sri Lanka had left Bangladesh confident of success on their spin-friendly pitches. Things went according to plan in the one-day series, with opener Imrul Kayes piling up 349 runs. And so it was a shock when Zimbabwe won the First Test at Sylhet, their first away victory since 2001 (also in Bangladesh). The home side bounced back at Mirpur, thanks to a huge stand between Mominul Haque and Mushfiqur Rahim, whose unbeaten 219 was Bangladesh's highest score. Shakib Al Hasan, the previous record-holder, missed the series with a finger injury, and the captaincy passed to Mahmudullah, whose second-innings century stretched the target over the horizon.

Zimbabwe were also without their best slow bowler, leg-spinner (and former captain) Graeme Cremer, who was recuperating from knee surgery. But it helped that several of their players were familiar with local conditions after stints in the Dhaka Premier League and the BPL. Of these, Sikandar Raza and Sean Williams were prominent at Sylhet, while Brendan Taylor scored twin hundreds in vain at Mirpur.

As expected, the spinners played the major role in the Tests. But it was a surprise that Zimbabwe's, which included two debutants – Brandon Mavuta and Wellington Masakadza, the captain's brother – outshone Bangladesh's in the First Test, sharing six second-innings wickets. They backed up Raza's flattish off-breaks, which produced three wickets in each innings. The pacemen had a part to play, too: the new-ball pair of Kyle Jarvis and Tendai Chatara shared five first-innings wickets. Slow left-armer Taijul Islam did take 11 at Sylhet and seven at Mirpur, but he had to send down more than 145 overs.

"It was tough sharing the Test series trophy," admitted Mahmudullah. "We played poorly in the First Test – we always try to win the home series." For Zimbabwe, any win is a triumph – success at Sylhet was only their third in an overseas Test – and they went home happy.

HIGHEST TEST SCORES FOR BANGLADESH

219*	**Mushfiqur Rahim**	**v Zimbabwe at Mirpur**	**2018-19**
217	Shakib Al Hasan	v New Zealand at Wellington	2016-17
206	Tamim Iqbal	v Pakistan at Khulna	2014-15
200	Mushfiqur Rahim	v Sri Lanka at Galle	2012-13
190	Mohammad Ashraful	v Sri Lanka at Galle	2012-13
181	Mominul Haque	v New Zealand at Chittagong (ZAC)	2013-14
176	Mominul Haque	v Sri Lanka at Chittagong (ZAC)	2017-18
161	**Mominul Haque**	**v Zimbabwe at Mirpur**	**2018-19**

ZIMBABWE TOURING PARTY

*H. Masakadza (T/50), R. P. Burl (T), R. W. Chakabva (T), B. B. Chari (T), T. L. Chatara (T/50), E. Chigumbura (50), C. R. Ervine (T/50), K. M. Jarvis (T/50), W. P. Masakadza (T), B. A. Mavuta (T/50), S. F. Mire (50), P. J. Moor (T/50), C. B. Mpofu (T), T. K. Musakanda (50), R. Ngarava (50), J. C. Nyumbu (T), Sikandar Raza (T/50), B. R. M. Taylor (T/50), D. T. Tiripano (T/50), S. C. Williams (T/50), C. Zhuwao (50). Coach: L. S. Rajput.

Sikandar Raza was not originally selected, but was added to the squad after settling contractual differences with the Zimbabwean board. Ngarava injured his groin during the third one-day international, and was replaced in the Test squad by Mpofu.

First one-day international   At Mirpur, October 21, 2018 (day/night). **Bangladesh won by 28 runs.** ‡**Bangladesh 271-8** (50 overs) (Imrul Kayes 144, Mithun Ali 37, Mohammad Saifuddin 50; K. M. Jarvis 4-37, T. L. Chatara 3-55); **Zimbabwe 243-9** (50 overs) (C. Zhuwao 35, S. C. Williams 50*, K. M. Jarvis 37; Mehedi Hasan 3-46). *MoM:* Imrul Kayes. *ODI debut:* Fazle Mahmud (Bangladesh). *Bangladesh, without the injured Tamim Iqbal and Shakib Al Hasan, were in trouble*

HIGHEST ODI SCORES FOR BANGLADESH

154	Tamim Iqbal.	v Zimbabwe at Bulawayo.	2009
144	**Mushfiqur Rahim.**	**v Sri Lanka at Dubai**	**2018-19**
144	**Imrul Kayes**	**v Zimbabwe at Mirpur.**	**2018-19**
134*	Shakib Al Hasan	v Canada at St John's, Antigua.	2006-07
132	Tamim Iqbal.	v Pakistan at Mirpur	2014-15
130*	Tamim Iqbal.	v West Indies at Providence	2018
129	Tamim Iqbal.	v Ireland at Mirpur	2007-08
128*	Mahmudullah.	v New Zealand at Hamilton	2014-15
128	Tamim Iqbal.	v England at The Oval	2017
127*	Soumya Sarkar.	v Pakistan at Mirpur	2014-15
127	Tamim Iqbal.	v Sri Lanka at Dambulla.	2016-17
125	Tamim Iqbal.	v England at Mirpur	2009-10

---

at 139-6 in the 30th over – but Imrul Kayes, who clobbered six sixes in his highest score, put on a national-record 127 for the seventh wicket with Mohammad Saifuddin, who hit a maiden international half-century. Brendan Taylor took five catches behind the stumps. Zimbabwe found it hard to push the scoring along, and when Sikandar Raza fell it was 88-4 after 21 overs. Sean Williams did his best, but some optimistic swinging from the tail only narrowed the margin of defeat. Kyle Jarvis hit 37 at No. 10, his highest score in ODIs, to follow his best bowling figures.

Second one-day international   At Chittagong, October 24, 2018 (day/night). **Bangladesh won by seven wickets. Zimbabwe 246-7** (50 overs) (B. R. M. Taylor 75, S. C. Williams 47, Sikandar Raza 49; Mohammad Saifuddin 3-45); ‡**Bangladesh 250-3** (44.1 overs) (Liton Das 83, Imrul Kayes 90, Mushfiqur Rahim 40*). *MoM:* Mohammad Saifuddin. *Bangladesh's victory – which clinched the series – never looked in doubt once Imrul and Liton Das raced out of the blocks with 148 in 24 overs. Fazle Mahmud's second duck in his first two ODIs, had little impact, although Kayes fell within sight of another century. Earlier, a bright innings from Taylor had given Zimbabwe some impetus, but only 58 came from the last 12 overs. Saifuddin followed a half-century in the first match with three wickets for his medium-pacers.*

Third one-day international   At Chittagong, October 26, 2018 (day/night). **Bangladesh won by seven wickets. Zimbabwe 286-5** (50 overs) (B. R. M. Taylor 75, S. C. Williams 129*, Sikandar Raza 40); ‡**Bangladesh 288-3** (42.1 overs) (Imrul Kayes 115, Soumya Sarkar 117). *MoM:* Soumya Sarkar. *MoS:* Imrul Kayes. *ODI debut:* Ariful Haque (Bangladesh). *Liton fell to the first ball of the chase, but then Imrul and Soumya Sarkar sprinted away: after the ten-over powerplay Bangladesh had 80-1 (Zimbabwe were 35-2), and they eventually put on 220, a national second-wicket record, beating 207 by Tamim Iqbal and Shakib Al Hasan against West Indies at Providence three months earlier. Imrul took his aggregate to 349 runs, the second-highest for any three-match ODI series, after Babar Azam's 360 for Pakistan v West Indies in the UAE in 2016-17. Sarkar's century was his* *second in ODIs, following only 47 runs in six innings. Bangladesh completed a 3–0 clean sweep with 47 balls to spare, even though Zimbabwe set a stiff target, thanks mainly to a third-wicket stand of 132 between Taylor and Williams, who also hit his second ODI hundred.*

BANGLADESH v ZIMBABWE

First Test

At Sylhet, November 3–6, 2018. Zimbabwe won by 151 runs. Toss: Zimbabwe. Test debuts: Ariful Haque, Nazmul Islam; W. P. Masakadza, B. A. Mavuta.

Zimbabwe will long remember the inaugural Test at the pretty Sylhet Stadium in the north-east of Bangladesh, not far from the Indian border. The 116th ground to stage a Test boasts a ceremonial tea garden, and there was even a Lord's-style bell to start proceedings with a flourish. Zimbabwe enjoyed the trappings, easing to their first victory in an overseas Test for 17 years, and only their 12th anywhere in 107 attempts. And they did it with spin, their inexperienced trio faring better than Bangladesh's much-hyped battalion. The hosts were handicapped by the absence of their leading wicket-taker Shakib Al Hasan – Mahmudullah captained instead – but had still been expected to rule the roost. Instead it was the skiddy off-breaks of Sikandar Raza, supported by the debutants Brandon Mavuta and Wellington Masakadza, which proved more incisive.

In their first Test of the year, Zimbabwe's batsmen also worked hard. Hamilton Masakadza made 52 in 32 overs after winning the toss, then Williams reined himself in for 88. While Moor and Chakabva were sharing a stand of 60, a big score looked in

---

HAVE A GO, BRO

Players who made their Test debut in a team captained by their brother:

Player	*Captain*		
E. J. Gregory	D. W. Gregory	Australia v England at Melbourne	1876-77
D. Taylor	H. W. Taylor	South Africa v England at Durban	1913-14
C. S. Nayudu	C. K. Nayudu	India v England at Calcutta	1933-34
R. S. Grant	G. C. Grant	West Indies v England at Bridgetown	1934-35
N. M. Parker	J. M. Parker	New Zealand v Pakistan at Karachi	1976-77
D. Ranatunga	A. Ranatunga	Sri Lanka v Australia at Brisbane	1989-90
S. Ranatunga	A. Ranatunga	Sri Lanka v Pakistan at Kandy	1994-95
W. P. Masakadza	**H. Masakadza**	**Zimbabwe v Bangladesh at Sylhet**	**2018-19**

Zulfiqar Ahmed made his debut for Pakistan under his brother-in-law, A. H. Kardar, against India at Lucknow in 1952-53. D. A. J. Holford's captain in his first Test for West Indies, against England at Manchester in 1966, was his cousin G. S. Sobers.

---

prospect, but when Chakabva fell – one of six victims for the hard-working slow left-armer Taijul Islam – the last five wickets added only 21. That looked plenty, though, when Bangladesh dipped to 19 for four, the lively new-ball pair of Jarvis and Chatara doing the damage. Mushfiqur Rahim and Ariful Haque – chosen for his debut a month after making 231 in a domestic game – papered over the cracks, but three wickets for Raza left Bangladesh staring at a deficit of 139.

Zimbabwe craved a big score to put themselves out of reach, but instead lost regular wickets to the spinners (Abu Jayed, the sole seamer, sent down just seven overs). Hamilton Masakadza led by example, gritting out 48 in 36 overs, but the innings was derailed by three wickets in five balls for Taijul, who finished with 11 for 170. Four others scraped to 20, and Bangladesh's eventual target was 321 – tough on a pitch taking turn, but not impossible.

Everything in the tea garden looked rosy as openers Liton Das and Imrul Kayes put on 56, but Raza pinned Liton, and Zimbabwe started to tighten the screw. Mominul Haque's indifferent run continued when he was castled by Jarvis, then Raza removed Imrul and Mahmudullah. Mavuta extracted four wickets with his leg-breaks as the slide continued. Finally, Wellington Masakadza persuaded Ariful to sky a catch, which keeper Chakabva clasped to spark Zimbabwean celebrations. Things were much quieter in the Bangladesh dressing-room.

Man of the Match: S. C. Williams.

Close of play: first day, Zimbabwe 236-5 (Moor 37, Chakabva 20); second day, Zimbabwe 1-0 (H. Masakadza 1, Chari 0); third day, Bangladesh 26-0 (Liton Das 14, Imrul Kayes 12).

Zimbabwe

*H. Masakadza lbw b Abu Jayed	52	– lbw b Mehedi Hasan	48
B. B. Chari b Taijul Islam	13	– b Mehedi Hasan	4
B. R. M. Taylor c Nazmul Hossain b Taijul Islam	6	– c Imrul Kayes b Taijul Islam	24
S. C. Williams c Mehedi Hasan b Mahmudullah	88	– b Taijul Islam	20
Sikandar Raza b Nazmul Islam	19	– b Taijul Islam	25
P. J. Moor not out	63	– c Liton Das b Taijul Islam	0
†R. W. Chakabva c Nazmul Hossain b Taijul Islam	28	– c Mahmudullah b Nazmul Islam	20
W. P. Masakadza c Mushfiqur Rahim b Taijul Islam	4	– lbw b Mehedi Hasan	17
B. A. Mavuta lbw b Nazmul Islam	3	– c Ariful Haque b Nazmul Islam	6
K. M. Jarvis c Mehedi Hasan b Taijul Islam	4	– not out	1
T. L. Chatara c Liton Das b Taijul Islam	0	– lbw b Taijul Islam	8
B 1, lb 1	2	B 4, lb 4	8

1/35 (2) 2/47 (3) 3/85 (1)   (117.3 overs) 282   1/19 (2) 2/47 (3)   (65.4 overs) 181
4/129 (5) 5/201 (4) 6/261 (7)   3/101 (1) 4/121 (4)
7/268 (8) 8/273 (9) 9/282 (10) 10/282 (11)   5/121 (6) 6/130 (5) 7/165 (8)
                                                             8/172 (7) 9/173 (9) 10/181 (11)

Abu Jayed 21–3–68–1; Taijul Islam 39.3–7–108–6; Ariful Haque 4–1–7–0; Mehedi Hasan 27–8–45–0; Nazmul Islam 23–6–49–2; Mahmudullah 3–0–3–1. *Second innings*—Taijul Islam 28.4–8–62–5; Nazmul Islam 6–1–27–2; Abu Jayed 7–1–25–0; Mehedi Hasan 19–7–48–3; Mahmudullah 4–1–7–0; Mominul Haque 1–0–4–0.

Bangladesh

Liton Das c Chakabva b Jarvis	9	– lbw b Sikandar Raza	23
Imrul Kayes b Chatara	5	– b Sikandar Raza	43
Mominul Haque c H. Masakadza b Sikandar Raza	11	– b Jarvis	9
Nazmul Hossain c Chakabva b Chatara	5	– (5) c Sikandar Raza b Mavuta	13
*Mahmudullah b Chatara	0	– (4) c sub (C. R. Ervine) b Sikandar Raza	16
†Mushfiqur Rahim c Chakabva b Jarvis	31	– c W. P. Masakadza b Mavuta	13
Ariful Haque not out	41	– c Chakabva b W. P. Masakadza	38
Mehedi Hasan c and b Williams	21	– c Chakabva b Mavuta	7
Taijul Islam c Chakabva b Sikandar Raza	8	– c Taylor b W. P. Masakadza	0
Nazmul Islam c Chari b Sikandar Raza	4	– lbw b Mavuta	0
Abu Jayed run out (Taylor/Chatara)	0	– not out	0
B 7, lb 1	8	B 5, lb 2	7

1/8 (2) 2/14 (1) 3/19 (4)   (51 overs) 143   1/56 (1) 2/67 (3)   (63.1 overs) 169
4/19 (5) 5/49 (3) 6/78 (6)   3/83 (2) 4/102 (4)
7/108 (8) 8/131 (9) 9/143 (10) 10/143 (11)   5/111 (5) 6/132 (6) 7/150 (8)
                                                        8/151 (9) 9/155 (10) 10/169 (7)

Jarvis 11–2–28–2; Chatara 10–4–19–3; Mavuta 6–0–27–0; Sikandar Raza 12–2–35–3; W. P. Masakadza 8–2–21–0; Williams 4–0–5–1. *Second innings*—Jarvis 14–5–29–1; Chatara 9–2–25–0; Sikandar Raza 17–1–41–3; Williams 8–2–13–0; Mavuta 10–2–21–4; W. P. Masakadza 5.1–0–33–2.

Umpires: R. A. Kettleborough and R. J. Tucker.   Third umpire: H. D. P. K. Dharmasena.
Referee: R. S. Madugalle.

BANGLADESH v ZIMBABWE

Second Test

At Mirpur, November 11–15, 2018. Bangladesh won by 218 runs. Toss: Bangladesh. Test debuts: Khaled Ahmed, Mithun Ali.

Bangladesh levelled the series with an emphatic victory at the Shere Bangla Stadium, which was fast becoming their stronghold: this was their fourth victory in the last seven Tests there, with another to come soon against West Indies. It was set up by big innings from Mominul Haque and Mushfiqur Rahim, and rammed home by the spinners, who shared 16 wickets to thwart a pair of hundreds from Taylor.

The Bangladeshis had not passed 200 in their previous eight Test innings, and looked on course for another disappointment when they lurched to 26 for three in the first hour. Jarvis removed both openers, while Tiripano had Mithun Ali caught behind for a debut duck. But that was the end of the good news for Zimbabwe. The spinners, so potent in Sylhet, were neutralised by a slower pitch, and Bangladesh's batsmen were soon doing as they pleased. Mominul, who had scored only 69 runs in eight Test innings since his twin hundreds against Sri Lanka at Chittagong in January, was quickly into his stride, showing improved footwork. He purred to his eighth Test century, and it was a surprise when he fell to the new ball shortly before stumps for a superb 161. His stand with Mushfiqur was eventually worth 266, a record for Bangladesh's fourth wicket in Tests, beating 180 by Mominul and Liton Das against Sri Lanka in that match at Chittagong.

Next day, after a careful start, Mushfiqur carried on serenely towards his second Test double-century. Not content with the fourth-wicket record, he broke the eighth-wicket record too, putting on 144 with Mehedi Hasan as Zimbabwe's bowlers proved toothless. They were without the parsimonious Chatara, whose match had ended when he tore a hamstring early on the second morning. Mahmudullah eventually called a halt after Mushfiqur reclaimed the record for Bangladesh's highest Test score, passing Shakib Al Hasan's 217 at Wellington in 2016-17.

Zimbabwe were up against it, but Taylor kept their heads above water with a defiant 110, his fifth Test century but first away from home. Reining in his attacking instincts – he hit only ten fours – he put on 139 for the sixth wicket with Moor, who made a Test-best 83. But the spinners worked their way through, Taijul finishing with a third successive five-for as the innings ended just before stumps on the third day. Zimbabwe had kept Bangladesh in the field for more than 105 overs, so Mahmudullah waived what would have been his side's first follow-on, despite a lead of 218. Embarrassment loomed at 25 for four, with both first-innings centurions sent packing by Tiripano, but Mithun and Mahmudullah stopped the rot with a stand of 118. The captain declared shortly after reaching his second Test century, nearly nine years after the first. It ended another drought: before this match he had managed only 86 runs in nine innings. Zimbabwe were left with a mountain to climb: 443 to win or, more realistically, 120 overs to draw.

TWIN HUNDREDS IN A TEST DEFEAT

H. Sutcliffe (176 and 127)	England v Australia at Melbourne	1924-25
G. A. Headley (106 and 107)	West Indies v England at Lord's	1939
V. S. Hazare (116 and 145)	India v Australia at Adelaide	1947-48
C. L. Walcott (155 and 110)	West Indies v Australia at Kingston	1954-55
S. M. Gavaskar (111 and 137)	India v Pakistan at Karachi	1978-79
A. Flower (142 and 199*)	Zimbabwe v South Africa at Harare	2001-02
B. C. Lara (221 and 130)	West Indies v Sri Lanka at Colombo (SSC)	2001-02
A. J. Strauss (123 and 108)	England v India at Chennai	2008-09
H. M. Amla (114 and 123*)	South Africa v India at Kolkata	2009-10
V. Kohli (115 and 141)	India v Australia at Adelaide	2014-15
B. R. M. Taylor (110 and 106*)	**Zimbabwe v Bangladesh at Mirpur**	**2018-19**

Taylor at least reached the foothills, and was still undefeated with 106 – it was the second time he had scored two hundreds in a Test, following Harare in April 2013, also against Bangladesh; the only other Zimbabwean to achieve the feat were the Flower brothers, Grant and Andy. But he was alone: after the openers put on 68, no one else managed more than 13. Off-spinner Mehedi winkled out the tail to finish with five for 38.

Man of the Match: Mushfiqur Rahim.   *Man of the Series:* Taijul Islam.

Close of play: first day, Bangladesh 303-5 (Mushfiqur Rahim 111, Mahmudullah 0); second day, Zimbabwe 25-1 (Chari 10, Tiripano 0); third day, Zimbabwe 304; fourth day, Zimbabwe 76-2 (Taylor 4, Williams 2).

Bangladesh

Liton Das c Mavuta b Jarvis	9	– b Jarvis	6
Imrul Kayes c Chakabva b Jarvis	0	– c Mavuta b Jarvis	3
Mominul Haque c Chari b Chatara	161	– c Chakabva b Tiripano	1
Mithun Ali c Taylor b Tiripano	0	– c Chakabva b Sikandar Raza	67
†Mushfiqur Rahim not out	219	– c Mavuta b Tiripano	7
Taijul Islam c Chakabva b Jarvis	4		
*Mahmudullah c Chakabva b Jarvis	36	– (6) not out	101
Ariful Haque c Chari b Jarvis	4	– (7) b Williams	5
Mehedi Hasan not out	68	– (8) not out	27
B 9, lb 8, w 1, nb 3	21	B 5, lb 1, w 1	7

1/13 (2) 2/16 (1)   (7 wkts dec, 160 overs) 522   1/9 (2)   (6 wkts dec, 54 overs) 224
3/26 (4) 4/292 (3)   2/10 (1) 3/10 (3)
5/299 (6) 6/372 (7) 7/378 (8)   4/25 (5) 5/143 (4) 6/151 (7)

Mustafizur Rahman and Khaled Ahmed did not bat.

Jarvis 28–6–71–5; Chatara 22.2–12–34–1; Sikandar Raza 22–1–111–0; Williams 30–4–80–0; Mavuta 31–1–137–0; Masakadza 2–0–7–0. *Second innings*—Jarvis 11–2–27–2; Tiripano 11–1–31–2; Williams 16–2–69–1; Sikandar Raza 7–0–39–1; Mavuta 9–0–52–0.

Zimbabwe

*H. Masakadza c Mehedi Hasan b Taijul Islam	14	– c Mominul Haque b Mehedi Hasan	25
B. B. Chari c Mominul Haque b Mehedi Hasan	53	– lbw b Taijul Islam	43
D. T. Tiripano c Mehedi Hasan b Taijul Islam	8	– (8) c Liton Das b Mehedi Hasan	0
B. R. M. Taylor c Taijul Islam b Mehedi Hasan	110	– (3) not out	106
S. C. Williams b Taijul Islam	11	– (4) b Mustafizur Rahman	13
Sikandar Raza b Taijul Islam	0	– (5) c and b Taijul Islam	12
P. J. Moor lbw b Ariful Haque	83	– (6) c Imrul Kayes b Mehedi Hasan	13
†R. W. Chakabva c Mominul Haque b Taijul Islam	10	– (7) run out (Mominul Haque/ Mushfiqur Rahim)	2
B. A. Mavuta c Ariful Haque b Mehedi Hasan	0	– c Taijul Islam b Mehedi Hasan	0
K. M. Jarvis not out	9	– c Khaled Ahmed b Mehedi Hasan	1
T. L. Chatara absent hurt		– absent hurt	
B 5, lb 1	6	B 1, lb 3, w 5	9

1/20 (1) 2/40 (3) 3/96 (2)   (105.3 overs) 304   1/68 (1) 2/70 (2)   (83.1 overs) 224
4/129 (5) 5/131 (6) 6/270 (7)   3/99 (4) 4/120 (5) 5/186 (6)
7/290 (4) 8/290 (9) 9/304 (8)   6/199 (7) 7/201 (8) 8/213 (9)
                                                                9/224 (10)

Mustafizur Rahman 21–8–58–0; Khaled Ahmed 18–7–48–0; Taijul Islam 40.3–10–107–5; Mehedi Hasan 20–3–61–3; Mahmudullah 2–0–14–0; Ariful Haque 4–2–10–1. *Second innings*—Mustafizur Rahman 10–2–19–1; Taijul Islam 37–5–93–2; Khaled Ahmed 12–4–45–0; Mehedi Hasan 18.1–5–38–5; Ariful Haque 3–1–7–0; Mahmudullah 1–0–1–0; Mominul Haque 2–0–17–0.

Umpires: H. D. P. K. Dharmasena and R. A. Kettleborough.   Third umpire: R. J. Tucker.
Referee: R. S. Madugalle.

BANGLADESH v WEST INDIES IN 2018-19

Mohammad Isam

Test matches (2): Bangladesh 2, West Indies 0
One-day internationals (3): Bangladesh 2, West Indies 1
Twenty20 internationals (3): Bangladesh 1, West Indies 2

West Indies had won both Tests easily when Bangladesh toured the Caribbean earlier in 2018, taking their overall record against them to ten victories out of 14. But the boot was firmly on the other foot when the teams reconvened on spin-friendly subcontinental surfaces.

The West Indians had expected a trial by turn, but the scale of it probably surprised them. Uniquely, the Bangladesh spinners took all 40 wickets in the two Tests, with the only pace bowling coming from Mustafizur Rahman, who sent down just four overs at Chittagong. The visiting batsmen kept trying to play the spinners off the back foot, with little success: on average, they lost a wicket every 29 deliveries. Only Shane Dowrich played an innings that lasted more than 100.

Off-spinner Mehedi Hasan led the way with 15 wickets, including 12 in the Second Test at Mirpur, where he broke his own national record for Bangladesh's best match figures. At Chittagong, 17-year-old off-spinner Nayeem Hasan had taken five for 61 in the first innings, watched by his parents and childhood coach. Mominul Haque chimed in with his sixth Test century on the ground, before Mahmudullah's 136 at Mirpur set up Bangladesh's first innings victory. They were held up only by Shimron Hetmyer, whose 93 contained one four and a remarkable nine sixes.

Bangladesh won the one-day series as well, as they had in July, but West Indies fought back to take a Twenty20 series marred by umpiring errors. The

YOUNGEST TO TAKE A FIVE-FOR IN A TEST

Yrs	Days		
16	307	Nasim-ul-Ghani (5-116†) ..	Pakistan v West Indies at Georgetown	1957-58
17	260	Mohammad Amir (5-79). . .	Pakistan v Australia at Melbourne	2009-10
17	**356**	**Nayeem Hasan (5-61‡)** . . .	**Bangladesh v W. Indies at Chittagong (ZAC)**	**2018-19**
18	36	Enamul Haque jnr (6-45) ..	Bangladesh v Zimbabwe at Chittagong (MAA)	2004-05
18	48	D. L. Vettori (5-84).	New Zealand v Sri Lanka at Hamilton	1996-97
18	196	P. J. Cummins (6-79‡)	Australia v South Africa at Johannesburg.	2011-12
18	236	Shahid Afridi (5-52‡)	Pakistan v Australia at Karachi.	1998-99
18	253	Wasim Akram (5-56)	Pakistan v New Zealand at Dunedin	1984-85
18	294	R. J. Shastri (5-125)	India v New Zealand at Auckland.	1980-81
18	301	E. Chigumbura (5-54).	Zimbabwe v Bangladesh at Chittagong (MAA)	2004-05
18	319	Shahid Nazir (5-53‡).	Pakistan v Zimbabwe at Sheikhupura.	1996-97
18	334	L. Sivaramakrishnan (6-64)	India v England at Bombay.	1984-85
18	361	Mehedi Hasan (6-80‡)	Bangladesh v England at Chittagong (ZAC) ..	2016-17

Only the first instance is shown for each player.
† *Nasim-ul-Ghani, a slow left-armer, took 6-67 in the next match, at Port-of-Spain, but never managed another five-for in a Test career that stretched to 1972-73.*
‡ *On debut.*

flashpoint came in the final match, when Tanvir Ahmed – standing in just his first men's series – wrongly no-balled seamer Oshane Thomas twice. Liton Das was caught from the second, and both free hits disappeared for six. The game was held up while West Indies' captain Carlos Brathwaite made his point to the officials, but the decision stood. "Oshane was under the pump," explained Brathwaite. "It messed his mindset." Brathwaite asked for a pause to regroup; oddly, it was Bangladesh's batsmen who seemed more affected, as the West Indians swept to their only series win out of six on their trip to the subcontinent, after drawing a blank in India.

Kraigg Brathwaite had led them in the Tests, after Jason Holder withdrew to rest an injured shoulder, but managed only 22 runs in four attempts. Shai Hope was also a disappointment, collecting 39, but he atoned in style, stroking successive one-day international centuries, then crashing 114 runs from 54 balls in the Twenty20s.

There was much interest in Bangladesh in the position of Mashrafe bin Mortaza, the long-serving one-day captain, who had announced his intention to run for parliament as part of the ruling Awami League just before the series; shortly after it, he was elected in his native Narail with 96% of the vote. Speculation was rife that he would bow out of international cricket to concentrate on his political career: if so, he finished on a high. His three for 30 earned him the match award in the first ODI, and he led the side shrewdly to claim the series.

WEST INDIES TOURING PARTY

*K. C. Brathwaite (T), F. A. Allen (50/20), S. W. Ambris (T/50), D. Bishoo (T/50), C. R. Brathwaite (50/20), D. M. Bravo (50/20), R. L. Chase (T/50), S. S. Cotterell (20), S. O. Dowrich (T), S. T. Gabriel (T), J. N. Hamilton (T), C. Hemraj (50), S. O. Hetmyer (T/50/20), S. D. Hope (T/50/20), E. Lewis (20), S. H. Lewis (T), K. M. A. Paul (T/50/20), K. A. Pierre (20), N. Pooran (20), K. O. A. Powell (T/50), R. Powell (50/20), D. Ramdin (20), R. A. Reifer (T), K. A. J. Roach (T/50), S. E. Rutherford (20), M. N. Samuels (50), O. R. Thomas (50/20), J. A. Warrican (T), K. O. K. Williams (20). *Coach:* N. Pothas.

J. O. Holder aggravated a shoulder injury on the preceding tour of India; he was replaced in the squad by Reifer, and as Test captain by K. C. Brathwaite. R. Powell led in the ODIs, and C. R. Brathwaite in the Twenty20s.

BANGLADESH v WEST INDIES

First Test

At Chittagong, November 22–24, 2018. Bangladesh won by 64 runs. Toss: Bangladesh. Test debut: Nayeem Hasan.

Bangladesh needed only three days to complete their first victory at home against West Indies, who had won five of the previous six encounters, to go with a watery draw at Chittagong in 2011-12. The spinners did all the damage, and also combined to score some important first-innings runs, when a collapse would have undone much of Mominul Haque's good work in making 120.

Mominul's century was his eighth in Tests, six of them on this ground, where he now averaged 83. He played conservatively, cashing in only when the bowlers pitched short or wide. Just before he was out, Bangladesh were riding high at 222 for three after winning the toss, but four wickets in 15 balls from the fiery Gabriel reduced them to 235 for seven. Earlier, he had been a bit too fiery, nudging Imrul Kayes twice as he ran between the wickets: Gabriel picked up two demerit points which, added to a similar offence in 2017, meant he was suspended for the next Test. Kayes was lucky to be there: Chase at second slip had grassed a regulation chance off Roach in the fifth over, which would have left Bangladesh 20 for two; later he was caught at deep square off a no-ball from slow left-armer Warrican, who still finished with a Test-best four for 62.

Nayeem Hasan, a local 17-year-old making his debut, hung around for more than two hours, sharing a ninth-wicket stand of 65 with Taijul Islam, who went on to his highest Test score as Bangladesh batted into the second day. Then began West Indies' trial by spin: Taijul started the slide, and before long it was 88 for five. Hetmyer counter-attacked spectacularly, adding 92 in 14 overs with Dowrich; they hit seven sixes in all. But it couldn't last: Hetmyer tickled Mehedi Hasan to the keeper and, although Dowrich inched the total to 246, a deficit of 78 was daunting on a turning pitch. Off-spinner Nayeem became the third-youngest to take a five-for in a Test. "He's a wonderful prospect," said Bangladesh's coach Steve Rhodes. "Five wickets on debut at that age is incredible."

MOST TEST CENTURIES ON ONE GROUND

100	T		
11	27	D. P. M. D. Jayawardene (Sri Lanka) . . .	Colombo (SSC)
9	11	D. G. Bradman (Australia)	Melbourne
9	22	J. H. Kallis (South Africa)	Cape Town
8	22	K. C. Sangakkara (Sri Lanka)	Colombo (SSC)
7	10	M. J. Clarke (Australia)	Adelaide
7	23	D. P. M. D. Jayawardene (Sri Lanka) . . .	Galle
7	23	K. C. Sangakkara (Sri Lanka)	Galle
6	**8**	**Mominul Haque (Bangladesh)**	**Chittagong (ZAC)**
6	10	M. L. Hayden (Australia)	Melbourne
6	12	M. P. Vaughan (England)	Lord's
6	16	R. T. Ponting (Australia)	Sydney
6	17	R. T. Ponting (Australia)	Adelaide
6	21	G. A. Gooch (England)	Lord's

J. B. Hobbs (England) made five centuries in ten Tests at Melbourne, the record away from home.

West Indies turned to their own spinners after a solitary over from Roach, which cost 11. Warrican soon removed Kayes, and the others struggled against Chase and Bishoo, who claimed seven for 44 between them. But for Mahmudullah, who resisted for 31, Bangladesh might not have made it to three figures. In all, 17 wickets tumbled on the second day.

A target of 204 looked attainable for West Indies – but not for long. They were soon in disarray at 11 for four, all to Taijul and Shakib Al Hasan, who nabbed Hope in single figures for the second time in the game. First to go was Powell, who missed a slog and was stumped first ball for a duck. That was a unique dismissal for an opener in Tests, and a landmark victim for Shakib in his 54th match: the first Bangladeshi to 200 Test wickets, and the fastest of any nationality to combine that with 3,000 runs, beating Ian Botham, who needed 55. Ambris dug in while Hetmyer hit out, taking two fours and a six off successive balls from Shakib, before lofting Mehedi to long-off after a quick 27; inside 22 overs West Indies were sunk at 75 for eight. Ambris continued to defy the spinners, giving his side brief hope during a stand of 63 with Warrican, but Mehedi put a stop to that.

Taijul finally had Ambris caught behind in the next over, although replays suggested he might not have touched the ball after 130 minutes of defiance. But it gave Taijul figures of six for 33, the best for Bangladesh in the fourth innings – and his fourth haul of five or more in 2018. It also meant their spinners had taken all 20 wickets for only the second time, following the win over England at Mirpur two years earlier.

Man of the Match: Mominul Haque.

Close of play: first day, Bangladesh 315-8 (Nayeem Hasan 24, Taijul Islam 32); second day, Bangladesh 55-5 (Mushfiqur Rahim 11, Mehedi Hasan 0).

Bangladesh

Imrul Kayes c Ambris b Warrican	44	– b Warrican	2
Soumya Sarkar c Dowrich b Roach	0	– c Brathwaite b Chase	11
Mominul Haque c Dowrich b Gabriel	120	– lbw b Chase	12
Mithun Ali c Dowrich b Bishoo	20	– b Bishoo	17
*Shakib Al Hasan b Gabriel	34	– c Gabriel b Warrican	1
†Mushfiqur Rahim lbw b Gabriel	4	– b Gabriel	19
Mahmudullah b Gabriel	3	– (8) c Hope b Bishoo	31
Mehedi Hasan b Warrican	22	– (7) c Dowrich b Bishoo	18
Nayeem Hasan c Hope b Warrican	26	– c Hope b Bishoo	5
Taijul Islam not out	39	– c Warrican b Chase	1
Mustafizur Rahman lbw b Warrican	0	– not out	2
B 3, lb 5, nb 4	12	B 2, lb 1, nb 3	6

1/1 (2) 2/105 (3) 3/153 (4)   (92.4 overs) 324   1/13 (1) 2/13 (2)   (35.5 overs) 125
4/222 (3) 5/226 (6) 6/230 (7)   3/32 (3) 4/35 (5)
7/235 (5) 8/259 (8) 9/324 (9) 10/324 (11)   5/53 (4) 6/69 (6) 7/106 (7)
                                     8/122 (9) 9/123 (8) 10/125 (10)

Roach 17–2–63–1; Gabriel 20–3–70–4; Chase 11–0–42–0; Warrican 21.4–6–62–4; Bishoo 15–0–60–1; Brathwaite 8–1–19–0. *Second innings*—Roach 1–0–11–0; Warrican 16–2–43–2; Chase 6.5–1–18–3; Bishoo 9–0–26–4; Gabriel 3–0–24–1.

West Indies

*K. C. Brathwaite c Soumya Sarkar b Shakib Al Hasan	13	– lbw b Taijul Islam	8
K. O. A. Powell lbw b Taijul Islam	14	– st Mushfiqur Rahim b Shakib Al Hasan	0
S. D. Hope b Shakib Al Hasan	1	– c Mushfiqur Rahim b Shakib Al Hasan	3
S. W. Ambris lbw b Nayeem Hasan	19	– c Mushfiqur Rahim b Taijul Islam	43
R. L. Chase c Imrul Kayes b Nayeem Hasan	31	– lbw b Taijul Islam	0
S. O. Hetmyer c Mushfiqur Rahim b Mehedi Hasan	63	– c Nayeem Hasan b Mehedi Hasan	27
†S. O. Dowrich not out	63	– lbw b Taijul Islam	5
D. Bishoo lbw b Nayeem Hasan	7	– b Taijul Islam	2
K. A. J. Roach lbw b Nayeem Hasan	2	– lbw b Taijul Islam	1
J. A. Warrican b Nayeem Hasan	12	– c Shakib Al Hasan b Mehedi Hasan	41
S. T. Gabriel c Mahmudullah b Shakib Al Hasan	6	– not out	0
B 6, lb 2, nb 2, p 5	15	B 9	9

1/29 (1) 2/30 (3) 3/31 (1)   (64 overs) 246   1/5 (2) 2/11 (3)   (35.2 overs) 139
4/77 (5) 5/88 (4) 6/180 (6)   3/11 (1) 4/11 (5)
7/199 (8) 8/205 (9) 9/225 (10) 10/246 (11)   5/44 (6) 6/51 (7) 7/69 (8)
                                    8/75 (9) 9/138 (10) 10/139 (4)

Mustafizur Rahman 2–1–4–0; Mehedi Hasan 15–0–67–1; Taijul Islam 20–3–51–1; Shakib Al Hasan 11–1–43–3; Nayeem Hasan 14–2–61–5; Mahmudullah 2–0–7–0. *Second innings*—Shakib Al Hasan 7–0–30–2; Nayeem Hasan 7–1–29–0; Taijul Islam 11.2–2–33–6; Mehedi Hasan 8–1–27–2; Mustafizur Rahman 2–0–11–0.

Umpires: Aleem Dar and R. K. Illingworth.   Third umpire: R. S. A. Palliyaguruge.
Referee: D. C. Boon.

BANGLADESH v WEST INDIES

Second Test

At Mirpur, November 30–December 2, 2018. Bangladesh won by an innings and 184 runs. Toss: Bangladesh. Test debut: Shadman Islam.

Bangladesh wrapped up the series with their first innings win, after 111 previous matches had brought only a dozen victories. This one, while pressed home by the spinners, was set up by a huge total in which West Indies' own spinners failed to make much impression.

First to lay down a marker was Shadman Islam, a solid 23-year-old opener, who became Bangladesh's eighth new cap in their eight Tests in 2018, after replacing the injured Imrul Kayes. He bedded down for most of the first two sessions, hitting just six fours from 199 balls in a patient display. It looked as if his good work might be in vain when Mushfiqur Rahim, just after completing 4,000 Test runs, fell to the Grenadian paceman Shermon Lewis, playing his second Test in place of the suspended Shannon Gabriel. But skipper Shakib Al Hasan put on 111 with Mahmudullah, who batted for more than six hours in all – his longest Test innings – before being last out for 136, his third and highest Test century. With everyone reaching double figures, Bangladesh made an imposing 508.

ALL 11 REACHING DOUBLE FIGURES IN TEST INNINGS

Total	Lowest		
475	11	England v Australia at Melbourne	1894-95
385	10	South Africa v England at Johannesburg	1905-06
636	11	England v Australia at Sydney	1928-29
358	10*	South Africa v Australia at Melbourne	1931-32
575-8 dec†	11	Australia v India at Melbourne	1947-48
397	11	India v Pakistan at Calcutta	1952-53
359	12	India v New Zealand at Dunedin	1967-68
524-9 dec	10*	India v New Zealand at Kanpur.	1976-77
471	10*	Australia v Sri Lanka at Colombo (SSC)	1992-93
470	10	England v West Indies at The Oval	2004
664	11	India v England at The Oval	2007
449-9 dec	10	West Indies v Australia at Bridgetown	2011-12
313	12	South Africa v England at Johannesburg	2015-16
508	**12***	**Bangladesh v West Indies at Mirpur**	**2018-19**

† *One batsman (D. G. Bradman) retired hurt after scoring 57.*

West Indies started their innings after tea on the second day, and by the close were in trouble at 75 for five. The top five were all bowled – the first such instance in a Test since 1890 – and Hope alone reached double figures; he was promptly out for ten. The procession continued next morning, when Mehedi Hasan finished with seven for 58 as West Indies were shot out for 111, their lowest against Bangladesh, undercutting 129 at Kingston four months previously.

A few weeks earlier, Bangladesh had batted again against Zimbabwe here, despite a lead of 218. Now, a massive 397 runs ahead, Shakib Al Hasan had no such qualms in enforcing the follow-on, the first time Bangladesh had done so. Brathwaite's poor series continued when he was out in the first over, and it was soon 29 for four. Total embarrassment for West Indies was averted by an astonishing innings from Hetmyer, who blasted nine sixes and a solitary four. Eight of the sixes came before that four, breaking the Test record of six, set barely a fortnight earlier by England's Sam Curran at Pallekele. Few would have begrudged Hetmyer a maiden century, but he holed out at long-on for 93, from 92 balls. He cleared the ropes three times in one Shakib over, during which he momentarily had 66 from 66, with six sixes. The only other West Indian to hit nine in an innings was Chris Gayle, during his 333 against Sri Lanka at Galle in 2010-11.

Hetmyer was one of 12 wickets in the match for Mehedi – an old adversary from Under-19 days – who improved his own national record for the best match figures (previously 12 for 157, against England here in 2016-17). Roach and Lewis enjoyed themselves in a last-gasp stand of 42 but, as in the First Test, it was Taijul who administered the *coup de grâce*, trapping Lewis for his 250th first-class scalp. "We obviously had a lot to prove after losing to them the way we did in July," said Shakib. "I think we have done that."

Man of the Match: Mehedi Hasan. *Man of the Series:* Shakib Al Hasan.

Close of play: first day, Bangladesh 259-5 (Shakib Al Hasan 55, Mahmudullah 31); second day, West Indies 75-5 (Hetmyer 32, Dowrich 17).

Bangladesh

Shadman Islam lbw b Bishoo	76	Mehedi Hasan c Dowrich b Warrican	18
Soumya Sarkar c Hope b Chase	19	Taijul Islam c Dowrich b Brathwaite	26
Mominul Haque c Chase b Roach	29	Nayeem Hasan not out	12
Mithun Ali b Bishoo	29	B 2, lb 8, w 1, nb 4	15
*Shakib Al Hasan c Hope b Roach	80		
†Mushfiqur Rahim b Lewis	14	1/42 (2) 2/87 (3) 3/151 (4) (154 overs) 508	
Mahmudullah b Warrican	136	4/161 (5) 5/190 (6) 6/301 (5)	
Liton Das b Brathwaite	54	7/393 (8) 8/416 (9) 9/472 (10) 10/508 (7)	

Roach 25–4–61–2; Lewis 20–2–69–1; Chase 28–0–111–1; Warrican 38–5–91–2; Bishoo 28–1–109–2; Brathwaite 15–0–57–2.

West Indies

*K. C. Brathwaite b Shakib Al Hasan	0	– lbw b Shakib Al Hasan	1
K. O. A. Powell b Mehedi Hasan	4	– st Mushfiqur Rahim b Mehedi Hasan	6
S. D. Hope b Mehedi Hasan	10	– c Shakib Al Hasan b Mehedi Hasan	25
S. W. Ambris b Shakib Al Hasan	7	– lbw b Taijul Islam	4
R. L. Chase b Mehedi Hasan	0	– c Mominul Haque b Taijul Islam	3
S. O. Hetmyer c and b Mehedi Hasan	39	– c Mithun Ali b Mehedi Hasan	93
†S. O. Dowrich lbw b Mehedi Hasan	37	– c Soumya Sarkar b Nayeem Hasan	3
D. Bishoo c Shadman Islam b Mehedi Hasan	1	– c Soumya Sarkar b Mehedi Hasan	12
K. A. J. Roach c Liton Das b Mehedi Hasan	1	– not out	37
J. A. Warrican not out	5	– c and b Mehedi Hasan	0
S. H. Lewis lbw b Shakib Al Hasan	0	– lbw b Taijul Islam	20
B 4, lb 3	7	B 6, lb 3	9

1/0 (1) 2/6 (2) 3/17 (4)	(36.4 overs) 111	1/2 (1) 2/14 (2)	(59.2 overs) 213
4/20 (5) 5/29 (3) 6/86 (6)		3/23 (4) 4/29 (5)	
7/88 (8) 8/92 (9) 9/110 (7) 10/111 (11)		5/85 (3) 6/96 (7) 7/143 (8)	
		8/166 (6) 9/171 (10) 10/213 (11)	

Shakib Al Hasan 15.4–4–27–3; Mehedi Hasan 16–1–58–7; Nayeem Hasan 3–0–9–0; Taijul Islam 1–0–10–0; Mahmudullah 1–1–0–0. *Second innings*—Shakib Al Hasan 14–3–65–1; Mehedi Hasan 20–2–59–5; Taijul Islam 10.2–1–40–3; Mahmudullah 1–0–6–0; Nayeem Hasan 14–2–34–1.

Umpires: Aleem Dar and R. S. A. Palliyaguruge.   Third umpire: R. K. Illingworth.
Referee: A. J. Pycroft.

First one-day international   At Mirpur, December 9, 2018 (day/night). **Bangladesh won by five wickets.** ‡**West Indies 195-9** (50 overs) (S. D. Hope 43, R. L. Chase 32, K. M. A. Paul 36; Mustafizur Rahman 3-35, Mashrafe bin Mortaza 3-30); **Bangladesh 196-5** (35.1 overs) (Liton Das 41, Mushfiqur Rahim 55*, Shakib Al Hasan 30). *MoM:* Mashrafe bin Mortaza. *West Indies' batting problems continued, against a combination of spin and the wily seam of Mashrafe bin Mortaza. They struggled to 127-6 in the 40th over, before Roston Chase and Keemo Paul put on 51. But Mustafizur*

Rahman, one of the best death bowlers around, took three wickets in nine balls to keep the total under 200. Liton Das gave the chase a quick start, then Mushfiqur Rahim eased Bangladesh home.

Second one-day international At Mirpur, December 11, 2018 (day/night). **West Indies won by four wickets. Bangladesh 255-7** (50 overs) (Tamim Iqbal 50, Mushfiqur Rahim 62, Shakib Al Hasan 65, Mahmudullah 30; O. R. Thomas 3-54); ‡**West Indies 256-6** (49.4 overs) (S. D. Hope 146*). *MoM:* S. D. Hope. *Bangladesh seemed to have the series in the bag when West Indies slipped to 185-6 after 39 overs, chasing 256. But Shai Hope was still there, approaching a third ODI century, and he dominated a seventh-wicket stand of 71* with Paul (18* from 31 balls), to pull off a sensational last-over victory. Hope's career-best 146* came from 144 deliveries. Bangladesh's total included half-centuries from their three senior batsmen, but only 64 came from the last ten overs.*

Third one-day international At Sylhet, December 14, 2018 (day/night). **Bangladesh won by eight wickets. West Indies 198-9** (50 overs) (S. D. Hope 108*; Mehedi Hasan 4-29); ‡**Bangladesh 202-2** (38.3 overs) (Tamim Iqbal 81*, Soumya Sarkar 80). *MoM:* Mehedi Hasan. *MoS:* S. D. Hope. *Bangladesh made sure of the ODI series with disciplined bowling, again restricting West Indies to under 200. That included another century from Hope, who batted through the 50 overs, but received little support: the next-highest score was 19, by Marlon Samuels. Mehedi Hasan took the first two wickets and finished with four, although the West Indians were annoyed about his dismissal of their captain, Rovman Powell, as they claimed there were too many fielders (six) on the leg side; the third umpire reviewed footage, but was unable to find a clear shot of the whole ground. Tamim Iqbal and Soumya Sarkar (who launched five sixes) made light of the chase with a second-wicket stand of 131 in 25 overs.*

First Twenty20 international At Sylhet, December 17, 2018. **West Indies won by eight wickets.** ‡**Bangladesh 129** (19 overs) (Shakib Al Hasan 61; S. S. Cotterell 4-28); **West Indies 130-2** (10.5 overs) (S. D. Hope 55). *MoM:* S. S. Cotterell. *Bangladesh misfired against the pacy left-armer Sheldon Cotterell, who performed his signature salute celebration (he was formerly in the Jamaican army) four times on a bouncy track. Hope then smashed six sixes from 23 balls as West Indies sauntered home. The start time was brought forward twice: first from 5pm to 2pm to avoid early-evening dew, then to 12.30 after a floodlight failed.*

Second Twenty20 international At Mirpur, December 20, 2018 (floodlit). **Bangladesh won by 36 runs. Bangladesh 211-4** (20 overs) (Liton Das 60, Soumya Sarkar 32, Shakib Al Hasan 42*, Mahmudullah 43*); ‡**West Indies 175** (19.2 overs) (S. D. Hope 36, R. Powell 50; Shakib Al Hasan 5-20). *MoM:* Shakib Al Hasan. *Bangladesh squared the series largely thanks to their captain Shakib Al Hasan, who followed a brisk 42* with 5-20, his country's second-best T20 figures, behind Elias Sunny's 5-13 against Ireland in Belfast in 2012. With Liton Das blazing 60 from 34 deliveries, Bangladesh's total proved more than enough, despite a dew-laden ball hampering their bowlers.*

Third Twenty20 international At Mirpur, December 22, 2018 (floodlit). **West Indies won by 50 runs. West Indies 190** (19.2 overs) (E. Lewis 89; Shakib Al Hasan 3-37, Mustafizur Rahman 3-33, Mahmudullah 3-18); ‡**Bangladesh 140** (17 overs) (Liton Das 43; K. M. A. Paul 5-15). *MoM:* E. Lewis. *MoS:* Shakib Al Hasan. *T20I debut:* S. E. Rutherford (West Indies). *West Indies took the series, after a match marred by umpiring errors. In the fourth over of the chase, Tanvir Ahmed called Oshane Thomas twice for overstepping, only for replays to show both were legal deliveries: Liton Das was caught at mid-off from the second, and both calls resulted in free hits that went for six. The game was held up for ten minutes while West Indies' captain Carlos Brathwaite queried the decisions with the umpires and match referee Jeff Crowe, but to no avail. West Indies regrouped well, sending Bangladesh plummeting from 65-1 to 96-8. Paul polished off the innings with his side's best T20 figures, and only their second five-for, after Darren Sammy's 5-26 against Zimbabwe at Port-of-Spain in 2009-10. Earlier, Evin Lewis had clattered 89 from 36 balls, with eight sixes.*

DOMESTIC CRICKET IN BANGLADESH IN 2017-18

UTPAL SHUVRO

Khulna won their third successive National Cricket League, and their fourth in the last six seasons. Though they had to wait until the final round, when they beat Dhaka by an innings and 49 runs, they were the only top-tier team to win any games, and led the table from the second round onwards.

Overall, it was their sixth first-class title, beating a record they had shared with Dhaka and Rajshahi, two teams with contrasting fortunes in 2017-18. That last-round defeat by Khulna relegated **Dhaka** to the second tier for the first time; they tied on points with Barisal, with an identical record, but went down because they had taken fewer wickets over the season. **Rajshahi**, who had spent the first three seasons of the split-league format in the lower tier, secured promotion after narrowly missing it the previous year; the first of their two victories came after they were bowled out for 79 in the first innings.

Khulna possessed the only two batsmen who reached 500 runs in the NCL. Anamul Haque, the former Test opener, made 619 at 77, and converted two of his three half-centuries into doubles – only the third batsman to score two double-hundreds in one NCL competition, after Rony Talukdar and Mosaddek Hossain in 2014-15. Mehedi Hasan (not the Test off-spinner) scored 501 at 83 and, more oddly, converted two of his three fifties into 177s. They shared a 295-run stand for Khulna's second wicket in the title-clinching victory over Dhaka, when the other Mehedi Hasan collected ten for 113 in his only appearance of the tournament. Slow left-armer Abdur Razzak, now 35, captured 20 wickets in six games.

Mizanur Rahman helped Rajshahi to promotion by scoring centuries in three consecutive innings, a feat previously achieved by Tamim Iqbal in 2012-13 and Talukdar in 2014-15. Seamer Farhad Reza's 21 victims made him the NCL's joint-leading wicket-taker with Dhaka Metropolis's slow left-armer Nehaduzzaman.

Razzak earned further glory in the Bangladesh Cricket League, the first-class franchise-based competition. His team, **South Zone**, won their third title when he took 11 for 101 in the final round, against defending champions North Zone, who started so far ahead on points that they needed only a draw. But Razzak skittled them for 187 and 115 to secure an innings victory. He was comfortably the most successful bowler in the tournament, with 43 wickets, including five hauls of five or more. In a second-round match against Central Zone, Razzak became the first Bangladeshi bowler to take 500 first-class wickets, two days after his team-mate Tushar Imran had become the first Bangladeshi batsman to score 10,000 first-class runs.

Tushar had a fabulous tournament, passing 50 in seven of his nine innings, with four centuries; even so, his 725 runs at 90 were exceeded by East Zone's Liton Das, with 779 at 97. But Tushar completed 1,000 in all first-class cricket for the second successive season. It was still not enough to win him an international return, ten years after he last played for Bangladesh, though Razzak was recalled for a lone Test against Sri Lanka, which enabled him to finish with 68 first-class wickets, a career-best.

In the one-day Dhaka Premier League, **Abahani** emerged as champions, thanks in part to one-day international captain Mashrafe bin Mortaza, who contributed 39 wickets. In the final week of the competition, they hit 393 for four and (after being put in) 374 for six, the two highest totals in one-day cricket in Bangladesh. Fifty centuries were scored in all, and Mohammad Ashraful became the second batsman to score five hundreds in a single List A tournament, after Alviro Petersen in South Africa's Momentum Cup in 2015-16. But four of them came in defeats, and his team, Kalabagan Krira Chakra, were relegated.

FIRST-CLASS AVERAGES IN 2017-18

BATTING (450 runs, average 40.00)

		M	I	NO	R	HS	100	Avge	Ct/St
1	Tushar Imran (*Khulna/South Zone*)	12	17	2	1,102	148	5	73.46	6
2	Liton Das (*Rangpur/EZ/Bangladesh*)...	9	15	2	953	274	3	73.30	10/3
3	Yasir Ali (*Chittagong/Bang A/E Zone*)	7	11	2	601	132	2	66.77	9
4	Mizanur Rahman (*Rajshahi/North Zone*)	11	17	2	931	175	5	62.06	7
5	Mehedi Hasan snr (*Khulna/Bang A/SZ*).	9	11	2	546	177	2	60.66	5
6	Anamul Haque (*Khulna/South Zone*) ...	9	13	0	782	216	2	60.15	6
7	Suhrawadi Shuvo (*Rangpur/North Zone*)	9	11	3	481	145	1	60.12	1
8	†Shadman Islam (*Dhaka Met/BangA/CZ*)	9	13	0	750	112	3	57.69	4
9	Raqibul Hasan (*Dhaka/Central Zone*) ..	10	13	3	551	105	1	55.10	7
10	Ariful Haque (*Rangpur/North Zone*) ...	12	15	3	657	162	4	54.75	5
11	†Mominul Haque (*Chittagong/EZ/Bang*)	8	14	0	752	258	4	53.71	3
12	Naeem Islam (*Rangpur/North Zone*) ...	10	11	1	532	216	2	53.20	6
13	Marshall Ayub (*Dhaka Met/C Zone*) ...	10	17	2	747	132	2	49.80	6
14	†Junaid Siddique (*Rajshahi/North Zone*)	11	16	1	687	150	2	45.80	7
15	Sohag Gazi (*Barisal/East Zone*)	12	14	3	480	99	0	43.63	13
16	†Nazmul Hossain (*Rajshahi/Bang A/NZ*)	10	17	1	698	194	1	43.62	6
17	Abdul Mazid (*Dhaka/Central Zone*)....	8	13	2	456	205	1	41.45	2
18	Tasamul Haque (*Chittagong/East Zone*)	8	14	2	497	108*	1	41.41	9
19	†Fazle Mahmud (*Barisal/South Zone*) ..	8	11	0	450	107	1	40.90	2
20	Jahurul Islam (*Rajshahi/North Zone*) ...	8	12	0	488	158	2	40.66	12/1
21	Nurul Hasan (*Khulna/Bang A/S Zone*)..	11	16	2	560	133	1	40.00	30/9

BOWLING (16 wickets)

		Style	O	M	R	W	BB	5I	Avge
1	Shoriful Islam (*Rajshahi/North Zone*)	LFM	140	24	420	20	4-33	0	21.00
2	Farhad Reza (*Rajshahi/North Zone*)..	RFM	262.1	69	734	32	5-57	1	22.93
3	Shafiul Islam (*Rajshahi/North Zone*)	RFM	155.5	28	513	20	4-58	0	25.65
4	Ebadat Hossain (*Bang A/Sylhet/CZ*)	RFM	144	23	490	19	4-32	0	25.78
5	Ariful Haque (*Rangpur/North Zone*) .	RFM	193	36	622	23	4-49	0	27.04
6	Iftekhar Sajjad (*Chittagong*)	RFM	202.1	47	515	18	5-43	2	28.61
7	Nehaduzzaman (*Dhaka Metropolis*) .	SLA	188	33	607	21	5-45	1	28.90
8	Mehedi Hasan Rana (*Chittagong/EZ*)	LFM	159.5	25	567	19	3-30	0	29.84
9	Abdur Razzak (*Khulna/S Zone/Bang*)	SLA	594	95	2,066	68	6-48	6	30.38
10	Saqlain Sajib (*Rajshahi/South Zone*)	SLA	228.5	51	631	20	3-26	0	31.55
11	Monir Hossain (*Barisal*)	SLA	195.2	39	542	17	7-85	1	31.88
12	Al-Amin Hossain (*Khulna/S Zone*)..	RFM	149	18	522	16	4-72	0	32.62
13	Abu Jayed (*Sylhet/East Zone*).......	RFM	243.4	32	932	28	5-71	1	33.28
14	Enamul Haque (*Sylhet/East Zone*) ...	SLA	182.4	23	685	19	5-63	2	36.05
15	Shuvagata Hom (*Dhaka/Central Zone*)	OB	255.2	35	943	24	4-62	0	39.29
16	Sohag Gazi (*Barisal/East Zone*)	OB	395	49	1,463	37	7-141	3	39.54
17	Taijul Islam (*Rajshahi/N Zone/Bang*)	SLA	352.4	55	1,156	29	5-105	1	39.86
18	Kamrul Islam (*Barisal/Bang A/SZ*) .	RFM	216	24	888	20	4-93	0	44.40
19	Mosharraf Hossain (*Dhaka/C Zone*)..	SLA	320.5	61	991	20	4-57	0	49.55

WALTON LED TV NATIONAL CRICKET LEAGUE IN 2017-18

Tier One	P	W	L	D	Pts	**Tier Two**	P	W	L	D	Pts
Khulna	6	2	0	4	25	Rajshahi	6	2	0	4	25
Rangpur	6	0	0	6	12						
Barisal.............	6	0	1	5	10	Sylhet	6	1	1	2†	16
						Chittagong	6	0	1	4*	10
Dhaka..............	6	0	1	5	10	Dhaka Metropolis.....	6	0	1	4*	10

*   *Plus one abandoned match.*   †   *Plus two abandoned matches.*

Outright win = 8pts; bonus for innings win = 1pt; draw = 2pts; abandoned = 2pts.

NATIONAL CRICKET LEAGUE WINNERS

†1999-2000	Chittagong	2005-06	Rajshahi	2012-13	Khulna
2000-01	Biman Bangladesh	2006-07	Dhaka	2013-14	Dhaka
	Airlines	2007-08	Khulna	2014-15	Rangpur
2001-02	Dhaka	2008-09	Rajshahi	2015-16	Khulna
2002-03	Khulna	2009-10	Rajshahi	2016-17	Khulna
2003-04	Dhaka	2010-11	Rajshahi	2017-18	Khulna
2004-05	Dhaka	2011-12	Rajshahi		

† *The National Cricket League was not first-class in 1999-2000.*

Khulna have won the title 6 times, Dhaka and Rajshahi 5, Biman Bangladesh Airlines, Chittagong and Rangpur 1.

BANGLADESH CRICKET LEAGUE IN 2017-18

					1st-inns	Bonus pts		
	P	*W*	*L*	*D*	*pts*	*Bat*	*Bowl*	*Pts*
South Zone	6	1	0	5	3	23	14	65
North Zone	6	2	1	3	2	17	14	62
East Zone	6	0	1	5	4	18	15	52
Central Zone.................	6	0	1	5	3	20	13	51

Outright win = 10pts; draw = 3pts; first-innings lead = 1pt.

DHAKA PREMIER LEAGUE IN 2017-18

50-over league plus Super League and Relegation League

Preliminary League	*P*	*W*	*L*	*Pts*
ABAHANI	11	8	3	16
LEGENDS OF RUPGANJ....	11	7	4	14
KHEL. SAMAJ KALYAN....	11	7	4	14
PRIME DOLESHWAR	11	6*	4	13
SJ DHANMONDI.	11	6	5	12
GAZI GRP CRICKETERS ...	11	6	5	12
Mohammedan	11	5*	5	11
Shinepukur	11	5	6	10
Prime Bank	11	5	6	10
Brothers Union	11	4	7	8
Agrani Bank	11	4	7	8
Kalabagan Krira Chakra	11	2	9	4

Super League	*P*	*W*	*L*	*Pts*
Abahani...................	16	12	4	24
Legends of Rupganj	16	10	6	20
Sheikh Jamal Dhanmondi.....	16	10	6	20
Prime Doleshwar............	16	8*	7	17
Khelaghar Samaj Kalyan	16	8	8	16
Gazi Group Cricketers	16	7	9	14

Relegation League	*P*	*W*	*L*	*Pts*
Brothers Union	13	6	7	12
Agrani Bank	13	5	8	10
Kalabagan Krira Chakra......	13	2	11	4

* *Plus one tie.*

The top six teams advanced to the Super League, carrying forward all their results from the Preliminary League, and then playing the other five qualifiers again. Teams tied on points were separated on head-to-head results.

The Bangladesh Premier League has its own section (page 1132).

INDIAN CRICKET IN 2018

Up, up and away

Sharda Ugra

If ever a blueprint were needed for Test teams to fashion histories and turnarounds, India's 2018 would serve handsomely. They adhered to the two basic principles of Test cricket: batsmen set up matches, bowlers win them. But it was in the fine print that they came of age as a touring team: a sorting-out and sweeping-up of the tiny, scattered, details, of selection, the reading of pitches, batting orders and fitness; even the toss began to fall their way. Eventually, at the end of 12 gruelling away Tests over 12 months, culminating in a historic win in Australia, they found themselves. As Virat Kohli, their captain, put it, they were "absolutely complete".

The limited-overs team swept through ten series and tournaments, and 48 completed matches, winning 14 and losing four across the board (there were also two one-day ties, against Afghanistan and West Indies). They lost

INDIA IN 2018

	Played	Won	Lost	Drawn/No result
Tests	14	7	7	–
One-day internationals	20	14	4	2
Twenty20 internationals	19	14	4	1

JANUARY / FEBRUARY	3 Tests, 6 ODIs and 3 T20Is (a) v South Africa	(page 966)
MARCH	T20 tri-series (in Sri Lanka) v Bangladesh and Sri Lanka	(page 1026)
APRIL		
MAY		
JUNE	1 Test (h) v Afghanistan	(page 877)
	2 T20Is (a) v Ireland	(page 905)
JULY / AUGUST / SEPTEMBER	5 Tests, 3 ODIs and 3 T20Is (a) v England	(page 317)
OCTOBER / NOVEMBER	2 Tests, 5 ODIs and 3 T20Is (h) v West Indies	(page 882)
DECEMBER / JANUARY	4 Tests, 3 ODIs and 3 T20Is (a) v Australia	(page 820)

For a review of Indian domestic cricket from the 2017-18 season, see page 889.

just once, 2–1 in England in a 50-over series. Not only did India end the year as the best team across the formats (they had 35 wins in all, six clear of England and Pakistan), they began 2019 by inflicting a rare ODI home defeat on Australia.

On their own turf, India had needed only eight days to wrap up three Tests against Afghanistan, on their debut, and West Indies. Instead, it was outside Asia – three series on three continents – where they sought validation, as a touring side who were not merely competitive, but successful. From a distance, seven defeats and four victories from those 12 games does not immediately seem like mission accomplished. Yet that is how it felt – not because of how the year took shape, but because of how it ended. Defeats in South Africa (1–2) and in England (1–4) threw cricket's slings and arrows at India. But in Australia they took up arms.

On a damp afternoon in Sydney, Kohli's men became the first Indian side to win a series in Australia in more than 70 years of trying. The Border–Gavaskar series finished 2–1, but the last two days were spoiled by rain, and 3–1 would have accurately represented the difference between the sides, not least in the quality of batsmanship and the response to crisis. Armed with the most potent fast-bowling pack in their history, India took advantage of an Australian batting line-up missing the banned Steve Smith and David Warner. After shuffling around their own batting, the Indians finally restored stability to their middle order, and gave the cold efficiency of their bowling enough runs to play with.

If one player symbolised their effort, it was Jasprit Bumrah. He went from white-ball specialism to a Test debut at Cape Town in January 2018, and finished the Australia series as their undeniable strike bowler, with 49 wickets at 21. Adjusting to conditions, he maintained his rattling speed, polished an outswinger, improvised lengths with the Kookaburra and the Dukes, and put his shoulder to work through the seaming tracks of South Africa, the damp swing of England, and Australia's hard drop-ins and soft outfields.

There were two batting anomalies in Australia that could have set India on the path to doubt and doom. They fielded three opening combinations in the four Tests and, apart from a stunning century in Perth, the talismanic Kohli – who had spent the summer exorcising personal demons in England – scored 159 runs in six other innings. Instead, the man who most reassured colleagues was Cheteshwar Pujara, who had responded to a poor start in South Africa with a stint at Yorkshire. He struggled there, too, and was left out of the First Test in England. But he was recalled for the Second, scored a century in the Fourth, at Southampton, and in Australia produced a performance for the ages: three centuries, 521 runs at 74, and the series award.

In a year of premier overseas opposition, India were grateful that Bumrah wasn't required to carry the pace attack: Mohammed Shami (49 wickets at 27 by the end of Sydney) and Ishant Sharma (41 at 21) had the best years of their careers. In all, India's seamers – Umesh Yadav contributed against West Indies, and Bhuvneshwar Kumar against South Africa, while Hardik Pandya claimed a five-for at Trent Bridge – took 179 wickets in the calendar year, a national record. The spin of Ravichandran Ashwin (38 at 25) and Ravindra Jadeja (27 at 23) remained effective, but for once it was not the story.

Darrian Traynor, Cricket Australia/Getty Images

Pride of India: Jasprit Bumrah earns the respect of India's captain, Virat Kohli.

In every country's Test development, several series become momentous markers. India had hoped one such series would come in England, but they were too reliant on the runs of Kohli, and the loss of five tosses condemned them to batting last in tricky conditions at Edgbaston and Southampton: 4–1 seemed an exaggeration, though it did say a little about England's edge in the pivotal moments.

Instead, India had to wait until Australia. After a dry 1990s, they had become competitive travellers only in the first decade of the 21st century, with series wins in the West Indies (their first for 35 years), Pakistan (their first ever), England (their first for 21) and New Zealand (41).

Kohli had watched on as a teenage batsman growing up in Delhi, and came to realise how precious away wins were for Indian cricket's sense of self. Early in his captaincy tenure, in 2015-16, he broke another drought – a first win in Sri Lanka for 22 years. For him, one-off away wins had become frequent. But, as he said before Australia: "If you want to win a series away from home, it has to be an obsession." By the end of 2018, he was one Test victory short of a record that will be hard to beat: having already equalled Sourav Ganguly as India's most successful overseas captain, with 11 wins, he needed one more to equal M. S. Dhoni's overall tally of 27.

Kohli's own batting will remain central to the challenge. In 2018 alone, he scored 2,735 runs in all international cricket, including 11 centuries. A few days after the victory in Australia, he said India's task was to become "a superpower in Test cricket". His reasoning was sound: "If Indian cricket and players respect Test cricket, then Test cricket will stay at the top." The world's most successful multi-format superstar has his mind on the big picture. Test cricket, Kohli wants us to know, is not going to die on his watch. It was the best message the Indian game could have sent the world for 2019.

In the offices of its governors, however, there were allegations of sexual harassment against the BCCI's first professionally hired CEO, Rahul Johri, and a cold war between two members of the Indian Supreme Court-appointed Committee of Administrators, the career bureaucrat Vinod Rai and former Indian captain Diana Edulji. The discord between Rai and Edulji followed differences about a badly handled investigation into the #MeToo allegations against Johri. The first came in the form of an anonymous tweet, later deleted. Within a month, two women – one from Johri's former place of work, the other at the BCCI – had testified against him before an independent investigation committee.

The panel reached bafflingly divergent conclusions. Two members, Justice Rakesh Sharma and Barkha Singh, former head of the National Commission for Women, called the allegations "false" and "baseless", and the charges "fabricated and manufactured with an ulterior motive to harm Mr Johri". A dissenting note from the third member, womens' rights lawyer Veena Gowda, said Johri's conduct was on occasion "unprofessional and inappropriate". It was essential, she said, that he be made to go through "gender-sensitivity counselling/training". Johri was eased back into his role without censure; there was no visible action around the gender-sensitivity counselling.

Early in 2019, things took an absurd twist. On January 7, Hardik Pandya indulged in some misogynistic lads' chatter on a popular TV talk show; K. L. Rahul sat beside him. Both were hauled back from the tour of Australia just before the start of the one-day series, suspended from all cricket, and issued show-cause notices to explain their "misconduct and indiscipline". The chief signatory of the notice? Rahul Johri.

INDIA v AFGHANISTAN IN 2018

ANAND VASU

Test match (1): India 1, Afghanistan 0

If you have grown up in a refugee camp, with row upon row of tarpaulin tents, in one of the least stable areas on the planet, cricket may not be the first thing on your mind. But if it is – despite never having smelled the freshly mown grass of summer, been to a coaching class or even watched a match on television – you must be from Afghanistan.

Their cricketers had already captured the world's attention with their compelling rise from the lower reaches of the global game. But there is a big difference between pulling off a Twenty20 upset, or doing well in a 50-over tournament among nations of a modest standard, and coming up against the top-ranked Test team in their own backyard. Afghanistan's arrival as Test cricket's 12th side involved a dive into the deep end.

They did not have to face Virat Kohli, India's regular captain, who had picked up a neck injury in the IPL, although he would probably have missed the match anyway because of a planned county stint with Surrey. Phil Simmons, Afghanistan's coach, did not set much store by Kohli's absence: "India is not Virat." But, in the one-off Test at Bangalore, India minus Virat were still far too good.

Afghanistan, like Ireland, had earned a shot at Test cricket by being better than virtually all their peers in the first-class Intercontinental Cup. They

Kabul TV: customers in an Afghan restaurant find the fare from India not quite to their taste.

deserved their moment in the sun, but the glare was too much, and they were shot out twice on the second day – not helped by warming up with three Twenty20 internationals against Bangladesh (see page 805). Afghanistan's poor showing didn't match the start Bangladesh had made in 2000-01, when they scored 400 in their first innings, against India, or the exploits a month earlier of Ireland, who extended Pakistan in friendly home conditions at Malahide (though both Bangladesh and Ireland eventually lost).

Still, how you begin does not always determine how far you go. Afghanistan's cricketers would have to marry enthusiasm with restraint as they negotiated the road ahead. In the next four years, they were scheduled to play 12 Tests, the same as Ireland and six fewer than Zimbabwe. Apart from a two-Test series against Zimbabwe in early 2021, all are one-offs. Some would be seen by touring teams as warm-ups before a longer series in India, Afghanistan's anointed home-from-home for Tests. At a time when the Indian board were in turmoil over their public image, they reached out to Afghanistan. Now they had to back up their good intentions and promises with action, to help the new boys find their feet.

AFGHANISTAN TOURING PARTY

*Asghar Stanikzai, Afsar Zazai, Hamza Hotak, Hashmatullah Shahidi, Ihsanullah Janat, Javed Ahmadi, Mohammad Nabi, Mohammad Shahzad, Mujeeb Zadran, Nasir Ahmadzai, Rahmat Shah, Rashid Khan, Sayed Shirzad, Wafadar Momand, Yamin Ahmadzai, Zahir Khan. *Coach:* P. V. Simmons.

AFGHANISTAN v INDIA

Only Test

At Bangalore, June 14–15, 2018. India won by an innings and 262 runs. Toss: India. Test debuts: Afghanistan (all).

When he walked out for the toss in his baggy scarlet cap, Asghar Stanikzai, Afghanistan's first Test captain, looked more like a film star than a cricketer. In his immaculate whites, he was more magisterial than Ajinkya Rahane, who was the leader – if temporarily, in the absence of Virat Kohli – of a country that had already played 521 Tests. An artist might have painted the proud Stanikzai as the incumbent and the shy Rahane as the ingénu.

But perceptions can differ from reality, and this became clear as the drama of the occasion, its political significance, and the pre-match razzmatazz gave way to more mundane things, such as the cricket. Yamin Ahmadzai ran in to bowl Afghanistan's first ball in Tests. But he stuttered, shuffled as he reached the crease, and pulled up short. Their first act was not a searing delivery that clattered into the stumps, or a wide one creamed to the ropes. It was a non-starter.

For a few overs, there was tension in the air. Yamin, eventually, did his job, and the 18-year-old seamer Wafadar Momand began reasonably well too. For India, Vijay was unconvincing at first, but Dhawan – perhaps the best flat-track flayer of wayward attacks in the world – cashed in. While Vijay survived, Dhawan thrived, and became the first Indian to score a century in the opening session of a Test.

As pace gave way to spin, expectations went through the roof. After all, Rashid Khan and Mujeeb Zadran had been misers in the IPL. But now Rashid sent down two full tosses in his first over, which Dhawan guided to the fence. He tried an ambitious googly fourth ball, and from there got cut to ribbons. Mujeeb, two years younger at 17, had become an IPL regular, but this was his maiden first-class match, and it showed. Before long, the

AFGHANISTAN'S INAUGURAL TEST
Flying the flag (or trying to)

ANAND VASU

The biggest problem Hazrat Shenwari faced on the morning of Afghanistan's first Test was that the counterfeiters hawking their dodgy merchandise outside Bangalore's Chinnaswamy Stadium had no Afghanistan jerseys, nor any flags. The locals had been creative enough to ditch the usual "Virat" shirts for ones that said "Ajinkya", for stand-in captain Rahane, but their ingenuity went no further.

Shenwari was at the ground with four friends, all from Afghanistan but now studying in India. They had returned home to spend Eid with their families – but the chance of being at Afghanistan's Test debut proved irresistible. "We go home every year at this time," said Shenwari. "But we had to cut the trip short to return for this match. There is one thing very interesting about cricket back home – it is the uniting factor, because it is the only thing both the people and the government support. Leave out cricket, and the people are against the government in almost every way."

Others made the trip too. Abdullah Abdullah, the chief executive of Afghanistan – not the cricket board, but the country itself – delivered a short address before the start. He was welcomed by India's minister for sport, Rajyavardhan Rathore, a former Olympic shooter who won the country's first individual silver medal, at Athens in 2004.

But while that touch of official pomp and splendour was to be expected, the real fun was in the stands. Despite being vastly outnumbered, Afghanistan's supporters found a way to make themselves heard. In particular, one supporter who had somehow unearthed a giant flag enjoyed exchanging banter with the Indian fans. Mujtaba Jalal, who had moved to Bangalore three years earlier in search of better prospects, explained that Afghans in India used a Facebook page to help them connect with other members of their community.

"There are more Afghans in north India, especially in Delhi, so they have regular events around festivals and things like that," he said. "Here we have to get together more informally, and the main attraction when we do is to share our love for Afghan food. I can show you a few places that serve excellent kebabs and bread."

As Afghanistan picked up a few wickets towards the end of the first day to peg India back, voices were in full cry. Rashid Khan was comfortably the most popular player. "I like watching Kohli, but I'm happy he's not there," said Anees, who had his hero's name painted on his cheeks. "That means I can just focus on Rashid."

By the end of the second day, though, after their side had been skittled twice in under two sessions, the Afghan fans were deflated. They made a beeline for the exits, having had enough of being surrounded by boisterous, triumphant Indians. Shenwari, who had been so eager to buy an Afghan flag, cut a forlorn figure at the same spot outside the ground, desperately pecking away at his smartphone, waiting for an Uber to spirit him away.

HUNDRED BEFORE LUNCH ON THE FIRST DAY OF A TEST

V. T. Trumper	103*	Australia v England at Manchester			1902
C. G. Macartney	112*	Australia v England at Leeds			1926
D. G. Bradman	105*	Australia v England at Leeds			1930
Majid Khan	108*	Pakistan v New Zealand at Karachi			1976-77
D. A. Warner	100*	Australia v Pakistan at Sydney			2016-17
S. Dhawan	**104***	**India v Afghanistan at Bangalore**			**2018**

All batsmen were openers except Macartney and Bradman, who batted at No. 3.

spinners Stanikzai had boldly declared were better than India's – conveniently overlooking the fact that Ashwin and Jadeja already had 476 Test wickets between them – were disappearing for several an over.

Dhawan departed soon after lunch for 107, carved from just 96 balls, having become the first to score a century in his first Test against five different opponents (Alastair Cook, Matthew Hayden, Kumar Sangakkara, Graeme Smith and Mark Taylor all did so against four). Vijay reached a more subdued hundred, his 12th in Tests, shortly after tea. Next morning, Pandya helped himself to the easiest 71 he is likely to make, and India were bowled out for 474 on the stroke of lunch. Rashid ended the innings by trapping Sharma in front – the previous day he had removed Rahane the same way – but finished with chastening figures of two for 154.

In came Afghanistan. Opener Mohammad Shahzad, unlikely to pass any fitness test but chosen because he often gives one-day innings a lightning start, was the first to go, run out by Pandya's direct hit from point in the fourth over. After that, on a benign Chinnaswamy pitch where nothing moved off the straight except in the first half-hour, Afghanistan approached Test batting as if they had forgotten what got them there in the first place. In a flash they were 35 for four, with Rahmat Shah becoming Yadav's 100th Test wicket. And when Stanikzai was drawn forward by Ashwin in the 13th over, and had his stumps rattled by a regulation off-break, the game was almost up. In around two hours, Afghanistan were shot out for 109, Ashwin taking four for 27.

Rahane enforced the follow-on after tea. Afghanistan had a good chance to drop anchor, and cheer up their supporters and lobbyists. But their batsmen again failed to live up to their own limited expectations. With Jadeja this time taking four wickets, they were hustled out in 38.4 overs; India did not need the extra half-hour to ensure a two-day finish, the 21st in all Tests, but only the seventh since the Second World War.

Statisticians had a field day. This was India's biggest innings win, the first two-day Test on the subcontinent, and only the fourth time a team had been bowled out twice in a day (it happened to India at Old Trafford in 1952, and twice to Zimbabwe against New Zealand, at Harare in 2005-06 and Napier in 2011-12). No day's play in a Test had seen as many wickets as the 24 that fell on the second day here since 1901-02, when 25 tumbled in the Ashes Test at Melbourne (the only higher casualty list was 27, on a rain-affected minefield at Lord's in 1888).

FIRST-CLASS DEBUT IN A TEST SINCE 1900

G. E. Vivian	New Zealand v India at Calcutta	1964-65
U. Ranchod	Zimbabwe v India at Delhi	1992-93
Mashrafe bin Mortaza	Bangladesh v Zimbabwe at Dhaka	2001-02
Yasir Ali	Pakistan v Bangladesh at Multan	2003-04
Nazmul Hossain	Bangladesh v India at Chittagong	2004-05
Mujeeb Zadran	**Afghanistan v India at Bangalore**	**2018**

A further 28 players made their first-class debut in a Test match in the 19th century, including all South Africa's team for their inaugural Test in 1888-89.

It was a shame, as the match should not have been about numbers. It should have been about how Afghanistan transcended bullets and bombs to collect runs and wickets. This was a fairytale without a happy ending.

Man of the Match: S. Dhawan.

Close of play: first day, India 347-6 (Pandya 10, Ashwin 7).

India

M. Vijay lbw b Wafadar Momand	105	R. Ashwin c Afsar Zazai b Yamin Ahmadzai	18
S. Dhawan c Mohammad Nabi b Yamin Ahmadzai	107	R. A. Jadeja c Rahmat Shah b Mohammad Nabi	20
K. L. Rahul b Yamin Ahmadzai	54	I. Sharma lbw b Rashid Khan	8
C. A. Pujara c Mohammad Nabi b Mujeeb Zadran	35	U. T. Yadav not out	26
*A. M. Rahane lbw b Rashid Khan	10	B 1, lb 12, w 2, nb 1	16
†K. D. Karthik run out (sub Nasir Ahmadzai/Afsar Zazai)	4		
H. H. Pandya c Afsar Zazai b Wafadar Momand	71	**(104.5 overs)**	**474**

1/168 (2) 2/280 (1) 3/284 (3) 4/318 (5) 5/328 (4) 6/334 (6) 7/369 (8) 8/436 (9) 9/440 (7) 10/474 (10)

Yamin Ahmadzai 19–7–51–3; Wafadar Momand 21–5–100–2; Mohammad Nabi 13–0–65–1; Rashid Khan 34.5–2–154–2; Mujeeb Zadran 15–1–75–1; Asghar Stanikzai 2–0–16–0.

Afghanistan

Mohammad Shahzad run out (Pandya)	14	– c Karthik b Yadav	13
Javed Ahmadi b Sharma	1	– c Dhawan b Yadav	3
Rahmat Shah lbw b Yadav	14	– c Rahane b Sharma	4
†Afsar Zazai b Sharma	6	– (7) b Jadeja	1
Hashmatullah Shahidi lbw b Ashwin	11	– not out	36
*Asghar Stanikzai b Ashwin	11	– c Dhawan b Jadeja	25
Mohammad Nabi c Sharma b Ashwin	24	– (4) lbw b Yadav	0
Rashid Khan c Yadav b Jadeja	7	– b Jadeja	12
Yamin Ahmadzai c Jadeja b Ashwin	0	– b Sharma	1
Mujeeb Zadran st Karthik b Jadeja	15	– c Yadav b Jadeja	3
Wafadar Momand not out	6	– b Ashwin	0
		B 4, lb 1	5
(27.5 overs)	**109**	**(38.4 overs)**	**103**

1/15 (1) 2/21 (2) 3/35 (3) 4/35 (4) 5/50 (6) 6/59 (5) 7/78 (8) 8/87 (9) 9/88 (7) 10/109 (10)

1/19 (1) 2/22 (2) 3/22 (4) 4/24 (3) 5/61 (6) 6/62 (7) 7/82 (8) 8/85 (9) 9/98 (10) 10/103 (11)

Yadav 6–1–18–1; Sharma 5–0–28–2; Pandya 5–0–18–0; Ashwin 8–1–27–4; Jadeja 3.5–1–18–2. *Second innings*—Sharma 7–2–17–2; Yadav 7–1–26–3; Pandya 4–2–6–0; Ashwin 11.4–3–32–1; Jadeja 9–3–17–4.

Umpires: C. B. Gaffaney and P. R. Reiffel.   Third umpire: R. J. Tucker.
Referee: A. J. Pycroft.

INDIA v WEST INDIES IN 2018-19

D EBASISH D ATTA

Test matches (2): India 2, West Indies 0
One-day internationals (5): India 3, West Indies 1
Twenty20 internationals (3): India 3, West Indies 0

Five years earlier, West Indies made a hastily arranged visit to India for the sole purpose of providing two matches in which Sachin Tendulkar could reach 200 Tests and bow out in front of his adoring public. With Ganguly, Laxman and Dravid already retired, it marked the end of a dynasty. Fast-forward to this series, and India had moved decisively into the Virat Kohli era.

For West Indies, however, nothing much seemed to have changed. In 2013, they were twice thrashed by an innings in three days; this time they lost by an innings and ten wickets. Green shoots are occasionally visible in West Indian cricket, but tours such as this mean they are usually trampled underfoot. Nor was there any solace in the limited-overs matches. They won one 50-over international and tied another, but otherwise were left with individual scraps: Roston Chase hit a century in the Second Test, Shimron Hetmyer and Shai Hope made white-ball runs, and Jason Holder again showed maturity as a leader.

YOUNGEST TO SCORE CENTURY ON TEST DEBUT

Yrs	Days			
16	364	Mohammad Ashraful (114)...	Bangladesh v Sri Lanka at Colombo (SSC).	2001-02
17	354	H. Masakadza (119)	Zimbabwe v West Indies at Harare	2001
18	328	Salim Malik (100*).........	Pakistan v Sri Lanka at Karachi	1981-82
18	**329**	**P. P. Shaw (134)...........**	**India v West Indies at Rajkot ....**	**2018-19**
19	108	Mohammad Wasim (109*)..	Pakistan v New Zealand at Lahore.......	1996-97
19	119	Javed Miandad (163).......	Pakistan v New Zealand at Lahore.......	1976-77
19	152	A. A. Jackson (164)	Australia v England at Adelaide..........	1928-29
19	184	Umar Akmal (129)	Pakistan v New Zealand at Dunedin	2009-10
19	228	A. B. Barath (104)..........	West Indies v Australia at Brisbane.......	2009-10
19	357	K. D. Walters (155).........	Australia v England at Brisbane..........	1965-66

Mohammad Ashraful's birthdate is disputed: some sources say he was 17 years 63 days.

If nothing else, the series underlined India's dominance at home. They had now won ten home Test series off the reel (including two single-Test visits by Bangladesh and Afghanistan), equalling the world record, set twice by Australia. And they had now won seven in a row, home and away, against West Indies, stretching back to 2002-03. Not since Kingston in May 2002 had they lost even a Test, a sequence of 21 matches.

West Indies coach Stuart Law was suspended from the first two ODIs: he was given three demerit points and fined his match fee for making "inappropriate comments" about the third and fourth umpires after Kieran Powell had been given out to a low catch by Ajinkya Rahane during the Second

Test in Hyderabad. Perhaps fired by indignation, the West Indian batsmen produced their best displays of the series.

For India, the victories served as a morale booster after their 4–1 Test defeat in England. Their batsmen were dominant – they lost just 19 wickets in the two Tests, and four players averaged over 90. It gave them a chance to hand a first cap to the 18-year-old opener Prithvi Shaw, who responded with a century on debut, and was comfortably the highest scorer, with 237 runs. Umesh Yadav was the most successful bowler with 11 wickets at 15, including a match-winning performance in the Second Test, when injury to his new-ball partner Shardul Thakur left him with extra responsibility. In the 50-over series, Kohli reeled off three hundreds, while Rohit Sharma proved as insatiable as he had been in the Asia Cup. The Tests were again played in front of largely empty stands, which led to questions about the scheduling of the tour, but India had at least built their confidence before the trip to Australia.

WEST INDIES TOURING PARTY

*J. O. Holder (T/50), F. A. Allen (50/20), S. W. Ambris (T/50), D. Bishoo (T/50), C. R. Brathwaite (20), K. C. Brathwaite (T), D. M. Bravo (20), R. L. Chase (T), S. O. Dowrich (T), S. T. Gabriel (T), J. N. Hamilton (T), C. Hemraj (50), S. O. Hetmyer (T/50/20), S. D. Hope (T/50/20), S. H. Lewis (T), O. C. McCoy (50/20), A. R. Nurse (50/20), K. M. A. Paul (T/50/20), K. A. Pierre (20), K. A. Pollard (20), N. Pooran (20), K. O. A. Powell (T/50), R. Powell (50/20), D. Ramdin (20), K. A. J. Roach (T/50), S. E. Rutherford (20), M. N. Samuels (50), O. R. Thomas (50/20), J. A. Warrican (T). *Coach:* S. G. Law.

C. R. Brathwaite captained in the Twenty20 matches. E. Lewis was originally selected in the ODI and Twenty20 squads, but withdrew for personal reasons. He was replaced by K. O. A. Powell in the 50-over squad and N. Pooran in the T20. A. S. Joseph was selected, but did not recover from injury and was replaced by S. H. Lewis in the Test squad and McCoy in the one-day squad. A. D. Russell was named for the T20s, but withdrew injured, and was replaced by Hope.

INDIA v WEST INDIES

First Test

At Rajkot, October 4–6, 2018. India won by an innings and 272 runs. Toss: India. Test debuts: P. P. Shaw; S. H. Lewis.

As the records piled up, the extent of India's dominance and West Indies' humiliation became ever starker. India's biggest innings win, and West Indies' second-heaviest defeat, never remotely resembled a contest. Kohli did not need to pull off any tactical masterstrokes: he won the toss, made the largest contribution to a huge total, then let his bowlers loose. Fourteen West Indies wickets fell on the third day – most in attempting ill-judged attacking shots – and their two innings did not add up to 100 overs.

West Indies were without captain Jason Holder, who had suffered an ankle injury at the pre-tour camp in Dubai, and Kemar Roach, who flew home after the death of his grandmother. It left their attack desperately short of experience. Kraigg Brathwaite took over the captaincy, but the seam bowling was entrusted to Gabriel, Keemo Paul, in only his second Test, and debutant Sherman Lewis. After opting not to blood him in England, India gave Prithvi Shaw a first cap. He disappointed no one.

After Rahul had been dismissed by Gabriel for a duck in the first over, Shaw eased towards his hundred as if it were preordained. Attacking mainly off the back foot, he reached 50 in 56 balls, and a century off 99. He became the fourth-youngest to hit a Test century on debut, and the third-fastest recorded by balls faced. Shaw received a

INDIA'S BIGGEST INNINGS VICTORIES

Inns & 272 runs	India (649-9 dec) v West Indies (181 & 196) at Rajkot	2018-19
Inns & 262 runs	India (474) v Afghanistan (109 & 103) at Bangalore	2018
Inns & 239 runs	India (610-3 dec) v Bangladesh (118 & 253) at Mirpur	2007
Inns & 239 runs	India (610-6 dec) v Sri Lanka (205 & 166) at Nagpur	2017-18
Inns & 219 runs	India (633-5 dec) v Australia (233 & 181) at Calcutta	1997-98
Inns & 198 runs	India (566-8 dec) v New Zealand (193 & 175) at Nagpur	2010-11
Inns & 171 runs	India (487) v Sri Lanka (135 & 181) at Pallekele	2017
Inns & 144 runs	India (642) v Sri Lanka (229 & 269) at Kanpur	2009-10
Inns & 140 runs	India (526) v Bangladesh (184 & 202) at Dhaka	2004-05
Inns & 135 runs	India (503) v Australia (237-9 dec & 131) at Hyderabad	2012-13

congratulatory message from Sachin Tendulkar, still India's youngest centurion, while coach Ravi Shastri did not shy away from comparisons: he said there "was a bit of Viru [Sehwag] and the Master" in his innings.

Shaw and Pujara added 206 for the second wicket to put India in control and, though Pujara fell 14 short of a century on his home ground, Kohli was ominously placed on 72 at the close. To no surprise, he completed his 24th Test hundred next day. In England, India had been let down by their lower-middle order, but there were no such failings here against a wilting attack. Pant freewheeled to 92, at one point looking as if he might beat Kohli to three figures, and Jadeja added an entertaining first Test hundred, at which point Kohli declared at India's highest score against West Indies, beating 644 for seven at Kanpur in 1978-79. The 217 conceded by Bishoo, while taking four wickets, was the second-most by a West Indies bowler, after Tommy Scott's five for 266 against England at Kingston in 1929-30.

With temperatures soaring, it was soon clear the tourists had no stomach for a fight: five batsmen were gone before the total reached 50. Ashwin regained some of the zip missing in England, and his four wickets included top-scorer Chase.

When the first innings was hurried to a conclusion on the third morning, with the deficit an eye-watering 468, the follow-on was a no-brainer for Kohli. Powell survived a skittish start to make 83, but most of his team-mates appeared to think the white-ball matches had already started. Kohli gave an extended bowl to Kuldeep Yadav, who was rewarded with his first Test five-for, and became the seventh to take international five-fors in three formats.

"I don't think you can compare the conditions with England," said Kohli. "That was a bigger challenge. We understand that, with the ability we have, we will dominate in these conditions. I'm happy we were clinical."

Man of the Match: P. P. Shaw.

Close of play: first day, India 364-4 (Kohli 72, Pant 17); second day, West Indies 94-6 (Chase 27, Paul 13).

India

P. P. Shaw c and b Bishoo	134	U. T. Yadav c Lewis b Brathwaite	22
K. L. Rahul lbw b Gabriel	0	Mohammed Shami not out	2
C. A. Pujara c Dowrich b Lewis	86		
*V. Kohli c Bishoo b Lewis	139	B 9, lb 1, nb 4	14
A. M. Rahane c Dowrich b Chase	41		
†R. R. Pant c Paul b Bishoo	92	1/3 (2) (9 wkts dec, 149.5 overs)	649
R. A. Jadeja not out	100	2/209 (3) 3/232 (1)	
R. Ashwin c Dowrich b Bishoo	7	4/337 (5) 5/470 (6) 6/534 (4)	
K. Yadav lbw b Bishoo	12	7/545 (8) 8/571 (9) 9/626 (10)	

Gabriel 21–1–84–1; Paul 15–1–61–0; Lewis 20–0–93–2; Bishoo 54–3–217–4; Chase 26–1–137–1; Brathwaite 13.5–1–47–1.

West Indies

	1st innings		2nd innings	
*K. C. Brathwaite b Mohammed Shami	....	2	– c Shaw b Ashwin	10
K. O. A. Powell lbw b Mohammed Shami	......	1	– c Shaw b K. Yadav..............	83
S. D. Hope b Ashwin	....	10	– lbw b K. Yadav	17
S. O. Hetmyer run out (Jadeja).	....	10	– c Rahul b K. Yadav..........	11
S. W. Ambris c Rahane b Jadeja	....	12	– st Pant b K. Yadav	0
R. L. Chase b Ashwin	....	53	– c Ashwin b K. Yadav........	20
†S. O. Dowrich b K. Yadav.	....	10	– not out	16
K. M. A. Paul c Pujara b U. T. Yadav	....	47	– c U. T. Yadav b Jadeja	15
D. Bishoo not out.	....	17	– c Pant b Ashwin	9
S. H. Lewis b Ashwin	....	0	– lbw b Jadeja	4
S. T. Gabriel st Pant b Ashwin.	....	1	– c K. Yadav b Jadeja	4
B 16, lb 2	....	18	B 5, lb 1, nb 1.............	7

1/2 (1)	2/7 (2)	3/21 (3)	(48 overs)	181	1/32 (1)	2/79 (3)	(50.5 overs)	196

1/2 (1) 2/7 (2) 3/21 (3)   (48 overs) 181   1/32 (1) 2/79 (3)   (50.5 overs) 196
4/32 (4) 5/49 (5) 6/74 (7)   3/97 (4) 4/97 (5)
7/147 (8) 8/159 (6) 9/159 (10) 10/181 (11)   5/138 (6) 6/151 (2) 7/172 (8)
                                                                         8/185 (9) 9/192 (10) 10/196 (11)

Mohammed Shami 9-2-22-2; U. T. Yadav 11-3-20-1; Ashwin 11-2-37-4; Jadeja 7-1-22-1; K. Yadav 10-1-62-1. *Second innings*—Mohammed Shami 3-0-11-0; Ashwin 18-2-71-2; U. T. Yadav 3-0-16-0; K. Yadav 14-2-57-5; Jadeja 12.5-1-35-3.

Umpires: I. J. Gould and N. J. Llong.   Third umpire: B. N. J. Oxenford.
Referee: B. C. Broad.

INDIA v WEST INDIES

Second Test

At Hyderabad, October 12–14, 2018. India won by ten wickets. Toss: West Indies. Test debut: S. N. Thakur.

Umesh Yadav joined elite company in another crushing victory that wrapped up the series in six days. He became only the third Indian seamer to take ten wickets in a home Test, after Kapil Dev (twice) and Javagal Srinath. Emerging from the wreckage of Rajkot, West Indies showed some overdue competitive spirit before collapsing in a heap.

Holder, their returning captain, deserved better than to be at the helm for another thrashing. Briefly, his team looked to have India under the cosh, but that was a distant memory by the time Shaw and Rahul completed the formalities on the third evening. Only six teams have won by ten wickets after gaining a smaller first-innings lead than India's 56.

On a pitch expected to help the spinners later on, Holder was happy to bat first. And when Shardul Thakur limped off with a groin injury ten balls into his debut, the cards seemed to be falling for West Indies. But their top order were again unable to find the right blend of attack and defence. They were saved from another lightweight total only by Chase and Holder, who put on 104 for the seventh wicket. Chase ended the day on 98 as West Indies passed 250 for the first time in four Tests in India. He quickly completed his fourth Test century next morning, but West Indies were in the field within 40 minutes of the start. Umesh finished with a Test-best six for 88.

Shaw picked up where he had left off in the First Test, with 70 off 53 balls, although the match then deviated from its expected course. When Holder removed Kohli for 45, India were 162 for four and by no means in command. Rahane, adapting his game to the pace of the pitch, and the more aggressive Pant put on 152 to steady the ship, with the help of some shoddy West Indies fielding: Pant was reprieved on 24 when substitute wicketkeeper Jahmar Hamilton, deputising for the injured Shane Dowrich, dropped a sitter off Gabriel. Holder kept his side in the hunt with three wickets on the third morning, and became the first West Indies seamer to take a five-for in India since Kenny Benjamin at Mohali in 1994-95. Pant departed for 92 for the second successive innings, and India's lead was a slender 28 when the ninth wicket fell. Thakur hobbled out to join Ashwin, and helped double the advantage and deflate West Indian morale.

Just how much was demonstrated when four wickets fell before they had wiped off the arrears. Umesh and Ashwin offered contrasting challenges with the new ball, and only Hope and Ambris held them up for long. With nine down, and India trying to secure two days off, Kohli summoned Umesh, who needed only one ball to complete his first ten-for. After two days in which 14 wickets fell, 16 had crashed on a frantic third. "We didn't expect that in the morning," said Kohli. "A three-day finish was not part of the plan."

Man of the Match: U. T. Yadav.   *Man of the Series:* P. P. Shaw.

Close of play: first day, West Indies 295-7 (Chase 98, Bishoo 2); second day, India 308-4 (Rahane 75, Pant 85).

West Indies

K. C. Brathwaite lbw b K. Yadav	14	– c Pant b U. T. Yadav	0
K. O. A. Powell c Jadeja b Ashwin	22	– c Rahane b Ashwin	0
S. D. Hope lbw b U. T. Yadav	36	– c Rahane b Jadeja	28
S. O. Hetmyer lbw b K. Yadav	12	– c Pujara b K. Yadav	17
S. W. Ambris c Jadeja b K. Yadav	18	– lbw b Jadeja	38
R. L. Chase b U. T. Yadav	106	– b U. T. Yadav	6
†S. O. Dowrich lbw b U. T. Yadav	30	– b U. T. Yadav	0
*J. O. Holder c Pant b U. T. Yadav	52	– c Pant b Jadeja	19
D. Bishoo b U. T. Yadav	2	– not out	10
J. A. Warrican not out	8	– b Ashwin	7
S. T. Gabriel c Pant b U. T. Yadav	0	– b U. T. Yadav	1
B 4, lb 7	11	Lb 1	1

1/32 (2) 2/52 (1) 3/86 (3)   (101.4 overs) 311   1/0 (1) 2/6 (2)   (46.1 overs) 127
4/92 (4) 5/113 (5) 6/182 (7)   3/45 (4) 4/45 (3)
7/286 (8) 8/296 (9) 9/311 (6) 10/311 (11)   5/68 (6) 6/70 (7) 7/108 (8)
                                                              8/109 (5) 9/126 (10) 10/127 (11)

U. T. Yadav 26.4–3–88–6; Thakur 1.4–0–9–0; Ashwin 24.2–7–49–1; K. Yadav 29–2–85–3; Jadeja 20–2–69–0. *Second innings*—U. T. Yadav 12.1–3–45–4; Ashwin 10–4–24–2; K. Yadav 13–1–45–1; Jadeja 11–5–12–3.

India

K. L. Rahul b Holder	4	– (2) not out	33
P. P. Shaw c Hetmyer b Warrican	70	– (1) not out	33
C. A. Pujara c sub (†J. N. Hamilton) b Gabriel	10		
*V. Kohli lbw b Holder	45		
A. M. Rahane c Hope b Holder	80		
†R. R. Pant c Hetmyer b Gabriel	92		
R. A. Jadeja lbw b Holder	0		
R. Ashwin b Gabriel	35		
K. Yadav b Holder	6		
U. T. Yadav c sub (†J. N. Hamilton) b Warrican	3		
S. N. Thakur not out	4		
B 12, lb 2, nb 5	19	B 6, lb 2, nb 1	9

1/61 (1) 2/98 (2) 3/102 (3)   (106.4 overs) 367   (no wkt, 16.1 overs) 75
4/162 (4) 5/314 (5) 6/314 (7)
7/322 (6) 8/334 (9) 9/339 (10) 10/367 (8)

Gabriel 20.4–1–107–3; Holder 23–5–56–5; Warrican 31–7–84–2; Chase 9–1–22–0; Bishoo 21–4–78–0; Brathwaite 2–0–6–0. *Second innings*—Holder 4–0–17–0; Warrican 4–0–17–0; Bishoo 4.1–0–19–0; Chase 4–0–14–0.

Umpires: I. J. Gould and B. N. J. Oxenford.   Third umpire: N. J. Llong.
Referee: B. C. Broad.

First one-day international At Guwahati, October 21, 2018 (day/night). **India won by eight wickets. West Indies** 322-8 (50 overs) (K. O. A. Powell 51, S. D. Hope 32, S. O. Hetmyer 106, J. O. Holder 38; Y. S. Chahal 3-41); ‡**India** 326-2 (42.1 overs) (R. G. Sharma 152*, V. Kohli 140). MoM: V. Kohli. *ODI debuts*: R. R. Pant (India); C. Hemraj, O. R. Thomas (West Indies). *A sell-out crowd for the Barsapara Stadium's first one-day international were treated to a thrilling match-winning partnership of 246 between Rohit Sharma and Virat Kohli. At times the batsmen appeared to be competing more with each other than the West Indies bowlers: it was their fifth double-century stand, improving their own world record, and India's highest for any wicket batting second. Kohli's 36th ODI century – his 20th in a successful chase – needed only 88 balls. Sharma became the fourth-fastest player to 20 hundreds, and the first to reach 150 six times, eclipsing Sachin Tendulkar and David Warner. Earlier, Shimron Hetmyer had taken advantage of the absence of Kuldeep Yadav, who had dismissed him three times in the Tests, to hit his third ODI century. Kieran Powell made 501 at the top of the order, but not even West Indies' highest score against India since January 2007 could prevent defeat.*

Second one-day international At Visakhapatnam, October 24, 2018 (day/night). **Tied.** ‡**India** 321-6 (50 overs) (V. Kohli 157*, A. T. Rayudu 73); **West Indies** 321-7 (50 overs) (C. Hemraj 32, S. D. Hope 123*, S. O. Hetmyer 94; K. Yadav 3-67). MoM: V. Kohli. *ODI debut*: O. C. McCoy (West Indies). *When Umesh Yadav ran in to bowl the last ball of the match to Shai Hope, West Indies needed five and appeared to have made a mess of the final stages of their chase. But Hope carved a full, wide delivery past point to secure the 37th ODI tie – India's second inside a month. The headlines seemed set to be about Kohli reaching 10,000 ODI runs, knocking 54 innings off Tendulkar's record. His second successive century came after a stand of 139 with Ambati Rayudu, who looked as if he might provide a solution to India's problem No. 4 spot. Kohli smashed 48 off his last 17 balls to complete what looked a formidable total. But with Hetmyer leading the charge, West Indies were not intimidated. He followed up his hundred in Guwahati with a fearless 94 off 64 balls, including seven sixes, and put on 143 with Hope. The run-out of Jason Holder, and a failure to take advantage of some gifts from the Indian spinners, put West Indies under pressure. Hope's century was his second in ODIs, but the first since his second appearance.*

FASTEST TO 10,000 ODI RUNS

Inns		Time
205	**V. Kohli (India)**	**10 yrs 67 days**
259	S. R. Tendulkar (India)	11 yrs 103 days
263	S. C. Ganguly (India/Asia)	13 yrs 204 days
266	R. T. Ponting (Australia/World)	12 yrs 37 days
272	J. H. Kallis (South Africa/Africa/World)	13 yrs 14 days
273	**M. S. Dhoni (India/Asia)**	**13 yrs 203 days**
278	B. C. Lara (West Indies/World)	16 yrs 37 days
287	R. Dravid (India/Asia/World)	10 yrs 317 days
293	T. M. Dilshan (Sri Lanka)	15 yrs 227 days
296	K. C. Sangakkara (Sri Lanka/Asia/World)	11 yrs 227 days

Third one-day international At Pune, October 27, 2018 (day/night). **West Indies won by 43 runs. West Indies** 283-9 (50 overs) (S. D. Hope 95, S. O. Hetmyer 37, J. O. Holder 32, A. R. Nurse 40; J. J. Bumrah 4-35); ‡**India** 240 (47.4 overs) (S. Dhawan 35, V. Kohli 107; M. N. Samuels 3-12). MoM: A. R. Nurse. *ODI debut*: F. A. Allen (West Indies). *It was either tactical genius or outrageous good fortune, but Holder's introduction of the part-time off-spin of Marlon Samuels in the 42nd over turned the match in West Indies' favour and squared the series. With his third ball, Samuels bowled the well-set Kohli – who had become the tenth man to score three successive ODI centuries, but the first for India – and added two more cheap wickets to complete his best ODI figures. Kohli's dismissal prompted an exodus from the stands. In all, the last seven wickets fell for 68. West Indies were once again indebted to the cool Hope, although they needed a late blast from Ashley Nurse – 40 off 22 balls – to set a challenging total. Jasprit Bumrah's four wickets included a beauty to remove Hope as he closed in on another hundred.*

Fourth one-day international At Mumbai (Brabourne), October 29, 2018 (day/night). **India won by 224 runs.** ‡**India** 377-5 (50 overs) (R. G. Sharma 162, S. Dhawan 38, A. T. Rayudu 100); **West Indies** 153 (36.2 overs) (J. O. Holder 54*; K. K. Ahmed 3-13, K. Yadav 3-42). MoM: R. G. Sharma.

India ruthlessly reasserted themselves to take a 2–1 lead into the final match. It was their third-largest win by runs – the biggest against a Full Member – and West Indies' second-heaviest defeat. Hosting its first men's ODI for 12 years, the Brabourne Stadium was reduced to silence when Kohli fell well short of a fourth successive hundred, but Sharma – going past 150 for the seventh time – and Rayudu raised spirits during a third-wicket partnership of 211 in 27.1 overs. Rayudu's century was the first for India by a batsman outside the top three in 21 months. Kohli's hunch that bowling under lights would help his seamers proved correct. There were three wickets for left-armer Khaleel Ahmed, after alert fielding had removed Hope and Powell. From 56-6, only Holder's 54* prevented an even bigger humiliation.

Fifth one-day international   At Thiruvananthapuram, November 1, 2018 (day/night). **India won by nine wickets.** ‡**West Indies 104** (31.5 overs) (R. A. Jadeja 4-34); **India 105-1** (14.5 overs) (R. G. Sharma 63*, V. Kohli 33*). *MoM:* R. A. Jadeja. *MoS:* V. Kohli. *The public at Greenfield Stadium's first ODI were entitled to feel cheated by a contest that lasted less than half its scheduled duration. With a chance to make it 2–2, West Indies folded limply after failing to come to terms with the slowness of the pitch. India won in less than 15 overs – an anticlimactic end to a series that had been boiling up nicely. India's seamers made West Indies in trouble from the start, but the main beneficiary of their befuddled approach was Ravindra Jadeja, who took his second four-wicket haul since returning to the team at the Asia Cup. Oshane Thomas provided a crumb of comfort for West Indies: his pace was too hot for Shikhar Dhawan, and he also had Kohli dropped.*

First Twenty20 international   At Kolkata, November 4, 2018 (floodlit). **India won by five wickets. West Indies 109-8** (20 overs) (K. Yadav 3-13); ‡**India 110-5** (17.5 overs) (K. D. Karthik 31*). *MoM:* K. Yadav. *T20I debuts:* K. K. Ahmed, K. H. Pandya (India); F. A. Allen, K. A. Pierre, O. R. Thomas (West Indies). *India's victory looked more comfortable than it was. Thomas, on debut, and captain Carlos Brathwaite had reduced them to 45-4, with Thomas making the top order jump around. But West Indies always had too few to defend, and Manish Pandey and Dinesh Karthik put on 38 for the fifth wicket to calm any flutters. In their first home T20 international without M. S. Dhoni, India could choose from two wicketkeepers: Karthik took the gloves, while Rishabh Pant fielded in the deep. West Indies were unable to fathom the Indian spinners, especially the miserly Kuldeep Yadav, although Fabian Allen top-scored on debut with 27 from No. 8.*

Second Twenty20 international   At Lucknow, November 6, 2018 (floodlit). **India won by 71 runs. India 195-2** (20 overs) (R. G. Sharma 111*, S. Dhawan 43); ‡**West Indies 124-9** (20 overs). *MoM:* R. G. Sharma. *Sharma illuminated India's first visit to the Ekana Stadium by becoming the first batsman to make four T20 international hundreds. He batted through the innings for 111*, hitting eight fours and seven sixes, having put on 123 for the first wicket with Dhawan, who could not find his usual fluency. West Indies' top order struggled again. The menacing Khaleel removed Hope and Hetmyer, and they only scraped into three figures.*

Third Twenty20 international   At Chennai, November 11, 2018 (floodlit). **India won by six wickets. West Indies 181-3** (20 overs) (D. M. Bravo 43*, N. Pooran 53*); **India 182-4** (20 overs) S. Dhawan 92, R. R. Pant 58). *MoM:* S. Dhawan. *MoS:* K. Yadav. *A last-ball howler by Allen denied West Indies the chance of a consolation victory. Bowling the final over, he had brought his team back into it with a fourth-ball dot, followed by the wicket of Dhawan. Needing one to win, Pandey hit the final delivery to Allen's right, but he failed to collect it cleanly, allowing Pandey and Karthik to scamper the winning single. West Indies had batted more sensibly than in previous matches. In a stand of 87*, Darren Bravo played conventionally, while Nicholas Pooran improvised for his first international fifty. The bedrock of India's response was a partnership of 130 for the third wicket between Dhawan and the innovative Pant. Brathwaite's apparent reluctance to use his spinners in the final overs remained a mystery.*

DOMESTIC CRICKET IN INDIA IN 2017-18

R. Mohan

Vidarbha became the fifth first-time winners of the Ranji Trophy in the 21st century, after Railways, Uttar Pradesh, Rajasthan and Gujarat. Their triumph reflected a greater spread of talent across India.

In their 60 previous seasons, Vidarbha had never reached the Ranji final. But they squeezed past Karnataka in the semi – winning by five runs after conceding a deficit of 116 – and then faced Delhi at Indore. Vidarbha captain Faiz Fazal bravely bowled first, and was justified when Rajneesh Gurbani's swing and seam picked up six first-innings wickets, including only the second hat-trick in a Ranji final, completed when he bowled Dhruv Shorey, who scored 145 of Delhi's 295. Solid batting, led by 133 from wicketkeeper Akshay Wadkar, enabled Vidarbha to pile up 547 across three days; Delhi left a target of just 29, which was knocked off with a day to spare. Gurbani won the match award in all three of the knockout games, in which he took 27 wickets at 14, including 12 for 162 against Karnataka.

One team-mate entirely used to Ranji finals was Wasim Jaffer, who had won eight with Mumbai before moving to Vidarbha in 2015-16. He played a valuable role as the senior pro, while the coach was another Mumbaikar, former Test keeper Chandrakant Pandit. Jaffer helped Vidarbha to a double when they won the Irani Cup match against the Rest of India on first-innings lead; on their home ground, they made the most of ideal batting conditions to score 800 for seven, an Irani record. Jaffer made 286, his 53rd century and eighth double, while Gurbani dented the Rest so badly with the new ball that they could not get even halfway to Vidarbha's total, despite 183 from Hanuma Vihari.

A revised format had divided the 28 Ranji teams into four groups, each providing two quarter-finalists, rather than two top-tier groups supplying three teams apiece, with two from a second tier; there was no promotion or relegation. Meanwhile the experiment with neutral venues for all Ranji matches ended after just one season. Home teams were directed to prepare fair surfaces, supervised by the grounds and pitches committee, and the balance between bat and ball improved a little. Mayank Agarwal of Karnataka was the tournament's most prolific scorer, with 1,160 (ahead of Fazal's 912 for Vidarbha); he made one of its three triple-centuries, alongside Vihari, for Andhra, and Prashant Chopra, in a first for Himachal Pradesh.

As in 2016-17, the Duleep Trophy was played as a selection trial by three combined teams rather than the traditional zonal sides. The final was dominated by Washington Sundar, a 17-year-old off-spinning all-rounder, who scored 88 and 42 and took 11 for 181, improving his career-best return twice, to seal **India Red's** 163-run win over India Blue with a day to spare; earlier, his team-mate Prithvi Shaw, also 17, scored the first of four centuries in five matches.

Poor umpiring remained a persistent problem, even in the IPL, though there it was mitigated by DRS. The BCCI served out warnings and took other measures trying to reduce the profusion of howlers.

In limited-overs cricket, **Karnataka** won their third Vijay Hazare Trophy, all in the last five years, after Agarwal hit 90 in 79 balls in the final against Saurashtra. Karnataka advanced to the Deodhar Trophy, but the double eluded them, as **India B** chased down 280 with minimum fuss. **Delhi** won the Syed Mushtaq Ali Twenty20 final against Rajasthan. Their campaign was spearheaded by Rishabh Pant, who scored 411 runs, including the second-fastest century in all T20 cricket – off 32 balls, two short of Chris Gayle's record in the 2013 IPL – to beat Himachal Pradesh in the North Zone.

Delhi experienced one of the oddest incidents of the season when a man drove his car across the pitch at Palam, during a Ranji game against Uttar Pradesh. The driver, who narrowly missed Gautam Gambhir at mid-on, claimed he had got lost looking for a short cut from the nearby airport.

FIRST-CLASS AVERAGES IN 2017-18

BATTING (600 runs)

		M	I	NO	R	HS	100	Avge	Ct/St
1	V. Kohli (*India*)	3	5	1	610	243	3	152.50	3
2	Anmolpreet Singh (*Punjab*)	5	7	1	753	267	3	125.50	4
3	M. A. Agarwal (*Karnataka/Rest*)	9	14	2	1,171	304*	5	97.58	4
4	G. H. Vihari (*Ind Bl/Ind A/And/Rest*) . . .	9	13	2	1,056	302*	4	96.00	13
5	Wasim Jaffer (*Vidarbha*)	10	14	2	881	286	2	73.41	14
6	C. A. Pujara (*Saurashtra/India*)	7	10	0	726	204	3	72.60	2
7	†F. Y. Fazal (*Vidarbha*)	10	15	1	1,001	206	5	71.50	17
8	†H. S. Bhatia (*Madhya Pradesh*)	7	14	5	629	107*	2	69.88	7
9	R. N. B. Indrajith (*Ind Red/Tamil Nadu*) .	8	12	2	692	200	2	69.20	14
10	S. R. Ramaswamy (*Vidarbha*)	10	16	3	855	182	3	65.76	8
11	P. K. Panchal (*Ind Red/Ind A/Gujarat*) . . .	11	16	2	895	152	4	63.92	13
12	G. Satish (*Vidarbha*)	10	13	1	758	164	3	63.16	2
13	K. K. Nair (*Ind Gr/Ind A/Karn/Rest*) . . .	11	16	2	853	153	4	60.92	13
14	S. D. Lad (*Mumbai*)	7	12	1	652	123	2	59.27	2
15	†G. Gambhir (*Delhi*)	9	12	0	683	144	3	56.91	1
16	†N. Rana (*Delhi*)	8	12	1	613	174	2	55.72	9
17	P. P. Shaw (*India Red/Mumbai/Rest*) . . .	8	15	1	773	154	4	55.21	5
18	S. V. Samson (*Kerala*)	7	12	0	627	175	2	52.25	15/2
19	P. Chopra (*Ind Gr/Himachal Pradesh*) . . .	7	13	0	672	338	1	51.69	3
20	A. R. Easwaran (*India Blue/Bengal*)	8	15	1	712	129	4	50.85	10
21	R. Samarth (*Ind Gr/Ind A/Karn/Rest*) . . .	12	18	1	791	129	3	46.52	14
22	†A. Raman (*Bengal*)	8	14	0	623	176	2	44.50	2
23	M. K. Tiwary (*India Blue/Bengal*)	11	18	1	622	123	1	36.58	9
24	†S. D. Chatterjee (*Ind Red/Ind A/Beng*) . . .	10	17	0	608	118	2	35.76	6

BOWLING (25 wickets)

		Style	O	M	R	W	BB	5I	Avge
1	J. S. Saxena (*Kerala*)	OB	319	74	753	44	8-85	3	17.11
2	R. N. Gurbani (*Vidarbha*)	RM	243.4	62	738	43	7-68	5	17.16
3	A. A. Sarwate (*Vidarbha*)	SLA	236.4	70	580	32	6-41	2	18.12
4	R. Vinay Kumar (*Karnataka*)	RM	179.2	40	495	27	6-34	2	18.33
5	I. Sharma (*India Blue/Delhi/India*)	RFM	211.3	61	557	29	5-38	1	19.20
6	C. T. Gaja (*Gujarat*)	RM	207.2	74	506	26	8-40	1	19.46
7	P. P. Chawla (*Gujarat*)	LB	198.5	27	667	32	5-44	3	20.84
8	K. V. Sharma (*Ind Red/Ind A/Vid*)	LB	299.4	59	938	45	6-94	3	20.84
9	K. Gowtham (*Karnataka*)	OB	283.5	59	826	39	7-72	3	21.17
10	A. B. Dinda (*India Red/Bengal*)	RFM	249.3	60	788	35	7-21	3	22.51
11	M. N. Hirwani (*Madhya Pradesh*)	LB	212.2	34	743	31	5-22	4	23.96
12	A. A. Wakhare (*Ind Blue/Vidarbha*)	OB	382.5	78	1,076	44	5-16	3	24.45
13	Parvez Rasool (*Ind Gr/Jammu & K*)	OB	277.4	58	813	33	6-70	4	24.63
14	V. Mishra (*Delhi*)	SLA	291.3	63	790	32	5-116	1	24.68
15	Mohammed Shami (*Bengal/India*)	RFM	240	54	822	33	6-61	4	24.90
16	D. A. Jadeja (*Saurashtra*)	SLA	232.1	42	885	34	6-68	3	26.02
17	N. A. Saini (*Ind Gr/Ind A/Delhi/Rest*) . . .	RM	355	92	1,006	36	5-135	1	27.94
18	D. Pathania (*Services*)	RM	253.2	43	833	28	7-41	1	29.75
19	M. Sharma (*Delhi*)	SLA	238.3	46	762	25	4-46	0	30.48
20	S. A. Desai (*Gujarat*)	SLA	273.1	46	885	29	6-80	3	30.51
21	S. Nadeem (*Ind Gr/Ind A/Jhar/Rest*) . . .	SLA	402.4	93	1,111	34	6-93	1	32.67
22	B. A. Bhatt (*India Blue/Andhra*)	SLA	423	91	1,205	36	4-40	0	33.47

DULEEP TROPHY IN 2017-18

	P	W	L	D	1st-inns pts	Pts	NRR
INDIA RED	2	1	0	1	1	7	−0.09
INDIA BLUE	2	0	0	2	4	4	0.22
India Green	2	0	1	1	1	1	−0.11

Outright win = 6pts; lead on first innings in a drawn match = 3pts; deficit on first innings in a drawn match = 1pt; no decision on first innings = 1pt.

Final   At Lucknow, September 25–28, 2017 (day/night). **India Red won by 163 runs. ‡India Red 483** (P. P. Shaw 154, K. D. Karthik 111) **and 208; India Blue 299** (A. R. Easwaran 127; V. D. Gohil 5-121, M. S. Washington Sundar 5-94) **and 229** (M. S. Washington Sundar 6-87). *Two 17-year-olds settled the Duleep final with a day to spare. Prithvi Shaw scored his second century, in his third first-class match; Washington Sundar followed a career-best 88 by collecting 11-181 with his off-spin.*

RANJI TROPHY IN 2017-18

Group A	P	W	L	D	1st-inns pts	Bonus	Pts	NRR
KARNATAKA	6	4	0	2	6	2	32	0.47
DELHI	6	3	0	3	7	2	27	0.33
Maharashtra	6	2	2	2*	4	0	16	0.08
Hyderabad	6	2	1	3†	3	1	16	−0.15
Railways	6	2	3	1	1	1	14	−0.31
Uttar Pradesh	6	0	3	3*	5	0	5	0.50
Assam	6	0	4	2	2	0	2	−0.97

Group B	P	W	L	D	1st-inns pts	Bonus	Pts	NRR
GUJARAT	6	5	0	1	1	3	34	0.09
KERALA	6	5	1	0	0	1	31	0.63
Saurashtra	6	3	1	2	6	2	26	0.24
Jammu & Kashmir	6	1	4	1	3	0	9	−0.07
Haryana	6	1	4	1	3	0	9	−0.50
Jharkhand	6	1	4	1	1	1	8	−0.04
Rajasthan	6	0	2	4	6	0	6	−0.29

Group C	P	W	L	D	1st-inns pts	Bonus	Pts	NRR
MADHYA PRADESH	6	3	1	2	2	1	21	−0.11
MUMBAI	6	2	0	4	8	1	21	0.22
Andhra	6	1	0	5	13	0	19	0.32
Baroda	6	1	1	4	10	0	16	0.50
Tamil Nadu	6	0	1	5	11	0	11	−0.11
Odisha	6	0	2	4	6	0	6	−0.64
Tripura	6	0	2	4	4	0	4	−0.42

Group D	P	W	L	D	1st-inns pts	Bonus	Pts	NRR
VIDARBHA	6	4	0	2	4	3	31	0.35
BENGAL	6	2	1	3	9	2	23	0.36
Punjab	6	2	2	2	4	2	18	0.60
Himachal Pradesh	6	1	1	4	8	0	14	0.30
Chhattisgarh	6	1	3	2	6	1	13	−0.51
Services	6	1	2	3	3	1	10	−0.27
Goa	6	0	2	4	6	0	6	−0.70

*   *Includes one abandoned match.*   †   *Includes two abandoned matches.*

Outright win = 6pts; bonus for winning by an innings or ten wickets = 1pt; lead on first innings in a drawn match = 3pts; deficit on first innings in a drawn match = 1pt; no decision on first innings = 1pt; abandoned = 1pt. Teams tied on points were ranked on most wins, and then on net run-rate.

The top two teams from each group advanced to the quarter-finals.

Quarter-finals Bengal drew with Gujarat but qualified on first-innings lead; Delhi beat Madhya Pradesh by seven wickets; Karnataka beat Mumbai by an innings and 20 runs; Vidarbha beat Kerala by 412 runs.

Semi-finals Delhi beat Bengal by an innings and 26 runs; Vidarbha beat Karnataka by five runs.

Final At Indore (Holkar), December 29, 2017–January 1, 2018. **Vidarbha won by nine wickets. Delhi 295** (D. Shorey 145; R. N. Gurbani 6-59) **and 280;** ‡**Vidarbha 547** (A. V. Wadkar 133; N. A. Saini 5-135) **and 32-1.** *Vidarbha claimed their first Ranji Trophy. Rajneesh Gurbani wound up Delhi's first innings with four wickets in seven balls, including centurion Dhruv Shorey, the third victim in a hat-trick. Akshay Wadkar hit a maiden century from No. 7, sharing stands of 169 and 132 with Aditya Sarwate and Siddhesh Neral to steer Vidarbha to a lead of 252; Delhi managed to make them bat again, but they raced past a target of 29 with a day in hand.*

RANJI TROPHY WINNERS

1934-35	Bombay	1962-63	Bombay	1990-91	Haryana
1935-36	Bombay	1963-64	Bombay	1991-92	Delhi
1936-37	Nawanagar	1964-65	Bombay	1992-93	Punjab
1937-38	Hyderabad	1965-66	Bombay	1993-94	Bombay
1938-39	Bengal	1966-67	Bombay	1994-95	Bombay
1939-40	Maharashtra	1967-68	Bombay	1995-96	Karnataka
1940-41	Maharashtra	1968-69	Bombay	1996-97	Mumbai
1941-42	Bombay	1969-70	Bombay	1997-98	Karnataka
1942-43	Baroda	1970-71	Bombay	1998-99	Karnataka
1943-44	Western India	1971-72	Bombay	1999-2000	Mumbai
1944-45	Bombay	1972-73	Bombay	2000-01	Baroda
1945-46	Holkar	1973-74	Karnataka	2001-02	Railways
1946-47	Baroda	1974-75	Bombay	2002-03	Mumbai
1947-48	Holkar	1975-76	Bombay	2003-04	Mumbai
1948-49	Bombay	1976-77	Bombay	2004-05	Railways
1949-50	Baroda	1977-78	Karnataka	2005-06	Uttar Pradesh
1950-51	Holkar	1978-79	Delhi	2006-07	Mumbai
1951-52	Bombay	1979-80	Delhi	2007-08	Delhi
1952-53	Holkar	1980-81	Bombay	2008-09	Mumbai
1953-54	Bombay	1981-82	Delhi	2009-10	Mumbai
1954-55	Madras	1982-83	Karnataka	2010-11	Rajasthan
1955-56	Bombay	1983-84	Bombay	2011-12	Rajasthan
1956-57	Bombay	1984-85	Bombay	2012-13	Mumbai
1957-58	Baroda	1985-86	Delhi	2013-14	Karnataka
1958-59	Bombay	1986-87	Hyderabad	2014-15	Karnataka
1959-60	Bombay	1987-88	Tamil Nadu	2015-16	Mumbai
1960-61	Bombay	1988-89	Delhi	2016-17	Gujarat
1961-62	Bombay	1989-90	Bengal	2017-18	Vidarbha

Bombay/Mumbai have won the Ranji Trophy 41 times, Karnataka 8, Delhi 7, Baroda 5, Holkar 4, Bengal, Hyderabad, Madras/Tamil Nadu, Maharashtra, Railways and Rajasthan 2, Gujarat, Haryana, Nawanagar, Punjab, Uttar Pradesh, Vidarbha and Western India 1.

IRANI CUP IN 2017-18

Ranji Trophy Champions (Vidarbha) v Rest of India

At Nagpur (VCA Stadium), March 14–18, 2018. **Drawn. Vidarbha won by virtue of their first-innings lead.** ‡**Vidarbha 800-7 dec** (Wasim Jaffer 286, G. Satish 120, A. V. Wankhade 157*) **and 79-0; Rest of India 390** (G. H. Vihari 183). *Wasim Jaffer batted ten hours and ten minutes for 286, his 53rd century and eighth double, out of 499 added while he was at the wicket; he put on 117 with Faiz Fazal (89) and 289 with Ganesh Satish. In reply, the Rest sank to 98-6, four dismissed by Rajneesh Gurbani. Hanuma Vihari and Jayant Yadav fought back with 216 for the seventh wicket, but Vidarbha secured the trophy through a 410-run lead.*

VIJAY HAZARE TROPHY IN 2017-18

Four 50-over leagues plus knockout

Quarter-finals Karnataka beat Hyderabad by 103 runs; Maharashtra beat Mumbai by seven wickets; Saurashtra beat Baroda by three wickets; Andhra beat Delhi by six wickets.

Semi-finals Karnataka beat Maharashtra by nine wickets; Saurashtra beat Andhra by 59 runs.

Final At Delhi, February 27, 2018. **Karnataka won by 41 runs.** Karnataka 253 (45.5 overs); ‡**Saurashtra 212** (46.3 overs). *Karnataka opener Mayank Agarwal set up their total with 90 in 79 balls, which took him to 723 for the tournament, at an average of 90 and strike-rate of 107; no one else reached 400.*

DEODHAR TROPHY IN 2017-18

50-over knockout for India A, India B and the winner of the Vijay Hazare Trophy

Final At Dharamsala, March 8, 2018 (day/night). **India B won by six wickets.** ‡**Karnataka 279-8** (50 overs) (R. Samarth 107); **India B 281-4** (48.2 overs). *Ravikumar Samarth was the only batsman in Karnataka's top five to pass 14, whereas four of India B's top five scored fifties.*

SYED MUSHTAQ ALI TROPHY IN 2017-18

Five 20-over leagues, two super leagues plus final

Final At Kolkata, January 26, 2018 (floodlit). **Delhi won by 41 runs.** ‡**Delhi 153-6** (20 overs); **Rajasthan 112** (19.1 overs). *Delhi's second final in four weeks brought them their first T20 title. The competition was contested throughout by state teams, after a single season in which the closing stages were played by combined zonal sides.*

The Vivo Indian Premier League has its own section (page 1135).

IRISH CRICKET IN 2018

Bigger Tests lie ahead

IAN CALLENDER

It was a landmark year with a historic match, but Ireland still face an uphill struggle to compete at the top level. Graham Ford's first year as national coach was always going to be dominated by the inaugural men's Test, against Pakistan, which produced Ireland's best performance of 2018. But failure to qualify for the World Cup was a massive blow.

Ireland should have 150 fixtures over the next four years, including a four-day Test against England at Lord's in July 2019. But the fear is that an inexperienced side are being forced to run before they can walk. The process will not be helped by the retirements of Ed Joyce and Niall O'Brien, who had more than 6,000 international runs between them: the batting department has been severely weakened for the challenges ahead.

The long-awaited first Test, at Malahide in May, did not start well: the Dublin weather washed out the opening day, costing Cricket Ireland around

IRELAND IN 2018

	Played	Won	Lost	Drawn/No result
Tests	1	–	1	–
One-day internationals	13	8	5	–
Twenty20 internationals	8	1	6	1

JANUARY	Triangular ODI tournament (in UAE) v Scotland and the UAE	(page 1106)
FEBRUARY		
MARCH	World Cup Qualifier (in Zimbabwe)	(page 790)
APRIL		
MAY	1 Test (h) v Pakistan	(page 897)
JUNE	Triangular T20 (in the Netherlands) v Netherlands and Scotland	(page 1098)
	2 T20Is (h) v India	(page 905)
JULY		
AUGUST	3 ODIs and 2 T20Is (h) v Afghanistan	(page 907)
SEPTEMBER		
OCTOBER		
NOVEMBER		
DECEMBER		

For a review of Irish domestic cricket from the 2018 season, see page 909.

Line and length: the Irish and Pakistan teams before the Malahide Test.

£65,000 in refunds. But the sun came out on the second morning, Tim Murtagh bowled the first ball, and Boyd Rankin took the first wicket. The following day, every past international was invited as Cricket Ireland's guests. They saw Joyce – who announced his retirement soon after the game – score Ireland's first Test run, but they were bowled out for a nervy 130. Sarfraz Ahmed enforced the follow-on, but Kevin O'Brien saved further embarrassment, hitting Ireland's first Test century. Pakistan needed 160 to win, and home hopes rocketed when Murtagh and Rankin reduced them to 14 for three. In the end, though, Imam-ul-Haq took them to a hard-earned five-wicket victory.

Ireland played 21 white-ball internationals in 2018, winning nine and losing 11. That might look a decent return, but only one of the victories was against a Test nation – a 50-over defeat of Afghanistan. They lost the other ten. A one-day century against the UAE helped the ever-present Paul Stirling lead the run-charts, with 684 in all matches; Andy Balbirnie came next with 594, although that included a pair in the Test. Joyce, who played only seven games, averaged 53, but no one else topped 30. Rankin took most wickets (28), just ahead of 37-year-old Murtagh (25 at 17), while Durham seamer Barry McCarthy flew the flag for the younger brigade with 20.

After straightforward victories against the UAE and Scotland in Dubai in January, Ireland had headed to the World Cup Qualifier in Zimbabwe. Controversially, there were only two places up for grabs. After convincing wins over the Netherlands, Papua New Guinea and the UAE, Ireland reduced West Indies to 83 for five – but Rovman Powell made the most of being dropped early on, and his century propelled his side to 257. Letting their opponents off the hook was a recurring theme of Ireland's year, and they fell 52 short.

After overwhelming the UAE, Ireland faced hosts Zimbabwe, who recovered from 139 for seven to reach 211, before Ireland collapsed to 104. Victory over

Scotland looked academic but, with the results going Ireland's way, the last qualifying game became a shoot-out for the final World Cup spot with Afghanistan. Ireland lost, and the jubilant Afghans joined West Indies in progressing to the tournament proper in England in 2019.

After the excitement of their maiden Test, Ireland went into Twenty20 mode. But a tri-series in the Netherlands in June – in which they beat and tied with Scotland, but lost both games to the Dutch – was insufficient preparation for the visit of India, who warmed up for their England tour with two huge wins, passing 200 in both matches. Ireland's batsmen were again exposed in the shortest format, but one of the bowlers at least gleaned some satisfaction: seamer Peter Chase dismissed Virat Kohli twice.

More worryingly, it was the same story when Afghanistan visited in August. They won both T20 internationals, and the 50-over series 2–1, Ireland having to make do with a consolation victory at Stormont, on pitches which had to be reused because of the demands of television. When asked how his team would prepare for the series against Afghanistan in India in early 2019, which will include both sides' second Test, captain William Porterfield said: "Playing out there [Stormont] would be a good start. We should never be playing three one-day internationals on used pitches."

The highlight of the women's year was taking on Bangladesh in front of a crowd of 10,000 at Malahide, part of a double-header with the men's game against India. Their year ended at the Twenty20 World Cup. Ireland lost all four games, and an era ended: Clare Shillington and Ciara Metcalfe, who first played for Ireland in the 20th century, and Ed Joyce's twin sisters, Isobel and Cecelia – who had been around almost as long – all announced their retirements. Like the men's team, the women face a tricky time ahead.

IRELAND v PAKISTAN IN 2018

LAWRENCE BOOTH

Test match (1): Ireland 0, Pakistan 1

The Pakistanis' detour to Dublin was perhaps a glimpse into the future. Not only did they contest Ireland's inaugural men's Test – the first addition to cricket's most prestigious club since Bangladesh in November 2000 – but they interrupted their tour of England to do so. Four days after seeing off Northamptonshire in early May, Pakistan were primed in Malahide, though rain delayed the contest by 24 hours. And nine days after completing a win that was less secure than the five-wicket margin suggested, they were lining up at Lord's against England. It felt like a sensible template for teams touring Britain and Ireland.

But the Irish refused to play the role of warm-up act. At one point, with Pakistan losing three quick wickets in pursuit of 160, it looked as if William

THE X-PERIENCE FACTOR

Number of first-class appearances for each team before their first Test:

1,574	England	1876-77	347	Sri Lanka	1981-82
1,103	**Ireland**	**2018**	295	India	1932
516	New Zealand	1929-30	**157**	**Afghanistan**	**2018**
407	West Indies	1928	109	Australia	1876-77
401	Pakistan	1952-53	57	Bangladesh	2000-01
384	Zimbabwe	1992-93	0	South Africa	1888-89

Research: Andrew Samson

Porterfield's side – boosted by a second-innings hundred from Kevin O'Brien – might become only the fourth to win a Test after following on. Ultimately, they had to settle for heroic failure, but their point had been made: Ireland had not been prematurely promoted to Test status. Far from it: seven of the team were in their thirties, with the 39-year-old Ed Joyce announcing his retirement a week later, and O'Brien's brother Niall in October, at the age of 36. In truth, Irish cricket had peaked before getting the chance to compete at the highest level.

There was no escaping the significance of the match. Tim Murtagh, their best bowler, suggested that several of his team-mates wore sunglasses during the presentation of caps, "in case there was a couple of tears rolling down". And, on the third day, over 100 former Ireland cricketers attended, which "added to the pressure", according to Kevin O'Brien: "We knew they were living and breathing every ball along with us." Cricket Ireland lost money staging the Test, but had budgeted to recoup some of this shortfall when they hosted India for two Twenty20 matches in late June.

Following page. Silver linings: Ireland lose their first men's Test, but win friends and admirers.

Charles McQuillan, Getty Images

PAKISTAN TOURING PARTY

*Sarfraz Ahmed, Asad Shafiq, Azhar Ali, Babar Azam, Fahim Ashraf, Fakhar Zaman, Haris Sohail, Hasan Ali, Imam-ul-Haq, Mohammad Abbas, Mohammad Amir, Rahat Ali, Saad Ali, Sami Aslam, Shadab Khan, Usman Salahuddin. *Coach:* J. M. Arthur.

IRELAND v PAKISTAN

Only Test

At Malahide, May 11–15, 2018. Pakistan won by five wickets. Toss: Ireland. Test debuts: A. Balbirnie, E. C. Joyce, T. E. Kane, T. J. Murtagh, K. J. O'Brien, N. J. O'Brien, W. T. S. Porterfield, P. R. Stirling, S. R. Thompson, G. C. Wilson; Fahim Ashraf, Imam-ul-Haq.

On the final morning of a beguiling game, Ireland's first men's Test was shaping up as a classic. Pakistan, chasing 160 after enforcing the follow-on, were 14 for three – and the Irish contemplating history. Forty-nine years earlier, up in Sion Mills, they had skittled the West Indians for 25; recent times had brought World Cup wins over Pakistan and England. But this would have topped the lot.

If Balbirnie had caught Babar Azam at third slip, with his score nine and the total 60, the papers might have been full of clichés about smiling eyes. Instead, Babar restored order in a stand of 126 with Imam-ul-Haq (nephew of Inzamam, now chairman of selectors), and Pakistan wriggled free. But their captain Sarfraz Ahmed admitted he had been worried. Ireland lost the game, yet won respect. Finally, they were on Test cricket's map.

Other than the first-day rain which delayed their formal coronation as the 11th Test nation, Malahide was the perfect host. A well-to-do coastal town half an hour north of Dublin, it had the feel of a county outground: convivial, pretty and – with a capacity of 6,000 – modest. In all, more than twice that number turned up, and it would have been above 15,000 without the washout. Attention wavered only on the second afternoon, a Saturday, when spectators went in search of TV screens to watch Leinster win rugby's European Champions Cup. Otherwise, the Test made gentle waves, nestled in the back pages alongside the rugby, plus football and the sports of the Gaelic Athletic Association,

Greens from ear to ear: the Ireland and Pakistan teams at the end of a fascinating battle.

which between 1902 and 1971 had banned cricket. When the Irish president Michael Higgins popped in on the third morning, his plan was to leave before lunch; he stayed until four. The setting invited relaxation. Perhaps that was part of the plan.

Shortly before the Test eventually began on the Saturday morning – as bright and blue as the Friday had been grim and grey – the teams lined up for the anthems. In the capital, Croke Park has seen more ferocious renditions, but there was emotion in the air and, after Porterfield chose to field, the first ball produced a manoeuvre straight from the scrum. Responding to Azhar Ali's call for a quick single, Imam collided with Tyrone Kane and wicketkeeper Niall O'Brien as they converged on the ball. For a few minutes, he lay winded on his back. It might have been the slowest opening over in Test history, but Ireland quickly made up for lost time.

Their first Test wicket went to a man who already had one: Rankin had removed Australian tailender Peter Siddle in his lone appearance for England, at Sydney in January 2014, and now squared up Azhar, who edged to second slip. Next ball, Murtagh – aged 36, born in Lambeth, and with 712 first-class wickets to his name – swung one into Imam's pads. Honestly, said a wag: you wait decades for Ireland to take a Test wicket, then two

---

TEST WICKETS FOR TWO COUNTRIES

		Debut
W. E. Midwinter	Australia (14), England (10)........................	1876-77
J. J. Ferris................	Australia (48), England (13)........................	1886-87
S. M. J. Woods............	Australia (5), England (5)..........................	1888
A. E. Trott..............	Australia (9), England (17).........................	1894-95
A. J. Traicos.............	South Africa (4), Zimbabwe (14)...................	1969-70
W. B. Rankin	**England (1), Ireland (3)**	**2013-14**

---

come along at once. Had Thompson's shy from backward point found its target seconds later, with Haris Sohail backing up too far, Pakistan would have been 13 for three.

They quietly regrouped, but after lunch Ireland hit back. Sohail squirted Thompson low to gully, and Babar edged the relentless Murtagh to second slip. Rankin went round the wicket and bounced Asad Shafiq, who spoiled nearly three hours of resistance by pulling him to midwicket. When Sarfraz Ahmed flashed Thompson into the cordon, Pakistan were 159 for six. But they batted deep – and Ireland made mistakes. Fahim Ashraf was dropped by Wilson at first slip on 24, and by Niall O'Brien on 36, and later that over completed a 52-ball half-century, the fastest on debut by a Pakistani. Next morning, Fahim was put down again, at third slip by sub fielder Andy McBrine on 72. Murtagh plugged away, before Pakistan sprang a surprise, declaring 40 minutes before lunch at 310 for nine – decent on a pitch tinged with emerald.

Their total quickly looked even better. Joyce scored Ireland's first Test run, a pragmatic nudge into the gully. But either side of the break, Mohammads Abbas and Amir – right-arm and left-arm, persistent and pernicious – reduced them to seven for four. The ball from Abbas which produced an lbw verdict against Joyce pitched a fraction outside leg, but there was no DRS: Cricket Ireland could not afford $10,000 a day.

Since rain had flattened out the four-day game, the follow-on deficit was 150 rather than 200. The party was falling flat. Kevin O'Brien hit 40, but at 73 for eight Ireland were in danger of undercutting South Africa's 84 against England at Port Elizabeth in 1888-89 as the lowest score in a maiden Test innings. Wilson, down at No. 9 and nursing an elbow badly bruised in the nets, averted that embarrassment, but not the follow-on. Pakistan had not enforced it since May 2002, but they had an eye on the forecast, and Ireland, 180 behind, were vulnerable.

The game might even have been over on the third evening, but Sarfraz spilled Joyce low to his left off Amir before he had scored, and Azhar dropped Porterfield at third slip,

GUERILLA CRICKET'S TEST DEBUT

By the people, for the people

LAWRENCE BOOTH

It's 12.30 on the fourth day at Malahide, and the arrival of two pints of lager signals a new commentary shift in a small box by the sightscreen. John Arlott preferred Beaujolais, Jim Swanton a glass of whisky. Guerilla Cricket are nothing if not democratic.

Sure enough, there is something for everyone. Nakul Pande, the non-drinker among a team of three, likens the beard of Ireland's Paul Stirling to a Viking berserker. Listeners are told that Gary Wilson averages 181 when playing the cut, and that Mohammad Amir's economy-rate is the ninth-best for a Pakistani who has bowled at least 50 balls in a Test. As if he's tuning in, Stirling carves Amir for four. "And that stat is immediately nullified," says Pande. Nigel Henderson spots something of Intikhab Alam in Pakistan's young leg-spinner Shadab Khan, but notes that Intikhab was "a little more roly-poly". Shadab drops short: "That's filth."

Guerilla Cricket, surprise winners of the global audio rights for this historic game, are laddish and erudite, geeky and mildly profane. "Pissed off" and "bloody" appear in one sentence; something stronger in another. *Test Match Special* would not approve, but the Guerillas are hardly playing to the traditional market. Jim sends in a ditty from Dublin – a limerick, as it happens. Another listener, Emmett, asks for the definition of a jaffa. And each player has his own jingle: Tyrone Kane, the Ireland seamer, gets Prince's "Purple Rain". Boundaries are greeted with a burst of Britney Spears and "Hit Me Baby One More Time". When the ball is deflected past the slips, we get "The Third Man" by Gertrud Huber. Arlott, you suspect, would raise his eyebrows – but then a glass of red.

How did it come to this? Essentially, the Guerillas – an off-shoot of the old Test Match Sofa, whose star commentator Dan Norcross graduated to the adult TMS – were in the right place at the right time. The BBC didn't bid, instead sending a lone reporter, Charlie Dagnall, to do bulletins. Irish radio weren't interested, and Talksport would have had too many ad breaks. Then there was an old friendship, between the Guerillas' David Brook, who once helped bring Test cricket to Channel 4 in the UK, and Cricket Ireland chief executive Warren Deutrom.

A week before the Test, Deutrom gave the Guerillas the nod. Their dozen-strong team found an Airbnb in Dublin, and jumped on the ferry at Holyhead. The accommodation cost £1,600, which was £600 more than for the rights. When they arrived at Malahide, they realised they needed more equipment: that was another £1,500. They took to JustGiving, a crowd-funding platform, in a bid to raise £5,000 to cover costs. By the fourth day, they were approaching £3,500; by early June, four years after they first broadcast "from a windowless room above a pub", they were there. "We're now in the tent, pissing out," says Nigel Walker, whose front room in Sydenham, south London, has often doubled up as the Guerilla studios.

Their audience wasn't bad at all. They reckoned they attracted a maximum of 60,000 listeners online at any one time during the Test, including around 10,000 a day on Facebook Live, where video streaming allows devotees to watch the commentators in action, as well as listen in. Their Twitter feed (@guerillacricket) picked up 500–600 new followers, lifting them towards 11,000.

The question was whether they could turn a one-off into a trend. The knowledge and passion are there, and the desire to reach out beyond cricket's traditional demographic chimes with the times. Guerilla Cricket are by the people, for the people. And if it all goes tits up – or, as Pande puts it live on air, "threatens to edge nipple skyward" – they'll always have the Dublin craic.

MOST FIRST-CLASS RUNS BEFORE TEST DEBUT

		M	*I*	*NO*	*HS*	*100*	*Avge*
21,308	W. G. Grace (England)	287	473	43	344	64	49.55
21,005	E. H. Bowley (England)	359	625	30	280*	36	35.30
20,173	R. G. A. Headley (West Indies)	392	708	59	187	29	31.08
19,318	A. R. Lewis (England)	377	652	67	223	29	33.02
19,309	S. J. Cook (South Africa)	246	432	49	313*	57	50.41
18,799	P. N. Kirsten (South Africa)	270	469	50	228	48	44.86
18,414	**E. C. Joyce (Ireland)**	**254**	**417**	**34**	**250**	**47**	**48.07**
17,926	J. Vine (England)	404	665	58	180	21	29.53
17,183	A. P. Wells (England)	299	498	74	253*	41	40.52
16,868	R. M. Prideaux (England)	300	543	47	202*	28	34.00
16,352	J. H. Parks (England)	371	596	54	197	30	30.16
16,255	G. A. Hick (England)	185	298	36	405*	57	62.04
16,208	H. W. Lee (England)	345	566	41	243*	32	30.87
15,942	C. T. Radley (England)	332	540	75	171	24	34.28
15,675	J. M. Brearley (England)	283	495	63	312*	23	36.28
15,401	D. Denton (England)	343	530	30	153*	20	30.80
15,313	M. E. K. Hussey (Australia)	176	317	27	331*	39	52.80

The most first-class wickets taken before Test debut is 1,527 by J. Southerton (England). T. J. Murtagh's 712 was a record for a team other than England, beating 585 by Imran Tahir (South Africa), and the most by any bowler since N. A. Mallender (817) in 1992.

again off Amir, on three. By now, Mick Jagger was in the crowd, ahead of a concert in Dublin. He posted a selfie on Twitter, and settled down to witness the fightback. As Amir struggled intermittently with a knee injury, Joyce and Porterfield survived 26 overs before stumps, reducing the deficit by 64. Joyce was run out next morning by Fahim, and Balbirnie lbw for a duck to Abbas for the second time in two days – the first pair in a country's inaugural Test since New Zealanders Ken James and Ted Badcock in 1929-30. Then, in successive overs, Amir swung one into Niall O'Brien (only leg stump was left standing), and moved one away from Porterfield. When he had Wilson caught at slip – his 100th Test wicket – Ireland were six down and still 23 behind.

Kevin O'Brien set about making a game of it. Seven years earlier, in that World Cup win over England, he had scored 100 off 50 balls; now he scored 50 off 100, bringing up the first Test half-century by a man for Ireland (Karen Young and Caitriona Beggs had beaten him to it by almost 18 years, in Ireland's only women's Test, also against Pakistan, at Trinity College, Dublin). Pakistan went on the defensive, even with the second new ball. By the time Shadab bowled Thompson for 53 with a big leg-break to end a stand of 114, Ireland led by 91. Soon after, O'Brien moved to a hundred – the fourth player to achieve the feat in his country's maiden Test, after Australia's Charles Bannerman, Zimbabwe's Dave Houghton and Bangladesh's Aminul Islam. It was only his second in first-class cricket, nearly a decade after his first, against Kenya. At stumps, he had 118 and, with Kane dropping anchor, Ireland were 139 in front.

Abbas cleaned up on the final morning – including O'Brien, who carved the first ball he faced to slip – and finished with five in the innings and nine in the match. But a small crowd had gathered, hoping for a miracle, and Murtagh played his part, removing Azhar and Shafiq. In between, Rankin took care of Sohail. But Imam knuckled down, and Babar exploited his reprieve. His run-out for 59, and the cheap removal of Sarfraz, slowed the procession, but at 3.45 on the fifth afternoon, Imam scored the winning runs – and Pakistan breathed again.

Man of the Match: K. J. O'Brien.   Attendance: 15,000.

Close of play: first day, no play; second day, Pakistan 268-6 (Shadab Khan 52, Fahim Ashraf 61); third day, Ireland 64-0 (Joyce 39, Porterfield 23); fourth day, Ireland 319-7 (K. J. O'Brien 118, Kane 8).

Pakistan

Azhar Ali c Porterfield b Rankin	4	– c Stirling b Murtagh	2
Imam-ul-Haq lbw b Murtagh	7	– not out	74
Haris Sohail c Porterfield b Thompson	31	– c Joyce b Rankin	7
Asad Shafiq c Balbirnie b Rankin	62	– b Murtagh	1
Babar Azam c Stirling b Murtagh	14	– run out (Balbirnie/Thompson)	59
*†Sarfraz Ahmed c Stirling b Thompson	20	– lbw b Thompson	8
Shadab Khan lbw b Murtagh	55	– not out	4
Fahim Ashraf c N. J. O'Brien b Thompson	83		
Mohammad Amir c N. J. O'Brien b Murtagh	13		
Mohammad Abbas not out	4		
Rahat Ali not out	0		
B 1, lb 10, w 2, nb 4	17	Nb 5	5

1/13 (1) 2/13 (2) (9 wkts dec, 96 overs) 310
3/71 (3) 4/104 (5) 5/153 (4)
6/159 (6) 7/276 (7) 8/304 (8) 9/306 (9)

1/2 (1) (5 wkts, 45 overs) 160
2/13 (3) 3/14 (4)
4/140 (5) 5/152 (6)

Murtagh 25–5–45–4; Rankin 21–3–75–2; Kane 20–2–86–0; Thompson 22–4–62–3; K. J. O'Brien 6–1–20–0; Stirling 2–0–11–0. *Second innings*—Murtagh 16–3–55–2; Rankin 12–1–57–1; Thompson 11–4–31–1; Kane 6–1–17–0.

Ireland

E. C. Joyce lbw b Mohammad Abbas	4	– run out (Fahim Ashraf)	43
*W. T. S. Porterfield b Mohammad Amir	1	– c Sarfraz Ahmed b Mohammad Amir	32
A. Balbirnie lbw b Mohammad Abbas	0	– lbw b Mohammad Abbas	0
†N. J. O'Brien b Mohammad Abbas	0	– b Mohammad Amir	18
P. R. Stirling c Babar Azam b Fahim Ashraf	17	– lbw b Mohammad Abbas	11
K. J. O'Brien b Imam-ul-Haq b Mohammad Amir	40	– c Haris Sohail b Mohammad Abbas	118
S. R. Thompson b Shadab Khan	3	– (8) b Shadab Khan	53
T. E. Kane c Babar Azam b Shadab Khan	0	– (9) b Mohammad Abbas	14
G. C. Wilson not out	33	– (7) c Haris Sohail b Mohammad Amir	12
W. B. Rankin c Sarfraz Ahmed b Mohammad Abbas	17	– b Mohammad Abbas	6
T. J. Murtagh c Imam-ul-Haq b Shadab Khan	5	– not out	5
B 8, lb 1, w 1	10	B 1, lb 20, w 4, nb 2	27

1/5 (1) 2/5 (3) 3/5 (2) (47.2 overs) 130
4/7 (4) 5/36 (5) 6/61 (7)
7/61 (8) 8/73 (6) 9/107 (10) 10/130 (11)

1/69 (1) 2/69 (3) (129.3 overs) 339
3/94 (4) 4/95 (2)
5/127 (5) 6/157 (7) 7/271 (8)
8/321 (6) 9/332 (10) 10/339 (9)

Mohammad Amir 10–5–9–2; Mohammad Abbas 11–4–44–4; Rahat Ali 7–0–18–0; Fahim Ashraf 5–2–18–1; Shadab Khan 13.2–3–31–3; Haris Sohail 1–0–1–0. *Second innings*—Mohammad Amir 29.2–9–63–3; Mohammad Abbas 28.3–10–66–5; Rahat Ali 23–3–75–0; Fahim Ashraf 18–3–51–0; Shadab Khan 30.4–7–63–1.

Umpires: R. K. Illingworth and N. J. Llong. Third umpire: M. Hawthorne.
Referee: B. C. Broad.

For Pakistan's matches in England, see page 289; for their games in Scotland, see page 1101.

IRELAND v INDIA IN 2018

Ian Callender

Twenty20 internationals (2): Ireland 0, India 2

Ireland's first two-match Twenty20 series against India was never going to be about the results. According to the rankings, it was 17th against third, and the margins of victory – 76 runs and 143 – reflected the gulf in class. While India were coming straight out of the IPL, Ireland had warmed up more modestly, with a tri-series against the Netherlands and Scotland. Above all, the Irish had no answer to the wrist-spin of Kuldeep Yadav and Yuzvendra Chahal, who shared 13 wickets in 14.3 overs.

The fans – the vast majority supporting India – packed out Malahide on both days, blessed by weather more in keeping with Delhi than Dublin. The real winner, though, was Cricket Ireland, who just six weeks earlier had hosted their inaugural Test, against Pakistan, at a financial loss. But 18,000 ticket sales for the two T20 games paid for their red-ball outlay. The proximity of the Test also allowed CI to keep infrastructure in place: five stands, the players' changing area and hospitality tents were all temporary.

SHORTEST COMPLETED INNINGS IN T20 INTERNATIONALS

Overs		
10.3	Netherlands (39) v Sri Lanka at Chittagong	2013-14
12.2	South Africa (100) v Pakistan at Centurion	2012-13
12.3	**Ireland (70) v India at Malahide**	**2018**
13.2	Scotland (91) v Kenya at Dubai (ICC Academy)	2013-14
13.2	Ireland (71) v Afghanistan at Dubai (Sports City)	2016-17
13.3	Afghanistan (93) v West Indies at Basseterre	2017
13.4	**West Indies (60) v Pakistan at Karachi**	**2017-18**
14.0	**Netherlands (106) v Scotland at Amstelveen**	**2018**

That said, chief executive Warren Deutrom stressed that the board would not be measuring success purely by the bottom line. "They're about cricket opportunities for our players, as well as putting our sport in the nation's shop window," he said. "Everything we do should be to serve that bigger vision for Irish cricket." India comfortably topped 200 in both matches, while Ireland batted out the overs in the first game, and were bowled out inside 13 in the second – their briefest innings and biggest defeat.

INDIAN TOURING PARTY

*V. Kohli, Bhuvneshwar Kumar, J. J. Bumrah, Y. S. Chahal, S. Dhawan, M. S. Dhoni, K. D. Karthik, S. Kaul, M. K. Pandey, H. H. Pandya, K. L. Rahul, S. K. Raina, R. G. Sharma, M. S. Washington Sundar, K. Yadav, U. T. Yadav. *Coach:* R. J. Shastri.

First Twenty20 international At Malahide, June 27. **India won by 76 runs. India 208-5** (20 overs) (R. G. Sharma 97, S. Dhawan 74; P. K. D. Chase 4-35); ‡Ireland 132-9 (20 overs) (J. N. K. Shannon 60; Y. S. Chahal 3-38, K. Yadav 4-21). *MoM:* K. Yadav. *An opening partnership* *of 160 in 16 overs set the tone, as India eased to victory in their first match in Ireland for 11 years. Their supporters turned out in force in glorious sunshine, cheering every entrance of their star batsmen, and every boundary. The openers, who hit five sixes apiece, did much as they pleased, and the mayhem continued after Shikhar Dhawan's dismissal for 74 from 45 balls, as 41 came from the next three overs. But the last belonged to Peter Chase who, in four balls, removed M. S. Dhoni, Rohit Sharma (whose 97 came from just 61) and Virat Kohli, to finish with his best figures for Ireland. In reply, James Shannon – who survived straightforward chances on nought and 17 – hit 60 from 35. But the next-best was Stuart Thompson's 12, and the Irish batsmen had no clue against the left-arm wrist-spin of Kuldeep Yadav, whose 4-21 was a career-best, and the leg-breaks of Yuzvendra Chahal.*

Second Twenty20 international   At Malahide, June 29. **India won by 143 runs. India 213-4** (20 overs) (K. L. Rahul 70, S. K. Raina 69, H. H. Pandya 32*; K. J. O'Brien 3-40); ‡**Ireland 70** (12.3 overs) (Y. S. Chahal 3-21, K. Yadav 3-16). *MoM:* K. L. Rahul. *T20I debut:* S. Kaul (India). *K. L. Rahul, one of four changes for India, top-scored with 70 from 36 balls as they passed 200 in successive T20 innings for the first time. Suresh Raina was a close second, with 69 from 45, before Hardik Pandya provided a late flourish, hitting four sixes in nine balls as 39 were plundered from the last two overs. Two of the other changes, Umesh Yadav (playing only his second T20I, after missing India's previous 65) and debutant seamer Siddharth Kaul, then reduced Ireland to 23-3, before Kuldeep and Chahal mopped up again, taking 6-37 between them. It was Ireland's second-lowest T20 total, behind 68 against West Indies in Guyana in April 2010. The Indian spectators lapped up the action once more, and not even the absence of Dhoni, who was rested, or another failure for Kohli at the hands of Chase, could dull their enthusiasm. India's previous-biggest win by runs had been 93, against Sri Lanka at Cuttack in 2017-18. There had been only one bigger win in all T20 internationals: 172 by Sri Lanka against Kenya at Johannesburg in September 2007, at the first World Twenty20.*

IRELAND v AFGHANISTAN IN 2018

Ian Callender

Twenty20 internationals (3): Ireland 0, Afghanistan 2
One-day internationals (3): Ireland 1, Afghanistan 2

The newest Test nations met across both white-ball formats, with Afghanistan comprehensively outflanking their hosts to complete their first series wins in Ireland. It proved a sobering end to a momentous summer for the home team. Captain William Porterfield took out his frustration on Cricket Ireland for ruling that the decisive one-day international at Belfast would be played on a reused surface. Officials blamed the demands of television, but Porterfield was unimpressed: "We can't turn pitches round in a week in Ireland. We have said that for the last six, seven, eight years, playing subcontinental teams. We shouldn't be producing pitches which spin as much as that."

Although Rashid Khan was the leading wicket-taker in the ODIs, it was no one-man show: he was well supported by off-spinner Mohammad Nabi, while seamers Aftab Alam and Gulbadeen Naib also made key contributions.

It was galling for Ireland, who felt they should have been 2–0 up: poor shots and careless running had cost them dear in the opener, when they ought to have chased 228. They fought back next game, with Andrew Balbirnie recording his second fifty of the series, and Tim Murtagh improving his best ODI figures for the second successive match. But if that suggested the sides were well matched, the statistics said otherwise: Afghanistan had four of the top six for runs and wickets in the ODIs. Ireland leaned too heavily on Murtagh and Boyd Rankin, who took 13 of the 18 to fall to bowlers.

The three-match Twenty20 series – the last was rained off – had already been won by Afghanistan. Opener Hazratullah Zazai hit 156 runs, 67 fewer than Ireland managed in total, while the second win was Afghanistan's seventh in a row over Ireland in the format. Spinners Rashid and Mujeeb Zadran took 12 wickets between them, while Ireland's eight bowlers took 14; their batting was too reliant on Paul Stirling. The gulf between the sides remained wide.

AFGHANISTAN TOURING PARTY

*Asghar Afghan (50/20), Aftab Alam (50/20), Dawlat Zadran (50), Fareed Ahmad (20), Gulbadeen Naib (50/20), Hashmatullah Shahidi (50), Hazratullah Zazai (20), Ihsanullah Janat (50), Javed Ahmadi (50), Mirwais Ashraf (20), Mohammad Nabi (50/20), Mohammad Shahzad (50/20), Mujeeb Zadran (50/20), Najibullah Zadran (50/20), Rahmat Shah (50), Rashid Khan (50/20), Samiullah Shenwari (20), Sayed Shirzad (50), Shafiqullah Shinwari (50/20), Usman Ghani (20), Wafadar Momand (50). *Coach:* P. V. Simmons.
Hazratullah Zazai, originally selected for Twenty20 games only, was added to the ODI squad.

First Twenty20 international At Bready, August 20 (floodlit). **Afghanistan won by 16 runs. Afghanistan 160-7** (18 overs) (Hazratullah Zazai 74, Asghar Afghan 31); ‡**Ireland 144-9** (18 overs) (G. C. Wilson 34; Rashid Khan 3-35). *Twenty-year-old Hazratullah Zazai's withering assault was the cornerstone of Afghanistan's win. Recalled for his first appearance since December 2016, he hit eight fours and six sixes in his 33-ball 74. That included 23 off a Tyrone Kane over and, by the time*

Hazratullah was dismissed in the eighth, his opening partner Mohammad Shahzad had been virtually reduced to the role of spectator. In a match reduced to 18 overs because of a wet outfield, Afghanistan were ticking along nicely at 151-2 after 15.1, before Ireland took five for nine from the final 17 balls. Mujeeb Zadran quickly removed Stuart Thompson and William Porterfield. Paul Stirling made 27 before being brilliantly caught on the square-leg boundary by a leaping Aftab Alam. And Ireland were on the ropes at 60-4, even before Rashid Khan was introduced, though captain Gary Wilson made a defiant 34.

Second Twenty20 international At Bready, August 22 (floodlit). **Afghanistan won by 81 runs.** ‡**Afghanistan 160-8** (20 overs) (Hazratullah Zazai 82, Asghar Afghan 37; P. K. D. Chase 3-35); **Ireland 79** (15 overs) (W. T. S. Porterfield 33; Mujeeb Zadran 3-17, Rashid Khan 4-17). *Afghanistan clinched the series with a thrashing. Hazratullah was again the star turn. This time he started slowly as Ireland took two early wickets, but blossomed to finish with 82 off 54. He and captain Asghar Afghan put on 116 in 13 overs, an Afghanistan record for any T20 wicket, with Hazratullah hitting three of his seven sixes in four balls off Stirling. But Ireland's bowlers were dogged, and it took Najibullah Zadran's 20* off ten balls to equal their total in the first game. Ireland's response was shambolic: after three overs they were 9-3, and only Porterfield – snared by another outstanding catch from Aftab – and Wilson reached double figures. Rashid and Mujeeb shared seven for 34.*

Third Twenty20 international At Bready, August 24. **Abandoned.** *MoS:* Hazratullah Zazai (Afghanistan).

First one-day international At Belfast, August 27. **Afghanistan won by 29 runs. Afghanistan 227-9** (50 overs) (Gulbadeen Naib 64, Hashmatullah Shahidi 54; T. J. Murtagh 4-31, W. B. Rankin 3-44); ‡**Ireland 198** (48.3 overs) (A. Balbirnie 55, G. C. Wilson 38). *ODI debut:* Hazratullah Zazai (Afghanistan). *On a sluggish pitch that made life awkward for batsmen, Afghanistan's bowling proved too good. When Rankin and Tim Murtagh each took an early wicket, Porterfield looked to have made the right move by asking Afghanistan to bat. First to go was Hazratullah, who was given his one-day debut after his T20 heroics, but was caught at cover off a leading edge after being surprised by Rankin's bounce. The recovery was led by Gulbadeen Naib, who shared stands of 53 with Rahmat Shah and 77 with Hashmatullah Shahidi. But when Rankin trapped Gulbadeen for 64, it was the signal for the Ireland bowlers – who did not concede a wide or no-ball – to reassert their early control. Murtagh's 4-31 were his best in ODIs, and Andrew Balbirnie became the first Ireland fielder to take four catches in this format. The last 15 overs yielded just 73, and 228 appeared an attainable target, but soft dismissals undermined the chase. Porterfield and Stirling were swiftly removed and – for the second time – Niall and Kevin O'Brien were both run out in the same ODI. Balbirnie battled to 55, but the spinners prevented any acceleration.*

Second one-day international At Belfast, August 29. **Ireland won by three wickets.** ‡**Afghanistan 182-9** (50 overs) (Rahmat Shah 32, Asghar Afghan 39, Najibullah Zadran 42; T. J. Murtagh 4-30); **Ireland 183-7** (43.5 overs) (P. R. Stirling 39, A. Balbirnie 60, S. Singh 36*; Rashid Khan 3-37). *Murtagh improved his best ODI figures for the second time in three days, then soothed fraying nerves by hitting the winning runs. The victory ended a run of 11 completed home games across all formats without a win for Ireland, stretching back to August 2016. Murtagh grabbed three wickets in his first 14 balls and, when Balbirnie's direct hit ran out Hashmatullah, Afghanistan were 16-4, and facing humiliation in their 100th ODI. But they mounted a fightback. Rahmat and Asghar painstakingly put on 56, and Najibullah top-scored with 42 from 52 balls to give them a glimmer. Mujeeb bowled Porterfield with the fourth ball of the reply, but Balbirnie's second successive half-century and Simi Singh's unbeaten 36 steadied the ship. Defending resolutely against the spinners and running sharp singles, they put on 47 for the fifth wicket before Balbirnie fell to a smart slip catch by Najibullah off Rashid. There was still time for Ireland to suffer an attack of the jitters. Wilson and Andy McBrine departed in quick succession, and Murtagh had some nervous moments waiting for the third umpire to adjudicate on a stumping. But he soon got the job done.*

Third one-day international At Belfast, August 31. **Afghanistan won by eight wickets.** ‡**Ireland 124** (36.1 overs) (Rashid Khan 3-18); **Afghanistan 127-2** (23.5 overs) (Ihsanullah Janat 57*, Rahmat Shah 33, Hashmatullah Shahidi 34*). *MoS:* Rashid Khan. *The decider was played on the same pitch as the first game four days earlier, making Porterfield fearful of batting second against Afghanistan's spinners. But as Ireland slumped to 39-4 inside 11 overs, it was seamers Aftab and Gulbadeen who inflicted the damage. Rashid then took two in two to end the rescue operation started by Singh and Kevin O'Brien. Wilson top-scored with 23, before becoming the fourth of five lbw victims. Rankin took a wicket with his first ball, but Afghanistan sprinted for the line: Hashmatullah put on 74 in 80 balls for the third wicket with Ihsanullah Janat, securing the series before the innings had reached its halfway point.*

DOMESTIC CRICKET IN IRELAND IN 2018

Ian Callender

It was the year of the bat in the Interprovincial Championship. The competition's sixth year – and the second with first-class status – produced five of its six highest totals and a record seven centuries. But it was also the year of **North West Warriors**, who claimed their inaugural three-day title after **Leinster Lightning** had won the previous five. They passed 440 in three of their four games, their international batsmen William Porterfield, Niall O'Brien and Stuart Thompson scored the four biggest hundreds, and seamers David Scanlon and Craig Young were the leading wicket-takers, with 36 between them. They were confirmed as champions after their second victory, over **Northern Knights**, in July; although Leinster had one more match against Northern, an over-rate penalty in an earlier fixture ensured they could not catch North West even with a maximum-points win, and they played out a high-scoring draw.

In the opening game in Dublin, North West had reached 509 for nine declared, an interprovincial record, thanks to a fourth-wicket stand of 308 between O'Brien and Thompson (the previous all-wicket best in the tournament was 196). There had been only one higher first-class total in Ireland, when the national team scored 524 for eight against Bermuda in 2007. Leinster found themselves following on, 223 behind, and at 137 for six they were staring at their first defeat in the competition. But Kevin O'Brien and captain George Dockrell dug in and saved the game.

The return match at Bready saw a remarkable turnaround. On the first day, North West were bowled out for 80 – the competition's second-lowest total – as Peter Chase claimed five for 24, the best figures of the season. Leinster took a first-innings lead of 193, only for Porterfield to hit a career-best 207, sharing century partnerships with Aaron Gillespie and David Rankin as North West piled up 460 for nine to earn the draw. They won their remaining games, against Northern, by ten wickets and 140 runs. Leinster also defeated Northern once; John Anderson's unbeaten 123 steered them home with two overs to spare.

Leinster did retain both limited-overs titles, though it looked as if North West might steal the 50-over Interprovincial Cup too after Andy Britton reduced the defending champions to 34 for five on the last day of the season, at Rathmines. But Lorcan Tucker and Tyrone Kane added 103 for the eighth wicket to help Leinster reach 253, and they bowled out North West for 195 to keep the cup in Dublin for a fifth successive year. Back in June, Leinster had set a List A world record when Simi Singh and Dockrell shared an unbroken stand of 215 for the seventh wicket to set up victory over Northern.

FIRST-CLASS AVERAGES IN 2018

BATTING (150 runs)

		M	I	NO	R	HS	100	Avge	Ct
1	K. J. O'Brien (*Leinster/Ireland*)	2	4	1	222	118	1	74.00	1
2	J. A. McCollum (*Northern*)	4	7	0	442	116	1	63.14	1
3	†W. T. S. Porterfield (*North West/Ireland*)	5	9	1	491	207	2	61.37	11
4	J. B. Tector (*Leinster*)	3	5	0	270	87	0	54.00	0
5	J. Anderson (*Leinster*)	4	6	1	256	123*	1	51.20	1
6	†N. J. O'Brien (*North West/Ireland*)	5	8	0	399	165	1	49.87	10
7	A. Balbirnie (*Leinster/Ireland*)	5	8	1	302	114*	1	43.14	5
8	D. A. Rankin (*North West*)	4	6	1	213	86	0	42.60	6
9	G. H. Dockrell (*Leinster*)	4	6	1	201	92	0	40.20	2
10	S. C. Getkate (*Northern*)	4	7	1	219	70	0	36.50	0
11	M. R. Adair (*Northern*)	3	5	0	176	91	0	35.20	2
12	†S. R. Thompson (*North West/Ireland*)	5	9	1	255	148	1	31.87	1

BOWLING (7 wickets)

		Style	O	M	R	W	BB	5I	Avge
1	Mohammad Abbas (*Pakistan*)	RFM	39.3	14	110	9	5-66	1	12.22
2	G. R. J. Kennedy (*North West*)	LM	50	10	133	8	3-36	0	16.62
3	D. Scanlon (*North West*)	RM	100.1	15	374	19	4-61	0	19.68
4	C. A. Young (*North West*)	RM	124.1	30	400	17	5-60	1	23.52
5	H. T. Tector (*Northern*)	OB	78	12	230	9	4-70	0	25.55
6	S. R. Thompson (*North West/Ireland*) . .	RM	122.2	29	386	15	3-62	0	25.73
7	S. Singh (*Leinster*)	OB	111	30	271	9	3-39	0	30.11
8	J. Cameron-Dow (*Northern*)	SLA	131.5	22	422	14	5-101	1	30.14
9	P. K. D. Chase (*Leinster*)	RFM	108.2	14	420	13	5-24	1	32.30
10	W. B. Rankin (*North West/Ireland*)	RFM	65	7	246	7	2-42	0	35.14
11	G. H. Dockrell (*Leinster*)	SLA	132.1	30	395	8	3-120	0	49.37

HANLEY ENERGY INTERPROVINCIAL CHAMPIONSHIP IN 2018

	P	W	L	D	Bonus pts		Pen	Pts
					Bat	*Bowl*		
North West	4	2	0	2	10	16	0	64
Leinster	4	1	0	3	13	12	–1	49
Northern	4	0	3	1	11	13	0	27

Win = 16pts; draw = 3pts. Bonus points awarded for the first 100 overs of each team's first innings: one batting point for the first 150 runs and then for 200, 250 and 300; one bowling point for the third wicket taken and for every subsequent two.

† *1pt deducted for slow over-rate.*

INTERPROVINCIAL CHAMPIONS

2013	Leinster	2015	Leinster	2017	Leinster
2014	Leinster	2016	Leinster	2018	North West

The Interprovincial Championship was not first-class between 2013 and 2016.

Leinster have won the title 5 times, North West 1.

HANLEY ENERGY INTERPROVINCIAL CUP IN 2018

50-over league

	P	W	L	NR	Bonus	Pts	NRR
Leinster	4	3	0	1	1	15	0.81
North West	4	1	2	1	0	6	–0.63
Northern	4	1	3	0	1	5	–0.14

The Hanley Energy Interprovincial Trophy appears on page 1148.

Winners of Irish Leagues and Cups
Irish Senior Cup **Waringstown.** Leinster Senior League **Merrion.** Leinster Senior Cup **Clontarf.** Munster Senior League **Cork County.** Munster Senior Cup **County Kerry.** Northern League **CIYMS.** Northern Challenge Cup **Waringstown.** North West League **Bready.** North West Senior Cup **Brigade.**

NEW ZEALAND CRICKET IN 2018

Crowe-funding

ANDREW ALDERSON

New Zealand's cricket offered bull- and bear-market returns to fans in 2018, depending on the colour of the ball. The Test team's stocks soared: they racked up four consecutive series victories for the first time, beating England, Pakistan and Sri Lanka (they had defeated West Indies at the end of 2017). They finished 2018 ranked third in the world. It was a shame that New Zealand played so infrequently: supply failed to meet demand. There were only seven Tests in the year, fewer than any of the established nations, Zimbabwe aside.

Still, there were plenty of individual highlights. Henry Nicholls averaged 73, the highest of anyone who played more than two Tests. Trent Boult and Tim Southee became the first Kiwi pair to bowl unchanged through an innings, during England's capitulation for 58 at Auckland; spinners Ajaz Patel and

NEW ZEALAND IN 2018

	Played	Won	Lost	Drawn/No result
Tests	7	4	1	2
One-day internationals	13	8	4	1
Twenty20 internationals	13	3	9	1

DECEMBER	2 Tests, 3 ODIs and 3 T20Is (h) v West Indies	(see *Wisden 2018*, page 914)
JANUARY	5 ODIs and 3 T20Is (h) v Pakistan	(page 914)
FEBRUARY	Trans-Tasman T20 tri-series (h/a) v Australia and England	(page 260)
MARCH	2 Tests and 5 ODIs (h) v England	(page 269)
APRIL		
MAY		
JUNE		
JULY		
AUGUST		
SEPTEMBER		
OCTOBER		
NOVEMBER	3 Tests, 3 ODIs and 3 T20Is (in the UAE) v Pakistan	(page 944)
DECEMBER		
JANUARY	2 Tests, 3 ODIs and 1 T20I (h) v Sri Lanka	(page 917)

For a review of New Zealand domestic cricket from the 2017-18 season, see page 924.

Hagen Hopkins, Getty Images

Armed attack: Trent Boult and Tim Southee bowled New Zealand to success in 2018.

Will Somerville helped win fluctuating Tests against Pakistan in Abu Dhabi on their respective debuts; Nicholls, Kane Williamson and B-J. Watling swung the momentum against Pakistan in the decider; and Tom Latham dominated Sri Lanka, with centuries at the Basin Reserve and Hagley Oval.

At Wellington, he became only the second New Zealander to carry his bat through a Test innings, after Glenn Turner, who did it twice. Latham finished with 264 not out, the highest by anyone achieving the feat, beating Alastair Cook's 244 a year earlier at Melbourne. He added 176 at Christchurch, where Boult ripped out six wickets in 15 balls, another Test record. And, finally, Colin de Grandhomme hit New Zealand's fastest Test fifty, from 28 balls.

Williamson's captaincy blossomed. He finished the year with 12 wins from his 22 Tests in charge, a percentage of 55; New Zealand's next-best is Geoff Howarth's 37% (11 wins from 30). Williamson also claimed the national record for most Test centuries, against England at Auckland. Since December 1987, Martin Crowe had held the record, but while he hit 17 from 131 innings, Williamson made it 18 from 114 – not that the milestone mattered much to a selfless player with an almost pathological desire to focus on team rather than individual achievements. Coincidentally, the bat Crowe had used for his final century – a magnificent 115 on one leg at Old Trafford in 1994 – was auctioned in April as part of his actor cousin Russell Crowe's divorce collection. Crowdfunding helped ensure the *taonga* (treasure) ended up in the NZ Cricket Museum at a cost of $A20,000.

New Zealand's blue-chip Test portfolio was countered by some mixed white-ball fortunes. The year started with a 5–0 win – only their second – at home to Pakistan, while the same teams shared the spoils in the UAE later in the year. In between, a strong England side shaded their series 3–2: it was all square going into the final match, after New Zealand had overhauled 335 to win at Dunedin, thanks to Ross Taylor's unbeaten 181, in which he flayed the bowlers, despite suffering from a groin strain that kept him out of the decider.

The Twenty20 record was patchy. New Zealand beat West Indies, but went down home and away to Pakistan, and also lost a final to Australia, after narrowly eliminating England in a novel triangular tournament contested both at home and in Australia. It led to some confusing TV scheduling, since different channels had the rights, depending on the venue.

The women's team dominated West Indies and Ireland, but lost to world champions England. The highlight of the year was the highest 50-over total by either gender, New Zealand's 490 for four in Dublin. They romped past 400 in the other two games against the outgunned Irish as well; in the last, Amelia Kerr, the 17-year-old grand-daughter of the former Test batsman Bruce Murray, clouted 232 not out, then added five for 17 with her leg-breaks. After six years, Suzie Bates relinquished the captaincy to Amy Satterthwaite, less than two months before the T20 World Cup in the Caribbean, where New Zealand failed to get out of their group after losing to India and eventual champions Australia.

The men's side also had a leadership shake-up. Mike Hesson, their longest-serving coach, resigned in June with a year left on his contract, wishing to spend more time at home. New Zealand's competitiveness and consistency, both home and away, reached a rare altitude during his tenure, which was notable for the use of sabermetrics and a humble approach. He oversaw a first World Cup final appearance, in 2015, seven successive undefeated Test series between 2013 and 2015, and a record-equalling 13 Tests without defeat at home (2012–16). And his last three years incorporated NZ's three longest winning streaks across all formats, including a 13-match sequence that ended during the Pakistan T20s.

Hesson's farewell, although it was not known as such at the time, was the Test series against England. New Zealand dominated the inaugural day/night match at Auckland, winning by an innings after England's sensational first-day collapse, then the lower order survived for a nailbiting draw in Christchurch. Gary Stead, a batsman who played five Tests in 1999 and later coached his old team Canterbury to several domestic titles, was named as Hesson's replacement. His first assignment ended with New Zealand's second Test series win over Pakistan away from home – the other was in 1969-70 – and was followed by victory over Sri Lanka.

New Zealand Cricket's budgeted $10.7m operating loss was restricted to $3.5m after a record home season of international cricket and a reduction in operating costs. There was also a new four-year agreement between the board and the players' association. The NZCPA negotiated a fixed revenue share of 26.5% for the players, an increase of 1.5%, meaning the incentives for players – male and female – have never been higher.

NEW ZEALAND v PAKISTAN IN 2017-18

Andrew Alderson

One-day internationals (5): New Zealand 5, Pakistan 0
Twenty20 internationals (3): New Zealand 1, Pakistan 2

Two questions preceded Pakistan's visit. How long could New Zealand's winning streak last, after seven straight victories against West Indies? And when would Sarfraz Ahmed's side replicate the white-ball form that had won them the Champions Trophy in 2017, then helped them to a 5–0 clean sweep over Sri Lanka in the UAE?

The second was answered eventually, although it took until the end of a trip that involved eight matches. By then, New Zealand had steamrollered to only their second 5–0 whitewash in a one-day series, 18 years after dispatching West Indies; Pakistan had not lost so heavily since visiting Australia eight years earlier. Another win in the first Twenty20 match extended New Zealand's sequence to a national-record 13 – and then Pakistan bit back.

At the end of the 50-over games, their coach Mickey Arthur told his men "not to fear anything, and play with freedom". He explained: "The bounce is considerably steeper than we're used to. Our guys are used to scoring off the front foot and square of the wicket – but in New Zealand you score predominantly off the back foot and, if you get on the front foot, you generally hit straight."

After a few days' osmosis, his advice had soaked in: Pakistan dominated the final two games to win the 20-over series, and once more topped the T20 rankings. But Arthur was unhappy with the way the tour had started: "Some players came back from T20 competitions far worse in all departments."

Before the tour, New Zealand's coach Mike Hesson had praised Pakistan's "aggressive and experienced batsmen, and as good a bowling attack as any in world cricket". He could easily have been talking about his own side. New Zealand applied a trusted blueprint to the 50-over matches: a fast start with the bat, usually led by Martin Guptill, who scored 310 runs; consolidation, so no more than two wickets had fallen at 30 overs, retaining resources to blast at the death; then tight powerplay overs with the ball, parsimonious spin bowling, and ruthless fielding. Rain at Nelson meant a change of approach, while at Hamilton Colin de Grandhomme batted as if stuck in the highlights reel. It helped that Babar Azam, one of Pakistan's new stars, had a nightmare in the 50-over games, managing just 31 runs. Finally, though, Pakistan's flair trumped New Zealand's methodology, and competitiveness was restored to a one-sided summer.

❝ For the new batsman, trying to hit Garner's yorker for eight an over was like trying to bench-press gravity."
The 1979 World Cup, page 122

PAKISTAN TOURING PARTY

*Sarfraz Ahmed (50/20), Aamer Yamin (50/20), Ahmed Shehzad (20), Azhar Ali (50), Babar Azam (50/20), Fahim Ashraf (50/20), Fakhar Zaman (50/20), Haris Sohail (50/20), Hasan Ali (50/20), Imam-ul-Haq (50), Mohammad Amir (50/20), Mohammad Hafeez (50/20), Mohammad Nawaz (50/20), Rumman Raees (50/20), Shadab Khan (50/20), Shoaib Malik (50), Umar Amin (50/20). *Coach:* J. M. Arthur.

Shoaib Malik was originally selected for the Twenty20 series as well, but suffered concussion during the fourth ODI and withdrew from the squad.

At Nelson, January 3, 2018. **Pakistanis won by 120 runs. Pakistanis 341-9** (50 overs) (Azhar Ali 104, Fakhar Zaman 106; A. A. Parikh 3-74); **‡New Zealand XI 221** (47.1 overs) (M. S. J. Davidson 54; Shadab Khan 4-52). *The match was as good as decided by the time Fakhar Zaman retired out, after 29 overs, having put on 206 with Azhar Ali, who retired himself on reaching three figures. Michael Davidson top-scored for a callow New Zealand XI, who included only one international – off-spinner Mark Craig, who had played the most recent of his 15 Tests in September 2016.*

First one-day international   At Wellington (Basin Reserve), January 6, 2018. **New Zealand won by 61 runs** (DLS). **New Zealand 315-7** (50 overs) (M. J. Guptill 48, C. Munro 58, K. S. Williamson 115, H. M. Nicholls 50; Hasan Ali 3-61); **‡Pakistan 166-6** (30.1 overs) (Fakhar Zaman 82*; T. G. Southee 3-22). *MoM:* K. S. Williamson. *More used to sunnier climes, Pakistan were greeted with a southerly wind that raged up Adelaide Road but might have come from Cape Horn. The first casualties were the bails, which the umpires dispensed with after gusts whisked them off several times in the first six overs. Pakistan's bowlers were next to be blown away: Kane Williamson's tenth one-day century helped New Zealand rack up the highest score in 28 ODIs at the Basin Reserve (though this was only the second there in 13 years). Hasan Ali celebrated his dismissal of the dangerous Colin Munro with a version of the haka. But inside four overs of the reply, Pakistan were done for at 13-3. Fakhar added 78 for the sixth wicket with Shadab Khan (28) but, when rain brought an early end, they were well adrift of a DLS target of 228.*

Second one-day international   At Nelson, January 9, 2018. **New Zealand won by eight wickets** (DLS). **‡Pakistan 246-9** (50 overs) (Mohammad Hafeez 60, Shadab Khan 52, Hasan Ali 51; L. H. Ferguson 3-39); **New Zealand 151-2** (23.5 overs) (M. J. Guptill 86*, L. R. P. L. Taylor 45*). *MoM:* M. J. Guptill. *After Tim Southee and Trent Boult made early inroads, Pakistan were floundering at 141-7. But Shadab and Hasan Ali – who belied his previous best score of 13 with a 30-ball half-century – dragged them close to 250, helped by 21 in an over from leg-spinner Todd Astle. Earlier, Mohammad Hafeez reached 6,000 ODI runs. After a downpour at 64-2 in the 14th over, New Zealand's target was revised to 151 in 25. Martin Guptill switched to T20 mode, putting on 104* with Taylor and finishing with 86* from 71, with five sixes.*

Third one-day international   At Dunedin (University Oval), January 13, 2018. **New Zealand won by 183 runs. ‡New Zealand 257** (50 overs) (M. J. Guptill 45, K. S. Williamson 73, L. R. P. L. Taylor 52, T. W. M. Latham 35; Rumman Raees 3-51, Hasan Ali 3-59); **Pakistan 74** (27.2 overs) (T. A. Boult 5-17). *MoM:* T. A. Boult. *Pakistan collapsed to their lowest total in ODIs against New Zealand – previously 116 at Dambulla in May 2003 – to hand them the series. Boult took three wickets in his first two overs, and at 32-8 Pakistan were in danger of eclipsing the lowest total in all ODIs, Zimbabwe's 35 against Sri Lanka at Harare in April 2004. Skipper Sarfraz Ahmed (14*) made sure they passed that, and the last pair's 22 was the highest partnership: Rumman Raees (16) became only the sixth No. 11 to top-score in an ODI innings. Earlier, New Zealand had declined from 209-3, losing seven for 48 after Williamson's calm 73. The day had started well for one local builder: when*

NO. 11 TOP-SCORING IN ODI INNINGS

C. Pringle (34*)	New Zealand (171-9) v West Indies at Guwahati	1994-95
P. J. Ongondo (36)	Kenya (192) v West Indies at Nairobi (Gymkhana).	2001
S. E. Bond (26).	New Zealand (132) v Australia at Colombo (SSC)	2002
Shoaib Akhtar (43)	Pakistan (134) v England at Cape Town	2002-03
Mohammad Amir (58)†	Pakistan (275) v England at Nottingham	2016
Rumman Raees (16) . .	**Pakistan (74) v New Zealand at Dunedin (University Oval)**	**2017-18**

† *Amir was the joint-top scorer with Sharjeel Khan. J. Garner made 37 from No. 11 for West Indies (228) v India at Manchester in the 1983 World Cup, but A. M. E. Roberts made 37* from No. 9.*

Guptill clubbed the fifth ball, from Mohammad Amir, over the fence, Craig Dougherty caught it one-handed to earn a $NZ50,000 prize from the sponsors, Tui Beer.

Fourth one-day international   At Hamilton, January 16, 2018 (day/night). **New Zealand won by five wickets.** ‡Pakistan 262-8 (50 overs) (Fakhar Zaman 54, Haris Sohail 50, Mohammad Hafeez 81, Sarfraz Ahmed 51; T. G. Southee 3-44); **New Zealand 263-5** (45.5 overs) (M. J. Guptill 31, C. Munro 56, K. S. Williamson 32, H. M. Nicholls 52*, C. de Grandhomme 74*; Shadab Khan 3-42). *MoM:* C. de Grandhomme. *Returning to the side after the death of his father, Colin de Grandhomme entered with New Zealand in trouble at 154-5, needing 109 from 15 overs; Shadab's best ODI figures had derailed the innings after openers Guptill and Munro put on 88. De Grandhomme responded by smacking a maiden ODI half-century from 25 balls. It was New Zealand's 11th successive victory in all formats (excluding a no-result), a national record. Earlier, Hafeez had guided Pakistan towards a decent total with a run-a-ball 81, before Sarfraz cracked 51 from 46. Shoaib Malik was hit on the back of the head by a fielder's throw; he continued batting, but was soon out for six. He did not field after showing signs of concussion, and played no further part in the tour.*

Fifth one-day international   At Wellington (Basin Reserve), January 19, 2018. **New Zealand won by 15 runs.** ‡New Zealand 271-7 (50 overs) (M. J. Guptill 100, C. Munro 34, L. R. P. L. Taylor 59; Rumman Raees 3-67); **Pakistan 256** (49 overs) (Haris Sohail 63, Shadab Khan 54, Aamer Yamin 32*; M. J. Henry 4-53, M. J. Santner 3-40). *MoM:* M. J. Guptill. *MoS:* M. J. Guptill. *After Guptill's 13th one-day hundred, and a half-century from Ross Taylor full of rasping cuts, Pakistan were set 272 – more than had ever been made batting second in an ODI at the Basin. They looked sunk at 57-5, three of them to Matt Henry (replacing the rested Boult), but Haris Sohail put on 105 with Shadab before both fell to Mitchell Santner. The lower order fought hard before Henry returned to seal New Zealand's second 5–0 ODI whitewash.*

First Twenty20 international   At Wellington (Westpac Stadium), January 22, 2018. **New Zealand won by seven wickets. Pakistan 105** (19.4 overs) (Babar Azam 41; S. H. A. Rance 3-26, T. G. Southee 3-13); ‡New Zealand 106-3 (15.5 overs) (C. Munro 49*). *MoM:* C. Munro. *Pakistan's miserable tour continued as they nosedived to 53-7, before Babar Azam piloted them past 100. Hasan Ali, whose 23 included three sixes, was the only other batsman to reach double figures. The new-ball pair of Seth Rance and Tim Southee – captaining while Williamson rested a stiff side – shared six wickets. New Zealand slipped to 8-2, but Munro ensured a modest target was reached with something to spare.*

Second Twenty20 international   At Auckland, January 25, 2018 (floodlit). **Pakistan won by 48 runs.** ‡Pakistan 201-4 (20 overs) (Fakhar Zaman 50, Ahmed Shehzad 44, Babar Azam 50*, Sarfraz Ahmed 41); **New Zealand 153** (18.3 overs) (M. J. Santner 37, B. M. Wheeler 30; Fahim Ashraf 3-22). *MoM:* Fakhar Zaman. *After nearly a month in New Zealand, Pakistan registered a victory, with their batsmen firing at last. Fakhar and Ahmed Shehzad put on 94, briefly the highest opening stand in T20 internationals at Eden Park, then Babar and Sarfraz took the target beyond 200. New Zealand quickly stumbled: by the ninth over it was 64-6. Santner and Ben Wheeler put on 54, but seamer Fahim wrapped things up.*

Third Twenty20 international   At Mount Maunganui, January 28, 2018 (floodlit). **Pakistan won by 18 runs.** ‡Pakistan 181-6 (20 overs) (Fakhar Zaman 46); **New Zealand 163-6** (20 overs) (M. J. Guptill 59). *MoM:* Shadab Khan. *MoS:* Mohammad Amir. *After surrendering the first six internationals of the tour, Pakistan rounded it off with two wins – and regained top spot in the T20 rankings. New Zealand had looked more likely winners when Guptill got going. He became the second batsman – after his former team-mate Brendon McCullum – to reach 2,000 runs in T20 internationals. Then, looking for a fifth six, he miscued Shadab to deep midwicket. Taylor and Tom Bruce fell in successive overs, and 48 off 15 balls proved too steep for the rest. Pakistan's top six had all reached 18: opener Fakhar top-scored with 46, while Umar Amin blasted three sixes in making 21 from seven balls.*

NEW ZEALAND v SRI LANKA IN 2018-19

Mark Geenty

Test matches (2): New Zealand 1, Sri Lanka 0
One-day internationals (3): New Zealand 3, Sri Lanka 0
Twenty20 international (1): New Zealand 1, Sri Lanka 0

Some belligerent and occasionally brutal Sri Lankan batting meant this tour didn't quite provide the mismatch expected. Even so, New Zealand assumed a familiarly dominant position at home in front of sun-drenched, holidaying crowds, leaving the tourists winless throughout their five-week visit.

It would be a stretch to say Sri Lanka's hopes were high, after a 3–0 home defeat by England. Then, early in the tour, news broke that batting coach Thilan Samaraweera was being shown the door after the Tests, to be replaced by the former Durham coach Jon Lewis. Kusal Mendis pointedly paid a glowing tribute to Samaraweera after he helped save the Wellington Test with an unbeaten 141, in concert with 120 not out from Angelo Mathews – the high point of Sri Lanka's trip.

New Zealand had returned less than a week before the First Test following a memorable 2–1 win over Pakistan in the UAE. Having scrapped hard on turning pitches, the batsmen relished home climes and true bounce – notably opener Tom Latham. He carried his bat for 264 on a friendly Wellington surface, and amassed 450 runs in the two games, nearly half Sri Lanka's entire tally of 909.

A fresher pitch at Christchurch showed up the visitors' technique against swing and bounce. New Zealand's new-ball duo, Trent Boult and Tim Southee, took 14 wickets, with Boult picking up six for four in 15 balls to destroy Sri Lanka's first innings. Latham and Henry Nicholls batted them out of the game, before New Zealand completed a fourth successive series win for the first time.

The one-day internationals reflected the rankings – New Zealand third, Sri Lanka eighth – despite some whirlwind hitting from Niroshan Dickwella, Kusal Perera and Tissara Perera, whose breathtaking 57-ball hundred got Sri Lanka within 22 runs in the second match. But the bowling, led by the veteran Lasith Malinga, was toothless on dream batting surfaces, and Ross Taylor led the run-feast as New Zealand averaged 351 across the three games. After himself averaging 91 in ODIs in 2018, Taylor began World Cup year with scores of 54, 90 and 137. The hundred, at Nelson, where he unleashed his power to demoralise Sri Lanka's bowlers at the death, made him the first New Zealander to hit 20 in a format.

Nicholls followed suit at Nelson to continue a remarkable few months, while the return of all-rounder Jimmy Neesham, 18 months after his last international, was a boost; his six-hitting duel with Tissara Perera was the abiding memory of the ODIs. Neesham crashed Perera's medium-pace over the rope five times in one over at Bay Oval, before Perera managed four off an over from Southee two days later. But Neesham's bowling was more effective, and helped New Zealand close out victories.

SRI LANKA TOURING PARTY

L. D. Chandimal (T/50/20), P. V. D. Chameera (T/50/20), D. M. de Silva (T/50/20), D. P. D. N. Dickwella (T/50/20), A. N. P. R. Fernando (T/50/20), D. A. S. Gunaratne (50/20), M. D. Gunathilleke (T/50/20), F. D. M. Karunaratne (T), C. B. R. L. S. Kumara (T/50/20), R. A. S. Lakmal (T), S. L. Malinga (50/20), A. D. Mathews (T), B. K. G. Mendis (T/50/20), M. D. K. Perera (T), M. D. K. J. Perera (50/20), N. L. T. C. Perera (50/20), S. Prasanna (50/20), C. A. K. Rajitha (T/50/20), W. S. R. Samarawickrama (T), P. A. D. L. R. Sandakan (T/50/20), M. D. Shanaka (50/20), A. R. S. Silva (T), H. D. R. L. Thirimanne (T). Coach: U. C. Hathurusinghe.

Malinga captained in the limited-overs matches. Mathews tore a hamstring in the Second Test, and missed the one-day games.

NEW ZEALAND v SRI LANKA

First Test

At Wellington (Basin Reserve), December 15–19, 2018. Drawn. Toss: New Zealand.

By the close on the third evening, it was one-way traffic, a finish apparently imminent as Sri Lanka's top order crumbled again. Teetering at 20 for three, they were still 276 behind. Latham's epic unbeaten 264 in 11 hours 34 minutes – the sixth-highest and third-longest by a New Zealander – looked certain to lead them to a tenth successive victory in an early-season (November or December) home Test.

Not so fast, said two Sri Lankans with a point to prove. Still just 23, Mendis had endured a lean trot against South Africa and England, his breakthrough 176 against Australia in 2016 a distant memory. Mathews, meanwhile, was still pained by his axing from the one-day captaincy amid questions over his fitness. His batting had a steely, defiant edge, and he had already top-scored with 83 in the first innings, when the pitch was at its trickiest. What followed was the first wicketless full day of Test cricket since South African openers Graeme Smith and Neil McKenzie batted through the first at Chittagong in February 2008. In almost 89 years of Tests in New Zealand, it had never happened before.

The Basin is usually a batsman's paradise on the third and fourth days, but offers enough bounce to keep the fast men interested. This pitch didn't start with as much moisture as usual, and what remained was sucked out by a strong wind, leaving an easy-paced featherbed that didn't break up. In recent years Wagner had frightened Bangladesh and West Indies with his well-directed bouncer barrage to a leg-theory field. This time it didn't work: the radar was slightly off, the bounce not as steep. Mendis and Mathews picked which short deliveries to take on and which to leave. Southee and Boult had no swing to assist them, left-arm spinner Ajaz Patel minimal turn in his first home Test.

The batsmen reined in their instincts and – as clouds gathered – the finish line came into sight. When the weather had the final say, 274 runs and nearly seven and a half hours after the pair united, they had secured a draw. It was Sri Lanka's highest second-innings stand,

HIGHEST SCORE WHEN CARRYING BAT

359*	S. B. Gohel	Gujarat (641) v Orissa at Jaipur	2016-17
357*	R. Abel	Surrey (811) v Somerset at The Oval	1899
318*	W. G. Grace	Gloucestershire (528) v Yorkshire at Cheltenham	1876
305*	W. H. Ashdown	Kent (560) v Derbyshire at Dover	1935
272*	R. R. Relf	Sussex (433) v Worcestershire at Eastbourne	1909
270*	C. F. Hughes	Derbyshire (475) v Yorkshire at Leeds	2013
265*	W. U. Tharanga	Ruhuna (450) v Basnahira South at Colombo (CCC)	2008-09
264*	**T. W. M. Latham**	**New Zealand (578) v Sri Lanka at Wellington**	**2018-19**
260*	D. S. Jadhav	India A (492) v Kenya at Nairobi (Simba)	2004

beating an unbroken 240 between Asanka Gurusinha and Arjuna Ranatunga against Pakistan at Colombo's P. Sara Oval in March 1986. Mendis had his sixth Test century, and Mathews his ninth, which he celebrated with a flurry of press-ups and a glare to the dressing-room.

New Zealand felt they hadn't bowled badly, but were frustrated by the pitch, after working hard to build a strong position. Southee had been outstanding early on, generating swing on a calm first day and defying a lean record on the ground to snare six for 68 and dismiss Sri Lanka for an undulating 282: Karunaratne and Mathews added 133 from the depths of nine for three, before Dickwella's unbeaten 80 prevented a collapse.

Then it was the Latham show. Only one other New Zealander – Glenn Turner (twice) – had carried his bat through a Test innings, and Latham was determined to play the long

---

ALL-DAY SPECIALS

Occasions when Sri Lanka batted through a complete day's play in a Test without losing a wicket:

Runs

240	A. P. Gurusinha/A. Ranatunga.........	v Pakistan at Colombo (PSO) (5th day)	1985-86
283†	S. T. Jayasuriya/R. S. Mahanama.......	v India at Colombo (RPS) (3rd).....	1997-98
265†	S. T. Jayasuriya/R. S. Mahanama.......	v India at Colombo (RPS) (4th).....	1997-98
257	K. C. Sangakkara/D. P. M. D. Jayawardene.	v South Africa at Colombo (SSC)...	2006
239	**B. K. G. Mendis/A. D. Mathews**.......	**v New Zealand at Wellington**.....	**2018-19**

† *Successive days.*

---

game. It was a classic opener's knock, leaving well, avoiding risk, and textbook cover-driving. Williamson unfurled another gem, an effortless 91 off 93 balls and, after he surprised everyone on a sun-drenched Sunday afternoon by getting out, Latham took over.

Kumara was lively and kept charging in – his reward was four wickets – but Latham was immovable. He reached 200 for the first time, in his 40th Test, and kept picking off the records as wickets gradually fell. When Boult was last out, he passed Alastair Cook's 244 at Melbourne in 2017-18 as the highest Test innings by an opener carrying his bat. It was no contest for the match award; all that was missing was the win. That would have to wait until Latham's home-town Test on Boxing Day.

Man of the Match: T. W. M. Latham.

Close of play: first day, Sri Lanka 275-9 (Dickwella 73); second day, New Zealand 311-2 (Latham 121, Taylor 50); third day, Sri Lanka 20-3 (Mendis 5, Mathews 2); fourth day, Sri Lanka 259-3 (Mendis 116, Mathews 117).

Sri Lanka

M. D. Gunathilleke lbw b Southee.............	1	– lbw b Boult.....................	3
F. D. M. Karunaratne c Watling b Wagner.......	79	– c Boult b Southee...............	10
D. M. de Silva c Watling b Southee.............	1	– b Southee......................	0
B. K. G. Mendis c Patel b Southee.............	2	– not out 141
A. D. Mathews c Watling b Southee.............	83	– not out 120
*L. D. Chandimal c Patel b Southee	6		
†D. P. D. N. Dickwella not out	80		
M. D. K. Perera c Watling b de Grandhomme.....	16		
R. A. S. Lakmal c Nicholls b Wagner...........	3		
C. A. K. Rajitha c Watling b Boult	2		
C. B. R. L. S. Kumara c de Grandhomme b Southee	0		
Lb 7, nb 2.........................	9	Lb 2, w 8, nb 3.............	13

1/5 (1) 2/7 (3) 3/9 (4) (90 overs) 282
4/142 (2) 5/167 (6) 6/187 (5)
7/223 (8) 8/240 (9) 9/275 (10) 10/282 (11)

1/5 (1) (3 wkts, 115 overs) 287
2/10 (3) 3/13 (2)

Boult 27–6–83–1; Southee 27–7–68–6; de Grandhomme 13–2–35–1; Wagner 20–2–75–2; Patel 3–0–14–0. *Second innings*—Southee 25–8–52–2; Boult 25–4–62–1; Wagner 23–4–100–0; de Grandhomme 13–4–24–0; Patel 28–10–46–0; Raval 1–0–1–0.

New Zealand

J. A. Raval c Dickwella b Kumara	43
T. W. M. Latham not out	264
*K. S. Williamson c Rajitha b de Silva	91
L. R. P. L. Taylor c Karunaratne b Kumara	50
H. M. Nicholls c Rajitha b Perera	50
†B-J. Watling c Dickwella b Kumara	0
C. de Grandhomme c Rajitha b de Silva . . .	49
T. G. Southee run out (Chandimal)	6
N. Wagner c de Silva b Lakmal	0

A. Y. Patel b Perera	6
T. A. Boult c Dickwella b Kumara	11
Lb 5, w 1, nb 2	8

1/59 (1) 2/221 (3) (157.3 overs) 578
3/312 (4) 4/426 (5)
5/426 (6) 6/499 (7) 7/520 (8)
8/520 (9) 9/549 (10) 10/578 (11)

Lakmal 31–6–88–1; Rajitha 34–5–144–0; Mathews 4–3–1–0; Perera 40–1–156–2; Kumara 31.3–2–127–4; de Silva 15–0–54–2; Gunathilleke 2–1–3–0.

Umpires: M. A. Gough and R. J. Tucker. Third umpire: R. K. Illingworth.
Referee: R. B. Richardson.

NEW ZEALAND v SRI LANKA

Second Test

At Christchurch, December 26–30, 2018. New Zealand won by 423 runs. Toss: Sri Lanka.
If the pitch at the Basin Reserve was not to New Zealand's liking, the one at Hagley Oval was the perfect Christmas present. Another Latham marathon – a mere nine and a half hours this time – was backed up by another busy century from Nicholls, his fellow Cantabrian, then by a swing clinic from Boult and an award-winning performance from Southee, whose all-round contribution evoked memories of his Napier debut against England as a teenager.

The result looked comprehensive, but it had taken a while for New Zealand to assert themselves – especially after Chandimal called correctly, and Lakmal and his fellow seamers got first gallop on a pitch so fresh and grassy they at times lost their footing. But Lakmal got it right in a superb display of swing bowling: around the wicket, and hooping it in to the left-handers, he swept through Raval, Latham, Williamson and Nicholls as New Zealand slipped to 36 for four. When Taylor was run out at the non-striker's end via Kumara's fingertips, 150 looked a lofty goal – and the series was on a knife edge.

Southee's first intervention was crucial. The unbeaten 77 he had made on that debut in March 2008 remained his highest Test score, since when his batting had been a regular source of angst. But his gung-ho approach always had the potential to damage opponents, and 68 off 65 balls was the most telling contribution of the first four sessions. By stumps, after Southee had quickly removed Sri Lanka's top three, 14 wickets had tumbled, though the tourists still looked likely to overhaul New Zealand's 178.

That all changed next morning in 15 balls from Boult. After ten wicketless overs on day one, he scythed through Sri Lanka with a stunning spell of six for four. The Kookaburra hadn't swung consistently for him, but this was the perfect storm: while he bowled full and fast, Sri Lanka's tailenders were clueless. The last four fell lbw for ducks as Boult's inswing looked almost unplayable, and he walked off saluting the crowd with Test-best figures of six for 30.

From there, Sri Lanka were never in it. By the second-day close, the Test was well advanced and Latham, on 74, in the driver's seat again; Lakmal, meanwhile, would remain wicketless in 30 overs. Latham's eighth Test century was a formality as the pitch flattened. Now it was a question of the size of New Zealand's lead. The answer was a mammoth

GOING CHEAP

Six wickets for fewest runs in a Test spell:

Spell	Balls			
6-0	15	J. J. C. Lawson (6-3)......	West Indies v Bangladesh at Dhaka.......	2001-02
6-1	25	C. E. L. Ambrose (7-25)...	West Indies v Australia at Perth..........	1992-93
6-2	25†	G. A. Lohmann (8-7).....	England v South Africa at Johannesburg...	1895-96
6-2	52	D. L. Underwood (8-51)...	England v Pakistan at Lord's	1974
6-3	32	V. D. Philander (6-21)....	South Africa v Australia at Johannesburg ..	2017-18
6-4	**15**	**T. A. Boult (6-30)**	**New Zealand v Sri Lanka at Christchurch**	**2018-19**
6-4	24	F. S. Trueman (7-44).....	England v West Indies at Birmingham	1963
6-4	31	Sarfraz Nawaz (9-86).....	Pakistan v Australia at Melbourne........	1978-79
6-4	33	P. C. R. Tufnell (6-25)....	England v West Indies at The Oval	1991
6-4	51	S. C. J. Broad (6-17).....	England v South Africa at Johannesburg...	2015-16
6-4	71	D. L. Underwood (7-32)...	England v New Zealand at Lord's	1969

† *Estimate. Ambrose took 7-1 in 32 balls, and Lohmann 8-4 in 44. Research: Charles Davis*

659, as Nicholls joined in the fun with his former schoolboy rival, notching his third century of a year in which he averaged 73. He and Latham, who were sharing a car to the ground each morning, added 214, before Latham finally went for 176. Nicholls and de Grandhomme, with an undefeated 71 off 45 balls, then rattled up 124 in less than 15 overs.

Sri Lanka were out on their feet – but faced more than two days to save the Test. They lasted 106 overs, but couldn't replicate their Wellington heroics on a bouncy Hagley surface. Mendis top-scored again, with 67, before an uppish shot off Wagner was brilliantly taken by substitute Matt Henry, diving forward at extra cover. When Mathews retired hurt with a hamstring injury, the end was nigh. New Zealand's big three finished the job, with Wagner on target and wearing Sri Lanka's batsmen down. It was easily New Zealand's biggest Test victory by runs, beating 254 against Zimbabwe at Bulawayo in August 2016. Boult finished with nine wickets in the match, and Southee five, but it was Southee's first-day batting that earned him the bottle of bubbly.

Man of the Match: T. G. Southee.

Close of play: first day, Sri Lanka 88-4 (Mathews 27, Silva 15); second day, New Zealand 231-2 (Latham 74, Taylor 25); third day, Sri Lanka 24-2 (Chandimal 14, Mendis 6); fourth day, Sri Lanka 231-6 (Perera 22, Lakmal 16).

New Zealand

J. A. Raval c Chandimal b Lakmal	6	– c Mendis b Perera................	74
T. W. M. Latham c Mendis b Lakmal	10	– c Dickwella b Chameera	176
*K. S. Williamson c Dickwella b Lakmal	2	– c Mendis b Kumara	48
L. R. P. L. Taylor run out (Kumara)	27	– lbw b Kumara....................	40
H. M. Nicholls b Lakmal	1	– not out	162
†B-J. Watling c Perera b Kumara...............	46		
C. de Grandhomme c Chameera b Kumara	1	– (6) not out......................	71
T. G. Southee c Gunathilleke b Perera..........	68		
N. Wagner c Mendis b Kumara	0		
A. Y. Patel c Lakmal b Kumara...............	2		
T. A. Boult not out.........................	1		
B 6, lb 7, nb 1..........	14	B 5, lb 3, w 3, nb 3.........	14

1/16 (1) 2/17 (2) 3/22 (3)   (50 overs) 178   1/121 (1)   (4 wkts dec, 153 overs) 585
4/36 (5) 5/57 (4) 6/64 (7)   2/189 (3) 3/247 (4)
7/172 (8) 8/175 (9) 9/177 (6) 10/178 (10)   4/461 (2)

Lakmal 19–5–54–5; Kumara 14–4–49–3; Mathews 4–1–6–0; Chameera 8–1–43–0; Perera 5–1–13–1. *Second innings*—Lakmal 30–6–96–0; Kumara 32–6–134–2; Chameera 30–5–147–1; Perera 41–3–149–1; Gunathilleke 16–2–45–0; Karunaratne 4–2–6–0.

Sri Lanka

M. D. Gunathilleke c Raval b Southee	8	– c Watling b Southee	4
F. D. M. Karunaratne c Williamson b Southee	7	– c Watling b Boult	0
*L. D. Chandimal c Watling b Southee	6	– c Nicholls b Wagner	56
B. K. G. Mendis c Watling b de Grandhomme	15	– sub (M. J. Henry) b Wagner	67
A. D. Mathews not out	33	– retired hurt	22
A. R. S. Silva c Southee b Boult	21	– c Watling b Wagner	18
†D. P. D. N. Dickwella c Southee b Boult	4	– b Southee	19
M. D. K. Perera lbw b Boult	0	– c Williamson b Wagner	22
R. A. S. Lakmal lbw b Boult	0	– b Boult	18
P. V. D. Chameera lbw b Boult	0	– lbw b Boult	3
C. B. R. L. S. Kumara lbw b Boult	0	– not out	0
B 5, lb 5	10	B 4, lb 2, w 1	7

1/10 (2) 2/20 (3) 3/21 (1)	(41 overs)	104
4/51 (4) 5/94 (6) 6/100 (7)		
7/100 (8) 8/100 (9) 9/104 (10) 10/104 (11)		

1/1 (2) 2/9 (1)	(106.2 overs)	236
3/126 (4) 4/158 (3)		
5/181 (7) 6/208 (6)		
7/233 (9) 8/233 (8) 9/236 (10)		

In the second innings Mathews retired hurt at 155-3.

Boult 15–8–30–6; Southee 15–5–35–3; de Grandhomme 6–0–19–1; Wagner 5–0–10–0. *Second innings*—Boult 28.2–11–77–3; Southee 27–13–61–2; de Grandhomme 10–1–23–0; Wagner 29–10–48–4; Patel 12–9–21–0.

Umpires: M. A. Gough and R. K. Illingworth.   Third umpire: R. J. Tucker.
Referee: R. B. Richardson.

First one-day international   At Mount Maunganui, January 3, 2019 (day/night). **New Zealand won by 45 runs.** ‡**New Zealand 371-7** (50 overs) (M. J. Guptill 138, K. S. Williamson 76, L. R. P. L. Taylor 54, J. D. S. Neesham 47*); **Sri Lanka 326** (49 overs) (D. P. D. N. Dickwella 76, M. D. Gunathilleke 43, M. D. K. J. Perera 102; J. D. S. Neesham 3-38). *MoM:* M. J. Guptill. *ODI debut:* T. L. Seifert (New Zealand). *Two returnees did most of the damage after New Zealand ran up 371, their fourth-highest ODI total at home and the biggest at the Bay Oval. Martin Guptill, missing through injury for ten months, hit a run-a-ball 138, which set the stage for a brutal late onslaught from Jimmy Neesham, out of form and favour since the 2017 Champions Trophy. He smashed the first five deliveries of a Tissara Perera over for six, but could manage only a single from the last; with the over including a no-ball, it cost 34 in all. Neesham's 47* needed only 13 deliveries. Sri Lanka replied boldly, with Niroshan Dickwella reverse-lapping the faster bowlers during a perky opening stand of 119 with Dhanushka Gunathilleke, who bounced back from a nightmare run in the Tests. But Neesham removed both in the space of four balls and, although Kusal Perera made his fourth one-day hundred, the mountain was too high to climb.*

Second one-day international   At Mount Maunganui, January 5, 2019 (day/night). **New Zealand won by 21 runs.** ‡**New Zealand 319-7** (50 overs) (C. Munro 87, L. R. P. L. Taylor 90, H. M. Nicholls 32, J. D. S. Neesham 64); **Sri Lanka 298** (46.2 overs) (M. D. Gunathilleke 71, N. L. T. C. Perera 140; I. S. Sodhi 3-55). *MoM:* N. L. T. C. Perera. *It's rare to score 140 from 74 balls and lose – but it happened to Tissara Perera. He arrived at 121-5, which soon became 128-7, but stunned spectators – and the New Zealand bowlers – by clouting 13 sixes and eight fours. The fielding disintegrated, with six chances going down; there were four sixes in the 46th over, bowled by Tim Southee. Perera put on 75 with Lasith Malinga (17), then 51 with Lakshan Sandakan (6), and 44 with last man Nuwan Pradeep Fernando (3*), before Trent Boult finally clung on to a catch. New Zealand were grateful they had again comfortably exceeded 300, mainly thanks to a third-wicket stand of 112 between Colin Munro and Ross Taylor, and another late blitz from Neesham (64 off 37 this time).*

Third one-day international   At Nelson, January 8, 2019. **New Zealand won by 115 runs. New Zealand 364-4** (50 overs) (K. S. Williamson 55, L. R. P. L. Taylor 137, H. M. Nicholls 124*; S. L. Malinga 3-93); ‡**Sri Lanka 249** (41.4 overs) (D. P. D. N. Dickwella 36, D. M. de Silva 36, M. D. K. J. Perera 43, N. L. T. C. Perera 80, M. D. Gunathilleke 31; L. H. Ferguson 4-40, I. S. Sodhi 3-40). *MoM:* L. R. P. L. Taylor. *New Zealand completed a clean sweep after a three-match run-fest that sometimes resembled a golf range-hitting competition. Taylor followed innings of 54 and 90 with a superb 137, his 20th one-day century, putting on 116 for the third wicket with Kane*

MOST SIXES IN AN ODI INNINGS

16	R. G. Sharma (209)......	India v Australia at Bangalore	2013-14
16	A. B. de Villiers (149)	South Africa v West Indies at Johannesburg	2014-15
16	C. H. Gayle (215)........	West Indies v Zimbabwe at Canberra	2014-15
15	S. R. Watson (185*)......	Australia v Bangladesh at Mirpur	2010-11
14	C. J. Anderson (131*).....	New Zealand v West Indies at Queenstown........	2013-14
13	**N. L. T. C. Perera (140)** ..	**Sri Lanka v New Zealand at Mount Maunganui...**	**2018-19**
12	X. M. Marshall (157*).....	West Indies v Canada at King City	2008
12	R. G. Sharma (208*)......	India v Sri Lanka at Mohali	2017-18

HIGHEST SCORE FROM No. 7 IN ODIs

170*	L. Ronchi	New Zealand v Sri Lanka at Dunedin	2014-15
146*	M. P. Stoinis..........	Australia v New Zealand at Auckland	2016-17
140	**N. L. T. C. Perera**	**Sri Lanka v New Zealand at Mount Maunganui...**	**2018-19**
139*	M. S. Dhoni	Asia XI v Africa XI at Chennai	2007
130	S. M. Pollock	Africa XI v Asia XI at Bangalore................	2007
121	J. C. Buttler..........	England v Sri Lanka at Lord's	2014
116	J. P. Faulkner.........	Australia v India at Bangalore	2013-14
113*	M. S. Dhoni	India v Pakistan at Chennai	2012-13
111*	M. Kaif	India v Zimbabwe at Colombo (RPS)	2002-03
111*	T. M. Odoyo..........	Kenya v Canada at Nairobi (Gymkhana)...........	2007-08

There have been eight further centuries from No. 7 in ODIs.

Williamson, and 154 for the fourth in 20 overs with Henry Nicholls, who reached his maiden ODI hundred from 71 balls. Malinga started with two early wickets, but lost the plot at the end, his first spell of 5–1–21–2 morphing into 10–1–93–3. Sri Lanka began well once more, and New Zealand were looking anxious when Tissara Perera got going again, on his way to 80 from 63 balls. But he fell to Lockie Ferguson, who unleashed a heady combination of raw pace, precision yorkers and slower bouncers to take four wickets. Leg-spinner Ish Sodhi claimed three, as Sri Lanka's last four wickets fell without addition.

Twenty20 international   At Auckland, January 11, 2019 (floodlit). **New Zealand won by 35 runs. New Zealand 179-7** (20 overs) (L. R. P. L. Taylor 33, D. A. J. Bracewell 44, S. C. Kuggeleijn 35*; C. A. K. Rajitha 3-44); ‡**Sri Lanka 144** (16.5 overs) (N. L. T. C. Perera 43; L. H. Ferguson 3-21, I. S. Sodhi 3-30). *MoM:* D. A. J. Bracewell. *T20I debuts:* S. C. Kuggeleijn (New Zealand); C. B. R. L. S. Kumara (Sri Lanka). *When New Zealand slipped to 55-5 after ten overs, bothered by the bounce at Eden Park, it seemed Sri Lanka might finally register a win. But Doug Bracewell, playing only because Neesham had tweaked a hamstring, crashed five sixes from 26 balls. Then the debutant Scott Kuggeleijn (whose father, Chris, played two Tests in 1988-89) added 35* from 15, with three sixes, swelling the target to 180 – still gettable on a small ground. But Bracewell removed the dangerous Dickwella, and caught Kusal and Tissara Perera, both centurions in the ODIs. The last six wickets tumbled for 26, and Sri Lanka had to contemplate their next assignment, two Tests in Australia, without a victory under their belt.*

DOMESTIC CRICKET IN NEW ZEALAND IN 2017-18

Mark Geenty

Ajaz Patel topped the Plunket Shield wicket-takers for the third successive season, and his durability, accuracy and skill helped **Central Districts** lift the title for the first time in five years. Coached by South African Heinrich Malan, Central had also reached both white-ball finals, losing to Northern Districts in the Super Smash, and Auckland in the Ford Trophy; then, in March, they pulled ahead of **Wellington**, who had led the four-day table for most of the season, to claim the Shield.

When the sides met in mid-March, Wellington started 11 points ahead, and reduced Central to 85 for eight chasing 372. But Central held on for a draw – they were unbeaten throughout the tournament – and beat defending champions Canterbury by an innings before drawing their last match, against Northern. Meanwhile, Wellington were rolled by both Northern and Auckland, and finished four points adrift.

Central opener Greg Hay and captain Will Young were among the top four Shield run-scorers, but Patel took his left-arm spin to a new level, twirling through 356 overs to collect 48 wickets at 21 apiece. He was named Domestic Cricketer of the Year, and – aged 30 – made a successful Test debut against Pakistan in November 2018. Born in Mumbai, Patel had emigrated as a child; he switched from seam to spin in his early twenties, realising his short stature would limit his future as a quick bowler.

Wellington supplied the next three leading wicket-takers: Logan van Beek, Hamish Bennett and the more familiar slow-bowling Patel, Jeetan (who tied on 36 with Auckland seamer Matt McEwan). But it was a newcomer, seamer Ollie Newton, who had given their season a sensational start. Making his first-class debut at 29, Newton struck with his first, third and fourth deliveries to reduce Auckland to two for three; a fourth victim made it 12 for seven, though they struggled on to 62. In reply, Michael Papps and Luke Woodcock plundered 432 – a New Zealand first-wicket record – to set up victory by an innings and 205. Papps scored a career-best 316 not out, and eventually headed the run-scorers' list with 814, to sign off a two-decade career with 12,294 first-class runs and 33 centuries.

Auckland finished a clear third and won the 50-over Ford Trophy final, beating Central, who had lost only one of nine previous matches. Fast bowler Lockie Ferguson and leg-spinner Tarun Nethula, the competition's top wicket-taker with 21, sparked a mid-innings Central collapse of five for seven. Mark Chapman made 480 runs, more than 100 clear of the next best. In the play-offs, Auckland had swept aside Canterbury after a bizarre moment when their opener Jeet Raval – who hit 149 – smashed one back at Andrew Ellis; it ricocheted off Ellis's head for six, but he passed a concussion test and appeared unharmed.

Reaching that play-off was **Canterbury's** highlight. A year after their four-day/one-day double, they finished bottom of the Shield. Injuries struck their attack, and Ken McClure was unavailable mid-season after a common assault charge; he pleaded guilty and was sentenced to 200 hours' community work, 12 months' supervision and financial reparation. After returning in March, he hit 210 against Auckland at Rangiora, in a match called off on the third morning when the ball reared dangerously. The umpires ruled the pitch unsafe, with Auckland 66 for six, trailing by 419.

Northern Districts won only two first-class games, but did better in 50-over cricket until a heavy loss to Canterbury in the play-offs. Seamer Brent Arnel, aged 39, collected 17 one-day wickets, second only to Nethula, but confirmed his retirement. **Otago** finished fifth in the Shield and bottom in both limited-overs competitions. South African coach Rob Walter had signed Rob Nicol from Auckland as captain, but he scored only 175 first-class runs, and joined Papps and Arnel at the exit. Neil Wagner and Jimmy Neesham moved on, to Northern and Wellington respectively, while Otago Cricket announced an independent review to address poor results over several years.

FIRST-CLASS AVERAGES IN 2017-18

BATTING (400 runs)

		M	I	NO	R	HS	100	Avge	Ct/St
1	†J. D. Ryder (*Central Districts*)	7	11	2	640	175	2	71.11	7
2	G. R. Hay (*Central Districts*)	9	15	2	786	140	3	60.46	3
3	T. C. Bruce (*Central Districts*)	6	10	2	434	89	0	54.25	9
4	M. H. W. Papps (*Wellington*)	10	18	2	814	316*	2	50.87	10
5	T. L. Seifert (*Northern Districts*)	9	15	1	703	167*	2	50.21	30/2
6	D. Cleaver (*Central Districts*).	8	13	1	560	88	0	46.66	29/2
7	W. A. Young (*Central Districts*)	10	17	1	686	162	1	42.87	6
8	†L. J. Woodcock (*Wellington*)	10	18	2	682	151	1	42.62	2
9	H. R. Cooper (*Northern Districts*)	7	11	0	450	136	1	40.90	1
10	†A. P. Devcich (*Northern Districts*).	7	13	1	462	116	2	38.50	3
11	D. C. de Boorder (*Otago*)	10	17	1	575	140*	1	35.93	34/2
12	†J. D. S. Neesham (*Otago*)	9	16	1	533	93	0	35.53	12
13	†S. M. Solia (*Auckland*)	7	13	0	428	72	0	32.92	5
14	C. D. Fletcher (*Canterbury*)	10	18	2	506	100*	1	31.62	27/2
15	K. J. McClure (*Canterbury*)	8	15	1	440	210	1	31.42	2
16	†D. R. Flynn (*Northern Districts*)	10	17	0	533	157	1	31.35	3
17	†H. D. Rutherford (*Otago*)	10	19	0	577	142	1	30.36	6
18	C. J. Bowes (*Wellington*)	10	19	0	570	93	0	30.00	5
19	A. K. Kitchen (*Otago*)	9	17	1	480	76	0	30.00	4
20	M. L. Guptill-Bunce (*Auckland*).	10	19	0	517	91	0	27.21	8
21	R. R. O'Donnell (*Auckland*)	9	17	1	413	93*	0	25.81	12
22	C. E. McConchie (*Canterbury*)	10	18	0	452	99	0	25.11	2
23	S. J. Murdoch (*Wellington*).	10	17	0	409	114	1	24.05	9

BOWLING (15 wickets)

		Style	O	M	R	W	BB	5I	Avge
1	W. D. Barnes (*Otago*)	RFM	62.4	17	178	15	6-64	1	11.86
2	L. V. van Beek (*Wellington*)	RFM	193	47	579	40	6-46	3	14.47
3	S. H. A. Rance (*Central Districts*).	RFM	149.4	32	429	28	6-26	3	15.32
4	H. K. Bennett (*Wellington*)	RFM	215.2	55	585	38	5-14	2	15.39
5	I. S. Sodhi (*Northern Districts/NZ*)	LB	177	28	467	28	7-30	4	16.67
6	L. H. Ferguson (*Auckland*)	RF	164	31	574	33	7-34	5	17.39
7	I. G. McPeake (*Wellington*)	RFM	200.4	41	677	35	5-21	3	19.34
8	B. G. Lister (*Auckland*)	LM	182.2	37	543	28	5-29	1	19.39
9	A. Y. Patel (*Central Districts*)	SLA	356.2	92	1,033	48	6-48	7	21.52
10	B. J. Arnel (*Northern Districts*) ...	RFM	229.1	69	565	26	5-73	2	21.73
11	J. S. Patel (*Wellington*)	OB	319.2	104	793	36	7-105	4	22.02
12	T. A. Boult (*N Districts/NZ*)	LFM	202.2	44	634	27	6-32	1	23.48
13	J. A. Duffy (*Otago*)	RFM	223	56	685	29	5-29	3	23.62
14	T. G. Southee (*N Districts/NZ*) ...	RFM	148	38	451	19	6-62	1	23.73
15	W. S. A. Williams (*Canterbury*) ..	RM	177.2	58	457	19	4-16	0	24.05
16	J. D. Baker (*Northern Districts*) ...	RFM	306	71	842	34	6-72	2	24.76
17	M. B. McEwan (*Auckland*)	RFM	270.3	52	892	36	6-48	2	24.77
18	M. D. Rae (*Otago*)	RFM	209.5	32	728	29	5-18	1	25.10
19	N. Wagner (*Otago/New Zealand*) .	LFM	372.1	89	1,090	43	7-39	2	25.34
20	M. J. G. Rippon (*Otago*)	SLW	154.3	26	485	19	4-30	0	25.52
21	C. S. Kuggeleijn (*N Districts*)	RFM	220.5	37	793	30	7-48	2	26.43
22	D. A. J. Bracewell (*C Districts*) ...	RFM	236.4	56	695	24	4-59	0	28.95
23	B. M. Tickner (*Central Districts*) .	RFM	232	40	871	30	5-23	1	29.03
24	O. R. Newton (*Wellington*)	RM	195.4	38	613	21	4-26	0	29.19
25	B. P. Coburn (*Canterbury*).	SLW	131.4	20	474	15	7-64	1	31.60
26	A. F. Milne (*Central Districts*). ...	RF	219	45	733	21	5-64	1	34.90
27	M. D. Craig (*Otago*).	OB	274.1	71	750	20	4-42	0	37.50

PLUNKET SHIELD IN 2017-18

	P	W	L	D	Bonus pts Bat	Bonus pts Bowl	Pts	NRPW runs/wkt
Central Districts.....	10	6	0	4	27	34	131†	11.59
Wellington.........	10	6	3	1	16	39	127	6.12
Auckland..........	10	5	3	2	14	31	105	–9.30
Northern Districts ...	10	2	4	4	20	36	80	2.01
Otago.............	10	2	7	1	18	37	79	–0.76
Canterbury.........	10	2	6	2	8	32	64	–8.79

†   *2pts deducted for slow over-rate.*

Outright win = 12pts. Bonus points were awarded as follows for the first 110 overs of each team's first innings: one batting point for the first 200 runs and then for 250, 300 and 350; one bowling point for the third wicket taken and then for the fifth, seventh and ninth. Net runs per wicket is calculated by subtracting average runs conceded per wicket from average runs scored per wicket.

PLUNKET SHIELD WINNERS

1921-22	Auckland	1957-58	Otago	1989-90	Wellington
1922-23	Canterbury	1958-59	Auckland	1990-91	Auckland
1923-24	Wellington	1959-60	Canterbury	1991-92	{ Central Districts
1924-25	Otago	1960-61	Wellington		{ Northern Districts
1925-26	Wellington	1961-62	Wellington	1992-93	Northern Districts
1926-27	Auckland	1962-63	Northern Districts	1993-94	Canterbury
1927-28	Wellington	1963-64	Auckland	1994-95	Auckland
1928-29	Auckland	1964-65	Canterbury	1995-96	Auckland
1929-30	Wellington	1965-66	Wellington	1996-97	Canterbury
1930-31	Canterbury	1966-67	Central Districts	1997-98	Canterbury
1931-32	Wellington	1967-68	Central Districts	1998-99	Central Districts
1932-33	Otago	1968-69	Auckland	1999-2000	Northern Districts
1933-34	Auckland	1969-70	Otago	2000-01	Wellington
1934-35	Canterbury	1970-71	Central Districts	2001-02	Auckland
1935-36	Wellington	1971-72	Otago	2002-03	Auckland
1936-37	Auckland	1972-73	Wellington	2003-04	Wellington
1937-38	Auckland	1973-74	Wellington	2004-05	Auckland
1938-39	Auckland	1974-75	Otago	2005-06	Central Districts
1939-40	Auckland	1975-76	Canterbury	2006-07	Northern Districts
1940–45	*No competition*	1976-77	Otago	2007-08	Canterbury
1945-46	Canterbury	1977-78	Auckland	2008-09	Auckland
1946-47	Auckland	1978-79	Otago	2009-10	Northern Districts
1947-48	Otago	1979-80	Northern Districts	2010-11	Canterbury
1948-49	Canterbury	1980-81	Auckland	2011-12	Northern Districts
1949-50	Wellington	1981-82	Wellington	2012-13	Central Districts
1950-51	Otago	1982-83	Wellington	2013-14	Canterbury
1951-52	Canterbury	1983-84	Canterbury	2014-15	Canterbury
1952-53	Otago	1984-85	Wellington	2015-16	Auckland
1953-54	Central Districts	1985-86	Otago	2016-17	Canterbury
1954-55	Wellington	1986-87	Central Districts	2017-18	Central Districts
1955-56	Canterbury	1987-88	Otago		
1956-57	Wellington	1988-89	Auckland		

Auckland have won the title outright 23 times, Wellington 20, Canterbury 19, Otago 13, Central Districts 9, Northern Districts 7. Central Districts and Northern Districts also shared the title once.

The tournament was known as the Shell Trophy from 1975-76 to 2000-01, and the State Championship from 2001-02 to 2008-09.

THE FORD TROPHY IN 2017-18

50-over league plus knockout

	P	W	L	NR/A	Bonus	Pts	NRR
CENTRAL DISTRICTS	8	6	1	1	3	29	1.02
AUCKLAND	8	4	3	1	2	20	0.19
NORTHERN DISTRICTS............	8	4	2	2	0	20	−0.11
CANTERBURY....................	8	2	4	2	0	12	−0.10
Wellington	8	2	5	1	0	10	−0.28
Otago............................	8	2	5	1	0	10	−0.73

Preliminary finals   1st v 2nd: Central Districts beat Auckland by seven wickets (DLS). **3rd v 4th:** Canterbury beat Northern Districts by 168 runs. **Final play-off:** Auckland beat Canterbury by 107 runs.

Final   At New Plymouth, February 24, 2018. **Auckland won by six wickets.** ‡**Central Districts 197** (46.4 overs); **Auckland 201-4** (32.4 overs). *Central were 128-2 in the 25th over before losing five for seven; needing only 198, Auckland swept home with more than 17 overs to spare.*

The Burger King Super Smash has its own section (page 1139).

PAKISTAN CRICKET IN 2018

The shorter the better

MAZHER ARSHAD

As some feared, Pakistan's one-day success in 2017, when they won the Champions Trophy and whitewashed Sri Lanka 5–0, proved a false dawn. Any sense they had found a winning 50-over formula was dispelled in the first series of 2018, when they suffered their own 5–0 hammering, in New Zealand.

Later in the year, at the Asia Cup in the UAE, Pakistan were twice thrashed by arch-rivals India, lost to Bangladesh, nearly lost to Afghanistan, and failed to reach the final. Throughout the year, their one-day batting was lightweight, typified by a collapse to 74 all out at Dunedin in January. Only an easy win in Zimbabwe in July, another 5–0, massaged their numbers, forming the bulk of their eight one-day wins in 2018, which included one against Hong Kong.

PAKISTAN IN 2018

	Played	Won	Lost	Drawn/No result
Tests	9	4	4	1
One-day internationals	18	8	9	1
Twenty20 internationals	19	17	2	–

JANUARY	5 ODIs and 3 T20Is (a) v New Zealand	(page 914)
FEBRUARY		
MARCH		
APRIL	3 T20Is (h) v West Indies	(page 931)
MAY	1 Test (a) v Ireland	(page 897)
JUNE	2 Tests (a) v England 2 T20Is (a) v Scotland	(page 289) (page 1102)
JULY	T20 tri-series (in Zimbabwe) v Australia and Zimbabwe 5 ODIs (a) v Zimbabwe	(page 1071) (page 1074)
AUGUST		
SEPTEMBER	Asia Cup (in the UAE)	(page 1110)
OCTOBER	2 Tests and 3 T20Is (in the UAE) v Australia	(page 933)
NOVEMBER	3 Tests, 3 ODIs and 3 T20Is (in the UAE) v New Zealand	(page 944)
DECEMBER		
JANUARY	3 Tests, 5 ODIs and 3 T20Is (a) v South Africa	(page 1007)
FEBRUARY		

For a review of Pakistan domestic cricket from the 2017-18 season, see page 959.

Sarah Ansell, Getty Images

Leap forward: Babar Azam and Hasan Ali celebrate at Lord's, where Pakistan thrashed England.

In Twenty20 cricket, however, Pakistan were invincible, winning six series (or tournaments) out of six, and – after losing at Wellington – 17 of their next 18 matches, the most by any team in a calendar year. They replaced New Zealand at the top of the rankings after coming from behind to win that series, then consolidated their position with victories over West Indies in Karachi (3–0), Scotland in Edinburgh (2–0), and Australia and New Zealand in the UAE (both 3–0). In between, they won a tri-series in Harare involving Australia and Zimbabwe. Pakistan had to go back to the World Twenty20 in India in early 2016 for the last time they failed to taste T20 success, since when they had won a world-record 11 series out of 11 under Sarfraz Ahmed, though the sequence ended in South Africa in early 2019, when he was banned for a racist remark.

Their success in the format has largely been credited to the Pakistan Super League, which in 2018 marked the return of big-time cricket to Karachi after an absence of nine years. The PCB have been using their T20 league as a launching pad for the full-time restoration of cricket to Pakistan, and the plan took a giant step when – after group matches in Dubai and Sharjah – Karachi staged the final, and Lahore the two eliminators. Soon after, Karachi also hosted the West Indians for that three-match T20 series.

For the purists, though, what mattered more was the inconsistency of the Test side. Apart from a memorable win at Lord's, where eight wickets for

Mohammad Abbas saw off England, Pakistan had little to write home about, and lost the Second Test at Leeds, squandering an opportunity to win their first series in England since 1996.

That came after a historic trip to Malahide, for Ireland's first men's Test. Despite following on, the Irish gave Pakistan a scare when they reduced them to 14 for three in pursuit of 160, before two youngsters – Imam-ul-Haq and Babar Azam, their best Test batsman of 2018 – came to the rescue. Although they beat Australia 1–0 in a two-Test series in the UAE, it felt like an underachievement given Australia's recent shortcomings in Asia, and the absence of four major players: Steve Smith and David Warner because of bans, Josh Hazlewood and Pat Cummins because of injuries. Against New Zealand, Pakistan twice failed to cope with fourth-innings pressure, and lost two Tests in Abu Dhabi (the first by four runs), despite a pair of 74-run leads. The upshot was New Zealand's first away win against them in 49 years.

There were a few moments of individual brilliance. Fakhar Zaman hit Pakistan's first one-day double-century, against Zimbabwe, and shared a world-record opening partnership of 304 with Imam. Then, in the Test series against Australia, Abbas became the first Pakistan seamer to claim ten in a match for over 12 years; his 36 wickets against Ireland, England and Australia cost just 12 apiece. Yasir Shah grabbed 14 to win the Dubai Test against New Zealand, and in the next game became the fastest to 200, his 33 Tests breaking a record set in 1936 by another leg-spinner, Australia's Clarrie Grimmett. But neither Abbas nor Yasir made much impact in South Africa at the end of the year, when Pakistan were thrashed 3–0 in the Tests.

Their Under-19 side had failed to beat India in the semi-final of the World Cup in New Zealand at the start of the year, but one of the stars of the tournament, left-arm seamer Shaheen Shah Afridi, was soon winning games at senior level. Aged just 18, he was Man of the Series for his nine wickets at 11 in the three-match one-day series against New Zealand in the UAE.

Off the field, Pakistan's administration went through some major changes after the country's most famous cricketer, World Cup-winning captain Imran Khan, became prime minister. That forced Najam Sethi, who had endured many political tussles with Imran, to resign as chairman of the Pakistan Cricket Board. Ehsan Mani, the former ICC president, was nominated by Imran to replace him, and elected by the board of governors. Mani then enticed Leicestershire chief executive Wasim Khan to be managing director, with the focus on overhauling the infrastructure of domestic cricket. Mani's first challenge came when the ICC's dispute resolution committee dismissed Pakistan's compensation claim against the BCCI for not honouring bilateral series agreements. The case had been filed by the Sethi-led regime.

But there was relief for the board when they raised $36m from a new broadcast and live-streaming rights agreement for the PSL over the next three years. That was 358% more than the previous deal, although a large part of it will go into the kitty for the six franchises.

PAKISTAN v WEST INDIES IN 2017-18

Mazher Arshad

Twenty20 internationals (3): Pakistan 3, West Indies 0

This whistle-stop tour was another stepping-stone in the revival of international cricket in Pakistan. Seven months after a World XI visited Lahore, West Indies played three matches on successive days in Karachi. They were without several big names because of the IPL, while others – including the Test and Twenty20 captains, Jason Holder and Carlos Brathwaite – opted out on security grounds, despite a massive police operation. Jason Mohammed stood in.

Pakistan won all three games easily, but to focus on the result would be to miss the point: the return of men's international cricket to Pakistan's biggest city after nine years. The series was shifted from Lahore when the ICC's security consultant Reg Dickason gave the all-clear after the National Stadium successfully hosted the Pakistan Super League final.

Karachi celebrated with great fervour: many roads, including the Shahrah-e-Faisal at the heart of the city, were decorated with cricket hoardings and pictures of the players. Even though the series was decided, the third match drew a full house, many of them seeing their team in action for the first time. Of Pakistan's 15-strong squad, only Sarfraz Ahmed and Shoaib Malik had played international cricket in Karachi before; in the case of Sarfraz, it was almost ten years since he had done so in his home town. "I don't think teams have any excuses for not coming to Pakistan any more," he said.

The matches were predictably lop-sided, with the world's top-ranked T20 side taking on a weakened team announced three days beforehand; most of the West Indians reached Pakistan just 24 hours ahead of the first game, while two arrived on the morning of the match itself. Babar Azam was named Man of the Series after scoring 165 runs, while there was a promising debut for Hussain Talat, a 22-year-old left-hander from Lahore. Mohammad Amir led the bowling attack, taking five for 25 in the first two matches before sitting out the third.

WEST INDIES TOURING PARTY

J. N. Mohammed, S. Badree, R. R. Emrit, A. D. S. Fletcher, A. M. McCarthy, K. M. A. Paul, V. Permaul, R. Powell, D. Ramdin, M. N. Samuels, O. F. Smith, C. A. K. Walton, K. O. K. Williams. Coach: S. G. Law.

First Twenty20 international   At Karachi, April 1, 2018 (floodlit). **Pakistan won by 143 runs. Pakistan 203-5** (20 overs) (Fakhar Zaman 39, Hussain Talat 41, Sarfraz Ahmed 38, Shoaib Malik 37*); ‡**West Indies 60** (13.4 overs). *MoM:* Hussain Talat. *T20I debuts:* Asif Ali, Hussain Talat (Pakistan); K. M. A. Paul, V. Permaul (West Indies). *Facing a jet-lagged attack containing two debutants, Pakistan equalled their biggest T20 total, against Bangladesh at Karachi in April 2008. Surprisingly, their highest score was only 41, from left-hander Hussain Talat, another debutant; Shoaib Malik, whose 37* came from just 14 balls, and Fahim Ashraf (16*) crashed 44 from the last two overs. Slow left-armer Veerasammy Permaul's tour came to a rapid end when he twisted his left ankle in his first over and was stretchered off; he had sent down only five deliveries, two of them* *wides. West Indies' batting was even more insipid than their bowling: Marlon Samuels top-scored with 18 as they equalled the lowest T20 total by a Test-playing country. Only once before, when Sri Lanka beat Kenya by 172 runs at Johannesburg in 2007-08, had a side won a T20 international by a wider margin.*

LARGEST VICTORIES BY RUNS IN T20 INTERNATIONALS

172	Sri Lanka (260-6) beat Kenya (88† in 19.3 overs) at Johannesburg	2007-08
143	**Pakistan (203-5) beat West Indies (60† in 13.4) at Karachi**	**2017-18**
143	**India (213-4) beat Ireland (70 in 12.3) at Malahide**	**2018**
130	South Africa (211-5) beat Scotland (81 in 15.4) at The Oval	2009
119	**New Zealand (243-5) beat West Indies (124† in 16.3) at Mount Maunganui** ..	**2017-18**
116	England (196-5) beat Afghanistan (80 in 17.2) at Colombo (RPS).............	2012-13
115	**Scotland (221-3) beat Netherlands (106† in 14) at Amstelveen**	**2018**
109	Zimbabwe (184-5) beat Canada (75 in 19.2) at King City	2008-09
106	Afghanistan (162-6) beat Kenya (56 in 18.4) at Sharjah	2013-14
103	Pakistan (183-6) beat New Zealand (80 in 15.5) at Christchurch	2010-11
103	Netherlands (172-4) beat Nepal (69 in 17.4) at Amstelveen	2015
102	Pakistan (203-5) beat Bangladesh (101 in 16) at Karachi	2007-08
100	England (179-8) beat Australia (79 in 14.3) at Southampton	2005
100	**Australia (229-2) beat Zimbabwe (129-9 in 20 overs) at Harare**	**2018**

† *One man absent. In all cases, the first innings lasted 20 overs.*

Second Twenty20 international   At Karachi, April 2, 2018 (floodlit). **Pakistan won by 82 runs.** ‡**Pakistan 205-3** (20 overs) (Babar Azam 97*, Hussain Talat 63); **West Indies 123** (19.2 overs) (C. A. K. Walton 40; Mohammad Amir 3-22). *MoM:* Babar Azam. *T20I debut:* O. F. Smith (West Indies). *About 20 hours after the first match ended, West Indies were back in the lions' den for another mauling. After equalling their T20 record total the day before, Pakistan now beat it, mainly thanks to Babar Azam, who cut and drove savagely on his way to 97* from 58 balls, and Talat. They put on 119 in 12.2 overs against a listless attack not helped by leaky fielding. West Indies did at least bat a little better, led by Chadwick Walton, whose dismissal inspired an over-the-top celebration from Shadab Khan, later fined 20% of his match fee. But three wickets in eight balls from Mohammad Amir scuppered any chance of a close result. Pakistan's win ensured they would remain top of the ICC's T20 rankings.*

Third Twenty20 international   At Karachi, April 3, 2018 (floodlit). **Pakistan won by eight wickets.** ‡**West Indies 153-6** (20 overs) (A. D. S. Fletcher 52, M. N. Samuels 31, D. Ramdin 42*); **Pakistan 154-2** (16.5 overs) (Fakhar Zaman 40, Babar Azam 51, Hussain Talat 31*). *MoS:* Fakhar Zaman. *MoS:* Babar Azam. *T20I debuts:* Shaheen Shah Afridi (Pakistan); A. M. McCarthy (West Indies). *Batting first, West Indies avoided early problems through a second-wicket stand of 72 between Andre Fletcher and Samuels, then Denesh Ramdin swelled the total with 42* from 18 balls. But it was not enough: Fakhar tore out of the blocks, making 40 (from 17) of an opening stand of 61 in 5.2 overs. Babar kept his foot down, and Pakistan sprinted to a clean sweep with 19 deliveries to spare. It was their seventh consecutive T20 series win (including a one-off match in England) since Sarfraz Ahmed took over as captain after the World Twenty20 in India in 2016.*

PAKISTAN v AUSTRALIA IN THE UAE IN 2018-19

Geoff Lemon

Test matches (2): Pakistan 1, Australia 0
Twenty20 internationals (3): Pakistan 3, Australia 0

It's safe to say no visit to the Gulf by Australia had ever been accorded as much significance. Their Test side took the field for the first time since the ball-tampering tour of South Africa six months earlier. Steve Smith and David Warner were suspended, and it was less a case of the new team containing a few holes, than of a series of holes being stitched together by a few new players. Tim Paine, Smith's replacement as captain, had promised a reformation of on-field behaviour. The times, they had a-changed, but no one knew what shape the new era would assume.

Australians often ignore Asian tours. Tucked away into quiet corners by pay TV and football seasons, these short trips to dustbowl arenas are given fleeting attention, or skipped over altogether. Their relevance can be dismissed whatever happens: if Australia win, it's against teams they expect to beat; if they lose, it's blamed on spin voodoo and doctored pitches.

That had held true in the UAE four years before, when a team that looked far better on paper – with Smith, Warner, Michael Clarke and Mitchell Johnson – lost both Tests, crushed by Younis Khan's three centuries, and disassembled by the spin of Yasir Shah and Zulfiqar Babar. But coming after Australia's 2013-14 Ashes whitewash and subsequent win in South Africa, it was chalked up Down Under as another Asian aberration to be forgotten.

By rights, the 2018-19 team should have been smashed as hard – harder, if that were actually possible under the laws of physics. It was a far more inexperienced team, with three of the top six making their debuts, two of the three first-choice pace bowlers injured, and a new coach, Justin Langer, in his first major engagement. All the distractions and ferment of the previous six

---

TEST CENTURY AGAINST COUNTRY OF BIRTH

C. Bannerman (165*)	Australia v England at Melbourne.	1876-77
P. S. McDonnell (147).	Australia v England at Sydney	1881-82
M. C. Cowdrey (160)	England v India at Leeds.	1959
V. Pollard (116).	New Zealand v England at Nottingham	1973
N. Hussain (128).	England v India at Birmingham	1996
G. A. Hick (101)	England v Zimbabwe at Lord's.	2000
A. Flower (142).	Zimbabwe v South Africa at Harare	2001-02
A. J. Strauss (126).	England v South Africa at Port Elizabeth	2004-05
A. Symonds (156).	Australia v England at Melbourne.	2006-07
K. P. Pietersen (152).	England v South Africa at Lord's	2008
B. A. Stokes (101).	England v New Zealand at Lord's	2015
U. T. Khawaja (141)	**Australia v Pakistan at Dubai**.	**2018-19**

Only the first century is shown in each case; Flower also made 199* in the second innings. Five players born in what was then India scored Test centuries against them for Pakistan. McDonnell (London) and Strauss (Johannesburg) scored Test centuries in the city of their birth.

Ryan Pierse, Getty Images

Aussie saviour: Usman Khawaja reverse-sweeps at Dubai.

months made it hard to focus on the cricket. This was an Australian team as green and unsteady as a newly hatched mantis; add in the punishing climate, and there should have been no chance to stand firm at all.

So to fight out a heroic draw from a hopeless position in Dubai was a superb performance, of the type even the great Australian teams of recent years had never produced in Asia. It was built around Usman Khawaja's epic century, but plenty of others contributed. Then, in the Second Test in Abu Dhabi, Australia's bowlers created a dominant position on the first day, and kept Pakistan's second innings in check. In the end, the blame belonged to Australia's double batting failure, which allowed Pakistan to complete their biggest win by runs.

For the hosts, the series – which marked the Wisden website's first foray into audio broadcasting, after securing commentary rights to the Tests and covering them live from the grounds – was no less important. Sarfraz Ahmed was still finding his way as Test captain, and recovering from a dire Asia Cup. After letting a win slip in Dubai, his side feared a Test series might vanish as well. But Sarfraz rallied them in Abu Dhabi with a fearless counter-attack, and his team carried on from there. Comeback wins don't come much more impressive. That gave Pakistan the momentum going into the Twenty20 series. Despite personnel changes and a powerful visiting line-up, they thrived in conditions perfectly suiting their style, and won all three matches.

The Australians did win once, meeting – and beating – the UAE for the first time. That apart, the good points were few and far between. But in truth they had done better than expected in the Tests: the Great Escape in Dubai would linger in the memory and, for some Australians, the fight they showed was a moment when they could start to feel proud of their team again.

AUSTRALIAN TOURING PARTY

*T. D. Paine (T), A. C. Agar (T/20), A. T. Carey (20), N. M. Coulter-Nile (20), B. J. Doggett (T), A. J. Finch (T/20), T. M. Head (T), J. M. Holland (T), U. T. Khawaja (T), M. Labuschagne (T), C. A. Lynn (20), N. M. Lyon (T/20), D. B. R. McDermott (20), M. R. Marsh (T), S. E. Marsh (T), G. J. Maxwell (T), M. G. Neser (T), M. T. Renshaw (T), D. J. M. Short (20), P. M. Siddle (T), B. Stanlake (20), M. A. Starc (T/20), A. J. Tye (20), A. Zampa (20). *Coach:* J. L. Langer.

Finch captained in the Twenty20 matches.

At Dubai (ICC Academy), September 29–October 2, 2018. **Drawn. ‡Pakistan A 278** (99.1 overs) (Sami Aslam 51, Abid Ali 85; J. M. Holland 5-79); **Australians 494-4 dec** (170 overs) (A. J. Finch 54, S. E. Marsh 94, M. R. Marsh 162, T. M. Head 90*). *The tourists dominated the first-class warm-up game, but couldn't quite force victory. Nathan Lyon wheeled down 39.1 overs as Pakistan A were restricted to 278 after being 224-5, then the Australian batsmen tucked in against an attack without any frontline spinners. Everyone who batted reached 36, with the Marsh brothers adding 207 for the third wicket and hitting 30 fours between them. Trailing by 216, Pakistan A batted through the final day, captain Asad Shafiq showing the way with 69 from 151 balls. Slow left-armer Jon Holland took five wickets, to win a Test recall after more than two years.*

PAKISTAN v AUSTRALIA

First Test

At Dubai, October 7–11, 2018. Drawn. Toss: Pakistan. Test debuts: Bilal Asif; A. J. Finch, T. M. Head, M. Labuschagne.

This match will be remembered for the heroic resistance of Usman Khawaja. His second innings ended at 141, but that does not convey the full scope of the 302 balls he faced, nor the nearly nine hours he spent at the crease in conditions so enervating he thought he had heatstroke on the final day, before carrying on for another session and a half. Such an innings had not seemed possible in a match Pakistan should have won inside four days.

On each of those days, they dominated two sessions before Australia found a way to pull things back. Winning the toss was a huge advantage, and the openers made the most of it on a placid surface. The first day belonged to Mohammad Hafeez, recalled to the Test team, at the age of 37, for the first time in two years after some blazing domestic form. His century, a mixture of doggedness and sporadic aggression, helped build an intimidating first-wicket partnership of 205 with Imam-ul-Haq. Australia broke it just after tea, and prised out two more wickets in the final session as Siddle and Lyon dried up the runs.

On the second day, it was Haris Sohail's turn for a century, his first in Tests, which mixed crease occupation with belligerence. Asad Shafiq played a stylish supporting hand. Pushed down the order in both innings by a nightwatchman, he joined Steve Waugh as one of just two to have reached 3,000 Test runs at No. 6. Marnus Labuschagne, the second man born in South Africa to play for Australia, after Kepler Wessels, took a wicket with his part-time leg-spin, and later ran out Babar Azam to start another post-tea slide. A big total was prevented from becoming a monster.

ONE OUT, ALL OUT

Fewest runs added after an opening stand of 100 or more in a Test:

Runs	From	To		
46	124-0	170	India v England at Manchester	1946
51	107-0	158	New Zealand v Australia at Auckland	1973-74
60	**142-0**	**202**	**Australia v Pakistan at Dubai**	**2018-19**
64	164-0	228†	Zimbabwe v West Indies at Bulawayo	2001
64	100-0	164	England v Bangladesh at Mirpur.	2016-17

† *One batsman absent hurt.*

BEST BOWLING ON TEST DEBUT FOR PAKISTAN

7-66	Mohammad Zahid	v New Zealand at Rawalpindi	1996-97
7-99	Mohammad Nazir.	v New Zealand at Karachi.	1969-70
6-36	**Bilal Asif**	**v Australia at Dubai**	**2018-19**
6-89	Arif Butt	v Australia at Melbourne.	1964-65
6-120	Tanvir Ahmed	v South Africa at Abu Dhabi.	2010-11
5-36	Mohammad Sami	v New Zealand at Auckland	2000-01
5-48	Shabbir Ahmed.	v Bangladesh at Karachi	2003-04
5-52	Shahid Afridi	v Australia at Karachi	1998-99
5-53	Shahid Nazir.	v Zimbabwe at Sheikhupura	1996-97
5-63	Wahab Riaz	v England at The Oval	2010
5-161	Yasir Arafat	v India at Bangalore	2007-08

Australia's openers reached stumps, then lunch next day, while adding a patient 142. Finch, making his Test debut after 135 white-ball internationals (and 13 centuries), scored 62, and Khawaja 85. But after they were parted, a shocking collapse saw all ten wickets cascade for 60. Mohammad Abbas's 80mph deliveries landed with suffocating accuracy and a touch of movement from a perfectly presented seam, while the 33-year-old Bilal Asif, Pakistan's own debutant, found huge bounce from an action that produced over-spin; he picked off the left-handers with turn. No one will ever bowl quite like Muttiah Muralitharan, but there were echoes in Bilal's rubbery flick, which made him almost a wrist-spinning off-breaker. He finished with six for 36, the best figures by a debutant against Australia, beating left-arm seamer Fred "Nutty" Martin's six for 50 for England at The Oval in 1890.

Instead of being deflated by such a brief rest, however, Australia's spinners went to the well again, taking three Pakistan wickets by stumps, then slowing them enough that the fourth day became a plod to the declaration rather than a charge. The eventual closure came after lunch, with the lead restricted to 461.

That still left Australia the best part of five sessions to survive – a big ask for a team with a dire Asian record, and against a bevy of spinners on a pitch starting to crumble, especially the footmarks. The first-wicket pair again started brightly but, when Finch fell for 49, the Marsh brothers did not manage a run between them. From 87 for three, another slide was averted by Travis Head, Australia's third debutant, who soaked up the pressure to reach the close. He changed his approach to Bilal, and scored brightly enough to keep his spirits up.

Head carried on past lunch on the fifth day, but was then done in by spin with the new ball. Labuschagne soon followed – but Khawaja was in the throes of a left-hander's masterclass. He drew yelps from commentators when he started reverse-sweeping Yasir Shah's leg-breaks out of the rough from round the wicket. But he played the stroke more than 20 times, and nailed almost every one. After only a couple of boundaries, Sarfraz posted a defensive third man, after which frequent singles there disrupted Yasir's line.

When Paine arrived with nearly four hours left, the draw was still unlikely. But he absorbed plenty of the strike, helping his exhausted partner push into the final hour.

BROTHERS MAKING DUCKS IN SAME TEST INNINGS

E. M. and G. F. Grace.	England v Australia at The Oval	1880
Hanif and Wazir Mohammad	Pakistan v England at The Oval	1954
D. R. and R. J. Hadlee	New Zealand v England at Nottingham	1973
J. J. and M. D. Crowe	New Zealand v England at The Oval	1983
A. and G. W. Flower	Zimbabwe v Pakistan at Rawalpindi	1993-94
B. C. and P. A. Strang	Zimbabwe v South Africa at Harare.	1995-96
M. E. and S. R. Waugh.	Australia v Pakistan at Colombo (PSS)	2002-03
M. R. and S. E. Marsh	**Australia v Pakistan at Dubai**	**2018-19**

Khawaja was finally trapped by Yasir after 522 minutes, equalling the second-longest vigil in the fourth innings of a Test, behind only Michael Atherton's 643 in Johannesburg in 1995-96. Hearts were in mouths through a tense final hour: Starc and Siddle were teased out by Yasir, with only the modest batting of Holland to come. But Paine saw out 220 minutes and 194 deliveries, while Lyon survived for 50 and 34.

At the end Paine was aware enough to gesture to his dressing-room to keep a lid on the celebrations: with a Test to play, he did not want to seem too joyful at a draw. But this was no ordinary draw. Until Khawaja fell late on, he had been on the field for all but an hour and a half of the match. His efforts were the bedrock of the most prolific innings any Australian team had produced batting last in Asia, both in terms of runs scored and overs faced. It was the fourth-longest by any team in Asia, not far short of South Africa's abstemious 143 in 143.1 overs at Delhi in 2015-16. This was a famous escape – and well worth celebrating.

Man of the Match: U. T. Khawaja.

Close of play: first day, Pakistan 255-3 (Haris Sohail 15, Mohammad Abbas 1); second day, Australia 30-0 (Khawaja 17, Finch 13); third day, Pakistan 45-3 (Imam-ul-Haq 23); fourth day, Australia 136-3 (Khawaja 50, Head 34).

Pakistan

Imam-ul-Haq c Paine b Lyon	76	– c and b Holland	48
Mohammad Hafeez lbw b Siddle	126	– c Labuschagne b Holland	17
Azhar Ali c Starc b Lyon	18	– (4) lbw b Holland	4
Haris Sohail c Paine b Lyon	110	– (5) lbw b Labuschagne	39
Mohammad Abbas b Siddle	1		
Asad Shafiq c Paine b Labuschagne	80	– c M. R. Marsh b Lyon	41
Babar Azam run out (Labuschagne/Paine)	4	– not out	28
*†Sarfraz Ahmed run out (Finch)	15		
Bilal Asif b Siddle	12	– (3) c Head b Lyon	0
Wahab Riaz not out	7		
Yasir Shah c Paine b Starc	3		
B 6, lb 21, nb 3	30	B 2, lb 2	4

1/205 (1) 2/222 (2) 3/244 (3)   (164.2 overs) 482   1/37 (2)   (6 wkts dec, 57.5 overs) 181
4/260 (5) 5/410 (6) 6/418 (7)   2/38 (3) 3/45 (4)
7/456 (4) 8/470 (8) 9/473 (9) 10/482 (11)   4/110 (1) 5/110 (5) 6/181 (6)

Starc 36.2–11–90–1; Siddle 29–11–58–3; Lyon 52–12–114–2; Holland 29–1–126–1; Labuschagne 8–0–29–1; M. R. Marsh 10–0–38–0. *Second innings*—Starc 6–1–18–0; Lyon 25.5–6–58–2; Siddle 2–1–3–0; Holland 20–3–83–3; Head 1–0–6–0; Labuschagne 3–0–9–1.

Australia

U. T. Khawaja c Imam-ul-Haq b Bilal Asif	85	– (2) lbw b Yasir Shah	141
A. J. Finch c Asad Shafiq b Mohammad Abbas	62	– (1) lbw b Mohammad Abbas	49
S. E. Marsh c Asad Shafiq b Bilal Asif	7	– c Sarfraz Ahmed b Mohammad Abbas	0
M. R. Marsh lbw b Mohammad Abbas	12	– lbw b Mohammad Abbas	0
T. M. Head c Haris Sohail b Bilal Asif	0	– lbw b Mohammad Hafeez	72
M. Labuschagne c Imam-ul-Haq b Bilal Asif	0	– lbw b Yasir Shah	13
*†T. D. Paine c Imam-ul-Haq b Bilal Asif	7	– not out	61
M. A. Starc c Sarfraz Ahmed b Mohammad Abbas	0	– c Babar Azam b Yasir Shah	1
P. M. Siddle b Mohammad Abbas	10	– lbw b Yasir Shah	0
N. M. Lyon c Imam-ul-Haq b Bilal Asif	6	– not out	5
J. M. Holland not out	0		
B 6, lb 7	13	B 13, lb 4, nb 3	20

1/142 (2) 2/160 (3) 3/167 (1)   (83.3 overs) 202   1/87 (1)   (8 wkts, 139.5 overs) 362
4/171 (5) 5/171 (6) 6/183 (4)   2/87 (3) 3/87 (4)
7/183 (7) 8/191 (8) 9/202 (9) 10/202 (10)   4/219 (5) 5/252 (6)
                                                       6/331 (2) 7/333 (8) 8/333 (9)

Mohammad Abbas 19–9–29–4; Wahab Riaz 11–2–39–0; Yasir Shah 28–6–80–0; Mohammad Hafeez 3–1–2–0; Bilal Asif 21.3–7–36–6; Azhar Ali 1–0–3–0. *Second innings*—Mohammad Abbas 27–7–56–3; Mohammad Hafeez 6–0–29–1; Yasir Shah 43.5–9–114–4; Wahab Riaz 16–3–42–0; Bilal Asif 37–8–87–0; Haris Sohail 9–1–16–0; Asad Shafiq 1–0–1–0.

Umpires: R. K. Illingworth and R. A. Kettleborough.   Third umpire: S. Ravi.
Referee: R. S. Madugalle.

PAKISTAN v AUSTRALIA

Second Test

At Abu Dhabi, October 16–19, 2018. Pakistan won by 373 runs. Toss: Pakistan. Test debuts: Fakhar Zaman, Mir Hamza.

If Dubai was Australia's get-out-of-jail card, Abu Dhabi was the equivalent for Pakistan and their captain. They looked doomed here following a spectacular collapse – but Sarfraz Ahmed hit back, and Australia's batting misfired again.

The groundsman, wanting to ensure a result, had produced a pitch with a thatch of grass down the middle and enough moisture to encourage bounce. Australia had to bowl first again, but Lyon produced a stunning pre-lunch spell of four wickets without conceding

---

MOST WICKETS IN FIRST TEN TESTS

		Balls	Runs	Avge	BB	5I	10M	Debut
71	T. Richardson (England).	3,371	1,636	23.04	7-168	10	3	1893
69	C. T. B. Turner (Australia)	2,905	895	12.97	7-43	9	2	1886-87
65	M. W. Tate (England).	3,832	1,305	20.07	6-42	6	1	1924
63	V. D. Philander (South Africa)	2,091	1,006	15.96	6-44	7	2	2011-12
62	A. L. Valentine (West Indies).	4,746	1,489	24.01	8-104	5	2	1950
61	J. J. Ferris (Australia/England†)	2,302	775	12.70	7-37	6	1	1886-87
61	Yasir Shah (Pakistan)	2,938	1,514	24.81	7-76	4	0	2014-15
60	R. Peel (England)	2,546	777	12.95	7-31	3	1	1884-85
60	A. M. E. Roberts (West Indies).	2,799	1,282	21.36	7-54	5	1	1973-74
59	H. Ironmonger (Australia)	3,224	925	15.67	7-23	4	2	1928-29
59	**Mohammad Abbas (Pakistan)**	**2,244**	**923**	**15.64**	**5-33**	**4**	**1**	**2016-17**

† *Ferris played only nine Tests in all – eight for Australia, and one for England, in 1891-92.*

---

a run: in the space of six balls, he caught and bowled Azhar Ali, had Haris Sohail held at silly point, and Asad Shafiq at short leg after a review, then bowled Babar Azam on the charge.

Pakistan had spiralled from 57 for one to 57 for five, and seemed on course for a trouncing against opponents buoyed by their First Test heroics. But Sarfraz countered without recklessness in a sparkling display. Rather than slamming boundaries, he kept the score ticking over by manipulating the field, backing away to cut off the stumps, or moving across to work to leg. His first 58 came at a run a ball, and relieved the pressure on Fakhar Zaman, who was making his debut after Imam-ul-Haq broke a finger fielding in Dubai. Better known for his attacking white-ball approach, Fakhar went to the opposite extreme. "I was not comfortable against the spinners," he said. "That's why I was blocking the ball and taking my time."

As the runs flowed in the middle session, Australia lost the plot. Although both batsmen fell for 94 – uniquely in a Test innings – their stand of 147 prevented the tourists from taking control. And the scale of the missed opportunity became obvious when Australia began their reply to a middling 282. If conditions had helped Lyon, they were a gift to

Francois Nel, Getty Images

Give him a Finch… and he'll take a mile. Mohammad Abbas celebrates the wicket of Aaron Finch on the fourth day.

Mohammad Abbas, a loaves-and-fishes kind of bowler, able to do so much with so little. He had been good on the flatness of Dubai, and the extra grass here made him almost unstoppable: he moved the ball away, swung it, reversed it, and produced a succession of edges and lbws. With Bilal Asif taking three wickets, including top-scorer Finch for 39, Australia tumbled to 145 an hour after lunch on the second day. Matters weren't helped by Labuschagne: he stood out of his ground at the non-striker's end, dozily watching the ball roll back on to his stumps after Yasir Shah, the bowler, had deflected a defensive shot from Starc.

The deficit was 137, which was fewer than in Dubai, but here there was more time left in the game. Fakhar and Sarfraz each made another half-century, while Azhar's own fifty ended in a run-out even more bizarre than Labuschagne's. After edging Siddle towards the third-man boundary, Azhar punched gloves and had a mid-pitch chat with Shafiq, unaware that the ball had stopped a few inches inside the rope. Paine was smart enough to play dumb as he waited for Starc's throw, before whipping off the bails.

Babar, meanwhile, had his own moment of drama. A star in limited-overs matches, he had yet to find a successful method in Tests, and had never scored a hundred. That remained the case when he was out for 99, trapped by Mitchell Marsh after becoming becalmed by a strangling field. Still, Babar had helped Pakistan towards a lead of 537 by the time Sarfraz declared late on the third day.

Australia had other problems: Khawaja, the saviour in Dubai, had injured his knee during the morning warm-up, and would not bat. Shaun Marsh moved up to open, and was

WINNING TEST DESPITE LOSING FOUR FOR NONE

West Indies (329-5 to 329-9, 1st inns) v Australia at Sydney	1960-61
England (234-6 to 234, 2nd inns) v Australia at Manchester	1972
Australia (74-1 to 74-5, 2nd inns) v Pakistan at Colombo (PSS)	2002-03
Pakistan (57-1 to 57-5, 1st inns) v Australia at Abu Dhabi	**2018-19**

Research: Andrew Samson

soon dismissed by Mir Hamza, a debutant left-armer who had replaced Wahab Riaz. He produced a perfect delivery that swung in, then seamed away and kissed off stump. Marsh finished the series with 14 runs in four innings.

On the fourth day Abbas feasted again, taking five more wickets to make it ten in the match. His ten-Test career had yielded 59 wickets at 15. At the same stage, only three bowlers – all from the 19th century – had lower averages.

The surface remained decent, but Australia had been unable to muster any resistance. For Pakistan, it was their biggest win by runs in Tests, eclipsing the thrashing by 356 of the Australians on the same ground four years previously. Sarfraz spent the fourth day resting after being concussed while batting, but from the comfort of his couch could savour a turnaround sparked by his own fighting innings.

Man of the Match: Mohammad Abbas. *Man of the Series:* Mohammad Abbas.

Close of play: first day, Australia 20-2 (Finch 13); second day, Pakistan 144-2 (Azhar Ali 54, Haris Sohail 17); third day, Australia 47-1 (Finch 24, Head 17).

Pakistan

Fakhar Zaman lbw b Labuschagne	94	– c and b Lyon	66
Mohammad Hafeez c Labuschagne b Starc	4	– c Head b Starc	6
Azhar Ali c and b Lyon	15	– run out (Starc/Paine)	64
Haris Sohail c Head b Lyon	0	– st Paine b Lyon	17
Asad Shafiq c Labuschagne b Lyon	0	– c sub (A. C. Agar) b Labuschagne	44
Babar Azam b Lyon	0	– lbw b M. R. Marsh	99
*†Sarfraz Ahmed c Siddle b Labuschagne	94	– lbw b Labuschagne	81
Bilal Asif c Paine b Labuschagne	12	– c Head b Lyon	15
Yasir Shah b M. R. Marsh	28	– lbw b Lyon	4
Mohammad Abbas b Starc	10	– not out	0
Mir Hamza not out	4	– not out	0
B 11, lb 6, nb 4	21	Lb 2, nb 2	4

1/5 (2) 2/57 (3) 3/57 (4)   (81 overs) 282   1/15 (2)   (9 wkts dec, 120 overs) 400
4/57 (5) 5/57 (6) 6/204 (1)   2/106 (1) 3/154 (4)
7/226 (8) 8/247 (7) 9/264 (9) 10/282 (10)   4/160 (3) 5/235 (5) 6/368 (6)
                                        7/390 (8) 8/394 (9) 9/400 (7)

Starc 12–3–37–2; Siddle 10–3–39–0; M. R. Marsh 7–2–21–1; Lyon 27–5–78–4; Holland 13–3–45–0; Labuschagne 12–2–45–3. *Second innings*—Starc 7–0–32–1; Siddle 23–4–68–0; Lyon 43–8–135–4; Holland 16–3–46–0; Labuschagne 16–1–74–2; M. R. Marsh 13–3–39–1; Head 2–0–4–0.

Australia

U. T. Khawaja c Sarfraz Ahmed b Mohammad Abbas	3	– absent hurt	
A. J. Finch c Fakhar Zaman b Bilal Asif	39	– (1) lbw b Mohammad Abbas	31
P. M. Siddle lbw b Mohammad Abbas	4	– (8) lbw b Yasir Shah	3
S. E. Marsh c Haris Sohail b Mohammad Abbas	3	– (2) lbw b Mir Hamza	4
T. M. Head c Asad Shafiq b Mohammad Abbas	14	– (3) c sub (†Mohammad Rizwan) b Mohammad Abbas	36
M. R. Marsh c Asad Shafiq b Yasir Shah	13	– (4) lbw b Mohammad Abbas	5
M. Labuschagne run out (Yasir Shah)	25	– (5) c sub (†Mohammad Rizwan) b Mohammad Abbas	43
*†T. D. Paine lbw b Bilal Asif	3	– (6) b Mohammad Abbas	0
M. A. Starc lbw b Mohammad Abbas	34	– (7) lbw b Yasir Shah	28
N. M. Lyon b Bilal Asif	2	– (9) not out	6
J. M. Holland not out	2	– (10) c Haris Sohail b Yasir Shah	3
Lb 3	3	Lb 5	5

1/16 (1) 2/20 (3) 3/36 (4)   (50.4 overs) 145   1/10 (2) 2/71 (3)   (49.4 overs) 164
4/56 (5) 5/75 (6) 6/85 (2)   3/77 (4) 4/78 (1)
7/91 (8) 8/128 (7) 9/132 (10) 10/145 (9)   5/78 (6) 6/145 (7)
                                          7/151 (8) 8/155 (5) 9/164 (10)

Mohammad Abbas 12.4–4–33–5; Mir Hamza 9–2–27–0; Yasir Shah 19–3–59–1; Bilal Asif 10–3–23–3. *Second innings*—Mohammad Abbas 17–2–62–5; Mir Hamza 6–0–40–1; Yasir Shah 21.4–5–45–3; Bilal Asif 5–2–12–0.

Umpires: R. K. Illingworth and S. Ravi.   Third umpire: R. A. Kettleborough.
Referee: R. S. Madugalle.

At Abu Dhabi, October 22, 2018. AUSTRALIA beat UNITED ARAB EMIRATES by seven wickets (see Cricket in the United Arab Emirates, page 1108).

PAKISTAN v AUSTRALIA

First Twenty20 International

At Abu Dhabi, October 24, 2018 (floodlit). Pakistan won by 66 runs. Toss: Australia.

Some say Twenty20 matches are meaningless, others argue they are the shape of cricket's future. A full three-match series did give some weight to the second point of view, although having a trophy shaped like a biscuit rather favoured the first. Even though the Tuc Cup was designed to reflect its snack-related sponsor, the first match was not exactly a cracker. Babar Azam and Mohammad Hafeez were criticised for a 73-run partnership that used up nearly ten overs, and was followed by a collapse of seven for 28 as new batsmen tried to tee off. But Babar remained unbeaten with 68 after some late blows, and a total of 155 would prove more than manageable. Australia had chosen to chase, but Imad Wasim bowled both openers in the first over. The rest couldn't work out their timing, several dismissed trying to force the pace on a relatively slow surface that needed Babar's calm. Australia were soon 22 for six, and limped to 89, which equalled their third-lowest in T20 internationals.

Man of the Match: Imad Wasim.

Pakistan

		B	4/6
1 Fakhar Zaman *c 8 b 11*	14	12	2
2 Babar Azam *not out*	68	55	5/1
3 Mohammad Hafeez *c 5 b 2*	39	30	2/2
4 Asif Ali *lbw b 9*	2	3	0
5 Hussain Talat *c 1 b 10*	9	6	1
6 Fahim Ashraf *c 4 b 10*	0	1	0
7 *†Sarfraz Ahmed *lbw b 11*	0	2	0
8 Shadab Khan *c 5 b 11*	1	2	0
9 Imad Wasim *c 1 b 10*	0	1	0
10 Hasan Ali *not out*	17	8	2/1
B 1, lb 3, w 1	5		

6 overs: 45-1   (20 overs) 155-8

1/32 2/105 3/110 4/130 5/130 6/131 7/133 8/133

11 Shaheen Shah Afridi did not bat.

Coulter-Nile 4–7–42–0; Stanlake 4–13–21–3; Tye 4–8–24–3; Agar 2–2–19–0; Zampa 4–5–32–1; Short 2–3–13–1.

Australia

		B	4/6
1 *A. J. Finch *b 9*	0	3	0
2 D. J. M. Short *b 9*	4	2	1
3 C. A. Lynn *b 6*	14	15	2
4 G. J. Maxwell *b 6*	2	7	0
5 B. R. McDermott *run out (1)*	0	2	0
6 †A. T. Carey *c 7 b 9*	1	3	0
7 A. C. Agar *c 7 b 10*	19	23	2
8 N. M. Coulter-Nile *b 8*	34	29	6
9 A. Zampa *c 10 b 11*	3	7	0
10 A. J. Tye *b 7*	6	3	1
11 B. Stanlake *not out*	2	7	0
B 1, lb 3	4		

6 overs: 26-6   (16.5 overs) 89

1/0 2/5 3/16 4/16 5/22 6/22 7/60 8/72 9/78

Imad Wasim 4–12–20–3; Fahim Ashraf 3–13–10–2; Hasan Ali 3–11–16–1; Shaheen Shah Afridi 3–9–23–2; Shadab Khan 3.5–13–16–1.

Umpires: Ahsan Raza and Shozab Raza.   Third umpire: Asif Yaqoob.
Referee: R. S. Madugalle.

PAKISTAN v AUSTRALIA

Second Twenty20 International

At Dubai, October 26, 2018 (floodlit). Pakistan won by 11 runs. Toss: Pakistan.

Pakistan chose to bat this time, but otherwise the match followed a similar script to the first. Babar Azam and Mohammad Hafeez put on 70 in ten overs, then a few wickets and some late hitting left Pakistan near 150. Coulter-Nile was the pick of the bowlers. Australia were set back by three tight overs at the start, which concluded with Short's controversial run-out; there was a debate about whether he had grounded his bat in time when Imad Wasim deflected a drive on to the stumps. Lynn hit one enormous six into the second tier, but surrendered his wicket after five dot balls and a wide from Imad Wasim, whose four overs cost just eight. There was a moment of magic when Fakhar Zaman collected the ball in his left hand at mid-off, and threw back-handed while swan-diving in mid-air, without looking at the stumps, to run out McDermott. At the other end was Maxwell, improvising his way to 52 from 37 balls. With support from Coulter-Nile, he dragged Australia back in the game. But the charge was never fully controlled. They needed 23 from Shaheen Shah Afridi's final over, but Maxwell fell to a mis-hit, and Coulter-Nile followed. Pakistan took the biscuit – and a tenth consecutive T20 series win.

Man of the Match: Imad Wasim.

Pakistan

		B	4/6
1 Babar Azam *c 2 b 1*	45	44	3
2 Fakhar Zaman *c 6 b 8*	11	12	1
3 Mohammad Hafeez *c 1 b 11*	40	34	3/2
4 Shoaib Malik *c 4 b 8*	14	12	1
5 Asif Ali *c 1 b 11*	9	6	0/1
6 Fahim Ashraf *not out*	17	10	1/1
7 Hasan Ali *c 4 b 8*	0	1	0
8 Imad Wasim *not out*	1	1	0
Lb 6, w 4	10		
6 overs: 46-1 (20 overs)	147-6		

1/29 2/99 3/106 4/117 5/131 6/131

9 *†Sarfraz Ahmed, 10 Shadab Khan and 11 Shaheen Shah Afridi did not bat.

Maxwell 1–3–5–0; Coulter-Nile 3–7–18–3; Stanlake 4–8–36–2; Tye 4–4–40–0; Marsh 1–4–5–0; Zampa 4–8–21–0; Short 3–4–16–1.

Australia

		B	4/6
1 D. J. M. Short *run out (8)*	2	12	0
2 *A. J. Finch *c 2 b 10*	3	10	0
3 C. A. Lynn *c 10 b 8*	7	12	0/1
4 M. R. Marsh *c 9 b 10*	21	23	1
5 G. J. Maxwell *c 4 b 11*	52	37	4/2
6 †A. T. Carey *c 2 b 3*	1	4	0
7 B. R. McDermott *run out (2)*	3	4	0
8 N. M. Coulter-Nile *c 5 b 11*	27	17	0/3
9 A. J. Tye *not out*	2	1	0
10 A. Zampa *not out*	0	0	0
Lb 13, w 5	18		
6 overs: 28-2 (20 overs)	136-8		

1/11 2/19 3/31 4/61 5/62 6/73 7/132 8/134

11 B. Stanlake did not bat.

Imad Wasim 4–17–8–1; Fahim Ashraf 3–11–14–0; Shadab Khan 4–8–30–2; Shaheen Shah Afridi 4–11–35–2; Hasan Ali 4–8–32–0; Mohammad Hafeez 1–3–4–1.

Umpires: Ahsan Raza and Asif Yaqoob.   Third umpire: Shozab Raza.
Referee: R. S. Madugalle.

PAKISTAN v AUSTRALIA

Third Twenty20 International

At Dubai, October 28, 2018 (floodlit). Pakistan won by 33 runs. Toss: Pakistan.

Another day, another mid-range total defended with ease. This time Babar Azam's accomplice was the 22-year-old Sahibzada Farhan, who had made a duck in his only other international. In for the injured Fakhar Zaman, he was the support act in an opening partnership of 93, which took nearly 13 overs. Babar made an even half-century, which left his average at 56, the best by anyone who had batted more than three times in T20 internationals. Lyon and Coulter-Nile suffered particular punishment. But once Zampa and Short slowed things up with their varying wrist-spin, the wickets began to drop; this time the final total was exactly 150. Australia had been unable to score off Imad Wasim in the first two games, but now the promoted wicketkeeper Carey savaged his first over for two sixes and two fours. But just as the tourists' fortunes seemed to have changed, Finch and Carey gave soft catches in the circle, and Lynn one to the deep, while McDermott was run out for the third time out of three. Shadab Khan removed Maxwell and Marsh, before Short – in a new role at No. 7 – holed out. Pakistan took ten wickets for the 27th time in T20 internationals (way ahead of the next best, Australia's 19) and the whitewash was complete.

Man of the Match: Shadab Khan.   *Man of the Series:* Babar Azam.

Pakistan

		B	4/6
1 Babar Azam *b 9*	50	40	5/1
2 Sahibzada Farhan *c 9 b 11*	39	38	2/3
3 Mohammad Hafeez *not out*	32	20	3/1
4 Shoaib Malik *c 2 b 10*	18	12	2
5 Asif Ali *c 8 b 6*	4	5	1
6 Fahim Ashraf *c 9 b 6*	0	1	0
7 Imad Wasim *not out*	3	4	0
W 4	4		

6 overs: 54-0   (20 overs)   150-5

1/93 2/97 3/126 4/140 5/141

8 *†Sarfraz Ahmed, 9 Shadab Khan, 10 Hasan
Ali and 11 Usman Shinwari did not bat.

Lyon 4–13–33–1; Coulter-Nile 3–6–29–0; Tye
4–8–30–1; Short 4–8–27–0; Zampa
4–9–25–1; Marsh 1–2–6–2.

Australia

		B	4/6
1 †A. T. Carey *c 6 b 3*	20	9	2/2
2 *A. J. Finch *c 3 b 6*	1	3	0
3 C. A. Lynn *c 6 b 9*	15	13	2
4 B. R. McDermott *run out (1/8)*	21	20	2/1
5 G. J. Maxwell *c 4 b 9*	4	8	0
6 M. R. Marsh *c 4 b 9*	21	24	0/1
7 D. J. M. Short *c 4 b 11*	10	15	1
8 N. M. Coulter-Nile *run out (9)*	0	1	0
9 A. J. Tye *c 8 b 10*	5	9	0
10 A. Zampa *c 7 b 10*	9	10	1
11 N. M. Lyon *not out*	4	4	0
Lb 5, w 1, nb 1	7		

6 overs: 53-2   (19.1 overs)   117

1/24 2/24 3/60 4/62 5/75 6/94 7/99 8/99 9/108

Imad Wasim 4–11–33–0; Fahim Ashraf
2–9–8–1; Mohammad Hafeez 2–4–16–1;
Hasan Ali 3.1–13–14–2; Shadab Khan
4–9–19–3; Usman Shinwari 4–12–22–1.

Umpires: Rashid Riaz and Shozab Raza.   Third umpire: Ahsan Raza.
Referee: R. S. Madugalle.

PAKISTAN v NEW ZEALAND IN THE UAE IN 2018-19

Mazher Arshad

Twenty20 internationals (3): Pakistan 3, New Zealand 0
One-day internationals (3): Pakistan 1, New Zealand 1
Test matches (3): Pakistan 1, New Zealand 2

New Zealand had not played for seven months before this tour. They showed some rust in the white-ball games, but atoned in the Tests, where they came from behind twice for stirring victories – the first by just four runs – to clinch their first away win over Pakistan for nearly half a century (Graham Dowling's side had triumphed 1–0 in 1969-70, Hanif Mohammad's final series).

Kane Williamson, New Zealand's captain, had a memorable time in the Tests. In three matches on sluggish pitches, he amassed 386 runs at 77, including a double of 89 and 139 in the Third Test, before a familiar last-day collapse by Pakistan. It moved Williamson up to second in the ICC rankings, not far behind Virat Kohli. "Beating Pakistan in their backyard is very tough," he said. "This will be one the guys remember for a long time."

Williamson's captaincy outshone Sarfraz Ahmed's: he bravely threw uncapped spinners Ajaz Patel and Will Somerville into the mix, and they responded with crucial performances in the two Test victories on their respective debuts. There were also important runs from left-hander Henry Nicholls, who made his first overseas century in the Third Test.

Sarfraz blamed the defeat on a lack of input from the tail. "Our lower order couldn't score runs," he lamented. "Even 50 or 60 from them could be handy." In the two defeats, both in Abu Dhabi, Pakistan lost six for 53, seven for 41, then seven for 62 and all ten for 137 on the final day of the series.

New Zealand's two victories sandwiched a huge Pakistan win in the Second Test, in Dubai, where leg-spinner Yasir Shah was unstoppable. Disconcerting the batsmen with bounce and extravagant turn, he claimed 14 wickets, and went on to zip past 200 in the final Test, his 33rd. Pakistan also unleashed an exciting prospect in Shaheen Shah Afridi, a slippery left-arm seamer. Only 18, he was fast-tracked into the Test squad after doing well in the limited-overs games. Although unrelated to Shahid Afridi, he does have a Test-playing brother – Riaz Afridi, who won a cap against Sri Lanka in 2004-05.

Mohammad Hafeez, 20 years Afridi's senior, announced his retirement from Test cricket before the decider, to concentrate on white-ball formats, in which he was an automatic selection. Although he narrowly missed a pair on his farewell, he made 132 runs for once out in the Twenty20 internationals, in which Pakistan continued their terrific run of form. It was their 11th successive T20 series win since Sarfraz took over the captaincy in 2016.

New Zealand hit back in the first one-day international – their 12th successive win over Pakistan in the format – but Fakhar Zaman ensured that run soon ended. Pakistan might have pinched the 50-over series in the decider, before rain made a rare appearance to force a no-result.

Beginner's pluck: Ajaz Patel, on debut, traps Azhar Ali, and New Zealand edge the First Test.

The PCB had hoped the T20 matches would be in Lahore or Karachi, but New Zealand declined on security grounds. It led to the one disappointment of an interesting tour: much of the cricket took place in front of empty stands.

NEW ZEALAND TOURING PARTY

*K. S. Williamson (T/50/20), C. J. Anderson (20), T. D. Astle (20), T. A. Blundell (T), T. A. Boult (T/50), M. S. Chapman (20), C. de Grandhomme (T/50/20), L. H. Ferguson (50/20), M. J. Henry (T/50), T. W. M. Latham (T/50), A. F. Milne (20), C. Munro (50/20), H. M. Nicholls (T/50), A. Y. Patel (T/50/20), G. D. Phillips (20), S. H. A. Rance (20), J. A. Raval (T), T. L. Seifert (20), I. S. Sodhi (T/50/20), W. E. R. Somerville (T), T. G. Southee (T/50/20), L. R. P. L. Taylor (T/50/20), N. Wagner (T), B-J. Watling (T/50), G. H. Worker (50). *Coach:* G. R. Stead.

Astle injured his knee just before the ODI series; he was replaced in the squad by Patel, and in the Test party by Somerville. Anderson was also originally named in the ODI squad, but injured his heel and was replaced by Ferguson and Worker.

TEST MATCH AVERAGES

PAKISTAN – BATTING AND FIELDING

	T	I	NO	R	HS	100	50	Avge	Ct/St
Babar Azam	3	5	1	267	127*	1	2	66.75	1
Azhar Ali	3	5	0	307	134	1	2	61.40	0
†Haris Sohail	3	5	0	232	147	1	0	46.40	1
Asad Shafiq	3	5	0	204	104	1	0	40.80	4
Sarfraz Ahmed	3	5	1	88	30*	0	0	22.00	10/2
†Imam-ul-Haq	3	5	0	73	27	0	0	14.60	1
Mohammad Hafeez	3	5	0	47	20	0	0	9.40	2
Bilal Asif	3	4	0	34	12	0	0	8.50	2
Yasir Shah	3	4	0	14	9	0	0	3.50	1
Hasan Ali	3	4	0	8	4	0	0	2.00	1

Played in two Tests: Mohammad Abbas 0*, 0*. Played in one Test: †Shaheen Shah Afridi 0*, 2*.

BOWLING

	Style	O	M	R	W	BB	5I	Avge
Yasir Shah	LB	190.5	37	552	29	8-41	3	19.03
Hasan Ali	RFM	98.4	32	274	13	5-45	1	21.07
Bilal Asif	OB	122.1	20	266	7	5-65	1	38.00
Shaheen Shah Afridi	LFM	43	11	137	3	2-85	0	45.66

Also bowled: Azhar Ali (LB) 1–0–2–0; Haris Sohail (SLA) 21–3–46–2; Mohammad Abbas (RFM) 58–28–91–2; Mohammad Hafeez (OB) 10–4–14–0.

NEW ZEALAND – BATTING AND FIELDING

	T	I	NO	R	HS	100	50	Avge	Ct/St
K. S. Williamson	3	6	1	386	139	1	2	77.20	3
†H. M. Nicholls	3	6	1	287	126*	1	2	57.40	1
B-J. Watling	3	6	1	174	77*	0	2	34.80	10/1
†J. A. Raval	3	6	0	131	46	0	0	21.83	1
L. R. P. L. Taylor	3	6	0	125	82	0	1	20.83	4
†T. W. M. Latham	3	6	0	99	50	0	1	16.50	3
C. de Grandhomme	3	6	0	63	26	0	0	10.50	1
†A. Y. Patel	3	5	2	27	6*	0	0	9.00	2
I. S. Sodhi.................	2	4	0	26	18	0	0	6.50	1
†N. Wagner	2	4	0	22	12	0	0	5.50	2
T. A. Boult.................	3	5	1	5	4*	0	0	1.25	0

Played in one Test: W. E. R. Somerville 12, 4; T. G. Southee 2, 15* (3 ct).

BOWLING

	Style	O	M	R	W	BB	5I	Avge
W. E. R. Somerville	OB	56	10	127	7	4-75	0	18.14
T. G. Southee	RFM	37	8	98	4	3-42	0	24.50
C. de Grandhomme	RFM	63	20	128	5	2-30	0	25.60
A. Y. Patel	SLA	135.5	22	385	13	5-59	1	29.61
T. A. Boult	LFM	91.2	24	262	7	4-54	0	37.42
N. Wagner	LFM	68	21	120	3	2-27	0	40.00
I. S. Sodhi.................	LB	44	1	141	3	2-37	0	47.00

Also bowled: K. S. Williamson (OB) 5–0–20–0.

First Twenty20 international   At Abu Dhabi, October 31, 2018 (floodlit). **Pakistan won by two runs.** ‡Pakistan 148-6 (20 overs) (Mohammad Hafeez 45, Sarfraz Ahmed 34); **New Zealand 146-6** (20 overs) (C. Munro 58, L. R. P. L. Taylor 42*; Hasan Ali 3-35). *MoM:* Mohammad Hafeez. *T20I debut:* A. Y. Patel (New Zealand). *The match would have gone to a super over if Ross Taylor had hit Shaheen Shah Afridi's last ball for six – but he could only despatch a full toss to long-off for four. Pakistan had been 10-2 in the fourth, but Asif Ali and Mohammad Hafeez added 67; later, from a dicey 123-6, they conjured 25 from the last two overs, with Imad Wasim (14*) carting Tim Southee for four and six to end the innings. Colin Munro ignited the chase with 58 from 42 balls before falling to leg-spinner Shadab Khan, who also ran out Colin de Grandhomme. After a miserly spell from Hafeez (3–10–13–0), the odds were stacked against New Zealand, especially when TIm Seifert fell for a golden duck to the final delivery of the 19th, which meant 17 were needed off the last. Taylor, whose 26-ball 42* contained only three boundaries, muscled them close.*

Second Twenty20 international   At Dubai, November 2, 2018 (floodlit). **Pakistan won by six wickets.** ‡New Zealand 153-7 (20 overs) (C. Munro 44, K. S. Williamson 37, C. J. Anderson 44*; Shaheen Shah Afridi 3-20); **Pakistan 154-4** (19.4 overs) (Babar Azam 40, Asif Ali 38, Mohammad

Hafeez 34*). *MoM:* Shaheen Shah Afridi. *The result was in the balance when Pakistan needed 40 from four overs, but Hafeez took 17 off the 17th, from Ish Sodhi. He finished with 34* from 21 balls, as Pakistan clinched their 11th series in a row with their 11th successful chase in a row. Munro had given New Zealand another turbocharged start – Glenn Phillips made only five of their opening stand of 50 – but, with Afridi bowling tightly (4–12–20–3), the runs dried up. It was 83-4 in the 13th over, before Corey Anderson clouted 44* from 25 to set up a more challenging target.*

Third Twenty20 international   At Dubai, November 4, 2018 (floodlit). **Pakistan won by 47 runs. ‡Pakistan 166-3** (20 overs) (Babar Azam 79, Mohammad Hafeez 53*); **New Zealand 119** (16.5 overs) (K. S. Williamson 60; Shadab Khan 3-30). *MoM:* Babar Azam. *MoS:* Mohammad Hafeez. T20I debut: Waqas Maqsood (Pakistan). *Pakistan completed a 3–0 sweep thanks mainly to Babar Azam. He consolidated his place on top of the T20 batting rankings with 79 from 58 balls during a second-wicket stand of 94 with Hafeez, who took his series aggregate to 132 for once out. Babar's 48th run was his 1,000th in T20Is in his 26th innings, beating Virat Kohli's record by one. New Zealand were always up against it once big hitters Munro and de Grandhomme fell in single figures. Kane Williamson crashed 60 from 38 balls, but his dismissal in the 13th over was the first of eight wickets to tumble for 23. Waqas Maqsood, a 31-year-old left-arm seamer, became the first man to make his T20I debut on his birthday; he ended the match with two wickets in his second over.*

First one-day international   At Abu Dhabi, November 7, 2018 (day/night). **New Zealand won by 47 runs. ‡New Zealand 266-9** (50 overs) (L. R. P. L. Taylor 80, T. W. M. Latham 68; Shaheen Shah Afridi 4-46, Shadab Khan 4-38); **Pakistan 219** (47.2 overs) (Imam-ul-Haq 34, Shoaib Malik 30, Sarfraz Ahmed 64, Imad Wasim 50; T. A. Boult 3-54, L. H. Ferguson 3-36). *MoM:* T. A. Boult. *A change of format worked wonders for New Zealand, who breezed to their 12th successive ODI victory over Pakistan. Their hero was Trent Boult, who set back the chase with a high-class hat-trick – Fakhar Zaman, Babar and Hafeez – to reduce Pakistan to 8-3. Only Danny Morrison (1993-94) and Shane Bond (2006-07) had previously taken ODI hat-tricks for New Zealand. Workmanlike innings from Sarfraz Ahmed and Imad patched things up, but there was too much to do. From 219-7, the last three wickets fell in four balls, the final two to the pacy Lockie Ferguson. A fourth-wicket partnership of 130 between Taylor and Tom Latham had been the bedrock of New Zealand's competitive total. Shadab just missed a hat-trick of his own, taking three wickets in four balls as New Zealand lurched from 208-3 to 210-7.*

Second one-day international   At Abu Dhabi, November 9, 2018 (day/night). **Pakistan won by six wickets. ‡New Zealand 209-9** (50 overs) (L. R. P. L. Taylor 86*, H. M. Nicholls 33; Shaheen Shah Afridi 4-38); **Pakistan 212-4** (40.3 overs) (Fakhar Zaman 88, Babar Azam 46; L. H. Ferguson 3-60). *MoM:* Shaheen Shah Afridi. *Fakhar's return to form, after a lacklustre Asia Cup, helped Pakistan end their losing run. He made an even 88, and put on 101 with Babar after Imam-ul-Haq (16*) retired hurt on being clonked on the helmet by Ferguson, who also took three wickets. But New Zealand's under-par total, in which the only substantial partnership was 75 between Taylor (who hit just three fours and a six from 120 balls) and Henry Nicholls, never looked enough. They were not helped when Williamson was run out for one by a fingertip deflection by Afridi, after a George Worker straight-drive.*

Third one-day international   At Dubai, November 11, 2018 (day/night). **No result. ‡Pakistan 279-8** (50 overs) (Fakhar Zaman 65, Babar Azam 92, Haris Sohail 60; L. H. Ferguson 5-45); **New Zealand 35-1** (6.5 overs). *MoM:* L. H. Ferguson. *MoS:* Shaheen Shah Afridi. *Pakistan gave themselves a chance of a series win after Babar thumped 92 and put on 108 for the third wicket with Haris Sohail. The hostile Ferguson completed his maiden international five-for, but Boult finished with chastening figures of 1-80. New Zealand's quest for 280 started badly, when Munro was bowled by Afridi for a duck, but the rain came before enough overs had been bowled to constitute a match. This was the 332nd official ODI in the UAE, but only the second to end without a result, after Ireland v Scotland in Dubai in January 2015.*

> **"** I looked up and saw some birds fly from a tree. I remember thinking how lucky they were. In that moment, I so wanted to be a bird."
> The 2014 Peshawar School Terrorist Attack, page 33

PAKISTAN v NEW ZEALAND

First Test

At Abu Dhabi, November 16–19, 2018. New Zealand won by four runs. Toss: New Zealand. Test debut: A. Y. Patel.

Pakistan were in control for much of this match, and seemed to be heading for a routine win as they chased just 176. But a headlong collapse, in which the last seven wickets crashed for 41, allowed New Zealand to pull off an improbable victory. It was only their fourth win away from home against Pakistan, who stumbled to their second defeat in 12 Tests at the Sheikh Zayed Stadium (another would soon follow).

The win was sealed by Ajaz Patel, an Indian-born slow left-armer making his debut, who claimed five for 59 in the second innings, the last four for seven in 41 balls. New Zealand had only ever successfully defended one lower target – 137, against England (who subsided for 64) at Wellington in 1977-78.

Pakistan had gone to lunch on the fourth day at 130 for four. Asad Shafiq had just departed, but they needed only 46 more. Instead, Babar Azam was run out from short fine

---

NARROWEST TEST VICTORIES BY RUNS

1	West Indies (252 and 146) beat Australia (213 and 184) at Adelaide	1992-93
2	England (407 and 182) beat Australia (308 and 279) at Birmingham	2005
3	Australia (299 and 86) beat England (262 and 120) at Manchester	1902
3	England (284 and 294) beat Australia (287 and 288) at Melbourne.	1982-83
4	**New Zealand (153 and 249) beat Pakistan (227 and 171) at Abu Dhabi**	**2018-19**
5	South Africa (169 and 239) beat Australia (292 and 111) at Sydney.	1993-94
6	Australia (181 and 165) beat England (133 and 207) at Sydney	1884-85
7	Australia (63 and 122) beat England (101 and 77) at The Oval.	1882
7	South Africa (253 and 231) beat Sri Lanka (308 and 169) at Kandy	2000
7	New Zealand (150 and 226) beat Australia (136 and 233) at Hobart.	2011-12
10	England (325 and 437) beat Australia (586 and 166) at Sydney	1894-95

As at January 14, 2019, there have been 12 one-wicket victories in Tests – and two ties.

---

leg after a mix-up with Azhar Ali, then Sarfraz Ahmed was given out on review, with New Zealand certain he had tickled Patel to Watling while trying to sweep. Panic set in, and the next three all failed to score: Bilal Asif missed a cross-batted heave, Yasir Shah prodded to slip, and Hasan Ali slog-swept to deep midwicket with 12 needed. Azhar had tried to farm the strike during the later stages of his fighting 65, but finally pushed forward to Patel and was struck on the pad. The umpire raised the finger: Azhar reviewed, but the ball was destined to clip the off bail. "That last hour was quite freakish," said Wagner, who had played his part with a testing 13-over spell in searing heat.

"It was a great advertisement for Test cricket," said Williamson. "An old-fashioned Test match, really slow in terms of scoring." The rate hovered around two and a half an over throughout, with Williamson himself making 63 from 112 balls on the first day as New Zealand struggled to 153, the lowest opening innings in a Test in Abu Dhabi. Mohammad Abbas conceded only 13 runs in 12 overs, while Yasir removed Taylor, who had been in good form in the white-ball games. Not long after lunch on the second day, Pakistan looked in total charge, already in front with only four wickets down, but once Asad Shafiq departed – one of four victims for Boult – the innings faded. The last six wickets fell for 53, most of them by Babar, last out for 62.

A lead of 74 looked decisive on a difficult surface which had offered turn from the start, especially after Latham went first ball, but Raval and Williamson dug deep. New Zealand got their noses in front on the third morning, but then Yasir deceived Williamson with a loopy leg-break that clipped the off bail, and Hasan Ali removed Taylor and Raval. A collapse was staved off by Nicholls and Watling, who shared the only century partnership of the match: they resisted for 51 overs in adding 112, before both fell to Yasir. New Zealand eventually clawed their way to 249 – Hasan and Yasir finished with five apiece – but Pakistan cleared off 37 of their target that evening without loss.

Three quick strikes from Patel and leg-spinner Sodhi on the fourth morning gave New Zealand hope, but Azhar and Shafiq seemed to snuff that out in a stand of 82, which ended on the stroke of lunch when Shafiq reached, firm-footed, for a Wagner awayswinger and was caught behind. And then came the sensational session. "This must rank as one of our best wins," said Williamson. Sarfraz lamented: "We should have finished it off. Some of the shots played by the tail were quite disappointing."

Man of the Match: A. Y. Patel.

Close of play: first day, Pakistan 59-2 (Azhar Ali 10, Haris Sohail 22); second day, New Zealand 56-1 (Raval 26, Williamson 27); third day, Pakistan 37-0 (Imam-ul-Haq 25, Mohammad Hafeez 8).

New Zealand

J. A. Raval c Sarfraz Ahmed b Mohammad Abbas .	7	– c Sarfraz Ahmed b Hasan Ali.......	46
T. W. M. Latham c Mohammad Hafeez b Yasir Shah	13	– b Hasan Ali	0
*K. S. Williamson c Sarfraz Ahmed b Hasan Ali ..	63	– b Yasir Shah	37
L. R. P. L. Taylor c Sarfraz Ahmed b Yasir Shah .	2	– lbw b Hasan Ali	19
H. M. Nicholls c Sarfraz Ahmed			
b Mohammad Abbas.	28	– c Sarfraz Ahmed b Yasir Shah......	55
†B-J. Watling lbw b Haris Sohail...............	10	– lbw b Yasir Shah	59
C. de Grandhomme lbw b Hasan Ali............	0	– lbw b Yasir Shah	3
I. S. Sodhi lbw b Haris Sohail	4	– b Hasan Ali	18
N. Wagner c Asad Shafiq b Bilal Asif	12	– b Yasir Shah	0
A. Y. Patel lbw b Yasir Shah	6	– not out	6
T. A. Boult not out.........................	4	– c Mohammad Hafeez b Hasan Ali ...	0
Lb 4	4	B 4, w 1, nb 1.............	6

1/20 (1) 2/35 (2) 3/39 (4)　　　　(66.3 overs) 153　　1/0 (2) 2/86 (3)　　　　(100.4 overs) 249
4/111 (5) 5/123 (3) 6/123 (7)　　　　　　　　　　　　3/105 (4) 4/108 (1)
7/128 (8) 8/133 (6) 9/149 (9) 10/153 (10)　　　　　5/220 (5) 6/224 (7) 7/227 (6)
　　　　　　　　　　　　　　　　　　　　　　　　8/227 (9) 9/249 (8) 10/249 (11)

Mohammad Abbas 12–7–13–2; Hasan Ali 16–6–38–2; Bilal Asif 13–1–33–1; Yasir Shah 16.3–2–54–3; Haris Sohail 8–2–11–2; Mohammad Hafeez 1–1–0–0. *Second innings*—Mohammad Abbas 22–10–31–0; Hasan Ali 17.4–3–45–5; Yasir Shah 37–6–110–5; Haris Sohail 7–1–12–0; Bilal Asif 14–3–43–0; Mohammad Hafeez 3–1–4–0.

Pakistan

Imam-ul-Haq c Williamson b de Grandhomme	6	– lbw b Patel	27
Mohammad Hafeez c Williamson b Boult........	20	– c de Grandhomme b Sodhi.........	10
Azhar Ali c Watling b Boult	22	– lbw b Patel	65
Haris Sohail c Latham b Sodhi................	38	– c and b Sodhi	4
Asad Shafiq b Boult........................	43	– c Watling b Wagner	45
Babar Azam c Watling b Boult	62	– run out (Sodhi/Patel)	13
*†Sarfraz Ahmed c Wagner b Patel	2	– c Watling b Patel	3
Bilal Asif st Watling b Patel.................	11	– b Patel.........................	0
Yasir Shah c Watling b Wagner...............	9	– c Taylor b Wagner...............	0
Hasan Ali c Taylor b de Grandhomme	4	– c sub (T. G. Southee) b Patel	0
Mohammad Abbas not out....................	0	– not out	0
B 4, lb 4, w 1, nb 1	10	B 4	4

1/27 (1) 2/27 (2) 3/91 (4)　　　　(83.2 overs) 227　　1/40 (1) 2/44 (2)　　　　(58.4 overs) 171
4/91 (3) 5/174 (5) 6/177 (7)　　　　　　　　　　　　3/48 (4) 4/130 (5)
7/195 (8) 8/220 (9) 9/227 (10) 10/227 (6)　　　　　5/147 (6) 6/154 (7) 7/154 (8)
　　　　　　　　　　　　　　　　　　　　　　　　8/155 (9) 9/164 (10) 10/171 (3)

Boult 18.2–6–54–4; de Grandhomme 13–6–30–2; Patel 24–4–64–2; Wagner 18–5–30–1; Sodhi 10–0–41–1. *Second innings*—Boult 7–0–29–0; de Grandhomme 3–0–15–0; Patel 23.4–4–59–5; Sodhi 12–0–37–2; Wagner 13–4–27–2.

Umpires: I. J. Gould and B. N. J. Oxenford.   Third umpire: P. R. Reiffel.
Referee: J. Srinath.

PAKISTAN v NEW ZEALAND

Second Test

At Dubai, November 24–27, 2018. Pakistan won by an innings and 16 runs. Toss: Pakistan.

After Pakistan's batsmen had made a hash of things in Abu Dhabi, Yasir Shah made sure they would not have the chance to do so in Dubai, taking 14 wickets in an innings victory. It was a superb performance, which answered critics who had wondered whether his powers were on the wane after a troublesome hip injury. Only Imran Khan, with 14 for 116 against Sri Lanka at Lahore in 1981-82, had returned better match figures for Pakistan.

Before Yasir got going, though, Pakistan's batsmen had given him a sizeable total to bowl at. De Grandhomme, handed the new ball, dismissed both openers cheaply, but Azhar Ali unrolled another patient innings; he and Haris Sohail ground out 126 in more than 61 overs. Then, after Patel struck for the only time, Sohail – dropped by Watling off Sodhi when 37 – and Babar Azam batted into the final session of the second day, adding 186 for the fifth wicket. Sohail reached his second Test century, and Babar his first, making up for being out for 99 against Australia in Abu Dhabi five weeks previously (he spent a nervous tea interval on 99 here). Sohail persisted to 147, hitting 13 fours from 421 balls.

MOST WICKETS BY A BOWLER ON ONE DAY IN A TEST

15-28	J. Briggs	England v South Africa at Cape Town	1888-89
14-80	H. Verity	England v Australia at Lord's	1934
12-120	J. Briggs	England v Australia at Adelaide	1891-92
11-110	M. H. Mankad	India v Pakistan at Delhi	1952-53
10-44	G. A. Lohmann	England v South Africa at Johannesburg	1895-96
10-54	J. C. Laker	England v Australia at Manchester	1956
10-67	S. F. Barnes	England v Australia at Melbourne	1902
10-74	A. Kumble	India v Pakistan at Delhi	1998-99
10-97	**Yasir Shah**	**Pakistan v New Zealand at Dubai**	**2018-19**

Wagner kept things tight, but he and Boult proved toothless on the sluggish surface, and the spinners found little assistance either.

New Zealand survived nine overs until the close, and reached 50 next day after the start was delayed for an hour by a shower. Then Yasir uncorked the genie. Raval was bowled off the thigh and the back of his bat, and Latham popped one that bounced to short leg. Williamson became a spectator, finishing with 28 not out from No. 3. There were a record-equalling six ducks as the last eight in the order managed just five runs between them. Hasan Ali combined with Yasir to run out Watling, then removed de Grandhomme, but Yasir – often spinning the ball the width of the stumps or more – took care of the rest; he had none for 24 before Raval fell, but then took eight for 17 in 42 balls, including a triple-wicket maiden.

Yasir's final figures were the best in Tests against New Zealand (previously the South African "Goofy" Lawrence's eight for 53 at Johannesburg in 1961-62), and the best in Dubai (Devendra Bishoo's eight for 49 for West Indies in October 2016). Only Sarfraz Nawaz and Abdul Qadir, who both took nine, had better Test figures for Pakistan. New Zealand equalled their own record for the worst collapse after an opening stand of at least 50: at Auckland in 2000-01, also against Pakistan, they had slid from 91 for none to 131.

And Yasir was not done. Pakistan enforced the follow-on (for the first time in seven UAE Tests in which they had the option), and he claimed two more wickets before the close, including Williamson, done in by one that spat sideways and kissed the outside edge. That gave him ten on the third day alone. "I haven't bowled as well as this," said Yasir. "When I came here this morning, I was thinking that I had to take ten wickets in the match. I didn't know I would end up taking ten in the day."

MOST DUCKS IN A TEST INNINGS

6	Pakistan (128) v West Indies at Karachi	....	1980-81
6	South Africa (105) v India at Ahmedabad	....	1996-97
6	Bangladesh (87) v West Indies at Dhaka	....	2002-03
6	India (140) v England at Manchester	....	2014
6	**New Zealand (90) v Pakistan at Dubai**	....	**2018-19**

There have been 35 instances of five ducks in a Test innings.

New Zealand batted much better second time around, but it was only a matter of time. Latham, Taylor and Nicholls ate up a fair bit during battling half-centuries, but Yasir – if not as irresistible as in the first innings – worked his way through, helped by three wickets from Hasan, as Pakistan squared the series late on the fourth day.

Man of the Match: Yasir Shah.
Close of play: first day, Pakistan 207-4 (Haris Sohail 81, Babar Azam 14); second day, New Zealand 24-0 (Raval 17, Latham 5); third day, New Zealand 131-2 (Latham 44, Taylor 49).

Pakistan

Imam-ul-Haq c Latham b de Grandhomme	9	Babar Azam not out	....	127
Mohammad Hafeez c Latham		*†Sarfraz Ahmed not out	....	30
b de Grandhomme .	9	B 2, nb 1	....	3
Azhar Ali run out (sub T. G. Southee/				
Watling) .	81	1/18 (2)	(5 wkts dec, 167 overs)	418
Haris Sohail c Watling b Boult	 147	2/25 (1) 3/151 (3)		
Asad Shafiq c Wagner b Patel	 12	4/174 (5) 5/360 (4)		

Bilal Asif, Yasir Shah, Hasan Ali and Mohammad Abbas did not bat.

Boult 34–7–106–1; de Grandhomme 30–11–44–2; Wagner 37–12–63–0; Patel 39–5–120–1; Sodhi 22–1–63–0; Williamson 5–0–20–0.

New Zealand

J. A. Raval b Yasir Shah	 31	– st Sarfraz Ahmed b Yasir Shah	 2
T. W. M. Latham c Imam-ul-Haq b Yasir Shah	 22	– c Sarfraz Ahmed b Hasan Ali	 50
*K. S. Williamson c Sarfraz Ahmed b Yasir Shah	... 28	– c Sarfraz Ahmed b Yasir Shah	 30
L. R. P. L. Taylor b Yasir Shah	 0	– c Yasir Shah b Bilal Asif	 82
H. M. Nicholls b Yasir Shah	 0	– b Hasan Ali	 77
†B-J. Watling run out (Hasan Ali/Yasir Shah)	 1	– lbw b Yasir Shah	 27
C. de Grandhomme lbw b Hasan Ali	 0	– b Hasan Ali	 14
I. S. Sodhi c Sarfraz Ahmed b Yasir Shah	 0	– b Yasir Shah	 4
N. Wagner lbw b Yasir Shah	 0	– c Hasan Ali b Yasir Shah	 10
A. Y. Patel lbw b Yasir Shah	 4	– not out	 5
T. A. Boult st Sarfraz Ahmed b Yasir Shah	 0	– c Sarfraz Ahmed b Yasir Shah	 0
Lb 3, nb 1	 4	B 9, lb 2	 11

1/50 (1) 2/61 (2) 3/61 (4)   (35.3 overs)   90   1/10 (1) 2/66 (3)   (112.5 overs) 312
4/61 (5) 5/63 (6) 6/69 (7)   3/146 (2) 4/198 (4)
7/72 (8) 8/72 (9) 9/90 (10) 10/90 (11)   5/255 (6) 6/270 (7) 7/285 (8)
                                                              8/301 (5) 9/311 (9) 10/312 (11)

Mohammad Abbas 9–4–18–0; Hasan Ali 10–5–25–1; Mohammad Hafeez 2–1–1–0; Yasir Shah 12.3–1–41–8; Bilal Asif 2–1–2–0. *Second innings*—Mohammad Abbas 15–7–29–0; Hasan Ali 19–7–46–3; Yasir Shah 44.5–9–143–6; Mohammad Hafeez 3–1–6–0; Bilal Asif 27–5–61–1; Haris Sohail 4–0–16–0.

Umpires: B. N. J. Oxenford and P. R. Reiffel.   Third umpire: I. J. Gould.
Referee: J. Srinath.

PAKISTAN v NEW ZEALAND

Third Test

At Abu Dhabi, December 3–7, 2018. New Zealand won by 123 runs. Toss: New Zealand. Test debuts: Shaheen Shah Afridi; W. E. R. Somerville.

In the First Test, New Zealand had overturned a first-innings deficit of 74 to win in Abu Dhabi. Now they did it again, to complete their first series victory over Pakistan away from home since 1969-70, and only the second by a visiting team, after Sri Lanka two years earlier, since Pakistan made the UAE their home in 2010. Like the first match, this one owed much to a debutant spinner: 34-year-old Will Somerville, who earlier in the year had been representing New South Wales. After returning to play for Auckland in his native New Zealand, he was called up as a replacement for this tour – and took seven wickets, including three important strikes as Pakistan's chase foundered.

Amid the Kiwi celebrations there was another landmark for Pakistan's leg-spinner Yasir Shah, whose fifth wicket in the match (Somerville in the second innings) was his 200th in Tests, in only his 33rd match. He was easily the fastest to the mark.

FASTEST TO 200 TEST WICKETS

T		*T*	
33	**Yasir Shah (Pakistan)**	42	M. D. Marshall (West Indies)
36	C. V. Grimmett (Australia)	42	M. Muralitharan (Sri Lanka)
37	R. Ashwin (India)	42	S. K. Warne (Australia)
38	D. K. Lillee (Australia)	44	A. V. Bedser (England)
38	Waqar Younis (Pakistan)	44	J. Garner (West Indies)
39	D. W. Steyn (South Africa)	44	R. J. Hadlee (New Zealand)
41	I. T. Botham (England)	45	C. E. L. Ambrose (West Indies)
41	S. C. G. MacGill (Australia)	45	Imran Khan (Pakistan)
42	A. A. Donald (South Africa)	45	G. D. McGrath (Australia)

As was the case for most of the series, runs were hard to come by. Williamson's determined 89, and a gritty unbeaten 77 from 250 balls by Watling, dragged New Zealand to 274. There were five wickets for off-spinner Bilal Asif, and a maiden scalp (Latham) for the debutant Shaheen Shah Afridi, an 18-year-old left-arm seamer with a searing yorker who had played only three previous first-class matches. Pakistan's reply had a poor start when Mohammad Hafeez, who had announced his Test retirement before the match, fell for a duck to Boult, who also removed Imam-ul-Haq in single figures. Azhar Ali and Asad Shafiq dropped anchor, eventually putting on 201 in 76 overs, by which time Pakistan were in the lead. But another tepid lower-order display kept the advantage within bounds, Somerville making an impressive start with four for 75.

New Zealand lost two quick wickets before the third-day close, and nightwatchman Somerville departed early next morning, but the fifth-wicket pair booked in for the rest of the day. They had a little luck: Williamson was dropped by Yasir on 80 and 106, while replays showed that Nicholls was lbw to Yasir on three, but Pakistan did not ask for a

NEW ZEALAND'S OLDEST TEST DEBUTANTS

Yrs	Days			
38	101	H. M. McGirr	v England at Auckland	1929-30
36	317	R. W. G. Emery	v West Indies at Christchurch	1951-52
36	120	N. Puna	v England at Christchurch	1965-66
36	89	A. F. Lissette	v West Indies at Dunedin	1955-56
34	295	S. G. Gedye	v South Africa at Wellington	1963-64
34	186	G. W. F. Overton	v South Africa at Durban	1953-54
34	161	M. Henderson	v England at Christchurch	1929-30
34	144	G. F. Cresswell	v England at The Oval	1949
34	**116**	**W. E. R. Somerville**	**v Pakistan at Abu Dhabi**	**2018-19**
34	36	L. Ronchi	v England at Leeds	2015
34	14	P. J. Petherick	v Pakistan at Lahore	1976-77

Only Somerville and Ronchi finished on the winning side.

---

review. Williamson took the eye, cover-driving off front foot and back during an excellent century, his 19th in Tests and one of the most valuable: it was a surprise when he fell first ball on the fifth morning, lbw to a ball clipping the top of the stumps. Nicholls marched on to his own hundred, his first away from home, before a declaration left Pakistan a tantalising 280 in 79 overs.

They never threatened. Hafeez narrowly avoided a farewell pair when he guided his first ball through Williamson's hands in the gully, but made only eight before he was bowled by Southee. Azhar nibbled at de Grandhomme's outswinger, then with successive deliveries Somerville removed Haris Sohail (a juggled catch by Taylor at slip) and Shafiq (a leg-side tickle, confirmed on review). Imam soon followed, making it 55 for five. Babar Azam and Sarfraz Ahmed resisted for an hour, before Somerville gated the captain with a quicker one. Southee and Patel helped wrap up the rest, including Babar, who spiralled a catch to mid-off after a defiant 51. It was the sixth time since August 2016 that Pakistan had surrendered all ten wickets on the final day to lose a Test.

Man of the Match: K. S. Williamson. *Man of the Series:* Yasir Shah.

Close of play: first day, New Zealand 229-7 (Watling 42, Somerville 12); second day, Pakistan 139-3 (Azhar Ali 62, Asad Shafiq 26); third day, New Zealand 26-2 (Williamson 14, Somerville 1); fourth day, New Zealand 272-4 (Williamson 139, Nicholls 90).

New Zealand

J. A. Raval lbw b Yasir Shah	45	– lbw b Shaheen Shah Afridi	0
T. W. M. Latham lbw b Shaheen Shah Afridi	4	– c Haris Sohail b Yasir Shah	10
*K. S. Williamson c Asad Shafiq b Hasan Ali	89	– lbw b Hasan Ali	139
L. R. P. L. Taylor b Yasir Shah	0	– (5) c Bilal Asif b Shaheen Shah Afridi	22
H. M. Nicholls b Yasir Shah	1	– (6) not out	126
†B-J. Watling not out	77	– (8) b Yasir Shah	0
C. de Grandhomme c Asad Shafiq b Bilal Asif	20	– c Bilal Asif b Yasir Shah	26
T. G. Southee c Babar Azam b Bilal Asif	2	– (9) not out	15
W. E. R. Somerville b Bilal Asif	12	– (4) lbw b Yasir Shah	4
A. Y. Patel c Asad Shafiq b Bilal Asif	6		
T. A. Boult b Bilal Asif	1		
B 11, lb 6	17	B 9, lb 1, nb 1	11

1/24 (2) 2/70 (1) 3/70 (4) (116.1 overs) 274
4/72 (5) 5/176 (3) 6/203 (7)
7/209 (8) 8/254 (9) 9/272 (10) 10/274 (11)

1/1 (1) (7 wkts dec, 113 overs) 353
2/24 (2) 3/37 (4)
4/60 (5) 5/225 (3) 6/334 (7) 7/334 (8)

Hasan Ali 20–6–58–1; Shaheen Shah Afridi 23–6–52–1; Yasir Shah 41–11–75–3; Bilal Asif 30.1–4–65–5; Haris Sohail 2–0–7–0. *Second innings*—Hasan Ali 16.5–5–62–1; Shaheen Shah Afridi 20–5–85–2; Yasir Shah 39.8–129–4; Bilal Asif 36–6–62–0; Azhar Ali 1–0–2–0; Mohammad Hafeez 1–0–3–0.

Pakistan

Imam-ul-Haq c Southee b Boult	9	– c Nicholls b Patel	22
Mohammad Hafeez c Southee b Boult	0	– b Southee	8
Azhar Ali c Patel b Somerville	134	– c Watling b de Grandhomme	5
Haris Sohail c Watling b Southee	34	– c Taylor b Somerville	9
Asad Shafiq lbw b Patel	104	– c Watling b Somerville	0
Babar Azam b Somerville	14	– c Southee b Patel	51
*†Sarfraz Ahmed c Raval b Somerville	25	– b Somerville	28
Bilal Asif c Taylor b Patel	11	– c Watling b Southee	12
Yasir Shah run out (de Grandhomme/Somerville)	1	– c Patel b Southee	4
Hasan Ali b Somerville	0	– c Williamson b Patel	4
Shaheen Shah Afridi not out	0	– not out	2
B 6, lb 9, nb 1	16	B 4, lb 6, nb 1	11

1/0 (2) 2/17 (1) 3/85 (4) (135 overs) 348 1/19 (2) 2/32 (3) (56.1 overs) 156
4/286 (3) 5/304 (5) 6/312 (6) 3/43 (4) 4/43 (5)
7/333 (8) 8/346 (9) 9/347 (10) 10/348 (7) 5/55 (1) 6/98 (7) 7/131 (8)
8/137 (9) 9/150 (6) 10/156 (10)

Southee 25–5–56–1; Boult 26–7–66–2; de Grandhomme 13–2–36–0; Patel 35–5–100–2; Somerville 36–8–75–4. *Second innings*—Southee 12–3–42–3; Boult 6–4–7–0; de Grandhomme 4–1–3–1; Patel 14.1–4–42–3; Somerville 20–2–52–3.

Umpires: I. J. Gould and P. R. Reiffel.   Third umpire: B. N. J. Oxenford.
Referee: J. Srinath.

PAKISTAN A v ENGLAND LIONS IN UAE IN 2018-19

A-team Test (1): Pakistan A 1, England Lions 0
A-team one-day internationals (5): Pakistan A 3, England Lions 2
A-team Twenty20 internationals (2): Pakistan A 0, England Lions 2

Earlier in 2018, the England Lions had endured a chastening tour of the Caribbean, losing all three A-team Tests and the one-day series. This trip was more of a success: although the solitary Test was lost, the one-dayers went down to the wire, and the Lions won both Twenty20 matches. Their coach, Graham Thorpe, called it "a really positive tour – we've been on the wrong end of one or two results, but the skills you develop as a result are crucial".

The bowlers led the way. Somerset's Lewis Gregory took nine wickets in the white-ball games, in which he was also captain. His fellow seamer, Lancashire's Saqib Mahmood, also claimed nine, after a late call-up when Josh Tongue was ruled out. Joe Clarke made a defiant century in the four-day match, and an equally valiant 60 not out in the deciding one-dayer, when he led the team because Gregory had an ankle injury. Lancashire's Alex Davies allied useful runs – often opening, a problem position for the seniors – to his unflashy wicketkeeping. The side were bolstered by the late inclusion of Ollie Pope, released early from the senior tour of Sri Lanka when it became obvious he was unlikely to feature in the Tests. He started with a duck in the four-day game, but crafted an unbeaten 93 in the third one-dayer – the innings of the tour, according to Gregory.

Pakistan A's batsmen were almost unstoppable when they got going. They clinched the four-day game by chasing down 312, and also won two of the one-dayers by huge margins after steaming well past 300. In the first of those, Shan Masood belted 161, and put on 276 with Abid Ali, who added 140 to his A-Test century a few days previously.

The Pakistanis rotated their line-up enthusiastically, using 27 players in all. This led to occasional confusion: in the T20s, they fielded three Mohammad Irfans, though the instantly recognisable 7ft 1in Test fast bowler was not among them. Gregory admitted: "The analyst had a bit of trouble working out which Irfan did what."

ENGLAND LIONS TOURING PARTY

*S. W. Billings (Kent; FC); D. M. Bess (Somerset; FC/50/20), D. R. Briggs (Hampshire; FC/50/20), J. M. Clarke (Worcestershire; FC/50/20), A. L. Davies (Lancashire; 50/20), L. Gregory (Somerset; 50/20), N. R. T. Gubbins (Middlesex; FC/50/20), S. R. Hain (Warwickshire; 50/20), M. D. E. Holden (Middlesex; FC/50/20), T. Köhler-Cadmore (Yorkshire; FC/50/20), L. S. Livingstone (Lancashire; FC/50/20), S. Mahmood (Lancashire; FC/50/20), J. Overton (Somerset; FC/50/20), O. J. D. Pope (Surrey; FC/50/20), J. A. Porter (Essex; FC/50/20), J. J. Roy (Surrey; FC), G. S. Virdi (Surrey; FC), M. A. Wood (Durham; FC/50/20). *Coach:* G. P. Thorpe.

Gregory captained in the white-ball matches. J. C. Tongue (Worcestershire) was originally selected for the first-class portion, but suffered a foot injury and was replaced by Mahmood. M. W. Parkinson

(Lancashire) was selected in all three squads, but withdrew with a lumbar stress fracture and was replaced by Briggs. C. Overton (Somerset) was also in all three squads, but returned home with back trouble before playing, but was not replaced. Pope joined the tour after being released from the senior squad in Sri Lanka.

PAKISTAN A v ENGLAND LIONS

A-Team Test

At Abu Dhabi, November 18–21, 2018. Pakistan A won by seven wickets. Toss: England Lions.

Pakistan A surged to victory despite a first-innings deficit of 45, chasing down a target of 312 with relative ease. In what would become a recurring theme of the tour, the Lions had to be rescued after an indifferent start: it was 58 for four once Pope and Clarke departed for ducks. But Billings, the captain, hung on grimly, sharing useful stands with Roy, Bess and Wood before the last four wickets fell for nine. Pakistan A's batting misfired too, against some testing seam bowling from Wood and Porter: only their captain, Mohammad Rizwan, and Ehsan Adil passed 22. The Lions' second innings resembled the first: after four quick wickets, one man stood defiant. This time it was Clarke, who completed a fighting century before Wood and Briggs stretched the advantage past 300. Shaheen Shah Afridi, a slippery 18-year-old left-armer soon to make his full Test debut, took seven wickets in the match, all bowled or caught behind. When Khurram Manzoor fell to the first ball of the chase, and Shan Masood soon followed, it was Lions rampant – but Abid Ali, an uncapped 31-year-old from Lahore, dug deep. He and Usman Salahuddin survived to the third-day close, and took their stand to 160 next morning, before Rizwan and Saud Shakil helped tick down the requirement. Abid finally fell with 16 wanted, one of three wickets for the persistent Bess, but by then a notable victory was all but assured.

Close of play: first day, Pakistan A 33-2 (Khurram Manzoor 11, Usman Salahuddin 1); second day, England Lions 144-4 (Clarke 61, Billings 32); third day, Pakistan A 132-2 (Abid Ali 58, Usman Salahuddin 59).

England Lions

M. D. E. Holden b Shaheen Shah Afridi	4	– c Mohammad Rizwan b Ehsan Adil . 19
N. R. T. Gubbins c Mohammad Irfan b Ali Shafiq .	20	– b Shaheen Shah Afridi 4
J. J. Roy c Khurram Manzoor b Mohammad Asghar	59	– run out (Shan Masood). 14
O. J. D. Pope c Mohammad Asghar b Ali Shafiq. . .	0	– b Shaheen Shah Afridi 10
J. M. Clarke b Mohammad Irfan	0	– c Mohammad Rizwan b Shaheen Shah Afridi . 107
*†S. W. Billings not out	74	– c Mohammad Rizwan b Shaheen Shah Afridi . 38
D. M. Bess st Mohammad Rizwan b Mohammad Irfan .	42	– c Mohammad Rizwan b Mohammad Asghar . 4
M. A. Wood b Shaheen Shah Afridi	22	– not out 36
D. R. Briggs c Usman Salahuddin b Mohammad Irfan .	5	– lbw b Ehsan Adil 21
J. Overton c Usman Salahuddin b Mohammad Irfan	0	– c Mohammad Rizwan b Ehsan Adil . 5
J. A. Porter b Shaheen Shah Afridi	0	– run out (Mohammad Rizwan) 0
Lb 6, w 1, nb 7	14	Lb 3, w 1, nb 4 8

1/10 (1) 2/54 (2) 3/57 (4)　　　　　(69 overs) 240　　　1/15 (1) 2/32 (1)　　　(85.2 overs) 266
4/58 (5) 5/107 (3) 6/186 (7)　　　　　　　　　　　　　3/42 (3) 4/55 (4)
7/231 (8) 8/238 (9) 9/238 (10) 10/240 (11)　　　　　5/164 (6) 6/186 (7) 7/204 (5)
　　　　　　　　　　　　　　　　　　　　　　　　　　8/257 (9) 9/263 (10) 10/266 (11)

Shaheen Shah Afridi 15–2–50–3; Ehsan Adil 7–0–35–0; Mohammad Irfan 25–2–80–4; Ali Shafiq 8–0–33–2; Mohammad Asghar 14–1–36–1. *Second innings*—Shaheen Shah Afridi 24–1–80–4; Mohammad Irfan 19–5–55–0; Ehsan Adil 14.2–1–55–3; Ali Shafiq 8–0–21–0; Mohammad Asghar 20–1–52–1.

Pakistan A

Khurram Manzoor c Billings b Porter	17	– lbw b Porter	0
Shan Masood c Overton b Wood	8	– b Wood	11
Abid Ali c Billings b Overton	11	– c Gubbins b Bess	113
Usman Salahuddin c Holden b Bess	18	– c Clarke b Bess	77
*†Mohammad Rizwan b Bess	58	– b Porter	47
Saud Shakil c Billings b Wood	4	– not out	47
Ehsan Adil c Roy b Wood	44	– c Billings b Bess	7
Mohammad Irfan jnr c Billings b Wood	22	– not out	2
Shaheen Shah Afridi c Wood b Porter	5		
Mohammad Asghar c Overton b Porter	0		
Ali Shafiq not out	1		
W 1, nb 6	7	Lb 2, w 1, nb 7	10

1/8 (2) 2/29 (3) 3/42 (1)   (58.2 overs) 195
4/101 (4) 5/120 (6) 6/120 (5)
7/184 (8) 8/189 (7) 9/192 (10) 10/195 (9)

1/0 (1)   (6 wkts, 97.4 overs) 314
2/12 (2) 3/172 (4)
4/247 (5) 5/296 (3) 6/306 (7)

Porter 12.2–4–22–3; Wood 17–0–67–4; Overton 9–1–23–1; Briggs 9–4–21–0; Bess 11–1–62–2.
Second innings—Porter 19–2–68–2; Wood 19–0–56–1; Bess 31–2–110–3; Overton 14.4–3–46–0; Briggs 14–2–32–0.

Umpires: Asif Yaqoob and Rashid Riaz.
Referee: Mohammed Anees.

First A-team one-day international   At Dubai (ICC Academy), November 25, 2018. **Pakistan A won by 187 runs. Pakistan A** 351-4 (50 overs) (Shan Masood 161, Abid Ali 140; L. Gregory 3-79); ‡**England Lions** 164 (32.5 overs) (Waqas Maqsood 4-34, Amad Butt 4-29). *MoM:* Shan Masood. *The Lions were blown away by a second-wicket stand of 276 between Shan Masood and Abid Ali, who both faced 134 balls. Needing to score at seven an over, the Lions were soon 58-4, and out of it. Left-armer Waqas Maqsood did most of the early damage, before Amad Butt, another seamer, took three wickets in five balls.*

Second A-team one-day international   At Dubai (ICC Academy), November 27, 2018. **England Lions won by six wickets.** ‡**Pakistan A** 289-7 (50 overs) (Mohammad Saad 117, Mohammad Rizwan 98; S. Mahmood 3-59); **England Lions** 290-4 (47.1 overs) (A. L. Davies 76, S. R. Hain 69). *MoM:* A. L. Davies. *The Lions squared the series after a much-improved batting performance, running down 290 with something to spare. Alex Davies put on 74 for the first wicket with Tom Köhler-Cadmore (30), and 76 for the second with Sam Hain. Mohammad Saad and Mohammad Rizwan had added 211 for Pakistan A's third wicket.*

Third A-team one-day international   At Abu Dhabi, November 29, 2018 (day/night). **England Lions won by 22 runs.** ‡**England Lions** 245 (50 overs) (O. J. D. Pope 93*; Khushdil Shah 3-37); **Pakistan A** 223-9 (50 overs) (Mohammad Rizwan 141*; D. M. Bess 3-35). *Ollie Pope worked hard to rescue the Lions from 57-4 – he hit only four boundaries from 109 balls – but 245 seemed underwhelming. However, Pakistan A crashed to 21-3, and fell short despite a superb 141* from skipper Rizwan; Adil Amin's 32 was the only other double-figure score.*

Fourth A-team one-day international   At Abu Dhabi, December 2, 2018. **Pakistan A won by 181 runs. Pakistan A** 335-4 (50 overs) (Shan Masood 61, Ali Imran 57, Adil Amin 120*, Mohammad Rizwan 73; L. Gregory 3-72); ‡**England Lions** 154 (31.4 overs) (Waqas Maqsood 5-32). *After Masood and Ali Imran opened with a patient stand of 113 in 23.5 overs, Amin (120* from 87 balls) and Rizwan (73 from 49) scorched 163 for the third wicket in 18. The Lions again made a poor start in the face of a big target and, when Joe Clarke and Lewis Gregory fell to successive deliveries in the 11th over, bowled by Maqsood, there was no escape from 42-5.*

Fifth A-team one-day international   At Dubai (Sports City), December 5, 2018. **Pakistan A won by seven wickets.** ‡**England Lions** 169 (45.1 overs) (J. M. Clarke 60*; Zohaib Khan 4-27); **Pakistan A** 170-3 (39.5 overs) (Israrullah 57, Mohammad Saad 67*). *Pakistan A pinched the series after another indifferent performance from the Lions, who stumbled from 101-3 to 108-8. There were four successive ducks, three caught behind by Mohammad Hasan off slow left-armer Zohaib Khan (there was also a run-out). Clarke, captaining in place of Gregory, who had an ankle niggle, put on 56 for the ninth wicket with Jamie Overton (33), but Pakistan A recovered from 4-2 to sail home.*

First A-team Twenty20 international   At Abu Dhabi, December 7, 2018. **England Lions won by four wickets. Pakistan A 131-8** (20 overs) (S. Mahmood 4-14); ‡**England Lions 135-6** (19.2 overs) (Mohammad Irfan 4-24). *After eight overs, Pakistan A were 37-5, but Umaid Asif organised a recovery of sorts. Things looked grim for the Lions at 88-6 in the 16th, but pacemen Mark Wood (27* from 18 balls) and Overton (24* from nine) added 47*. Saqib Mahmood had earlier taken 4-14 in three overs. The Pakistan A-team included three Mohammad Irfans, none of them the tall Test player of the same name. The one who took four wickets is a leg-spinner who plays for Multan.*

Second A-team Twenty20 international   At Abu Dhabi, December 8, 2018. **England Lions won by four wickets. ‡Pakistan A 139-9** (20 overs) (L. S. Livingstone 3-24, J. Overton 3-24); **England Lions 145-6** (18.5 overs). *Tight bowling restricted Pakistan A, whose captain Shan Masood top-scored with 42. Liam Livingstone, armed with the new ball, took three wickets with his leg-breaks, while Overton – the sixth bowler tried – claimed three in seven deliveries. The Lions again made heavy weather of the chase: it was 98-5 in the 15th over, but Livingstone's 35* from 19 ensured they won the T20 series 2–0.*

DOMESTIC CRICKET IN PAKISTAN IN 2017-18

Abid Ali Kazi

There was a unusually familiar look to domestic cricket. The format of the Quaid-e-Azam Trophy identical for the third consecutive season – unprecedented in the 21st century – and the final contested by **Sui Northern Gas** and **WAPDA**, who between them had won the previous three titles. Defending champions WAPDA had the upper hand when they reduced their opponents to 21 for four in their second innings, only nine ahead, but Iftikhar Ahmed and Mohammad Rizwan fought back with a stand of 193, and Sui Northern collected their third trophy in four seasons when Samiullah demolished the run-chase with eight for 62.

One of the most frequent changes in the Quaid-e-Azam format has been the regular shift between including departmental teams alongside the regional sides, and splitting the two into separate first-class tournaments. When the two are combined, as at present, the departmental teams are dominant, as they can afford the best talent. In an attempt to improve the balance and build up a stronger set of second-string cricketers, the Pakistan Cricket Board introduced a draft system. Regional teams were to pick 12 local players, two of whom had to be under 19, plus a further eight from a pool chosen by the national selection committee. The board planned to monitor the players' progress over the year.

But departmental sides were also feeling the pinch. In July, United Bank confirmed it was disbanding its team after a steep decline in profits. The **United Bank** team, by contrast, had enjoyed a successful season. They just missed the Quaid-e-Azam final – finishing one point behind WAPDA in their Super Eight group – and claimed the departmental one-day cup after winning all seven group games, as well as two in the knockouts. They coasted to victory in the final against WAPDA, their last match for the foreseeable future. (The bank had pulled out once before, re-establishing a team in 2011-12 after 14 seasons' absence.) It was particularly disappointing because United Bank had a reputation for developing young talent through the academy housed at their own first-class ground. National Bank, who had won only one match in 2017-18 and lost all their one-day games, said they would hire any United Bank players needing a job.

Easily the most successful batsman of the season was United Bank's Saad Ali. He scored 957 runs at 68, more than 200 ahead of Sui Northern's Iftikhar Ahmed, and comfortably headed the averages; his haul included the highest individual score, 232, against Pakistan Television. Only Mohammad Saad of WAPDA matched his three centuries. But it was not a good season for batsmen. Some blamed the adoption of the Dukes ball, though it was eventually accepted as more consistent and better at retaining its shape than previous models. Former Test captain Misbah-ul-Haq, who appeared for Sui Northern, pointed to the poor quality of pitches, which was exacerbated by a busy schedule cramming the entire first-class tournament – ten rounds plus a final – into three months interrupted by a three-week Twenty20 competition for regional sides. Five of the 68 pool and Super Eight games ended in two days.

Seam bowlers had a better time of it. Aizaz Cheema of Lahore Blues was the leading wicket-taker, with 60 at nine. Saad Altaf achieved the best first-class match return by a Pakistani bowler when he took 16 for 141 for Rawalpindi against the Federally Administered Tribal Areas. Another left-arm seamer, 17-year-old Shaheen Shah Afridi, claimed eight for 39, the best innings return by a Pakistani on first-class debut (though he finished on the losing side when Rawalpindi bowled KRL out for 77). Three more seamers – Rumman Raees, Waqas Maqsood and Ahmed Jamal – took nine in an innings.

In the national tournaments for the regions, the one-day final was won by Karachi Whites, who beat Islamabad in a high-scoring game, while the T20 final was an all-Lahore affair, the Blues defeating the Whites.

FIRST-CLASS AVERAGES IN 2017-18

BATTING (400 runs)

		M	I	NO	R	HS	100	Avge	Ct/St
1	†Saad Ali (*United Bank*)	10	15	1	957	232	3	68.35	10
2	Abid Ali (*Islamabad*)	7	13	2	541	231*	1	49.18	9
3	Faisal Iqbal (*Karachi Whites*)	7	12	3	413	100*	1	45.88	10
4	Hammad Azam (*United Bank*)	9	13	3	439	128	1	43.90	5
5	Faizan Riaz (*Islamabad*)	7	12	1	479	114*	1	43.54	6
6	†Fawad Alam (*Sui Southern Gas*)	10	17	3	570	124	2	40.71	7
7	†Ali Asad (*National Bank*)	7	14	2	487	90	0	40.58	4
8	Mohammad Mohsin (*Lahore Whites*)	8	14	2	469	96*	0	39.08	4
9	Iftikhar Ahmed (*Sui Northern Gas*)	11	21	2	735	106	2	38.68	14
10	Mohammad Saad (*WAPDA*)	11	20	3	650	134*	1	38.23	3
11	†Umar Amin (*Sui Southern Gas*)	8	14	0	533	145	2	38.07	9
12	Usman Salahuddin (*Lahore Whites*)	7	13	2	417	101*	1	37.90	3
13	†Saud Shakil (*Pakistan Television*)	7	13	0	488	108	1	37.53	5
14	†Sami Aslam (*Sui Southern Gas*)	7	12	1	407	133*	1	37.00	4
15	Aamer Sajjad (*WAPDA*)	10	18	2	591	106*	1	36.93	13
16	Rameez Raja (*National Bank*)	7	13	0	470	150	1	36.15	0
17	Rizwan Hussain (*Lahore Whites*)	8	14	0	497	138	1	35.50	4
18	Saad Nasim (*Lahore Blues*)	10	16	0	561	123	2	35.06	8
19	Mohammad Rizwan (*Sui Northern Gas*)	10	19	2	596	109*	1	35.05	33/4
20	Yasir Hameed (*FATA*)	7	14	0	459	157	1	32.78	9
21	Kamran Akmal (*WAPDA*)	8	14	1	418	139	1	32.15	30/1
22	†Umar Siddiq (*United Bank*)	9	14	0	444	115	1	31.71	10
23	†Raza Ali Dar (*Lahore Blues*)	10	16	1	464	87	0	30.93	5
24	†Imran Farhat (*Habib Bank*)	10	18	0	494	105	1	27.44	7
25	Waqas Saleem (*Lahore Blues*)	10	19	2	429	52	0	25.23	17
26	†Salman Butt (*WAPDA*)	11	20	1	437	66	0	23.00	5

BOWLING (30 wickets)

		Style	O	M	R	W	BB	5I	Avge
1	Aizaz Cheema (*Lahore Blues*)	RFM	233	68	577	60	7-52	5	9.61
2	Mir Hamza (*United Bank*)	LFM	226.4	60	565	42	7-68	5	13.45
3	Sohail Khan (*United Bank*)	RFM	259.4	62	705	51	6-59	5	13.82
4	Mohammad Asif (*WAPDA*)	RFM	220.1	54	609	44	6-23	5	13.84
5	Mohammad Abbas (*Sui Northern Gas*)	RFM	196	54	529	37	6-24	3	14.29
6	Sadaf Hussain (*KRL*)	LFM	264	66	706	47	7-85	2	15.02
7	Azizullah (*Sui Northern Gas*)	RFM	183.1	43	523	34	6-27	3	15.38
8	Zulfiqar Babar (*WAPDA*)	SLA	201.2	52	498	32	7-41	2	15.56
9	Amad Butt (*Habib Bank*)	RFM	195.1	43	627	39	6-106	3	16.07
10	Kashif Bhatti (*Sui Southern Gas*)	SLA	288.2	69	790	49	8-50	4	16.12
11	Yasir Ali (*KRL*)	RFM	170	43	507	31	6-50	2	16.35
12	Waqas Maqsood (*WAPDA*)	LFM	201.3	45	563	33	9-32	1	17.06
13	Nazar Hussain (*Rawalpindi*)	LFM	176.2	40	603	35	7-80	4	17.22
14	Umar Gul (*Habib Bank*)	RFM	209	32	641	37	5-19	4	17.32
15	Waqas Ahmed (*Lahore Whites*)	RF	274	51	910	52	7-79	5	17.50
16	Tabish Khan (*Pakistan Television*)	RFM	234.2	53	670	37	8-32	3	18.10
17	Mohammad Irfan (*Lahore Whites*)	SLA	330.4	97	856	44	6-99	3	19.45
18	Bilawal Iqbal (*Lahore Blues*)	RFM	288.5	69	843	43	6-38	1	19.60
19	Umaid Asif (*Lahore Whites*)	RFM	280	62	867	44	6-28	3	19.70
20	Taj Wali (*Peshawar*)	LFM	204.4	30	711	34	7-50	3	20.91
21	Abdur Rehman (*Habib Bank*)	SLA	238.2	49	737	35	7-50	1	21.05
22	Asif Afridi (*FATA*)	LFM	251.2	73	641	30	5-64	2	21.36
23	Hamza Nadeem (*Islamabad*)	RFM	232.5	50	713	32	4-35	0	22.28
24	Shehzad Azam (*Islamabad*)	RFM	213.2	26	814	36	6-64	4	22.61
25	Raza Hasan (*National Bank*)	SLA	275.5	61	829	32	8-76	3	25.90

QUAID-E-AZAM TROPHY IN 2017-18

PRELIMINARY GROUPS

Pool A	P	W	L	D	Pts	Pool B	P	W	L	D	Pts
SUI NORTHERN GAS ..	7	6	0	1	51	UNITED BANK	7	6	1	0	57
SUI SOUTHERN GAS ..	7	4	1	2	43	HABIB BANK	7	5	2	0	46
LAHORE BLUES	7	4	3	0	34	KRL................	7	4	2	1	33
WAPDA.............	7	4	2	1	33	LAHORE WHITES.....	7	3	2	2	33
Peshawar	7	3	3	1*	29	Rawalpindi..........	7	3	4	0	24
National Bank	7	1	4	2	12	Karachi Whites	7	2	4	1	18
Islamabad...........	7	1	4	2	12	Pakistan Television ...	7	1	5	1	12
Faisalabad	7	0	6	1*	1	FATA..............	7	1	5	1	9

SUPER EIGHT

Group A	P	W	L	D	Pts	Group B	P	W	L	D	Pts
SUI NORTHERN GAS ..	3	2	0	1	21	WAPDA.............	3	2	1	0	16
Habib Bank...........	3	1	1	1	10	United Bank	3	2	1	0	15
Lahore Blues	3	1	2	0	9	Sui Southern Gas	3	2	1	0	12
Lahore Whites	3	1	2	0	6	KRL................	3	0	3	0	0

FATA = Federally Administered Tribal Areas; KRL = Khan Research Laboratories; WAPDA = Water and Power Development Authority.

*   *Includes one abandoned match.*

Outright win = 6pts; win by an innings = 1pt extra; lead on first innings in a won or drawn game = 3pts; draw after following on = 1pt; no result on first innings = 1pt. Teams tied on points were ranked on most wins, then fewest losses, then net run-rate.

The top four teams from the preliminary groups advanced to the Super Eight groups, but did not carry forward their earlier results. Faisalabad were relegated for 2018-19, with Multan and ZTBL (Zarai Taraqiati Bank Ltd) promoted from the regional and departmental non-first-class competitions; FATA would also have been relegated, but were reprieved when United Bank disbanded their team.

Final At Karachi (National), December 21–25, 2017. **Sui Northern Gas won by 103 runs. Sui Northern Gas 259 and 268** (Iftikhar Ahmed 106); **‡WAPDA 271 and 153** (Samiullah Khan 8-62). *In a low-scoring match, Kamran Akmal (67) steered WAPDA to a 12-run lead on first innings, and they had high hopes of retaining the trophy when they reduced Sui Northern to 21-4 on the third day. But Iftikhar Ahmed and Mohammad Rizwan (91) added 193, and left-arm seamer Samiullah Khan skittled WAPDA second time round, finishing with 11-129 to ensure Sui Northern's third title in four seasons.*

QUAID-E-AZAM TROPHY WINNERS

1953-54	Bahawalpur	1973-74	Railways	1988-89	ADBP
1954-55	Karachi	1974-75	Punjab A	1989-90	PIA
1956-57	Punjab	1975-76	National Bank	1990-91	Karachi Whites
1957-58	Bahawalpur	1976-77	United Bank	1991-92	Karachi Whites
1958-59	Karachi	1977-78	Habib Bank	1992-93	Karachi Whites
1959-60	Karachi	1978-79	National Bank	1993-94	Lahore City
1961-62	Karachi Blues	1979-80	PIA	1994-95	Karachi Blues
1962-63	Karachi A	1980-81	United Bank	1995-96	Karachi Blues
1963-64	Karachi Blues	1981-82	National Bank	1996-97	Lahore City
1964-65	Karachi Blues	1982-83	United Bank	1997-98	Karachi Whites
1966-67	Karachi	1983-84	National Bank	1998-99	Peshawar
1968-69	Lahore	1984-85	United Bank	1999-2000	PIA
1969-70	PIA	1985-86	Karachi	2000-01	Lahore City Blues
1970-71	Karachi Blues	1986-87	National Bank	2001-02	Karachi Whites
1972-73	Railways	1987-88	PIA	2002-03	PIA

2003-04	Faisalabad	2008-09	Sialkot	2013-14	Rawalpindi
2004-05	Peshawar	2009-10	Karachi Blues	2014-15	Sui Northern Gas
2005-06	Sialkot	2010-11	Habib Bank	2015-16	Sui Northern Gas
2006-07	Karachi Urban	2011-12	PIA	2016-17	WAPDA
2007-08	Sui Northern Gas	2012-13	Karachi Blues	2017-18	Sui Northern Gas

The competition has been contested sometimes by regional teams, sometimes by departments, and sometimes by a mixture of the two. Karachi teams have won the Quaid-e-Azam Trophy 20 times, PIA 7, National Bank 5, Lahore teams, Sui Northern Gas and United Bank 4, Bahawalpur, Habib Bank, Peshawar, Punjab, Railways and Sialkot 2, ADBP, Faisalabad, Rawalpindi and WAPDA 1.

DEPARTMENTAL ONE-DAY CUP IN 2017-18

50-over league plus knockout

Semi-finals   United Bank beat Sui Southern Gas by seven wickets; WAPDA beat Pakistan Television by nine wickets.

Final   At Karachi (UBL), January 14, 2018. **United Bank won by six wickets. WAPDA 218** (48.3 overs); ‡**United Bank 220-4** (43 overs). *United Bank completed their ninth straight win in this tournament in what they were later told was their last match. WAPDA, playing their second final in three weeks, subsided to 113-7 before Khalid Usman and Wahab Riaz got them past 200; United won with seven overs to spare, their chase revolving around Sohaib Maqsood's 63.*

REGIONAL ONE-DAY CUP IN 2017-18

50-over league plus knockout

Semi-finals   Karachi Whites beat Peshawar by five wickets; Islamabad beat Rawalpindi by 13 runs.

Final   At Rawalpindi (Cricket), February 11, 2018. **Karachi Whites won by five wickets.** ‡**Islamabad 347-4** (50 overs) (Babar Azam 105); **Karachi Whites 349-5** (49.3 overs) (Fawad Alam 149). *Fawad Alam's career-best 149 from 130 balls took Karachi Whites to the brink of victory; they needed seven when he was caught by fellow centurion Babar Azam at the end of the penultimate over. Anwar Ali sealed victory with a six.*

PAKISTAN CUP IN 2018

50-over league plus final

Final   At Faisalabad (Iqbal), May 6, 2018 (day/night). **Federal Areas won by five wickets. Khyber Pakhtunkhwa 252** (43.4 overs) (Babar Azam 105); ‡**Federal Areas 254-5** (41 overs). *Federal Areas retained their title with nine overs to spare, after left-arm seamer Usman Shinwari restricted Khyber Pakhtunkhwa with three tight spells earning 3-34.*

NATIONAL T20 CUP IN 2017-18

20-over league plus knockout

Semi-finals   Lahore Whites beat Faisalabad by ten runs; Lahore Blues beat FATA by ten runs.

Final   At Rawalpindi (Cricket), November 30, 2017 (floodlit). **Lahore Blues won by seven wickets.** ‡**Lahore Whites 127-5** (20 overs); **Lahore Blues 131-3** (17.3 overs). *In this Lahore derby, Whites were 66-4 by the 11th over, though captain Salman Butt batted through the innings for 62*. But Blues opener Imam-ul-Haq secured the cup with 59*.*

The HBL Pakistan Super League has its own section (page 1141).

SOUTH AFRICAN CRICKET IN 2018

Atmospheric disturbance

COLIN BRYDEN

Faf du Plessis's mission to take South Africa back to the top of the Test rankings made progress during the year, with the exception of a trip to Sri Lanka. Back in August 2016, when he first captained the Test team, they were languishing in seventh place. By January 2019, when du Plessis was suspended for the final Test against Pakistan because of a second over-rate infraction in 12 months, South Africa had won 17 of his 27 matches in charge, and were about to move second, behind India. Catching them may be a step too far for du Plessis, who turns 35 in July, but his leadership has been inspiring.

Recent successes have largely come at home, and on surfaces tailored to an outstanding battery of fast bowlers. Both du Plessis and the coach, Ottis

SOUTH AFRICA IN 2018

	Played	Won	Lost	Drawn/No result
Tests	10	6	4	–
One-day internationals	17	9	8	–
Twenty20 internationals	7	4	3	–

JANUARY } FEBRUARY	3 Tests, 6 ODIs and 3 T20Is (h) v India	(page 966)
MARCH } APRIL	4 Tests (h) v Australia	(page 985)
MAY		
JUNE		
JULY } AUGUST	2 Tests, 5 ODIs and 1 T20I (a) v Sri Lanka	(page 1029)
SEPTEMBER } OCTOBER	3 ODIs and 2 T20Is (h) v Zimbabwe	(page 1005)
NOVEMBER	3 ODIs and 1 T20I (a) v Australia	(page 815)
DECEMBER } JANUARY } FEBRUARY	3 Tests, 5 ODIs and 3 T20Is (h) v Pakistan	(page 1007)

For a review of South African domestic cricket from the 2017-18 season, see page 1018.

Gibson, have unashamedly called for pitches that played to their strengths, and some have done so excessively. The captain's home record has been impressive: 13 wins, two defeats and a draw, when a Test against New Zealand was abandoned because of a waterlogged Kingsmead. And those two defeats, by India and Australia, came in series South Africa won.

The pitches for the India series at the start of 2018, though, were disappointing, with groundsmen struggling to produce surfaces that were friendly to pace and still provided a fair contest. The strip for the Third Test, at Johannesburg, was rated poor by the ICC after the ball deviated unpredictably, even dangerously, off several cracks.

If the pitches for the Australia series were better, the atmosphere between the teams was awful. The ill-feeling started with a clash between David Warner and Quinton de Kock at Durban, and escalated. There were several confrontations in the Second Test, at Port Elizabeth, culminating in Kagiso Rabada being suspended for two matches after bumping shoulders with Steve Smith, the Australian captain. Then, to Smith's undisguised dismay, the verdict was overturned on appeal.

Australian coach Darren Lehmann complained about the "disgusting" behaviour of the crowd towards Warner during the Third Test at Newlands, the day before the sandpaper scandal. With Smith, Warner and Cameron Bancroft banned, a demoralised Australia were thrashed in the Fourth Test, as South Africa triumphed 3–1. They were yet to play Ireland or Afghanistan, but it completed a full set of home-and-away series wins against the other ten Test countries since South Africa returned to international cricket in 1991-92.

Their bowling was insatiable – led by Rabada, with excellent support from Vernon Philander, Morne Morkel and the exciting Lungi Ngidi. The (brief) return of A. B. de Villiers to Test cricket invigorated the batting, while Aiden Markram proved an accomplished opening partner for the gritty Dean Elgar. On the down side, Hashim Amla, who turned 35 in March, had a poor year by his high standards.

There were other clouds. Both de Villiers and Morkel retired from international cricket – de Villiers's return lasted only eight Tests – while the great disappointment of the year was how South Africa capitulated twice in Sri Lanka, prompting du Plessis to acknowledge that his players badly needed to rediscover their fight away from home. They had done it before: between 2006 and 2015, they did not lose a series abroad.

At the turn of 2019, South Africa disposed easily of Pakistan, despite a knee injury ruling out Ngidi. A rejuvenated Dale Steyn became the country's all-time leading wicket-taker, and Duanne Olivier made full use of an opportunity to show off his pace and hostility, taking 24 wickets at 14 in three matches.

At the start of a World Cup year, however, South Africa's one-day form was patchy. They were thrashed 5–1 at home by India, but beat Sri Lanka and Australia away. No longer blessed with a constant supply of all-rounders, they had seemingly settled on a strategy of picking the four best available bowlers, but had yet to identify a No. 7 able to score runs and take wickets.

After the embarrassment of the cancellation of the much-hyped Global T20 League in 2017, Cricket South Africa finally entered the competitive city-based franchise market with the Mzansi Super League. It was a modest success,

Insatiable, but not invulnerable: Lungi Ngidi gave Faf du Plessis another potent weapon, but was injured for the Pakistan series.

and offered a lucrative windfall for local players and a handful of overseas names. But it was shown on free-to-air television, with neither a major sponsor nor a lucrative rights deal. CSA budgeted for a loss of R40m (about £2.2m).

In challenging economic times, only one of the three major domestic competitions attracted sponsorship, while a backer for the home Test season was announced only 13 days before the opening match. The deal was for one season only. Income from television remained the key to financial stability.

Thabang Moroe, 35, was appointed CSA chief executive in July, though he had fulfilled the role in an acting capacity since the departure of Haroon Lorgat in the wake of the Global League fiasco in 2017. He had attended King Edward VII School – the alma mater of Ali Bacher, Graeme Smith, de Kock and others – on a cricket scholarship, after being introduced to the game at his Soweto primary school through Bacher's development programme. He rose rapidly through the administrative ranks, and was elected vice-president of CSA in 2016.

Moroe's self-proclaimed passion for transformation included the elevation of women's cricket, as well as a continuing push for greater black African participation. The national women's team did not build on reaching the semi-finals of the 2017 World Cup, and failed to reach the knockout stages of the World T20 in the West Indies. Black interest in cricket, though, did seem to be growing, both through participation and spectator attendance, notably at big games in Johannesburg.

Initially, Moroe's relationship with the SA Cricketers' Association was frosty. A memorandum of agreement between CSA and the players was signed four months after the deadline, with revenue-sharing apparently the stumbling block.

SOUTH AFRICA v INDIA IN 2017-18

Neil Manthorp

Test matches (3): South Africa 2, India 1
One-day internationals (6): South Africa 1, India 5
Twenty20 internationals (3): South Africa 1, India 2

For the second successive tour of South Africa, India cut short the proposed itinerary. They declined to take part in the traditional Boxing Day Test but, by way of compensation, stretched the one-day series to six games. The changes were forced not by BCCI animosity – in 2013-14, their issues with Cricket South Africa's then chief executive Haroon Lorgat had threatened the entire trip – but by a home series against Sri Lanka that ran until Christmas Eve.

India headed straight to Cape Town, forgoing a warm-up in favour of a week's training at the Western Province club, one of the best equipped in the city. "We have prepared the pitches we want and have been able to practise like we want," said an upbeat Virat Kohli, India's captain. "It's much better than playing a two- or three-day game where the batsmen score 30 or 40 and give someone else a chance."

Faf du Plessis, his opposite number, had unashamedly called for seamer-friendly pitches with pace and bounce. And when Newlands delivered to such an extent that neither team could exert much control, Kohli had the grace to say he had no problem with the surface: "It was what we expected, and it was an exciting match."

The Second Test should have been India's for the taking. An inexperienced groundsman at Centurion had struggled with extreme heat the week before, and the pitch was dry, quickly turning dusty. Yet Kohli's brilliant 153 – the only century of the series on either side – was not quite enough to keep India in contention. For South Africa, Lungi Ngidi – a tall 21-year-old of genuine pace making his Test debut – took six for 39 in the second innings, including Kohli for five.

The drama and courage of India's consolation win at the Wanderers swept them into the one-day series, which they dominated. Kohli's leadership was

MOST RUNS IN A BILATERAL ONE-DAY SERIES

			M	I	HS	100	Avge	SR	
558	**V. Kohli**	**I v SA†**	**6**	**6**	**160***	**3**	**186.00**	**99.46**	**2017-18**
515	Fakhar Zaman	P v Z†	5	5	210*	2	257.50	111.47	2018
491	R. G. Sharma	I v A	6	6	209	2	122.75	108.62	2013-14
478	G. J. Bailey	A v I†	6	6	156	1	95.60	116.01	2013-14
467	H. Masakadza	Z v Ken	5	5	178*	2	116.75	97.29	2009-10
455	C. H. Gayle	WI v I†	7	7	140	3	65.00	94.98	2002-03
454	K. P. Pietersen	E v SA†	7	6	116	3	151.33	105.58	2004-05
454	K. C. Sangakkara	SL v E	7	7	112	1	75.66	82.69	2014-15
453	**V. Kohli**	**I v WI**	**5**	**5**	**157***	**3**	**151.00**	**112.96**	**2018-19**
451	Salman Butt	P v B	5	5	136	2	90.20	97.19	2007-08

† *Away.*

Only connect: Virat Kohli cracks another boundary during his unbeaten 160 in the third ODI.

almost as irrepressible as his breathtaking batting: his 558 runs at a shade under one a ball were unprecedented for a bilateral series. By its end, he had scored 19 hundreds in successful chases, another runaway record.

The other startling feature of the one-day series was the influence of wrist-spin. Kuldeep Yadav (17 wickets at 13) and Yuzvendra Chahal (16 at 16) helped themselves – and at times it really looked like that – to 33 of the 51 taken by Indian bowlers. South Africa were hampered by finger injuries: du Plessis played only the first game, while A. B. de Villiers missed the first three, giving the middle order an inexperienced look. But the spinners – Kuldeep left-arm and Chahal right, often bowling in tandem – were mesmerising.

India's success in the limited-overs legs – they prevailed in the Twenty20s too – prompted many to question the wisdom of arriving just a week before the Tests. With hindsight, Kohli and coach Ravi Shastri admitted that acclimatisation had come too late to achieve the goal of winning a first Test series in South Africa, which Shastri had said would have helped "define this Indian team as the best ever".

THE HUNDRED GAMES

Most centuries in successful ODI chases:

100		I	Avge	100		I	Avge
20	**V. Kohli (I)**	**79**	**98.93**	8	A. C. Gilchrist (A)	90	46.87
14	S. R. Tendulkar (I)	124	55.45	8	R. T. Ponting (A)	104	57.34
9	Saeed Anwar (P)	59	63.04	7	**S. Dhawan (I)**	**45**	**53.30**
9	T. M. Dilshan (SL)	60	62.23	7	M. E. Waugh (A)	61	51.37
9	S. T. Jayasuriya (SL)	103	39.92	7	S. P. Fleming (NZ)	62	60.50
8	**C. H. Gayle (WI)**	**62**	**57.50**	7	B. C. Lara (WI)	78	68.58
8	**R. G. Sharma (I)**	**74**	**63.20**	7	H. H. Gibbs (SA)	80	40.64

On countless occasions Kohli's desire and determination manifested themselves in displays of petulance, most obviously in the Second Test, when he railed against the umpires for halting play in persistent light rain. Some thought his celebrations at the fall of a wicket provocative; others considered them merely exuberant. At all times, however, he either was – or appeared to be – at the centre of the action.

That South Africa felt the need to prepare pitches that so favoured their strengths was a reflection both of the extreme conditions they had encountered in India two years earlier, and of the threat they felt from an unusually inflated Test squad of 17, which covered every position with more skill and depth than any other. Had they been better prepared for the First Test, Shastri might have got his wish.

INDIA TOURING PARTY

*V. Kohli (T/50/20), R. Ashwin (T), Bhuvneshwar Kumar (T/50/20), J. J. Bumrah (T/50/20), Y. S. Chahal (50/20), S. Dhawan (T/50/20), M. S. Dhoni (50/20), S. S. Iyer (50), R. A. Jadeja (T), K. M. Jadhav (50), K. D. Karthik (T/50/20), Mohammed Shami (T/50), M. K. Pandey (50/20), H. H. Pandya (T/50/20), A. R. Patel (50/20), P. A. Patel (T), A. M. Rahane (T/50), K. L. Rahul (T/20), S. K. Raina (20), W. P. Saha (T), I. Sharma (T), R. G. Sharma (T/50/20), S. N. Thakur (50/20), J. D. Unadkat (20), M. Vijay (T), K. Yadav (50/20), U. T. Yadav (T). *Coach:* R. J. Shastri.

Saha injured a hamstring in training and was replaced in the Test squad by Karthik.

TEST MATCH AVERAGES

SOUTH AFRICA – BATTING AND FIELDING

	T	I	NO	R	HS	100	50	Avge	Ct
†D. Elgar	3	6	1	207	86*	0	2	41.40	2
A. B. de Villiers	3	6	0	211	80	0	2	35.16	6
H. M. Amla	3	6	0	203	82	0	3	33.83	1
F. du Plessis	3	6	0	183	63	0	2	30.50	7
A. K. Markram	3	6	0	140	94	0	1	23.33	2
K. A. Maharaj	2	4	0	74	35	0	0	18.50	1
V. D. Philander	3	6	0	94	35	0	0	15.66	1
†K. Rabada	3	6	0	76	30	0	0	12.66	3
†Q. de Kock	3	6	0	71	43	0	0	11.83	17
†M. Morkel	3	6	2	29	10*	0	0	7.25	3
L. T. Ngidi	2	4	1	6	4	0	0	2.00	0

Played in one Test: †A. L. Phehlukwayo 9, 0 (1 ct); D. W. Steyn 16*, 0* (1 ct).

BOWLING

	Style	O	M	R	W	BB	5I	Avge
V. D. Philander	RFM	96.2	33	238	15	6-42	1	15.86
L. T. Ngidi	RFM	53.2	14	155	9	6-39	1	17.22
M. Morkel	RF	98.1	26	260	13	4-60	0	20.00
K. Rabada	RF	104.2	21	304	15	3-34	0	20.26

Also bowled: K. A. Maharaj (SLA) 36–3–125–1; A. L. Phehlukwayo (RFM) 10–1–40–2; D. W. Steyn (RFM) 17.3–6–51–2.

INDIA – BATTING AND FIELDING

	T	I	NO	R	HS	100	50	Avge	Ct
V. Kohli	3	6	0	286	153	1	1	47.66	3
Bhuvneshwar Kumar	2	4	1	101	33	0	0	33.66	2
R. Ashwin	2	4	0	90	38	0	0	22.50	0
H. H. Pandya	3	6	0	119	93	0	1	19.83	3
R. G. Sharma	2	4	0	78	47	0	0	19.50	1
M. Vijay	3	6	0	102	46	0	0	17.00	4
C. A. Pujara	3	6	0	100	50	0	1	16.66	1
Mohammed Shami	3	6	1	72	28	0	0	14.40	0
†P. A. Patel	2	4	0	56	19	0	0	14.00	10
K. L. Rahul	2	4	0	30	16	0	0	7.50	1
I. Sharma	2	4	2	14	7*	0	0	7.00	0
J. J. Bumrah	3	6	2	4	2	0	0	1.00	2

Played in one Test: †S. Dhawan 16, 16; A. M. Rahane 9, 48 (2 ct); W. P. Saha 0, 8 (10 ct).

BOWLING

	Style	O	M	R	W	BB	5I	Avge
Mohammed Shami	RFM	83.3	16	256	15	5-28	1	17.06
I. Sharma	RFM	69	12	150	8	3-46	0	18.75
Bhuvneshwar Kumar	RFM	67	22	203	10	4-87	0	20.30
J. J. Bumrah	RFM	112.1	16	353	14	5-54	1	25.21
R. Ashwin	OB	76.3	17	215	7	4-113	0	30.71
H. H. Pandya	RFM	51	7	162	3	2-27	0	54.00

SOUTH AFRICA v INDIA

First Test

At Cape Town, January 5–8, 2018. South Africa won by 72 runs. Toss: South Africa. Test debut: J. J. Bumrah.

For three pulsating days, this Test hummed along at such a rollicking pace it seemed impossible for either team to keep up – as if the winners would be the side who simply kept the car on the road. The non-stop action left spectators breathless, and the players emotionally and physically spent – despite the third day being washed out.

South Africa picked five bowlers, yet chose to bat on an obviously seam-friendly pitch. Within 22 minutes, Bhuvneshwar Kumar had reduced them to 12 for three. But de Villiers, playing his first serious Test match for two years following his self-imposed unavailability (and the five-session demolition of Zimbabwe a week earlier), raced to a 55-ball half-century with ten boundaries. Four came in a single over from Bhuvneshwar.

The South Africans went on to 286, thanks to consistent scoring down the order, and India knew they had missed their opportunity. At the end of a gripping first day, they closed on 28 for three, with Dhawan having fallen to Steyn, whose emotional return after a year out with a shoulder injury had been as keenly anticipated as de Villiers's. Not long after lunch on the second day India were battered, bruised and, at 92 for seven, apparently already beaten.

Later, though, Steyn limped out of the attack. He had bowled with speed and accuracy, but in his 18th over landed awkwardly in a footmark and bruised his heel. It was worse than first thought, and he arrived at the ground next day with his foot in a moonboot, and a prognosis of at least four weeks on the sidelines.

On the second afternoon, Pandya flipped the game upside down with a thrilling combination of authentic drives and comical hooks and pulls, which – though he had little to lose – still required courage. Bhuvneshwar proved a vital ally, defending stoutly before getting off the mark from his 34th ball. He contributed a stubborn 25 to an eighth-wicket stand of 99. Compared with what might have been, India's deficit of 77 felt almost like a victory. Openers Elgar and Markram put on 52, before late blows from Pandya removed both. At the end of another hectic day, South Africa were two down and 142 ahead.

The third day was lost to rain – badly needed in the drought-stricken Western Cape. Speculation about a declaration seemed logical on the fourth, until the covers were removed to reveal a pitch that had resumed its first-day appearance. It took India's seamers barely 20 overs to claim eight at a cost of just 65. Their target was 208, and would have been fewer but for de Villiers's breezy 35. He was briefly joined by a hobbling Steyn – batting against medical advice – before holing out to deep midwicket. Kohli sprinted off with arms raised and fists clenched as if in premature triumph. To be fair, others also believed India were on the verge of a victory that would have ranked among their greatest. Some, though, pointed at the trajectory described by the first three innings: 286, 209 and 130.

An opening stand of 30, in which Vijay was twice reprieved on review, suggested it could yet be India's moment of history – only for all ten to cascade for 105. Morkel claimed two of the first three, and Rabada the sixth and seventh, including Pandya, who

---

MOST DISMISSALS IN A TEST FOR INDIA

11 (11 ct)	**R. R. Pant**	v Australia at Adelaide	**2018-19**
10 (10 ct)	**W. P. Saha**	v South Africa at Cape Town	**2017-18**
9 (8 ct, 1 st)	M. S. Dhoni	v Australia at Melbourne	2014-15
8 (8 ct)	N. R. Mongia	v South Africa at Durban	1996-97
8 (8 ct)	N. R. Mongia	v Pakistan at Kolkata	1998-99
8 (7 ct, 1st)	M. S. Dhoni	v Australia at Perth	2007-08
8 (6 ct, 2 st)	M. S. Dhoni	v Bangladesh at Mirpur	2009-10
8 (6 ct, 2 st)	M. S. Dhoni	v West Indies at Mumbai	2011-12

---

was far less bold with the match on the line. In the absence of Steyn, the rest belonged to Philander, who owns his beloved Newlands turf when it offers so much. The apex of his career-best six for 42 (which he bettered nearly three months later) was the wicket of Kohli: with the game in the balance at 71 for three, he departed for 28.

Philander had teased him with three overs of awayswingers which he had left, responsibly and maturely. He knew the nip-backer was inevitable, but was powerless to prevent it thudding into his pad, and the review was more in desperation than hope. When the verdict was confirmed, his head slumped, and he left to several words of farewell from the fielders.

The moisture in the pitch had been tempered by the afternoon sun, and conditions might have eased had Kohli not asked for the heavy roller. It was a fatal error. Visiting captains have often sought advice from groundsmen at South Africa's capricious coastal venues, but he did not. His request prompted a quiet intake of breath. The dampness was squeezed back into the surface, and Philander did what he does best. He took the last three wickets in four balls.

India's selection, whether bizarre, courageous or both, did not pay off. Vice-captain Ajinkya Rahane, whose overseas Test average was 53, had made way for seamer Jasprit Bumrah, making his Test debut despite not having played a first-class game for a year. Credit to Kohli in one respect, however: he described the Newlands pitch as excellent for Test cricket.

Man of the Match: V. D. Philander.

Close of play: first day, India 28-3 (Pujara 5, Sharma 0); second day, South Africa 65-2 (Rabada 2, Amla 4); third day, no play.

South Africa

D. Elgar c Saha b Bhuvneshwar Kumar	0	– (2) c Saha b Pandya	25
A. K. Markram lbw b Bhuvneshwar Kumar	5	– (1) c Bhuvneshwar Kumar b Pandya	34
H. M. Amla c Saha b Bhuvneshwar Kumar	3	– (4) c Sharma b Mohammed Shami	4
A. B. de Villiers b Bumrah	65	– (5) c Bhuvneshwar Kumar b Bumrah	35
*F. du Plessis c Saha b Pandya	62	– (6) c Saha b Bumrah	0
†Q. de Kock c Saha b Bhuvneshwar Kumar	43	– (7) c Saha b Bumrah	8
V. D. Philander b Mohammed Shami	23	– (8) lbw b Mohammed Shami	0
K. A. Maharaj run out (Ashwin)	35	– (9) c Saha b Bhuvneshwar Kumar	15
K. Rabada c Saha b Ashwin	26	– (3) c Kohli b Mohammed Shami	5
D. W. Steyn not out	16	– (11) not out	0
M. Morkel lbw b Ashwin	2	– (10) c Saha b Bhuvneshwar Kumar	2
B 2, lb 3, nb 1	6	W 2	2

1/0 (1) 2/7 (2) 3/12 (3)   (73.1 overs)   286   1/52 (1) 2/59 (2)   (41.2 overs)   130
4/126 (4) 5/142 (5) 6/202 (6)   3/66 (4) 4/73 (3)
7/221 (7) 8/258 (8) 9/280 (9) 10/286 (11)   5/82 (6) 6/92 (7) 7/95 (8)
                                                   8/122 (9) 9/130 (10) 10/130 (5)

Bhuvneshwar Kumar 19–4–87–4; Mohammed Shami 16–6–47–1; Bumrah 19–1–73–1; Pandya 12–1–53–1; Ashwin 7.1–1–21–2. *Second innings*—Bhuvneshwar Kumar 11–5–33–2; Bumrah 11.2–1–39–3; Mohammed Shami 12–3–28–3; Pandya 6–0–27–2; Ashwin 1–0–3–0.

India

M. Vijay c Elgar b Philander	1	– c de Villiers b Philander	13
S. Dhawan c and b Steyn	16	– c sub (C. H. Morris) b Morkel	16
C. A. Pujara c du Plessis b Philander	26	– c de Kock b Morkel	4
*V. Kohli c de Kock b Morkel	5	– lbw b Philander	28
R. G. Sharma lbw b Rabada	11	– b Philander	10
R. Ashwin c de Kock b Philander	12	– (8) c de Kock b Philander	37
H. H. Pandya c de Kock b Rabada	93	– c de Villiers b Rabada	1
†W. P. Saha lbw b Steyn	0	– (6) lbw b Rabada	8
Bhuvneshwar Kumar c de Kock b Morkel	25	– not out	13
Mohammed Shami not out	4	– c du Plessis b Philander	4
J. J. Bumrah c Elgar b Rabada	2	– c du Plessis b Philander	0
B 1, lb 13	14	Lb 1	1

1/16 (1) 2/18 (2) 3/27 (4)   (73.4 overs)   209   1/30 (2) 2/30 (1)   (42.4 overs)   135
4/57 (5) 5/76 (3) 6/81 (6)   3/39 (3) 4/71 (4)
7/92 (8) 8/191 (9) 9/199 (7) 10/209 (11)   5/76 (5) 6/77 (7) 7/82 (6)
                                                   8/131 (8) 9/135 (10) 10/135 (11)

Philander 14.3–8–33–3; Steyn 17.3–6–51–2; Morkel 19–6–57–2; Rabada 16.4–4–34–3; Maharaj 6–0–20–0. *Second innings*—Philander 15.4–4–42–6; Morkel 11–1–39–2; Rabada 12–2–41–2; Maharaj 4–1–12–0.

Umpires: M. A. Gough and R. A. Kettleborough.   Third umpire: P. R. Reiffel.
Referee: B. C. Broad.

SOUTH AFRICA v INDIA

Second Test

At Centurion, January 13–17, 2018. South Africa won by 135 runs. Toss: South Africa. Test debut: L. T. Ngidi.

Kohli's self-belief, his determination to keep India in the series, and his mastery of the art of batting produced an innings of immense skill and raw intensity. An astonishing 153 from 217 balls belied another awkward pitch, whose dry and cracked appearance was more subcontinental than sub-Saharan. And it deserved better. The problem was, none of his team-mates made a half-century.

He might have brought victory had India not conceded 335 after du Plessis chose to bat. The seamers, unable to adapt to a surface that had roasted for a week under a fierce sun, were guilty of wayward and ill-considered bowling, while Ashwin, the sole spinner, strove too hard for wickets when patience was required. South Africa went two up with one to play.

Markram enjoyed the best of the conditions on day one, and punished the pace attack for bowling too full or too short with a range of drives and cuts. Eventually he feathered an Ashwin delivery on 94. Amla was just as ruthless on the loose deliveries, and it took a brilliant swivel-and-shy airborne run-out from the bowler, Pandya, to dismiss him at the non-striker's end, stretching for what he believed was an easy single.

Alarmed by the rate of the pitch's deterioration, du Plessis took as much satisfaction from the length of time he batted (more than three and a half hours) as the runs he scored. He was ninth out for 63, missing a reversing inswinger, but convinced the eventual total was "at least 100 runs better than it looks". Maharaj bowled the only over before lunch, the first time a South African spinner had opened in a first innings of a Test since Aubrey Faulkner against Australia at Old Trafford, in the 1912 triangular tournament. And du

---

BEST BOWLING ON TEST DEBUT FOR SOUTH AFRICA

8-64	L. Klusener	v India at Calcutta	1996-97
7-29	K. J. Abbott	v Pakistan at Centurion	2012-13
7-63	A. E. Hall	v England at Cape Town	1922-23
7-81	M. de Lange	v Sri Lanka at Durban	2011-12
7-95	W. H. Ashley	v England at Cape Town	1888-89
6-38	P. M. Pollock	v New Zealand at Durban	1961-62
6-39	**L. T. Ngidi**	**v India at Centurion**	**2017-18**
6-43	C. N. McCarthy	v England at Durban	1948-49
6-99	A. J. Bell	v England at Lord's	1929
6-128	S. F. Burke	v New Zealand at Cape Town	1961-62
6-152	G. M. Parker	v England at Birmingham	1924

Hall and Burke took 11 in the match; no one else managed ten.

Plessis's view was corroborated as India struggled to 164 for five not long before stumps on the second day. One of those five was the first-ball dismissal of Pujara, run out by a direct hit from mid-on by the debutant fast bowler, Lungi Ngidi.

Next morning, the rebuild was progressing steadily until a sauntering Pandya, sent back by Kohli, became the game's fourth run-out victim. A speculative throw from Philander at mid-on hit the stumps and, although Pandya was comfortably over the line, he had grounded neither bat nor boot. The carelessness of the dismissal added to Kohli's rage, which he focused on South Africa's bowlers.

A more reliable partner arrived in Ashwin, and they whittled the deficit to 55 before being separated. Du Plessis aimed to frustrate Kohli, placing up to eight men on the boundary when he was on strike. Sometimes the wise man backs away from the challenge rather than accept it. Fire burned in Kohli, and du Plessis knew a handful of boundaries could make the difference.

India kept the arrears to 28, before Bumrah trapped Markram and Amla, South Africa's first-innings top-scorers, for singles. A bloody-minded Elgar entrenched himself, and de Villiers all but won the game with an innings of 80 that seemed to be crafted on an entirely different surface – despite the frontline seamers hitting a consistent and more appropriate length. (On the third evening, Kohli was enraged by the umpires allowing play in light rain; after complaining to Michael Gough, he aggressively threw the ball into the ground, costing him 25% of his match fee and a demerit point.)

India had more than four sessions to score 287 – no team had made as many to win a Test at Centurion – but they did not begin well. The most telling blow was struck by Ngidi, whose nip-backer from wide of the crease crashed into Kohli's knee. He optimistically reviewed, but the ball was knocking over middle, and India limped to 35 for three by the end of the fourth day. Next morning, Pujara became the first player to be run out twice in a Test for India, after de Villiers tore from slip to third man and hurled in a precision throw as the batsmen aimed for a third. From 49 for four, India staggered to 87 for seven, a home win now inevitable. Sharma briefly offered some pleasing resistance before Ngidi hastened the conclusion. Strong and powerful, he ripped into the lower order with remarkable control for a 21-year-old. On a last-day pitch he was a terror, his pace so fiery that his victims seemed as relieved as they were disappointed.

Man of the Match: L. T. Ngidi.

Close of play: first day, South Africa 269-6 (du Plessis 24, Maharaj 10); second day, India 183-5 (Kohli 85, Pandya 11); third day, South Africa 90-2 (Elgar 36, de Villiers 50); fourth day, India 35-3 (Pujara 11, Patel 5).

South Africa

D. Elgar c Vijay b Ashwin	31	– (2) c Rahul b Mohammed Shami 61
A. K. Markram c Patel b Ashwin	94	– (1) lbw b Bumrah................... 1
H. M. Amla run out (Pandya)	82	– lbw b Bumrah..................... 1
A. B. de Villiers b I. Sharma	20	– c Patel b Mohammed Shami 80
*F. du Plessis b I. Sharma	63	– c and b Bumrah................... 48
†Q. de Kock c Kohli b Ashwin	0	– c Patel b Mohammed Shami 12
V. D. Philander run out (Patel/Pandya)	0	– c Vijay b I. Sharma.............. 26
K. A. Maharaj c Patel b Mohammed Shami	18	– c Patel b I. Sharma.............. 6
K. Rabada c Pandya b I. Sharma	11	– c Kohli b Mohammed Shami 4
M. Morkel c Vijay b Ashwin	6	– not out......................... 10
L. T. Ngidi not out	1	– c Vijay b Ashwin................ 1
Lb 8, nb 1	9	B 2, lb 5, w 1................. 8

1/85 (1) 2/148 (2) 3/199 (4)   (113.5 overs) 335   1/1 (1) 2/3 (3)   (91.3 overs) 258
4/246 (3) 5/250 (6) 6/251 (7)   3/144 (4) 4/151 (2)
7/282 (8) 8/324 (9) 9/333 (10) 10/335 (10)   5/163 (6) 6/209 (7)
                                           7/215 (8) 8/245 (9)
                                           9/245 (5) 10/258 (11)

Bumrah 22–6–60–0; Mohammed Shami 15–2–58–1; I. Sharma 22–4–46–3; Pandya 16–4–50–0; Ashwin 38.5–10–113–4. *Second innings*—Ashwin 29.3–6–78–1; Bumrah 20–3–70–3; I. Sharma 17–3–40–2; Mohammed Shami 16–3–49–4; Pandya 9–1–14–0.

India

M. Vijay c de Kock b Maharaj	46	– b Rabada........................ 9
K. L. Rahul c and b Morkel	10	– c Maharaj b Rabada.............. 4
C. A. Pujara run out (Ngidi)	0	– run out (Ngidi/de Villiers/de Kock).. 19
*V. Kohli c de Villiers b Morkel	153	– lbw b Morkel.................... 5
R. G. Sharma lbw b Rabada	10	– (6) c de Villiers b Rabada....... 47
†P. A. Patel c de Kock b Ngidi	19	– (5) c Morkel b Rabada........... 19
H. H. Pandya run out (Philander)	15	– c de Kock b Ngidi............... 6
R. Ashwin c du Plessis b Philander	38	– c de Kock b Ngidi............... 3
Mohammed Shami c Amla b Morkel	1	– c Morkel b Ngidi................ 28
I. Sharma c Markram b Morkel	3	– not out......................... 4
J. J. Bumrah not out	0	– c Philander b Ngidi............. 2
B 8, lb 1, w 2, nb 1	12	B 4, w 1...................... 5

1/28 (2) 2/28 (3) 3/107 (1)   (92.1 overs) 307   1/11 (1) 2/16 (2)   (50.2 overs) 151
4/132 (5) 5/164 (6) 6/209 (7)   3/26 (4) 4/49 (3)
7/280 (8) 8/281 (9) 9/306 (10) 10/307 (4)   5/65 (5) 6/83 (7)
                                           7/87 (8) 8/141 (6)
                                           9/145 (9) 10/151 (11)

Maharaj 20–1–67–1; Morkel 22.1–5–60–4; Philander 16–3–46–1; Rabada 20–1–74–1; Ngidi 14–2–51–1. *Second innings*—Philander 10–3–25–0; Rabada 14–3–47–3; Ngidi 12.2–3–39–6; Morkel 8–3–10–0; Maharaj 6–1–26–0.

Umpires: M. A. Gough and P. R. Reiffel.   Third umpire: R. A. Kettleborough.
Referee: B. C. Broad.

SOUTH AFRICA v INDIA

Third Test

At Johannesburg, January 24–27, 2018. India won by 63 runs. Toss: India.

India were almost denied the opportunity to complete one of their finest Test victories when the match came close to being abandoned because of an unsafe pitch. But after ending play 19 minutes early on the third evening, the officials gave it one last chance next day, and India completed a gripping and hard-fought consolation win.

As South Africa chased an unlikely target of 241, Elgar and Amla began to inch their way up the mountain, scoring at barely two an over and collecting nearly as many bruises as runs. They took the score to 124 for one but, once Amla was caught by a diving Pandya at square leg, the floodgates opened, and the last nine wickets clattered for 53; Mohammed Shami claimed five yet, such was the unpredictability of the surface, anybody could have benefited.

The pitch had been prepared by Bethuel Buthelezi and Chris Scott, who between them had more than 70 years' experience. But even they were at a loss to follow du Plessis's apparent request for "pace and bounce with seam movement, but no spin". He later claimed he had asked for nothing more than a typical South African wicket. Maharaj and Ashwin were omitted, and not an over of spin was bowled.

LONGEST TIME SPENT ON NOUGHT IN TESTS

Mins

103	S. C. J. Broad	England v New Zealand at Auckland	2012-13
101	G. I. Allott	New Zealand v South Africa at Auckland	1998-99
97	T. G. Evans	England v Australia at Adelaide	1946-47
84	R. K. Chauhan	India v Sri Lanka at Ahmedabad	1993-94
82	P. I. Pocock	England v West Indies at Georgetown	1967-68
81	J. M. Anderson	England v Sri Lanka at Leeds	2014
79	**C. A. Pujara . . . . .**	**India v South Africa at Johannesburg**	**2017-18**
74	J. T. Murray	England v Australia at Sydney	1962-63
72	C. G. Rackemann . .	Australia v England at Sydney	1990-91
72	P. M. Such	England v New Zealand at Manchester	1999
72	Manjural Islam	Bangladesh v Sri Lanka at Colombo (SSC)	2002

Kohli's decision to bat seemed crazy – the skies were thunderously grey – but it was spectacularly vindicated. The openers departed quickly, before the captain joined Pujara, who despite a poor series looked up for a fight. The score had crept to 27 for two when Philander dropped Kohli on 11, a moment that perhaps cost South Africa a clean sweep: he went on to top score with 54. Pujara's innings was extraordinary for its patience. He required 54 balls to get off the mark: for India, only Rajesh Chauhan, who took 57 against Sri Lanka in 1993-94, had spent longer on nought. And although he eventually collected eight fours, Pujara's 50 comprised 179 deliveries of unshakeable concentration.

Both will have scored far easier and less valuable hundreds than the half-centuries they chiselled out here, yet a total of 187 seemed at least 50 short. By the close, South Africa had lost Markram. Next morning, Bumrah and Bhuvneshwar Kumar took regular wickets once the skilful resistance of nightwatchman Rabada had been broken. Amla, though, was in a class of his own, adopting a new trigger movement that took him outside off stump, so lessening the chance of an outside edge. The two innings had the same shape – single figures from all bar Nos 3, 4 and 8 – though South Africa secured a gossamer lead.

Runs became even harder to acquire, and survival was always likely to be short-lived, so Kohli and Rahane chanced their arm, each accruing half a dozen boundaries in precious forties. Equally impressive was Bhuvneshwar, who struck twin thirties in the classic style of many a No. 8: block the straight balls and swing at the others with a healthy disregard for aesthetics. Shami swung at pretty much everything, and the brace of sixes in his rapid 27 had the feeling of nails in the South African coffin.

So did the delivery from Shami that crashed into Elgar's grille on the third evening, bringing the umpires, Ian Gould and Aleem Dar, together for a third time to discuss the pitch. While balls had been bouncing erratically and dangerously from a good length for much of the day, this was a perfect bouncer with a normal trajectory: in light that was beginning to fade, Elgar simply didn't see it. But by then everyone had grown jittery about the possibility of a serious injury, and match referee Andy Pycroft joined the debate in the middle. Ceding to safety concerns, the officials agreed to adjourn for the day, and consult about the next move. South Africa were 17 for one needing a further 224.

When play did resume on the fourth morning, the pitch was on its final warning and, although fingers and ribs remained at risk, nothing threatened neck or head. Amla and Elgar accepted the pain, and clawed their way to a point where the improbable seemed distinctly possible – only for the collapse to ensue. Amid it all, Elgar remained unbowed and unbeaten, the second time he had carried his bat. His was an innings of rare, memorable courage, symbolic of an approach that places team considerations above individual achievement – and well above personal pain.

The Wanderers pitch was rated poor by the umpires and given three demerit points by the ICC. Du Plessis said he would not be interfering again in the future.

Man of the Match: Bhuvneshwar Kumar.   *Man of the Series:* V. D. Philander.

Close of play: first day, South Africa 6-1 (Elgar 4, Rabada 0); second day, India 49-1 (Vijay 13, Rahul 16); third day, South Africa 17-1 (Elgar 11, Amla 2).

India

M. Vijay c de Kock b Rabada	8	– b Rabada	25
K. L. Rahul c de Kock b Philander	0	– (3) c du Plessis b Philander	16
C. A. Pujara c de Kock b Phehlukwayo	50	– (4) c du Plessis b Morkel	1
*V. Kohli c de Villiers b Ngidi	54	– (5) b Rabada	41
A. M. Rahane lbw b Morkel	9	– (6) c de Kock b Morkel	48
†P. A. Patel c de Kock b Morkel	2	– (2) c Markram b Philander	16
H. H. Pandya c de Kock b Phehlukwayo	0	– c and b Rabada	4
Bhuvneshwar Kumar c Phehlukwayo b Rabada	30	– c de Kock b Morkel	33
Mohammed Shami c Rabada b Philander	8	– c de Villiers b Ngidi	27
I. Sharma c du Plessis b Rabada	0	– not out	7
J. J. Bumrah not out	0	– c Rabada b Philander	0
B 11, lb 7, w 6, nb 2	26	B 5, lb 12, w 12	29

1/7 (2) 2/13 (1) 3/97 (4)   (76.4 overs) 187   1/17 (1) 2/51 (3)   (80.1 overs) 247
4/113 (5) 5/144 (3) 6/144 (6)   3/57 (4) 4/100 (1)
7/144 (8) 8/163 (9) 9/166 (10) 10/187 (8)   5/134 (5) 6/148 (7) 7/203 (6)
                                            8/238 (9) 9/240 (8) 10/247 (11)

Morkel 17–5–47–2; Philander 19–10–31–2; Rabada 18.4–6–39–3; Ngidi 15–7–27–1; Phehlukwayo 7–1–25–2. *Second innings*—Philander 21.1–5–61–3; Rabada 23–5–69–3; Morkel 21–6–47–3; Ngidi 12–2–38–1; Phehlukwayo 3–0–15–0.

South Africa

D. Elgar c Patel b Bhuvneshwar Kumar	4	– (2) not out	86
A. K. Markram c Patel b Bhuvneshwar Kumar	2	– (1) c Patel b Mohammed Shami	4
K. Rabada c Rahane b Sharma	30	– (9) c Pujara b Bhuvneshwar Kumar	0
H. M. Amla c Pandya b Bumrah	61	– (3) c Pandya b Sharma	52
A. B. de Villiers b Bhuvneshwar Kumar	5	– (4) c Rahane b Bumrah	6
*F. du Plessis b Bumrah	8	– (5) b Sharma	2
†Q. de Kock c Patel b Bumrah	8	– (6) lbw b Bumrah	0
V. D. Philander c Bumrah b Mohammed Shami	35	– (7) b Mohammed Shami	10
A. L. Phehlukwayo lbw b Bumrah	9	– (8) b Mohammed Shami	0
M. Morkel not out	9	– b Mohammed Shami	0
L. T. Ngidi c Patel b Bumrah	0	– c †sub (K. D. Karthik) b Mohammed Shami	4
Lb 14, w 9	23	B 7, w 6	13

1/3 (2) 2/16 (1) 3/80 (3)   (65.5 overs) 194 1/5 (1) 2/124 (3)   (73.3 overs) 177
4/92 (5) 5/107 (6) 6/125 (7)   3/131 (4) 4/144 (5)
7/169 (4) 8/175 (8) 9/194 (9) 10/194 (11)   5/145 (6) 6/157 (7) 7/157 (8)
                     8/160 (9) 9/161 (10) 10/177 (11)

Bhuvneshwar Kumar 19–9–44–3; Bumrah 18.5–2–54–5; Sharma 14–2–33–1; Mohammed Shami 12–0–46–1; Pandya 2–0–3–0. *Second innings*—Bhuvneshwar Kumar 18–4–39–1; Mohammed Shami 12.3–2–28–5; Bumrah 21–3–57–2; Sharma 16–3–31–2; Pandya 6–1–15–0.

Umpires: Aleem Dar and I. J. Gould. Third umpire: M. A. Gough.
Referee: A. J. Pycroft.

SOUTH AFRICA v INDIA

First One-Day International

At Durban, February 1, 2018 (day/night). India won by six wickets. Toss: South Africa.

Kohli's extraordinary record in successful run-chases shone even more brightly after one of his most ruthless batting performances yet. He was so clinical, and scored so easily, that in the second half of his innings he ostentatiously admonished himself after each rare dot ball. Even so, Rahane matched him shot for shot in a stand of 189, a third-wicket record in this fixture, and looked particularly comfortable against the fast bowlers, making his omission from two of the three Tests the more curious. South Africa had earlier been heavily dependent on their own captain. In an otherwise modest batting performance, du Plessis stood out: his ninth one-day international hundred was of the highest quality, though he admitted a total of 269 was 50 or 60 short of competitive. In large part that was down to South Africa's historical weakness against wrist-spin. Between them, the right–left pair of Chahal and Yadav claimed five for 79, despite the pitch offering little turn or bounce. The news that du Plessis would miss the rest of the series after breaking a finger trying to catch Kohli – a similar injury sustained in identical circumstances during the Third Test had already sidelined de Villiers – did not improve the mood in the home camp.

Man of the Match: V. Kohli.

South Africa

†Q. de Kock lbw b Chahal	34	K. Rabada run out (Dhoni/Bhuvneshwar Kumar) . 1
H. M. Amla lbw b Bumrah	16	M. Morkel not out . 0
*F. du Plessis c Pandya b Bhuvneshwar Kumar	120	Lb 3, w 2, nb 1 . 6
A. K. Markram c Pandya b Chahal	9	
J-P. Duminy b Yadav	12	1/30 (2) 2/83 (1) (8 wkts, 50 overs) 269
D. A. Miller c Kohli b Yadav	7	3/103 (4) 4/122 (5)
C. H. Morris b Yadav	37	5/134 (6) 6/208 (7)
A. L. Phehlukwayo not out	27	7/264 (3) 8/268 (9) 10 overs: 49-1

Imran Tahir did not bat.

Bhuvneshwar Kumar 10–1–71–1; Bumrah 10–0–56–1; Pandya 7–0–41–0; Chahal 10–0–45–2; Yadav 10–0–34–3; Jadhav 3–0–19–0.

India

R. G. Sharma c de Kock b Morkel	20	†M. S. Dhoni not out	4
S. Dhawan run out (Markram)	35	Lb 6, w 11	17
*V. Kohli c Rabada b Phehlukwayo	112		
A. M. Rahane c Imran Tahir b Phehlukwayo	79	1/33 (1) 2/67 (2) (4 wkts, 45.3 overs)	270
H. H. Pandya not out	3	3/256 (4) 4/262 (3) 10 overs: 49-1	

K. M. Jadhav, Bhuvneshwar Kumar, K. Yadav, J. J. Bumrah and Y. S. Chahal did not bat.

Morkel 7–0–35–1; Rabada 9.3–0–48–0; Morris 7–0–52–0; Imran Tahir 10–0–51–0; Phehlukwayo 8–0–42–2; Duminy 2–0–16–0; Markram 2–0–20–0.

Umpires: I. J. Gould and B. P. Jele.   Third umpire: Aleem Dar.
Referee: A. J. Pycroft.

SOUTH AFRICA v INDIA

Second One-Day International

At Centurion, February 4, 2018. India won by nine wickets. Toss: India. One-day international debut: K. Zondo.

If South Africa had been in a muddle against wrist-spin in the first match, they were in utter chaos in the second. The Chahal–Yadav pairing this time managed eight for 42, dismissing the hosts for their lowest total on home soil. And, as in Durban three days earlier, it had nothing to do with the pitch. So mesmerised were South Africa by pace and dip that minimal turn hardly mattered. In front

---

LOWEST ODI TOTALS BY SOUTH AFRICA

69 (28 overs) .	v Australia at Sydney	1993-94
83 (23) .	v England at Nottingham	2008
101 (26.5) .	v Pakistan at Sharjah	1999-2000
106 (38.3) .	v Australia at Sydney	2001-02
107 (32.1) .	v England at Lord's	2003
108 (34.1) .	v New Zealand at Mumbai (Brabourne)	2006-07
117 (48) .	v India at Nairobi	1999-2000
118 (32.2) .	**v India at Centurion**	**2017-18**
119 (36.5) .	v England at Port Elizabeth	2009-10

---

of a capacity crowd, de Kock and stand-in captain Markram (playing only his third ODI) both pulled long hops to midwicket, Miller deflected a better ball to slip, debutant Khaya Zondo top-edged a slog-sweep, and Duminy missed a more orthodox one. At the scheduled break India required 26 more, so an extra 15 minutes – a minimum of four overs – were allowed. It did not quite prove enough: with two runs needed, lunch was taken. Kohli appealed for common sense, but the umpires applied the letter of the law. Dhawan and Kohli had been so dominant in what passed for a chase it seemed the guillotine would descend sooner, but the South African attack stuck to their forlorn task. Even so, the entire embarrassment was complete in 52.5 overs.

Man of the Match: Y. S. Chahal.

South Africa

H. M. Amla c Dhoni b Bhuvneshwar Kumar	23
†Q. de Kock c Pandya b Chahal	20
*A. K. Markram c Bhuvneshwar Kumar b Yadav	8
J-P. Duminy lbw b Chahal	25
D. A. Miller c Rahane b Yadav	0
K. Zondo c Pandya b Chahal	25
C. H. Morris c Bhuvneshwar Kumar b Chahal	14
K. Rabada lbw b Yadav	1
M. Morkel lbw b Chahal	1
Imran Tahir b Bumrah	0
T. Shamsi not out	0
W 1	1

1/39 (1) 2/51 (2) 3/51 (3)   (32.2 overs) 118
4/51 (5) 5/99 (6) 6/107 (4)
7/110 (8) 8/117 (9) 9/118 (10)
10/118 (7)   10 overs: 39-1

Bhuvneshwar Kumar 5–1–19–1; Bumrah 5–1–12–1; Pandya 5–0–34–0; Chahal 8.2–1–22–5; Yadav 6–0–20–3; Jadhav 3–0–11–0.

India

R. G. Sharma c Morkel b Rabada	15
S. Dhawan not out	51
*V. Kohli not out	46
Lb 1, w 6	7

1/26 (1)   (1 wkt, 20.3 overs) 119
                  10 overs: 57-1

A. M. Rahane, H. H. Pandya, †M. S. Dhoni, K. M. Jadhav, Bhuvneshwar Kumar, K. Yadav, J. J. Bumrah and Y. S. Chahal did not bat.

Morkel 4–0–30–0; Rabada 5–0–24–1; Morris 3–0–16–0; Imran Tahir 5.3–0–30–0; Shamsi 3–1–18–0.

Umpires: Aleem Dar and A. T. Holdstock.   Third umpire: I. J. Gould.
Referee: A. J. Pycroft.

SOUTH AFRICA v INDIA

Third One-Day International

At Cape Town, February 7, 2018 (day/night). India won by 124 runs. Toss: South Africa. One-day international debuts: H. Klaasen, L. T. Ngidi.

Rarely has a batsman held sway in a one-day international innings as magnificently as Kohli during his unbeaten 160. He and a carefree Dhawan added 140 for the second wicket but, with the bowlers fighting back, no one else passed 16. Matters might have been different: Kohli, on nought, was given lbw to Rabada. He consulted Dhawan before opting to review – suggesting he thought the ball was missing leg. But Snickometer revealed a sound as it passed the bat, and he lived again. While Dhawan flashed and wafted entertainingly (until he fell to a stunning one-handed catch at full stretch by Markram), Kohli was so precise that another Indian victory appeared inevitable long before it came. Even the acceleration in the closing overs – a pulled six and cover-drive for four off the last two balls, from Rabada – seemed premeditated. "You kind of know, mostly, what they will bowl at that stage of the innings," he said. In need of a large century, but missing the injured trio of de Kock, de Villiers and du Plessis, South Africa lost Amla to the seventh ball, lbw to Bumrah. A useful stand of 78 between Markram and Duminy was ended by Yadav, the first of eight wickets he shared with Chahal. For the first time, South Africa had lost the first three ODIs of a home series.

Man of the Match: V. Kohli.

India

R. G. Sharma c Klaasen b Rabada........	0	Bhuvneshwar Kumar not out...........	16	
S. Dhawan c Markram b Duminy........	76			
*V. Kohli not out......................	160	Lb 3, w 12	15	
A. M. Rahane c Phehlukwayo b Duminy ..	11			
H. H. Pandya c Klaasen b Morris.......	14	1/0 (1) 2/140 (2) (6 wkts, 50 overs)	303	
†M. S. Dhoni c Ngidi b Imran Tahir.......	10	3/160 (4) 4/188 (5)		
K. M. Jadhav c Klaasen b Phehlukwayo...	1	5/228 (6) 6/236 (7)	10 overs: 50-1	

K. Yadav, J. J. Bumrah and Y. S. Chahal did not bat.

Rabada 10–1–54–1; Ngidi 6–0–47–0; Morris 9–0–45–1; Phehlukwayo 6–0–42–1; Imran Tahir 9–0–52–1; Duminy 10–0–60–2.

South Africa

H. M. Amla lbw b Bumrah	1	Imran Tahir c Kohli b Chahal	8	
*A. K. Markram st Dhoni b Yadav	32	L. T. Ngidi lbw b Yadav	6	
J-P. Duminy lbw b Chahal	51			
†H. Klaasen lbw b Chahal	6	Lb 2, w 2	4	
D. A. Miller c Dhoni b Bumrah..........	25			
K. Zondo c sub (M. K. Pandey) b Chahal ..	17	1/1 (1) 2/79 (2) 3/88 (4) (40 overs)	179	
C. H. Morris lbw b Yadav..............	14	4/95 (3) 5/129 (5) 6/150 (7)		
A. L. Phehlukwayo c Kohli b Yadav......	3	7/150 (6) 8/158 (8) 9/167 (10)		
K. Rabada not out	12	10/179 (11)	10 overs: 48-1	

Bhuvneshwar Kumar 7–0–41–0; Bumrah 7–0–32–2; Pandya 8–0–35–0; Chahal 9–0–46–4; Yadav 9–1–23–4.

Umpires: I. J. Gould and A. T. Holdstock.   Third umpire: Aleem Dar.
Referee: A. J. Pycroft.

SOUTH AFRICA v INDIA

Fourth One-Day International

At Johannesburg, February 10, 2018 (day/night). South Africa won by five wickets (DLS). Toss: India.

A lively capacity crowd, many wearing pink for South Africa's annual breast-cancer awareness match, helped bring a change in fortune. But arguably the real assistance came from a storm that reduced the chase to 202 in 28 overs. Earlier, Dhawan hit a freewheeling 109 (the ninth to score a century in his 100th ODI), while Kohli continued his relentless unpicking of the South African attack. The biggest surprise came when he was caught at cover for 75. That made it 178 for two with 19 overs left, so the seamers did well to keep India to 289. The rain, which had interrupted their innings, returned in the eighth over of the reply, with South Africa 43 for one. A fit-again de Villiers helped take 17 off a Chahal over, though when he departed for 26 they still needed 100 from 11. Miller, who went on to a brisk 39, was given two lives: dropped off a leading edge and, three deliveries later, bowled by a Chahal no-ball. But it was Heinrich Klaasen who did most to win the game. His mixture of power and unorthodoxy unsettled the wrist-spinners, who together conceded more than ten an over. If the closing stages had an element of hit-and-hope, there was also a positive approach unseen in the three previous games: Phehlukwayo's phenomenal 23 came from just five balls.

Man of the Match: H. Klaasen.

India

R. G. Sharma c and b Rabada	5	K. Yadav not out			0
S. Dhawan c de Villiers b Morkel	109				
*V. Kohli c Miller b Morris	75				
A. M. Rahane c Rabada b Ngidi	8	Lb 6, w 12			18
S. S. Iyer c Morris b Ngidi	18				
†M. S. Dhoni not out	42	1/20 (1) 2/178 (3)	(7 wkts, 50 overs)		289
H. H. Pandya c Markram b Rabada	9	3/206 (2) 4/210 (4)			
Bhuvneshwar Kumar run out (Duminy/		5/247 (5) 6/262 (7)			
Morris)	5	7/282 (8)	10 overs: 53-1		

J. J. Bumrah and Y. S. Chahal did not bat.

Morkel 10–0–55–1; Rabada 10–0–58–2; Ngidi 10–0–52–2; Morris 10–0–60–1; Phehlukwayo 6–0–38–0; Duminy 4–0–20–0.

South Africa

*A. K. Markram lbw b Bumrah	22	A. L. Phehlukwayo not out			23
H. M. Amla c Bhuvneshwar Kumar b Yadav	33	Lb 3, w 6, nb 2			11
J-P. Duminy lbw b Yadav	10				
A. B. de Villiers c Sharma b Pandya	26	1/43 (1) 2/67 (3)	(5 wkts, 25.3 overs)		207
D. A. Miller lbw b Chahal	39	3/77 (2) 4/102 (4)			
†H. Klaasen not out	43	5/174 (5)	7.2 overs: 43-1		

C. H. Morris, K. Rabada, M. Morkel and L. T. Ngidi did not bat.

Bhuvneshwar Kumar 4–0–27–0; Bumrah 5–0–21–1; Yadav 6–0–51–2; Pandya 5–0–37–1; Chahal 5.3–0–68–1.

Umpires: Aleem Dar and B. P. Jele.　　Third umpire: I. J. Gould.
Referee: A. J. Pycroft.

SOUTH AFRICA v INDIA

Fifth One-Day International

At Port Elizabeth, February 13, 2018 (day/night). India won by 73 runs. Toss: South Africa.

Yet again one of India's top four built the platform for a competitive score. Having made little impression until now, Sharma began cautiously – unlike Dhawan, who hit eight fours from 23 balls. And once Sharma's hesitation over a single had resulted in Kohli's dismissal, there was greater need than ever for him to bat deep. He avoided all further risk until he fell for a classy 115, the first of four victims for Ngidi, whose pace and guile in the last ten overs held India to 274. But it proved plenty. Markram chipped to midwicket off the toe of the bat to end an opening stand of 52 and, when de Villiers feathered a cut behind, South Africa were 65 for three. Their last hope evaporated when a direct hit from Pandya accounted for Amla. No one, neither fielder nor batsman, believed it was out, and everyone returned to their positions to await the third-umpire formalities. But Amla's bat was on the line. That allowed Yadav and Chahal to run through a hapless lower order, and the series was comfortably India's.

Man of the Match: R. G. Sharma.

India

S. Dhawan c Phehlukwayo b Rabada	34	Bhuvneshwar Kumar not out			19
R. G. Sharma c Klaasen b Ngidi	115	K. Yadav not out			2
*V. Kohli run out (Duminy)	36	B 1, lb 9, w 7			17
A. M. Rahane run out (Morkel/Klaasen)	8				
S. S. Iyer c Klaasen b Ngidi	30	1/48 (1) 2/153 (3)	(7 wkts, 50 overs)		274
H. H. Pandya c Klaasen b Ngidi	0	3/176 (4) 4/236 (2)			
†M. S. Dhoni c Markram b Ngidi	13	5/236 (6) 6/238 (5) 7/265 (7)	10 overs: 61-1		

J. J. Bumrah and Y. S. Chahal did not bat.

Morkel 10–2–44–0; Rabada 9–0–58–1; Ngidi 9–1–51–4; Phehlukwayo 8–0–34–0; Duminy 4–0–29–0; Shamsi 10–0–48–0.

South Africa

H. M. Amla run out (Pandya)	71	T. Shamsi c Pandya b Yadav		0
*A. K. Markram c Kohli b Bumrah	32	L. T. Ngidi not out		4
J-P. Duminy c Sharma b Pandya	1			
A. B. de Villiers c Dhoni b Pandya	6	Lb 6, w 2		8
D. A. Miller b Chahal	36			
†H. Klaasen st Dhoni b Yadav	39	1/52 (2) 2/55 (3) 3/65 (4)	(42.2 overs)	201
A. L. Phehlukwayo b Yadav	0	4/127 (5) 5/166 (1) 6/168 (7)		
K. Rabada c Chahal b Yadav	3	7/196 (8) 8/197 (6) 9/197 (10)		
M. Morkel lbw b Chahal	1	10/201 (9)	10 overs: 52-1	

Bhuvneshwar Kumar 7–0–43–0; Bumrah 7–0–22–1; Pandya 9–0–30–2; Yadav 10–0–57–4; Chahal 9.2–0–43–2.

Umpires: S. George and I. J. Gould.   Third umpire: Aleem Dar.
Referee: A. J. Pycroft.

SOUTH AFRICA v INDIA

Sixth One-Day International

At Centurion, February 16, 2018 (day/night). India won by eight wickets. Toss: India.

Kohli rounded off his astounding series with a brutal century that sped India to another largely unchallenged win. His unbeaten 129 from just 96 deliveries – in essence one extended fist pump in celebration of a famous 5–1 victory – was the most clinical of his three centuries. Across six innings, he had totalled 558 runs at near enough one a ball. De Villiers, on his home ground, had earlier borne the brunt of a beleaguered crowd's expectations. He applied himself with dedication, but on 30 stepped back to cut a Chahal delivery that turned out to be a googly. Initially, Zondo fared well, but he grew indecisive as wickets tumbled, and perished failing to lift an inside-out drive over cover. Phehlukwayo walloped a couple of sixes but, while passing 200 from the depths of 151 for seven might have felt like an achievement, it was popgun stuff to India. For South Africa, two wickets for Ngidi was as good as it got. The remainder of the game assumed a familiar guise: another episode of the Kohli show.

Man of the Match: V. Kohli.   *Man of the Series:* V. Kohli.

South Africa

*A. K. Markram c Iyer b Thakur	24	Imran Tahir c Kohli b Bumrah		2
H. M. Amla c Dhoni b Thakur	10	L. T. Ngidi not out		0
A. B. de Villiers b Chahal	30			
K. Zondo c Pandya b Chahal	54	W 3		3
†H. Klaasen c Kohli b Bumrah	22			
F. Behardien c Bumrah b Thakur	1	1/23 (2) 2/43 (1) 3/105 (3)	(46.5 overs)	204
C. H. Morris c Dhawan b Yadav	4	4/135 (5) 5/136 (6) 6/142 (7)		
A. L. Phehlukwayo c and b Thakur	34	7/151 (4) 8/187 (9) 9/192 (10)		
M. Morkel c Iyer b Pandya	20	10/204 (8)	10 overs: 44-2	

Thakur 8.5–0–52–4; Bumrah 8–1–24–2; Pandya 10–0–39–1; Yadav 10–0–51–1; Chahal 10–0–38–2.

India

S. Dhawan c Zondo b Ngidi	. . . .	18
R. G. Sharma c Klaasen b Ngidi	. . . .	15
*V. Kohli not out	. . . .	129
A. M. Rahane not out	. . . .	34
B 4, lb 1, w 5	. . . .	10

1/19 (2) 2/80 (1)   (2 wkts, 32.1 overs) 206
10 overs: 63-1

S. S. Iyer, H. H. Pandya, †M. S. Dhoni, K. Yadav, S. N. Thakur, J. J. Bumrah and Y. S. Chahal did
not bat.

Morkel 7–0–42–0; Ngidi 8–1–54–2; Morris 6–0–36–0; Phehlukwayo 4–0–27–0; Imran Tahir
7.1–0–42–0.

Umpires: Aleem Dar and S. George.   Third umpire: I. J. Gould.
Referee: A. J. Pycroft.

SOUTH AFRICA v INDIA

First Twenty20 International

At Johannesburg, February 18, 2018. India won by 28 runs. Toss: South Africa. Twenty20
international debuts: C. J. Dala, H. Klaasen.

A hugely experienced India overwhelmed an experimental South African line-up who fought hard,
but were never in serious contention. On one of the world's highest-scoring grounds, Kohli's side
enjoyed a lightning start thanks to Sharma and then Raina, their combined 36 occupying just 16 balls
and seizing the initiative. With Dhawan continuing his form from the one-dayers, India seemed set
for untold riches at 98 for two after eight overs. The middle order, though, could not maintain the
tempo, and they settled for a decent 203. Hendricks anchored the chase with style and composure,
but there was insufficient oomph from his colleagues. Bhuvneshwar Kumar compensated for the
absence of swing by varying his pace or angle – or both – and claimed a career-best five for 24.

Man of the Match: Bhuvneshwar Kumar.

India

		B	4/6
1 R. G. Sharma c 6 b 10	21	9	2/2
2 S. Dhawan c 6 b 7	72	39	10/2
3 S. K. Raina c and b 10	15	7	2/1
4 *V. Kohli lbw b 11	26	20	2/1
5 M. K. Pandey not out	29	27	0/1
6 †M. S. Dhoni b 8	16	11	2
7 H. H. Pandya not out	13	7	2
Lb 2, w 9	11		

6 overs: 78-2   (20 overs) 203-5

1/23 2/49 3/108 4/155 5/183

8 Bhuvneshwar Kumar, 9 J. D. Unadkat, 10 J. J.
Bumrah and 11 Y. S. Chahal did not bat.

Paterson 4–3–48–0; Dala 4–8–47–2; Morris
4–8–39–1; Shamsi 4–8–37–1; Smuts
2–2–14–0; Phehlukwayo 2–4–16–1.

South Africa

		B	4/6
1 J. T. Smuts c 2 b 8	14	9	3
2 R. R. Hendricks c 6 b 8	70	50	8/1
3 *J-P. Duminy c 3 b 8	3	7	0
4 D. A. Miller c 2 b 7	9	5	0/1
5 F. Behardien c 5 b 11	39	27	3/2
6 †H. Klaasen c 3 b 8	16	8	1/1
7 A. L. Phehlukwayo c 11 b 9	13	8	2
8 C. H. Morris c 3 b 8	0	1	0
9 D. Paterson run out (7/6)	1	1	0
10 C. J. Dala not out	2	3	0
11 T. Shamsi not out	0	2	0
B 1, lb 1, w 5, nb 1	8		

6 overs: 41-2   (20 overs) 175-9

1/29 2/38 3/48 4/129 5/154 6/158 7/158 8/159
9/175

Bhuvneshwar Kumar 4–10–24–5; Unadkat
4–11–33–1; Bumrah 4–9–32–0; Pandya
4–5–45–1; Chahal 4–5–39–1.

Umpires: S. George and A. T. Holdstock.   Third umpire: B. P. Jele.
Referee: A. J. Pycroft.

SOUTH AFRICA v INDIA

Second Twenty20 International

At Centurion, February 21, 2018 (floodlit). South Africa won by six wickets. Toss: South Africa. Twenty20 international debut: S. N. Thakur.

A frenzied display of hitting from Klaasen helped level the series. The omens were good for South Africa early on: Zambia-born seamer Junior Dala had Sharma lbw first ball; Dhawan miscued a Duminy full toss to mid-on; and in the next over Dala removed Kohli for a single. India were 45 for three in the powerplay. Raina began the recovery, before Pandey and Dhoni shared an unbroken stand of 98 against determined, intelligent bowling. Dhoni's 27-ball half-century confirmed he still

MOST RUNS CONCEDED IN A TWENTY20 INTERNATIONAL

69	B. J. McCarthy	Ireland v Afghanistan at Greater Noida..............	2016-17
68	K. J. Abbott.........	South Africa v West Indies at Johannesburg..........	2014-15
64	J. M. Anderson.....	England v Australia at Sydney....................	2006-07
64	S. T. Jayasuriya......	Sri Lanka v Pakistan at Johannesburg...............	2007-08
64	**A. J. Tye........**	**†Australia v New Zealand at Auckland......**	**2017-18**
64‡	**B. M. Wheeler......**	**†New Zealand v Australia at Auckland......**	**2017-18**
64	**Y. S. Chahal.......**	**India v South Africa at Centurion...........**	**2017-18**
63	Rubel Hossain......	Bangladesh v West Indies at Mirpur................	2012-13
63	Mashrafe bin Mortaza .	Bangladesh v Pakistan at Mirpur...................	2013-14
61	L. N. Onyango......	Kenya v Sri Lanka at Johannesburg................	2007-08
61	S. I. Mahmood......	England v South Africa at Centurion	2009-10
61	A. N. P. R. Fernando..	Sri Lanka v India at Lahore......................	2017-18

† *In the same match.* ‡ *From 3.1 overs; all others from four.*

had the ability to hit yorkers to the boundary. At 38 for two after five, South Africa were slipping behind, but Klaasen hauled them back: a switch hit for six, reverse sweeps for four, and an outrageous back-foot punch over extra cover all brought gasps from the crowd. Duminy ended the match with successive sixes off Unadkat.

Man of the Match: H. Klaasen.

India		B	4/6
1 S. Dhawan *c 6 b 3*	24	14	3/2
2 R. G. Sharma *lbw b 10*.......	0	1	0
3 S. K. Raina *lbw b 8*	31	24	5
4 *V. Kohli *c 4 b 10*	1	5	0
5 M. K. Pandey *not out*	79	48	6/3
6 †M. S. Dhoni *not out*	52	28	4/3
W 1		1	

6 overs: 45-3   (20 overs) 188-4

1/0 2/44 3/45 4/90

7 H. H. Pandya, 8 Bhuvneshwar Kumar, 9 J. D. Unadkat, 10 S. N. Thakur and 11 Y. S. Chahal did not bat.

Morris 4–11–42–0; Dala 4–14–28–2; Paterson 4–4–51–0; Duminy 2–4–13–1; Shamsi 2–3–24–0; Phehlukwayo 2–3–15–1; Smuts 2–3–15–0.

South Africa		B	4/6
1 R. R. Hendricks *c 7 b 10*	26	17	5
2 J. T. Smuts *c 3 b 9*	2	9	0
3 *J-P. Duminy *not out*	64	40	4/3
4 †H. Klaasen *c 6 b 9*	69	30	3/7
5 D. A. Miller *c 10 b 7*	5	6	0
6 F. Behardien *not out*	16	10	0/1
Lb 2, w 5	7		

6 overs: 50-2   (18.4 overs) 189-4

1/24 2/38 3/131 4/141

7 C. H. Morris, 8 A. L. Phehlukwayo, 9 D. Paterson, 10 C. J. Dala and 11 T. Shamsi did not bat.

Bhuvneshwar Kumar 3–7–19–0; Thakur 4–6–31–1; Unadkat 3.4–9–42–2; Pandya 4–6–31–1; Chahal 4–4–64–0.

Umpires: B. P. Jele and A. Paleker.   Third umpire: S. George.
Referee: A. J. Pycroft.

SOUTH AFRICA v INDIA

Third Twenty20 International

At Cape Town, February 24, 2018 (floodlit). India won by seven runs. Toss: South Africa. Twenty20 international debut: C. Jonker.

A painfully slow start to the chase left South Africa almost out of the game at 45 for one after nine overs; it was as if Miller and Duminy had forgotten the target was 173. The experiment of opening with Miller and Duminy failed when he pulled a long hop to deep midwicket, while Duminy – who struck three sixes in a desperate bid to catch up – sliced a slower ball to mid-off. That asked a lot of Christiaan Jonker, the 31-year-old debutant, but he did what he had been doing domestically for years: dig his bat underneath yorkers and manufacture boundaries from the unlikeliest deliveries. He rattled along, but 53 from the last three proved just beyond him. India had enjoyed their usual flyer thanks to Raina, even if Dhawan endured one of those days when the ball eluded both the middle of his bat and the hands of the fielders. Karthik gave the innings a rousing finish with 13 from six deliveries, turning an average total into a winning one.

Man of the Match: S. K. Raina.   *Man of the Series:* Bhuvneshwar Kumar.

India

		B	4/6
1 *R. G. Sharma *lbw b 10*	11	8	2
2 S. Dhawan *run out (10)*	47	40	3
3 S. K. Raina *c 7 b 11*	43	27	5/1
4 M. K. Pandey *c 2 b 10*	13	10	0/1
5 H. H. Pandya *c 4 b 6*	21	17	0/1
6 †M. S. Dhoni *c 2 b 10*	12	11	1
7 K. D. Karthik *lbw b 6*	13	6	3
8 A. R. Patel *not out*	1	1	0
9 Bhuvneshwar Kumar *not out*	3	1	0
Lb 2, w 5, nb 1	8		

6 overs: 57-1   (20 overs) 172-7

1/14 2/79 3/111 4/126 5/151 6/163 7/168

10 S. N. Thakur and 11 J. J. Bumrah did not bat.

Morris 4–6–43–2; Dala 4–8–35–3; Duminy 3–4–22–0; Phehlukwayo 3–4–26–0; Shamsi 4–5–31–1; Phangiso 2–3–13–0.

South Africa

		B	4/6
1 R. R. Hendricks *c 2 b 9*	7	13	1
2 D. A. Miller *c 8 b 3*	24	23	2/1
3 *J-P. Duminy *c 1 b 10*	55	41	2/3
4 †H. Klaasen *c 9 b 5*	7	10	0
5 C. Jonker *c 1 b 9*	49	24	5/2
6 C. H. Morris *b 11*	4	3	1
7 F. Behardien *not out*	15	6	3
B 1, lb 1, w 2	4		

6 overs: 25-1   (20 overs) 165-6

1/10 2/45 3/79 4/109 5/114 6/165

8 A. L. Phehlukwayo, 9 A. M. Phangiso, 10 C. J. Dala and 11 T. Shamsi did not bat.

Bhuvneshwar Kumar 4–10–24–2; Bumrah 4–7–39–1; Thakur 4–11–35–1; Pandya 4–10–22–1; Raina 3–4–27–1; Patel 1–1–16–0.

Umpires: S. George and B. P. Jele.   Third umpire: A. T. Holdstock.
Referee: A. J. Pycroft.

SOUTH AFRICA v AUSTRALIA IN 2017-18

FIRDOSE MOONDA

Test matches (4): South Africa 3, Australia 1

It was billed as a battle between the best bowling attacks in the game, but became a battle about everything else. This contest had it all: on-field scuffles, off-field altercations, ambush marketing, expulsions and sackings, a resignation, a retirement, a rewriting of the history books – and a small piece of sandpaper.

South Africa defeated Australia at home for the first time since 1969-70, finally completing a full set of post-readmission series wins against every Test team, home and away. But the Australia they beat at the Wanderers were very different from the side who had beaten them in Durban four weeks earlier. The first version, cocksure and cunning, had just won the Ashes; the second, disgraced and disintegrating, returned home having lost more than a few games of cricket.

Across the four Tests there were eight breaches of the ICC's code of conduct, equalling Sri Lanka v England in 2000-01 as the most ill-tempered series since the code was drawn up in 1991. In between electrifying spells of bowling, Kagiso Rabada committed two offences in one match. But it was Australia's misdemeanours which defined the tour.

On the third afternoon of the Third Test at Newlands, Cameron Bancroft was caught on camera hiding something small and yellow down the front of his trousers. That evening, he and Australian captain Steve Smith told the press it was sticky tape, which Bancroft – apparently under instructions from the team's leadership group – was using to capture grains of sand and roughen the ball. Both men apologised, but played down the incident as isolated and impulsive. Cricket Australia were not convinced. Before the game resumed next morning, Smith and his vice-captain David Warner had been stripped of their positions, and the captaincy handed to wicketkeeper Tim Paine. A few hours later, Australia lost the match – and the players involved faced grave consequences.

Smith was given four demerit points – triggering a one-Test ban – and fined his entire match fee by the ICC, Bancroft three points and 75% of his. Meanwhile, CA launched their own investigation. Iain Roy, their head of integrity, flew to South Africa, followed by chief executive James Sutherland. They concluded that the tape was in fact sandpaper, that only Smith, Warner and Bancroft knew of the plan, and that the Australians had not previously tampered with the ball. Smith and Warner were banned from cricket – in or involving Australia – for a year, and Bancroft for nine months. All three were sent home and, in the days that followed, held tearful press conferences; they said they would not contest the sanctions. Coach Darren Lehmann promised to lead the changes Australian cricket needed. But, on the eve of the final Test at Johannesburg, he announced he would resign when it ended, after five years in charge. Australia's new-look top order struggled horribly, and South Africa romped home by 492 runs to complete a 3–1 triumph.

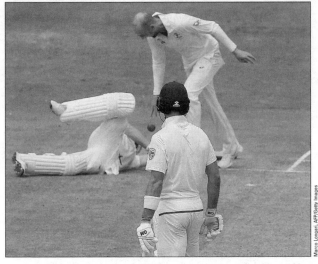

Marco Longari, AFP/Getty Images

A drop too much: after running out A. B. de Villiers at Durban, Nathan Lyon deliberately lets the ball land on him – a display of petulance that brought censure and a fine from the ICC.

Australia had misbehaved from the start. At Durban, they tried to get the stump microphones turned down by loudly naming brands in direct competition with official sponsors – a cynical attempt to allow them to sledge the South Africans without being heard. They failed, but the verbals still flowed, and Aiden Markram and Quinton de Kock were subjected to hours of taunts as they battled to avoid defeat on the fourth day. Markram was mocked for his part in the run-out of A. B. de Villiers, and de Kock insulted over his weight, fitness and personal life. Warner led the abuse, and was heard calling de Kock "a fucken' sook", Australian slang for wimp, as the players left the field for tea on the fourth day. Walking up the stairs to the dressing-rooms, de Kock finally responded, making a derogatory comment about Warner's wife, Candice, and her tryst with New Zealand rugby player Sonny Bill Williams in 2007, before she had met her husband. CCTV footage showed Warner being physically restrained by team-mates.

Each side blamed the other. Australia maintained they had not aimed a personal insult at de Kock, while South African team manager Mohammed Moosajee said they "definitely, definitely, definitely" did. A debate ensued: what exactly was "personal"? South Africa said it was anything attacking someone's character; Australia limited it to comments about families and significant others, and insisted there was a line that could not be crossed. Bemused, the South Africans called for clarity. "Who does the line belong to?"

SANDPAPERGATE – WHAT THEY SAID

"A shocking disappointment"

The Australian cricket team has always believed it could win in any situation against any opposition, by playing combative, skilful and fair cricket, driven by our pride in the fabled Baggy Green. I have no doubt the current Australian team continues to believe in this mantra. However, some have now failed our culture, making a serious error of judgment in the Cape Town Test match." **Steve Waugh**

To hear that the Australian cricket team had been involved in premeditated cheating is something that is embarrassing. But the jump to hysteria is something that has elevated the offence beyond what they actually did. **Shane Warne**

There is this unrealistic belief [in Australia] that Australian cricketers are above the underhanded tactics the public perceive other countries stoop to in order to win. This image was shattered in Cape Town. **Ian Chappell**

I've got the experience to help these young players and that's where our focus should be right now until the other guys come back… We're not talking about the next five years. It's the next six months and we need to fix it now. If Cricket Australia ask me, I'd drop everything to help out. **Michael Clarke**

I think the reaction back in Australia was as big as it was because the public felt the Australian players hadn't played the game in a fair way. **Ricky Ponting**

I've hated this talk about 'the line'. What is the line? Who sets it? Who dictates how it is enforced? It is totally different culture to culture, yet the Australians believe they're the ones who should be setting it? That it's OK to intimidate a person from another country, another culture, during the day, and be buddies with him afterwards? Nonsense. The Aussies have played the victim when they deem the other team has overstepped the mark. And when they've been in the ascendancy and behaved badly, everything is OK because they have determined as much. **Mickey Arthur**

It's almost like teams and people around the world have been waiting for them to stuff up so they can lay the boot in. As an Australian, I'm embarrassed. Steve is a lovely young bloke who has made a terrible mistake. **England's coach Trevor Bayliss**

To say that a bowler has got a ball in his hands, and anybody else in the field does not know that it has been tampered with, is absolute nonsense. **Andrew Flintoff**

I saw Steve Smith say it's the first time they've tried it. To me it seems really surprising they've changed a method that's been working. Look at the Ashes series we've just played, look through all of those Test matches and they reverse-swing the ball sometimes in conditions you wouldn't expect the ball to reverse. **Stuart Broad**

I look at the amount of tape some of the fielders have worn, particularly during the Ashes series, at mid-on and mid-off. I am pretty sure it was going on throughout the Ashes series – but it was not the reason England lost 4–0. They still would have lost the series. **Michael Vaughan**

This has been an eye-opener. We've come to realise that the world – not only Australia – regards ball-tampering in a very serious light. It goes to the spirit of the game. We need to look at the penalty imposed, specific to ball-tampering. **ICC chief executive Dave Richardson**

What I did has lived with me ever since and it will be the same for Smith and Bancroft. They will struggle for the rest of their lives, and be known as the ones who brought Australian cricket into disrepute. I haven't been able to shake off what happened to me in 37 years. I come up on Google as the man who took the lead role in Australian cricket's darkest day. It's a real relief I can finally drop that title." **Trevor Chappell, who bowled underarm against New Zealand in 1980-81**

To the whole nation, who hold those who wear the Baggy Green up on a pedestal – about as high as you can get in Australia – this is a shocking disappointment. **Australian prime minister Malcolm Turnbull**

asked coach Ottis Gibson. Amid the philosophical conundrums, Australia's 1–0 lead was almost forgotten.

By now, the dispute had spread beyond the players. Cricket South Africa were wrong not to condemn supporters who tried to shame Candice Warner, and two board officials unthinkingly posed for photos with fans who were wearing Williams masks. At Newlands, Warner needed a minder while he fielded on the boundary. His wife was severely affected by events, and later blamed herself for his part in the tampering plot, implying that he had been driven to cheat because of his anger about the mockery she had endured. Warner was contrite, and said he held only "a tiny ray of hope that I may one day be given the privilege of playing for my country again".

South Africa were not mere bystanders. Rabada, the leading wicket-taker in the series with 23 at 19, was both sublime and naive. He entered the series on five demerit points, then earned four more in the Second Test, after brushing shoulders with Smith and screaming at Warner. It meant he would be suspended for the final two Tests, but a nine-day break before the Third meant CSA could throw their weight behind an appeal. They hired a powerful seven-strong team, including high-profile advocate Dali Mpofu and sports lawyer David Becker, the ICC's former head of legal. Hearing the case, New Zealand's Michael Heron agreed Rabada had made inappropriate contact with Smith, but was not "comfortably satisfied" it was deliberate, and reduced his punishment to one demerit point. That left him free to play at Cape Town. The Australians were unimpressed, and Smith suggested they would consider contesting ICC sanctions in future, though he conceded they wanted to compete against the best. Handed a lifeline, Rabada vowed to control his temper.

All the while, two sides who routinely bring out the best – and worst – in each other were playing some engrossing cricket. Mitchell Starc seemed to scar South Africa with nine wickets in the opening Test, but they regrouped, and he took only three more before missing the last through injury. Instead, Pat Cummins shone, finishing just one behind Rabada. Australia's batting was a concern throughout: they passed 255 only once, in the first innings of the series, while no one made a hundred, and no partnership reached three figures.

Markram hit most runs, with 480 and two centuries, and underlined his potential by bringing up 1,000 runs in his first season as a Test batsman.

PLUMBING THE DEPTHS

Australia's lowest collective batting averages in series of four or more Tests:

Avge		T	I	NO	R	HS
17.70	v England (a) in 1956	5	99	12	1,540	97
17.99	v England (h) in 1978-79	6	132	12	2,159	129
18.68	v England (a) in 1902	5	81	9	1,345	119
19.31	v England (h) in 1884-85	5	102	11	1,758	128
20.60	v South Africa (a) in 1969-70	4	88	8	1,648	83
21.00	**v South Africa (a) in 2017-18**	**4**	**88**	**8**	**1,680**	**96**
22.15	v England (a) in 1905	5	91	12	1,750	146
22.47	v West Indies (h) in 1984-85	5	96	9	1,955	173
22.70	v West Indies (a) in 1983-84	5	109	12	2,202	120
23.39	v England (h) in 1903-04	5	110	10	2,339	185*

THE SANDPAPER SCANDAL

Scratching the surface

Mar 2   First Test, second day: Australian players name sponsors' rivals near stump mikes in unsuccessful attempt to have them turned down.

Mar 4   Nathan Lyon fined 15% of his match fee for dropping the ball on A. B. de Villiers after running him out. David Warner and Quinton de Kock are involved in an argument after leaving the field for tea. Both are disciplined by the ICC.

Mar 6   Australia wicketkeeper Tim Paine denies de Kock suffered personal abuse at Durban: "That's completely false. At no stage was Quinton's family mentioned. We were trying to make it an uncomfortable place for Quinton to bat, no doubt, but we didn't cross the line. We spoke about cricket stuff and a few little things with his fitness."

Mar 9   Second Test, first day: Kagiso Rabada brushes shoulders with Steve Smith after dismissing him; banned from two Tests, but allowed to play on appeal.

Mar 12   Mitchell Marsh fined for swearing at Rabada, who had just claimed his wicket.

Mar 23   After some Australian players are abused by spectators, coach Darren Lehmann labels the Newlands crowd disgraceful. "As soon as they cross the line and talk about players' families, it's just not on."

Mar 24   Third Test, third day: TV cameras show fielder Cameron Bancroft working vigorously on the ball. Lehmann sends twelfth man Peter Handscomb to speak with Bancroft, who is soon filmed hiding something down the front of his trousers.

    At the press conference, Smith admits a plan by the "leadership group" to alter the condition of the ball, as Australia were behind in the match. Bancroft says he used a small piece of yellow adhesive tape, which he had dragged in the soil to create an abrasive surface. Smith says it was "a big mistake", but will not stand down as captain. ICC fine Bancroft 75% of match fee and three demerit points for attempting to alter the condition of the ball, while Smith is fined his whole match fee and banned from the Fourth Test for "conduct contrary to the spirit of the game".

Mar 25   Amid worldwide outrage, Australia's prime minister Malcolm Turnbull calls Smith's admission "a shocking disappointment". In Melbourne, Cricket Australia chief executive James Sutherland apologises to fans, launches an investigation, and announces that captain Smith and vice-captain Warner – who suggested the plan to Bancroft – will lose their roles for the remainder of the Test (an unprecedented move), with Paine taking charge.

Mar 27   CA find Smith, Warner and Bancroft guilty of bringing the game into disrepute, and send them home.

Mar 28   The board suspend Smith and Warner from international and Australian domestic cricket for a year, and Bancroft for nine months. Smith and Bancroft will not be considered for leadership positions for a further year, while Warner will not be considered again. The inquiry finds that Bancroft had used sandpaper, not yellow tape.

    CA's investigation is satisfied Lehmann did not know of the plan and – to some scepticism – says no other players were involved. The board announce a review of the culture and conduct of the team; it would be chaired by former Test batsman Rick McCosker. Ex-captain Allan Border admits: "The Australian cricket team is not a popular one, and their antics on the field have upset a lot of people." Smith and Warner lose IPL contracts, while Somerset cancel Bancroft's county deal.

Mar 29   Smith gives a tearful press conference in Sydney, conceding it was a serious error of judgment: "I know I will regret this for the rest of my life." On seeing the footage of this, and Bancroft's press conference in Perth, Lehmann decides to resign as coach. "Australian cricket needs to move forward," he says, "and this is the right thing to do."

    The Magellan Financial Group terminate their naming-rights agreement with CA two years early. Many other sponsors express concerns, while the three players lose several lucrative personal contracts.

Mar 31   Warner speaks to the press, apologises for his part in the imbroglio and says he is resigned to not playing for Australia again.

Apr 4   Smith, Bancroft and (next day) Warner say they will not challenge the sanctions.

May 23   Warner's wife, Candice, reveals that she miscarried their baby after the furore.

De Villiers was second, with 427, and – after nearly two years' sabbatical – appeared to demonstrate a renewed passion for the longest format. But less than two months after the series finished he surprised everyone by announcing his retirement from international cricket. Aged 34, he said he had "run out of gas", though his batting was as classy as ever.

While Rabada stood out with the ball, the 33-year-old Morne Morkel marked his penultimate appearance for South Africa with a career-best match haul of nine at Newlands. He believed he could still play for two or three years, but chose to do so on a Kolpak deal at Surrey. Vernon Philander had none of the injury concerns that blighted his tour of England in 2017, and sealed the series with a spell of six for three on the final morning.

And so South Africa capped a sparkling summer, with eight wins in ten Tests, and triumphs over India and Australia. They put their success down, in part, to an inclusive culture that ensured younger players felt more at home than before: where once they had carried seniors' bags or cleaned their shoes, they were now their equals.

Paine said Australia would learn to listen as they entered a new era, but admitted: "We've now got a fine line between being really respectful of opposition and the game, and also being at a level that is really competitive. It's going to be a different style to what a lot of the guys have been used to, but I think we'll find it pretty quickly." And there was a note of relief in his voice when he added: "It will be good to get home, have a rest and think about it."

AUSTRALIA TOURING PARTY

*S. P. D. Smith, C. T. Bancroft, J. A. Burns, P. J. Cummins, P. S. P. Handscomb, J. R. Hazlewood, J. M. Holland, U. T. Khawaja, N. M. Lyon, M. R. Marsh, S. E. Marsh, G. J. Maxwell, T. D. Paine, M. T. Renshaw, J. A. Richardson, C. J. Sayers, M. A. Starc, D. A. Warner. *Coach:* D. S. Lehmann.

J. M. Bird was originally selected, but injured a hamstring and was replaced by Sayers. Warner arrived late after captaining Australia's Twenty20 side. Smith, Bancroft and Warner were sent home after the ball-tampering incident, and replaced by Burns, Maxwell and Renshaw. Paine took over as captain.

TEST MATCH AVERAGES

SOUTH AFRICA – BATTING AND FIELDING

	T	I	NO	R	HS	100	50	Avge	Ct/St
A. B. de Villiers	4	8	2	427	126*	1	4	71.16	11
T. Bavuma	2	4	2	136	95*	0	1	68.00	1
A. K. Markram	4	8	0	480	152	2	1	60.00	2
†D. Elgar	4	8	1	333	141*	1	2	47.57	8
†Q. de Kock	4	7	0	223	83	0	3	31.85	18/1
V. D. Philander	4	7	2	155	52*	0	1	31.00	1
F. du Plessis	4	8	1	175	120	1	0	25.00	1
H. M. Amla	4	8	0	196	56	0	1	24.50	4
T. B. de Bruyn	2	4	1	58	36	0	0	19.33	2
K. A. Maharaj	4	6	0	83	45	0	0	13.83	0
†K. Rabada	4	6	0	74	29	0	0	12.33	1
†M. Morkel	3	5	1	13	6	0	0	3.25	1

Played in one Test: L. T. Ngidi 5 (1 ct).

BOWLING

	Style	O	M	R	W	BB	5I	Avge
L. T. Ngidi	RFM	26.3	8	75	5	3-51	0	15.00
V. D. Philander	RFM	129	48	269	16	6-21	1	16.81
K. Rabada	RF	140.5	40	443	23	6-54	2	19.26
M. Morkel	RF	90.4	25	294	15	5-23	1	19.60
K. A. Maharaj	SLA	161.2	22	572	17	5-123	1	33.64

Also bowled: T. Bavuma (RM) 1–0–10–0; T. B. de Bruyn (RFM) 2–0–6–0; D. Elgar (SLA) 4–1–16–1; A. K. Markram (OB) 6.4–1–11–0.

AUSTRALIA – BATTING AND FIELDING

	T	I	NO	R	HS	100	50	Avge	Ct/St
T. D. Paine	4	8	3	215	62	0	1	43.00	15/1
C. T. Bancroft	3	6	0	223	77	0	2	37.16	6
†D. A. Warner	3	6	0	217	63	0	2	36.16	1
S. P. D. Smith	3	6	0	142	56	0	1	23.66	7
M. R. Marsh	4	8	0	176	96	0	1	22.00	3
‡J. R. Hazlewood	4	8	5	63	17	0	0	21.00	2
†U. T. Khawaja	4	8	0	165	75	0	2	20.62	2
†S. E. Marsh	4	8	0	147	40	0	0	18.37	2
N. M. Lyon	4	8	0	100	47	0	0	12.50	2
P. J. Cummins	4	8	0	89	50	0	1	11.12	3
†M. A. Starc	3	6	0	60	35	0	0	10.00	1

Played in one Test: J. A. Burns 4, 42; P. S. P. Handscomb 0, 24 (4 ct); †M. T. Renshaw 8, 5 (1 ct); C. J. Sayers 0, 0 (1 ct).

BOWLING

	Style	O	M	R	W	BB	5I	Avge
P. J. Cummins	RF	155.4	32	472	22	5-83	1	21.45
M. A. Starc	LF	109.2	18	413	12	5-34	1	34.41
J. R. Hazlewood	RFM	160	30	471	12	3-61	0	39.25
M. R. Marsh	RFM	42	6	169	4	2-26	0	42.25
N. M. Lyon	OB	210.5	39	681	16	3-50	0	42.56

Also bowled: M. T. Renshaw (OB) 4–0–13–0; C. J. Sayers (RFM) 49–11–146–2; S. P. D. Smith (LB) 7–4–9–0.

At Benoni, February 22–24, 2018. **Australians won by five wickets.** ‡South Africa A **220** (58.5 overs) (J. R. Hazlewood 3-40, P. J. Cummins 4-32) **and 248** (72.5 overs) (S. von Berg 52; M. A. Starc 4-46); **Australians 329** (90.4 overs) (P. J. Cummins 59*; B. E. Hendricks 5-83) **and 140-5** (29.3 overs) (D. Olivier 4-74). *The Australians fielded their Test side minus David Warner (who had led the T20 team in Auckland the previous day), and their pace attack ran through the home batsmen on the opening day. They advanced to a 109-run lead, though – thanks to left-arm seamer Beuran Hendricks – no one reached 50 except Pat Cummins at No. 8. The match's only other* *half-century came from Shaun von Berg, also at No. 8, in South Africa A's second innings. Mitchell Starc took four wickets, including his 300th in first-class cricket, to leave a straightforward target, though Duanne Olivier gave the tourists some nervous moments.*

SOUTH AFRICA v AUSTRALIA

First Test

At Durban, March 1–5, 2018. Australia won by 118 runs. Toss: Australia.

An underprepared South Africa were overwhelmed by the incisiveness of an Australian attack led by the reverse swing of Starc. His first-innings five-for crippled the hosts, and he took nine for 109 in all. From 150 for five in response to Australia's 351, South Africa were shot out for 162, and never recovered. But instead of feeling deflated they harnessed a sense of indignation at Australia's behaviour, following a spat between Warner and de Kock.

On the final morning, with Australia needing one wicket for victory, video footage from the stairwell leading to the dressing-rooms was leaked. Taken during the tea break the previous day, it showed Warner being restrained by team-mates as he tried to confront de Kock. Australia claimed he had made an insulting personal comment about Warner's wife, Candice. South Africa insisted he had been provoked by a prolonged verbal campaign, with Warner front and centre. Whatever the reality, neither player emerged with credit. The clash set the tone for a foul-tempered series.

The fourth day had begun with Australia expecting to wrap things up before long. Instead, they were made to work. Markram crafted a century that properly announced him on the biggest stage, while de Kock's 83 was his best Test score for nearly a year. Their sixth-wicket partnership of 147 couldn't prevent an Australian victory, but it certainly got up their noses.

Warner it was who had given Australia a sound start on the first morning, with a sixth score above 50 in his seven Test innings in South Africa, before Smith built on it with his fifth consecutive half-century, following his bountiful Ashes. But neither reached 60, and on the second day it was left to Mitchell Marsh to tip the balance Australia's way. The last five wickets all but doubled the score, to 351, with Marsh ninth out for 96. Left-arm spinner Maharaj collected his fourth five-for.

Not satisfied with the pressure they applied with the bat, Australia tried to impose themselves via other means. As they took to the field for the South African reply, several mentioned the names of official sponsors' rivals, such as Qantas (rival airline Emirates back the ICC) and Castlemaine XXXX (Castle Lager has long been associated with South African cricket). They wanted the stump microphones turned down, and to sledge with impunity, but host broadcaster SuperSport refused to play ball.

With early turn on offer, Lyon was introduced in the eighth over and instantly dismissed Elgar and Amla to leave South Africa 27 for two. De Villiers alone seemed capable of repairing the damage, producing a fluent unbeaten 71 while the rest crumbled. Du Plessis, rusty after four weeks out with a broken finger, became Starc's first victim, and de Bruyn, picked as an extra batsman ahead of a fourth seamer, quickly followed. With Starc finding prodigious movement, the tail stood little chance. Australia led by 189, and even a more disciplined South African bowling effort could not drag the game back. Bancroft reached his second Test half-century, but no one else passed 38, and Maharaj finished with career-best match figures of nine for 225.

BEST FIGURES FOR AUSTRALIA IN SOUTH AFRICA

13-173	C. V. Grimmett (7-100, 6-73) at Durban	1935-36
12-127	M. G. Johnson (7-68, 5-59) at Centurion	2013-14
10-88	C. V. Grimmett (5-32, 5-56) at Cape Town	1935-36
10-110	C. V. Grimmett (3-70, 7-40) at Johannesburg (Old Wanderers)	1935-36
9-66	J. V. Saunders (2-32, 7-34) at Johannesburg (Old Wanderers)	1902-03
9-82	A. K. Davidson (4-44, 5-38) at Port Elizabeth	1957-58
9-89	S. R. Clark (5-55, 4-34) at Cape Town	2005-06
9-99	W. P. Howell (4-18, 5-81) at Cape Town	1902-03
9-109	**M. A. Starc (5-34, 4-75) at Durban**	**2017-18**
9-141	**P. J. Cummins (5-83, 4-58) at Johannesburg**	**2017-18**
9-144	R. Benaud (4-95, 5-49) at Cape Town	1957-58
9-154	R. Benaud (4-70, 5-84) at Johannesburg	1957-58

The three instances by Grimmett, aged 44, were in successive Tests, the last of his career.

Set 417, South Africa quickly found themselves 49 for four, encouraging talk of a 4–0 defeat. In particular, the run-out of de Villiers for a duck sent Australia into a frenzy. Warner, who threw the ball in for Lyon to break the stumps, screamed in the direction of Markram, who had sent de Villiers back after suggesting a single. To add insult to injury, Lyon – rushing towards his team-mates after completing the run-out – deliberately dropped the ball on to de Villiers, who had dived for the crease and lay sprawled on the ground. It was an undignified vignette.

That Markram was able to keep out the Australian bowlers and their sledging earned him respect. He also showed off a full range of strokes on his way to a century, prompting former South African captain Ali Bacher to declare him "a new star". Only Mike Atherton, in his famous vigil at Johannesburg in 1995-96, had made more in the fourth innings of a Test in South Africa since readmission. But Markram was dismissed late on the fourth day, and Australia needed little time on the fifth to remove de Kock and take a 1–0 lead. The games, though, had only just begun.

Man of the Match: M. A. Starc.

Close of play: first day, Australia 225-5 (M. R. Marsh 32, Paine 21); second day, South Africa 162; third day, Australia 213-9 (Cummins 17, Hazlewood 4); fourth day, South Africa 293-9 (de Kock 81, Morkel 0).

Australia

C. T. Bancroft c de Kock b Philander	5	– st de Kock b Maharaj	53
D. A. Warner c de Villiers b Philander	51	– c sub (P. W. A. Mulder) b Rabada . . .	28
U. T. Khawaja c de Kock b Rabada	14	– c de Kock b Maharaj	6
*S. P. D. Smith c de Villiers b Maharaj	56	– lbw b Elgar	38
S. E. Marsh c de Villiers b Maharaj	40	– c de Villiers b Morkel	33
M. R. Marsh c Morkel b Philander	96	– c Amla b Rabada	6
†T. D. Paine c de Kock b Rabada	25	– c de Villiers b Maharaj	14
P. J. Cummins b Maharaj	3	– b Maharaj	26
M. A. Starc b Maharaj	35	– c Elgar b Morkel	7
N. M. Lyon c de Bruyn b Maharaj	12	– c Amla b Morkel	2
J. R. Hazlewood not out	0	– not out	9
B 4, lb 8	12	Lb 5	5

1/15 (1) 2/39 (3) 3/95 (2)	(110.4 overs) 351	1/56 (2) 2/71 (3)	(74.4 overs) 227
4/151 (4) 5/177 (5) 6/237 (7)		3/108 (1) 4/146 (4)	
7/251 (8) 8/300 (9) 9/341 (6) 10/351 (10)		5/156 (6) 6/175 (7) 7/185 (5)	
		8/203 (9) 9/209 (10) 10/227 (8)	

Morkel 22–3–75–0; Philander 27–12–59–3; Maharaj 33.4–5–123–5; Rabada 25–7–74–2; Markram 1–0–2–0; de Bruyn 2–0–6–0. *Second innings*—Morkel 15–4–47–3; Philander 14–4–35–0; Maharaj 29.4–4–102–4; Rabada 13–5–28–2; Elgar 3–1–10–1.

South Africa

D. Elgar c and b Lyon	7	– (2) c Paine b Starc	9
A. K. Markram c Bancroft b Cummins	32	– (1) c Paine b M. R. Marsh	143
H. M. Amla c Bancroft b Lyon	0	– lbw b Hazlewood	8
A. B. de Villiers not out	71	– run out (Warner/Lyon)	0
*F. du Plessis c Paine b Starc	15	– b Cummins	4
T. B. de Bruyn c Paine b Starc	6	– c Paine b Hazlewood	36
†Q. de Kock b Lyon	20	– lbw b Hazlewood	83
V. D. Philander c Paine b Starc	8	– c Paine b Starc	6
K. A. Maharaj b Hazlewood	0	– b Starc	0
K. Rabada lbw b Starc	3	– b Starc	0
M. Morkel b Starc	0	– not out	3
		B 2, lb 3, nb 1	6

1/27 (1) 2/27 (3) 3/55 (2)   (51.4 overs) 162   1/29 (2) 2/39 (3)   (92.4 overs) 298
4/92 (5) 5/108 (6) 6/150 (7)   3/39 (4) 4/49 (5)
7/158 (8) 8/159 (9) 9/162 (10) 10/162 (11)   5/136 (6) 6/283 (1) 7/290 (8)
                                                      8/290 (9) 9/290 (10) 10/298 (7)

Starc 10.4–3–34–5; Hazlewood 13–5–31–1; Lyon 16–3–50–3; Cummins 12–2–47–1. *Second innings*—Starc 18–2–75–4; Hazlewood 15.4–2–61–3; Lyon 32–7–86–0; Cummins 15–3–47–1; M. R. Marsh 7–2–21–1; Smith 5–3–3–0.

Umpires: H. D. P. K. Dharmasena and S. Ravi.   Third umpire: C. B. Gaffaney.
Referee: J. J. Crowe.

SOUTH AFRICA v AUSTRALIA

Second Test

At Port Elizabeth, March 9–12, 2018. South Africa won by six wickets. Toss: Australia.

South Africa's resolve had strengthened after their Durban defeat and the stairwell saga. They were no longer merely motivated, said captain du Plessis: they were now "motivated-slash-angry". Australia continued to support Warner following the set-to with de Kock, insisting he was defending his wife. And while the South African management never publicly confirmed whether the comment from de Kock that so enraged Warner had been about Candice and a long-ago fling with rugby player Sonny Bill Williams, neither did they deny it. Some said de Kock had gone too far.

To avoid an escalation, match referee Jeff Crowe spoke to both captains before the Test, instructing them to keep their players under control. But he could not demand the same of the Port Elizabeth crowd, some of whom hatched a plan to antagonise Warner and shame his wife, who was at the game. They made Williams masks, and printed songsheets containing lewd lyrics. The masks were not allowed into the ground at first, but – incredibly – CSA officials intervened to ensure they were.

When the cricket began, Bancroft and Warner put on 98 after Smith had won the toss, only for all ten wickets to tumble for 145. The damage was done by Rabada, who either side of tea took five for 13 in 18 balls, including three in an over. The first of the five was Smith, whose shoulder Rabada brushed in his follow-through; it really was little more than that, although Smith's reaction seemed designed to make it look worse. Rabada was later charged with a Level Two offence, which would incur a ban.

But before South Africa could concern themselves with the misdemeanour of one of their players, they had to deal with unbecoming conduct from their officials. A photograph of CSA's communication manager Altaaf Kazi and commercial manager Clive Eksteen posing with three fans wearing Sonny Bill masks was published in the Australian press. Kazi and Eksteen were suspended and sent back to CSA headquarters in Johannesburg (Kazi subsequently resigned), while the board issued an apology to Cricket Australia and the Warners. Masks were not allowed for the rest of the match.

That was not the end of spectator involvement. On the second day, the umpires asked the St George's Park brass band to play only between overs, prompting them to leave the ground in protest. Other fans objected to the fussiness, and the band returned before the day was out. The cricket was more subdued. Elgar and Amla crawled through the second session, scoring 43 in 26 overs. On a tricky pitch, their dismissals started a mini-collapse of five for 72, but de Villiers was on hand to complete what he had started in Durban,

---

BEST FIGURES FOR SOUTH AFRICA AT HOME TO AUSTRALIA

11-150	**K. Rabada (5-96, 6-54) at Port Elizabeth**	**2017-18**
10-116	C. B. Llewellyn (5-43, 5-73) at Johannesburg (Old Wanderers)	1902-03
10-178	M. Ntini (6-100, 4-78) at Johannesburg	2005-06
9-51	**V. D. Philander (3-30, 6-21) at Johannesburg**	**2017-18**
9-103	M. J. Procter (3-30, 6-73) at Port Elizabeth	1969-70
9-110	**M. Morkel (4-87, 5-23) at Cape Town**	**2017-18**
9-161	P. L. Harris (3-34, 6-127) at Cape Town	2008-09
9-167	H. J. Tayfield (7-23, 2-144) at Durban	1949-50
9-216	C. B. Llewellyn (6-92, 3-124) at Johannesburg (Old Wanderers)	1902-03
9-225	**K. A. Maharaj (5-123, 4-102) at Durban**	**2017-18**

---

scoring his 22nd Test hundred – though his first since January 2015. It was a reprise of the previous 21, full of signature strokes: the slice behind square, the audacious front-foot pull, the reverse sweep. He put on 84 for the eighth wicket with Philander and 58 for the ninth with Maharaj, and was left undefeated on 126, his sixth Test century against Australia. It was, he said, "right up there with the best feeling ever". And it meant South Africa were 139 in front.

Just as Australia's lead at Durban had proved enough, so did South Africa's here. Knowing this could be his last Test of the series, Rabada ran in like a man possessed. When he bowled Warner, he screamed in his face, earning yet another demerit point. But he was undeterred, adding two wickets later on the third afternoon, including top-scorer Khawaja, and three on the fourth morning, as Australia tried to retaliate. When Rabada bowled Mitchell Marsh, the batsman mouthed an obscenity in his direction. It was just the latest incident to incur Crowe's displeasure.

Rabada finished with six for 54, and 11 for 150 in all, but described his success as "bittersweet", and said his behaviour had "let the team down". Even so, he was the reason South Africa's target was a relatively straightforward 101, polished off for the loss of four wickets. But their celebrations were short-lived. A few hours after they had squared the series, Rabada was found guilty of nudging Smith, fined 50% of his match fee and given three demerit points, taking his total to eight – nine after the Warner incident. It added up to a two-Test suspension.

Then came another twist. As South Africa's cricketers prepared for Cape Town, their lawyers got to work. Two days before the start of the next Test, Rabada's punishment was downgraded from three points to one, freeing him up to play. Incensed, the Australians turned up at Newlands nursing dark thoughts.

Man of the Match: K. Rabada.

Close of play: first day, South Africa 39-1 (Elgar 11, Rabada 17); second day, South Africa 263-7 (de Villiers 74, Philander 14); third day, Australia 180-5 (M. R. Marsh 39, Paine 5).

Australia

C. T. Bancroft c de Kock b Philander	38	– b Ngidi	24
D. A. Warner b Ngidi	63	– b Rabada	13
U. T. Khawaja c de Kock b Philander	4	– lbw b Rabada	75
*S. P. D. Smith lbw b Rabada	25	– c de Kock b Maharaj	11
S. E. Marsh lbw b Rabada	24	– c de Kock b Rabada	1
†T. D. Paine b Ngidi	36	– (7) not out	28
M. R. Marsh c de Kock b Rabada	4	– (6) b Rabada	45
P. J. Cummins c de Kock b Rabada	0	– c de Bruyn b Rabada	5
M. A. Starc b Rabada	8	– c de Kock b Rabada	1
N. M. Lyon b Ngidi	17	– b Ngidi	5
J. R. Hazlewood not out	10	– c Ngidi b Maharaj	17
Lb 14	14	B 2, lb 10, w 2	14

1/98 (1) 2/104 (3) 3/117 (2)   (71.3 overs) 243
4/161 (4) 5/166 (5) 6/170 (7)
7/170 (6) 8/182 (9) 9/212 (10) 10/243 (6)

1/27 (1) 2/62 (1)   (79 overs) 239
3/77 (4) 4/86 (5)
5/173 (3) 6/186 (6) 7/202 (8)
8/204 (9) 9/211 (10) 10/239 (11)

Philander 18–7–25–2; Rabada 21–2–96–5; Ngidi 13.3–3–51–3; Maharaj 18–1–51–0; Elgar 1–0–6–0. *Second innings*—Philander 18–5–56–0; Rabada 22–9–54–6; Maharaj 23–2–90–2; Ngidi 13–5–24–2; Markram 3–1–3–0.

South Africa

D. Elgar c Paine b Hazlewood	57	– (2) c and b Lyon	5
A. K. Markram lbw b Cummins	11	– (1) c Smith b Hazlewood	21
K. Rabada b Cummins	29		
H. M. Amla b Starc	56	– (3) c Paine b Cummins	27
A. B. de Villiers not out	126	– (4) c Bancroft b Lyon	28
*F. du Plessis lbw b M. R. Marsh	9	– (5) not out	2
T. B. de Bruyn lbw b M. R. Marsh	1	– (6) not out	15
†Q. de Kock b Lyon	9		
V. D. Philander c Bancroft b Cummins	36		
K. A. Maharaj b Hazlewood	30		
L. T. Ngidi run out (Smith)	5		
B 9, lb 2, w 2	13	B 4	4

1/22 (2) 2/67 (3) 3/155 (4)   (118.4 overs) 382
4/155 (1) 5/179 (6) 6/183 (7)
7/227 (8) 8/311 (9) 9/369 (10) 10/382 (11)

1/22 (2)   (4 wkts, 22.5 overs) 102
2/32 (1) 3/81 (3)
4/81 (4)

Starc 33.4–5–110–1; Hazlewood 30–5–98–2; Cummins 24–6–79–3; Lyon 22–5–58–1; M. R. Marsh 9–1–26–2. *Second innings*—Starc 3–0–15–0; Hazlewood 6–0–26–1; Lyon 9–0–44–2; Cummins 4.5–0–13–1.

Umpires: H. D. P. K. Dharmasena and C. B. Gaffaney.   Third umpire: S. Ravi.
Ravi replaced Gaffaney from the second day, and B. P. Jele replaced Ravi as third umpire.
Referee: J. J. Crowe.

> **❝** The game began to resemble a variety show: Short smashed a hospitality-box window, another six knocked a beer from a spectator's grasp, and a fan earned $50,000 for a one-handed catch."
>
> The Trans-Tasman T20 Tri-Series in 2017-18, page 265

SOUTH AFRICA v AUSTRALIA

Third Test

At Cape Town, March 22–25, 2018. South Africa won by 322 runs. Toss: South Africa.

On the third afternoon of a Test that was drifting away from Australia, TV cameras spotted Bancroft, stationed in the covers, applying something to the ball. It wasn't quite clear what: the item was small and yellow, and soon disappeared into his pocket. Over in the dug-out, twelfth man Peter Handscomb chatted smilingly on a walkie-talkie, apparently to coach Darren Lehmann up in the dressing-room. Handscomb came out on as a substitute fielder and spoke to Bancroft, who hid the object down the front of his trousers. The umpires, Nigel Llong and Richard Illingworth, approached him. Smith joined the conversation, and Bancroft produced a black cloth from his pocket by way of explanation. The umpires seemed satisfied, and the ball was not changed. But the series, and the careers of three players, had been irrevocably altered.

That evening, with South Africa in command, Smith and Bancroft turned up at the press conference. Smith began by turning to Bancroft to ask: "Do you want to explain?" Bancroft confessed to tampering with the ball, but claimed he had used sticky tape to collect granules of earth, which he rubbed on one side of the ball to hasten reverse swing. The tape, it later emerged, was in reality a piece of yellow sandpaper. He looked sheepish, while Smith mixed remorse with self-preservation. He said he was "embarrassed", and called the incident "deeply regrettable"; he claimed tampering had never previously occurred under his leadership, and said he remained the right person to captain Australia. Four months earlier, he and Bancroft had sat side by side after the First Ashes Test at Brisbane and ridiculed Jonny Bairstow about his infamous headbutt. They were smiling no longer.

Next morning, neither Smith nor vice-captain Warner – part of the leadership group Smith said had orchestrated the plan – was in post. It was reported that Warner had initiated the ruse, showing Bancroft how to tamper with the ball, while Smith turned a blind eye. The captaincy passed to Paine, who had only recently returned to the Test side after a seven-year absence. And that afternoon, the ICC announced Smith had been banned for the series finale. But the recriminations were not over.

Egged on by prime minister Malcolm Turnbull, Cricket Australia launched their own probe. Their results, made public three days after the Test finished, were pitiless: year-long bans for Smith and Warner, and nine months for Bancroft. All three were sent home before the Fourth Test, while CA chief executive James Sutherland promised an independent review into "the conduct and culture" of the side. Meanwhile, rumours spread about rifts in the Australian camp, with the bowling members of the leadership group – Hazlewood, Lyon and Starc – said to be unhappy that Smith had implicated them. Once home, the banned trio all broke down in separate press conferences. After seeing Smith and Bancroft in distress (Warner's mea culpa came later), Lehmann announced the Johannesburg Test would be his last in charge. These were spectacular falls from grace – and they utterly overshadowed an excellent performance by South Africa.

The game had been set up by Elgar, who held them together with one of his more free-flowing knocks. De Villiers contributed 64, but of the rest only Amla passed 22. Bavuma, picked ahead of Theunis de Bruyn despite a broken hand keeping him out since January, was one of four middle-order victims for Cummins, as South Africa collapsed from 220 for two to 257 for eight. But on the second morning Elgar dragged them over 300, batting for seven and a quarter hours and becoming the first man in Test history to carry his bat twice in a calendar year (he had made an unbeaten 86 out of 177 against India at Johannesburg two months earlier). He and West Indies' Desmond Haynes were now the only players to do it three times in all.

Attention turned to Rabada, reprieved and refreshed after his brush with the law – and Smith's shoulder. His battle with Warner proved a microcosm of the series: hard-hitting,

THE VIEW FROM SOUTH AFRICA
"They've got the evidence"

NEIL MANTHORP

When A. B. de Villiers suggested that Graeme Smith, his old friend and captain – and now a TV commentator – might engineer closer scrutiny of the Australian team's maintenance of the ball during the Second Test, he didn't realise he had been beaten to the punch. The umpires and match referee had already spoken informally to host broadcasters SuperSport after the First, and wondered if a cameraman had spotted anything unusual as the ball made its way back to the bowler.

And so, when David Warner, Australia's ball-shiner-in-chief, took the field at Port Elizabeth sporting elaborate bandaging on his left hand, close-ups appeared repeatedly on the giant screen. Towards the end of the game, he decorated the bandages with the names of his wife, Candice, and his daughters, Ivy Mae and Indi Rae. That did nothing to allay South African suspicions: at Cape Town, they believed it was instructive that Warner was relieved of his polishing duties.

On the third afternoon of that Third Test, an electric buzz went through the commentary boxes like an item of breaking news. "They've got the evidence," said Smith off-air, as if breathless after a quick single. "They're editing it now and will play it in the next few minutes." The cameramen had been searching for an hour and a half. And what they had found changed everything.

When the events were replayed, culminating with the sight of Cameron Bancroft thrusting something down his trousers, Smith – still off-air – emitted a theatrical "Sandpaper!" He turned slightly pale, before his cheeks flushed red. "This does not look good for Australia," he said, aware of the understatement. Smith was not alone in his interpretation of the sequence of clips, which included coach Darren Lehmann on the walkie-talkie, and the arrival on the field of twelfth man Peter Handscomb. He suspected a greater conspiracy than Bancroft and Steve Smith would claim at that evening's press conference.

The scandal gripped South Africa, making headlines in places never normally featuring sport. The players and management took a keen interest in the outcome of Cricket Australia's hastily organised investigation. And when, back in Sydney, a tearful Warner dodged a question about whether Australia had previously tampered with the ball, no one missed his evasiveness.

Faf du Plessis admitted before the final Test at Johannesburg that his team had harboured suspicions of tampering as far back as the fractious series opener at Durban, but conceded there was no evidence. He was also happy to admit that both teams had been "looking to get reverse", but insisted his side had done so legally: "We certainly weren't walking around with sandpaper in our pockets."

There was barely a cricket follower in the country who hadn't seen Bancroft's panic or Warner's bandages. But the sight of Smith being hustled through Johannesburg airport by armed police to a background of taunts and jeers took things to an unacceptable level of nastiness.

South Africans easily forgave Quinton de Kock for his remark to Warner about his wife's liaison with Sonny Bill Williams, because they felt de Kock had reached a tipping point after two hours of almost non-stop taunting by Warner. But a nation familiar with real crime winced at the sight of cheating cricketers being treated like terror suspects. It had all spiralled out of control.

Gianluigi Guercia, AFP/Getty Images

Cape destroyer: Kagiso Rabada castles David Warner, whose predicament soon became worse.

spiteful, engrossing, and ultimately won by South Africa. Warner was hit on the arm by Rabada's second ball, and square-drove his third for four. Then, in five deliveries spread across two overs, he scythed four fours and hooked a six over fine leg. Rabada's next ball took out off stump. As Warner walked back, he was confronted by a member of the public, who landed an insult before security intervened. Inevitably, a small section of the crowd wore Sonny Bill Williams masks, prompting Lehmann – who had once encouraged Australian fans to send Stuart Broad home from the Ashes in tears – to label them a "disgrace". Cricket Australia lodged a complaint with CSA, who upped the security presence.

Bancroft prospered, but the cheap removal of Khawaja and Smith by Morkel – back in the side after Lungi Ngidi injured a toe – meant Australia needed a big effort from their middle order. They were stable on 150 for three, until Shaun Marsh chased a wide one to give Morkel his 300th Test wicket. It was the first of five to fall for 25, as Philander and Rabada made hay. Paine and Lyon resisted but, when Hazlewood fell to Rabada on the third morning, South Africa led by 56. Cummins quickly removed Elgar, but the pitch had flattened, allowing Markram and de Villiers to dig in. With the score on 129 for two, and Australia desperate for a breakthrough, the cameras zoomed in on Bancroft.

The rest of the innings passed in a blur. Markram fell for 84, and de Villiers for his second sixty of the match; du Plessis failed again, and Bavuma once more looked rusty. But it was incidental. All that mattered was the contents of Bancroft's trousers.

The morning after the press conference had a sombre air. De Kock and Philander registered half-centuries, and Lyon his 300th Test wicket (Rabada, stumped). It left Australia needing 430 – implausible even if they had been in the mood. They reached 57, before Bancroft was run out, sparking a collapse of ten for 50 in 19 overs. Morkel's five for 23 gave him a Test-best haul of nine for 110, and ensured South Africa could not lose the series. He called it "the highlight of my life". In the other dressing-room, Australia were experiencing the other end of the scale.

Man of the Match: M. Morkel.

Close of play: first day, South Africa 266-8 (Elgar 121, Rabada 6); second day, Australia 245-9 (Paine 33, Hazlewood 1); third day, South Africa 238-5 (de Villiers 51, de Kock 29).

THE VIEW FROM AUSTRALIA

Brazen, blatant and inept

GREG BAUM

Sandpapergate triggered two unprecedented outpourings in Australia. The first was anger towards the team. It was instant, visceral and almost universal. Compounded by the fissile power of social media, it engulfed the country. Backlash was followed by further lash, in the form of draconian suspensions for the three central players. Australia felt betrayed.

The second outpouring also came from deep inside. It was from the cricketers themselves, as the gravity of their situation dawned on them, and their country's horror hit them in the face. It had already been a testy and turbulent tour, but if they had thought this would be just one more incident to sleep on and ride out, they were quickly and wholly disabused. Shock followed upon shock, tripping over further shock: ours at them, them at our reaction, and finally them at themselves.

Hysterical receptions, sleepless nights, and long, lonely trips on separate planes followed for the protagonists, before the cascade of bewilderment pooled in four wrenching and macabre media conferences. Ricky Ponting, who must have thought he had seen everything in cricket, said he couldn't bring himself to watch.

Steve Smith and David Warner were both moved to free-flowing tears, Cameron Bancroft to the point of them. Even coach Darren Lehmann, as he announced his resignation back in South Africa, found his voice catching; when done, he rubbed his eyes vigorously with balled fists. In a country where the sight of men crying still causes discomfort, the tears were the thing. Here, literally, was an outpouring. Here was the scandal hitting home.

We watched and listened in fascination, but didn't learn much. Bancroft made a gaffe about how what hurt him most was to have given up so easily his hard-won place in the team. It might not have sounded as he intended. Otherwise, the search for nitty-gritty yielded nothing, and Warner retreated over and over to a mantra-like line about how he was shouldering full and personal responsibility.

The four ransacked the thesaurus to convey variations on embarrassment, regret and apology, to ask for forgiveness and to pledge to make it up to Australia. Punctuation took the form of pauses, gulps, deep breaths and long exhalations, lowered heads, distant stares, and ever more reedy voices, choked off by tears.

For all four, the tripwire was family and kids. Themselves, they would have to live with; the public were at arm's length. But families were right there, helpless and innocent, not asking but wanting to know. It was a question about what kids should make of it all that led Smith's thoughts to his parents, and overwhelmed him. His father, Peter, stepped in to put a hand on his shoulder as his son dissolved into tears – a defining and indelible image. Soon after, the briefing was halted.

An ocean away in South Africa, the watching Lehmann felt a pang. He says it played no part in his decision to resign, and yet you wonder. If the press conferences answered few questions, the whole episode did pose one to the country. Ball-tampering was not new, nor really secret. Previous penalties had been minimal. Why did this instance catalyse such national outrage, and result in the self-administered decimation of the Australian cricket team, and for three of them, the 21st-century equivalent of being put in the stocks?

It can only be that their handiwork was so brazen, so blatant and so inept, and the attempt to cover it up so laughable. All summer long, as the Australians gabbled on about not crossing "the line", they had been accused of making it up as they went along. Now they had lost the plot altogether.

South Africa

D. Elgar not out	141	– (2) c Smith b Cummins	14
A. K. Markram c Smith b Hazlewood	0	– (1) c Cummins b Starc	84
H. M. Amla c Cummins b Hazlewood	31	– c Bancroft b Cummins	31
A. B. de Villiers c Warner b Cummins	64	– c S. E. Marsh b Hazlewood	63
*F. du Plessis c Smith b Cummins	5	– lbw b Lyon	20
T. Bavuma c Smith b Cummins	1	– c sub (P. S. P. Handscomb) b Hazlewood	5
†Q. de Kock c Paine b Cummins	3	– c Paine b Cummins	65
V. D. Philander c Paine b M. R. Marsh	8	– not out	52
K. A. Maharaj c Bancroft b Starc	3	– (10) c Cummins b Lyon	5
K. Rabada c Smith b Lyon	22	– (9) st Paine b Lyon	20
M. Morkel c Smith b Lyon	4	– c Khawaja b Hazlewood	6
B 13, lb 11, w 2, nb 3	29	B 4, lb 1, w 2, nb 1	8

1/6 (2) 2/92 (3) 3/220 (4) (97.5 overs) 311
4/234 (5) 5/236 (6) 6/242 (7)
7/254 (8) 8/257 (9) 9/307 (10) 10/311 (11)

1/28 (2) 2/104 (3) (112.2 overs) 373
3/151 (1) 4/196 (5)
5/201 (6) 6/269 (4) 7/324 (7)
8/354 (9) 9/362 (10) 10/373 (11)

Starc 21–3–81–1; Hazlewood 23–4–59–2; Lyon 19.5–6–43–2; Cummins 26–6–78–4; M. R. Marsh 7–2–26–1; Smith 1–1–0–0. *Second innings*—Starc 23–5–98–1; Hazlewood 25.2–5–69–3; Cummins 27–5–67–3; Lyon 31–2–102–3; Smith 1–0–6–0; M. R. Marsh 5–0–26–0.

Australia

C. T. Bancroft lbw b Philander	77	– run out (du Plessis)	26
D. A. Warner b Rabada	30	– c de Villiers b Rabada	32
U. T. Khawaja c Rabada b Morkel	5	– c de Villiers b Maharaj	1
*S. P. D. Smith c Elgar b Morkel	5	– c Elgar b Morkel	7
S. E. Marsh c de Kock b Morkel	26	– c Markram b Maharaj	4
M. R. Marsh c de Kock b Philander	5	– c de Villiers b Morkel	16
†T. D. Paine not out	34	– not out	9
P. J. Cummins c de Villiers b Rabada	4	– c Elgar b Morkel	0
M. A. Starc c de Villiers b Rabada	2	– c Markram b Morkel	7
N. M. Lyon c Elgar b Morkel	47	– run out (Bavuma/de Kock)	0
J. R. Hazlewood c Amla b Rabada	10	– c Philander b Morkel	5
B 1, lb 5, nb 4	10	B 4	4

1/43 (2) 2/61 (3) 3/72 (4) (69.5 overs) 255
4/150 (5) 5/150 (1) 6/156 (6)
7/173 (8) 8/175 (9) 9/241 (10) 10/255 (11)

1/57 (1) 2/59 (2) (39.4 overs) 107
3/59 (3) 4/59 (5)
5/75 (4) 6/86 (6) 7/86 (8)
8/94 (9) 9/94 (10) 10/107 (11)

Philander 15–5–26–2; Rabada 20.5–1–91–4; Morkel 21–7–87–4; Maharaj 12–3–35–0; Bavuma 1–0–10–0. *Second innings*—Rabada 12–6–31–1; Philander 6–2–17–0; Morkel 9.4–3–23–5; Maharaj 12–2–32–2.

Umpires: R. K. Illingworth and N. J. Llong.   Third umpire: I. J. Gould.
Referee: A. J. Pycroft.

> **"**He was an unconventional batsman who would occasionally switch to being a left-hander in the middle of an over: despite this, or perhaps because of it, he failed to reach double figures in his nine first-class matches."
> Obituaries, page 207

SOUTH AFRICA v AUSTRALIA

Fourth Test

At Johannesburg, March 30–April 3, 2018. South Africa won by 492 runs. Toss: South Africa. Test debut: C. J. Sayers.

With South Africa needing only a draw to clinch the series, and Morkel set to retire from the international prevailing stage, the Fourth Test should have been about celebration. But that was far from the prevailing mood. After announcing he would resign as Australian coach, Lehmann said he had not slept for days, while both camps admitted they were emotionally drained. Du Plessis even likened the series to a soap opera, and said it had been a challenge to keep his players focused. Above all, the teams promised to bury the hatchet. Inspired by football, Paine suggested they shake hands after the national anthems. South Africa agreed. But the whole thing was rather disconcerting, and Elgar later said he had never encountered such a "docile" Australian side.

Events at Cape Town meant recalls for Queenslanders Renshaw and Burns, who had arrived from the Sheffield Shield final less than 48 hours earlier, and Handscomb (Glenn Maxwell was also added to the squad). Australia had to make a fourth change when Mitchell Starc suffered a stress fracture of the shin, also ruling him out of the IPL. In came the 30-year-old South Australian seamer Chadd Sayers for his debut. Australia looked ripe for the plucking.

Sure enough, on a Wanderers pitch more placid than usual – it had been rated poor following the Test against India, so groundsman Bethuel Buthelezi played it safe – they were made to toil after South Africa chose to bat. Markram struck a majestic career-best

FEWEST TESTS TO REACH 1,000 RUNS

		I	NO	HS	100	50	Avge
7	D. G. Bradman (Australia)	13	1	334	5	2	99.66
9	H. Sutcliffe (England).	12	1	176	5	4	92.27
9	E. D. Weekes (West Indies)	13	0	194	5	2	82.46
9	G. A. Headley (West Indies).	18	1	223	6	0	61.11
10	R. N. Harvey (Australia).	15	4	178	6	2	95.00
10	F. M. M. Worrell (West Indies)	16	2	261	3	3	72.00
10	G. S. Ballance (England)	17	2	156	4	5	67.93
10	M. A. Taylor (Australia).	18	1	219	3	5	64.00
10	**A. K. Markram (South Africa)**	**18**	**0**	**152**	**4**	**3**	**55.55**
10	A. J. Strauss (England)	20	2	137	4	4	58.61

Figures shown to the end of the match in which the player reached 1,000.

152, adding 89 with Amla and 105 with de Villiers, who passed 50 for the eighth time in 14 Test innings since three successive ducks against England in January 2016. Du Plessis fell first ball to Cummins, leaving him with 65 runs in nine, but Bavuma consolidated on the second day, before speeding up. Maharaj threw the bat at everything during a ninth-wicket stand of 76, but – with Bavuma on 95 – fell slashing at a wide one from Cummins. Morkel fended the next delivery to second slip to leave Bavuma stranded, and Cummins with a hard-earned five-for. Even so, the last four wickets had contributed 189. South Africa's 488 was the highest total of the series.

Australia's revamped top order made no impression. Burns and Renshaw departed quickly; Handscomb was bowled first ball by Philander. When the Marsh brothers succumbed in successive overs shortly before the close, it was 96 for six. Shaun Marsh might have been out earlier had de Kock not fluffed a stumping. He had a valid excuse: a bee stung him as he collected the ball.

Paine, batting with a hairline fracture of his right thumb, and Cummins mounted a mini-revival on the third morning, adding 99 as Cummins made his first Test fifty, but South Africa secured a lead of 267. A variety of niggles among his bowlers, however, dissuaded du Plessis from enforcing the follow-on: Morkel had a side strain, Philander a heavily strapped groin, and Rabada lower-back trouble, later found to be a stress fracture. South Africa batted and batted, for over seven and a half hours, and their lead grew, past 400, past 500, past 600. Elgar ground out 81 at slower than a run an over, while du Plessis overcame a blow from Sayers to the finger he had broken against India ending his drought by scoring his eighth Test hundred.

By tea on the fourth day, he decided South Africa had run Australia out of the series, and his bowlers – fit or not – were ready for a final flourish. They turned in an inspired display. Morkel bowled off two-thirds of his normal run-up, at reduced pace, but still removed both openers that evening; in between, Maharaj pinned Khawaja. But, on the final morning, it was Philander who woke up raring to go.

He had Shaun Marsh held at gully with the first ball of the day, and Mitchell Marsh caught behind with the fourth – his 200th Test wicket. After that, it was a procession: Handscomb dragged on trying to leave, Paine edged behind, Cummins was bowled shouldering arms, and Sayers drove to third slip, completing a pair. In 32 balls, Philander had taken six for three. His overall figures of six for 21 were a Test-best – and the joint-third-cheapest haul of six or more against Australia, behind England's Stuart Broad (eight for 15 at Trent Bridge in 2015) and Wilfred Rhodes (seven for 17 at Edgbaston in 1902). Soon after, the run-out of Lyon confirmed South Africa's first home series win against Australia since the 4–0 whitewash of 1969-70, and their biggest win by runs against anyone, surpassing 358 against New Zealand at the same ground more than a decade earlier. It was Australia's second-biggest defeat, after 675 against England at Brisbane in 1928-29.

Du Plessis called the performance their "most complete" of the series, and praised his team for maintaining a sense of calm. Paine was matter-of-fact as he looked ahead to a year without Smith and Warner. He added: "A lot of us have got to step up and take the slack." The rest of the sport looked on, unsure whether to laugh or cry.

Man of the Match: V. D. Philander.   *Man of the Series:* K. Rabada.

Close of play: first day, South Africa 313-6 (Bavuma 25, de Kock 7); second day, Australia 110-6 (Paine 5, Cummins 7); third day, South Africa 134-3 (Elgar 39, du Plessis 34); fourth day, Australia 88-3 (Handscomb 23, S. E. Marsh 7).

South Africa

D. Elgar c Sayers b Lyon	19	– (2) c S. E. Marsh b Lyon 81
A. K. Markram c M. R. Marsh b Cummins	152	– (1) c Handscomb b Cummins 37
H. M. Amla c Handscomb b Cummins	27	– c M. R. Marsh b Lyon 16
A. B. de Villiers c Paine b Sayers	69	– c Paine b Cummins 6
*F. du Plessis lbw b Cummins	0	– c Handscomb b Cummins 120
T. Bavuma not out	95	– not out 35
K. Rabada c Renshaw b Sayers	0	
†Q. de Kock c M. R. Marsh b Lyon	39	– (7) lbw b Cummins 4
V. D. Philander c Khawaja b Lyon	12	– (8) not out 33
K. A. Maharaj c Paine b Cummins	45	
M. Morkel c Handscomb b Cummins	0	
B 13, lb 12, w 5	30	B 4, lb 8 12
	——	——

1/53 (1) 2/142 (3) 3/247 (2)   (136.5 overs) 488   1/54 (1)   (6 wkts dec, 105 overs) 344
4/247 (5) 5/299 (4) 6/299 (7)   2/79 (3) 3/94 (4)
7/384 (8) 8/412 (9) 9/488 (10) 10/488 (11)   4/264 (5) 5/266 (2) 6/273 (7)

Hazlewood 26–3–86–0; Sayers 35–9–78–2; Cummins 28.5–5–83–5; Lyon 40–3–182–3; M. R. Marsh 6–1–30–0; Renshaw 1–0–4–0. *Second innings*—Hazlewood 21–6–41–0; Sayers 14–2–68–0; Lyon 41–13–116–2; Cummins 18–5–58–4; M. R. Marsh 8–0–40–0; Renshaw 3–0–9–0.

Australia

M. T. Renshaw c de Kock b Philander	8	– lbw b Morkel	5
J. A. Burns c du Plessis b Rabada	4	– lbw b Morkel	42
U. T. Khawaja c de Kock b Philander	53	– lbw b Maharaj	7
P. S. P. Handscomb b Philander	0	– b Philander	24
S. E. Marsh c de Villiers b Maharaj	16	– c Bavuma b Philander	7
M. R. Marsh b Morkel	4	– c de Kock b Philander	0
*†T. D. Paine c Elgar b Rabada	62	– c de Kock b Philander	7
P. J. Cummins lbw b Maharaj	50	– b Philander	1
N. M. Lyon c Elgar b Rabada	8	– run out (Markram/de Kock)	9
C. J. Sayers c Amla b Maharaj	0	– c Elgar b Philander	0
J. R. Hazlewood not out	1	– not out	9
B 3, lb 9, nb 3	15	Lb 1, nb 7	8

1/10 (2) 2/34 (1) 3/38 (4)	(70 overs)	221
4/90 (3) 5/96 (6) 6/96 (5)		
7/195 (8) 8/206 (9) 9/207 (10) 10/221 (7)		

1/21 (1) 2/34 (3)	(46.4 overs)	119
3/68 (2) 4/88 (5)		
5/88 (6) 6/95 (4) 7/99 (7)		
8/100 (8) 9/100 (10) 10/119 (9)		

Philander 18–8–30–3; Rabada 19–7–53–3; Morkel 12.2–3–34–1; Maharaj 20–3–92–3; Markram 0.4–0–0–0. *Second innings*—Rabada 8–3–16–0; Philander 13–5–21–6; Maharaj 13–2–47–1; Morkel 10.4–5–28–2; Markram 2–0–6–0.

Umpires: I. J. Gould and N. J. Llong.   Third umpire: R. K. Illingworth.
Referee: A. J. Pycroft.

SOUTH AFRICA v ZIMBABWE IN 2018-19

Lungani Zama

One-day internationals (3): South Africa 3, Zimbabwe 0
Twenty20 internationals (3): South Africa 2, Zimbabwe 0

As thoughts turned towards the World Cup in England in 2019, South Africa took the chance to test their one-day bench strength during this low-key series against their neighbours. Zimbabwe competed bravely at times, but were predictably outclassed, and saved from a 6–0 whitewash only by the rain that ruined the final match, in Benoni.

South Africa faced the task of replacing A. B. de Villiers, who had announced his retirement from international cricket four months previously. They were also lacking Hashim Amla, who had injured a finger during the Caribbean Premier League, and Quinton de Kock, who was rested from the one-day series. David Miller also skipped the 50-over matches, although he and de Kock returned for the Twenty20s. All this meant a white-ball recall for Test opener Dean Elgar, a rare chance for reserve wicketkeeper Heinrich Klaasen, and another for the 32-year-old Warriors finisher Christiaan Jonker.

South Africa also welcomed back two key bowlers. Leg-spinner Imran Tahir, 39 but still full of beans, returned after a county stint and a CPL contract. But the latest comeback of Dale Steyn – injury-free after a spell with Hampshire – was even more heartening for the locals. Steyn entered the series with a point to prove to those who had written off his international prospects, and did well with the ball. He also turned one game with the bat.

The matches were spread around South Africa's lesser international venues, but the early-season pitches could have been better: the highest total in the 50-over series was a modest 231. The track at Kimberley, especially, was capricious – low and slow one minute, wicked bounce the next.

In front of small crowds, South Africa prevailed, but the tenacious Zimbabweans gave them more headaches than they might have expected. Without Steyn's surprise batting intervention – and a hat-trick from Tahir – Zimbabwe might well have won the second ODI, and they had their moments in the other matches. Kyle Jarvis was a threat, while his new-ball partner Tendai Chatara took six wickets in the one-day series. Tahir, though, matched that in one game, finished with 15 at 7.60 in all and won both series awards.

ZIMBABWE TOURING PARTY

*H. Masakadza (50/20), T. L. Chatara (50/20), C. J. Chibhabha (20), E. Chigumbura (50/20), T. S. Chisoro (20), C. R. Ervine (50), K. M. Jarvis (50/20), T. S. Kamunhukamwe (50), N. Madziva (20), W. P. Masakadza (50/20), B. A. Mavuta (50/20), S. F. Mire (50/20), P. J. Moor (50/20), C. B. Mpofu (20), R. C. Murray (50), T. K. Musakanda (20), R. Ngarava (50), B. R. M. Taylor (50/20), D. T. Tiripano (50), S. C. Williams (50/20). *Coach:* L. S. Rajput.

First one-day international At Kimberley, September 30, 2018. **South Africa won by five wickets. Zimbabwe 117** (34.1 overs) (L. T. Ngidi 3-19); ‡**South Africa 119-5** (26.1 overs) (H. Klaasen 44). *MoM:* L. T. Ngidi. *ODI debuts:* C. Jonker (South Africa); B. A. Mavuta (Zimbabwe).

The groundsman at Diamond Oval might have been tempted to disappear into the nearby Big Hole of Kimberley after producing a tricky pitch. J.-P. Duminy, captain while Faf du Plessis missed the first two matches with a shoulder injury, had no hesitation in bowling first, and Lungi Ngidi was soon exploiting a fuller length. Zimbabwe limped into three figures only thanks to Elton Chigumbura, who top-scored with 27 from No. 7. With Tendai Chatara removing both openers, South Africa wobbled to 40-3 after ten overs, but even on this surface the target was too small to cause real problems. Duminy (16*) passed 5,000 ODI runs just before the end.

Second one-day international   At Bloemfontein, October 3, 2018 (day/night). **South Africa won by 120 runs.** ‡**South Africa 198** (47.3 overs) (A. K. Markram 35, D. W. Steyn 60; T. L. Chatara 3-42); **Zimbabwe 78** (24 overs) (Imran Tahir 6-24). *MoM:* D. W. Steyn. *On another testing track, South Africa started indifferently again – 9-2 after 13 balls – and when they declined further to 101-7 in the 26th, Zimbabwe looked odds-on to square the series. But Dale Steyn, in his first ODI for two years, clobbered a maiden fifty, in his 117th match. He put on 75 with Andile Phehlukwayo (28) to give himself something to bowl at – then ripped out two quick wickets. Zimbabwe made it to 43-2, only to lose eight for 35, six to Imran Tahir, whose haul included South Africa's fourth ODI hat-trick. For the second time in two matches, Zimbabwe undercut their lowest score against South Africa, which before this series had been 119 at Centurion in November 2009.*

ODI HAT-TRICKS FOR SOUTH AFRICA

C. K. Langeveldt.	v West Indies at Bridgetown	2004-05
J.-P. Duminy	v Sri Lanka at Sydney	2014-15
K. Rabada†	v Bangladesh at Mirpur	2015
Imran Tahir.	**v Zimbabwe at Bloemfontein**	**2018-19**

†   *On debut.   Langeveldt's hat-trick ended the match when West Indies needed two runs to win.*

Third one-day international   At Paarl, October 6, 2018 (day/night). **South Africa won by four wickets.** ‡**Zimbabwe 228** (49.3 overs) (B. R. M. Taylor 40, S. C. Williams 69; D. W. Steyn 3-29, K. Rabada 3-32); **South Africa 231-6** (45.5 overs) (A. K. Markram 42, R. R. Hendricks 66, H. Klaasen 59). *MoM:* H. Klaasen. *MoS:* Imran Tahir. *South Africa swept the one-day series despite an improved batting performance from Zimbabwe. Sean Williams struck ten fours in his 69, and shared a careful fourth-wicket partnership of 73 with Brendan Taylor – but the later batsmen managed only 46 from the last ten overs. South Africa's openers began with a stand of 75 and, although the result deserted du Plessis (26) and Duminy fell in the space of 11 deliveries, the result was never in much doubt. Reeza Hendricks lasted 82 balls for his 66, then wicketkeeper Heinrich Klaasen made 59 from 67.*

First Twenty20 international   At East London, October 9, 2018 (floodlit). **South Africa won by 34 runs.** ‡**South Africa 160-6** (20 overs) (F. du Plessis 34, H. E. van der Dussen 56, D. A. Miller 39; K. M. Jarvis 3-37); **Zimbabwe 126** (17.2 overs) (P. J. Moor 44; Imran Tahir 5-23). *MoM:* Imran Tahir. *T20I debuts:* G. L. Cloete, H. E. van der Dussen (South Africa). *Both sides shuffled the pack from the 50-over series, but the results stayed the same. Quinton de Kock and David Miller returned for South Africa, but there was also a dream start for Rassie van der Dussen, who smacked 56 from 44 balls. Three quick strikes from Tahir, who took the new ball, reduced Zimbabwe to 11-3, and they were never on terms, despite an eighth-wicket stand of 53 between Peter Moor and Brendan Mavuta (28).*

Second Twenty20 international   At Potchefstroom, October 12, 2018 (floodlit). **South Africa won by six wickets.** ‡**Zimbabwe 132-7** (20 overs) (S. C. Williams 41); **South Africa 135-4** (15.4 overs) (J.-P. Duminy 33*). *MoM:* D. Paterson. *Zimbabwe did not make the most of the best batting pitch of their trip, throttled by testing seam bowling from Ngidi (2-36), Dane Paterson (2-22, with 17 dot balls), Robbie Frylinck (2-20) and Phehlukwayo (0-15, with 14 dots). South Africa had 51-1 after the powerplay and Duminy took them home with plenty to spare.*

Third Twenty20 international   At Benoni, October 14, 2018. **South Africa v Zimbabwe. Abandoned.** *MoS:* Imran Tahir.

SOUTH AFRICA v PAKISTAN IN 2018-19

Lungani Zama

Test matches (3): South Africa 3, Pakistan 0
One-day internationals (5): South Africa 3, Pakistan 2
Twenty20 internationals (2): South Africa 2, Pakistan 1

A year on from the high-profile visit of India and the shenanigans of the Australians in Cape Town, Pakistan arrived hoping to create drama of their own – and become the first side from the subcontinent to win a Test series in South Africa. They were adamant they were up to the task, with a fast-bowling attack capable of blowing holes in any line-up, and a coach – Mickey Arthur – who knew local conditions better than most. They had serious skill, and the chutzpah of youth.

But there was a caveat: Pakistan would have to score enough runs for their bowlers to work with – and South Africa has become the most unforgiving country in the world for batsmen. That view was only strengthened by what happened here. Hard though they fought, Pakistan couldn't overcome a barrage of nasty quick bowling. Dale Steyn had begun the series with a bit of history, overhauling Shaun Pollock's national-record 421 Test wickets on the first morning at Centurion. But the real damage was done by Duanne Olivier, whose previous five Tests had been spread across two years. He made himself undroppable, and finished with 24 wickets at 14, one short of the national record for a three-Test series (by Charles Llewellyn against Australia in 1902-03). Rapid, mean and partial to the bouncer, Olivier was central to South Africa's 3–0 win. It was their seventh Test series victory in a row at home, equalling the national record, set between March 1998 and November 2001.

But they didn't have it all their own way. In that First Test, they needed the calm head of Hashim Amla to chase down a potentially tricky total on a poor surface, while the Second, at Newlands, was settled by a partnership between Faf du Plessis and Temba Bavuma. South Africa left out spinner Keshav Maharaj after Centurion, with their pace attack clearly troubling a Pakistan top order that had talent, if not quite the temperament in testing conditions.

Even so, Babar Azam had a good tour, and Shan Masood was belligerent. Imam-ul-Haq occasionally sparkled – mainly in the one-dayers, where he was the Man of the Series – but South Africa always won the big moments. The result was tough on Pakistan, but they bowled better than they batted, with left-arm quicks Mohammad Amir and newcomer Shaheen Shah Afridi especially impressive.

The 50-over series turned into an exciting five-match fling. The find for South Africa was Rassie van der Dussen, who struck three half-centuries to complicate selection for the World Cup. His Lions team-mate Reeza Hendricks also showed class at the top of the order. It boiled down to a decider in Cape Town, where South Africa again seized the day, thanks to a brutal 83 from Quinton de Kock.

Gianluigi Guercia, AFP/Getty Images

Bloemfontein Bone Collector: Duanne Olivier takes to the stage as to the manner born.

For a while, the cricket took a back seat, as the authorities considered how to deal with comments made during the second game, at Durban, by Pakistan's captain, Sarfraz Ahmed. With Andile Phehlukwayo leading South Africa's chase, Sarfraz was caught on the stump mike referring to him, in Urdu, as "black guy". He later apologised, both to Phehlukwayo and to "the people of South Africa", prompting du Plessis to say: "We forgive him because he said sorry." But the ICC punished Sarfraz anyway, banning him for four white-ball matches.

The T20 series was a bit of a hit-and-giggle affair. South Africa rested most of their big guns, and gave chances to the talent that had came through their long-awaited Mzansi Super League. Pakistan ended a tough but entertaining visit by winning the last of the three games, but not before they had suffered their first series defeat in the format since visiting New Zealand early in 2016.

PAKISTAN TOURING PARTY

*Sarfraz Ahmed (T/50), Asad Shafiq (T), Asif Ali (20), Azhar Ali (T), Babar Azam (T/50/20), Fahim Ashraf (T/50/20), Fakhar Zaman (T/50/20), Haris Sohail (T), Hasan Ali (T/50/20), Hussain Talat (50/20), Imad Wasim (50/20), Imam-ul-Haq (T/50), Mohammad Abbas (T), Mohammad Amir (T/ 50/20), Mohammad Hafeez (50/20), Mohammad Rizwan (T/50/20), Sahibzada Farhan (20), Shadab Khan (T/50/20), Shaheen Shah Afridi (T/50/20), Shan Masood (T/50), Shoaib Malik (50/20), Usman Shinwari (50/20), Yasir Shah (T). *Coach:* J. M. Arthur.

Sarfraz Ahmed was suspended for the last two ODIs and the first two Twenty20s, and went home; Shoaib Malik captained instead, while Mohammad Rizwan was added to the T20 squad.

TEST MATCH AVERAGES

SOUTH AFRICA – BATTING AND FIELDING

	T	I	NO	R	HS	100	50	Avge	Ct
†Q. de Kock	3	4	0	251	129	1	1	62.75	17
H. M. Amla	3	6	2	209	71	0	2	52.25	3
T. Bavuma	3	5	1	172	75	0	2	43.00	1
A. K. Markram	3	5	0	201	90	0	2	40.20	3
F. du Plessis	2	4	1	106	103	1	0	35.33	4
†D. Elgar	3	6	1	126	50	0	1	25.20	5
D. W. Steyn	3	4	2	38	23	0	0	19.00	0
T. B. de Bruyn	3	6	0	112	49	0	0	18.66	3
†K. Rabada	3	4	0	51	21	0	0	12.75	5
V. D. Philander	2	3	0	31	16	0	0	10.33	1
D. Olivier	3	4	2	11	10*	0	0	5.50	0

Played in one Test: M. Z. Hamza 41, 0 (2 ct); K. A. Maharaj 4 (1 ct).

BOWLING

	Style	O	M	R	W	BB	5I	Avge
D. Olivier	RFM	88	16	353	24	6-37	3	14.70
K. Rabada	RF	86.2	14	318	17	4-61	0	18.70
V. D. Philander	RFM	57	17	171	6	3-43	0	28.50
D. W. Steyn	RFM	94.1	16	348	12	4-85	0	29.00

Also bowled: D. Elgar (SLA) 0.4–0–1–0; K. A. Maharaj (SLA) 14–3–44–0.

PAKISTAN – BATTING AND FIELDING

	T	I	NO	R	HS	100	50	Avge	Ct/St
Hasan Ali	2	4	3	54	22	0	0	54.00	2
†Shan Masood	3	6	0	228	65	0	2	38.00	0
Babar Azam	3	6	0	221	72	0	2	36.83	3
Asad Shafiq	3	6	0	186	88	0	2	31.00	4
†Imam-ul-Haq	3	6	0	149	57	0	1	24.83	0
Sarfraz Ahmed	3	6	0	112	56	0	1	18.66	18/1
Mohammad Abbas	2	4	1	30	11	0	0	10.00	2
Azhar Ali	3	6	0	59	36	0	0	9.83	1
†Mohammad Amir	3	6	1	49	22*	0	0	9.80	0
†Fakhar Zaman	2	4	0	32	12	0	0	8.00	2
†Shaheen Shah Afridi	2	4	0	21	14	0	0	5.25	0
Yasir Shah	2	4	0	14	5	0	0	3.50	0

Played in one Test: †Fahim Ashraf 0, 15; Shadab Khan 5, 47* (1 ct).

BOWLING

	Style	O	M	R	W	BB	5I	Avge
Fahim Ashraf	RFM	29	5	99	6	3-42	0	16.50
Shadab Khan	LB	21.3	2	80	4	3-41	0	20.00
Mohammad Amir	LFM	105.4	26	283	12	4-62	0	23.58
Shaheen Shah Afridi	LFM	60.1	5	240	9	4-44	0	26.66
Hasan Ali	RFM	65	14	267	6	2-70	0	44.50
Mohammad Abbas	RFM	74	17	231	5	2-44	0	46.20

Also bowled: Asad Shafiq (LB) 6–0–25–0; Azhar Ali (LB) 0.5–0–8–0; Shan Masood (RFM) 8–2–25–2; Yasir Shah (LB) 32.4–2–123–1.

SOUTH AFRICA v PAKISTAN

First Test

At Centurion, December 26–28, 2018. South Africa won by six wickets. Toss: Pakistan.

After several seasons of trying to resuscitate interest in the Boxing Day Test, South Africa moved the fixture from Durban to the high veld. The shift allowed Steyn the opportunity to break Shaun Pollock's national record of 421 Test wickets on the ground where his career first took flight. After Pakistan elected to bat, Rabada trapped Imam-ul-Haq in the second over, before Steyn had Fakhar Zaman taken at third slip, to spark celebrations from the players and an appreciative audience.

But the remaining headlines belonged to another South African fast bowler. Olivier, drafted in to the squad after Lungi Ngidi suffered a knee injury in Australia, then selected here when Vernon Philander broke his right thumb, quickly made his presence felt in his first Test for over a year. Bowling fast and short, he helped himself to six for 37 – his first Test haul of more than three – and confirmed the rise of the Bloemfontein Bone Collector, a nickname bestowed by his team-mate, Elgar. Pakistan were shot out for 181 in 47 overs, and only made that many thanks to a ninth-wicket stand of 67 in less than ten overs between Babar Azam and Hasan Ali.

In response, South Africa faced a skilful Pakistani attack, even without the injured Mohammad Abbas. Locating good lengths and meticulous lines, left-armers Mohammad Amir and – in only his second Test – Shaheen Shah Afridi struck regularly, and the hosts required a resolute 53 from Bavuma and a typically breezy 45 from de Kock to gain a first-innings lead of 42. The match was rattling along: shots were played, cordons kept busy.

For a while, Imam and Shan Masood, back after more than a year out of the side, bucked the trend, adding 57 for the second wicket as Pakistan moved 59 in front with nine wickets in hand. For South Africa, a tricky chase loomed. But Olivier rushed through the defences of Imam, before bouncing out Azhar Ali in his next over, a taste of what awaited him in the rest of the series. Olivier had prised open the middle order, and the rest of his gang poured through.

Steyn accounted for Asad Shafiq and later Masood, ninth out for 65, while three wickets for Rabada – including Sarfraz Ahmed for a six-ball pair – made him Test cricket's leading wicket-taker in 2018, with 52. From 101 for one, Pakistan had limped to 190. Olivier finished with five in the innings, and 11 for 96 in all – only Rabada and Australia's Mitchell Johnson had better match figures in a Centurion Test.

South Africa were unlikely to be pushed by a target of 149, but there were a few hairy moments. Markram fell for a duck, leg-before to Hasan for the second time in the game, before the out-of-form Amla was dropped at third slip on eight by Fakhar. In the next over Pakistan were fuming when third umpire Joel Wilson ruled Azhar had failed to get his fingers under the ball at first slip after Elgar edged Afridi. Coach Mickey Arthur stormed into Wilson's room to remonstrate, earning a demerit point for his troubles.

Slowly, the batsmen asserted themselves. Elgar took several blows, but fought his way to 50, before providing the medium-pace of Masood with a first Test wicket. Amla found his rhythm again, spraying some delightful square punches, and sucking any lingering drama from the match with his first half-century in 11 Test innings, equalling his longest drought. His stand of 119 with Elgar was a South African record for the second wicket against Pakistan – for a fortnight. One quirk remained: when du Plessis swung Afridi to long leg for a duck, it meant both captains had completed a pair in the same Test for the first time. But it couldn't deny South Africa.

Man of the Match: D. Olivier.

Close of play: first day, South Africa 127-5 (Bavuma 38, Steyn 13); second day, Pakistan 190.

Pakistan

Imam-ul-Haq lbw b Rabada	0	– b Olivier	57
Fakhar Zaman c Elgar b Steyn	12	– c Rabada b Olivier	12
Shan Masood b Olivier	19	– c Maharaj b Steyn	65
Azhar Ali c de Bruyn b Olivier	36	– c Rabada b Olivier	0
Asad Shafiq lbw b Olivier	7	– c de Kock b Steyn	6
Babar Azam c du Plessis b Rabada	71	– b Rabada	6
*†Sarfraz Ahmed b Olivier	0	– c du Plessis b Rabada	0
Mohammad Amir b Olivier	1	– b Rabada	12
Yasir Shah lbw b Rabada	4	– c de Kock b Olivier	0
Hasan Ali not out	21	– not out	11
Shaheen Shah Afridi c de Kock b Olivier	0	– c Markram b Olivier	4
B 7, lb 2, w 1	10	B 6, lb 10, w 1	17

1/1 (1) 2/17 (2) 3/54 (3) (47 overs) 181
4/62 (5) 5/86 (4) 6/86 (7)
7/96 (8) 8/111 (9) 9/178 (6) 10/181 (11)

1/44 (2) 2/101 (1) (56 overs) 190
3/103 (4) 4/134 (5)
5/142 (6) 6/142 (7) 7/158 (8)
8/159 (9) 9/185 (3) 10/190 (11)

Steyn 13–1–66–1; Rabada 17–4–59–3; Olivier 14–3–37–6; Maharaj 3–1–10–0. *Second innings—*
Steyn 15–4–34–2; Rabada 15–4–47–3; Olivier 15–3–59–5; Maharaj 11–2–34–0.

South Africa

A. K. Markram lbw b Hasan Ali	12	– (2) lbw b Hasan Ali	0
D. Elgar c Azhar Ali b Shaheen Shah Afridi	22	– (1) c Sarfraz Ahmed b Shan Masood	50
H. M. Amla c Babar Azam b Mohammad Amir	8	– not out	63
T. B. de Bruyn c Sarfraz Ahmed b Mohammad Amir	29	– st Sarfraz Ahmed b Yasir Shah	10
*F. du Plessis c Babar Azam b Shaheen Shah Afridi	0	– c Hasan Ali b Shaheen Shah Afridi	0
T. Bavuma c Sarfraz Ahmed b Shaheen Shah Afridi	53	– not out	13
D. W. Steyn c Sarfraz Ahmed b Mohammad Amir	23		
†Q. de Kock c Fakhar Zaman b Mohammad Amir	45		
K. A. Maharaj lbw b Hasan Ali	4		
K. Rabada c Asad Shafiq b Shaheen Shah Afridi	19		
D. Olivier not out	0		
Lb 3, w 2, nb 3	8	B 4, lb 5, w 6	15

1/19 (1) 2/43 (3) 3/43 (2) (60 overs) 223
4/43 (5) 5/112 (4) 6/146 (7)
7/170 (6) 8/189 (9) 9/220 (10) 10/223 (8)

1/0 (2) (4 wkts, 50.4 overs) 151
2/119 (1) 3/136 (4)
4/137 (5)

Mohammad Amir 20–6–62–4; Hasan Ali 18–4–70–2; Shaheen Shah Afridi 18–1–64–4; Yasir
Shah 4–0–24–0. *Second innings—*Mohammad Amir 12–5–24–0; Hasan Ali 13–6–39–1; Shaheen
Shah Afridi 15–1–53–1; Yasir Shah 7.4–1–20–1; Shan Masood 3–1–6–1.

Umpires: B. N. J. Oxenford and S. Ravi. Third umpire: J. S. Wilson.
Referee: D. C. Boon.

SOUTH AFRICA v PAKISTAN

Second Test

At Cape Town, January 3–6, 2019. South Africa won by nine wickets. Toss: South Africa.
South Africa had selection headaches to remedy as they sought to close out the series.
Newlands traditionally brings spinners into the game, but that didn't stop them from
plumping for their traditional strengths of seam and speed, sacrificing slow left-armer
Keshav Maharaj for the fit-again Philander. And while he managed only two wickets, a
four-pronged pace attack proved too strong for Pakistan.

Du Plessis hadn't hesitated to bowl on a pitch that looked as if it would help the quicks.
Sure enough, Steyn and Philander both struck in their first spells, and – with contributions

from Rabada and Olivier – Pakistan were 54 for five inside 20 overs. That included Azhar Ali, fending another short ball from Olivier to slip. A stand of 60 ended when Rabada had Shan Masood caught behind for 44, before Sarfraz Ahmed showed what was possible during a roguish 56. Mohammad Amir helped his captain with a determined 22, but Pakistan were all out for 177 by tea, Olivier bagging four.

South Africa's openers walked out to brilliant sunshine, and Markram made up for lost time at Centurion with 78, before he was bowled by the last ball of the day, from the innocuous Masood – a horror delivery, barely rising above ankle height. Unpredictable bounce would become a theme of the match, and was revisited by Mickey Arthur at a press conference.

Amla and de Bruyn didn't last long next morning but, from 149 for four, the innings was rebuilt by du Plessis and Bavuma. It wasn't always pretty, as balls spat from a length, but their alliance of 156 in 53 overs sealed the series. Du Plessis went to his ninth century in Tests, but first score over 41 against Pakistan in ten innings – while Bavuma might have felt that his 75 was even more satisfying than his maiden hundred against England on the same ground three years earlier. De Kock added gloss with 59 and, although Amir and Shaheen Shah Afridi both claimed first-innings four-fors for the second match running, South Africa led by 254.

Having given a breather of 124 overs, their fast bowlers charged in once more. Steyn and Rabada made early breaches, before Masood and Asad Shafiq added a spirited 132. But just as they seemed set to make South Africa suffer in the sun, Steyn induced an edge from Masood; eight overs later, Philander did the same to Shafiq. The Pakistan crumble was on and, despite a brilliant innings from Babar Azam – whose 72 included 15 fours – their last seven fell for 100. Had Philander not overstepped when Mohammad Abbas slogged him to mid-off, South Africa might have completed another three-day win.

Instead, their pursuit of 41 on the fourth morning was scrappy. De Bruyn opened in place of Markram, who had injured his thigh in the field, but without success. Amla then retired hurt, struck on the biceps by a snarling Amir. And while du Plessis could celebrate a series win and the match award, he was suspended from the Third Test because of a slow over-rate.

A tetchy Sarfraz was left to bemoan the difference in pace between his bowlers and South Africa's, suggesting the hosts' attack were "fitter than us", and admitting: "We're playing worse in Tests than all other forms."

Man of the Match: F. du Plessis.

Close of play: first day, South Africa 123-2 (Amla 24); second day, South Africa 382-6 (de Kock 55, Philander 6); third day, Pakistan 294.

Pakistan

Imam-ul-Haq lbw b Philander	8	– c Elgar b Steyn	6
Fakhar Zaman c Bavuma b Steyn	1	– (6) c and b Rabada	7
Shan Masood c de Kock b Rabada	44	– (2) c de Kock b Steyn	61
Azhar Ali c Amla b Olivier	2	– (3) lbw b Rabada	6
Asad Shafiq c Elgar b Rabada	20	– (4) c de Kock b Philander	88
Babar Azam c du Plessis b Olivier	2	– (5) c Amla b Rabada	72
*†Sarfraz Ahmed c de Kock b Olivier	56	– lbw b Olivier	6
Mohammad Amir not out	22	– c de Kock b Steyn	0
Yasir Shah c du Plessis b Olivier	5	– c sub (M. Z. Hamza) b Steyn	5
Mohammad Abbas c de Kock b Rabada	0	– not out	10
Shaheen Shah Afridi c de Kock b Steyn	3	– c Philander b Rabada	14
B 8, lb 2, w 3, nb 1	14	B 9, lb 4, w 2, nb 4	19

1/9 (2) 2/13 (1) 3/19 (4)   (51.1 overs) 177   1/10 (1) 2/27 (3)   (70.4 overs) 294
4/51 (5) 5/54 (6) 6/114 (3)   3/159 (2) 4/194 (4)
7/156 (7) 8/162 (9) 9/163 (10) 10/177 (11)   5/201 (6) 6/220 (7) 7/221 (8)
                                                        8/247 (9) 9/270 (5) 10/294 (11)

Steyn 15.1–3–48–3; Philander 11–3–36–1; Rabada 10.2–2–35–2; Olivier 15–3–48–4. *Second innings*—Philander 19–6–51–1; Steyn 19.2–2–85–4; Olivier 16–3–84–1; Rabada 16.4–2–61–4.

South Africa

A. K. Markram b Shan Masood	78		
D. Elgar c Sarfraz Ahmed b Mohammad Amir	20	– (1) not out	24
H. M. Amla b Mohammad Abbas	24	– retired hurt	2
T. B. de Bruyn c Babar Azam b Shaheen Shah Afridi	13	– (2) c Sarfraz Ahmed b Mohammad Abbas	4
*F. du Plessis c Sarfraz Ahmed b Shaheen Shah Afridi	103	– (4) not out	3
T. Bavuma c Sarfraz Ahmed b Shaheen Shah Afridi	75		
†Q. de Kock c Asad Shafiq b Mohammad Amir	59		
V. D. Philander b Mohammad Amir	16		
K. Rabada b Mohammad Amir	11		
D. W. Steyn c Fakhar Zaman b Shaheen Shah Afridi	13		
D. Olivier not out	10		
B 5, lb 1, nb 3	9	B 4, w 5, nb 1	10

1/56 (2) 2/123 (1) 3/126 (3)   (124.1 overs) 431   1/4 (2)   (1 wkt, 9.5 overs) 43
4/149 (4) 5/305 (6) 6/356 (5)
7/394 (7) 8/407 (8) 9/408 (9) 10/431 (10)

In the second innings Amla retired hurt at 23-1.

Mohammad Amir 33–9–88–4; Mohammad Abbas 34–8–100–1; Shaheen Shah Afridi 27.1–3–123–4; Yasir Shah 21–1–79–0; Shan Masood 5–1–19–1; Asad Shafiq 4–0–16–0. *Second innings*—Mohammad Amir 5–2–17–0; Mohammad Abbas 4–0–14–1; Azhar Ali 0.5–0–8–0.

Umpires: B. N. J. Oxenford and J. S. Wilson.   Third umpire: S. Ravi.
Referee: D. C. Boon.

SOUTH AFRICA v PAKISTAN

Third Test

At Johannesburg, January 11–14, 2019. South Africa won by 107 runs. Toss: South Africa. Test debut: M. Z. Hamza.

South Africa made it seven home Test wins in a row against Pakistan, and 11 out of 12, as their fast bowlers again outgunned the tourists' batsmen. With du Plessis suspended, the captaincy passed to Elgar for the second time, following Lord's 2017, when du Plessis had returned home for the birth of his first child, and South Africa lost by 211 runs.

And while Elgar, after winning the toss under sunny skies, was caught behind off Mohammad Abbas in the second over, Markram cover-drove imperiously during a second-wicket stand of 126 with Amla. It was a surprise when he fell not long after lunch, caught behind down the leg side for 90 off Fahim Ashraf, who had replaced the injured Shaheen Shah Afridi. Still, at 229 for three, South Africa had a chance to bat Pakistan out of the game, but the last seven fell for 33 in 15 overs – including the debutant middle-order batsman Zubayr Hamza, their 100th Test cricketer since readmission.

Thanks to Philander and his trademark relentlessness, however, Pakistan's top order were in the mire before the first-day close, Shan Masood and the hapless Azhar Ali both caught behind from consecutive balls. Imam-ul-Haq and nightwatchman Abbas resisted next morning, as South Africa missed five chances of varying difficulty, before Olivier removed Abbas and Asad Shafiq in the same over. Sarfraz Ahmed got his one-day practice in early, spanking eight fours in a 40-ball 50, and adding 78 for the sixth wicket in ten overs with Babar Azam, but the last five crashed for 16, leaving Olivier with another five-for. If Pakistan, 77 behind, wanted a consolation victory, as India had secured here a year earlier, they would have to bowl well.

Instead, they ran into de Kock, one of the game's most outrageous talents. Apparently oblivious to the match situation when he walked out to bat – South Africa were 93 for five, only 170 in front – he fought fire with fire. Amla stood vigil, methodically grinding down the bowlers' resolve, but de Kock dazzled, striding to his first Test century in two years. Rarely prone to emotion, he let his frustration out as he punched down the ground to reach three figures. By the time he fell for a startling 129 off 138 balls to Shadab Khan, who had replaced his ineffective fellow leg-spinner Yasir Shah, the game was beyond Pakistan's reach.

To their credit, they went down fighting. Set 381, they even flirted with a heist. Shafiq spanked a sprightly 65, and Shadab an entertaining 47 not out against a tiring attack, but South Africa had enough to play with. Olivier had started the fourth morning by going for the jugular of Babar, who gloved a snorter, then bluffed Sarfraz with a full delivery next ball, when the field suggested a short one. It was the third time in the Test he had taken two in an over. Three for Rabada helped hustle out the lower order, before Pakistan's innings, and series, ended before lunch with the comical run-out of Abbas. For South Africa's coach, Ottis Gibson, it was "mission accomplished".

Man of the Match: Q. de Kock. *Man of the Series:* D. Olivier.

Close of play: first day, Pakistan 17-2 (Imam-ul-Haq 10, Mohammad Abbas 0); second day, South Africa 135-5 (Amla 42, de Kock 34); third day, Pakistan 153-3 (Asad Shafiq 48, Babar Azam 17).

South Africa

A. K. Markram c Sarfraz Ahmed b Fahim Ashraf . .	90	– (2) c Sarfraz Ahmed b Mohammad Abbas .	21
*D. Elgar c Sarfraz Ahmed b Mohammad Abbas . . .	5	– (1) c Sarfraz Ahmed b Mohammad Amir .	5
H. M. Amla c Asad Shafiq b Shadab Khan	41	– c Sarfraz Ahmed b Hasan Ali	71
T. B. de Bruyn lbw b Mohammad Abbas	49	– c Asad Shafiq b Fahim Ashraf	7
M. Z. Hamza c Sarfraz Ahmed b Mohammad Amir .	41	– lbw b Fahim Ashraf	0
T. Bavuma c Sarfraz Ahmed b Mohammad Amir . .	8	– c Sarfraz Ahmed b Shadab Khan	23
†Q. de Kock c Mohammad Abbas b Fahim Ashraf . .	18	– c Hasan Ali b Shadab Khan	129
V. D. Philander lbw b Hasan Ali	1	– lbw b Mohammad Amir	14
K. Rabada c Sarfraz Ahmed b Hasan Ali	0	– c Shadab Khan b Fahim Ashraf	21
D. W. Steyn not out	2	– not out	0
D. Olivier c Mohammad Abbas b Fahim Ashraf . . .	1	– c Sarfraz Ahmed b Shadab Khan	1
Lb 2, w 1, nb 4	7	B 2, lb 6, w 1, nb 2	11

1/6 (2) 2/132 (1) 3/154 (3)   (77.4 overs) 262   1/24 (1) 2/29 (2)   (80.3 overs) 303
4/229 (4) 5/238 (6) 6/244 (5)   3/45 (4) 4/45 (5)
7/249 (8) 8/257 (9) 9/262 (7) 10/262 (11)   5/93 (6) 6/195 (3) 7/223 (8)
                                               8/302 (9) 9/302 (9) 10/303 (11)

Mohammad Amir 15.4–2–36–2; Mohammad Abbas 18–6–44–2; Hasan Ali 17–3–75–2; Fahim Ashraf 15–2–57–3; Shadab Khan 10–2–39–1; Asad Shafiq 2–0–9–0. *Second innings*—Mohammad Amir 20–2–56–2; Mohammad Abbas 18–3–73–1; Hasan Ali 17–1–83–1; Fahim Ashraf 14–3–42–3; Shadab Khan 11.3–0–41–3.

Pakistan

Imam-ul-Haq c Elgar b Philander	43	– c de Kock b Steyn	35
Shan Masood c de Kock b Philander	2	– c de Kock b Steyn	37
Azhar Ali c de Kock b Philander	0	– c de Kock b Olivier	15
Mohammad Abbas c de Bruyn b Olivier	11	– (11) run out (Markram/de Kock)	9
Asad Shafiq c de Kock b Olivier	0	– (4) c Elgar b Philander	65
Babar Azam c Rabada b Olivier	49	– (5) c de Kock b Olivier	21
*†Sarfraz Ahmed c Amla b Rabada	50	– (6) b Olivier	0
Shadab Khan c de Bruyn b Rabada	5	– (7) not out	47
Fahim Ashraf c Hamza b Olivier	0	– (8) c Markram b Rabada	15
Mohammad Amir c Hamza b Olivier	10	– (9) c Markram b Rabada	4
Hasan Ali not out	0	– (10) c and b Rabada	22
B 5, lb 10	15	Lb 2, nb 1	3

1/6 (2) 2/6 (3) 3/53 (4)   (49.4 overs) 185   1/67 (1) 2/74 (2)   (65.4 overs) 273
4/53 (5) 5/91 (1) 6/169 (7)   3/104 (3) 4/162 (5)
7/169 (6) 8/169 (9) 9/185 (10) 10/185 (8)   5/162 (6) 6/179 (4) 7/204 (8)
                                              8/208 (9) 9/242 (10) 10/273 (11)

Steyn 12–4–35–0; Philander 13–4–43–3; Rabada 11.4–0–41–2; Olivier 13–2–51–5. *Second innings*—Steyn 20–2–80–2; Philander 14–4–41–1; Olivier 15–2–74–3; Rabada 16–2–75–3; Elgar 0.4–0–1–0.

Umpires: S. Ravi and J. S. Wilson.   Third umpire: B. N. J. Oxenford.
Referee: D. C. Boon.

First one-day international   At Port Elizabeth, January 19, 2019 (day/night). **Pakistan won by five wickets. ‡South Africa 266-2** (50 overs) (H. M. Amla 108*, R. R. Hendricks 45, H. E. van der Dussen 93); **Pakistan 267-5** (49.1 overs) (Imam-ul-Haq 86, Babar Azam 49, Mohammad Hafeez 71*). *MoM:* Mohammad Hafeez. *ODI debuts:* D. Olivier, H. E. van der Dussen (South Africa). *The 50-over series was expected to be a good test for both sides, given their strength in depth, but it was Pakistan who better read the St George's Park surface. Before that, one of South Africa's call-ups, 29-year-old Rassie van der Dussen, a stalwart of domestic cricket, wasted little time getting*

FEWEST WICKETS DOWN FOR A SIDE LOSING AN ODI

1	Sri Lanka (138-1) lost to New Zealand (203-6) at Hambantota (*D/L*).............	2013-14
1	Zimbabwe (104-1) lost to India (203-7) at Hamilton (*revised target*).............	1991-92
2	West Indies (304-2) lost to South Africa (310-6) at Johannesburg	2003-04
2	**South Africa (266-2) lost to Pakistan (267-5) at Port Elizabeth**	**2018-19**
2	Pakistan (220-2) lost to West Indies (221-0) at Melbourne	1991-92
2†	India (183-2) v Pakistan (205-7) at Sahiwal...................................	1978-79
2	New Zealand (167-2) lost to Australia (239-6) at Auckland (*revised target*).......	1989-90

† *India's captain, B. S. Bedi, conceded the match in protest at Pakistan's short-pitched bowling.*

comfortable: he made an even-paced 93 before falling to a full toss, and put on 155 for the second wicket with Hashim Amla, who reached his 27th ODI century. But, on a slow surface, neither could quite hit the accelerator in the final ten overs. With powerhouses like David Miller lying in wait, South Africa's 266-2 felt like a missed opportunity, especially as only one wicket had fallen in the first 46 overs. Their total was soon looking as pedestrian. The arrival for the one-day matches of Mohammad Hafeez and Shoaib Malik had galvanised Pakistan and, after Imam-ul-Haq hit 86, adding 94 for the second wicket with Babar Azam, Hafeez struck a pugnacious 71* from 63 balls to lead his side home with five balls to spare. This was Pakistan's highest successful chase away to South Africa, beating 235 at Durban nearly six years earlier.

Second one-day international   At Durban, January 22, 2019 (day/night). **South Africa won by five wickets. Pakistan 203** (45.5 overs) (Sarfraz Ahmed 41, Hasan Ali 59; A. L. Phehlukwayo 4-22, T. Shamsi 3-56); **‡South Africa 207-5** (42 overs) (H. E. van der Dussen 80*, D. A. Miller 31, A. L. Phehlukwayo 69*; Shaheen Shah Afridi 3-44). *MoM:* A. L. Phehlukwayo. *ODI debut:* Hussain Talat (Pakistan). *South Africa's series-squaring win was overshadowed by comments made in the field by Sarfraz Ahmed to Andile Phehlukwayo, who was riding his luck as he took his side to victory with a maiden ODI fifty. Speaking in Urdu during the 37th over of the chase, Sarfraz was overheard by the stump mike saying: "Hey black guy, where's your mother sitting today? What [prayer] what have you got her to say for you today?" On Twitter the following day, he denied his remarks had been "directed towards anyone in particular". On his home ground, Phehlukwayo had helped rescue South Africa from 80-5 in pursuit of 204, putting on 124* with van der Dussen after three early wickets for Shaheen Shah Afridi, and two in two balls for Shadab Khan. Earlier, Phehlukwayo had made good use of the slower ball on a clammy Kingsmead surface to help reduce Pakistan to 112-8. Their eventual 203 owed much to a cheeky 59 from 45 balls by No. 10 Hasan Ali, who added 90 with Sarfraz before becoming Phehlukwayo's fourth victim – also an ODI best. Left-arm wrist-spinner Tabraiz Shamsi ended with 3-56, throwing the ball up and finding purchase.*

Third one-day international   At Centurion, January 25, 2019 (day/night). **South Africa won by 13 runs** (DLS). **‡Pakistan 317-6** (50 overs) (Imam-ul-Haq 101, Babar Azam 69, Mohammad Hafeez 52, Shoaib Malik 31, Imad Wasim 43*); **South Africa 187-2** (33 overs) (Q. de Kock 33, R. R. Hendricks 83*, F. du Plessis 40*). *MoM:* R. R. Hendricks. *ODI debut:* B. E. Hendricks (South Africa). *Centurion lived up to its billing as the best batting ground in the country – only for a savage Gauteng storm to interrupt an engaging match, with South Africa ahead on DLS. The day had begun*

GOOD DAY AT THE OFFICE

Career best batting and best bowling in the same one-day international:

J. K. Lever (27*, 4-29)	England v Australia at Birmingham.	1977
Tauseef Ahmed (27*, 4-38)	Pakistan v New Zealand at Sialkot.	1984-85
Aamer Malik (90, 2-35)	Pakistan v Australia at Perth (WACA).	1988-89
D. J. Callaghan (169* and 3-32).	Pakistan v New Zealand at Centurion	1994-95
A. Kuruvilla (7, 4-43).	India v Sri Lanka at Colombo (SSC)	1997-98
R. C. Irani (53*, 5-26)	England v India at The Oval	2003
Y. K. Pathan (123*, 3-49)	India v New Zealand at Bangalore	2010-11
H. Patel (62, 4-28)	Canada v Afghanistan at King City	2011
M. W. Machan (114, 3-42).	Scotland v Bangladesh at Aberdeen.	2013
Javed Ahmadi (81, 4-37)	Afghanistan v Ireland at Dubai	2014-15
Rohan Mustafa (109, 5-25)	UAE v Papua New Guinea at Abu Dhabi	2016-17
K. M. Jarvis (37, 4-37)	**Zimbabwe v Bangladesh at Mirpur**	**2018-19**
A. L. Phehlukwayo (69, 4-22)	**South Africa v Pakistan at Durban**.	**2018-19**

Minimum: 20 ODIs played.   *Research: Aslam Siddiqui*

---

with another tweet from Sarfraz, this time a photo of him shaking hands with, and apologising to, Phehlukwayo for his comments during the second ODI. Two days later, Sarfraz was found guilty by the ICC of breaching their anti-racism code, and banned for four matches. Before all that, Imam celebrated a brilliant century by making a chatting gesture with his hands, then putting a finger to his lips. It was aimed, he said, at those who believed he owed his place in the side to his uncle, Pakistan's chief selector Inzamam-ul-Haq, a suggestion which had "really pissed me off". Babar made a sweet 69, and there was a second half-century of the series from Hafeez. Imad Wasim then clubbed 43 from 23 balls at the death, as the ball flew in the thin high-veal air. Amid the carnage, Dale Steyn took 2-43, bowling as fast and accurately as ever. South Africa initially needed 318 on a good track, before rain interrupted the innings at 88-2 in the 17th. An hour's break didn't cost any overs, but Reeza Hendricks decided it would be best to stay ahead on DLS, in case bad weather returned. When it did, after 33, Hendricks had added 58 from 57 balls, and 108* for the third wicket with Faf du Plessis, and South Africa claimed a 2–1 lead.

Fourth one-day international At Johannesburg, January 27, 2019. **Pakistan won by eight wickets. South Africa 164** (41 overs) (H. M. Amla 59, F. du Plessis 57; Usman Shinwari 4-35); ‡**Pakistan 168-2** (31.3 overs) (Imam-ul-Haq 71, Fakhar Zaman 44, Babar Azam 41*). MoM: Usman Shinwari. *The Pink Day fixture is a red-letter day in South African cricket, raising funds for breast-cancer research and charities. This was the eighth such game – and the first lost by the hosts, who rolled over for 164. Left-arm seamer Usman Shinwari took 4-35, including three in four balls, as South Africa failed to build on half-centuries from Amla and du Plessis, who added 101 for the third wicket; the last eight went down for 45. Pakistan, whose four previous ODIs against South Africa at the Wanderers had all been lost, were in no mood for charity. Imam put on 70 for the first wicket with Fakhar Zaman, and 94 for the second with Babar, before falling with the scores level. Mohammad Rizwan pumped his first ball past point as Pakistan squared the series with 111 deliveries to spare. Shoaib Malik had walked out for the toss, leading his country in an ODI for the first time for ten years as details of Sarfraz's ban emerged.*

Fifth one-day international At Cape Town, January 30, 2019 (day/night). **South Africa won by seven wickets. Pakistan 240-8** (50 overs) (Fakhar Zaman 70, Shoaib Malik 31, Imad Wasim 47*); ‡**South Africa 241-3** (40 overs) (Q. de Kock 83, R. R. Hendricks 34, F. du Plessis 50*, H. E. van der Dussen 50*). MoM: Q. de Kock. MoS: Imam-ul-Haq. *At the end of a fluctuating series, it was South Africa who prevailed, after a disciplined performance from their bowlers was followed by a reminder of the talents of Quinton de Kock. Du Plessis had backed his team to bowl first, despite most teams at Newlands preferring to chase, but the only real threat came from Fakhar, who made a run-a-ball 70 before top-edging Phehlukwayo to fine leg, where Imran Tahir did well to stay inside the boundary. With that went Pakistan's best hope of setting a testing target. Imad gave them a late boost with 47* off 31, but middle-order sluggishness – their Nos 4-7 managed only 77 off 144 balls between them – meant they had to settle for 240. De Kock was caught at cover off Shinwari on 12, only for replays to reveal a no-ball. He went on to a fearless 83 from 58, before du Plessis and van der Dussen each hit 50* as South Africa cantered to a 3–2 victory with ten overs to spare.*

First Twenty20 international   At Cape Town, February 1, 2019 (floodlit). **South Africa won by six runs. South Africa 192-6** (20 overs) (R. R. Hendricks 74, F. du Plessis 78; Usman Shinwari 3-31); ‡**Pakistan 186-9** (20 overs) (Babar Azam 38, Hussain Talat 40, Shoaib Malik 49). *MoM:* D. A. Miller. *After his grafting century in the Test series, du Plessis pummelled 78 from 45 balls. Adding a festive 131 in 12 overs with the in-form Reeza Hendricks (74 from 41), du Plessis paved the way for a record T20I score at Newlands – though South Africa lost five for 35 from the last 29 balls, three to Shinwari. Set more than 9.5 an over, Pakistan nearly won. Babar (38 from 27) and Hussain Talat (40 from 32) got the ball rolling, before Shoaib took the chase deep. But with 14 needed off three balls, he swung wildly into the Cape night to provide a fourth catch for Miller, who also ran out Babar and Rizwan, and won the match award for his fielding (he was earlier out for ten). South Africa were grateful for the nerve of Phehlukwayo (1-27), whose slower balls kept Pakistan guessing.*

Second Twenty20 international   At Johannesburg, February 3, 2019. **South Africa won by seven runs. South Africa 188-3** (20 overs) (J. N. Malan 33, H. E. van der Dussen 45, D. A. Miller 65*); ‡**Pakistan 181-7** (20 overs) (Babar Azam 90, Hussain Talat 55; A. L. Phehlukwayo 3-36). *MoM:* D. A. Miller. *T20I debuts:* J. N. Malan, L. L. Sipamla (South Africa). *The teams played out another cliffhanger, at a partisan Wanderers. South Africa began by clattering 188-3, the acceleration coming first from van der Dussen (45 from 27 balls, with four sixes), then – more spectacularly – from Miller, who was captaining his country for the first time while du Plessis sat out the final two games. He blasted 65* from 29, with five sixes, three in a traumatic 20th over from Shinwari that included a no-ball and cost 29. His four overs leaked 63, in contrast to the left-arm spin of Imad, who had gone for just nine and claimed the wicket of debutant Janneman Malan. Chasing another big total, Pakistan needed instant aggression. Babar supplied it, with a blistering 90 from 58 balls, while Talat (55 from 41) helped add 102 for the second wicket. But the middle order had no answer to Phehlukwayo's relish for the death overs and the knuckle ball. He took three as Pakistan lost six for 33, to slump to their first T20 series defeat in 12. There was a promising international debut for seamer Lutho Sipamla, who conceded only 23.*

Third Twenty20 international   At Centurion, February 6, 2019 (floodlit). **Pakistan won by 27 runs. Pakistan 168-9** (20 overs) (B. E. Hendricks 4-14); ‡**South Africa 141-9** (20 overs) (H. E. van der Dussen 41, C. H. Morris 55*; Mohammad Amir 3-27). *MoM:* Shadab Khan. *MoS:* D. A. Miller. *Centurion provided Pakistan with a happy send-off, in another frenzy of fun. Babar drilled five fours in an 11-ball 23 – one of seven scores between 17 and 26 as they reached 168-9. Beuran Hendricks returned career-best figures of 4-14, and Chris Morris chipped in with 2-27. The others came in for stick, though, as Pakistan took advantage of an inexperienced attack. South Africa's chase never got going. Imad was tidy again, going for 19 from four overs. And, with a rash of established stars rested, only van der Dussen stood firm in the top order, with 41 from 35. That left too much to do at the back end, though Morris blazed a maiden T20I half-century, from 29 balls.*

DOMESTIC CRICKET IN SOUTH AFRICA IN 2017-18

Colin Bryden

When former Test wicketkeeper Mark Boucher was appointed to run the **Titans** in 2016, many had doubts about his lack of coaching credentials. But over the next two seasons he vindicated the decision, juggling an embarrassment of riches to win four out of the six titles on offer. First time round, he had collected the two limited-overs trophies. In 2017-18, he followed that by retaining the Twenty20 Challenge, where he could field a team of near-international strength, and then scored a less predictable triumph in the first-class Sunfoil Series, played mainly without the Titans' national players. With call-ups by South Africa and several injuries, Boucher's biggest challenge was trying to achieve consistency in selection, particularly in the four-day competition.

Only a slip-up in the semi-finals of the 50-over Momentum One-Day Cup prevented the Titans from achieving a hat-trick. They finished on top in the round robin, but were surprisingly beaten by the fourth-placed **Warriors**, who went on to share the title with the **Dolphins** when two attempts to play the final were spoiled by rain – the third time in six seasons the weather had thwarted the emergence of an outright one-day champion.

An unprecedented 23 of the 30 Sunfoil Series matches ended in draws. In the first half of the tournament, running from September to October, it was 14 out of 15 – the exception being the Titans' win over the Lions in the final round before the break for white-ball cricket. The number of outright results picked up slightly when the competition resumed in February, but the final total of seven was half the previous low of 14 since the current franchise format arrived in 2004-05. One theory was that groundsmen had begun preparing batsman-friendly pitches earlier than usual, in anticipation of the planned city-based Global T20 league – called off less than a month before the scheduled start in November – and that natural grass growth had been stunted.

As the final round of the Sunfoil Series began in March, only the Warriors had won two games; they led the table, but all teams except the Lions were close enough to have a chance of overtaking them. Titans were fourth, less than seven points behind, and the first two days of their match against defending champions the Knights were rained off – as were the first two days at Durban, where the Warriors were playing the Dolphins. That game ended in another draw, but at Centurion the Titans and the Knights, both hoping to leapfrog the Warriors, agreed to restrict both first innings to 40 overs to contrive a result. A batting rampage shaped by Heino Kuhn and Heinrich Klaasen rushed the Titans to a 100-run lead; Chris Morris claimed six for 55 in the Knights' second innings, and the Titans won by four wickets to take the title by 1.52 points.

The Warriors, with far fewer resources, finished second in the Sunfoil Series, shared the one-day trophy and reached the semis in the T20 challenge, while the Dolphins showed improvement, particularly in the limited-overs formats, where they reached both finals. The **Cape Cobras** finished in the top three in all competitions, but the **Knights** had no first-class wins and finished bottom of both white-ball tables, and the **Lions** struggled in all formats.

Despite that, the leading run-scorer in the Sunfoil Series was the Lions' Rassie van der Dussen, with 959 at 73 in a tournament predictably dominated by batsmen. Former Test off-spinner Simon Harmer followed up his success as a Kolpak player for Essex by taking 47 wickets for the Warriors – 14 more than anyone else in the competition.

KwaZulu-Natal won the first-class provincial competition, with **North West** winning the 50-over final, and **KwaZulu-Natal Inland** the Africa T20 Cup. In the three-day competition, Marco Marais scored the season's only triple-hundred, in 191 balls, for Border against Eastern Province, adding 428 with Bradley Williams.

FIRST-CLASS AVERAGES IN 2017-18

BATTING (675 runs)

		M	I	NO	R	HS	100	Avge	Ct/St
1	A. J. Pienaar (*South Western Districts*)	10	15	6	909	186	4	101.00	6
2	J. N. Malan (*North West*)	10	15	4	1,046	208*	4	95.09	7
3	H. E. van der Dussen (*Lions*)	10	18	5	959	163	3	73.76	5
4	M. Marais (*Border*)	9	15	4	810	300*	3	73.63	6
5	A. P. Agathangelou (*Northerns/Titans*)	8	15	3	806	251	2	67.16	7
6	D. J. Vilas (*Dolphins*)	8	14	3	734	161	3	66.72	14/1
7	R. S. Second (*Knights/Free State/SA A*)	12	17	4	865	203*	3	66.53	31
8	A. K. Markram (*Titans/South Africa*)	13	23	1	1,439	152	5	65.40	11
9	G. Roelofsen (*KwaZulu-Natal Inland*)	10	14	2	781	224*	3	65.08	30/5
10	M. Z. Hamza (*Cape Cobras/WP/SA A*)	14	22	3	1,203	121	4	63.31	9
11	†D. Elgar (*Titans/South Africa*)	15	26	3	1,425	237*	5	61.95	16
12	G. J. Snyman (*Northern Cape*)	7	12	0	695	209	2	57.91	4
13	T. B. de Bruyn (*Knights/SA A/S Africa*)	9	14	2	677	195	2	56.41	10
14	†P. Botha (*Free State*)	10	17	4	716	119*	3	55.07	5
15	†V. B. van Jaarsveld (*Dolphins*)	10	18	1	898	110	4	52.82	8
16	D. G. Bedingham (*Boland*)	8	15	0	790	147	3	52.66	8
17	K. Verreynne (*Cape Cobras/W Prov*)	12	18	3	762	88	0	50.80	25/1
18	K. Rapulana (*North West/Lions*)	11	18	3	755	259*	1	50.33	2
19	A. B. de Villiers (*Titans/South Africa*)	9	17	2	728	126*	1	48.53	27
20	H. M. Amla (*Cape Cobras/S Africa*)	11	20	0	946	189	3	47.30	11
21	P. J. Malan (*Cape Cobras/WP/SA A*)	15	24	0	1,114	195	4	46.41	2
22	F. du Plessis (*Titans/South Africa*)	10	18	3	696	135*	2	46.40	11
23	K. D. Petersen (*Knights/Northern Cape*)	11	18	3	683	141	2	45.53	6
24	†S. Muthusamy (*Dolphins/KZN/SA A*)	17	30	4	957	127	1	36.80	14
25	†E. M. Moore (*Warriors/E Province*)	16	28	1	883	115	3	32.70	9

BOWLING (30 wickets, average 30.00)

		Style	O	M	R	W	BB	5I	Avge
1	G. I. Hume (*KwaZulu-Natal Inland*)	RFM	249.3	82	571	40	7-23	3	14.27
2	V. D. Philander (*Cape Cobras/SA*)	RFM	272.2	100	582	38	6-21	2	15.31
3	M. Morkel (*Titans/SA/Easterns*)	RF	289.5	85	834	49	5-20	3	17.02
4	R. R. Richards (*Titans/Easterns*)	LFM	200.5	36	678	39	6-20	3	17.38
5	C. J. August (*Easterns/Titans*)	LFM	259.	62	765	41	6-52	2	18.65
6	K. Rabada (*Lions/South Africa*)	RF	355.1	89	1,053	56	6-54	4	18.80
7	B. M. Scholtz (*Namibia*)	SLA	260.4	65	711	35	5-54	1	20.31
8	C. P. Savage (*Dolphins/KZ-Natal*)	RF	223.3	48	687	33	5-45	1	20.81
9	S. R. Harmer (*Warriors*)	OB	338.2	66	1,027	47	6-47	4	21.85
10	S. Nhlebela (*KwaZulu-Natal*)	SLA	233.5	54	767	35	6-96	2	21.91
11	B. L. Barends (*North West*)	RM	240.1	64	703	32	4-37	0	21.96
12	Z. Pongolo (*Gauteng/Lions*)	RFM	240.3	55	761	34	5-105	1	22.38
13	M. Arnold (*Easterns*)	RF	232.3	48	725	32	5-51	1	22.65
14	S. Muthusamy (*Dolphins/KZN/SA A*)	SLA	449.2	110	1,248	54	7-83	4	23.11
15	Z. C. Qwabe (*Boland*)	RFM	266.5	58	814	34	4-55	0	23.94
16	K. J. Dudgeon (*KZ-Natal/Dolphins*)	RFM	227.1	30	843	35	5-32	1	24.08
17	T. Bokako (*Warriors/E Province*)	RF	298.3	73	1,048	43	5-30	1	24.37
18	M. A. R. Cohen (*Cape Cobras/WP*)	LFM	205.4	24	858	34	5-40	2	25.23
19	S. H. Jamison (*Gauteng/Lions*)	RFM	296	63	969	37	5-65	1	26.18
20	M. N. Piedt (*South Western Districts*)	RFM	290.4	75	823	31	5-79	1	26.54
21	M. Pretorius (*Titans/Northerns*)	RF	260.4	56	829	31	5-41	1	26.74
22	T. P. Kaber (*Northerns*)	SLW	209.3	16	843	31	6-81	2	27.19
23	D. Olivier (*Knights/SA/FS/SA A*)	RFM	283.1	65	946	33	4-74	0	28.66
24	K. A. Maharaj (*Dolphins/S Africa*)	SLA	400.3	65	1,343	45	7-76	4	29.84

Averages include CSA Provincial Three-Day Challenge matches played in Namibia.

SUNFOIL SERIES IN 2017-18

	P	W	L	D	Bonus pts Bat	Bonus pts Bowl	Pts
Titans.................	10	2	1	7	37.96	32	143.96
Warriors..............	10	2	1	7	34.44	34	142.44
Cape Cobras	10	1	1	8	43.36	26	133.36
Knights	10	0	1	9	43.70	29	126.70
Dolphins	10	1	1	8	33.66	29	126.66
Lions	10	1	2	7	34.46	28	120.46

Outright win = 16pts; draw = 6pts. Bonus points awarded for the first 100 overs of each team's first innings: one batting point for the first 150 runs and 0.02 of a point for every subsequent run; one bowling point for the third wicket taken and for every subsequent two.

CHAMPIONS

1889-90	Transvaal	1954-55	Natal
1890-91	Kimberley	1955-56	Western Province
1892-93	Western Province	1958-59	Transvaal
1893-94	Western Province	1959-60	Natal
1894-95	Transvaal	1960-61	Natal
1896-97	Western Province	1962-63	Natal
1897-98	Western Province	1963-64	Natal
1902-03	Transvaal	1965-66 {	Natal
1903-04	Transvaal		Transvaal
1904-05	Transvaal	1966-67	Natal
1906-07	Transvaal	1967-68	Natal
1908-09	Western Province	1968-69	Transvaal
1910-11	Natal	1969-70 {	Transvaal
1912-13	Natal		Western Province
1920-21	Western Province	1970-71	Transvaal
	Transvaal	1971-72	Transvaal
1921-22 {	Natal	1972-73	Transvaal
	Western Province	1973-74	Natal
1923-24	Transvaal	1974-75	Western Province
1925-26	Transvaal	1975-76	Natal
1926-27	Transvaal	1976-77	Natal
1929-30	Transvaal	1977-78	Western Province
1931-32	Western Province	1978-79	Transvaal
1933-34	Natal	1979-80	Transvaal
1934-35	Transvaal	1980-81	Natal
1936-37	Natal	1981-82	Western Province
1937-38 {	Natal	1982-83	Transvaal
	Transvaal	1983-84	Transvaal
1946-47	Natal	1984-85	Transvaal
1947-48	Natal	1985-86	Western Province
1950-51	Transvaal	1986-87	Transvaal
1951-52	Natal	1987-88	Transvaal
1952-53	Western Province	1988-89	Eastern Province

1989-90 {	Eastern Province
	Western Province
1990-91	Western Province
1991-92	Eastern Province
1992-93	Orange Free State
1993-94	Orange Free State
1994-95	Natal
1995-96	Western Province
1996-97	Natal
1997-98	Free State
1998-99	Western Province
1999-2000	Gauteng
2000-01	Western Province
2001-02	KwaZulu-Natal
2002-03	Easterns
2003-04	Western Province
2004-05 {	Dolphins
	Eagles
2005-06 {	Dolphins
	Titans
2006-07	Titans
2007-08	Eagles
2008-09	Titans
2009-10	Cape Cobras
2010-11	Cape Cobras
2011-12	Titans
2012-13	Cape Cobras
2013-14	Cape Cobras
2014-15	Lions
2015-16	Titans
2016-17	Knights
2017-18	Titans

Transvaal/Gauteng have won the title outright 25 times, Natal/KwaZulu-Natal 21, Western Province 18, Titans 5, Cape Cobras 4, Orange Free State/Free State 3, Eagles/Knights and Eastern Province 2, Easterns, Kimberley and Lions 1. The title has been shared seven times as follows: Transvaal 4, Natal and Western Province 3, Dolphins 2, Eagles, Eastern Province and Titans 1.

The tournament was the Currie Cup from 1889-90 to 1989-90, the Castle Cup from 1990-91 to 1995-96, the SuperSport Series from 1996-97 to 2011-12, and the Sunfoil Series from 2012-13.

From 1971-72 to 1990-91, the non-white South African Cricket Board of Control (later the South African Cricket Board) organised their own three-day tournaments. These are now recognised as first-class (see *Wisden 2006*, pages 79–80). A list of winners appears in *Wisden 2007*, page 1346.

SUNFOIL THREE-DAY CUP IN 2017-18

Pool A	P	W	L	D	Pts	Pool B	P	W	L	D	Pts
KZ-NATAL........	10	6	2	2	178.90	NAMIBIA........	10	5	3	2	153.68
Western Province ..	10	5	2	3	159.22	Free State........	10	3	1	6	151.72
Border...........	10	3	2	5	133.54	KZN Inland......	10	3	2	5	142.80
Northerns........	10	2	3	4*	122.50	Easterns........	10	3	3	4	142.44†
North West	10	0	2	8	122.26	Eastern Province ..	10	2	3	5	124.30
SW Districts......	10	0	1	9	117.00	Boland.........	10	3	5	2	121.40
Northern Cape.....	10	1	4	5	111.48	Gauteng.........	10	1	4	4*	94.38

*　 *Includes one abandoned match.* 　　†　 *2pts deducted for slow over-rate.*

Outright win = 16pts; draw = 6pts; abandoned = 6pts. Bonus points awarded for the first 100 overs of each team's first innings: one batting point for the first 150 runs and 0.02 of a point for every subsequent run; one bowling point for the third wicket taken and for every subsequent two.

The teams were divided into two pools of seven. Each played the other six in their pool, plus four teams from the other pool; all results counted towards the final table. The two pool leaders met in a final.

Final　 At Durban, April 12–13, 2018. **KwaZulu-Natal won by an innings and 25 runs. Namibia 132** (C. P. Savage 5-45, S. Muthusamy 5-18) **and 177** (K. J. Dudgeon 5-32); ‡**KwaZulu-Natal 334-4 dec** (M. N. Erlank 139). *KwaZulu-Natal rolled over Namibia inside two days, with slow left-arm Senuran Muthusamy reaching 50 first-class wickets for the season.*

MOMENTUM ONE-DAY CUP IN 2017-18

50-over league plus knockout

	P	W	L	T	Bonus	Pts	NRR
TITANS..............	10	7	3	0	5	33	1.01
CAPE COBRAS	10	7	3	0	3	31	0.33
DOLPHINS	10	6	3	1	2	29	0.33
WARRIORS	10	4	6	0	1	17	−0.38
Lions	10	3	6	1	1	16	−0.18
Knights..............	10	1	7	2	1	11	−1.12

Semi-finals　 Warriors beat Titans by eight wickets; Dolphins beat Cape Cobras by 49 runs.

Final　 At Durban, February 2, 2018 (day/night). **No result. Dolphins 154-6** (39.4 overs) v ‡**Warriors.** *The teams shared the trophy after rain interrupted the first innings and washed out an attempt to play a new game the following day.*

The Ram Slam T20 Challenge has its own section (page 1143).

CSA PROVINCIAL 50-OVER CHALLENGE IN 2017-18

50-over league

Pool A	P	W	L	NR	Pts	Pool B	P	W	L	NR	Pts
NORTH WEST.......	10	7	3	0	33	GAUTENG	10	8	1	1	36
KwaZulu-Natal	10	6	4	0	27	KwaZulu-Natal Inland..	10	6	4	0	28
Border	10	6	4	0	25	Namibia............	10	6	4	0	26
South Western Districts	10	5	4	1	23	Easterns...........	10	5	4	1	24
Northerns...........	10	4	3	3	23	Free State.........	10	4	5	1	21
Western Province	10	3	6	1	15	Eastern Province	10	3	7	0	13
Northern Cape.......	10	1	7	2	8	Boland.............	10	1	9	0	5

Final　 At Johannesburg, April 8, 2018. **North West won by 34 runs.** ‡**North West 179** (49.2 overs); **Gauteng 145** (41.3 overs). *North West opener Janneman Malan scored 69 in a match where no one else reached 40.*

AFRICA T20 CUP IN 2017-18

20-over league plus semi-finals and final

Pool A	P	W	L	NR	Pts	Pool B	P	W	L	NR	Pts
NAMIBIA	3	3	0	0	12	GAUTENG	3	2	1	0	10
SW Districts	3	2	1	0	8	Eastern Province	3	2	1	0	9
Easterns	3	1	2	0	4	North West	3	1	2	0	5
Western Province	3	0	3	0	0	Northerns	3	1	2	0	4

Pool C	P	W	L	NR	Pts	Pool D	P	W	L	NR	Pts
FREE STATE	3	2	1	0	10	KZN INLAND	3	2	0	1	10
Kenya	3	2	1	0	8	Boland	3	1	0	2	9
KwaZulu-Natal	3	1	2	0	5	Border	3	0	1	2	4
Northern Cape	3	1	2	0	4	Zimbabwe	3	0	2	1	2

Semi-finals KwaZulu-Natal Inland beat Gauteng by eight wickets; Free State beat Namibia by ten wickets.

Final At Kimberley, September 25, 2017. **KwaZulu-Natal Inland won by six wickets. Free State 128-5** (20 overs); ‡**KwaZulu-Natal Inland 129-4** (17.5 overs). *Karabo Mogotsi batted throughout Free State's innings, but scored only 42* in 60 balls. KwaZulu-Natal kept up a steady rate, and Kyle Nipper completed victory with 38* in 31.*

SRI LANKAN CRICKET IN 2018

Minister with portfolio

SA'ADI THAWFEEQ

It was a desperate year for Sri Lankan cricket. Results were poor, but that paled beside the scandals that engulfed players, former players and officials. While the elections that were supposed to deliver a new set of administrators were mired in red tape and squabbles, the organisation drifted. The running of the game was taken over by Harin Fernando, the minister of sport, who made sensational allegations about levels of corruption in the Sri Lankan game.

The most shocking news came in October, when Sanath Jayasuriya, one of the country's greatest players and a national hero, was suspended by the ICC and charged with two counts of breaching their anti-corruption code. It was alleged he had failed to co-operate with an investigation into match-fixing in Sri Lanka during his second term as chairman of selectors, in 2016 and 2017. Later Nuwan Zoysa, the former fast bowler, who had been the national bowling

SRI LANKA IN 2018

	Played	Won	Lost	Drawn/No result
Tests	12	4	5	3
One-day internationals	17	6	10	1
Twenty20 internationals	8	4	4	–

JANUARY	ODI tri-series (in Bangladesh) v Bangladesh and Zimbabwe	(page 849)
FEBRUARY	2 Tests and 2 T20Is (a) v Bangladesh	(page 852)
MARCH	T20 tri-series (h) v Bangladesh and India	(page 1026)
APRIL		
MAY		
JUNE	3 Tests (a) v West Indies	(page 1043)
JULY / AUGUST	2 Tests, 5 ODIs and 1 T20I (h) v South Africa	(page 1029)
SEPTEMBER	Asia Cup (in the UAE)	(page 1110)
OCTOBER / NOVEMBER	3 Tests, 5 ODIs and 1 T20I (h) v England	(page 359)
DECEMBER / JANUARY	2 Tests, 3 ODIs and 1 T20I (a) v New Zealand	(page 917)

For a review of Sri Lankan domestic cricket from the 2017-18 season, see page 1036.

Ishara S. Kodikara, AFP/Getty Images

Yes, minister: coach Chandika Hathurusinghe talks to Harin Fernando, who took charge of Sri Lankan cricket, during the Test defeat in Australia in February 2019.

coach, was also charged with match-fixing, and all-rounder Dilhara Lokuhettige with corruption in the T10 league in the UAE in 2017. Soon after, the touring England team administered a 3–0 Test whitewash to deepen the sense of crisis.

Fernando did not mince his words. After a meeting with Alex Marshall, head of the ICC's Anti-Corruption Unit, he said he had seen a confidential report which gave a damning view of the levels of corruption in Sri Lankan cricket. The ACU continued their inquiry in January 2019 by announcing a 15-day amnesty for Sri Lankan players to come forward and said a "number of people" had provided "new and important information". Meanwhile, Fernando continued to be the voice of reform. In February, he flew to Australia – at his own expense, he stressed – to meet the players after two heavy Test defeats.

Some of the lurid headlines were even about the cricket. In St Lucia in June, Sri Lanka refused to take the field on the third morning of the Second Test after learning they were being punished for ball-tampering. Captain Dinesh Chandimal had been caught on camera the previous day putting a sweet in his mouth, then applying saliva to the ball. Chandimal, coach Chandika Hathurusinghe and manager Asanka Gurusinha were locked in lengthy discussions with match referee Javagal Srinath, before play began two hours late. Chandimal was banned from the Third Test, which Sri Lanka won under Suranga Lakmal to level the series.

It was not the end of it. Captain, coach and manager were all charged with bringing the game into disrepute, and suspended for both Tests and four one-day internationals when South Africa toured in July. With Hathurusinghe absent, the team had their best result of the year, winning the Tests 2–0. In his first year in the job, he had stepped into the vacuum caused by the chaos among administrators, and often appeared to be the sport's highest-profile figure. The problem was that results did not match his visibility.

Defeats outnumbered wins across the formats. Sri Lanka squeezed into the automatic qualifying spots for the World Cup by virtue of their eighth-placed ranking, but their luck ran out when they failed to secure direct qualification for the World T20 in Australia in 2020. World champions as recently as 2014, they will have to negotiate the qualifying tournament. In Test series, the bright spots were the home win over South Africa, an away victory in Bangladesh, and that draw in the Caribbean. But the whitewash by England – only the third time they had lost every Test of a home series – underlined the paucity of resources. More thrashings followed in New Zealand and Australia at the start of 2019.

Another disappointment was being knocked out of the Asia Cup in the first round, after losing to Afghanistan and Bangladesh. In an effort to find a solution, the Australian Steve Rixon was appointed fielding coach, and Jon Lewis, the former Durham coach, given responsibility for batting. Both appointments were until the end of the 2019 World Cup.

After the Asia Cup debacle, Angelo Mathews was dropped and sacked as one-day captain. Hathurusinghe questioned his fitness, and criticised his running between the wickets. Mathews claimed he had been made a scapegoat, and pointed out it had been Hathurusinghe's decision to reappoint him as captain. After Mathews reached a match-saving hundred against New Zealand at Wellington in December, he performed dips and push-ups, and flexed his right arm in the direction of the dressing-room.

It was a shame that politics overshadowed the farewell to a Sri Lankan great. Spinner Rangana Herath retired at the end of the First Test against England at Galle, after taking 433 wickets, more than any left-armer in history. Uneasily, Sri Lanka moved into a new era.

NIDAHAS TROPHY IN 2017-18

Sa'adi Thawfeeq

1 India   2 Bangladesh   3 Sri Lanka

Sri Lanka were excluded from their own party when they failed to reach the final of a Twenty20 tournament organised to celebrate 70 years of independence (*nidahas* is the Sinhala word for freedom). India left five leading players at home, but underlined their bench strength by winning a pulsating final against Bangladesh. The hosts, in their first home assignment under new coach Chandika Hathurusinghe, could only look on enviously.

India were without Virat Kohli, M. S. Dhoni, Bhuvneshwar Kumar, Jasprit Bumrah and Hardik Pandya, but were led smartly by Rohit Sharma. Once they had recovered from losing their opening match against Sri Lanka, they looked unstoppable. Bangladesh battled hard, but made themselves deeply unpopular at the conclusion of their victory over Sri Lanka in the last game of the league stage. It was marred by ugly scenes, in part a result of bad feeling during the series in Bangladesh the previous month.

The teams riled each other by trading versions of the *nagin* snake dance at the fall of wickets, and the rancour spilled over in the last over of what amounted to a semi-final. With Bangladesh needing 12 off four balls, Shakib Al Hasan – in charge for the first time in the tournament after injury – briefly tried to call his batsmen off in protest at the umpires' failure to award a no-ball on height. Bangladesh substitute Nurul Hasan exchanged angry words with Sri Lanka's stand-in captain Tissara Perera, before Mahmudullah channelled his fury, rounding off his 43 from 18 balls with a match-winning six off the penultimate delivery.

> Washington Sundar, an 18-year-old off-spinner, was the Player of the Tournament

It also emerged that a glass door in the Bangladesh dressing-room had been smashed after the match. Shakib and Nurul were fined and given demerit points, while the Bangladesh board issued a statement rebuking the players. The kerfuffle meant India received enthusiastic support in the final.

Sharma proved good at extracting the most from his players. Washington Sundar, an 18-year-old off-spinner with just two previous international appearances, was the Player of the Tournament, with eight wickets at 14. Shikhar Dhawan anchored the batting with 198 runs at just under 40, and Sharma was also consistent. In the final, Dinesh Karthik supplied the fireworks, after India left themselves needing 34 off the last two overs.

Bangladesh's surprise progress owed much to some explosive batting. In the first of their wins over Sri Lanka, Liton Das opened with 43 in 19 balls, before Mushfiqur Rahim thumped 72 off 35 to round off Bangladesh's highest T20 total. In Kusal Perera, Sri Lanka had the tournament's top run-scorer, with 204 at 51, but that was small consolation.

NATIONAL SQUADS

Sri Lanka *L. D. Chandimal, M. A. Aponso, P. V. D. Chameera, A. Dananjaya, D. M. de Silva, A. N. P. R. Fernando, M. D. Gunathilleke, R. A. S. Lakmal, B. K. G. Mendis, B. M. A. J. Mendis, M. D. K. J. Perera, N. L. T. C. Perera, M. D. Shanaka, W. U. Tharanga, I. Udana. *Coach:* U. C. Hathurusinghe.

N. L. T. C. Perera took over as captain when Chandimal was suspended after two matches.

Bangladesh *Mahmudullah, Abu Haider, Abu Jayed, Ariful Haque, Imrul Kayes, Liton Das, Mehedi Hasan, Mushfiqur Rahim, Mustafizur Rahman, Nazmul Islam, Nurul Hasan, Rubel Hossain, Sabbir Rahman, Soumya Sarkar, Tamim Iqbal, Taskin Ahmed. *Coach:* C. A. Walsh.

Shakib Al Hasan joined the squad before the final group game and took over the captaincy.

India *R. G. Sharma, Y. S. Chahal, S. Dhawan, D. Hooda, K. D. Karthik, M. K. Pandey, R. R. Pant, A. R. Patel, K. L. Rahul, S. K. Raina, V. Shankar, M. Siraj, S. N. Thakur, J. D. Unadkat, M. S. Washington Sundar. *Coach:* R. J. Shastri.

At Colombo (RPS), March 6, 2018 (floodlit). **Sri Lanka won by five wickets. India 174-5** (20 overs) (S. Dhawan 90, M. K. Pandey 37); ‡**Sri Lanka 175-5** (18.3 overs) (M. D. K. J. Perera 66). MoM: M. D. K. J. Perera. *T20I debut:* V. Shankar (India). *Sri Lanka launched their campaign with an assured victory, with Kusal Perera hogging the headlines for his 66 off 37 balls. He slammed 26 off the third over of the chase, from seamer Shardul Thakur, while Tissara Perera calmed nerves at the death with a well-judged 22*. India had slipped to 9-2 after two overs, and a modest 40 after the powerplay, but they reached a challenging total thanks to Shikhar Dhawan's 90 off 49 balls, his best T20I score.*

At Colombo (RPS), March 8, 2018 (floodlit). **India won by six wickets. Bangladesh 139-8** (20 overs) (Liton Das 34, Sabbir Rahman 30; J. D. Unadkat 3-38); ‡**India 140-4** (18.4 overs) (S. Dhawan 55). MoM: V. Shankar. *Dhawan's second successive fifty guided India to a comfortable win in a lacklustre encounter. Bangladesh's total would have been feebler but for some generous Indian fielding: three catches were dropped from off-spinner Vijay Shankar, including one by the bowler himself. He still won the match award, after removing the dangerous duo of Mushfiqur Rahim and Mahmudullah. Liton Das was put down twice on his way to a top-score of 34 but, from 107-4 after 15 overs, Bangladesh seemed likely to make more than 139.*

At Colombo (RPS), March 10, 2018 (floodlit). **Bangladesh won by five wickets. Sri Lanka 214-6** (20 overs) (B. K. G. Mendis 57, M. D. K. J. Perera 74, W. U. Tharanga 32*; Mustafizur Rahman 3-48); ‡**Bangladesh 215-5** (19.4 overs) (Tamim Iqbal 47, Liton Das 43, Mushfiqur Rahim 72*). MoM: Mushfiqur Rahim. *Set 215, which was 22 higher than they had ever made in a T20 innings, Bangladesh were given a flying start by Tamim Iqbal and Das, promoted to open, who hammered 74 inside six overs. After Tamim departed, Mushfiqur made a dazzling 72* off 35 balls, equally severe on seam and spin. Even the departures of Mahmudullah and Sabbir Rahman in quick succession did not halt Mushfiqur, who secured the fourth-highest successful chase in T20Is in the final over. Sri Lanka's total, their fourth-highest, had leaned heavily on Kusal Mendis (57 off 30) and Kusal Perera (74 off 48).*

At Colombo (RPS), March 12, 2018 (floodlit). **India won by six wickets. Sri Lanka 152-9** (19 overs) (B. K. G. Mendis 55; S. N. Thakur 4-27); ‡**India 153-4** (17.3 overs) (M. K. Pandey 42*, K. D. Karthik 39*). MoM: S. N. Thakur. *Thakur bounced back from his mauling in the opening match to take four wickets and put India within touching distance of the final. He deployed his variations to good effect, while teenage off-spinner Washington Sundar claimed two victims in four inexpensive overs. In a match reduced to 19, Sri Lanka – without captain Dinesh Chandimal, suspended for two matches because of a slow over-rate – moved brightly to 96-2 in the 11th over after a partnership of 62 between Kusal Mendis and Upul Tharanga. India stumbled to 85-4, but Manish Pandey and Dinesh Karthik guided them home.*

At Colombo (RPS), March 14, 2018 (floodlit). **India won by 17 runs. India 176-3** (20 overs) (R. G. Sharma 89, S. Dhawan 35, S. K. Raina 47); ‡**Bangladesh 159-6** (20 overs) (Mushfiqur Rahim 72*; M. S. Washington Sundar 3-22). MoM: R. G. Sharma. *India continued their improvement since their opening defeat and booked their place in the final. On a slow pitch, they advanced cautiously, before going at ten an over in the second half of their innings. Rohit Sharma top-scored with 89 off 61 balls, including five sixes, and received good support from Dhawan and Suresh Raina. Bangladesh's response was holed below the waterline by Sundar, who struck three times in the powerplay.*

Mushfiqur continued his rich vein with 72* off 55, but lacked assistance. This was the only instance in the tournament of victory for the team batting first.

At Colombo (RPS), March 16, 2018 (floodlit). **Bangladesh won by two wickets. Sri Lanka 159-7** (20 overs) (M. D. K. J. Perera 61, N. L. T. C. Perera 58); ‡**Bangladesh 160-8** (19.5 overs) (Tamim Iqbal 50, Mahmudullah 43*). *MoM:* Mahmudullah. *In a feverish atmosphere, Mahmudullah remained the coolest man in the stadium, steering Bangladesh into the final with a six off the penultimate ball. Earlier in the over, captain Shakib Al Hasan emerged from the dressing-room and tried to take his batsmen off in protest at the umpires' failure to call a no-ball on height. Substitute Nurul Hasan traded verbals with Tissara, and there was pushing and shoving. When things calmed down, Mahmudullah hit Isuru Udana for four, two and six to round off a match-winning 43* off 18 balls. Sri Lanka's 159-7 had owed much to the Pereras – Kusal Perera hit 61 and Tissara 58. Shakib and Nurul were fined 25% of their match fees.*

India 6pts, Bangladesh 4pts, Sri Lanka 2pts.

Final   At Colombo (RPS), March 18, 2018 (floodlit). **India won by four wickets. Bangladesh 166-8** (20 overs) (Sabbir Rahman 77; Y. S. Chahal 3-18); ‡**India 168-6** (20 overs) (R. G. Sharma 56). *MoM:* K. D. Karthik. *MoS:* M. S. Washington Sundar. *Karthik ensured that India added the Nidahas Trophy to their cabinet by hitting the last ball of the match for six. The win sparked jubilation in the stands, where a big crowd were now motivated by intense dislike of Bangladesh. "We didn't feel we were playing outside India," said Sharma, their stand-in leader, who shrewdly held back Karthik's finishing expertise. India needed 34 from two overs after a wicket maiden from Mustafizur Rahman, but Karthik caned Rubel Hossain for 22 in the 19th. Shakib employed part-timer Soumya Sarkar for the final over and, although he removed Shankar with the fifth ball, Karthik carved a wide half-volley over extra cover to seal the win. His 29* came off eight deliveries. Bangladesh's total had been built around 77 from 50 by Sabbir, who had to supervise a rebuilding operation from 68-4.*

SRI LANKA v SOUTH AFRICA IN 2018

FIDEL FERNANDO

Test matches (2): Sri Lanka 2, South Africa 0
One-day internationals (5): Sri Lanka 2, South Africa 3
Twenty20 international (1): Sri Lanka 1, South Africa 0

This was a topsy-turvy tour. South Africa recorded their lowest Test total since readmission in the first match of the trip, and ended it with their lowest Twenty20 total – but in between collected some rollicking one-day wins to take the 50-over series. Their batting had glaring weaknesses against the red ball, but their spinners performed hearteningly well with the white.

Sri Lanka, meanwhile, followed a trend: specialists in Tests at home, but awful at one-day internationals anywhere. It was a minor surprise that they regrouped to win the Twenty20 game that rounded off the tour, as they had been consistently modest in the shortest format for two years.

In recent times, the world's Test teams have seemingly organised themselves into two groups: those who can barely play spin, and those who would rather self-destruct against it. South Africa proved emphatic members of the second lot, crashing to totals of 126, 73 and 124 in their first three innings of the series.

The turn on offer was substantial, but hardly alarming. South Africa had decent spinners themselves, but the Sri Lankans played them well, especially opener Dimuth Karunaratne. And although 40-year-old Rangana Herath – playing in his penultimate series – had been swallowing visiting top orders whole for years, his support acts, Dilruwan Perera and Akila Dananjaya, had tended to be feisty rather than fearsome. But the South African batsmen were apparently incapable of distinguishing between balls that would turn from those that slid on.

The Galle Test was especially embarrassing: the tourists' match aggregate of 199 was bettered by Karunaratne alone. He went on to enjoy a golden series, making 158 not out, 60, 53 and 85 before any of the South Africans managed even a half-century. He scored 195 more runs than anyone else in the Tests, and won both match awards.

South Africa banked on seam bowling, despite the dusty tracks, but could not find any of the reverse swing that had envenomed Dale Steyn and his partners on their previous visit, in 2014. This time, Steyn was returning from another long injury lay-off. He went into the series just two wickets behind Shaun Pollock's South African Test record of 421 – but couldn't break it, drawing level at Galle, before going wicketless on an unforgiving pitch at the Sinhalese Sports Club in Colombo.

When the one-day internationals started, the script changed abruptly. Even without their leading spinner, Imran Tahir, South Africa won the first three with a casual arrogance. Pacemen Lungi Ngidi and Andile Phehlukwayo were outstanding, as was the inexperienced left-arm wrist-spinner Tabraiz Shamsi.

Having a ball: Dimuth Karunaratne enjoys a golden series.

He took four for 33 in the first one-dayer, and made a case for consideration as Tahir's partner in the 2019 World Cup.

South Africa tinkered with their line-up after clinching the series, which helped Sri Lanka win the final two games. The tourists did go back to their best XI for the solitary T20, but had one final nightmare against the spinners, sliding to 98 all out. Sri Lanka wobbled but won, which allowed them to claim they had had the better of the exchanges overall.

SOUTH AFRICA TOURING TEAM

*F. du Plessis (T/50), H. M. Amla (T/50/20), T. Bavuma (T), C. J. Dala (50/20), T. B. de Bruyn (T), Q. de Kock (T/50/20), J-P. Duminy (50/20), D. Elgar (T), R. R. Hendricks (50/20), H. Klaasen (T), K. A. Maharaj (T/50/20), A. K. Markram (T/50/20), D. A. Miller (50/20), P. W. A. Mulder (50/20), L. T. Ngidi (T/50/20), A. L. Phehlukwayo (50/20), V. D. Philander (T), K. Rabada (T/50/20), T. Shamsi (T/50/20), D. W. Steyn (T), S. von Berg (T). *Coach:* O. D. Gibson.

Shamsi briefly returned home for personal reasons, and missed the Second Test. Du Plessis injured his shoulder in the third ODI, and left the tour; de Kock captained in the last two ODIs, and Duminy in the T20 international.

SRI LANKA v SOUTH AFRICA

First Test

At Galle, July 12–14, 2018. Sri Lanka won by 278 runs. Toss: Sri Lanka.

The last time South Africa had played in Galle, in 2014, centuries from Dean Elgar and J-P. Duminy set up a comfortable victory. But now, in a meek performance, many of the same batsmen were stiff and jerky, like puppets. And it was the Sri Lankan spinners who were pulling the strings.

Before South Africa's batting nosedived, however, Karunaratne produced a sublime lone hand. He became only the fourth Sri Lankan to carry his bat in a Test, following Sidath Wettimuny, Marvan Atapattu and Russel Arnold, and extended his eighth century to 158, in a total of 287. While the rest struggled – the next best was fellow opener Gunathilleke's 26 – Karunaratne's innings was a masterclass, scored at a strike-rate of around 70. He started securely against the pacy Rabada, then manoeuvred the spinners adroitly, taking calculated risks to force du Plessis to adopt fields he was comfortable with. "I tried to get them to drop the ball where I wanted it dropped," he said. On a difficult track, it seemed at times as if he had arranged with the bowler where the delivery would land, because he was so often in the right place to meet it.

The South Africans had hoped their five-man attack – three frontline quicks and two spinners – would be more penetrative than Sri Lanka's. In that 2014 victory, Steyn had scythed through the middle order twice with the old ball, while Philander copped a fine for picking the seam. But now neither Steyn nor Rabada – two notable movers of the old ball in the past – could get the thing to reverse, in this Test or the next.

Sri Lanka went down a different route. While South Africa's seamers sent down 35 overs in the first innings, Lakmal gave himself only 4.3 in the match (but still took three cheap wickets to polish off South Africa's disappointing first innings). He was in charge because Dinesh Chandimal, the regular captain, was serving a suspension for a ball-tampering incident during the tour of the West Indies.

With Dilruwan Perera taking four wickets, South Africa were demolished for 126, the only sustained resistance coming from du Plessis and Philander in a seventh-wicket stand of 64 that occupied 28 overs. Then Karunaratne sparkled for another half-century as Sri Lanka tried to build on their lead of 161. Again he had little support; slow left-armer Maharaj took four wickets in an uninspiring total of 190. Rabada claimed three this time, including his 150th in Tests, and also ran out Roshen Silva by deflecting Mathews's drive into the stumps.

Still, South Africa needed 352 to win on a spinners' paradise. It was a tough task – but no one was prepared for quite how hopeless they would be. Both openers were stumped for the first time in South African history, and no one reached 23 or lasted more than 50 balls. Within 29 overs they were all out for 73 – their lowest total since 1956-57, when England skittled them for 72 in successive Tests at Johannesburg and Cape Town. Perera tweaked his way to career-best match figures of ten for 78, due reward for attacking the stumps. It was his second haul of ten, after the Galle Test against Australia two years earlier.

Man of the Match: F. D. M. Karunaratne.

Close of play: first day, South Africa 4-1 (Elgar 4, Maharaj 0); second day, Sri Lanka 111-4 (Mathews 14, Silva 10).

Sri Lanka

M. D. Gunathilleke c de Kock b Rabada	26	– c Rabada b Maharaj 17
F. D. M. Karunaratne not out	158	– c Amla b Rabada 60
D. M. de Silva b Shamsi	11	– b Maharaj 9
B. K. G. Mendis c Rabada b Steyn	24	– lbw b Maharaj 0
A. D. Mathews c de Kock b Rabada	1	– b Maharaj 35
A. R. S. Silva c Markram b Rabada	0	– run out (Rabada) 13
†D. P. D. N. Dickwella c Amla b Shamsi	18	– c de Kock b Rabada 9
M. D. K. Perera c de Kock b Philander	1	– lbw b Rabada 2
H. M. R. K. B. Herath run out (Philander/de Kock)	1	– (10) lbw b Shamsi 0
*R. A. S. Lakmal c de Kock b Rabada	10	– (9) not out 33
P. A. D. L. R. Sandakan st de Kock b Shamsi ...	25	– c Bavuma b Steyn 6
B 7, lb 1, w 2, nb 2	12	B 2, lb 4 6

1/44 (1) 2/70 (3) 3/115 (4)   (78.4 overs) 287   1/51 (1) 2/64 (3)   (57.4 overs) 190
4/119 (5) 5/119 (6) 6/161 (7)   3/64 (4) 4/92 (2)
7/164 (8) 8/176 (9) 9/224 (10) 10/287 (11)   5/117 (6) 6/132 (7) 7/134 (8)
                                                                 8/156 (5) 9/163 (10) 10/190 (11)

Philander 8–1–28–1; Steyn 13–0–54–1; Rabada 14–1–50–4; Maharaj 17–3–49–0; Shamsi 25.4–2–91–3; Elgar 1–0–7–0. *Second innings*—Rabada 12–0–44–3; Steyn 11.4–1–35–1; Maharaj 20–5–58–4; Shamsi 11–0–37–1; Philander 3–0–10–0.

South Africa

D. Elgar c Mathews b Perera	8	– (2) st Dickwella b Perera	4
A. K. Markram c Mathews b Herath	0	– (1) st Dickwella b Herath	19
K. A. Maharaj lbw b Herath	3	– (8) c Sandakan b Perera	9
H. M. Amla c Mendis b Perera	15	– (3) c de Silva b Perera	0
T. Bavuma b Sandakan	17	– (4) c de Silva b Perera	2
*F. du Plessis b Lakmal	49	– (5) c Mathews b Herath	1
†Q. de Kock b Perera	3	– (6) lbw b Perera	10
V. D. Philander lbw b Perera	18	– (7) not out	22
K. Rabada b Lakmal	2	– b Perera	0
D. W. Steyn c Mathews b Lakmal	8	– c and b Herath	2
T. Shamsi not out	0	– lbw b Sandakan	2
B 2, nb 1	3	B 2	2

1/1 (2)　2/9 (3)　3/13 (1)　　　　　　　(54.3 overs)　126　　1/12 (2)　2/16 (3)　　　(28.5 overs)　73
4/40 (4)　5/48 (5)　6/51 (7)　　　　　　　　　　　　　　　　3/24 (4)　4/25 (5)
7/115 (8)　8/115 (6)　9/123 (9)　10/126 (10)　　　　　　　5/32 (1)　6/36 (6)　7/58 (8)
　　　　　　　　　　　　　　　　　　　　　　　　　　　　8/58 (9)　9/67 (10)　10/73 (11)

Herath 19–5–39–2; Perera 23–8–46–4; Sandakan 8–1–18–1; Lakmal 4.3–0–21–3. *Second innings*—Herath 14–4–38–3; Perera 14–4–32–6; Sandakan 0.5–0–1–1.

Umpires: P. R. Reiffel and R. J. Tucker.　Third umpire: N. J. Llong.
Referee: R. B. Richardson.

SRI LANKA v SOUTH AFRICA

Second Test

At Colombo (SSC), July 20–23, 2018. Sri Lanka won by 199 runs. Toss: Sri Lanka.

Sri Lanka romped to a 2–0 win, helped by a tactical blunder from South Africa, who chose only one spinner on a pitch that neutered the seamers. Maharaj, their slow left-armer, made the best of a bad situation by claiming nine for 129 in the first innings, South Africa's best figures away from home, but the quicker bowlers managed only two wickets in the match. With Maharaj the sole threat, it meant the Sri Lankan batsmen were rarely under pressure. He was only the fifth bowler to take nine in the opening innings of any Test, following Subhash Gupte, Richard Hadlee, Abdul Qadir and Muttiah Muralitharan.

Sri Lanka's openers put on 116, Karunaratne adding 53 to his pile of runs from the first match. Gunathilleke and Dhananjaya de Silva also made half-centuries, but they all eventually fell to Maharaj, bowling slightly quicker than he had at Galle, and looking far more dangerous as a result. His perseverance – only Roshen Silva, yorked by Rabada, escaped his clutches – allowed South Africa to keep the scoring within bounds, at least until Dananjaya and Herath enjoyed a feisty last-wicket partnership of 74, which stretched the total to 338 on a pitch expected to take increasing amounts of turn.

South Africa's batsmen, though, did not hold Sri Lanka up for long. The new ball was taken by the spinners – Lakmal gave himself only two overs this time, both in the second innings – and by the ninth it was 15 for three, Elgar adding a duck to his two failures at Galle. Du Plessis tried to counter-attack, hitting 48 from 51 balls, but of the rest only de Kock passed 20. South Africa were skittled for 124, taking their series aggregate to 323 for 30. Dananjaya, in his first home Test, collected five wickets and Perera four, but the batting was so shaky that any spinner on the island might have fancied their chances.

With three days and a session left, Chandimal waived the follow-on, which gave Karunaratne one last chance to showcase his talent. He played second fiddle to Gunathilleke in an opening stand of 91, but then took control; it was a surprise when he nicked a wide one from Ngidi within sight of another century. The lead stretched to 489 before the inevitable declaration. Maharaj plugged away, bowling throughout the innings save for a change of ends, and finished with 12 for 283, South Africa's best match figures in Asia.

The task was impossible, but at last the visiting batsmen showed some fight. Elgar made a gritty 37, then de Bruyn made his mark. With a highest score of 48 from five Tests, he seemed too high at No. 3 but, after surviving two drops before reaching double figures, he

---

BEST BOWLING FIGURES FOR SOUTH AFRICA

9-113	H. J. Tayfield (OB)	v England at Johannesburg		1956-57
9-129	**K. A. Maharaj (SLA)**	**v Sri Lanka at Colombo (SSC)**		**2018**
8-53	G. B. Lawrence (RFM)	v New Zealand at Johannesburg		1961-62
8-64†	L. Klusener (RFM)	v India at Calcutta		1996-97
8-69	H. J. Tayfield (OB)	v England at Durban		1956-57
8-70	S. J. Snooke (RFM)	v England at Johannesburg		1905-06
8-71	A. A. Donald (RF)	v Zimbabwe at Harare		1995-96

† *On debut. Tayfield's performances were in successive Tests.*

---

applied himself to make a maiden Test century. There was a wobble towards the end of the third day when du Plessis and nightwatchman Maharaj fell to successive balls from Dananjaya, but de Bruyn and Bavuma did well next morning with a stand of 123.

The resistance lasted until halfway through the fourth day, when the last rites were administered by Herath, as ever a handful in the fourth innings. He finished with six for 98, his 34th five-for in his 92nd Test. He then quietly announced his intention to retire later in the year: "There comes a time for every cricketer, when they have to stop playing. I think that time has come for me."

Man of the Match: F. D. M. Karunaratne. *Man of the Series:* F. D. M. Karunaratne.

Close of play: first day, Sri Lanka 277-9 (Dananjaya 16, Herath 5); second day, Sri Lanka 151-3 (Karunaratne 59, Mathews 12); third day, South Africa 139-5 (de Bruyn 45, T. Bavuma 14).

Sri Lanka

M. D. Gunathilleke c Rabada b Maharaj	57	– c Elgar b Maharaj		61
F. D. M. Karunaratne c de Kock b Maharaj	53	– c de Kock b Ngidi		85
D. M. de Silva lbw b Maharaj	60	– lbw b Maharaj		0
B. K. G. Mendis c Rabada b Maharaj	21	– run out (Markram/de Kock)		18
A. D. Mathews c du Plessis b Maharaj	10	– c du Plessis b Maharaj		71
A. R. S. Silva b Rabada	22	– not out		32
†D. P. D. N. Dickwella c du Plessis b Maharaj	5	– not out		7
M. D. K. Perera c Ngidi b Maharaj	17			
A. Dananjaya not out	43			
*R. A. S. Lakmal c Markram b Maharaj	0			
H. M. R. K. B. Herath c Elgar b Maharaj	35			
B 4, lb 2, w 8, nb 1	15	Nb 1		1

1/116 (2) 2/117 (1) 3/153 (4)   (104.1 overs) 338   1/91 (1)   (5 wkts dec, 81 overs) 275
4/169 (5) 5/223 (6) 6/238 (7)   2/102 (3) 3/136 (4)
7/247 (3) 8/264 (8) 9/264 (10) 10/338 (11)   4/199 (2) 5/263 (5)

Steyn 17–3–60–0; Rabada 20–3–55–1; Ngidi 14.2–1–54–0; Maharaj 41.1–10–129–9; Markram 8.4–1–24–0; Elgar 3–1–10–0. *Second innings*—Maharaj 40–4–154–3; Rabada 8–0–42–0; Markram 7–1–18–0; de Bruyn 5–0–20–0; Steyn 11–2–30–0; Ngidi 9–5–9–1; Elgar 1–0–2–0.

South Africa

A. K. Markram lbw b Herath	7	– (2) lbw b Herath	14
D. Elgar c de Silva b Dananjaya	0	– (1) lbw b Perera	37
T. B. de Bruyn c Dickwella b Dananjaya	3	– b Herath	101
H. M. Amla c Mendis b Perera	19	– b Herath	6
*F. du Plessis c Dickwella b Perera	48	– c Mathews b Dananjaya	7
T. Bavuma c Mendis b Perera	11	– (7) c Dickwella b Herath	63
†Q. de Kock lbw b Dananjaya	32	– (8) b Herath	8
K. A. Maharaj c Karunaratne b Dananjaya	2	– (6) lbw b Dananjaya	0
K. Rabada c Mathews b Perera	1	– c Mathews b Perera	18
D. W. Steyn lbw b Dananjaya	0	– c Gunathilleke b Herath	6
L. T. Ngidi not out	0	– not out	4
Nb 1	1	B 16, lb 5, w 1, nb 4	26

1/4 (2) 2/8 (3) 3/15 (1)   (34.5 overs) 124   1/23 (2) 2/80 (1)   (86.5 overs) 290
4/70 (4) 5/85 (5) 6/114 (6)   3/100 (4) 4/113 (5)
7/119 (8) 8/124 (7) 9/124 (10) 10/124 (9)   5/113 (6) 6/236 (7) 7/246 (8)
                                                               8/280 (3) 9/280 (9) 10/290 (10)

Perera 12.5–1–40–4; Dananjaya 13–2–52–5; Herath 9–1–32–1. *Second innings*—Herath 32.5–5–98–6; Perera 30–4–90–2; Dananjaya 19–2–67–2; Lakmal 2–0–8–0; de Silva 2–0–5–0; Gunathilleke 1–0–1–0.

Umpires: N. J. Llong and R. J. Tucker.   Third umpire: P. R. Reiffel.

Referee: R. B. Richardson.

First one-day international   At Dambulla, July 29, 2018. **South Africa won by five wickets. ‡Sri Lanka 193** (34.3 overs) (M. D. K. J. Perera 81, N. L. T. C. Perera 49; K. Rabada 4-41, T. Shamsi 4-33); **South Africa 196-5** (31 overs) (Q. de Kock 47, F. du Plessis 47, J-P. Duminy 53*; A. Dananjaya 3-50). MoM: T. Shamsi. *The game was effectively won in the first nine overs, with Kagiso Rabada and Lungi Ngidi blasting out four between them to leave Sri Lanka 36-5 (there was also a run-out). That they managed a semi-respectable 193 was thanks to a pair of Pereras, who put on 92 for the sixth wicket in less than nine overs: Kusal hit 11 fours and a six in his 81 from 72 balls, while Tissara clobbered eight fours from 30. South Africa stuttered when Hashim Amla and Aiden Markram were dismissed by consecutive deliveries from Akila Dananjaya in the fifth over. But Quinton de Kock and Faf du Plessis regained control, putting on 86 before J-P. Duminy rushed his side home with 19 overs to spare with 53* from 32.*

Second one-day international   At Dambulla, August 1, 2018 (day/night). **South Africa won by four wickets. ‡Sri Lanka 244-8** (50 overs) (D. P. D. N. Dickwella 69, A. D. Mathews 79*; L. T. Ngidi 3-50, A. L. Phehlukwayo 3-45); **South Africa 246-6** (42.5 overs) (Q. de Kock 87, H. M. Amla 43, F. du Plessis 49, J-P. Duminy 32; A. Dananjaya 3-60). MoM: Q. de Kock. *ODI debuts: N. G. R. P. Jayasuriya, C. A. K. Rajitha (Sri Lanka). Sri Lanka's batsmen put up stiffer resistance, but not enough to threaten another comfortable South African win. Ngidi and Andile Phehlukwayo were the primary destroyers this time. Niroshan Dickwella made 69, and Angelo Mathews 79*, but no one else reached 20. The chase began confidently, de Kock and Amla putting on 91 before Dananjaya struck twice. But de Kock carried on, eventually falling for 87 to the debutant seamer Kasun Rajitha with victory in sight. Tissara Perera took his 150th ODI wicket, and Suranga Lakmal his 100th.*

Third one-day international   At Pallekele, August 5, 2018. **South Africa won by 78 runs. South Africa 363-7** (50 overs) (H. M. Amla 59, R. R. Hendricks 102, J-P. Duminy 92, D. A. Miller 51; N. L. T. C. Perera 4-75); **‡Sri Lanka 285** (45.2 overs) (B. K. G. Mendis 31, A. D. Mathews 32, D. M. de Silva 84, A. Dananjaya 37; L. T. Ngidi 4-57, A. L. Phehlukwayo 3-74). MoM: R. R. Hendricks. *ODI debut: R. R. Hendricks (South Africa). Mathews chose to bowl, hoping the pitch would improve as the day progressed. But South Africa showed it was already pretty good, rattling up their highest ODI total in Sri Lanka (previously 339-5 at Hambantota in 2014). Reeza Hendricks led the way, becoming only the third South African (after Colin Ingram and Temba Bavuma) to score a century in his first ODI. Although he hit only nine boundaries, it took him just 88 balls – faster than any other debut hundred. Duminy slapped 92 from 70, with four sixes, as Tissara Perera collected four expensive wickets. Sri Lanka were never in touch, despite a late burst from Dhananjaya de Silva, who cracked an ODI-best 84 from 66 balls from No. 7 to give the crowd something to cheer after his side had slipped to 155-6.*

Fourth one-day international   At Pallekele, August 8, 2018 (day/night). **Sri Lanka won by three runs** (DLS). **Sri Lanka 306-7** (39 overs) (D. P. D. N. Dickwella 34, W. U. Tharanga 36, M. D. K. J. Perera 51, N. L. T. C. Perera 51*, M. D. Shanaka 65); ‡**South Africa 187-9** (21 overs) (H. M. Amla 40, J-P. Duminy 38; R. A. S. Lakmal 3-46). *MoM:* M. D. Shanaka. *ODI debut:* C. J. Dala (South Africa). *This was reduced to a 45-over match after a late start, then further shortened by two showers during Sri Lanka's innings and a downpour two overs into South Africa's reply; their eventual target was 191 in 21. South Africa rested Rabada and Tabraiz Shamsi, and were also without du Plessis, who had returned home after injuring his shoulder in the previous match (de Kock captained instead). Sri Lanka finally put together a decent batting performance, with a seventh-wicket stand of 109 in 11 overs between Tissara Perera (51* from 45 balls) and Dasun Shanaka (65 from 34, with five sixes) propelling them past 300. The final total included a dozen sixes. At 108-2 in the tenth, South Africa looked like chasing down their revised target, but were pegged back, despite the bowlers being handicapped by a wet ball. Eight were needed from the final over, but Suranga Lakmal conceded only four. It was Sri Lanka's first victory in the last 12 ODIs against South Africa.*

Fifth one-day international   At Colombo (RPS), August 12, 2018 (day/night). **Sri Lanka won by 178 runs.** ‡**Sri Lanka 299-8** (50 overs) (A. D. Mathews 97*, D. M. de Silva 30); **South Africa 121** (24.4 overs) (Q. de Kock 54; A. Dananjaya 6-29). *MoM:* A. Dananjaya. *MoS:* J-P. Duminy. *Mathews's run-a-ball 97* formed the spine of a useful total, before off-spinner Dananjaya completed a huge win with a career-best 6-29, Sri Lanka's best one-day figures against South Africa. Three of those wickets came as they limped to 48-4 in the ten-over powerplay, and only de Kock survived for long. South Africa left more than half their overs unused as they slumped to their second-biggest defeat by Sri Lanka.*

Twenty20 international   At Colombo (RPS), August 14, 2018 (floodlit). **Sri Lanka won by three wickets.** ‡**South Africa 98** (16.4 overs) (P. A. D. L. R. Sandakan 3-19); **Sri Lanka 99-7** (16 overs) (L. D. Chandimal 36*, D. M. de Silva 31). *MoM:* D. M. de Silva. *South Africa's batsmen were befuddled by spin one last time: left-arm wrist-spinner Lakshan Sandakan (who had been left out of the ODIs), Dananjaya (2-15) and part-time offie de Silva (2-22) claimed seven wickets between them. South Africa lost their last five for 29, to crash to their lowest total in T20 internationals (previously 100 against Pakistan at Centurion in 2012-13). Rabada dismissed both openers in the first over of the chase, before Dinesh Chandimal and de Silva added 53. Shamsi and Junior Dala shared four wickets to set nerves jangling at 88-7, but Chandimal stayed calm.*

DOMESTIC CRICKET IN SRI LANKA IN 2017-18

Sa'adi Thawfeeq

Chilaw Marians, one of the youngest clubs in Sri Lanka's first-class Premier League, won the title for the second time in their brief history. Founded in 1975, they clinched it by beating reigning champions Sinhalese (established 1899) in their last match. They left Sinhalese a daunting target of 540, and bundled them out for 275; all-rounder Shehan Jayasuriya scored 146 and 88, and picked up four wickets in each innings with his off-spin.

Chilaw won nine of their ten group and Super Eight games, and tied the other, entering the final round on top of the table, just as they had the previous season. Then, they had faltered, and were overtaken by Sinhalese; this time, they made no mistake. The captain, left-arm spinner Malinda Pushpakumara, was the tournament's leading wicket-taker, with 70 at 16, and for the second year running claimed the most in all first-class cricket. Chilaw also had three of the top four run-scorers in Tier A – Sachithra Serasinghe and Oshada Fernando, with three centuries apiece, and Jayasuriya, with two. Serasinghe later scored a fourth, for Galle District, and ended the season the only batsman to reach 1,000 first-class runs.

In Tier B of the Premier League, **Negombo** made their first-class debut, a year later than they had expected. They had originally won promotion when Sebastianites, who beat them in the qualifying Sara Trophy final, were disqualified for fielding ineligible players; Negombo were then excluded after a legal wrangle, and had sought redress against Sri Lanka Cricket when they were also kept out of a limited-overs competition. Despite drawing six of their eight matches, Negombo won Tier B by a fraction of a point from Lankan, to gain immediate promotion to Tier A. They tied a game against Kalutara Town when their left-arm spinner Umega Chaturanga completed match figures of 12 for 191 – the second-best return of the season, after 12 for 73 by another slow left-armer, Chanaka Komasaru, for Ports Authority against Badureliya in Tier A. Ports Authority fielded former England batsman Nick Compton, who scored 489 runs in seven matches, and Pakistanis Adeel Malik (brother of Test player Shoaib Malik) and Shoaib Nasir.

Sinhalese had their revenge on Chilaw when they beat them in the semi-finals of the Premier limited-overs tournament, and went on to win the final against their old rivals Nondescripts. Both sides fielded five current internationals but, despite Sri Lanka captain Dinesh Chandimal's 103, Nondescripts managed only 236; powered by Test opener Dhanushka Gunathilleke's 119, Sinhalese cruised home.

The four district teams – Colombo, Dambulla, Galle and Kandy – who were introduced in a 50-over provincial tournament in April 2017 returned to play in all three formats between March and August 2018. The first-class Super Four Provincial Tournament included a round of day/night games with pink balls (to prepare leading players for the day/night Test in the West Indies in June), though it was disrupted by rain. **Galle District** contrived to win the competition without a single outright victory, pushing Dambulla – the only team who did record a win – into second place; the points system meant that Galle's 24, for taking the first-innings lead in all their three matches, outweighed Dambulla's 20, for a win plus one first-innings lead.

Galle owed much to the 535 runs piled up by Roshen Silva (the next-best was 315 from Kandy's Niroshan Dickwella). He scored 231 not out against Colombo – coming in at 22 for four – and 168 against Kandy, ending the season with 887 at 73. Galle also won the final of the limited-overs Super Four in June, when Upul Tharanga helped them reach a decisive 320 for seven against Colombo District. But by August, Tharanga was playing for Colombo in the Twenty20 Super Four, and his unbeaten 104 from 55 balls steered them to victory over Dambulla in the final.

FIRST-CLASS AVERAGES IN 2017-18

BATTING (550 runs, average 35.00)

		M	I	NO	R	HS	100	Avge	Ct/St
1	A. R. S. Silva (*Ragama/Galle District*) .	9	16	4	887	231*	3	73.91	4
2	Kashif Naved (*Panadura*)	8	14	2	805	192	3	67.08	5
3	J. K. Silva (*Sinhalese/Colombo District*)	11	15	2	827	202*	3	63.61	9
4	M. H. P. Gunathilake (*Kurunegala Youth*)	7	13	4	560	154*	1	62.22	7
5	M. D. Shanaka (*Sinhalese/Galle District*)	7	10	1	559	114*	1	62.11	6
6	P. Nissanka (*Badureliya/Kandy District*)	10	18	3	832	188*	3	55.46	7
7	R. T. M. Wanigamuni (*Bloomfield*).....	9	15	4	591	137*	2	53.72	3
8	L. P. C. Silva (*Moors/Colombo Dist*) ..	10	15	1	742	134	3	53.00	19
9	D. M. Sarathchandra (*Dambul/Tamil U*)	12	21	5	835	119*	4	52.18	26/8
10	†G. S. N. F. G. Jayasuriya (*Chilaw M/Col*)	11	17	0	873	146	2	51.35	10
11	L. Abeyratne (*Colombo/Colombo Dist*) .	9	14	0	707	115	3	50.50	17/4
12	†F. D. M. Karunaratne (*Sinhalese/Damb*)	9	16	1	738	143	3	49.20	6
13	†H. D. R. L. Thirimanne (*Ragama/Colom*)	11	20	3	830	166*	2	48.82	21
14	M. S. Warnapura (*Colombo/Galle Dist*) .	12	18	4	680	138*	2	48.57	3
15	B. O. P. Fernando (*Chilaw M/Galle Dist*)	11	19	2	820	196	3	48.23	7
16	S. C. Serasinghe (*Chilaw M/Dambulla*) .	13	23	0	1,108	145	4	48.17	16
17	D. V. B. Hasaranga (*Navy*)	8	12	0	572	93	0	47.66	11
18	A. K. Perera (*Nondescripts*)...........	9	16	1	680	129*	1	45.33	2
19	S. M. A. Priyanjan (*Colombo/Dambulla*)	12	19	0	825	156	2	43.42	8
20	S. A. D. U. Mihiran (*Air Force*)	8	15	1	603	115	2	43.07	7
21	S. Ashan (*Sinhalese*)	10	15	2	551	107	1	42.38	5
22	A. B. L. D. Rodrigo (*Lankan*)	8	15	0	616	121	2	41.06	5
23	†T. A. M. Siriwardene (*Sinhal/Dambulla*)	12	19	2	681	137*	1	40.05	11
24	P. A. R. P. Perera (*Colts/Kandy District*)	13	23	2	830	92	0	39.52	13
25	A. V. L. Madushan (*Army*)	8	16	2	552	151*	1	39.42	4
26	†W. P. S. Fernando (*Negombo*).........	8	15	0	564	86	0	37.60	9
27	†M. L. Udawatte (*Nondescripts/Kandy*)..	13	23	1	817	106	2	37.13	15
28	†K. P. N. M. Karunanayake (*Bloom/Dam*)	10	18	1	619	122	1	36.41	5

BOWLING (35 wickets, average 30.00)

		Style	O	M	R	W	BB	5I	Avge
1	N. C. Komasaru (*Ports Authority*)	SLA	425	108	1,074	69	7-49	7	15.56
2	A. M. Fernando (*Chil M/Dambulla*) ..	RFM	172.3	28	604	36	5-34	2	16.77
3	P. M. Pushpakumara (*Chil M/Galle*).	SLA	425.4	89	1,305	73	6-56	7	17.87
4	G. S. N. F. G. Jayasuriya (*Chil M/Col*)	OB	212.2	34	663	36	7-22	1	18.41
5	R. M. G. K. Sirisoma (*Galle*).......	SLA	395	94	1,024	55	7-115	6	18.61
6	L. Embuldeniya (*Nondescripts/Col*) .	SLA	375.4	51	1,212	65	6-59	7	18.64
7	M. A. Liyanapathiranage (*Ports Auth*)	SLA	289.4	57	747	40	5-52	2	18.67
8	C. N. V. Silva (*Police*).............	SLA	333.2	69	980	50	6-103	5	19.60
9	K. D. V. Wimalasekara (*Army*)	RFM	281	54	879	43	9-108	4	20.44
10	S. C. Serasinghe (*Chil M/Dambulla*)	OB	228	42	760	37	4-31	0	20.54
11	S. M. S. M. Senanayake (*Sinha/Dam*)	OB	470.4	99	1,339	63	7-82	2	21.25
12	J. U. Chaturanga (*Negombo*)	SLA	398.5	96	1,157	54	7-79	5	21.42
13	K. M. M. de Silva (*Bloomfield*)	SLA	373.4	77	1,018	47	5-56	5	21.65
14	N. G. R. P. Jayasuriya (*Colts/Kandy*)	SLA	451.1	74	1,425	62	7-26	3	22.98
15	D. R. F. Weerasinghe (*Lankan*)	OB	299.5	48	888	37	5-43	2	24.00
16	S. Randiv (*Burgher*)..............	OB	318.2	44	1,059	43	6-90	3	24.62
17	A. A. S. Silva (*Badureliya*)	OB	339.4	43	1,136	45	7-79	4	25.24
18	N. T. Gamage (*Colts/Galle District*).	RFM	231	21	983	37	6-71	3	26.56
19	N. M. Kavikara (*Lankan*)..........	SLA	286.3	38	965	36	4-51	0	26.80
20	G. D. Bandara (*Panadura*)........	LB	284.2	45	991	36	5-51	2	27.52
21	B. M. A. J. Mendis (*Tamil U/Kandy*)	LB	268.1	38	968	35	6-100	1	27.65
22	K. N. Peiris (*Ragama/Galle District*)	OB	273	35	1,056	36	6-67	2	29.33
23	D. K. R. C. Jayatissa (*Saracens*)	OB	306.5	30	1,040	35	5-51	1	29.71

PREMIER LEAGUE TOURNAMENT TIER A IN 2017-18

Group A	P	W	L	D	Pts	Group B	P	W	L	D	Pts
SINHALESE	6	1	0	5	71.155	CHIL MARIANS...	6	5	0	0†	101.445
RAGAMA	6	0	0	6	66.925	BURGHER........	6	1	1	3†	69.720
COLTS........	6	2	1	3	66.760	NONDESCRIPTS .	6	3	3	0	63.325
SARACENS......	6	0	2	4	49.130	PTS AUTHORITY .	6	2	3	1	58.505
Colombo..........	6	1	0	5	46.760	Tamil Union	6	1	2	3	54.780
Moors	6	0	0	6	33.410	Army	6	1	2	3	36.370
Bloomfield	6	0	1	5	32.815	Badureliya	6	1	3	2	35.575

Super Eight	P	W	L	D	Pts	Plate	P	W	L	D	Pts
Chilaw Marians	7	6	0	0†	118.925	Moors	5	1	0	4	52.300
Sinhalese	7	4	1	2	93.260	Badureliya	5	1	0	4	48.330
Ports Authority	7	4	3	0	82.130	Tamil Union	5	0	0	5	46.480
Burgher............	7	3	3	0†	74.060	Colombo..........	5	0	1	4	44.960
Nondescripts.......	7	3	4	0	72.125	Army	5	1	2	1†	40.850
Colts	7	2	3	2	60.425	Bloomfield	5	0	0	4†	36.850
Ragama............	7	1	3	3	53.605						
Saracens	7	0	6	1	30.990						

† *Plus one tie.*

The top four teams from each group advanced to the Super Eight, carrying forward their results against fellow qualifiers, then played the other four qualifiers. The bottom three from each group entered the Plate competition, run on the same principles. The bottom-placed Plate team, Bloomfield, were relegated and replaced by Negombo, the winners of Tier B.

Outright win = 12pts; win by an innings = 2pts extra; tie = 6pts; lead on first innings in a drawn game = 8pts; tie on first innings in a drawn game = 4pts. Bonus points were awarded as follows: 0.15pt for each wicket taken and 0.005pt for each run scored, up to 400 runs per innings.

CHAMPIONS

1988-89	{ Nondescripts / Sinhalese	1997-98	Sinhalese	2008-09	Colts
		1998-99	Bloomfield	2009-10	Chilaw Marians
1989-90	Sinhalese	1999-2000	Colts	2010-11	Bloomfield
1990-91	Sinhalese	2000-01	Nondescripts	2011-12	Colts
1991-92	Colts	2001-02	Colts	2012-13	Sinhalese
1992-93	Sinhalese	2002-03	Moors	2013-14	Nondescripts
1993-94	Nondescripts	2003-04	Bloomfield	2014-15	Ports Authority
1994-95	{ Bloomfield / Sinhalese	2004-05	Colts	2015-16	Tamil Union
		2005-06	Sinhalese	2016-17	Sinhalese
1995-96	Colombo	2006-07	Colombo	2017-18	Chilaw Marians
1996-97	Bloomfield	2007-08	Sinhalese		

Sinhalese have won the title outright 8 times, Colts 6, Bloomfield 4, Nondescripts 3, Chilaw Marians and Colombo 2, Moors, Ports Authority and Tamil Union 1. Sinhalese have shared it twice, Bloomfield and Nondescripts once each.

The tournament was known as the Lakspray Trophy from 1988-89 to 1989-90, the P. Saravanamuttu Trophy from 1990-91 to 1997-98, and the Premier League from 1998-99.

PREMIER LEAGUE TOURNAMENT TIER B IN 2017-18

	P	W	L	T	D	Pts
Negombo	8	1	0	1	6	87.665
Lankan	8	2	0	0	6	86.895
Galle......................	8	1	2	0	5	76.380
Kalutara Town	8	1	0	1	6	75.620
Air Force	8	2	3	0	3	71.685
Kurunegala Youth	8	0	1	0	7	66.205
Panadura..................	8	1	1	0	6	64.330
Navy.....................	8	1	0	0	7	63.165
Police	8	0	2	0	6	58.540

SUPER FOUR PROVINCIAL TOURNAMENT IN 2017-18

50-over league plus final

	P	W	L	D	Bonus	Pts
GALLE DISTRICT	3	0	0	3	14.020	38.020
DAMBULLA DISTRICT	3	1	0	2	15.545	35.545
Kandy District	3	0	0	3	14.540	22.540
Colombo District	3	0	1	2	11.310	11.310

Outright win = 12pts; win by an innings = 2pts extra; lead on first innings in a drawn game = 8pts. Bonus points were awarded as follows: 0.15pt for each wicket taken and 0.005pt for each run scored, up to 400 runs per innings.

PREMIER LIMITED-OVERS TOURNAMENT IN 2017-18

Four 50-over mini-leagues plus knockout

Quarter-finals Chilaw Marians beat Burgher by 30 runs; Nondescripts beat Colts by five wickets; Sinhalese beat Ragama by eight wickets; Saracens beat Tamil Union by four wickets.

Semi-finals Sinhalese beat Chilaw Marians by eight wickets; Nondescripts beat Saracens by 89 runs.

Final At Colombo (SSC), March 25, 2018. **Sinhalese won by four wickets. Nondescripts 236** (48.2 overs) (L. D. Chandimal 103); ‡**Sinhalese 239-6** (45.5 overs) (M. D. Gunathilleke 119). *Dinesh Chandimal batted through most of Nondescripts' innings, with little support, but was outdone by Dhanushka Gunathilleke, whose 119 came at almost a run a ball.*

SUPER FOUR PROVINCIAL LIMITED-OVERS TOURNAMENT IN 2018

50-over league plus final

Final At Colombo (RPS), June 10. **Galle District won by 75 runs. ‡Galle District 320-7** (50 overs) (W. U. Tharanga 124); **Colombo District 245** (44.2 overs). *Upul Tharanga hit 124 in 122 balls, and added 125 with Sadeera Samarawickrama to set up a formidable target.*

SUPER FOUR PROVINCIAL TWENTY20 TOURNAMENT IN 2018

50-over league plus final

Final At Colombo (RPS), September 2 (floodlit). **Colombo Districts won by seven wickets. ‡Dambulla District 163-8** (20 overs); **Colombo District 167-3** (18.2 overs) (W. U. Tharanga 104*). *Upul Tharanga batted throughout Colombo's chase for 104* in 55 balls, including nine sixes.*

The SLC Twenty20 tournament in 2017-18 has its own section (page 1147).

WEST INDIES CRICKET IN 2018

Not quite as miserable as it seemed

VANEISA BAKSH

During India's tour of Australia in December, Viv Richards gushed over Virat Kohli (and perhaps himself). He enjoyed paddling through a bit of nostalgia as he recalled the aggressive style he and Kohli share, and speculated about the strength of a batting line-up that included the two of them. Such musing was a diversion from the dismal saga that West Indies cricket had become – at least until the arrival of England in January 2019.

The year dawned with the conclusion of a Twenty20 series against New Zealand, which West Indies lost heavily, so maintaining a pattern. In two Tests, three ODIs and three T20s, New Zealand won the lot, except the rain-ruined second T20. In March came the World Cup Qualifiers in Zimbabwe, where West Indies at least did what was required, and ensured they would be at the party in 2019. But their opponents reflected the state to which their one-day cricket had fallen. World champions at Lord's in 1975 and 1979, they had

WEST INDIES IN 2018

	Played	Won	Lost	Drawn/No result
Tests	9	3	5	1
One-day internationals	18	8	9	1
Twenty20 internationals	15	4	10	1

DECEMBER / JANUARY	2 Tests, 3 ODIs and 3 T20Is (a) v New Zealand	(see *Wisden 2018*, page 914)
FEBRUARY		
MARCH	World Cup Qualifier (in Zimbabwe)	(page 790)
APRIL	3 T20Is (a) v Pakistan	(page 931)
MAY	1 T20I (in England) v World XI	(page 707)
JUNE	3 Tests (h) v Sri Lanka	(page 1043)
JULY / AUGUST	2 Tests, 3 ODIs and 3 T20Is (h) v Bangladesh	(page 1053)
SEPTEMBER		
OCTOBER / NOVEMBER	2 Tests, 5 ODIs and 3 T20Is (a) v India	(page 882)
DECEMBER	2 Tests, 3 ODIs and 3 T20Is (a) v Bangladesh	(page 863)

For a review of West Indian domestic cricket from the 2017-18 season, see page 1065.

A YEAR TO REMEMBER

Bowlers taking 30 Test wickets at under 14 in a calendar year:

	T	O	M	R	W	BB	5I	10M	Avge	
G. A. Lohmann (E)	4	114.1	50	255	38	9-28	4	2	6.71	1896
R. Peel (E)	4	108.1	71	239	33	7-31	2	1	7.24	1888
J. C. Laker (E)	6	314.3	138	480	48	10-53	4	2	10.00	1956
C. T. B. Turner (A)	4	168	112	348	33	7-43	6	2	10.54	1888
G. A. R. Lock (E)	7	236	105	373	35	7-35	3	1	10.65	1958
C. V. Grimmett (A)	3	193.1	77	371	33	7-40	5	3	11.24	1936
Shoaib Akhtar (P)	4	144.5	29	371	30	6-30	3	2	12.36	2003
J. O. Holder (WI)	**6**	**150.1**	**38**	**409**	**33**	**6-59**	**4**	**1**	**12.39**	**2018**
R. J. Hadlee (NZ)	6	227.4	81	462	35	5-28	3	1	13.20	1984
Imran Khan (P)	9	393.1	112	824	62	8-58	5	2	13.29	1982
H. Ironmonger (A)	7	267	122	473	35	7-23	2	1	13.51	1931
Mohammad Abbas (P)	**7**	**230.1**	**82**	**523**	**38**	**5-33**	**3**	**1**	**13.76**	**2018**
D. L. Underwood (A)	8	309	139	525	38	7-32	4	2	13.81	1969

to scrap for the right to return, against teams from the lower rungs of world cricket. They won all their games, except against Afghanistan, who beat them twice, including the final – and they were lucky to see off Scotland.

Next came a lightning trip to Karachi, where Pakistan strolled to victory in all three T20 internationals; in late May, West Indies beat a World XI in a fundraiser at Lord's. After hotfooting it back to the Caribbean, they hosted Sri Lanka. Jason Holder's team won the First Test, at Port-of-Spain, before going downhill, drawing in St Lucia, and losing in Barbados. Still, there was compensation in the form of Shannon Gabriel, whose electric pace snatched 20 wickets at 14 apiece. Holder's own form was also exceptional in this series, and the one that followed.

Bangladesh represented sterner opponents than in the past. But in July, Kemar Roach ripped them apart for 43 in the First Test in Antigua, with figures of five for eight. Gabriel took five more in the second innings to deliver a crushing victory. Kraigg Brathwaite hit a hundred, and added another in the next Test as West Indies claimed the series 2–0. Bangladesh exacted revenge in the white-ball contests, in both formats edging the hosts 2–1.

At the end of the year, it was West Indies' turn to visit Bangladesh, where they were bested in the Tests, and allowed the hosts their first innings victory. Things looked up a fraction as they approached Christmas: although West Indies again lost the ODI series 2–1, they did shade the Twenty20s. It was not sweetness and light, however. Carlos Brathwaite, the captain, complained to the match referee after the second game about the standard of umpiring, reportedly prompting Tanvir Ahmed, one of the on-field officials, to concede he had enjoyed better days. There had been controversy in the one-day series as well, with the deciding game played in a sour atmosphere.

Sandwiched between the home-and-away contests with Bangladesh was a difficult trip to India. Again, West Indies came off worse, losing three of the 50-over internationals, tying one and winning another. There were glimmers of optimism in the batting of Shai Hope and Shimron Hetmyer, though neither fared well in the Tests, which West Indies lost by sickeningly familiar margins: an innings and 272, and ten wickets. Holder maintained his prowess with the

Shaun Botterill/Getty Images

New year, new direction: Richard Pybus and Jason Holder talk tactics for 2019.

ball, but had little support. The only batsman to prosper was Roston Chase. India took the T20 series 3–0.

The Caribbean Premier League, played in August and September, threw up some encouraging new names, such as batsman Sherfane Rutherford and left-arm spinner Khary Pierre. Both made their international debuts before 2018 was out. They may be part of the West Indies team of the future: Dwayne Bravo announced he was no longer available, though would be happy to continue in various T20 leagues. And with Chris Gayle turning 40 in September, a changing of the guard was starting. It didn't just involve the players: head coach Stuart Law resigned to take a post with Middlesex.

Not that there was much sign of change at Cricket West Indies. In a radio interview, Dave Cameron, the president, said the board had been spending millions to develop players, only for them to show little loyalty. And he claimed franchise cricket was a distraction: "Everybody wants the game to be over in three hours, and we all want to get rich very, very quickly."

He had already told *The Sunday Gleaner* that cricket in Jamaica was being held back because PE teachers were predominantly women who "don't know the history and neither are they interested". While Cameron was trying to explain what he saw as one cause of the waning affection for the game, preparations were continuing for the women's World T20 in November, held for the first time in the Caribbean. West Indies, the defending champions, warmed up against South Africa, and drew their 20-over series 2–2. In the tournament, though, they lost to eventual winners Australia in the semi-final.

At the end of the year, there seemed no cause for optimism. But Richard Pybus was drafted in as a temporary coach for the men's team, and – under the inspirational Holder – England were beaten. Who'd have thought it?

WEST INDIES v SRI LANKA IN 2018

Revatha Silva

Test matches (3): West Indies 1, Sri Lanka 1

This series came to a boil during the Second Test in St Lucia. Before play could start on the third morning, with West Indies 118 for two in reply to Sri Lanka's 253, it was announced that the ball would be changed. Footage recorded the previous evening showed Sri Lankan captain Dinesh Chandimal placing a sweet in his mouth, before applying saliva to the ball, which umpires Aleem Dar and Ian Gould spent some time inspecting. It also emerged that West Indies would resume on 123, their overnight total boosted by five penalty runs.

That sanction enraged the tourists, and heated discussions ensued between Javagal Srinath, the match referee, and the Sri Lankans – especially Chandimal, coach Chandika Hathurusinghe and team manager Asanka Gurusinha. In chaotic scenes, the captain marched his side on and off the field as revised start times came and went. Eventually the Test, scheduled to begin at 9.30 – half an hour early, because rain had interrupted the second day – resumed at 11.30. As it turned out, those two hours might have enabled Sri Lanka to win the match, which instead ended in a draw.

After the game, Srinath fined Chandimal his entire match fee and imposed two suspension points, which ruled him out of the last Test. Chandimal promptly contested the punishment. Michael Beloff QC, chairman of the ICC's code of conduct commission, heard the appeal and upheld the decision. Suranga Lakmal took over as captain, and guided his side to a series-levelling victory.

With the furore of Australia's ball-tampering scandal in Cape Town still in the public consciousness, the ICC were keen to stamp their authority on this affair. In July, after the Sri Lankans had left the Caribbean, Chandimal, Hathurusinghe and Gurusinha were charged with bringing the game into disrepute by refusing to take the field. The three admitted breaching the ICC's code, and agreed not to take part in the home series against South Africa pending the outcome of the ICC hearing. It ruled that they should be banned for two Tests and four one-dayers.

The three Caribbean Tests were dominated by pace. Of the 102 wickets claimed by bowlers, 86 fell to seam (though the unavailability of Rangana Herath, rested for the second match and injured for the last, did not help the spinners' cause). Shannon Gabriel, who took 13 wickets at St Lucia, led the way, claiming 20 at under 15; Jason Holder and Kemar Roach, with 23 between them, gave useful support. If West Indies' reliance on speed was nothing new, the fact that the Sri Lankans could match their battery was less foreseeable. Lahiru Kumara, a 21-year-old seamer from Kandy, took 17 wickets, confirming him as one of their brightest prospects. Lakmal chipped in with 12, while Kasun Rajitha, who made his debut in St Lucia, claimed 11.

Leading run-makers in the series were the West Indies wicketkeeper Shane Dowrich, with 288, and Kusal Mendis, with 285. Dowrich's hundred at Port-of-Spain helped set up victory (and he contributed fifties in the other two matches). Chandimal's classy century in the Second Test might also have brought Sri Lanka level, had time allowed. Forced to play at Bridgetown with a stand-in captain, the visitors showed resilience in squaring the series. In a low-scoring match, their seam attack proved fractionally the stronger.

By way of an unwelcome footnote to the events of St Lucia, Sri Lanka sent leg-spinner Jeffrey Vandersay home for a breach of team discipline. The evening after the end of the Test, he and three team-mates went out to a nightclub. His companions made it back to the hotel in time for a seven o'clock departure for Barbados, but not Vandersay, who was reportedly unable to remember anything after 2am. Already in Sri Lanka Cricket's bad books after turning up 45 minutes late for the pre-tour team photograph, he was given a one-year ban, suspended for 12 months.

SRI LANKA TOURING PARTY

*L. D. Chandimal, A. Dananjaya, D. M. de Silva, D. P. D. N. Dickwella, A. M. Fernando, P. L. S. Gamage, M. D. Gunathilleke, H. M. R. K. B. Herath, C. B. R. L. S. Kumara, R. A. S. Lakmal, A. D. Mathews, B. K. G. Mendis, M. D. K. Perera, M. D. K. J. Perera, C. A. K. Rajitha, M. D. Shanaka, A. R. S. Silva, M. L. Udawatte, J. D. F. Vandersay. *Coach:* U. C. Hathurusinghe.

De Silva joined the tour late, after his father was shot dead near Columbo. Gamage and Mathews withdrew after the First Test – Gamage with a finger injury and Mathews for personal reasons. They were replaced by Gunathilleke and Shanaka. Vandersay was sent home after staying out late in St Lucia. Lakmal captained in the Third Test after Chandimal was suspended.

TEST MATCH AVERAGES

WEST INDIES – BATTING AND FIELDING

	T	I	NO	R	HS	100	50	Avge	Ct
S. O. Dowrich	3	6	1	288	125*	1	2	57.60	13
K. A. J. Roach	3	5	3	97	39	0	0	48.50	0
J. O. Holder	3	6	1	198	74	0	1	39.60	4
†K. O. A. Powell	3	6	0	166	88	0	1	27.66	1
K. C. Brathwaite	3	6	1	104	59*	0	1	20.80	1
R. L. Chase	3	6	0	123	41	0	0	20.50	3
S. D. Hope	3	6	0	114	44	0	0	19.00	4
†D. S. Smith	3	6	0	91	61	0	1	15.16	4
†D. Bishoo	3	5	1	58	40	0	0	14.50	4
†M. L. Cummins	3	4	2	24	14	0	0	12.00	0
S. T. Gabriel	3	3	0	11	6	0	0	3.66	0

BOWLING

	Style	O	M	R	W	BB	5I	Avge
R. L. Chase	OB	19.2	2	55	4	4-15	0	13.75
S. T. Gabriel	RF	88.4	15	299	20	8-62	2	14.95
J. O. Holder	RFM	80.2	26	193	12	5-41	1	16.08
K. A. J. Roach	RFM	86	23	281	11	4-49	0	25.54
D. Bishoo	LB	56	7	151	4	3-48	0	37.75
M. L. Cummins	RFM	77.4	21	221	3	3-39	0	73.66

Also bowled: K. C. Brathwaite (OB) 1–0–4–0.

SRI LANKA – BATTING AND FIELDING

	T	I	NO	R	HS	100	50	Avge	Ct
L. D. Chandimal.............	2	4	1	229	119*	1	0	76.33	1
M. D. K. Perera	2	4	3	57	23*	0	0	57.00	1
B. K. G. Mendis.............	3	6	0	285	102	1	1	47.50	8
†D. P. D. N. Dickwella........	3	6	0	176	62	0	1	29.33	9
†M. D. K. J. Perera............	3	6	1	92	32	0	0	18.40	1
A. R. S. Silva	3	6	0	85	48	0	0	14.16	1
D. M. de Silva	2	4	0	40	17	0	0	10.00	6
R. A. S. Lakmal	3	5	0	33	15	0	0	6.60	2
†M. L. Udawatte	2	4	0	23	19	0	0	5.75	2
†C. B. R. L. S. Kumara	3	5	1	8	8	0	0	2.00	0
C. A. K. Rajitha	2	3	0	4	4	0	0	1.33	0

Played in one Test: †A. Dananjaya 2, 23; P. L. S. Gamage 0*, 3; †M. D. Gunathilleke 29, 21 (1 ct); †H. M. R. K. B. Herath 5, 0; A. D. Mathews 11, 31 (1 ct).

BOWLING

	Style	O	M	R	W	BB	5I	Avge
C. A. K. Rajitha	RFM	60	11	160	11	3-20	0	14.54
C. B. R. L. S. Kumara	RF	108.2	17	338	17	4-58	0	19.88
R. A. S. Lakmal	RFM	113	30	262	12	3-25	0	21.83
H. M. R. K. B. Herath	SLA	56	14	119	3	2-52	0	39.66
M. D. K. Perera	OB	60.3	9	163	3	1-13	0	54.33

Also bowled: A. Dananjaya (OB) 44–14–114–2; D. M. de Silva (OB) 4–0–15–0; P. L. S. Gamage (RFM) 41–9–110–0; B. K. G. Mendis (LB) 1–0–12–0.

At Tarouba, Trinidad, May 30–June 1, 2018. **Drawn.** ‡Sri Lankans **428** (119.4 overs) (M. D. K. J. Perera 65, L. D. Chandimal 108, D. P. D. N. Dickwella 74; J. A. Warrican 4-81, R. R. S. Cornwall 3-124) **and 135-0** (33 overs) (B. K. G. Mendis 60*, M. D. K. J. Perera 50*); **West Indies Board President's XI 272** (77 overs) (J. D. Campbell 62, K. O. A. Powell 60, R. R. S. Cornwall 54*; M. D. K. Perera 3-50, C. B. R. L. S. Kumara 3-47, A. Dananjaya 3-46). *Despite losing Kusal Mendis to the first ball of the match, the Sri Lankans gained useful practice: the rest of the top nine made double figures – and Mendis hit 60* at the second attempt. Their bowlers shared the wickets around after John Campbell's 52-ball half-century gave the President's XI a brisk start. Spinners Jomel Warrican and Rahkeem Cornwall took seven between them.*

WEST INDIES v SRI LANKA

First Test

At Port-of-Spain, Trinidad, June 6–10, 2018. West Indies won by 226 runs. Toss: West Indies.

When Mahela Jayawardene had led the last Sri Lankan team to play a Test in the Caribbean, in 2008, he could call on the services of several greats, including Muttiah Muralitharan, Kumar Sangakkara and Chaminda Vaas. The series was drawn, but it included Sri Lanka's solitary away victory over West Indies, in Guyana. The only survivor from that match was Herath, who had gone wicketless back then. He fared a little better now, picking up three, but could not prevent a defeat so resounding it suggested West Indies – who had lost 2–0 in Sri Lanka in 2015 – might have turned a corner. Retaining the Sobers–Tissera Trophy was going to prove a challenge for the tourists.

After Holder chose to bat, West Indies lost openers Brathwaite and Devon Smith – playing his first Test for three years – within 12 overs. Kumara was not always the most accurate member of the attack, but he was the speediest and most threatening, dismissing Powell and Hope after both had seemingly bedded in. On a slowish first day, neither the over-rate nor the scoring matched Kumara's pace: despite 32 overs of spin, Sri Lanka sent down only 84, while West Indies finished on 246 for six – a distinct improvement on 147 for five. Dowrich was unbeaten on 46, and Bishoo yet to score from 32 deliveries.

Next day, the pair dodged showers and progressed steadily. Moments after they raised a century stand, Bishoo edged his 160th ball to gully, and departed for a diligent 40. Dowrich, though, kept going, now in partnership with Roach, whose 39 was the seventh contribution to the scorecard of between 38 and 44. When the declaration came at 414 for eight, Dowrich was unbeaten on a career-best 125, spanning 325 deliveries and almost eight hours.

In a flash, the West Indies quicks had Sri Lanka in disarray: 31 for three on the second evening became 43 for four next morning. Chandimal and Dickwella imposed some order in a stand of 78, but poor late-order batting against a short-ball assault from Cummins saw them dismissed 229 behind. Holder declined the follow-on.

After Smith was bowled twice in two deliveries by Lakmal – the first a big no-ball – West Indies relied on a sharp 88 from Powell. Kumara again proved the most potent of the Sri Lankan bowlers. There were signs of spin, but not enough to cause undue worry, and generally their runs came at a healthier rate. Holder, trapped by Herath after walloping a run-a-ball 39, declared again, 452 ahead and with nearly five sessions left.

Thanks to a battling innings from Kusal Mendis, Sri Lanka made it to stumps at 176 for three, and with a glimmer of hope. Chandimal had retired ill with heat exhaustion but would return; Mendis was taking the game to West Indies and was 94 not out. He moved to his fifth Test century on the last morning, but not far beyond. Slow bowlers Chase and Bishoo found increasing turn, and took the last five wickets for eight giving West Indies victory shortly after lunch.

Man of the Match: S. O. Dowrich.

Close of play: first day, West Indies 246-6 (Dowrich 46, Bishoo 0); second day, Sri Lanka 31-3 (Chandimal 3, Silva 1); third day, West Indies 131-4 (Powell 64, Dowrich 11); fourth day, Sri Lanka 176-3 (Mendis 94, Gamage 0).

West Indies

K. C. Brathwaite c Dickwella b Lakmal	3	– c Dickwella b Kumara	16
D. S. Smith run out (Kumara/Dickwella)	7	– b Lakmal	20
K. O. A. Powell b Kumara	38	– c sub (J. D. F. Vandersay)	
		b M. D. K. Perera	88
S. D. Hope c Dickwella b Kumara	44	– c Mendis b Kumara	1
R. L. Chase c Mathews b Herath	38	– b Herath	12
†S. O. Dowrich not out	125	– lbw b Kumara	13
*J. O. Holder c Dickwella b Kumara	40	– lbw b Herath	39
D. Bishoo c Silva b Lakmal	40	– not out	16
K. A. J. Roach c Chandimal b Kumara	39	– not out	11
M. L. Cummins not out	0		
B 14, lb 20, w 2, nb 4	40	B 4, lb 2, nb 1	7

1/4 (1) 2/40 (2) (8 wkts dec, 154 overs) 414 1/36 (2) (7 wkts dec, 72 overs) 223
3/80 (3) 4/134 (4) 5/147 (5) 2/55 (1) 3/75 (4)
6/237 (7) 7/339 (8) 8/414 (9) 4/119 (5) 5/149 (6)
  6/191 (3) 7/203 (7)

S. T. Gabriel did not bat.

Lakmal 29–11–55–2; Gamage 26–6–67–0; M. D. K. Perera 35–5–84–0; Kumara 31–4–95–4; Herath 32–9–67–1; Mendis 1–0–12–0. *Second innings*—Lakmal 12–2–32–1; Gamage 15–3–43–0; Herath 24–5–52–2; Kumara 9–0–40–3; M. D. K. Perera 12–1–50–1.

Sri Lanka

B. K. G. Mendis c Holder b Gabriel	4	– c Dowrich b Gabriel	102
M. D. K. J. Perera c Chase b Roach	0	– c Smith b Gabriel	12
*L. D. Chandimal c Chase b Gabriel	44	– c Brathwaite b Chase	27
A. D. Mathews c Chase b Holder	11	– c Dowrich b Holder	31
A. R. S. Silva b Roach	5	– c and b Bishoo	14
†D. P. D. N. Dickwella run out (Brathwaite)	31	– (7) lbw b Chase	19
M. D. K. Perera c Hope b Bishoo	20	– (8) not out	3
H. M. R. K. B. Herath c sub (S. O. Hetmyer) b Cummins	5	– (9) c Hope b Bishoo	0
R. A. S. Lakmal c Bishoo b Cummins	15	– (10) c Dowrich b Chase	1
P. L. S. Gamage not out	0	– (6) lbw b Bishoo	3
C. B. R. L. S. Kumara c Dowrich b Cummins	8	– c Dowrich b Chase	0
B 8, lb 16, w 12, nb 6	42	B 3, lb 4, nb 7	14

1/2 (2) 2/16 (1) 3/30 (4) (55.4 overs) 185   1/21 (2) 2/123 (4) (83.2 overs) 226
4/43 (5) 5/121 (3) 6/140 (6)   3/175 (5) 4/189 (1)
7/148 (8) 8/156 (7) 9/175 (9) 10/185 (11)   5/195 (6) 6/218 (3) 7/222 (7)
                                                     8/225 (9) 9/226 (10) 10/226 (11)

In the second innings Chandimal, when 15, retired ill at 49-1 and resumed at 189-4.

Roach 10–3–34–2; Gabriel 13–0–48–2; Cummins 12.4–4–39–3; Holder 7–1–15–1; Bishoo 13–2–25–1. *Second innings*—Roach 15–3–57–0; Gabriel 15–2–52–2; Holder 14–6–24–1; Cummins 12–4–23–0; Bishoo 19–2–48–3; Chase 8.2–1–15–4.

Umpires: Aleem Dar and R. A. Kettleborough.   Third umpire: I. J. Gould.
Referee: J. Srinath.

WEST INDIES v SRI LANKA

Second Test

At Gros Islet, St Lucia, June 14–18, 2018. Drawn. Toss: Sri Lanka. Test debuts: C. A. K. Rajitha, M. L. Udawatte.

A match disrupted by rain was the setting for another ball-tampering controversy. Coming less than three months after the furore that overwhelmed the Australian tour of South Africa, it gained widespread attention – though since the agent used on the ball was sugary saliva rather than sandpaper, the offence was deemed less severe. What made the sorry business more serious, however, was the refusal of Chandimal, perpetrator as well as captain, to resume play on the third morning. All told, two hours were lost – two rainless hours that might have been enough for Sri Lanka to secure victory.

After Chandimal opted to bat on a pitch that gave seamers more help than expected, Mahela Udawatte was superbly caught in the slips by Holder. It was Udawatte's second ball in Test cricket – his debut had come a decade after his first one-day international – and the first of 13 wickets for Gabriel, whose express pace unsettled the Sri Lankans once again. Perera and Mendis offered some resistance, but the real fight came from Chandimal, who made a responsible unbeaten 119, the backbone of his team's 253. Gabriel finished with five wickets, and Roach four, as West Indies looked to win successive Tests against major opponents for the first time since beating New Zealand in 2012. Their openers survived a couple of overs before stumps.

The following day, a Friday, brought showers, 42 overs, 116 runs, two wickets and – though it wasn't clear at the time – controversy. The umpires were suspicious about how the Sri Lankans had been polishing the ball late in the day, and asked to review footage. Next morning, officials and batsmen made their way to the middle, but not the Sri Lankans. Television focused on their dressing-room, where Chandimal, coach Chandika Hathuru-singhe and team manager Asanka Gurusinha were in discussion with match referee Javagal

BEST INNINGS FIGURES FOR WEST INDIES IN A TEST...

9-95	J. M. Noreiga	v India at Port-of-Spain	1970-71
8-29	C. E. H. Croft	v Pakistan at Port-of-Spain	1976-77
8-38	L. R. Gibbs	v India at Bridgetown	1961-62
8-45	C. E. L. Ambrose	v England at Bridgetown	1989-90
8-49	D. Bishoo	v Pakistan at Dubai	2016-17
8-62	**S. T. Gabriel**	**v Sri Lanka at Gros Islet**	**2018**
8-92	M. A. Holding	v England at The Oval	1976
8-104	A. L. Valentine	v England at Manchester	1950

Srinath. After 80 minutes, and with everyone on the pitch, it was announced that the batsmen would choose a new ball, and that West Indies' overnight score would be swollen by five penalty runs. That set the cat back among the pigeons, and more discussions ensued near the boundary. Eventually, the Sri Lankans, who claimed the penalty runs came as a shock, said they would resume the game "under protest".

A fired-up Kumara promptly unleashed three successive bouncers at Smith. A sense of injustice spurred on the seamers, and they kept the batsmen on their toes throughout. Smith hit 61, Dowrich followed his Port-of-Spain hundred with a fifty, and Chase made 41, but spirited pace bowling dragged Sri Lanka back into contention. Kumara reached 93mph, Kasun Rajitha made a promising – and aggressive – debut, and the last six wickets fell for 59. They limited the deficit to 47 and, by the close, had reduced that to 13, for the loss of Perera. The game was nicely poised.

Sunday morning brought more details of the ball-tampering incident. In a press release, the ICC said: "The officials laid the charge after television footage from the final session's play on Friday appeared to show the Sri Lanka captain taking sweets out from his left pocket and putting these in his mouth, before applying the artificial substance to the ball which the umpires viewed as an attempt to change its condition." Chandimal denied the allegations, though the evidence looked damning.

Sunday also confirmed this had become a cracker of a Test. Gabriel tore in, and in no time helped reduce Sri Lanka to 48 for four – a lead of just one. But despite his gusto, the middle order fought back: Mendis scored heavily to leg, sweeping the spinners and pulling the seamers, and there were consistent scores down the card.

Gabriel polished off the last two wickets on the final morning to complete figures of eight for 62, and a match return of 13 for 121, West Indies' best at home. Even so, they needed a tricky but mouth-watering 296 in a minimum of 85 overs – if the weather held. Rajitha and Lakmal struck three times before lunch, and Kumara forced Hope to retire hurt after he took a blow in the ribs. Dowrich went soon after the break, and it needed a rearguard from Brathwaite and the injured Hope to stop the rot. In the fourth over after tea, Lakmal got one to lift; it clonked Hope on the elbow and clattered into the stumps. Rain drove the players off shortly afterwards at 137 for five and, though they came back on briefly, bad light brought the Test to a permanent end.

...AND BEST MATCH FIGURES FOR WEST INDIES IN A TEST

14-149	M. A. Holding	v England at The Oval	1976
13-55	C. A. Walsh	v New Zealand at Wellington	1994-95
13-121	**S. T. Gabriel**	**v Sri Lanka at Gros Islet**	**2018**
12-121	A. M. E. Roberts	v India at Madras	1974-75
11-84	C. E. L. Ambrose	v England at Port-of-Spain	1993-94
11-89	M. D. Marshall	v India at Port-of-Spain	1988-89
11-103	**J. O. Holder**	**v Bangladesh at Kingston**	**2018**
11-107	M. A. Holding	v Australia at Melbourne	1981-82
11-120	M. D. Marshall	v New Zealand at Bridgetown	1984-85
11-126	W. W. Hall	v India at Kanpur	1958-59

The waiting game: with batsmen and officials kicking their heels, Dinesh Chandimal belatedly leads out his Sri Lankan team.

At the hearing after the match, Chandimal claimed he could not remember what sweets he had been eating. Srinath found him guilty all the same, and handed him a one-Test ban, meaning he would miss the upcoming day/night match in Barbados. Chandimal's appeal fell on deaf ears.

Man of the Match: S. T. Gabriel.

Close of play: first day, West Indies 2-0 (Brathwaite 2, Smith 0); second day, West Indies 118-2 (Smith 53, Hope 2); third day, Sri Lanka 34-1 (Udawatte 11, Rajitha 0); fourth day, Sri Lanka 334-8 (Dananjaya 16, Lakmal 7).

Sri Lanka

M. D. K. J. Perera c Holder b Roach	32	– c Dowrich b Gabriel	20
M. L. Udawatte c Holder b Gabriel	0	– c Bishoo b Roach	19
D. M. de Silva b Gabriel	12	– (4) c Smith b Gabriel	3
B. K. G. Mendis c Dowrich b Holder	45	– (5) b Gabriel	87
*L. D. Chandimal not out	119	– (6) c Dowrich b Roach	39
A. R. S. Silva c Holder b Gabriel	6	– (7) c Dowrich b Gabriel	48
†D. P. D. N. Dickwella c Hope b Gabriel	16	– (8) c Powell b Gabriel	62
A. Dananjaya c Dowrich b Roach	2	– (9) b Gabriel	23
R. A. S. Lakmal lbw b Gabriel	10	– (10) lbw b Gabriel	7
C. A. K. Rajitha c Dowrich b Roach	4	– (3) lbw b Gabriel	0
C. B. R. L. S. Kumara c Hope b Roach	0	– not out	0
B 1, lb 2, w 2, nb 2	7	B 12, lb 8, w 3, nb 11	34

1/0 (2) 2/15 (3) 3/59 (1)   (79 overs) 253
4/126 (4) 5/148 (6) 6/179 (7)
7/190 (8) 8/206 (9) 9/237 (10) 10/253 (11)

1/32 (1) 2/34 (3)   (91.4 overs) 342
3/44 (4) 4/48 (2)
5/165 (6) 6/199 (5) 7/298 (7)
8/307 (8) 9/334 (10) 10/342 (9)

Roach 18–8–49–4; Gabriel 16–4–59–5; Cummins 19–5–69–0; Holder 14–2–56–1; Bishoo 11–3–15–0; Chase 1–0–2–0. *Second innings*—Roach 21–3–78–2; Gabriel 20.4–6–62–8; Holder 15–3–38–0; Cummins 13–1–44–0; Bishoo 11–0–58–0; Chase 10–1–38–0; Brathwaite 1–0–4–0.

West Indies

K. C. Brathwaite c Dickwella b Rajitha	22	– not out	59
D. S. Smith lbw b Dananjaya	61	– c de Silva b Rajitha	1
K. O. A. Powell c Mendis b Kumara	27	– c Udawatte b Rajitha	2
S. D. Hope c de Silva b Lakmal	19	– b Lakmal	39
R. L. Chase c Lakmal b Kumara	41	– b Lakmal	13
†S. O. Dowrich c Dickwella b Lakmal	55	– c de Silva b Dananjaya	8
*J. O. Holder c Dickwella b Rajitha	15	– not out	15
D. Bishoo c Mendis b Rajitha	2		
K. A. J. Roach lbw b Kumara	13		
M. L. Cummins not out	8		
S. T. Gabriel c de Silva b Kumara	3		
B 11, lb 8, w 9, nb 1, p 5	34	B 10	10

1/59 (1) 2/115 (3) 3/149 (4) (100.3 overs) 300   1/6 (2) (5 wkts, 60.3 overs) 147
4/163 (2) 5/241 (5) 6/254 (6)   2/8 (3) 3/55 (5)
7/261 (8) 8/279 (7) 9/292 (9) 10/300 (11)   4/64 (6) 5/117 (4)

In the second innings Hope, when 6, retired hurt at 25-2 and resumed at 64-4.

Lakmal 24–6–50–2; Dananjaya 25–7–81–1; Rajitha 22–6–49–3; Kumara 26.3–4–86–4; de Silva 3–0–10–0. *Second innings*—Lakmal 17.3–3–48–2; Rajitha 13–3–23–2; Kumara 10–3–28–0; Dananjaya 19–7–33–1; de Silva 1–0–5–0.

Umpires: Aleem Dar and I. J. Gould.   Third umpire: R. A. Kettleborough.
Referee: J. Srinath.

WEST INDIES v SRI LANKA

Third Test

At Bridgetown, Barbados (day/night), June 23–26, 2018. Sri Lanka won by four wickets.
Toss: West Indies.
  West Indies began the first day/night Test in the Caribbean with hopes of securing their first series victory over Sri Lanka since 2003. They were one up with one to play – and their opponents were in some confusion. Lahiru Gamage had broken a finger at Port-of-Spain and gone home; Angelo Mathews had also returned, for personal reasons. Then Rangana Herath, rested for St Lucia, was ruled out after splitting the webbing on his right hand in practice. And there was the small matter of the fall-out from the ball-tampering episode: Dinesh Chandimal was banned, so Gunathilleke came in for his third Test, and the captaincy passed to Lakmal. By contrast, West Indies fielded the same team for the third game running.
  On a rain-interrupted opening day, the Sri Lankan seamers made life almost impossible for the batsmen on a pitch that Jeff Dujon described as the greenest he had seen at

---

WEST INDIES' LOWEST TEST TOTALS AT HOME

47	v England at Kingston	2003-04
51	v Australia at Port-of-Spain	1998-99
93	**v Sri Lanka at Bridgetown**	**2018**
94	v England at Bridgetown	2003-04
102	v England at Bridgetown	1934-35
102	v South Africa at Port-of-Spain	2010
103	v India at Kingston	2005-06
107	v New Zealand at Bridgetown	2002
108	v India at Gros Islet	2016
109	v Australia at Georgetown	1972-73

Bridgetown. Aided by a hard pink ball and windy, overcast conditions, the bowlers ripped into the upper order. If Smith prodded feebly, Brathwaite and Powell were less culpable: the ball was swinging and bouncing at pace, and the fielders held on to smart catches. Eight for three became 24 for four, then 53 for five.

Once again, Dowrich strode to the rescue. Riding his luck early on, he knuckled down to forge a steadying partnership with Holder, who might have questioned the wisdom of his decision at the toss. They were still there at the end of a stop–start floodlit evening, though, and they fought on next day, until Dowrich was trapped by Kumara, ending their stand on 115. Holder fell for a gritty 74 – undone by a superb one-handed diving catch by Dilruwan Perera at gully – and the total had reached 204 when Kumara removed Gabriel with disconcerting bounce. For the third match running, he had taken four wickets in West Indies' first innings.

Then it was the Sri Lankans' turn to face a barrage of fast bowling under lights, and they too were quickly in tatters, Roach removing the openers by the seventh over. Gunathilleke and Mendis orchestrated a recovery of their own amid the rain but, from 75 for two, Sri Lanka stumbled to stumps at 99 for five.

Next day, 20 wickets fell – a record for a Caribbean Test, surpassing the 18 on the second day when England lost on this ground in May 2015. Roshen Silva departed quickly,

TEST WINS FOR AWAY TEAMS AT KENSINGTON OVAL

	Winning captain	Losing captain	
England won by four wickets	R. E. S. Wyatt	G. C. Grant	1934-35
England won by 208 runs	M. A. Atherton	R. B. Richardson	1993-94
Australia won by ten wickets	M. A. Taylor	R. B. Richardson	1994-95
New Zealand won by 204 runs	S. P. Fleming	C. L. Hooper	2002
Australia won by nine wickets	S. R. Waugh	B. C. Lara	2002-03
England won by eight wickets	M. P. Vaughan	B. C. Lara	2003-04
South Africa won by inns and 86 runs	G. C. Smith	S. Chanderpaul	2004-05
Australia won by 87 runs	R. T. Ponting	C. H. Gayle	2007-08
South Africa won by seven wickets	G. C. Smith	C. H. Gayle	2010
Australia won by three wickets	M. J. Clarke	D. J. G. Sammy	2011-12
New Zealand won by 53 runs	B. B. McCullum	D. Ramdin	2014
Sri Lanka won by four wickets	**R. A. S. Lakmal**	**J. O. Holder**	**2018**

India have played nine Tests at Bridgetown, Pakistan seven and Zimbabwe one.

but Dickwella, handed a reprieve when Dowrich fumbled a leg-side chance, steered Sri Lanka to 147 for six before Holder found his edge. The remaining batsmen came and went in a flash – though it would have been even quicker if Holder, who finished with four victims, had not overstepped a split second before rearranging Dilruwan Perera's stumps. It was the sixth time in the series a West Indian had denied himself a wicket by bowling a no-ball.

Even so, a lead of 50 put the home team in the box seat – if not for long. An inspired performance from Lakmal and Kumara, the explosive Sri Lankan opening pair, reduced West Indies to 14 for five. Rajitha then demolished the middle order with three wickets in ten balls and, when Gabriel was run out, the whole innings had lasted less than 32 overs.

Sri Lanka had done wonders to get back into the game, but now they had to bat under lights – a tricky proposition while Roach, Gabriel and Holder were swinging the ball round corners. Needing 144 to level the series, they were an unsteady 81 for five at the end of a frenetic third day. If it was even-steven on the resumption next afternoon, the odds favoured West Indies when Holder despatched Mendis without addition.

That brought Kusal Perera to the crease. He had been rushed to hospital in an ambulance the previous evening after colliding with an advertising hoarding, but suffered no lasting injury. Getting by on nerves and good fortune – he and Dilruwan Perera did not always have full control of their shots – they whittled away at the target, and ultimately, they made it without further loss. The scale of Sri Lanka's victory was clear from the fact that no other subcontinental team had won at Bridgetown. They also retained the Sobers–Tissera Trophy. Given their travails, it was quite an achievement.

Man of the Match: J. O. Holder.   *Man of the Series:* S. O. Dowrich.

Close of play: first day, West Indies 132-5 (Dowrich 60, Holder 33); second day, Sri Lanka 99-5 (Silva 3, Dickwella 13); third day, Sri Lanka 81-5 (Mendis 25, M. D. K. Perera 1).

West Indies

K. C. Brathwaite c Gunathilleke b Lakmal	2	– c Udawatte b Lakmal	2
D. S. Smith c de Silva b Lakmal	2	– b Lakmal	0
K. O. A. Powell c Mendis b Kumara	4	– c Dickwella b Kumara	7
S. D. Hope c Mendis b Rajitha	11	– b Kumara	0
R. L. Chase b Rajitha	14	– c M. D. K. J. Perera b Lakmal	5
†S. O. Dowrich lbw b Kumara	71	– c Lakmal b Rajitha	16
*J. O. Holder c M. D. K. Perera b Rajitha	74	– c Mendis b Rajitha	15
D. Bishoo c Mendis b Kumara	0	– b Rajitha	0
K. A. J. Roach not out	11	– not out	23
M. L. Cummins c Mendis b M. D. K. Perera	2	– c de Silva b M. D. K. Perera	14
S. T. Gabriel c Dickwella b Kumara	2	– run out (Rajitha/Dickwella)	6
B 4, lb 6, w 1	11	Lb 4, w 1	5

1/3 (2)   2/8 (1)   3/8 (3)   (69.3 overs) 204
4/24 (5)   5/53 (4)   6/168 (6)
7/183 (8)   8/189 (7)   9/201 (10)   10/204 (11)

1/1 (2)   2/8 (1)   (31.2 overs) 93
3/9 (4)   4/14 (5)
5/14 (3)   6/41 (6)   7/41 (8)
8/56 (7)   9/82 (10)   10/93 (11)

Lakmal 19–5–52–2; Kumara 23.3–5–58–4; Rajitha 17–1–68–3; M. D. K. Perera 10–3–16–1. *Second innings*—Lakmal 11.3–3–25–3; Kumara 8.2–1–31–2; Rajitha 8–1–20–3; M. D. K. Perera 3.3–0–13–1.

Sri Lanka

M. D. K. J. Perera c Dowrich b Roach	0	– (8) not out	28
M. L. Udawatte lbw b Roach	4	– lbw b Roach	0
M. D. Gunathilleke lbw b Holder	29	– (1) c Bishoo b Holder	21
B. K. G. Mendis b Gabriel	22	– lbw b Holder	25
D. M. de Silva lbw b Gabriel	8	– (3) b Holder	17
A. R. S. Silva c Dowrich b Gabriel	11	– (5) c Smith b Holder	1
†D. P. D. N. Dickwella c Smith b Holder	42	– (6) b Holder	6
M. D. K. Perera not out	11	– (7) not out	23
*R. A. S. Lakmal c sub (K. M. A. Paul) b Holder	0		
C. A. K. Rajitha b Holder	0		
C. B. R. L. S. Kumara run out (Holder)	0		
B 9, lb 14, w 1, nb 3	27	B 8, lb 15	23

1/0 (1)   2/16 (2)   3/75 (4)   (59 overs) 154
4/81 (3)   5/85 (5)   6/118 (6)
7/147 (7)   8/147 (9)   9/150 (10)   10/154 (11)

1/9 (2)   (6 wkts, 40.2 overs) 144
2/30 (1)   3/48 (3)
4/50 (5)   5/74 (6)   6/81 (4)

Roach 12–5–30–2; Gabriel 15–2–52–3; Cummins 15–6–29–0; Holder 16–8–19–4; Bishoo 1–0–1–0. *Second innings*—Roach 10–1–33–1; Gabriel 9–1–26–0; Holder 14.2–4–41–5; Cummins 6–1–17–0; Bishoo 1–0–4–0.

Umpires: I. J. Gould and R. A. Kettleborough.   Third umpire: Aleem Dar.
Referee: J. Srinath.

WEST INDIES v BANGLADESH IN 2018

Craig Cozier

Test matches (2): West Indies 2, Bangladesh 0
One-day internationals (3): West Indies 1, Bangladesh 2
Twenty20 internationals (3): West Indies 1, Bangladesh 2

West Indies and Bangladesh swapped identities like characters in a spy thriller. In the Tests, the West Indians were dominant, securing their first home series win since they beat the same opponents in 2014, mainly thanks to the potency of their seam attack. Bangladesh were dreadful, raising questions about their appetite for the longest format. But once the white-ball matches started, they rediscovered their mojo, and won both series.

Their new coach Steven Rhodes's first day at the office could hardly have been worse: Bangladesh were bowled out for 43 at North Sound, their lowest Test total. Pitches were prepared to assist the West Indies quicks, but this was no throwback to the bouncer barrages of the 1980s. The Bangladesh batsmen were found wanting technically and, faced with the relentlessness of Kemar Roach, Miguel Cummins and Jason Holder, seemed unwilling to tough it out.

At Sabina Park, West Indies were just as authoritative, with Kraigg Brathwaite hitting his second hundred of the series, and Holder taking 11 wickets. Bangladesh's failure to pass 168 in either game brought criticism from BCB president Nazmul Hassan. It wasn't as if the team could cite a lack of experience: Shakib Al Hasan, Tamim Iqbal and Mushfiqur Rahim were the only players on either side with 50 caps.

In the white-ball matches, Bangladesh dusted themselves off and came out fighting. Mashrafe bin Mortaza's astute leadership and seam-bowling variations helped reinvigorate the team. Tamim forgot his Test woes with scores of 130, 54 and 103. It was Bangladesh's first one-day overseas series win in nine years.

The T20 games began more brightly for West Indies, the world champions, with a DLS victory in St Kitts. But when the action switched to Florida, Bangladesh – inspired by large expat support – recovered impressively.

BANGLADESH TOURING PARTY

*Shakib Al Hasan (T/50/20), Abu Haider (50/20), Anamul Haque (50), Abu Jayed (T/50/20), Ariful Haque (20), Imrul Kayes (T), Kamrul Islam (T), Liton Das (T/50/20), Mahmudullah (T/50/20), Mashrafe bin Mortaza (50), Mehedi Hasan (T/50/20), Mominul Haque (T), Mosaddek Hossain (50/20), Mushfiqur Rahim (T/50/20), Mustafizur Rahman (50/20), Nazmul Hossain (T/50/20), Nazmul Islam (50/20), Nurul Hasan (T), Rubel Hossain (T/50/20), Sabbir Rahman (50/20), Soumya Sarkar (20), Shafiul Islam (T), Taijul Islam (T), Tamim Iqbal (T/50/20). *Coach:* S. J. Rhodes.

Mashrafe captained in the ODIs.

WEST INDIES v BANGLADESH

First Test

At North Sound, Antigua, July 4–6, 2018. West Indies won by an innings and 219 runs. Toss: West Indies. Test debut: Abu Jayed.

With fast-bowling knights Andy Roberts and Curtly Ambrose looking on, Roach produced one of the most devastating bursts in Test history. He took five wickets in 12 balls as Bangladesh staggered to 18 for five within nine overs of the start. It was a feat matched only by Monty Noble, for Australia against England at Melbourne in 1901-02, and Jacques Kallis, for South Africa against Bangladesh at Potchefstroom in 2002-03.

Roach, who had turned 30 four days earlier, expertly probed off stump, and the Bangladeshis proved easy prey. Four fell to catches behind the wicket, as their lack of practice, and technical deficiencies against pace and bounce, were ruthlessly exposed. By the time he took his second wicket, Roach was already hobbling with a hamstring strain, but he kept going, and at one point claimed four for none in six balls. Cummins and Holder ensured there was no recovery. Only opener Liton Das reached double figures – scoring 58% of his side's total, a national record – and the innings was done and dusted in 18.4 overs. Bangladesh's 43 was their lowest Test score, behind 62 against Sri Lanka in Colombo in 2007, and the lowest against West Indies, undercutting England's 46 at Port-of-Spain in 1993-94. It was also the lowest by anyone since India's 42 at Lord's in 1974.

FEWEST BALLS FACED IN A TEST BY ONE TEAM

Balls	Runs		
248	123	South Africa v England at Port Elizabeth	1895-96
303	90	South Africa v England at Cape Town	1888-89
329	81	South Africa v Australia at Melbourne	1931-32
335	151	Australia v England at Manchester	1888
349	140	India v England at Manchester	1952
354	**187**	**Bangladesh v West Indies at North Sound**	**2018**
360	233	Australia v England at Melbourne	1903-04
388	115	England v Australia at Lord's	1888
396	163	Australia v England at The Oval	1896
399	**212**	**Afghanistan v India at Bangalore**	**2018**

West Indies were batting before lunch, and soon showed it was possible to cope with whatever demons lurked in the pitch. By the close they were 201 for two, with Brathwaite in sight of his seventh Test century. He had put on 113 for the first wicket with Smith, who ended speculation about his place with 58, before becoming seamer Abu Jayed's first Test victim. On the second morning, a trademark cut to third man completed Brathwaite's hundred. Shai Hope piled on the misery for Bangladesh with a stylish 67, his first half-century in 13 innings. Mehedi Hasan's off-breaks troubled some West Indies batsmen, to offer the tourists a slice of cheer. But, trailing by 363, they were soon in trouble again. Roach was resting his injury in the hope of returning for the Second Test, but Gabriel swiftly made up for a wicketless first innings with two in his second over; Tamim departed two runs after becoming the first Bangladeshi to pass 4,000 in Tests.

A two-day finish looked possible, but Bangladesh found just enough resolve to extend the match into the third morning. Even so, they would have fallen short of three figures again if not for the defiance of wicketkeeper Nurul Hasan. Showing better judgment than the senior batsmen, he treated the pitched-up delivery with respect, and dealt severely with anything short. He made Bangladesh's fastest overseas fifty, from 36 balls, and put on 55 for the ninth wicket with Rubel Hossain, before falling to a smart return catch by Cummins, who then bowled Rubel to seal victory. It was the first time in 2,310 Tests that four bowlers from one side all finished with five wickets.

Man of the Match: K. A. J. Roach.

Close of play: first day, West Indies 201-2 (Brathwaite 88, Bishoo 1); second day, Bangladesh 62-6 (Mahmudullah 15, Nurul Hasan 7).

Bangladesh

Tamim Iqbal c Dowrich b Roach	4	– c Hope b Gabriel	13
Liton Das c Chase b Cummins	25	– c Brathwaite b Holder	2
Mominul Haque c Hope b Roach	1	– b Gabriel	0
Mushfiqur Rahim lbw b Roach	0	– b Gabriel	8
*Shakib Al Hasan c Holder b Roach	0	– c Holder b Gabriel	12
Mahmudullah c Dowrich b Roach	0	– c Chase b Holder	15
†Nurul Hasan c Holder b Cummins	4	– (8) c and b Cummins	64
Mehedi Hasan c Smith b Cummins	1	– (7) c Dowrich b Holder	2
Kamrul Islam c Dowrich b Holder	0	– b Gabriel	7
Rubel Hossain not out	6	– b Cummins	16
Abu Jayed b Holder	2	– not out	0
		B 1, w 3, nb 1	5

1/10 (1) 2/16 (3) 3/18 (4)   (18.4 overs) 43   1/14 (1) 2/14 (3)   (40.2 overs) 144
4/18 (5) 5/18 (6) 6/34 (2)   3/16 (2) 4/36 (4)
7/34 (7) 8/35 (8) 9/35 (9) 10/43 (11)   5/43 (5) 6/50 (7) 7/63 (6)
                                      8/88 (9) 9/143 (8) 10/144 (10)

Roach 5–1–8–5; Gabriel 5–0–14–0; Holder 4.4–0–10–2; Cummins 4–2–11–3. *Second innings*—Holder 15.3–3–30–3; Gabriel 12.3–3–77–5; Cummins 7.2–2–16–2; Bishoo 5–1–16–0; Chase 1–0–4–0.

West Indies

K. C. Brathwaite c Mehedi Hasan		K. A. J. Roach lbw b Mehedi Hasan	33
b Shakib Al Hasan	121	M. L. Cummins not out	1
D. S. Smith c Nurul Hasan b Abu Jayed	58	S. T. Gabriel c Shakib Al Hasan b Abu Jayed	5
K. O. A. Powell c Liton Das b Mahmudullah	48		
D. Bishoo b Kamrul Islam	19	B 3, lb 8, w 3, nb 1	15
S. D. Hope c Tamim Iqbal b Abu Jayed	67		
R. L. Chase lbw b Mehedi Hasan	2	1/113 (2) 2/194 (3) (137.3 overs) 406
†S. O. Dowrich c Liton Das		3/246 (4) 4/272 (1)
b Shakib Al Hasan	4	5/281 (6) 6/288 (7) 7/338 (8)
*J. O. Holder c Liton Das b Mehedi Hasan	33	8/394 (9) 9/400 (5) 10/406 (11)

Abu Jayed 26.3–7–84–3; Rubel Hossain 17–3–44–0; Kamrul Islam 20–3–69–1; Shakib Al Hasan 27–2–71–2; Mehedi Hasan 34–6–101–3; Mahmudullah 11–1–18–1; Mominul Haque 2–0–8–0.

Umpires: R. K. Illingworth and R. A. Kettleborough.   Third umpire: S. Ravi.
Referee: B. C. Broad.

WEST INDIES v BANGLADESH

Second Test

At Kingston, Jamaica, July 12–14, 2018. West Indies won by 166 runs. Toss: Bangladesh. Test debut: K. M. A. Paul.

West Indies survived a second-innings scare to record another three-day win and secure the series. As in Antigua, this was a victory built on a resolute century by Brathwaite and an incisive display by the seamers. In the absence of the injured Kemar Roach, Holder provided the cutting edge with 11 for 103, his best Test figures, and the seventh-best for West Indies.

The teams came to different conclusions on how the pitch would play – West Indies left out leg-spinner Devendra Bishoo, and bolstered the batting with Hetmyer; Bangladesh called up slow left-armer Taijul Islam. The 20-year-old Keemo Paul made his debut in place of Roach, while Mushfiqur Rahim, in his 62nd Test, became Bangladesh's most capped player.

Perhaps still scarred by the First Test, Shakib Al Hasan opted to bowl. After a cursory over of seam, his spinners gave West Indies a searching examination, and when Taijul removed Hope at 138 for three, Bangladesh glimpsed an opening. But Hetmyer, fresh from a century in the tour warm-up, proved the perfect foil for the unflappable Brathwaite. They added 109, though Brathwaite might have been stumped on 82, and was reprieved on 98 when Shakib failed to review after umpire Ravi turned down a leg-before shout off Taijul.

Runs flowed more freely in the final session, giving West Indies command. On the second morning, Hetmyer seemed set for a first Test century until he feathered a catch behind to provoke a flurry of wickets, but Holder and Gabriel hit out for the last wicket to take them past 350. Mehedi Hasan's perseverance was rewarded with five for 93.

Gabriel struck two early blows and, although Tamim Iqbal and Shakib put on 59, Holder bowled his opposite number, and Paul claimed a notable first Test wicket by knocking back Tamim's off stump. Holder snuffed out any hopes of a recovery with superb spells either side of tea, to earn him the luxury of considering the follow-on. He decided against it, but might have harboured doubts as the Bangladesh spinners got to work. West Indies were soon in trouble, and it needed 32 from Chase to take them into three figures. Their eventual 129 was comfortably their lowest total against Bangladesh, while Shakib's six for 33 were his country's best overseas figures.

But a target of 335 was too steep. Holder was again the executioner, with a career-best six for 59, all bowled or lbw. He took the key wickets of Tamim, for a duck, Shakib, after a defiant 54, and Mushfiqur, who made a rapid 31, and took his Test bowling average below 30.

Man of the Match: J. O. Holder.   *Man of the Series:* J. O. Holder.

Close of play: first day, West Indies 295-4 (Hetmyer 84, Chase 16); second day, West Indies 19-1 (Smith 8, Paul 0).

West Indies

K. C. Brathwaite c Taijul Islam b Mehedi Hasan	110	– b Shakib Al Hasan	8
D. S. Smith c Mominul Haque b Mehedi Hasan	2	– st Nurul Hasan b Shakib Al Hasan	16
K. O. A. Powell lbw b Mehedi Hasan	29	– (4) lbw b Shakib Al Hasan	18
S. D. Hope c Nurul Hasan b Taijul Islam	29	– (5) lbw b Taijul Islam	4
S. O. Hetmyer c Nurul Hasan b Abu Jayed	86	– (6) lbw b Abu Jayed	18
R. L. Chase lbw b Abu Jayed	20	– (7) b Mehedi Hasan	32
†S. O. Dowrich c Mehedi Hasan b Taijul Islam	6	– (8) not out	12
*J. O. Holder not out	33	– (9) st Nurul Hasan b Mehedi Hasan	1
K. M. A. Paul c Mominul Haque b Mehedi Hasan	0	– (3) st Nurul Hasan b Shakib Al Hasan	13
M. L. Cummins lbw b Mehedi Hasan	0	– b Shakib Al Hasan	1
S. T. Gabriel b Abu Jayed	12	– b Shakib Al Hasan	0
B 20, lb 7	27	B 1, lb 2, w 1, nb 2	6

1/9 (2) 2/59 (3) 3/138 (4)   (112 overs) 354
4/247 (1) 5/297 (5) 6/302 (6)
7/318 (7) 8/319 (9) 9/319 (10) 10/354 (11)

1/19 (1) 2/28 (2)   (45 overs) 129
3/53 (3) 4/60 (4)
5/64 (5) 6/97 (6) 7/122 (7)
8/124 (9) 9/129 (10) 10/129 (11)

Abu Jayed 18–7–38–3; Shakib Al Hasan 22–3–60–0; Mehedi Hasan 29–9–93–5; Taijul Islam 25–4–82–2; Kamrul Islam 10–1–34–0; Mahmudullah 8–1–20–0. *Second innings*—Abu Jayed 8–1–21–1; Mehedi Hasan 11–2–45–2; Kamrul Islam 2–0–3–0; Shakib Al Hasan 17–5–33–6; Taijul Islam 7–0–24–1.

Bangladesh

Tamim Iqbal b Paul	47	– lbw b Holder	0
Liton Das lbw b Gabriel	12	– c Hope b Paul	33
Mominul Haque c Hope b Gabriel	0	– lbw b Chase	15
*Shakib Al Hasan b Holder	32	– b Holder	54
Mahmudullah lbw b Holder	0	– c Hope b Chase	4
Mushfiqur Rahim c Hope b Holder	24	– b Holder	31
†Nurul Hasan lbw b Paul	0	– lbw b Holder	0
Mehedi Hasan lbw b Cummins	3	– c Smith b Gabriel	10
Taijul Islam b Holder	18	– not out	13
Kamrul Islam not out	0	– lbw b Holder	0
Abu Jayed b Holder	0	– b Holder	0
Lb 5, nb 8	13	B 4, lb 2, nb 2	8

1/20 (2) 2/20 (3) 3/79 (4)   (46.1 overs) 149
4/79 (5) 5/117 (1) 6/117 (7)
7/128 (6) 8/135 (8) 9/149 (9) 10/149 (11)

1/2 (1) 2/40 (2)   (42 overs) 168
3/52 (3) 4/67 (5)
5/121 (4) 6/121 (7) 7/138 (8)
8/162 (4) 9/168 (10) 10/168 (11)

Gabriel 10–3–19–2; Paul 9–2–25–2; Cummins 9–1–34–1; Holder 10.1–1–44–5; Chase 8–0–22–0. *Second innings*—Holder 13–3–59–6; Gabriel 9–2–29–1; Paul 7–0–34–1; Cummins 5–1–20–0; Chase 8–4–20–2.

Umpires: R. K. Illingworth and S. Ravi.   Third umpire: R. A. Kettleborough.
Referee: B. C. Broad.

First one-day international   At Providence, Guyana, July 22, 2018. **Bangladesh won by 48 runs.** ‡**Bangladesh 279-4** (50 overs) (Tamim Iqbal 130*, Shakib Al Hasan 97, Mushfiqur Rahim 30); West Indies 231-9 (50 overs) (C. H. Gayle 40, S. O. Hetmyer 52; Mashrafe bin Mortaza 4-37). *MoM: Tamim Iqbal. A heavyweight partnership between Tamim Iqbal and Shakib Al Hasan set up Bangladesh's victory. Despite surviving several chances and not always scoring fluently, they put on 207 – the second-highest for any Bangladeshi wicket – after coming together at 1-1. At 146 balls, Tamim's tenth ODI hundred was his country's slowest, and it needed Mushfiqur Rahim's 30 off 11, and 43 off the last two overs, to put meat on the bones. West Indies lost Chris Gayle – run out in a mix-up with Shimron Hetmyer – just when he seemed to have just got the measure of the surface. But with 15 overs to go, they needed 140 with six wickets in hand, and were still in with a shout. Mashrafe bin Mortaza's four victims included the dangerous Evin Lewis and the captain Jason Holder.*

Second one-day international   At Providence, Guyana, July 25, 2018 (day/night). **West Indies won by three runs. West Indies 271** (49.3 overs) (S. O. Hetmyer 125, R. Powell 44; Rubel Hossain 3-61); ‡**Bangladesh 268-6** (50 overs) (Tamim Iqbal 54, Shakib Al Hasan 56, Mushfiqur Rahim 68, Mahmudullah 39). *MoM: S. O. Hetmyer. A nerveless final over from Holder ensured Hetmyer's outstanding century was not in vain – and squared the series. Bangladesh needed eight, but Mushfiqur was caught at deep midwicket off the first ball. His next five conceded only four, sealing what had appeared an unlikely triumph. Asked to bat, West Indies were struggling at 102-4 before Hetmyer and Rovman Powell put on 103. The rebuilding began cautiously, but Hetmyer provided late acceleration: his 125 off 93 balls included seven sixes. Bangladesh started at a gallop, Holder's first over costing 20 as Anamul Haque launched him on to the pavilion roof. The 50 arrived inside five overs, but the charge slowed after the tenth. A stand of 87 between Mushfiqur and Mahmudullah put them back on track, but the run-out of Mahmudullah in the 46th over proved critical. Alzarri Joseph was given an official reprimand and a demerit point for sending off Anamul.*

Third one-day international   At Basseterre, St Kitts, July 28, 2018. **Bangladesh won by 18 runs.** ‡**Bangladesh 301-6** (50 overs) (Tamim Iqbal 103, Shakib Al Hasan 37, Mahmudullah 67*, Mashrafe bin Mortaza 36); West Indies 283-6 (50 overs) (C. H. Gayle 73, S. D. Hope 64, S. O. Hetmyer 30, R. Powell 74*). *MoM: Tamim Iqbal. MoS: Tamim Iqbal. Bangladesh clinched the series with their highest total against West Indies. It was built on Tamim's second century of the series, and a late flourish from Mahmudullah and Mashrafe, who added 100 off the final 66 balls. For a while, it seemed Gayle would make short work of the target. He hit 73 off 66, and the last of his five sixes was his 476th in internationals, level with Shahid Afridi's record. But, in trying to go one better, he hit Rubel Hossain's slower ball to Mehedi Hasan at long-on. Hope compiled a sedate 64 off 94 deliveries, but West Indies were given fresh impetus when Ricardo Powell's clean striking took him* to 50 off 27. Bangladesh held their nerve, Mustafizur Rahman and Rubel bowling well-directed yorkers to frustrate Powell. The result left Holder still awaiting his first ODI series win.

First Twenty20 international   At Basseterre, St Kitts, July 31, 2018 (floodlit). **West Indies won by seven wickets** (DLS). **Bangladesh 143-9** (20 overs) (Mahmudullah 35; K. O. K. Williams 4-28); ‡**West Indies 93-3** (9.1 overs) (A. D. Russell 35*). *MoM:* A. D. Russell. *Andre Russell eased West Indies past a stiff DLS target of 91 in 11 overs with 11 balls to spare, but Kesrick Williams was at least as worthy of the match award. After completing an athletic juggling catch at third man to remove the dangerous Shakib, he took 4-28, his best T20 international figures, and showed off his celebratory dance moves. His victims included top-scorer Mahmudullah, deceived by a dipping slower-ball yorker. Bangladesh had lost both openers for nought in the opening over, from off-spinner Ashley Nurse, who did not bowl again – "tactics", said captain Carlos Brathwaite. Rain during the interval handed a revised target to West Indies, who were without Gayle, rested for the start of the Caribbean Premier League. They lost two early wickets, but Samuels got them back on track, and Russell's 35* off 21 balls completed the job.*

Second Twenty20 international   At Lauderhill, Florida, August 4, 2018 (floodlit). **Bangladesh won by 12 runs. Bangladesh 171-5** (20 overs) (Tamim Iqbal 74, Shakib Al Hasan 60); ‡**West Indies 159-9** (20 overs) (A. D. S. Fletcher 43, R. Powell 43; Mustafizur Rahman 3-50, Nazmul Islam 3-28). *MoM:* Tamim Iqbal. *Bangladesh marked West Indies' 100th Twenty20 international by levelling the series. Backed by the majority of a vociferous Florida crowd numbering around 5,000, Bangladesh held their nerve: entrusted with defending 15 in the final over, slow left-armer Nazmul Islam conceded just two. Nurse took two early wickets again, but Tamim, with 74 off 44 balls, and Shakib, with 60 off 38 – his first fifty since the 2016 World Twenty20 – turned things around in a stand of 90. West Indies also lost early wickets, and found scoring tough, but Andre Fletcher and Marlon Samuels, both with 43, kept them interested until the last over. Nazmul's 3-28 were his best T20 international figures. Tamim quickly rediscovered his one-day form, while Shakib starred with bat and ball as Bangladesh ruined West Indies' 100th match in this format.*

Third Twenty20 international   At Lauderhill, Florida, August 5, 2018 (floodlit). **Bangladesh won by 19 runs** (DLS). ‡**Bangladesh 184-5** (20 overs) (Liton Das 61, Mahmudullah 32*); **West Indies 135-7** (17.1 overs) (A. D. Russell 47; Mustafizur Rahman 3-31). *MoM:* Liton Das. *MoS:* Shakib Al Hasan. *Bangladesh completed a mixed tour by coming from behind to win the T20 series. Brathwaite's decision to give the new ball to Nurse backfired this time, as Liton Das and Tamim blasted 61 in less than five overs. Liton went to his first white-ball international fifty, off 24 balls. Bangladesh stalled, but Mahmudullah, with 32* off 20, steered them to a challenging total. West Indies never got going, and were 32-3 after the powerplay. Nazmul had to be replaced in mid-over when his left hand was injured by Chadwick Walton's spikes as he dived to make a stop; Soumya Sarkar replaced him, and dismissed Walton with his third ball. Russell briefly raised West Indian hopes, hitting six sixes in his 47 off 21. Rain confirmed Bangladesh's win, which was greeted enthusiastically by the expats. "It felt like playing at home," said Shakib.*

WEST INDIES A v ENGLAND LIONS IN 2017-18

RICHARD WHITEHEAD

A-Team Test matches (3): West Indies A 3, England Lions 0
A-Team one-day internationals (3): West Indies A 2, England Lions 1

It would have been a good moment to have excelled. As England reflected on an Ashes thrashing, and prepared for what would be an equally fruitless Test series in New Zealand, the Lions tour of the West Indies offered a perfect opportunity for the fringe performers to make a case for promotion. But, with the exception of Somerset left-arm spinner Jack Leach, they fluffed their lines: whitewashed in the Test series, the Lions were then beaten in the one-dayers.

Head coach Andy Flower pointed out the long-term benefits of the experience. But he was disappointed his batsmen did not adapt more quickly to the challenges presented by a West Indies A-team sprinkled with Test players. Once, the Caribbean provided a test of reflexes and bravery, and encouraged an instinct for self-preservation. But this tour became a daily trial by spin: the combination of slow left-armer Jomel Warrican and heavyweight off-spinner Rahkeem Cornwall bamboozled the Lions repeatedly. "We have to be harsh and honest with ourselves, and try and pull our games forward," said their captain, Keaton Jennings.

On pitches that often helped slow bowlers from the start, Leach performed superbly, with 18 wickets at 21 in the three Tests. Leach believed he had benefited from studying Nathan Lyon in the Ashes during a Lions training camp in Australia: "I changed a few things to try and get a bit more energy on the ball." In the third game, his Somerset team-mate Dom Bess took five second-innings wickets with his off-breaks.

None of the batsmen made an impact. Haseeb Hameed showed glimpses of the class that was apparent during his introduction to Test cricket in India in 2016-17, and was the Lions' leading run-scorer, though with a modest 167 at 27. Elsewhere there were innings of promise rather than substance from Jennings, Nick Gubbins, Paul Coughlin, Joe Clarke and Liam Livingstone. No one made a century, and there were only three fifties.

As with the seniors, the Lions were prone to match-defining collapses. On the third evening of the first Test at Trelawny, the last six wickets fell for 14 in eight overs, effectively settling the outcome of what had been a close contest. In the second match, at Sabina Park, the first six departed for the addition of 29 either side of lunch on the first day. In the third, in Antigua – played in day/night conditions with a pink ball – the last nine fell to Warrican and Cornwall for 53.

The one-day series was lost 2–1, the Lions' victory coming only after the outcome had been decided. With England's white-ball cricket in rude health, this seemed less of a missed opportunity for the young pretenders. In the first match, Warwickshire's Sam Hain made a superb century and came within a boundary of taking his team to victory. He also played a prominent role in the long-awaited win, with an unbeaten 54; Matt Parkinson, the 21-year-old Lancashire leg-spinner, took four wickets. But there could be no quibbling with Flower's assessment: "The tour has allowed us to learn a great deal about the players, but the results are extremely disappointing."

ENGLAND LIONS TOURING PARTY

*K. K. Jennings (Lancashire; FC/50), D. M. Bess (Somerset; FC/50), J. M. Clarke (Worcestershire; FC/50), P. Coughlin (Nottinghamshire; FC/50), M. S. Crane (Hampshire; FC), M. J. J. Critchley (Derbyshire; 50), S. M. Curran (Surrey; 50), A. L. Davies (Lancashire; FC/50), L. A. Dawson (Hampshire; 50), B. T. Foakes (Surrey; FC), G. H. S. Garton (Sussex; 50), R. J. Gleeson (Northamptonshire; FC/50), N. R. T. Gubbins (Middlesex; FC/50), S. R. Hain (Warwickshire; 50), H. Hameed (Lancashire; FC), T. G. Helm (Middlesex; 50), D. W. Lawrence (Essex; FC/50), M. J. Leach (Somerset; FC), L. S. Livingstone (Lancashire; FC/50), S. Mahmood (Lancashire; FC/50), S. A. Northeast (Hampshire; FC/50), M. W. Parkinson (Lancashire; 50), J. A. Porter (Essex; FC/50), T. S. Roland-Jones (Middlesex; FC/50). *Head coach:* A. Flower.

J. C. Tongue (Worcestershire) withdrew from the first-class squad with an ankle injury and was replaced by Bess, originally part of the one-day squad only. Crane left after the second A-Team Test to prepare for England's tour of New Zealand. Roland-Jones was originally selected for the first-class squad only.

At Kingston, Jamaica, February 5–7, 2018 (not first-class). **Drawn. England Lions 263-8 dec** (75.3 overs) (K. K. Jennings 129*, A. L. Davies 53) **and 230** (57.4 overs) (J. M. Clarke 87; J. H. Merchant 5-35); ‡**Jamaica 236** (68.3 overs) (A. O. Thomas 109; J. A. Porter 3-24, T. S. Roland-Jones 3-37) **and 131-4** (45 overs). *England Lions named 16 players and Jamaica 15, but only 11 from each side batted in the solitary warm-up match. In the first innings, Keaton Jennings hit an unbeaten century and put on 97 with Alex Davies, but the others struggled. In the second there were runs for Joe Clarke, but Aldane Thomas took a hundred off the England attack.*

WEST INDIES A v ENGLAND LIONS

First A-Team Test

At Trelawny Greenfields, Jamaica, February 11–14, 2018. West Indies A won by two wickets. Toss: West Indies A.

For much of an absorbing game, the Lions went toe to toe with West Indies A. Then, in the last session of the third day, Cornwall and Warrican got to work, turning the match decisively in the home team's favour. It was to the Lions' credit that, thanks to Leach, they came close to pulling off an unlikely victory. Just as crucial as the efforts of the West Indian spinners was a first-innings century from Dowrich, who dug his side out of a hole at 114 for eight. He put on 161 with the ubiquitous Warrican, whose patient unbeaten 71 was his maiden senior fifty. Coach Andy Flower had praised the vigilance of Gubbins and Coughlin in the first innings, but their application was not repeated, as the Lions tumbled to 132, with Warrican claiming seven for 33. Only Hameed was up to the challenge. A target of 106 appeared routine, but from 51 for one West Indies A crashed to 98 for eight, as Leach's five-for induced anxiety in a small but vocal crowd. Cornwall steered them home, however, hitting Crane for the winning boundary. The Lions could at least point to a disparity in experience: the hosts had 84 Test caps to their 14.

Man of the Match: J. A. Warrican.

Close of play: first day, England Lions 233-6 (Coughlin 51, Roland-Jones 18); second day, West Indies A 232-8 (Dowrich 90, Warrican 54); third day, West Indies A 31-1 (Powell 16).

England Lions

*K. K. Jennings c Blackwood b Cornwall	49	– c Dowrich b Cornwall	0
H. Hameed lbw b Warrican	13	– b Warrican	39
N. R. T. Gubbins lbw b Cornwall	50	– c Blackwood b Warrican	20
J. M. Clarke c Singh b Joseph	1	– c Dowrich b Warrican	31
L. S. Livingstone b Cornwall	21	– b Warrican	1
†B. T. Foakes c Dowrich b Louis	16	– c Powell b Cornwall	20
P. Coughlin c Singh b Cornwall	60	– lbw b Warrican	11
T. S. Roland-Jones c Campbell b Reifer	18	– lbw b Cornwall	2
M. J. Leach lbw b Cornwall	3	– not out	0
M. S. Crane b Brooks b Reifer	1	– c Singh b Warrican	0
J. A. Porter not out	0	– c Dowrich b Warrican	0
B 6, lb 6, w 1, nb 7	20	B 2, lb 1, nb 5	8

1/38 (2) 2/94 (1) 3/101 (4) (107.5 overs) 252 1/8 (1) 2/60 (3) (59.3 overs) 132
4/129 (3) 5/149 (5) 6/182 (6) 3/75 (2) 4/81 (5)
7/233 (8) 8/250 (7) 9/251 (10) 10/252 (9) 5/118 (4) 6/120 (6) 7/124 (8)
8/132 (7) 9/132 (10) 10/132 (11)

Reifer 18–4–50–2; Joseph 13–4–39–1; Louis 9–1–27–1; Cornwall 37.5–10–68–5; Warrican 29–9–54–1; Campbell 1–0–2–0. *Second innings*—Cornwall 25–5–55–3; Reifer 4–1–13–0; Warrican 23.3–12–33–7; Joseph 2–0–7–0; Louis 1–0–5–0; Campbell 4–0–16–0.

West Indies A

*K. O. A. Powell c Jennings b Porter	0	– c Gubbins b Livingstone	30
J. D. Campbell c Jennings b Roland-Jones	0	– c Livingstone b Leach	15
J. Blackwood c Livingstone b Porter	35	– b Leach	4
S. S. J. Brooks st Foakes b Leach	12	– lbw b Leach	16
V. A. Singh c Foakes b Coughlin	10	– c Porter b Leach	18
†S. O. Dowrich c Gubbins b Livingstone	119	– b Leach	3
R. A. Reifer c Hameed b Leach	6	– c Hameed b Livingstone	3
R. R. S. Cornwall run out (Hameed)	4	– not out	14
J. S. Louis lbw b Leach	6	– (10) not out	1
J. A. Warrican not out	71	– (9) c and b Crane	0
K. A. Joseph b Livingstone	0		
B 8, lb 2, w 1, nb 5	16	B 3, nb 1	4

1/0 (1) 2/2 (2) 3/50 (3) (96 overs) 279 1/31 (2) (8 wkts, 29.5 overs) 108
4/54 (4) 5/76 (5) 6/89 (7) 2/51 (1) 3/57 (3) 4/80 (4)
7/94 (8) 8/114 (9) 9/275 (6) 10/279 (11) 5/86 (6) 6/91 (7) 7/97 (5) 8/98 (9)

Porter 16–2–47–2; Roland-Jones 14–2–48–1; Leach 34–7–84–3; Coughlin 8–2–17–1; Crane 10–0–43–0; Livingstone 14–1–30–2. *Second innings*—Porter 2–0–11–0; Livingstone 12–1–53–2; Leach 13–2–28–5; Crane 2.5–0–13–1.

Umpires: V. M. Smith and C. O. Wright.

WEST INDIES A v ENGLAND LIONS

Second A-Team Test

At Kingston, Jamaica, February 18–20, 2018. West Indies A won by an innings and 17 runs. Toss: West Indies A.

Warrican topped his efforts in the previous game, taking 12 wickets as West Indies A wrapped up the series inside three days. The Lions struggled from the moment Powell brought on his spinners inside the first hour, after Jennings and Hameed had taken their opening stand past 50. Clarke made 56, but Warrican ran through a feeble innings with a career-best eight for 34. By the close, West Indies A were already 14 ahead, although four wickets had given the Lions a sniff. It disappeared on a dreadful second day. Hamilton, dropped on four off Livingstone on the first evening, hit 100, and added 72 with Dowrich and 102 with Reifer, who made 95. Leach was a beacon amid the gloom with six for 138. Facing a deficit of 277, the Lions made a better fist of things second time around. Jennings and Hameed looked composed, until Hameed was needlessly run out. Only Livingstone and Coughlin got to 30, with Cornwall and Warrican proving irresistible.

Man of the Match: J. A. Warrican.

Close of play: first day, West Indies A 159-4 (Hamilton 17, Dowrich 20); second day, England Lions 34-0 (Jennings 11, Hameed 18).

England Lions

*K. K. Jennings lbw b Cornwall	28	– lbw b Cornwall	20
H. Hameed st Dowrich b Warrican	23	– run out (Louis)	18
N. R. T. Gubbins c Blackwood b Warrican	0	– lbw b Warrican	22
J. M. Clarke b Warrican	56	– b Reifer	6
L. S. Livingstone b Warrican	0	– c Louis b Cornwall	48
†A. L. Davies c Brooks b Warrican	4	– c Hamilton b Warrican	21
P. Coughlin c Blackwood b Warrican	0	– lbw b Cornwall	47
T. S. Roland-Jones c Cornwall b Warrican	4	– lbw b Cornwall	2
M. J. Leach b Cornwall	1	– b Warrican	29
M. S. Crane c Cornwall b Warrican	12	– not out	25
J. A. Porter not out	0	– lbw b Warrican	0
B 7, lb 4, w 1, nb 5	17	B 5, lb 1, nb 16	22

1/56 (1) 2/56 (3) 3/76 (1)   (57 overs) 145   1/43 (2) 2/65 (1)   (100.2 overs) 260
4/77 (5) 5/85 (6) 6/85 (7)   3/77 (4) 4/80 (3)
7/101 (8) 8/106 (9) 9/144 (10) 10/145 (4)   5/102 (6) 6/185 (5) 7/188 (8)
                                                    8/215 (7) 9/258 (9) 10/260 (11)

Reifer 7–1–30–0; Joseph 5–0–16–0; Louis 4–1–10–0; Cornwall 21–7–44–2; Warrican 20–6–34–8. *Second innings*—Reifer 13–5–25–1; Louis 9–1–27–0; Joseph 13–5–45–0; Cornwall 38–10–88–4; Warrican 27.2–9–69–4.

West Indies A

J. D. Campbell c Hameed b Leach	47	J. S. Louis c Jennings b Coughlin	14
*K. O. A. Powell c and b Livingstone	59	K. A. Joseph not out	5
J. Blackwood c Jennings b Leach	6		
S. S. J. Brooks b Livingstone	1	B 4, lb 10, w 3, nb 3	20
J. N. Hamilton c Clarke b Roland-Jones	100		
†S. O. Dowrich c Gubbins b Leach	43	1/72 (1) 2/78 (3) (110.4 overs) 422
R. A. Reifer b Leach	95	3/87 (4) 4/128 (2)
R. R. S. Cornwall b Leach	25	5/200 (6) 6/302 (5) 7/351 (8)
J. A. Warrican st Davies b Leach	7	8/371 (9) 9/410 (10) 10/422 (7)

Porter 11–2–51–0; Roland-Jones 10–1–42–1; Livingstone 23–4–83–2; Leach 41.4–6–138–6; Crane 14–1–59–0; Coughlin 11–1–35–1.

Umpires: V. M. Smith and C. O. Wright.

WEST INDIES A v ENGLAND LIONS

Third A-Team Test

At North Sound, Antigua, February 26–March 1, 2018 (day/night). West Indies A won by 212 runs. Toss: West Indies A.

Another thumping victory for the hosts left the Lions seeking crumbs of consolation. And, in a day/night game played with a pink ball, there were one or two. Bess joined forces with Somerset team-mate Leach and took five for 88 in West Indies A's second innings; and there were three first-innings wickets for another debutant, Lancashire's Saqib Mahmood, while his county team-mate Hameed made a composed 48. But others found it hard going once more. "This series has given us the opportunity to learn about the batsmen in difficult circumstances," said Flower. Yet again, the

Lions' chief tormentor was Warrican, who took 11 for 88, to finish the series with 31 wickets at nine. The opening day had belonged to the Lions, with Mahmood and Northamptonshire's Richard Gleeson sharing five wickets, and Leach adding three. But a position of strength was surrendered on the second morning, when seven wickets fell. Cornwall and Warrican picked up nine and, although Bess made inroads, West Indies A closed 291 ahead, scenting a whitewash. Set an improbable 408 after Hamilton had made 79 and Dowrich 71, the Lions subsided for 195.

Man of the Match: J. A. Warrican.

Close of play: first day, England Lions 20-0 (Jennings 9, Hameed 8); second day, West Indies A 157-4 (Hamilton 36, Dowrich 13); third day, England Lions 132-6 (Davies 15, Leach 5).

West Indies A

J. D. Campbell lbw b Mahmood	33	– c Jennings b Bess	22
*K. O. A. Powell c Davies b Gleeson	11	– lbw b Bess	28
J. Blackwood c Gubbins b Leach	28	– c Gubbins b Leach	10
S. S. J. Brooks lbw b Gleeson	63	– lbw b Bess	37
J. N. Hamilton lbw b Mahmood	20	– c Davies b Bess	79
†S. O. Dowrich c Davies b Mahmood	0	– c Northeast b Coughlin	71
R. A. Reifer c Leach b Jennings	27	– c Davies b Coughlin	14
R. R. S. Cornwall c Gubbins b Coughlin	33	– lbw b Bess	1
K. M. A. Paul c Northeast b Leach	0	– not out	0
J. A. Warrican not out	2	– c Davies b Coughlin	0
K. A. Joseph lbw b Leach	0		
B 5, lb 2, w 8, nb 4	19	B 4, lb 5, nb 2	11

1/29 (2) 2/75 (1) 3/77 (3)   (76.2 overs) 236   1/54 (1)   (9 wkts dec, 88.3 overs) 273
4/150 (5) 5/154 (6) 6/187 (4)   2/57 (2) 3/73 (3)
7/228 (7) 8/229 (9) 9/235 (8) 10/236 (11)   4/127 (4) 5/239 (5) 6/272 (7)
                                                         7/273 (6) 8/273 (6) 9/273 (10)

Mahmood 17–6–50–3; Gleeson 18–5–43–2; Coughlin 14–3–54–1; Leach 21.2–5–58–3; Bess 5–1–24–0; Jennings 1–1–0–1. *Second innings*—Mahmood 3–0–17–0; Gleeson 11–4–42–0; Coughlin 15.3–1–44–3; Bess 34–8–88–5; Leach 25–2–73–1.

England Lions

*K. K. Jennings lbw b Reifer	16	– c Reifer b Paul	14
H. Hameed lbw b Warrican	48	– st †Hamilton b Warrican	26
N. R. T. Gubbins lbw b Cornwall	4	– b Cornwall	21
J. M. Clarke lbw b Warrican	0	– b Warrican	22
S. A. Northeast c Hamilton b Cornwall	3	– run out (Reifer)	6
†A. L. Davies b Warrican	8	– c Paul b Warrican	23
P. Coughlin c Blackwood b Cornwall	11	– b Warrican	4
M. J. Leach c Cornwall b Warrican	0	– c †Hamilton b Cornwall	14
D. M. Bess st Dowrich b Warrican	4	– c †Hamilton b Paul	18
R. J. Gleeson c and b Warrican	0	– not out	12
S. Mahmood not out	4	– lbw b Warrican	9
B 1, nb 3	4	B 10, lb 5, w 5, nb 6	26

1/38 (1) 2/49 (3) 3/52 (4)   (54.1 overs) 102   1/35 (1) 2/78 (3)   (70.3 overs) 195
4/63 (5) 5/72 (6) 6/92 (2)   3/80 (2) 4/102 (5)
7/92 (8) 8/96 (7) 9/97 (10) 10/102 (9)   5/118 (4) 6/126 (7) 7/153 (6)
                                                         8/153 (8) 9/180 (9) 10/195 (11)

Reifer 7–2–16–1; Paul 3–1–3–0; Joseph 2–0–3–0; Cornwall 24–8–46–3; Warrican 18.1–5–33–6. *Second innings*—Reifer 4–0–22–0; Joseph 9–0–29–0; Paul 7–0–25–2; Cornwall 23–7–49–2; Warrican 27.3–13–55–5.

Umpires: D. K. Butler and C. M. Tuckett.

At North Sound, Antigua, March 4, 2018 (day/night). **England Lions won by 246 runs. ‡England Lions 328-9** (50 overs) (A. L. Davies 78, S. M. Curran 119; J. Spencer 4-6, O. Peters 3-50); **Antigua Masterblasters 82** (30.3 overs) (S. M. Curran 3-24, R. J. Gleeson 3-15). *Sam Curran produced an* *impressive all-round display as the Lions won their first match of the tour. They were 80-5 when Curran and Davies began a stand of 141 in 21 overs. Curran made 119, then grabbed three wickets as the Masterblasters were shot out; Gleeson also took three. The hosts named 15 and the Lions 14, but only 11 batted.*

First A-Team one-day international   At Coolidge, Antigua, March 6, 2018 (day/night). **West Indies A won by five runs.** ‡West Indies A 272 (49.5 overs) (J. Blackwood 99); **England Lions 267** (49.4 overs) (N. R. T. Gubbins 54, S. R. Hain 144; K. M. A. Paul 5-49). MoM: J. Blackwood. *Sam Hain took the Lions to the brink of victory in a thrilling opening to the one-day series. Six were needed off three balls when – having added 102 for the last wicket with Matt Parkinson – he was well caught at long-on by Raymon Reifer off Roston Chase. After Keemo Paul had cut through the Lions' middle order, Hain did not find anyone to stay with him until Gleeson arrived at No. 10. When he fell, they still needed 108, but Parkinson was defiant, and Hain went on the offensive; in all, his 144 – a List A best – came from 122 balls, and he hit five sixes. West Indies A's total had been built around 99 from Jermaine Blackwood, after opener Chanderpaul Hemraj had retired hurt without facing after tweaking a hamstring. He returned at No. 9 and made 12.*

Second A-Team one-day international   At Coolidge, Antigua, March 9, 2018 (day/night). **West Indies A won by 25 runs.** ‡West Indies A 256-9 (50 overs) (J. Blackwood 53, K. M. A. Paul 55; R. J. Gleeson 3-52, S. M. Curran 3-41); **England Lions 231** (48.4 overs) (K. M. A. Paul 3-55, J. A. Warrican 3-41). MoM: K. M. A. Paul. *A familiar collapse handed the series to West Indies A. The Lions appeared in control of the chase at 173-4 in the 40th over but, after Jennings was dismissed for 33, and Curran next over, they folded. In all, the last six fell for 58. Earlier, despite Blackwood's half-century, the West Indians looked as if they might struggle to post a challenging total after Gleeson and Curran removed the top order. They were in danger of being bowled out at 153-7 in the 36th over, but Paul made the first of his key contributions with 55, and a match-changing stand of 97 with Reifer (45*). Paul then secured the match award with 3-55.*

Third A-Team one-day international   At Coolidge, Antigua, March 11, 2018 (day/night). **England Lions won by seven wickets.** ‡West Indies A 170 (38.1 overs) (R. L. Chase 67; M. W. Parkinson 4-26); **England Lions 171-3** (31.1 overs) (S. R. Hain 54*). MoM: M. W. Parkinson. *The Lions finally won an international fixture. Hain underlined the good impression he made in the opening match with an unbeaten 54, soothing anxieties after another wobble. Davies and Nick Gubbins had put on an aggressive 87 in 11.4 overs, but then three wickets fell for four, giving the West Indians a potential way back into the match. However, Hain put on 80* with Sam Northeast to complete a consolation win. Parkinson had another good game, taking four wickets after Gleeson and Curran had again teamed up impressively with the new ball.*

DOMESTIC CRICKET IN THE WEST INDIES IN 2017-18

HAYDN GILL

After four seasons of the franchise system in the West Indies, there were small signs that the initiative was beginning to bear some fruit. But concerns remained about the standard of the game in the Caribbean.

The franchise set-up has produced only one first-class champion: **Guyana**, who romped to the title for the fourth time running. Only Barbados, with four successive first-class titles in the 1970s, and Jamaica, with five up to 2011-12, have been as consistently dominant in West Indian regional cricket. Guyana secured the trophy with two rounds to go, on completing the sixth of their seven victories, and finished more than 50 points ahead of runners-up Barbados, who won three matches. It underlined a significant gap between them and their rivals, and robbed the competition of excitement in the closing rounds.

The authorities could take some comfort: more matches were going the distance, teams were batting longer and scoring more runs, and a few fast bowlers emerged. The competition produced 35 centuries, a notable increase from 21 the previous season. There were nine totals of 400-plus (up from four), and only one under 100 (down from seven) – and that was 99, by Jamaica when they visited Guyana in the opening round. While 11 matches in 2016-17 had concluded with a day to spare, the number dipped to six, plus one lasting just two days. Overall, there were 20 outright results in 30 games, including a tie between Guyana and Windward Islands – three fewer than the previous season.

There were two standouts in Guyana's attack. The left-arm spinner Veerasammy Permaul continued to mesmerise Caribbean batsmen, and was the only bowler to reach 50 wickets in the competition, though his attempts to translate that success to international level have been disappointing. But Guyana also unearthed a potential star in fast bowler Keemo Paul, who had played in the West Indies team that won the Under-19 World Cup in 2015-16. An exciting all-rounder, Paul grabbed 42 wickets at 18, and scored a maiden century. The selectors were quick to acknowledge a rare talent. He made his international debut in March, a few weeks after his 20th birthday, and had appeared for West Indies in all three formats by July.

Paul was one of two seamers to break into the tournament's top five wicket-takers, the most since 2006-07; in seven of the intervening ten seasons, all five had been spinners. The other was 21-year-old Jeremiah Louis, who collected 40 wickets for Leeward Islands. The presence of Paul and Louis was the first sign that a rule introduced in 2016-17, awarding teams 0.2 bonus points for each wicket taken by fast bowlers, might be starting to play a positive role. Almost 60% of Guyana's wickets fell to pace, though for Jamaica the proportion was less than 30%.

With the leading players frequently absent on tour with West Indies, a few discards took the opportunity to dominate. None did so more emphatically than Devon Smith, Windwards' opening batsman. He scored 1,095 runs with six centuries, both records for the West Indian domestic competition, and in his final innings shared an unbroken stand of 323 with Tyrone Theophile against Leewards, a tournament-best for the second wicket. His form earned him yet another Test recall, at the age of 36. The next-highest run-scorer was another experienced campaigner, Denesh Ramdin, who hit three centuries on the way to an aggregate of 799, and returned to West Indies' Twenty20 side. Both Chanderpauls, father Shivnarine and son Tagenarine, scored a hundred for Guyana, but rarely batted together.

Smith was also one of the leading scorers in the Super50 competition, where **Windward Islands** captured their first title since 2012-13. They won the final against the previous one-day champions, Barbados, for whom Roston Chase scored 558 in all. Hampshire and Kent – and the USA – took part, with Kent reaching the semi-finals.

FIRST-CLASS AVERAGES IN 2017-18

BATTING (300 runs, average 25.00)

		M	I	NO	R	HS	100	Avge	Ct/St
1	†D. S. Smith (*Windward Islands*)	10	18	5	1,095	185*	6	84.23	11
2	D. Ramdin (*Trinidad & Tobago*).	10	18	5	799	132*	3	61.46	9
3	K. A. R. Hodge (*Windward Islands*) . . .	7	11	1	535	128	1	53.50	7
4	A. Bramble (*Guyana*)	10	15	2	613	196*	1	47.15	42/3
5	†T. Chanderpaul (*Guyana*)	9	16	4	459	101*	1	38.25	4
6	†V. A. Singh (*West Indies A/Guyana*) . . .	12	21	3	687	119	2	38.16	11
7	S. E. Rutherford (*Guyana*).	9	12	3	343	93	0	38.11	8
8	†S. A. R. Moseley (*Barbados*)	10	19	2	643	117	2	37.82	4
9	F. A. Allen (*Jamaica*)	8	14	2	446	169*	1	37.16	5
10	S. S. J. Brooks (*West Indies A/Barbados*)	14	24	1	854	166	1	37.13	10
11	†C. Hemraj (*Guyana*)	10	18	1	623	90	0	36.64	8
12	D. C. Thomas (*Leeward Islands*)	10	17	0	616	172	1	36.23	19
13	†J. D. Campbell (*West Indies A/Jamaica*)	14	25	1	803	156	1	33.45	12
14	†S. Chanderpaul (*Guyana*)	7	11	0	363	109	1	33.00	2
15	A. Saunders (*Leeward Islands*)	7	13	0	419	101	1	32.23	3
16	†J. L. Carter (*Barbados*)	10	17	0	527	103	1	31.00	18
17	J. P. Greaves (*Barbados*)	10	14	1	399	79*	0	30.69	8
18	K. U. Carty (*Leeward Islands*)	7	10	0	305	82	0	30.50	5
19	†P. Palmer (*Jamaica*)	10	18	2	483	136	1	30.18	8
20	R. O. Cato (*Windward Islands*).	9	15	0	450	90	0	30.00	12
21	J. Blackwood (*Jamaica/West Indies A*) .	6	11	0	327	81	0	29.72	12
22	†L. R. Johnson (*Guyana*).	10	17	0	475	165	1	27.94	15
23	M. V. Hodge (*WI A/Leeward Islands*) . .	11	19	0	530	91	0	27.89	4
24	T. Webster (*Trinidad & Tobago*)	9	16	1	414	178	1	27.60	4
25	†A. A. Jangoo (*Trinidad & Tobago*).	10	19	1	490	96	0	27.22	16/1
26	B. A. King (*Jamaica*)	9	16	0	427	98	0	26.68	3

BOWLING (15 wickets, average 30.00)

		Style	O	M	R	W	BB	5I	Avge
1	P. M. Pushpakumara (*Sri Lanka A*) . .	SLA	111.3	26	288	23	6-46	2	12.52
2	N. O. Miller (*Jamaica*).	SLA	243.5	74	504	36	8-54	4	14.00
3	J. A. Warrican (*Barbados/W Indies A*)	SLA	453.3	134	1,090	67	8-34	6	16.26
4	K. M. A. Paul (*Guyana/West Indies A*)	RFM	274.2	63	813	44	5-59	1	18.47
5	V. Permaul (*Guyana*).	SLA	414.1	121	945	50	6-29	4	18.90
6	K. D. Williams (*Barbados*)	OB	149.5	39	394	19	5-50	1	20.73
7	M. J. Leach (*England Lions*)	SLA	135	22	381	18	6-138	2	21.16
8	D. St Clair (*Trinidad & Tobago*)	LM	179.4	42	551	26	6-62	1	21.19
9	G. Motie (*Guyana*).	SLA	202.3	59	451	21	4-39	0	21.47
10	R. Shepherd (*Guyana*)	RFM	110	25	324	15	5-40	1	21.60
11	S. H. Lewis (*Windward Islands*)	RFM	216.5	42	650	30	5-64	1	21.66
12	S. Berridge (*Leeward Islands*)	RFM	138.5	20	543	24	5-59	1	22.62
13	D. K. Jacobs (*West Indies A/Jamaica*)	LB	348.5	64	926	40	7-74	3	23.15
14	S. E. Rutherford (*Guyana*)	RFM	148.5	33	511	22	6-32	1	23.22
15	D. E. Johnson (*Windward Islands*). . .	LF	122	33	361	15	3-45	0	24.06
16	J. S. Louis (*Leeward Islands/WI A*)	RFM	319.2	67	1,007	41	6-69	1	24.56
17	S. Shillingford (*Windward Islands*) . .	OB	392.1	85	951	38	7-94	3	25.02
18	K. R. Mayers (*Windward Islands*) . . .	RM	212	65	581	23	5-92	1	25.26
19	I. Khan (*Trinidad & Tobago*).	LB	424.1	82	1,226	48	6-59	3	25.54
20	R. R. S. Cornwall (*WI A/Leeward Is*)	OB	539.5	111	1,487	58	5-68	3	25.63
21	D. C. Green (*Jamaica*).	RM	243	53	697	27	4-45	0	25.81
22	J. D. Campbell (*W Indies A/Jamaica*)	OB	181	33	510	19	4-40	0	26.84
23	K. A. Stoute (*Barbados*)	RFM	175.3	53	431	16	4-58	0	26.93
24	K. A. Joseph (*West Indies A/Guyana*)	RFM	218.1	47	689	25	4-38	0	27.56
25	J. P. Greaves (*Barbados*)	RM	186.4	44	522	18	4-67	0	29.00

Averages do not include tours by Sri Lanka and Bangladesh in June and July 2018.

WICB PROFESSIONAL CRICKET LEAGUE IN 2017-18

					Bonus points		
	P	W	L	D	Bat	Bowl	Pace	Pts
Guyana	10	7	0	2†	22	28	20.8	166.8
Barbados	10	3	2	5	21	29	13.4	114.4
Leeward Islands	10	2	4	4	11	29	18.8	94.8
Jamaica	10	3	4	3	15	25	8.6	93.6
Windward Islands	10	2	4	3†	8	23	15.6	85.6
Trinidad & Tobago	10	2	5	3	18	21	10.4	82.4

† *Plus one tie.*

Win = 12pts; draw = 3pts; tie = 6pts. Bonus points were awarded as follows for the first 110 overs of each team's first innings: one batting point for the first 200 runs and then for 250, 300, 350 and 400; one bowling point for the third wicket taken and then for the sixth and ninth. In addition, 0.2pts awarded for every wicket taken by a pace bowler, across both innings.

REGIONAL CHAMPIONS

1965-66	Barbados	1983-84	Barbados	2001-02	Jamaica
1966-67	Barbados	1984-85	Trinidad & Tobago	2002-03	Barbados
1967-68	*No competition*	1985-86	Barbados	2003-04	Barbados
1968-69	Jamaica	1986-87	Guyana	2004-05	Jamaica
1969-70	Trinidad	1987-88	Jamaica	2005-06	Trinidad & Tobago
1970-71	Trinidad	1988-89	Jamaica	2006-07	Barbados
1971-72	Barbados	1989-90	Leeward Islands	2007-08	Jamaica
1972-73	Guyana	1990-91	Barbados	2008-09	Jamaica
1973-74	Barbados	1991-92	Jamaica	2009-10	Jamaica
1974-75	Guyana	1992-93	Guyana	2010-11	Jamaica
1975-76 {	Trinidad	1993-94	Leeward Islands	2011-12	Jamaica
	Barbados	1994-95	Barbados	2012-13	Barbados
1976-77	Barbados	1995-96	Leeward Islands	2013-14	Barbados
1977-78	Barbados	1996-97	Barbados	2014-15	Guyana
1978-79	Barbados	1997-98 {	Leeward Islands	2015-16	Guyana
1979-80	Barbados		Guyana	2016-17	Guyana
1980-81	Combined Islands	1998-99	Barbados	2017-18	Guyana
1981-82	Barbados	1999-2000	Jamaica		
1982-83	Guyana	2000-01	Barbados		

Barbados have won the title outright 21 times, Jamaica 12, Guyana 9, Trinidad/Trinidad & Tobago 4, Leeward Islands 3, Combined Islands 1. Barbados, Guyana, Leeward Islands and Trinidad have also shared the title.

The tournament was known as the Shell Shield from 1965-66 to 1986-87, the Red Stripe Cup from 1987-88 to 1996-97, the President's Cup in 1997-98, the Busta Cup from 1998-99 to 2001-02, the Carib Beer Cup from 2002-03 to 2007-08, the Headley–Weekes Trophy from 2008-09 to 2012-13, the President's Trophy in 2013-14 and the WICB Professional Cricket League from 2014-15, though it was sponsored by Digicel in 2016-17.

REGIONAL SUPER50 IN 2017-18

50-over league plus knockout

Zone A	P	W	L	BP	Pts		**Zone B**	P	W	L	BP	Pts
BARBADOS	8	6	2	3	27		GUYANA	8	6	2	2	26
WINDWARD ISLANDS	8	5	3	2	22		KENT	8	6	2	1	25
Trinidad & Tobago	8	4	3†	4	22		Jamaica	8	5	3	4	24
Campuses/Colleges	8	2	5†	1	11		Leeward Islands	8	2	6	1	9
Hampshire	8	2	6	1	9		USA	8	1	7	1	5

† *Plus one abandoned match.*

Semi-finals Barbados beat Kent by 13 runs (DLS); Windward Islands beat Guyana by 52 runs (DLS).

Final At Coolidge, February 24, 2018 (day/night). **Windward Islands won by three wickets.** ‡**Barbados 232-9** (50 overs); **Windward Islands 236-7** (49.3 overs). *Jonathan Carter (80) led Barbados to 140-2, but they struggled in the final ten overs, losing five for 45. Roland Cato responded with 54 in 64, his maiden List A half-century, and a run-a-ball 23 from Alick Athanaze ensured Windwards scraped home with three deliveries to spare.*

The Caribbean Premier League has its own section (page 1145).

ZIMBABWE CRICKET IN 2018

Tears and fears

LIAM BRICKHILL

Zimbabwe's dreams were dashed, after an emotional, rain-swept end to their attempts to qualify for the 2019 World Cup. In late March, in front of an all-singing, all-dancing Harare Sports Club filled to capacity, Craig Ervine needed to hit the last ball against the UAE for six to send Zimbabwe through. But his attempted slug died lamely over backward point – along with the team's hopes.

It felt like the end of an era for Zimbabwean cricket, and tears were shed as all-rounder Sikandar Raza delivered a heart-rending speech after receiving his Player of the Tournament award. "It's very painful," said captain Graeme Cremer, whose side had in fact had two cracks at qualifying, losing to West Indies before the defeat by the UAE. "The guys are shattered. I'm sure most Zimbabweans are."

The players who had seen the team through the previous decade, Ervine and Raza among them, are all in their thirties now. The events of 2018 gave an

ZIMBABWE IN 2018

	Played	Won	Lost	Drawn/No result
Tests	2	1	1	–
One-day internationals	26	5	20	1
Twenty20 internationals	8	–	8	–

JANUARY	ODI tri-series (in Sri Lanka) v Bangladesh and Sri Lanka	(page 849)
FEBRUARY	5 ODIs and 2 T20Is (in the UAE) v Afghanistan	(page 803)
MARCH	World Cup Qualifier (h)	(page 790)
APRIL		
MAY		
JUNE		
JULY	T20 tri-series (h) v Australia and Pakistan	(page 1071)
	5 ODIs (h) v Pakistan	(page 1074)
AUGUST		
SEPTEMBER	} 3 ODIs and 2 T20Is (a) v South Africa	(page 1005)
OCTOBER		
NOVEMBER	} 2 Tests and 3 ODIs (a) v Bangladesh	(page 857)
DECEMBER		

For a review of Zimbabwe domestic cricket from the 2017-18 season, see page 1077.

indication of who would lead them through the next, and ensure Zimbabwe are represented at future global events. Batsmen Peter Moor and Tarisai Musakanda are both captaincy material, and leg-spinner Brandon Mavuta has already turned enough heads to raise attention on the T20 market. Richard Ngarava, while raw, has new-ball potential, and the likes of Ryan Murray, Ryan Burl and Liam Roche wait in the wings. But Zimbabwe also lost one of their youngest and brightest lights, as 6ft 8in fast bowler Blessing Muzarabani opted to end his international career at 21 and head for the stability of a county deal with Northamptonshire. While many in the Zimbabwean fraternity were sad to see him go, few begrudged his decision to make the most of his talent.

Zimbabwe sorely missed him in their early-summer trip to South Africa, where they had their hosts 58 for four and 101 for seven in two of the three ODIs, but were unable to land the knockout blow, and left winless. A couple of the squad did at least earn contracts in the inaugural Mzansi Super League in South Africa, with Raza and Sean Williams joining A. B. de Villiers's Tshwane Spartans, and Mavuta being picked up by Durban Heat. All three were sparingly used, but the exposure did them good.

At least Zimbabwe ended the year with a rare Test success, holding Bangladesh to a 1–1 draw in their own backyard – no mean feat against a team who had won home Tests against England and Australia in recent years. Zimbabwe's previous win anywhere other than Harare had come at Chittagong in November 2001. The success in Sylhet, by 151 runs, offered some succour for the disappointment of the Qualifiers and the subsequent capitulation to Pakistan, when Zimbabwe were dire, even by their standards. While Pakistan reached 300 or more three times in five 50-over games, Zimbabwe managed 200 only once, disintegrating for 67 in the third, and claimed just 14 wickets. They seemed in danger of giving up completely as they were handed thrashings of increasing severity, culminating in Fakhar Zaman's double-century in one of the most one-sided contests in living memory.

Zimbabwe were without many of their best players during that series. Brendan Taylor – who led the one-day run-charts with 898 at 42, and scored twin centuries in the Test defeat by Bangladesh at Mirpur – Raza, Williams and Ervine all made themselves unavailable because of unpaid wages during a fallout with the board over the failure to qualify for the World Cup. Tatenda Taibu was sacked as national selector, along with every coach in the country, including those of the Under-19 and A-teams. None of the national backroom staff escaped the purge, with national coach Heath Streak accused of racism as the spat took on a nasty tone. It was a charge dismissed as opportunistic by fans and followers of Zimbabwean cricket across the racial spectrum.

By September, the absent players were all back in the fold, while Lalchand Rajput, who played two Tests for India in the 1980s, had taken over as national coach. Rajput quickly put optimism at the centre of his strategy – just as well, since the team had lost their last 13 ODIs of 2018, and all eight completed Twenty20 internationals. They will need plenty of Rajput's good cheer in 2019, with another qualifying tournament, this time for the T20 World Cup, on the horizon.

ZIMBABWE TRI-NATIONS T20 SERIES IN 2018

Adam Collins

1 Pakistan   2 Australia   3 Zimbabwe

The signs were not promising: seven Twenty20 matches in eight days, all on the same ground in the middle of the southern winter, and with the hosts ravaged by a pay row. Two weeks before the first game, there was even a suggestion the competition might be cancelled, since it was not exactly an appetising prospect. But things turned out rather better than expected. The brisk timetable, the all-round excellence of Pakistan, Zimbabwe's heartening improvement and the batting of Aaron Finch combined to produce a tournament that felt worth repeating.

It helped that the final was a cracker. Pakistan cemented their No. 1 ranking by making their highest successful T20 run-chase, as Fakhar Zaman showed his fondness for the big occasion with a match-winning 91 to deny Australia in a tight finish. He took the match award and, with 278 runs at 55, was also Man of the Tournament. In winning their ninth successive T20 series (beginning with a one-off match against England in 2016), Sarfraz Ahmed's team underlined their mastery of the format. Even so, their attack could not match the potency of Australia's, but Mohammad Amir and 18-year-old Shaheen Shah Afridi were among the leading bowlers.

For Australia there was the balm of recording their first victories since the seismic events in South Africa, especially after their miserable white-ball results in England. Finch led the side impressively, and in the first group match against Zimbabwe surpassed his own T20 international record by bludgeoning 172 off 76 balls. He ended as leading run-scorer, with 306 at 76, and a strike-rate of 201. They also had the most successful bowler: Andrew Tye took 12 wickets at 12.

Zimbabwe were without five senior players after a pay dispute crippled their preparation. Hamilton Masakadza was appointed captain only a couple of days before the start, so it was little wonder they lost their first two matches heavily. But they were encouraged later in the group stages, when they took Pakistan and Australia to the final over. Two fifties from Solomon Mire demonstrated his class.

However, that could not disguise continued administrative chaos. During the first game against Australia, the players suffered the ignominy of being jeered by their own fans in the vocal Castle Corner area of the Harare Sports Club.

Despite paltry crowds and the occasional brutal wind-chill, the series was given positive feedback by players and backroom staff: the consensus was that it was preferable to the 19-day equivalent played between Australia, New Zealand and England in February. If its legacy was that more countries could be persuaded to visit Zimbabwe, the game there would get a much-needed boost.

NATIONAL SQUADS

Zimbabwe *H. Masakadza, R. P. Burl, B. B. Chari, C. J. Chibhabha, E. Chigumbura, T. S. Chisoro, K. M. Jarvis, W. P. Masakadza, B. A. Mavuta, S. F. Mire, P. J. Moor, C. B. Mpofu, R. C. Murray, T. K. Musakanda, B. Muzarabani, J. C. Nyumbu, D. T. Tiripano, M. N. Waller, C. Zhuwao. *Coach:* L. S. Rajput.

Jarvis withdrew after breaking his thumb in the first game, and was replaced by Tiripano.

Australia *A. J. Finch, A. C. Agar, A. T. Carey, T. M. Head, N. J. Maddinson, G. J. Maxwell, J. A. Richardson, K. W. Richardson, D. J. M. Short, B. Stanlake, M. P. Stoinis, M. J. Swepson, A. J. Tye, J. D. Wildermuth. *Coach:* J. L. Langer.

Pakistan *Sarfraz Ahmed, Asif Ali, Fahim Ashraf, Fakhar Zaman, Haris Sohail, Hasan Ali, Hussain Talat, Mohammad Amir, Mohammad Hafeez, Mohammad Nawaz, Sahibzada Farhan, Shadab Khan, Shaheen Shah Afridi, Shoaib Malik, Usman Shinwari. *Coach:* J. M. Arthur.

At Harare, July 1. **Pakistan won by 74 runs. Pakistan 182-4** (20 overs) (Fakhar Zaman 61, Shoaib Malik 37*, Asif Ali 41*); ‡**Zimbabwe 108** (17.5 overs) (T. K. Musakanda 43). *MoM: Asif Ali. T20I debuts: T. K. Musakanda, J. C. Nyumbu (Zimbabwe). A modest 78-3 at halfway, Pakistan looked as if they might struggle to deliver the predicted thrashing. Then Fakhar Zaman, Shoaib Malik and Asif Ali moved up a gear. Asif's career-best 41* came off 21 balls, with six sixes, as Pakistan added 61 from the last five overs. Kyle Jarvis bowled his first two for nine, but in the 14th broke a thumb trying to catch Fakhar at long-on, and was ruled out of the tournament. Zimbabwe appeared resigned to their fate, and only a fluent 43 from Tarisai Musakanda on debut cheered the locals.*

At Harare, July 2. **Australia won by nine wickets. Zimbabwe 116** (19.5 overs) (B. Stanlake 4-8, A. J. Tye 3-38); ‡**Australia 117-1** (10.5 overs) (A. J. Finch 68*). *MoM: B. Stanlake. A stunning opening burst from Billy Stanlake settled a one-sided encounter. Using his height to full effect, he confirmed the good impression he had made in the one-dayers in England. Aaron Finch, who shrewdly let him bowl four overs off the reel, accounted for three of the victims at slip, but Fakhar – caught behind attempting to hook – might have been reprieved if there had been the budget for DRS. Stanlake's figures were the second-best for Australia in T20s, with the best four-over economy-rate. Pakistan were not allowed to rebuild: Shoaib, in his 100th T20 international, ran himself out, and Andrew Tye took three late wickets. Finch looked keen to secure an early finish: his 68* included six sixes. It was 119 days since Australia's previous victory in any format, in the First Test against South Africa at Durban.*

At Harare, July 3. **Australia won by 100 runs. Australia 229-2** (20 overs) (A. J. Finch 172, D. J. M. Short 46); ‡**Zimbabwe 129-9** (20 overs) (A. J. Tye 3-12). *MoM: A. J. Finch. With a blistering assault on a feeble Zimbabwe attack, Finch set a T20 international record. In hitting 172 from 76 balls (16 fours, ten sixes), he passed his own 156 against England at Southampton in 2013. After being put in, Australia galloped to 75-0 in the powerplay. Finch reached his 50 in 22 balls, and his hundred in 50. D'Arcy Short sensibly assumed a supporting role as they established a record all-wicket partnership in T20 internationals of 223 – thrashing the previous mark by 52. Both fell in the final over, Finch hitting his wicket trying to smash a six that would have taken him past Chris Gayle's T20-record 175*, for Royal Challengers Bangalore in the IPL in 2013. Amid the carnage, Tendai Chisoro went for just 19. Zimbabwe were never in the hunt, Ashton Agar and Tye both performing impressively. It was Australia's biggest win by runs – and Zimbabwe's heaviest defeat.*

At Harare, July 4. **Pakistan won by seven wickets. Zimbabwe 162-4** (20 overs) (S. F. Mire 94, T. K. Musakanda 33); ‡**Pakistan 163-3** (19.1 overs) (Fakhar Zaman 47, Hussain Talat 44, Sarfraz Ahmed 38*). *MoM: S. F. Mire. There were crumbs of comfort for Zimbabwe in taking Pakistan to the last over. But defeat extinguished any hope of making the final. Solomon Mire, who had top-scored in the futile chase against Australia, prospered again, with 94 from 63 balls, a Zimbabwean T20 record. He received good support from Musakanda in a stand of 64. Pakistan appeared in control until Fakhar was removed by Mire for 47. They needed 28 off three overs, but the experience of Sarfraz Ahmed and Shoaib saw them through with five balls in hand.*

At Harare, July 5. **Pakistan won by 45 runs. Pakistan 149-7** (20 overs) (Fakhar Zaman 73, Hussain Talat 30, Asif Ali 37*; A. J. Tye 3-35); ‡**Australia 149-7** (20 overs) (A. T. Carey 37*; Shaheen Shah Afridi 3-37). *MoM: Fakhar Zaman. In midwinter conditions, and in front of a crowd of less than 100, Pakistan thwarted Australia's attempt to seize their No. 1 ranking. A straightforward victory also put them in good heart for their meeting in the final three days later. Fakhar again assumed command after Finch had put them in. He hit 73 in 42 balls, and others chipped in before*

Asif clobbered 37* off 18. Pakistan's seamers undermined Australia from the start, with Shaheen Shah Afridi fulfilling – he later claimed – a premonition that his first two international wickets would be Finch and Glenn Maxwell. Alex Carey prevented a rout, but Australia were left to reconsider their plans for the final.

At Harare, July 6. **Australia won by five wickets.** ‡**Zimbabwe 151-9** (20 overs) (S. F. Mire 63, P. J. Moor 30; A. J. Tye 3-28); **Australia 154-5** (19.5 overs) (T. M. Head 48, G. J. Maxwell 56; B. Muzarabani 3-21). *MoM:* A. J. Tye. *T20I debuts:* B. A. Mavuta (Zimbabwe); J. D. Wildermuth (Australia). *Marcus Stoinis struck the winning boundary off Donald Tiripano with a ball to spare after Australia threatened to make a mess of what had appeared a stroll. Zimbabwe were again left with nothing to show from a much improved performance. Mire shone with 63 off 52, but Tye underlined his status as the best bowler in the tournament with his fourth successive three-wicket haul. There were no Finch fireworks this time; instead Travis Head and Maxwell, who hit five sixes, added 103. Maxwell's dismissal prompted a stumble which almost cost Australia dearly. Blessing Muzarabani bowled superbly at the beginning and end of the innings.*

Australia 12pts, Pakistan 12pts, Zimbabwe 0pts.

Final At Harare, July 8. **Pakistan won by six wickets.** ‡**Australia 183-8** (20 overs) (D. J. M. Short 76, A. J. Finch 47; Mohammad Amir 3-33); **Pakistan 187-4** (19.2 overs) (Fakhar Zaman 91, Shoaib Malik 43*). *MoM:* Fakhar Zaman. *MoS:* Fakhar Zaman. *T20I debut:* Sahibzada Farhan (Pakistan). *Pakistan recovered from a calamitous start to complete their highest T20 chase. Not for the first time, Asif provided the cool head with 17* off 11 balls, concluding with a pull through midwicket off Stoinis to take Pakistan over the line. In the opening over, Maxwell had snaffled two wickets, leaving Fakhar and Sarfraz with a rebuilding operation. They soon hit him out of the attack, only for Sarfraz to be carelessly run out. Fakhar's partnership of 107 with Shoaib proved crucial, especially a six-over spell yielding 78. Australia had been on course for a commanding total when Finch and Short put on 95 inside ten overs. But they failed to maintain the momentum, and wickets fell regularly, three to the excellent Mohammad Amir. Short was exempt from criticism with 76 off 53 balls.*

ZIMBABWE v PAKISTAN IN 2018

Liam Brickhill

One-day internationals (5): Zimbabwe 0, Pakistan 5

Rarely can a bilateral series between two Test-playing nations have been so uncompetitive. Even at full strength, Zimbabwe would probably have struggled against an increasingly assertive Pakistan limited-overs side, fresh from their triumph in the T20 tri-series in Harare. But injury and infighting depleted their resources, and a team that might charitably have been called second-string was flattened without mercy.

Mayhem on the field was matched by ineptitude off it. Pakistan's travel plans were put back several days when it emerged that Zimbabwe Cricket had been unable to come up with the money for their hotel booking in Bulawayo. And the Zimbabweans lost their eighth senior squad member when Malcolm Waller pulled out, citing untenable working conditions, via a lawyer's letter to the board.

They had already lost Kyle Jarvis and Solomon Mire to injury at either end of the tri-series, and there seemed no resolution in sight to the stand-off between ZC and five leading players, including former captains Graeme Cremer and Brendan Taylor, and key all-rounder Sikandar Raza. They refused to play unless they received the money owed to them, unpaid fees dating back to the tour of Sri Lanka in July 2017.

Those who remained were hopelessly out of their depth. You could be forgiven for losing track of the various records broken during the series, many of them by Fakhar Zaman, who reached statistical heights he may never again scale. There were personal-bests aplenty in a feeding frenzy of bat and ball, but no one feasted quite as heavily as the openers – Fakhar and the bespectacled Imam-ul-Haq – who scored more than two-thirds of Pakistan's runs. Their four century stands, including a world-record triple in the fourth game, were part of an aggregate partnership of 704. Imam helped himself to three centuries in five innings, while Fakhar scored 515 runs in all, including 455 between dismissals, another record. He averaged a stunning 257, smashed Pakistan's first ODI double-century, and became the quickest from anywhere to reach 1,000 runs, in just 18 innings. Zimbabwe's highest score, by contrast, was a measly 59, by the beleaguered stand-in skipper Hamilton Masakadza.

Each game only added to the dread in the home camp, and Zimbabwe went about the thankless task of bowling to Fakhar and Imam with an impotent

WINNING AN ODI SERIES 5–0 AWAY FROM HOME

West Indies in India	1983-84	Australia in the West Indies	2008
England in Zimbabwe	2001-02	Sri Lanka in Zimbabwe	2008-09
Pakistan in Zimbabwe	2002-03	Zimbabwe in Kenya	2008-09
Sri Lanka in Zimbabwe	2004	South Africa in the West Indies	2010
Australia in New Zealand	2004-05	India in Zimbabwe	2013
South Africa in the West Indies	2005	India in Sri Lanka	2017
Sri Lanka in England	2006	**Pakistan in Zimbabwe**	**2018**

nihilism. The crowds that had filled the grounds during the World Cup Qualifier were nowhere to be seen, and even the sun refused to shine: the whole series was played out under grey skies, in frigid midwinter temperatures.

Pakistan had been whitewashed themselves in their previous one-day series, in New Zealand in January, so gave no quarter this time: they did not remove their collective boot from Zimbabwe's throat until the closing moments of the final match. With the 5–0 scoreline safely in the bag, perhaps the deepest ignominy came with the sight of wicketkeeper Sarfraz Ahmed taking off his pads to deliver two overs of gentle throwdowns to the shell-shocked Zimbabweans. The sacking of Bulawayo was complete.

PAKISTAN TOURING PARTY

Sarfraz Ahmed, Asif Ali, Babar Azam, Fahim Ashraf, Fakhar Zaman, Haris Sohail, Hasan Ali, Imam-ul-Haq, Junaid Khan, Mohammad Amir, Mohammad Hafeez, Mohammad Nawaz, Shadab Khan, Shoaib Malik, Usman Shinwari, Yasir Shah. Coach: J. M. Arthur.

First one-day international At Bulawayo, July 13, 2018. **Pakistan won by 201 runs. Pakistan 308-7** (50 overs) (Imam-ul-Haq 128, Fakhar Zaman 60, Babar Azam 30, Asif Ali 46); ‡**Zimbabwe 107** (35 overs) (R. C. Murray 32*; Shadab Khan 4-32). MoM: Imam-ul-Haq. *ODI debuts:* R. C. Murray, L. N. Roche (Zimbabwe); Asif Ali (Pakistan). *Pakistan's openers took a little time to get going on a cold morning, but eventually added 113 in 24 overs before Fakhar Zaman sent a return catch to the 18-year-old debutant off-spinner Liam Roche. Imam-ul-Haq went on to a 109-ball century, then Pakistan's own debutant, Asif Ali, sped them towards 300 by cracking 46 from 25. Zimbabwe were soon in trouble, dipping to 55-5 against disciplined seam bowling. Another new cap, 20-year-old wicketkeeper Ryan Murray, hung on for over an hour, easily beating his previous-best List A score of 18. But Shadab Khan's leg-spin confounded the tail as Pakistan romped to their first ODI victory of 2018, at the sixth attempt. Zimbabwe's total was the lowest in ODIs at Queens Club – for five days.*

Second one-day international At Bulawayo, July 16, 2018. **Pakistan won by nine wickets. ‡Zimbabwe 194** (49.2 overs) (H. Masakadza 59, P. J. Moor 50; Usman Shinwari 4-36, Hasan Ali 3-32); **Pakistan 195-1** (36 overs) (Imam-ul-Haq 44, Fakhar Zaman 117*). MoM: Fakhar Zaman. *Pakistan's seamers set up a comfortable victory. Usman Shinwari disposed of both openers in single figures, and later took two wickets with successive balls as he and Hasan Ali turned Zimbabwe's 140-4 into 194 all out, aided by some inept running. The game was up as Pakistan's openers purred to 119 in the 21st over, and they were separated only when Imam failed to ground his bat properly while diving for a single. But Fakhar sailed on to his second ODI century during a partnership of 76* with Babar Azam (29*), and the match was won with 14 overs to spare.*

Third one-day international At Bulawayo, July 18, 2018. **Pakistan won by nine wickets. ‡Zimbabwe 67** (25.1 overs) (Fahim Ashraf 5-22); **Pakistan 69-1** (9.5 overs) (Fakhar Zaman 43*). MoM: Fahim Ashraf. *ODI debut:* P. S. Masvaure (Zimbabwe). *Zimbabwe's series lurched from bad to worse as they subsided to their lowest ODI total against Pakistan (previously 94 at Sharjah in April 1997) and the lowest by anyone at Bulawayo. Opener Chamu Chibhabha made 16, but no one else passed ten as Fahim Ashraf demolished the middle order with his skiddy seamers. Imam fended the first ball of the chase, a snorter from Blessing Muzarabani, through to keeper Murray, but that was the only good news for Zimbabwe. Although Fakhar was clanged on the helmet by Richard Ngarava, he and Babar sealed victory (and the series) inside ten overs, with 241 balls to spare, the most for Pakistan. The match ended well before the scheduled mid-innings break.*

Fourth one-day international At Bulawayo, July 20, 2018. **Pakistan won by 244 runs. ‡Pakistan 399-1** (50 overs) (Imam-ul-Haq 113, Fakhar Zaman 210*, Asif Ali 50*); **Zimbabwe 155** (42.4 overs) (E. Chigumbura 37, D. T. Tiripano 44; Shadab Khan 4-28). MoM: Fakhar Zaman. *ODI debut:* T. S. Kamunhukamwe (Zimbabwe). *If Zimbabwe thought things could only get better, they reckoned without Fakhar, who scorched to Pakistan's first double-century in ODIs, beating Saeed Anwar's national record of 194, against India at Chennai in May 1997. Fakhar clattered 24 fours and five sixes from 156 balls, and put on 304 with Imam, a first-wicket record in ODIs. With Asif Ali smacking a 22-ball half-century, Pakistan just missed reaching 400 for the first time; they still eclipsed their*

HIGHEST PARTNERSHIPS IN ODIs

Runs	Wkt			
372	2nd	C. H. Gayle/M. N. Samuels..........	WI v Z at Canberra......	2014-15
331	2nd	S. R. Tendulkar/R. Dravid...........	I v NZ at Hyderabad.....	1999-2000
318	2nd	S. C. Ganguly/R. Dravid............	I v SL at Taunton.......	1999
304	**1st**	**Imam-ul-Haq/Fakhar Zaman**.......	**P v Z at Bulawayo**......	**2018**
286	1st	W. U. Tharanga/S. T. Jayasuriya......	SL v E at Leeds........	2006
284	1st	D. A. Warner/T. M. Head...........	A v P at Adelaide.......	2016-17
282*	1st	Q. de Kock/H. M. Amla............	SA v B at Kimberley.....	2017-18
282	1st	W. U. Tharanga/T. M. Dilshan.......	SL v Z at Pallekele.....	2010-11
275*	4th	M. Azharuddin/A. Jadeja...........	I v Z at Cuttack........	1997-98
274	1st	J. A. H. Marshall/B. B. McCullum....	NZ v Ire at Aberdeen....	2008

previous-highest, 385-7 against Bangladesh at Dambulla in 2010. Facing a hopeless task, Zimbabwe were soon 67-5, before Elton Chigumbura and Donald Tiripano doubled the score. Even so, with Shadab taking four more wickets, Zimbabwe slid to their second-heaviest defeat, after a 272-run thrashing by South Africa at Benoni in 2010-11.

Fifth one-day international At Bulawayo, July 22, 2018. **Pakistan won by 131 runs. ‡Pakistan 364-4** (50 overs) (Imam-ul-Haq 110, Fakhar Zaman 85, Babar Azam 106*); **Zimbabwe 233-4** (50 overs) (H. Masakadza 34, T. S. Kamunhukamwe 34, P. S. Masvaure 39, R. C. Murray 47, P. J. Moor 44*). *MoM:* Babar Azam. *MoS:* Fakhar Zaman. *This was the most competitive match of the series – but Pakistan still won easily, to complete their 5–0 whitewash. The openers motored to 168 before Fakhar was out in the 25th over: it took his aggregate to 515, exceeded in a five-match bilateral rubber only by India's Virat Kohli (558) in South Africa earlier in the year. Fakhar broke two major ODI records: he reached 1,000 runs in his 18th innings (three quicker than anyone), and had also made 455 runs between dismissals, beating 405 by another Pakistani, Mohammad Yousuf, in 2002. Imam made his third hundred of the series, while Babar scorched to three figures in 72 balls, the second fifty needing only 17. Shoaib Malik passed 7,000 runs in ODIs during his 18. Zimbabwe made a better fist of another unlikely chase: openers Hamilton Masakadza and newcomer Tinashe Kamunhukamwe put on 66, then Prince Masvaure added 78 with Murray. But the asking-rate kept climbing and, in the end, Moor and Chigumbura (25*) batted out time.*

FASTEST TO 1,000 RUNS IN ODIs

I		M	HS	100	Avge
18	**Fakhar Zaman (Pakistan)**....................	**18**	**210***	**3**	**76.07**
21	I. V. A. Richards (West Indies)..................	22	153*	3	70.60
21	K. P. Pietersen (England).......................	27	116	3	67.00
21	I. J. L. Trott (England).........................	21	137	3	54.11
21	Babar Azam (Pakistan).........................	21	123	3	51.85
21	Q. de Kock (South Africa)......................	21	135	5	47.67
23	R. N. ten Doeschate (Netherlands)..............	24	109*	2	64.13
23	C. G. Greenidge (West Indies)..................	23	106*	2	53.65
23	Azhar Ali (Pakistan)...........................	23	102	2	51.85
24	G. M. Turner (New Zealand)....................	25	171*	2	58.94
24	H. M. Amla (South Africa)......................	25	140	2	51.00
24	V. Kohli (India)...............................	27	107	2	50.75
24	S. Dhawan (India).............................	24	116	4	45.45
24	Yasir Hameed (Pakistan).......................	24	127*	2	44.35

DOMESTIC CRICKET IN ZIMBABWE IN 2017-18

JOHN WARD

The domestic game continued to suffer from Zimbabwe Cricket's huge debts, as well as poor planning and budgeting. The first-class Logan Cup began in October, but halted abruptly in early December, after 14 matches, when the money to stage it ran out. Plans to restart in January fell through, and the remaining six games, plus the one-day Pro50 Championship – which had managed only two before the enforced break – were eventually squeezed into April and May. For the fourth time in five seasons, the Twenty20 tournament was scrapped. Domestic cricket was also disrupted by the international programme, training camps and the unavailability of players; on top of injuries, some refused to continue as they had not been paid, and others had to leave to fulfil overseas contracts.

The four regular provincial sides were joined by **Rising Stars**, a team of young players, most of whom had visited England in 2017 on a non-first-class tour organised by former Test captain Tatenda Taibu. Despite a promising pace attack, inexperience meant they finished last in the Logan Cup, though they beat Bulawayo Tuskers by 268 runs, with a maiden century from Somerset's Harare-born Ed Byrom. (He advanced past 150, which earned his side an extra batting point under a new system.) But they came into their own in the Pro50, where their fire and enthusiasm overcame weakened opposition; they headed the table and beat Mountaineers in the final. Several players appeared for the national team: the tall fast bowler Blessing Muzarabani soon became Zimbabwe's spearhead (though in September 2018 he signed a three-year Kolpak deal with Northamptonshire). Among the batsmen, the steady Ryan Burl, the brilliant but profligate Tarisai Musakanda and explosive opener Tinashe Kamunhukamwe also played for Zimbabwe, along with seamer Richard Ngarava, leg-spinner Brandon Mavuta and Ryan Murray, a wicketkeeper-batsman studying at Cape Town University.

Overall, though, the most powerful team remained **Manicaland Mountaineers**, whose strength in depth meant they were less affected by injuries and international call-ups. The season's outstanding domestic cricketer was Donald Tiripano, who captained the side when Tino Mawoyo was unavailable. One of only four players to appear in all Logan Cup matches, he scored 678 at 75 to head the averages, and took 30 wickets at 21. Another seamer, Victor Nyauchi, claimed 31 at 22. Mohammad Eqlakh, an Indian from rural Uttar Pradesh, scored 153 not out against Rising Stars – only to be deported for outstaying his visa. In their final game, 28-year-old Ngoni Mupamba scored a century on debut.

Perhaps the match of the season was Mountaineers' opening fixture, against Midlands Rhinos. Needing 328, a depleted Rhinos reached 321 for six, after a magnificent century from Prince Masvaure. But three wickets in 12 balls from Nyauchi, plus a run-out, saw Mountaineers win by two runs. Their main enemy was complacency: another second-string Rhinos side inflicted their only defeat, in April.

Runners-up **Harare Metropolitan Eagles** were led by Tino Mutombodzi, who enjoyed his best season with the bat and revived his leg-spin. Opener Cephas Zhuwao, just short of his 33rd birthday, turned a maiden century into 265, a Logan Cup record, against Rhinos, bludgeoning 12 sixes. He was recalled by Zimbabwe, but found international bowling a stiffer challenge.

Bulawayo Metropolitan Tuskers had a strong all-round attack, led by medium-pacer Ernest Masuku, who took 32 wickets at 23, but too often inconsistent batting proved their downfall. **Midlands Rhinos** had 11 national players – including Brendan Taylor, Kyle Jarvis and Solomon Mire, who had recently returned to resume their international careers – but five played only once. The capable wicketkeeper Nyasha Mayavo finally found his confidence as a batsman, averaging 50.

Zimbabwe has plenty of raw talent, but the tribulations of the governing body and the country itself have robbed them of several top players, while many who remain are afflicted by lethargy and a lack of cricketing nous.

FIRST-CLASS AVERAGES IN 2017-18

BATTING (350 runs)

		M	I	NO	R	HS	100	Avge	Ct/St
1	D. T. Tiripano (*Manicaland Mountaineers*)	8	14	5	678	121	1	75.33	3
2	C. T. Mutombodzi (*Harare Met Eagles*)...	7	12	2	654	122	2	65.40	5
3	R. Nyathi (*Midlands Rhinos*).	4	7	1	372	131	1	62.00	1
4	†C. Zhuwao (*Harare Metropolitan Eagles*)	7	14	0	821	265	2	58.64	4
5	Sikandar Raza (*Bul Met Tuskers/Zim*)	4	8	0	414	110	1	51.75	1
6	†R. P. Burl (*Rising Stars*)	5	9	1	401	134	1	50.12	6
7	N. P. Mayavo (*Midlands Rhinos*)	7	12	1	550	149	2	50.00	14/1
8	R. Mutumbami (*Bulawayo Met Tuskers*) ..	7	12	3	442	92*	0	49.11	8
9	F. Mutizwa (*Manicaland Mountaineers*)...	6	10	1	439	124*	1	48.77	6
10	†C. R. Ervine (*Bulawayo Met Tuskers/Zim*).	6	11	1	481	98*	0	48.10	7
11	R. W. Chakabva (*Harare Met Eagles/Zim*)	7	14	2	553	138	1	46.08	13/3
12	†B. M. Chapungu (*Midlands Rhinos*)	6	12	1	496	128	1	45.09	7
13	†P. S. Masvaure (*Midlands Rhinos*)	6	12	0	506	124	3	42.16	7
14	B. B. Chari (*Bulawayo Met Tuskers*)......	6	12	1	432	127	1	39.27	3
15	T. K. Musakanda (*Rising Stars*)	6	10	0	374	80	0	37.40	7
16	K. O. Maunze (*Harare Met Eagles*)	6	12	1	405	78	0	36.81	2
17	C. Ncube (*Bulawayo Metropolitan Tuskers*)	7	13	0	357	136	1	27.46	5/1

BOWLING (15 wickets)

		Style	O	M	R	W	BB	5I	Avge
1	B. Muzarabani (*Rising Stars*)............	RFM	91.1	17	324	18	5-32	1	18.00
2	Sikandar Raza (*Bul Met Tuskers/Zim*).....	OB	121.5	29	318	17	5-99	1	18.70
3	D. T. Tiripano (*Mountaineers*)..........	RFM	216.2	47	641	30	4-23	0	21.36
4	A. G. Cremer (*Midlands Rhinos/Zim*).....	LB	146.4	27	421	19	5-40	2	22.15
5	V. M. Nyauchi (*Mountaineers*)...........	RFM	215.1	49	707	31	4-41	0	22.80
6	C. T. Mutombodzi (*Harare Met Eagles*)...	LB	130.1	20	483	21	5-60	1	23.00
7	E. Masuku (*Bulawayo Met Tuskers*).......	RM	186.4	36	738	32	5-69	1	23.06
8	J. C. Nyumbu (*Bulawayo Met Tuskers*)	OB	216.5	55	513	21	4-49	0	24.42
9	B. A. Mavuta (*Rising Stars*)............	LB	175.4	21	661	27	4-35	0	24.48
10	S. C. Williams (*Bul Met Tuskers/Zim*)....	SLA	130.2	24	415	16	4-26	0	25.93
11	T. S. Chisoro (*Midlands Rhinos/Zim*)....	SLA/LFM	259.5	65	822	31	8-94	3	26.51
12	C. B. Mpofu (*Bul Met Tuskers/Zim*)......	RFM	178.3	52	419	15	5-32	1	27.93
13	T. L. Chatara (*Mountaineers*)...........	RFM	150.5	30	497	15	4-73	0	33.13
14	M. T. Chinouya (*Midlands Rhinos*)	RFM	189.1	43	595	17	4-25	0	35.00
15	W. P. Masakadza (*Mountaineers*)..........	SLA	161.2	27	543	15	6-132	1	36.20
16	N. Ncube (*Rising Stars*)	RFM	155.5	23	612	15	5-109	1	40.80
17	T. Mufudza (*Harare Met Eagles*).........	OB	263.1	42	933	19	5-205	1	49.10

LOGAN CUP IN 2017-18

					1st-	Bonus pts		
	P	W	L	D	inns	Bat	Bowl	Pts
Manicaland Mountaineers	8	4	1	3	7	8	12	57
Harare Metropolitan Eagles	8	3	2	3	2	12	11	49
Bulawayo Metropolitan Tuskers	8	3	3	2	3	7	12	44
Midlands Rhinos.............	8	2	3	3	5	4	10	37
Rising Stars.................	8	1	4	3	3	5	9	29

Win = 6pts; draw = 2pts; lead on first innings = 1pt. Bonus points were awarded as follows in either innings: one batting point for a team reaching 300 and for each subsequent 100, one batting point for a batsman scoring 150, and one bowling point for a team taking ten wickets.

LOGAN CUP WINNERS

1993-94	Mashonaland U24		2006-07	Easterns
1994-95	Mashonaland		2007-08	Northerns
1995-96	Mashonaland		2008-09	Easterns
1996-97	Mashonaland		2009-10	Mashonaland Eagles
1997-98	Mashonaland		2010-11	Matabeleland Tuskers
1998-99	Mashonaland		2011-12	Matabeleland Tuskers
1999-2000	Mashonaland		2012-13	Matabeleland Tuskers
2000-01	Mashonaland		2013-14	Mountaineers
2001-02	Mashonaland		2014-15	Matabeleland Tuskers
2002-03	Mashonaland		2015-16	Mashonaland Eagles
2003-04	Mashonaland		2016-17	Manicaland Mountaineers
2004-05	Mashonaland		2017-18	Manicaland Mountaineers
2005-06	*No competition*			

PRO50 CHAMPIONSHIP IN 2017-18

50-over league

	P	W	L	NR	Bonus	Pts	NRR
Rising Stars.....................	8	5	2	1	3	25	0.95
Manicaland Mountaineers	8	4	3	1	3	21	0.28
Bulawayo Metropolitan Tuskers........	8	4	3	1	2	20	0.08
Harare Metropolitan Eagles	8	3	5	0	0	12	−0.61
Midlands Rhinos...................	8	2	5	1	1	11	−0.55

Final At Harare (Takashinga), June 2, 2018. **Rising Stars won by 144 runs. Rising Stars 281-9** (50 overs) ((D. T. Tiripano 6-55); ‡**Manicaland Mountaineers 137** (30.1 overs) (B. A. Mavuta 8-38). *Leg-spinner Brandon Mavuta clinched the title and became the first man to take eight in a List A game in Zimbabwe – eclipsing the earlier performance of Donald Tiripano, who claimed a career-best six as Rising Stars lost five late wickets for 23.*

INTERNATIONAL RESULTS IN 2018

TEST MATCHES

	Tests	W	L	D	% won	% lost	% drawn
England	13	8	4	1	**61.53**	30.76	7.69
South Africa..........	10	6	4	0	**60.00**	40.00	0.00
New Zealand	7	4	1	2	**57.14**	14.28	28.57
India.................	14	7	7	0	**50.00**	50.00	0.00
Zimbabwe	2	1	1	0	**50.00**	50.00	0.00
Pakistan	9	4	4	1	**44.44**	44.44	11.11
Bangladesh............	8	3	4	1	**37.50**	50.00	12.50
Sri Lanka	12	4	5	3	**33.33**	41.66	25.00
West Indies...........	9	3	5	1	**33.33**	55.55	11.11
Australia.............	10	3	6	1	**30.00**	60.00	10.00
Ireland	1	0	1	0	**0.00**	100.00	0.00
Afghanistan	1	0	1	0	**0.00**	100.00	0.00
Totals	48	43	43	5	**89.58**	89.58	10.41

ONE-DAY INTERNATIONALS (Full Members only)

	ODIs	W	L	T	NR	% won	% lost
England	23	17	5	0	1	**77.27**	22.72
India.................	19	13	4	2	0	**73.68**	26.31
Afghanistan	17	11	5	1	0	**67.64**	32.35
New Zealand	13	8	4	0	1	**66.66**	33.33
Bangladesh............	20	13	7	0	0	**65.00**	35.00
South Africa..........	17	9	8	0	0	**52.94**	47.05
Pakistan	17	7	9	0	1	**43.75**	56.25
Sri Lanka	17	6	10	0	1	**37.50**	62.50
West Indies...........	15	5	9	1	0	**36.66**	63.33
Zimbabwe	23	4	19	0	0	**17.39**	82.60
Ireland	6	1	5	0	0	**16.66**	83.33
Australia.............	13	2	11	0	0	**15.38**	84.61
Totals	100	96	96	2	2		

Matches between Full Members only. The % won/lost excludes no-results; ties count as half a win.
The following also played official ODIs in 2018, some against Full Members (not included above):
Scotland (P11 W5 L5 T1); Netherlands (P2 W1 L1); UAE (P11 W4 L7); Nepal (P3 W1 L2); Papua New Guinea (P4 W1 L3); Hong Kong (P6 W1 L5).

TWENTY20 INTERNATIONALS (Full Members only)

	T20Is	W	L	NR	% won	% lost
Afghanistan	7	7	0	0	**100.00**	0.00
Pakistan	17	15	2	0	**88.23**	11.76
India.................	19	14	4	1	**77.77**	22.22
South Africa..........	7	4	3	0	**57.14**	42.85
Australia.............	18	9	8	1	**52.94**	47.05
Sri Lanka	8	4	4	0	**50.00**	50.00
England	9	4	5	0	**44.44**	55.55
Bangladesh............	16	5	11	0	**31.25**	68.75
New Zealand	13	3	9	1	**25.00**	75.00
West Indies...........	14	3	10	1	**23.07**	76.92
Ireland	4	0	4	0	**0.00**	100.00
Zimbabwe	8	0	8	0	**0.00**	100.00
Totals	70	68	68	2		

Matches between Full Members only. The % won/lost excludes no-results.
The following also played official T20Is in 2018, some against Full Members (not included above):
Netherlands (P5 W2 L2 NR1); Scotland (P6 W2 L3 T1); UAE (P1 L1); World XI (P1 L1); Nepal (P1 NR1).

MRF TYRES ICC TEAM RANKINGS

TEST CHAMPIONSHIP (As at January 14, 2019)

		Matches	Points	Rating
1	India	43	5,007	116
2	South Africa	39	4,280	110
3	England	49	5,310	108
4	New Zealand	30	3,213	107
5	Australia	41	4,143	101
6	Sri Lanka	45	4,103	91
7	Pakistan	32	2,803	88
8	West Indies	35	2,463	70
9	Bangladesh	25	1,727	69
10	Zimbabwe	11	138	13

Afghanistan and Ireland each had a rating of 0 from one Test, insufficient to achieve a ranking.

ONE-DAY CHAMPIONSHIP (As at December 31, 2018)

		Matches	Points	Rating
1	England	55	6,918	126
2	India	58	7,000	121
3	New Zealand	43	4,803	112
4	South Africa	45	4,985	111
5	Pakistan	43	4,370	102
6	Australia	40	3,980	100
7	Bangladesh	39	3,608	93
8	Sri Lanka	54	4,240	79
9	West Indies	40	2,899	72
10	Afghanistan	36	2,394	67
11	Zimbabwe	48	2,497	52
12	Ireland	23	904	39
13	Scotland	16	535	33
14	United Arab Emirates	14	298	21

The Netherlands had a rating of 8 and Nepal 5; neither had played enough matches for a ranking.

TWENTY20 CHAMPIONSHIP (As at December 31, 2018)

		Matches	Points	Rating
1	Pakistan	36	4,979	138
2	India	42	5,298	126
3	England	22	2,586	118
4	Australia	28	3,266	117
5	South Africa	22	2,502	114
6	New Zealand	25	2,803	112
7	West Indies	27	2,725	101
8	Afghanistan	27	2,490	92
9	Sri Lanka	29	2,518	87
10	Bangladesh	30	2,321	77
11	Scotland	15	927	62
12	Zimbabwe	20	1,097	55
13	United Arab Emirates	13	649	50
14	Netherlands	12	598	50
15	Hong Kong	10	420	42
16	Oman	7	270	39
17	Ireland	19	638	34

Nepal had a rating of 26, but had not played enough matches for a ranking.

The ratings are based on all Test series, one-day and Twenty20 internationals since May 1, 2015.

MRF TYRES ICC PLAYER RANKINGS

Introduced in 1987, the rankings have been backed by various sponsors, but were taken over by the ICC in January 2005. They rank cricketers on a scale up to 1,000 on their performances in Tests. The rankings take into account playing conditions, the quality of the opposition and the result of the matches. In August 1998, a similar set of rankings for one-day internationals was launched, and Twenty20 rankings were added in October 2011.

The leading players in the Test rankings on January 14, 2019, were:

	Batsmen	Points		Bowlers	Points
1	V. Kohli (I)	922	1	K. Rabada (SA)	882
2	K. S. Williamson (NZ)	897	2	J. M. Anderson (E)	874
3	C. A. Pujara (I)	881	3	V. D. Philander (SA)	809
4	S. P. D. Smith (A)	874	4	P. J. Cummins (A)	804
5	J. E. Root (E)	807	5	R. A. Jadeja (I)	794
6	D. A. Warner (A)	772	6	T. A. Boult (NZ)	771
7	H. M. Nicholls (NZ)	763	7	Mohammad Abbas (P)	770
8	A. K. Markram (SA)	741	8	T. G. Southee (NZ)	767
9	F. D. M. Karunaratne (SL)	715	9	R. Ashwin (I)	763
10	H. M. Amla (SA)	711	10	J. O. Holder (WI)	751

The leading players in the one-day international rankings on December 31, 2018, were:

	Batsmen	Points		Bowlers	Points
1	V. Kohli (I)	899	1	J. J. Bumrah (I)	841
2	R. G. Sharma (I)	871	2	Rashid Khan (Afg)	788
3	L. R. P. L. Taylor (NZ)	808	3	K. Yadav (I)	723
4	J. E. Root (E)	807	4	K. Rabada (SA)	702
5	Babar Azam (P)	802	5	Mustafizur Rahman (B)	695
6	D. A. Warner (A)	791	6	Y. S. Chahal (I)	683
7	F. du Plessis (SA)	785		A. U. Rashid (E)	683
8	S. D. Hope (WI)	780	8	T. A. Boult (NZ)	682
9	S. Dhawan (I)	767	9	Mujeeb Zadran (Afg)	679
10	K. S. Williamson (NZ)	756	10	J. R. Hazlewood (A)	675

The leading players in the Twenty20 international rankings on December 31, 2018, were:

	Batsmen	Points		Bowlers	Points
1	Babar Azam (P)	858	1	Rashid Khan (Afg)	793
2	C. Munro (NZ)	815	2	Shadab Khan (P)	752
3	A. J. Finch (A)	806	3	K. Yadav (I)	714
4	E. Lewis (WI)	751	4	A. U. Rashid (E)	676
5	Fakhar Zaman (P)	749	5	A. Zampa (A)	670
6	G. J. Maxwell (A)	745	6	I. S. Sodhi (NZ)	668
7	K. L. Rahul (I)	719	7	Shakib Al Hasan (B)	658
8	M. J. Guptill (NZ)	703	8	Fahim Ashraf (P)	652
9	A. D. Hales (E)	697	9	Imad Wasim (P)	651
10	R. G. Sharma (I)	689	10	Imran Tahir (SA)	640

TEST AVERAGES IN CALENDAR YEAR 2018

BATTING (350 runs)

	T	I	NO	R	HS	100	50	Avge	SR	Ct/St
1 †H. M. Nicholls (NZ)	7	12	3	658	162*	3	3	73.11	48.66	7
2 †T. W. M. Latham (NZ)	7	12	1	658	264*	2	2	59.81	43.06	6
3 K. S. Williamson (NZ)	7	12	1	651	139	2	3	59.18	54.47	7
4 Babar Azam (P)	8	14	3	616	127*	1	6	56.00	54.46	6
5 V. Kohli (I)	13	24	0	1,322	153	5	5	55.08	54.33	12
6 A. B. de Villiers (SA)	7	14	2	638	126*	1	6	53.16	64.44	17
7 A. D. Mathews (SL)	8	16	3	640	120*	1	5	49.23	46.07	10
8 B. K. G. Mendis (SL)	12	23	1	1,023	196	3	4	46.50	54.64	21
9 †F. D. M. Karunaratne (SL)	9	17	1	743	158*	1	7	46.43	56.63	6
10 †Mominul Haque (B)	8	15	0	673	176	4	0	44.86	66.30	7
11 J. C. Buttler (E)	10	18	1	760	106	1	6	44.70	68.10	9
12 J. E. Root (E)	13	24	1	948	125	2	6	41.21	53.19	9
13 L. D. Chandimal (SL)	7	12	1	448	119*	1	2	40.72	40.87	5
14 †U. T. Khawaja (A)	10	18	0	732	171	2	4	40.66	43.33	8
15 Mahmudullah (B)	8	13	3	476	136	2	1	39.66	54.71	3
16 †Haris Sohail (P)	8	15	1	550	147	2	0	39.28	43.17	8
17 †R. R. Pant (I)	8	14	0	537	114	1	2	38.35	71.22	40/2
18 C. A. Pujara (I)	13	23	1	837	132*	3	4	38.04	38.46	5
19 †S. O. Hetmyer (WI)	5	10	0	376	93	0	3	37.60	83.74	2
20 †S. M. Curran (E)	7	12	1	404	78	0	3	36.72	57.87	0
21 †D. Elgar (SA)	10	20	2	661	141*	1	5	36.72	38.95	13
22 S. O. Dowrich (WI)	9	17	4	474	125*	1	3	36.46	43.13	26
23 A. R. S. Silva (SL)	10	19	2	616	109	1	4	36.23	41.70	2
24 B-J. Watling (NZ)	7	11	1	355	85	0	3	35.50	37.36	29/1
25 T. D. Paine (A)	10	19	5	493	62	0	2	35.21	41.39	41/2
26 Mushfiqur Rahim (B)	8	15	1	490	219*	1	1	35.00	49.24	8/2
27 A. K. Markram (SA)	10	20	0	672	152	2	3	33.60	61.14	7
28 Asad Shafiq (P)	9	16	0	536	104	1	3	33.50	48.99	13
29 A. M. Rahane (I)	12	21	0	644	81	0	5	30.66	44.04	14
30 J. M. Bairstow (E)	11	20	0	609	110	2	3	30.45	53.51	29/2
31 Azhar Ali (P)	9	17	0	517	134	1	4	30.41	39.89	1
32 †Imam-ul-Haq (P)	8	15	2	391	76	0	3	30.07	48.09	7
33 †A. N. Cook (E)	10	18	0	516	147	1	2	28.66	44.06	19
34 †K. K. Jennings (E)	9	16	1	425	146*	1	0	28.33	47.59	12
35 †B. A. Stokes (E)	10	20	0	537	66	0	4	26.85	46.09	11
36 H. M. Amla (SA)	10	20	1	510	82	0	5	26.84	41.29	7
37 D. M. de Silva (SL)	10	19	0	509	173	1	3	26.78	59.32	18
38 †D. P. D. N. Dickwella (SL)	12	22	2	519	80*	0	3	25.95	66.36	30/6
39 †S. E. Marsh (A)	10	19	0	492	156	1	1	25.89	42.01	3
40 H. H. Pandya (I)	8	15	1	354	93	0	3	25.28	63.78	3
41 K. C. Brathwaite (WI)	9	17	1	391	121	2	1	24.43	34.63	3
42 F. du Plessis (SA)	10	20	1	463	120	1	2	24.36	52.91	13
43 R. L. Chase (WI)	9	17	0	396	106	1	1	23.29	52.17	6
44 †K. O. A. Powell (WI)	9	17	0	391	88	0	2	23.00	66.15	1
45 K. L. Rahul (I)	12	22	1	468	149	1	1	22.28	59.01	17
46 †Q. de Kock (SA)	10	18	0	392	83	0	2	21.77	67.70	45/2

BOWLING (12 wickets)

	Style	O	M	R	W	BB	5I	Avge	SR
1 J. O. Holder (WI)	RFM	150.1	38	409	33	6-59	4	12.39	27.30
2 Mohammad Abbas (P)	RFM	230.1	82	523	38	5-33	2	13.76	36.34
3 V. D. Philander (SA)	RFM	236.2	82	545	32	6-21	2	17.03	44.31
4 T. G. Southee (NZ)	RFM	212	59	552	29	6-62	2	19.03	43.86

		Style	O	M	R	W	BB	5I	Avge	SR
5	Mohammad Amir (P)	LFM	126.3	36	307	16	4-36	0	19.18	47.43
6	Shakib Al Hasan (B)......	SLA	113.4	18	329	17	6-33	1	19.35	40.11
7	L. T. Ngidi (SA)	RFM	103.1	28	293	15	6-39	1	19.53	41.26
8	S. T. Gabriel (WI)	RF	189.2	28	723	37	8-62	3	19.54	30.70
9	M. Morkel (SA)..........	RF	188.5	51	554	28	5-23	1	19.78	40.46
10	P. J. Cummins (A)........	RF	314.1	65	879	44	6-27	2	19.97	42.84
11	K. Rabada (SA)..........	RF	331.1	73	1,044	52	6-54	2	20.07	38.21
12	J. J. Bumrah (I)	RFM	379.4	89	1,009	48	6-33	3	21.02	47.45
13	U. T. Yadav (I)	RF	126.5	17	428	20	6-88	1	21.40	38.05
14	I. Sharma (I)	RFM	335	71	894	41	5-51	1	21.80	49.02
15	Mehedi Hasan (B)........	OB	299.1	53	907	41	7-58	4	22.12	43.78
16	K. A. J. Roach (WI)	RFM	134	30	424	19	5-8	1	22.31	42.31
17	R. A. Jadeja (I)	SLA	197.4	30	558	25	4-17	0	22.32	47.44
18	J. M. Anderson (E)	RFM	391.4	113	968	43	5-20	1	22.51	54.65
19	Taijul Islam (B).........	SLA	333.1	57	988	43	6-33	4	22.97	46.48
20	Yasir Shah (P)...........	LB	315	61	894	38	8-41	3	23.52	49.73
21	T. A. Boult (NZ).........	LFM	281.1	75	789	33	6-30	2	23.90	51.12
22	A. Dananjaya (SL)	OB	168.5	26	655	27	6-115	3	24.25	37.51
23	M. J. Leach (E)	SLA	193.4	34	498	20	5-83	1	24.90	58.10
24	S. M. Curran (E).........	LFM	106.5	15	352	14	4-74	0	25.14	45.78
25	R. Ashwin (I)............	OB	386	88	964	38	4-27	0	25.36	60.94
26	Hasan Ali (P)............	RFM	184.2	51	574	22	5-45	1	26.09	50.27
27	Bilal Asif (P)............	OB	195.4	40	424	16	6-36	2	26.50	73.37
28	Mohammed Shami (I).....	RFM	383.5	68	1,268	47	6-56	2	26.97	49.00
29	B. A. Stokes (E).........	RFM	179.2	31	602	22	4-40	0	27.36	48.90
30	R. A. S. Lakmal (SL)......	RFM	304.2	67	859	31	5-54	1	27.70	58.90
31	S. C. J. Broad (E)........	RFM	331.2	79	990	35	6-54	1	28.28	56.80
32	C. B. R. L. S. Kumara (SL).	RF	206.5	30	743	26	4-58	0	28.57	47.73
33	H. M. R. K. B. Herath (SL).	SLA	267.2	44	773	27	6-98	2	28.62	59.40
34	M. M. Ali (E)............	OB	265	34	922	32	5-63	1	28.81	49.68
35	P. A. D. L. R. Sandakan (SL)	SLW	86.5	5	346	12	5-95	1	28.83	43.41
36	C. R. Woakes (E)	RFM	108	20	347	12	3-55	0	28.91	54.00
37	M. D. K. Perera (SL)......	OB	470	64	1,466	50	6-32	3	29.32	56.40
38	A. U. Rashid (E)	LB	186	17	647	22	5-49	1	29.40	50.72
39	J. R. Hazlewood (A)......	RFM	317.2	80	865	26	3-52	0	33.26	73.23
40	K. A. Maharaj (SA).......	SLA	329.3	50	1,131	34	9-129	2	33.26	58.14
41	H. H. Pandya (I)	RFM	124.1	16	433	13	5-28	1	33.30	57.30
42	M. A. Starc (A)	LF	320.3	69	1,034	31	5-34	1	33.35	62.03
43	N. M. Lyon (A)..........	OB	615.3	114	1,667	49	6-122	2	34.02	75.36
44	A. Y. Patel (NZ)	SLA	178.5	41	466	13	5-59	1	35.84	82.53
45	N. Wagner (NZ)	LFM	219.4	58	550	14	4-48	0	39.28	94.14
46	D. Bishoo (WI)	LB	192.1	16	676	15	4-26	0	45.06	76.86

MOST DISMISSALS BY A WICKETKEEPER

Dis		T			Dis		T		
47	(45ct, 2st)	10	Q. de Kock (SA)		32	(29ct, 3st)	9	Sarfraz Ahmed (P)	
43	(41ct, 2st)	10	T. D. Paine (A)		31	(29ct, 2st)	9	J. M. Bairstow (E)	
42	(40ct, 2st)	8	R. R. Pant (I)		30	(29ct, 1st)	7	B-J. Watling (NZ)	
36	(30ct, 6st)	12	D. P. D. N. Dickwella (SL)						

Bairstow played two further Tests when not keeping wicket, but took no catches.

MOST CATCHES IN THE FIELD

Ct	T			Ct	T	
21	12	B. K. G. Mendis (SL)		17	7	A. B. de Villiers (SA)
19	10	A. N. Cook (E)		17	12	K. L. Rahul (I)
18	10	D. M. de Silva (SL)		16	9	S. D. Hope (WI)

ONE-DAY INTERNATIONAL AVERAGES
IN CALENDAR YEAR 2018

BATTING (400 runs)

		M	I	NO	R	HS	100	50	Avge	SR	4	6
1	V. Kohli (I)	14	14	5	1,202	160*	6	3	133.55	102.55	123	13
2	L. R. P. L. Taylor (NZ) . .	11	10	3	639	181*	2	4	91.28	88.87	48	7
3	†Tamim Iqbal (B)	12	12	4	684	130*	2	5	85.50	76.33	57	9
4	Rameez Shahzad (UAE) . .	8	8	2	472	121*	2	3	78.66	87.08	43	10
5	R. G. Sharma (I)	19	19	5	1,030	162	5	3	73.57	100.09	104	39
6	†Fakhar Zaman (P)	17	17	4	875	210*	2	6	67.30	96.47	101	13
7	S. D. Hope (WI)	18	18	5	875	146*	3	3	67.30	74.59	60	15
8	Imrul Kayes (B)	8	8	1	436	144	2	2	62.28	90.45	38	8
9	F. du Plessis (SA)	8	8	1	434	125	2	0	62.00	96.23	44	6
10	†Imam-ul-Haq (P)	13	13	2	672	128	3	3	61.09	83.06	47	4
11	†S. E. Marsh (A)	7	7	0	416	131	3	0	59.42	101.96	28	12
12	C. S. MacLeod (Scot) . . .	11	11	2	534	157*	2	2	59.33	99.81	65	6
13	J. E. Root (E)	24	24	8	946	113*	3	5	59.12	83.93	65	6
14	Mushfiqur Rahim (B)	19	19	5	770	144	1	5	55.00	82.35	55	15
15	J. C. Buttler (E)	23	18	5	671	110*	2	4	51.61	113.53	60	19
16	†S. Dhawan (I)	19	19	1	897	127	3	2	49.83	102.28	127	11
17	†S. C. Williams (Z)	11	11	2	448	129*	1	3	49.77	85.00	40	3
18	M. J. Guptill (NZ)	10	10	1	423	100	1	2	47.00	73.18	38	10
19	K. S. Williamson (NZ) . . .	11	11	1	468	115	2	1	46.80	75.97	31	4
20	J. M. Bairstow (E)	22	22	0	1,025	139	4	2	46.59	118.22	124	31
21	A. J. Finch (A)	11	11	0	493	107	3	1	44.81	89.47	38	13
22	B. R. M. Taylor (Z)	21	21	0	898	138	2	4	42.76	87.60	83	22
23	†E. J. G. Morgan (E)	22	22	4	756	92	0	7	42.00	93.79	70	21
24	J. J. Roy (E)	22	22	0	894	180	3	4	40.63	105.05	98	21
25	†S. O. Hetmyer (WI)	18	18	0	727	127	3	2	40.38	109.65	47	30
26	Sikandar Raza (Z)	18	18	2	633	92	0	5	39.56	82.31	47	20
27	†Shakib Al Hasan (B)	15	13	0	497	97	0	5	38.23	83.95	47	1
28	Rahmat Shah (Afg)	20	19	0	722	114	1	6	38.00	74.74	66	7
29	A. Balbirnie (Ire)	13	13	0	489	105	2	3	37.61	71.80	50	2
30	Babar Azam (P)	18	17	3	509	106*	1	2	36.35	81.18	43	5
31	Mohammad Shahzad (Afg)	18	18	1	607	124	1	4	35.70	81.47	70	17
32	A. D. Hales (E)	14	14	1	457	147	1	3	35.15	91.76	51	10
33	†W. T. S. Porterfield (Ire) . .	13	13	0	450	139	2	1	34.61	76.66	49	5
34	P. R. Stirling (Ire)	13	13	0	450	126	1	2	34.61	80.93	51	7
35	D. P. D. N. Dickwella (SL)	14	12	0	415	95	0	3	34.58	85.92	55	0
36	†N. L. T. C. Perera (SL) . .	17	15	3	415	64	0	2	34.58	115.59	30	15
37	J. O. Holder (WI)	15	15	3	405	99*	0	3	33.75	87.28	24	13
38	Mahmudullah (B)	20	16	3	419	76	0	3	32.23	75.35	27	12
39	Mohammad Nabi (Afg) . . .	20	17	2	463	84	0	3	30.86	91.86	26	16
40	H. Masakadza (Z)	26	26	0	581	84	0	3	22.34	68.11	63	11

BOWLING (15 wickets)

		Style	O	M	R	W	BB	4I	Avge	SR	ER
1	Rashid Khan (Afg)	LB	178	12	694	48	5-24	3	14.45	22.25	3.89
2	J. J. Bumrah (I)	RFM	100.5	9	366	22	4-35	1	16.63	27.50	3.62
3	Ehsan Khan (HK)	OB	53	0	255	15	4-33	1	17.00	21.20	4.81
4	T. J. Murtagh (Ire)	RFM	81	10	329	19	4-30	3	17.31	25.57	4.06
5	K. Yadav (I)	SLW	172.2	4	800	45	6-25	3	17.77	22.97	4.64
6	S. M. Sharif (Scot)	RFM	89.1	4	429	22	5-33	1	19.50	24.31	4.81
7	Mujeeb Zadran (Afg)	OB	188	16	723	37	5-50	2	19.54	30.48	3.84
8	W. B. Rankin (Ire)	RFM	112.4	13	460	23	4-15	1	20.00	29.39	4.08
9	L. H. Ferguson (NZ)	RF	76.2	0	392	19	5-45	1	20.63	24.10	5.13
10	N. L. T. C. Perera (SL) . . .	RFM	89.3	0	518	25	5-55	3	20.72	21.48	5.78

		Style	O	M	R	W	BB	4I	Avge	SR	ER
11	Mustafizur Rahman (B) ..	LFM	149.5	10	630	29	4-43	1	21.72	31.00	4.20
12	Fahim Ashraf (P)	RFM	80.1	6	350	16	5-22	1	21.87	30.06	4.36
13	Rubel Hossain (B)	RFM	101.2	4	508	23	4-46	1	22.08	26.43	5.01
14	A. Dananjaya (SL)......	OB	123.1	0	644	28	6-29	2	23.00	26.39	5.22
15	L. T. Ngidi (SA).......	RFM	107.4	9	599	26	4-51	2	23.03	24.84	5.56
16	Mohammad Naveed (UAE)	RM	94.5	1	553	24	5-28	1	23.04	23.70	5.83
17	A. G. Cremer (Z)	LB	137	4	606	25	4-32	2	24.24	32.88	4.42
18	Shadab Khan (P)	LB	129.1	3	567	23	4-28	3	24.65	33.69	4.38
19	Y. S. Chahal (I)	LB	156.1	3	754	29	5-22	2	26.00	32.31	4.82
20	K. Rabada (SA)	RF	124	8	602	23	4-41	2	26.17	32.34	4.85
21	C. R. Woakes (E).......	RFM	99	5	506	19	3-26	0	26.63	31.26	5.11
22	T. K. Curran (E).......	RFM	72.4	2	453	17	5-35	1	26.64	25.64	6.23
23	A. L. Phehlukwayo (SA).	RFM	91	3	533	20	3-33	0	26.65	27.30	5.85
24	Shakib Al Hasan (B)	SLA	125.4	5	563	21	4-42	1	26.80	35.90	4.48
25	T. L. Chatara (Z)	RFM	154.5	10	811	30	4-33	1	27.03	30.96	5.23
26	L. E. Plunkett (E)......	RFM	82.3	2	522	19	4-46	2	27.47	26.05	6.32
27	A. U. Rashid (E)	LB	213	1	1,154	42	4-36	2	27.47	30.42	5.41
28	T. A. Boult (NZ)	LFM	107.2	5	636	22	5-17	1	28.90	29.27	5.92
29	Mohammad Nabi (Afg)..	OB	171.2	11	699	24	3-48	0	29.12	42.83	4.07
30	Sikandar Raza (Z)	OB	136	5	649	22	3-30	0	29.50	37.09	4.77
31	Mehedi Hasan (B)	OB	134	7	535	18	4-29	1	29.72	44.66	3.99
32	Mashrafe bin Mortaza (B)	RFM	164	7	806	26	4-37	1	31.00	37.84	4.91
33	J. O. Holder (WI)......	RFM	123	1	685	21	5-53	2	32.61	35.14	5.56
34	K. M. Jarvis (Z)	RFM	119.5	6	591	18	4-37	1	32.83	39.94	4.93
35	Hasan Ali (P)..........	RFM	113.1	3	646	19	3-32	0	34.00	35.73	5.70
36	M. M. Ali (E).........	OB	195.5	3	1,000	29	4-46	1	34.48	40.51	5.10
37	K. A. J. Roach (WI).....	RFM	103	7	530	15	4-27	1	35.33	41.20	5.14
38	B. Muzarabani (Z)	RFM	131	4	733	18	4-47	1	40.72	43.66	5.59

MOST DISMISSALS BY A WICKETKEEPER

Dis		M			Dis		M	
35	(26ct, 9st)	23	J. C. Buttler (E)		26	(23ct, 3st)	12	N. J. O'Brien (Ire)
29	(20ct, 9st)	21	B. R. M. Taylor (Z)		25	(24ct, 1st)	10	Q. de Kock (SA)
27	(17ct, 10st)	20	M. S. Dhoni (I)		23	(21ct, 2st)	19	Mushfiqur Rahim (B)

O'Brien played one further one-day international when not keeping wicket, but took no catches.

MOST CATCHES IN THE FIELD

Ct	M			Ct	M	
13	22	J. J. Roy (E)		11	16	Najibullah Zadran (Afg)
12	24	J. E. Root (E)		11	19	R. G. Sharma (I)
11	13	B. A. Stokes (E)				

TWENTY20 INTERNATIONAL AVERAGES IN CALENDAR YEAR 2018

BATTING (250 runs)

		M	I	NO	R	HS	100	50	Avge	SR	4	6
1	†C. Munro (NZ)	12	12	1	500	104	1	4	45.45	178.57	41	35
2	†N. L. T. C. Perera (SL/Wld) .	9	9	2	283	61	0	1	40.42	177.98	20	19
3	A. J. Finch (A)...........	17	17	4	531	172	1	2	40.84	176.41	45	31
4	J. J. Roy (E)............	9	9	0	271	69	0	2	30.11	169.37	28	15
5	Shoaib Malik (P/Wld)......	16	15	6	369	53	0	1	41.00	164.00	26	17
6	B. K. G. Mendis (SL)	8	8	0	259	70	0	4	32.37	158.89	23	13
7	K. L. Rahul (I)...........	13	11	2	324	101*	1	1	36.00	149.30	26	16

		M	I	NO	R	HS	100	50	Avge	SR	4	6
8	†Fakhar Zaman (P)	17	17	0	576	91	0	4	33.88	**148.83**	67	19
9	R. G. Sharma (I)	19	18	2	590	111*	2	3	36.87	**147.50**	51	31
10	†S. Dhawan (I)	18	17	0	689	92	0	6	40.52	**147.22**	70	25
11	M. J. Guptill (NZ)	10	10	0	410	105	1	4	41.00	**146.95**	26	24
12	Liton Das (B)	14	14	0	333	61	0	2	23.78	**146.69**	29	17
13	Sarfraz Ahmed (P)	19	14	3	354	89*	0	1	32.18	**145.08**	37	10
14	†S. K. Raina (I)	13	11	0	298	69	0	1	27.09	**143.96**	29	11
15	G. J. Maxwell (A)	19	18	4	506	103*	1	2	36.14	**143.75**	35	23
16	Mahmudullah (B)	16	16	4	414	45	0	0	34.50	**138.00**	39	13
17	Mohammad Hafeez (P)	8	8	3	250	53*	0	1	50.00	**134.40**	18	12
18	Mushfiqur Rahim (B)	16	16	3	397	72*	0	3	30.53	**132.33**	37	9
19	Babar Azam (P)	12	12	3	563	97*	0	6	62.55	**126.51**	54	7
20	†Tamim Iqbal (B/Wld)	16	16	0	356	74	0	2	22.25	**121.91**	35	12
21	†D. J. M. Short (A)	18	18	2	515	76	0	4	32.18	**121.17**	55	15
22	M. K. Pandey (I)	13	11	7	299	79*	0	1	74.75	**121.05**	21	7
23	†Hussain Talat (P)	11	11	1	273	63	0	1	27.30	**117.67**	23	4
24	K. S. Williamson (NZ)	12	12	1	251	72	0	2	22.81	**115.66**	19	7

BOWLING (10 wickets)

		Style	O	D	R	W	BB	4I	Avge	SR	ER
1	K. Yadav (I)	SLW	34.3	104	206	21	5-24	1	9.80	9.85	**5.97**
2	Rashid Khan (Afg/Wld)	LB	30	76	191	22	4-12	2	8.68	8.18	**6.36**
3	Bhuvneshwar Kumar (I)	RFM	40.4	111	266	12	5-24	1	22.16	20.33	**6.54**
4	Mohammad Amir (P)	LFM	33	90	217	14	3-22	0	15.50	14.14	**6.57**
5	Shadab Khan (P)	LB	73.4	178	488	28	3-19	0	17.42	15.78	**6.62**
6	Shakib Al Hasan (B)	SLA	40	107	266	15	5-20	1	17.73	16.00	**6.65**
7	A. U. Rashid (E)	LB	36	79	246	12	3-11	0	20.50	18.00	**6.83**
8	Fahim Ashraf (P)	RFM	51.1	154	361	15	3-5	0	24.06	20.46	**7.05**
9	B. Stanlake (A)	RF	59	176	460	25	4-8	1	18.40	14.16	**7.79**
10	Shaheen Shah Afridi (P)	LFM	26	58	203	11	3-20	0	18.45	14.18	**7.80**
11	T. G. Southee (NZ)	RFM	39	96	307	12	3-13	0	25.58	19.50	**7.87**
12	Y. S. Chahal (I)	LB	52	115	411	18	3-18	0	22.83	17.33	**7.90**
13	K. M. A. Paul (WI)	RFM	48.4	111	394	17	5-15	1	23.17	17.17	**8.09**
14	H. H. Pandya (I)	RFM	30	60	243	10	4-38	1	24.30	18.00	**8.10**
15	C. J. Dala (SA)	RFM	19	52	157	11	3-35	0	14.27	10.36	**8.26**
16	I. S. Sodhi (NZ)	LB	45	91	374	10	2-25	0	37.40	27.00	**8.31**
17	Hasan Ali (P)	RFM	97	114	391	15	3-35	0	26.06	18.80	**8.31**
18	A. J. Tye (A)	RFM	68.3	147	587	31	4-23	1	18.93	13.25	**8.56**
19	Rubel Hossain (B)	RFM	41.1	86	370	13	2-24	0	28.46	19.00	**8.98**
20	T. A. Boult (NZ)	LFM	29.5	74	278	12	3-50	0	25.27	16.27	**9.31**
21	Mustafizur Rahman (B)	LFM	45.1	99	445	21	3-31	0	21.19	12.90	**9.85**
22	J. D. Unadkat (I)	LFM	21.4	50	214	10	3-38	0	21.40	13.00	**9.87**
23	K. O. K. Williams (WI)	RFM	23.4	36	240	10	4-28	1	24.00	14.20	**10.14**

MOST DISMISSALS BY A WICKETKEEPER

Dis		M		Dis		M	
20	(15ct, 5st)	19	Sarfraz Ahmed (P)	11	(7ct, 4st)	7	M. S. Dhoni (I)
16	(11ct, 5st)	19	A. T. Carey (A)	9	(6ct, 3st)	9	K. D. Karthik (I)
12	(8ct, 4st)	16	Mushfiqur Rahim (B)	7	(6ct, 1st)	10	D. Ramdin (WI)

Karthik played five further Twenty20 internationals when not keeping wicket, taking one catch.

MOST CATCHES IN THE FIELD

Ct	M			Ct	M	
13	17	A. J. Finch (A)		10	16	Shoaib Malik (P/Wld)
11	19	G. J. Maxwell (A)		10	17	Fakhar Zaman (P)
10	13	S. K. Raina (I)				

OTHER FIRST-CLASS TOURS IN 2018

SRI LANKA A IN BANGLADESH IN 2018

Sri Lanka A played three A-team Tests and three one-day internationals during a month-long tour of Bangladesh. Dimuth Karunaratne led them to a 1–0 victory in the four-day games, then Tissara Perera took charge for the one-dayers. Lahiru Thirimanne earned a recall to the full Test squad with 347 runs in the first-class matches, including two centuries, while Karunaratne and Shehan Jayasuriya also reached three figures. Slow left-armer Malinda Pushpakumara took nine wickets in the third match. Perera's thunderous hundred from No. 7 squared the one-day series, but the decider was ruined by rain.

At Chittagong (ZAC), June 26–29, 2018. **Drawn. ‡Sri Lanka A 449-8 dec** (131.1 overs) (F. D. M. Karunaratne 60, H. D. R. L. Thirimanne 168, K. I. C. Asalanka 90, S. Ashan 70; Khaled Ahmed 4-92) **and 262-2** (57 overs) (F. D. M. Karunaratne 161, H. D. R. L. Thirimanne 67*); **Bangladesh A 414** (135 overs) (Mosaddek Hossain 135, Sabbir Rahman 165; N. G. R. P. Jayasuriya 3-83, P. A. D. L. R. Sandakan 5-108). *MoM:* H. D. R. L. Thirimanne. *Lahiru Thirimanne, who batted 558 minutes for his highest score, put on 156 for the fifth wicket with Charith Asalanka. Bangladesh A replied in kind, with their captain Mosaddek Hossain adding 209 for the fourth with Sabbir Rahman, who went on to his own career-best.*

At Chittagong (ZAC), July 3–6, 2018. **Drawn. ‡Sri Lanka A 281-5 dec** (80 overs) (H. D. R. L. Thirimanne 100*, S. M. A. Priyanjan 57); **Bangladesh A 59-1** (16 overs). *MoM:* H. D. R. L. Thirimanne. *No play was possible on the first two days, and only 15 overs on the third. Thirimanne occupied another 321 minutes in scoring 100*.*

At Sylhet, July 10–12, 2018. **Sri Lanka A won by an innings and 38 runs. ‡Bangladesh A 167** (62.3 overs) (G. S. N. F. G. Jayasuriya 3-47, P. M. Pushpakumara 3-48, N. G. R. P. Jayasuriya 3-12) **and 107** (45.3 overs) (P. M. Pushpakumara 6-46); **Sri Lanka A 312** (81.1 overs) (G. S. N. F. G. Jayasuriya 142, S. Ashan 60; Mustafizur Rahman 3-44, Sanjamul Islam 4-104). *MoM:* G. S. N. F. G. Jayasuriya. *A three-day victory gave Sri Lanka A the series 1–0, with slow left-armer Malinda Pushpakumara – who had missed the first two games – taking nine wickets. Off-spinner Shehan Jayasuriya snared five, to add to an important century that rescued his side from 78-4.*

At Sylhet, July 17, 2018. **Bangladesh A won by two runs. Bangladesh A 280-7** (50 overs) (Mizanur Rahman 67, Fazle Mahmud 59); **‡Sri Lanka A 278** (50 overs) (M. D. Shanaka 78; Khaled Ahmed 4-72, Shoriful Islam 3-54). *MoM:* Ariful Haque. *A late burst from Ariful Haque, who clobbered 47 from 22 deliveries, with four sixes, gave Bangladesh A just enough to play with, despite Dasun Shanaka's run-a-ball 78, which included six sixes. Seamer Khaled Ahmed was entrusted with the final over: it boiled down to three required off the last ball, but Shehan Madushanka Kumara, who had hurtled to 21 from 11 with three sixes, missed it and was bowled.*

At Sylhet, July 19, 2018. **Sri Lanka A won by 67 runs. ‡Sri Lanka A 275** (49.4 overs) (N. L. T. C. Perera 111; Nayeem Hasan 3-42); **Bangladesh A 208** (44.3 overs) (P. M. Pushpakumara 3-32, K. N. Peiris 3-39). *MoM:* N. L. T. C. Perera. *The Sri Lankan captain Tissara Perera entered in the 21st over, with his side in bother at 103-5 – and smashed 111 in 88 balls, with five sixes, to set up a target that proved too much. Bangladesh A's top seven all reached double figures, but the highest score was Al-Amin's 46. Pushpakumara and off-spinner Nishan Peiris shared six wickets as the Sri Lankans squared the series.*

At Sylhet, July 22, 2018. **No result. ‡Sri Lanka A 240-9** (45 overs) (W. S. R. Samarawickrama 75, S. M. A. Priyanjan 53; Sanjamul Islam 4-24); **Bangladesh A 12-0** (3.4 overs). *Bangladesh A's target was revised to 243 in 45 overs, but further rain ended the match, so the series stayed at 1–1.*

BANGLADESH A IN IRELAND IN 2018

Bangladesh A, captained by seasoned Test batsmen Mominul Haque in the 50-over matches and Soumya Sarkar in the Twenty20s, visited Ireland in August. The one-dayers were drawn 2–2, and the tourists edged a rain-hit T20 series 2–1. The home team included few first-choice players, although Kevin O'Brien and William Porterfield were drafted in for the 20-over games. Mominul smashed 182 in the fourth one-dayer, but Andy Balbirnie, the Wolves' captain, turned the tables with an equally dominant 160 not out to win the final game, and squared the series.

At Oak Hill, August 1, 2018. **No result. Ireland Wolves 37-1** (5 overs) v **‡Bangladesh A.** *A game already reduced to 28 overs was called off after only five, when the rain returned to County Wicklow.*

At Oak Hill, August 3, 2018. **Bangladesh A won by 87 runs. Bangladesh A 289-6** (50 overs) (Zakir Hasan 92, Fazle Mahmud 53; P. K. D. Chase 3-63, T. E. Kane 3-67); **‡Ireland Wolves 202** (46.3 overs) (Shoriful Islam 3-40). *A run-a-ball 92 from opener Zakir Hasan was followed by late urgency from Al-Amin (47 from 49) and Fazle Mahmud (53 from 41) as Bangladesh A got close to 300, helped by indisciplined bowling which gave away 26 in wides. Ireland Wolves slipped to 14-3, and never recovered; Tyrone Kane top-scored with 49 from No. 8.*

At Oak Hill, August 5, 2018. **Ireland Wolves won by 34 runs. Ireland Wolves 245** (49.3 overs) (S. R. Thompson 68, A. R. McBrine 59; Khaled Ahmed 4-42); **‡Bangladesh A 211** (46.3 overs) (A. R. McBrine 3-37, T. E. Kane 4-24, B. J. McCarthy 3-37). *A much better bowling performance helped Ireland Wolves make it 1–1. Off-spinner Andy McBrine took the new ball and finished with three wickets, while seamers Kane and Barry McCarthy shared seven. The backbone of the Wolves' innings came in a fourth-wicket stand of 103 between Stuart Thompson and McBrine, and the eventual total was more than enough: Bangladesh A slid to 149-7, and didn't really threaten.*

At Dublin (The Vineyard), August 8, 2018. **Bangladesh A won by 85 runs. ‡Bangladesh A 386-4** (50 overs) (Zakir Hasan 79, Mominul Haque 182, Mithun Ali 87*); **Ireland Wolves 301** (46.1 overs) (A. Balbirnie 106, S. Singh 53; Khaled Ahmed 3-73, Fazle Mahmud 3-47). *A career-best 182 from the visiting captain Mominul Haque put the match well beyond the Irish. He stroked 27 fours and three sixes from only 133 balls, and put on 210 for the second wicket with Zakir and 112 for the third with Mithun Ali. Balbirnie's sparky 106 and a 32-ball 53 from Simi Singh ensured the Wolves reached 300, but the margin was still substantial.*

At Dublin (Clontarf), August 10, 2018. **Ireland Wolves won by eight wickets. ‡Bangladesh A 283-8** (50 overs) (Mithun Ali 73, Fazle Mahmud 74; P. K. D. Chase 3-57); **Ireland Wolves 285-2** (46.4 overs) (A. Balbirnie 160*, A. R. McBrine 89). *Balbirnie had warmed up in the previous match, and now spanked a glorious 160* from 144 balls as his side swept to a series-levelling victory; he put on 197 with McBrine. "When you wake up, you never expect to make a score like that in a one-day game," said Balbirnie.*

At Dublin (Clontarf), August 13, 2018. **Bangladesh A won by four wickets. ‡Ireland Wolves 152** (20 overs); **Bangladesh A 155-6** (18 overs) (Soumya Sarkar 57; A. R. McBrine 3-23). *Only Singh, with 41 from 37, got going for Ireland Wolves and, although Zakir fell to the first ball of the chase, skipper Soumya Sarkar (57 from 41) and Nazmul Hossain (38 from 23) put Bangladesh A in charge.*

At Dublin (Clontarf), August 15, 2018. **‡Ireland Wolves v Bangladesh A. Abandoned.**

At Malahide, August 16, 2018. **Ireland Wolves won by 51 runs** (DLS). **Ireland Wolves 202-6** (20 overs) (Mohammad Saifuddin 3-33); **‡Bangladesh A 104-7** (15 overs). *This match was added after the previous day's washout at Clontarf. Thompson hit 47 from 38 balls, and William Porterfield 45 from 34 as Ireland Wolves sprinted past 200. Bangladesh A's target was revised to 156 in 15 overs, and they were soon adrift at 62-7. Umpire Mary Waldron, a current international, stood in a men's representative match for the first time.*

At Malahide, August 17, 2018. **Bangladesh A won by six wickets. ‡Ireland Wolves 183-5** (18 overs) (W. T. S. Porterfield 78, S. Singh 67*; Mohammad Saifuddin 4-28); **Bangladesh A 187-4** (16.5 overs) (Mithun Ali 80; S. C. Getkate 3-36). *In a match reduced to 18 overs after a late start, Ireland Wolves did well to reach 183: Porterfield (78 from 39, with 60 in boundaries) and Singh (67* from 41) put on 111 for the fourth wicket. But Bangladesh A always looked in charge, with Mithun (80 from 39) and Sarkar (47 from 30) cracking a rapid opening stand of 117.*

SOUTH AFRICA A IN INDIA IN 2018

South Africa A, captained by Khaya Zondo, played two A-team Tests in India in August, before a quadrangular one-day series. Mayank Agarwal's double-century set up a thumping home win in the first match, but the second was drawn. The Indian seamer Mohammed Siraj took 14 wickets, including ten in the victory at Bangalore. Fast bowler Duanne Olivier took ten in the series for South Africa A, whose wicketkeeper Rudi Second scored 94, 94 and 47.

At Bangalore, August 4–7, 2018. **India A won by an innings and 30 runs. ‡South Africa A 246** (88.3 overs) (R. S. Second 94; M. Siraj 5-56) **and 308** (128.5 overs) (M. Z. Hamza 63, R. S. Second 94, S. von Berg 50; M. Siraj 5-73); **India A 584-8 dec** (129.4 overs) (P. P. Shaw 136, M. A. Agarwal

220, G. H. Vihari 54, K. Srikar Bharat 64; B. E. Hendricks 3-98). *South Africa A batted reasonably well – especially in their long second innings – but were flattened when the Indians ran up 584. Prithvi Shaw and Mayank Agarwal shared an opening stand of 277 in four hours, then Agarwal added a further 118 with Ravikumar Samarth en route to 220. Trailing by 338, South Africa A were soon 6-3, all the wickets going to Mohammed Siraj, who finished with ten in the match, but some determined resistance almost forced the hosts to bat again. Rudi Second survived for five and a half hours, and scored his second 94 of the match.*

At Alur, August 10–13, 2018. **Drawn. India A 345** (101 overs) (G. H. Vihari 148, A. R. Bawne 80; D. Olivier 6-63) **and 181-4** (51 overs) (S. S. Iyer 65, A. R. Bawne 64*); ‡**South Africa A 319** (98.2 overs) (S. J. Erwee 58, M. Z. Hamza 93; M. Siraj 4-72, A. Rajpoot 3-52). *Shaw and Agarwal were separated in the first over this time – the first of six wickets for the impressive Duanne Olivier – but Hanuma Vihari starred instead, sharing a fourth-wicket stand of 177 with Ankit Bawne. Rain allowed only 32.4 overs on the third day, and the match petered out on the fourth.*

QUADRANGULAR A-TEAM SERIES IN INDIA IN 2018

India showed off their impressive bench strength in this four-way series, as their B-team – supposedly the third-best national XI – beat Australia A in the final after earlier walloping India A. The first week was bedevilled by incessant rain in Andhra, which eventually caused the tournament to be moved. Manish Pandey, the India B captain, finished as the leading run-scorer with 306, without being dismissed; his team-mate Mayank Agarwal was next with 236. India B led the wicket-takers, too: leg-spinner Shreyas Gopal had nine, and seamer Prasidh Krishna eight, although the only five-for was claimed by the South African fast bowler Dane Paterson.

At Mulapadu (DVRP), August 17, 2018. **India A v Australia A. Abandoned.** *India A 2pts, Australia A 2pts.*

At Mulapadu (Chukkapalli Pitchaiah), August 17, 2018. **India B v South Africa A. Abandoned.** *India B 2pts, South Africa A 2pts.*

At Mulapadu (Chukkapalli Pitchaiah), August 19, 2018. **Australia A v South Africa A. Abandoned.** *Australia A 2pts, South Africa A 2pts.*

At Mulapadu (DVRP), August 19, 2018. **India A v India B. Abandoned.** *India A 2pts, India B 2pts.*

At Mulapadu (DVRP), August 21, 2018. **India A v South Africa A. Abandoned.** *India A 2pts, South Africa A 2pts.*

At Mulapadu (Chukkapalli Pitchaiah), August 21, 2018. **India B v Australia A. Abandoned.** *India B 2pts, Australia A 2pts. Following incessant rain in Andhra, the remaining games were shifted to Bangalore and Alur in Karnataka.*

At Bangalore, August 23, 2018. **India A won by five wickets.** ‡**Australia A 151** (31.4 overs) (M. Siraj 4-68, K. Gowtham 3-31); **India A 152-5** (38.3 overs) (A. T. Rayudu 62*; J. A. Richardson 3-27). *MoM:* A. T. Rayudu. *India A 5pts. After the teams had kicked their heels for a week, the tournament finally got under way. India A started with a bonus-point victory, although they were in trouble at 29-4 in reply to a modest 151. But Ambati Rayudu (62*) and Krunal Pandya (49) ended the jitters by putting on 109.*

At Alur, August 23, 2018. **India B won by 30 runs** (DLS). **South Africa A 231** (47.3 overs) (S. Muthusamy 55; P. M. Krishna 4-49, R. Shreyas Gopal 3-42); ‡**India B 214-5** (40.3 overs) (M. K. Pandey 95*). *India B 4pts. Rain followed the teams from Andhra, but held off just long enough: when the final downpour came, India B needed to have scored 185. Their captain Manish Pandey, with one eye on the clouds, made 95*.*

At Bangalore, August 25, 2018. **Australia A won by 32 runs.** ‡**Australia A 322-5** (50 overs) (T. M. Head 110, M. Labuschagne 65); **South Africa A 290** (48.4 overs) (G. L. Cloete 50, K. Zondo 117; M. J. Swepson 3-40). *MoM:* T. M. Head. *Australia A 4pts. Both captains scored centuries, but Travis Head's measured 110 secured the laurels. His third-wicket partnership of 136 with Marnus Labuschagne set up a total beyond South Africa A, despite Khaya Zondo's 117, which included seven sixes. Leg-spinner Mitch Swepson filleted the middle order with three wickets in 12 balls.*

At Alur, August 25, 2018. **India B won by seven wickets.** ‡**India A 217** (49 overs) (P. M. Krishna 4-50); **India B 218-3** (41.1 overs) (M. A. Agarwal 124). *MoM:* M. A. Agarwal. *India B 4pts. A rapid 124 from Mayank Agarwal helped India B tweak the noses of their supposedly senior countrymen,* *who had been hamstrung by a good opening spell from seamer Prasidh Krishna: he took all the wickets as the A team slipped to 45-3 in the 11th.*

At Bangalore, August 27, 2018. **South Africa A won by four wickets. India A 157** (37.3 overs) (D. Paterson 5-19); ‡**South Africa A 159-6** (37.4 overs) (K. K. Ahmed 3-45). *MoM:* D. Paterson. *South Africa A 5pts. South Africa A were already unlikely to progress, but their victory also eliminated India A, who slipped to 31-4. Two went to seamer Dane Paterson, who returned to chop off the tail and finish with 9.3–2–19–5. "That was a South African wicket put out today," he said of the greenish surface. Despite a wobble to 111-5, South Africa A completed a bonus-point win.*

At Alur, August 27, 2018. **Australia A won by five wickets** (DLS). **India B 276-6** (50 overs) (M. K. Pandey 117*; M. G. Neser 3-47); ‡**Australia A 248-5** (40 overs) (U. T. Khawaja 101*, J. D. Wildermuth 62*). *Australia A 4pts. Usman Khawaja anchored Australia A to a stunning win that confirmed their place in the final, against the side they conquered here. Pandey's 117* from 109 balls was the foundation of India B's total. The Australians were set 247 in 40 overs after a rain break, and dipped to 155-5 in the 39th. Although the sixth-wicket pair pulled things back – Khawaja faced 93 balls for his 101* – a win looked almost impossible when nine were needed from the last two balls. But Jack Wildermuth (62* from 42) creamed Krishna to the cover boundary, then hit the last ball over long-on for six.*

India B 14pts, Australia A 14pts, South Africa A 11pts, India A 11pts.

Third Place Play-off   At Alur, August 29, 2018. **India A won by 124 runs. India A 275-7** (50 overs) (S. S. Iyer 67, A. T. Rayudu 66; B. E. Hendricks 3-39); ‡**South Africa A 151** (37.1 overs) (Bhuvneshwar Kumar 3-33).

Final   At Bangalore, August 29, 2018. **India B won by nine wickets. Australia A 225** (47.5 overs) (D. J. M. Short 72, A. T. Carey 53; R. Shreyas Gopal 3-50); ‡**India B 230-1** (36.3 overs) (M. A. Agarwal 69, S. Gill 66*, M. K. Pandey 73*). *MoM:* M. K. Pandey. *Another imposing batting performance swept India B to the title, after their bowlers had restricted Australia A to 225. Agarwal made 69 from 67 balls, then Shubman Gill piled on 120* for the second wicket in 16 overs with Pandey, whose 73* took his tournament aggregate to 306, in four not-out innings.*

AUSTRALIA A IN INDIA IN 2018

After reaching the final of the quadrangular one-day series in India, Australia A – now captained by Mitchell Marsh – played two four-day representative matches in September. Usman Khawaja's century set up victory in the first, despite 11 wickets for Mohammed Siraj, but India A outbatted them in the second.

At Bangalore, September 2–5, 2018. **Australia A won by 98 runs.** ‡**Australia A 243** (75.3 overs) (U. T. Khawaja 127, M. Labuschagne 60; M. Siraj 8-59) **and 292** (83.5 overs) (T. M. Head 87; M. Siraj 3-77); **India 274** (83.1 overs) (A. R. Bawne 91*; M. G. Neser 4-61, J. M. Holland 3-89) **and 163** (59.3 overs) (M. A. Agarwal 80; J. M. Holland 6-81). *Slow left-armer Jon Holland spun Australia A to victory on the fourth day, as India A fell well short of a target of 262: from 124-3, they lost seven for 39. Australia's other hero was Usman Khawaja, last out for 127 after opening in the first innings. He shared a first-wicket stand of 78 with Kurtis Patterson (31), and 114 for the fifth with Marnus Labuschagne, but no one else made more than four – there were five ducks, four lbw to seamer Mohammed Siraj, who finished with a career-best 8-59. Ankit Bawne played the Khawaja role as India A chiselled out a lead of 31, then an improved batting performance – with 87 from Travis Head and tenacious performances from the tail – dragged Australia A to 292.*

At Alur, September 8–11, 2018. **India A won by six wickets.** ‡**Australia A 346** (109 overs) (T. M. Head 68, M. R. Marsh 113*; K. Yadav 5-91, S. Nadeem 3-90) **and 213** (102.5 overs) (P. S. P. Handscomb 56; K. Gowtham 3-39, K. Yadav 3-46); **India 505** (144 overs) (R. Samarth 83, A. R. Easwaran 86, S. Gill 50, K. Srikar Bharat 106, K. Yadav 52; C. P. Tremain 3-41, A. C. Agar 3-87) **and 55-4** (6.2 overs). *Australia A defended grimly in their second innings, which lasted 102.5 overs – Peter Handscomb faced 153 balls for his 56, and tailender Michael Neser 112 for 17 – but were winkled out with around 45 minutes left on the final day. Needing 55 in eight overs, India A squared the series with ten balls remaining. The spadework was done in their first innings of 505, which meant they led by 159 despite Mitchell Marsh's fighting century. Wicketkeeper Srikar Bharat's hundred built on an opening stand of 174 between Ravikumar Samarth and Abhimanyu Easwaran.*

PAKISTAN A v NEW ZEALAND A IN THE UAE IN 2018-19

Just before the full New Zealand side took on Pakistan in all formats in the UAE, their A-team made a reconnaissance visit. Captained by Corey Anderson, they won the T20 series 2–1, despite being shot out for 65 in the first match, but Pakistan A shaded all three 50-over games, with wicketkeeper Mohammad Rizwan making 256 runs for once out. For New Zealand A, Will Young scored 134 in the third match, but the unfortunate Glenn Phillips made three ducks in the space of seven balls: he was out in the first over of all three games. The tour concluded with two four-day matches, both drawn. Jeet Raval captained in those, and was one of several players kept on for the full series. For Pakistan A, Shan Masood earned a Test recall with innings of 167, 100 and 73.

At Dubai (ICC Academy), October 12, 2018. **Pakistan A won by eight wickets. ‡New Zealand A 65** (12.2 overs) (Umaid Asif 5-20); **Pakistan A 66-2** (12.5 overs). *A helter-skelter match lasted just 25.1 overs: New Zealand A were shot out for 65, with only Corey Anderson (16) and Tim Seifert (26) reaching double figures. The left-arm new-ball pair of Waqas Maqsood (2-7) and Shaheen Shah Afridi (2-12) did the early damage, then the 34-year-old seamer Umaid Asif took 5-20.*

At Dubai (ICC Academy), October 15, 2018. **New Zealand A won by seven wickets. ‡Pakistan A 142-7** (20 overs) (Hussain Talat 51; A. Y. Patel 3-30); **New Zealand A 146-3** (19.5 overs) (G. D. Phillips 53, G. H. Worker 52). *While New Zealand A's openers were adding 107, a comfortable victory looked on the cards – but two wickets in a Hussain Talat over set nerves jangling, and in the end the winning run came with one ball to spare, when Tom Bruce hit Talat for four.*

At Dubai (ICC Academy), October 17, 2018. **New Zealand A won by five wickets. ‡Pakistan A 156-6** (20 overs); **New Zealand A 159-5** (19 overs) (G. D. Phillips 69*). *With Glenn Phillips making 69* from 50 balls, with four sixes, New Zealand A came from behind to take the series.*

At Abu Dhabi, October 21, 2018. **Pakistan A won by one wicket. New Zealand A 222** (49.3 overs) (T. D. Astle 51; Aamer Yamin 3-27); **‡Pakistan A 223-9** (49.3 overs) (Mohammad Rizwan 105*; L. H. Ferguson 4-28). *Pakistan A almost threw away what had looked a regulation victory when they were 163-3, chasing 223: with Lockie Ferguson taking three wickets in the 39th over, they nosedived to 182-9. But Mohammad Rizwan was well set, and put on 41* with last man Rahat Ali, whose contribution was 3* from 15 balls.*

At Abu Dhabi, October 24, 2018. **Pakistan A won by five wickets. New Zealand A 224** (48.4 overs) (B-J. Watling jnr 4-37); **‡Pakistan A 225-5** (49 overs) (Mohammad Saad 51, Saud Shakil 65*). *B-J. Watling's 76 lifted New Zealand A to 224, but it never looked enough. Although Pakistan A were 101-4 in the 25th over, a patient stand of 112 between Mohammad Saad and Saud Shakil took them within sight of victory. The Mohammad Irfan who took four wickets was not the 7ft 1in Test bowler, but a 6ft 6in seamer from Punjab.*

At Abu Dhabi, October 26, 2018. **Pakistan A won by seven wickets. ‡New Zealand A 265-8** (50 overs) (W. A. Young 134; Mohammad Irfan jnr 3-49, Mohammad Asghar 4-29); **Pakistan A 267-3** (48.2 overs) (Mohammad Rizwan 117*). *Will Young's career-best 134 – after his side had been 11-2 in the seventh over – was trumped by another century from Rizwan, who took his series tally to 256 for once out as Pakistan A swept the one-dayers 3–0. Slow left-armer Mohammad Asghar took four wickets.*

At Dubai (ICC Academy), October 30–November 2, 2018. **Drawn. ‡Pakistan A 346-9 dec** (94 overs) (Shan Masood 167, Abid Ali 83; S. C. Kuggeleijn 4-54, K. A. Jamieson 3-46) **and 241-3 dec** (58 overs) (Shan Masood 100, Abid Ali 61, Usman Salahuddin 50*); **New Zealand A 278-9 dec** (102 overs) (R. Ravindra 70, L. V. van Beek 56*; Kashif Bhatti 3-67) **and 163-4** (63 overs) (W. A. Young 74*). *Shan Masood batted for 523 minutes in the first innings, and four hours in the second. New Zealand A were staring at a big deficit at 196-9 in their first innings, but Nos 10 and 11 Logan van Beek (56*) and Blair Tickner (22* from 88 balls) put on 82*. After Masood's second century, the New Zealanders had little interest in chasing 310 in what became 63 overs, once both openers were out for single figures.*

At Abu Dhabi, November 6–9, 2018. **Drawn. ‡Pakistan A 427-8 dec** (123.3 overs) (Shan Masood 73, Usman Salahuddin 125, Saad Ali 144; N. Wagner 3-60) **and 206-2 dec** (63 overs) (Abid Ali 104*, Usman Salahuddin 64*); **New Zealand A 380-8 dec** (117.1 overs) (J. A. Raval 97, R. Ravindra 64, N. Wagner 53*; Mohammad Asghar 4-127) **and 68-5** (25 overs) (Ehsan Adil 3-21). *A stalemate – and a 0–0 draw – was all but assured by solid first-innings batting by both sides. Usman Salahuddin and Saad Ali shared a fifth-wicket stand of 230, then the New Zealand A captain Jeet*

Raval led a consistent reply, lasting more than five hours for 97: the top nine all scored 19 or more. They continued late into the third day, and there was little likelihood of a result after that, despite a clatter of wickets when the New Zealanders batted again after Abid Ali's six-hour century.

INDIA A IN NEW ZEALAND IN 2018-19

India A, captained by Ajinkya Rahane, drew all three four-day matches in New Zealand, then Manish Pandey took over for three 50-over games, all of which were won. He scored the Indians' only century of the tour, an unbeaten 111 in the second one-dayer. Hamish Rutherford marked his recall to New Zealand representative teams with 114 in the first four-day game, while Will Young – fresh from a successful time against Pakistan – impressed with his good form with a century in each series.

At Mount Maunganui, November 16–19, 2018. **Drawn. ‡India A 467-8 dec** (122.1 overs) (P. P. Shaw 62, M. A. Agarwal 65, G. H. Vihari 86, P. A. Patel 94, V. Shankar 62; B. M. Tickner 4-80) **and 247-3** (65 overs) (P. P. Shaw 50, M. Vijay 60, G. H. Vihari 51*); **New Zealand A 458-9 dec** (134 overs) (H. D. Rutherford 114, D. Cleaver 53, S. H. A. Rance 69*; K. Gowtham 3-107). *A run-soaked match at the Bay Oval ended in a quiet draw. Wicketkeeper Parthiv Patel top-scored for India A before becoming one of four wickets for hard-working seamer Blair Tickner. Hamish Rutherford and Will Young kicked off the reply with a stand of 121; Rutherford went on to his 13th first-class century, five and a half years after hitting 171 on Test debut against England. A last-wicket stand of 83 between Seth Rance and Tickner (30*) closed the deficit to nine. India A faced only eight overs on the third evening, and batted out the fourth day for a draw.*

At Hamilton, November 23–26, 2018. **Drawn. New Zealand A 303-7 dec** (106 overs) (W. A. Young 123, T. F. van Woerkom 54; M. Siraj 4-50); **‡India A 159-2** (46 overs) (R. Samarth 50*). *Bad weather allowed only 62 overs after a full first day, on which Young made a patient century.*

At Whangarei, November 30–December 3, 2018. **Drawn. ‡India A 323** (89 overs) (A. R. Easwaran 56, S. Gill 62, V. Shankar 71; D. A. J. Bracewell 5-78, L. H. Ferguson 4-88) **and 38-1** (14 overs); **New Zealand A 398** (131.4 overs) (T. L. Seifert 86, C. D. Fletcher 103, D. A. J. Bracewell 55, K. A. Jamieson 53; K. Gowtham 6-139). *Rain curtailed the first two days, and washed out the last. A result was already unlikely, after wicketkeeper Cameron Fletcher led a recovery from 165-5, with a career-best 103 in five and a half hours. Off-spinner Krishna Gowtham prised out six wickets.*

At Mount Maunganui, December 7, 2018. **India A won by four wickets. New Zealand A 308-6** (50 overs) (H. D. Rutherford 70, T. L. Seifert 59, J. D. S. Neesham 79*); **‡India A 311-6** (49 overs) (S. S. Iyer 54, V. Shankar 87*). *Boosted by 59 from Tom Seifert and a 48-ball 79* from Jimmy Neesham, New Zealand A set a steep target of 309 – but India A breezed past it with an over to spare. It could have gone either way at 159-4 in the 26th, but Vijay Shankar and Ishan Kishan thumped 116 for the fifth wicket.*

At Mount Maunganui, December 9, 2018. **India A won by five wickets. New Zealand A 299-9** (50 overs) (G. H. Worker 99, W. A. Young 102); **‡India A 300-5** (49 overs) (S. S. Iyer 59, M. K. Pandey 111*, V. Shankar 59). *George Worker, who was bowled by slow left-armer Akshar Patel for 99, put on 190 for the second wicket with Young, and ensured India A would again be chasing 300. But for the second time in three days they got there with an over left, captain Manish Pandey making 111* at better than a run a ball. He put on 90 for the third wicket with Shreyas Iyer, and 123 for the fourth with Shankar.*

At Mount Maunganui, December 11, 2018. **India A won by 75 runs. ‡India A 275-8** (50 overs) (Anmolpreet Singh 71; S. H. A. Rance 3-49); **New Zealand A 200** (44.2 overs) (T. L. Seifert 55; S. Kaul 4-37). *India A completed a one-day clean sweep, with seamer Siddharth Kaul taking four wickets, including top-scorer Seifert. India A had rejigged their side after going 2–0 up: 20-year-old opener Anmolpreet Singh made 71 and Ankit Bawne 48 in their only outings of the series.*

For India A and West Indies A in England in 2018, see page 691. For England Lions in the West Indies in 2017-18, see page 1059, and for the Lions against Pakistan A in the UAE in 2018-19, see page 955.

ICC INTERCONTINENTAL CUP

The four-day tournament for Associate Members, whose seventh instalment had been won by Afghanistan in 2017, took a break last year. It was expected to resume in 2019, but in October 2018 the ICC asked for "expressions of interest" from countries, adding that "a structured multi-day competition on a cost-sharing basis will be proposed, giving members the choice of playing longer-form cricket". It remains to be seen how many will be able to afford to participate in a tournament which, while undoubtedly ambitious and beneficial, was also expensive.

At the same time, the **World Cricket League**, the one-day championship which ran alongside the Intercontinental Cup, was reorganised. The Netherlands, who won the last instalment in 2017, will play in the new CWC (Cricket World Cup) Super League, alongside the 12 Test nations: that competition will run until 2022, and produce the direct qualifiers for the 2023 World Cup in India. The next seven in the rankings will contest League Two, which will start in July 2019. Each team should play 36 one-day internationals over a 30-month period; the top three in the final table will progress straight to the World Cup Qualifier, while the remainder will face play-offs, also involving the top teams from the division below, to reach the Qualifier.

CRICKET IN HONG KONG IN 2018

Downward curve

Nazvi Careem

In Bulawayo on March 8, Hong Kong beat Afghanistan in their second match of the World Cup qualifying tournament. Victory over a newly created Test nation brought a mixture of joy and relief to everyone involved with Hong Kong cricket, especially administrators who had committed significant sums to contracts for the senior players. Some dared to dream of a World Cup place.

Four games later, it had all gone horribly wrong. Defeat by Zimbabwe was followed by another, against Nepal. Hong Kong were condemned to bottom place in their group, and the repercussions were enormous: demotion to the second tier of Associate Member cricket, the loss of one-day international status, and a big cut in funding, of roughly HK$8m (around £800,000).

It did not take long for the impact to be felt. Cricket Hong Kong retained players on contracts but some, including off-spinner Ehsan Khan, who had performed well in Zimbabwe, were forced to look for coaching work to supplement their incomes. Wicketkeeper-batsman Chris Carter, born in Hong Kong but raised in Perth, quit as a contracted player to pursue his ambition of becoming a pilot. Even before the qualifying competition, they had lost Hong Kong-born batsman Mark Chapman, who switched to New Zealand, where his father was born. Leading players Babar Hayat, Nizakat Khan and Anshuman Rath found employment in Twenty20 tournaments in the UAE and Nepal.

Aside from reduced ICC funding, the cricketers have also been cut off from the Hong Kong Sports Institute, an elite training academy that had provided cash, coaching and facilities to the senior team. The arrangement ended in the spring of 2018 because cricket was no longer part of the Asian Games roster – a requirement for central government financial support.

Involvement in the Asia Cup in September was brief, and brought defeats by Pakistan and India. But the India match almost produced a sensational victory. Chasing 286, Hong Kong reached 174 for no wicket, before losing by 26 runs. "We really showed the world what we can do," said the captain, Rath. "But we had India by the horns and really should have finished it off."

More seriously, the scourge of match-fixing threatened to destabilise the squad. In October, all-rounder Irfan Ahmed, his brother Nadeem Ahmed and Haseeb Amjad were suspended and charged with 19 counts of breaking the ICC's code of conduct. Irfan had only just ended a 30-month ban for failing to report an illegal approach.

While the national team struggled, the two international tournaments held in Hong Kong the previous year disappeared: in 2018-19, neither the World Sixes nor the T20 Blitz took place. Cricket Hong Kong promised that both events would be combined into a week-long cricket festival in October 2019.

CRICKET IN NEPAL IN 2018

The miracle workers

UJJWAL ACHARYA

After waiting years for a miracle, three came along at once. Nepal claimed one-day international status for the first time. Teenage leg-spinner Sandeep Lamichhane became a hot Twenty20 property. And a domestic T20 league was launched.

Nepal did just enough at the World Cup Qualifier in Zimbabwe in March to be granted ODI status. They lost four matches, but victories over Hong Kong and Papua New Guinea secured the last available spot, even if the World Cup was a step too far. Just being in Zimbabwe was a minor miracle, as Nepal had endured a seat-of-the-pants campaign in World Cricket League Division Two. They beat hosts Namibia by one wicket, and Kenya from the last ball, before Nepal's tenth-wicket pair conjured 51 from 47 deliveries to overcome Canada, and qualify.

Lamichhane took 17 wickets in the tournament, shortly after signing an IPL contract, and made an impressive start for Delhi Daredevils. He then represented the World XI in a charity international at Lord's, before becoming a globe-trotting T20 hired gun: he played in Canada for Montreal Tigers, in the Caribbean for St Kitts & Nevis Patriots, in Afghanistan for Nangrahar Leopards, in Bangladesh for Sylhet Sixers, and in Australia for Melbourne Stars (he conceded just 16 runs in the 2019 final, which they lost).

If Lamichhane was the rising star, the established one – Paras Khadka – proved an inspirational captain. He supervised a 1–1 draw in Nepal's first official ODI series, against the Netherlands in August, and started 2019 with 2–1 wins over the UAE in ODIs and T20s. Other precocious talent emerged: Rohit Kumar Paudel, just 16, became the youngest man to score an ODI half-century, breaking Shahid Afridi's record, while Sundeep Jora – a year older – annexed the equivalent T20 record. Nepal's next target is the T20 World Cup, in Australia in 2020. They began by winning all their matches with a confident display at the Asia Region Qualifier in Malaysia in October, demolishing China for 26, and knocking off the runs in 11 balls.

The administrative story was less wonderful. The Cricket Association of Nepal remained suspended from the ICC for a third year, because of irregularities in the board elections. The game was kept alive by private franchise cricket. There were three such competitions – the Dhangadi, Pokhara and Everest Premier Leagues – which attracted players from Associate nations, and were broadcast live. Some of the locals were fast-tracked into the national squad, such as seamer Abinash Bohara, who won the T20 series award against the UAE.

CRICKET IN THE NETHERLANDS IN 2018

Hungry for more

DAVE HARDY

The euphoria at the end of 2017 that accompanied winning the World Cricket League – and regaining ODI status – did not live long. In March 2018, the Dutch suffered a serious disappointment at the World Cup Qualifier in Zimbabwe. They lost their first two group matches, against Ireland and the UAE, but beat Papua New Guinea; going into the last round, they had a slim chance of progressing. Had they overcome West Indies, and the UAE suffered a heavy defeat by Ireland, net run-rate might have been enough. Ireland did their bit and, with Wesley Barresi and Ryan ten Doeschate going nicely as rain threatened, the Dutch dared to hope. But four quick wickets – including two run-outs and a stumping – meant West Indies won on DLS.

The failure in Zimbabwe was perhaps a factor in Peter Borren being relieved of the captaincy in April – a "mutual decision". At the age of 34, Borren announced his retirement as a Netherlands international. He had been in charge for nearly a decade, and left an indelible mark, not only on the Dutch game, but on Associate cricket in general. He was a talented all-rounder, a world-class fielder and a magnificent captain, who combined nous with motivational qualities. He is the only Dutch international to have played 100 white-ball matches. He was a tireless champion of Associate cricket, and will be remembered as a fearless critic of the ICC – not that he managed to persuade them of the folly of reducing the 2019 World Cup to ten teams.

Left-arm spinner Pieter Seelaar replaced him and enjoyed an ideal start, winning two Twenty20s against Ireland. Once again, the elation was soon punctured, following two heavy defeats by Scotland. Just as dispiriting was the lack of opportunity to exploit the regained ODI status. The Netherlands played only two matches in 2018, both at home to Nepal; the series finished 1–1.

The national team are in a transitional phase, with many of the experienced players who served so well in recent years not always available. Two of the newer recruits, both seamers, are hoping to gain valuable county experience: the 23-year-old Shane Snater has already played four white-ball matches for Essex, while Fred Klaassen, 26, has signed for Kent. More impressive still was Sterre Kalis who, aged 18, had gained an "Associate Rookie" contract with Sydney Thunder for the 2017-18 season of the Women's Big Bash.

VOC of Rotterdam won the national 50-over title for the first time since 1994. Seelaar had an outstanding all-round season for them, hitting 555 runs at 50 and taking 22 wickets at 13. HBS of The Hague won their first national trophy since 1980, triumphing in the T20 competition, the first played with a white ball rather than a pink. After nearly a decade, VCC of Voorburg clinched promotion to the *Topklasse*; Punjab of Rotterdam were relegated after two seasons in the top flight.

NETHERLANDS TRI-NATION SERIES IN 2018

IAN CALLENDER

1 Scotland   2 Netherlands   3 Ireland

Scotland bounced back from an opening defeat by Ireland to claim the T20 Tri-Nation Series in the Netherlands in style. They had to win the last two matches against the hosts, who had beaten the Irish twice, and did so comfortably – by seven wickets and a record-breaking 115 runs. Scotland had three of the tournament's top four run-scorers, in George Munsey (204), captain Kyle Coetzer (153) and Richie Berrington (146 for once out). Yet they had arrived in Deventer after two chastening defeats by Pakistan in Edinburgh, and appeared to be feeling the effects when they immediately leaked 205 to Ireland. But they tied their second game, also against Ireland – the officials ought to have enforced a super over, but misunderstood the regulations – and ended with 221 for three, their highest T20 total, against the Netherlands.

The hosts won two low-scoring games against Ireland in Rotterdam, but failed to adjust to a quicker pitch against Scotland in Amstelveen; the closest any of their batsmen came to totalling 100 was Auckland-born Max O'Dowd's 90. It didn't help that Somerset's Roelof van der Merwe was available for only one match, in which he took two for 24 and scored 37 off 26 balls against Ireland.

The Irish were playing their first T20 internationals for 15 months and, against the Dutch, it showed. The batting of Paul Stirling was an exception – he was the only player in the tournament to score two fifties – while Andy Balbirnie hit 74 off 40 balls in their only win, their first in seven T20Is. Boyd Rankin, Ireland's best bowler, was fit to play just one match, while William Porterfield, who gave up the T20 captaincy to Gary Wilson, sat out the Scotland games.

NATIONAL SQUADS

Netherlands *P. M. Seelaar, W. Barresi, B. N. Cooper, B. F. W. de Leede, S. A. Edwards, Q. W. M. Gunning, F. J. Klaassen, M. P. O'Dowd, Saqib Zulfiqar, Sikander Zulfiqar, S. Snater, T. van der Gugten, R. E. van der Merwe, P. A. van Meekeren, T. P. Visée. *Coach:* R. J. Campbell.

Ireland *G. C. Wilson, A. Balbirnie, P. K. D. Chase, G. H. Dockrell, B. J. McCarthy, K. J. O'Brien, W. T. S. Porterfield, S. W. Poynter, W. B. Rankin, J. N. K. Shannon, S. Singh, P. R. Stirling, S. R. Thompson, C. A. Young. *Coach:* G. X. Ford.

Scotland *K. J. Coetzer, R. D. Berrington, M. H. Cross, D. E. Budge, A. C. Evans, M. A. Leask, C. S. MacLeod, H. G. Munsey, S. M. Sharif, C. B. Sole, H. Tahir, C. D. Wallace, M. R. J. Watt, B. T. J. Wheal, S. G. Whittingham. *Coach:* G. E. Bradburn.

At Rotterdam, June 12, 2018. **Netherlands won by four runs. Netherlands 144** (19.5 overs) (B. F. W. de Leede 33, P. M. Seelaar 36; B. J. McCarthy 3-26, S. Singh 3-23); ‡**Ireland 140-8** (20 overs) (S. Singh 57*; P. M. Seelaar 3-25). *T20I debuts: B. F. W. de Leede, S. A. Edwards, F. J. Klaassen, Saqib Zulfiqar, S. Snater (Netherlands); S. Singh (Ireland). Ireland needed 34 off two overs, and got close when the 19th, bowled by Fred Klaassen (born in Haywards Heath), disappeared for 22. But seamer Paul van Meekeren, the Netherlands' best bowler, restricted the batsmen to seven off the 20th, to give the hosts a winning start. Ireland had enjoyed a good 19th over with the ball too: the Dutch lost two wickets as their last four fell for eight, and were grateful for a fifth-wicket* *stand of 64 between Bas de Leede and Pieter Seelaar. A confident team would have chased 145 without a problem, but Ireland found themselves 63-7 in the 14th, before a 29-ball 57* from the debutant Simi Singh – who had earlier taken three wickets – ensured some late excitement. He needed to hit van Meekeren's last ball for six, but could manage only a single off a yorker.*

At Rotterdam, June 13, 2018. **Netherlands won by four wickets. ‡Ireland 158-6** (20 overs) (J. N. K. Shannon 51, G. C. Wilson 45*); **Netherlands 159-6** (19 overs) (M. P. O'Dowd 39, R. E. van der Merwe 37). *The Netherlands pulled off a fifth successive T20 win over Ireland. James Shannon was promoted to open with Paul Stirling, and Ireland hit 58 off the first five overs. But when those two were dismissed in successive overs, the innings lost its way. From 84-3 at halfway, they struggled to 158-6, with just six boundaries from the last ten. Roelof van der Merwe, in his only match of the series, dismissed Singh and Kevin O'Brien. Max O'Dowd then powered 39 in 24 balls, before a fifth-wicket stand of 39 between van der Merwe and Seelaar kept the Dutch in control. Requiring 23 from the last three overs, they completed the job in two, culminating in successive fours by Scott Edwards off Barry McCarthy.*

At Deventer, June 16, 2018. **Ireland won by 46 runs. ‡Ireland 205-5** (20 overs) (P. R. Stirling 51, A. Balbirnie 74, G. C. Wilson 58); **Scotland 159-5** (20 overs) (H. G. Munsey 41, K. J. Coetzer 33). *T20I debuts: P. K. D. Chase (Ireland); S. G. Whittingham (Scotland). Ireland equalled their third-highest T20 total on their way to victory over a Scotland team containing ten of the side that had beaten England in an ODI six days earlier (Stuart Whittingham had replaced fellow seamer Safyaan Sharif). But the Scots had no answer to Stirling, who smacked eight fours in the first four overs en route to a 27-ball half-century. In his first match of the tournament, Andrew Balbirnie maintained the momentum with 74 from 40 – his maiden T20I fifty – before Gary Wilson took over, finishing with 58 from 38. Scotland threatened to compete while George Munsey and Kyle Coetzer were hitting 60 off the first six overs, but the Irish slow bowlers applied the squeeze, and the innings dribbled away.*

At Deventer, June 17, 2018. **Tied. ‡Scotland 185-4** (20 overs) (H. G. Munsey 46, K. J. Coetzer 54, C. S. MacLeod 46*); **Ireland 185-6** (20 overs) (P. R. Stirling 81). *The ICC apologised to both sides after match officials failed to implement a super over following the tenth T20I tie, which thus became the first to remain tied. The captains were reportedly told before the tournament that, contrary to the regulations, super overs would not be used. It left the ICC to admit that match referee David Jukes and umpires Allan Haggo and Pim van Liemt had "misinterpreted" the rubric. Ireland had needed seven off the last over with six wickets in hand, but lost Kevin O'Brien to the first ball, brilliantly caught by Dylan Budge at long-off. Only four runs came from the next four deliveries, so Stuart Thompson needed three off the last; he managed two to long-on. Ireland's pursuit of 186 had been given a flying start by Stirling's 41-ball 81, which broke his own national T20I record (79 against Afghanistan in Dubai in 2011-12), before O'Brien thrashed three sixes in a 17-ball 28. Scotland had flown out of the blocks too, Munsey (46 off 25) and Coetzer (54 off 41) battering 93 in eight overs.*

At Amstelveen, June 19, 2018. **Scotland won by seven wickets. ‡Netherlands 160-6** (20 overs) (M. P. O'Dowd 31, W. Barresi 53*); **Scotland 161-3** (17.4 overs) (H. G. Munsey 46, K. J. Coetzer 42, R. D. Berrington 49*). *Scotland won their first match of the tournament to set up a final-day decider against the hosts. After their bowlers restricted the Netherlands to 160, Munsey and Coetzer continued their excellent form by blasting 74 inside six overs, and the rest of the chase proved straightforward; Richie Berrington finished things off with his ninth four. The Dutch had also made a fast start – 43 in 3.5 overs, before Mark Watt, who went for just 18 in his four, bowled Tobias Visée for 25. Wesley Barresi batted for the rest of the innings, but his 53* ate up 51 deliveries, and the last seven balls brought three wickets.*

At Amstelveen, June 20, 2018. **Scotland won by 115 runs. ‡Scotland 221-3** (20 overs) (H. G. Munsey 71, M. H. Cross 50, R. D. Berrington 64*); **Netherlands 106** (14 overs) (S. A. Edwards 31*; H. Tahir 3-26). *Scotland's first T20 total over 200 (their previous best was 189-3 against Hong Kong at Abu Dhabi in 2016-17) turned the decider into a cakewalk. Their biggest win, by far, was also the Netherlands' biggest defeat. The openers began with their fourth consecutive stand of 50 or more, before Munsey went on to a 34-ball 71, Scotland's second-highest T20 score, behind Berrington's 100 against Bangladesh at The Hague in 2012. Munsey added 84 in eight overs with Matt Cross, who in turn put on 78 with Berrington (64* off 30). The Netherlands lost two wickets in the first seven balls, and only three reached double figures as they were bowled out in 14 overs, though the injured Saqib Zulfiqar did not bat.*

Scotland 5pts, Netherlands 4pts, Ireland 3pts.

NETHERLANDS v NEPAL

One-day internationals (2): Netherlands 1, Nepal 1

First one-day international   At Amstelveen, August 1. **Netherlands won by 55 runs.**
‡Netherlands 189 (47.4 overs) (B. F. W. de Leede 30, M. J. G. Rippon 51; S. Kami 3-34, P. Khadka
4-26); **Nepal 134** (41.5 overs) (G. Malla 51, D. S. Airee 33; F. J. Klaassen 3-30, M. J. G. Rippon
3-23, P. M. Seelaar 3-20). *MoM*: M. J. G. Rippon. *ODI debuts*: B. F. W. de Leede, S. A. Edwards,
F. J. Klaassen, S. Snater, D. J. ter Braak (Netherlands); D. S. Airee, S. P. Gauchan, S. Kami, K. C.
Karan, P. Khadka, S. Lamichhane, G. Malla, B. Regmi, A. K. Sah, A. Sheikh, S. Vesawkar (Nepal).
*This was Nepal's first official one-day international, and the Netherlands' first since regaining the
ODI status they lost in 2014. Nepal looked set for victory at 85-1 in the 19th over, but the dismissal
of Paras Khadka, their captain, heralded a collapse. Three left-arm bowlers shared nine wickets:
seamer Fred Klaassen, wrist-spinner Michael Rippon (who had earlier top-scored with 51), and
orthodox spinner Pieter Seelaar, the Dutch captain. After the match, Shakti Gauchan – who first
played for Nepal as a 17-year-old in 2001 – confirmed his retirement, having fulfilled his ambition
of playing an official ODI. "He's one of the most hard-working cricketers I've ever seen or known,"
said Khadka.*

Second one-day international   At Amstelveen, August 3. **Nepal won by one run.** ‡Nepal 216
(48.5 overs) (P. Khadka 51, S. Kami 61; F. J. Klaassen 3-38); **Netherlands 215** (50 overs) (D. J. ter
Braak 39, W. Barresi 71; S. Lamichhane 3-41). *MoM*: S. Kami. *ODI debuts*: L. S. Bhandari, S. P.
Khakurel, R. K. Paudel (Nepal). *Nepal pulled off their maiden victory – and squared the series – in
an exciting match. After Khadka made 51, No. 8 Sompal Kami boosted Nepal's total with 61 from
46. It looked all over when the Netherlands declined to 185-9 in the 44th over, with the highly rated
leg-spinner Sandeep Lamichhane taking three wickets, but Klaassen and Paul van Meekeren put on
30. Khadka took the ball for the last over, with six required, and it boiled down to two from the final
delivery: Klaassen timed a meaty straight-drive – but it was too straight, and clattered into the
stumps at the non-striker's end. Khadka had time to collect the ball and uproot a stump, to run
Klaassen out and complete a famous victory. Nepal's Rohit Kumar Paudel, a month short of his 16th
birthday, became the fourth-youngest man to appear in an ODI.*

CRICKET IN SCOTLAND IN 2018

Back down to earth

WILLIAM DICK

It was the best of times and the worst of times for Scottish cricket in 2018 – triumphant and tear-filled in equal measure. Undoubtedly the highlight of the year – arguably of any year – came at Edinburgh in June, when Calum MacLeod's unbeaten 140 inspired the national side to a historic and thrilling one-day victory over No. 1-ranked England. Yet even amid the euphoria of that win, later voted Sporting Moment of the Year at the Team Scotland Scottish Sports Awards, there was a realisation that future opportunities to repeat the feat were likely to be rare.

By the time Eoin Morgan's side arrived at The Grange, Scotland had failed – in heart-breaking circumstances – to claim one of the two coveted World Cup spots on offer at the qualifying tournament in Zimbabwe in March. Needing victory over West Indies in Harare, the Scots looked on course when they dismissed them for 198. With storm clouds gathering, Richie Berrington and George Munsey manoeuvred them ahead on DLS, only for an umpiring error to send Berrington on his way. When the rain arrived, Scotland were five short – and utterly crestfallen.

Having missed out to the Netherlands in December 2017 on a place in the ICC's new one-day international league, starting in 2020, this was another crushing blow for a team capable of competing at the highest level. Rather than dine at the top table, Scotland will have to content themselves with Cricket World Cup League Two, which will at least guarantee 36 matches over two and a half years.

These matches, though, will be against similarly ambitious nations, such as Nepal and the UAE, but not England or Australia – or even Afghanistan, whom Scotland beat in Zimbabwe, or Ireland. This year brings the small consolation of two ODIs each against Sri Lanka and Afghanistan as they prepare for the World Cup. But with doubt over the future structure of the multi-day Intercontinental Cup, it was little surprise when head coach Grant Bradburn moved on, to become fielding coach of Pakistan. His parting message, in which he reminded the ICC of their "obligation to recognise the very success they have invested in over many years", and to ensure Scotland and other leading Associates play more games, highlighted the conundrum facing Cricket Scotland.

Having come back down to earth with two T20I defeats by Pakistan shortly after the England game, Scotland headed across the North Sea for a T20 tri-series against the Netherlands and Ireland. They recovered from an opening defeat by the Irish to tie the return match, before twice trouncing the hosts to take the title. The last of those matches took place on June 20 – before mid-summer's day – yet represented Scotland's last competitive action of the year.

However, 2019 began on a positive note with the appointment of Bradburn's successor – Shane Burger, a former coach of KwaZulu-Natal Inland. There was also an upbeat pronouncement from Cricket Scotland's chief executive Malcolm Cannon, who remains committed to "the strategic goal of achieving ICC Full Member status".

The women's game continued to make significant progress. Scotland came third at the World T20 Qualifier in the Netherlands in July, and finished the year 11th in the new 47-team table. But the Scots lost one of their most talented players when left-arm spinner Kirstie Gordon was selected to play for England at the T20 World Cup. Along with fellow Scot Leigh Kasperek, now of New Zealand, Gordon was named in the Team of the Tournament.

Grange, coached by John Blain, returned to the forefront of the club game by winning the treble of Eastern Premiership, Grand Final and Scottish Cup. Blain, who has established a successful Academy at the club, has ambitious plans: this summer, Grange will take on Minor County opposition. Unsurprisingly, they provided many of the Eastern Knights team who retained the regional Pro50 Cup and recaptured the T20 Blitz title. In future, the regional structure will include a List A-accredited competition, which will be central to hopes of full membership. Elsewhere, Ferguslie were Western Premier champions, while Heriot's lifted the T20 Cup.

For Scotland's one-day international against England, see page 304.

Winners of Scottish Leagues and Cups
Eastern Premier Division **Grange**. Western Premier Division **Ferguslie**. National Champions **Grange**. Citylets Scottish Cup **Grange**. Murgitroyd T20 Cup **Heriot's**. Tilney Pro50 Cup **Eastern Knights**. Tilney T20 Blitz **Eastern Knights**. Women's Premier League **Edinburgh South/Stewart's Melville**. Beyond Boundaries Women's T20 Cup **The West**.

SCOTLAND v PAKISTAN IN 2018

Mazher Arshad

Twenty20 internationals (2): Scotland 0, Pakistan 2

It's not often cricket has knocked Donald Trump off the front pages, but that was the case in Scotland as Pakistan arrived for two Twenty20 games. The hosts' recent ODI victory over England was deemed more important by some editors than the summit in Singapore between Trump and North Korean leader Kim Jong-un. Pictures of seamer Safyaan Sharif displaced the politicians.

The coverage at least alerted Pakistan to the dangers of cruising towards the end of their tour of Britain and Ireland. "We were not taking them lightly even before the England match," said captain Sarfraz Ahmed. The series offered an opportunity for Scotland, ranked No. 11, to edge into top ten, qualify for the World T20 in Australia in 2020, and nudge Pakistan out of the No. 1 position. But perhaps it was expecting too much of the Scots to switch formats immediately after their famous victory: Pakistan won both games clinically, and travelled home on a winning note.

First Twenty20 international At Edinburgh, June 12. **Pakistan won by 48 runs.** ‡Pakistan 204-4 (20 overs) (Sarfraz Ahmed 89*, Shoaib Malik 53; A. C. Evans 3-23); **Scotland 156-6** (20 overs) (K. J. Coetzer 31, M. A. Leask 38*). *MoM:* Sarfraz Ahmed. *T20I debuts:* D. E. Budge, H. Tahir (Scotland). *When Scotland openers Henry Munsey and Kyle Coetzer crashed 53 off the first five overs, thoughts turned to the possibility of another top-ranked white-ball side being embarrassed in Edinburgh. But Pakistan spinners Mohammad Nawaz and Shadab Khan had other ideas. Coetzer was removed by Nawaz for 31 off 18, Shadab took care of Richie Berrington and Calum MacLeod, hero of the victory over England, and the outcome was not in doubt again, although Michael Leask top-scored with 38*. An excellent effort in the middle overs by Scotland had seen Pakistan poised uncertainly at 124-3 after 15. But 80 were plundered off the last five: Sarfraz Ahmed finished with 89*, and Shoaib Malik hit five sixes in a 27-ball 53. Scotland's debutant slow left-armer Hamza Tahir went for 57 off his four overs.*

Second Twenty20 international At Edinburgh, June 13. **Pakistan won by 84 runs.** ‡Pakistan 166-6 (20 overs) (Fakhar Zaman 33, Shoaib Malik 49*; M. A. Leask 3-31); **Scotland 82** (14.4 overs) (Fahim Ashraf 3-5). *MoM:* Usman Shinwari. *Good work by the Pakistan seamers, and dreadful running between the wickets, condemned Scotland to a heavy defeat. The arrival of Shoaib late in the innings transformed Pakistan's prospects. He hammered 49* off 22, including five sixes, as 34 came off the last two overs. Usman Shinwari knocked a dent in Scotland's hopes by removing Munsey and Coetzer early on. MacLeod tried to rebuild, but became one of three victims for Fahim Ashraf. Scotland suffered three run-outs, and lost their last four wickets for six.*

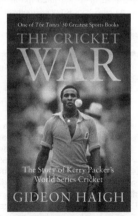

CRICKET IN THE UNITED ARAB EMIRATES IN 2018

On the retained list

PAUL RADLEY

Rain is not usually a factor in the lives of the UAE's cricketers: time is more often lost to sandstorms. So it was bizarre how often rain made an appearance at the tipping points of their year. In Namibia in February, with the future of the newly professional game in the UAE on the line, they dodged the showers for just long enough to win the World Cricket League Division Two, beating Nepal by seven runs in the final. That earned them the chance to play for World Cup qualification – and, perhaps more pertinently, to retain one-day international status – in Zimbabwe a month later.

In Harare, the pressure remained acute. A structure that has a small band of professionals on central contracts is hugely dependent on the ICC funding that comes with that ODI status, which was first awarded when they qualified for the 2015 World Cup. Retaining it is vital. With two wins – against Papua New Guinea and the Netherlands – they made it to the second stage and, in the process, achieved their objective. Reaching the World Cup, however, proved beyond Rohan Mustafa's side, although they did manage their first win over a Full Member. In the last match of the Super Six stage, they took advantage of Zimbabwe's jangling nerves and, with the help of a rain interruption that worked against the hosts, recorded a three-run DLS win. Rameez Shahzad hit 59 off 61 balls and put on 74 with Ghulam Shabbir, while Mohammad Naveed took three wickets. Rameez and Naveed were the UAE's best performers throughout the competition.

With the Asia Cup switched to the UAE from India, there was extra incentive to reach the final stages. Four wins out of five meant they finished top of the table in the qualifying competition in Malaysia. In the final against Hong Kong, Ashfaq Ahmed's aggressive 79 from 51 balls put them in a strong position. But this time rain arrived at the wrong moment, and Hong Kong pinched the prize with three balls to spare.

Frustration boiled over at the Emerging Teams Asia Cup in Pakistan in December, which pitched together players from Asia's five Test nations and the UAE, Oman and Hong Kong. The UAE bowlers were on top against Hong Kong in a key match when water seeped under the covers during a short rain break. The no-result meant Pakistan and Bangladesh went through at the UAE's expense. Mustafa, Rameez and Ahmed Raza all expressed annoyance in social-media posts, and criticised the Asian Cricket Council and the Pakistan Cricket Board. The Emirates Cricket Board, keen to maintain good relations with the PCB, imposed fines and eight-week bans on each, unimpressed by their subsequent apologies. It seemed harsh, especially given that, in a squad containing many expats, all three have a long-standing affinity with the country.

T10 LEAGUE IN 2017-18

Paul Radley

1 Kerala Kings   2 Punjabi Legends

The new T10 League in Sharjah in December 2017 was always going to be a bit different. And, sure enough, it was won by a team nominally representing a state in India, despite not having one Indian on the books (their leading player was from Belfast), and being owned by a perfume tycoon from Yemen.

The event was dreamed up by Shaji Ul Mulk, a billionaire building magnate born in India but based in the UAE for most of his adult life, a lot of which had been spent bowling off-spin. He feels he might even have made the UAE side for the 1996 World Cup had business not consumed him. Ul Mulk conceived the T10 idea while watching Brazil play football on TV. Impressed by the intensity, he sought a way of fitting cricket into 90 minutes – the simplest method was to cut a Twenty20 match in half.

In practice, the matches lasted longer than a game of football, thanks in part to the addition of strategic time-outs after five overs of each innings, tailored for ad breaks. The tournament itself was unashamedly commercial; even dot balls were sponsored, by Ul Mulk's manufacturing company.

The snappy format actually made for longer days than at the average Test. To maximise the chances of attracting the leading players, needed for the credibility of the concept, the six-team competition was squeezed into four days. With quarter-finals and a fifth-place play-off, that meant four games on both Friday and Saturday, and the schedule proved rather elastic: at one point TV commentator Rameez Raja finished a toss interview before hurrying back to the boundary to complete a post-match presentation.

But the event proved a hit at the box office. The Sharjah Cricket Stadium was sold out, with 15,000 capacity crowds on two of the four days, and close to full on the others. Friday cricket in Sharjah is usually a hot ticket, especially when Shahid Afridi is involved – but the fact that finals night sold out was unexpected. Sunday, when the two semi-finals and the final were played, is the first day of the working week in the UAE, and usually a tough sell. But at around 11pm the ground authorities proudly flashed up a message on the big screen: "Full house, thank you Sharjah fans."

Even though Afridi's team, the Pakhtoons, went out in the semi, most supporters stayed until the end, in the small hours of Monday morning. Eoin Morgan, who captained Kerala Kings, was still talking to the media at 1.30am after his side won the final against Punjabi Legends. Ireland opener Paul Stirling was Kerala's leading light, carrying on his form from the one-day series against Afghanistan. He hit 181 runs in the five matches while being dismissed only twice, with a strike-rate of 196. "In ten-over cricket, it can't go too wrong," he said. "I just like to watch the ball and hit it." The format was brutal on bowlers, but Kerala had the pick of those, too: Pakistanis Wahab Riaz and Sohail Tanvir both conceded less than eight an over.

T10 CRICKET LEAGUE IN 2017-18

10-over leagues plus knockouts

	P	W	L	NR	Pts	NRR
Pakhtoons.........	2	2	0	0	4	2.60
Maratha Arabians	2	1	0	1	2	−0.95
Team Sri Lanka......	2	0	2	0	0	−1.65

	P	W	L	NR	Pts	NRR
Kerala Kings........	2	1	0	1	2	0.75
Punjabi Legends	2	1	0	1	2	−0.06
Bengal Tigers	2	1	0	1	2	−0.62

Final At Sharjah, December 17, 2017 (floodlit). **Punjabi Legends 120-3** (10 overs) (L. Ronchi 70); ‡**Kerala Kings 121-2** (8 overs) (P. R. Stirling 52*, E. J. G. Morgan 63). *The Legends set a steep target, thanks to Luke Ronchi's 34-ball 70, which contained five sixes: it gave him 197 runs in five matches in the tournament, at a strike-rate of 185. His team-mate Shoaib Malik made 191 at 217. Despite losing Chadwick Walton to the first ball of the chase, the Kings strolled home, with the Middlesex pair of Paul Stirling and Eoin Morgan smashing 113 from the next 41 deliveries.*

UNITED ARAB EMIRATES TRI-SERIES IN 2017-18

Paul Radley

1 Ireland   2 Scotland   3 United Arab Emirates

Ireland made full use of a competition arranged at short notice as a warm-up for the World Cup Qualifier in Zimbabwe in March. They won all four of their matches, while their batsmen enjoyed valuable time in the middle, to the evident satisfaction of coach Graham Ford, who welcomed the chance to escape indoor nets. It also provided a handy workout for Scotland and, in particular, the United Arab Emirates, who went on to reach Zimbabwe via the second division of the World Cricket League.

Ireland realised they were there to be shot at. "I think there has been a target on our back in the past three or four years, and not because of this full membership stuff," said their long-serving opener Ed Joyce. The UAE and Scotland, meanwhile, shared the honours in their two meetings. The UAE's Rameez Shahzad was the tournament's leading run-scorer, with 258 at 86, while three bowlers took eight wickets – Ireland's Kevin O'Brien and Barry McCarthy, and the UAE's Mohammad Naveed.

NATIONAL SQUADS

United Arab Emirates *Rohan Mustafa, Adnan Mufti, Ahmed Raza, Amir Hayat, Ashfaq Ahmed, Ghulam Shabbir, Imran Haider, Mohammad Boota, Mohammad Naveed, Mohammad Usman, Qadeer Ahmed, Rameez Shahzad, Shaiman Anwar, Zahoor Khan. *Coach:* D. R. Brown.

Ireland *W. T. S. Porterfield, A. Balbirnie, P. K. D. Chase, G. H. Dockrell, E. C. Joyce, A. R. McBrine, B. J. McCarthy, J. I. Mulder, K. J. O'Brien, N. J. O'Brien, S. W. Poynter, W. B. Rankin, S. Singh, P. R. Stirling, G. C. Wilson. *Coach:* G. X. Ford.

Scotland *K. J. Coetzer, R. D. Berrington, S. J. Cameron, M. H. Cross, A. C. Evans, M. A. Jones, M. A. Leask, C. S. MacLeod, H. G. Munsey, S. M. Sharif, T. B. Sole, C. D. Wallace, M. R. J. Watt, S. G. Whittingham. *Coach:* G. E. Bradburn.

At Dubai (ICC Academy), January 11, 2018. **Ireland won by four wickets. United Arab Emirates 222-9** (50 overs) (Rameez Shahzad 75); ‡**Ireland 226-6** (49.2 overs) (E. C. Joyce 116*, G. C. Wilson 53). *MoM:* E. C. Joyce. *ODI debuts:* Ashfaq Ahmed, Mohammad Boota (UAE). *The UAE squandered a golden opportunity to record a first victory over a Full Member. After making 222-9 on the back of a dogged 75 off 111 balls from Rameez Shahzad, they had Ireland in a corner at 91-5, only to miss a chance to remove Ed Joyce. He and Gary Wilson added 131 to take Ireland to the brink of victory. Joyce passed 10,000 List A runs during his sixth ODI century.*

At Dubai (ICC Academy), January 13, 2018. **Ireland won by 67 runs.** ‡**Ireland 301-5** (50 overs) (W. T. S. Porterfield 139, A. Balbirnie 102); **United Arab Emirates 234** (48.4 overs) (Rameez Shahzad 50; K. J. O'Brien 4-41). *MoM:* W. T. S. Porterfield. *Ireland captain William Porterfield showed his relish for the ICC Academy ground by making the highest of his ten ODI centuries. In four matches there, he had now scored 343 runs. Andrew Balbirnie also hit a hundred, his first in ODIs, as they put on 201 for the second wicket. The UAE began sluggishly and never threatened Ireland's total, although Rameez made another half-century. Kevin O'Brien finished with four wickets.*

At Dubai (ICC Academy), January 16, 2018. **Ireland won by six wickets. Scotland 219** (49.2 overs) (M. A. Jones 87; W. B. Rankin 3-49); ‡**Ireland 223-4** (34.5 overs) (A. Balbirnie 67, N. J. O'Brien 55). *MoM:* A. Balbirnie. *ODI debut:* M. A. Jones, T. B. Sole (Scotland). *Led by Balbirnie's 67 off 55 balls, Ireland made short work of overhauling an inadequate total for their third successive win. Their bowlers exerted such a stranglehold on Scotland's top order that, by the time the third wicket fell in the 20th over, only 63 had been scored. Boyd Rankin took 3-49, and spinners George Dockrell and Andy McBrine tightened the grip. Scotland's total would have been even lower but for Michael Jones, their 20-year-old debutant opener, who batted into the 44th over for 87. After Porterfield fell to the second ball of the reply, Balbirnie and Paul Stirling put on 104 in 16 overs, then Niall O'Brien eased to 55.*

At Dubai (ICC Academy), January 18, 2018. **Ireland won by 24 runs.** ‡**Ireland 331-6** (50 overs) (P. R. Stirling 74, N. J. O'Brien 51; S. G. Whittingham 3-58); **Scotland 307-9** (50 overs) (M. A. Jones 74, C. S. MacLeod 58, M. A. Leask 59). *MoM:* P. R. Stirling. *ODI debut:* S. J. Cameron (Scotland). *Ireland ensured they would finish top of the table after scoring their joint-highest ODI total – matching 331-8 against Zimbabwe at Hobart during the 2015 World Cup. They flew home before Scotland or the UAE had registered a point. Six Irish batsmen reached 40, though only two passed 50; Stirling led the way with 74, sharing a second-wicket partnership of 117 with the in-form Balbirnie (47). Niall O'Brien chipped in with 51, and brother Kevin 46 off 24 balls. For Scotland, Jones underlined his promise with 74, and there were half-centuries from Calum MacLeod and Michael Leask, who put on 95 for the sixth wicket. But Ireland always had enough.*

At Dubai (ICC Academy), January 21, 2018. **Scotland won by 31 runs. Scotland 249-8** (50 overs) (M. H. Cross 107*; Shaiman Anwar 3-61); ‡**United Arab Emirates 218** (46.3 overs) (Ghulam Shabbir 90). *MoM:* M. H. Cross. *A first ODI hundred by Matthew Cross steered Scotland to victory over the hosts. Batting at No. 3, Cross glued Scotland's innings together after the UAE had reduced them to 73-4. He put on 59 with George Munsey (45) and 41* for the ninth wicket with Alasdair Evans, who made just four but hung around for the final four overs. Cross took 18 off the last four balls of the innings, from Mohammad Naveed. The UAE looked in control of the chase at 142-3, but folded against Scotland's miserly attack. Ghulam Shabbir hit 90 off 83 balls, an ODI best, but no one offered much after he was run out. The result was disappointing for the UAE coach Dougie Brown, in charge against his homeland for the first time.*

At Dubai (ICC Academy), January 23, 2018. **United Arab Emirates won by four wickets.** ‡**Scotland 299-9** (50 overs) (K. J. Coetzer 75, R. D. Berrington 90; Mohammad Naveed 3-47, Zahoor Khan 3-62); **United Arab Emirates 300-6** (49.1 overs) (Ashfaq Ahmed 92, Rameez Shahzad 121*). *MoM:* Rameez Shahzad. *ODI debut:* Amir Hayat (UAE). *Rameez hit the UAE's second-highest ODI score – following Khurram Khan's 132* against Afghanistan on the same ground in 2014-15 – to steer his team to their only win of the series. He came in at 50-2 in the 11th over, put on 125 with Ashfaq Ahmed and 75 with Adnan Mufti (38), and eased his team home off* *the first ball of the final over; in all, Rameez faced just 115 deliveries. It was the first time the UAE had made 300 in an ODI. Naveed took 3-47 in Scotland's innings, in which Richie Berrington's 90 came from 95 balls.*

Ireland 8pts, Scotland 2pts, United Arab Emirates 2pts.

UNITED ARAB EMIRATES v AUSTRALIA

Twenty20 international (1): UAE 0, Australia 1

Twenty20 international   At Abu Dhabi (Nursery No. 2), October 22, 2018. **Australia won by seven wickets.** ‡**United Arab Emirates 117-6** (20 overs) (Shaiman Anwar 41); **Australia 119-3** (16.1 overs) (D. J. M. Short 68*). *MoM:* D. J. M. Short. *T20I debuts:* Amir Hayat, Ashfaq Ahmed, Chirag Suri (UAE); B. R. McDermott (Australia). *In between the Test and T20 series against Pakistan, Australia recorded the only win of their tour, in their first official international against the UAE. It was upgraded from a warm-up game a few days before and, as there was not enough time to produce a pitch at the Sheikh Zayed Stadium, was played on the No. 2 Nursery Oval. A mismatch looked on the cards when the UAE slumped to 0-2 after seven balls, with debutant Ashfaq Ahmed and captain Rohan Mustafa both bagging ducks, but 39-year-old Shaiman Anwar anchored a modest recovery, his 41 including two straight sixes. Aaron Finch fell for a single, but D'Arcy Short made sure of victory with 68* from 53 balls. Ben McDermott, the son of the former Test fast bowler Craig, marked his international debut by hitting the winning boundary.*   GEOFF LEMON

ASIA CUP QUALIFIER IN 2018

1   Hong Kong   2   United Arab Emirates

Six teams convened in Kuala Lumpur in August 2018 to squabble over the final spot in the Asia Cup proper, to be held in the United Arab Emirates a few weeks later. When the UAE topped the qualifying table – after beating Oman by 13 runs in a final-game shoot-out – they looked set to join their own party. But Hong Kong scuppered that in a rain-affected final, overhauling a revised target with two wickets and three balls to spare.

It was reward for Hong Kong's consistent batting throughout the tournament: Anshuman Rath made 209 runs and Babar Hayat 196, although the leading scorer was Singapore's Anish Param, with 218. Hong Kong's off-spinner Nadeem Ahmed claimed 14 wickets, two more than the UAE slow left-armer Ahmed Raza, who took six for 20 against Singapore. Every team had something to cheer: hosts Malaysia upset Hong Kong in the opening match, while 100 from Param helped Singapore beat Malaysia.

The group game between Nepal and the UAE was an official one-day international, as both teams had the required status. The final, oddly, was not, as Hong Kong had lost their ODI status after the World Cup Qualifier earlier in the year. However, their matches in the Asia Cup itself would be deemed official by the ICC.

GROUP TABLE

	P	W	L	NR	Pts	NRR
UNITED ARAB EMIRATES	5	4	1	0	8	1.28
HONG KONG	5	3	1	1	7	1.53
Oman	5	3	1	1	7	0.58
Nepal	5	2	3	0	4	−0.25
Malaysia..................	5	1	4	0	2	−0.99
Singapore	5	1	4	0	2	−2.17

One-day international   At Kuala Lumpur, August 30, 2018. **United Arab Emirates won by 78 runs. United Arab Emirates** 254-9 (50 overs) (Ashfaq Ahmed 45, Chirag Suri 65, Rameez Shahzad 35, Adnan Mufti 57*; S. Lamichhane 4-24); ‡**Nepal** 176 (48.5 overs) (S. P. Khakurel 50, D. S. Airee 40; Mohammad Naveed 3-48, Ahmed Raza 4-37). *MoM:* Ahmed Raza. *ODI debut:* S. Pun (Nepal). *Left-arm spinner Ahmed Raza's four wickets included the vital scalp of Paras Khadka, Nepal's captain, for 16.*

Final   At Kuala Lumpur, September 6, 2018. **Hong Kong won by two wickets (DLS). United Arab Emirates** 176-9 (24 overs) (Ashfaq Ahmed 79; Aizaz Khan 5-28, Nadeem Ahmed 3-28); ‡**Hong Kong** 179-8 (23.3 overs) (Nizakat Khan 38, C. J. Carter 33). *MoM:* Aizaz Khan. *A long rain interruption when the UAE were 65-3 in the 16th reduced this to a 24-over match. Medium-pacer Aizaz Khan collected five wickets as the UAE hit out wildly on resumption: opener Ashfaq Ahmed hammered 79 from 51 balls, with nine fours and six sixes. Hong Kong's target was revised to 179, and they scraped home in the final over to claim the place at the Asia Cup.*

THE ASIA CUP IN 2018

Anand Vasu

1 India   2 Bangladesh

The international calendar leaves little scope for quiet reflection. Seventeen days after they left The Oval at the conclusion of a chastening 4–1 Test series defeat by England, India were triumphantly lifting the Asia Cup in Dubai following a last-ball thriller against Bangladesh. It was breathless in more ways than one. Virat Kohli put his feet up at home, handing the reins to Rohit Sharma, but this was still a formidable India squad, and they proved too strong for their rivals. "We ticked all the boxes," said Sharma.

The tournament was scheduled to have been held in India but, with political tensions making it impossible for Pakistan to travel, it was switched to the UAE. That did not prevent Sharma's team accruing a significant gain. Thanks to a tweak of the regulations after the competition began, they played all their games in Dubai, while other teams had to play some matches in Abu Dhabi.

If India's final victory was predictable, much else was not. Traditionally the competition had been dominated by them, Pakistan and Sri Lanka, but there was evidence of a new order emerging. While five-times winners Sri Lanka headed home early, Bangladesh came agonisingly close to a maiden triumph. And the most compelling side to watch were Afghanistan. Meticulous, street-smart and canny, they gave everyone a run for their money. They also had the best bowler: leg-spinner Rashid Khan took ten wickets at 17.

Sharma revelled in the extra responsibility. He topped the averages with 317 at 105, and was the tournament's second-highest run-scorer. Only team-mate Shikhar Dhawan, recovering from a tough time in England, managed more, with 342 at 68. Kuldeep Yadav, whose fortunes had fluctuated on that tour, was the joint-highest wicket-taker, with ten. Until the drama of the final, India were seriously extended only by Afghanistan, in their last Super Four game. It may have been a dead rubber, but it was still the best match of the lot – finishing in the 36th ODI tie. Bangladesh leaned heavily on the batting of Mushfiqur Rahim, who scored 302 at 60. Mustafizur Rahman was the leading seamer, with ten wickets.

One disappointment was that no matches were played in Sharjah, the venue that first brought international cricket to the Middle East. Overall, though, the short, sharp format ensured interest did not flag, and attendances were healthy.

NATIONAL SQUADS

*   *Captain*   ‡   *Did not play*

Afghanistan   *Asghar Afghan, Aftab Alam, Gulbadeen Naib, Hashmatullah Shahidi, Ihsanullah Janat, Javed Ahmadi, Mohammad Nabi, Mohammad Shahzad, Mujeeb Zadran, ‡Munir Ahmad, Najibullah Zadran, Rahmat Shah, Rashid Khan, Samiullah Shenwari, ‡Sayed Shirzad, ‡Wafadar Momand. *Coach:* P. V. Simmons.

Bangladesh *Mashrafe bin Mortaza, Abu Haider, ‡Ariful Haque, Imrul Kayes, Liton Das, Mahmudullah, Mehedi Hasan, Mithun Ali, Mosaddek Hossain, Mushfiqur Rahim, Mustafizur Rahman, Nazmul Hossain, Nazmul Islam, Shalkib Al Hasan, Soumya Sarkar, Tamim Iqbal. *Coach:* S. J. Rhodes.

Tamim Iqbal did not play after the first game because of a wrist injury. Imrul Kayes and Soumya Sarkar joined the squad after the first Super Four match.

Hong Kong *A. Rath, Aizaz Khan, ‡Arshad Mohammad, Babar Hayat, C. J. Carter, Ehsan Khan, Ehsan Nawaz, ‡R. Kapur, ‡C. L. McAuslan, S. S. McKechnie, Nadeem Ahmed, Nizakat Khan, K. D. Shah, ‡Tanveer Ahmed, Tanvir Afzal, ‡Waqas Khan. *Coach:* S. J. Cook.

India *R. G. Sharma, K. K. Ahmed, Bhuvneshwar Kumar, J. J. Bumrah, Y. S. Chahal, D. L. Chahar, S Dhawan, M. S. Dhoni, R. A. Jadeja, K. M. Jadhav, K. D. Karthik, S. Kaul, M. K. Pandey, H. H. Pandya, ‡A. R. Patel, K. L. Rahul, A. T. Rayudu, S. N. Thakur, K. Yadav. *Coach:* R. J. Shastri.

Thakur suffered a hip injury against Hong Kong. Patel was injured while fielding as a substitute in the group match against Pakistan. Pandya suffered a back injury in the same match. They were replaced by Kaul, Jadeja and Chahar respectively.

Pakistan *Sarfraz Ahmed, Asif Ali, Babar Azam, Fahim Ashraf, Fakhar Zaman, Haris Sohail, Hasan Ali, Imam-ul-Haq, Junaid Khan, Mohammad Amir, Mohammad Nawaz, Shadab Khan, Shaheen Shah Afridi, ‡Shan Masood, Shoaib Malik, Usman Shinwari. *Coach:* J. M. Arthur.

Sri Lanka *A. D. Mathews, M. A. Aponso, P. V. D. Chameera, D. M. de Silva, D. P. D. N. Dickwella, G. S. N. F. G. Jayasuriya, R. A. S. Lakmal, S. L. Malinga, B. K. G. Mendis, M. D. K. Perera, M. D. K. J. Perera, M. K. P. A. D. Perera, N. L. T. C. Perera, ‡C. A. K. Rajitha, M. D. Shanaka, W. U. Tharanga. *Coach:* U. C. Hathurusinghe.

L. D. Chandimal (finger injury) was replaced by Dickwella, and M. D. Gunathilleke (lower back) by Jayasuriya before the tournament began.

Group A

At Dubai (Sports City), September 16. **Pakistan won by eight wickets.** ‡**Hong Kong 116** (37.1 overs) (Usman Shinwari 3-19); **Pakistan 120-2** (23.4 overs) (Imam-ul-Haq 50*, Babar Azam 33). *MoM:* Usman Shinwari. *Hong Kong captain Anshuman Rath raised eyebrows when he decided to bat in searing heat, but when Nizakat Khan took 11 off Mohammad Amir's first over there was hope the minnows might make a match of it. The natural order was soon restored. Hong Kong were five down before the score had reached 50, and only Kinchit Shah and Aizaz Khan took them into three figures. Pakistan knocked off the runs in leisurely fashion. Imam-ul-Haq – under fire because of whispers that he owed his place to his uncle, Inzamam, who was chairman of selectors – bolstered his credentials with an unbeaten half-century.*

At Dubai (Sports City), September 18. **India won by 26 runs. India 285-7** (50 overs) (S. Dhawan 127, A. T. Rayudu 60, K. D. Karthik 33; K. D. Shah 3-39); ‡**Hong Kong 259-8** (50 overs) (Nizakat Khan 92, A. Rath 73; K. K. Ahmed 3-48, Y. S. Chahal 3-46). *MoM:* S. Dhawan. *ODI debut:* K. K. Ahmed (India). *When Hong Kong reached 174-0 at the start of the 35th over, 112 from victory, one of cricket's greatest upsets looked possible. Then the openers Nizakat and Rath were dismissed in quick succession, and talk of a fairytale evaporated. Hong Kong did not fold, but the outcome was never again in doubt. India's total had been built on Shikhar Dhawan's 14th ODI hundred. There was also a solid 60 from Ambati Rayudu, returning after a two-year absence, although the Hong Kong attack persevered, and conceded just 48 in the last ten overs. Nizakat and Rath launched the reply in style, fearlessly taking on the India seamers. It needed the spinners to apply the brakes.*

At Dubai (Sports City), September 19. **India won by eight wickets.** ‡**Pakistan 162** (43.1 overs) (Babar Azam 47, Shoaib Malik 43; Bhuvneshwar Kumar 3-15, K. M. Jadhav 3-23); **India 164-2** (29 overs) (R. G. Sharma 52, S. Dhawan 46, A. T. Rayudu 31*, K. D. Karthik 31*). *MoM:* Bhuvneshwar Kumar. *In terms of hype, atmosphere and expectation, this was the match the tournament had been waiting for. In all other respects, it was a damp squib: India beefed up their seam attack and won easily. Jasprit Bumrah's pace and accuracy caused concern among the Pakistan top order, and Bhuvneshwar Kumar reaped the benefits at the other end. Pakistan had picked themselves up from 3-2 but, when Babar Azam and Shoaib Malik were removed, the rest followed meekly. Sharma made a half-century, and Dhawan again looked in good touch as India cruised with 21 overs to spare.*

Group B

At Dubai (Sports City), September 15. **Bangladesh won by 137 runs.** ‡**Bangladesh 261** (49.3 overs) (Mushfiqur Rahim 144, Mithun Ali 63; S. L. Malinga 4-23); **Sri Lanka 124** (35.2 overs). *MoM:* Mushfiqur Rahim. *An innings that evolved into a masterclass from Mushfiqur Rahim guided Bangladesh towards their biggest victory by runs away from home. The match had begun well enough for Sri Lanka: Lasith Malinga, in his first international appearance in more than a year, removed Liton Das and Shakib Al Hasan in the first over and, when Tamim Iqbal retired after being hit on the wrist by Suranga Lakmal, Bangladesh were effectively 3-3. They did not panic: with the sprightly Mithun Ali, Mushfiqur put on 132 in 24 overs. Mithun went for 63, his highest ODI score, and Mushfiqur organised the rest of the innings brilliantly. After the ninth wicket fell at 229, Tamim came back out with his hand in a cast, and Mushfiqur flayed three sixes and three fours. His career-best 144 was Bangladesh's second-highest individual score, and his 55% of the total a national record. Sri Lanka were never in the hunt, and needed runs from the tail to avoid an even more comprehensive thrashing.*

At Abu Dhabi, September 17. **Afghanistan won by 91 runs.** ‡**Afghanistan 249** (50 overs) (Mohammad Shahzad 34, Ihsanullah Janat 45, Rahmat Shah 72, Hashmatullah Shahidi 37; N. L. T. C. Perera 5-55); **Sri Lanka 158** (41.2 overs) (W. U. Tharanga 36). *MoM:* Rahmat Shah. *Sri Lanka slunk home to lick their wounds after a result that underlined Afghanistan's progress. They did not rely on pyrotechnics or one outstanding bowling performance: instead, it was a solid, all-round effort that took them into the Super Four stage. After opting to bat, they built slowly, reaching 109-2 at halfway; top-scorer Rahmat Shah did not hit a boundary until his 44th ball. There was no late charge, but it quickly became clear that 249 was enough against a shambolic Sri Lanka. They lost Kusal Mendis in the first over and, although Upul Tharanga and Dhananjaya de Silva tried to mount a recovery, they slipped from 54-1 to 108-5. "Afghanistan outplayed us – it was a shocking performance by the whole team," said captain Angelo Mathews.*

At Abu Dhabi, September 20. **Afghanistan won by 136 runs.** ‡**Afghanistan 255-7** (50 overs) (Mohammad Shahzad 37, Hashmatullah Shahidi 58, Gulbadeen Naib 42*, Rashid Khan 57*; Shakib Al Hasan 4-42); **Bangladesh 119** (42.1 overs) (Shakib Al Hasan 32). *MoM:* Rashid Khan. *ODI debuts: Abu Haider, Nazmul Hossain (Bangladesh). Afghanistan tucked another scalp under their belts and again demonstrated how to win on the sluggish surfaces of the UAE. Putting aside their customary no-holds-barred approach, they grafted for runs, and trusted their spinners to do the rest. Hashmatullah Shahidi took 92 balls to make 58, but their total was given a late boost by the eighth-wicket pair of Gulbadeen Naib and Rashid Khan, who added 95* in 9.1 overs. Bangladesh were soon in trouble, and the impressive Rashid, on his 20th birthday, removed both their leading scorers in a miserly spell. For good measure he ran out Abu Haider with a direct hit.*

FINAL GROUP TABLES

GROUP A

	P	W	L	Pts	NRR
INDIA	2	2	0	4	1.47
PAKISTAN	2	1	1	2	−0.28
Hong Kong	2	0	2	0	−1.74

GROUP B

	P	W	L	Pts	NRR
AFGHANISTAN	2	2	0	4	2.27
BANGLADESH	2	1	1	2	−0.01
Sri Lanka	2	0	2	0	−2.28

Super Four

At Dubai (Sports City), September 21. **India won by seven wickets. Bangladesh 173** (49.1 overs) (Mehedi Hasan 42; Bhuvneshwar Kumar 3-32, J. J. Bumrah 3-37, R. A. Jadeja 4-29); ‡**India 174-3** (36.2 overs) (R. G. Sharma 83*, S. Dhawan 40, M. S. Dhoni 33). *MoM:* R. A. Jadeja. *In his first ODI* *for more than a year, Ravindra Jadeja produced a stellar performance to put India on track for a place in the final. Flown in to replace the injured Akshar Patel, he took four wickets for the first time since August 2014 to justify Sharma's decision to chase. After the new-ball pair of Bhuvneshwar and Bumrah had removed the openers, Jadeja took the key wickets of Shakib, Mithun and Mushfiqur. There was a hint of defiance down the order from Mehedi Hasan in a partnership of 66 with captain Mashrafe bin Mortaza, but Bangladesh had nowhere near enough. Sharma and Dhawan knocked off the first 50 in the powerplay, and Sharma was still there when India eased home in the 37th over.*

At Abu Dhabi, September 21. **Pakistan won by three wickets. ‡Afghanistan 257-6** (50 overs) (Rahmat Shah 36, Hashmatullah Shahidi 97*; Asghar Afghan 67; Mohammad Nawaz 3-57); **Pakistan 258-7** (49.3 overs) (Imam-ul-Haq 80, Babar Azam 66, Shoaib Malik 51*; Rashid Khan 3-46). *MoM:* Shoaib Malik. *ODI debut:* Shaheen Shah Afridi (Pakistan). *In the most absorbing match of the tournament so far, Afghanistan stuck to the plan that had served them well – and almost won again. Pakistan arrived at the final over needing ten, but Shoaib Malik was well set and smashed the second ball from a nervy Aftab Alam for six, then the third for four. It was more than they deserved after a shoddy performance in the field, and some panicky batting against Mujeeb Zadran and Rashid. After a poor start, Hashmatullah had assumed responsibility for rebuilding Afghanistan's innings. He played magnificently for 97*, which included just seven fours, and added 94 with Asghar Afghan, who hit five sixes in a brisk 67. Shaheen Shah Afridi, making his debut in place of Mohammad Amir, took two wickets but saw three catches go down off his bowling. Pakistan lost Fakhar Zaman in the first over, before Babar and Imam-ul-Haq batted with impressive maturity to add 153. Rashid's three wickets dragged Afghanistan back into it, but Shoaib would not be budged.*

At Abu Dhabi, September 23. **Bangladesh won by three runs. ‡Bangladesh 249-7** (50 overs) (Liton Das 41, Mushfiqur Rahim 33, Imrul Kayes 72*; Mahmudullah 74; Aftab Alam 3-54); **Afghanistan 246-7** (50 overs) (Mohammad Shahzad 53, Hashmatullah Shahidi 71, Asghar Afghan 39, Mohammad Nabi 38). *MoM:* Mahmudullah. *ODI debut:* Nazmul Islam (Bangladesh). *Afghanistan's tournament ended in a heartbreaking final over after they failed to scrape together the seven they needed to win. Mustafizur Rahman enhanced his reputation as one of the leading death bowlers, conceding just two runs off the bat, and dismissing Rashid. Batting second for the first time in the competition, Afghanistan were grateful for Hashmatullah's 71 and a solid 53 from Mohammad Shahzad. But the asking-rate mounted as Bangladesh applied pressure, and Mohammad Nabi was dismissed in the penultimate over. Afghanistan had taken an early grip by reducing Bangladesh to 87-5 in the 21st. It took a stand of 128, a national sixth-wicket record, between Imrul Kayes, who had only just arrived to reinforce the squad, and Mahmudullah to set a challenging total. They showed a mastery of Rashid which few had managed.*

At Dubai (Sports City), September 23. **India won by nine wickets. ‡Pakistan 237-7** (50 overs) (Fakhar Zaman 31, Sarfraz Ahmed 44, Shoaib Malik 78, Asif Ali 30); **India 238-1** (39.3 overs) (R. G. Sharma 111*; S. Dhawan 114). *MoM:* S. Dhawan. *Another India–Pakistan encounter, another India cruise, another crushing anticlimax. Pakistan were easily outmanoeuvred by opponents who punished all their mistakes: coach Mickey Arthur called it a reality check. With one eye on bowling in cooler conditions, Pakistan had batted first, but India responded with a cohesive effort as Sharma handled his attack adroitly. A partnership of 107 for the fourth wicket between Sarfraz Ahmed and Shoaib briefly disturbed India's wellbeing, but they were never able to proceed quickly enough to build a threatening total. Continuing their rich vein, Sharma and Dhawan turned the chase into a stroll. They put on 210 largely untroubled runs – a record opening partnership for India against Pakistan – and were not parted until the finish line was in sight. The win secured India's place in the final.*

At Dubai (Sports City), September 25. **Tied. ‡Afghanistan 252-8** (50 overs) (Mohammad Shahzad 124, Mohammad Nabi 64; R. A. Jadeja 3-46); **India 252** (49.5 overs) (K. L. Rahul 60, A. T. Rayudu 57, K. D. Karthik 44). *MoM:* Mohammad Shahzad. *ODI debut:* D. L. Chahar (India). *With India heading for the final and Afghanistan heading home, it should have been a non-event. Instead it turned into a gripping battle that demonstrated again Afghanistan's determination to slug it out with the elite. Shahzad's fifth ODI century, his first against a leading nation, dominated the early part of the Afghanistan innings. Faced with an attack lacking some of its big guns, he reached three figures in 88 balls, with ten fours and six sixes. Nabi's 64 provided ballast down the order. With the top three all contributing, India eased into a position of command, but they were on the wrong side of some questionable decisions – including an lbw against stand-in captain M. S. Dhoni in his 100th ODI in charge. After a superb penultimate over by Aftab, India needed seven off six balls. With two left and India nine down, the scores were level: Rashid bowled an inviting long hop, but Jadeja picked out Najibullah Zadran at deep midwicket. "When you tie with a team like India, it's like winning," said Asghar Afghan.*

At Abu Dhabi, September 26. **Bangladesh won by 37 runs.** ‡Bangladesh 239 (48.5 overs) (Mushfiqur Rahim 99, Mithun Ali 60; Junaid Khan 4-19); **Pakistan 202-9** (50 overs) (Imam-ul-Haq 83, Shoaib Malik 30, Asif Ali 31; Mustafizur Rahman 4-43). *MoM:* Mushfiqur Rahim. *The final match of the Super Four became a semi-final shoot-out, but Pakistan never looked good enough to seize the opportunity. At 12-3, Bangladesh – without Shakib and Tamim, both injured – were teetering. It took Mushfiqur to ride to the rescue with 99 off 166 balls, and his salvage operation with Mithun – 144 for the fourth wicket – allowed them to set a challenging total. Pakistan also got off to a calamitous start and, although Imam battled to 83, they were unable to recover. Mustafizur, perhaps the only seamer in the tournament who got the ball to move, was the star of an impressive bowling effort.*

SUPER FOUR TABLE

	P	W	L	T	Pts	NRR
INDIA	3	2	0	1	5	0.86
BANGLADESH	3	2	1	0	4	−0.15
Pakistan	3	1	2	0	2	−0.59
Afghanistan	3	0	2	1	1	−0.04

Final　At Dubai (Sports City), September 28. **India won by three wickets. Bangladesh 222** (48.3 overs) (Liton Das 121, Mehedi Hasan 32, Soumya Sarkar 33; K. Yadav 3-45); ‡India 223-7 (50 overs) (R. G. Sharma 48, K. D. Karthik 37, M. S. Dhoni 36). *MoM:* Liton Das. *MoS:* S. Dhawan. *Kedar Jadhav shrugged off a hamstring tear to steer India to the title with a scampered leg-bye off the last ball. They had needed six off six, but Jadhav – who had hobbled off earlier and returned only in the 48th over when India looked like making a hash of it – and Kuldeep Yadav held their nerve. Bangladesh's total had owed everything to Liton's first ODI hundred, from 87 balls. They were rewarded for their enterprise in promoting Mehedi to open for the first time in any format – only to lose all ten for 102. India were then guilty of dawdling against a hard-working attack. Jadeja seemed set to take them over the line, but 11 were still needed when Rubel Hossain removed him. "The boys should feel proud, but we have to learn so many things," said Mashrafe.*

CRICKET ROUND THE WORLD IN 2018

COMPILED BY JAMES COYNE AND TIMOTHY ABRAHAM

ICC WORLD CRICKET LEAGUE

The ICC have been known to move the goalposts after the whistle – and never more so than for their Associate nations. The abolition of the World Cricket League in its 11th year was felt keenly by Associate aficionados, though the longer league format which was to replace it (see page 1480) would hopefully end some of the uncertainties for individual boards.

The WCL's promotion-and-relegation divisional structure – two up, two survive, two down – had proved exciting, expensive and extreme. And in late 2017 the ICC introduced new eligibility criteria: non-passport holders could now qualify after just three years' residency in a country, down from seven. This played into the hands of countries with more liberal immigration policies, or with sizable South Asian populations.

The penultimate round of qualifying for the 2019 World Cup – Division Two in Namibia in February 2018 – was a classic. UAE coach Dougie Brown said, given the funds at stake, he had been more nervous about promotion there than his side's performance at the World Cup Qualifier in Zimbabwe.

Nepal's tigerish bowling and flaky but explosive batting was in full evidence during three last-over wins, all in run-chases, two with their last pair at the crease. They lost to relegated Oman, and could easily have been demoted themselves. Instead, they topped the table to reach the Qualifier, while last-round defeats for Canada and Namibia cost them each a place. Nepal captain Paras Khadka struck 51 and 42 in winning causes, followed by a century in a defeat by the UAE in the final; video of the 17 wickets taken by 17-year-old leg-spinner Sandeep Lamichhane vaulted him to the attention of IPL franchises.

The ICC had for some time considered T20 the "global growth vehicle" to popularise the game, which raised concerns over the next cycle of 50-over cricket. But the ICC initially kickstarted 2023 World Cup qualification with WCL Division Four in Malaysia in April 2018.

One beneficiary of the eligibility changes was Shahid Afridi's 33-year-old nephew, Irfan, who had recently moved to Uganda to work in the import–export business. He produced a performance against Vanuatu right out of uncle's playbook: a 17-ball fifty followed by three wickets with his leg-spin. Uganda had been beaten by Malaysia by nine runs in a controversial finish, when Deusdedit Muhumuza was adjudged run out by a direct hit, despite home footage from the sidelines suggesting wicketkeeper Shafiq Sharif had removed the bails with his gloves. But Uganda fought back to win the title: Roger Mukasa took the ball for the first time in the last over of a rain-reduced match, with Denmark needing five to win – and four wickets fell for three runs. The Ugandans also defended 90 against Jersey.

A lack of professionalism continued to plague Bermuda, who were relegated for the fourth time in six tournaments. A spat in the nets led to star batsman

Kamau Leverock being banned from the first two games, both lost. When he came back, against Jersey, his 66 off 43 balls produced the Bermudians' only win. Leverock, based in the UK, stepped away from national duty later in the year. "We don't have a players' union," he said, "so players are not able to defend themselves when things happen on tour. I was just handed a two-match ban without even being able to speak to the coaches."

News of the ICC's overhaul came shortly before Division Three, held at the Al Amerat complex in Oman. The tournament had been pushed back to November to allow the USA to participate in the West Indies Regional Super 50 – not the only favour many felt the Americans were getting, in order to nudge them closer to a maiden World Cup. In Uganda's match against the USA, Mukasa was told by an umpire that if he kept Afridi on after his first over he would be no-balled – even though ICC officials are supposed to report suspect actions *after* play. It turned out that the USA coach Pubudu Dassanayake had complained to the organisers about Afridi's action after seeing him bowl in the previous game. The USA won – and Afridi failed subsequent ICC testing.

Oman and the USA – each containing just two players who had come through their youth systems – snapped up the promotion spots and headed to Division Two in Windhoek in April 2019, the last WCL event. For the top four, there would be a guaranteed 36 one-day internationals over two years in the new Cricket World Cup League 2, the kind of exposure that the WCL, for all its decade of drama, could not provide.   JAMES COYNE

QUALIFYING FOR THE T20 WORLD CUP IN 2020

There was a pleasant surprise for the Associates when the ICC board voted to expand T20 international status to all men's and women's teams in member nations by the start of 2019. It allowed cricket to introduce a comprehensive global T20 ranking system – the first attempt to match football and both rugby codes.

David Kendix, the actuary who devised and oversees the ICC's ranking systems, admitted T20 standings would not be completely reliable at the lower end, since many smaller Associates never played teams outside their region. But ICC staff hoped that full world rankings would encourage more bilateral fixtures, lead to greater awareness among native populations, unlock government funding and increase commercial opportunities. Some of the smaller Associates had not contested ICC-run tournaments for nine years, having been instructed to direct their modest funds towards development.

In the men's game, impending T20I status came on the heels of a new T20 sub-regional qualification process beginning in February 2018, giving all members a theoretical opportunity to qualify for the T20 World Cup in Australia in 2020. Later in the year, the ICC scrapped the entry fee, which had deterred some smaller Associates from taking part in 2018.

The geographical pooling in some regions led to inevitable mismatches. In Americas Northern, Panama and Belize were bowled out by Canada for 42 or fewer on all four occasions. In Asia Eastern, Myanmar were nine for eight when rain came in Kuala Lumpur; Malaysia knocked off a revised target of six in eight balls. But promotion slots were carefully allocated to present the obviously stronger sides with a clear path to qualifying, unless there was a genuine upset.

Lowering the threshold for T20Is meant some matches would be played on artificial pitches. And in Colombia – not an ICC member – the South American Championships, including the first women's T20Is for Brazil, Chile and Mexico, were played on the hastily shaven grass of a polo field. "We obviously can't expect all our members to produce grounds of Test-match standard, or televise games," said ICC general manager of cricket Geoff Allardice. "It's not feasible for them all to put in blocks of turf wickets. Associates will run matches to a set of standards that is reasonable, but not as exacting."

There were worries, though, that some boards lacked the staff to rigorously implement the anti-corruption measures the ICC would usually demand for full internationals. If games took place without adequate regulation, but with TV coverage or live-streaming, they ran the risk of infiltration by illegal betting markets.

Statisticians – grappling with endless T20I debutants and the prospect of a slew of records – voiced concerns that many Associates were not yet reliably collating scorecards or other data. So while Twitter soon suggested Botsogo Mpedi of Botswana had taken women's T20I-record figures of six for eight against Lesotho – overhauling New Zealand's Amy Satterthwaite – it took months for confirmation to appear in online record sections.   JAMES COYNE

BHUTAN

Like Nepal, Bhutan has never been colonised – not even by the cricket-playing British. But the arrival of cable TV in 1999 enabled Bhutanese to watch the World Cup, and led to humble beginnings with gully cricket. "One day I found cricket gear belonging to my physics teacher from India lying in the lab," says Tshering Dorji. "I borrowed it and became the first person in Bhutan to possess cricket gear." Seventeen years after the Bhutan Cricket Council Board were formed, a survey found that cricket was the country's third-most popular sport, after archery and football. There are now eight clubs: four in the capital Thimpu, and others in the districts of Punakha, Wangdi, Paro and Sarpang. In the last BCCB Super League, Suprit Pradhan of Bhutan Tourism Corporation Ltd CC established a record for the fastest double-hundred (221 not out, 95 balls). There are inter-school age-group tournaments, and Bhutan have been finalists in Asian Cricket Council Under-15 and Under-19 Challenge Cups. The women's team, who played in their first international tournament in 2008, reached the finals of the ACC Under-19 Championships in 2010, and the first domestic tournaments have shown encouraging results. But most cricket is played at football grounds on jute matting or astroturf. The exception is Sarpang, who have access to the facilities over the Indian border in Assam, where the authorities have assisted in installing a cricket academy and a turf wicket at Sarpang's ground. The BCCI have helped develop a fully fledged ground near Thimpu, and offered technical support for cricket in all 20 districts of the country. In February 2018, Bhutan's men claimed their first international title by winning the ACC T20 Eastern Region. In the subsequent T20 World Cup Qualifier Asia B in Malaysia, they beat China and Myanmar, and gave the host nation a fright in the opening match when Sanjeevan Gurung, a bustling medium-pacer, took a hat-trick. All this has been achieved with an entirely Bhutanese set-up, which marks them out from expat-dominated Associate countries.   RAVI CHATURVEDI

CANADA

Valentine's Day heartbreak at WCL Division Two in Namibia, where Canada missed out on reaching the World Cup qualifier after losing by one wicket to Nepal, was followed by a more encouraging development. In midsummer, King City, just outside Toronto, hosted the country's own franchise tournament – the Global T20 Canada. It immediately drew attention with the announcement that Steve Smith and David Warner, banned for a year by Australia, would be playing their first professional cricket since the infamy of Cape Town.

In a few weeks, the league, owned by Mercuri Canada, locked in player contracts, sorted the logistics, and succeeded where Cricket Canada had long failed by securing corporate sponsorship. The tournament gave a glimpse of what is possible for cricket in the Greater Toronto Area. But, barring the opening day and the final, a ground with temporary capacity of 7,000 was never more than half full; a clash with the football World Cup may not have helped. Despite drainage issues, all but one of the 22 matches went ahead without a hitch.

While the league and Cricket Canada were happy, the domestic player pool were decidedly muted. Each of the five teams named after Canadian cities were required to have two Associate players and four locals in their squad, but were under no compulsion to play any. The majority of Canadians were taken blind, many with slim experience, and spent three weeks on drinks duty. Rizwan Cheema, Canada's most experienced and celebrated T20 player, suited up for every game for Winnipeg Hawks – captained by Warner – but never made it into the XI, a frustrating scenario for a player who has spent his career clobbering sixes at King City. Those who did get an extended run justified their places, most notably the Vancouver Knights all-rounder Saad Bin Zafar, who in the final grabbed the opportunity of promotion up the order by hitting an unbeaten title-winning 79 off 48 balls in front of a full house.

A few weeks later, King City was the venue for CricketFest Canada, which comprised West Indies B and three teams of locals. Inexplicably, the matches were not advertised during the Global T20 Canada, and the attendance was of the two-men-and-a-dog variety, while the dismantling of the seating and video screens made the ground look forlorn. The Canada Broadcasting Corporation were brought in to stream CricketFest on their website – the equivalent of showcasing a house the morning after a riotous party in which the guests have walked off with the furniture.

In October, Toronto-born 24-year-old golden boy Nitish Kumar was replaced as national captain for the West Indies Regional Super 50 by 36-year-old newly qualified South African Davy Jacobs. Oddly, the move was branded as a "rebuild". There was a solitary win against the Windward Islands, though left-arm seamer Romesh Eranga was a revelation, topping the bowling with 17 wickets in six matches at an average of 12.   FARAZ SARWAT

ESTONIA

Lembit Öpik once quipped that Estonians knew as much about cricket as visiting teams knew about the national delicacy of pickled herring. Öpik, a former Liberal Democrat MP whose parents are from Estonia, might have to think again after the country made it a hat-trick of titles at the fourth edition of the Continental European Natives Cup, held in Warsaw. Skipper Marko Vaik finished the top run-scorer, while stocky medium-pacer Kalle Vislapuu scooped the bowling award and Player of the Tournament. "We now have around 20 Estonians playing cricket," Vaik said. "The best part was we had a 13-year-old and two women in our team." Two decades after Kristian Garancis, an Estonian who became fixated with cricket on a business trip to Australia, kickstarted the game in Tallinn, the Estonian Cricket Association are building a new ground. A 30-acre site has been purchased ten minutes' drive from downtown Tallinn, and will be home to both the national cricket and rugby union teams. It is set to become the first ground in continental Europe to have permanent floodlights. "We'll also have an indoor centre, gym, sauna, cafe/bar, and even a room for video analysis," says Estonia cricket stalwart Tim Heath. It is a far cry from the days when matches were played on a bumpy football ground in a forest. Back then, winter ice-cricket matches were played at the Jeti Arena – a former Soviet missile factory converted into an ice rink – or on a frozen lake outside Tallinn, with perplexed curlers looking on. This proved popular with boozy touring sides from the UK, who happily supped vintage Crimean champagne and munched on bear steaks as part of the post-match hospitality. An artificial wicket laid at Tallinn's hippodrome in the early 2000s ensured cricket had a more serious presence in summer although, when the racetrack's groundsman once covered the field with horse manure to tackle a problem with rabbit holes, the cricketers were left with the malodorous task of clearing it with spades. In 2012, Shane Warne and Elizabeth Hurley dropped by for ICC European Division Three. Warne's involvement had been organised by a gambling company who sponsored the Estonia team – earning the ECA a slap on the wrists from the ICC for breach of regulations – though it was his companion who piqued the interest of daily newspaper *Postimees*. "Hurley could not say anything about the average Estonian man," they reported. "But she said that the cricket guys appeared to be very hot types." Vaik, Vislapuu and team-mates have proved they can play a bit too.   TIMOTHY ABRAHAM

KENYA

After a World Cup semi-final in 1996, and ODI status, Kenya were spoken of as the next Test nation. Now they find themselves marooned in international cricket's third tier. Continued calamity on the field has been matched by chaos off it: Kenya spent much of 2018 without a properly constituted board, and facing the risk of sanction by the ICC. The latest shenanigans were sparked by a winless campaign at WCL Division Two, where relegation prompted the resignations of captain Rakep Patel, coach Thomas Odoyo – who called the tournament "a week of mental anguish" – and Cricket Kenya chairman Jackie Janmohamed. The board did not long survive her: fresh elections were forestalled when a committee of former players and administrators appealed to the sports minister to launch an investigation into alleged incompetence and misappropriation of funds at CK and a number of provincial associations, and asserted that the constitution was in conflict with Kenyan law. In April, the ministry dissolved the board, replacing them with a nine-member interim committee charged with overseeing the game and drafting a new constitution ahead of fresh elections within three months. Those elections never materialised, and the interim committee fell to infighting, with rival factions wrestling for control of CK finances. Kenyan cricket found itself in a state of financial paralysis, with unpaid players boycotting MCC's tour and threatening strike action. Cricket South Africa are understood to have provided a loan to cover the costs of participating in the Africa T20 tournament; Janmohamed personally raised £12,200 to cover player pay for WCL Division Three. Her intervention ensured CK avoided immediate ICC sanction, though a fourth-place finish in Oman meant reclaiming ODI status was off the table in the next World Cup cycle. Merely avoiding suspension from the ICC ought to be Kenya's first goal.   Bertus de Jong

MALAYSIA

The spiritual home of Malaysian cricket is in danger of being turned into a commercial development by its owners. The Kinrara Academy Oval is a key reason Malaysia have been a favoured host for ICC events, with the ground welcoming WCL Division Four, the Asia Cup Qualifier and a Twenty20 World Cup regional qualifying event in 2018 alone. The ground has hosted more WCL matches than any other in the world. With the market for cricket in the UAE increasingly crowded, Kinrara was well situated as an alternative neutral venue for Pakistan matches. Though there are a number of other grounds in Malaysia, now recognised as a Tier A country on the ICC's development scorecard, the facilities at Kinrara, which has a hostel for players and the Malaysian Cricket Association offices, cannot easily be replaced. Singapore and Hong Kong (which have only limited access to their own facilities) have made regular use of Kinrara for training and development tours. A grassroots campaign to save the ground met with some success, with Brian Lara – who captained West Indies there in the 2006-07 DLF Cup – lending his support, and the ICC, which had invited the MCA to bid to host next year's T20 World Cup Qualifier, publicly expressing their concern. The venue represents a significant investment not only for the MCA but also the Malaysian state, which spent considerable money upgrading the venue during its 15-year lease, which expired on October 31. The National Sports Council stepped in to moderate, with the ground granted a stay of execution. The developers,

Perumahan Kinrara Bhd, seem unlikely to budge, as the urbanisation of the surrounding area has seen the value of the land increase dramatically; they also allege that MCA's rent payments are in significant arrears. For now, cricket continues – Kinrara held an Under-12s tournament for local schoolchildren in November – but each competition could be the last. Following the recent series there between Pakistan and Australia women, the deputy sports minister Steven Sim vowed that Malaysian cricket "would always have a home." But it seems doubtful it will be Kinrara.   BERTUS DE JONG

NEUTRAL MORESNET

More than a century after Dr Wilhelm Molly attempted to make this Northern European territory of just 1.4 square miles the world's first Esperanto-speaking state, a *kriketo-matĉo* (cricket match) was held on its soil. Between 1816 and 1920, Neutral Moresnet – *Amikejo*, in Esperanto – occupied a patch of land where the Netherlands, Belgium and Germany meet. It was created at the Congress of Vienna after the Napoleonic Wars, largely to solve the prickly issue of access to the Vieille Montagne zinc mine; in 1863, the mine appointed Molly, an avid Esperantist, as its doctor. A national anthem was composed, and in 1908 Neutral Moresnet was proclaimed the home of Esperanto. Under the Treaty of Versailles, however, it was annexed to Belgium, and in 1920 lost its neutrality. A six-hit away from the house of 103-year-old Catharina Meessen – the last surviving Moresnetter – veterans of the Fellowship of Fairly Odd Places Cricket Club, wearing candy-striped blazers, added another odd place to their collection. They lost to fellow Dutch side The Zamigo's in the grounds of the Park Hotel, which stands on the site of the old zinc mine, now in the Belgian town of Kelmis. In its self-governing heyday, Moresnet had levied low taxes on alcohol, which encouraged a thriving liquor trade, plus gambling dens and casinos. "Players from both sides honoured those traditions in the third innings," explained FFOPCC's Dr Michel Bakker. "But we raised €3,000 for local good causes as well." After respects were paid at Molly's grave, Hans van Beurten of FFOPCC gave a speech in Esperanto, though Dutch was more prevalent once play started. Cricket's complex lexicon has long been translated into the language: *palisetaro* (wicket), *bastoneto* (bail), and *preteraĵo* (bye) are all terms included in the most widely used dictionary. Its compiler, Professor John Wells, said: "They are attempts to render the meaning of the cricketing terms using ordinary Esperanto roots, suffixes, and endings. A wicket is a set (*ar*) of small (*et*) wooden stakes (*palis*), hence *palisetaro*."   TIMOTHY ABRAHAM

URUGUAY

A rivalry older than the Ashes has risen anew, and cricket is being played again on both sides of the River Plate. It is 150 years since Montevideo CC first hosted Buenos Aires CC, but since the 1960s there had been little cricket in Uruguay, and Montevideo CC are primarily a rugby club. An influx from

India has reignited interest, however, and there are now 100 active players. In August, the national team secured second place in the South American Championships in Bogotá, and the Uruguayan Cricket Association have been repopulated with ten committee members. Funds raised from 27 donors have enabled an artificial pitch to be bought and shipped to Montevideo to restore hard-ball cricket. For several years, tapeball has been played on La Rambla seafront in the optimistically named Uruguayan Premier League, to the amusement and bemusement of locals. In December, the first match on the new pitch was played between a UPL XI and a UCA President's XI. Uruguay enhanced cricketing relations with Argentina by celebrating the sesquicentenary with two T20s at the Belgrano Athletic Club in Buenos Aires. Future goals are to broaden participation, and earn ICC associate membership.   ROB SHARP

UNITED STATES OF AMERICA

If anyone expected a fairytale after the USA Cricket Association were expelled from the ICC in 2017, the first full year of the ICC-piloted USA Cricket proved there was still a mountain to climb. (In January 2019, however, came news of a few steps on the ascent, when USA Cricket were granted associate membership.)

A promise to revive the national championship – a core element of USACA's domestic structure – never materialised. And the inaugural elections for the new governing body, originally targeted for April but postponed until August, earned as many detractors as supporters. There were allegations of duplicate or improper registrations, such as organisations claiming to be a league for voting purposes, despite playing just a handful of matches a year. These bore a resemblance to complaints of sham leagues during the USACA days. Others said the website was too complicated to fill out the registration.

It has been argued that the USA has a potential cricket market of between 10m–20m players and fans. But the number who registered to vote in a free membership sign-up period totalled a little over 5,000 – well below the 38,000 players reported in the ICC data census under USACA in 2014.

The elections produced a new leadership. Just one of the seven chosen officials – Southern California Cricket Association president Atul Rai, USACA president from 2001 to 2003 – had held a position in the old USACA or American Cricket Federation regimes. The new board chairman, San Francisco 49ers executive vice-president Paraag Marathe, also on the board of Leeds United, was one of three independent directors.

The ICC's revised eligibility guidelines opened the door to a number of potential new USA players. Former West Indies international Xavier Marshall had made his debut in January, along with ex-India Under-19s Sunny Sohal and Saurabh Netravalkar. In recent years, ICC Americas regional trials had unearthed talents such as Ali Khan, who made his name in 2018 with Winnipeg Hawks in the inaugural Global T20 Canada, before helping Trinbago Knight Riders to the CPL title. This time the trials helped put Monank Patel in the frame. A former Gujarat junior player, he had been toiling away in relative anonymity in New Jersey, but scored a sensational 80-ball hundred after being invited to national squad trials in Houston, and added three more centuries in the year for the USA.

Marshall was dropped in June, ostensibly as punishment for skipping portions of the New York regional combine, which was a USA Cricket guideline for selection. Yet in October, the selectors called up the Barbados-contracted pair of Aaron Jones and Hayden Walsh jr to make their USA debuts at WCL Division Three, even though neither had shown up for the combines. Then there was the controversial sacking of captain Ibrahim Khaleel, after he led the USA to the T20 World Cup sub-regional qualifier title at a new facility in North Carolina. In the end, the Bajan duo played instrumental roles under new captain Netravalkar as the USA sealed promotion to Division Two after four previous failed attempts, putting them one good tournament away from one-day international status.

At the end of 2018, USA Cricket announced plans for their own T20 franchise tournament. Nine years earlier, USACA had drawn 102 expressions of interest from potential bidders. USA Cricket elicited "more than 20" by their initial deadline – an indication that the T20 franchise market might have reached saturation point. They need only look north of the border, where the Global T20 Canada was run at a considerable loss after operating costs of $10.5m, to see the potential pitfalls.   PETER DELLA PENNA

VANUATU

When the Manaro Voui volcano erupted for a second consecutive year last July, it led to a full evacuation of the tiny island of Ambae. With the 11,500 residents taken to the safety of Espiritu Santo – the largest of Vanuatu's 82 islands – potential tragedy was averted. There was also an unlikely benefit. During the residents' initial displacement, Vanuatu Cricket development officers ran taster sessions for evacuated children. The initiative was one of many launched since the arrival of chief executive Shane Deitz, a former South Australia batsman. In conjunction with the Australian government, the Vanuatu cricketing authorities are using the sport to tackle diabetes, from which 11% of the adult population suffers; in many rural and indigenous regions, the figure is worse. Island cricket – close to the Samoan sport of *kilikiti*, played with a hard rubber ball and wooden sticks – has been introduced as one of a number of measures. The game is being aimed at local "mamas", the villages' older women, many of whom suffer from poor health and a lack of education, and the intention is to supplement sport with cookery classes and health checks. Deitz hopes the initiative will take current playing numbers beyond the current 20,000. Since 2012, the men's side have achieved four WCL promotions. The implementation of paid contracts has been crucial. Each squad member earns a full-time wage, allowing a group of professional cricketers to train all day, every day – a rarity at this level of the international ladder. Still, Vanuatu need Deitz's know-how: five days before his 43rd birthday, seven months after a hip replacement and ten years after leaving the professional game, he made his debut for his adopted country at WCL Division Four, Vanuatu's highest stage of competition yet. He top-scored with 164 runs at 54, but could not prevent their relegation. Professionalism comes with its own challenges in an archipelago still steeped in local custom. Deitz drives a ramshackle minibus across Santo each day to take his entire squad to training, and repeats the trip to drop them home – a 12-hour routine at the heart of one of Associate cricket's most uplifting stories.   NICK FRIEND

GLOBAL TOURNAMENTS

ICC WORLD CRICKET LEAGUE

	Date	Promoted	Survived	Relegated
Division Two	Feb	UAE, Nepal	Canada, Namibia	Oman, Kenya
Division Three	Nov	Oman, USA	Singapore, Kenya, Uganda, Denmark	
Division Four	Apr/May	Uganda, Denmark	Malaysia, Jersey	Vanuatu, Bermuda

ICC T20 WORLD CUP SUB-REGIONAL QUALIFIERS

	Date	Promoted	Others
Africa North-Western	Apr	Ghana, Nigeria	Sierra Leone, Gambia
Africa Eastern	Jul	Kenya, Uganda	Tanzania, Rwanda
Africa Southern	Oct/Nov	Botswana, Namibia	St Helena, Mozambique, Malawi, Lesotho, eSwatini
Americas Southern	Feb/Mar	Bermuda, Cayman Is	Argentina
Americas Northern	Sep	USA, Canada	Panama, Belize
Asia Western	Apr	UAE, Qatar, Kuwait	Saudi Arabia, Bahrain, Maldives
Asia Eastern	Oct	Nepal, Singapore, Malaysia	Thailand, Bhutan, Myanmar, China
East Asia–Pacific A	Aug	PNG, Vanuatu	Samoa, Fiji
East Asia–Pacific B	Dec	Philippines	South Korea, Japan, Indonesia
Europe A	Aug/Sep	Denmark, Germany	Austria, France, Portugal, Cyprus
Europe B	Aug/Sep	Italy, Jersey	Belgium, Spain, Finland, Isle of Man
Europe C	Aug/Sep	Norway, Guernsey	Sweden, Israel, Czech Republic, Gibraltar

OTHER TOURNAMENTS

	Date	Promoted	Others
Asia Cup Qualifier	Aug/Sep	Hong Kong	UAE, Oman, Nepal, Malaysia, Singapore
S. American Champ.	Aug	Mexico	Uruguay, Costa Rica, Brazil, Argentina A, Chile, Peru, Colombia

WOMEN'S TOURNAMENTS

	Date	Promoted	Others
World T20 Qualifier	Jul	Bangladesh, Ireland	Scotland, PNG, Thailand, Uganda, UAE, Netherlands

	Date	Winner	Others
S. American Champ.	Aug	Brazil	Chile, Peru, Mexico

PART SIX

Overseas Domestic Twenty20 Cricket

OVERSEAS DOMESTIC T20 CRICKET IN 2017-18

FREDDIE WILDE

Twenty20 cricket spent the year challenging assumptions. Australia's Big Bash League had been dominated by chasing teams over the previous two seasons, but Adelaide Strikers won the title despite never once choosing to bat second. And in an era when analysis suggests sides should take advantage of the field restrictions in the powerplay, only one team in the BBL scored more slowly in the first six overs than they did.

Elsewhere, the Chennai Super Kings were roundly criticised for assembling an ageing squad at the Indian Premier League auction, but went on to win the title, with 36-year-old Shane Watson scoring a century in the final. Less than six months later, the Worcestershire Rapids – with the youngest squad in the competition – won the T20 Blast for the first time, with 19-year-old fast bowler Pat Brown a star. It seemed there was no golden rule for Twenty20.

Well, maybe one: sign Rashid Khan. His teams finished top of the table in the Bangladesh Premier League, won the BBL and the Shpageeza Cricket League (Afghanistan's domestic competition), and reached the finals of the IPL and the T20 Blast. Rashid's brilliance remained undimmed by familiarity; he took more wickets at a lower strike-rate – 76 at 16.43 – than in the corresponding previous 12 months (50 at 16.68). Of the major leagues, he has only the Pakistan Super League to conquer, probably because he hasn't played in it yet.

If any player was worth breaking the bank for at the IPL auction it was Rashid, but no one went over the top, with team owners keeping a tighter grip on the purse strings. The triennial "mega auction", in which most players are released into the pool, was the first since the £1.97bn broadcast deal. It was a chance for the IPL to flex its financial muscle but, even though the salary cap was increased by 21% for 2018, the auction was largely defined by prudence.

The real story of the IPL was the triumphant return of CSK, marshalled by the canny M. S. Dhoni. But the tournament was also shaped by the brilliance of runners-up Sunrisers Hyderabad, whose attack defended three scores below 150. The young Delhi Daredevils squad finished bottom, but the emergence of Prithvi Shaw and the progress of Rishabh Pant provided hope.

ROLL OF HONOUR

Winner

Bangladesh Premier League	Rangpur Riders	Nov–Dec 2017
CSA T20 Challenge (South Africa)	Titans	Nov–Dec 2017
Super Smash (New Zealand)	Northern Districts	Dec 2017–Jan 2018
Big Bash League (Australia)	Adelaide Strikers	Dec 2017–Feb 2018
Pakistan Super League (UAE/Pakistan)	Islamabad United	Feb–March 2018
Indian Premier League	Chennai Super Kings	April–May 2018
T20 Blast (England)	Worcestershire	July–Sept 2018
Caribbean Premier League (West Indies)	Trinbago Knight Riders	Aug–Sept 2018

The success of the Sunrisers' attack was mirrored in the BBL and the Blast, where Adelaide and Sussex, both coached by Jason Gillespie, finished as winners and runners-up respectively. The BBL featured two extra matches per team, but this expansion did not significantly affect attendances or television ratings. Growth to a full home-and-away schedule in 2018-19 would test the depth of the league's popularity. Runners-up Hobart Hurricanes rode on the wave of superb seasons for D'Arcy Short and Jofra Archer, who were rewarded handsomely at the IPL auction a few weeks later.

The Pakistan Super League was deservedly won by Islamabad United, whose impressive scouting – five of their emerging players were subsequently selected in national squads – was overshadowed by a phenomenal performance from the New Zealander Luke Ronchi, who blasted 435 runs at a strike-rate of 182. On slow pitches, his powerplay pyrotechnics broke the back of low-scoring matches. The high standard of fielding – unusual in Pakistan cricket – was another conspicuous feature. Most of the tournament was once again played in the United Arab Emirates, but the play-offs took place in Pakistan.

Few places have contributed more to Twenty20 cricket than the West Indies, and that looks set to continue after the region's next generation was showcased in both the Global T20 Canada League and the Caribbean Premier League. The Canadian tournament took place in front of largely empty stands in Toronto, and its long-term viability remained uncertain – but it did provide a platform for the West Indies B squad, whose young team embarked on a spectacular run to the final, where they lost to a Vancouver Knights side captained by Chris Gayle. The league also allowed Steve Smith and David Warner to make low-key comebacks during their international bans.

The CPL was retained by Trinbago Knight Riders – comfortably the best team again – but the season was marked by the emergence of Guyanese left-handers Shimron Hetmyer and Sherfane Rutherford, Jamaican quick Oshane Thomas, all-rounder Fabian Allen, and slow left-armer Khary Pierre.

In October 2017, the BPL was due to go head-to-head with South Africa's T20 Global League, but it was indicative of cricket's balance of power that the BPL attracted the higher-profile overseas players, even before the South African competition was postponed, mainly for financial reasons. Fewer than half the contracted players in the BPL were from Bangladesh, and the league boasted a cast of overseas cricketers second only to the IPL.

Gayle had struggled for much of 2017, but ended a spell of 56 innings without a hundred with two in the BPL play-offs in December, to propel Rangpur Raiders to the title. Comilla Victorians and Dhaka Dynamites were the standout teams in the round-robin phase, but they were swept aside by Gayle's brilliance. With leagues and trends coming and going, Twenty20 cricket often appears to be in a state of flux, but one phenomenon remains: somewhere in the world, Chris Gayle is hitting sixes.

THE LEADING TWENTY20 CRICKETER IN 2018

Rashid Khan

Alan Gardner

Achieving success is one thing, but sustaining it can be another trick entirely – particularly for a young sportsman in an era of saturation coverage and in-depth analysis. But Rashid Khan, the Afghanistan leg-spinner who was still a teenager at the start of 2018, not only maintained his phenomenal record in the shortest form of the game, he surpassed himself.

In doing so, he made the leap from prodigy to superstar. The ICC's top-ranked T20 bowler for most of the year – he also shared top spot in the one-day international rankings, and played in Afghanistan's Test debut – Rashid was the closest thing to a banker in the high-rolling world of franchise T20. He took his wickets with a smile, seemingly grateful for every opportunity that came his way. When his father died on December 30, months from being able to watch his son play in the 2019 World Cup, Rashid stayed on at the Big Bash League in Australia rather than return home.

While supposedly having as many as seven variations, he is no mystery spinner. He is open about his methods, relying on accuracy, a fast arm and a well-disguised googly. In a masterclass for Sky, he revealed an unconventional approach to leg-spin: "I don't use my wrist. Mostly I use the top of my fingers. I think that puts more speed on the ball." Opposing batsmen might know what is coming – they're just not sure what to do.

If the global T20 circuit can seem repetitive, a wall-to-wall spread of itinerant six-hitters and sponsored time outs, there was nothing humdrum about Rashid. No player was more in demand in 2018, when he lined up 61 times for seven teams in five countries – including the Afghanistan national side and a World XI at Lord's. No player came close to his 96 wickets, beating the previous T20 best for a calendar year: Dwayne Bravo's 87 in 2016, from 72 matches. (Rashid is also third in the list, with 80 in 2017, from 56.)

He collected plaudits and accolades wherever he went: joint-leading wicket-taker at the 2017-18 Big Bash, where his Adelaide Strikers lifted the trophy; joint-second in the 2018 IPL, where his Sunrisers Hyderabad lost in the final. With Sussex, in the Vitality Blast, he linked up again with Jason Gillespie, his coach at the Strikers, and helped them to their first finals day appearance since 2012. At the inaugural Afghanistan Premier League, he was Man of the Tournament. And he was reliably among the most parsimonious bowlers in every competition he played.

All this from a 20-year-old who had converted from an opening batsman to a spin bowler only four years earlier, who taught himself through endless hours in the nets, and whose country was barely an Affiliate Member of the ICC when he was born. Afghan hero, IPL millionaire, T20 smash hit – the Rashid story was one for all of cricket to savour.

KFC T20 BIG BASH LEAGUE IN 2017-18

Daniel Cherny

1 Adelaide Strikers   2 Hobart Hurricanes

This was the year the Bash got bigger. The BBL had become a runaway success, not least because of the acclaimed coverage of Network Ten. And in the final summer of Ten's five-year deal, the league expanded – not in terms of teams, though that had been discussed, but games. Each side played an extra two, with many of the new fixtures held at regional venues such as Geelong, Alice Springs and Launceston. But there were public complaints from several overseas players that gaps between games were too long. And, as it turned out, there was a decline in attendances and television ratings.

The drop in crowds could be attributed to the awful campaign of **Melbourne Stars**. Although they had not won any of the competition's first six editions, they had been perennial semi-finalists. This time they plummeted to the bottom of the table, winning just twice. Their plight was typified by a new recruit, Ben Dunk. Twice the competition's leading run-scorer, he endured a miserable campaign, averaging just 11. It was also the final season in the Stars' green for Kevin Pietersen, who bowed out after an indifferent summer. **Sydney Sixers** struggled too, and both sides were out of the semi-final running relatively early. With more games than before, that made for a lot of dead rubbers.

It could have been worse. **Hobart Hurricanes** looked likely to be in the mix for the wooden spoon, but their season turned around dramatically in early January, when they won five games in a row, including a controversial victory over **Brisbane Heat**, who lost Alex Ross for obstructing the field. Hobart were powered by the destructive batting of D'Arcy Short, a player of Indigenous background who had taken a circuitous route via the Northern Territory and Western Australia to become an overnight sensation in Tasmania. He made 572 runs all told, 129 more than Adelaide's Alex Carey, at a strike-rate of 148. Despite losing their last three games, the Hurricanes crept into fourth spot, before toppling **Perth Scorchers** at their new Optus Stadium. It was an ignominious end for the Scorchers, who had done well to finish top of the ladder, despite being plagued by injuries and call-ups.

The other semi-final was a thriller, as **Adelaide Strikers** edged **Melbourne Renegades** by one run at Adelaide Oval to book a home final. The Renegades had enjoyed a much better season than usual, with the veteran Cameron White leading the way. They stumbled but recovered, beating **Sydney Thunder** and Brisbane on the road in their last two games to book a play-off spot for the first time in five years. The Heat and the Thunder had their moments, but neither was consistent enough to warrant a semi-final berth.

Adelaide Strikers' standout performer was the Afghanistan leg-spinner Rashid Khan, whose 18 victims made him the joint-leading wicket-taker with Dwayne Bravo of the Renegades. But Rashid was forced to depart after the semi for international duty. The Strikers were at least able to call on captain

Travis Head and wicketkeeper-batsman Carey after Cricket Australia cleared them and Short to play in the final. That followed an outcry over scheduling which had Australia playing a Twenty20 tri-series with England and New Zealand right at the pointy end of the BBL. Head made 44 not out in the final, but it was a century from opener Jake Weatherald which led the Strikers to their first title.

Things were set to look different again in 2018-19, with the teams all playing each other home and away – 14 qualifying games apiece. The matches will be shared between Channel Seven and Fox Sports as part of a new broadcast deal. It was perhaps fitting that Adelaide's win in the final – the last game to be shown by Ten – was played in an unusual twilight slot to lead in to the reality show *I'm a Celebrity… Get Me Out of Here!* Television talks.

BIG BASH LEAGUE IN 2017-18

	P	W	L	Pts	NRR
PERTH SCORCHERS	10	8	2	16	0.15
ADELAIDE STRIKERS	10	7	3	14	0.80
MELBOURNE RENEGADES	10	6	4	12	0.29
HOBART HURRICANES	10	5	5	10	−0.29
SydneySixers	10	4	6	8	0.33
Sydney Thunder	10	4	6	8	−0.03
Brisbane Heat	10	4	6	8	−0.43
Melbourne Stars	10	2	8	4	−0.92

1st v 4th   At Perth Stadium, February 1, 2018 (floodlit). **Hobart Hurricanes won by 71 runs.** **Hobart Hurricanes** 210-4 (20 overs) (M. S. Wade 71, B. R. McDermott 67*, D. T. Christian 37); ‡**Perth Scorchers** 139 (17.5 overs) (S. E. Marsh 30, T. T. Bresnan 43; T. S. Rogers 3-31, D. T. Christian 4-17). *MoM:* M. S. Wade. *Three-time winners (and defending champions) Perth Scorchers came badly unstuck against the Hurricanes, who eased to their first final since 2013-14. Matthew Wade gave them a flying start with 71 from 45 balls, then Ben McDermott and Dan Christian piled on 88 for the fourth wicket in 39. From 41-1 after five overs, the Scorchers slumped to 68-7 in the tenth. Christian mopped up.*

2nd v 3rd   At Adelaide, February 2, 2018 (floodlit). **Adelaide Strikers won by one run.** ‡**Adelaide Strikers** 178-5 (20 overs) (J. B. Weatherald 57, T. M. Head 85*); **Melbourne Renegades** 177-4 (20 overs) (M. S. Harris 45, T. L. W. Cooper 36*). *MoM:* T. M. Head. *Adelaide Strikers reached the final for the first time when, with three needed, the Renegades' Kieron Pollard missed the last delivery, from Ben Laughlin, and could manage only a bye. The Renegades had looked likely winners at 87-2 after nine overs, but Rashid Khan dismissed Tim Ludeman for 28, and the other bowlers kept the brakes on. Earlier, Travis Head's 85* from 57 balls had underpinned the Strikers' solid innings.*

FINAL

ADELAIDE STRIKERS v HOBART HURRICANES

At Adelaide, February 4, 2018 (floodlit). Adelaide Strikers won by 25 runs. Toss: Adelaide Strikers.

A sell-out home crowd acclaimed the Strikers' first Big Bash title, achieved without leg-spinner Rashid Khan or the tall seamer Billy Stanlake, both absent on international duty. Instead it was the unsung opener Jake Weatherald who set up their victory with a superb 115 – his first T20 century – much of it during a second-wicket partnership of 140 with Travis Head. Weatherald clouted eight sixes and nine fours, and helped his side to only the third total above 200 in this season's competition (the Strikers previous-best was 187, also against the Hurricanes). After Paine fell in the first over of the chase, a lively stand of 81 between Short and Bailey kept the Hurricanes in the hunt – but three wickets for Siddle ended their hopes. Wade, run out without facing as the end loomed, was fined \$A6,000 after hitting a seat in the dug-out with his bat as he stomped off.

Man of the Match: J. B. Weatherald.   *Attendance:* 40,732.

Player of the Tournament: D. J. M. Short.

Adelaide Strikers

	B	4/6
1 †A. T. Carey *b 8* 18	16	3
2 J. B. Weatherald *c 3 b 5*.......115	70	9/8
3 *T. M. Head *not out* 44	29	2/1
4 C. A. Ingram *not out* 14	6	1/1
Lb 4, w 6, nb 1 11		

6 overs: 53-1   (20 overs) 202-2

1/41 2/181

5 J. R. Dean, 6 J. W. Wells, 7 J. S. Lehmann, 8 M. G. Neser, 9 L. N. O'Connor, 10 P. M. Siddle and 11 B. Laughlin did not bat.

Rose 3–3–30–0; Archer 4–8–46–1; Rogers 4–8–30–0; Meredith 3–8–34–0; Short 2–4–20–0; Christian 4–7–38–1.

Hobart Hurricanes

	B	4/6
1 †T. D. Paine *c 1 b 3*......... 5	4	1
2 D. J. M. Short *c 1 b 10*........ 68	44	6/4
3 *G. J. Bailey *c 7 b 10* 46	33	2/2
4 B. R. McDermott *lbw b 10* 9	13	0
5 D. T. Christian *not out*........ 29	19	3/1
6 M. S. Wade *run out (1)* 0	0	0
7 S. A. Milenko *not out* 9	7	1
Lb 8, w 3.................. 11		

6 overs: 60-1   (20 overs) 177-5

1/6 2/87 3/120 4/145 5/145

8 J. C. Archer, 9 C. A. Rose, 10 T. S. Rogers and 11 R. P. Meredith did not bat.

Head 3–5–30–1; Neser 4–6–34–0; Laughlin 4–7–43–0; Siddle 4–15–17–3; O'Connor 4–6–27–0; Ingram 1–1–18–0.

Umpires: S. A. J. Craig and P. J. Gillespie. Third umpire: G. C. Joshua.
Referee: P. L. Marshall.

BIG BASH FINALS

2011-12	SYDNEY SIXERS beat Perth Scorchers by seven wickets at Perth.	
2012-13	BRISBANE HEAT beat Perth Scorchers by 34 runs at Perth.	
2013-14	PERTH SCORCHERS beat Hobart Hurricanes by 39 runs at Perth.	
2014-15	PERTH SCORCHERS beat Sydney Sixers by four wickets at Canberra.	
2015-16	SYDNEY THUNDER beat Melbourne Stars by three wickets at Melbourne.	
2016-17	PERTH SCORCHERS beat Sydney Sixers by nine wickets at Perth.	
2017-18	ADELAIDE STRIKERS beat Hobart Hurricanes by 25 runs at Adelaide.	

THE AKS BANGLADESH PREMIER LEAGUE IN 2017-18

MOHAMMAD ISAM

1 Rangpur Riders   2 Dhaka Dynamites

Like all great showmen, Chris Gayle understands the value of keeping the audience waiting for the routine that brings the house down. For the first few weeks of the Bangladesh Premier League he seemed content to hide in the chorus line, with just two fifties in eight innings for **Rangpur Riders**. Then came the knockouts – and Gayle moved centre stage. In the first qualifier he hit 126. That was just the warm-up for a brutal 146 – including 18 sixes, breaking his own world record – in the final to dethrone **Dhaka Dynamites** and deliver Rangpur's first title. With customary modesty, Gayle anointed himself "the greatest batsman of all time".

His pyrotechnics made for an entertaining conclusion to a generally disappointing competition. Players complained that pitches were often too stodgy for high scoring. Brendon McCullum, Mashrafe bin Mortaza and Tamim Iqbal were among the critics, and Tamim was censured by the Bangladesh board for speaking out. It was the first BPL not to be shown on Indian television, which lowered its profile; coverage at home, meanwhile, was marred by technical difficulties.

MOST SIXES IN A T20 INNINGS

18	C. H. Gayle (146*)	**Rangpur Riders v Dhaka Dynamites at Mirpur**	**2017-18**
17	C. H. Gayle (175*)	RC Bangalore v Pune Warriors at Bangalore	2012-13
16	G. R. Napier (152*)	Essex v Sussex at Chelmsford.	2008
16	M. D. Shanaka (123)	Sinhalese v Saracens at Colombo (Colts)	2015-16
15	C. H. Gayle (151*)	Somerset v Kent at Taunton	2015
14	C. G. Williams (116)	Namibia v Scotland at Windhoek	2011-12
14	A. J. Finch (156)	Australia v England at Southampton.	2013
14	**C. H. Gayle (126*)**	**Rangpur Riders v Khulna Titans at Mirpur**	**2017-18**

Rangpur needed their barnstorming finish after a sluggish start. They lost three of their first four league games, and squeezed into the knockouts. But they showed a mastery of tight finishes, beating **Chittagong Vikings** when Tissara Perera hit the last ball for six, and **Sylhet Sixers** with two deliveries to spare.

Early on, the headlines had belonged to **Comilla Victorians** and **Khulna Titans**. Comilla won nine of their 12 league matches to finish top of the table. Afghanistan leg-spinner Rashid Khan produced some eye-catching perform-ances before leaving for international duty, and conceded just seven in four overs against **Rajshahi Kings**. Comilla's stellar batting line-up also contributed, with regular runs from Jos Buttler, the highest-profile English player on view, Marlon Samuels and Tamim. But their oversized squad became an issue, with some talented players, notably Pakistan opener Fakhar Zaman, spending too much time on the bench. Khulna were rewarded for putting faith in less well-known names: Abu Jayed, the Bangladeshi seamer, was the second-highest wicket-taker, with 18 at 20. They finished third in the league, but were blown away by Gayle in the first qualifier.

Defending champions Dhaka were impressive in the league games, winning seven to finish second, and had some stand-out performers: Evin Lewis was the competition's second-highest run-scorer behind Gayle, with 396 at 36, and a strike-rate of 159. And Shakib Al Hasan topped the wickets list with 22 at 13, including five for 16 against Rangpur.

Sylhet won their first three games, but Yorkshire imports Liam Plunkett and Tim Bresnan could not help them into the knockouts. Rajshahi, runners-up in 2016-17, were hampered by injuries to captain Darren Sammy, Luke Wright and Lendl Simmons. Chittagong had a miserable time and finished bottom. Luke Ronchi regularly gave them good starts, but their bowling was too dependent on Sikandar Raza.

BANGLADESH PREMIER LEAGUE IN 2017-18

	P	W	L	A	Points	NRR
COMILLA VICTORIANS..	12	9	3	0	18	0.57
DHAKA DYNAMITES	12	7	4	1	15	1.63
KHULNA TITANS........	12	7	4	1	15	0.07
RANGPUR RIDERS	12	6	6	0	12	−0.26
Sylhet Sixers	12	4	7	1	9	−0.42
Rajshahi Kings............	12	4	8	0	8	−1.09
Chittagong Vikings	12	3	8	1	7	−0.47

Teams tied on points were separated by head-to-head record.

3rd v 4th At Mirpur, December 8, 2017. **Rangpur Riders won by eight wickets. Khulna Titans 167-6** (20 overs); ‡**Rangpur Riders 171-2** (15.2 overs). (C. H. Gayle 126*, Mithun Ali 30*). *MoM:* C. H. Gayle. *A stunning assault from Chris Gayle powered Rangpur Riders into the final play-off with 28 balls to spare. His 126* included 14 sixes and six fours, and was briefly the highest score in five seasons of the BPL. Rangpur were 25-2 after Jofra Archer had removed Sohag Gazi and Brendon McCullum, before Gayle and Mithun Ali put on 146*. Five Khulna batsmen reached 20, without building anything more substantial.*

1st v 2nd At Mirpur, December 8, 2017 (floodlit). **Dhaka Dynamites won by 95 runs. ‡Dhaka Dynamites 191-7** (20 overs) (E. Lewis 47, J. L. Denly 32, K. A. Pollard 31, Shahid Afridi 30; Hasan Ali 3-16); **Comilla Victorians 96** (18 overs) (Tamim Iqbal 31; Shahid Afridi 3-16). *MoM:* Shahid Afridi. *The holders cruised into the final after a vintage performance by Shahid Afridi. Comilla were flummoxed by Dhaka's four-pronged spin attack and, chasing a stiff target, could not recapture the zest of their early displays. By the time Afridi removed top-scorer Tamim Iqbal and Dwayne Bravo in the tenth over they were 55-6, and the contest was over. Evin Lewis's 47 had set the tone for Dhaka: he put on 69 with Joe Denly, before Kieron Pollard and Afridi ensured there was no slackening off.*

Final play-off At Mirpur, December 10–11, 2017 (floodlit). **Rangpur Riders won by 36 runs. Rangpur Riders 192-3** (20 overs) (J. Charles 105*, B. B. McCullum 78); ‡**Comilla Victorians 156** (20 overs) (Tamim Iqbal 36, Liton Das 39; Rubel Hossain 3-34). *MoM:* J. Charles. *Rain after seven overs of Rangpur's innings brought the possibility of an abandonment, which would have taken Comilla into the final because of a superior qualifying record. But the regulations were hazy and, after prolonged discussions, the captains agreed to resume next evening. Tamim, the Comilla skipper, said: "Any team in our shoes would have done the same." His generosity went unrewarded thanks to Johnson Charles's hundred and 78 from McCullum, his first significant contribution. They added 151 for the second wicket. Tamim and Liton Das got Comilla off to a flyer, but once they were parted the chase stalled. A revival was nipped in the bud when Ravi Bopara dismissed Jos Buttler and Marlon Samuels.*

Final At Mirpur, December 12, 2017 (floodlit). **Rangpur Riders won by 57 runs. Rangpur Riders 206-1** (20 overs) (C. H. Gayle 146*, B. B. McCullum 51*); ‡**Dhaka Dynamites 149-9** (20 overs) (Jahurul Islam 50). *MoM:* C. H. Gayle. *MoS:* C. H. Gayle. *Gayle raised the bar again with an explosive 146* off 69 balls, including a world-record 18 sixes –. the highest Twenty20 score on Bangladeshi soil. Dhaka, the holders and favourites, were shell-shocked by a bruising partnership of 201* between him and McCullum, who had both kept their powder dry until the tournament's sharp end. Shakib Al Hasan had removed Charles in the second over, but then dropped Gayle at cover on 22. The final five overs produced 75, Gayle hitting three of the last four balls for six. Dhaka's hopes had crumbled by the ninth over, when Shakib's dismissal left them 71-5.*

BPL FINALS

2011-12   DHAKA GLADIATORS beat Barisal Burners by eight wickets at Mirpur.
2012-13   DHAKA GLADIATORS beat Chittagong Kings by 43 runs at Mirpur.
2015-16   COMILLA VICTORIANS beat Barisal Bulls by three wickets at Mirpur.
2016-17   DHAKA DYNAMITES beat Rajshahi Kings by 56 runs at Mirpur.
2017-18   RANGPUR RIDERS beat Dhaka Dynamites by 57 runs at Mirpur.

There was no tournament in 2013-14 or 2014-15, following a match-fixing scandal and pay disputes.

VIVO INDIAN PREMIER LEAGUE IN 2017-18

BHARAT SUNDARESAN

1 Chennai Super Kings   2 Sunrisers Hyderabad

In April 2016, the West Indies team – especially Carlos Brathwaite's savage hitting – debunked theories that Twenty20 was based on intricate strategy and high-octane energy. They conquered the world through brute force. Two years on, M. S. Dhoni's **Chennai Super Kings** put to pasture another vaunted notion, that athleticism and youth are prerequisites for winning the IPL. Dhoni's "Daddy Army" waltzed to the title at the Wankhede, with the help of a scintillating unbeaten hundred from one of their most experienced members, Australian all-rounder Shane Watson. It was a theme of the tournament: one or other of Chennai's thirtysomethings kept playing the match-winner. They finished joint-top of the league, and beat their fellow finalists (and table toppers) **Sunrisers Hyderabad** in all four of their encounters.

Victory for Chennai was the sweeter for coming after two years in the wilderness: they had been suspended from the IPL when a senior official, Gurunath Meiyappan, was found guilty on corruption and betting charges. It wasn't quite the perfect return to the fold, though. A dispute between Tamil Nadu and Karnataka over the use of water from the Kaveri river had sparked political unrest in Chennai and, after playing their first home game at the M. A. Chidambaram Stadium, CSK were forced to move their base more than 1,000km to Pune, which no longer had a team in the tournament. (To their displeasure, neither Rising Pune Supergiant nor Gujarat Lions, the sides who had replaced the exiled franchises, were allowed to stay in the league.)

While the ageing warriors walked away with the trophy, IPL11 also saw the emergence of talented young Indian players. **Delhi Daredevils** boasted Rishabh Pant, aged 20, who was outscored only by Hyderabad's Kane Williamson. Meanwhile **Rajasthan Royals** – who had also been suspended for two seasons – benefited from the 23-year-old Sanju Samson's skills either side of the stumps. His form suggested the gloves would be on safe hands after the Dhoni era. A slew of Indian pace bowlers, such as Siddharth Kaul, Shivam Mavi and Aavesh Khan, all took significant strides. And, for CSK, Deepak Chahar regained his swing, making him difficult to hit.

The IPL was now into its second decade. Some felt that, with age, its attractions had faded, that it all seemed a little passé. But Indian cricket fans, a species with indefatigable loyalty, dispelled any doubts. Stadiums were fuller, with gate receipts and TV audiences both up. And CSK provided the perfect illustration of the IPL's claim to be "wholesome family entertainment" when the children of their superstars – Dhoni's young daughter, Ziva, leading the way – enacted a scene from every Indian wedding reception: as the lengthy presentation ceremony rumbled on, they ran joyously around the Wankhede.

Another talking point was Delhi welcoming back their prodigal son Gautam Gambhir, after he had led Kolkata Knight Riders to titles in 2012 and 2014.

But his reign was short-lived and, after the first six games brought five defeats, he dropped himself. Delhi's form improved, though they had to settle for another wooden spoon. The previous year's bottom side, **Royal Challengers Bangalore**, inched themselves up the table, but not into the knockouts.

Another development was the influx of English talent. After years of the ECB obstructing players keen to hone their skills (and earn a little cash), attitudes had softened. It meant that for the first time there were more Englishmen (12) than New Zealanders or West Indians – unthinkable a few seasons earlier. Jos Buttler was a singular success for Rajasthan, though not until he moved to the top of the order. Seven innings at No. 5 or 6 had brought 120 runs at 20; six as an opener 428 at 107 (and a strike-rate of 165). His blistering form helped revive his Test career, and he started to open in Twenty20 internationals, too.

The number of Australians was down. In the wake of the ball-tampering episode in South Africa, Steve Smith and David Warner had their invitations rescinded, while influential seamers Mitchell Starc and Pat Cummins – to the chagrin of **Kolkata Knight Riders** and **Mumbai Indians** – opted out at the eleventh hour because of injury. It felt as though the new broadcasters – Star Sports had paid a staggering $2.55bn for the rights until 2022 – were fielding more Australians in the commentary box. One player who did excel was Andrew Tye, whose 24 wickets for **Kings XI Punjab** made him the most penetrative bowler of the tournament.

For Tye and many others, the knuckle ball had shifted from novelty to necessity, though it was wrist-spin that confirmed its place as the T20 world's preferred currency. The stocks are high in Afghanistan, which provided two of the IPL's youngest stars. Mujeeb Zadran, a 17-year-old whose ability to mix off-spin with leg-breaks had persuaded Kings XI to shell out more than $600,000, shared the spotlight with Rashid Khan, a couple of years older and uprooting trees with Hyderabad. And it was a glorious Mujeeb wrong'un – perhaps the ball of the tournament – that dismissed Bangalore's Virat Kohli. Another teenage leg-spinner, Delhi's Sandeep Lamichhane, was further proof of how quickly the game is travelling. He was the first cricketer from Nepal to play in the IPL, and was praised by Indian prime minister Narendra Modi for enhancing the relationship between the countries.

In a competition brimming with spin, Sunil Narine showed there was more to his game than a sackful of variations. For several years a useful pinch-hitter, he now proved himself a genuine all-rounder for Kolkata. He was in the top 20 for wickets (seventh-equal with 17), economy (13th among frontline bowlers with 7.65) and runs (20th with 357). And no one with 150 or more could match his outrageous strike-rate of 189. He was named Player of the Tournament.

> **❝**
> Smith and Warner prepared to become the grandstand performers at a ground with no grandstand."
> Australia's Ball-Tampering Farrago, page 40

VIVO INDIAN PREMIER LEAGUE IN 2017-18

	P	W	L	Pts	NRR
SUNRISERS HYDERABAD	14	9	5	18	0.28
CHENNAI SUPER KINGS	14	9	5	18	0.25
KOLKATA KNIGHT RIDERS ...	14	8	6	16	−0.07
RAJASTHAN ROYALS	14	7	7	14	−0.25
Mumbai Indians.	14	6	8	12	0.31
Royal Challengers Bangalore	14	6	8	12	0.12
Kings XI Punjab	14	6	8	12	−0.50
Delhi Daredevils	14	5	9	10	−0.22

1st v 2nd At Mumbai, May 22, 2018 (floodlit). **Chennai Super Kings won by two wickets. Sunrisers Hyderabad 139-7** (20 overs) (C. R. Brathwaite 43*); ‡**Chennai Super Kings 140-8** (19.1 overs) (F. du Plessis 67*). *MoM:* F. du Plessis. *Hyderabad lost Shikhar Dhawan first ball, chopping on, and run-scoring was always tricky against a disciplined attack, exemplified by Ravi Jadeja's 4–14–13–1. A spirited 43* from Carlos Brathwaite lifted them from 88-6 after 15, and a target of 140 assumed bigger proportions once three Chennai wickets had fallen in four overs. M. S. Dhoni never settled – his first runs came from his ninth ball – and he departed for nine from 18, leaving them 39-4. But Faf du Plessis bided his time with greater success: 20 came from the 18th over, bowled by Brathwaite, and the job was almost done.*

3rd v 4th At Kolkata, May 23, 2018 (floodlit). **Kolkata Knight Riders won by 25 runs. Kolkata Knight Riders 169-7** (20 overs) (K. D. Karthik 52, A. D. Russell 49*); ‡**Rajasthan Royals 144-4** (20 overs) (A. M. Rahane 46, S. V. Samson 50). *MoM:* A. D. Russell. *Rajasthan had made it this far thanks to the electric form of Jos Buttler, but he and Ben Stokes had gone back to England and from 87-1 after ten overs, they let the opportunity slip. Neither Ajinkya Rahane nor Sanju Samson could find the middle of the bat, and Kolkata ran out comfortable winners. That had seemed unlikely after losing three of their top four in single figures. But Andre Russell smote 49* from 25 balls, and his fluency proved the difference.*

Final play-off At Kolkata, May 25, 2018 (floodlit). **Sunrisers Hyderabad won by 14 runs. Sunrisers Hyderabad 174-7** (20 overs) (W. P. Saha 35, S. Dhawan 34, Rashid Khan 34*); ‡**Kolkata Knight Riders 160-9** (20 overs) (C. A. Lynn 48, S. Gill 30, Rashid Khan 3-19). *MoM:* Rashid Khan. *There was no agonising over the winner of the match award: Rashid Khan walloped four sixes and two fours in a savage ten-ball 34*, then followed it up with three wickets, two catches and a run-out. His was the perfect flourish at the end of Hyderabad's largely steady innings, while the three victims of his leg-spin – Robin Uthappa, Chris Lynn and Russell – were all Kolkata dangermen.*

FINAL

CHENNAI SUPER KINGS v SUNRISERS HYDERABAD

At Mumbai, May 27, 2018. Chennai Super Kings won by eight wickets. Toss: Chennai Super Kings.
  Shane Watson, at 36 the embodiment of Dhoni's mature Chennai team, showed that even in Twenty20 cricket there could be time to play yourself in. Despite a target of 179, Watson took 11 deliveries to get off the mark; he gave the utmost respect to Bhuvneshwar Kumar and Rashid Khan, who together conceded 17 from the 20 balls they bowled him. Against the others, it was a case of man versus boys: Watson's remaining 100 cascaded from 37, as victory came with an over and a half to spare. Raina gave solid support, but it was essentially the Shane show. Earlier, Hyderabad had never quite clicked; 44 came from the last four but, on a true pitch and against the most confident of batting sides, they needed 200-plus. Tight lines from Chahar and Ngidi, who bowled a maiden to Williamson, the tournament's leading run-scorer, had given Chennai a momentum they never quite lost.
  Man of the Match: S. R. Watson. *Man of the Tournament:* S. P. Narine (Kolkata Knight Riders).

Sunrisers Hyderabad

		B	4/6
1 †S. P. Goswami *run out (9/5)* ..	5	5	0
2 S. Dhawan *b 7*	26	25	2/1
3 *K. S. Williamson *st 5 b 9*....	47	36	5/2
4 Shakib Al Hasan *c 3 b 6*	23	15	2/1
5 Y. K. Pathan *not out*	45	25	4/2
6 D. J. Hooda *c 12 b 11*	3	4	0
7 C. R. Brathwaite *c 4 b 10*	21	11	0/3
Lb 1, w 6, nb 1	8		

6 overs: 42-1   (20 overs) 178-6

1/13 2/64 3/101 4/133 5/144 6/178

8 Rashid Khan, 9 Bhuvneshwar Kumar, 10 S. Kaul and 11 S. Sharma did not bat.

Chahar 4–10–25–0; Ngidi 4–11–26–1; Thakur 3–4–31–1; Sharma 3–7–25–1; Bravo 4–5–46–1; Jadeja 2–2–24–1.

Chennai Super Kings

		B	4/6
1 S. R. Watson *not out*	117	57	11/8
2 F. du Plessis *c and b 11*	10	11	1
3 S. K. Raina *c 1 b 7*	32	24	3/1
4 A. T. Rayudu *not out*	16	19	1/1
Lb 3, w 3	6		

6 overs: 35-1   (18.3 overs) 181-2

1/16 2/133

5 *†M. S. Dhoni, 6 D. J. Bravo, 7 R. A. Jadeja, 8 D. L. Chahar, 9 K. V. Sharma, 10 S. N. Thakur and 11 L. T. Ngidi did not bat.

12th man: D. R. Shorey.

Bhuvneshwar Kumar 4–16–17–0; Sharma 4–9–52–1; Kaul 3–2–43–0; Rashid Khan 4–9–24–0; Shakib Al Hasan 1–1–15–0; Brathwaite 2.3–3–27–1.

Umpires: M. Erasmus and S. Ravi.   Third umpire: N. N. Menon.
Referee: A. J. Pycroft.

RECENT IPL FINALS

2013-14   KOLKATA KNIGHT RIDERS beat Kings XI Punjab by three wickets at Bangalore.
2014-15   MUMBAI INDIANS beat Chennai Super Kings by 41 runs at Kolkata.
2015-16   SUNRISERS HYDERABAD beat Royal Challengers Bangalore by eight runs at Bangalore.
2016-17   MUMBAI INDIANS beat Rising Pune Supergiant by one run at Hyderabad.
2017-18   CHENNAI SUPER KINGS beat Sunrisers Hyderabad by eight wickets at Mumbai.

BURGER KING SUPER SMASH IN 2017-18

M ARK G EENTY

1 Knights   2 Central Stags

Even Twenty20 has room for a throwback. Grinning through beards bushy enough to have graced WG's chin, **Knights** captain Dean Brownlie and Player of the Tournament Anton Devcich clutched the Super Smash trophy as their uniforms glowed in the Hamilton sun. Hirsute in pink, the team formerly known as Northern Districts had a unique look, and backed it up on the pitch. They cruised into the final – a healthy six points clear after the regular season – then demolished **Central Stags**, knocking off a small target inside nine overs.

Their second T20 title, four years after the first, became a stroll in Seddon Park as Devcich followed three wickets for his left-arm spin with a rapid half-century to cap a dominant all-round tournament. The appointment of the former Test wicketkeeper Gareth Hopkins as a specialist T20 coach had paid immediate dividends. For the Stags, it was a second successive defeat in the final, which extended their T20 drought to eight seasons.

At 32, Devcich burnished his reputation as a power-hitting, abrasive competitor. He had played 16 white-ball internationals for New Zealand without quite cracking the top level but now felt able to decline a domestic contract and instead start a career as a T20 freelance. He was rarely out of the headlines, starting in the opening match, when he was fined $NZ900 for swearing and berating the third umpire while providing on-field comments live on television.

Knights lost that game, to defending champions Wellington Firebirds, but suffered only one more defeat. Next evening, Devcich's opening partner Tim Seifert smacked a century in 40 balls – a New Zealand T20 record – against Auckland Aces at Mount Maunganui as they amassed 214, and their roll began.

The openers were dominant. The left-handed Devcich headed the run-charts with 343 at a strike-rate of 168, while Seifert – a busy young wicketkeeper-batsman – earned a New Zealand call-up after 323 runs at 146. Stags captain Will Young split them with 331 at 145. Often opening the bowling, Devcich snared 15 wickets at an impressive economy-rate of 6.39; only the Stags' tall seamer Blair Tickner took more, with 21, but cost eight an over.

Big-name imports were thin on the ground, as the Super Smash again ran up against Australia's Big Bash, but Ben Stokes's three-match cameo for **Canterbury Kings** – he was missing the Ashes because of the brawl in Bristol in September – was a notable headline act. His presence got people talking in Christchurch, the city of his birth, and one spectacular knock of 93 off 47 balls against Otago Volts justified his presence. But it was one of just four wins for the Kings, who finished fourth and missed the play-offs.

The Knights rotated two overseas seamers, Ben Laughlin of Australia and England's Chris Jordan, while Surrey's Sam Curran was a tidy all-round contributor for **Auckland Aces**, whose star batsman Mark Chapman made 307 runs at a strike-rate of 171. The Aces finished second in the table, but their title charge was derailed by the Stags in the preliminary final.

Samit Patel, from the 2017 English Twenty20 champions Nottinghamshire, collected 185 runs and 11 wickets for **Wellington Firebirds**, but back-to-back defeats by the Stags ended their title defence. The Knights had their own Nottinghamshire connection: leg-spinner Ish Sodhi, another cog in the side that had won the T20 Blast, took 12 wickets in seven matches, including a miserly two for 15 in the final.

Otago Volts finished bottom again, winning just twice, but their fast bowler Warren Barnes generated attention when he donned a custom-made baseball-style facemask to protect his head from white Kookaburra missiles in his follow-through.

The title sponsors changed again: appropriately for the game's quickest format, it was a fast-food swap, Burger King replacing McDonald's after just one season.

SUPER SMASH IN 2017-18

	P	W	L	A	Pts	NRR
KNIGHTS	10	7	2	1	30	0.75
AUCKLAND ACES	10	5	3	2	24	0.20
CENTRAL STAGS	10	5	4	1	22	1.04
Canterbury Kings	10	4	5	1	18	0.95
Wellington Firebirds	10	3	5	2	16	−0.28
Otago Volts	10	2	7	1	10	−2.70

2nd v 3rd At Auckland (Eden Park Outer Oval), January 17, 2018 (floodlit). **Central Stags won by 36 runs. Central Stags 163-6** (20 overs) (D. Cleaver 54); ‡**Auckland Aces 127** (17.3 overs) (C. Cachopa 38; S. H. A. Rance 3-22, A. Y. Patel 3-26). *The Stags started circumspectly – 39-2 in the six-over powerplay, with Sam Curran taking the second wicket. But Tom Bruce lit the blue touchpaper with 28 off 13 balls, then Dane Cleaver took over with 54 from 33. Auckland never really got going, and were 73-6 a ball after halfway. The Mumbai-born left-arm spinner Ajaz Patel collected three wickets, then seamer Seth Rance hustled out the last three in eight deliveries.*

Final At Hamilton, January 20, 2018 (floodlit). **Knights won by nine wickets.** ‡**Central Stags 99-8** (20 overs) (G. H. Worker 37; A. P. Devcich 3-16); **Knights 103-1** (8.5 overs) (A. P. Devcich 51*). *MoS:* A. P. Devcich. *Anton Devcich starred with ball and bat in a one-sided final. First he took three wickets with his slow left-armers as the Stags were throttled in the middle overs – only 31 came from eight by Devcich and leg-spinner Ish Sodhi – and the target was a modest 100. The Knights shot out of the blocks in the chase, taking ten from each of the first three overs. Ajaz Patel's first cost only three, but skipper Dean Brownlie hit five fours off Blair Tickner's next, then Devcich hit every delivery from Patel to the boundary.*

SUPER SMASH FINALS

2005-06	CANTERBURY WIZARDS beat Auckland Aces by six wickets at Auckland.
2006-07	AUCKLAND ACES beat Otago Volts by 60 runs at Auckland.
2007-08	CENTRAL STAGS beat Northern Knights by five wickets at New Plymouth.
2008-09	OTAGO VOLTS headed the table; the final against Canterbury Wizards at Dunedin was washed out.
2009-10	CENTRAL STAGS beat Auckland Aces by 78 runs at New Plymouth.
2010-11	AUCKLAND ACES beat Central Stags by four runs at Auckland.
2011-12	AUCKLAND ACES beat Canterbury Wizards by four wickets at Auckland.
2012-13	OTAGO VOLTS beat Wellington Firebirds by four wickets at Dunedin.
2013-14	NORTHERN KNIGHTS beat Otago Volts by five wickets at Hamilton.
2014-15	WELLINGTON FIREBIRDS beat Auckland Aces by six runs at Hamilton.
2015-16	AUCKLAND ACES beat Otago Volts by 20 runs at New Plymouth.
2016-17	WELLINGTON FIREBIRDS beat Central Stags by 14 runs at New Plymouth.
2017-18	KNIGHTS beat Central Stags by nine wickets at Hamilton.

HBL PAKISTAN SUPER LEAGUE IN 2017-18

CHARLES REYNOLDS

1 Islamabad United   2 Peshawar Zalmi

The third edition of the Pakistan Super League built on the success of its predecessors. While the first, held entirely in the Gulf, was important simply because it happened, the second began the process of reintroducing high-profile cricket to Pakistan by holding the final at Lahore's Gaddafi Stadium. For the third, it hosted two of the PSL's three qualifying play-offs, before the bandwagon moved on to Karachi for the final. Most non-Pakistani members of the teams chose to travel. If PSL2 had dipped a toe in the water, PSL3 risked a whole foot. The aim was that the entire competition would be on home soil within a few years.

Islamabad United's mixture of overseas pros and youthful home-grown talent earned them their second title. While injuries to a few key figures, such as Rumman Raees and Andre Russell, might have derailed some, Islamabad were fortunate to have the red-hot New Zealand opener Luke Ronchi. He hit five fifties in 11 innings, including a blistering 52 in the final. He was named Player of the Tournament. Invaluable support came from Islamabad's crop of promising youngsters: Hussain Talat, Asif Ali, Fahim Ashraf and teenage leg-spinner Shadab Khan.

The holders, **Peshawar Zalmi**, had to settle for second. They took their time to come good, securing their play-off spot thanks to wins in their last two group games, but were fearsome in the knockouts. Their influential captain, Darren Sammy, was at the heart of their success, even if injuries meant he hobbled through some matches; Kamran Akmal struck vital runs, ending with four fifties and the tournament's only century.

In a welcome move, the number of franchises increased from five to six, imbuing the group stage with a little more jeopardy, since two teams would now fail to progress. Unfortunately for the new boys – the excellently named **Multan Sultans** – they were one of the two to miss the cut, despite winning four of their first five completed matches. **Lahore Qalandars** finished last for the third year running. They did at least usher another exciting left-arm fast bowler on to the stage: Shaheen Shah Afridi, then aged 17, claimed the extraordinary figures of five for four against Multan.

Karachi Kings were much improved, but injuries to skipper Imad Wasim and new signing Shahid Afridi did not help, and a lack of composure meant they lost both play-off games – a disappointment after finishing second in the table. Two-time runners-up **Quetta Gladiators** were spared a hat-trick of heartbreaks. Once again, they were disadvantaged by their overseas players' unwillingness to fly to Pakistan, including Australian all-rounder Shane Watson, their star in the group games. It prompted Quetta coach Moin Khan to call for sides not to pick players unprepared to make the trip. Given the likelihood of more games on home soil, that seemed a reasonable suggestion.

HBL PAKISTAN SUPER LEAGUE IN 2017-18

	P	W	L	A	Pts	NRR
ISLAMABAD UNITED	10	7	3	0	14	0.29
KARACHI KINGS	10	5	4	1	11	0.02
PESHAWAR ZALMI	10	5	5	0	10	0.46
QUETTA GLADIATORS	10	5	5	0	10	0.31
Multan Sultans	10	4	5	1	9	−0.19
Lahore Qalandars	10	3	7	0	6	−0.93

1st v 2nd At Dubai (Sports City), March 18, 2018 (floodlit). **Islamabad United won by eight wickets. ‡Karachi Kings 154-4** (20 overs) (J. L. Denly 51, C. A. Ingram 68*); **Islamabad United 155-2** (12.3 overs) (L. Ronchi 94*). MoM: L. Ronchi. *On an excellent batting surface, Luke Ronchi made mincemeat of a modest target. He reached his fifty from 19 deliveries – the fastest in the tournament's three years – hit 12 fours and five sixes in his 39-ball 94*, and sped Islamabad to the final with oceans of time to spare. Ronchi was facing an experienced attack, but paid no heed to reputation: all five bowlers cost at least ten an over. Karachi had begun at a subdued rate, their powerplay score of 29-2 as revealing as Islamabad's 75-0.*

3rd v 4th At Lahore, March 20, 2018 (floodlit). **Peshawar Zalmi won by one run. Peshawar Zalmi 157** (20 overs) (L. A. Dawson 62; Rahat Ali 4-16); **‡Quetta Gladiators 156-9** (20 overs) (Mohammad Nawaz 35, Sarfraz Ahmed 35). MoM: Hasan Ali. *In the first two editions of the PSL, Quetta had reached the final after beating Peshawar by a single. The margin remained the same, but it was third time unlucky for Quetta, who were without Kevin Pietersen and Shane Watson after they declined to fly to Pakistan. Peshawar's innings had relied on Liam Dawson – his resourcefulness at odds with his team-mates' one-dimensional hitting – until he became the last of left-arm seamer Rahat Ali's four wickets. Hasan Ali (2-21) then helped keep Quetta quiet and, after Wahab Riaz conceded just three runs (and snatched two wickets) from the 19th, they needed a seemingly impossible 25 from the last, bowled by Dawson. Anwar Ali crashed 22 off five, but his partner, Mir Hamza, was run out aiming for the second that would have meant a super over.*

Final play-off At Lahore, March 21, 2018 (floodlit). **Peshawar Zalmi won by 13 runs. Peshawar Zalmi 170-7** (16 overs) (Kamran Akmal 77, A. D. S. Fletcher 34; R. S. Bopara 3-35); **‡Karachi Kings 157-2** (16 overs) (J. L. Denly 79*, Babar Azam 63). MoM: Kamran Akmal. *Thanks to the electric hitting of Kamran Akmal, who launched eight, mainly leg-side, sixes from 27 balls, Peshawar simply had too many runs in a contest reduced to 16 overs by rain. He reached fifty in 17, beating Ronchi's record from three days earlier. Ravi Bopara took three wickets, including Kamran, though it needed Mohammad Amir (4–13–16–0) to keep any sort of lid on the scoring: he did not concede a boundary. Rarely do a team lose because they have wickets intact, but Karachi needed Colin Ingram, their power hitter, to arrive before the penultimate over. Joe Denly was brisk – 79* from 46 – but not brisk enough.*

Final At Karachi, March 25, 2018 (floodlit). **Islamabad United won by three wickets. ‡Peshawar Zalmi 148-9** (20 wickets) (C. J. Jordan 36, L. A. Dawson 33; Shadab Khan 3-25); **Islamabad United 154-7** (16.5 overs) (L. Ronchi 52, Sahibzada Farhan 44). MoM: L. Ronchi. MoS: L. Ronchi. *Billed as the battle of the in-form openers, Kamran and Ronchi, this contest was, except for five overs, a one-sided affair. Kamran faced nine balls for a single, and Peshawar never enjoyed much fluency until No. 10 Wahab smashed 28 from 14. By the time Islamabad were 96-0 in the ninth over of the reply, the issue looked settled. But Ronchi's departure for his fifth fifty of the tournament gave them the jitters and, at 116-6 after 14, Karachi briefly had a sniff. They didn't help their cause, though, when Kamran, the keeper, dropped a skyer; fine leg then hurled the ball past the stumps and to the boundary. What should have been a wicket cost six runs. Reprieved, Asif Ali ended on 26* from six.*

PSL FINALS

2015-16 ISLAMABAD UNITED beat Quetta Gladiators by six wickets at Dubai.
2016-17 PESHAWAR ZALMI beat Quetta Gladiators by 58 runs at Lahore.
2017-18 ISLAMABAD UNITED beat Peshawar Zalmi by three wickets at Karachi.

RAM SLAM T20 CHALLENGE IN 2017-18

TRISTAN HOLME

1 Titans   2 Dolphins

The embarrassing collapse of Cricket South Africa's grand Global League provided an unexpected shot in the arm for the T20 Challenge. Restored at short notice to its prime slot in the calendar, and including South African internationals, it enjoyed an increase in attendances and viewing figures. Sponsors Ram, who quit after the 2015-16 match-fixing scandal, came back on board. CSA officials must have heaved a sigh of relief.

The tournament might have lacked a sprinkling of stardust, but it proved that South African fans identify strongly with their own: Dale Steyn's return from injury with the Titans was an ongoing story.

Not everything was rosy. A **Titans** squad boasting most of the international talent were predictably too strong for everyone else, thus removing any tension. And the weather was too intrusive. Durban was so wet that the **Dolphins** completed just one of their five home matches in the league stage. Their home semi-final was also washed out, but they had scraped together enough points to advance to the final, where they were hammered by the Titans.

In search of their third successive title, the Titans had begun with 13 players who had appeared for South Africa and, by the end of the season, Junior Dala and Heinrich Klaasen had joined them. It exposed a key flaw: nationally contracted players choose which franchise they represent, and most opted for the team reputed to be the best run. CSA's acting-chief executive Thabang Moroe suggested a draft system to level things up.

The Titans were simply unstoppable, winning their first six completed games to secure a home semi-final. Coach Mark Boucher rested important players for the final league games, which were lost to the Cobras and the Dolphins. But they were firing on all cylinders again to blitz the **Warriors** by eight wickets in the semi-final, then demolish the Dolphins.

Cape Cobras, who had lost key players after a dispute with the management, benefited from larger home crowds. But a poor start ultimately cost them a place in the final, when their semi against the Dolphins was rained off. The Warriors, runners-up the previous year, continued to punch above their weight, but were unable to win a trophy for coach Malibongwe Maketa before he left to become assistant coach of the national side. The **Lions**, who finished fifth, were still reeling from the fixing scandal of two seasons earlier, and the loss of big names, while the **Knights**, bottom again, faced their usual struggle to attract talent to Bloemfontein.

Reeza Hendricks, of the Lions, was the leading run-scorer, with 361 in only seven innings at a strike-rate of 137; he hit one of two centuries in the competition. The other was scored by the Dolphins' Sarel Erwee, the only player with no international experience to make a mark. The Titans' left-arm wrist-spinner Tabraiz Shamsi was the leading wicket-taker, with 16.

RAM SLAM T20 CHALLENGE IN 2017-18

	P	W	L	NR/A	Bonus pts	Pts	NRR
TITANS	10	6	2	2	4	32	1.10
DOLPHINS	10	3	2	5	1	23	1.22
CAPE COBRAS	10	5	4	1	0	22	−0.39
WARRIORS	10	4	5	1	0	18	−0.73
Lions	10	2	4	4	0	16	−0.38
Knights	10	2	5	3	0	14	−0.32

Semi-final   At Centurion, December 13, 2017 (floodlit). **Titans won by eight wickets. Warriors 143** (18.1 overs) (C. A. Ingram 41, C. N. Ackermann 48; T. Shamsi 4-32); ‡**Titans 145-2** (15.2 overs) (A. K. Markram 56*, A. B. de Villiers 54*). *Batsman of the Match: A. K. Markram. Bowler of the Match: T. Shamsi. The Titans overcame a hiccup in their two final league matches and cruised into the final. Colin Ingram and Colin Ackermann had put on 63 for the third wicket as the Warriors recovered from a poor start, before Tabraiz Shamsi snared four victims in his third and fourth overs. His celebration – an imaginary walkie-talkie cupped to his ear – mimicked the officials consulting the third umpire. The Warriors were briefly back in the game when the Titans were 44-2, but Aiden Markram and A. B. de Villiers added 101* in less than 11 overs.*

Semi-final   At Durban, December 14, 2017 (floodlit). **Dolphins v Cape Cobras. Abandoned.** *The Dolphins progressed after finishing above the Cobras in the group stages.*

Final   At Centurion, December 16, 2017 (floodlit). **Titans won by seven wickets. Dolphins 100** (18.3 overs) (C. H. Morris 4-13); ‡**Titans 101-3** (11.1 overs) (Q. de Kock 39). *Batsman of the Match: Q. de Kock. Bowler of the Match: C. H. Morris. An outstanding performance in the field by the Titans set up their hat-trick of titles. Having earned a home final, they were backed by a near-capacity crowd, and the Dolphins, whose progress had been assisted by washouts, looked undercooked and overawed. In the absence of Dale Steyn and Morne Morkel, Chris Morris took four cheap wickets after the Dolphins had been put in. He was well supported by Lungi Ngidi, who removed Sarel Erwee, a century-maker on the same ground earlier in the competition, and by Malusi Siboto. The Dolphins' faint hopes receded further when Imran Tahir was hit on the hand while batting, and could not bowl. A simple run-chase was clinically executed, with Quinton de Kock playing himself back into form after a poor tournament.*

CSA T20 CHALLENGE FINALS

2003-04	EAGLES beat Eastern Cape by seven runs (D/L).
2004-05	TITANS beat Warriors by eight wickets.
2005-06	EAGLES beat Cape Cobras by six wickets.
2006-07	LIONS beat Cape Cobras by six wickets.
2007-08	TITANS beat Dolphins by 18 runs.
2008-09	CAPE COBRAS beat Eagles by 22 runs.
2009-10	WARRIORS beat Lions by 82 runs.
2010-11	CAPE COBRAS beat Warriors by 12 runs.
2011-12	TITANS beat Lions by 45 runs.
2012-13	LIONS beat Titans by 30 runs.
2013-14	DOLPHINS beat Cape Cobras by two runs.
2014-15	CAPE COBRAS beat Knights by 33 runs.
2015-16	TITANS beat Dolphins by seven wickets.
2016-17	TITANS beat Warriors by six runs.
2017-18	TITANS beat Dolphins by seven wickets.

Titans have won the title 6 times, Cape Cobras 3, Eagles/Knights and Lions 2, Dolphins and Warriors/Eastern Cape 1.

The tournament was the Standard Bank Pro20 Series from 2003-04 to 2010-11, the MiWay T20 Challenge in 2011-12 and the Ram Slam T20 Challenge from 2012-13 (excluding 2016-17 when there was no headline sponsor).

THE HERO CARIBBEAN PREMIER LEAGUE IN 2018

Peter Miller

1 Trinbago Knight Riders   2 Guyana Amazon Warriors

Trinbago Knight Riders secured back-to-back CPL titles, after topping the group table with seven victories. Boasting the tournament's leading run-scorer (New Zealander Colin Munro, with 567) and the leading wicket-taker (Australian leg-spinner Fawad Ahmed, with 22), they were worthy champions.

The runners-up in both the qualifying table and the final were **Guyana Amazon Warriors**. While the Knight Riders were replete with big names, the Warriors were workmanlike, with contributions throughout the squad. The rise of some talented young West Indians was one of the features of the sixth edition of the CPL and, in Shimron Hetmyer (440 runs) and Sherfane Rutherford (171), the Warriors had two exciting examples. Their breakout star, though, was the New South Wales off-spinner Chris Green, who made a rapid transition from late replacement and relative unknown to team captain and a favourite with the fans.

Another local youngster to shine was Oshane Thomas, who claimed 18 wickets for **Jamaica Tallawahs**. Bowling with pace and late movement, he was a constant threat, and it was no surprise when he made his international debut in India later in the year. Andre Russell, who had missed the 2017 tournament while serving a ban for missing a drugs test, found captaincy tough – but underlined his ability with a hat-trick against the Knight Riders at Port-of-Spain, before hitting 121 from 49 balls as the Tallawahs overhauled 224. He was one of four centurions in the tournament, along with Hetmyer, Kieron Pollard and the New Zealander Glenn Phillips.

The previous year's runners-up, **St Kitts & Nevis Patriots**, made it to the final play-off this time, before losing to the eventual champions. Their most impressive bowler was Nepal leg-spinner Sandeep Lamichhane. But Evin Lewis, one of 2017's most consistent performers, averaged 11. His opening partner, 38-year-old Chris Gayle, was the Patriots' leading scorer with 283.

Even with some outstanding talent, **St Lucia Stars** had another season to forget, though – unlike in 2017 – they did at least win a game. Pollard replaced Darren Sammy as captain, and hit 330 runs, including a maiden T20 century. Despite playing in a stadium named after him, Sammy endured a difficult time: he managed just 39 runs in five innings – 36 in one knock – and didn't bowl.

Barbados Tridents lost seven successive matches, including all five at home, and propped up the table. They had some big-name players, including Hashim Amla and Martin Guptill, but never found the right combination. Even when the towering Mohammad Irfan produced the most economical four-over spell in T20 history – 4–23–1–2, the solitary run coming off his final delivery – the Tridents still managed to lose. One player who did enhance his reputation in the format was Shai Hope, who had missed the 2017 CPL on Test duty. He finished with 288 runs, including 88 against the Warriors in one of the Tridents' rare victories, helped by left-arm seamer Raymon Reifer, whose five for 20 was the competition's best return.

The tournament saw the return to high-profile cricket of the Australians Steve Smith and David Warner, who were still banned from the international game following the Cape Town sandpaper incident. Neither set the world alight. Warner made 220 runs for the Stars, and Smith 185 for the Tridents.

CARIBBEAN PREMIER LEAGUE IN 2018

	P	W	L	NR	Pts	NRR
TRINBAGO KNIGHT RIDERS	10	7	3	0	14	0.82
GUYANA AMAZON WARRIORS	10	6	4	0	12	0.29
JAMAICA TALLAWAHS	10	6	4	0	12	0.22
ST KITTS & NEVIS PATRIOTS	10	5	4	1	11	0.25
St Lucia Stars	10	3	6	1	7	−0.94
Barbados Tridents	10	2	8	0	4	−0.71

1st v 2nd   At Providence, Guyana, September 11 (floodlit). **Guyana Amazon Warriors won by two wickets. Trinbago Knight Riders 122-7** (20 overs); ‡**Guyana Amazon Warriors 126-8** (19.5 overs) (S. O. Hetmyer 39, S. E. Rutherford 30). *MoM:* S. O. Hetmyer. *The Warriors made it to the final, winning a low-scoring match when Sohail Tanvir smashed the penultimate ball, from Dwayne Bravo, for a straight six. The Knight Riders never recovered from losing Brendon McCullum – to a questionable lbw – and Colin Munro for ducks; Colin Ingram's 25 was the highest score in their underwhelming total. The Warriors struggled in turn to 52-5 after 12 overs, then Shimron Hetmyer and Sherfane Rutherford put on 50 before falling to successive deliveries. It was left to Tanvir and Romario Shepherd to save the day with a ninth-wicket stand of 21*.*

3rd v 4th   At Providence, Guyana, September 12, 2018 (floodlit). **St Kitts & Nevis Patriots won by two wickets. Jamaica Tallawahs 191-5** (20 overs) (G. D. Phillips 103, L. R. P. L. Taylor 33); ‡**St Kitts & Nevis Patriots 193-8** (19.5 overs) (A. P. Devcich 50; O. R. Thomas 3-43, I. S. Sodhi 3-36). *MoM:* A. P. Devcich. *For the second day running the match was won by a six off the fifth ball of the final over, Ben Cutting (17*) belting Rovman Powell over midwicket. The Patriots had been energised by Anton Devcich's 23-ball half-century. It was bad luck on the New Zealander Glenn Phillips, whose 103 from 63 for the Tallawahs, which included six sixes, was his second T20 century, both coming in defeats.*

Final play-off   At Tarouba, Trinidad, September 14, 2018 (floodlit). **Trinbago Knight Riders won by 20 runs. Trinbago Knight Riders 165-6** (20 overs) (B. B. McCullum 43); ‡**St Kitts & Nevis Patriots 145-8** (20 overs) (D. C. Thomas 35, B A. King 33, F. A. Allen 32*; Fawad Ahmed 3-13). *MoM:* Fawad Ahmed. *The Knight Riders grabbed their second chance of a place in the final thanks to tight bowling, especially from the Australian leg-spinner Fawad Ahmed, whose 4–14–14–3 included the wickets of Devcich and Cutting, the Patriots' batting heroes from the previous match. Earlier, Chris Gayle had fallen for a duck in the first over. Dwayne Bravo, the Knight Riders' captain, smacked 24 late runs from eight balls to swell their total, which proved crucial.*

Final   At Tarouba, Trinidad, September 16, 2-18 (floodlit). **Trinbago Knight Riders won by eight wickets. Guyana Amazon Warriors 147-9** (20 overs) (L. Ronchi 44; K. A. Pierre 3-29); ‡**Trinbago Knight Riders 150-2** (17.3 overs) (B. B. McCullum 39, C. Munro 68*). *MoM:* K. A. Pierre. *MoS:* C. Munro. *The Pakistan-born USA international Ali Khan started the match by removing Cameron Delport's off stump first ball. It kicked off a tight bowling display that allowed the Knight Riders to retain their title. Sunil Narine (1-31) was the most expensive of their quintet, while slow left-armer Khary Pierre's 3-29 included top-scorer Luke Ronchi for 44. After a burst from McCullum (39 from 24 balls), Munro wrapped up the trophy with 68* from 39, his sixth half-century of the tournament.*

OTHER DOMESTIC T20 COMPETITIONS

SHPAGEEZA T20 TOURNAMENT IN 2017-18

It was a wonder Afghanistan's Twenty20 tournament happened at all. In May 2017, a car bomb outside the German embassy in Kabul killed 90 people, forcing the tournament to be postponed from July to September. But violence struck again: during the match between Boost Defenders and Mis Ainak Knights, a suicide attacker detonated a bomb outside the Kabul International Stadium, killing three and injuring 12.

Adam Hollioake, the former England one-day captain who was coaching Boost, told *The Daily Telegraph*: "The noise after was so deep and rumbling, and kept going for such a long time, that I felt it going through my whole body... I could see the guys sprinting off the pitch. I would say it was 75-100 metres from the changing-room. You could see all the windows had been blown out."

After a security sweep, the match continued. And so did the tournament, with every remaining fixture taking place at the same ground. That evening, Wais Barmak, Afghanistan's interior minister, met with all the teams and told them the government would ensure their safety. A clutch of foreign players left for home – including the South African Cameron Delport, who that day had hit the only century of the competition – but the majority remained, and helped the local heroes produce a successful tournament.

The Knights, coached by former Warwickshire opener Andy Moles, gritted their teeth and made it to the final. But **Band-e-Amir Dragons** took the trophy, after seamer Tendai Chatara, later named best bowler, defended 12 off the last over. Chatara was one of four Zimbabweans in the final, alongside Ryan Burl, Sikandar Raza and Vusi Sibanda, who all ended on the losing side. It was tough on the Knights' 18-year-old left-arm wrist-spinner Zahir Khan, whose three for 31 left him as the top wicket-taker. But his performances, together with those of winning captain Rashid Khan, showed Afghanistan's slow bowling to be in rude health.

	P	W	L	Pts	NRR
Band-e-Amir Dragons	5	4	1	12	1.68
Mis Ainak Knights.........	5	4	1	12	0.43
Kabul Eagles	5	3	2	9	0.33
Boost Defenders...........	5	2	3	6	−0.17
Speen Ghar Tigers	5	2	3	6	−1.01
Amo Sharks	5	0	5	0	−1.44

Final At Kabul, September 22, 2017. **Band-e-Amir Dragons won by four runs. ‡Band-e-Amir Dragons 158-7** (20 overs) (Javed Ahmadi 55, Hazratullah Zazai 35; Zahir Khan 3-31); **Mis Ainak Knights 154-7** (20 overs) (Sikandar Raza 40). *MoM:* Javed Ahmadi.

SRI LANKA CRICKET T20 TOURNAMENT IN 2017-18

In Sri Lanka, the domestic T20 competition was squeezed into a fortnight in February and March 2018. Colts and Moors were the only teams with 100% records in the four qualifying groups, but they both lost in the quarter-finals.

Nondescripts came out on top in the end, beating Colombo CC in a high-scoring final at the P. Sara Oval. Sri Lanka's veteran fast bowler Lasith Malinga took 17 wickets for the champions, a number matched only by his team-mate Chaturanga de Silva, a slow left-armer. Ruvindu Gunasekara of Saracens was the leading run-scorer with 272.

Final At Colombo (PSO), March 8, 2018. **Nondescripts won by six runs. Nondescripts 183-7** (20 overs) (P. B. B. Rajapaksa 79, M. L. Udawatte 68; I. D. N. Thushara 4-32); ‡**Colombo** 177 (19.3 overs) (S. S. Pathirana 47, P. W. H. de Silva 42; C. B. R. L. S. Kumara 3-31, C. Karunaratne 4-28). *Nondescripts recovered from 7-2 thanks to a 126-run stand between Bhanuka Rajapaksa and Mahela Udawatte. Colombo's batsmen twice reached good positions, but three-wicket bursts from Chamika Karunaratne (in eight balls) and Lahiru Kumara (in six) dashed their hopes.*

HANLEY ENERGY INTER-PROVINCIAL TROPHY IN 2018

A week after Ireland's inaugural Test at Malahide, their domestic Twenty20 tournament kicked off. Defending champions **Leinster Lightning** shot out of the blocks by monstering Munster by 80 runs, and won their next four games as well to retain the title, their fifth in six seasons. Leinster had the leading run-scorer in Andy Balbirnie (262), while Tyrone Kane topped the bowling averages with 11 wickets at ten. Nine came in the two games against Northern Knights – four for 23 in Belfast and five for 22 in Dublin. Slow left-armer George Dockrell also took 11 for the Lightning, but the leading wicket-taker was leg-spinner Yaqoob Ali, with 12 for Munster Reds. Taking part for the second year, the Reds finished bottom again, but did taste victory for the first time. After beating North West Warriors, they ended by inflicting the Lightning's only defeat, by two runs under lights at Dublin's Sydney Parade. It was the closest margin of a tournament in which the results were usually clear-cut, although the Lightning did edge the Warriors by four runs in a low-scoring contest at Bready, restricting them to 95 for eight.

	P	W	L	NR	Bonus	Pts	NRR
Leinster Lightning	6	5	1	0	3	23	1.56
Northern Knights	6	3	3	0	3	15	0.30
North West Warriors	6	2	4	0	0	8	−0.72
Munster Reds	6	2	4	0	8	8	−1.17

In tournaments without official status, the Arabian Cricket Carnival in Bahrain was won by **Dubai Destroyers**, who included the former West Indian all-rounder Ricardo Powell, now 40. The evocatively named Everest Premier League, in Nepal, was won by **Biratnagar Warriors**. Led by the national captain Paras Khadka, and also including Hong Kong's Babar Hayat, they pipped Bhairahawa Gladiators by one run in the final in Kirtipur. Hong Kong's own competition, the T20 Blitz, was won by the **Hung Hom Jaguars**, who edged out Galaxy Gladiators Lantau on net run-rate, even though the Gladiators possessed the leading scorer in Kumar Sangakkara (311 in five matches). Scotland's captain Kyle Coetzer made the only century of the tournament, for City Kaitak.

PART SEVEN

Women's Cricket

WOMEN'S INTERNATIONAL CRICKET IN 2018

MELINDA FARRELL

It was all aboard the fast train for women's cricket, with the growing success of the two major Twenty20 leagues in Australia and England, a high-profile exhibition match in India and – most importantly – the first standalone World T20, in the Caribbean. But as the women's game zips along the track to higher standards and greater popularity, it carries a warning: mind the gap.

The gap is not new, of course: there has long been a divide between countries with more resources and experience, and those where women's involvement has come later and with less support. But a landmark Women's Global Employment Market Report & Survey, carried out by the Federation of International Cricketers' Associations, concluded that only Australia and to a lesser extent England could offer a genuine professional career path to women.

While professionalism has developed rapidly, FICA found there were still no more than 120 women players worldwide on full-time contracts, although that number will rise significantly in Australia over the next few years under the 2017 Memorandum of Understanding negotiated with Cricket Australia. And while the BCCI dipped their toes in the water with an IPL women's challenge match, featuring many of the world's best players, the reality of a women's IPL still seemed distant.

Three tiers have emerged among the ten teams who have one-day international status, with results largely reflecting investment at domestic level. Australia sit at the top, with the world's only professional domestic structure, and England are not far behind, thanks to the semi-professional Super League. The second group – India, New Zealand, South Africa and West Indies – have invested in central contracts but rely heavily on academies to develop talent. Of the remainder, only Pakistan and Ireland offer central contracts, but there are caveats: Pakistan's players weren't paid their monthly retainers for more than six months leading up to the World T20, because of administrative changes within the PCB, while Ireland, in a welcome move, announced they were implementing contracts after the tournament ended. There is no indication when the situation may improve for Bangladesh and Sri Lanka.

That Australia were victorious in the WT20 final over England, the 50-over world champions, ran true to FICA's findings; that India and West Indies completed the semi-final quartet reinforced them. To complete the picture, South Africa and New Zealand each won two WT20 matches, Pakistan and Sri Lanka one, and Ireland and Bangladesh none.

England's other results throughout 2018 also reflected their place in the hierarchy. They won two home bilateral series, against South Africa and New Zealand, and when all three teams played a T20 tri-series they defeated New Zealand in the final. Earlier in the year England had lost to Australia in the final of another T20 tri-series, in India.

Despite that result, England and India remained the only teams to defeat Australia in any format since February 2017. And yet there was still a significant gap between Australia and England, and it threatened to widen amid the lack of clarity surrounding the English domestic structure. In 2015, when the ECB announced the formation of the T20 Kia Super League, they said it would soon be joined by a 50-over competition. But, although the KSL has had three largely successful seasons, the ECB's plans to implement The Hundred in 2020 mean it will be dropped after one more, while the one-day competition has been indefinitely shelved.

England remain reliant on the Loughborough Academy for new talent, but the benefits of investing in the domestic game were illustrated by the emergence of Linsey Smith, Sophia Dunkley and Kirstie Gordon, who earned WT20 call-ups after flourishing in the KSL. Although each was known within the ECB high performance system, playing in front of decent crowds and television cameras helped prepare them for their international debuts. Gordon, in particular, was a revelation. A former Scotland player, she changed her national status, had an outstanding season for Loughborough Lightning, took eight WT20 wickets and was named one of the ICC's five breakout performers for 2018.

But the fact that England had to blood three debutants in the Caribbean, in the forced absence of some senior players, highlighted the lack of depth in their ranks compared with Australia. Other countries with wholly amateur domestic set-ups have even smaller margins for injuries or retirements. And it is hard to ignore the likely upshot of the success of the Australian WBBL, and the increasing revenue set aside for domestic cricketers there: if other countries don't act, the gap could soon become a canyon and, bar the odd upset, all but impossible to bridge.

Barely in sight were the Associate Members' teams, who were elevated en masse to Twenty20 international status from the Asia Cup in June. The standard of their game could be judged from the fact that, within six months, 30 of the 37 lowest totals – in a format running back to 2004 – had been made by Associate sides.

ICC WOMEN'S WORLD TWENTY20 IN 2018-19

RAF NICHOLSON

1 Australia   2 England   3= India, West Indies

The first standalone women's World Twenty20 was a success, despite inauspicious beginnings, when unseasonal rainfall in St Lucia led to England's match with Sri Lanka being washed out, and caused the ICC to consider relocating games. But for the first time at a global women's event, every match was broadcast live, and public interest was high: 10% of the populations of St Lucia and Antigua turned up to watch.

Australia reclaimed the title, winning their fourth World T20 out of six in front of a buzzing crowd at the Sir Vivian Richards Stadium. The victory was built on a brilliant run of form by Alyssa Healy, whose 225 runs were 42 more than anyone else, and won her the Player of the Tournament award. Australia's only defeat came after she sustained concussion against India, and was unable to bat. Ellyse Perry was also a key contributor, finishing with nine wickets and an economy-rate of 5.56. Her spell in the semi-final against West Indies, when she took two for two, was ferocious. There were also ten wickets apiece for seamer Megan Schutt and off-spinner Ashleigh Gardner, who both went for less than a run a ball.

In the final, Australia demolished **England**, whose crestfallen coach Mark Robinson said his side's lack of game-time had cost them. After the washout against Sri Lanka, the batsmen were reduced to practising under the stands; only Amy Jones, with 107, ended up among the tournament's top ten run-scorers. England missed Katherine Brunt, who could not shake off a back injury, and Sarah Taylor, who stayed at home as her treatment for anxiety issues continued. Their absence gave opportunities to Sophia Dunkley and Linsey Smith, while 21-year-old Kirstie Gordon, a slow left-armer who had previously played for Scotland, finished as England's leading wicket-taker, with eight, only four months after her first professional match.

That the two finalists were Australia and England raised concerns about the lopsided funding of the women's game: the gap between the two best-resourced nations and the rest seemed to be widening. During the tournament, it emerged that Pakistan's players had not been paid their monthly retainers by the PCB for over six months.

Although they lost, **India** reached the semi-finals for the first time since 2010, testament to their progress under coach Ramesh Powar. Their batsmen provided two of the tournament's highlights: captain Harmanpreet Kaur's 103 off 51 balls on the opening day against New Zealand, and Smriti Mandhana's 83 off 55 during the memorable win over Australia, which unexpectedly allowed India to top their group.

But all this was overshadowed by a spat between Powar and the former captain Mithali Raj. After making half-centuries against Pakistan and Ireland, she missed the game against Australia with a knee injury, and then – after

There she goes again: Alyssa Healy guides Australia to glory.

declaring herself fit again – was not chosen for the semi-final: the Indian camp said they wanted to stick with a winning combination. Annisha Gupta, a consultant who had lined up commercial deals for Raj, among others, took to Twitter to denounce Kaur as a "manipulative, lying, immature, undeserving captain". Gupta's Twitter account was later deleted, and Raj denied suggestions she had thrown tantrums during the tournament.

Semi-final defeat for defending champions **West Indies** was at least an improvement on their poor showing at the 50-over World Cup in 2017. Against **Sri Lanka** they made 187 for five, their second-highest T20 total, and they successfully defended low scores against Bangladesh and South Africa, thanks to career-best figures from Deandra Dottin and Stafanie Taylor; Dottin's five for five as Bangladesh were shot out for 46 was a competition record. They also took down England by four wickets to top their group.

Predictions of mammoth totals in the new era of women's power-hitting did not come to pass. The pitches were generally low and slow, and the highest total was India's Harmanpreet-inspired 194 for five on the first day; in ten of the 22 completed games, the side batting first failed to reach 110. Poor technique had to take some of the blame.

New Zealand's tournament was effectively over after five days, following defeats by India and Australia; coach Haidee Tiffen's decision not to select the explosive opener Rachel Priest, who was dumped in 2017 on fitness grounds, continued to raise eyebrows. **South Africa** also suffered several collapses: they were bowled out for 76 by West Indies and, two days later, for 85 by England. They did manage a last-ditch win, against Bangladesh, to avoid the indignity of having to qualify for the next tournament, in 2020.

Upsets were non-existent, too. On the opening day, **Bangladesh** limited West Indies to 106 for eight, but folded horribly. **Pakistan's** only win came against Ireland, with Javeria Khan hitting a national-record 74 not out. Sana Mir's stunning leg-break to Laura Delany – pitching outside leg and hitting the top of middle and leg – was voted Play of the Tournament. In that game, **Ireland** achieved the first successful DRS review in a World T20. But they failed to win a match, and Delany, their captain, broke down in the press conference after the Pakistan defeat: "It's so incredibly frustrating, because if we were professional I wonder what the score would have been out there today." Long-serving players Ciara Metcalfe and Clare Shillington joined the Joyce twins, Cecelia and Isobel, in retiring after Ireland's last match.

Concern over the quality and consistency of the umpiring was another theme, not least the penalties handed out after batsmen supposedly ran on the pitch – Ireland were docked five runs against Australia, and Pakistan ten against India. The umpires failed to call out any further incidents.

But the good news was that, by and large, the tournament took place in front of singing, dancing crowds: almost 10,000 – a record for a women's international in the West Indies – packed into the Darren Sammy Stadium in St Lucia to witness the hosts' win over England. The local interest caused Pete Russell, the chief operating officer of the Caribbean Premier League, to declare that a women's CPL was "no longer a question of if, but when".

NATIONAL SQUADS

* Captain.   ‡ Did not play.

Australia **M. M. Lanning, ‡N. E. Bolton, ‡N. J. Carey, A. K. Gardner, R. L. Haynes, A. J. Healy, ‡J. L. Jonassen, D. M. Kimmince, S. G. Molineux, B. L. Mooney, E. A. Perry, M. L. Schutt, E. J. Villani, T. J. Vlaeminck, G. L. Wareham. *Coach:* M. P. Mott.*

Bangladesh **Salma Khatun, Ayasha Rahman, Fahima Khatun, Farzana Haque, Jahanara Alam, Khadija Tul Kobra, Lata Mondal, Nahida Akter, Nigar Sultana, ‡Panna Ghosh, Ritu Moni, Rumana Ahmed, Sanjida Islam, Shamima Sultana, Sharmin Akter. *Coach:* A. Jain.*

England **H. C. Knight, T. T. Beaumont, S. I. R. Dunkley, S. Ecclestone, ‡N. E. Farrant, K. L. Gordon, ‡J. L. Gunn, D. Hazell, A. E. Jones, N. R. Sciver, A. Shrubsole, L. C. N. Smith, ‡F. C. Wilson, L. Winfield, D. N. Wyatt. *Coach:* M. A. Robinson.*

K. H. Brunt was originally selected, but withdrew with a back injury and was replaced with Wilson.

India **H. Kaur, T. Bhatia, ‡E. K. Bisht, D. Hemalatha, M. Joshi, V. Krishnamurthy, S. S. Mandhana, A. A. Patil, M. D. Raj, A. Reddy, J. I. Rodrigues, D. B. Sharma, ‡D. B. Vaidya, P. Yadav, R. P. Yadav. *Coach:* R. R. Powar.*

P. Vastrakar was originally selected, but withdrew with a knee injury and was replaced by Vaidya.

Ireland **L. K. Delany, K. J. Garth, C. N. I. M. Joyce, I. M. H. C. Joyce, S. M. Kavanagh, ‡A. J. Kenealy, G. H. Lewis, L. Maritz, C. J. Metcalfe, L. A. O'Reilly, C. Raack, E. A. J. Richardson, C. M. A. Shillington, ‡R. Stokell, M. V. Waldron. *Coach:* A. Hamilton.*

New Zealand **A. E. Satterthwaite, S. W. Bates, B. M. Bezuidenhout, S. F. M. Devine, ‡K. E. Ebrahim, M. L. Green, ‡H. R. Huddleston, H. N. K. Jensen, L. M. Kasperek, A. C. Kerr, K. J. Martin, A. M. Peterson, H. M. Rowe, L. M. Tahuhu, J. M. Watkin. *Coach:* H. M. Tiffen.*

Pakistan **Javeria Khan, Aimen Anwar, Aliya Riaz, Anam Amin, Ayesha Zafar, Bismah Maroof, Diana Baig, Muneeba Ali, Nahida Khan, Nashra Sandhu, ‡Natalia Pervaiz, Nida Dar, Sana Mir, Sidra Nawaz, Umaima Sohail. *Coach:* M. J. Coles.*

Sidra Ameen was originally named, but replaced when Bismah Maroof was passed fit after a sinus operation.

South Africa *D. van Niekerk, M. R. Daniels, M. du Preez, Y. Fourie, S. Ismail, M. Kapp, M. M. Klaas, L. Lee, S. E. Luus, Z. Mali, ‡R. Searle, T. S. Sekhukhune, C. L. Tryon, F. Tunnicliffe, L. Wolvaardt. *Coach:* H. K. Moreeng.

T. Chetty and S. Smith were originally selected, but withdrew with back and finger injuries, and were replaced by Tunnicliffe and Daniels. A. R. Ntozakhe was also chosen, but was suspended after her bowling action was deemed illegal; she was replaced by Fourie.

Sri Lanka *A. M. C. Jayangani, N. N. D. de Silva, W. K. Dilhari, S. I. P. Fernando, K. A. D. A. Kanchana, L. E. Kaushalya, B. M. S. M. Kumari, B. Y. A. Mendis, G. W. H. M. Perera, K. D. U. Prabodhani, O. U. Ranasinghe, H. A. S. D. Siriwardene, M. A. D. D. Surangika, ‡R. S. Vandort, S. S. Weerakkody. *Coach:* H. de Silva.

West Indies *S. R. Taylor, ‡M. R. Aguilleira, S. A. Campbelle, S. S. Connell, B. Cooper, D. J. S. Dottin, A. S. S. Fletcher, C. A. Henry, ‡Q. Joseph, Kycia A. Knight, N. Y. McLean, H. K. Matthews, A. Mohammed, ‡C. N. Nation, S. C. Selman. *Coach:* H. W. D. Springer.

S. S. Grimmond was originally selected, but withdrew with a leg injury and was replaced by Joseph.

Group A

At Providence, Guyana, November 9, 2018 (floodlit). **West Indies won by 60 runs. West Indies 106-8** (20 overs) (K. A. Knight 32; Jahanara Alam 3-23); ‡**Bangladesh 46** (14.4 overs) (D. J. S. Dottin 5-5). *PoM:* D. J. S. Dottin. *Bangladesh sniffed an upset when they reduced the hosts to 50-5; Jahanara Alam removed Hayley Matthews and Deandra Dottin with her first two deliveries, and added a third off the last ball of the innings when she stuck out her left hand to clasp a return catch from Kycia Knight. But Knight and captain Stafanie Taylor (29) had given West Indies something to defend, and Bangladesh's batting proved incapable of attacking it. Dottin blasted them out to claim the third-best figures in all women's T20Is – 3.4–18–5–5, one a return catch, the rest bowled. No one reached ten as they folded for 46, the lowest total in six women's World T20 tournaments.*

At Gros Islet, St Lucia, November 10, 2018 (floodlit). **England v Sri Lanka. Abandoned.** *Heavy rain allowed no chance of play. Worries about the weather in St Lucia led to preliminary discussions about moving the group games elsewhere, but in the end they stayed put.*

At Gros Islet, St Lucia, November 12, 2018 (floodlit). **England won by seven wickets** (DLS). **Bangladesh 76-9** (20 overs) (Ayasha Rahman 39; K. L. Gordon 3-16); ‡**England 64-3** (9.3 overs). *PoM:* K. L. Gordon. *T20I debuts:* S. I. R. Dunkley, K. L. Gordon, L. C. N. Smith (England). *In their delayed debut, England looked understandably rusty before securing the points. But they could not completely escape the soggy weather: a downpour and a 28-minute hold-up during the chase saw their target revised to 64 in 16 overs. Slow left-armer Kirstie Gordon, one of three debutants, took the match award for three cheap wickets. Bangladesh seemed unsure whether to proceed with caution or all-out aggression: Ayasha Rahman was the only batsman to score a run in the first nine overs (she had 23* of 24-3, which included a wide). England's reply began uncertainly, and they would have been 16-3 had wicketkeeper Shamima Sultana not dropped Amy Jones.*

At Gros Islet, St Lucia, November 12, 2018 (floodlit). **South Africa won by seven wickets. Sri Lanka 99-8** (20 overs) (S. Ismail 3-10); ‡**South Africa 102-3** (18.3 overs) (M. Kapp 38, D. van Niekerk 33*). *PoM:* S. Ismail. *Sri Lanka's first match had been washed out, and now they found themselves put in on a damp pitch, with little answer to the pace of Shabnim Ismail and Marizanne Kapp. Dilani Manodara Surangika thumped 20* from 12 balls, but could not quite lift them into three figures. South Africa lost both openers in their first seven deliveries, before Udeshika Prabodhani hit Kapp's stumps, only for the bails to stay put. Kapp and her wife, captain Dane van Niekerk, rebuilt the innings, and South Africa completed their opening win with nine balls to spare.*

At Gros Islet, St Lucia, November 14, 2018 (floodlit). **Sri Lanka won by 25 runs. Sri Lanka 97-7** (20 overs) (H. A. S. D. Siriwardene 31; Jahanara Alam 3-21); ‡**Bangladesh 72** (20 overs) (A. M. C. Jayangani 3-17). *PoM:* H. A. S. D. Siriwardene. *The all-round prowess of Shashikala Siriwardene condemned Bangladesh to an early exit. First she made 31 to boost a Sri Lankan innings that had been flagging at 30-3 after nine overs. Then she took 2-10 with her off-breaks to help strangle a lifeless Bangladeshi response, which contained just three fours and 75 dot balls. Both innings had begun with a wicket: Yasoda Mendis was bowled first ball by Jahanara; and, from the first ball of Bangladesh's reply, Sanjida Islam trapped by Prabodhani, who quickly inflicted the same fate on Farzana Haque.*

At Gros Islet, St Lucia, November 14, 2018 (floodlit). **West Indies won by 31 runs. West Indies 107-7** (20 overs) (K. A. Knight 32; S. Ismail 3-12); ‡**South Africa 76** (18.4 overs) (S. R. Taylor 4-12). PoM: S. R. Taylor. *The holders delighted another packed house and moved closer to the semi-finals, but they were given a scare before South Africa lost nine for 28. Backed by brilliant fielding, Taylor's off-breaks bewildered the lower-middle order after the earlier batsmen had built the foundations for a successful chase. Ismail made an explosive start with a wind-assisted 3-12, before Knight and Natasha McLean rebuilt.*

At Gros Islet, St Lucia, November 16, 2018 (floodlit). **England won by seven wickets. ‡South Africa 85** (19.3 overs) (N. R. Sciver 3-4, A. Shrubsole 3-11); **England 87-3** (14.1 overs). PoM: N. R. Sciver. *England took a step closer to the semi-finals after South Africa suffered another shambolic collapse: defeat spelled the end of their tournament. At 55-4, they retained hopes of a decent total, but it all went horribly wrong. Six wickets tumbled for 30, and Anya Shrubsole ended the innings with a hat-trick; Nat Sciver's 3-4 included 20 dots. Danni Wyatt and Tammy Beaumont looked like breezing past the target on their own before England carelessly lost three wickets. "I haven't worked these pitches out yet," said Shrubsole. "They look really good but nobody's scoring a lot of runs on them."*

HAT-TRICKS IN WOMEN'S TWENTY20 INTERNATIONALS

Asmavia Iqbal	Pakistan v England at Loughborough	2012
E. K. Bisht	India v Sri Lanka at Colombo (Nondescripts)	2012-13
M. Kapp	South Africa v Bangladesh at Potchefstroom	2013-14
N. R. Sciver	England v New Zealand at Bridgetown	2013-14
Sana Mir	Pakistan v Sri Lanka at Sharjah	2014-15
A. M. Peterson	New Zealand v Australia at Geelong	2016-17
M. L. Schutt	Australia v India at Mumbai (Brabourne)	2017-18
Fahima Khatun	Bangladesh v United Arab Emirates at Utrecht	2018
A. Mohammed	West Indies v South Africa at Tarouba	2018-19
A. Shrubsole	**England v South Africa at Gros Islet**	**2018-19**

At Gros Islet, St Lucia, November 16, 2018 (floodlit). **West Indies won by 83 runs. ‡West Indies 187-5** (20 overs) (H. K. Matthews 62, D. J. S. Dottin 49, S. R. Taylor 41); **Sri Lanka 104** (17.4 overs) (A. M. C. Jayangani 44; H. K. Matthews 3-16). PoM: H. K. Matthews. *Matthews shone with bat and ball to help West Indies into the last four; with Sri Lanka eliminated, the result meant England were through, too. Matthews began with 62 off 36 deliveries in a raucous opening stand of 94 with Dottin, then claimed three wickets as the Sri Lankans – chasing an unlikely 188 – lost their last six for 16. Only opener Chamari Atapattu Jayangani made more than 11.*

At Gros Islet, St Lucia, November 18, 2018 (floodlit). **West Indies won by four wickets. England 115-8** (20 overs) (S. I. R. Dunkley 35); ‡**West Indies 117-6** (19.3 overs) (D. J. S. Dottin 46, S. A. Campbelle 45; A. Shrubsole 3-10). PoM: D. J. S. Dottin. *Both teams had already qualified for the semi-finals, and Australia's surprise defeat the previous day meant the winners of this match would face them, while the losers would play India. West Indies took charge by reducing England to 50-6 in the 11th over, before 20-year-old Sophia Dunkley, in only her second international innings, and Shrubsole saved face with a stand of 58. Shrubsole, who had ended the previous game with a hat-trick, then struck twice in her first four balls as West Indies slipped to 3-2, but Dottin (who hit four sixes) and Shemaine Campbelle righted the ship. A tight spell from Gordon (4–16–24–1) ensured the match went down to the final over, but England's fielders missed three late chances as West Indies squeezed over the line.*

At Gros Islet, St Lucia, November 18, 2018 (floodlit). **South Africa won by 30 runs. South Africa 109-9** (20 overs) (Salma Khatun 3-20); ‡**Bangladesh 79-5** (20 overs) (Rumana Ahmed 34*). PoM: M. Kapp. *South Africa went home after a cathartic victory, but without providing any answers about their batting frailties. There were runs at the top of the order, Kapp making 25 off 19 balls before being brilliantly caught by Farzana Haque at deep midwicket. But the expected acceleration did not materialise, as five wickets tumbled for 14. Bangladesh needed to win inside 13 overs to ensure automatic qualification for the next tournament, but they crawled along, apparently uninterested.*

Group B

At Providence, Guyana, November 9, 2018. **India won by 34 runs.** ‡**India 194-5** (20 overs) (J. I. Rodrigues 59, H. Kaur 103); **New Zealand 160-9** (20 overs) (S. W. Bates 67, K. J. Martin 39; D. Hemalatha 3-26, P. Yadav 3-33). *PoM:* H. Kaur. *T20I debut:* D. Hemalatha (India). *A record-breaking 103 from 51 balls by Harmanpreet Kaur took India to the highest total at a women's World Twenty20, and victory in the tournament opener. After a slow start – five from 13 balls – she finished with eight sixes, having added 134 in 12.4 overs for the fourth wicket with the 18-year-old Jemimah Rodrigues, an Indian all-wicket T20 record. It was only the third century in the competition's history, following Meg Lanning and Deandra Dottin, and the highest T20 score for India, beating Mithali Raj's 97* against Malaysia in Kuala Lumpur five months earlier. Suzie Bates managed 67 from 50 balls in reply but, from 52-0 in the seventh over, New Zealand lost wickets regularly.*

At Providence, Guyana, November 9, 2018 (floodlit). **Australia won by 52 runs.** ‡**Australia 165-5** (20 overs) (A. J. Healy 48, B. L. Mooney 48, M. M. Lanning 41); **Pakistan 113-8** (20 overs). *PoM:* A. J. Healy. *They were not quite at their best, but Australia still exuded intent. Alyssa Healy was in command of the Pakistan spinners in a classy 48, a score matched by opening partner Beth Mooney. Aliya Riaz, Pakistan's only seamer, was the pick of their attack with 2-25. Facing their record chase, Pakistan opted for practice, but 21-year-old Umaima Sohail looked an exciting prospect.*

At Providence, Guyana, November 11, 2018. **India won by seven wickets. Pakistan 133-7** (20 overs) (Bismah Maroof 53, Nida Dar 52); ‡**India 137-3** (19 overs) (M. D. Raj 56). *PoM:* M. D. Raj. *India continued their assured start with a convincing victory over Pakistan – but there was room for improvement. Their fielding was lamentable: five catches went down in the Pakistan innings, giving India a stiffer total to chase. Bismah Maroof and Nida Dar hit fifties and put on 90 for the fourth wicket, but Pakistan were penalised ten runs for two separate incidents of batsmen running on the pitch. Raj was in ominously good form, stroking 56 off 47.*

At Providence, Guyana, November 11, 2018 (floodlit). **Australia won by nine wickets.** ‡**Ireland 93-6** (20 overs); **Australia 94-1** (9.1 overs) (A. J. Healy 56*). *PoM:* A. J. Healy. *Healy smashed a 21-ball half-century as Australia massaged their net run-rate. Only New Zealand's Sophie Devine had got there faster in women's T20 internationals – 18 balls against India at Bangalore in 2015. Ireland's openers had put on 30 before five fell for 16, Ellyse Perry (2-12) proving especially hard to get away. They were not helped when captain Laura Delany was adjudged by umpire Langton Rusere to have run on the danger zone as she took a single off Delissa Kimmince, handing Australia five penalty runs to kickstart their own innings. Non-striker Gaby Lewis had just been warned for a similar breach, and was run out in the same over; it didn't help that, in her attempt to avoid the pitch, she took a wider route than usual. Healy and Mooney began Australia's reply with 71 inside six overs, and victory came with almost 11 to spare.*

At Providence, Guyana, November 13, 2018 (floodlit). **Pakistan won by 38 runs.** ‡**Pakistan 139-6** (20 overs) (Javeria Khan 74*; L. A. O'Reilly 3-19); **Ireland 101-9** (20 overs) (I. M. H. C. Joyce 30). *PoM:* Javeria Khan. *T20I debut:* C. Raack (Ireland). *In what was already promising to be the battle to avoid the group's wooden spoon, Pakistan owed much to their captain Javeria Khan's 74* from 52 balls: she made the lion's share as 110 came from the last ten overs. It was Pakistan's highest T20I score, beating Bismah Maroof's 65* against Bangladesh in Karachi in 2015-16. The turning point came in the ninth over, when Javeria should have been caught at long-on – but Clare Shillington had strayed too far in from the rope, denying Sydney-born leg-spinner Celeste Raack a wicket in her third international delivery. Medium-pacer Lucy O'Reilly, who turned 19 on the first day of the tournament, took three wickets in the final over. The experienced pair of Shillington and Isobel Joyce made 27 and 30, but Ireland crashed from 76-3 to 101-9. Slow left-armer Nashra Sandhu kept things quiet with 4–19–8–2.*

At Providence, Guyana, November 13, 2018 (floodlit). **Australia won by 33 runs.** ‡**Australia 153-7** (20 overs) (A. J. Healy 53; L. M. Kasperek 3-25); **New Zealand 120** (17.3 overs) (S. W. Bates 48; M. L. Schutt 3-12). *PoM:* A. J. Healy. *Australia maintained their 100% record, but their batsmen were set some questions by New Zealand. Healy continued her rich run of form with a third successive half-century in an opening stand of 71 with Mooney. But the innings got stuck in second gear, with Leigh Kasperek's off-breaks proving particularly effective. At 13-3, New Zealand were reeling, but Bates and Katey Martin hauled them briefly back into contention with a stand of 66.*

At Providence, Guyana, November 15, 2018. **India won by 52 runs. India 145-6** (20 overs) (M. D. Raj 51, S. S. Mandhana 33); ‡**Ireland 93-8** (20 overs) (I. M. H. C. Joyce 33; R. P. Yadav 3-25). *PoM:* M. D. Raj. *India secured a place in the semi-finals with an efficient win. Asked to bat in damp conditions, Raj and Smriti Mandhana opened with 67 in ten overs before both fell to Kim Garth.*

Mandhana later said India should have got 170 – but 145 turned out to be plenty. Again, only Shillington (23) and Isobel Joyce reached double figures; Radha Yadav picked up three wickets, and Taniya Bhatia three stumpings, as Ireland limited their ambitions to batting out their 20 overs.

At Providence, Guyana, November 15, 2018 (floodlit). **New Zealand won by 54 runs. New Zealand 144-6** (20 overs) (S. F. M. Devine 32, S. W. Bates 35); ‡**Pakistan 90** (18 overs) (Javeria Khan 36; A. C. Kerr 3-21, J. M. Watkin 3-9). *PoM:* J. M. Watkin. *New Zealand already knew they could not reach the semi-finals, but finally managed a win, reaching 120-2 after 18 overs before a clatter of wickets. Pakistan struggled against the spinners, and were never in touch once Javeria departed in the ninth. Jess Watkin returned 4–17–9–3 with her off-breaks, and fellow spinners Kasperek and Amelia Kerr 4-43 between them.*

At Providence, Guyana, November 17, 2018. **India won by 48 runs.** ‡**India 167-8** (20 overs) (S. S. Mandhana 83, H. Kaur 43; E. A. Perry 3-16); **Australia 119** (19.4 overs) (E. A. Perry 39*; A. A. Patil 3-15). *PoM:* S. S. Mandhana. *T20I debut:* T. J. Vlaeminck (Australia). *India ensured they finished on top of the group with a surprisingly easy victory. Mandhana offered belligerence from the start, unsettling the bowlers with her footwork, and dealing severely with anything pitched up; she passed 1,000 T20I runs on her way to a career-best 83. Australia lost Healy after she received a blow to the head in a collision with Megan Schutt in the 19th over of the Indian innings. She did not bat, and her team failed to master a battery of spinners.*

At Providence, Guyana, November 17, 2018 (floodlit). **New Zealand won by eight wickets.** ‡**Ireland 79-9** (20 overs) (G. H. Lewis 39; L. M. Kasperek 3-19); **New Zealand 81-2** (7.3 overs) (S. F. M. Devine 51). *PoM:* S. F. M. Devine. *It was too late for New Zealand to revive their prospects, but they maintained their dominance over Ireland, established in Dublin in June. They needed only 45 deliveries to knock off 80; Devine's 21-ball fifty was three short of her own T20 record, but matched Alyssa Healy six days before. As in their earlier games, Ireland survived 20 overs, but 79 was the lowest of their four totals. Four senior players made this their last international appearance: Shillington scored 12, but the Joyce twins and Ciara Metcalfe managed one run and a catch between them. Three of them had played international cricket before the birth of Lewis, now 17, who provided Ireland's brightest moments with 39 from 36 balls.*

GROUP TABLES

Group A	P	W	L	A	Pts	NRR
WEST INDIES	4	4	0	0	8	2.24
ENGLAND	4	2	1	1	5	1.31
South Africa	4	2	2	0	4	–0.27
Sri Lanka	4	1	2	1	3	–1.17
Bangladesh	4	0	4	0	0	–1.98

Group B	P	W	L	A	Pts	NRR
INDIA	4	4	0	0	8	1.82
AUSTRALIA	4	3	1	0	6	1.51
New Zealand	4	2	2	0	4	1.03
Pakistan	4	1	3	0	2	–0.98
Ireland	4	0	4	0	0	–3.52

Semi-finals

At North Sound, Antigua, November 22, 2018 (floodlit). **Australia won by 71 runs. Australia 142-5** (20 overs) (A. J. Healy 46, M. M. Lanning 31); ‡**West Indies 71** (17.3 overs). *PoM:* A. J. Healy. *West Indies had won all four group games, but crashed when it most mattered. Hoping to replicate their triumph in the 2015-16 final, when they chased down Australia's 148, they got only halfway to the target. Healy returned after her concussion scare in the defeat by India and scored 46 in 38 balls, taking her tournament aggregate past 200, at an average of 67. Lanning kept up the good work, and Haynes provided the final acceleration with 25 from 15. Healy was soon back in action, running out Matthews when she left her crease, and Perry followed up by dismissing Dottin and Campbelle in her first two overs. Taylor's 16 was the only double-figure score; Gardner had figures of 4–13–15–2. All six Australian bowlers claimed at least one wicket as they progressed into their fifth successive World T20 final.*

At North Sound, Antigua, November 22, 2018 (floodlit). **England won by eight wickets.** ‡**India 112** (19.3 overs) (S. S. Mandhana 34; H. C. Knight 3-9); **England 116-2** (17.1 overs) (A. E. Jones

53*, N. R. Sciver 52*). *PoM:* A. E. Jones. *England's assured performance booked a place in the final, with Jones and Sciver steering them past their target in a third-wicket stand of 92*. India made a controversial start even before they got on the field, when it was announced that Mithali Raj, who had missed their victory over Australia, had been left out despite recovering from her knee injury. Her experience might have been useful on a slow pitch. Mandhana scored 34 out of 43 before she was caught and bowled by Ecclestone at the end of the powerplay, and Rodrigues hit a run-a-ball 26, but no one outside the top four passed seven. There were three run-outs, and England's four spinners took 7-71. Their only wobble came when both openers fell cheaply, but Jones and Sciver, allowed a steady stream of singles between occasional boundaries, did the rest.*

FINAL

AUSTRALIA v ENGLAND

Raf Nicholson

At North Sound, Antigua, November 24 (floodlit). Australia won by eight wickets. Toss: England.

Australia's third victory over England in the last four World Twenty20 finals was the easiest of the lot, as Gardner and Lanning made light work of a modest chase. After England chose to bat, they lost wickets regularly, despite Wyatt being dropped three times on her way to a 37-ball 43: clumsy fielding was a feature of the match, with the ball quickly becoming coated in heavy dew under the lights. Knight made 25, but no one else passed six. Jones was brilliantly run out by a direct hit from midwicket by Wareham, whose leg-breaks then removed Winfield and Dunkley with successive deliveries. The wicket of Winfield came after the first DRS review in a women's World T20 final: she was given not out, but technology showed the ball would have hit middle stump. Having recorded career-best figures in the semi-final, Gardner improved them again, removing Wyatt, Knight and Shrubsole with her off-breaks. In reply, Ecclestone bowled Player of the Tournament Healy for 22 during a tidy spell, and when Mooney fell to Hazell, Australia were 44 for two in the eighth over. But they always looked in control, and Gardner hurried them to their fourth World T20 trophy with a pair of sixes back over Gordon's head. Lanning's unbeaten 28 helped seal victory with 29 balls to spare, and she described the result as the "most satisfying" of her career, following Australian disappointments at the last tournament, in India in 2016, and at the 50-over World Cup in 2017. "The last couple of World Cup exits for us hurt our team a lot," she said. "We spoke about not hiding away from that fact."

Player of the Match: A. K. Gardner.   *Player of the Tournament:* A. J. Healy.

England

		B	4/6
1 D. N. Wyatt *c 4 b 3*	43	37	5/1
2 T. T. Beaumont *c 5 b 11*	4	9	0
3 †A. E. Jones *run out (10)*	4	4	1
4 N. R. Sciver *lbw b 7*	1	3	0
5 *H. C. Knight *c 10 b 3*	25	28	1/1
6 L. Winfield *lbw b 10*	6	9	0
7 S. I. R. Dunkley *b 10*	0	1	0
8 A. Shrubsole *c 7 b 3*	5	11	0
9 D. Hazell *lbw b 11*	6	9	0
10 S. Ecclestone *run out (7/1)*	4	6	0
11 K. L. Gordon *not out*	1	1	0
B 2, lb 1, w 3	6		

6 overs: 36-2   (19.4 overs)   105

1/18 2/30 3/41 4/64 5/74 6/74 7/84 8/98 9/104

Molineux 3–7–23–0; Schutt 3.4–10–13–2; Perry 3–8–23–1; Kimmince 3–11–10–0; Wareham 3–11–11–2; Gardner 4–10–22–3.

Australia

		B	4/6
1 †A. J. Healy *b 10*	22	20	4
2 B. L. Mooney *c 3 b 9*	14	15	1
3 A. K. Gardner *not out*	33	26	1/3
4 *M. M. Lanning *not out*	28	30	3
Lb 2, w 7	9		

6 overs: 37-1   (15.1 overs)   106-2

1/29 2/44

5 E. J. Villani, 6 R. L. Haynes, 7 E. A. Perry, 8 S. G. Molineux, 9 D. M. Kimmince, 10 G. L. Wareham and 11 M. L. Schutt did not bat.

Sciver 1.1–4–3–0; Shrubsole 3–7–30–0; Ecclestone 4–16–12–1; Hazell 3–7–19–1; Gordon 3–4–30–0; Knight 1–2–10–0.

Umpires: S. George and L. Rusere.   Third umpire: G. O. Brathwaite.
Referee: R. B. Richardson.

WOMEN'S INTERNATIONAL SERIES IN 2018

SOUTH AFRICA v INDIA IN 2017-18

One-day internationals (3): South Africa 1, India 2
Twenty20 internationals (5): South Africa 1, India 3

India completed their first away double, building their 50-over success on the attractive batting of Smriti Mandhana (219 runs in three innings, including a duck), and their Twenty20 win on the consistency of Mithali Raj, who made three of their four fifties. Veda Krishnamurthy flourished with the bat in both formats. Too often, South Africa lacked the firepower to compete.

First one-day international   At Kimberley, February 5, 2018. **India won by 88 runs.** ‡India 213-7 (50 overs) (S. S. Mandhana 84, M. D. Raj 45); **South Africa 125** (43.2 overs) (D. van Niekerk 41; J. N. Goswami 4-24, S. S. Pandey 3-23). *PoM:* S. S. Mandhana. *Three two-wicket bursts – from Shikha Pandey at the start of South Africa's chase, and from Jhulan Goswami at the end – took India to an easy win. It had been set up by a second-wicket stand of 99 between Smriti Mandhana and captain Mithali Raj, although from 154-1 in the 36th over India might have managed more.*

Second one-day international   At Kimberley, February 7, 2018. **India won by 178 runs. India 302-3** (50 overs) (S. S. Mandhana 135, H. Kaur 55*, V. Krishnamurthy 51*); ‡**South Africa 124** (30.5 overs) (L. Lee 73; P. Yadav 4-24). *PoM:* S. S. Mandhana. *A career-best 135 from 129 balls by Mandhana helped lift India to a series-clinching total – only their second over 300, after 358-2 against Ireland at Potchefstroom in May 2017. She smashed seamer Ayabonga Khaka for four fours and a six in five legitimate balls (either side of a delivery that sped away for five wides), before Harmanpreet Kaur and Veda Krishnamurthy (51* off 33) added 61* in the last 6.4 overs. Goswami became the first woman to reach 200 ODI wickets when she removed Laura Wolvaardt cheaply, and only Lizelle Lee (73 off 75) flourished against India's slow bowlers, of whom leg-spinner Poonam Yadav was the pick. Of the other batsmen, only No. 8 Marizanne Kapp (17*) reached double figures.*

Third one-day international   At Potchefstroom, February 10, 2018. **South Africa won by seven wickets. ‡India 240** (50 overs) (D. B. Sharma 79, V. Krishnamurthy 56, S. S. Pandey 31*; S. Ismail 4-30); **South Africa 241-3** (49.2 overs) (L. Wolvaardt 59, A. Steyn 30, M. du Preez 90*, D. van Niekerk 41*). *PoM:* M. du Preez. *PoS:* S. S. Mandhana. *ODI debut:* P. Vastrakar (India). *South Africa punished a sloppy fielding display by India to prevent a whitewash. Mignon du Preez added 118 for the third wicket with Wolvaardt, before she and Dane van Niekerk (41* off 30) exploited dropped catches and overthrows to take their side home with four balls to spare. India had lost Mandhana to a third-ball duck, and needed half-centuries from Deepti Sharma and Krishnamurthy to help them to 240.*

Women's Championship: India 4pts, South Africa 2pts.

First Twenty20 international   At Potchefstroom, February 13, 2018. **India won by seven wickets. South Africa 164-4** (20 overs) (D. van Niekerk 38, M. du Preez 31, C. L. Tryon 32*); ‡India 168-3 (18.5 overs) (M. D. Raj 54*, J. I. Rodrigues 37, V. Krishnamurthy 37*). *PoM:* M. D. Raj. *T20I debuts:* N. de Klerk, A. R. Ntozakhe (South Africa); T. Bhatia, J. I. Rodrigues, P. Vastrakar, R. P. Yadav (India). *Raj anchored India's chase with 54* from 48 balls, leaving the fireworks to 17-year-old debutant Jemimah Rodrigues (37 off 27) and the in-form Krishnamurthy (37* off 22). Earlier, Chloe Tryon had battered 32* off seven to give South Africa something to defend.*

Second Twenty20 international   At East London, February 16, 2018. **India won by nine wickets. South Africa 142-7** (20 overs) (S. E. Luus 33); ‡**India 144-1** (19.1 overs) (M. D. Raj 76*, S. S. Mandhana 57). *PoM:* M. D. Raj. *India waltzed home as Raj became the first woman to score four successive T20I fifties. She and Mandhana, both dropped twice before reaching 50, put on 106 in 14.2 overs to break the back of a modest chase. Seven South Africans had reached double figures, but none managed more than Sune Luus's 33.*

Third Twenty20 international   At Johannesburg, February 18, 2018. **South Africa won by five wickets. India 133** (17.5 overs) (S. S. Mandhana 37, H. Kaur 48; S. Ismail 5-30); ‡**South Africa 134-5** (19 overs) (S. E. Luus 41, C. L. Tryon 34). PoM: S. Ismail. *South Africa reduced the deficit to 2–1 with two to play thanks to a maiden T20I five-for from seamer Shabnim Ismail. She induced an Indian collapse from 93-2 to 133, before Luus top-scored again, with 41 off 34. Tryon provided late impetus with 34 off 15.*

Fourth Twenty20 international   At Centurion, February 21, 2018. **No result. South Africa 130-3** (15.3 overs) (L. Lee 58*, D. van Niekerk 55) v ‡**India.** *High-veld rain left India with an unassailable lead after South Africa looked poised to set a testing target. Openers Lee (58* off 38, with five sixes) and van Niekerk (55 off 47) had begun with 103 in 12.3 overs, before the fall of three quick wickets – and the rain.*

Fifth Twenty20 international   At Cape Town, February 24, 2018. **India won by 54 runs. India 166-4** (20 overs) (M. D. Raj 62, J. I. Rodrigues 44); ‡**South Africa 112** (18 overs) (S. S. Pandey 3-16, R. A. Dhar 3-26, R. S. Gayakwad 3-26). PoM: M. D. Raj. PoS: M. D. Raj. *India completed a 3–1 win largely thanks to a second-wicket stand of 98 between the consistent Raj and the precocious Rodrigues. South Africa's chase never got going, with 34-year-old seamer Rumeli Dhar one of a trio to take three wickets – her first in international cricket after six years out of the team.*

NEW ZEALAND v WEST INDIES IN 2017-18

One-day internationals (3): New Zealand 3, West Indies 0
Twenty20 internationals (5): New Zealand 4, West Indies 0

Bad weather in New Plymouth, which wiped out the fourth T20 international, denied New Zealand the chance to complete an 8–0 hammering across the two formats. But their 3–0 win in the 50-over matches took them top of the ICC World Championship, and confirmed their batting strength. Sophie Devine (261 runs at 130) and Suzie Bates (234 at 117) dominated those games, before Katey Martin (180 at 60, including three fifties) and Amy Satterthwaite (160 at 80) took charge in the T20s, in which Leigh Kasperek claimed ten wickets with her off-breaks. Stafanie Taylor did her best to hold West Indies' batting together, and there were some bright cameos from Hayley Matthews, but otherwise the tourists were dismal.

First one-day international   At Lincoln (Bert Sutcliffe Oval), March 4, 2018. **New Zealand won by one run. New Zealand 278-9** (50 overs) (S. W. Bates 44, S. F. M. Devine 108; A. S. S. Fletcher 3-55, S. R. Taylor 3-54); ‡**West Indies 277-9** (50 overs) (Kycia A. Knight 38, S. R. Taylor 90, Kyshona A. Knight 44*). PoM: S. F. M. Devine. *ODI debut: L. R. Down (New Zealand). Needing 11 off the last over, bowled by Leigh Kasperek, West Indies could manage only nine, leaving Kyshona Knight stranded. But the crucial wicket had been Stafanie Taylor, dismissed by Kate Ebrahim (the wife of the former Zimbabwe Test batsman Dion) for a high-class 90, to leave the visitors 215-6 in pursuit of 279. Earlier, Sophie Devine's third ODI century had formed the bedrock of New Zealand's highest total against West Indies (for a week, at least), although a last-wicket stand of 27* between Kasperek and Holly Huddleston proved vital.*

Second one-day international   At Lincoln (Bert Sutcliffe Oval), March 8, 2018. **New Zealand won by eight wickets. West Indies 194** (48.1 overs) (S. R. Taylor 86, C. N. Nation 35; L. M. Tahuhu 3-42, L. M. Kasperek 4-44); ‡**New Zealand 195-2** (30.4 overs) (S. F. M. Devine 80, S. W. Bates 101*). PoM: S. W. Bates. *An opening stand of 175 inside 29 overs between Devine and Suzie Bates, who made an 86-ball 101*, her ninth ODI century, allowed New Zealand to claim the series at a canter. West Indies had slid from 95-2 to 194, with Taylor top-scoring once more. Kasperek collected four wickets.*

Third one-day international   At Christchurch (Hagley Oval), March 11, 2018. **New Zealand won by 205 runs. New Zealand 310-5** (50 overs) (S. W. Bates 89, A. E. Satterthwaite 69, S. F. M. Devine 73*); ‡**West Indies 105** (34.5 overs) (S. F. M. Devine 3-24). PoM: S. F. M. Devine. *Devine shone with bat and ball as New Zealand passed 300 for the first time against West Indies, en route* *to their biggest win by runs against them (previously 198, at Chandigarh in the 1997-98 World Cup). After clumping 73* off 58 balls to back up a second-wicket stand of 151 between Bates and Amy Satterthwaite, Devine picked up three cheap wickets as West Indies succumbed hopelessly to a whitewash. Taylor top-scored for the third game in a row, but only with 26.*

Women's Championship: New Zealand 6pts, West Indies 0pts.

First Twenty20 international   At Mount Maunganui, March 14, 2018. **New Zealand won by eight runs. New Zealand 167-6** (20 overs) (S. W. Bates 49, K. J. Martin 54, A. E. Satterthwaite 36); ‡**West Indies 159-6** (20 overs) (H. K. Matthews 53, S. R. Taylor 51*; L. M. Kasperek 3-35). *PoM:* K. J. Martin. *T20I debut:* R. Boyce (West Indies). *Taylor was left frustrated after being unable to get the strike as the game climaxed in New Zealand's favour. With West Indies needing 22 off two overs, Taylor hit Kasperek for a six and a single, but faced only two of the last ten balls. Meanwhile, Kasperek removed the Knight twins – Kyshona and Kycia – in three deliveries, before Akeira Peters failed to score from the first three balls of the final over, delivered by Devine. Earlier, Hayley Mathews had blasted ten fours in a 31-ball 53, made out of 60 while she was at the wicket. But New Zealand had enough, thanks in part to Katey Martin's 54 off 35.*

Second Twenty20 international   At Mount Maunganui, March 16, 2018 (floodlit). **New Zealand won by 106 runs. New Zealand 185-3** (20 overs) (K. J. Martin 65, A. E. Satterthwaite 71*); ‡**West Indies 79-8** (20 overs) (S. F. M. Devine 3-12). *PoM:* A. E. Satterthwaite. *T20I debut:* K. A. Heffernan (New Zealand). *New Zealand achieved their biggest T20 win by runs, eclipsing 102 against Sri Lanka at Christchurch in 2015-16, after good work from Martin (65 off 61) and fireworks from Satterthwaite (71* off 42). They put on 124 for the third wicket at ten an over. The West Indian reply was again feeble. They managed only four fours and two sixes, with Devine picking up 3-12 and leg-spinner Amelia Kerr conceding just four runs in three overs.*

Third Twenty20 international   At New Plymouth, March 20, 2018. **New Zealand won by one run. New Zealand 134-7** (20 overs) (S. F. M. Devine 41, S. W. Bates 52*; H. K. Matthews 3-24); ‡**West Indies 133-7** (20 overs) (M. R. Aguilleira 38*; L. M. Kasperek 3-31). *PoM:* H. K. Matthews. *West Indies seemed certain to complete their form of win of the tour when they began the final over needing five, with six wickets in hand. But off-spinner Anna Peterson had Kycia Knight caught off her first ball, before conceding two runs from her next two. Britney Cooper was then stumped, and Peters run out. Needing three off the last, Merissa Aguilleira could manage only a leg-bye. New Zealand ought to have made certain when they batted, but couldn't build on an opening stand of 52 in 5.3 overs between Devine and Bates. Despite that, they now led 3–0 with two to play.*

Fourth Twenty20 international   At New Plymouth, March 22, 2018. **New Zealand v West Indies. Abandoned.**

Fifth Twenty20 international   At Hamilton, March 25, 2018. **New Zealand won by seven wickets. West Indies 139-5** (20 overs) (H. K. Matthews 40, S. R. Taylor 42, D. J. S. Dottin 33); ‡**New Zealand 143-3** (16.2 overs) (K. J. Martin 54*, A. E. Satterthwaite 43*; S. S. Connell 3-35). *PoM:* K. J. Martin. *New Zealand completed a 4–0 rout after yet more runs from Martin, whose 41-ball 54* contained ten fours, and Satterthwaite, who settled for a run-a-ball 43*. They rebuilt after Shamilia Connell reduced the hosts to 27-3 en route to a career-best 3-35. West Indies had been kickstarted by Matthews's 40 off 28, but never looked likely to force victory.*

INDIA v AUSTRALIA IN 2017-18

One-day internationals (3): India 0, Australia 3

Australia travelled to India in March, for three ODIs ahead of a T20 tri-series also involving England. The tour marked the return of Meg Lanning, Australia's captain, who had been out with shoulder trouble since the 2017 World Cup semi-final at Derby, which India had won. Australia avenged that defeat with three comfortable victories here. Nicole Bolton hit a century in the first, and 84 in the second; in the third, Alyssa Healy made a blistering 133. Slow left-armer Jess Jonassen took eight wickets, and went top of the ODI bowling rankings.

First one-day international At Vadodara (Reliance), March 12, 2018. **Australia won by eight wickets.** ‡**India 200** (50 overs) (P. G. Raut 37, S. Verma 41, P. Vastrakar 51; A. Wellington 3-24, J. L. Jonassen 4-30); **Australia 202-2** (32.1 overs) (N. E. Bolton 100*, A. J. Healy 38, M. M. Lanning 33). *PoM:* N. E. Bolton. *ODI debuts:* J. I. Rodrigues (India); N. J. Carey (Australia). *Australia's spinners took an early hold: Ashleigh Gardner (off-breaks), Amanda-Jade Wellington (leg-spin) and Jess Jonassen (slow left-arm) had 8-88 between them, as India – missing captain Mithali Raj, down with a fever – struggled to 200. They got that far only because of an enterprising Indian-record eighth-wicket stand of 76 between wicketkeeper Sushma Verma and 18-year-old Pooja Vastrakar, who made 51 from No. 9. But it was nowhere near enough. After Australia's openers sprinted to 60 in nine overs, Meg Lanning's first run took her to 3,000 in ODIs. When she left at 128, Nicole Bolton assumed control, completing her fourth ODI century shortly before Ellyse Perry (25*) stroked the winning boundary with 107 balls to spare.*

Second one-day international At Vadodara (Reliance), March 15, 2018. **Australia won by 60 runs. Australia 287-9** (50 overs) (N. E. Bolton 84, E. A. Perry 70*, B. L. Mooney 56; S. S. Pandey 3-61); ‡**India 227** (49.2 overs) (S. S. Mandhana 67, P. Vastrakar 30; J. L. Jonassen 3-51). *PoM:* N. E. Bolton. *Another attacking innings from Bolton, who hit 12 fours from 88 balls before being adjudged lbw despite an edge, gave Australia a good start. Perry and Beth Mooney then added 96 for the fourth wicket in 14 overs. Mooney had a lucky escape when 37, after nicking a Poonam Yadav googly to the keeper, but again the umpire missed the edge. India looked in with a chance as openers Punam Raut (27 off 61 balls) and Smriti Mandhana put on 88, but the returning Raj was out for 15, and two wickets apiece for Jonassen and Wellington meant 155-3 became 170-7.*

Third one-day international At Vadodara (Reliance), March 18, 2018. **Australia won by 97 runs.** ‡**Australia 332-7** (50 overs) (A. J. Healy 133, E. A. Perry 32, R. L. Haynes 43, B. L. Mooney 34*, A. K. Gardner 35); **India 235** (44.4 overs) (J. I. Rodrigues 42, S. S. Mandhana 52, D. B. Sharma 37; A. K. Gardner 3-40). *PoM:* A. J. Healy. *Australia's clean sweep rarely looked in doubt once opener Alyssa Healy had blasted 133 from 115 balls. Rapid contributions down the order – Mooney clattered 34* from 19 balls, and Gardner 35 from 20 – lifted the total to 332. No side had chased 300 to win a women's ODI, but India made a decent start, with Jemimah Rodrigues and Mandhana adding 101. But both fell to successive balls from Gardner in the 14th over, and scoreboard pressure told on the rest.*

Women's Championship: Australia 6pts, India 0pts.

SRI LANKA v PAKISTAN IN 2017-18

One-day internationals (3): Sri Lanka 0, Pakistan 3
Twenty20 internationals (3): Sri Lanka 1, Pakistan 2

Pakistan had not won a series in either format since a pair of 2–0 victories against Bangladesh three years earlier. Now they followed a facile one-day whitewash with a more harder-fought victory in the Twenty20s. Javeria Khan was the mainstay of their batting, while in the ODIs Sana Mir averaged 35 with the bat and eight with the ball. Sri Lanka's highest total in six games was 181.

First one-day international At Dambulla, March 20, 2018. **Pakistan won by 69 runs. Pakistan 250-6** (50 overs) (Javeria Khan 113*, Nida Dar 34); ‡**Sri Lanka 181** (45.2 overs) (A. M. C. Jayangani 46, H. A. S. D. Siriwardene 44; Bismah Maroof 3-17). *PoM:* Javeria Khan. *ODI debuts: W. K. Dilhari (Sri Lanka); Muneeba Ali, Natalia Pervaiz (Pakistan). Javeria Khan's second ODI hundred proved decisive after Pakistan had staggered to 72-4. She added 72 with Nida Dar, 46 with Sana Mir (27) and 60* with the debutant Natalia Pervaiz (21*) to ensure a total that always looked beyond Sri Lanka. Three wickets in five overs for Bismah Maroof confirmed Pakistan's superiority.*

Second one-day international At Dambulla, March 22, 2018. **Pakistan won by 94 runs.** ‡**Pakistan 250-6** (50 overs) (Muneeba Ali 31, Bismah Maroof 89, Nida Dar 38); **Sri Lanka 156** (37 overs) (Sana Mir 4-32). *PoM:* Bismah Maroof. *Pakistan matched their total of two days earlier, but this time extended their margin of victory, to claim the series with a game to spare. Bismah's 89* *was the cornerstone of their innings, before Mir's off-breaks winkled out four batsmen. Without a last-wicket stand of 50, Sri Lanka would have lost even more heavily.*

Third one-day international   At Dambulla, March 24, 2018. **Pakistan won by 108 runs. ‡Pakistan 215-9** (50 overs) (Nahida Khan 46, Javeria Khan 30); **Sri Lanka 107** (41.3 overs) (M. D. N. Hansika 35; Sana Mir 4-27, Nashra Sandhu 3-18). *PoM:* Sana Mir. *An alarming collapse handed Pakistan a 3–0 clean sweep. Set fair at 49-0 in pursuit of 216, Sri Lanka cascaded to 107 all out, with Pakistan's spinners – led by Mir's second successive four-for – taking all ten. The visitors ought to have made more than 215: eight reached double figures, but the highest was opener Nahida Khan's 46.*

Women's Championship: Pakistan 6pts, Sri Lanka 0pts.

First Twenty20 international   At Colombo (SSC), March 28, 2018. **Pakistan won by one wicket. Sri Lanka 129-6** (20 overs) (M. A. A. Sanjeewani 61, N. N. D. de Silva 35*); **‡Pakistan 133-9** (19.5 overs) (Bismah Maroof 42, Javeria Khan 52; B. M. S. M. Kumari 3-23). *PoM:* Javeria Khan. *T20I debuts:* H. I. S. Mendis (Sri Lanka); Fareeha Mehmood, Ghulam Fatima (Pakistan). *Pakistan spluttered over the line when debutant No. 11 Ghulam Fatima hit the penultimate ball of the match for four to complete their highest successful chase (previously 123-0, chasing 120, against Ireland at Solihull in 2013). At 79-2, with Bismah and Javeria together, they were easing home, but seven fell for 48, including Nashra Sandhu to the second ball of the last over, with three needed. Javeria's 33-ball half-century was the quickest by a Pakistani woman, though they were not helped when the umpires added five penalty runs to Sri Lanka's total because a batsman had run on the pitch. Sri Lanka had recovered from 38-5 thanks to 61 from Anushka Sanjeewani, whose previous seven T20I innings had produced a best of 16, and 35* from Nilakshi de Silva, whose previous seven had produced a best of 12.*

Second Twenty20 international   At Colombo (Nondescripts), March 30, 2018. **Sri Lanka won by seven wickets. ‡Pakistan 72** (18.4 overs) (H. A. S. D. Siriwardene 4-9); **Sri Lanka 73-3** (14.2 overs). *PoM:* H. A. S. D. Siriwardene. *Sri Lanka squared the series after Pakistan crumbled from 37-1 to 72 all out in 11 overs, with off-spinner Shashikala Siriwardene picking up a career-best 4-9. They then cruised home with 34 balls to spare, a national record.*

Third Twenty20 international   At Colombo (SSC), March 31, 2018. **Pakistan won by 38 runs. Pakistan 113-6** (20 overs) (Javeria Khan 38); **‡Sri Lanka 75-8** (20 overs). *PoM:* Javeria Khan. *The decider turned into a damp squib, as Sri Lanka made a hash of chasing 114. Four of their top six were run out as they staggered to 36-7; Imalka Mendis hung around for 25*, but consumed 49 balls. Nida Dar conceded only six runs in her four overs. Pakistan's own underwhelming 113-6 centred on Javeria's run-a-ball 38.*

TWENTY20 TRI-SERIES IN INDIA IN 2017-18

1 Australia   2 England   3 India

A switch of formats did not impede Australia's momentum after they had thrashed India in the ODI series. Despite the talent in the Indian and England line-ups, Australia simply looked the best team in the world, shrugging off a heavy defeat by England in the second match. Their captain, Meg Lanning, oozed authority, scoring 175 runs in all from 108 balls without being dismissed, and was well supported by Elyse Villani and Beth Mooney. The Australians also had the three leading bowlers, led by Player of the Tournament Megan Schutt. Despite the brilliance of Smriti Mandhana, India's bowling lacked penetration, and they managed just one win, in a dead rubber. Danni Wyatt shone with the bat for England, scoring a century in a world-record chase, but they faded, losing their last three, including a one-sided final against Australia.

At Mumbai (Brabourne), March 22, 2018. **Australia won by six wickets. India 152-5** (20 overs) (S. S. Mandhana 67, A. A. Patil 35); **‡Australia 156-4** (18.1 overs) (B. L. Mooney 45, E. J. Villani 39, M. M. Lanning 35*; J. N. Goswami 3-30). *PoM:* A. K. Gardner (Australia). *T20I debut:* S. G. Molineux (Australia). *Australia needed 41 from 41 when Meg Lanning walked out, but they cruised* *home as she hit four fours and a six in a stand of 44* with Rachael Haynes. India had made a strong start: Smriti Mandhana carried on her good form from the ODIs, reaching India's fastest T20 fifty, from 30 balls, with a pulled six off Ellyse Perry. But her team-mates could not find the accelerator.*

At Mumbai (Brabourne), March 23, 2018. **England won by eight wickets. Australia 149-8** (20 overs) (A. J. Healy 31, R. L. Haynes 65; J. L. Gunn 3-26); ‡**England 150-2** (17 overs) (T. T. Beaumont 58*, N. R. Sciver 68*). *PoM:* N. R. Sciver. *T20I debuts:* N. J. Carey (Australia); A. N. Davidson-Richards, K. L. George, B. F. Smith (England). Nat Sciver's dominant all-round performance inflicted Australia's first defeat of their tour. She hit her first T20I fifty, and put on 116* for the third wicket with Tammy Beaumont as England eased home with three overs to spare. Sciver had also taken two wickets in a skittish Australia innings. Jenny Gunn was the best of the bowlers, though Katie George – one of three England debutants – produced a stunning pick-up-and-throw off her own bowling to run out Beth Mooney. Haynes (65 off 45) lacked support.*

At Mumbai (Brabourne), March 25, 2018. **England won by seven wickets. India 198-4** (20 overs) (M. D. Raj 53, S. S. Mandhana 76, H. Kaur 30); ‡**England 199-3** (18.4 overs) (D. N. Wyatt 124, T. T. Beaumont 35). *PoM:* D. N. Wyatt. *Danni Wyatt slammed England's highest T20 score in a world-record chase, beating their own 181-6 against Australia at Canberra four months earlier. Wyatt, who said she had been working on "playing straight and hitting the sightscreens", made 124 – two short of Lanning's world record – off 64 balls, cracking 15 fours and five sixes in a dazzling exhibition. She put on 61 in 5.2 overs with Bryony Smith, and 96 with Beaumont. When Wyatt was dismissed off the last ball of the 17th over, England needed only 16. She had eclipsed her own national record of 100, in that same Canberra game. She dedicated the innings to her father, Steve, who had flown in to watch. Earlier, India had posted their biggest T20 total, surpassing 168-3 against South Africa at Potchefstroom the previous month. Mithali Raj and Mandhana added 129 in 12.5 overs for the first wicket, while Mandhana hit India's fastest fifty – from 25 balls – for the second time in four days.*

At Mumbai (Brabourne), March 26, 2018. **Australia won by 36 runs. Australia 186-5** (20 overs) (B. L. Mooney 71, E. J. Villani 61); ‡**India 150-5** (20 overs) (J. I. Rodrigues 50, H. Kaur 33, A. A. Patil 38*; M. L. Schutt 3-31). *PoM:* M. L. Schutt. *India's third defeat meant Australia and England were in the final with two matches to go. Mooney (71 off 46) and Elyse Villani (61 off 42) provided the backbone of Australia's total by adding 114, a national third-wicket record, before Megan Schutt bowled Mandhana and Raj with successive balls – then completed a hat-trick by removing Deepti Sharma with the first delivery of her next over. At 17 years 202 days, opener Jemimah Rodrigues had become the youngest Indian to score a T20I half-century.*

At Mumbai (Brabourne), March 28, 2018. **Australia won by eight wickets. England 96** (17.4 overs) (D. M. Kimmince 3-20); ‡**Australia 97-2** (11.3 overs) (E. A. Perry 47*, M. M. Lanning 41*). *PoM:* E. A. Perry. England *messed up their lines in a dress rehearsal for the final. This time their entry in the record book was unwanted: 96 was their joint-second-lowest T20 total. Wyatt was dismissed off the fourth ball of the innings, and no one could halt the decline; the highest score was 24 by Alice Davidson-Richards. Seamer Delissa Kimmince grabbed a career-best 3-20. Lanning became the first Australian – man or woman – to pass 2,000 T20I runs as they raced to their target.*

At Mumbai (Brabourne), March 29, 2018. **India won by eight wickets. ‡England 107** (18.5 overs) (D. N. Wyatt 31; A. A. Patil 3-21); **India 108-2** (15.4 overs) (S. S. Mandhana 62*). *PoM:* A. A. Patil. *India finally got off the mark, against an England team who had mislaid their swagger. Mandhana was again imperious: she hit George for three successive fours in the second over, when she was also dropped by Beaumont on 13, and finished with 62* from 41. England had looked well set at 59-1 in the seventh but, when Wyatt fell to a superb return catch by Sharma, they imploded.*

Final At Mumbai (Brabourne), March 31, 2018. **Australia won by 57 runs. Australia 209-4** (20 overs) (A. J. Healy 33, A. K. Gardner 33, M. M. Lanning 88*, E. J. Villani 51); ‡**England 152-9** (20 overs) (D. N. Wyatt 34, N. R. Sciver 50, A. E. Jones 30; M. L. Schutt 3-14). *PoM:* M. M. Lanning. *PoT:* M. L. Schutt. *Australia pummelled the highest total in a women's T20I to win the trophy with ease. Lanning led the way with 88*, taking her tournament aggregate to 175 without being dismissed. Tash Farrant had removed Mooney in the first over, but England's control was fleeting, and Lanning and Villani added 139 for the fourth wicket in 12 overs. Australia hit 32 fours, the highest in a women's or men's T20I. England, led by Danielle Hazell in the absence of the injured Heather Knight, got off to a poor start, and looked remotely threatening only during a stand of 51 between Sciver and Amy Jones. Schutt's three cheap wickets, which gave her nine overall, secured the Player of the Tournament award.*

INDIA v ENGLAND IN 2017-18

One-day internationals (3): India 2, England 1

When England's spinners, Danielle Hazell and Sophie Ecclestone, helped them level the series, captain Heather Knight's thoughts strayed to history. "I only found out this morning that we haven't won a series here," she said. "That will keep us motivated for the third game." Motivation may not have been lacking, but runs were: India won at a canter. They had held most of the aces across a week in Nagpur. With 181 runs for twice out, Smriti Mandhana appeared to be playing a different game to the others. Amy Jones was England's top-scorer, but they all came in one innings. In a series dominated by spin – only seven wickets fell to seamers – Ecclestone, the leading wicket-taker on either side, and Hazell performed superbly. Poonam Yadav and Ekta Bisht proved just as dangerous for India.

ENGLAND TOURING PARTY

*H. C. Knight (Berkshire), T. T. Beaumont (Kent), K. L. Cross (Lancashire), A. N. Davidson-Richards (Kent), S. Ecclestone (Lancashire), G. A. Elwiss (Sussex), N. E. Farrant (Kent), K. L. George (Hampshire), J. L. Gunn (Warwickshire), A. Hartley (Middlesex), D. Hazell (Yorkshire), A. E. Jones (Warwickshire), N. R. Sciver (Surrey), A. Shrubsole (Somerset), B. F. Smith (Surrey), F. C. Wilson (Middlesex), D. N. Wyatt (Sussex). *Coach:* M. A. Robinson.

First one-day international   At Nagpur, April 6, 2018. **India won by one wicket. ‡England 207** (49.3 overs) (T. T. Beaumont 37, F. C. Wilson 45, D. Hazell 33; E. K. Bisht 3-49, P. Yadav 4-30); **India 208-9** (49.1 overs) (S. S. Mandhana 86; S. Ecclestone 4-37). *PoM:* S. S. Mandhana. *ODI debut:* A. N. Davidson-Richards (England). *In their first meeting since the 2017 World Cup final at Lord's, India and England served up another thriller – and this time India edged it. When last pair Ekta Bisht and Poonam Yadav, who had shared seven wickets, came together, they needed 18 off three overs. They managed only four off the 48th, but 12 came off the 49th, from Anya Shrubsole – who had stolen the World Cup from India's grasp eight months earlier – and they were almost there. A single and a Nat Sciver wide completed the job. India had been cruising after Smriti Mandhana's 86: they needed 37 off 72, but then managed just 13 off 46. Sophie Ecclestone cashed in on the anxiety with 4-37, her best ODI figures. England's innings had been launched by a stand of 71 between Danni Wyatt and Tammy Beaumont, but they lost six for 53, before Fran Wilson's patient 45.*

Second one-day international   At Nagpur, April 9, 2018. **England won by eight wickets. ‡India 113** (37.2 overs) (S. S. Mandhana 42; D. Hazell 4-32, S. Ecclestone 4-14); **England 117-2** (29 overs) (D. N. Wyatt 47, T. T. Beaumont 39*). *PoM:* S. Ecclestone. *In their contrasting styles, England's spinners drove India to distraction. Danielle Hazell removed Mithali Raj and Harmanpreet Kaur with her off-breaks, while Ecclestone's slow left-armers accounted for Veda Krishnamurthy and, crucially, Mandhana, although she still top-scored. Both had career-bests, Ecclestone for the second successive match. Wyatt slammed 47 off 43, before Beaumont finished the job.*

Third one-day international   At Nagpur, April 12, 2018. **India won by eight wickets. ‡England 201-9** (50 overs) (A. E. Jones 94, H. C. Knight 36); **India 202-2** (45.2 overs) (S. S. Mandhana 53*, M. D. Raj 74*, D. B. Sharma 54*). *PoM:* D. B. Sharma. *PoS:* S. S. Mandhana. *India wheeled out their big guns to clinch the series with something to spare. Raj's 74* in a partnership of 103* with Deepti Sharma was a world-record 56th ODI score of 50 or more, taking her past Charlotte Edwards. England knew their total was lightweight and, although Shrubsole raised hopes by removing Jemimah Rodrigues and Sharma, India were soon in the driving seat. Player of the Series Mandhana made her usual contribution before retiring ill, but Raj and Sharma powered on, Sharma completing the job with a six. England were indebted to wicketkeeper Amy Jones, who followed two ducks with a battling career-best 94.*

SOUTH AFRICA v BANGLADESH IN 2018

One-day internationals (5): South Africa 5, Bangladesh 0
Twenty20 internationals (3): South Africa 3, Bangladesh 0

South Africa completed their first 5–0 one-day whitewash, before equalling their best Twenty20 series result, during a desperately one-sided encounter with Bangladesh. Seven South Africans conceded three an over or less during the 50-over matches, while only one Bangladeshi – slow left-armer Nahida Akter – conceded less than four. Chloe Tryon, who battered 134 ODI runs at a strike-rate of 141, embodied the difference between the sides.

First one-day international   At Potchefstroom, May 4. **South Africa won by 106 runs.** ‡South Africa 270-9 (50 overs) (L. Lee 54, D. van Niekerk 44, C. L. Tryon 65); **Bangladesh 164** (49.3 overs) (Sanjida Islam 35, Farzana Haque 69*; D. van Niekerk 3-23). *PoM:* C. L. Tryon. *ODI debut:* Murshida Khatun (Bangladesh). *South Africa overwhelmed the Bangladeshis in every department. Chloe Tryon's 65 off 42 demonstrated power well beyond her opponents, while the leg-spin of Dane van Niekerk and the off-breaks of Raisibe Ntozakhe (10–1–21–1) were all but unhittable. Chasing an unlikely 271, Bangladesh had a stand of 63 for the second wicket, and 52 for the tenth, but nothing else above 13. Farzana Haque, their No. 3, hung around for 69*, but used up 146 balls.*

Second one-day international   At Potchefstroom, May 6. **South Africa won by nine wickets.** ‡**Bangladesh 89** (39.5 overs) (A. Khaka 3-13, R. Ntozakhe 3-16); South Africa 90-1 (17.1 overs) (L. Lee 32, L. Wolvaardt 37*). *PoM:* A. Khaka. *ODI debut:* Jannatul Ferdus (Bangladesh). *The whole affair was done and dusted in 57 overs after Bangladesh collapsed to 89 against the seam of Ayabonga Khaka and the spin of Ntozakhe, who both returned career-bests. From 45-8, it was something of a recovery. South Africa brushed aside the target for the loss of Lizelle Lee.*

Third one-day international   At Kimberley, May 9. **South Africa won by nine wickets. Bangladesh 71** (36.5 overs) (Nigar Sultana 33*; A. Khaka 3-16); ‡**South Africa 72-1** (14.2 overs) (L. Lee 44*). *PoM:* L. Lee. *ODI debut:* Z. Mali (South Africa). *Bangladesh suffered a repeat of the previous game – only worse. Once more, they succumbed to what became their third-lowest total, and South Africa's series-clinching win was complete in 51.1 overs. From 6-4, Bangladesh had no way back, though wicketkeeper Nigar Sultana scratched out 33* from 97 balls. Khaka completed another cheap three-for. Lee led a one-sided chase.*

Fourth one-day international   At Kimberley, May 11. **South Africa won by 154 runs.** ‡South Africa 230-7 (50 overs) (L. Lee 70, L. Wolvaardt 32, T. Chetty 31, C. L. Tryon 60); **Bangladesh 76** (33.2 overs). *PoM:* C. L. Tryon. *Lee became the third South African, after Mignon du Preez and Trisha Chetty, to score 2,000 ODI runs during another simple win. Her 70 was followed by Tryon's brutal 60 off 42, before Bangladesh folded once more. Their five lowest ODI totals had now all come against South Africa.*

Fifth one-day international   At Bloemfontein, May 14. **South Africa won by six wickets. Bangladesh 166-9** (50 overs) (Shamima Sultana 53, Rumana Ahmed 74; S. Ismail 3-17); ‡**South Africa 169-4** (35 overs) (L. Lee 44, L. Wolvaardt 70*; Khadija Tul Kobra 3-37). *PoM:* L. Wolvaardt. *PoS:* L. Lee. *ODI debut:* Sobhana Mostary (Bangladesh). *Bangladesh lasted the full 50 overs for the first time in the series, but could not prevent a whitewash. Wicketkeeper Shamima Sultana and captain Rumana Ahmed threatened respectability during a fourth-wicket stand of 85, before the tourists settled for 166-9. Laura Wolvaardt supervised the chase with 70*. Earlier, Chetty became the first female wicketkeeper to complete 150 dismissals in ODIs.*

First Twenty20 international   At Kimberley, May 17. **South Africa won by 17 runs.** ‡South Africa 127-6 (20 overs) (L. Lee 46, L. Wolvaardt 30; Khadija Tul Kobra 3-23); **Bangladesh 110-5** (20 overs) (Rumana Ahmed 36, Farzana Haque 35; S. Ismail 3-19). *PoM:* S. Ismail. *T20I debut:* S. Lackay (South Africa). *South Africa continued their dominance from the 50-over series, thanks mainly to an opening stand of 77 inside ten overs between Lee (46 off 38) and Wolvaardt (30 off 22).*

Off-spinner Khadija Tul Kubra induced a collapse of four for nine, before a late injection from Sune Luus (28 off 23). In reply, Rumana and Farzana put on 72 for the third wicket, but Shabnim Ismail gave Bangladesh nothing to hit.*

Second Twenty20 international   At Bloemfontein, May 19. **South Africa won by 32 runs. South Africa 169-4** (20 overs) (S. E. Luus 71, D. van Niekerk 66); ‡**Bangladesh 137-5** (20 overs) (Shamima Sultana 50, Farzana Haque 37). PoM: D. van Niekerk. *T20I debut*: T. Brits (South Africa). *Bangladesh succumbed to another defeat, handing South Africa the series, but came away with two national records: their highest T20 total and, thanks to Shamima, their first half-century. But they were chasing shadows after Luus's career-best 71 from 57 and van Niekerk's 42-ball 66.*

Third Twenty20 international   At Bloemfontein, May 20. **South Africa won by 23 runs. South Africa 64-4** (9 overs); ‡**Bangladesh 41-6** (9 overs) (A. Khaka 3-10). PoM: A. Khaka. PoS: S. Ismail. *T20I debuts*: Z. Mali (South Africa); Jannatul Ferdus, Murshida Khatun (Bangladesh). *South Africa made it eight white-ball wins out of eight in 17 days in a game reduced to nine overs a side by rain. The day after her international debut, Tazmin Brits top-scored for the hosts with 29 off 22, before Ismail began with a maiden. Bangladesh were soon floundering at 25-5.*

ASIA CUP IN MALAYSIA IN 2018

1 Bangladesh   2 India

Bangladesh spoiled India's plans for a seventh successive Asia Cup, beating them both in the group stage and in a gripping final, when Jahanara Alam scampered two off the last ball. It was the greatest moment in the history of Bangladesh women's cricket, and social-media footage emerged of their men's team, watching on a dressing-room TV, cheering them to victory. The week-long tournament took place in Kuala Lumpur, a month before the ICC gave official T20I status to all women's matches between Associate Members; they then retrospectively gave official status to all 16 games in this tournament. There were some grim statistics for Malaysia, the hosts, who managed a best of 60 for nine, against Bangladesh, and were dismissed for 30 by Pakistan and for 27 by India. Thailand, the other outsiders, beat Malaysia by nine wickets, then stunned Sri Lanka, chasing down 105 to win off the last ball after off-spinner Wongpaka Liengprasert took five for 12, the tournament's best figures. India's Harmanpreet Kaur top-scored, with 215 runs at 53, while the leading wicket-taker was Pakistan's off-spinner Nida Dar, who claimed 11 at seven. Liengprasert finished with nine at 4.46.

INDIA 8pts, BANGLADESH 8pts, Pakistan 6pts, Sri Lanka 4pts, Thailand 4pts, Malaysia 0pts.

Final   At Kuala Lumpur, June 10. **Bangladesh won by three wickets. India 112-9** (20 overs) (H. Kaur 56); ‡**Bangladesh 113-7** (20 overs) (P. Yadav 4-9). PoM: Rumana Ahmed. *Bangladesh stunned India in a last-ball victory – but almost made a mess of it. Needing three off three with five wickets in hand, they lost Sanjida Islam, caught at long-on, and Rumana Ahmed, run out attempting a second. But Jahanara Alam heaved Harmanpreet Kaur, bowling because seamer Shikha Pandey had limped off with a knee injury after only four balls, to deep midwicket, and dived home for the winning two. Kaur had held India's below-par innings together, hitting 56 from 42 balls in a total of 112-9. No one else passed 11, while Anuja Patil was given out obstructing the field after the umpires ruled she had changed course trying to make her ground. Opening the bowling, slow left-armer Nahida Akter conceded only 12 in her four overs. Poonam Yadav picked up a career-best 4-9 with her leg-breaks, but each of Bangladesh's top five reached double figures, to set up the nervy climax.*

IRELAND v NEW ZEALAND IN 2018

Twenty20 international (1): Ireland 0, New Zealand 1
One-day internationals (3): Ireland 0, New Zealand 3

New Zealand's visit to Dublin produced a string of records, all at the expense of Ireland's bowlers. After a ten-wicket win in the lone T20 international, the tourists – uniquely – racked up three successive one-day totals of 400-plus, and finished the three-match series with three of the four highest in ODIs, and an eye-watering 1,348 runs for 17 wickets. Ireland managed 391 for 30. In the final game, 17-year-old Amelia Kerr combined a world-record 232 not out with five cheap wickets for her leg-spin.

Twenty20 international   At Dublin (YMCA), June 6. **New Zealand won by ten wickets. ‡Ireland 136-8** (20 overs) (C. N. I. M. Joyce 30, G. H. Lewis 61; L. M. Kasperek 3-25); **New Zealand 142-0** (11 overs) (S. W. Bates 63*, J. M. Watkin 77*). *T20I debuts:* R. Delaney, L. Maritz, C. Murray (Ireland); J. M. Watkin (New Zealand). *A sparkling 77* from 38 balls on international debut by Jess Watkin hastened New Zealand to their first ten-wicket T20 win, with nine overs to spare. Her stand of 142* with Suzie Bates (63* off 29) was a national all-wicket record – for a fortnight. Seventeen-year-old Gaby Lewis's maiden T20I fifty had lifted Ireland to 136-8.*

First one-day international   At Dublin (YMCA), June 8. **New Zealand won by 346 runs. ‡New Zealand 490-4** (50 overs) (S. W. Bates 151, J. M. Watkin 62, M. L. Green 122, A. C. Kerr 81*, Extras 31); **Ireland 144** (35.3 overs) (L. K. Delany 37, J. Gray 35; L. M. Kasperek 4-17). *ODI debuts:* C. Murray; J. M. Watkin (New Zealand). *In a match of unmitigated carnage, New Zealand broke their own world-record total (previously 455-5 against Pakistan at Christchurch in 1996-97) – and the hearts of Ireland's bowlers. Bates led the way with her tenth ODI hundred, 151 from 94 balls, overhauling Debbie Hockley's national-record tally of 4,064 runs. She put on 172 inside 19 overs with Watkin (62 off 59) and 116 in 11 with Maddy Green, who converted a maiden ODI half-century into a 77-ball 122. Amelia Kerr (81* off 45) twisted the knife. The bowling figures deserved a PG certificate: Cara Murray, a 17-year-old leg-spinner on international debut, took 2-119, the most expensive analysis in ODI history, while Louise Little (0-92), Lara Maritz (1-93) and Lewis (1-92) ensured that four of the five worst analyses now featured in one innings. Ireland, a batsman short after Isobel Joyce hit her head on the ground while fielding, subsided to 144, with Leigh Kasperek collecting a career-best 4-17.*

Second one-day international   At Dublin (The Vineyard), June 10. **New Zealand won by 306 runs. ‡New Zealand 418** (49.5 overs) (S. F. M. Devine 108, M. L. Green 50, A. E. Satterthwaite 48, B. M. Bezuidenhout 43, A. M. Peterson 46, Extras 32; L. Maritz 4-58); **Ireland 112** (35.3 overs) (L. K. Delany 33). *A merciless New Zealand flicked Ireland aside once more after Sophie Devine's 61-ball 108, which included 13 of her side's 50 fours, and six of their nine sixes. Four others passed 40, while Maritz, a 17-year-old seamer, did well to finish with four wickets in her fourth ODI. Two days after one mauling, Murray suffered another: 2-96 from eight overs. Ireland reached 87-3 in the 26th over, only to lose seven for 25.*

Third one-day international   At Dublin (Clontarf), June 13. **New Zealand won by 305 runs. ‡New Zealand 440-3** (50 overs) (A. E. Satterthwaite 61, A. C. Kerr 232*, L. M. Kasperek 113, Extras 30); **Ireland 135** (44 overs) (U. Raymond-Hoey 43; A. C. Kerr 5-17). *PoS:* A. C. Kerr. *Amelia Kerr produced one of the most devastating all-round performances in the game's history, following a world-record 232* from 145 balls – only the second double-century in women's ODIs – with figures of 5-17 as New Zealand unleashed a third straight thrashing. After adding 113 in 14 overs with Amy Satterthwaite (61 off 45), she put on 295 in 33 with Kasperek, an ODI record for the second wicket, and eventually eclipsed Belinda Clark's 229* for Australia against Denmark in Mumbai in 1997-98. Kasperek's 105-ball 113 dwarfed her previous ODI best of 21*, while Kerr had never scored more than 30. At 17 years 243 days, she became international cricket's youngest double-centurion of either gender, beating Javed Miandad (19 years 140 days for Pakistan). Her 31 fours was also a record for a women's ODI. She then bowled all five of her victims for a career-best haul, as Ireland slipped to another harrowing defeat.*

ENGLAND v SOUTH AFRICA IN 2018

MARTIN DAVIES

One-day internationals (3): England 2, South Africa 1

A busy summer of international cricket for England, the World Cup holders, started with a visit from South Africa, the team they had beaten with two balls to spare in the semi-final at Bristol 11 months earlier. The tourists' captain, Dane van Niekerk, spoke of revenge, and an upset was on the cards when they comfortably defeated a lacklustre England in the first of the three one-day internationals. It was the first time in 15 years South Africa had beaten them on English soil, in any format, and they had never won a series against England, home or away. But they had four bowlers (Shabnim Ismail, Marizanne Kapp, Ayabonga Khaka and van Niekerk) ranked in the ICC's top ten, while England had only Anya Shrubsole. They were one win from history.

But England's batting – so abject at Worcester, with the exception of Katherine Brunt's unbeaten 72 – sparked into life at Hove, ignited by hundreds from opener Tammy Beaumont and the mercurial Sarah Taylor. For Beaumont, it was the start of a golden run against the South Africans in the white-ball formats: in 12 days, she scored three successive centuries, and 393 runs in all from 343 deliveries, with 52 fours and five sixes. The hard-hitting Lizelle Lee, who had batted responsibly for 92 in the first game, replied with a hundred of her own, at Hove, but it was in vain.

The champagne moment of the decider at Canterbury came when Taylor showed off her electric glovework with a leg-side stumping to end van Niekerk's innings on 95. Another Beaumont century took England to a 2–1 win, and four much-needed points in the ICC Women's Championship.

SOUTH AFRICA TOURING PARTY

*D. van Niekerk, T. Brits, S. Ismail, M. Kapp, A. Khaka, M. M. Klaas, S. Lackay, L. Lee, S. E. Luus, Z. Mali, A. R. Ntozakhe, M. du Preez, A. Steyn, C. L. Tryon, L. Wolvaardt. *Coach:* H. K. Moreeng.

First one-day international   At Worcester, June 9. **South Africa won by seven wickets. ‡England 189-9** (50 overs) (K. H. Brunt 72*; S. Ismail 3-25, A. Khaka 3-42); **South Africa 193-3** (45.3 overs) (L. Lee 92*, D. van Niekerk 58, M. du Preez 36*). *PoM:* L. Lee. *ODI debut:* S. Lackay (South Africa). *England were undone by the pace of Shabnim Ismail and Marizanne Kapp, and the swing of Ayabonga Khaka. After they chose to bat on an overcast day, Amy Jones scored 19 out of 20 for the first wicket but, once she was bowled attempting to pull a full ball, chaos ensued. None of England's big guns fired and, when Khaka struck twice in the 17th over, they were reeling at 64-6. The score stagnated: over the next hour, Jenny Gunn and then Anya Shrubsole hung around with Katherine Brunt, scoring just 11 between them, and at 97-8 England were heading for a miserable total. But Brunt was not finished. She and Laura Marsh lifted the tempo with 51 in ten overs, before Sophie Ecclestone helped add 41 off the last 33 balls; Brunt reached a career-best 72*. Two early South African wickets, one an outrageous leg-side stumping from Sarah Taylor, standing up to Shrubsole, gave England a glimmer of hope, but a restrained 92* from Lizelle Lee, who added 113 with Dane van Niekerk, took the game away. Lee finished it by hitting Marsh for six.*

Second one-day international   At Hove, June 12 (day/night). **England won by 69 runs. England 331-6** (50 overs) (T. T. Beaumont 101, S. J. Taylor 118); ‡**South Africa 262-9** (50 overs) (L. Lee 117, L. Wolvaardt 32, C. L. Tryon 44; S. Ecclestone 3-54). *PoM:* S. J. Taylor. *Hoping for a repeat* *performance from their bowlers, South Africa put England in, but found little swing or seam movement. Beaumont and Jones shared a rollicking opening stand of 71, before Jones slapped a short ball from Ismail to midwicket – but that brought in Taylor, who was determined not to miss out on her home ground. Beaumont, given a couple of lives by the lack of DRS, went to her fourth international century, and Taylor her seventh, as the pair added 156. Cameos from Knight and Danni Wyatt took England to 331-6. After a measured start with Laura Wolvaardt, Lee cut loose and brought up South Africa's first ODI hundred against England, out of 140-0 in 25 overs. It was a good platform, but they lost four quick wickets, with Lee falling to a smart catch by Wyatt at cover. Chloe Tryon threatened to steal the game with 44 off 26 balls, hitting four huge sixes, but when she became the third victim of Sophie Ecclestone, who had conceded 30 off her first three overs, South Africa's chase dribbled away.*

Third one-day international   At Canterbury, June 15 (day/night). **England won by seven wickets.** ‡**South Africa 228** (49.5 overs) (L. Wolvaardt 64, D. van Niekerk 95; K. H. Brunt 3-52); **England 232-3** (44 overs) (T. T. Beaumont 105, H. C. Knight 80*). *PoM:* T. T. Beaumont. *Seeking their first series win over England, South Africa elected to bat, but the early loss of the prolific Lee put them on the back foot. Wolvaardt and van Niekerk shared a third-wicket stand of 103, and they were 197-3 with 31 balls to go – only for the innings to subside to 228 all out. Brunt claimed three in eight deliveries, including a wide which brought a lightning leg-side stumping by Taylor, while there were two run-outs and another stumping off successive balls in the final over. After England's openers had seen off Ismail and Kapp, Khaka removed Jones with her first delivery and Taylor with her 12th; she could have added Knight but squandered a straightforward return catch. It allowed Knight to accompany Beaumont to her second consecutive hundred. Though Beaumont fell in sight of victory, Knight wrapped up the series in the 44th over with four fours off Khaka, lifting England to fourth in the Women's Championship.*

Women's Championship: England 4pts, South Africa 2pts.

TWENTY20 TRI-SERIES IN ENGLAND IN 2018

RAF NICHOLSON

1 England   2 New Zealand   3 South Africa

This series showcased a new style of women's Twenty20 cricket, marking a move towards the dominance of bat over ball. The first day at Taunton epitomised this, when the world-record total in women's T20Is was beaten twice: first by New Zealand, who hit 216, then by England, who made 250. Both sides made the final, won by England, both times at South Africa's expense.

With scores of 116, 71, 23, 11 and 35, England's Tammy Beaumont continued her purple patch. New Zealand's Suzie Bates hit her maiden T20I century in the first match, and finished second to Beaumont in the run-list. But New Zealand's real problem was their middle order, which failed to fire – openers Bates and Sophie Devine hit over two-thirds of the team's runs.

For England, there was also the exciting emergence of 19-year-old slow left-armer Sophie Ecclestone, who finished as the tournament's leading wicket-taker, with ten. For South Africa, the unexplained absence of wicketkeeper Trisha Chetty raised eyebrows – Lizelle Lee's glovework cost her side vital wickets and runs.

The experimental format – with each side playing two back-to-back matches on the same day – was designed for the convenience of broadcasters and spectators rather than the players. South Africa probably came off worst, their tired attack eventually conceding 466 runs across 40 overs on the first day, at

Taunton. Crowds were good but not spectacular – over 2,500 on both days at
Taunton, but just 1,880 for the final at Chelmsford.

At Taunton, June 20. **New Zealand won by 66 runs. New Zealand 216-1** (20 overs) (S. W. Bates
124*, S. F. M. Devine 73); ‡**South Africa 150-6** (20 overs) (D. van Niekerk 58, M. du Preez 36;
H. N. K. Jensen 3-28). PoM: S. W. Bates. *South Africa's decision to bowl backfired on a beautiful
batting track. New Zealand motored to a record 216-1 thanks to Suzie Bates's ferocious 124* from
66 balls, as she and Sophie Devine shared an opening stand of 182 – a record for any wicket in
men's or women's T20 internationals. While Bates fell two short of the highest score in women's
T20Is, she did pass Charlotte Edwards's record for most career runs (2,605). South Africa's hopes
were quickly dashed when Lizelle Lee was bounced out by Devine. Three more wickets fell in seven
balls, leaving them 41-4 at the end of the powerplay. Dane van Niekerk and Mignon du Preez averted
humiliation by adding 77, with van Niekerk hitting a 39-ball fifty. But it came too late.*

At Taunton, June 20 (floodlit). **England won by 121 runs. ‡England 250-3** (20 overs) (D. N. Wyatt
56, T. T. Beaumont 116, N. R. Sciver 33, K. H. Brunt 42*); **South Africa 129-6** (20 overs) (D. van
Niekerk 72). PoM: T. T. Beaumont. *A demoralised South African attack faced another onslaught as
England reached 147-0 in 13 overs. Tammy Beaumont's 47-ball century, containing four sixes and
18 fours, was a remarkable feat from a player whose T20 game had been regarded as a weakness.
She eventually spooned a catch back to Stacy Lackay, but Katherine Brunt (42* off 16) ensured
England's innings never stalled; they finished with 250-3, smashing the record set by New Zealand
hours earlier. Anya Shrubsole sent down two early maidens, and finished with 4–17–8–0. Another
half-century from van Niekerk was the only highlight of the South African reply.*

At Taunton, June 23. **South Africa won by six wickets. ‡England 160-5** (20 overs) (T. T. Beaumont
71, H. C. Knight 35*); **South Africa 166-4** (19.3 overs) (L. Lee 68, S. E. Luus 63*). PoM: S. E.
Luus. *England again chose to bat, this time less effectively. Danni Wyatt soon fell to the off-spin of
Raisibe Ntozakhe. Beaumont cashed in again, reaching 71 off 59 balls, though she was dropped
three times. Despite 35* from Heather Knight, England finished 20 short of a par score. South Africa
lost Laura Wolvaardt for a duck, but Sune Luus, promoted to No. 3 after Lackay was taken ill, joined
Lee to power South Africa towards the target, putting on 103. Lee holed out to Nat Sciver at deep
midwicket for a 37-ball 68, but Luus continued apace, hitting Brunt for two fours and a six in the
last over. It capped a poor display by England in the field, with at least five straightforward catches
going begging.*

At Taunton, June 23 (floodlit). **England won by 54 runs. ‡England 172-8** (20 overs) (N. R. Sciver
59; L. M. Kasperek 3-35); **New Zealand 118** (18.3 overs) (S. Ecclestone 4-18). PoM: S. Ecclestone.
*For the first time in five innings Beaumont failed to make 50, bowled for 23 by Hayley Jensen
attempting a scoop, but Sciver took up the reins to smash a 31-ball half-century. Her departure
sparked a small collapse – three in six balls in the 17th and 18th overs – but late slogging from
Shrubsole (22 off 11) turned a reasonable total into a good one. Chasing 173, New Zealand lost
their three best batsmen – Bates, Devine and Amy Satterthwaite – in eight overs, Tash Farrant
making her mark on her return by having Devine caught at point in her first. Slow left-armer
Ecclestone wrapped up the tail to finish with a career-best 4-18.*

At Bristol, June 28. **New Zealand won by eight wickets. ‡South Africa 148-6** (20 overs) (C. L.
Tryon 35); **New Zealand 151-2** (15.2 overs) (S. W. Bates 62, S. F. M. Devine 68*). PoM: S. F. M.
Devine. *New Zealand dominated what was in effect a semi-final. They had started waywardly,
donating six wides and several overthrows in the first three overs, but South Africa failed to take
advantage. A late 35 from 15 balls from Chloe Tryon felt like an afterthought. In reply, Bates and
Devine – aided by the absence of injured seamer Shabnim Ismail – put on 130 for the first wicket in
13 overs. Bates eventually edged Marizanne Kapp to Lee, but Devine was unfazed.*

At Bristol, June 28 (floodlit). **England won by seven wickets. ‡New Zealand 129** (18.1 overs)
(S. F. M. Devine 52, A. E. Satterthwaite 37; A. Shrubsole 3-16); **England 130-3** (15.5 overs) (S. J.
Taylor 51, N. R. Sciver 39*). PoM: A. Shrubsole. *From 86-2 at halfway, New Zealand lost eight for
43 amid some reckless slogging. That included a first international scalp for 19-year-old left-arm
seamer Katie George, who trapped Satterthwaite with a full-length inswinger. England lost both
openers early, off-spinner Jess Watkin striking twice in seven balls in her first game of the series.
But from there, they made short work of the target, thanks to a beautiful half-century from Sarah
Taylor, and unbeaten contributions from Sciver and Knight (24*).*

ENGLAND 6pts, NEW ZEALAND 4pts, South Africa 2pts.

Final   At Chelmsford, July 1. **England won by seven wickets.** ‡New Zealand 137-9 (20 overs) (S. F. M. Devine 31, S. W. Bates 31); **England 141-3** (17.1 overs) (D. N. Wyatt 50, T. T. Beaumont 35). *PoM:* K. H. Brunt. *New Zealand raced to 55-0 in five overs, before Brunt trapped Devine. Two balls later she got rid of Katey Martin, before the tourists' middle order again struggled: from 84-2 they surrendered seven for 52, starting when Bates lost her middle stump to Ecclestone's arm-ball. England made it to 77-0 in ten overs, with Danni Wyatt hitting a 35-ball half-century, including the only six of the innings. The only nervous moment came when 17-year-old leg-spinner Amelia Kerr dismissed Beaumont and Taylor with successive balls in the 13th, but Sciver and Knight ensured England would lift the trophy.*

IRELAND v BANGLADESH IN 2018

Twenty20 internationals (3): Ireland 1, Bangladesh 2

Although Bangladesh won the series, Ireland regained some confidence after their shellackings by New Zealand earlier in June. The first and third matches went down to the last ball, and the second to the last over. The Bangladesh seamer Jahanara Alam was named Player of the Series for her seven wickets, five in the first game.

First Twenty20 international   At Dublin (YMCA), June 28. **Bangladesh won by four wickets.** Ireland 134-8 (20 overs) (I. M. H. C. Joyce 41; Jahanara Alam 5-28); ‡Bangladesh 135-6 (20 overs) (Nigar Sultana 46). *Ireland's innings was derailed by Jahanara Alam, who claimed Bangladesh's best figures in T20Is. Sanjida Islam perished going for the winning run off the penultimate ball, but Fahima Khatun (26*) squeezed one off the last.*

Second Twenty20 international   At Malahide, June 29. **Bangladesh won by four wickets.** ‡Ireland 124-8 (20 overs) (C. N. I. M. Joyce 60); **Bangladesh 125-6** (19.1 overs) (Shamima Sultana 51, Farzana Haque 36). *Cecelia Joyce's 47-ball 60 ensured Ireland set a reasonable target. Bangladesh were cruising at 96-1 in the 14th, but slipped to 117-6 before limping over the line. The match, a double-header with the men's game against India, was watched by nearly 10,000.*

Third Twenty20 international   At Dublin (Sydney Parade), July 1. **Ireland won by six wickets.** Bangladesh 151-4 (20 overs) (Shamima Sultana 30, Farzana Haque 66*); ‡Ireland 152-4 (20 overs) (G. H. Lewis 50, L. K. Delany 46). *PoS:* Jahanara Alam. *Ireland ended a 16-match losing streak in white-ball internationals when Isobel Joyce (22*) hit the last two balls of Jahanara's final over for four and one. Gaby Lewis and captain Laura Delany had put on 93 for the third wicket in 9.3 overs. Bangladesh's total owed much to Farzana Haque, whose 66* came from 47 balls.*

WORLD TWENTY20 QUALIFIER IN THE NETHERLANDS IN 2018

1 Bangladesh   2 Ireland   3 Scotland   4 Papua New Guinea
5 Thailand   6 Uganda   7 United Arab Emirates   8 Netherlands

The two places available at the World Twenty20 in the Caribbean were claimed by Bangladesh, who were unbeaten throughout, and Ireland, who lost only in the final. Ireland's Clare Shillington, 37, was named Player of the Tournament for her 126 runs at a strike-rate of 115; that included 47 in an important victory over Scotland. Her team-mate Lucy O'Reilly topped the wicket-takers, with 11, although the Bangladesh leg-spinner Rumana Ahmed took ten at an average of 4.2. The surprise packets were Thailand, who finished fifth, and beat the UAE and Uganda. But it was a disappointing competition for the hosts: the Netherlands came last, losing all their matches, including the seventh-place play-off, following a super over. Oddly, however, the Dutch had easily the highest scorer, Sterre Kalis (231, including two of the tournament's three half-centuries). Next came the Scottish sisters, Sarah and Kathryn Bryce, with 162 and 129.

Final At Utrecht, July 14. **Bangladesh won by 25 runs. Bangladesh 122-9** (20 overs) (Ayasha Rahman 46; L. A. O'Reilly 4-28); ‡**Ireland 97** (18.4 overs) (Panna Ghosh 5-16). *PoM:* Panna Ghosh. *PoT:* C. M. A. Shillington (Ireland). *Bangladesh completed their fifth straightforward victory out of five. Fellow qualifiers Ireland looked in with a chance when Bangladesh slipped from 80-1 to 122-9, medium-pacer Lucy O'Reilly finishing with four wickets. But Ireland's batsmen struggled: only three reached double figures, with Gaby Lewis's 26 the top score, as seamer Panna Ghosh improved Bangladesh's best T20I analysis.*

ENGLAND v NEW ZEALAND IN 2018

RAF NICHOLSON

One-day internationals (3): England 2, New Zealand 1

England had just beaten New Zealand three times during the T20 triangular, and continued to boss them around when the 50-over games began. They won the first two by huge margins, before New Zealand hit back to pinch a couple of ICC Championship points.

The opening pair were key to England's success, with stands of 104, 40 and 111. Tammy Beaumont continued her form with 160 runs in total, which helped her beat Jan Brittin's record for the most international runs in an English summer (596 in 1984); she finished with 628. Her partner, Amy Jones, finally made good on her promise, and outscored Beaumont by one run.

New Zealand's flakiness fuelled concerns they were standing still in an era when other teams were becoming more professional. Their batting looked weak, particularly against the spinners, with Sophie Devine's century in the third match the only saving grace; she finished with 164 in the series, 100 more than any of her team-mates. A slump by Suzie Bates – her best score was 28 – did not help. Senior bowler Lea Tahuhu also had a poor series, and was left out of the final match. But New Zealand's coach, Haidee Tiffen, said she had been pleased with the exposure given to younger players, particularly 20-year-old Jess Watkin, whose scalps included Beaumont, Jones and Danni Wyatt. Nonetheless, questions remained about the absence of Rachel Priest, omitted from the team since 2017 over fitness concerns; her runs were sorely missed.

The series started with the first women's one-day international at Headingley. It attracted a crowd of 2,100 on a day when the England men's football team were playing their World Cup quarter-final, and helped answer criticisms previously levelled at the ECB about the lack of women's internationals in the north of England.

NEW ZEALAND TOURING PARTY

*S. W. Bates, B. M. Bezuidenhout, S. F. M. Devine, K. E. Ebrahim, M. L. Green, H. R. Huddleston, H. N. K. Jensen, L. M. Kasperek, A. C. Kerr, K. J. Martin, A. M. Peterson, H. M. Rowe, A. E. Satterthwaite, L. M. Tahuhu, J. M. Watkin. *Coach:* H. M. Tiffen.

First one-day international At Leeds, July 7. **England won by 142 runs.** ‡England 290-5 (50 overs) (A. E. Jones 63, T. T. Beaumont 40, H. C. Knight 63, N. R. Sciver 37, K. H. Brunt 30*); **New Zealand 148** (35.3 overs) (S. F. M. Devine 33; N. R. Sciver 3-18, L. A. Marsh 3-24). *PoM:* N. R. Sciver. *ODI debut:* K. L. George (England). *England's innings got off to a flyer as Amy Jones and Tammy Beaumont put on 111, punishing some wayward bowling from the seamers. Jones reached her first international half-century on home soil, from 56 balls. Amelia Kerr then struck twice – Jones stumped and Sarah Taylor bowled, both bamboozled by her googly. But England finished strongly: 76 came from the last ten overs. In reply, Suzie Bates and Sophie Devine reached 50-0 in ten overs, but both were caught at mid-off, part of a collapse of four for five in 17 balls. Laura Marsh finished off the tail.*

Second one-day international At Derby, July 10 (day/night). **England won by 123 runs.** ‡England 241 (48 overs) (T. T. Beaumont 67, N. R. Sciver 54); **New Zealand 118** (38 overs) (K. L. George 33, S. Ecclestone 3-14). *PoM:* T. T. Beaumont. *Beaumont continued her remarkable run, top-scoring with 63 and adding 57 with Nat Sciver before falling lbw to Jess Watkin. Katherine Brunt (25) and Georgia Elwiss (18) helped keep some momentum in the death overs, though England were bowled out with two unused. In only her second ODI, left-arm seamer Katie George set up another New Zealand collapse, quickly removing Devine and Amy Satterthwaite in successive overs. Bates top-scored with 24 but, by the time Marsh deceived her in the 19th over with a turning ball that knocked back middle stump, any hope of a recovery was gone. Kate Ebrahim and Holly Huddleston saved some face with 26 for the last wicket, but England completed a huge win.*

Third one-day international At Leicester, July 13 (day/night). **New Zealand won by four wickets.** ‡England 219 (47.4 overs) (A. E. Jones 78, T. T. Beaumont 53; L. M. Kasperek 5-39); **New Zealand 224-6** (44.4 overs) (S. F. M. Devine 117*). *PoM:* S. F. M. Devine. *PoS:* A. E. Jones. *After Knight won her third toss out of three, Beaumont and Jones shared another century opening stand. But England failed to make the most of that good start, losing their last eight for 63; seven fell to spinners, Leigh Kasperek the star with her first ODI five-for. Watkin, promoted to open in place of Bates, was lbw to Brunt in the first over, but Devine built a solid platform with half-century partnerships for the second and fourth wickets with Maddy Green and Satterthwaite. There was a mid-innings wobble to 150-5, but Devine brought up a 101-ball century in the 38th over, and clinched victory by smashing Brunt over long leg for six.*

Women's Championship: England 4pts, New Zealand 2pts.

SRI LANKA v INDIA IN 2018-19

One-day internationals (3): Sri Lanka 1, India 2
Twenty20 internationals (5): Sri Lanka 0, India 4

India ventured across the Palk Strait for three matches in the 50-over Championship, and then played five 20-over matches to warm up for the World Twenty20. Sri Lanka pulled off a surprise victory in the final ODI, in which the two captains, Mithali Raj and Chamari Atapattu Jayangani, traded centuries in a high-scoring match. In the T20 series, India were unstoppable – except by the weather, which ruined the second game. Their star was Jemimah Rodrigues, who had just turned 18: she hit 191 runs at 63, almost twice as many as anyone else. She had been less successful in the ODIs, bagging a duck in her only innings.

First one-day international At Galle, September 11, 2018. **India won by nine wickets.** ‡Sri Lanka 98 (35.1 overs) (A. M. C. Jayangani 33; M. Joshi 3-16); **India 100-1** (19.5 overs) (S. S. Mandhana 73*). *ODI debuts:* T. Bhatia, D. Hemalatha (India). *India needed little more than half the available time to polish off Sri Lanka, bowling them out for 98. Seamer Mansi Joshi led the rout with* *career-best figures in her first international for 14 months after a knee injury. Smriti Mandhana, whose 73* included 56 in boundaries, then dominated an opening stand of 96 with Punam Raut (24).*

Second one-day international   At Galle, September 13, 2018. **India won by seven runs. ‡India 219** (50 overs) (M. D. Raj 52, T. Bhatia 68, D. Hemalatha 35; A. M. C. Jayangani 3-42); **Sri Lanka 212** (48.1 overs) (A. M. C. Jayangani 57, H. A. S. D. Siriwardene 49, N. N. D. de Silva 31). *Chasing 220, Sri Lanka looked sunk when Sripali Weerakkoddy and Anushka Sanjeewani fell to successive balls in the 42nd over, which made it 165-5. But Nilakshi de Silva and Udeshika Prabodhani added 40, before the last three wickets fell for seven, and India could breathe again. Their innings had featured 52 from Mithali Raj, in 121 balls, and a sprightlier 68 from 66 by Taniya Bhatia, in only her second ODI; she later took two good catches and ended the match with a stumping.*

Third one-day international   At Katunayake (FTZ), September 16, 2018. **Sri Lanka won by three wickets. India 253-5** (50 overs) (S. S. Mandhana 51, M. D. Raj 125*, D. B. Sharma 38); **‡Sri Lanka 257-7** (49.5 overs) (G. W. H. M. Perera 45, A. M. C. Jayangani 115). *Raj, who entered at 0-1 and stayed to the end for 125* – her seventh and highest ODI century – seemed to have done enough to ensure India's whitewash. She put on 102 for the second wicket with Mandhana, and 92 for the fifth in 14 overs with Deepti Sharma. But one captain's innings was trumped by another. Chamari Atapattu Jayangani hit four sixes in her 115 and, although she departed at 193-3, the later batsmen were up to the task: 17-year-old Kavisha Dilhari drove the fifth ball of the last over, from Sharma, straight for four to complete Sri Lanka's victory, which ended a run of ten defeats by India dating back to February 2013.*

Women's Championship: India 4pts, Sri Lanka 2pts.

First Twenty20 international   At Katunayake (FTZ), September 19, 2018. **India won by 13 runs. India 168-8** (20 overs) (J. I. Rodrigues 36, T. Bhatia 46, A. A. Patil 36); **‡Sri Lanka 155** (19.3 overs) (B. Y. A. Mendis 32, L. E. Kaushalya 45; P. Yadav 4-26). *T20I debuts:* W. K. Dilhari (Sri Lanka); A. Reddy (India). *India survived Mandhana's golden duck to post a competitive total. They hurtled to 70-2 after five overs, before Jemimah Rodrigues was out for a 15-ball 36. Sri Lanka also started quickly, the openers taking 39 from three overs, and later Eshani Kaushalya gave India a fright with 45 from 31. But the unrelated Yadavs – leg-spinner Poonam and 18-year-old slow left-armer Radha – shared six wickets to keep a lid on the scoring, and skipper Harmanpreet Kaur made up for a duck with the last two wickets.*

Second Twenty20 international   At Colombo (Colts), September 21, 2018. **No result. Sri Lanka 49-3** (7.5 overs) **v ‡India.**

Third Twenty20 international   At Colombo (Colts), September 22, 2018. **India won by five wickets. Sri Lanka 131-8** (20 overs) (H. A. S. D. Siriwardene 35, N. N. D. de Silva 31); **‡India 132-5** (18.2 overs) (J. I. Rodrigues 57). *A tight spell plus two run-outs from seamer Arundhati Reddy (4–14–19–2) helped restrict Sri Lanka to 131, despite de Silva's late 20-ball burst. India had 38-2 after 6.1 overs, with Raj and Mandhana both out, but Rodrigues spanked 57 from 40.*

Fourth Twenty20 international   At Colombo (CCC), September 24, 2018. **India won by seven wickets. Sri Lanka 134-5** (17 overs) (A. M. C. Jayangani 31, H. A. S. D. Siriwardene 40; A. A. Patil 3-36); **‡India 137-3** (15.4 overs) (J. I. Rodrigues 52*, A. A. Patil 54*; O. U. Ranasinghe 3-33). *India clinched the series after another powerful performance from Rodrigues, whose 52* needed only 37 balls. She had been peeved to fall within sight of victory in the previous match and, from 41-3 after four overs, made sure this time in a stand of 96* with Anuja Patil (54* from 42). Patil had earlier taken three wickets as Sri Lanka were held to 134 in a match reduced to 17 overs.*

Fifth Twenty20 international   At Katunayake (FTZ), September 25, 2018. **India won by 51 runs. India 156** (18.3 overs) (J. I. Rodrigues 46, H. Kaur 63; H. A. S. D. Siriwardene 3-19, S. I. P. Fernando 3-24); **‡Sri Lanka 105** (17.4 overs) (P. Yadav 3-18). *India sealed a 4–0 victory with another dominant display, despatching Sri Lanka for 105 with three more scalps for Poonam Yadav, who finished the series as the leading wicket-taker on either side, with eight. At 105-2 in the 12th over, India had threatened to set a much larger target – but after Rodrigues departed for 46 off 31, no one could stay with Kaur, whose 38-ball 63 included five sixes.*

WEST INDIES v SOUTH AFRICA IN 2018-19

One-day internationals (3): West Indies 1, South Africa 1
Twenty20 internationals (5): West Indies 2, South Africa 2

The hardest-fought tour in women's cricket in 2018 ended with a pair of draws. West Indies came from behind to level the 50-over games in Barbados, thanks to a century from opener Hayley Matthews, before South Africa turned around a 2–0 deficit in the Twenty20 matches – the last four of them at Brian Lara's academy in Tarouba, Trinidad. In the second, West Indian off-spinner Anisa Mohammed took a hat-trick. West Indies finished the one-dayers fourth in the ICC Championship, while South Africa were stuck in seventh.

First one-day international At Bridgetown, Barbados, September 16, 2018. **South Africa won by 40 runs. South Africa 201-9** (50 overs) (L. Wolvaardt 45, S. E. Luus 58, D. van Niekerk 46*; S. R. Taylor 3-37); ‡**West Indies 161** (46 overs) (S. A. Campbelle 46; M. Kapp 3-14). PoM: S. E. Luus. *ODI debut: T. S. Sekhukhune (South Africa). Marizanne Kapp made sure of a comfortable victory with 9–2–14–3, becoming the third South African, after Dane van Niekerk and Shabnim Ismail, to take 100 ODI wickets. Kapp had Hayley Matthews caught behind second ball as West Indies set off in pursuit of 202, then removed Merissa Aguilleira and Afy Fletcher in the same over to make it 85-7. South Africa's innings has been built around a patient half-century for Sune Luus, though from 104-1 in the 28th over the innings fell away, leaving No. 4 van Niekerk stranded.*

Second one-day international At Bridgetown, Barbados, September 19, 2018. **No result. South Africa 177-8** (38 overs) (D. van Niekerk 53, C. L. Tryon 37; D. J. S. Dottin 3-29) v ‡**West Indies.** *Rain meant a point each in the ICC Championship, though South Africa had stuttered after reaching 152-4. Van Niekerk was run out soon after passing 50, while Chloe Tryon made an enterprising 37.*

Third one-day international At Bridgetown, Barbados, September 22, 2018 (day/night). **West Indies won by 115 runs.** ‡**West Indies 292-5** (50 overs) (H. K. Matthews 117, S. R. Taylor 46, D. J. S. Dottin 59, Extras 35; M. Kapp 4-55); **South Africa 177** (42.3 overs) (L. Wolvaardt 54, D. van Niekerk 77; D. J. S. Dottin 4-36). PoM: H. K. Matthews. PoS: D. van Niekerk. *A maiden international hundred for Matthews inspired West Indies to their second-highest total (behind 368-8 against Sri Lanka at Mumbai in February 2013) and a share of the Championship points. She dominated a second-wicket stand of 176 with her captain, Stafanie Taylor (46), before Deandra Dottin weighed in with 59 off 44. Only Kapp escaped punishment, taking 4-55, compared with six colleagues' combined 1-235. South Africa slipped to 10-2, before Laura Wolvaardt and the in-form van Niekerk put on 108. But Dottin's seamers claimed four wickets as the last eight tumbled for 59.*

Women's Championship: West Indies 3pts, South Africa 3pts.

First Twenty20 international At Bridgetown, Barbados, September 24, 2018. **West Indies won by 17 runs.** ‡**West Indies 124-6** (20 overs) (N. Y. McLean 38); **South Africa 107-7** (20 overs) (M. Kapp 30; S. R. Taylor 3-16). PoM: N. Y. McLean. *T20I debuts: R. Searle, T. S. Sekhukhune, S. Smith, F. Tunnicliffe (South Africa). South Africa were scuppered by tight bowling from West Indies, and their own inexperienced batting, as they fell well short in a modest chase. Taylor and Fletcher, off-spinner and leg-spinner, claimed 5-33 between them, while two of South Africa's four debutants, Robyn Searle and Faye Tunnicliffe, contributed a combined 28 off 59 balls. Kapp's 30 from No. 7 was in vain. Natasha McLean had made a steady 38 off 41 for West Indies, but South Africa's two other newcomers fared better with the bat: seamer Tumi Sekhukhune conceded only 12 in her four overs, and off-spinner Saarah Smith collected 2-17.*

Second Twenty20 international At Tarouba, Trinidad, September 28, 2018 (floodlit). **West Indies won by nine wickets. South Africa 101-8** (20 overs) (D. van Niekerk 36; A. Mohammed 5-24); ‡**West Indies 102-1** (15.3 overs) (N. Y. McLean 42*, S. R. Taylor 35*). PoM: A. Mohammed. *Off-spinner Anisa Mohammed claimed West Indies' first T20 hat-trick, removing Kapp, Smith and Masabata Klaas with the last three balls of the South African innings. That made it four wickets in the over (van Niekerk had fallen to its second ball), and completed her third format haul of five. From 82-3, South Africa lost 5-19 in their last 16 deliveries. They had begun poorly too, when*

Matthews inflicted ducks on Lizelle Lee, who ate up 12 balls, and Luus. West Indies cantered to a 2–0 lead, thanks to a second-wicket stand of 72* in 9.1 overs between McLean and Taylor.

Third Twenty20 international   At Tarouba, Trinidad, September 30, 2018 (floodlit). **West Indies v South Africa. Abandoned.**

Fourth Twenty20 international   At Tarouba, Trinidad, October 4, 2018. **South Africa won by eight wickets. West Indies 135-3** (20 overs) (N. Y. McLean 57*); ‡**South Africa 136-2** (18.3 overs) (L. Lee 54, L. Wolvaardt 55*). PoM: L. Wolvaardt. *South Africa pulled one back after their openers, Lee and Wolvaardt, broke open the chase with a stand of 89 in 12 overs. Lee made 54 off 38, while Wolvaardt batted through for 55* off 57. For West Indies, opener McLean consumed 61 deliveries for her 57*; Kapp was as tidy as ever, going for just 13 from her four overs.*

Fifth Twenty20 international   At Tarouba, Trinidad, October 6, 2018 (floodlit). **South Africa won by three wickets. West Indies 155-5** (20 overs) (H. K. Matthews 70); ‡**South Africa 156-7** (19.5 overs) (L. Lee 42, C. L. Tryon 31). PoM: L. Lee. PoS: N. Y. McLean. *A solid chase earned South Africa a 2–2 share of the series. Lee, whose 24-ball 42 included ten fours, got them off to a flyer, before Tryon – captain for the third time in the series because van Niekerk had an ankle injury – hit 31 off 22. Despite a late stumble, Smith got them over the line with a ball to spare. West Indies' 155 had centred on Matthews's powerful 70 off 52.*

AUSTRALIA v NEW ZEALAND IN 2018-19

Twenty20 internationals (3); Australia 3, New Zealand 0

Australia warmed up for the World Twenty20 in the Caribbean with a trio of straightforward run-chases. The whitewash helped address their recent struggles against New Zealand, who had won nine of the previous 13 T20 games between the sides. Australia boasted both the outstanding batsman and bowler: Alyssa Healy's tally of 138 included two fifties, while Ellyse Perry claimed six wickets at 12.

First Twenty20 international   At North Sydney, September 29, 2018 (floodlit). **Australia won by six wickets. New Zealand 162-5** (20 overs) (S. F. M. Devine 43, K. J. Martin 56*); ‡**Australia 164-4** (17.4 overs) (M. M. Lanning 56*, R. L. Haynes 69*). PoM: R. L. Haynes. T20I debut: G. L. Wareham (Australia). *Meg Lanning and Rachael Haynes rescued Australia from 45-4, and extended their T20 record at North Sydney Oval to six wins out of six. Lanning hit 56* off 44 balls, and Haynes 69* off 40 (with 50 in boundaries), as they put on 119*, a fifth-wicket record in T20Is, to secure victory with 14 deliveries to spare. New Zealand had been boosted by a late surge from Katey Martin (56* off 34) and Bernadine Bezuidenhout (20* off 13), who thrashed 42* off the last 3.2 overs. This was the first home televised international not broadcast by Channel Nine for nearly 40 years, after Cricket Australia's new deal with Seven, a free-to-air channel.*

Second Twenty20 international   At Brisbane (Allan Border Field), October 1, 2018. **Australia won by six wickets. New Zealand 145-8** (20 overs) (S. W. Bates 77; M. L. Schutt 3-15); ‡**Australia 149-4** (18.5 overs) (A. J. Healy 57, E. J. Villani 50*). PoM: M. L. Schutt. *A stunning 52-ball 77 from Suzie Bates wasn't enough to stretch Australia. Amy Satterthwaite was the only other New Zealander to find the boundary, as an attack led by Megan Schutt kept the rate under control. Beth Mooney fell third ball in reply, but Alyssa Healy's 57 off 41 was followed by Elyse Villani's 50* off 39 as Australia cruised to a series victory.*

Third Twenty20 international   At Canberra, October 5, 2018 (floodlit). **Australia won by nine wickets. New Zealand 103** (19 overs) (K. J. Martin 35*; E. A. Perry 4-21, S. G. Molineux 3-11); ‡**Australia 105-1** (12.3 overs) (A. J. Healy 67). PoM: E. A. Perry. PoS: A. J. Healy. *Australia's third win was the easiest, after New Zealand lost five for eight in 15 balls from 68-3, leaving Martin stranded. Four were out for ducks, and both Ellyse Perry and left-arm spinner Sophie Molineux found themselves on hat-tricks. Healy took care of the chase, thrashing 54 in boundaries in a 44-ball 67, and dominating an opening stand of 98 with Mooney.*

BANGLADESH v PAKISTAN IN 2018-19

Twenty20 internationals (4): Bangladesh 0, Pakistan 3
One-day international (1): Bangladesh 1, Pakistan 0

Pakistan outgunned neighbours Bangladesh in the Twenty20 internationals, humbling them for 30 in the second match (the first was washed out) and keeping them below 100 in the other two. Medium-pacer Anam Amin started with three for nought en route to series figures of five for 23 in 11 overs; off-spinner Nida Dar was not far behind, with five for 38. Bangladesh did manage a consolation victory in the one-day international, with their own off-spinner, Khadija Tul Kobra, claiming a national record six for 20.

First Twenty20 international At Cox's Bazar, October 2, 2018. **Bangladesh v Pakistan. Abandoned.**

Second Twenty20 international At Cox's Bazar, October 3, 2018. **Pakistan won by 58 runs. Pakistan 88-5** (14 overs); ‡**Bangladesh 30** (12.5 overs) (Anam Amin 3-0). PoM: Anam Amin. *A wet outfield meant a late start, and a 14-over match – but Pakistan needed less than that to demolish Bangladesh for 30, the lowest T20I total by an established nation, undercutting their own 44, also against Pakistan, in Bangkok in 2016-17. Rumana Ahmed top-scored with nine from No. 7; slow left-armer Anam Amin took three wickets in three overs without conceding a run.*

Third Twenty20 international At Cox's Bazar, October 5, 2018. **Pakistan won by seven wickets.** ‡**Bangladesh 81-8** (20 overs); **Pakistan 85-3** (18.1 overs) (Nahida Khan 33, Javeria Khan 31*). PoM: Nahida Khan. *Bangladesh fared better than in the first match, but still no one could reach 20 as they crept along at four an over. After Nahida Khan kicked off the chase with 33, skipper Javeria Khan anchored her side with 31*.*

Fourth Twenty20 international At Cox's Bazar, October 6, 2018. **Pakistan won by seven wickets.** ‡**Bangladesh 77** (20 overs) (Natalia Pervaiz 3-20); **Pakistan 78-3** (14.5 overs) (Javeria Khan 36). PoM: Natalia Pervaiz. *Pakistan completed a 3–0 victory, again throttling the Bangladesh scoring-rate. Seamer Natalia Pervaiz started the procession, before Diana Baig (2-12) and off-spinner Sana Mir (2-10) joined in.*

One-day international At Cox's Bazar, October 8, 2018. **Bangladesh won by six wickets.** ‡**Pakistan 94** (34.5 overs) (Khadija Tul Kobra 6-20); **Bangladesh 95-4** (29 overs) (Farzana Haque 48, Rumana Ahmed 34). PoM: Khadija Tul Kobra. ODI debut: Umaima Sohail (Pakistan). *Bangladesh atoned for their poor showing in the T20s with a comprehensive victory in the solitary ODI. It looked unlikely when Pakistan reached 50-1 in the 16th over, but they lost their last nine for 44, six to off-spinner Khadija Tul Kobra, who returned Bangladesh's best ODI figures, beating 4-20 by Rumana Ahmed against India at Ahmedabad in April 2013. A target of 95 was no certainty, as Bangladesh had not made that many in the T20s, but after dipping to 6-2 they made sure through a partnership of 81 between Farzana Haque and Rumana.*

PAKISTAN v AUSTRALIA IN MALAYSIA IN 2018-19

One-day internationals (3): Pakistan 0, Australia 3
Twenty20 internationals (3): Pakistan 0, Australia 3

Australia asserted their superiority over Pakistan with a pair of clean sweeps in Kuala Lumpur, and moved four points clear at the top of the ICC Women's Championship. Wicketkeeper Alyssa Healy shone with the bat, making 260 runs across the six games, while Sophie Molineux, a left-arm spinner, took 13 wickets in all at just seven apiece; her 37 overs cost only 91. Pakistan scored a respectable 235 in the third ODI, but were otherwise outclassed.

First one-day international   At Kuala Lumpur, October 18, 2018. **Australia won by five wickets** (DLS). ‡**Pakistan 95** (37.2 overs) (M. L. Schutt 3-17, N. J. Carey 3-19); **Australia 95-5** (22.2 overs) (Sana Mir 3-26). *PoM:* M. L. Schutt. *ODI debuts:* S. G. Molineux, G. L. Wareham (Australia). *Australia won a scrappy, rain-affected game after Pakistan collapsed from 52-2 to 95 all out with 22 balls of their allotted 41 overs unused. Seamers Megan Schutt and Nicola Carey shared six cheap wickets, while two young spinners made telling debuts: 19-year-old Georgia Wareham claimed two with her leg-breaks, while slow left-armer Sophie Molineux, 20, returned 7–2–9–1. Alyssa Healy and Nicole Bolton began with 40 in seven, though Australia then lost five wickets – three to the off-breaks of Sana Mir, who had earlier top-scored for Pakistan with 21* (Javeria Khan was dismissed for 21).*

Second one-day international   At Kuala Lumpur, October 20, 2018. **Australia won by 150 runs.** ‡**Australia 273-7** (50 overs) (M. M. Lanning 124, R. L. Haynes 79; Nashra Sandhu 3-54); **Pakistan 123** (40.1 overs) (Nahida Khan 66; S. G. Molineux 4-14). *PoM:* M. M. Lanning. *Meg Lanning's 12th ODI hundred, but her first against Pakistan – completing a full set of centuries against the seven teams she had played against – took Australia clear at the top of the ICC Women's Championship. She added 181 with Rachael Haynes (79 off 82), an Australian fourth-wicket record, and faced only 106 balls for her 124. Pakistan never got going. Opener Nahida Khan was ninth out for 66, Pakistan's highest score against Australia, but was part of a surrender in which the last five fell for two. Molineux followed her impressive debut with 4-14.*

Third one-day international   At Kuala Lumpur, October 22, 2018. **Australia won by 89 runs.** ‡**Australia 324-7** (50 overs) (A. J. Healy 97, E. A. Perry 32, R. L. Haynes 30, B. L. Mooney 38, A. K. Gardner 62*; Sana Mir 3-53); **Pakistan 235-7** (50 overs) (Nahida Khan 37, Sidra Ameen 41, Nida Dar 30, Aliya Riaz 51; A. K. Gardner 3-44). *PoM:* A. K. Gardner. *PoS:* Sana Mir and M. M. Lanning. *ODI debut:* T. J. Vlaeminck (Australia). *Ashleigh Gardner starred as Australia made it 3–0. First she bludgeoned 62* off 37 balls to lift her side to their highest score against Pakistan for over 21 years. Then she took three wickets with her off-breaks, though the Pakistanis at least managed their first total of 200-plus against the Australians, with Aliya Riaz scoring a maiden ODI fifty. The tone had been set by Healy, who made 97 off 75.*

Women's Championship: Australia 6pts, Pakistan 0pts.

First Twenty20 international   At Kuala Lumpur, October 25, 2018. **Australia won by 64 runs.** ‡**Australia 195-3** (20 overs) (B. L. Mooney 38, A. J. Healy 59, A. K. Gardner 63*); **Pakistan 131-7** (20 overs) (Nahida Khan 43; S. G. Molineux 4-16). *PoM:* S. G. Molineux. *T20I debut:* Umaima Sohail (Pakistan). *Healy (59 off 35) and Gardner (63* off 37) prospered again, as they had three days earlier in the final ODI. Set an imposing 196, Pakistan reached 82-2 in the 11th over, but couldn't kick on. Yet again, Molineux proved both incisive and economical, finishing with 4-16.*

Second Twenty20 international   At Kuala Lumpur, October 27, 2018 (floodlit). **Australia won by six wickets. Pakistan 101** (19.5 overs) (Umaima Sohail 43; S. G. Molineux 3-4, G. L. Wareham 3-12); ‡**Australia 104-4** (17 overs). *PoM:* G. L. Wareham. *Australia claimed the series after Pakistan folded in a heap – from 55-1 in the ninth to 101. Umaima Sohail made 43 in her second T20I, from No. 3, but no one below her passed six, as Molineux and Wareham took 6-26 between them. Australia lost four wickets in reply, but the result was never in doubt.*

Third Twenty20 international   At Kuala Lumpur, October 29, 2018. **Australia won by nine wickets. Pakistan 97-8** (20 overs) (Bismah Maroof 34); ‡**Australia 98-1** (10.2 overs) (A. J. Healy 67*). *PoM:* A. J. Healy. *PoS:* Umaima Sohail and A. J. Healy. *Australia's sixth win out of six followed a ruthless display in the field, which included four run-outs. Healy then battered 67* off 41 balls as they knocked off a small target with nearly half their overs in hand.*

> **"** She once recalled her mother telling her: 'You'll never meet nice men if you play cricket.' Rheinberg said: 'She was quite right in a way. I won't say I didn't meet nice men – but I didn't marry.'"
> The Netta Rheinberg Diaries, Page 45

THE EXPANSION OF OFFICIAL T20 INTERNATIONALS
Botsogo blooms in Botswana

STEVEN LYNCH

The ICC's decision to give full international status to all women's Twenty20 matches between member nations, which came into force in July 2018, led to some exotic entries in the records.

The matches at the Asia Cup involving Thailand and hosts Malaysia were retrospectively deemed official, but the first tournament after the change was in Botswana in August. Its capital, Gaborone, is probably best known as the setting for the *No. 1 Ladies' Detective Agency* books – and their heroine, Precious Ramotswe, might have been briefly befuddled as six other African teams joined in the fun down at the local Oval.

Fifteen-year-old Botsogo Mpedi took a format-best six for eight for Botswana against Lesotho in the first match, and finished as the leading wicket-taker, with 14 at 5.57. Eventual winners Namibia bowled Mozambique out for 25 – briefly the lowest in T20 internationals – then later that day restricted Lesotho to 31 for seven, chasing 211. Ann Marie Kamara, of runners-up Sierra Leone, was the leading scorer, with 199. Malawi also took part.

At around the same time, the South American Championship was played at the Los Pinos Polo Club in Bogotà. Brazil won all their group games, then skittled Chile in the final for 45. Amazingly, that was the highest total they conceded in seven matches; they undercut the T20I record (set in Botswana the day before) by bowling out Mexico for 18, of which 12 came from Anjuli Ladron. Brazil's Roberta Moretti Avery, also an accomplished golfer, took nine for 22 in all. "We knew we were going into the record books," she said. "All the procedures were in place – more paperwork, official umpires. Very exciting." Her team-mate Renata Sousa took nine for 24, and Denise Souza nine for 42. Sousa (143 runs) and 41-year-old Narayana Reinehr Ribeiro (156) were the leading batsmen. Ribeiro's twin sister, Erika, also played for Brazil. The host nation, Colombia, did not enter, although they did have a team in the men's tournament: Mexico won that, after dismissing Uruguay for 44 in the final.

Another unlikely location featured in November, when China visited South Korea and triumphed 2–1 at the Yeonhui ground in Incheon, which had also hosted matches during the 2014 Asian Games. China fared less well early in 2019, being bowled out for 14 – a new low – by the UAE in Bangkok.

There may yet be another addition from 2018. Malaysia beat Singapore 4–2 in August but, possibly misunderstanding the new regulations, failed to inform the ICC. They have now asked for the series to be considered official. And there will soon be more unfamiliar names in the mix: at the start of 2019, the rule change was extended to men's T20 internationals.

ICC WOMEN'S CHAMPIONSHIP 2017–2020

In 2014, the ICC introduced a Women's Championship as a qualifying tournament for the World Cup, and to create a more meaningful programme for the leading teams. Australia won the first edition, which ended in November 2016, and the second cycle began late in 2017. Each of the eight sides from the previous World Cup play each other in three one-day internationals over two and a half years (they can arrange more games if they choose, but only the designated three carry points). The top four in the final table will advance directly to the next World Cup, while the bottom four will contest a further qualifying tournament with six other teams. By the end of 2018, Australia led the way again, having lost only one of their nine matches, and were due to take on second-placed New Zealand at home early in 2019. England, in third, were scheduled to face India away in February, Sri Lanka away in March, and West Indies at home in June.

CHAMPIONSHIP TABLE

	P	W	L	NR	Pts	NRR
Australia	9	8	1	0	16	1.55
New Zealand	9	6	3	0	12	0.40
England	9	5	4	0	10	0.57
West Indies	9	4	4	1	9	−0.25
India	9	4	5	0	8	0.38
Pakistan	9	4	5	0	8	−0.37
South Africa	9	3	5	1	7	−1.04
Sri Lanka	9	1	8	0	2	−1.21

As at December 31, 2018.

MRF TYRES ICC WOMEN'S RANKINGS

In 2015, the ICC introduced a table of women's international rankings, which combined results from Tests, one-day and Twenty20 internationals. In 2018, after Twenty20 international status was extended to all Associate women's teams, this was replaced by separate rankings for one-day and Twenty20 cricket.

ONE-DAY INTERNATIONAL TEAM RANKINGS

(As at December 31, 2018)

		Matches	Points	Rating
1	Australia...............	22	3,110	141
2	England	24	2,963	123
3	India..................	27	3,212	119
4	New Zealand	27	3,126	116
5	South Africa...........	36	3,538	98
6	West Indies	19	1,754	92
7	Pakistan	23	1,652	72
8	Sri Lanka	23	1,335	58
9	Bangladesh............	13	632	49
10	Ireland	10	211	21

TWENTY20 INTERNATIONAL TEAM RANKINGS

(As at December 31, 2018)

		Matches	Points	Rating
1	Australia...............	28	7,937	283
2	England	24	6,567	274
3	New Zealand	29	7,925	273
4	West Indies	24	6,320	263
5	India..................	32	8,157	255
6	South Africa...........	25	6,052	242
7	Pakistan	31	6,972	225
8	Sri Lanka	26	5,403	208
9	Bangladesh............	31	5,913	191
10	Ireland	17	3,153	185

Remaining rankings 11 Scotland (150), 12 Thailand (146), 13 Zimbabwe (145), 14 United Arab Emirates (130), 15 Uganda (127), 16 Kenya (121), 17 Papua New Guinea (120), 18 Nepal (117), 19 Samoa (106), 20 Tanzania (89), 21 Hong Kong (81), 22 Indonesia (80), 23 Netherlands (76), 24 Qatar (74), 25 China (68), 26 Namibia (63), 27 Japan (57), 28 Botswana (49), 29 Argentina (48), 30 Sierra Leone (44), 31 Malaysia (43), 32 Germany (43), 33 Oman (36), 34 Brazil (33), 35 Vanuatu (29), 36 South Korea (27), 37 France (25), 38 Mozambique (21), 39 Denmark (20), 40 Zambia (11), 41 Malawi (10), 42 Belgium (9), 43 Chile (7), 44 Peru (0), 45 Lesotho (0), 46 Swaziland (0), 47 Singapore (0).

> " He could bowl one ball that would go down the leg side for four wides, but the next would be a perfect outswinger at 100 miles an hour... and the next would be at your throat. That was hard."
> Cricket's Windrush Generation, page 53

PLAYER RANKINGS

In October 2008, the ICC launched a set of rankings for women cricketers, on the same principles as those for men, based on one-day international performances. Twenty20 rankings were added in September 2012. There are no Test rankings.

The leading players in the women's one-day international rankings on December 31, 2018, were:

	Batsmen	Points			Bowlers	Points
1	E. A. Perry (A)	681		1	Sana Mir (P)	663
2	M. M. Lanning (A)	675		2	M. L. Schutt (A)	660
3	M. D. Raj (I)	674		3	M. Kapp (SA)	643
4	S. S. Mandhana (I)	672		4	J. L. Jonassen (A)	636
5	L. Lee (SA)	659		5	J. N. Goswami (I)	609
6	T. T. Beaumont (E)	657		6	S. Ismail (SA)	603
7	S. W. Bates (NZ)	656		7	K. H. Brunt (E)	592
8	S. R. Taylor (WI)	632		8	S. R. Taylor (WI)	573
9	A. M. C. Jayangani (SL)	628		9	E. A. Perry (A)	568
10	S. F. M. Devine (NZ)	619		10	A. Khaka (SA)	562

The leading players in the women's Twenty20 international rankings on December 31, 2018, were:

	Batsmen	Points			Bowlers	Points
1	S. W. Bates (NZ)	694		1	M. L. Schutt (A)	728
2	S. R. Taylor (WI)	656		2	P. Yadav (I)	662
3	H. Kaur (I)	632		3	L. M. Kasperek (NZ)	647
4	M. M. Lanning (A)	623		4	S. Ecclestone (E)	643
5	D. J. S. Dottin (WI)	614		5	E. A. Perry (A)	641
6	J. I. Rodrigues (I)	607		6	A. Shrubsole (E)	638
7	B. L. Mooney (A)	601		7	A. C. Kerr (NZ)	612
8	A. J. Healy (A)	575		8	D. M. Kimmince (A)	606
9	M. D. Raj (I)	570		9	Nida Dar (P)	596
10	S. S. Mandhana (I)	567		10	Nashra Sandhu (P)	587
					S. Ismail (SA)	587

WOMEN'S ONE-DAY INTERNATIONAL AVERAGES IN CALENDAR YEAR 2018

BATTING (200 runs)

		M	I	NO	R	HS	100	50	Avge	SR	4	6
1	S. F. M. Devine (NZ) ...	7	7	2	533	117*	3	2	106.60	109.89	52	10
2	A. C. Kerr (NZ)	7	7	3	374	232*	1	1	93.50	133.09	48	5
3	S. W. Bates (NZ)	8	7	1	438	151	2	1	73.00	102.09	52	2
4	†S. S. Mandhana (I)	12	12	2	669	135	1	7	66.90	91.02	80	10
5	T. T. Beaumont (E).	9	9	1	452	105	2	2	56.50	74.09	54	1
6	D. van Niekerk (SA).	13	11	2	500	95	0	4	55.55	74.18	54	3
7	A. J. Healy (A)	6	6	0	329	133	1	1	54.83	109.66	47	6
8	S. R. Taylor (WI)	6	5	0	254	90	0	2	50.80	76.04	21	2
9	L. Lee (SA).	14	14	2	565	117	1	4	47.08	80.25	69	13
10	N. E. Bolton (A)	6	6	1	235	100*	1	1	47.00	82.45	28	0
11	†A. M. C. Jayangani (SL).	6	6	0	275	115	1	1	45.83	67.56	34	6
12	M. D. Raj (I).	11	11	3	360	125*	1	2	45.00	62.06	35	1
13	H. C. Knight (E)	8	8	2	264	80*	0	2	44.00	83.80	25	0
14	L. Wolvaardt (SA)	13	13	2	458	70*	0	4	41.63	61.31	40	1
15	†D. B. Sharma (I)	12	10	2	320	79	0	2	40.00	68.08	32	3
16	Javeria Khan (P)	7	7	1	227	113*	1	0	37.83	73.94	28	0
17	A. E. Jones (E)	9	9	0	327	94	0	3	36.33	76.76	36	2
18	M. M. Lanning (A)......	6	6	0	217	124	1	0	36.16	93.13	33	0
19	M. L. Green (NZ)	9	7	0	253	122	1	1	36.14	94.75	25	4
20	Nahida Khan (P)	6	6	0	208	66	0	1	34.66	62.65	32	0
21	†A. E. Satterthwaite (NZ).	9	9	0	257	69	0	2	28.55	97.34	30	1
22	M. du Preez (SA)	12	10	2	213	90*	0	1	26.62	71.23	21	0
23	†C. L. Tryon (SA).	14	10	0	265	65	0	2	26.50	121.00	24	11

BOWLING (8 wickets)

		Style	O	M	R	W	BB	4I	Avge	SR	ER
1	Sana Mir (P).	OB	64	13	224	19	4-27	2	11.78	20.21	3.50
2	Khadija Tul Kobra (B).	OB	32.5	2	112	9	6-20	1	12.44	21.88	3.41
3	J. L. Jonassen (A).....	SLA	30	1	121	8	4-30	1	15.12	22.50	4.03
4	L. M. Kasperek (NZ) ..	SLA	68.1	1	306	20	5-39	3	15.30	20.45	4.48
5	S. Ecclestone (E)	SLA	85	12	281	18	4-14	1	15.61	28.33	3.30
6	A. K. Gardner (A).....	OB	45.1	4	175	11	3-40	0	15.90	24.63	3.87
7	J. N. Goswami (I)....	RFM	56.2	8	191	12	4-24	1	15.91	28.16	3.39
8	D. J. S. Dottin (WI) ...	RFM	46.3	0	202	12	4-36	1	16.83	23.25	4.34
9	M. L. Schutt (A)......	RM	45	9	157	9	3-17	0	17.44	30.00	3.48
10	R. S. Gayakwad (I)....	SLA	44	4	145	8	2-14	0	18.12	33.00	3.29
11	M. Kapp (SA)........	RFM	89	9	337	18	4-55	1	18.72	29.66	3.78
12	A. C. Kerr (NZ)	LB	60	4	251	13	5-17	1	19.30	27.69	4.18
13	S. Ismail (SA).	RFM	76	10	283	14	4-30	1	20.21	32.57	3.72
14	K. H. Brunt (E).	RFM	48.4	5	184	9	3-52	0	20.44	32.44	3.78
15	P. Yadav (I)	LB	104.5	6	454	20	4-24	2	22.70	31.45	4.33
16	A. Khaka (SA)	RFM	78.5	6	388	17	3-13	0	22.82	27.82	4.92
17	Nashra Sandhu (P)	SLA	53.3	8	210	9	3-18	0	23.33	35.66	3.92
18	C. L. Tryon (SA).	LFM	43.1	3	187	8	2-14	0	23.37	32.37	4.33
19	L. M. Tahuhu (NZ). ...	RFM	42.1	0	217	9	3-42	0	24.11	28.11	5.14
20	L. A. Marsh (E)	OB/RFM	49.2	1	248	9	3-24	0	27.55	32.88	5.02
21	S. S. Pandey (I).......	RM	59.2	2	303	10	3-23	0	30.30	35.60	5.10
22	A. R. Ntozakhe (SA) ...	OB	91	8	321	10	3-16	0	32.10	54.60	3.52
23	E. K. Bisht (I).	SLA	54	4	271	8	3-49	0	33.87	40.50	5.01
24	D. B. Sharma (I)......	OB	93	5	408	9	2-25	0	45.33	62.00	4.38

WOMEN'S TWENTY20 INTERNATIONAL AVERAGES
IN CALENDAR YEAR 2018

BATTING (300 runs)

		M	I	NO	R	HS	100	50	Avge	SR	4	6
1	A. J. Healy (A)	17	16	2	578	67*	0	6	41.28	145.95	88	11
2	†C. L. Tryon (SA)	18	17	4	300	35	0	0	23.07	144.92	26	15
3	S. F. M. Devine (NZ)	16	16	1	473	73	0	4	31.53	144.20	48	21
4	D. N. Wyatt (E)	15	15	0	416	124	1	2	27.73	143.44	57	9
5	N. R. Sciver (E)	15	15	5	406	68*	0	4	40.60	135.78	47	4
6	S. W. Bates (NZ)	17	16	3	670	124*	1	5	51.53	135.35	89	9
7	†S. S. Mandhana (I)	25	23	1	622	83	0	5	28.27	130.67	78	18
8	H. K. Matthews (WI)	13	13	0	304	70	0	3	23.38	129.91	42	7
9	K. J. Martin (NZ)	16	16	5	414	65	0	4	37.63	129.78	58	4
10	J. I. Rodrigues (I)	19	15	1	461	59	0	4	32.92	129.13	50	11
11	T. T. Beaumont (E)	15	15	1	430	116	1	2	30.71	126.47	58	5
12	H. Kaur (I)	25	22	6	663	103	1	2	41.43	126.28	58	25
13	M. M. Lanning (A)	15	13	6	385	88*	0	2	55.00	120.31	52	3
14	†B. L. Mooney (A)	16	16	1	370	71	0	1	24.66	118.58	49	1
15	†Bismah Maroof (P)	14	14	1	323	62	0	3	24.84	117.45	31	0
16	L. Lee (SA)	20	20	1	436	68	0	3	22.94	117.20	49	19
17	Javeria Khan (P)	18	18	3	454	74*	0	2	30.26	112.37	54	1
18	†A. E. Satterthwaite (NZ)	15	15	4	302	71*	0	1	27.45	112.26	32	4
19	D. van Niekerk (SA)	16	16	1	490	72	0	4	32.66	108.88	56	9
20	M. D. Raj (I)	22	19	3	575	97*	0	7	35.93	105.89	69	6
21	Shamima Sultana (B)	23	22	0	396	51	0	2	18.00	91.87	57	1
22	Farzana Haque (B)	23	21	4	348	66*	0	2	20.47	84.87	30	4
23	Ayasha Rahman (B)	21	21	1	318	46	0	0	15.90	77.37	28	9

BOWLING (15 wickets)

		Style	O	M	R	W	BB	4I	Avge	SR	ER
1	Nida Dar (P)	OB	63.3	1	300	22	5-21	2	13.63	17.31	4.72
2	Nashra Sandhu (P)	SLA	50.5	1	243	15	2-7	0	16.20	20.33	4.78
3	Rumana Ahmed (B)	LB	76	5	364	30	3-2	0	12.13	15.20	4.78
4	Salma Khatun (B)	OB	78.5	2	382	20	3-20	0	19.10	23.65	4.84
5	Nahida Akter (B)	SLA	68	4	334	20	2-2	0	16.70	20.40	4.91
6	Khadija Tul Kobra (B)	OB	59	1	293	17	3-13	0	17.23	20.82	4.96
7	M. L. Schutt (A)	RM	62.1	2	322	28	3-12	0	11.50	13.32	5.17
8	O. U. Ranasinghe (SL)	RFM	44.4	2	243	15	3-33	0	16.20	17.86	5.44
9	Jahanara Alam (B)	RM	67	3	372	19	5-28	1	19.57	21.15	5.55
10	H. A. S. D. Siriwardene (SL)	RFM	52.1	0	290	18	4-9	1	16.11	17.38	5.55
11	P. Yadav (I)	LB	90	2	522	35	4-9	2	14.91	15.42	5.80
12	L. A. O'Reilly (Ire)	RM	25.2	1	147	15	4-28	1	9.80	10.13	5.80
13	S. G. Molineux (A)	SLA	51.3	2	301	15	4-16	1	20.06	20.60	5.84
14	R. P. Yadav (I)	SLA	46.5	0	294	17	3-25	0	17.29	16.52	6.27
15	D. B. Sharma (I)	OB	62.2	1	400	18	2-15	0	22.22	20.77	6.41
16	A. K. Gardner (A)	OB	47	1	303	20	3-22	0	15.15	14.10	6.44
17	D. M. Kimmince (A)	RFM	63	0	411	20	3-20	0	20.55	18.90	6.52
18	S. Ecclestone (E)	SLA	52.3	1	350	17	4-18	1	20.58	18.52	6.66
19	A. A. Patil (I)	OB	71	0	480	20	3-15	0	24.00	21.30	6.76
20	E. A. Perry (A)	RM	51	2	348	20	4-21	1	17.40	15.30	6.82
21	D. J. S. Dottin (WI)	RFM	38	1	261	16	5-5	1	16.31	14.25	6.86
22	S. F. M. Devine (NZ)	RM	47	3	331	17	3-12	0	19.47	16.58	7.04
23	L. M. Kasperek (NZ)	OB	52	0	367	27	3-19	0	13.59	11.55	7.05
24	S. Ismail (SA)	RFM	47	3	348	20	5-30	1	17.40	14.10	7.40

WOMEN'S BIG BASH LEAGUE IN 2017-18

Adam Collins

1 Sydney Sixers   2 Perth Scorchers

"More to do, but heading in the right direction." An old NSW Labor Party slogan summed up the third Women's Big Bash League. It remained the marquee T20 competition for women, bolstered by its partnership with a free-to-air broadcaster happy to give it prominent slots. On the park, **Sydney Sixers** claimed back-to-back pennants; off it, the tournament ticked along. For all that, there was a sense that it needed to mature further.

Players cleared the ropes 206 times in 2017-18, compared with 111 two years before. Ash Gardner belted 21 sixes, ten in a devastating 52-ball 114 in the Sixers' first match. That was the high-water mark of a spectacular opening weekend, when six games netted 2,023 runs, including five of the six biggest WBBL totals to date. Better still, Gardner's century was in prime time on Saturday night, watched by 629,000 viewers. Along with Ellyse Perry, who clubbed 91 from 49, she helped the Sixers reach 242 for four against **Melbourne Stars**, the highest Big Bash total for either gender, beating the Hobart men's 223 for eight.

The gap between bat and ball soon narrowed – Sarah Aley and Katherine Brunt, with 23 wickets apiece, saw the Sixers and **Perth Scorchers** into the final – but that first weekend won't be forgotten, especially by the 9,000 fans at North Sydney Oval. All told, 151,931 spectators attended a WBBL game, 25% up on 2016-17.

TV audiences averaged 223,000 across a dozen games, and Cricket Australia reported 1.8m clicks on their website's live streams. Under a new deal in 2018-19, the number of broadcast matches jumped to 23, simulcast by both free and subscription networks.

With that comes a responsibility to iron out kinks. The most glaring is that the knockout venues are still dictated by which *men's* teams have qualified, to set up double-headers. This meant the two Sydney sides – who finished first and second – had to play away semis, with **Sydney Thunder** soundly beaten in a tired showing after flying across the continent to Perth.

In May, CA chief executive James Sutherland announced that the fifth competition would have its own window in October 2019. This is a welcome move, and it would be still better if the WBBL could be given similar status to the IPL to avoid clashes with international cricket, which removed South Africans Marizanne Kapp and Dane van Niekerk from the climax.

CA could also study the ECB's strategy for balancing teams. Sydney's dominance is predictable, given that New South Wales have won 19 of the 22 seasons of the Women's National Cricket League. In England's Kia Super League, the best local talent is distributed between squads. That **Hobart Hurricanes**, who boasted no Australian internationals, won just two of their 14 fixtures was no surprise.

The Sixers made up for the loss of Kapp and van Niekerk by drafting former Australia seamer Sarah Coyte back into the game. She had walked away a year earlier to treat an eating disorder, but returned at the end of January; eight days later, she won the match award in the final. Sixers captain Perry was the leading scorer, with 552, followed by Perth's Australian mainstays, Elyse Villani and Nicole Bolton. When reinforced by national captain Meg Lanning – who defected from the Stars, only to miss the season because of shoulder surgery – Perth should be as formidable as the Sydney teams.

For the first time **Adelaide Strikers**, led brilliantly by New Zealand's Suzie Bates and fielding the game's best swing bowler, Megan Schutt, reached the final four. But Gardner and Aley ensured they were outmuscled at home in the semi-final. **Brisbane Heat** and **Melbourne Renegades** both spent more time in the top four than the bottom half, before faltering late on. Brisbane were too reliant on Beth Mooney, the ICC's T20 international player of 2017, while the Renegades made an art form of losing the fixtures they needed to win.

WOMEN'S BIG BASH LEAGUE IN 2017-18

	P	W	L	Pts	NRR
SYDNEY SIXERS	14	10	4	20	0.89
SYDNEY THUNDER	14	10	4	20	0.68
PERTH SCORCHERS	14	8	6	16	0.26
ADELAIDE STRIKERS.	14	8	6	16	0.25
Brisbane Heat	14	7	7	14	0.14
Melbourne Renegades.	14	6	8	12	0.09
Melbourne Stars	14	5	9	10	−0.63
Hobart Hurricanes	14	2	12	4	−1.73

Semi-final   At Perth (Optus), February 1, 2018. **Perth Scorchers won by 27 runs. Perth Scorchers 148-2** (20 overs) (E. J. Villani 38, N. E. Bolton 37, N. R. Sciver 38*); ‡**Sydney Thunder 121-8** (20 overs) (F. C. Wilson 46; E. L. King 3-17). PoM: N. E. Bolton. *Granted a home semi in Perth's new headquarters because their male equivalents had topped the BBL table, the third-placed Scorchers ensured another final. Elyse Villani and Nicole Bolton had given them a solid start, followed up by Nat Sciver's 28-ball 38*, and their winning margin might have been greater. But with Sydney Thunder 46-5 in the 11th over, Fran Wilson hit 46 in 28 deliveries.*

Semi-final   At Adelaide, February 2, 2018. **Sydney Sixers won by 17 runs.** ‡**Sydney Sixers 138-5** (20 overs) (A. K. Gardner 72); **Adelaide Strikers 121-9** (20 overs) (T. T. Beaumont 50; S. E. Aley 4-18). PoM: S. E. Aley. *Megan Schutt and Sophie Devine kept the Sixers quiet for four overs – just 9-1 – before Ash Gardner hit the accelerator, passing 50 with her sixth six on the way to 72 in 45 balls. By contrast, Adelaide Strikers were 20-0 from three overs – then slumped to 23-6, with four ducks, as Sarah Aley took 4-1 in her first 12 deliveries, and Kim Garth 2-2 in six. Tammy Beaumont pushed the total towards three figures, but could not stop the Sixers reaching their third final in three tournaments.*

FINAL

PERTH SCORCHERS v SYDNEY SIXERS

At Adelaide, February 4, 2018. Sydney Sixers won by nine wickets. Toss: Perth Scorchers.

In a replay of the previous final, Sydney Sixers won again, but far more easily. The woman of the moment was Sarah Coyte, in only her fourth game of the tournament; she had retired from the Adelaide Strikers 12 months earlier to deal with anorexia, but was invited on board by Sixers coach Ben Sawyer after making a comeback in grade cricket. Coyte had Elyse Villani stumped off her third delivery, then – after three more wickets fell in three overs as Ellyse Perry juggled her attack – returned to claim another two, reducing the Scorchers to 66 for six. Perth were all out off the final ball, leaving the Sixers chasing only 100 to retain the trophy. Alyssa Healy and Perry knocked off 64 by the halfway mark; Ash Gardner arrived to smash her 21st six of the tournament, and Perry hit successive fours off Emma King to complete victory with five overs to spare.

Player of the Match: S. J. Coyte.

Player of the Tournament: A. E. Satterthwaite (Melbourne Renegades).

Perth Scorchers

		B	4/6
1 *E. J. Villani *st 1 b 10*	16	29	3
2 N. E. Bolton *lbw b 11*	5	13	0
3 N. R. Sciver *c 1 b 2*	2	4	0
4 M. P. Banting *c 9 b 4*	5	9	0
5 T. M. M. Newton *lbw b 10*.....	12	17	0
6 H. L. Graham *b 10*...........	14	16	0
7 K. H. Brunt *c 3 b 8*..........	10	13	0
8 L. K. Ebsary *c 1 b 4*	4	4	1
9 P. M. Cleary *not out*.........	18	14	2
10 E. L. King *run out (3/4)*	2	2	0
11 †E. J. Smith *run out (3/4)*.....	0	0	0
Lb 2, w 8, nb 1	11		

6 overs: 22-0   (20 overs)   99

1/23 2/26 3/29 4/41 5/61 6/66 7/71 8/90 9/94

Gardner 4–11–19–0; Perry 2–6–9–1; Aley 4–14–19–1; Garth 2–9–7–1; Coyte 4–13–17–3; Burns 4–7–26–2.

Sydney Sixers

		B	4/6
1 †A. J. Healy *st 11 b 10*	41	32	5/1
2 *E. A. Perry *not out*..........	36	42	5
3 A. K. Gardner *not out*	22	16	2/1
W 1.....................	1		

6 overs: 39-0   (15 overs)   100-1

1/64

4 E. A. Burns, 5 S. J. McGlashan, 6 A. E. Jones, 7 A. R. Reakes, 8 S. E. Aley, 9 L. G. Smith, 10 S. J. Coyte and 11 K. J. Garth did not bat.

Brunt 3–10–20–0; Bolton 2–5–20–0; Graham 4–13–17–0; Cleary 2–4–17–0; King 4–10–26–1.

Umpires: G. J. Davidson and J. D. Ward.   Third umpire: M. W. Graham-Smith.
Referee: D. J. Harper.

WOMEN'S BIG BASH FINALS

2015-16   SYDNEY THUNDER beat Sydney Sixers by three wickets at Melbourne.
2016-17   SYDNEY SIXERS beat Perth Scorchers by seven runs at Perth.
2017-18   SYDNEY SIXERS beat Perth Scorchers by nine wickets at Adelaide.

KIA SUPER LEAGUE IN 2018

S YD E GAN

1 Surrey Stars   2 Loughborough Lightning   3 Western Storm

In its third year, the Kia Super League appeared to be in rude health. An expanded format meant teams played each other home and away, doubling the number of matches in the group stages. But appearances were deceptive. When the ECB announced the launch of The Hundred in 2020, the KSL became collateral damage. The 2019 edition was scheduled to be the last.

On the positive side, eight teams will be created for a women's version of the 100-ball tournament, to run alongside the men's. Eight fixtures will be double headers. "To build the women's and the men's competitions' identities together, is a prospect that few sports ever have," said Clare Connor, the ECB's director of women's cricket. "It will attract more women and girls to the game." Connor has set out her ambition for a fully professional domestic structure for women's cricket by 2025, and pledged to deliver an "equally worthwhile" Twenty20 tournament, in addition to The Hundred. But details remained sketchy.

The 2018 KSL produced its third winner in three years: **Surrey Stars** got it right on finals day, after finishing third in the group stage. You would have got long odds on them after the opening day, when they were crushed by **Southern Vipers**; Tammy Beaumont, making her Vipers debut against her old team, hit an unbeaten 62 in a seven-wicket win. But they won only one more game, and finished bottom.

Loughborough Lightning were neck-and-neck with defending champions **Western Storm** through most of the group stages, but pulled ahead in the penultimate round with a nine-wicket win over the Storm, Rachael Haynes hitting 66 not out, and slow left-armer Kirstie Gordon claiming three for 19, which included Player of the Tournament Smriti Mandhana and England captain Heather Knight with successive balls.

With the Lightning qualifying directly for the final, and the Storm easing into their third successive play-off, the race for third came down to the final match. In a nailbiter at The Oval, the Stars beat the Storm with two balls to spare, and squeezed in front of **Lancashire Thunder**, who had their best season yet, with five wins. **Yorkshire Diamonds** finished fifth for the third year running.

Mandhana lived up to her star billing, hitting 421 runs at 60 and making a hundred in 61 balls against the Thunder at Old Trafford. The other century-maker was the Stars' overseas player Lizelle Lee, in the final. Gordon, in her first Super League season, was the leading bowler, with 17 wickets at 12. She was called up for England's World Twenty20 squad, and made her international debut less than six months after her first professional match. Others who made the step up were left-arm spinner Linsey Smith, who had taken 11 wickets for the Lightning, and Stars' all-rounder Sophia Dunkley – further proof of the Super League's role in developing talent for England.

KIA SUPER LEAGUE IN 2018

20-over league plus play-off and final

	P	W	L	NR	Bonus	Pts	NRR
LOUGHBOROUGH LIGHTNING	10	7	3	0	5	33	1.36
WESTERN STORM	10	6	3	1	4	30	0.91
SURREY STARS	10	5	4	1	2	24	–0.40
Lancashire Thunder	10	5	5	0	1	21	–0.82
Yorkshire Diamonds	10	3	6	1	1	15	–0.29
Southern Vipers	10	2	7	1	0	10	–0.49

Play-off At Hove, August 27. **Surrey Stars won by nine runs. Surrey Stars 162-5 (20 overs)** (N. R. Sciver 72*, M. Kapp 32*); ‡**Western Storm 153-6 (20 overs)** (H. C. Knight 34, F. C. Wilson 58*). PoM: N. R. Sciver. *A stellar all-round performance from captain Nat Sciver carried Surrey Stars into the final. She made 72*, and put on 90* in 9.5 overs with Marizanne Kapp, just when it looked as if the Stars were struggling to set a competitive targt. Sciver then took two wickets, and led an impressive performance in the field. In the absence of Smriti Mandhana, who had left for an Indian training camp, Heather Knight and Fran Wilson stepped up for the Storm, but Wilson's 58* was not quite enough.*

FINAL

LOUGHBOROUGH LIGHTNING v SURREY STARS

At Hove, August 27. Surrey Stars won by 66 runs. Toss: Loughborough Lightning.

Surrey Stars carried their play-off form triumphantly into the final to ensure Loughborough Lightning, the group winners, finished empty-handed. It was a victory built on a brutal 55-ball century from South African opener Lee, who hit six sixes and 13 fours, and made the most of being dropped on the boundary by Adams off Gordon on 37. Lee put on 111 for the third wicket with Sciver, who once again lifted the total to an intimidating level, with 40 off 31 balls. The Lightning were soon in trouble, and were down and out at 63 for six at the halfway stage. Leg-spinner van Niekerk took three key wickets, and 19-year-old off-spinner Mady Villiers disposed of the lower order.

Player of the Match: L. Lee. Player of the Tournament: S. S. Mandhana.

Surrey Stars

		B	4/6
1 L. Lee c l b 10	104	58	13/6
2 B. F. Smith run out (8)	2	8	0
3 †S. J. Taylor c l b 5	5	8	1
4 *N. R. Sciver c 6 b 11	40	31	6
5 D. van Niekerk not out	15	10	0/1
6 S. I. R. Dunkley c 6 b 7	2	3	0
7 M. Kapp c l b 5	1	2	0
8 L. A. Marsh not out	0	1	0
B 5, lb 2, w 6, nb 1	14		

6 overs: 44-2 (20 overs) **183-6**

1/16 2/44 3/155 4/164 5/169 6/178

9 A. Cranstone, 10 M. K. Villiers and 11 E. Gray did not bat.

Gunn 4–8–37–1; Devine 3–7–37–0; Smith 4–12–26–1; Elwiss 4–12–29–2; Gordon 3–6–30–1; Glenn 2–5–17–0.

Loughborough Lightning

		B	4/6
1 R. L. Haynes c l b 6	17	20	3
2 S. F. M. Devine lbw b 7	5	3	1
3 †A. E. Jones b 5	5	3	1
4 E. J. Villani b 7	2	6	0
5 *G. A. Elwiss c 4 b 5	18	16	2
6 G. L. Adams b 5	11	12	1
7 J. L. Gunn not out	23	21	2
8 L. F. Higham b 10	1	3	0
9 S. Glenn b 10	18	12	3
10 K. L. Gordon b 10	6	8	1
11 L. C. N. Smith st 3 b 8	3	8	0
Lb 1, w 6, nb 1	8		

6 overs: 36-3 (18.3 overs) **117**

1/13 2/18 3/26 4/40 5/63 6/63 7/66 8/90 9/104

Marsh 3.3–12–16–1; Kapp 3–12–14–2; van Niekerk 4–7–37–3; Dunkley 3–6–19–1; Sciver 1–1–8–0; Villiers 4–11–22–3.

Umpires: N. L. Bainton and S. Redfern. Third umpire: J. W. Lloyds.

ENGLISH DOMESTIC CRICKET IN 2018

After quarter of a century in which the women's County Championship was dominated by three teams – initially Yorkshire, then Sussex and Kent – the Royal London Women's One-Day Cup threw up first-time winners for the second season running.

Though **Hampshire** had never laid hands on the trophy, their captain knew it well: former England batsman Charlotte Edwards had won it seven times with Kent. She had led Hampshire to the Division Two title in 2017, and helped them lift the top prize a year later – the same path taken by the previous champions, Lancashire. Hampshire also fielded Suzie Bates of New Zealand, the tournament's leading run-scorer with 358 at 89, including two centuries. She picked up ten wickets, too, in support of off-spinner Fi Morris, who took 15, and 19-year-old England seamer Katie George, with 11.

They began the final round in June four points ahead of Yorkshire, with five wins apiece. Both completed a sixth victory, and Hampshire guaranteed the title by collecting a maximum 18 points against Middlesex – whose defeat relegated them, along with Somerset. **Sussex** won Division Two, to bounce straight back after their shock relegation in 2017, with Surrey also returning after two seasons.

Despite their disappointment in the 50-over competition, **Middlesex** secured the Vitality Twenty20 Cup, winning seven of their eight matches to keep ahead of Sussex and Kent. In the second division, Hampshire and Wales earned promotion on net run-rate, after finishing level on points with Scotland. **Lancashire** won the Under-17 County Cup final, dismissing Staffordshire for 80 – after rain revised their target to 90 – and **Yorkshire** the Under-15 Cup, beating Sussex by 103 runs.

In January 2019, news emerged that the ECB were discussing a radical reform of women's county cricket from 2020, which would establish a professional tier of up to ten teams playing 50- and 20-over cricket (ensuring the survival of a Twenty20 competition for top players once the Super League was replaced by The Hundred). There would be no promotion or relegation; counties in the lower tier would act as feeders to the top level.

In club cricket, there was a new tournament with a familiar champion, as the National Knockout Cup was replaced by the Vitality Women's Club T20 Cup, split into a Cup and a Plate competition (which picked up the Cup's first-round losers). The regional winners in both sections advanced to the national finals at Newport, where **Finchley Gunns** (who last won the longer-format knockout in 2016) swept aside semi-finalists Berkswell by ten wickets and finalists Hursley Park by 52 runs. Bridgwater won the Plate.

VITALITY WOMEN'S TWENTY20 CUP IN 2018

Division One: Middlesex 28pts, Sussex 24, Kent 20, Warwickshire 16, Nottinghamshire 16, Lancashire 16, Surrey 13, Yorkshire 8, Worcestershire 1.

Division Two: Hampshire 28, Wales 28, Scotland 28, Durham 20, Somerset 16, Cheshire 8, Berkshire 8, Northamptonshire 4, Gloucestershire 4.

Division Three: *Group A:* Devon 32, Oxfordshire 20, Cornwall 20, Dorset 16, Buckinghamshire 8, Wiltshire 0; *Group B:* Derbyshire 28, Staffordshire 24, Leicestershire 20, Shropshire 8, Northumberland 8, Cumbria 8; *Group C:* Essex 28, Lincolnshire 24, Hertfordshire 16, Norfolk 16, Suffolk 12, Cambridgeshire 0.

ROYAL LONDON WOMEN'S ONE-DAY CUP IN 2018

50-over league

Division One	P	W	L	T	A	Bonus pts Bat	Bonus pts Bowl	Pts	Avge pts
Hampshire........	7	6	1	0	0	23	26	109	15.57
Yorkshire........	7	6	1	0	0	22	24	106	15.14
Kent............	7	4	3	0	0	22	21	83	11.85
Lancashire.......	7	3	4	0	0	22	19	71	10.14
Warwickshire	7	1	3	2	1	18	19	57	9.50
Nottinghamshire ..	7	2	4	1	0	19	19	63	9.00
Middlesex	7	2	4	0	1	17	15	52	8.66
Somerset	7	1	5	1	0	9	22	46	6.57

Division Two	P	W	L	T	A	Bonus pts Bat	Bonus pts Bowl	Pts	Avge pts
SUSSEX	7	5	1	0	1	21	24	95	15.83
SURREY........	7	6	1	0	0	25	24	109	15.57
Wales..........	7	4	2	0	1	18	24	82	13.66
Devon	7	3	4	0	0	20	24	74	10.57
Berkshire.......	7	3	3	0	1	13	14	57	9.50
Essex	7	3	3	0	1	12	13	55	9.16
Derbyshire......	7	2	5	0	0	13	21	54	7.71
Northamptonshire .	7	0	7	0	0	12	20	32	4.57

Division Three

Group A DURHAM avge pts 15.33, Scotland 15.00, Cumbria 8.50, Northumberland 2.50.
Group B CORNWALL 15.50, Netherlands 15.33, Wiltshire 4.50, Dorset 4.50.
Group C OXFORDSHIRE 15.50, Gloucestershire 13.33, Buckinghamshire 10.66, Hertfordshire 3.66.
Group D SUFFOLK 15.33, Lincolnshire 12.00, Norfolk 7.50, Cambs & Hunts 4.50.
Group E WORCESTERSHIRE 15.40, Staffordshire 13.40, Leicestershire 11.20, Shropshire 3.60.
Play-offs Essex beat Suffolk by 293 runs and remained in Division Two; Durham beat Oxfordshire by 85 runs; Worcestershire beat Cornwall by 97 runs. Durham and Worcestershire were promoted to Division Two, replacing Derbyshire and Northamptonshire.

Win = 10pts; tie = 5pts. Up to four batting and four bowling points are available to each team in each match. Final points are divided by the number of matches played (excluding no-results and abandoned games) to calculate the average number of points.

DIVISION ONE AVERAGES

BATTING (170 runs)

	M	I	NO	R	HS	100	50	Avge	SR	Ct/St
T. T. Beaumont (*Kent*)...........	4	4	2	261	98	0	3	130.50	74.35	1
S. W. Bates (*Hants*)............	6	6	2	358	148	2	1	89.50	86.47	3
L. Winfield (*Yorks*).............	4	4	1	197	69	0	2	65.66	90.78	1/3
E. L. Lamb (*Lancs*).............	7	7	1	339	91	0	3	56.50	81.68	1
A. N. Davidson-Richards (*Kent*) ..	7	7	2	223	61*	0	2	44.60	57.77	4
A. E. Jones (*Warwicks*)	5	5	0	193	68	0	1	38.60	99.48	3/4
L. M. Kasperek (*Yorks*)	7	5	0	179	68	0	2	35.80	69.64	0
M. E. Bouchier (*Middx*)	6	6	1	172	76	0	1	34.40	75.43	0
†E. Jones (*Lancs*)	7	7	1	193	61*	0	1	32.16	55.78	4
S. B. Odedra (*Notts*)	7	7	0	196	88	0	2	28.00	48.75	2

BOWLING (11 wickets)

	Style	O	M	R	W	BB	4I	Avge	SR	ER
K. C. Thompson (*Yorks*)	SLW	43	16	73	11	5-14	0	6.63	23.45	1.69
K. L. Gordon (*Notts*)	SLA	68.2	11	180	23	5-18	2	7.82	17.82	2.63
L. M. Kasperek (*Yorks*)	OB	65.1	10	176	15	3-13	0	11.73	26.06	2.70
F. M. K. Morris (*Hants*)	OB	59.4	10	179	15	4-12	1	11.93	23.86	3.00
K. L. George (*Hants*).......	LM	57.3	11	150	11	4-13	1	13.63	31.36	2.60
L. A. Marsh (*Kent*)	RFM/OB	46	2	157	11	3-18	0	14.27	25.09	3.41
N. Richards (*Somerset*)	LB	48.2	5	173	11	3-21	0	15.72	26.36	3.57
M. S. Belt (*Kent*)..........	OB	54.2	5	184	11	3-15	0	16.72	29.63	3.38
L. E. Szczepanski (*Somerset*)	LB	55.4	2	193	11	3-25	0	17.54	30.36	3.46

VITALITY WOMEN'S CLUB T20 FINALS IN 2018

Cup final   At Newport, June 24. **Finchley Gunns won by 52 runs.** ‡**Finchley Gunns 144-5** (20 overs) (C. C. Dalton 75); **Hursley Park 92-8** (20 overs) (C. D. Lowman 32; R. Tyson 3-12). *Former Ireland international Cat Dalton followed up 70* in the semi-final against Berkswell with 75, sharing an opening stand of 81 with her captain, Kylie White, one of three Finchley players who were run out. Chasing 145, Hursley Park struggled; only two reached double figures, though they did bat out their 20 overs.*

Plate final   At Newport, June 24. **Bridgwater won by 86 runs. Bridgwater 185-4** (20 overs) (B. Forge 114*, Extras 31); ‡**Cottingham 99** (19.3 overs) (L. Connelley 39; T. Bond 3-10, J. Poole 3-2). *Bridgwater opener Bernadette Forge smashed 114* from 68 balls, and it mattered little that only two of her partners got past four. Tilly Bond and Jennifer Poole reduced Cottingham to 17-3 and, with one woman retiring hurt, they barely got halfway to the target.*

THE UNIVERSITY MATCHES IN 2018

At Oxford, May 18. **Oxford University won by 106 runs. Oxford University 187-1** (20 overs) (V. M. Picker 74*, I. N. Brown 50, S. Kelly 41*); ‡**Cambridge University 81-5** (20 overs) (F. R. Barber 31). *Vanessa Picker and Imogen Brown opened with 103 in 12.3 overs for Oxford, before Sian Kelly plundered 41* off 20 balls. Cambridge managed less than half the required scoring-rate, as three of the home bowlers conceded only 12 off their four overs.*

At Lord's (Nursery), June 22. **Oxford University won by 188 runs.** ‡**Oxford University 283** (48.1 overs) (V. M. Picker 37, S. Kelly 55, S. E. G. Taylor 57, Extras 33; C. N. Allison 3-40); **Cambridge University 95** (33 overs) (I. N. Brown 6-18). *Oxford completed a Varsity double with another massive victory. Fifties from Kelly and Sophie Taylor left a challenging target of 284, and again Cambridge could not reach even 100. Their openers put on 41 before all ten fell for 54; Brown grabbed 6-18 in her ten overs, while Helen Baxendale and Surabhi Shukla conceded ten runs in six overs between them.*

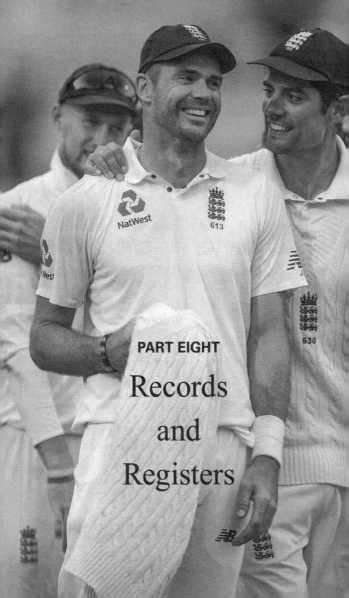

PART EIGHT

Records
and
Registers

FEATURES OF 2018

This section now covers the calendar year. Some of the features listed occurred in series and seasons reported in *Wisden 2018*, and some in series and seasons that will be reported in *Wisden 2020*; these items are indicated by [W18] or [W20].

Double-Hundreds (60)

	Mins	Balls	4	6		
343		332	53	1	P. Bisht	Meghalaya v Sikkim at Bhubaneswar.[W20]
286	610	431	34	1	Wasim Jaffer	Vidarbha v Rest of India at Nagpur.
274	496	293	35	2	‡Liton Das	East Zone v Central Zone at Rajshahi.
268	513	328	29	4	S. Gill	Punjab v Tamil Nadu at Mohali.[W20]
267*		345	21	5	A. R. Rohera	Madhya Pradesh v Hyderabad at Indore.[W20]
265	643	464	30	1	Shehzar Mohammad . .	Karachi Whites v Multan at Multan.[W20]
264*	694	489	21	1	T. W. M. Latham	NZ v Sri Lanka (1st Test) at Wellington.
261		331	39	3	‡Milind Kumar	Sikkim v Manipur at Kolkata.[W20]
258	484	344	23	3	Mominul Haque.	East Zone v South Zone at Savar.
253		244	30	7	P. Dogra.	Puducherry v Sikkim at Wayanad.[W20]
250*	594	403	22	1	A. L. Davies	Victoria v NSW at Melbourne.[W20]
250*	580	364	26	2	R. van Tonder	Free State v Gauteng at Bloemfontein.[W20]
250		480	22	3	P. Akshath Reddy . . .	Hyderabad v Tamil Nadu at Tirunelveli.[W20]
249	386	271	29	6	‡Darwish Rasooli	Amo v Speen Ghar at Ghazi Am Kh Town.
243	430	311	30	0	W. J. Pucovski	Victoria v Western Australia at Perth.[W20]
235*	533	363	27	4	D. J. Vilas	Lancashire v Somerset at Manchester.
231*		392	17	0	A. R. S. Silva	Galle Dist v Colombo Dist at Hambantota.
231	472	325	21	4	Ariful Haque	Rangpur v Barisal at Bogra.
228*	379	252	18	7	Rony Talukdar	Dhaka v Chittagong at Fatullah.[W20]
228	431	287	27	0	S. van Zyl	Cape Cobras v Lions at Paarl.
228		269	25	10	M. Raghav	Manipur v Nagaland at Dimapur.[W20]
226	621	461	26	0	G. R. Hay.	Central Districts v Otago at Alexandra.[W20]
224*	415	276	29	0	G. Roelofsen	KZN Inland v Namibia at Pietermaritzburg.
224		336	29	3	K. H. Devdhar	Baroda v Saurashtra at Rajkot.[W20]
224		215	31	3	‡Milind Kumar	Sikkim v Nagaland at Dimapur.[W20]
222		266	30	3	Indrajit Kumar	Bihar v Arunachal Pradesh at Patna.[W20]
221*	441	349	19	1	Asad Shafiq	Sui N Gas v Islamabad at Islamabad.[W20]
220	372	251	31	4	M. A. Agarwal.	India A v South Africa A at Bangalore.[W20]
220		381	14	6	S. A. S. Rawat	Uttarakhand v Sikkim at Bhubaneswar.[W20]
219*		421	18	1	Mushfiqur Rahim. . . .	Bangladesh v Zim (2nd Test) at Mirpur.
219	380	277	27	4	M. M. Ali	Worcestershire v Yorkshire at Scarborough.
214*	384	290	26	2	C. D. J. Dent	Gloucestershire v Leicestershire at Bristol.
213	493	327	26	2	Mohammad Hafeez . .	Sui N Gas v Peshawar at Faisalabad.[W20]
212*		340	24	2	R. Bhatia	Uttarakhand v Meghalaya at Dehradun.[W20]
211*	426	345	22	0	Adil Amin	Sui Southern Gas v ZTBL at Islamabad.[W20]
211	444	320	23	0	Zakir Hasan	East Zone v Central Zone at Khulna.
210	538	414	22	0	K. J. McClure	Canterbury v Auckland at Rangiora.
210	346	302	30	1	Munir Ahmad	Boost v Speen Ghar at Khost.
210		313	26	1	J. K. Silva	Sinhalese v Negombo at Colombo.[W20]
209	294	222	26	2	G. J. Snyman	N Cape v Free State at Bloemfontein.
208*		308	19	0	K. Joshi	Uttarakhand v Arunachal P at Goalpara.[W20]
207	564	442	25	2	W. T. S. Porterfield . .	North West v Leinster at Bready.
206*		247	26	0	P. Nissanka	Nondescripts v Army at Colombo.[W20]
206*		481	19	2	P. A. R. P. Perera	Colts v Badureliya at Colombo.[W20]
206		371	23	1	P. K. Garg	Uttar Pradesh v Tripura at Lucknow.[W20]
205	376	246	22	8	Abdul Mazid	Central Zone v East Zone at Rajshahi.
204	455	331	24	2	I. R. Bell	Warwickshire v Glamorgan at Colwyn Bay.
203*	531	389	26	2	D. P. Conway	Wellington v Otago at Wellington.[W20]
203	220	142	32	4	‡Liton Das	Rangpur v Rajshahi at Rajshahi.[W20]
202*		506	16	1	V. A. Saxena	Uttarakhand v Meghalaya at Dehradun.[W20]

	Mins	Balls	4	6		
202	382	302	24	0	M. A. Naylor	Oxford Univ v Cambridge Univ at Oxford.
201*	514	437	28	0	J. M. Vince	Hampshire v Somerset at Taunton.
201*		279	20	4	M. K. Tiwary	Bengal v Madhya Pradesh at Kolkata.[W20]
201		369	22	2	B. B. Ghosh	Tripura v Services at Agartala.[W20]
200*	275	182	20	6	‡Darwish Rasooli	Amo v Boost at Ghazi Am Khan Town.
200*		364	26	1	J. M. D. B. M. P. Jayamanna	Negombo v Kurunegala Youth at Kurunegala.
200*	103	89	11	22	Shafiqullah Shinwari .	Kabul v Boost at Asadabad.
200*		215	22	1	A. A. Kazi	Nagaland v Mizoram at Dimapur.[W20]
200		302	28	1	M. M. M. S. Cooray .	Colts v Moors at Colombo.
200	292	223	23	4	Imran Janat	Kabul v Band-e-Amir at Asadabad.

‡   *Liton Das, Milind Kumar and Darwish Rasooli each scored two double-hundreds.*

Hundred on First-Class Debut

154	Darwish Rasooli	Amo v Band-e-Amir at Asadabad.
104	F. D. de Beer	Boland v KwaZulu-Natal Inland at Paarl.
117*	P. K. Garg	Uttar Pradesh v Goa at Kanpur.[W20]
103	C. R. Gnaneshwar	Andhra v Himachal Pradesh at Amtar.[W20]
177	M. U. Mahrour	Bihar v Nagaland at Patna.[W20]
158	N. Mupamba	Manicaland Mountaineers v Rising Stars at Harare.
138	Nabi Gul	Peshawar v Islamabad at Islamabad.[W20]
135	Omair Bin Yousuf	Karachi Whites v ZTBL at Karachi.[W20]
228	M. Raghav	Manipur v Nagaland at Dimapur.[W20]
104	J. M. Richards	Gauteng v KwaZulu-Natal Inland at Johannesburg.[W20]
138	Rohail Nazir	Islamabad v Habib Bank at Islamabad.[W20]
267*	A. R. Rohera	Madhya Pradesh v Hyderabad at Indore.[W20]
138	D. Rohit.	Puducherry v Meghalaya at Puducherry.[W20]
110	Sanvir Singh	Punjab v Andhra at Visakhapatnam.[W20]
103	B. R. Sharath	Karnataka v Vidarbha at Nagpur.[W20]

Three or More Hundreds in Successive Innings

R. Bhatia (Uttarakhand)	121	v Sikkim at Bhubaneswar.[W20]	
	152*	v Arunachal Pradesh at Goalpara.[W20]	
	212*	v Meghalaya at Dehradun.[W20]	
Milind Kumar (Sikkim)	261	v Manipur at Kolkata.[W20]	
	224	v Nagaland at Dimapur.[W20]	
	133	v Uttarakhand at Bhubaneswar.[W20]	
Tushar Imran (South Zone).	148	v North Zone at Rajshahi.	
	130 and 103*	v East Zone at Sylhet.	

Hundred in Each Innings of a Match

I. R. Bell	106*	115*	Warwickshire v Glamorgan at Birmingham.
Junaid Siddique.	137	150	North Zone v South Zone at Rajshahi.
B. K. E. L. Milantha	112	150*	Ragama v Moors at Colombo.
Milind Kumar	117	127*	Sikkim v Meghalaya at Bhubaneswar.[W20]
D. K. H. Mitchell	118	163	Worcestershire v Lancashire at Worcester.
Mohammad Hasan	125	100*	Karachi Whites v Sui Southern Gas at Karachi.[W20]
Mominul Haque	176	105	Bangladesh v Sri Lanka (1st Test) at Chittagong.
K. H. Pandya	160	104	Baroda v Railways at Delhi.[W20]
J. M. Richards	132	118	Gauteng v Northern Cape at Kimberley.[W20]
Sami Aslam	100	100*	Sui Southern Gas v Rawalpindi at Rawalpindi.[W20]
Shan Masood.	167	100	Pakistan A v New Zealand A at Dubai.[W20]
B. R. M. Taylor	110	106*	Zimbabwe v Bangladesh (2nd Test) at Mirpur.

Tushar Imran	130	103*	South Zone v East Zone at Sylhet.
Tushar Imran	104	159	Khulna v Rajshahi at Rajshahi.[W20]
A. A. Waghmode	103	102*	Baroda v Vidarbha at Nagpur.[W20]
Zahidullah	118	106	Speen Ghar v Amo at Ghazi Amanullah Khan Town.

Carrying Bat through Completed Innings

J. J. F. Dreyer	97*	Free State (183) v KwaZulu-Natal Inland at Pietermaritzburg.[W20]
D. Elgar	86*	South Africa (177) v India (3rd Test) at Johannesburg.
D. Elgar	141*	South Africa (311) v Australia (3rd Test) at Cape Town.
B. A. Godleman	105*	Derbyshire (210) v Middlesex at Lord's.
F. D. M. Karunaratne	158*	Sri Lanka (287) v South Africa (1st Test) at Galle.
T. W. M. Latham	264*	New Zealand (578) v Sri Lanka (1st Test) at Wellington.
T. G. Mokoena	154*	Knights (363) v Titans at Bloemfontein.
E. M. Moore	116*	Warriors (307) v Titans at Centurion.[W20]
J. R. Murphy	39*	Glamorgan (94) v Kent at Cardiff.
Omair Bin Yousuf	92*	Karachi Whites (158) v Sui Southern Gas at Karachi.[W20]
W. A. A. M. Silva	168*	Chilaw Marians (427) v Ports Authority at Colombo.

Hundred before Lunch

S. Dhawan	104*	India v Afghanistan (Only Test) at Bangalore on day 1.
Rahmatullah Sahaq	103*	Mis Ainak v Amo at Ghazi Amanullah Khan on day 3.
M. T. Renshaw	111*	Somerset v Yorkshire at Taunton on day 2 (no play on day 1).
A. B. L. D. Rodrigo	106*	Lankan v Kalutara Town at Maggona on day 1.
D. Wiese	103*	Sussex v Warwickshire at Birmingham on day 4.

Fast Double-Hundreds

| Shafiqullah Shinwari | 89 balls† | Kabul v Boost at Asadabad. |
| Liton Das | 140 balls | Rangpur v Rajshahi at Rajshahi.[W20] |

† *World record.*

Most Sixes in an Innings

22	Shafiqullah Shinwari (200*)	Kabul v Boost at Asadabad.
12	Hazratullah Zazai (121)	Band-e-Amir v Amo at Asadabad.
12	V. J. Kushwah (159)	Chhattisgarh v Gujarat at Valsad.[W20]
11	S. S. Iyer (178)	Mumbai v Baroda at Mumbai.[W20]
10	R. Jonathan (131)	Nagaland v Arunachal Pradesh at Dimapur.[W20]
10	S. Prasanna (89)	Army v Ports Authority at Panagoda.[W20]
10	M. Raghav (228)	Manipur v Nagaland at Dimapur.[W20]
9	Alok Kapali (165*)	East Zone v Central Zone at Khulna.
9	S. O. Hetmyer (93)	West Indies v Bangladesh (2nd Test) at Mirpur.
9	Karim Janat (102*)	Kabul v Boost at Asadabad.
9	H. J. Kotze (153*)	South Western Districts v Border at Oudtshoorn.
9	Muslim Musa (166)	Band-e-Amir v Kabul at Asadabad.

Most Runs in Boundaries

	4	6		
218	53	1	P. Bisht (343)	Meghalaya v Sikkim at Bhubaneswar.[W20]

Most Runs off an Over

| 30 | S. R. Dubey (666660) off Swapnil Singh | Mumbai v Baroda at Mumbai.[W20] |

Longest Innings

Mins
694	T. W. M. Latham (264*)	New Zealand v Sri Lanka (1st Test) at Wellington.
685	P. J. Malan (180)	Cape Cobras v Titans at Paarl.
643	Shehzar Mohammad (265).	Karachi Whites v Multan at Multan.[W20]
640	Usman Salahuddin (153*)	Lahore Whites v Sui Northern Gas at Lahore.[W20]
621	G. R. Hay (226)	Central Districts v Otago at Alexandra.[W20]
610	Wasim Jaffer (286).	Vidarbha v Rest of India at Nagpur.

Unusual Dismissals

Obstructing the Field
R. P. Burl (134) . . . . Rising Stars v Harare Metropolitan Eagles at Harare.

First-Wicket Partnership of 100 in Each Innings

121	140	B. M. Chapungu/T. P. Maruma, Midlands Rhinos v Manicaland Mountaineers at Mutare.
124	130	J. N. Malan/P. J. Malan, Cape Cobras v Warriors at Port Elizabeth. [W20]

Highest Wicket Partnerships

First Wicket
350	Abdul Mazid/Rony Talukdar, Dhaka v Chittagong at Fatullah.[W20]
311	Nazmul Hossain/Mizanur Rahman, Rajshahi v Rangpur at Rajshahi.[W20]
304	Khurram Manzoor/Omair Bin Yousuf, Karachi Whites v ZTBL at Karachi.[W20]
278	D. R. Flynn/H. R. Cooper, Northern Districts v Canterbury at Whangarei.
277	P. P. Shaw/M. A. Agarwal, India A v South Africa A at Bangalore.[W20]
274	F. D. M. Karunaratne/J. K. Silva, Sinhalese v Moors at Colombo.
273	L. U. Igalagamage/P. B. B. Rajapaksa, Nondescripts v Colts at Galle.

Second Wicket
332	Omair Bin Yousuf/Shehzar Mohammad, Karachi Whites v Multan at Multan.[W20]
325	A. P. Agathangelou/N. Brand, Northerns v Northern Cape at Pretoria.[W20]
323*	T. Theophile/D. S. Smith, Windward Islands v Leeward Islands at Basseterre.
308	B. K. G. Mendis/D. M. de Silva, Sri Lanka v Bangladesh (1st Test) at Chittagong.
308	Rizwan Ali/Ali Sarfraz, Islamabad v FATA at Islamabad.[W20]
300	F. Y. Fazal/Wasim Jaffer, Vidarbha v Baroda at Nagpur.[W20]

Third Wicket
433	R. R. Biswa/P. Bisht, Meghalaya v Sikkim at Bhubaneswar.[W20]
338*	Farhan Zakhil/Darwish Rasooli, Amo v Boost at Ghazi Amanullah Khan Town.
289	Wasim Jaffer/G. Satish, Vidarbha v Rest of India at Nagpur.
287	S. C. Cook/H. E. van der Dussen, Lions v Cape Cobras at Paarl.
283	S. D. Lad/S. S. Iyer, Mumbai v Baroda at Mumbai.[W20]
259	A. N. Cook/J. E. Root, England v India (5th Test) at The Oval.

Fourth Wicket
350	W. J. Lubbe/H. E. van der Dussen, Lions v Titans at Potchefstroom.[W20]
308	N. J. O'Brien/S. R. Thompson, North West v Leinster at Dublin.
298	Liton Das/Afif Hossain, East Zone v Central Zone at Rajshahi.
289	U. T. Khawaja/K. S. Carlson, Glamorgan v Derbyshire at Swansea.
274*	B. K. G. Mendis/A. D. Mathews, Sri Lanka v New Zealand (1st Test) at Wellington.
272	F. Y. Fazal/A. V. Wadkar, Vidarbha v Chhattisgarh at Naya Raipur.[W20]

Fifth Wicket
399*	V. A. Saxena/R. Bhatia, Uttarakhand v Meghalaya at Dehradun.[W20]
294	R. S. Bopara/R. N. ten Doeschate, Essex v Somerset at Chelmsford.
284*	A. R. Rohera/Y. Dubey, Madhya Pradesh v Hyderabad at Indore.[W20]

267   D. A. Escott/M. A. Naylor, Oxford University v Cambridge University at Oxford.
265   Muslim Musa/Asif Musazai, Band-e-Amir v Kabul at Asadabad.

Sixth Wicket
278   M. J. Richardson/S. W. Poynter, Durham v Derbyshire at Derby.
273   Kamran Ghulam/Hammad Azam, National Bank v Islamabad at Islamabad.[W20]
247   L. J. Woodcock/M. J. Nofal, Wellington v Central Districts at Wellington.
233   Mominul Haque/Zakir Hasan, East Zone v South Zone at Savar.
231   M. S. Warnapura/S. S. Pathirana, Colombo v Bloomfield at Colombo.
231   S. A. S. Rawat/V. Bhatt, Uttarakhand v Sikkim at Bhubaneswar.[W20]

Seventh Wicket
216   G. H. Vihari/J. Yadav, Rest of India v Vidarbha at Nagpur.
199   S. Baby/V. Vinod, Kerala v Madhya Pradesh at Thumba.[W20]
188   J. N. Shah/D. A. Jadeja, Saurashtra v Baroda at Rajkot.
171   I. R. Jaggi/S. Nadeem, Jharkhand v Uttar Pradesh at Lucknow.[W20]
161   R. A. Reifer/S. E. Rutherford, Guyana v Trinidad & Tobago at Providence.

Eighth Wicket
177   V. J. Kushwah/Shivendra Singh, Chhattisgarh v Gujarat at Valsad.[W20]
172   S. R. Hain/D. M. Bess, MCC v Essex at Bridgetown.
171   R. A. Jadeja/K. R. Makwana, Saurashtra v Railways at Rajkot.[W20]
167   R. S. S. S. de Zoysa/H. I. A. Jayaratne, Ragama v Nondescripts at Colombo.[W20]

Ninth Wicket
171   G. S. Ballance/J. A. Brooks, Yorkshire v Worcestershire at Worcester.
161   S. O. Dowrich/J. A. Warrican, West Indies A v England Lions at Greenfields.

Tenth Wicket
152   Rahmanullah/Nawaz Khan, Mis Ainak v Kabul at Asadabad.
136   A. G. Milton/S. J. Magoffin, Worcestershire v Somerset at Worcester.
124   Abdul Mazid/Shahidul Islam, Central Zone v South Zone at Sylhet.[W20]
123   G. R. J. Kennedy/D. Scanlon, North West v Northern at Comber.
121   R. T. M. Wanigamuni/C. A. K. Rajitha, Bloomfield v Tamil Union at Colombo.
120   Ibrahim Zadran/Nijat Masood, Band-e-Amir v Kabul at Asadabad.
104   Ikram Ali Khil/Qais Ahmad, Speen Ghar v Mis Ainak at Asadabad.
103*   H. L. P. Maduwantha/E. M. C. D. Edirisinghe, Saracens v Badureliya at Maggona.[W20]
103   H. D. R. L. Thirimanne/S. I. Fernando, Ragama v Colombo at Colombo.
100*   P. A. R. P. Perera/R. S. Tillakaratne, Colts v Badureliya at Colombo.[W20]
100   G. Stewart/I. A. A. Thomas, Kent v Middlesex at Canterbury.

Most Wickets in an Innings

9-53   B. M. A. J. Mendis . . . .   Tamil Union v Ports Authority at Colombo.[W20]
9-108   K. D. V. Wimalasekara. . . .   Army v Nondescripts at Panagoda.
9-129   K. A. Maharaj. . . . .   South Africa v Sri Lanka (2nd Test) at Colombo.
8-34   J. A. Warrican. . . . .   West Indies A v England Lions at Kingston.
8-41   Yasir Shah. . . . .   Pakistan v New Zealand (2nd Test) at Dubai.
8-41   Tabish Khan. . . . .   Pakistan Television v Lahore Blues at Faisalabad.[W20]
8-45   J. S. Saxena. . . . .   Kerala v Andhra at Thumba.[W20]
8-47   Nayeem Hasan . . . .   East Zone v Central Zone at Sylhet.[W20]
8-47   J. A. Richardson. . . . .   Western Australia v New South Wales at Perth.[W20]
8-51   C. Rushworth . . . .   Durham v Sussex at Chester-le-Street.
8-51   A. Aman . . . .   Bihar v Meghalaya at Shillong.[W20]
8-57   B. A. Hutton . . . .   Northamptonshire v Gloucestershire at Northampton.
8-59   M. Siraj. . . . .   India A v Australia A at Bangalore.[W20]
8-61   W. R. C. Fernando . . . .   Negombo v Panadura at Panadura.
8-62   S. T. Gabriel . . . .   West Indies v Sri Lanka (2nd Test) at Gros Islet.
8-70   Abdur Rehman . . . .   Habib Bank v Karachi Whites at Karachi.[W20]
8-70   Ali Shafiq . . . .   KRL v FATA at Abbottabad.[W20]

8-76   Abdul Baqi . . . .   Boost v Amo at Ghazi Amanullah Khan Town.
8-77   S. N. J. O'Keefe . . . .   New South Wales v Victoria at Melbourne.
8-80   H. G. S. Dakshina . . . .   Navy v Galle at Dambulla.
8-80   O. P. Stone . . . .   Warwickshire v Sussex at Birmingham.
8-85   M. J. Leach . . . .   Somerset v Essex at Taunton.
8-85   Parvez Rasool . . . .   Jammu & Kashmir v Services at Delhi.[W20]
8-89   J. A. Warrican . . . .   Barbados v Jamaica at Cave Hill.[W20]
8-94   T. S. Chisoro . . . .   Midlands Rhinos v Manicaland Mountaineers at Mutare.
8-103   N. M. Lyon . . . .   Australians v Pakistan A at Dubai.[W20]
8-106   Nayeem Hasan . . . .   Chittagong v Dhaka at Cox's Bazar.[W20]
8-130   D. L. Piedt. . . . .   Cape Cobras v Warriors at Port Elizabeth.[W20]
8-148   M. A. Aponso . . . .   Ragama v Chilaw Marians at Katunayake.[W20]
8-148   S. A. Desai . . . .   Gujarat v Vidarbha at Nagpur.[W20]
8-184   G. P. D. S. Pathirana . . . . . .   Moors v Colts at Colombo.

Most Wickets in a Match

14-65   Saurabh Kumar . . . .   Uttar Pradesh v Haryana at Lahli.[W20]
14-68   A. Aman. . . . .   Bihar v Meghalaya at Shillong.[W20]
14-119   Abdul Baqi . . . .   Boost v Amo at Ghazi Amanullah Khan Town.
14-120   Abdur Rehman . . . .   Habib Bank v Karachi Whites at Karachi.[W20]
14-125   K. T. H. Ratnayake . . . . . .   Sinhalese v Colombo at Colombo.[W20]
14-184   Yasir Shah . . . .   Pakistan v New Zealand (2nd Test) at Dubai.
13-121   S. T. Gabriel. . . . .   West Indies v Sri Lanka (2nd Test) at Gros Islet.
13-175   T. S. Chisoro . . . .   Midlands Rhinos v Manicaland Mountaineers at Mutare.
13-234   M. A. Aponso . . . .   Ragama v Chilaw Marians at Katunayake.[W20]
12-54   Aavesh Khan . . . .   Madhya Pradesh v Hyderabad at Indore.[W20]
12-62   I. S. Sodhi. . . . .   Northern Districts v Wellington at Wellington.
12-71   V. Mishra . . . .   Delhi v Madhya Pradesh at Delhi.[W20]
12-73   M. J. Henry . . . .   Kent v Durham at Chester-le-Street.
12-94   Mohammad Abbas . . . .   Sui Northern Gas v WAPDA at Karachi.[W20]
12-96   D. Dhapola . . . .   Uttarakhand v Manipur at Dehradun.[W20]
12-96   A. Aman. . . . .   Bihar v Nagaland at Patna.[W20]
12-100   C. Rushworth . . . .   Durham v Sussex at Chester-le-Street.
12-102   M. J. Leach. . . . .   Somerset v Lancashire at Taunton.
12-103   J. A. Warrican . . . .   West Indies A v England Lions at Kingston.
12-114   Nauman Ali . . . .   KRL v Peshawar at Rawalpindi.[W20]
12-116   J. A. Warrican . . . .   Barbados v Jamaica at Cave Hill.[W20]
12-117   Mehedi Hasan . . . .   Bangladesh v West Indies (2nd Test) at Mirpur.
12-120   Ali Shafiq . . . .   KRL v FATA at Abbottabad.[W20]
12-126   A. C. Mishra. . . . .   Railways v Baroda at Delhi.[W20]
12-144   Abdur Razzak. . . . .   South Zone v North Zone at Chittagong.[W20]
12-147   S. Shillingford . . . .   Windward Islands v Trinidad & Tobago at Tarouba.[W20]
12-148   S. R. Harmer . . . .   Warriors v Dolphins at Port Elizabeth.
12-157   D. K. Jacobs. . . . .   Jamaica v Leeward Islands at Kingston.
12-159   B. M. A. J. Mendis. . . . . . .   Tamil Union v Ports Authority at Colombo.[W20]
12-283   K. A. Maharaj . . . .   South Africa v Sri Lanka (2nd Test) at Colombo.

Outstanding Innings Analyses

3.5–2–5–6   R. S. Patel . . . .   Surrey v Somerset at Guildford.
2.3–2–0–4   W. S. Rangika . . . .   Air Force v Panadura at Panadura.

Four Wickets in Four Balls

Mohammad Mudhasir . . . .   Jammu & Kashmir v Rajasthan at Jaipur.[W20]

Hat-Tricks (16)

K. J. Abbott	Hampshire v Worcestershire at Worcester.
Abdur Rehman	Habib Bank v Karachi Whites at Karachi.[W20]
T. B. Abell	Somerset v Nottinghamshire at Nottingham.
Aizaz Cheema	Lahore Blues v Pakistan Television at Faisalabad.[W20]
J. Clark	Lancashire v Yorkshire at Manchester.
Delwar Hossain	Rajshahi v Rangpur at Rangpur.[W20]
P. C. de Silva	Nondescripts v Moors at Colombo (Moors).[W20]
D. Dhapola	Uttarakhand v Meghalaya at Dehradun.[W20]
Enamul Haque	Sylhet v Dhaka at Khulna.[W20]
R. J. Gleeson	MCC v Essex at Bridgetown.
M. B. McEwan	Auckland v Northern Districts at Auckland.
Mohammad Mudhasir	Jammu & Kashmir v Rajasthan at Jaipur.[W20]
M. Mohammed	Tamil Nadu v Madhya Pradesh at Dindigul.[W20]
Monir Hossain	Barisal v Rajshahi at Rajshahi.[W20]
C. Overton	Somerset v Nottinghamshire at Nottingham.
T. A. Rahman	Nagaland v Manipur at Dimapur.[W20]

Wicket with First Ball in First-Class Career

P. A. D. Lakshan	Colts v Colombo at Colombo (Colts).[W20]

Match Double (100 runs and 10 wickets)

A. Aman	89, 17*; 5-19, 5-22	Bihar v Sikkim at Patna.[W20]
B. M. A. J. Mendis	106; 9-53, 3-106	Tamil U v Ports Authority at Colombo.[W20]
Parvez Rasool	11, 115; 8-85, 2-18	Jammu & Kashmir v Services at Delhi.[W20]

Most Wicketkeeping Dismissals in an Innings

8 (7ct, 1st)	M. A. R. S. Fernando	Chilaw Marians v Colts at Colombo.
7 (7ct)	C. D. Bist	Rajasthan v Jharkhand at Ranchi.[W20]
7 (7ct)	M. Malika	Border v North West at East London.[W20]
6 (7ct, 1st)	Umair Masood	Rawalpindi v Karachi Whites at Karachi.[W20]
6 (6ct)	T. R. Ambrose	Warwickshire v Sussex at Birmingham.
6 (6ct)	B. C. Brown	Sussex v Gloucestershire at Cheltenham.
6 (6ct)	T. Chiecktey	Western Province v Northern Cape at Kimberley.
6 (6ct)	Dhiman Ghosh	North Zone v Central Zone at Sylhet.
6 (6ct)	B. J. Horne	Auckland v Central Districts at Auckland.[W20]
6 (6ct)	J. P. Inglis	Western Australia v South Australia at Adelaide.[W20]
6 (6ct)	Jamal Anwar	Habib Bank v National Bank at Faisalabad.[W20]
6 (6ct)	Mahidul Islam	East Zone v Central Zone at Bogra.[W20]
6 (6ct)	Maqbool Ahmed	Sui Southern Gas v ZTBL at Islamabad.[W20]
6 (6ct)	R. R. Pant	India v Australia (1st Test) at Adelaide.
6 (6ct)	J. J. Peirson	Queensland v Tasmania at Hobart.[W20]
6 (6ct)	A. Rawat	Delhi v Bengal at Kolkata.[W20]
6 (5ct, 1st)	A. P. Tare	Mumbai v Saurashtra at Mumbai.[W20]
6 (5ct, 1st)	D. J. Vilas	Lancashire v Yorkshire at Manchester.

Most Wicketkeeping Dismissals in a Match

11 (11ct)	Maqbool Ahmed	Sui Southern Gas v ZTBL at Islamabad.[W20]
11 (11ct)	R. R. Pant	India v Australia (1st Test) at Adelaide.
10 (10ct)	T. R. Ambrose	Warwickshire v Durham at Chester-le-Street.
10 (8ct, 2st)	M. Mosehle	Lions v Warriors at East London.
10 (10ct)	W. P. Saha	India v South Africa (1st Test) at Cape Town.
10 (10ct)	K. Srikar Bharat	India A v South Africa A at Bangalore.[W20]

9 (8ct, 1st)	M. A. R. S. Fernando...	Chilaw Marians v Colts at Colombo.
9 (9ct)	B. T. Foakes	Surrey v Nottinghamshire at The Oval.
9 (9ct)	Z. E. Green	Namibia v Eastern Province at Port Elizabeth.
9 (9ct)	B. J. Horne..........	Auckland v Central Districts at Auckland.[W20]

Most Catches in an Innings in the Field

| 5 | Jahurul Islam .... | North Zone v Central Zone at Sylhet. |
| 5 | S. P. D. Smith .... | Australia v South Africa (3rd Test) at Cape Town. |

Most Catches in a Match in the Field

7	P. S. P. Handscomb	Victoria v South Australia at Adelaide.
7	K. L. Rahul	India v England (3rd Test) at Nottingham.
6	C. N. Ackermann............	Warriors v Titans at East London.
6	M. Q. Adams	Western Province v Gauteng at Rondebosch.
6	K. B. Arun Karthik	Kerala v Tamil Nadu at Chennai.[W20]
6	D. G. Brownlie.............	Northern Districts v Canterbury at Christchurch.[W20]
6	K. K. Jennings	England v Sri Lanka at Colombo.
6	D. K. H. Mitchell..........	Worcestershire v Hampshire at Worcester.
6	T. M. N. Sampath	Burgher v Ragama at Katunayake.
6	S. P. D. Smith	Australia v South Africa (3rd Test) at Cape Town.
6	H. D. R. L. Thirimanne	Ragama v Nondescripts at Colombo.
6	M. L. Udawatte	Nondescripts v Badureliya at Colombo.
6	B. J. Webster	Tasmania v Queensland at Brisbane.

No Byes Conceded in Total of 500 or More

K. S. K. Chaitnay	Hyderabad v Andhra (502-7 dec) at Visakhapatnam.[W20]
S. M. Davies	Somerset v Essex (517-5 dec) at Chelmsford.
A. K. N. de Silva............	Army v Nondescripts (500-5 dec) at Colombo.[W20]
D. P. D. N. Dickwella.......	Sri Lanka v Bangladesh (513) (1st Test) at Chittagong.
D. P. D. N. Dickwella.......	Sri Lanka v New Zealand (578) (1st Test) at Wellington.
B. T. Foakes	Surrey v Worcestershire (526) at The Oval.
J. P. Inglis	Western Australia v Victoria (504) at Perth.[W20]
Jaker Ali	East Zone v Central Zone (546) at Rajshahi.
H. J. Kotze	South Western Districts v North West (569-6) at Oudtshoorn.
M. Mosehle..............	Lions v Knights (500-8 dec) at Kimberley.
Nurul Hasan	South Zone v East Zone (546) at Savar.
Nurul Hasan	Khulna v Rajshahi (552) at Rajshahi.[W20]
S. K. Patel	Tripura v Uttar Pradesh (552-7 dec) at Lucknow.[W20]
S. S. Patel	Saurashtra v Baroda (533-9) at Rajkot.[W20]
J. J. Peirson	Queensland v South Australia (505) at Adelaide.[W20]
Shamsul Islam..............	Barisal v Rangpur (502) at Bogra.[W20]
A. P. Tare	Mumbai v Vidarbha (511) at Nagpur.[W20]
K. A. Vaz	Goa v Uttar Pradesh (564-4 dec) at Kanpur.[W20]

Highest Innings Totals

826-7 dec	Meghalaya v Sikkim at Bhubaneswar.[W20]
800-7 dec	Vidarbha v Rest of India at Nagpur.
735-6 dec	East Zone v Central Zone at Khulna.
713-9 dec	Sri Lanka v Bangladesh (1st Test) at Chittagong.
711-8 dec	East Zone v Central Zone at Rajshahi.
649-7 dec	Australia v England (5th Test) at Sydney.[W18]
649-9 dec	India v West Indies (1st Test) at Rajkot.
647-8 dec	Puducherry v Sikkim at Wayanad.[W20]

618-9 dec	Nondescripts v Colts at Galle.
609-6 dec	India A v West Indies A at Beckenham.
603	Peshawar v FATA at Abbottabad.[W20]
600-6 dec	Karachi Whites v Multan at Multan.[W20]

Lowest Innings Totals

35	Sui Northern Gas v Habib Bank at Faisalabad.[W20]
36	Panadura v Air Force at Panadura.
43	Bangladesh v West Indies (1st Test) at North Sound.
44	National Bank v Sui Northern Gas at Faisalabad.[W20]
45	Mizoram v Puducherry at Puducherry.[W20]
46	Meghalaya v Bihar at Shillong.[W20]
50	Yorkshire v Essex at Chelmsford.
53	Canterbury v Wellington at Christchurch.
56	Middlesex v Kent at Canterbury.
57	Ragama v Chilaw Marians at Colombo.
58	England v New Zealand (1st Test) at Auckland.
60	Bihar v Uttarakhand at Dehradun.[W20]
60†	Tripura v Uttar Pradesh at Lucknow.[W20]

† *One man absent.*

Highest Fourth-Innings Totals

466-8	Kabul v Band-e-Amir at Asadabad (set 492).
445	Warwickshire v Kent at Tunbridge Wells (set 519).
414-6	Queensland v Tasmania at Hobart (set 414).[W20]

Match Aggregate of 1,500 Runs

1,645 for 37	Band-e-Amir (577 and 258-9 dec) v Kabul (344 and 466-8) at Asadabad.
1,533 for 24	Bangladesh (513 and 307-5 dec) v Sri Lanka (713-9 dec) (1st Test) at Chittagong.

Matches Dominated by Batting (1,200 runs at 80 runs per wicket)

1,389-16 (86.81)   East Zone (735-6 dec and 226-0) v Central Zone (428) at Khulna.

Four Individual Hundreds in an Innings

East Zone (735-6 dec) v Central Zone at Khulna.
Nondescripts (618-9 dec) v Colts at Galle.
Habib Bank (490-6 dec) v National Bank at Faisalabad.[W20]
Meghalaya (826-7 dec) v Sikkim at Bhubaneswar.[W20]

Six or More Individual Fifties in an Innings

7	Band-e-Amir (577) v Kabul at Asadabad.
6	Band-e-Amir (503-6) v Speen Ghar at Khost.
6	Western Province (502-4 dec) v Northern Cape at Cape Town.[W20]
6	Gujarat (538-7 dec) v Chhattisgarh at Valsad.[W20]

Large Margin of Victory

Nondescripts (330 and 367-7 dec) beat Moors (81 and 73) at Colombo by 543 runs.[W20]
S Africa (488 and 344-6 dec) beat Australia (221 and 119) (4th Test) at Johannesburg by 492 runs.
Peshawar (235 and 603) beat FATA (171 and 183) at Abbottabad by 484 runs.[W20]
NZ (178 and 585-4 dec) beat Sri Lanka (104 and 236) (2nd Test) at Christchurch by 423 runs.

Win after Following On

Leicestershire (440 and 101) lost to Durham (184 and 403) at Chester-le-Street by 46 runs.
Northamptonshire (346 and 184) lost to Middlesex (187 and 374) at Northampton by 31 runs.

Tied Matches

Bloomfield (163 and 206) v Army (171 and 198) at Colombo.
Lancashire (99 and 170) v Somerset (192 and 77) at Taunton.

Eleven Bowlers in an Innings

Central Zone v East Zone (226-0) at Khulna.

Most Extras in an Innings

b	*lb*	*w*	*nb*	*p*	
81	34	23	2	22		Durham (376) v Derbyshire at Chester-le-Street.
61	28	15	3	10	5	Queensland (438-9 dec) v New South Wales at Wollongong.
61	30	27	0	4		North West (446) v Northern at Comber.
58	35	0	19	4		India A (321-5) v West Indies A at Taunton.
57	22	2	14	19		India A (609-6 dec) v West Indies A at Beckenham.
56	14	23	4	15		Cape Cobras (428) v Titans at Benoni.
56	28	16	3	4	5	Middlesex (374) v Northamptonshire at Northampton.
51	17	23	2	9		West Indies A (302) v India A at Taunton.
51	23	13	1	14		KwaZulu-Natal Inland (397) v Gauteng at Johannesburg.[W20]
50	5	17	12	16		Warwickshire (299) v Sussex at Birmingham.

Career Aggregate Milestones

20,000 runs	I. R. Bell.
15,000 runs	G. Gambhir, D. I. Stevens.
10,000 runs	G. S. Ballance, R. Clarke, E. J. M. Cowan, Khurram Manzoor, H. G. Kuhn, D. J. Malan, S. E. Marsh, J. E. Root, M. D. Stoneman, R. N. ten Doeschate, Tushar Imran, S. van Zyl, C. L. White, K. S. Williamson.
500 wickets	Abdur Razzak, Aizaz Cheema, Asad Ali, R. Ashwin, S. R. Harmer, N. C. Komasaru, N. M. Lyon, N. O. Miller, M. Morkel, S. Prasanna, A. U. Rashid, S. M. S. M. Senanayake, P. M. Siddle, Yasir Shah, Zulfiqar Babar.
500 dismissals	S. M. Davies, Sarfraz Ahmed.

RECORDS

Compiled by Philip Bailey

This section covers
- first-class records to December 31, 2018 (page 1215).
- List A one-day records to December 31, 2018 (page 1243).
- List A Twenty20 records to December 31, 2018 (page 1246).
- All-format career records to December 31, 2018 (page 1248).
- Test records to January 14, 2019, the end of the South Africa v Pakistan series (page 1249).
- Test records series by series (page 1283).
- one-day international records to December 31, 2018 (page 1327).
- World Cup records (page 1338).
- Twenty20 international records to December 31, 2018 (page 1344).
- miscellaneous other records to December 31, 2018 (page 1350).
- women's Test records, one-day international and Twenty20 international records to December 31, 2018 (page 1354).

The sequence
- Test series records begin with those involving England, arranged in the order their opponents entered Test cricket (Australia, South Africa, West Indies, New Zealand, India, Pakistan, Sri Lanka, Zimbabwe, Bangladesh, Ireland, Afghanistan). Next come all remaining series involving Australia, then South Africa – and so on until Zimbabwe v Bangladesh records appear on page 1323.

Notes
- Unless otherwise stated, all records apply only to first-class cricket. This is considered to have started in 1815, after the Napoleonic War.
- mid-year seasons taking place outside England are given simply as 2017, 2018, etc.
- (E), (A), (SA), (WI), (NZ), (I), (P), (SL), (Z), (B), (Ire), (Afg) indicates the nationality of a player or the country in which a record was made.
- in career records, dates in italic indicate seasons embracing two different years (i.e. non-English seasons). In these cases, only the first year is given, e.g. *2018* for 2018-19.

See also
- up-to-date records on www.wisdenrecords.com.
- Features of 2018 (page 1197).

CONTENTS

FIRST-CLASS RECORDS

BATTING RECORDS

BOWLING RECORDS

ALL-ROUND RECORDS

WICKETKEEPING RECORDS

FIELDING RECORDS

TEAM RECORDS

LIST A ONE-DAY RECORDS

LIST A TWENTY20 RECORDS

ALL-FORMAT CAREER RECORDS

TEST RECORDS

BATTING RECORDS

BOWLING RECORDS

ALL-ROUND RECORDS

WICKETKEEPING RECORDS

FIELDING RECORDS

TEAM RECORDS

PLAYERS

UMPIRES

TEST SERIES

ONE-DAY INTERNATIONAL RECORDS

TWENTY20 INTERNATIONAL RECORDS

MISCELLANEOUS RECORDS

WOMEN'S TEST AND OTHER INTERNATIONAL RECORDS

NOTES ON RECORDS

The new faces

STEVEN LYNCH

Some unfamiliar names have muscled their way into this section. For the first time since 1877, two countries played their inaugural Tests: both lost – Afghanistan in a sobering two days – but Kevin O'Brien's debut hundred ensured some joy for Ireland.

The Afghans had more luck in domestic cricket: Shafiqullah Shinwari belted a double-century for Kabul in 103 minutes, beating Ravi Shastri's previous mark by ten, and 24 sixes in the match, another record. In India in December 2018, Ajay Rohera of Madhya Pradesh hit the highest score on first-class debut, an unbeaten 267 against Hyderabad.

By then, Alastair Cook had returned to his farm, clutching several major England records: most caps, runs, centuries and catches, not to mention least sweat. He did lose one: New Zealander Tom Latham made the highest score by an opener carrying his bat, 264 against Sri Lanka. Cook's retirement meant there was no current batsman with 10,000 Test runs – Hashim Amla was closest, with 9,231 by the end of South Africa's series against Pakistan.

Cook's England team-mates claimed records, too. They shot past their own, for the highest ODI total, with 481 at Trent Bridge in the course of inflicting their first 5–0 whitewash of Australia in any format. And, with the last delivery of Cook's farewell game, Jimmy Anderson became the most successful fast bowler in Tests, passing Glenn McGrath's 563 wickets. Elsewhere, Pakistan's Yasir Shah hurried to 200 in only his 33rd Test, three quicker than another leg-spinner, Clarrie Grimmett.

This year, for the first time, *Wisden* includes a page of all-format records, aggregating performances in first-class, List A and T20 matches. Jack Hobbs has topped the first-class table for three-quarters of a century, but his 61,237 runs are trumped overall by Graham Gooch (67,057) and Graeme Hick (64,372). For the bowlers, Derek Underwood rises to fifth.

Yet more unfamiliar names featured for the first time as a result of the ICC's decision to award official status to all women's Twenty20 internationals between member countries. It had an immediate effect in some areas: of the 36 lowest totals, 35 have come since the category was thrown open in June 2018, along with the best bowling figures in the format. Expect more red ink: the decision was extended to men's T20 internationals from the start of 2019.

ROLL OF DISHONOUR

The following players have either been banned after being found guilty of breaching anti-corruption codes, or have admitted to some form of on-field corruption:

Amit Singh (I), Ata-ur-Rehman (P), M. Azharuddin (I), A. Bali (I), G. H. Bodi (SA), A. Chandila (I), A. A. Chavan (I), P. Cleary (A), W. J. Cronje (SA), Danish Kaneria (P), H. H. Gibbs (SA), C. L. Hall (A), Irfan Ahmed (HK), Irfan Ansari (UAE), A. Jadeja (I), H. N. K. Jensen (NZ), Khalid Latif (P), J. Logan (A), K. S. Lokuarachchi (SL), P. Matshikwe (SA), N. E. Mbhalati (SA), M. D. Mishra (I), Mohammad Amir (P), Mohammad Ashraful (B), Mohammad Asif (P), Mohammad Irfan (P), Mohammad Nawaz (P), Nasir Jamshed (P), Naved Arif (P), M. O. Odumbe (Ken), A. N. Petersen (SA), M. Prabhakar (I), Salim Malik (P), Salman Butt (P), M. N. Samuels (WI), M. N. Shah (I), Shariful Haque (B), Sharjeel Khan (P), Ajay Sharma (I), S. Sreesanth (I), S. J. Srivastava (I), T. P. Sudhindra (I), J. Symes (SA), S. K. Trivedi (I), T. L. Tsolekile (SA), L. L. Tsotsobe (SA), L. Vincent (NZ), M. S. Westfield (E), H. S. Williams (SA), A. R. Yadav (I).

FIRST-CLASS RECORDS

This section covers first-class cricket to December 31, 2018. Bold type denotes performances in the calendar year 2018 or, in career figures, players who appeared in first-class cricket in that year.

BATTING RECORDS

HIGHEST INDIVIDUAL INNINGS

In all first-class cricket, there have been **221** individual scores of 300 or more. The highest are:

501*	B. C. Lara	Warwickshire v Durham at Birmingham	1994
499	Hanif Mohammad	Karachi v Bahawalpur at Karachi	1958-59
452*	D. G. Bradman	NSW v Queensland at Sydney	1929-30
443*	B. B. Nimbalkar	Maharashtra v Kathiawar at Poona	1948-49
437	W. H. Ponsford	Victoria v Queensland at Melbourne	1927-28
429	W. H. Ponsford	Victoria v Tasmania at Melbourne	1922-23
428	Aftab Baloch	Sind v Baluchistan at Karachi	1973-74
424	A. C. MacLaren	Lancashire v Somerset at Taunton	1895
405*	G. A. Hick	Worcestershire v Somerset at Taunton	1988
400*	B. C. Lara	West Indies v England at St John's	2003-04
394	Naved Latif	Sargodha v Gujranwala at Gujranwala	2000-01
390	S. C. Cook	Lions v Warriors at East London	2009-10
385	B. Sutcliffe	Otago v Canterbury at Christchurch	1952-53
383	C. W. Gregory	NSW v Queensland at Brisbane	1906-07
380	M. L. Hayden	Australia v Zimbabwe at Perth	2003-04
377	S. V. Manjrekar	Bombay v Hyderabad at Bombay	1990-91
375	B. C. Lara	West Indies v England at St John's	1993-94
374	D. P. M. D. Jayawardene	Sri Lanka v South Africa at Colombo (SSC)	2006
369	D. G. Bradman	South Australia v Tasmania at Adelaide	1935-36
366	N. H. Fairbrother	Lancashire v Surrey at The Oval	1990
366	M. V. Sridhar	Hyderabad v Andhra at Secunderabad	1993-94
365*	C. Hill	South Australia v NSW at Adelaide	1900-01
365*	G. S. Sobers	West Indies v Pakistan at Kingston	1957-58
364	L. Hutton	England v Australia at The Oval	1938
359*	V. M. Merchant	Bombay v Maharashtra at Bombay	1943-44
359*	S. B. Gohel	Gujarat v Orissa at Jaipur	2016-17
359	R. B. Simpson	NSW v Queensland at Brisbane	1963-64
357*	R. Abel	Surrey v Somerset at The Oval	1899
357	D. G. Bradman	South Australia v Victoria at Melbourne	1935-36
356	B. A. Richards	South Australia v Western Australia at Perth	1970-71
355*	G. R. Marsh	Western Australia v South Australia at Perth	1989-90
355*	K. P. Pietersen	Surrey v Leicestershire at The Oval	2015
355	B. Sutcliffe	Otago v Auckland at Dunedin	1949-50
353	V. V. S. Laxman	Hyderabad v Karnataka at Bangalore	1999-2000
352	W. H. Ponsford	Victoria v NSW at Melbourne	1926-27
352	C. A. Pujara	Saurashtra v Karnataka at Rajkot	2012-13
351*	S. M. Gugale	Maharashtra v Delhi at Mumbai	2016-17
351	K. D. K. Vithanage	Tamil Union v Air Force at Katunayake	2014-15
350	Rashid Israr	Habib Bank v National Bank at Lahore	1976-77

A fuller list can be found in Wisdens *up to 2011.*

DOUBLE-HUNDRED ON DEBUT

227	T. Marsden	Sheffield & Leicester v Nottingham at Sheffield	1826
207	N. F. Callaway†	New South Wales v Queensland at Sydney	1914-15
240	W. F. E. Marx	Transvaal v Griqualand West at Johannesburg	1920-21
200*	A. Maynard	Trinidad v MCC at Port-of-Spain	1934-35
232*	S. J. E. Loxton	Victoria v Queensland at Melbourne	1946-47

215*	G. H. G. Doggart	Cambridge University v Lancashire at Cambridge . . .	1948
202	J. Hallebone	Victoria v Tasmania at Melbourne	1951-52
230	G. R. Viswanath	Mysore v Andhra at Vijayawada	1967-68
260	A. A. Muzumdar	Bombay v Haryana at Faridabad	1993-94
209*	A. Pandey	Madhya Pradesh v Uttar Pradesh at Bhilai	1995-96
210*	D. J. Sales	Northamptonshire v Worcestershire at Kidderminster	1996
200*	M. J. Powell	Glamorgan v Oxford University at Oxford	1997
201*	M. C. Juneja	Gujarat v Tamil Nadu at Ahmedabad	2011-12
213	Jiwanjot Singh	Punjab v Hyderabad at Mohali	2012-13
202	A. Gupta	Punjab v Himachal Pradesh at Dharamsala.	2017-18
256*	Bahir Shah	Speen Ghar v Amo at Ghazi Amanullah Town	2017-18
203	B. D. Schmulian	C. Districts v N. Districts at Mount Maunganui	2017-18
228	**M. Raghav**	**Manipur v Nagaland at Dimapur**	**2018-19**
267*	**A. R. Rohera**	**Madhya Pradesh v Hyderabad at Indore**	**2018-19**

†   *In his only first-class innings. He was killed in action in France in 1917.*

TWO SEPARATE HUNDREDS ON DEBUT

148	and 111	A. R. Morris	New South Wales v Queensland at Sydney	1940-41
152	and 102*	N. J. Contractor	Gujarat v Baroda at Baroda	1952-53
132*	and 110	Aamer Malik	Lahore A v Railways at Lahore	1979-80
130	and 100*	Noor Ali	Afghanistan v Zimbabwe XI at Mutare	2009
158	and 103*	K. H. T. Indika	Police v Seeduwa Raddoluwa at Colombo (Police)	2010-11
126	and 112	V. S. Awate	Maharashtra v Vidarbha at Nagpur.	2012-13
154*	and 109*	T. J. Dean	Victoria v Queensland at Melbourne	2015-16
102	and 142	Haji Murad	Amo v Speen Ghar at Ghazi Amanullah Town . .	2017-18

TWO DOUBLE-HUNDREDS IN A MATCH

A. E. Fagg   244   202*   Kent v Essex at Colchester   1938

In February 2019, after the deadline for this section, A. K. Perera scored 201 and 231 for Nondescripts v Sinhalese at Colombo.

TRIPLE-HUNDRED AND HUNDRED IN A MATCH

G. A. Gooch	333	123	England v India at Lord's	1990
K. C. Sangakkara	319	105	Sri Lanka v Bangladesh at Chittagong.	2013-14

DOUBLE-HUNDRED AND HUNDRED IN A MATCH

In addition to Fagg, Gooch and Sangakkara, there have been **62** further instances of a batsman scoring a double-hundred and a hundred in the same first-class match. The most recent are:

C. J. L. Rogers.	200	140*	Derbyshire v Surrey at The Oval.	2010
M. R. Ramprakash	223	103*	Surrey v Middlesex at The Oval	2010
N. V. Ojha	219*	101*	India A v Australia A at Brisbane	2014
S. D. Robson	231	106	Middlesex v Warwickshire at Lord's	2016
G. S. Ballance	108	203*	Yorkshire v Hampshire at Southampton	2017

Zaheer Abbas achieved the feat four times, for Gloucestershire between 1976 and 1981, and was not out in all eight innings. M. R. Hallam did it twice for Leicestershire, in 1959 and 1961; N. R. Taylor twice for Kent, in 1990 and 1991; G. A. Gooch for England in 1990 (see above) and Essex in 1994; M. W. Goodwin twice for Sussex, in 2001 and 2007; and C. J. L. Rogers for Northamptonshire in 2006 and for Derbyshire in 2010.

TWO SEPARATE HUNDREDS IN A MATCH MOST TIMES

R. T. Ponting	8	J. B. Hobbs.	6	M. L. Hayden.	5
Zaheer Abbas	8	G. M. Turner	6	G. A. Hick	5
W. R. Hammond	7	C. B. Fry	5	C. J. L. Rogers	5
M. R. Ramprakash	7	G. A. Gooch	5		

W. Lambert scored 107 and 157 for Sussex v Epsom at Lord's in 1817, a feat not repeated until W. G. Grace's 130 and 102* for South of the Thames v North of the Thames at Canterbury in 1868.

FIVE HUNDREDS OR MORE IN SUCCESSION

D. G. Bradman (1938-39)	6	B. C. Lara (1993-94–1994)	5
C. B. Fry (1901)	6	P. A. Patel (2007–2007-08)	5
M. J. Procter (1970-71)	6	K. C. Sangakkara (2017)	5
M. E. K. Hussey (2003)	5	E. D. Weekes (1955-56)	5

Bradman also scored four hundreds in succession twice, in 1931-32 and 1948–1948-49; W. R. Hammond did it in 1936-37 and 1945–1946, and H. Sutcliffe in 1931 and 1939.

T. W. Hayward (Surrey v Nottinghamshire and Leicestershire), D. W. Hookes (South Australia v Queensland and New South Wales) and V. Sibanda (Zimbabwe XI v Kenya and Mid West v Southern Rocks) are the only players to score two hundreds in each of two successive matches. Hayward scored his in six days, June 4–9, 1906.

The most fifties in consecutive innings is ten – by E. Tyldesley in 1926, by D. G. Bradman in the 1947-48 and 1948 seasons, and by R. S. Kaluwitharana in 1994-95.

MOST HUNDREDS IN A SEASON

D. C. S. Compton (1947)	18	W. R. Hammond (1937)	13
J. B. Hobbs (1925)	16	T. W. Hayward (1906)	13
W. R. Hammond (1938)	15	E. H. Hendren (1923)	13
H. Sutcliffe (1932)	14	E. H. Hendren (1927)	13
G. Boycott (1971)	13	E. H. Hendren (1928)	13
D. G. Bradman (1938)	13	C. P. Mead (1928)	13
C. B. Fry (1901)	13	H. Sutcliffe (1928)	13
W. R. Hammond (1933)	13	H. Sutcliffe (1931)	13

Since 1969 (excluding G. Boycott – above)

G. A. Gooch (1990)	12	M. R. Ramprakash (1995)	10
S. J. Cook (1991)	11	M. R. Ramprakash (2007)	10
Zaheer Abbas (1976)	11	G. M. Turner (1970)	10
G. A. Hick (1988)	10	Zaheer Abbas (1981)	10
H. Morris (1990)	10		

*The most outside England is nine by V. Sibanda in Zimbabwe (2009-10), followed by eight by D. G. Bradman in Australia (1947-48), D. C. S. Compton (1948-49), R. N. Harvey and A. R. Morris (both 1949-50) all three in South Africa, M. D. Crowe in New Zealand (1986-87), Asif Mujtaba in Pakistan (1995-96), V. V. S. Laxman in India (1999-2000), M. G. Bevan in Australia (2004-05) and **Zia-ul-Haq in Afghanistan (2017-18)**.*

The most double-hundreds in a season is six by D. G. Bradman (1930), five by K. S. Ranjitsinhji (1900) and E. D. Weekes (1950), and four by Arun Lal (1986-87), C. B. Fry (1901), W. R. Hammond (1933 and 1934), E. H. Hendren (1929-30), V. M. Merchant (1944-45), C. A. Pujara (2012-13) and G. M. Turner (1971-72).

MOST DOUBLE-HUNDREDS IN A CAREER

D. G. Bradman	37	W. G. Grace	13	Younis Khan	12
W. R. Hammond	36	B. C. Lara	13	J. W. Hearne	11
E. H. Hendren	22	C. P. Mead	13	L. Hutton	11
M. R. Ramprakash	17	W. H. Ponsford	13	D. S. Lehmann	11
H. Sutcliffe	17	K. C. Sangakkara	13	V. M. Merchant	11
C. B. Fry	16	J. T. Tyldesley	13	C. J. L. Rogers	11
G. A. Hick	16	P. Holmes	12	A. Sandham	11
J. B. Hobbs	16	Javed Miandad	12	G. Boycott	10
C. G. Greenidge	14	J. L. Langer	12	R. Dravid	10
K. S. Ranjitsinhji	14	**C. A. Pujara**	**12**	M. W. Gatting	10
G. A. Gooch	13	R. B. Simpson	12	S. M. Gavaskar	10

J. Hardstaff jnr.	10	D. P. M. D. Jayawardene	10	R. T. Simpson	10
V. S. Hazare	10	I. V. A. Richards	10	G. M. Turner	10
B. J. Hodge	10	A. Shrewsbury	10	Zaheer Abbas	10

MOST HUNDREDS IN A CAREER

(100 or more)

		Total	Total Inns	100th 100 Season	Inns	400+	300+	200+
1	J. B. Hobbs	197	1,315	1923	821	0	1	16
2	E. H. Hendren	170	1,300	1928-29	740	0	1	22
3	W. R. Hammond	167	1,005	1935	680	0	4	36
4	C. P. Mead	153	1,340	1927	892	0	0	13
5	G. Boycott	151	1,014	1977	645	0	0	10
6	H. Sutcliffe	149	1,088	1932	700	0	1	17
7	F. E. Woolley	145	1,532	1929	1,031	0	1	9
8	G. A. Hick	136	871	1998	574	1	3	16
9	L. Hutton	129	814	1951	619	0	1	11
10	G. A. Gooch	128	990	1992-93	820	0	1	13
11	W. G. Grace	126	1,493	1895	1,113	0	3	13
12	D. C. S. Compton	123	839	1952	552	0	1	9
13	T. W. Graveney	122	1,223	1964	940	0	0	7
14	D. G. Bradman	117	338	1947-48	295	1	6	37
15	I. V. A. Richards	114	796	1988-89	658	0	1	10
	M. R. Ramprakash	114	764	2008	676	0	1	17
17	Zaheer Abbas	108	768	1982-83	658	0	0	10
18	A. Sandham	107	1,000	1935	871	0	1	11
	M. C. Cowdrey	107	1,130	1973	1,035	0	1	3
20	T. W. Hayward	104	1,138	1913	1,076	0	1	8
21	G. M. Turner	103	792	1982	779	0	1	10
	J. H. Edrich	103	979	1977	945	0	1	4
23	L. E. G. Ames	102	951	1950	916	0	0	9
	E. Tyldesley	102	961	1934	919	0	0	7
	D. L. Amiss	102	1,139	1986	1,081	0	0	3

In the above table, 200+, 300+ and 400+ include all scores above those figures.

G. A. Gooch's record includes his century in South Africa in 1981-82, which is no longer accepted by the ICC. Zaheer Abbas and G. Boycott scored their 100th hundreds in Test matches.

Current Players

The following who played in 2018 have scored 40 or more hundreds.

S. Chanderpaul	77	H. M. Amla	52	J. C. Hildreth	44
M. E. Trescothick	66	E. C. Joyce	47	G. Gambhir	43
A. N. Cook	63	C. A. Pujara	47	Misbah-ul-Haq	43
I. R. Bell	57	S. C. Cook	46	J. K. Silva	40
Wasim Jaffer	56	I. J. L. Trott	46		

MOST RUNS IN A SEASON

	Season	I	NO	R	HS	100	Avge
D. C. S. Compton	1947	50	8	3,816	246	18	90.85
W. J. Edrich	1947	52	8	3,539	267*	12	80.43
T. W. Hayward	1906	61	8	3,518	219	13	66.37
L. Hutton	1949	56	6	3,429	269*	12	68.58
F. E. Woolley	1928	59	4	3,352	198	12	60.94
H. Sutcliffe	1932	52	7	3,336	313	14	74.13
W. R. Hammond	1933	54	5	3,323	264	13	67.81
E. H. Hendren	1928	54	7	3,311	209*	13	70.44
R. Abel	1901	68	8	3,309	247	7	55.15

3,000 in a season has been surpassed on 19 other occasions (a full list can be found in Wisden 1999 *and earlier editions). W. R. Hammond, E. H. Hendren and H. Sutcliffe are the only players to achieve the feat three times. K. S. Ranjitsinhji was the first batsman to reach 3,000 in a season, with 3,159 in 1899. M. J. K. Smith (3,245 in 1959) and W. E. Alley (3,019 in 1961) are the only players except those listed above to have reached 3,000 since World War II.*

W. G. Grace scored 2,739 runs in 1871 – the first batsman to reach 2,000 in a season. He made ten hundreds including two double-hundreds, with an average of 78.25 in all first-class matches.

The highest aggregate in a season since the reduction of County Championship matches in 1969 was 2,755 by S. J. Cook (42 innings) in 1991, and the last batsman to achieve 2,000 in England was M. R. Ramprakash (2,026 in 2007); C. A. Pujara scored 2,064 in India in 2016-17.

2,000 RUNS IN A SEASON MOST TIMES

J. B. Hobbs 17	F. E. Woolley 13	C. P. Mead 11
E. H. Hendren 15	W. R. Hammond 12	T. W. Hayward 10
H. Sutcliffe 15	J. G. Langridge 11	

Since the reduction of County Championship matches in 1969, G. A. Gooch is the only batsman to have reached 2,000 runs in a season five times.

1,000 RUNS IN A SEASON MOST TIMES

Includes overseas tours and seasons

W. G. Grace 28	A. Jones 23	G. Gunn 20
F. E. Woolley 28	T. W. Graveney 22	T. W. Hayward 20
M. C. Cowdrey 27	W. R. Hammond 22	G. A. Hick 20
C. P. Mead 27	D. Denton 21	James Langridge 20
G. Boycott 26	J. H. Edrich 21	J. M. Parks 20
J. B. Hobbs 26	G. A. Gooch 21	M. R. Ramprakash 20
E. H. Hendren 25	W. Rhodes 21	A. Sandham 20
D. L. Amiss 24	D. B. Close 20	M. J. K. Smith 20
W. G. Quaife 24	K. W. R. Fletcher 20	C. Washbrook 20
H. Sutcliffe 24	M. W. Gatting 20	

F. E. Woolley reached 1,000 runs in 28 consecutive seasons (1907–1938), C. P. Mead in 27 (1906–1936).

Outside England, 1,000 runs in a season has been reached most times by D. G. Bradman (in 12 seasons in Australia).

Three batsmen have scored 1,000 runs in a season in each of four different countries: G. S. Sobers in West Indies, England, India and Australia; M. C. Cowdrey and G. Boycott in England, South Africa, West Indies and Australia.

HIGHEST AGGREGATES OUTSIDE ENGLAND

	Season	I	NO	R	HS	100	Avge
In Australia							
D. G. Bradman	1928-29	24	6	1,690	340*	7	93.88
In South Africa							
J. R. Reid	1961-62	30	2	1,915	203	7	68.39
In West Indies							
E. H. Hendren	1929-30	18	5	1,765	254*	6	135.76
In New Zealand							
M. D. Crowe	1986-87	21	3	1,676	175*	8	93.11
In India							
C. A. Pujara	2016-17	29	4	2,064	256*	7	82.56
In Pakistan							
Saadat Ali	1983-84	27	1	1,649	208	4	63.42

	Season	I	NO	R	HS	100	Avge
In Sri Lanka							
R. P. Arnold..............	1995-96	24	3	1,475	217*	5	70.23
In Zimbabwe							
V. Sibanda................	2009-10	26	4	1,612	215	9	73.27
In Bangladesh							
Tushar Imran............	2016-17	16	2	1,249	220	5	89.21
In Afghanistan							
Zia-ul-Haq	**2017-18**	**31**	**4**	**1,616**	**148**	**8**	**59.85**

Excluding Pujara in India (above), the following aggregates of over 2,000 runs have been recorded in more than one country:

M. Amarnath (P/I/WI).......	1982-83	34	6	2,234	207	9	79.78
J. R. Reid (SA/A/NZ)	1961-62	40	2	2,188	203	7	57.57
S. M. Gavaskar (I/P)	1978-79	30	6	2,121	205	10	88.37
R. B. Simpson (I/P/A/WI)....	1964-65	34	4	2,063	201	8	68.76
M. H. Richardson (Z/SA/NZ) .	2000-01	34	3	2,030	306	4	65.48

The only other player to hit ten hundreds in an overseas season was V. V. S. Laxman in India and Australia in 1999-2000.

LEADING BATSMEN IN AN ENGLISH SEASON

(Qualification: 8 completed innings)

Season	Leading scorer	Runs	Avge	Top of averages	Runs	Avge
1946	D. C. S. Compton	2,403	61.61	W. R. Hammond.......	1,783	84.90
1947	D. C. S. Compton	3,816	90.85	D. C. S. Compton	3,816	90.85
1948	L. Hutton............	2,654	64.73	D. G. Bradman........	2,428	89.92
1949	L. Hutton............	3,429	68.58	J. Hardstaff	2,251	72.61
1950	R. T. Simpson........	2,576	62.82	E. D. Weekes	2,310	79.65
1951	J. D. Robertson.......	2,917	56.09	P. B. H. May	2,339	68.79
1952	L. Hutton............	2,567	61.11	D. S. Sheppard	2,262	64.62
1953	W. J. Edrich	2,557	47.35	R. N. Harvey.........	2,040	65.80
1954	D. Kenyon...........	2,636	51.68	D. C. S. Compton	1,524	58.61
1955	D. J. Insole	2,427	42.57	D. J. McGlew	1,871	58.46
1956	T. W. Graveney.......	2,397	49.93	K. Mackay	1,103	52.52
1957	T. W. Graveney......	2,361	49.18	P. B. H. May	2,347	61.76
1958	P. B. H. May	2,231	63.74	P. B. H. May	2,231	63.74
1959	M. J. K. Smith.......	3,245	57.94	V. L. Manjrekar	755	68.63
1960	M. J. K. Smith.......	2,551	45.55	R. Subba Row........	1,503	55.66
1961	W. E. Alley	3,019	56.96	W. M. Lawry	2,019	61.18
1962	J. H. Edrich	2,482	51.70	R. T. Simpson	867	54.18
1963	J. B. Bolus	2,190	41.32	G. S. Sobers	1,333	47.60
1964	T. W. Graveney.......	2,385	54.20	K. F. Barrington	1,872	62.40
1965	J. H. Edrich	2,319	62.67	M. C. Cowdrey	2,093	63.42
1966	A. R. Lewis	2,198	41.47	G. S. Sobers	1,349	61.31
1967	C. A. Milton	2,089	46.42	K. F. Barrington	2,059	68.63
1968	B. A. Richards.......	2,395	47.90	G. Boycott	1,487	64.65
1969	J. H. Edrich	2,238	69.93	J. H. Edrich	2,238	69.93
1970	G. M. Turner........	2,379	61.00	G. S. Sobers	1,742	75.73
1971	G. Boycott...........	2,503	100.12	G. Boycott	2,503	100.12
1972	Majid Khan..........	2,074	61.00	G. Boycott	1,230	72.35
1973	G. M. Turner........	2,416	67.11	G. M. Turner........	2,416	67.11
1974	R. T. Virgin.........	1,936	56.94	C. H. Lloyd.........	1,458	63.39
1975	G. Boycott...........	1,915	73.65	R. B. Kanhai........	1,073	82.53
1976	Zaheer Abbas	2,554	75.11	Zaheer Abbas	2,554	75.11
1977	I. V. A. Richards.....	2,161	65.48	G. Boycott	1,701	68.04

Season	Leading scorer	Runs	Avge	Top of averages	Runs	Avge
1978	D. L. Amiss	2,030	53.42	C. E. B. Rice	1,871	66.82
1979	K. C. Wessels	1,800	52.94	G. Boycott	1,538	102.53
1980	P. N. Kirsten	1,895	63.16	A. J. Lamb	1,797	66.55
1981	Zaheer Abbas	2,306	88.69	Zaheer Abbas	2,306	88.69
1982	A. I. Kallicharran	2,120	66.25	G. M. Turner	1,171	90.07
1983	K. S. McEwan	2,176	64.00	I. V. A. Richards	1,204	75.25
1984	G. A. Gooch	2,559	67.34	C. G. Greenidge	1,069	82.23
1985	G. A. Gooch	2,208	71.22	I. V. A. Richards	1,836	76.50
1986	C. G. Greenidge	2,035	67.83	C. G. Greenidge	2,035	67.83
1987	G. A. Hick	1,879	52.19	M. D. Crowe	1,627	67.79
1988	G. A. Hick	2,713	77.51	R. A. Harper	622	77.75
1989	S. J. Cook	2,241	60.56	D. M. Jones	1,510	88.82
1990	G. A. Gooch	2,746	101.70	G. A. Gooch	2,746	101.70
1991	S. J. Cook	2,755	81.02	C. L. Hooper	1,501	93.81
1992	P. D. Bowler	2,044	65.93	Salim Malik	1,184	78.93
	M. A. Roseberry	2,044	56.77			
1993	G. A. Gooch	2,023	63.21	D. C. Boon	1,437	75.63
1994	B. C. Lara	2,066	89.82	J. D. Carr	1,543	90.76
1995	M. R. Ramprakash	2,258	77.86	M. R. Ramprakash	2,258	77.86
1996	S. G. Law	1,944	67.03	S. C. Ganguly	762	95.25
1997	S. P. James	1,775	68.26	G. A. Hick	1,524	69.27
1998	J. P. Crawley	1,851	74.04	J. P. Crawley	1,851	74.04
1999	S. G. Law	1,833	73.32	S. G. Law	1,833	73.32
2000	D. S. Lehmann	1,477	67.13	M. G. Bevan	1,124	74.93
2001	M. E. K. Hussey	2,055	79.03	D. R. Martyn	942	104.66
2002	I. J. Ward	1,759	62.82	R. Dravid	773	96.62
2003	S. G. Law	1,820	91.00	S. G. Law	1,820	91.00
2004	R. W. T. Key	1,896	79.00	R. W. T. Key	1,896	79.00
2005	O. A. Shah	1,728	66.46	M. E. K. Hussey	1,074	76.71
2006	M. R. Ramprakash	2,278	103.54	M. R. Ramprakash	2,278	103.54
2007	M. R. Ramprakash	2,026	101.30	M. R. Ramprakash	2,026	101.30
2008	S. C. Moore	1,451	55.80	T. Frost	1,003	83.58
2009	M. E. Trescothick	1,817	75.70	M. R. Ramprakash	1,350	90.00
2010	M. R. Ramprakash	1,595	61.34	J. C. Hildreth	1,440	65.45
2011	M. E. Trescothick	1,673	79.66	I. R. Bell	1,091	90.91
2012	N. R. D. Compton	1,494	99.60	N. R. D. Compton	1,494	99.60
2013	C. J. L. Rogers	1,536	51.20	S. M. Katich	1,097	73.13
2014	A. Lyth	1,619	70.39	J. E. Root	1,052	75.14
2015	J. C. Hildreth	1,758	56.70	J. M. Bairstow	1,226	72.11
2016	K. K. Jennings	1,602	64.08	S. A. Northeast	1,402	82.47
2017	K. C. Sangakkara	1,491	106.50	K. C. Sangakkara	1,491	106.50
2018	**R. J. Burns**	**1,402**	**60.95**	**O. J. D. Pope**	**1,098**	**61.00**

The highest average recorded in an English season was 115.66 (2,429 runs, 26 innings) by D. G. Bradman in 1938.

In 1953, W. A. Johnston averaged 102.00 from 17 innings, 16 not out.

MOST RUNS

Dates in italics denote the first half of an overseas season; i.e. *1945* denotes the 1945-46 season.

		Career	R	I	NO	HS	100	Avge
1	J. B. Hobbs	1905–1934	61,237	1,315	106	316*	197	50.65
2	F. E. Woolley	1906–1938	58,969	1,532	85	305*	145	40.75
3	E. H. Hendren	1907–1938	57,611	1,300	166	301*	170	50.80
4	C. P. Mead	1905–1936	55,061	1,340	185	280*	153	47.67
5	W. G. Grace	1865–1908	54,896	1,493	105	344	126	39.55
6	W. R. Hammond	1920–1951	50,551	1,005	104	336*	167	56.10
7	H. Sutcliffe	1919–1945	50,138	1,088	123	313	149	51.95
8	G. Boycott	1962–1986	48,426	1,014	162	261*	151	56.83
9	T. W. Graveney	1948–*1971*	47,793	1,223	159	258	122	44.91

		Career	R	I	NO	HS	100	Avge
10	G. A. Gooch	1973–2000	44,846	990	75	333	128	49.01
11	T. W. Hayward	1893–1914	43,551	1,138	96	315*	104	41.79
12	D. L. Amiss	1960–1987	43,423	1,139	126	262*	102	42.86
13	M. C. Cowdrey	1950–1976	42,719	1,130	134	307	107	42.89
14	A. Sandham	1911–*1937*	41,284	1,000	79	325	107	44.82
15	G. A. Hick	*1983*–2008	41,112	871	84	405*	136	52.23
16	L. Hutton	1934–1960	40,140	814	91	364	129	55.51
17	M. J. K. Smith	1951–1975	39,832	1,091	139	204	69	41.84
18	W. Rhodes	1898–1930	39,802	1,528	237	267*	58	30.83
19	J. H. Edrich	1956–1978	39,790	979	104	310*	103	45.47
20	R. E. S. Wyatt	1923–1957	39,405	1,141	157	232	85	40.04
21	D. C. S. Compton	1936–1964	38,942	839	88	300	123	51.85
22	E. Tyldesley	1909–1936	38,874	961	106	256*	102	45.46
23	J. T. Tyldesley	1895–1923	37,897	994	62	295*	86	40.66
24	K. W. R. Fletcher	1962–1988	37,665	1,167	170	228*	63	37.77
25	C. G. Greenidge	1970–1992	37,354	889	75	273*	92	45.88
26	J. W. Hearne	1909–1936	37,252	1,025	116	285*	96	40.98
27	L. E. G. Ames	1926–1951	37,248	951	95	295	102	43.51
28	D. Kenyon	1946–1967	37,002	1,159	59	259	74	33.63
29	W. J. Edrich	1934–1958	36,965	964	92	267*	86	42.39
30	J. M. Parks	1949–1976	36,673	1,227	172	205*	51	34.76
31	M. W. Gatting	1975–1998	36,549	861	123	258	94	49.52
32	D. Denton	1894–1920	36,479	1,163	70	221	69	33.37
33	G. H. Hirst	1891–1929	36,323	1,215	151	341	60	34.13
34	I. V. A. Richards	*1971*–1993	36,212	796	63	322	114	49.40
35	A. Jones	1957–1983	36,049	1,168	72	204*	56	32.89
36	W. G. Quaife	1894–1928	36,012	1,203	185	255*	72	35.37
37	R. E. Marshall	*1945*–1972	35,725	1,053	59	228*	68	35.94
38	M. R. Ramprakash	1987–2012	35,659	764	93	301*	114	53.14
39	G. Gunn	1902–1932	35,208	1,061	82	220	62	35.96

Some works of reference provide career figures which differ from those in this list, owing to the exclusion or inclusion of matches recognised or not recognised as first-class by Wisden. *A fuller list can be found in* Wisdens *up to 2011.*

Current Players with 20,000 Runs

	Career	R	I	NO	HS	100	Avge
S. Chanderpaul	1991–2018	27,545	626	108	303*	77	53.17
M. E. Trescothick	1993–2018	26,089	665	36	284	66	41.47
A. N. Cook	2003–2018	22,604	513	36	294	63	47.38
I. R. Bell	1999–2018	20,256	516	55	262*	57	43.93

HIGHEST CAREER AVERAGE

(Qualification: 10,000 runs)

Avge		Career	I	NO	R	HS	100
95.14	D. G. Bradman	*1927*–1948	338	43	28,067	452*	117
71.22	V. M. Merchant	*1929*–1951	229	43	13,248	359*	44
67.46	Ajay Sharma	*1984*–2000	166	16	10,120	259*	38
65.18	W. H. Ponsford	*1920*–1934	235	23	13,819	437	47
64.99	W. M. Woodfull	*1921*–1934	245	39	13,388	284	49
58.24	A. L. Hassett	*1932*–1953	322	32	16,890	232	59
58.19	V. S. Hazare	*1934*–1966	365	45	18,621	316*	60
57.84	S. R. Tendulkar	1988–2013	490	51	25,396	248*	81
57.83	D. S. Lehmann	1987–2007	479	33	25,795	339	82
57.32	M. G. Bevan	1989–2006	400	66	19,147	216	68
57.27	**S. P. D. Smith**	**2007–2017**	**208**	**26**	**10,424**	**239**	**37**
57.22	A. F. Kippax	*1918*–1935	256	33	12,762	315*	43
56.83	G. Boycott	1962–1986	1,014	162	48,426	261*	151

Avge		*Career*	*I*	*NO*	*R*	*HS*	*100*
56.55	C. L. Walcott	*1941–1963*	238	29	11,820	314*	40
56.37	K. S. Ranjitsinhji	*1893–1920*	500	62	24,692	285*	72
56.22	R. B. Simpson	*1952–1977*	436	62	21,029	359	60
56.10	W. R. Hammond	*1920–1951*	1,005	104	50,551	336*	167
56.08	**Fawad Alam**	*2003–2018*	**245**	**41**	**11,441**	**296***	**30**
56.02	M. D. Crowe	*1979–1995*	412	62	19,608	299	71
55.90	R. T. Ponting	*1992–2013*	494	62	24,150	257	82
55.51	L. Hutton	*1934–1960*	814	91	40,140	364	129
55.34	E. D. Weekes	*1944–1964*	241	24	12,010	304*	36
55.33	R. Dravid	*1990–2011*	497	67	23,794	270	68
55.11	S. V. Manjrekar	*1984–1997*	217	31	10,252	377	31

G. A. Headley scored 9,921 runs, average 69.86, between 1927-28 and 1954.

FASTEST FIFTIES

Minutes

11	C. I. J. Smith (66)	Middlesex v Gloucestershire at Bristol	1938
13	Khalid Mahmood (56)	Gujranwala v Sargodha at Gujranwala.	2000-01
14	S. J. Pegler (50)	South Africans v Tasmania at Launceston.	1910-11
14	F. T. Mann (53)	Middlesex v Nottinghamshire at Lord's.	1921
14	H. B. Cameron (56)	Transvaal v Orange Free State at Johannesburg.	1934-35
14	C. I. J. Smith (52)	Middlesex v Kent at Maidstone	1935

The number of balls taken to achieve fifties was rarely recorded until recently. C. I. J. Smith's two fifties (above) may have taken only 12 balls each. Khalid Mahmood reached his fifty in 15 balls.

Fifties scored in contrived circumstances and with the bowlers' compliance are excluded from the above list, including the fastest of them all, in 8 minutes (13 balls) by C. C. Inman, Leicestershire v Nottinghamshire at Nottingham, 1965, and 10 minutes by G. Chapple, Lancashire v Glamorgan at Manchester, 1993.

FASTEST HUNDREDS

Minutes

35	P. G. H. Fender (113*)	Surrey v Northamptonshire at Northampton	1920
40	G. L. Jessop (101)	Gloucestershire v Yorkshire at Harrogate	1897
40	Ahsan-ul-Haq (100*)	Muslims v Sikhs at Lahore.	1923-24
42	G. L. Jessop (191)	Gentlemen of South v Players of South at Hastings .	1907
43	A. H. Hornby (106)	Lancashire v Somerset at Manchester	1905
43	D. W. Hookes (107)	South Australia v Victoria at Adelaide.	1982-83
44	R. N. S. Hobbs (100)	Essex v Australians at Chelmsford.	1975

The fastest recorded authentic hundred in terms of balls received was scored off 34 balls by D. W. Hookes (above). Research of the scorebook has shown that P. G. H. Fender scored his hundred from between 40 and 46 balls. He contributed 113 to an unfinished sixth-wicket partnership of 171 in 42 minutes with H. A. Peach.

E. B. Alletson (Nottinghamshire) scored 189 out of 227 runs in 90 minutes against Sussex at Hove in 1911. It has been estimated that his last 139 runs took 37 minutes.

Hundreds scored in contrived circumstances and with the bowlers' compliance are excluded, including the fastest of them all, in 21 minutes (27 balls) by G. Chapple, Lancashire v Glamorgan at Manchester, 1993; 24 minutes (27 balls) by M. L. Pettini, Essex v Leicestershire at Leicester, 2006; and 26 minutes (36 balls) by T. M. Moody, Warwickshire v Glamorgan at Swansea, 1990.

FASTEST DOUBLE-HUNDREDS

Minutes

103	**Shafiqullah Shinwari (200*)**	**Kabul v Boost at Asadabad**	**2017-18**
113	R. J. Shastri (200*)	Bombay v Baroda at Bombay	1984-85
120	G. L. Jessop (286)	Gloucestershire v Sussex at Hove	1903
120	C. H. Lloyd (201*)	West Indians v Glamorgan at Swansea	1976
130	G. L. Jessop (234)	Gloucestershire v Somerset at Bristol	1905
131	V. T. Trumper (293)	Australians v Canterbury at Christchurch	1913-14

Shafiqullah faced 89 balls, which was also a record.

FASTEST TRIPLE-HUNDREDS

Minutes

181	D. C. S. Compton (300)	MCC v North Eastern Transvaal at Benoni	1948-49
205	F. E. Woolley (305*)	MCC v Tasmania at Hobart	1911-12
205	C. G. Macartney (345)	Australians v Nottinghamshire at Nottingham	1921
213	D. G. Bradman (369)	South Australia v Tasmania at Adelaide	1935-36

The fastest triple-hundred in terms of balls received was scored off 191 balls by M. Marais for Border v Eastern Province at East London in 2017-18.

MOST RUNS IN A DAY BY ONE BATSMAN

390*	B. C. Lara	Warwickshire v Durham at Birmingham	1994
345	C. G. Macartney	Australians v Nottinghamshire at Nottingham	1921
334	W. H. Ponsford	Victoria v New South Wales at Melbourne	1926-27
333	K. S. Duleepsinhji	Sussex v Northamptonshire at Hove	1930
331*	J. D. Robertson	Middlesex v Worcestershire at Worcester	1949
325*	B. A. Richards	South Australia v Western Australia at Perth	1970-71

These scores do not necessarily represent the complete innings. See page 1215.

*There have been another **14** instances of a batsman scoring 300 in a day, most recently 319 by R. R. Rossouw, Eagles v Titans at Centurion in 2009-10 (see Wisden 2003, page 278, for full list).*

LONGEST INNINGS

Hrs	Mins			
16	55	R. Nayyar (271)	Himachal Pradesh v Jammu&Kashmir at Chamba	1999-2000
16	10	Hanif Mohammad (337)	Pakistan v West Indies at Bridgetown	1957-58
		Hanif believed he batted 16 hours 39 minutes.		
16	4	S. B. Gohel (359*)	Gujarat v Orissa at Jaipur	2016-17
15	7	V. A. Saxena (257)	Rajasthan v Tamil Nadu at Chennai	2011-12
14	38	G. Kirsten (275)	South Africa v England at Durban	1999-2000
14	32	K. K. Nair (328)	Karnataka v Tamil Nadu at Mumbai	2014-15
13	58	S. C. Cook (390)	Lions v Warriors at East London	2009-10
13	56	A. N. Cook (263)	England v Pakistan at Abu Dhabi	2015-16
13	43	T. Kohli (300*)	Punjab v Jharkhand at Jamshedpur	2012-13
13	41	S. S. Shukla (178*)	Uttar Pradesh v Tamil Nadu at Nagpur	2008-09
13	32	A. Chopra (301*)	Rajasthan v Maharashtra at Nasik	2010-11

1,000 RUNS IN MAY

	Runs	*Avge*
W. G. Grace, May 9 to May 30, 1895 (22 days)	1,016	112.88
Grace was 46 years old.		
W. R. Hammond, May 7 to May 31, 1927 (25 days)	1,042	74.42
Hammond scored his 1,000th run on May 28, thus equalling		
Grace's record of 22 days.		
C. Hallows, May 5 to May 31, 1928 (27 days)	1,000	125.00

1,000 RUNS IN APRIL AND MAY

	Runs	*Avge*
T. W. Hayward, April 16 to May 31, 1900	1,074	97.63
D. G. Bradman, April 30 to May 31, 1930	1,001	143.00
On April 30 Bradman was 75 not out.		

	Runs	Avge
D. G. Bradman, April 30 to May 31, 1938	1,056	150.85
Bradman scored 258 on April 30, and his 1,000th run on May 27.		
W. J. Edrich, April 30 to May 31, 1938	1,010	84.16
Edrich was 21 not out on April 30. All his runs were scored at Lord's.		
G. M. Turner, April 24 to May 31, 1973	1,018	78.30
G. A. Hick, April 17 to May 29, 1988	1,019	101.90
Hick scored a record 410 runs in April, and his 1,000th run on May 28.		

MOST RUNS SCORED OFF AN OVER

(All instances refer to six-ball overs)

36	G. S. Sobers	off M. A. Nash, Nottinghamshire v Glam at Swansea (six sixes)....	1968
36	R. J. Shastri	off Tilak Raj, Bombay v Baroda at Bombay (six sixes)............	1984-85
34	E. B. Alletson	off E. H. Killick, Notts v Sussex at Hove (46604446 inc 2 nb)	1911
34	F. C. Hayes	off M. A. Nash, Lancashire v Glamorgan at Swansea (646666)	1977
34†	A. Flintoff	off A. J. Tudor, Lancs v Surrey at Manchester (64444660 inc 2 nb) .	1998
34	C. M. Spearman	off S. J. P. Moreton, Gloucestershire v Oxford UCCE at Oxford (666646) *Moreton's first over in first-class cricket.*............	2005
32	C. C. Smart	off G. Hill, Glamorgan v Hampshire at Cardiff (664664)	1935
32	I. R. Redpath	off N. Rosendorff, Australians v OFS at Bloemfontein (666644) ...	1969-70
32	P. W. G. Parker	off A. I. Kallicharran, Sussex v Warwicks at Birmingham (466664).	1982
32	I. T. Botham	off I. R. Snook, England XI v C Dists at Palmerston North (466466)	1983-84
32	Khalid Mahmood	off Naved Latif, Gujranwala v Sargodha at Gujranwala (666662)...	2000-01

† *Altogether 38 runs were scored off this over, the two no-balls counting for two extra runs each under ECB regulations.*

The following instances have been excluded because of the bowlers' compliance: 34 – M. P. Maynard off S. A. Marsh, Glamorgan v Kent at Maidstone, 1992; 34 – G. Chapple off P. A. Cottey, Lancashire v Glamorgan at Manchester, 1993; 34 – F. B. Touzel off F. J. J. Viljoen, Western Province B v Griqualand West at Kimberley, 1993-94. Chapple scored a further 32 off Cottey's next over.

There were 35 runs off an over received by A. T. Reinholds off H. T. Davis, Auckland v Wellington at Auckland 1995-96, but this included 16 extras and only 19 off the bat.

In a match against KwaZulu-Natal at Stellenbosch in 2006-07, W. E. September (Boland) conceded 34 in an over: 27 to M. Bekker, six to K. Smit, plus one no-ball.

In a match against Canterbury at Christchurch in 1989-90, R. H. Vance (Wellington) deliberately conceded 77 runs in an over of full tosses which contained 17 no-balls and, owing to the umpire's understandable miscalculation, only five legitimate deliveries.

The greatest number of runs scored off an eight-ball over is 34 (40446664) by R. M. Edwards off M. C. Carew, Governor-General's XI v West Indians at Auckland, 1968-69.

MOST SIXES IN AN INNINGS

23	C. Munro (281)	Auckland v Central Districts at Napier..............	2014-15
22	**Shafiqullah Shinwari (200*)**	**Kabul v Boost at Asadabad**	**2017-18**
16	A. Symonds (254*)	Gloucestershire v Glamorgan at Abergavenny	1995
16	G. R. Napier (196)	Essex v Surrey at Croydon	2011
16	J. D. Ryder (175)	New Zealanders v Australia A at Brisbane..........	2011-12
16	Mukhtar Ali (168)	Rajshahi v Chittagong at Savar...................	2013-14
15	J. R. Reid (296)	Wellington v Northern Districts at Wellington......	1962-63
15	Ziaur Rahman (152*)	South Zone v Central Zone at Mirpur..............	2012-13
15	H. G. Kumara (200*)	Saracens v Air Force at Katunayake	2014-15
15	K. P. Pietersen (355*)	Surrey v Leicestershire at The Oval	2015
15	A. H. T. Donald (234)	Glamorgan v Derbyshire at Colwyn Bay	2016

*There have been **nine** further instances of 14 or more sixes in an innings.*

MOST SIXES IN A MATCH

24	**Shafiqullah Shinwari (22, 200*)**	**Kabul v Boost at Asadabad**	**2017-18**
23	C. Munro (281)	Auckland v Central Districts at Napier	2014-15
21	R. R. Pant (117, 131)	Delhi v Jharkhand at Thumba	2016-17
20	A. Symonds (254*, 76)	Gloucestershire v Glam at Abergavenny	1995
18	**Hazratullah Zazai (121, 62)**	**Band-e-Amir v Amo at Asadabad**	**2017-18**
17	W. J. Stewart (155, 125)	Warwickshire v Lancashire at Blackpool	1959
17	K. P. S. P. Karunanayake (52, 150*)	Army v Ports Authority at Colombo (CCC)	2014-15

MOST SIXES IN A SEASON

80	I. T. Botham	1985	51	A. W. Wellard	1933
66	A. W. Wellard	1935	49	I. V. A. Richards	1985
65	**Najeeb Tarakai**	**2017-18**	48	A. W. Carr	1925
57	A. W. Wellard	1936	48	J. H. Edrich	1965
57	A. W. Wellard	1938	48	A. Symonds	1995

MOST BOUNDARIES IN AN INNINGS

	4/6			
72	62/10	B. C. Lara (501*)	Warwickshire v Durham at Birmingham	1994
68	68/–	P. A. Perrin (343*)	Essex v Derbyshire at Chesterfield	1904
65	64/1	A. C. MacLaren (424)	Lancashire v Somerset at Taunton	1895
64	64/–	Hanif Mohammad (499)	Karachi v Bahawalpur at Karachi	1958-59
57	52/5	J. H. Edrich (310*)	England v New Zealand at Leeds	1965
57	52/5	Naved Latif (394)	Sargodha v Gujranwala at Gujranwala	2000-01
56	54/2	K. M. Jadhav (327)	Maharashtra v Uttar Pradesh at Pune	2012-13
55	55/–	C. W. Gregory (383)	NSW v Queensland at Brisbane	1906-07
55	53/2	G. R. Marsh (355*)	W. Australia v S. Australia at Perth	1989-90
55	51/3†	S. V. Manjrekar (377)	Bombay v Hyderabad at Bombay	1990-91
55	52/3	D. S. Lehmann (339)	Yorkshire v Durham at Leeds	2006
55	54/1	D. K. H. Mitchell (298)	Worcestershire v Somerset at Taunton	2009
55	54/1	S. C. Cook (390)	Lions v Warriors at East London	2009-10
55	47/8	R. R. Rossouw (319)	Eagles v Titans at Centurion	2009-10

† *Plus one five.*

PARTNERSHIPS OVER 500

624	for 3rd	K. C. Sangakkara (287)/D. P. M. D. Jayawardene (374), Sri Lanka v South Africa at Colombo (SSC)	2006
594*	for 3rd	S. M. Gugale (351*)/A. R. Bawne (258*), Maharashtra v Delhi at Mumbai	2016-17
580	for 2nd	Rafatullah Mohmand (302*)/Aamer Sajjad (289), WAPDA v Sui Southern Gas at Sheikhupura	2009-10
577	for 4th	V. S. Hazare (288)/Gul Mahomed (319), Baroda v Holkar at Baroda	1946-47
576	for 2nd	S. T. Jayasuriya (340)/R. S. Mahanama (225), Sri Lanka v India at Colombo (RPS)	1997-98
574*	for 4th	F. M. M. Worrell (255*)/C. L. Walcott (314*), Barbados v Trinidad at Port-of-Spain	1945-46
561	for 1st	Waheed Mirza (324)/Mansoor Akhtar (224*), Karachi Whites v Quetta at Karachi	1976-77
555	for 1st	P. Holmes (224*)/H. Sutcliffe (313), Yorkshire v Essex at Leyton	1932
554	for 1st	J. T. Brown (300)/J. Tunnicliffe (243), Yorks v Derbys at Chesterfield	1898
539	for 3rd	S. D. Jogiyani (282)/R. A. Jadeja (303*), Saurashtra v Gujarat at Surat	2012-13
523	for 3rd	M. A. Carberry (300*)/N. D. McKenzie (237), Hants v Yorks at Southampton	2011
520*	for 5th	C. A. Pujara (302*)/R. A. Jadeja (232*), Saurashtra v Orissa at Rajkot	2008-09
503	for 1st	R. G. L. Carters (209)/A. J. Finch (288*), Cricket Australia XI v New Zealanders at Sydney	2015-16
502*	for 4th	F. M. M. Worrell (308*)/J. D. C. Goddard (218*), Barbados v Trinidad at Bridgetown	1943-44
501	for 3rd	A. N. Petersen (286)/A. G. Prince (261), Lancs v Glam at Colwyn Bay	2015

HIGHEST PARTNERSHIPS FOR EACH WICKET

First Wicket

561	Waheed Mirza/Mansoor Akhtar, Karachi Whites v Quetta at Karachi.........	1976-77
555	P. Holmes/H. Sutcliffe, Yorkshire v Essex at Leyton......................	1932
554	J. T. Brown/J. Tunnicliffe, Yorkshire v Derbyshire at Chesterfield	1898
503	R. G. L. Carters/A. J. Finch, Cricket Australia XI v New Zealanders at Sydney .	2015-16
490	E. H. Bowley/J. G. Langridge, Sussex v Middlesex at Hove	1933

Second Wicket

580	Rafatullah Mohmand/Aamer Sajjad, WAPDA v Sui S. Gas at Sheikhupura	2009-10
576	S. T. Jayasuriya/R. S. Mahanama, Sri Lanka v India at Colombo (RPS).......	1997-98
480	D. Elgar/R. R. Rossouw, Eagles v Titans at Centurion......................	2009-10
475	Zahir Alam/L. S. Rajput, Assam v Tripura at Gauhati	1991-92
465*	J. A. Jameson/R. B. Kanhai, Warwicks v Gloucestershire at Birmingham......	1974

Third Wicket

624	K. C. Sangakkara/D. P. M. D. Jayawardene, Sri Lanka v SA at Colombo (SSC)	2006
594*	S. M. Gugale/A. R. Bawne, Maharashtra v Delhi at Mumbai	2016-17
539	S. D. Jogiyani/R. A. Jadeja, Saurashtra v Gujarat at Surat	2012-13
523	M. A. Carberry/N. D. McKenzie, Hampshire v Yorks at Southampton	2011
501	A. N. Petersen/A. G. Prince, Lancashire v Glamorgan at Colwyn Bay	2015

Fourth Wicket

577	V. S. Hazare/Gul Mahomed, Baroda v Holkar at Baroda....................	1946-47
574*	C. L. Walcott/F. M. M. Worrell, Barbados v Trinidad at Port-of-Spain........	1945-46
502*	F. M. M. Worrell/J. D. C. Goddard, Barbados v Trinidad at Bridgetown	1943-44
470	A. I. Kallicharran/G. W. Humpage, Warwicks v Lancs at Southport	1982
462*	D. W. Hookes/W. B. Phillips, South Australia v Tasmania at Adelaide	1986-87

Fifth Wicket

520*	C. A. Pujara/R. A. Jadeja, Saurashtra v Orissa at Rajkot	2008-09
494	Marshall Ayub/Mehrab Hossain, Central Zone v East Zone at Bogra	2012-13
479	Misbah-ul-Haq/Usman Arshad, Sui N. Gas v Lahore Shalimar at Lahore	2009-10
464*	M. E. Waugh/S. R. Waugh, New South Wales v Western Australia at Perth....	1990-91
428*	B. C. Williams/M. Marais, Border v Eastern Province at East London	2017-18

Sixth Wicket

487*	G. A. Headley/C. C. Passailaigue, Jamaica v Lord Tennyson's XI at Kingston..	1931-32
428	W. W. Armstrong/M. A. Noble, Australians v Sussex at Hove	1902
417	W. P. Saha/L. R. Shukla, Bengal v Assam at Kolkata	2010-11
411	R. M. Poore/E. G. Wynyard, Hampshire v Somerset at Taunton	1899
399	B. A. Stokes/J. M. Bairstow, England v South Africa at Cape Town..........	2015-16

Seventh Wicket

460	Bhupinder Singh jnr/P. Dharmani, Punjab v Delhi at Delhi.................	1994-95
371	M. R. Marsh/S. M. Whiteman, Australia A v India A at Brisbane............	2014
366*	J. M. Bairstow/T. T. Bresnan, Yorkshire v Durham at Chester-le-Street	2015
347	D. St E. Atkinson/C. C. Depeiza, West Indies v Australia at Bridgetown	1954-55
347	Farhad Reza/Sanjamul Islam, Rajshahi v Chittagong at Savar...............	2013-14

Eighth Wicket

433	A. Sims and V. T. Trumper, A. Sims' Aust. XI v Canterbury at Christchurch...	1913-14
392	A. Mishra/J. Yadav, Haryana v Karnataka at Hubli	2012-13
332	I. J. L. Trott/S. C. J. Broad, England v Pakistan at Lord's	2010
313	Wasim Akram/Saqlain Mushtaq, Pakistan v Zimbabwe at Sheikhupura	1996-97
292	R. Peel/Lord Hawke, Yorkshire v Warwickshire at Birmingham	1896

Ninth Wicket

283	A. Warren/J. Chapman, Derbyshire v Warwickshire at Blackwell	1910
268	J. B. Commins/N. Boje, South Africa A v Mashonaland at Harare	1994-95
261	W. L. Madsen/T. Poynton, Derbyshire v Northants at Northampton	2012
251	J. W. H. T. Douglas/S. N. Hare, Essex v Derbyshire at Leyton	1921
249*†	A. S. Srivastava/K. Seth, Madhya Pradesh v Vidarbha at Indore	2000-01

† *276 unbeaten runs were scored for this wicket in two separate partnerships; after Srivastava retired hurt, Seth and N. D. Hirwani added 27.*

Tenth Wicket

307	A. F. Kippax/J. E. H. Hooker, New South Wales v Victoria at Melbourne	1928-29
249	C. T. Sarwate/S. N. Banerjee, Indians v Surrey at The Oval	1946
239	Aqeel Arshad/Ali Raza, Lahore Whites v Hyderabad at Lahore	2004-05
235	F. E. Woolley/A. Fielder, Kent v Worcestershire at Stourbridge	1909
233	Ajay Sharma/Maninder Singh, Delhi v Bombay at Bombay	1991-92

There have been only 13 last-wicket stands of 200 or more.

UNUSUAL DISMISSALS

Handled the Ball

There have been **63** instances in first-class cricket. The most recent are:

W. S. A. Williams	Canterbury v Otago at Dunedin	2012-13
E. Lewis	Trinidad & Tobago v Leeward Islands at Port-of-Spain	2013-14
C. A. Pujara	Derbyshire v Leicestershire at Derby	2014
I. Khan	Dolphins v Lions at Johannesburg	2014-15
K. Lesporis	Windward Islands v Barbados at Bridgetown	2015-16
S. R. Dickson	Kent v Leicestershire at Leicester	2016
M. Z. Hamza	Cape Cobras v Knights at Bloemfontein	2016-17

Under the 2017 revision of the Laws, Handled the Ball was subsumed under Obstructing the Field.

Obstructing the Field

There have been **30** instances in first-class cricket. T. Straw of Worcestershire was given out for obstruction v Warwickshire in both 1899 and 1901. The most recent are:

W. E. Bell	Northern Cape v Border at Kimberley	2015-16
Jahid Ali	Pakistan A v Zimbabwe A at Bulawayo	2016-17
Ghamai Zadran	Mis Ainak v Boost at Ghazi Amanullah Town	2017-18
Rashid Zadran	Mis Ainak v Band-e-Amir at Kabul	2017-18
Zia-ur-Rehman	Mis Ainak v Amo at Khost	2017-18
R. P. Burl	**Rising Stars v Harare Metropolitan Eagles at Harare**	**2017-18**

Hit the Ball Twice

There have been **21** instances in first-class cricket. The last occurrence in England involved J. H. King of Leicestershire v Surrey at The Oval in 1906. The most recent are:

Aziz Malik	Lahore Division v Faisalabad at Sialkot....................	1984-85
Javed Mohammad	Multan v Karachi Whites at Sahiwal	1986-87
Shahid Pervez	Jammu & Kashmir v Punjab at Srinagar	1986-87
Ali Naqvi	PNSC v National Bank at Faisalabad.......................	1998-99
A. George	Tamil Nadu v Maharashtra at Pune	1998-99
Maqsood Raza	Lahore Division v PNSC at Sheikhupura..................	1999-2000
D. Mahajan	Jammu & Kashmir v Bihar at Jammu	2005-06

Timed Out

There have been **six** instances in first-class cricket:

A. Jordaan	Eastern Province v Transvaal at Port Elizabeth (SACB match)....	1987-88
H. Yadav	Tripura v Orissa at Cuttack................................	1997-98
V. C. Drakes	Border v Free State at East London	2002-03
A. J. Harris	Nottinghamshire v Durham UCCE at Nottingham.	2003
R. A. Austin	Combined Campuses & Colleges v Windward Is at Arnos Vale ...	2013-14
C. Kunje	Bulawayo Met Tuskers v Manica Mountaineers at Bulawayo.....	2017-18

BOWLING RECORDS

TEN WICKETS IN AN INNINGS

In the history of first-class cricket, there have been **80** instances of a bowler taking all ten wickets in an innings, plus a further three instances of ten wickets in 12-a-side matches. Occurrences since the Second World War:

	O	M	R		
*W. E. Hollies (Warwickshire)....	20.4	4	49	v Notts at Birmingham	1946
J. M. Sims (East)...............	18.4	2	90	v West at Kingston	1948
T. E. Bailey (Essex)	39.4	9	90	v Lancashire at Clacton.........	1949
J. K. Graveney (Glos.)	18.4	2	66	v Derbyshire at Chesterfield	1949
R. Berry (Lancashire)	36.2	9	102	v Worcestershire at Blackpool ...	1953
S. P. Gupte (President's XI)	24.2	7	78	v Combined XI at Bombay	1954-55
J. C. Laker (Surrey)............	46	18	88	v Australians at The Oval	1956
J. C. Laker (England)	51.2	23	53	v Australia at Manchester	1956
G. A. R. Lock (Surrey)	29.1	18	54	v Kent at Blackheath...........	1956
K. Smales (Nottinghamshire)	41.3	20	66	v Gloucestershire at Stroud	1956
P. M. Chatterjee (Bengal)	19	11	20	v Assam at Jorhat..............	1956-57
J. D. Bannister (Warwickshire)...	23.3	11	41	v Comb. Services at Birmingham†	1959
A. J. G. Pearson (Cambridge U.) .	30.3	8	78	v Leics at Loughborough	1961
N. I. Thomson (Sussex)	34.2	19	49	v Warwickshire at Worthing.....	1964
P. J. Allan (Queensland)........	15.6	3	61	v Victoria at Melbourne	1965-66
I. J. Brayshaw (W. Australia)	17.6	4	44	v Victoria at Perth.............	1967-68
Shahid Mahmood (Karachi Whites) .	25	5	58	v Khairpur at Karachi...........	1969-70
E. E. Hemmings (International XI)	49.3	14	175	v West Indies XI at Kingston	1982-83
P. Sunderam (Rajasthan)........	22	5	78	v Vidarbha at Jodhpur..........	1985-86
S. T. Jefferies (W. Province)....	22.5	7	59	v Orange Free State at Cape Town .	1987-88
Imran Adil (Bahawalpur)	22.5	3	92	v Faisalabad at Faisalabad	1989-90
G. P. Wickremasinghe (Sinhalese) .	19.2	5	41	v Kalutara PCC at Colombo (SSC)	1991-92
R. L. Johnson (Middlesex)	18.5	6	45	v Derbyshire at Derby..........	1994
Naeem Akhtar (Rawalpindi B)...	21.3	10	28	v Peshawar at Peshawar	1995-96
A. Kumble (India).............	26.3	9	74	v Pakistan at Delhi	1998-99

	O	M	R		
D. S. Mohanty (East Zone)	19	5	46	v South Zone at Agartala	2000-01
O. D. Gibson (Durham)	17.3	1	47	v Hampshire at Chester-le-Street	2007
M. W. Olivier (Warriors)	26.3	4	65	v Eagles at Bloemfontein	2007-08
Zulfiqar Babar (Multan)	39.4	3	143	v Islamabad at Multan	2009-10

* *W. E. Hollies bowled seven and had three lbw. The only other instance of a bowler achieving the feat without the direct assistance of a fielder came in 1850 when J. Wisden bowled all ten, for North v South at Lord's.*

† *Mitchells & Butlers Ground.*

OUTSTANDING BOWLING ANALYSES

	O	M	R	W		
H. Verity (Yorkshire)	19.4	16	10	10	v Nottinghamshire at Leeds	1932
G. Elliott (Victoria)	19	17	2	9	v Tasmania at Launceston	1857-58
Ahad Khan (Railways)	6.3	4	7	9	v Dera Ismail Khan at Lahore	1964-65
J. C. Laker (England)	14	12	2	8	v The Rest at Bradford	1950
D. Shackleton (Hampshire)	11.1	7	4	8	v Somerset at Weston-s-Mare	1955
E. Peate (Yorkshire)	16	11	5	8	v Surrey at Holbeck	1883
K. M. Dabengwa (Westerns)	4.4	3	1	7	v Northerns at Harare	2006-07
F. R. Spofforth (Australians)	8.3	6	3	7	v England XI at Birmingham	1884
W. A. Henderson (NE Transvaal)	9.3	7	4	7	v OFS at Bloemfontein	1937-38
Rajinder Goel (Haryana)	7	4	4	7	v Jammu & Kashmir at Chandigarh	1977-78
N. W. Bracken (NSW)	7	5	4	7	v South Australia at Sydney	2004-05
V. I. Smith (South Africans)	4.5	3	1	6	v Derbyshire at Derby	1947
S. Costick (Victoria)	21.1	20	1	6	v Tasmania at Melbourne	1868-69
Israr Ali (Bahawalpur)	11	10	1	6	v Dacca U. at Bahawalpur	1957-58
A. D. Pougher (MCC)	3	3	0	5	v Australians at Lord's	1896
G. R. Cox (Sussex)	6	6	0	5	v Somerset at Weston-s-Mare	1921
R. K. Tyldesley (Lancashire)	5	5	0	5	v Leicestershire at Manchester	1924
P. T. Mills (Gloucestershire)	6.4	6	0	5	v Somerset at Bristol	1928

MOST WICKETS IN A MATCH

19-90	J. C. Laker	England v Australia at Manchester	1956
17-48†	C. Blythe	Kent v Northamptonshire at Northampton	1907
17-50	C. T. B. Turner	Australians v England XI at Hastings	1888
17-54	W. P. Howell	Australians v Western Province at Cape Town	1902-03
17-56	C. W. L. Parker	Gloucestershire v Essex at Gloucester	1925
17-67	A. P. Freeman	Kent v Sussex at Hove	1922
17-89	W. G. Grace	Gloucestershire v Nottinghamshire at Cheltenham	1877
17-89	F. C. L. Matthews	Nottinghamshire v Northants at Nottingham	1923
17-91	H. Dean	Lancashire v Yorkshire at Liverpool	1913
17-91†	H. Verity	Yorkshire v Essex at Leyton	1933
17-92	A. P. Freeman	Kent v Warwickshire at Folkestone	1932
17-103	W. Mycroft	Derbyshire v Hampshire at Southampton	1876
17-106	G. R. Cox	Sussex v Warwickshire at Horsham	1926
17-106†	T. W. J. Goddard	Gloucestershire v Kent at Bristol	1939
17-119	W. Mead	Essex v Hampshire at Southampton	1895
17-137	W. Brearley	Lancashire v Somerset at Manchester	1905
17-137	J. M. Davison	Canada v USA at Fort Lauderdale	2004
17-159	S. F. Barnes	England v South Africa at Johannesburg	1913-14
17-201	G. Giffen	South Australia v Victoria at Adelaide	1885-86
17-212	J. C. Clay	Glamorgan v Worcestershire at Swansea	1937

† *Achieved in a single day.*

H. Arkwright took 18-96 for MCC v Gentlemen of Kent in a 12-a-side match at Canterbury in 1861.
    There have been **59** *instances of a bowler taking 16 wickets in an 11-a-side match, the most recent being 16-141 by Saad Altaf for Rawalpindi v FATA at Mirpur, 2017-18.*

FOUR WICKETS WITH CONSECUTIVE BALLS

There have been **44** instances in first-class cricket. R. J. Crisp achieved the feat twice, for Western Province in 1931-32 and 1933-34. A. E. Trott took four in four balls and another hat-trick in the same innings for Middlesex v Somerset in 1907, his benefit match. Occurrences since 2007:

Tabish Khan	Karachi Whites v ZTBL at Karachi.	2009-10
Kamran Hussain	Habib Bank v Lahore Shalimar at Lahore.	2009-10
N. Wagner	Otago v Wellington at Queenstown.	2010-11
Khalid Usman	Abbottabad v Karachi Blues at Karachi	2011-12
Mahmudullah	Central Zone v North Zone at Savar	2013-14
A. C. Thomas	Somerset v Sussex at Taunton.	2014
Taj Wali	Peshawar v Port Qasim Authority at Peshawar	2015-16
N. G. R. P. Jayasuriya	Colts v Badureliya at Maggona	2015-16
K. R. Smuts	Eastern Province v Boland at Paarl	2015-16

In their match with England at The Oval in 1863, Surrey lost four wickets in the course of a four-ball over from G. Bennett.

Sussex lost five wickets in the course of the final (six-ball) over of their match with Surrey at Eastbourne in 1972. P. I. Pocock, who had taken three wickets in his previous over, captured four more, taking in all seven wickets with 11 balls, a feat unique in first-class matches. (The eighth wicket fell to a run-out.)

In 1996, K. D. James took four in four balls for Hampshire against Indians at Southampton and scored a century, a feat later emulated by Mahmudullah and Smuts.

HAT-TRICKS

Double Hat-Trick

Besides Trott's performance, which is mentioned in the preceding section, the following instances are recorded of players having performed the hat-trick twice in the same match, Rao doing so in the same innings.

A. Shaw	Nottinghamshire v Gloucestershire at Nottingham	1884
T. J. Matthews	Australia v South Africa at Manchester.	1912
C. W. L. Parker	Gloucestershire v Middlesex at Bristol	1924
R. O. Jenkins	Worcestershire v Surrey at Worcester.	1949
J. S. Rao	Services v Northern Punjab at Amritsar	1963-64
Amin Lakhani	Combined XI v Indians at Multan	1978-79
M. A. Starc	New South Wales v Western Australia at Sydney (Hurstville). .	2017-18

Five Wickets in Six Balls

W. H. Copson	Derbyshire v Warwickshire at Derby	1937
W. A. Henderson	NE Transvaal v Orange Free State at Bloemfontein	1937-38
P. I. Pocock	Surrey v Sussex at Eastbourne	1972
Yasir Arafat	Rawalpindi v Faisalabad at Rawalpindi	2004-05
N. Wagner	Otago v Wellington at Queenstown	2010-11

Yasir Arafat's five wickets were spread across two innings and interrupted only by a no-ball. Wagner was the first to take five wickets in a single over.

Most Hat-Tricks

D. V. P. Wright	7	R. G. Barlow	4	T. G. Matthews	4
T. W. J. Goddard	6	Fazl-e-Akbar	4	M. J. Procter	4
C. W. L. Parker	6	A. P. Freeman	4	T. Richardson	4
S. Haigh	5	J. T. Hearne	4	F. R. Spofforth	4
V. W. C. Jupp	5	J. C. Laker	4	F. S. Trueman	4
A. E. G. Rhodes.	5	G. A. R. Lock	4		
F. A. Tarrant	5	G. G. Macaulay	4		

Hat-Trick on Debut

There have been **18** instances in first-class cricket. Occurrences since 2000:

S. M. Harwood	Victoria v Tasmania at Melbourne	2002-03
P. Connell	Ireland v Netherlands at Rotterdam	2008
A. Mithun	Karnataka v Uttar Pradesh at Meerut	2009-10
Zohaib Shera	Karachi Whites v National Bank at Karachi	2009-10

R. R. Phillips (Border) took a hat-trick in his first over in first-class cricket (v Eastern Province at Port Elizabeth, 1939-40) having previously played in four matches without bowling.

250 WICKETS IN A SEASON

	Season	O	M	R	W	Avge
A. P. Freeman	1928	1,976.1	423	5,489	304	18.05
A. P. Freeman	1933	2,039	651	4,549	298	15.26
T. Richardson	1895‡	1,690.1	463	4,170	290	14.37
C. T. B. Turner	1888†	2,427.2	1,127	3,307	283	11.68
A. P. Freeman	1931	1,618	360	4,307	276	15.60
A. P. Freeman	1930	1,914.3	472	4,632	275	16.84
T. Richardson	1897‡	1,603.4	495	3,945	273	14.45
A. P. Freeman	1929	1,670.5	381	4,879	267	18.27
W. Rhodes.	1900	1,553	455	3,606	261	13.81
J. T. Hearne.	1896‡	2,003.1	818	3,670	257	14.28
A. P. Freeman	1932	1,565.5	404	4,149	253	16.39
W. Rhodes.	1901	. 1,565	505	3,797	251	15.12

†   *Indicates 4-ball overs.*   ‡   *5-ball overs.*

In four consecutive seasons (1928–1931), A. P. Freeman took 1,122 wickets, and in eight consecutive seasons (1928–1935), 2,090 wickets. In each of these eight seasons he took over 200 wickets.

T. Richardson took 1,005 wickets in four consecutive seasons (1894–1897).

The earliest date by which any bowler has taken 100 in an English season is June 12, achieved by J. T. Hearne in 1896 and C. W. L. Parker in 1931, when A. P. Freeman did it on June 13.

100 WICKETS IN A SEASON MOST TIMES

(Includes overseas tours and seasons)

W. Rhodes	23	C. W. L. Parker	16	G. H. Hirst	15
D. Shackleton.	20	R. T. D. Perks.	16	A. S. Kennedy	15
A. P. Freeman.	17	F. J. Titmus	16	
T. W. J. Goddard	16	J. T. Hearne	15	

D. Shackleton reached 100 wickets in 20 successive seasons – 1949–1968.

Since the reduction of County Championship matches in 1969, D. L. Underwood (five times) and J. K. Lever (four times) are the only bowlers to have reached 100 wickets in a season more than twice. The highest aggregate in a season since 1969 is 134 by M. D. Marshall in 1982.

The most instances of 200 wickets in a season is eight by A. P. Freeman, who did it in eight successive seasons – 1928 to 1935 – including 304 in 1928. C. W. L. Parker did it five times, T. W. J. Goddard four times, and J. T. Hearne, G. A. Lohmann, W. Rhodes, T. Richardson, M. W. Tate and H. Verity three times each.

The last bowler to reach 200 wickets in a season was G. A. R. Lock (212 in 1957).

An expanded and regularly updated online version of the Records can be found at www.wisdenrecords.com

100 WICKETS IN A SEASON OUTSIDE ENGLAND

W		Season	Country	R	Avge
116	M. W. Tate	1926-27	India/Ceylon	1,599	13.78
113	Kabir Khan	1998-99	Pakistan	1,706	15.09
107	Ijaz Faqih	1985-86	Pakistan	1,719	16.06
106	C. T. B. Turner	1887-88	Australia	1,441	13.59
106	R. Benaud	1957-58	South Africa	2,056	19.39
105	Murtaza Hussain	1995-96	Pakistan	1,882	17.92
104	S. F. Barnes...............	1913-14	South Africa	1,117	10.74
104	Sajjad Akbar	1989-90	Pakistan	2,328	22.38
103	Abdul Qadir	1982-83	Pakistan	2,367	22.98
101	**Zia-ur-Rehman**	**2017-18**	**Afghanistan**	**1,995**	**19.75**

LEADING BOWLERS IN AN ENGLISH SEASON

(Qualification: 10 wickets in 10 innings)

Season	Leading wicket-taker	Wkts	Avge	Top of averages	Wkts	Avge
1946	W. E. Hollies	184	15.60	A. Booth.............	111	11.61
1947	T. W. J. Goddard	238	17.30	J. C. Clay	65	16.44
1948	J. E. Walsh	174	19.56	J. C. Clay	41	14.17
1949	R. O. Jenkins	183	21.19	T. W. J. Goddard	160	19.18
1950	R. Tattersall	193	13.59	R. Tattersall	193	13.59
1951	R. Appleyard	200	14.14	R. Appleyard	200	14.14
1952	J. H. Wardle.........	177	19.54	F. S. Trueman.........	61	13.78
1953	B. Dooland..........	172	16.58	C. J. Knott	38	13.71
1954	B. Dooland..........	196	15.48	J. B. Statham	92	14.13
1955	G. A. R. Lock........	216	14.49	R. Appleyard	85	13.01
1956	D. J. Shepherd	177	15.36	G. A. R. Lock........	155	12.46
1957	G. A. R. Lock........	212	12.02	G. A. R. Lock........	212	12.02
1958	G. A. R. Lock........	170	12.08	H. L. Jackson	143	10.99
1959	D. Shackleton	148	21.55	J. B. Statham	139	15.01
1960	F. S. Trueman........	175	13.98	J. B. Statham	135	12.31
1961	J. A. Flavell	171	17.79	J. A. Flavell	171	17.79
1962	D. Shackleton........	172	20.15	C. Cook	58	17.13
1963	D. Shackleton........	146	16.75	C. C. Griffith	119	12.83
1964	D. Shackleton........	142	20.40	J. A. Standen	64	13.00
1965	D. Shackleton........	144	16.08	H. J. Rhodes.........	119	11.04
1966	D. L. Underwood	157	13.80	D. L. Underwood	157	13.80
1967	T. W. Cartwright	147	15.52	D. L. Underwood	136	12.39
1968	R. Illingworth........	131	14.36	O. S. Wheatley........	82	12.95
1969	R. M. H. Cottam......	109	21.04	A. Ward.............	69	14.82
1970	D. J. Shepherd	106	19.16	Majid Khan	11	18.81
1971	L. R. Gibbs..........	131	18.89	G. G. Arnold	83	17.12
1972 {	T. W. Cartwright	98	18.64	I. M. Chappell	10	10.60
	B. Stead	98	20.38			
1973	B. S. Bedi..........	105	17.94	T. W. Cartwright	89	15.84
1974	A. M. E. Roberts	119	13.62	A. M. E. Roberts	119	13.62
1975	P. G. Lee	112	18.45	A. M. E. Roberts	57	15.80
1976	G. A. Cope...........	93	24.13	M. A. Holding	55	14.38
1977	M. J. Procter........	109	18.04	R. A. Woolmer........	19	15.21
1978	D. L. Underwood	110	14.49	D. L. Underwood	110	14.49
1979 {	D. L. Underwood	106	14.85	J. Garner............	55	13.83
	J. K. Lever	106	17.30			
1980	R. D. Jackman	121	15.40	J. Garner............	49	13.93
1981	R. J. Hadlee	105	14.89	R. J. Hadlee	105	14.89
1982	M. D. Marshall	134	15.73	R. J. Hadlee	61	14.57
1983 {	J. K. Lever	106	16.28	Imran Khan	12	7.16
	D. L. Underwood	106	19.28			

Season	Leading wicket-taker	Wkts	Avge	Top of averages	Wkts	Avge
1984	R. J. Hadlee	117	14.05	R. J. Hadlee	117	14.05
1985	N. V. Radford	101	24.68	R. M. Ellison	65	17.20
1986	C. A. Walsh	118	18.17	M. D. Marshall	100	15.08
1987	N. V. Radford	109	20.81	R. J. Hadlee	97	12.64
1988	F. D. Stephenson	125	18.31	M. D. Marshall	42	13.16
1989	{ D. R. Pringle	94	18.64	T. M. Alderman	70	15.64
	{ S. L. Watkin	94	25.09			
1990	N. A. Foster	94	26.61	I. R. Bishop	59	19.05
1991	Waqar Younis	113	14.65	Waqar Younis	113	14.65
1992	C. A. Walsh	92	15.96	C. A. Walsh	92	15.96
1993	S. L. Watkin	92	22.80	Wasim Akram	59	19.27
1994	M. M. Patel	90	22.86	C. E. L. Ambrose	77	14.45
1995	A. Kumble	105	20.40	A. A. Donald	89	16.07
1996	C. A. Walsh	85	16.84	C. E. L. Ambrose	43	16.67
1997	A. M. Smith	83	17.63	A. A. Donald	60	15.63
1998	C. A. Walsh	106	17.31	V. J. Wells	36	14.27
1999	A. Sheriyar	92	24.70	Saqlain Mushtaq	58	11.37
2000	G. D. McGrath	80	13.21	C. A. Walsh	40	11.42
2001	R. J. Kirtley	75	23.32	G. D. McGrath	40	15.60
2002	{ M. J. Saggers	83	21.51	C. P. Schofield	18	18.38
	{ K. J. Dean	83	23.50			
2003	Mushtaq Ahmed	103	24.65	Shoaib Akhtar	34	17.05
2004	Mushtaq Ahmed	84	27.59	D. S. Lehmann	15	17.40
2005	S. K. Warne	87	22.50	M. Muralitharan	36	15.00
2006	Mushtaq Ahmed	102	19.91	Naved-ul-Hasan	35	16.71
2007	Mushtaq Ahmed	90	25.66	Harbhajan Singh	37	18.54
2008	J. A. Tomlinson	67	24.76	M. Davies	41	14.63
2009	Danish Kaneria	75	23.69	G. Onions	69	19.95
2010	A. R. Adams	68	22.17	J. K. H. Naik	35	17.68
2011	D. D. Masters	93	18.13	T. T. Bresnan	29	17.68
2012	G. Onions	72	14.73	G. Onions	72	14.73
2013	G. Onions	73	18.92	T. A. Copeland	45	18.26
2014	M. H. A. Footitt	84	19.19	G. R. Napier	52	15.63
2015	C. Rushworth	90	20.54	R. J. Sidebottom	43	18.09
2016	{ G. R. Napier	69	22.30	J. M. Anderson	45	17.00
	{ J. S. Patel	69	24.02			
2017	J. A. Porter	85	16.74	J. L. Pattinson	32	12.06
2018	**O. E. Robinson**	**81**	**17.43**	**O. P. Stone**	**43**	**12.30**

MOST WICKETS

Dates in italics denote the first half of an overseas season; i.e. *1970* denotes the 1970-71 season.

		Career	W	R	Avge
1	W. Rhodes	1898–1930	4,187	69,993	16.71
2	A. P. Freeman	1914–1936	3,776	69,577	18.42
3	C. W. L. Parker	1903–1935	3,278	63,817	19.46
4	J. T. Hearne	1888–1923	3,061	54,352	17.75
5	T. W. J. Goddard	1922–1952	2,979	59,116	19.84
6	W. G. Grace	1865–1908	2,876	51,545	17.92
7	A. S. Kennedy	1907–1936	2,874	61,034	21.23
8	D. Shackleton	1948–1969	2,857	53,303	18.65
9	G. A. R. Lock	1946–*1970*	2,844	54,709	19.23
10	F. J. Titmus	1949–1982	2,830	63,313	22.37
11	M. W. Tate	1912–1937	2,784	50,571	18.16
12	G. H. Hirst	1891–1929	2,739	51,282	18.72
13	C. Blythe	1899–1914	2,506	42,136	16.81

Some works of reference provide career figures which differ from those in this list, owing to the exclusion or inclusion of matches recognised or not recognised as first-class by Wisden. *A fuller list can be found in* Wisdens *up to 2011.*

Current Players with 750 Wickets

	Career	W	R	Avge
H. M. R. K. B. Herath	1996–2018	1,071	26,984	25.19
D. S. Hettiarachchi	1994–2017	947	22,238	23.48
J. M. Anderson.	2002–2018	910	23,201	25.49
J. S. Patel	1999–2018	822	27,215	33.10
S. Weerakoon.	1995–2017	816	17,967	22.01
T. J. Murtagh	2000–2018	760	19,613	25.80
M. D. K. Perera	2000–2018	756	19,836	26.23

ALL-ROUND RECORDS

REMARKABLE ALL-ROUND MATCHES

V. E. Walker	20*	108	10-74	4-17	England v Surrey at The Oval	1859
W. G. Grace	104		2-60	10-49	MCC v Oxford University at Oxford .	1886
G. Giffen	271		9-96	7-70	South Australia v Victoria at Adelaide	1891-92
B. J. T. Bosanquet	103	100*	3-75	8-53	Middlesex v Sussex at Lord's	1905
G. H. Hirst	111	117*	6-70	5-45	Yorkshire v Somerset at Bath	1906
F. D. Stephenson	111	117	4-105	7-117	Notts v Yorkshire at Nottingham.	1988

E. M. Grace, for MCC v Gentlemen of Kent in a 12-a-side match at Canterbury in 1862, scored 192* and took 5-77 and 10-69.

HUNDRED AND HAT-TRICK

G. Giffen, Australians v Lancashire at Manchester	1884
*W. E. Roller, Surrey v Sussex at The Oval	1885
W. B. Burns, Worcestershire v Gloucestershire at Worcester	1913
V. W. C. Jupp, Sussex v Essex at Colchester	1921
R. E. S. Wyatt, MCC v Ceylonese at Colombo (Victoria Park)	1926-27
L. N. Constantine, West Indians v Northamptonshire at Northampton	1928
D. E. Davies, Glamorgan v Leicestershire at Leicester	1937
V. M. Merchant, Dr C. R. Pereira's XI v Sir Homi Mehta's XI at Bombay	1946-47
M. J. Procter, Gloucestershire v Essex at Westcliff-on-Sea.	1972
M. J. Procter, Gloucestershire v Leicestershire at Bristol	1979
†K. D. James, Hampshire v Indians at Southampton.	1996
J. E. C. Franklin, Gloucestershire v Derbyshire at Cheltenham.	2009
Sohag Gazi, Barisal v Khulna at Khulna	2012-13
Sohag Gazi, Bangladesh v New Zealand at Chittagong	2013-14
†Mahmudullah, Central Zone v North Zone at Savar	2013-14
†K. R. Smuts, Eastern Province v Boland at Paarl	2015-16

* *W. E. Roller is the only player to combine 200 with a hat-trick.*

† *K. D. James, Mahmudullah and K. R. Smuts all combined 100 with four wickets in four balls (Mahmudullah's were split between two innings).*

THE DOUBLE

The double was traditionally regarded as 1,000 runs and 100 wickets in an English season. The feat became exceptionally rare after the reduction of County Championship matches in 1969.

Remarkable Seasons

	Season	R	W		Season	R	W
G. H. Hirst	1906	2,385	208	J. H. Parks	1937	3,003	101

1,000 Runs and 100 Wickets

W. Rhodes	16	W. G. Grace	8	F. J. Titmus	8
G. H. Hirst	14	M. S. Nichols	8	F. E. Woolley	7
V. W. C. Jupp	10	A. E. Relf	8	G. E. Tribe	7
W. E. Astill	9	F. A. Tarrant	8		
T. E. Bailey	8	M. W. Tate	8†		

† *M. W. Tate also scored 1,193 runs and took 116 wickets on the 1926-27 MCC tour of India and Ceylon.*

R. J. Hadlee (1984) and F. D. Stephenson (1988) are the only players to perform the feat since the reduction of County Championship matches in 1969. A complete list of those performing the feat before then may be found on page 202 of the 1982 Wisden. T. E. Bailey (1959) was the last player to achieve 2,000 runs and 100 wickets in a season; M. W. Tate (1925) the last to reach 1,000 runs and 200 wickets. Full lists may be found in Wisdens up to 2003.

Wicketkeeper's Double

The only wicketkeepers to achieve 1,000 runs and 100 dismissals in a season were L. E. G. Ames (1928, 1929 and 1932, when he scored 2,482 runs) and J. T. Murray (1957).

WICKETKEEPING RECORDS

MOST DISMISSALS IN AN INNINGS

9 (8ct, 1st)	Tahir Rashid	Habib Bank v PACO at Gujranwala	1992-93
9 (7ct, 2st)	W. R. James*	Matabeleland v Mashonaland CD at Bulawayo	1995-96
8 (8ct)	A. T. W. Grout	Queensland v Western Australia at Brisbane	1959-60
8 (8ct)†	D. E. East	Essex v Somerset at Taunton	1985
8 (8ct)	S. A. Marsh‡	Kent v Middlesex at Lord's	1991
8 (6ct, 2st)	T. J. Zoehrer	Australians v Surrey at The Oval	1993
8 (7ct, 1st)	D. S. Berry	Victoria v South Australia at Melbourne	1996-97
8 (7ct, 1st)	Y. S. S. Mendis	Bloomfield v Kurunegala Y at Colombo (Bloomfield)	2000-01
8 (7ct, 1st)	S. Nath§	Assam v Tripura at Guwahati	2001-02
8 (8ct)	J. N. Batty¶	Surrey v Kent at The Oval	2004
8 (8ct)	Golam Mabud	Sylhet v Dhaka at Dhaka	2005-06
8 (8ct)	A. Z. M. Dyili	Eastern Province v Free State at Port Elizabeth	2009-10
8 (8ct)	D. C. de Boorder	Otago v Wellington at Wellington	2009-10
8 (8ct)	R. S. Second	Free State v North West at Bloemfontein	2011-12
8 (8ct)	T. L. Tsolekile	South Africa A v Sri Lanka A at Durban	2012
8 (7ct, 1st)	**M. A. R. S. Fernando**	**Chilaw Marians v Colts at Colombo (SSC)**	**2017-18**

There have been 110 further instances of seven dismissals in an innings. R. W. Taylor achieved the feat three times, and G. J. Hopkins, Kamran Akmal, I. Khaleel, S. A. Marsh, K. J. Piper, Shahin Hossain, T. L. Tsolekile and Wasim Bari twice. Khaleel did it twice in the same match. Marsh's and Tsolekile's two instances both included one of eight dismssals – see above. H. Yarnold made six stumpings and one catch in an innings for Worcestershire v Scotland at Dundee in 1951. A fuller list can be found in Wisdens before 2004.

*　W. R. James also scored 99 and 99 not out.*	† *The first eight wickets to fall.*
‡　*S. A. Marsh also scored 108 not out.*	§ *On his only first-class appearance.*
¶　*J. N. Batty also scored 129.*	

WICKETKEEPERS' HAT-TRICKS

W. H. Brain, Gloucestershire v Somerset at Cheltenham, 1893 – three stumpings off successive balls from C. L. Townsend.

K. R. Meherhomji, Freelooters v Nizam's State Railway A at Secunderabad, 1931-32 – three catches off successive balls from L. Ramji.

G. O. Dawkes, Derbyshire v Worcestershire at Kidderminster, 1958 – three catches off successive balls from H. L. Jackson.

R. C. Russell, Gloucestershire v Surrey at The Oval, 1986 – three catches off successive balls from C. A. Walsh and D. V. Lawrence (2).

T. Frost, Warwickshire v Surrey at Birmingham, 2003 – three catches off successive balls from G. G. Wagg and N. M. Carter (2).

MOST DISMISSALS IN A MATCH

14 (11ct, 3st)	I. Khaleel	Hyderabad v Assam at Guwahati	2011-12
13 (11ct, 2st)	W. R. James*	Matabeleland v Mashonaland CD at Bulawayo	1995-96
12 (8ct, 4st)	E. Pooley	Surrey v Sussex at The Oval	1868
12 (9ct, 3st)	D. Tallon	Queensland v New South Wales at Sydney	1938-39
12 (9ct, 3st)	H. B. Taber	New South Wales v South Australia at Adelaide	1968-69
12 (12ct)	P. D. McGlashan	Northern Districts v Central Districts at Whangarei	2009-10
12 (11ct, 1st)	T. L. Tsolekile	Lions v Dolphins at Johannesburg	2010-11
12 (12ct)	Kashif Mahmood	Lahore Shalimar v Abbottabad at Abbottabad	2010-11
12 (12ct)	R. S. Second	Free State v North West at Bloemfontein	2011-12

* *W. R. James also scored 99 and 99 not out.*

100 DISMISSALS IN A SEASON

128 (79ct, 49st)	L. E. G. Ames	1929	104 (82ct, 22st)	J. T. Murray	1957
122 (70ct, 52st)	L. E. G. Ames	1928	102 (69ct, 33st)	F. H. Huish	1913
110 (63ct, 47st)	H. Yarnold	1949	102 (95ct, 7st)	J. T. Murray	1960
107 (77ct, 30st)	G. Duckworth	1928	101 (62ct, 39st)	F. H. Huish	1911
107 (96ct, 11st)	J. G. Binks	1960	101 (85ct, 16st)	R. Booth	1960
104 (40ct, 64st)	L. E. G. Ames	1932	100 (91ct, 9st)	R. Booth	1964

L. E. G. Ames achieved the two highest stumping totals in a season: 64 in 1932, and 52 in 1928.

MOST DISMISSALS

Dates in italics denote the first half of an overseas season; i.e. *1914* denotes the 1914-15 season.

			Career	M	Ct	St
1	R. W. Taylor	1,649	1960–1988	639	1,473	176
2	J. T. Murray	1,527	1952–1975	635	1,270	257
3	H. Strudwick	1,497	1902–1927	675	1,242	255
4	A. P. E. Knott	1,344	1964–1985	511	1,211	133
5	R. C. Russell	1,320	1981–2004	465	1,192	128
6	F. H. Huish	1,310	1895–1914	497	933	377
7	B. Taylor	1,294	1949–1973	572	1,083	211
8	S. J. Rhodes	1,263	1981–2004	440	1,139	124
9	D. Hunter	1,253	1888–1909	548	906	347

Current Players with 500 Dismissals

		Career	M	Ct	St
901	J. S. Foster	2000–2018	289	839	62
884	Kamran Akmal	*1997–2018*	233	820	64
679	T. R. Ambrose	2001–2018	239	639	40
540	N. J. O'Brien	2004–2018	176	492	48
539	Adnan Akmal	*2003–2018*	158	508	31
537	P. A. Patel	*2001–2018*	185	461	76
514	S. M. Davies	2005–2018	210	484	30
506	Sarfraz Ahmed	*2005–2018*	147	454	52

Some of these figures include catches taken in the field.

FIELDING RECORDS

excluding wicketkeepers

MOST CATCHES IN AN INNINGS

7	M. J. Stewart	Surrey v Northamptonshire at Northampton	1957
7	A. S. Brown	Gloucestershire v Nottinghamshire at Nottingham	1966
7	R. Clarke	Warwickshire v Lancashire at Liverpool.	2011

MOST CATCHES IN A MATCH

10	W. R. Hammond†	Gloucestershire v Surrey at Cheltenham	1928
9	R. Clarke	Warwickshire v Lancashire at Liverpool.	2011
8	W. B. Burns	Worcestershire v Yorkshire at Bradford	1907
8	F. G. Travers	Europeans v Parsees at Bombay	1923-24
8	A. H. Bakewell	Northamptonshire v Essex at Leyton.	1928
8	W. R. Hammond	Gloucestershire v Worcestershire at Cheltenham	1932
8	K. J. Grieves	Lancashire v Sussex at Manchester	1951
8	C. A. Milton	Gloucestershire v Sussex at Hove	1952
8	G. A. R. Lock	Surrey v Warwickshire at The Oval	1957
8	J. M. Prodger	Kent v Gloucestershire at Cheltenham	1961
8	P. M. Walker	Glamorgan v Derbyshire at Swansea.	1970
8	Masood Anwar	Rawalpindi v Lahore Division at Rawalpindi	1983-84
8	M. C. J. Ball	Gloucestershire v Yorkshire at Cheltenham	1994
8	J. D. Carr	Middlesex v Warwickshire at Birmingham.	1995
8	G. A. Hick	Worcestershire v Essex at Chelmsford	2005
8	Naved Yasin	State Bank v Bahawalpur Stags at Bahawalpur.	2014-15
8	A. M. Rahane	India v Sri Lanka at Galle	2015-16

† *Hammond also scored a hundred in each innings.*

MOST CATCHES IN A SEASON

78	W. R. Hammond	1928	71	P. J. Sharpe	1962
77	M. J. Stewart	1957	70	J. Tunnicliffe.	1901
73	P. M. Walker	1961			

The most catches by a fielder since the reduction of County Championship matches in 1969 is 59 by G. R. J. Roope in 1971.

MOST CATCHES

Dates in italics denote the first half of an overseas season; i.e. *1970* denotes the 1970-71 season.

		Career	M			Career	M
1,018	F. E. Woolley	1906–1938	979	784	J. G. Langridge . . .	1928–1955	574
887	W. G. Grace	1865–1908	879	764	W. Rhodes	1898–1930	1,107
830	G. A. R. Lock	1946–*1970*	654	758	C. A. Milton	1948–1974	620
819	W. R. Hammond .	1920–1951	634	754	E. H. Hendren. . . .	1907–1938	833
813	D. B. Close	1949–1986	786				

*The most catches by a current player is 550 by **M. E. Trescothick** between 1993 and 2018 (including two taken while deputising as wicketkeeper).*

TEAM RECORDS

HIGHEST INNINGS TOTALS

1,107	Victoria v New South Wales at Melbourne	1926-27
1,059	Victoria v Tasmania at Melbourne	1922-23
952-6 dec	Sri Lanka v India at Colombo (RPS)	1997-98
951-7 dec	Sind v Baluchistan at Karachi.	1973-74
944-6 dec	Hyderabad v Andhra at Secunderabad	1993-94
918	Holkar v Mysore at Indore	1945-46
912-8 dec	New South Wales v South Australia at Sydney	1900-01
912-6 dec†	Tamil Nadu v Goa at Panjim	1988-89
910-6 dec	Railways v Dera Ismail Khan at Lahore.	1964-65
903-7 dec	England v Australia at The Oval.	1938
900-6 dec	Queensland v Victoria at Brisbane	2005-06

† *Tamil Nadu's total of 912-6 dec included 52 penalty runs from their opponents' failure to meet the required bowling rate.*

The highest total in a team's second innings is 770 by New South Wales v South Australia at Adelaide in 1920-21.

HIGHEST FOURTH-INNINGS TOTALS

654-5	England v South Africa at Durban	1938-39
	After being set 696 to win. The match was left drawn on the tenth day.	
604	Maharashtra (*set 959 to win*) v Bombay at Poona.	1948-49
576-8	Trinidad (*set 672 to win*) v Barbados at Port-of-Spain	1945-46
572	New South Wales (*set 593 to win*) v South Australia at Sydney.	1907-08
541-7	West Zone (*won*) v South Zone at Hyderabad	2009-10
529-9	Combined XI (*set 579 to win*) v South Africans at Perth	1963-64
518	Victoria (*set 753 to win*) v Queensland at Brisbane	1926-27
513-9	Central Province (*won*) v Southern Province at Kandy.	2003-04
507-7	Cambridge University (*won*) v MCC and Ground at Lord's.	1896
506-6	South Australia (*won*) v Queensland at Adelaide	1991-92
503-4	South Zone (*won*) v England A at Gurgaon	2003-04
502-6	Middlesex (*won*) v Nottinghamshire at Nottingham.	1925
502-8	Players (*won*) v Gentlemen at Lord's	1900
500-7	South African Universities (*won*) v Western Province at Stellenbosch	1978-79

MOST RUNS IN A DAY (ONE SIDE)

721	Australians (721) v Essex at Southend (1st day).	1948
651	West Indians (651-2) v Leicestershire at Leicester (1st day)	1950
649	New South Wales (649-7) v Otago at Dunedin (2nd day)	1923-24
645	Surrey (645-4) v Hampshire at The Oval (1st day).	1909
644	Oxford U. (644-8) v H. D. G. Leveson Gower's XI at Eastbourne (1st day) . . .	1921
640	Lancashire (640-8) v Sussex at Hove (1st day).	1937
636	Free Foresters (636-7) v Cambridge U. at Cambridge (1st day).	1938
625	Gloucestershire (625-6) v Worcestershire at Dudley (2nd day)	1934

MOST RUNS IN A DAY (BOTH SIDES)

(excluding the above)

685	North (169-8 and 255-7), South (261-8 dec) at Blackpool (2nd day).	1961
666	Surrey (607-4), Northamptonshire (59-2) at Northampton (2nd day).	1920
665	Rest of South Africa (339), Transvaal (326) at Johannesburg (1st day).	1911-12
663	Middlesex (503-4), Leicestershire (160-2) at Leicester (2nd day)	1947
661	Border (201), Griqualand West (460) at Kimberley (1st day).	1920-21
649	Hampshire (570-8), Somerset (79-3) at Taunton (2nd day)	1901

HIGHEST AGGREGATES IN A MATCH

Runs	Wkts		
2,376	37	Maharashtra v Bombay at Poona	1948-49
2,078	40	Bombay v Holkar at Bombay	1944-45
1,981	35	South Africa v England at Durban	1938-39
1,945	18	Canterbury v Wellington at Christchurch	1994-95
1,929	39	New South Wales v South Australia at Sydney	1925-26
1,911	34	New South Wales v Victoria at Sydney	1908-09
1,905	40	Otago v Wellington at Dunedin	1923-24

In Britain

Runs	Wkts		
1,815	28	Somerset v Surrey at Taunton	2002
1,808	20	Sussex v Essex at Hove	1993
1,795	34	Somerset v Northamptonshire at Taunton	2001
1,723	31	England v Australia at Leeds	1948
1,706	23	Hampshire v Warwickshire at Southampton	1997

LOWEST INNINGS TOTALS

12†	Oxford University v MCC and Ground at Oxford		1877
12	Northamptonshire v Gloucestershire at Gloucester		1907
13	Auckland v Canterbury at Auckland		1877-78
13	Nottinghamshire v Yorkshire at Nottingham		1901
14	Surrey v Essex at Chelmsford		1983
15	MCC v Surrey at Lord's		1839
15†	Victoria v MCC at Melbourne		1903-04
15†	Northamptonshire v Yorkshire at Northampton		1908
15	Hampshire v Warwickshire at Birmingham		1922
	Following on, Hampshire scored 521 and won by 155 runs.		
16	MCC and Ground v Surrey at Lord's		1872
16	Derbyshire v Nottinghamshire at Nottingham		1879
16	Surrey v Nottinghamshire at The Oval		1880
16	Warwickshire v Kent at Tonbridge		1913
16	Trinidad v Barbados at Bridgetown		1942-43
16	Border v Natal at East London (first innings)		1959-60
17	Gentlemen of Kent v Gentlemen of England at Lord's		1850
17	Gloucestershire v Australians at Cheltenham		1896
18	The Bs v England at Lord's		1831
18†	Kent v Sussex at Gravesend		1867
18	Tasmania v Victoria at Melbourne		1868-69
18†	Australians v MCC and Ground at Lord's		1896
18	Border v Natal at East London (second innings)		1959-60
18†	Durham MCCU v Durham at Chester-le-Street		2012

† *One man absent.*

At Lord's in 1810, The Bs, with one man absent, were dismissed by England for 6.

LOWEST TOTALS IN A MATCH

34	(16 and 18) Border v Natal at East London	1959-60
42	(27† and 15†) Northamptonshire v Yorkshire at Northampton	1908

† *Northamptonshire batted one man short in each innings.*

LOWEST AGGREGATE IN A COMPLETED MATCH

Runs	Wkts		
85	11†	Quetta v Rawalpindi at Islamabad............................	2008-09
105	31	MCC v Australians at Lord's.............................	1878

† *Both teams forfeited their first innings.*

The lowest aggregate in a match in which the losing team was bowled out twice since 1900 is 157 for 22 wickets, Surrey v Worcestershire at The Oval, 1954.

LARGEST VICTORIES

Largest Innings Victories

Inns and 851 runs	Railways (910-6 dec) v Dera Ismail Khan at Lahore............	1964-65
Inns and 666 runs	Victoria (1,059) v Tasmania at Melbourne	1922-23
Inns and 656 runs	Victoria (1,107) v New South Wales at Melbourne	1926-27
Inns and 605 runs	New South Wales (918) v South Australia at Sydney	1900-01
Inns and 579 runs	England (903-7 dec) v Australia at The Oval.................	1938
Inns and 575 runs	Sind (951-7 dec) v Baluchistan at Karachi..................	1973-74
Inns and 527 runs	New South Wales (713) v South Australia at Adelaide	1908-09
Inns and 517 runs	Australians (675) v Nottinghamshire at Nottingham	1921

Largest Victories by Runs Margin

685 runs	New South Wales (235 and 761-8 dec) v Queensland at Sydney ..	1929-30
675 runs	England (521 and 342-8 dec) v Australia at Brisbane	1928-29
638 runs	New South Wales (304 and 770) v South Australia at Adelaide ..	1920-21
609 runs	Muslim Comm. Bank (575 and 282-0 dec) v WAPDA at Lahore ..	1977-78

Victory Without Losing a Wicket

Lancashire (166-0 dec and 66-0) beat Leicestershire by ten wickets at Manchester......	1956
Karachi A (277-0 dec) beat Sind A by an innings and 77 runs at Karachi	1957-58
Railways (236-0 dec and 16-0) beat Jammu & Kashmir by ten wickets at Srinagar......	1960-61
Karnataka (451-0 dec) beat Kerala by an innings and 186 runs at Chikmagalur.........	1977-78

*There have been **30** wins by an innings and 400 runs or more, the most recent being an innings and 413 runs by Dhaka v Barisal at Mirpur in 2014-15.*

*There have been 24 wins by 500 runs or more, the most recent being **543 runs by Nondescripts v Moors at Colombo (Moors) in 2018-19**.*

There have been 33 wins by a team losing only one wicket, the most recent being by KwaZulu-Natal Inland v Namibia at Pietermaritzburg in 2015-16.

TIED MATCHES

Since 1948, a tie has been recognised only when the scores are level with all the wickets down in the fourth innings. There have been **40** instances since then, including two Tests (see Test record section); Sussex have featured in five of those, Essex and Kent in four each.

The most recent instances are:

Police v Kalutara PCC at Colombo (BRC)	2016-17
Guyana v Windward Islands at Providence...........................	2017-18
Chilaw Marians v Burgher at Katunayake...........................	2017-18
Negombo v Kalutara Town at Gampaha.............................	2017-18
Bloomfield v Army at Colombo (Moors)	**2017-18**
Somerset v Lancashire at Taunton.............................	**2018**

MATCHES COMPLETED ON FIRST DAY

(Since 1946)

Derbyshire v Somerset at Chesterfield, June 11....................................	1947
Lancashire v Sussex at Manchester, July 12	1950
Surrey v Warwickshire at The Oval, May 16	1953
Somerset v Lancashire at Bath, June 6 (H. F. T. Buse's benefit)...................	1953
Kent v Worcestershire at Tunbridge Wells, June 15	1960
Griqualand West v Easterns at Kimberley, March 10	2010-11

SHORTEST COMPLETED MATCHES

Balls

121	Quetta (forfeit and 41) v Rawalpindi (forfeit and 44-1) at Islamabad	2008-09
350	Somerset (35 and 44) v Middlesex (86) at Lord's	1899
352	Victoria (82 and 57) v Tasmania (104 and 37-7) at Launceston	1850-51
372	Victoria (80 and 50) v Tasmania (97 and 35-2) at Launceston	1853-54

An expanded and regularly updated online version of the Records can be found at
www.wisdenrecords.com

LIST A ONE-DAY RECORDS

List A is a concept intended to provide an approximate equivalent in one-day cricket of first-class status. It was introduced by the Association of Cricket Statisticians and Historians and is now recognised by the ICC, with a separate category for Twenty20 cricket. Further details are available at stats.acscricket.com/ListA/Description.html. List A games comprise:

(a) One-day internationals.
(b) Other international matches (e.g. A-team internationals).
(c) Premier domestic one-day tournaments in Test-playing countries.
(d) Official tourist matches against the main first-class teams (e.g. counties, states and Board XIs).

The following matches are excluded:

(a) Matches originally scheduled as less than 40 overs per side (e.g. Twenty20 games).
(b) World Cup warm-up games.
(c) Tourist matches against teams outside the major domestic competitions (e.g. universities).
(d) Festival games and pre-season friendlies.

This section covers one-day cricket to December 31, 2018. Bold type denotes performances in the calendar year 2018 or, in career figures, players who appeared in List A cricket in that year.

BATTING RECORDS

HIGHEST INDIVIDUAL INNINGS

268	A. D. Brown	Surrey v Glamorgan at The Oval	2002
264	R. G. Sharma	India v Sri Lanka at Kolkata	2014-15
257	**D. J. M. Short**	**Western Australia v Queensland at Sydney**	**2018-19**
248	S. Dhawan	India A v South Africa A at Pretoria	2013
237*	M. J. Guptill	New Zealand v West Indies at Wellington	2014-15
229*	B. R. Dunk	Tasmania v Queensland at Sydney	2014-15
222*	R. G. Pollock	Eastern Province v Border at East London	1974-75
222	J. M. How	Central Districts v Northern Districts at Hamilton	2012-13
220*	B. M. Duckett	England Lions v Sri Lanka A at Canterbury	2016
219	V. Sehwag	India v West Indies at Indore	2011-12
215	C. H. Gayle	West Indies v Zimbabwe at Canberra	2014-15
210*	**Fakhar Zaman**	**Pakistan v Zimbabwe at Bulawayo**	**2018**
209*	**Abid Ali**	**Islamabad v Peshawar at Peshawar**	**2017-18**
209	R. G. Sharma	India v Australia at Bangalore	2013-14
208*	R. G. Sharma	India v Sri Lanka at Mohali	2017-18
207	Mohammad Ali	Pakistan Customs v DHA at Sialkot	2004-05
206	A. I. Kallicharran	Warwickshire v Oxfordshire at Birmingham	1984
204*	Khalid Latif	Karachi Dolphins v Quetta Bears at Karachi	2008-09
203	A. D. Brown	Surrey v Hampshire at Guildford	1997
202*	A. Barrow	Natal v SA African XI at Durban	1975-76
202*	P. J. Hughes	Australia A v South Africa A at Darwin	2014
202	T. M. Head	South Australia v Western Australia at Sydney	2015-16
202	**K. V. Kaushal**	**Uttarakhand v Sikkim at Nadiad**	**2018-19**
201*	R. S. Bopara	Essex v Leicestershire at Leicester	2008
201	V. J. Wells	Leicestershire v Berkshire at Leicester	1996
200*	S. R. Tendulkar	India v South Africa at Gwalior	2009-10
200	**Kamran Akmal**	**WAPDA v Habib Bank at Hyderabad**	**2017-18**

MOST RUNS

	Career	M	I	NO	R	HS	100	Avge
G. A. Gooch	1973–1997	614	601	48	22,211	198*	44	40.16
G. A. Hick	1983–2008	651	630	96	22,059	172*	40	41.30
S. R. Tendulkar	1989–2011	551	538	55	21,999	200*	60	45.54
K. C. Sangakkara	1997–2017	528	500	54	19,453	169	39	43.61
I. V. A. Richards	1973–1993	500	466	61	16,995	189*	26	41.96

	Career	M	I	NO	R	HS	100	Avge
R. T. Ponting	1992–2013	456	445	53	16,363	164	34	41.74
C. G. Greenidge	1970–1992	440	436	33	16,349	186*	33	40.56
S. T. Jayasuriya	1989–2011	557	542	25	16,128	189	31	31.19
A. J. Lamb	1972–1995	484	463	63	15,658	132*	19	39.14
D. L. Haynes	1976–1996	419	416	44	15,651	152*	28	42.07
S. C. Ganguly	1989–2011	437	421	43	15,622	183	31	41.32
K. J. Barnett	1979–2005	527	500	54	15,564	136	17	34.89
D. P. M. D. Jayawardene . .	1995–2016	546	509	51	15,364	163*	21	33.54
R. Dravid	1992–2011	449	416	55	15,271	153	21	42.30
M. G. Bevan	1989–2006	427	385	124	15,103	157*	13	57.86

HIGHEST PARTNERSHIP FOR EACH WICKET

367*	for 1st	M. N. van Wyk/C. S. Delport, Dolphins v Knights at Bloemfontein	2014-15
372	for 2nd	C. H. Gayle/M. N. Samuels, West Indies v Zimbabwe at Canberra	2014-15
309*	for 3rd	T. S. Curtis/T. M. Moody, Worcestershire v Surrey at The Oval	1994
276	for 4th	Mominul Haque/A. R. S. Silva, Prime Doleshwar v Abahani at Bogra . .	2013-14
267*	for 5th	Minhazul Abedin/Khaled Mahmud, Bangladeshis v Bahawalpur at Karachi	1997-98
267*	for 6th	G. D. Elliott/L. Ronchi, New Zealand v Sri Lanka at Dunedin	2014-15
215*	**for 7th**	**S. Singh/G. H. Dockrell, Leinster v Northern at Dublin**	**2018**
203	for 8th	Shahid Iqbal/Haaris Ayaz, Karachi Whites v Hyderabad at Karachi	1998-99
155	for 9th	C. M. W. Read/A. J. Harris, Notts v Durham at Nottingham	2006
128	for 10th	A. Ashish Reddy/M. Ravi Kiran, Hyderabad v Kerala at Secunderabad .	2014-15

BOWLING RECORDS

BEST BOWLING ANALYSES

8-10	**S. Nadeem**	**Jharkhand v Rajasthan at Chennai**	**2018-19**
8-15	R. L. Sanghvi	Delhi v Himachal Pradesh at Una	1997-98
8-19	W. P. U. J. C. Vaas	Sri Lanka v Zimbabwe at Colombo (SSC)	2001-02
8-20*	D. T. Kottehewa	Nondescripts v Ragama at Colombo (Moors)	2007-08
8-21	M. A. Holding	Derbyshire v Sussex at Hove	1988
8-26	K. D. Boyce	Essex v Lancashire at Manchester	1971
8-30	G. D. R. Eranga	Burgher v Army at Colombo (Colts)	2007-08
8-31	D. L. Underwood	Kent v Scotland at Edinburgh	1987
8-38	**B. A. Mavuta**	**Rising Stars v Manicaland Mountaineers at Harare** . . .	**2017-18**
8-40	**Yeasin Arafat**	**Gazi Group Cricketers v Abahani at Fatullah**	**2017-18**
8-43	S. W. Tait	South Australia v Tasmania at Adelaide	2003-04
8-52	K. A. Stoute	West Indies A v Lancashire at Manchester	2010
8-66	S. R. G. Francis	Somerset v Derbyshire at Derby	2004

* *Including two hat-tricks.*

MOST WICKETS

	Career	M	B	R	W	BB	4I	Avge
Wasim Akram	1984–2003	594	29,719	19,303	881	5-10	46	21.91
A. A. Donald	1985–2003	458	22,856	14,942	684	6-15	38	21.84
M. Muralitharan	1991–2010	453	23,734	15,270	682	7-30	29	22.39
Waqar Younis	1988–2003	412	19,841	15,098	675	7-36	44	22.36
J. K. Lever	1968–1990	481	23,208	13,278	674	5-8	34	19.70
J. E. Emburey	1975–2000	536	26,399	16,811	647	5-23	26	25.98
I. T. Botham	1973–1993	470	22,899	15,264	612	5-27	18	24.94

WICKETKEEPING AND FIELDING RECORDS

MOST DISMISSALS IN AN INNINGS

8	(8 ct)	D. J. S. Taylor	Somerset v Combined Universities at Taunton ...	1982
8	(5ct, 3st)	S. J. Palframan	Boland v Easterns at Paarl	1997-98
8	(8ct)	D. J. Pipe	Worcestershire v Hertfordshire at Hertford	2001
8	(6ct, 2st)	P. M. Nevill	New South Wales v Cricket Aus XI at Sydney ...	2017-18

There have been 14 instances of seven dismissals in an innings, the most recent being K. A. Vaz (6ct, 1st) for Goa v Gujarat at Chennai in 2017-18 and L. R. Johns (7ct) for Wellington v Canterbury at Wellington in 2018-19.

MOST CATCHES IN AN INNINGS IN THE FIELD

There have been **15** instances of a fielder taking five catches in an innings. The most recent are:

5	A. R. McBrine	Ireland v Sri Lanka A at Belfast	2014
5	**Farhad Hossain**	**Prime Doleshwar v Sheikh Jamal Dhanmondi at Fatullah**	**2017-18**
5	**Zahid Zakhail**	**Amo v Boost at Kabul**.............................	**2018**

TEAM RECORDS

HIGHEST INNINGS TOTALS

496-4	(50 overs)	Surrey v Gloucestershire at The Oval	2007
481-6	**(50 overs)**	**England v Australia at Nottingham**......................	**2018**
458-4	**(50 overs)**	**India A v Leicestershire at Leicester**	**2018**
445-8	(50 overs)	Nottinghamshire v Northamptonshire at Nottingham.........	2016
444-3	(50 overs)	England v Pakistan at Nottingham	2016
443-9	(50 overs)	Sri Lanka v Netherlands at Amstelveen	2006
439-2	(50 overs)	South Africa v West Indies at Johannesburg................	2014-15
438-4	(50 overs)	South Africa v India at Mumbai	2014-15
438-5	(50 overs)	Surrey v Glamorgan at The Oval	2002
438-9	(49.5 overs)	South Africa v Australia at Johannesburg..................	2005-06
434-4	(50 overs)	Australia v South Africa at Johannesburg..................	2005-06
434-4	(50 overs)	Jamaica v Trinidad & Tobago at Coolidge	2016-17
433-3	(50 overs)	India A v South Africa A at Pretoria......................	2013

LOWEST INNINGS TOTALS

18	(14.3 overs)	West Indies Under-19 v Barbados at Blairmont	2007-08
19	(10.5 overs)	Saracens v Colts at Colombo (Colts)	2012-13
23	(19.4 overs)	Middlesex v Yorkshire at Leeds	1974
30	(20.4 overs)	Chittagong v Sylhet at Dhaka	2002-03
31	(13.5 overs)	Border v South Western Districts at East London...........	2007-08
34	(21.1 overs)	Saurashtra v Mumbai at Mumbai	1999-2000
35	(18 overs)	Zimbabwe v Sri Lanka at Harare	2003-04
35	(20.2 overs)	Cricket Coaching School v Abahani at Fatullah	2013-14
35	(15.3 overs)	Rajasthan v Railways at Nagpur	2014-15
36	(25.4 overs)	Leicestershire v Sussex at Leicester	1973
36	(18.4 overs)	Canada v Sri Lanka at Paarl	2002-03

An expanded and regularly updated online version of the Records can be found at
www.wisdenrecords.com

LIST A TWENTY20 RECORDS

This section covers Twenty20 cricket to December 31, 2018. Bold type denotes performances in the calendar year 2018 or, in career figures, players who appeared in Twenty20 cricket in that year.

BATTING RECORDS

HIGHEST INDIVIDUAL INNINGS

175*	C. H. Gayle	RC Bangalore v Pune Warriors at Bangalore	2012-13
172	**A. J. Finch**	**Australia v Zimbabwe at Harare**	**2018**
162*	H. Masakadza	Mountaineers v Mashonaland Eagles at Bulawayo ...	2015-16
161	A. Lyth	Yorkshire v Northamptonshire at Leeds	2017
158*	B. B. McCullum	Kolkata Knight Riders v RC Bangalore at Bangalore .	2007-08
158*	B. B. McCullum	Warwickshire v Derbyshire at Birmingham.	2015
156	A. J. Finch	Australia v England at Southampton	2013
153*	L. J. Wright	Sussex v Essex at Chelmsford	2014
152*	G. R. Napier	Essex v Sussex at Chelmsford	2008
151*	C. H. Gayle	Somerset v Kent at Taunton	2015
150*	Kamran Akmal	Lahore Whites v Islamabad at Rawalpindi	2017-18

MOST RUNS

	Career	M	I	NO	R	HS	100	Avge	SR
C. H. Gayle............	2005–*2018*	357	349	46	12,095	175*	21	39.91	148.07
B. B. McCullum.......	2004–*2018*	358	353	33	9,628	158*	7	30.08	137.20
K. A. Pollard.........	2006–*2018*	434	390	107	8,532	104	1	30.14	150.44
Shoaib Malik	2004–*2018*	329	309	84	8,347	95*	0	37.09	125.48
S. K. Raina...........	2006–*2018*	296	280	44	7,928	126*	4	33.59	139.23
D. A. Warner	2006–*2018*	252	251	27	7,888	135*	6	35.21	142.38
V. Kohli..............	2006–*2018*	250	236	45	7,809	113	4	40.88	133.32
D. R. Smith...........	2005–*2018*	326	318	26	7,777	110*	5	26.63	127.63
R. G. Sharma	2006–*2018*	295	282	45	7,701	118	6	32.49	133.51
A. J. Finch	2008–*2018*	243	238	27	7,607	172	6	34.50	143.50
B. J. Hodge...........	2003–*2017*	277	261	60	7,405	106	2	36.84	131.27
L. J. Wright	2004–*2018*	300	279	26	7,200	153*	7	28.45	144.17
S. R. Watson	2004–*2018*	277	269	30	7,100	124*	5	29.70	139.37

HIGHEST PARTNERSHIP FOR EACH WICKET

223	**for 1st**	**A. J. Finch/D. J. M. Short, Australia v Zimbabwe at Harare**	**2018**
229	for 2nd	V. Kohli/A. B. de Villiers, RC Bangalore v Gujarat Lions at Bangalore ...	2015-16
171	**for 3rd**	**I. R. Bell/A. J. Hose, Warwickshire v Northants at Birmingham**	**2018**
202*	for 4th	M. C. Juneja/A. Malik, Gujarat v Kerala at Indore	2012-13
150	for 5th	H. M. Amla/D. J. Bravo, Trinbago KR v Barb. Tridents at Port-of-Spain..	2016
161	**for 6th**	**K. Lewis/A. D. Russell, Jamaica T v Trinbago KR at Port-of-Spain** ...	**2018**
107*	for 7th	L. Abeyratne/P. S. R. Anurudhda, Colombo v Chilaw Marians at Colombo	2015-16
120	for 8th	Azhar Mahmood/I. Udana, Wayamba v Uva at Colombo (RPS)	2012
69	for 9th	C. J. Anderson/J. H. Davey, Somerset v Surrey at The Oval............	2017
63	for 10th	G. D. Elliott/Zulfiqar Babar, Quetta Glad. v Peshawar Zalmi at Sharjah ...	2015-16

BOWLING RECORDS

BEST BOWLING ANALYSES

6-5	A. V. Suppiah	Somerset v Glamorgan at Cardiff......................	2011
6-6	Shakib Al Hasan	Barbados v Trinidad & Tobago at Bridgetown	2013
6-7	S. L. Malinga	Melbourne Stars v Perth Scorchers at Perth	2012-13
6-8	B. A. W. Mendis	Sri Lanka v Zimbabwe at Hambantota.................	2012-13
6-9	P. Fojela	Border v Easterns at East London....................	2014-15

6-11	I. S. Sodhi	Adelaide Strikers v Sydney Thunder at Sydney	2016-17
6-14	Sohail Tanvir	Rajasthan Royals v Chennai Superstars at Jaipur	2007-08
6-14	D. Punia	Services v Haryana at Delhi	2014-15
6-15	S. R. Abeywardene	Panadura v Air Force at Colombo (BRC)	2005-06

MOST WICKETS

	Career	*M*	*B*	*R*	*W*	*BB*	*4I*	*Avge*	*ER*
D. J. Bravo	*2005–2018*	419	8,116	11,202	460	5-23	11	24.35	8.28
S. L. Malinga	*2004–2018*	262	5,777	6,669	352	6-7	12	18.94	6.92
S. P. Narine	*2010–2018*	299	6,840	6,784	342	5-19	11	19.83	5.95
Shakib Al Hasan	*2006–2018*	280	5,870	6,689	321	6-6	11	20.83	6.83
Shahid Afridi	*2004–2018*	282	6,084	6,792	307	5-7	11	22.12	6.69
Sohail Tanvir	*2004–2018*	303	6,345	7,756	302	6-14	7	25.68	7.33
Yasir Arafat	*2005–2016*	226	4,702	6,344	281	4-5	10	22.57	8.09
Imran Tahir	*2005–2018*	231	4,899	5,778	276	5-23	9	20.93	7.07
Saeed Ajmal	*2004–2017*	195	4,338	4,706	271	4-14	8	17.36	6.50
A. C. Thomas	*2003–2015*	225	4,558	5,739	263	5-24	5	21.82	7.55
Azhar Mahmood	2003–2016	230	4,825	6,143	258	5-24	4	23.81	7.63
D. P. Nannes	*2007–2014*	215	4,624	5,719	257	5-31	9	22.25	7.42
K. A. Pollard	*2006–2018*	434	4,510	6,153	255	4-15	5	24.12	8.18

WICKETKEEPING AND FIELDING RECORDS

MOST DISMISSALS IN AN INNINGS

| 7 (7ct) | E. F. M. U. Fernando | Lankan v Moors at Colombo (Bloomfield) | 2005-06 |

MOST CATCHES IN AN INNINGS IN THE FIELD

5	Manzoor Ilahi	Jammu & Kashmir v Delhi at Delhi	2010-11
5	J. M. Vince	Hampshire v Leeward Islands at North Sound	2010-11
5	J. L. Ontong	Cape Cobras v Knights at Cape Town	2014-15
5	A. K. V. Adikari	Chilaw Marians v Bloomfield at Colombo (SSC)	2014-15
5	P. G. Fulton	Canterbury v Northern Districts at Hamilton	2015-16
5	M. W. Machan	Sussex v Glamorgan at Hove	2016

TEAM RECORDS

HIGHEST INNINGS TOTALS

263-3	(20 overs)	Australia v Sri Lanka at Pallekele	2016
263-5	(20 overs)	RC Bangalore v Pune Warriors at Bangalore	2012-13
262-4	**(20 overs)**	**North West v Limpopo at Paarl**	**2018-19**
260-4	(20 overs)	Yorkshire v Northamptonshire at Leeds	2017
260-5	(20 overs)	India v Sri Lanka at Indore	2017-18
260-6	(20 overs)	Sri Lanka v Kenya at Johannesburg	2007-08
254-3	(20 overs)	Gloucestershire v Trinidad & Tobago at Uxbridge	2011
251-6	(20 overs)	Sinhalese v Saracens at Colombo (Colts)	2015-16
250-3	(20 overs)	Somerset v Gloucestershire at Taunton	2006
250-6	**(20 overs)**	**Surrey v Kent at Canterbury**	**2018**

LOWEST INNINGS TOTALS

30	(11.1 overs)	Tripura v Jharkhand at Dhanbad	2009-10
39	(10.3 overs)	Netherlands v Sri Lanka at Chittagong	2013-14
44	(12.5 overs)	Leeward Islands v Trinidad & Tobago at North Sound	2011-12
44	(14.4 overs)	Boland v North West at Potchefstroom	2014-15
44	(12.1 overs)	Assam v Delhi at Vadodara	2015-16
44	(10.4 overs)	Khulna Titans v Rangpur Riders at Mirpur	2016-17

ALL-FORMAT CAREER RECORDS

This section covers combined records in first-class, List A and Twenty20 cricket to December 31, 2018. Bold type denotes a player who appeared in 2018. Daggers denote players who appeared in first-class and List A formats, and double daggers players who appeared in all three; all other players appeared only in first-class cricket.

MOST RUNS

	Career	M	I	NO	R	HS	100	Avge
G. A. Gooch†	1973–2000	1,195	1,591	123	67,057	333	172	45.67
G. A. Hick‡	1983–2008	1,214	1,537	183	64,372	405*	178	47.54
J. B. Hobbs	1905–1934	826	1,315	106	61,237	316*	197	50.65
F. E. Woolley	1906–1938	979	1,532	85	58,969	305*	145	40.75
G. Boycott†	1962–1986	922	1,316	206	58,521	261*	159	52.72
E. H. Hendren	1907–1938	833	1,300	166	57,611	301*	170	50.80
D. L. Amiss†	1960–1987	1,062	1,530	160	55,942	262*	117	40.83
C. P. Mead	1905–1936	814	1,340	185	55,061	280*	153	47.67
W. G. Grace	1865–1908	880	1,493	105	54,896	344	126	39.55
C. G. Greenidge†	1970–1992	963	1,325	108	53,703	273*	125	44.12

MOST WICKETS

	Career	M	B	R	W	BB	5I	Avge
W. Rhodes	1898–1930	1,107	184,940	69,993	4,187	9-24	287	16.71
A. P. Freeman	1914–1936	592	154,658	69,577	3,776	10-53	386	18.42
C. W. L. Parker	1903–1935	635	157,328	63,819	3,278	10-79	277	19.46
J. T. Hearne	1888–1923	639	144,470	54,352	3,061	9-32	255	17.75
D. L. Underwood†	1963–1987	1,089	159,571	61,111	3,037	9-28	161	20.12
F. J. Titmus†	1949–1982	941	180,576	67,396	2,989	9-52	171	22.54
T. W. J. Goddard	1922–1952	593	142,186	59,116	2,979	10-113	251	19.84
D. Shackleton†	1948–1973	684	161,071	54,175	2,898	9-30	194	18.69
W. G. Grace	1865–1908	880	126,056	51,545	2,876	10-49	246	17.92
A. S. Kennedy	1907–1936	677	150,917	61,034	2,874	10-37	225	21.23

The figure for balls bowled by Grace is uncertain.

MOST DISMISSALS

	Career	M	Dis	Ct	St
R. W. Taylor†	1960–1988	972	2,070	1,819	251
S. J. Rhodes‡	1981–2004	920	1,929	1,671	258
R. C. Russell‡	1981–2004	946	1,885	1,658	227
A. P. E. Knott†	1964–1985	829	1,741	1,553	188
J. T. Murray†	1952–1975	784	1,724	1,432	292
C. M. W. Read‡	1995–2017	801	1,583	1,430	153
Kamran Akmal‡	*1997–2018*	798	1,557	1,304	253
P. A. Nixon‡	1989–*2011*	862	1,549	1,360	189
D. L. Bairstow†	1970–1990	888	1,545	1,372	173
A. C. Gilchrist‡	*1992–2013*	648	1,498	1,356	142

Total dismissals include catches taken when not keeping wicket.

MOST CATCHES IN THE FIELD

	Career	M	Ct		Career	M	Ct
F. E. Woolley	1906–1938	979	1,018	G. A. Hick‡	1983–2008	1,214	1,008

TEST RECORDS

This section covers all Tests up to January 14, 2019. Bold type denotes performances since January 1, 2018, or, in career figures, players who have appeared in Test cricket since that date.

BATTING RECORDS

HIGHEST INDIVIDUAL INNINGS

400*	B. C. Lara	West Indies v England at St John's	2003-04
380	M. L. Hayden.	Australia v Zimbabwe at Perth.	2003-04
375	B. C. Lara	West Indies v England at St John's	1993-94
374	D. P. M. D. Jayawardene . .	Sri Lanka v South Africa at Colombo (SSC)	2006
365*	G. S. Sobers.	West Indies v Pakistan at Kingston	1957-58
364	L. Hutton	England v Australia at The Oval	1938
340	S. T. Jayasuriya.	Sri Lanka v India at Colombo (RPS)	1997-98
337	Hanif Mohammad	Pakistan v West Indies at Bridgetown	1957-58
336*	W. R. Hammond	England v New Zealand at Auckland.	1932-33
334*	M. A. Taylor	Australia v Pakistan at Peshawar	1998-99
334	D. G. Bradman.	Australia v England at Leeds	1930
333	G. A. Gooch.	England v India at Lord's	1990
333	C. H. Gayle	West Indies v Sri Lanka at Galle	2010-11
329*	M. J. Clarke	Australia v India at Sydney	2011-12
329	Inzamam-ul-Haq	Pakistan v New Zealand at Lahore	2002
325	A. Sandham	England v West Indies at Kingston	1929-30
319	V. Sehwag	India v South Africa at Chennai	2007-08
319	K. C. Sangakkara.	Sri Lanka v Bangladesh at Chittagong	2013-14
317	C. H. Gayle	West Indies v South Africa at St John's.	2004-05
313	Younis Khan	Pakistan v Sri Lanka at Karachi	2008-09
311*	H. M. Amla	South Africa v England at The Oval	2012
311	R. B. Simpson	Australia v England at Manchester	1964
310*	J. H. Edrich	England v New Zealand at Leeds.	1965
309	V. Sehwag	India v Pakistan at Multan	2003-04
307	R. M. Cowper	Australia v England at Melbourne	1965-66
304	D. G. Bradman.	Australia v England at Leeds	1934
303*	K. K. Nair	India v England at Chennai	2016-17
302*	Azhar Ali	Pakistan v West Indies at Dubai	2016-17
302	L. G. Rowe	West Indies v England at Bridgetown	1973-74
302	B. B. McCullum	New Zealand v India at Wellington	2013-14

*There have been **64** further instances of 250 or more runs in a Test innings.*

The highest innings for the countries not mentioned above are:

266	D. L. Houghton	Zimbabwe v Sri Lanka at Bulawayo	1994-95
219*	**Mushfiqur Rahim**	**Bangladesh v Zimbabwe at Mirpur**	**2018-19**
118	**K. J. O'Brien**	**Ireland v Pakistan at Malahide**	**2018**
36*	**Hashmatullah Shahidi** . . .	**Afghanistan v India at Bangalore**	**2018**

HUNDRED ON TEST DEBUT

C. Bannerman (165*)	Australia v England at Melbourne	1876-77
W. G. Grace (152)	England v Australia at The Oval	1880
H. Graham (107)	Australia v England at Lord's	1893
†K. S. Ranjitsinhji (154*)	England v Australia at Manchester.	1896
†P. F. Warner (132*).	England v South Africa at Johannesburg	1898-99
†R. A. Duff (104).	Australia v England at Melbourne	1901-02
§R. E. Foster (287).	England v Australia at Sydney	1903-04
G. Gunn (119)	England v Australia at Sydney	1907-08
†R. J. Hartigan (116)	Australia v England at Adelaide.	1907-08

†H. L. Collins (104)	Australia v England at Sydney	1920-21
W. H. Ponsford (110)	Australia v England at Sydney	1924-25
A. A. Jackson (164)	Australia v England at Adelaide	1928-29
†G. A. Headley (176)	West Indies v England at Bridgetown	1929-30
J. E. Mills (117)	New Zealand v England at Wellington	1929-30
Nawab of Pataudi snr (102)	England v Australia at Sydney	1932-33
B. H. Valentine (136)	England v India at Bombay	1933-34
†L. Amarnath (118)	India v England at Bombay	1933-34
†P. A. Gibb (106)	England v South Africa at Johannesburg	1938-39
S. C. Griffith (140)	England v West Indies at Port-of-Spain	1947-48
A. G. Ganteaume (112)	West Indies v England at Port-of-Spain	1947-48
†J. W. Burke (101*)	Australia v England at Adelaide	1950-51
P. B. H. May (138)	England v South Africa at Leeds	1951
R. H. Shodhan (110)	India v Pakistan at Calcutta	1952-53
B. H. Pairaudeau (115)	West Indies v India at Port-of-Spain	1952-53
†O. G. Smith (104)	West Indies v Australia at Kingston	1954-55
A. G. Kripal Singh (100*)	India v New Zealand at Hyderabad	1955-56
C. C. Hunte (142)	West Indies v Pakistan at Bridgetown	1957-58
C. A. Milton (104*)	England v New Zealand at Leeds	1958
†A. A. Baig (112)	India v England at Manchester	1959
Hanumant Singh (105)	India v England at Delhi	1963-64
Khalid Ibadulla (166)	Pakistan v Australia at Karachi	1964-65
B. R. Taylor (105)	New Zealand v India at Calcutta	1964-65
K. D. Walters (155)	Australia v England at Brisbane	1965-66
J. H. Hampshire (107)	England v West Indies at Lord's	1969
†G. R. Viswanath (137)	India v Australia at Kanpur	1969-70
G. S. Chappell (108)	Australia v England at Perth	1970-71
‡§L. G. Rowe (214, 100*)	West Indies v New Zealand at Kingston	1971-72
A. I. Kallicharran (100*)	West Indies v New Zealand at Georgetown	1971-72
R. E. Redmond (107)	New Zealand v Pakistan at Auckland	1972-73
†F. C. Hayes (106*)	England v West Indies at The Oval	1973
†C. G. Greenidge (107)	West Indies v India at Bangalore	1974-75
†L. Baichan (105*)	West Indies v Pakistan at Lahore	1974-75
G. J. Cosier (109)	Australia v West Indies at Melbourne	1975-76
S. Amarnath (124)	India v New Zealand at Auckland	1975-76
Javed Miandad (163)	Pakistan v New Zealand at Lahore	1976-77
†A. B. Williams (100)	West Indies v Australia at Georgetown	1977-78
†D. M. Wellham (103)	Australia v England at The Oval	1981
†Salim Malik (100*)	Pakistan v Sri Lanka at Karachi	1981-82
K. C. Wessels (162)	Australia v England at Brisbane	1982-83
W. B. Phillips (159)	Australia v Pakistan at Perth	1983-84
¶M. Azharuddin (110)	India v England at Calcutta	1984-85
D. S. B. P. Kuruppu (201*)	Sri Lanka v New Zealand at Colombo (CCC)	1986-87
†M. J. Greatbatch (107*)	New Zealand v England at Auckland	1987-88
M. E. Waugh (138)	Australia v England at Adelaide	1990-91
A. C. Hudson (163)	South Africa v West Indies at Bridgetown	1991-92
R. S. Kaluwitharana (132*)	Sri Lanka v Australia at Colombo (SSC)	1992-93
D. L. Houghton (121)	Zimbabwe v India at Harare	1992-93
P. K. Amre (103)	India v South Africa at Durban	1992-93
†G. P. Thorpe (114*)	England v Australia at Nottingham	1993
G. S. Blewett (102*)	Australia v England at Adelaide	1994-95
S. C. Ganguly (131)	India v England at Lord's	1996
†Mohammad Wasim (109*)	Pakistan v New Zealand at Lahore	1996-97
Ali Naqvi (115)	Pakistan v South Africa at Rawalpindi	1997-98
Azhar Mahmood (128*)	Pakistan v South Africa at Rawalpindi	1997-98
M. S. Sinclair (214)	New Zealand v West Indies at Wellington	1999-2000
†Younis Khan (107)	Pakistan v Sri Lanka at Rawalpindi	1999-2000
Aminul Islam (145)	Bangladesh v India at Dhaka	2000-01
†H. Masakadza (119)	Zimbabwe v West Indies at Harare	2001
T. T. Samaraweera (103*)	Sri Lanka v India at Colombo (SSC)	2001
Taufeeq Umar (104)	Pakistan v Bangladesh at Multan	2001-02

†Mohammad Ashraful (114)	Bangladesh v Sri Lanka at Colombo (SSC)	2001-02
V. Sehwag (105)	India v South Africa at Bloemfontein.	2001-02
L. Vincent (104)	New Zealand v Australia at Perth.	2001-02
S. B. Styris (107)	New Zealand v West Indies at St George's	2002
J. A. Rudolph (222*)	South Africa v Bangladesh at Chittagong	2003
‡Yasir Hameed (170, 105).	Pakistan v Bangladesh at Karachi	2003
†D. R. Smith (105*)	West Indies v South Africa at Cape Town	2003-04
A. J. Strauss (112)	England v New Zealand at Lord's	2004
M. J. Clarke (151)	Australia v India at Bangalore	2004-05
†A. N. Cook (104*)	England v India at Nagpur	2005-06
M. J. Prior (126*).	England v West Indies at Lord's	2007
M. J. North (117)	Australia v South Africa at Johannesburg	2008-09
†Fawad Alam (168)	Pakistan v Sri Lanka at Colombo (PSS)	2009
†I. J. L. Trott (119)	England v Australia at The Oval	2009
Umar Akmal (129).	Pakistan v New Zealand at Dunedin	2009-10
†A. B. Barath (104)	West Indies v Australia at Brisbane	2009-10
A. N. Petersen (100)	South Africa v India at Kolkata	2009-10
S. K. Raina (120).	India v Sri Lanka at Colombo (SSC)	2010
K. S. Williamson (131)	New Zealand v India at Ahmedabad	2010-11
†K. A. Edwards (110)	West Indies v India at Roseau	2011
S. E. Marsh (141).	Australia v Sri Lanka at Pallekele	2011-12
Abul Hasan (113).	Bangladesh v West Indies at Khulna	2012-13
†F. du Plessis (110*)	South Africa v Australia at Adelaide	2012-13
H. D. Rutherford (171)	New Zealand v England at Dunedin.	2012-13
S. Dhawan (187).	India v Australia at Mohali.	2012-13
R. G. Sharma (177)	India v West Indies at Kolkata	2013-14
†J. D. S. Neesham (137*)	New Zealand v India at Wellington	2013-14
S. van Zyl (101*).	South Africa v West Indies at Centurion	2014-15
A. C. Voges (130*)	Australia v West Indies at Roseau	2015
S. C. Cook (115)	South Africa v England at Centurion	2015-16
K. K. Jennings (112)	England v India at Mumbai	2016-17
T. A. Blundell (107*)	New Zealand v West Indies at Wellington.	2017-18
†K. J. O'Brien (118).	**Ireland v Pakistan at Malahide**	**2018**
P. P. Shaw (134).	**India v West Indies at Rajkot**	**2018-19**
B. T. Foakes (107)	**England v Sri Lanka at Galle**	**2018-19**

† *In his second innings of the match.*
‡ *L. G. Rowe and Yasir Hameed are the only batsmen to score a hundred in each innings on debut.*
§ *R. E. Foster (287, 19) and L. G. Rowe (214, 100*) are the only batsmen to score 300 on debut.*
¶ *M. Azharuddin is the only batsman to score hundreds in each of his first three Tests.*

L. and S. Amarnath were father and son.
Ali Naqvi and Azhar Mahmood achieved the feat in the same innings.
Only Bannerman, Houghton, Aminul Islam and O'Brien scored hundreds in their country's first Test.

TWO SEPARATE HUNDREDS IN A TEST

Triple-Hundred and Hundred in a Test

G. A. Gooch (England)	333 and 123 v India at Lord's	1990
K. C. Sangakkara (Sri Lanka)	319 and 105 v Bangladesh at Chittagong	2013-14

The only instances in first-class cricket. M. A. Taylor (Australia) scored 334 and 92 v Pakistan at Peshawar in 1998-99.*

Double-Hundred and Hundred in a Test

K. D. Walters (Australia).	242 and 103 v West Indies at Sydney	1968-69
S. M. Gavaskar (India).	124 and 220 v West Indies at Port-of-Spain	1970-71
†L. G. Rowe (West Indies)	214 and 100* v New Zealand at Kingston	1971-72
G. S. Chappell (Australia)	247* and 133 v New Zealand at Wellington	1973-74
B. C. Lara (West Indies)	221 and 130 v Sri Lanka at Colombo (SSC)	2001-02

† *On Test debut.*

Two Hundreds in a Test

There have been **84** instances of a batsman scoring two separate hundreds in a Test, including the seven listed above. The most recent was by **B. R. M. Taylor for Zimbabwe v Bangladesh at Mirpur in 2018-19.**

S. M. Gavaskar (India), R. T. Ponting (Australia) and D. A. Warner (Australia) all achieved the feat three times. C. L. Walcott scored twin hundreds twice in one series, for West Indies v Australia in 1954-55. L. G. Rowe and Yasir Hameed both did it on Test debut.

MOST DOUBLE-HUNDREDS

D. G. Bradman (A)	12	M. S. Atapattu (SL)	6	S. R. Tendulkar (I)	6
K. C. Sangakkara (SL)	11	Javed Miandad (P)	6	Younis Khan (P)	6
B. C. Lara (WI)	9	**V. Kohli (I)**	**6**	**A. N. Cook (E)**	**5**
W. R. Hammond (E)	7	R. T. Ponting (A)	6	R. Dravid (I)	5
D. P. M. D. Jayawardene (SL)	7	V. Sehwag (I)	6	G. C. Smith (SA)	5

M. J. Clarke (Australia) scored four double-hundreds in the calendar year 2012.

MOST HUNDREDS

S. R. Tendulkar (I)	51	M. J. Clarke (A)	28	I. R. Bell (E)	22
J. H. Kallis (SA)	45	A. R. Border (A)	27	G. Boycott (E)	22
R. T. Ponting (A)	41	G. C. Smith (SA)	27	M. C. Cowdrey (E)	22
K. C. Sangakkara (SL)	38	G. S. Sobers (WI)	26	**A. B. de Villiers (SA)**	**22**
R. Dravid (I)	36	Inzamam-ul-Haq (P)	25	W. R. Hammond (E)	22
S. M. Gavaskar (I)	34	**V. Kohli (I)**	**25**	D. C. Boon (A)	21
D. P. M. D. Jayawardene (SL)	34	G. S. Chappell (A)	24	R. N. Harvey (A)	21
B. C. Lara (WI)	34	Mohammad Yousuf (P)	24	G. Kirsten (SA)	21
Younis Khan (P)	34	I. V. A. Richards (WI)	24	A. J. Strauss (E)	21
A. N. Cook (E)	**33**	Javed Miandad (P)	23	**D. A. Warner (A)**	**21**
S. R. Waugh (A)	32	J. L. Langer (A)	23	K. F. Barrington (E)	20
S. Chanderpaul (WI)	30	K. P. Pietersen (E)	23	P. A. de Silva (SL)	20
M. L. Hayden (A)	30	V. Sehwag (I)	23	G. A. Gooch (E)	20
D. G. Bradman (A)	29	**S. P. D. Smith (A)**	**23**	M. E. Waugh (A)	20
H. M. Amla (SA)	**28**	M. Azharuddin (I)	22		

*The most hundreds for New Zealand is **19** by **K. S. Williamson**, the most for Zimbabwe is 12 by A. Flower, and the most for Bangladesh is 8 by **Mominul Haque** and **Tamim Iqbal**.*

MOST HUNDREDS AGAINST ONE TEAM

D. G. Bradman	19	Australia v England	K. C. Sangakkara	10	Sri Lanka v Pakistan
S. M. Gavaskar	13	India v West Indies	G. S. Sobers	10	West Indies v England
J. B. Hobbs	12	England v Australia	S. R. Waugh	10	Australia v England
S. R. Tendulkar	11	India v Australia			

MOST DUCKS

	0s	Inns		0s	Inns
C. A. Walsh (WI)	43	185	C. E. L. Ambrose (WI)	26	145
C. S. Martin (NZ)	36	104	Danish Kaneria (P)	25	84
G. D. McGrath (A)	35	138	D. K. Morrison (NZ)	24	71
S. K. Warne (A)	34	199	**J. M. Anderson (E)**	**24**	**202**
M. Muralitharan (SL/World)	33	164	B. S. Chandrasekhar (I)	23	80
I. Sharma (I)	**30**	**124**	**H. M. R. K. B. Herath (SL)**	**23**	**144**
S. C. J. Broad (E)	**30**	**180**	**M. Morkel (SA)**	**22**	**104**
Zaheer Khan (I)	29	127	M. S. Atapattu (SL)	22	156
M. Dillon (WI)	26	68	S. R. Waugh (A)	22	260

	0s	Inns		0s	Inns
S. J. Harmison (E/World)	21	86	B. S. Bedi (I)	20	101
M. Ntini (SA)	21	116	D. L. Vettori (NZ/World)	20	174
Waqar Younis (P)	21	120	M. A. Atherton (E)	20	212
M. S. Panesar (E)	20	68			

CARRYING BAT THROUGH TEST INNINGS

(Figures in brackets show team's total)

A. B. Tancred	26*	(47)	South Africa v England at Cape Town	1888-89
J. E. Barrett	67*	(176)†	Australia v England at Lord's	1890
R. Abel	132*	(307)	England v Australia at Sydney	1891-92
P. F. Warner	132*	(237)†	England v South Africa at Johannesburg	1898-99
W. W. Armstrong	159*	(309)	Australia v South Africa at Johannesburg	1902-03
J. W. Zulch	43*	(103)	South Africa v England at Cape Town	1909-10
W. Bardsley	193*	(383)	Australia v England at Lord's	1926
W. M. Woodfull	30*	(66)§	Australia v England at Brisbane	1928-29
W. M. Woodfull	73*	(193)‡	Australia v England at Adelaide	1932-33
W. A. Brown	206*	(422)	Australia v England at Lord's	1938
L. Hutton	202*	(344)	England v West Indies at The Oval	1950
L. Hutton	156*	(272)	England v Australia at Adelaide	1950-51
Nazar Mohammad¶	124*	(331)	Pakistan v India at Lucknow	1952-53
F. M. M. Worrell	191*	(372)	West Indies v England at Nottingham	1957
T. L. Goddard	56*	(99)	South Africa v Australia at Cape Town	1957-58
D. J. McGlew	127*	(292)	South Africa v New Zealand at Durban	1961-62
C. C. Hunte	60*	(131)	West Indies v Australia at Port-of-Spain	1964-65
G. M. Turner	43*	(131)	New Zealand v England at Lord's	1969
W. M. Lawry	49*	(107)	Australia v India at Delhi	1969-70
W. M. Lawry	60*	(116)‡	Australia v England at Sydney	1970-71
G. M. Turner	223*	(386)	New Zealand v West Indies at Kingston	1971-72
I. R. Redpath	159*	(346)	Australia v New Zealand at Auckland	1973-74
G. Boycott	99*	(215)	England v Australia at Perth	1979-80
S. M. Gavaskar	127*	(286)	India v Pakistan at Faisalabad	1982-83
Mudassar Nazar¶	152*	(323)	Pakistan v India at Lahore	1982-83
S. Wettimuny	63*	(144)	Sri Lanka v New Zealand at Christchurch	1982-83
D. C. Boon	58*	(103)	Australia v New Zealand at Auckland	1985-86
D. L. Haynes	88*	(211)	West Indies v Pakistan at Karachi	1986-87
G. A. Gooch	154*	(252)	England v West Indies at Leeds	1991
D. L. Haynes	75*	(176)	West Indies v England at The Oval	1991
A. J. Stewart	69*	(175)	England v Pakistan at Lord's	1992
D. L. Haynes	143*	(382)	West Indies v Pakistan at Port-of-Spain	1992-93
M. H. Dekker	68*	(187)	Zimbabwe v Pakistan at Rawalpindi	1993-94
M. A. Atherton	94*	(228)	England v New Zealand at Christchurch	1996-97
G. Kirsten	100*	(239)	South Africa v Pakistan at Faisalabad	1997-98
M. A. Taylor	169*	(350)	Australia v South Africa at Adelaide	1997-98
G. W. Flower	156*	(321)	Zimbabwe v Pakistan at Bulawayo	1997-98
Saeed Anwar	188*	(316)	Pakistan v India at Calcutta	1998-99
M. S. Atapattu	216*	(428)	Sri Lanka v Zimbabwe at Bulawayo	1999-2000
R. P. Arnold	104*	(231)	Sri Lanka v Zimbabwe at Harare	1999-2000
Javed Omar	85*	(168)†‡	Bangladesh v Zimbabwe at Bulawayo	2000-01
V. Sehwag	201*	(329)	India v Sri Lanka at Galle	2008
S. M. Katich	131*	(268)	Australia v New Zealand at Brisbane	2008-09
C. H. Gayle	165*	(317)	West Indies v Australia at Adelaide	2009-10
Imran Farhat	117*	(223)	Pakistan v New Zealand at Napier	2009-10
R. Dravid	146*	(300)	India v England at The Oval	2011
T. M. K. Mawoyo	163*	(412)	Zimbabwe v Pakistan at Bulawayo	2011-12
D. A. Warner	123*	(233)	Australia v New Zealand at Hobart	2011-12
C. A. Pujara	145*	(312)	India v Sri Lanka at Colombo (SSC)	2015-16
D. Elgar	118*	(214)	South Africa v England at Durban	2015-16
K. C. Brathwaite	142*	(337)	West Indies v Pakistan at Sharjah	2016-17

A. N. Cook	244*	(491)	England v Australia at Melbourne	2017-18
D. Elgar	**86***	**(177)**	**South Africa v India at Johannesburg**	**2017-18**
D. Elgar	**141***	**(311)**	**South Africa v Australia at Cape Town**	**2017-18**
F. D. M. Karunaratne	**158***	**(287)**	**Sri Lanka v South Africa at Galle**	**2018**
T. W. M. Latham	**264***	**(578)**	**New Zealand v Sri Lanka at Wellington**	**2018-19**

† *On debut.* ‡ *One man absent.* § *Two men absent.* ¶ *Father and son.*

T. W. M. Latham (264) holds the record for the highest score by a player carrying his bat in a Test.*
　　D. L. Haynes and D. Elgar have achieved the feat on three occasions; Haynes also opened the batting and was last man out in each innings for West Indies v New Zealand at Dunedin, 1979-80.
　　G. M. Turner was the youngest at 22 years 63 days old when he first did it in 1969.

MOST RUNS IN A SERIES

	T	I	NO	R	HS	100	Avge		
D. G. Bradman	5	7	0	974	334	4	139.14	A v E	1930
W. R. Hammond	5	9	1	905	251	4	113.12	E v A	1928-29
M. A. Taylor	6	11	1	839	219	2	83.90	A v E	1989
R. N. Harvey	5	9	0	834	205	4	92.66	A v SA	1952-53
I. V. A. Richards	4	7	0	829	291	3	118.42	WI v E	1976
C. L. Walcott	5	10	0	827	155	5	82.70	WI v A	1954-55
G. S. Sobers	5	8	2	824	365*	3	137.33	WI v P	1957-58
D. G. Bradman	5	9	0	810	270	3	90.00	A v E	1936-37
D. G. Bradman	5	5	1	806	299*	4	201.50	A v SA	1931-32

MOST RUNS IN A CALENDAR YEAR

	T	I	NO	R	HS	100	Avge	Year
Mohammad Yousuf (P)	11	19	1	1,788	202	9	99.33	2006
I. V. A. Richards (WI)	11	19	0	1,710	291	7	90.00	1976
G. C. Smith (SA)	15	25	2	1,656	232	6	72.00	2008
M. J. Clarke (A.)	11	18	3	1,595	329*	5	106.33	2012
S. R. Tendulkar (I.)	14	23	3	1,562	214	7	78.10	2010
S. M. Gavaskar (I)	18	27	1	1,555	221	5	59.80	1979
R. T. Ponting (A.)	15	28	5	1,544	207	6	67.13	2005
R. T. Ponting (A.)	11	18	3	1,503	257	6	100.20	2003

M. Amarnath reached 1,000 runs in 1983 on May 3, in his ninth Test of the year.
　　The only case of 1,000 in a year before World War II was C. Hill of Australia: 1,060 in 1902.
　　M. L. Hayden (Australia) scored 1,000 runs in each year from 2001 to 2005.

MOST RUNS

		T	I	NO	R	HS	100	Avge
1	S. R. Tendulkar (India)	200	329	33	15,921	248*	51	53.78
2	R. T. Ponting (Australia)	168	287	29	13,378	257	41	51.85
3	J. H. Kallis (South Africa/World)	166	280	40	13,289	224	45	55.37
4	R. Dravid (India/World)	164	286	32	13,288	270	36	52.31
5	**A. N. Cook (England)**	**161**	**291**	**16**	**12,472**	**294**	**33**	**45.35**
6	K. C. Sangakkara (Sri Lanka)	134	233	17	12,400	319	38	57.40
7	B. C. Lara (West Indies/World)	131	232	6	11,953	400*	34	52.88
8	S. Chanderpaul (West Indies)	164	280	49	11,867	203*	30	51.37
9	D. P. M. D. Jayawardene (SL)	149	252	15	11,814	374	34	49.84
10	A. R. Border (Australia)	156	265	44	11,174	205	27	50.56
11	S. R. Waugh (Australia)	168	260	46	10,927	200	32	51.06
12	S. M. Gavaskar (India)	125	214	16	10,122	236*	34	51.12
13	Younis Khan (Pakistan)	118	213	19	10,099	313	34	52.05
14	G. C. Smith (South Africa/Wld)	117	205	13	9,265	277	27	48.25
15	**H. M. Amla (South Africa)**	**122**	**211**	**16**	**9,231**	**311***	**28**	**47.33**
16	G. A. Gooch (England)	118	215	6	8,900	333	20	42.58
17	Javed Miandad (Pakistan)	124	189	21	8,832	280*	23	52.57

		T	I	NO	R	HS	100	Avge
18	Inzamam-ul-Haq (Pakistan/World)	120	200	22	8,830	329	25	49.60
19	V. V. S. Laxman (India)	134	225	34	8,781	281	17	45.97
20	**A. B. de Villiers (South Africa)** .	**114**	**191**	**18**	**8,765**	**278***	**22**	**50.66**
21	M. J. Clarke (Australia)	115	198	22	8,643	329*	28	49.10
22	M. L. Hayden (Australia)	103	184	14	8,625	380	30	50.73
23	V. Sehwag (India/World)	104	180	6	8,586	319	23	49.34
24	I. V. A. Richards (West Indies) . . .	121	182	12	8,540	291	24	50.23
25	A. J. Stewart (England)	133	235	21	8,463	190	15	39.54
26	D. I. Gower (England)	117	204	18	8,231	215	18	44.25
27	K. P. Pietersen (England)	104	181	8	8,181	227	23	47.28
28	G. Boycott (England)	108	193	23	8,114	246*	22	47.72
29	G. S. Sobers (West Indies)	93	160	21	8,032	365*	26	57.78
30	M. E. Waugh (Australia)	128	209	17	8,029	153*	20	41.81
31	M. A. Atherton (England)	115	212	7	7,728	185*	16	37.69
32	I. R. Bell (England)	118	205	24	7,727	235	22	42.69
33	J. L. Langer (Australia)	105	182	12	7,696	250	23	45.27
34	M. C. Cowdrey (England)	114	188	15	7,624	182	22	44.06
35	C. G. Greenidge (West Indies) . . .	108	185	16	7,558	226	19	44.72
36	Mohammad Yousuf (Pakistan) . . .	90	156	12	7,530	223	24	52.29
37	M. A. Taylor (Australia)	104	186	13	7,525	334*	19	43.49
38	C. H. Lloyd (West Indies)	110	175	14	7,515	242*	19	46.67
39	D. L. Haynes (West Indies)	116	202	25	7,487	184	18	42.29
40	D. C. Boon (Australia)	107	190	20	7,422	200	21	43.65
41	G. Kirsten (South Africa)	101	176	15	7,289	275	21	45.27
42	W. R. Hammond (England).	85	140	16	7,249	336*	22	58.45
43	C. H. Gayle (West Indies)	103	182	11	7,214	333	15	42.18
44	S. C. Ganguly (India)	113	188	17	7,212	239	16	42.17
45	S. P. Fleming (New Zealand)	111	189	10	7,172	274*	9	40.06
46	G. S. Chappell (Australia).	87	151	19	7,110	247*	24	53.86
47	A. J. Strauss (England)	100	178	6	7,037	177	21	40.91
48	D. G. Bradman (Australia)	52	80	10	6,996	334	29	99.94
49	S. T. Jayasuriya (Sri Lanka)	110	188	14	6,973	340	14	40.07
50	L. Hutton (England)	79	138	15	6,971	364	19	56.67

MOST RUNS FOR EACH COUNTRY

ENGLAND

A. N. Cook **12,472**	A. J. Stewart 8,463	K. P. Pietersen 8,181
G. A. Gooch 8,900	D. I. Gower 8,231	G. Boycott 8,114

AUSTRALIA

R. T. Ponting 13,378	S. R. Waugh 10,927	M. L. Hayden 8,625
A. R. Border 11,174	M. J. Clarke 8,643	M. E. Waugh 8,029

SOUTH AFRICA

J. H. Kallis† 13,206	**H. M. Amla** **9,231**	G. Kirsten 7,289
G. C. Smith† 9,253	**A. B. de Villiers** **8,765**	H. H. Gibbs 6,167

† *J. H. Kallis also scored 44 and 39* and G. C. Smith 12 and 0 for the World XI v Australia (2005-06 Super Series Test).*

WEST INDIES

B. C. Lara† 11,912	I. V. A. Richards 8,540	C. G. Greenidge. 7,558
S. Chanderpaul 11,867	G. S. Sobers 8,032	C. H. Lloyd 7,515

† *B. C. Lara also scored 5 and 36 for the World XI v Australia (2005-06 Super Series Test).*

NEW ZEALAND

S. P. Fleming	7,172	B. B. McCullum	6,453	M. D. Crowe	5,444
L. R. P. L. Taylor	**6,523**	**K. S. Williamson**	**5,865**	J. G. Wright	5,334

INDIA

S. R. Tendulkar	15,921	S. M. Gavaskar	10,122	V. Sehwag†	8,503
R. Dravid†	13,265	V. V. S. Laxman	8,781	S. C. Ganguly	7,212

† *R. Dravid also scored 0 and 23 and V. Sehwag 76 and 7 for the World XI v Australia (2005-06 Super Series Test).*

PAKISTAN

Younis Khan	10,099	Inzamam-ul-Haq†	8,829	Salim Malik	5,768
Javed Miandad	8,832	Mohammad Yousuf	7,530	**Azhar Ali**	**5,669**

† *Inzamam-ul-Haq also scored 1 and 0 for the World XI v Australia (2005-06 Super Series Test).*

SRI LANKA

K. C. Sangakkara	12,400	S. T. Jayasuriya	6,973	**A. D. Mathews**	**5,554**
D. P. M. D. Jayawardene	11,814	P. A. de Silva	6,361	M. S. Atapattu	5,502

ZIMBABWE

A. Flower	4,794	A. D. R. Campbell	2,858	G. J. Whittall	2,207
G. W. Flower	3,457	**H. Masakadza**	**2,223**	H. H. Streak	1,990

BANGLADESH

Tamim Iqbal	**4,049**	**Shakib Al Hasan**	**3,807**	Mohammad Ashraful	2,737
Mushfiqur Rahim	**4,006**	Habibul Bashar	3,026	**Mominul Haque**	**2,513**

IRELAND

No player has scored 1,000 Test runs for Ireland. The highest total is **158**, by **K. J. O'Brien**.

AFGHANISTAN

No player has scored 1,000 Test runs for Afghanistan. The highest total is **47**, by **Hashmatullah Shahidi**.

HIGHEST CAREER AVERAGE

(Qualification: 20 innings)

Avge		T	I	NO	R	HS	100
99.94	D. G. Bradman (A)	52	80	10	6,996	334	29
61.87	A. C. Voges (A)	20	31	7	1,485	269*	5
61.37	**S. P. D. Smith (A)**	**64**	**117**	**16**	**6,199**	**239**	**23**
60.97	R. G. Pollock (SA)	23	41	4	2,256	274	7
60.83	G. A. Headley (WI)	22	40	4	2,190	270*	10

Avge		*T*	*I*	*NO*	*R*	*HS*	*100*
60.73	H. Sutcliffe (E)	54	84	9	4,555	194	16
59.23	E. Paynter (E)	20	31	5	1,540	243	4
58.67	K. F. Barrington (E)	82	131	15	6,806	256	20
58.61	E. D. Weekes (WI)	48	81	5	4,455	207	15
58.45	W. R. Hammond (E).	85	140	16	7,249	336*	22
57.78	G. S. Sobers (WI)	93	160	21	8,032	365*	26
57.40	K. C. Sangakkara (SL)	134	233	17	12,400	319	38
56.94	J. B. Hobbs (E)	61	102	7	5,410	211	15
56.68	C. L. Walcott (WI)	44	74	7	3,798	220	15
56.67	L. Hutton (E).	79	138	15	6,971	364	19
55.37	J. H. Kallis (SA/World)	166	280	40	13,289	224	45
55.00	E. Tyldesley (E)	14	20	2	990	122	3

S. G. Barnes (A) scored 1,072 runs at 63.05 from 19 innings.

BEST CAREER STRIKE-RATES

(Runs per 100 balls. Qualification: 1,000 runs)

SR		*T*	*I*	*NO*	*R*	*100*	*Avge*
88.31	**T. G. Southee (NZ)**.	**63**	**95**	**9**	**1,550**	**0**	**18.02**
86.97	Shahid Afridi (P).	27	48	1	1,716	5	36.51
82.22	V. Sehwag (I).	104	180	6	8,586	23	49.34
81.98	A. C. Gilchrist (A).	96	137	20	5,570	17	47.60
76.49	G. P. Swann (E).	60	76	14	1,370	0	22.09
74.50	**D. A. Warner (A)**.	**74**	**137**	**5**	**6,363**	**21**	**48.20**
71.81	**Q. de Kock (SA)**.	**38**	**62**	**5**	**2,176**	**4**	**38.17**
70.98	**Sarfraz Ahmed (P)**.	**49**	**86**	**13**	**2,657**	**3**	**36.39**
70.28	M. Muralitharan (SL)	133	164	56	1,261	0	11.67
70.01	**D. P. D. N. Dickwella (SL)**.	**27**	**51**	**4**	**1,436**	**0**	**30.55**
67.88	D. J. G. Sammy (WI).	38	63	2	1,323	1	21.68
66.94	**S. Dhawan (I)**.	**34**	**58**	**1**	**2,315**	**7**	**40.61**
66.68	**M. A. Starc (A)**.	**49**	**77**	**14**	**1,351**	**0**	**21.44**

Comprehensive data on balls faced has been available only in recent decades, and its introduction varied from country to country. Among earlier players for whom partial data is available, Kapil Dev (India) had a strike-rate of 80.91 and I. V. A. Richards (West Indies) 70.19 in those innings which were fully recorded.

HIGHEST PERCENTAGE OF TEAM'S RUNS OVER TEST CAREER

(Qualification: 20 Tests)

	Tests	*Runs*	*Team Runs*	*% of Team Runs*
D. G. Bradman (Australia)	52	6,996	28,810	24.28
G. A. Headley (West Indies)	22	2,190	10,239	21.38
B. C. Lara (West Indies)	131	11,953	63,328	18.87
L. Hutton (England)	79	6,971	38,440	18.13
J. B. Hobbs (England).	61	5,410	30,211	17.90
A. D. Nourse (South Africa)	34	2,960	16,659	17.76
E. D. Weekes (West Indies)	48	4,455	25,667	17.35
S. P. D. Smith (Australia)	**64**	**6,199**	**35,998**	**17.22**
B. Mitchell (South Africa)	42	3,471	20,175	17.20
H. Sutcliffe (England)	54	4,555	26,604	17.12
K. C. Sangakkara (Sri Lanka)	134	12,400	72,779	17.03
B. Sutcliffe (New Zealand)	42	2,727	16,158	16.87

The percentage shows the proportion of a team's runs scored by that player in all Tests in which he played, including team runs in innings in which he did not bat.

FASTEST FIFTIES

Minutes

24	Misbah-ul-Haq	Pakistan v Australia at Abu Dhabi	2014-15
27	Mohammad Ashraful	Bangladesh v India at Mirpur	2007
28	J. T. Brown	England v Australia at Melbourne	1894-95
29	S. A. Durani	India v England at Kanpur	1963-64
30	E. A. V. Williams	West Indies v England at Bridgetown	1947-48
30	B. R. Taylor	New Zealand v West Indies at Auckland	1968-69

The fastest fifties in terms of balls received (where recorded) are:

Balls

21	Misbah-ul-Haq	Pakistan v Australia at Abu Dhabi	2014-15
23	D. A. Warner.	Australia v Pakistan at Sydney	2016-17
24	J. H. Kallis	South Africa v Zimbabwe at Cape Town	2004-05
25	S. Shillingford.	West Indies v New Zealand at Kingston.	2014
26	Shahid Afridi.	Pakistan v India at Bangalore	2004-05
26	Mohammad Ashraful	Bangladesh v India at Mirpur	2007
26	D. W. Steyn.	South Africa v West Indies at Port Elizabeth .	2014-15

FASTEST HUNDREDS

Minutes

70	J. M. Gregory	Australia v South Africa at Johannesburg. . . .	1921-22
74	Misbah-ul-Haq	Pakistan v Australia at Abu Dhabi	2014-15
75	G. L. Jessop.	England v Australia at The Oval.	1902
78	R. Benaud	Australia v West Indies at Kingston	1954-55
80	J. H. Sinclair	South Africa v Australia at Cape Town	1902-03
81	I. V. A. Richards	West Indies v England at St John's.	1985-86
86	B. R. Taylor.	New Zealand v West Indies at Auckland	1968-69

The fastest hundreds in terms of balls received (where recorded) are:

Balls

54	B. B. McCullum	New Zealand v Australia at Christchurch	2015-16
56	I. V. A. Richards	West Indies v England at St John's.	1985-86
56	Misbah-ul-Haq	Pakistan v Australia at Abu Dhabi	2014-15
57	A. C. Gilchrist.	Australia v England at Perth	2006-07
67	J. M. Gregory	Australia v South Africa at Johannesburg. . . .	1921-22
69	S. Chanderpaul	West Indies v Australia at Georgetown	2002-03
69	D. A. Warner.	Australia v India at Perth.	2011-12
70	C. H. Gayle	West Indies v Australia at Perth	2009-10

FASTEST DOUBLE-HUNDREDS

Minutes

214	D. G. Bradman	Australia v England at Leeds	1930
217	N. J. Astle	New Zealand v England at Christchurch.	2001-02
223	S. J. McCabe	Australia v England at Nottingham.	1938
226	V. T. Trumper.	Australia v South Africa at Adelaide.	1910-11
234	D. G. Bradman	Australia v England at Lord's	1930
240	W. R. Hammond	England v New Zealand at Auckland	1932-33

The fastest double-hundreds in terms of balls received (where recorded) are:

Balls

153	N. J. Astle	New Zealand v England at Christchurch.	2001-02
163	B. A. Stokes	England v South Africa at Cape Town	2015-16
168	V. Sehwag.	India v Sri Lanka at Mumbai (BS)	2009-10
182	V. Sehwag.	India v Pakistan at Lahore	2005-06
186	B. B. McCullum	New Zealand v Pakistan at Sharjah.	2014-15
194	V. Sehwag.	India v South Africa at Chennai	2007-08

FASTEST TRIPLE-HUNDREDS

Minutes

| 288 | W. R. Hammond | England v New Zealand at Auckland | 1932-33 |
| 336 | D. G. Bradman | Australia v England at Leeds | 1930 |

The fastest triple-hundred in terms of balls received (where recorded) is:

Balls

| 278 | V. Sehwag | India v South Africa at Chennai | 2007-08 |

MOST RUNS SCORED OFF AN OVER

28	B. C. Lara (466444)	off R. J. Peterson	WI v SA at Johannesburg .	2003-04
28	G. J. Bailey (462466)	off J. M. Anderson	A v E at Perth	2013-14
27	Shahid Afridi (666621)	off Harbhajan Singh	P v I at Lahore	2005-06
26	C. D. McMillan (444464)	off Younis Khan	NZ v P at Hamilton	2000-01
26	B. C. Lara (406664)	off Danish Kaneria	WI v P at Multan	2006-07
26	M. G. Johnson (446066)	off P. L. Harris	A v SA at Johannesburg .	2009-10
26	B. B. McCullum (466046)	off R. A. S. Lakmal	NZ v SL at Christchurch .	2014-15
26	H. H. Pandya (446660)	off P. M. Pushpakumara	I v SL at Pallekele	2017

MOST RUNS IN A DAY

309	D. G. Bradman	Australia v England at Leeds	1930
295	W. R. Hammond	England v New Zealand at Auckland	1932-33
284	V. Sehwag	India v Sri Lanka at Mumbai	2009-10
273	D. C. S. Compton	England v Pakistan at Nottingham	1954
271	D. G. Bradman	Australia v England at Leeds	1934

MOST SIXES IN A CAREER

B. B. McCullum (NZ)	107		A. Flintoff (E/World)	82
A. C. Gilchrist (A)	100		M. L. Hayden (A)	82
C. H. Gayle (WI)	98		Misbah-ul-Haq (P)	81
J. H. Kallis (SA/World)	97		K. P. Pietersen (E)	81
V. Sehwag (I/World)	91		M. S. Dhoni (I)	78
B. C. Lara (WI)	88		R. T. Ponting (A)	73
C. L. Cairns (NZ)	87		C. H. Lloyd (WI)	70
I. V. A. Richards (WI)	84		Younis Khan (P)	70

SLOWEST INDIVIDUAL BATTING

0	in 101 minutes	G. I. Allott, New Zealand v South Africa at Auckland	1998-99
4*	in 110 minutes	Abdul Razzaq, Pakistan v Australia at Melbourne	2004-05
6	in 137 minutes	S. C. J. Broad, England v New Zealand at Auckland	2012-13
9*	in 184 minutes	Arshad Khan, Pakistan v Sri Lanka at Colombo (SSC)	2000
18	in 194 minutes	W. R. Playle, New Zealand v England at Leeds	1958
19*	in 217 minutes	M. D. Crowe, New Zealand v Sri Lanka at Colombo (SSC)	1983-84
25	in 289 minutes	H. M. Amla, South Africa v India at Delhi	2015-16
35	in 332 minutes	C. J. Tavaré, England v India at Madras	1981-82
43	in 354 minutes	A. B. de Villiers, South Africa v India at Delhi	2015-16
60	in 390 minutes	D. N. Sardesai, India v West Indies at Bridgetown	1961-62
62	in 408 minutes	Ramiz Raja, Pakistan v West Indies at Karachi	1986-87
68	in 458 minutes	T. E. Bailey, England v Australia at Brisbane	1958-59
86	in 474 minutes	Shoaib Mohammad, Pakistan v West Indies at Karachi	1990-91
99	in 505 minutes	M. L. Jaisimha, India v Pakistan at Kanpur	1960-61
104	in 529 minutes	S. V. Manjrekar, India v Zimbabwe at Harare	1992-93

105	in 575 minutes	D. J. McGlew, South Africa v Australia at Durban............	1957-58
114	in 591 minutes	Mudassar Nazar, Pakistan v England at Lahore	1977-78
120*	in 609 minutes	J. J. Crowe, New Zealand v Sri Lanka at Colombo (CCC).....	1986-87
136*	in 675 minutes	S. Chanderpaul, West Indies v India at St John's	2001-02
163	in 720 minutes	Shoaib Mohammad, Pakistan v New Zealand at Wellington ...	1988-89
201*	in 777 minutes	D. S. B. P. Kuruppu, Sri Lanka v NZ at Colombo (CCC)....	1986-87
275	in 878 minutes	G. Kirsten, South Africa v England at Durban	1999-2000
337	in 970 minutes	Hanif Mohammad, Pakistan v West Indies at Bridgetown	1957-58

SLOWEST HUNDREDS

557 minutes	Mudassar Nazar, Pakistan v England at Lahore.....................	1977-78
545 minutes	D. J. McGlew, South Africa v Australia at Durban	1957-58
535 minutes	A. P. Gurusinha, Sri Lanka v Zimbabwe at Harare	1994-95
516 minutes	J. J. Crowe, New Zealand v Sri Lanka at Colombo (CCC)	1986-87
500 minutes	S. V. Manjrekar, India v Zimbabwe at Harare	1992-93
488 minutes	P. E. Richardson, England v South Africa at Johannesburg...........	1956-57

The slowest hundred for any Test in England is 458 minutes (329 balls) by K. W. R. Fletcher, England v Pakistan, The Oval, 1974.
The slowest double-hundred in a Test was scored in 777 minutes (548 balls) by D. S. B. P. Kuruppu for Sri Lanka v New Zealand at Colombo (CCC), 1986-87, on his debut.

PARTNERSHIPS OVER 400

624	for 3rd	K. C. Sangakkara (287)/			
		D. P. M. D. Jayawardene (374)	SL v SA	Colombo (SSC)	2006
576	for 2nd	S. T. Jayasuriya (340)/R. S. Mahanama (225)	SL v I	Colombo (RPS)	1997-98
467	for 3rd	A. H. Jones (186)/M. D. Crowe (299)......	NZ v SL	Wellington	1990-91
451	for 2nd	W. H. Ponsford (266)/D. G. Bradman (244) .	A v E	The Oval	1934
451	for 3rd	Mudassar Nazar (231)/Javed Miandad (280*)	P v I	Hyderabad	1982-83
449	for 4th	A. C. Voges (269*)/S. E. Marsh (182)......	A v WI	Hobart	2015-16
446	for 2nd	C. C. Hunte (260)/G. S. Sobers (365*)	WI v P	Kingston	1957-58
438	for 2nd	M. S. Atapattu (249)/K. C. Sangakkara (270)	SL v Z	Bulawayo	2003-04
437	for 4th	D. P. M. D. Jayawardene (240)/			
		T. T. Samaraweera (231)	SL v P	Karachi	2008-09
429*	for 3rd	J. A. Rudolph (222*)/H. H. Dippenaar (177*)	SA v B	Chittagong	2003
415	for 1st	N. D. McKenzie (226)/G. C. Smith (232) ...	SA v B	Chittagong	2007-08
413	for 1st	M. H. Mankad (231)/Pankaj Roy (173).....	I v NZ	Madras	1955-56
411	for 4th	P. B. H. May (285*)/M. C. Cowdrey (154)..	E v WI	Birmingham	1957
410	for 1st	V. Sehwag (254)/R. Dravid (128*)	I v P	Lahore	2005-06
405	for 5th	S. G. Barnes (234)/D. G. Bradman (234)....	A v E	Sydney	1946-47

415 runs were added for the third wicket for India v England at Madras in 1981-82 by D. B. Vengsarkar (retired hurt), G. R. Viswanath and Yashpal Sharma. 408 runs were added for the first wicket for India v Bangladesh at Mirpur in 2007 by K. D. Karthik (retired hurt), Wasim Jaffer (retired hurt), R. Dravid and S. R. Tendulkar.

HIGHEST PARTNERSHIPS FOR EACH WICKET

First Wicket

415	N. D. McKenzie (226)/G. C. Smith (232).........	SA v B	Chittagong	2007-08
413	M. H. Mankad (231)/Pankaj Roy (173)	I v NZ	Madras	1955-56
410	V. Sehwag (254)/R. Dravid (128*)..............	I v P	Lahore	2005-06
387	G. M. Turner (259)/T. W. Jarvis (182)	NZ v WI	Georgetown	1971-72
382	W. M. Lawry (210)/R. B. Simpson (201).........	A v WI	Bridgetown	1964-65

Second Wicket

576	S. T. Jayasuriya (340)/R. S. Mahanama (225)	SL v I	Colombo (RPS)	1997-98
451	W. H. Ponsford (266)/D. G. Bradman (244).	A v E	The Oval	1934
446	C. C. Hunte (260)/G. S. Sobers (365*)	WI v P	Kingston	1957-58
438	M. S. Atapattu (249)/K. C. Sangakkara (270).	SL v Z	Bulawayo	2003-04
382	L. Hutton (364)/M. Leyland (187)	E v A	The Oval	1938

Third Wicket

624	K. C. Sangakkara (287)/ D. P. M. D. Jayawardene (374)	SL v SA	Colombo (SSC)	2006
467	A. H. Jones (186)/M. D. Crowe (299).	NZ v SL	Wellington	1990-91
451	Mudassar Nazar (231)/Javed Miandad (280*)	P v I	Hyderabad	1982-83
429*	J. A. Rudolph (222*)/H. H. Dippenaar (177*)	SA v B	Chittagong	2003
397	Qasim Omar (206)/Javed Miandad (203*)	P v SL	Faisalabad	1985-86

Fourth Wicket

449	A. C. Voges (269*)/S. E. Marsh (182)	A v WI	Hobart	2015-16
437	D. P. M. D. Jayawardene (240)/ T. T. Samaraweera (231).	SL v P	Karachi	2008-09
411	P. B. H. May (285*)/M. C. Cowdrey (154)	E v WI	Birmingham	1957
399	G. S. Sobers (226)/F. M. M. Worrell (197*).	WI v E	Bridgetown	1959-60
388	W. H. Ponsford (181)/D. G. Bradman (304).	A v E	Leeds	1934

Fifth Wicket

405	S. G. Barnes (234)/D. G. Bradman (234)	A v E	Sydney	1946-47
385	S. R. Waugh (160)/G. S. Blewett (214)	A v SA	Johannesburg	1996-97
376	V. V. S. Laxman (281)/R. Dravid (180)	I v A	Kolkata	2000-01
359	Shakib Al Hasan (217)/Mushfiqur Rahim (159).	B v NZ	Wellington	2016-17
338	G. C. Smith (234)/A. B. de Villiers (164).	SA v P	Dubai	2013-14

Sixth Wicket

399	B. A. Stokes (258)/J. M. Bairstow (150*).	E v SA	Cape Town	2015-16
352	B. B. McCullum (302)/B-J. Watling (124).	NZ v I	Wellington	2013-14
351	D. P. M. D. Jayawardene (275)/ H. A. P. W. Jayawardene (154*).	SL v I	Ahmedabad	2009-10
346	J. H. Fingleton (136)/D. G. Bradman (270)	A v E	Melbourne	1936-37

Seventh Wicket

347	D. St E Atkinson (219)/C. C. Depeiza (122)	WI v A	Bridgetown	1954-55
308	Waqar Hassan (189)/Imtiaz Ahmed (209)	P v NZ	Lahore	1955-56
280	R. G. Sharma (177)/R. Ashwin (124).	I v WI	Kolkata	2013-14
259*	V. V. S. Laxman (143*)/M. S. Dhoni (132*)	I v SA	Kolkata	2009-10
248	Yousuf Youhana (203)/Saqlain Mushtaq (101*)	P v NZ	Christchurch	2000-01

Eighth Wicket

332	I. J. L. Trott (184)/S. C. J. Broad (169).	E v P	Lord's	2010
313	Wasim Akram (257)/Saqlain Mushtaq (79)	P v Z	Sheikhupura	1996-97
256	S. P. Fleming (262)/J. E. C. Franklin (122*)	NZ v SA	Cape Town	2005-06
253	N. J. Astle (156*)/A. C. Parore (110)	NZ v A	Perth	2001-02
246	L. E. G. Ames (137)/G. O. B. Allen (122)	E v NZ	Lord's	1931

Ninth Wicket

195	M. V. Boucher (78)/P. L. Symcox (108).	SA v P	Johannesburg	1997-98
190	Asif Iqbal (146)/Intikhab Alam (51).	P v E	The Oval	1967
184	Mahmudullah (76)/Abul Hasan (113).	B v WI	Khulna	2012-13
180	J-P. Duminy (166)/D. W. Steyn (76)	SA v A	Melbourne	2008-09
163*	M. C. Cowdrey (128*)/A. C. Smith (69*)	E v NZ	Wellington	1962-63

Tenth Wicket

198	J. E. Root (154*)/J. M. Anderson (81)	E v I	Nottingham	2014
163	P. J. Hughes (81*)/A. C. Agar (98).	A v E	Nottingham	2013
151	B. F. Hastings (110)/R. O. Collinge (68*)	NZ v P	Auckland	1972-73
151	Azhar Mahmood (128*)/Mushtaq Ahmed (59)	P v SA	Rawalpindi	1997-98
143	D. Ramdin (107*)/T. L. Best (95).	WI v E	Birmingham	2012

HIGHEST PARTNERSHIPS FOR EACH COUNTRY

ENGLAND

359	for 1st	L. Hutton (158)/C. Washbrook (195).	v SA	Johannesburg	1948-49
382	for 2nd	L. Hutton (364)/M. Leyland (187)	v A	The Oval	1938
370	for 3rd	W. J. Edrich (189)/D. C. S. Compton (208) . . .	v SA	Lord's	1947
411	for 4th	P. B. H. May (285*)/M. C. Cowdrey (154) . . .	v WI	Birmingham	1957
254	for 5th	K. W. R. Fletcher (113)/A. W. Greig (148) . . .	v I	Bombay	1972-73
399	for 6th	B. A. Stokes (258)/J. M. Bairstow (150*)	v SA	Cape Town	2015-16
197	for 7th	M. J. K. Smith (96)/J. M. Parks (101*).	v WI	Port-of-Spain	1959-60
332	for 8th	I. J. L. Trott (184)/S. C. J. Broad (169).	v P	Lord's	2010
163*	for 9th	M. C. Cowdrey (128*)/A. C. Smith (69*)	v NZ	Wellington	1962-63
198	for 10th	J. E. Root (154*)/J. M. Anderson (81)	v I	Nottingham	2014

AUSTRALIA

382	for 1st	W. M. Lawry (210)/R. B. Simpson (201).	v WI	Bridgetown	1964-65
451	for 2nd	W. H. Ponsford (266)/D. G. Bradman (244). . .	v E	The Oval	1934
315	for 3rd	R. T. Ponting (206)/D. S. Lehmann (160)	v WI	Port-of-Spain	2002-03
449	for 4th	A. C. Voges (269*)/S. E. Marsh (182)	v WI	Hobart	2015-16
405	for 5th	S. G. Barnes (234)/D. G. Bradman (234)	v E	Sydney	1946-47
346	for 6th	J. H. Fingleton (136)/D. G. Bradman (270) . . .	v E	Melbourne	1936-37
217	for 7th	K. D. Walters (250)/G. J. Gilmour (101)	v NZ	Christchurch	1976-77
243	for 8th	R. J. Hartigan (116)/C. Hill (160).	v E	Adelaide	1907-08
154	for 9th	S. E. Gregory (201)/J. McC. Blackham (74) . .	v E	Sydney	1894-95
163	for 10th	P. J. Hughes (81*)/A. C. Agar (98).	v E	Nottingham	2013

SOUTH AFRICA

415	for 1st	N. D. McKenzie (226)/G. C. Smith (232).	v B	Chittagong	2007-08
315*	for 2nd	H. H. Gibbs (211*)/J. H. Kallis (148*).	v NZ	Christchurch	1998-99
429*	for 3rd	J. A. Rudolph (222*)/H. H. Dippenaar (177*) .	v B	Chittagong	2003
308	for 4th	H. M. Amla (208)/A. B. de Villiers (152).	v WI	Centurion	2014-15
338	for 5th	G. C. Smith (234)/A. B. de Villiers (164). . . .	v P	Dubai	2013-14
271	for 6th	A. G. Prince (162*)/M. V. Boucher (117)	v B	Centurion	2008-09
246	for 7th	D. J. McGlew (255*)/A. R. A. Murray (109) . .	v NZ	Wellington	1952-53
150	for 8th {	N. D. McKenzie (103)/S. M. Pollock (111) . .	v SL	Centurion	2000-01
		G. Kirsten (130)/M. Zondeki (59).	v E	Leeds	2003
195	for 9th	M. V. Boucher (78)/P. L. Symcox (108).	v P	Johannesburg	1997-98
107*	for 10th	A. B. de Villiers (278*)/M. Morkel (35*).	v P	Abu Dhabi	2010-11

WEST INDIES

298	for 1st	C. G. Greenidge (149)/D. L. Haynes (167). . . .	v E	St John's	1989-90
446	for 2nd	C. C. Hunte (260)/G. S. Sobers (365*).	v P	Kingston	1957-58
338	for 3rd	E. D. Weekes (206)/F. M. M. Worrell (167). . .	v E	Port-of-Spain	1953-54
399	for 4th	G. S. Sobers (226)/F. M. M. Worrell (197*). . .	v E	Bridgetown	1959-60
322	for 5th†	B. C. Lara (213)/J. C. Adams (94)	v A	Kingston	1998-99
282*	for 6th	B. C. Lara (400*)/R. D. Jacobs (107*).	v E	St John's	2003-04
347	for 7th	D. St E Atkinson (219)/C. C. Depeiza (122). .	v A	Bridgetown	1954-55
212	for 8th	S. O. Dowrich (103)/J. O. Holder (110)	v Z	Bulawayo	2017-18
161	for 9th	C. H. Lloyd (161*)/A. M. E. Roberts (68)	v I	Calcutta	1983-84
143	for 10th	D. Ramdin (107*)/T. L. Best (95).	v E	Birmingham	2012

† *344 runs were added between the fall of the 4th and 5th wickets: P. T. Collins retired hurt when he and Lara had added 22 runs.*

NEW ZEALAND

387	for 1st	G. M. Turner (259)/T. W. Jarvis (182)	v WI	Georgetown	1971-72
297	for 2nd	B. B. McCullum (202)/K. S. Williamson (192)	v P	Sharjah	2014-15
467	for 3rd	A. H. Jones (186)/M. D. Crowe (299)	v SL	Wellington	1990-91
271	for 4th	L. R. P. L. Taylor (151)/J. D. Ryder (201). . . .	v I	Napier	2008-09
222	for 5th	N. J. Astle (141)/C. D. McMillan (142)	v Z	Wellington	2000-01
365*	for 6th	K. S. Williamson (242*)/B-J. Watling (142*) .	v SL	Wellington	2014-15
225	for 7th	C. L. Cairns (158)/J. D. P. Oram (90).	v SA	Auckland	2003-04
256	for 8th	S. P. Fleming (262)/J. E. C. Franklin (122*) . .	v SA	Cape Town	2005-06
136	for 9th	I. D. S. Smith (173)/M. C. Snedden (22)	v I	Auckland	1989-90
151	for 10th	B. F. Hastings (110)/R. O. Collinge (68*) . . .	v P	Auckland	1972-73

INDIA

413	for 1st	M. H. Mankad (231)/Pankaj Roy (173)	v NZ	Madras	1955-56
370	for 2nd	M. Vijay (167)/C. A. Pujara (204).	v A	Hyderabad	2012-13
336	for 3rd†	V. Sehwag (309)/S. R. Tendulkar (194*).	v P	Multan	2003-04
365	for 4th	V. Kohli (211)/A. M. Rahane (188).	v NZ	Indore	2016-17
376	for 5th	V. V. S. Laxman (281)/R. Dravid (180).	v A	Kolkata	2000-01
298*	for 6th	D. B. Vengsarkar (164*)/R. J. Shastri (121*). .	v A	Bombay	1986-87
280	for 7th	R. G. Sharma (177)/R. Ashwin (124).	v WI	Kolkata	2013-14
241	for 8th	V. Kohli (235)/J. Yadav (104)	v E	Mumbai	2016-17
149	for 9th	P. G. Joshi (52*)/R. B. Desai (85)	v P	Bombay	1960-61
133	for 10th	S. R. Tendulkar (248*)/Zaheer Khan (75) . . .	v B	Dhaka	2004-05

† *415 runs were scored for India's 3rd wicket v England at Madras in 1981-82, in two partnerships: D. B. Vengsarkar and G. R. Viswanath put on 99 before Vengsarkar retired hurt, then Viswanath and Yashpal Sharma added a further 316.*

PAKISTAN

298	for 1st	Aamir Sohail (160)/Ijaz Ahmed snr (151)	v WI	Karachi	1997-98
291	for 2nd	Zaheer Abbas (274)/Mushtaq Mohammad (100)	v E	Birmingham	1971
451	for 3rd	Mudassar Nazar (231)/Javed Miandad (280*) .	v I	Hyderabad	1982-83
350	for 4th	Mushtaq Mohammad (201)/Asif Iqbal (175) . .	v NZ	Dunedin	1972-73
281	for 5th	Javed Miandad (163)/Asif Iqbal (166)	v NZ	Lahore	1976-77
269	for 6th	Mohammad Yousuf (223)/Kamran Akmal (154)	v E	Lahore	2005-06
308	for 7th	Waqar Hassan (189)/Imtiaz Ahmed (209)	v NZ	Lahore	1955-56
313	for 8th	Wasim Akram (257*)/Saqlain Mushtaq (79) . .	v Z	Sheikhupura	1996-97
190	for 9th	Asif Iqbal (146)/Intikhab Alam (51).	v E	The Oval	1967
151	for 10th	Azhar Mahmood (128*)/Mushtaq Ahmed (59)	v SA	Rawalpindi	1997-98

SRI LANKA

335	for 1st	M. S. Atapattu (207*)/S. T. Jayasuriya (188) .	v P	Kandy	2000
576	for 2nd	S. T. Jayasuriya (340)/R. S. Mahanama (225) .	v I	Colombo (RPS)	1997-98
624	for 3rd	K. C. Sangakkara (287)/			
		D. P. M. D. Jayawardene (374).	v SA	Colombo (SSC)	2006
437	for 4th	D. P. M. D. Jayawardene (240)/			
		T. T. Samaraweera (231)	v P	Karachi	2008-09
280	for 5th	T. T. Samaraweera (138)/T. M. Dilshan (168) .	v B	Colombo (PSS)	2005-06
351	for 6th	D. P. M. D. Jayawardene (275)/			
		H. A. P. W. Jayawardene (154*)	v I	Ahmedabad	2009-10
223*	for 7th	H. A. P. W. Jayawardene (120*)/			
		W. P. U. J. C. Vaas (100*)	v B	Colombo (SSC)	2007
170	for 8th	D. P. M. D. Jayawardene (237)/			
		W. P. U. J. C. Vaas (69)	v SA	Galle	2004
118	for 9th	T. T. Samaraweera (83)/B. A. W. Mendis (78) .	v I	Colombo (PSS)	2010
79	for 10th	W. P. U. J. C. Vaas (68*)/M. Muralitharan (43)	v A	Kandy	2003-04

ZIMBABWE

164	for 1st	D. D. Ebrahim (71)/A. D. R. Campbell (103) .	v WI	Bulawayo	2001
160	for 2nd	Sikandar Raza (82)/H. Masakadza (81)	v B	Chittagong	2014-15
194	for 3rd	A. D. R. Campbell (99)/D. L. Houghton (142).	v SL	Harare	1994-95
269	for 4th	G. W. Flower (201*)/A. Flower (156)	v P	Harare	1994-95
277*	for 5th	M. W. Goodwin (166*)/A. Flower (100*)	v P	Bulawayo	1997-98
165	for 6th	D. L. Houghton (121)/A. Flower (59).	v I	Harare	1992-93
154	for 7th	H. H. Streak (83*)/A. M. Blignaut (92)	v WI	Harare	2001
168	for 8th	H. H. Streak (127*)/A. M. Blignaut (91)	v WI	Harare	2003-04
87	for 9th	P. A. Strang (106*)/B. C. Strang (42)	v P	Sheikhupura	1996-97
97*	for 10th	A. Flower (183*)/H. K. Olonga (11*)	v I	Delhi	2000-01

BANGLADESH

312	for 1st	Tamim Iqbal (206)/Imrul Kayes (150)	v P	Khulna	2014-15
232	for 2nd	Shamsur Rahman (106)/Imrul Kayes (115) . . .	v SL	Chittagong	2013-14
236	**for 3rd**	**Mominul Haque (176)/Mushfiqur Rahim (92)**	**v SL**	**Chittagong**	**2017-18**
266	**for 4th**	**Mominul Haque (161)/**			
		Mushfiqur Rahim (219*)	**v Z**	**Mirpur**	**2018-19**
359	for 5th	Shakib Al Hasan (217)/Mushfiqur Rahim (159)	v NZ	Wellington	2016-17
191	for 6th	Mohammad Ashraful (129*)/			
		Mushfiqur Rahim (80).	v SL	Colombo (PSS)	2007
145	for 7th	Shakib Al Hasan (87)/Mahmudullah (115) . . .	v NZ	Hamilton	2009-10
144*	**for 8th**	**Mushfiqur Rahim (219*)/Mehedi Hasan (68*)**	**v Z**	**Mirpur**	**2018-19**
184	for 9th	Mahmudullah (76)/Abul Hasan (113)	v WI	Khulna	2012-13
69	for 10th	Mohammad Rafique (65)/Shahadat Hossain (3*)	v A	Chittagong	2005-06

IRELAND

69	**for 1st**	E. C. Joyce (43)/W. T. S. Porterfield (32) . . .	**v P**	**Malahide**	**2018**
0	**for 2nd** {	W. T. S. Porterfield (1)/A. Balbirnie (0)	**v P**	**Malahide**	**2018**
	{	W. T. S. Porterfield (32)/A. Balbirnie (0)	**v P**	**Malahide**	**2018**
25	**for 3rd**	W. T. S. Porterfield (32)/N. J. O'Brien (18) .	**v P**	**Malahide**	**2018**
2	**for 4th**	N. J. O'Brien (0)/P. R. Stirling (17)	**v P**	**Malahide**	**2018**
32	**for 5th**	P. R. Stirling (11)/K. J. O'Brien (118).	**v P**	**Malahide**	**2018**
30	**for 6th**	K. J. O'Brien (118)/G. C. Wilson (12).	**v P**	**Malahide**	**2018**
114	**for 7th**	K. J. O'Brien (118)/S. R. Thompson (53)	**v P**	**Malahide**	**2018**
50	**for 8th**	K. J. O'Brien (118)/T. E. Kane (14).	**v P**	**Malahide**	**2018**
34	**for 9th**	G. C. Wilson (33*)/W. B. Rankin (17).	**v P**	**Malahide**	**2018**
23	**for 10th**	G. C. Wilson (33*)/T. J. Murtagh (5)	**v P**	**Malahide**	**2018**

AFGHANISTAN

19	for 1st	Mohammad Shahzad (13)/Javed Ahmadi (3)	v I	Bangalore	2018
6	for 2nd	Javed Ahmadi (1)/Rahmat Shah (14)	v I	Bangalore	2018
14	for 3rd	Rahmat Shah (14)/Afsar Zazai (6).........	v I	Bangalore	2018
2	for 4th	Rahmat Shah (4)/Hashmatullah Shahidi(36*)	v I	Bangalore	2018
37	for 5th	Hashmatullah Shahidi (36*)/ .... Asghar Stanikzai (25)	v I	Bangalore	2018
9	for 6th	Hashmatullah Shahidi (11)/ .... Mohammad Nabi (24).	v I	Bangalore	2018
20	for 7th	Hashmatullah Shahidi (36*)/ Rashid Khan (12)	v I	Bangalore	2018
9	for 8th	Mohammad Nabi (24)/Yamin Ahmadzai (0)	v I	Bangalore	2018
13	for 9th	Hashmatullah Shahidi (36*)/ .... Mujeeb Zadran (3)	v I	Bangalore	2018
21	for 10th	Mujeeb Zadran (15)/Wafadar Momand (6*)	v I	Bangalore	2018

UNUSUAL DISMISSALS

Handled the Ball

W. R. Endean	South Africa v England at Cape Town	1956-57
A. M. J. Hilditch	Australia v Pakistan at Perth	1978-79
Mohsin Khan	Pakistan v Australia at Karachi	1982-83
D. L. Haynes	West Indies v India at Bombay	1983-84
G. A. Gooch	England v Australia at Manchester	1993
S. R. Waugh	Australia v India at Chennai	2000-01
M. P. Vaughan	England v India at Bangalore	2001-02

Obstructing the Field

L. Hutton	England v South Africa at The Oval.	1951

There have been no cases of Hit the Ball Twice or Timed Out in Test cricket.

BOWLING RECORDS

MOST WICKETS IN AN INNINGS

10-53	J. C. Laker	England v Australia at Manchester.	1956
10-74	A. Kumble	India v Pakistan at Delhi.	1998-99
9-28	G. A. Lohmann	England v South Africa at Johannesburg	1895-96
9-37	J. C. Laker	England v Australia at Manchester.	1956
9-51	M. Muralitharan.	Sri Lanka v Zimbabwe at Kandy	2001-02
9-52	R. J. Hadlee	New Zealand v Australia at Brisbane	1985-86
9-56	Abdul Qadir.	Pakistan v England at Lahore	1987-88
9-57	D. E. Malcolm	England v South Africa at The Oval.	1994
9-65	M. Muralitharan.	Sri Lanka v England at The Oval	1998
9-69	J. M. Patel	India v Australia at Kanpur.	1959-60
9-83	Kapil Dev	India v West Indies at Ahmedabad	1983-84
9-86	Sarfraz Nawaz	Pakistan v Australia at Melbourne	1978-79
9-95	J. M. Noreiga.	West Indies v India at Port-of-Spain	1970-71
9-102	S. P. Gupte.	India v West Indies at Kanpur	1958-59
9-103	S. F. Barnes	England v South Africa at Johannesburg	1913-14
9-113	H. J. Tayfield	South Africa v England at Johannesburg	1956-57
9-121	A. A. Mailey	Australia v England at Melbourne	1920-21
9-127	H. M. R. K. B. Herath . . .	Sri Lanka v Pakistan at Colombo (SSC).	2014
9-129	**K. A. Maharaj**	**South Africa v Sri Lanka at Colombo (SSC)**	**2018**

There have been 78 instances of eight wickets in a Test innings.

The best bowling figures for the countries not mentioned above are:

8-39	Taijul Islam	Bangladesh v Zimbabwe at Mirpur	2014-15
8-109	P. A. Strang	Zimbabwe v New Zealand at Bulawayo	2000-01
4-45	**T. J. Murtagh**	**Ireland v Pakistan at Malahide**	**2018**
3-51	**Yamin Ahmadzai**	**Afghanistan v India at Bangalore**	**2018**

OUTSTANDING BOWLING ANALYSES

	O	M	R	W		
J. C. Laker (E)	51.2	23	53	10	v Australia at Manchester	1956
A. Kumble (I)	26.3	9	74	10	v Pakistan at Delhi	1998-99
G. A. Lohmann (E)	14.2	6	28	9	v South Africa at Johannesburg . . .	1895-96
J. C. Laker (E)	16.4	4	37	9	v Australia at Manchester	1956
G. A. Lohmann (E)	9.4	5	7	8	v South Africa at Port Elizabeth . . .	1895-96
J. Briggs (E)	14.2	5	11	8	v South Africa at Cape Town	1888-89
S. C. J. Broad (E)	9.3	5	15	8	v Australia at Nottingham	2015
S. J. Harmison (E)	12.3	8	12	7	v West Indies at Kingston	2003-04
J. Briggs (E)	19.1	11	17	7	v South Africa at Cape Town	1888-89
M. A. Noble (A)	7.4	2	17	7	v England at Melbourne	1901-02
W. Rhodes (E)	11	3	17	7	v Australia at Birmingham	1902

WICKET WITH FIRST BALL IN TEST CRICKET

Batsman dismissed

T. P. Horan	W. W. Read	A v E	Sydney	1882-83
A. Coningham	A. C. MacLaren	A v E	Melbourne	1894-95
W. M. Bradley	F. Laver	E v A	Manchester	1899
E. G. Arnold	V. T. Trumper	E v A	Sydney	1903-04
A. E. E. Vogler	E. G. Hayes	SA v E	Johannesburg	1905-06
J. N. Crawford	A. E. E. Vogler	E v SA	Johannesburg	1905-06
G. G. Macaulay	G. A. L. Hearne	E v SA	Cape Town	1922-23
M. W. Tate	M. J. Susskind	E v SA	Birmingham	1924
M. Henderson	E. W. Dawson	NZ v E	Christchurch	1929-30
H. D. Smith	E. Paynter	NZ v E	Christchurch	1932-33
T. F. Johnson	W. W. Keeton	WI v E	The Oval	1939
R. Howorth	D. V. Dyer	E v SA	The Oval	1947
Intikhab Alam	C. C. McDonald	P v A	Karachi	1959-60
R. K. Illingworth	P. V. Simmons	E v WI	Nottingham	1991
N. M. Kulkarni	M. S. Atapattu	I v SL	Colombo (RPS)	1997-98
M. K. G. C. P. Lakshitha	Mohammad Ashraful	SL v B	Colombo (SSC)	2002
N. M. Lyon	K. C. Sangakkara	A v SL	Galle	2011-12
R. M. S. Eranga	S. R. Watson	SL v A	Colombo (SSC)	2011-12
D. L. Piedt	M. A. Vermeulen	SA v Z	Harare	2014-15
G. C. Viljoen	A. N. Cook	SA v E	Johannesburg	2015-16

HAT-TRICKS

Most Hat-Tricks

S. C. J. Broad	**2**	H. Trumble	2
T. J. Matthews†	2	Wasim Akram‡	2

† *T. J. Matthews did the hat-trick in each innings of the same match.*

‡ *Wasim Akram did the hat-trick in successive matches.*

Hat-Tricks

There have been **43** hat-tricks in Tests, including the above. Occurrences since 2007:

R. J. Sidebottom	England v New Zealand at Hamilton.	2007-08
P. M. Siddle.	Australia v England at Brisbane	2010-11
S. C. J. Broad.	England v India at Nottingham	2011
Sohag Gazi†	Bangladesh v New Zealand at Chittagong.	2013-14
S. C. J. Broad.	England v Sri Lanka at Leeds	2014
H. M. R. K. B. Herath	Sri Lanka v Australia at Galle	2016
M. M. Ali.	England v South Africa at The Oval	2017

† *Sohag Gazi also scored 101 not out.*

M. J. C. Allom, P. J. Petherick and D. W. Fleming did the hat-trick on Test debut. D. N. T. Zoysa took one in the second over of a Test (his first three balls); I. K. Pathan in the first over of a Test.

FOUR WICKETS IN FIVE BALLS

M. J. C. Allom.	England v New Zealand at Christchurch.	1929-30
	On debut, in his eighth over: W-WWW	
C. M. Old.	England v Pakistan at Birmingham	1978
	Sequence interrupted by a no-ball: WW-WW	
Wasim Akram	Pakistan v West Indies at Lahore (*WW-WW*)	1990-91

MOST WICKETS IN A TEST

19-90	J. C. Laker	England v Australia at Manchester.	1956
17-159	S. F. Barnes	England v South Africa at Johannesburg	1913-14
16-136†	N. D. Hirwani.	India v West Indies at Madras.	1987-88
16-137†	R. A. L. Massie.	Australia v England at Lord's.	1972
16-220	M. Muralitharan.	Sri Lanka v England at The Oval	1998

† *On Test debut.*

There have been 18 further instances of 14 or more wickets in a Test match.

The best bowling figures for the countries not mentioned above are:

15-123	R. J. Hadlee	New Zealand v Australia at Brisbane	1985-86
14-116	Imran Khan	Pakistan v Sri Lanka at Lahore.	1981-82
14-149	M. A. Holding	West Indies v England at The Oval	1976
13-132	M. Ntini	South Africa v West Indies at Port-of-Spain. . . .	2004-05
12-117	**Mehedi Hasan. . . . .**	**Bangladesh v West Indies at Mirpur. . . . .**	**2018-19**
11-255	A. G. Huckle.	Zimbabwe v New Zealand at Bulawayo	1997-98
6-100	**T. J. Murtagh . . . .**	**Ireland v Pakistan at Malahide . . . .**	**2018**
3-51	**Yamin Ahmadzai . . . . . .**	**Afghanistan v India at Bangalore . . . .**	**2018**

MOST BALLS BOWLED IN A TEST

S. Ramadhin (West Indies) sent down 774 balls in 129 overs against England at Birmingham, 1957, the most delivered by any bowler in a Test, beating H. Verity's 766 for England against South Africa at Durban, 1938-39. In this match Ramadhin also bowled the most balls (588) in any first-class innings, since equalled by Arshad Ayub, Hyderabad v Madhya Pradesh at Secunderabad, 1991-92.

MOST WICKETS IN A SERIES

	T	R	W	Avge		
S. F. Barnes	4	536	49	10.93	England v South Africa	1913-14
J. C. Laker	5	442	46	9.60	England v Australia	1956
C. V. Grimmett	5	642	44	14.59	Australia v South Africa	1935-36
T. M. Alderman	6	893	42	21.26	Australia v England	1981
R. M. Hogg	6	527	41	12.85	Australia v England	1978-79
T. M. Alderman	6	712	41	17.36	Australia v England	1989
Imran Khan	6	558	40	13.95	Pakistan v India	1982-83
S. K. Warne	5	797	40	19.92	Australia v England	2005

The most for South Africa is 37 by H. J. Tayfield against England in 1956-57, for West Indies 35 by M. D. Marshall against England in 1988, for India 35 by B. S. Chandrasekhar against England in 1972-73 (all in five Tests), for New Zealand 33 by R. J. Hadlee against Australia in 1985-86, for Sri Lanka 30 by M. Muralitharan against Zimbabwe in 2001-02, for Zimbabwe 22 by H. H. Streak against Pakistan in 1994-95 (all in three Tests), and for Bangladesh 19 by Mehedi Hasan against England in 2016-17 (two Tests).

MOST WICKETS IN A CALENDAR YEAR

	T	R	W	5I	10M	Avge	Year
S. K. Warne (Australia)	15	2,114	96	6	2	22.02	2005
M. Muralitharan (Sri Lanka)	11	1,521	90	9	5	16.89	2006
D. K. Lillee (Australia)	13	1,781	85	5	2	20.95	1981
A. A. Donald (South Africa)	14	1,571	80	7	–	19.63	1998
M. Muralitharan (Sri Lanka)	12	1,699	80	7	4	21.23	2001
J. Garner (West Indies)	15	1,604	77	4	–	20.83	1984
Kapil Dev (India)	18	1,739	75	5	1	23.18	1983
M. Muralitharan (Sri Lanka)	10	1,463	75	7	3	19.50	2000

MOST WICKETS

		T	Balls	R	W	5I	10M	Avge	SR
1	M. Muralitharan (SL/World)	133	44,039	18,180	800	67	22	22.72	55.04
2	S. K. Warne (Australia)	145	40,704	17,995	708	37	10	25.41	57.49
3	A. Kumble (India)	132	40,850	18,355	619	35	8	29.65	65.99
4	**J. M. Anderson (England)**	**145**	**31,746**	**15,245**	**565**	**26**	**3**	**26.98**	**56.18**
5	G. D. McGrath (Australia)	124	29,248	12,186	563	29	3	21.64	51.95
6	C. A. Walsh (West Indies)	132	30,019	12,688	519	22	3	24.44	57.84
7	Kapil Dev (India)	131	27,740	12,867	434	23	2	29.64	63.91
8	D. W. Steyn (South Africa)	**91**	**18,272**	**9,881**	**433**	**26**	**5**	**22.81**	**42.19**
	H. M. R. K. B. Herath (SL)	**93**	**25,993**	**12,157**	**433**	**34**	**9**	**28.07**	**60.03**
	S. C. J. Broad (SL)	**124**	**25,341**	**12,575**	**433**	**16**	**2**	**29.04**	**58.52**
11	R. J. Hadlee (New Zealand)	86	21,918	9,611	431	36	9	22.29	50.85
12	S. M. Pollock (South Africa)	108	24,353	9,733	421	16	1	23.11	57.84
13	Harbhajan Singh (India)	103	28,580	13,537	417	25	5	32.46	68.53
14	Wasim Akram (Pakistan)	104	22,627	9,779	414	25	5	23.62	54.65
15	C. E. L. Ambrose (WI)	98	22,103	8,501	405	22	3	20.99	54.57
16	M. Ntini (South Africa)	101	20,834	11,242	390	18	4	28.82	53.42
17	I. T. Botham (England)	102	21,815	10,878	383	27	4	28.40	56.95
18	M. D. Marshall (West Indies)	81	17,584	7,876	376	22	4	20.94	46.76
19	Waqar Younis (Pakistan)	87	16,224	8,788	373	22	5	23.56	43.49
20	Imran Khan (Pakistan)	88	19,458	8,258	362	23	6	22.81	53.75
	D. L. Vettori (NZ/World)	113	28,814	12,441	362	20	3	34.36	79.59
22	D. K. Lillee (Australia)	70	18,467	8,493	355	23	7	23.92	52.01
	W. P. U. J. C. Vaas (SL)	111	23,438	10,501	355	12	2	29.58	66.02
24	**R. Ashwin (India)**	**65**	**18,372**	**8,700**	**342**	**26**	**7**	**25.43**	**53.71**
25	**N. M. Lyon (Australia)**	**84**	**21,534**	**10,883**	**339**	**14**	**2**	**32.10**	**63.52**
26	A. A. Donald (South Africa)	72	15,519	7,344	330	20	3	22.25	47.02
27	R. G. D. Willis (England)	90	17,357	8,190	325	16	–	25.20	53.40

		T	Balls	R	W	5I	10M	Avge	SR
28	M. G. Johnson (Australia)...	73	16,001	8,891	313	12	3	28.40	51.12
29	Zaheer Khan (India)	92	18,785	10,247	311	11	1	32.94	60.40
30	B. Lee (Australia)	76	16,531	9,554	310	10	–	30.81	53.32
31 {	**M. Morkel (South Africa)..**	**86**	**16,498**	**8,550**	**309**	**8**	**–**	**27.66**	**53.39**
	L. R. Gibbs (West Indies) ...	79	27,115	8,989	309	18	2	29.09	87.75
33	F. S. Trueman (England)....	67	15,178	6,625	307	17	3	21.57	49.43

MOST WICKETS FOR EACH COUNTRY

ENGLAND

J. M. Anderson	**565**	I. T. Botham	383	F. S. Trueman	307
S. C. J. Broad	**433**	R. G. D. Willis	325	D. L. Underwood	297

AUSTRALIA

S. K. Warne	708	D. K. Lillee	355	M. G. Johnson	313
G. D. McGrath	563	**N. M. Lyon**	339	B. Lee..............	**310**

SOUTH AFRICA

D. W. Steyn.........	**433**	M. Ntini	390	**M. Morkel**...........	**309**
S. M. Pollock	421	A. A. Donald	330	J. H. Kallis†	291

† *J. H. Kallis also took 0-35 and 1-3 for the World XI v Australia (2005-06 Super Series Test).*

WEST INDIES

C. A. Walsh	519	M. D. Marshall.......	376	J. Garner............	259
C. E. L. Ambrose	405	L. R. Gibbs..........	309	M. A. Holding	249

NEW ZEALAND

R. J. Hadlee	431	**T. G. Southee**	**237**	C. S. Martin	233
D. L. Vettori†	361	**T. A. Boult**..........	**233**	C. L. Cairns	218

† *D. L. Vettori also took 1-73 and 0-38 for the World XI v Australia (2005-06 Super Series Test).*

INDIA

A. Kumble	619	Harbhajan Singh......	417	Zaheer Khan..........	311
Kapil Dev...........	434	**R. Ashwin**	**342**	**I. Sharma**...........	**267**

PAKISTAN

Wasim Akram	414	Imran Khan	362	Abdul Qadir	236
Waqar Younis	373	Danish Kaneria.......	261	Saqlain Mushtaq......	208

SRI LANKA

M. Muralitharan†	795	W. P. U. J. C. Vaas ...	355	**R. A. S. Lakmal**	**127**
H. M. R. K. B. Herath	**433**	**M. D. K. Perera**	**151**	S. L. Malinga	101

† *M. Muralitharan also took 2-102 and 3-55 for the World XI v Australia (2005-06 Super Series Test).*

ZIMBABWE

H. H. Streak	216	P. A. Strang	70	A. G. Cremer	57
R. W. Price	80	H. K. Olonga	68	B. C. Strang	56

BANGLADESH

Shakib Al Hasan	**205**	**Taijul Islam**	**97**	Mashrafe bin Mortaza	78
Mohammad Rafique	100	**Mehedi Hasan**	**84**	Shahadat Hossain	72

IRELAND

No player has taken ten wickets for Ireland. The highest total is **six** by **T. J. Murtagh**.

AFGHANISTAN

No player has taken ten wickets for Afghanistan. The highest total is **three** by **Yamin Ahmadzai**.

BEST CAREER AVERAGES

(Qualification: 75 wickets)

Avge		T	W	Avge		T	W
10.75	G. A. Lohmann (E)	18	112	18.63	C. Blythe (E)	19	100
16.43	S. F. Barnes (E)	27	189	20.39	J. H. Wardle (E)	28	102
16.53	C. T. B. Turner (A)	17	101	20.53	A. K. Davidson (A)	44	186
16.98	R. Peel (E)	20	101	20.94	M. D. Marshall (WI)	81	376
17.75	J. Briggs (E)	33	118	20.97	J. Garner (WI)	58	259
18.41	F. R. Spofforth (A)	18	94	20.99	C. E. L. Ambrose (WI)	98	405
18.56	F. H. Tyson (E)	17	76				

BEST CAREER STRIKE-RATES

(Balls per wicket. Qualification: 75 wickets)

SR		T	W	SR		T	W
34.19	G. A. Lohmann (E)	18	112	45.42	F. H. Tyson (E)	17	76
38.42	**K. Rabada (SA)**	**35**	**168**	45.46	C. Blythe (E)	19	100
38.75	S. E. Bond (NZ)	18	87	45.74	Shoaib Akhtar (P)	46	178
41.65	S. F. Barnes (E)	27	189	46.76	M. D. Marshall (WI)	81	376
42.19	**D. W. Steyn (SA)**	**91**	**433**	47.02	A. A. Donald (SA)	72	330
43.49	Waqar Younis (P)	87	373	48.78	Mohammad Asif (P)	23	106
44.52	F. R. Spofforth (A)	18	94	**48.87**	**V. D. Philander (SA)**	**57**	**211**
45.12	J. V. Saunders (A)	14	79	49.32	C. E. H. Croft (WI)	27	125
45.18	J. Briggs (E)	33	118	49.43	F. S. Trueman (E)	67	307

BEST CAREER ECONOMY-RATES

(Runs per six balls. Qualification: 75 wickets)

ER		T	W	ER		T	W
1.64	T. L. Goddard (SA)	41	123	1.94	W. J. O'Reilly (A)	27	144
1.67	R. G. Nadkarni (I)	41	88	1.94	H. J. Tayfield (SA)	37	170
1.88	H. Verity (E)	40	144	1.95	A. L. Valentine (WI)	36	139
1.88	G. A. Lohmann (E)	18	112	1.95	F. J. Titmus (E)	53	153
1.89	J. H. Wardle (E)	28	102	1.97	S. Ramadhin (WI)	43	158
1.91	R. Illingworth (E)	61	122	1.97	R. Peel (E)	20	101
1.93	C. T. B. Turner (A)	17	101	1.97	A. K. Davidson (A)	44	186
1.94	M. W. Tate (E)	39	155	1.98	L. R. Gibbs (WI)	79	309

HIGHEST PERCENTAGE OF TEAM'S WICKETS OVER TEST CAREER

(Qualification: 20 Tests)

	Tests	Wkts	Team Wkts	% of Team Wkts
M. Muralitharan (Sri Lanka/World)............	133	800	2,070	38.64
S. F. Barnes (England).......................	27	189	494	38.25
R. J. Hadlee (New Zealand)..................	86	431	1,255	34.34
C. V. Grimmett (Australia)	37	216	636	33.96
Fazal Mahmood (Pakistan)	34	139	410	33.90
Yasir Shah (Pakistan)	**35**	**203**	**600**	**33.83**
W. J. O'Reilly (Australia)	27	144	446	32.28
S. P. Gupte (India)	36	149	470	31.70
Saeed Ajmal (Pakistan)	35	178	575	30.95
Mohammad Rafique (Bangladesh)............	33	100	328	30.48
A. V. Bedser (England)......................	51	236	777	30.37
R. Ashwin (India).........................	**65**	**342**	**1,139**	**30.02**

Excluding the Super Series Test, Muralitharan took 795 out of 2,050 wickets in his 132 Tests for Sri Lanka, a percentage of 38.78.

The percentage shows the proportion of a team's wickets taken by that player in all Tests in which he played, including team wickets in innings in which he did not bowl.

ALL-ROUND RECORDS

HUNDRED AND FIVE WICKETS IN AN INNINGS

England

A. W. Greig	148	6-164	v West Indies	Bridgetown.....	1973-74
I. T. Botham	103	5-73	v New Zealand....	Christchurch	1977-78
I. T. Botham	108	8-34	v Pakistan.........	Lord's	1978
I. T. Botham	114	6-58, 7-48	v India	Bombay........	1979-80
I. T. Botham	149*	6-95	v Australia	Leeds..........	1981
I. T. Botham	138	5-59	v New Zealand....	Wellington	1983-84

Australia

C. Kelleway	114	5-33	v South Africa	Manchester	1912
J. M. Gregory	100	7-69	v England........	Melbourne......	1920-21
K. R. Miller	109	6-107	v West Indies	Kingston	1954-55
R. Benaud	100	5-84	v South Africa	Johannesburg ...	1957-58

South Africa

J. H. Sinclair	106	6-26	v England........	Cape Town	1898-99
G. A. Faulkner	123	5-120	v England........	Johannesburg ...	1909-10
J. H. Kallis	110	5-90	v West Indies	Cape Town	1998-99
J. H. Kallis	139*	5-21	v Bangladesh	Potchefstroom...	2002-03

West Indies

D. St E. Atkinson	219	5-56	v Australia	Bridgetown.....	1954-55
O. G. Smith	100	5-90	v India	Delhi..........	1958-59
G. S. Sobers	104	5-63	v India	Kingston	1961-62
G. S. Sobers	174	5-41	v England........	Leeds..........	1966
R. L. Chase	137*	5-121	v India	Kingston	2016

New Zealand

B. R. Taylor†	105	5-86	v India	Calcutta........	1964-65

India

M. H. Mankad	184	5-196	v England	Lord's	1952
P. R. Umrigar	172*	5-107	v West Indies	Port-of-Spain	1961-62
R. Ashwin	103	5-156	v West Indies	Mumbai	2011-12
R. Ashwin	113	7-83	v West Indies	North Sound	2016

Pakistan

Mushtaq Mohammad	201	5-49	v New Zealand	Dunedin	1972-73
Mushtaq Mohammad	121	5-28	v West Indies	Port-of-Spain	1976-77
Imran Khan	117	6-98, 5-82	v India	Faisalabad	1982-83
Wasim Akram	123	5-100	v Australia	Adelaide	1989-90

Zimbabwe

P. A. Strang	106*	5-212	v Pakistan	Sheikhupura	1996-97

Bangladesh

Shakib Al Hasan	144	6-82	v Pakistan	Mirpur	2011-12
Sohag Gazi	101*	6-77‡	v New Zealand	Chittagong	2013-14
Shakib Al Hasan	137	5-80, 5-44	v Zimbabwe	Khulna	2014-15

† *On debut.*   ‡ *Including a hat-trick; Sohag Gazi is the only player to score a hundred and take a hat-trick in the same Test.*

HUNDRED AND FIVE DISMISSALS IN AN INNINGS

D. T. Lindsay	182	6ct	SA v A	Johannesburg	1966-67
I. D. S. Smith	113*	4ct, 1st	NZ v E	Auckland	1983-84
S. A. R. Silva	111	5ct	SL v I	Colombo (PSS)	1985-86
A. C. Gilchrist	133	4ct, 1st	A v E	Sydney	2002-03
M. J. Prior	118	5ct	E v A	Sydney	2010-11
A. B. de Villiers	103*	6ct and 5ct	SA v P	Johannesburg	2012-13
M. J. Prior	110*	5ct	E v NZ	Auckland	2012-13
B-J. Watling	124	5ct	NZ v I	Wellington	2013-14
B-J. Watling	142*	4ct, 1st	NZ v SL	Wellington	2014-15
J. M. Bairstow	140	5ct	E v SL	Leeds	2016
J. M. Bairstow	**101**	**5ct**	**E v NZ**	**Christchurch**	**2017-18**

100 RUNS AND TEN WICKETS IN A TEST

A. K. Davidson	44 80	5-135 6-87 }	A v WI	Brisbane	1960-61
I. T. Botham	114	6-58 7-48 }	E v I	Bombay	1979-80
Imran Khan	117	6-98 5-82 }	P v I	Faisalabad	1982-83
Shakib Al Hasan	137 6	5-80 5-44 }	B v Z	Khulna	2014-15

Wicketkeeper A. B. de Villiers scored 103* and held 11 catches for South Africa against Pakistan at Johannesburg in 2012-13.

2,000 RUNS AND 200 WICKETS

	Tests	Runs	Wkts	Tests for 1,000/100 Double
R. Ashwin (India)	65	2,361	342	24
R. Benaud (Australia)	63	2,201	248	32
†I. T. Botham (England)	102	5,200	383	21
S. C. J. Broad (England)	**124**	**3,064**	**433**	**35**

	Tests	Runs	Wkts	Tests for 1,000/100 Double
C. L. Cairns (New Zealand)..............	62	3,320	218	33
A. Flintoff (England/World)	79	3,845	226	43
R. J. Hadlee (New Zealand)..............	86	3,124	431	28
Harbhajan Singh (India)..................	103	2,224	417	62
Imran Khan (Pakistan)	88	3,807	362	30
M. J. Johnson (Australia)................	73	2,065	313	37
†J. H. Kallis (South Africa/World)	166	13,289	292	53
Kapil Dev (India)	131	5,248	434	25
A. Kumble (India)	132	2,506	619	56
S. M. Pollock (South Africa).............	108	3,781	421	26
Shakib Al Hasan (Bangladesh)	**55**	**3,807**	**205**	**54**
†G. S. Sobers (West Indies).............	93	8,032	235	48
W. P. U. J. C. Vaas (Sri Lanka)	111	3,089	355	47
D. L. Vettori (New Zealand/World).......	113	4,531	362	47
†S. K. Warne (Australia)................	145	3,154	708	58
Wasim Akram (Pakistan)................	104	2,898	414	45

H. H. Streak scored 1,990 runs and took 216 wickets in 65 Tests for Zimbabwe.

† *J. H. Kallis also took 200 catches, S. K. Warne 125, I. T. Botham 120 and G. S. Sobers 109. These four and C. L. Hooper (5,762 runs, 114 wickets and 115 catches for West Indies) are the only players to have achieved the treble of 1,000 runs, 100 wickets and 100 catches in Test cricket.*

WICKETKEEPING RECORDS

MOST DISMISSALS IN AN INNINGS

7 (7ct)	Wasim Bari..........	Pakistan v New Zealand at Auckland	1978-79
7 (7ct)	R. W. Taylor.........	England v India at Bombay...............	1979-80
7 (7ct)	I. D. S. Smith	New Zealand v Sri Lanka at Hamilton	1990-91
7 (7ct)	R. D. Jacobs	West Indies v Australia at Melbourne......	2000-01

The first instance of seven wicketkeeping dismissals in a Test innings was a joint effort for Pakistan v West Indies at Kingston in 1976-77. Majid Khan made four catches, deputising for the injured wicketkeeper Wasim Bari, who made three more catches on his return.

There have been 31 instances of players making six dismissals in a Test innings, the most recent being R. R. Pant (6ct) for India v Australia at Adelaide in 2018-19.

MOST STUMPINGS IN AN INNINGS

5	K. S. More	India v West Indies at Madras	1987-88

MOST DISMISSALS IN A TEST

11 (11ct)	R. C. Russell.........	England v South Africa at Johannesburg ...	1995-96
11 (11ct)	A. B. de Villiers	South Africa v Pakistan at Johannesburg ...	2012-13
11 (11ct)	**R. R. Pant ....**	**India v Australia at Adelaide ....**	**2018-19**
10 (10ct)	R. W. Taylor.........	England v India at Bombay...............	1979-80
10 (10ct)	A. C. Gilchrist	Australia v New Zealand at Hamilton......	1999-2000
10 (10ct)	**W. P. Saha ....**	**India v South Africa at Cape Town .....**	**2017-18**
10 (10ct)	**Sarfraz Ahmed .....**	**Pakistan v South Africa at Johannesburg..**	**2018-19**

There have been 26 instances of players making nine dismissals in a Test, the most recent being J. M. Bairstow (9 ct) for England v Sri Lanka at Leeds in 2016. S. A. R. Silva made 18 in two successive Tests for Sri Lanka against India in 1985-86.

The most stumpings in a match is 6 by K. S. More for India v West Indies at Madras in 1987-88.

J. J. Kelly (8ct) for Australia v England in 1901-02 and L. E. G. Ames (6ct, 2st) for England v West Indies in 1933 were the only keepers to make eight dismissals in a Test before World War II.

MOST DISMISSALS IN A SERIES

(Played in 5 Tests unless otherwise stated)

29 (29ct)	B. J. Haddin	Australia v England	2013
28 (28ct)	R. W. Marsh	Australia v England	1982-83
27 (25ct, 2st)	R. C. Russell	England v South Africa	1995-96
27 (25ct, 2st)	I. A. Healy	Australia v England (6 Tests)	1997

S. A. R. Silva made 22 dismissals (21ct, 1st) in three Tests for Sri Lanka v India in 1985-86.

H. Strudwick, with 21 (15ct, 6st) for England v South Africa in 1913-14, was the only wicketkeeper to make as many as 20 dismissals in a series before World War II.

MOST DISMISSALS

			T	Ct	St
1	M. V. Boucher (South Africa/World)		555	147	532	23
2	A. C. Gilchrist (Australia)		416	96	379	37
3	I. A. Healy (Australia).		395	119	366	29
4	R. W. Marsh (Australia)		355	96	343	12
5	M. S. Dhoni (India).		294	90	256	38
6	B. J. Haddin (Australia)		270	66	262	8
	P. J. L. Dujon (West Indies)		270	79	265	5
8	A. P. E. Knott (England).		269	95	250	19
9	M. J. Prior (England).		256	79	243	13
10	A. J. Stewart (England).		241	82	227	14
11	Wasim Bari (Pakistan)		228	81	201	27
12	R. D. Jacobs (West Indies)		219	65	207	12
	T. G. Evans (England).		219	91	173	46
14	D. Ramdin (West Indies).		217	74	205	12
15	Kamran Akmal (Pakistan).		206	53	184	22
16	A. C. Parore (New Zealand)		201	67	194	7

The record for P. J. L. Dujon excludes two catches taken in two Tests when not keeping wicket; A. J. Stewart's record likewise excludes 36 catches taken in 51 Tests and A. C. Parore's three in 11 Tests.

Excluding the Super Series Test, M. V. Boucher made 553 dismissals (530ct, 23st in 146 Tests) for South Africa, a national record.

W. A. Oldfield made 52 stumpings, a Test record, in 54 Tests for Australia; he also took 78 catches.

The most dismissals by a wicketkeeper playing for the countries not mentioned above are:

		T	Ct	St
K. C. Sangakkara (Sri Lanka)		151	48	131	20
A. Flower (Zimbabwe).		151	55	142	9
Mushfiqur Rahim (Bangladesh)		**112**	**54**	**97**	**15**
N. J. O'Brien (Ireland).		**2**	**1**	**2**	**0**
Afsar Zazai (Afghanistan)		**2**	**1**	**2**	**0**

K. C. Sangakkara's record excludes 51 catches taken in 86 matches when not keeping wicket but includes two catches taken as wicketkeeper in a match where he took over when the designated keeper was injured; A. Flower's record excludes nine catches in eight Tests when not keeping wicket, and Mushfiqur Rahim's five catches in 12 Tests when not keeping wicket.

FIELDING RECORDS

(Excluding wicketkeepers)

MOST CATCHES IN AN INNINGS

5	V. Y. Richardson	Australia v South Africa at Durban	1935-36
5	Yajurvindra Singh	India v England at Bangalore	1976-77
5	M. Azharuddin.	India v Pakistan at Karachi.	1989-90
5	K. Srikkanth.	India v Australia at Perth	1991-92
5	S. P. Fleming.	New Zealand v Zimbabwe at Harare	1997-98

5	G. C. Smith	South Africa v Australia at Perth	2012-13
5	D. J. G. Sammy	West Indies v India at Mumbai	2013-14
5	D. M. Bravo	West Indies v Bangladesh at Arnos Vale	2014-15
5	A. M. Rahane	India v Sri Lanka at Galle	2015-16
5	J. Blackwood	West Indies v Sri Lanka at Colombo (PSO)	2015-16
5	**S. P. D. Smith**	**Australia v South Africa at Cape Town**	**2017-18**

MOST CATCHES IN A TEST

8	A. M. Rahane	India v Sri Lanka at Galle	2015-16
7	G. S. Chappell	Australia v England at Perth	1974-75
7	Yajurvindra Singh	India v England at Bangalore	1976-77
7	H. P. Tillekeratne	Sri Lanka v New Zealand at Colombo (SSC)	1992-93
7	S. P. Fleming	New Zealand v Zimbabwe at Harare	1997-98
7	M. L. Hayden	Australia v Sri Lanka at Galle	2003-04
7	**K. L. Rahul**	**India v England at Nottingham**	**2018**

There have been 31 instances of players taking six catches in a Test, the most recent being K. K. Jennings for England v Sri Lanka at Colombo (SSC) in 2018-19.

MOST CATCHES IN A SERIES

(Played in 5 Tests unless otherwise stated)

15	J. M. Gregory	Australia v England	1920-21
14	G. S. Chappell	Australia v England (6 Tests)	1974-75
13	R. B. Simpson	Australia v South Africa	1957-58
13	R. B. Simpson	Australia v West Indies	1960-61
13	B. C. Lara	West Indies v England (6 Tests)	1997-98
13	R. Dravid	India v Australia (4 Tests)	2004-05
13	B. C. Lara	West Indies v India (4 Tests)	2005-06

MOST CATCHES

Ct	T		Ct	T	
210	164†	R. Dravid (India/World)	157	104	M. A. Taylor (Australia)
205	149	D. P. M. D. Jayawardene (SL)	156	156	A. R. Border (Australia)
200	166‡	J. H. Kallis (SA/World)	139	118	Younis Khan (Pakistan)
196	168	R. T. Ponting (Australia)	135	134	V. V. S. Laxman (India)
181	128	M. E. Waugh (Australia)	134	115	M. J. Clarke (Australia)
175	**161**	**A. N. Cook (England)**	**131**	**90**	**L. R. P. L. Taylor (New Zealand)**
171	151	S. P. Fleming (New Zealand)	128	103	M. L. Hayden (Australia)
169	117†	G. C. Smith (SA/World)	125	145	S. K. Warne (Australia)
164	131†	B. C. Lara (West Indies/World)			

† *Excluding the Super Series Test, Dravid made 209 catches in 163 Tests for India, Kallis 196 in 165 Tests for South Africa, and Lara 164 in 130 Tests for West Indies, all national records. G. C. Smith made 166 catches in 116 Tests for South Africa.*

The most catches in the field for other countries are Zimbabwe 60 in 60 Tests (A. D. R. Campbell); Bangladesh 36 in 43 Tests (Mahmudullah); Ireland 3 in 1 Test (P. R. Stirling); Afghanistan 2 in 1 Test (Mohammad Nabi).

TEAM RECORDS

HIGHEST INNINGS TOTALS

952-6 dec	Sri Lanka v India at Colombo (RPS)	1997-98
903-7 dec	England v Australia at The Oval	1938
849	England v West Indies at Kingston	1929-30
790-3 dec	West Indies v Pakistan at Kingston	1957-58

765-6 dec	Pakistan v Sri Lanka at Karachi	2008-09
760-7 dec	Sri Lanka v India at Ahmedabad.....................................	2009-10
759-7 dec	India v England at Chennai...	2016-17
758-8 dec	Australia v West Indies at Kingston	1954-55
756-5 dec	Sri Lanka v South Africa at Colombo (SSC)	2006
751-5 dec	West Indies v England at St John's.................................	2003-04

The highest innings totals for the countries not mentioned above are:

690	New Zealand v Pakistan at Sharjah..................................	2014-15
682-6 dec	South Africa v England at Lord's	2003
638	Bangladesh v Sri Lanka at Galle	2012-13
563-9 dec	Zimbabwe v West Indies at Harare...................................	2001
339	**Ireland v Pakistan at Malahide**	**2018**
109	**Afghanistan v India at Bangalore**	**2018**

HIGHEST FOURTH-INNINGS TOTALS

To win

418-7	West Indies (needing 418) v Australia at St John's.................	2002-03
414-4	South Africa (needing 414) v Australia at Perth....................	2008-09
406-4	India (needing 403) v West Indies at Port-of-Spain	1975-76
404-3	Australia (needing 404) v England at Leeds	1948

To tie

347	India v Australia at Madras	1986-87

To draw

654-5	England (needing 696 to win) v South Africa at Durban	1938-39
450-7	South Africa (needing 458 to win) v India at Johannesburg..........	2013-14
429-8	India (needing 438 to win) v England at The Oval	1979
423-7	South Africa (needing 451 to win) v England at The Oval	1947

To lose

451	New Zealand (lost by 98 runs) v England at Christchurch	2001-02
450	Pakistan (lost by 39 runs) v Australia at Brisbane.................	2016-17
445	India (lost by 47 runs) v Australia at Adelaide....................	1977-78
440	New Zealand (lost by 38 runs) v England at Nottingham..............	1973
431	New Zealand (lost by 121 runs) v England at Napier	2007-08

MOST RUNS IN A DAY (BOTH SIDES)

588	England (398-6), India (190-0) at Manchester (2nd day)	1936
522	England (503-2), South Africa (19-0) at Lord's (2nd day)	1924
509	Sri Lanka (509-9) v Bangladesh at Colombo (PSS) (2nd day)..........	2002
508	England (221-2), South Africa (287-6) at The Oval (3rd day)	1935

MOST RUNS IN A DAY (ONE SIDE)

509	Sri Lanka (509-9) v Bangladesh at Colombo (PSS) (2nd day)..........	2002
503	England (503-2) v South Africa at Lord's (2nd day)	1924
494	Australia (494-6) v South Africa at Sydney (1st day)...............	1910-11
482	Australia (482-5) v South Africa at Adelaide (1st day).............	2012-13
475	Australia (475-2) v England at The Oval (1st day)..................	1934

MOST WICKETS IN A DAY

27	England (18-3 to 53 all out and 62) v Australia (60) at Lord's (2nd day)	1888
25	Australia (112 and 48-5) v England (61) at Melbourne (1st day)	1901-02
24	England (69-1 to 145 and 60-5) v Australia (119) at The Oval (2nd day)	1896
24	**India (347-6 to 474) v Afghanistan (109 and 103) at Bangalore (2nd day) . . .**	**2018**

HIGHEST AGGREGATES IN A TEST

Runs	Wkts			Days played
1,981	35	South Africa v England at Durban	1938-39	10†
1,815	34	West Indies v England at Kingston	1929-30	9‡
1,764	39	Australia v West Indies at Adelaide	1968-69	5
1,753	40	Australia v England at Adelaide	1920-21	6
1,747	25	Australia v India at Sydney	2003-04	5
1,723	31	England v Australia at Leeds	1948	5
1,702	28	Pakistan v India at Faisalabad	2005-06	5

† *No play on one day.* ‡ *No play on two days.*

LOWEST INNINGS TOTALS

26	New Zealand v England at Auckland	1954-55
30	South Africa v England at Port Elizabeth	1895-96
30	South Africa v England at Birmingham	1924
35	South Africa v England at Cape Town	1898-99
36	Australia v England at Birmingham	1902
36	South Africa v Australia at Melbourne	1931-32
42	Australia v England at Sydney	1887-88
42	New Zealand v Australia at Wellington	1945-46
42†	India v England at Lord's	1974
43	South Africa v England at Cape Town	1888-89
43	**Bangladesh v West Indies at North Sound . . . .**	**2018**
44	Australia v England at The Oval	1896
45	England v Australia at Sydney	1886-87
45	South Africa v Australia at Melbourne	1931-32
45	New Zealand v South Africa at Cape Town	2012-13

The lowest innings totals for the countries not mentioned above are:

47	West Indies v England at Kingston	2003-04
49	Pakistan v South Africa at Johannesburg	2012-13
51	Zimbabwe v New Zealand at Napier	2011-12
71	Sri Lanka v Pakistan at Kandy	1994-95
103	**Afghanistan v India at Bangalore . . . .**	**2018**
130	**Ireland v Pakistan at Malahide . . . .**	**2018**

FEWEST RUNS IN A FULL DAY'S PLAY

95	Australia (80), Pakistan (15-2) at Karachi (1st day, 5$\frac{1}{2}$ hrs)	1956-57
104	Pakistan (0-0 to 104-5) v Australia at Karachi (4th day, 5$\frac{1}{2}$ hrs)	1959-60
106	England (92-2 to 198) v Australia at Brisbane (4th day, 5 hrs)	1958-59
	England were dismissed five minutes before the close of play, leaving no	
	time for Australia to start their second innings.	
111	S. Africa (48-2 to 130-6 dec), India (29-1) at Cape Town (5th day, 5$\frac{1}{2}$ hrs) . . .	1992-93
112	Australia (138-6 to 187), Pakistan (63-1) at Karachi (4th day, 5$\frac{1}{2}$ hrs)	1956-57
115	Australia (116-7 to 165 and 66-5 after following on) v Pakistan at Karachi (4th	
	day, 5$\frac{1}{2}$ hrs)	1988-89
117	India (117-5) v Australia at Madras (1st day, 5$\frac{1}{2}$ hrs)	1956-57
117	New Zealand (6-0 to 123-4) v Sri Lanka at Colombo (SSC) (5th day, 5$\frac{3}{4}$ hrs) .	1983-84

In England

151	England (175-2 to 289), New Zealand (37-7) at Lord's (3rd day, 6 hrs)	1978
158	England (211-2 to 369-9) v South Africa at Manchester (5th day, 6 hrs)	1998
159	Pakistan (208-4 to 350), England (17-1) at Leeds (3rd day, 6 hrs)	1971

LOWEST AGGREGATES IN A COMPLETED TEST

Runs	Wkts			Days played
234	29	Australia v South Africa at Melbourne	1931-32	3†
291	40	England v Australia at Lord's	1888	2
295	28	New Zealand v Australia at Wellington	1945-46	2
309	29	West Indies v England at Bridgetown	1934-35	3
323	30	England v Australia at Manchester	1888	2

† *No play on one day.*

LARGEST VICTORIES

Largest Innings Victories

Inns & 579 runs	England (903-7 dec) v Australia (201 & 123†) at The Oval	1938
Inns & 360 runs	Australia (652-7 dec) v South Africa (159 & 133) at Johannesburg . .	2001-02
Inns & 336 runs	West Indies (614-5 dec) v India (124 & 154) at Calcutta.	1958-59
Inns & 332 runs	Australia (645) v England (141 & 172) at Brisbane.	1946-47
Inns & 324 runs	Pakistan (643) v New Zealand (73 & 246) at Lahore.	2002
Inns & 322 runs	West Indies (660-5 dec) v New Zealand (216 & 122) at Wellington . .	1994-95
Inns & 310 runs	West Indies (536) v Bangladesh (139 & 87) at Dhaka.	2002-03
Inns & 301 runs	New Zealand (495-7 dec) v Zimbabwe (51 & 143) at Napier	2011-12

† *Two men absent in both Australian innings.*

Largest Victories by Runs Margin

675 runs	England (521 & 342-8 dec) v Australia (122 & 66†) at Brisbane.	1928-29
562 runs	Australia (701 & 327) v England (321 & 145‡) at The Oval	1934
530 runs	Australia (328 & 578) v South Africa (205 & 171§) at Melbourne	1910-11
492 runs	**South Africa (488 & 344-6 dec) v Australia (221 and 119) at Johannesburg**	**2017-18**
491 runs	Australia (381 & 361-5 dec) v Pakistan (179 & 72) at Perth.	2004-05
465 runs	Sri Lanka (384 and 447-6 dec) v Bangladesh (208 and 158) at Chittagong . .	2008-09
425 runs	West Indies (211 & 411-5 dec) v England (71 & 126) at Manchester	1976
423 runs	**New Zealand (178 & 585-4 dec) v Sri Lanka (104 & 236) at Christchurch**	**2018-19**
409 runs	Australia (350 & 460-7 dec) v England (215 & 186) at Lord's.	1948
408 runs	West Indies (328 & 448) v Australia (203 & 165) at Adelaide.	1979-80
405 runs	Australia (566-8 dec & 254-2 dec) v England (312 & 103) at Lord's.	2015

† *One man absent in Australia's first innings; two men absent in their second.*
‡ *Two men absent in England's first innings; one man absent in their second.*
§ *One man absent in South Africa's second innings.*

TIED TESTS

West Indies (453 & 284) v Australia (505 & 232) at Brisbane	1960-61
Australia (574-7 dec & 170-5 dec) v India (397 & 347) at Madras.	1986-87

MOST CONSECUTIVE TEST VICTORIES

16 Australia	1999-2000 to 2000-01		9 South Africa	2001-02 to 2003
16 Australia	2005-06 to 2007-08		8 Australia	1920-21 to 1921
11 West Indies	1983-84 to 1984-85		8 England	2004 to 2004-05
9 Sri Lanka	2001 to 2001-02			

MOST CONSECUTIVE TESTS WITHOUT VICTORY

44	New Zealand	1929-30 to 1955-56	23 New Zealand	1962-63 to 1967-68
34	Bangladesh.	2000-01 to 2004-05	22 Pakistan	1958-59 to 1964-65
31	India.	1981-82 to 1984-85	21 Sri Lanka	1985-86 to 1992-93
28	South Africa.	1935 to 1949-50	20 West Indies	1968-69 to 1972-73
24	India.	1932 to 1951-52	20 West Indies	2004-05 to 2007
24	Bangladesh.	2004-05 to 2008-09		

WHITEWASHES

Teams winning every game in a series of four Tests or more:

Five-Test Series

Australia beat England	1920-21	West Indies beat England	1985-86
Australia beat South Africa.	1931-32	South Africa beat West Indies	1998-99
England beat India	1959	Australia beat West Indies	2000-01
West Indies beat India.	1961-62	Australia beat England	2006-07
West Indies beat England	1984	Australia beat England	2013-14

Four-Test Series

Australia beat India.	1967-68	England beat India	2011
South Africa beat India.	1969-70	Australia beat India.	2011-12
England beat West Indies	2004	India beat Australia.	2012-13

The winning team in each instance was at home, except for West Indies in England, 1984.

PLAYERS

YOUNGEST TEST PLAYERS

Years	Days			
15	124	Mushtaq Mohammad	Pakistan v West Indies at Lahore	1958-59
16	189	Aqib Javed	Pakistan v New Zealand at Wellington	1988-89
16	205	S. R. Tendulkar.	India v Pakistan at Karachi	1989-90

The above table should be treated with caution. All birthdates for Bangladesh and Pakistan (after Partition) must be regarded as questionable because of deficiencies in record-keeping. Hasan Raza was claimed to be 14 years 227 days old when he played for Pakistan against Zimbabwe at Faisalabad in 1996-97; this age was rejected by the Pakistan Cricket Board, although no alternative has been offered. Suggestions that Enamul Haque jnr was 16 years 230 days old when he played for Bangladesh against England in Dhaka in 2003-04 have been discounted by well-informed local observers, who believe he was 18.

The youngest Test players for countries not mentioned above are:

17	**78**	**Mujeeb Zadran**	**Afghanistan v India at Bangalore**	**2018**
17	122	J. E. D. Sealy.	West Indies v England at Bridgetown	1929-30
17	128	Mohammad Sharif	Bangladesh v Zimbabwe at Bulawayo	2000-01
17	189	C. D. U. S. Weerasinghe .	Sri Lanka v India at Colombo (PSS).	1985-86
17	239	I. D. Craig	Australia v South Africa at Melbourne	1952-53
17	352	H. Masakadza	Zimbabwe v West Indies at Harare.	2001
18	10	D. L. Vettori	New Zealand v England at Wellington	1996-97
18	149	D. B. Close	England v New Zealand at Manchester	1949
18	340	P. R. Adams	South Africa v England at Port Elizabeth	1995-96
23	**307**	**T. E. Kane**	**Ireland v Pakistan at Malahide**	**2018**

OLDEST PLAYERS ON TEST DEBUT

Years	Days			
49	119	J. Southerton	England v Australia at Melbourne	1876-77
47	284	Miran Bux.	Pakistan v India at Lahore	1954-55
46	253	D. D. Blackie	Australia v England at Sydney	1928-29
46	237	H. Ironmonger.	Australia v England at Brisbane	1928-29
42	242	N. Betancourt	West Indies v England at Port-of-Spain	1929-30
41	337	E. R. Wilson	England v Australia at Sydney	1920-21
41	27	R. J. D. Jamshedji	India v England at Bombay	1933-34
40	345	C. A. Wiles	West Indies v England at Manchester.	1933
40	295	O. Henry	South Africa v India at Durban	1992-93
40	216	S. P. Kinneir	England v Australia at Sydney	1911-12
40	110	H. W. Lee	England v South Africa at Johannesburg	1930-31
40	56	G. W. A. Chubb	South Africa v England at Nottingham.	1951
40	37	C. Ramaswami	India v England at Manchester	1936

*The oldest Test player on debut for Ireland was **E. C. Joyce, 39 years 231 days**, v Pakistan at Malahide, 2018; for New Zealand, H. M. McGirr, 38 years 101 days, v England at Auckland, 1929-30; for Sri Lanka, D. S. de Silva, 39 years 251 days, v England at Colombo (PSS), 1981-82; for Zimbabwe, A. C. Waller, 37 years 84 days, v England at Bulawayo, 1996-97; for Bangladesh, Enamul Haque snr, 35 years 58 days, v Zimbabwe at Harare, 2000-01; for Afghanistan, **Mohammad Nabi, 33 years 99 days**, v India at Bangalore, 20018. A. J. Traicos was 45 years 154 days old when he made his debut for Zimbabwe (v India at Harare, 1992-93) having played three Tests for South Africa in 1969-70.*

OLDEST TEST PLAYERS

(Age on final day of their last Test match)

Years	Days			
52	165	W. Rhodes	England v West Indies at Kingston.	1929-30
50	327	H. Ironmonger.	Australia v England at Sydney	1932-33
50	320	W. G. Grace	England v Australia at Nottingham.	1899
50	303	G. Gunn	England v West Indies at Kingston.	1929-30
49	139	J. Southerton	England v Australia at Melbourne	1876-77
47	302	Miran Bux	Pakistan v India at Peshawar	1954-55
47	249	J. B. Hobbs	England v Australia at The Oval.	1930
47	87	F. E. Woolley	England v Australia at The Oval.	1934
46	309	D. D. Blackie	Australia v England at Adelaide	1928-29
46	206	A. W. Nourse	South Africa v England at The Oval.	1924
46	202	H. Strudwick	England v Australia at The Oval.	1926
46	41	E. H. Hendren	England v West Indies at Kingston.	1934-35
45	304	A. J. Traicos	Zimbabwe v India at Delhi	1992-93
45	245	G. O. B. Allen	England v West Indies at Kingston.	1947-48
45	215	P. Holmes	England v India at Lord's	1932
45	140	D. B. Close	England v West Indies at Manchester.	1976

MOST TEST APPEARANCES

200	S. R. Tendulkar (India)	**145**	**J. M. Anderson (England)**
168	R. T. Ponting (Australia)	145	S. K. Warne (Australia)
168	S. R. Waugh (Australia)	134	V. V. S. Laxman (India)
166	J. H. Kallis (South Africa/World)	134	K. C. Sangakkara (Sri Lanka)
164	S. Chanderpaul (West Indies)	133	M. Muralitharan (Sri Lanka/World)
164	R. Dravid (India/World)	133	A. J. Stewart (England)
161	**A. N. Cook (England)**	132	A. Kumble (India)
156	A. R. Border (Australia)	132	C. A. Walsh (West Indies)
149	D. P. M. D. Jayawardene (Sri Lanka)	131	Kapil Dev (India)
147	M. V. Boucher (South Africa/World)	131	B. C. Lara (West Indies/World)

128	M. E. Waugh (Australia)		124	G. D. McGrath (Australia)
125	S. M. Gavaskar (India)		**122**	**H. M. Amla (South Africa)**
124	**S. C. J. Broad (England)**		121	I. V. A. Richards (West Indies)
124	Javed Miandad (Pakistan)		120	Inzamam-ul-Haq (Pakistan/World)

Excluding the Super Series Test, J. H. Kallis has made 165 appearances for South Africa, a national record. The most appearances for New Zealand is 112 by D. L. Vettori; for Zimbabwe, 67 by G. W. Flower; and for Bangladesh 61 by Mohammad Ashraful.

MOST CONSECUTIVE TEST APPEARANCES FOR A COUNTRY

159	**A. N. Cook (England)**.....................	**May 2006 to September 2018**
153	A. R. Border (Australia)......................	March 1979 to March 1994
107	M. E. Waugh (Australia)......................	June 1993 to October 2002
106	S. M. Gavaskar (India).......................	January 1975 to February 1987
101†	B. B. McCullum (New Zealand).............	March 2004 to February 2016
98	A. B. de Villiers (South Africa)...............	December 2004 to January 2015
96†	A. C. Gilchrist (Australia)...................	November 1999 to January 2008
93	R. Dravid (India)	June 1996 to December 2005
93	D. P. M. D. Jayawardene (Sri Lanka)	November 2002 to January 2013

The most consecutive Test appearances for the countries not mentioned above (excluding Afghanistan and Ireland) are:

85	G. S. Sobers (West Indies)....................	April 1955 to April 1972
64	**Asad Shafiq (Pakistan)**......................	**October 2011 to January 2019**
56	A. D. R. Campbell (Zimbabwe)................	October 1992 to September 2001
53	Javed Miandad (Pakistan)	December 1977 to January 1984
49	Mushfiqur Rahim (Bangladesh)................	July 2007 to January 2017

†   *Complete Test career.*

Bold type denotes sequence which was still in progress after January 1, 2018.

MOST TESTS AS CAPTAIN

	P	W	L	D		P	W	L	D
G. C. Smith (SA/World)	109	53	29*	27	Misbah-ul-Haq (P)	56	26	19	11
A. R. Border (A)	93	32	22	38†	A. Ranatunga (SL)	56	12	19	25
S. P. Fleming (NZ)	80	28	27	25	M. A. Atherton (E)	54	13	21	20
R. T. Ponting (A)	77	48	16	13	W. J. Cronje (SA)	53	27	11	15
C. H. Lloyd (WI)	74	36	12	26	M. P. Vaughan (E)	51	26	11	14
M. S. Dhoni (I)	60	27	18	15	I. V. A. Richards (WI)	50	27	8	15
A. N. Cook (E)	59	24	22	13	M. A. Taylor (A)	50	26	13	11
S. R. Waugh (A)	57	41	9	7	A. J. Strauss (E)	50	24	11	15

*   *Includes defeat as World XI captain in Super Series Test against Australia.*   †   *One tie.*

Most Tests as captain of other countries:

	P	W	L	D
Mushfiqur Rahim (B)	34	7	18	9
A. D. R. Campbell (Z)	21	2	12	7
W. T. S. Porterfield (Ire)	**1**	**0**	**1**	**0**
Asghar Stanikzai (Afg)	**1**	**0**	**1**	**0**

A. R. Border captained Australia in 93 consecutive Tests.

W. W. Armstrong (Australia) captained his country in the most Tests without being defeated: ten matches with eight wins and two draws.

Mohammad Ashraful (Bangladesh) captained his country in the most Tests without ever winning: 12 defeats and one draw.

UMPIRES

MOST TESTS

		First Test	Last Test
128	S. A. Bucknor (West Indies)	1988-89	2008-09
123	**Aleem Dar (Pakistan)**................	**2003-04**	**2018-19**
108	R. E. Koertzen (South Africa)	1992-93	2010
95	D. J. Harper (Australia)	1998-99	2011
92	D. R. Shepherd (England)	1985	2004-05
84	B. F. Bowden (New Zealand)	1999-2000	2014-15
78	D. B. Hair (Australia).................	1991-92	2008
74	S. J. A. Taufel (Australia)	2000-01	2012
73	**I. J. Gould (England)**.................	**2008-09**	**2018-19**
73	S. Venkataraghavan (India)	1992-93	2003-04
66	H. D. Bird (England)	1973	1996
65	**R. J. Tucker (Australia)**...............	**2009-10**	**2018-19**
58	**H. D. P. K. Dharmasena (Sri Lanka)**	**2010-11**	**2018-19**
57	S. J. Davis (Australia)	1997-98	2014-15
57	**R. A. Kettleborough (England)**..........	**2010-11**	**2018-19**
55	**N. J. Llong (England)**.................	**2007-08**	**2018-19**
55	**B. N. Oxenford (Australia)**	**2010-11**	**2018-19**
54	**M. Erasmus (South Africa)**	**2009-10**	**2018-19**

SUMMARY OF TESTS

1876-77 to January 14, 2019

	Opponents	Tests	E	A	SA	WI	NZ	I	P	SL	Z	B	Ire	Afg	Wld	Tied	Drawn
								Won by									
England	Australia	346	108	144	–	–	–	–	–	–	–	–	–	–	–	–	94
	South Africa	149	61	–	33	–	–	–	–	–	–	–	–	–	–	–	55
	West Indies	154	48	–	–	55	–	–	–	–	–	–	–	–	–	–	51
	New Zealand	103	48	–	–	–	10	–	–	–	–	–	–	–	–	–	45
	India	122	47	–	–	–	–	26	–	–	–	–	–	–	–	–	49
	Pakistan	83	25	–	–	–	–	–	21	–	–	–	–	–	–	–	37
	Sri Lanka	34	15	–	–	–	–	–	–	8	–	–	–	–	–	–	11
	Zimbabwe	6	3	–	–	–	–	–	–	–	0	–	–	–	–	–	3
	Bangladesh	10	9	–	–	–	–	–	–	–	–	1	–	–	–	–	0
Australia	South Africa	98	–	52	26	–	–	–	–	–	–	–	–	–	–	–	20
	West Indies	116	–	58	–	32	–	–	–	–	–	–	–	–	–	1	25
	New Zealand	57	–	31	–	–	8	–	–	–	–	–	–	–	–	–	18
	India	98	–	42	–	–	–	28	–	–	–	–	–	–	–	1	27
	Pakistan	64	–	31	–	–	–	–	15	–	–	–	–	–	–	–	18
	Sri Lanka	29	–	17	–	–	–	–	–	4	–	–	–	–	–	–	8
	Zimbabwe	3	–	3	–	–	–	–	–	–	0	–	–	–	–	–	0
	Bangladesh	6	–	5	–	–	–	–	–	–	–	1	–	–	–	–	0
	ICC World XI	1	–	1	–	–	–	–	–	–	–	–	–	–	0	–	0
South Africa	West Indies	28	–	–	18	3	–	–	–	–	–	–	–	–	–	–	7
	New Zealand	45	–	–	25	–	4	–	–	–	–	–	–	–	–	–	16
	India	36	–	–	15	–	–	11	–	–	–	–	–	–	–	–	10
	Pakistan	26	–	–	15	–	–	–	4	–	–	–	–	–	–	–	7
	Sri Lanka	27	–	–	14	–	–	–	–	7	–	–	–	–	–	–	6
	Zimbabwe	9	–	–	8	–	–	–	–	–	0	–	–	–	–	–	1
	Bangladesh	12	–	–	10	–	–	–	–	–	–	0	–	–	–	–	2
West Indies	New Zealand	47	–	–	–	13	15	–	–	–	–	–	–	–	–	–	19
	India	96	–	–	–	30	–	20	–	–	–	–	–	–	–	–	46
	Pakistan	52	–	–	–	17	–	–	20	–	–	–	–	–	–	–	15
	Sri Lanka	20	–	–	–	4	–	–	–	9	–	–	–	–	–	–	7
	Zimbabwe	10	–	–	–	7	–	–	–	–	0	–	–	–	–	–	3
	Bangladesh	16	–	–	–	10	–	–	–	–	–	4	–	–	–	–	2
New Zealand	India	57	–	–	–	–	10	21	–	–	–	–	–	–	–	–	26
	Pakistan	58	–	–	–	–	12	–	25	–	–	–	–	–	–	–	21
	Sri Lanka	34	–	–	–	–	15	–	–	8	–	–	–	–	–	–	11
	Zimbabwe	17	–	–	–	–	11	–	–	–	0	–	–	–	–	–	6
	Bangladesh	13	–	–	–	–	10	–	–	–	–	0	–	–	–	–	3
India	Pakistan	59	–	–	–	–	–	9	12	–	–	–	–	–	–	–	38
	Sri Lanka	44	–	–	–	–	–	20	–	7	–	–	–	–	–	–	17
	Zimbabwe	11	–	–	–	–	–	7	–	–	2	–	–	–	–	–	2
	Bangladesh	9	–	–	–	–	–	7	–	–	–	0	–	–	–	–	2
	Afghanistan	1	–	–	–	–	–	1	–	–	–	–	–	0	–	–	0
Pakistan	Sri Lanka	53	–	–	–	–	–	–	19	16	–	–	–	–	–	–	18
	Zimbabwe	17	–	–	–	–	–	–	10	–	3	–	–	–	–	–	4
	Bangladesh	10	–	–	–	–	–	–	9	–	–	0	–	–	–	–	1
	Ireland	1	–	–	–	–	–	–	1	–	–	–	0	–	–	–	0
Sri Lanka	Zimbabwe	18	–	–	–	–	–	–	–	13	0	–	–	–	–	–	5
	Bangladesh	20	–	–	–	–	–	–	–	16	–	1	–	–	–	–	3
Zimbabwe	Bangladesh	16	–	–	–	–	–	–	–	–	7	6	–	–	–	–	3
		2,341	364	384	164	171	95	150	136	88	12	13	0	0	0	2	762

RESULTS SUMMARY OF TESTS

1876-77 to January 14, 2018 (2,341 matches)

	Tests	Won	Lost	Drawn	Tied	% Won	Toss Won
England	1,007†	364	298	345	–	36.14	493
Australia	818†	384†	222	210	2	46.94	409
South Africa	430	164	142	124	–	38.13	209
West Indies	539	171	192	175	1	31.72	276
New Zealand	431	95	171	165	–	22.04	215
India	533	150	165	217	1	28.14	267

	Tests	Won	Lost	Drawn	Tied	% Won	Toss Won
Pakistan	423	136	128	159	–	32.15	201
Sri Lanka	279	88	105	86	–	31.54	151
Zimbabwe	107	12	68	27	–	11.21	58
Bangladesh	112	13	83	16	–	11.60	61
Ireland	1	0	1	0	–	0.00	1
Afghanistan	1	0	1	0	–	0.00	0
ICC World XI	1	0	1	0	–	0.00	0

† Includes Super Series Test between Australia and ICC World XI.

ENGLAND v AUSTRALIA

Captains

Season	England	Australia	T	E	A	D
1876-77	James Lillywhite	D. W. Gregory	2	1	1	0
1878-79	Lord Harris	D. W. Gregory	1	0	1	0
1880	Lord Harris	W. L. Murdoch	1	1	0	0
1881-82	A. Shaw	W. L. Murdoch	4	0	2	2
1882	A. N. Hornby	W. L. Murdoch	1	0	1	0

THE ASHES

Captains

Season	England	Australia	T	E	A	D	Held by
1882-83	Hon. Ivo Bligh	W. L. Murdoch	4*	2	2	0	E
1884	Lord Harris[1]	W. L. Murdoch	3	1	0	2	E
1884-85	A. Shrewsbury	T. P. Horan[2]	5	3	2	0	E
1886	A. G. Steel	H. J. H. Scott	3	3	0	0	E
1886-87	A. Shrewsbury	P. S. McDonnell	2	2	0	0	E
1887-88	W. W. Read	P. S. McDonnell	1	1	0	0	E
1888	W. G. Grace[3]	P. S. McDonnell	3	2	1	0	E
1890†	W. G. Grace	W. L. Murdoch	2	2	0	0	E
1891-92	W. G. Grace	J. McC. Blackham	3	1	2	0	A
1893	W. G. Grace[4]	J. McC. Blackham	3	1	0	2	E
1894-95	A. E. Stoddart	G. Giffen[5]	5	3	2	0	E
1896	W. G. Grace	G. H. S. Trott	3	2	1	0	E
1897-98	A. E. Stoddart[6]	G. H. S. Trott	5	1	4	0	A
1899	A. C. MacLaren[7]	J. Darling	5	0	1	4	A
1901-02	A. C. MacLaren	J. Darling[8]	5	1	4	0	A
1902	A. C. MacLaren	J. Darling	5	1	2	2	A
1903-04	P. F. Warner	M. A. Noble	5	3	2	0	E
1905	Hon. F. S. Jackson	J. Darling	5	2	0	3	E
1907-08	A. O. Jones[9]	M. A. Noble	5	1	4	0	A
1909	A. C. MacLaren	M. A. Noble	5	1	2	2	A
1911-12	J. W. H. T. Douglas	C. Hill	5	4	1	0	E
1912	C. B. Fry	S. E. Gregory	3	1	0	2	E
1920-21	J. W. H. T. Douglas	W. W. Armstrong	5	0	5	0	A
1921	Hon. L. H. Tennyson[10]	W. W. Armstrong	5	0	3	2	A
1924-25	A. E. R. Gilligan	H. L. Collins	5	1	4	0	A
1926	A. W. Carr[11]	H. L. Collins[12]	5	1	0	4	E
1928-29	A. P. F. Chapman[13]	J. Ryder	5	4	1	0	E
1930	A. P. F. Chapman[14]	W. M. Woodfull	5	1	2	2	A
1932-33	D. R. Jardine	W. M. Woodfull	5	4	1	0	E
1934	R. E. S. Wyatt[15]	W. M. Woodfull	5	1	2	2	A
1936-37	G. O. B. Allen	D. G. Bradman	5	2	3	0	A
1938†	W. R. Hammond	D. G. Bradman	4	1	1	2	A
1946-47	W. R. Hammond[16]	D. G. Bradman	5	0	3	2	A
1948	N. W. D. Yardley	D. G. Bradman	5	0	4	1	A
1950-51	F. R. Brown	A. L. Hassett	5	1	4	0	A
1953	L. Hutton	A. L. Hassett	5	1	0	4	E

Captains

Season	England	Australia	T	E	A	D	Held by
1954-55	L. Hutton	I. W. Johnson[17]	5	3	1	1	E
1956	P. B. H. May	I. W. Johnson	5	2	1	2	E
1958-59	P. B. H. May	R. Benaud	5	0	4	1	A
1961	P. B. H. May[18]	R. Benaud[19]	5	1	2	2	A
1962-63	E. R. Dexter	R. Benaud	5	1	1	3	A
1964	E. R. Dexter	R. B. Simpson	5	0	1	4	A
1965-66	M. J. K. Smith	R. B. Simpson[20]	5	1	1	3	A
1968	M. C. Cowdrey[21]	W. M. Lawry[22]	5	1	1	3	A
1970-71†	R. Illingworth	W. M. Lawry[23]	6	2	0	4	E
1972	R. Illingworth	I. M. Chappell	5	2	2	1	E
1974-75	M. H. Denness[24]	I. M. Chappell	6	1	4	1	A
1975	A. W. Greig[25]	I. M. Chappell	4	0	1	3	A
1976-77‡	A. W. Greig	G. S. Chappell	1	0	1	0	—
1977	J. M. Brearley	G. S. Chappell	5	3	0	2	E
1978-79	J. M. Brearley	G. N. Yallop	6	5	1	0	E
1979-80‡	J. M. Brearley	G. S. Chappell	3	0	3	0	—
1980‡	I. T. Botham	G. S. Chappell	1	0	0	1	—
1981	J. M. Brearley[26]	K. J. Hughes	6	3	1	2	E
1982-83	R. G. D. Willis	G. S. Chappell	5	1	2	2	A
1985	D. I. Gower	A. R. Border	6	3	1	2	E
1986-87	M. W. Gatting	A. R. Border	5	2	1	2	E
1987-88‡	M. W. Gatting	A. R. Border	1	0	0	1	—
1989	D. I. Gower	A. R. Border	6	0	4	2	A
1990-91	G. A. Gooch[27]	A. R. Border	5	0	3	2	A
1993	G. A. Gooch[28]	A. R. Border	6	1	4	1	A
1994-95	M. A. Atherton	M. A. Taylor	5	1	3	1	A
1997	M. A. Atherton	M. A. Taylor	6	2	3	1	A
1998-99	A. J. Stewart	M. A. Taylor	5	1	3	1	A
2001	N. Hussain[29]	S. R. Waugh[30]	5	1	4	0	A
2002-03	N. Hussain	S. R. Waugh	5	1	4	0	A
2005	M. P. Vaughan	R. T. Ponting	5	2	1	2	E
2006-07	A. Flintoff	R. T. Ponting	5	0	5	0	A
2009	A. J. Strauss	R. T. Ponting	5	2	1	2	E
2010-11	A. J. Strauss	R. T. Ponting[31]	5	3	1	1	E
2013	A. N. Cook	M. J. Clarke	5	3	0	2	E
2013-14	A. N. Cook	M. J. Clarke	5	0	5	0	A
2015	A. N. Cook	M. J. Clarke	5	3	2	0	E
2017-18	**J. E. Root**	**S. P. D. Smith**	**5**	**0**	**4**	**1**	**A**

		T	E	A	D
In Australia	....	180	57	95	28
In England	....	166	51	49	66
Totals	....	**346**	**108**	**144**	**94**

* *The Ashes were awarded in 1882-83 after a series of three matches which England won 2–1. A fourth match was played and this was won by Australia.*

† *The matches at Manchester in 1890 and 1938 and at Melbourne (Third Test) in 1970-71 were abandoned without a ball being bowled and are excluded.*

‡ *The Ashes were not at stake in these series.*

The following deputised for the official touring captain or were appointed by the home authority for only a minor proportion of the series:

[1]A. N. Hornby (First). [2]W. L. Murdoch (First), H. H. Massie (Third), J. McC. Blackham (Fourth). [3]A. G. Steel (First). [4]A. E. Stoddart (First). [5]J. McC. Blackham (First). [6]A. C. MacLaren (First, Second and Fifth). [7]W. G. Grace (First). [8]H. Trumble (Fourth and Fifth). [9]F. L. Fane (First, Second and Third). [10]J. W. H. T. Douglas (First and Second). [11]A. P. F. Chapman (Fifth). [12]W. Bardsley (Third and Fourth). [13]J. C. White (Fifth). [14]R. E. S. Wyatt (Fifth). [15]C. F. Walters (First). [16]N. W. D. Yardley (Fifth). [17]A. R. Morris (Second). [18]M. C. Cowdrey (First and Second). [19]R. N. Harvey (Second). [20]B. C. Booth (First and Third). [21]T. W. Graveney (Fourth). [22]B. N. Jarman (Fourth) [23]I. M. Chappell (Seventh). [24]J. H. Edrich (Fourth). [25]M. H. Denness (First). [26]I. T. Botham (First and Second). [27]A. J. Lamb (First). [28]M. A. Atherton (Fifth and Sixth). [29]M. A. Atherton (Second and Third). [30]A. C. Gilchrist (Fourth). [31]M. J. Clarke (Fifth).

HIGHEST INNINGS TOTALS

For England in England: 903-7 dec at The Oval   1938
            in Australia: 644 at Sydney   2010-11

For Australia in England: 729-6 dec at Lord's   1930
            in Australia: 662-9 dec at Perth **2017-18**

LOWEST INNINGS TOTALS

For England in England: 52 at The Oval   1948
            in Australia: 45 at Sydney   1886-87

For Australia in England: 36 at Birmingham   1902
            in Australia: 42 at Sydney   1887-88

DOUBLE-HUNDREDS

For England (14)

364	L. Hutton at The Oval	1938	231*	W. R. Hammond at Sydney	1936-37
287	R. E. Foster at Sydney	1903-04	227	K. P. Pietersen at Adelaide	2010-11
256	K. F. Barrington at Manchester	1964	216*	E. Paynter at Nottingham	1938
251	W. R. Hammond at Sydney	1928-29	215	D. I. Gower at Birmingham	1985
244*	**A. N. Cook at Melbourne**	**2017-18**	207	N. Hussain at Birmingham	1997
240	W. R. Hammond at Lord's	1938	206	P. D. Collingwood at Adelaide . .	2006-07
235*	A. N. Cook at Brisbane	2010-11	200	W. R. Hammond at Melbourne .	1928-29

For Australia (25)

334	D. G. Bradman at Leeds	1930	232	S. J. McCabe at Nottingham	1938
311	R. B. Simpson at Manchester . . .	1964	225	R. B. Simpson at Adelaide	1965-66
307	R. M. Cowper at Melbourne	1965-66	219	M. A. Taylor at Nottingham	1989
304	D. G. Bradman at Leeds	1934	215	S. P. D. Smith at Lord's	2015
270	D. G. Bradman at Melbourne . . .	1936-37	212	D. G. Bradman at Adelaide	1936-37
266	W. H. Ponsford at The Oval	1934	211	W. L. Murdoch at The Oval	1884
254	D. G. Bradman at Lord's	1930	207	K. R. Stackpole at Brisbane	1970-71
250	J. L. Langer at Melbourne	2002-03	206*	W. A. Brown at Lord's	1938
244	D. G. Bradman at The Oval	1934	206	A. R. Morris at Adelaide	1950-51
239	**S. P. D. Smith at Perth**	**2017-18**	201*	J. Ryder at Adelaide	1924-25
234	S. G. Barnes at Sydney	1946-47	201	S. E. Gregory at Sydney	1894-95
234	D. G. Bradman at Sydney	1946-47	200*	A. R. Border at Leeds	1993
232	D. G. Bradman at The Oval	1930			

INDIVIDUAL HUNDREDS

In total, England have scored **242** hundreds against Australia, and Australia have scored **313** against England. The players with at least five hundreds are as follows:

For England

12: J. B. Hobbs.
 9: D. I. Gower, W. R. Hammond.
 8: H. Sutcliffe.
 7: G. Boycott, J. H. Edrich, M. Leyland.
 5: K. F. Barrington, D. C. S. Compton, **A. N. Cook**, M. C. Cowdrey, L. Hutton, F. S. Jackson, A. C. MacLaren.

For Australia

19: D. G. Bradman.
10: S. R. Waugh.
9: G. S. Chappell.
8: A. R. Border, A. R. Morris, R. T. Ponting, **S. P. D. Smith**.
7: D. C. Boon, M. J. Clarke, W. M. Lawry, M. J. Slater.
6: R. N. Harvey, M. A. Taylor, V. T. Trumper, M. E. Waugh, W. M. Woodfull.
5: M. L. Hayden, J. L. Langer, C. G. Macartney, W. H. Ponsford.

RECORD PARTNERSHIPS FOR EACH WICKET

For England

323 for 1st	J. B. Hobbs and W. Rhodes at Melbourne......................	1911-12
382 for 2nd†	L. Hutton and M. Leyland at The Oval	1938
262 for 3rd	W. R. Hammond and D. R. Jardine at Adelaide	1928-29
310 for 4th	P. D. Collingwood and K. P. Pietersen at Adelaide	2006-07
237 for 5th	**D. J. Malan and J. M. Bairstow at Perth**.....................	**2017-18**
215 for 6th	⎰ L. Hutton and J. Hardstaff jnr at The Oval	1938
	⎱ G. Boycott and A. P. E. Knott at Nottingham	1977
143 for 7th	F. E. Woolley and J. Vine at Sydney	1911-12
124 for 8th	E. H. Hendren and H. Larwood at Brisbane	1928-29
151 for 9th	W. H. Scotton and W. W. Read at The Oval...............	1884
130 for 10th	R. E. Foster and W. Rhodes at Sydney	1903-04

For Australia

329 for 1st	G. R. Marsh and M. A. Taylor at Nottingham............	1989
451 for 2nd†	W. H. Ponsford and D. G. Bradman at The Oval	1934
276 for 3rd	D. G. Bradman and A. L. Hassett at Brisbane	1946-47
388 for 4th	W. H. Ponsford and D. G. Bradman at Leeds	1934
405 for 5th‡	S. G. Barnes and D. G. Bradman at Sydney	1946-47
346 for 6th†	J. H. Fingleton and D. G. Bradman at Melbourne.......	1936-37
165 for 7th	C. Hill and H. Trumble at Melbourne	1897-98
243 for 8th†	R. J. Hartigan and C. Hill at Adelaide	1907-08
154 for 9th†	S. E. Gregory and J. McC. Blackham at Sydney	1894-95
163 for 10th†	P. J. Hughes and A. C. Agar at Nottingham	2013

† *Record partnership against all countries.* ‡ *World record.*

MOST RUNS IN A SERIES

England in England	............732 (average 81.33)	D. I. Gower	1985
England in Australia	...........905 (average 113.12)	W. R. Hammond........	1928-29
Australia in England	............974 (average 139.14)	D. G. Bradman	1930
Australia in Australia	...........810 (average 90.00)	D. G. Bradman	1936-37

MOST WICKETS IN A MATCH

In total, England bowlers have taken ten or more wickets in a match **40** times against Australia, and Australian bowlers have done it **43** times against England. The players with at least 12 in a match are as follows:

For England

19-90 (9-37, 10-53)	J. C. Laker at Manchester	1956
15-104 (7-61, 8-43)	H. Verity at Lord's.................................	1934
15-124 (7-56, 8-68)	W. Rhodes at Melbourne	1903-04
14-99 (7-55, 7-44)	A. V. Bedser at Nottingham	1953
14-102 (7-28, 7-74)	W. Bates at Melbourne	1882-83
13-163 (6-42, 7-121)	S. F. Barnes at Melbourne	1901-02
13-244 (7-168, 6-76)	T. Richardson at Manchester........................	1896
13-256 (5-130, 8-126)	J. C. White at Adelaide	1928-29

12-102 (6-50, 6-52)†	F. Martin at The Oval	1890
12-104 (7-36, 5-68)	G. A. Lohmann at The Oval	1886
12-136 (6-49, 6-87)	J. Briggs at Adelaide	1891-92

There are a further 12 instances of 11 wickets in a match, and 17 instances of ten.

For Australia

16-137 (8-84, 8-53)†	R. A. L. Massie at Lord's	1972
14-90 (7-46, 7-44)	F. R. Spofforth at The Oval	1882
13-77 (7-17, 6-60)	M. A. Noble at Melbourne	1901-02
13-110 (6-48, 7-62)	F. R. Spofforth at Melbourne	1878-79
13-148 (6-97, 7-51)	B. A. Reid at Melbourne	1990-91
13-236 (4-115, 9-121)	A. A. Mailey at Melbourne	1920-21
12-87 (5-44, 7-43)	C. T. B. Turner at Sydney	1887-88
12-89 (6-59, 6-30)	H. Trumble at The Oval	1896
12-107 (5-57, 7-50)	S. C. G. MacGill at Sydney	1998-99
12-173 (8-65, 4-108)	H. Trumble at The Oval	1902
12-175 (5-85, 7-90)†	H. V. Hordern at Sydney	1911-12
12-246 (6-122, 6-124)	S. K. Warne at The Oval	2005

There are a further 13 instances of 11 wickets in a match, and 18 instances of ten.

† *On first appearance in England–Australia Tests.*

A. V. Bedser, J. Briggs, J. C. Laker, T. Richardson, R. M. Hogg, A. A. Mailey, H. Trumble and C. T. B. Turner took ten wickets or more in successive Tests.

MOST WICKETS IN A SERIES

England in England	46 (average 9.60)	J. C. Laker	1956
England in Australia	38 (average 23.18)	M. W. Tate	1924-25
Australia in England	42 (average 21.26)	T. M. Alderman (6 Tests)	1981
Australia in Australia	41 (average 12.85)	R. M. Hogg (6 Tests)	1978-79

WICKETKEEPING – MOST DISMISSALS

	M	Ct	St	Total
†R. W. Marsh (Australia)	42	141	7	148
I. A. Healy (Australia)	33	123	12	135
A. P. E. Knott (England)	34	97	8	105
A. C. Gilchrist (Australia)	20	89	7	96
†W. A. Oldfield (Australia)	38	59	31	90
A. A. Lilley (England)	32	65	19	84
B. J. Haddin (Australia)	20	79	1	80
A. J. Stewart (England)	26	76	2	78
A. T. W. Grout (Australia)	22	69	7	76
T. G. Evans (England)	31	64	12	76

† *The number of catches by R. W. Marsh (141) and stumpings by W. A. Oldfield (31) are respective records in England–Australia Tests.*

Stewart held a further six catches in seven matches when not keeping wicket.

SCORERS OF OVER 2,500 RUNS

	T	I	NO	R	HS	100	Avge
D. G. Bradman (Australia)	37	63	7	5,028	334	19	89.78
J. B. Hobbs (England)	41	71	4	3,636	187	12	54.26
A. R. Border (Australia)	47	82	19	3,548	200*	8	56.31
D. I. Gower (England)	42	77	4	3,269	215	9	44.78
S. R. Waugh (Australia)	46	73	18	3,200	177*	10	58.18
G. Boycott (England)	38	71	9	2,945	191	7	47.50
W. R. Hammond (England)	33	58	3	2,852	251	9	51.85

	T	I	NO	R	HS	100	Avge
H. Sutcliffe (England)	27	46	5	2,741	194	8	66.85
C. Hill (Australia)	41	76	1	2,660	188	4	35.46
J. H. Edrich (England)	32	57	3	2,644	175	7	48.96
G. A. Gooch (England)	42	79	0	2,632	196	4	33.31
G. S. Chappell (Australia) . .	35	65	8	2,619	144	9	45.94

BOWLERS WITH 100 WICKETS

	T	Balls	R	W	5I	10M	Avge
S. K. Warne (Australia)	36	10,757	4,535	195	11	4	23.25
D. K. Lillee (Australia).	29	8,516	3,507	167	11	4	21.00
G. D. McGrath (Australia)	30	7,280	3,286	157	10	0	20.92
I. T. Botham (England)	36	8,479	4,093	148	9	2	27.65
H. Trumble (Australia).	31	7,895	2,945	141	9	3	20.88
R. G. D. Willis (England).	35	7,294	3,346	128	7	0	26.14
M. A. Noble (Australia)	39	6,895	2,860	115	9	2	24.86
R. R. Lindwall (Australia)	29	6,728	2,559	114	6	0	22.44
W. Rhodes (England)	41	5,790	2,616	109	6	1	24.00
S. F. Barnes (England)	20	5,749	2,288	106	12	1	21.58
C. V. Grimmett (Australia).	22	9,224	3,439	106	11	2	32.44
D. L. Underwood (England).	29	8,000	2,770	105	4	2	26.38
A. V. Bedser (England)	21	7,065	2,859	104	7	2	27.49
J. M. Anderson (England)	**31**	**7,027**	**3,594**	**104**	**5**	**1**	**34.55**
G. Giffen (Australia)	31	6,391	2,791	103	7	1	27.09
W. J. O'Reilly (Australia)	19	7,864	2,587	102	8	3	25.36
C. T. B. Turner (Australia)	17	5,179	1,670	101	11	2	16.53
R. Peel (England).	20	5,216	1,715	101	5	1	16.98
T. M. Alderman (Australia)	17	4,717	2,117	100	11	1	21.17
J. R. Thomson (Australia)	21	4,951	2,418	100	5	0	24.18

RESULTS ON EACH GROUND

In England

	Matches	England wins	Australia wins	Drawn
The Oval.	37	16	7	14
Manchester.	29	7	7	15†
Lord's.	36	7	15	14
Nottingham	22	6	7	9
Leeds	24	7	9	8
Birmingham.	14	6	3	5
Sheffield.	1	0	1	0
Cardiff	2	1	0	1
Chester-le-Street.	1	1	0	0

† *Excludes two matches abandoned without a ball bowled.*

In Australia

	Matches	England wins	Australia wins	Drawn
Melbourne	56	20	28	8†
Sydney	56	22	27	7
Adelaide.	32	9	18	5
Brisbane				
Exhibition Ground	1	1	0	0
Woolloongabba	21	4	12	5
Perth.	14	1	10	3

† *Excludes one match abandoned without a ball bowled.*

ENGLAND v SOUTH AFRICA

Captains

Season	England	South Africa	T	E	SA	D
1888-89	C. A. Smith[1]	O. R. Dunell[2]	2	2	0	0
1891-92	W. W. Read	W. H. Milton	1	1	0	0
1895-96	Lord Hawke[3]	E. A. Halliwell[4]	3	3	0	0
1898-99	Lord Hawke	M. Bisset	2	2	0	0
1905-06	P. F. Warner	P. W. Sherwell	5	1	4	0
1907	R. E. Foster	P. W. Sherwell	3	1	0	2
1909-10	H. D. G. Leveson Gower[5]	S. J. Snooke	5	2	3	0
1912	C. B. Fry	F. Mitchell[6]	3	3	0	0
1913-14	J. W. H. T. Douglas	H. W. Taylor	5	4	0	1
1922-23	F. T. Mann	H. W. Taylor	5	2	1	2
1924	A. E. R. Gilligan[7]	H. W. Taylor	5	3	0	2
1927-28	R. T. Stanyforth[8]	H. G. Deane	5	2	2	1
1929	J. C. White[9]	H. G. Deane	5	2	0	3
1930-31	A. P. F. Chapman	H. G. Deane[10]	5	0	1	4
1935	R. E. S. Wyatt	H. F. Wade	5	0	1	4
1938-39	W. R. Hammond	A. Melville	5	1	0	4
1947	N. W. D. Yardley	A. Melville	5	3	0	2
1948-49	F. G. Mann	A. D. Nourse	5	2	0	3
1951	F. R. Brown	A. D. Nourse	5	3	1	1
1955	P. B. H. May	J. E. Cheetham[11]	5	3	2	0
1956-57	P. B. H. May	C. B. van Ryneveld[12]	5	2	2	1
1960	M. C. Cowdrey	D. J. McGlew	5	3	0	2
1964-65	M. J. K. Smith	T. L. Goddard	5	1	0	4
1965	M. J. K. Smith	P. L. van der Merwe	3	0	1	2
1994	M. A. Atherton	K. C. Wessels	3	1	1	1
1995-96	M. A. Atherton	W. J. Cronje	5	0	1	4
1998	A. J. Stewart	W. J. Cronje	5	2	1	2
1999-2000	N. Hussain	W. J. Cronje	5	1	2	2
2003	M. P. Vaughan[13]	G. C. Smith	5	2	2	1

THE BASIL D'OLIVEIRA TROPHY

Captains

Season	England	South Africa	T	E	SA	D	Held by
2004-05	M. P. Vaughan	G. C. Smith	5	2	1	2	E
2008	M. P. Vaughan[14]	G. C. Smith	4	1	2	1	SA
2009-10	A. J. Strauss	G. C. Smith	4	1	1	2	SA
2012	A. J. Strauss	G. C. Smith	3	0	2	1	SA
2015-16	A. N. Cook	H. M. Amla[15]	4	2	1	1	E
2017	J. E. Root	F. du Plessis[16]	4	3	1	0	E

			T	E	SA	D
In South Africa			81	31	19	31
In England			68	30	14	24
Totals.............................			149	61	33	55

The following deputised for the official touring captain or were appointed by the home authority for only a minor proportion of the series:

[1]M. P. Bowden (Second). [2]W. H. Milton (Second). [3]Sir Timothy O'Brien (First). [4]A. R. Richards (Third). [5]F. L. Fane (Fourth and Fifth). [6]L. J. Tancred (Second and Third). [7]J. W. H. T. Douglas (Fourth). [8]G. T. S. Stevens (Fifth). [9]A. W. Carr (Fourth and Fifth). [10]E. P. Nupen (First), H. B. Cameron (Fourth and Fifth). [11]D. J. McGlew (Third and Fourth). [12]D. J. McGlew (Second). [13]N. Hussain (First). [14]K. P. Pietersen (Fourth). [15]A. B. de Villiers (Third and Fourth). [16]D. Elgar (First).

SERIES RECORDS

Highest score	E	258	B. A. Stokes at Cape Town	2015-16
	SA	311*	H. M. Amla at The Oval	2012
Best bowling	E	9-28	G. A. Lohmann at Johannesburg.	1895-96
	SA	9-113	H. J. Tayfield at Johannesburg	1956-57
Highest total	E	654-5	at Durban.	1938-39
	SA	682-6 dec	at Lord's	2003
Lowest total	E	76	at Leeds	1907
	SA {	30	at Port Elizabeth	1895-96
		30	at Birmingham.	1924

ENGLAND v WEST INDIES

Captains

Season	England	West Indies	T	E	WI	D
1928	A. P. F. Chapman	R. K. Nunes	3	3	0	0
1929-30	Hon. F. S. G. Calthorpe	E. L. G. Hoad[1]	4	1	1	2
1933	D. R. Jardine[2]	G. C. Grant	3	2	0	1
1934-35	R. E. S. Wyatt	G. C. Grant	4	1	2	1
1939	W. R. Hammond	R. S. Grant	3	1	0	2
1947-48	G. O. B. Allen[3]	J. D. C. Goddard[4]	4	0	2	2
1950	N. W. D. Yardley[5]	J. D. C. Goddard	4	1	3	0
1953-54	L. Hutton	J. B. Stollmeyer	5	2	2	1
1957	P. B. H. May	J. D. C. Goddard	5	3	0	2
1959-60	P. B. H. May[6]	F. C. M. Alexander	5	1	0	4

THE WISDEN TROPHY

Captains

Season	England	West Indies	T	E	WI	D	Held by
1963	E. R. Dexter	F. M. M. Worrell	5	1	3	1	WI
1966	M. C. Cowdrey[7]	G. S. Sobers	5	1	3	1	WI
1967-68	M. C. Cowdrey	G. S. Sobers	5	1	0	4	E
1969	R. Illingworth	G. S. Sobers	3	2	0	1	E
1973	R. Illingworth	R. B. Kanhai	3	0	2	1	WI
1973-74	M. H. Denness	R. B. Kanhai	5	1	1	3	WI
1976	A. W. Greig	C. H. Lloyd	5	0	3	2	WI
1980	I. T. Botham	C. H. Lloyd[8]	5	0	1	4	WI
1980-81†	I. T. Botham	C. H. Lloyd	4	0	2	2	WI
1984	D. I. Gower	C. H. Lloyd	5	0	5	0	WI
1985-86	D. I. Gower	I. V. A. Richards	5	0	5	0	WI
1988	J. E. Emburey[9]	I. V. A. Richards	5	0	4	1	WI
1989-90‡	G. A. Gooch[10]	I. V. A. Richards[11]	4	1	2	1	WI
1991	G. A. Gooch	I. V. A. Richards	5	2	2	1	WI
1993-94	M. A. Atherton	R. B. Richardson[12]	5	1	3	1	WI
1995	M. A. Atherton	R. B. Richardson	6	2	2	2	WI
1997-98§	M. A. Atherton	B. C. Lara	6	1	3	2	WI
2000	N. Hussain[13]	J. C. Adams	5	3	1	1	E
2003-04	M. P. Vaughan	B. C. Lara	4	3	0	1	E
2004	M. P. Vaughan	B. C. Lara	4	4	0	0	E
2007	M. P. Vaughan[14]	R. R. Sarwan[15]	4	3	0	1	E
2008-09§	A. J. Strauss	C. H. Gayle	5	0	1	4	WI
2009	A. J. Strauss	C. H. Gayle	2	2	0	0	E
2012	A. J. Strauss	D. J. G. Sammy	3	2	0	1	E
2014-15	A. N. Cook	D. Ramdin	3	1	1	1	E
2017	J. E. Root	J. O. Holder	3	2	1	0	E

	In England.	86	34	30	22	
	In West Indies.	68	14	25	29	
	Totals	154	48	55	51	

†   *The Second Test, at Georgetown, was cancelled owing to political pressure and is excluded.*
‡   *The Second Test, at Georgetown, was abandoned without a ball being bowled and is excluded.*
§   *The First Test at Kingston in 1997-98 and the Second Test at North Sound in 2008-09 were called off on their opening days because of unfit pitches and are shown as draws.*

The following deputised for the official touring captain or were appointed by the home authority for only a minor proportion of the series:

[1]N. Betancourt (Second), M. P. Fernandes (Third), R. K. Nunes (Fourth). [2]R. E. S. Wyatt (Third). [3]K. Cranston (First). [4]G. A. Headley (First), G. E. Gomez (Second). [5]F. R. Brown (Fourth). [6]M. C. Cowdrey (Fourth and Fifth). [7]M. J. K. Smith (First), D. B. Close (Fifth). [8]I. V. A. Richards (Fifth). [9]M. W. Gatting (First), C. S. Cowdrey (Fourth), G. A. Gooch (Fifth). [10]A. J. Lamb (Fourth and Fifth). [11]D. L. Haynes (Third). [12]C. A. Walsh (Fifth). [13]A. J. Stewart (Second). [14]A. J. Strauss (First). [15]D. Ganga (Third and Fourth).

SERIES RECORDS

Highest score	E	325	A. Sandham at Kingston	1929-30
	WI	400*	B. C. Lara at St John's..................	2003-04
Best bowling	E	8-53	A. R. C. Fraser at Port-of-Spain	1997-98
	WI	8-45	C. E. L. Ambrose at Bridgetown	1989-90
Highest total	E	849	at Kingston	1929-30
	WI	751-5 dec	at St John's	2003-04
Lowest total	E	46	at Port-of-Spain	1993-94
	WI	47	at Kingston	2003-04

ENGLAND v NEW ZEALAND

	Captains					
Season	England	New Zealand	T	E	NZ	D
1929-30	A. H. H. Gilligan	T. C. Lowry	4	1	0	3
1931	D. R. Jardine	T. C. Lowry	3	1	0	2
1932-33	D. R. Jardine[1]	M. L. Page	2	0	0	2
1937	R. W. V. Robins	M. L. Page	3	1	0	2
1946-47	W. R. Hammond	W. A. Hadlee	1	0	0	1
1949	F. G. Mann[2]	W. A. Hadlee	4	0	0	4
1950-51	F. R. Brown	W. A. Hadlee	2	1	0	1
1954-55	L. Hutton	G. O. Rabone	2	2	0	0
1958	P. B. H. May	J. R. Reid	5	4	0	1
1958-59	P. B. H. May	J. R. Reid	2	1	0	1
1962-63	E. R. Dexter	J. R. Reid	3	3	0	0
1965	M. J. K. Smith	J. R. Reid	3	3	0	0
1965-66	M. J. K. Smith	B. W. Sinclair[3]	3	0	0	3
1969	R. Illingworth	G. T. Dowling	3	2	0	1
1970-71	R. Illingworth	G. T. Dowling	2	1	0	1
1973	R. Illingworth	B. E. Congdon	3	2	0	1
1974-75	M. H. Denness	B. E. Congdon	2	1	0	1
1977-78	G. Boycott	M. G. Burgess	3	1	1	1
1978	J. M. Brearley	M. G. Burgess	3	3	0	0
1983	R. G. D. Willis	G. P. Howarth	4	3	1	0
1983-84	R. G. D. Willis	G. P. Howarth	3	0	1	2
1986	M. W. Gatting	J. V. Coney	3	0	1	2
1987-88	M. W. Gatting	J. J. Crowe[4]	3	0	0	3
1990	G. A. Gooch	J. G. Wright	3	1	0	2
1991-92	G. A. Gooch	M. D. Crowe	3	2	0	1
1994	M. A. Atherton	K. R. Rutherford	3	1	0	2
1996-97	M. A. Atherton	L. K. Germon[5]	3	2	0	1
1999	N. Hussain[6]	S. P. Fleming	4	1	2	1
2001-02	N. Hussain	S. P. Fleming	3	1	1	1
2004	M. P. Vaughan[7]	S. P. Fleming	3	3	0	0
2007-08	M. P. Vaughan	D. L. Vettori	3	2	1	0

		Captains				
Season	England		New Zealand	T	E	NZ	D
2008	M. P. Vaughan		D. L. Vettori	3	2	0	1
2012-13	A. N. Cook		B. B. McCullum	3	0	0	3
2013	A. N. Cook		B. B. McCullum	2	2	0	0
2015	A. N. Cook		B. B. McCullum	2	1	1	0
2017-18	**J. E. Root**		**K. S. Williamson**	**2**	**0**	**1**	**1**
	In New Zealand			**49**	**18**	**5**	**26**
	In England			54	30	5	19
	Totals			**103**	**48**	**10**	**45**

The following deputised for the official touring captain or were appointed by the home authority for only a minor proportion of the series:

[1]R. E. S. Wyatt (Second). [2]F. R. Brown (Third and Fourth). [3]M. E. Chapple (First). [4]J. G. Wright (Third). [5]S. P. Fleming (Third). [6]M. A. Butcher (Third). [7]M. E. Trescothick (First).

SERIES RECORDS

Highest score	E	336*	W. R. Hammond at Auckland..............	1932-33
	NZ	222	N. J. Astle at Christchurch	2001-02
Best bowling	E	7-32	D. L. Underwood at Lord's...............	1969
	NZ	7-74	B. L. Cairns at Leeds....................	1983
Highest total	E	593-6 dec	at Auckland...........................	1974-75
	NZ	551-9 dec	at Lord's	1973
Lowest total	E	58	at Auckland...........................	**2017-18**
	NZ	26	at Auckland...........................	1954-55

ENGLAND v INDIA

		Captains				
Season	England	India	T	E	I	D
1932	D. R. Jardine	C. K. Nayudu	1	1	0	0
1933-34	D. R. Jardine	C. K. Nayudu	3	2	0	1
1936	G. O. B. Allen	Maharajkumar of Vizianagram	3	2	0	1
1946	W. R. Hammond	Nawab of Pataudi snr	3	1	0	2
1951-52	N. D. Howard[1]	V. S. Hazare	5	1	1	3
1952	L. Hutton	V. S. Hazare	4	3	0	1
1959	P. B. H. May[2]	D. K. Gaekwad[3]	5	5	0	0
1961-62	E. R. Dexter	N. J. Contractor	5	0	2	3
1963-64	M. J. K. Smith	Nawab of Pataudi jnr	5	0	0	5
1967	D. B. Close	Nawab of Pataudi jnr	3	3	0	0
1971	R. Illingworth	A. L. Wadekar	3	0	1	2
1972-73	A. R. Lewis	A. L. Wadekar	5	1	2	2
1974	M. H. Denness	A. L. Wadekar	3	3	0	0
1976-77	A. W. Greig	B. S. Bedi	5	3	1	1
1979	J. M. Brearley	S. Venkataraghavan	4	1	0	3
1979-80	J. M. Brearley	G. R. Viswanath	1	1	0	0
1981-82	K. W. R. Fletcher	S. M. Gavaskar	6	0	1	5
1982	R. G. D. Willis	S. M. Gavaskar	3	1	0	2
1984-85	D. I. Gower	S. M. Gavaskar	5	2	1	2
1986	M. W. Gatting[4]	Kapil Dev	3	0	2	1
1990	G. A. Gooch	M. Azharuddin	3	1	0	2
1992-93	G. A. Gooch[5]	M. Azharuddin	3	0	3	0
1996	M. A. Atherton	M. Azharuddin	3	1	0	2
2001-02	N. Hussain	S. C. Ganguly	3	0	1	2
2002	N. Hussain	S. C. Ganguly	4	1	1	2
2005-06	A. Flintoff	R. Dravid	3	1	1	1
2007	M. P. Vaughan	R. Dravid	3	0	1	2
2008-09	K. P. Pietersen	M. S. Dhoni	2	0	1	1

Captions

Season	England	India	T	E	I	D
2011	A. J. Strauss	M. S. Dhoni	4	4	0	0
2012-13	A. N. Cook	M. S. Dhoni	4	2	1	1
2014	A. N. Cook	M. S. Dhoni	5	3	1	1
2016-17	A. N. Cook	V. Kohli	5	0	4	1
2018	**J. E. Root**	**V. Kohli**	**5**	**4**	**1**	**0**

		T	E	I	D
In England		62	34	7	21
In India		60	13	19	28
Totals		122	47	26	49

* *Since 1951-52, series in India have been for the De Mello Trophy. Since 2007, series in England have been for the Pataudi Trophy.*

The following deputised for the official touring captain or were appointed by the home authority for only a minor proportion of the series:
[1]D. B. Carr (Fifth). [2]M. C. Cowdrey (Fourth and Fifth). [3]Pankaj Roy (Second). [4]D. I. Gower (First). [5]A. J. Stewart (Second).

The 1932 Indian touring team was led by the Maharajah of Porbandar, but he did not play in the Test.

SERIES RECORDS

Highest score	E	333	G. A. Gooch at Lord's	1990
	I	303*	K. K. Nair at Chennai	2016-17
Best bowling	E	8-31	F. S. Trueman at Manchester..............	1952
	I	8-55	M. H. Mankad at Madras..................	1951-52
Highest total	E	710-7 dec	at Birmingham...........................	2011
	I	759-7 dec	at Chennai	2016-17
Lowest total	E	101	at The Oval	1971
	I	42	at Lord's	1974

ENGLAND v PAKISTAN

Captains

Season	England	Pakistan	T	E	P	D
1954	L. Hutton[1]	A. H. Kardar	4	1	1	2
1961-62	E. R. Dexter	Imtiaz Ahmed	3	1	0	2
1962	E. R. Dexter[2]	Javed Burki	5	4	0	1
1967	D. B. Close	Hanif Mohammad	3	2	0	1
1968-69	M. C. Cowdrey	Saeed Ahmed	3	0	0	3
1971	R. Illingworth	Intikhab Alam	3	1	0	2
1972-73	A. R. Lewis	Majid Khan	3	0	0	3
1974	M. H. Denness	Intikhab Alam	3	0	0	3
1977-78	J. M. Brearley[3]	Wasim Bari	3	0	0	3
1978	J. M. Brearley	Wasim Bari	3	2	0	1
1982	R. G. D. Willis[4]	Imran Khan	3	2	1	0
1983-84	R. G. D. Willis[5]	Zaheer Abbas	3	0	1	2
1987	M. W. Gatting	Imran Khan	5	0	1	4
1987-88	M. W. Gatting	Javed Miandad	3	0	1	2
1992	G. A. Gooch	Javed Miandad	5	1	2	2
1996	M. A. Atherton	Wasim Akram	3	0	2	1
2000-01	N. Hussain	Moin Khan	3	1	0	2
2001	N. Hussain[6]	Waqar Younis	2	1	1	0
2005-06	M. P. Vaughan[7]	Inzamam-ul-Haq	3	0	2	1
2006†	A. J. Strauss	Inzamam-ul-Haq	4	3	0	1
2010	A. J. Strauss	Salman Butt	4	3	1	0

		Captains				
Season	England	Pakistan	T	E	P	D
2011-12*U*	A. J. Strauss	Misbah-ul-Haq	3	0	3	0
2015-16*U*	A. N. Cook	Misbah-ul-Haq	3	0	2	1
2016	A. N. Cook	Misbah-ul-Haq	4	2	2	0
2018	**J. E. Root**	**Sarfraz Ahmed**	**2**	**1**	**1**	**0**
	In England		53	23	12	18
	In Pakistan		24	2	4	18
	In United Arab Emirates		6	0	5	1
	Totals...........................		83	25	21	37

† *In 2008, the ICC changed the result of the forfeited Oval Test of 2006 from an England win to a draw, in contravention of the Laws of Cricket, only to rescind their decision in January 2009.*

U Played in United Arab Emirates.

The following deputised for the official touring captain or were appointed by the home authority for only a minor proportion of the series:
[1]D. S. Sheppard (Second and Third). [2]M. C. Cowdrey (Third). [3]G. Boycott (Third). [4]D. I. Gower (Second). [5]D. I. Gower (Second and Third). [6]A. J. Stewart (Second). [7]M. E. Trescothick (First).

SERIES RECORDS

Highest score	E	278	D. C. S. Compton at Nottingham.............	1954
	P	274	Zaheer Abbas at Birmingham	1971
Best bowling	E	8-34	I. T. Botham at Lord's.....................	1978
	P	9-56	Abdul Qadir at Lahore.....................	1987-88
Highest total	E	598-9 dec	at Abu Dhabi	2015-16
	P	708	at The Oval	1987
Lowest total	E	72	at Abu Dhabi	2011-12
	P	72	at Birmingham...........................	2010

ENGLAND v SRI LANKA

		Captains				
Season	England	Sri Lanka	T	E	SL	D
1981-82	K. W. R. Fletcher	B. Warnapura	1	1	0	0
1984	D. I. Gower	L. R. D. Mendis	1	0	0	1
1988	G. A. Gooch	R. S. Madugalle	1	1	0	0
1991	G. A. Gooch	P. A. de Silva	1	1	0	0
1992-93	A. J. Stewart	A. Ranatunga	1	0	1	0
1998	A. J. Stewart	A. Ranatunga	1	0	1	0
2000-01	N. Hussain	S. T. Jayasuriya	3	2	1	0
2002	N. Hussain	S. T. Jayasuriya	3	2	0	1
2003-04	M. P. Vaughan	H. P. Tillekeratne	3	0	1	2
2006	A. Flintoff	D. P. M. D. Jayawardene	3	1	1	1
2007-08	M. P. Vaughan	D. P. M. D. Jayawardene	3	0	1	2
2011	A. J. Strauss	T. M. Dilshan[1]	3	1	0	2
2011-12	A. J. Strauss	D. P. M. D. Jayawardene	2	1	1	0
2014	A. N. Cook	A. D. Mathews	2	0	1	1
2016	A. N. Cook	A. D. Mathews	3	2	0	1
2018-19	**J. E. Root**	**R. A. S. Lakmal[2]**	**3**	**3**	**0**	**0**
	In England		18	8	3	7
	In Sri Lanka		16	7	5	4
	Totals...........................		34	15	8	11

The following deputised for the official touring captain or was appointed by the home authority for only a minor proportion of the series:
[1]K. C. Sangakkara (Third). [2]L. D. Chandimal (First).

SERIES RECORDS

Highest score	E	203	I. J. L. Trott at Cardiff	2011
	SL	213*	D. P. M. D. Jayawardene at Galle	2007-08
Best bowling	E	7-70	P. A. J. DeFreitas at Lord's	1991
	SL	9-65	M. Muralitharan at The Oval..............	1998
Highest total	E	575-9 dec	at Lord's.................................	2014
	SL	628-8 dec	at Colombo (SSC)	2003-04
Lowest total	E	81	at Galle.................................	2007-08
	SL	81	at Colombo (SSC)	2000-01

ENGLAND v ZIMBABWE

		Captains				
Season	England	Zimbabwe	T	E	Z	D
1996-97	M. A. Atherton	A. D. R. Campbell	2	0	0	2
2000	N. Hussain	A. Flower	2	1	0	1
2003	N. Hussain	H. H. Streak	2	2	0	0
	In England		4	3	0	1
	In Zimbabwe		2	0	0	2
	Totals		6	3	0	3

SERIES RECORDS

Highest score	E	137	M. A. Butcher at Lord's	2003
	Z	148*	M. W. Goodwin at Nottingham...............	2000
Best bowling	E	6-33	R. L. Johnson at Chester-le-Street.............	2003
	Z	6-87	H. H. Streak at Lord's......................	2000
Highest total	E	472	at Lord's	2003
	Z	376	at Bulawayo............................	1996-97
Lowest total	E	147	at Nottingham	2000
	Z	83	at Lord's	2000

ENGLAND v BANGLADESH

		Captains				
Season	England	Bangladesh	T	E	B	D
2003-04	M. P. Vaughan	Khaled Mahmud	2	2	0	0
2005	M. P. Vaughan	Habibul Bashar	2	2	0	0
2009-10	A. N. Cook	Shakib Al Hasan	2	2	0	0
2010	A. J. Strauss	Shakib Al Hasan	2	2	0	0
2016-17	A. N. Cook	Mushfiqur Rahim	2	1	1	0
	In England		4	4	0	0
	In Bangladesh....................		6	5	1	0
	Totals		10	9	1	0

SERIES RECORDS

Highest score	E	226	I. J. L. Trott at Lord's	2010
	B	108	Tamim Iqbal at Manchester................	2010
Best bowling	E	5-35	S. J. Harmison at Dhaka	2003-04
	B	6-77	Mehedi Hasan at Mirpur	2016-17
Highest total	E	599-6 dec	at Chittagong	2009-10
	B	419	at Mirpur	2009-10
Lowest total	E	164	at Mirpur	2016-17
	B	104	at Chester-le-Street	2005

AUSTRALIA v SOUTH AFRICA

Captains

Season	Australia	South Africa	T	A	SA	D
1902-03S	J. Darling	H. M. Taberer[1]	3	2	0	1
1910-11A	C. Hill	P. W. Sherwell	5	4	1	0
1912E	S. E. Gregory	F. Mitchell[2]	3	2	0	1
1921-22S	H. L. Collins	H. W. Taylor	3	1	0	2
1931-32A	W. M. Woodfull	H. B. Cameron	5	5	0	0
1935-36S	V. Y. Richardson	H. F. Wade	5	4	0	1
1949-50S	A. L. Hassett	A. D. Nourse	5	4	0	1
1952-53A	A. L. Hassett	J. E. Cheetham	5	2	2	1
1957-58S	I. D. Craig	C. B. van Ryneveld[3]	5	3	0	2
1963-64A	R. B. Simpson[4]	T. L. Goddard	5	1	1	3
1966-67S	R. B. Simpson	P. L. van der Merwe	5	1	3	1
1969-70S	W. M. Lawry	A. Bacher	4	0	4	0
1993-94A	A. R. Border	K. C. Wessels[5]	3	1	1	1
1993-94S	A. R. Border	K. C. Wessels	3	1	1	1
1996-97S	M. A. Taylor	W. J. Cronje	3	2	1	0
1997-98A	M. A. Taylor	W. J. Cronje	3	1	0	2
2001-02A	S. R. Waugh	S. M. Pollock	3	3	0	0
2001-02S	S. R. Waugh	M. V. Boucher	3	2	1	0
2005-06A	R. T. Ponting	G. C. Smith	3	2	0	1
2005-06S	R. T. Ponting	G. C. Smith[6]	3	3	0	0
2008-09A	R. T. Ponting	G. C. Smith	3	1	2	0
2008-09S	R. T. Ponting	G. C. Smith[7]	3	2	1	0
2011-12S	M. J. Clarke	G. C. Smith	2	1	1	0
2012-13A	M. J. Clarke	G. C. Smith	3	0	1	2
2013-14S	M. J. Clarke	G. C. Smith	3	2	1	0
2016-17A	S. P. D. Smith	F. du Plessis	3	1	2	0
2017-18S	**S. P. D. Smith[8]**	**F. du Plessis**	**4**	**1**	**3**	**0**

			T	A	SA	D
	In South Africa		54	29	16	9
	In Australia		41	21	10	10
	In England		3	2	0	1
	Totals		**98**	**52**	**26**	**20**

S   Played in South Africa.   A   Played in Australia.   E   Played in England.

The following deputised for the official touring captain or were appointed by the home authority for only a minor proportion of the series:
[1]J. H. Anderson (Second), E. A. Halliwell (Third). [2]L. J. Tancred (Third). [3]D. J. McGlew (First). [4]R. Benaud (First). [5]W. J. Cronje (Third). [6]J. H. Kallis (Third). [7]J. H. Kallis (Third). [8]T. D. Paine (Fourth).

SERIES RECORDS

Highest score	A	299*	D. G. Bradman at Adelaide	1931-32
	SA	274	R. G. Pollock at Durban	1969-70
Best bowling	A	8-61	M. G. Johnson at Perth	2008-09
	SA	7-23	H. J. Tayfield at Durban	1949-50
Highest total	A	652-7 dec	at Johannesburg	2001-02
	SA	651	at Cape Town	2008-09
Lowest total	A	47	at Cape Town	2011-12
	SA	36	at Melbourne	1931-32

AUSTRALIA v WEST INDIES

Captains

Season	Australia	West Indies	T	A	WI	T	D
1930-31A	W. M. Woodfull	G. C. Grant	5	4	1	0	0
1951-52A	A. L. Hassett[1]	J. D. C. Goddard[2]	5	4	1	0	0
1954-55W	I. W. Johnson	D. St E. Atkinson[3]	5	3	0	0	2

THE FRANK WORRELL TROPHY

Captains

Season	Australia	West Indies	T	A	WI	T	D	Held by
1960-61A	R. Benaud	F. M. M. Worrell	5	2	1	1	1	A
1964-65W	R. B. Simpson	G. S. Sobers	5	1	2	0	2	WI
1968-69A	W. M. Lawry	G. S. Sobers	5	3	1	0	1	A
1972-73W	I. M. Chappell	R. B. Kanhai	5	2	0	0	3	A
1975-76A	G. S. Chappell	C. H. Lloyd	6	5	1	0	0	A
1977-78W	R. B. Simpson	A. I. Kallicharran[4]	5	1	3	0	1	WI
1979-80A	G. S. Chappell	C. H. Lloyd[5]	3	0	2	0	1	WI
1981-82A	G. S. Chappell	C. H. Lloyd	3	1	1	0	1	WI
1983-84W	K. J. Hughes	C. H. Lloyd[6]	5	0	3	0	2	WI
1984-85A	A. R. Border[7]	C. H. Lloyd	5	1	3	0	1	WI
1988-89A	A. R. Border	I. V. A. Richards	5	1	3	0	1	WI
1990-91A	A. R. Border	I. V. A. Richards	5	1	2	0	2	WI
1992-93A	A. R. Border	R. B. Richardson	5	1	2	0	2	WI
1994-95W	M. A. Taylor	R. B. Richardson	4	2	1	0	1	A
1996-97A	M. A. Taylor	C. A. Walsh	5	3	2	0	0	A
1998-99W	S. R. Waugh	B. C. Lara	4	2	2	0	0	A
2000-01A	S. R. Waugh[8]	J. C. Adams	5	5	0	0	0	A
2002-03W	S. R. Waugh	B. C. Lara	4	3	1	0	0	A
2005-06A	R. T. Ponting	S. Chanderpaul	3	3	0	0	0	A
2007-08W	R. T. Ponting	R. R. Sarwan[9]	3	2	0	0	1	A
2009-10A	R. T. Ponting	C. H. Gayle	3	2	0	0	1	A
2011-12W	M. J. Clarke	D. J. G. Sammy	3	2	0	0	1	A
2015W	M. J. Clarke	D. Ramdin	2	2	0	0	0	A
2015-16A	S. P. D. Smith	J. O. Holder	3	2	0	0	1	A
	In Australia		66	37	18	1	10	
	In West Indies		50	21	14	0	15	
	Totals		116	58	32	1	25	

A Played in Australia.   W Played in West Indies.

The following deputised for the official touring captain or were appointed by the home authority for only a minor proportion of the series:

[1]A. R. Morris (Third). [2]J. B. Stollmeyer (Fifth). [3]J. B. Stollmeyer (Second and Third). [4]C. H. Lloyd (First and Second). [5]D. L. Murray (First). [6]I. V. A. Richards (Second). [7]K. J. Hughes (First and Second). [8]A. C. Gilchrist (Third). [9]C. H. Gayle (Third).

SERIES RECORDS

Highest score	A	269*	A. C. Voges at Hobart.....................	2015-16
	WI	277	B. C. Lara at Sydney	1992-93
Best bowling	A	8-71	G. D. McKenzie at Melbourne	1968-69
	WI	7-25	C. E. L. Ambrose at Perth	1992-93
Highest total	A	758-8 dec	at Kingston	1954-55
	WI	616	at Adelaide...........................	1968-69
Lowest total	A	76	at Perth..............................	1984-85
	WI	51	at Port-of-Spain.......................	1998-99

AUSTRALIA v NEW ZEALAND

Captains

Season	Australia	New Zealand	T	A	NZ	D
1945-46N	W. A. Brown	W. A. Hadlee	1	1	0	0
1973-74A	I. M. Chappell	B. E. Congdon	3	2	0	1
1973-74N	I. M. Chappell	B. E. Congdon	3	1	1	1
1976-77N	G. S. Chappell	G. M. Turner	2	1	0	1
1980-81A	G. S. Chappell	G. P. Howarth[1]	3	2	0	1
1981-82N	G. S. Chappell	G. P. Howarth	3	1	1	1

TRANS-TASMAN TROPHY

		Captains					
Season	Australia	New Zealand	T	A	NZ	D	Held by
1985-86A	A. R. Border	J. V. Coney	3	1	2	0	NZ
1985-86N	A. R. Border	J. V. Coney	3	0	1	2	NZ
1987-88A	A. R. Border	J. J. Crowe	3	1	0	2	A
1989-90A	A. R. Border	J. G. Wright	1	0	0	1	A
1989-90N	A. R. Border	J. G. Wright	1	0	1	0	NZ
1992-93N	A. R. Border	M. D. Crowe	3	1	1	1	NZ
1993-94A	A. R. Border	M. D. Crowe[2]	3	2	0	1	A
1997-98A	M. A. Taylor	S. P. Fleming	3	2	0	1	A
1999-2000N	S. R. Waugh	S. P. Fleming	3	3	0	0	A
2001-02A	S. R. Waugh	S. P. Fleming	3	0	0	3	A
2004-05A	R. T. Ponting	S. P. Fleming	2	2	0	0	A
2004-05N	R. T. Ponting	S. P. Fleming	3	2	0	1	A
2008-09A	R. T. Ponting	D. L. Vettori	2	2	0	0	A
2009-10N	R. T. Ponting	D. L. Vettori	2	2	0	0	A
2011-12A	M. J. Clarke	L. R. P. L. Taylor	2	1	1	0	A
2015-16A	S. P. D. Smith	B. B. McCullum	3	2	0	1	A
2015-16N	S. P. D. Smith	B. B. McCullum	2	2	0	0	A
	In Australia		31	17	3	11	
	In New Zealand		26	14	5	7	
	Totals		57	31	8	18	

A Played in Australia.   N Played in New Zealand.

The following deputised for the official touring captain: [1]M. G. Burgess (Second). [2]K. R. Rutherford (Second and Third).

SERIES RECORDS

Highest score	A	253	D. A. Warner at Perth	....	2015-16
	NZ	290	L. R. P. L. Taylor at Perth	....	2015-16
Best bowling	A	6-31	S. K. Warne at Hobart	....	1993-94
	NZ	9-52	R. J. Hadlee at Brisbane	....	1985-86
Highest total	A	607-6 dec	at Brisbane	....	1993-94
	NZ	624	at Perth	....	2015-16
Lowest total	A	103	at Auckland	....	1985-86
	NZ	42	at Wellington	....	1945-46

AUSTRALIA v INDIA

		Captains					
Season	Australia	India	T	A	I	T	D
1947-48A	D. G. Bradman	L. Amarnath	5	4	0	0	1
1956-57I	I. W. Johnson[1]	P. R. Umrigar	3	2	0	0	1
1959-60I	R. Benaud	G. S. Ramchand	5	2	1	0	2
1964-65I	R. B. Simpson	Nawab of Pataudi jnr	3	1	1	0	1
1967-68A	R. B. Simpson[2]	Nawab of Pataudi jnr[3]	4	4	0	0	0
1969-70I	W. M. Lawry	Nawab of Pataudi jnr	5	3	1	0	1
1977-78A	R. B. Simpson	B. S. Bedi	5	3	2	0	0
1979-80I	K. J. Hughes	S. M. Gavaskar	6	0	2	0	4
1980-81A	G. S. Chappell	S. M. Gavaskar	3	1	1	0	1
1985-86A	A. R. Border	Kapil Dev	3	0	0	0	3
1986-87I	A. R. Border	Kapil Dev	3	0	0	1	2
1991-92A	A. R. Border	M. Azharuddin	5	4	0	0	1

THE BORDER–GAVASKAR TROPHY

		Captains						
Season	*Australia*	*India*	*T*	*A*	*I*	*T*	*D*	*Held by*
1996-97*I*	M. A. Taylor	S. R. Tendulkar	1	0	1	0	0	I
1997-98*I*	M. A. Taylor	M. Azharuddin	3	1	2	0	0	I
1999-2000*A*	S. R. Waugh	S. R. Tendulkar	3	3	0	0	0	A
2000-01*I*	S. R. Waugh	S. C. Ganguly	3	1	2	0	0	I
2003-04*A*	S. R. Waugh	S. C. Ganguly	4	1	1	0	2	I
2004-05*I*	R. T. Ponting[4]	S. C. Ganguly[5]	4	2	1	0	1	A
2007-08*A*	R. T. Ponting	A. Kumble	4	2	1	0	1	A
2008-09*I*	R. T. Ponting	A. Kumble[6]	4	0	2	0	2	I
2010-11*I*	R. T. Ponting	M. S. Dhoni	2	0	2	0	0	I
2011-12*A*	M. J. Clarke	M. S. Dhoni[7]	4	4	0	0	0	A
2012-13*I*	M. J. Clarke[8]	M. S. Dhoni	4	0	4	0	0	I
2014-15*A*	M. J. Clarke[9]	M. S. Dhoni[10]	4	2	0	0	2	A
2016-17*I*	S. P. D. Smith	V. Kohli[11]	4	1	2	0	1	I
2018-19*A*	**T. D. Paine**	**V. Kohli**	**4**	**1**	**2**	**0**	**1**	**I**
	In Australia..................		48	29	7	0	12	
	In India.......................		50	13	21	1	15	
	Totals........................		98	42	28	1	27	

A Played in Australia.   I Played in India.

The following deputised for the official touring captain or were appointed by the home authority for only a minor proportion of the series:

[1]R. R. Lindwall (Second). [2]W. M. Lawry (Third and Fourth). [3]C. G. Borde (First). [4]A. C. Gilchrist (First, Second and Third). [5]R. Dravid (Third and Fourth). [6]M. S. Dhoni (Second and Fourth). [7]V. Sehwag (Fourth). [8]S. R. Watson (Fourth). [9]S. P. D. Smith (Second, Third and Fourth). [10]V. Kohli (First and Fourth). [11]A. M. Rahane (Fourth).

SERIES RECORDS

Highest score	A	329*	M. J. Clarke at Sydney	. . . .	2011-12
	I	281	V. V. S. Laxman at Kolkata.	. . . .	2000-01
Best bowling	A	8-50	N. M. Lyon at Bangalore.	. . . .	2016-17
	I	9-69	J. M. Patel at Kanpur.	. . . .	1959-60
Highest total	A	674	at Adelaide.	. . . .	1947-48
	I	705-7 dec	at Sydney.	. . . .	2003-04
Lowest total	A	83	at Melbourne.	. . . .	1980-81
	I	58	at Brisbane.	. . . .	1947-48

AUSTRALIA v PAKISTAN

		Captains					
Season	*Australia*	*Pakistan*	*T*	*A*	*P*	*D*	
1956-57*P*	I. W. Johnson	A. H. Kardar	1	0	1	0	
1959-60*P*	R. Benaud	Fazal Mahmood[1]	3	2	0	1	
1964-65*P*	R. B. Simpson	Hanif Mohammad	1	0	0	1	
1964-65*A*	R. B. Simpson	Hanif Mohammad	1	0	0	1	
1972-73*A*	I. M. Chappell	Intikhab Alam	3	3	0	0	
1976-77*A*	G. S. Chappell	Mushtaq Mohammad	3	1	1	1	
1978-79*A*	G. N. Yallop[2]	Mushtaq Mohammad	2	1	1	0	
1979-80*P*	G. S. Chappell	Javed Miandad	3	0	1	2	
1981-82*A*	G. S. Chappell	Javed Miandad	3	2	1	0	
1982-83*P*	K. J. Hughes	Imran Khan	3	0	3	0	
1983-84*A*	K. J. Hughes	Imran Khan[3]	5	2	0	3	
1988-89*P*	A. R. Border	Javed Miandad	3	0	1	2	
1989-90*A*	A. R. Border	Imran Khan	3	1	0	2	

Season	Australia	Captains Pakistan	T	A	P	D
1994-95*P*	M. A. Taylor	Salim Malik	3	0	1	2
1995-96*A*	M. A. Taylor	Wasim Akram	3	2	1	0
1998-99*P*	M. A. Taylor	Aamir Sohail	3	1	0	2
1999-2000*A*	S. R. Waugh	Wasim Akram	3	3	0	0
2002-03*S*/*U*	S. R. Waugh	Waqar Younis	3	3	0	0
2004-05*A*	R. T. Ponting	Inzamam-ul-Haq[4]	3	3	0	0
2009-10*A*	R. T. Ponting	Mohammad Yousuf	3	3	0	0
2010*E*	R. T. Ponting	Shahid Afridi[5]	2	1	1	0
2014-15*U*	M. J. Clarke	Misbah-ul-Haq	2	0	2	0
2016-17*A*	S. P. D. Smith	Misbah-ul-Haq	3	3	0	0
2018-19*U*	**T. D. Paine**	**Sarfraz Ahmed**	**2**	**0**	**1**	**1**
In Pakistan			20	3	7	10
In Australia....................			35	24	4	7
In Sri Lanka			1	1	0	0
In United Arab Emirates.............			**6**	**2**	**3**	**1**
In England			2	1	1	0
Totals...........................			**64**	**31**	**15**	**18**

P   Played in Pakistan.   A   Played in Australia.
S/U   First Test played in Sri Lanka, Second and Third Tests in United Arab Emirates.
U   Played in United Arab Emirates.   E   Played in England.

The following deputised for the official touring captain or were appointed by the home authority for only a minor proportion of the series:
[1]Imtiaz Ahmed (Second). [2]K. J. Hughes (Second). [3]Zaheer Abbas (First, Second and Third).
[4]Yousuf Youhana *later known as Mohammad Yousuf* (Second and Third). [5]Salman Butt (Second).

SERIES RECORDS

Highest score	A	334*	M. A. Taylor at Peshawar	1998-99
	P	237	Salim Malik at Rawalpindi	1994-95
Best bowling	A	8-24	G. D. McGrath at Perth	2004-05
	P	9-86	Sarfraz Nawaz at Melbourne................	1978-79
Highest total	A	624-8 dec	at Melbourne..........................	2016-17
	P	624	at Adelaide...........................	1983-84
Lowest total	A	80	at Karachi............................	1956-57
	P	53	at Sharjah............................	2002-03

AUSTRALIA v SRI LANKA

Season	Australia	Captains Sri Lanka	T	A	SL	D
1982-83*S*	G. S. Chappell	L. R. D. Mendis	1	1	0	0
1987-88*A*	A. R. Border	R. S. Madugalle	1	1	0	0
1989-90*A*	A. R. Border	A. Ranatunga	2	1	0	1
1992-93*S*	A. R. Border	A. Ranatunga	3	1	0	2
1995-96*A*	M. A. Taylor	A. Ranatunga[1]	3	3	0	0
1999-2000*S*	S. R. Waugh	S. T. Jayasuriya	3	0	1	2
2003-04*S*	R. T. Ponting	H. P. Tillekeratne	3	3	0	0
2004*A*	R. T. Ponting[2]	M. S. Atapattu	2	1	0	1

THE WARNE–MURALITHARAN TROPHY

		Captains						
Season	Australia	Sri Lanka	T	A	SL	D	Held by
2007-08A	R. T. Ponting	D. P. M. D. Jayawardene	2	2	0	0	A
2011-12S	M. J. Clarke	T. M. Dilshan	3	1	0	2	A
2012-13A	M. J. Clarke	D. P. M. D. Jayawardene	3	3	0	0	A
2016S	S. P. D. Smith	A. D. Mathews	3	0	3	0	SL
	In Australia...................		13	11	0	2	
	In Sri Lanka...................		16	6	4	6	
	Totals........................		29	17	4	8	

A   Played in Australia.   S   Played in Sri Lanka.

The following deputised for the official touring captain or was appointed by the home authority for only a minor proportion of the series:
   [1]P. A. de Silva (Third). [2]A. C. Gilchrist (First).

SERIES RECORDS

Highest score	A	219	M. J. Slater at Perth........................	1995-96
	SL	192	K. C. Sangakkara at Hobart................	2007-08
Best bowling	A	7-39	M. S. Kasprowicz at Darwin................	2004
	SL	7-64	H. M. R. K. B. Herath at Colombo (SSC).....	2016
Highest total	A	617-5 dec	at Perth....................................	1995-96
	SL	547-8 dec	at Colombo (SSC).........................	1992-93
Lowest total	A	106	at Galle....................................	2016
	SL	97	at Darwin..................................	2004

AUSTRALIA v ZIMBABWE

		Captains				
Season	Australia	Zimbabwe	T	A	Z	D
1999-2000Z	S. R. Waugh	A. D. R. Campbell	1	1	0	0
2003-04A	S. R. Waugh	H. H. Streak	2	2	0	0
	In Australia...................		2	2	0	0
	In Zimbabwe...................		1	1	0	0
	Totals........................		3	3	0	0

A   Played in Australia.   Z   Played in Zimbabwe.

SERIES RECORDS

Highest score	A	380	M. L. Hayden at Perth...................	2003-04
	Z	118	S. V. Carlisle at Sydney..................	2003-04
Best bowling	A	6-65	S. M. Katich at Sydney...................	2003-04
	Z	6-121	R. W. Price at Sydney....................	2003-04
Highest total	A	735-6 dec	at Perth....................................	2003-04
	Z	321	at Perth....................................	2003-04
Lowest total	A	403	at Sydney..................................	2003-04
	Z	194	at Harare..................................	1999-2000

AUSTRALIA v BANGLADESH

Season	Australia	*Captains* Bangladesh	T	A	B	D
2003*A*	S. R. Waugh	Khaled Mahmud	2	2	0	0
2005-06*B*	R. T. Ponting	Habibul Bashar	2	2	0	0
2017-18*B*	S. P. D. Smith	Mushfiqur Rahim	2	1	1	0
	In Australia......................		2	2	0	0
	In Bangladesh....................		4	3	1	0
	Totals		6	5	1	0

A   Played in Australia.   B   Played in Bangladesh.

SERIES RECORDS

Highest score	A	201*	J. N. Gillespie at Chittagong	2005-06
	B	138	Shahriar Nafees at Fatullah	2005-06
Best bowling	A	8-108	S. C. G. MacGill at Fatullah	2005-06
	B	5-62	Mohammad Rafique at Fatullah..............	2005-06
Highest total	A	581-4 dec	at Chittagong	2005-06
	B	427	at Fatullah	2005-06
Lowest total	A	217	at Mirpur	2017-18
	B	97	at Darwin...............................	2003

AUSTRALIA v ICC WORLD XI

Season	Australia	ICC World XI	T	A	ICC	D
2005-06*A*	R. T. Ponting	G. C. Smith	1	1	0	0

A   Played in Australia.

SERIES RECORDS

Highest score	A	111	M. L. Hayden at Sydney	2005-06
	Wld	76	V. Sehwag at Sydney........................	2005-06
Best bowling	A	5-43	S. C. G. MacGill at Sydney	2005-06
	Wld	4-59	A. Flintoff at Sydney	2005-06
Highest total	A	345	at Sydney	2005-06
	Wld	190	at Sydney	2005-06
Lowest total	A	199	at Sydney	2005-06
	Wld	144	at Sydney	2005-06

SOUTH AFRICA v WEST INDIES

Season	South Africa	*Captains* West Indies	T	SA	WI	D
1991-92*W*	K. C. Wessels	R. B. Richardson	1	0	1	0
1998-99*S*	W. J. Cronje	B. C. Lara	5	5	0	0

SIR VIVIAN RICHARDS TROPHY

Captains

Season	South Africa	West Indies	T	SA	WI	D	Held by
2000-01W	S. M. Pollock	C. L. Hooper	5	2	1	2	SA
2003-04S	G. C. Smith	B. C. Lara	4	3	0	1	SA
2004-05W	G. C. Smith	S. Chanderpaul	4	2	0	2	SA
2007-08 S	G. C. Smith	C. H. Gayle[1]	3	2	1	0	SA
2010W	G. C. Smith	C. H. Gayle	3	2	0	1	SA
2014-15S	H. M. Amla	D. Ramdin	3	2	0	1	SA
	In South Africa		15	12	1	2	
	In West Indies		13	6	2	5	
	Totals		28	18	3	7	

S   Played in South Africa.   W   Played in West Indies.

The following deputised for the official touring captain:
[1]D. J. Bravo (Third).

SERIES RECORDS

Highest score	SA	208	H. M. Amla at Centurion..................	2014-15
	WI	317	C. H. Gayle at St John's	2004-05
Best bowling	SA	7-37	M. Ntini at Port-of-Spain.................	2004-05
	WI	7-84	F. A. Rose at Durban.....................	1998-99
Highest total	SA	658-9 dec	at Durban	2003-04
	WI	747	at St John's	2004-05
Lowest total	SA	141	at Kingston	2000-01
	WI	102	at Port-of-Spain.........................	2010

SOUTH AFRICA v NEW ZEALAND

Captains

Season	South Africa	New Zealand	T	SA	NZ	D
1931-32N	H. B. Cameron	M. L. Page	2	2	0	0
1952-53N	J. E. Cheetham	W. M. Wallace	2	1	0	1
1953-54S	J. E. Cheetham	G. O. Rabone[1]	5	4	0	1
1961-62S	D. J. McGlew	J. R. Reid	5	2	2	1
1963-64N	T. L. Goddard	J. R. Reid	3	0	0	3
1994-95S	W. J. Cronje	K. R. Rutherford	3	2	1	0
1994-95N	W. J. Cronje	K. R. Rutherford	1	1	0	0
1998-99N	W. J. Cronje	D. J. Nash	3	1	0	2
2000-01S	S. M. Pollock	S. P. Fleming	3	2	0	1
2003-04N	G. C. Smith	S. P. Fleming	3	1	1	1
2005-06S	G. C. Smith	S. P. Fleming	3	2	0	1
2007-08S	G. C. Smith	D. L. Vettori	2	2	0	0
2011-12N	G. C. Smith	L. R. P. L. Taylor	3	1	0	2
2012-13S	G. C. Smith	B. B. McCullum	2	2	0	0
2016S	F. du Plessis	K. S. Williamson	2	1	0	1
2016-17N	F. du Plessis	K. S. Williamson	3	1	0	2
	In New Zealand		20	8	1	11
	In South Africa..................		25	17	3	5
	Totals		45	25	4	16

N   Played in New Zealand.   S   Played in South Africa.

The following deputised for the official touring captain:
[1]B. Sutcliffe (Fourth and Fifth).

SERIES RECORDS

Highest score	SA	275*	D. J. Cullinan at Auckland	1998-99
	NZ	262	S. P. Fleming at Cape Town	2005-06
Best bowling	SA	8-53	G. B. Lawrence at Johannesburg.	1961-62
	NZ	6-60	J. R. Reid at Dunedin	1963-64
Highest total	SA	621-5 dec	at Auckland	1998-99
	NZ	595	at Auckland	2003-04
Lowest total	SA	148	at Johannesburg	1953-54
	NZ	45	at Cape Town	2012-13

SOUTH AFRICA v INDIA

		Captains					
Season	*South Africa*		*India*	*T*	*SA*	*I*	*D*
1992-93*S*	K. C. Wessels	M. Azharuddin		4	1	0	3
1996-97*I*	W. J. Cronje	S. R. Tendulkar		3	1	2	0
1996-97*S*	W. J. Cronje	S. R. Tendulkar		3	2	0	1
1999-2000*I*	W. J. Cronje	S. R. Tendulkar		2	2	0	0
2001-02*S*†	S. M. Pollock	S. C. Ganguly		2	1	0	1
2004-05*I*	G. C. Smith	S. C. Ganguly		2	0	1	1
2006-07*S*	G. C. Smith	R. Dravid		3	2	1	0
2007-08*I*	G. C. Smith	A. Kumble[1]		3	1	1	1
2009-10*I*	G. C. Smith	M. S. Dhoni		2	1	1	0
2010-11*S*	G. C. Smith	M. S. Dhoni		3	1	1	1
2013-14*S*	G. C. Smith	M. S. Dhoni		2	1	0	1

THE FREEDOM TROPHY

		Captains						
Season	*South Africa*		*India*	*T*	*SA*	*I*	*D*	*Held by*
2015-16*I*	H. M. Amla		V. Kohli	4	0	3	1	I
2017-18*S*	**F. du Plessis**		**V. Kohli**	**3**	**2**	**1**	**0**	**SA**
	In South Africa			**20**	**10**	**3**	**7**	
	In India			16	5	8	3	
	Totals			**36**	**15**	**11**	**10**	

S   Played in South Africa.   I   Played in India.

†   *The Third Test at Centurion was stripped of its official status by the ICC after a disciplinary dispute and is excluded.*

The following was appointed by the home authority for only a minor proportion of the series:
  [1]M. S. Dhoni (Third).

SERIES RECORDS

Highest score	SA	253*	H. M. Amla at Nagpur	2009-10
	I	319	V. Sehwag at Chennai	2007-08
Best bowling	SA	8-64	L. Klusener at Calcutta	1996-97
	I	7-66	R. Ashwin at Nagpur	2015-16
Highest total	SA	620-4 dec	at Centurion	2010-11
	I	643-6 dec	at Kolkata	2009-10
Lowest total	SA	79	at Nagpur	2015-16
	I	66	at Durban	1996-97

SOUTH AFRICA v PAKISTAN

		Captains				
Season	*South Africa*	*Pakistan*	*T*	*SA*	*P*	*D*
1994-95*S*	W. J. Cronje	Salim Malik	1	1	0	0
1997-98*P*	W. J. Cronje	Saeed Anwar	3	1	0	2
1997-98*S*	W. J. Cronje[1]	Rashid Latif[2]	3	1	1	1
2002-03*S*	S. M. Pollock	Waqar Younis	2	2	0	0
2003-04*P*	G. C. Smith	Inzamam-ul-Haq[3]	2	0	1	1
2006-07*S*	G. C. Smith	Inzamam-ul-Haq	3	2	1	0
2007-08*P*	G. C. Smith	Shoaib Malik	2	1	0	1
2010-11*U*	G. C. Smith	Misbah-ul-Haq	2	0	0	2
2012-13*S*	G. C. Smith	Misbah-ul-Haq	3	3	0	0
2013-14*U*	G. C. Smith	Misbah-ul-Haq	2	1	1	0
2018-19*S*	**F. du Plessis**[4]	**Sarfraz Ahmed**	**3**	**3**	**0**	**0**
	In South Africa...................		15	12	2	1
	In Pakistan.......................		7	2	1	4
	In United Arab Emirates		4	1	1	2
	Totals........................		26	15	4	7

S   Played in South Africa.   P   Played in Pakistan.   U   Played in United Arab Emirates.

The following deputised for the official touring captain or were appointed by the home authority for only a minor proportion of the series:
[1]G. Kirsten (First). [2]Aamir Sohail (First and Second). [3]Yousuf Youhana *later known as Mohammad Yousuf* (First). [4]D. Elgar (Third).

SERIES RECORDS

Highest score	SA	278*	A. B. de Villiers at Abu Dhabi	2010-11
	P	146	Khurram Manzoor at Abu Dhabi.............	2013-14
Best bowling	SA	7-29	K. J. Abbott at Centurion	2012-13
	P {	6-78	Mushtaq Ahmed at Durban.................	1997-98
		6-78	Waqar Younis at Port Elizabeth	1997-98
Highest total	SA	620-7 dec	at Cape Town	2002-03
	P	456	at Rawalpindi	1997-98
Lowest total	SA	124	at Port Elizabeth	2006-07
	P	49	at Johannesburg.......................	2012-13

SOUTH AFRICA v SRI LANKA

		Captains				
Season	*South Africa*	*Sri Lanka*	*T*	*SA*	*SL*	*D*
1993-94*SL*	K. C. Wessels	A. Ranatunga	3	1	0	2
1997-98*SA*	W. J. Cronje	A. Ranatunga	2	2	0	0
2000*SL*	S. M. Pollock	S. T. Jayasuriya	3	1	1	1
2000-01*SA*	S. M. Pollock	S. T. Jayasuriya	3	2	0	1
2002-03*SA*	S. M. Pollock	S. T. Jayasuriya[1]	2	2	0	0
2004*SL*	G. C. Smith	M. S. Atapattu	2	0	1	1
2006*SL*	A. G. Prince	D. P. M. D. Jayawardene	2	0	2	0
2011-12*SA*	G. C. Smith	T. M. Dilshan	3	2	1	0
2014*SL*	H. M. Amla	A. D. Mathews	2	1	0	1

Season	South Africa	*Captains* Sri Lanka	T	SA	SL	D
2016-17*SA*	F. du Plessis	A. D. Mathews	3	3	0	0
2018*SL*	**F. du Plessis**	**R. A. S. Lakmal**	**2**	**0**	**2**	**0**
	In South Africa............................		13	11	1	1
	In Sri Lanka		**14**	**3**	**6**	**5**
	Totals............................		27	14	7	6

SA   Played in South Africa.   SL   Played in Sri Lanka.

The following deputised for the official captain:
   [1]M. S. Atapattu (Second).

SERIES RECORDS

Highest score	SA	224	J. H. Kallis at Cape Town	2011-12
	SL	374	D. P. M. D. Jayawardene at Colombo (SSC)...	2006
Best bowling	SA	**9-129**	**K. A. Maharaj at Colombo (SSC)**	**2018**
	SL	7-84	M. Muralitharan at Galle	2000
Highest total	SA	580-4 dec	at Cape Town.................	2011-12
	SL	756-5 dec	at Colombo (SSC)	2006
Lowest total	SA	**73**	**at Galle**	**2018**
	SL	95	at Cape Town...........................	2000-01

SOUTH AFRICA v ZIMBABWE

Season	South Africa	*Captains* Zimbabwe	T	SA	Z	D
1995-96*Z*	W. J. Cronje	A. Flower	1	1	0	0
1999-2000*S*	W. J. Cronje	A. D. R. Campbell	1	1	0	0
1999-2000*Z*	W. J. Cronje	A. Flower	1	1	0	0
2001-02*Z*	S. M. Pollock	H. H. Streak	2	1	0	1
2004-05*S*	G. C. Smith	T. Taibu	2	2	0	0
2014-15*Z*	H. M. Amla	B. R. M. Taylor	1	1	0	0
2017-18*S*	A. B. de Villiers	A. G. Cremer	1	1	0	0
	In Zimbabwe		5	4	0	1
	In South Africa...................		4	4	0	0
	Totals		9	8	0	1

S   Played in South Africa.   Z   Played in Zimbabwe.

SERIES RECORDS

Highest score	SA	220	G. Kirsten at Harare.....................	2001-02
	Z	199*	A. Flower at Harare.....................	2001-02
Best bowling	SA	8-71	A. A. Donald at Harare	1995-96
	Z	5-101	B. C. Strang at Harare	1995-96
Highest total	SA	600-3 dec	at Harare	2001-02
	Z	419-9 dec	at Bulawayo.......................	2001-02
Lowest total	SA	346	at Harare	1995-96
	Z	54	at Cape Town.....................	2004-05

SOUTH AFRICA v BANGLADESH

		Captains					
Season	*South Africa*		*Bangladesh*	*T*	*SA*	*B*	*D*
2002-03*S*	S. M. Pollock[1]		Khaled Mashud	2	2	0	0
2003*B*	G. C. Smith		Khaled Mahmud	2	2	0	0
2007-08*B*	G. C. Smith		Mohammad Ashraful	2	2	0	0
2008-09*S*	G. C. Smith		Mohammad Ashraful	2	2	0	0
2015*B*	H. M. Amla		Mushfiqur Rahim	2	0	0	2
2017-18*S*	F. du Plessis		Mushfiqur Rahim	2	2	0	0
	In South Africa..................			6	6	0	0
	In Bangladesh...................			6	4	0	2
	Totals..........................			12	10	0	2

S   Played in South Africa.   B   Played in Bangladesh.

The following deputised for the official captain:
[1]M. V. Boucher (First).

SERIES RECORDS

Highest score	SA	232	G. C. Smith at Chittagong	2007-08
	B	77	Mominul Haque at Potchefstroom...........	2017-18
Best bowling	SA	5-19	M. Ntini at East London	2002-03
	B	6-27	Shahadat Hossain at Mirpur................	2007-08
Highest total	SA	583-7 dec	at Chittagong	2007-08
	B	326	at Chittagong	2015
Lowest total	SA	170	at Mirpur	2007-08
	B	90	at Potchefstroom	2017-18

WEST INDIES v NEW ZEALAND

		Captains					
Season	*West Indies*		*New Zealand*	*T*	*WI*	*NZ*	*D*
1951-52*N*	J. D. C. Goddard		B. Sutcliffe	2	1	0	1
1955-56*N*	D. St E. Atkinson		J. R. Reid[1]	4	3	1	0
1968-69*N*	G. S. Sobers		G. T. Dowling	3	1	1	1
1971-72*N*	G. S. Sobers		G. T. Dowling[2]	5	0	0	5
1979-80*N*	C. H. Lloyd		G. P. Howarth	3	0	1	2
1984-85*N*	I. V. A. Richards		G. P. Howarth	4	2	0	2
1986-87*N*	I. V. A. Richards		J. V. Coney	3	1	1	1
1994-95*N*	C. A. Walsh		K. R. Rutherford	2	1	0	1
1995-96*N*	C. A. Walsh		L. K. Germon	2	1	0	1
1999-2000*N*	B. C. Lara		S. P. Fleming	2	0	2	0
2002*W*	C. L. Hooper		S. P. Fleming	2	0	1	1
2005-06*N*	S. Chanderpaul		S. P. Fleming	3	0	2	1
2008-09*N*	C. H. Gayle		D. L. Vettori	2	0	0	2
2012*W*	D. J. G. Sammy		L. R. P. L. Taylor	2	2	0	0
2013-14*N*	D. J. G. Sammy		B. B. McCullum	3	0	2	1
2014*W*	D. Ramdin		B. B. McCullum	3	1	2	0

Season	West Indies	*Captains* New Zealand	T	WI	NZ	D
2017-18*N*	J. O. Holder[3]	K. S. Williamson	2	0	2	0
		In New Zealand..................	29	7	12	10
		In West Indies...................	18	6	3	9
		Totals	47	13	15	19

N Played in New Zealand.   W Played in West Indies.

The following deputised for the official touring captain or were appointed by the home authority for only a minor proportion of the series:
[1]H. B. Cave (First). [2]B. E. Congdon (Third, Fourth and Fifth). [3]K. C. Brathwaite (Second).

SERIES RECORDS

Highest score	WI	258	S. M. Nurse at Christchurch		1968-69
	NZ	259	G. M. Turner at Georgetown.............		1971-72
Best bowling	WI	7-37	C. A. Walsh at Wellington		1994-95
	NZ	7-27	C. L. Cairns at Hamilton		1999-2000
Highest total	WI	660-5 dec	at Wellington........................		1994-95
	NZ	609-9 dec	at Dunedin (University).................		2013-14
Lowest total	WI	77	at Auckland		1955-56
	NZ	74	at Dunedin...........................		1955-56

WEST INDIES v INDIA

Season	West Indies	*Captains* India	T	WI	I	D
1948-49*I*	J. D. C. Goddard	L. Amarnath	5	1	0	4
1952-53*W*	J. B. Stollmeyer	V. S. Hazare	5	1	0	4
1958-59*I*	F. C. M. Alexander	Ghulam Ahmed[1]	5	3	0	2
1961-62*W*	F. M. M. Worrell	N. J. Contractor[2]	5	5	0	0
1966-67*I*	G. S. Sobers	Nawab of Pataudi jnr	3	2	0	1
1970-71*W*	G. S. Sobers	A. L. Wadekar	5	0	1	4
1974-75*I*	C. H. Lloyd	Nawab of Pataudi jnr[3]	5	3	2	0
1975-76*W*	C. H. Lloyd	B. S. Bedi	4	2	1	1
1978-79*I*	A. I. Kallicharran	S. M. Gavaskar	6	0	1	5
1982-83*W*	C. H. Lloyd	Kapil Dev	5	2	0	3
1983-84*I*	C. H. Lloyd	Kapil Dev	6	3	0	3
1987-88*I*	I. V. A. Richards	D. B. Vengsarkar[4]	4	1	1	2
1988-89*W*	I. V. A. Richards	D. B. Vengsarkar	4	3	0	1
1994-95*I*	C. A. Walsh	M. Azharuddin	3	1	1	1
1996-97*W*	C. A. Walsh[5]	S. R. Tendulkar	5	1	0	4
2001-02*W*	C. L. Hooper	S. C. Ganguly	5	2	1	2
2002-03*I*	C. L. Hooper	S. C. Ganguly	3	0	2	1
2005-06*W*	B. C. Lara	R. Dravid	4	0	1	3
2011*W*	D. J. G. Sammy	M. S. Dhoni	3	0	1	2
2011-12*I*	D. J. G. Sammy	M. S. Dhoni	3	0	2	1
2013-14*I*	D. J. G. Sammy	M. S. Dhoni	2	0	2	0

Captains

Season	West Indies	India	T	WI	I	D
2016W	J. O. Holder	V. Kohli	4	0	2	2
2018-19*I*	**J. O. Holder**[6]	**V. Kohli**	**2**	**0**	**2**	**0**
	In India		47	14	13	20
	In West Indies		49	16	7	26
	Totals		96	30	20	46

I   Played in India.   W   Played in West Indies.

The following deputised for the official touring captain or were appointed by the home authority for only a minor proportion of the series:
[1]P. R. Umrigar (First), M. H. Mankad (Fourth), H. R. Adhikari (Fifth). [2]Nawab of Pataudi jnr (Third, Fourth and Fifth). [3]S. Venkataraghavan (Second). [4]R. J. Shastri (Fourth). [5]B. C. Lara (Third). [6]K. C. Brathwaite (First).

SERIES RECORDS

Highest score	WI	256	R. B. Kanhai at Calcutta		1958-59
	I	236*	S. M. Gavaskar at Madras		1983-84
Best bowling	WI	9-95	J. M. Noreiga at Port-of-Spain		1970-71
	I	9-83	Kapil Dev at Ahmedabad		1983-84
Highest total	WI	644-8 dec	at Delhi		1958-59
	I	**649-9 dec**	**at Rajkot. . . . .**		**2018-19**
Lowest total	WI	103	at Kingston		2005-06
	I	75	at Delhi		1987-88

WEST INDIES v PAKISTAN

Captains

Season	West Indies	Pakistan	T	WI	P	D
1957-58W	F. C. M. Alexander	A. H. Kardar	5	3	1	1
1958-59P	F. C. M. Alexander	Fazal Mahmood	3	1	2	0
1974-75P	C. H. Lloyd	Intikhab Alam	2	0	0	2
1976-77W	C. H. Lloyd	Mushtaq Mohammad	5	2	1	2
1980-81P	C. H. Lloyd	Javed Miandad	4	1	0	3
1986-87P	I. V. A. Richards	Imran Khan	3	1	1	1
1987-88W	I. V. A. Richards[1]	Imran Khan	3	1	1	1
1990-91P	D. L. Haynes	Imran Khan	3	1	1	1
1992-93W	R. B. Richardson	Wasim Akram	3	2	0	1
1997-98P	C. A. Walsh	Wasim Akram	3	0	3	0
1999-2000W	J. C. Adams	Moin Khan	3	1	0	2
2001-02U	C. L. Hooper	Waqar Younis	2	0	2	0
2004-05W	S. Chanderpaul	Inzamam-ul-Haq[2]	2	1	1	0
2006-07P	B. C. Lara	Inzamam-ul-Haq	3	0	2	1
2010-11W	D. J. G. Sammy	Misbah-ul-Haq	2	1	1	0
2016-17U	J. O. Holder	Misbah-ul-Haq	3	1	2	0
2016-17W	J. O. Holder	Misbah-ul-Haq	3	1	2	0
	In West Indies		26	12	7	7
	In Pakistan		21	4	9	8
	In United Arab Emirates		5	1	4	0
	Totals		52	17	20	15

P   Played in Pakistan.   W   Played in West Indies.   U   Played in United Arab Emirates.

The following were appointed by the home authority or deputised for the official touring captain for a minor proportion of the series:
[1]C. G. Greenidge (First). [2]Younis Khan (First).

SERIES RECORDS

Highest score	WI	365*	G. S. Sobers at Kingston	1957-58
	P	337	Hanif Mohammad at Bridgetown	1957-58
Best bowling	WI	8-29	C. E. H. Croft at Port-of-Spain	1976-77
	P	7-80	Imran Khan at Georgetown.	1987-88
Highest total	WI	790-3 dec	at Kingston	1957-58
	P	657-8 dec	at Bridgetown	1957-58
Lowest total	WI	53	at Faisalabad	1986-87
	P	77	at Lahore	1986-87

WEST INDIES v SRI LANKA

		Captains					
Season	West Indies		Sri Lanka	T	WI	SL	D
1993-94S	R. B. Richardson		A. Ranatunga	1	0	0	1
1996-97W	C. A. Walsh		A. Ranatunga	2	1	0	1
2001-02S	C. L. Hooper		S. T. Jayasuriya	3	0	3	0
2003W	B. C. Lara		H. P. Tillekeratne	2	1	0	1
2005S	S. Chanderpaul		M. S. Atapattu	2	0	2	0
2007-08W	C. H. Gayle		D. P. M. D. Jayawardene	2	1	1	0
2010-11S	D. J. G. Sammy		K. C. Sangakkara	3	0	0	3

THE SOBERS–TISSERA TROPHY

		Captains						
Season	West Indies		Sri Lanka	T	WI	SL	D	Held by
2015-16S	J. O. Holder		A. D. Mathews	2	0	2	0	SL
2018W	**J. O. Holder**		**L. D. Chandimal[1]**	**3**	**1**	**1**	**1**	**SL**
	In West Indies.			**9**	**4**	**2**	**3**	
	In Sri Lanka			11	0	7	4	
	Totals.			**20**	**4**	**9**	**7**	

W Played in West Indies. S Played in Sri Lanka.

The following deputised for the official touring captain:
  [1]R. A. S. Lakmal (Third).

SERIES RECORDS

Highest score	WI	333	C. H. Gayle at Galle	2010-11
	SL	204*	H. P. Tillekeratne at Colombo (SSC)	2001-02
Best bowling	WI	**8-62**	**S. T. Gabriel at Gros Islet**	**2018**
	SL	8-46	M. Muralitharan at Kandy.	2005
Highest total	WI	580-9 dec	at Galle	2010-11
	SL	627-9 dec	at Colombo (SSC)	2001-02
Lowest total	WI	**93**	**at Bridgetown**.	**2018**
	SL	150	at Kandy	2005

WEST INDIES v ZIMBABWE

		Captains					
Season	West Indies		Zimbabwe	T	WI	Z	D
1999-2000W	J. C. Adams		A. Flower	2	2	0	0

THE CLIVE LLOYD TROPHY

		Captains					
Season	*West Indies*	*Zimbabwe*	*T*	*WI*	*Z*	*D*	*Held by*
2001Z	C. L. Hooper	H. H. Streak	2	1	0	1	WI
2003-04Z	B. C. Lara	H. H. Streak	2	1	0	1	WI
2012-13W	D. J. G. Sammy	B. R. M. Taylor	2	2	0	0	WI
2017-18Z	J. O. Holder	A. G. Cremer	2	1	0	1	WI
	In West Indies		4	4	0	0	
	In Zimbabwe		6	3	0	3	
	Totals		10	7	0	3	

W   Played in West Indies.   Z   Played in Zimbabwe.

SERIES RECORDS

Highest score	WI	191	B. C. Lara at Bulawayo		2003-04
	Z	147	H. Masakadza at Bulawayo		2017-18
Best bowling	WI	6-49	S. Shillingford at Bridgetown		2012-13
	Z	6-73	R. W. Price at Harare		2003-04
Highest total	WI	559-6 dec	at Bulawayo		2001
	Z	563-9 dec	at Harare		2001
Lowest total	WI	128	at Bulawayo		2003-04
	Z	63	at Port-of-Spain		1999-2000

WEST INDIES v BANGLADESH

		Captains				
Season	*West Indies*	*Bangladesh*	*T*	*WI*	*B*	*D*
2002-03B	R. D. Jacobs	Khaled Mashud	2	2	0	0
2003-04W	B. C. Lara	Habibul Bashar	2	1	0	1
2009W	F. L. Reifer	Mashrafe bin Mortaza[1]	2	0	2	0
2011-12B	D. J. G. Sammy	Mushfiqur Rahim	2	1	0	1
2012-13B	D. J. G. Sammy	Mushfiqur Rahim	2	2	0	0
2014-15W	D. Ramdin	Mushfiqur Rahim	2	2	0	0
2018W	**J. O. Holder**	**Shakib Al Hasan**	**2**	**2**	**0**	**0**
2018-19B	**K. C. Brathwaite**	**Shakib Al Hasan**	**2**	**0**	**2**	**0**
	In West Indies		8	5	2	1
	In Bangladesh		8	5	2	1
	Totals		**16**	**10**	**4**	**2**

B   Played in Bangladesh.   W   Played in West Indies.

The following deputised for the official touring captain for a minor proportion of the series:
  [1]Shakib Al Hasan (Second).

SERIES RECORDS

Highest score	WI	261*	R. R. Sarwan at Kingston		2003-04
	B	**136**	**Mahmudullah at Mirpur**		**2018-19**
Best bowling	WI	6-3	J. J. C. Lawson at Dhaka		2002-03
	B	**7-58**	**Mehedi Hasan at Mirpur**		**2018-19**
Highest total	WI	648-9 dec	at Khulna		2012-13
	B	556	at Mirpur		2012-13
Lowest total	WI	111	**at Mirpur**		**2018-19**
	B	**43**	**at North Sound**		**2018**

NEW ZEALAND v INDIA

	Captains					
Season	*New Zealand*	*India*	*T*	*NZ*	*I*	*D*
1955-56*I*	H. B. Cave	P. R. Umrigar[1]	5	0	2	3
1964-65*I*	J. R. Reid	Nawab of Pataudi jnr	4	0	1	3
1967-68*N*	G. T. Dowling[2]	Nawab of Pataudi jnr	4	1	3	0
1969-70*I*	G. T. Dowling	Nawab of Pataudi jnr	3	1	1	1
1975-76*N*	G. M. Turner	B. S. Bedi[3]	3	1	1	1
1976-77*I*	G. M. Turner	B. S. Bedi	3	0	2	1
1980-81*N*	G. P. Howarth	S. M. Gavaskar	3	1	0	2
1988-89*I*	J. G. Wright	D. B. Vengsarkar	3	1	2	0
1989-90*N*	J. G. Wright	M. Azharuddin	3	1	0	2
1993-94*N*	K. R. Rutherford	M. Azharuddin	1	0	0	1
1995-96*I*	L. K. Germon	M. Azharuddin	3	0	1	2
1998-99*N*†	S. P. Fleming	M. Azharuddin	2	1	0	1
1999-2000*I*	S. P. Fleming	S. R. Tendulkar	3	0	1	2
2002-03*N*	S. P. Fleming	S. C. Ganguly	2	2	0	0
2003-04*I*	S. P. Fleming	S. C. Ganguly[4]	2	0	0	2
2008-09*N*	D. L. Vettori	M. S. Dhoni[5]	3	0	1	2
2010-11*I*	D. L. Vettori	M. S. Dhoni	3	0	1	2
2012-13*I*	L. R. P. L. Taylor	M. S. Dhoni	2	0	2	0
2013-14*N*	B. B. McCullum	M. S. Dhoni	2	1	0	1
2016-17*I*	K. S. Williamson[6]	V. Kohli	3	0	3	0
	In India................................		34	2	16	16
	In New Zealand		23	8	5	10
	Totals..................................		57	10	21	26

I   Played in India.   N   Played in New Zealand.

†   *The First Test at Dunedin was abandoned without a ball being bowled and is excluded.*

The following deputised for the official touring captain or were appointed by the home authority for a minor proportion of the series:
[1]Ghulam Ahmed (First). [2]B. W. Sinclair (First). [3]S. M. Gavaskar (First). [4]R. Dravid (Second). [5]V. Sehwag (Second). [6]L. R. P. L. Taylor (Second).

SERIES RECORDS

Highest score	*NZ*	302	B. B. McCullum at Wellington...........	2013-14
	I	231	M. H. Mankad at Madras	1955-56
Best bowling	*NZ*	7-23	R. J. Hadlee at Wellington	1975-76
	I	8-72	S. Venkataraghavan at Delhi...........	1964-65
Highest total	*NZ*	680-8 dec	at Wellington.........................	2013-14
	I	583-7 dec	at Ahmedabad	1999-2000
Lowest total	*NZ*	94	at Hamilton	2002-03
	I	81	at Wellington.........................	1975-76

NEW ZEALAND v PAKISTAN

	Captains					
Season	*New Zealand*	*Pakistan*	*T*	*NZ*	*P*	*D*
1955-56*P*	H. B. Cave	A. H. Kardar	3	0	2	1
1964-65*N*	J. R. Reid	Hanif Mohammad	3	0	0	3
1964-65*P*	J. R. Reid	Hanif Mohammad	3	0	2	1
1969-70*P*	G. T. Dowling	Intikhab Alam	3	1	0	2
1972-73*N*	B. E. Congdon	Intikhab Alam	3	0	1	2
1976-77*P*	G. M. Turner[1]	Mushtaq Mohammad	3	0	2	1
1978-79*N*	M. G. Burgess	Mushtaq Mohammad	3	0	1	2
1984-85*P*	J. V. Coney	Zaheer Abbas	3	0	2	1

		Captains					
Season	*New Zealand*		*Pakistan*	*T*	*NZ*	*P*	*D*
1984-85*N*	G. P. Howarth		Javed Miandad	3	2	0	1
1988-89*N*†	J. G. Wright		Imran Khan	2	0	0	2
1990-91*P*	M. D. Crowe		Javed Miandad	3	0	3	0
1992-93*N*	K. R. Rutherford		Javed Miandad	1	0	1	0
1993-94*N*	K. R. Rutherford		Salim Malik	3	1	2	0
1995-96*N*	L. K. Germon		Wasim Akram	1	0	1	0
1996-97*P*	L. K. Germon		Saeed Anwar	2	1	1	0
2000-01*N*	S. P. Fleming		Moin Khan[2]	3	1	1	1
2002*P*‡	S. P. Fleming		Waqar Younis	1	0	1	0
2003-04*N*	S. P. Fleming		Inzamam-ul-Haq	2	0	1	1
2009-10*N*	D. L. Vettori		Mohammad Yousuf	3	1	1	1
2010-11*N*	D. L. Vettori		Misbah-ul-Haq	2	0	1	1
2014-15*U*	B. B. McCullum		Misbah-ul-Haq	3	1	1	1
2016-17*N*	K. S. Williamson		Misbah-ul-Haq[3]	2	2	0	0
2018-19*U*	**K. S. Williamson**		**Sarfraz Ahmed**	**3**	**2**	**1**	**0**

		T	*NZ*	*P*	*D*
In Pakistan		21	2	13	6
In New Zealand		31	7	10	14
In United Arab Emirates		**6**	**3**	**2**	**1**
Totals		**58**	**12**	**25**	**21**

N   Played in New Zealand.   P   Played in Pakistan.   U   Played in United Arab Emirates.

†   The First Test at Dunedin was abandoned without a ball being bowled and is excluded.
‡   The Second Test at Karachi was cancelled owing to civil disturbances.

The following were appointed by the home authority for only a minor proportion of the series or deputised for the official touring captain:
[1]J. M. Parker (Third). [2]Inzamam-ul-Haq (Third). [3]Azhar Ali (Second).

SERIES RECORDS

Highest score	NZ	204*	M. S. Sinclair at Christchurch	2000-01
	P	329	Inzamam-ul-Haq at Lahore	2002
Best bowling	NZ	7-52	C. Pringle at Faisalabad	1990-91
	P	**8-41**	**Yasir Shah at Dubai**	**2018-19**
Highest total	NZ	690	at Sharjah	2014-15
	P	643	at Lahore	2002
Lowest total	NZ	70	at Dacca	1955-56
	P	102	at Faisalabad	1990-91

NEW ZEALAND v SRI LANKA

		Captains					
Season	*New Zealand*		*Sri Lanka*	*T*	*NZ*	*SL*	*D*
1982-83*N*	G. P. Howarth		D. S. de Silva	2	2	0	0
1983-84*S*	G. P. Howarth		L. R. D. Mendis	3	2	0	1
1986-87*S*†	J. J. Crowe		L. R. D. Mendis	1	0	0	1
1990-91*N*	M. D. Crowe[1]		A. Ranatunga	3	0	0	3
1992-93*S*	M. D. Crowe		A. Ranatunga	2	0	1	1
1994-95*N*	K. R. Rutherford		A. Ranatunga	2	0	1	1
1996-97*N*	S. P. Fleming		A. Ranatunga	2	2	0	0
1997-98*S*	S. P. Fleming		A. Ranatunga	3	1	2	0
2003*S*	S. P. Fleming		H. P. Tillekeratne	2	0	0	2
2004-05*N*	S. P. Fleming		M. S. Atapattu	2	1	0	1
2006-07*N*	S. P. Fleming		D. P. M. D. Jayawardene	2	1	1	0
2009*S*	D. L. Vettori		K. C. Sangakkara	2	0	2	0
2012-13*S*	L. R. P. L. Taylor		D. P. M. D. Jayawardene	2	1	1	0
2014-15*N*	B. B. McCullum		A. D. Mathews	2	2	0	0

Season	New Zealand	*Captains* Sri Lanka	T	NZ	SL	D
2015-16N	B. B. McCullum	A. D. Mathews	2	2	0	0
2018-19N	**K. S. Williamson**	**L. D. Chandimal**	**2**	**1**	**0**	**1**
	In New Zealand		19	11	2	6
	In Sri Lanka		15	4	6	5
	Totals		**34**	**15**	**8**	**11**

N   Played in New Zealand.   S   Played in Sri Lanka.

†   *The Second and Third Tests were cancelled owing to civil disturbances.*

The following was appointed by the home authority for only a minor proportion of the series:
[1]I. D. S. Smith (Third).

SERIES RECORDS

Highest score	NZ	299	M. D. Crowe at Wellington	1990-91
	SL	267	P. A. de Silva at Wellington	1990-91
Best bowling	NZ	7-130	D. L. Vettori at Wellington	2006-07
	SL	6-43	H. M. R. K. B. Herath at Galle	2012-13
Highest total	NZ	671-4	at Wellington	1990-91
	SL	498	at Napier	2004-05
Lowest total	NZ	102	at Colombo (SSC)	1992-93
	SL	93	at Wellington	1982-83

NEW ZEALAND v ZIMBABWE

Season	New Zealand	*Captains* Zimbabwe	T	NZ	Z	D
1992-93Z	M. D. Crowe	D. L. Houghton	2	1	0	1
1995-96N	L. K. Germon	A. Flower	2	0	0	2
1997-98Z	S. P. Fleming	A. D. R. Campbell	2	0	0	2
1997-98N	S. P. Fleming	A. D. R. Campbell	2	2	0	0
2000-01Z	S. P. Fleming	H. H. Streak	2	2	0	0
2000-01N	S. P. Fleming	H. H. Streak	1	0	0	1
2005-06Z	S. P. Fleming	T. Taibu	2	2	0	0
2011-12Z	L. R. P. L. Taylor	B. R. M. Taylor	1	1	0	0
2011-12N	L. R. P. L. Taylor	B. R. M. Taylor	1	1	0	0
2016Z	K. S. Williamson	A. G. Cremer	2	2	0	0
	In New Zealand		6	3	0	3
	In Zimbabwe		11	8	0	3
	Totals		17	11	0	6

N   Played in New Zealand.   Z   Played in Zimbabwe.

SERIES RECORDS

Highest score	NZ	173*	L. R. P. L. Taylor at Bulawayo	2016
	Z	203*	G. J. Whittall at Bulawayo	1997-98
Best bowling	NZ	6-26	C. S. Martin at Napier	2011-12
	Z	8-109	P. A. Strang at Bulawayo	2000-01
Highest total	NZ	582-4 dec	at Bulawayo.	2016
	Z	461	at Bulawayo.	1997-98
Lowest total	NZ	207	at Harare	1997-98
	Z	51	at Napier	2011-12

NEW ZEALAND v BANGLADESH

		Captains				
Season	*New Zealand*	*Bangladesh*	*T*	*NZ*	*B*	*D*
2001-02*N*	S. P. Fleming	Khaled Mashud	2	2	0	0
2004-05*B*	S. P. Fleming	Khaled Mashud	2	2	0	0
2007-08*N*	D. L. Vettori	Mohammad Ashraful	2	2	0	0
2008-09*B*	D. L. Vettori	Mohammad Ashraful	2	1	0	1
2009-10*N*	D. L. Vettori	Shakib Al Hasan	1	1	0	0
2013-14*B*	B. B. McCullum	Mushfiqur Rahim	2	0	0	2
2016-17*N*	K. S. Williamson	Mushfiqur Rahim[1]	2	2	0	0
	In New Zealand		7	7	0	0
	In Bangladesh		6	3	0	3
	Totals		13	10	0	3

B   Played in Bangladesh.   N   Played in New Zealand.

The following deputised for the official touring captain for only a minor proportion of the series:
   [1]Tamim Iqbal (Second).

SERIES RECORDS

Highest score	*NZ*	202	S. P. Fleming at Chittagong	2004-05
	B	217	Shakib Al Hasan at Wellington	2016-17
Best bowling	*NZ*	7-53	C. L. Cairns at Hamilton	2001-02
	B	7-36	Shakib Al Hasan at Chittagong	2008-09
Highest total	*NZ*	553-7 dec	at Hamilton	2009-10
	B	595-8 dec	at Wellington	2016-17
Lowest total	*NZ*	171	at Chittagong	2008-09
	B	108	at Hamilton	2001-02

INDIA v PAKISTAN

		Captains				
Season	*India*	*Pakistan*	*T*	*I*	*P*	*D*
1952-53*I*	L. Amarnath	A. H. Kardar	5	2	1	2
1954-55*P*	M. H. Mankad	A. H. Kardar	5	0	0	5
1960-61*I*	N. J. Contractor	Fazal Mahmood	5	0	0	5
1978-79*P*	B. S. Bedi	Mushtaq Mohammad	3	0	2	1
1979-80*I*	S. M. Gavaskar[1]	Asif Iqbal	6	2	0	4
1982-83*P*	S. M. Gavaskar	Imran Khan	6	0	3	3
1983-84*I*	Kapil Dev	Zaheer Abbas	3	0	0	3
1984-85*P*	S. M. Gavaskar	Zaheer Abbas	2	0	0	2
1986-87*I*	Kapil Dev	Imran Khan	5	0	1	4
1989-90*P*	K. Srikkanth	Imran Khan	4	0	0	4
1998-99*I*	M. Azharuddin	Wasim Akram	2	1	1	0
1998-99*I*†	M. Azharuddin	Wasim Akram	1	0	1	0
2003-04*P*	S. C. Ganguly[2]	Inzamam-ul-Haq	3	2	1	0
2004-05*I*	S. C. Ganguly	Inzamam-ul-Haq	3	1	1	1
2005-06*P*	R. Dravid	Inzamam-ul-Haq[3]	3	0	1	2

Captains

Season	India	Pakistan	T	I	P	D
2007-08*I*	A. Kumble	Shoaib Malik[4]	3	1	0	2
	In India		33	7	5	21
	In Pakistan......................		26	2	7	17
	Totals...........................		59	9	12	38

I Played in India. P Played in Pakistan.

† *This Test was part of the Asian Test Championship and was not counted as part of the preceding bilateral series.*

The following were appointed by the home authority for only a minor proportion of the series or deputised for the official touring captain:
[1]G. R. Viswanath (Sixth). [2]R. Dravid (First and Second). [3]Younis Khan (Third). [4]Younis Khan (Second and Third).

SERIES RECORDS

Highest score	*I*	309	V. Sehwag at Multan......................	2003-04
	P	280*	Javed Miandad at Hyderabad	1982-83
Best bowling	*I*	10-74	A. Kumble at Delhi	1998-99
	P	8-60	Imran Khan at Karachi	1982-83
Highest total	*I*	675-5 dec	at Multan	2003-04
	P	699-5	at Lahore	1989-90
Lowest total	*I*	106	at Lucknow	1952-53
	P	116	at Bangalore............................	1986-87

INDIA v SRI LANKA

Captains

Season	India	Sri Lanka	T	I	SL	D
1982-83*I*	S. M. Gavaskar	B. Warnapura	1	0	0	1
1985-86*S*	Kapil Dev	L. R. D. Mendis	3	0	1	2
1986-87*I*	Kapil Dev	L. R. D. Mendis	3	2	0	1
1990-91*I*	M. Azharuddin	A. Ranatunga	1	1	0	0
1993-94*S*	M. Azharuddin	A. Ranatunga	3	1	0	2
1993-94*I*	M. Azharuddin	A. Ranatunga	3	3	0	0
1997-98*S*	S. R. Tendulkar	A. Ranatunga	2	0	0	2
1997-98*I*	S. R. Tendulkar	A. Ranatunga	3	0	0	3
1998-99*S*†	M. Azharuddin	A. Ranatunga	1	0	0	1
2001*S*	S. C. Ganguly	S. T. Jayasuriya	3	1	2	0
2005-06*I*	R. Dravid[1]	M. S. Atapattu	3	2	0	1
2008*S*	A. Kumble	D. P. M. D. Jayawardene	3	1	2	0
2009-10*I*	M. S. Dhoni	K. C. Sangakkara	3	2	0	1
2010*S*	M. S. Dhoni	K. C. Sangakkara	3	1	1	1
2015-16*S*	V. Kohli	A. D. Mathews	3	2	1	0
2017*S*	V. Kohli	L. D. Chandimal[2]	3	3	0	0
2017-18*I*	V. Kohli	L. D. Chandimal	3	1	0	2
	In India...................................		20	11	0	9
	In Sri Lanka		24	9	7	8
	Totals		44	20	7	17

I Played in India. S Played in Sri Lanka.

† *This Test was part of the Asian Test Championship.*

The following were appointed by the home authority for only a minor proportion of the series:
[1]V. Sehwag (Third). [2]H. M. R. K. B. Herath (First).

SERIES RECORDS

Highest score	*I*	293	V. Sehwag at Mumbai (BS)................	2009-10
	SL	340	S. T. Jayasuriya at Colombo (RPS).........	1997-98
Best bowling	*I*	7-51	Maninder Singh at Nagpur	1986-87
	SL	8-87	M. Muralitharan at Colombo (SSC)	2001
Highest total	*I*	726-9 dec	at Mumbai (BS)......................	2009-10
	SL	952-6 dec	at Colombo (RPS)	1997-98
Lowest total	*I*	112	at Galle...........................	2015-16
	SL	82	at Chandigarh.......................	1990-91

INDIA v ZIMBABWE

		Captains					
Season	*India*		*Zimbabwe*	*T*	*I*	*Z*	*D*
1992-93*Z*	M. Azharuddin		D. L. Houghton	1	0	0	1
1992-93*I*	M. Azharuddin		D. L. Houghton	1	1	0	0
1998-99*Z*	M. Azharuddin		A. D. R. Campbell	1	0	1	0
2000-01*I*	S. C. Ganguly		H. H. Streak	2	1	0	1
2001*Z*	S. C. Ganguly		H. H. Streak	2	1	1	0
2001-02*I*	S. C. Ganguly		S. V. Carlisle	2	2	0	0
2005-06*Z*	S. C. Ganguly		T. Taibu	2	2	0	0
	In India............................			5	4	0	1
	In Zimbabwe			6	3	2	1
	Totals			11	7	2	2

I Played in India.   Z Played in Zimbabwe.

SERIES RECORDS

Highest score	*I*	227	V. G. Kambli at Delhi	1992-93
	Z	232*	A. Flower at Nagpur	2000-01
Best bowling	*I*	7-59	I. K. Pathan at Delhi	2005-06
	Z	6-73	H. H. Streak at Harare	2005-06
Highest total	*I*	609-6 dec	at Nagpur	2000-01
	Z	503-6	at Nagpur	2000-01
Lowest total	*I*	173	at Harare...........................	1998-99
	Z	146	at Delhi............................	2001-02

INDIA v BANGLADESH

		Captains					
Season	*India*		*Bangladesh*	*T*	*I*	*B*	*D*
2000-01*B*	S. C. Ganguly		Naimur Rahman	1	1	0	0
2004-05*B*	S. C. Ganguly		Habibul Bashar	2	2	0	0
2007*B*	R. Dravid		Habibul Bashar	2	1	0	1
2009-10*B*	M. S. Dhoni[1]		Shakib Al Hasan	2	2	0	0
2015*B*	V. Kohli		Mushfiqur Rahim	1	0	0	1
2016-17*I*	V. Kohli		Mushfiqur Rahim	1	1	0	0
	In Bangladesh.....................			8	6	0	2
	In India...........................			1	1	0	0
	Totals			9	7	0	2

B Played in Bangladesh.   I Played in India.

The following deputised for the official touring captain for a minor proportion of the series:
    [1]V. Sehwag (First).

SERIES RECORDS

Highest score	*I*	248*	S. R. Tendulkar at Dhaka	2004-05
	B	158*	Mohammad Ashraful at Chittagong	2004-05
Best bowling	*I*	7-87	Zaheer Khan at Mirpur	2009-10
	B	6-132	Naimur Rahman at Dhaka.................	2000-01
Highest total	*I*	687-6 dec	at Hyderabad	2016-17
	B	400	at Dhaka............................	2000-01
Lowest total	*I*	243	at Chittagong	2009-10
	B	91	at Dhaka............................	2000-01

INDIA v AFGHANISTAN

Season	India	Captains Afghanistan	T	I	Afg	D
2018*I*	**A. M. Rahane**	**Asghar Stanikzai**	1	1	0	0
	In India		1	1	0	0
	Totals............................		1	1	0	0

I Played in India.

SERIES RECORDS

Highest score	*I*	107	**S. Dhawan at Bangalore**	**2018**
	Afg	36*	**Hashmatullah Shahidi at Bangalore**	**2018**
Best bowling	*I*	4-17	**R. A. Jadeja at Bangalore**.....................	**2018**
	Afg	3-51	**Yamin Ahmadzai at Bangalore**	**2018**
Highest total	*I*	474	**at Bangalore**................................	**2018**
	Afg	109	**at Bangalore**................................	**2018**
Lowest total	*I*	474	**at Bangalore**................................	**2018**
	Afg	103	**at Bangalore**................................	**2018**

PAKISTAN v SRI LANKA

Season	Pakistan	Captains Sri Lanka	T	P	SL	D
1981-82*P*	Javed Miandad	B. Warnapura[1]	3	2	0	1
1985-86*P*	Javed Miandad	L. R. D. Mendis	3	2	0	1
1985-86*S*	Imran Khan	L. R. D. Mendis	3	1	1	1
1991-92*P*	Imran Khan	P. A. de Silva	3	1	0	2
1994-95*S*†	Salim Malik	A. Ranatunga	2	2	0	0
1995-96*P*	Ramiz Raja	A. Ranatunga	3	1	2	0
1996-97*S*	Ramiz Raja	A. Ranatunga	2	0	0	2
1998-99*P*‡	Wasim Akram	H. P. Tillekeratne	1	0	0	1
1998-99*B*‡	Wasim Akram	P. A. de Silva	1	1	0	0
1999-2000*P*	Saeed Anwar[2]	S. T. Jayasuriya	3	1	2	0
2000*S*	Moin Khan	S. T. Jayasuriya	3	2	0	1
2001-02*P*‡	Waqar Younis	S. T. Jayasuriya	1	0	1	0
2004-05*P*	Inzamam-ul-Haq	M. S. Atapattu	2	1	1	0
2005-06*S*	Inzamam-ul-Haq	D. P. M. D. Jayawardene	2	1	0	1
2008-09*P*§	Younis Khan	D. P. M. D. Jayawardene	2	0	0	2
2009*S*	Younis Khan	K. C. Sangakkara	3	0	2	1
2011-12*U*	Misbah-ul-Haq	T. M. Dilshan	3	1	0	2
2012*S*	Misbah-ul-Haq[3]	D. P. M. D. Jayawardene	3	0	1	2
2013-14*U*	Misbah-ul-Haq	A. D. Mathews	3	1	1	1

Captains

Season	Pakistan	Sri Lanka	T	P	SL	D
2014*S*	Misbah-ul-Haq	A. D. Mathews	2	0	2	0
2015*S*	Misbah-ul-Haq	A. D. Mathews	3	2	1	0
2017-18*U*	Sarfraz Ahmed	L. D. Chandimal	2	0	2	0
	In Pakistan		21	8	6	7
	In Sri Lanka		23	8	7	8
	In Bangladesh........................		1	1	0	0
	In United Arab Emirates		8	2	3	3
	Totals		53	19	16	18

P   Played in Pakistan.   *S*   Played in Sri Lanka.   *B*   Played in Bangladesh.
U   Played in United Arab Emirates.

†   *One Test was cancelled owing to the threat of civil disturbances following a general election.*
‡   *These Tests were part of the Asian Test Championship.*
§   *The Second Test ended after a terrorist attack on the Sri Lankan team bus on the third day.*

The following deputised for the official touring captain or were appointed by the home authority for only a minor proportion of the series:
[1]L. R. D. Mendis (Second). [2]Moin Khan (Third). [3]Mohammad Hafeez (First).

SERIES RECORDS

Highest score	*P*	313	Younis Khan at Karachi		2008-09
	SL	253	S. T. Jayasuriya at Faisalabad		2004-05
Best bowling	*P*	8-58	Imran Khan at Lahore		1981-82
	SL	9-127	H. M. R. K. B. Herath at Colombo (SSC).....		2014
Highest total	*P*	765-6 dec	at Karachi................................		2008-09
	SL	644-7 dec	at Karachi................................		2008-09
Lowest total	*P*	90	at Colombo (PSS)		2009
	SL	71	at Kandy..................................		1994-95

PAKISTAN v ZIMBABWE

Captains

Season	Pakistan	Zimbabwe	T	P	Z	D
1993-94*P*	Wasim Akram[1]	A. Flower	3	2	0	1
1994-95*Z*	Salim Malik	A. Flower	3	2	1	0
1996-97*P*	Wasim Akram	A. D. R. Campbell	2	1	0	1
1997-98*Z*	Rashid Latif	A. D. R. Campbell	2	1	0	1
1998-99*P*†	Aamir Sohail[2]	A. D. R. Campbell	2	0	1	1
2002-03*Z*	Waqar Younis	A. D. R. Campbell	2	2	0	0
2011-12*Z*	Misbah-ul-Haq	B. R. M. Taylor	1	1	0	0
2013-14*Z*	Misbah-ul-Haq	B. R. M. Taylor[3]	2	1	1	0
	In Pakistan		7	3	1	3
	In Zimbabwe		10	7	2	1
	Totals		17	10	3	4

P   Played in Pakistan.   *Z*   Played in Zimbabwe.

†   *The Third Test at Faisalabad was abandoned without a ball being bowled and is excluded.*

The following were appointed by the home authority for only a minor proportion of the series:
[1]Waqar Younis (First). [2]Moin Khan (Second). [3]H. Masakadza (First).

SERIES RECORDS

Highest score	P	257*	Wasim Akram at Sheikhupura	1996-97
	Z	201*	G. W. Flower at Harare	1994-95
Best bowling	P	7-66	Saqlain Mushtaq at Bulawayo..............	2002-03
	Z	6-90	H. H. Streak at Harare	1994-95
Highest total	P	553	at Sheikhupura	1996-97
	Z	544-4 dec	at Harare	1994-95
Lowest total	P	103	at Peshawar	1998-99
	Z	120	at Harare	2013-14

PAKISTAN v BANGLADESH

			Captains				
Season	*Pakistan*		*Bangladesh*	*T*	*P*	*B*	*D*
2001-02*P*†	Waqar Younis		Naimur Rahman	1	1	0	0
2001-02*B*	Waqar Younis		Khaled Mashud	2	2	0	0
2003-04*P*	Rashid Latif		Khaled Mahmud	3	3	0	0
2011-12*B*	Misbah-ul-Haq		Mushfiqur Rahim	2	2	0	0
2014-15*B*	Misbah-ul-Haq		Mushfiqur Rahim	2	1	0	1
	In Pakistan			4	4	0	0
	In Bangladesh...................			6	5	0	1
	Totals...........................			10	9	0	1

P   Played in Pakistan.   B   Played in Bangladesh.

†   *This Test was part of the Asian Test Championship.*

SERIES RECORDS

Highest score	P	226	Azhar Ali at Mirpur	2014-15
	B	206	Tamim Iqbal at Khulna	2014-15
Best bowling	P	7-77	Danish Kaneria at Dhaka	2001-02
	B	6-82	Shakib Al Hasan at Mirpur	2011-12
Highest total	P	628	at Khulna	2014-15
	B	555-6	at Khulna	2014-15
Lowest total	P	175	at Multan	2003-04
	B	96	at Peshawar	2003-04

PAKISTAN v IRELAND

			Captains				
Season	*Pakistan*		*Ireland*	*T*	*P*	*Ire*	*D*
2018*Ire*	Sarfraz Ahmed		W. T. S. Porterfield	1	1	0	0
	In Ireland			**1**	**1**	**0**	**0**
	Totals...........................			**1**	**1**	**0**	**0**

Ire   Played in Ireland.

SERIES RECORDS

Highest score	P	**83**	**Fahim Ashraf at Malahide**.................	**2018**
	Ire	**118**	**K. J. O'Brien at Malahide**.................	**2018**
Best bowling	P	**5-66**	**Mohammad Abbas at Malahide**	**2018**
	Ire	**4-45**	**T. J. Murtagh at Malahide**.................	**2018**
Highest total	P	**310-9 dec**	**at Malahide**..............................	**2018**
	Ire	**339**	**at Malahide**	**2018**
Lowest total	Ire	**130**	**at Malahide**	**2018**

SRI LANKA v ZIMBABWE

Captains

Season	Sri Lanka	Zimbabwe	T	SL	Z	D
1994-95Z	A. Ranatunga	A. Flower	3	0	0	3
1996-97S	A. Ranatunga	A. D. R. Campbell	2	2	0	0
1997-98S	A. Ranatunga	A. D. R. Campbell	2	2	0	0
1999-2000Z	S. T. Jayasuriya	A. Flower	3	1	0	2
2001-02S	S. T. Jayasuriya	S. V. Carlisle	3	3	0	0
2003-04Z	M. S. Atapattu	T. Taibu	2	2	0	0
2016-17Z	H. M. R. K. B. Herath	A. G. Cremer	2	2	0	0
2017S	L. D. Chandimal	A. G. Cremer	1	1	0	0
	In Sri Lanka		8	8	0	0
	In Zimbabwe		10	5	0	5
	Totals		18	13	0	5

S Played in Sri Lanka.   Z Played in Zimbabwe.

SERIES RECORDS

Highest score	SL	270	K. C. Sangakkara at Bulawayo		2003-04
	Z	266	D. L. Houghton at Bulawayo		1994-95
Best bowling	SL	9-51	M. Muralitharan at Kandy		2001-02
	Z	5-106	P. A. Strang at Colombo (RPS)		1996-97
Highest total	SL	713-3 dec	at Bulawayo		2003-04
	Z	462-9 dec	at Bulawayo		1994-95
Lowest total	SL	218	at Bulawayo		1994-95
	Z	79	at Galle		2001-02

SRI LANKA v BANGLADESH

Captains

Season	Sri Lanka	Bangladesh	T	SL	B	D
2001-02S†	S. T. Jayasuriya	Naimur Rahman	1	1	0	0
2002S	S. T. Jayasuriya	Khaled Mashud	2	2	0	0
2005-06S	M. S. Atapattu	Habibul Bashar	2	2	0	0
2005-06B	D. P. M. D. Jayawardene	Habibul Bashar	2	2	0	0
2007S	D. P. M. D. Jayawardene	Mohammad Ashraful	3	3	0	0
2008-09B	D. P. M. D. Jayawardene	Mohammad Ashraful	2	2	0	0
2012-13S	A. D. Mathews	Mushfiqur Rahim	2	1	0	1
2013-14B	A. D. Mathews	Mushfiqur Rahim	2	1	0	1
2016-17S	H. M. R. K. B. Herath	Mushfiqur Rahim	2	1	1	0
2017-18B	**L. D. Chandimal**	**Mahmudullah**	**2**	**1**	**0**	**1**
	In Sri Lanka		12	10	1	1
	In Bangladesh		**8**	**6**	**0**	**2**
	Totals		20	16	1	3

S Played in Sri Lanka.   B Played in Bangladesh.

† This Test was part of the Asian Test Championship.

SERIES RECORDS

Highest score	SL	319	K. C. Sangakkara at Chittagong		2013-14
	B	200	Mushfiqur Rahim at Galle		2012-13
Best bowling	SL	7-89	H. M. R. K. B. Herath at Colombo (RPS)		2012-13
	B	5-70	Shakib Al Hasan at Mirpur		2008-09
Highest total	SL	730-6 dec	at Mirpur		2013-14
	B	638	at Galle		2012-13
Lowest total	SL	**222**	**at Mirpur**		**2017-18**
	B	62	at Colombo (PSS)		2007

ZIMBABWE v BANGLADESH

		Captains				
Season	*Zimbabwe*	*Bangladesh*	*T*	*Z*	*B*	*D*
2000-01Z	H. H. Streak	Naimur Rahman	2	2	0	0
2001-02B	B. A. Murphy[1]	Naimur Rahman	2	1	0	1
2003-04Z	H. H. Streak	Habibul Bashar	2	1	0	1
2004-05B	T. Taibu	Habibul Bashar	2	0	1	1
2011-12Z	B. R. M. Taylor	Shakib Al Hasan	1	1	0	0
2012-13Z	B. R. M. Taylor	Mushfiqur Rahim	2	1	1	0
2014-15B	B. R. M. Taylor	Mushfiqur Rahim	3	0	3	0
2018-19B	**H. Masakadza**	**Mahmudullah**	**2**	**1**	**1**	**0**
	In Zimbabwe		7	5	1	1
	In Bangladesh		**9**	**2**	**5**	**2**
	Totals...........................		16	7	6	3

Z   Played in Zimbabwe.   B   Played in Bangladesh.

The following deputised for the official touring captain:

[1]S. V. Carlisle (Second).

SERIES RECORDS

Highest score	Z	171	B. R. M. Taylor at Harare	2012-13
	B	**219***	**Mushfiqur Rahim at Mirpur**	**2018-19**
Best bowling	Z	6-59	D. T. Hondo at Dhaka	2004-05
	B	8-39	Taijul Islam at Mirpur	2014-15
Highest total	Z	542-7 dec	at Chittagong	2001-02
	B	**522-7 dec**	**at Mirpur**	**2018-19**
Lowest total	Z	114	at Mirpur	2014-15
	B	107	at Dhaka	2001-02

TEST GROUNDS

in chronological order

	City and Ground	*First Test Match*		*Tests*
1	**Melbourne, Melbourne Cricket Ground**	**March 15, 1877**	A v E	**111**
2	**London, Kennington Oval**	**September 6, 1880**	E v A	**101**
3	**Sydney, Sydney Cricket Ground (No. 1)**	**February 17, 1882**	A v E	**107**
4	Manchester, Old Trafford	July 11, 1884	E v A	78
5	**London, Lord's**	**July 21, 1884**	E v A	**137**
6	Adelaide, Adelaide Oval	December 12, 1884	A v E	77
7	**Port Elizabeth, St George's Park**	**March 12, 1889**	SA v E	**29**
8	**Cape Town, Newlands**	**March 25, 1889**	SA v E	**57**
9	Johannesburg, Old Wanderers	March 2, 1896	SA v E	22
	Now the site of Johannesburg Railway Station.			
10	**Nottingham, Trent Bridge**	**June 1, 1899**	E v A	**63**
11	**Leeds, Headingley**	**June 29, 1899**	E v A	**77**
12	**Birmingham, Edgbaston**	**May 29, 1902**	E v A	**51**
13	Sheffield, Bramall Lane	July 3, 1902	E v A	1
	Sheffield United Football Club have built a stand over the cricket pitch.			
14	Durban, Lord's	January 21, 1910	SA v E	4
	Ground destroyed and built on.			
15	**Durban, Kingsmead**	**January 18, 1923**	SA v E	**43**
16	Brisbane, Exhibition Ground	November 30, 1928	A v E	2
	No longer used for cricket.			
17	Christchurch, Lancaster Park	January 10, 1930	NZ v E	40
	Also known under sponsors' names.			

	City and Ground	First Test Match		Tests
18	**Bridgetown, Kensington Oval**	**January 11, 1930**	WI v E	53
19	**Wellington, Basin Reserve**	**January 24, 1930**	NZ v E	62
20	**Port-of-Spain, Queen's Park Oval**	**February 1, 1930**	WI v E	61
21	**Auckland, Eden Park**	**February 14, 1930**	NZ v E	50
22	Georgetown, Bourda	February 21, 1930	WI v E	30
23	**Kingston, Sabina Park**	**April 3, 1930**	WI v E	51
24	Brisbane, Woolloongabba	November 27, 1931	A v SA	60
25	Bombay, Gymkhana Ground	December 15, 1933	I v E	1
	No longer used for first-class cricket.			
26	Calcutta (*now Kolkata*), Eden Gardens	January 5, 1934	I v E	41
27	Madras (*now Chennai*),	February 10, 1934	I v E	32
	Chepauk (Chidambaram Stadium)			
28	Delhi, Feroz Shah Kotla	November 10, 1948	I v WI	34
29	Bombay (*now Mumbai*), Brabourne Stadium	December 9, 1948	I v WI	18
	Rarely used for first-class cricket.			
30	Johannesburg, Ellis Park	December 27, 1948	SA v E	6
	Mainly a football and rugby stadium, no longer used for cricket.			
31	Kanpur, Green Park (Modi Stadium)	January 12, 1952	I v E	22
32	Lucknow, University Ground	October 25, 1952	I v P	1
	Ground destroyed, now partly under a river bed.			
33	Dacca (*now Dhaka*),	January 1, 1955	P v I	17
	Dacca (*now Bangabandhu*) Stadium			
	Originally in East Pakistan, now Bangladesh, no longer used for cricket.			
34	Bahawalpur, Dring (*now Bahawal*) Stadium	January 15, 1955	P v I	1
	Still used for first-class cricket.			
35	Lahore, Lawrence Gardens (Bagh-e-Jinnah)	January 29, 1955	P v I	3
	Still used for club and occasional first-class matches.			
36	Peshawar, Services Ground	February 13, 1955	P v I	1
	Superseded by new stadium.			
37	Karachi, National Stadium	February 26, 1955	P v I	41
38	Dunedin, Carisbrook	March 11, 1955	NZ v E	10
39	Hyderabad, Fateh Maidan (Lal Bahadur Stadium)	November 19, 1955	I v NZ	3
40	Madras, Corporation Stadium	January 6, 1956	I v NZ	9
	Superseded by rebuilt Chepauk Stadium.			
41	**Johannesburg, Wanderers**	**December 24, 1956**	SA v E	40
42	Lahore, Gaddafi Stadium	November 21, 1959	P v A	40
43	Rawalpindi, Pindi Club Ground	March 27, 1965	P v NZ	1
	Superseded by new stadium.			
44	Nagpur, Vidarbha CA Ground	October 3, 1969	I v NZ	9
	Superseded by new stadium.			
45	Perth, Western Australian CA Ground	December 11, 1970	A v E	44
	Superseded by new stadium.			
46	Hyderabad, Niaz Stadium	March 16, 1973	P v E	5
47	**Bangalore, Karnataka State CA Ground**	**November 22, 1974**	I v WI	23
	(Chinnaswamy Stadium)			
48	Bombay (*now Mumbai*), Wankhede Stadium	January 23, 1975	I v WI	25
49	Faisalabad, Iqbal Stadium	October 16, 1978	P v I	24
50	Napier, McLean Park	February 16, 1979	NZ v P	10
51	Multan, Ibn-e-Qasim Bagh Stadium	December 30, 1980	P v WI	1
	Superseded by new stadium.			
52	St John's (Antigua), Recreation Ground	March 27, 1981	WI v E	22
53	Colombo, P. Saravanamuttu Stadium/	February 17, 1982	SL v E	21
	P. Sara Oval			
54	Kandy, Asgiriya Ground	April 22, 1983	SL v A	21
	Superseded by new stadium at Pallekele.			
55	Jullundur, Burlton Park	September 24, 1983	I v P	1
56	Ahmedabad, Sardar Patel (Gujarat) Stadium	November 12, 1983	I v WI	12
57	**Colombo, Sinhalese Sports Club Ground**	**March 16, 1984**	SL v NZ	43
58	Colombo, Colombo Cricket Club Ground	March 24, 1984	SL v NZ	3
59	Sialkot, Jinnah Stadium	October 27, 1985	P v SL	4

	City and Ground	First Test Match		Tests
60	Cuttack, Barabati Stadium	January 4, 1987	I v SL	2
61	Jaipur, Sawai Mansingh Stadium	February 21, 1987	I v P	1
62	Hobart, Bellerive Oval	December 16, 1989	A v SL	13
63	Chandigarh, Sector 16 Stadium	November 23, 1990	I v SL	1
	Superseded by Mohali ground.			
64	Hamilton, Seddon Park	February 22, 1991	NZ v SL	24
	Also known under various sponsors' names.			
65	Gujranwala, Municipal Stadium	December 20, 1991	P v SL	1
66	Colombo, R. Premadasa (Khettarama) Stadium	August 28, 1992	SL v A	9
67	Moratuwa, Tyronne Fernando Stadium	September 8, 1992	SL v A	4
68	Harare, Harare Sports Club	October 18, 1992	Z v I	34
69	Bulawayo, Bulawayo Athletic Club	November 1, 1992	Z v NZ	1
	Superseded by Queens Sports Club ground.			
70	Karachi, Defence Stadium	December 1, 1993	P v Z	1
71	Rawalpindi, Rawalpindi Cricket Stadium	December 9, 1993	P v Z	8
72	Lucknow, K. D. "Babu" Singh Stadium	January 18, 1994	I v SL	1
73	Bulawayo, Queens Sports Club	October 20, 1994	Z v SL	23
74	Mohali, Punjab Cricket Association Stadium	December 10, 1994	I v WI	13
75	Peshawar, Arbab Niaz Stadium	September 8, 1995	P v SL	6
76	**Centurion (*ex Verwoerdburg*), Centurion Park**	**November 16, 1995**	**SA v E**	**24**
77	Sheikhupura, Municipal Stadium	October 17, 1996	P v Z	2
78	St Vincent, Arnos Vale	June 20, 1997	WI v SL	3
79	**Galle, International Stadium**	**June 3, 1998**	**SL v NZ**	**32**
80	Bloemfontein, Springbok Park	October 29, 1999	SA v Z	5
	Also known under various sponsors' names.			
81	Multan, Multan Cricket Stadium	August 29, 2001	P v B	5
82	Chittagong, Chittagong Stadium	November 15, 2001	B v Z	8
	Also known as M. A. Aziz Stadium.			
83	Sharjah, Sharjah Cricket Association Stadium	January 31, 2002	P v WI	9
84	St George's, Grenada, Queen's Park New Stadium	June 28, 2002	WI v NZ	3
85	East London, Buffalo Park	October 18, 2002	SA v B	1
86	Potchefstroom, North West Cricket Stadium	October 25, 2002	SA v B	2
	Now known under sponsor's name.			
87	Chester-le-Street, Riverside Ground	June 5, 2003	E v Z	6
	Also known under sponsor's name.			
88	**Gros Islet, St Lucia, Beausejour Stadium**	**June 20, 2003**	**WI v SL**	**6**
	Now known as Darren Sammy Stadium.			
89	Darwin, Marrara Cricket Ground	July 18, 2003	A v B	2
90	Cairns, Cazaly's Football Park	July 25, 2003	A v B	2
	Also known under sponsor's name.			
91	**Chittagong, Chittagong Divisional Stadium**	**February 28, 2006**	**B v SL**	**18**
	Also known as Bir Shrestha Shahid Ruhul Amin Stadium/Zohur Ahmed Chowdhury Stadium.			
92	Bogra, Shaheed Chandu Stadium	March 8, 2006	B v SL	1
93	Fatullah, Narayanganj Osmani Stadium	April 9, 2006	B v A	2
94	Basseterre, St Kitts, Warner Park	June 22, 2006	WI v I	3
95	**Mirpur (Dhaka), Shere Bangla Natl Stadium**	**May 25, 2007**	**B v I**	**19**
96	Dunedin, University Oval	January 4, 2008	NZ v B	8
97	Providence Stadium, Guyana	March 22, 2008	WI v SL	2
98	**North Sound, Antigua, Sir Vivian Richards Stadium**	**May 30, 2008**	**WI v A**	**6**
99	Nagpur, Vidarbha CA Stadium, Jamtha	November 6, 2008	I v A	6
100	Cardiff, Sophia Gardens	July 8, 2009	E v A	3
	Now known under sponsor's name.			
101	**Hyderabad, Rajiv Gandhi Intl Stadium**	**November 12, 2010**	**I v NZ**	**5**
102	**Dubai, Dubai Sports City Stadium**	**November 12, 2010**	**P v SA**	**13**
103	**Abu Dhabi, Sheikh Zayed Stadium**	**November 20, 2010**	**P v SA**	**13**
104	**Pallekele, Muttiah Muralitharan Stadium**	**December 1, 2010**	**SL v WI**	**7**
105	**Southampton, Rose Bowl**	**June 16, 2011**	**E v SL**	**3**
	Now known under sponsor's name.			
106	Roseau, Dominica, Windsor Park	July 6, 2011	WI v I	5

	City and Ground	First Test Match		Tests
107	Khulna, Khulna Division Stadium	November 21, 2012	B v WI	3

Also known as Bir Shrestha Shahid Flight Lt Motiur Rahman/Shaikh Abu Naser Stadium.

	City and Ground	First Test Match		Tests
108	**Christchurch, Hagley Oval**	**December 26, 2014**	**NZ v SL**	**6**
109	Indore, Maharani Usharaje Trust Ground	October 8, 2016	I v NZ	1
110	**Rajkot, Saurashtra CA Stadium**	**November 9, 2016**	**I v E**	**2**
111	Visakhapatnam, Andhra CA-Visakhapatnam DCA Stadium	November 17, 2016	I v E	1
112	Pune (Gahunje), Subrata Roy Sahara Stadium	February 23, 2017	I v A	1
113	Ranchi, Jharkhand State CA Oval Ground	March 16, 2017	I v A	1
114	Dharamsala, Himachal Pradesh CA Stadium	March 25, 2017	I v A	1
115	**Malahide (Dublin), The Village**	**May 11, 2018**	**Ire v P**	**1**
116	**Sylhet, Sylhet Stadium**	**November 3, 2018**	**B v Z**	**1**
117	**Perth, Optus Stadium**	**December 14, 2018**	**A v I**	**1**

Bold type denotes grounds used for Test cricket since January 1, 2018.

ONE-DAY INTERNATIONAL RECORDS

Matches in this section do not have first-class status.

This section covers one-day international cricket to December 31, 2018. Bold type denotes performances since January 1, 2018, or, in career figures, players who have appeared in one-day internationals since that date.

SUMMARY OF ONE-DAY INTERNATIONALS

1970-71 to December 31, 2018

	Opponents	Matches	Won by														Tied	NR
			E	A	SA	WI	NZ	I	P	SL	Z	B	Afg	Ire	Ass	Oth		
England	Australia	147	61	81	–	–	–	–	–	–	–	–	–	–	–	–	2	3
	South Africa	59	26	–	29	–	–	–	–	–	–	–	–	–	–	–	1	3
	West Indies	96	49	–	–	42	–	–	–	–	–	–	–	–	–	–	–	5
	New Zealand	89	40	–	–	–	43	–	–	–	–	–	–	–	–	–	2	4
	India	99	41	–	–	–	–	53	–	–	–	–	–	–	–	–	2	3
	Pakistan	82	49	–	–	–	–	–	31	–	–	–	–	–	–	–	–	2
	Sri Lanka	74	36	–	–	–	–	–	–	35	–	–	–	–	–	–	1	2
	Zimbabwe	30	21	–	–	–	–	–	–	–	8	–	–	–	–	–	–	1
	Bangladesh	20	16	–	–	–	–	–	–	–	–	4	–	–	–	–	–	–
	Afghanistan	1	1	–	–	–	–	–	–	–	–	–	0	–	–	–	–	–
	Ireland	9	7	–	–	–	–	–	–	–	–	–	–	1	–	–	–	1
	Associates	15	13	–	–	–	–	–	–	–	–	–	–	–	1	–	–	1
Australia	South Africa	99	–	48	47	–	–	–	–	–	–	–	–	–	–	–	3	1
	West Indies	139	–	73	–	60	–	–	–	–	–	–	–	–	–	–	3	3
	New Zealand	136	–	90	–	–	39	–	–	–	–	–	–	–	–	–	–	7
	India	128	–	73	–	–	–	45	–	–	–	–	–	–	–	–	–	10
	Pakistan	98	–	62	–	–	–	–	32	–	–	–	–	–	–	–	1	3
	Sri Lanka	96	–	60	–	–	–	–	–	32	–	–	–	–	–	–	–	4
	Zimbabwe	30	–	27	–	–	–	–	–	–	2	–	–	–	–	–	–	1
	Bangladesh	20	–	18	–	–	–	–	–	–	–	1	–	–	–	–	–	1
	Afghanistan	2	–	2	–	–	–	–	–	–	–	–	0	–	–	–	–	–
	Ireland	5	–	4	–	–	–	–	–	–	–	–	–	0	–	–	–	1
	Associates	16	–	16	–	–	–	–	–	–	–	–	–	–	0	–	–	–
	ICC World XI	3	–	3	–	–	–	–	–	–	–	–	–	–	–	0	–	–
South Africa	West Indies	61	–	–	44	15	–	–	–	–	–	–	–	–	–	–	1	1
	New Zealand	70	–	–	41	–	24	–	–	–	–	–	–	–	–	–	–	5
	India	83	–	–	46	–	–	34	–	–	–	–	–	–	–	–	–	3
	Pakistan	73	–	–	47	–	–	–	25	–	–	–	–	–	–	–	–	1
	Sri Lanka	71	–	–	38	–	–	–	–	31	–	–	–	–	–	–	1	1
	Zimbabwe	41	–	–	38	–	–	–	–	–	2	–	–	–	–	–	–	1
	Bangladesh	20	–	–	17	–	–	–	–	–	–	3	–	–	–	–	–	–
	Ireland	5	–	–	5	–	–	–	–	–	–	–	–	0	–	–	–	–
	Associates	18	–	–	18	–	–	–	–	–	–	–	–	–	0	–	–	–
West Indies	New Zealand	64	–	–	–	30	27	–	–	–	–	–	–	–	–	–	–	7
	India	126	–	–	–	62	–	59	–	–	–	–	–	–	–	–	2	3
	Pakistan	133	–	–	–	70	–	–	60	–	–	–	–	–	–	–	3	–
	Sri Lanka	56	–	–	–	28	–	–	–	25	–	–	–	–	–	–	–	3
	Zimbabwe	48	–	–	–	36	–	–	–	–	10	–	–	–	–	–	1	1
	Bangladesh	34	–	–	–	21	–	–	–	–	–	11	–	–	–	–	–	2
	Afghanistan	5	–	–	–	1	–	–	–	–	–	–	3	–	–	–	–	1
	Ireland	7	–	–	–	5	–	–	–	–	–	–	–	1	–	–	–	1
	Associates	19	–	–	–	18	–	–	–	–	–	–	–	–	1	–	–	–
New Zealand	India	101	–	–	–	–	44	51	–	–	–	–	–	–	–	–	1	5
	Pakistan	106	–	–	–	–	48	–	54	–	–	–	–	–	–	–	1	3
	Sri Lanka	95	–	–	–	–	45	–	–	41	–	–	–	–	–	–	1	8
	Zimbabwe	38	–	–	–	–	27	–	–	–	9	–	–	–	–	–	1	1
	Bangladesh	31	–	–	–	–	21	–	–	–	–	10	–	–	–	–	–	–
	Afghanistan	1	–	–	–	–	1	–	–	–	–	–	0	–	–	–	–	–
	Ireland	4	–	–	–	–	4	–	–	–	–	–	–	0	–	–	–	–
	Associates	12	–	–	–	–	12	–	–	–	–	–	–	–	0	–	–	–

	Opponents	Matches	E	A	SA	WI	NZ	I	P	SL	Z	B	Afg	Ire	Ass	Oth	Tied	NR
													Won by					
India	Pakistan	131	–	–	–	–	–	54	73	–	–	–	–	–	–	–	–	4
	Sri Lanka	158	–	–	–	–	–	90	–	56	–	–	–	–	–	–	1	11
	Zimbabwe	63	–	–	–	–	–	51	–	–	10	–	–	–	–	–	2	–
	Bangladesh	35	–	–	–	–	–	29	–	–	–	5	–	–	–	–	–	1
	Afghanistan	2	–	–	–	–	–	1	–	–	–	–	0	–	–	–	1	–
	Ireland	3	–	–	–	–	–	3	–	–	–	–	–	0	–	–	–	–
	Associates	24	–	–	–	–	–	22	–	–	–	–	–	–	2	–	–	–
Pakistan	Sri Lanka	153	–	–	–	–	–	–	90	58	–	–	–	–	–	–	1	4
	Zimbabwe	59	–	–	–	–	–	–	52	–	4	–	–	–	–	–	1	2
	Bangladesh	36	–	–	–	–	–	–	31	–	–	5	–	–	–	–	–	–
	Afghanistan	3	–	–	–	–	–	–	3	–	–	–	0	–	–	–	–	–
	Ireland	7	–	–	–	–	–	–	5	–	–	–	–	1	–	–	1	–
	Associates	21	–	–	–	–	–	–	21	–	–	–	–	–	0	–	–	–
Sri Lanka	Zimbabwe	57	–	–	–	–	–	–	–	44	11	–	–	–	–	–	–	2
	Bangladesh	45	–	–	–	–	–	–	–	36	–	7	–	–	–	–	–	2
	Afghanistan	3	–	–	–	–	–	–	–	2	–	–	1	–	–	–	–	–
	Ireland	4	–	–	–	–	–	–	–	4	–	–	–	0	–	–	–	–
	Associates	16	–	–	–	–	–	–	–	15	–	–	–	–	1	–	–	–
Zimbabwe	Bangladesh	72	–	–	–	–	–	–	–	–	28	44	–	–	–	–	–	–
	Afghanistan	25	–	–	–	–	–	–	–	–	10	–	15	–	–	–	–	–
	Ireland	10	–	–	–	–	–	–	–	–	6	–	–	3	–	–	1	–
	Associates	44	–	–	–	–	–	–	–	–	34	–	–	–	7	–	1	2
Bangladesh	Afghanistan	7	–	–	–	–	–	–	–	–	–	4	3	–	–	–	–	–
	Ireland	9	–	–	–	–	–	–	–	–	–	6	–	2	–	–	–	1
	Associates	26	–	–	–	–	–	–	–	–	–	18	–	–	8	–	–	–
Afghanistan	Ireland	20	–	–	–	–	–	–	–	–	–	–	10	10	–	–	–	–
	Associates	37	–	–	–	–	–	–	–	–	–	–	23	–	13	–	–	1
Ireland	Associates	56	–	–	–	–	–	–	–	–	–	–	–	43	9	–	1	3
Associates	Associates	125	–	–	–	–	–	–	–	–	–	–	–	–	120	–	–	5
Asian CC XI	ICC World XI	1	–	–	–	–	–	–	–	–	–	–	–	–	–	1	–	–
	African XI	6	–	–	–	–	–	–	–	–	–	–	–	–	–	5	–	1
		4,073	360	557	370	388	335	492	477	379	134	118	55	61	162	6	37	142

Associate and Affiliate Members of ICC who have played one-day internationals are Afghanistan, Bermuda, Canada, East Africa, Hong Kong, Ireland, Kenya, Namibia, Netherlands, Papua New Guinea, Scotland, United Arab Emirates and USA. Sri Lanka, Zimbabwe, Bangladesh, Afghanistan and Ireland played one-day internationals before gaining Test status; these are not counted as Associate results.

RESULTS SUMMARY OF ONE-DAY INTERNATIONALS

1970-71 to December 31, 2018 (4,073 matches)

	Matches	Won	Lost	Tied	No Result	% Won (excl. NR)
South Africa	600	370	208	6	16	63.86
Australia	919	557	319	9	34	63.44
Pakistan...................	902	477	398	8	19	54.47
India	953	492	412	9	40	54.38
Afghanistan...............	106	55	48	1	2	53.36
England...................	721	360	328	8	25	52.29
West Indies	788	388	363	10	27	51.64
Sri Lanka	828	379	407	5	37	48.23
New Zealand..............	747	335	366	6	40	47.80
Ireland...................	139	61	68	3	7	47.34
Bangladesh	355	118	230	–	7	33.90
Zimbabwe	517	134	365	7	11	27.17
Asian Cricket Council XI	7	4	2	–	1	66.66
Netherlands...............	78	29	45	1	3	39.33
Scotland	106	38	61	1	6	38.50

	Matches	Won	Lost	Tied	No Result	% Won (excl. NR)
Hong Kong	26	9	16	–	1	36.00
Papua New Guinea	18	6	12	–	–	33.33
Nepal	3	1	2	–	–	33.33
United Arab Emirates	46	13	33	–	–	28.26
Kenya	154	42	107	–	5	28.18
ICC World XI	4	1	3	–	–	25.00
Canada	77	17	58	–	2	22.66
Bermuda	35	7	28	–	–	20.00
African XI	6	1	4	–	1	20.00
USA	2	–	2	–	–	0.00
East Africa	3	–	3	–	–	0.00
Namibia	6	–	6	–	–	0.00

Matches abandoned without a ball bowled are not included except (from 2004) where the toss took place, in accordance with an ICC ruling. Such matches, like those called off after play began, are now counted as official internationals in their own right, even when replayed on another day. In the percentages of matches won, ties are counted as half a win.

BATTING RECORDS

HIGHEST INDIVIDUAL INNINGS

264	R. G. Sharma	India v Sri Lanka at Kolkata	2014-15
237*	M. J. Guptill	New Zealand v West Indies at Wellington	2014-15
219	V. Sehwag	India v West Indies at Indore	2011-12
215	C. H. Gayle	West Indies v Zimbabwe at Canberra	2014-15
210*	**Fakhar Zaman**	**Pakistan v Zimbabwe at Bulawayo**	**2018**
209	R. G. Sharma	India v Australia at Bangalore	2013-14
208*	R. G. Sharma	India v Sri Lanka at Mohali	2017-18
200*	S. R. Tendulkar	India v South Africa at Gwalior	2009-10
194*	C. K. Coventry	Zimbabwe v Bangladesh at Bulawayo	2009
194	Saeed Anwar	Pakistan v India at Chennai	1997-97
189*	I. V. A. Richards	West Indies v England at Manchester	1984
189*	M. J. Guptill	New Zealand v England at Southampton	2013
189	S. T. Jayasuriya	Sri Lanka v India at Sharjah	2000-01
188*	G. Kirsten	South Africa v UAE at Rawalpindi	1995-96
186*	S. R. Tendulkar	India v New Zealand at Hyderabad	1999-2000
185*	S. R. Watson	Australia v Bangladesh at Mirpur	2010-11
185	F. du Plessis	South Africa v Sri Lanka at Cape Town	2016-17
183*	M. S. Dhoni	India v Sri Lanka at Jaipur	2005-06
183	S. C. Ganguly	India v Sri Lanka at Taunton	1999
183	V. Kohli	India v Pakistan at Mirpur	2011-12
181*	M. L. Hayden	Australia v New Zealand at Hamilton	2006-07
181*	**L. R. P. L. Taylor**	**New Zealand v England at Dunedin (University)**	**2017-18**
181	I. V. A. Richards	West Indies v Sri Lanka at Karachi	1987-88
180*	M. J. Guptill	New Zealand v South Africa at Hamilton	2016-17
180	**J. J. Roy**	**England v Australia at Melbourne**	**2017-18**

The highest individual scores for other Test countries are:

177	P. R. Stirling	Ireland v Canada at Toronto	2010
154	Tamim Iqbal	Bangladesh v Zimbabwe at Bulawayo	2009
131*	Mohammad Shahzad	Afghanistan v Zimbabwe at Sharjah	2015-16

MOST HUNDREDS

S. R. Tendulkar (I)	49	Saeed Anwar (P)	20	V. Sehwag (I/Wld/Asia)	15
V. Kohli (I)	**38**	D. P. M. D. Jayawardene		**W. U. Tharanga (SL)**	**15**
R. T. Ponting (A/World)	30	(SL/Asia)	19		
S. T. Jayasuriya (SL/Asia)	28	B. C. Lara (WI/World)	19	*Most hundreds for other*	
H. M. Amla (SA)	**26**	**L. R. P. L. Taylor (NZ)**	**19**	*Test countries:*	
A. B. de Villiers (SA)	**25**	M. E. Waugh (A)	18	**J. E. Root (E)**	**13**
K. C. Sangakkara (SL)	25	D. L. Haynes (WI)	17	**W. T. S. Porterfield (Ire)**	**11**
C. H. Gayle (WI/World)	**23**	J. H. Kallis (SA/Wld/Af)	17	**Tamim Iqbal (B)**	**11**
T. M. Dilshan (SL)	22	N. J. Astle (NZ)	16	**B. R. M. Taylor (Z)**	**10**
S. C. Ganguly (I/Asia)	22	A. C. Gilchrist (A/World)	16	**Mohammad Shahzad (Afg)**	**5**
H. H. Gibbs (SA)	21	**S. Dhawan (I)**	**15**		
R. G. Sharma (I)	**21**	Mohammad Yousuf (P/As)	15		

Ponting's total includes one for the World XI, the only hundred for a combined team.

MOST RUNS

		M	I	NO	R	HS	100	Avge
1	S. R. Tendulkar (India)	463	452	41	18,426	200*	49	44.83
2	K. C. Sangakkara (SL/Asia/World)	404	380	41	14,234	169	25	41.98
3	R. T. Ponting (Australia/World)	375	365	39	13,704	164	30	42.03
4	S. T. Jayasuriya (Sri Lanka/Asia)	445	433	18	13,430	189	28	32.36
5	D. P. M. D. Jayawardene (SL/Asia)	448	418	39	12,650	144	19	33.37
6	Inzamam-ul-Haq (Pakistan/Asia)	378	350	53	11,739	137*	10	39.52
7	J. H. Kallis (S. Africa/World/Africa)	328	314	53	11,579	139	17	44.36
8	S. C. Ganguly (India/Asia)	311	300	23	11,363	183	22	41.02
9	R. Dravid (India/World/Asia)	344	318	40	10,889	153	12	39.16
10	B. C. Lara (West Indies/World)	299	289	32	10,405	169	19	40.48
11	T. M. Dilshan (Sri Lanka)	330	303	41	10,290	161*	22	39.57
12	**V. Kohli (India)**	**216**	**208**	**37**	**10,232**	**183**	**38**	**59.83**
13	**M. S. Dhoni (India/Asia)**	**332**	**282**	**79**	**10,173**	**183***	**10**	**50.11**

The leading aggregates for players who have appeared for other Test countries are:

	M	I	NO	R	HS	100	Avge
S. P. Fleming (New Zealand/World)	280	269	21	8,037	134*	8	32.40
A. Flower (Zimbabwe)	213	208	16	6,786	145	4	35.34
E. J. G. Morgan (Ireland/England)	**212**	**199**	**29**	**6,557**	**124***	**11**	**38.57**
Tamim Iqbal (Bangladesh)	**186**	**184**	**8**	**6,450**	**154**	**11**	**36.64**
Mohammad Shahzad (Afghanistan)	**76**	**76**	**3**	**2,508**	**131***	**5**	**34.35**

Excluding runs for combined teams, the record aggregate for Sri Lanka is 13,975 in 397 matches by K. C. Sangakkara; for Australia, 13,589 in 374 matches by R. T. Ponting; for Pakistan, 11,701 in 375 matches by Inzamam-ul-Haq; for South Africa, 11,550 in 323 matches by J. H. Kallis; for West Indies, 10,348 in 295 matches by B. C. Lara; for New Zealand, 8,007 in 279 matches by S. P. Fleming; for England, 5,813 in 189 matches by E. J. G. Morgan; and for Ireland, 3,722 in 122 matches by W. T. S. Porterfield.

BEST CAREER STRIKE-RATES BY BATSMEN

(Runs per 100 balls. Qualification: 1,000 runs)

SR		Position	M	I	R	Avge
121.05	G. J. Maxwell (A)	5/6	87	78	2,242	32.02
117.00	Shahid Afridi (P/World/Asia)	2/7	398	369	8,064	23.57
116.97	**J. C. Buttler (E)**	**6/7**	**122**	**101**	**3,176**	**39.70**
114.50	L. Ronchi (A/NZ)	7	85	68	1,397	23.67
109.88	**N. L. T. C. Perera (SL)**	**7/8**	**112**	**112**	**1,867**	**19.44**
108.72	C. J. Anderson (NZ)	6	49	44	1,109	27.72

SR		Position	M	I	R	Avge
104.64	**M. M. Ali (E)**	**2/7**	**87**	**71**	**1,621**	**26.57**
104.56	**J. M. Bairstow (E)**	**2/6**	**54**	**50**	**2,017**	**48.02**
104.33	V. Sehwag (I/World/Asia)	1/2	251	245	8,273	35.05
104.24	J. P. Faulkner (A)	7/8	69	52	1,032	34.40
104.23	**J. J. Roy (E)**	**1**	**70**	**69**	**2,536**	**37.85**
101.57	**D. A. Miller (SA)**	**5/6**	**112**	**100**	**2,780**	**38.61**
101.09	**A. B. de Villiers (SA/Africa)**	**4/5**	**228**	**218**	**9,577**	**53.50**
100.05	D. J. G. Sammy (WI)	7/8	126	105	1,871	24.94

Position means a batsman's most usual position(s) in the batting order.

FASTEST ONE-DAY INTERNATIONAL FIFTIES

Balls

16	A. B. de Villiers......	South Africa v West Indies at Johannesburg	2014-15
17	S. T. Jayasuriya......	Sri Lanka v Pakistan at Singapore	1995-96
17	M. D. K. J. Perera	Sri Lanka v Pakistan at Pallekele	2015
17	M. J. Guptill	New Zealand v Sri Lanka at Christchurch	2015-16
18	S. P. O'Donnell	Australia v West Indies at Sharjah	1989-90
18	Shahid Afridi........	Pakistan v Sri Lanka at Nairobi	1996-97
18	Shahid Afridi........	Pakistan v Netherlands at Colombo (SSC)...........	2002
18	G. J. Maxwell	Australia v India at Bangalore	2013-14
18	Shahid Afridi........	Pakistan v Bangladesh at Mirpur	2013-14
18	B. B. McCullum	New Zealand v England at Wellington...............	2014-15
18	A. J. Finch	Australia v Sri Lanka at Dambulla	2016

FASTEST ONE-DAY INTERNATIONAL HUNDREDS

Balls

31	A. B. de Villiers	South Africa v West Indies at Johannesburg	2014-15
36	C. J. Anderson.......	New Zealand v West Indies at Queenstown..........	2013-14
37	Shahid Afridi........	Pakistan v Sri Lanka at Nairobi	1996-97
44	M. V. Boucher.......	South Africa v Zimbabwe at Potchefstroom	2006-07
45	B. C. Lara	West Indies v Bangladesh at Dhaka.............	1999-2000
45	Shahid Afridi........	Pakistan v India at Kanpur	2004-05
46	J. D. Ryder	New Zealand v West Indies at Queenstown..........	2013-14
46	J. C. Buttler	England v Pakistan at Dubai	2015-16
48	S. T. Jayasuriya	Sri Lanka v Pakistan at Singapore	1995-96

HIGHEST PARTNERSHIP FOR EACH WICKET

304	**for 1st**	Imam-ul-Haq/Fakhar Zaman	P v Z	Bulawayo.........	**2018**
372	for 2nd	C. H. Gayle/M. N. Samuels	WI v Z	Canberra	2014-15
258	for 3rd	D. M. Bravo/D. Ramdin	WI v Z	Basseterre	2014-15
275*	for 4th	M. Azharuddin/A. Jadeja	I v Z	Cuttack	1997-98
256*	for 5th	D. A. Miller/J.-P. Duminy	SA v Z	Hamilton	2014-15
267*	for 6th	G. D. Elliott/L. Ronchi	NZ v SL	Dunedin	2014-15
177	for 7th	J. C. Buttler/A. U. Rashid	E v NZ	Birmingham	2015
138*	for 8th	J. M. Kemp/A. J. Hall	SA v I	Cape Town	2006-07
132	for 9th	A. D. Mathews/S. L. Malinga	SL v A	Melbourne........	2010-11
106*	for 10th	I. V. A. Richards/M. A. Holding	WI v E	Manchester	1984

BOWLING RECORDS

BEST BOWLING ANALYSES

8-19	W. P. U. J. C. Vaas	Sri Lanka v Zimbabwe at Colombo (SSC)	2001-02
7-12	Shahid Afridi	Pakistan v West Indies at Providence	2013
7-15	G. D. McGrath	Australia v Namibia at Potchefstroom...........	2002-03
7-18	Rashid Khan	Afghanistan v West Indies at Gros Islet	2017

7-20	A. J. Bichel	Australia v England at Port Elizabeth	2002-03
7-30	M. Muralitharan	Sri Lanka v India at Sharjah	2000-01
7-33	T. G. Southee	New Zealand v England at Wellington	2014-15
7-34	T. A. Boult	New Zealand v West Indies at Christchurch	2017-18
7-36	Waqar Younis	Pakistan v England at Leeds	2001
7-37	Aqib Javed	Pakistan v India at Sharjah...................	1991-92
7-45	Imran Tahir	South Africa v West Indies at Basseterre.......	2016
7-51	W. W. Davis	West Indies v Australia at Leeds	1983

The best analyses for other Test countries are:

6-4	S. T. R. Binny	India v Bangladesh at Mirpur	2014
6-19	H. K. Olonga	Zimbabwe v England at Cape Town	1999-2000
6-26	Mashrafe bin Mortaza	Bangladesh v Kenya at Nairobi	2006
6-26	Rubel Hossain	Bangladesh v New Zealand at Mirpur	2013-14
6-31	P. D. Collingwood	England v Bangladesh at Nottingham	2005
6-55	P. R. Stirling	Ireland v Afghanistan at Greater Noida........	2016-17

HAT-TRICKS

Four Wickets in Four Balls

S. L. Malinga   Sri Lanka v South Africa at Providence..................... 2006-07

Four Wickets in Five Balls

Saqlain Mushtaq   Pakistan v Zimbabwe at Peshawar......................... 1996-97

Most Hat-Tricks

| S. L. Malinga .... | 3 | W. P. U. J. C. Vaas†..... | 2 |
| Saqlain Mushtaq........ | 2 | Wasim Akram .... | 2 |

† *W. P. U. J. C. Vaas took the second of his two hat-tricks, for Sri Lanka v Bangladesh at Pietermaritzburg in 2002-03, with the first three balls of the match.*

Hat-Tricks

There have been **46** hat-tricks in one-day internationals, including the above. Those since 2016-17:

Taskin Ahmed	Bangladesh v Sri Lanka at Dambulla......................	2016-17
P. W. H. de Silva	Sri Lanka v Zimbabwe at Galle	2017
K. Yadav	India v Australia at Kolkata	2017-18
D. S. M. Kumara	**Sri Lanka v Bangladesh at Mirpur**......................	**2017-18**
Imran Tahir	**South Africa v Zimbabwe at Bloemfontein**	**2018-19**
T. A. Boult	**New Zealand v Pakistan at Abu Dhabi**..................	**2018-19**

MOST WICKETS

		M	Balls	R	W	BB	4I	Avge
1	M. Muralitharan (SL/World/Asia)......	350	18,811	12,326	534	7-30	25	23.08
2	Wasim Akram (Pakistan).............	356	18,186	11,812	502	5-15	23	23.52
3	Waqar Younis (Pakistan).............	262	12,698	9,919	416	7-36	27	23.84
4	W. P. U. J. C. Vaas (SL/Asia)........	322	15,775	11,014	400	8-19	13	27.53
5	Shahid Afridi (Pakistan/World/Asia) ...	398	17,670	13,635	395	7-12	13	34.51
6	S. M. Pollock (SA/World/Africa)......	303	15,712	9,631	393	6-35	17	24.50
7	G. D. McGrath (Australia/World)......	250	12,970	8,391	381	7-15	16	22.02
8	B. Lee (Australia)	221	11,185	8,877	380	5-22	23	23.36
9	A. Kumble (India/Asia).............	271	14,496	10,412	337	6-12	10	30.89
10	S. T. Jayasuriya (Sri Lanka/Asia).....	445	14,874	11,871	323	6-29	12	36.75
11	J. Srinath (India)	229	11,935	8,847	315	5-23	10	28.08
12	**S. L. Malinga (Sri Lanka)**..........	**210**	**10,094**	**8,929**	**311**	**6-38**	**18**	**28.71**

		M	Balls	R	W	BB	4I	Avge
13	D. L. Vettori (New Zealand/World)	295	14,060	9,674	305	5-7	10	31.71
14	S. K. Warne (Australia/World)	194	10,642	7,541	293	5-33	13	25.73
15	Saqlain Mushtaq (Pakistan)..........	169	8,770	6,275	288	5-20	17	21.78
	A. B. Agarkar (India)................	191	9,484	8,021	288	6-42	12	27.85
17	Zaheer Khan (India/Asia)	200	10,097	8,301	282	5-42	8	29.43
18	J. H. Kallis (S. Africa/World/Africa)....	328	10,750	8,680	273	5-30	4	31.79
19	A. A. Donald (South Africa)..........	164	8,561	5,926	272	6-23	13	21.78
20	J. M. Anderson (England)	194	9,584	7,861	269	5-23	13	29.22
	Abdul Razzaq (Pakistan/Asia)........	265	10,941	8,564	269	6-35	11	31.83
	Harbhajan Singh (India/Asia)	236	12,479	8,973	269	5-31	5	33.35
23	M. Ntini (South Africa/World)	173	8,687	6,559	266	6-22	12	24.65
24	**Mashrafe bin Mortaza (Bang/Asia)...**	**202**	**10,102**	**8,093**	**258**	**6-26**	**8**	**31.38**
25	Kapil Dev (India)...................	225	11,202	6,945	253	5-43	4	27.45

The leading aggregates for players who have appeared for other Test countries are:

H. H. Streak (Zimbabwe)	189	9,468	7,129	239	5-32	8	29.82
C. A. Walsh (West Indies)	205	10,822	6,918	227	5-1	7	30.47
Rashid Khan (Afghanistan)	**52**	**2,623**	**1,708**	**118**	**7-18**	**8**	**14.47**
K. J. O'Brien (Ireland)	**128**	**4,089**	**3,576**	**112**	**4-13**	**5**	**31.92**

Excluding wickets taken for combined teams, the record for Sri Lanka is 523 in 343 matches by M. Muralitharan; for South Africa, 387 in 294 matches by S. M. Pollock; for Australia, 380 in 249 matches by G. D. McGrath; for India, 334 in 269 matches by A. Kumble; for New Zealand, 297 in 291 matches by D. L. Vettori; for Bangladesh, 257 in 200 matches by Mashrafe bin Mortaza; and for Zimbabwe, 237 in 187 matches by H. H. Streak.

BEST CAREER STRIKE-RATES BY BOWLERS

(Balls per wicket. Qualification: 1,500 balls)

SR		M	W
22.22	**Rashid Khan (Afg)**	**52**	**118**
25.43	**K. Yadav (I)**.....................	**33**	**67**
25.93	**M. A. Starc (A)**	**75**	**145**
26.93	**Mustafizur Rahman (B)**	**40**	**73**
26.95	Mohammed Shami (I).............	47	87
26.98	**M. J. Henry (NZ)**	**36**	**68**
27.10	Hamid Hassan (Afg)...............	32	56
27.22	S. W. Tait (A)....................	35	62
27.32	B. A. W. Mendis (SL).............	87	152
28.13	**Mohammed Shami (I)**.............	**52**	**94**
28.35	**J. J. Bumrah (I)**..................	**44**	**78**
28.48	M. J. McClenaghan (NZ)	48	82
28.72	R. N. ten Doeschate (Netherlands)	33	55

BEST CAREER ECONOMY-RATES

(Runs conceded per six balls. Qualification: 50 wickets)

ER		M	W
3.09	J. Garner (WI)...................	98	146
3.28	R. G. D. Willis (E)	64	80
3.30	R. J. Hadlee (NZ)	115	158
3.32	M. A. Holding (WI)	102	142
3.40	A. M. E. Roberts (WI)	56	87
3.48	C. E. L. Ambrose (WI)............	176	225

WICKETKEEPING AND FIELDING RECORDS

MOST DISMISSALS IN AN INNINGS

6 (6 ct)	A. C. Gilchrist	Australia v South Africa at Cape Town	1999-2000
6 (6 ct)	A. J. Stewart	England v Zimbabwe at Manchester	2000
6 (5ct, 1st)	R. D. Jacobs	West Indies v Sri Lanka at Colombo (RPS)	2001-02
6 (5ct, 1st)	A. C. Gilchrist	Australia v England at Sydney	2002-03
6 (6 ct)	A. C. Gilchrist	Australia v Namibia at Potchefstroom	2002-03
6 (6 ct)	A. C. Gilchrist	Australia v Sri Lanka at Colombo (RPS)	2003-04
6 (6 ct)	M. V. Boucher	South Africa v Pakistan at Cape Town	2006-07
6 (5ct, 1st)	M. S. Dhoni	India v England at Leeds	2007
6 (6 ct)	A. C. Gilchrist	Australia v India at Vadodara	2007-08
6 (5ct, 1st)	A. C. Gilchrist	Australia v India at Sydney	2007-08
6 (6 ct)	M. J. Prior	England v South Africa at Nottingham	2008
6 (6 ct)	J. C. Buttler	England v South Africa at The Oval	2013
6 (6 ct)	M. H. Cross	Scotland v Canada at Christchurch	2013-14
6 (5ct, 1st)	Q. de Kock	S. Africa v N. Zealand at Mount Maunganui	2014-15
6 (6 ct)	Sarfraz Ahmed	Pakistan v South Africa at Auckland	2014-15

MOST DISMISSALS

			M	Ct	St
1	482	K. C. Sangakkara (Sri Lanka/World/Asia)	360	384	98
2	472	A. C. Gilchrist (Australia/World)	282	417	55
3	**425**	**M. S. Dhoni (India/Asia)**	**332**	**310**	**115**
4	424	M. V. Boucher (South Africa/Africa)	294	402	22
5	287	Moin Khan (Pakistan)	219	214	73
6	242	B. B. McCullum (New Zealand)	185	227	15
7	234	I. A. Healy (Australia)	168	195	39
8	220	Rashid Latif (Pakistan)	166	182	38
9	206	R. S. Kaluwitharana (Sri Lanka)	186	131	75
10	204	P. J. L. Dujon (West Indies)	169	183	21
	204	**Mushfiqur Rahim (Bangladesh)**	**186**	**162**	**42**

The leading aggregates for players who have appeared for other Test countries are:

178	**J. C. Buttler (England)**	**121**	**153**	**25**
165	A. Flower (Zimbabwe)	186	133	32
96	**N. J. O'Brien (Ireland)**	**80**	**82**	**14**
82	**Mohammad Shahzad (Afghanistan)**	**75**	**58**	**24**

*Excluding dismissals for combined teams, the most for Sri Lanka is 473 (378ct, 95st) in 353 matches by K. C. Sangakkara; for Australia, 470 (416ct, 54st) in 281 matches by A. C. Gilchrist; for India, 419 (307ct, 112st) in 329 matches by **M. S. Dhoni**; and for South Africa, 415 (394ct, 21st) in 289 matches by M. V. Boucher.*

K. C. Sangakkara's list excludes 19 catches taken in 44 one-day internationals when not keeping wicket; M. V. Boucher's record excludes one in one; B. B. McCullum's excludes 35 in 75; R. S. Kaluwitharana's one in three; Mushfiqur Rahim's two in 72; A. Flower's eight in 27; N. J. O'Brien's eight in 23; and Mohammad Shahzad's one in one. A. C. Gilchrist played five one-day internationals and J. C. Buttler one without keeping wicket, but they made no catches in those games. R. Dravid (India) made 210 dismissals (196ct, 14st) in 344 one-day internationals but only 86 (72ct, 14st) in 74 as wicketkeeper (including one where he took over during the match).

MOST CATCHES IN AN INNINGS IN THE FIELD

5	J. N. Rhodes	South Africa v West Indies at Bombay	1993-94

*There have been **38** instances of four catches in an innings.*

MOST CATCHES

Ct	M		Ct	M	
218	448	D. P. M. D. Jayawardene (SL/Asia)	127	398	Shahid Afridi (Pak/World/Asia)
160	375	R. T. Ponting (Australia/World)			
156	334	M. Azharuddin (India)			*Most catches for other Test countries:*
140	463	S. R. Tendulkar (India)	120	227	C. L. Hooper (West Indies)
133	280	S. P. Fleming (New Zealand/World)	**120**	**281**	**C. H. Gayle (WI/World)**
131	**207**	**L. R. P. L. Taylor (New Zealand)**	108	197	P. D. Collingwood (England)
131	328	J. H. Kallis (SA/World/Africa)	86	221	G. W. Flower (Zimbabwe)
130	262	Younis Khan (Pakistan)	**58**	**202**	**Mashrafe bin Mortaza (Ban/As)**
130	350	M. Muralitharan (SL/World/Asia)	**57**	**122**	**W. T. S. Porterfield (Ireland)**
127	273	A. R. Border (Australia)	**50**	**106**	**Mohammad Nabi (Afghanistan)**

Excluding catches taken for combined teams, the record aggregate for Sri Lanka is 213 in 442 matches by D. P. M. D. Jayawardene; for Australia, 158 in 374 by R. T. Ponting; for New Zealand, 132 in 279 by S. P. Fleming; for South Africa, 131 in 323 by J. H. Kallis; and for Bangladesh, 57 in 200 by Mashrafe bin Mortaza.

Younis Khan's record excludes five catches made in three one-day internationals as wicketkeeper.

TEAM RECORDS

HIGHEST INNINGS TOTALS

481-6	**(50 overs)**	**England v Australia at Nottingham**	**2018**
444-3	(50 overs)	England v Pakistan at Nottingham	2016
443-9	(50 overs)	Sri Lanka v Netherlands at Amstelveen	2006
439-2	(50 overs)	South Africa v West Indies at Johannesburg	2014-15
438-4	(50 overs)	South Africa v India at Mumbai	2015-16
438-9	(49.5 overs)	South Africa v Australia at Johannesburg	2005-06
434-4	(50 overs)	Australia v South Africa at Johannesburg	2005-06
418-5	(50 overs)	South Africa v Zimbabwe at Potchefstroom	2006-07
418-5	(50 overs)	India v West Indies at Indore	2011-12
417-6	(50 overs)	Australia v Afghanistan at Perth	2014-15
414-7	(50 overs)	India v Sri Lanka at Rajkot	2009-10
413-5	(50 overs)	India v Bermuda at Port-of-Spain	2006-07
411-4	(50 overs)	South Africa v Ireland at Canberra	2014-15
411-8	(50 overs)	Sri Lanka v India at Rajkot	2009-10
408-5	(50 overs)	South Africa v West Indies at Sydney	2014-15
408-9	(50 overs)	England v New Zealand at Birmingham	2015
404-5	(50 overs)	India v Sri Lanka at Kolkata	2014-15
402-2	(50 overs)	New Zealand v Ireland at Aberdeen	2008
401-3	(50 overs)	India v South Africa at Gwalior	2009-10

The highest totals by other Test countries are:

399-1	**(50 overs)**	**Pakistan v Zimbabwe at Bulawayo**	**2018**
372-2	(50 overs)	West Indies v Zimbabwe at Canberra	2014-15
351-7	(50 overs)	Zimbabwe v Kenya at Mombasa	2008-09
338	(50 overs)	Afghanistan v Ireland at Greater Noida	2016-17
331-6	**(50 overs)**	**Ireland v Scotland at Dubai**	**2017-18**
331-8	(50 overs)	Ireland v Zimbabwe at Hobart	2014-15
329-6	(50 overs)	Bangladesh v Pakistan at Mirpur	2014-15

HIGHEST TOTALS BATTING SECOND

438-9	(49.5 overs)	South Africa v Australia at Johannesburg (*Won by 1 wicket*) . .	2005-06
411-8	(50 overs)	Sri Lanka v India at Rajkot (*Lost by 3 runs*)	2009-10
372-6	(49.2 overs)	South Africa v Australia at Durban (*Won by 4 wickets*)	2016-17
366-8	(50 overs)	England v India at Cuttack (*Lost by 15 runs*)	2016-17
365-9	(45 overs)	England v New Zealand at The Oval (*Lost by 13 runs DLS*) . . .	2015
365	**(48.5 overs)**	**England v Scotland at Edinburgh (*Lost by 6 runs*)**	**2018**

362-1	(43.3 overs)	India v Australia at Jaipur (*Won by 9 wickets*)	2013-14
356-7	(48.1 overs)	India v England at Pune (*Won by 3 wickets*)	2016-17
351-4	(49.3 overs)	India v Australia at Nagpur (*Won by 6 wickets*).	2013-14
350-3	(44 overs)	England v New Zealand at Nottingham (*Won by 7 wickets*) . . .	2015
350-9	(49.3 overs)	New Zealand v Australia at Hamilton (*Won by 1 wicket*)	2006-07

HIGHEST MATCH AGGREGATES

872-13	(99.5 overs)	South Africa v Australia at Johannesburg	2005-06
825-15	(100 overs)	India v Sri Lanka at Rajkot	2009-10
763-14	(96 overs)	England v New Zealand at The Oval	2015
747-14	(100 overs)	India v England at Cuttack	2016-17
743-12	(99.2 overs)	South Australia v Australia at Durban	2016-17
736-15	**(98.5 overs)**	**Scotland v England at Edinburgh.**	**2018**
730-9	(100 overs)	South Africa v West Indies at Johannesburg	2014-15
726-14	(95.1 overs)	New Zealand v India at Christchurch	2008-09
721-6	(93.3 overs)	India v Australia at Jaipur	2013-14
720-16	**(87 overs)**	**England v Australia at Nottingham**	**2018**

LOWEST INNINGS TOTALS

35	(18 overs)	Zimbabwe v Sri Lanka at Harare	2003-04
36	(18.4 overs)	Canada v Sri Lanka at Paarl	2002-03
38	(15.4 overs)	Zimbabwe v Sri Lanka at Colombo (SSC)	2001-02
43	(19.5 overs)	Pakistan v West Indies at Cape Town	1992-93
43	(20.1 overs)	Sri Lanka v South Africa at Paarl	2011-12
44	(24.5 overs)	Zimbabwe v Bangladesh at Chittagong	2009-10
45	(40.3 overs)	Canada v England at Manchester	1979
45	(14 overs)	Namibia v Australia at Potchefstroom	2002-03

The lowest totals by other Test countries are:

54	(26.3 overs)	India v Sri Lanka at Sharjah	2000-01
54	(23.2 overs)	West Indies v South Africa at Cape Town	2003-04
58	(18.5 overs)	Bangladesh v West Indies at Mirpur	2010-11
58	(17.4 overs)	Bangladesh v India at Mirpur	2014
58	(16.1 overs)	Afghanistan v Zimbabwe at Sharjah	2015-16
64	(35.5 overs)	New Zealand v Pakistan at Sharjah	1985-86
69	(28 overs)	South Africa v Australia at Sydney	1993-94
70	(25.2 overs)	Australia v England at Birmingham	1977
70	(26.3 overs)	Australia v New Zealand at Adelaide	1985-86
77	(27.4 overs)	Ireland v Sri Lanka at St George's	2006-07
86	(32.4 overs)	England v Australia at Manchester	2001

LARGEST VICTORIES

290 runs	New Zealand (402-2 in 50 overs) v Ireland (112 in 28.4 ov) at Aberdeen	2008
275 runs	Australia (417-6 in 50 overs) v Afghanistan (142 in 37.3 overs) at Perth	2014-15
272 runs	South Africa (399-6 in 50 overs) v Zimbabwe (127 in 29 overs) at Benoni . . .	2010-11
258 runs	South Africa (301-8 in 50 overs) v Sri Lanka (43 in 20.1 overs) at Paarl	2011-12
257 runs	India (413-5 in 50 overs) v Bermuda (156 in 43.1 overs) at Port-of-Spain	2006-07
257 runs	South Africa (408-5 in 50 overs) v West Indies (151 in 33.1 overs) at Sydney .	2014-15
256 runs	Australia (301-6 in 50 overs) v Namibia (45 in 14 overs) at Potchefstroom . . .	2002-03
256 runs	India (374-4 in 50 overs) v Hong Kong (118 in 36.5 overs) at Karachi	2008
255 runs	Pakistan (337-6 in 47 overs) v Ireland (82 in 23.4 overs) at Dublin	2016

*There have been **53** instances of victory by ten wickets.*

TIED MATCHES

There have been **37** tied one-day internationals. Australia have tied nine matches; Bangladesh are the only Test country never to have tied. The most recent ties are:

South Africa (230-6 in 31 overs) v West Indies (190-6 in 26.1 overs) at Cardiff (D/L)	2013
Ireland (268-5 in 50 overs) v Netherlands (268-9 in 50 overs) at Amstelveen	2013
Pakistan (229-6 in 50 overs) v West Indies (229-9 in 50 overs) at Gros Islet	2013
Pakistan (266-5 in 47 overs) v Ireland (275-5 in 47 overs) at Dublin (D/L)	2013
New Zealand (314 in 50 overs) v India (314-9 in 50 overs) at Auckland	2013-14
Sri Lanka (286-9 in 50 overs) v England (286-8 in 50 overs) at Nottingham	2016
Zimbabwe (257 in 50 overs) v West Indies (257-8 in 50 overs) at Bulawayo.	2016-17
Zimbabwe (210 in 46.4 overs) v Scotland (210 in 49.1 overs) at Bulawayo	**2017-18**
Afghanistan (252-8 in 50 overs) v India (252 in 49.5 overs) at Dubai	**2018-19**
India (321-6 in 50 overs) v West Indies (321-7 in 50 overs) at Visakhapatnam	**2018-19**

OTHER RECORDS

MOST APPEARANCES

463	S. R. Tendulkar (I)		**332**	**M. S. Dhoni (I/Asia)**
448	D. P. M. D. Jayawardene (SL/Asia)		330	T. M. Dilshan (SL)
445	S. T. Jayasuriya (SL/Asia)		328	J. H. Kallis (SA/World/Africa)
404	K. C. Sangakkara (SL/World/Asia)		325	S. R. Waugh (A)
398	Shahid Afridi (P/World/Asia)		322	W. P. U. J. C. Vaas (SL/Asia)
378	Inzamam-ul-Haq (P/Asia)		311	S. C. Ganguly (I/Asia)
375	R. T. Ponting (A/World)		308	P. A. de Silva (SL)
356	Wasim Akram (P)		304	Yuvraj Singh (I/Asia)
350	M. Muralitharan (SL/World/Asia)		303	S. M. Pollock (SA/World/Africa)
344	R. Dravid (I/World/Asia)		300	T. M. Dilshan (SL)
334	M. Azharuddin (I)			

*Excluding appearances for combined teams, the record for Sri Lanka is 441 by S. T. Jayasuriya; for Pakistan, 393 by Shahid Afridi; for Australia, 374 by R. T. Ponting; for South Africa, 323 by J. H. Kallis; for West Indies, 295 by B. C. Lara; for New Zealand, 291 by D. L. Vettori; for Zimbabwe, 221 by G. W. Flower; for Bangladesh, **200** by **Mashrafe bin Mortaza**; for England, 197 by P. D. Collingwood; for Ireland, **128** by **K. J. O'Brien**; and for Afghanistan, **106** by **Mohammad Nabi**.*

MOST MATCHES AS CAPTAIN

	P	W	L	T	NR		P	W	L	T	NR
R. T. Ponting (A/World)	230	165	51	2	12	S. C. Ganguly (I/Asia) .	147	76	66	0	5
S. P. Fleming (NZ)	218	98	106	1	13	Imran Khan (P).......	139	75	59	1	4
M. S. Dhoni (I)	**200**	**110**	**74**	**5**	**11**	W. J. Cronje (SA)......	138	99	35	1	3
A. Ranatunga (SL)....	193	89	95	1	8	D. P. M. D.	138	99	35	1	3
A. R. Border (A)	178	107	67	1	3	Jayawardene (SL/As)..	129	71	49	1	8
M. Azharuddin (I)	174	90	76	2	6	B. C. Lara (WI)	125	59	59	1	7
G. C. Smith (SA/Af) ..	150	92	51	1	6						

An expanded and regularly updated online version of the Records can be found at www.wisdenrecords.com

WORLD CUP RECORDS

WORLD CUP FINALS

1975	WEST INDIES (291-8) beat Australia (274) by 17 runs	Lord's
1979	WEST INDIES (286-9) beat England (194) by 92 runs	Lord's
1983	INDIA (183) beat West Indies (140) by 43 runs	Lord's
1987	AUSTRALIA (253-5) beat England (246-8) by seven runs	Calcutta
1992	PAKISTAN (249-6) beat England (227) by 22 runs.	Melbourne
1996	SRI LANKA (245-3) beat Australia (241-7) by seven wickets	Lahore
1999	AUSTRALIA (133-2) beat Pakistan (132) by eight wickets.	Lord's
2003	AUSTRALIA (359-2) beat India (234) by 125 runs	Johannesburg
2007	AUSTRALIA (281-4) beat Sri Lanka (215-8) by 53 runs (D/L method)	Bridgetown
2011	INDIA (277-4) beat Sri Lanka (274-6) by six wickets	Mumbai
2015	AUSTRALIA (186-3) beat New Zealand (183) by seven wickets	Melbourne

TEAM RESULTS

	Rounds reached			Matches				
	W	F	SF	P	W	L	T	NR
Australia (11).............	5	7	7	84	62	20	1	1
New Zealand (11)	–	1	7	79	48	30	–	1
India (11)	2	3	6	75	46	27	1	1
England (11)	–	3	5	72	41	29	1	1
West Indies (11).	2	3	4	71	41	29	–	1
Pakistan (11)	1	2	6	71	40	29	–	2
South Africa (7)..........	–	–	4	55	35	18	2	–
Sri Lanka (11)	1	3	4	73	35	35	1	2
Bangladesh (5)............	–	–	–	32	11	20	–	1
Zimbabwe (9)	–	–	–	57	11	42	1	3
Ireland (3)	–	–	–	21	7	13	1	–
Kenya (5)................	–	–	1	29	6	22	–	1
Canada (4)...............	–	–	–	18	2	16	–	–
Netherlands (4)	–	–	–	20	2	18	–	–
Afghanistan (1)	–	–	–	6	1	5	–	–
United Arab Emirates (2).....	–	–	–	11	1	10	–	–
Bermuda (1)..............	–	–	–	3	–	3	–	–
East Africa (1)	–	–	–	3	–	3	–	–
Namibia (1)	–	–	–	6	–	6	–	–
Scotland (3)	–	–	–	14	–	14	–	–

The number of tournaments each team has played in is shown in brackets. Matches abandoned or cancelled without a ball bowled are not included.

BATTING RECORDS

Highest Scores

237*	M. J. Guptill	New Zealand v West Indies at Wellington	2014-15
215	C. H. Gayle	West Indies v Zimbabwe at Canberra	2014-15
188*	G. Kirsten	South Africa v United Arab Emirates at Rawalpindi ...	1995-96
183	S. C. Ganguly	India v Sri Lanka at Taunton.	1999
181	I. V. A. Richards	West Indies v Sri Lanka at Karachi.	1987-88
178	D. A. Warner	Australia v Afghanistan at Perth	2014-15
175*	Kapil Dev	India v Zimbabwe at Tunbridge Wells	1983
175	V. Sehwag	India v Bangladesh at Mirpur	2010-11
172*	C. B. Wishart	Zimbabwe v Namibia at Harare	2002-03
171*	G. M. Turner†	New Zealand v East Africa at Birmingham	1975
162*	A. B. de Villiers	South Africa v West Indies at Sydney	2014-15

161*	T. M. Dilshan	Sri Lanka v Bangladesh at Melbourne	2014-15
161	A. C. Hudson	South Africa v Netherlands at Rawalpindi	1995-96
160	Imran Nazir	Pakistan v Zimbabwe at Kingston.	2006-07

Highest scores for other Test-playing countries:

158	A. J. Strauss	England v India at Bangalore	2010-11
128*	Mahmudullah	Bangladesh v New Zealand at Hamilton.	2014-15
115*	J. P. Bray	Ireland v Zimbabwe at Kingston.	2006-07
96	Samiullah Shenwari	Afghanistan v Scotland at Dunedin (University Oval) . .	2014-15

† Turner scored 171* on the opening day of the inaugural World Cup in 1975.

Most Hundreds

6, S. R. Tendulkar (I); 5, R. T. Ponting (A) and K. C. Sangakkara (SL); 4, A. B. de Villiers (SA),
T. M. Dilshan (SL), S. C. Ganguly (I), D. P. M. D. Jayawardene (SL) and M. E. Waugh (A); 3, M. L.
Hayden (A), S. T. Jayasuriya (SL), Ramiz Raja (P), I. V. A. Richards (WI) and Saeed Anwar (P).

Most Runs in a Tournament

673, S. R. Tendulkar (I) 2002-03; 659, M. L. Hayden (A) 2006-07; 548, D. P. M. D. Jayawardene
(SL) 2006-07; 547, M. J. Guptill (NZ) 2014-15; 541, K. C. Sangakkara (SL) 2014-15; 539, R. T.
Ponting (A) 2006-07; 523, S. R. Tendulkar (I) 1995-96; 500, T. M. Dilshan (SL) 2010-11.

Most Runs

	M	I	NO	R	HS	100	Avge
S. R. Tendulkar (India).	45	44	4	2,278	152	6	56.95
R. T. Ponting (Australia)	46	42	4	1,743	140*	5	45.86
K. C. Sangakkara (Sri Lanka) . . .	37	35	8	1,532	124	5	56.74
B. C. Lara (West Indies)	34	33	4	1,225	116	2	42.24
A. B. de Villiers (South Africa) . .	23	22	3	1,207	162*	4	63.52
S. T. Jayasuriya (Sri Lanka).	38	37	3	1,165	120	3	34.26
J. H. Kallis (South Africa)	36	32	7	1,148	128*	1	45.92
T. M. Dilshan (Sri Lanka) . . .	27	25	4	1,112	161*	4	52.95
D. P. M. D. Jayawardene (SL) . . .	40	34	3	1,100	115*	4	35.48
A. C. Gilchrist (Australia)	31	31	1	1,085	149	1	36.16
Javed Miandad (Pakistan)	33	30	5	1,083	103*	1	43.32
S. P. Fleming (New Zealand). . . .	33	33	3	1,075	134*	2	35.83
H. H. Gibbs (South Africa)	25	23	4	1,067	143	2	56.15
P. A. de Silva (Sri Lanka)	35	32	3	1,064	145	2	36.68
I. V. A. Richards (West Indies) . .	23	21	5	1,013	181	3	63.31
S. C. Ganguly (India).	21	21	3	1,006	183	4	55.88
M. E. Waugh (Australia)	22	22	3	1,004	130	4	52.84

Highest Partnership for Each Wicket

282	for 1st	W. U. Tharanga and T. M. Dilshan.	SL v Z	Pallekele	2010-11
372	for 2nd	C. H. Gayle and M. N. Samuels	WI v Z	Canberra	2014-15
237*	for 3rd	R. Dravid and S. R. Tendulkar.	I v K	Bristol	1999
204	for 4th	M. J. Clarke and B. J. Hodge	A v Neth	Basseterre	2006-07
256*	for 5th	D. A. Miller and J-P. Duminy.	SA v Z	Hamilton	2014-15
162	for 6th	K. J. O'Brien and A. R. Cusack	Ire v E	Bangalore	2010-11
107	for 7th {	Shaiman Anwar and Amjad Javed	UAE v Ire	Brisbane	2014-15
		Amjad Javed and Nasir Aziz.	UAE v WI	Napier	2014-15
117	for 8th	D. L. Houghton and I. P. Butchart	Z v NZ	Hyderabad (India)	1987-88
126*	for 9th	Kapil Dev and S. M. H. Kirmani	I v Z	Tunbridge Wells	1983
71	for 10th	A. M. E. Roberts and J. Garner.	WI v I	Manchester	1983

BOWLING RECORDS

Best Bowling

7-15	G. D. McGrath	Australia v Namibia at Potchefstroom	2002-03
7-20	A. J. Bichel	Australia v England at Port Elizabeth	2002-03
7-33	T. G. Southee	New Zealand v England at Wellington	2014-15
7-51	W. W. Davis	West Indies v Australia at Leeds	1983
6-14	G. J. Gilmour	Australia v England at Leeds	1975
6-23	A. Nehra	India v England at Durban	2002-03
6-23	S. E. Bond	New Zealand v Australia at Port Elizabeth	2002-03
6-25	W. P. U. J. C. Vaas	Sri Lanka v Bangladesh at Pietermaritzburg	2002-03
6-27	K. A. J. Roach	West Indies v Netherlands at Delhi	2010-11
6-28	M. A. Starc	Australia v New Zealand at Auckland	2014-15
6-38	S. L. Malinga	Sri Lanka v Kenya at Colombo (RPS)	2010-11
6-39	K. H. MacLeay	Australia v India at Nottingham	1983

Best analyses for other Test-playing countries:

5-16	Shahid Afridi	Pakistan v Kenya at Hambantota	2010-11
5-18	A. J. Hall	South Africa v England at Bridgetown	2006-07
5-21	P. A. Strang	Zimbabwe v Kenya at Patna.	1995-96
5-39	V. J. Marks	England v Sri Lanka at Taunton.	1983
4-21	Shafiul Islam	Bangladesh v Ireland at Mirpur	2010-11
4-32	A. R. Cusack	Ireland v Zimbabwe at Hobart	2014-15
4-38	Shapoor Zadran	Afghanistan v Scotland at Dunedin (University Oval) .	2014-15

Other Bowling Records

Hat-tricks: Chetan Sharma, India v New Zealand at Nagpur, 1987-88; Saqlain Mushtaq, Pakistan v Zimbabwe at The Oval, 1999; W. P. U. J. C. Vaas, Sri Lanka v Bangladesh at Pietermaritzburg, 2002-03 (the first three balls of the match); B. Lee, Australia v Kenya at Durban, 2002-03; S. L. Malinga, Sri Lanka v South Africa at Providence, 2006-07 (four wickets in four balls); K. A. J. Roach, West Indies v Netherlands at Delhi, 2010-11; S. L. Malinga, Sri Lanka v Kenya at Colombo (RPS), 2010-11; S. T. Finn, England v Australia at Melbourne, 2014-15; J-P. Duminy, South Africa v Sri Lanka at Sydney, 2014-15.

Most economical bowling (minimum 10 overs): 12–8–6–1, B. S. Bedi, India v East Africa at Leeds, 1975.

Most expensive bowling (minimum 10 overs): 12–1–105–2, M. C. Snedden, New Zealand v England at The Oval, 1983; 10–2–104–1, J. O. Holder, West Indies v South Africa at Sydney, 2014-15; 10–1–101–2, Dawlat Zadran, Afghanistan v Australia at Perth, 2014-15.

Most Wickets in a Tournament

26, G. D. McGrath (A) 2006-07; 23, M. Muralitharan (SL) 2006-07, S. W. Tait (A) 2006-07 and W. P. U. J. C. Vaas (SL) 2002-03; 22, T. A. Boult (NZ) 2014-15, B. Lee (A) 2002-03, M. A. Starc (A) 2014-15; 21, G. B. Hogg (A) 2006-07, G. D. McGrath (A) 2002-03, Shahid Afridi (P) 2010-11 and Zaheer Khan (I) 2010-11; 20, G. I. Allott (NZ) 1999 and S. K. Warne (A) 1999.

Most Wickets

	M	B	R	W	BB	4I	Avge
G. D. McGrath (Australia). . . .	39	1,955	1,292	71	7-15	2	18.19
M. Muralitharan (Sri Lanka) . .	40	2,061	1,335	68	4-19	4	19.63
Wasim Akram (Pakistan).	38	1,947	1,311	55	5-28	3	23.83
W. P. U. J. C. Vaas (Sri Lanka)	31	1,570	1,040	49	6-25	2	21.22
Zaheer Khan (India).	23	1,193	890	44	4-42	1	20.22
J. Srinath (India)	34	1,700	1,224	44	4-30	2	27.81
S. L. Malinga (Sri Lanka)	22	1,024	908	43	6-38	2	21.11
A. A. Donald (South Africa) . .	25	1,313	913	38	4-17	2	24.02
J. D. P. Oram (New Zealand) .	23	1,094	768	36	4-39	2	21.33

	M	B	R	W	BB	41	Avge
D. L. Vettori (New Zealand) ..	32	1,689	1,168	36	4-18	2	32.44
B. Lee (Australia)	17	825	629	35	5-42	3	17.97
G. B. Hogg (Australia).......	21	951	654	34	4-27	2	19.23
Imran Khan (Pakistan).......	28	1,017	655	34	4-37	2	19.26
S. W. Tait (Australia)........	18	819	731	34	4-39	1	21.50
T. G. Southee (New Zealand) .	17	920	784	33	7-33	1	23.75
S. K. Warne (Australia)	28	1,166	624	32	4-29	4	19.50
C. Z. Harris (New Zealand) ...	17	977	861	32	4-7	1	26.90

WICKETKEEPING RECORDS

Most Dismissals in an Innings

6 (6ct)	A. C. Gilchrist	Australia v Namibia at Potchefstroom	2002-03
6 (6ct)	Sarfraz Ahmed	Pakistan v South Africa at Auckland	2014-15
5 (5ct)	S. M. H. Kirmani	India v Zimbabwe at Leicester	1983
5 (4ct, 1st)	J. C. Adams	West Indies v Kenya at Pune	1995-96
5 (4ct, 1st)	Rashid Latif	Pakistan v New Zealand at Lahore	1995-96
5 (5ct)	R. D. Jacobs	West Indies v New Zealand at Southampton	1999
5 (4ct, 1st)	N. R. Mongia	India v Zimbabwe at Leicester	1999
5 (5ct)	Umar Akmal........	Pakistan v Zimbabwe at Brisbane.............	2014-15

Most Dismissals in a Tournament

21, A. C. Gilchrist (A) 2002-03; 17, A. C. Gilchrist (A) 2006-07 and K. C. Sangakkara (SL) 2002-03; 16, R. Dravid (I) 2002-03, P. J. L. Dujon (WI) 1983, B. J Haddin (A) 2014-15 and Moin Khan (P) 1999; 15, M. S. Dhoni (I) 2014-15, D. J. Richardson (SA) 1991-92, K. C. Sangakkara (SL) 2006-07.

Most Dismissals

K. C. Sangakkara (SL) 54 (41ct, 13st)	D. Ramdin (WI) .... 26 (26 ct)
A. C. Gilchrist (A) 52 (45ct, 7st)	A. J. Stewart (E)............ 23 (21ct, 2st)
M. S. Dhoni (I) 32 (27ct, 5st)	R. D. Jacobs (WI)........... 22 (21ct, 1st)
B. B. McCullum (NZ)....... 32 (30ct, 2st)	Wasim Bari (P)............ 22 (18ct, 4st)
M. V. Boucher (SA)........ 31 (31 ct)	A. Bagai (Canada) 21 (19ct, 2st)
Moin Khan (P) 30 (23ct, 7st)	I. A. Healy (A) 21 (18ct, 3st)
B. J Haddin (A)............. 29 (29 ct)	P. J. L. Dujon (WI)......... 20 (19ct, 1st)

B. B. McCullum took a further two catches in nine matches when not keeping wicket.

FIELDING RECORDS

Most Catches

28, R. T. Ponting (A); 18, S. T. Jayasuriya (SL); 16, C. L. Cairns (NZ), Inzamam-ul-Haq (P), D. P. M D. Jayawardene (SL) and B. C. Lara (WI); 15, G. C. Smith (SA); **14**, P. A. de Silva (SL), A. Kumble (I), W. T. S. Porterfield (Ire) and S. R. Waugh (A).

MOST APPEARANCES

46, R. T. Ponting (A); 45, S. R. Tendulkar (I); 40, D. P. M D. Jayawardene (SL) and M. Muralitharan (SL); 39, G. D. McGrath (A); 38, S. T. Jayasuriya (SL) and Wasim Akram (P); 37, K. C. Sangakkara (SL); 36, J. H. Kallis (SA); 35, P. A. de Silva (SL) and Inzamam-ul-Haq (P); 34, B. C. Lara (WI),

B. B. McCullum (NZ) and J. Srinath (I); 33, S. P. Fleming (NZ), Javed Miandad (P) and S. R. Waugh (A); 32, D. L. Vettori (NZ).

TEAM RECORDS

Highest Totals

417-6	(50 overs)	Australia v Afghanistan at Perth	2014-15
413-5	(50 overs)	India v Bermuda at Port-of-Spain	2006-07
411-4	(50 overs)	South Africa v Ireland at Canberra	2014-15
408-5	(50 overs)	South Africa v West Indies at Sydney	2014-15
398-5	(50 overs)	Sri Lanka v Kenya at Kandy	1995-96
393-6	(50 overs)	New Zealand v West Indies at Wellington	2014-15
377-6	(50 overs)	Australia v South Africa at Basseterre.	2006-07
376-9	(50 overs)	Australia v Sri Lanka at Sydney	2014-15
373-6	(50 overs)	India v Sri Lanka at Taunton	1999
372-2	(50 overs)	West Indies v Zimbabwe at Canberra	2014-15
370-4	(50 overs)	India v Bangladesh at Mirpur	2010-11

Highest totals for other Test-playing countries:

349	(49.5 overs)	Pakistan v Zimbabwe at Kingston	2006-07
340-2	(50 overs)	Zimbabwe v Namibia at Harare.	2002-03
338-8	(50 overs)	England v India at Bangalore	2010-11
331-8	(50 overs)	Ireland v Zimbabwe at Hobart.	2014-15
322-4	(48.1 overs)	Bangladesh v Scotland at Nelson	2014-15
232	(49.4 overs)	Afghanistan v Sri Lanka at Dunedin (University Oval)	2014-15

Highest total batting second:

338-8	(50 overs)	England v India at Bangalore	2010-11

Lowest Totals

36	(18.4 overs)	Canada v Sri Lanka at Paarl	2002-03
45	(40.3 overs)	Canada v England at Manchester	1979
45	(14 overs)	Namibia v Australia at Potchefstroom.	2002-03
58	(18.5 overs)	Bangladesh v West Indies at Mirpur	2010-11
68	(31.3 overs)	Scotland v West Indies at Leicester.	1999
69	(23.5 overs)	Kenya v New Zealand at Chennai	2010-11
74	(40.2 overs)	Pakistan v England at Adelaide.	1991-92
77	(27.4 overs)	Ireland v Sri Lanka at St George's	2006-07
78	(24.4 overs)	Bermuda v Sri Lanka at Port-of-Spain	2006-07
78	(28 overs)	Bangladesh v South Africa at Mirpur	2010-11

Highest Aggregate

688-18	(96.2 overs)	Australia v Sri Lanka at Sydney	2014-15

RESULTS

Largest Victories

10 wkts	India beat East Africa at Leeds	1975
10 wkts	West Indies beat Zimbabwe at Birmingham	1983
10 wkts	West Indies beat Pakistan at Melbourne	1991-92
10 wkts	South Africa beat Kenya at Potchefstroom	2002-03
10 wkts	Sri Lanka beat Bangladesh at Pietermaritzburg	2002-03
10 wkts	South Africa beat Bangladesh at Bloemfontein	2002-03
10 wkts	Australia beat Bangladesh at North Sound	2006-07
10 wkts	New Zealand beat Kenya at Chennai	2010-11
10 wkts	New Zealand beat Zimbabwe at Ahmedabad	2010-11

10 wkts	Pakistan beat West Indies at Mirpur	2010-11
10 wkts	Sri Lanka beat England at Colombo (RPS)	2010-11
275 runs	Australia beat Afghanistan at Perth	2014-15
257 runs	India beat Bermuda at Port-of-Spain	2006-07
257 runs	South Africa beat West Indies at Sydney	2014-15
256 runs	Australia beat Namibia at Potchefstroom	2002-03

Narrowest Victories

1 wkt	West Indies beat Pakistan at Birmingham	1975
1 wkt	Pakistan beat West Indies at Lahore	1987-88
1 wkt	South Africa beat Sri Lanka at Providence	2006-07
1 wkt	England beat West Indies at Bridgetown	2006-07
1 wkt	Afghanistan beat Scotland at Dunedin	2014-15
1 wkt	New Zealand beat Australia at Auckland	2014-15
1 run	Australia beat India at Madras	1987-88
1 run	Australia beat India at Brisbane	1991-92
2 runs	Sri Lanka beat England at North Sound	2006-07

Ties

Australia v South Africa at Birmingham	1999
South Africa v Sri Lanka (D/L) at Durban	2002-03
Ireland v Zimbabwe at Kingston	2006-07
India v England at Bangalore	2010-11

TWENTY20 INTERNATIONAL RECORDS

Matches in this section do not have first-class status.

This section covers Twenty20 international cricket to December 31, 2018. Bold type denotes performances since January 1, 2018, or, in career figures, players who have appeared in Twenty20 internationals since that date.

RESULTS SUMMARY OF TWENTY20 INTERNATIONALS

2004-05 to December 31, 2018 (717 matches)

	Matches	Won	Lost	No Result	% Won (excl. NR)
Afghanistan...............	68	46	22	–	67.64
India.....................	110	70*	37	3	65.42
Pakistan..................	139	90*	49†	–	64.74
South Africa..............	107	63	43	1	59.43
Australia.................	114	58	54†	2	51.78
Sri Lanka................	110	56*	53	1	51.37
England..................	105	51*	50	4	50.49
New Zealand.............	114	56†	55‡	3	50.45
West Indies..............	107	51†	52*	4	49.51
Ireland..................	69	27§	35	6	43.65
Bangladesh..............	85	26	57	2	31.32
Zimbabwe................	62	14*	48	–	22.58
Netherlands..............	50	26	21	3	55.31
Scotland	50	20§	26	3	43.61
Hong Kong..............	24	10	14	–	41.66
Kenya	29	10	19	–	34.48
United Arab Emirates..........	27	9	18	–	33.33
Papua New Guinea...........	9	3	6	–	33.33
Oman	17	5	11	1	31.25
Nepal....................	12	3	8	1	27.27
World XI.................	4	1	3	–	25.00
Canada	19	4	15*	–	21.05
Bermuda	3	–	3	–	0.00

* *Includes one game settled by a tie-break.*		† *Includes two settled by a tie-break.*	
‡ *Includes three settled by a tie-break.*		§ *Plus one tie.*	

Apart from Ireland v Scotland, ties were decided by bowling contests or one-over eliminators.

Matches abandoned without a ball bowled are not included except where the toss took place, when they are shown as no result. In the percentages of matches won, ties are counted as half a win.

BATTING RECORDS

HIGHEST INDIVIDUAL INNINGS

172	**A. J. Finch**	**Australia v Zimbabwe at Harare**.....................	**2018**
156	A. J. Finch	Australia v England at Southampton	2013
145*	G. J. Maxwell	Australia v Sri Lanka at Pallekele.....................	2016
125*	E. Lewis	West Indies v India at Kingston	2017
124*	S. R. Watson	Australia v India at Sydney...........................	2015-16
123	B. B. McCullum	New Zealand v Bangladesh at Pallekele.................	2012-13
122	Babar Hayat	Hong Kong v Oman at Fatullah	2015-16
119	F. du Plessis	South Africa v West Indies at Johannesburg	2014-15
118*	Mohammad Shahzad	Afghanistan v Zimbabwe at Sharjah....................	2015-16
118	R. G. Sharma	India v Sri Lanka at Indore...........................	2017-18
117*	R. E. Levi	South Africa v New Zealand at Hamilton................	2011-12

117*	Shaiman Anwar	United Arab Emirates v Papua New Guinea at Abu Dhabi	2016-17
117	C. H. Gayle	West Indies v South Africa at Johannesburg	2007-08
116*	B. B. McCullum	New Zealand v Australia at Christchurch	2009-10
116*	A. D. Hales	England v Sri Lanka at Chittagong	2013-14
114*	M. N. van Wyk	South Africa v West Indies at Durban	2014-15
111*	Ahmed Shehzad	Pakistan v Bangladesh at Mirpur	2013-14
111*	**R. G. Sharma**	**India v West Indies at Lucknow**	**2018-19**
110*	K. L. Rahul	India v West Indies at Lauderhill	2016

MOST RUNS

		M	I	NO	R	HS	100	Avge	SR
1	**M. J. Guptill (New Zealand)**	75	73	7	2,271	105	2	34.40	132.88
2	**R. G. Sharma (India)**	90	82	14	2,237	118	4	32.89	138.17
3	**Shoaib Malik (Pakistan/World)**	108	101	30	2,190	75	0	30.84	123.24
4	**V. Kohli (India)**	65	60	16	2,167	90*	0	49.25	136.11
5	B. B. McCullum (New Zealand)	71	70	10	2,140	123	2	35.66	136.21
6	Mohammad Shahzad (Afghanistan)	65	65	3	1,936	118*	1	31.22	134.81
7	Mohammad Hafeez (Pakistan)	89	86	8	1,908	86	0	24.46	116.12
8	T. M. Dilshan (Sri Lanka)	80	79	12	1,889	104*	1	28.19	120.67
9	J-P. Duminy (South Africa)	78	72	23	1,858	96*	0	37.91	124.36
10	D. A. Warner (Australia)	70	70	3	1,792	90*	0	26.74	140.10
11	E. J. G. Morgan (England)	77	74	13	1,734	85*	0	28.42	131.16
12	Umar Akmal (Pakistan)	82	77	14	1,690	94	0	26.82	122.90
13	A. B. de Villiers (South Africa)	78	75	11	1,672	79*	0	26.12	135.16
14	A. J. Finch (Australia)	50	50	7	1,663	172	2	38.67	156.29
15	Tamim Iqbal (Bangladesh/World)	75	75	5	1,613	103*	1	23.04	116.63
16	M. N. Samuels (West Indies)	67	65	10	1,611	89*	0	29.29	116.23
17	C. H. Gayle (West Indies)	56	52	4	1,607	117	2	33.47	143.09
18 {	A. D. Hales (England)	57	57	7	1,605	116*	1	32.10	136.24
	S. K. Raina (India)	78	66	11	1,605	101	1	29.18	134.87
20	H. Masakadza (Zimbabwe)	58	58	2	1,516	93*	0	27.07	117.06
21	D. P. M. D. Jayawardene (Sri Lanka)	55	55	8	1,493	100	1	31.76	133.18
22	M. S. Dhoni (India)	93	80	40	1,487	56	0	37.17	127.09
23	Shakib Al Hasan (Bangladesh)	72	72	9	1,471	84	0	23.34	122.99
24	L. R. P. L. Taylor (New Zealand)	84	76	18	1,467	63	0	25.29	121.23
25	S. R. Watson (Australia)	58	56	6	1,462	124*	1	29.24	145.32
26	Ahmed Shehzad (Pakistan)	57	57	2	1,454	111*	1	26.43	115.67
27	K. S. Williamson (New Zealand)	54	52	7	1,424	73*	0	31.64	121.08
28	Shahid Afridi (Pakistan)	99	91	12	1,416	54*	0	17.92	150.00

The leading aggregates for players who have appeared for other Test countries are:

	P. R. Stirling (Ireland)	52	51	4	1,181	81	0	25.12	135.90

Excluding runs for the World XI, the record aggregate for Bangladesh is 1,556 in 71 matches by Tamim Iqbal.

FASTEST TWENTY20 INTERNATIONAL FIFTIES

Balls

12	Yuvraj Singh	India v England at Durban	2007-08
14	C. Munro	New Zealand v Sri Lanka at Auckland	2015-16
16	**S. D. Hope**	**West Indies v Bangladesh at Sylhet**	**2018-19**
17	P. R. Stirling	Ireland v Afghanistan at Dubai	2011-12
17	S. J. Myburgh	Netherlands v Ireland at Sylhet	2013-14
17	C. H. Gayle	West Indies v South Africa at Cape Town	2014-15
18	D. A. Warner	Australia v West Indies at Sydney	2009-10
18	G. J. Maxwell	Australia v Pakistan at Mirpur	2013-14
18	G. J. Maxwell	Australia v Sri Lanka at Pallekele	2016
18	**C. Munro**	**New Zealand v West Indies at Mount Maunganui**	**2017-18**
18	**C. Munro**	**New Zealand v England at Hamilton**	**2017-18**
18	**E. Lewis**	**West Indies v Bangladesh at Mirpur**	**2018-19**

FASTEST TWENTY20 INTERNATIONAL HUNDREDS

Balls

35	D. A. Miller	South Africa v Bangladesh at Potchefstroom.	2017-18
35	R. G. Sharma	India v Sri Lanka at Indore.	2017-18
45	R. E. Levi	South Africa v New Zealand at Hamilton	2011-12
46	F. du Plessis	South Africa v West Indies at Johannesburg	2014-15
46	K. L. Rahul.	India v West Indies at Lauderhill	2016
47	A. J. Finch	Australia v England at Southampton	2013
47	C. H. Gayle.	West Indies v England at Mumbai	2015-16
47	**C. Munro. . . . .**	**New Zealand v West Indies at Mount Maunganui . .**	**2017-18**
48	E. Lewis	West Indies v India at Lauderhill	2016
49	G. J. Maxwell	Australia v Sri Lanka at Pallekele.	2016
49	**M. J. Guptill . . . .**	**New Zealand v Australia at Auckland . . . .**	**2017-18**

HIGHEST PARTNERSHIP FOR EACH WICKET

223	for 1st	A. J. Finch/D. J. M. Short	A v Z	**Harare**	**2018**
166	for 2nd	D. P. M. D. Jayawardene/K. C. Sangakkara	SL v WI	Bridgetown	2010
152	for 3rd	A. D. Hales/E. J. G. Morgan.	E v SL	Chittagong	2013-14
161	for 4th	D. A. Warner/G. J. Maxwell.	A v SA	Johannesburg	2015-16
119*	for 5th	Shoaib Malik/Misbah-ul-Haq.	P v A	Johannesburg	2007-08
101*	for 6th	C. L. White/M. E. K. Hussey	A v SL	Bridgetown	2010
91	for 7th	P. D. Collingwood/M. H. Yardy.	E v WI	The Oval	2007
80	for 8th	P. L. Mommsen/S. M. Sharif	Scot v Neth	Edinburgh	2015
66	for 9th	D. J. Bravo/J. E. Taylor	WI v P	Dubai	2016-17
31*	for 10th	Wahab Riaz/Shoaib Akhtar	P v NZ	Auckland	2010-11

BOWLING RECORDS

BEST BOWLING ANALYSES

6-8	B. A. W. Mendis	Sri Lanka v Zimbabwe at Hambantota	2012-13
6-16	B. A. W. Mendis	Sri Lanka v Australia at Pallekele.	2011-12
6-25	Y. S. Chahal	India v England at Bangalore	2016-17
5-3	H. M. R. K. B. Herath	Sri Lanka v New Zealand at Chittagong	2013-14
5-3	Rashid Khan	Afghanistan v Ireland at Greater Noida	2016-17
5-6	Umar Gul	Pakistan v New Zealand at The Oval	2009
5-6	Umar Gul	Pakistan v South Africa at Centurion	2012-13
5-13	Elias Sunny	Bangladesh v Ireland at Belfast	2012
5-13	Samiullah Shenwari	Afghanistan v Kenya at Sharjah	2013-14
5-14	Imad Wasim	Pakistan v West Indies at Dubai	2016-17
5-15	**K. M. A. Paul**	**West Indies v Bangladesh at Mirpur**	**2018-19**
5-18	T. G. Southee	New Zealand v Pakistan at Auckland.	2010-11
5-19	R. McLaren	South Africa v West Indies at North Sound	2010
5-19	M. A. A. Jamil	Netherlands v South Africa at Chittagong	2013-14
5-20	N. N. Odhiambo	Kenya v Scotland at Nairobi.	2009-10

HAT-TRICKS

B. Lee	Australia v Bangladesh at Cape Town	2007-08
J. D. P. Oram	New Zealand v Sri Lanka at Colombo (RPS).	2009
T. G. Southee	New Zealand v Pakistan at Auckland.	2010-11
N. L. T. C. Perera	Sri Lanka v India at Ranchi	2015-16
S. L. Malinga	Sri Lanka v Bangladesh at Colombo (RPS)	2016-17
Fahim Ashraf	Pakistan v Sri Lanka at Abu Dhabi	2017-18

Southee took four wickets in five balls.

MOST WICKETS

		M	B	R	W	BB	4I	Avge	ER
1	**Shahid Afridi (Pakistan/World)**.....	99	2,168	2,396	98	4-11	3	24.44	6.63
2	S. L. Malinga (Sri Lanka)..........	69	1,475	1,810	92	5-31	2	19.67	7.36
3	Shakib Al Hasan (Bangladesh)......	72	1,571	1,775	88	4-15	3	20.17	6.77
4 {	Umar Gul (Pakistan)	60	1,203	1,443	85	5-6	6	16.97	7.19
	Saeed Ajmal (Pakistan)............	64	1,430	1,516	85	4-19	4	17.83	6.36
6	**Mohammad Nabi (Afghanistan)**....	65	1,366	1,625	67	4-10	3	24.25	7.13
7 {	B. A. W. Mendis (Sri Lanka)........	39	885	952	66	6-8	5	14.42	6.45
	K. M. D. N. Kulasekara (Sri Lanka) ..	58	1,231	1,530	66	4-31	2	23.18	7.45
9	S. C. J. Broad (England)...........	56	1,173	1,491	65	4-24	1	22.93	7.62
10	Rashid Khan (Afghanistan/World)...	35	792	794	64	4-10	3	12.40	6.01
11	T. G. Southee (New Zealand) ..	54	1,140	1,629	63	5-18	1	25.85	8.57
12	Imran Tahir (South Africa/World) ..	37	821	927	62	5-24	3	14.95	6.77
13	G. H. Dockrell (Ireland)	54	1,030	1,132	59	4-20	1	19.18	6.59
14 {	D. W. Steyn (South Africa)..........	42	901	1,009	58	4-9	2	17.39	6.71
	K. J. O'Brien (Ireland)	67	891	1,099	58	4-45	1	18.94	7.40
	N. L. McCullum (New Zealand)	63	1,123	1,278	58	4-16	2	22.03	6.82
17	S. Badree (West Indies/World)......	52	1,146	1,180	56	4-15	1	21.07	6.17
18 {	**Mohammad Hafeez (Pakistan)**.....	89	1,117	1,226	54	4-10	1	22.70	6.58
	Sohail Tanvir (Pakistan)	57	1,214	1,454	54	3-12	0	26.92	7.18
20 {	**Mohammad Amir (Pakistan)**	41	912	1,039	52	4-13	1	19.98	6.83
	R. Ashwin (India)	46	1,026	1,193	52	4-8	2	22.94	6.97
	D. J. Bravo (West Indies)	66	1,042	1,470	52	4-28	2	28.26	8.46
23	G. P. Swann (England)	39	810	859	51	3-13	0	16.84	6.36
24 {	S. P. Narine (West Indies)	48	1,030	1,034	50	4-12	1	20.68	6.02
	N. L. T. C. Perera (Sri Lanka/World)	75	1,012	1,541	50	3-24	0	30.82	9.13

The leading aggregates for other Test countries are:

	S. R. Watson (Australia)	58	930	1,187	48	4-15	1	24.72	7.65
	A. G. Cremer (Zimbabwe)	29	570	660	35	3-11	0	18.85	6.94

*Excluding the World XI, the record aggregate for Pakistan is 97 in 98 matches by **Shahid Afridi**; for South Africa **60** in 34 by **Imran Tahir**; and for West Indies **54** in 50 matches by **S. Badree**.*

WICKETKEEPING AND FIELDING RECORDS

MOST DISMISSALS IN AN INNINGS

5 (3ct, 2st)	Mohammad Shahzad	Afghanistan v Oman at Abu Dhabi	2015-16
5 (5ct)	**M. S. Dhoni**	**India v England at Bristol**	**2018**

There have been 18 instances of four dismissals in an innings.

MOST DISMISSALS

			M	Ct	St
1	87	M. S. Dhoni (India).............................	93	54	33
2	60	Kamran Akmal (Pakistan)	53	28	32
3 {	58	D. Ramdin (West Indies)	68	38	20
	58	Mushfiqur Rahim (Bangladesh)	73	30	28
5	54	Mohammad Shahzad (Afghanistan)	64	26	28
6	45	K. C. Sangakkara (Sri Lanka)	56	25	20
7	44	Q. de Kock (South Africa)	35	35	9
8	42	Sarfraz Ahmed (Pakistan)	54	32	10

Mushfiqur Rahim's record excludes one catch in four matches when not keeping wicket. Kamran Akmal played five matches and Mohammad Shahzad one in which they did not keep wicket or take a catch.

MOST CATCHES IN AN INNINGS IN THE FIELD

4	D. J. G. Sammy	....	West Indies v Ireland at Providence	2010
4	Babar Hayat	....	Hong Kong v Afghanistan at Mirpur............	2015-16

MOST CATCHES

Ct	M			Ct	M	
47	**108**	**Shoaib Malik (Pakistan/World)**		38	62	Umar Akmal (Pakistan)
44	52	A. B. de Villiers (South Africa)		35	66	D. J. Bravo (West Indies)
44	84	L. R. P. L. Taylor (New Zealand)		34	65	**Mohammad Nabi (Afghanistan)**
42	78	S. K. Raina (India)		34	77	E. J. G. Morgan (England)
41	70	D. A. Warner (Australia)		34	78	J-P. Duminy (South Africa)
40	64	D. A. Miller (South Africa/World)		33	65	V. Kohli (India)
39	75	M. J. Guptill (New Zealand)		33	90	R. G. Sharma (India)

A. B. de Villiers' record excludes 28 dismissals (21ct, 7st) in 26 matches when keeping wicket; Umar Akmal's excludes 13 (11ct, 2st) in 20 matches.

TEAM RECORDS

HIGHEST INNINGS TOTALS

263-3	(20 overs)	Australia v Sri Lanka at Pallekele........................	2016
260-5	(20 overs)	India v Sri Lanka at Indore........................	2017-18
260-6	(20 overs)	Sri Lanka v Kenya at Johannesburg	2007-08
248-6	(20 overs)	Australia v England at Southampton	2013
245-5	**(18.5 overs)**	**Australia v New Zealand at Auckland**	**2017-18**
245-6	(20 overs)	West Indies v India at Lauderhill	2016
244-4	(20 overs)	India v West Indies at Lauderhill	2016
243-5	**(20 overs)**	**New Zealand v West Indies at Mount Maunganui**	**2017-18**
243-6	**(20 overs)**	**New Zealand v Australia at Auckland**	**2017-18**
241-6	(20 overs)	South Africa v England at Centurion	2009-10
236-6	(19.2 overs)	West Indies v South Africa at Johannesburg	2014-15
233-8	(20 overs)	Afghanistan v Ireland at Greater Noida	2016-17
231-7	(20 overs)	South Africa v West Indies at Johannesburg	2014-15
230-8	(19.4 overs)	England v South Africa at Mumbai	2015-16

LOWEST INNINGS TOTALS

39	(10.3 overs)	Netherlands v Sri Lanka at Chittagong	2013-14
53	(14.3 overs)	Nepal v Ireland at Belfast........................	2015
56	(18.4 overs)	Kenya v Afghanistan at Sharjah.......................	2013-14
60†	(15.3 overs)	New Zealand v Sri Lanka at Chittagong	2013-14
60†	**(13.4 overs)**	**West Indies v Pakistan at Karachi**	**2017-18**
67	(17.2 overs)	Kenya v Ireland at Belfast	2008
68	(16.4 overs)	Ireland v West Indies at Providence......................	2010
69	(17 overs)	Hong Kong v Nepal at Chittagong....................	2013-14
69	(17.4 overs)	Nepal v Netherlands at Amstelveen	2015
70	(20 overs)	Bermuda v Canada at Belfast	2008
70	(15.4 overs)	Bangladesh v New Zealand at Kolkata	2015-16
70	**(12.3 overs)**	**Ireland v India at Malahide**................................	**2018**

†   *One man absent.*

OTHER RECORDS

MOST APPEARANCES

108	**Shoaib Malik (Pakistan/World)**	80	T. M. Dilshan (Sri Lanka)
99	**Shahid Afridi (Pakistan/World)**	78	A. B. de Villiers (South Africa)
93	**M. S. Dhoni (India)**	78	**J-P. Duminy (South Africa)**
90	**R. G. Sharma (India)**	78	**S. K. Raina (India)**
89	**Mohammad Hafeez (Pakistan)**	77	**E. J. G. Morgan (England)**
84	**L. R. P. L. Taylor (New Zealand)**	77	**Mushfiqur Rahim (Bangladesh)**
82	Umar Akmal (Pakistan)	76	**Mahmudullah (Bangladesh)**

WORLD TWENTY20 FINALS

2007-08	INDIA (157-5) beat Pakistan (152) by five runs....................	Johannesburg
2009	PAKISTAN (139-2) beat Sri Lanka (138-6) by eight wickets	Lord's
2010	ENGLAND (148-3) beat Australia (147-6) by seven wickets	Bridgetown
2012-13	WEST INDIES (137-6) beat Sri Lanka (101) by 36 runs.............	Colombo (RPS)
2013-14	SRI LANKA (134-4) beat India (130-4) by six wickets..............	Mirpur
2015-16	WEST INDIES (161-6) beat England (155-9) by four wickets	Kolkata

MISCELLANEOUS RECORDS

LARGE ATTENDANCES

Test Series

943,000	Australia v England (5 Tests)	1936-37

In England

549,650	England v Australia (5 Tests)	1953

Test Matches

†‡465,000	India v Pakistan, Calcutta	1998-99
350,534	Australia v England, Melbourne (Third Test)	1936-37

Attendance at India v England at Calcutta in 1981-82 may have exceeded 350,000.

In England

158,000+	England v Australia, Leeds	1948
140,111	England v India, Lord's....................................	2011
137,915	England v Australia, Lord's................................	1953

Test Match Day

‡100,000	India v Pakistan, Calcutta (first four days)..................	1998-99
91,112	Australia v England, Melbourne (Fourth Test, first day).........	2013-14
90,800	Australia v West Indies, Melbourne (Fifth Test, second day)......	1960-61
89,155	Australia v England, Melbourne (Fourth Test, first day)..........	2006-07

Other First-Class Matches in England

93,000	England v Australia, Lord's (Fourth Victory Match, 3 days)	1945
80,000+	Surrey v Yorkshire, The Oval (3 days)	1906
78,792	Yorkshire v Lancashire, Leeds (3 days)......................	1904
76,617	Lancashire v Yorkshire, Manchester (3 days)	1926

One-Day Internationals

‡100,000	India v South Africa, Calcutta.............................	1993-94
‡100,000	India v West Indies, Calcutta..............................	1993-94
‡100,000	India v West Indies, Calcutta..............................	1994-95
‡100,000	India v Sri Lanka, Calcutta (World Cup semi-final)	1995-96
‡100,000	India v Australia, Kolkata	2003-04
93,013	Australia v New Zealand, Melbourne (World Cup final)	2014-15
‡90,000	India v Pakistan, Calcutta	1986-87
‡90,000	India v South Africa, Calcutta.............................	1991-92
87,182	England v Pakistan, Melbourne (World Cup final)	1991-92
86,133	Australia v West Indies, Melbourne	1983-84

Twenty20 International

84,041	Australia v India, Melbourne...............................	2007-08

† *Estimated.*
‡ *No official attendance figures were issued for these games, but capacity at Calcutta (now Kolkata) is believed to have reached 100,000 following rebuilding in 1993.*

LORD'S CRICKET GROUND

Lord's and the Marylebone Cricket Club were founded in London in 1787. The Club has enjoyed an uninterrupted career since that date, but there have been three grounds known as Lord's. The first (1787–1810) was situated where Dorset Square now is; the second (1809–13), at North Bank, had to be abandoned owing to the cutting of the Regent's Canal; and the third, opened in 1814, is the present one at St John's Wood. It was not until 1866 that the freehold of Lord's was secured by MCC. The present Pavilion was erected in 1890 at a cost of £21,000.

MINOR CRICKET

HIGHEST INDIVIDUAL SCORES

1,009*	P. P. Dhanawade, K. C. Gandhi English School v Arya Gurukul at Kalyan	2015-16
	Dhanawade faced 327 balls in 6 hours 36 minutes and hit 129 fours and 59 sixes	
628*	A. E. J. Collins, Clark's House v North Town at Clifton College.	1899
	Junior house match. He batted 6 hours 50 minutes spread over four afternoons	
566	C. J. Eady, Break-o'-Day v Wellington at Hobart	1901-02
556*	**P. Moliya, Mohinder Lal Amarnath C Ac U14 v Yogi C Ac U14 at Vadodara**	**2018-19**
546	P. P. Shaw, Rizvi Springfield School v St Francis D'Assisi School at Mumbai . .	2013-14
515	D. R. Havewalla, B. B. and C. I. Railways v St Xavier's at Bombay	1933-34
506*	J. C. Sharp, Melbourne GS v Geelong College at Melbourne	1914-15
502*	Chaman Lal, Mohindra Coll., Patiala v Government Coll., Rupar at Patiala.	1956-57
498	Arman Jaffer, Rizvi Springfield School v IES Raja Shivaji School at Mumbai. . .	2010-11
490	S. Dadswell, North West University v Potchefstroom at Potchefstroom	2017-18
486*	S. Sankruth Sriram, JSS Intl School U16 v Hebron School U16 at Ootacamund .	2014-15
485	A. E. Stoddart, Hampstead v Stoics at Hampstead.	1886
475*	Mohammad Iqbal, Muslim Model HS v Government HS, Sialkot at Gujranwala.	1958-59
473	Arman Jaffer, Rizvi Springfield School v IES VN Sule School at Mumbai.	2012-13
466*	G. T. S. Stevens, Beta v Lambda (Univ Coll School house match) at Neasden. . .	1919
	Stevens scored his 466 and took 14 wickets on one day	
461*	Ali Zorain Khan, Nagpur Cricket Academy v Reshimbagh Gymkhana at Nagpur	2010-11
459	J. A. Prout, Wesley College v Geelong College at Geelong	1908-09
451*	V. H. Mol, Maharashtra Under-19 v Assam Under-19 at Nasik	2011-12

The highest score in a Minor County match is 323* by F. E. Lacey for Hampshire v Norfolk at Southampton in 1887; the highest in the Minor Counties Championship is 282 by E. Garnett for Berkshire v Wiltshire at Reading in 1908.

HIGHEST PARTNERSHIPS

721* for 1st	B. Manoj Kumar and M. S. Tumbi, St Peter's High School v St Philip's High School at Secunderabad	2006-07
664* for 3rd	V. G. Kambli and S. R. Tendulkar, Sharadashram Vidyamandir School v St Xavier's High School at Bombay.	1987-88

Manoj Kumar and Tumbi reportedly scored 721 in 40 overs in an Under-13 inter-school match; they hit 103 fours between them, but no sixes. Their opponents were all out for 21 in seven overs.
Kambli was 16 years old, Tendulkar 14. Tendulkar made his Test debut 21 months later.

MOST WICKETS WITH CONSECUTIVE BALLS

There are **two** recorded instances of a bowler taking nine wickets with consecutive balls. Both came in school games: Paul Hugo, for Smithfield School v Aliwal North at Smithfield, South Africa, in 1930-31, and Stephen Fleming (not the future Test captain), for Marlborough College A v Bohally School at Blenheim, New Zealand, in 1967-68. There are five further verified instances of eight wickets in eight balls, the most recent by Mike Walters for the Royal Army Educational Corps v Joint Air Transport Establishment at Beaconsfield in 1979.

TEN WICKETS FOR NO RUNS

There are **26** recorded instances of a bowler taking all ten wickets in an innings for no runs, the most recent **Akash Choudhary**, for Disha Cricket Academy v Pearl Academy in the Late Bahwer Singh T20 Tournament in Jaipur 2017-18. When Jennings Tune did it, for the Yorkshire club Cliffe v Eastrington at Cliffe in 1923, all ten of his victims were bowled.

NOUGHT ALL OUT

In minor matches, this is more common than might be imagined. The historian Peter Wynne-Thomas says the first recorded example was in Norfolk, where an Eleven of Fakenham, Walsingham and Hempton were dismissed for nought by an Eleven of Licham, Dunham and Brisley in July 1815.

MOST DISMISSALS IN AN INNINGS

The only recorded instance of a wicketkeeper being involved in all ten dismissals in an innings was by Welihinda Badalge Bennett, for Mahinda College against Richmond College in Ceylon (now Sri Lanka) in 1952-53. His feat comprised six catches and four stumpings. There are three other known instances of nine dismissals in the same innings, one of which – by H. W. P. Middleton for Priory v Mitre in a Repton School house match in 1930 – included eight stumpings. Young Rangers' innings against Bohran Gymkhana in Karachi in 1969-70 included nine run-outs.

The widespread nature – and differing levels of supervision – of minor cricket matches mean that record claims have to be treated with caution. Additions and corrections to the above records for minor cricket will only be considered for inclusion in Wisden *if they are corroborated by independent evidence of the achievement.*

Research: Steven Lynch

RECORD HIT

The Rev. W. Fellows, while at practice on the Christ Church ground at Oxford in 1856, reportedly drove a ball bowled by Charles Rogers 175 yards from hit to pitch; it is claimed that the feat was matched by J. W. Erskine in a match at Galle in 1902.

BIGGEST HIT AT LORD'S

The only known instance of a batsman hitting a ball over the present pavilion at Lord's occurred when A. E. Trott, appearing for MCC against Australians on July 31, August 1, 2, 1899, drove M. A. Noble so far and high that the ball struck a chimney pot and fell behind the building.

THROWING THE CRICKET BALL

140 yards 2 feet	Robert Percival, on the Durham Sands racecourse, Co. Durham	c1882
140 yards 9 inches	Ross Mackenzie, at Toronto	1872
140 yards	"King Billy" the Aborigine, at Clermont, Queensland	1872

Extensive research by David Rayvern Allen has shown that these traditional records are probably authentic, if not necessarily wholly accurate. Modern competitions have failed to produce similar distances although Ian Pont, the Essex all-rounder who also played baseball, was reported to have thrown 138 yards in Cape Town in 1981. There have been speculative reports attributing throws of 150 yards or more to figures as diverse as the South African Test player Colin Bland, the Latvian javelin thrower Janis Lusis, who won a gold medal for the Soviet Union in the 1968 Olympics, and the British sprinter Charley Ransome. The definitive record is still awaited.

COUNTY CHAMPIONSHIP

MOST APPEARANCES

762	W. Rhodes	Yorkshire	1898–1930
707	F. E. Woolley	Kent	1906–1938
668	C. P. Mead	Hampshire	1906–1936
617	N. Gifford	Worcestershire (484), Warwickshire (133)	1960–1988
611	W. G. Quaife	Warwickshire	1895–1928
601	G. H. Hirst	Yorkshire	1891–1921

MOST CONSECUTIVE APPEARANCES

423	K. G. Suttle	Sussex	1954–1969
412	J. G. Binks	Yorkshire	1955–1969

J. Vine made 417 consecutive appearances for Sussex in all first-class matches (399 of them in the Championship) between July 1900 and September 1914.

J. G. Binks did not miss a Championship match for Yorkshire between making his debut in June 1955 and retiring at the end of the 1969 season.

UMPIRES

MOST COUNTY CHAMPIONSHIP APPEARANCES

570	T. W. Spencer	1950–1980		517	H. G. Baldwin	1932–1962
531	F. Chester	1922–1955		511	A. G. T. Whitehead	1970–2005
523	D. J. Constant	1969–2006				

MOST SEASONS ON ENGLISH FIRST-CLASS LIST

38	D. J. Constant	1969–2006		27	B. Dudleston	1984–2010
36	A. G. T. Whitehead	1970–2005		27	J. W. Holder	1983–2009
31	K. E. Palmer	1972–2002		27	J. Moss	1899–1929
31	T. W. Spencer	1950–1980		26	W. A. J. West	1896–1925
30	R. Julian	1972–2001		25	H. G. Baldwin	1932–1962
30	P. B. Wight	1966–1995		25	A. Jepson	1960–1984
29	H. D. Bird	1970–1998		25	J. G. Langridge	1956–1980
28	F. Chester	1922–1955		25	B. J. Meyer	1973–1997
28	B. Leadbeater	1981–2008		25	D. R. Shepherd	1981–2005
28	R. Palmer	1980–2007				

An expanded and regularly updated online version of the Records can be found at www.wisdenrecords.com

WOMEN'S TEST RECORDS

This section covers all women's Tests to December 31, 2018. No Tests were played in the calendar year 2018.

BATTING RECORDS

HIGHEST INDIVIDUAL INNINGS

242	Kiran Baluch............	Pakistan v West Indies at Karachi............	2003-04
214	M. D. Raj	India v England at Taunton.................	2002
213*	E. A. Perry	Australia v England at North Sydney	2017-18
209*	K. L. Rolton	Australia v England at Leeds	2001
204	K. E. Flavell	New Zealand v England at Scarborough.......	1996
204	M. A. J. Goszko	Australia v England at Shenley..............	2001
200	J. Broadbent	Australia v England at Guildford	1998

1,000 RUNS IN A CAREER

R	T		R	T	
1,935	27	J. A. Brittin (England)	1,110	13	S. Agarwal (India)
1,676	23	C. M. Edwards (England)	1,078	12	E. Bakewell (England)
1,594	22	R. Heyhoe-Flint (England)	1,030	15	S. C. Taylor (England)
1,301	19	D. A. Hockley (New Zealand)	1,007	14	M. E. Maclagan (England)
1,164	18	C. A. Hodges (England)	1,002	14	K. L. Rolton (Australia)

BOWLING RECORDS

BEST BOWLING ANALYSES

8-53	N. David	India v England at Jamshedpur	1995-96
7-6	M. B. Duggan	England v Australia at Melbourne...............	1957-58
7-7	E. R. Wilson	Australia v England at Melbourne	1957-58
7-10	M. E. Maclagan	England v Australia at Brisbane	1934-35
7-18	A. Palmer...........	Australia v England at Brisbane	1934-35
7-24	L. Johnston	Australia v New Zealand at Melbourne...........	1971-72
7-34	G. E. McConway.....	England v India at Worcester...................	1986
7-41	J. A. Burley	New Zealand v England at The Oval..............	1966

MOST WICKETS IN A MATCH

13-226	Shaiza Khan.........	Pakistan v West Indies at Karachi	2003-04

50 WICKETS IN A CAREER

W	T		W	T	
77	17	M. B. Duggan (England)	60	19	S. Kulkarni (India)
68	11	E. R. Wilson (Australia)	57	16	R. H. Thompson (Australia)
63	20	D. F. Edulji (India)	55	15	J. Lord (New Zealand)
60	13	C. L. Fitzpatrick (Australia)	50	12	E. Bakewell (England)
60	14	M. E. Maclagan (England)			

WICKETKEEPING RECORDS

SIX DISMISSALS IN AN INNINGS

8 (6ct, 2st)	L. Nye...........	England v New Zealand at New Plymouth	1991-92
6 (2ct, 4st)	B. A. Brentnall	New Zealand v South Africa at Johannesburg.......	1971-72

25 DISMISSALS IN A CAREER

		T	*Ct*	*St*
58	C. Matthews (Australia)	20	46	12
43	J. Smit (England)...................	21	39	4
36	S. A. Hodges (England).............	11	19	17
28	B. A. Brentnall (New Zealand)	10	16	12

TEAM RECORDS

HIGHEST INNINGS TOTALS

569-6 dec	Australia v England at Guildford...................................	1998
525	Australia v India at Ahmedabad....................................	1983-84
517-8	New Zealand v England at Scarborough	1996
503-5 dec	England v New Zealand at Christchurch	1934-35

LOWEST INNINGS TOTALS

35	England v Australia at Melbourne	1957-58
38	Australia v England at Melbourne	1957-58
44	New Zealand v England at Christchurch	1934-35
47	Australia v England at Brisbane	1934-35

WOMEN'S ONE-DAY INTERNATIONAL RECORDS

This section covers women's one-day international cricket to December 31, 2018. Bold type denotes performances in the calendar year 2018 or, in career figures, players who appeared in that year.

BATTING RECORDS

HIGHEST INDIVIDUAL INNINGS

232*	**A. C. Kerr**	**New Zealand v Ireland at Dublin**..................	**2018**
229*	B. J. Clark	Australia v Denmark at Mumbai....................	1997-98
188	D. B. Sharma	India v Ireland at Potchefstroom	2017
178*	A. M. C. Jayangani ...	Sri Lanka v Australia at Bristol....................	2017
173*	C. M. Edwards.......	England v Ireland at Pune	1997-98
171*	H. Kaur	India v Australia at Derby	2017
171	S. R. Taylor	West Indies v Sri Lanka at Mumbai	2012-13
168*	T. T. Beaumont	England v Pakistan at Taunton	2016
168	S. W. Bates	New Zealand v Pakistan at Sydney	2008-09
157	R. H. Priest	New Zealand v Sri Lanka at Lincoln................	2015-16
156*	L. M. Keightley......	Australia v Pakistan at Melbourne.................	1996-97
156*	S. C. Taylor	England v India at Lord's	2006
154*	K. L. Rolton........	Australia v Sri Lanka at Christchurch	2000-01
153*	J. Logtenberg........	South Africa v Netherlands at Deventer	2007
152*	M. M. Lanning.......	Australia v Sri Lanka at Bristol....................	2017
151	K. L. Rolton........	Australia v Ireland at Dublin	2005
151	**S. W. Bates**	**New Zealand v Ireland at Dublin**..................	**2018**

MOST RUNS IN A CAREER

R	*M*		*R*	*M*	
6,550	**197**	**M. D. Raj (India)**	**4,245**	**115**	**S. W. Bates (New Zealand)**
5,992	191	C. M. Edwards (England)	4,101	126	S. C. Taylor (England)
4,844	118	B. J. Clark (Australia)	4,064	118	D. A. Hockley (New Zealand)
4,814	141	K. L. Rolton (Australia)	**3,945**	**118**	**S. J. Taylor (England)**
4,284	**114**	**S. R. Taylor (West Indies)**			

BOWLING RECORDS

BEST BOWLING ANALYSES

7-4	Sajjida Shah............	Pakistan v Japan at Amsterdam................	2003
7-8	J. M. Chamberlain......	England v Denmark at Haarlem...............	1991
7-14	A. Mohammed.........	West Indies v Pakistan at Mirpur	2011-12
7-24	S. Nitschke............	Australia v England at Kidderminster...........	2005
6-10	J. Lord...............	New Zealand v India at Auckland..............	1981-82
6-10	M. Maben	India v Sri Lanka at Kandy	2003-04
6-10	S. Ismail..............	South Africa v Netherlands at Savar...........	2011-12

MOST WICKETS IN A CAREER

W	M		W	M	
207	171	**J. N. Goswami (India)**	136	112	Sana Mir (Pakistan)
180	109	C. L. Fitzpatrick (Australia)	135	143	**J. L. Gunn (England)**
146	115	**A. Mohammed (W. Indies)**	134	114	**S. R. Taylor (West Indies)**
146	125	L. C. Sthalekar (Australia)	131	100	E. A. Perry (Australia)
141	97	N. David (India)	126	98	D. van Niekerk (S. Africa)
136	112	**K. H. Brunt (England)**	125	86	S. Ismail (South Africa)

WICKETKEEPING RECORDS

MOST DISMISSALS IN AN INNINGS

6 (4ct, 2st)	S. L. Illingworth	New Zealand v Australia at Beckenham........	1993
6 (1ct, 5st)	V. Kalpana..........	India v Denmark at Slough	1993
6 (2ct, 4st)	Batool Fatima	Pakistan v West Indies at Karachi.............	2003-04
6 (4ct, 2st)	Batool Fatima	Pakistan v Sri Lanka at Colombo (PSO).........	2010-11

MOST DISMISSALS IN A CAREER

		M	Ct	St
153	T. Chetty (South Africa)	105	108	45
133	R. J. Rolls (New Zealand)	104	90	43
129	S. J. Taylor (England)	118	81	48
114	J. Smit (England)	109	69	45
105	M. R. Aguilleira (West Indies)......	112	78	27
100	Batool Fatima (Pakistan)	83	54	46
100	J. C. Price (Australia).............	84	70	30

Chetty's total includes two catches in two matches, Taylor's and Aguilleira's each include two in eight matches and Batool Fatima's three in 15 while not keeping wicket; Price's includes one taken in the field after giving up the gloves mid-game. Rolls did not keep wicket in three matches and Smit in one; neither took any catches in these games.

TEAM RECORDS

HIGHEST INNINGS TOTALS

491-4	**New Zealand v Ireland at Dublin**	**2018**
455-5	New Zealand v Pakistan at Christchurch	1996-97
440-3	**New Zealand v Ireland at Dublin**	**2018**
418	**New Zealand v Ireland at Dublin**	**2018**
412-3	Australia v Denmark at Mumbai	1997-98
397-4	Australia v Pakistan at Melbourne	1996-97
378-5	England v Pakistan at Worcester	2016
377-7	England v Pakistan at Leicester	2017
376-2	England v Pakistan at Vijayawada	1997-98
375-5	Netherlands v Japan at Schiedam.......................	2003

LOWEST INNINGS TOTALS

22	Netherlands v West Indies at Deventer	2008
23	Pakistan v Australia at Melbourne..	1996-97
24	Scotland v England at Reading...	2001
26	India v New Zealand as St Saviour	2002
27	Pakistan v Australia at Hyderabad (India)................................	1997-98
28	Japan v Pakistan at Amsterdam	2003
29	Netherlands v Australia at Perth	1988-89

WOMEN'S WORLD CUP WINNERS

1973	England		1993	England		2008-09	England
1977-78	Australia		1997-98	Australia		2012-13	Australia
1981-82	Australia		2000-01	New Zealand		2017	England
1988-89	Australia		2004-05	Australia			

WOMEN'S TWENTY20 INTERNATIONAL RECORDS

This section covers women's T20 international cricket to December 31, 2018. Bold type denotes performances in the calendar year 2018 or, in career figures, players who appeared in that year. In 2018, the ICC gave T20I status to all future matches between Members, Full or Associate.

BATTING RECORDS

HIGHEST INDIVIDUAL INNINGS

126	M. M. Lanning.......	Australia v Ireland at Sylhet	2013-14
124*	**S. W. Bates**	**New Zealand v South Africa at Taunton**...........	**2018**
124	**D. N. Wyatt**........	**England v India at Mumbai (BS)**..................	**2017-18**
117*	B. L. Mooney........	Australia v England at Canberra	2017-18
116*	S. A. Fritz.........	South Africa v Netherlands at Potchefstroom	2010-11
116	**T. T. Beaumont**	**England v South Africa at Taunton**...............	**2018**

MOST RUNS IN A CAREER

R	M		R	M	
3,007	**108**	**S. W. Bates (New Zealand)**	2,175	89	S. J. Taylor (England)
2,748	93	S. R. Taylor (West Indies)	**1,886**	**93**	**H. Kaur (India)**
2,605	95	C. M. Edwards (England)	**1,802**	**80**	**S. F. M. Devine (New Zealand)**
2,315	**85**	**M. M. Lanning (Australia)**	**1,701**	**92**	**Bismah Maroof (Pakistan)**
2,283	**85**	**M. D. Raj (India)**	1,557	73	D. van Niekerk (South Africa)
2,210	107	D. J. S. Dottin (West Indies)			

BOWLING RECORDS

BEST BOWLING ANALYSES

6-8	**B. Mpedi**............	**Botswana v Lesotho at Gaborone**	**2018**
6-17	A. E. Satterthwaite.......	New Zealand v England at Taunton	2007
5-5	**D. J. S. Dottin**.........	**West Indies v Bangladesh at Providence**.......	**2018-19**
5-8	S. E. Luus	South Africa v Ireland at Chennai...............	2015-16
5-10	A. Mohammed.........	West Indies v South Africa at Cape Town	2009-10
5-10	M. R. Strano	Australia v New Zealand at Geelong.............	2016-17
5-11	J. N. Goswami.........	India v Australia at Visakhapatnam	2011-12
5-11	A. Shrubsole	England v New Zealand at Wellington	2011-12
5-12	A. Mohammed.........	West Indies v New Zealand at Bridgetown.......	2013-14
5-12	**W. Liengprasert**........	**Thailand v Sri Lanka at Kuala Lumpur**	**2018**
5-13	A. S. S. Fletcher	West Indies v Sri Lanka at Coolidge...........	2017-18
5-15	S. F. Daley............	West Indies v Sri Lanka at Colombo (RPS)	2012-13

MOST WICKETS IN A CAREER

W	M		W	M	
113	99	A. Mohammed (West Indies)	81	59	A. Shrubsole (England)
100	102	E. A. Perry (Australia)	81	97	Sana Mir (Pakistan)
85	85	D. Hazell (England)	78	72	S. Ismail (South Africa)
82	88	Nida Dar (Pakistan)	76	80	S. F. M. Devine (New Zealand)
82	93	S. R. Taylor (West Indies)	75	104	J. L. Gunn (England)

WICKETKEEPING RECORDS

MOST DISMISSALS IN AN INNINGS

5 (1ct, 4st)	Kycia A. Knight......	West Indies v Sri Lanka at Colombo (RPS)	2012-13
5 (1ct, 4st)	Batool Fatima	Pakistan v Ireland at Dublin	2013
5 (1ct, 4st)	Batool Fatima	Pakistan v Ireland at Dublin (semi-final)........	2013
5 (3ct, 2st)	**B. M. Bezuidenhout..**	**New Zealand v Ireland at Dublin**	**2018**

MOST DISMISSALS IN A CAREER

		M	Ct	St
73	S. J. Taylor (England)	87†	23	50
72	A. J. Healy (Australia)	92†	30	42
68	R. H. Priest (New Zealand)	68†	38	30
67	M. R. Aguilleira (West Indies)......	92†	35	32
58*	J. L. Gunn (England)	104	58	
57	T. Chetty (South Africa)...........	68	34	23
54*	L. S. Greenway (England)	85	54	
53*	S. W. Bates (New Zealand)	108	53	
50	Batool Fatima (Pakistan)	45	11	39

* *Catches made by non-wicketkeeper in the field.*

† *Taylor's total includes two matches and Priest's one in the field where they made no catches; Healy's total includes 15 matches in the field where she made two catches, and Aguilleira's ten in the field where she made two catches.*

TEAM RECORDS

HIGHEST INNINGS TOTALS

250-3	**England v South Africa at Taunton**	2018
216-1	**New Zealand v South Africa at Taunton**	2018
210-5	**Namibia v Lesotho at Gaborone**	2018
209-4	**Australia v England at Mumbai (BS)**	2017-18
205-1	South Africa v Netherlands at Potchefstroom	2010-11
199-3	**England v India at Mumbai (BS)**	2017-18
198-4	**India v England at Mumbai (BS)**	2017-18
195-3	**Australia v Pakistan at Kuala Lumpur**	2018-19
194-5	**India v New Zealand at Providence**	2018-19
191-4	West Indies v Netherlands at Potchefstroom	2010-11
191-4	Australia v Ireland at Sylhet..	2013-14

LOWEST INNINGS TOTALS

18†	**Mexico v Brazil at Bogota**..	**2018-19**
25	**Mozambique v Namibia at Gaborone**	**2018**
27	**Malaysia v India at Kuala Lumpur**	**2018**
30	**Malaysia v Pakistan at Kuala Lumpur**	**2018**
30	**Bangladesh v Pakistan at Cox's Bazar**.............................	**2018-19**

† *One woman absent.*

WOMEN'S WORLD TWENTY20 WINNERS

2009	England	2012-13	Australia	2015-16	West Indies
2010	Australia	2013-14	Australia	**2018-19**	**Australia**

BIRTHS AND DEATHS

TEST CRICKETERS

Full list from 1876-77 to January 14, 2019

In the Test career column, dates in italics indicate seasons embracing two different years (i.e. non-English seasons). In these cases, only the first year is given, e.g. *1876* for 1876-77. Some non-English series taking place outside the host country's normal season are dated by a single year.

The Test career figures are complete up to January 14, 2019; the one-day international and Twenty20 international totals up to December 31, 2018. Career figures are for one national team only; those players who have appeared for more than one Test team are listed on page 1448, and for more than one one-day international or Twenty20 international team on page 1451.

The forename by which a player is known is underlined if it is not his first name.

Family relationships are indicated by superscript numbers; where the relationship is not immediately apparent from a shared name, see the notes at the end of this section. (*CY 1889*) signifies that the player was a Wisden Cricketer of the Year in the 1889 Almanack. The 5/10 column indicates instances of a player taking five wickets in a Test innings and ten wickets in a match. O/T signifies number of one-day and Twenty20 internationals played.

¹ *Father and son(s).*   ² *Brothers.*   ³ *Grandfather, father and son.*   ⁴ *Grandfather and grandson.*   ⁵ *Great-grandfather and great-grandson.*
† *Excludes matches for another ODI or T20I team.*   ‡ *Excludes matches for another Test team.*

ENGLAND (689 players)

	Born	Died	Tests	Test Career	Runs	HS	100s	Avge	Wkts	BB	5/10	Avge	Ct/St	O/T
Abel Robert (*CY 1890*)	30.11.1857	10.12.1936	13	1888–1902	744	132*	2	37.20	–	–	–/–	–	13	–
Absolom Charles Alfred	7.6.1846	30.7.1889	1	*1878*	58	52	0	29.00	–	–	–/–	–	0	
Adams Christopher John (*CY 2004*)	6.5.1970		5	1999	104	31	0	13.00	1	1-42	0/0	59.00	6	5
Afzaal Usman	9.6.1977		3	2001	83	54	0	16.60	1	1-49	0/0	49.00	6	
Agnew Jonathan Philip MBE (*CY 1988*)	4.4.1960		3	1984–1985	10	5	0	10.00	4	2-51	0/0	93.25	0	3
Ali Kabir	24.11.1980		1	2003	10	9	0	5.00	5	3-80	0/0	27.20	0	14
Ali Moeen Munir (*CY 2015*)	18.6.1987		55	2014–2018	2,692	155*	5	30.94	163	6-53	5/1	37.44	31	87/25
Allen David Arthur	29.10.1935	24.5.2014	39	1959–1966	918	88	0	25.50	122	5-30	4/0	30.97	10	
Allen Sir George Oswald Browning ("Gubby")	31.7.1902	29.11.1989	25	1930–1947	750	122	1	24.19	81	7-80	5/1	29.37	20	
Allom Maurice James Carrick	23.3.1906	8.4.1995	5	1929–1930	14	8*	0	14.00	14	5-38	1/0	18.92	0	
Allott Paul John Walter	14.9.1956		13	1981–1985	213	52*	0	14.20	26	6-61	1/0	41.69	4	13
Ambrose Timothy Raymond	1.12.1982		11	2007–2008	447	102	1	29.80	–	–	–/–	–	31	5/1

Name	Born	Died	Tests	Test Career	Runs	HS	100s	Avge	Wkts	BB	5/10	Avge	Ct/St	O/T
Ames Leslie Ethelbert George CBE (CY 1929)	3.12.1905	27.2.1990	47	1929–1938	2,434	149	8	40.56	–	–	–/–	–	74/23	
Amiss Dennis Leslie MBE (CY 1975)	7.4.1943		50	1966–1977	3,612	262*	11	46.30	–	–	–/–	–	24	18
Anderson James Michael OBE (CY 2009)	30.7.1982		145	2003–2018	1,169	81	0	9.66	565	7-42	26/3	26.98	87	194/19
Andrew Keith Vincent	15.12.1929	27.12.2010	2	1954–1963	29	15	0	9.66	–	–	–/–	–	1	
Ansari Zafar Shahaan	10.12.1991		3	2016	49	32	0	9.80	5	2-76	0/0	55.00	1	1
Appleyard Robert MBE (CY 1952)	27.6.1924	17.3.2015	9	1954–1956	51	19*	0	17.00	31	5-51	1/0	17.87	4	
Archer Alfred German	6.12.1871	15.7.1935	1	1898	31	24*	0	31.00	0	–	–/–	–	0	
Armitage Thomas	25.4.1848	21.9.1922	2	1876	33	21	0	11.00	0	0-15	0/0	–	0	
Arnold Edward George	7.11.1876	25.10.1942	10	1903–1907	160	40	0	13.33	31	5-37	1/0	25.41	8	
Arnold Geoffrey Graham (CY 1972)	3.9.1944		34	1967–1975	421	59	0	12.02	115	6-45	6/0	28.29	8	14
Arnold John	30.11.1907	4.4.1984	1	1931	34	34	0	17.00	–	–	–/–	–	0	
Astill William Ewart (CY 1933)	1.3.1888	10.2.1948	9	1927–1929	190	40	0	12.66	25	4-58	0/0	34.24	7	
Atherton Michael Andrew OBE (CY 1991)	23.3.1968		115	1989–2001	7,728	185*	16	37.69	2	1-20	0/0	151.00	83	54
Athey Charles William Jeffrey	27.9.1957		23	1980–1988	919	123	0	22.97	0	–	–/–	–	13	31
Attewell William (CY 1892)	12.6.1861	11.6.1927	10	1884–1891	150	43*	0	16.66	28	4-42	0/0	22.35	9	
Bailey Robert John	28.10.1963		4	1988–1989	119	43	0	14.87	0	–	–/–	–	0	4
Bailey Trevor Edward CBE (CY 1950)	3.12.1923	10.2.2011	61	1949–1958	2,290	134*	1	29.74	132	7-34	5/1	29.21	32	
Bairstow David Leslie	1.9.1951	5.1.1998	4	1979–1980	125	59	0	20.83	0	–	–/–	–	12/1	21
Bairstow Jonathan Marc (CY 2016)	26.9.1989		60	2012–2018	3,696	167*	6	37.71	–	–	–/–	–	157/9	54/27
Bakewell Alfred Harry (CY 1934)	2.11.1908	23.1.1983	6	1931–1935	409	107	1	45.44	0	–	–/–	–	3	
Balderstone John Christopher	16.11.1940	6.3.2000	2	1976	39	35	0	9.75	1	1-80	0/0	80.00	1	
Ball Jacob Timothy	14.3.1991		4	2016–2017	67	31	0	8.37	3	1-47	0/0	114.33	1	18/2
Ballance Gary Simon (CY 2015)	22.11.1989		23	2013–2017	1,498	156	4	37.45	–	–	–/–	–	22	16
Barber Robert William (CY 1967)	26.9.1935		28	1960–1968	1,495	185	1	35.59	42	4-132	0/0	43.00	21	
Barber Wilfred	18.4.1901	10.9.1968	2	1935	83	44	0	20.75	1	1-0	0/0	0.00	0	
Barlow Graham Derek	26.3.1950		3	1976–1977	17	7*	0	4.25	0	–	–/–	–	2	6
Barlow Richard Gorton	28.5.1851	31.7.1919	17	1881–1886	591	62	0	22.73	34	7-40	3/0	22.55	14	
Barnes Sydney Francis (CY 1910)	19.4.1873	26.12.1967	27	1901–1913	242	38*	0	8.06	189	9-103	24/7	16.43	12	
Barnes William (CY 1890)	27.5.1852	24.3.1899	21	1880–1890	725	134	0	23.38	51	6-28	3/0	15.54	19	
Barnett Charles Stowe (CY 1937)	3.7.1910	28.5.1993	20	1933–1948	1,098	129	2	35.41	0	0-1	0/0	–	14	
Barnett Kim John (CY 1989)	17.7.1960		4	1988–1989	207	80	0	29.57	0	0-32	0/0	–	2	
Barratt Fred	12.4.1894	29.1.1947	5	1929–1929	28	17	0	9.33	5	1-8	0/0	47.00	17	1
Barrington Kenneth Frank (CY 1960)	24.11.1930	14.3.1981	82	1955–1968	6,806	256	20	58.67	29	3-4	0/0	44.82	58	
Barton Victor Alexander	6.10.1867	23.3.1906	1	1891	23	23	0	23.00	0	–	–/–	–	0	
Bates Willie	19.11.1855	8.1.1900	15	1881–1886	656	64	0	27.33	50	7-28	4/1	16.42	9	
Batty Gareth Jon	13.10.1977		9	2003–2016	149	38	0	14.90	15	3-55	0/0	60.93	3	10/1

	Born	Died	Tests	Test Career	Runs	HS	100s	Avge	Wkts	BB	5/10	Avge	Ct/St	OIT
Bean George	7.3.1864	16.3.1923	3	1891	92	50	0	18.40	–	–	–/–	–	4	–
Bedser *Sir* Alec Victor CBE (CY 1947)	4.7.1918	4.4.2010	51	1946–1955	714	79	0	12.75	236	7-44	15/5	24.89	26	4
Bell Ian Ronald MBE (CY 2008)	11.4.1982	–	118	2004–2015	7,727	235	22	42.69	1	1-33	0/0	76.00	100	161/8
Benjamin Joseph Emmanuel	2.2.1961	–	1	1994	0	0	0	0.00	4	4-42	0/0	20.00	0	2
Benson Mark Richard	6.7.1958	–	1	1986	51	30	0	25.50	–	–	–/–	–	0	1
Berry Robert	29.1.1926	2.12.2006	2	1950	6	4*	0	3.00	9	5-63	1/0	25.33	2	–
Bess Dominic Mark	22.7.1997	–	2	2018	111	57	0	37.00	9	4-84	0/0	40.33	1	–
Bicknell Martin Paul (CY 2001)	14.1.1969	–	4	1993–2003	45	15	0	6.42	14	3-33	0/0	38.78	1	7
Binks James Graham (CY 1969)	5.10.1935	–	2	1963	91	55	0	22.75	–	–	–/–	–	8	–
Bird Morice Carlos	25.3.1888	9.12.1933	10	1909–1913	280	61	0	18.66	8	3-11	0/0	15.00	5	–
Birkenshaw Jack MBE	13.11.1940	–	5	1972–1973	148	64	0	21.14	13	5-57	1/0	36.07	3	–
Blackwell Ian David	10.6.1978	–	1	2005	4	4	0	4.00	0	0-28	0/0	–	0	34
Blakey Richard John	15.1.1967	–	2	1992	4	4	0	1.75	–	–	–/–	–	2	3
Bligh *Hon.* Ivo Francis Walter	13.3.1859	10.4.1927	4	1882	62	19	0	10.33	–	–	–/–	–	7	–
Blythe Colin (CY 1904)	30.5.1879	8.11.1917	19	1901–1909	183	27	0	9.63	100	8-59	9/4	18.63	6	–
Board John Henry	23.2.1867	15.4.1924	6	1898–1905	108	29	0	10.80	–	–	–/–	–	8/3	–
Bolus John Brian	31.1.1934	–	7	1963–1963	496	88	0	41.33	0	0-16	0/0	–	2	–
Booth Major William (CY 1914)	10.12.1886	1.7.1916	2	1913	46	32	0	23.00	7	4-49	0/0	18.57	0	–
Bopara Ravinder Singh	4.5.1985	–	13	2007–2012	575	143	3	31.94	1	1-39	0/0	290.00	6	120/38
Borthwick Scott George	19.4.1990	–	1	2013	5	4	0	2.50	4	3-33	0/0	20.50	2	2/1
Bosanquet Bernard James Tindal (CY 1905)	13.10.1877	12.10.1936	7	1903–1905	147	27	0	13.36	25	8-107	2/0	24.16	9	–
Botham *Sir* Ian Terence OBE (CY 1978)	24.11.1955	–	102	1977–1992	5,200	208	14	33.54	383	8-34	27/4	28.40	120	116
Bowden Montague Parker	1.11.1865	19.2.1892	2	1888	25	25	0	12.50	–	–	–/–	–	1	–
Bowes William Eric (CY 1932)	25.7.1908	4.9.1987	15	1932–1946	28	10*	0	4.66	68	6-33	6/0	22.33	2	–
Bowley Edward Henry (CY 1930)	6.6.1890	–	5	1929–1929	252	109	1	36.00	0	0-7	0/0	–	2	–
Boycott Geoffrey OBE (CY 1965)	21.10.1940	–	108	1964–1981	8,114	246*	22	47.72	7	3-47	0/0	54.57	33	36
Bradley Walter Morris	2.1.1875	19.6.1944	2	1899	23	23*	0	23.00	6	5-67	1/0	38.83	1	–
Braund Leonard Charles (CY 1902)	18.10.1875	23.12.1955	23	1901–1907	987	104	3	25.97	47	8-81	3/0	38.51	39	–
Brearley John Michael OBE (CY 1977)	28.4.1942	–	39	1976–1981	1,442	91	0	22.88	–	–	–/–	–	52	25
Brearley Walter (CY 1909)	11.3.1876	30.1.1937	4	1905–1912	21	11*	0	7.00	17	5-110	1/0	21.11	0	–
Brennan Donald Vincent	10.2.1920	9.1.1985	2	1951	16	16	0	8.00	–	–	–/–	–	0/1	–
Bresnan Timothy Thomas (CY 2012)	28.2.1985	–	23	2009–2013	575	91	0	26.13	72	5-48	1/0	32.73	8	85/34
Briggs John (CY 1889)	3.10.1862	11.1.1902	33	1884–1899	815	121	0	18.11	118	8-11	9/4	17.75	12	–
Broad Brian Christopher	29.9.1957	–	25	1984–1989	1,661	162	6	39.54	0	0-4	0/0	–	10	34
Broad Stuart Christopher John MBE (CY 2010)	24.6.1986	–	124	2007–2018	3,064	169	1	19.39	433	8-15	16/2	29.04	40	121/56
Brockwell William (CY 1895)	21.1.1865	30.6.1935	7	1893–1899	202	49	0	16.83	5	3-33	0/0	61.80	6	–

	Born	Died	Tests	Test Career	Runs	HS	100s	Avge	Wkts	BB	5/10	Avge	Ct/St	O/T
Bromley-Davenport Hugh Richard	18.8.1870	23.5.1954	4	1895–1898	128	84	0	21.33	4	2-46	0/0	24.50	1	
Brookes Dennis (CY 1957)	29.10.1915	9.3.2006	1	1947	17	10	0	8.50	–	–	–/–	–	1	
Brown Alan	17.10.1935		2	1961	3	3*	0	–	3	3-27	0/0	50.00	1	
Brown David John	30.1.1942		26	1965–1969	342	44*	0	11.79	79	5-42	2/0	28.31	7	
Brown Frederick Richard MBE (CY 1933)	16.12.1910	24.7.1991	22	1931–1953	734	79	0	25.31	45	5-49	1/0	31.06	22	
Brown George	6.10.1887	3.12.1964	7	1921–1922	299	84	0	29.90	0	–	–/–	–	9/3	
Brown John Thomas (CY 1895)	20.8.1869	4.11.1904	8	1894–1899	470	140	1	36.15	0	0-22	0/0	69.00	7	1
Brown Simon John Emmerson	29.6.1969		1	1996	11	10*	0	11.00	2	1-60	0/0	28.23	1	
Buckenham Claude Percival	16.1.1876	23.2.1937	4	1909	43	17	0	6.14	21	5-115	1/0	–	2	
Burns Rory Joseph (CY 2019)	26.8.1990		3	2018	155	59	0	25.83	0	–	–/–	–	1	
Butcher Alan Raymond (CY 1991)	7.1.1954		1	1979	34	20	0	17.00	0	0-9	0/0	–	0	1
Butcher Mark Alan	23.8.1972		71	1997–2004	4,288	173*	8	34.58	15	4-42	0/0	36.06	61	3
Butcher Roland Orlando	14.10.1953		3	1980	71	32	0	14.20	0	–	–/–	–	3	
Butler Harold James	12.3.1913	17.7.1991	2	1947–1947	15	15*	0	15.00	12	4-34	0/0	17.91	1	
Butt Henry Rigden	27.12.1865	21.12.1928	3	1895	22	13	0	7.33	–	–	–/–	–	1/1	
Butler Joseph Charles (CY 2019)	8.9.1990		28	2014–2018	1,544	106	8	36.76	–	–	–/–	–	63	122/66
Caddick Andrew Richard (CY 2001)	21.11.1968		62	1993–2002	861	49*	0	10.37	234	7-46	13/1	29.91	21	54
Calthorpe *Hon.* Frederick Somerset Gough	27.5.1892	19.11.1935	4	1929	129	49	0	18.42	1	1-38	0/0	91.00	2	
Capel David John	6.2.1963		15	1987–1989	374	98	0	15.58	21	3-88	0/0	50.66	6	23
Carberry Michael Alexander	29.9.1980		6	2009–2013	345	60	0	28.75	0	–	–/–	–	7	6/1
Carr Arthur William (CY 1923)	21.5.1893	7.2.1963	11	1922–1929	237	63	0	19.75	–	–	–/–	–	3	
Carr Donald Bryce OBE (CY 1960)	28.12.1926	12.6.2016	2	1951	135	76	0	33.75	2	2-84	0/0	70.00	0	
Carr Douglas Ward (CY 1910)	17.3.1872	23.3.1950	1	1909	0	0	0	0.00	7	5-146	2/1	40.28	0	
Cartwright Thomas William MBE	22.7.1935	30.4.2007	5	1964–1965	26	9	0	5.20	15	6-94	1/0	36.26	2	
Chapman Arthur Percy Frank (CY 1919)	3.9.1900	16.9.1961	26	1924–1930	925	121	1	28.90	0	0-10	0/0	–	32	
Charlwood Henry Rupert James	19.12.1846	6.6.1888	2	1876	63	36	0	15.75	–	–	–/–	–	1	
Chatterton William	27.12.1861	19.3.1913	1	1891	48	48	0	48.00	–	–	–/–	–	0	
Childs John Henry (CY 1987)	15.8.1951		2	1988	2	2*	0	–	3	1-13	0/0	61.00	0	
Christopherson Stanley	11.11.1861	6.4.1949	1	1884	17	17	0	17.00	1	1-52	0/0	69.00	0	
Clark Edward Winchester	9.8.1902	28.4.1982	8	1929–1934	36	10	0	9.00	32	5-98	1/0	28.09	1	
Clarke Rikki	29.9.1981		2	2003	96	55	0	32.00	4	2-7	0/0	15.00	1	20
Clay John Charles	18.3.1898	11.8.1973	1	1935	–	–	–	–	0	0-30	0/0	–	0	
Close Dennis Brian CBE (CY 1964)	24.2.1931	14.9.2015	22	1949–1976	887	70	0	25.34	18	4-35	0/0	29.55	24	3
Coldwell Leonard John	10.1.1933	6.8.1996	7	1962–1964	9	6*	0	4.50	22	6-85	1/0	27.72	1	
Collingwood Paul David MBE (CY 2007)	26.5.1976		68	2003–2010	4,259	206	10	40.56	17	3-23	0/0	59.88	96	197/35‡
[4]Compton Denis Charles Scott CBE (CY 1939)	23.5.1918	23.4.1997	78	1937–1956	5,807	278	17	50.06	25	5-70	1/0	56.40	49	

Name	Born	Died	Tests	Test Career	Runs	HS	100s	Avge	Wkts	BB	5/10	Avge	Ct/St	OIT
[4]Compton Nicholas Richard Denis (CY 2013)	26.6.1983		16	2012–2016	775	117	2	28.70	—	—	–/–	—	7	
Cook Sir Alastair Nathan CBE (CY 2012)	25.12.1984		161	2005–2018	12,472	294	33	45.35	1	1-6	0/0	7.00	175	92/4
Cook Cecil ("Sam")	23.8.1921	5.9.1996	1	1947	4	4	0	2.00	0	0-40	0/0	—	0	
Cook Geoffrey	9.10.1951		7	1981–1982	203	66	0	15.61	0	0-4	0/0	—	9	6
Cook Nicholas Grant Billson	17.6.1956		15	1983–1989	179	31	0	8.52	52	6-65	4/1	32.48	5	3
Cope Geoffrey Alan	23.2.1947		3	1977	40	22	0	13.33	8	3-102	0/0	34.62	1	3
Copson William Henry (CY 1937)	27.4.1908	13.9.1971	3	1939–1947	6	6	0	6.00	15	5-85	1/0	19.80	1	
Cork Dominic Gerald (CY 1996)	7.8.1971		37	1995–2002	864	59	0	18.00	131	7-43	5/0	29.81	18	32
Cornford Walter Latter	25.12.1900	6.2.1964	4	1929	36	18	0	9.00	—	—	–/–	—	5/3	
Cottam Robert Michael Henry	16.10.1944		4	1968–1972	27	13	0	6.75	14	4-50	0/0	23.35	2	
Coventry Hon. Charles John	26.2.1867	2.6.1929	2	1888	13	12	0	13.00	—	—	–/–	—	0	
Cowans Norman George	17.4.1961		19	1982–1985	175	36	0	7.95	51	6-77	2/0	39.27	9	23
[1]Cowdrey Christopher Stuart	20.10.1957		6	1984–1988	101	38	0	14.42	4	2-65	0/0	77.25	5	3
[1]Cowdrey Lord [Michael Colin] CBE (CY 1956)	24.12.1932	4.12.2000	114	1954–1974	7,624	182	22	44.06	0	0-1	0/0	—	120	1
Coxon Alexander	18.1.1916	22.1.2006	1	1948	19	19	0	9.50	3	2-90	0/0	57.33	0	
Crane Mason Sidney	18.02.1997		1	2017	6	4	0	3.00	1	1-193	0/0	193.00	1	0/2
Cranston James	9.1.1859	10.12.1904	1	1890	31	16	0	15.50	—	—	–/–	—	0	
Cranston Kenneth	20.10.1917	8.1.2007	8	1947–1948	209	45	0	14.92	18	4-12	0/0	25.61	3	
Crapp John Frederick	14.10.1912	13.2.1981	7	1948–1948	319	56	0	29.00	—	—	–/–	—	7	
Crawford John Neville (CY 1907)	1.12.1886	2.5.1963	12	1905–1907	469	74	1	22.33	39	5-48	3/0	29.48	13	
Crawley John Paul	21.9.1971		37	1994–2002	1,800	156*	4	34.61	—	—	–/–	—	29	13
Croft Robert Damien Bale MBE	25.5.1970		21	1996–2001	421	37*	0	16.19	49	5-95	0/0	37.24	10	50
[2]Curran Samuel Matthew (CY 2019)	3.6.1998		2	2018–2018	404	78	0	36.72	14	4-74	0/0	25.14	0	2
[2]Curran Thomas Kevin	12.03.1995		2	2017	66	39	0	33.00	2	1-65	0/0	100.00	2	11/7
Curtis Timothy Stephen	15.1.1960		5	1988–1989	140	41	0	15.55	0	0-7	0/0	—	3	
Cuttell Willis Robert (CY 1898)	13.9.1863	9.12.1929	2	1898	65	21	0	16.25	6	3-17	0/0	12.16	2	
Dawson Edward William	13.2.1904	4.6.1979	5	1927–1929	175	55	0	19.44	—	—	–/–	—	3	
Dawson Liam Andrew	1.3.1990		3	2016–2017	84	66*	0	21.00	7	2-34	0/0	42.57	2	3/6
Dawson Richard Kevin James	4.8.1980		2	2001–2002	114	19*	0	11.40	11	4-134	0/0	61.54	3	
Dean Harry	13.8.1884	12.3.1957	3	1912	10	8	0	5.00	11	4-19	0/0	13.90	0	
DeFreitas Phillip Anthony Jason (CY 1992)	18.2.1966		44	1986–1995	934	88	0	14.82	140	7-70	4/0	33.57	14	103
Denness Michael Henry OBE (CY 1975)	1.12.1940	19.4.2013	28	1969–1975	1,667	188	4	39.69	—	—	–/–	—	28	12
Denton David (CY 1906)	4.7.1874	16.2.1950	11	1905–1909	424	104	1	20.19	—	—	–/–	—	8	
Dewes John Gordon	11.10.1926	12.5.2015	5	1948–1950	121	67	0	12.10	—	—	–/–	—	0	
Dexter Edward Ralph CBE (CY 1961)	15.5.1935	5.10.2011	62	1958–1968	4,502	205	9	47.89	66	4-10	0/0	34.93	29	
Dilley Graham Roy	18.5.1959		41	1979–1989	521	56	0	13.35	138	6-38	6/0	29.76	10	36

	Born	Died	Tests	Test Career	Runs	HS	100s	Avge	Wkts	BB	5/10	Avge	Ct/St	O/T
Dipper Alfred Ernest	9.11.1885	7.11.1945	1	1921	51	40	0	25.50	–	–	–/–	–	–	–
Doggart George Hubert Graham OBE	18.7.1925	16.2.2018	2	1950	76	29	0	19.00	–	–	–/–	–	3	–
D'Oliveira Basil Lewis CBE (CY 1967)	4.10.1931	18.11.2011	44	1966–1972	2,484	158	5	40.06	47	3-46	0/0	39.55	29	4
Dollery Horace Edgar ("Tom") (CY 1952)	14.10.1914	20.1.1987	4	1947–1950	72	37	0	10.28	–	–	–/–	–	1	–
Dolphin Arthur	24.12.1885	23.10.1942	1	1920	1	1	0	0.50	–	–	–/–	–	1	–
Douglas John William Henry Tyler (CY 1915)	3.9.1882	19.12.1930	23	1911–1924	962	119	1	29.15	45	5-46	1/0	33.02	9	–
Downton Paul Rupert	4.4.1957		30	1980–1988	785	74	0	19.62	–	–	–/–	–	70/5	28
Druce Norman Frank (CY 1898)	1.1.1875	27.10.1954	5	1897	252	64	0	28.00	–	–	–/–	–	5	–
Ducat Andrew (CY 1920)	16.2.1886	23.7.1942	1	1921	5	3	0	2.50	–	–	–/–	–	1	–
Duckett Ben Matthew (CY 2017)	17.10.1994		4	2016	110	56	0	15.71	–	–	–/–	–	1	3
Duckworth George (CY 1929)	9.5.1901	5.1.1966	24	1924–1936	234	39*	0	14.62	0	0-7	–/–	–	45/15	–
Duleepsinhji Kumar Shri (CY 1930)	13.6.1905	5.12.1959	12	1929–1931	995	173	3	58.52	0	0-7	0/0	–	10	–
Durston Frederick John	11.7.1893	8.4.1965	1	1921	8	6*	0	8.00	5	4-102	0/0	27.20	4	–
Ealham Mark Alan	27.8.1969		8	1996–1998	210	53*	0	21.00	17	4-21	0/0	28.70	4	64
Edmonds Philippe-Henri	8.3.1951		51	1975–1987	875	64	0	17.50	125	7-66	2/0	34.18	42	29
Edrich John Hugh MBE (CY 1966)	21.6.1937		77	1963–1976	5,138	310*	12	43.54	0	0-6	0/0	–	43	7
Edrich William John (CY 1940)	26.3.1916	24.4.1986	39	1938–1954	2,440	219	6	40.00	41	4-68	0/0	41.29	39	–
Elliott Harry	2.11.1891	2.2.1976	4	1927–1933	61	37*	0	15.25	–	–	–/–	–	8/3	–
Ellison Richard Mark (CY 1986)	21.9.1959		11	1984–1986	202	41	0	13.46	35	6-77	3/1	29.94	2	14
Emburey John Ernest (CY 1984)	20.8.1952		64	1978–1995	1,713	75	0	22.53	147	7-78	6/0	38.40	34	61
Emmett George Malcolm	2.12.1912	18.12.1976	1	1948	10	10	0	5.00	–	–	–/–	–	–	–
Emmett Thomas	3.9.1841	29.6.1904	7	1876–1881	160	48	0	13.33	9	7-68	1/0	31.55	9	–
Evans Alfred John	1.5.1889	18.9.1960	1	1921	18	14	0	9.00	–	–	–/–	–	–	–
Evans Thomas Godfrey CBE (CY 1951)	18.8.1920	3.5.1999	91	1946–1959	2,439	104	2	20.49	0	–	–/–	–	173/46	–
Fagg Arthur Edward	18.6.1915	13.9.1977	5	1936–1939	150	39	0	18.75	0	–	–/–	–	5	–
Fairbrother Neil Harvey	9.9.1963		10	1987–1992	219	83	0	15.64	0	0-9	0/0	–	4	75
Fane Frederick Luther	27.4.1875	27.11.1960	14	1905–1909	682	143	1	26.23	–	–	–/–	–	6	–
Farnes Kenneth (CY 1939)	8.7.1911	20.10.1941	15	1934–1938	58	20	0	4.83	60	6-96	3/1	28.65	1	–
Farrimond William	23.5.1903	15.11.1979	4	1930–1935	116	35	0	16.57	–	–	–/–	–	5/2	–
Fender Percy George Herbert (CY 1915)	22.8.1892	15.6.1985	13	1920–1929	380	60	0	19.00	29	5-90	2/0	40.86	14	–
Ferris John James	21.5.1867	17.11.1900	1†	1891	16	16	0	16.00	13	7-37	2/1	7.00	–	–
Fielder Arthur (CY 1907)	19.7.1877	30.8.1949	6	1903–1907	78	20	0	11.14	26	6-82	1/0	27.34	4	–
Finn Steven Thomas	4.4.1989		36	2009–2016	279	56	0	11.16	125	6-79	5/0	30.40	8	69/21
Fishlock Laurence Barnard (CY 1947)	2.1.1907	25.6.1986	4	1936–1946	47	19*	0	11.75	–	–	–/–	–	–	–
Flavell John Alfred (CY 1965)	15.5.1929	25.2.2004	4	1961–1964	31	14	0	7.75	7	2-65	0/0	52.42	2	–
Fletcher Keith William Robert OBE (CY 1974)	20.5.1944		59	1968–1981	3,272	216	7	39.90	2	1-6	0/0	96.50	54	24

	Born	Died	Tests	Test Career	Runs	HS	100s	Avge	Wkts	BB	5/10	Avge	Ct/St	O/T
Flintoff Andrew MBE (CY 2004)	6.12.1977		78§	1998–2009	3,795	167	5	31.89	219	5-58	3/0	33.34	52	138‡/7
Flowers Wilfred	7.12.1856	1.11.1926	8	1884–1893	254	56	0	18.14	14	5-46	1/0	21.14	2	
Foakes Benjamin Thomas	15.2.1993		5	2018	277	107	1	69.25					8/2	
Ford Francis Gilbertson Justice	14.12.1866	7.2.1940	5	1894	168	48	0	18.66	1	1-47	0/0	129.00	5	
Foster Frank Rowbotham (CY 1912)	31.1.1889	3.5.1958	11	1911–1912	330	71	0	23.57	45	6-91	4/0	20.57	11	11/5
Foster James Savin	15.4.1980		7	2001–2002	226	48	0	25.11					17/1	
Foster Neil Alan (CY 1988)	6.5.1962		29	1983–1993	446	39	0	11.73	88	8-107	5/1	32.85	7	48
Foster Reginald Erskine ("Tip") (CY 1900)	16.4.1878	13.5.1914	8	1903–1907	602	287	1	46.30					13	
Fothergill Arnold James	26.8.1854	1.8.1932	2	1888	33	32	0	16.50	8	4-19	0/0	11.25	0	
Fowler Graeme	20.4.1957		21	1982–1984	1,307	201	3	35.32					10	
Fraser Angus Robert Charles MBE (CY 1996)	8.8.1965		46	1989–1998	388	32	0	7.46	177	8-53	13/2	27.32	9	26
Freeman Alfred Percy ("Tich") (CY 1923)	17.5.1888	28.1.1965	12	1924–1929	154	50*	0	14.00	66	7-71	5/3	25.86	4	42
French Bruce Nicholas	13.8.1959		16	1986–1987	308	59	0	18.11					38/1	13
Fry Charles Burgess (CY 1895)	25.4.1872	7.9.1956	26	1895–1912	1,223	144	2	32.18	0	0-3	0/0	–	17	
Gallian Jason Edward Riche	25.6.1971		3	1995–1995	74	28	0	12.33	0	0-6	0/0	–	1	
Gatting Michael William OBE (CY 1984)	6.6.1957		79	1977–1994	4,409	207	10	35.55	4	1-14	0/0	79.25	59	92
Gay Leslie Hewitt	24.3.1871	1.11.1949	1	1894	37	33	0	18.50					3/1	
Geary George (CY 1927)	9.7.1893	6.3.1981	14	1924–1934	249	66	0	15.56	46	7-70	4/1	29.41	13	
Gibb Paul Antony	11.7.1913	7.12.1977	8	1938–1946	581	120	2	44.69					3/1	
Giddins Edward Simon Hunter	20.7.1971		4	1999–2000	10	7	0	2.50	12	5-15	1/0	20.00	0	
Gifford Norman MBE (CY 1975)	30.3.1940		15	1964–1973	179	25*	0	16.27	33	5-55	1/0	31.09	8	2
Giles Ashley Fraser MBE (CY 2005)	19.3.1973		54	1998–2006	1,421	59	0	20.89	143	5-57	5/0	40.60	33	62
Gilligan Alfred Herbert Harold	29.6.1896	5.5.1978	4	1929	71	32	0	17.75					3	
²**Gilligan** Arthur Edward Robert (CY 1924)	23.12.1894	5.9.1976	11	1922–1924	209	39*	0	16.07	36	6-7	2/1	29.05	3	
Gimblett Harold (CY 1953)	19.10.1914	30.3.1978	3	1936–1939	129	67*	0	32.25					1	
Gladwin Clifford	3.4.1916	9.4.1988	8	1947–1949	170	51*	0	28.33	15	3-21	0/0	38.06	2	
Goddard Thomas William John (CY 1938)	1.10.1900	22.5.1966	8	1930–1939	13	8	0	6.50	22	6-29	1/0	26.72	3	
Gooch Graham Alan OBE (CY 1980)	23.7.1953		118	1975–1994	8,900	333	20	42.58	23	3-39	0/0	46.47	103	125
Gough Darren (CY 1999)	18.9.1970		58	1998–2003	855	65	0	12.57	229	6-42	9/0	28.39	13	158‡/2
Gover Alfred Richard MBE (CY 1937)	29.2.1908	7.10.2001	4	1936–1946	2	2*	0	–	8	3-85	0/0	44.87	–	
Gower David Ivon OBE (CY 1979)	1.4.1957		117	1978–1992	8,231	215	18	44.25	1	1-1	0/0	20.00	74	114
Grace Edward Mills	28.11.1841	20.5.1911	1	1880	36	36	0	18.00					1	
²**Grace** George Frederick	13.12.1850	22.9.1880	1	1880	0	0	0	0.00					–	
²**Grace** William Gilbert (CY 1896)	18.7.1848	23.10.1915	22	1880–1899	1,098	170	2	32.29	9	2-12	0/0	26.22	39	
Graveney Thomas William OBE (CY 1953)	16.6.1927	3.11.2015	79	1951–1969	4,882	258	11	44.38	1	1-34	0/0	167.00	80	

§ *Flintoff's figures exclude 50 runs and seven wickets for the ICC World XI v Australia in the Super Series Test in 2005-06.*

	Born	Died	Tests	Test Career	Runs	HS	100s	Avge	Wkts	BB	5/10	Avge	Ct/St	O/T
Greenhough Thomas	9.11.1931	15.9.2009	4	1959–1960	4	2	0	1.33	16	5-35	1/0	22.31	1	
Greenwood Andrew	20.8.1847	12.2.1889	2	1876	77	49	0	19.25	–	–	–/–	–	2	
[2] Greig Anthony William (CY 1975)	6.10.1946	29.12.2012	58	1972–1977	3,599	148	8	40.43	141	8-86	6/2	32.20	87	22
[2] Greig Ian Alexander	8.12.1955		2	1982	26	14	0	6.50	4	4-53	0/0	28.50	0	
Grieve Basil Arthur Firebrace	28.5.1864	19.11.1917	2	1888	40	14*	0	40.00	–	–	–/–	–	0	
Griffith Stewart Cathie CBE ("Billy")	16.6.1914	7.4.1993	3	1947–1948	157	140	1	31.40	–	–	–/–	–	5	
[2] Gunn George (CY 1914)	13.6.1879	29.6.1958	15	1907–1929	1,120	122*	2	40.00	0	0-8	0/0	–	15	
[2] Gunn John Richmond (CY 1904)	19.7.1876	21.8.1963	6	1901–1905	85	24	0	10.62	18	5-76	1/0	21.50	3	
[2] Gunn William (CY 1890)	4.12.1858	29.1.1921	11	1886–1899	392	102*	1	21.77	–	–	–/–	–	5	
Habib Aftab	7.2.1972		2	1999	26	19	0	8.66	–	–	–/–	–	0	
Haig Nigel Esmé	12.12.1887	27.10.1966	5	1921–1929	126	47	0	14.00	13	3-73	0/0	34.46	8	
Haigh Schofield (CY 1901)	19.3.1871	27.2.1921	11	1898–1912	113	25	0	7.53	24	6-11	1/0	25.91	8	
Hales Alexander Daniel	3.1.1989		11	2015–2016	573	94	0	27.28	–	–	–/–	–	8	67/57
Hallows Charles (CY 1928)	4.4.1895	10.11.1972	2	1921–1928	42	26	0	42.00	–	–	–/–	–	0	
Hameed Haseeb	17.1.1997		3	2016	219	82	0	43.80	–	–	–/–	–	4	
Hamilton Gavin Mark	16.9.1974		1	1999	0	0	0	0.00	0	0-63	0/0	–	0	0‡
Hammond Walter Reginald (CY 1928)	19.6.1903	1.7.1965	85	1927–1946	7,249	336*	22	58.45	83	5-36	2/0	37.80	110	
Hampshire John Harry	10.2.1941	1.3.2017	8	1969–1975	403	107	1	26.86	–	–	–/–	–	9	3
Hardinge Harold Thomas William ("Wally") (CY 1915)	25.2.1886	8.5.1965	1	1921	30	25	0	15.00	–	–	–/–	–	0	
[1] Hardstaff Joseph snr.	9.11.1882	2.4.1947	5	1907	311	72	0	31.10	–	–	–/–	–	1	
[1] Hardstaff Joseph jnr (CY 1938)	3.7.1911	1.1.1990	23	1935–1948	1,636	205*	4	46.74	–	–	–/–	–	9	
Harmison Stephen James MBE (CY 2005)	23.10.1978		62§	2002–2009	742	49*	0	12.16	222	7-12	8/1	31.94	7	58/2
Harris Lord [George Robert Canning]	3.2.1851	24.3.1932	4	1878–1884	145	52	0	29.00	0	0-14	0/0	–	2	
Hartley John Cabourn	15.11.1874	8.3.1963	2	1905	15	9	0	3.75	1	1-62	0/0	115.00	2	
Hawke Lord [Martin Bladen] (CY 1909)	16.8.1860	10.10.1938	5	1895–1898	55	30	0	7.85	–	–	–/–	–	3	
Hayes Ernest George (CY 1907)	6.11.1876	2.12.1953	5	1905–1912	86	35	0	10.75	–	–	–/–	–	2	
Hayes Frank Charles	6.12.1946		9	1973–1976	244	106*	1	15.25	–	–	–/–	–	7	
Hayward Thomas Walter (CY 1895)	29.3.1871	19.7.1939	35	1895–1909	1,999	137	3	34.46	14	4-22	0/0	36.71	19	6
[3] Headley Dean Warren	27.1.1970		15	1997–1999	186	31	0	8.45	60	6-60	1/0	27.85	7	13
Hearne Alec (CY 1894)	22.7.1863	16.5.1952	1	1891	9	9	0	4.50	–	–	–/–	–	1	
[1,2] Hearne Frank	23.11.1858	14.7.1949	2†	1888	47	27	0	23.50	–	–	–/–	–	1	
Hearne George Gibbons	7.7.1856	13.2.1932	1	1891	0	0	0	0.00	–	–	–/–	–		
Hearne John Thomas (CY 1892)	3.5.1867	17.4.1944	12	1891–1899	126	40	0	9.00	49	6-41	4/1	22.08	4	
[2] Hearne John William (CY 1912)	11.2.1891	14.9.1965	24	1911–1926	806	114	1	26.00	30	5-49	1/0	48.73	13	

§ *Harmison's figures exclude one run and four wickets for the ICC World XI v Australia in the Super Series Test in 2005-06.*

	Born	Died	Tests	Test Career	Runs	HS	100s	Avge	Wkts	BB	5/10	Avge	Ct/St	OIT
Hegg Warren Kevin	23.2.1968	–	2	1998	30	30	0	7.50	–	–	–/–	–	8	
Hemmings Edward Ernest	20.2.1949	–	16	1982–1990	383	95	0	22.52	43	6-58	1/0	32.44	5	33
Hendren Elias Henry ("Patsy") (CY 1920)	5.2.1889	4.10.1962	51	1920–1934	3,525	205*	7	47.63	1	1-27	0/0	31.00	33	
Hendrick Michael (CY 1978)	22.10.1948	–	30	1974–1981	128	15	0	6.40	87	4-28	0/0	25.83	25	22
Heseltine Christopher	26.11.1869	13.6.1944	2	1895	18	18	0	9.00	5	5-38	1/0	16.80	3	
Hick Graeme Ashley MBE (CY 1987)	23.5.1966	–	65	1991–2000	3,383	178	6	31.32	23	4-126	0/0	56.78	90	120
Higgs Kenneth (CY 1968)	14.1.1937	–	15	1965–1968	185	63	0	11.56	71	6-91	2/0	20.74	4	
Hill Allen	14.11.1843	7.9.2016	2	1876	101	49	0	50.50	7	4-27	0/0	18.57	1	
Hill Arthur James Ledger	26.7.1871	28.8.1910	2	1895	251	124	0	62.75	4	4-8	0/0	2.00	1	
Hilton Malcolm Jameson (CY 1957)	2.8.1928	6.9.1950	4	1950–1951	37	15	0	7.40	14	5-61	1/0	34.07	1	
Hirst George Herbert (CY 1901)	7.9.1871	8.7.1990	24	1897–1909	790	85	0	22.57	59	5-48	3/0	30.00	18	
Hitch John William (CY 1914)	7.5.1886	10.5.1965	7	1911–1921	103	51*	0	14.71	7	2-31	0/0	46.42	4	
Hobbs Sir John Berry (CY 1909)	16.12.1882	21.12.1963	61	1907–1930	5,410	211	15	56.94	1	1-19	0/0	165.00	17	
Hobbs Robin Nicholas Stuart	8.5.1942	–	7	1967–1971	34	15*	0	6.80	12	3-25	0/0	40.08	8	
Hoggard Matthew James MBE (CY 2006)	31.12.1976	–	67	2000–2007	473	38	0	7.27	248	7-61	7/1	30.50	24	26
Hollies William Eric (CY 1955)	5.6.1912	16.4.1981	13	1934–1950	37	18*	0	5.28	44	7-50	5/0	30.27	2	
[2]Hollioake Adam John (CY 2003)	5.9.1971	–	4	1997–1997	65	45	0	10.83	4	2-31	0/0	33.50	4	35
Hollioake Benjamin Caine	11.11.1977	23.3.2002	2	1997–1998	44	28	0	11.00	2	2-105	0/0	49.75	2	20
Holmes Errol Reginald Thorold (CY 1936)	21.8.1905	16.8.1960	5	1934–1935	114	85*	0	16.28	2	1-10	0/0	38.00	4	
Holmes Percy (CY 1920)	25.11.1886	3.9.1971	7	1921–1932	357	88	0	27.46	–	–	–/–	–	3	
Hone Leland	30.11.1853	31.12.1896	1	1878	13	7	0	6.50					2	
Hopwood John Leonard	30.10.1903	15.6.1985	2	1934	12	8	0	6.00	0	0-16	0/0	–	0	
Hornby Albert Neilson ("Monkey")	10.2.1847	17.12.1925	3	1878–1884	21	9	0	3.50	1	1-0	0/0	0.00	0	
Horton Martin John	21.4.1934	3.4.2011	2	1959	60	58	0	30.00	2	2-24	0/0	29.50	4	
Howard Nigel David	18.5.1925	31.5.1979	4	1951	86	23	0	17.20	–	–	–/–	–	0	
Howell Henry	29.11.1890	9.7.1932	5	1920–1924	15	5	0	7.50	7	4-115	0/0	79.85	0	
Howorth Richard	26.4.1909	2.4.1980	5	1947–1947	145	45*	0	18.12	19	6-124	1/0	33.42	2	
Humphries Joseph	19.5.1876	7.5.1946	3	1907	44	16	0	8.80	0	–	–/–	–	7	
Hunter Joseph	3.8.1855	4.1.1891	5	1884	93	39*	0	18.60	–	–	–	–	8/3	
Hussain Nasser OBE (CY 2003)	28.3.1968	–	96	1989–2004	5,764	207	14	37.18	0	0-15	0/0	–	67	88
Hutchings Kenneth Lotherington (CY 1907)	7.12.1882	3.9.1916	7	1907–1909	341	126	1	28.41	1	1-5	0/0	81.00	9	
[1]Hutton Sir Leonard (CY 1938)	23.6.1916	6.9.1990	79	1937–1954	6,971	364	19	56.67	3	1-2	0/0	77.33	57	
[1]Hutton Richard Anthony	6.9.1942	–	5	1971	219	81	0	36.50	9	3-72	0/0	28.55	9	
Iddon John	8.1.1902	17.4.1946	5	1934–1935	170	73	0	28.33	0	0-3	0/0	–	5	
Igglesden Alan Paul	8.10.1964	–	3	1989–1993	6	3*	0	3.00	6	2-91	0/0	54.83	0	4
Ikin John Thomas	7.3.1918	15.9.1984	18	1946–1955	606	60	0	20.89	3	1-38	0/0	118.00	31	

	Born	Died	Tests	Test Career	Runs	HS	100s	Avge	Wkts	BB	5/10	Avge	Ct/St	O/T
Illingworth Raymond CBE (CY 1960)	8.6.1932		61	1958–1973	1,836	113	2	23.24	122	6-29	3/0	31.20	45	3
Illingworth Richard Keith	23.8.1963		9	1991–1995	128	28	0	18.28	19	4-96	0/0	32.36	5	25
Ilott Mark Christopher	27.8.1970		5	1993–1995	28	15	0	7.00	12	3-48	0/0	45.16	0	
Insole Douglas John CBE (CY 1956)	18.4.1926	5.8.2017	9	1950–1957	408	110*	0	27.20					8	
Irani Ronald Charles	26.10.1971		3	1996–1999	86	41	0	17.20	3	1-22	0/0	37.33	2	31
Jackman Robin David (CY 1981)	13.8.1945		4	1980–1982	42	17	0	7.00	14	4-110	0/0	31.78	0	15
Jackson Sir Francis Stanley (CY 1894)	21.11.1870	9.3.1947	20	1893–1905	1,415	144*	5	48.79	24	5-52	1/0	33.29	10	
Jackson Herbert Leslie (CY 1959)	5.4.1921	25.4.2007	2	1949–1961	15	8	0	15.00	7	2-26	0/0	22.14	1	
James Stephen Peter	7.9.1967		2	1998	71	36	0	17.75					1	
Jameson John Alexander	30.6.1941		4	1971–1973	214	82	0	26.75	1	1-17	0/0	17.00	0	3
Jardine Douglas Robert (CY 1928)	23.10.1900	18.6.1958	22	1928–1933	1,296	127	1	48.00	0	0-10	0/0	–	26	
Jarvis Paul William	29.6.1965		9	1987–1992	132	29*	0	10.15	21	4-107	0/0	45.95	2	16
Jenkins Roland Oliver (CY 1950)	24.11.1918	22.7.1995	9	1948–1952	198	39	0	18.00	32	5-116	1/0	34.31	4	
Jennings Keaton Kent	19.6.1992		15	2016–2018	719	146*	2	26.62	0	0-2	0/0	–	15	
Jessop Gilbert Laird (CY 1898)	19.5.1874	11.5.1955	18	1899–1912	569	104	1	21.88	10	4-68	0/0	35.40	11	
Johnson Richard Leonard	29.12.1974		3	2003–2003	59	26	0	14.75	16	6-33	2/0	17.18	2	10
Jones Arthur Owen	16.8.1872	21.12.1914	12	1899–1909	291	34	0	13.85	3	3-73	0/0	44.33	15	
Jones Geraint Owen MBE	14.7.1976		34	2003–2006	1,172	100	1	23.91					128/5	49½/2
Jones Ivor Jeffrey	10.2.1941		15	1963–1967	38	16	0	4.75	44	6-118	1/0	40.20	4	
Jones Simon Philip MBE (CY 2006)	25.12.1978		18	2002–2005	205	44	0	15.76	59	6-53	3/0	28.23	4	8
Jordan Christopher James	4.10.1988		8	2014–2014	180	35	0	18.00	21	4-18	0/0	35.80	14	31/35
Jupp Henry	19.11.1841	8.4.1889	2	1876	68	63	0	17.00					2	
Jupp Vallance William Crisp (CY 1928)	27.3.1891	9.7.1960	8	1921–1928	208	38	0	17.33	28	4-37	0/0	22.00	5	
Keeton William Walter (CY 1940)	30.4.1905	10.10.1980	2	1934–1939	57	25	0	14.25					2	
Kennedy Alexander Stuart (CY 1933)	24.1.1891	15.11.1959	5	1922	93	41*	0	15.50	31	5-76	2/0	19.32	5	
Kenyon Donald	15.5.1924	12.11.1996	8	1951–1955	192	87	0	12.80					5	
Kerrigan Simon Christopher	10.5.1989		1	2013	–	1*	–	–	0	0-53	0/0	–	0	
Key Robert William Trevor (CY 2005)	12.5.1979		15	2002–2004	775	221	1	31.00	–	–	–/–	–	11	5/1
Khan Amjad	14.10.1980		1	2008	–	–	–	–	1	1-111	0/0	122.00	0	0/1
Killick Rev. Edgar Thomas	9.5.1907	18.5.1953	2	1929	81	31	0	20.25					2	
Kilner Roy (CY 1924)	17.10.1890	5.4.1928	9	1924–1926	233	74	0	33.28	24	4-51	0/0	30.58	6	
King John Herbert	16.4.1871	18.11.1946	1	1909	64	60	0	32.00	1	1-99	0/0	99.00	0	
Kinneir Septimus Paul (CY 1912)	13.5.1871	16.10.1928	1	1911	52	30	0	26.00					0	
Kirtley Robert James	10.1.1975		4	2003–2003	32	12	0	5.33	19	6-34	1/0	29.52	3	11/1
Knight Albert Ernest (CY 1904)	8.10.1872	25.4.1946	3	1903	81	70*	0	16.20					1	
Knight Barry Rolfe	18.2.1938		29	1961–1969	812	127	2	26.19	70	4-38	0/0	31.75	14	

	Born	Died	Tests	Test Career	Runs	HS	100s	Avge	Wkts	BB	5/10	Avge	Ct/St	O/T
Knight Donald John (CY 1915)	12.5.1894	5.1.1960	2	1921	54	38	0	13.50	–	–	–/–	–	1	
Knight Nicholas Verity	28.11.1969		17	1995–2001	719	113	1	23.96	–	–	–/–	–	26	100
Knott Alan Philip Eric (CY 1970)	9.4.1946		95	1967–1981	4,389	135	5	32.75	–	–	–/–	–	250/19	20
Knox Neville Alexander (CY 1907)	10.10.1884	3.3.1935	2	1907	24	8*	0	8.00	3	2-39	0/0	35.00	–	
Laker James Charles (CY 1952)	9.2.1922	23.4.1986	46	1947–1958	676	63	0	14.08	193	10-53	9/3	21.24	12	
Lamb Allan Joseph (CY 1981)	20.6.1954		79	1982–1992	4,656	142	14	36.09	1	1-6	0/0	23.00	75	122
Langridge James (CY 1932)	10.7.1906	10.9.1966	8	1933–1946	242	70	0	26.88	19	7-56	2/0	21.73	6	
Larkins Wayne	22.11.1953		13	1979–1990	493	64	0	20.54	–	–	–/–	–	8	25
Larter John David Frederick	24.4.1940		10	1962–1965	16	10	0	3.20	37	5-57	2/0	25.43	5	
Larwood Harold MBE (CY 1927)	14.11.1904	22.7.1995	21	1926–1932	485	98	0	19.40	78	6-32	4/1	28.35	15	
Lathwell Mark Nicholas	26.12.1971		2	1993	78	33	0	19.50	–	–	–/–	–	–	
Lawrence David Valentine ("Syd")	28.11.1964		5	1988–1991	60	34	0	10.00	18	5-106	1/0	37.55	2	1
Leach Matthew Jack	22.6.1991		4	2017–2018	55	16	0	9.16	20	5-83	1/0	24.90	2	
Leadbeater Edric	15.8.1927	17.4.2011	2	1951	40	38	0	20.00	2	1-38	0/0	109.00	3	
Lee Henry William	26.10.1890	21.4.1981	1	1930	19	18	0	9.50	–	–	–/–	–	2	
Lees Walter Scott (CY 1906)	25.12.1875	10.9.1924	5	1905	66	25*	0	11.00	26	6-78	2/0	17.96	2	
Legge Geoffrey Bevington	26.1.1903	21.11.1940	5	1927–1929	299	196	1	49.83	0	0-34	0/0	–	1	
Leslie Charles Frederick Henry	8.12.1861	12.2.1921	4	1882	106	54	0	15.14	4	3-31	0/0	11.00	1	
Lever John Kenneth MBE (CY 1979)	24.2.1949		21	1976–1986	306	53	0	11.76	73	7-46	3/1	26.72	11	22
Lever Peter	17.9.1940		17	1970–1975	350	88*	0	21.87	41	6-38	2/0	36.80	11	10
Leveson Gower Sir Henry Dudley Gresham	8.5.1873	1.2.1954	3	1909	95	31	0	23.75	–	–	–/–	–	1	
Levett William Howard Vincent ("Hopper")	25.1.1908	1.12.1995	1	1933	7	5	0	7.00	–	–	–/–	–	3	
Lewis Anthony Robert CBE	6.7.1938		9	1972–1973	457	125	1	32.64	–	–	–/–	–	0	
Lewis Clairmonte Christopher	14.2.1968		32	1990–1996	1,105	117	0	23.02	93	6-111	3/0	37.52	25	53
Lewis Jonathan	26.8.1975		1	2006	27	20	0	13.50	3	3-68	0/0	40.66	0	13/2
Leyland Maurice (CY 1929)	20.7.1900	1.1.1967	41	1928–1938	2,764	187	9	46.06	6	3-91	0/0	97.50	13	
Lilley Arthur Frederick Augustus ("Dick") (CY 1897)	28.11.1866	17.11.1929	35	1896–1909	903	84	0	20.52	1	1-23	0/0	23.00	70/22	
Lillywhite James	23.2.1842	25.10.1929	2	1876	16	10	0	8.00	8	4-70	0/0	15.75	1	
Lloyd David	18.3.1947		9	1974–1974	552	214*	1	42.46	0	0-4	0/0	–	11	8
Lloyd Timothy Andrew	5.11.1956		1	1984	10	10*	0	–	–	–	–/–	–	0	3
Loader Peter James (CY 1958)	25.10.1929	15.3.2011	13	1954–1958	76	17	0	5.84	39	6-36	1/0	22.51	2	
Lock Graham Anthony Richard (CY 1954)	5.7.1929	30.3.1995	49	1952–1967	742	89	0	13.74	174	7-35	9/3	25.58	59	
Lockwood William Henry (CY 1899)	25.3.1868	26.4.1932	12	1893–1902	231	52*	0	17.76	43	7-71	5/1	20.53	4	
Lohmann George Alfred (CY 1889)	2.6.1865	1.12.1901	18	1886–1896	213	62*	0	8.87	112	9-28	9/5	10.75	28	
Lowson Frank Anderson	1.7.1925	8.9.1984	7	1951–1955	245	68	0	18.84	–	–	–/–	–	5	

Name	Born	Died	Tests	Test Career	Runs	HS	100s	Avge	Wkts	BB	5/10	Avge	Ct/St	O/T
Lucas Alfred Perry	20.2.1857	12.10.1923	5	1878–1884	157	55	0	19.62	0	0-23	0/0	–	14	
Luckhurst Brian William (CY 1971)	5.2.1939	1.3.2005	21	1970–1974	1,298	131	4	36.05	1	1-9	0/0	32.00	14	3
Lyth Adam (CY 2015)	25.9.1987		7	2015	265	107	1	20.38	0	0-0	0/0	–	8	
Lyttelton Hon. Alfred	7.2.1857	5.7.1913	4	1880–1884	94	31	0	15.66	4	4-19	0/0	4.75	2	
Macaulay George Gibson (CY 1924)	7.12.1897	13.12.1940	8	1922–1933	112	76	0	18.66	24	5-64	1/0	27.58	5	
MacBryan John Crawford William (CY 1925)	22.7.1892	14.7.1983	1	1924	–	–	–	–	–	–	–/–	–	0	
McCague Martin John	24.5.1969		3	1993–1994	21	11	0	4.20	6	4-121	0/0	65.00	1	
McConnon James Edward	21.6.1922	26.1.2003	2	1954	18	11	0	9.00	4	3-19	0/0	18.50	4	
McGahey Charles Percy (CY 1902)	12.2.1871	10.1.1935	2	1901	38	18	0	9.50	–	–	–/–	–	1	
McGrath Anthony	6.10.1975		4	2003	201	81	0	40.20	4	3-16	0/0	14.00	3	14
MacGregor Gregor (CY 1891)	31.8.1869	20.8.1919	8	1890–1893	96	31	0	12.00	–	–	–/–	–	14/3	
McIntyre Arthur John William (CY 1958)	14.5.1918	26.12.2009	3	1950–1955	19	7	0	3.16	–	–	–/–	–	8	
MacKinnon Francis Alexander	9.4.1848	27.2.1947	1	1878	5	5	0	2.50	–	–	–/–	–	0	
MacLaren Archibald Campbell (CY 1895)	1.12.1871	17.11.1944	35	1894–1909	1,931	140	5	33.87	–	–	–/–	–	29	
McMaster Joseph Emile Patrick	16.3.1861	1888	1	1888	0	0	0	0.00	–	–	–/–	–	0	
Maddy Darren Lee	23.5.1974		3	1999–1999	46	24	0	11.50	0	0-40	0/0	–	4	8/4
Mahmood Sajid Iqbal	21.12.1981		8	2006–2006	81	34	0	8.10	20	4-22	0/0	38.10	0	26/4
Makepeace Joseph William Henry	22.8.1881	19.12.1952	4	1920	279	117	0	34.87	–	–	–/–	–	11	
Malan David Johannes	03.09.1987		15	2017–2018	724	140	0	27.84	0	0-7	0/0	–	1	0/5
Malcolm Devon Eugene (CY 1995)	22.2.1963		40	1989–1997	236	29	0	6.05	128	9-57	5/2	37.09	3	10
Mallender Neil Alan	13.8.1961		2	1992	26	4	0	2.66	10	5-50	1/0	21.50	3	
Mann Francis George CBE	6.9.1917	8.8.2001	7	1948–1949	376	136*	0	37.60	–	–	–/–	–	4	
Mann Francis Thomas	3.3.1888	6.10.1964	5	1922	281	84	0	35.12	–	–	–/–	–	1	
Marks Victor James	25.6.1955		6	1982–1983	249	83	0	27.66	11	3-78	0/0	44.00	2	34
Marriott Charles Stowell ("Father")	14.9.1895	13.10.1966	1	1933	0	0	0	0.00	11	6-59	2/1	8.72	4	
Martin Frederick (CY 1892)	12.10.1861	13.12.1921	2	1890–1891	14	13	0	7.00	14	6-50	2/1	10.07	1	
Martin John William	16.2.1917	4.1.1987	1	1947	26	29	0	13.00	1	1-111	0/0	129.00	2	
Martin Peter James	15.11.1968		8	1995–1997	115	29	0	8.84	17	4-60	0/0	34.11	1	20
Mason John Richard (CY 1898)	26.3.1874	15.10.1958	5	1897	129	32	0	12.90	2	1-8	0/0	74.50	6	
Matthews Austin David George	3.5.1904	29.7.1977	1	1937	2	2*	0	–	2	1-13	0/0	32.50	3	
May Peter Barker Howard CBE (CY 1952)	31.12.1929	27.12.1994	66	1951–1961	4,537	285*	13	46.77	–	–	–/–	–	42	
Maynard Matthew Peter (CY 1998)	21.3.1966		4	1988–1993	87	35	0	10.87	–	–	–/–	–	3	14
Mead Charles Philip (CY 1912)	9.3.1887	26.3.1958	17	1911–1928	1,185	182*	4	49.37	–	–	–/–	–	4	
Mead Walter (CY 1904)	1.4.1868	18.3.1954	2	1899	7	7	0	3.50	1	1-91	0/0	91.00	1	
Midwinter William Evans	19.6.1851	3.12.1890	4†	1881	95	36	0	13.57	10	4-81	0/0	27.20	5	
Milburn Colin ("Ollie") (CY 1967)	23.10.1941	28.2.1990	9	1966–1968	654	139	2	46.71	–	–	–/–	–	7	

	Born	Died	Tests	Test Career	Runs	HS	100s	Avge	Wkts	BB	5/10	Avge	Ct/St	OT
Miller Audley Montague	19.10.1869	26.6.1959	1	1895	24	20*	0	–	–	–	–/–	–	0	25
Miller Geoffrey OBE	8.9.1952		34	1976–1984	1,213	98*	0	25.80	60	5-44	1/0	30.98	17	
Milligan Frank William	19.3.1870	31.3.1900	2	1898	58	38	0	14.50	0	0-0	0/0	–	1	
Millman Geoffrey	2.10.1934	6.4.2005	6	1961–1962	60	32*	0	12.00	–	–	–/–	–	13/2	
Milton Clement Arthur (CY 1959)	10.3.1928	25.4.2007	6	1958–1959	204	104*	1	25.50	0	0-12	0/0	–	5	
Mitchell Arthur	13.9.1902	25.12.1976	6	1933–1936	298	72	0	29.80	0	0-4	0/0	–	9	
Mitchell Frank (CY 1902)	13.8.1872	11.10.1935	2†	1898	88	41	0	22.00	0	–	–/–	–	2	
Mitchell Thomas Bignall	4.9.1902	27.1.1996	5	1932–1935	20	9	0	5.00	8	2-49	0/0	62.25	1	
Mitchell-Innes Norman Stewart ("Mandy")	7.9.1914	28.12.2006	1	1935	5	5	0	5.00	0	–	–/–	–	0	
Mold Arthur Webb (CY 1892)	27.5.1863	29.4.1921	3	1893	0	0*	0	0.00	7	3-44	0/0	33.42	1	
Moon Leonard James	9.2.1878	23.11.1916	4	1905	182	36	0	22.75	–	–	–/–	–	4	
Morgan Eoin Joseph Gerard (CY 2011)	10.9.1986		16	2010–2011	700	130	2	30.43	–	–	–/–	–	11	189‡/77
Morley Frederick	16.12.1850	28.9.1884	4	1880–1882	6	2*	0	1.50	16	5-56	1/0	18.50	4	
Morris Hugh	5.10.1963		3	1991	115	44	0	19.16	0	–	–/–	–	3	
Morris John Edward	1.4.1964		3	1990	71	32	0	23.66	0	–	–/–	–	3	8
Mortimore John Brian	14.5.1933	13.2.2014	9	1958–1964	243	73*	0	24.30	13	3-36	0/0	56.38	3	
Moss Alan Edward	14.11.1930		9	1953–1960	61	26	0	10.16	21	4-35	0/0	29.80	1	
Moxon Martyn Douglas (CY 1993)	4.5.1960		10	1986–1989	455	99	0	28.43	0	0-3	0/0	–	10	8
Mullally Alan David	12.7.1969		19	1996–2001	127	24	0	5.52	58	5-105	1/0	31.24	6	50
Munton Timothy Alan (CY 1995)	30.7.1965		2	1992	25	25*	0	25.00	4	2-22	0/0	50.00	0	
Murdoch William Lloyd	18.10.1854	18.2.1911	1†	1891	12	12	0	12.00	–	–	–/–	–	0/1	
Murray John Thomas MBE (CY 1967)	1.4.1935	24.7.2018	21	1961–1967	506	112	0	22.00	–	–	–/–	–	52/3	
Newham William	12.12.1860	26.6.1944	1	1887	26	17	0	13.00	–	–	–/–	–	0	
Newport Philip John	11.10.1962		3	1988–1990	110	40*	0	27.50	10	4-87	0/0	41.70	1	
Nichols Morris Stanley (CY 1934)	6.10.1900	26.1.1961	14	1929–1939	355	78*	0	29.58	41	6-35	2/0	28.09	11	
Oakman Alan Stanley Myles	20.4.1930	6.9.2018	2	1956	14	10	0	7.00	0	0-21	0/0	–	7	
O'Brien Sir Timothy Carew	5.11.1861	9.12.1948	5	1884–1895	59	20	0	7.37	–	–	–/–	–	4	
O'Connor Jack	6.11.1897	22.2.1977	4	1929–1929	153	51	0	21.85	1	1-31	0/0	72.00	2	
Old Christopher Middleton (CY 1979)	22.12.1948		46	1972–1981	845	65	0	14.82	143	7-50	4/0	28.11	22	32
Oldfield Norman	5.5.1911	19.4.1996	1	1939	99	80	0	49.50	–	–	–/–	–	0	
Onions Graham (CY 2010)	9.9.1982		9	2009–2012	30	17*	0	10.00	32	5-38	1/0	29.90	0	4
Ormond James	20.8.1977		2	2001–2001	38	18	0	12.66	2	1-70	0/0	92.50	0	
Overton Craig	10.04.1994		3	2017	98	41*	0	24.50	7	3-105	0/0	42.28	1	1
Padgett Douglas Ernest Vernon	20.7.1934		2	1960	51	31	0	12.75	0	0-8	0/0	–	0	
Paine George Alfred Edward (CY 1935)	11.6.1908	30.3.1978	4	1934	97	49	0	16.16	17	5-168	1/0	27.47	5	
Palairet Lionel Charles Hamilton (CY 1893)	27.5.1870	27.3.1933	2	1902	49	20	0	12.25	–	–	–/–	–	2	

	Born	Died	Tests	Test Career	Runs	HS	100s	Avge	Wkts	BB	5/10	Avge	Ct/St	O/T
Palmer Charles Henry CBE	15.5.1919	31.3.2005	1	1953	22	22	0	11.00	0	0-15	0/0	189.00	0	—
Palmer Kenneth Ernest MBE	22.4.1937		1	1964	10	10	0	10.00	1	1-113	0/0	—	0	26/1
Panesar Mudhsuden Singh ("Monty")(CY 2007)	25.4.1982		50	2005–2013	220	26	0	4.88	167	6-37	12/2	34.71	10	—
Parfitt Peter Howard (CY 1963)	8.12.1936		37	1961–1972	1,882	131*	7	40.91	12	2-5	0/0	47.83	42	—
Parker Charles Warrington Leonard (CY 1923)	14.10.1882	11.7.1959	1	1921	—	—	—	—	2	2-32	0/0	16.00	0	—
Parker Paul William Giles	15.1.1956		1	1981	13	13	0	6.50	—		—	—	0	—
Parkhouse William Gilbert Anthony	12.10.1925	10.8.2000	7	1950–1959	373	78	0	28.69	—		—/—	—	3	—
Parkin Cecil Harry (CY 1924)	18.2.1886	15.6.1943	10	1920–1924	160	36	0	12.30	32	5-38	2/0	35.25	3	—
Parks James Horace (CY 1938)	12.5.1903	21.11.1980	1	1937	29	22	0	14.50	3	2-26	0/0	12.00		—
Parks James Michael (CY 1968)	21.10.1931		46	1954–1967	1,962	108*	2	32.16	1	1-43	0/0	51.00	103/11	—
Pataudi Iftikhar Ali Khan, Nawab of (CY 1932)	16.3.1910	5.1.1952	3†	1932–1934	144	102	1	28.80	—		—/—	—	0	—
Patel Minal Mahesh	7.7.1970		2	1996	45	27	0	22.50	1	1-101	0/0	180.00	0	—
Patel Samit Rohit	30.11.1984		6	2011–2015	151	42	0	16.77	7	2-27	0/0	60.14	2	36/18
Pattinson Darren John	2.8.1979		1	2008	21	13	0	10.50	2	2-95	0/0	48.00	0	—
Paynter Edward (CY 1938)	5.11.1901	5.2.1979	20	1931–1939	1,540	243	4	59.23	—		—/—	—	7	—
Peate Edmund	2.3.1855	11.3.1900	9	1881–1886	70	13	0	11.66	31	6-85	2/0	22.03	2	—
Peebles Ian Alexander Ross (CY 1931)	20.1.1908	27.2.1980	13	1927–1931	98	26	0	10.88	45	6-63	3/0	30.91	2	—
Peel Robert (CY 1889)	12.2.1857	12.8.1941	20	1884–1896	427	83	0	14.72	101	7-31	5/1	16.98	17	—
Penn Frank	7.3.1851	26.12.1916	1	1880	50	27*	0	50.00	—		—/—	—	0	—
Perks Reginald Thomas David	4.10.1911	22.11.1977	2	1938–1939	3	2*	0	—	11	5-100	2/0	32.27	1	—
Philipson Hylton	8.6.1866	4.12.1935	5	1891–1894	63	30	0	9.00	—		—/—	—	8/3	—
Pietersen Kevin Peter MBE (CY 2006)	27.6.1980		104	2005–2013	8,181	227	23	47.28	10	3-52	0/0	88.60	62	134‡/37
Pigott Anthony Charles Shackleton	4.6.1958		2	1983	12	8*	0	12.00	2	2-75	0/0	37.50		—
Pilling Richard (CY 1891)	11.8.1855	28.3.1891	8	1881–1888	91	23	0	7.58	—		—/—	—	10/4	—
Place Winston	7.12.1914	25.1.2002	3	1947	144	107	1	28.80	—		—/—	—		—
Plunkett Liam Edward	6.4.1985		13	2005–2014	238	55*	0	15.86	41	5-64	1/0	37.46	3	74/20
Pocock Patrick Ian	24.9.1946		25	1967–1984	206	33	0	6.24	67	6-79	3/0	44.41	15	1
Pollard Richard	19.6.1912	16.12.1985	4	1946–1948	13	10*	0	13.00	15	5-24	1/0	25.20	3	—
Poole Cyril John	13.3.1921	11.2.1996	3	1951	161	69*	0	40.25	0	0-9	0/0	—	1	—
Pope George Henry	27.1.1911	29.10.1993	1	1947	8	8*	0	—	1	1-49	0/0	85.00		—
Pope Oliver John Douglas	2.1.1998		2	2018	54	28	0	18.00	—		—/—	—	2	—
Pougher Arthur Dick	19.4.1865	20.5.1926	1	1891	17	17	0	17.00	3	3-26	0/0	8.66	1	—
Price John Sidney Ernest	22.7.1937		15	1963–1972	66	32	0	7.33	40	5-73	1/0	35.02	2	—
Price Wilfred Frederick Frank	25.4.1902	13.1.1969	1	1938	6	6	0	3.00	—		—/—	—	7	—
Prideaux Roger Malcolm	31.7.1939		3	1968–1968	102	64	0	20.40	0	0-0	0/0	—	2	—
Pringle Derek Raymond	18.9.1958		30	1982–1992	695	63	0	15.10	70	5-95	3/0	35.97	10	44

	Born	Died	Tests	Test Career	Runs	HS	100s	Avge	Wkts	BB	5/10	Avge	Ct/St	O/T
Prior Matthew James (CY 2010)	26.2.1982	–	79	2007–2014	4,099	131*	7	40.18	0	1-1	–/–	–	243/13	68/10
Pullar Geoffrey (CY 1960)	1.8.1935	26.12.2014	28	1959–1962	1,974	175	4	43.86	1	1-1	0/0	37.00	2	4
Quaife William George (CY 1902)	17.3.1872	13.10.1951	7	1899–1901	228	68	0	19.00	0	0-6	0/0	–	4	–
Radford Neal Victor (CY 1986)	7.6.1957	–	3	1986–1987	21	12*	0	7.00	4	2-131	0/0	87.75	4	6
Radley Clive Thornton MBE (CY 1979)	13.5.1944	–	8	1977–1978	481	158	2	48.10	–	–	–/–	–	4	4
Ramprakash Mark Ravin MBE (CY 2007)	5.9.1969	–	52	1991–2001	2,350	154	2	27.32	4	1-2	0/0	119.25	39	18
Randall Derek William (CY 1980)	24.2.1951	–	47	1976–1984	2,470	174	7	33.37	0	0-1	0/0	–	31	49
Ranjitsinhji Kumar Shri (CY 1897)	10.9.1872	2.4.1933	15	1896–1902	989	175	2	44.95	1	1-23	0/0	39.00	13	–
Rankin William Boyd	5.7.1984	–	1†	2013	13	13	0	6.50	1	1-47	0/0	81.00	0	7†/2‡
Rashid Adil Usman	17.2.1988	–	18	2015–2018	527	61	0	20.26	60	5-49	2/0	37.88	4	78/33
Read Christopher Mark Wells (CY 2011)	10.8.1978	–	15	1999–2006	360	55	0	18.94	–	–	–/–	–	48/6	36/1
Read Holcombe Douglas ("Hopper")	28.1.1910	5.1.2000	1	1935	–	–	–	–	6	4-136	0/0	33.33	–	–
Read John Maurice (CY 1890)	9.2.1859	17.2.1929	17	1882–1893	461	57	0	17.07	0	0-27	0/0	–	8	–
Read Walter William (CY 1893)	23.11.1855	6.1.1907	18	1882–1893	720	117	1	27.69	0	1-4	0/0	–	16	–
Reeve Dermot Alexander OBE (CY 1996)	2.4.1963	–	3	1991	124	59	0	24.80	2	1-4	0/0	30.00	1	29
Relf Albert Edward (CY 1914)	26.6.1874	26.3.1937	13	1903–1913	416	63	0	23.11	25	5-85	1/0	24.96	14	–
Rhodes Harold James	22.7.1936	–	2	1959	0	0*	0	–	9	4-50	0/0	27.11	0	–
Rhodes Steven John (CY 1995)	17.6.1964	–	11	1994–1994	294	65*	0	24.50	–	–	–/–	–	46/3	9
Rhodes Wilfred (CY 1899)	29.10.1877	8.7.1973	58	1899–1929	2,325	179	2	30.19	127	8-68	6/1	26.96	60	–
Richards Clifton James ("Jack")	10.8.1958	–	8	1986–1988	285	133	1	21.92	–	–	–/–	–	20/1	22
² **Richardson Derek Walter** ("Dick")	3.11.1934	–	1	1957	33	33	0	33.00	–	–	–/–	–	1	–
Richardson Peter Edward (CY 1957)	4.7.1931	16.2.2017	34	1956–1963	2,061	126	5	37.47	3	2-10	0/0	16.00	6	–
² **Richardson Thomas** (CY 1897)	11.8.1870	2.7.1912	14	1893–1897	177	25*	0	11.06	88	8-94	11/4	25.22	5	–
Richmond Thomas Leonard	23.6.1890	29.12.1957	1	1921	6	4	0	3.00	2	2-69	0/0	43.00	0	–
Ridgway Frederick	10.8.1923	26.9.2015	5	1951	49	24	0	8.16	7	4-83	0/0	54.14	3	–
Robertson John David Benbow (CY 1948)	22.2.1917	12.10.1996	11	1947–1951	881	133	2	46.36	2	2-17	0/0	29.00	6	–
Robins Walter Vivian (CY 1930)	3.6.1906	12.12.1968	19	1929–1937	612	108	1	26.60	64	6-32	1/0	27.46	12	–
Robinson Robert Timothy (CY 1986)	21.11.1958	–	29	1984–1989	1,601	175	4	36.38	0	0-0	0/0	–	8	26
Robson Samuel David	1.7.1989	–	7	2014	336	127	1	30.54	0	–	–/–	–	5	–
Roland-Jones Tobias Skelton	29.01.1988	–	4	2017	82	25	0	20.50	17	5-57	1/0	19.64	0	1
Roope Graham Richard James (CY 1972)	12.7.1946	26.11.2006	21	1972–1978	860	77	0	30.71	8	0-2	0/0	24.25	35	8
Root Charles Frederick	16.4.1890	20.1.1954	3	1926	–	–	–	–	8	4-84	0/0	–	1	–
Root Joseph Edward (CY 2014)	30.12.1990	–	77	2012–2018	6,508	254	15	50.44	20	2-9	0/0	46.95	85	121/28
Rose Brian Charles (CY 1980)	4.6.1950	–	9	1977–1980	358	70	0	25.57	0	–	–/–	–	4	2
Royle Vernon Peter Fanshawe Archer	29.1.1854	21.5.1929	1	1878	21	18	0	10.50	0	0-6	0/0	–	2	–
Rumsey Frederick Edward	4.12.1935	–	5	1964–1965	30	21*	0	15.00	17	4-25	0/0	27.11	0	–

Name	Born	Died	Tests	Test Career	Runs	HS	100s	Avge	Wkts	BB	5/10	Avge	Ct/St	O/T
Russell Albert Charles ("Jack") (CY 1923)	7.10.1887	23.3.1961	10	1920–1922	910	140	2	56.87	0	—	-/-	—	8	
Russell Robert Charles ("Jack") (CY 1990)	15.8.1963		54	1988–1997	1,897	128*	5	27.10	0	—	-/-	—	153/12	40
Russell William Eric	3.7.1936		10	1961–1967	362	70	0	21.29	1	0-19	0/0	—	4	
Saggers Martin John	23.5.1972		3	2003–2004	1	1	0	0.33	7	2-29	0/0	35.28	1	
Salisbury Ian David Kenneth (CY 1993)	21.11.1970		15	1992–2000	368	50	0	16.72	20	4-163	0/0	76.95	5	4
Sandham Andrew (CY 1923)	6.7.1890	20.4.1982	14	1921–1929	879	325	2	38.21	0	—	-/-	—	4	04
Schofield Christopher Paul	6.10.1978		2	2000	67	57	0	22.33	0	0-73	0/0	—	0	
Schultz Sandford Spence	29.8.1857	18.12.1937	1	1878	20	20	0	20.00	1	1-16	0/0	26.00	0	
Scotton William Henry	15.1.1856	9.7.1893	15	1881–1886	510	90	0	22.17	0	0-20	0/0	—	4	
Selby John	1.7.1849	11.3.1894	6	1876–1881	256	70	0	23.27	0	—	-/-	—	1	
Selvey Michael Walter William	25.4.1948		3	1976–1976	15	5*	0	7.50	6	4-41	0/0	57.16	1	
Shackleton Derek (CY 1959)	12.8.1924	28.9.2007	7	1950–1963	113	42	0	18.83	18	4-72	0/0	42.66	1	
Shah Owais Alam	22.10.1978		6	2005–2008	269	88	0	26.90	0	0-12	0/0	—	2	71/17
Shahzad Ajmal	27.7.1985		1	2010	5	5	0	5.00	4	3-45	0/0	15.75	2	11/3
Sharp John	15.2.1878	28.1.1938	3	1909	188	105	1	47.00	3	3-67	0/0	37.00	2	
Sharpe John William (CY 1892)	9.12.1866	19.6.1936	3	1890–1891	44	26	0	22.00	11	6-84	1/0	27.72	2	
Sharpe Philip John (CY 1963)	27.12.1936	19.5.2014	12	1963–1969	786	85	1	46.23	0	—	-/-	—	17	
Shaw Alfred	29.8.1842	16.1.1907	7	1876–1881	111	40	0	10.09	12	5-38	1/0	23.75	4	
Sheppard Rt Rev. Lord [David Stuart] (CY 1953)	6.3.1929	5.3.2005	22	1950–1962	1,172	119	3	37.80	0	—	-/-	—	12	
Sherwin Mordecai (CY 1891)	26.2.1851	3.7.1910	3	1886–1888	30	21*	0	15.00	0	—	-/-	—	5/2	
Shrewsbury Arthur (CY 1890)	11.4.1856	19.5.1903	23	1881–1893	1,277	164	3	35.47	0	0-2	0/0	—	29	
Shuter John	9.2.1855	5.7.1920	1	1888	28	28	0	28.00	0	—	-/-	—	1	
Shuttleworth Kenneth	13.11.1944		5	1970–1971	46	21	0	7.66	12	5-47	1/0	35.58	0	
Sidebottom Arnold	1.4.1954		1	1985	2	2	0	2.00	1	1-65	0/0	65.00	0	
Sidebottom Ryan Jay (CY 2008)	15.1.1978		22	2001–2009	313	31	0	15.65	79	7-47	5/1	28.24	5	25/18
Silverwood Christopher Eric Wilfred	5.3.1975		6	1996–2002	29	10	0	7.25	11	5-91	1/0	40.36	5	7
Simpson Reginald Thomas (CY 1950)	27.2.1920	24.11.2013	27	1948–1954	1,401	156*	4	33.35	2	2-4	0/0	11.00	5	
Simpson-Hayward George Hayward Thomas	7.6.1875	2.10.1936	5	1909	105	29*	0	15.00	23	6-43	2/0	18.26	1	
Sims James Morton	13.5.1903	27.4.1973	4	1935–1936	16	12	0	4.00	11	5-73	2/0	43.63	6	
Sinfield Reginald Albert	24.12.1900	17.3.1988	1	1938	6	6	0	6.00	2	1-51	0/0	61.50	6	
Slack Wilfred Norris	12.12.1954	15.11.1989	3	1985–1986	81	52	0	13.50	0	—	-/-	—	3	2
Smailes Thomas Francis	27.3.1910	1.12.1970	1	1946	25	25	0	25.00	3	3-44	1/0	20.66	0	
Small Gladstone Cleophas	18.10.1961		17	1986–1990	263	59	0	15.47	55	5-48	2/0	34.01	9	53
Smith Alan Christopher CBE	25.10.1936		6	1962	118	69*	0	29.50	0	—	-/-	—	20	
Smith Andrew Michael	1.10.1967		1	1997	4	4*	0	4.00	0	0-89	0/0	—	0	
Smith Cedric Ivan James (CY 1935)	25.8.1906	8.2.1979	5	1934–1937	102	27	0	10.20	15	5-16	1/0	26.20	1	

	Born	Died	Tests	Test Career	Runs	HS	100s	Avge	Wkts	BB	5/10	Avge	Ct/St	O/T
Smith *Sir Charles Aubrey*	21.7.1863	20.12.1948	1	1888	3	3	0	3.00	7	5-19	1/0	8.71	5	4
[2]**Smith** *Christopher Lyall (CY 1984)*	15.10.1958		8	1983–1986	392	91	0	30.15	3	2-31	0/0	13.00	5	2
Smith *David Mark*	9.1.1956		2	1985	80	47	0	20.00					0	
Smith *David Robert*	5.10.1934	17.12.2003	5	1961	38	34	0	9.50	6	2-60	0/0	59.83	2	
Smith *Denis (CY 1935)*	24.1.1907	12.9.1979	2	1935	128	57	0	32.00					1	
Smith *Donald Victor*	14.6.1923		3	1957	25	16*	0	8.33	1	1-12	0/0	97.00	0	
Smith *Edward Thomas*	19.7.1977		3	2003	87	64	0	17.40					5	
Smith *Ernest James ("Tiger")*	6.2.1886	31.8.1979	11	1911–1913	113	22	0	8.69	1	1-10	–/–	128.00	17/3	
Smith *Harry*	21.5.1891	12.11.1937	1	1928	7	7	0	7.00					1	
Smith *Michael John Knight OBE (CY 1960)*	30.6.1933		50	1958–1972	2,278	121	3	31.63	1	1-10	0/0	–	53	
[2]**Smith** *Robin Arnold (CY 1990)*	13.9.1963		62	1988–1995	4,236	175	9	43.67	0	0-6	–/–	–	39	71
Smith *Thomas Peter Bromley (CY 1947)*	30.10.1908	4.8.1967	4	1946–1946	33	24	0	6.60	3	2-172	0/0	106.33	1	
Smithson *Gerald Arthur*	1.11.1926	6.9.1970	2	1947	70	35	0	23.33					1	
Snow *John Augustine (CY 1973)*	13.10.1941		49	1965–1976	772	73	0	13.54	202	7-40	8/1	26.66	16	9
Southerton *James*	16.11.1827	16.6.1880	2	1876	7	6	0	3.50	7	4-46	0/0	15.28	2	
Spooner *Reginald Herbert (CY 1905)*	21.10.1880	2.10.1961	10	1905–1912	481	119	1	32.06					4	
Spooner *Richard Thompson*	30.12.1919	20.12.1997	7	1951–1955	354	92	0	27.23					10/2	
Stanyforth *Ronald Thomas*	30.5.1892	20.2.1964	4	1927	13	6*	0	2.60					7/2	
Staples *Samuel James (CY 1929)*	18.9.1892	4.6.1950	3	1927	65	39	0	13.00	15	3-50	0/0	29.00	1	
Statham *John Brian CBE (CY 1955)*	17.6.1930	10.6.2000	70	1950–1965	675	38	0	11.44	252	7-39	9/1	24.84	28	1
Steel *Allan Gibson*	24.9.1858	15.6.1914	13	1880–1888	600	148	2	35.29	29	3-27	0/0	20.86	5	
Steele *David Stanley OBE (CY 1976)*	29.9.1941		8	1975–1976	673	106	1	42.06	2	1-1	0/0	19.50	7	1
Stephenson *John Patrick*	14.3.1965		1	1989	36	25	0	18.00	0		–/–	–	0	
Stevens *Greville Thomas Scott (CY 1918)*	7.1.1901	19.9.1970	10	1922–1929	263	69	0	15.47	20	5-90	2/1	32.40	9	
Stewart *Graham Barry*	16.12.1955	21.1.2014	2	1979–1980	28	27*	0	28.00	5	3-111	0/0	36.60	0	4
[1]**Stewart** *Alec James OBE (CY 1993)*	8.4.1963		133	1989–2003	8,463	190	15	39.54	0	0-5	–/–	–	263/14	170
Stewart *Michael James OBE (CY 1958)*	16.9.1932		8	1962–1963	385	87	0	35.00					6	
Stoddart *Andrew Ernest (CY 1893)*	11.3.1863	3.4.1915	16	1887–1897	996	173	2	35.57	2	1-10	0/0	47.00	6	
Stokes *Benjamin Andrew (CY 2016)*	4.6.1991		49	2013–2018	2,966	258	6	33.70	117	6-22	4/0	32.70	49	75/23
Stoneman *Mark Daniel*	26.06.1987		11	2017–2018	526	60	0	27.68					0	
Storer *William (CY 1899)*	25.1.1867	28.2.1912	6	1897–1899	215	51	0	19.54	2	1-24	0/0	54.00	11	
Strauss *Andrew John OBE (CY 2005)*	2.3.1977		100	2004–2012	7,037	177	21	40.91	0		–/–	–	121	127/4
Street *George Benjamin*	6.12.1889	24.4.1924	1	1922	11	7*	0	11.00					0/1	
Strudwick *Herbert (CY 1912)*	28.1.1880	14.2.1970	28	1909–1926	230	24	0	7.93					61/12	
[2]**Studd** *Charles Thomas*	2.12.1860	16.7.1931	5	1882–1882	160	48	0	20.00	3	2-35	0/0	32.66	5	
[2]**Studd** *George Brown*	20.10.1859	13.2.1945	4	1882	31	9	0	4.42					8	

Name	Born	Died	Tests	Test Career	Runs	HS	100s	Avge	Wkts	BB	Avge	5/10	Ct/St	O/T
Subba Row Raman CBE (CY 1961)	29.1.1932	–	13	1958–1961	984	137	3	46.85	0	0-2	–	0/0	5	–
Such Peter Mark	12.6.1964	–	11	1993–1999	67	14*	0	6.09	37	6-67	33.56	2/0	4	–
Sugg Frank Howe (CY 1890)	11.1.1862	29.5.1933	2	1888	55	31	0	27.50	–	–	–	–/–	0	–
Sutcliffe Herbert (CY 1920)	24.11.1894	22.1.1978	54	1924–1935	4,555	194	16	60.73	–	–	–	–/–	23	–
Swann Graeme Peter (CY 2010)	24.3.1979	–	60	2008–2013	1,370	85	1	22.09	255	6-65	29.96	17/3	54	79/39
Swetman Roy	25.10.1933	–	11	1958–1959	254	65	0	16.93	–	–	–	–/–	24/2	–
[1]Tate Frederick William	24.7.1867	24.2.1943	1	1902	9	5*	0	9.00	2	2-7	25.50	0/0	2	–
[1]Tate Maurice William (CY 1924)	30.5.1895	18.5.1956	39	1924–1935	1,198	100*	1	25.48	155	6-42	26.16	7/1	11	–
Tattersall Roy	17.8.1922	9.12.2011	16	1950–1954	50	10*	0	5.00	58	7-52	26.08	4/1	8	–
Tavaré Christopher James	27.10.1954	–	31	1980–1989	1,755	149	2	32.50	0	0-0	–	–/–	20	29
Taylor James William Arthur	6.1.1990	–	7	2012–2015	312	76	0	26.00	–	–	–	–/–	7	27/1
Taylor Jonathan Paul	8.8.1964	–	2	1992–1994	34	17*	0	17.00	3	1-18	52.00	0/0	1	–
Taylor Kenneth	21.8.1935	–	3	1959–1964	57	24	0	11.40	0	0-6	–	–/–	–	–
Taylor Leslie Brian	25.10.1953	–	2	1985	–	1*	0	–	4	2-34	44.50	0/0	–	2
Taylor Robert William MBE (CY 1977)	17.7.1941	–	57	1970–1983	1,156	97	0	16.28	–	–	–	–/–	167/7	27
Tennyson *Lord* Lionel Hallam (CY 1914)	7.11.1889	6.6.1951	9	1913–1921	345	74*	0	31.36	0	0-1	–	–/–	6	–
Terry Vivian Paul	14.11.1959	–	2	1984	16	8	0	5.33	–	–	–	–/–	2	–
Thomas John Gregory	12.8.1960	–	5	1985–1986	83	31*	0	13.83	10	4-70	50.40	0/0	–	3
Thompson George Joseph (CY 1906)	27.10.1877	3.3.1943	6	1909–1909	273	63	0	30.33	23	4-50	27.73	0/0	5	–
Thomson Norman Ian	23.11.1929	–	5	1964	69	39	0	23.00	9	2-55	63.11	0/0	–	–
Thorpe Graham Paul MBE (CY 1998)	1.8.1969	–	100	1993–2005	6,744	200*	16	44.66	0	0-0	–	0/0	105	82
Titmus Frederick John MBE (CY 1963)	24.11.1932	23.3.2011	53	1955–1974	1,449	84*	0	22.29	153	7-79	32.22	7/0	35	2
Tolchard Roger William	15.6.1946	–	4	1976	129	67	0	25.80	–	–	–	–/–	5	1
[1]Townsend Charles Lucas (CY 1899)	7.11.1876	17.10.1958	2	1899	51	38	0	17.00	3	3-50	25.00	0/0	–	–
Townsend David Charles Humphrey	20.4.1912	27.1.1997	3	1934	77	36	0	12.83	0	0-9	–	0/0	1	–
Townsend Leslie Fletcher (CY 1934)	8.6.1903	17.2.1993	4	1929–1933	97	40	0	16.16	6	2-22	34.16	0/0	2	–
Tredwell James Cullum	27.2.1982	–	2	2009–2014	45	37	0	22.50	11	4-47	29.18	0/0	2	45/17
[4]Tremlett Christopher Timothy	2.9.1981	–	12	2007–2013	113	25*	0	10.27	53	6-48	27.00	2/0	4	15/1
[4]Tremlett Maurice Fletcher	5.7.1923	30.7.1984	3	1947	20	18*	0	6.66	4	2-98	56.50	0/0	2	–
Trescothick Marcus Edward MBE (CY 2005)	25.12.1975	–	76	2000–2006	5,825	219	14	43.79	1	1-34	155.00	0/0	95	123/3
[2]Trott Albert Edwin (CY 1899)	6.2.1873	30.7.1914	2‡	1898	23	16	0	5.75	17	5-49	11.64	1/0	4	–
[2]Trott Ian Jonathan Leonard (CY 2011)	22.4.1981	–	52	2009–2014	3,835	226	9	44.08	5	1-5	80.00	0/0	29	68/7
Trueman Frederick Sewards OBE (CY 1953)	6.2.1931	1.7.2006	67	1952–1965	981	39*	0	13.81	307	8-31	21.57	17/3	64	–
Tudor Alex Jeremy	23.10.1977	–	10	1998–2002	229	99*	0	19.08	28	5-44	34.39	1/0	3	3
Tufnell Neville Charsley	13.6.1887	3.8.1951	1	1909	14	14	0	14.00	–	–	–	–/–	0/1	–
Tufnell Philip Clive Roderick	29.4.1966	–	42	1990–2001	153	22*	0	5.10	121	7-47	37.68	5/2	12	20

Name	Born	Died	Tests	Test Career	Runs	HS	100s	Avge	Wkts	BB	5/10	Avge	Ct/St	O/T
Turnbull Maurice Joseph Lawson (CY 1931)	16.3.1906	5.8.1944	9	1929–1936	224	61	0	20.36	–	–	–/–	–	1	–
[2]Tyldesley [George] Ernest (CY 1920)	5.2.1889	5.5.1962	14	1921–1928	990	122	3	55.00	0	0-2	0/0	–	2	–
[2]Tyldesley John Thomas (CY 1902)	22.11.1873	27.11.1930	31	1898–1909	1,661	138	4	30.75	–	–	–/–	–	16	–
Tyldesley Richard Knowles (CY 1925)	11.3.1897	17.9.1943	7	1924–1930	47	29	0	7.83	19	3-50	0/0	32.57	1	–
Tylecote Edward Ferdinando Sutton	23.6.1849	15.3.1938	6	1882–1886	152	66	0	19.00	0	–	–/–	–	5/5	–
Tyler Edwin James	13.10.1864	25.1.1917	1	1895	0	0	0	0.00	4	3-49	0/0	16.25	–	–
Tyson Frank Holmes (CY 1956)	6.6.1930	27.9.2015	17	1954–1958	230	37*	0	10.95	76	7-27	4/1	18.56	4	11
Udal Shaun David	18.3.1969		4	2005	109	33*	0	18.16	8	4-14	0/0	43.00	–	
Ulyett George	21.10.1851	18.6.1898	25	1876–1890	949	149	1	24.33	50	7-36	1/0	20.40	19	
Underwood Derek Leslie MBE (CY 1969)	8.6.1945		86	1966–1981	937	45*	0	11.56	297	8-51	17/6	25.83	44	26
Valentine Bryan Herbert	17.1.1908	2.2.1983	7	1933–1938	454	136	1	64.85	–	–	–/–	–		
Vaughan Michael Paul OBE (CY 2003)	29.10.1974		82	1999–2008	5,719	197	18	41.44	6	2-71	0/0	93.50	44	86/2
Verity Hedley (CY 1932)	18.5.1905	31.7.1943	40	1931–1939	669	66*	0	20.90	144	8-43	5/2	24.37	30	
Vernon George Frederick	20.6.1856	10.8.1902	1	1882	14	11*	0	14.00	0	0-11	0/0	–		
Vince James Michael	14.3.1991		13	2016–2017	548	83	0	24.90	0	0-8	0/0	–	8	
Vine Joseph (CY 1906)	15.5.1875	25.4.1946	2	1911	46	36	0	46.00	–	–	–/–	–	0	
Voce William (CY 1933)	8.8.1909	6.6.1984	27	1929–1946	308	66	0	13.39	98	7-70	3/2	27.88	15	
Waddington Abraham	4.2.1893	28.10.1959	2	1920	16	7	0	4.00	1	1-35	0/0	119.00		
Wainwright Edward (CY 1894)	8.4.1865	28.10.1919	5	1893–1897	132	49	0	14.66	–	–	–/–	–	2	
Walker Peter Michael	17.2.1936		3	1960	128	52	0	32.00	–	–	–/–	–	5	6/7
Walters Cyril Frederick (CY 1934)	28.8.1905	23.12.1992	11	1933–1934	784	102	1	52.26	–	–	–/–	–	6	
Ward Alan	10.8.1947		5	1969–1976	40	21	0	8.00	14	4-61	0/0	32.35	3	
Ward Albert (CY 1890)	21.11.1865	6.11.1939	7	1893–1894	487	117	1	37.46	–	–	–/–	–	1	
Ward Ian James	30.9.1972		5	2001	129	39	0	16.12	–	–	–/–	–		
Wardle John Henry (CY 1954)	8.1.1923	23.7.1985	28	1947–1957	653	66	0	19.78	102	7-36	5/1	20.39	12	
Warner Sir Pelham Francis (CY 1904)	2.10.1873	30.1.1963	15	1898–1912	622	132*	1	23.92	–	–	–/–	–	3	
Warr John James	16.7.1927	9.5.2016	2	1950	4	4	0	1.00	1	1-76	0/0	281.00	1	
Warren Arnold	2.4.1875	3.9.1951	1	1905	7	7	0	7.00	6	5-57	1/0	18.83		
Washbrook Cyril CBE (CY 1947)	6.12.1914	27.4.1999	37	1937–1956	2,569	195	6	42.81	1	1-25	0/0	33.00	12	4
Watkin Steven Llewellyn (CY 1994)	15.9.1964		1	1991–1993	25	13	0	5.00	11	4-65	0/0	27.72		
Watkins Albert John ("Allan")	21.4.1922	3.8.2011	15	1948–1952	810	137*	2	40.50	11	3-20	0/0	50.36	17	1
Watkinson Michael	1.8.1961		4	1995–1995	167	82*	0	33.40	10	3-64	0/0	34.80		
Watson Willie (CY 1954)	7.3.1920	24.4.2004	23	1951–1958	879	116	2	25.85	–	–	–/–	–	8	
Webbe Alexander Josiah	16.1.1855	19.2.1941	1	1878	4	4	0	2.00	–	–	–/–	–	2	
Wellard Arthur William (CY 1936)	8.4.1902	31.12.1980	2	1937–1938	47	38	0	11.75	7	4-81	0/0	33.85	2	
Wells Alan Peter	2.10.1961		1	1995	3	3*	0	3.00	–	–	–/–	–	0	1

	Born	Died	Tests	Test Career	Runs	HS	100s	Avge	Wkts	BB 0-12	5/10	Avge	Ct/St	O/T
Westley Thomas	13.03.1989		5	2017	193	59	0	24.12	0	–	–	–	1	
Wharton Alan	30.4.1923	26.8.1993	1	1949	20	13	0	10.00	–	–	–	–	1	
Whitaker John James (CY 1987)	5.5.1962		1	1986	11	11	0	11.00	–	–	–	–	0	
White Craig	16.12.1969		30	1994–2002	1,052	121	0	24.46	59	5-32	3/0	37.62	14	2
White David William ("Butch")	14.12.1935	1.8.2008	2	1961	0	0	0	0.00	4	3-65	0/0	29.75	0	51
White John Cornish (CY 1929)	19.2.1891	2.5.1961	15	1921–1930	239	29	0	18.38	49	8-126	3/1	32.26	6	
Whysall William Wilfrid (CY 1925)	31.10.1887	11.11.1930	4	1924–1930	209	76	0	29.85					7	
Wilkinson Leonard Litton	5.11.1916	3.9.2002	3	1938	3	2	0	3.00	7	2-12	0/0	38.71	0	
Willey Peter	6.12.1949		26	1976–1986	1,184	102*	2	26.90	7	2-73	0/0	65.14	3	26
Williams Neil FitzGerald	2.7.1962	27.3.2006	1	1990	38	38	0	38.00	2	2-148	0/0	74.00	0	
Willis Robert George Dylan MBE (CY 1978)	30.5.1949		90	1970–1984	840	28*	0	11.50	325	8-43	16/0	25.20	39	64
[2] Wilson Clement Eustace Macro	15.5.1875	8.2.1944	2	1898	42	18	0	14.00					0	
Wilson Donald	7.8.1937	21.7.2012	6	1963–1970	75	42	0	12.50	11	2-17	0/0	42.36	1	
[2] Wilson Evelyn Rockley	25.3.1879	21.7.1957	1	1920	10	5	0	5.00	3	2-28	0/0	12.00	0	
Woakes Christopher Roger (CY 2017)	2.3.1989		26	2013–2018	1,012	137*	1	30.66	72	6-70	2/1	32.94	12	808
Wood Arthur (CY 1939)	25.8.1898	1.4.1973	4	1938–1939	80	53	0	20.00					10/1	
Wood Barry	26.12.1942		12	1972–1978	454	90	0	21.61	0	0-2	–/–	–	6	13
Wood George Edward Charles	22.8.1893	18.3.1971	3	1924	7	6	0	3.50					5/1	
Wood Henry (CY 1891)	14.12.1853	30.4.1919	4	1888–1891	204	134*	0	68.00	0	–	–/–	–	2/1	
Wood Mark Andrew	11.1.1990		12	2015–2018	291	52	0	17.11	30	3-39	0/0	41.73	4	35/4
Wood Reginald	7.3.1860	6.1.1915	1	1886	6	6	0	3.00					0	
Woods Samuel Moses James (CY 1889)	13.4.1867	30.4.1931	3†	1895	122	53	0	30.50	5	3-28	0/0	25.80	4	
Woolley Frank Edward (CY 1911)	27.5.1887	18.10.1978	64	1909–1934	3,283	154	5	36.07	83	7-76	4/1	33.91	64	
Woolmer Robert Andrew (CY 1976)	14.5.1948	18.3.2007	19	1975–1981	1,059	149	3	33.09	4	1-8	0/0	74.75	10	6
Worthington Thomas Stanley (CY 1937)	21.8.1905	31.8.1973	9	1929–1936	321	128	1	29.18	8	2-19	0/0	39.50	8	
Wright Charles William	27.5.1863	10.1.1936	3	1895	125	71	0	31.25					0	
Wright Douglas Vivian Parson (CY 1940)	21.8.1914	13.11.1998	34	1938–1950	289	45	0	11.11	108	7-105	6/1	39.11	10	
Wyatt Robert Elliott Storey (CY 1930)	2.5.1901	20.4.1995	40	1927–1936	1,839	149	2	31.70	18	3-4	0/0	35.66	16	
Wynyard Edward George	1.4.1861	30.10.1936	3	1896–1905	72	30	0	12.00	0	0-2	0/0	–	0	
Yardley Norman Walter Dransfield (CY 1948)	19.3.1915	3.10.1989	20	1938–1950	812	99	0	25.37	21	3-67	0/0	33.66	14	
Young Harding Isaac ("Sailor")	5.2.1876	12.12.1964	2	1899	43	43	0	21.50	12	4-30	0/0	21.83	1	
Young John Albert	14.10.1912	5.2.1993	8	1947–1949	28	10*	0	5.60	17	3-65	0/0	44.52	5	
Young Richard Alfred	16.9.1885	1.7.1968	2	1907	27	13	0	6.75					6	

AUSTRALIA (456 players)

	Born	Died	Tests	Test Career	Runs	HS	100s	Avge	Wkts	BB	5/10	Avge	Ct/St	O/T
a'Beckett Edward Lambert	11.8.1907	2.6.1989	4	1928–1931	143	41	0	20.42	3	1-41	0/0	105.66	4	
Agar Ashton Charles	14.10.1993		4	2013–2017	195	98	0	32.50	9	3-46	0/0	45.55	4	9/15
Alderman Terence Michael (CY 1982)	12.6.1956		41	1981–1990	203	26*	0	6.54	170	6-47	14/1	27.15	27	65
Alexander George	22.4.1851	6.11.1930	2	1880–1884	52	33	0	13.00	2	2-69	0/0	46.50	2	
Alexander Harry Houston	9.6.1905	15.4.1993	1	1932	17	17*	0	17.00	1	1-129	0/0	154.00	0	
Allan Francis Erskine	2.12.1849	9.2.1917	1	1878	5	5	0	5.00	4	2-30	0/0	20.00	0	
Allan Peter John	31.12.1935		1	1965	–	–	–	–	2	2-58	0/0	41.50	0	
Allen Reginald Charles	2.7.1858	2.5.1952	1	1886	44	30	0	22.00	–	–	–	–	0	
Andrews Thomas James Edwin	26.8.1890	28.1.1970	16	1921–1926	592	94	0	26.90	1	1-23	0/0	116.00	12	
² Angel Jo	22.4.1968		4	1992–1994	35	11	0	5.83	10	3-54	0/0	46.30	1	3
Archer Kenneth Alan	17.1.1928		5	1950–1951	234	48	0	26.00	–	–	–	–	20	
² Archer Ronald Graham	25.10.1933	27.5.2007	19	1952–1956	713	128	1	24.58	48	5-53	1/0	27.45	20	
Armstrong Warwick Windridge (CY 1903)	22.5.1879	13.7.1947	50	1901–1921	2,863	159*	6	38.68	87	6-35	3/0	33.59	44	
Badcock Clayvel Lindsay ("Jack")	10.4.1914	13.12.1982	7	1936–1938	160	118	1	14.54	–	–	–	–	3	
Bailey George John	7.9.1982		5	2013	183	53	0	26.14	–	–	–	–	3	90/29‡
Bancroft Cameron Timothy	19.11.1992		8	2017	402	82*	0	30.92	–	–	–	–	10	0/1
² Bannerman Alexander Chalmers	21.3.1854	19.9.1924	28	1878–1893	1,108	94	0	23.08	4	3-111	0/0	40.75	21	
Bannerman Charles	23.7.1851	20.8.1930	3	1876–1878	239	165*	1	59.75	–	–	–	–	11	
Bardsley Warren (CY 1910)	6.12.1882	20.1.1954	41	1909–1926	2,469	193*	6	40.47	–	–	–	–	12	
² Barnes Sidney George	5.6.1916	16.12.1973	13	1938–1948	1,072	234	3	63.05	4	2-25	0/0	54.50	14	
Barnett Benjamin Arthur	23.3.1908	29.6.1979	4	1938	195	57	0	27.85	–	–	–	–	3/2	
Barrett John Edward	15.10.1866	6.2.1916	2	1890	80	67*	0	26.66	–	–	–	–	1	
Beard Graeme Robert	19.8.1950		3	1979	114	49	0	22.80	1	1-26	0/0	109.00	1	2
Beer Michael Anthony	9.6.1984		2	2010–2011	6	2*	0	3.00	3	2-56	0/0	59.33	1	
² Benaud John	11.5.1944		3	1972	223	142	0	44.60	2	2-12	0/0	6.00	0	
Benaud Richard OBE (CY 1962)	6.10.1930	10.4.2015	63	1951–1963	2,201	122	3	24.45	248	7-72	16/1	27.03	65	
Bennett Murray John	6.10.1956		3	1984–1985	71	23	0	23.66	6	3-79	0/0	54.16	5	8
Bevan Michael Gwyl	8.5.1970		18	1994–1997	785	91	0	29.07	29	6-82	1/0	24.24	8	232
Bichel Andrew John	27.8.1970		19	1996–2003	355	71	0	16.90	58	5-60	1/0	32.24	16	67
Bird Jackson Munro	11.12.1986		8	2012–2017	43	19*	0	14.33	34	5-59	1/0	30.64	2	
Blackham John McCarthy (CY 1891)	11.5.1854	28.12.1932	35	1876–1894	800	74	0	15.68	–	–	–	–	37/24	
Blackie Donald Dearness	5.4.1882	18.4.1955	3	1928	24	11*	0	8.00	14	6-94	1/0	31.71	2	
Blewett Gregory Scott	28.10.1971		46	1994–1999	2,552	214	4	34.02	14	2-9	0/0	51.42	45	32

	Born	Died	Tests	Test Career	Runs	HS	100s	Avge	Wkts	BB	5/10	Avge	Ct/St	O/T
Bollinger Douglas Erwin	24.7.1981		12	2008–2010	54	21	0	7.71	50	5-28	2/0	25.92	2	39/9
Bonnor George John	25.2.1855	27.6.1912	17	1880–1888	512	128	1	17.06	2	1-5	0/0	42.00	16	
Boon David Clarence MBE (CY 1994)	29.12.1960		107	1984–1995	7,422	200	21	43.66	–	0-0	0/0	–	99	181
Booth Brian Charles MBE	19.10.1933		29	1961–1965	1,773	169	5	42.21	3	2-33	0/0	48.66	17	
Border Allan Robert (CY 1982)	27.7.1955		156	1978–1993	11,174	205	27	50.56	39	7-46	2/1	39.10	156	273
Boyle Henry Frederick	10.12.1847	21.11.1907	12	1878–1884	153	36*	0	12.75	32	6-42	1/0	20.03	10	
Bracken Nathan Wade	12.9.1977		5	2003–2005	70	37	0	17.50	12	4-48	0/0	42.08	2	116/19
Bradman Sir Donald George AC (CY 1931)	27.8.1908	25.2.2001	52	1928–1948	6,996	334	29	99.94	2	1-8	0/0	36.00	32	
Bright Raymond James	13.7.1954		25	1977–1986	445	33	0	14.35	53	7-87	4/1	41.13	13	11
Bromley Ernest Harvey	2.9.1912	1.2.1967	2	1932–1934	38	26	0	9.50	0	0-19	0/0	–	2	
Brown William Alfred (CY 1939)	31.7.1912	16.3.2008	22	1934–1948	1,592	206*	4	46.82	–	–	–/–	–	14	
Bruce William	22.5.1864	3.8.1925	14	1884–1894	702	80	0	29.25	12	3-88	0/0	36.66	12	
Burge Peter John Parnell (CY 1965)	17.5.1932	5.10.2001	42	1954–1965	2,290	181	4	38.16	–	–	–/–	–	23	
Burke James Wallace (CY 1957)	12.6.1930	2.2.1979	24	1950–1958	1,280	189	3	34.59	8	4-37	0/0	28.75	18	
Burn Edwin James Kenneth (K. E.)	17.9.1862	20.7.1956	2	1890	41	19	0	10.25	–	–	–/–	–	0	
Burns Joseph Antony	6.9.1989		14	2014–2017	919	170	3	36.76	–	–	–/–	–	15	6
Burton Frederick John	2.11.1865	25.8.1929	2	1886–1887	4	2*	0	2.00	–	–	–/–	–	1/1	
Callaway Sydney Thomas	6.2.1868	25.11.1923	3	1891–1894	87	41	0	17.40	6	5-37	1/0	23.66	1	
Callen Ian Wayne	2.5.1955		1	1977	26	22*	0	26.00	6	3-83	0/0	31.83	1	5
Campbell Gregory Dale	10.3.1964		4	1989–1989	10	5	0	2.50	13	3-79	0/0	38.69	1	12
Carkeek William ("Barlow")	17.10.1878	20.2.1937	6	1912	16	6*	0	5.33	–	–	–/–	–	6	
Carlson Phillip Henry	8.8.1951		2	1978	23	21	0	5.75	2	2-41	0/0	49.50	2	4
Carter Hanson	15.3.1878	8.6.1948	28	1907–1921	873	72	0	22.97	–	–	–/–	–	44/21	
Cartwright Hilton William Raymond	14.2.1992		3	2016–2017	55	37	0	27.50	0	0-15	0/0	–	2	2
Casson Beau	7.12.1982		1	2007	10	10	0	10.00	3	3-86	0/0	43.00	0	2
[2,4] **Chappell Gregory Stephen** MBE (CY 1973)	7.8.1948		87	1970–1983	7,110	247*	24	53.86	47	5-61	1/0	40.70	122	74
[2,4] **Chappell Ian Michael** (CY 1976)	26.9.1943		75	1964–1979	5,345	196	14	42.42	20	2-21	0/0	65.80	105	16
[2,4] **Chappell Trevor Martin**	21.10.1952		3	1981	79	27	0	15.80	–	–	–/–	–	2	20
Charlton Percie Chater	9.4.1867	30.9.1954	2	1890	29	11	0	7.25	3	3-18	0/0	8.00	2	
Chipperfield Arthur Gordon	17.11.1905	29.7.1987	14	1934–1938	552	109	1	32.47	5	3-91	0/0	87.40	15	
Clark Stuart Rupert	28.9.1975		24	2005–2009	248	39	0	13.05	94	5-32	2/0	23.86	4	39/9
Clark Wayne Maxwell	19.9.1953		10	1977–1978	98	33	0	5.76	44	4-46	0/0	28.75	4	2
Clarke Michael John (CY 2010)	2.4.1981		115§	2004–2015	8,643	329*	28	49.10	31	6-9	2/0	38.19	134	245/34
Colley David John	15.3.1947		3	1972	84	54	0	21.00	6	3-83	0/0	52.00	1	1
Collins Herbert Leslie	21.11.1888	28.5.1959	19	1920–1926	1,352	203	4	45.06	4	2-47	0/0	63.00	13	

§ *Clarke's figures include 44 runs and one catch for Australia v the ICC World XI in the Super Series Test in 2005-06.*

	Born	Died	Tests	Test Career	Runs	HS	100s	Avge	Wkts	BB	5/10	Avge	Ct/St	O/T
Coningham Arthur	14.7.1863	13.6.1939	1	1894	13	10	0	6.50	2	2-17	0/0	38.00	0	1
Connolly Alan Norman	29.6.1939		29	1963–1970	260	37	0	10.40	102	6-47	4/0	29.22	17	
Cook Simon Hewitt	29.1.1972		2	1997	7	3*	0	–	7	5-39	1/0	20.28	0	
Cooper Bransby Beauchamp	15.3.1844	7.8.1914	1	1876	18	15	0	9.00	0	–	–/–	–	2	
Cooper William Henry	11.9.1849	5.4.1939	2	1881–1884	13	7	0	6.50	9	6-120	1/0	25.11	1	
Copeland Trent Aaron	14.3.1986		3	2011	39	23*	0	13.00	6	2-24	0/0	37.83	2	
Corling Grahame Edward	13.7.1941		5	1964	5	3	0	1.66	12	4-60	0/0	37.25	1	
Cosier Gary John	25.4.1953		18	1975–1978	897	168	2	28.93	5	2-26	0/0	68.20	14	9
Cottam John Thomas	5.9.1867	30.1.1897	1	1886	4	3	0	2.00	–	–	–/–	–	1	
Cotter Albert ("Tibby")	3.12.1883	31.10.1917	21	1903–1911	457	45	0	13.05	89	7-148	7/0	28.64	8	
Coulthard George	1.8.1856	22.10.1883	1	1881	6	6*	0	–	–	–	–/–	–	0	
Cowan Edward James McKenzie	16.6.1982		18	2011–2013	1,001	136	1	31.28	–	–	–/–	–	24	
Cowper Robert Maskew	5.10.1940		27	1964–1968	2,061	307	5	46.84	36	4-48	0/0	31.63	21	
Craig Ian David	12.6.1935	16.11.2014	11	1952–1957	358	53	0	19.88	–	–	–/–	–	2	
Crawford William Patrick Anthony	3.8.1933	21.1.2009	4	1956–1956	53	34	0	17.66	7	3-28	0/0	15.28	1	
Cullen Daniel James	10.4.1984		1	2005	–	–	0	–	1	1-25	0/0	54.00	0	5
Cummins Patrick James	8.5.1993		11	2011–2018	528	63	0	21.12	80	6-27	3/0	24.51	8	42/18
Dale Adam Craig	30.12.1968		2	1997–1998	6	5	0	2.00	6	3-71	0/0	31.16	0	30
Darling Joseph (CY 1900)	21.11.1870	2.1.1946	34	1894–1905	1,657	178	3	28.56	–	–	–/–	–	27	
Darling Leonard Stuart	14.8.1909	24.6.1992	12	1932–1936	474	85	0	27.88	0	0-3	0/0	–	8	
Darling Warrick Maxwell	1.5.1957		14	1977–1979	697	91	0	26.80	–	–	–/–	–	5	18
Davidson Alan Keith MBE (CY 1962)	14.6.1929		44	1953–1962	1,328	80	0	24.59	186	7-93	14/2	20.53	42	
Davis Ian Charles	25.6.1953		15	1973–1977	692	105	1	26.61	–	–	–/–	–	9	3
Davis Simon Peter	8.11.1959		1	1985	0	0	0	0.00	0	0-70	0/0	–	0	39
De Courcy James Harry	18.4.1927	20.6.2000	3	1953	81	41	0	16.20	–	–	–/–	–	3	
Dell Anthony Ross	6.8.1947		2	1970–1973	6	3*	0	–	6	3-65	0/0	26.66	0	
Dodemaide Anthony Ian Christopher	5.10.1963		10	1987–1992	202	50	0	22.44	34	6-58	1/0	28.02	6	24
Doherty Xavier John	22.12.1982		4	2010–2012	51	18*	0	12.75	7	3-131	0/0	78.28	2	60/11
Donnan Henry	12.11.1864	13.8.1956	5	1891–1896	75	15	0	8.33	0	0-22	0/0	–	1	
Doolan Alexander James	29.11.1985		4	2013–2014	191	89	0	23.87	–	–	–/–	–	2	
Dooland Bruce (CY 1955)	1.11.1923	8.9.1980	3	1946–1947	76	29	0	19.00	9	4-69	0/0	46.55	3	
Duff Reginald Alexander	17.8.1878	13.12.1911	22	1901–1905	1,317	146	2	35.59	4	2-43	0/0	21.25	14	
Duncan John Ross Frederick	25.3.1944		1	1970	3	3	0	3.00	0	0-30	0/0	–	0	
Dyer Gregory Charles	16.3.1959		6	1986–1987	131	60	0	21.83	–	–	–/–	–	22/2	23
Dymock Geoffrey	21.7.1945		21	1973–1979	236	31*	0	9.44	78	7-67	5/1	27.12	15	15
Dyson John	11.6.1954		30	1977–1984	1,359	127*	2	26.64	–	–	–/–	–	10	29

	Born	Died	Tests	Test Career	Runs	HS	100s	Avge	Wkts	BB	5/10	Avge	Ct/St	O/T
Eady Charles John	29.10.1870	20.12.1945	2	1896–1901	20	10*	–	6.66	7	3-30	0/0	16.00	0	–
Eastwood Kenneth Humphrey	23.11.1935		1	1970	5	5	–	2.50	–	1-21	0/0	21.00	0	–
Ebeling Hans Irvine	1.1.1905	12.1.1980	1	1934	43	41	–	21.50	3	3-74	0/0	29.66	0	–
Edwards John Dunlop	12.6.1860	31.7.1911	1	1888	48	26	–	9.60	–	–	–	–	1	–
Edwards Ross	1.12.1942		20	1972–1975	1,171	170*	2	40.37	0	0-20	0/0	–	7	9
Edwards Walter John	23.12.1949		3	1974	68	30	–	11.33	–	–	–	–	0	1
Elliott Matthew Thomas Gray (CY 1998)	28.9.1971		21	1996–2004	1,172	199	3	33.48	–	–	–	–	14	–
Emery Philip Allan	25.6.1964		1	1994	8	8*	–	–	–	–	–	–	5/1	1
Emery Sidney Hand	15.10.1885	7.1.1967	4	1912	6	5	–	3.00	5	2-46	0/0	49.80	2	–
Evans Edwin	26.3.1849	2.7.1921	6	1881–1886	82	33	–	10.25	7	3-64	0/0	47.42	5	–
Fairfax Alan George	16.6.1906	17.5.1955	10	1928–1930	410	65	–	51.25	21	4-31	0/0	30.71	15	–
Faulkner James Peter	29.4.1990		1	2013	45	23	–	22.50	6	4-51	0/0	16.33	0	69/24
Favell Leslie Ernest MBE	6.10.1929	14.6.1987	19	1954–1960	757	101	1	27.03	–	–	–	–	9	–
Ferguson Callum James	21.11.1984		1	2016	4	3	–	2.00	–	–	–	–	0	30/3
Ferris John James (CY 1889)	21.5.1867	17.11.1900	8†	1886–1890	98	20	–	8.16	48	5-26	4/0	14.25	4	–
Finch Aaron James	17.11.1986		5	2018	278	62	–	27.80	0	0-8	0/0	–	7	96/50
Fingleton John Henry Webb OBE	28.4.1908	22.11.1981	18	1931–1938	1,189	136	5	42.46	–	–	–	–	13	–
Fleetwood-Smith Leslie O'Brien ("Chuck")	30.3.1908	16.3.1971	10	1935–1938	54	16*	–	9.00	42	6-110	2/1	37.38	0	–
Fleming Damien William	24.4.1970		20	1994–2000	305	71*	–	19.06	75	5-30	3/0	25.89	9	88
Francis Bruce Colin	18.2.1948		3	1972	52	27	–	10.40	–	–	–	–	1	–
Freeman Eric Walter	13.7.1944		11	1967–1969	345	76	–	19.16	34	4-52	0/0	33.17	5	–
Freer Frederick Alfred William	4.12.1915	2.11.1998	1	1946	28	28*	–	–	3	2-49	0/0	24.66	0	–
Gannon John Bryant ("Sam")	8.2.1947		3	1977	3	3*	–	3.00	11	4-77	0/0	32.81	3	–
Garrett Thomas William	26.7.1858	6.8.1943	19	1876–1887	339	51*	–	12.55	36	6-78	2/0	26.94	7	–
Gaunt Ronald Arthur	26.2.1934	30.3.2012	3	1957–1963	6	3	–	3.00	7	3-53	0/0	44.28	1	–
Gehrs Donald Raeburn Algernon	29.11.1880	25.6.1953	6	1903–1910	221	67	–	20.09	0	0-4	0/0	–	6	–
George Peter Robert	16.10.1986		1	2010	1	1	–	1.00	2	2-48	0/0	38.50	0	–
²Giffen George (CY 1894)	27.3.1859	29.11.1927	31	1881–1896	1,238	161	1	23.35	103	7-117	7/1	27.09	24	–
²Giffen Walter Frank	20.9.1861	28.6.1949	3	1886–1891	11	3	–	1.83	–	–	–	–	0	–
Gilbert David Robert	29.12.1960		9	1985–1986	57	15	–	7.12	16	3-48	0/0	52.68	0	14
Gilchrist Adam Craig (CY 2002)	14.11.1971		96§	1999–2007	5,570	204*	17	47.60	–	–	–	–	379/37	286§/13
Gillespie Jason Neil (CY 2002)	19.4.1975		71	1996–2005	1,218	201*	2	18.73	259	7-37	8/0	26.13	27	97/1
Gilmour Gary John	26.6.1951	10.6.2014	15	1973–1976	483	101	1	23.00	54	6-85	3/0	26.03	8	5
Gleeson John William	14.3.1938	8.10.2016	29	1967–1972	395	45	–	10.39	93	5-61	3/0	36.20	17	–
Graham Henry	22.11.1870	7.2.1911	6	1893–1896	301	107	2	30.10	–	–	–	–	3	–

§ *Gilchrist's figures include 95 runs, five catches and two stumpings for Australia v the ICC World XI in the Super Series Test in 2005-06.*

	Born	Died	Tests	Test Career	Runs	HS	100s	Avge	Wks	BB	5/10	Avge	Ct/St	O/T
[2]Gregory David William	15.4.1845	4.8.1919	3	1876-1878	60	43	0	20.00	0	0-9	0/0	–	0	–
[1,2]Gregory Edward James	29.5.1839	22.4.1899	1	1876	11	11	0	5.50	0	–	–/–	–	1	–
Gregory Jack Morrison (CY 1922)	14.8.1895	7.8.1973	24	1920-1928	1,146	119	2	36.96	85	7-69	4/0	31.15	37	–
Gregory Ross Gerald	28.2.1916	10.6.1942	2	1936	153	80	0	51.00	0	0-14	0/0	–	1	–
[1]Gregory Sydney Edward (CY 1897)	14.4.1870	31.7.1929	58	1890-1912	2,282	201	4	24.53	0	0-4	0/0	–	25	–
Grimmett Clarence Victor (CY 1931)	25.12.1891	2.5.1980	37	1924-1935	557	50	0	13.92	216	7-40	21/7	24.21	17	–
Groube Thomas Underwood	2.9.1857	5.8.1927	1	1880	11	11	0	5.50	–	–	–/–	–	0	–
Grout Arthur Theodore Wallace	30.3.1927	9.11.1968	51	1957-1965	890	74	0	15.08	–	–	–/–	–	163/24	–
Guest Colin Ernest John	7.10.1937	8.12.2018	1	1962	11	11	0	11.00	0	0-8	0/0	–	0	–
Haddin Bradley James	23.10.1977		66	2007-2015	3,265	169	4	32.97	–	–	–/–	–	262/8	126/34
Hamence Ronald Arthur	25.11.1915	24.3.2010	3	1946-1947	81	30*	0	27.00	–	–	–/–	–	1	–
Hammond Jeffrey Roy	19.4.1950		5	1972	28	19	0	9.33	15	4-38	0/0	32.53	2	1
Handscomb Peter Stephen Patrick	26.4.1991		16	2016-2018	934	110	2	38.91	0	–	–/–	–	28	8
Harris Marcus Sinclair	21.7.1992		4	2018	258	79	0	36.85	–	–	–/–	–	6	–
Harris Ryan James (CY 2014)	11.10.1979		27	2009-2014	603	74	0	21.53	113	7-117	5/0	23.52	13	21/3
Harry John	1.8.1857	27.10.1919	1	1894	8	6	0	4.00	0	0-7	–/–	–	1	–
Hartigan Roger Joseph	12.12.1879	7.6.1958	2	1907	170	116	1	42.50	0	0-7	0/0	–	2	–
Hartkopf Albert Ernst Victor	28.12.1889	20.5.1968	1	1924	80	80	0	40.00	1	1-120	0/0	134.00	0	–
[2]Harvey Mervyn Roye	29.4.1918	18.3.1995	1	1946	43	31	0	21.50	–	–	–/–	–	0	–
[2]Harvey Robert Neil MBE (CY 1954)	8.10.1928	16.6.1993	79	1947-1962	6,149	205	21	48.41	3	1-8	0/0	40.00	64	–
Hassett Arthur Lindsay MBE (CY 1949)	28.8.1913	16.6.1993	43	1938-1953	3,073	198*	10	46.56	0	0-1	0/0	–	30	–
Hastings John Wayne	4.11.1985		1	2012	52	32	0	26.00	1	1-51	0/0	153.00	2	29/9
Hauritz Nathan Michael	18.10.1981		17	2004-2010	426	75	0	25.05	63	5-53	2/0	34.98	3	58/3
Hawke Neil James Napier	27.6.1939	25.12.2000	27	1962-1968	365	45*	0	16.59	91	7-105	6/1	29.41	9	–
Hayden Matthew Lawrence (CY 2003)	29.10.1971		103§	1993-2008	8,625	380	30	50.73	0	0-7	0/0	–	128	161/9
Hazlewood Josh Reginald	8.1.1991		44	2014-2018	388	39	0	12.51	164	6-67	6/0	27.14	15	44/7
Hazlitt Gervys Rignold	4.9.1888	30.10.1915	9	1907-1912	89	34*	0	11.12	23	7-25	1/0	27.08	4	–
Head Travis Michael	29.12.1993		6	2018	359	72	0	32.63	0	0-2	0/0	–	5	42/16
Healy Ian Andrew (CY 1994)	30.4.1964		119	1988-1999	4,356	161*	4	27.39	–	–	–/–	–	366/29	168
Hendry Hunter Scott Thomas Laurie ("Stork")	24.5.1895	16.12.1988	11	1921-1928	335	112	1	20.93	16	3-36	0/0	40.00	10	–
Henriques Moises Constantino	1.2.1987		4	2012-2016	164	81*	0	23.42	2	1-48	0/0	82.00		11/11
Hibbert Paul Anthony	23.7.1952	27.11.2008	1	1977	15	13	0	7.50	0	–	–/–	–		–
Higgs James Donald	11.7.1950		22	1977-1980	111	16	0	5.55	66	7-143	2/0	31.16	3	–
Hilditch Andrew Mark Jefferson	20.5.1956		18	1978-1985	1,073	119	2	31.55	0	–	–/–	–	13	8
Hilfenhaus Benjamin William	15.3.1983		27	2008-2012	355	56*	0	13.65	99	5-75	2/0	28.50	8	25/7

§ Hayden's figures include 188 runs and three catches, for Australia v the ICC World XI in the Super Series Test in 2005-06.

	Born	Died	Tests	Test Career	Runs	HS	100s	Avge	Wkts	BB	5/10	Avge	Ct/St	O/T
Hill Clement (CY 1900)	18.3.1877	5.9.1945	49	1896–1911	3,412	191	7	39.21	–	–	–/–	–	33	
Hill John Charles	25.6.1923	11.8.1974	3	1953–1954	21	8*	0	7.00	8	3-35	0/0	34.12	2	
Hoare Desmond Edward	19.10.1934		1	1960	35	35*	0	17.50	2	2-68	0/0	78.00	2	25/15
Hodge Bradley John	29.12.1974		6	2005–2007	503	203*	1	55.88	0	0-8	0/0	–	9	
Hodges John Robart	11.8.1855	d unknown	2	1876	10	8	0	3.33	6	2-7	0/0	14.00	2	
Hogan Tom George	23.9.1956		7	1982–1983	205	42*	0	18.63	15	5-66	1/0	47.06	0	16
Hogg George Bradley	6.2.1971		7	1996–2007	186	79	0	26.57	17	2-40	0/0	54.88	7	123/15
Hogg Rodney Malcolm	5.3.1951		38	1978–1984	439	52	0	9.75	123	6-74	6/2	28.47	7	71
Hohns Trevor Victor	23.1.1954		18	1988–1989	136	40	0	22.66	17	3-59	0/0	34.11	3	
Hole Graeme Blake	6.1.1931	14.2.1990	18	1950–1954	789	66	0	25.45	3	1-9	0/0	42.00	21	
Holland Jonathan Mark	29.5.1987		4	2016–2018	6	3	0	3.00	9	3-83	0/0	63.77	1	
Holland Robert George	19.10.1946	17.9.2017	11	1984–1985	35	10	0	3.18	34	6-54	3/2	39.76	5	2
Hookes David William	3.5.1955	19.1.2004	23	1976–1985	1,306	143*	1	34.36	1	1-4	0/0	41.00	12	
Hopkins Albert John Young	3.5.1874	25.4.1931	20	1901–1909	509	43	0	16.41	26	4-81	0/0	26.76	11	39
Horan Thomas Patrick	8.3.1854	16.4.1916	15	1876–1884	471	124	1	18.84	11	6-40	1/0	13.00	6	
Hordern Herbert Vivian MBE	10.2.1883	17.6.1938	7	1910–1911	254	50	0	23.09	46	7-90	5/2	23.36	6	
Hornibrook Percival Mitchell	27.7.1899	25.8.1976	6	1928–1930	60	26	0	10.00	17	7-92	1/0	39.05	7	
Howell William Peter	29.12.1869	14.7.1940	18	1897–1903	158	35	0	7.52	49	5-81	1/0	28.71	12	
Hughes Kimberley John (CY 1981)	26.1.1954		70	1977–1984	4,415	213	9	37.41	0	0-0	0/0	–	50	97
Hughes Mervyn Gregory (CY 1994)	23.11.1961		53	1985–1993	1,032	72*	0	16.64	212	8-87	7/1	28.38	23	33
Hughes Phillip Joel	30.11.1988	27.11.2014	26	2008–2013	1,535	160	3	32.65	0	–	–/–	–	15	25/1
Hunt William Alfred	26.8.1908	30.12.1983	1	1931	0	0	0	0.00	0	0-14	0/0	–	1	
Hurst Alan George	15.7.1950		12	1973–1979	102	26	0	6.00	43	5-28	2/0	27.90	3	8
Hurwood Alexander	17.6.1902	26.9.1982	2	1930	5	5	0	2.50	11	4-22	0/0	15.45	1	
Hussey Michael Edward Killeen	27.5.1975		79	2005–2012	6,235	195	19	51.52	7	1-0	0/0	43.71	85	185/38
Inverarity Robert John	31.1.1944		6	1968–1972	174	56	0	17.40	4	3-26	0/0	23.25	4	
Iredale Francis Adams	19.6.1867	15.4.1926	14	1894–1899	807	140	2	36.68	0	0-3	0/0	–	16	
Ironmonger Herbert	7.4.1882	31.5.1971	14	1928–1932	42	12	0	2.62	74	7-23	4/2	17.97	3	
Iverson John Brian	27.7.1915	24.10.1973	5	1950	3	1*	0	0.75	21	6-27	1/0	15.23	2	
Jackson Archibald Alexander	5.9.1909	16.2.1933	8	1928–1930	474	164	1	47.40	0	–	–/–	–	7	
Jaques Philip Anthony	3.5.1979		11	2005–2007	902	150	3	47.47	–	–	–/–	–	7	6
Jarman Barrington Noel	17.2.1936		19	1959–1968	400	78	0	14.81	–	–	–/–	–	50/4	
Jarvis Arthur Harwood	19.10.1860	15.11.1933	11	1884–1894	303	82	0	16.83	–	–	–/–	–	9/9	
Jenner Terrence James	8.9.1944	25.5.2011	9	1970–1975	208	74	0	23.11	24	5-90	1/0	31.20	5	
Jennings Claude Burrows	5.6.1884	20.6.1950	6	1912	107	32	0	17.83	0	–	–/–	–	5	1
Johnson Ian William Geddes CBE	8.12.1917	9.10.1998	45	1945–1956	1,000	77	0	18.51	109	7-44	3/0	29.19	30	

	Born	Died	Tests	Test Career	Runs	HS	100s	Avge	Wkts	BB	5/10	Avge	Ct/St	O/T
Johnson Leonard Joseph	18.3.1919	20.4.1977	1	1947	25	25*	0	–	6	3-8	0/0	12.33	–	
Johnson Mitchell Guy	2.11.1981		73	2007–2015	2,065	123*	1	22.20	313	8-61	12/3	28.40	27	153/30
Johnson William Arras (CY 1949)	26.2.1922	25.5.2007	40	1947–1954	273	29	0	11.37	160	6-44	7/0	23.91	16	
Jones Dean Mervyn (CY 1990)	24.3.1961		52	1983–1992	3,631	216	11	46.55	1	1-5	0/0	64.00	34	164
Jones Ernest	30.9.1869	23.11.1943	19	1894–1902	126	20	0	5.04	64	7-88	3/1	29.01	21	
Jones Samuel Percy	1.8.1861	14.7.1951	12	1881–1887	428	87	0	21.40	6	4-47	0/0	18.66	12	
Joslin Leslie Ronald	13.12.1947		1	1967	9	7	0	4.50	–	–	–/–	–	0	
Julian Brendon Paul	10.8.1970		7	1993–1995	128	56*	0	16.00	15	4-36	0/0	39.93	4	25
Kasprowicz Michael Scott	10.2.1972		38	1996–2005	445	25	0	10.59	113	7-36	4/0	32.88	16	43/2
Katich Simon Mathew	21.8.1975		56§	2001–2010	4,188	157	10	45.03	21	6-65	1/0	30.23	39	45/3
Kelleway Charles	25.4.1886	16.11.1944	26	1910–1928	1,422	147	3	37.42	52	5-33	1/0	32.36	24	
Kelly James Joseph (CY 1903)	10.5.1867	14.8.1938	36	1896–1905	664	46*	0	17.02	–	–	–/–	–	43/20	
Kelly Thomas Joseph Dart	3.5.1844	20.7.1893	2	1876–1878	64	35	0	21.33	–	–	–/–	–	1	
Kendall Thomas Kingston	24.8.1851	17.8.1924	2	1876	39	17*	0	13.00	14	7-55	1/0	15.35	2	
Kent Martin Francis	23.11.1953		3	1981	171	17	0	28.50	–	–	–/–	–	6	5
Kerr Robert Byers	16.6.1961		2	1985	31	17	0	7.75	–	–	–/–	–	1	4
Khawaja Usman Tariq	18.12.1986		39	2010–2018	2,653	174	8	42.11	0	0-1	0/0	–	31	18/9
Kippax Alan Falconer	25.5.1897	5.9.1972	22	1924–1934	1,192	146	2	36.12	0	0-2	0/0	–	13	
Kline Lindsay Francis	29.9.1934	2.10.2015	13	1957–1960	58	15*	0	8.28	34	7-75	1/0	22.82	9	
Krejza Jason John	14.11.1983		2	2008	71	32	0	23.66	13	8-215	1/1	43.23	4	8
Labuschagne Marnus	22.6.1994		5	2018	119	43	0	23.80	7	3-45	0/0	33.28	6	
Laird Bruce Malcolm	21.11.1950		21	1979–1982	1,341	92	0	35.28	0	0-3	0/0	–	16	23
Langer Justin Lee (CY 2001)	21.11.1970		105§	1992–2006	7,696	250	23	45.27	0	0-3	0/0	–	73	8
Langley Gilbert Roche Andrews (CY 1957)	14.9.1919	14.5.2001	26	1951–1956	374	53	0	14.96	–	–	–/–	–	83/15	
Laughlin Trevor John	30.1.1951		3	1977–1978	87	35	0	17.40	6	5-101	1/0	43.66	3	6
Laver Frank Jonas	7.12.1869	24.9.1919	15	1899–1909	196	45	0	11.52	37	8-31	2/0	26.05	8	
Law Stuart Grant (CY 1998)	18.10.1968		1	1995	54	54*	0	–	–	–	–/–	–	–	54
Lawry William Morris (CY 1962)	11.2.1937		67	1961–1970	5,234	210	13	47.15	0	0-6	0/0	–	30	1
Lawson Geoffrey Francis	7.12.1957		46	1980–1989	894	74	0	15.96	180	8-112	11/2	30.56	10	79
Lee Brett (CY 2006)	8.11.1976		76§	1999–2008	1,451	64	0	20.15	310	5-30	10/0	30.81	23	221/25
Lee Philip Keith	15.9.1904	9.8.1980	2	1931–1932	57	42	0	19.00	5	4-111	0/0	42.40	–	
Lehmann Darren Scott (CY 2001)	5.2.1970		27	1997–2004	1,798	177	5	44.95	15	3-42	0/0	27.46	11	117
Lillee Dennis Keith MBE (CY 1973)	18.7.1949		70	1970–1983	905	73*	0	13.71	355	7-83	23/7	23.92	23	63
Lindwall Raymond Russell MBE (CY 1949)	3.10.1921	23.6.1996	61	1945–1959	1,502	118	2	21.15	228	7-38	12/0	23.03	26	

§   Katich's figures include two runs and one catch, Langer's 22 runs and one catch, and Lee's four runs, two wickets and one catch for Australia v the ICC World XI in the Super Series Test in 2005-06.

	Born	Died	Tests	Test Career	Runs	HS	100s	Avge	Wkts	BB	5/10	Avge	Ct/St	O/T
Love Hampden Stanley Bray	10.8.1895	22.7.1969	1	1932	8	5	0	4.00	–	–	–/–	–	3	
Love Martin Lloyd	30.3.1974		5	2002–2003	233	100*	1	46.60					7	
Loxton Samuel John Everett OBE	29.3.1921	3.12.2011	12	1947–1950	554	101	1	36.93	8	3-55	0/0	43.62	7	15/2
Lyon Nathan Michael	20.11.1987		84	2011–2018	922	47	0	12.13	339	8-50	14/2	32.10	41	
Lyons John James	21.5.1863	21.7.1927	14	1886–1897	731	134	1	27.07	6	5-30	1/0	24.83	3	
McAlister Peter Alexander	11.7.1869	10.5.1938	8	1903–1909	252	41	0	16.80			–/–		10	
Macartney Charles George (CY 1922)	27.6.1886	9.9.1958	35	1907–1926	2,131	170	7	41.78	45	7-58	2/1	27.55	17	
McCabe Stanley Joseph (CY 1935)	16.7.1910	25.8.1968	39	1930–1938	2,748	232	6	48.21	36	4-13	0/0	42.86	41	
McCool Colin Leslie	9.12.1916	5.4.1986	14	1945–1949	459	104*	1	35.30	36	5-41	3/0	26.61	14	
McCormick Ernest Leslie	16.5.1906	28.6.1991	12	1935–1938	54	17*	0	6.00	36	4-101	0/0	29.97	8	
McCosker Richard Bede (CY 1976)	11.12.1946		25	1974–1979	1,622	127	4	39.56			–/–		21	14
McDermott Craig John (CY 1986)	14.4.1965		71	1984–1995	940	42*	0	12.20	291	8-97	14/2	28.63	19	138
McDonald Andrew Barry	15.6.1981		4	2008	107	68	0	21.40	9	3-25	0/0	33.33	2	
McDonald Colin Campbell	17.11.1928		47	1951–1961	3,107	170	5	39.32	0	0-3	0/0	–	14	
McDonald Edgar Arthur (CY 1922)	6.1.1891	22.7.1937	11	1920–1921	116	36	0	16.57	43	5-32	2/0	33.27	3	
McDonnell Percy Stanislaus	13.11.1858	24.9.1896	19	1880–1888	955	147	3	28.93	0	0-11	0/0	–	6	
McGain Bryce Edward	25.3.1972		1	2008	2	2	0	1.00	0	0-149	0/0	–	–	
MacGill Stuart Charles Glyndwr	25.2.1971		44§	1997–2007	349	43	0	9.69	208	8-108	12/2	29.02	16	3
McGrath Glenn Donald (CY 1998)	9.2.1970		124§	1993–2006	641	61	0	7.36	563	8-24	29/3	21.64	38	249§/2
McIlwraith John	7.9.1857	5.7.1938	1	1886	9	7	0	4.50					1	
McIntyre Peter Edward	27.4.1966		2	1994–1996	22	16	0	7.33	5	3-103	0/0	38.80	0	
McKay Clinton James	22.2.1983		1	2009	10	10	0	10.00	1	1-56	0/0	101.00	1	59/6
Mackay Kenneth Donald MBE	24.10.1925	13.6.1982	37	1956–1962	1,507	89	0	33.48	50	6-42	2/0	34.42	16	
McKenzie Graham Douglas (CY 1965)	24.6.1941		60	1961–1970	945	76	0	12.27	246	8-71	16/3	29.78	34	1
McKibbin Thomas Robert	10.12.1870	15.12.1939	5	1894–1897	88	28*	0	14.66	17	3-35	0/0	29.17	4	
McLaren John William	22.12.1886	17.11.1921	1	1911	0	0*	0	–	1	1-23	0/0	70.00	0	
Maclean John Alexander	27.4.1946		4	1978	79	33*	0	11.28			–/–		18	2
McLeod Charles Edward	24.10.1869	26.11.1918	17	1894–1905	573	112	1	23.87	33	5-65	2/0	40.15	9	
McLeod Robert William	19.1.1868	14.6.1907	6	1891–1893	146	31	0	13.27	12	5-53	1/0	31.83	3	
McShane Patrick George	18.4.1858	11.12.1903	3	1884–1887	26	12*	0	5.20	1	1-39	0/0	48.00	2	
Maddinson Nicolas James	21.12.1991		3	2016	27	22	0	6.75	0	0-9	0/0	–	2	0/6
Maddocks Leonard Victor	24.5.1926	27.8.2016	7	1954–1956	177	69	0	17.70			–/–		19/1	
Maguire John Norman	15.9.1956		3	1983	28	15*	0	7.00	10	4-57	0/0	32.30	2	23
Mailey Arthur Alfred	3.1.1886	31.12.1967	21	1920–1926	222	46*	0	11.10	99	9-121	6/2	33.91	14	
Mallett Ashley Alexander	13.7.1945		38	1968–1980	430	43*	0	11.62	132	8-59	6/1	29.84	30	9

§ MacGill's figures include no runs and nine wickets and McGrath's two runs and three wickets for Australia v the ICC World XI in the Super Series Test in 2005-06.

Name	Born	Died	Tests	Test Career	Runs	HS	100s	Avge	Wkts	BB	5/10	Avge	Ct/St	O/T
Malone Michael Francis	9.10.1950		1	1977	46	46	–	46.00	6	5-63	1/0	12.83	0	10
Mann Anthony Longford	8.11.1945		4	1977	189	105	1	23.62	4	3-12	0/0	79.00	2	–
Manou Graham Allan	23.4.1979		1	2009	21	13*	–	21.00	0	–	–/–	–	3	4
Marr Alfred Percy	28.3.1862	15.3.1940	1	1884	5	5	–	2.50	0	0-3	0/0	–	0	–
Marsh Geoffrey Robert	31.12.1958		50	1985–1991	2,854	138	4	33.18	–	–	–/–	–	38	117
Marsh Mitchell Ross	20.10.1991		31	2014–2018	1,219	181	3	25.39	35	4-61	0/0	43.91	15	53/11
Marsh Rodney William MBE (CY 1982)	4.11.1947		96	1970–1983	3,633	132	3	26.51	0	0-3	0/0	–	343/12	92
Marsh Shaun Edward	9.7.1983		38	2011–2018	2,265	182	6	34.31	–	–	–/–	–	23	60/15
Martin John Wesley	28.7.1931	16.7.1992	8	1960–1966	214	55	0	17.83	17	3-56	0/0	48.94	5	–
Martyn Damien Richard (CY 2002)	21.10.1971		67	1992–2006	4,406	165	13	46.37	2	1-0	0/0	84.00	36	208/4
Massie Hugh Hamon	11.4.1854	12.10.1938	9	1881–1884	249	55	0	15.56	–	–	–/–	–	5	–
Massie Robert Arnold Lockyer (CY 1973)	14.4.1947		6	1972–1972	78	42	0	11.14	31	8-53	2/1	20.87	1	3
Matthews Christopher Darrell	22.9.1962		3	1986–1988	54	32	0	10.80	6	3-95	0/0	52.16	1	–
Matthews Gregory Richard John	15.12.1959		33	1983–1992	1,849	130	4	41.08	61	5-103	2/1	48.22	17	59
Matthews Thomas James	3.4.1884	14.10.1943	8	1911–1912	153	53	0	17.00	16	4-29	0/0	26.18	7	–
Maxwell Glenn James	14.10.1988		7	2012–2017	339	104	1	26.07	8	4-127	0/0	42.62	5	87/57
May Timothy Brian Alexander	26.1.1962		24	1987–1994	225	42*	0	14.06	75	5-9	3/0	34.74	6	47
Mayne Edgar Richard	27.7.1882	26.10.1961	4	1912–1921	64	25*	0	21.33	0	0-1	0/0	–	2	–
Mayne Lawrence Charles	23.1.1942		6	1964–1969	76	13	0	9.50	19	4-43	0/0	33.05	3	–
Meckiff Ian	6.1.1935		18	1957–1963	154	45*	0	11.84	45	6-38	2/0	31.62	9	–
Mennie Joe Matthew	24.12.1988		1	2016	10	10	0	5.00	1	1-85	0/0	85.00	0	2
Meuleman Kenneth Douglas	5.9.1923	10.9.2004	1	1945	0	0	0	0.00	–	–	–/–	–	0	–
Midwinter William Evans	19.6.1851	3.12.1890	8†	1876–1886	174	37	0	13.38	14	5-78	1/0	23.78	5	–
Miller Colin Reid	6.2.1964		18	1998–2000	174	43	0	8.28	69	5-32	3/1	26.15	6	–
Miller Keith Ross MBE (CY 1954)	28.11.1919	11.10.2004	55	1945–1956	2,958	147	7	36.97	170	7-60	7/1	22.97	38	–
Minnett Roy Baldwin	13.6.1888	21.10.1955	9	1911–1912	391	90	0	26.06	11	4-34	0/0	26.36	6	–
Misson Francis Michael	19.11.1938		5	1960–1961	38	25*	0	19.00	16	4-58	0/0	38.50	6	–
Moody Thomas Masson (CT 2000)	2.10.1965		8	1989–1992	456	106	2	32.57	2	1-17	0/0	73.50	9	76
Moroney John	24.7.1917	1.7.1999	7	1949–1951	383	118	2	34.81	–	–	–/–	–	0	–
Morris Arthur Robert MBE (CY 1949)	19.1.1922	22.8.2015	46	1946–1954	3,533	206	12	46.48	2	1-5	0/0	25.00	15	–
Morris Samuel	22.6.1855	20.9.1931	1	1884	14	10*	0	14.00	2	2-73	0/0	36.50	1	–
Moses Henry	13.2.1858	7.12.1938	6	1886–1894	198	33	0	19.80	–	–	–/–	–	1	–
Moss Jeffrey Kenneth	29.6.1947		1	1978	60	38*	0	60.00	0	–	–/–	–	0	1
Moule William Henry	31.1.1858	24.8.1939	1	1880	40	34	0	20.00	3	3-23	0/0	7.66	2	–
Muller Scott Andrew	11.7.1971		2	1999	6	6*	0	–	7	3-68	0/0	36.85	2	–
Murdoch William Lloyd	18.10.1854	18.2.1911	18†	1876–1890	896	211	2	32.00	–	–	–/–	–	14	–

	Born	Died	Tests	Test Career	Runs	HS	100s	Avge	Wkts	BB	5/10	Avge	Ct/St	O/T
Musgrove Henry Alfred.	27.11.1858	2.11.1931	1	1884	13	9	0	6.50	–	–	–/–	–	0	
Nagel Lisle Ernest.	6.3.1905	23.11.1971	1	1932	21	21*	0	21.00	2	2-110	0/0	55.00	0	
Nash Laurence John.	2.5.1910	24.7.1986	2	1931–1936	30	17	0	15.00	10	4-18	0/0	12.60	6	0/9
Nevill Peter Michael.	13.10.1985		17	2015–2016	468	66	0	22.28	–	–	–/–	–	61/2	
Nicholson Matthew James.	2.10.1974		1	1998	14	9	0	7.00	4	3-56	0/0	28.75	0	
Nitschke Homesdale Carl ("Jack").	14.4.1905	29.9.1982	2	1931	53	47	0	26.50	–	–	–/–	–	3	
Noble Montague Alfred (CY 1900).	28.1.1873	22.6.1940	42	1897–1909	1,997	133	1	30.25	121	7-17	9/2	25.00	26	
Noblet Geffery.	14.9.1916	16.8.2006	3	1949–1952	22	13*	0	7.33	7	3-21	0/0	26.14	1	
North Marcus James.	28.7.1979		21	2008–2010	1,171	128	5	35.48	14	6-55	1/0	42.21	17	2/1
Nothling Otto Ernest.	1.8.1900	26.9.1965	1	1928	52	44	0	26.00	0	0-12	0/0	–	0	
O'Brien Leo Patrick Joseph.	2.7.1907	13.3.1997	5	1932–1936	211	61	0	26.37	–	–	–/–	–	3	
O'Connor John Denis Alphonsus.	9.9.1875	23.8.1941	4	1907–1909	86	20	0	12.28	13	5-40	1/0	26.15	3	
O'Donnell Simon Patrick.	26.1.1963		6	1985–1985	206	48	0	29.42	6	3-37	0/0	84.00	4	87
Ogilvie Alan David.	3.6.1951		5	1977	178	47	0	17.80	–	–	–/–	–	5	
O'Keeffe Stephen Norman John.	9.12.1984		9	2014–2017	86	25	0	9.55	35	6-35	2/1	29.40	4	0/7
O'Keeffe Kerry James.	25.11.1949		24	1970–1977	644	85	0	25.76	53	5-101	1/0	38.07	15	2
Oldfield William Albert Stanley MBE (CY 1927).	9.9.1894	10.8.1976	54	1920–1936	1,427	65*	0	22.65	–	–	–/–	–	78/52	
O'Neill Norman Clifford Louis (CY 1962).	19.2.1937	3.3.2008	42	1958–1964	2,779	181	6	45.55	17	4-41	0/0	39.23	21	
O'Reilly William Joseph OBE (CY 1935).	20.12.1905	6.10.1992	27	1931–1945	410	56*	0	12.81	144	7-54	11/3	22.59	7	
Oxenham Ronald Keven.	28.7.1891	16.8.1939	7	1928–1931	151	48	0	15.10	14	4-39	0/0	37.28	4	
Paine Timothy David.	8.12.1984		19	2010–2018	939	92	0	34.77	–	–	–/–	–	77/4	35/10‡
Palmer George Eugene.	22.2.1859	22.8.1910	17	1880–1886	296	48	0	14.09	78	7-65	6/2	21.51	13	
Park Roy Lindsay.	30.7.1892	23.1.1947	1	1920	0	0	0	0.00	0	0-9	0/0	–	0	
Pascoe Leonard Stephen.	13.2.1950		14	1977–1981	106	30*	0	10.60	64	5-59	1/0	26.06	2	29
§Pattinson James Lee.	3.5.1990		17	2011–2015	332	42	0	27.66	70	5-27	4/0	26.15	4	15/4
Pellew Clarence Everard ("Nip").	21.9.1893	9.5.1981	10	1920–1921	484	116	2	37.23	0	0-3	0/0	–	4	
Phillips Wayne Bentley.	1.3.1958		27	1983–1985	1,485	159	2	32.28	–	–	–/–	–	52	48
Phillips Wayne Norman.	7.11.1962		1	1991	22	14	0	11.00	–	–	–/–	–	0	
Philpott Peter Ian.	21.11.1934		8	1964–1965	93	22	0	10.33	26	5-90	1/0	38.46	5	
Ponsford William Harold MBE (CY 1935).	19.10.1900	6.4.1991	29	1924–1934	2,122	266	7	48.22	–	–	–/–	–	21	
Ponting Ricky Thomas (CY 2006).	19.12.1974		1688	1995–2012	13,378	257	41	51.85	5	1-0	0/0	55.20	196	374‡/17
Pope Roland James.	18.2.1864	27.7.1952	1	1884	3	3	0	1.50	–	–	–/–	–	0	
Quiney Robert John.	20.8.1982		2	2012	9	9	0	3.00	0	0-3	0/0	–	0	5
Rackemann Carl Gray.	3.6.1960		12	1982–1990	53	15*	0	5.30	39	6-86	3/1	29.15	2	52
Ransford Vernon Seymour (CY 1910).	20.3.1885	19.3.1958	20	1907–1911	1,211	143*	1	37.84	1	1-9	0/0	28.00	10	

§ *Ponting's figures include 100 runs and one catch for Australia v the ICC World XI in the Super Series Test in 2005–06.*

	Born	Died	Tests	Test Career	Runs	HS	100s	Avge	Wkts	BB	5/10	Avge	Ct/St	O/T
Redpath Ian Ritchie MBE.	11.5.1941		66	1963–1975	4,737	171	8	43.45	0	0-0	0/0	–	83	5
Reedman John Cole	9.10.1865	25.3.1924	1	1894	21	17	0	10.50	1	1-12	0/0	24.00	1	
Reid Bruce Anthony	14.3.1963		27	1985–1992	93	13	0	4.65	113	7-51	5/2	24.63	5	61
Reiffel Paul Ronald.	19.4.1966		35	1991–1997	955	79*	0	26.52	104	6-71	5/0	26.96	15	92
Renneberg David Alexander	23.9.1942		8	1966–1967	22	9	0	3.66	23	5-39	2/0	36.08	2	
Renshaw Matthew Thomas	28.3.1996		11	2016–2017	636	184	1	33.47	0	0-4	0/0	–	8	
Richardson Arthur John	24.7.1888	23.12.1973	9	1924–1926	403	100	1	31.00	12	2-20	0/0	43.41	1	
[4]Richardson Victor York OBE	7.9.1894	30.10.1969	19	1924–1935	706	138	1	23.53			–/–	–	24	
Rigg Keith Edward	21.5.1906	28.2.1995	8	1930–1936	401	127	1	33.41			–/–	–	5	
Ring Douglas Thomas	14.10.1918	23.6.2003	13	1947–1953	426	67	0	22.42	35	6-72	2/0	37.28	5	
Ritchie Gregory Michael	23.1.1960		30	1982–1986	1,690	146	3	35.20	0	0-10	0/0	–	14	44
Rixon Stephen John.	25.2.1954		13	1977–1984	394	54	0	18.76			0/0	–	42/5	6
Robertson Gavin Ron.	28.5.1966		4	1997–1998	140	57	0	20.00	13	4-72	0/0	39.61	1	13
Robertson William Roderick	6.10.1861	24.6.1938	1	1884	2	2	0	1.00	0	0-24	0/0	–	–	
Robinson Richard Daryl	8.6.1946		3	1977	100	34	0	16.66			–/–	–	4	
Robinson Rayford Harold	26.3.1914	10.8.1965	1	1936	5	3	0	2.50			–/–	–	1	2
Rogers Christopher John Llewellyn (CY 2014)	31.8.1977		25	2007–2015	2,015	173	5	42.87			–/–	–	15	
Rorke Gordon Frederick	27.6.1938		4	1958–1959	9	7	0	4.50	10	3-23	0/0	20.30	1	
Rutherford John Walter	25.9.1929		1	1956	30	30	0	30.00	1	1-11	0/0	15.00	–	
Ryder John	8.8.1889	3.4.1977	20	1920–1928	1,394	201*	3	51.62	17	2-20	0/0	43.70	17	
Saggers Ronald Arthur	15.5.1917	17.3.1987	6	1948–1949	30	14	0	10.00			–/–	–	16/8	
Saunders John Victor	21.3.1876	21.12.1927	14	1901–1907	39	11*	0	2.29	79	7-34	6/0	22.73	5	
Sayers Chadd James	31.8.1987		1	2017	2	2	0	0.00	2	2-78	0/0	73.00	–	
Scott Henry James Herbert	26.12.1858	23.9.1910	8	1884–1886	359	102	1	27.61	0	0-9	0/0	–	8	
Sellers Reginald Hugh Durning	20.8.1940		1	1964	0	0	0	0.00	0	0-17	0/0	–	–	
Serjeant Craig Stanton	1.11.1951		12	1977–1977	522	124	1	23.72			–/–	–	13	3
[5]Sheahan Andrew Paul	30.9.1946		31	1967–1973	1,594	127	2	33.91			–/–	–	17	3
Shepherd Barry Kenneth	23.4.1937	17.9.2001	9	1962–1964	502	96	0	41.83	0	0-3	0/0	–	2	
Siddle Peter Matthew	25.11.1984		64	2008–2018	1,080	51	0	14.21	214	6-54	8/0	30.28	17	17/2
Sievers Morris William	13.4.1912	10.5.1968	3	1936	67	25*	0	13.40	9	5-21	1/0	17.88	4	
Simpson Robert Baddeley (CY 1965).	3.2.1936		62	1957–1977	4,869	311	10	46.81	71	5-57	2/0	42.26	110	2
Sincock David John.	1.2.1942		3	1964–1965	80	29	0	26.66	8	3-67	0/0	51.25	2	
Slater Keith Nichol.	12.3.1936		1	1958	1	1*	0	–	2	2-40	0/0	50.50	1	
Slater Michael Jonathon	21.2.1970		74	1993–2001	5,312	219	14	42.83	1	1-4	0/0	10.00	33	42
Sleep Peter Raymond.	4.5.1957		14	1978–1989	483	90	0	24.15	31	5-72	1/0	45.06	4	
Slight James.	20.10.1855	9.12.1930	1	1880	11	11	0	5.50			–/–	–	0	

Name	Born	Died	Tests	Test Career	Runs	HS	100s	Avge	Wkts	BB	5/10	Avge	Ct/St	O/T
Smith David Bertram Miller	14.9.1884	29.1.1963	2	1912	30	24*	0	15.00	–	–	–/–	–	1	–
Smith Steven Barry	18.10.1961		3	1983	41	12	0	8.20	–	–	–/–	–		28
Smith Steven Peter Devereux (CY 2016)	2.6.1989		64	2010–2017	6,199	239	23	61.37	17	3-18	0/0	54.88	96	108/30
Spofforth Frederick Robert	9.9.1853	4.6.1926	18	1876–1886	217	50	0	9.43	94	7-44	7/4	18.41	11	–
Stackpole Keith Raymond MBE (CY 1973)	10.7.1940		43	1965–1973	2,807	207	7	37.42	15	2-33	0/0	66.73	47	6
Starc Mitchell Aaron	13.1.1990		49	2011–2018	1,351	99	0	21.44	199	6-50	9/1	28.91	24	75/23
Stevens Gavin Byron	29.2.1932		4	1959	112	28	0	16.00	–	–	–/–	–	1	–
Symonds Andrew	9.6.1975		26	2003–2008	1,462	162*	2	40.61	24	3-50	0/0	37.33	22	198/14
Taber Hedley Brian	29.4.1940		16	1966–1969	353	48	0	16.04	–	–	–/–	–	56/4	–
Tait Shaun William	22.2.1983		3	2005–2007	20	8	0	6.66	5	3-97	0/0	60.40	1	35/21
Tallon Donald (CY 1949)	17.2.1916	7.9.1984	21	1945–1953	394	92	0	17.13	–	–	–/–	–	50/8	–
Taylor John Morris	10.10.1895	12.5.1971	20	1920–1926	997	108	1	35.60	1	1-25	0/0	45.00	11	–
Taylor Mark Anthony (CY 1990)	27.10.1964		104	1988–1998	7,525	334*	19	43.49	1	1-11	0/0	26.00	157	113
Taylor Peter Laurence	22.8.1956		13	1986–1991	431	87	0	26.93	27	6-78	1/0	39.55	10	83
Thomas Grahame	21.3.1938	29.8.2003	8	1964–1965	325	61	0	29.54	–	–	–/–	–	3	–
Thoms George Ronald	22.3.1927		1	1951	44	28	0	22.00	–	–	–/–	–	0	–
Thomson Alan Lloyd ("Froggy")	2.12.1945		4	1970	22	12*	0	22.00	12	3-79	0/0	54.50	0	1
Thomson Jeffrey Robert	16.8.1950		51	1972–1985	679	49	0	12.81	200	6-46	8/0	28.00	20	50
Thomson Nathaniel Frampton Davis	29.5.1839	2.9.1896	2	1876	67	41	0	16.75	1	1-14	0/0	31.00	3	–
Thurlow Hugh Motley ("Pud")	10.11.1903	3.12.1975	1	1931	0	0	0	0.00	1	0-33	0/0	–	0	–
Toohey Peter Michael	20.4.1954		15	1977–1979	893	122	1	31.89	0	0-4	0/0	–	9	5
Toshack Ernest Raymond Herbert	8.12.1914	11.5.2003	12	1945–1948	73	20*	0	14.60	47	6-29	4/1	21.04	4	–
Travers Joseph Patrick Francis	10.1.1871	15.9.1942	1	1901	10	9	0	5.00	1	1-14	0/0	14.00	1	–
Tribe George Edward (CY 1955)	4.10.1920	5.4.2009	3	1946	35	25*	0	17.50	2	2-48	0/0	165.00	0	–
[2]**Trott** Albert Edwin (CY 1899)	6.2.1873	30.7.1914	3†	1894	205	85*	0	102.50	9	8-43	1/0	21.33	4	–
[2]**Trott** George Henry Stevens (CY 1894)	5.8.1866	10.11.1917	24	1888–1897	921	143	1	21.92	29	4-71	0/0	35.13	21	–
[2]**Trumble** Hugh (CY 1897)	12.5.1867	14.8.1938	32	1890–1903	851	70	0	19.79	141	8-65	9/3	21.78	45	–
[2]**Trumble** John William	16.9.1863	17.8.1944	7	1884–1886	243	59	0	20.25	10	3-29	0/0	22.20	3	–
Trumper Victor Thomas (CY 1903)	2.11.1877	28.6.1915	48	1899–1911	3,163	214*	8	39.04	8	3-60	0/0	39.62	31	–
Turner Alan	23.7.1950		14	1975–1976	768	136	1	29.53	–	–	–/–	–	15	6
Turner Charles Thomas Biass (CY 1889)	16.11.1862	1.1.1944	17	1886–1894	323	29	0	11.53	101	7-43	11/2	16.53	8	–
Veivers Thomas Robert	6.4.1937		21	1963–1966	813	88	0	31.26	33	4-68	0/0	41.66	7	–
Veletta Michael Robert John	30.10.1963		8	1987–1989	207	39	0	18.81	–	–	–/–	–	12	20
Voges Adam Charles	4.10.1979		20	2015–2016	1,485	269*	5	61.87	0	0-3	0/0	–	15	31/7
Wade Matthew Scott	26.12.1987		22	2011–2017	886	106	2	28.58	0	0-0	0/0	–	63/11	94/26
Waite Mervyn George	7.1.1911	16.12.1985	2	1938	11	8	0	3.66	1	1-150	0/0	190.00	1	–

	Born	Died	Tests	Test Career	Runs	HS	100s	Avge	Wkts	BB	5/10	Avge	Ct/St	O/T
Walker Maxwell Henry Norman ("Tim")	12.9.1948	28.9.2016	34	1972–1977	586	78*	0	19.53	138	8-143	6/0	27.47	12	17
Wall Thomas Welbourn ("Tim")	13.5.1904	26.3.1981	18	1928–1934	121	20	0	6.36	56	5-14	3/0	35.89	11	
Walters Francis Henry	9.2.1860	1.6.1922	1	1884	12	7	0	6.00					1	
Walters Kevin Douglas MBE	21.12.1945		74	1965–1980	5,357	250	15	48.26	49	5-66	1/0	29.08	43	28
Ward Francis Anthony	23.2.1906	25.3.1974	4	1936–1938	36	18	0	6.00	11	6-102	1/0	52.18	1	
Warne Shane Keith (CY 1994)	13.9.1969		145§	1991–2006	3,154	99	0	17.32	708	8-71	37/10	25.41	125	193‡
Warner David Andrew	27.10.1986		74	2011–2017	6,363	253	21	48.20	4	2-45	0/0	67.25	54	106/70
Watkins John Russell	16.4.1943		1	1972	39	36	0	39.00	6	0-21	0/0	–	1	
Watson Graeme Donald	8.3.1945		5	1966–1972	97	50	0	10.77	6	2-67	0/0	42.33	1	2
Watson Shane Robert	17.6.1981		59§	2004–2015	3,731	176	4	35.19	75	6-33	3/0	33.68	45	190/58
Watson William James	31.1.1931		4	1954	106	30	0	17.66	0	0-5	0/0	–	1	
Waugh Mark Edward (CY 1991)	2.6.1965		128	1990–2002	8,029	153*	20	41.81	59	5-40	0/0	41.16	181	244
Waugh Stephen Rodger (CY 1989)	2.6.1965		168	1985–2003	10,927	200	32	51.06	92	5-28	3/0	37.44	112	325
Wellham Dirk Macdonald	13.3.1959		6	1981–1986	257	103	1	23.36	0	0-2	0/0	–	5	17
Wessels Kepler Christoffel (CY 1995)	14.9.1957		24†	1982–1985	1,761	179	4	42.95	0	0-11	0/0	–	18	54‡
Whatmore Davenell Frederick	16.3.1954		7	1978–1979	293	77	0	22.53	0	0-11	0/0	–	13	1
White Cameron Leon	18.8.1983		4	2008	146	46	0	29.20	5	2-71	0/0	68.40	1	91/47
Whitney Michael Roy	24.2.1959		12	1981–1992	68	13	0	6.18	39	7-27	2/1	33.97	2	38
Whitty William James	15.8.1886	30.1.1974	14	1909–1912	161	39*	0	13.41	65	6-17	3/0	21.12	4	
Wiener Julien Mark	1.5.1955		6	1979	281	93	0	25.54	0	0-19	0/0	–	4	7
Williams Brad Andrew	20.11.1974		4	2003	23	10*	0	7.66	9	4-53	0/0	45.11	4	25
Wilson John William	20.8.1921	13.10.1985	1	1956	–	–	–	–	1	1-25	0/0	64.00	0	
Wilson Paul	12.1.1972		1	1997	0	0*	0	–	1	0-50	0/0	–	0	11
Wood Graeme Malcolm	6.11.1956		59	1977–1988	3,374	172	9	31.83	0	–	–/–	–	41	83
Woodcock Ashley James	27.2.1947		1	1973	27	27	0	27.00	–			–	1	1
Woodfull William Maldon OBE (CY 1927)	22.8.1897	11.8.1965	35	1926–1934	2,300	161	7	46.00					7	
Woods Samuel Moses James (CY 1889)	13.4.1867	30.4.1931	3†	1888	32	18	0	5.33	5	2-35	0/0	24.20	1	
Woolley Roger Douglas	16.9.1954		2	1982–1983	21	13	0	10.50				–	13/4	4
Worrall John	20.6.1860	17.11.1937	11	1884–1899	478	76	0	25.15	1	1-97	0/0	127.00	13	
Wright Kevin John	27.12.1953		10	1978–1979	219	55*	0	16.84				–	31/4	5
Yallop Graham Neil	7.10.1952		39	1975–1984	2,756	268	8	41.13	1	1-21	0/0	116.00	23	30
Yardley Bruce	5.9.1947		33	1977–1982	978	74	0	19.56	126	7-98	6/1	31.63	31	7
Young Shaun	13.6.1970		1	1997	4	4*	0	4.00	0	0-5	0/0	–	0	
Zoehrer Timothy Joseph	25.9.1961		10	1985–1986	246	52*	0	20.50				–	18/1	22

§ *Warne's figures include 12 runs and six wickets, and Watson's 34 runs and no wicket, for Australia v the ICC World XI in the Super Series Test in 2005-06.*

Births and Deaths of Test Cricketers – South Africa   1393

SOUTH AFRICA (335 players)

	Born	Died	Tests	Test Career	Runs	HS	100s	Avge	Wkts	BB	5/10	Avge	Cl/St	O/T
Abbott Kyle John	18.6.1987		11	2012–2016	95	17	0	6.78	39	7-29	3/0	22.71	4	28/21
Ackerman Hylton Deon	14.2.1973		4	1997	161	57	0	20.12	–	–	–/–	–	1	
Adams Paul Regan	20.1.1977		45	1995–2003	360	35	0	9.00	134	7-128	4/1	32.87	29	24
Adcock Neil Amwin Treharne (CY 1961)	8.3.1931	6.1.2013	26	1953–1961	146	24	0	5.40	104	6-43	5/0	21.10	4	–
Amla Hashim Mahomed (CY 2013)	31.3.1983		122	2004–2018	9,231	311*	28	47.33	0	0-4	0/0	–	108	169/41‡
Anderson James Henry	26.4.1874	11.3.1926	1	1902	43	32	0	21.50	–	–	–/–	–	–	
Ashley William Hare	10.2.1862	14.7.1930	1	1888	1	1	0	0.50	7	7-95	1/0	13.57	0	
Bacher Adam Marc	29.10.1973		19	1996–1999	833	96	0	26.03	0	0-4	0/0	–	11	
Bacher Aron ("Ali")	24.5.1942		12	1965–1969	679	73	0	32.33	–	–	–/–	–	10	13
Balaskas Xenophon Constantine	15.10.1910	12.5.1994	9	1930–1938	174	122*	1	14.50	22	5-49	1/0	36.63	5	
Barlow Edgar John	12.8.1940	30.12.2005	30	1961–1969	2,516	201	6	45.74	40	5-85	1/0	34.05	35	
Baumgartner Harold Vane	17.11.1883	8.4.1938	1	1913	19	16	0	9.50	2	2-99	0/0	49.50	0	
Bavuma Temba	17.5.1990		34	2014–2018	1,660	102*	0	34.58	1	1-29	0/0	61.00	16	2
Beaumont Rolland	4.2.1884	25.5.1958	5	1912–1913	70	31	0	7.77	0	0-0	0/0	–	2	
Begbie Denis Warburton	12.12.1914	10.3.2009	5	1948–1949	138	48	0	19.71	1	1-38	0/0	130.00	2	
Bell Alexander John	15.4.1906	1.8.1985	16	1929–1935	69	26*	0	6.27	48	6-99	4/0	32.64	6	
Bisset Sir Murray	14.4.1876	24.10.1931	3	1898–1909	103	35	0	25.75	–	–	–/–	–	2/1	
Bisset George Finlay	5.11.1905	14.11.1965	4	1927	38	23	0	19.00	25	7-29	2/0	18.76	3	
Blanckenberg James Manuel	31.12.1892	d unknown	18	1913–1924	455	59*	0	19.78	60	6-76	4/0	30.28	9	
Bland Kenneth Colin (CY 1966)	5.4.1938	14.4.2018	21	1961–1966	1,669	144*	3	49.08	2	2-16	0/0	62.50	10	
Bock Ernest George	17.9.1908	5.9.1961	1	1935	11	9*	0	–	0	0-42	0/0	–	0	
Boje Nico	20.3.1973		43	1999–2006	1,312	85	0	25.23	100	5-62	3/0	42.65	18	113‡/1
Bond Gerald Edward	5.4.1909	27.8.1965	1	1938	0	0	0	0.00	1	0-16	0/0	–	0	
Rosch Tertius	14.3.1966	14.2.2000	1	1991	5	5*	0	–	3	2-61	0/0	34.66	0	2
Botha Johan	2.5.1982		5	2005–2010	83	25	0	20.75	17	4-56	0/0	33.70	3	76‡/40
Botten James Thomas ("Jackie")	21.6.1938	14.5.2006	3	1965	65	33	0	10.83	8	2-56	0/0	42.12	1	
Boucher Mark Verdon (CY 2009)	3.12.1976		146§	1997–2011	5,498	125	5	30.54	1	1-6	0/0	6.00	530/23	290‡/25
Brann William Henry	4.4.1899	22.9.1953	3	1922	71	50	0	14.20	–	–	–/–	–	2	
Briscoe Arthur Wellesley ("Dooley")	6.2.1911	22.4.1941	2	1935–1938	33	16	0	11.00	0	–	–/–	–	0	
Bromfield Harry Dudley	26.6.1932		9	1961–1965	59	21	0	11.80	17	5-88	1/0	35.23	13	
Brown Lennox Sidney	24.11.1910	1.9.1983	2	1931	17	8	0	5.66	3	1-30	0/0	63.00	0	
Burger Christopher George de Villiers	12.7.1935	5.6.2014	2	1957	62	37*	0	20.66	–	–	–/–	–	1	

§ Boucher's figures exclude 17 runs and two catches for the ICC World XI v Australia in the Super Series Test in 2005-06.

	Born	Died	Tests	Test Career	Runs	HS	100s	Avge	Wkts	BB	5/10	Avge	Ct/St	O/T
Burke Sydney Frank	11.3.1934	3.4.2017	2	1961–1964	42	20	0	14.00	11	6-128	2/1	23.36	0	
Buys Isaac Daniel	4.2.1895	d unknown	1	1922	4	4*	0	4.00	0	0-20	0/0	–	0	
Cameron Horace Brakenridge ("Jock") (CY 1936)	5.7.1905	2.11.1935	26	1927–1935	1,239	90	0	30.21	–	–	–/–	–	39/12	
Campbell Thomas	9.2.1882	5.10.1924	5	1909–1912	90	48	0	15.00	–	–	–/–	–	7/1	
Carlstein Peter Rudolph	28.10.1938		8	1957–1963	190	42	0	14.61	–	–	–/–	–	3	
Carter Claude Paglett	23.4.1881	8.11.1952	10	1912–1924	181	45	0	18.10	28	6-50	2/0	24.78	2	
Catterall Robert Hector (CY 1925)	10.7.1900	3.1.1961	24	1922–1930	1,555	120	3	37.92	7	3-15	0/0	23.14	12	
Chapman Horace William	30.6.1890	1.12.1941	2	1913–1921	39	17	0	13.00	1	1-51	0/0	104.00		
Cheetham John Erskine	26.5.1920	21.8.1980	24	1948–1955	883	89	0	23.86	0	0-2	0/0	–	13	
Chevalier Grahame Anton	9.3.1937	14.11.2017	1	1969	0	0*	0	0.00	5	3-68	0/0	20.00	1	
Christy James Alexander Joseph	12.12.1904	1.2.1971	10	1929–1931	618	103	1	34.33	5	1-15	0/0	46.00	3	
Chubb Geoffrey Walter Ashton	12.4.1911	28.8.1982	5	1951	63	15*	0	10.50	21	6-51	2/0	27.47	1	
Cochran John Alexander Kennedy	15.7.1909	15.6.1987	1	1930	4	4	0	4.00	0	0-47	0/0	–		
Coen Stanley Keppel ("Shunter")	14.10.1902	29.1.1967	2	1927	101	41*	0	50.50	0	0-7	0/0	–	1	
Commaille John McIllwaine Moore ("Mick")	21.2.1883	28.7.1956	12	1909–1927	355	47	0	16.90	–	–	–/–	–		
Commins John Brian	19.2.1965		3	1994	125	45	0	25.00	–	–	–/–	–	2	
Conyngham Dalton Parry	10.5.1897	7.7.1979	1	1922	7	6*	0	3.50	2	1-40	0/0	51.50	1	
Cook Frederick James	1870	30.11.1915	1	1895	7	7	0	3.50	–	–	–/–	–		
Cook Stephen Craig	29.11.1982		11	2015–2016	632	117	3	33.26	0	0-16	0/0	–	6	
Cook Stephen James (CY 1990)	31.7.1953		3	1992–1993	107	43	0	17.83	–	–	–/–	–	0	4
Cooper Alfred Henry Cecil	2.9.1893	18.7.1963	1	1913	6	6	0	3.00	–	–	–/–	–		
Cox Joseph Lovell	28.6.1886	4.7.1971	3	1913	17	12*	0	3.40	4	2-74	0/0	61.25	1	
Cripps Godfrey	19.10.1865	27.7.1943	1	1891	21	18	0	10.50	0	–	0/0	–		
Crisp Robert James	28.5.1911	2.3.1994	9	1935–1936	123	35	0	10.25	20	5-99	1/0	37.35	3	
Cronje Wessel Johannes ("Hansie")	25.9.1969	1.6.2002	68	1991–1999	3,714	135	6	36.41	43	3-14	0/0	29.95	33	188
Cullinan Daryll John	4.3.1967		70	1992–2000	4,554	275*	14	44.21	2	1-10	0/0	35.50	67	138
Curnow Sydney Harry	16.12.1907	28.7.1986	7	1930–1931	168	47	0	12.00	–	–	–/–	–	5	
Dalton Eric Londesbrough	2.12.1906	3.6.1981	15	1929–1938	698	117	2	31.72	12	4-59	0/0	40.83	5	
Davies Eric Quail	26.8.1909	11.11.1976	5	1935–1938	9	3	0	1.80	10	4-75	0/0	68.71		
Dawson Alan Charles	27.11.1969		5	2003	10	10	0	10.00	5	2-20	0/0	23.40	1	19
Dawson Oswald Charles	1.9.1919	22.12.2008	9	1947–1948	293	55	0	20.92	5	2-57	0/0	57.80	10	
Deane Hubert Gouvaine ("Nummy")	21.7.1895	21.10.1939	17	1924–1930	628	93	0	25.12	0	0-6	0/0	–	8	
de Bruyn Theunis Booysen	8.10.1992		9	2016–2018	346	101	1	20.35	–	–	–/–	–	10	
de Bruyn Zander	5.7.1975		3	2004	155	83	0	38.75	3	2-32	0/0	30.66	0	0/2
de Kock Quinton	17.12.1992		38	2013–2018	2,176	129*	4	38.17	–	–	–/–	–	158/9	98/35

Name	Born	Died	Tests	Test Career	Runs	HS	100s	Avge	Wkts	BB	5/10	Avge	Ct/St	O/T
de Lange Marchant	13.10.1990		2	2011	9	9	0	4.50	9	7-81	1/0	30.77	1	4/6
de Villiers Abraham Benjamin	17.2.1984		114	2004–2017	8,765	278*	22	50.66	–	–	–/–	52.00	222/5	223†/78
de Villiers Petrus Stephanus ("Fanie")	13.10.1964		18	1993–1997	359	67*	0	18.89	85	6-23	5/2	24.27	11	83
de Wet Friedel	26.6.1980		4	2009	20	20	0	10.00	6	4-55	0/0	31.00	1	
Dippenaar Hendrik Human ("Boeta")	14.6.1977		38	1999–2006	1,718	177*	3	30.14	0	0-1	0/0	–	27	101‡/1
Dixon Cecil Donovan	12.2.1891	9.9.1969	1	1913	0	0	0	0.00	3	2-62	0/0	39.33	1	
Donald Allan Anthony (CY 1992)	20.10.1966		72	1991–2001	652	37	0	10.68	330	8-71	20/3	22.25	18	164
Dower Robert Reid	4.6.1876	15.9.1964	1	1898	9	9	0	4.50			–/–		0	
Draper Ronald George	24.12.1926		2	1949	25	15	0	8.33					2	
Duckworth Christopher Anthony Russell	22.3.1933	16.5.2014	2	1956	28	13	0	7.00					0	
Dumbrill Richard	19.11.1938		5	1965–1966	153	36	0	15.30	9	4-30	0/0	37.33	3	
Duminy Jacobus Petrus	16.12.1897	31.1.1980	3	1927–1929	30	12	0	5.00	1	1-17	0/0	39.00	3	
Duminy Jean-Paul	14.4.1984		46	2008–2017	2,103	166	6	32.85	42	4-47	0/0	38.11	38	192†/8
Dunell Owen Robert	15.7.1856	21.10.1929	1	1888	42	26*	0	14.00			–/–		–	
du Plessis Francois	13.7.1984		56	2012–2018	3,408	137	9	42.07	0	0-1	0/0	–	49	124†/39‡
du Preez John Harcourt	14.11.1942		2	1966	0	0	0	0.00	3	2-22	0/0	17.00	2	
du Toit Jacobus Francois	2.4.1869	10.7.1909	1	1891	2	2*	0	–	1	1-47	0/0	47.00	0	
Dyer Dennis Victor	2.5.1914	16.6.1990	3	1947	96	62	0	16.00			–/–		–	
Eksteen Clive Edward	2.12.1966		7	1993–1999	91	22	0	10.11	8	3-12	0/0	61.75	5	6
Elgar Dean	11.6.1987		54	2012–2018	3,369	199	11	40.10	14	4-22	0/0	44.14	58	8
Elgie Michael Kelsey ("Kim")	6.3.1933		3	1961	75	56	0	12.50	0	0-18	0/0	–	4	
Elworthy Steven BEM	23.2.1965		4	1998–2002	72	48	0	18.00	13	4-66	0/0	34.15	2	39
Endean William Russell	31.5.1924	28.6.2003	28	1951–1957	1,630	162*	3	33.95	–	–	–/–	–	41	
Farrer William Stephen ("Buster")	8.12.1936		6	1961–1963	221	40	0	27.62					0	
Faulkner George Aubrey	17.12.1881	10.9.1930	25	1905–1924	1,754	204	4	40.79	82	7-84	4/0	26.58	20	
Fellows-Smith Jonathan Payn	3.2.1932	28.9.2013	4	1960	166	35	0	27.66	0	0-13	0/0	–	2	
Fichardt Charles Gustav	20.3.1870	30.5.1923	2	1891–1895	15	10	0	3.75					2	
Finlason Charles Edward	19.2.1860	31.7.1917	1	1888	6	6	0	3.00	0	0-7	0/0	–	0	
Floquet Claude Eugene	3.11.1884	22.11.1963	1	1909	12	11*	0	12.00	0	0-24	0/0	–	0	
Francis Howard Henry	26.5.1868	7.1.1936	2	1898	39	29	0	9.75					2	
Francois Cyril Matthew	20.6.1897	26.5.1944	5	1922	252	72	0	31.50	6	3-23	0/0	37.50	5	
Frank Charles Newton	27.1.1891	25.12.1961	3	1921	236	152	1	39.33					2	
Frank William Hughes Bowker	23.11.1872	16.2.1945	1	1895	7	5	0	3.50	1	1-52	0/0	52.00	0	
Fuller Edward Russell Henry	2.8.1931	19.7.2008	7	1952–1957	64	17	0	8.00	22	5-66	1/0	30.36	3	
Fullerton George Murray	8.12.1922	19.11.2002	7	1947–1951	325	88	0	25.00			–/–		10/2	
Funston Kenneth James	3.12.1925	15.4.2005	18	1952–1957	824	92	0	25.75			–/–		7	

	Born	Died	Tests	Test Career	Runs	HS	100s	Avge	Wkts	BB	5/10	Avge	Ct/St	O/T
Gamsy Dennis	17.2.1940	–	2	1969	39	30*	0	19.50	0	–	–/–	–	5	–
Gibbs Herschelle Herman	23.2.1974	–	90	1996–2007	6,167	228	14	41.95	0	0-4	–/–	–	94	248/23
Gleeson Robert Anthony	6.12.1873	27.9.1919	1	1895	4	3	0	4.00	–	–	–/–	–	2	–
Glover George Keyworth	13.5.1870	15.11.1938	1	1895	21	18*	0	21.00	1	1-28	0/0	28.00	0	–
Goddard Trevor Leslie	1.8.1931	25.11.2016	41	1955–1969	2,516	112	1	34.46	123	6-53	5/0	26.22	48	–
Gordon Norman	6.8.1911	2.9.2014	5	1938	8	7*	0	2.00	20	5-103	2/0	40.35	1	–
Graham Robert	16.9.1877	21.4.1946	2	1898	6	4	0	1.50	3	2-22	0/0	42.33	2	–
Grieveson Ronald Eustace	24.8.1909	24.7.1998	2	1938	114	75	0	57.00	0	–	–/–	–	7/3	–
Griffin Geoffrey Merton	12.6.1939	16.11.2006	2	1960	25	14	0	6.25	8	4-87	0/0	24.00	0	–
Hall Alfred Ewart	23.1.1896	1.1.1964	7	1922–1930	11	5	0	1.83	40	7-63	3/1	22.15	4	–
Hall Andrew James	31.7.1975	–	21	2001–2006	760	163	1	26.20	45	3-1	0/0	35.93	16	88/2
Hall Glen Gordon	24.5.1938	26.6.1987	1	1964	0	0	0	0.00	1	1-94	0/0	94.00	0	–
Halliwell Ernest Austin (CY 1905)	7.9.1864	2.10.1919	8	1891–1902	188	57	0	12.53	–	–	–/–	–	102	–
Halse Clive Gray	28.2.1935	28.5.2002	3	1963	30	19*	0	–	6	3-50	0/0	43.33	1	–
Hamza Mogammad Zubayr	19.6.1995	–	1	2018	41	41	0	20.50	0	–	–/–	–	2	–
[2] Hands Philip Albert Myburgh	18.3.1890	27.4.1951	7	1913–1924	300	83	0	25.00	0	0-1	0/0	–	3	–
Hands Reginald Harry Myburgh	26.7.1888	20.4.1918	1	1913	7	7	0	3.50	–	–	–/–	–	0	–
Hanley Martin Andrew	10.11.1918	2.6.2000	1	1948	0	0	0	0.00	1	1-57	0/0	88.00	0	–
Harmer Simon Ross	10.2.1989	–	5	2014–2015	58	13	0	11.60	20	4-61	0/0	29.40	5	–
Harris Paul Lee	2.11.1978	–	37	2006–2010	460	46	0	10.69	103	6-127	3/0	37.87	16	3
Harris Terence Anthony	27.8.1916	7.3.1993	3	1947–1948	100	60	0	25.00	0	–	–/–	–	1	–
Hartigan Gerald Patrick Desmond	30.12.1884	7.1.1955	5	1912–1913	114	51	0	11.40	1	1-72	0/0	141.00	0	–
Harvey Robert Lyon	14.9.1911	20.7.2000	2	1935	51	28	0	12.75	–	–	–/–	–	0	–
Hathorn Christopher Maitland Howard	7.4.1878	17.5.1920	12	1902–1910	325	102	1	17.10	–	–	–/–	–	5	–
Hayward Frank ("Nantie")	20.3.1977	–	16	1999–2004	66	14	0	7.33	54	5-56	1/0	29.79	4	21
[1] Hearne Frank	23.11.1858	14.7.1949	4†	1891–1895	121	30	0	15.12	2	2-40	0/0	20.00	2	–
[1] Hearne George Alfred Lawrence	27.3.1888	13.11.1978	3	1922–1924	59	28	0	11.80	–	–	–/–	–	3	–
Heine Peter Samuel	28.6.1928	4.2.2005	14	1955–1961	209	31	0	9.95	58	6-58	4/0	25.08	8	–
Henderson Claude William	14.6.1972	–	7	2001–2002	65	30	0	9.28	22	4-116	0/0	42.18	8	–
Henry Omar	23.1.1952	–	3	1992	53	34	0	17.66	3	1-20	0/0	63.00	2	–
Hime Charles Frederick William	24.10.1869	6.12.1940	1	1895	8	8	0	4.00	–	–	–/–	–	0	–
Hudson Andrew Charles	17.3.1965	–	35	1991–1997	2,007	163	4	33.45	–	–	–/–	–	36	89
Hutchinson Philip	25.1.1862	30.9.1925	2	1888	14	11	0	3.50	–	–	–/–	–	3	–
Imran Tahir	27.3.1979	–	20	2011–2015	130	29*	0	9.28	57	5-32	2/0	40.24	8	91/34‡
Ironside David Ernest James	2.5.1925	21.8.2005	3	1953	37	13	0	18.50	15	5-51	1/0	18.33	1	–
Irvine Brian Lee	9.3.1944	–	4	1969	353	102	1	50.42	–	–	–/–	–	2	–

	Born	Died	Tests	Test Career	Runs	HS	100s	Avge	Wkts	BB	5/10	Avge	Ct/St	O/T
Jack Steven Douglas	4.8.1970		2	1994	7	7	0	3.50	8	4-69	0/0	24.50	1	2
Johnson Clement Lecky	31.3.1871	31.5.1908	1	1895	10	7	0	5.00	0	0-57	0/0	—	1	—
Kallis Jacques Henry (CY 2013)	16.10.1975		165§	1995-2013	13,206	224	45	55.25	291	6-54	5/0	32.63	196	323‡/25
Keith Headley James	25.10.1927	17.11.1997	8	1952-1956	318	73	0	21.20	0	0-19	0/0	—	3	—
Kemp Justin Miles	2.10.1977		4	2000-2005	80	55	0	13.33	9	3-33	0/0	24.66	3	79‡/8
Kempis Gustav Adolph	4.8.1865	19.5.1890	1	1888	0	0*	0	0.00	4	3-53	0/0	19.00	0	—
Khan Imran	27.4.1984		1	2008	20	20	0	20.00	—	—	—/—	—	—	—
²Kirsten Gary (CY 2004)	23.11.1967		101	1993-2003	7,289	275	21	45.27	2	1-0	0/0	71.00	83	185
²Kirsten Peter Noel	14.5.1955		12	1991-1994	626	104	1	31.30	0	0-5	0/0	—	8	40
Kleinveldt Rory Keith	15.3.1983		4	2012	27	17*	0	9.00	10	3-65	0/0	42.20	2	10/6
Klusener Lance (CY 2000)	4.9.1971		49	1996-2004	1,906	174	4	32.86	80	8-64	1/0	37.91	34	171
Kotze Johannes Jacobus ("Kodgee")	7.8.1879	7.7.1931	3	1902-1907	2	2	0	0.40	6	3-64	0/0	40.50	3	—
Kuhn Heino Gunther	1.4.1984		4	2017	113	34	0	14.12	—	—	—/—	—	2	0/7
Kuiper Adrian Paul	24.8.1959		1	1991	34	34	0	17.00	2	2-31	0/0	15.50	0	25
Kuys Frederick	21.3.1870	12.9.1953	1	1898	26	26	0	13.00	0	0-31	0/0	—	0	—
Lance Herbert Roy ("Tiger")	6.6.1940	10.11.2010	13	1961-1969	591	70	0	28.14	12	3-30	0/0	39.91	7	—
Langeveldt Charl Kenneth	17.12.1974		6	2004-2005	16	10	0	8.00	16	5-46	1/0	37.06	8	72/9
Langton Arthur Chudleigh Beaumont ("Chud")	2.3.1912	27.11.1942	15	1935-1938	298	73*	0	15.68	40	5-58	1/0	45.67	8	—
Lawrence Godfrey Bernard	31.3.1932		5	1961	141	43	0	17.62	28	8-53	2/0	18.28	2	—
le Roux Frederick Louis	5.2.1882	22.9.1963	1	1913	1	1	0	0.50	0	0-5	0/0	—	0	—
Lewis Percy Tyson	2.10.1884	30.1.1976	1	1913	0	0	0	0.00	—	—	—/—	—	0	—
Liebenberg Gerhardus Frederick Johannes	7.4.1972		5	1997-1998	104	45	0	13.00	—	—	—/—	—	0	4
¹Lindsay Denis Thomson	4.9.1939	30.11.2005	19	1963-1969	1,130	182	3	37.66	—	—	—/—	—	57/2	—
¹Lindsay John Dixon	8.9.1908	31.8.1990	3	1947	21	9*	0	7.00	—	—	—/—	—	4/1	—
Lindsay Nevil Vernon	30.7.1886	2.2.1976	1	1921	35	29	0	17.50	0	0-20	0/0	—	2	—
Ling William Victor Stone	3.10.1891	26.9.1960	6	1921-1922	168	38	0	16.80	0	0-20	0/0	—	1	—
Llewellyn Charles Bennett (CY 1911)	26.9.1876	7.6.1964	15	1895-1912	544	90	0	20.14	48	6-92	4/1	29.60	7	—
Lundie Eric Balfour	15.3.1888	12.9.1917	1	1913	1	1	0	1.00	4	4-101	0/0	26.75	0	—
Macaulay Michael John	19.4.1939		1	1964	33	21	0	16.50	4	2-73	0/0	36.50	2	—
McCarthy Cuan Neil	24.3.1929	14.8.2000	15	1948-1951	28	5	0	3.11	36	6-43	2/0	41.94	6	—
McGlew Derrick John ("Jackie") (CY 1956)	11.3.1929	9.6.1998	34	1951-1961	2,440	255*	7	42.06	0	0-7	0/0	—	18	—
McKenzie Neil Douglas (CY 2009)	24.11.1975		58	2000-2008	3,253	226	5	37.39	0	0-1	0/0	—	54	64/2
McKinnon Atholl Henry	20.8.1932	2.12.1983	8	1960-1966	107	27	0	17.83	26	4-128	0/0	35.57	1	—
McLaren Ryan	9.2.1983		2	2009-2013	47	33*	0	23.50	3	2-72	0/0	54.00	0	54/12
McLean Roy Alastair (CY 1961)	9.7.1930	26.8.2007	40	1951-1964	2,120	142	5	30.28	0	0-1	0/0	—	23	—

§ *Kallis's figures exclude 83 runs, one wicket and four catches for the ICC World XI v Australia in the Super Series Test in 2005-06.*

	Born	Died	Tests	Test Career	Runs	HS	100s	Avge	Wkts	BB	Avge	5/10	Ct/St	O/T
McMillan Brian Mervin	22.12.1963		38	1992–1998	1,968	113	3	39.36	75	4-65	33.82	0/0	49	78
McMillan Quintin	23.6.1904	3.7.1948	13	1929–1931	306	50*	0	18.00	36	5-66	34.52	2/0	8	
Maharaj Keshav Athmanand	7.2.1990		23	2016–2018	407	45	0	14.53	90	9-129	28.14	5/1	6	4
Mann Norman Bertram Fleetwood ("Tufty")	28.12.1920	31.7.1952	19	1947–1951	400	52	0	13.33	58	6-59	33.10	1/0	3	
Mansell Percy Neville Frank MBE	16.3.1920	9.5.1995	13	1951–1955	355	90	0	17.75	11	3-58	66.90	0/0	15	
Markham Lawrence Anderson	12.9.1924	5.8.2000	1	1948	20	20	0	20.00	1	1-34	72.00	0/0	0	
Markram Aiden Kyle	4.10.1994		15	2017–2018	1,241	152	4	45.96	0	0-0	–	–/–	13	16
Marx Waldemar Frederick Eric	4.7.1895	2.6.1974	3	1921	125	36	0	20.83	4	3-85	36.00	0/0	0	
Matthews Craig Russell	15.2.1965		18	1992–1995	348	62*	0	18.31	52	5-42	28.88	2/0	4	56
Meintjes Douglas James	9.6.1890	17.7.1979	2	1922	43	21	0	14.33	6	3-38	19.16	0/0	3	
Melle Michael George	3.6.1930	28.12.2003	7	1949–1952	68	17	0	8.50	26	6-71	32.73	2/0	4	
Melville Alan (CY 1948)	19.5.1910	18.4.1983	11	1938–1948	894	189	4	52.58	–	–	–	–/–	8	
Middleton James	30.9.1895	23.12.1913	6	1895–1902	52	22	0	7.42	24	5-51	18.41	2/0		
Mills Charles Henry	26.11.1867	26.7.1948	1	1891	25	21	0	12.50	2	2-83	41.50	0/0	1	
Milton Sir William Henry	3.12.1854	6.3.1930	3	1888–1891	68	21	0	11.33	2	1-5	24.00	0/0	2	
Mitchell Bruce (CY 1936)	8.1.1909	1.7.1995	42	1929–1948	3,471	189*	8	48.88	27	5-87	51.11	1/0	56	
Mitchell Frank (CY 1902)	13.8.1872	11.10.1935	3†	1912	28	12	0	4.66	–	–	–	–/–		
Morkel Denijs Paul Beck	25.1.1906	6.10.1980	16	1927–1931	663	88	4	24.55	18	4-93	45.61	0/0	13	
²Morkel Johannes Albertus	10.6.1981		1	2008	58	58	0	58.00	1	1-44	132.00	0/0	1	56½/50
²Morkel Morne	6.10.1984		86	2006–2017	944	40	0	11.65	309	6-23	27.66	8/0	25	114½/41‡
Morris Christopher Henry	30.4.1987		4	2015–2017	173	69	0	24.71	12	3-38	38.25	0/0	5	34/18
Murray Anton Ronald Andrew	30.4.1922	17.4.1995	10	1952–1953	289	109	1	22.23	18	4-169	39.44	0/0	3	
Nel Andre	15.7.1977		36	2001–2008	337	34	0	9.91	123	6-32	31.86	3/1	16	79/2
Nel John Desmond	10.7.1928	13.1.2018	6	1949–1957	150	38	0	13.63	–	–	–	–/–	3	
Newberry Claude	1889	1.8.1916	4	1913	62	16	0	7.75	11	4-72	24.36	0/0	3	
Newson Edward Serrurier OBE	2.12.1910	24.4.1988	3	1930–1938	30	16	0	7.50	4	2-58	66.25	0/0	1	
Ngam Mfuneko	29.1.1979		3	2000	0	0*	0	–	11	3-26	17.18	0/0	1	
Ngidi Lungisani True-man	29.03.1996		4	2017–2018	15	5	0	3.75	15	6-39	19.53	1/0	2	13/7
Nicholson Frank	17.9.1909	30.7.1982	4	1935	76	29	0	10.85	0	0-5	–	0/0	3	
Nicolson John Fairless William	19.7.1899	13.12.1935	3	1927	179	78	0	35.80	0	0-3	–	0/0	0	
Norton Norman Ogilvie	11.5.1881	27.6.1968	1	1909	9	7	0	4.50	4	4-47	11.75	0/0	0	
³Nourse Arthur Dudley (CY 1948)	12.11.1910	14.8.1981	34	1935–1951	2,960	231	9	53.81	0	0-0	–	0/0	12	
³Nourse Arthur William ("Dave")	25.1.1879	8.7.1948	45	1902–1924	2,234	111	1	29.78	41	4-25	37.87	0/0	43	
Ntini Makhaya	6.7.1977		101	1997–2009	699	32*	0	9.84	390	7-37	28.82	18/4	25	172£/10
Nupen Eiulf Peter ("Buster")	1.11.1902	29.1.1977	17	1921–1935	348	69	0	14.50	50	6-46	35.76	5/1	9	
Ochse Arthur Edward	11.3.1870	11.4.1918	2	1888	16	8	0	4.00	–	–	–	–/–	0	

	Born	Died	Tests	Test Career	Runs	HS	100s	Avge	Wkts	BB	5/10	Avge	Ct/St	O/T
Ochse Arthur Lennox	11.10.1899	5.5.1949	3	1927–1929	11	4*	0	3.66	10	4-79	0/0	36.20	1	
O'Linn Sidney	5.5.1927	11.12.2016	7	1960–1961	297	98	0	27.00	—			—	4	
Olivier Duanne	9.5.1992		8	2016–2018	18	10*	0	3.60	41	6-37	3/1	18.19	0	
Ontong Justin Lee	4.1.1980		2	2001–2004	57	32	0	19.00	1	1-79	0/0	133.00	1	27‡/14
Owen-Smith Harold Geoffrey ("Tuppy") (CY 1930)	18.2.1909	28.2.1990	5	1929	252	129	1	42.00	0	0-3	0/0	—	4	
Palm Archibald William	8.6.1901	18.1.1966	1	1927	15	13	0	7.50	—			—	—	
Parker George Macdonald	27.5.1899	1.5.1969	2	1924	3	2*	0	1.50	8	6-152	1/0	34.12	1	
Parkin Durant Clifford	20.2.1873	20.3.1936	1	1891	6	6	0	3.00	3	3-82	0/0	27.33	2	
Parnell Wayne Dillon	30.7.1989		6	2009–2017	67	23	0	16.75	15	4-51	0/0	27.60	3	65/40
Partridge Joseph Titus	9.12.1932	6.6.1988	11	1963–1964	73	13*	0	10.42	44	7-91	3/0	31.20	6	
Pearse Charles Ormerod Cato	10.10.1884	7.5.1953	3	1910	55	31	0	9.16	3	3-56	0/0	35.33	1	
Pegler Sidney James	28.7.1888	10.9.1972	16	1909–1924	356	35*	0	15.47	47	7-65	2/0	33.44	5	
Peterson Alviro Nathan	25.11.1980		36	2009–2014	2,093	182	5	34.88	1	1-2	0/0	62.00	31	21/2
Peterson Robin John	4.8.1979		15	2003–2013	464	84	0	17.92	38	5-33	1/0	37.26	9	79/21
Phehlukwayo Andile Lucky	3.3.1996		4	2017	19	9	0	9.50	11	3-13	0/0	13.36	2	34/16
Philander Vernon Darryl	24.6.1985		57	2011–2018	1,516	74	0	24.45	211	6-21	13/2	21.73	17	30/7
Piedt Dane Lee-Roy	6.3.1990		7	2014–2016	48	19	0	6.85	24	5-153	1/0	36.04	4	
[2] Pithey Anthony John	17.7.1933		17	1956–1964	819	154	1	31.50	0	0-5	0/0	—	12	
[2] Pithey David Bartlett	4.10.1936	17.11.2006	8	1963–1966	138	55	0	12.54	12	6-58	1/0	48.08	6	
Plimsoll Jack Bruce	27.10.1917	21.11.2018	1	1947	16	8*	0	16.00	3	3-128	0/0	47.66	0	
[1,2] Pollock Peter Maclean (CY 1966)	30.6.1941	11.11.1999	28	1961–1969	607	75*	0	21.67	116	6-38	9/1	24.18	9	
[1] Pollock Robert Graeme (CY 1966)	27.2.1944		23	1963–1969	2,256	274	7	60.97	4	2-50	0/0	51.00	17	
[1] Pollock Shaun Maclean (CY 2003)	16.7.1973		108	1995–2007	3,781	111	2	32.31	421	7-87	16/1	23.11	72	294‡/12
Poore Robert Montagu (CY 1900)	20.3.1866	14.7.1938	3	1895	76	20	0	12.66	1	1-4	0/0	4.00	3	
Podhecary James Edward	6.12.1933	11.5.2016	1	1960	26	12	0	6.50	9	4-58	0/0	39.33	2	
Powell Albert William	18.7.1873	11.9.1948	1	1898	16	11	0	8.00	1	1-10	0/0	10.00	2	
Pretorius Dewald	6.12.1977		4	2001–2003	22	11	0	7.33	6	4-115	0/0	71.66	0	49‡/1
Prince Ashwell Gavin	28.5.1977		66	2001–2011	3,665	162*	11	41.64	1	1-2	0/0	47.00	47	
Prince Charles Frederick Henry	11.9.1874	2.2.1949	1	1898	6	5	0	3.00	—			—	0	
Pringle Meyrick Wayne	22.6.1966		4	1991–1995	67	33	0	16.75	10	2-62	0/0	54.00	0	17
Procter Michael John (CY 1970)	15.9.1946		7	1966–1969	226	48	0	25.11	41	6-73	1/0	15.02	4	
Promnitz Henry Louis Ernest	23.2.1904	7.9.1983	2	1927	14	5	0	3.50	8	5-58	1/0	20.12	2	
Quinn Neville Anthony	21.2.1908	5.8.1934	12	1929–1931	90	28	0	6.00	35	6-92	1/0	32.71	1	
Rabada Kagiso	25.5.1995		35	2015–2018	482	34	0	12.35	168	7-112	9/4	21.41	21	57/18
Reid Norman	26.12.1890	6.6.1947	1	1921	17	11	0	8.50	2	2-63	0/0	31.50	0	

	Born	Died	Tests	Test Career	Runs	HS	100s	Avge	Wkts	BB	5/10	Avge	Ct/St	O/T
Rhodes Jonathan Neil (CY 1999)	27.7.1969		52	1992–2000	2,532	117	3	35.66	0	0-0	00	–	34	245
² Richards Alfred Renfrew	14.12.1867	9.1.1904	1	1895	6	6	0	3.00	–	–	–/–	–	0	–
Richards Barry Anderson (CY 1969)	21.7.1945		4	1969	508	140	2	72.57	1	1-12	00	26.00	3	–
Richards William Henry Matthews	26.3.1862	4.1.1903	1	1888	4	4	0	2.00	–	–	–/–	–	3	–
Richardson David John	16.9.1959		42	1991–1997	1,359	109	1	24.26	–	–	–/–	–	150/2	122
Robertson John Benjamin	5.6.1906	5.7.1985	3	1935	51	17	0	10.20	6	3-143	00	53.50	2	–
Rose-Innes Albert	16.2.1868	22.11.1946	2	1888	14	13	0	3.50	5	5-43	1/0	17.80	2	–
Routledge Thomas William	18.4.1867	9.5.1927	4	1891–1895	72	24	0	9.00	–	–	–/–	–	2	–
² Rowan Athol Matthew Burchell	7.2.1921	22.2.1998	15	1947–1951	290	41	0	17.05	54	5-68	4/0	38.59	2	–
² Rowan Eric Alfred Burchell (CY 1952)	20.7.1909	30.4.1993	26	1935–1951	1,965	236	3	43.66	0	0-0	00	–	14	–
Rowe George Alexander	15.6.1874	8.1.1950	5	1895–1902	26	13*	0	4.33	15	5-115	1/0	30.40	4	–
Rudolph Jacobus Andries	4.5.1981		48	2003–2012	2,622	222*	6	35.43	4	1-1	00	108.00	29	43‡/1
Rushmere Mark Weir	7.1.1965		1	1991	6	3	0	3.00	–	–	–/–	–	0	4
Samuelson Sivert Vause	21.11.1883	18.11.1958	1	1909	22	15	0	11.00	0	0-64	00	–	1	–
Schultz Brett Nolan	26.8.1970		9	1992–1997	9	6	0	1.50	37	5-48	2/0	20.24	2	1
Schwarz Reginald Oscar (CY 1908)	4.5.1875	18.11.1918	20	1905–1912	374	61	0	13.85	55	6-47	2/0	25.76	18	–
Seccull Arthur William	14.9.1868	20.7.1945	1	1895	23	17*	0	23.00	2	2-37	00	18.50	1	–
Seymour Michael Arthur ("Kelly")	5.6.1936		7	1963–1969	84	36	0	12.00	9	3-80	00	65.33	2	–
Shalders William Alfred	12.2.1880	18.3.1917	12	1898–1907	355	42	0	16.13	1	1-6	00	6.00	9	–
Shamsi Tabraiz	18.2.1990		2	2016–2018	20	18*	0	20.00	6	3-91	00	46.33	0	11/9
Shepstone George Harold	9.4.1876	3.7.1940	2	1895–1898	38	21	0	9.50	0	0-8	00	–	1	–
Sherwell Percy William	17.8.1880	17.4.1948	13	1905–1910	427	115	1	23.72	–	–	–/–	–	20/16	–
Siedle Ivan Julian ("Jack")	11.1.1903	24.8.1982	18	1927–1935	977	141	1	28.73	1	1-7	00	7.00	7	–
Sinclair James Hugh	16.10.1876	23.2.1913	25	1895–1910	1,069	106	3	23.23	63	6-26	1/0	31.68	9	–
Smith Charles James Edward	25.12.1872	27.3.1947	1	1902	106	45	0	21.20	–	–	–/–	–	0	–
Smith Frederick William	31.3.1861	17.4.1914	3	1888–1895	45	12	0	9.00	–	–	–/–	–	2	–
§ Smith Graeme Craig (CY 2004)	1.2.1981		1168	2001–2013	9,253	277	27	48.70	8	2-145	00	110.62	166	196‡/33
Smith Vivian Ian	23.2.1925	25.8.2015	9	1947–1957	39	11*	0	3.90	12	4-143	00	64.08	3	–
Snell Richard Peter	12.9.1968		5	1991–1994	95	48	0	13.57	19	4-74	00	28.31	1	42
² Snooke Sibley John ("Tip")	1.2.1881	14.8.1966	26	1905–1922	1,008	103	1	22.40	35	8-70	1/1	20.05	24	–
Snooke Stanley de la Courtte	11.11.1878	6.4.1959	1	1907	4	2	0	0.00	–	–	–/–	–	2	–
Solomon William Rodger Thomson	23.4.1872	13.7.1964	1	1898	4	2	0	2.00	–	–	–/–	–	1	–
Stewart Robert Burnard	3.9.1856	12.9.1913	1	1888	13	9	0	6.50	–	–	–/–	–	2	–
Steyn Dale Willem (CY 2013)	27.6.1983		91	2004–2018	1,232	76	0	13.84	433	7-51	26/5	22.81	23	119‡/42
Steyn Philippus Jeremia Rudolf	30.6.1967		3	1994	127	46	0	21.16	–	–	–/–	–	0	1

§ *G. C. Smith's figures exclude 12 runs and three catches for the ICC World XI v Australia in the Super Series Test in 2005-06.*

	Born	Died	Tests	Test Career	Runs	HS	100s	Avge	Wkts	BB	5/10	Avge	Ct/St	O/T
Stricker Louis Anthony	26.5.1884	5.2.1960	13	1909–1912	344	48	0	14.33	0	1-36	0/0	105.00	3	–
Strydom Pieter Coenraad	10.6.1969		2	1999	35	30	0	11.66	0	0-27	–/–	–	1	10
Susskind Manfred John	8.6.1891	9.7.1957	5	1924	268	65	0	33.50	0	–	–	–	1	–
Symcox Patrick Leonard	14.4.1960		20	1993–1998	741	108	1	28.50	37	4-69	0/0	43.32	5	80
Taberer Henry Melville	7.10.1870	5.6.1932	1	1902	2	2	0	2.00	1	1-25	0/0	48.00	–	–
[2]Tancred Augustus Bernard	20.8.1865	23.11.1911	2	1888	87	29	0	29.00	0	–	–/–	–	2	–
[2]Tancred Louis Joseph	7.10.1876	28.7.1934	14	1902–1913	530	97	0	21.20	–	–	–	–	3	–
[2]Tancred Vincent Maximillian	7.7.1875	3.6.1904	1	1898	25	18	0	12.50	0	–	–	–	–	–
[2]Tapscott George Lancelot ("Dusty")	7.11.1889	13.12.1940	1	1913	5	4	0	2.50	0	–	–	–	1	–
[2]Tapscott Lionel Eric ("Doodles")	18.3.1894	8.7.1934	2	1922	58	50*	0	29.00	0	0-2	0/0	–	0	–
Tayfield Hugh Joseph (CY 1956)	30.1.1929	24.2.1994	37	1949–1960	862	75	0	16.90	170	9-113	14/2	25.91	26	–
Taylor Alistair Innes ("Scotch")	25.7.1925	7.2.2004	1	1956	18	12	0	9.00	0	–	–/–	–	0	–
[2]Taylor Daniel	9.1.1887	24.1.1957	2	1913	85	36	0	21.25	–	–	–	–	0	–
Taylor Herbert Wilfred (CY 1925)	5.5.1889	8.2.1973	42	1912–1931	2,936	176	7	40.77	5	3-15	0/0	31.20	19	4
Terbrugge David John	31.1.1977		4	1998–2003	16	4*	0	5.33	20	5-46	1/0	25.85	4	–
Theunissen Nicolaas Hendrik Christiaan de Jong	4.5.1867	9.11.1929	1	1888	2	2*	0	2.00	0	0-51	0/0	–	1	–
Thornton George	24.12.1867	31.11.1939	1	1902	1	1*	0	–	1	1-20	0/0	20.00	0	–
Tomlinson Denis Stanley	4.9.1910	11.7.1993	1	1935	9	9*	0	9.00	0	0-38	0/0	–	1	–
Traicos Athanasios John	17.5.1947		3†	1969	8	5*	0	4.00	4	2-70	0/0	51.75	4	0‡
Trimborn Patrick Henry Joseph	18.5.1940		4	1966–1969	13	11*	0	6.50	11	3-12	0/0	23.36	7	–
Tsolekile Thami Lungisa	9.10.1980		3	2004	47	22	0	9.40	–	–	–	–	6	–
Tsotsobe Lonwabo Lennox	7.3.1984		5	2010–2010	19	8*	0	6.33	9	3-43	0/0	49.77	1	61/23
¹Tuckett Thomas Delville	6.2.1919	5.9.2016	9	1947–1948	131	40*	0	11.90	19	5-68	2/0	51.57	9	–
¹Tuckett Lindsay Richard ("Len")	19.4.1885	8.4.1963	1	1913	0	0*	0	0.00	0	0-24	0/0	–	2	–
Twentyman-Jones Percy Sydney	13.9.1876	8.3.1954	1	1902	0	0	0	0.00	–	–	–	–	0	–
van der Bijl Pieter Gerhard Vintcent	21.10.1907	16.2.1973	5	1938	460	125	1	51.11	–	–	–	–	1	–
van der Merwe Edward Alexander	9.11.1903	26.2.1971	2	1929–1935	27	19	0	9.00	–	–	–	–	3	–
van der Merwe Peter Laurence	14.3.1937	23.1.2013	15	1963–1966	533	76	0	25.38	1	1-6	0/0	22.00	11	–
van Jaarsveld Martin	18.6.1974		9	2002–2004	397	73	0	30.53	0	0-28	0/0	–	11	11
van Ryneveld Clive Berrange	19.3.1928	29.1.2018	19	1951–1957	724	83	0	26.81	17	4-67	0/0	39.47	14	–
van Zyl Stiaan	19.9.1987		12	2014–2016	395	101*	0	26.33	6	3-20	0/0	24.66	6	0/1
Varnals George Derek	24.7.1935		3	1964	97	23	0	16.16	0	0-2	0/0	–	6	–
Vilas Dane James	10.6.1985		6	2015–2015	94	26	0	10.44	–	–	–	–	13	–
Viljoen G. C. ("Hardus")	6.3.1989		1	2015	26	20*	0	26.00	1	1-79	0/0	94.00	0	–
Viljoen Kenneth George	14.5.1910	21.1.1974	27	1930–1948	1,365	124	2	28.43	0	0-10	0/0	–	5	–
Vincent Cyril Leverton	16.2.1902	24.8.1968	25	1927–1935	526	60	0	20.23	84	6-51	3/0	31.32	27	–

	Born	Died	Tests	Test Career	Runs	HS	100s	Avge	Wkts	BB	5/10	Avge	Ct/St	O/T
Vincent Charles Henry	2.9.1866	28.9.1943	3	1888–1891	26	9	0	4.33	4	3-88	0/0	48.25	1	—
Vogler Albert Edward Ernest (CY 1908)	28.11.1876	9.8.1946	15	1905–1910	340	65	0	17.00	64	7-94	5/1	22.73	20	
²Wade Herbert Frederick	14.9.1905	23.11.1980	10	1935–1935	327	40*	0	20.43	–	–	–/–	–	4	
Wade Walter Wareham ("Billy")	18.6.1914	31.5.2003	11	1938–1949	511	125	1	28.38	–	–	–/–	–	15/2	
Waite John Henry Bickford	19.1.1930	22.6.2011	50	1951–1964	2,405	134	4	30.44	–	–	–/–	–	124/17	
Walter Kenneth Alexander	5.11.1939	13.9.2003	2	1961	11	10	0	3.66	6	4-63	0/0	32.83	3	
Ward Thomas Alfred	2.8.1887	16.2.1936	23	1912–1924	459	64	0	13.90	–	–	–/–	–	19/13	
Watkins John Cecil	10.4.1923		15	1949–1956	612	92	0	23.53	29	4-22	0/0	28.13	12	
Wesley Colin	5.9.1937		3	1960	49	35	0	9.80	–	–	–/–	–	1	
Wessels Kepler Christoffel (CY 1995)	14.9.1957		16†	1991–1994	1,027	118	2	38.03	–	–	–/–	–	12	55‡
Westcott Richard John	19.9.1927	16.1.2013	5	1953–1957	166	62	0	18.44	–	–	–/–	–	0	
White Gordon Charles	5.2.1882	17.10.1918	17	1905–1912	872	147	2	30.06	9	4-47	0/0	33.44	10	
Willoughby Charl Myles	3.12.1974		2	2003	–	–	–	–	1	1-47	0/0	125.00	0	3
Willoughby Joseph Thomas	7.11.1874	11.3.1952	2	1895	8	5	0	2.00	6	2-37	0/0	26.50	0	
Wimble Clarence Skelton	22.4.1861	28.11.1901	1	1891	0	0	0	0.00	–	–	–/–	–	0	
Winslow Paul Lyndhurst	21.5.1929	24.5.2011	5	1949–1955	186	108	1	20.66	–	–	–/–	–	1	
Wynne Owen Edgar	1.6.1919	13.7.1975	6	1948–1949	219	50	0	18.25	–	–	–/–	–	3	
Zondeki Monde	25.7.1982		6	2003–2008	82	59	0	16.40	19	6-39	1/0	25.26	1	11‡/1
Zulch Johan Wilhelm	2.1.1886	19.5.1924	16	1909–1921	983	150	2	32.76	0	0-2	0/0	–	4	

WEST INDIES (316 players)

	Born	Died	Tests	Test Career	Runs	HS	100s	Avge	Wkts	BB	5/10	Avge	Ct/St	O/T
Achong Ellis Edgar	16.2.1904	30.8.1986	6	1929–1934	81	22	0	8.10	8	2-64	0/0	47.25	6	
Adams James Clive	9.1.1968		54	1991–2000	3,012	208*	6	41.26	27	5-17	1/0	49.48	48	127
Alexander Franz Copeland Murray ("Gerry")	2.11.1928	16.4.2011	25	1957–1960	961	108	0	30.03	–	–	–/–	–	85/5	
Ali Imtiaz	28.7.1954		1	1975	1	1*	0	–	2	2-37	0/0	44.50	0	
Ali Inshan	25.9.1949	24.6.1995	12	1970–1976	172	25	0	10.75	34	5-59	1/0	47.67	7	
Allan David Walter	5.11.1937		5	1961–1966	75	40*	0	12.50	–	–	–/–	–	15/3	
Allen Ian Basil Alston	6.10.1965		2	1991	5	4*	0	–	5	2-69	0/0	36.00	1	
Ambris Sunil Walford	23.3.1993		6	2017–2018	166	43	0	15.09	–	–	–/–	–	2	1
Ambrose Sir Curtly Elconn Lynwall (CY 1992)	21.9.1963		98	1988–2000	1,439	53	0	12.40	405	8-45	22/3	20.99	18	176
Arthurton Keith Lloyd Thomas	21.2.1965		33	1988–1995	1,382	157*	2	30.71	1	1-17	0/0	183.00	22	105
Asgarali Nyron Sultan	28.12.1920	5.11.2006	2	1957	62	29	0	15.50	–	–	–/–	–	0	
²Atkinson Denis St Eval	9.8.1926	9.11.2001	22	1948–1957	922	219	1	31.79	47	7-53	3/0	35.04	11	

	Born	Died	Tests	Test Career	Runs	HS	100s	Avge	Wkts	BB	5/10	Avge	Ct/St	O/T
² Atkinson Eric St Eval	6.11.1927	29.5.1998	8	1957–1958	126	37	0	15.75	25	5-42	1/0	23.56	2	—
Austin Richard Arkwright	5.9.1954	7.2.2015	2	1977	22	20	0	11.00	0	0-5	0/0	—	2	1
Austin Ryan Anthony	15.11.1981		2	2009	39	19	0	9.75	3	1-29	0/0	51.66	3	—
Bacchus Sheik Faoud Ahamul Fasiel	31.11.1954		19	1977–1981	782	250	1	26.06	0	0-3	0/0	—	17	29
Baichan Leonard	12.5.1946		3	1974–1975	184	105*	1	46.00	—	—	—/—	—	2	—
Baker Lionel Sionne	6.9.1984		4	2008–2009	23	18	0	11.50	5	2-39	0/0	79.00	1	10/3
Banks Omari Ahmed Clemente	17.7.1982		10	2002–2005	318	50*	0	26.50	28	4-87	0/0	48.82	6	5
Baptiste Eldine Ashworth Elderfield	12.3.1960		10	1983–1989	233	87*	0	23.30	16	3-31	0/0	35.18	2	43
Barath Adrian Boris	14.4.1990		15	2009–2012	657	104	1	23.46	0	0-3	0/0	—	13	14/2
Barrett Arthur George	4.4.1944	6.3.2018	6	1970–1974	40	19	0	6.66	13	3-43	0/0	46.38	3	—
Barrow Ivanhoe Mordecai	16.1.1911	2.4.1979	11	1929–1939	276	105	1	16.23	—	—	—/—	—	17/5	—
Bartlett Edward Lawson	10.3.1906	21.12.1976	5	1928–1930	131	84	0	18.71					2	—
Baugh Carlton Seymour	23.6.1982		21	2002–2011	610	68	0	17.94	—	—	—/—	—	43/5	47/3
Benjamin Kenneth Charlie Griffith	8.4.1967		26	1991–1997	222	43*	0	7.92	92	6-66	4/1	30.27	2	26
Benjamin Winston Keithroy Matthew	31.12.1964		21	1987–1994	470	85	0	18.80	61	4-46	0/0	27.01	12	85
Benn Sulieman Jamaal	22.7.1981		26	2007–2014	486	42	0	14.29	87	6-81	6/0	39.10	14	47/24
Bernard David Eddison	19.7.1981		3	2002–2009	202	69	0	40.40	4	2-30	0/0	46.25	0	20/1
Bess Brandon Jeremy	13.12.1987		1	2010	11	11*	0	11.00	1	1-65	0/0	92.00	0	—
Best Carlisle Alonza	14.5.1959		8	1985–1990	342	164	1	28.50	0	0-2	0/0	—	8	24
Best Tino la Bertram	26.8.1981		25	2002–2013	401	95	0	12.53	57	6-40	2/0	40.19	6	26/6
Betancourt Nelson	4.6.1887	12.10.1947	1	1929	52	39	0	26.00					0	—
Binns Alfred Phillip	24.7.1929	29.12.2017	5	1952–1955	64	27	0	9.14	—	—	—/—	—	14/3	—
Birkett Lionel Sydney	14.4.1905	16.1.1998	4	1930	136	64	0	17.00	1	1-16	0/0	71.00	4	—
Bishoo Devendra	6.11.1985		36	2010–2018	707	45	0	15.36	117	8-49	4/1	37.17	20	37/5
Bishop Ian Raphael	24.10.1967		43	1988–1997	632	48	0	12.15	161	6-40	6/0	24.27	8	84
Black Marlon Ian	7.6.1975		6	2000–2001	21	6	0	2.62	12	4-83	0/0	49.75	0	5
Blackwood Jermaine	20.11.1991		27	2014–2017	1,324	112*	1	30.09	2	2-14	0/0	97.00	24	5
Boyce Keith David (CY 1974)	11.10.1943	11.10.1996	21	1971–1975	657	95*	0	24.33	60	6-77	2/1	30.01	5	8
Bradshaw Ian David Russell	9.7.1974		5	2005	96	33	0	13.71	9	3-73	0/0	60.00	3	62/1
Brathwaite Carlos Ricardo	18.7.1988		3	2015–2016	181	69	0	45.25	1	1-30	0/0	242.00	0	28/35
Brathwaite Kraigg Clairmonte	1.12.1992		53	2010–2018	3,311	212	8	35.22	17	6-29	1/0	56.70	25	10
² Bravo Dwayne John	7.10.1983		40	2004–2010	2,200	113	3	31.42	86	6-55	2/0	39.83	41	164/66
² Bravo Darren Michael	6.2.1989		49	2010–2016	3,400	218	8	40.00	0	0-2	0/0	—	47	97/17
Breese Gareth Rohan	9.1.1976		1	2002	5	5	0	2.50	2	2-108	0/0	67.50	0	—
Browne Courtney Oswald	7.12.1970		20	1994–2004	387	68	0	16.12	—	—	—/—	—	79/2	46
Browne Cyril Rutherford	8.10.1890	12.1.1964	4	1928–1929	176	70*	0	25.14	6	2-72	0/0	48.00	1	—

Name	Born	Died	Tests	Test Career	Runs	HS	100s	Avge	Wkts	BB	5/10	Avge	Ct/St	O/T
Butcher Basil Fitzherbert (CY 1970)	3.9.1933		44	1958–1969	3,104	209*	7	43.11	5	5-34	1/0	18.00	15	
Butler Lennox Stephen	9.2.1929	1.9.2009	1	1954	16	16	0	16.00	2	2-151	0/0	75.50	0	
Butts Clyde Godfrey	8.7.1957		7	1984–1987	108	38	0	15.42	10	4-73	0/0	59.50	2	
Bynoe Michael Robin	23.2.1941		4	1958–1966	111	48	0	18.50	1	1-5	0/0	5.00	4	
Camacho George Stephen	15.10.1945	2.10.2015	11	1967–1970	640	87	0	29.09	0	0-12	0/0	–	4	
Cameron Francis James	22.6.1923	10.6.1994	5	1948	151	75*	0	25.16	3	2-74	0/0	92.66	4	
[2] Cameron John Hemsley	8.4.1914	13.2.2000	2	1939	6	5	0	2.00	3	3-66	0/0	29.33	0	
Campbell Sherwin Legay	1.11.1970		52	1994–2001	2,882	208	4	32.38	0	–	–/–	–	47	90
Carew George McDonald	4.6.1910	9.12.1974	4	1934–1948	170	107	1	28.33	0	0-2	0/0	–	1	
Carew Michael Conrad ("Joey")	15.9.1937	8.1.2011	19	1963–1971	1,127	109	1	34.15	8	1-11	0/0	54.62	13	
Challenor George	28.6.1888	30.7.1947	3	1928	101	46	0	16.83	–	–	–/–	–	0	
Chanderpaul Shivnarine (CY 2008)	16.8.1974		164	1993–2014	11,867	203*	30	51.37	9	1-2	–/–	98.11	66	268/22
Chandrika Rajindra	8.8.1989		5	2015–2016	140	37	0	14.00	–	–	–/–	–	2	
Chang Herbert Samuel	2.7.1952		2	1978	8	6	0	4.00	–	–	–/–	–	0	
Chase Roston Lamar	22.3.1992		26	2016–2018	1,461	137*	4	32.46	42	5-121	1/0	47.61	13	11
Chattergoon Sewnarine	3.4.1981		4	2007–2008	127	46	0	18.14	–	–	–/–	–	1	18
[2] Christiani Cyril Marcel	28.10.1913	4.4.1938	4	1934	98	32*	0	19.60	–	–	–/–	–	6/1	
[2] Christiani Robert Julian	19.7.1920	4.1.2005	22	1947–1953	896	107	1	26.35	3	3-52	0/0	36.00	19/2	
Clarke Carlos Bertram OBE	7.4.1918	14.10.1993	3	1939	3	2	0	1.00	6	3-59	0/0	29.83	2	
Clarke Sylvester Theophilus	11.12.1954	4.12.1999	11	1977–1981	172	35*	0	15.63	42	5-126	1/0	27.85	2	10
[2] Collins Pedro Tyrone	12.8.1976		32	1998–2005	235	24	0	5.87	106	6-53	3/0	34.63	7	30
Collymore Corey Dalanelo	21.12.1977		30	1998–2007	197	16*	0	7.88	93	7-57	4/1	32.30	6	84
Constantine Lord [Learie Nicholas] MBE (CY 1940)	21.9.1901	1.7.1971	18	1928–1939	635	90	0	19.24	58	5-75	2/0	30.10	28	
Cotterell Sheldon Shane	19.8.1989		2	2013–2014	11	5	0	2.75	5	1-72	0/0	73.00	0	6/10
Croft Colin Everton Hunte	15.3.1953		27	1976–1981	158	33	0	10.53	125	8-29	3/0	23.30	8	19
Cuffy Cameron Eustace	8.2.1970		15	1994–2002	58	15	0	4.14	43	4-82	0/0	33.83	5	41
Cummins Anderson Cleophas	7.5.1966		5	1992–1994	98	50	0	19.60	8	4-54	0/0	42.75	1	63‡
Cummins Miguel Lamar	5.9.1990		13	2016–2018	95	24*	0	6.78	27	6-48	1/0	37.59	2	11
Da Costa Oscar Constantine	16.1.1907	1.10.1936	5	1929–1934	153	39	0	19.12	3	1-14	0/0	58.33	5	
Daniel Wayne Wendell	16.1.1956		10	1975–1983	46	11	0	6.57	36	5-39	1/0	25.27	4	18
[2] Davis Bryan Allan	2.5.1940		4	1964	245	68	0	30.62	–	–	–/–	–	4	
[2] Davis Charles Allan	1.1.1944		15	1968–1972	1,301	183	4	54.20	2	1-27	0/0	165.00	4	
Davis Winston Walter	18.9.1958		15	1982–1987	202	77	0	15.53	45	4-19	1/0	32.71	10	35
de Caires Francis Ignatius	12.5.1909	2.2.1959	3	1929	232	80	0	38.66	0	0-9	0/0	–	4	
Deonarine Narsingh	16.8.1983		18	2004–2013	725	82	0	25.89	24	4-37	0/0	29.70	16	31/8

	Born	Died	Tests	Test Career	Runs	HS	100s	Avge	Wkts	BB	5/10	Avge	Ct/St	O/T
Depeiza Cyril Claimonte	10.10.1928	10.11.1995	5	1954–1955	187	122	1	31.16	0	0-3	00	–	7/4	
Dewdney David Thomas	23.10.1933		9	1954–1957	17	5*	0	2.42	21	5-21	1/0	38.42	0	
Dhanraj Rajindra	6.2.1969		4	1994–1995	17	9	0	4.25	8	2-49	00	74.37	1	6
Dillon Mervyn	5.6.1974		38	1996–2003	549	43	0	8.44	131	5-71	2/0	33.57	16	108
Dowe Uton George	29.3.1949		4	1970–1972	8	8*	0	8.00	12	4-69	00	44.50	3	
Dowlin Travis Montague	24.2.1977		6	2009–2010	343	95	0	31.18	0	0-3	00	–	5	11/2
Dowrich Shane Omari	30.10.1991		27	2015–2018	1,198	125*	2	27.86	–	–	–/–	–	66/5	
Drakes Vasbert Conniel	5.8.1969		12	2002–2003	386	67	0	21.44	33	5-93	1/0	41.27	2	34
Dujon Peter Jeffrey Leroy (CY 1989)	28.5.1956		81	1981–1991	3,322	139	5	31.94	0	0-19	–/–	–	267/5	169
²**Edwards** Fidel Henderson	6.2.1982		55	2003–2012	394	30	0	6.56	165	7-87	12/0	37.87	10	50/20
Edwards Kirk Anton	3.11.1984		17	2011–2014	986	121	2	31.80	0	0-19	00	–	15	16
Edwards Richard Martin	3.6.1940		5	1968	65	22	0	9.28	18	5-84	1/0	34.77	0	
Ferguson Wilfred	14.12.1917	23.2.1961	8	1947–1953	200	75	0	28.57	34	6-92	3/1	34.26	11	
Fernandes Maurius Pacheco	12.8.1897	8.5.1981	2	1928–1929	49	22	0	12.25	–	–	–/–	–	4	
Findlay Thaddeus Michael MBE	19.10.1943		10	1969–1972	212	44*	0	16.30	–	–	–/–	–	19/2	
Foster Maurice Linton Churchill	9.5.1943		14	1969–1977	580	125	1	30.52	9	2-41	00	66.66	3	2
Francis George Nathaniel	11.12.1897	12.1.1942	10	1928–1933	81	19*	0	5.78	23	4-40	00	33.17	7	
Frederick Michael Campbell	6.5.1927	18.6.2014	1	1953	30	30	0	15.00	–	–	–/–	–	0	
Fredericks Roy Clifton (CY 1974)	11.11.1942	5.9.2000	59	1968–1976	4,334	169	8	42.49	7	1-12	00	78.28	62	12
Fudadin Assad Badyr	1.8.1985		3	2012	122	55	0	30.50	0	0-11	00	–	4	
Fuller Richard Livingston	30.1.1913	3.5.1987	1	1934	1	1	0	1.00	0	0-2	00	–	0	
Furlonge Hammond Allan	19.6.1934		3	1954–1955	99	64	0	19.80	–	–	–/–	–	0	
Gabriel Shannon Terry	28.4.1988		40	2012–2018	190	20*	0	4.87	120	8-62	5/1	29.73	15	18/2
Ganga Daren	14.1.1979		48	1998–2007	2,160	135	3	25.71	1	1-20	00	106.00	30	35/1
Ganteaume Andrew Gordon	22.1.1921	17.2.2016	1	1947	112	112	1	112.00	–	–	–/–	–	0	
Garner Joel MBE (CY 1980)	16.12.1952		58	1976–1986	672	60	0	12.44	259	6-56	7/0	20.97	42	98
Garrick Leon Vivian	11.11.1976		2	2000	27	27	0	13.50	–	–	–/–	–	1	3
Gaskin Berkeley Bertram McGarrell	21.3.1908	2.5.1979	2	1947	17	10	0	5.66	2	1-15	00	79.00	1	
Gayle Christopher Henry	21.9.1979		103	1999–2014	7,214	333	15	42.18	73	5-34	2/0	42.73	96	281/56
Gibbs Glendon Lionel	27.12.1925	21.2.1979	1	1954	12	12	0	6.00	0	0-2	00	–	0	
Gibbs Lancelot Richard (CY 1972)	29.9.1934		79	1957–1975	488	25	0	6.97	309	8-38	18/2	29.09	52	3
Gibson Ottis Delroy (CY 2008)	16.3.1969		2	1995–1998	93	37	0	23.25	3	2-81	00	91.66	3	15
Gilchrist Roy	28.6.1934	18.7.2001	13	1957–1958	60	12	0	5.45	57	6-55	1/0	26.68	4	
Gladstone Morais George	14.1.1901	19.5.1978	1	1929	12	12*	0	–	1	1-139	00	189.00	0	
Goddard John Douglas Claude OBE	21.4.1919	26.8.1987	27	1947–1957	859	83*	0	30.67	33	5-31	1/0	31.81	22	
Gomes Hilary Angelo ("Larry") (CY 1985)	13.7.1953		60	1976–1986	3,171	143	9	39.63	15	2-20	00	62.00	18	83

Name	Born	Died	Tests	Test Career	Runs	HS	100s	Avge	Wkts	BB	5/10	Avge	Ct/St	O/T
Gomez Gerald Eldridge	10.10.1919	6.8.1996	29	1939–1953	1,243	101	1	30.31	58	7-55	1/1	27.41	18	–
[2] Grant George Copeland ("Jackie")	9.5.1907	26.10.1978	12	1930–1934	413	71*	0	25.81	0	0-1	00	–	10	–
[2] Grant Rolph Stewart	15.12.1909	18.10.1977	7	1934–1939	220	77	0	22.00	11	3-68	00	32.09	13	25
Gray Anthony Hollis	23.5.1963		5	1986	48	12*	0	8.00	22	4-39	00	17.13	6	5
Greenidge Alvin Ethelbert	20.8.1956		6	1977–1978	222	69	0	22.20	0	–	–/–	–	5	1
Greenidge Cuthbert Gordon MBE (CY 1977)	1.5.1951		108	1974–1990	7,558	226	19	44.72	0	0-0	00	–	96	128
Greenidge Geoffrey Alan	26.5.1948		5	1971–1972	209	50	0	29.85	0	0-2	00	–	3	–
Grell Mervyn George	18.12.1899	11.1.1976	1	1929	34	21	0	17.00	0	0-7	00	–	1	–
Griffith Adrian Frank Gordon	19.11.1971		14	1996–2000	638	114	1	24.53	–	–	–/–	–	16	9
[2] Griffith Charles Christopher (CY 1964)	14.12.1938		28	1959–1968	530	54	0	16.56	94	6-36	5/0	28.54	16	–
Griffith Herman Clarence	1.12.1893	18.3.1980	13	1928–1933	91	18	0	5.05	44	6-103	2/0	28.25	4	–
Guillen Simpson Clairmonte ("Sammy")	24.9.1924	2.3.2013	5†	1951	104	54	0	26.00	–	–	–/–	–	9/2	–
Hall Sir Wesley Winfield	12.9.1937		48	1958–1968	818	50*	0	15.73	192	7-69	9/1	26.38	11	–
Harper Roger Andrew	17.3.1963		25	1983–1993	535	74	0	18.44	46	6-57	1/0	28.06	36	105
Haynes Desmond Leo (CY 1991)	15.2.1956		116	1977–1993	7,487	184	18	42.29	1	1-2	00	8.00	65	238
[3] Headley George Alphonso MBE (CY 1934)	30.5.1909	30.11.1983	22	1929–1953	2,190	270*	10	60.83	0	0-0	00	–	14	–
[3] Headley Ronald George Alphonso	29.6.1939		2	1973	62	42	0	15.50	–	–	–/–	–	2	–
Hendriks John Leslie	21.12.1933		20	1961–1969	447	64	0	18.62	–	–	–/–	–	42/5	–
Hetmyer Shimron Odilon	26.12.1996		10	2016–2018	594	93	0	29.70	–	–	–/–	–	7	20/8
Hinds Ryan O'Neal	17.2.1981		15	2001–2009	505	84	0	21.04	13	2-45	00	66.92	4	14
Hinds Wavell Wayne	7.9.1976		45	1999–2005	2,608	213	2	33.01	16	3-79	00	36.87	32	119/5
Hoad Edward Lisle Goldsworthy	29.1.1896	5.3.1986	4	1928–1933	98	36	0	12.25	–	–	–/–	–	1	–
Holder Jason Omar	5.11.1991		35	2014–2018	1,554	110	2	30.47	86	6-59	5/1	28.50	25	85/8
Holder Roland Irwin Christopher	22.12.1967		11	1996–1998	380	91	0	25.33	–	–	–/–	–	16	37
Holding Michael Anthony (CY 1977)	16.2.1954		60	1975–1986	910	73	0	14.20	249	8-92	13/2	23.68	22	102
Holford David Anthony Jerome	16.4.1940	3.6.1997	24	1966–1976	768	105*	0	13.78	51	5-23	1/0	39.39	18	–
Holt John Kenneth Constantine	12.8.1923		17	1953–1958	1,066	166	2	36.75	1	1-20	00	20.00	8	–
Hooper Carl Llewellyn	15.12.1966		102	1987–2002	5,762	233	13	36.46	114	5-26	4/0	49.42	115	227
[2] Hope Kyle Antonio	20.11.1988		5	2017–2017	101	43	0	11.22	–	–	–/–	–	3	–
Hope Shai Diego (CY 2018)	10.11.1993		26	2014–2018	1,340	147	2	28.51	–	–	–/–	–	32	44/9
Howard Anthony Bourne	27.8.1946		1	1971	–	–	–	–	2	2-140	00	70.00	–	–
Hunte Sir Conrad Cleophas (CY 1964)	9.5.1932	3.12.1999	44	1957–1966	3,245	260	8	45.06	2	1-17	00	55.00	16	–
Hunte Errol Ashton Clairmore	3.10.1905	26.6.1967	3	1929	166	58	0	33.20	–	–	–/–	–	5	–
Hylton Leslie George	29.3.1905	17.5.1955	6	1934–1939	70	19	0	11.66	16	4-27	00	26.12	1	–
Jacobs Ridley Detamore	26.11.1967		65	1998–2004	2,577	118	3	28.31	–	–	–/–	–	207/12	147

Name	Born	Died	Tests	Test Career	Runs	HS	100s	Avge	Wkts	BB	5/10	Avge	Ct/St	O/T
Jaggernauth Amit Sheldon	16.11.1983		1	2007	0	0*	0	0.00	0	1-74	0/0	96.00		
Johnson Hophnie Hobah Hines	13.7.1910	24.6.1987	3	1947–1950	38	22	0	9.50	13	5-41	2/1	18.30	0	6
Johnson Leon Rayon	8.8.1987		9	2014–2016	403	66	0	25.18	0	0-9	0/0	–	7	
Johnson Tyrell Fabian	10.1.1917	5.4.1985	1	1939	9	9*	0	–	3	2-53	0/0	43.00	1	
Jones Charles Ernest Llewellyn	3.11.1902	10.12.1959	4	1929–1934	63	19	0	9.00	0	0-2	0/0	–	3	
Jones Prior Erskine Waverley	6.6.1917	21.11.1991	9	1947–1951	47	10*	0	5.22	25	5-85	1/0	30.04	4	
Joseph Alzarri Shaheim	20.11.1996		6	2016–2017	41	8	0	3.72	15	3-53	0/0	38.86	2	16
Joseph David Rolston Emmanuel	15.11.1969		4	1998	141	50	0	20.14			-/-	–	10	
Joseph Sylvester Cleofoster	5.9.1978		5	2004–2007	147	45	0	14.70	1	0-8	0/0	–	3	13
Julien Bernard Denis	13.3.1950		24	1973–1976	866	121	2	30.92	50	5-57	1/0	37.36	14	12
Jumadeen Raphick Rasif	12.4.1948		12	1971–1978	84	56	0	21.00	29	4-72	0/0	39.34	4	
Kallicharran Alvin Isaac BEM (CY 1983)	21.3.1949		66	1971–1980	4,399	187	12	44.43	4	2-16	0/0	39.50	51	31
Kanhai Rohan Bholalall (CY 1964)	26.12.1935		79	1957–1973	6,227	256	15	47.53	0	0-1	0/0	–	50	7
Kentish Esmond Seymour Maurice	21.11.1916	10.6.2011	2	1947–1953	1	1*	0	1.00	8	5-49	1/0	22.25	1	
King Collis Llewellyn	11.6.1951		9	1976–1980	418	100*	1	32.15	3	1-30	0/0	94.00	5	18
King Frank McDonald	14.12.1926	23.12.1990	14	1952–1955	116	21	0	8.28	29	5-74	1/0	39.96	5	
King Lester Anthony	27.2.1939	9.7.1998	2	1961–1967	41	20	0	10.25	9	5-46	1/0	17.11	2	
King Reon Dane	6.10.1975		19	1998–2004	66	12*	0	3.47	53	5-51	1/0	32.69	2	50
Lambert Clayton Benjamin	10.2.1962		5	1991–1998	284	104	1	31.55	1	1-4	0/0	5.00	8	11‡
Lara Brian Charles (CY 1995)	2.5.1969		130§	1990–2006	11,912	400*	34	53.17	0	0-0	0/0	–	164	295‡
Lashley Patrick Douglas ("Peter")	11.2.1937		4	1960–1966	159	49	0	22.71	1	1-1	0/0	1.00	4	
Lawson Jermaine Jay Charles	13.1.1982		13	2002–2005	52	14	0	3.46	51	7-78	2/0	29.64	8	13
Legall Ralph Archibald	1.12.1925	2003	4	1952	50	23	0	10.00	0	–	-/-	–	8/1	
Lewis Desmond Michael	1.12.1946	25.3.2018	3	1970	259	88	0	86.33	0	–	-/-	–	8	
Lewis Rawl Nicholas	5.9.1974		5	1997–2007	89	40	0	8.90	4	2-42	0/0	114.00	8	28‡
Lewis Sherman Hakim	21.10.1995		5	2018	24	20	0	6.00	3	2-93	0/0	54.00	1	
Lloyd Clive Hubert CBE (CY 1971)	31.8.1944		110	1966–1984	7,515	242*	19	46.67	10	2-13	0/0	62.20	90	87
Logie Augustine Lawrence	28.9.1960		52	1982–1991	2,470	130	2	35.79	0	0-0	0/0	–	57	158
McGarrell Neil Christopher	12.7.1972		4	2000–2001	61	33	0	15.25	17	4-23	0/0	26.64	2	17
McLean Nixon Alexei McNamara	20.7.1973		19	1997–2000	368	46	0	12.26	44	3-53	0/0	42.56	5	45
McMorris Easton Dudley Ashton St John	4.4.1935		13	1957–1966	564	125	1	26.85			-/-	–	5	
McWatt Clifford Aubrey	1.2.1922	20.7.1997	6	1953–1954	202	54	0	28.85	1	1-16	0/0	16.00	9/1	
Madray Ivan Samuel	2.7.1934	23.4.2009	2	1957	3	2	0	1.00	0	0-12	0/0	–	5	
Marshall Malcolm Denzil (CY 1983)	18.4.1958	4.11.1999	81	1978–1991	1,810	92	0	18.85	376	7-22	22/4	20.94	25	136
Marshall Norman Edgar	27.2.1924	11.8.2007	1	1954	8	8	0	4.00	2	1-22	0/0	31.00		

§ *Lara's figures exclude 41 runs for the ICC World XI v Australia in the Super Series Test in 2005-06.*

	Born	Died	Tests	Test Career	Runs	HS	100s	Avge	Wkts	BB	5/10	Avge	Ct/St	O/T
[2] Marshall Roy Edwin (CY 1959)	25.4.1930	27.10.1992		1951	143	30	0	20.42	0	0-3	0/0	–	1	–
Marshall Xavier Melbourne	27.3.1986		7	2005–2008	243	85	0	20.25	0	0-0	0/0	–	2	246
Martin Frank Reginald	12.10.1893	23.11.1967	9	1928–1930	486	123*	1	28.58	8	3-91	0/0	77.37	2	–
Martindale Emmanuel Alfred	25.11.1909	17.3.1972	10	1933–1939	58	22	0	5.27	37	5-22	3/0	21.72	5	–
Mattis Everton Hugh	11.4.1957		4	1980	145	71	0	29.00	0	0-4	0/0	–	3	2
Mendonca Ivor Leon	13.7.1934	14.6.2014	2	1961	81	78	0	40.50	–	–	–/–	–	8/2	–
Merry Cyril Arthur	20.1.1911	19.4.1964	2	1933	34	13	0	8.50	0	–	0/0	–	1	509
Miller Nikita O'Neil	16.5.1982		1	2009	5	5	0	2.50	0	0-27	0/0	–	0	–
Miller Roy Samuel	24.12.1924		1	1952	23	23	0	23.00	0	0-28	0/0	–	1	–
Mohammed Dave	8.10.1979		5	2003–2006	225	52	0	32.14	13	3-98	0/0	51.38	1	7
Moodie George Horatio	26.11.1915	8.6.2002	1	1934	5	5	0	5.00	3	2-23	0/0	13.33	0	–
Morton Runako Shakur	22.7.1978	4.3.2012	15	2005–2007	573	70*	0	22.03	0	0-4	0/0	–	20	567
Moseley Ezra Alphonsa	5.1.1958		2	1989	35	26	0	8.75	6	2-70	0/0	43.50	1	9
Murray David Anthony	29.5.1950		19	1977–1981	601	84	0	21.46	0	–	–/–	–	57/5	10
Murray Deryck Lance	20.5.1943		62	1963–1980	1,993	91	0	22.90	0	–	–/–	–	181/8	26
Murray Junior Randalph	20.1.1968		33	1992–2001	918	101*	1	22.39	0	–	–/–	–	99/3	55
Nagamootoo Mahendra Veeren	9.10.1975		5	2000–2002	185	68	0	26.42	12	3-119	0/0	53.08	2	24
Nanan Rangy	29.5.1953	23.3.2016	1	1980	16	8	0	8.00	4	2-37	0/0	22.75	2	–
Narine Sunil Philip	26.5.1988		6	2012–2013	40	22*	0	8.00	21	6-91	2/0	40.52	2	65/48
Nash Brendan Paul	14.12.1977		21	2008–2011	1,103	114	2	33.42	2	1-21	0/0	123.50	6	9
Neblett James Montague	13.11.1901	28.3.1959	1	1934	16	11*	0	16.00	1	1-44	0/0	75.00	0	
Noreiga Jack Mollinson	15.4.1936	8.8.2003	4	1970	11	9	0	3.66	17	9-95	2/0	29.00	0	
Nunes Robert Karl	7.6.1894	23.7.1958	4	1928–1929	245	92	0	30.62	–	–	–/–	–	2	
Nurse Seymour MacDonald (CY 1967)	10.11.1933		29	1959–1968	2,523	258	6	47.60	0	0-0	0/0	–	21	
Padmore Albert Leroy	17.12.1946		2	1975–1976	8	8*	0	8.00	1	1-36	0/0	135.00	0	
Pagon Donovan Jomo	13.9.1982		2	2004	37	35	0	12.33	0	–	–/–	–	0	
Pairaudeau Bruce Hamilton	14.4.1931		13	1952–1957	454	115	1	21.61	0	0-3	0/0	–	6	
Parchment Brenton Anthony	24.6.1982		2	2007	55	20	0	13.75	0	–	–/–	–	4	7/1
Parry Derick Recaldo	22.12.1954		12	1977–1979	381	65	0	22.41	23	5-15	1/0	40.69	4	6
Pascal Nelon Troy	25.4.1987		2	2010–2010	12	10	0	6.00	0	0-27	0/0	–	1	1
Passailaigue Charles Clarence	4.8.1901	7.1.1972	1	1929	46	44	0	46.00	0	0-15	0/0	–	0	
Patterson Balfour Patrick	15.9.1961		28	1985–1992	145	21*	0	6.59	93	5-24	5/0	30.90	3	59
Paul Keemo Mandela Angus	21.2.1997		3	2018–2018	75	47	0	18.75	3	2-25	0/0	40.00	1	11/13
Payne Thelston Rodney O'Neale	13.2.1957		1	1985	5	5	0	5.00	–	–	–/–	–	5	7
Permaul Veerasammy	11.8.1989		6	2012–2015	98	23*	0	12.25	18	3-32	0/0	43.77	2	7/1
Perry Nehemiah Odolphus	16.6.1968		4	1998–1999	74	26	0	12.33	10	5-70	1/0	44.60	1	21

	Born	Died	Tests	Test Career	Runs	HS	100s	Avge	Wkts	BB	5/10	Avge	Ct/St	O/T
Peters Keon Kenroy	24.2.1982		1	2014		0	0	0.00	0	2-69	0/0	34.50	0	1
Phillips Norbert	12.6.1948		9	1977–1978	297	47	0	29.70	28	4-48	0/0	37.17	5	
Phillips Omar Jamel	12.10.1986		2	2009	160	94	0	40.00	0	–	–/–		1	
Pierre Lancelot Richard	5.6.1921	14.4.1989	1	1947	–	–	–		0	0-9	0/0	–	0	
Powell Daren Brentlyle	15.4.1978		37	2002–2008	407	36*	0	7.82	85	5-25	1/0	47.85	8	55/5
Powell Kieran Omar Akeem	6.3.1990		40	2011–2018	2,011	134	2	26.81	0	0-0	0/0		29	46/1
Powell Ricardo Lloyd	16.12.1978		2	1999–2003	53	30	0	17.66	0	0-13	0/0	–	–	109
Rae Allan Fitzroy	30.9.1922	27.2.2005	15	1948–1952	1,016	109	4	46.18	0	–	–/–	–	10	
Ragoonath Suruj	22.3.1968		1	1998	13	9	0	4.33	0	–	–/–	–	–	
Ramadhin Sonny (CY 1951)	1.5.1929		43	1950–1960	361	44	0	8.20	158	7-49	10/1	28.98	9	
Ramdass Ryan Rakesh	3.7.1983		1	2005	26	23	0	13.00	0	–	–/–	–	2	1
Ramdin Denesh	13.3.1985		74	2005–2015	2,898	166	4	25.87	0	0-0	0/0	–	205/12	139/68
Ranmarine Dinanath	4.6.1975		12	1997–2001	106	35*	0	6.23	45	5-78	1/0	30.73	8	4
Rampaul Ravindranath	15.10.1984		18	2009–2012	335	40*	0	14.56	49	4-48	0/0	34.79	3	92/23
Reifer Floyd Lamonte	23.7.1972		6	1996–2009	111	29	0	9.25	0	–	–/–	–	6	8/1
Reifer Raymon Anton	11.5.1991		1	2017	52	29	0	52.00	2	1-36	0/0	44.00	0	
Richards Dale Maurice	16.7.1976		3	2009–2010	125	69	0	20.83	0	–	–/–	–	4	8/1
Richards Sir Isaac Vivian Alexander (CY 1977)	7.3.1952		121	1974–1991	8,540	291	24	50.23	32	2-17	0/0	61.37	122	187
Richardson Sir Richard Benjamin (CY 1992)	12.1.1962		86	1983–1995	5,949	194	16	44.39	0	0-0	0/0	–	90	224
Rickards Kenneth Roy	22.8.1923	21.8.1995	2	1947–1951	104	67	0	34.66	0	–	–/–	–	–	
Roach Clifford Archibald	13.3.1904	16.4.1988	16	1928–1934	952	209	2	30.70	2	1-18	0/0	51.50	5	
Roach Kemar Andre Jamal	30.6.1988		50	2009–2018	776	41	0	11.93	166	6-48	8/1	28.61	12	80/11
Roberts Alphonso Theodore	18.9.1937	24.7.1996	1	1955	28	28	0	14.00	0	0-0	0/0	–	2	
Roberts Sir Anderson Montgomery Everton CBE (CY 1975)	29.1.1951		47	1973–1983	762	68	0	14.94	202	7-54	11/2	25.61	9	56
Roberts Lincoln Abraham	4.9.1974		1	1998	0	0	0	0.00	0	–	–/–	–	0	
Rodriguez William Vicente	25.6.1934		5	1961–1967	96	50	0	13.71	7	3-51	0/0	53.42	3	27
Rose Franklyn Albert	1.2.1972		19	1996–2000	344	69	0	13.23	53	7-84	2/0	30.88	4	11
Rowe Lawrence George	8.1.1949		30	1971–1979	2,047	302	7	43.55	0	0-1	0/0	–	17	
Russell Andre Dwayne	29.4.1988		1	2010	18	12	0	2.00	1	1-73	0/0	104.00	1	52/47
[20] **St Hill Edwin Lloyd**	9.3.1904	21.5.1957	2	1929	2	12	0	4.50	3	2-110	0/0	73.66	–	
St Hill Wilton H.	6.7.1893	d unknown	3	1928–1929	117	38	0	19.50	0	0-9	0/0	–	0	
Sammy Darren Julius Garvey	20.12.1983		38	2007–2013	1,323	106	1	21.68	84	7-66	4/0	35.79	65	126/66‡
[21] **Samuels Marlon Nathaniel** ‡	5.1.1981		71	2000–2016	3,917	260	7	32.64	41	4-13	0/0	59.63	28	207/67
[22] **Samuels Robert George**	13.3.1971		6	1995–1996	372	125	0	37.20	0	–	–/–	–	4	8
Sanford Adam	12.7.1975		11	2001–2003	72	18*	0	4.80	30	4-132	0/0	43.86	0	

	Born	Died	Tests	Test Career	Runs	HS	100s	Avge	Wkts	BB	5/10	Avge	Ct/St	O/T
Sarwan Rammaresh Ronnie	23.6.1980		87	1999–2011	5,842	291	15	40.01	23	4-37	0/0	50.56	53	181/18
Scarlett Reginald Osmond	15.8.1934	15.6.1961	3	1959	54	29*	0	18.00	2	1-46	0/0	104.50	2	
‡**Scott Alfred Homer Patrick**	29.7.1934	12.9.1963	1	1952	5	5	0	5.00	0	0-52	0/0	–	0	
Scott Oscar Charles ("Tommy")	14.8.1892	3.1.1982	8	1928–1930	171	35	0	17.10	22	5-266	1/0	42.04	0	
Sealey Benjamin James	12.8.1899		1	1933	41	29	0	20.50	1	1-10	0/0	10.00	0	
Sealy James Edward Derrick	11.9.1912		11	1929–1939	478	92	0	28.11	3	2-7	0/0	31.33	6/1	
Shepherd John Neil (*CY 1979*)	9.11.1943		5	1969–1970	77	32	0	9.62	19	5-104	1/0	25.21	4	
Shillingford Grayson Cleophas	25.9.1944	23.12.2009	7	1969–1971	57	25	0	8.14	15	3-63	0/0	35.80	2	
Shillingford Irvine Theodore	18.4.1944		4	1976–1977	218	120	1	31.14	–	–	–	–	1	2
Shillingford Shane	22.2.1983		16	2010–2014	266	53*	0	13.30	70	6-49	6/2	34.55	9	
Shivnarine Sewdatt	13.5.1952		8	1977–1978	379	63	0	29.15	1	1-13	0/0	167.00	6	1
Simmons Lendl Mark Platter	25.1.1985		8	2008–2011	278	49	0	17.37	1	1-60	0/0	147.00	5	68/45
Simmons Philip Verant (*CY 1997*)	18.4.1963		26	1987–1997	1,002	110	1	22.26	4	2-34	0/0	64.25	26	143
Singh Charran Kamkaran	27.11.1935	19.11.2015	2	1959	11	11	0	3.66	5	2-28	0/0	33.20	2	
Singh Vishaul Anthony	12.11.1989		3	2016	63	32	0	10.50	–	–	–	–	2	
Small Joseph A.	3.11.1892	26.4.1958	3	1928–1929	79	52	0	13.16	3	2-67	0/0	61.33	3	
Small Milton Anthony	12.2.1964		2	1983–1984	3	3*	0	–	4	3-40	0/0	38.25	0	2
Smith Cameron Wilberforce	29.7.1933		5	1960–1961	222	55	0	24.66	–	–	–	–	4/1	
Smith Devon Sheldon	21.10.1981		43	2002–2018	1,760	108	1	23.78	0	0-3	0/0	–	36	47/6
Smith Dwayne Romel	12.4.1983		10	2003–2005	320	105*	1	24.61	7	3-71	0/0	49.14	9	105/33
Smith O'Neil Gordon ("Collie") (*CY 1958*)	5.5.1933	9.9.1959	26	1954–1958	1,331	168	4	31.69	48	5-90	1/0	33.85	9	
Sobers Sir Garfield St Aubrun (*CY 1964*)	28.7.1936		93	1953–1973	8,032	365*	26	57.78	235	6-73	6/0	34.03	109	1
Solomon Joseph Stanislaus	26.8.1930		27	1958–1964	1,326	100*	1	34.00	4	1-20	0/0	67.00	13	
Stayers Sven Conrad ("Charlie")	9.6.1937	6.1.2005	4	1961	58	35*	0	19.33	9	3-65	0/0	40.44	0	
‡**Stollmeyer Jeffrey Baxter**	11.3.1921	10.9.1989	32	1939–1954	2,159	160	4	42.33	13	3-32	0/0	39.00	20	
Stollmeyer Victor Humphrey	24.1.1916	21.9.1999	1	1939	96	96	0	96.00	–	–	–	–	0	
Stuart Colin Ellsworth Laurie	28.9.1973		6	2000–2001	24	12*	0	3.42	20	3-33	0/0	31.40	2	5
Taylor Jaswick Ossie	3.1.1932	13.11.1999	3	1957–1958	4	4*	0	2.00	10	5-109	1/0	27.30	0	
Taylor Jerome Everton	22.6.1984		46	2003–2015	856	106	1	12.96	130	6-47	4/0	34.46	8	90/30
Thompson Patterson Ian Chesterfield	26.9.1971		2	1995–1996	17	10*	0	8.50	5	2-58	0/0	43.00	0	2
Tonge Gavin Courtney	13.2.1983		1	2009	25	23*	1	25.00	1	1-28	0/0	113.00	0	5/1
Trim John	25.1.1915	12.11.1960	4	1947–1951	21	12	0	5.25	18	5-34	1/0	16.16	2	
Valentine Alfred Louis (*CY 1951*)	28.4.1930	11.5.2004	36	1950–1961	141	14	0	4.70	139	8-104	8/2	30.32	13	
Valentine Vincent Adolphus	4.4.1908	6.7.1972	2	1933	35	19*	0	11.66	1	1-55	0/0	104.00	0	
Walcott Sir Clyde Leopold (*CY 1958*)	17.1.1926	26.8.2006	44	1947–1959	3,798	220	15	56.68	11	3-50	0/0	37.09	53/11	
Walcott Leslie Arthur	18.1.1894	27.2.1984	1	1929	40	24	0	40.00	1	1-17	0/0	32.00	0	

Name	Born	Died	Tests	Test Career	Runs	HS	100s	Avge	Wkts	BB	5/10	Avge	Ct/St	O/T
Wallace Philo Alphonso	2.8.1970		7	1997–1998	279	92	0	21.46			–/–		9	33
Walsh Courtney Andrew (CY 1987)	30.10.1962		132	1984–2000	936	30*	0	7.54	519	7-37	22/3	24.44	29	205
Walton Chadwick Antonio Kirkpatrick	3.7.1985		2	2009	13	10	0	3.25			–/–		10	9/119
Warrican Jomel Andrel	20.5.1992		7	2015–2018	138	41	0	27.60	21	4-62	00	38.38	2	
Washington Dwight Marlon	5.3.1938		1	2004	7	7*	0	–		0-20	00	–	3	
Watson Chester Donald	1.7.1938		7	1959–1961	12	5	0	2.40	19	4-62	00	38.10		
Weekes Sir Everton de Courcy (CY 1951)	26.2.1925		48	1947–1957	4,455	207	15	58.61			–/–		49	
Weekes Kenneth Hunnell	24.1.1912	9.2.1998	2	1939	173	137	1	57.66	1	1-8	00	77.00	1	
White Anthony Wilbur	20.11.1938		2	1964	71	57*	0	23.66	3	2-34	00	50.66	1	
Wight Claude Vibart	28.7.1902	4.10.1969	4	1928–1929	67	23	0	22.33		0-6	00	–	0	
Wight George Leslie	28.5.1929	4.1.2004	2	1952	21	21	0	21.00			–/–		0	
Wiles Charles Archibald	11.8.1892	4.11.1957	1	1933	2	2	0	1.00			–/–		0	
Willett Elquemedo Tonito	1.5.1953		5	1972–1974	74	26	0	14.80	11	3-33	00	43.81	0	
Williams Alvadon Basil	21.11.1949	25.10.2015	7	1977–1978	469	111	2	39.08			–/–		5	
Williams David	4.11.1963		11	1991–1997	242	65	0	13.44			–/–		40/2	36
Williams Ernest Albert Vivian ("Foffie")	10.4.1914	13.4.1997	10	1939–1947	113	72	0	18.83	9	3-51	00	26.77	2	
Wishart Stuart Clayton	12.8.1969		31	1992–2001	1,183	128	1	24.14		0-19	00	–	27	57
Wishart Kenneth Leslie	28.11.1908	18.10.1972	2	1934	52	52	0	26.00			–/–		0	
Worrell Sir Frank Mortimer Maglinne (CY 1951)	1.8.1924	13.3.1967	51	1947–1963	3,860	261	9	49.48	69	7-70	2/0	38.72	43	

NEW ZEALAND (275 players)

Name	Born	Died	Tests	Test Career	Runs	HS	100s	Avge	Wkts	BB	5/10	Avge	Ct/St	O/T
Adams Andre Ryan	17.7.1975		1	2001	18	11	0	9.00	6	3-44	00	17.50	1	42/4
Alabaster John Chaloner	11.7.1930		21	1955–1971	272	34	0	9.71	49	4-46	00	38.02	3	
Allcott Cyril Francis Walter	7.10.1896	19.11.1973	6	1929–1931	113	33	0	22.60	6	2-102	00	90.16	3	
Allott Geoffrey Ian	24.12.1971		10	1995–1999	27	8*	0	3.37	19	4-74	00	58.47	2	31
Anderson Corey James	13.12.1990		13	2013–2015	683	116	1	32.52	16	3-47	00	41.18	7	49/31
Anderson Robert Wickham	2.10.1948		9	1976–1978	423	92	0	23.50			–/–		1	2
Anderson William McDougall	8.10.1919	21.12.1979	1	1945	5	4	0	2.50			–/–		0	
Andrews Bryan	4.4.1945		2	1973	22	17	0	22.00	2	2-40	00	77.00	0	
Arnel Brent John	3.1.1979		9	2009–2011	45	8*	0	5.62	9	4-95	00	62.88	3	
Astle Nathan John	15.9.1971		81	1995–2006	4,702	222	11	37.02	51	3-27	00	42.01	70	223/4
Astle Todd Duncan	24.9.1986		4	2012–2017	56	35	0	14.00	4	3-39	00	37.00	2	6/2
Badcock Frederick Theodore ("Ted")	9.8.1897	19.9.1982	7	1929–1932	137	64	0	19.57	16	4-80	00	38.12	1	

	Born	Died	Tests	Test Career	Runs	HS	100s	Avge	Wkts	BB	5/10	Avge	Ct/St	O/T
Barber Richard Trevor	3.6.1925	7.8.2015	1	1955	17	12	0	8.50	—	—	—/—	—	1	
Bartlett Gary Alex	3.2.1941		10	1961–1967	263	40	0	15.47	24	6-38	1/0	33.00	8	
Barton Paul Thomas	9.10.1935		7	1961–1962	285	109	1	20.35	—	—	—/—	—	4	
Beard Donald Derek	14.1.1920	15.7.1982	9	1951–1955	101	31	0	20.20	9	3-22	0/0	33.55	2	
Beck John Edward Francis	1.8.1934	23.4.2000	8	1953–1955	394	99	0	26.26	—	—	—/—	—	0	
Bell Matthew David	25.2.1977		18	1998–2007	729	107	2	24.30	—	—	—/—	—	19	7
Bell William	5.9.1931		2	1953	21	21*	0	—	2	1-54	0/0	117.50	0	
Bennett Hamish Kyle	22.2.1987		1	2010	4	4	0	4.00	0	0-47	0/0	—	1	16
Bilby Grahame Paul	7.5.1941		2	1965	55	28	0	13.75	—	—	—/—	—	3	
Blain Tony Elston	17.2.1962		11	1986–1993	456	78	0	26.82	—	—	—/—	—	19/2	38
Blair Robert William	23.6.1932		19	1952–1963	189	64*	0	6.75	43	4-85	0/0	35.23	5	
Blundell Thomas Ackland	1.9.1990			2017	136	107*	0	68.00	—	—	—/—	—	5	0/3
Blunt Roger Charles (CY 1928)	3.11.1900	22.6.1966	9	1929–1931	330	96	0	27.50	12	3-17	0/0	39.33	5	
Bolton Bruce Alfred	31.5.1935		2	1958	59	33	0	19.66	—	—	—/—	—	—	
Bond Shane Edward	7.6.1975		18	2001–2009	168	41*	0	12.92	87	6-51	5/1	22.09	8	82/20
Boock Stephen Lewis	20.9.1951		30	1977–1988	207	37	0	6.27	74	7-87	4/0	34.64	14	14
Boult Trent Alexander	22.7.1989		59	2011–2018	562	52*	0	14.41	233	6-30	7/1	27.90	30	69/25
[1,2] **Bracewell Brendon Paul**	14.9.1959		6	1978–1984	24	8	0	2.40	14	3-110	0/0	41.78	—	1
[2] **Bracewell Douglas Alexander John**	28.9.1990		27	2011–2016	568	47	0	13.85	72	6-40	2/0	38.83	10	16/17
[2] **Bracewell John Garry**	15.4.1958		41	1980–1990	1,001	110	1	20.42	102	6-32	4/1	35.81	31	53
[1] **Bradburn Grant Eric**	26.5.1966		7	1990–2000	105	30*	0	13.12	6	3-134	0/0	76.66	6	11
Bradburn Wynne Pennell	24.11.1938	25.9.2008	2	1963	62	32	0	15.50	—	—	—/—	—	2	
[1] **Broom Neil Trevor**	20.11.1983		2	2016	32	20	0	10.66	—	—	—/—	—	0	39/11
Brown Vaughan Raymond	3.11.1959		2	1985	51	36*	0	25.50	1	1-17	0/0	176.00	3	3
Browning Dean Graham	30.7.1984		14	2011–2013	711	109	1	29.62	1	1-13	0/0	52.00	17	16/5
Burgess Mark Gordon	17.7.1944		50	1967–1980	2,684	119*	5	31.20	6	3-23	0/0	35.33	34	26
Burke Cecil	27.3.1914	4.8.1997	1	1945	4	3	0	2.00	2	2-30	0/0	15.00	0	
Burtt Thomas Browning	22.1.1915	24.5.1988	10	1946–1952	252	42	0	21.00	33	6-162	3/0	35.45	2	
Butler Ian Gareth	24.11.1981		8	2001–2004	76	26	0	9.50	24	6-46	1/0	36.83	4	26/19
Butterfield Leonard Arthur	29.8.1913	5.7.1999	1	1945	0	0	0	0.00	0	0-24	0/0	—	0	
[1] **Cairns Bernard Lance**	10.10.1949		43	1973–1985	928	64	0	16.28	130	7-74	6/1	32.91	30	78
[1] **Cairns Christopher Lance (CY 2000)**	13.6.1970		62	1989–2004	3,320	158	5	33.53	218	7-27	13/1	29.40	14	2142/2
Cameron Francis James MBE	1.6.1932		19	1961–1965	116	27*	0	11.60	62	5-34	3/0	29.82	1	
Cave Henry Butler	10.10.1922	15.9.1989	19	1949–1958	229	22*	0	8.80	34	4-21	0/0	43.14	8	
Chapple Murray Ernest	25.7.1930	31.7.1985	14	1952–1965	497	76	0	19.11	1	1-24	0/0	84.00	10	
Chatfield Ewen John MBE	3.7.1950		43	1974–1988	180	21*	0	8.57	123	6-73	3/1	32.17	7	114

	Born	Died	Tests	Test Career	Runs	HS	100s	Avge	Wkts	BB	5/10	Avge	Ct/St	O/T
Cleverley Donald Charles	23.12.1909	16.2.2004	2	1931–1945	19	10*	0	19.00	0	0-51	0/0	–		
Collinge Richard Owen	2.4.1946		35	1964–1978	533	68*	0	14.40	116	6-63	3/0	29.25	10	15
Colquhoun Ian Alexander	8.6.1924	26.2.2005	2	1954	1	1*	0	0.50					4	
Coney Jeremy Vernon MBE (CY 1984)	21.6.1952		52	1973–1986	2,668	174*	3	37.57	27	3-28	0/0	35.77	64	88
Congdon Bevan Ernest OBE (CY 1974)	11.2.1938	10.2.2018	61	1964–1978	3,448	176	7	32.22	59	5-65	1/0	36.50	44	11
Cowie John OBE	30.3.1912	3.6.1994	9	1937–1949	90	45	0	10.00	45	6-40	4/1	21.53	3	
Craig Mark Donald	23.3.1987		15	2014–2016	589	67	0	36.81	50	7-94	1/1	46.52	14	
Cresswell George Fenwick	22.3.1915	10.1.1966	3	1949–1950	14	12*	0	7.00	13	6-168	1/0	22.46	0	
Cromb Ian Burns	25.6.1905	6.3.1984	5	1931–1931	123	51*	0	20.50	8	3-113	0/0	55.25	1	
[2] Crowe Jeffrey John	14.9.1958		39	1982–1989	1,601	128	3	26.24	0	0-0	0/0	–	41	75
[2] Crowe Martin David MBE (CY 1985)	22.9.1962		77	1981–1995	5,444	299	17	45.36	14	2-25	0/0	48.28	71	143
Cumming Craig Derek	31.8.1975		11	2004–2007	441	74	0	25.94					3	13
Cunis Robert Smith	5.1.1941	9.8.2008	20	1963–1971	295	51	0	12.82	51	6-76	1/0	37.00		
D'Arcy John William	23.4.1936		5	1958	136	33	0	13.60						
Davis Heath Te-Ihi-O-Te-Rangi	30.11.1971		5	1994–1997	20	8*	0	6.66	17	5-63	1/0	29.35	4	11
de Grandhomme Colin	22.7.1986		15	2016–2018	721	105	1	32.77	31	6-41	1/0	29.96	10	22/22
de Groen Richard Paul	5.8.1962		5	1993–1994	45	26	0	7.50	11	3-40	0/0	45.90	2	12
Dempster Charles Stewart (CY 1932)	15.11.1903	14.2.1974	10	1929–1932	723	136	2	65.72	0	0-10	0/0	–	2	
Dempster Eric William MBE	25.1.1925	15.8.2011	5	1952–1953	106	47	0	17.66	2	1-24	0/0	109.50		
Dick Arthur Edward	10.10.1936		17	1961–1965	370	50*	0	14.23					47/4	
Dickinson George Ritchie	11.3.1903	17.3.1978	3	1929–1931	31	11	0	6.20	8	3-66	0/0	30.62	3	
Donnelly Martin Paterson (CY 1948)	17.10.1917	22.10.1999	7	1937–1949	582	206	1	52.90	0	0-20	0/0	–	7	
Doull Simon Blair	6.8.1969		32	1992–1999	570	46	0	14.61	98	7-65	6/0	29.30	16	42
Dowling Graham Thorne OBE	4.3.1937		39	1961–1971	2,306	239	3	31.16	1	1-19	0/0	19.00	23	
Drum Christopher James	10.7.1974		5	2000–2001	10	4	0	3.33	16	3-36	0/0	30.12	4	5
Dunning John Angus	6.2.1903	24.6.1971	4	1932–1937	38	19	0	7.60	5	2-35	0/0	98.60	2	
Edgar Bruce Adrian	23.11.1956		39	1978–1986	1,958	161	3	30.59	0	0-3	0/0	–	14	64
Edwards Graham Neil ("Jock")	27.5.1955		8	1976–1980	377	55	0	25.13					7	6
Elliott Grant David	21.3.1979		5	2007–2009	86	25	0	10.75	4	2-8	0/0	35.00	2	83/16‡
Emery Raymond William George	28.3.1915	18.12.1982	2	1951	46	28	0	11.50	2	2-52	0/0	26.00	0	
Fisher Frederick Eric	28.7.1924	19.6.1996	1	1952	23	14	0	11.50	1	1-78	0/0	78.00	0	
Fleming Stephen Paul	1.4.1973		111	1993–2007	7,172	274*	9	40.06	0	0-0	0/0	–	171	279¼/5
Flynn Daniel Raymond	16.4.1985		24	2008–2012	1,038	95	0	25.95					10	20/5
Foley Henry	28.11.1906	16.10.1948	1	1929	4	2*	0	2.00						
Franklin James Edward Charles	7.11.1980		31	2000–2012	808	122*	1	20.71	82	6-119	3/0	33.97	12	110/38
Franklin Trevor John	15.3.1962		21	1983–1990	828	101	1	23.00					8	3

	Born	Died	Tests	Test Career	Runs	HS	100s	Avge	Wkts	BB	5/10	Avge	Ct/St	O/T
Freeman Douglas Linford	8.9.1914	31.5.1994	1	1932	2	1	0	1.00	-	-	-/-	-	0	-
Fulton Peter Gordon	1.2.1979		23	2005–2014	967	136	2	25.44	1	1-91	0/0	169.00	25	49/12
Gallichan Norman	3.6.1906	25.3.1969	1	1937	32	30	0	16.00	3	3-99	0/0	37.66	0	-
Gedye Sidney Graham	2.5.1929	10.8.2014	4	1963–1964	193	55	0	24.12	-	-	-/-	-	0	-
Germon Lee Kenneth	4.11.1968		12	1995–1996	382	55	0	21.22	-	-	-/-	-	27/2	37
Gillespie Mark Raymond	17.10.1979		5	2007–2011	76	27	0	10.85	22	6-113	3/0	28.68	1	32/11
Gillespie Stuart Ross	2.3.1957		1	1985	28	28	0	28.00	-	-	-/-	-	0	19
Gray Evan John	18.11.1954		10	1983–1988	248	50	0	15.50	17	1-79	0/0	79.00	6	10
Greatbatch Mark John	11.12.1963		41	1987–1996	2,021	146*	3	30.62	0	3-73	0/0	52.11	27	84
Guillen Simpson Clairmonte ("Sammy")	24.9.1924	2.3.2013	3†	1955	98	41	0	16.33	-	-	-/-	-	4/1	-
Guptill Martin James	30.9.1986		47	2008–2016	2,586	189	3	29.38	8	3-11	0/0	37.25	50	159/75
Guy John William	29.8.1934		12	1955–1961	440	102	1	20.95	-	-	-/-	-	2	-
[1,2] Hadlee Dayle Robert	6.1.1948		26	1969–1977	530	56	0	14.32	71	4-30	0/0	33.64	8	11
[1,2] Hadlee Sir Richard John (CY 1982)	3.7.1951		86	1972–1990	3,124	151*	2	27.16	431	9-52	36/9	22.29	39	115
Hadlee Walter Arnold CBE	4.6.1915	29.9.2006	11	1937–1950	543	116	0	30.16	-	-	-/-	-	6	
Harford Noel Sherwin	30.8.1930	30.3.1981	8	1955–1958	229	93	0	15.26	-	-	-/-	-	0	
Harford Roy Ivan	30.5.1936		3	1967	7	6	0	2.33	-	-	-/-	-	11	
Harris Chris Zinzan	20.11.1969		23	1992–2002	777	71	0	20.44	16	2-16	0/0	73.12	14	250
Harris Parke Gerald Zinzan	18.7.1927	1.12.1991	9	1955–1964	378	101	0	22.23	0	0-14	0/0	-	6	
Harris Roger Meredith	27.7.1933		2	1958	31	13	0	10.33	-	-	-/-	-	0	
Hart Matthew Norman	16.5.1972		14	1993–1995	353	45	0	17.65	29	5-77	1/0	49.58	9	13
[2] Hart Robert Garry	2.12.1974		11	2002–2003	260	57*	0	16.25	-	-	-/-	-	29/1	2
Hartland Blair Robert	22.10.1966		9	1991–1994	303	52	0	16.83	-	-	-/-	-	5	16
Haslam Mark James	26.9.1972		4	1992–1995	4	3	0	4.00	2	1-33	0/0	122.50	1	1
Hastings Brian Frederick	23.3.1940		31	1968–1975	1,510	117*	4	30.20	0	0-3	0/0	-	23	11
Hayes John Arthur	11.1.1927	25.12.2007	15	1950–1958	73	19	0	4.86	30	4-36	0/0	40.56	3	
Henderson Matthew	2.8.1895	17.6.1970	1	1929	8	6	0	8.00	2	2-38	0/0	32.00	1	
Henry Matthew James	14.12.1991		9	2015–2017	216	66	0	19.63	25	4-93	0/0	46.52	5	36/6
Hopkins Gareth James	24.11.1976		4	2008–2010	71	15	0	11.83	-	-	-/-	-	9/17	25/10
[2] Horne Matthew Jeffery	5.12.1970		35	1996–2003	1,788	157	4	28.38	0	0-4	0/0	-	3	50
Horne Philip Andrew	21.1.1960		4	1986–1990	71	27	0	10.14	-	-	-/-	-		
Hough Kenneth William	24.10.1928	20.9.2009	2	1958	62	31*	0	62.00	6	3-79	0/0	29.16		4
How Jamie Michael	19.5.1981		19	2005–2008	772	92	0	22.70	0	0-0	0/0	-	18	41/5
[2] Howarth Geoffrey Philip OBE	29.3.1951		47	1974–1984	2,531	147	6	32.44	3	1-13	0/0	90.33	29	70
[2] Howarth Hedley John	25.12.1943	7.11.2008	30	1969–1976	291	61	0	12.12	86	5-34	2/0	36.95	33	9
Ingram Peter John	25.10.1978		2	2009	61	42	0	15.25	-	-	-/-	-	0	8/3

Name	Born	Died	Tests	Test Career	Runs	HS	100s	Avge	Wkts	BB	5/10	Avge	Ct/St	O/T
James Kenneth Cecil	12.3.1904	21.8.1976	11	1929–1932	52	14	0	4.72	0	0-0	0/0	–	11/5	
Jarvis Terrence Wayne	29.7.1944		13	1964–1972	625	182	1	29.76	–		–/–		3	
Jones Andrew Howard	9.5.1959		39	1986–1994	2,922	186	7	44.27	1	1-40	0/0	194.00	25	87
Jones Richard Andrew	22.10.1973		1	2003	23	16	0	11.50	–		–/–		0	5
Kennedy Robert John	3.6.1972		4	1995	28	22	0	7.00	6	3-28	0/0	63.33	2	7
Kerr John Lambert	28.12.1910	27.5.2007	7	1931–1937	212	59	0	19.27	–		–/–		4	
Kuggeleijn Christopher Mary	10.5.1956		2	1988	7	7	0	1.75	1	1-50	0/0	67.00		16
Larsen Gavin Rolf	27.9.1962		8	1994–1995	127	26*	0	14.11	24	3-57	0/0	28.70	5	121
[1]Latham Rodney Terry	12.6.1961		4	1991–1992	219	119	0	31.28	0	0-6	0/0	–	1	33
Latham Thomas William Maxwell	2.4.1992		41	2013–2018	2,953	264*	8	41.59	–		–/–		41	77/13
Lees Warren Kenneth MBE	19.3.1952		21	1976–1983	778	152	0	23.57	0	0-4	0/0	–	52/7	31
Leggat Ian Bruce	7.6.1930		1	1953	0	0	0	0.00	0	0-6	0/0	–	2	
Leggat John Gordon	27.5.1926	9.3.1973	9	1951–1955	351	61	0	21.93	3	2-73	0/0	41.33		
Lissette Allen Fisher	6.11.1919	24.1.1973	1	1955	2	1*	0	1.00	–		–/–			
Loveridge Greg Riaka	15.1.1975		1	1995	4	4*	0	–	–		–/–			
Lowry Thomas Coleman	17.2.1898	20.7.1976	7	1929–1931	223	80	0	27.87	0	0-0	0/0	–	8	
McCullum Brendon Barrie (CY 2016)	27.9.1981		101	2003–2015	6,453	302	12	38.64	1	1-1	0/0	88.00	198/11	260/71
McEwan Paul Ernest	19.12.1953		4	1979–1984	96	40*	0	16.00	0	0-6	0/0	–	5	17
MacGibbon Anthony Roy	28.8.1924	6.4.2010	26	1950–1958	814	66	0	19.85	70	5-64	1/0	30.85	13	
McGirr Herbert Mendelson	5.11.1891	14.4.1964	2	1929	51	51	0	51.00	1	1-65	0/0	115.00		
McGregor Spencer Noel	18.12.1931	21.11.2007	25	1954–1964	892	111	1	19.82	–		–/–		9	
McIntosh Timothy Gavin	4.12.1979		17	2008–2010	854	136	1	27.54	–		–/–		10	19/2
McKay Andrew John	17.4.1980		1	2010	25	20*	0	25.00	1	1-120	0/0	120.00		
McLeod Edwin George	14.10.1900	14.9.1989	1	1929	18	16	0	18.00	–		–/–			
McMahon Trevor George	8.11.1929		5	1955	7	4*	0	2.33	–		–/–		7/1	
McMillan Craig Douglas	13.9.1976		55	1997–2004	3,116	142	6	38.46	28	3-48	0/0	44.89	22	197/8
McRae Donald Alexander Noel	25.12.1912	10.8.1986	1	1945	8	8	0	4.00	0	0-44	0/0	–		
[2]Marshall Hamish John Hamilton	15.2.1979		13	2000–2005	652	160	1	38.35	0	0-4	0/0	–	1	66/3
Marshall James Andrew Hamilton	15.2.1979		7	2004–2008	218	52	0	19.81	–		–/–		5	10/3
Martin Bruce Philip	25.4.1980		5	2012–2013	74	41	0	14.80	12	4-43	0/0	53.83		
Martin Christopher Stewart	10.12.1974		71	2000–2012	123	12*	0	2.36	233	6-26	10/1	33.81	14	20/6
Mason Michael James	27.8.1974		1	2003	3	3	0	1.50	0	0-32	0/0	–		26/3
Matheson Alexander Malcolm	27.2.1906	31.12.1985	2	1929–1931	7	7	0	7.00	2	2-7	0/0	68.00	2	
Meale Trevor	11.11.1928	21.5.2010	1	1958	21	10	0	5.25	–		–/–		2	
Merritt William Edward	18.8.1908	9.6.1977	6	1929–1931	73	19	0	10.42	12	4-104	0/0	51.41	2	
Meuli Edgar Milton	20.2.1926	15.4.2007	1	1952	38	23	0	19.00	–		–/–		0	

Name	Born	Died	Tests	Test Career	Runs	HS	100s	Avge	Wkts	BB	5i10	Avge	Ct/St	O/T
Milburn Barry Douglas	24.11.1943	17.12.1996	3	1968	8	4*	0	8.00	0	–	–	–	6/2	–
Miller Lawrence Somerville Martin	31.3.1923	11.12.1996	13	1952–1958	346	47	0	13.84	0	–	–/–	–	1	–
Mills John Ernest	3.9.1905	11.12.1972	7	1929–1932	241	117	1	26.77	0	0–1	0/0	–	1	–
Mills Kyle David	15.3.1979		19	2004–2008	289	57	0	11.56	44	4-16	0/0	33.02	4	170/42
Moir Alexander McKenzie	17.7.1919	17.6.2000	17	1950–1958	327	41*	0	14.86	28	6-155	2/0	50.64	2	–
Moloney Denis Andrew Robert ("Sonny")	11.8.1910	15.7.1942	3	1937	156	64	0	26.00	0	0-9	0/0	–	3	–
Mooney Francis Leonard Hugh	26.5.1921		14	1949–1953	343	46	0	17.15	0	–	–	–	22/8	–
Morgan Ross Winston	12.2.1941		20	1964–1971	734	97	0	22.24	5	1-16	0/0	121.80	10	–
Morrison Bruce Donald	17.12.1933		1	1962	10	10	0	5.00	2	2-129	0/0	64.50	1	–
Morrison Daniel Kyle	3.2.1966		48	1987–1996	379	42	0	8.42	160	7-89	10/0	34.68	14	96
Morrison John Francis MacLean	27.8.1947		17	1973–1981	656	117	1	22.62	2	2-52	0/0	35.50	9	18
Motz Richard Charles (CY 1966)	12.1.1940	29.4.2007	32	1961–1969	612	60	0	11.54	100	6-63	5/0	31.48	9	–
Munro Colin	11.3.1987		1	2012	15	15	0	7.50	2	2-40	0/0	20.00	0	43/48
Murray Bruce Alexander Grenfell	18.9.1940		13	1967–1970	598	90	0	23.92	1	1-0	0/0	0.00	21	–
Murray Darrin James	4.9.1967		8	1994	303	52	0	20.20	0	–	–/–	–	6	1
Nash Dion Joseph	20.11.1971		32	1992–2001	729	89*	0	23.51	93	6-27	3/1	28.48	13	81
Neesham James Douglas Sheehan	17.9.1990		12	2013–2016	709	137*	2	33.76	14	3-42	0/0	48.21	12	41/15
Newman Sir Jack	3.7.1902	23.9.1996	3	1931–1932	33	19	0	8.25	2	2-76	0/0	127.00	0	–
Nicholls Henry Michael	15.11.1991		23	2015–2018	1,350	162*	4	43.54	0	–	–	–	17	3/4
Nicol Robert James	28.5.1983		2	2011	28	19	0	7.00	0	0-0	0/0	–	2	22/21
O'Brien Iain Edward	10.7.1976		10	2004–2009	219	31	0	7.55	73	6-75	1/0	33.27	6	10/4
O'Connor Shayne Barry	15.11.1973		19	1997–2001	103	20	0	5.72	53	5-51	1/0	32.52	6	38
Oram Jacob David Philip	28.7.1978		33	2002–2009	1,780	133	5	36.32	60	4-41	0/0	33.05	15	160/36
O'Sullivan David Robert	16.11.1944		11	1972–1976	158	23*	0	9.29	18	5-148	1/0	67.83	2	3
Overton Guy William Fitzroy	8.6.1919	7.9.1993	3	1953	8	3*	0	1.60	9	3-65	0/0	28.66	–	–
Owens Michael Barry	11.11.1969		8	1992–1994	16	8*	0	2.66	17	4-99	0/0	34.41	3	1
Page Milford Laurenson ("Curly")	8.5.1902	13.2.1987	14	1929–1937	492	104	1	24.60	5	2-21	0/0	46.20	6	–
Papps Michael Hugh William	2.7.1979		8	2003–2007	246	86	0	16.40	0	–	–/–	–	11	6
Parker John Morton	21.2.1951		36	1972–1980	1,498	121	3	24.55	1	1-24	0/0	24.00	30	24
²Parker Norman Murray	28.8.1948		3	1976	89	40	0	14.83	0	–	–/–	–	4	–
Parore Adam Craig	23.1.1971		78	1990–2001	2,865	110	2	26.28	0	–	–	–	197/7	179
Patel Ajaz Yunus	21.10.1988		5	2018	35	6*	0	7.00	13	5-59	1/0	35.84	4	0/2
Patel Dipak Narshibhai	25.10.1958		37	1986–1996	1,200	99	0	20.68	75	6-50	3/0	42.05	15	75
Patel Jeetan Shashi (CY 2015)	7.5.1980		24	2005–2016	381	47	0	12.70	65	5-110	1/0	47.35	13	43/11
Petherick Peter James	25.9.1942	7.6.2015	6	1976	34	13	0	4.85	16	3-90	0/0	42.81	4	–
Petrie Eric Charlton	22.5.1927	14.8.2004	14	1955–1965	258	55	0	12.90	–	–	–/–	–	25	–

	Born	Died	Tests	Test Career	Runs	HS	100s	Avge	Wkts	BB	5/10	Avge	Ct/St	O/T
Playle William Rodger	1.12.1938	7.6.1996	8	1958–1962	151	65	0	10.06	0	—	–/–	—	4	—
Pocock Blair Andrew	18.6.1971		15	1993–1997	665	85	0	22.93	0	0-10	0/0	—	5	—
Pollard Victor	7.9.1945		32	1964–1973	1,266	116	2	24.34	40	3-3	0/0	46.32	19	3
Poore Matt Beresford	1.6.1930		14	1952–1955	355	45	0	15.43	9	2-28	0/0	40.77	1	—
Priest Mark Wellings	12.8.1961		3	1990–1997	56	26	0	14.00	3	2-42	0/0	52.66	1	18
Pringle Christopher	26.1.1968		14	1990–1994	175	30	0	10.29	30	7-52	1/1	46.30	3	64
Puna Narotam ("Tom")	28.10.1929	7.6.1996	3	1965	31	18*	0	15.50	4	2-40	0/0	60.00	1	—
Rabone Geoffrey Osborne	6.11.1921	19.1.2006	12	1949–1954	562	107	1	31.22	16	6-68	1/0	39.68	5	—
Raval Jeet Ashokbhai	22.5.1988		16	2016–2018	902	88	0	34.69	0	0-1	0/0	—	16	—
Redmond Aaron James	23.9.1979		8	2008–2013	325	83	0	21.66	3	2-47	0/0	26.66	5	67
Redmond Rodney Ernest	29.12.1944		1	1972	163	107	1	81.50	0	—	–/–	—	—	2
Reid John Fulton	3.3.1956		19	1978–1985	1,296	180	6	46.28	0	0-0	0/0	—	9	25
Reid John Richard OBE *(CY 1959)*	3.6.1928		58	1949–1965	3,428	142	6	33.28	85	6-60	1/0	33.35	43/1	—
Richardson Mark Hunter	11.6.1971		38	2000–2004	2,776	145	4	44.77	1	1-16	0/0	21.00	26	4
Roberts Albert William	20.8.1909	13.5.1978	5	1929–1937	248	66*	0	27.55	7	4-101	0/0	29.85	4	—
Roberts Andrew Duncan Glenn	6.5.1947	26.10.1989	7	1975–1976	254	84*	0	23.09	4	1-12	0/0	45.50	4	1
Robertson Gary Keith	15.7.1960		1	1985	12	12	0	12.00	1	1-91	0/0	91.00	—	10
Ronchi Luke	23.4.1981		4	2015–2016	319	88	0	39.87	—	—	–/–	—	5	81†/29‡
Rowe Charles Gordon	30.6.1915	9.6.1995	1	1945	0	0	0	0.00	—	—	–/–	—	—	—
Rutherford Hamish Duncan	27.4.1989		16	2012–2014	755	171	1	26.96	0	0-2	0/0	—	11	4/7
Rutherford Kenneth Robert	26.10.1965		56	1984–1994	2,465	107*	3	27.08	1	1-38	0/0	161.00	32	121
Ryder Jesse Daniel	6.8.1984		18	2008–2011	1,269	201	3	40.93	5	2-7	0/0	56.00	12	48/22
Santner Mitchell Josef	5.2.1992		17	2015–2017	535	73	0	25.47	34	3-60	0/0	37.05	12	53/27
Scott Roy Hamilton	6.3.1917	5.8.2005	1	1946	18	18	0	18.00	1	1-74	0/0	74.00	—	—
Scott Verdun John	31.7.1916	2.8.1980	10	1945–1951	458	84	0	28.62	0	0-5	0/0	—	7	—
Sewell David Graham	20.10.1977		1	1997	1	1*	0	—	0	0-9	0/0	—	—	—
Shrimpton Michael John Froud	23.6.1940	13.6.2015	10	1962–1973	265	46	0	13.94	5	3-35	0/0	31.60	2	—
Sinclair Barry Whitley	23.10.1936		21	1962–1967	1,148	138	3	29.43	2	2-32	0/0	16.00	8	—
Sinclair Ian McKay	1.6.1933		2	1955	25	18*	0	8.33	1	1-79	0/0	120.00	—	—
Sinclair Mathew Stuart	9.11.1975		33	1999–2009	1,635	214	3	32.05	0	0-1	0/0	—	31	54/2
Smith Frank Brunton	13.3.1922	6.7.1997	4	1946–1951	237	96	0	47.40	1	1-113	0/0	113.00	0	—
Smith Horace Dennis	8.1.1913	25.11.1986	1	1932	4	4	0	4.00	0	0-113	0/0	—	2	—
Smith Ian David Stockley MBE	28.2.1957		63	1980–1991	1,815	173	2	25.56	—	—	–/–	—	168/8	98
Snedden Colin Alexander MBE	7.1.1918	23.4.2011	1	1946	—	—	—	—	0	0-46	0/0	—	0	—
Snedden Martin Colin	23.11.1958		25	1980–1990	327	33*	0	14.86	58	5-68	1/0	37.91	7	93
Sodhi Inderbir Singh ("Ish")	31.10.1992		17	2013–2018	448	63	0	21.33	41	4-60	1/0	48.58	11	25/29

	Born	Died	Test Career	Tests	Runs	HS	100s	Avge	Wkts	BB	5/10	Avge	Ct/St	OIT
Somerville William Edgar Richard	9.8.1984		2018	1	16	16		8.00	7	4-75	0/0	18.14	0	135/54
Southee Timothy Grant	11.12.1988		2007–2018	63	1,550	77*		18.02	237	7-64	8/1	29.93	43	
Sparling John Trevor	24.7.1938		1958–1963	11	229	50		12.72	5	1-9	0/0	65.40	4	
Spearman Craig Murray	4.7.1972		1995–2000	19	922	112	1	26.34					21	51
Stead Gary Raymond	9.1.1972		1998–1999	5	278	78		34.75		0-1			2	
Stirling Derek Alexander	5.10.1961		1984–1986	6	108	26		15.42	13	4-88	0/0	46.23	1	6
Styris Scott Bernard	10.7.1975		2002–2007	29	1,586	170	5	36.04	20	3-28	0/0	50.75	23	188/31
Su'a Murphy Logo	7.11.1966		1991–1994	13	165	44		12.69	36	5-73	2/0	38.25	8	12
Sutcliffe Bert MBE (CY 1950)	17.11.1923	20.4.2001	1946–1965	42	2,727	230*	5	40.10	4	2-38	0/0	86.00	20	
Taylor Bruce Richard	12.7.1943		1964–1973	30	898	124	2	20.40	111	7-74	4/0	26.60	10	2
Taylor Donald Dougald	2.3.1923	5.12.1980	1946–1955	3	159	77		31.80					2	
Taylor Luteru Ross Poutoa Lote	8.3.1984		2007–2018	90	6,523	290	17	45.93	2	2-4	0/0	24.00	131	207/84
Thomson Keith	26.2.1941		1967	2	94	69		31.33	1	1-9	0/0	9.00	2	
Thomson Shane Alexander	27.1.1969		1989–1995	19	958	120*	1	30.90	19	3-63	0/0	50.15	7	56
Tindill Eric William Thomas	18.12.1910	1.8.2010	1937–1946	5	73	37*		9.12					6/1	
Troup Gary Bertram	3.10.1952		1976–1985	15	55	13*		4.58	39	6-95	1/1	37.28	2	22
Truscott Peter Bennetts	14.8.1941		1964	1	29	26		14.50					2	
Tuffey Daryl Raymond	11.6.1978		1999–2009	26	427	80*		16.42	77	6-54	2/0	31.75	15	94/3
Turner Glenn Maitland (CY 1971)	26.5.1947		1968–1982	41	2,991	259	7	44.64	0	0-5	0/0		42	41
Twose Roger Graham	17.4.1968		1995–1999	16	628	94		25.12	3	2-36	0/0	43.33	5	87
Vance Robert Howard	31.3.1955		1987–1989	4	207	68		29.57	0				0	8
Van Wyk Cornelius Francois Kruger	7.2.1980		2011–2012	9	341	71		21.31					23/1	
Vaughan Justin Thomas Caldwell	30.8.1967		1992–1996	6	201	44		18.27	11	4-27	0/0	40.90	0	18
Vettori Daniel Luca	27.1.1979		1996–2014	112§	4,523	140	6	30.15	361	7-87	20/3	34.15	58	291±/34
Vincent Lou	11.11.1978		2001–2007	23	1,332	224	3	34.15	1	0-2	0/0	107.00	19	102/9
Vivian Graham Ellery	28.2.1946		1964–1971	5	110	43		18.33	1	1-14	0/0		3	
Vivian Henry Gifford	4.11.1912	12.8.1983	1931–1937	7	421	100	1	42.10	17	4-58	0/0	37.23	4	13
Wadsworth Kenneth John	30.11.1946	19.8.1976	1969–1975	33	1,010	80		21.48					92/4	
Wagner Neil	13.3.1986		2012–2018	40	464	37		11.60	158	7-39	5/0	28.88	10	13
Walker Brooke Graeme Keith	25.3.1977		2000–2002	5	118	27*		19.66	5	2-92	0/0	79.80	0	11
Wallace Walter Mervyn	19.12.1916	21.3.2008	1937–1952	13	439	66		20.90	0	0-5	0/0		5	
Walmsley Kerry Peter	23.8.1973		1994–2000	3	13	5		2.60	9	3-70	0/0	43.44	0	2
Ward John Thomas	11.3.1937		1963–1967	8	75	35*		12.50	0				16/1	
Watling Bradley-John	9.7.1985		2009–2018	59	3,057	142*	6	37.74					200/7	28/5
Watson William	31.8.1965		1986–1993	15	60	11		5.00	40	6-78	1/0	34.67	4	61

§ Vettori's figures exclude eight runs and one wicket for the ICC World XI v Australia in the Super Series Test in 2005-06.

	Born	Died	Tests	Test Career	Runs	HS	100s	Avge	Wkts	BB	5/10	Avge	Ct/St	O/T
Watt Leslie	17.9.1924	15.11.1996	3	1954	2	2	0	1.00	—	—	—/—	—	0	0
Webb Murray George	22.6.1947		3	1970–1973	12	12	0	6.00	4	2-114	0/0	117.75	0	0
Webb Peter Neil	14.7.1957		2	1979	11	5	0	3.66	—	—	—/—	—	2	5
Weir Gordon Lindsay	2.6.1908	31.10.1984	11	1929–1937	416	74*	0	29.71	7	3-38	0/0	29.85	3	
White David John	26.6.1961		2	1990	31	18	0	7.75	5	0-5	0/0	—	1	3
Whitelaw Paul Erskine	10.2.1910	28.8.1988	2	1932	64	30	0	32.00	—	—	—/—	—	0	3
Williamson Kane Stuart (CY 2016)	8.8.1990		70	2010–2018	5,865	242*	19	51.44	29	4-44	0/0	39.65	63	129/54
Wiseman Paul John	4.5.1970		25	1997–2004	366	36	0	14.07	61	5-82	2/0	47.59	11	15
Wright John Geoffrey MBE	5.7.1954		82	1977–1992	5,334	185	12	37.82	—	0-1	0/0	—	38	149
Young Bryan Andrew	3.11.1964		35	1993–1998	2,034	267*	2	31.78	—	—	—/—	—	54	74
Young Reece Alan	15.9.1979		5	2010–2011	169	57	0	24.14	—	—	—/—	—	8	
Yuile Bryan William	29.10.1941		17	1962–1969	481	64	0	17.81	34	4-43	0/0	35.67	12	

INDIA (295 players)

	Born	Died	Tests	Test Career	Runs	HS	100s	Avge	Wkts	BB	5/10	Avge	Ct/St	O/T
Aaron Varun Raymond	29.10.1989		9	2011–2015	35	9	0	3.88	18	3-97	0/0	52.61	1	9
Abid Ali Syed	9.9.1941		29	1967–1974	1,018	81	0	20.36	47	6-55	1/0	42.12	32	5
Adhikari Hemchandra Ramachandra	31.7.1919	25.10.2003	21	1947–1958	872	114*	1	31.14	3	3-68	0/0	27.33	8	
Agarkar Ajit Bhalchandra	4.12.1977		26	1998–2005	571	109*	1	16.79	58	6-41	1/0	47.32	6	191/4
Agarwal Mayank Anurag	16.2.1991		2	2018	195	77	0	65.00	—	—	—/—	—	3	
2 Amar Singh Ladha	4.12.1910	21.5.1940	7	1932–1936	292	51	0	22.46	28	7-86	2/0	30.64	3	
1,2 Amarnath Mohinder (CY 1984)	24.9.1950		69	1969–1987	4,378	138	11	42.50	32	4-63	0/0	55.68	47	85
1 Amarnath Nanik ("Lala")	11.9.1911	5.8.2000	24	1933–1952	878	118	1	24.38	45	5-96	2/0	32.91	13	
1,2 Amarnath Surinder	30.12.1948		10	1975–1978	550	124	1	30.55	1	1-5	0/0	5.00	4	3
Amir Elahi	1.9.1908	28.12.1980	1†	1947	17	13	0	8.50	—	—	—/—	—	0	
Amre Pravin Kalyan	14.8.1968		11	1992–1993	425	103	1	42.50	—	—	—/—	—	9	37
Ankola Salil Ashok	1.3.1968		1	1989	6	6	0	6.00	2	1-35	0/0	64.00	0	20
2 Apte Arvindrao Laxmanrao	24.10.1934	5.8.2014	1	1959	15	8	0	7.50	0	0-3	0/0	—	0	
2 Apte Madhavrao Laxmanrao	5.10.1932		7	1952	542	163*	1	49.27	—	—	—/—	—	2	
Arshad Ayub	2.8.1958		13	1987–1989	257	57	0	17.13	41	5-50	3/0	35.07	2	32
Arun Bharathi	14.12.1962		2	1986	4	2*	0	4.00	4	3-76	0/0	29.00	2	4
Arun Lal	1.8.1955		16	1982–1988	729	93	0	26.03	0	0-0	0/0	—	13	13
Ashwin Ravichandran	17.9.1986		65	2011–2018	2,361	124	4	29.14	342	7-59	26/7	25.43	23	111/46
Azad Kirtivardhan	2.1.1959		7	1980–1983	135	24	0	11.25	3	2-84	0/0	124.33	3	25

	Born	Died	Tests	Test Career	Runs	HS	100s	Avge	Wkts	BB	5/10	Avge	Ct/St	O/T
Azharuddin Mohammad (CY 1991)	8.2.1963		99	1984–1999	6,215	199	22	45.03	0	0-4	0/0	–	105	334
Badani Hemang Kamal	14.11.1976		4	2001	94	38	0	15.66	0	0-17	0/0	–	6	40
Badrinath Subramaniam	30.8.1980		2	2009	63	56	0	21.00		–	–/–	–	2	7/1
Bahutule Sairaj Vasant	6.1.1973		2	2000–2001	39	21*	0	13.00	3	1-32	0/0	67.66	1	8
Baig Abbas Ali	19.3.1939		10	1959–1966	428	112	1	23.77	0	0-2	0/0	–	6	–
Balaji Lakshmipathy	27.9.1981		8	2003–2004	51	31	0	5.66	27	5-76	1/0	37.18	1	305
Banerjee Sarodindu Nath ("Shute")	3.10.1911	14.10.1980	1	1948	13	8	0	6.50	5	4-54	0/0	25.40	0	–
Banerjee Subroto Tara	13.2.1969		1	1991	3	3	0	3.00	3	3-47	0/0	15.66	0	6
Banerjee Sudangsu Abinash	1.11.1917	14.9.1992	1	1948	0	0	0	0.00	5	4-120	0/0	36.20	3	–
Bangar Sanjay Bapusaheb	11.10.1972		12	2001–2002	470	100*	1	29.37	7	2-23	0/0	49.00	4	15
Baqa Jilani Mohammad	20.7.1911	2.7.1941	1	1936	16	12	0	16.00	0	0-55	0/0	–	0	–
Bedi Bishan Singh	25.9.1946		67	1966–1979	656	50*	0	8.98	266	7-98	14/1	28.71	26	10
Bhandari Prakash	27.11.1935		3	1954–1956	77	39	0	19.25	0	0-12	0/0	–	3	–
Bharadwaj Raghvendrarao Vijay	15.8.1975		3	1999	28	22	0	9.33	1	1-26	0/0	107.00	3	10
Bhat Adwai Raghuram	16.4.1958		2	1983	6	6	0	3.00	4	2-65	0/0	37.75	0	–
Bhuvneshwar Kumar	5.2.1990		21	2012–2017	552	63*	0	22.08	63	6-82	4/0	26.09	8	95/34
Binny Roger Michael Humphrey	19.7.1955		27	1979–1986	830	83*	0	23.05	47	6-56	2/0	32.63	11	72
Binny Stuart Terence Roger	3.6.1984		6	2014–2015	194	78	0	21.55	3	2-24	0/0	86.00	4	14/3
Borde Chandrakant Gulabrao	21.7.1934		55	1958–1969	3,061	177*	5	35.59	52	5-88	1/0	46.48	37	–
Bunrah Jasprit Jasbrisingh	6.12.1993		10	2017–2018	14	6	0	1.55	49	6-33	3/0	21.89	3	44/40
Chandrasekhar Bhagwat Subramanya (CY 1972)	17.5.1945		58	1963–1979	167	22	0	4.07	242	8-79	16/2	29.74	25	–
Chauhan Chetandra Pratap Singh	21.7.1947		40	1969–1980	2,084	97	0	31.57	2	1-4	0/0	53.00	38	7
Chauhan Rajesh Kumar	19.12.1966		21	1992–1997	98	23	0	7.00	47	4-48	0/0	39.51	12	35
Chawla Piyush Pramod	24.12.1988		3	2005–2012	6	4	0	2.00	7	4-69	0/0	38.57	1	25/7
Chopra Aakash	19.9.1977		10	2003–2004	437	60	0	23.00		–	–/–	–	15	–
Chopra Nikhil	26.12.1973		1	1999	7	4	0	3.50	0	0-78	0/0	–	0	39
Chowdhury Nirode Ranjan	23.5.1923	14.12.1979	2	1948–1951	3	3*	0	3.00	1	1-130	0/0	205.00	0	–
Colah Sorabji Hormasji Munchersha	22.9.1902	11.9.1950	2	1932–1933	69	31	0	17.25	1	1-9	0/0	80.00	2	–
Contractor Nariman Jamshedji	7.3.1934		31	1955–1961	1,611	108	1	31.58		–	–/–	–	18	19
Dahiya Vijay	10.5.1973		2	2000	2	2*	0	–		–	–/–	–	6	–
Dani Hemchandra Tukaram	24.5.1933	19.12.1999	1	1952	–	–	–	–	1	1-9	0/0	19.00		–
Das Shiv Sunder	5.11.1977		23	2000–2001	1,326	110	2	34.89	0	0-7	0/0	–	34	4
Dasgupta Deep	7.6.1977		8	2001	344	100	1	28.66	0	–	–/–	–	13	5
Desai Ramakant Bhikaji	20.6.1939	27.4.1998	28	1958–1967	418	85	0	13.48	74	6-56	2/0	37.31	9	–
Dhawan Shikhar (CY 2014)	5.12.1985		34	2012–2018	2,315	190	7	40.61	0	0-0	0/0	–	28	115/46

	Born	Died	Tests	Test Career	Runs	HS	100s	Avge	Wkts	BB	5/10	Avge	Ct/St	O/T
Dhoni Mahendra Singh	7.7.1981		90	2005–2014	4,876	224	6	38.09	0	0-1	–/–	–	256/38	329§/93
Dighe Sameer Sudhakar	8.10.1968		6	2000–2001	141	47	0	15.66					12/2	23
Dilawar Hussain	19.3.1907	26.8.1967	3	1933–1936	254	59	0	42.33					6/1	
Divecha Ramesh Vithaldas	18.10.1927		5	1951–1952	60	26	0	12.00	11	3-102	0/0	32.81	5	
Doshi Dilip Rasiklal	22.12.1947		33	1979–1983	129	20	0	4.60	114	6-102	6/0	30.71	10	15
Dravid Rahul (CY 2000)	11.1.1973		163§	1996–2011	13,265	270	36	52.63	1	1-18	0/0	39.00	209	340§/1
Durani Salim Aziz	11.12.1934		29	1959–1972	1,202	104	1	25.04	75	6-73	3/1	35.42	14	
Engineer Farokh Maneksha	25.2.1938		46	1961–1974	2,611	121	2	31.08					66/16	5
Gadkari Chandrasekhar Vaman	3.2.1928	11.1.1998	6	1952–1954	129	50*	0	21.50	0	0-8	0/0	–	6	
¹ Gaekwad Anshuman Dattajirao	23.9.1952		40	1974–1984	1,985	201	2	30.07	2	1-4	0/0	93.50	15	15
Gaekwad Dattajirao Krishnarao	27.10.1928		11	1952–1960	350	52	0	18.42	0	0-4	0/0	–	5	
Gaekwad Hiralal Ghasilal	29.8.1923	2.1.2003	1	1952	22	14	0	11.00	0	0-47	0/0	–	–	
Gambhir Gautam	14.10.1981		58	2004–2016	4,154	206	9	41.95	0	0-4	0/0	–	38	147/37
Gandhi Devang Jayant	6.9.1971		4	1999	204	88	0	34.00					3	3
Gandotra Ashok	24.11.1948		2	1969	54	18	0	13.50					1	
Ganesh Doddanarasiah	30.6.1973		4	1996	25	8	0	6.25	5	0-5	0/0	57.40	1	1
Ganguly Sourav Chandidas	8.7.1972		113	1996–2008	7,212	239	16	42.17	32	3-28	0/0	52.53	71	308‡
Gavaskar Sunil Manohar (CY 1980)	10.7.1949		125	1970–1986	10,122	236*	34	51.12	1	1-34	0/0	206.00	108	108
Ghavri Karsan Devjibhai	28.2.1951		39	1974–1980	913	86	0	21.23	109	5-33	4/0	33.54	16	19
Ghorpade Jayasinghrao Mansinghrao	2.10.1930	29.3.1978	8	1952–1959	229	41	0	15.26	0	0-17	0/0	–	4	
Ghulam Ahmed	4.7.1922	28.10.1998	22	1948–1958	192	50	0	8.72	68	7-49	4/1	30.17	11	
Gopalan Morappakam Joysam	6.6.1909	21.12.2003	1	1933	18	11*	0	18.00	1	1-39	0/0	39.00	3	
Gopinath Coimbatarao Doraikannu	1.3.1930		8	1951–1959	242	50*	0	22.00	1	1-11	0/0	11.00	2	
Guard Ghulam Mustafa	12.12.1925	13.3.1978	2	1958–1959	11	7	0	5.50	3	2-69	0/0	60.66	2	
Guha Subrata	31.1.1946	5.11.2003	4	1967–1969	17	6	0	3.40	3	2-55	0/0	103.66	2	
Gul Mahomed	15.10.1921	8.5.1992	8†	1946–1952	166	34	0	11.06	2	2-21	0/0	12.00	3	
² Gupte Balkrishna Pandharinath	30.8.1934	5.7.2005	3	1960–1964	28	17*	0	28.00	3	1-54	0/0	116.33	0	
² Gupte Subhashchandra Pandharinath ("Fergie")	11.12.1929	31.5.2002	36	1951–1961	183	21	0	6.31	149	9-102	12/1	29.55	14	
Gursharan Singh	8.3.1963		1	1989	18	18	0	18.00					2	1
Hafeez Abdul (see Kardar)														
Hanumant Singh	29.3.1939	29.11.2006	14	1963–1969	686	105	1	31.18	0	0-5	0/0	–	11	
Harbhajan Singh	3.7.1980		103	1997–2015	2,224	115	2	18.22	417	8-84	25/5	32.46	42	234‡/28
Hardikar Manohar Shankar	8.2.1936	4.2.1995	2	1958	56	32*	0	18.66	1	1-9	0/0	55.00	3	
Harvinder Singh	23.12.1977		3	1997–2001	6	6	0	2.00	4	2-62	0/0	46.25	0	16
Hazare Vijay Samuel	11.3.1915	18.12.2004	30	1946–1952	2,192	164*	7	47.65	20	4-29	0/0	61.00	11	

§ *Dravid's figures exclude 23 runs and one catch for the ICC World XI v Australia in the Super Series Test in 2005-06.*

	Born	Died	Tests	Test Career	Runs	HS	100s	Avge	Wkts	BB	5/10	Avge	Ct/St	O/T
Hindlekar Dattaram Dharmaji	1.1.1909	30.3.1949	4	1936–1946	71	26	0	14.20	0	–	–/–	–	3	
Hirwani Narendra Deepchand	18.10.1968		17	1987–1996	54	17	0	5.40	66	8-61	4/1	30.10	5	18
Ibrahim Khanmohammad Cassumbhoy	26.1.1919	12.11.2007	4	1948	169	85	0	21.12	0	–	–/–	–	5	
Indrajitsinhji Kumar Shri	15.6.1937	12.3.2011	4	1964–1969	51	23	0	8.50	0	–	–/–	–	6/3	
Irani Jamshed Khudadad	18.8.1923	25.2.1982	2	1947	3	2*	0	3.00	0	–	–/–	–	2/1	
Jadeja Ajaysinhji	1.2.1971		15	1992–1999	576	96	0	26.18		–	–/–	–	5	196
Jadeja Ravindrasinh Anirudhsinh	6.12.1988		41	2012–2018	1,485	100*	1	32.28	192	7-48	9/1	23.68	31	144/40
[3]Jahangir Khan Mohammad	1.2.1910	23.7.1988	4	1932–1936	39	13	0	5.57	4	4-60	0/0	63.75	4	
Jai Laxmidas Purshottamdas	1.4.1902	29.1.1968	1	1933	19	19	0	9.50	0	–	–/–	–	0	
Jaisimha Motganhalli Laxmanarsu	3.3.1939	6.7.1999	39	1959–1970	2,056	129	3	30.68	9	2-54	0/0	92.11	17	125
Jamshedji Rustomji Jamshedji Dorabji	18.11.1892	5.4.1976	1	1933	5	4*	0	5.00	3	3-137	0/0	45.66	0	
Jayantilal Kenia	13.1.1948		1	1970	5	5	0	5.00	0	–	–/–	–	0	
Johnson David Jude	16.10.1971		2	1996	8	5	0	4.00	3	2-52	0/0	47.66	0	
Joshi Padmanabh Govind	27.10.1926	8.1.1987	12	1951–1960	207	52*	0	10.89	0	–	–/–	–	18/9	
Joshi Sunil Bandacharya	6.6.1970		15	1996–2000	352	92	0	20.70	41	5-142	1/0	35.85	7	69
Kaif Mohammad	1.12.1980		13	2000–2005	624	148*	1	32.84	0	0-4	0/0	–	14	125
Kambli Vinod Ganpat	18.1.1972		17	1992–1995	1,084	227	4	54.20	0	–	–/–	–	7	104
Kanitkar Hrishikesh Hemant	14.11.1974		2	1999	74	45	0	18.50	0	0-2	0/0	–	0	34
[1]Kanitkar Hemant Shamsunder	8.12.1942	9.6.2015	2	1974	111	65	0	27.75	0	–	–/–	–	0	
Kapil Dev (CY 1983)	6.1.1959		131	1978–1993	5,248	163	8	31.05	434	9-83	23/2	29.64	64	225
Kapoor Aashish Rakesh	25.3.1971		4	1994–1996	97	42	0	19.40	6	2-19	0/0	42.50	1	17
Kardar Abdul Hafeez	17.1.1925	21.4.1996	3†	1946	80	43	0	16.00	0	–	–/–	–	1	
Karim Syed Saba	14.11.1967		1	2000	15	15	0	15.00	0	–	–/–	–	3	34
Karthik Krishankumar Dinesh	1.6.1985		26	2004–2018	1,025	129	1	25.00	0	–	–/–	–	57/6	86/26‡
Kartik Murali	11.9.1976		8	2000–2004	88	43	0	9.77	24	4-44	0/0	34.16	4	37/1
Kenny Ramnath Baburao	29.9.1930	21.11.1985	5	1958–1959	245	62	0	27.22	1	1-9	0/0	13.00	1	
Kirmani Syed Mujtaba Hussein	29.12.1949		88	1975–1985	2,759	102	2	27.04		–	–/–	–	160/38	49
Kishenchand Gogumal	14.4.1925	16.4.1997	5	1947–1952	89	44	0	8.90	0	–	–/–	–	1	
Kohli Virat (CY 2019)	5.11.1988		77	2011–2018	6,613	243	25	53.76	0	0-0	0/0	–	72	216/65
[2]Kripal Singh Amritsar Govindsingh	6.8.1933	22.7.1987	14	1955–1964	422	100*	1	28.13	10	3-43	0/0	58.40	4	
Krishnamurthy Pochiah	12.7.1947	28.1.1999	5	1970	33	20	0	5.50	0	–	–/–	–	7/1	
Kulkarni Nilesh Moreshwar	3.4.1973		3	1997–2000	5	4	0	5.00	2	1-70	0/0	166.00	1	10
Kulkarni Rajiv Ramesh	25.9.1962		3	1986	2	2	0	1.00	5	3-85	0/0	45.40	1	10
Kulkarni Umesh Narayan	7.3.1942		4	1967	13	7	0	4.33	5	2-37	0/0	47.60	0	
Kumar Praveen	2.10.1986		6	2011	149	40	0	14.90	27	5-106	1/0	25.81	2	68/10
Kumar Vaman Viswanath	22.6.1935		2	1960–1961	6	6	0	3.00	7	5-64	1/0	28.85	2	

	Born	Died	Tests	Test Career	Runs	HS	100s	Avge	Wkts	BB	5/10	Avge	Ct/St	O/T
Kumble Anil (CY 1996)	17.10.1970		132	1990–2008	2,506	110*	0	17.77	619	10-74	35/8	29.65	60	269‡
Kunderan Budhisagar Krishnappa	2.10.1939	23.6.2006	18	1959–1967	981	192	2	32.70	0	0-13	0/0		23/7	
Kuruvilla Abey	8.8.1968		10		66	35*	0	6.60	25	5-68	1/0	35.68		25
Lall Singh	16.12.1909	19.11.1985	1	1932	44	29	0	22.00	–	–	–/–	–	1	
Lamba Raman	2.11.1960	22.2.1998	4	1986–1987	102	53	0	20.40	–	–	–/–	–	5	32
Laxman Vangipurappu Venkata Sai (CY 2002)	1.11.1974		134	1996–2011	8,781	281	17	45.97	2	1-2	0/0	63.00	135	86
Madan Lal	20.3.1951		39	1974–1986	1,042	74	0	22.65	71	5-23	4/0	40.08	15	67
Maka Ebrahim Suleman	5.3.1922	7.9.1994	2	1952	2	2*	0	2.00	–	–	–/–	–	2/1	
Malhotra Ashok Omprakash	26.1.1957		7	1981–1984	226	72*	0	25.11	0	0-0	–/–	–	2	20
Maninder Singh	13.6.1965		35	1982–1992	99	15	0	3.80	88	7-27	3/2	37.36	9	59
¹**Manjrekar Sanjay Vijay**	12.7.1965		37	1987–1996	2,043	218	4	37.14	1	0-4	0/0	44.00	25/1	74
¹**Manjrekar Vijay Laxman**	26.9.1931	18.10.1983	55	1951–1964	3,208	189*	7	39.12	1	1-16	0/0	–	19/2	
Mankad Ashok Vinoo	12.10.1946	1.8.2008	22	1969–1977	991	97	0	25.41	0	0-0	0/0	–	12	1
²**Mankad Mulvantrai Himmatlal ("Vinoo") (CY 1947)**	12.4.1917	21.8.1978	44	1946–1958	2,109	231	5	31.47	162	8-52	8/2	32.32	33	
Mantri Madhav Krishnaji	1.9.1921	23.5.2014	4	1951–1954	67	39	0	9.57	–	–	–/–	–	8/1	
Meherhomji Khershedji Rustomji	9.8.1911	10.2.1982	1	1936	0	0*	0		–	–			1	
Mehra Vijay Laxman	12.3.1938	25.8.2006	8	1955–1963	329	62	0	25.30	0	0-1		–	1	
Merchant Vijay Madhavji (CY 1937)	12.10.1911	27.10.1987	10	1933–1951	859	154	3	47.72	0	0-17	0/0	–	7	
²**Mhambrey Paras Laxmikant**	20.6.1972		2	1996	58	28	0	29.00	2	1-43	0/0	74.00	1	3
Milkha Singh Amritsar Govindsingh	31.12.1941	10.11.2017	4	1959–1961	92	35	0	15.33	0	0-2	0/0	–	2	
²**Mishra Amit**	24.11.1982		22	2008–2016	648	84	0	21.60	76	5-71	1/0	35.72	8	36/10
Mithun Abhimanyu	25.10.1989		4	2010–2011	120	46	0	24.00	9	4-105	0/0	50.66	3	5
Modi Rustomji Sheryar	11.11.1924	17.5.1996	10	1946–1952	736	112	1	46.00	0	0-14	0/0	–	3	
²**Mohammed Shami**	3.9.1990		40	2013–2018	433	51*	0	11.10	144	6-56	4/0	29.54	9	52/7
Mohanty Debasis Sarbeswar	20.7.1976		2	1997	0	0*	0	–	4	4-78	–/–	59.75	9	45
Mongia Nayan Ramlal	19.12.1969		44	1993–2000	1,442	152	1	24.03	–	–		–	99/8	140
More Kiran Shankar	4.9.1962		49	1986–1993	1,285	73	0	25.70	–	–		–	110/20	94
Muddiah Venkatappa Musandra	8.6.1929	1.10.2009	2	1959–1960	11	11	0	5.50	3	2-40	0/0	44.66	0	
Mukund Abhinav	6.1.1990		7	2011–2017	320	81	0	22.85	0	0-14	0/0	–	6	
Mushtaq Ali Syed	17.12.1914	18.6.2005	11	1933–1951	612	112	2	32.21	3	1-45	0/0	67.33	7	
Nadkarni Rameshchandra Gangaram ("Bapu")	4.4.1933		41	1955–1967	1,414	122*	1	25.70	88	6-43	4/1	29.07	22	
Naik Sudhir Sakharam	21.2.1945		3	1974–1974	141	77	0	23.50	–	–		–	6	
Nair Karun Kaladharan	6.12.1991		6	2016	374	303*	1	62.33	–	0-4		–	0	
Naoomal Jeoomal	17.4.1904	28.7.1980	3	1932–1933	108	43	0	27.00	2	1-4	0/0	34.00	2	2
Narasimha Rao Modireddy Venkateshwar	11.8.1954		4	1978–1979	46	20*	0	9.20	3	2-46	0/0	75.66	8	2

	Born	Died	Tests	Test Career	Runs	HS	100s	Avge	Wkts	BB	5/10	Avge	Ct/St	OIT
Navle Janaradan Gyanoba	7.12.1902	7.9.1979	2	1932–1933	42	13	0	10.50	–	–	–	–	1	–
Nayak Surendra Vithal	20.10.1954		2	1982	19	11	0	9.50	1	1-16	0/0	132.00	1	4
² **Nayudu Cottari Kanakaiya (CY 1933)**	31.10.1895	14.11.1967	7	1932–1936	350	81	0	25.00	9	3-40	0/0	42.88	4	–
² **Nayudu Cottari Subbanna**	18.4.1914	22.11.2002	11	1933–1951	147	36	0	9.18	2	1-19	0/0	179.50	3	–
² **Nazir Ali Syed**	8.6.1906	18.2.1975	2	1932–1933	30	13	0	7.50	4	4-83	0/0	20.75	0	–
Nehra Ashish	29.4.1979		17	1998–2003	77	19	0	5.50	44	4-72	0/0	42.40	5	117‡27
Nissar Mohammad	1.8.1910	11.3.1963	6	1932–1936	55	14	0	6.87	25	5-90	3/0	28.28	2	–
Nyalchand Sukhlal Shah	14.9.1915	3.1.1997	1	1952	7	6*	0	7.00	3	3-97	0/0	32.33	0	–
Ojha Naman Vijaykumar	20.7.1983		1	2015	56	35	0	28.00	–	–	–/–	–	4/1	1/2
Ojha Pragyan Prayish	5.9.1986		24	2009–2013	89	18*	0	8.90	113	6-47	7/1	30.26	10	18/6
Pai Ajit Manohar	28.4.1945		1	1969	10	9	0	5.00	2	2-29	0/0	15.50	0	–
Palia Phiroze Edulji	5.9.1910	9.9.1981	2	1932–1936	29	16	0	9.66	0	0-2	–/–	–	1	–
Pandit Chandrakant Sitaram	30.9.1961		5	1986–1991	171	39	0	24.42	–	–	–/–	–	14/2	36
Pandya Hardik Himanshu	11.10.1993		11	2017–2018	532	108	1	31.29	17	5-28	1/0	31.05	7	42/35
Pankaj Singh	6.5.1985		2	2014	10	9	0	3.33	2	2-113	0/0	146.00	1	1
Pant Rishabh Rajendra	4.10.1997		9	2018–2018	696	159*	2	49.71	–	–	–/–	–	40/2	3/10
Parkar Ghulam Ahmed	25.10.1955		1	1982	7	6	0	3.50	–	–	–/–	–	1	10
Parkar Ramnath Dhondu	31.10.1946	11.8.1999	2	1972	80	35	0	20.00	–	–	–/–	–	1	–
Parsana Dhiraj Devshibhai	2.12.1947		2	1978	1	1	0	0.50	1	1-32	0/0	50.00	0	–
Patankar Chandrakant Trimbak	24.11.1930		1	1955	14	13	0	14.00	–	–	–/–	–	3/1	–
² **Pataudi Iftikhar Ali Khan, Nawab of (CY 1932)**	16.3.1910	5.1.1952	3†	1946	55	22	0	11.00	–	–	–/–	–	0	–
Pataudi Mansur Ali Khan, Nawab of (CY 1968)	5.1.1941	22.9.2011	46	1961–1974	2,793	203*	6	34.91	1	1-10	0/0	88.00	27	–
Patel Brijesh Pursuram	24.11.1952		21	1974–1977	972	115*	1	29.45	–	–	–/–	–	17	10
Patel Jasubhai Motibhai	26.11.1924	12.12.1992	7	1954–1959	25	12	0	2.77	29	9-69	2/1	21.96	2	–
Patel Munaf Musa	12.7.1983		13	2005–2011	60	15*	0	7.50	35	4-25	0/0	38.54	6	70/3
Patel Parthiv Ajay	9.3.1985		25	2002–2017	934	71	0	31.13	–	–	–/–	–	62/10	38/2
Patel Rashid	1.6.1964		1	1988	0	0	0	0.00	–	0-14	0/0	–	0	1
Pathan Irfan Khan	27.10.1984		29	2003–2007	1,105	102	1	31.57	100	7-59	7/2	32.26	8	120/24
Patiala Maharajah of (Yadavendra Singh)	17.1.1913	17.6.1974	1	1933	84	60	0	42.00	–	–	–/–	–	2	–
Patil Sadashiv Raoji	10.10.1933		1	1955	14	14*	0	–	2	1-15	0/0	25.50	1	–
Patil Sandeep Madhusudan	18.8.1956		29	1979–1984	1,588	174	4	36.93	9	2-28	0/0	26.66	12	45
Phadkar Dattatraya Gajanan	12.12.1925	17.3.1985	31	1947–1958	1,229	123	2	32.34	62	7-159	3/0	36.85	21	–
Powar Ramesh Rajaram	20.5.1978		2	2007	13	7	0	6.50	6	3-33	0/0	19.66	0	31
Prabhakar Manoj	15.4.1963		39	1984–1995	1,600	120	1	32.65	96	6-132	3/0	37.30	20	130
Prasad Bapu Krishnarao Venkatesh	5.8.1969		33	1996–2001	203	30*	0	7.51	96	6-33	7/1	35.00	6	161
Prasad Mannava Sri Kanth	24.4.1975		6	1999	106	19	0	11.77	–	–	–/–	–	15	17

	Born	Died	Tests	Test Career	Runs	HS	100s	Avge	Wkts	BB	5/10	Avge	Ct/St	O/T
Prasanna Erapalli Anatharao Srinivas	22.5.1940		49	1961–1978	735	37	0	11.48	189	8-76	10/2	30.38	18	–
Pujara Cheteshwar Arvind	25.1.1988		68	2010–2018	5,426	206*	18	51.18	0	0-2	0/0	–	45	5
Punjabi Panamnal Hotchand	20.9.1921	4.10.2011	5	1954	164	33	0	16.40	–			–	–	
Rahane Ajinkya Madhukar	6.6.1988		56	2012–2018	3,488	188	9	40.55	–			–	73	90/20
Rahul Kamrur Lokesh	18.4.1992		34	2014–2018	1,905	199	5	35.27	–			–	43	13/25
Rai Singh Kanwar	24.2.1922	12.11.1993	1	1947	26	24	0	13.00	–			–	–	
Raina Suresh Kumar	27.11.1986		18	2010–2014	768	120	1	26.48	13	2-1	0/0	46.38	23	226/78
Rajinder Pal	18.11.1937		1	1963	6	3*	0	6.00	0	0-3	0/0	–	0	
Rajindernath Vijay	7.1.1928	9.5.2018	1	1952	–			–				–	0/4	
Rajput Lalchand Sitaram	18.12.1961		2	1985	105	61	0	26.25	–			–	1	4
Raju Sagi Lakshmi Venkatapathy	9.7.1969		28	1989–2000	240	31	0	10.00	93	6-12	5/1	30.72	6	53
Raman Woorkeri Venkat	23.5.1965		11	1987–1996	448	96	0	24.88	2	1-7	0/0	64.50	6	27
Ramaswami Cotar	16.6.1896	1.1990	1	1936	170	60	0	56.66	–			–	–	
²Ramchand Gulabrai Sipahimalani	26.7.1927	8.9.2003	33	1952–1959	1,180	109	2	24.58	41	6-49	1/0	46.31	20	
Ramesh Sadagoppan	16.10.1975		19	1998–2001	1,367	143	2	37.97	0	0-5	0/0	–	18	
²Ramji Ladha	10.2.1900	20.12.1948	1	1933	1	1	0	0.50	0	0-64	0/0	–	0	
Rangachari Commandur Rajagopalachari	14.4.1916	9.10.1993	4	1947–1948	8	8*	0	2.66	9	5-107	1/0	54.77	1	
Rangnekar Khanderao Moreshwar	27.6.1917	11.10.1984	3	1947	33	18	0	5.50	–			–	–	
Ranjane Vasant Baburao	22.7.1937	22.12.2011	7	1958–1964	40	16	0	6.66	19	4-72	0/0	34.15	1	
Rathore Vikram	26.3.1969		6	1996–1996	131	44	0	13.10	–			–	12	7
Ratra Ajay	13.12.1981		6	2001–2002	163	115*	1	18.11	–			–	11/2	12
Razdan Vivek	25.8.1969		2	1989	6	6*	0	6.00	5	5-79	0/0	28.20	0	3
Reddy Bharath	12.11.1954		4	1979	38	21	0	9.50	–			–	9/2	3
Rege Madhusudan Ramachandra	18.3.1924	16.12.2013	1	1948	15	15	0	7.50	–			–	–	
Roy Ambar	5.6.1945	19.9.1997	4	1969	91	48	0	13.00	–			–	0	
Roy Pankaj	31.5.1928	4.2.2001	43	1951–1960	2,442	173	5	32.56	1	1-6	0/0	66.00	16	
²Roy Pranab	10.2.1957		2	1981	71	60*	0	35.50	–			–	0	
Saha Wriddhaman Prasanta	24.10.1984		32	2009–2017	1,164	117	3	30.63	–			–	75/10	9
Sandhu Balwinder Singh	3.8.1956		8	1982–1983	214	71	0	30.57	10	3-87	0/0	55.70	1	22
Sanghvi Rahul Laxman	3.9.1974		1	2000	2	2	0	1.00	2	2-67	0/0	39.00	0	10
Sarandeep Singh	21.10.1979		3	2000–2001	43	39*	0	43.00	10	4-136	0/0	34.00	0	5
Sardesai Dilip Narayan	8.8.1940	2.7.2007	30	1961–1972	2,001	212	5	39.23	0	0-3	0/0	–	4	
Sarwate Chandrasekhar Trimbak	22.7.1920	23.12.2003	9	1946–1951	208	37	0	13.00	3	1-16	0/0	124.66	0	
Saxena Ramesh Chandra	20.9.1944	16.8.2011	1	1967	25	16	0	12.50	0	0-11	0/0	–	0	
Sehwag Virender	20.10.1978		103§	2001–2012	8,503	319	23	49.43	40	5-104	1/0	47.35	90	241½/19

§ *Sehwag's figures exclude 83 runs and one catch for the ICC World XI v Australia in the Super Series Test in 2005-06.*

	Born	Died	Tests	Test Career	Runs	HS	100s	Avge	Wkts	BB	5/10	Avge	Ct/St	O/T
Sekhar Thirumalai Ananthanpillai	28.3.1956		2	1982	0	0*	0		0		—/—		0	4
Sen Probir Kumar ("Khokhan")	31.5.1926	27.1.1970	14	1947–1952	165	25	0	11.78	0	0-43	-/-		20/11	
Sen Gupta Apoorva Kumar	3.8.1939	14.9.2013	1	1958	9	8	0	4.50	0		-/-		0	
Sharma Ajay Kumar	3.4.1964		1	1987	53	30	0	26.50	0		0/0		1	31
Sharma Chetan	3.1.1966		23	1984–1988	396	54	0	22.00	61	6-58	4/1	35.45	7	65
Sharma Gopal	3.8.1960		5	1984–1990	11	10*	0	3.66	10	2-95	0/0	41.80	2	11
Sharma Ishant	2.9.1988		90	2007–2018	627	31*	0	7.74	267	7-74	8/1	34.28	19	80/14
Sharma Karan Vinod	23.10.1987		2	2014	8	4*	0	8.00	4	2-95	0/0	59.50	0	2/1
Sharma Parthasarathy Harishchandra	5.1.1948	20.10.2010	5	1974–1976	187	54	0	18.70	0	0-2	0/0		1	
Sharma Rohit Gurunath	30.4.1987		27	2013–2018	1,585	177	3	39.62	2	1-26	0/0	101.00	25	193/90
Sharma Sanjeev Kumar	25.8.1965		2	1988–1990	56	38	0	28.00	6	3-37	0/0	41.16	1	23
Shastri Ravishankar Jayadritha	27.5.1962		80	1980–1992	3,830	206	11	35.79	151	5-75	2/0	40.96	36	150
Shaw Prithvi Pankaj	9.11.1999		2	2018	237	134	1	118.50	0		—/—		2	
Shinde Sadashiv Ganpatrao	18.8.1923	22.6.1955	7	1946–1952	85	14	0	14.16	12	6-91	1/0	59.75		
Shodhan Roshan Harshadlal ("Deepak")	18.10.1928	16.5.2016	3	1952	181	110	1	60.33	0	0-1	0/0		2	
Shukla Rakesh Chandra	4.2.1948		1	1982	29	24	0		2	2-82	0/0	76.00	2	
Siddiqui Iqbal Rashid	26.12.1974		1	2001	27	15	0	29.00	1	1-32	0/0	48.00	0	
Sidhu Navjot Singh	20.10.1963		51	1983–1998	3,202	201	9	42.13	0	0-9	0/0			136
Singh Rabindra Ramanarayan ("Robin")	14.9.1963		1	1998	27	15	0	13.50	0	0-16	0/0		5	136
Singh Robin	1.1.1970		1	1998	0	0	0	0.00	0		0/0			
Singh Rudra Pratap	6.12.1985		14	2005–2011	116	30	0	7.25	40	5-59	1/0	42.05	6	58/10
Singh Vikram Rajvir	17.9.1984		5	2005–2007	47	29	0	11.75	8	3-48	0/0	53.37	1	2
Sivaramakrishnan Laxman	31.12.1965		9	1982–1985	130	25	0	16.25	26	6-64	3/1	44.03	9	16
Sohoni Sriranga Wasudev	5.3.1918	19.5.1993	4	1946–1951	83	29*	0	16.60	2	1-16	0/0	58.66	2	
Solkar Eknath Dhondu	18.3.1948	26.6.2005	27	1969–1976	1,068	102	1	25.42	18	3-28	0/0	59.44	53	7
Sood Man Mohan	6.7.1939		1	1959	3	3	0	1.50	0		—/—			
Sreesanth Shanthakumaran	6.2.1983		27	2005–2011	281	35	0	10.40	87	5-40	3/0	37.59	2	53/10
Srikkanth Krishnamachari	21.12.1959		43	1981–1991	2,062	123	2	29.88	0	0-1	0/0		40	146
Srinath Javagal	31.8.1969		67	1991–2002	1,009	76	0	14.21	236	8-86	10/1	30.49	22	229
Srinivasan Thirumalai Echambadi	26.10.1950	6.12.2010	1	1980	48	29	0	24.00	0		—/—			2
Subramanya Venkataraman	16.7.1936		9	1964–1967	263	75	0	18.78	3	2-32	0/0	67.00	9	
Sunderam Gundibail Rama	29.3.1930	20.6.2010	2	1955	3	3*	0		2	2-46	0/0	55.33	0	
Surendranath Raman	4.1.1937	5.5.2012	11	1958–1960	136	27	0	10.46	26	5-75	2/0	40.50	4	
Surti Rusi Framroze	25.5.1936	13.1.2013	26	1960–1969	1,263	99	1	28.70	42	5-74	1/0	46.71	26	
Swamy Venkatraman Narayan	23.5.1924	1.5.1983	1	1955					0	0-15	—/—			
Tamhane Narendra Shankar	4.8.1931	19.3.2002	21	1954–1960	225	54*	0	10.22	0		-/-		35/16	

Name	Born	Died	Tests	Test Career	Runs	HS	Avge	100s	Wkts	BB	Avge	5/10	Ct/St	O/T
Tarapore Keki Khurshedji	17.12.1910	15.6.1986	1	1948	2	2	2.00	0	0	0-72	–	0/0	0	
Tendulkar Sachin Ramesh (CY 1997)	24.4.1973		200	1989–2013	15,921	248*	53.78	51	46	3-10	54.17	0/0	115	463/1
Thakur Shardul Narendra	16.10.1991		1	2018	4	4*	–	0	0	0-9	–	0/0	0	5/7
Umrigar Pahlanji Ratanji ("Polly")	28.3.1926	7.11.2006	59	1948–1961	3,631	223	42.22	12	35	6-74	42.08	2/0	33	
Unadkat Jaydev Dipakbhai	18.10.1991		1	2010	2	1*	2.00	0	0	0-101	–	0/0	0	7/10
Vengsarkar Dilip Balwant (CY 1987)	6.4.1956		116	1975–1991	6,868	166	42.13	17	0	0-3	–	0/0	78	129
Venkataraghavan Srinivasaraghavan	21.4.1945		57	1964–1983	748	64	11.68	0	156	8-72	36.11	3/1	44	15
Venkataramana Margashayam	24.4.1966		1	1988	0	0*	–	0	1	1-10	58.00	0/0	1	
Vihari Gade Hanuma	13.10.1993		1	2018–2018	167	56	23.85	0	5	3-37	26.40	0/0	1	
Vijay Murali	1.4.1984		61	2008–2018	3,982	167	38.28	12	1	1-12	198.00	0/0	49	17/9
Vinay Kumar Ranganath	12.2.1984		1	2011	11	6	5.50	0	1	1-73	73.00	0/0	0	31/9
Viswanath Gundappa Rangnath	12.2.1949		91	1969–1982	6,080	222	41.93	14	1	1-11	46.00	0/0	63	25
Viswanath Sadanand	29.11.1962		3	1985	31	20	6.20	0	–	–	–	–/–	11	22
Vizianagram Maharajkumar of (Sir Vijaya Anand)	28.12.1905	2.12.1965	3	1936	33	19*	8.25	0	–	–	–	–/–	–	
Wadekar Ajit Laxman	1.4.1941	15.8.2018	37	1966–1974	2,113	143	31.07	1	0	0-0	–	0/0	46	2
Wasim Jaffer	16.2.1978		31	2000–2007	1,944	212	34.10	5	2	2-18	9.00	0/0	27	2
Wassan Atul Satish	23.3.1968		4	1989–1990	94	53	23.50	0	10	4-108	50.40	0/0	1	9
[1,2] Wazir Ali Syed	15.9.1903	17.6.1950	7	1932–1936	237	42	16.92	0	0	0-0	–	0/0	1	
Yadav Jayant	22.11.1990		4	2016	228	104	45.60	1	11	3-30	33.36	0/0	–	1
Yadav Kuldeep	14.12.1994		6	2016–2018	51	26	8.50	0	24	5-57	24.12	3/0	3	33/17
Yadav Nandlal Shivlal	26.1.1957		35	1979–1986	403	43	14.39	0	102	5-76	35.09	3/0	10	7
Yadav Umeshkumar Tilak	25.10.1987		41	2011–2018	283	30	10.88	0	119	6-88	33.47	2/1	14	75/6
Yadav Vijay	14.3.1967		4	1992	30	30	30.00	0	–	–	–	–/–	1/2	19
Yajurvindra Singh	1.8.1952		4	1976–1979	109	43*	18.16	0	0	0-2	–	0/0	11	
Yashpal Sharma	11.8.1954		37	1979–1983	1,606	140	33.45	2	1	1-6	17.00	0/0	16	42
[1] Yograj Singh	25.3.1958		1	1980	10	6	5.00	0	1	1-63	63.00	0/0	0	6
Yohannan Tinu	18.2.1979		3	2001–2002	13	8*	–	0	5	2-56	51.20	0/0	3	3
[1] Yuvraj Singh	12.12.1981		40	2003–2012	1,900	169	33.92	3	9	2-9	60.77	0/0	31	301±/58
Zaheer Khan (CY 2008)	7.10.1978		92	2000–2013	1,231	75	11.95	0	311	7-87	32.94	11/1	19	194±/17

PAKISTAN (236 players)

	Born	Died	Tests	Test Career	Runs	HS	100s	Avge	Wkts	BB	5/10	Avge	Ct/St	OIT
Aamer Malik	3.1.1963		14	1987–1994	565	117	2	35.31		1-0	0/0	89.00	15/1	24
Aamir Nazir	2.1.1971		6	1992–1995	31	11	0	6.20	20	5-46	1/0	29.85	2	9
Aamir Sohail	14.9.1966		47	1992–1999	2,823	205	5	35.28	25	4-54	0/0	41.96	36	156
Abdul Kadir	10.5.1944	12.3.2002	4	1964	272	95	0	34.00	–	–	–/–	–	0/1	
Abdul Qadir	15.9.1955		67	1977–1990	1,029	61	0	15.59	236	9-56	15/5	32.80	15	104
Abdul Razzaq	2.12.1979		46	1999–2006	1,946	134	3	28.61	100	5-35	1/0	36.94	15	261¼/32
Abdur Rauf	9.12.1978		3	2009–2009	52	31	0	8.66	6	2-59	0/0	46.33	0	4/1
Abdur Rehman	1.3.1980		22	2007–2014	395	60	0	14.10	99	6-25	2/0	29.39	8	31/8
Adnan Akmal	13.3.1985		21	2010–2013	591	64	0	24.62	–	–	–/–	–	66/11	5
Afaq Hussain	31.12.1939	25.2.2002	2	1961–1964	66	35*	0	–	1	1-40	0/0	106.00	2	
Aftab Baloch	1.4.1953		2	1969–1974	97	60*	0	48.50	0	0-2	0/0	–	0	
Aftab Gul	31.3.1946		6	1968–1971	182	33	0	22.75	0	0-4	0/0	–	3	
Agha Saadat Ali	21.6.1929	25.10.1995	1	1955	8	8*	0	–	–	–	–/–	–	3	
Agha Zahid	7.1.1953		1	1974	15	14	0	7.50	–	–	–/–	–	0	
Ahmed Shehzad	23.11.1991		13	2013–2016	982	176	3	40.91	0	0-8	0/0	–	3	81/57
Aizaz Cheema	5.9.1979		7	2011–2012	1	1*	0	–	20	4-24	0/0	31.90	1	14/5
Akram Raza	22.11.1964		9	1989–1994	153	32	0	15.30	13	3-46	0/0	56.30	8	49
Ali Hussain Rizvi	6.1.1974		1	1997	–	–	–	–	2	2-72	0/0	36.00	0	
Ali Naqvi	19.3.1977		5	1997	242	115	1	30.25	–	0-11	0/0	–	8	
Alim-ud-Din	15.12.1930	12.7.2012	25	1954–1962	1,091	109	2	25.37	1	1-17	0/0	75.00	8	
Amir Elahi	1.9.1908	28.12.1980	5†	1952	65	47	0	10.83	7	4-134	0/0	35.42	4	
Anil Dalpat	20.9.1963		9	1983–1984	167	52	0	15.18	–	–	–/–	–	22/3	15
Anwar Hussain	16.7.1920	9.10.2002	4	1952	42	17	0	7.00	1	1-25	0/0	29.00	0	
Anwar Khan	24.12.1955		1	1978	15	12	0	15.00	0	0-12	0/0	–	0	
Aqib Javed	5.8.1972		22	1988–1998	101	28*	0	5.05	54	5-84	1/0	34.70	2	163
Arif Butt	17.5.1944	10.7.2007	3	1964	59	20	0	11.80	14	6-89	1/0	20.57	2	
Arshad Khan	22.3.1971		9	1997–2004	31	9*	0	5.16	32	5-38	1/0	30.00	0	58
Asad Shafiq	28.1.1986		69	2010–2018	4,323	137	12	38.94	2	1-7	0/0	76.00	67	60/10
Ashfaq Ahmed	6.6.1973		1	1993	1	1*	0	1.00	2	2-31	0/0	26.50	0	3
Ashraf Ali	22.4.1958		8	1981–1987	229	65	0	45.80	–	–	–/–	–	17/5	16
Asif Iqbal (CY 1968)	6.6.1943		58	1964–1979	3,575	175	11	38.85	53	5-48	2/0	28.33	36	10
Asif Masood	23.1.1946		16	1968–1976	93	30*	0	10.33	38	5-111	1/0	41.26	5	7
Asif Mujtaba	4.11.1967		25	1986–1996	928	65*	0	24.42	4	1-0	0/0	75.75	19	66

	Born	Died	Tests	Test Career	Runs	HS	100s	Avge	Wkts	BB	5/10	Avge	Ct/St	O/T
Asim Kamal	31.5.1976		12	2003–2005	717	99	0	37.73			–/–	–	10	30
Ata-ur-Rehman	28.3.1975		13	1992–1996	76	19	0	8.44	31	4-50	0/0	34.54	2	
Atif Rauf	3.3.1964		1	1993	25	16	0	12.50	–	–	–/–	–	5	
Atiq-uz-Zaman	20.7.1975		1	1999	26	25	0	13.00	–	–	–/–	–	6	3
Azam Khan	1.3.1969		1	1996	14	14	0	14.00	–	–	–/–	–	0	6
Azeem Hafeez	29.7.1963		18	1983–1984	134	24	0	8.37	63	6-46	4/0	34.98	1	15
Azhar Ali	19.2.1985		73	2010–2018	5,669	302*	15	43.27	8	2-35	0/0	75.25	61	53
Azhar Khan	7.9.1955		1	1979	14	14	0	14.00	1	1-1	0/0	2.00	2	
Azhar Mahmood	28.2.1975		21	1997–2001	900	136	3	30.00	39	4-50	0/0	35.94	14	143
2 Azmat Rana	3.11.1951	30.5.2015	1	1979	49	49	0	49.00	–	–	–/–	–	0	2
Babar Azam	15.10.1994		21	2016–2018	1,235	127*	1	35.28	–	–	–/–	–	16	54/26
Basit Ali	13.12.1970		19	1992–1995	858	103	1	26.81	0	0-6	0/0	–	6	50
3 Bazid Khan	25.3.1981		1	2004	32	23	0	16.00	–	–	–/–	–	1	5
Bilal Asif	24.9.1985		2	2018	73	15	0	9.12	16	6-36	2/0	26.50	2	3
Bilawal Bhatti	17.9.1991		2	2013	70	32	0	35.00	6	3-65	0/0	48.50	2	109
Danish Kaneria	16.12.1980		61	2000–2010	360	29	0	7.05	261	7-77	15/2	34.79	18	18
D'Souza Antao	17.1.1939		3	1958–1962	76	23*	0	38.00	17	5-112	1/0	43.82	3	
Ehsan Adil	15.3.1993		3	2012–2015	21	12	0	5.25	5	2-54	0/0	52.60	0	6
Ehtesham-ud-Din	4.9.1950		5	1979–1982	2	2	0	1.00	16	5-47	1/0	23.43	2	
Fahim Ashraf	16.1.1994		4	2018–2018	138	83	0	23.00	11	3-42	0/0	26.09	4	16/23
Faisal Iqbal	30.12.1981		26	2000–2009	1,124	139	1	26.76	–	–	–/–	–	22	18
Fakhar Zaman	10.4.1990		1	2018	192	94	0	32.00	–	–	–/–	–	3	26/26
Farhan Adil	25.9.1977		1	2003	33	25	0	16.50	–	–	–/–	–	2	
Farooq Hamid	3.3.1945		1	1964	3	3	0	1.50	1	1-82	0/0	107.00	0	
Farrukh Zaman	2.4.1956		1	1976	–	–	–	–	0	0-7	0/0	–	0	
Fawad Alam	8.10.1985		3	2009–2009	250	168	1	41.66	–	–	–/–	–	3	38/24
Fazal Mahmood (CY 1955)	18.2.1927	30.5.2005	34	1952–1962	620	60	0	14.09	139	7-42	13/4	24.70	11	
Fazl-e-Akbar	20.10.1980		5	1997–2003	52	25	0	13.00	11	3-85	0/0	46.45	2	2
Ghazali Mohammad Ebrahim Zainuddin	15.6.1924	26.4.2003	2	1954	32	18	0	8.00	0	0-18	0/0	–	0	
Gulam Abbas	1.5.1947		1	1967	12	12	0	6.00	–	–	–/–	–	0	
Gul Mahomed	15.10.1921	8.5.1992	1†	1956	39	27*	0	39.00	1	1-1	0/0	95.00	0	40
1,2 Hanif Mohammad (CY 1968)	21.12.1934	11.8.2016	55	1952–1969	3,915	337	12	43.98	1	1-1	0/0	95.00	40	269
Haris Sohail	9.1.1989		10	2017–2018	726	147	2	40.33	7	3-1	0/0	22.28	8	12
Haroon Rashid	25.3.1953		23	1976–1982	1,217	153	3	34.77	0	0-3	0/0	–	16	41/27
Hasan Ali	7.2.1994		9	2016–2018	155	29	0	15.50	31	5-45	1/0	28.90	4	16
Hasan Raza	11.3.1982		7	1996–2005	235	68	0	26.11	0	0-1	0/0	–	5	

	Born	Died	Tests	Test Career	Runs	HS	100s	Avge	Wkts	BB	5/10	Avge	Ct/St	O/T
Haseeb Ahsan	15.7.1939	8.3.2013	12	1957–1961	61	14	0	6.77	27	6-202	2/0	49.25	1	
Humayun Farhat [1]	24.1.1981		1	2000	54	28	0	27.00			—/—		1	5
Ibadulla Khalid ("Billy") [2]	20.12.1935		4	1964–1967	253	166	1	31.62	1	1-42	0/0	99.00	3	
Iftikhar Ahmed	3.9.1990		1	2016	4	4	0	4.00	1	1-1	0/0	13.00	1	2/1
Iftikhar Anjum	1.12.1980		1	2005	9	9*			0	0-8	0/0			62/2
Ijaz Ahmed snr	20.9.1968		60	1986–2000	3,315	211	12	37.67	2	1-9	0/0	38.50	45	250
Ijaz Ahmed jnr	2.2.1969		2	1995	29	16	0	9.66	0	0-1	0/0		3	2
Ijaz Butt	10.3.1938		8	1958–1962	279	58	0	19.92			—/—		5	
Ijaz Faqih	24.3.1956		5	1980–1987	183	105	1	26.14	4	1-38	0/0	74.75	3	27
Imam-ul-Haq	12.12.1995		10	2018–2018	483	76	0	28.41			—/—		7	16
Imran Farhat [2]	20.5.1982		40	2000–2012	2,400	128	3	32.00	3	2-69	0/0	94.66	40	58/7
Imran Khan (CY 1983) [2]	25.11.1952		88	1971–1991	3,807	136	6	37.69	362	8-58	23/6	22.81	28	175
Mohammad Imran Khan	15.7.1987		9	2014–2016	6	6	0	1.00	28	5-58	1/0	30.14	0	
Imran Nazir	16.12.1981		8	1998–2002	427	131	2	32.84	0	0-0	0/0		4	79/25
Imtiaz Ahmed	5.1.1928	31.12.2016	41	1952–1962	2,079	209	3	29.28	0	0-0	0/0		77/16	
Intikhab Alam	28.12.1941		47	1959–1976	1,493	138	1	22.28	125	7-52	5/2	35.95	20	4
Inzamam-ul-Haq	3.3.1970		119§	1992–2007	8,829	329	25	50.16	0	0-8	0/0		81	375‡/1
Iqbal Qasim	6.8.1953		50	1976–1988	549	56	0	13.07	171	7-49	8/2	28.11	42	15
Irfan Fazil	2.11.1981		1	1999	4	3	0	4.00	2	1-30	0/0	32.50	1	
Israr Ali	1.5.1927	1.2.2016	4	1952–1959	33	10	0	4.71	6	2-29	0/0	27.50	1	
Jalal-ud-Din	12.6.1959		6	1982–1985	3	2	0	3.00	11	3-77	0/0	48.81	1	8
Javed Akhtar	21.11.1940	8.7.2016	1	1962	4	2*	0	4.00	0	0-52	0/0		0	
Javed Burki	8.5.1938		25	1960–1969	1,341	140	3	30.47	0	0-2	0/0		7	
Javed Miandad (CY 1982) [2]	12.6.1957		124	1976–1993	8,832	280*	23	52.57	17	3-74	0/0	40.11	93/1	233
Junaid Khan	24.12.1989		22	2011–2015	122	17	0	7.17	71	5-38	5/0	31.73	4	71/9
Kabir Khan	12.4.1974		4	1994	24	10	0	8.00	9	3-26	0/0	41.11	1	10
Kamran Akmal [2]	13.1.1982		53	2002–2010	2,648	158*	6	30.79			—/—		184/22	157/58
Kardar Abdul Hafeez	17.1.1925	21.4.1996	23†	1952–1957	847	93	0	24.91	21	3-35	0/0	45.42	15	
Khalid Hassan	14.7.1937	3.12.2013	1	1954	17	10	0	17.00	2	2-116	0/0	58.00	0	
Khalid Wazir [1]	27.4.1936		2	1954	14	9*	0	7.00			—/—		0	
Khan Mohammad	1.1.1928	4.7.2009	13	1952–1957	100	26*	0	10.00	54	6-21	4/0	23.92	4	
Khurram Manzoor	10.6.1986		16	2008–2014	817	146	1	28.17	0	0-0	0/0		8	7/3
Liaqat Ali	21.5.1955		5	1974–1978	28	12	0	7.00	6	3-80	0/0	59.83	1	3
Mahmood Hussain	2.4.1932	25.12.1991	27	1952–1962	336	35	0	10.18	68	6-67	2/0	38.64	5	
Majid Jahangir Khan (CY 1970) [1]	28.9.1946		63	1964–1982	3,931	167	8	38.92	27	4-45	0/0	53.92	70	23

§ Inzamam-ul-Haq's figures exclude one run for the ICC World XI v Australia in the Super Series Test in 2005-06.

Name	Born	Died	Tests	Test Career	Runs	HS	100s	Avge	Wkts	BB	5/10	Avge	Ct/St	O/T
Mansoor Akhtar	25.12.1957		19	1980-1989	655	111	1	25.19	7	2-38	0/0	27.71	9	41
[2] Manzoor Elahi	15.4.1963		6	1984-1994	123	52	0	15.37	7	2-12	0/0	63.66	7	54
Maqsood Ahmed	26.3.1925	4.1.1999	16	1952-1955	507	99	0	19.50	3	2-59	0/0	34.00	13	
Masood Anwar	12.12.1967		1	1990	39	37	0	19.50	1	1-40	0/0	40.00	0	
Mathias Wallis	4.2.1935	1.9.1994	21	1955-1962	783	77	0	23.72			-/-		22	
Mir Hamza	10.9.1992		1	2018	4	4*	0	–	0	0-20	0/0	–	–	
Miran Bux	20.4.1907	8.2.1991	2	1954	4	1*	0	1.00	2	2-82	0/0	57.50	0	
Misbah-ul-Haq (CY 2017)	28.5.1974		75	2000-2016	5,222	161*	10	46.62	–		-/-		50	162/39
Mohammad Abbas	10.3.1990		14	2016-2018	63	11	0	6.30	66	5-33	4/1	18.86	4	
Mohammad Akram	10.9.1974		9	1995-2000	24	10*	0	2.66	17	5-138	1/0	50.52	4	23
Mohammad Amir	13.4.1992		36	2009-2018	751	48	0	13.41	119	6-44	4/0	30.47	5	46/41
(formerly Mohammad Aamer)														
Mohammad Asif	20.12.1982		23	2004-2010	141	29	0	5.64	106	6-41	7/1	24.36	0	38/11
Mohammad Ayub	13.9.1979		1	2012	34	18	0	17.00			-/-		1	
Mohammad Aslam Khokhar	5.1.1920	22.1.2011	1	1954	47	25	0	23.50			-/-		0	
Mohammad Farooq	8.4.1938		7	1960-1964	85	47	0	17.00	21	4-70	0/0	32.47	1	
Mohammad Hafeez	17.10.1980		55	2003-2018	3,652	224	10	37.64	53	4-16	0/0	34.11	45	203/89
Mohammad Hussain	8.10.1976		2	1996-1998	18	17	0	6.00	5	2-66	0/0	29.00	1	14
Mohammad Ilyas	19.3.1946		10	1964-1968	441	126	1	23.21	0	0-1	0/0		6	
Mohammad Irfan	6.6.1982		4	2012-2013	28	14	0	5.60	10	3-44	0/0	38.90	0	60/20
Mohammad Khalil	11.11.1982		4	2004	9	5	0	3.00	0	0-38	0/0		0	3
Mohammad Munaf	2.11.1935		4	1959-1961	63	25	0	12.60	11	4-42	0/0	31.00	0	
Mohammad Nawaz	21.3.1994		3	2016	50	25	0	12.50	5	2-32	0/0	29.40	2	14/16
Mohammad Nazir	8.3.1946		14	1969-1983	144	29*	0	18.00	34	7-99	3/0	33.05	4	4
Mohammad Ramzan	25.12.1970		1	1997	36	29	0	18.00			-/-			
Mohammad Rizwan	1.6.1992		2	2016	13	13*	0	13.00			-/-		2/1	25/10
Mohammad Salman	7.8.1981		2	2010	25	13	0	6.25			-/-		7/1	
Mohammad Sami	24.2.1981		36	2000-2012	487	49	0	11.59	85	5-36	2/0	52.74		87/13
Mohammad Talha	15.10.1988		4	2008-2014	34	19	0	8.50	9	3-65	0/0	56.00		3
Mohammad Wasim	8.8.1977		18	1996-2000	783	192	1	30.11	0	0-3	0/0			25
Mohammad Yousuf (CY 2007)	27.8.1974		90	1997-2010	7,530	223	24	52.29	0	0-0	-/-		65	288/3
(formerly Yousuf Youhana)														
Mohammad Zahid	2.8.1976		5	1996-2002	7	6*	0	1.40	15	7-66	1/1	33.46	0	11
Mohsin Kamal	16.6.1963		19	1983-1994	37	13*	0	9.25	24	4-116	0/0	34.25	4	19
Mohsin Khan	15.3.1955		48	1977-1986	2,709	137	7	37.10	0	0-0	0/0		34	75
[2] Moin Khan	23.9.1971		69	1990-2004	2,741	137	4	28.55			-/-		128/20	219

	Born	Died	Tests	Test Career	Runs	HS	100s	Avge	Wkts	BB	5/10	Avge	Ct/St	O/T
¹Mudassar Nazar	6.4.1956		76	1976–1988	4,114	231	10	38.09	66	6-32	1/0	38.36	48	122
Mufasir-ul-Haq	16.8.1944	27.7.1983	1	1964	8	8*	0	–	3	2-50	–	–	1	
Munir Malik	10.7.1934	30.11.2012	3	1959–1962	7	4	0	2.33	9	5-128	1/0	39.77	1	
Mushtaq Ahmed (CY 1997)	28.6.1970		52	1989–2003	656	59	0	11.71	185	7-56	10/3	32.97	23	144
²Mushtaq Mohammad (CY 1963)	22.11.1943		57	1958–1978	3,643	201	10	39.17	79	5-28	3/0	29.22	42	10
Nadeem Abbasi	15.4.1964		3	1989	46	36	0	23.00			–/–		6	
Nadeem Ghauri	12.10.1962		1	1989	0	0	0	0.00	0	0-20	0/0	–	0	6
²Nadeem Khan	10.12.1969		2	1992–1998	34	25	0	17.00	2	2-147	0/0	115.00	0	2
Nasim-ul-Ghani	14.5.1941		29	1957–1972	747	101	1	16.60	52	6-67	2/0	37.67	11	1
Nasir Jamshed	6.12.1989		2	2012	51	46	0	12.75		–	–	–	1	48/18
Naushad Ali	1.10.1943		6	1964	156	39	0	14.18	1	–	–	–	9	
Naved Anjum	27.7.1963		2	1989–1990	44	22	0	14.66	4	2-57	–/–	40.50	1	13
Naved Ashraf	4.9.1974		2	1998–1999	64	32	0	21.33			–/–		0	
Naved Latif	21.2.1976		1	2001	20	20	0	10.00			–/–		0	11
Naved-ul-Hasan	28.2.1978		9	2004–2006	239	42*	0	19.91	18	3-30	0/0	58.00	3	74/4
¹Nazar Mohammad	5.3.1921	12.7.1996	5	1952	277	124*	1	39.57	0	0.4	0/0	–	7	
Niaz Ahmed	11.11.1945	12.4.2000	2	1967–1968	17	16*	0	–	3	2-72	0/0	31.33	1	
²Pervez Sajjad	30.8.1942		19	1964–1972	123	24	0	13.66	59	7-74	3/0	23.89	9	
Qaiser Abbas	7.5.1982		1	2000	2	2	0	2.00	0	–	–/–	–	0	
Qasim Omar	9.2.1957		26	1983–1986	1,502	210	3	36.63	0	0-0	0/0	–	15	31
Rahat Ali	12.9.1988		21	2012–2018	136	35*	0	7.55	58	6-127	2/0	39.03	9	14
²Ramiz Raja	14.8.1962		57	1983–1996	2,833	122	2	31.83	0	–	–	–	34	198
²Rashid Khan	15.12.1959		4	1981–1984	155	59	0	51.66	8	3-129	0/0	45.00	2	29
²Rashid Latif	14.10.1968		37	1992–2003	1,381	150	0	28.77	0	0-10	0/0	–	119/11	166
Rehman Sheikh Fazalur	11.6.1935		1	1957	10	8	0	5.00	1	1-43	0/0	99.00	0	
²Riaz Afridi	21.1.1985		1	2004	9	9	0	9.00	2	2-42	0/0	43.50	0	
Rizwan-uz-Zaman	4.9.1961		11	1981–1988	345	60	0	19.16	4	3-26	0/0	11.50	4	3
²Sadiq Mohammad	3.5.1945		41	1969–1980	2,579	166	5	35.81	0	0-0	0/0	–	28	19
Saeed Ahmed	1.10.1937		41	1957–1972	2,991	172	5	40.41	22	4-64	0/0	36.45	13	
Saeed Ajmal	14.10.1977		35	2009–2014	451	50	0	11.00	178	7-55	10/4	28.10	11	113/64
Saeed Anwar (CY 1997)	6.9.1968		55	1990–2001	4,052	188*	11	45.52	0	0-0	0/0	–	18	247
Salah-ud-Din	14.2.1947		5	1964–1969	117	34*	0	19.50	7	2-36	0/0	26.71	3	
Saleem Jaffer	19.11.1962		14	1986–1991	42	10*	0	5.25	36	5-40	1/0	31.63	2	39
Salim Altaf	19.4.1944		21	1967–1978	276	53*	0	14.52	46	4-11	0/0	37.17	3	6
²Salim Elahi	21.11.1976		13	1995–2002	436	72	0	18.95			–/–		10/1	48
Salim Malik (CY 1988)	16.4.1963		103	1981–1998	5,768	237	15	43.69	5	1-3	0/0	82.80	65	283

	Born	Died	Tests	Test Career	Runs	HS	100s	Avge	Wkts	BB	5/10	Avge	Ct/St	O/T
Salim Yousuf	7.12.1959		32	1981–1990	1,055	91*	0	27.05			–/–		91/13	86
Salman Butt	7.10.1984		33	2003–2010	1,889	122	3	30.46	1	1-36	0/0	106.00	12	78/24
Sami Aslam	12.12.1995		13	2014–2017	758	91	0	31.58					15	4
Saqlain Mushtaq (CY 2000)	29.12.1976		49	1995–2003	927	101*	0	14.48	208	8-164	13/3	29.83	15	169
Sarfraz Ahmed	22.5.1987		49	2009–2018	2,657	112	3	36.39			–/–		146/21	98/54
Sarfraz Nawaz	1.12.1948		55	1968–1983	1,045	90	0	17.71	177	9-86	4/1	32.75	26	45
Shabbir Ahmed	21.4.1976		10	2003–2005	88	24*	0	8.80	51	5-48	2/0	23.03	3	32/1
Shadab Kabir	12.11.1977		5	1996–2001	148	55	0	21.14		0-9	0/0		3	3
Shadab Khan	4.10.1998		6	2016–2018	240	56	0	34.28	12	3-31	0/0	38.83	11	29/29
Shafiq Ahmed	28.3.1949		6	1974–1980	99	27*	0	11.00	0	0-1	0/0		1	3
²Shafqat Rana	10.8.1943		5	1964–1969	221	95	0	31.57	1	1-2	0/0	9.00	5	
²Shaheen Shah Afridi	6.4.2000		3	2018	23	14	0	5.75	12	4-64	0/0	31.41	0	6/7
Shahid Afridi	1.3.1980		27	1998–2010	1,716	156*	5	36.51	48	5-52	1/0	35.60	10	393‡/98‡
Shahid Israr	1.3.1950	29.4.2013	1	1976	7	7*	0	–					2	
Shahid Mahboob	25.8.1962		1	1989	–	–	–	–	2	2-131	0/0	65.50	0	10
Shahid Mahmood	17.3.1939		1	1962	25	16	0	12.50	0	0-23	0/0	–	0	
Shahid Nazir	4.12.1977		15	1996–2006	194	40	0	12.12	36	5-53	1/0	35.33	5	17
Shahid Saeed	6.1.1966		1	1989	12	12	0	12.00	0	0-7	0/0	–	0	10
Shakeel Ahmed snr.	12.2.1966		1	1998	1	1	0	1.00	4	4-91	0/0	34.75	0	
Shakeel Ahmed jnr.	12.11.1971		3	1992–1994	74	33	0	14.80			–/–		4	2
Shan Masood	14.10.1989		15	2013–2018	793	125	1	26.43	2	1-6	0/0	22.00	10	
Sharpe Duncan Albert	3.8.1937		3	1959	44	40	0	22.00					2	25/15
Shoaib Akhtar	13.8.1975		46	1997–2007	544	47	0	10.07	178	6-11	12/2	25.69	12	158‡/15
Shoaib Malik	1.2.1982		35	2001–2015	1,898	245	3	35.14	32	4-33	0/0	47.46	18	274‡/117‡
¹Shoaib Mohammad	8.1.1961		45	1983–1995	2,705	203*	7	44.34	5	2-8	0/0	34.00	22	63
Shuja-ud-Din Butt	10.4.1930	7.2.2006	19	1954–1961	395	47	0	15.19	20	3-18	0/0	40.05	8	
Sikander Bakht	25.8.1957		26	1976–1982	146	22*	0	6.34	67	8-69	3/1	36.00	7	27
Sohail Khan	6.3.1984		9	2008–2016	252	65	0	25.20	27	5-68	2/0	41.66	2	13/5
Sohail Tanvir	12.12.1984		2	2007	17	13	0	5.66	5	5-83	1/0	63.20	2	62/57
Tahir Naqqash	6.6.1959		15	1981–1984	300	57	0	21.42	34	5-40	2/0	41.11	3	40
Talat Ali Malik	29.5.1950		10	1972–1978	370	61	0	23.12	0	0-1	0/0	–	4	
Tanvir Ahmed	20.12.1978		5	2010–2012	170	57	0	34.00	17	6-120	1/0	26.64	1	2/1
Taslim Arif	1.5.1954	13.3.2008	6	1979–1980	501	210*	1	62.62	1	1-28	0/0	28.00	6/3	2
Taufeeq Umar	20.6.1981		44	2001–2014	2,963	236	6	37.98	0	0-0	0/0	–	48	2
Tauseef Ahmed	10.5.1958		34	1979–1993	318	35*	0	17.66	93	6-45	3/0	31.72	9	70

	Born	Died	Tests	Test Career	Runs	HS	100s	Avge	Wkts	BB	5/10	Avge	Ct/St	O/T
[2] Umar Akmal	26.5.1990		16	2009–2011	1,003	129	1	35.82	–	–	–/–	–	12	116/82
Umar Amin	16.10.1989		4	2010	99	33	0	12.37	3	1-7	00	21.00	11	16/14
Umar Gul	14.4.1984		47	2003–2012	577	65*	0	9.94	163	6-135	4/0	34.06	11	130/60
Usman Salahuddin	2.12.1990		1	2018	37	33	0	18.50	–	–	–/–	–	0	2
Wahab Riaz	28.6.1985		27	2010–2018	306	39	0	8.50	83	5-63	2/0	34.50	5	79/27
Wajahatullah Wasti	11.11.1974		6	1998–1999	329	133	2	36.55	0	0-0	00	–	7	15
Waqar Hassan	12.9.1932		21	1952–1959	1,071	189	3	31.50	0	0-10	00	–	10	
Waqar Younis (CY 1992)	16.11.1971		87	1989–2002	1,010	45	0	10.20	373	7-76	22/5	23.56	18	262
Wasim Akram (CY 1993)	3.6.1966		104	1984–2001	2,898	257*	3	22.64	414	7-119	25/5	23.62	44	356
Wasim Bari	23.3.1948		81	1967–1983	1,366	85	0	15.88	0	0-2	00	–	201/27	51
[2] Wasim Raja	3.7.1952		57	1972–1984	2,821	125	4	36.16	51	4-50	00	35.80	20	54
[2] Wazir Mohammad	22.12.1929	23.8.2006	20	1952–1959	801	189	2	27.62	0	0-2	00	–	0	
Yasir Ali	15.10.1985		1	2003	1	1*		–	2	1-12	00	27.50	0	
Yasir Arafat	12.3.1982		3	2007–2008	94	50*	0	47.00	9	5-161	1/0	48.66	5	11/13
Yasir Hameed	28.2.1978		25	2003–2010	1,491	170	2	32.41	0	0-0	00	–	20	56
Yasir Shah	2.5.1986		35	2014–2018	508	38*	0	11.04	203	8-41	16/3	28.72	19	19/2
[2] Younis Ahmed	20.10.1947		4	1969–1986	177	62	0	29.50	0	0-6	00	–	5	2
Younis Khan (CY 2017)	29.11.1977		118	2000–2017	10,099	313	34	52.05	9	2-23	00	54.55	139	265/25
Yousuf Youhana (see Mohammad Yousuf)														
Zaheer Abbas (CY 1972)	24.7.1947		78	1969–1985	5,062	274	12	44.79	3	2-21	00	44.00	34	62
Zahid Fazal	10.11.1973		9	1990–1995	288	78	0	18.00	1	–	–/–	–	5	19
[2] Zahoor Elahi	1.3.1971		2	1996	30	22	0	10.00	–	–	–/–	–	1	14
Zakir Khan	3.4.1963		2	1985–1989	9	9*	0		5	3-80	00	51.80	1	17
Zulfiqar Ahmed	22.11.1926	3.10.2008	9	1952–1956	200	63*	0	33.33	20	6-42	2/1	18.30	4	
Zulfiqar Babar	10.12.1978		15	2013–2016	144	56	0	16.00	54	5-74	2/0	39.42	8/2	5/7
Zulqarnain	25.5.1962		3	1985	24	13	0	6.00	–	–	–/–	–	2	16
Zulqarnain Haider	23.4.1986		1	2010	88	88	0	44.00	–	–	–/–	–		4/3

SRI LANKA (147 players)

	Born	Died	Tests	Test Career	Runs	HS	100s	Avge	Wkts	BB	5/10	Avge	Ct/St	O/T
Ahangama Franklyn Saliya	14.9.1959		3	1985	11	11	0	5.50	18	5-52	1/0	19.33	1	1
Amalean Kaushik Naginda	7.4.1965		2	1985–1987	9	7*	0	9.00	7	4-97	00	22.28	1	8
Amerasinghe Amerasinghe Mudalige Jayantha Gamini	2.2.1954		2	1983	54	34	0	18.00	3	2-73	00	50.00	3	
Amerasinghe Merenna Koralage Don Ishara	5.3.1978		1	2007	0	0*	0	–	1	1-62	00	105.00	0	8

	Born	Died	Tests	Test Career	Runs	HS	100s	Avge	Wkts	BB	5/10	Avge	Ct/St	OIT
Anurasiri Sangarange Don	25.2.1966		18	1985–1997	91	24	0	5.35	41	4-71	0/0	37.75	4	45
Arnold Russel Premakumaran	25.10.1973		44	1996–2004	1,821	123	3	28.01	11	3-76	0/0	54.36	51	180/1
Atapattu Marvan Samson	22.11.1970		90	1990–2007	5,502	249	16	39.02	1	1-9	0/0	24.00	58	268/2
Bandara Herath Mudiyanselage Charitha Malinga	31.12.1979		8	1997–2005	124	43	0	15.50	16	3-84	0/0	39.56	4	31/4
Bandaratilleke Mapa Rallage Chandima Niroshan	16.5.1975		7	1997–2001	93	25	0	11.62	23	5-36	1/0	30.34	0	3
Chameera Pathira Vasan Dushmantha	11.1.1992		7	2015–2018	64	19	0	5.33	23	5-47	1/0	39.82	4	22/19
Chandana Umagiliya Durage Upul	7.5.1972		16	1998–2004	616	92	0	26.78	37	6-179	3/1	41.48	7	147
Chandimal Lokuge Dinesh	18.11.1989		51	2011–2018	3,744	164	11	43.53	–	–	–/–	–	76/10	144/54
Dananjaya Akila (Mahamarakkala Kurukulasooriya Patabendige Akila Dananjaya Perera)	4.10.1993		5	2017–2018	135	43*	0	19.28	27	6-115	3/0	24.25	1	30/16
Dassanayake Pubudu Bathiya	11.7.1970		11	1993–1994	196	36	0	13.06	–	–	–/–	–	19/5	16
de Alwis Ronald Guy	15.2.1959	12.1.2013	11	1982–1987	152	28	0	8.00	–	–	–/–	–	21/2	31
de Mel Ashantha Lakdasa Francis	9.5.1959		17	1981–1986	326	34	0	14.17	59	6-109	3/0	36.94	9	57
de Saram Samantha Indika	2.9.1973		4	1999	117	39	0	23.40	–	–	–/–	–	9	15/1
de Silva Ashley Matthew	3.12.1963		3	1992–1993	10	9	0	3.33	–	–	–/–	–	4/1	4
de Silva Dandeniyage Somachandra	11.6.1942		12	1981–1984	406	61	0	21.36	37	5-59	1/0	36.40	5	41
de Silva Dhananjaya Maduranga	6.9.1991		21	2016–2018	1,355	173	4	34.74	9	2-54	0/0	71.55	25	27/9
de Silva Ellawalakankanamge Asoka Ranjit	28.3.1956		10	1985–1990	185	50	0	15.41	8	2-67	0/0	129.00	4	28
de Silva Ginigalgodage Ramba Ajit	12.12.1952		4	1981–1982	41	14	0	8.20	7	2-38	0/0	55.00	0	6
de Silva Karunakalage Sajeewa Chanaka	11.9.1971		8	1996–1998	65	27	0	9.28	16	5-85	1/0	55.56	5	38
de Silva Pinnaduwage Aravinda (CY 1996)	17.10.1965		93	1984–2002	6,361	267	20	42.97	29	3-30	0/0	41.65	43	308
de Silva Sanjeewa Kumara Lanka	29.7.1975		3	1997	36	20*	0	18.00	–	–	–/–	–	1	11
de Silva Weddikkara Ruwan Sujeewa	7.10.1979		3	2002–2007	10	5*	0	10.00	11	4-35	0/0	19.00	1	
Dharmasena Handunnettige Deepthi Priyantha Kumar	24.4.1971		31	1993–2003	868	62*	0	19.72	69	6-72	3/0	42.31	14	141
Dias Roy Luke	18.10.1952		20	1981–1986	1,285	109	3	36.71	0	0-17	0/0	–	6	58
Dickwella Dickwella Patabandige Dilantha Niroshan	23.6.1993		27	2014–2018	1,436	83	0	30.55	–	–	–/–	–	66/17	46/14
Dilshan Tillekeratne Mudiyanselage	14.10.1976		87	1999–2012	5,492	193	16	40.98	39	4-10	0/0	43.87	88	330/80
Dunusinghe Chamara Iroshan	19.10.1970		5	1994–1995	160	91	0	16.00	–	–	–/–	–	13/2	1
Eranga Ranaweera Mudiyanselage Shaminda	23.6.1986		21	2011–2016	193	45*	0	12.86	57	4-49	0/0	37.50	5	19/3
Fernando Aththachchi Nuwan Pradeep Roshan	19.10.1986		28	2011–2017	132	17*	0	4.00	70	6-132	1/0	42.90	5	31/9
Fernando Congenige Randhi Dilhara	19.7.1979		40	2000–2012	249	39*	0	8.30	100	5-42	3/0	37.84	10	146/18

Name	Born	Died	Test Career	Tests	Runs	HS	100s	Avge	Wkts	BB	5/10	Avge	Ct/St	O/T
Fernando Ellekutige Rufus Nemesion Susil	19.12.1955		1982–1983	5	112	46	0	11.20		–	–/–		1	7
Fernando Kandage Hasantha Ruwan Kumara	14.10.1979		2002	2	38	24	0	9.50	4	3-63	0/0	27.00	0	7
Fernando Kandana Arachchige Dinusha Manoj	10.8.1979		2003	2	56	51*	0	28.00	3	1-29	0/0	107.00	0	1
Fernando Muthuhanthrige Vishwa Thilina	18.9.1991		2016–2017	2	4	4*	0	2.00	3	2-87	0/0	34.33	4	6/1
Fernando Thudellage Charitha Buddhika	22.8.1980		2001–2002	9	132	45	0	26.40	18	4-27	0/0	44.00	0	17
Gallage Indika Sanjeewa	22.11.1975		1999	1	3	3	0	3.00	0	0-24	0/0		0	3
Gamage Panagamuwa Lahiru Sampath	5.4.1988		2017–2018	3	6	3	0	1.50	10	2-38	0/0	57.30	0	9
Goonatillake Hettiarachige Mahes	16.8.1952		1981–1982	5	177	56	0	22.12		–	–/–		10/3	6
Gunaratne Downdegedara Asela Sampath	8.1.1986		2016–2017	6	455	116	1	56.87	3	2-28	0/0	38.00	6	29/12
Gunasekera Yohan	8.11.1957		1982	1	48	23	0	12.00		–	–/–		0	3
Gunatilleke Mashtayage Dhanushka	17.03.1991		2017–2018	8	299	61	0	18.68	1	1-16	0/0	111.00	6	33/15
Gunawardene Dihan Avishka	26.5.1977		1998–2005	6	181	43	0	16.45		–	–/–		2	61
Guneratne Roshan Punyajith Wijesinghe	26.1.1962	21.7.2005	1982	1	0	0*	0		0	0-84	0/0		–	–
Gurusinha Asanka Pradeep	16.9.1966		1985–1996	41	2,452	143	7	38.92	20	2-7	0/0	34.05	33	147
Hathurusinghe Upul Chandika	13.9.1968		1990–1998	26	1,274	83	0	29.62	17	4-66	0/0	46.41	7	35
Herath Herath Mudiyanselage Rangana Keerthi Bandara	19.3.1978		1999–2018	93	1,699	80*	0	14.64	433	9-127	34/9	28.07	24	71/17
Hettiarachchi Dinuka Sulaksana	15.7.1976		2000	1	0	0*	0	0.00	2	2-36	0/0	20.50	0	–
Jayasekera Rohan Stanley Amarasiriwardene	7.12.1957		1981	1	2	2	0	1.00		–	–/–		0	2
Jayasundera Maduravelage Don Udara Supeksha	3.1.1991		2015	2	30	26	0	7.50	0	–	–/–		2	–
Jayasuriya Sanath Teran (CY 1997)	30.6.1969		1990–2007	110	6,973	340	14	40.07	98	5-34	2/0	34.34	78	441‡/31
Jayawardene Denagamage Proboth Mahela de Silva (CY 2007)	27.5.1977		1997–2014	149	11,814	374	34	49.84	6	2-32	0/0	51.66	205	443‡/55
Jayawardene Hewasandatchige Asiri Prasanna Wishvanath	9.10.1979		2000–2014	58	2,124	154*	4	29.50		–	–/–		124/32	6
Jeganathan Sridharan	11.7.1951		1982	1	19	8	0	4.75	0	–	–/–		2	5
John Vinothen Bede	27.5.1960	14.5.1996	1982–1984	6	53	27*	0	10.60	28	5-60	2/0	21.92	2	45
Jurangpathy Baba Roshan	25.6.1967		1985–1986	2	1	1	0	0.25		–	–/–			–
Kalavitigoda Shantha	23.12.1977		2004	1	8	7	0	4.00	1	1-69	0/0	93.00		–
Kalpage Ruwan Senani	19.2.1970		1993–1998	11	294	63	0	18.37	12	2-27	0/0	64.50	10	86
Kaluhalamulla H. K. S. R. (see Randiv, Suraj)														
[2] Kaluperuma Lalith Wasantha Silva	25.6.1949		1981	2	12	11*	0	4.00	0	0-24	0/0		2	4
[2] Kaluperuma Sanath Mohan Silva	22.10.1961		1983–1987	4	88	23	0	11.00	2	2-17	0/0	62.00	4	–
Kaluwitharana Romesh Shantha	24.11.1969		1992–2004	49	1,933	132*	3	26.12	0	0-9	0/0		93/26	189
Kapugedera Chamara Kantha	24.2.1987		2006–2009	8	418	96	0	34.83		–	–/–		6	102/43

Name	Born	Died	Tests	Test Career	Runs	HS	100s	Avge	Wkts	BB	5/10	Avge	Ct/St	O/T
Karunaratne Frank Dimuth Madushanka	28.4.1988		56	2012-2018	3,894	196	8	37.08		1-31	0/0	103.00	46	17
Kaushal Paskuwal Handi Tharindu	5.3.1993		7	2014-2015	106	18	0	10.60	25	5-42	2/0	44.20	3	1
Kulasekara Chamith Kosala Bandara	15.7.1985		1	2011	22	15	0	11.00	1	1-65	0/0	80.00	0	
Kulasekara Kulasekara Mudiyanselage Dinesh Nuwan	22.7.1982		21	2004-2014	391	64	0	14.48	48	4-21	0/0	37.37	8	184/58
Kumara Chandradasa Brahammana Ralalage Lahiru Sudesh	13.2.1997		14	2016-2018	44	10	0	3.38	49	6-122	1/0	36.42	3	8
Kuruppu Don Sardha Brendon Priyantha	5.1.1962		4	1986-1991	320	201*	1	53.33					3	54
Kuruppuarachchi Ajith Kosala	1.11.1964		2	1985-1986	0	0*	0	–	8	5-44	1/0	18.62	1	44
Labrooy Graeme Fredrick	7.6.1964		9	1986-1990	158	70*	0	14.36		5-133	1/0	44.22	0	81/10
Lakmal Ranasinghe Arachchige Suranga	10.3.1987		54	2010-2018	698	42	0	11.25	127	5-54	2/0	40.74	15	
Lakshitha Materba Kanatha Gamage Chamila Premanath	4.1.1979		2	2002-2002	42	40	0	14.00	5	2-33	0/0	31.60	1	7
Liyanage Dulip Kapila	6.6.1972		9	1992-2001	69	23	0	7.66	17	4-56	0/0	39.17		16
Lokuarachchi Kaushal Samaraweera	20.5.1982		3	2003-2003	94	28*	0	23.50	5	2-47	0/0	59.00	3	21/2
Madugalle Ranjan Senerath	22.4.1959		21	1981-1988	1,029	103	1	29.40	0	0-0	0/0	–		63
Madurasinghe Madurasinghe Arachchige Wijayasiri Ranjith	30.1.1961		3	1988-1992	24	11	0	4.80	3	3-60	0/0	57.33		12
Mahanama Roshan Siriwardene	31.5.1966		52	1985-1997	2,576	225	4	29.27		0-3	0/0	–	56	213
Maharoof Mohamed Farveez	7.9.1984		22	2003-2011	556	72	0	18.53	25	4-52	0/0	65.24	7	109/8
Malinga Separamadu Lasith	28.8.1983		30	2004-2010	275	64	0	11.45	101	5-50	3/0	33.15	7	210/69
Mathews Angelo Davis (CY 2015)	2.6.1987		80	2009-2018	5,554	160	9	44.79	33	4-44	0/0	52.87	65	203/72
Mendis Balapuwaduge Ajantha Winslo	11.3.1987		19	2008-2014	213	78	0	16.38	70	6-99	4/1	34.77	2	87/39
Mendis Balapuwaduge Kusal Gimhan	2.2.1995		34	2015-2018	2,464	196	6	37.90		1-10	0/0	55.00	50	54/16
Mendis Louis Rohan Duleep	25.8.1952		24	1981-1988	1,329	124	4	31.64				–		79
Mirando Magina Thilan Thushara	1.3.1981		10	2003-2010	94	15*	0	8.54	28	5-83	1/0	37.14	3	38/6
Mubarak Jehan	10.11.1981		13	2002-2015	385	67	0	17.50	1	0-1	0/0	–	15	40/16
Muralitharan Muttiah (CY 1999)	17.4.1972		132§	1992-2010	1,259	67	0	11.87	795	9-51	67/22	22.67	72	343½/12
Nawaz Mohamed Naveed	20.9.1973		4	2002	99	78*	0	99.00				–	0	3
Nissanka Ratnayake Arachchige Prabath	25.10.1980		3	2003	18	12*	0	6.00	10	5-64	1/0	36.60	0	23
Paranavitana Nishad Tharanga	15.4.1982		32	2008-2012	1,792	111	2	32.58	1	1-26	0/0	86.00	27	20
Perera Anhettige Suresh Asanka	16.2.1978		3	1998-2001	77	43*	0	25.66	1	1-104	0/0	180.00		13/3
Perera Mahawaduge Dilruwan Kamalaneth	22.7.1982		36	2013-2018	1,103	95	0	19.35	151	6-32	8/2	32.76	19	82/35
Perera Mathurage Don Kusal Janith	17.8.1990		13	2013-2018	657	110	1	28.56				–	17/8	
Perera M. K. P. A. D. (*see* Dananjaya, Akila)														

§ *Muralitharan's figures exclude two runs, five wickets and two catches for the ICC World XI v Australia in the Super Series Test in 2005-06.*

	Born	Died	Tests	Test Career	Runs	HS	100s	Avge	Wkts	BB	5/10	Avge	Ct/St	O/T
Perera Narangoda Liyanaarachchilage Tissara Chirantha	3.4.1989		6	2011–2012	203	75	0	20.30	11	4-63	0/0	59.36	1	145/71‡
Perera Panagodage Don Kuchira Laksiri	6.4.1977		8	1998–2002	33	11*	0	11.00	17	3-40	0/0	38.88	2	19/2
Prasad Kariyawasam Tirana Gamage Dammika	30.5.1983		25	2008–2015	476	47	0	12.86	75	5-50	1/0	35.97	6	24/1
Prasanna Seekkuge	27.6.1985		1	2011	5	5	0	5.00	0	0-80	0/0	–	0	38/20
Pushpakumara Karuppiahyage Ravindra	21.7.1975		23	1994–2001	166	44	0	8.73	58	7-116	4/0	38.65	10	31
Pushpakumara Paulage Malinda	24.3.1987		4	2017–2018	102	42*	0	17.00	14	3-28	0/0	37.14	2	2
Rajitha Chandrasekara Arachchilage Kasun	1.6.1993		3	2018–2018	6	4	0	1.50	11	3-20	0/0	27.63	3	3/4
Ramanayake Champaka Priyadarshana Hewage	8.1.1965		18	1987–1993	143	34*	0	9.53	44	5-82	1/0	42.72	6	62
Ramyakumara Wijekoon Mudiyanselage Gayan	21.12.1976		2	2005	38	14	0	12.66	2	2-49	0/0	33.00	0	0/3
Ranasinghe Anura Nandana	13.10.1956	9.11.1998	2	1981–1982	88	77	0	22.00	1	1-23	0/0	69.00	0	9
Ranatunga Arjuna (CY 1999)	1.12.1963		93	1981–2000	5,105	135*	4	35.69	16	2-17	0/0	65.00	47	269
Ranatunga Dammika	12.10.1962		1	1989	87	45	0	43.50	–	–	–	–	0	4
Ranatunga Sanjeeva	25.4.1969		9	1994–1996	531	118	2	33.18	–	–	–	–		13
Randiv Suraj (Hewa Kaluhalamullage Suraj Randiv Kaluhalamulla; formerly M. M. M. Suraj)	30.1.1985		12	2010–2012	147	39	0	9.18	43	5-82	1/0	37.51	1	31/7
Ratnayake Rumesh Joseph	2.1.1964		23	1982–1991	433	56	0	14.43	73	6-66	5/0	35.10	9	70
Ratnayake Joseph Ravindran	2.5.1960		22	1981–1989	807	93	0	25.21	56	8-83	4/0	35.21	1	78
Samarasekera Maitipage Athula Rohitha	5.8.1961		4	1988–1991	118	57	0	16.85	3	2-38	0/0	34.66	3	39
Samaraweera Dulip Prasanna	12.2.1972		7	1993–1994	211	42	0	15.07	–	–	–	–	5	5
Samaraweera Thilan Thusara	22.9.1976		81	2001–2012	5,462	231	14	48.76	15	4-49	0/0	45.93	45	53
Samarawickrama Wedagedara Sadeera Rashen	30.8.1995		4	2017	125	38	0	15.62	–	–	–	–	4	6/5
Sandakan Paththamperuma Arachchige Don Lakshan Rangika	10.6.1991		11	2016–2018	117	25	0	10.63	37	5-95	2/0	34.48	6	165
Sangakkara Kumar Chokshanada (CY 2012)	27.10.1977		134	2000–2015	12,400	319	38	57.40	0	0-4	0/0	–	182/20	397‡/56
Senanayake Charith Panduka	19.12.1962		3	1990	97	64	0	19.40	0	0-30	0/0	–	2	7
Senanayake Senanayake Mudiyanselage Sachithra Madhushanka	9.2.1985		1	2013	5	5	0	5.00	0	–	–	–	1	49/24
Shanaka Madagamagamage Dasun	9.9.1991		11	2016–2017	29	17	0	5.80	9	3-46	0/0	29.00		18/26
Silva Athege Roshen Shivanka	17.11.1988		11	2017–2018	690	109	1	38.33	–	–	–	–	2	
Silva Jayan Kaushal	27.5.1986		39	2011–2018	2,099	139	3	28.36	–	–	–	–	34	1
Silva Kelaniyage Jayantha	2.6.1973		7	1995–1997	6	6*	0	2.00	20	4-16	1/0	32.35		
Silva Lindamullage Prageeth Chamara	14.12.1979		11	2006–2007	537	152*	1	33.56	1	1-57	0/0	65.00	7	75/16
Silva Sampathawaduge Amal Rohitha	12.12.1960		9	1982–1988	353	111	1	25.21	–	–	–	–	33/1	20

	Born	Died	Tests	Test Career	Runs	HS	100s	Avge	Wkts	BB	5/10	Avge	Ct/St	O/T
Siriwardene Tissa Appuhamilage Milinda	4.12.1985		5	2015–2016	298	68	0	33.11	11	3-25	0/0	23.36	3	26/22
Tharanga Warushavithana Upul	2.2.1985		31	2005–2017	1,754	165	3	31.89	–	–	–/–	–	24	231+/26
Thirimanne Hettige Don Rumesh Lahiru	8.9.1989		29	2011–2017	1,153	155*	1	23.06	0	0-5	0/0	–	15	117/26
Tillekeratne Hashan Prasantha	14.7.1967		83	1989–2003	4,545	204*	11	42.87	0	0-0	0/0	–	122/2	200
Udawatte Mahela Lakmal	19.7.1986		2	2018	23	19	0	5.75	0	–	–/–	–	2	9/8
Upashantha Kalutarage Eric Amila	10.6.1972		2	1998–2002	10	6	0	3.33	4	2-41	0/0	50.00	0	12
Vaas Warnakulasuriya Patabendige Ushantha Joseph Chaminda	27.1.1974		111	1994–2009	3,089	100*	0	24.32	355	7-71	12/2	29.58	31	321+/6
Vandort Michael Graydon	19.1.1980		20	2001–2008	1,144	140	3	36.90	–	–	–/–	–	6	1
Vithanage Kasun Disi Kithuruwan	26.2.1991		10	2012–2015	370	103*	1	26.42	1	1-73	0/0	133.00	10	6/3
Warnapura Bandula	1.3.1953		4	1981–1982	96	38	0	12.00	0	0-1	0/0	–	2	12
Warnapura Basnayake Shalith Malinda	26.5.1979		14	2007–2009	821	120	2	35.69	0	0-40	0/0	–	14	3
Warnaweera Kahakatchchi Patabandige Jayananda	23.11.1960		10	1985–1994	39	20	0	4.33	32	4-25	0/0	31.90	0	6
Weerasinghe Colombage Don Udesh Sanjeewa	1.3.1968		1	1985	3	3	0	3.00	0	0-8	0/0	–	0	–
Welagedara Uda Walawwe Mahim Bandaralage Chanaka Asanka	20.3.1981		21	2007–2014	218	48	0	9.08	55	5-52	2/0	41.32	5	10/2
² **Wettimuny** Mithra de Silva	11.6.1951		2	1982	28	17	0	7.00	0	–	–/–	–	2	1
² **Wettimuny** Sidath (CY 1985)	12.8.1956	20.1.2019	23	1981–1986	1,221	190	2	29.07	0	0-16	0/0	–	10	35
Wickremasinghe Angupitige Gamini Dayantha	27.12.1965		3	1989–1992	17	13*	0	8.50	1	6-60	3/0	–	9/1	4
Wickremasinghe Gallage Pramodya	14.8.1971		40	1991–2000	555	51	0	9.40	85	6-60	3/0	41.87	18	134
Wijegunawardene Kapila Indaka Weerakkody	23.11.1964		2	1991–1991	14	6*	0	4.66	7	4-51	0/0	21.00	0	26
Wijesuriya Roger Gerard Christopher Ediriweera	18.2.1960		4	1981–1985	22	8	0	4.40	1	1-68	0/0	294.00	1	8
Wijetunge Piyal Kashyapa	6.8.1971		1	1993	10	10	0	5.00	2	1-58	0/0	59.00	0	–
Zoysa Demuni Nuwan Tharanga	13.5.1978		30	1996–2004	288	28*	0	8.47	64	5-20	1/0	33.70	4	9

ZIMBABWE (107 players)

	Born	Died	Tests	Test Career	Runs	HS	100s	Avge	Wkts	BB	5/10	Avge	Ct/St	O/T
Arnott Kevin John	8.3.1961		4	1992	302	101*	0	43.14	–	–	–/–	–	4	13
Blignaut Arnoldus Mauritius ('Andy')	1.8.1978		19	2000–2005	886	92	0	26.84	53	5-73	3/0	37.05	13	54/1
Brain David Hayden	4.10.1964		9	1992–1994	115	28	0	10.45	30	5-42	0/0	30.50	1	23
Brandes Eddo André	5.3.1963		10	1992–1999	121	39	0	10.08	26	3-45	0/0	36.57	4	59
Brent Gary Bazil	13.1.1976		4	1999–2001	35	25	0	5.83	7	3-21	0/0	44.85	1	70/3

	Born	Died	Tests	Test Career	Runs	HS	100s	Avge	Wkts	BB	5/10	Avge	Ct/St	O/T
Briant Gavin Aubrey	11.4.1969		1	1992	17	16	0	8.50	–	–	–/–	–	0	5
Bruk-Jackson Glen Keith	25.4.1969		2	1993	39	31	0	9.75	–	–	–/–	–	0	1
Burl Ryan Ponsonby	15.4.1994		1	2017	16	16	0	8.00	–	–	–/–	–	1	13/4
Burmester Mark Greville	24.1.1968		3	1992	54	30*	0	27.00	3	3-78	0/0	75.66	1	8
Butchart Iain Peter	9.5.1960		1	1994	23	15	0	11.50	0	0-11	0/0	–	–	20
Campbell Alistair Douglas Ross	23.9.1972		60	1992–2002	2,858	103	2	27.21	0	0-1	0/0	–	60	188
Carlisle Stuart Vance	10.5.1972		37	1994–2005	1,615	118	2	26.91	–	–	–/–	–	34	111
Chakabva Regis Wiriranai	20.9.1987		14	2011–2018	678	101	1	26.07	–	–	–/–	–	25/3	34/5
Chari Brian Bara	14.2.1991		7	2014–2018	254	80	0	18.14	–	0-3	0/0	–	8	10
Chatara Tendai Larry	28.2.1991		9	2012–2018	90	22	0	6.42	24	5-61	1/0	27.62	0	62/13
Chibhabha Chamunorwa Justice	6.9.1986		2	2016–2017	124	60	0	20.66	1	1-44	0/0	162.00	0	103/33
Chigumbura Elton	14.3.1986		14	2003–2014	569	88	0	21.07	21	5-54	1/0	46.00	6	210†/53
Chinouya Michael Tawanda	9.6.1986		2	2016	1	1	0	0.50	3	1-45	0/0	62.66	0	2
Chisoro Tendai Sam	12.2.1988		1	2017	9	9	0	9.00	3	3-113	0/0	37.66	0	18/12
Coventry Charles Kevin	8.3.1983		2	2005	88	37	0	22.00	–	–	–/–	–	3	39/13
Cremer Alexander Graeme	19.9.1986		19	2004–2017	540	102*	0	16.36	57	5-125	1/0	45.68	12	96/29
Crocker Gary John	16.5.1962		3	1992	69	33	0	23.00	3	2-65	0/0	72.33	0	6
Dabengwa Keith Mbusi	17.8.1980		3	2005	90	35	0	15.00	5	3-127	0/0	49.80	1	37/8
Dekker Mark Hamilton	5.12.1969		14	1993–1996	333	68*	0	15.85	0	0-5	0/0	–	12	23
Duffin Terrence	20.3.1982		2	2005	80	56	0	20.00	–	–	–/–	–	2	23
Ebrahim Dion Digby	7.8.1980		29	2000–2005	1,226	94	0	22.70	–	–	–/–	–	16	82
[2]Ervine Craig Richard	19.8.1985		15	2011–2017	941	160	2	33.60	–	–	–/–	–	15	84/16
[2]Ervine Sean Michael	6.12.1982		5	2003–2003	261	86	0	32.62	9	4-146	0/0	43.11	7	42
Evans Craig Neil	29.11.1969		3	1996–2003	52	22	0	8.66	2	0-8	0/0	–	5	53
Ewing Gavin Mackie	21.11.1981		1	2003–2005	108	71	0	18.00	2	1-27	0/0	130.00	1	7
Ferreira Neil Robert	3.6.1979		1	2005	21	16	0	10.50	–	–	–/–	–	1	–
[2]Flower Andrew OBE (CY 2002)	28.4.1968		63	1992–2002	4,794	232*	12	51.54	0	0-0	0/0	–	151/9	213
[2]Flower Grant William	20.12.1970		67	1992–2003	3,457	201*	6	29.54	25	4-41	1/0	61.48	43	221
Friend Travis John	7.1.1981		13	2001–2003	447	81	0	29.80	25	5-31	1/0	43.60	2	51
Goodwin Murray William	11.12.1972		19	1997–2000	1,414	166*	3	42.84	0	0-3	0/0	–	10	71
Gripper Trevor Raymond	28.12.1975		20	1999–2003	809	112	1	21.86	6	2-91	0/0	84.83	14	8
Hondo Douglas Tafadzwa	7.7.1979		9	2001–2004	83	19	0	9.22	21	6-59	1/0	36.85	5	56
Houghton David Laud	23.6.1957		22	1992–1997	1,464	266	4	43.05	0	0-0	0/0	–	17	63
Huckle Adam George	21.9.1971		8	1997–1998	74	28*	0	6.72	25	6-109	2/1	34.88	3	19
James Wayne Robert	27.8.1965		4	1993–1994	61	33	0	15.25	–	–	–/–	–	16	11
[1]Jarvis Kyle Malcolm	16.2.1989		12	2011–2018	126	25*	0	10.50	46	5-54	3/0	27.60	3	40/14

	Born	Died	Tests	Test Career	Runs	HS	100s	Avge	Wkts	BB	5/10	Avge	Ct/St	O/T
[1] Jarvis Malcolm Peter	6.12.1955		5	1992–1994	4	2*	0	2.00	11	3-30	00	35.72	2	12
Johnson Neil Clarkson	24.1.1970		13	1998–2000	532	107	1	24.18	15	4-77	00	39.60	12	48
Kamungozi Tafadzwa Paul	8.6.1987		1	2014	5	5	0	2.50	1	1-51	00	58.00	0	14/1
Lamb Gregory Arthur	4.3.1980		1	2011	46	39	0	23.00	3	3-120	00	47.00	2	15/5
Lock Alan Charles Ingram	10.9.1962		1	1995	8	8*	0	8.00	5	3-68	00	21.00		8
Madondo Trevor Nyasha	22.11.1976	11.6.2001	3	1997–2000	90	74*	0	30.00		–	–/–			13
Mahwire Ngonidzashe Blessing	31.7.1982		10	2002–2005	147	50*	0	13.36	18	4-92	00	50.83	1	23
Maregwede Alester	5.8.1981		2	2003	74	28	0	18.50		–	–/–		1	11
Marillier Douglas Anthony	24.4.1978		5	2000–2001	185	73	0	30.83	11	4-57	00	29.27	2	48
Maruma Timycen	19.4.1988		2	2012	20	10	0	10.00		–	–/–	1	17/10
[2] Masakadza Hamilton	9.8.1983		38	2001–2018	2,223	158	5	30.04	16	3-24	00	30.56	29	204/58
Masakadza Shingirai Winston	4.9.1986		5	2011–2014	88	24	0	11.00	16	4-32	00	32.18	2	16/7
[2] Masakadza Wellington Pedzisai	4.10.1993		2	2018	21	17	0	10.50	2	2-33	00	27.00		17/9
Masvaure Prince Spencer	7.10.1988		3	2016	55	42	0	13.75	0	0-23	00	–		7
Matambanadzo Everton Zvikomborero	13.4.1976		3	1996–1999	17	7	0	4.25	4	2-62	00	62.50		2
Matsikenyeri Stuart	3.5.1983		8	2003–2004	351	57	0	23.40	2	1-58	00	172.50	7	113/10
Mavuta Brandon Anesu	4.3.1997		2	2018	9	10*	0	2.25	4	4-21	00	59.25	3	5/3
Mawoyo Tinotenda Mbiri Kanayi	8.1.1986		11	2011–2016	615	163*	1	29.28		–	–/–	7	7
Mbangwa Mpumelelo ("Pommie")	26.6.1976		15	1996–2000	34	8	0	2.00	32	3-23	00	31.43	2	29
Meth Keegan Orry	8.2.1988		2	2012	72	31*	0	24.00	4	2-41	00	24.50	2	11/2
Mire Solomon Farai	21.8.1989		2	2017	78	47	0	19.50	1	1-22	00	32.00	0	40/7
Moor Peter Joseph	2.2.1991		8	2016–2018	533	83	0	35.53		–	–/–	9/1	42/16
Mpofu Christopher Bobby	27.11.1985		15	2004–2017	105	33	0	5.83	29	4-92	00	48.00	4	80/24
Mumba Carl Tapfuma	6.5.1995		2	2016	14	10*	0	4.66	8	4-50	00	37.25		4
Mupariwa Tawanda	16.4.1985		2	2003	15	14	0	15.00	0	0-136	00	–	0	4/4
Murphy Brian Andrew	1.12.1976		11	1999–2001	123	30	0	10.25	18	3-32	00	61.83	11	31
Musakanda Tarisai Kenneth	31.10.1994		1	2017	6	6	0	3.00		–	–/–	2	15/6
Mushangwe Natsai	9.2.1991		2	2014	8	8	0	2.00	7	4-82	00	62.14	2	6/5
Mutendera David Travolta	25.1.1979		1	2000	10	10	0	5.00	0	0-29	00	–	0	9
Mutizwa Forster	24.8.1985		1	2011	24	18	0	12.00		–	–/–	0	17/3
Mutumbami Richmond	11.6.1989		6	2012–2014	217	43	0	19.72		–	–/–	17/2	31/14
Muzarabani Blessing	2.10.1996		1	2017	14	14	0	14.00	0	0-48	00	–	0	18/6
Mwayenga Waddington	20.6.1984		1	2005	15	14*	0	15.00	1	1-79	00	79.00	0	3
Ncube Njabulo	14.10.1989		1	2011	17	14	0	8.50	1	1-80	00	121.00	1	6
Nkala Mluleki Luke	14.1.1981		10	2000–2004	187	47	0	14.38	11	3-82	00	66.09	4	50/1
Nyumbu John Curtis	1.3.1983		3	2014–2016	38	14	0	7.60	5	5-157	1/0	75.80	2	19/2

	Born	Died	Tests	Test Career	Runs	HS	100s	Avge	Wkts	BB	5/10	Avge	Ct/St	O/T
Olonga Henry Khaaba	3.7.1976		30	1994–2002	184	24	0	5.41	68	5-70	2/0	38.52	10	50
Panyangara Tinashe	21.10.1985		9	2003–2014	201	40*	0	16.75	31	5-59	1/0	26.22	3	65/14
Peall Stephen Guy	2.9.1969		4	1993–1994	60	30	0	15.00	4	2-89	0/0	75.75	1	21
Price Raymond William	12.6.1976		22	1999–2012	261	36	0	8.70	80	6-73	5/1	36.06	4	102/16
Pycroft Andrew John	6.6.1956		3	1992	152	60	0	30.40	–	–	–/–	–	2	20
Ranchod Ujesh	17.5.1969		1	1992	8	7	0	4.00	1	1-45	0/0	45.00	0	3
2 Rennie Gavin James	12.1.1976		23	1997–2001	1,023	93	0	22.73	1	1-40	0/0	84.00	13	40
2 Rennie John Alexander	29.7.1970		4	1993–1997	62	22	0	12.40	3	2-22	0/0	97.66	1	44
Rogers Barney Guy	20.8.1982		4	2004	90	29	0	11.25	0	0-17	0/0	–	1	15
Shah Ali Hassimshah	7.8.1959		3	1992–1996	122	62	0	24.40	1	1-46	0/0	125.00	0	28
Sibanda Vusimuzi	10.10.1983		14	2003–2014	591	93	0	21.10	–	–	–/–	–	16	125‡/26
Sikandar Raza	24.4.1986		12	2013–2018	818	127	–	34.08	20	5-99	1/0	49.45	11	88/28
2 Strang Bryan Colin	9.6.1972		26	1994–2001	465	53	0	12.91	56	5-101	1/0	39.33	11	49
Strang Paul Andrew	28.7.1970		24	1994–2001	839	106*	1	27.06	70	8-109	4/1	36.02	15	95
Streak Heath Hilton	16.3.1974		65	1993–2005	1,990	127*	1	22.35	216	6-73	7/0	28.14	17	187‡
Taibu Tatenda	14.5.1983		28	2001–2011	1,546	153	1	30.31	1	1-27	0/0	27.00	57/5	149‡/17
Taylor Brendan Ross Murray	6.2.1986		28	2003–2018	1,840	171	6	35.38	0	0-6	0/0	–	27	188/30
Tiripano Donald Tatenda	17.3.1988		7	2014–2018	227	49*	0	20.63	13	3-91	0/0	46.61	4	249
1 Traicos Athanasios John	17.5.1947		4‡	1992	11	5	0	2.75	14	5-86	1/0	40.14	4	27
Utseya Prosper	26.3.1985		2	2003–2013	107	45	0	15.28	10	3-60	0/0	41.00	2	164/35
Vermeulen Mark Andrew	2.3.1979		9	2002–2014	449	118	1	24.94	0	0-5	0/0	–	6	43
Viljoen Dirk Peter	11.3.1977		2	1997–2000	57	38	0	14.25	1	1-14	0/0	53.00	1	53
Vitori Brian Vitalis	22.2.1990		4	2011–2013	52	19*	0	10.40	12	5-61	1/0	38.66	2	24/11
Waller Andrew Christopher	25.9.1959		2	1996	69	50	0	23.00	–	–	–/–	–	2	39
1 Waller Malcolm Noel	28.9.1984		14	2011–2017	577	72*	0	21.37	8	4-59	0/0	27.25	10	79/32
Watambwa Brighton Tonderai	9.6.1977		6	2000–2001	11	4*	0	3.66	14	4-64	0/0	35.00	0	
Whittall Andrew Richard	28.3.1973		10	1996–1999	114	17	0	7.60	7	3-73	0/0	105.14	8	63
Whittall Guy James	5.9.1972		46	1993–2002	2,207	203*	4	29.42	51	4-18	0/0	40.94	19	147
Williams Sean Colin	26.9.1986		10	2012–2018	553	119	1	27.65	17	3-20	0/0	45.41	9	122/26
Wishart Craig Brian	9.1.1974		27	1995–2005	1,098	114	1	22.40	–	–	–/–	–	15	90

BANGLADESH (94 players)

	Born	Died	Tests	Test Career	Runs	HS	100s	Avge	Wkts	BB	5/10	Avge	Ct/St	O/T
Abdur Razzak	15.6.1982		13	2005–2017	248	43	0	15.50	28	4-63	0/0	59.75	4	153/34
Abu Jayed	2.8.1993		2	2018–2018	2	2	0	0.50	3	3-38	0/0	29.50	0	0/3
Abul Hasan	5.8.1992		1	2012	165	113	0	82.50	3	2-80	0/0	123.66	3	7/5
Aftab Ahmed	10.11.1985		16	2004–2009	582	82*	0	20.78	5	2-31	0/0	47.40	7	85/11
Akram Khan	1.11.1968		8	2000–2003	259	44	0	16.18	–	–	–/–	–	3	44
Al-Amin Hossain	1.1.1990		6	2013–2014	68	32*	0	22.66	6	3-80	0/0	76.66	0	14/25
Al Sahariar	23.4.1978		15	2000–2003	683	71	0	22.76	–	–	–/–	–	10	29
Alamgir Kabir	10.1.1981		3	2002–2003	8	4	0	2.00	0	0-39	0/0	–	0	–
Alok Kapali	1.1.1984		17	2002–2005	584	85	0	17.69	6	3-3	0/0	118.16	5	69/7
Aminul Islam	2.2.1968		13	2000–2002	530	145	1	21.20	1	1-66	0/0	149.00	5	39
Anamul Haque	16.12.1992		4	2012–2014	73	22	0	9.12	–	–	–/–	–	2	37/13
Anwar Hossain Monir	31.12.1981		3	2003–2005	22	13	0	7.33	0	0-95	0/0	–	1	1
Anwar Hossain Piju	10.12.1983		2	2002	14	12	0	7.00	–	–	–/–	–	0	–
Ariful Haque	18.11.1992		2	2018	88	41*	0	29.33	1	1-10	0/0	24.00	2	1/9
Bikash Ranjan Das	14.7.1982		1	2000	2	2*	0	1.00	1	1-64	0/0	72.00	0	–
Ehsanul Haque	1.12.1979		1	2002	7	5	0	3.50	0	0-18	0/0	–	1	6
Elias Sunny	2.8.1986		4	2011–2012	38	20*	0	7.60	12	6-94	1/0	43.16	1	4/7
Enamul Haque snr.	27.2.1966		10	2000–2003	180	24*	0	12.00	18	4-136	0/0	57.05	1	29
Enamul Haque jnr.	5.12.1986		15	2003–2012	59	13	0	5.90	44	7-95	3/1	40.61	3	10
Fahim Muntasir	1.11.1980		3	2001–2002	52	33	0	8.66	5	3-131	0/0	68.40	1	3
Faisal Hossain	26.10.1978		1	2003	7	5	0	3.50	–	–	–/–	–	0	6
Habibul Bashar	17.8.1972		50	2000–2007	3,026	113	3	30.87	0	0-1	0/0	–	22	111
Hannan Sarkar	1.12.1982		17	2002–2004	662	76	0	20.06	0	0-1	0/0	–	7	20
Hasibul Hossain	3.6.1977		5	2000–2001	97	31	0	10.77	6	2-125	0/0	95.16	1	32
Imrul Kayes	12.12.1986		37	2008–2018	1,776	150	3	25.37	0	0-1	0/0	–	35	78/14
Jahurul Islam	12.12.1986		7	2009–2012	347	48	0	26.69	–	–	–/–	–	7	14/3
Javed Omar Belim	25.11.1976		40	2000–2007	1,720	119	1	22.05	0	0-12	0/0	–	10	59
Jubair Hossain	12.9.1995		6	2014–2015	13	7*	0	4.33	16	5-96	1/0	30.81	2	3/1
Junaid Siddique	30.10.1987		19	2007–2012	969	106	1	26.18	0	0-2	0/0	–	11	54/7
Kamrul Islam	10.12.1991		7	2016–2018	51	25*	0	5.66	8	3-87	0/0	63.00	0	–
Khaled Ahmed	20.9.1992		1	2018	–	–	–	–	–	0-45	0/0	–	0	–
Khaled Mahmud	26.7.1971		12	2001–2003	266	45	0	12.09	13	4-37	0/0	64.00	2	77
Khaled Mashud	8.2.1976		44	2000–2007	1,409	103*	1	19.04	–	–	–/–	–	78/9	126

	Born	Died	Tests	Test Career	Runs	HS	100s	Avge	Wkts	BB	5/10	Avge	Ct/St	O/T
Liton Das	13.10.1994		13	2015–2018	558	94	0	25.36	–	–	–/–	62.80	22/2	24/18
Mahbubul Alam	1.12.1983		4	2008	5	2	0	1.25	1	2-62	–/–	–	0	5
Mahmudullah	4.2.1986		43	2009–2018	2,407	136	3	31.67	41	5-51	1/0	46.51	36/1	168/76
Manjural Islam	7.11.1979		17	2000–2003	81	21	0	3.68	28	6-81	1/0	57.32	4	34
Manjural Islam Rana	4.5.1984		6	2003–2004	257	69	0	25.70	8	3-84	0/0	80.20	3	25
Marshall Ayub	5.12.1988		3	2013	125	41	0	20.83	0	0-15	0/0	–	2	–
Mashrafe bin Mortaza	5.10.1983		36	2001–2009	797	79	0	12.85	78	4-60	0/0	41.52	9	200‡/54
Mehedi Hasan	25.10.1997		18	2016–2018	543	68*	0	19.39	84	7-58	7/2	29.78	17	22/13
Mehrab Hossain snr	22.9.1978		9	2000–2003	241	71	0	13.38	0	0-5	0/0	–	6	18
Mehrab Hossain jnr	8.7.1987		7	2007–2008	243	83	0	20.25	4	2-29	0/0	70.25	2	18/2
Mithun Ali	3.2.1990		3	2018	133	67	0	26.60	–	–	–/–	–	1	13/13
Mohammad Ashraful	9.9.1984		61	2001–2012	2,737	190	6	24.00	21	2-42	0/0	60.52	25	175‡/23
Mohammad Rafique	5.9.1970		33	2000–2007	1,059	111	1	18.57	100	6-77	7/0	40.76	7	123‡/1
Mohammad Salim	15.10.1981		2	2003	49	26	0	16.33	–	–	–/–	–	3/1	1
Mohammad Shahid	1.11.1988		5	2014–2015	57	25	0	11.40	5	2-23	0/0	57.60	0	1
Mohammad Sharif	12.12.1983		10	2000–2007	122	24*	0	7.17	14	4-98	0/0	79.00	5	9
Mominul Haque	29.9.1991		33	2012–2018	2,513	181	8	44.08	4	3-27	0/0	70.25	25	28/6
Mosaddek Hossain	10.12.1995		2	2016–2017	104	75	0	34.66	0	0-10	0/0	–	2	24/8
Mushfiqur Rahim	1.9.1988		66	2005–2018	4,006	219*	6	35.14	–	–	–/–	63.30	102/15	198/77
Mushfiqur Rahman	1.1.1980		10	2000–2004	232	46*	0	13.64	13	4-65	0/0	33.74	6	28
Mustafizur Rahman	6.9.1995		12	2015–2018	40	10*	0	3.63	27	4-37	0/0	303.00	1	40/30
Naeem Islam	31.12.1986		8	2008–2012	416	108	1	32.00	1	1-11	0/0	–	2	59/10
² Nafis Iqbal	31.1.1985		11	2004–2005	518	121	1	23.54	–	–	–/–	–	2	16
Naimur Rahman	19.9.1974		8	2000–2002	210	48	0	15.00	12	6-132	1/0	59.83	2	29
Nasir Hossain	30.11.1991		19	2011–2017	1,044	100	1	34.80	8	3-52	0/0	55.25	10	65/31
Nayeem Hasan	2.12.2000		3	2018	43	26	0	21.50	6	5-61	1/0	22.16	1	–
Nazimuddin	1.10.1985		3	2011–2012	125	78	0	20.83	0	–	–/–	–	1	11/7
Nazmul Hossain	5.10.1987		2	2004–2011	16	8*	0	8.00	5	2-61	0/0	38.80	0	38/4
Nazmul Hossain Shanto	25.5.1998		2	2016–2018	48	18	0	12.00	0	0-13	0/0	–	0	3
Nazmul Islam	21.3.1991		1	2018	4	4	0	2.00	4	2-27	0/0	19.00	0	5/13
Nurul Hasan	21.11.1993		3	2016–2018	115	64	0	19.16	–	–	–/–	–	5/3	2/9
Rafiqul Islam	7.11.1977		1	2002	7	6	0	3.50	–	–	–/–	–	0	–
Rajin Saleh	20.11.1983		24	2003–2008	1,141	89	0	25.93	2	1-9	0/0	134.00	15	43
Raqibul Hasan	8.10.1987		9	2008–2011	336	65	0	19.76	1	1-0	0/0	17.00	9	55/5
Robiul Islam	20.10.1986		9	2010–2014	99	33	0	9.00	25	6-71	2/0	39.68	5	3/1
Rubel Hossain	1.1.1990		26	2009–2018	259	45*	0	9.96	33	5-166	1/0	80.33	11	95/27

Died column entry: Manjural Islam Rana — 16.3.2007

	Born	Died	Tests	Test Career	Runs	HS	100s	Avge	Wks	BB	5/10	Avge	Ct/St	O/T
Sabbir Rahman	20.8.1991		11	2016–2017	481	66	0	24.05	0	0-9	0/0	–	3	54/41
Sajidul Islam	18.11.1988		3	2007–2012	18	6	0	3.00	3	2-71	0/0	77.33	0	0/1
Sanjamul Islam	17.1.1990		1	2017	24	24	0	24.00	1	1-153	0/0	153.00	0	3
Sanwar Hossain	5.8.1973		9	2001–2003	345	49	0	19.16	5	2-128	0/0	62.00	1	27
Shadman Islam	18.5.1995		1	2018	76	76	0	76.00	–	–	–/–	–	1	–
Shafiul Islam	6.10.1989		11	2009–2017	211	53	0	10.55	17	3-86	0/0	55.41	2	56/12
Shahadat Hossain	7.8.1986		38	2005–2014	521	40	0	10.01	72	6-27	4/0	51.81	9	51/6
Shahriar Hossain	1.6.1976		3	2000–2003	99	48	0	19.80	–	–	–/–	–	0/1	20
Shahriar Nafees	1.5.1985		24	2005–2012	1,267	138	1	26.39	–	–	–/–	–	19	75/1
Shakib Al Hasan	24.3.1987		55	2007–2018	3,807	217	5	39.65	205	7-36	18/2	31.29	22	195/72
Shamsur Rahman	5.6.1988		6	2013–2014	305	106	1	25.41	0	0-5	0/0	–	7	109
Shuvagata Hom	11.11.1986		8	2014–2016	244	50	0	22.18	8	2-66	0/0	63.25	8	4/5
Sohag Gazi	5.8.1991		10	2012–2013	325	101*	1	21.66	38	6-74	2/0	42.07	5	20/10
Soumya Sarkar	25.2.1993		12	2014–2018	588	86	0	26.72	1	1-45	0/0	159.00	15	38/41
Subashis Roy	28.11.1988		4	2016–2017	14	12*	0	14.00	9	3-118	0/0	51.66	0	17/1
Suhrawadi Shuvo	21.11.1988		1	2011	15	15	0	7.50	4	3-73	0/0	36.50	0	52/8
Syed Rasel	3.7.1984		6	2005–2007	37	19	0	4.62	12	4-129	0/0	47.75	0	4
Taijul Islam	7.2.1992		23	2014–2018	334	39*	0	10.43	97	8-39	7/1	30.65	12	
Talha Jubair	10.12.1985		7	2002–2004	52	31	0	6.50	14	3-135	0/0	55.07	1	6
²Tamim Iqbal (*CY 2011*)	20.3.1989		56	2007–2018	4,049	206	8	37.84	0	0-1	0/0	–	14	186/71‡
Tapash Baisya	25.12.1982		21	2002–2005	384	66	0	11.29	36	4-72	0/0	59.36	6	56
Tareq Aziz	4.9.1983		3	2003–2004	22	10*	0	11.00	1	1-76	0/0	261.00	1	10
Taskin Ahmed	3.4.1995		5	2016–2017	68	33	0	8.90	7	2-43	0/0	97.42	1	32/19
Tushar Imran	10.12.1983		5	2002–2007	89	28	0	8.90	0	0-48	0/0	–	1	41
Ziaur Rahman	2.12.1986		1	2012	14	14	0	7.00	4	4-63	0/0	17.75	0	13/14

IRELAND (11 players)

	Born	Died	Tests	Test Career	Runs	HS	100s	Avge	Wkts	BB	5/10	Avge	Ct/St	O/T
Balbirnie Andrew	28.12.1990		1	2018	0	0	0	0.00	–	–	–/–	–	1	50/16
Joyce Edmund Christopher	22.9.1978		1	2018	47	43	0	23.50	–	–	–/–	–	1	61½/16‡
Kane Tyrone Edward	8.7.1994		1	2018	14	14	0	7.00	0	0-17	0/0	–	0	0/6
Murtagh Timothy James	2.8.1981		1	2018	10	5*	0	10.00	6	4-45	0/0	16.66	0	45/14
2 O'Brien Kevin Joseph	4.3.1984		1	2018	158	118	1	79.00	0	0-20	0/0	–	2	128/67
2 O'Brien Niall John	8.11.1981		1	2018	18	18	0	9.00	–	–	–/–	–	2	103/30
Porterfield William Thomas Stuart	6.9.1984		1	2018	33	32	0	16.50	–	–	–/–	–	2	122/61
Rankin William Boyd	5.7.1984		1†	2018	23	17	0	11.50	3	2-75	0/0	44.00	0	53‡/28‡
Stirling Paul Robert	3.9.1990		1	2018	28	17	0	14.00	0	0-11	0/0	–	3	100/52
Thompson Stuart Robert	15.8.1991		1	2018	56	53	0	28.00	4	3-62	0/0	23.25	0	20/28
Wilson Gary Craig	5.2.1986		1	2018	45	33*	0	45.00	–	–	–/–	–	0	99/61

AFGHANISTAN (11 players)

	Born	Died	Tests	Test Career	Runs	HS	100s	Avge	Wkts	BB	5/10	Avge	Ct/St	O/T
Afsar Zazai	10.8.1993		1	2018	7	6	0	3.50	–	–	–/–	–	2	17/1
Asghar Afghan Stanikzai	27.2.1987		1	2018	36	25	0	18.00	0	0-16	0/0	–	0	94/56
Hashmatullah Shahidi	4.11.1994		1	2018	47	36*	0	47.00	–	–	–/–	–	0	25/1
Javed Ahmadi	2.1.1992		1	2018	4	3	0	2.00	–	–	–/–	–	2	40/3
Mohammad Nabi	7.3.1985		1	2018	24	24	0	12.00	1	1-65	0/0	65.00	2	106/65
Mohammad Shahzad	15.7.1991		1	2018	27	14	0	13.50	–	–	–/–	–	1	76/65
Mujeeb Ur Rahman Zadran	28.3.2001		1	2018	18	15	0	9.00	1	1-75	0/0	75.00	0	23/7
Rahmat Shah	6.7.1993		1	2018	18	14	0	9.00	–	–	–/–	–	1	53
Rashid Khan	20.9.1998		1	2018	19	12	0	9.50	2	2-154	0/0	77.00	0	52/34‡
Wafadar Momand	1.2.2000		1	2018	6	6*	0	6.00	2	2-100	0/0	50.00	0	
Yamin Ahmadzai	25.7.1992		1	2018	1	1	0	0.50	3	3-51	0/0	17.00	0	3/2

Notes

Family relationships in the above lists are indicated by superscript numbers; the following list
contains only those players whose relationship is not apparent from a shared name.

In one Test, A. and G. G. Hearne played for England; their brother, F. Hearne, for South Africa.

The Waughs and New Zealand's Marshalls are the only instance of Test-playing twins.

Adnan Akmal: brother of Kamran and Umar Akmal.

Amar Singh, L.: brother of L. Ramji.

Azmat Rana: brother of Shafqat Rana.

Bazid Khan (Pakistan): son of Majid Khan (Pakistan) and grandson of M. Jahangir Khan (India).

Bravo, D. J. and D. M.: half-brothers.

Chappell, G. S., I. M. and T. M.: grandsons of V. Y. Richardson.

Collins, P. T.: half-brother of F. H. Edwards.

Cooper, W. H.: great-grandfather of A. P. Sheahan.

Edwards, F. H.: half-brother of P. T. Collins.

Hanif Mohammad: brother of Mushtaq, Sadiq and Wazir Mohammad; father of Shoaib Mohammad.

Headley, D. W (England): son of R. G. A. and grandson of G. A. Headley (both West Indies).

Hearne, F. (England and South Africa): father of G. A. L. Hearne (South Africa).

Jahangir Khan, M. (India): father of Majid Khan and grandfather of Bazid Khan (both Pakistan).

Kamran Akmal: brother of Adnan and Umar Akmal.

Khalid Wazir (Pakistan): son of S. Wazir Ali (India).

Kirsten, G. and P. N.: half-brothers.

Majid Khan (Pakistan): son of M. Jahangir Khan (India) and father of Bazid Khan (Pakistan).

Manzoor Elahi: brother of Salim and Zahoor Elahi.

Moin Khan: brother of Nadeem Khan.

Mudassar Nazar: son of Nazar Mohammad.

Murray, D. A.: son of E. D. Weekes.

Mushtaq Mohammad: brother of Hanif, Sadiq and Wazir Mohammad.

Nadeem Khan: brother of Moin Khan.

Nafis Iqbal: brother of Tamim Iqbal.

Nazar Mohammad: father of Mudassar Nazar.

Nazir Ali, S.: brother of S. Wazir Ali.

Pattinson, D. J. (England): brother of J. L. Pattinson (Australia).

Pervez Sajjad: brother of Waqar Hassan.

Ramiz Raja: brother of Wasim Raja.

Ramji, L.: brother of L. Amar Singh.

Riaz Afridi: brother of Shaheen Shah Afridi.

Richardson, V. Y.: grandfather of G. S., I. M. and T. M. Chappell.

Sadiq Mohammad: brother of Hanif, Mushtaq and Wazir Mohammad.

Saeed Ahmed: brother of Younis Ahmed.

Salim Elahi: brother of Manzoor and Zahoor Elahi.

Shafqat Rana: brother of Azmat Rana.

Shaheen Shah Afridi: brother of Riaz Afridi.

Sheahan, A. P.: great-grandson of W. H. Cooper.

Shoaib Mohammad: son of Hanif Mohammad.

Tamim Iqbal: brother of Nafis Iqbal.

Umar Akmal: brother of Adnan and Kamran Akmal.

Waqar Hassan: brother of Pervez Sajjad.

Wasim Raja: brother of Ramiz Raja.

Wazir Ali, S. (India): brother of S. Nazir Ali (India) and father of Khalid Wazir (Pakistan).

Wazir Mohammad: brother of Hanif, Mushtaq and Sadiq Mohammad.

Weekes, E. D.: father of D. A. Murray.

Yograj Singh: father of Yuvraj Singh.

Younis Ahmed: brother of Saeed Ahmed.

Yuvraj Singh: son of Yograj Singh.

Zahoor Elahi: brother of Manzoor and Salim Elahi.

Teams are listed only where relatives played for different sides.

PLAYERS APPEARING FOR MORE THAN ONE TEST TEAM

Fifteen cricketers have appeared for two countries in Test matches, namely:

Amir Elahi (India 1, Pakistan 5)
J. J. Ferris (Australia 8, England 1)
S. C. Guillen (West Indies 5, New Zealand 3)
Gul Mahomed (India 8, Pakistan 1)
F. Hearne (England 2, South Africa 4)
A. H. Kardar (India 3, Pakistan 23)
W. E. Midwinter (England 4, Australia 8)
F. Mitchell (England 2, South Africa 3)

W. L. Murdoch (Australia 18, England 1)
Nawab of Pataudi snr (England 3, India 3)
W. B. Rankin (England 1, Ireland 1)
A. J. Traicos (South Africa 3, Zimbabwe 4)
A. E. Trott (Australia 3, England 2)
K. C. Wessels (Australia 24, South Africa 16)
S. M. J. Woods (Australia 3, England 3)

Rankin also played seven one-day internationals and two Twenty20 internationals for England and 53 ODIs and 28 T20Is for Ireland; Wessels played 54 ODIs for Australia and 55 for South Africa.

The following players appeared for the ICC World XI against Australia in the Super Series Test in 2005-06: M. V. Boucher, R. Dravid, A. Flintoff, S. J. Harmison, Inzamam-ul-Haq, J. H. Kallis, B. C. Lara, M. Muralitharan, V. Sehwag, G. C. Smith, D. L. Vettori.

In 1970, England played five first-class matches against the Rest of the World after the cancellation of South Africa's tour. Players were awarded England caps, but the matches are no longer considered to have Test status. Alan Jones (born 4.11.1938) made his only appearance for England in this series, scoring 5 and 0; he did not bowl and took no catches.

ONE-DAY AND TWENTY20 INTERNATIONAL CRICKETERS

The following players had appeared for Test-playing countries in one-day internationals or Twenty20 internationals by December 31, 2018, but had not represented their countries in Test matches by January 14, 2019. (Numbers in brackets signify number of ODIs for each player: where a second number appears, e.g. (5/1), it signifies the number of T20Is for that player.)

By January 2018, D. A. Miller (112 ODIs/61 T20Is, including three for the World XI) was the most experienced international player never to have appeared in Test cricket. R. G. Sharma held the record for most international appearances before making his Test debut, with 108 ODIs and 36 T20Is. S. Badree had played a record 52 T20Is (including two for the World XI) without a Test or ODI appearance.

England

M. W. Alleyne (10), I. D. Austin (9), S. W. Billings (15/17), D. R. Briggs (1/7), A. D. Brown (16), D. R. Brown (9), G. Chapple (1), J. W. M. Dalrymple (27/3), S. M. Davies (8/5), J. L. Denly (9/6), J. W. Dernbach (24/34), M. V. Fleming (11), P. J. Franks (1), I. J. Gould (18), A. P. Grayson (2), H. F. Gurney (10/2), G. W. Humpage (3), T. E. Jesty (10), E. C. Joyce (17/2), C. Kieswetter (46/25), L. S. Livingstone (0/2), G. D. Lloyd (6), A. G. R. Loudon (1), J. D. Love (3), M. B. Loye (7), M. J. Lumb (3/27), M. A. Lynch (3), A. D. Mascarenhas (20/14), S. C. Meaker (2/2), T. S. Mills (0/4), P. Mustard (10/2), P. A. Nixon (19/1), S. D. Parry (2/5), J. J. Roy (70/32), M. J. Smith (5), N. M. K. Smith (7), J. N. Snape (10/1), V. S. Solanki (51/3), O. P. Stone (4), R. J. W. Topley (10/6), J. O. Troughton (6), C. M. Wells (2), V. J. Wells (9), A. G. Wharf (13), D. J. Willey (42/24), L. J. Wright (50/51), M. H. Yardy (28/14).

D. R. Brown also played 16 ODIs for Scotland, and E. C. Joyce one Test, 61 ODIs and 16 T20Is for Ireland.

Australia

S. A. Abbott (1/3), J. P. Behrendorff (0/5), T. R. Birt (0/4), G. A. Bishop (2), S. M. Boland (14/3), C. J. Boyce (0/7), R. J. Campbell (2), A. T. Carey (6/19), D. T. Christian (19/16), M. J. Cosgrove (3), N. M. Coulter-Nile (22/26), B. C. J. Cutting (4/4), M. J. Di Venuto (9), B. R. Dorey (4), B. R. Dunk (0/5), Fawad Ahmed (3/2), P. J. Forrest (15), B. Geeves (2/1), S. F. Graf (11), I. J. Harvey (73), S. M. Harwood (1/3), S. D. Heazlett (1), J. R. Hopes (84/12), D. J. Hussey (69/39), M. Klinger (0/3), B. Laughlin (5/3), S. Lee (45), M. L. Lewis (7/2), C. A. Lynn (4/18), R. J. McCurdy (11), B. R. McDermott (0/8), K. H. MacLeay (16), P. Maher (26), J. M. Muirhead (0/5), D. P. Nannes (1/15), M. G. Neser (2), A. A. Noffke (1/2), J. S. Paris (2), L. A. Pomersbach (0/1), G. D. Porter (2), N. J. Reardon (0/2), J. A. Richardson (4/7), K. W. Richardson (18/9), B. J. Rohrer (0/1), L. Ronchi (4/3), G. S. Sandhu (2), D. J. M. Short (4/18), J. D. Siddons (1), B. Stanlake (6/17), M. P. Stoinis (21/17),

A. M. Stuart (3), M. J. Swepson (0/1), C. P. Tremain (4), G. S. Trimble (2), A. J. Turner (0/3), A. J. Tye (7/26), J. D. Wildermuth (0/2), D. J. Worrall (3), B. E. Young (6), A. Zampa (33/20), A. K. Zesers (2).

R. J. Campbell also played three T20Is for Hong Kong, D. P. Nannes two T20Is for the Netherlands, and L. Ronchi four Tests, 72 ODIs and 26 T20Is for New Zealand..

South Africa

Y. A. Abdulla (0/2), S. Abrahams (1), F. Behardien (59/38), D. M. Benkenstein (23), G. H. Bodi (2/1), L. E. Bosman (13/14), R. E. Bryson (7), D. J. Callaghan (29), G. L. Cloete (0/1), D. N. Crookes (32), C. J. Dala (2/5), H. Davids (2/9), R. Frylinck (0/3), T. Henderson (0/1), B. E. Hendricks (0/7), R. R. Hendricks (9/14), C. A. Ingram (31/9), C. Jonker (2/2), J. C. Kent (2), H. Klaasen (12/6), L. J. Koen (5), G. J-P. Kruger (3/1), E. Leie (0/2), R. E. Levi (0/13), J. Louw (3/2), D. A. Miller (112/61), M. Mosehle (0/7), P. V. Mpitsang (2), P. W. A. Mulder (7), S. J. Palframan (7), D. Paterson (3/8), A. M. Phangiso (21/16), N. Pothas (3), D. Pretorius (14/2), A. G. Puttick (1), C. E. B. Rice (3), M. J. R. Rindel (22), R. R. Rossouw (36/15), D. B. Rundle (2), T. G. Shaw (9), M. Shezi (1), E. O. Simons (23), J. T. Smuts (0/8), E. L. R. Stewart (6), R. Telemachus (37/3), J. Theron (4/9), A. C. Thomas (0/1), T. Tshabalala (4), H. E. van der Dussen (0/2), R. E. van der Merwe (13/13), J. J. van der Wath (10/8), V. B. van Jaarsveld (2/3), M. N. van Wyk (17/8), C. J. P. G. van Zyl (2), D. Wiese (6/20), H. S. Williams (7), M. Yachad (1), K. Zondo (5).

R. E. van der Merwe also played 12 T20Is for the Netherlands.

West Indies

F. A. Allen (4/6), H. A. G. Anthony (3), S. Badree (0/50), C. D. Barnwell (0/6), M. C. Bascombe (0/1), R. R. Beaton (2), N. E. Bonner (0/2), D. Brown (3), B. St A. Browne (4), P. A. Browne (5), H. R. Bryan (15), D. C. Butler (5/1), J. L. Carter (28), J. Charles (48/34), D. O. Christian (0/2), R. T. Crandon (1), R. R. Emrit (2/4), S. E. Findlay (9/2), A. D. S. Fletcher (25/42), R. S. Gabriel (11), R. C. Haynes (8), C. Hemraj (6), R. O. Hurley (9), D. P. Hyatt (9/5), K. C. B. Jeremy (6), E. Lewis (35/20), A. M. McCarthy (0/1), O. C. McCoy (2), A. Martin (9/1), G. E. Mathurin (0/3), J. N. Mohammed (28/9), A. R. Nurse (40/12), W. K. D. Perkins (0/1), K. A. Pierre (0/3), K. A. Pollard (101/59), N. Pooran (0/8), R. Powell (34/20), M. R. Pydanna (3), A. C. L. Richards (1/1), S. E. Rutherford (0/1), K. Santokie (0/12), K. F. Semple (7), O. F. Smith (0/2), D. C. Thomas (21/3), O. R. Thomas (4/6), C. M. Tuckett (1), K. O. K. Williams (8/18), L. R. Williams (15).

New Zealand

G. W. Aldridge (2/1), M. D. Bailey (1), M. D. Bates (2/3), B. R. Blair (14), T. C. Bruce (0/14), C. E. Bulfin (4), T. K. Canning (4), M. S. Chapman (3/5), P. G. Coman (3), A. P. Devcich (12/4), B. J. Diamanti (1/1), M. W. Douglas (6), A. M. Ellis (15/5), L. H. Ferguson (19/2), B. G. Hadlee (2), L. J. Hamilton (2), R. T. Hart (1), K. A. Hayes (1), R. M. Hira (0/15), P. A. Hitchcock (14/1), L. G. Howell (2), A. K. Kitchen (0/5), S. C. Kuggeleijn (2), M. J. McClenaghan (48/28), N. L. McCullum (84/63), P. D. McGlashan (4/11), B. J. McKechnie (14), E. B. McSweeney (16), A. W. Mathieson (1), J. P. Millmow (5), A. F. Milne (40/21), T. S. Nethula (5), J. A. J. Penn (5), R. G. Petrie (12), G. D. Phillips (0/11), S. H. A. Rance (2/5), R. B. Reid (9), S. J. Roberts (2), T. L. Seifert (0/7), S. L. Stewart (4), L. W. Stott (1), G. P. Sulzberger (3), A. R. Tait (5), E. P. Thompson (1/1), M. D. J. Walker (3), R. J. Webb (3), B. M. Wheeler (6/6), J. W. Wilson (3), W. A. Wisneski (3), L. J. Woodcock (4/3), G. H. Worker (10/2).

M. S. Chapman also played 2 ODIs and 19 T20Is for Hong Kong.

India

K. K. Ahmed (6/6), S. Aravind (0/1), P. Awana (0/2), A. C. Bedade (13), A. Bhandari (2), Bhupinder Singh snr (2), G. Bose (1), Y. S. Chahal (34/27), D. L. Chahar (1/1), V. B. Chandrasekhar (7), U. Chatterjee (3), N. A. David (4), P. Dharmani (1), R. Dhawan (3/1), A. B. Dinda (13/9), F. Y. Fazal (1), R. S. Gavaskar (11), R. S. Ghai (6), M. S. Gony (2), Gurkeerat Singh (3), S. S. Iyer (6/6), K. M. Jadhav (48/9), Joginder Sharma (4/4), A. V. Kale (1), S. Kaul (3/2), S. C. Khanna (10), G. K. Khoda (2), A. R. Khurasiya (12), D. S. Kulkarni (12/2), T. Kumaran (8), Mandeep Singh (0/3), J. J. Martin (10), D. Mongia (57/1), S. P. Mukherjee (3), A. M. Nayar (3), P. Negi (0/1), G. K. Pandey (2), M. K. Pandey (23/28), K. H. Pandya (0/6), J. V. Paranjpe (4), Parvez Rasool (1/1), A. K. Patel (8), A. R. Patel (38/11), Y. K. Pathan (57/22), Randhir Singh (2), S. S. Raul (2), A. T. Rayudu (45/6), A. M. Salvi (3), S. V. Samson (0/1), V. Shankar (0/5), M. Sharma (26/8), R. Sharma (4/2), S. Sharma (0/2), L. R. Shukla (3), R. P. Singh (3), M. Siraj (0/3), R. S. Sodhi (18), S. Somasunder (2), B. B. Sran (6/2), S. Sriram (8), Sudhakar Rao (1), M. K. Tiwary (12/3), S. S. Tiwary (3), S. Tyagi (4/1),

R. V. Uthappa (46/13), P. S. Vaidya (4), Y. Venugopal Rao (16), M. S. Washington Sundar (1/7), Jai P. Yadav (12).

Pakistan

Aamer Hameed (2), Aamer Hanif (5), Aamer Yamin (4/2), Akhtar Sarfraz (4), Anwar Ali (22/16), Arshad Pervez (2), Asad Ali (4/2), Asif Ali (11/16), Asif Mahmood (2), Awais Zia (0/5), Faisal Athar (1), Ghulam Ali (3), Haafiz Shahid (3), Hammad Azam (11/5), Hasan Jamil (6), Hussain Talat (0/11), Imad Wasim (32/31), Imran Abbas (2), Imran Khan jnr (0/3), Iqbal Sikandar (4), Irfan Bhatti (1), Javed Qadir (1), Junaid Zia (4), Kamran Hussain (2), Kashif Raza (1), Khalid Latif (5/13), Mahmood Hamid (1), Mansoor Amjad (1/1), Mansoor Rana (2), Manzoor Akhtar (7), Maqsood Rana (1), Masood Iqbal (1), Moin-ul-Atiq (5), Mujahid Jamshed (4), Mukhtar Ahmed (0/6), Naeem Ahmed (1), Naeem Ashraf (2), Najaf Shah (1), Naseer Malik (3), Nauman Anwar (0/1), Naumanullah (1), Parvez Mir (3), Rafatullah Mohmand (0/3), Rameez Raja (0/2), Raza Hasan (1/10), Rizwan Ahmed (1), Rumman Raees (9/8), Saad Nasim (3/3), Saadat Ali (8), Saeed Azad (4), Sahibzada Farhan (0/3), Sajid Ali (13), Sajjad Akbar (2), Salim Pervez (1), Samiullah Khan (2), Shahid Anwar (1), Shahzaib Hasan (3/10), Shakeel Ansar (0/2), Shakil Khan (1), Shoaib Khan (0/1), Sohaib Maqsood (26/20), Sohail Fazal (2), Tanvir Mehdi (1), Usman Shinwari (9/13), Waqas Maqsood (0/1),Wasim Haider (3), Zafar Gohar (1), Zafar Iqbal (8), Zahid Ahmed (2).

Sri Lanka

M. A. Aponso (9/3), J. R. M. W. S. Bandara (0/8), K. M. C. Bandara (1/1), J. W. H. D. Boteju (2), D. L. S. de Silva (2), G. N. de Silva (4), P. C. de Silva (7/2), P. W. H. de Silva (9), S. N. T. de Silva (0/3), L. H. D. Dilhara (9/2), A. M. Fernando (1), B. Fernando (0/2), E. R. Fernando (3), T. L. Fernando (1), U. N. K. Fernando (2), W. I. A. Fernando (1), J. C. Gamage (4), W. C. A. Ganegama (4), F. R. M. Goonatilleke (1), P. W. Gunaratne (23), A. A. W. Gunawardene (1), P. D. Heyn (2), W. S. Jayantha (17), P. S. Jayaprakashdaran (1), C. U. Jayasinghe (0/5), S. A. Jayasinghe (2), G. S. N. F. G. Jayasuriya (9/11), N. G. R. P. Jayasuriya (2), S. H. T. Kandamby (39/5), S. H. U. Karnain (19), H. G. J. M. Kulatunga (0/2), D. S. M. Kumara (1/2), L. D. Madushanka (4), B. M. A. J. Mendis (54/22), C. Mendis (1), P. H. K. D. Mendis (0/1), A. M. N. Munasinghe (5), E. M. D. Y. Munaweera (2/13), H. G. D. Nayanakantha (3), A. R. M. Opatha (5), S. P. Pasqual (2), S. S. Pathirana (18/5), A. K. Perera (4/2), K. G. Perera (1), H. S. M. Pieris (3), S. M. A. Priyanjan (23/3), M. Pushpakumara (3/1), R. L. B. Rambukwella (0/2), S. K. Ranasinghe (4), N. Ranatunga (2), N. L. K. Ratnayake (2), R. J. M. G. M. Rupasinghe (0/2), A. P. B. Tennekoon (4), M. H. Tissera (3), I. Udana (2/18), J. D. F. Vandersay (11/7), D. M. Vonhagt (1), A. P. Weerakkody (1), D. S. Weerakkody (3), S. Weerakoon (2), K. Weeraratne (15/5), S. R. D. Wettimuny (3), R. P. A. H. Wickremaratne (3).

Zimbabwe

R. D. Brown (7), K. M. Curran (11), S. G. Davies (4), K. G. Duers (6), E. A. Essop-Adam (1), D. A. G. Fletcher (6), T. N. Garwe (1), J. G. Heron (6), R. S. Higgins (11), V. R. Hogg (2), A. J. Ireland (26/1), L. M. Jongwe (22/8), R. Kaia (1), T. S. Kamunhukamwe (2), F. Kasteni (3), A. J. Mackay (3), N. Madziva (12/9), G. C. Martin (5), M. A. Meman (1), T. V. Mufambisi (6), R. C. Murray (5), T. K. Musakanda (1), C. T. Mutombodzi (11/5), T. Muzarabani (8/9), R. Ngarava (9), I. A. Nicolson (2), G. A. Paterson (10), G. E. Peckover (3), E. C. Rainsford (39/2), P. W. E. Rawson (10), H. P. Rinke (18), L. N. Roche (3), R. W. Sims (3), G. M. Strydom (12), C. Zhuwao (9/7).

Bangladesh

Abu Haider (2/13), Afif Hossain (0/1), Ahmed Kamal (1), Alam Talukdar (2), Aminul Islam jnr (1), Anisur Rahman (2), Arafat Sunny (16/10), Ather Ali Khan (19), Azhar Hussain (7), Dhiman Ghosh (14/1), Dolar Mahmud (7), Farhad Reza (34/13), Faruq Ahmed (7), Fazle Mahmud (2), Gazi Ashraf (7), Ghulam Faruq (5), Ghulam Nausher (9), Hafizur Rahman (2), Harunur Rashid (2), Jahangir Alam (3), Jahangir Badshah (5), Jamaluddin Ahmed (1), Mafizur Rahman (4), Mahbubur Rahman (2), Mazharul Haque (1), Mehedi Hasan snr (0/1), Minhazul Abedin (27), Mohammad Saifuddin (7/9), Moniruzzaman (2), Morshed Ali Khan (3), Mosharraf Hossain (5), Mukhtar Ali (0/1), Nadif Chowdhury (0/3), Nasir Ahmed (7), Nazmus Sadat (0/1), Neeyamur Rashid (2), Nurul Abedin (4), Rafiqul Alam (2), Raqibul Hasan snr (2), Rony Talukdar (0/1), Saiful Islam (7), Sajjad Ahmed (2), Samiur Rahman (2), Saqlain Sajib (0/1), Shafiuddin Ahmed (11), Shahidur Rahman (2), Shariful Haq (1), Sheikh Salahuddin (6), Tanveer Haider (2), Wahidul Gani (1), Zahid Razzak (3), Zakir Hasan (0/1), Zakir Hassan (2).

Ireland

J. Anderson (8/4), A. C. Botha (42/14), J. P. Bray (15/2), S. A. Britton (1), K. E. D. Carroll (6), P. K. D. Chase (25/6), P. Connell (13/9), A. R. Cusack (59/37), G. H. Dockrell (77/54), P. S. Eaglestone (1/1), M. J. Fourie (7), P. G. Gillespie (5), R. S. Haire (2), J. D. Hall (3), D. T. Johnston (67/30), N. G. Jones (14/5), D. I. Joyce (3), G. E. Kidd (6/1), D. Langford-Smith (22), J. B. Little (0/4), A. R. McBrine (33/19), W. K. McCallan (39/9), R. D. McCann (8/3), G. J. McCarter (1/3), B. J. McCarthy (23/6), J. F. Mooney (64/27), P. J. K. Mooney (4), E. J. G. Morgan (23), J. Mulder (4/8), A. D. Poynter (19/19), S. W. Poynter (16/19), D. A. Rankin (0/2), E. J. Richardson (2), J. N. K. Shannon (1/8), S. Singh (10/8), M. C. Sorensen (13/26), R. Strydom (9/4), S. P. Terry (5/1), G. J. Thompson (3/8), L. J. Tucker (0/4), A. van der Merwe (9), R. M. West (10/5), R. K. Whelan (2), A. R. White (61/18), C. A. Young (13/16).

E. J. G. Morgan also played 16 Tests, 189 ODIs and 77 T20Is for England.

Afghanistan

Abdullah Mazari (2), Aftab Alam (20/12), Ahmed Shah (1), Dawlat Ahmadzai (3/2), Dawlat Zadran (72/33), Fareed Ahmad (5/9), Gulbadeen Naib (49/38), Hamid Hassan (32/22), Hamza Hotak (31/31), Hasti Gul (2), Hazratullah Zazai (2/3), Ihsanullah Janat (16), Izatullah Dawlatzai (5/4), Karim Janat (1/14), Karim Sadiq (24/36), Khaliq Dad (6), Mirwais Ashraf (46/25), Mohibullah Paak (2), Najeeb Tarakai (1/9), Najibullah Zadran (50/47), Nasim Baras (0/3), Nasir Ahmadzai (16), Naveen-ul-Haq (2), Nawroz Mangal (49/32), Noor Ali Zadran (46/20), Noor-ul-Haq (2), Raees Ahmadzai (5/8), Rokhan Barakzai (1/3), Samiullah Shenwari (79/60), Sayed Shirzad (0/3), Shabir Noori (10/1), Shafiqullah Shinwari (24/41), Shapoor Zadran (43/34), Sharafuddin Ashraf (14/6), Usman Ghani (15/17), Zakiullah (1), Zamir Khan (0/1).

PLAYERS APPEARING FOR MORE THAN ONE ONE-DAY/TWENTY20 INTERNATIONAL TEAM

The following players have played ODIs for the **African XI** in addition to their national side:

N. Boje (2), L. E. Bosman (1), J. Botha (2), M. V. Boucher (5), E. Chigumbura (3), A. B. de Villiers (5), H. H. Dippenaar (6), J. H. Kallis (3), J. M. Kemp (6), J. A. Morkel (2), M. Morkel (3), T. M. Odoyo (5), P. J. Ongondo (1), J. L. Ontong (1), S. M. Pollock (3), A. G. Prince (3), J. A. Rudolph (2), V. Sibanda (2), G. C. Smith (1), D. W. Steyn (2), H. H. Streak (2), T. Taibu (1), S. O. Tikolo (4), M. Zondeki (2). (Odoyo, Ongondo and Tikolo played for Kenya, who do not have Test status.)

The following players have played ODIs for the **Asian Cricket Council XI** in addition to their national side:

Abdul Razzaq (4), M. S. Dhoni (3), R. Dravid (1), C. R. D. Fernando (1), S. C. Ganguly (3), Harbhajan Singh (2), Inzamam-ul-Haq (3), S. T. Jayasuriya (4), D. P. M. D. Jayawardene (5), A. Kumble (2), Mashrafe bin Mortaza (2), Mohammad Ashraful (2), Mohammad Asif (3), Mohammad Rafique (2), Mohammad Yousuf (7), M. Muralitharan (4), A. Nehra (3), K. C. Sangakkara (4), V. Sehwag (7), Shahid Afridi (3), Shoaib Akhtar (3), W. U. Tharanga (1), W. P. U. J. C. Vaas (1), Yuvraj Singh (3), Zaheer Khan (6).

The following players have played ODIs for an **ICC World XI** in addition to their national side:

C. L. Cairns (1), R. Dravid (1), S. P. Fleming (1), A. Flintoff (3), C. H. Gayle (3), A. C. Gilchrist (1), D. Gough (1), M. L. Hayden (1), J. H. Kallis (3), B. C. Lara (4), G. D. McGrath (1), M. Muralitharan (3), M. Ntini (1), K. P. Pietersen (2), S. M. Pollock (3), R. T. Ponting (1), K. C. Sangakkara (3), V. Sehwag (3), Shahid Afridi (2), Shoaib Akhtar (3), D. L. Vettori (4), S. K. Warne (1).

The following players have played T20Is for a **World XI** in addition to their national side:

H. M. Amla (3), S. Badree (2), G. J. Bailey (1), S. W. Billings (1), P. D. Collingwood (1), B. C. J. Cutting (3), F. du Plessis (3), G. D. Elliott (1), Imran Tahir (3), K. D. Karthik (1), S. Lamichhane (1), M. J. McClenaghan (1), D. A. Miller (3), T. S. Mills (1), M. Morkel (3), T. D. Paine (2), N. L. T. C. Perera (1), Rashid Khan (1), L. Ronchi (1), D. J. G. Sammy (2), Shahid Afridi (1), Shoaib Malik (1), Tamim Iqbal (4).

K. C. Wessels played Tests and ODIs for both Australia and South Africa. **D. R. Brown** played ODIs for England plus ODIs and T20Is for Scotland. **C. B. Lambert** played Tests and ODIs for West Indies and one ODI for USA. **E. C. Joyce** played ODIs and T20Is for England and all three formats for Ireland; **E. J. G. Morgan** ODIs for Ireland and all three formats for England; and **W. B. Rankin** all three formats for Ireland and England. **A. C. Cummins** played Tests and ODIs for West

Indies and ODIs for Canada. **G. M. Hamilton** played Tests for England and ODIs for Scotland. **D. P. Nannes** played ODIs and T20Is for Australia and T20Is for the Netherlands. **L. Ronchi** played ODIs and T20Is for Australia and all three formats for New Zealand. **G. O. Jones** played all three formats for England and ODIs for Papua New Guinea. **R. E. van der Merwe** played ODIs and T20Is for South Africa and T20Is for the Netherlands. **R. J. Campbell** played ODIs for Australia and T20Is for Hong Kong. **M. S. Chapman** played ODIs and T20Is for Hong Kong and New Zealand.

ELITE TEST UMPIRES

The following umpires were on the ICC's elite panel in February 2019. The figures for Tests, one-day internationals and Twenty20 internationals and the Test Career dates refer to matches in which they have officiated as on-field umpires (excluding abandoned games). The totals of Tests are complete up to January 14, 2019, the totals of one-day internationals and Twenty20 internationals up to December 31, 2018.

	Country	*Born*	*Tests*	*Test Career*	*ODIs*	*T20Is*
Aleem Dar	P	6.6.1968	123	*2003–2018*	196	43
Dharmasena Handunnettige Deepthi						
Priyantha <u>Kumar</u>	SL	24.4.1971	58	*2010–2018*	89	22
Erasmus Marais	SA	27.2.1964	54*	*2009–2018*	81	26
Gaffaney Christopher Blair	NZ	30.11.1975	25	*2014–2018*	60	20
Gould Ian James	E	19.8.1957	73	*2008–2018*	135	37
Illingworth Richard Keith	E	23.8.1963	39*	*2012–2018*	59	16
Kettleborough Richard Allan	E	15.3.1973	57	*2010–2018*	75	22
Llong Nigel James	E	11.2.1969	55	*2007–2018*	121	32
Oxenford Bruce Nicholas James	A	5.3.1960	55	*2010–2018*	88	20
Ravi Sundaram	I	22.4.1966	32	*2013–2018*	35	18
Reiffel Paul Ronald	A	19.4.1966	41	*2012–2018*	58	16
Tucker Rodney James	A	28.8.1964	65	*2009–2018*	78	35

* *Includes one Test where he took over mid-match.*

BIRTHS AND DEATHS

OTHER CRICKETING NOTABLES

The following list shows the births and deaths of cricketers, and people associated with cricket, who have *not* played in men's Test matches.

Criteria for inclusion All non-Test players who have either (1) scored 20,000 first-class runs, or (2) taken 1,500 first-class wickets, or (3) achieved 750 dismissals, or (4) reached both 15,000 runs and 750 wickets. Also included are (5) the leading players who flourished before the start of Test cricket, (6) *Wisden* Cricketers of the Year who did not play Test cricket, and (7) others of merit or interest.

Names Where players were normally known by a name other than their first, this is underlined.

Teams Where only one team is listed, this is normally the one for which the player made most first-class appearances. Additional teams are listed only if the player appeared for them in more than 20 first-class matches, or if they are especially relevant to their career. School and university teams are not given unless especially relevant (e.g. for the schoolboys chosen as wartime Cricketers of the Year in the 1918 and 1919 *Wisdens*).

		Born	*Died*
Adams Percy Webster	Cheltenham College; *CY 1919*	5.9.1900	28.9.1962
Aird Ronald MC Hampshire; sec. MCC 1953–62, pres. MCC 1968–69		4.5.1902	16.8.1986
Aislabie Benjamin	Surrey, secretary of MCC 1822–42	14.1.1774	2.6.1842
Alcock Charles William	Secretary of Surrey 1872–1907	2.12.1842	26.2.1907
Editor, Cricket magazine, 1882–1907. Captain of Wanderers and England football teams.			
Aleem Dar	Umpire in 117 Tests by January 2018	6.6.1968	
Alley William Edward	NSW, Somerset; Test umpire; *CY 1962*	3.2.1919	26.11.2004
Alleyne Mark Wayne	Gloucestershire; *CY 2001*	23.5.1968	
Altham Harry Surtees CBE Surrey, Hants; historian; pres. MCC 1959–60		30.11.1888	11.3.1965
Arlott Leslie Thomas John OBE	Broadcaster and writer	25.2.1914	14.12.1991
Arthur John Michael	Griq. W, OFS; South Africa coach 2005–10,		17.5.1968	
	Australia coach 2011–13, Pakistan coach 2016–		
Ashdown William Henry	Kent	27.12.1898	15.9.1979
The only player to appear in English first-class cricket before and after the two world wars.			
Ash Eileen (*née* Whelan)	England women	30.10.1911	
Believed to be the longest-lived international cricketer.			
Ashley-Cooper Frederick Samuel	Historian	22.3.1877	31.1.1932
Ashton *Sir* Hubert KBE MC Cam U, Essex; pres. MCC 1960–61; *CY 1922*		13.2.1898	17.6.1979
Austin *Sir* Harold Bruce Gardiner	Barbados	15.7.1877	27.7.1943
Austin Ian David	Lancashire; *CY 1999*	30.5.1966	
Bailey Jack Arthur	Essex; secretary of MCC 1974–87	22.6.1930	12.7.2018
Bainbridge Philip	Gloucestershire, Durham; *CY 1986*	16.4.1958	
Bakewell Enid (*née* Turton) MBE	England women	16.12.1940	
Bannister John David	Warwickshire; writer and broadcaster	23.8.1930	23.1.2016
Barker Gordon	Essex	6.7.1931	10.2.2006
Bartlett Hugh Tryon	Sussex; *CY 1939*	7.10.1914	26.6.1988
Bates Suzannah Wilson	New Zealand women	16.9.1987	
Bayliss Trevor Harley	NSW; SL coach 2007–11; Eng. coach 2015–	21.12.1962	
Beauclerk *Rev. Lord* Frederick	Middlesex, Surrey, MCC	8.5.1773	22.4.1850
Beaumont Tamsin Tilley	England women; *CY 2019*	11.3.1991	
Beldam George William	Middlesex; photographer	1.5.1868	23.11.1937
Beldham William ("Silver Billy")	Hambledon, Surrey	5.2.1766	26.2.1862
Beloff Michael Jacob QC	Head of ICC Code of Conduct Commission	18.4.1942	
Benkenstein Dale Martin	KwaZulu-Natal, Durham; *CY 2009*	9.6.1974	
Berry Anthony Scyld Ivens	Editor of *Wisden* 2008–11	28.4.1954	
Berry Leslie George	Leicestershire	28.4.1906	5.2.1985
Bird Harold Dennis ("Dickie") OBE Yorkshire, Leics; umpire in 66 Tests		19.4.1933	
Blofeld Henry Calthorpe OBE	Cambridge Univ; broadcaster	23.9.1939	
Bond John David	Lancashire; *CY 1971*	6.5.1932	
Booth Roy	Yorkshire, Worcestershire	1.10.1926	24.9.2018
Bowden Brent Fraser ("Billy")	Umpire in 84 Tests	11.4.1963	

		Born	Died
Bowley Frederick Lloyd	Worcestershire	9.11.1873	31.5.1943
Bradshaw Keith Tasmania; secretary/chief executive MCC 2006–11		2.10.1963	
Brewer Derek Michael Secretary/chief executive MCC 2012–17		2.4.1958	
Briers Nigel Edwin	Leicestershire; *CY 1993*	15.1.1955	
Brittin Janette Ann MBE	England women	4.7.1959	11.9.2017
Brookes Wilfrid H.	Editor of *Wisden* 1936–39	5.12.1894	28.5.1955
Bryan John Lindsay	Kent; *CY 1922*	26.5.1896	23.4.1985
Buchanan John Marshall Queensland; Australia coach 1999–2007		5.4.1953	
Bucknor Stephen Anthony Umpire in a record 128 Tests		31.5.1946	
Bull Frederick George	Essex; *CY 1898*	2.4.1875	16.9.1910
Buller John Sydney MBE	Worcestershire; Test umpire	23.8.1909	7.8.1970
Burnup Cuthbert James	Kent; *CY 1903*	21.11.1875	5.4.1960
Caine Charles Stewart	Editor of *Wisden* 1926–33	28.10.1861	15.4.1933
Calder Harry Lawton	Cranleigh School; *CY 1918*	24.1.1901	15.9.1995
Cardus *Sir* John Frederick Neville	Writer	3.4.1888	27.2.1975
Chalke Stephen Robert	Writer	5.6.1948	
Chapple Glen	Lancashire; *CY 2012*	23.1.1974	
Chester Frank	Worcestershire; Test umpire	20.1.1895	8.4.1957
Stood in 48 Tests between 1924 and 1955, a record that lasted until 1992.			
Clark Belinda Jane	Australia women	10.9.1970	
Clark David Graham	Kent; president MCC 1977–78	27.1.1919	8.10.2013
Clarke Charles Giles CBE Chairman ECB, 2007–15, pres. ECB, 2015–18		29.5.1953	
Clarke William Nottinghamshire; founded the All-England XI		24.12.1798	25.8.1856
Collier David Gordon OBE Chief executive of ECB, 2005–14		22.4.1955	
Collins Arthur Edward Jeune	Clifton College	18.8.1885	11.11.1914
Made 628* in a house match in 1899, the highest score in any cricket until 2016.			
Conan Doyle *Dr Sir* Arthur Ignatius	MCC	22.5.1859	7.7.1930
Creator of Sherlock Holmes; his only victim in first-class cricket was W. G. Grace.			
Connor Clare Joanne CBE England women; administrator		1.9.1976	
Constant David John Kent, Leics; first-class umpire 1969–2006		9.11.1941	
Cook Thomas Edwin Reed	Sussex	5.1.1901	15.1.1950
Cox George jnr	Sussex	23.8.1911	30.3.1985
Cox George snr	Sussex	29.11.1873	24.3.1949
Cozier Winston Anthony Lloyd	Broadcaster and writer	10.7.1940	11.5.2016
Dalmiya Jagmohan Pres. BCCI 2001–04, 2015, pres. ICC 1997–2000		30.5.1940	20.9.2015
Davies Emrys	Glamorgan; Test umpire	27.6.1904	10.11.1975
Davison Brian Fettes Rhodesia, Leics, Tasmania, Gloucestershire		21.12.1946	
Dawkes George Owen	Leicestershire, Derbyshire	19.7.1920	10.8.2006
Day Arthur Percival	Kent; *CY 1910*	10.4.1885	22.1.1969
de Lisle Timothy John March Phillipps	Editor of *Wisden* 2003	25.6.1962	
Dennett Edward George	Gloucestershire	27.4.1880	14.9.1937
Deutrom Warren Robert Chief executive, Cricket Ireland 2006–		13.1.1970	
Dhanawade Pranav Prashant K. C. Gandhi English School		13.5.2000	
Made the highest score in any cricket, 1,009*, in a school match in Mumbai in January 2016.			
Di Venuto Michael James Tas., Derbys, Durham; Surrey coach 2016–		12.12.1973	
Eagar Edward Patrick	Photographer	9.3.1944	
Eddings Earl Robert Chairman of Cricket Australia 2018–		10.12.1967	
Edwards Charlotte Marie CBE	England women; *CY 2014*	17.12.1979	
Ehsan Mani President ICC 2003–06; Chairman PCB 2018–		23.3.1945	
Engel Matthew Lewis Editor of *Wisden* 1993–2000, 2004–07		11.6.1951	
Farbrace Paul Kent, Middx; SL coach 2014; Eng. asst coach 2014–19		7.7.1967	
"Felix" (Nicholas Wanostrocht) Kent, Surrey, All-England		4.10.1804	3.9.1876
Batsman, artist, author (Felix on the Bat) and inventor of the Catapulta bowling machine.			
Ferguson William Henry BEM	Scorer	6.6.1880	22.9.1957
Scorer and baggage-master for five Test teams on 43 tours over 52 years and "never lost a bag".			
Findlay William Oxford U, Lancs; sec. MCC 1926–36		22.6.1880	19.6.1953
Firth John D'Ewes Evelyn	Winchester College; *CY 1918*	21.2.1900	21.9.1957
Fitzpatrick Cathryn Lorraine	Australia women	4.3.1968	
Fletcher Duncan Andrew Gwynne OBE Zimbabwe; England coach 1999–2007; India coach 2011–15		27.9.1948	

		Born	Died
Ford Graham Xavier	Natal B; South Africa coach 1999–2002;	16.11.1960	
	SL coach 2012–14, 2016–17; Ireland coach 2017–		
Foster Henry Knollys	Worcestershire; *CY 1911*	30.10.1873	23.6.1950
Frindall William Howard MBE	Statistician	3.3.1939	30.1.2009
Frith David Edward John	Writer	16.3.1937	
Gibbons Harold Harry Ian Haywood	Worcestershire	8.10.1904	16.2.1973
Gibson Clement Herbert	Eton, Cam. U, Sussex, Argentina; *CY 1918*	23.8.1900	31.12.1976
Gibson Norman Alan Stanley	Writer	28.5.1923	10.4.1997
Gore Adrian Clements	Eton College; *CY 1919*	14.5.1900	7.6.1990
Gould Ian James	Middlesex, Sussex; Test umpire	19.8.1957	
Grace *Mrs* Martha	Mother and cricketing mentor of WG	18.7.1812	25.7.1884
Grace William Gilbert jnr	Gloucestershire; son of WG	6.7.1874	2.3.1905
Graveney David Anthony	Gloucestershire, Somerset, Durham	2.1.1953	
Chairman of England selectors 1997–2008.			
Graves Colin James	Chairman of ECB, 2015–	22.1.1948	
Gray James Roy	Hampshire	19.5.1926	31.10.2016
Gray Malcolm Alexander	President of ICC 2000–03	30.5.1940	
Green David Michael	Lancashire, Gloucestershire; *CY 1969*	10.11.1939	19.3.2016
Grieves Kenneth James	New South Wales, Lancashire	27.8.1925	3.1.1992
Griffith Mike Grenville	Sussex, Camb. Univ; president MCC 2012–13	25.11.1943	
Haigh Gideon Clifford Jeffrey Davidson	Writer	29.12.1965	
Hair Darrell Bruce	Umpire in 78 Tests	30.9.1952	
Hall Louis	Yorkshire; *CY 1890*	1.11.1852	19.11.1915
Hallam Albert William	Lancashire, Nottinghamshire; *CY 1908*	12.11.1869	24.7.1940
Hallam Maurice Raymond	Leicestershire	10.9.1931	1.1.2000
Hallows James	Lancashire; *CY 1905*	14.11.1873	20.5.1910
Hamilton Duncan	Writer	24.12.1958	
Harper Daryl John	Umpire in 95 Tests	23.10.1951	
Harrison Tom William	Derbyshire; chief executive of ECB 2015–	11.12.1971	
Hartley Alfred	Lancashire; *CY 1911*	11.4.1879	9.10.1918
Harvey Ian Joseph	Victoria, Gloucestershire; *CY 2004*	10.4.1972	
Hedges Lionel Paget	Tonbridge School, Kent, Glos; *CY 1919*	13.7.1900	12.1.1933
Henderson Robert	Surrey; *CY 1890*	30.3.1865	28.1.1931
Hesson Michael James	New Zealand coach 2012–18	30.10.1974	
Hewett Herbert Tremenheere	Somerset; *CY 1893*	25.5.1864	4.3.1921
Heyhoe Flint *Baroness* [Rachael] OBE	England women	11.6.1939	18.1.2017
Hide Mary Edith ("Molly")	England women	24.10.1913	10.9.1995
Hodson Richard Phillip	Cambridge Univ; president MCC 2011–12	26.4.1951	
Horton Henry	Hampshire	18.4.1923	2.11.1998
Howard Cecil Geoffrey	Middlesex; administrator	14.2.1909	8.11.2002
Hughes David Paul	Lancashire; *CY 1988*	13.5.1947	
Huish Frederick Henry	Kent	15.11.1869	16.3.1957
Humpage Geoffrey William	Warwickshire; *CY 1985*	24.4.1954	
Hunter David	Yorkshire	23.2.1860	11.1.1927
Ingleby-Mackenzie Alexander Colin David OBE	Hants; pres. MCC 1996–98	15.9.1933	9.3.2006
Iremonger James	Nottinghamshire; *CY 1903*	5.3.1876	25.3.1956
Isaac Alan Raymond	Chair NZC 2008–10; president ICC 2012–14	20.1.1952	
Jackson Victor Edward	NSW, Leicestershire	25.10.1916	30.1.1965
James Cyril Lionel Robert ("Nello")	Writer	4.1.1901	31.5.1989
Jesty Trevor Edward	Hants, Griq W., Surrey, Lancs; umpire; *CY 1983*	2.6.1948	
Johnson Paul	Nottinghamshire	24.4.1965	
Johnston Brian Alexander CBE MC	Broadcaster	24.6.1912	5.1.1994
Jones Alan MBE	Glamorgan; *CY 1978*	4.11.1938	
Played once for England, against Rest of World in 1970, regarded at the time as a Test match.			
Kerr Amelia Charlotte	New Zealand women	13.10.2000	
Scored 232, the highest score in women's ODIs, against Ireland in 2018, aged 17.*			
Kilburn James Maurice	Writer	8.7.1909	28.8.1993
King John Barton	Philadelphia	19.10.1873	17.10.1965
"Beyond question the greatest all-round cricketer produced by America" – Wisden.			

		Born	Died
Knight Heather Clare OBE	England women; *CY 2018*	26.12.1990	
Knight Roger David Verdon OBE	Surrey, Glos, Sussex; sec. MCC 1994–2005, pres. MCC 2015–16	6.9.1946	
Knight W. H.	Editor of *Wisden* 1864–79	29.11.1812	16.8.1879
Koertzen Rudolf Eric	Umpire in 108 Tests	26.3.1949	
Lacey *Sir* Francis Eden	Hants; secretary of MCC 1898–1926	19.10.1859	26.5.1946
Lamb Timothy Michael Middx, Northants; ECB chief exec 1997–2004		24.3.1953	
Langridge John George MBE	Sussex; Test umpire; *CY 1950*	10.2.1910	27.6.1999
Lanning Meghann Moira	Australia women	25.3.1992	
Lavender Guy William	Secretary/chief executive MCC 2017–	8.7.1967	
Lee Peter Granville	Northamptonshire, Lancashire; *CY 1976*	27.8.1945	
Lillywhite Frederick William	Sussex	13.6.1792	21.8.1854
Long Arnold	Surrey, Sussex	18.12.1940	
Lord Thomas	Middlesex; founder of Lord's	23.11.1755	13.1.1832
Lorgat Haroon	Chief executive of ICC 2008–12	26.5.1960	
Lovett Ian Nicholas	President of ECB 2018–	6.9.1944	
Lyon Beverley Hamilton	Gloucestershire; *CY 1931*	19.1.1902	22.6.1970
McEwan Kenneth Scott	Eastern Province, Essex; *CY 1978*	16.7.1952	
McGilvray Alan David MBE	NSW; broadcaster	6.12.1909	17.7.1996
Maclagan Myrtle Ethel	England women	2.4.1911	11.3.1993
MacLaurin *Lord* [Ian Charter] Chair of ECB 1997–2002, pres. MCC 2017–18		30.3.1937	
Mandhana Smriti Shriniwas	India women	18.7.1996	
Manners John Errol DSC	Hampshire	25.9.1914	

Believed to be the longest-lived first-class cricketer; in 2018 he overtook Jim Hutchinson of Derbyshire (103 years 344 days).

		Born	Died
Manohar Shashank Vyankatesh Pres. BCCI 2008–11, 2015–16; ICC chairman 2015–		29.9.1957	
Marlar Robin Geoffrey	Sussex; writer; pres. MCC 2005–06	2.1.1931	
Marshal Alan	Surrey; *CY 1909*	12.6.1883	23.7.1915
Martin-Jenkins Christopher Dennis Alexander MBE Writer; broadcaster; pres. MCC 2010–11		20.1.1945	1.1.2013
Maxwell James Edward	Commentator	28.7.1950	
Mendis Gehan Dixon	Sussex, Lancashire	20.4.1955	
Mercer John Sussex, Glamorgan; coach and scorer; *CY 1927*		22.4.1893	31.8.1987
Meyer Rollo John Oliver OBE	Somerset	15.3.1905	9.3.1991
Modi Lalit Kumar	Chairman, Indian Premier League 2008–10	29.11.1963	
Moles Andrew James	Warwickshire, NZ coach 2008–09	12.2.1961	
Moores Peter Sussex; England coach 2007–09, 2014–15		18.12.1962	
Moorhouse Geoffrey	Writer	29.11.1931	26.11.2009
Morgan Derek Clifton	Derbyshire	26.2.1929	4.11.2017
Morgan Frederick David OBE Chair ECB 2003–07, pres. ICC 2008–10, pres. MCC 2014–15		6.10.1937	
Mynn Alfred	Kent, All-England	19.1.1807	1.11.1861
Neale Phillip Anthony OBE Worcestershire; England manager; *CY 1989*		5.6.1954	
Newman John Alfred	Hampshire	12.11.1884	21.12.1973
Newstead John Thomas	Yorkshire; *CY 1909*	8.9.1877	25.3.1952
Nicholas Mark Charles Jefford	Hampshire; broadcaster	29.9.1957	
Nicholls Ronald Bernard	Gloucestershire	4.12.1933	21.7.1994
Nixon Paul Andrew	Leicestershire, Kent	21.10.1970	
Nyren John Hants; author of *The Young Cricketer's Tutor*, 1833		15.12.1764	28.6.1837
Nyren Richard Hants; Landlord Bat & Ball, Broadhalfpenny Down		1734	25.4.1797
Ontong Rodney Craig	Border, Glamorgan, N. Transvaal	9.9.1955	
Ormrod Joseph Alan	Worcestershire, Lancashire	22.12.1942	
Pardon Charles Frederick	Editor of *Wisden* 1887–90	28.3.1850	18.4.1890
Pardon Sydney Herbert	Editor of *Wisden* 1891–1925	23.9.1855	20.11.1925
Parks Henry William	Sussex	18.7.1906	7.5.1984
Parr George Notts, captain/manager of All-England XI		22.5.1826	23.6.1891
Partridge Norman Ernest Malvern College, Warwickshire; *CY 1919*		10.8.1900	10.3.1982
Pawar Sharadchandra Govindrao Pres. BCCI 2005–08, ICC 2010–12		12.12.1940	

		Born	Died
Payton Wilfred Richard Daniel	Nottinghamshire	13.2.1882	2.5.1943
Pearce Thomas Neill	Essex; administrator	3.11.1905	10.4.1994
Pearson Frederick	Worcestershire	23.9.1880	10.11.1963
Perrin Percival Albert ("Peter")	Essex; *CY 1905*	26.5.1876	20.11.1945
Perry Ellyse Alexandra	Australia women	3.11.1990	
Pilch Fuller	Norfolk, Kent	17.3.1804	1.5.1870
"The best batsman that has ever yet appeared" – Arthur Haygarth, 1862.			
Porter James Alexander	Essex; *CY 2018*	25.5.1993	
Preston Hubert	Editor of *Wisden* 1944–51	16.12.1868	6.8.1960
Preston Norman MBE	Editor of *Wisden* 1952–80	18.3.1903	6.3.1980
Pritchard Thomas Leslie	Wellington, Warwickshire, Kent	10.3.1917	22.8.2017
Pybus Richard Alexander	Coach Pak 1999–2003, Bang 2012, WI 2019	5.7.1964	
Rait Kerr *Col.* Rowan Scrope	Europeans; sec. MCC 1936–52	13.4.1891	2.4.1961
Raj Mithali Dorai	India women	3.12.1982	
Reeves William	Essex; Test umpire	22.1.1875	22.3.1944
Rheinberg Netta MBE	England women; writer and administrator	24.10.1911	18.6.2006
Rice Clive Edward Butler	Transvaal, Nottinghamshire; *CY 1981*	23.7.1949	28.7.2015
Richardson Alan	Warwicks, Middx, Worcs; *CY 2012*	6.5.1975	
Roberts Kevin Joseph	New South Wales; CEO Cricket Australia 2018–	25.7.1972	
Robertson-Glasgow Raymond Charles	Somerset; writer	15.7.1901	4.3.1965
Robins Derrick Harold	Warwickshire; tour promoter	27.6.1914	3.5.2004
Robinson Mark Andrew OBE	Northants, Yorkshire, Sussex, coach	23.11.1966	
Robinson Raymond John	Writer	8.7.1905	6.7.1982
Roebuck Peter Michael	Somerset; writer; *CY 1988*	6.3.1956	12.11.2011
Rotherham Gerard Alexander	Rugby School, Warwickshire; *CY 1918*	28.5.1899	31.1.1985
Sainsbury Peter James	Hampshire; *CY 1974*	13.6.1934	12.7.2014
Samson Andrew William	Statistician	17.2.1964	
Sawhney Manu	Chief Executive of ICC 2019–	1.11.1966	
Sciver Natalie Ruth	England women; *CY 2018*	20.8.1992	
Scott Stanley Winckworth	Middlesex; *CY 1893*	24.3.1854	8.12.1933
Sellers Arthur Brian MBE	Yorkshire; *CY 1940*	5.3.1907	20.2.1981
Seymour James	Kent	25.10.1879	30.9.1930
Shepherd David Robert MBE	Gloucestershire; umpire in 92 Tests	27.12.1940	27.10.2009
Shepherd Donald John	Glamorgan; *CY 1970*	12.8.1927	18.8.2017
Shrubsole Anya MBE	England women; *CY 2018*	7.12.1991	
Silk Dennis Raoul Whitehall CBE	Somerset; pres. MCC 1992–94	8.10.1931	
Simmons Jack MBE	Lancashire, Tasmania; *CY 1985*	28.3.1941	
Skelding Alexander	Leics; first-class umpire 1931–58	5.9.1886	17.4.1960
Smith Sydney Gordon	Northamptonshire; *CY 1915*	15.1.1881	25.10.1963
Smith William Charles ("Razor")	Surrey; *CY 1911*	4.10.1877	15.7.1946
Solanki Vikram Singh	Worcestershire, Surrey, England	1.4.1976	
Southerton Sydney James	Editor of *Wisden* 1934–35	7.7.1874	12.3.1935
Speed Malcolm Walter	Chief executive of ICC 2001–08	14.9.1948	
Spencer Thomas William OBE	Kent; Test umpire	22.3.1914	1.11.1995
Srinivasan Narayanaswami	Pres. BCCI 2011–14; ICC chair 2014–15	3.1.1945	
Stephenson Franklyn Dacosta	Nottinghamshire, Sussex; *CY 1989*	8.4.1959	
Stephenson Harold William	Somerset	18.7.1920	23.4.2008
Stephenson Heathfield Harman	Surrey, All-England	3.5.1832	17.12.1896
Captained first English team to Australia, 1861-62; umpired first Test in England, 1880.			
Stephenson *Lt.-Col.* John Robin CBE	Secretary of MCC 1987–93	25.2.1931	2.6.2003
Studd *Sir* John Edward Kynaston	Middlesex	26.7.1858	14.1.1944
Lord Mayor of London 1928–29; president of MCC 1930.			
Surridge Walter Stuart	Surrey; *CY 1953*	3.9.1917	13.4.1992
Sutherland James Alexander	Victoria; CEO Cricket Australia 2001–18	14.7.1965	
Suttle Kenneth George	Sussex	25.8.1928	25.3.2005
Swanton Ernest William ("Jim") CBE	Middlesex; writer	11.2.1907	22.1.2000
Tarrant Francis Alfred	Victoria, Middlesex; *CY 1908*	11.12.1880	29.1.1951
Taufel Simon James Arnold	Umpire in 74 Tests	21.1.1971	
Taylor Brian ("Tonker")	Essex; *CY 1972*	19.6.1932	12.6.2017
Taylor Samantha Claire MBE	England women; *CY 2009*	25.9.1975	

		Born	Died
Taylor Stafanie Roxann	West Indies women	11.6.1991	
Taylor Tom Launcelot	Yorkshire; *CY 1901*	25.5.1878	16.3.1960
Thornton Charles Inglis ("Buns")	Middlesex	20.3.1850	10.12.1929
Timms John Edward	Northamptonshire	3.11.1906	18.5.1980
Todd Leslie John	Kent	19.6.1907	20.8.1967
Tunnicliffe John	Yorkshire; *CY 1901*	26.8.1866	11.7.1948
Turner Francis <u>Michael</u> MBE	Leicestershire; administrator	8.8.1934	21.7.2015
Turner Robert Julian	Somerset	25.11.1967	
Ufton Derek Gilbert	Kent	31.5.1928	
van der Bijl Vintcent Adriaan Pieter	Natal, Middx, Transvaal; *CY 1981*	19.3.1948	
van Niekerk Dane	South Africa women	14.5.1993	
Virgin Roy Thomas	Somerset, Northamptonshire; *CY 1971*	26.8.1939	
Ward William	Hampshire	24.7.1787	30.6.1849
Scorer of the first recorded double-century: 278 for MCC v Norfolk, 1820.			
Wass Thomas George	Nottinghamshire; *CY 1908*	26.12.1873	27.10.1953
Watson Frank	Lancashire	17.9.1898	1.2.1976
Webber Roy	Statistician	23.7.1914	14.11.1962
Weigall Gerald John Villiers	Kent; coach	19.10.1870	17.5.1944
West George H.	Editor of *Wisden* 1880–86	1851	6.10.1896
Wheatley Oswald Stephen CBE	Warwickshire, Glamorgan; *CY 1969*	28.5.1935	
Whitaker Edgar <u>Haddon</u> OBE	Editor of *Wisden* 1940–43	30.8.1908	5.1.1982
Wight Peter Bernard	Somerset; umpire	25.6.1930	31.12.2015
Wilson Elizabeth Rebecca ("Betty")	Australia women	21.11.1921	22.1.2010
Wilson John <u>Victor</u>	Yorkshire; *CY 1961*	17.1.1921	5.6.2008
Wisden John	Sussex	5.9.1826	5.4.1884
"The Little Wonder"; founder of Wisden Cricketers' Almanack, *1864.*			
Wood Cecil John Burditt	Leicestershire	21.11.1875	5.6.1960
Woodcock John Charles OBE	Writer; editor of *Wisden* 1981–86	7.8.1926	
Wooller Wilfred	Glamorgan	20.11.1912	10.3.1997
Wright Graeme Alexander	Editor of *Wisden* 1987–92, 2001–02	23.4.1943	
Wright Levi George	Derbyshire; *CY 1906*	15.1.1862	11.1.1953
Wright Luke James	Leicestershire, Sussex, England	7.3.1985	
Young Douglas <u>Martin</u>	Worcestershire, Gloucestershire	15.4.1924	18.6.1993

CRICKETERS OF THE YEAR, 1889–2019

1889	*Six Great Bowlers of the Year:* J. Briggs, J. J. Ferris, G. A. Lohmann, R. Peel, C. T. B. Turner, S. M. J. Woods.

1889   *Six Great Bowlers of the Year:* J. Briggs, J. J. Ferris, G. A. Lohmann, R. Peel, C. T. B. Turner, S. M. J. Woods.

1890   *Nine Great Batsmen of the Year:* R. Abel, W. Barnes, W. Gunn, L. Hall, R. Henderson, J. M. Read, A. Shrewsbury, F. H. Sugg, A. Ward.

1891   *Five Great Wicketkeepers:* J. M. Blackham, G. MacGregor, R. Pilling, M. Sherwin, H. Wood.

1892   *Five Great Bowlers:* W. Attewell, J. T. Hearne, F. Martin, A. W. Mold, J. W. Sharpe.

1893   *Five Batsmen of the Year:* H. T. Hewett, L. C. H. Palairet, W. W. Read, S. W. Scott, A. E. Stoddart.

1894   *Five All-Round Cricketers:* G. Giffen, A. Hearne, F. S. Jackson, G. H. S. Trott, E. Wainwright.

1895   *Five Young Batsmen of the Season:* W. Brockwell, J. T. Brown, C. B. Fry, T. W. Hayward, A. C. MacLaren.

1896   W. G. Grace.

1897   *Five Cricketers of the Season:* S. E. Gregory, A. A. Lilley, K. S. Ranjitsinhji, T. Richardson, H. Trumble.

1898   *Five Cricketers of the Year:* F. G. Bull, W. R. Cuttell, N. F. Druce, G. L. Jessop, J. R. Mason.

1899   *Five Great Players of the Season:* W. H. Lockwood, W. Rhodes, W. Storer, C. L. Townsend, A. E. Trott.

1900   *Five Cricketers of the Season:* J. Darling, C. Hill, A. O. Jones, M. A. Noble, Major R. M. Poore.

1901   *Mr R. E. Foster and Four Yorkshiremen:* R. E. Foster, S. Haigh, G. H. Hirst, T. L. Taylor, J. Tunnicliffe.

1902   L. C. Braund, C. P. McGahey, F. Mitchell, W. G. Quaife, J. T. Tyldesley.

1903   W. W. Armstrong, C. J. Burnup, J. Iremonger, J. J. Kelly, V. T. Trumper.

1904   C. Blythe, J. Gunn, A. E. Knight, W. Mead, P. F. Warner.

1905   B. J. T. Bosanquet, E. A. Halliwell, J. Hallows, P. A. Perrin, R. H. Spooner.

1906   D. Denton, W. S. Lees, G. J. Thompson, J. Vine, L. G. Wright.

1907   J. N. Crawford, A. Fielder, E. G. Hayes, K. L. Hutchings, N. A. Knox.

1908   A. W. Hallam, R. O. Schwarz, F. A. Tarrant, A. E. E. Vogler, T. G. Wass.

1909   *Lord Hawke and Four Cricketers of the Year:* W. Brearley, Lord Hawke, J. B. Hobbs, A. Marshal, J. T. Newstead.

1910   W. Bardsley, S. F. Barnes, D. W. Carr, A. P. Day, V. S. Ransford.

1911   H. K. Foster, A. Hartley, C. B. Llewellyn, W. C. Smith, F. E. Woolley.

1912   *Five Members of MCC's team in Australia:* F. R. Foster, J. W. Hearne, S. P. Kinneir, C. P. Mead, H. Strudwick.

1913   *Special Portrait:* John Wisden.

1914   M. W. Booth, G. Gunn, J. W. Hitch, A. E. Relf, Hon. L. H. Tennyson.

1915   J. W. H. T. Douglas, P. G. H. Fender, H. T. W. Hardinge, D. J. Knight, S. G. Smith.

1916–17   No portraits appeared.

1918   *School Bowlers of the Year:* H. L. Calder, J. D. E. Firth, C. H. Gibson, G. A. Rotherham, G. T. S. Stevens.

1919   *Five Public School Cricketers of the Year:* P. W. Adams, A. P. F. Chapman, A. C. Gore, L. P. Hedges, N. E. Partridge.

1920   *Five Batsmen of the Year:* A. Ducat, E. H. Hendren, P. Holmes, H. Sutcliffe, E. Tyldesley.

1921   *Special Portrait:* P. F. Warner.

1922   H. Ashton, J. L. Bryan, J. M. Gregory, C. G. Macartney, E. A. McDonald.

1923   A. W. Carr, A. P. Freeman, C. W. L. Parker, A. C. Russell, A. Sandham.

1924   *Five Bowlers of the Year:* A. E. R. Gilligan, R. Kilner, G. G. Macaulay, C. H. Parkin, M. W. Tate.

1925   R. H. Catterall, J. C. W. MacBryan, H. W. Taylor, R. K. Tyldesley, W. W. Whysall.

1926   *Special Portrait:* J. B. Hobbs.

1927   G. Geary, H. Larwood, J. Mercer, W. A. Oldfield, W. M. Woodfull.

1928   R. C. Blunt, C. Hallows, W. R. Hammond, D. R. Jardine, V. W. C. Jupp.

1929   L. E. G. Ames, G. Duckworth, M. Leyland, S. J. Staples, J. C. White.

1930   E. H. Bowley, K. S. Duleepsinhji, H. G. Owen-Smith, R. W. V. Robins, R. E. S. Wyatt.

1931   D. G. Bradman, C. V. Grimmett, B. H. Lyon, I. A. R. Peebles, M. J. Turnbull.

1932   W. E. Bowes, C. S. Dempster, James Langridge, Nawab of Pataudi snr, H. Verity.
1933   W. E. Astill, F. R. Brown, A. S. Kennedy, C. K. Nayudu, W. Voce.
1934   A. H. Bakewell, G. A. Headley, M. S. Nichols, L. F. Townsend, C. F. Walters.
1935   S. J. McCabe, W. J. O'Reilly, G. A. E. Paine, W. H. Ponsford, C. I. J. Smith.
1936   H. B. Cameron, E. R. T. Holmes, B. Mitchell, D. Smith, A. W. Wellard.
1937   C. J. Barnett, W. H. Copson, A. R. Gover, V. M. Merchant, T. S. Worthington.
1938   T. W. J. Goddard, J. Hardstaff jnr, L. Hutton, J. H. Parks, E. Paynter.
1939   H. T. Bartlett, W. A. Brown, D. C. S. Compton, K. Farnes, A. Wood.
1940   L. N. Constantine, W. J. Edrich, W. W. Keeton, A. B. Sellers, D. V. P. Wright.
1941–46 No portraits appeared.
1947   A. V. Bedser, L. B. Fishlock, V. (M. H.) Mankad, T. P. B. Smith, C. Washbrook.
1948   M. P. Donnelly, A. Melville, A. D. Nourse, J. D. Robertson, N. W. D. Yardley.
1949   A. L. Hassett, W. A. Johnston, R. R. Lindwall, A. R. Morris, D. Tallon.
1950   T. E. Bailey, R. O. Jenkins, John Langridge, R. T. Simpson, B. Sutcliffe.
1951   T. G. Evans, S. Ramadhin, A. L. Valentine, E. D. Weekes, F. M. M. Worrell.
1952   R. Appleyard, H. E. Dollery, J. C. Laker, P. B. H. May, E. A. B. Rowan.
1953   H. Gimblett, T. W. Graveney, D. S. Sheppard, W. S. Surridge, F. S. Trueman.
1954   R. N. Harvey, G. A. R. Lock, K. R. Miller, J. H. Wardle, W. Watson.
1955   B. Dooland, Fazal Mahmood, W. E. Hollies, J. B. Statham, G. E. Tribe.
1956   M. C. Cowdrey, D. J. Insole, D. J. McGlew, H. J. Tayfield, F. H. Tyson.
1957   D. Brookes, J. W. Burke, M. J. Hilton, G. R. A. Langley, P. E. Richardson.
1958   P. J. Loader, A. J. McIntyre, O. G. Smith, M. J. Stewart, C. L. Walcott.
1959   H. L. Jackson, R. E. Marshall, C. A. Milton, J. R. Reid, D. Shackleton.
1960   K. F. Barrington, D. B. Carr, R. Illingworth, G. Pullar, M. J. K. Smith.
1961   N. A. T. Adcock, E. R. Dexter, R. A. McLean, R. Subba Row, J. V. Wilson.
1962   W. E. Alley, R. Benaud, A. K. Davidson, W. M. Lawry, N. C. O'Neill.
1963   D. Kenyon, Mushtaq Mohammad, P. H. Parfitt, P. J. Sharpe, F. J. Titmus.
1964   D. B. Close, C. C. Griffith, C. C. Hunte, R. B. Kanhai, G. S. Sobers.
1965   G. Boycott, P. J. Burge, J. A. Flavell, G. D. McKenzie, R. B. Simpson.
1966   K. C. Bland, J. H. Edrich, R. C. Motz, P. M. Pollock, R. G. Pollock.
1967   R. W. Barber, B. L. D'Oliveira, C. Milburn, J. T. Murray, S. M. Nurse.
1968   Asif Iqbal, Hanif Mohammad, K. Higgs, J. M. Parks, Nawab of Pataudi jnr.
1969   J. G. Binks, D. M. Green, B. A. Richards, D. L. Underwood, O. S. Wheatley.
1970   B. F. Butcher, A. P. E. Knott, Majid Khan, M. J. Procter, D. J. Shepherd.
1971   J. D. Bond, C. H. Lloyd, B. W. Luckhurst, G. M. Turner, R. T. Virgin.
1972   G. G. Arnold, B. S. Chandrasekhar, L. R. Gibbs, B. Taylor, Zaheer Abbas.
1973   G. S. Chappell, D. K. Lillee, R. A. L. Massie, J. A. Snow, K. R. Stackpole.
1974   K. D. Boyce, B. E. Congdon, K. W. R. Fletcher, R. C. Fredericks, P. J. Sainsbury.
1975   D. L. Amiss, M. H. Denness, N. Gifford, A. W. Greig, A. M. E. Roberts.
1976   I. M. Chappell, P. G. Lee, R. B. McCosker, D. S. Steele, R. A. Woolmer.
1977   J. M. Brearley, C. G. Greenidge, M. A. Holding, I. V. A. Richards, R. W. Taylor.
1978   I. T. Botham, M. Hendrick, A. Jones, K. S. McEwan, R. G. D. Willis.
1979   D. I. Gower, J. K. Lever, C. M. Old, C. T. Radley, J. N. Shepherd.
1980   J. Garner, S. M. Gavaskar, G. A. Gooch, D. W. Randall, B. C. Rose.
1981   K. J. Hughes, R. D. Jackman, A. J. Lamb, C. E. B. Rice, V. A. P. van der Bijl.
1982   T. M. Alderman, A. R. Border, R. J. Hadlee, Javed Miandad, R. W. Marsh.
1983   Imran Khan, T. E. Jesty, A. I. Kallicharran, Kapil Dev, M. D. Marshall.
1984   M. Amarnath, J. V. Coney, J. E. Emburey, M. W. Gatting, C. L. Smith.
1985   M. D. Crowe, H. A. Gomes, G. W. Humpage, J. Simmons, S. Wettimuny.
1986   P. Bainbridge, R. M. Ellison, C. J. McDermott, N. V. Radford, R. T. Robinson.
1987   J. H. Childs, G. A. Hick, D. B. Vengsarkar, C. A. Walsh, J. J. Whitaker.
1988   J. P. Agnew, N. A. Foster, D. P. Hughes, P. M. Roebuck, Salim Malik.
1989   K. J. Barnett, P. J. L. Dujon, P. a. Neale, F. D. Stephenson, S. R. Waugh.
1990   S. J. Cook, D. M. Jones, R. C. Russell, R. A. Smith, M. A. Taylor.
1991   M. A. Atherton, M. Azharuddin, A. R. Butcher, D. L. Haynes, M. E. Waugh.
1992   C. E. L. Ambrose, P. A. J. DeFreitas, A. A. Donald, R. B. Richardson, Waqar Younis.
1993   N. E. Briers, M. D. Moxon, I. D. K. Salisbury, A. J. Stewart, Wasim Akram.
1994   D. C. Boon, I. A. Healy, M. G. Hughes, S. K. Warne, S. L. Watkin.
1995   B. C. Lara, D. E. Malcolm, T. A. Munton, S. J. Rhodes, K. C. Wessels.
1996   D. G. Cork, P. A. de Silva, A. R. C. Fraser, A. Kumble, D. A. Reeve.
1997   S. T. Jayasuriya, Mushtaq Ahmed, Saeed Anwar, P. V. Simmons, S. R. Tendulkar.

1998	M. T. G. Elliott, S. G. Law, G. D. McGrath, M. P. Maynard, G. P. Thorpe.
1999	I. D. Austin, D. Gough, M. Muralitharan, A. Ranatunga, J. N. Rhodes.
2000	C. L. Cairns, R. Dravid, L. Klusener, T. M. Moody, Saqlain Mushtaq.

Cricketers of the Century D. G. Bradman, G. S. Sobers, J. B. Hobbs, S. K. Warne, I. V. A. Richards.

2001	M. W. Alleyne, M. P. Bicknell, A. R. Caddick, J. L. Langer, D. S. Lehmann.
2002	A. Flower, A. C. Gilchrist, J. N. Gillespie, V. V. S. Laxman, D. R. Martyn.
2003	M. L. Hayden, A. J. Hollioake, N. Hussain, S. M. Pollock, M. P. Vaughan.
2004	C. J. Adams, A. Flintoff, I. J. Harvey, G. Kirsten, G. C. Smith.
2005	A. F. Giles, S. J. Harmison, R. W. T. Key, A. J. Strauss, M. E. Trescothick.
2006	M. J. Hoggard, S. P. Jones, B. Lee, K. P. Pietersen, R. T. Ponting.
2007	P. D. Collingwood, D. P. M. D. Jayawardene, Mohammad Yousuf, M. S. Panesar, M. R. Ramprakash.
2008	I. R. Bell, S. Chanderpaul, O. D. Gibson, R. J. Sidebottom, Zaheer Khan.
2009	J. M. Anderson, D. M. Benkenstein, M. V. Boucher, N. D. McKenzie, S. C. Taylor.
2010	S. C. J. Broad, M. J. Clarke, G. Onions, M. J. Prior, G. P. Swann.
2011	E. J. G. Morgan, C. M. W. Read, Tamim Iqbal, I. J. L. Trott.
2012	T. T. Bresnan, G. Chapple, A. N. Cook, A. Richardson, K. C. Sangakkara.
2013	H. M. Amla, N. R. D. Compton, J. H. Kallis, M. N. Samuels, D. W. Steyn.
2014	S. Dhawan, C. M. Edwards, R. J. Harris, C. J. L. Rogers, J. E. Root.
2015	M. M. Ali, G. S. Ballance, A. Lyth, A. D. Mathews, J. S. Patel.
2016	J. M. Bairstow, B. B. McCullum, S. P. D. Smith, B. A. Stokes, K. S. Williamson.
2017	B. M. Duckett, Misbah-ul-Haq, T. S. Roland-Jones, C. R. Woakes, Younis Khan.
2018	S. D. Hope, H. C. Knight, J. A. Porter, N. R. Sciver, A. Shrubsole.
2019	T. T. Beaumont, R. J. Burns, J. C. Buttler, S. M. Curran, V. Kohli.

From 2001 to 2003 the award was made on the basis of all cricket round the world, not just the English season. This ended in 2004 with the start of Wisden's *Leading Cricketer in the World award. Sanath Jayasuriya was chosen in 1997 for his influence on the English season, stemming from the 1996 World Cup. In 2011, only four were named after the Lord's spot-fixing scandal made the selection of one of the five unsustainable.*

CRICKETERS OF THE YEAR: AN ANALYSIS

The special portrait of John Wisden in 1913 marked the 50th anniversary of his retirement as a player – and the 50th edition of the Almanack. Wisden died in 1884. The special portraits of P. F. Warner in 1921 and J. B. Hobbs in 1926 were in addition to their earlier selection as a Cricketer of the Year in 1904 and 1909 respectively. These three special portraits and the Cricketers of the Century in 2000 are excluded from the following analysis.

The five players selected to be Cricketers of the Year for 2019 bring the number chosen since selection began in 1889 to 600. They have been chosen from 41 different teams, as follows:

Derbyshire	13	Nottinghamshire	29	Australians	73	Cranleigh School	1
Durham	8	Somerset	20	South Africans	28	Eton College	2
Essex	25	Surrey	52	West Indians	27	Malvern College	1
Glamorgan	12	Sussex	21	New Zealanders	10	Rugby School	1
Gloucestershire	17	Warwickshire	26	Indians	16	Tonbridge School	1
Hampshire	16	Worcestershire	17	Pakistanis	14	Univ Coll School	1
Kent	28	Yorkshire	47	Sri Lankans	7	Uppingham School	1
Lancashire	35	Cambridge Univ	10	Zimbabweans	1	Winchester College	1
Leicestershire	8	Oxford Univ	7	Bangladeshis	1		
Middlesex	30	Berkshire	1	England Women	6		
Northamptonshire	15	Staffordshire	1	Cheltenham College	1		

Schoolboys were chosen in 1918 and 1919 when first-class cricket was suspended due to war. The total of sides comes to 631 because 31 players appeared for more than one side (excluding England men) in the year for which they were chosen.

Types of Player

Of the 600 Cricketers of the Year, 299 are best classified as batsmen, 162 as bowlers, 99 as all-rounders and 40 as wicketkeepers or wicketkeeper-batsmen.

Research: Robert Brooke

PART NINE

The Almanack

OFFICIAL BODIES

INTERNATIONAL CRICKET COUNCIL

The ICC are world cricket's governing body. They are responsible for managing the playing conditions and Code of Conduct for international fixtures, expanding the game and organising the major tournaments, including the World Cup and World Twenty20. Their mission statement says the ICC "will lead by providing a world-class environment for international cricket, delivering major events across three formats, providing targeted support to members and promoting the global game".

Twelve national governing bodies are currently Full Members of the ICC; full membership qualifies a nation (or geographic area) to play official Test matches. A candidate for full membership must meet a number of playing and administrative criteria, after which elevation is decided by a vote among existing Full Members. With the former categories of associate and affiliate membership merging in 2017, there are currently 93 Associate Members.

The ICC were founded in 1909 as the Imperial Cricket Conference by three Foundation Members: England, Australia and South Africa. Other countries (or geographic areas) became Full Members and thus acquired Test status as follows: India, New Zealand and West Indies in 1926, Pakistan in 1952, Sri Lanka in 1981, Zimbabwe in 1992, Bangladesh in 2000, and Afghanistan and Ireland in 2017. South Africa ceased to be a member on leaving the Commonwealth in 1961, but were re-elected as a Full Member in 1991.

In 1965, "Imperial" was replaced by "International", and countries from outside the Commonwealth were elected for the first time. The first Associate Members were Ceylon (later Sri Lanka), Fiji and the USA. Foundation Members retained a veto over all resolutions. In 1989, the renamed International Cricket Council (rather than "Conference") adopted revised rules, aimed at producing an organisation which could make a larger number of binding decisions, rather than simply make recommendations to national governing bodies. In 1993, the Council, previously administered by MCC, gained their own secretariat and chief executive. The category of Foundation Member was abolished.

In 1997, the Council became an incorporated body, with an executive board, and a president instead of a chairman. The ICC remained at Lord's, with a commercial base in Monaco, until August 2005, when after 96 years they moved to Dubai in the United Arab Emirates, which offered organisational and tax advantages.

In 2014, the ICC board approved a new structure, under which they were led by a chairman again, while India, Australia and England took permanent places on key committees. But in 2016 the special privileges given to these three were dismantled and, in early 2017, the board agreed to revise the constitution on more egalitarian lines.

Officers

Chairman: S. V. Manohar. *Deputy Chairman:* I. Khwaja. *Chief Executive:* D. J. Richardson. M. Sawhney was due to succeed Richardson in July 2019.

Chairs of Committees – Chief Executives' Committee: D. J. Richardson. *Cricket:* A. Kumble. *Audit:* Y. Narayan. *Finance and Commercial Affairs:* C. J. Graves. *Nominations Committee:* S. V. Manohar. *Code of Conduct Commission:* M. J. Beloff QC. *Women's Committee:* C. J. Connor. *Development:* I. Khwaja. *Disputes Resolution Committee:* M. J. Beloff QC. *Membership:* I. Khwaja. *Medical Advisory:* Dr P. Harcourt. *Anti-Corruption Oversight:* D. Howman. *HR & Remuneration:* G. J. Barclay. *Anti-Corruption Unit Chairman:* Sir Ronnie Flanagan. *ICC Ethics Officer:* P. Nicholson.

ICC Board: The chairman and chief executive sit on the board *ex officio*. They are joined by I. K. Nooyi (independent female director), Azizullah Fazli (Afghanistan), G. J. Barclay (New Zealand), A. G. S. Brian (Scotland), W. O. Cameron (West Indies), A. Choudhary (India), E. R. Eddings (Australia), Ehsan Mani (Pakistan), C. J. Graves (England), I. Khwaja (Singapore), R. A. McCollum

T. Mukuhlani (Zimbabwe), Nazmul Hassan (Bangladesh), C. Nenzani (South Africa), A. S. S. Silva (Sri Lanka), M. Vallipuram (Malaysia).

Chief Executives' Committee: The chief executive, chairman and the chairs of the committee and women's committees sit on this committee *ex officio*. They are joined by the chief executives of the 12 Full Member boards and three Associate Member boards: Asadullah Khan (Afghanistan), S. Damodar (Botswana), A. M. de Silva (Sri Lanka), W. R. Deutrom (Ireland), J. M. Grave (West Indies), T. W. Harrison (England), R. Johri (India), W. G. Khan (Pakistan), G. Makoni (Zimbabwe), T. G. Moroe (South Africa), Nizam Uddin Chowdhury (Bangladesh), K. J. Roberts (Australia), N. Speight (Bermuda), B. Timmer (Netherlands), D. J. White (New Zealand).

Cricket Committee: The chief executive and chairman sit on the committee *ex officio*. They are joined by A. Kumble (*chairman*), B. J. Clark, K. J. Coetzer, R. Dravid, D. P. M. D. Jayawardene, R. A. Kettleborough, R. S. Madugalle, T. B. A. May, S. M. Pollock, J. P. Stephenson, A. J. Strauss, D. J. White (with one coaches' representative to be nominated).

General Manager – Cricket: G. J. Allardice. *General Manager – Commercial:* D. C. Jamieson. *General Manager – Anti-Corruption Unit:* A. J. Marshall. *General Manager – Strategic Communications:* C. Furlong. *General Manager – Development:* W. Glenwright. *Chief Financial Officer:* A. Khanna. *Chief Operating Officer/General Counsel:* I. Higgins. *Head of Events:* C. M. B. Tetley. *Head of Media Rights, Broadcast & Digital:* A. Dabas. *Head of Internal Audit:* Muhammad Ali.

Membership

Full Members (12): Afghanistan, Australia, Bangladesh, England, India, Ireland, New Zealand, Pakistan, South Africa, Sri Lanka, West Indies and Zimbabwe.

Associate Members* (93):

Africa (20): Botswana (2005), Cameroon (2007), Gambia (2002), Ghana (2002), Kenya (1981), Lesotho (2001), Malawi (2003), Mali (2005), Morocco (1999), Mozambique (2003), Namibia (1992), Nigeria (2002), Rwanda (2003), St Helena (2001), Seychelles (2010), Sierra Leone (2002), Swaziland (2007), Tanzania (2001), Uganda (1998), Zambia (2003).

Americas (16): Argentina (1974), Bahamas (1987), Belize (1997), Bermuda (1966), Brazil (2002), Canada (1968), Cayman Islands (2002), Chile (2002), Costa Rica (2002), Falkland Islands (2007), Mexico (2004), Panama (2002), Peru (2007), Suriname (2002), Turks & Caicos Islands (2002), USA (1965/2019).

Asia (16): Bahrain (2001), Bhutan (2001), China (2004), Hong Kong (1969), Iran (2003), Kuwait (2005), Malaysia (1967), Maldives (2001), Myanmar (2006), Nepal (1996), Oman (2000), Qatar (1999), Saudi Arabia (2003), Singapore (1974), Thailand (2005), United Arab Emirates (1990).

East Asia Pacific (9): Cook Islands (2000), Fiji (1965), Indonesia (2001), Japan (2005), Papua New Guinea (1973), Philippines (2000), Samoa (2000), South Korea (2001), Vanuatu (1995).

Europe (32): Austria (1992), Belgium (2005), Bulgaria (2008), Croatia (2001), Cyprus (1999), Czech Republic (2000), Denmark (1966), Estonia (2008), Finland (2000), France (1998), Germany (1999), Gibraltar (1969), Greece (1995), Guernsey (2005), Hungary (2012), Isle of Man (2004), Israel (1974), Italy (1995), Jersey (2007), Luxembourg (1998), Malta (1998), Netherlands (1966), Norway (2000), Portugal (1996), Romania (2013), Russia (2012), Scotland (1994), Serbia (2015), Slovenia (2005), Spain (1992), Sweden (1997), Turkey (2008).

* *Year of election shown in parentheses. Switzerland (1985) were removed in 2012 for failing to comply with the ICC's membership criteria; Cuba (2002) and Tonga (2000) in 2013 for failing to demonstrate a suitable administrative structure; Brunei in 2014; and the USA in 2017, though a new USA body were admitted in 2019. Nepal were suspended in 2016, and the Falkland Islands in 2017.*

Full Members are the governing bodies for cricket of a country recognised by the ICC, or nations associated for cricket purposes, or a geographical area, from which representative teams are qualified to play official Test matches.

Associate Members are the governing bodies for cricket of a country recognised by the ICC, or countries associated for cricket purposes, or a geographical area, which does not qualify as a Full Member, but where cricket is firmly established and organised.

Addresses

ICC Street 69, Dubai Sports City, Sh Mohammed Bin Zayed Road, PO Box 500 070, Dubai, United Arab Emirates (+971 4382 8800; www.icc-cricket.com; enquiry@icc-cricket.com).

Afghanistan Afghanistan Cricket Board, Alokozay Kabul International Cricket Stadium, Kabul Nandari, District 8, Kabul (+93 78 813 3144; www.cricket.af; info@afghancricket.af).

Australia Cricket Australia, 60 Jolimont Street, Jolimont, Victoria 3002 (+61 3 9653 9999; www.cricket.com.au; public.enquiries@cricket.com.au).

Bangladesh Bangladesh Cricket Board, Sher-e-Bangla National Cricket Stadium, Mirpur, Dhaka 1216 (+880 2 803 1001; www.tigercricket.com.bd; info@tigercricket.com.bd).

England England and Wales Cricket Board (see below).

India Board of Control for Cricket in India, Cricket Centre, 4th Floor, Wankhede Stadium, D Road, Churchgate, Mumbai 400 020 (+91 22 2289 8800; www.bcci.tv; office@bcci.tv).

Ireland Cricket Ireland, Unit 22, Grattan Business Park, Clonshaugh, Dublin 17 (+353 1 894 7914; www.cricketireland.ie; info@cricketireland.ie).

New Zealand New Zealand Cricket, PO Box 8353, Level 4, 8 Nugent Street, Grafton, Auckland 1023 (+64 9 972 0605; www.nzc.nz; info@nzcricket.org.nz).

Pakistan Pakistan Cricket Board, Gaddafi Stadium, Ferozpur Road, Lahore 54600 (+92 42 3571 7231; www.pcb.com.pk; info@pcb.com.pk).

South Africa Cricket South Africa, PO Box 55009 Northlands 2116; 86, 5th & Glenhove St, Melrose Estate, Johannesburg (+27 11 880 2810; www.cricket.co.za; info@cricket.co.za).

Sri Lanka Sri Lanka Cricket, 35 Maitland Place, Colombo 07000 (+94 112 681 601; www.srilankacricket.lk; info@srilankacricket.lk).

West Indies West Indies Cricket Board, PO Box 616 W, Factory Road, St John's, Antigua (+1 268 481 2450; www.windiescricket.com; wicb@windiescricket.com).

Zimbabwe Zimbabwe Cricket, PO Box 2739, 28 Maiden Drive, Highlands, Harare (+263 4 788 090; www.zimcricket.org; info@zimcricket.org).

Associate Members' addresses may be found on the ICC website, www.icc-cricket.com

ENGLAND AND WALES CRICKET BOARD

The England and Wales Cricket Board (ECB) are responsible for the administration of all cricket – professional and recreational – in England and Wales. In 1997, they took over the functions of the Cricket Council, the Test and County Cricket Board and the National Cricket Association, which had run the game since 1968. In 2005, a streamlined constitution replaced a Management Board of 18 with a 12-strong Board of Directors, three appointed by the first-class counties, two by the county boards. In 2010, this expanded to 14, and added the ECB's first women directors. After a governance review, it returned to 12, including four independent non-executive directors, in 2018.

Officers

President: I. N. Lovett. *Chairman:* C. J. Graves. *Chief Executive Officer:* T. W. Harrison.

Board of Directors: D. M. Bushell, M. Darlow, A. P. Dickinson, C. J. Graves, T. W. Harrison, B. J. O'Brien, Lord Patel of Bradford, L. C. Pearson, S. Smith, J. Stichbury, B. D. H. Trenowden, J. Wood.

Committee Chairs – Executive Committee: T. W. Harrison. *Anti-Corruption:* M. Darlow. *Audit & Risk:* A. P. Dickinson. *Governance:* Lord Patel. *Cricket:* P. G. Wright. *Discipline:* T. J. G. O'Gorman. *Recreational Assembly:* J. Wood. *Regulatory:* N. I. Coward. *Remuneration:* C. J. Graves. *Chief Operating Officer:* D. Mahoney. *Chief Financial Officer:* S. Smith. *Chief Commercial Officer:* T. Singh. *Managing Director, World Cup 2019:* S. Elworthy. *Managing Director, County Cricket:* G. M. Hollins. *Managing Director, New Competition:* S. Patel. *Managing Director, England Men's Cricket:* A. F. Giles. *Managing Director, England Women's Cricket:* C. J. Connor. *Director, Communications:* C. Haynes. *Director, England Cricket Operations:* J. D. Carr. *Director, Participation & Growth:* N. Pryde. *Commercial Director:* R. Calder. *People Director:* R. Ranganathan. *Performance Director:* D. Parsons. *Head of Information Technology:* D. Smith. *National Selector:* E. T. Smith. *Other Selectors:* T. H. Bayliss and J. W. A. Taylor.

ECB: Lord's Ground, London NW8 8QZ (020 7432 1200; www.ecb.co.uk).

THE MARYLEBONE CRICKET CLUB

The Marylebone Cricket Club evolved out of the White Conduit Club in 1787, when Thomas Lord laid out his first ground in Dorset Square. Their members revised the Laws in 1788 and gradually took responsibility for cricket throughout the world. However, they relinquished control of the game in the UK in 1968, and the International Cricket Council finally established their own secretariat in 1993. MCC still own Lord's and remain the guardian of the Laws. They call themselves "a private club with a public function" and aim to support cricket everywhere, especially at grassroots level and in countries where the game is least developed.

Patron: HER MAJESTY THE QUEEN

Officers

President: 2018–19 – A. W. Wreford. *Club Chairman:* G. M. N. Corbett. *Treasurer:* A. B. Elgood. *Trustees:* P. A. B. Beecroft, M. G. Griffith, R. S. Leigh. *Hon. Life Vice-Presidents:* Lord Bramall, E. R. Dexter, C. A. Fry, A. R. Lewis, Sir Oliver Popplewell, D. R. W. Silk, M. O. C. Sturt, J. C. Woodcock.

Chief Executive and Secretary: G. W. Lavender. *Assistant Secretaries – Cricket:* J. P. Stephenson. *Membership and Operations:* J. A. S. Clifford. *Estates:* R. J. Ebdon. *Finance:* A. D. Cameron. *Legal:* H. A. Roper-Curzon.

MCC Committee: J. M. Brearley, I. S. Duncan, A. R. C. Fraser, W. R. Griffiths, S. P. Hughes, P. L. O. Leaver, H. J. H. Loudon, M. C. J. Nicholas, J. O. D. Orders, N. M. Peters, N. E. J. Pocock, S. C. Taylor. The president, club chairman, treasurer and committee chairmen are also on the committee.

Chairmen of Committees – Arts and Library: D. J. C. Faber. *Cricket:* M. V. Fleming. *Estates:* D. C. Brooks Wilson. *Finance:* A. B. Elgood. *Membership and General Purposes:* Sir Ian Magee. *World Cricket:* M. W. Gatting.

MCC: The Chief Executive and Secretary, Lord's Ground, London NW8 8QN (020 7616 8500; www.lords.org; reception@mcc.org.uk. Tickets 020 7432 1000; ticketing@mcc.org.uk).

PROFESSIONAL CRICKETERS' ASSOCIATION

The Professional Cricketers' Association were formed in 1967 (as the Cricketers' Association) to be the collective voice of first-class professional players, and enhance and protect their interests. During the 1970s, they succeeded in establishing pension schemes and a minimum wage. In recent years their strong commercial operations and greater funding from the ECB have increased their services to current and past players, including education, legal and financial help. In 2011, these services were extended to England's women cricketers.

President: G. A. Gooch. *Chairman:* D. K. H. Mitchell. *President – Professional Cricketers' Trust:* D. A. Graveney. *Non-Executive Chairman:* J. R. Metherell. *Non-Executive Directors:* I. T. Guha and P. G. Read. *Chief Executive:* D. A. Leatherdale. *Director of Development and Welfare:* I. J. Thomas. *Financial Director:* P. Garrett. *Business Development Manager:* G. M. Hamilton. *Commercial Manager:* A. Phipps. *Head of Events and Fundraising:* E. Lewis. *Head of Commercial Rights:* E. M. Reid. *Player Rights Manager:* E. Caldwell. *Communications Manager:* L. Reynolds. *Member Services Manager:* A Prosser.

PCA: *London Office* – The Laker Stand, The Oval, Kennington, London SE11 5SS (0207 449 4226; www.thepca.co.uk; communications@thepca.co.uk). *Birmingham Office* – Box 108–9, R. E. S. Wyatt Stand, Warwickshire CCC, Edgbaston, Birmingham B5 7QU.

CRIME AND PUNISHMENT

ICC Code of Conduct – Breaches and Penalties in 2017-18 to 2018-19

V. Kohli   India v South Africa, Second Test at Centurion.
Repeatedly complained of state of ball and threw it on ground. 25% fine / 1 demerit pt – B. C. Broad.

Mashrafe bin Mortaza   Bangladesh v Sri Lanka, one-day tri-series final at Mirpur.
Ran towards dismissed batsman B. K. G. Mendis yelling loudly. 20% fine / 1 demerit pt – D. C. Boon.

M. D. Gunathilleke   Sri Lanka v Bangladesh, one-day tri-series final at Mirpur.
Ran towards dismissed batsman Tamim Iqbal, shouting. Reprimand / 1 demerit pt – D. C. Boon.

Sikandar Raza   Zimbabwe v Afghanistan, third one-day international at Sharjah.
Raised arms in protest and delayed leaving when lbw. 15% fine / 1 demerit pt – R. B. Richardson.

K. Rabada   South Africa v India, fifth one-day international at Port Elizabeth.
After dismissing S. Dhawan, waved and said "bye" to him. 15% fine / 1 demerit pt – A. J. Pycroft.

D. A. Warner   Australia v South Africa, First Test at Durban.
Heated exchange with Q. de Kock on leaving the field; had to be restrained by team-mates. 75% fine / 3 demerit pts – J. J. Crowe.

Q. de Kock   South Africa v Australia, First Test at Durban.
Heated exchange with D. A. Warner on leaving the field. 25% fine / 1 demerit pt – J. J. Crowe.

N. M. Lyon   Australia v South Africa, First Test at Durban.
Dropped ball on fallen A. B. de Villiers after running him out. 15% fine / 1 demerit pt – J. J. Crowe.

Mohammad Shahzad   Afghanistan v Zimbabwe, World Cup Qualifier ODI at Bulawayo.
Struck divot from ground on dismissal. Banned for two games / 15% fine / 1 demerit pt – D. T. Jukes.

Mujeeb Zadran   Afghanistan v Zimbabwe, World Cup Qualifier ODI at Bulawayo.
Threw the ball dangerously close to B. R. M. Taylor. 50% fine / 3 demerit pts – D. T. Jukes.

B. R. M. Taylor   Zimbabwe v Afghanistan, World Cup Qualifier ODI at Bulawayo.
Dissent at umpire's decision. 15% fine / 1 demerit pt – D. T. Jukes.

K. Rabada   South Africa v Australia, Second Test at Port Elizabeth.
Barged into S. P. D. Smith after dismissing him. Originally charged with inappropriate deliberate contact, leading to 50% fine / 3 demerit pts, which would have taken him to eight in total, meaning a two-Test ban – J. J. Crowe. On appeal, M. Heron QC ruled contact was inappropriate but not necessarily deliberate; reduced to 25% fine / 1 demerit pt.

K. Rabada   South Africa v Australia, Second Test at Port Elizabeth.
Aggressive send-off after dismissing D. A. Warner. 15% fine / 1 demerit pt – J. J. Crowe.

M. R. Marsh   Australia v South Africa, Second Test at Port Elizabeth.
Swore at K. Rabada, who had just bowled him. 20% fine / 1 demerit pt – J. J. Crowe.

Shakib Al Hasan   Bangladesh v Sri Lanka, Nidahas Trophy T20I at Colombo (RPS).
Called his batsmen off the field in protest at umpire's decision. 25% fine / 1 demerit pt – B. C. Broad.

Nurul Hasan (twelfth man)   Bangladesh v Sri Lanka, Nidahas Trophy T20I at Colombo (RPS).
Argued with Sri Lankan captain N. L. T. C. Perera after being sent on with message for batsmen. 25% fine / 1 demerit pt – B. C. Broad.

M. N. Samuels   West Indies v Zimbabwe, World Cup Qualifier ODI at Harare.
Struck a fielding disc with his bat when out. Reprimand / 1 demerit pt – G. F. Labrooy.

S. C. Williams   Zimbabwe v UAE, World Cup Qualifier ODI at Harare.
Swore at Rohan Mustafa, who had just dismissed him. 15% fine / 1 demerit pt – D. T. Jukes.

Rohan Mustafa   UAE v Zimbabwe, World Cup Qualifier ODI at Harare.
Swore at S. C. Williams after dismissing him. 15% fine / 1 demerit pt – D. T. Jukes.

S. P. D. Smith   Australia v South Africa, Third Test at Cape Town.
Conspiracy to tamper with the ball. Banned for one Test / 100% fine / 4 demerit pts – A. J. Pycroft.

C. T. Bancroft   Australia v South Africa, Third Test at Cape Town.
Admitted tampering with the ball. 75% fine/3 demerit pts – A. J. Pycroft.

Diana Baig   Pakistan v Sri Lanka, first Twenty20 international at Colombo (SSC).
Damaged the pitch while batting; five penalty runs. Reprimand/1 demerit pt – W. C. Labrooy.

M. J. Coles (coach)   Pakistan v Sri Lanka, firstTwenty20 international at Colombo (SSC).
Entered the field after match to shout at the umpires. Reprimand/1 demerit pt – W. C. Labrooy.

Shadab Khan   Pakistan v West Indies, second Twenty20 international at Karachi.
Swore and pointed at C. A. K. Walton after dismissing him. 20% fine/1 demerit pt – D. C. Boon.

Rubel Hossain   Bangladesh v Afghanistan, second Twenty20 at Dehradun.
Gestured and shook his head when appeal was turned down. Reprimand/1 demerit pt – A. J. Pycroft.

L. D. Chandimal   Sri Lanka v West Indies, Second Test at Gros Islet, St Lucia.
Tampering with the ball. Banned for one Test/100% fine/4 demerit pts – J. Srinath.

L. D. Chandimal   Sri Lanka v West Indies, Second Test at Gros Islet, St Lucia.
Refused to take team on field on third day. Banned for two Tests and four ODIs/100% fine/6 demerit pts – J. Srinath.

U. C. Hathurusinghe (coach) and A. P. Gurusinha (manager)   Sri Lanka v West Indies, Second Test at Gros Islet, St Lucia.
Joined Chandimal in keeping team off field. Banned for two Tests and four ODIs/6 demerit pts each – J. Srinath.

A. S. Joseph   West Indies v Bangladesh, second one-day international at Providence.
Pointed at pavilion after dismissing Anamul Haque. Reprimand/1 demerit pt – B. C. Broad.

Rubel Hossain   Bangladesh v West Indies, third one-day international at Basseterre.
Swore loudly after S. O. Hetmyer hit him for four. Reprimand/1 demerit pt – B. C. Broad.

I. Sharma   India v England, First Test at Birmingham.
Provocative send-off after dismissing D. J. Malan. 15% fine/1 demerit pt – J. J. Crowe.

Abu Haider   Bangladesh v West Indies, second Twenty20 international at Lauderhill.
Swore repeatedly after R. Powell hit him for six. 20% fine/1 demerit pt – B. C. Broad.

A. R. Nurse   West Indies v Bangladesh, third Twenty20 international at Lauderhill.
Swore loudly after Liton Das hit him for two sixes and a four. Reprimand/1 demerit pt – B. C. Broad.

S. C. J. Broad   England v India, Third Test at Nottingham.
Aggressive language towards R. R. Pant after bowling him. 15% fine/1 demerit pt – J. J. Crowe.

J. M. Anderson   England v India, Fifth Test at The Oval.
Aggression towards umpire after V. Kohli survived review. 15% fine/1 demerit pt – A. J. Pycroft.

Hasan Ali   Pakistan v Afghanistan, Asia Cup one-day international at Abu Dhabi.
Threatened to throw ball at striker Hashmatullah Shahidi. 15% fine/1 demerit pt – A. J. Pycroft.

Asghar Afghan   Afghanistan v Pakistan, Asia Cup one-day international at Abu Dhabi.
Brushed shoulders with bowler Hasan Ali while taking a run. 15% fine/1 demerit pt – A. J. Pycroft.

Rashid Khan   Afghanistan v Pakistan, Asia Cup one-day international at Abu Dhabi.
Gave batsman Asif Ali send-off on dismissing him. 15% fine/1 demerit pt – A. J. Pycroft.

A. L. Phehlukwayo   South Africa v Zimbabwe, second one-day international at Bloemfontein.
Raised his arms in dissent when given out caught behind. Reprimand/1 demerit pt – J. J. Crowe.

S. G. Law (coach)   West Indies v India, Second Test at Hyderabad.
Accused Indians of cheating in front of fourth umpire. 100% fine/3 demerit pts – B. C. Broad.

K. K. Ahmed   India v West Indies, fourth one-day international at Mumbai.
Aggressive behaviour after dismissing M. N. Samuels. Reprimand/1 demerit pt – B. C. Broad.

J. M. Anderson   England v Sri Lanka, First Test at Galle.
Threw ball at pitch when cautioned for running on it. Reprimand/1 demerit pt – A. J. Pycroft.

J. E. Root   England v Sri Lanka, Second Test at Pallekele.
Shook his head and kicked turf when appeal turned down. Reprimand/1 demerit pt – A. J. Pycroft.

S. T. Gabriel West Indies v Bangladesh, First Test at Chittagong.
Inappropriate deliberate contact with batsman Imrul Kayes. 30% fine/2 demerit pts – D. C. Boon.

C. B. R. L. S. Kumara Sri Lanka v New Zealand, First Test at Wellington.
Swore loudly after being edged for four. 15% fine/1 demerit pt – R. B. Richardson.

Shakib Al Hasan Bangladesh v West Indies, first Twenty20 international at Sylhet.
While batting, yelled at umpire that ball should be called wide. 15% fine/1 demerit pt – J. J. Crowe.

J. M. Arthur (coach) Pakistan v South Africa, First Test at Centurion.
Entered third umpire's room to question decision. Reprimand/1 demerit pt – D. C. Boon.

Sarfraz Ahmed Pakistan v South Africa, second one-day international at Durban.
Made racist remark to A. L. Phehlukwayo. Charged under Anti-Racism Code rather than Code of Conduct; banned for four ODIs/T20Is and ordered to undergo an education programme. No fine or demerit points applied.

Twenty-eight further breaches took place in Associate Member or Under-19 internationals during this period.

Under ICC regulations on minor over-rate offences, players are fined 10% of their match fee for every over their side fails to bowl in the allotted time, with the captain fined double that amount. There were 13 instances in this period in men's internationals, and two in women's:

F. du Plessis/South Africa v India, 2nd Test at Centurion, 40%/20% – B. C. Broad.

A. K. Markram/South Africa v India, 4th ODI at Johannesburg, 20%/10% – A. J. Pycroft.

L. D. Chandimal/Sri Lanka v Bangladesh, Nidahas Trophy T20I, 0%/60% – B. C. Broad.
  Chandimal was not fined, but was suspended for two matches.

Mahmudullah/Bangladesh v Sri Lanka, Nidahas Trophy T20I, 20%/10% – B. C. Broad.

Sarfraz Ahmed/Pakistan v England, 1st Test at Lord's, 60%/30% – J. J. Crowe.

J. O. Holder/West Indies v Sri Lanka, 3rd Test at Bridgetown, 60%/30% – J. Srinath.

H. Masakadza/Zimbabwe v Pakistan, tri-series T20I at Harare, 20%/10% – J. J. Crowe.

Mashrafe bin Mortaza/Bangladesh v India, Asia Cup ODI final at Dubai, 40%/20% – D. C. Boon.

A. E. Satterthwaite/NZ v Australia, Women's WT20I at Providence, 20%/10% – R. B. Richardson.

M. M. Lanning/Australia v India, Women's WT20I at Providence, 20%/10% – R. B. Richardson.

A. J. Finch/Australia v India, 1st T20I at Brisbane, 20%/10% – J. J. Crowe.

C. R. Brathwaite/West Indies v Bangladesh, 2nd T20I at Mirpur, 40%/20% – J. J. Crowe.

Shakib Al Hasan/Bangladesh v West Indies, 2nd T20I at Mirpur, 20%/10% – J. J. Crowe.

S. L. Malinga/Sri Lanka v NZ, 1st ODI at Mount Maunganui, 20%/10% – R. B. Richardson.

F. du Plessis/South Africa v Pakistan, 2nd Test at Cape Town, 20%/10% – D. C. Boon.
  Du Plessis was suspended for one Test as it was his second offence within 12 months.

There were two further instances in Associate Member internationals.

INTERNATIONAL UMPIRES' PANELS

In 1993, the ICC formed an international umpires' panel, containing at least two officials from each Full Member. A third-country umpire from this panel stood with a home umpire in every Test from 1994 onwards. In 2002, an elite panel was appointed: two elite umpires – both independent – were to stand in all Tests, and at least one in every ODI, where one home umpire was allowed. A supporting panel of international umpires was created to provide cover at peak times in the Test schedule, second umpires in one-day internationals, and third umpires to give rulings from TV replays. The panels are sponsored by Emirates Airlines.

The elite panel at the start of 2019: Aleem Dar (P), H. D. P. K. Dharmasena (SL), M. Erasmus (SA), C. B. Gaffaney (NZ), I. J. Gould (E), R. K. Illingworth (E), R. A. Kettleborough (E), N. J. Llong (E), B. N. J. Oxenford (A), S. Ravi (I), P. R. Reiffel (A), R. J. Tucker (A).

The international panel: G. A. Abood (A), Ahmed Shah Durrani (Afg), Ahmed Shah Pakteen (Afg), Ahsan Raza (P), Asif Yaqoob (P), R. J. Bailey (E), Bismillah Shinwari (Afg), R. E. Black (Ire), G. O. Brathwaite (WI), C. M. Brown (NZ), I. Chabi (Z), A. K. Chowdhury (I), N. Duguid (WI), S. D. Fry (A), Gazi Sohel (B), S. George (SA), M. A. Gough (E), S. B. Haig (NZ), L. E. Hannibal (SL), M. Hawthorne (Ire), A. T. Holdstock (SA), P. B. Jele (SA), W. R. Knights (NZ), R. E. J. Martinesz (SL), Masudur Rahman (B), T. J. Matibiri (Z), N. N. Menon (I), C. K. Nandan (I), A. J. Neill (Ire), S. J. Nogajski (A), A. Paleker (SA), R. S. A. Palliyaguruge (SL), Rashid Riaz (P), L. S. Reifer (WI), P. A. Reynolds (Ire), R. T. Robinson (E), L. Rusere (Z), C. Shamshuddin (I), Sharfuddoula (B), Shozab Raza (P), Tanvir Ahmed (B), R. B. Tiffin (Z), A. G. Wharf (E), J. S. Wilson (WI), P. Wilson (A), R. R. Wimalasiri (SL).

ICC development panel: Akbar Ali (UAE), V. R. Angara (Botswana), S. N. Bandekar (USA), K. D. Cotton (NZ), R. D'Mello (Kenya), A. J. T. Dowdalls (Scotland), D. A. Haggo (Scotland), Iftikhar Ali (UAE), H. K. G. Jansen (Netherlands), V. K. Jha (Nepal), A. Kapa (PNG), H. E. Kearns (Jersey), A. W. Louw (Namibia), L. Oala (PNG), D. Odhiambo (Kenya), I. O. Oyieko (Kenya), C. A. Polosak (A), B. B. Pradhan (Nepal), S. S. Prasad (Singapore), Rahul Asher (Oman), I. N. Ramage (Scotland), S. Redfern (E), Rizwan Akram (Netherlands), D. N. Subedi (Nepal), Tabarak Dar (Hong Kong), I. A. Thomson (Hong Kong), C. H. Thorburn (Namibia), W. P. M. van Liemt (Netherlands), K. Viswanadan (Malaysia), J. M. Williams (WI).

ICC REFEREES' PANEL

In 1991, the ICC formed a panel of referees to enforce their Code of Conduct for Tests and one-day internationals, and to support the umpires in upholding the game's conduct. In 2002, the ICC launched an elite panel, on full-time contracts, for all international cricket, sponsored by Emirates Airlines. At the start of 2019, it consisted of D. C. Boon (A), B. C. Broad (E), J. J. Crowe (NZ), R. S. Madugalle (SL), A. J. Pycroft (Z), R. B. Richardson (WI), J. Srinath (I).

A further panel of international referees consisted of Akhtar Ahmad (B), Anis Sheikh (P), G. A. V. Baxter (NZ), S. R. Bernard (A), O. Chirombe (Z), D. Cooke (Ire), E. T. Dube (Z), R. A. Dykes (NZ), K. Gallagher (Ire), D. Govindjee (SA), Hamim Talwar (Afg), D. O. Hayles (WI), D. T. Jukes (E), R. D. King (WI), G. F. Labrooy (SL), W. C. Labrooy (SL), Mohammad Javed (P), V. Narayanan Kutty (I), M. Nayyar (I), Neeyamur Rashid (B), W. M. Noon (E), G. H. Pienaar (SA), R. W. Stratford (A), S. Wadvalla (SA), P. Whitticase (E), Zarab Shah Zaheer (Afg).

ENGLISH UMPIRES FOR 2019

First-class: R. J. Bailey, N. L. Bainton, P. K. Baldwin, I. D. Blackwell, M. Burns, N. G. B. Cook, B. J. Debenham, J. H. Evans, M. A. Gough, I. J. Gould, P. J. Hartley, R. K. Illingworth, R. A. Kettleborough, N. J. Llong, G. D. Lloyd, J. W. Lloyds, N. A. Mallender, D. J. Millns, S. J. O'Shaughnessy, P. R. Pollard, R. T. Robinson, M. J. Saggers, B. V. Taylor, R. J. Warren, A. G. Wharf. *Reserves:* Hasan Adnan, T. Lungley, J. D. Middlebrook, M. Newell, N. Pratt, I. N. Ramage, C. M. Watts, R. A. White.

National Panel for Second XI, Minor Counties and MCCU games: R. G. B. Allen, J. S. Beckwith, S. Beswick, T. Caldicott, G. I. Callaway, S. Cobb, K. Coburn, J. R. Cousins, N. G. C. Cowley, D. Daniels, A. Davies, H. Davies, N. Davies, M. P. Dobbs, C. Dunn, R. G. Eagleton, R. C. Ellis, P. Evans, J. Farrell, K. Fergusson, M. M. French, R. R. Garland, D. J. Gower, N. J. Hall, R. C. Hampshire, A. C. Harris, I. L. Herbert, A. Hicks, S. Hollingshead, C. Johnson, M. Johnson, B. Jones, I. P. Laurence, S. E. Lavis, K. A. Little, A. Lunn, G. W. Marshall, J. Marshall, R. P. Medland, B. Morris, P. Mustard, Naeem Ashraf, J. K. H. Naik, P. D. Nicholls, R. Parker, A. P. Payne, D. N. Pedley, B. J. Peverall, N. E. Piddock, J. Pitcher, M. Pointer, D. Price, J. P. Prince, M. Qureshi, S. Redfern, I. G. Rich, P. Richardson, S. Richardson, G. M. Roberts, S. J. Ross, A. Shaikh, S. Shanmugam, J. D. Shantry, P. Smith, P. J. Sparshott, M. J. Spenceley, R. W. Tolchard, J. R. Tomsett, J. C. Tredwell, C. J. Viljoen, D. M. Warburton, I. G. Warne, M. D. Watton, A. J. Wheeler, S. Widdup.

THE DUCKWORTH/LEWIS/STERN METHOD

In 1997, the ECB's one-day competitions adopted a new method to revise targets in interrupted games, devised by Frank Duckworth of the Royal Statistical Society and Tony Lewis of the University of the West of England. The method was gradually taken up by other countries and, in 1999, the ICC decided to incorporate it into the standard playing conditions for one-day internationals.

The system aims to preserve any advantage that one team have established before the interruption. It uses the idea that teams have two resources from which they make runs – an allocated number of overs, and ten wickets. It also takes into account when the interruption occurs, because of the different scoring-rates typical of different stages of an innings. Traditional run-rate calculations relied only on the overs available, and ignored wickets lost.

It uses one table with 50 rows, covering matches of up to 50 overs, and ten columns, from nought to nine wickets down. Each figure gives the percentage of the total runs that would, on average, be scored with a certain number of overs left and wickets lost. If a match is shortened before it begins, to, say, 33 overs a side, the figure for 33 overs and ten wickets remaining would be the starting point.

If overs are lost, the table is used to calculate the percentage of runs the team would be expected to score in those missing overs. This is obtained by reading the figure for the number of overs left, and wickets down, when play stops, and subtracting the figure for the number of overs left when it resumes. If the delay occurs between innings, and the second team's allocation of overs is reduced, then their target is obtained by calculating the appropriate percentage for the reduced number of overs with all ten wickets standing. For instance, if the second team's innings halves from 50 overs to 25, the table shows that they still have 66.5% of their resources left, so have to beat two-thirds of the first team's total, rather than half. If the first innings is complete and the second innings interrupted or prematurely terminated, the score to beat is reduced by the percentage of the innings lost.

The version known as the "Professional Edition" was introduced into one-day internationals from 2003, and subsequently into most national one-day competitions. Using a more advanced mathematical formula (it is entirely computerised), it adjusts the tables to allow for the different scoring-rates that emerge in matches with above-average first-innings scores. In 2014, analysis by Steven Stern, an Australian professor of statistics who became responsible for the method after Duckworth and Lewis retired, indicated further modification was needed. The Duckworth/Lewis/Stern method is now used in all one-day and Twenty20 internationals, as well as most national competitions. The original "Standard Edition" is used where computers are unavailable, and at lower levels of the game.

The system also covers first-innings interruptions, multiple interruptions and innings ended by rain. The tables are revised slightly every two years, taking account of changing scoring-rates; the average total in a 50-over international is now 263 (up from 225 in 1999).

In the World Cup semi-final between South Africa and New Zealand at Auckland in March 2015, South Africa were 216 for three from 38 overs when seven overs were lost to rain; after the innings resumed, they finished on 281. With three wickets down, the lost overs constituted 14.85% of South Africa's scoring resources, meaning they used only 85.15%. By contrast, New Zealand's 43-over chase constituted 90% of the resources of a full innings. Their revised target was determined by multiplying South Africa's total, 281, by 90% divided by 85.15% and adding one run: 281 x (90/85.15) + 1 = 298. New Zealand scored 299 for six in 42.5 overs to win, with a six off the penultimate delivery. Had South Africa been two down at the interruption, the lost overs would have constituted a higher percentage of their scoring resources; the revised target would have been 301, and New Zealand would have needed two more runs off the final ball.

A similar system, usually known as the VJD method, is used in some domestic matches in India. It was devised by V. Jayadevan, a civil engineer from Kerala.

POWERPLAYS

In one-day and Twenty20 internationals, two semi-circles of 30-yard (27.43 metres) radius are drawn on the field behind each set of stumps, joined by straight lines parallel to the pitch.

At the instant of delivery in the first ten overs of an uninterrupted one-day international innings (the first six overs in a Twenty20 international), only two fielders may be positioned outside this 30-yard area. During the next 30 overs no more than four fielders may be stationed outside the 30-yard area; and in the final ten overs, no more than five. (In Twenty20 internationals, no more than five may be positioned outside the area for the last 14 overs.) In matches affected by the weather, the number of overs in each powerplay stage is reduced in proportion to the overall reduction of overs.

In July 2015, the one-day international requirement for two close fielders in the first ten overs, and the five-over batting powerplay, to be claimed between the 11th and 40th overs, was abolished.

MEETINGS AND DECISIONS IN 2018

MCC WORLD CRICKET COMMITTEE

The MCC World Cricket Committee met in Sydney on January 9–10, chaired for the first time by Mike Gatting.

They discussed how a proper wage structure and longer central contracts would entice more players to commit to international cricket, rather than opting out for domestic Twenty20 leagues. Players in the poorer nations were not paid enough, and accountability was needed on where member boards spent ICC funds.

The committee believed the upcoming World Test Championship was the key to safeguarding Test cricket's future against the threat from global T20 leagues, but asked the ICC and member boards to research fans' expectations of Test cricket. Most committee members favoured simultaneous matches towards the end of the Championship cycle, to maximise interest, and five-day Tests.

The committee had long supported the inclusion of Twenty20 cricket in the Olympic Games, and now felt the primary barrier was India's reluctance; they urged India to join in lobbying the International Olympic Committee to adopt cricket, ideally in Paris in 2024 but, if not, at Los Angeles in 2028.

The committee believed player associations had an important role to play in fighting corruption. Some players were reluctant to report approaches because of concerns about anonymity; player associations could act as a trusted third party, passing information on to the ICC's Anti-Corruption Unit. The education process needed improvement; the best method was to use players with personal experience of the problem.

The committee praised the successful women's World Cup in England in 2017. It was crucial that the momentum was not lost; each ICC Full Member should invest in developing women's and girls' cricket. More than 180m people were estimated to have watched the World Cup, with every match broadcast on television or via live-streaming, and streaming T20 leagues in Australia and England also helped fans follow the game. Venues must create the right spectacle, with good pace in the pitch. The committee were concerned by the imbalance in women's international cricket. To be really successful, it needed at least eight competing nations, but only six were realistic contenders; some form of minimum wage and payment structure was required. There should be windows in the international calendar for the Big Bash and Kia Super Leagues, to ensure the best cricketers took part.

The committee encouraged MCC to promote education on concussion through their free eLearning platform. The Laws allowed for a replacement, but this was not always practical, and players must not feel obliged to carry on to avoid leaving the team short. On the other hand, there were concerns about replacements, including players sitting idle, and exploitable loopholes. MCC would monitor trials in the professional game. The committee also recommended mandatory helmets, with stem guards, in all professional cricket, while every international team should have a trained medic to assess head injuries.

With the arrival of the World Test Championship in 2019, the committee recommended standardising DRS technology across the competition. The ICC should be prepared to fund the technology to assist hosts unable to afford it.

The committee praised MCC's work with young players from Pakistan who have suffered from the lack of international cricket there; Yasir Jan had been invited to train with MCC Young Cricketers at Lord's. MCC were reviewing their overseas tour strategy to identify countries where their tours could have most impact – such as Zimbabwe, Nepal and Germany.

The committee confirmed that, in extreme heat, Law 2.7.1 empowered umpires to suspend play, as it fell into the category of unreasonable or dangerous conditions.

ECB SPONSORSHIP DEAL

On February 7, the ECB announced that health and life insurance company Vitality had signed a four-year deal to sponsor the domestic T20 Blast competition, men's and women's home T20 internationals, the men's and women's Club T20 competitions and the Under-19 Club T20 tournament until 2021.

ICC BOARD

The ICC Board met in Dubai on February 9, and announced that Indra Nooyi, the chair and chief executive of PepsiCo, had been appointed as the board's first independent female director under the revised constitution, to serve an initial two years from June.

They agreed a revised financial model with increased allocations for new Full Members Ireland and Afghanistan, projected to be worth $40m each over the eight-year cycle.

The board expressed concern that the Indian government did not offer a tax exemption for ICC events in India. Talks with the government would continue, but the ICC would explore alternative hosts for the 2021 Champions Trophy.

A delegation who had visited Nepal, currently suspended from ICC associate membership, reported that a general meeting in March was expected to adopt an amended constitution and hold elections, with a view to being reinstated in June.

There was also an update on the new national governing body in the USA, set up after the expulsion of USACA in 2017. USA Cricket should hold elections by June 2018, enabling them to apply for associate membership at the ICC annual conference.

ENGLAND MEN'S SELECTION PANEL

On March 12, the ECB announced that England national selector James Whitaker was stepping down after a decade as a selector and five years in the top job. This coincided with a new approach to scouting, assessing and selecting England players. Designated discipline-specific scouts, including the current national lead coaches, would provide information to a new selection panel, made up of the national selector, an independent England selector and the England head coach.

On April 20, Ed Smith, the journalist and former Kent and Middlesex captain who played three Tests in 2003, was appointed as the national selector. On July 13, former Nottinghamshire and England batsman James Taylor was added as the second selector, completing the panel with Smith and coach Trevor Bayliss.

ECB MEETINGS

Chairmen and representatives of the 18 first-class counties and MCC met the ECB chairman Colin Graves, chief executive Tom Harrison and several ECB directors at Lord's on March 26. They discussed the controversial payment of £2.5m to Glamorgan as compensation for not applying to stage Test cricket between 2020 and 2024, and the principles around any future payments to counties. Two days later, the ECB commissioned an external review into the process leading to the Glamorgan payment, while Richard Thompson stood down as a director, reportedly because of misgivings about it; earlier in March, another director, Andy Nash, had resigned, citing similar payments to Test grounds as one of his reasons.

The ECB later announced the formation of a board to develop their new eight-team short-format competition for 2020, first proposed in March 2017. Chaired by Graves, it included independent members from the business and entertainment sectors, as well as representatives of the county game and ECB senior management.

On April 19, the ECB unveiled a new approach to the eight-team competition, based on the format of 100 balls for each team, to differentiate it from the Blast and other T20 tournaments. Men's and women's teams would share a common format, brands and identities in their respective leagues. The ECB said The Hundred's simplicity would appeal to families and a diverse audience. It would occupy a five-week window in the summer and be promoted across Sky and the BBC.

On April 25, the ECB appointed Leicestershire chief executive Wasim Khan to chair a working group on the structure of men's county cricket. He was joined by three county directors of cricket, Keith Greenfield, Ashley Giles and Martyn Moxon; two chief executives, Derek Bowden and Hugh Morris; Mark Wallace and Ian Thomas from the Professional Cricketers' Association; and Andrew Strauss, John Carr and Alan Fordham from the ECB.

ICC BOARD

The ICC Board met in Kolkata on April 25–26, and agreed that all Twenty20 matches between ICC Members should have full international status, in order to use the T20 format to globalise the game. All women's teams from Associate Members would be awarded T20I status from July 2018, and men's teams from the start of 2019.

The board and chief executives discussed a review of the Code of Conduct, and supported stricter sanctions for ball-tampering, abusive language, send-offs and dissent. They also wanted a culture of respect embodying the spirit of cricket, on and off the field.

A new Future Tours Programme for 2019–2023 was signed off, incorporating two cycles of the new World Test Championship, plus an extra World T20 event to replace the Champions Trophy in 2021, and a World Cup Qualification League.

There had been a sharp increase in the number of domestic T20 leagues seeking ICC approval. Though the board agreed these were good for the global game, a working group was set up to consider how to regulate them and ensure international cricket remained attractive to players.

Concussion guidelines developed by the Medical Advisory Committee were adopted.

The board agreed a process for electing the next ICC chairman, after Shashank Manohar's first two-year term expired. They ratified Belinda Clark of Australia as the women's representative on the Cricket Committee, replacing Clare Connor of England. In May, two further appointments to the Cricket Committee were announced: Scotland captain Kyle Coetzer replaced Ireland's Kevin O'Brien as the Associate Member representative (Ireland were now a Full Member), and New Zealand coach Mike Hesson replaced Darren Lehmann, who had resigned as Australia's coach.

MCC AGM AND GROUND REDEVELOPMENT

The 231st AGM of the Marylebone Cricket Club was held at Lord's on May 2, with president Lord MacLaurin of Knebworth in the chair. He announced that his successor, from October, would be Anthony Wreford, the businessman and former non-executive chairman of the Professional Cricketers' Association, who had played a key role in opening up MCC membership to women from 1998.

Resolutions were passed increasing members' entrance fees and annual subscriptions, changing the basis for the outer-town subscription concession and re-opening the senior membership class. The number of membership candidates the committee may elect out of turn was doubled to 12 a year. Members also accepted that they should pay for admission to the five matches Lord's was to host in the 2019 men's World Cup.

Membership on December 31, 2017, totalled 23,652, made up of 17,848 full members, 5,268 associate members, 370 honorary members, 39 senior members and 127 out-match members. There were 12,081 candidates awaiting election to full membership; 537 vacancies arose in 2017.

On June 6, MCC unveiled architects WilkinsonEyre's designs for the new three-tier Compton and Edrich Stands, which would accommodate around 11,500 spectators, an increase of 2,500, expanding the ground capacity to 31,000. A walkway overlooking the Nursery Ground would link the two stands, and the top tier of both would be partially covered. There would be debenture seating and restaurants in the middle tier, and 3% of all seating would be for wheelchair users or those with restricted mobility. If the planning application was approved by Westminster City Council, MCC members would be asked to vote on the plans in May 2019. Demolition of the existing stands should begin after the Ashes Test in August, with this phase of the ground redevelopment completed in 2021.

ECB MEETINGS

On May 4, the ECB approved the nominations' committee recommendations for four new board directors – two independent non-executives (Brenda Trenowden and Delia Bushell) and two cricket non-executives (Barry O'Brien and Alan Dickinson). This was part of the move towards a fully independent board, agreed in 2017. O'Brien and Dickinson would be required to step down from their current roles as Glamorgan chairman and Surrey treasurer under Sport England's Code for Sports Governance.

At the AGM on May 9, the ECB's 41 members (the chairs of the 39 first-class and Minor Counties, and of MCC and the Minor Counties Cricket Association) approved the new board, ratifying the appointments of Trenowden, Bushell, O'Brien and Dickinson, and the addition of chief financial officer Scott Smith. Existing board members Colin Graves (the chairman), Tom Harrison (the chief executive), Martin Darlow, Lord Patel, Lucy Pearson, Jane Stichbury and Jim Wood were also approved, while Giles Clarke, Matthew Fleming, Ian Lovett and Peter Wright stood down.

ECB SOUTH ASIAN ACTION PLAN

On May 10, the ECB announced a plan to engage with South Asian communities and draw in more players, fans and volunteers. It was to launch with events in three core cities, including a street tape-ball competition in Birmingham, a schools' competition in Bradford, and a women's and girls' session at Leyton. An advisory group had found that the single biggest barrier to South Asian participation was lack of facilities in urban areas; others were a lack of scouting, the cost of travel and equipment, a lack of female coaches, poor access to cricket at school and a lack of cultural considerations.

Recommended actions included the creation of 20-plus urban cricket centres and the development of 1,000 non-turf pitches and 100 turf pitches by 2024; finding community talent champions to scout talent previously missed; delivering cricket sessions to 6,000 primary schools in deprived urban communities through Chance to Shine; supporting the progression of BAME coaches, and training 200 female coaches; and bursaries for talented young South Asian players.

In an update on June 2, the ECB reported that they had formed a partnership with the Royal National Children's SpringBoard Foundation to run a pilot cricket scholarship project in 2019, connecting four young South Asian players from urban areas with schools offering strong cricket. This could be expanded to give young cricketers life-changing bursaries. They were also working with the British Asian Trust and National Asian Cricket Council, and inviting applications for three pilot urban cricket centres.

In a further update on November 20, the ECB announced £1.2m of funding via a National Lottery grant to develop a network of South Asian female coaches and mentors, who would support All Stars Cricket, ECB's entry-level programme for five-to-eight-year-olds. Leyton Cricket Club had been chosen for the first urban cricket centre, and 58 non-turf pitches installed, while the ECB T20 City Cup had expanded to 16 cities.

ICC CHAIRMAN

On May 15, the ICC announced that Shashank Manohar, the board's first independent chairman, would serve a second two-year term. He was the sole nominee for the position.

UNIVERSITY CRICKET

On May 17, the ECB announced that from 2020 they would resume funding university cricket. This had been undertaken by MCC since 2004, when it took over the University Centres of Cricketing Excellence programme established by the ECB in 2000. MCC had invested over £7.5m in the six "MCC Universities", based at Cambridge, Cardiff, Durham, Leeds/Bradford, Loughborough and Oxford; 18 MCCU cricketers had gone on to represent their countries, and 119 had secured first-class county contracts.

The ECB and MCC were working on a new scheme with input from the existing MCCUs, additional universities, British Universities & Colleges Sport and the first-class counties. They hoped to enhance white-ball university cricket and increase support for elite women cricketers in higher education.

ICC WORLD CUP MEDIA RIGHTS

On May 24, the ICC confirmed that the BBC's *Test Match Special* had secured rights to broadcast ball-by-ball coverage of the 2019 World Cup, to be held in England and Wales. It would broadcast via BBC Radio 5 Live Sports Extra, Radio 4 Long Wave and the BBC Sport website. The deal ensured that *TMS* would cover all major ICC events through to the 2023 World Cup in India, including the women's World Cup in New Zealand in 2021 and the men's and women's World T20 events.

ICC CRICKET COMMITTEE

The ICC Cricket Committee met in Mumbai on May 28–29, and supported the ICC Board's commitment to improve player behaviour and develop a culture of respect. They discussed what member boards could do to create a better atmosphere and provide for a fair contest; what it means to play in the spirit of cricket; and the specific offences to be covered by the Code, the level of sanctions and the consistent handling of charges. They recommended giving greater authority to match officials; greater leadership accountability for boards and team support staff; clear expectations for the treatment of visiting teams, particularly around practice facilities, warm-up games and logistical arrangements; and greater education for young players on the history and spirit of the game. They also recommended increasing sanctions for ball-tampering; creating a new offence for offensive, personal, insulting or orchestrated abuse; considering a new offence of attempting to gain an unfair advantage; creating a Code of Respect; and giving referees the authority to downgrade or upgrade a level of offence.

On the World Test Championship, the committee discussed whether to award the toss automatically to the visiting team, but felt it was an integral part of Test cricket. Acknowledging that the biased preparation of pitches could threaten the tournament's competitiveness, they urged members to focus on providing a better balance between bat and ball. They recommended that points should be awarded for each match, but not for a series win, and a draw should give each team a third of the available points. It was agreed to propose a reserve day for the final, to make up any time lost to bad weather.

ICC MARKET RESEARCH

On June 27, the ICC released the results of a global market research project, based on over 19,000 interviews with cricket fans by Nielsen Sports. Results suggested cricket had over a billion fans in the surveyed 16–69 age group, with 34 the average age; 39% were female. Two-thirds of fans interviewed were interested in all three formats, with the World Cup and World T20 the most popular events. Two-thirds were interested in women's cricket and wanted more live coverage. Test cricket was most popular in England and Wales, where 86% of fans were interested. Globally, T20 internationals were the most popular format, with 92% interest; 87% said they would like the Olympics to include T20 cricket.

The research suggested that cricket has the potential to grow in traditional and non-traditional markets. Sports fans not currently interested in cricket wanted a better understanding of the cricket calendar, making it easier to follow, which the ICC were seeking to address in their global strategy.

ICC ANNUAL MEETINGS

The ICC annual conference and associated meetings were in Dublin on June 28–July 2.

Chairman Shashank Manohar welcomed Indra Nooyi, the ICC board's first independent female director. Imran Khwaja of Singapore, the Associate Members' chairman, was unanimously reappointed ICC vice-chairman following his re-election as an Associate representative (alongside Malaysia's Mahinda Vallipuram and Scotland's Tony Brian).

The board allowed a representative of the Sri Lankan sports minister to attend as an observer, but requested that elections for Sri Lanka Cricket should be held within six months; if not, SLC's membership status would come into question.

A package of measures was agreed to enable Zimbabwe Cricket to stabilise their business. ZC's funding would be rearranged to help them service existing debts, and the rest of the funding released on a controlled basis. ICC management would work with ZC on their cricketing, management and financial structures.

The board approved changes to the Code of Conduct recommended by the Cricket Committee and the Chief Executives' Committee, including the introduction of new offences: attempting to gain an unfair advantage (other than by ball-tampering); audible obscenity; and disobeying an umpire's instructions. Ball-tampering was upgraded to a Level 3 offence, earning a maximum 12 suspension points (equivalent to six Tests or 12 one-day internationals). Players or support staff appealing against a decision would be required to lodge a fee (refundable if they succeeded). Stump microphone guidelines were changed to allow the audio to be broadcast at any time. The board also agreed to consider how member boards can be held liable for players' behaviour, through sanctions for a certain threshold of accumulated offences.

The Chief Executives' Committee agreed to changes in the conduct of tours to build a culture of respect. Touring teams should be treated as guests, with a standard of accommodation, travel and catering equal to that for the home team, and the opportunity to mix socially. They should be able to prepare for international matches under conditions similar to those expected during the series, including the same standard and variety of net bowlers and training pitches.

The committee approved playing conditions for the World Test Championship, including the points structure and a reserve day for the final. All Tests in the Championship must be scheduled for five days, but it was confirmed that bilateral four-day Tests were allowed.

Following the decision at the April board meeting to award international status to all women's Twenty20 matches between ICC members after July 1, it was agreed that all games at the recent Women's T20 Asia Cup should be given the status retrospectively.

A working group of member chief executives and representatives of the Federation of International Cricketers' Associations, set up to look at the sanctioning of tournaments and player release, met to outline their objectives. These included preserving international cricket as the pinnacle of competition and ensuring that the best players are available; preserving domestic T20 competition as a means of developing the game globally without compromising international cricket; ensuring events are played to a single set of rules; protecting player health, safety and welfare; protecting the sport's integrity; protecting the game's grassroots development, with revenues reinvested; encouraging the development of home-grown players; and acknowledging that there are a finite number of playing dates in the calendar.

After the AGM, it was announced that ICC chief executive David Richardson would step down at the end of the World Cup in July 2019, after seven years in the post.

MCC WORLD CRICKET COMMITTEE

The MCC World Cricket Committee met at Lord's on August 6–7.

The committee agreed that ICC measures had created a more positive environment for Zimbabwe Cricket, and noted the successful World Cup qualifying tournament staged there in March. MCC had taken advice from the Foreign Office and ECB about a possible tour of Zimbabwe, and no objections were received. The committee agreed that MCC should monitor the situation, and consider sending a team once conditions were right.

They were interested by the statistics from the ICC's recent global market research project – in particular that 64% of cricket fans support all three formats of the sport, and 87% support cricket at the Olympic Games. The committee noted moves to have women's cricket included in the 2022 Commonwealth Games in Birmingham.

They debated the future of cricket's culture in the light of the ball-tampering incident during the South Africa–Australia series in March, and escalating misconduct on the field. They believed in a holistic approach, with boards taking responsibility for their teams' conduct, and touring programmes arranged to ensure adequate preparation for visiting teams.

The committee heard about the inclusion of women's cricket in the ICC's global strategy and welcomed news of a reformed women's committee to be responsible for all playing conditions and activity; they recognised the need to grow the base below international cricket, to address the widening of the gap between the nations who can and can't afford to pay players.

The committee thanked the ICC for sharing their invaluable statistical trends data. They were concerned that Test over-rates over the past 12 months were the lowest for 11 years, and in the T20 format they were the lowest ever, and discussed measures to improve the pace, including a "shot clock" from the moment a bowler reached the top of his mark to the moment the over was completed.

They discussed feedback on Law 41.7 concerning full tosses above waist height. This 2017 amendment, under which a bowler is removed after two such deliveries, had been poorly received, and was often ignored or overwritten by playing conditions. It was recommended that MCC should review this Law.

The committee viewed footage of recent accidents where bowlers were hit by powerful straight-drives after completing their delivery. They supported a proposal from the ECB and MCC for manufacturers to develop head protection for bowlers, and also felt existing protection for batsmen and fielders should be reviewed.

MCC were to work with ICC to identify countries that would benefit from the MCC touring programme, coaching, pitch preparation and umpire tuition. The club were also willing to share resources such as the eLearning platform for umpires.

Sanjay Patel, the managing director for the ECB's new competition, addressed the committee on the concept of The Hundred, due to launch in 2020; he reassured them that it would still be a recognisable form of cricket.

This was Rod Marsh's final meeting after six years on the committee; he recalled key topics during that time, including day/night Test cricket, corruption, governance, universal adoption of DRS and limiting the size of bats. In October, Shane Warne was appointed to take Marsh's place.

ENGLAND PLAYER CONTRACTS

The ECB currently award separate contracts for Test and white-ball cricket; players on Test contracts have their salaries paid in full by the ECB, while those on white-ball contracts receive a supplement to their county salary.

On September 28, the ECB awarded ten Test contracts to run for 12 months from October 2018. They went to Moeen Ali, James Anderson, Jonny Bairstow, Stuart Broad, Jos Buttler, Sam Curran, Adil Rashid, Joe Root, Ben Stokes and Chris Woakes. They also awarded 13 white-ball contracts, to Ali, Bairstow, Buttler, Rashid, Root, Stokes, Woakes, plus Alex Hales, Eoin Morgan, Liam Plunkett, Jason Roy, David Willey and Mark Wood. In addition, Tom Curran was given an incremental contract.

Compared with the previous year, Alastair Cook had retired from Test cricket; Buttler and Rashid added Test contracts to their white-ball contracts; Jake Ball lost his white-ball contract; and the Curran brothers gained contracts for the first time.

ICC BOARD

The ICC Board met in Singapore on October 15–20, and approved a simplified league-based qualification structure for the 50-over men's World Cup.

From 2019, there would be three qualifying leagues: the CWC Super League for the 12 Full Members plus the Netherlands, the CWC League 2 for the next seven Associate Members in the current World Cricket League rankings; and the CWC Challenge League, for the next 12 Associates in the WCL rankings, divided into two groups. From the Super League, the host country (India) and the other top seven would advance straight to the 2023 World Cup. The remaining two places at the World Cup would go to the finalists from a ten-team CWC qualifying tournament to be held in 2022. The qualifying tournament would be contested by the bottom five from the Super League, the top three from League 2, and the top two from a qualifier play-off; the six-team qualifier play-off would be contested by the bottom four from League 2 and the two Challenge League group winners.

The board relaxed the criteria for the World T20 qualification pathway (men's and women's). To take part, member countries would have to have eight (down from ten) unique domestic teams playing a minimum of five matches over the last two years. Entry fees were abolished.

The ICC agreed to seek expressions of interest from Associate Members who had previously competed in the Intercontinental Cup and/or World Cricket League and were keen to continue playing a multi-day format, with a view to proposing a new competition on a cost-sharing basis.

For women's global tournaments, it was confirmed there would be a qualifying event in all five ICC regions, with the top team in each region progressing to the World Cup Qualifier and World T20 Qualifier. For the 2021 World Cup, the hosts plus the top four teams from the Women's Championship would qualify directly, while the bottom three joined Bangladesh, Ireland and the five regional winners in the Qualifier. The next edition of the Women's Championship would expand from eight teams to ten, to include all women's sides with ODI status.

The four top events were officially renamed to specify the gender of participants: the ICC Men's Cricket World Cup, the ICC Women's Cricket World Cup, the ICC Men's World T20 and the ICC Women's World T20. (In November, after the latest Women's World T20, there was a further name change, with the Twenty20 tournaments renamed the ICC Women's T20 World Cup and the ICC Men's T20 World Cup.)

The board agreed to improve procedures protecting children and vulnerable adults, and those tackling sexual harassment, bullying and inappropriate behaviour, and improving off-field behaviour at ICC events.

New Zealand barrister David Howman, the former director of the World Anti-Doping Agency, was appointed as the new chair of the Independent Anti-Corruption Oversight Group, succeeding John Abbott.

The board approved a change to the remit and composition of the Women's Committee to incorporate a broader range of stakeholders. The new committee, meeting twice a year, would consist of a chair appointed by the board (who must be female); two Full Member chief executives; two Full Member representatives with expertise in developing the women's game; one Associate Member representative; one independent member with expertise in marketing, broadcast or media, not directly employed by a member board; two current players (one a from FICA-represented country, one not); one women's national team coach; and one media representative.

ECB DOMESTIC STRUCTURE

On October 31, the ECB announced that the 18 first-class counties had agreed to changes in the men's domestic structure from 2020, as recommended by the working group chaired by Wasim Khan.

In the County Championship, teams would continue to play 14 matches each, but Division One would expand from eight teams to ten, and Division Two contract from ten to eight. To achieve this, one team would be relegated in 2019 and three promoted, though the system would revert to two-up, two-down in 2020. This change would increase the security of teams in Division One and the opportunities for those in Division Two, with a smaller percentage of one set relegated, and a greater percentage of the other promoted. A seeding system was being explored to address the imbalance of ten-team divisions playing 14 matches each, as not all can meet home and away.

From 2020, the county 50-over competition would be played during the new short-form competition (The Hundred), in July and August; overseas players would be excluded. The counties would be in two groups of nine (not necessarily the existing North and South groups), playing eight matches each before the top three qualified for a knockout stage.

The Twenty20 Blast would retain its current format, with North and South Groups of nine counties each, all teams playing 14 games, with the top four from each group qualifying for quarter-finals, leading to the finals day at Edgbaston.

From 2020, there would be a round of 50-over fixtures in July before the domestic one-day competition, with each first-class county visiting a Minor County.

ECB PRESIDENT

On November 2, the ECB announced that Ian Lovett had been ratified as their new president, succeeding Giles Clarke. Lovett had been chairman of Middlesex from 2007 to 2016, and was on the ECB board from 2009 to May 2018, serving as deputy chairman for the last three years, during which he oversaw the governance reforms which led to a fully independent board.

ICC DISPUTES PANEL

On November 20, after a three-day hearing, an ICC disputes panel dismissed the Pakistan Cricket Board's claim against the Board of Control for Cricket in India. The PCB had claimed damages from the BCCI after India failed to tour Pakistan in November 2014 or December 2015, citing a letter written by the BCCI secretary in 2014 listing seven bilateral series to be played between 2014 and 2023. The BCCI argued that this was merely the first step of arranging a programme, and that it did not constitute a legal agreement as it did not reach the final stage of being agreed as part of the Future Tours Programme; the PCB regarded the FTP agreement stage as a formality. The panel ruled that the letter was no more than a declaration of intent, and there had been no obligation on the BCCI to tour.

COMMONWEALTH GAMES

On November 26, the ICC confirmed they had submitted a bid in partnership with the ECB for Twenty20 women's cricket to be included in the Commonwealth Games at Birmingham in 2022. They proposed an eight-team event in two pools of four, with 16 matches over eight days. Cricket's only previous appearance at the Games was in 1998, when men's teams played in Kuala Lumpur; South Africa won gold.

ENGLAND PLAYER QUALIFICATION

On November 29, the ECB agreed updated regulations for qualification to play for England, bringing the rules closer to those of the ICC. From the start of 2019, players must be (a) British citizens; (b) either born in England/Wales, or resident for three years (for a total of 210 days a year); (c) not have appeared as a local player in professional international or domestic cricket in another Full Member country in the last three years.

Previously seven years' residence was required by players moving from another Full Member country after their 18th birthday, or four if moving from an Associate Member country or arriving before their 18th birthday, and there were similar seven- and four-year qualification periods after playing professional international or domestic cricket in another Full Member country.

MANAGING DIRECTOR OF ENGLAND MEN'S CRICKET

On December 14, Ashley Giles was appointed as managing director of England men's cricket, succeeding Andrew Strauss, who stepped down in October for family reasons. Giles had played 54 Tests for England, and later served as director of cricket for Warwickshire and Lancashire. He had also had a spell as England's limited-overs coach from 2012 to 2014.

DATES IN CRICKET HISTORY

c. 1550	Evidence of cricket being played in Guildford, Surrey.
1610	Reference to "cricketing" between Weald & Upland and North Downs near Chevening, Kent.
1611	Randle Cotgrave's French–English dictionary translates the French word "crosse" as a cricket staff. Two youths fined for playing cricket at Sidlesham, Sussex.
1624	Jasper Vinall becomes first man known to be killed playing cricket: hit by a bat while trying to catch the ball – at Horsted Green, Sussex.
1676	First reference to cricket being played abroad, by British residents in Aleppo, Syria.
1694	Two shillings and sixpence paid for a "wagger" (wager) on a match at Lewes.
1697	First reference to "a great match" with 11 players a side for 50 guineas, in Sussex.
1700	Cricket match announced on Clapham Common.
1709	First recorded inter-county match: Kent v Surrey.
1710	First reference to cricket at Cambridge University.
1727	Articles of Agreement written governing the conduct of matches between the teams of the Duke of Richmond and Mr Brodrick of Peperharow, Surrey.
1729	Date of earliest surviving bat, belonging to John Chitty, now in the Oval pavilion.
1730	First recorded match at the Artillery Ground, off City Road, central London, still the cricketing home of the Honourable Artillery Company.
1744	Kent beat All-England by one wicket at the Artillery Ground. First known version of the Laws of Cricket, issued by the London Club, formalising the pitch as 22 yards long.
c. 1767	Foundation of the Hambledon Club in Hampshire, the leading club in England for the next 30 years.
1769	First recorded century, by John Minshull for Duke of Dorset's XI v Wrotham.
1771	Width of bat limited to $4^1/_4$ inches, which it has remained ever since.
1774	Lbw law devised.
1776	Earliest known scorecards, at the Vine Club, Sevenoaks, Kent.
1780	The first six-seamed cricket ball, manufactured by Dukes of Penshurst, Kent.
1787	First match at Thomas Lord's first ground, Dorset Square, Marylebone – White Conduit Club v Middlesex. Formation of Marylebone Cricket Club by members of the White Conduit Club.
1788	First revision of the Laws of Cricket by MCC.
1794	First recorded inter-school match: Charterhouse v Westminster.
1795	First recorded case of a dismissal "leg before wicket".
1806	First Gentlemen v Players match at Lord's.
1807	First mention of "straight-armed" (i.e. roundarm) bowling: by John Willes of Kent.
1809	Thomas Lord's second ground opened, at North Bank, St John's Wood.
1811	First recorded women's county match: Surrey v Hampshire at Ball's Pond, London.
1814	Lord's third ground opened on its present site, also in St John's Wood.
1827	First Oxford v Cambridge match, at Lord's: a draw.
1828	MCC authorise the bowler to raise his hand level with the elbow.

1833	John Nyren publishes *Young Cricketer's Tutor* and *The Cricketers of My Time*.
1836	First North v South match, for years regarded as the principal fixture of the season.
c. **1836**	Batting pads invented.
1841	General Lord Hill, commander-in-chief of the British Army, orders that a cricket ground be made an adjunct of every military barracks.
1844	First official international match: Canada v United States.
1845	First match played at The Oval.
1846	The All-England XI, organised by William Clarke, begin playing matches, often against odds, throughout the country.
1849	First Yorkshire v Lancashire match.
c. **1850**	Wicketkeeping gloves first used.
1850	John Wisden bowls all ten batsmen in an innings for North v South.
1853	First mention of a champion county: Nottinghamshire.
1858	First recorded instance of a hat being awarded to a bowler taking wickets with three consecutive balls.
1859	First touring team to leave England, captained by George Parr, draws enthusiastic crowds in the US and Canada.
1864	"Overhand bowling" authorised by MCC. John Wisden's *The Cricketer's Almanack* first published.
1868	Team of Australian Aboriginals tour England.
1873	W. G. Grace becomes the first player to record 1,000 runs and 100 wickets in a season. First regulations restricting county qualifications, regarded by some as the official start of the County Championship.
1877	First Test match: Australia beat England by 45 runs at Melbourne.
1880	First Test in England: a five-wicket win against Australia at The Oval.
1882	Following England's first defeat by Australia in England, an "obituary notice" to English cricket in the *Sporting Times* leads to the tradition of the Ashes.
1889	Work begins on present Lord's Pavilion. South Africa's first Test match. Declarations first authorised, but only on the third day, or in a one-day match.
1890	County Championship officially constituted.
1895	W. G. Grace scores 1,000 runs in May, and reaches his 100th hundred.
1899	A. E. J. Collins scores 628 not out in a junior house match at Clifton College, the highest recorded individual score in any game – until 2016. Selectors choose England team for home Tests, instead of host club issuing invitations.
1900	In England, six-ball over becomes the norm, instead of five.
1909	Imperial Cricket Conference (ICC – now the International Cricket Council) set up, with England, Australia and South Africa the original members.
1910	Six runs given for any hit over the boundary, instead of only for a hit out of the ground.
1912	First and only triangular Test series played in England, involving England, Australia and South Africa.
1915	W. G. Grace dies, aged 67.
1926	Victoria score 1,107 v New South Wales at Melbourne, still a first-class record.
1928	West Indies' first Test match. A. P. Freeman of Kent and England becomes the only player to take more than 300 first-class wickets in a season: 304.

1930	New Zealand's first Test match. Donald Bradman's first tour of England: he scores 974 runs in five Tests, still a record for any series.
1931	Stumps made higher (28 inches not 27) and wider (nine inches not eight – this was optional until 1947).
1932	India's first Test match. Hedley Verity of Yorkshire takes ten wickets for ten runs v Nottinghamshire, the best innings analysis in first-class cricket.
1932-33	The Bodyline tour of Australia in which England bowl at batsmen's bodies with a packed leg-side field to neutralise Bradman's scoring.
1934	Jack Hobbs retires, with 197 centuries and 61,237 runs, both records. First women's Test: Australia v England at Brisbane.
1935	MCC condemn and outlaw Bodyline.
1947	Denis Compton (Middlesex and England) hits a record 3,816 runs in an English season.
1948	First five-day Tests in England. Bradman concludes Test career with a second-ball duck at The Oval and an average of 99.94 – four runs would have made it 100.
1952	Pakistan's first Test match.
1953	England regain the Ashes after a 19-year gap, the longest ever.
1956	Jim Laker of England takes 19 wickets for 90 v Australia at Manchester, the best match analysis in first-class cricket.
1960	First tied Test: Australia v West Indies at Brisbane.
1963	Distinction between amateurs and professionals abolished in English cricket. The first major one-day tournament begins in England: the Gillette Cup.
1968	Garry Sobers becomes first man to hit six sixes in an over, for Nottinghamshire against Glamorgan at Swansea.
1969	Limited-over Sunday league inaugurated for first-class counties.
1970	Proposed South African tour of England cancelled; South Africa excluded from international cricket because of their government's apartheid policies.
1971	First one-day international: Australia beat England at Melbourne by five wickets.
1973	First women's World Cup: England are the winners.
1975	First men's World Cup: West Indies beat Australia in final at Lord's.
1976	First women's match at Lord's: England beat Australia by eight wickets.
1977	Centenary Test at Melbourne, with identical result to the first match: Australia beat England by 45 runs. Australian media tycoon Kerry Packer signs 51 of the world's leading players in defiance of the cricketing authorities.
1978	Graham Yallop of Australia is the first batsman to wear a protective helmet in a Test.
1979	Packer and official cricket agree peace deal.
1981	England beat Australia in Leeds Test, after following on with bookmakers offering odds of 500-1 against them winning.
1982	Sri Lanka's first Test match.
1991	South Africa return, with a one-day international in India.
1992	Zimbabwe's first Test match. Durham become first county since Glamorgan in 1921 to attain first-class status.
1993	The ICC cease to be administered by MCC, becoming an independent organisation.

1994 Brian Lara becomes the first player to pass 500 in a first-class innings: 501 not out for Warwickshire v Durham.

2000 South Africa's captain Hansie Cronje banned from cricket for life after admitting receiving bribes from bookmakers in match-fixing scandal.
Bangladesh's first Test match.
County Championship split into two divisions, with promotion and relegation.

2001 Sir Donald Bradman dies, aged 92.

2003 First Twenty20 game played, in England.

2004 Lara is the first to score 400 in a Test innings, for West Indies v England in Antigua.

2005 England regain the Ashes after 16 years.

2006 Pakistan become first team to forfeit a Test, for refusing to resume at The Oval.
Shane Warne becomes the first man to take 700 Test wickets.

2007 Australia complete 5–0 Ashes whitewash for the first time since 1920-21.
Australia win the World Cup for the third time running.
India beat Pakistan in the final of the inaugural World Twenty20.

2008 Indian Premier League of 20-over matches launched.
Sachin Tendulkar becomes the leading scorer in Tests, passing Lara.

2009 Terrorists in Lahore attack buses containing Sri Lankan team and match officials.

2010 Tendulkar scores the first double-century in a one-day international, against South Africa; later in the year, he scores his 50th Test century.
Muttiah Muralitharan retires from Test cricket, after taking his 800th wicket.
Pakistan bowl three deliberate no-balls in Lord's Test against England; the ICC ban the three players responsible.

2011 India become the first team to win the World Cup on home soil.
Salman Butt, Mohammad Asif and Mohammad Amir are given custodial sentences of between six and 30 months for their part in the Lord's spot-fix.

2012 Tendulkar scores his 100th international century, in a one-day game against Bangladesh at Mirpur.

2013 150th edition of *Wisden Cricketers' Almanack*.
Tendulkar retires after his 200th Test match, with a record 15,921 runs.

2014 Australia complete only the third 5–0 Ashes whitewash.
India's Rohit Sharma hits 264 in one-day international against Sri Lanka at Kolkata.
Australian batsman Phillip Hughes, 25, dies after being hit on the neck by a bouncer.

2015 Australia win World Cup for fifth time, beating New Zealand in final at Melbourne.

2016 Pranav Dhanawade, 15, makes 1,009 not out – the highest recorded individual score in any match – in a school game in Mumbai.
McCullum hits Test cricket's fastest hundred, from 54 balls, in his final match, against Australia at Christchurch.

2017 England women beat India by nine runs to win the World Cup at Lord's.
England play their first day/night home Test, against West Indies at Edgbaston.
Australia and England play first day/night Ashes Test, at Adelaide.

2018 Three Australians are banned after sandpaper is used on the ball in a Test in South Africa.
Afghanistan and Ireland's men play their first Test matches.
Alastair Cook retires after 161 Tests, 12,472 runs and 33 centuries.
James Anderson takes his 564th Test wicket, unprecedented by a pace bowler.
ECB announce new franchise 100-ball tournament, to start in 2020.

ANNIVERSARIES IN 2019–20

COMPILED BY STEVEN LYNCH

2019

Apr 21   John Goddard (Barbados) born, 1919.
Captained West Indies to their first series victory in England, in 1950.

May 2   Brian Lara (Trinidad) born, 1969.
Silky left-hander whose 400* and 501* are records for Test and first-class cricket.

May 15   Charles Palmer (Leicestershire and Worcestershire) born, 1919.
Amateur all-rounder who took eight for seven against Surrey in 1955.

May 16   County cricket resumes after the Great War, 1919.
The Championship restarts with matches at Lord's and The Oval.

May 23   Colin Milburn (England) loses eye in car accident, 1969.
He had scored a Test century two months earlier, but never played for England again.

Jun 30   Sanath Jayasuriya (Sri Lanka) born, 1969.
Hard-hitting batsman and teasing slow bowler who played 110 Tests and 445 ODIs.

Jul 13   Tom Emmett (Yorkshire) takes 16 wickets in a day at Hunslet, 1869.
Left-armer Emmett demolishes Cambridgeshire for 40 and 46.

Jul 22   Jack White (Somerset) takes 16 wickets in a day at Bath, 1919.
Worcestershire are skittled for 67 and 78 by slow left-armer White.

Jul 27   Jonty Rhodes (South Africa) born, 1969.
Perhaps the greatest fielder of his generation – and a perky batsman.

Jul 31   Dick Barlow (Lancashire) dies aged 68, 1919.
Obdurate batsman, later umpire, immortalised in Francis Thompson's poem "At Lord's".

Jul 31   Hemu Adhikari (India) born, 1919.
Military man who captained (later managed) India, and hit a Test century v West Indies.

Aug 1   Graham Thorpe (Surrey) born, 1969.
Nuggety left-hander who played 100 Tests for England.

Aug 2   Ken Suttle left out by Sussex, 1969.
He had played in all Sussex's previous 423 Championship matches, a record.

Aug 4   Dave Gregory (Australia) dies aged 74, 1919.
Captained in the very first Test, at Melbourne in March 1877.

Aug 20   Jack Brown (Yorkshire) born, 1869.
Opener who struck a 28-minute half-century, still the fastest in a Test, in 1894-95.

Aug 20   Gregor MacGregor (Middlesex) dies aged 49, 1919.
Amateur wicketkeeper who played for England, and also rugby for Scotland.

Sep 5   Mark Ramprakash (Middlesex and Surrey) born, 1969.
Prolific batsman who scored 114 first-class centuries.

Sep 13   Shane Warne (Australia) born, 1969.
The best leg-spinner of them all: finished with 708 Test wickets.

Sep 14   Gil Langley (South Australia) born, 1919.
Wicketkeeper who played 26 Tests in the 1950s, and later became a politician.

Sep 18   Herbert Sutcliffe (Yorkshire) ends his first summer with 1,839 runs, 1919.
Elegant batsman sets the record for a maiden first-class season.

Sep 30   Ernie Jones (Australia) born, 1869.
Fast bowler who, legend has it, fired a bouncer through W. G. Grace's beard in 1896.

Oct 10   Gerry Gomez (Trinidad) born, 1919.
          Hard-working all-rounder who played for West Indies from 1939 to 1953-54.

Oct 30   Vic Richardson (Australia) dies aged 75, 1969.
          Combative batsman – and grandfather of the Chappell brothers.

Nov 28   Keith Miller (Australia) born, 1919.
          Charismatic all-rounder who formed a fearsome new-ball partnership with Ray Lindwall.

Nov 28   Nick Knight (England) born, 1969.
          Left-hander who played 17 Tests and 100 ODIs for England; now a commentator.

Dec 20   Dick Spooner (Warwickshire) born, 1919.
          Wicketkeeper who won seven Test caps despite starting his first-class career at 28.

2020

Feb 5   Darren Lehmann (Australia) born, 1970.
          Left-hand batsman – and coach – who supplied the coup de grâce *in two World Cup finals.*

Feb 9   Glenn McGrath (Australia) born, 1970.
          Metronomic seamer who finished with 563 Test wickets, and three World Cup medals.

Feb 11   Alistair Brown (Surrey) born, 1970.
          Hard-hitting batsman whose 268 against Glamorgan in 2002 remains a List A record.

Feb 12   Percy Tarilton scores the first triple-century in the West Indies, 1920.
          Tarilton made 304* for Barbados against Trinidad at Bridgetown.

Feb 27   Reg Simpson (Nottinghamshire) born, 1920.
          Prolific opening batsman who played 27 Tests for England.

Mar 3   Inzamam-ul-Haq (Pakistan) born, 1970.
          Stately batsman whose 25 Test hundreds included a triple against New Zealand.

Mar 7   Willie Watson (Yorkshire and Leicestershire) born, 1920.
          Talented all-round sportsman who played cricket and football for England.

Mar 10   South Africa complete 4–0 whitewash of Australia, 1970.
          South Africa's last official Test for 22 years, as opposition to apartheid grew.

ONE HUNDRED AND FIFTY YEARS AGO

Wisden Cricketers' Almanack 1870

ETON v HARROW, AT LORD'S, 1869   That this, the most attractive match of the season, annually increases in popularity with the fair and fashionable portion of English society, Lord's ground bore brilliant testimony on Friday, the 9th of last July, on which day £100 more was taken at the gates for admission than was ever taken before in one day at Lord's. The weather was fortunately fine; the attendance was marvellous, both in numbers and quality; and the old ground, as it that day appeared, a fitting subject for a companion picture to Frith's *Derby Day* [a large-scale painting, by William Powell Frith, completed in 1858]. One writer described the Grand Stand as being "as gay as a bank of summer flowers", and so it was, for two-thirds of the occupants were The Ladies of England, whose gay, varied and brilliant-hued attires pleasantly contrasted with the dark, sombre-clad, dense mass of the humanity that thronged the seats and roof of the Pavilion, a majority of whom had been public school boys, many of whom are distinguished members of the highest and most honoured institutions of the country. As many of the drags of The Four-In-Hand Club [a coach-driving club] as could gain admission to the ground were grouped together at the north-west end of the Pavilion. Around the ground, flanking the ropes, closely clustered (at most parts six deep) were 600 carriages of the nobility and gentry, each vehicle fully, most of them fairly freighted. The tops of the wood-stacks had occupants, so had the windowsills of the Racket Court, and the top of Mr Dark's garden wall; and how vast was the number of visitors each day may be estimated from the facts that on the Friday, about £770, and on Saturday, nearly £500, was taken at the gates for admission money. In fact, the Eton and Harrow match at Lord's has now become one of the prominent events of the London Season; for years and years to come it may it so continue to be, and thus materially aid in keeping alive the interest for the fine old game, at present so manifest and general, among its very best supporters, The Gentlemen of England.

THE NOTTINGHAMSHIRE BATSMAN OF 1869: RICHARD DAFT   Daft's two great not out innings for his county… form one of the prominent batting features of the London Cricketing Season 1869… both innings being great displays of rare judgment, backed up by scientific defence, resulting in large not out innings for himself, great success for his county, and one of the highest county averages yet made. [Daft hit 103 not out at Lord's v MCC, and 93 not out at The Oval v Surrey. He played seven matches for Nottinghamshire in 1869, and totalled 471 runs at 67.]

NOTTINGHAMSHIRE BOWLING IN 1869   Out of 5,835 balls or (not to make too fine a point of it) 1,458 overs bowled by the Nottingham men in their seven matches last season only one wide and one no-ball was bowled… More than half the overs bowled by J. C. Shaw were maidens… Wootton's bowling tells well, and Howitt's is a rarely [*sic*] good all-round display, as more than a moiety of the overs are maidens, the runs analyse but a shade more than one per over, and out of the 11 wickets due to him nine were bowled. Alfred Shaw kept the runs down well… and Daft's "little lot of lobs" in the Oval match formed one of the leading sensational features of the Surrey season.

MCC AND GROUND v THE COUNTY OF HERTS, AT CHORLEYWOOD, 1869   For the score of this match, the compiler is indebted to a report in *Bell's Life in London*, a most lucid, crisp and compact cricket report that commented on "King Charles II and Nell Gwynne; Macauley; The Evangelisation of the Heathen; Mary-la-Bonne; Warpaint; A Straight Derby Tip; Knaves of Herts; Small Boys; A County Policeman, and Stricken Herts". MCC and Ground won by 22 runs.

ONE HUNDRED YEARS AGO

From Wisden Cricketers' Almanack 1920

NOTES BY THE EDITOR [Sydney Pardon]   The season of 1919 proved, beyond all question or dispute, that cricket had lost nothing of its attraction for the public. Indeed, one may go further than that. Despite a break of four years and the fact that at all grounds the charge for admission – in view of the entertainment tax and vastly increased expenses – was doubled, county matches drew far larger crowds than in ordinary seasons before the war. The faint hearts who, without evidence on the point, had jumped to the conclusion that cricket would never again be its old self, were utterly confuted… Such being the pleasant state of affairs in the first year of peace, I trust we shall hear no more about the need for drastic alterations in the game. Looking back on the events of the season it is quaint to think that we were asked to shorten the boundaries, to penalise the batting side for every maiden over played, to banish the left-handed batsman, and to limit to three, or at most four, the number of professionals in every county eleven. All these fatuous suggestions and others just as foolish were, it will be remembered, put forward quite seriously. Happily we shall not be worried by them again.

THE LEADING COUNTIES IN 1919   The decision to restrict all county matches in 1919 to two days, and to let the result be determined by the percentage of actual wins to matches played, robbed the Championship of much of its significance… Even with the extended hours of play sides strong in batting found it extremely difficult to arrive at a definite result. Out of 124 matches 56, including the unfortunate tie at Taunton, were left drawn… The disadvantages of the new scheme, more especially the long hours of play, soon became obvious, and before the season ended it was resolved to return in 1920 to the old order of things. Yorkshire won the Championship, but the result hung in the balance right up to the finish.

SOMERSET v SUSSEX, AT TAUNTON, 1919   An extraordinary and in some respects very regrettable incident marked the first of the Taunton matches last season. On the second afternoon, Sussex, with the score at a tie, had a wicket to fall, the remaining batsman being Heygate, who was crippled by rheumatism. It was understood when the innings began that he would not be able to bat, and as there was some doubt as to whether he would come in, one of the Somerset players – not J. C. White, the acting-captain – appealed to Street, the umpire, on the ground that the limit of two minutes had been exceeded. Street pulled up the stumps and the match was officially recorded as a tie… Whether or not Heygate would have been able to crawl to the wicket, it was very unsportsmanlike that such a point should have been raised when there remained ample time to finish the match.

YORKSHIRE v AUSTRALIANS, AT SHEFFIELD, 1919   The Australians gained an astonishing victory by one wicket. They had 170 to get in the last innings, and when their ninth wicket went down at 116 it seemed any odds against them. Gregory was joined by Long and the two batsmen, playing with great nerve, steadily hit off the remaining 54 runs and won the match. They were heartily congratulated by the Yorkshire team on their performance and loudly applauded by the crowd. Gregory had a great match, taking 13 wickets, and scoring 30 and not out 41.

HAMPSHIRE v GLOUCESTERSHIRE, AT SOUTHAMPTON, 1919   A very curious incident marked this drawn match of heavy scoring. On the second day, just at the close of Hampshire's first innings, Pothecary played a ball into the top of his pad and shook it out into the hands of Smith, the wicketkeeper. He was given out caught, contrary to Law 33b, which states "if the ball, whether struck by the bat or not, lodges in the batsman's clothing, the ball shall become dead". All through the game the batting on a beautiful wicket completely beat the bowling, 1,167 runs being scored in the two days.

FIFTY YEARS AGO

From Wisden Cricketers' Almanack 1970

NOTES BY THE EDITOR [Norman Preston]   As we move into the 1970s, cricket in England tries to keep pace with the times. Among the recent better innovations were... the restricted immediate registration of overseas players, and in 1969 the new John Player's Sunday County League... There can be no question that the Player's Sunday League was an instant success. The Gillette Cup had already whetted the public's appetite for this kind of cricket. It is liked because both sides are seen batting, bowling and fielding on the same afternoon and at the end there is a definite result. Moreover every ball counts; it is a vital part of the day's sport; the batsmen have to sharpen up their strokes; go for the risky single – there were countless run-outs – and the fielders have to be on their toes. The majority of these games produced wonderful fielding in the way runs were saved as well as superb catching. This was a feverish tempo and something no one could expect in a three-day Championship match let alone a five-day Test. Nevertheless, this one-day instant cricket must never be regarded as a substitute for genuine first-class cricket... The sense of urgency which the one-day game breeds must stimulate the players, particularly the younger batsmen, by encouraging them to forsake ultra-defensive methods and to go for their strokes.

IRISH CRICKET IN 1969, by Derek Scott   When the history of Irish Cricket is next written 1969 may well, in retrospect, be considered a turning point, a watershed, the beginning of a new era. In that single year Ireland bowled out the West Indies for 25, won two matches in a season for the first time in 12 years, played more matches than in any season since 1947, won an away match for the first time since 1949 and at last found a good captain [D. E. Goodwin], and a team of Pakistan Test players toured Ireland... July 2, at Sion Mills, was the big day. West Indies on a slow, green wicket were bowled out for 25 (Goodwin five for six, O'Riordan four for 18), after being 12 for none. There was not much world news that day, so this remarkable feat made the front pages with colour pictures, interviews, cartoons and even poems.

GLAMORGAN IN 1969   Watching Glamorgan's last-wicket pair engaged in a tense struggle to avoid defeat in their first match of the season against Yorkshire at Swansea, not even the most optimistic Welshman would have prophesied that Glamorgan would not only win the County Championship but complete a memorable summer unbeaten – a notable double which had not been achieved since Lancashire's record in 1930... After a not-so-merry month of May, when Glamorgan were actually perched perilously at the foot of the table, the team, always potentially strong, found their real strength. They... went on to play some glorious cricket with the right touch of adventure in the batting to take full advantage of the bonus points scoring system. Indeed towards the close of the season Glamorgan were playing like real champions, and... the thrilling last-over wins against Middlesex and Essex at Swansea will be long remembered as one of the most wonderful weeks in Glamorgan's history... It should be added that Glamorgan went through a crowded season with only 13 players... The same 11 formed the side in most matches, and without any Test commitment it enabled the team rhythm to be maintained. Although first-class cricket has rarely been self-supporting, financially it was also a good season for Glamorgan. During their last three matches, when the Championship fight was in its most exciting phase, gate receipts reached a record £7,000 – more money than Glamorgan have taken in a full season in some years of their stormy past.

Compiled by Christopher Lane

HONOURS AND AWARDS IN 2018-19

In 2018-19, the following were decorated for their services to cricket:

Order of Ikhamanga (South Africa), 2018: H. M. Amla (excellent achievement in the sport of cricket) Silver Award.

Queen's Birthday Honours, 2018: J. A. Bowron (Templepatrick CC; services to cricket in County Antrim) BEM; J. W. Donaldson (Frenchay CC; services to cricket in Bristol) BEM; S. Elworthy (South Africa, managing director of 2019 World Cup; services to cricket) BEM; S. Redfern (England Women, umpire; services to cricket in the UK and abroad) MBE.

Queen's Birthday Honours (Australia), 2018: R. J. Bache (Southern District CC, South Australia; services to cricket and Australian Rules football) OAM; J. Broadbent (Australia Women, coach; services to cricket) OAM; R. N. Harvey (Victoria, NSW and Australia; services to cricket) OAM; G. S. Hudson (Hunter Valley, NSW; services to cricket and community) OAM; R. J. Inverarity (Western Australia, South Australia and Australia; services to cricket as player, captain, coach and selector, and to education) AM; I. H. Ravenscroft (player, coach, administrator in South Australia; services to cricket) OAM; A. Wells (Bathurst, NSW; services to cricket) OAM.

Queen's Birthday Honours (New Zealand), 2018: R. H. Mettrick (founder of Riverbend Camp Cricket Tournament in Hawke's Bay; services to cricket) QSM.

New Year's Honours, 2019: E. Bakewell (England Women; services to women's cricket) MBE; A. N. Cook (Essex and England; services to cricket) Knight; R. P. Hill (services to disability cricket) MBE; A. I. Kallicharran (West Indies; services to cricket and charity) BEM; P. Wynne-Thomas (statistician, historian; services to cricket and community in Nottinghamshire) BEM.

New Year's Honours (New Zealand), 2019: L. H. Kerr (Canterbury Country CA, umpire; services to sport) QSM.

Padma Awards (India), 2019: G. Gambhir (Delhi and India) Padma Shri.

Australia Day Honours, 2019: M. G. Gandy (Tasmania, umpire and writer; services to cricket) OAM; R. Horder (Parramatta DCC; services to cricket) OAM; M. Jones (Australia Women, commentator; services to cricket and community) OAM; N. G. Marks (New South Wales, state selector; services to cricket) OAM; T. Y. Pellew umpire in South Australia; services to cricket) OAM.

ICC AWARDS

The ICC's 14th annual awards, selected by a panel of 23, were announced in January 2019.

Cricketer of the Year (Sir Garfield Sobers Trophy)	**Virat Kohli (I)**
Test Player of the Year	**Virat Kohli (I)**
One-Day International Player of the Year	**Virat Kohli (I)**
Twenty20 International Performance of the Year	**Aaron Finch (A)**
Emerging Player of the Year	**Rishabh Pant (I)**
Associate Player of the Year	**Calum MacLeod (Scot)**
Umpire of the Year (David Shepherd Trophy)	**Kumar Dharmasena (SL)**
Spirit of Cricket Award	**Kane Williamson (NZ)**
Fans' Moment of the Year	**India win Under-19 World Cup**

The panel also selected two men's World XIs from the previous 15 months:

ICC World Test team	*ICC World one-day team*
1 Tom Latham (NZ)	1 Rohit Sharma (I)
2 Dimuth Karunaratne (SL)	2 Jonny Bairstow (E)
3 Kane Williamson (NZ)	3 *Virat Kohli (I)
4 *Virat Kohli (I)	4 Joe Root (E)
5 Henry Nicholls (NZ)	5 Ross Taylor (NZ)
6 †Rishabh Pant (I)	6 †Jos Buttler (E)
7 Jason Holder (WI)	7 Ben Stokes (E)
8 Kagiso Rabada (SA)	8 Mustafizur Rahman (B)
9 Nathan Lyon (A)	9 Rashid Khan (Afg)
10 Jasprit Bumrah (I)	10 Kuldeep Yadav (I)
11 Mohammad Abbas (P)	11 Jasprit Bumrah (I)

Previous Cricketers of the Year were Rahul Dravid (2004), Andrew Flintoff and Jacques Kallis (jointly in 2005), Ricky Ponting (2006 and 2007), Shivnarine Chanderpaul (2008), Mitchell Johnson (2009 and 2014), Sachin Tendulkar (2010), Jonathan Trott (2011), Kumar Sangakkara (2012), Michael Clarke (2013), Steve Smith (2015) and Ravichandran Ashwin (2016). Virat Kohli, the first man to win all three top awards, was also Cricketer of the Year in 2017.

The women's awards and World XIs, selected by a panel of 15, were announced in December 2018:

Women's Cricketer of the Year (Rachael Heyhoe Flint Trophy)	**Smriti Mandhana (I)**
Women's One-Day International Cricketer of the Year	**Smriti Mandhana (I)**
Women's Twenty20 International Cricketer of the Year	**Alyssa Healy (A)**
Women's Emerging Player of the Year	**Sophie Ecclestone (E)**

ICC ODI Team of the Year		*ICC T20I Team of the Year*	
1	Smriti Mandhana (I)	1	Smriti Mandhana (I)
2	Tammy Beaumont (E)	2	†Alyssa Healy (A)
3	*Suzie Bates (NZ)	3	Suzie Bates (NZ)
4	Dane van Niekerk (SA)	4	*Harmanpreet Kaur (I)
5	Sophie Devine (NZ)	5	Nat Sciver (E)
6	†Alyssa Healy (A)	6	Ellyse Perry (A)
7	Marizanne Kapp (SA)	7	Ashleigh Gardner (A)
8	Deandra Dottin (WI)	8	Leigh Kasperek (NZ)
9	Sana Mir (P)	9	Megan Schutt (A)
10	Sophie Ecclestone (E)	10	Rumana Ahmed (B)
11	Poonam Yadav (I)	11	Poonam Yadav (I)

ICC CRICKET HALL OF FAME

The ICC Cricket Hall of Fame was launched in 2009 in association with the Federation of International Cricketers' Associations to recognise legends of the game. In the first year, 60 members were inducted: 55 from the earlier FICA Hall of Fame, plus five new players elected in October 2009 by a voting academy made up of the ICC president, 11 ICC member representatives, a FICA representative, a women's cricket representative, ten journalists, a statistician, and all living members of the Hall of Fame. Candidates must have retired from international cricket at least five years ago.

The members elected in 2018 were Rahul Dravid (India), Ricky Ponting (Australia) and Claire Taylor (England), who brought the total to 87.

ICC DEVELOPMENT PROGRAMME AWARDS

The ICC announced the global winners of their 2017 Development Programme Awards in July 2018. The Best Overall Cricket Development Programme won £3,500 worth of equipment.

Best Overall Cricket Development Programme	**Emirates Cricket Board**
Best Women's Cricket Initiative	**Rwanda Cricket Association**
Spirit of Cricket Award	**Rwanda Cricket Association**
Image of the Year	**Vanuatu Cricket Association**
Lifetime Service Award	**Brian Fell (Germany)**
Volunteer of the Year	**Craig White (Mexico)**

ALLAN BORDER MEDAL

Steve Smith won the Allan Border Medal, for the best Australian international player of the previous 12 months, in February 2018. The award has also been won by Glenn McGrath, Steve Waugh, Matthew Hayden, Adam Gilchrist, Ricky Ponting (four times), Michael Clarke (four times), Brett Lee, Shane Watson (twice), Mitchell Johnson, and David Warner (twice). Smith received 246 votes from team-mates, umpires and journalists, well ahead of Warner's 162, and was also named Test Player of the Year; he had previously won both titles in 2015. **David Warner** retained One-day International Player of the Year, and **Aaron Finch** was Twenty20 International Player of the Year. **George Bailey** of Tasmania was Men's Domestic Player of the Year, and **Jhye Richardson** of Western Australia was the Bradman Young Player of the Year. Australia all-rounder **Ellyse Perry** won her second Belinda Clark Award for the Women's International Cricketer of the Year. **Beth Mooney** of Queensland was Female Domestic Player of the Year, and **Georgia Redmayne** of Tasmania was the Betty Wilson Female Young Player of the Year.

SHEFFIELD SHIELD PLAYER OF THE YEAR

The Sheffield Shield Player of the Year Award for 2017-18 was **Chris Tremain**, who took 51 wickets for Victoria. The award, instituted in 1975-76, is adjudicated by umpires over the season. The Lord's Taverners Indigenous Cricketer of the Year was **D'Arcy Short** of Western Australia, and **Paul Wilson** was Umpire of the Year. The Benaud Spirit of Cricket Awards for fair play went to **Queensland's** men and **Victoria's** women.

CRICKET SOUTH AFRICA AWARDS

South African fast bowler **Kagiso Rabada** won six CSA awards in June 2018 – just as he had done two years before. He was the South African Cricketer of the Year, Test Cricketer of the Year, One-Day International Cricketer of the Year, Players' Player of the Year and Fans' Player of the Year. He also won the Delivery of the Year award for the ball that bowled David Warner in the Third Test at Cape Town. **A. B. de Villiers**, who had just announced his retirement from international cricket, was the Twenty20 International Cricketer of the Year. **David Miller** won the Always Original award for his 35-ball century against Bangladesh – a Twenty20 international record. The Women's Cricketer of the Year was national captain **Dane van Niekerk**, and the Women's Players' Player was **Laura Wolvaardt**, who was also the Women's ODI Cricketer of the Year, while **Chloe Tryon** was the Women's T20 Cricketer of the Year. The International Newcomer of the Year was **Aiden Markram** (a year after he won the domestic equivalent). In the domestic categories, the Titans collected three awards (down from four in 2017): **Tabraiz Shamsi** was One-Day Cup Cricketer and T20 Challenge Player of the Year, and **Mark Boucher** was Coach of the Year again. **Simon Harmer** of the Warriors was Sunfoil Series Cricketer of the Year, **Pieter Malan** of the Cape Cobras was the Domestic Players' Player of the Season, and his team-mate **Kyle Verreynne** Domestic Newcomer of the Year. **Jon-Jon Smuts** of the Warriors won the SACA Most Valuable Player award, and the Africa T20 Cup Player of the Tournament was **Sarel Erwee** of KwaZulu-Natal Inland. **Shaun George** retained the CSA Umpire of the Year, **Adrian Holdstock** was the CSA Umpires' Umpire, and **Evan Flint** of Newlands in Cape Town was Groundsman of the Year.

PROFESSIONAL CRICKETERS' ASSOCIATION AWARDS

The following awards were announced at the PCA's annual dinner in October 2018.

Reg Hayter Cup (NatWest PCA Players' Player of the Year)	**Joe Denly** (Kent)
John Arlott Cup (NatWest PCA Young Player of the Year)	**Ollie Pope** (Surrey)
Specsavers Test Player of the Summer	**James Anderson**
Royal London One-Day International Player of the Summer	**Jos Buttler**
NatWest Women's Player of the Summer	**Sophie Ecclestone**
PCA County Championship Player of the Year	**Tom Bailey** (Lancashire)
Vitality Blast Player of the Year	**Joe Denly** (Kent)
Royal London One-Day Cup Player of the Year	**Joe Denly** (Kent)
Greene King PCA England Masters Player of the Year	**Ali Brown**
Harold Goldblatt Award (PCA Umpire of the Year)	**Michael Gough**
ECB Special Award	**Mick Hunt**

PCA Team of the Year: ***Rory Burns, Alex Davies, Joe Denly, Ian Bell, James Vince, Moeen Ali, †Dane Vilas, Rikki Clarke, Ed Barnard, Matt Henry, Morne Morkel**.

CHRISTOPHER MARTIN-JENKINS SPIRIT OF CRICKET AWARDS

MCC and the BBC introduced the Spirit of Cricket awards in memory of Christopher Martin-Jenkins, the former MCC president and *Test Match Special* commentator, in 2013. In September 2018 the Award went to **Dan Bowser** and **Chris Edwards** of the England Learning Disability cricket team. On a tour of the Netherlands, England had Denmark Under-17 nine down, needing eight to win, when seamer Alex Jervis thought he had found an edge, and the umpire gave it out. But the captain, Edwards, withdrew the appeal after Bowser, at slip, told him the batsman had hit the ground rather than the ball. Denmark added four more runs before Jervis found the edge again and England won by three.

WALTER LAWRENCE TROPHY

The Walter Lawrence Trophy for the fastest century in 2018 went to **Martin Guptill**, who reached a hundred in 35 balls for Worcestershire against Northamptonshire in a floodlit Vitality Blast game at Northampton on July 27. He won the trophy plus £3,000. Since 2008, the Trophy has been available for innings in all senior cricket in England; traditionally, it was reserved for the fastest first-class hundred against authentic bowling (in 2018, Grant Stewart's maiden century from 71 deliveries, scored from No. 10 for Kent against Middlesex at Canterbury). England all-rounder **Nat Sciver** won the Women's Award for the highest score by a woman, her unbeaten 98-ball 180 for Surrey against Derbyshire at Spondon in the Royal London One-Day Women's Cup. The MCCU Universities Award went to **Sam Evans**, who made 217 for Loughborough MCCU against Leeds/Bradford MCCU at the Haslegrave ground. Sciver and Evans each received a silver medallion and £500. The award for the highest score by a schoolboy against MCC went to **Will Buttleman**, who scored 140 in 123 balls for Felsted School in Essex; he received a medallion and a Gray-Nicolls bat.

CRICKET WRITERS' CLUB AWARDS

In October 2018, Surrey swept the board in the Cricket Writers' Club's awards for players. **Sam Curran** was voted Young Cricketer of the Year; he had made his Test debut against Pakistan two days before his 20th birthday, and was later named England's Man of the Series in the Tests against India. **Rory Burns** was County Championship Player of the Year after leading Surrey to the title; he was easily the leading scorer in the competition, with 1,359 runs. Another Surrey captain, **Nat Sciver**, was named the third CWC Women's Cricketer of the Year for her all-round role as the Surrey Stars won the Kia Super League for the first time. The Peter Smith Memorial Award "for services to the presentation of cricket to the public" went to the **Stewart family**, including Micky and his sons, Alec and Neil. The Cricket Book of the Year was *Arlott, Swanton and the Soul of English Cricket* by **Stephen Fay** and **David Kynaston**.

A list of Young Cricketers from 1950 to 2004 appears in Wisden 2005, *page 995. A list of Peter Smith Award winners from 1992 to 2004 appears in* Wisden 2005, *page 745.*

SPORTS BOOK AWARDS

At the Sports Book Awards ceremony in June 2018, **John Woodcock**, who edited *Wisden Cricketers' Almanack* from 1981 to 1986 and was *The Times'* cricket correspondent from 1954 to 1988, received a lifetime achievement award for his sports writing.

SECOND XI PLAYER OF THE YEAR

The Association of Cricket Statisticians and Historians named Essex all-rounder **Paul Walter** as the Les Hatton Second XI Player of the Year for 2018. Walter scored 592 at 65 in six matches in the Second XI Championship, reaching 219 not out against Somerset and 176 against Gloucestershire, and also took 26 wickets at 17. In the Twenty20 tournament, his scores included 103 in 50 balls against Glamorgan.

GROUNDSMEN OF THE YEAR

Lee Fortis was named ECB Groundsman of the Year for his four-day pitches at The Oval; the previous winner, **Steve Birks** (Trent Bridge), was runner-up, with commendations for Gary Barwell of Edgbaston and Karl McDermott at the Rose Bowl. **McDermott** shared the one-day award with Taunton's **Simon Lee**, while Robin Saxton (Cardiff) and Sean Williams (Bristol) were commended. **Adrian Long** (Beckenham) took the award for the best outground, with **Christian Brain** runner-up for Cheltenham, and Nick Searle commended for Radlett. The MCCU groundsman award, which is now the responsibility of MCC, was shared by **Richard Robinson** for Leeds/Bradford's Weetwood ground, and **Paul Derrick** at the Racecourse ground in Durham.

CRICKET SOCIETY AWARDS

Wetherell Award for Leading First-class All-rounder	**Moeen Ali** (Worcestershire)
Wetherell Award for Leading Schools All-rounder	**George Hill** (Sedbergh School)
Most Promising Young Male Cricketer	**Pat Brown** (Worcestershire)
Most Promising Young Woman Cricketer	**Sophia Dunkley** (Middx/Surrey Stars)
Sir John Hobbs Silver Jubilee Memorial Prize (for Outstanding Under-16 Schoolboy)	**Jacob Bethell** (Rugby School)
A. A. Thomson Fielding Prize (for Best Schoolboy Fielder)	**James Cronie** (Stowe School)
Christopher Box-Grainger Memorial Trophy (for schools promoting cricket to the underprivileged)	**Brent Knoll School, Lewisham**
Don Rowan Memorial Trophy (for schools promoting cricket for disabled children)	**Orchard Hill College, Camberwell**
Ian Jackson Award for Services to Cricket	**John Holder**
The Perry-Lewis/Kershaw Trophy (for contribution to the Cricket Society XI)	**Andy Graham and Andrew Moss**

WOMBWELL CRICKET LOVERS' SOCIETY AWARDS

George Spofforth Cricketer of the Year	**Moeen Ali** (Worcestershire/England)
Brian Sellers Captain of the Year	**Rory Burns** (Surrey)
C. B. Fry Young Cricketer of the Year	**Sam Curran** (Surrey/England)
Arthur Wood Wicketkeeper of the Year	**Tim Ambrose** (Yorkshire)
Learie Constantine Fielder of the Year	**Sean Dickson** (Kent)
Denis Compton Memorial Award for Flair	**Jos Buttler** (Lancashire/England)
Denzil Batchelor Award for Services to English Cricket	**Paul Collingwood** (Durham)
Dr Leslie Taylor Award (best Roses performance)	**Tom Köhler-Cadmore** (Yorkshire)
Les Bailey Most Promising Young Yorkshire Player	**Jonathan Tattersall**
Ted Umbers Award – Services to Yorkshire Cricket	**Bryan Stott***
J. M. Kilburn Cricket Writer of the Year	**Chris Waters** (*Yorkshire Post*)
Jack Fingleton Cricket Commentator of the Year	**Daniel Norcross**

* *A Yorkshire player from 1952 to 1963.*

ECB BUSINESS OF CRICKET AWARDS

The ECB announced the BOCA awards, designed to celebrate Marketing and PR excellence across domestic and international cricket, in November 2018. **Durham** picked up three prizes: David Jackson from their marketing and comms team was named Rising Star, and they also won the Best Commercial Partnership and Most Improved Match Day Experience awards. **Worcestershire's** Carrie Lloyd was the Unsung Hero of Match Operations, and they were also judged to have the Best Growth Strategy. **Nottinghamshire** won the awards for the Warmest Welcome and Inspiring Fan Loyalty, while **Yorkshire** had the Best Domestic Campaign for increasing membership numbers. **Hampshire** were recognised for Welcoming Families, and **Leicestershire** for Unleashing Cricket in the Community by linking cricket with Bollywood dancing. **Warwickshire's** podcast, "The Bears Podblast", earned the Club Innovation Award. **MCC** won the Volunteer of the Season award for their Lord's Outfielders match-day volunteer programme, and **Mick Hunt**, who was retiring as Lord's groundsman after 49 years, received the Appreciation of Service Award.

ECB OSCAs

The ECB presented the 2018 NatWest Outstanding Service to Cricket Awards to volunteers from recreational cricket in October. The winners were:

NatWest CricketForce Club Award	**Stiffkey CC** (Norfolk)

Davy Jackson organised clearing the pavilion, redecorating, repairing floors, improving toilets.

Heartbeat of the Club	**Alison Slack** (Yorkshire)

Co-ordinated Fishlake's All Stars programme for juniors and has raised regular funding.

Leagues and Boards Award	**Peter Wreford** (Arden League)

Developed the Arden Sunday Cricket League in Warwickshire, growing it from 29 to 43 teams.

Officiating – umpires and scorers **Heather Vernon** (Warwickshire)
County scorers' officer for Warwickshire, who runs courses and a support group for scorers.

Coach of the Year **Anna Tunnicliff** (Town Malling)
Organised two women's teams at Town Malling and the first Tonbridge & Malling Girls' Festival.

Young Coach of the Year **Erica Turner** (Northamptonshire)
Managed the U15 County Girls and coached the Kettering & Corby and East Northants hubs.

Outstanding Contribution to Coaching **Jonathan Caldecott** (Shropshire)
Lead coach for Shropshire's disability sides, as well as coaching at club and county level.

Young Volunteer Award (for under-25s) **Amy Carnwell** (Staffordshire)
Oakamoor committee member, Level 2 coach and junior co-ordinator, and won funding for nets.

Lifetime Achiever **Tony Banks** (Staffordshire)
Over 50 years, has served Springhill CC as player, captain, groundsman and financial backer.

Outstanding Contribution to Disability Cricket **British Association for Cricketers with Disabilities**
Formed in 1991 and started what became the ECB National Disabled County Championship, which now has over 500 players with physical and learning disabilities in four competitions.

Vitality Under-19 Twenty20 Club of the Year **Oakley CC** (Hampshire)
Their season ended with fireworks, a new electronic scoreboard, a beer tent and a barbecue.

Women's Soft Ball Cricket Festival of the Year **Asian Sports Association** (Leicestershire)
A day-long event for 92 women and girls, with ten teams and a bhangra-blaze warm-up.

All Stars Cricket Centre of the Year **Downend CC** (Bristol)
Ran coaching sessions for 86 children after arranging training for parents and teenage coaches.

CRICKET COMMUNITY CHAMPION AWARD

MCC and *The Cricketer* introduced a new award in 2017 recognising individuals working to build, maintain and support the game at grassroots level. The second winner, announced in May, was **Chris Mainstone** from Ketton CC in Rutland, for "his relentless commitment to the junior section" over 14 years. He was invited to ring the bell at Lord's at the start of the one-day international between England and India in July.

ACS STATISTICIAN OF THE YEAR

In March 2019, the Association of Cricket Statisticians and Historians awarded the Brooke–Lambert Statistician of the Year trophy to **Jeremy Lonsdale** for his book *A game taken seriously: The foundations of Yorkshire's cricketing power*, which was also shortlisted by the British Society of Sports History for the Lord Aberdare Literary Prize.

WORLD CUP FIXTURES

Thu May 30	England v South Africa	The Oval	
Fri May 31	Pakistan v West Indies	Nottingham	
Sat Jun 1	New Zealand v Sri Lanka	Cardiff	
	Afghanistan v Australia	Bristol	♀
Sun Jun 2	South Africa v Bangladesh	The Oval	
Mon Jun 3	England v Pakistan	Nottingham	
Tue Jun 4	Afghanistan v Sri Lanka	Cardiff	
Wed Jun 5	India v South Africa	Southampton	
	Bangladesh v New Zealand	The Oval	♀
Thu Jun 6	Australia v West Indies	Nottingham	
Fri Jun 7	Pakistan v Sri Lanka	Bristol	
Sat Jun 8	England v Bangladesh	Cardiff	
	Afghanistan v New Zealand	Taunton	♀
Sun Jun 9	Australia v India	The Oval	
Mon Jun 10	South Africa v West Indies	Southampton	
Tue Jun 11	Bangladesh v Sri Lanka	Bristol	
Wed Jun 12	Australia v Pakistan	Taunton	
Thu Jun 13	India v New Zealand	Nottingham	
Fri Jun 14	England v West Indies	Southampton	
Sat Jun 15	Australia v Sri Lanka	The Oval	
	Afghanistan v South Africa	Cardiff	♀
Sun Jun 16	India v Pakistan	Manchester	
Mon Jun 17	Bangladesh v West Indies	Taunton	
Tue Jun 18	England v Afghanistan	Manchester	
Wed Jun 19	New Zealand v South Africa	Birmingham	
Thu Jun 20	Australia v Bangladesh	Nottingham	
Fri Jun 21	England v Sri Lanka	Leeds	
Sat Jun 22	Afghanistan v India	Southampton	
	New Zealand v West Indies	Manchester	♀
Sun Jun 23	Pakistan v South Africa	Lord's	
Mon Jun 24	Afghanistan v Bangladesh	Southampton	
Tue Jun 25	England v Australia	Lord's	
Wed Jun 26	New Zealand v Pakistan	Birmingham	
Thu Jun 27	India v West Indies	Manchester	
Fri Jun 28	South Africa v Sri Lanka	Chester-le-Street	
Sat Jun 29	Afghanistan v Pakistan	Leeds	
	Australia v New Zealand	Lord's	♀
Sun Jun 30	England v India	Birmingham	
Mon Jul 1	Sri Lanka v West Indies	Chester-le-Street	
Tue Jul 2	Bangladesh v India	Birmingham	
Wed Jul 3	England v New Zealand	Chester-le-Street	
Thu Jul 4	Afghanistan v West Indies	Leeds	
Fri Jul 5	Bangladesh v Pakistan	Lord's	
Sat Jul 6	India v Sri Lanka	Leeds	
	Australia v Sri Lanka	Manchester	♀
Tue Jul 9	Semi-final – First v Fourth	Manchester	
Thu Jul 11	Semi-final – Second v Third	Birmingham	
Sun Jul 14	Final	Lord's	

♀ = Day/night or floodlit game.
All games start at 10.30 or 1.30 (floodlit).

2019 FIXTURES

SS Test	Specsavers Test match			
RL ODI	Royal London one-day international			
VT20I	Vitality Twenty20 international			
KW Test	Kia Women's Test			
RL WODI	Royal London Women's one-day international			
WVT20I	Women's Vitality Twenty20 international			
SSCC D1/2	Specsavers County Championship Division 1/Division 2			
RLODC	Royal London One-Day Cup			
VB T20	The Vitality Blast			
KSL WT20	Women's Kia Super League			
Univs	First-class university match			
Univs (nfc)	Non-first-class university match			
♀	Day/night or floodlit game			

Sun Mar 24–Wed 27	Friendly	MCC	v Surrey	Dubai
Tue Mar 26–Thu 28	Univs	Cambridge MCCU	v Essex	Cambridge
		Derbyshire	v Leeds/Brad MCCU	Derby
		Durham	v Durham MCCU	Chester-le-Street
		Leicestershire	v Loughboro MCCU	Leicester
		Middlesex	v Oxford MCCU	Northwood
		Somerset	v Cardiff MCCU	Taunton
Sun Mar 31– Tue Apr 2	Univs	Cambridge MCCU	v Nottinghamshire	Cambridge
		Kent	v Loughboro MCCU	Canterbury
		Leeds/Brad MCCU	v Yorkshire	Weetwood
		Northamptonshire	v Durham MCCU	Northampton
		Oxford MCCU	v Hampshire	Oxford
		Sussex	v Cardiff MCCU	Hove
Thu Apr 4–Sat 6	Univs (nfc)	Surrey	v Durham MCCU	The Oval
Fri Apr 5–Mon 8	SSCC D1	Hampshire	v Essex	Southampton
		Nottinghamshire	v Yorkshire	Nottingham
		Somerset	v Kent	Taunton
	SSCC D2	Derbyshire	v Durham	Derby
		Northamptonshire	v Middlesex	Northampton
		Sussex	v Leicestershire	Hove
Fri Apr 5–Sun 7	Univs (nfc)	Cambridge MCCU	v Worcestershire	Cambridge
		Glamorgan	v Cardiff MCCU	Cardiff
		Gloucestershire	v Oxford MCCU	Bristol
		Loughboro MCCU	v Lancashire	Loughborough
		Warwickshire	v Leeds/Brad MCCU	Birmingham
Thu Apr 11–Sun 14	SSCC D1	Hampshire	v Yorkshire	Southampton
		Nottinghamshire	v Somerset	Nottingham
		Surrey	v Essex	The Oval
		Warwickshire	v Kent	Birmingham
	SSCC D2	Durham	v Sussex	Chester-le-Street
		Glamorgan	v Northamptonshire	Cardiff
		Gloucestershire	v Derbyshire	Bristol
		Leicestershire	v Worcestershire	Leicester
		Middlesex	v Lancashire	Lord's
Wed Apr 17	RLODC	Durham	v Northamptonshire	Chester-le-Street
		Glamorgan	v Essex	Cardiff
		Gloucestershire	v Surrey	Bristol
		Kent	v Hampshire	Canterbury ♀
		Lancashire	v Worcestershire	Manchester
		Yorkshire	v Leicestershire	Leeds

Fri Apr 19	RLODC	Derbyshire	v Northamptonshire	Derby
		Durham	v Leicestershire	Chester-le-Street
		Essex	v Middlesex	Chelmsford
		Hampshire	v Glamorgan	Southampton
		Nottinghamshire	v Lancashire	Nottingham
		Somerset	v Kent	Taunton
		Sussex	v Surrey	Hove
		Warwickshire	v Yorkshire	Birmingham
Sun Apr 21	RLODC	Derbyshire	v Nottinghamshire	Derby
		Glamorgan	v Somerset	Cardiff
		Kent	v Sussex	Beckenham
		Leicestershire	v Worcestershire	Leicester
		Middlesex	v Gloucestershire	Lord's
		Northamptonshire	v Warwickshire	Northampton
		Yorkshire	v Lancashire	Leeds
Tue Apr 23	RLODC	Gloucestershire	v Kent	Bristol
		Hampshire	v Middlesex	Southampton
		Surrey	v Essex	The Oval
		Warwickshire	v Nottinghamshire	Birmingham
Wed Apr 24	RLODC	Lancashire	v Northamptonshire	Manchester
		Leicestershire	v Derbyshire	Leicester
		Sussex	v Somerset	Hove
		Worcestershire	v Durham	Worcester
Thu Apr 25	RLODC	Glamorgan	v Kent	Cardiff
		Surrey	v Middlesex	The Oval
Fri Apr 26	RLODC	Hampshire	v Gloucestershire	Southampton
		Northamptonshire	v Worcestershire	Northampton
		Nottinghamshire	v Leicestershire	Nottingham
		Somerset	v Essex	Taunton ♀
		Warwickshire	v Durham	Birmingham
		Yorkshire	v Derbyshire	Leeds
Sat Apr 27	Tour (o-d)	Kent	v Pakistanis	Beckenham
	RLODC	Middlesex	v Sussex	Lord's
Sun Apr 28	RLODC	Durham	v Derbyshire	Chester-le-Street
		Essex	v Hampshire	Chelmsford
		Glamorgan	v Surrey	Cardiff
		Gloucestershire	v Somerset	Bristol
		Lancashire	v Leicestershire	Manchester
		Nottinghamshire	v Yorkshire	Nottingham
		Worcestershire	v Warwickshire	Worcester
Mon Apr 29	Tour (o-d)	Northamptonshire	v Pakistanis	Northampton
Tue Apr 30	RLODC	Derbyshire	v Warwickshire	Derby
		Durham	v Lancashire	Gosforth
		Essex	v Sussex	Chelmsford
		Gloucestershire	v Glamorgan	Bristol
		Surrey	v Hampshire	The Oval
Wed May 1	Tour (o-d)	Leicestershire	v Pakistanis	Leicester ♀
	RLODC	Middlesex	v Somerset	Radlett
		Northamptonshire	v Yorkshire	Northampton
		Worcestershire	v Nottinghamshire	Worcester
Thu May 2	RLODC	Hampshire	v Sussex	Southampton
		Lancashire	v Derbyshire	Manchester
		Surrey	v Kent	The Oval
Fri May 3	ODI	**IRELAND**	**v ENGLAND**	**Malahide**
	RLODC	Nottinghamshire	v Durham	Grantham

Sat May 4	RLODC	Leicestershire	v Northamptonshire	Leicester	
		Warwickshire	v Lancashire	Birmingham	
		Worcestershire	v Yorkshire	Worcester	
Sun May 5	VT20I	**ENGLAND**	**v PAKISTAN**	**Cardiff**	
	Tri-series	**IRELAND**	**v WEST INDIES**	**Clontarf**	
	RLODC	Kent	v Essex	Beckenham	
		Middlesex	v Glamorgan	Lord's	
		Somerset	v Hampshire	Taunton	
		Sussex	v Gloucestershire	Eastbourne	
Mon May 6	RLODC	Derbyshire	v Worcestershire	Derby	
		Leicestershire	v Warwickshire	Leicester	
		Northamptonshire	v Nottinghamshire	Northampton	
		Yorkshire	v Durham	Leeds	
Tue May 7	Tri-series	**WEST INDIES**	**v BANGLADESH**	**Clontarf**	
	RLODC	Essex	v Gloucestershire	Chelmsford	♀
		Kent	v Middlesex	Canterbury	♀
		Somerset	v Surrey	Taunton	♀
		Sussex	v Glamorgan	Hove	♀
Wed May 8	RL ODI	**ENGLAND**	**v PAKISTAN**	**The Oval**	♀
	ODI	**SCOTLAND**	**v AFGHANISTAN**	**Edinburgh**	
Thu May 9	Tri-series	**IRELAND**	**v BANGLADESH**	**Malahide**	
Fri May 10	ODI	**SCOTLAND**	**v AFGHANISTAN**	**Edinburgh**	
	RLODC	**Quarter-final**			
	RLODC	**Quarter-final**			♀
Sat May 11	RL ODI	**ENGLAND**	**v PAKISTAN**	**Southampton**	
	Tri-series	**IRELAND**	**v WEST INDIES**	**Malahide**	
Sun May 12	RLODC	**Semi-final**			
	RLODC	**Semi-final**			
Mon May 13	Tri-series	**WEST INDIES**	**v BANGLADESH**	**Malahide**	
Tue May 14	RL ODI	**ENGLAND**	**v PAKISTAN**	**Bristol**	♀
Tue May 14–Fri 17	SSCC D1	Essex	v Nottinghamshire	Chelmsford	
		Kent	v Yorkshire	Canterbury	
		Somerset	v Surrey	Taunton	
		Warwickshire	v Hampshire	Birmingham	
	SSCC D2	Glamorgan	v Gloucestershire	Newport	
		Lancashire	v Northamptonshire	Manchester	
		Middlesex	v Leicestershire	Lord's	
		Worcestershire	v Durham	Worcester	
Wed May 15	Tri-series	**IRELAND**	**v BANGLADESH**	**Clontarf**	
Fri May 17	RL ODI	**ENGLAND**	**v PAKISTAN**	**Nottingham**	♀
	Tri-series	**FINAL**		**Malahide**	
	Varsity T20	Cambridge U	v Oxford U	Cambridge	
	W Varsity T20	Cambridge U	v Oxford U	Cambridge	
Sat May 18	ODI	**SCOTLAND**	**v SRI LANKA**	**Edinburgh**	
Sun May 19	RL ODI	**ENGLAND**	**v PAKISTAN**	**Leeds**	
	ODI	**IRELAND**	**v AFGHANISTAN**	**Stormont**	
Sun May 19–Wed 22	SSCC D2	Derbyshire	v Glamorgan	Derby	
Mon May 20–Thu 23	SSCC D1	Hampshire	v Nottinghamshire	Newclose, IoW	
		Kent	v Surrey	Beckenham	
		Somerset	v Warwickshire	Taunton	
	SSCC D2	Durham	v Gloucestershire	Chester-le-Street	
		Lancashire	v Worcestershire	Manchester	
		Northamptonshire	v Sussex	Northampton	

Tue May 21	ODI ODI	IRELAND SCOTLAND	v AFGHANISTAN v SRI LANKA	Stormont Edinburgh	
Sat May 25	RLODC	Final			
Mon May 27–Thu 30	SSCC D1	Essex Warwickshire Yorkshire	v Kent v Surrey v Hampshire	Chelmsford Birmingham Leeds	
	SSCC D2	Gloucestershire Leicestershire Sussex Worcestershire	v Lancashire v Derbyshire v Glamorgan v Middlesex	Cheltenham Leicester Hove Worcester	
Tue May 28	Varsity (o-d)	Cambridge U	v Oxford U	Lord's	
Sun Jun 2–Wed 5	SSCC D2	Middlesex Northamptonshire	v Sussex v Glamorgan	Lord's Northampton	
Mon Jun 3–Thu 6	SSCC D1	Surrey Warwickshire Yorkshire	v Somerset v Nottinghamshire v Essex	Guildford Birmingham Leeds	
	SSCC D2	Durham Lancashire	v Derbyshire v Leicestershire	Chester-le-Street Liverpool	
Thu Jun 6	RL WODI	ENGLAND WOMEN	v WEST INDIES WOMEN	Leicester	♀
Sun Jun 9	RL WODI	ENGLAND WOMEN	v WEST INDIES WOMEN	Worcester	♀
Sun Jun 9–Wed 12	SSCC D1	Nottinghamshire	v Hampshire	Sookholme	
Mon Jun 10–Thu 13	SSCC D1	Kent Surrey	v Somerset v Yorkshire	Canterbury Guildford	
	SSCC D2	Durham Leicestershire Worcestershire Glamorgan Sussex	v Northamptonshire v Middlesex v Lancashire v Derbyshire v Gloucestershire	Chester-le-Street Leicester Worcester Swansea Arundel	
Thu Jun 13	RL WODI	ENGLAND WOMEN	v WEST INDIES WOMEN	Chelmsford	♀
Sun Jun 16–Wed 19	SSCC D1 SSCC D2	Essex Middlesex	v Hampshire v Glamorgan	Chelmsford Radlett	
Mon Jun 17–Thu 20	SSCC D1	Kent Yorkshire	v Nottinghamshire v Warwickshire	Tunbridge Wells York	
	SSCC D2	Derbyshire Leicestershire Worcestershire	v Lancashire v Gloucestershire v Sussex	Derby Leicester Worcester	
Tue Jun 18	WVT20I	ENGLAND WOMEN	v WEST INDIES WOMEN	Northampton	♀
Thu Jun 20	Tour (o-d)	Northamptonshire	v Australia A	Northampton	♀
Fri Jun 21	WVT20I	ENGLAND WOMEN	v WEST INDIES WOMEN	Northampton	♀
Sun Jun 23	Tour (o-d)	Derbyshire	v Australia A	Derby	
Sun Jun 23–Wed 26	SSCC D1	Essex Surrey	v Somerset v Warwickshire	Chelmsford The Oval	
	SSCC D2	Gloucestershire	v Glamorgan	Bristol	
Mon Jun 24–Thu 27	SSCC D2 SSCC D2	Northamptonshire Sussex	v Leicestershire v Durham	Northampton Hove	
Tue Jun 25	WVIT20 Tour (o-d)	ENGLAND WOMEN Worcestershire	v WEST INDIES WOMEN v Australia A	Derby Worcester	♀

Sun Jun 30–Wed Jul 3	SSCC D1	Kent	v Warwickshire	Canterbury	
		Nottinghamshire	v Essex	Nottingham	
		Somerset	v Hampshire	Taunton	
		Yorkshire	v Surrey	Scarborough	
	SSCC D2	Derbyshire	v Middlesex	Derby	
		Glamorgan	v Worcestershire	Cardiff	
		Lancashire	v Durham	Sedbergh School	
		Sussex	v Northamptonshire	Hove	
Sun Jun 30	Tour (o-d)	Gloucestershire	v Australia A	Bristol	
Mon Jul 1	ODI	**IRELAND**	**v ZIMBABWE**	**Bready**	
Tue Jul 2	RL WODI	**ENGLAND WOMEN**	**v AUSTRALIA WOMEN**	**Leicester**	♀
	Tour (o-d)	Gloucestershire	v Australia A	Bristol	
Tue Jul 2–Fri 5	Varsity	Cambridge U	v Oxford U	Cambridge	
Thu Jul 4	RL WODI	**ENGLAND WOMEN**	**v AUSTRALIA WOMEN**	**Leicester**	♀
	ODI	**IRELAND**	**v ZIMBABWE**	**Stormont**	
Sat Jul 6–Tue 9	SSCC D1	Hampshire	v Warwickshire	Southampton	
Sun Jul 7	RL WODI	**ENGLAND WOMEN**	**v AUSTRALIA WOMEN**	**Canterbury**	
	ODI	**IRELAND**	**v ZIMBABWE**	**Stormont**	
Sun Jul 7–Wed 10	Tour	Sussex	v Australia A	Arundel	
	SSC D1	Essex	v Yorkshire	Chelmsford	
		Somerset	v Nottinghamshire	Taunton	
		Surrey	v Kent	The Oval	
	SSCC D2	Leicestershire	v Durham	Leicester	
		Middlesex	v Gloucestershire	Northwood	
		Northamptonshire	v Lancashire	Northampton	
		Worcestershire	v Derbyshire	Worcester	
Wed Jul 10	T20I	**IRELAND**	**v ZIMBABWE**	**Stormont**	
Fri Jul 12	T20I	**IRELAND**	**v ZIMBABWE**	**Bready**	
Sat Jul 13	T20I	**IRELAND**	**v ZIMBABWE**	**Bready**	
Sat Jul 13–Tue 16	SSCC D1	Hampshire	v Kent	Southampton	
		Nottinghamshire	v Surrey	Nottingham	
		Warwickshire	v Essex	Worcester	
		Yorkshire	v Somerset	Leeds	
	SSCC D2	Durham	v Worcestershire	Chester-le-Street	
		Glamorgan	v Middlesex	Cardiff	
		Lancashire	v Sussex	Manchester	
Sun Jul 14–Wed 17	Tour	England Lions	v Australia/Australia A	Canterbury	
	SSCC D2	Derbyshire	v Northamptonshire	Chesterfield	
Mon Jul 15–Thu 18	SSCC D2	Gloucestershire	v Leicestershire	Cheltenham	
Thu Jul 18–Sun 21	KW Test	**ENGLAND WOMEN**	**v AUSTRALIA WOMEN**	**Taunton**	
Thu Jul 18	VB T20	Glamorgan	v Somerset	Cardiff	♀
		Middlesex	v Essex	Lord's	♀
		Nottinghamshire	v Worcestershire	Nottingham	♀
Fri Jul 19	VB T20	Durham	v Northamptonshire	Chester-le-Street	♀
		Essex	v Surrey	Chelmsford	♀
		Gloucestershire	v Glamorgan	Cheltenham	
		Hampshire	v Sussex	Southampton	
		Leicestershire	v Lancashire	Leicester	♀ ♀
		Worcestershire	v Warwickshire	Worcester	
		Yorkshire	v Nottinghamshire	Leeds	♀
Sat Jul 20	VB T20	Derbyshire	v Yorkshire	Chesterfield	
		Kent	v Somerset	Canterbury	♀

Sun Jul 21–Wed 24	SSCC D2	Gloucestershire	v Worcestershire	Cheltenham	
Sun Jul 21	VB T20	Hampshire	v Kent	Southampton	
		Lancashire	v Durham	Manchester	
		Warwickshire	v Leicestershire	Birmingham	
	U19 Tri-series	England U19	v India U19	Worcester	
Mon Jul 22	U19 Tri-series	England U19	v Bangladesh U19	Worcester	
Tue Jul 23–Fri 26	Tour	Australians	v Australia A	Southampton	
	VB T20	Leicestershire	v Yorkshire	Leicester	♀
		Surrey	v Middlesex	The Oval	♀
Wed Jul 24–Sat 27	SS Test	**ENGLAND**	**v IRELAND**	**Lord's**	
Wed Jul 24	VB T20	Nottinghamshire	v Northamptonshire	Nottingham	♀
		Sussex	v Hampshire	Hove	♀
		Warwickshire	v Derbyshire	Birmingham	♀
	U19 Tri-series	Bangladesh U19	v India U19	Worcester	
Thu Jul 25		Gloucestershire	v Middlesex	Cheltenham	
		Surrey	v Glamorgan	The Oval	♀
		Yorkshire	v Lancashire	Leeds	♀
Fri Jul 26	WVT20I	**ENGLAND WOMEN**	**v AUSTRALIA WOMEN**	**Chelmsford**	♀
	VB T20	Derbyshire	v Nottinghamshire	Derby	♀
		Glamorgan	v Middlesex	Cardiff	♀
		Kent	v Essex	Canterbury	♀
		Lancashire	v Worcestershire	Manchester	♀
		Leicestershire	v Durham	Leicester	♀
		Northamptonshire	v Warwickshire	Northampton	♀
		Somerset	v Hampshire	Taunton	♀
		Sussex	v Surrey	Hove	♀
	U19 Tri-series	England	v India	Cheltenham	
Sat Jul 27	VB T20	Essex	v Gloucestershire	Chelmsford	♀
		Nottinghamshire	v Leicestershire	Nottingham	
	U19 Tri-series	India U19	v Bangladesh U19	Cheltenham	
Sun Jul 28	WVT20I	**ENGLAND WOMEN**	**v AUSTRALIA WOMEN**	**Hove**	
	VB T20	Derbyshire	v Lancashire	Derby	
		Northamptonshire	v Yorkshire	Northampton	
		Somerset	v Sussex	Taunton	
		Worcestershire	v Durham	Worcester	
	U19 Tri-series	England U19	v Bangladesh U19	Cheltenham	
Tue Jul 30	VB T20	Surrey	v Kent	The Oval	♀
	U19 Tri-series	Bangladesh U19	v India U19	Billericay	
Wed Jul 31	WVT20I	**ENGLAND WOMEN**	**v AUSTRALIA WOMEN**	**Bristol**	♀
	VB T20	Durham	v Leicestershire	Chester-le-Street	♀
		Worcestershire	v Derbyshire	Worcester	
Thu Aug 1–Mon 5	1st Test	**ENGLAND**	**v AUSTRALIA**	**Birmingham**	
Thu Aug 1	VB T20	Essex	v Hampshire	Chelmsford	♀
		Glamorgan	v Gloucestershire	Cardiff	♀
		Middlesex	v Kent	Lord's	♀
	U19 Tri-series	England U19	v Bangladesh U19	Billericay	
Fri Aug 2	VB T20	Durham	v Lancashire	Chester-le-Street	♀
		Gloucestershire	v Essex	Bristol	♀
		Hampshire	v Glamorgan	Southampton	♀
		Northamptonshire	v Derbyshire	Northampton	♀
		Nottinghamshire	v Warwickshire	Nottingham	♀
		Somerset	v Surrey	Taunton	♀
		Sussex	v Kent	Hove	♀
		Yorkshire	v Worcestershire	Leeds	♀

Sat Aug 3	**VB T20**	Lancashire	v Nottinghamshire	Manchester	♀
	U19 Tri-series	England U19	v India U19	Chelmsford	
Sun Aug 4	**VB T20**	Gloucestershire	v Sussex	Bristol	
		Kent	v Hampshire	Beckenham	
		Middlesex	v Somerset	Richmond	
		Worcestershire	v Leicestershire	Worcester	
		Yorkshire	v Warwickshire	Leeds	
Mon Aug 5	**U19 Tri-series**	England U19	v Bangladesh U19	Beckenham	
Tue Aug 6	**VB T20**	Sussex	v Glamorgan	Hove	♀
	KSL W20	Lancashire T	v Southern V	Liverpool	
		Loughboro L	v Western S	Loughborough	
		Yorkshire D	v Surrey S	Leeds	♀
Wed Aug 7–Fri 9	**Tour**	Worcestershire	v Australians	Worcester	
Wed Aug 7	**VB T20**	Essex	v Somerset	Chelmsford	♀
		Gloucestershire	v Kent	Bristol	♀
		Leicestershire	v Warwickshire	Leicester	♀
		Northamptonshire	v Durham	Northampton	♀
	U19 Tri-series	Bangladesh U19	v India U19	Beckenham	
Thu Aug 8	**VB T20**	Middlesex	v Surrey	Lord's	♀
	KSL W20	Loughboro L	v Southern V	Loughborough	
		Surrey S	v Lancashire T	Guildford	
Fri Aug 9	**VB T20**	Derbyshire	v Durham	Derby	♀
		Glamorgan	v Essex	Cardiff	♀
		Hampshire	v Somerset	Southampton	♀
		Lancashire	v Yorkshire	Manchester	♀
		Leicestershire	v Northamptonshire	Leicester	♀
		Surrey	v Gloucestershire	The Oval	♀
		Sussex	v Middlesex	Hove	♀
		Warwickshire	v Nottinghamshire	Birmingham	♀
	U19 Tri-series	England U19	v India U19	Beckenham	
Sat Aug 10	**VB T20**	Somerset	v Kent	Taunton	♀
	KSL W20	Western S	v Lancashire T	Taunton	
Sun Aug 11	**VB T20**	Durham	v Nottinghamshire	Chester-le-Street	
		Glamorgan	v Surrey	Cardiff	
		Middlesex	v Gloucestershire	Radlett	
		Warwickshire	v Lancashire	Birmingham	
		Worcestershire	v Northamptonshire	Worcester	
		Yorkshire	v Derbyshire	Leeds	
	KSL W20	Southern V	v Western S	Southampton	
		Yorkshire D	v Loughboro L	Leeds	
	U-19 Tri-series	Final		Hove	
Mon Aug 12	**KSL W20**	Surrey S	v Southern V	The Oval	♀
Tue Aug 13	**VB T20**	Derbyshire	v Worcestershire	Derby	♀
		Gloucestershire	v Hampshire	Bristol	♀
	KSL W20	Lancashire T	v Yorkshire D	Liverpool	
		Western S	v Loughboro L	Bristol	
Wed Aug 14–Sun 18 2nd Test		**ENGLAND**	**v AUSTRALIA**	**Lord's**	
Wed Aug 14	**VB T20**	Kent	v Glamorgan	Canterbury	♀
		Northamptonshire	v Lancashire	Northampton	♀
Thu Aug 15	**VB T20**	Derbyshire	v Leicestershire	Derby	♀
		Durham	v Worcestershire	Chester-le-Street	♀
		Surrey	v Sussex	The Oval	♀

Thu Aug 15	KSL W20	Southern V	v Lancashire T	Hove	♀
		Surrey S	v Loughboro L	Guildford	
		Yorkshire D	v Western S	York	
Fri Aug 16	VB T20	Essex	v Glamorgan	Chelmsford	♀
		Hampshire	v Surrey	Southampton	♀
		Kent	v Sussex	Canterbury	♀
		Lancashire	v Warwickshire	Manchester	♀
		Northamptonshire	v Leicestershire	Northampton	♀
		Nottinghamshire	v Derbyshire	Nottingham	♀
		Somerset	v Gloucestershire	Taunton	♀
		Yorkshire	v Durham	Leeds	♀
Sun Aug 18–Wed 21	SSCC D1	Kent	v Essex	Canterbury	
		Surrey	v Hampshire	The Oval	
		Warwickshire	v Somerset	Birmingham	
		Yorkshire	v Nottinghamshire	Scarborough	
	SSCC D2	Derbyshire	v Gloucestershire	Derby	
		Durham	v Leicestershire	Chester-le-Street	
		Glamorgan	v Lancashire	Colwyn Bay	
		Northamptonshire	v Worcestershire	Northampton	
		Sussex	v Middlesex	Hove	
Sun Aug 18	KSL W20	Lancashire T	v Western S	Chester Boughton H	
		Loughboro L	v Yorkshire D	Loughborough	
		Southern V	v Surrey S	Arundel	
Tue Aug 20	KSL W20	Lancashire T	v Loughboro L	Manchester	♀
		Surrey S	v Yorkshire D	Guildford	
		Western S	v Southern V	Bristol	
Wed Aug 21	KSL W20	Southern V	v Yorkshire D	Southampton	♀
		Western S	v Surrey S	Taunton	♀
Thu Aug 22–Mon 26	3rd Test	**ENGLAND**	**v AUSTRALIA**	**Leeds**	
Thu Aug 22	VB T20	Sussex	v Essex	Hove	♀
Fri Aug 23	VB T20	Derbyshire	v Northamptonshire	Derby	♀
		Durham	v Yorkshire	Chester-le-Street	♀
		Gloucestershire	v Somerset	Bristol	♀
		Kent	v Surrey	Canterbury	♀
		Leicestershire	v Nottinghamshire	Leicester	♀
		Warwickshire	v Worcestershire	Birmingham	♀
	KSL W20	Loughboro L	v Surrey S	Loughborough	
		Yorkshire D	v Lancashire T	Scarborough	
Sat Aug 24	VB T20	Middlesex	v Sussex	Uxbridge	
		Somerset	v Glamorgan	Taunton	♀
Sun Aug 25	VB T20	Hampshire	v Essex	Southampton	
		Leicestershire	v Derbyshire	Leicester	
		Nottinghamshire	v Yorkshire	Nottingham	
		Warwickshire	v Northamptonshire	Birmingham	
		Worcestershire	v Lancashire	Worcester	
	KSL W20	Loughboro L	v Lancashire T	Nottingham	
		Surrey S	v Western S	Guildford	
		Yorkshire D	v Southern V	York	
Mon Aug 26	VB T20	Glamorgan	v Sussex	Cardiff	
		Lancashire	v Derbyshire	Manchester	
Tue Aug 27	VB T20	Durham	v Warwickshire	Chester-le-Street	♀
		Surrey	v Somerset	The Oval	♀
Wed Aug 28	T20	Worcestershire	v Nottinghamshire	Worcester	
	KSL W20	Lancashire T	v Surrey S	Manchester	♀
		Southern V	v Loughboro L	Southampton	♀
		Western S	v Yorkshire D	Taunton	♀

Thu Aug 29–Sat 31	**Tour**	Derbyshire	v Australians	Derby
Thu Aug 29	**VB T20**	Hampshire	v Middlesex	Southampton ♀
		Kent	v Gloucestershire	Canterbury ♀
		Surrey	v Essex	The Oval ♀
		Yorkshire	v Northamptonshire	Leeds ♀
Fri Aug 30	**VB T20**	Essex	v Kent	Chelmsford ♀
		Glamorgan	v Hampshire	Cardiff ♀
		Lancashire	v Leicestershire	Manchester ♀
		Northamptonshire	v Worcestershire	Northampton ♀
		Nottinghamshire	v Durham	Nottingham ♀
		Somerset	v Middlesex	Taunton ♀
		Sussex	v Gloucestershire	Hove ♀
		Warwickshire	v Yorkshire	Birmingham ♀
Sun Sep 1	**KSL W20**	**Semi-final and final**		Hove
Wed Sep 4–Sun 8	**4th Test**	**ENGLAND**	**v AUSTRALIA**	**Manchester**
Wed Sep 4	**VB T20**	**Quarter-final**		♀
Thu Sep 5	**VB T20**	**Quarter-final**		♀
Fri Sep 6	**VB T20**	**Quarter-final**		♀
Sat Sep 7	**VB T20**	**Quarter-final**		♀
Tue Sep 10–Fri 13	**SSCC D1**	Essex	v Warwickshire	Chelmsford
		Hampshire	v Surrey	Southampton
		Nottinghamshire	v Kent	Nottingham
		Somerset	v Yorkshire	Taunton
	SSCC D2	Gloucestershire	v Sussex	Bristol
		Lancashire	v Derbyshire	Manchester
		Leicestershire	v Northamptonshire	Leicester
		Middlesex	v Durham	Lord's
		Worcestershire	v Glamorgan	Worcester
Thu Sep 12–Mon 16	**5th Test**	**ENGLAND**	**v AUSTRALIA**	**The Oval**
Sun Sep 15		*The Cricketer* Village Cup final		Lord's
Mon Sep16–Thu 19	**SSCC D1**	Essex	v Surrey	Chelmsford
		Hampshire	v Somerset	Southampton
		Nottinghamshire	v Warwickshire	Nottingham
		Yorkshire	v Kent	Leeds
	SSCC D2	Derbyshire	v Sussex	Derby
		Glamorgan	v Leicestershire	Cardiff
		Lancashire	v Middlesex	Manchester
		Northamptonshire	v Durham	Northampton
		Worcestershire	v Gloucestershire	Worcester
Mon Sep 16		National Clubs final		Lord's
Sat Sep 21	**VB T20**	**Semi-finals and final**		Birmingham
Mon Sep 23–Thu 26	**SSCC D1**	Kent	v Hampshire	Canterbury
		Somerset	v Essex	Taunton
		Surrey	v Nottinghamshire	The Oval
		Warwickshire	v Yorkshire	Birmingham
	SSCC D2	Durham	v Glamorgan	Chester-le-Street
		Gloucestershire	v Northamptonshire	Bristol
		Leicestershire	v Lancashire	Leicester
		Middlesex	v Derbyshire	Lord's
		Sussex	v Worcestershire	Hove

CRICKET TRADE DIRECTORY

BOOKSELLERS

BOUNDARY BOOKS, The Haven, West Street, Childrey OX12 9UL. Tel: 01235 751021; email: mike@boundarybooks.com; website: boundarybooks.com. Rare books, cricket antiques, artworks, autographs and memorabilia bought and sold. Please register to receive regular email catalogues. Oxfordshire showroom open by appointment. Unusual and scarce items always available.

CHRISTOPHER SAUNDERS, Kingston House, High Street, Newnham-on-Severn, Gloucs GL14 1BB. Tel: 01594 516030; email: chris@cricket-books.com; website: cricket-books.com. Office/bookroom open by appointment. Second-hand/antiquarian cricket books and memorabilia bought and sold. Regular catalogues issued containing selections from over 12,000 items in stock.

GRACE BOOKS AND CARDS (Ted Kirwan), Donkey Cart Cottage, Main Street, Bruntingthorpe, Lutterworth, Leics LE17 5QE. Tel: 0116 247 8417; email: ted@gracecricketana.co.uk. Second-hand and antiquarian cricket books, *Wisdens*, autographed material and cricket ephemera of all kinds. Now also modern postcards of current international cricketers.

JOHN JEFFERS, The Old Mill, Aylesbury Road, Wing, Leighton Buzzard LU7 0PG. Tel: 01296 688543 or 07846 537692; e-mail: edgwarerover@live.co.uk. *Wisden* specialist. Immediate decision and top settlement for purchase of *Wisden* collections. Why wait for the next auction? Why pay the auctioneer's commission anyway?

J. W. McKENZIE, 12 Stoneleigh Park Road, Ewell, Epsom, Surrey KT19 0QT. Tel: 020 8393 7700; email: mckenziecricket@btconnect.com; website: mckenzie-cricket.co.uk. Old cricket books and memorabilia specialist since 1972. Free catalogues issued regularly. Large shop premises open 9–4.30 Monday–Friday. Thirty minutes from London Waterloo. Please phone before visiting.

KEN FAULKNER, 65 Brookside, Wokingham, Berkshire RG41 2ST. Tel: 0118 978 5255; email: kfaulkner@bowmore.demon.co.uk; website: bowmore.demon.co.uk. Bookroom open by appointment. My stall, with a strong *Wisden* content, will be operating at the 2019 Cheltenham Cricket Festival. We purchase *Wisden* collections which include pre-1946 editions.

KEN PIESSE CRICKET BOOKS, PO Box 868, Mt Eliza, Victoria 3930, Australia. Tel: (+61) 419 549 458; email: kenpiesse@ozemail.com.au; website: cricketbooks.com.au. Australian cricket's internet specialists. Quality cricket books bought and sold. We also stock photographs and ephemera. Publishers of quality limited editions, including the new Cec Pepper biography.

ROGER PAGE, 10 Ekari Court, Yallambie, Victoria 3085, Australia. Tel: (+61) 3 9435 6332; email: rpcricketbooks@unite.com.au; website: rpcricketbooks.com.au. Australia's only full-time dealer in new and second-hand cricket books. Distributor of overseas cricket annuals and magazines. Agent for Association of Cricket Statisticians and Cricket Memorabilia Society.

ST MARY'S BOOKS & PRINTS, 9 St Mary's Hill, Stamford, Lincolnshire PE9 2DP. Tel: 01780 763033; email: info@stmarysbooks.com; website: stmarysbooks.com. Dealers in *Wisdens* 1864–2018, second-hand, rare cricket books and *Vanity Fair* prints. Book-search service offered.

SPORTSPAGES, 7 Finns Business Park, Mill Lane, Farnham, Surrey GU10 5RX. Tel: 01252 851040; email: info@sportspages.com; website: sportspages.com. Large stock of *Wisdens*, fine sports books and sports memorabilia, including cricket, rugby, football and golf. Books and sports memorabilia also purchased, please offer. Visitors welcome to browse by appointment.

TIM BEDDOW, 66 Oak Road, Oldbury, West Midlands B68 0BD. Tel: 0121 421 7117 or 07956 456112; email: wisden1864@hotmail.com. Wanted: any items of sporting memorabilia. Cricket, motor racing, TT, F1, stock cars, speedway, ice hockey, football, rugby, golf, boxing, horse racing, athletics and *all* other sports. Top prices paid for vintage items.

WILLIAM H. ROBERTS, Long Low, 27 Gernhill Avenue, Fixby, Huddersfield, West Yorkshire HD2 2HR. Tel: 01484 654463; email: william@roberts-cricket.co.uk; website: williamroberts-cricket.com. Second-hand/antiquarian cricket books, *Wisdens*, autographs and memorabilia bought and sold. Many thanks for your continued support.

WISDEN DIRECT: wisdenalmanack.com/books. Various editions of *Wisden Cricketers' Almanack* since 2001 and other Wisden publications, all at discounted prices.

WISDEN REPRINTS, Tel: 0800 7 999 501; email: wisdenauction@cridler.com; website: wisdenauction.com. Limited-edition Willows *Wisden* reprints still available for various years at wisdenauction.com.

WISDENS.ORG, Tel: 07793 060706; email: wisdens@cridler.com; website: wisdens.org; Twitter: @Wisdens. The unofficial *Wisden* collectors' website. Valuations, guide, discussion forum, all free to use. *Wisden* prices updated constantly. We also buy and sell *Wisdens* for our members. Email us for free advice about absolutely anything to do with collecting *Wisdens*.

WISDENWORLD.COM, Tel: 01480 819272 or 07966 513171; email: bill.wisden@gmail.com; website: wisdenworld.com. A unique and friendly service; quality *Wisdens* bought and sold at fair prices, along with free advice on the value of your collection. The world's largest *Wisden*-only seller; licensed by Wisden.

AUCTIONEERS

CHRISTIE'S, 8 King Street, St. James's, London SW1Y 6QT. Tel: 0207 389 2157; email: jwilson@christies.com; website: christies.com. Christie's sells valuable cricket books and collections. They hold the world record for an individual edition of *Wisden* (6th edition – 1869 – sold for £32,500 in July 2018). For valuations of all cricketana, contact Julian Wilson, senior specialist.

DOMINIC WINTER, Specialist Auctioneers & Valuers, Mallard House, Broadway Lane, South Cerney, Gloucestershire GL7 5UQ. Tel: 01285 860006; website: dominicwinter.co.uk. Check our website for forthcoming specialist sales.

GRAHAM BUDD AUCTIONS in association with Sotheby's, PO Box 47519, London N14 6XD. Tel: 020 8366 2525; website: grahambuddauctions.co.uk. Specialist auctioneer of sporting memorabilia.

KNIGHTS WISDEN, Norfolk. Tel: 01263 768488; email: tim@knights.co.uk; website: knightswisden.co.uk. Established and respected auctioneers. World-record *Wisden* prices achieved in 2007. Four major cricket/sporting memorabilia auctions per year including specialist *Wisden* sale in May. Entries invited.

WISDENAUCTION.COM. Tel: 0800 7 999 501; email: wisdenauction@cridler.com; website: wisdenauction.com. A specially designed auction website for buying and selling *Wisdens*. List your spares today and bid live for that missing year. Every original edition for sale including all hardbacks. Built by collectors for collectors, with the best descriptions on the internet. See advert facing page 1536.

CRICKET DATABASES

CRICKETARCHIVE: cricketarchive.com. The most comprehensive searchable database on the internet with scorecards of all first-class, List A, pro T20 and major women's matches, as well as a wealth of league and friendly matches. The database currently has more than 1.25m players and over 700,000 full and partial scorecards.

CRICVIZ: cricviz.com; email: marketing@cricviz.com. CricViz is the official analytics provider to the ICC, and operates the largest cricket database, selling predictive modelling and analysis of the sport to broadcasters, teams and media clients, including wisden.com.

CSW DATABASE FOR PCs. Contact Ric Finlay, email: ricf@netspace.net.au; website: tastats.com.au. Men's and women's international, T20, Australian, NZ and English domestic. Full scorecards and 2,500 searches. Suitable for professionals and hobbyists alike.

WISDEN RECORDS: wisdenrecords.com. Up-to-date and in-depth cricket records from *Wisden*.

CRICKET COLLECTING, MEMORABILIA AND MUSEUMS

CRICKET MEMORABILIA SOCIETY. *See entry in Cricket Societies section.*

LORD'S TOURS & MUSEUM, Lord's Cricket Ground, St John's Wood, London NW8 8QN. Tel: 020 7616 8595; email: tours@mcc.org.uk; website: lords.org/tours. A tour of Lord's provides a fascinating behind-the-scenes insight into the world's most famous cricket ground. See the original Ashes urn, plus an outstanding collection of art, cricketing memorabilia and much more.

SIR DONALD BRADMAN'S CHILDHOOD HOME, 52 Shepherd Street, Bowral, NSW 2576, Australia. Tel: (+61) 478 779 642; email: hello@52shepherdstreet.com.au; website: 52shepherdstreet.com. The house where Don Bradman developed his phenomenal cricketing skills by throwing a golf ball against the base of a tank stand. Open for tours and special events.

WILLOW STAMPS, 10 Mentmore Close, Harrow, Middlesex HA3 0EA. Tel: 020 8907 4200; email: willowstamps@tinyonline.co.uk. Standing order service for new cricket stamp issues, comprehensive back stocks of most earlier issues.

WISDEN COLLECTORS' CLUB: Tel: 01480 819272 or 07966 513171; email: bill.wisden@gmail.com; website: wisdencollectorsclub.co.uk. Free and completely impartial advice on *Wisdens*. We also offer *Wisdens* and other cricket books to our members, usually at no charge except postage. Quarterly newsletter, discounts on publications and a great website. Licensed by Wisden.

CRICKET EQUIPMENT

ACUMEN BOOKS, Pennyfields, New Road, Bignall End, Stoke-on-Trent ST7 8QF. Tel: 01782 720753; email: wca@acumenbooks.co.uk; website: acumenbooks.co.uk. Everything for umpires, scorers, officials, etc. MCC Lawbooks, open-learning manuals, Tom Smith and other textbooks, Duckworth/Lewis, scorebooks, equipment, over & run counters, gauges, heavy and Hi-Vis bails, etc; import/export.

BOLA MANUFACTURING LTD, 6 Brookfield Road, Cotham, Bristol BS6 5PQ. Tel: 0117 924 3569; email: info@bola.co.uk; website: bola.co.uk. Manufacturer of bowling machines and ball-throwing machines for all sports. Machines for professional and all recreational levels for sale to the UK and overseas.

CHASE CRICKET, Dummer Down Farm, Basingstoke, Hampshire RG25 2AR. Tel: 01256 397499; email: info@chasecricket.co.uk; website: chasecricket.co.uk. Chase Cricket specialises in handmade bats and hi-tech soft goods. Established 1996. "Support British Manufacturing."

CRICKET SOCIETIES

CRICKET MEMORABILIA SOCIETY, Honorary Secretary: Steve Cashmore, 4 Stoke Park Court, Stoke Road, Bishops Cleeve, Cheltenham, Gloucestershire GL52 8US. Email: cms87@btinternet.com; website: cricketmemorabilia.org. To promote and support the collection and appreciation of all cricket memorabilia. Four meetings annually at first-class grounds, with two auctions. Meetings attended by former Test players. Regular members' magazine. Research and valuations undertaken.

THE CRICKET SOCIETIES' ASSOCIATION, Secretary: Dave Taylor, 16 Leech Brook Close, Audenshaw, Manchester M34 5PL. Tel: 0161 336 8536; email: taylor_d2@sky.com; website: cricketsocietiesassociation.com. For cricket lovers in the winter – join a local society and enjoy speaker evenings with fellow enthusiasts for the summer game.

THE CRICKET SOCIETY, c/o David Wood, Membership Secretary, PO Box 6024, Leighton Buzzard, LU7 2ZS. Email: david.wood@cricketsociety.com; website: cricketsociety.com. A worldwide society which promotes cricket through its awards, acclaimed publications, regular meetings, dinners and special events.

CRICKET TOUR OPERATORS

GULLIVERS SPORTS TRAVEL, Ground Floor, Ashvale 2, Ashchurch Business Centre, Alexandra Way, Tewkesbury, Gloucs GL20 8NB. Tel: 01684 879221; email: gullivers@ gulliverstravel.co.uk; website: gulliverstravel.co.uk. The UK's longest-established cricket tour operator offers a great choice of supporter packages for the world's most exciting events – including the Ashes in Australia – and playing tours for schools, clubs, universities and military teams.

PITCHES AND GROUND EQUIPMENT

DT6 3UX. ... ~~Gore Cross Business Park, Corbin Way, Bradpole, Bridport, Dorset~~
Alongside manufacturing **Gore Cross Business Park, Corbin Way, Bradpole, Bridport, Dorset** ~~mail:~~ **sales@huckcricket.co.uk; website: huckcricket.co.uk.** the complete portfolio of ground and club equ~~...~~ high-quality polypropylene cricket netting, we offer ~~...~~cessary for cricket clubs of all levels.

PLUVIUS, Willow Cottage, Canada Lane, Norton Lindsey, Warwick CV35 8JH. Tel: 07966 597203; email: pluviusltd@aol.com; website: pluvius.uk.com. Manufacturers of value-for-money pitch covers and sightscreens, currently used on Test, county, school and club grounds throughout the UK.

ERRATA

Wisden 1885	Page 138	The match against Surrey on August 18–20 was not Mr H. B. Steel's first appearance for Lancashire; he had played nine previous first-class matches in 1883 and 1884, though this was his first century.
	Page 181	In Lancashire's match with Gloucestershire on July 24–25, P. Barlow is said to have been bowled, but the scorecard can was he was caught by E. M. Grace.
Wisden 1962	Page 728	In South African Fezela's match ... against Combined Services, D. T. Lindsay captain and D. T. Linds... the keeper. ...(not G...
Wisden 1973	Page 90	Barry Woo... a mere 29 years 228 days, not 30, when he made his Test debut in the final Ashes Test of 1972.
Wisden 1977	Page 1039	Research suggests that George Emmett probably worked with the Gloucestershire groundstaff as a winter job while still playing in the 1950s, rather than becoming a groundsman after his retirement. He would also have been responsible for the groundstaff in his later role as secretary at the Imperial Athletic Club in Bristol.
Wisden 2012	Page 866	New Zealand's victory at Hobart in December 2011 was their first over Australia since Auckland (not Wellington) in March 1993.
Wisden 2018	Page 188	Jan Brittin averaged 129 in England's ODI series with New Zealand in 1984.
	Page 227	In the photo of Don Shepherd, the non-striker is John Prodger rather than Bob Wilson.
	Page 508	In Kent's match with Leicestershire, it was Adam Milne who had Pillans caught behind.
	Page 655	In the T20 Blast averages, M. J. Santner should be SLA not LB.
	Page 665	In the list of players hitting six sixes in an over, G. S. Sobers was playing for Nottinghamshire v Glamorgan.
	Page 669	In Hampshire's game with Kent on August 1, it was Mitch Claydon who bowled the last over.
	Page 880	In Tripura's match against Himachal Pradesh on October 20–23, it was Bishal Ghosh not Rana Bishal Ghosh who shared a stand of 230 with Smit Patel.
	Page 948	In the Departmental One-Day Cup semi-final, Sui Southern Gas won with 15.3 overs to spare.
	Page 1037	Windward Islands' match against Guyana on November 26–29 was played at the Darren Sammy Stadium at Gros Islet, St Lucia.
	Page 1213	Nottinghamshire's 429-9 against Somerset was at Taunton.

CHARITIES IN 2018

...L CASTLE CRICKET FOUNDATION – more than 300,000 disadvantaged youngsters, ... with special needs, mainly from inner-city areas, have received instruction and encouragement at Arundel since 1986. In 2018, there were more than 60 days devoted to activities, and over 2,000 young people benefited. Donations can be made at www.justgiving.com/arundelcastlecricket. Director of cricket: John Barclay, Arundel Park, West Sussex BN18 9LH. Tel: 01903 882602; www.arundelcastlecricketfoundation.co.uk.

THE BRIAN JOHNSTON MEMORIAL TRUST supports cricket for the blind, and aims to ease the financial worries of talented young cricketers through scholarships. Registered Charity No. 1045946. Trust administrator: Richard Anstey, 178 Manor Drive North, Worcester Park, Surrey KT4 7RU; raganstey@btinternet.com; www.lordstaverners.org/brian-johnston-memorial-trust.

BUNBURY CRICKET CLUB has raised over £17m for national charities and worthwhile causes since 1987. A total of 1,792 boys have played in the Bunbury Festival; a thousand have gone on to play first-class cricket, and 94 for England. The 33rd ECB David English Bunbury Festival, in August 2019, will be at Felsted School. The Bunburys also presented the only two Under-15 World Cups (1996 and 2000), and an Under-15 tour of India is being planned. Contact: Dr David English CBE, 1 Highwood Cottages, Nan Clark's Lane, London NW7 4HJ; davidenglishbunbury@gmail.com; www.bunburycricket.co.uk.

CAPITAL KIDS CRICKET, which celebrates its 30th anniversary in 2019, aims to improve the physical, social and emotional development of children. It is a fully inclusive organisation providing sporting and social opportunities in the more deprived areas of London, and organises activities in state schools, hospitals, community centres, local parks, and residential centres away from London: the Spirit of Cricket is at the heart of what we do. Around 10,000 young people are involved every year. Chairman: Haydn Turner; haydn.turner@yahoo.co.uk. Chief executive: Shahidul Alam Ratan; 07748 114811; shahidul.alam@capitalkidscricket.org.uk; www.capitalkidscricket.org.uk.

CHANCE TO SHINE is a national children's charity on a mission to spread the power of cricket throughout schools and communities. Since launching in 2005, Chance to Shine has reached over 4m children across more than 14,000 state schools. Contact: The Kia Oval, London SE11 5SW. Tel: 020 7735 2881; www.chancetoshine.org.

THE CHANGE FOUNDATION is an award-winning UK-based charity that uses cricket and other sports to create transformational change in the lives of marginalised and vulnerable young people. The charity has been designing sport-for-development initiatives for 37 years and has worked in 35 countries with a range of partners, including the ICC and UNICEF. We pioneered disability cricket, setting up and running the England Blind Cricket Team. Our cricket centre in the London Borough of Sutton was built – with the help of our president, Phil Tufnell – to cater for cricketers with a disability, and is home to many projects, including our new "walking cricket" programme. Chief Executive: Andy Sellins, The Cricket Centre, Plough Lane, Wallington, Surrey SM6 8JQ. Tel: 020 8669 2177; office@thechangefoundation.org.uk; www.thechangefoundation.org.uk.

CRICKET BUILDS HOPE, formerly the Rwanda Cricket Stadium Foundation, successfully completed efforts in 2017 to raise £1m to build a new cricket facility in Rwanda's capital, Kigali. The charity now plans more cricketing projects. Partnership head: Jon Surtees, The Kia Oval, London SE11 5SS. Tel: 020 7820 5780.

THE CRICKET SOCIETY TRUST aims to support schools and organisations to encourage enjoyment of the game, particularly by children with special needs, through programmes arranged with the Arundel Castle Cricket Foundation and the Belvoir Castle Cricket Trust. The Trust is also supporting the MCC Foundation's Training Hubs Programme. Hon. secretary: Ken Merchant, 16 Louise Road, Rayleigh, Essex SS6 8LW. Tel: 01268 747414; www.cricketsocietytrust.org.uk.

THE DICKIE BIRD FOUNDATION, set up by the former umpire in 2004, helps financially disadvantaged young people under the age of 18 to participate in the sport of their choice. Grants are made towards the cost of equipment and clothing. Trustee: Ted Cowley, 3 The Tower, Tower Drive, Arthington Lane, Pool-in-Wharfedale, Otley, Yorkshire LS21 1NQ. Tel: 07503 641457; www.thedickiebirdfoundation.co.uk.

THE ENGLAND AND WALES CRICKET TRUST was established in 2005 to aid community participation in cricket, with a fund for interest-free loans to amateur cricket clubs. In the financial year to January 2018, it spent £13.4m on charitable activities – primarily grants to c. and amateur cricket clubs, and to county boards to support their programmes. Contact: Cricket Ground, London NW8 8QZ. Tel: 020 7432 1200; feedback@ecb.co.uk.

THE EVELINA LONDON CHILDREN'S HOSPITAL is the official charity partner o. CCC and The Kia Oval. Ten minutes from the ground, Evelina is one of the country's leading children's hospitals, treating patients from all over south-east England. Partnership head: Jon Surtees, The Kia Oval, London SE11 5SS. Tel: 020 7820 5780; www.kiaoval.com.

FIELDS IN TRUST is a UK charity that actively champions parks and green spaces by protecting them in perpetuity. Green spaces do good, do good and need to be protected for good. Over 2,800 spaces have been protected since our foundation in 1925. Chief executive: Helen Griffiths, 36 Woodstock Grove, London W12 8LE. Tel: 020 7427 2110; www.fieldsintrust.org; www.facebook.com/fieldsintrust. Twitter: @FieldsInTrust.

THE HORNSBY PROFESSIONAL CRICKETERS' FUND supports former professional cricketers "in necessitous circumstances", or their dependants, through regular financial help or one-off grants towards healthcare or similar essential needs. Where appropriate it works closely with the PCA and a player's former county. The Trust was established in 1928 from a bequest from the estate of J. H. J. Hornsby (Middlesex, MCC and the Gentlemen), augmented more recently by a bequest from Sir Alec and Eric Bedser, and by a merger with the Walter Hammond Memorial Fund. Secretary: The Rev. Prebendary Mike Vockins OBE, The Chantry, Charlton Musgrove, Wincanton, Somerset BA9 8HG. Tel: 01963 34837.

THE LEARNING FOR A BETTER WORLD (LBW) TRUST, established in 2006, provides tertiary education to disadvantaged students in the cricket-playing countries of the developing world. In 2018 it assisted over 2,000 students in India, Pakistan, Nepal, Uganda, Afghanistan, Sri Lanka, South Africa, Jamaica, Kenya and Tanzania. Chairman: David Vaux, GPO Box 3029, Sydney, NSW 2000, Australia; www.lbwtrust.com.au.

THE LORD'S TAVERNERS is the UK's leading youth cricket and disability sports charity, dedicated to giving disadvantaged and disabled young people a sporting chance. In 2019, it will donate over £4m to help young people of all abilities and backgrounds to participate in cricket and other sporting activities. Registered Charity No. 306054. The Lord's Taverners, 90 Chancery Lane, London WC2A 1EU. Tel: 020 7025 0000; contact@lordstaverners.org; www.lordstaverners.org.

THE MARYLEBONE CRICKET CLUB FOUNDATION's flagship programme is a network of 50 Cricket Hubs that provide a free, ten-week coaching programme to state-educated 11–15-year-olds across the country. In 2017, 2,500 hours of intensive coaching and matchplay were delivered to over 2,000 youngsters. Contact: MCC Foundation, Lord's Ground, London NW8 8QN. Tel: 020 7616 8529; info@mccfoundation.org.uk; www.lords.org/mccfoundation.

THE PRIMARY CLUB provides sporting facilities for the blind and partially sighted. Membership is nominally restricted to those dismissed first ball in any form of cricket; almost 10,000 belong. In total, the club has raised £3m, helped by sales of its tie, popularised by *Test Match Special*. Andrew Strauss is president of the Primary Club Juniors. Hon. secretary: Chris Larlham, PO Box 12121, Saffron Walden, Essex CB10 2ZF. Tel: 01799 586507; www.primaryclub.org.

THE PRINCE'S TRUST helps disadvantaged young people get their lives on track. Founded by HRH The Prince of Wales in 1976, it supports 11–30-year-olds who are struggling at school or unemployed. The Trust's programmes use a variety of activities, including cricket, to engage young people and help them gain skills, confidence and qualifications. Prince's Trust House, 9 Eldon Street, London EC2M 7LS. Tel: 0800 842842; www.princes-trust.org.uk.

THE PROFESSIONAL CRICKETERS' TRUST was created to support the lifelong health and wellbeing of PCA members and their immediate families. We look out for players throughout their active careers and long afterwards, funding life-changing medical assistance, crisis helplines and educational programmes in England and Wales. Director of development and welfare: Ian Thomas, PCA, The Kia Oval, Laker Stand, London SE11 5SS. Tel: 07920 575578; www.thepca.co.uk.

THE TOM MAYNARD TRUST – formed in 2012 after Tom's death – covers two main areas: helping aspiring young professionals with education projects, currently across six sports; and providing grants to help with travel, kit, coaching, training and education. From 2014 to 2018, we also ran an academy in Spain for young county cricketers. Contact: Mike Fatkin, 67a Radnor Road, Canton, Cardiff CF5 1RA; www.tommaynardtrust.com.

CHRONICLE OF 2018

OUTLOOK INDIA   January 8
Four youths from the village of Arin, in the disputed Indian state of Jammu &
Kashmir, were arrested for playing the Pakistan national anthem before a local
cricket match.

INDIAN EXPRESS   January 9
Babulal Briya, a 63-year-old retired railwayman, set himself on fire with
kerosene after Indian captain Virat Kohli was out for five in the Cape Town
Test. He died four days later.

TIMES OF INDIA   January 9
Bangladesh is setting up special courts inside grounds to stage on-the-spot
trials for spectators in the stands suspected of betting on major matches.

SUNDAY TIMES, SRI LANKA   January 14
Security at the Russian embassy in Colombo has been tightened because
youngsters, said to be from a squatter camp, pelted stones at the compound
after their ball landed inside and the staff evidently refused to return it.

NOTTINGHAM POST   January 16
Conmen in Nottinghamshire have been trying to defraud cricket clubs by
sending their treasurers emails purporting to come from their chairman
requesting a transfer of funds. "Always check the email address from someone
asking you for money; it will normally be a giveaway if fraudulent," advised
Nottinghamshire Police. "Also, look out for strange spellings or formal
language like 'Dear Sir'."

THE COURIER, DUNDEE   January 16
Freuchie CC from Fife, the national village champions in 1985, are campaigning
against local dog owners whose pets foul their pitch. "Umpteen times we've
put notices up on Facebook, but it just keeps on happening," said president
Robbie Birrell. "We're fed up with this."

COAST CITY WEEKLY MESSENGER   January 17
South Road CC's Fourth XI were bowled out for two by Sheidow Park, the
lowest score ever in the Adelaide and Suburban Cricket Association. It beat
six all out by Keswick in 1959-60. South Road had passed 100 only once in
nine previous innings. Vice-captain Peter Fosdike said that playing the top side
with an inexperienced line-up on a windy day offering late swing was a
"perfect storm". Club president Aaron Schmidt added: "They're not the most
skilled lads, but they're definitely the most passionate we've got at the club."
(See also November 10.)

THE AVENUE MAIL/GULF NEWS   January 22/23

A cricketer died of a heart attack while celebrating his team's win in Jamshedpur, eastern India. Shivam Kumar Dubey had scored 55 in a Twenty20 game and was fielding at long-off when the opposition failed to score off the final ball, giving victory to his side, the World Truck Cab Drop department of Tata Motors. Dubey took off his T-shirt and raced in to join his team-mates but then collapsed. He was 34, about to be married.

PRESS TRUST OF INDIA   January 31

Tanishq Gavate, 14, broke the world record for all cricket by scoring 1,045 in an innings, his coach claimed. The innings took place over two days in a tournament in the satellite city of Navi Mumbai, in the semi-final of a tournament at the Yashwantrao Chavan English Medium School; it contained 149 fours and 67 sixes. Gavate was playing for a team arranged by the organisers against a school side. A Mumbai Cricket Association official said the tournament was not recognised, but the coach, named only as Manish, insisted the game was played with a leather ball, overarm bowling and a minimum boundary of 50 yards. [By the start of 2019, the score had not been ratified by the Association of Cricket Statisticians and Historians, due to a lack of corroboration.]

OUTLOOK INDIA/ICC-CRICKET.COM   February 1

The Ajman All Stars, a privately run Twenty20 league in the UAE, has been discontinued after a video went viral showing bizarre batting by Dubai Stars against Sharjah Warriors. Five were stumped and three run out in Dubai's 46 all out. "We consider there to be strong evidence to indicate this was a corrupt event," said Alex Marshall of the ICC Anti-Corruption Unit.

ESPNCRICINFO   February 5

Indian cricket's official website went blank for the weekend that included the Under-19 team's World Cup victory. The BCCI blamed former official Lalit Modi for registering domains in his own name instead of the board's. Modi's lawyer said the board should have been more proactive.

MAIL ONLINE AUSTRALIA   February 5

Jasmine Dunlop, 12, earned her father's team a draw after being called from the crowd at Apollo Bay, Victoria, to bat out the final two overs when the home team were a player short. Her dad Darren described one of the bowlers as "Tumble Guts from the bar", but said neither he nor Jasmine was worried: "The guys look after the younger kids and slow the balls down."

ESPNCRICINFO   February 8

In Antigua, Kent batsman Zak Crawley was denied a maiden List A century by alleged unsportsmanlike behaviour from the opposition. Kent, who had been invited to take part in the Caribbean Super 50, needed four to beat the Leeward Islands, with Crawley 98 not out. Sheeno Berridge bowled two wides before Crawley chased a similar ball for a single. The fielders then let a shot from the other batsman, Sean Dickson, who was refusing to run, go for the winning four.

HINDUSTAN TIMES   February 19
Cricketer-turned-politician Imran Khan, 65, has married his "spiritual adviser" Bushra Wattoo in a low-key ceremony. His two previous marriages ended in divorce.

EVENING STANDARD   February 22
Wandsworth Council, south London, has unanimously passed new park rules which critics say could lead to children being fined £500 for climbing trees, flying kites – or playing cricket. Councillor Jonathan Cook insisted the updated guidelines would be applied in a "common sense" way.

SUNDAY GLEANER, JAMAICA   February 25
Dave Cameron, president of Cricket West Indies, said the revival of cricket is being hampered by the prevalence of female PE teachers. "Most of them don't know cricket," he said. "They don't know the history, and neither are they interested."

NINE.COM.AU   March 19
Playing on the Masters course at Augusta National, Shane Warne hit his first ever hole-in-one, at the 16th: 155 yards and into the wind. "Can't believe it !!!!!!!!!!" he tweeted.

March 19

HINDUSTAN TIMES March 24

Indian Test player Wriddhaman Saha hit 102 off 20 balls in the JC Mukherjee Trophy, a Twenty20 tournament in Kolkata.

CRICBUZZ April 4

Newlands, Cape Town's Test match ground, was burgled for the third time in three years over the Easter weekend. At least 15 men, some armed, forced their way in and demanded the keys to the presidential suite, where they stole TV sets, alcohol and other items.

ABC, AUSTRALIA April 13

A group of farmers in drought-stricken western New South Wales took a day off and played cricket in the dried-up bed of the Darling River.

DAILY MAIL
April 20

The British submarine HMS *Trenchant* pushed through the Arctic Ocean ice near the North Pole as part of a major exercise to prepare for possible Arctic warfare. In the absence of an immediate enemy, the crew played cricket.

SUNDAY TELEGRAPH
April 22

Britain's oldest Asian cricket club, the Indian Gymkhana, founded in 1916, want to recruit players of other ethnic backgrounds. The club, based near Hounslow, west London, have never operated a colour bar, and first expressed a wish to become multi-racial during their golden jubilee in 1966. They have now recruited Charlie Puckett, former secretary of the Middlesex League, and are looking for more. "We want people from other communities to join," said cricket secretary Sanjay Sood. "Hounslow is a very multicultural area, and we want to reflect modern Britain, which is so mixed now."

INDIAN EXPRESS
April 22

The Pakistan player Hasan Ali gatecrashed the nightly flag-lowering ceremony on the country's border with India at Wagah, walking on to the road to demonstrate his wicket-taking celebrations, to the fury of the Indian authorities. "The act has hit the sanctity of the parade. We will lodge a protest," said a senior border official. The ritualised ceremony, held at sunset every day, has become a tourist attraction, and is seen as a symbol of both the rivalry and the co-operation between the nations.

LIFE 365, PUNE
May 1

The charity Cricket Without Borders have been to refugee camps in Jordan to teach the game to Syrian refugees.

DAILY TELEGRAPH May 8

Five-year-old Harry Butt was saying goodbye to friends on the driveway of a house near Poole Grammar School in Dorset when he was hit by a six struck out of the grounds. He was left with severe concussion, two black eyes and a swollen nose. "I just feel really upset that they've been told about the balls going over, and nothing has been done," said his mother, Michelle. The school was very apologetic but said perimeter netting could be impractical because of high winds. Headmaster Andy Baker did say he would move first-team matches to a pitch further from the fence.

TVNZ May 9

Cricketers in Glenavy, New Zealand, called at a house and confronted a group of squatters to demand the return of items stolen from their clubrooms. "We just want our cricket gear back, mate – just give us the cricket gear and that's it," one said, and later claimed success. Sergeant Kevin Reynolds criticised the players: "Vigilante action such as this can harm police investigations. Thankfully, the tenant of the property was co-operative and the situation didn't escalate."

ESPNCRICINFO May 10

England bowler Stuart Broad beat almost six million other contestants to win Week 37 of the Fantasy Premier League, said to be the world's biggest such football game.

TIMES OF INDIA May 16

A two-day interdistrict Under-16 match at the Medical College Ground in Kottayam, Kerala, was abandoned after college staff drove their cars on to the pitch and said they wanted to play tennis-ball cricket there. "This could have been avoided if the cricket association had given the college authorities the fixtures," said one staff member.

DAILY TELEGRAPH May 18
The private bank Coutts & Co, used by the Royal Family, have taken "appropriate action" against members of their cricket team after a player was videoed wearing "an inappropriate and insensitive item" on a tour of Rwanda. The item was a hat adorned with a novelty penis.

RADIO FREE EUROPE/WISDEN INDIA May 19
Eight people were killed and 45 wounded by rocket explosions at a sports stadium in the Afghan city of Jalalabad, which has become a stronghold for Taliban and Islamic State militants. The stadium was hosting a cricket match at the start of Ramadan. Officials said the match organiser, Hidayatullah Zaheer, was among the dead. A suicide bomber killed three people at a game in Kabul in September 2017.

IRISH TIMES May 23
A cricketer was arrested in his whites as he strolled off the pitch at Hills CC, near Dublin. Mohammed "Romi" Ramzan was then deported for organising sham marriages for Asian men who paid up to €20,000 each to marry Latvian women and gain the right to stay in the EU. A deportation order had been in force for some time. Unable to find him, police focused on Ramzan's love of cricket, and eventually tracked him down.

DAILY EXPRESS   May 25

Prime minister Theresa May has leapfrogged the 27-year waiting list and been fast-tracked into MCC. "The prime minister's nomination for membership was considered in accordance with MCC's rules, which allow for a limited number of candidates for membership to be elected out of turn," said a spokesman. [Her two Conservative predecessors are both members. John Major, who later became a committee member before resigning in disgust, was elected to MCC under the same procedure. There are conflicting reports as to whether David Cameron queued up or not.]

THE TIMES   May 26

The village cricket club at Hoveringham, Nottinghamshire (population: 359), have been bequeathed £250,000 by a former member, Derek Wright. The club had been struggling to find players, but believed they would now be able to attract recruits. Wright was a member for 53 years and served as player, captain, groundsman, secretary and president, before he died in 2017, aged 82. Chairman David Armitage said Wright had no close relatives and was "an unassuming, lovely man". He added: "The cricket club were his family."

ESPNCRICINFO   June 3

Pakistani batsmen Fawad Alam broke a dressing-room window with his bat after being timed out. Fawad was playing for Clitheroe against Colne in a Lancashire League T20 match. He later admitted he was furious, but said the breakage was accidental: he was trying to throw the bat into his kitbag.

MID-DAY, MUMBAI   June 6

Vilas Godbole, 76, discovered he was a first-class cricketer 53 years late, when he learned he was an answer in a quiz on Facebook. He also found out this entitled him to a 20,000 rupee (£240) monthly pension. Godbole played a single match for Bombay against Ceylon in January 1965 without realising it had first-class status: in his only innings, he hit a six off his first ball, before being out for 15. He has started receiving the pension, but not the 12 years' unpaid arrears he believes he is owed.

AGENCE FRANCE-PRESSE   June 8

A wax effigy of Indian cricket captain Virat Kohli required repairs immediately after going on display at Madame Tussauds in Delhi after star-struck fans swamped the statue. Part of his ear had been clipped off.

CRICKETYORKSHIRE.COM   June 14

Ouseburn Second XI were six for four against Hampthswaite of Division Four of the Nidderdale League, with their captain John Moorhouse thinking of digging in to achieve a half-respectable score. He actually took the total to 272 for nine, making 225 not out and sharing an unbeaten last-wicket stand of 106 with 12-year-old Charlie Raine – enough for a 67-run win. "I hit 22 sixes across the three houses behind the bowler's arm," said Moorhouse. "I'm not an arrogant man, but I've played cricket since the age of five and I've never experienced so much fun."

WESTON MERCURY June 14

Congresbury CC in Somerset have pleaded with dog owners to take their pets elsewhere, to protect young players from excrement-related infections. Parish Council chairman Di Hassan agreed: "We're asking dog owners to realise there are plenty of other areas where they can exercise their dogs. Even though legally they are allowed, morally they might reconsider where they go."

MUMBAI MIRROR June 20

Six people were arrested for allegedly hacking a man to death in a cricket match "between friends" near Bangalore. The dead man, named Mani, aged 22, was said to have refused to fetch a ball hit out of the ground.

SOUTH LONDON GUARDIAN/THE GUARDIAN June 22/August 19

Mitcham Green, believed to have been a cricket ground since 1685, and thus the world's oldest, is now under threat from developers. Mitcham CC have been in dispute with an investment company who a decade ago bought the freehold of the pavilion, a car park and a closed-down pub and now want to build a 70-room hotel. The club believe this will make cricket on the green untenable. "We are stressing to them that there's no intention of taking them off the site," said architect Marcus Beale. The club say the company, Phoenix Investments, do not answer letters.

WAKEFIELD EXPRESS June 29

Thieves stole a £1,000 defibrillator from Sandal CC, Yorkshire. "The cabinet is apparently unbreakable, but they've got into it using their hands or a stick," said club treasurer David Dansfield.

INDEPENDENT.CO.UK July 3

Three men, including an umpire, were reportedly taken to hospital after a cricket match in Gothenburg, Sweden, turned into a brawl in which bats were used as weapons. Between 15 and 20 people from the two teams were involved in the fight, which police said left the umpire with a broken arm.

DAILY MAIL July 5

Richard Symmonds, a 30-year-old vending-machine supervisor, scored an unbeaten 343 in a 40-over total of 457 for five for Burnt Yates in a Second XI match against Darley. It was the highest innings in the 125-year history of Yorkshire's Nidderdale League. Symmonds hit 30 sixes, including six in an over. "It's not about me getting that score," he said. "It's about getting the other team out afterwards." That happened too: Burnt Yates won by 289 runs. Symmonds celebrated by taking his wife out for fish and chips.

BOLTON NEWS July 6

The Bolton League have allowed clubs to postpone tomorrow's matches because of a clash with England's World Cup football quarter-final against Sweden. However, the neighbouring Greater Manchester League refused, which annoyed Michael Farley, the captain of Radcliffe. "It's a shame because it makes the game meaningless," said Farley. "Everyone wants to win a game of cricket, but they want to win the World Cup more."

SKY SPORTS July 8

Former England goalkeeper Joe Hart, 31, decided not to watch England play Sweden and turned out instead for Shrewsbury CC for the first time in 13 years. Hart was omitted from the World Cup squad, despite having played in nine of the ten qualifying matches. Against Knowle & Dorridge in the Birmingham Premier League, he scored six and took a catch.

SUNDAY INDEPENDENT, PLYMOUTH July 8

In Division Three (West) of the Cornwall League, the game between Goldsithney and Mullion ended at 11.38am after Goldsithney were bowled out for 39 and lost by nine wickets. The league had allowed teams to vary their timings so they could watch England v Sweden. These players made it with more than three hours to spare.

ESPNCRICINFO July 8

South Africa women's captain Dane van Niekerk and fast-bowling all-rounder Marizanne Kapp became the second set of current international team-mates to get married after New Zealand's Amy Satterthwaite and Lea Tahuhu last year. (Lynsey Askew of England married Alex Blackwell of Australia in 2015.)

TIMES OF INDIA   July 10

Harmanpreet Kaur, the Indian women's Twenty20 captain, has lost her rank as a deputy superintendent of police four months after being offered the position. She was said to have submitted a false graduation certificate, and could therefore join the force only as a constable. She insisted her degree was genuine.

SOUTHERN DAILY ECHO   July 12

The Hampshire League match between Hythe & Dibden Fourths and Fawley Thirds was abandoned when an umpire lost a tooth, having allegedly been assaulted by a Fawley player after turning down an lbw appeal.

CLUB-CRICKET.CO.UK   July 12

Ollie Churchill-Coleman scored the first triple-century in the Northamptonshire League: an unbeaten 303 with 39 sixes for Irthlingborough Town Third XI against Horton House Fourths in Division 11. However, some players thought he had "gone too far" against a callow attack including a 13-year-old. The scorebooks suggested Churchill-Coleman was on 299 when Irthlingborough had declared on 432 for seven. However, an extra four was discovered. Irthlingborough won by 361 runs.

CAMBRIDGE NEWS   July 13

After 49 years of club cricket, Kevin Clement of Godmanchester Town CC, near Huntingdon, has taken his 2,000th wicket, to add to more than 20,000 runs. Clement, 63, says he has always recorded his tallies. "I kept the celebrations to a few subdued handshakes – it's an age thing – but we had a few beers in the clubhouse later."

DAILY TELEGRAPH   July 16

Former West Indian Test player Collis King, still a legend in league cricket aged 67, has been deported from the UK for a breach of the entry rules. King, whose wife is British, tried to apply for a spousal visa while in the UK on a visitor's visa; he was told he could apply only from his native Barbados, and then given 14 days to leave. King is a hero in Dunnington, Yorkshire for his continuing skill on the field, and his coaching. [At the start of 2019, King remained in Barbados, awaiting an appeal.]

DAILY TELEGRAPH   July 17

Former Middlesex fast bowler Wes Stewart has been granted British citizenship 63 years after arriving from Jamaica as a ten-year-old. Stewart was among those caught up in the Windrush scandal when it emerged that the status of many migrants of that era remained unclear. Stewart had been told that if he left the country he might not be allowed back. However, the Home Office have now relented. "It is a massive relief, and great news," he said. "I can now go to Jamaica with my son."

DEVONLIVE.COM   July 17

A tree at Barton CC, Torquay – known locally as the Agatha Christie oak – has collapsed. Hercule Poirot's creator, who lived nearby before her death in 1976, used to sit in its shade to watch matches.

YORKSHIRE POST   July 26

Tom Collins and Mark Holmes batted throughout a 20-over innings for Carlton Towers CC in an unbroken partnership of 340 against Eggborough Power Station. Collins scored 200 and Holmes 112. It was the highest total in the Snaith Evening League's 87-year history.

DAILY TELEGRAPH   July 26

BBC's "Newsnight" programme have apologised for showing a clip of Wasim Akram instead of his former Pakistan team-mate Imran Khan, as part of a piece documenting Imran's journey from cricketer to potential prime minister.

THE TIMES   July 26

Eddie Stokoe was reunited with his wedding ring 52 years after he took it off before going out to bat in 1966. It was found by a spectator who fell over while walking her dog on the nearby riverbank during a match, dislodging the ring from its hiding place in the mud at Shotley Bridge, County Durham. The woman then bumped into Stokoe's brother, who recognised the inscription "Edward–Jean Oct 16 1965". The couple were thrilled, and Eddie now wears the ring again, but on his little finger, since it no longer fits as it did when he was 21.

METRO.CO.UK   July 26

An air ambulance landed on the pitch at Earls Colne CC, Essex, to treat a fielder who had split the skin between his thumb and forefinger. "In a small percentage of missions, crews attend incidents that are, thankfully, less serious than at first thought," said a spokesman.

SYDNEY MORNING HERALD   July 29

Cricket Australia have sacked an employee for campaigning against restrictions on abortion in Tasmania on social media. Angela Williamson, 39, began tweeting on the subject after she had to go to Melbourne to have a pregnancy terminated when the state's only abortion clinic closed. Williamson, who was employed as a lobbyist, was told her tweets had damaged her relationship with the Tasmanian government.

THE CRICKETER   August 2

Mike Simpson, a building engineer, scored 237 not out from 62 balls for Sheffield Collegiate against Khan in the Sheffield Alliance Midweek League. Unfortunately, he had no chance of excitedly telling his workmates next morning. "They don't really have any interest," he said. "No one really cares."

OLDHAM TIMES   August 2

Two South Africans playing for Shaw CC in the Greater Manchester League were seriously hurt when they were attacked outside an Oldham nightclub. Justin Watson, 20, had a badly broken jaw, and Shaw's professional, Marques Ackerman, suffered severe concussion. Shaw were unable to find a substitute pro for their Saturday match because the attack happened after the 48-hour deadline for replacements. The league refused to waive the rule until it was too late. Asked if he was aggrieved at the league's attitude, Shaw captain Steve Whiston said that was "an understatement".

INDIAN EXPRESS   August 3

Lights installed on a beach as a security measure have had an unexpected consequence, allowing cricket to be played between 10.30 and midnight. The players, at Gamdevi, Mumbai, have agreed not to play at weekends, when the beach is crowded.

THE SUN   August 7

A furious father clouted a man having sex with a naked woman in front of cricket-playing children, after police took 45 minutes to respond to 999 calls. The incident – videoed and widely watched on YouTube – happened on a hot afternoon in Roundhay Park, Leeds.

EXMOUTH JOURNAL   August 8

Sam Corney, 17, and his 14-year-old sister Emma put on an unbroken 197 for Exmouth Third XI against Topsham Seconds in the Devon League. Sam made 108 and Emma 67. Their father Russell was scoring.

DAILY MAIL   August 9

Jay Darrell of Minehead Second XI was two away from his maiden century with five to win, when the bowler chucked the ball out of reach towards the boundary, conceding five extras. After being monstered on Twitter, Decland Redwood of Purnell apologised, describing his decision as "ill-judged and impulsive". He was banned for nine matches by the Somerset League.

KBTX-TV, Bryan, Texas   August 10

Texas businessman Tanweer Ahmed is building a 90-acre cricket complex with ten separate pitches, by a highway on the outskirts of Houston. "We have over 30 teams that play in the Houston area, but we just don't have enough fields," said Houston Cricket League president Iqra Farooqui. "This facility will allow us to play and help grow the game." The region's South Asian population has almost doubled since 2000.

Mail Online   August 11

The Derbyshire Premier League match between Chesterfield and Denby had to be called off because the ground at Queen's Park had been taken over by travellers.

Burnley Express   August 14

Lancashire League club Nelson have been hit by a £6,000 water bill – originally £12,000 before they appealed – due to a leak in a hut on a disused bowling green. "We are relieved that the bill has been reduced," said chairman David Heap. "But this is still five years' worth of money that has literally washed down the drain."

Kent Online   August 16

Anton O'Sullivan and Ben Tomkinson took hat-tricks in the same innings for Marden against Weald in the Kent Village League. Tomkinson also took two wickets with the last two balls, to finish with five for nought.

Sidmouth Herald   August 17

Day-tripper Barbara Tummey, 80, needed about a dozen stitches after she was struck on the head by a ball hit over the wall from the seafront ground at Sidmouth, Devon. An earlier six had been caught by a nearby pedestrian. "Good job it didn't hit anyone on the head," said Mrs Tummey's daughter. Then came the next. When the victim missed the coach back, club official Fionn Wardrop made the 300-mile round trip to get her home. "I can't praise the cricket club enough – they were wonderful," Mrs Tummey said. "I feel sorry for the cricketers – it wasn't intentional." The club said they had applied to install netting, but their plans had been rejected by the council as "out of keeping".

LORDS.ORG   August 23

The MCC Foundation, the charitable arm of MCC, claimed a world record for the longest continuous indoor cricket match. Two teams from Cross Arrows CC, who normally use the Nursery Ground, played in the Lord's school for 31 hours, 27 minutes and 12 seconds. The same players took part throughout, with five-minute breaks permitted every hour. The previous best, 25 hours 59 minutes, was set in South Africa in 2014. [The feat was yet to be recognised by Guinness in early 2019.]

COVENTRY TELEGRAPH   August 24

Wasim Lodgi, 54, was resuscitated by a team-mate after suffering a cardiac arrest, having taken four wickets for Pak Shaheen against Peugeot in the Warwickshire League. Wasim's team-mate Asad Khan saved his life using CPR, which he had learned on an ECB training course.

WHITEHAVEN NEWS   August 27

Mary Smith, an umpire for 40 years, was knocked out after being hit in the face while standing in a potential title decider between Cockermouth and Cleator in the North Lancashire & Cumbria League. After consultation, the match continued. "It was a cracking game, but marred by the terrible accident to Mary," said her colleague, Gordon McCullough.

TIMES OF INDIA   August 31

A 23-year-old man, identified as Rizwan, died in hospital after being shot during a scuffle between boys playing cricket in Noida near Delhi.

MORNINGTON PENINSULA LEADER   September 3

French Island CC, based off the coast of Victoria, have offered free ferry rides, food and performance-based incentives to recruit players from the mainland and avert the 120-year-old club's closure. Captain Matthew Spark said the club, which until recently fielded two teams, were down to seven regulars. The island, which once housed a prison, has only 100 residents. The cricket teas have a particularly good reputation.

THE CRICKETER   September 5

Christian Silkstone scored 316 off 116 balls for Triangle against Thornton in the Halifax League, but said he couldn't remember much about it. "I have a shocking short-term memory, so I'm used to not remembering too much about an innings," he said. He managed to escape buying the drinks, as it had been agreed that all the fines for the season were to be put behind the bar that night.

HEREFORD TIMES   September 5

Vandals who broke into the pavilion at Eastnor CC, Herefordshire, sprayed tomato ketchup over the floors, walls and furniture.

LEICESTER MERCURY   September 6

A parrot stopped play at Hinckley, Leicestershire. After squawking from the trees and circling the ground, a large macaw landed on 67-year-old Tom Flannery, playing for Hinckley Amateur Thirds, and refused to budge. "It just perched on his shoulder like he was Long John Silver or something," said Tim David, captain of opponents Hathern Old Seconds. "We had to stop the game because this bird was big enough to take someone's finger off." The bird's owners eventually arrived to remove him. "It seems to have just taken a shine to Tom," said Hinckley chairman Phil York. "He doesn't look much like a pirate – he has a bit of a beard but no eyepatch or wooden leg."

SUNDAY TIMES   September 16

Two pupils at Millfield School (fees: £40,000 per year) were suspended after an initiation rite, involving beating newcomers with cricket bats and a belt, was videoed.

BBC   September 18

Durham's Riverside ground at Chester-le-Street is to become the first British sports venue to install sanitary bins in gents' toilets so that men suffering from bladder problems can dispose of incontinence products.

WORCESTER OBSERVER   September 21

Basil D'Oliveira was posthumously awarded the freedom of his adopted home city of Worcester, six years after his death and 50 years after the D'Oliveira Affair. The mayor, councillor Jabba Riaz, presented the honour to Basil's son Shaun.

INDIAN EXPRESS   September 22

Shopkeeper and weekend cricketer Saiju Titus, 36, had to make a 1,400-mile dash by plane and taxi to ensure his List A debut, with 24 hours' notice. This followed a decision by the BCCI to revoke a dispensation allowing associate members Puducherry (formerly Pondicherry) to field extra imported players in the Hazare Trophy. Along with five others, he rushed to Anand for the match against Uttarakhand, where four of the six made their debut. "A dream has come true," he said. "But I hardly got any sleep. Not even the two hours the others managed." Titus scored ten and held a catch. (He later played another match in the tournament, and made his first-class debut.)

NEWCASTLE CHRONICLE   September 27/28

Langley Park CC, where football manager Sir Bobby Robson used to play, have found a new ground six weeks after being expelled from their home of 100 years by landowner Alan Cassidy. They will now move to Bearpark, which had been derelict since the closure of the club based there. Cassidy said the cricketers had broken the rules by bringing in their own drinks, an allegation denied by officials.

HINDUSTAN TIMES   October 14

Shehzar Mohammad, grandson of the great Hanif, became the sixth member of his family to score a first-class double-century when he made 265 for Karachi Whites against Multan in a Quaid-e-Azam Trophy match at Multan. Shehzar, 26, followed Hanif, his own father Shoaib, his great-uncles Mushtaq and Sadiq, and Sadiq's son Imran.

THE GUARDIAN   October 23

Andrew Flintoff has been named a host of the BBC motoring show "Top Gear", which has seen its domestic audience halve since the departure of Jeremy Clarkson. Flintoff is to share duties with fellow Lancastrian Paddy McGuinness. The BBC say the programme still has a worldwide audience of 350 million in 200 countries and territories, many of which have not heard of Flintoff – yet.

TIMES OF INDIA   October 31

Priyanshu Moliya, 14, scored an unbeaten 556 in a two-day Under-14 fixture for the Mohinder Amarnath Cricket Academy in Vadodara. Before he batted, Moliya had taken four wickets with his off-breaks as the Yogi Cricket Academy were all out for 52. He then hit 98 fours and a six off 319 balls before the declaration came at 826 for four. He took two more wickets in a victory by an innings and 689. "When I saw him for the first time, I knew I was seeing something special," Amarnath said. "He is a fine talent and he will get better with exposure. I like his passion as well." Moliya had scored 254 in the same tournament in 2017.

DAILY NEWS, SRI LANKA   November 1

Left-arm fast bowler Kalana Perera took eight for one as St Thomas' College, Mount Lavinia, dismissed St Mary's College, Kegalle, for six in the Sri Lankan Inter Schools tournament. Only two runs came off the bat. Perera had already taken eight for 17 when St Mary's were 72 all out in the first innings, giving him match figures of 16 for 18.

ROAD RAGE (South Road CC magazine)   November 10

South Road's troubled fourth team (see January 17) fielded only seven players against Happy Valley, but in a "stellar" effort bowled the opposition out for 127. Unfortunately, they were then skittled for eight in the first innings, before almost making the opposition bat again by scoring 116. [In December, the club decided to field three teams for the rest of the season.]

THE TIMES   November 12

Wales scored their first rugby win over Australia in their last 14 attempts, having brought in the 2005 Ashes star Simon Jones to address the forwards about "the belief and mindset" needed to beat the Aussies.

DAWN, PAKISTAN/AGENCE FRANCE-PRESSE   November 24

At least seven people were killed when rival groups exchanged fire at a police post where they had come to register a case against each other following a row between their children during a cricket match. The incident happened in Havelian, near Abbottabad, in Pakistan. Two pairs of brothers were among the dead.

MAIL ONLINE   December 1

England captain Joe Root, 27, married Carrie Cotterell, a medical rep, in Sheffield before flying off to play for Sydney Thunder in the Big Bash. The couple have been together for four years and have a son of nearly two.

MAIL ONLINE   December 4

The day before facing an ECB disciplinary committee over his 2017 late-night fracas, England star Ben Stokes spent six hours having four lions tattooed on his back. It will require another 18 before completion. He now has seven lions about his person, including the three of the England crest on his shoulder.

THE STATESMAN, CALCUTTA   December 5

A goat being offered as the prize in a cricket tournament in the remote Indian settlement of Dangi was mauled to death by a leopard 48 hours before the event. Village elders had to shell out 50,000 rupees (£60) to buy a new goat.

THE HINDU   December 12

Rex Rajkumar Singh of Manipur had figures of 9.5–6–11–10 when Arunachal Pradesh were bowled out for 36 in the Under-19 Cooch Behar Trophy at Anantapur.

We are always grateful for contributions for this section, especially stories from local or non-UK media. Items from club and school websites are also welcome. Please send newspaper cuttings to Matthew Engel at Fair Oak, Bacton, Herefordshire HR2 0AT (always including the paper's name and date) and URLs to editors@wisdenalmanack.com.

INDEX OF TEST MATCHES

Eight earlier men's Test series in 2017-18 – Bangladesh v Australia, Pakistan v Sri Lanka, South Africa v Bangladesh, Zimbabwe v West Indies, India v Sri Lanka, Australia v England, New Zealand v West Indies, South Africa v Zimbabwe – and the Australia v England women's Test appeared in *Wisden 2018*.

INDEX OF UNUSUAL OCCURRENCES

INDEX OF ADVERTISEMENTS

PART TITLES